Consumer and Trading Standards:
Law and Practice 2022

Tenth Edition

Consumer and Trading Standards: Law and Practice 2022

Tenth Edition

Jonathan Kirk, QC
LLB (Hons), Barrister-at-law
Member of the Honourable Society of Lincoln's Inn

Bryan Lewin, MBE
DCA, DMS, FCTSI

LexisNexis® UK & Worldwide

United Kingdom	RELX (UK) Limited trading as LexisNexis®, 1–3 Strand, London WC2N 5JR
LNUK Global Partners	LexisNexis® encompasses authoritative legal publishing brands dating back to the 19th century including: Butterworths® in the United Kingdom, Canada and the Asia-Pacific region; Les Editions du Juris Classeur in France; and Matthew Bender® worldwide. Details of LexisNexis® locations worldwide can be found at www.lexisnexis.com

ISBN 978-1-7847-3480-0

9 781784 734800

ISBN for this volume: 9781784734800

Printed and bound by Hobbs the Printers, Hampshire, SO40 3WX

Visit LexisNexis at http://www.lexisnexis.co.uk

Foreword to the Tenth Edition

When it was suggested that I write this foreword I was told that nobody from the business sector had written the piece before. I was, of course, both honoured and pleased to accept but there is a caveat that I worked for many years in local government before moving into the private sector.

Looking back on some of the previous contributions to this publication I noticed some familiar themes, concerning resource reductions, job cuts and a skills gap. Those concerns are even more pertinent today. I was fortunate to be invited to the CTSI Symposium in September 2021 and while there was much discussion about job losses and increased responsibilities, I also sensed a real enthusiasm for change and for sharing expertise.

The 'Pink Book' provides us with an invaluable and comprehensive directory of consumer law but it is, I believe, relevant and considered enforcement of those laws that is key to consumer protection. I have always maintained that to regulate a business effectively it is vital to have a thorough understanding of its operation. It is also arguable that enforcement is at least half communication and half legal knowledge.

We have been through almost two years of the Covid pandemic and without underestimating how tough it has been, I have been amazed by just how agile and resilient some businesses have proven to be. Enforcement officers too have been faced with a tough time, with an ever changing and sometimes confusing range of guidance documents to be assessed and monitored – often dealing with business owners who, already, feel beleaguered by obstacles to trading. In those situations, effective communication and understanding business pressure has made things easier for everybody.

Industry is constantly changing and adapting to meet both consumer demands and shifts in global markets. Cybercrime is an increasing threat with the potential to disrupt distribution chains or amend formulations of manufactured items. Food fraud is also a huge threat and, potentially, a highly lucrative option for organised crime. Quite apart from substitution of inferior or unregulated ingredients, the risk of introduction of unknown allergens is very real. Sharing intelligence between agencies and also businesses is the best way to combat those threats.

The year ahead will doubtless bring more challenges, further financial constraints, and additional responsibilities, but I am confident that cross functional working and flexibility will allow those challenges to be met.

Alan Lacey
November 2021

Preface to the Tenth Edition

'It was the best of times, it was the worst of times.'
Charles Dickens – A Tale of Two Cities

As we trudge towards the end of 2021, the covid storm clouds are again cumulating, warning us now of the omicron variant waiting around our Christmas corner. The pandemic has indeed provided us with the best and worst of times in 2021. As restrictions relaxed with the vaccine roll-out, our lives began to resemble a normality that had become dim in the collective memory. Pubs and restaurants filled, and airplanes were booked for hopeful holidays in the sun. But, with a familiar ebb and flow, the pandemic strikes back and we anxiously await the next tide of public health restrictions.

The story of Covid 19 will be talked about for decades, but a feature we hope is not lost to time is the great human triumph in all of this, and a regulatory triumph at that. It is not an exaggeration to say that the UK's lightning authorisation of vaccines has led the world and saved thousands of lives. It has shown how a regulator, not previously lauded for its agility, was able to adapt and work with industry to smash the normal times for producing a safe vaccine. Although Plato told us that necessity is the mother of invention, the child must still be nurtured and we are all grateful that the MHRA was able to show a safe pathway through those regulatory thickets.

The Pink Book is now rather an old publication, in its tenth edition and well into its third decade in existence, but progress continues apace. Given what we have all experienced of the vaccine programme, it is perhaps appropriate that, in the 2022 Edition, we welcome a brand new chapter on health and medicine. All of the other chapters have been carefully updated, and we remain grateful for the work undertaken by our contributing editors. We would, again, like to thank our excellent developer, Evelyn Reid and veteran editor, Tracy Robinson.

Lucy Florence (14) and Sophie Matilda (11, but nearly 12) are both now in and around that delightful time of life for parents, the teen years. And the apple does not fall far from the tree, as they have both become vocal specialists on the meaning of the term 'unfair'. Despite their sometimes spirited submissions, Jonathan remains incredibly proud of them both. Bryan continues to be inspired by the efforts and achievements of his five grandchildren – Finbar, Orla, Joseph, Elsa and Nellie and their parents.

Preface to the Tenth Edition

We have agreed that royalties from the publication of *Consumer and Trading Standards: Law and Practice* (Tenth Edition) will again be donated to Meningitis Now and the British Heart Foundation.

The law is stated as at 15 November 2021.

Jonathan and Bryan

Contributors

Advertising
Anna Medvinskaia
LLB (Hons), LLM (Cantab), Barrister
With an additional contribution from the Advertising Standards Authority

Age-restricted Products
Sabrina Goodchild
BA (Oxon), Barrister

Animal Health and Welfare
Jonathan Goulding
LLB (Hons), Barrister
Stephanie Young
BA (Hons) MCTSI, CTSP

Civil Enforcement
Jason Freeman
MA (Cantab), Barrister

Consumer Credit
Daniel Brayley
MA (Cantab), Barrister
Lee Finch
LLB (Hons), LLM Barrister

Contributors

Fred Philpott
LLB (Hons), Barrister

Consumer Rights

Elizabeth Tyler
BA (Hons), Barrister

Anna Medvinskaia
LLB (Hons), LLM (Cantab), Barrister

Lee Finch
LLB (Hons), LLM Barrister

Criminal Enforcement

Jonathan Spicer
MA (Cantab), Barrister

Miles Bennett
LLB (Hons), Barrister

Lee Reynolds
LLB (Hons), Barrister

Louise Baxter
MBE, FCTSI

Criminal Precedents Committee

Kevin Barry (Chairman)
LLB (Hons), Barrister

Jonathan Goulding
LLB (Hons), Barrister

Miles Bennett
LLB (Hons), Barrister

Adam Pearson
LLB (Nott), Barrister

Alex Greenwood
LLB (Hons), Barrister

Lee Reynolds
LLB (Hons), Barrister
Alison Lambert
LLB (Hons), Barrister
Andrew Johnson
LLB (Hons), Barrister
Michael Coley
LLB (Lond), Barrister
Alison Hollis
LLB (Hons), LLM, Barrister
Robin Kingham
BA (Oxon), Barrister
Sabrina Goodchild
BA (Oxon), Barrister
George Spence-Jones
MEng (Hons), Barrister

Environmental Standards
Robin Kingham
BA (Oxon), Barrister

Food and Feed
Adam Pearson
LLB (Nott), Barrister
Sukh Gill
LLB(Hons), DTS, MCTSI
Stuart Jessop
BSC (Psych), Barrister

Fraud and Money Laundering
John Vincent
DTS, DMS, MCTSI

Contributors

Cameron Crowe
BA (Hons), Barrister

Health and Medicine
Andrew Johnson
LLB (Hons), Barrister
Bramble Badenach-Nicolson
BA (Hons), Barrister

Health and Safety
Hayley Saunders
BA (Hons), Solicitor
Cameron Crowe
BA (Hons), Barrister

Introduction and Primary Authority
Iain MacDonald
BA (Oxon), Barrister
Helen Kirkman
BSC (Hons), DTS

Information
Michael Coley
LLB (Hons) (Lond), Barrister

Intellectual Property
Richard Roberts
BA (Oxon), Barrister
Alex Greenwood
LLB (Hons), Barrister

Interpretation of Consumer Law

Bradley Say
LLB (Hons), Barrister

Metrology and Hallmarking

George Spence-Jones
MEng (Hons), Barrister

Northern Ireland

Kevin McNamara
BTech (Hons), DTS, MCTSI

Prices

Wendy Potts
BA, DCA, CTSP, MCTSI

Product Safety

Christine Heemskerk
BSC (Econ), DTS, DMS, Chair CTSI 2012–13, 2015–16

Scotland

Neil Coltart
BSC, LLB, DTS, ILM, MAPEA, MCTSI

Territorial Jurisdiction

Kevin De Hann QC
MA (Cantab), Barrister
Ben Lloyd
LLB (Hons), LLM Barrister

Contributors

Jason Freeman
MA (Cantab), Barrister

Travel
Thomas Samuels
MA (Oxon), Barrister
Anna Medvinskaia
LLB (Hons), LLM (Cantab), Barrister
Michael Coley
LLB (Hons) (Lond), Barrister

Unfair Commercial Practices
Jason Freeman
MA (Cantab), Barrister
Jonathan Goulding
LLB (Hons), Barrister

Unfair Contract Terms
Jason Freeman
MA (Cantab), Barrister

Unfair Trading
Alison Lambert
LLB (Hons), Barrister
Alison Hollis
LLB (Hons), LLM Barrister

Wales
Timothy Keohane
DBA, DTS, FCTSI, MICA

First Edition

HHJ Ben Gumpert QC

MA (Cantab), Barrister

Chapters

Contents

Contents

Contents

Contents

Contents

Contents

Contents

Contents

Contents

Contents

Contents

Contents

Contents

Contents

Contents

Contents

l

Table of Abbreviations

ABA 2003	Anti-social Behaviour Act 2003
AB(S)A 2004	Antisocial Behaviour etc (Scotland) Act 2004
ASA	Advertising Standards Authority
ASBO	Anti-social behaviour order
ATOL	Air Travel Organisers' Licensing
AWA 2006	Animal Welfare Act 2006
AHW(S)A 2006	Animal Health and Welfare (Scotland) Act 2006
BBFC	British Board of Film Classification
BEIS	Department of Business, Energy and Industrial Strategy
BERR	Department for Business, Enterprise and Regulatory Reform
BIS	Department for Business, Innovation and Skills
BPR 2008	Business Protection from Misleading Marketing Regulations 2008
BRDO	Better Regulation Delivery Office
CA 2006	Companies Act 2006
CCA 1974	Consumer Credit Act 1974
CCA 2006	Consumer Credit Act 2006
CFA 2014	Children and Families Act 2014
CHIS	Covert human intelligence sources
CJA 1988	Criminal Justice Act 1988
CJEU	Court of Justice of the European Union
CLR(S)R 1999	Cigarette Lighter Refill (Safety) Regulations 1999
CMA	Competition and Markets Authority
CPA 1987	Consumer Protection Act 1987

CDPA 1988	Copyright, Designs and Patents Act 1988
CPR	Civil Procedure Rules
CPUTR 2008	Consumer Protection from Unfair Trading Regulations 2008
CRA 2015	Consumer Rights Act 2015
CTSI	Chartered Trading Standards Institute
CYPA 1933	Children and Young Persons Act 1933
DEA 2017	Digital Economy Act 2017
DECC	Department of Energy and Climate Change
Defra	Department for Environment Food and Rural Affairs
DETI	Department of Enterprise, Trade and Investment
DfE	Department for the Economy
EnA 2002	Enterprise Act 2002
EA 2016	Enterprise Act 2016
ECHR	European Convention for the Protection of Human Rights and Fundamental Freedoms
ECR 2002	Electronic Commerce (EC Directive) Regulations 2002
EIR 2011	Energy Information Regulations 2011
ETSD	European Technical Standards Directive
EU	European Union
EU(W)A 2018	European Union (Withdrawal) Act 2018
EU(WA)A 2020	European Union (Withdrawal Agreement) Act 2020
FA 2006	Fraud Act 2006
FCA	Financial Conduct Authority
FSA	Food Standards Agency
FSA 1990	Food Safety Act 1990
FSMA 2000	Financial Services and Markets Act 2000
GA 2005	Gambling Act 2005
HSE	Health and Safety Executive
H(TNC)(S)A 2016	Health (Tobacco, Nicotine etc and Care) (Scotland) Act 2016
LA 2003	Licensing Act 2003
LBRO	Local Better Regulation Office
LLP	Limited Liability Partnership

MCAD 2006	Misleading and Comparative Advertising Directive
MID	Directive 2004/22/EC of the European Parliament and of the Council on measuring instruments (Measuring Instruments Directive)
NAWI Directive	Council Directive 90/384/EEC relating to non-automatic weighing instruments
NIP 2015	Nicotine Inhaling Products (Age of Sale and Proxy Purchasing) Regulations 2015
Ofcom	Office of Communications
OFT	Office of Fair Trading
OS(P)A 1995	Olympic Symbol etc (Protection) Act 1995
PACE 1984	Police and Criminal Evidence Act 1984
PA(S)R 2015	Pyrotechnic Articles (Safety) Regulations 2015
PERR 2015	Packaging (Essential Requirements) Regulations 2015
PMO 2004	Price Marking Order 2004
POCA 2002	Proceeds of Crime Act 2002
PSA 2016	Psychoactive Substances Act 2016
PTLAR 2018	Package Travel and Linked Arrangements Regulations 2018
RESA 2008	Regulatory Enforcement and Sanctions Act 2008
RIPA 2000	Regulation of Investigatory Powers Act 2000
RIP(S)A 2000	Regulation of Investigatory Powers (Scotland) Act 2000
SECCI	Standard European Consumer Credit Information
SMDA 2013	Scrap Metal Dealers Act 2013
S(R)A 2010	Sunbeds (Regulation) Act 2010
TDA 1968	Trade Descriptions Act 1968
TPMS(S)A 2010	Tobacco and Primary Medical Services (Scotland) Act 2010
UCPD	Unfair Commercial Practices Directive
UGSA 1971	Unsolicited Goods and Services Act 1971
UTCCR 1999	Unfair Terms in Consumer Contracts Regulations 1999
VRA 1984	Video Recordings Act 1984
WMA 1985	Weights and Measures Act 1985

Table of Statutes

Other Jurisdiction

USA

Table of Statutory Instruments

Table of Retained EU Material

Table of EU Material

Table of Cases

A

B

E

F

G

H

K

M

N

P

Q

R

S

T

U

V

W

X

Y

Chapter 1

INTRODUCTION AND
PRIMARY AUTHORITY

Contents

INTRODUCTION

1.1 The origins of Inspectors of Weights and Measures in the United Kingdom can be traced to Magna Carta.

Magna Carta Clause 35

'Let there be one measure of wine throughout the whole kingdom, and one measure of ale; and one measure of corn; and one width of cloth.'

1.2 Before the last century the predominant interest of weights and measures inspectors was largely to ensure that customers buying essential products were not cheated by unscrupulous merchants and to ensure that dangerous goods were stored safely. For example, by the thirteenth century, there were local Assizes of Bread and Ale that inspected the quality and quantity of these common items. Bread had to be weighed against the King's standard pound and if a brewer or baker was found to have given a short measure they could be fined, put in the pillory or flogged. Bread was such an essential item of the British diet that its price was controlled from the twelfth century until 1815.

1.3 An important function of inspectors was to ensure that scales used by merchants were accurate. For example, the Weights and Measures Act 1889 legislated that every scale used for selling in trade had to be stamped and verified. However, there was still great inconsistency in practice because of local custom and inspectors found it difficult to enforce standard measures when faced with a local unit. For example the 'Scotch pint' of milk was actually half a gallon.

1

1.4 In the early twentieth century, inspectors spent a considerable amount of time lobbying Government to legislate against the practice of merchants including the wrapper in the weight of packets of tea. It was estimated in 1908 that some £1million was spent buying paper rather than tea. In the second part of the twentieth century a perennial problem was the practice of 'clocking' second-hand cars (reducing the odometer reading) by dishonest second-hand car traders and numerous prosecutions were brought against such traders. Whilst the fraudulent practice has been reduced by the DVLA compiling data of mileage of cars on a transfer of ownership a national survey carried out in 2017 found that a quarter of UK dealers expressed concern that clocking and mileage discrepancies had worsened.

1.5 It is arguable, however, that the primary rationale for the Pink Book was founded sixty years ago when the Committee on Consumer Protection (the 'Molony Committee') was appointed by the Government to review the working of the existing legislation relating to merchandise marks and certification trade marks, and to consider and report what changes in the law and what other measures, if any, were desirable for the further protection of the consuming public. In Chapter 2 of its Final Report, published in 1962, the Molony Committee sought to explain the meaning of 'consumer protection, but concluded that it was:

> 'an amorphous conception that cannot be defined. It consists of those instances where the law intervenes to impose safeguards in favour of purchasers and hire-purchasers, together with the activities of a number of organisations, variously inspired, the object or effect of which is to procure fair and satisfying treatment for the domestic buyer. From another viewpoint 'consumer protection' may be regarded as those measures which contribute, directly or indirectly, to the consumers assurance that he will buy goods of suitable quality appropriate to his purpose; that they will give him reasonable use, and that if he has just complaint there will be a means of redress[1].'

[1] The scale of this task can be illustrated by some local eccentricities which persisted well into the fourteenth century – in Devon, for example, there were 18 ounces to the pound and 16 pounds to the stone when measuring cheese or butter (*Tavistock Abbey: A Study in the Social and Economic History of Devon*, HPR Finberg, cited in *The Time Traveller's Guide to Medieval England*, Ian Mortimer).

1.6 The Trade Descriptions Act 1968 ('TDA 1968') flowed from the Molony Committee's recommendations for reform and together with the Food and Drugs Act 1955 and the Weights and Measures Act 1963 was considered to provide 'comprehensive protection of the public, and trade and commerce in those dealings in goods which concern everyone of us'[1]. This 'consumerism' period also saw the introduction of the Fair Trading Act in 1973 and the Consumer Credit Act in 1974 which followed the Crowther Committee Report.

[1] Preface to 'The Trade Descriptions Act 1968' – JA O'Keefe (Butterworths 1968).

1.7 Whilst modern-day trading standards services still have, as their main objectives, consumer protection and fair-trading, the areas which they have become either obliged or expected to enforce have increased both in size and complexity. Local authority trading standards and regulatory departments are now required to enforce standards in a wide variety of other disciplines. Copyright, trademarks and counterfeit goods investigations are now part of the staple diet of trading standards officers' work. The Consumer Protection from Unfair Trading Regulations 2008 ('CPUTR 2008') have forced investigators and prosecutors to embrace a European jurisprudential approach which was unfamiliar to many. The reality is that the work of trading standards services now impacts on nearly all aspects of a consumer's daily life.

1.8 The increased regulation faced by businesses small and large caused concern within the business community and there was extensive press commentary about how the burdens of red tape were causing a drag on enterprise. This fed into the political process and resulted in the Regulatory Enforcement and Sanctions Act 2008 which had the objective of ensuring that sanctions sought against business were proportionate to the offence committed and sought to provide consistency of decision making by the Primary Authority scheme, which is of considerable importance and discussed in greater detail below.

Brexit

1.9 In order to effect the departure of the UK from the EU, Parliament passed the European Union (Withdrawal) Act 2018 ('EU(W)A 2018') and the European Union (Withdrawal Agreement) Act 2020 ('EU(WA)A 2020'), which provided the UK Government with, among other things, powers to ensure the continued effectiveness of EU laws retained after Brexit. Section 8 of EU(W)A 2018 provides Government departments with the powers to produce delegated legislation to 'prevent, remedy or mitigate . . . . any failure of retained EU law to operate effectively, or . . . any other deficiency'.

1.10 There are a substantial number of Exit Regulations designed to ensure that retained EU laws will continue to have effect. Implementation of the Northern Ireland Protocol (part of the Withdrawal Agreement) also required the passing and amendment of Exit Regulations. These provisions took effect from 'IP completion day' (currently 31 December 2020). All Exit Regulations which contained commencement provisions referring to 'exit day' (which was 31 January 2020) are to be read as referring to IP completion day[3].

[3]   Paragraph 1(1) of Sch 5(1) to the EU(WA)A 2020.

1.11 The Exit Regulations do not seek to make substantive changes to the purposes of the laws they amend. Their primary purpose is to amend EU references in UK legislation that implement EU law, for example by replacing the words 'Member States' with the 'UK'. However, the Exit Regulations also transfer functions, that were previously conferred on EU entities, onto UK institutions and revoke certain pan-European consumer schemes that will no longer operate after the UK has left the EU, such as the EU online dispute resolution platform.

1.12 An example of a consumer law Exit Regulation is the Consumer Protection (Amendment etc.) (EU Exit) Regulations 2018[1], which, for example, replaces references to the 'European Economic Area' with the 'United Kingdom'[2]. The Exit Regulations apply in all areas of consumer law that implement EU law. In addition to general consumer protection measures (see above) there are Exit Regulations in relation to intellectual property[3], consumer credit[4], metrology[5], travel[6], product safety[7], age-restricted sales[8], food[9], environmental standards[10] and animal health and welfare[11]. The volume of Exit Regulations is, as will be seen, considerable and the measures referred to above do not provide a comprehensive or exhaustive list. It therefore remains important for practitioners to consider carefully whether statutory provisions implementing, or connected with, retained EU law have been amended.

1   SI 2018/1326, which also amends the Consumer Rights Act 2015; Consumer Rights (Payment Surcharges) Regulations 2012; Consumer Contracts (Information, Cancellation and Additional Charges) Regulations 2013; Crystal Glass (Descriptions) Regulations 1973; Footwear (Indication of Composition) Labelling Regulations 1995; Alternative Dispute Resolution for Consumer Disputes (Competent Authorities and Information) Regulations 2015 and revokes Regulation (EU) 524/2013 – Online Dispute Resolution).

2   For example, see reg 6(2) amending reg 27(5) of the CPUTR.

3   Trade Marks (Amendment etc.) (EU Exit) Regulations 2019; Intellectual Property (Copyright and Related Rights) (Amendment) (EU Exit) Regulations 2019; Designs and International Trade Marks (Amendment etc.) (EU Exit) Regulations 2019. Each of these provisions is subject to amendment by the (currently) draft Intellectual Property (Amendment etc.) (EU Exit) Regulations 2020.

4   Consumer Credit (Amendment) (EU Exit) Regulations 2018.

5   Weighing and Measuring Equipment and Meters (Amendment of Secondary Legislation) (EU Exit) Regulations 2018.

6   Timeshare, Holiday Products, Resale and Exchange Contracts (Amendment etc.) (EU Exit) Regulations 2018; Package Travel and Linked Travel Arrangements (Amendment) (EU Exit) Regulations 2018; Air Passenger Rights and Air Travel Organisers' Licensing (Amendment) (EU Exit) Regulations 2019. The latter two of these Regulations have certain definitions substituted from 1 September 2020 by the Road Vehicles (Approval) Regulations 2020, but these will not take effect until IP completion day,

7   See, for example, Product Safety and Metrology etc. (Amendment etc.) (EU Exit) Regulations 2019 but see also the significant amendments made as to geographical application (exclusion of Northern Ireland) by the Product Safety and Metrology etc. (Amendment to Extent and Meaning of Market) (EU Exit) Regulations 2020; Construction Products (Amendment etc.) (EU Exit) Regulations 2019.

8   Tobacco Products and Nicotine Inhaling Products (Amendment etc.) (EU Exit) Regulations 2019.

9   General Food Law (Amendment etc.) (EU Exit) Regulations 2019; Nutrition (Amendment) (EU Exit) Regulations 2019; Food (Amendment) (EU Exit) Regulations 2019; Food Additives, Flavourings, Enzymes and Extraction Solvents (Amendment etc) (EU Exit) Regulations 2019; Genetically Modified Food and Feed (Amendment etc.) (EU Exit) Regulations 2019; Materials and Articles in Contact with Food (Amendment) (EU Exit) Regulations 2019; Novel Food (Amendment) (EU Exit) Regulations 2019; Contaminants in Food (Amendment) (EU Exit) Regulations 2019; Quick-frozen Foodstuffs (Amendment) (EU Exit) Regulations 2019.

10 Ecodesign for Energy-Related Products and Energy Information (Amendment) (EU Exit) Regulations 2019; Detergents (Amendment) (EU Exit) Regulations 2019.

11 Animal Health and Welfare (Miscellaneous Amendments) (England) (EU Exit) Regulations 2018; Animal Health and Welfare (Miscellaneous Amendments) (Wales) (EU Exit) Regulations 2019 (as amended); Livestock (Records, Identification and Movement) (Amendment) (EU Exit) Regulations 2019 (and see also the various regional Regulations); Official Controls (Animals, Feed and Food) (England) (Amendment) (EU Exit) Regulations 2018; Official Controls (Animals, Feed and Food) (Northern Ireland) (Amendment) (EU Exit) Regulations 2019; Transmissible Spongiform Encephalopathies and Animal By-Products (Amendment etc.) (EU Exit) Regulations 2019; Veterinary Surgeons and Animal Welfare (Amendment) (EU Exit) Regulations 2019; Farriers and Animal Health (Amendment) (EU Exit) Regulations 2019; Animal Health, Plant Health, Seeds and Seed Potatoes (Amendment) (EU Exit) Regulations 2019; Animal Health, Alien Species in Aquaculture and Invasive Non-native Species (Amendment) (EU Exit) Regulations 2019; Animal Welfare (Amendment) (EU Exit) Regulations 2019; Trade in Animals and Related Products (Amendment) (EU Exit) Regulations 2019; Zoonotic Disease Eradication and Control (Amendment) (EU Exit) Regulations 2019; Official Controls for Feed, Food and Animal Health and Welfare (Amendment etc) (EU Exit) Regulations 2019; Equine (Records, Identification and Movement) (Amendment) (EU Exit) Regulations 2019; Animals (Legislative Functions) (EU Exit) Regulations 2019.

Wales

1.13 Currently, laws made by the Welsh Parliament (Senedd Cymru)[1], which are, ostensibly, only applicable to Wales, still form part of the law of England and Wales. This is because England and Wales – unlike Scotland and Northern Ireland – share a single legal jurisdiction. Following a referendum in March 2011, the National Assembly for Wales was granted further powers to make laws known as Assembly Bills. Acts may include subordinate legislation. The Senedd's approach to legislation is that it is made bilingually rather than made first in English and then translated into Welsh.

1   The 'National Assembly for Wales' or 'Welsh Assembly' changed its name in May 2020 to the 'Welsh Parliament' or in Welsh, 'Senedd Cymru' (see the Government of Wales Act 2006, s 1(1)).

1.14 The 20 areas in which the Senedd has competence to make laws are listed in the Government of Wales Act 2006, Sch 7A. They include:

- animal health and welfare;
- consumer protection, including the sale and supply of goods to consumers, consumer guarantees, hire purchase, trade descriptions, advertising and price indications, apart from in relation to food (including packaging and other materials which come into contact with food), agricultural and horticultural products, animals and animal products, seeds, fertilisers and pesticides (and things treated by virtue of any enactment as pesticides);
- food and food products: food safety (including packaging and other materials which come into contact with food); protection of interests of consumers in relation to food.

The Wales Act 2017 is an enabling Act which changes the basis of the legislative competence of the Senedd, moving from a conferred powers model to a reserved powers model. The Act devolves additional executive powers to Welsh Ministers and includes provisions which set out the constitutional relationship of the Senedd and Welsh Government within the United Kingdom's constitutional arrangements.

1.15 The first major piece of regulatory legislation, using the new powers, was the Food Hygiene Rating (Wales) Act 2013 which saw Wales become the first country in the UK to introduce a mandatory scheme requiring food businesses to openly display their hygiene rating. However, the National Assembly had previously introduced Wales-only laws in a variety of areas such as sunbeds (under the Sunbeds (Regulation) Act 2010), charges for single use carrier bags (under the Climate Change Act 2008) and prohibiting the use of collars designed to administer an electric shock on cats and dogs (under the Animal Welfare Act 2006).

1.16 The Wales Bill was introduced into the House of Commons on 7 June 2016. It amends the Government of Wales Act 2006 and makes provision about the functions of the Welsh Ministers giving effect to the Government's policy of establishing a 'reserved powers' model for devolution to Wales.

Scotland

1.17 Although the majority of offences in Scotland are common law (for example there is no Theft Act) most of the offences reported to trading standards services have a statutory basis. Many of these offences derive from legislation that applies across the United Kingdom; however, it is important to note that the processes and evidential rules are quite different in Scotland. An illustration of this can be seen in a passage from *Hamilton v HMA*[1] in relation to the Trade Descriptions Act 1968 ('TDA 1968'):

> 'No analogy can usefully be drawn as to what may be the correct application of the wording of section 19(1) to Scottish procedure for what may happen South of the border.'

[1] 1997 SLT 31 per Lord Justice General Hope at pp 34G–34H.

1.18 Perhaps the best known evidential rule in Scotland is the requirement for corroboration, this requirement was classically set out in *Morton v HMA*[1]:

> 'No person can be convicted of a crime or a statutory offence except where the legislature otherwise directs, unless there is evidence of at least two witnesses implicating the person accused with the commission of the crime or offence with which he is charged. This rule has proved an invaluable safeguard in the practice of our criminal courts against unjust convictions and it is a rule from which the courts ought not to depart.'

[1] 1938 JC 50 per Lord Justice Clerk Aitchison.

1.19 Nowadays this statement might perhaps be better read as 'at least two independent sources' given the development of forensic science and the reliance on documentary evidence in many cases. The consequence of this evidential rule is that not only the offence but every essential fact in relation to it requires to be corroborated.

1.20 The terms of reference of the 2011 Review of Scottish Law and Practice – the *Carloway Review* – required it to consider issues relating to the right of access to legal advice, police questioning of suspects, the operation of the current system of detention, evidence (including corroboration and adverse inference) and issues arising from the Criminal Procedure (Legal Assistance, Detention and Appeals) (Scotland) Act 2010. On the issue of corroboration, the Review was 'in no doubt that the requirement of corroboration should be entirely abolished for all categories of crime'. In December 2012 the Scottish Government sought views, in a public consultation, on additional safeguards required following the removal of the requirement for corroboration.

1.21 The successful prosecution of an accused will always rely on the care with which the investigation is carried out and the subsequent report to the Procurator Fiscal. This means that anyone investigating offences must be sure that they have followed the correct procedures and recorded their compliance. Some investigations may require the use of covert surveillance techniques such as directed surveillance or the use of covert human intelligence sources, the proper use of these is regulated by the Regulation of Investigatory Powers (Scotland) Act 2000. The Act requires that these techniques are only used when it is proportionate and necessary for the purposes of preventing or detecting crime or preventing disorder, in the interests of public safety or for the purpose of protecting public health.

1.22 Each local authority will have adopted processes that allow for these covert techniques to be considered and if appropriate authorised. The admissibility of any evidence gathered using these covert techniques relies on the investigating officer following these procedures so it is vital that they are followed and compliance with them properly recorded. If the investigation requires it the Regulation of Investigatory Powers Act 2000 outlines the requirements for acquiring communications data.

1.23 Another significant difference in the criminal justice process is the fact that all prosecutions in Scotland are dealt with through the Crown Office and Procurator Fiscal's Service. The majority of trading standards cases are prosecuted by Procurators Fiscal, for the area in which the offence has allegedly taken place, although cases heard in the High Court of Justiciary will be prosecuted by Advocates Depute.

1.24 Once a report, alleging that offence/s have been committed, has been submitted for consideration by the Procurator Fiscal, they determine whether or not the report should be accepted and, if so, in which court and whether under summary or solemn procedure. In a formal sense it is the Procurator Fiscal who directs investigations although in most cases that are dealt with by trading standards services the investigating officer will have presented a report covering all the necessary evidential elements.

1.25 In assessing whether or not to proceed to prosecution the Procurator Fiscal will consider a number of matters. Most obviously whether the alleged offence is known in the law of Scotland, whether there is sufficient evidence to prove a crime has taken place and who committed it, whether there is a reasonable prospect of securing a conviction and, perhaps most importantly, whether the prosecution is in the public interest?

1.26 The Criminal Procedure (Scotland) Act 1995 covers a large number of procedural matters including the submission of documentary evidence, however in most instances a witness will be required to speak to any evidence that is being led and indeed except in the instance of expert evidence, two witnesses will be required.

1.27 Although the majority of the offences reported to the Procurator Fiscal by trading standards services will be tried under summary procedure, where they are conducted under solemn procedure the jury will consist of 15 members. There are a number of other differences in Scotland, including the vocabulary of the criminal justice process and perhaps, most famously, there are three verdicts in Scottish Courts including 'not proven'.

1.28 The Scottish Parliament is able to make laws – see the Scotland Act 1998, s 29 – but this section limits the competence of the Scottish Parliament to do so. The Scotland Act 1998, s 29(2) provides that a provision is outside the legislative competence of the Scottish Parliament if certain criteria apply – one of which is that a provision is outside that competence if it would form part of the law of any country or territory other than Scotland. This provision, therefore, prevents the Scottish Parliament from legislating matters affecting the law in England, Wales or elsewhere.

Northern Ireland

1.29 When the Northern Ireland Executive was formed under Devolution in 1998, it gave, through its Programme for Government, a commitment to publish a Consumer Strategy for Northern Ireland. Underpinning that strategy was an agreed policy position requiring that consumers and law-abiding businesses in Northern Ireland should be afforded a level of protection which was at least on a par with that enjoyed by their counterparts in England, Scotland and Wales.

1.30 Among the devolved administrations, only in Northern Ireland is consumer protection a transferred (or devolved) function. In Northern Ireland, trading standards, in contrast to Great Britain's local authority model, is a *central government* function, and, as a consequence, a national service[1]. The Trading Standards Service comprises some 60 staff with headquarters in Belfast and regional offices in Londonderry, Ballymena, Armagh and Enniskillen, covering the North, East, South and West of the country respectively. The Service is now positioned as a business area within the Department for the Economy (DfE)[2]. The staff are civil servants and like their 'mainstream' departmental colleagues, accountable to the Minister for the Economy.

[1]   With the exception of certain trading standards functions such as product safety, which are delivered by district councils.
[2]   It was formerly a part of the Department for Enterprise, Trade and Investment ('DETI').

1.31 The Service's enforcement agenda has, therefore, been shaped largely by legislation covering areas such as trade descriptions (though the 1968 Act has now been largely repealed and replaced by a successor regime dealing with unfair commercial practices); weights and measures; fair trading; unfair terms in consumer contracts; consumer credit; hallmarking; estate agency; property misdescriptions; prices and price marking; trademarks and timeshare.

1.32 Trading Standards Officers in Northern Ireland, however, unlike many of their counterparts in Great Britain, have no rights of audience in any courts and, as a result, all of the Service's prosecutions are processed by Northern Ireland's Public Prosecution Service ('PPS') which is part of the Department of the Director of Public Prosecutions. Cases are sent to the PPS from the Trading Standards Service with a recommendation for the commencement of legal proceedings, and, if proceedings are directed, the case will be prosecuted by a PPS official or, more commonly, counsel instructed by the PPS.

1.33 The PPS, in contrast to, for example, the Crown Prosecution Service in Great Britain, has no investigative function. It acts solely to direct (or not) on the evidence compiled by the Trading Standards Service, and to process the investigation through to a hearing, and to an appeal if required. The Trading Standards Officer's role in court – in most cases the magistrates court – is to assist the prosecutor and to act as a witness for DfE, in whose name all trading standards cases are taken.

1.34 The Trading Standards function in Northern Ireland is positioned, in notable contrast to Great Britain, within the same central government structure as DfE's other consumer affairs functions. The Northern Ireland Government's functions, therefore, relating to enforcement: advice; intervention: outreach: marketing: policy, legislation, and sponsorship of the Northern Ireland Consumer Council, are all positioned (and accommodated) together within DfE's Consumer Affairs Branch.

1.35 Along with the Northern Ireland Executive's desire to maintain parity of consumer protection with Great Britain, the UK-wide transposition of European Instruments has had the effect of not merely harmonising the consumer protection provisions across the European Union, but in addition, has significantly reinforced the commonality of the consumer protection framework within the United Kingdom. Although there may be equivalence, or even mirroring, of protection, there will inevitably be minor differences in the section or article numbers referencing the particular provision. There may also be more significant differences arising from the implementation of the Northern Ireland Protocol, a process which at the time of drafting remained subject to political deadlock in certain areas. Drafting nuances and preferences should, therefore, be represented accurately in, for example, drafting summonses, informations or other legal instruments. On occasions there have been drafting anomalies in the transposition of a directive into Northern Ireland-specific law. The unique position of Northern Ireland is also reflected in the application of other EU measures, such as EU Regulation 2019/1020 on Market Surveillance and Compliance of Products[1].

[1] Guidance as to the application of the Regulation, produced by the Office for Product Safety & Standards, can be found at https://assets.publishing.service.gov.uk/government/uploads/system/uploads/attachment_data/file/993170/guidance-msc-regulation-article-4-msas.pdf. Note that Regulation (EU) No 2019/1020 has been implemented in relation to Northern Ireland by the Market Surveillance (Northern Ireland) Regulations 2021.

Local weights and measures authorities

1.36 There are now a wide variety of criminal offences and civil infringements that apply across the spectrum of commercial practices. Although legislation is principally concerned with the protection of consumers, some of the statutes enshrine the rights and interests of traders and their intellectual property. The responsibility for enforcing this criminal legislation is usually the statutory duty of 'local weights and measures authorities' through their trading standards service.

1.37 'Local weights and measures authorities' are defined in the Weights and Measures Act 1985, s 69:

69 Local weights and measures authorities

(1) In England, the local weights and measures authority shall be—

    (a) for each non-metropolitan county, metropolitan district and London borough, the council of that county, district or borough,

    (b) for the City of London and the Inner and Middle Temples, the Common Council of the City of London, and

    (c) for the Isles of Scilly, the Council of the Isles of Scilly.

(2)   In Wales, the local weights and measures authority for each county shall be the county council and for each county borough shall be the county borough council.

(3)   In Scotland, the local weights and measures authority for the area of each council constituted under section 2 of the Local Government etc. (Scotland) Act 1994 shall be the council for that area.

1.38 There are now over 200 local authorities exercising trading standards functions. They have duties and responsibilities for enforcing a wide range of national and European laws through both criminal and civil law processes. In addition to regulatory activities, most services provide advice, information and education to consumers and businesses in order to make them aware of their rights and obligations – although there are no powers, as such, to intervene or negotiate on behalf of consumers in disputes.

CONSUMER LAW INSTITUTIONS

Government

1.39 The majority of legislation enforced by Trading Standards (from July 2016) falls under the Department for Business, Energy and Industrial Strategy ('BEIS') which was formed by the merger of the Department for Business, Innovation and Skills ('BIS') and the Department of Energy and Climate Change ('DECC'). BIS was itself created by the merger of the Department for Business, Enterprise and Regulatory Reform and the Department of Innovation, Universities and Skills in 2009.

1.40 The BEIS legislation primarily comprises areas concerned with fair trading, product safety, weights and measures, prices, consumer credit, estate agents, package travel, timeshare, video recordings and intellectual property. BEIS does not have a responsibility towards areas such as age restricted sales, food and animal health. Environmental matters – covering waste, energy and climate change were previously spread across a number of Departments. For example, the Single Use Carrier Bags Charges (England) Order 2015[1] was the responsibility of the Department for the Environment, Food and Rural Affairs ('Defra'). The Scottish Government has responsibility for some of the non-BEIS legislative functions, for example the Single Use Carrier Bag Charge (Scotland) Regulations 2014[2].

[1]   SI 2015/776.
[2]   SSI 2014/161.

1.41 No government minister has a remit specifically dedicated to consumer matters. On 13 February 2020, Paul Scully MP was appointed as the Parliamentary under Secretary of State for Small Business, Consumers, and Labour Markets. This post has responsibility for a wide range of issues including consumer and competition, labour markets, postal affairs and the retail sector. The Government's wide-ranging reforms to the consumer, competition and credit regimes which started in 2011 were completed by March 2014 and resulted in the establishment of a number of new or revamped organisations, changed responsibilities and a Consumer Protection Partnership.

The Competition and Markets Authority

1.42 The Competition and Markets Authority ('CMA'), which was established under the Enterprise and Regulatory Reform Act 2013, came into being in shadow form in October 2013 and took on its full powers from April 2014 taking over many of the functions of the Competition Commission and the Office of Fair Trading ('OFT'). The CMA is an independent non-ministerial department. The OFT, which had responsibility for both protecting consumers and promoting competition, was a non-ministerial department. It was established under the Fair Trading Act 1973 and ceased to exist on 31 March 2014.

Citizens Advice

1.43 From April 2012 a Citizens Advice consumer service took over from the OFT-run Consumer Direct. This contact centre service provided free, practical advice on a range of consumer matters, including information on consumer rights and practical guidance on individual problems and how to gain redress. The responsibility for the operation of the consumer helpline in Scotland was transferred to Advice Direct Scotland in April 2019. Citizens Advice has also undertaken consumer advocacy responsibilities for representing consumers' interests in areas such as gas, electricity and postal services as well as unregulated sectors. Consumer Futures, which was formerly Consumer Focus, and represented consumers across regulated markets, was abolished in April 2014, with all its functions transferred to other bodies (Citizens Advice, Citizens Advice Scotland and Consumer Council for Northern Ireland). Citizens Advice also took responsibility from the OFT for the national coordination of consumer education in Great Britain.

The Financial Conduct Authority

1.44 The Financial Services Act 2012 'abolished' the Financial Services Authority, renaming it as the Financial Conduct Authority ('FCA'). The FCA regulates the financial services industry in the UK. In 2014, the FCA took over the OFT's regulatory responsibility for the consumer credit industry. The OFT's anti-money laundering powers and responsibilities passed to the FCA in respect of consumer credit financial institutions, and to HMRC, in respect of estate agents. The Prudential Regulation Authority ('PRA') is a part of the Bank of England and responsible for the prudential regulation and supervision of banks, building societies, credit unions, insurers and major investment firms.

The National Trading Standards Estate Agency Team

1.45 The OFT's functions and powers to prohibit or warn estate agents, and to authorise estate agents redress schemes, under the Estate Agents Act 1979, were transferred in 2014 to Powys County Council[1], as 'the lead enforcement authority'.

[1] Public Bodies (Abolition of The National Consumer Council and Transfer of The Office of Fair Trading's Functions in Relation to Estate Agents Etc) Order 2014, SI 2014/631.

Consumer Protection Partnership

1.46 The Consumer Protection Partnership ('CPP'), formerly known as the Strategic Intelligence, Prevention and Enforcement Partnership ('SIPEP') was formed in April 2012 and includes the National Trading Standards Board, Trading Standards Scotland, the Department for the Economy in Northern Ireland, the Financial Conduct Authority, the Chartered Trading Standards Institute, Consumer Council for Northern Ireland, and the Citizens Advice Service. Its purpose is to identify areas where there is a risk that consumers will face harm and, where action is not already in place, to agree actions to tackle the issues as necessary. The fourth report on the Partnership's work to date and planned future activities was published in October 2017.

Local authority advisory bodies

1.47 Local Authorities Coordination of Trading Standards ('LACOTS') was originally established in 1978 with the aim of supporting and attempting to ensure that uniform enforcement was conducted by Trading Standards departments. LACOTS subsequently expanded to cover other areas such as food safety, gambling, civil registration and a number of other enforcement functions and, as a result, changed its title to Local Authorities Coordinators of Regulatory Services ('LACORS'). LACORS was renamed Local Government Regulation ('LGR') in 2010 but was disbanded a year later by the Local Government Association.

Better regulation bodies

1.48 The Local Better Regulation Office ('LBRO') was established in 2007, initially set up as a private company limited by guarantee. LBRO became an executive non-departmental public body and given a range of statutory duties and powers (including the operation of the Primary Authority scheme) under the Regulatory Enforcement and Sanctions Act 2008. LBRO was dissolved in April 2012, and its functions taken over by the Better Regulation Delivery Office ('BRDO'). BRDO was then incorporated into a new structure in April 2016, combining with the National Measurement and Regulation Office, known as Regulatory Delivery ('RD'), a directorate of BEIS. The Office for Product Safety and Standards ('OPSS') was created in January 2018 by BEIS and now carries on the work formerly undertaken by RD.

British Hallmarking Council

1.49 Following the structural changes referred to above, OPSS now also has policy (legislative) responsibility for the hallmarking of precious metal articles. The British Hallmarking Council, established and governed by the Hallmarking Act 1973, is an Executive Non-Departmental Public Body established by the Hallmarking Act 1973. The Council is funded by the UK's four Assay Offices.

Chartered Trading Standards Institute

1.50 In 2013 the Chartered Trading Standards Institute ('CTSI') took over the OFT's role in providing (most) business information to retailers. The CMA retains primary responsibility for business education on unfair contract terms. The OFT-managed consumer code approval scheme was succeeded by a self-funding model established by the CTSI as from April 2013.

National Trading Standards and Trading Standards Scotland

1.51 National Trading Standards was set up in 2012 by the Government as part of changes to the consumer protection landscape. It brings together representatives of Trading Standards from England and Wales to prioritise, fund and coordinate national and regional enforcement cases. With effect from April 2013, the NTS took over some coordination and database-management functions previously undertaken by the OFT. Trading Standards Scotland fulfils a similar function to NTS in Scotland.

Designated enforcers

1.52 Under the Enterprise Act 2002 a designated enforcer is any public or private body in the UK which the Secretary of State designates in a Statutory Instrument, having identified that the person or body has the protection of the collective interests of consumers as one of its purposes. The following bodies are designated: the Civil Aviation Authority, the Financial Conduct Authority, Ofcom, Ofwat, the Gas and Electricity Markets Authority (Ofgem), the Information Commissioner's Office, the Office of Road and Rail, the Consumer's Association (Which?) and the Northern Ireland Authority for Utility Regulation ('UREGNI').

Food

1.53 The Food Standards Agency ('FSA') is an independent Government department established by the Food Standards Act 1999. In 2010 Machinery of Government changes resulted in the Department of Health ('DoH') taking over nutrition policy in England but in Scotland and Northern Ireland the FSA stayed in control. Responsibility for nutrition policy in Wales lies with the Welsh Government. The DoH and Department for Environment, Food and Rural Affairs ('Defra') took over food labelling policy in England, where this does not relate to food safety or nutrition, but the FSA continued to be in charge of labelling policy matters in Wales, Scotland and Northern Ireland.

1.54 In 2015 Food Standards Scotland ('FSS') replaced the FSA in Scotland. FSS was established by the Food (Scotland) Act 2015 as a non-ministerial office, part of the Scottish Administration, alongside, but separate from, the Scottish Government. The FSA maintains overall responsibility for food safety and food hygiene for the remainder of the UK. The FSA in Wales is based in Cardiff and the FSA in Northern Ireland is based in Belfast. The Welsh Food Advisory Committee and the Northern Ireland Food Advisory Committee provide advice or information to the FSA about matters connected with its functions, including, in particular, matters affecting or otherwise relating to Wales and Northern Ireland, respectively.

1.55 The FSA's National Food Crime Unit ('NFCU') works with partners to protect consumers from serious criminal activity that impacts on the safety or authenticity of food.

PRIMARY AUTHORITY

Introduction

1.56 Part 2 of the Regulatory Enforcement and Sanctions Act 2008 ('RESA 2008') established a Primary Authority Scheme ('PA Scheme') with the aim of securing co-ordination and consistency of regulatory enforcement by local authorities. The PA Scheme is described as enabling 'business to form a legal partnership with a local authority (known as the primary authority) which can provide . . . assured, consistent regulatory advice that makes it simpler and easier to comply with environmental health, trading standards and fire safety legislation. Enforcing authorities should respect this advice . . . '[1]. The PA Scheme was introduced to address concerns regarding local authority regulatory enforcement, including inconsistent advice, wasted resources, duplication of effort and the absence of an effective dispute resolution mechanism when two local authorities cannot agree on a regulatory approach.

[1] Primary Authority: A guide for businesses.

1.57 The PA Scheme has been expanded by the amendments made in the Enterprise Act 2016 ('EA 2016'), which came into force substantively from 1 October 2017. The most important changes were to extend eligibility to more businesses and pre-start-up businesses; to make it easier for businesses in regulated groups to participate and to establish a role for certain national regulators. The amended Pt 2 should be considered alongside the Co-ordination of Regulatory Enforcement Regulations 2017 (the 'CORE Regulations')[1], which contain important provision on the definition of enforcement action and the statutory referral process under RESA 2008, Sch 4A.

[1] SI 2017/835; the Regulations replace the Co-ordination of Regulatory Enforcement (Enforcement Action) Order 2009, SI 2009/665 (as amended), the Co-ordination of Regulatory Enforcement (Regulatory Functions in Scotland and Northern Ireland) Order 2009, SI 2009/669 and the Co-ordination of Regulatory Enforcement (Procedure for References to LBRO) Order 2009, SI 2009/670.

1.58 Part 1 of RESA 2008 established the Local Better Regulation Office ('LBRO') which was the statutory body that was originally the operator of the scheme. The LBRO was quickly replaced by the Better Regulation Delivery Office ('BRDO') in 2012. In April 2016 BRDO was incorporated into Regulatory Delivery ('RD'), a directorate of the Department for Business, Energy and Industrial Strategy, now the Office for Product Safety and Standards ('OPSS'). OPSS operates the PA Scheme[1] and is responsible for issuing guidance on how the scheme operates[2], maintaining the primary authority register and operating the review mechanism under RESA 2008, Sch 4A. New statutory guidance on the PA Scheme was issued by RD in October 2017[3]. A handbook on Primary Authority (the 'PA Handbook') giving further guidance on the operation of the scheme was previously maintained by RD, but the Handbook was withdrawn in October 2017. Current guidance appears on the OPSS web pages.

[1] OPSS's functions under Pt 2 apply in Scotland and Northern Ireland in respect of matters that are reserved. The Regulatory Reform (Scotland) Act 2014 creates a legal framework for implementation of Primary Authority arrangements relating to the Devolved regulatory responsibilities of Local Authorities in Scotland, however, this is not yet in force.
[2] Where OPSS exercises the Secretary of State's function of giving guidance, provision is made for it to consult Welsh Ministers.
[3] Given under the Regulatory Enforcement and Sanctions Act 2008, s 30A.

Background to primary authority

1.59 The rationale underpinning the PA Scheme can principally be found in the Hampton Review on reducing administrative burdens[1], which reported that 'A highly fragmented system means that business is more likely to be on the receiving end of conflicting advice' which could 'impose undue burdens'[2].

[1] *Reducing administrative burdens effective inspection and enforcement.* This report, and the subsequent Macrory Review, *Regulatory Justice: Making Sanctions Effective*, November 2006, formed the foundation for the Regulatory Enforcement and Sanctions Act 2008.
[2] Paragraph 4.11.

1.60 In the Explanatory Notes to RESA 2008 it is stated that 'Uncoordinated action means that businesses receive unnecessary inspections and conflicting advice, while a lack of communication amongst local authorities results in duplication of effort'. It is stated that the PA Scheme 'makes provision for more consistent and co-ordinated regulatory enforcement by local authorities'.

1.61 The Government Consultation on the draft RESA 2008 Bill disclosed the thrust of the PA Scheme[1]:

'The Primary Authority principle is based on the core idea that a business operating across the UK should be able to rely on a single local authority for regulatory advice and support. For example, a multi-site retailer who seeks guidance from one local authority on product labelling should feel assured that if the guidance is followed, it will not be challenged in any of its individual outlets by other local authorities.'

[1] Better Regulation Executive, Consultation on the Draft Regulatory Enforcement and Sanctions Bill, May 2007, para 3.7.

1.62 The most important and contentious aspect of the PA Scheme is the capacity of a local authority PA to block enforcement action, by another enforcer, against a business that it has a PA relationship with. The argument that this was undemocratic because it centralises enforcement power with a PA, thereby removing local control of enforcement decision-making[1], was rejected during the passage of RESA 2008 through Parliament. A proposed amendment, removing the power of a PA to direct that enforcement action should not be taken, was rejected by Government on the basis that its removal 'would not deliver the certainty that businesses have the right to expect'[2].

[1] Advanced in the House of Lords by Baroness Turner of Camden 'For one council, or LBRO, to direct another council not to take enforcement action is undemocratic, and an interference in the principles of the judicial system. In the case of LBRO directing a council not to take action this also amounts to a centralisation of power' (House of Lords, 28 November 2007).
[2] HL Deb 28 January 2008 c GC235.

Scope of the Primary Authority Scheme

1.63 The scope of the scheme is set out in ss 22A–22C of RESA 2008, which defines the key elements of the PA relationship by reference to the PA, the regulated business and any qualifying enforcer. In general terms, there are five questions that need to be considered in determining whether proposed enforcement action falls within the scope of the PA Scheme.

(a)   Is the person to be enforced against a 'regulated person' or a member of a 'regulated group' under the PA Scheme?

(b) Is the enforcement action proposed by a qualifying regulator?

(c) Does the proposed enforcement action concern a 'relevant function' covered by RESA 2008?

(d) Has 'advice and guidance' been given to the regulated person or member of a 'regulated group' under the PA Scheme?

(e) Does the proposed action amount to 'enforcement action' for the purposes of RESA 2008?

It will also be necessary to consider, in relation to the enforcer's duties to notify in advance, whether one of the statutory exceptions applies (see RESA 2008, s 25D).

1.64 The PA Scheme should be distinguished from non-statutory schemes that local authorities have historically engaged in. Home and lead authority agreements[1] have existed for many years between local authority regulators and business enterprises. These relationships are now increasingly rare and do not attract the same statutory protections as the PA Scheme.

[1] Historically, home authority was the term used for trading standards and food safety matters, whereas lead authority was the term used for health and safety matters.

Regulated person

1.65 A regulated person is defined widely as any person that carries on, or proposes to carry on, an activity in relation to which a qualified regulator has a relevant function under RESA 2008[1]. This encompasses all local authorities (including fire and rescue authorities) and the wide variety of statutory duties they have in relation to the enforcement of consumer protection, environmental health, food, licensing and fire safety legislation. A business and local authority may agree to engage in a PA relationship, however that must be approved by the Secretary of State. This is referred to as 'nomination'[2]. OPSS administers the 'nomination' process through which a PA relationship is ratified. The rule that the PA Scheme could only apply where a business carried out its own regulated activities in two or more local authority areas has now been repealed by the EA 2016. The PA Scheme can now apply even if the business operates in only one local authority area, or it is yet to start its regulated activities[3].

[1] Regulatory Enforcement and Sanctions Act 2008, s 22A(1).
[2] Regulatory Enforcement and Sanctions Act 2008, ss 23A–23D.
[3] Explanatory Notes 113–144 to the EA 2016.

1.66 All PA relationships should be recorded on the PA public register which is administered by OPSS and is accessible online[1]. The PA Register has a secure part that is not accessible to the public where enforcers can see further information on partnerships and communicate with primary authorities.

[1] https://primary-authority.beis.gov.uk/par.

Regulated group

1.67 RESA 2008, s 22A(2) provides:

(2) A group of persons is a "regulated group" for the purposes of this Part if the Secretary of State is satisfied that—

(a)   a member of the group carries on, or proposes to carry on, an activity, and

(b)   a qualifying regulator has a relevant function which is, or would be, exercisable in relation to the member in respect of the activity.

1.68 A major extension of the PA Scheme, introduced in 2013 and amended by the EA 2016, is the possibility for regulated groups that permit many businesses to receive advice and guidance through a single PA relationship. This is aimed at trade associations, franchises and other groups of businesses. The co-ordinator of the regulated group must ultimately be 'nominated' by the Secretary of State; who also has a statutory obligation to secure that the PA register records the name of the co-ordinator of a regulated group and any person nominated to exercise the co-ordinator's functions[1]. The co-ordinator must maintain an up-to-date list of members of the group that should be available to the PA, OPSS and any qualifying regulator or supporting regulator. This is important because a regulator will not be bound by the PA group relationship in relation to one of its members, in relation to notification of enforcement action, unless the regulator is 'aware the member belongs to the group'[2]. The coordinator also has a duty to pass any advice or guidance given to it by the primary authority on to regulated group members who the co-ordinator considers might find it relevant[3]. A similar duty exists in respect of an inspection plan[4].

[1]   Regulatory Enforcement and Sanctions Act 2008, s 23C.
[2]   Regulatory Enforcement and Sanctions Act 2008, s 25C(1)(b).
[3]   Regulatory Enforcement and Sanctions Act 2008, s 24A(4).
[4]   Regulatory Enforcement and Sanctions Act 2008, s 26A(9).

Qualifying regulators under Pt 2 of RESA 2008

1.69 There are now four different types of PA regulator for the purposes of Pt 2 of RESA 2008: 'qualifying regulators', 'specified regulators', 'supporting regulators' and 'complementary regulators'. Under RESA 2008, s 22B all local authorities (including fire and rescue authorities) are 'qualifying regulators' and are therefore capable of acting as a PA. The Secretary of State now has the power, by secondary legislation, to make any other regulator with a relevant regulatory function a 'specified regulator'[1]. In the Explanatory Notes to the EA 2016 it is stated that the power would 'enable the Secretary of State to make legislation that will bring regulators other than local authorities within the scope of the scheme' such that regulators, other than local authorities may be able to act as a PA[2].

[1]   As at November 2021 there were no such 'specified regulators'.
[2]   Notes 107 and 110.

1.70 The amendments to RESA 2008 in the EA 2016 introduced 'supporting regulators' as a part of the PA Scheme[1]. This was aimed at national regulators that have responsibility for relevant functions under RESA 2008. A supporting regulator may assist a PA in the preparation of advice, guidance or inspection plans. Importantly, the supporting regulator must now exercise its own functions in relation to a regulated person, 'consistently with any advice or guidance under RESA 2008, s 24A, or any inspection plan' which it has supported and consented to[2]. This is qualified by the words 'so far as it is possible for the supporting regulator to do so in accordance with its other functions'[3]. The CORE Regulations have specified the CMA, FSA, Gambling Commission, the

HSE and the Secretary of State as supporting regulators[4]. Statutory guidance clarifies that the Secretary of State is specified in respect of regulatory functions concerning weights and measures and product safety regulation[5].

[1] Regulatory Enforcement and Sanctions Act 2008, s 28A.
[2] Regulatory Enforcement and Sanctions Act 2008, s 28A(3).
[3] Regulatory Enforcement and Sanctions Act 2008, s 28A(5).
[4] Schedule to the CORE Regulations.
[5] Primary Authority Statutory Guidance, para 31.1.

1.71 'Complementary regulators' are defined broadly in RESA 2008, s 28B(1) as any person with a relevant regulatory function that the Secretary of State specifies in secondary legislation[1]. This must set out the designated functions[2] of the complementary regulator, which must 'so far as is possible' act consistently with PA advice and guidance[3]. The distinction between a 'complementary regulator' and a 'specified regulator' is that the former may not be nominated to act as a PA in relation to the designated function.

[1] As at November 2021 this power had not been exercised.
[2] Regulatory Enforcement and Sanctions Act 2008, s 28B(1)(b) and (9).
[3] Regulatory Enforcement and Sanctions Act 2008, s 28B(2)–(4).

Relevant function

1.72 RESA 2008, s 4 provides:

4 "Relevant function"

(1)   In this Part "relevant function", in relation to a local authority in England or Wales, means—

(a)   a function under a relevant enactment of imposing requirements, restrictions or conditions, or setting standards or giving guidance, in relation to any activity, or

(b)   a function which relates to the securing of compliance with, or the enforcement of, requirements, restrictions, conditions, standards or guidance which under or by virtue of a relevant enactment relate to any activity.

(2)   In subsection (1) "relevant enactment" means—

(a)   an enactment specified in Schedule 3 or an enactment made under such an enactment;

(b)   an enactment to which subsection (3) applies.

(3)   This subs. applies to any enactment made under section 2(2) of the European Communities Act 1972 with respect to any of the following matters—

(a)   agricultural produce (quality standards and labelling);
(b)   animal health and welfare;
(c)   animal feed;
(d)   consumer protection;
(e)   environmental protection;
(f)   food hygiene and standards;
(g)   public health and safety;
(h)   weights and measures (including measuring instruments).

1.73 The definition of a relevant function is set out by RESA 2008, s 4, which lists a broad range of regulatory statutes in RESA 2008, Sch 3, which can be amended by statutory instrument. These include most of the consumer protection provisions that are commonly enforced by local authority trading standards departments and extend into a variety of other regulatory areas, such as fire safety, food hygiene and environmental standards. The definition of relevant function in s 4 also encompasses secondary legislation made under the European Communities Act 1972 in a number of specified areas, including consumer protection. Secondary legislation made under the European Communities Act 1972, prior to 31 December 2020, is preserved by the European Union (Withdrawal) Act 2018, s 2.

1.74 Relevant functions in Scotland are specified by reg 3 of the CORE Regulations as listed provisions that are applicable in Scotland that relate to reserved matters. Relevant functions in Northern Ireland are specified by reg 4 of the CORE Regulations as listed provisions that are applicable in Northern Ireland that do not relate to transferred matters.

Advice and guidance

1.75 RESA 2008, s 24A provides:

24 A Primary authority advice and guidance

(1)   The primary authority, if it is a direct primary authority, has the function of—

 (a)   giving advice and guidance to the regulated person in relation to each partnership function;

 (b)   giving advice and guidance, in relation to each partnership function, to other qualifying regulators as to how they should exercise it in relation to the regulated person.

(2)   The primary authority, if it is a co-ordinated primary authority, has the function of—

 (a)   giving advice and guidance to the co-ordinator of the regulated group in relation to each partnership function;

 (b)   giving advice and guidance, in relation to each partnership function, to other qualifying regulators as to how they should exercise it in relation to a member of the group.

1.76 In *R (Kingston Upon Hull CC) v BRDO, Newcastle CC, Greggs plc*[1] the High Court emphasised the importance of a PA getting right the law that underpins any advice and guidance given to a business. This was particularly important when considering discretionary enforcement powers that might result in other competing businesses being treated less advantageously. The court rejected PA guidance, which suggested that there may be more than one lawful construction of a statute. Kerr J stated that[2]:

'First, the statutory definition cannot have more than one correct construction. Second, the correct construction is a matter for the court. Third, if the construction adopted is materially different from what the court decides is the law, the advice cannot be correct. The guidance documents are wrong to suggest otherwise . . .
Fourth, it is critical that the primary authority gets the law right; otherwise the regulated person is subjected to different law from that which applies to its competitors and colleagues in the market place. That would violate the principle of equality before the law.'

The guidance documents referred to in this judgment were subsequently revised to take account of the effect of the decision.

¹   [2016] PTSR 967, [2016] CTLC 63, [2016] ACD 94.
²   Paragraphs 54–56.

Inspection plans

1.77 One of the criticisms made against enforcement authorities concerned inconsistency in the frequency and standards of local authority inspections carried out at business premises. There is now provision in RESA 2008, ss 26A–26C for a PA to make an inspection plan that sets out the scope, frequency and circumstances in which an inspection can be carried out by other local authority regulators. When an inspection plan has been consented to and other regulators have been notified about it, they may not exercise the inspection function 'otherwise than in accordance with the plan' unless the PA has consented to the way the other regulator wants to exercise the inspection function¹. The sanction for breaching this prohibition is not set out in RESA 2008. However, the mandatory language of RESA 2008, s 26B(2) suggests that an inspection that was not in accordance with the PA inspection plan would be unlawful, even if the criteria for exercising the specific statutory power was met.

¹   Regulatory Enforcement and Sanctions Act 2008, s 26(B(2) or, in relation to a regulated group, the member's name is not included on the list notified to the inspecting regulator.

Prohibition against enforcement action

1.78 The most difficult question that arises under the PA Scheme is whether a PA should prohibit enforcement action taken by another enforcer because it is inconsistent with advice and guidance that the PA has given a business. The decision-making process can be broken down into three separate stages of 'notification', 'prohibition' and 'referral'. Each of these stages have automatic prohibition periods that apply.

1.79 The effect of *notification* under the PA Scheme is to impose a moratorium of five working days¹ on the enforcer taking any enforcement action. During that period the PA has the opportunity of *prohibiting* the enforcement action because it is inconsistent with PA advice and guidance. Following that decision an application may be made by the business or the enforcing authority involved to *refer* it to the Secretary of State for a review, during which time enforcement action is also stayed. If the regulated person or member of a regulated group applies to refer the matter during that period, the enforcement action is prohibited until the referral has been determined. These prohibition periods are not to be included when calculating specific statutory time limits applicable for an offence (see also CHAPTER 4, Criminal Enforcement)².

¹   For the limited circumstances in which the period may differ, see Primary Authority statutory guidance, para 21.10.
²   Regulatory Enforcement and Sanctions Act 2008, ss 25B(4) and 25C(8) also referring to referral prohibition under para 5(7) of Regulatory Enforcement and Sanctions Act 2008, Sch 4A.

Enforcement action

1.80 Enforcement action is defined in RESA 2008, s 25A and supplemented by the Co-ordination of Regulatory Enforcement Regulations 2017 (the 'CORE Regulations')[1].

> **25A "Enforcement action"**
>
> (1) In this Part, "enforcement action" means—
>
> (a) action which relates to securing compliance with a restriction, requirement or condition in the event of breach (or putative breach) of a restriction, requirement or condition;
>
> (b) action taken with a view to, or in connection with, the imposition of a sanction (criminal or otherwise) in respect of an act or omission;
>
> (c) action taken in connection with the pursuit of a remedy conferred by an enactment in respect of an act or omission.

[1] SI 2017/835, the Regulations replace the Co-ordination of Regulatory Enforcement (Enforcement Action) Order 2009, SI 2009/665 (as amended).

1.81 Under the CORE Regulations the service of all statutory notices, orders and civil penalties[1] will amount to enforcement action for the purposes of the PA Scheme. Commencing proceedings in a court or tribunal is also enforcement action, as is the imposition of a civil or criminal sanction, administering a caution or accepting an undertaking. It would appear from this definition that investigation and the exercise of statutory investigation powers, that fall outside the CORE Regulations, will not amount to enforcement action[2]. This would suggest that the exercise of search and seizure powers and the questioning of suspects would not amount to enforcement action.

[1] SI 2017/835, reg 5(1)(a) '(i) an abatement notice, (ii) an alterations notice, (iii) a compliance notice, (iv) a demolition order, (v) a detention notice, (vi) an enforcement notice, (vii) a fixed monetary penalty, (viii) a hazard awareness notice, (ix) an improvement notice, (x) a premises order, (xi) a prohibition notice (including an emergency prohibition notice), (xii) a prohibition order, (xiii) a remedial action notice (including an emergency remedial action notice), (xiv) a request to fulfil a discretionary requirement, (xv) a stop notice, (xvi) a suspension notice, or (xvii) any other notice or order'.

[2] See para 24.21 of the PA Statutory Guidance.

Duty to notify

1.82 An enforcer must formally notify the PA, subject to the exceptions[1], where it 'proposes to take enforcement action' against a person that is a party to a PA relationship[2]. RESA 2008, s 29B makes provision for what the enforcing authority must do where there is more than one PA. Notification must be in writing 'before taking the proposed enforcement action'. In relation to regulated groups, the notification obligation applies only if the enforcer is aware that the business that is the subject of enforcement is a member of the group. The effect of the notification is that the enforcing authority 'may not take the action during the relevant period'. The PA statutory guidance requires that notification should be made via the PA register. It should be itemised to include multiple enforcement actions and should include the detail required by the notification template[3]. The enforcing authority should also be available to provide further information or clarification during the relevant period.

[1] See **1.63** above.

3   Paragraphs 24.22–24.31 of the PA Statutory Guidance. At para 21.11, the Guidance makes clear that in considering an application by the primary authority to extend the relevant period, the Secretary of State will take account of any evidence that the enforcing authority has failed to provide adequate information to enable the primary authority to make an informed decision.

1.83 Where the enforcer does not inform the PA of proposed enforcement action, but the PA is informed by the regulated person, the PA has a separate duty to inform the enforcer in writing that it cannot take any enforcement action during the relevant period[1].

1   Regulatory Enforcement and Sanctions Act 2008, s 25C(3).

The relevant period

1.84 The relevant period during which an enforcer is prohibited from taking enforcement action is defined by RESA 2008, s 25C(9) to be a period of five working days[1] after the date on which either:

(a)   the enforcer informs the primary authority it proposes to take action, or if this does not happen;

(b)   when the primary authority notifies the enforcer under RESA 2008, s 25C(3).

A 'working day' excludes Saturdays, Sundays and all bank holidays in the relevant part of the UK[2]. RESA 2008, s 30B gives the Secretary of State the power to amend time periods by secondary legislation.

1   'the fifth working day after the day on which the period begins' Regulatory Enforcement and Sanctions Act 2008, s 25C(9)(b)(i). For the limited circumstances in which the period may differ, see Primary Authority statutory guidance, para 21.10.
2   Regulatory Enforcement and Sanctions Act 2008, s 30D(2).

Prohibition during relevant period

1.85 Taking enforcement action during the 5-day relevant period is statutorily prohibited and therefore unlawful. That prohibition is triggered solely by the existence of the PA relationship rather than its relevance to the particular enforcement action that is proposed. It is likely that the prohibition will be strictly interpreted and it is unlikely to depend on whether the enforcer was actually aware that a PA relationship existed. It would appear that the provision would expressly state any requirement that knowledge was necessary, as it does in RESA 2008, s 25B(1)(b).

1.86 The effect of commencing proceedings in contravention of this prohibition is potentially serious. Both civil and criminal proceedings would be vulnerable to legal arguments concerning lack of jurisdiction and abuse of process.

Prohibition for inconsistency

1.87 The heart of PA is the power to stop enforcement proceedings taken by another local authority. It is this power that is key to the protection of business against inconsistent regulation envisaged by the legislation. It is also contentious because it undermines local decision making. The prohibition power has also been criticised on the grounds that it inevitably risks bias because the decision is taken by those engaged in the PA relationship, about advice and guidance given by the PA.

1.88 RESA 2008, s 25C(4) states:

> (4) If the primary authority determines, within the relevant period, that the proposed enforcement action is inconsistent with advice or guidance previously given by it (generally or specifically), it may direct the enforcing authority in writing not to take the action.

1.89 RESA 2008, s 25C(4) provides the PA with a discretion to direct that the enforcing authority does not take the enforcement action. The use of the word 'may' rather than 'shall' suggests that the PA has a broader discretion not to direct that enforcement action be prohibited, even if it would be inconsistent. It is likely that the PA should consider a wide range of circumstances relevant to the exercise of that discretion including any specific local enforcement considerations or relevant change in circumstances. It may also be important for the PA to consider the further grounds upon which the Secretary of State may review the decision, that the advice and guidance is both 'correct' and 'properly given'.

1.90 The PA Handbook (which, as noted above, was withdrawn in October 2017 and accordingly may now be considered as of historic interest only) purported to give some guidance on how the decision under RESA 2008, s 25C(4) should be exercised[1]:

> 'Where relevant Primary Authority Advice has been given, the primary authority's responsibility is to decide whether the proposed enforcement action is inconsistent with that advice. Whilst this will often be straightforward where the advice relates to interpretation, or the applicability of legislation, it will inevitably be more complex where the advice relates to business systems or controls, or to the checks that the business carries out on implementation of those systems or controls.
>
> Where the proposed enforcement action relates to a local failure to implement the business' controls, the primary authority is unlikely to be able to determine whether the action would be inconsistent with Primary Authority Advice that it has given on those controls without having a detailed picture of the local failure and its causes.
>
> Ideally, the primary authority will have had an opportunity to work through these issues prior to the formal notification. However, where this has not happened, this may mean that the primary authority will need to request further information from the enforcing authority and the business. In this situation, the deadline of five working days to respond to the notification is likely to be challenging.'

[1] Pages 153–154.

1.91 In *R (Kingston Upon Hull CC) v BRDO, Newcastle CC, Greggs plc*[1] a judicial review challenge was made by Kingston upon Hull City Council to PA advice given by Newcastle City Council to Greggs plc regarding the latter's obligations to provide toilets in its bakery shops. Newcastle had advised Greggs that it did not need to provide toilets where there were ten or less seats in a store. The High Court agreed that the advice was unlawful and quashed the decision of the BRDO to affirm it. Kerr J set out how he considered that the PA Scheme should operate by reference to the facts of the case[2]:

> 'How then should Hull reconcile its retention of s. 20 functions in relation to Greggs' branches in Hull, with its obvious, although unstated, obligation to take account of Newcastle's advice about how to exercise those same functions? The interaction of statutory functions leads to the following division. I will use the facts of this case as an example of how the scheme should operate, in this case and in other cases.
>
> First, it is for Newcastle to give advice and guidance to Hull, as it did. In doing so, it must get the law right; see above. It is crucial that it does so because the law must be the same for everyone in the relevant market, to avoid unlawful distortion of competition. You cannot have one law for Greggs and another for its competitors. That proposition alone is sufficient to defeat the objection founded on immateriality.
>
> Secondly, in advising and giving guidance on the exercise of discretionary powers, Newcastle may suggest what weight should be given to particular factors. These may include matters such as the number of seats and the proportions of take away and sit-down customers. Those discretionary matters must be clearly separated from, and seen to be separated from, statements of what the law is. For the reasons I have already given, that is not a matter that is merely cosmetic or immaterial. It is fundamental.
>
> Third, the advice and guidance must obviously be taken very seriously by Hull. In practice, it is advice that should be followed unless there is a good reason not to do so, because otherwise either the primary authority (here, Newcastle) or the regulated person (here, Greggs) can, albeit ultimately subject to the consent of the BDRO, stop the enforcement action by using the s. 28 and Sch 4 machinery.'

1   [2016] PTSR 967, [2016] CTLC 63, [2016] ACD 94.
2   Paragraphs 70–75.

1.92 An interesting question arises about whether a PA could prohibit enforcement action on the basis that it would be inconsistent with changes implemented since an infringement. For example, a business that has breached a regulation may subsequently agree a comprehensive due diligence system with its PA to ensure the breach is not repeated and take substantial steps to implement that system. Can it be argued that a prosecution for the original breach is inconsistent with the advice and guidance given because the enforcement action occurs after the problem has been rectified? It seems unlikely that this was Parliament's intention. The business would not have relied on PA advice at the time of the breach and subsequent changes are likely to be considered mitigation, rather than a reason for a PA to prevent enforcement action.

1.93 In circumstances where the PA has decided not to direct against the enforcement action or to refer the matter to the Secretary of State, it also has a duty under RESA 2008, s 29C(2) to take reasonable steps to ascertain whether another PA has given advice and guidance that might be inconsistent with proposed enforcement action. In those circumstances the first PA has a duty to refer the proposed enforcement action to the other PA. When this happens the 5 working days' time moratorium on enforcement action will restart on the referral to the other PA[1].

1   Explanatory Note 173 to the EA 2016 'In practice, this means that the relevant period (during which time the enforcing authority cannot take enforcement action) will restart'.

1.94 An enforcement authority would be acting unlawfully if it took enforcement action in contravention of a prohibition under RESA 2008, s 25C(4). Commencing any civil or criminal proceedings would plainly be vulnerable to legal arguments on both jurisdiction and abuse of process.

Prohibition during the referral period

1.95 If the PA decides not to exercise its discretion to prohibit the enforcement action under RESA 2008, s 25C(4), the regulated person may apply for consent to refer the matter to the Secretary of State for review (see below). The enforcing authority must inform the business that it intends to continue with the enforcement action and it may not take the enforcement action during the 10-day 'referral period'[1] during which the regulated person may refer the decision of the PA to the Secretary of State for review[2].

1   RESA 2008, Sch 4A, para 5(4).
2   RESA 2008, s 25C(6).

1.96 If the regulated person makes a referral application during the referral period, the enforcing authority 'may not take the proposed enforcement action at any time after the making of the reference and before its determination'[1]. It is not entirely clear how this provision would be affected in circumstances where an application is made out of time under the 'exceptional circumstances' provision in reg 8 of the CORE Regulations, but it may be that a decision to allow such an application would be treated as having the effect of extending the referral period, and therefore the prohibition.

1   RESA 2008, Sch 4A, para 5(7).

Sequence of prohibition periods

1.97 It is important for an enforcement authority to understand the sequence of mandatory prohibition periods that apply when a PA considers its decision under RESA 2008, s 25C(4) to prohibit enforcement action. The scheme of the legislation provides the regulated person with protection from enforcement during the 5-day relevant period when the PA is making its decision (plus, potentially, a further 5 days if referral to a second PA is necessary) and also in the 10-day referral period when the regulated person decides whether to refer the matter to the Secretary of State. If there is actually then an application for a referral by the regulated person, that prohibition continues until the referral has been determined.

1.98 Sequence of prohibition periods is shown in the table below.

Relevant Decision	Prohibition on enforcement action	Provision
Notification to PA by EA of proposed enforcement action or notification of PA to EA.	5 working days[1] prohibition against taking the enforcement action for PA to make decision about prohibition under s 25C(4)	s 25C(2)(b) and (3)

(If applicable) Notification by first PA to second PA	5 working days prohibition against taking the enforcement action for second PA to make a decision about prohibition	s 25C(2)(b) by operation of s29C(4)
Decision by PA not to exercise its discretion to prohibit enforcement action under s 25C(4)	Further 10 working days[2] prohibition from the time that the EA indicates it intends to continue prosecution	s 25C(6) and para 5(4) of Sch 4A
Regulated person makes an application to refer the matter to the Secretary of State for review.	Prohibition from the time of making the referral application until the referral has been determined	para 5(7) of Sch 4A RESA 2008

RESA 2008, s 30B gives the Secretary of State the power to amend time periods by secondary legislation.

[1] For the limited circumstances in which the period may differ, see Primary Authority statutory guidance, para 21.10.

[2] For the limited circumstances in which the period may differ, see Primary Authority statutory guidance, para 24.43.

Exceptions

1.99 Section 5D of RESA 2008 provides the Secretary of State with the power, using secondary legislation, to make exceptions to the duty of a regulator to notify PA of intended enforcement action, the power of a PA to prevent that action and the capacity of any party to refer the matter to the Secretary of State. The wording of s 25D is important because the power is to prescribe the circumstances when RESA 2008, ss 25B, 25C and Sch 4A 'do not apply'. The effect of this is to permit enforcement action by a regulator where that is required urgently or prior notification would be wholly disproportionate. In these circumstances notification must be made to the PA retrospectively.

1.100 The exemptions are now set out in reg 6 of the CORE Regulations which mirrors the wording of RESA 2008, s 25D. Regulation 6[1] states:

6 Enforcement action

In accordance with section 25D of the Act, sections 25B and 25C of the Act do not apply where—

    (a)   the enforcement action is required urgently to avoid a significant risk of serious harm to—
        (i)   human health,
        (ii)   the environment (including the health of animals or plants), or
        (iii)   the financial interests of consumers; or
    (b)   the application of sections 25B or 25C of the Act would be wholly disproportionate.

[1] SI 2017/835, reg 6.

1.101 There is a requirement in RESA 2008, s 25D(3) that a qualifying regulator must 'inform the primary authority of the action as soon as it reasonably can' if acting under reg 6(b) on the basis that notification 'would be wholly disproportionate'. The purpose of this notification appears to relate to the desirability of ensuring that a PA is kept informed of all matters relevant to the regulated business[1], rather than to afford any protection to the business in relation to the enforcement action, because a PA notified in that way would not appear to have any power under RESA 2008, s 25C(4) to prevent the enforcement action or to refer the matter to the Secretary of State for review.

[1]   Paragraph 21.26 of the PA Statutory Guidance.

Referral to the Secretary of State

1.102 RESA 2008, Sch 4A permits all three of the affected parties to refer a decision made under the PA Scheme to the Secretary of State for review. This is effectively a review of the decision under RESA 2008, s 25C(4) about whether enforcement action should be prohibited because it is inconsistent with advice and guidance given and whether it was also both correct and properly given.

1.103 When a PA has prohibited the enforcement action, the enforcer may apply for consent to the matter being referred. When the PA has refused to prohibit the enforcement action, the regulated business may apply for consent. Additionally, if the PA is unsure about whether to prohibit the enforcement action, it may ask the Secretary of State to take the decision[1]. Regulation 7 of the CORE Regulations sets out the information and documentary support that should be provided in an application for consent to a referral.

[1]   RESA 2008, Sch 4A, paras 1–4. Paragraph 1 applies where the PA brings its own enforcement action.

Time limit for referrals

1.104 RESA 2008, Sch 4A, para 5 provides:

5 Timing

(1)   Any reference under this Schedule must be made as soon as is reasonably practicable, and in any event within the referral period.

1.105 This provision provides a strict time limit on when a referral may be made. The length of the 'referral period' is 10 working days.

(a)   For an enforcer, time runs from the date of notification by the PA that the enforcement action is to be prohibited[1].
(b)   For a business, the time runs from the date the business is told that the enforcing authority will proceed with the enforcement action[2].

If the PA asks the Secretary of State to make the decision, it must do so within the same 5-day period it would ordinarily have for making that decision (see above). Any decision on the referral must be made by the Secretary of State within 28 days from the date the reference is made[3]. Regulation 8 of the CORE Regulations provides the Secretary of State with a residual discretion to allow an application for consent outside those time limits 'in exceptional circumstances'.

[1]   SI 2017/835, reg 8(1).
[2]   SI 2017/835, reg 8(2).

[3]   RESA 2008, Sch 4A, para 5(7).

Consent

1.106 The review process under RESA 2008, Sch 4A requires the Secretary of State to give 'consent' to the referral. Guidance as to the manner in which this decision will be taken is set out in *References for Determination: Policy and Procedure*[1]. At para 7.4, the following matters are said to constitute reasons to refuse consent:

(a)   an application is incomplete or has otherwise been improperly made;
(b)   the subject of an application is not an appropriate question for Safety and Standards to determine;
(c)   consent has already been given to another party relating to the same question;
(d)   consent has already been given to another applicant making a related application;
(e)   Safety and Standards is not satisfied that the applicant has provided sufficient and appropriate reasons for making the application; or
(f)   the application is frivolous or vexatious.

[1]   BEIS, October 2018.

Standard of review

1.107 On referral the standard of review is the same whether the application is made by the PA, enforcer or regulated business. The Secretary of State must be satisfied of the matters identified (in paras 2(3) or 3(3) or 4(3) to RESA 2008, Sch 4A) in determining whether the PA decision should be confirmed or revoked.

1.108 The matters identified in RESA 2008, Sch 4A, paras 2(3) or 3(3) or 4(3) are:

(a)   the proposed enforcement action is inconsistent with advice or guidance previously given by the primary authority (generally or specifically), and
(b)   the advice or guidance was correct and properly given.

1.109 In *R (Kingston Upon Hull CC) v BRDO, Newcastle CC, Greggs plc*[1] the High Court gave guidance on the meaning of 'correct' in this context. The submission had been made that there could be more than one tenable construction of a statutory provision, such that both constructions were 'correct' for the purposes of the test applied on a referral. This was robustly rejected. Kerr J stated that:

'The notion of more than one correct construction, taken to its logical limit, would be subversive of the rule of law. It would make the executive and not the courts responsible for deciding what the law is. For that reason, at the very least crystal clear words would be needed to confer on an executive body the function of deciding on the meaning of statutory provisions and giving the body a choice about which of more than one possible meaning it prefers. In the absence of such clear words, the term "correct" should be taken to mean what it says, ie "right" or, if you prefer, "not wrong".'

[1]   [2016] PTSR 967, [2016] CTLC 63, [2016] ACD 94.

Power to charge a fee

1.110 RESA 2008, s 27A permits the charging of regulated persons' or co-ordinators' fees for the operation of the PA Scheme.

27A Power to charge

(1) The primary authority—

(a) may, in the case of a regulated person, charge the person such fees as the authority considers to represent the costs reasonably incurred by it in the exercise of its functions under this Part in relation to the person;

(b) may, in the case of a regulated group, charge the co-ordinator such fees as the authority considers to represent the costs reasonably incurred by it in the exercise of its functions under the Part in relation to the regulated group.

1.111 The provision enables a PA to charge both the regulated person or the co-ordinator of a regulated group for the work it has done. The primary authority is entitled to recover such costs as it has reasonably incurred in the exercise of its functions. Under RESA 2008, s 30A the Secretary of State may issue guidance about the charging of fees. That guidance is incorporated in the Primary Authority Statutory Guidance.

Chapter 2

INTERPRETATION
OF CONSUMER LAW

Contents

INTRODUCTION

2.1 Virtually all consumer protection laws in the UK are to be found in statutes and delegated legislation. The interpretation of these provisions can be complex, with layers of regulation that typically implemented European Union ('EU') laws sometimes drafted in unfamiliar terms. The interpretation of domestic measures implementing EU law usually required consideration of both domestic and EU law principles of interpretation and is now subject to detailed rules under the European Union (Withdrawal) Act 2018 ('EU(W)A 2018')[1].

[1]   See **2.42** et seq.

GENERAL PRINCIPLES OF STATUTORY INTERPRETATION

Parliamentary intention

2.2 The primary purpose of statutory interpretation is to ascertain the intention of the legislature as expressed in a statutory provision. In *Regina (Spath Holme Ltd) v Secretary of State for the Environment*, Lord Nicholls of Birkenhead set out the process by which Parliamentary intention should be ascertained[1]:

'Statutory interpretation is an exercise which requires the court to identify the meaning borne by the words in question in the particular context. The task of the court is often said to be to ascertain the intention of Parliament expressed in the language under consideration. This is correct and may be helpful, so long as it is remembered that the "intention of Parliament" is an objective concept, not subjective. The phrase is a shorthand reference to the intention which the court reasonably imputes to Parliament in respect of the language used. It is not the subjective intention of the minister or other persons who promoted the legislation. Nor is it the subjective intention of the draftsman, or of individual members or even of a majority of individual members of either House. These individuals will often have widely varying intentions. Their understanding of the legislation and the words used may be impressively complete or woefully inadequate. Thus, when courts say that such-and-such a meaning "cannot be what Parliament intended", they are saying only that the words under consideration cannot reasonably be taken as used by Parliament with that meaning.'

[1]   [2001] 2 AC 349, at 398–9.

2.3 In ascertaining Parliamentary intention an important constitutional principle must be observed. Those who are subject to the law ought to be able to read and understand those laws, without having to look into the process by which they were made. Lord Diplock expressed this aspect of the rule of law in *Fothergill v Monarch Airlines Ltd*[1]:

'The source to which Parliament must have intended the citizen to refer is the language of the Act itself. These are the words which Parliament has itself approved as accurately expressing its intentions. If the meaning of those words is clear and unambiguous and does not lead to a result that is manifestly absurd or unreasonable, it would be a confidence trick by Parliament and destructive of all legal certainty if the private citizen could not rely upon that meaning but was required to search through all that had happened before and in the course of the legislative process in order to see whether there was anything to be found from which it could be inferred that

Parliament's real intention had not been accurately expressed by the actual words that Parliament had adopted to communicate it to those affected by the legislation.'

[1] *Fothergill v Monarch Airlines Ltd* [1981] AC 251, 279–280.

Plain meaning

2.4 The starting point for interpreting the words used in a statutory provision is that generally a court should follow the natural or ordinary meaning of the language used: its plain meaning. In *Pinner v Everett*, Lord Reid expressed this as[1]:

> 'In determining the meaning of any word or phrase in a statue the first question to ask always is what is the natural or ordinary meaning of that word or phrase in its context in the statute. It is only when that meaning leads to some result which cannot reasonably be supposed to have been the intention of the legislature that it is proper to look for some other possible meaning of the word or phrase.'

[1] [1969] 1 WLR 1266 at 1273.

2.5 Evidence is generally not admissible about the meaning of an ordinary word[1], although may be admissible in relation to other more specialist terms[2]. The citation of a 'well known and authoritative' dictionary meaning is permissible, although the court remains free to arrive at its own conclusion.

[1] *Marquis of Camden v IRC* [1914] 1 KB 641.
[2] *Blankley v Godley* [1952] 1 All ER 436.

2.6 This approach to interpretation, although sometimes distinguished from purposive interpretation, is better viewed as a reflection of the general principle that statutory interpretation is always the process of ascertaining the legislator's intention. That intention can most easily be identified by a consideration of the natural or ordinary meaning of the words that Parliament has chosen to use.

2.7 There are numerous reasons that can be given for a court to depart from the plain meaning of a statutory provision. In recent times, the most commonly cited reasons include:

- The ordinary and natural meaning might lead to an absurd result[1], or one not intended by Parliament[2].
- The language used is ambiguous or obscure, for example it is capable of more than one grammatical meaning.
- The ordinary and natural meaning would lead to a result that is incompatible with an established common law principle of interpretation.
- The ordinary and natural meaning is incompatible with a statutory obligation, such as the Human Rights Act 1998, s 3 or the ECA 1972, s 2.

[1] Lord Wensleydale's 'golden rule', *River Wear Comrs v Adamson* (1877) 2 App Cas 743 at 764–5 HL.
[2] For example, *Stock v Frank Jones (Tipton) Ltd* [1978] 1 All ER 948 HL, per Lord Simon of Glaisdale.

Established common law principles

2.8 There are a vast number of presumptions that have developed through the common law about how legislation should be interpreted by the courts. Many of these have their justification in public policies, such as the protection of a citizen's rights. Although there have been attempts to codify these principles to strict rules, they are probably best analysed as merely assumptions that can reasonably be attributed to the intention of Parliament when enacting legislation. For example, Parliament would not ordinarily intend to deprive a person of their liberty by criminal sanction without expressly saying so. It follows that these interpretative principles are rarely, if ever, immutable and may be displaced by the circumstances, context or express language in a piece of legislation. There are many such principles to be found in the textbooks on statutory interpretation, however, we have referred only to those that are most likely to be of use to consumer law practitioners analysed as merely assumptions that can reasonably be attributed to the intention of Parliament when enacting legislation. For example, Parliament would not ordinarily intend to deprive a person of their liberty by criminal sanction without expressly saying so. It follows that these interpretative principles are rarely, if ever, immutable and may be displaced by the circumstances, context or express language in a piece of legislation. There are many such principles to be found in the textbooks on statutory interpretation, however, we have referred only to those that are most likely to be of use to consumer law practitioners.

Presumption against doubtful penalisation

2.9 It is to be presumed that a provision is not intended to have penal consequences unless that purpose is unambiguous and clearly stated. The presumption dates back to the rule of law set out in Magna Carta 1215, that a person must not be imprisoned or stripped of rights without lawful judgment or by the law of the land.

2.10 The Court of Appeal has recently stated the principle to be that an obscure provision should be 'construed narrowly' because of its potentially penal consequences[1]. The principle exists even though there are potentially circumstances where it will be outweighed by other factors[2].

[1] Per Dyson LJ, *Aggasi v Robinson (Inspector of Taxes)* [2005] EWCA Civ 1507, [2006] 1 All ER 900 at [56].
[2] *R v Dowds* [2012] EWCA Crim 281 at [37]–[38].

2.11 The presumption is particularly strong in cases where imprisonment is a potential outcome. In *R v Hallstrom ex parte W (No 2)* it was stated that there is a 'canon of construction that Parliament is presumed not to enact legislation which interferes with the liberty of the subject without making it clear that this was its intention'[1]. However, the principle is not confined to criminal sanction and extends to any laws that inflict 'hardship or deprivation of any kind on a person'[2]. It has been applied, for example, in relation the deprivation of property rights without compensation (see below)[3]. It has been applied, for example, in relation the deprivation of property rights without compensation (see below).

¹ [1986] QB 1090 per McCullough J at [1104]. Note, *Hallstrom* was subject to criticism in *R v BHB Community Healthcare NHS Trust Ex p B* [1999] 1 FLR 106, Times, October 14 1998, CA (Civ Div) 30 July 1998, although the general principle quoted in the text is likely to be followed.
² *Bennion on Statutory Interpretation* (6th edn), referring to Bennion in *Halsbury's Laws*.
³ *AG v Horner* (1884) 14 QBD 245 at 256–7; *Bond v Nottingham Corpn* [1940] Ch 429 at 435.

2.12 In many consumer protection measures, the criminal offence is clearly set out together with the applicable sentence. An area of difficulty may be the drafting of charges for general provisions that define the criminal offence by reference to the breach of a standard not set out in the statute. For example, the Consumer Protection Act 1987, s 12(1) creates an offence of supplying goods that contravene a safety regulation. In such cases it will be important that the offence is drafted clearly by focussing on its ingredients, setting out in simple terms the nature of the alleged contravention focussing on its ingredients, setting out in simple terms the nature of the alleged contravention.

Presumption in favour of property rights

2.13 There is a general principle of interpretation that the property rights and other economic interests of private persons should be respected. This principle is similar to the presumption against doubtful penalisation in that it assumes that Parliament intends to protect a citizen's economic rights, unless Parliament's intention to interfere is unambiguous and clearly stated. It is also to be assumed that Parliament would not ordinarily intend to deprive a citizen of property without adequate compensation. An Act should not be construed to prejudice established private rights under contracts¹, or title to property unless it is clearly intended to do so. This presumption is now reflected in the ECHR qualified right to the peaceful enjoyment of possessions².

¹ *Allen v Thorn Electrical Industries* [1968] 1 QB 487.
² ECHR Protocol, Art 1. 'No one shall be deprived of his possessions except in the public interest and subject to the conditions. Every natural or legal person is entitled to the peaceful enjoyment of his possessions. No one shall be deprived of his possessions except in the public interest and subject to the conditions provided for by law and by the general principles of international law'.

Presumption of positive effect

2.14 There is a general rule of statutory construction that it is better for a measure to be given effect rather than be considered void. This is really an application of the courts heeding the intention of Parliament that laws should be given effect. In *R (Hasani) v Blackfriars Crown Court*, Hooper LJ stated that it was a 'well-known rule of statutory interpretation that, if it is possible, the provisions of an Act must be construed so as to give them a sensible meaning'¹. *Blackfriars Crown Court*, Hooper LJ stated that it was a 'well-known rule of statutory interpretation that, if it is possible, the provisions of an Act must be construed so as to give them a sensible meaning'.

¹ [2005] EWHC 3016 (Admin), [2006] 1 All ER 817 at [14].

Statutory materials

2.15 It follows from the principle that citizens should be able to know their law by reading it, that any approach to statutory interpretation must be cautious when using statutory material that is 'external' to the plain meaning of the words in a provision. In *R (Spath Holme Ltd) v Secretary of State for the Environment*, it was accepted that the courts were not 'confined to looking solely at the language in question in its context within the statute' and might consider the context and background. However, Lord Nicholls made it clear that[1]: confined to looking solely at the language in question in its context within the statute' and might consider the context and background. However, Lord Nicholls made it clear that:

> 'External aids differ significantly from internal aids. Unlike internal aids, external aids are not found within the statute in which Parliament has expressed its intention in the words in question. This difference is of constitutional importance. Citizens, with the assistance of their advisers, are intended to be able to understand parliamentary enactments, so that they can regulate their conduct accordingly. They should be able to rely upon what they read in an Act of Parliament . . . courts should . . . approach the use of external aids with circumspection. Judges frequently turn to external aids for confirmation of views reached without their assistance. That is unobjectionable. But the constitutional implications point to a need for courts to be slow to permit external aids to displace meanings which are otherwise clear and unambiguous and not productive of absurdity.'

1   [2001] 2 AC 349, at 398–9.

Headings, cross headings and side-notes

2.16 The heading in a statutory provision may be used as a tool for interpretation, but only insofar as the heading provides a reliable guide to the material to which it is attached[1]. It must be remembered that a heading, by its nature, is only likely to represent a brief summary of the relevant sections. It is not as important as the wording of the provision itself. A cross-heading may also indicate the scope of the sections that follow it, however caution should be adopted in relation to sections that have since been amended[2]. Side-notes are no longer used in Acts of the UK Parliament. In older statutes where side-notes still appear, it is permissible to use sidenotes to construe the legislation with some caution[3]. In *DPP v Schildkamp*, Lord Reid stated[4]:

> 'The question which has arisen in this case is whether and to what extent it is permissible to give weight to punctuation, cross-headings and side-notes to sections in the Act . . . it may be more realistic to accept the Act as printed as being the product of the whole legislative process, and to give due weight to everything found in the printed Act. I say more realistic because in very many cases the provision before the court was never even mentioned in debate in either House, and it may be that its wording was never closely scrutinised by any member of either House. In such a case it is not very meaningful to say that the words of the Act represent the intention of Parliament but that punctuation, cross-headings and side-notes do not . . . I would not object to taking all these matters into account, provided that we realise that they cannot have equal weight with the words of the Act. Punctuation can be of some assistance in construction. A cross-heading ought to indicate the scope of the sections which follow it but there is always a possibility that the scope of one of these sections may be widened by amendment. But a side-note is a poor guide to the scope of a section, for it can do no more than indicate the main subject with which the

section deals' scrutinised by any member of either House. In such a case it is not very meaningful to say that the words of the Act represent the intention of Parliament but that punctuation, cross-headings and side-notes do not . . . I would not object to taking all these matters into account, provided that we realise that they cannot have equal weight with the words of the Act. Punctuation can be of some assistance in construction. A cross-heading ought to indicate the scope of the sections which follow it but there is always a possibility that the scope of one of these sections may have been widened by amendment. But a side-note is a poor guide to the scope of a section, for it can do no more than indicate the main subject with which the section deals.'

1   *DPP v Schildkamp* [1971] AC 1 per Lord Reid at 10.
2   *DPP v Schildkamp* [1971] AC 1, per Lord Reid.
3   *Stephens v Cuckfield RDC* [1960] 2 QB 373 at 383.
4   *DPP v Schildkamp* [1971] AC 1, at 10.

Explanatory notes

2.17 Most statutory provisions are now accompanied by a set of explanatory notes. In complex regulatory provisions, these notes are often valuable in determining the purpose of the legislation. Explanatory notes are usually prepared by the Government department responsible for the legislation. They do not form part of a Bill or draft statutory instrument during its passage through Parliament and are not, consequently, endorsed by Parliament. It follows that they cannot be amended by Parliament. In *R (Westminster City Council) v National Asylum Support Service*, Lord Steyn observed[1]:

> 'The notes are intended to be neutral in political tone: they aim to explain the effect of the text and not to justify it. The purpose is to help the reader to get his bearings and to ease the task of assimilating the law.'

1   [2002] UKHL 38, [2002] 4 All ER 654, [2002] 1 WLR 2956 at para [4].

2.18 It is not necessary to show ambiguity before an explanatory note is used. They are admissible aids to construction as long as they 'cast light on the objective setting or contextual scene of the statute, and the mischief at which it is aimed'[1].

1   *National Asylum Support Service*, per Lord Steyn at para [6]; see also *R v Montila* [2004] UKHL 50 at [35] and *Flora v Wakom (Heathrow) Ltd* [2006] EWCA Civ 1103 at [14]–[18].

Green papers, white papers and other reports

2.19 Green papers are consultation documents produced by the Government with the aim of generating feedback. They sometimes include different legislative options and are often the first step in the legislative process. White papers are policy documents produced by the Government setting out proposals for future legislation in a more concrete form. White papers sometimes include a draft version of a planned Bill, but remain consultative in nature. Where this type of Parliamentary material is useful to explain a legislative project, it may be relied on by the court when considering the resulting legislation[1].

1   *Duke v GEC Reliance Ltd* [1988] AC 618 at 637.

2.20 Reports made by the Law Commission and other committees of inquiry, such as a Royal Commission or parliamentary select committee, are to be considered a part of the enacting history of any Act that is based upon the report. Such a report can be cited and taken into consideration by a court when interpreting the Act's statutory provisions[1].

[1] *Black-Clawson International Ltd v Papierwerke Waldhof-Aschaffenburg AG* [1975] AC 591 at 647.

Hansard

2.21 The rule in *Pepper v Hart*[1] is a rule of practice that permits the use of certain parliamentary materials to aid the interpretation of a statute. Where the legal meaning of an enactment is *ambiguous* or *obscure*, or *its literal meaning leads to an absurdity*, a court may have regard to any statement on the Bill for the Act containing the enactment, as set out in the official report or record of debates. The record may only be used if:

- it is clear;
- was made by or on behalf of the minister or other person who was the promoter of the Bill[2]; and
- discloses the legislative intention underlying the statutory provision.

[1] *Pepper (Inspector of Taxes) v Hart* [1993] AC 593, [1992] 1 All ER 42 HL.
[2] See *R v Secretary of State for Foreign and Commonwealth Affairs, ex parte Rees-Mogg* [1994] 1 All ER 457 DC.

2.22 Although the rule was stated strictly in *Pepper v Hart*, in modern appellate advocacy it would appear that greater flexibility is applied in practice, with Hansard material regularly considered without applying the letter of the limitation[1]. This can be founded on the basis that *Pepper v Hart* is merely a rule of practice rather than an absolute rule of law. It is also arguable that a court has a residuary inherent jurisdiction to consider such material when required, even though it would not meet the strict criteria set out in *Pepper v Hart*.

[1] See for example *R v Warwickshire CC ex parte Johnson* [1993] AC 583, 592.

Executive guidance

2.23 Government departments and agencies often give guidance on the meaning of legislation after it has been enacted. This is sometimes provided as a consequence of a statutory duty[1]. On other occasions it is designed to provide practical advice. In *Governors of the Peabody Trust v Reeve* the High Court considered the OFT Guidance on unfair terms in tenancy agreements. It was stated that[2]:

> 'Although the court is in no sense bound by the guidance provided by the Office of Fair Trading . . . that guidance does give landlords helpful common-sense indications of what is likely to be considered to be fair and should be carefully taken into account when drafting a variation clause in a tenancy agreement.'

[1] For example, the Regulatory Enforcement and Sanctions Act 2008, s 30A (as amended).
[2] [2008] EWHC 1432 (Ch), [2009] L & TR 6 at para [54].

2.24 The cardinal principle when considering such guidance, in the context of statutory interpretation, is that it remains the constitutional responsibility of the courts to determine the legal meaning of a statutory provision. It is only a court that has the role of authoritatively interpreting legislation as far as it is necessary to do in deciding a case. Executive, investigative and prosecution agencies offering guidance on the construction of legislation remain subject to the determination of a court. In *Regina v London Transport Executive, ex parte Greater London Council*, Kerr LJ stated the principle[1], Kerr LJ stated the principle:

> 'The interpretation of the intention of Parliament as expressed in our statutes is a matter for the courts. Once the meaning of an Act of Parliament has been authoritatively interpreted . . . that interpretation is the law, unless and until it is thereafter changed by Parliament.'

[1]   [1983] QB 484 at 490.

2.25 The weight that should be given to guidance will depend on the circumstances in which it is given. In *R (Ali) v Newham LBC*[1], Parker J stated that:

> 'the weight that should be given to particular guidance depends upon the specific context in which the guidance has been produced. In particular (without intending to create an exhaustive list) I believe that it is necessary to give due regard to the authorship of the guidance, the quality and intensity of the work done in the production of the guidance, the extent to which the (possibly competing) interests of those who are likely to be affected by the guidance have been recognised and weighed, the importance of any more general public policy that the guidance has sought to promote, and the express terms of the guidance itself.'

[1]   [2012] EWHC 2970 (Admin) (30 October 2012) at para [39].

LINGUISTIC CANONS OF CONSTRUCTION

2.26 The linguistic canons of construction apply equally to statutory provisions as they would to any text.

Consistent use of terms

2.27 The use of a particular word in a statute is presumed to be consistent throughout, unless the context otherwise requires. This can be important when analysing specific provisions in the context of an Act, however, care should be taken with statutes that cover a variety of different legislative topics. This rule applies in relation to delegated legislation as a consequence of the Interpretation Act 1978, s 11.

Associated words principle

2.28 It is a contextual canon of construction that words should be construed by reference to associated words, unless the context requires otherwise, *noscitur a sociis*. The *noscitur a sociis* principle is that words should not be read in isolation, but should take colour from the words that surround them. For example, in the phrase 'crane, winch, hoist or block and tackle', the word 'crane' plainly does not refer to a large bird. The principle is not confined to words in the same string or sentence and may extend to other passages within the text[1].

1   *City Index Ltd v Leslie* [1992] QB 98, per Lord Donaldson MR at 105.

2.29 In *Bourne (Inspector of Taxes) v Norwich Crematorium Ltd*, the principle was stated by the High Court as[1]:

'English words derive colour from those which surround them. Sentences are not mere collections of words to be taken out of the sentence, defined separately by reference to the dictionary or decided cases, and then put back into the sentence with the meaning which you have assigned to them as separate words.'

1   [1967] 1 WLR 691, per Stamp J at 696.

2.30 In *Miller v FA Sadd & Son Ltd*[1] the High Court considered in the Trade Descriptions Act 1968, s 6 (now repealed), which extended the meaning of 'offering to supply' goods to include 'having goods in [the trader's] possession for supply'. The defendant had contracted to supply schools with foodstuffs at a particular price, but later delivered the goods together with an invoice for a false price that was higher than agreed. The Prosecution argued that the defendant was deemed to have offered to supply goods with a false trade description because the goods were in the defendant's possession for supply, together with the false invoice, before being delivered.

1   [1981] 3 All ER 265 at 269.

2.31 The High Court rejected this interpretation of the Trade Descriptions Act 1968, s 6 on the basis that the words 'in his possession for supply' must be read alongside (*'sui generis')* 'exposing' for supply. It followed that a trader could not offer for supply goods that had already been the subject of a concluded contractual agreement. This is perhaps an example of a court using a canon of linguistic construction to avoid following the literal meaning of a phrase.

Restricting wide words, *ejusdem generis*

2.32 The *ejusdem generis* principle is really a specific application of the associative words principle. It suggests that in a string of words, a general or wide word should have its meaning restricted to the genus or class of the narrower words in the string, unless the context requires otherwise. For example, the meaning of 'other items' in the phrase 'watches, clocks, timers, chronometers and other items' is likely to be restricted to items of the same class or type as the others.

2.33 In *Westminster CC v Ray Alan (Manshops)* the High Court considered the word 'facilities' in the Trade Descriptions Act 1968, s 14(1) (now repealed) which penalised false statements as to the nature of 'any services, accommodation or facilities'[1]. It found that the word 'facilities' was limited by reference to the words 'service' and 'accommodation' and therefore did not include a closing down sale of goods.

1   [1982] 1 WLR 382 at 387.

2.34 The principle is most applied when the more general word is used at the end of a list, but may also apply when the wider word is within the list or string of narrower words[1]. The principle is, however, unlikely to have any application where the general word is first and then followed by a string of narrower words[2].

[1]   *Scales v Pickering* (1828) 4 Bing 448; *Shaw v Ruddin* (1858) 9 Ir CLR 214.
[2]   *Wellsted's Will Trusts* [1949] Ch 296 at 318.

STATUTORY RULES OF INTERPRETATION

The Interpretation Act 1978

2.35 The Interpretation Act 1978 sets out various general rules for interpreting statutory materials. The following definitions are of particular relevance to consumer law practitioners.

5 Definitions

In any Act, unless the contrary intention appears, words and expressions listed in schedule 1 to this Act are be construed according to that schedule.

Schedule 1

"Month" means calendar month . . .

"Person" includes a body of persons corporate or unincorporated . . .

"Secretary of State" means one of Her Majesty's Principal Secretaries of State;

"Statutory maximum", with reference to a fine or penalty on summary conviction for an offence—

(a)   in relation to England and Wales, means the prescribed sum within the meaning of section 32 of the Magistrates' Courts Act 1980;

(b)   in relation to Scotland, means the prescribed sum within the meaning of section 225(8) of the Criminal Procedure (Scotland) Act 1995; and

(c)   in relation to Northern Ireland, means the prescribed sum within the meaning of Article 4 of the Fines and Penalties (Northern Ireland) Order 1984 . . .

"Writing" includes typing, printing, lithography, photography, and any other modes of representing reproducing words in a visible form, and expressions referring to writing are construed accordingly.

. . .

6 Construction of certain expressions relating to offences

In relation to England and Wales—

(a)   "indictable offence" means an offence which, if committed by an adult, is triable on indictment, whether it is exclusively so triable or triable either way;

(b)   "summary offence" means an offence which, if committed by an adult, is triable only summarily;

(c)   "offence triable either way" means an offence . . . .which, if committed by an adult, is triable either on indictment or summarily;

and the terms "indictable", "summary" and "triable either way", in their application to offences, are to be construed accordingly.

In the above definitions references to the way or ways in which an offence is triable are to be construed without regard to the effect, if any . . . on the mode of trial in a particular case.

7 Gender and number

In any Act, unless the contrary intention appears—

  (a)   words importing the masculine gender include the feminine;
  (b)   words importing the feminine gender include the masculine;
  (c)   words in the singular include the plural and words in the plural include the singular.

8 References to service by post.

Where an Act authorises or requires any document to be served by post (whether the expression "serve" or the expression "give" or "send" or any other expression is used) then, unless the contrary intention appears, the service is deemed to be effected by properly addressing, pre-paying and posting a letter containing the document and, unless the contrary is proved, to have been effected at the time at which the letter would be delivered in the ordinary course of post.

9 References to distance

In the measurement of any distance for the purposes of an Act, that distance shall, unless the contrary intention appears, be measured in a straight line on a horizontal plane.

10 References to time of day

Subject to section 3 of the Summer Time Act 1972 (construction of references to points of time during the period of summer time), whenever an expression of time occurs in an Act, the time referred to shall, unless it is otherwise specifically stated, be held to be Greenwich mean time.

Territorial jurisdiction

2.36 Territorial jurisdiction is now covered in Chapter 3.

Delegated legislation

2.37 Consumer protection laws are often introduced in the form of secondary, or delegated, legislation. This allows Parliament to pass framework legislation, allowing the more detailed regulation to be introduced by Government departments, usually in the form of orders, regulations and rules under the Statutory Instruments Act 1946. The term 'statutory instrument' applies to all 'orders, rules, regulations or other subordinate legislation'[1]. Subordinate legislation is introduced in a variety of forms[2], largely governed by convention. However, there is no hierarchy of subordinate legislation. In consumer protection measures, the most common are *regulations* and *orders*. Each clause of an order is referred to as an 'article'; in regulations each clause is referred to as a 'regulation'. Clauses within the schedules to both are referred to as 'paragraphs'. It is conventional to refer to the revocation of a statutory instruments, whereas statutes are 'repealed'.

[1]   Statutory Instruments Act 1946, s 1.
[2]   'Orders in Council, orders, rules, regulations, schemes, warrants, byelaws and other instruments made or to be made under any Act': Interpretation Act 1978, s 21.

2.38 The ambit and scope of a statutory instrument is limited to the power conferred by the delegating statute (the 'parent provision')[1]. Subordinate legislation that goes beyond the scope of the parent provision is vulnerable to a finding that it is *ultra vires* (beyond power). Expressions used in the Interpretation Act 1978 conferring power to make subordinate legislation have a consistent meaning in the subordinate legislation.

11 Construction of subordinate legislation

Where an Act confers power to make subordinate legislation, expressions used in that legislation have, unless the contrary intention appears, the meaning which they bear in the Act.

[1]   See for example *R v Secretary of State the Home Department, ex parte Leech* (No 2) [1994] QB 198; *Raymond v Honey* [1983] 1 AC 1, per Lord Wilberforce.

2.39 It was historically considered that any disobedience of subordinate legislation was an indictable misdemeanour at common law[1]. An offence occurred even if the criminality was not expressly set out in the delegated legislation or parent statute. It seems highly unlikely that such a rule exists today[2].

[1]   *R v Walker* (1875) LR 10 QB 355; *R v Hall* [1891] 1 QB 747 at 765; *Willingale v Norris* [1909] 1 KB at 64 DC.

[2]   See *R v Horseferry Road Magistrates' Court, ex parte Independent Broadcasting Authority* [1987] QB 54 DC, where it was said that disobedience of a statute was not of itself an offence and in modern times, no more than a rule of construction.

Human rights

2.40 At the time of writing, the UK government has refused to commit to the UK's continued adherence to the ECHR after exit from the EU. On the other hand, neither has it stated that the UK will withdraw from the Convention; therefore for present purposes, we will assume the UK's continued adherence to the Convention.

3 Interpretation of legislation

(1)   So far as it is possible to do so, primary legislation and subordinate legislation must be read and given effect in a way which is compatible with the Convention rights.

(2)   This section—

    (a)   applies to primary legislation and subordinate legislation whenever enacted;

    (b)   does not affect the validity, continuing operation or enforcement of any incompatible primary legislation; and

    (c)   does not affect the validity, continuing operation or enforcement of any incompatible subordinate legislation if (disregarding any possibility of revocation) primary legislation prevents removal of the incompatibility.

2.41 It is beyond the scope of this chapter to consider the interpretative obligations required by the Human Rights Act 1998, s 3 and the European Convention on Human Rights. A comprehensive guide to these obligations is to be found in *Lester, Pannick & Herberg: Human Rights Law and Practice*.

STATUS, APPLICATION AND INTERPRETATION OF EU LAW POST-BREXIT

Introduction

2.42 Before turning to consider the general principles of interpretation of EU law, it is first necessary to consider the status, application and interpretation of EU law post-Brexit. This is a short guide to a complex legal framework.

Overview

2.43 On 31 January 2020 (exit day), the UK left the EU, the UK-EU withdrawal agreement came into force, and s 1 of the EU(W)A 2018 repealed the European Communities Act 1972 (ECA 1972), which had previously enabled EU law to apply to the UK. However, s 1A of the EEU(W)A 2018 immediately saved much of the effect of the ECA 1972 (in modified form) for the duration of the transition period[1], and s 1B saved UK legislation that implemented EU requirements ('EU-derived domestic legislation'). These savings preserved business as usual for most purposes during the transition period, and postponed substantive legal changes until the end of that period. At the end of the transition period, ss 2 to 4 of the EU(W)A 2018 created a new body of UK law, known as retained EU law, based on the EU law that applied to the UK at the end of the transition period.

[1] The transitional period came to an end on 31 December 2020.

Retained EU law

2.44 EU law was retained as follows:

- Section 2 retained EU-derived domestic legislation, as it had effect in UK law at the end of the transition period, although some exceptions apply. The definition of EU-derived domestic legislation is broad enough to catch most UK legislation made before the end of the transition period that had an EU connection.
- Section 3 saved and converted into UK law most (but not all) directly applicable EU law (such as EU regulations) as it had effect in EU law immediately before the end of the transition period, but only so far as it applied to the UK under the transitional arrangements in Part Four of the withdrawal agreement, and subject to various other exceptions.
- Section 4 saved and converted into UK law most of the EU rights, powers, liabilities, obligations, restrictions, remedies and procedures which before the end of the transition period were recognised and available in UK law through the s 1A savings and modifications to s 2(1) of the ECA 1972 (such as directly effective rights in EU treaties).

Interpretation of retained EU law

2.45 The EU(W)A 2018 includes rules relating to the interpretation of retained EU law as follows:

- Section 5(1) to 5(3) gives retained EU law under ss 3 and 4 priority over conflicting UK law passed or made before the end of the transition period, but not over UK law passed or made afterwards, with certain provisos.
- Section 6 sets out the rules that courts must apply when interpreting retained EU law, including their use of CJEU decisions that had effect before the end of the transition period, and their ability to depart from such decisions.

Section 6 rules on interpreting retained EU law

2.46 By s 6:

- UK courts must (with exceptions for the Supreme Court, the High Court of Justiciary where it is acting as a final court of appeal, and the Court of Appeal and equivalent courts) decide any question about the validity, meaning or effect of retained EU law (so far as it remains unmodified, and so far as relevant to it) in accordance with retained domestic case law, retained EU case law, and retained general principles of EU law, and having regard to the limits of EU competences immediately before the end of the transition period (s 6(3)).
- UK courts interpreting unmodified retained EU law must therefore continue to follow the CJEU decisions that applied before the end of the transition period until one of the courts above departs from the CJEU decision (subject to the usual rules of precedent between decisions of UK courts), or until UK legislation modifies the retained EU law.
- Where retained EU law has been modified[1] after the end of the transition period, s 6(3) 'does not prevent' UK courts from deciding its validity, meaning or effect in accordance with relevant retained domestic and retained EU case law and retained general principles of EU law, and having regard to the limits of EU competences immediately before the end of the transition period, if doing so is 'consistent with the intention of the modifications' (s 6(6)).
- In deciding whether to depart from any retained EU case law, the Supreme Court and the High Court of Justiciary in Scotland apply the same test they would apply in deciding whether to depart from their own case law (s 6(5)).
- The European Union (Withdrawal) Act 2018 (Relevant Court) (Retained EU Case Law) Regulations 2020[2], extended the power to depart from retained EU case law to the Court of Appeal and equivalent courts across the UK (such as the Inner House of the Court of Session in Scotland).
- The terms of the withdrawal agreement (as implemented into UK law by UK legislation) take precedence over the requirements of s 6 (s 6(6A), EU(W)A 2018).

[1] Modify includes to amend, repeal or revoke: see EU(W)A 2018, s 20.
[2] SI 2020/1525.

Status of retained EU law

2.47 At the end of the transition period, retained EU law under s 2 of the EU(W)A 2018 (EU-derived domestic legislation) already had the status of primary or secondary legislation in UK law. However, there was no comparable pre-existing legal status for retained EU law under ss 3 or 4 of the EU(W)A 2018. Section 7(1) to 7(4) of the EU(W)A 2018 clarifies the status of retained EU law as primary or secondary legislation for the purposes of amendment by other UK legislation. Section 7(5) of the EU(W)A 2018 lists EUWA provisions that address the status of retained EU law for other purposes.

CJEU jurisdiction and case law after end of transition period

2.48 From the end of the transition period, the withdrawal agreement specifies certain limited circumstances in which the CJEU has jurisdiction, the UK must comply with CJEU rulings, and UK courts can refer cases to the CJEU. For instance, post-transition:

- The CJEU continues to have jurisdiction in respect of proceedings brought, or requests for preliminary rulings referred, before the end of the transition period (Art 86, withdrawal agreement).
- For four years post-transition, the European Commission can bring cases before the CJEU relating to UK breaches during transition. The European Commission can also bring cases before the CJEU relating to the UK's failure to comply with EU decisions (whether adopted before the end of the transition period, or post-transition under Art 95(1)) within four years of the decision date (Art 87).
- A UK court or tribunal can request a preliminary ruling from the CJEU on the interpretation of Part Two of the withdrawal agreement (citizens' rights), where the court or tribunal considers that a decision is necessary for it to give judgment. In general, the case must have commenced at first instance within eight years from the end of the transition period, although earlier deadlines apply in some circumstances (Art 158).

Lipton v BA City Flyer Ltd

2.49 In *Lipton*[1] the Court of Appeal had to consider the status of EU Regulation 261/04 following the UK's exit from the EU. The CA held as follows:

- The Regulation had been adopted before the UK's exit from the EU and the expiry of the transitional period and was directly applicable.
- After the UK's exit from the EU, the regulation became 'retained legislation' pursuant to s 3 of the EU(W)A 2018 and formed part of UK domestic law, taking effect as amended by the Air Passenger Rights and Air Travel Organisers' Licensing (Amendment) (EU Exit) Regulations 2019.
- The principle of supremacy of EU law applies by virtue of s 5(2) of EU(W)A 2018[2] which provides that the principle: 'continues to apply on or after IP completion day so far as relevant to the interpretation,

disapplication or quashing of any enactment or rule of law passed or made before IP completion day'.

- The regulation had to be given a purposive construction which took into account its recital and other principles, and its effect was to be determined by reference to case law of the CJEU made before 23.00 on 31st December 2020.

- Paragraph 2 of Sch 1 of EU(W)A 2018, entitled 'General principles of EU law', makes general principles part of domestic law provided they were recognised in relevant case law prior to IP completion day.

[1]   [2021] EWCA Civ 454, [2021] 1 WLR 2545, [2021] 1 Lloyd's Rep 484.
[2]   SI 2019/278.

GENERAL PRINCIPLES OF INTERPRETATION OF EU LAW

Purposive interpretation

2.50 The CJEU's approach to statutory interpretation is rather different to that of English courts. As noted by the late Bingham J in *Customs and Excise Commissioners v Samex ApS*[1]:

> 'The interpretation of Community instruments involves very often not the process familiar to common lawyers of laboriously extracting the meaning from words used but the more creative process of supplying flesh to a spare and loosely constructed skeleton.'

[1]   *Customs and Excise Commissioners v Samex ApS* [1983] 3 CMLR 194 (QBD), at 211.

2.51 Thus, the CJEU seeks to reveal and advance the purpose of the particular provision and in so doing does not consider itself bound by the provision's precise wording[1]. This is understandable when EU law is drafted in general terms and in pursuit of broad aims and purposes. Accordingly, the CJEU approach to interpretation 'involves placing the provision in question in its context and interpreting it in relation to the broader scheme of which it forms a part'[2]. This is why, whilst the preamble of a particular EU legislative measure has no binding legal force, it is often resorted to as providing the context within which the particular provision is to be read[3].

[1]   See, for instance, Sir Patrick Neill *The European Court of Justice: a case study in judicial activism* (European Policy Forum, 1995) 47.
[2]   J Millet 'Rules of Interpretation of EEC Legislation' (1989) 11 *Statute Law Review* 163.
[3]   See, for instance, Case C-562/08 *Muller Fleisch GmbH v Land Baden-Wurttemberg* [2010] ECR I-1391 at para 40, Case C-134/08 *Tyson Parketthandel* [2009] ECR I-2875 at para 16.

2.52 In the *CILFIT* judgment[1], the CJEU noted that one of the features that needed to be borne in mind in the process of interpretation of EU law is the multilingual nature of EU law; EU law is drafted in several languages with each version being equally authentic. There is an overriding imperative for uniform interpretation across the Union and the CJEU will seek to interpret the provision in question in accordance with the different language versions. Divergences between language versions are resolved by reference to the provision's purpose and the general scheme of the rules of which it forms part[2]. The court's 'teleological' approach to interpretation is not dissimilar to the common law 'purposive approach'. However, whilst the purposive approach is only resorted to in common law systems where provision is ambiguous or lacks clarity, the CJEU sees such an approach as a primary interpretative tool.

[1]   In this regard, see Case 283/81 *CILFIT v Ministry of Health* [1982] ECR 3415 at paras 17–20.
[2]   Case 30/77 *Bouchereau* [1977] ECR 1999 at para 14.

2.53 In the first English case to consider the CPUTR 2008 in any detail, *OFT v Purely Creative*[1], the High Court reminded practitioners that the canons of construction of EU law are of paramount importance when interpreting legislation with an EU basis. This is of particular significance when the legislation has implemented a Directive that is expressly designed to harmonise laws throughout the Member States (such as the UCPD).

[1]   [2011] EWHC 106 (Ch).

No binding precedents

2.54 A further important difference in approach between common law systems and that of the CJEU is the absence of the doctrine of binding precedent at EU level[1], albeit in practice the CJEU rarely departs from principles laid down in its previous cases, often repeating passages verbatim. The absence of an explicit doctrine of binding precedent has a number of consequences[2]. It means, first of all, that the national courts remain entitled to refer questions previously dealt with by the CJEU to it a second time[3]. Secondly, the distinction between the *ratio* of a judgment of the CJEU and *obiter* remarks is not recognised in EU law. The entirety of the judgment is seen as an expression of the will of the court. Finally, the absence of a formal doctrine of binding precedent means that the CJEU does not always indicate whether it is developing, distinguishing, departing from or altogether overruling its previous decisions[4], causing occasional confusion on the part of practitioners.

[1]   This is not to say that the judgments of the CJEU do not constitute a 'source of law'. Indeed, in Case C-224/01 *Kobler* [2003] ECR I-10239 the Court has held that a 'manifest breach' of its case law by a national authority of a Member State may render the Member State liable in damages to an injured party (para 56).
[2]   Aidan O'Neill QC *EU Law for UK Lawyers* (Hart Publishing, 2011), pp 48–53.
[3]   See, for instance, Case C-91/92 *Dori v Recreb* [1994] ECR I-3325.
[4]   See, for instance, Case C-368/95 *Familiapress v Bauer Verlag* [1997] ECR I-3689, which failed to make any reference to its previous ruling which pointed the other way (Joined Cases 60 and 61/84 *Cinetheque SA and Others v Federation Nationale des Cinemas Français* [1985] ECR 2605). The CJEU has only expressly overruled its decisions in a small number of cases. See, for instance, Case C-267, 268/91 *Criminal Proceedings against Keck and Mithouard* [1993] ECR I-6097.

Minimum and maximum harmonisation

2.55 Article 114 was used to harmonise national laws in the context and functioning of the internal market, enabling the EU to choose the relevant standards that become applicable across the Union[1]. There has been a proliferation of harmonised standards in the past few decades, with EU measures affecting such things as doorstep selling[2], the labelling of foodstuffs[3] and the safety of toys[4].

[1]   Weatherill *EU Consumer Law and Policy* (Elgar European Law, 2005), p 2.

2   Directive 2011/83/EU which repealed Directive 85/577/EEC and which lays down a set of
    uniform rules to protect consumers in distance and off-premises contracts.
3   Regulation 1169/2011/EU which repealed Directive 2000/13/EEC relating to labelling, presen-
    tation and advertising of foodstuffs.
4   Directive 2009/48/EC on toy safety.

2.56 Minimum harmonisation measures act as minimum standards. Member States are allowed to maintain or introduce more stringent rules than those contained in the EU measure[1]. For instance, in *Buet*[2], the CJEU upheld the French ban on doorstep selling, which gave consumers more protection than that laid down by the Doorstep Selling Directive, on the ground that the Union measure was one of minimum harmonisation. Hence, on the minimum harmonisation model, the EU measure acts as a floor below which national legislation cannot fall.

1   For an example of a minimum harmonisation measure, see Directive 93/13 on unfair terms in
    consumer contracts ([1993] OJ L 95/29).
2   Case 382/87 *Buet v Ministère Public* [1989] ECR 1235.

2.57 Maximum harmonisation, on the other hand, prevents Member States from maintaining or adopting measures that are more restrictive than the harmonising measure[1]. The *Plus*[2] and *Total*[3] cases under the UCPD illustrate this point. In both cases, Member States had unilaterally introduced blanket bans on commercial practices that were not listed in Annex I to the UCPD, which sets out the practices that are prohibited in all circumstances. The CJEU held that because the UCPD was a measure of maximum harmonisation, Member States were pre-empted from adopting more restrictive measures. If a practice was not in the Annex, then it had to be assessed individually in the light of the general clauses. The blanket bans were therefore found to be illegal. Under the maximum harmonisation model the harmonising measure acts as both floor and ceiling. This is not to say that any act on the part of the Member State which goes further than the maximum harmonising measure is necessarily illegal. In such instances of 'gold plating'[4] it becomes necessary to assess the reach of the Directive in question; 'gold plating' will only breach EU law if the national measure overlaps with the Directive and goes beyond it.

1   See, for instance, Case C-44/01 *Hartlauer* [2003] ECR I-3095 on Directive 84/450 on mislead-
    ing advertising (superseded by Directive 2006/114/EEC).
2   Joint cases C-261/07 and C-299/07 *VTB-VAB NV v Total Belgium NV* and *Galatea BVBA v
    Sanoma Magazines Belgium NV* [2010] All ER (EC) 694.
3   Case C-304/08 *Zentrale zur Bekämpfung unlauteren Wettbewerbs eV v Plus Warenhandelsge-
    sellschaft mbH* [2011] All ER (EC) 338.
4   The term 'gold plating' is used to describe the process whereby a Member State goes beyond an
    EU harmonising measure. It has been defined by the European Commission as the act of
    'transposition of EU legislation, which goes beyond what is required by that legislation, while
    staying within legality. If not illegal, 'gold plating' is usually presented as a bad practice because
    it imposes costs that could have been avoided'.

Sector-specific legislation

2.58 Wide-reaching harmonisation measures are often accompanied by a caveat: where sector-specific EU legislation is in place and its provisions overlap with the general provisions of the harmonising measure, the sector-specific legislation shall take precedence. For instance, Art 3(4) UCPD states:

In the case of conflict between the provisions of this Directive and other Community rules regulating specific aspects of unfair commercial practices, the latter shall prevail and apply to those specific aspects.

2.59 Recital 10 of the Preamble provides as follows:

'It is necessary to ensure that the relationship between this Directive and exist-ing Community law is coherent, particularly where detailed provisions on unfair commercial practices apply to specific sectors . . . This Directive accordingly applies only in so far as there are no specific Community law provisions regulating specific aspects of unfair commercial practices, such as information requirements and rules on the way the information is presented to the consumer. It provides protection for consumers where there is no specific sectoral legislation at Community level and prohibits traders from creating a false impression of the nature of products . . . '

2.60 It will be interesting to see what significance the courts attribute to the word 'conflict' in Art 3(4). A broad view of Art 3(4) would suggest that where a specific sectoral measure applies to the commercial practice in question, it ousts the application of the UCPD. It could therefore be said that rather than meaning 'incompatibility', it could be argued that the word 'conflict' is used in the same way as in the 'conflict of laws', where the question is which system of laws applies to a given dispute. This appears to accord with the Commission Guidance on the Directive[1]:

'Where sectoral legislation is in place and its provisions overlap with the Direc-tive's general provisions, the corresponding provisions of the *lex specialis* will prevail . . . Often, such conflicts arise from the fact that the *lex specialis* contains more detailed precontractual information requirements, or stricter rules on the way the information is presented to consumers (see Recital 10 of the Directive).'

[1]   Guidance on the Implementation/Application of Directive 2005/29/EC on Unfair Commercial Practices.

Time periods under EU law

2.61 EC Regulation 1182/71 determining the rules applicable to periods, dates and time limits:

Article 4

1. Subject to the provisions of this Article, the provisions of Article 3 shall, with the exception of paragraphs 4 and 5, apply to the times and periods of entry into force, taking effect, application, expiry of validity, termination of effect or cessation of application of acts of the Council or Commission or of any provisions of such acts.

Article 3

4. Where the last day of a period expressed otherwise than in hours is a public holiday, Sunday or Saturday, the period shall end with the expiry of the last hour of the following working day.

2.62 This provision may be important when construing provisions that imple-ment EU law, such as the Consumer Contracts (Information, Cancellation and Additional Charges) Regulations 2013, which provides for 14-day cancellation periods, see CHAPTER 6, Consumer Rights.

Definition of consumer

2.63 European directives[1] generally define a consumer to be any natural person who is acting for purposes which are outside his trade, business, craft or profession. The definition of consumer in UK legislation has been modified to include the words 'wholly or mainly' in recent enactments[2].

1   Article 2 of the UCPD/ Consumer Rights Act 2015.
2   CCR 2013, SI 2013/3134, the CPUTR 2008, substituted by the Consumer Protection (Amendment) Regulations 2014, SI 2014/870, reg 2(3) and Consumer Rights Act 2015.

2.64 Consumer Rights Act 2015, s 76(2) and s 2(3):

'consumer' means an individual acting for purposes that are wholly or mainly outside that individual's trade, business, craft or profession.

2.65 A consumer is an individual, not a legal entity, such as a company[1]. The courts look to the substance of a transaction. An individual who purchased a house to live in using an investment company was found to be a consumer. However, the result would have been different if the purchase had been for investment purposes[2]. In claims under the CRA 2015, a trader who claims an individual is *not* a consumer must prove it[3].

1   CJEU *Cape v Idealservice* (C-541/99) at paras 15–16.
2   *Heifer International Inc v Christiansen* [2008] Bus LR D49 at para 250. See also *R&B Customs Brokers Co Ltd v United Dominions Trust Ltd* [1988] 1 All ER 847. The CJEU case of *Condominio di Milano, via Meda v Eurothermo SpA* (C-329/19) casts some doubt on these decisions, but the Court in that case was clear that member states may extend protection to associations which act on behalf of consumers, so arguably this is what the UK has done here through the common law process and there is no need for express statutory wording to that effect.
3   See for example Consumer Rights Act 2015, s 76(3).

2.66 There are three types of situation in which it is not always easy to assess whether an individual is acting outside their trade, business, craft or profession: where a business use is in the future or the past, where the individual is engaged in an activity which may be profitable, and where the purposes of the contract are a mixture of business and consumer.

2.67 The courts have set out some general principles to be applied.

*   The focus must be on the person's role in the context of *that* contract, rather than their general situation. A person may be a consumer for some transactions and 'an economic operator' in others. The nature and aim of the contract, and all its facts, must be considered[1].
*   'contracts concluded for the purpose of satisfying an individual's **own needs in terms of private consumption** come under the provisions designed to protect the consumer as the party deemed to be the weaker party economically'[2].
*   However the scale of the activities may not be determinative because wealthy consumers are consumers nonetheless[3].
*   'consumption' equates to 'enjoyment' or 'use of' the product[4].
*   Where an individual acts 'in such a way as to give the other party to the contract the legitimate impression that he was active for the purposes of his business' he may forfeit his consumer protection[5]. However, this

principle should not be overstated exaggerating one's experience of investing for example is not an indication of being in business[6].

- The fact that a consumer develops expertise in a field, holds out their expertise to others, and seeks to organize others to challenge a trader does not mean they are professional[7]. 'The question is not the knowledge, experience, skill or expertise of the putative consumer, but the purpose of the contract[8].'

- It is irrelevant and inappropriate to consider whether the contracting party in question is 'in need of protection' or is unlike the 'paradigm of the average' consumer[9].

[1] *Dentalkit* at para 16. See also CJEU *Costea* (C110/14) at para 20: an individual's personal technical skill or ability (eg if they are a lawyer) does not mean they are not a consumer if they enter a contract for non-business purposes (paras 26–27). It is also not relevant that a loan is secured on their business premises (para 28), since the consumer is presumed to be the weaker party when acting in a personal capacity.

[2] *Dentalkit* at para 17. See also *Standard Bank London Ltd v Apostolakis (No 1)* [2002] CLC 933.

[3] *Ang v Reliantco Investments Ltd* [2019] EWHC 879 at para 62. See also *CJEU Pillar Securitisation Sarl v Arnadottir* C-694/17 para 45 'a consumer who has concluded a credit agreement for more than [€75,000] is not any less deserving of the protection set out' in the Lugano II Convention than a consumer who has taken a loan for less.

[4] *Standard Bank London Ltd v Apostolakis (No 1)* [2002] CLC 933. See also the decision in *Turner and Co (GB) Ltd v Abi* [2010] EWHC 2078 (QB) at paras 41 and 42.

[5] *Gruber v BayWa AG* (C-464–01) at para 54. See also *Overy v PayPal* [2012] EWHC 2659 (QB) at para 169.

[6] *Ang v Reliantco Investments Ltd* [2019] EWHC 879 at para 58.

[7] CJEU *Schrems v Facebook Ireland Ltd* C-498/16 para 39–41. Specifically, the CJEU ruled that activities such as publishing books, lecturing, setting up websites, fundraising and being assigned other consumers' claims may not make a person lose their consumer status.

[8] *Ang v Reliantco Investments Ltd* [2019] EWHC 879 at para 41(i). Knowledge or skill might help the court to decide whether a person is running a business, but is not determinative in itself. In this case, the consumer, who was the wife of a person who developed Bitcoin, was engaged in Bitcoin investments, and was found not to be acting in the course of business.

[9] *Ang v Reliantco Investments Ltd* [2019] EWHC 879 at para 41(iii)–(iv).

Future and past business purpose

2.68 In *Benincasa v Dentalkit Srl*[1], the CJEU considered a jurisdictional argument about an individual who made purchases intended for use in a future dentistry business, which ultimately never traded. It held that the fact that the business purpose lies in the future does not divest the contract of its trade or professional character[2]. A person may be a consumer at the start of a long contract, but move to professional status later on[3].

[1] [1998] All ER (EC) 135, [1997] ECR I-3767.
[2] *Dentalkit* at para 17.
[3] CJEU *Schrems v Facebook Ireland Ltd* C-498/16 at paras 37–38.

2.69 Similarly in *Turner & Co (GB) Ltd v Abi* the High Court found that a person selling their shares in the business that they ran was not a consumer[1]:

'Owning and running printing companies was his business. It was how he made his living. This contract was made for the purposes of that business. This was not, to use the words of the European Court of Justice, something for his family or personal use. It was a business decision made in the course of running the business through which he earned his living. I do not think it right to import into that factual analysis concepts of English company law differentiating the business of the company from the business of its owners.'

¹ [2010] EWHC 2078 (QB). The judge ruled at para 42 that the approach taken in *Turner* is consistent with that of the CJEU in *France v Di Pinto* [1993] 1 CMLR 399 where it held that a person selling their business is not a consumer in that transaction. This appears to be at odds with the older decision *Davies v Sumner* [1984] 1 WLR 1301, which focussed almost exclusively on the need for regularity before a person is to be regarded as a trader.

Profit making activities

2.70 The mere fact that an individual hopes to profit from a transaction does not necessarily remove their consumer status[1]. There are many squarely consumer transactions which aim to generate money, such as ISA investments or private pensions[2]. This approach can be contrasted to earlier suggestions that account must be taken of the extent to which they have a profit seeking motive, the number, amount and frequency of transactions, the seller's sales turnover and whether they purchase products in order to resell them[3]. The fact that a consumer develops expertise in a field, holds out their expertise to others, and seeks to organise others to challenge a trader does not mean they are professional[4]. Specifically, the CJEU ruled that activities such as publishing books, lecturing, setting up websites, fundraising and being assigned other consumers' claims will not make a person lose their consumer status[5].

¹ *Standard Bank London Ltd v Apostolakis (No 1)* [2002] CLC 933.
² Investment by a private individual of their personal surplus wealth, in the hope of generating good returns, is not a business activity, but a private consumption need: *Ang v Reliantco Investments Ltd* [2019] EWHC 879 at para 63.
³ See also the views of the European Commission in Commission Guidance [COM (2016) 320] para 2.1, and also Commission Communication *A European Agenda for the Collaborative Economy* [COM (2016) 356] para 2.3.
⁴ CJEU *Schrems v Facebook Ireland Ltd* C-498/16 at paras 39–41.
⁵ CJEU *Schrems v Facebook Ireland Ltd* C-498/16.

2.71 In *Reliantco*, the CJEU ruled that the critical question is whether a person enters the transaction within the scope of their actual profession[1]. However, previous decisions have generally set out a range of criteria to be considered[2]. In light of *Reliantco*, those decisions may need to be revisited. The sorts of criteria which have previously been considered to be relevant include:

- The regularity of the transactions[3], although this factor is now less likely to be determinative having regard to the *Reliantco* cases[4].
- The scale of the transaction, bearing in mind that even very large transactions have been held still to be consumer contracts[5].
- Whether they in fact derive their living from it – whether it is a business that they carry on[6].
- Whether it in fact relates to their main business[7].
- Whether they bring expertise to the transaction[8]. This is another factor that may now need to be reconsidered after the *Reliantco* cases[9].
- Whether the transaction is part of a lifestyle choice, savings scheme or driven by personal circumstances[10].

¹ This approach finds support in the CJEU decision of *Jana Petruchova* (C-208/18), in the context of Regulation 1215/2012, Art 17(1).

2   See CJEU *Komisia za zashtita na potrebitelite v Kamenova* (C-105/17) paras 38–39 which sets
     out a non exhaustive and non exclusive list of criteria to be considered. See also *AMT
     Futures Ltd v Marzillier* [2015] 2 WLR 187 at para 58.
3   See *R&B Customs Brokers Co Ltd v United Dominions Trust Ltd* [1988] 1 All ER 847.
4   *Ang v Reliantco Investments Ltd* [2019] EWHC 879 at para 65: 'spread, regularity and value
     of investment activity cannot . . . determine the issue'.
5   In *Ang v Reliantco Investments Ltd* [2019] EWHC 879 at para 62 large scale speculative
     investments in Bitcoin were held to be consumer transactions. In *Spreadex v Cochrane* [2012]
     EWHC 1290 (Comm), an individual signed up to a website of a spread betting bookmaker to
     make bets on the movements in the prices of stocks, shares and commodities. He built up a
     credit balance of more than £60,000 with the bookmaker, which was regulated by the Financial
     Services Authority. The court found that he was 'plainly a consumer within the meaning of the
     UTCCR'.
6   See *FSA v Asset LI Inc* [2013] EWHC 178 (Ch) at para 127, purchasers of plots of land as
     investments were consumers. However, see also *Allied Irish Bank Plc v Higgins and Ors* [2010]
     IEHC 219.
7   *Maple Leaf Macro Volatility Master Fund and Another v Rouvroy and Another* [2009] 1
     Lloyd's Rep 475 at para 209.
8   *Ghandour v Arab Bank (Switzerland)* [2008] ILPr 35. However, this must now be treated with
     caution given the CJEU's ruling in *Costea* (C110/14) at para 20.
9   *Ang v Reliantco Investments Ltd* [2019] EWHC 879 at paras 41(i) and 68–69: it is not relevant
     to consider whether the individual investor relies on their own expertise, or trades through
     intermediaries, as 'investment of private wealth is an intensely personal matter'.
10   *The Office of Fair Trading v Foxtons* [2009] EWHC 1681 (Ch) at para 28. See also *Smith and
     Smith v Mortgage Express* [2007] CTLC 134 – purchaser of buy-to-let property a consumer,
     and *Parker v NFU Mutual Insurance Society Ltd* [2012] EWHC 2156 (Comm), where property
     was let out but the UTCCR 1999 still applied.

Mixed purpose contracts

2.72 The CRA 2015, in defining a consumer as someone acting for purposes
that are 'wholly or mainly' outside their business, has extended protection
beyond that which existed previously. The leading case was *Gruber v BayWa
AG*[1], concerning an Austrian farmer who purchased roof tiles from a German
supplier for a building which contained not only his home, but also premises he
used for his business. He brought a claim alleging the tiles were defective in the
Austrian courts, relying on his status as a consumer under Art 15 of the Brussels
Regulation. In that case, the CJEU held that an individual would only be
protected if the business purpose *was* 'so limited as to be negligible in the overall
context of the supply. The fact that the private element is predominant is
irrelevant in that respect'[2]. Under the CRA 2015 the burden of proof is,
however, on the trader to establish that the consumer purpose is not predominant[3].

1   C-464–01, [2006] QB 204.
2   See also *Evans v Cherry Tree Finance* [2008] EWCA Civ 331 and [2007] EWHC 3523 (Ch) at
     paras 48–49 and 52. Applied in *Alfred Overy v Paypal Europe* [2012] EWHC 2659 (QB).
3   See Consumer Rights Act 2015, s 76(3).

Definition of trader

2.73 The term *'trader'* is now used in most EU consumer protection directives[1].
This is reflected in the CRA 2015, s 2(2) which sought to align key terms in the
implementation of EU consumer legislation in the UK[2]. The basic definition of
trader focuses on the 'purpose' for which a person[3] is acting.

CRA 2015, s 2(2):

(2) "Trader" means a person acting for purposes relating to that person's trade, business, craft or profession, whether acting personally or through another person acting in the trader's name or on the trader's behalf.

1   An exception is the Unfair Terms Directive (93/13/EEC) which uses the term 'seller or supplier' defined in Article 2(c) as 'acting for purposes relating to his trade, business or profession, whether publicly owned or privately owned'.

2   For example, the Consumer Contracts (Information, Cancellation and Additional Charges) Regulations 2013, SI 2013/3134, the Alternative Dispute Resolution for Consumer Disputes (Competent Authorities and Information) Regulations 2015, SI 2015/542 and the Consumer Protection from Unfair Trading Regulations 2008, SI 2008/1277.

3   'Person' includes a body of persons corporate or unincorporated, Interpretation Act 1978, Sch 1.

2.74 In *R (Khatun) v Newham LBC*[1] the Court of Appeal considered whether a local authority was acting for purposes relating to its 'trade, business or profession' when letting property to a homeless person under a statutory duty, for the purposes of the unfair terms legislation. A broad construction of 'trader' was applied to include, 'every entity engaged in an economic activity, regardless of the legal status of the entity and the way in which it is financed'. It was appropriate to ask whether the entity 'is engaged in activity which could, at least in principle, be carried out by a private undertaking in order to make profits'. This broad approach is consistent with that taken by the CJEU in considering the application of various consumer directives to bodies such as publicly owned entities and education providers[2].

1   [2005] QB 37, [2004] 3 WLR 417, [2004] HLR 29, [2004] L & TR 18.

2   CJEU *Karel de Grote v Kuijpers* (C-147/16) para 42. The Court in this case also ruled that any body engaged in professional activities, whether publicly or privately owned, or run on a not for profit basis, is within scope (para 51). A higher education establishment can therefore be a trader in particular where it offers additional services, ancillary to education (para 57). See also CJEU *Siba v Devenas* C-573/13 paras 25, 28–30 a lawyer or other public body may be a trader; and *Asbeek Brusse v Jahani* (C-488/11) paras 28–30. The CJEU held the test is whether the contracting parties are acting for purposes relating to their trade, business or profession. The directive does not restrict its scope solely to contracts concluded between a seller and a consumer.

2.75 The term 'trader' is to be given a similarly broad construction for the purposes of the CPUTR 2008, which implements the Unfair Commercial Practices Directive ('UCPD') in the UK, see **CHAPTER 8** Unfair Commercial Practices. In the *BKK Mobil Oil Case*[1] the CJEU stated that the drafting of 'trader' in the UCPD had 'conferred a particularly broad meaning on the term'. In *Surrey Trading Standards v Scottish and Southern Energy PLC*[2] the Court of Appeal (Criminal Division) also gave a broad construction to the concept of 'trader' placed in the context of the 'commercial practices' definition under the UCPD. Davis LJ stated that:

'It is important to bear in mind that "trader", for the purpose of [CPUTR 2008], extends to any person who in relation to a commercial practice is acting for purposes relating to his business. The words "any", "in relation to", "acting" and "relating to" are all words of width and elasticity.'

1   *BP Mobile Oil Körperschaft des öffentlichen Rechts v Zentrale zur Bekämpfung unlauteren Wettbewerbs eV* Case C-59/12.

2   [2012] EWCA Crim 539.

2.76 EU Guidance[1] on the meaning of trader in the UCPD states that:

'Whether a seller qualifies as a "trader" or a consumer must be assessed on a case-by-case basis. Different criteria could be relevant, such as:

–   whether the seller has a profit-seeking motive, including the fact that he/she might have received remuneration or other compensation for acting on behalf of a given trader;
–   the number, amount and frequency of transactions;
–   the seller's sales turnover;
–   whether the seller purchases products in order to resell them.'

[1]   *Guidance on the implementation /application of directive 2005/29/EC on unfair commercial practices.*

2.77 In the case of online sales and the UCPD the CJEU decided that it is for the national courts to decide whether a person is a trader by adopting a case-by-case approach having regard to the following (non-exhaustive) factors[1]:

*   whether the sale was intended to generate profit;
*   whether the seller had technical information and expertise relating to the products which he offered for sale which the consumer did not necessarily have, with the result that he was placed in a more advantageous position than the consumer;
*   whether the seller had a legal status which enabled him to engage in commercial activities and to what extent the online sale was connected to the seller's commercial or professional activity;
*   whether the seller was subject to VAT;
*   whether the seller, acting on behalf of a particular trader or on his own behalf or through another person acting in his name and on his behalf, received remuneration or an incentive;
*   whether the seller purchased new or second-hand goods in order to resell them, thus making that a regular, frequent and/or simultaneous activity in comparison with his usual commercial or business activity;
*   whether the goods for sale were all of the same type or of the same value, and, in particular, whether the offer was concentrated on a small number of goods.

[1]   *Komisia za zashtita na potrebitelite v Evelina Kamenova and Okrazhna prokuratura,* C-105/17.

Agents, representatives and employees

2.78 The agent or representative of a trader will usually be acting for the purposes of trade, business, craft or a profession. However, the question of whether that agent or representative is also a 'trader' will depend on the particular provision concerned. There is a difference between the definition of 'trader' in the UCPD and in other EU consumer protection measures that are primarily concerned with the legal effect of a contractual relationship[1], such as consumer contract information and cancellation. In the UCPD the definition of 'trader' expressly extends both to traders 'and anyone acting in the name or on behalf of the trader' (emphasis added). It follows that a trader's agent or representative is also bound, as a trader, not to engage in unfair commercial practices against consumers. This makes obvious policy sense as many such bad practices are committed by a principal trader's agents or representatives, for example, self-employed door-to-door salesmen.

[1]   Consumer Rights Act 2015, the Consumer Contracts (Information, Cancellation and Additional Charges) Regulations 2013, SI 2013/3134, the Alternative Dispute Resolution for Consumer Disputes (Competent Authorities and Information) Regulations 2015, SI 2015/542.

2.79 The position is different for provisions focussing on contractual relationships, such as those implemented as a consequence of the EU Consumer Rights Directive[1]. These provisions do not expressly make the trader's agent or representative responsible for compliance with the relevant regulatory obligation. However, they do make the trader responsible for those obligations 'whether acting personally or through another person acting in the trader's name or on the trader's behalf'. This reflects the contractual nature of the obligations concerned in these provisions. It plainly makes sense for the party contracting with a consumer, rather than an agent or representative, to be fixed with regulatory obligations affecting the contract, such as its cancellation. Of course this does not mean that a trader's agent or representative will never have regulatory obligations under this type of consumer protection provision. Their responsibility will simply depend on whether they themselves engage in the particular practice covered, for example, if they contract with the consumer on their own behalf.

[1]   Consumer Rights Act 2015 and the Consumer Contracts (Information, Cancellation and Additional Charges) Regulations 2013, SI 2013/3134.

2.80 This distinction is also relevant when considering the liability of a trader's employee as a 'trader'. In implementing the UCPD, the CPUTR 2008 expressly defined 'trader' additionally to include those acting 'in the name of or on behalf of a trader'. As the primary purpose of the UCPD is consumer protection, it seems likely that this creates liability for the employees of a trader. For example, it would not be logical for the UCPD liability of a door-to-door salesman to depend on whether he was engaged as an employee or self-employed agent. That is not to say that it will always be proportionate to bring proceedings against the employee of a trader. In many circumstances that may be disproportionate, however, the question is likely to be one of enforcement discretion, rather than actual liability.

2.81 An employee is unlikely, however, to be responsible for the obligations of a trader under the EU measures focussing on contractual obligations, for the same reason that agents and representatives ordinarily are not. Equally, the employees of a trader are not liable to pay consumer redress for unfair commercial practices under Pt 4A of the CPUTR 2008, even if they are criminally liable for them[1].

[1]   See CPUTR 2008, SI 2008/1277, reg 2.

Public bodies

2.82 It is now clear that most UK consumer protection measures will apply to public authorities, to the extent that they engage in the practices covered by them[1]. For example, the CRA 2015, s 2(7) expressly states that 'business' includes the activities of public authorities[2].

CRA 2015, s 2(7):

(7) "Business" includes the activities of any government department or local or public authority.

¹ An exception is the Alternative Dispute Resolution for Consumer Disputes (Competent Authorities and Information) Regulation 2015, SI 2015/542.
² See also CPUTR 2008, SI 2008/1277, reg 2 and Consumer Contracts (Information, Cancellation and Additional Charges) Regulations 2013, SI 2013/3134, reg 5.

Charities

2.83 It is very likely that charities and other not-for-profit organisations, such as NGOs, mutuals and cooperatives, will also be considered traders if they engage in the commercial practices covered by EU consumer protection laws. It is likely that the courts will apply the broad test used in *Khatun* and ask whether the activity could, in principle, be undertaken by a private body for profit. The fact that an organisation is structured as 'non-profit' is therefore likely to be immaterial to the assessment of whether it qualifies as a trader. These EU directives typically state expressly that a particular sector is excluded from the ambit of the measure. For example, the Consumer Rights Directive expressly excludes certain social services and healthcare provision¹. There are no such express exclusions for charities or other not-for-profit organisations.

¹ CRD 2011/83/EC, Art 3(3).

JUDICIAL PRECEDENT

Introduction

2.84 The courts of England and Wales exist in a hierarchical structure with the Supreme Court (formerly the judicial committee of the House of Lords) at its head. Judicial precedent is the mechanism by which that structure operates. Its aim is to produce consistency and to avoid the chaos that would ensue if judges at all levels felt free to arrive at decisions without reference to decisions of other courts of the same or superior level.

2.85 The obligation imposed by precedent is to follow statements of law forming the reasoning that led to the decision (the *ratio decidendi*) of the superior court, not other remarks or observations that are made in passing which are not causative of the decision in question (*obiter dicta*), which nonetheless may have persuasive force.

The position of the CJEU within the hierarchy

2.86 The position of the CJEU was an oddity. It was not formally part of the hierarchy but the Supreme Court/House of Lords and all other courts were obliged to follow its rulings on matters concerning EU law and make references to it where the court in question was the final court of appeal¹. That was the position until 31 December 2020. After 31 December 2020 the position is as follows:

(1) decisions of the CJEU made prior to 31 December 2020 are binding insofar as they relate to retained EU law;

(2) save that the Supreme Court, Court of Appeal and the High Court sitting as an appeal court, may depart from decisions of the CJEU on the same basis as they may depart from their own previous decisions[2]; and

(3) any decisions of the CJEU handed down after 31 December 2020 will have persuasive force only[3].

It should be noted that the CJEU is not obliged to follow its own decisions and therefore there may be conflicting, co-existing decisions of that court. Until 31 December 2020 a UK court faced with conflicting decisions could refer the case before it to the CJEU; after that date, save for some limited exceptions, the UK court is free to choose between the conflicting decisions.

[1] See the ECA 1972, ss 2 and 3; and *R v Secretary State of Transport ex p Factortame (No 1)* [1990] AC 85.
[2] See below.
[3] See generally **2.48** above.

The Supreme Court

2.87 The Supreme Court lies at the head of the hierarchy and its decisions must be followed by all other UK courts. It is free to depart from its own decisions in the circumstances set out in its Practice Direction of 1966[1], that is, while treating its former decisions as normally binding, it may depart from a previous decision when it appears right to do so. The Practice Direction makes clear that the power would be used cautiously, especially where such may impact retrospectively on contracts, settlements of property and fiscal arrangements and where it may undermine certainty as to the criminal law[2].

[1] [1966] 1 WLR 1234.
[2] For an example of the exercise of the power, see *Kleinwort Benson Ltd v Lincoln City Council* [1999] 2 AC 349.

The Court of Appeal (Civil Division)

2.88 The Court of Appeal must follow decisions of the Supreme Court/House of Lords and is generally bound by its own previous decisions and those of older courts of co-ordinate jurisdiction[1], except it may depart from such prior decisions where:

(a) the court has to decide between two conflicting decisions;

(b) its previous decision cannot stand with a decision of the House of Lords[2];

(c) its prior decision was given *per incuriam*, eg where a statute or a rule having statutory effect which would have affected the decision was not brought to the attention of the earlier court[3].

[1] Eg the Exchequer Chamber.
[2] Now the Supreme Court. Presumably the same principle applies to binding decisions of the CJEU.
[3] See *Young v Bristol Aeroplane Co Ltd* [1946] AC 163.

The Court of Appeal (Criminal Division)

2.89 The position of the Criminal Division of the Court of Appeal is similar to that of the Civil Division save that the principles laid out in *Young* are subject to the gloss that the court may depart from prior decisions where such is necessary in the interests of justice[1] This reflects the fact that the Criminal Division is often concerned with the liberty of the subject, and that doing justice in the instant case is paramount.

[1]   See *R v Spencer* [1985] QB 771, per May LJ at 779.

The Divisional Courts

2.90 Divisional Courts of whichever division are bound by the decisions of the Supreme Court/House of Lords, Court of Criminal Appeal[1], and by either division of the Court of Appeal[2]. So far as their own previous decisions are concerned:

(1)   In their supervisory jurisdiction, they will follow their previous decisions as a matter of judicial comity; however, they may depart from a prior decision if convinced it is wrong[3].

(2)   In their appellate jurisdiction, such as a review by way of case stated, they are bound by it[4]. Presumably they may depart from prior decisions on the same grounds as the Court of Appeal can as set out in *Young*.

[1]   See *Ruse v Reed* [1949] 1 KB 370.
[2]   See *Carr v Mercantile Products Ltd* [1949] 2 KB 601 and *Reed v Joannon* (1890) 25 QBD 300.
[3]   See *R v H M Coroner for Greater Manchester ex p Tal* [1985] 1 QB 67.
[4]   See *Tal's Case* (above) and *USA v McCafferty* [1984] 1 WLR 867, 873.

2.91 Divisional Courts often sit as two member courts. This raises the issue of the status of split decisions. This is not a problem that is likely to arise in a modern times as the practice is to re-constitute as a three member court where a two member court is divided[1]. In the case of a historical split decision, the answer probably is as follows:

(1)   Where the court is exercising its appellate jurisdiction, the decision which is in line with the court below stands[2].

(2)   Where the court is exercising its supervisory jurisdiction, the decision is not binding and the court may choose which judgment to follow if there is no other binding authority on the point, or, arrive at its own decision.

[1]   See for instance *Sheldrake v DPP* [2004] QB 487.
[2]   Adopting the practice of House of Lords as illustrated by *Beamish v Beamish* (1861) 9 HLC 274.

The High Court

2.92 The High Court is bound by decisions of the Supreme Court/House of Lords, Court of Appeal and, for all practical purposes[1], the Divisional Courts. So far as its own previous decisions are concerned the same principles apply as with the Divisional Courts, viz. it is bound by its previous decisions arrived at in an appellate capacity and will only depart from a decision arrived at under its original jurisdiction if convinced it is wrong.

1   See Robert Goff LJ in *Tal's Case* (above) at p 81 where he says: 'we find it difficult to imagine that a single judge exercising this jurisdiction [ie a supervisory jurisdiction] would ever depart from a decision of a divisional court'.

The Upper Tribunal

2.93 The Upper Tribunal was created in 2008 as part of a programme, set out in the Tribunals, Courts and Enforcement Act 2007, to rationalise the tribunal system, and to provide a common means of handling appeals against the decisions of lower tribunals. The Upper Tribunal is a superior court of record, giving it equivalent status to the High Court. The same principles apply to it as apply to the High Court (see above).

The Crown Court

2.94 The Crown Court was instituted by the Courts Act 1971 as a superior court of record, as the successor to assizes or quarter sessions, However, in the absence of any systematic reporting of its decisions, its rulings do not bind other Crown Courts or the magistrates' court[1]. It is bound by decisions of the Supreme Court/House of Lords, Court of Appeal and High Court.

1   See Andrew Ashworth, 'The Binding Effect of Crown Court Decisions', cr LR (1980) 502.

Inferior courts and First-tier Tribunals

2.95 The inferior courts consist of the county court and magistrates' courts. They are incapable of setting binding precedent but county court judges will tend to follow other decisions of the county court to promote judicial comity. District judges in the magistrates' court do likewise. The inferior courts and first-tier tribunals are bound by decisions of superior courts of record other than the Crown Court.

Chapter 3

TERRITORIAL JURISDICTION

Contents

INTRODUCTION

3.1 The stratospheric rise of the internet as a medium for traders selling to United Kingdom ('UK') consumers has substantially increased the importance of territorial jurisdiction in consumer law. It is now commonplace for traders selling products to UK consumers to operate entirely from overseas. In a textbook of this size and type it is not possible to deal comprehensively with all of the complex legal issues involved in litigation in many different territorial jurisdictions. Instead we have attempted to provide a practical guide to the issues that are likely to be faced by UK enforcers and consumers in three different scenarios:

(a) Private civil litigation between a UK consumer and an overseas trader.
(b) Public enforcement by a UK regulator against an overseas trader selling products to UK consumers.
(c) Criminal enforcement against an overseas trader in relation to the commission of offences against UK consumers.

3.2 Most UK consumer protection provisions now have a European Union ('EU') law basis and there is a significant level of cooperation by EU Members States in relation to both public enforcement and private civil litigation of consumer law issues. Many of the relevant international treaties were negotiated and agreed as a part of the UK's EU membership, and these will continue to apply to many pieces of litigation even after the UK's exit from the EU (which was completed on 31 December 2020). Consequently, we have distinguished in our scenarios between an overseas trader based in the EU and a trader based outside the EU. The position from 1 January 2021 in relation to civil jurisdiction and applicable law is that:

- Jurisdiction of cases already commenced in court will continue to be governed by the Brussels Recast Regulation or Lugano Convention (as the case may be)[1].

- Jurisdiction of cases which are commenced in the UK on or after 1 January 2021 will be governed by the domestic law of each UK jurisdiction – the UK will cease to be bound by the EU regime on jurisdiction[2].

- The law applicable to a contract concluded on or before 31 December 2020 will continue to be governed by the Rome I Regulation (EC 593/2008)[3].

- The law applicable to torts and delicts where the event giving rise to the damage occurred on or before 31 December 2020 will continue to be governed by the Rome II Regulation (EC 864/2007)[4].

- The law applicable to contracts concluded and harmful events which occur from 1 January 2021 onwards will be governed by the Rome I and Rome II Regulations as retained EU law, and as amended by the Law Applicable to Contractual Obligations and Non-Contractual Obligations (Amendment etc) (EU Exit) Regulations 2019.

---

[1] See Arts 67 and 69 of the Withdrawal Agreement and reg 92 of the Civil Jurisdiction and Judgements (Amendment) (EU Exit) Regulations 2019.
[2] The UK has applied to accede to the Lugano Convention 2007 as a sovereign state, but at the time of writing is still waiting for the other contracting countries to agree to this.
[3] Art 66 of the Withdrawal Agreement.
[4] Art 66 of the Withdrawal Agreement.

GENERAL PRINCIPLES

Territorial extent of UK legislation

3.3 UK consumer law is largely, although not entirely, statute based. Unless the contrary intention appears, it is presumed that an Act of Parliament extends to the whole of the UK[1], but not to any territory outside the UK[2]. The presumption applies equally to delegated legislation, which has the same territorial effect as the parent provision under which it was made. It is presumed that Parliament does not intend to outlaw conduct which takes place exclusively overseas unless it clearly says so on the face of the legislation, or that can be implied from the scheme, context and subject matter of the legislation, since to do otherwise would breach the principle of comity[3]. It is therefore important to look carefully in the legislation for the provision setting out the territorial extent of the law, although this may not be decisive[4]. Where an overseas trader establishes itself within the UK, it will be subject to UK law, in the same way as any other British citizen is[5]. Likewise, an overseas trader's property in the UK is subject to UK law[6].

---

[1] *Bennion on Statutory Interpretation* (7th edn), 4.6.
[2] *King v Director of the Serious Fraud Office* [2009] 1 WLR 718 at 725.

3   See *R (on the application of KBR, Inc) (Appellant) v Director of the Serious Fraud Office (Respondent)* [2021] UKSC 2 para 28–29. In assessing whether the SFO was able to apply powers to a person outside the UK, the Supreme Court considered the wording and purpose of the legislation, the legislative history of the statute, including the pre-legislative report, the later legislative developments, and analogies with similar legislative schemes.

4   *R (on the application of KBR, Inc) (Appellant) v Director of the Serious Fraud Office (Respondent)* [2021] UKSC 2 para 29, where a statement that legislation 'extends to England and Wales only' was not to be read as determining whether it had extra-territorial effect. Further, not all provisions in a statute have the same territorial ambit.

5   *Re Sawyers, ex p Blain* (1879) 12 Ch D 522 per James LJ at 526.

6   *Gold Star Publications Ltd v DPP* [1981] 2 All ER 257, [1981] 1 WLR 732 per Lord Wilberforce at 734.

3.4 Legislation in the UK may not apply to all parts of the UK. Territorial limits are defined in the Interpretation Act 1978, Sch 1:

> "England" means, subject to any alteration of boundaries under Pt IV of the Local Government Act 1972, the area consisting of the counties established by section 1 of that Act, Greater London and the Isles of Scilly.

> "Wales" means the combined area of the counties which were created by section 20 of the Local Government Act 1972, as originally enacted, but subject to any alteration made under section 73 of that Act (consequential alteration of boundary following alteration of watercourse).

> "United Kingdom" means Great Britain and Northern Ireland.

> "British Islands" means the United Kingdom, the Channel Islands and the Isle of Man.

Overseas traders and UK consumers

3.5 It is very likely that UK laws will apply to an overseas trader selling products to UK consumers in the UK. Otherwise, the consumer protection purpose of such legislation would be substantially undermined[1]. This is particularly important in the modern trading era, where overseas businesses can easily reach UK consumers without being physically present within the territory, for example by online trading, mail order, telephone sales etc[2]. Parliament must be taken to protect consumers within the UK at the time they transact, no matter where the trader is based. This is so even where the territorial extent of a statute is ostensibly limited to the UK or a part thereof.

1   It is likely that the presumption against extra-territorial effect is displaced by implication, *Jeffreys v Boosey* (1854) 4 HL Cas 815 at 970.

2   *Cox v Ergo Versicherung AG* [2014] UKSC 22 per Lord Sumption 'Implied extraterritorial effect is certainly possible, and there are a number of examples of it. But, in most if not all cases, it will arise only if (i) the terms of the legislation cannot effectually be applied or its purpose cannot effectually be achieved unless it has extraterritorial effect; or (ii) the legislation gives effect to a policy so significant in the law of the forum that Parliament must be assumed to have intended that policy to apply to any one resorting to an English court regardless of the law that would otherwise apply.'

Territorial extent of EU law

3.6 Where the law applicable to the trader's conduct is derived from an EU directive or regulation, as much consumer law is, the position is shaped by the jurisprudence of the CJEU. In the context of whether EU intellectual property law applied to traders outside the territory, the CJEU has ruled that it is important to consider whether the purpose of the legislation could be achieved otherwise. In the case of *L'Oreal SA v eBay International AG*, the court ruled that EU law must apply where a trader *targets* consumers in the EU, since otherwise,

> 'operators which use electronic commerce by offering for sale, on an online market place targeted at consumers within the EU, trademarked goods located in a third State, which it is possible to view on the screen and to order via that marketplace, would, so far as offers for sale of that type are concerned, have no obligation to comply with the EU intellectual property rules. Such a situation would have an impact on the effectiveness *(effet utile)* of those rules.'[1]

[1]   Case C-324/09 *L'Oreal SA v eBay International AG*, para 62.

CIVIL PROCEEDINGS

3.7 The capacity of a UK consumer to bring proceedings against an overseas trader in the UK courts has for many years been substantially governed by EU law in the form of the Brussels and Rome Regimes. The former is set out in the 2012 Brussels Recast Regulation. This provides a general rule that a defendant should be sued in the Member State it is domiciled. However, that rule is displaced where the dispute is between a consumer and an overseas trader. Where the trader was based in an EU Member State, a UK consumer has been able to use the UK courts to bring proceedings against the trader in contract or tort, where the trader's activity was targeted at UK consumers. Since 2015, by virtue of the Consumer Rights Act 2015, a UK consumer can now also bring contractual proceedings in the UK courts against any overseas trader across the world if their activities were targeted at UK consumers. Although the enforcement of any UK judgment in a non-EU country would depend on the reciprocal arrangements in place between the UK and that country. There is mutual enforcement of civil judgments between EU countries, which UK consumers can continue to take advantage of where they had already commenced proceedings against the trader on or before 31 December 2020[1].

[1]   Art 67 of the Withdrawal Agreement.

3.8 The capacity for consumers to bring proceedings against overseas traders in the UK courts does not necessarily mean that UK law will govern the dispute. The consequence of the Rome Regime is that the parties may agree that a different country's laws will apply. However, the overseas trader is not permitted to contract out of the consumer's mandatory legal rights in their country of domicile. For example, the right to reject under s 20 of the Consumer Rights Act 2015 ('CRA 2015') can be relied on by a UK consumer, even if it had been agreed that the laws of a different country should apply[1]. The consumer jurisdiction rules in the Brussels and Rome Regimes are largely replicated in the Lugano Convention, which applies in relation to the EFTA countries: Iceland, Norway and Switzerland[2].

[1]   From 1 January 2021, the Rome I regime as it applies to UK consumers has been altered so that UK consumers cannot lose key rights under the Consumer Rights Act where they enter into a contract which applies the law of any country apart from the UK – see reg 3 of the Consumer Protection (Amendment etc) (EU Exit) Regulations 2018.
[2]   The UK has applied to accede to the Lugano Convention as a sovereign state, but until this process is completed, consumers will not be able to benefit from its provisions in relation to litigation which commences on or after 1 January 2021.

3.9 Within the European regime, the rules governing jurisdiction in relation to contractual and non-contractual matters are set out in different instruments. However where the consumer contract regime applies, the consumer's state courts may also have jurisdiction over non-contractual matters that arose in relation to entering into the contract, and which are inseparably linked to it. This is to ensure that the consumer is able to have all these connected matters resolved in one set of proceedings. Issues which are likely to be sufficiently connected include alleged breaches of pre-contract information requirements, and misleading statements[1].

---
[1] CJEU *AU v Reliantco Investments Ltd* (C-500/18) paras 60–71.

3.10 The effect of the Brussels and Rome Regimes is that a UK consumer could largely rely on UK consumer rights in the UK courts to bring civil proceedings against an overseas trader that has targeted the UK. Likewise, a consumer domiciled in another EU state could not be pursued in the courts of the UK, where a UK based trader directs their activities towards them[1]. The significant exception to this position was when there was a non-contractual dispute with a trader outside the EU or Lugano Convention countries[2]. In order to bring a civil claim in those circumstances, domestic legal principles about the appropriate forum for resolving the dispute will apply. In English law, these are primarily engaged by the Civil Procedure Rules in relation to the service of proceedings overseas, and these are the rules which will apply to all civil litigation commenced in England and Wales on or after 1 January 2021.

---
[1] *Herriot Watt University v Schlamp* [2020] SC Edin 15, para 15.
[2] There is also an exception in relation to contracts for transport (see below).

Issues

3.11 From a procedural standpoint the most important questions for any UK consumer wishing to sue a non-UK trader following a cross-border purchase of goods or services are:

(a)   Can I bring proceedings against the trader in the UK courts or must I do so in the jurisdiction where the trader is established or in some other jurisdiction?

(b)   What system of law will the court apply in order to determine the dispute?

(c)   If successful, how do I enforce the judgment against a trader who is outside the UK?

Commencing civil proceedings in a UK court

EU law regimes – litigation which commenced up to 31 December 2020

3.12 In relation to litigation which commenced before the end of the EU exit implementation period, namely 31 December 2020, the EU regime on jurisdiction and will continue to apply. The EU regime on applicable law continues to apply to contracts which were entered into before this date, and to harmful events which occurred before this date[1]. EU law has long applied special jurisdictional and choice of law rules to consumer contracts. This is because EU law recognises the inequality of bargaining power between traders and consumers. The latter frequently find themselves in a Hobson's Choice situation, onerous or disadvantageous trading terms being imposed by the trader who buries them in the small print of terms and conditions. The EU rules are set out in the Brussels and Rome regimes to be discussed in more detail below. Essentially, the Brussels regime governs jurisdictional competence whereas the Rome regime governs applicable law. The synergy between them is not complete but works well in practice. Rome determines issues relating to choice-of-law in consumer contracts by reference to the Member State in which the consumer is 'habitually resident', whereas under the Brussels regime the determining factor for jurisdiction is the Member State where he is 'domiciled'. Habitual residence and domicile are not identical concepts for the purposes of private international law but in practice this presents few difficulties.

[1] See Withdrawal Agreement Arts 66, 67 and 69.

Choice of forum – the Brussels Regime

3.13 Until 10 January 2015 the position as regards jurisdiction in the EU was governed by Council Regulation (EC) No 44/2001 of 22 December 2000 on jurisdiction and the recognition and enforcement of judgments in civil and commercial matters ('Brussels I'). Brussels I contained provisions applicable to consumer contracts designed to protect consumers from being forced to sue in distant, unfamiliar jurisdictions as a result of choice of forum clauses imposed by traders in standard form contracts similar to those provided under the Rome I regime for choice of law.

3.14 Under the Brussels I regime, however, the protective provisions were only engaged where both the trader and the consumer were domiciled in an EU Member State[1]. They were not applicable where the trader was domiciled outside the EU. This was seen as placing EU consumers dealing with non-EU traders via the Internet at an unfair disadvantage. Accordingly, in its Proposal for an Amended Jurisdiction Regulation[2] the Commission noted:

> 'Access to justice in the EU is overall unsatisfactory in disputes involving defendants from outside the EU. With some exceptions, the current Regulation only applies where the defendant is domiciled inside the EU. Otherwise jurisdiction is governed by national law. The diversity of national law leads to unequal access to justice for EU companies in transactions with partners from third countries: some can easily litigate in the EU, others cannot, even in situations where no other court guaranteeing a fair trial is competent. In addition, where national legislation does not grant access to court in disputes with parties outside the EU, the enforcement of mandatory EU law protecting eg consumers, employees or commercial agents is not guaranteed . . .
> More specifically, the amendment will ensure that the protective jurisdiction rules available for consumers, employees and insured will also apply if the defendant is domiciled outside the EU.'

[1] See eg recital 9, Art 4.
[2] Published in December 2010 (COM (2010) 748 (final).

3.15 Regulation (EU) No 1215/2012 of the European Parliament and of the Counsel of 12 December 2012 on jurisdiction and the recognition and enforcement of judgments in civil and commercial matters (recast) ('Brussels I Recast') applies to legal proceedings instituted on or after 10 January 2015 (Art 66). The effective date is therefore the date on which proceedings are commenced rather than the date on which the cause of action arose. Whilst Recital (13) recognises that there must be a connection between proceedings to which the Regulation applies and the territory of the Member States with the result that the common rules of jurisdiction should only apply when the defendant is domiciled in a Member State, Recital (14) states that in order to ensure the protection of consumers, certain rules of jurisdiction in the Regulation should apply irrespective of the defendant's domicile. Recitals (18) and (19) state that the consumer, as the 'weaker party', should be protected by rules of jurisdiction more favourable to his interests than provided by the general rules, as an exception to the principal of respect for the autonomy of the parties to a contract to choose the forum for themselves.

3.16 Section 4 of the Recast Regulation therefore lays down special rules for determining jurisdiction in the context of consumer contracts. Article 17 applies the jurisdictional rules of the section to contracts between a 'consumer' and a party who pursues commercial or professional activities in the Member State of the consumer's domicile or by any means directs such activities to the Member State of the consumer's domicile or to several States including that state and the contract falls within the scope of such activities. As will be seen, these provisions are very similar to those contained in Art 6 of Rome I.

3.17 There is an important exception contained in Art 17(3) which provides that Art 17 does not apply to a contract of transport other than a contract which, for an inclusive price, provides for a combination of travel and accommodation. Thus, whilst it would apply to a contract for a package holiday it would not, for example, apply to a contract for flight only, a simple rail or bus journey, etc.

3.18 Article 18 makes it clear that the place where the trader is domiciled is irrelevant and therefore provides that:

> A consumer may bring proceedings against the other party to a contract either in the courts of the Member State in which that party is domiciled or, regardless of the domicile of the other party, in the courts for the place where the consumer is domiciled.

3.19 By virtue of Art 19 the provisions of section 4 can only be departed from by agreement in very limited circumstances eg one entered into after the dispute has arisen. The mere fact that a standard form contract contains a choice of forum provision stipulating the courts of a Member State other than that where the consumer is domiciled will not affect the latter's ability to sue in the courts of his domicile. Article 17 was clearly drafted with e-commerce in mind as cross-border contracts for the sale of goods and the provision of services are, *par excellence*, likely to give rise to conflict of laws issues in the sense of being likely to have a link to more than one system of law. Its provisions will apply even if the trader merely 'directs' professional or commercial activities towards the Member State in which the consumer is domiciled or towards several states including that state.

The concept of a consumer

3.20 An important preliminary matter is whether a person is engaging as a consumer. In many cases this will be uncontroversial, however, there has been litigation where the individual's status as a consumer has been challenged on the basis that they are engaging in money making or other professional activities. The CJEU has ruled that the person's status as a consumer is determined by the nature and objective of the contract (ie whether the contract is intended to satisfy personal needs). Factors that are not necessarily decisive include expertise, regularity of contracting and whether the person has made a large amount of money from the contract[1].

[1]   *CJEU AB v Personal Exchange International Ltd* (C-774/19) (10 December 2020) para 29–50, a contract concerning online gambling.

3.21 For the purposes of the Brussels I Recast regime, the concept of 'consumer' must be strictly construed because it is an exception to the general rule that a defendant should be sued in their own domicile. Therefore it may be narrower in scope than for other legislation, such that a person may be a consumer for the purposes of, for example, unfair terms, but not for the Brussels regime[1]. In particular, where a contract is for a mixture of business and consumer purposes, a person may only be a consumer under the Brussels regime where the business use is not more than 'negligible'. However, they may be afforded the protection of the unfair terms provisions, where the business use does not predominate[2].

[1]   See for example *Heriot-Watt University v Christian Schlamp* [2021] SAC (Civ) 12 para 30.
[2]   *Heriot-Watt University v Christian Schlamp* [2021] SAC (Civ) 12 paras 27–29 & 33. The person seeking to rely on their status as a consumer bears the burden of proving this (para 27). CF *AB v Personal Exchange International Ltd* (C-774/19) (10 December 2020) para 44, where the CJEU stated that the court must take account of the definition of consumer in other areas of EU law.

Directing commercial activities

3.22 Unless access to a website is blocked to persons located in particular jurisdictions either by the trader himself or the authorities in that jurisdiction (a common practice for example in the context of gambling websites) that website will be a window to the world on the trader's goods or services. The question will therefore arise, what level of permissible interactivity will be required before a trader will be found to be 'directing' commercial activities at a particular Member State. A website might be entirely passive, amounting to no more than a virtual billboard for the trader's products. On the other hand, it might permit varying degrees of interactivity from, say, requesting further information to actively permitting the consumer to purchase goods and/or services.

3.23 In combined cases *Pammer and Hotel Alpenhof*[1] the Court of Justice of the European Union (CJEU) was concerned with cross-border travel and accommodation services purchased online by a consumer in one Member State from a trader established in another Member State. Although the cases concerned parallel provisions in Brussels I the principles are equally applicable under Brussels I Recast. The court noted that the Internet is an inherently international communication medium with a worldwide reach. In the result, advertising on a trader's website is, in principle, accessible throughout the EU irrespective of any intention on the part of the trader to target customers outside the state in which he is established. It cannot therefore follow from the mere fact that a trader's website is accessible by persons in a Member State means that he is directing his commercial activities at that Member State.

[1]   Cases C-585/08 and C-144/09 [2010] ECR I 12527.

3.24 The court in *Alpenhof* further remarked:

'Consequently, it must be held that, in order for Article 15(1)(c) of Regulation No 44/2001 to be applicable, the trader must have manifested its intention to establish commercial relations with consumers from one or more other Member States, including that of the consumer's domicile. It must therefore be determined, in the case of a contract between a trader and a given consumer, whether, before any contract with that consumer was concluded, there was evidence demonstrating that the trader was envisaging doing business with consumers domiciled in other Member States, including the Member State of that consumer's domicile, in the sense that it was minded to conclude a contract with those consumers.'

3.25 Advocate General Trstenjak said in her Opinion[1]:

'It can be established from a literal interpretation that the customary meaning of the concept of the directing of activities to a Member State or several Member States is that the undertaking actively endeavours to conclude contracts with consumers from that Member State or those Member States. It is therefore essential for there to be active conduct on the part of the undertaking, the objective and outcome of which is to win customers from other Member States. An interpretation whereby mere access in the Member State of the consumer's domicile to a website would suffice for the directing of activities to that State would ultimately undermine the significance of the concept of 'directing'. It can therefore be established on the basis of the normal meaning of the concept of the directing of activities that the mere fact that a website can be consulted on the internet is not sufficient to justify a finding that the undertaking is directing its activities to the Member State of the consumer's domicile. Nor, on a literal interpretation, can any support be found for the view that, when interpreting this concept, a distinction is to be drawn between interactive and passive websites, as the wording of this article does not make any mention of different kinds of websites.'

[1]   Para 63, Opinion dated 18 May 2010.

3.26 Based on the decision of the court and the opinion of the Advocate General with which the court agreed, the following factors will be relevant to establish that a trader is directing his commercial activity either worldwide or to a specific jurisdiction or jurisdictions:

- The trader's website invites distance contracts and enables such contracts to be concluded via the website.
- The nature of the trader's commercial activity carried on via the website is inherently cross-border or international.
- It is clear that the trader had in mind doing business with consumers domiciled in one or more Member States including that where the consumer is domiciled.
- The website boasts of or refers to an international clientele and/or provides reviews from customers in particular jurisdictions and/or refers to services provided to customers in particular jurisdictions[1].
- The website is in multiple languages and/or or accepts multiple currencies.
- The website uses an international language such as English or Spanish.

- The general appearance of the website suggests that the trader is inviting international transactions or transactions from specific jurisdictions.
- Telephone numbers are listed with an international dialling code.
- The website advertises a local helpline number in the jurisdiction where the consumer is habitually resident/domiciled.
- A domain name is used which is not that of the member state of the business.
- Country specific domain names are used.
- An internet referencing service eg Google is paid to facilitate access to the website either internationally or from particular jurisdictions.
- The trader advertises his goods and/or services in conventional media in the consumer's jurisdiction.

Advocate General Trstenjak took the view that if a trader used the top-level domain names of particular States for example '.de', '.co.uk' etc that would be conclusive evidence that commercial activities were being directed towards consumers in those States[1].

[1] See for example the French Supreme Court decision in *LY v PWC Landwell-PriceWaterhouseCoopers Tax & Legal Services* [2021] ILPr 9 at paras 23–24.
[1] See para 84.

3.27 In *Daniela Mühlleitner v Ahmad Yusufi and Wadat Yusufi*[1] the court took matters a stage further in holding that it was not a precondition for the application of the special rules[2] that the contract between the trader and the consumer was concluded at a distance. In that case a consumer domiciled in Austria followed up an advertisement for the sale of a car placed on the internet on behalf of an auto trader based in Germany. The advertisement gave an international dialling code for the trader's business number. Although the car referred to in the advertisement had already been sold by the time the consumer contacted the trader, she was offered another vehicle by his staff, the details of which were sent to her by email. She was told, in terms, that her Austrian nationality would not prevent her from purchasing that vehicle. Shortly afterwards she travelled to the trader's premises in Germany where she signed the contract of sale, took possession of the car and drove it back to Austria.

[1] Case C-190/11.
[2] Prescribed in section 4 of Brussels I.

3.28 The car proved to be seriously defective. The trader refused to remedy the defects so the consumer sued in the Regional Court (Landesgericht) for Wels in Austria where she was domiciled. She failed at first instance and in her initial appeals, the courts accepting the trader's arguments that she should have brought the proceedings in Germany on the grounds that:

(i)   the trader was not directing its activities at Austrian Consumers; and
(ii)   the contract was not concluded at a distance, being signed face to face at the trader's business premises in Germany.

She appealed further to the Oberster Gerichthof (appeal court) which appears to have found that despite the essentially passive nature of the website on which the advertisement for the vehicle appeared the trader was, as a matter of fact, directing its commercial activities towards consumers in Austria.

3.29 As far as the second ground was concerned the Oberster Gerichthof referred the following question to the Court of Justice for a preliminary ruling '*Does the application of Article 15(1)(c) of Regulation (EC) No 44/2001 (the Brussels I Regulation) presuppose that the contract between the consumer and the undertaking has been concluded at a distance?*' The Court of Justice held that considering:

(a) the legislative history of Art 15(1)(c);

(b) the fact that it did not specify that its application was limited to cases where relevant contracts were concluded at a distance; and

(c) its legislative purpose (protecting the weaker party to a contract with a trader),

the application of Art 15(1)(c) did not require relevant contracts to have been concluded at a distance.

3.30 In *Maletic v lastminute.com GmbH & TUI Österreich GmbH*[1] the claimant consumers who were domiciled in Austria booked a package holiday to Egypt via the website of lastminute.com a company with its registered office in Munich. The website stated that lastminute.com acted as agent for TUI a company with its registered office in Vienna who would operate the holiday. The booking as confirmed to the consumers by lastminute.com was for a particular hotel in Hurghada, Egypt. However, due to mismanagement of the booking by TUI the consumers were booked into a different hotel in the same resort that had a similar sounding name. The consumers did not notice the mistake until they arrived in Egypt. Wishing to stay at the hotel they believed they had booked, they incurred substantial additional expenditure in order to be able to do so. They subsequently instituted proceedings before their local court, the *Bezirksgericht* Bludenz, Austria, to recover that expenditure from lastminute.com and TUI on the basis that they were jointly and severally liable for what had occurred.

[1] Case C-478/12.

3.31 The *Bezirksgericht* accepted jurisdiction insofar as lastminute.com was concerned in reliance upon Art 15(1)(c) of Brussels I. However, it dismissed the action against TUI on the basis that the situation as between that company and the consumers was an entirely domestic one. Accordingly, proceedings against TUI should have been instituted in accordance with Austrian law in the relevant court of the defendant's domicile in Vienna. The consumers appealed that part of the *Bezirksgericht's* decision to the *Landgericht* Feldkirch (appeal court) which referred the question whether the situation as regards TUI was a purely domestic situation to the Court of Justice for a preliminary ruling.

3.32 The Court of Justice stated that it was necessary to determine whether, in the circumstances of this, section 4 of Brussels I was applicable to a contracting partner such as TUI, and whether there was a sufficient international element capable of justifying its application. The court went on to hold that even on the basis that a single transaction, such as that which led the consumers to book and pay for their holiday on lastminute.com's website, may be divided into two separate contractual relationships, one with the online travel agency lastminute.com and, the second with the travel operator TUI, the second contractual relationship could not be classified as 'purely' domestic since it was inseparably linked to the first contractual relationship which was made through a travel agency situated in another Member State.

3.33 The court again emphasised the clear legislative purposes that under-pinned the Regulation namely to protect the consumer as the weaker party to the contract and to minimise the possibility of concurrent proceedings so as to ensure that irreconcilable judgments will not be given in two Member States. Those objectives precluded a solution which required the Maletics to pursue parallel proceedings in Bludenz and Vienna, by way of connected actions against two operators both of whom were involved in the booking and the arrangements for the package holiday at issue in the main proceedings. The court therefore took a very liberal view of the requisite cross-border element required to bring section 4 into play. This ruling by the Court of Justice runs very much true to form. The goal of protecting the consumer as the party with weaker bargaining power has, once again, been pushed very much to the forefront of its reasoning.

3.34 Although all of the cases referred to above were decided under section 4 of Brussels I, they apply with equal force to section 4 of Brussels I Recast since the effective provisions of that section in both Regulations are identical.

The domestic regime

3.35 Where the Brussels I Recast Regime does not apply, the English courts may still have jurisdiction. In relation to litigation which commences on or after 1 January 2021, jurisdiction will be determined by the domestic regime. Of particular note is the new provisions of ss 15A to 15E of the Civil Jurisdiction and Judgments Act 1982, which came into effect on 1 January 2021. These have the effect of overriding any exclusive jurisdiction clause in a consumer contract, where the consumer is domiciled in the UK. They effectively reproduce the Brussels I Recast regime in the UK, and the case law which is described above in relation to the Brussels regime is relevant to interpretation of ss 15A to 15E[1]. The procedural steps in establishing this are more cumbersome than under the EU regime and there is more scope for the defendant to challenge the juris-diction, by applying for a stay on the basis that some other jurisdiction is more appropriate (arguing *forum non conveniens*). Jurisdiction under the common law rules is based on one of either the service of proceedings on the defendant, or the submission to the jurisdiction by the defendant. A person may be said to submit to the jurisdiction by taking any step in the proceedings which is inconsistent with the right to contest jurisdiction, and having been served with proceedings, will be taken to have submitted if he fails to apply to challenge it within 14 days after filing an acknowledgment of service[2].

---

[1] See *George Bitar v Banque Libano-Francaise SAL* [2021] EWHC 2787 (QB) at para 10, citing the *Pammer* case with approval and applying it. Key concepts remain that of 'consumer', 'consumer contract' and 'directing activities' to the UK. The court considered that taken individually, merely using the English language in marketing, providing an option for persons in the UK to contact the bank, and having some customers who live in the UK, would not be sufficient to show that a bank directed its activities towards consumers in the UK. However these were relevant, and it was significant that the bank had a strategy to target the market in Europe, and referred in its annual report to a residential mortgage business with London clients

(para 64). Further, it is not necessary to show the trader 'intended' to direct its activities towards the UK, and instead website pages should be viewed objectively to assess whether they give the impression that the trader was interested in securing business from people in the UK.
2   CPR 11.4.

Jurisdiction through service of proceedings

3.36 There are three main ways in which service may be effected, which are likely to be relevant.

(a)   The first is to serve on the defendant when they are physically within the jurisdiction, even though they are domiciled in a state which is not part of the European Regime. This step could still be challenged, however, on the basis that there is another more appropriate forum.

(b)   The second is to serve on a company under the Companies Act 2006, if they have some place of business within the UK. A place of business is anywhere they regularly conduct business, or any premises which indicate the company may be contacted there[1].

(c)   The third is to obtain permission to serve under one of the Civil Procedure Rules gateways under CPR 6.36 and PD 6B 3.1. Under the rules, the claimant must demonstrate that the claim falls within one of the listed gateways, that the claim has a reasonable prospect of success and that England is the proper place to bring the claim.

1   Companies Act 2006, s 1139(2)(b).

Securing permission under the CPR to serve proceedings

3.37 The claimant should make an application without notice under CPR 23, supported by a witness statement which includes the specific gateways relied on, the draft particulars of claim setting out the substantive case, the evidence that England is the proper place to bring the claim, and make *full and frank disclosure* of all the material facts in relation to the prospects of success, including anything detrimental. Failure to make full disclosure may result in the court later setting aside the order granting permission. In assessing whether to accept jurisdiction, the court must be satisfied that there is a 'plausible evidential basis' for the application of the relevant gateway. If there is doubt, it is sufficient for the court to be satisfied there is a good arguable case for the application of the gateway -it does not have to resolve the evidential dispute fully[1].

1   See *Goldman Sachs International v Novo Banco SA* [2018] UKSC 34 para 9, *Kaefer Aislamientos SA de CV v AMS Drilling Mexico SA* [2019] EWCA Civ 10 paras 73–80 and *Bitar v Banqu Libano-Francaise SAL* [2021] EWHC 2787 QB paras 12–14.

3.38 There are a number of gateways which may be relevant to consumer protection enforcement, depending on the facts[1]. Where a trader has caused or is causing harm in the UK, a claimant could rely on gateway 9. This could include a situation where a consumer has suffered loss because they were misled by a distance seller, but also where they are suffering harm in the UK as a result of a transaction or event which occurred overseas. It simply needs to be shown that 'damage' occurs in the UK – not that 'the damage', or 'direct damage' occurred there – and in this respect this gateway is much wider than the corresponding ground in the Brussels regime[2]. In the classic case where the defendant is outside the jurisdiction, and it is proposed to restrain them from carrying out acts outside the jurisdiction which impact on consumers in the UK, another possible gateway is gateway 20[3]. This covers claims made under various enactments which allow proceedings to be brought and those proceedings are not covered by any of the other gateways.

[1] For example, gateway 2 – a claim for an injunction ordering the defendant to do or refrain from doing an act within the jurisdiction; gateway 9 – a claim in tort where damage was sustained, or will be sustained, within the jurisdiction.

[2] See *FS Cairo (Nile Plaza) LLC v Lady Brownlie (as Dependent and Executrix of Professor Sir Ian Brownlie CBE QC)* [2021] UKSC 45.

[3] PD 6B 3.1(20).

3.39 This gateway was relied on successfully by the Competition and Markets Authority to secure permission to serve proceedings on Viagogo AG, a company domiciled in Switzerland, which was threatening to challenge the application of the European Regime[1]. Morgan J ruled that the Enterprise Act 2002, the Consumer Rights Act 2015, the Consumer Contracts (Information, Cancellation and Additional Charges) Regulations 2013, the Consumer Protection from Unfair Trading Regulations 2008 and the Electronic Commerce (EC Directive) Regulations 2002 were all enactments that fell within this gateway. It should be noted in passing that although it would be unusual to seek permission to serve out of the jurisdiction where the European Regime applies, because of the stance taken by the defendant in correspondence, namely to challenge the application of the European Regime, Morgan J ruled it was proper to grant permission on this alternative basis[2].

[1] *Competition and Markets Authority v Viagogo AG* [2018] EWHC 2525 (Ch).

[2] *Competition and Markets Authority v Viagogo AG* [2018] EWHC 2525 (Ch) at para 7.

3.40 If there is a suitable gateway, the claimant must, secondly, show they have a reasonable prospect of success in relation to the claim, which means 'whether the claimant can show a serious issue to be tried in respect of each cause of action in respect of which permission to serve out is sought.'[1] In the *Viagogo AG* application this involved taking the judge through the causes of action and the underlying law, and satisfying him that there was 'at the very least a serious issue to be tried in relation to the claimant's contentions that it is able to seek enforcement orders in relation to the activities of the defendant in so far as those activities have their impact and effect within this jurisdiction.'[2]

[1] *Competition and Markets Authority v Viagogo AG* [2018] EWHC 2525 (Ch) at para 9 and White Book CPR 6.37.15.2.

[2] *Competition and Markets Authority v Viagogo AG* [2018] EWHC 2525 (Ch) at para 10.

3.41 The third step in the application process is to satisfy the court that England is the most appropriate forum, or the 'proper place', for bringing the claim[1]. The sorts of factors the court will have regard to include:

* the law which applies to the claim;
* where the business transactions took place;
* the location of witnesses and other evidence;
* the convenience of the parties;
* expense; and
* whether the proceedings are part of a larger dispute which could lead to irreconcilable judgments if fragmented (especially if relevant proceedings have already been commenced abroad).

Where another jurisdiction may be more appropriate, the court could still give permission if there is a real risk that substantial justice will not be obtained in the foreign jurisdiction[2].

1   *Spiliada Maritime Corp v Cansulex Ltd* [1987] AC 460.
2   *Vedanta Resources plc v Lungowe* [2019] UKSC 20.

The practicalities of serving proceedings

SERVICE WITHIN THE EU

3.42 In relation to proceedings which have already commenced before 31 December 2020, and documents have already been received by a service agency in the receiving state, the following EU regime continues to apply into 2021[1]. Because this regime relies on reciprocity, and the application of agreed jurisdiction rules, it is unlikely that UK litigants will continue to benefit from the EU special procedure. Where the defendant is in an EU member state (but not the Lugano Convention states of Iceland, Switzerland and Norway), and the claimant is able to give their address, they may be served under the EU Service Regulation[2]. Indeed this is mandatory in relation to civil and commercial matters, which consumer enforcement appears to be. The most convenient is likely to be the transmission method (Art 4), which is service via the authorities designated under the Service Regulation for this purpose[3]. In England and Wales, the transmission agency is the Foreign Process Section, which sends the material to the receiving agency in the relevant Member State.

1   Art 68 of the Withdrawal Agreement.
2   (EC) (1393/2007).
3   Other methods of service provided for are post (Art 14), direct service (where permitted under the law of the receiving state) (Art 15) and diplomatic or consular agents (Art 13). The particular service requirements of each member state are set out on the e-justice portal.

3.43 The documents being served need to be translated into a language the defendant understands (at the claimant's expense). This is only required if actually necessary, which it may well not be if the pre-litigation correspondence has been conducted in English[1]. If the documents are not translated there is a risk the addressee may refuse to accept service. The receiving agency must effect service within 1 month of receipt, failing which they must notify the claimant and continue to attempt service if this seems possible within a reasonable period of time[2].

1   Service Regulation Art 8 and Art 5 and *Alta Realitat SL v Erlock Film ApS* (C-384/14).
2   Service Regulation Art 7.

SERVICE UNDER THE HAGUE SERVICE CONVENTION

3.44 Where the defendant is in a contracting state, such as Switzerland, service may be effected under the Hague Convention. This applies to civil and commercial matters. The rules for service under the Hague Convention are set out in CPR 6.42(1) and 6.43. Further guidance can be found in the Practical Handbook on the Operation of the Hague Service Convention. It is important to note that transmission under the Hague Convention can take time, as long as 6 months in some cases.

SERVICE WHERE NO TREATY OR CONVENTION IS IN PLACE

3.45 The procedure applicable is set out in CPR 6.43. The main complication is that it is generally necessary to seek local legal advice on the methods of service that are valid.

ALTERNATIVE METHODS OF SERVICE

3.46 Given the complexity of service out of the jurisdiction and the time it takes, especially in the absence of international agreement on effecting service, it is sensible to consider whether, while seeking permission to serve out of the jurisdiction, there is reason to request an order for alternative service. This is provided for in CPR 6.15(1). The test is whether there is good reason to order that steps taken to bring the claim form to the attention of the defendant amount to good service. Such an application was successfully made by the Competition and Markets Authority to serve proceedings on Viagogo AG's London based solicitors, who had been instructed not to accept service[1]. The application was to some extent unusual because the claimant's primary case was that the matter was covered by the Hague Convention. However the judge was persuaded that this was reasonably doubtful given the defendant's stance that the litigation was not a civil or commercial matter under the Lugano Convention, as they would therefore also be likely to challenge service under the Hague Convention[2].

[1] *Competition and Markets Authority v Viagogo AG* [2018] EWHC 2525 (Ch) at paras 15–24.
[2] See *Cecil v Bayat* [2011] 1 WLR 3086 at para 68 for authority as to why alternative service may be permitted even where the Hague Convention applies.

3.47 In order to grant an order for alternative service the judge had to devise a method of service which was fair to the defendant and did not infringe the obligation of comity to Switzerland. In deciding that service on London lawyers achieved this, Morgan J considered the following factors:

(a)   Service on solicitors in London could not in any way infringe the law of Switzerland[1].

(b)   The intention of the Applicant to move to secure an interim enforcement order due to changes which Viagogo's competitors in the market had already promised to make.

(c)   The close involvement of the defendant's solicitors in the conduct of correspondence to date, which led the judge to consider that service on those solicitors would enable the proceedings to be brought to the defendant's attention without delay, and so enable the defendant to engage with and react to the proceedings without delay.

The judge also granted an order excusing translation of the documents, given the manifest ability of the defendants to engage in English, it would be a distraction, and merely add to the costs.

[1] See CPR 6.40(4) which provides: '(4) Nothing in . . . any court order authorises or requires any person to do anything which is contrary to the law of the country where the claim form or other document is to be served.'.

3.48 It is also possible, in exceptional circumstances, to obtain an order dispensing with service of proceedings entirely. This is governed by CPR 6.16, which provides that such an application must be supported by evidence, but may be made at any time and without notice to the proposed defendant. It should also be noted that CPR 6.28 makes a similar provision for service of any other document to be dispensed with.

3.49 Such an application was successfully made in the case of *Lonestar Communications Corp LLC v Daniel Kaye (and others)*[1]. The test applied was whether there were exceptional circumstances, and whether it was fair and just to make the order. The steps which the claimant had taken, which satisfied the exceptional circumstances test were (1) attempting the serve the defendant in Israel under the Hague Convention, and (2) making six attempts to contact the defendant through the internet and using social media. The judge found that it could be inferred from the defendant's behaviour that he knew of the proceedings and was evading service, for example after various attempts were made to contact him, he dis-instructed his solicitors, closed his Facebook Messenger account, took down his website, and declined to accept a request for connection through LinkedIn.

[1]   [2019] EWHC 3008.

3.50 In relation to whether an order was fair and just, the judge went on to find that without an order dispensing with service the claimant would suffer prejudice by being unable to pursue its claim. By contrast, the defendant suffered none, as he was simply trying to evade service. Further, the claimant undertook to continue to take steps to inform the defendant of the proceedings.

Applicable law

3.51 Various expressions are used to describe the system of law that regulates the rights and obligations of the parties to a contract eg applicable law, governing law, proper law etc. 'Applicable law' is probably most apt because that is the expression used in Regulation EC No 593/2008 of the European Parliament and of the Council of 17 June 2008 on the law applicable to contractual obligations (Rome I). The UK opted into Rome I which, as a Regulation, was automatically incorporated into domestic law without the need for implementing legislation. Since choice of law issues will often arise in tandem with jurisdiction issues Rome I must be interpreted consistently with Brussels I and its successor Brussels I Recast with which it shares a number of provisions in common. This is of particular importance in the context of consumer transactions. Going forwards, the Rome I regime will continue to apply to contracts which were concluded before the end of the EU exit implementation period (31 December 2020)[1]. Where a contract is concluded on or after 1 January 2021, questions of applicable law will be determined by the Rome I Regulation as retained EU law, and as amended by the Law Applicable to Contractual Obligations and Non-Contractual Obligations (Amendment etc) (EU Exit) Regulations 2019. This is likely in substance to preserve the EU regime on applicable law post Brexit, albeit that future CJEU rulings on the scope and meaning of the Rome I and Rome II Regulations will no longer be binding on UK courts (although they can be taken into account). In practical terms however it is likely that in most consumer cases, UK judges will simply apply UK law, especially given that consumers cannot contract out of their mandatory statutory protections. This is because the courts will apply the default rule that if no specific law is pleaded, UK law applies, and even if some other law is referred to, the courts will presume UK law gives the same result, unless a party proves the contrary[2].

1   Art 66 of the Withdrawal Agreement.
2   *FS Cairo (Nile Plaza) LLC v Lady Brownlie (as Dependent and Executrix of Professor Sir Ian Brownlie CBE QC)* [2021] UKSC 45.

3.52 Article 1 applies the provisions of Rome I to contractual obligations in civil and commercial matters where a conflict of laws issue arises. Article 2 establishes a principle of universal application with the result that any law specified by virtue thereof must be applied:

(i)   whether or not it is the law of a Member State of the EU; and
(ii)   irrespective of whether one or more (or indeed all) of the parties to a dispute before the courts of a Member State is/are based outside the EU.

3.53 The basic principle underpinning Rome I is that any choice of law made by the parties to a contract will be respected (Art 3). That is, however, subject to various exceptions. Most importantly for our purposes, the Regulation also incorporates a 'protective' principle which recognises that certain contracts should be 'protected' from the general principle of free choice of applicable law because one of the parties may be in a weaker bargaining position. Thus Recital 23 states:

> As regards contracts concluded with parties regarded as being weaker, those parties should be protected by conflict-of-law rules that are more favourable to their interests than the general rules.

3.54 Business-to-consumer contracts are given protected status by Rome I for the very reason that consumers are frequently confronted with standard terms and conditions imposed by traders, which they cannot individually negotiate. They must accept them if they want the trader's goods or services or leave them – Hobson's Choice. Most often they cannot source the goods or services elsewhere because competitors will impose similar terms and conditions. Thus Recital 25 provides:

> Consumers should be protected by such rules of the country of their habitual residence that cannot be derogated from by agreement, provided that the consumer contract has been concluded as a result of the professional pursuing his commercial or professional activities in that particular country. The same protection should be guaranteed if the professional, while not pursuing his commercial or professional activities in the country where the consumer has his habitual residence, directs his activities by any means to that country or to several countries, including that country, and the contract is concluded as a result of such activities.

As has been seen with Brussels I and Brussels I Recast this is in effect identical to the principle that underpins those Regulations.

3.55 Business-to-consumer contracts therefore benefit from a special regime set out in Art 6. This provides (where relevant) as follows:

(1)   Without prejudice to Arts 5 and 7, a contract concluded by a natural person for a purpose which can be regarded as being outside his trade or

profession (the consumer) with another person acting in the exercise of his trade or profession (the professional) shall be governed by the law of the country where the consumer has his habitual residence, provided that the professional:

(a)   pursues his commercial or professional activities in the country where the consumer has his habitual residence, or

(b)   by any means, directs such activities to that country or to several countries including that country,

and the contract falls within the scope of such activities.

(2)   Notwithstanding paragraph 1, the parties may choose the law applicable to a contract which fulfils the requirements of paragraph 1, in accordance with Art 3. Such a choice may not, however, have the result of depriving the consumer of the protection afforded to him by provisions that cannot be derogated from by agreement by virtue of the law which, in the absence of choice, would have been applicable on the basis of paragraph 1.

(3)   If the requirements in points (a) or (b) of paragraph 1 are not fulfilled, the law applicable to a contract between a consumer and a professional shall be determined pursuant to Arts 3 and 4.

Whilst respecting a consumer's freedom to choose a system of law other than that of his habitual residence, Rome I ensures that in so doing he retains the protections of such 'mandatory' provisions of the latter as are imposed by operation of the local law and cannot, for that reason, be contracted out of.

3.56 In the context of business-to-consumer contracts, if the consumer is habitually resident in the UK Art 6 will apply irrespective of where the professional selling goods or providing services is located provided that the professional was either:

(a)   pursuing its commercial activities in the UK; or

(b)   by any means directing those activities to the UK or to several countries including the UK

and the contact was concluded as the result of those activities.

3.57 It should be recalled that where Art 6 applies to a contract between a trader and a consumer that contains a choice of law clause nominating a system of law other than that of the Member State in which the consumer is habitually resident, that choice will be respected but only to the extent that it does not deprive the consumer of protective provisions that cannot be contracted out of under the laws of the Member State in which he is habitually resident. This means that potentially more than one system of law may apply to determine eg the validity of a contract and the interpretation of its terms. Protections contained, for example, in the Consumer Rights Act 2015 would apply since these are imposed by operation of law and cannot be contracted out of. Further, provided the consumer is habitually resident for example in England and Wales, the fact that the defendant to the proceedings is a corporation established and habitually resident in a non-EU jurisdiction will not preclude the application of Rome I for the purposes of determining the applicable law[1].

[1] It should be noted that where a contract is entered into on or after 1 January 2021, UK consumer law ceases to differentiate between clauses applying EU/EEA laws and those applying any other legal regime – see Consumer Rights Act 2015, s 32 and s 74, as amended by the Consumer Protection (Amendment etc) (EU Exit) Regulations 2018, reg 3.

3.58 In practice, it would not matter if the consumer habitually resided in eg Scotland because Art 22 makes special provision for Member States such as the UK that comprise several territorial units, each having its own system of law governing contractual obligations. Article 22(1) treats each such unit as a country in its own right for the purposes of identifying the applicable law under the Regulation. By virtue of Art 28, Rome I applies to all relevant contracts concluded after 17 December 2009.

3.59 The principle that the Rome I and the Brussels I regimes should be interpreted in a harmonious manner is retained for the purposes of the Recast Regulation. Accordingly the case law applicable to the question whether a trader is directing his commercial activities to the Member State of the consumer's habitual residence decided under Art 6 of Rome I will be equally applicable in the context of Art 17 of Brussels I Recast albeit that the relevant Member State will be that of the consumer's domicile.

Enforcement of judgments

3.60 Having secured a successful outcome in the UK courts the next stage for the consumer will be to enforce the judgment in the country where the trader has his business establishment and where his assets are located. Within the UK, the procedure for enforcing English judgments in Scotland or Northern Ireland is set out in the Civil Jurisdiction and Judgments Act 1982[1], and in essence it requires the claimant to obtain a certificate from the English court (including a certified copy of a non-money judgment), and then to apply to the local court to register the judgment, within 6 months of the date of the certificate. The judgment then has the same force and effect as a local judgment.

[1] Sections 18, 19 and Sch 6 and 7.

3.61 In the case of traders established within the EU the consumer can continue to invoke the special regime for the enforcement of judgments prescribed in section 2 of Chapter II of Brussels I Recast[1], in relation to court proceedings which were commenced before the end of the EU exit implementation period (31 December 2020)[2]. Given the length of time that some proceedings take to be concluded, this regime may remain important to UK litigants for several years. The Recast Brussels regime effectively abolishes the exequatur (the legal document issued by a sovereign authority that permits enforcement) for all judgments given in proceedings to which it applies commenced after 10 January 2015. Article 39 provides that a judgment given in a Member State which is enforceable in that Member State is automatically enforceable in all other Member States without the requirement to obtain a declaration of enforceability. The judgment creditor obtains a certificate from the English court in a standard form[3], it is then served on the judgment debtor with the judgment and any translation.

[1] For proceedings issued before 10 January 2015, in the 2001 Brussels Regulation and within the EFTA states (Iceland, Norway and Switzerland) it is governed by the Lugano Convention 2007.
[2] Arts 67 and 69 of the Withdrawal Agreement.
[3] See Annex 1 to the Recast Brussels Regulation.

3.62 The judgment becomes enforceable as though it had been given in the courts of the Member State in which enforcement is sought. There are very limited grounds the judgment debtor can rely on to resist enforcement. The burden falls on the defendant to contest enforcement in the courts of that member state. Article 45 severely circumscribes the grounds[1] on which recognition of the judgment can be refused. An example would be where it would be manifestly contrary to public policy to do so. Article 46 limits the grounds on which the court can refuse to enforce the judgment to those prescribed in Art 45.

[1] Where it would be manifestly contrary to public policy to do so; in the case of a judgment in default, the defendant was not served with the claim in time to prepare his defence (but to rely on this the defendant must have brought proceedings to challenge the judgment); the judgment is irreconcilable with a judgement given in the enforcing state (or with an enforceable judgment given in another state) in a dispute between the same parties; the judgment is in conflict with the protections offered to the weaker party in consumer, insurance and employment disputes in the Brussels Regulation itself.

3.63 If the trader is established outside the EU and has no presence within the EU, or where litigation against an EU trader commences on or after 1 January 2021, enforcement will be governed by the national rules of the state where the judgment is to be enforced. Success may depend upon whether the there is some reciprocal arrangement in place between the UK and the country of the trader's domicile. In a chapter of this length, it is not possible to record each of these agreements. However, there are bilateral arrangements between the UK and a number of Commonwealth countries, such as Canada, Australia, India, Jersey, New Zealand and Nigeria.

The European Small Claims Procedure

3.64 The European Small Claims Procedure[1] ('ESCP') is available as an alternative to other procedures established by the laws of the EU Member States where the claim is brought if the value of the claim is less than €5000[2]. It continues to apply to small claims commenced in the UK before the end of the EU exit implementation period (31 December 2020)[3]. It is no longer applicable to claims launched from 1 January 2021. The scope of the ESCP includes civil and commercial cases, which includes claims in respect of the sale of goods and supply of services to consumers. Any consumer who is able to invoke the protections available by virtue of Brussels I Recast can use the ESCP. The procedure is decidedly fast-track, being essentially a written procedure which is subject to a tight timetable for completion. A hearing will only be directed if it is deemed to be necessary or if one party requests it.

[1] Was established by Regulation 861/2007 establishing the European Small Claims Procedure (OJ 2007 L 191/1 (the ESCP Regulation).
[2] Increased from €2000 with effect from 14 July 2017.
[3] Art 67 of the Withdrawal Agreement.

CIVIL REGULATORY ENFORCEMENT

3.65 In the UK, consumer infringements may be enforced by public enforcers using the civil courts. This is primarily undertaken using the enforcement provisions in Pt 8 of the Enterprise Act 2002. These are covered in detail in CHAPTER 5 (Civil Enforcement). Enforcers frequently encounter situations in which UK consumers are being harmed by traders based overseas, for example where consumers are misled, goods fail to arrive or a contract contains unfair terms. These situations pose legal and practical challenges to enforcement that can be complex. Generally the rules of jurisdiction and applicable law which apply to regulatory enforcement brought under the Enterprise Act on or after 1 January 2021 will be the same as those described above which apply to private claims. A claim for an Enterprise Act order is most likely to be treated either as a tortious matter or a statutory claim for the purpose of jurisdictional gateways. However where the case commenced before this date, or is brought by an EU enforcer against a trader directing their activities towards consumers in the EU, the rules will continue to be governed by the EU regime, which is described below.

Regulatory enforcement by EU enforcers

3.66 Where an infringing trader is based in the EU the Brussels Recast and Rome regimes were able to be invoked to assist an application for an enforcement order under the Enterprise Act 2002, or an injunction under the CRA 2015, on the basis that consumer law infringements are a *'civil or commercial matter'* relating to a tort. Where a trader is based in EFTA (Iceland, Norway or Switzerland) the 2007 Lugano Convention, the provisions of which are very similar, apply. Before 1 January 2021, where the European Regime applied, the permission of the English courts was not required to serve proceedings on the defendant in their domicile in the EU[1]. However it is a precondition that there must be no proceedings between the parties concerning the same claim, which are pending in another part of the UK or the EU[2]. The Brussels Recast regime does not apply to claims commenced on or after 1 January 2021. However the Rome regime continues to apply where the harmful event occurred on or before 31 December 2020, and in relation to harm which occurs after this date, the UK retained EU law version of the Rome regime will apply.

[1]   CPR 6.31 and 6.33.
[2]   CPR 6.33(2)(a).

Civil or commercial matter

3.67 The Brussels and Rome Regimes apply to *'civil or commercial matters'* but not to *'administrative matters'*. A question arises about whether a claim by a UK public enforcer under Pt 8 of the EA 2002 would be considered a 'civil or commercial matter'. In this context it is important to recognise that these concepts are European in origin, where Member States have both common law and civil legal systems. The CJEU rulings in *Henkel*[1] and *Amazon*[2] involved enforcement by a private Austrian consumer protection body against traders established outside Austria that were allegedly using unfair terms. The CJEU found that the enforcement of consumer law was generally a civil or commercial matter, rather than an administrative matter[3]. The CJEU has also ruled that enforcement of infringements of the Unfair Commercial Practices Directive may be a civil or commercial matter, including where the order seeks not only an order for the cessation of those practices, but also an order for publicity and the imposition of a penalty payment[4].

1   Case C-167/00 *Verein für Konsumenteninformation v Henkel.*
2   Case C-191/15 *Verein für Konsumenteninformation v Amazon EU Sàrl.*
3   See Art 1 of each Regulation.
4   Case C-73/19 *Directeur-Generaal van de Algemene Directie Controle en Bemiddeling van de FOD Economie v Movic.*

3.68 The enforcer in *Henkel* was a private body, however, the judgment suggests that the critical factor in determining whether the action is a 'civil or commercial matter' is the character of the obligation owed by the defendant rather than the public or private nature of the enforcer[1]. The CJEU stated that:

> 'Not only is a consumer protection organisation such as the VKI a private body, but in addition, as the German Government correctly observed, the subject matter of the main proceedings is not an exercise of public powers, since those proceedings do not in any way concern the exercise of powers derogating from the rules of law applicable to relations between private individuals. On the contrary, the action pending before the national court concerns the prohibition on traders' using unfair terms in their contracts with consumers and thus seeks to make relationships governed by private law subject to review by the courts. Hence, an action of that kind is a civil matter within the meaning of the first paragraph of Article 1 of the Brussels Convention.'[2]

This approach was confirmed in the more recent decision in *Movic*, where the CJEU ruled that the public status of claimant did not matter, where they were taking action which in principle a trade or consumer body could take[3]. Further, the Court confirmed that acting in the general interests of consumers is not an exercise of public power, and it was not determinative either that the evidence the case was founded on was obtained using public powers[4]. Where the remedies sought include some which only a public body could obtain (such as being granted the power to declare the existence of infringements by swearing an oath), which would not themselves be civil or commercial matters, this would not invalidate the whole proceedings, since as long as the primary claim may be brought under the Brussels Regulation, ancillary claims may be brought along with it[5].

1   Examples of other matters brought by public bodies, which were ruled to be civil or commercial matters include: *Land Berlin v Ellen Mirjam Sapir and others* (Case C-645/11) – recovery of overpayment of compensation paid to victim of illegal expropriation of land; *The Commissioners for Her Majesty's Revenue and Customs v Sunico Aps and others* (Case C-49/12) – claim for damages caused by conspiracy to commit VAT fraud. By contrast, where a public body is acting in the exercise of its public powers to punish infringements of competition law, this has been ruled to be an administrative matter (*Gazdasagi Versenyhivatal v Siemens Aktiengesellschaft Osterreich* (Case C-102/15)).
2   *Henkel* at para 30.
3   CJEU *Movic* (C-73/19) para 49.
4   CJEU *Movic* (C-73/19) paras 53, 56.
5   CJEU *Movic* (C-73/19) para 63.

Contract or tort

3.69 It is also important to understand whether a public enforcement application is to be considered a claim arising from breach of contract or a matter relating to tort. In *Amazon* the CJEU ruled that the cause of action is of a tortious nature, even where an enforcer is seeking to tackle an unfair contract term. This is because actions seeking to establish liability are not related to a contract[1]. Further, the nature of a preventative action to protect the collective interests of consumers is tortious in nature[2]. It follows that enforcement action taken under Pt 8 of the EA 2002 or the CRA 2015 is likely to fall within the Art 7.2 exception to the general rule[3], provides that a defendant may be sued 'in matters relating to tort, delict or quasi-delict, in the courts for the place where the harmful event occurred or may occur'.

[1]   See *Amazon* para 37.
[2]   *Amazon* paras 39–42.
[3]   The general rule of the European Regime is that a defendant should be sued in their own country of domicile, and where the regime applies the rules must be followed strictly, see Art 4.1 Recast Brussels Regulation.

Where the harmful event occurred

3.70 For public enforcement against a trader in another EU country the crucial question is likely to be where the harmful event occurred. In the *Henkel* case, the ECJ considered that this was the place where consumers sustained damage personally, and also the place where unfair terms are being used, thus undermining the legal stability of that place[1]. Therefore the Austrian consumer protection body was able to bring proceedings in Austria against a German trader using allegedly unfair terms in contracts with Austrian consumers. It is likely that the same reasoning would apply in relation to other consumer protection law, for example the CJEU has ruled that where a car is manufactured with a defect, the place where the harmful event occurs is every place where it is sold to consumers (which could be in many different states)[2].

[1]   *Henkel* para 42.
[2]   CJEU *Verein fur Konsumenteninformation v Volkswagen AG* (C-343/19).

3.71 Where a trader creates a misleading document for example, which is never published in the consumer's domicile, it is unlikely that a consumer has suffered harm. Consequently, any litigation for the illegal conduct that has occurred may need to take place in the trader's domicile. By contrast, once a misleading document is read by a consumer, the harm occurs in the place where the consumer was when they read it[1]. There is, however, a distinction between the place where the harm occurs, whose courts do have jurisdiction, and any place where consequential harm is suffered, which will not have any special jurisdictional rights[2].

[1]   See by analogy the ruling in *Wintersteiger AG* (C-523/10) paras 21–39, where it was ruled that where a trademark infringement arose from an advert displayed on Google, the place where the harmful event occurred was the state in which the trade mark was registered.
[2]   See CJEU *Verein fur Konsumenteninformation v Volkswagen AG* (C-343/19). The Court rejected the idea that the impact on consumers was purely financial damage, but material damage resulting from the loss in value of the vehicle purchased (at para 34). While the manufacturer thus faces litigation in potential multiple jurisdictions, it has to anticipate that this will happen when it contravenes the statutory requirements imposed on it (para 37).

Applicable law

3.72 The Rome II Regulation is likely to apply to a public enforcement action against a trader in a Member State, when that action is based on tort. In

Amazon the CJEU ruled that the law[1] applicable to the dispute between the enforcer and the trader is determined by Art 6.1, which provides that:

'The law applicable to a non-contractual obligation arising out of an act of unfair competition shall be the law of the country where competitive relations or the collective interests of consumers are, or are likely to be, affected.'

This means that UK law will apply where a trader is dealing with consumers in the UK. It follows that proceedings may be brought under Pt 8 of the EA 2002, rather than under the enforcement rules of the trader's domicile. In principle, the substantive infringement should also be governed by UK law. Art 6.1 will not apply when there is a valid choice of law clause that selects the law of a different jurisdiction[2]. However, Art 6.2 requires that a consumer is not deprived of the mandatory provisions of their own state law and indeed these mandatory provisions must be made clear to consumers in the contractual terms. Even where overseas law applies, this does not mean that the claimant must plead this. Rather, if proceedings are brought in England and Wales, the courts will presume English law would give the same result as the relevant foreign law where it is fair and reasonable to do so. A party which wishes to argue there is a material difference would need to produce evidence to prove this[3].

[1]   Additionally the place the harm occurred is likely to be the consumers' domicile for the purposes of Art 4.1.
[2]   Article 3.1 of Rome I (see also *Amazon*).
[3]   *FS Cairo (Nile Plaza) LLC v Lady Brownlie (as Dependent and Executrix of Professor Sir Ian Brownlie CBE QC)* [2021] UKSC 45.

Enforcement action within the EU Member States

The Injunctions Directive

3.73 The Injunctions Directive[1] permits enforcers who are listed in the Official Journal as 'qualified entities' to commence proceedings in another Member State to seek an order requiring the cessation or prohibition of an infringement of one of the laws listed in the annex to the Injunctions Directive[2]. It applies where there is harm to the collective interests of consumers, and for further information on this concept, and the UK implementation of the Injunctions Directive, see the CHAPTER 5 (Civil Enforcement). UK entities are not able to take such action as of 1 January 2021[3], but those who were able to take action before this date include every trading standards department, as well as sectoral regulators such as the FCA, CAA and Ofgem, and the Competition and Markets Authority[4].

[1]   2009/22/EC.
[2]   Injunctions Directive Article 2.1.
[3]   The Consumer Protection (Enforcement) (Amendment etc) (EU Exit) Regulations 2019, SI 2019/203, regs.3, 9 & 10.
[4]   For a full list of current qualified entities see https://eur-lex.europa.eu/legal-content/EN/TXT/?uri=celex:52016XC0930(03).

3.74 The advantage of the Injunctions Directive is that it gives qualified entities standing to bring proceedings in the member state where the trader is domiciled. This means that there are unlikely to be the same complications around service of proceedings and enforcement of the ultimate judgment. From the enforcer's perspective, however, these actions can be complicated and costly because they often require detailed knowledge of local procedural rules and the ability to operate in the local language. This invariably requires instruction of local lawyers and translation of all the documentation, which can be costly and risk legal points being misunderstood. The question of which law applies may also be unclear. The discussion above on applicable law suggests that the overseas court should apply UK law, which would add a further level of complexity. There have only ever been two cases brought under the Injunctions Directive in the cross-border context envisaged. These were both brought by the Office of Fair Trading – one against a Belgian company (Duchesne trading as TV Direct)[1], and the other against a Dutch company (Best Sales)[2]. In the Duchesne case Belgian law was applied, whereas in Best Sales, UK law was applied.

[1] See the OFT web archive: https://webarchive.nationalarchives.gov.uk/20131101202510/http://www.oft.gov.uk/news-and-updates/press/2005/234-05.

[2] https://webarchive.nationalarchives.gov.uk/20140402175544/http://oft.gov.uk/news-and-updates/press/2008/86-08.

Enforcement under the Consumer Protection Co-operation Regulation

3.75 A far simpler method of taking action against a trader in their own domicile is to make a request for enforcement assistance under the CPC Regulation[1]. The CPC Regulation creates an enforcement network across the EU, and also includes enforcers in the EEA. The UK, having left the EU, no longer participates in the CPC enforcement network, and so is unable to benefit from the features described here. As of 1 January 2021, the UK has withdrawn from the CPC regime and revoked the CPC Regulation[2]. However given that UK businesses may find themselves facing enforcement under the CPC regime if they deal with EU consumers, it is helpful to set out here how the system operates. The CPC Regulation requires member state to designate Competent Authorities for enforcing each piece of law listed in the Annex to the Regulation. These enforcers are listed for each member state in the Official Journal[3]. The UK implementation was Pt 8 of the EA 2002, which is covered in detail in CHAPTER 5 (Civil Enforcement). Each enforcer must have a minimum set of investigatory powers and be competent to achieve a minimum set of enforcement outcomes when they receive a request for cross border enforcement assistance[4]. In the UK, the investigatory powers required by the CPC Regulation were conferred on relevant enforcers by Sch 5 of the CRA 2015. The Regulation also provides for CPC enforcers to take 'joint actions' to deal with infringements which are occurring in multiple Member States, and for the Commission to take a role in co-ordinating actions against the most widespread infringements[5].

[1] Currently Regulation (EU) 2017/2394. This replaced Regulation (EC) 2006/2004 on 17 January 2020.

[2] Reg 3(7) of the Consumer Protection (Enforcement) (Amendment etc) (EU Exit) Regulations 2020, SI 2020/1347.

[3] https://ec.europa.eu/info/sites/info/files/list_of_cpc_authorities_update_17-05-2019.pdf.

[4] The powers are set out in Arts 9 and 10 of the 2017 Regulation, and in Art 4.6 of the 2006 Regulation.

[5] See Chapter IV of the 2017 Regulation.

Bilateral enforcement assistance

3.76 The CPC Regulation sets out a system for bilateral enforcement assistance. In order to make a request for assistance, the relevant competent authority directs their request through the Single Liaison Office ('SLO') for their member state. The request, together with any supporting evidence, is sent to the relevant SLO in the other Member State, through a secure online portal[1]. The receiving SLO then identifies the relevant Competent Authority to take action. In the case of an investigation request, the Competent Authority must take the appropriate steps promptly to gather the required information[2]. In the case of an enforcement request, the requested authority must take all necessary and proportionate enforcement measures to bring about the cessation or prohibition of the infringement without delay[3]. They may instruct another body to do this under Art 8.3 of the 2017 Regulation. Even without a request for assistance, a competent authority must provide information to its counterparts in the EEA proactively, wherever it becomes aware of an intra-Union infringement[4].

[1]   Art 28 of the 2017 Regulation. The portal is created and maintained by the Commission under Art 35 of the current Regulation.
[2]   Art 11 of the 2017 Regulation.
[3]   Art 12 of the 2017 Regulation.
[4]   Art 26 of the current Regulation.

Joint enforcement

3.77 In addition to the ability to secure bilateral assistance, the CPC Regulation requires enforcers to co-ordinate their investigation and enforcement activities, in particular where there is a cross border infringement[1].

This builds on the power, contained in Art 9.1 and 9.2 of the 2006 Regulation, which allowed the CPC enforcers, with the assistance of the European Commission, to take several 'joint actions' to tackle problems affecting consumers across the EU/EEA. These have included work to prevent unauthorised transactions in the context of children's apps, improvements to the transparency of car rental terms and conditions and requiring social media sites to provide a 'notice and takedown' mechanism for enforcers to remove illegal content. More details may be found on the Europa website[2]. The CPC Regulation makes provision for the EU to enter into co-operation arrangements with enforcers outside the EU[3]. Therefore there is a basis for continued co-operation between the UK and EU, which could prevent traders exploiting any enforcement gap to harm consumers.

[1]   Chapter IV of the 2017 Regulation.
[2]   https://ec.europa.eu/info/live-work-travel-eu/consumers/enforcement-consumer-protection/co ordinated-actions_en.
[3]   Art 32 of the 2017 Regulation.

Enforcement involving third countries

3.78 Where a competent authority receives relevant intelligence from an authority in a country outside the EU/EEA, it is required to notify other enforcers in the EU/EEA, if it is permitted to do so by any bilateral assistance agreement between it and the third country authority[1]. Further, competent authorities may also share intelligence they receive under the CPC Regulation with authorities in third countries, where they have a bilateral assistance agreement with them, provided they obtain the consent of the authority which originally communicated the information[2]. Under Art 32, the network as a whole must co-operate with third countries in the consumer protection areas covered by the CPC Regulation in order to enhance the protection of consumers' economic interests. To this end, the Community may establish mutual assistance arrangements with the third country concerned[3].

[1]   Art 32.3 of the 2017 Regulation.
[2]   Art 32.4 of the 2017 Regulation.
[3]   These provisions were slightly extended by Art 32 of the 2017 Regulation.

International enforcement co-operation

3.79 Besides the formal mechanisms provided for within the EU, there exists also the less formal framework created by the International Consumer Protection Enforcement Network ('ICPEN'). This is a group of approximately 60 countries which have agreed to co-operate in the area of consumer protection. These countries have all signed the ICPEN Memorandum of Understanding, by which they agree to share intelligence on consumer protection issues, share best practices in enforcement, work together to combat cross border consumer law infringements, and promote more effective consumer protection enforcement[1]. In practical terms, ICPEN organises an annual websweep to identify infringements in particular sectors, holds biannual conferences to facilitate joint working, and engages in various joint enforcement projects throughout the year. It also facilitates bilateral co-operation by maintaining an up to date contact list.

[1]   The ICPEN MoU can be reviewed here: https://www.icpen.org/sites/default/files/2017-08/Me morandum_on_the_Establishment_and_Operation_of_ICPEN_2016.pdf.

Bilateral international enforcement co-operation

3.80 Certain countries have made detailed provisions in their law to enable local enforcers to investigate and secure outcomes for the benefit of foreign consumers and enforcers. Providing a full list of these states is beyond the scope of this chapter. It is worth noting that two such states are the United States of America, and Canada. Restrictions on space prevent a full discussion of both jurisdictions, but there follows a brief description of the powers available to the US Federal Trade Commission, which UK enforcers may be able to take advantage of in order to protect the interests of UK consumers.

Federal Enforcement in the USA

3.81 Federal enforcement of consumer law is governed by US Federal Trade Commission Act[1] ('the FTC Act'). Section 5(a) of the FTC Act prohibits 'unfair or deceptive acts or practices in or affecting commerce.'[2] This expressly includes acts or practices involving foreign commerce that either cause reasonably foreseeable injury in the USA or involve 'material conduct occurring within' the USA[3]. The scope of 'unfair or deceptive practices in or affecting commerce' expressly includes false advertisements in relation to food, drugs, medical devices, services or cosmetics[4].

[1] 15 USC para 41 et seq, as amended by the US SAFE WEB Act.
[2] Under s 4 of the FTC Act 'commerce' is defined to include commerce with foreign nations.
[3] Section 5((a)(4)(A)).
[4] Section 12 and 15 FTC Act.

3.82 The FTC defines 'unfair' practices by reference to any one of three criteria: (1) the practice injures consumers; (2) it violates established public policy; (3) it is unethical or unscrupulous[1]. According to the FTC's policy statement on 'deceptive' practices, the FTC requires three factors to be present[2]:

- there must be a representation, omission or practice that is likely to mislead the consumer[3];
- the practice must be misleading from the perspective of a consumer acting reasonably in the circumstances. If the representation or practice affects or is directed primarily to a particular group, the Commission examines reasonableness from the perspective of that group;
- the representation, omission, or practice must be a 'material' one[4].

[1] https://www.ftc.gov/public-statements/1980/12/ftc-policy-statement-unfairness.
[2] https://www.ftc.gov/system/files/documents/public_statements/410531/831014deceptionstmt. pdf. Further discussion of each of these criteria may be found in the FTC policy statement.
[3] Practices that have been found misleading or deceptive in specific cases include false oral or written representations, misleading price claims, sales of hazardous or systematically defective products or services without adequate disclosures, failure to disclose information regarding pyramid sales, use of bait and switch techniques, failure to perform promised services, and failure to meet warranty obligations.
[4] The FTC explains that 'the basic question is whether the act or practice is likely to affect the consumer's conduct or decision with regard to a product or service. If so, the practice is material, and consumer injury is likely, because consumers are likely to have chosen differently but for the deception. In many instances, materiality, and hence injury, can be presumed from the nature of the practice. In other instances, evidence of materiality may be necessary.'.

3.83 In all cases the FTC can only act against unfair or deceptive practices in or affecting commerce where the consumer injury is substantial; it must not be outweighed by any countervailing benefits to consumers or competition that the practice produces; and it must be an injury that consumers themselves could not reasonably have avoided[1]. The FTC is also empowered to make rules which 'define with specificity acts or practices which are unfair or deceptive.'[2] For example the FTC has issued rules governing care labels on clothing[3], cooling off period information in relation to door to door selling[4], deceptive pricing[5], disclosures that must be made by funeral providers[6], delivery times for distance selling[7], practices of telemarketers[8], use of endorsements and testimonials in advertising[9], and negative option selling[10]. These are just a selection of the rules the FTC has made[11]; the FTC also issues guidance applying to commercial practices to help traders to understand their obligations, such as in relation to leather products[12], bait advertising[13], green claims[14], and use of the word 'free'[15].

[1] TC Act s 5 (n). For further discussion see the FTC policy statement on unfairness: https://www.ftc.gov/public-statements/1980/12/ftc-policy-statement-unfairness.
[2] Section 18 FTC Act.
[3] 16 CFR 423.
[4] 16 CFR Pt 429.
[5] 16 CFR Pt 233.

6   16 CFR 453.
7   16 CFR Pt 435.
8   16 CFR 310.
9   16 CFR 255.
10   16 CFR Pt 425.
11   A full list with links to all the rules and guides may be found at https://www.ftc.gov/enforcem
     ent/rules/rules-and-guides.
12   16 CFR Pt 24.
13   16 CFR Pt 238.
14   16 CFR Pt 260.
15   16 CFR Pt 251.

Federal relief available

3.84 Where a person engages in unfair or deceptive acts or practices, the FTC may issue a cease and desist order under s 5(b) of the FTC Act or bring civil proceedings against them under s 19[1]. The relief available includes providing redress to injured consumers[2], including foreign victims[3].

1   It is noteworthy that where the FTC makes a final cease and desist order, which it has cause to enforce through the courts, all of the findings of fact made by the FTC are treated as conclusive – FTC Act s 19(c)(1).
2   Section 19(b).
3   Section 5(a)(4)(B).

FTC investigatory powers

3.85 The FTC has a general power to investigate any legal or natural person who is engaged in commerce or whose business affects commerce[1]. Specifically, the FTC may require access to documentation, may subpoena testimony from witnesses, and require production of documentary evidence[2]. The FTC may also, where it has reason to believe a person has any information relevant to unfair or deceptive practices, serve on that person a civil investigative demand requiring them to produce documents, file written reports, answer questions or give oral testimony[3]. There are detailed provisions governing the confidentiality of such evidence[4].

1   Section 6(a). It is not allowed to investigate banks – but may require such institutions to provide information about other traders under investigation (see *Proviso* to s 6).
2   Section 9.
3   Section 20(c)(1).
4   See s 21(b),(c) and (f), and s 6(f).

Assistance for overseas enforcers

3.86 A foreign law enforcement agency[1] may send a written request to the FTC for investigative assistance, where the enforcer is investigating possible infringements of laws prohibiting 'fraudulent or deceptive practices' or any other practices which are 'substantially similar to practices prohibited by any provision of the laws' administered by the FTC[2]. The practice does not have to infringe US law[3]. Such a request empowers the FTC to conduct such investigation as it deems necessary to collect the pertinent information and evidence, using all the investigative powers at its disposal[4]. The FTC is not under an obligation to provide assistance however, and its Commissioners must first consider whether the requesting agency has agreed to provide or will provide reciprocal assistance to the FTC; whether compliance with the request would prejudice the public interest of the USA; and whether the foreign investigation concerns acts or practices that cause or are likely to cause injury to a significant number of persons[5].

1   Defined in s 4 as 'any agency or judicial authority of a foreign government . . . or a multinational organization constituted by and comprised of foreign states, that is vested with law enforcement or investigative authority in civil, criminal or administrative matters.'
2   This would include rules promulgated by the FTC, as well as a number of other laws the FTC enforcers connected with privacy protection, but not anti-trust. Anti trust co-operation is provided for elsewhere.
3   Section 6(j)(1).
4   Section 6(j)(2).
5   Section 6(j)(3).

Co-operation between the UK and US

3.87 In order to facilitate cross border enforcement co-operation, in 2019 the FTC and the CMA entered into a Memorandum of Understanding. This enables the FTC Commissioners to be satisfied that UK enforcers have agreed to provide reciprocal assistance. It provides a framework for UK enforcers to channel requests through the CMA, or to approach the FTC directly or assistance. The MOU includes (at Annex 1) a model request form, which helps enforcers to provide all the information the FTC needs to decide whether it can provide assistance, and sets out various other declarations the enforcer should give in order to ensure confidentiality of evidence exchanged under the MoU (at Annex 4)[1].

1   A full text of the MoU can be found at https://www.gov.uk/government/publications/cma-and -ftc-memorandum-of-understanding.

CRIMINAL ENFORCEMENT AGAINST OVERSEAS TRADERS

3.88 Trading standards departments do not generally have a good record in prosecuting traders that are based overseas but nonetheless commit consumer law offences against UK consumers. This is largely because local authorities are reluctant to engage in potentially difficult and expensive litigation in circumstances where they have both finite resources and limited experience of such cases. This is increasingly becoming a significant problem, leaving a gaping hole in the armoury of consumer law regulators. In the internet age it has become all too easy for traders to target UK consumers with criminal practices by operating from a foreign jurisdiction. It is undoubtedly a significant benefit to such traders, and an encouragement to operate remotely, that they are generally beyond the radar of most consumer law regulators. This regulatory fear of pursuing overseas traders may also be unwarranted. The law in this area has developed over the last decade and the procedures in place for service overseas and extradition no longer present the same level of complexity and difficulty for prosecutors.

3.89 Prosecuting an overseas trader in the English courts for committing a criminal offence against a UK consumer requires consideration of three specific topics:

(a)   territorial jurisdiction for a domestic criminal offence;

(b)   service of process under the Criminal Procedure Rules; and
(c)   extraditing a defendant from overseas.

This part is not applicable in Scotland or Northern Ireland.

Territorial jurisdiction for domestic criminal offences

3.90 The starting point for domestic prosecutions in England and Wales is that the courts are not concerned with conduct abroad and only have jurisdiction over acts committed in England and Wales[1]. In determining territorial jurisdiction for criminal offences, it is important to establish where the offence was actually committed. This may not be the same as the location of the defendant. The courts have traditionally asked the question whether the 'essence' or 'gist'[2] of the offence occurred within the jurisdiction, sometimes known as the 'last act' rule[3]. However, the modern approach is to ask where a 'substantial measure' of the activities constituting a crime took place[4]. Where the offending occurred across borders then prosecuting authorities should also give consideration to whether any issues of concurrent jurisdiction arise. The Director of Public Prosecutions has published guidance on the handling of cases which may be of assistance[5] and the CPS has published guidance on jurisdiction[6].

1   *Cox v Army Council* [1963] AC 48.
2   *R v Harden* [1963] 1 QB 8 46 Cr App R 90.
3   *R v Manning* [1998] 2 Cr App R 461, CA.
4   *R v Smith (Wallace Duncan) (no 4)* [2004] 2 Cr App R 17, CA.
5   *Director's Guidance on the handling of cases where the jurisdiction to prosecute is shared with prosecuting authorities overseas*: https://www.cps.gov.uk/publication/directors-guidance-hand ling-cases-where-jurisdiction-prosecute-shared-prosecuting.
6   https://www.cps.gov.uk/legal-guidance/jurisdiction.

3.91 In our opinion the courts are likely to consider that a 'substantial measure' of an offence was committed within the UK jurisdiction, if the victim was a consumer in the UK at the time it occurred. This is likely to be the position even if the offence was committed remotely by somebody outside the jurisdiction, for example using the internet or acting through an agent[1]. The rationale for this is the consumer protection nature of these offences. They are primarily designed to protect UK consumers and it seems unlikely that Parliament would have intended that purpose to be jurisdictionally frustrated because a trader was selling to, or otherwise dealing with, UK consumers from abroad. The courts have taken a less restrictive approach where the defendant's conduct, or the consequences of the conduct, take place in England[2].

1   See also *R v Baxter* [1972] QB 1, Cr App R 214 on agency.
2   See *Treacy v DPP* [1971] AC 537 and also importantly the decision of the Privy Council in *Liagsiriprasert v Government of the United States of America* [1991] 1 AC 225.

3.92 Specific provisions apply to offences committed on board a UK Ship[1] or UK aircraft in flight.[2]

1   Merchant Shipping Act 1995, ss 280–282.
2   Civil Aviation Act 1982, s 92 (as amended).

Service of process overseas

3.93 The procedural requirements for serving criminal process overseas are particularly important when the defendant is a company and cannot, as an incorporeal body, be extradited. The procedure for serving overseas process is governed by s 3 of the Crime (International Co-operation) Act 2003 ('C(IC)A 2003') and Pt 49 of the Criminal Procedure Rules ('Crim PR') and applies to any 'summons or order'[1] 'made for the purposes of criminal proceedings by a court in England and Wales or Northern Ireland.'[2] The process can be 'issued or made in spite of the fact that the person on whom it is to be served is outside the UK.'

[1]   Section 51 Interpretation 'Process' includes any other document issued or made by a court for service on parties or witnesses; and any document issued by a prosecuting authority outside the UK for the purposes of criminal proceedings.
[2]   Section 3(1).

3.94 There are two primary rules that apply under the section 3 procedure. The first and most important is that the effect of serving process on an overseas defendant does not subsequently give a domestic court power to order arrest following a failure to attend or comply[1]. The effect of service creates no legal obligation to comply. The process of arrest in a foreign jurisdiction is governed by extradition treaties agreed between sovereign states. For reasons of comity, a UK court cannot exercise such a jurisdiction over a party or witness in another country. It follows that, unlike a domestic warrant, process served under section 3 must not contain a penal notice[2].

[1]   Section 3(6).
[2]   Section 3(4).

3.95 The second rule in s 3 is procedural. Where the process is to be served outside the UK, if it is believed that the person it will be served upon does not understand English, the process must be 'translated into an appropriate language' and served on the court[1]. Service must ordinarily be effected by post, however, s 4 provides an alternative where arrangements between the UK and a foreign country have been agreed. Alternative service may apply when the correct address of the person to be served is not known; it has not been possible to serve the process by post or there are good reasons for thinking that postal service will not be effective or is inappropriate. Section 4A of the C(IC)A 2003 sets out a procedure for serving overseas the new 'charge' and 'requisition' documents that permit certain prosecutors to start criminal proceedings without first issuing in a court. At the time of writing, the new provisions[2] had not been brought into force and it is not clear whether the power will extend to local authority prosecutors.

[1]   Section 3(3).
[2]   Criminal Justice and Courts Act 2015, by amendment to s 29 of the Criminal Justice Act 2003.

3.96 An overseas defendant that has been served under these procedures may nonetheless choose not to attend for criminal trial or other relevant hearings. Although there is no power to compel attendance in these circumstances, the criminal courts have the capacity to try a defendant in absence. In summary proceedings, there is a presumption in s 11 of the Magistrates' Court Act 1981 that the trial should take place unless to do so would be 'contrary to the interests of justice'. In the Crown Court there is also a discretion to try an absent defendant, although that is applied more sparingly[1].

[1]   See *R v Jones (Anthony)* [2003] 1 AC 1 HL.

Enforcement of fines

3.97   When a trader is based within another EU country, a fine can usually be enforced under the EU Framework Decision on the mutual recognition of fines[1], which was implemented by Pt 6 of the Criminal Justice and Immigration Act 2008[2] ('CJIA 2008'). This provides for the reciprocal enforcement, within the EU, of criminal fines (including criminal costs and compensation orders) imposed after 1 October 2009[3]. Part 6 permits the fines officer[4] in a magistrates' court[5] to issue a certificate requesting that an unpaid fine, that is not subject to appeal, be enforced in the Member State where a defendant 'is normally resident, or has property or income'[6]. For a corporate defendant, 'normally resident' is taken to mean where the company has its registered office. In the event of a no-deal Brexit, these mutual recognition provisions will no longer apply[7]. However, it may also be possible to enforce a fine as a civil judgment debt[8].

[1]   2005/214/JHA.
[2]   In England, Wales and Northern Ireland. In Scotland by the Mutual Recognition of Criminal Financial Penalties in the European Union (Scotland) Order 2009, SI 2009/342.
[3]   Section 80(5).
[4]   Section 81(2)(a).
[5]   A magistrates' court in England and Wales, a Sheriff Court or JP Court in Scotland and a court of petty sessions in Northern Ireland.
[6]   Para 38(4)(b) in Sch 5 of the Courts Act 2003.
[7]   The Criminal Justice (Amendment etc.) (EU Exit) Regulations 2018.
[8]   See s 87 of the Magistrates' Court Act 1981.

Extradition

3.98   Extradition is the legal process by which persons accused or convicted of criminal offences are surrendered by one State or 'judicial authority' to another for the purposes of being prosecuted, being sentenced following conviction, or serving a sentence already imposed. For those responsible for the investigation and prosecution of criminal offences in England and Wales the main purpose of extradition will be to secure a person's return to the jurisdiction in three circumstances:

(a)   where that person is abroad and is accused of committing an offence in the UK;

(b)   a person convicted in the UK but who is abroad having absconded after conviction but before sentence; and

(c)   a person convicted and sentenced in the UK but who is abroad having absconded from their sentence.

As such, extradition cases are often described either as 'accusation' cases or 'conviction' cases. Some cases can involve a 'mixed' request for extradition where a person is both accused of some offences and convicted of others.

3.99 The exact procedure followed to secure extradition will depend on the country within which the requested person (the 'RP') is located, if indeed that information is known. At present, there are broadly two types of extradition request made by UK authorities: (i) the issuance by a judge in the UK of a 'Part 3 warrant' (or 'Arrest Warrant') to be circulated amongst the Member States of the EU; and (ii) the issuance of an extradition request by the Home Office to States not within the EU on the basis of other treaty or bilateral arrangements. Arrest Warrants are issued and executed between judicial authorities whereas extradition requests are issued and executed between sovereign States.

3.100 Following the UK's departure from the EU, the UK is no longer part of the 'European Arrest Warrant' or 'EAW' scheme. Title VII of Pt 3 of the TCA governs surrender agreements between the UK and EU. This was implemented at the domestic level through the European Union (Future Relationship) Act 2020 (EUFRA 2020). The new arrangement closely replicates the Framework Decision on the European Arrest Warrant and the surrender scheme in place between the EU, Norway and Iceland. However, there are some key differences, including the fact that a State may refuse to execute an arrest warrant on grounds of nationality and that cooperation is subject to the principle of proportionality. The TCA also provides for additional safeguards for a requested person, in particular, the right to be informed of their right to appoint a lawyer in the issuing State for the purpose of assisting the lawyer in the executing State.

3.101 Due to the similarities between the TCA and the Framework Decision, few legislative changes to the EA 2003 were required. The transition period, as defined by the Withdrawal Agreement, ended at 11pm on 31 December 2020. In cases where no arrest has been made, the TCA states that EAWs issued under the Framework Decision during the transition period shall be treated as Arrest Warrants for the purpose of the new surrender arrangements. With regard to those arrested, or provisionally arrested, pursuant to EAWs during the transition period but not surrendered before that date, the amendments made by the 2019 Regulations do not apply (reg 57).

3.102 The new agreement refers to an extradition requests simply as an 'arrest warrant'. Strictly speaking they are not 'European Arrest Warrants', but no doubt the terminology will continue to be used interchangeably. For the purposes of this Chapter, arrests warrants issued within the new European Union scheme will be referred to as 'Arrest Warrants' or 'AWs'. They are also known as 'Part 3 Warrants' as they are issued under Pt 3 of the 2003 Act. Given that much of the Extradition Act 2003 has not required amendment, the essential steps to be followed in England and Wales to obtain an Arrest Warrant remain the same.

The first steps in any extradition process

3.103 The first step in any extradition process will be the same regardless of the foreign state concerned.

Charging decision and domestic warrant

3.104 A request for a person's extradition to the UK can only be made once a formal charging decision has been taken by the relevant prosecuting authority. In other words, extradition can only be sought in an accusation case where a decision has been taken that the RP is to be prosecuted (ie where he is formally 'accused' of a criminal offence). In *Re Ismail*[1], the House of Lords determined that 'mere suspicion' of criminality is not sufficient to found a request. Indeed, it would be an abuse of process to seek a person's return where they are merely suspected of an offence and with a view to interview them before a charging decision is taken.

[1] [1999] 1 AC 320.

3.105 Forcibly returning a person to the UK in disregard of formal extradition processes where available is also capable of amounting to an abuse of process[1]. Therefore, it is important to note that any request for extradition is predicated on there being extant criminal proceedings against the RP. In other words, unless criminal proceedings are formally underway there can be no request for extradition.

[1] *Horseferry Road Magistrates' Court, ex parte Bennett* [1994] 1 AC 42.

3.106 Once a charging decision has been made in an accusation case the next step is to obtain a domestic warrant for the person's arrest. A domestic warrant is a warrant issued pursuant to any of the following provisions:

(a)   Section 1 of the Magistrates' Courts Act 1980 ('MCA 1980');
(b)   Section 72 of the Criminal Justice Act 1967 ('CJA 1967'); or
(c)   Section 7 of the Bail Act 1976 ('BA 1976').

In most cases, the relevant provision will be s 1 MCA 1980. Section 72 CJA 1967 deals with escaped prisoners and s 7 BA 1976 relates to someone already on bail but failing to attend court.

3.107 A warrant can be sought pursuant to s 1 MCA 1980 upon an information being laid before a justice of the peace (or district judge) that a person has, or is suspected of having, committed an offence. A warrant can only be issued if the information is in writing[1]. Where the offence charged is an indictable offence, a warrant may be issued at any time notwithstanding that a summons has previously been issued[2]. A warrant can only be issued where the offence to which it relates is an indictable offence or is punishable with imprisonment[3].

[1] Section 1(3) MCA 1980.
[2] Section 1(6) MCA 1980.
[3] Section 1(4) MCA 1980.

3.108 Part 7 of the Criminal Procedure Rules ('Crim PR') governs the procedure to be followed in obtaining a warrant pursuant to s 1. MCA 1980. A prosecutor who wants the court to issue a warrant must serve on the court officer a written application, or a copy of a written charge that has been issued; or present to the court either of those documents. The application must set out the allegation or allegations made by the applicant in terms that comply with rule 7.3 (allegation of offence in application or charge); and demonstrate that the application is made in time; if legislation imposes a time limit, and that the applicant has the necessary consent, if legislation requires it. The application must also demonstrate that the offence or offences alleged can be tried in the Crown Court and that the offence or offences alleged can be punished with imprisonment. It must concisely outline the applicant's grounds for asserting that the defendant's address is not sufficiently established for a summons to be served where applicable.

3.109 Rule 7.3 provides that an allegation of an offence in an application for the issue of a summons or warrant or must contain: (a) a statement of the offence that describes the offence in ordinary language, and identifies any legislation that creates it; and (b) such particulars of the conduct constituting the commission of the offence as to make clear what the prosecutor alleges against the defendant. It is common for suspects not to have been interviewed by investigators before they leave the UK and therefore before extradition is sought. That is not a bar to extradition provided a charging decision has been made.

3.110 For conviction cases, where a RP has been convicted in absence or failed to attend on bail following conviction the court is likely to have issued a domestic arrest warrant (or if not, such a warrant ought to be sought) and that can be used to found a request for extradition, together with the relevant certificate of conviction. Where a serving prisoner absconds from a prison sentence they will be unlawfully at large and they can be arrested without an arrest warrant. However, if they are to be prosecuted for a new offence (such as escape from lawful custody) a fresh domestic warrant will be required for that offence.

Location of the conduct

3.111 In the majority of cases, the RP is accused of committing an offence the conduct of which occurred within the UK. For the purposes of extradition, it is not necessary for all of the conduct to have occurred within the UK; rather, it is necessary to show that *some* of the conduct occurred in the jurisdiction. In *Cando Armas*, Lord Hope said, that in relation to the location of a defendant[1]:

> 'It is now well established that the physical presence of the defendant in the territory is not required so long as the effects of his actions were intentionally felt there. That rule is matched by its corollary which is that, if the effects of those actions were intentionally felt here, criminal jurisdiction can be exercised in respect of their effect irrespective of where the actions took place which gave rise to them.'

[1] *Cando Armas*, Per Lord Hope [2006] 2 AC 1 at 35; see also *R (Bermingham) v Director of the Serious Fraud Office* [2007] QB 727 and *Norris v Government of the United States* [2008] 2 WLR 673.

The steps required to obtain an arrest warrant

3.112 Extradition between the UK and countries within the EU operates on the basis of the TCA scheme. The procedure for obtaining an Arrest Warrant in England and Wales for the return of a person to the jurisdiction is governed by Pt 3 EA 2003 (such warrants are known as 'Part 3 warrants'). Part 3 warrants are in effect Arrest Warrants issued by the courts in the UK. A Pt 3 warrant can only be issued by an 'appropriate judge', ie a district judge (magistrates' court), a justice of the peace or a Crown Court judge[1], and only upon application by a constable or an 'appropriate person'. An appropriate person is either any member of the Serious Fraud Office designated by the Director of the SFO or the Director of Public Prosecutions and any Crown Prosecutor[2].

[1]   Section 149 EA 2003.
[2]   See para 2 of the Extradition Act 2003 (Part 3 Designation) Order 2003.

3.113   Therefore, it should be noted that the trading standards department of a local authority ('Trading Standards') does not have the power itself to apply for an Arrest Warrant (ie a Pt 3 warrant). Current CPS policy is that it does not make AW applications on behalf of other UK prosecutors and it must have conduct itself of domestic proceedings in order to make an application[1]. Therefore, National Trading Standards may want to consider approaching the police with a view to a constable obtaining an EAW. However, it should be noted that although a constable may apply for an EAW, in accordance with a Memorandum of Understanding between the CPS, NCA and ACPO, no application should be made without the approval of the responsible CPS prosecutor in the relevant CPS area. Again, Trading Standards ought to consult the relevant bodies for early advice or assistance as such cooperation cannot be guaranteed.

[1]   https://www.cps.gov.uk/legal-guidance/extradition, accessed on 14 September 2021.

3.114   In order to apply for an AW it is necessary to demonstrate, in an accusation case, that there are reasonable grounds for believing that the person has committed an extradition offence and that a domestic warrant has been issued in respect of the person[1]. In a conviction case, it is necessary to demonstrate that the person has been convicted of an extradition offence and his extradition is sought for the purpose of his being sentenced for the offence or of his serving a sentence of imprisonment or another form of detention imposed in respect of the offence; and either a domestic warrant has been issued in respect of the person or the person may be arrested without a warrant. Separate accusation and conviction cases against the same defendant can be included in a single AW, but the different matters must clearly be set out to avoid confusion.

[1]   Section 142(2) EA 2003.

3.115   Once a domestic warrant has been obtained a Pt 3 warrant (AW) can be sought. In practice, a domestic arrest warrant pursuant to s 1 MCA 1980 could be obtained at the same time as a Pt 3 warrant. A Pt 3 warrant in an accusation case has to contain a statement that the person in respect of whom the warrant is issued is accused in the UK of the commission of an extradition offence specified in the warrant, and the warrant is issued with a view to his arrest and extradition to the UK for the purpose of being prosecuted for the offence[1].

[1]   Section 142(4) EA 2003.

3.116   In a conviction case, the AW has to state that the person in respect of whom the warrant is issued has been convicted of an 'extradition offence' specified in the warrant and the warrant is issued with a view to his arrest and extradition to the UK for the purpose of being sentenced for the offence or serving a sentence of imprisonment or another form of detention imposed in respect of it. Conduct constitutes an 'extradition offence' in relation to the UK if the conduct occurs in the UK and the conduct is punishable under the law of the relevant part of the UK with imprisonment or another form of detention for a term of 12 months or a greater punishment[1].

1   Sections 142, 148 EA 2003.

3.117 The Pt 3 warrant must also certify whether the conduct constituting the extradition offence specified in the warrant falls within the Trade and Cooperation Agreement list; whether the offence is an extra-territorial offence; and what is the maximum punishment that may be imposed on conviction of the offence[1]. The conduct which falls within the TCA list must be taken to include conduct which constitutes an attempt, conspiracy or incitement to carry out conduct falling within the list, or aiding, abetting, counselling or procuring the carrying out of conduct falling within the list.

1   Section 142(6) EA 2003.

3.118 The judicial authority executing the AW will have to be satisfied that the UK offences (and in particular the conduct relied upon) would amount to offences in their jurisdiction if committed there (the principal of 'dual criminality'). This requirement is dispensed with if the offences come within the TCA list of offences[1]. Where the conduct does not fall within the AW list of offence categories, the executing Member State may need to establish dual criminality (ie that there is an equivalent, if not identical, offence in their domestic legislation).

1   See Sch 2, EA 2003.

3.119 Included within a Pt 3 warrant (AW) is a summary of the allegation against the individual(s) and so, before obtaining a Pt 3 warrant it would be necessary for Trading Standards to draft such a summary for inclusion within. The summary need not be lengthy but clearly must contain the relevant essential allegations upon which the proceedings have been brought. A *pro forma* AW form can be found at Annex 43 to the TCA and ought to be used as a template for the information required for a Pt 3 warrant[1].

1   https://eur-lex.europa.eu/legal-content/EN/TXT/HTML/?uri=CELEX:22021A0430(01)&from=EN#d1844e32-2069-1.

3.120 Where a person is arrested upon a Pt 3 warrant (AW), that person will be entitled to resist their extradition in accordance with the law of the foreign state. Whilst a EU country is obliged to uphold a valid AW it cannot be guaranteed that extradition will be successful. Trading Standards may be called upon by the authorities of the foreign state to provide further information to support the case or to address any questions that they may have. Whilst the process is supposed to be speedy no particular time-scale can be guaranteed.

Provisional arrests

3.121 In exceptional circumstances a request can be made for provisional arrest. Typically the need arises where a wanted person has been located and there not enough time to obtain an AW. Such a request must be necessary and proportionate. Those seeking such an arrest must believe that an AW will immediately follow. An application is made through the National Crime Agency (again, for a non-CPS prosecuting body this step could only be taken in consultation with the CPS and/or the police). An AW must be issued and received by the EU member state in question within 48 hours of provisional arrest. For some states the time limit is 24 hours.

Seizure of property

3.122 It is possible for property to be seized at the time an AW is executed if that property is listed in the AW. Any such items are not normally provided until the RP is extradited upon the AW. The precise powers will vary as between various Member States. If evidence is required pre-charge or more urgently then use ought to be made of other mutual legal assistance powers.

Extradition outside the EU

3.123 Extradition requests to jurisdictions outside of the EU (and therefore not a party to the AW scheme) are not made pursuant to a statutory scheme but rather are made by the Secretary of State for the Home Department pursuant to Royal Prerogative. Such requests are made on a State to State basis and typically on the basis of a multilateral treaty[1] or bilateral treaty[2]. Countries such as the United States of America, Australia, Canada, and Norway fall into this category of case. As with an AW, a charging decision will already have been made in an accusation case before an extradition request is sought.

[1]   Eg the European Convention on Extradition 1957.
[2]   Eg extradition treaty between the United States of America and the United Kingdom 2003.

3.124 Extradition will only be possible in respect of extradition offences, the precise definition of which will vary depending upon the international treaty in question. In general, the offence must be a criminal offence that is punishable in both States with at least 12 months' imprisonment. In conviction cases a sentence of at least 4 months' imprisonment must usually have been imposed. The dual criminality exercise will again be undertaken by the requested State (as with AW cases, although here there is no equivalent of the TCA list of offences and so dual criminality is always required).

3.125 The precise content of the extradition request will again depend on the country and international arrangement in question. Typically, an extradition request in an accusation case will need to include a copy of the domestic arrest warrant; a document setting out a summary of facts of the case; details of the legislation creating the offence together with maximum sentences available and details of the requested person. Some jurisdictions still require the UK to provide evidence of a prima facie case, if so copies of witness statements will need to be included. It is often the case that authenticated copies of such documents are required and so often a hearing is held *ex parte* before a magistrates' court for such documents to be authenticated on oath.

3.126 Usually, in cases being prosecuted by the CPS, it will draft the extradition request and advise the police as to what documents are required to be included. Once drafted, the request is sent by the CPS to the Home Office for onward transmission to the relevant State. As with AWs, National Trading Standards ought to consult the CPS as to whether it can assist with the drafting of such extradition requests. The Home Office could also be approached to see whether it is also willing to deal directly with National Trading Standards where NTS is conducting a prosecution.

Other matters that can arise in either an AW or non-AW case

SURRENDER TO THE UK

3.127 The NCA will be notified if a person is to be extradited to the UK pursuant to an AW and it will then liaise with the relevant UK enforcement authority in relation to the collection of the RP. Where the Home Office has made an extradition request it will likewise be notified of any decisions upon return to the UK. A person returned to the UK ought to be produced before the relevant court that issued the domestic arrest warrant as soon as possible.

DISCLOSURE

3.128 It is important to note ordinary statutory disclosure obligations will apply where a criminal prosecution is underway, see CHAPTER 4 Criminal Enforcement. However, whilst there are no formal statutory disclosure obligations relating to extradition proceedings, there exists a duty of candour in relation to the content of the extradition request itself. The contents of an AW or extradition request must be accurate and fair and ought to be reviewed against any unused material (either before the application is made or shortly thereafter).

3.129 Disclosure is a continuing obligation and any material that comes to a prosecutor's attention after an extradition request has been made ought to be subject to such a review. Clearly if such material renders the AW or any extradition request inaccurate or means there is no longer a realistic prospect of conviction then the AW or extradition request ought to be withdrawn. Any material generated as a result of the extradition request (for example in relation to investigations to locate a RP) will need to be reviewed for disclosure purposes. An AW or extradition request itself is likely to be become unused material.

3.130 A judicial authority (in an AW case) or requested State is entitled to ask for further information to address any questions they may have about the case. These should be dealt with by the prosecutor and should also be reviewed for disclosure purposes. In the same way, any decision issued by the judicial authority or requested State upon the request itself ought to be obtained at the point the RP is handed over to the UK authorities and retention and review for disclosure purposes. It may be necessary to refer to such documents subsequently to ascertain the precise basis of the decision to extradite the RP. In short, any material created during the extradition process ought to be gathered and reviewed for the purposes of disclosure.

Withdrawing an AW or request for extradition

3.131 An AW can only be withdrawn by a district judge, a justice of the peace or a Crown Court judge. If an AW is withdrawn investigators should also consider applying to withdraw any domestic warrants. The Home Office is responsible for withdrawing any extradition requests it has made to other States and the same considerations would apply to any domestic warrants.

Specialty

3.132 The principle of 'specialty' (or 'speciality') essentially provides that an extradited individual can only be prosecuted in the UK for the offences upon which he or she was extradited or an offence disclosed by the information provided to the extraditing territory in respect of that offence[1]. In an AW case, following extradition the RP may only be dealt with for offences in respect of which they were extradited and cannot face proceedings for other offences that pre-date extradition[2]. Specialty does not prevent prosecution for the offence in respect of which the person was extradited[3]; an offence disclosed by the information in the AW; an extradition offence in respect of which consent to the person being dealt with is given on behalf of the territory in response to a request made by the UK judge; an offence which is not punishable with imprisonment or another form of detention; an offence in respect of which the person will not be detained in connection with his trial, sentence or appeal; and an offence in respect of which the person waives the right that he would have (but for this paragraph) not to be dealt with for the offence.

[1] See s 146 EA 2003 in respect of a Part 3 warrant.
[2] Sections 146–147 EA 2003.
[3] Pursuant to s 146 EA 2003.

3.133 Where a person has been arrested pursuant to an AW and consented to their surrender, the person will also be asked if he agrees to waive his right to specialty. Such waiver is usually irrevocable, subject to the law of the particular EU state. If consent has been provided then ordinarily specialty does not apply[1]. Specialty is also dispensed with if a person is given an opportunity to leave the UK following their return and then does not do so, or does so but subsequently returns[2].

[1] Section 147 EA 2003.
[2] See ss 146, 150, 151A EA 2003.

3.134 A person may usually be dealt with for lesser included offences pursuant to s 146 EA 2003, for example preferring assault occasioning actual bodily harm instead of grievous bodily harm[1]. Where a 'new' offence is very closely related to the original offence it might be possible to prosecute for the new offence. Such an instance would require very close consideration of the facts of the case to ensure that the nature of the of the offence has not changed[2]. Therefore, in AW accusation cases, the AW should set out all of the offences that the RP will be prosecuted for. In conviction cases, the AW should refer to all offences of which the RP has been convicted of (whether or not sentence has yet been imposed and including offences for which a suspended sentence has been passed).

[1] *R v Seddon* [2009] EWCA Crim 483, [2009] 1 WLR 2342, [2009] 2 Cr App R 9.
[2] See the decision of the CJEU in *Leymann and Pustovarov* C-388/08 PPU.

3.135 In non-AW cases the rules on specialty will be contained within the relevant international treaty governing the extradition process and in s 150 and s 151A EA 2003. The rules are broadly similar: a person can only be dealt with in the UK for offences that were expressly the subject of the request for extradition (or lesser included offences) and upon which extradition was granted. Specialty can also be waived if the RP consents to his extradition to the UK or if the State in question provides its consent post-extradition.

3.136 Post-extradition consent can be obtained for the prosecution of other offences but it can be a cumbersome process. In practice Trading Standards ought to ensure that where possible the Part 3 warrant or extradition request is sufficiently detailed to include all key facts that underpin any charge or potential charges. Following the RP's return to the UK, it is important that the indictment properly reflects the charges that were included within the AW or extradition request. It is important to note that the speciality rule is concerned with offences, as opposed to evidence. The rule operates to prevent the UK courts from dealing with a RP for an offence different in its essential nature from the charge(s) upon which he was extradited. Therefore, the rule does not limit a prosecution as regards the evidence (or additional evidence) it is entitled to adduce to establish guilt[1].

1   *GW v Serious Fraud Office* [2018] EWCA Crim 1155, [2018] 4 WLR 129.

Bail Act offences

3.137 A Bail Act offence of failing to surrender to bail must be included in an extradition request as a separate offence, otherwise a RP returned to the UK cannot be prosecuted for it (unless post-surrender consent is obtained). The preferred practice is to include such an offence within an AW or extradition request[1].

1   See *R v Seddon* [2009] EWCA Crim 483; *R v Jones (Royston)* [2011] EWCA Crim 107 and *R. v Shepherd (Jack Sebastian)* [2019] EWCA Crim 1062, [2019] 2 Cr App R 26.

Return of person acquitted or not tried

3.138 Proceedings must begin against a person returned to the UK within 6 months of the day of their arrival (s 156 EA 2003). If not, and upon the RP's application within 3 months of the end of that period, the Secretary of State must arrange for the RP's return to the extraditing territory. The RP can also request his return following his acquittal or discharge and again such application must be made within 3 months of the date of acquittal or discharge.

Crediting periods of remand

3.139 If the RP is convicted following extradition, the UK court will need to be told the amount of time spent in custody abroad during any extradition proceedings. The provisions of ss 240ZA and 243 CJA 2003 will determine whether or not time spent in custody abroad during the extradition process will be credited towards any sentence of imprisonment. Where a person who was unlawfully at large from a sentence has been returned to the UK pursuant to an AW to serve that sentence, the Secretary of State count any time spent in custody solely awaiting extradition against the sentence. If the RP was also on remand in relation to a domestic charge then that time would not count.

Chapter 4

CRIMINAL ENFORCEMENT

Contents

INTRODUCTION

4.1 Although consumer law often provides criminal sanction for its breach, the number of criminal prosecutions taken annually has been decreasing for a number of years. For example, around 300 cases under the Consumer Protection from Unfair Trading Regulations 2008[1] ('CPUTR 2008') reach the courts each year whereas the number taken under the legislation that the CPUTR 2008 replaced was three times that figure. Despite this reduction more cases are being dealt with by the Crown Court, indicating that local authorities have actively embraced the Macrory philosophy that 'criminal prosecution and the criminal courts . . . should largely be preserved for the truly egregious offenders'[2].

[1] SI 2008/1277.
[2] The Macrory Review of Regulatory Penalties, 28 November 2006.

4.2 A central and fundamental criticism highlighted by the Macrory Review was the allegedly heavy reliance placed on criminal prosecution by regulators as a primary, core sanctioning tool. The Regulatory Enforcement and Sanctions Act 2008 ('RESA 2008', see CHAPTER 1) provided a framework of civil sanctions in areas where criminal sanctions exist, although the Government was not convinced that this regime would be effective in consumer law. Recently enacted legislative controls on letting agents and secondary ticketing, in the Consumer Rights Act 2015, only provide for civil sanctions. Local authorities and their officers also need to have regard to the Principles of Good Regulation set out in the Legislative and Regulatory Reform Act 2006, and the Regulators' Code made under the Act. In particular regulators should publish service standards, which should include clear information on their enforcement policy, explaining how they respond to non-compliance – see **4.13**.

4.3 Criminal prosecutions are considered by many local authorities to be an appropriate and proportionate response against those who flout the law or act irresponsibly, particularly given that there is a range of out-of-court disposals that may also be employed.

4.4 At a time when funding for local authorities is a real issue, some trading standards departments may be more inclined to commence criminal proceedings if they believe that there is a chance of getting a share of any confiscation order under the Proceeds of Crime Act 2002 ('POCA 2002'). However, although prosecutors should consider proceeds of crime at various stages of a case – when considering the public interest in charging a suspect; when selecting charges; when making submissions on court venue; and when considering a defendant's offer of a plea – a body given the power to prosecute should not consider the possible financial advantage to itself as a relevant factor in the decision to prosecute. See **4.202** et seq.

CRIMINAL PROSECUTIONS

Introduction

4.5 Although there are various methods by which legislation can be enforced, the duty of enforcement frequently entails the prosecution of offences through the criminal courts. In Scotland all criminal prosecutions are conducted through the Crown Office and Procurator Fiscal Office. There was once thought to be a potential difficulty with an enforcement authority prosecuting cases in which there had been police involvement: *R v Ealing Justices ex parte Dixon*[1]. However the case of *R v Croydon Justices ex p Holmberg*[2] approved such a course after an operation involving collaboration between a trading standards department and the police.

[1] [1990] 2 QB 91, DC.
[2] (1992) 157 JP 277, CO/1391/1, QBD.

4.6 The Court of Appeal in *Scopelight Ltd & Others v Chief of Police for Northumbria*[1], went further still. It found that prohibiting the use in private prosecutions of property seized and retained by the police would 'substantially . . . erode' the role of private prosecutions. Consequently, a decision whether detention is necessary in each case should made in light of its individual facts and circumstances, including the identity and motive of the prosecutor.

[1]   [2009] EWCA Civ 1156.

Territorial jurisdiction

4.7 Territorial jurisdiction in relation to criminal prosecution is now covered in CHAPTER 3.

The right to bring a criminal prosecution

4.8 The Prosecution of Offences Act 1985 specifically preserves the right, in England and Wales, of a private citizen to bring a criminal prosecution[1]. There will usually be a right for a private citizen to bring a private prosecution for the criminal offences concerning consumer and trading standards.

[1]   Prosecution of Offences Act 1985, s 6(1).

4.9 For example, any person can bring a prosecution under the CPUTR 2008. In *House of Cars Ltd v Derby Car and Van Contracts Ltd*[1] a private prosecution under the CPUTR 2008 was brought after the Office of Fair Trading ('OFT') and the relevant local authority had declined to do so. However, there are exceptions[2] and the terms of the criminal provision should be considered carefully before any private prosecution is commenced.

[1]   [2012] CTLC 62.
[2]   Certain provisions, however, do not permit private prosecutions such as the Weights and Measures Act 1985, s 83(1).

4.10 The powers of entry and other rights to facilitate the gathering of evidence may not, however, be exercised by a private prosecutor, but only by a duly appointed officer. In *Media Protection Services Ltd v Crawford*[1] it was found that the laying of an information is a reserved legal activity under the Legal Services Act 2007 and can only be undertaken by a private prosecutor himself, or by a person authorised to carry out such a reserved legal activity.

[1]   [2012] EWHC 2373 (Admin), [2013] 1 WLR 1068.

Restrictions on proceedings for certain offences

4.11 The Enterprise Act 2002, s 230 requires local weights and measures authorities to give notice to the Competition and Markets Authority (CMA) of intended prosecutions, a summary of the evidence relied upon and their outcome, after they are finally determined. Paragraph 101 of Sch 2 to CPUTR 2008 amends the Enterprise Act 2002 (Pt 8 Notice to OFT of Intended Prosecution Specified Enactments, Revocation and Transitional Provision)

Order 2003[1] to include intended prosecutions under the CPUTR 2008. Proceedings are not invalid by reason only of the failure of the authority to comply with the Enterprise Act 2002, s 230.

[1]   SI 2003/1376.

4.12 The prosecution of some offences can only be instituted by, or with the consent of the Director of Public Prosecutions, for example, Unsolicited Goods and Services Act 1971, s 4 – an offence where a person sends or causes to be sent to another person any book, magazine or leaflet (or advertising material for any such publication) which he knows or ought reasonably to know is unsolicited and which describes or illustrates human sexual techniques. Under Weights and Measures Act 1985, s 83 proceedings for any offence under the Act or any instrument made under it can only be instituted except by or on behalf of a local weights and measures authority or the chief officer of police for a police area. Proceedings in under Health and Safety at Work etc Act 1974, s 38 for certain specified offences, in England and Wales, can only be instituted by an inspector the Environment Agency or the Natural Resources Body for Wales by or with the consent of the Director of Public Prosecutions.

Principles of good regulation

4.13 When exercising a regulatory function specified by the Legislative and Regulatory Reform (Regulatory Functions) Order 2007[1], local authorities, and their officers, must also have regard to the Principles of Good Regulation and the Regulators' Code, which came into force as a statutory Code of Practice in April 2014[2]. The Legislative and Regulatory Reform Act 2006, s 21 sets out the five principles – regulatory activities should be carried out in a way that is transparent, accountable, proportionate, and consistent and should be targeted only at cases in which action is needed.

[1]   SI 2007/3544.
[2]   Replacing the Regulators' Compliance Code.

4.14 The Legislative and Regulatory Reform Act 2006, s 22 provides for the issuing of a Code of Practice, with Legislative and Regulatory Reform Act 2006, s 23 providing detail on the issuing and revision of a code of practice. The Legislative and Regulatory Reform (Regulatory Functions) (Amendment) Order 2009[1] extends the duty to have regard to the Regulators' Code to local authorities in Scotland, Wales and Northern Ireland in respect of specified functions which are reserved, not devolved or not transferred. In addition, it extends the duty to have regard to the Regulators' Code to those who regulate private businesses and third sector operators carrying out 'public sector' functions for or on behalf of the public sector.

[1]   SI 2009/2981.

4.15 The Code contains the following principles (which persons exercising regulatory functions must have regard to, under the Legislative and Regulatory Reform Act 2006, s 21):

(i)   regulators should carry out their activities in a way that supports those they regulate to comply and grow;

(ii)   regulators should provide simple and straightforward ways to communication with those they regulate;

(iii)   regulators should base their regulatory activities on risk;

(iv)   regulators should share information about compliance and risk;

(v)   regulators should ensure clear information, guidance and advice is available to help those they regulate meet their responsibilities to comply; and

(vi)   regulators should ensure that their approach to their regulatory activities is transparent.

Enforcement policies

4.16 The Regulators' Code, made under the Legislative and Regulatory Reform Act 2006, provides:

'6.2 Regulators' published service standards should include clear information on:

. . .

d)   their enforcement policy, explaining how they respond to non-compliance;

6.4 Regulators should have mechanisms in place to ensure that their officers act in accordance with their published service standards, including their enforcement policy.'

'2.3 Regulators should provide an impartial and clearly explained route to appeal against a regulatory decision or a failure to act in accordance with this Code. Individual officers of the regulator who took the decision or action against which the appeal is being made should not be involved in considering the appeal. This route to appeal should be publicised to those who are regulated.'

4.17 In *R v Glen Adaway*[1] the Court of Appeal emphasised the importance of regulators considering the terms of their own enforcement policy before embarking on a criminal prosecution. The extent to which this will amount to an abuse of process, however, was doubted in *R v Golding*[2] where Tracey LJ said[3]:

'In the absence of oppression or misconduct the decision to prosecute is for the prosecutor and an erroneous failure to apply policy or guidance will not affect the position. The task of the Crown Court, and this court if the matter goes to appeal, is to deal with the case on the merits. If the failure to adhere to policy guidance means that there is an insufficiency of evidence, then the remedy is in the court's hands.'

[1]   [2004] EWCA Crim 2831, [2005] LLR 142.
[2]   [2014] EWCA Crim 889.
[3]   The court also referred to *R v A* [2012] EWCA Crim 434 (paras 79–87 per Judge LCJ) and *R (Barons Pub Company Limited) v Staines Magistrates' Court* [2013] EWHC 898 (Admin).

4.18 A recent example of the courts' reluctance to interfere with the decision to prosecute can be found in the case of *R v Connors Building and Restoration Ltd*[1]. A company's conviction for failing to comply with the Health and Safety at Work etc. Act 1974, Pt I, s 2(1) after an employee had been injured whilst using a rip saw was upheld as it was a serious offence which caused serious harm. The fact that the Health and Safety Executive could have issued an Improvement Notice instead of deciding to prosecute did not mean that the decision to prosecute amounted to an abuse of process. The company had argued, by reference to the Enforcement Policy Statement (EPS) and Enforcement Management Model (EMM) of the HSE, that the public interest for prosecution had not been met and that prosecution was not a proportionate response. The Court of Appeal rejected that argument, finding that it would be highly undesirable for a different standard of review in abuse of process applications to apply to challenges to decisions by the HSE to prosecute than the standard applied to such decisions by the CPS[2].

---

[1]   [2020] EWCA Crim 868.

[2]   Paragraph 23, applying *Moss & Son Ltd v Crown Prosecution Service* [2012] EWHC 3658 (Admin).

Local authority borders

4.19 The statutory limit to a local authority's power to bring proceedings in relation to matters occurring outside its own geographical area, in Local Government Act 1972 ('LGA 1972'), s 222, has historically raised difficult legal questions. These have primarily focused on the uncertainty of what was meant by 'expedient for the promotion or protection of the interests of the inhabitants' of the local authority's own area in s 222(1)(a). A Consultation on consolidating and modernising consumer law enforcement powers by the Department for Business, Innovation and Skills ('BIS'), launched in March 2012, commented that 'the current law enabling Trading Standards Services to work across local authority boundaries is open to different interpretations. The result is uncertainty and administrative costs for enforcers'.

4.20 These concerns led to the enactment of para 46 of Sch 5 to the CRA 2015[1], which came into force on 1 October 2015 and states that:

46 Criminal proceedings

(1)   A local weights and measures authority in England or Wales may bring proceedings for a consumer offence allegedly committed in a part of England or Wales which is outside that authority's area.

Paragraph 46 applies to the listed 'consumer offences'[2] and obstruction offences[3] in Sch 5 CRA 2015. Importantly, the power is also extended to the prosecution of an offence not referred to in Sch 5, where it originated 'from an investigation into a breach' of consumer legislation[4]. BIS Guidance on the exercise of the paragraph 46 power suggests that 'Enforcers operating across their local authority boundaries are encouraged to liaise with enforcers in the relevant local authorities and primary authorities when considering operating outside their local area. This will help to avoid any likelihood of duplication of enforcement activities.' The power extends to district councils in England, Wales and Northern Ireland[5]. It does not apply in Scotland where prosecutions are instituted by the Procurator Fiscal.

---

[1]   Came into force on 1 October 2015, art 3 of the Consumer Rights Act 2015 (Commencement No 3, Transitional Provisions, Savings and Consequential Amendments) Order 2015/1630.

[2]   Listed in paras 11 and 12 of Sch 5 to the CRA 2015.

[3]   Listed in paras 36 or 37 of Sch 5 to the CRA 2015.

[4]   Paragraphs 46(2)(d), 46(4)(d) and 46(6)(c).

[5]   Paragraphs 46(3) and (5).

Section 222

4.21 In relation to local authority prosecutions falling within CRA 2015, Sch 5, para 46, it is likely that LGA 1972, s 222 is now largely redundant. However, it will remain of relevance where a local authority prosecutes for offences falling outside that provision, such as where the prosecuted offences are not listed as consumer offences and do not originate from an investigation into such offences. In relation to the bringing of either criminal or civil proceedings in the name of a local authority the LGA 1972, s 222 provides:

> **222 Power of local authorities to prosecute or defend legal proceedings**
>
> (1)   Where a local authority consider it expedient for the promotion or protection of the interests of the inhabitants of their area—
>
>   (a)   they may prosecute or defend or appear in any legal proceedings and, in the case of civil proceedings, may institute them in their own name, and
>
>   (b)   they may, in their own name, make representations in the interests of the inhabitants at any public inquiry held by or on behalf of any Minister or public body under any enactment.

4.22 In determining challenges to the exercise of the s 222 discretion, the courts have adopted a limited supervisory approach. In *Stoke on Trent City Council v B & Q Retail Limited*, it was made clear that challenges should be governed by public law principles:

> 'Section 222 requires that a local authority shall only act if they "consider it expedient for the promotion or protection of the interests of the inhabitants of their area". Any exercise by the local authority of this statutory power is subject to the control of judicial review and the application of the principles enunciated in *Associated Provincial Picture Houses Ltd v Wednesbury Corporation* [1948] 1 KB 223. In considering the exercise of their powers the local authority must take into account matters which they ought to take into account, ignore matters which they ought not to take into account and then reach a decision which is not so unreasonable that no reasonable local authority could have come to it.'[1]

[1]   [1984] 1 AC 754, p 775 F–G.

4.23 A challenge to the s 222 discretion will ordinarily turn on its own facts and the courts are likely to be slow to interfere[1] where a local authority 'considers' that the expediency criterion is met[2]. The test is subjective, with potentially relevant considerations being wide and not limited strictly by geography[3]. In *Oldham Metropolitan Borough Council v Worldwide Marketing Solutions Ltd* it was stated that there was:

> 'no basis for limiting the matters the local authority may consider to activities taking place within the relevant area or directly affecting its inhabitants . . . a local authority can properly take into account broader considerations of how to promote or protect the interests of its inhabitants, not limited to situations where unlawful activity is continuing or contemplated within its area.'[4]

[1]   *R v AB & Ors* [2017] EWCA Civ 534 – courts have jurisdiction to 'review' an authority's decision, albeit 'sparingly' [43].

[2]   This follows the decisions in *Mole Valley District Council v Smith* [1994] 24 HLR 442 where the Court of Appeal stated in relation to civil proceedings that 'where the balance of the public interest lies is for the respondent councils to determine and not for this court.' See also *Barking & Dagenham London Borough Council v Jones* [1999] All ER (D) 923 'It is for the local authority to make that judgment'.

3   The decision in *R (on the application of Donnachie) v Cardiff Magistrates' Court* [2009] 489 (Admin) was approved, however, questioned the decision in *Brighton and Hove City Council v Woolworths plc* to the extent that it found the prosecution of breaches of a suspension notice that occurred outside the authority's area 'could not ex hypothesi be expedient' to protect inhabitants' interests.

4   [2014] EWHC 1910 [28].

4.24 In *R v AB*[1], the Court of Appeal considered the decision of Thurrock Council to create an external prosecution service in relation to frauds against the legal aid fund. This was found effectively to be a parallel to the Crown Prosecution Service. The particular defendants in *AB* were employees of a London-based solicitors' practice specialising in immigration. They had allegedly conspired to defraud the Legal Aid Agency of approximately £4 million by submitting claims for payment in respect of fabricated work. The Court of Appeal held that the prosecution was not *expedient for the promotion or protection of the interests of the inhabitants of Thurrock* and had therefore been commenced unlawfully. It was stated that:

'As for the suggestion that it could be considered in the inhabitants of Thurrock that the legal aid system, from which all may benefit, should not be defrauded, the alleged criminality to be prosecuted must have an actual or potential impact on the inhabitants of Thurrock as inhabitants of Thurrock, not just as UK taxpayers more generally. For the requirements of s 222 to be met, the interests of the inhabitants of Thurrock must be engaged over and above their interests merely as ordinary citizens of the nation.[2]'

1   [2017] EWCA Crim 534, [2017] 1 WLR 4071, [2017] C App R 25.

2   Paragraph 54.

4.25 In *Lee Qualter Commercial Reduction Services Ltd & Anor v Preston Crown Court*[1] it was argued that a local authority had acted beyond its powers (ultra vires) by commencing a region-wide investigation into rogue trading in the energy sector. The investigation was a part of the regional and national coordination of cases by National Trading Standards. The local authority had made court applications for production orders under the Proceeds of Crime Act 2002, which it was argued did not satisfy the s 222(1)(a) test. The High Court rejected a judicial review application brought on this basis. It found that the requirement under s 222(1) LGA 1972 did not apply at the investigatory stage of a criminal investigation because it encompassed only local authority decisions to 'prosecute' or to 'appear' in legal proceedings. This did not include court applications for investigatory purposes. The broad power set out in Pt 1 of Chapter 1 to the Localism Act 2011[2] ('LA 2011') was sufficient to encompass an investigation or court application for investigatory purposes.

1   [2019] EWHC 2563 (Admin), [2019] 10 WLUK 49.

2   Section 1(1) 'A local authority has power to do anything that individuals generally may do.' This provision must be read together with limitations in ss 1–8 of the Localism Act 2011.

4.26 The decision in *Qualter* places a surprising gloss on the meaning of 'appear in any proceedings' in s 222(1)(a) by distinguishing between substantive criminal 'proceedings' and those concerning a court application for investigatory purposes. The s 222(1)(a) test has previously been accepted to apply in relation to a variety of different court proceedings, including both civil applications[1] and criminal prosecutions. It seems unlikely that the very general provision in s 1 of the LA 2011 was designed to provide a basis for such a fine statutory distinction. The High Court in *Qualter* did not consider the application of the paras 44–46 of Sch 5 to the CRA 2015 because that issue was not raised until a late stage in the judicial review proceedings. In our view that is regrettable because that provision would have provided a proper legal basis for rejecting what was clearly an unmeritorious judicial review application.

1 See for example: *Mole Valley District Council v Smith* [1994] 24 HLR 442; *Stoke on Trent v B & Q Retail Limited* [1984] 1 AC 754; *Oldham Metropolitan Borough Council v Worldwide Marketing Solutions Ltd* [2014] EWHC 1910.

Section 101 agreements

4.27 Under s 101(1)(b) of the LGA 1972 a local authority may arrange for the discharge of any of its functions by another local authority[1]. In *R (on the application of Donnachie) v Cardiff Magistrates' Court*[2] a case brought under the Trade Descriptions Act 1968 (TDA 1968) – the court observed that, in future, it would be wise for a local authority to enter into s 101 agreements with other local authorities before laying informations alleging offences committed outside of its administrative area[3]. This may still be prudent for offences committed under legislation not covered by para 46 to Sch 5 of the CRA 2015.

1 See also Pt 1A of the Local Government Act 2000 and Pts 2 and 3 of the Local Authorities (Arrangements for the Discharge of Functions) (England) Regulations 2012, SI 1019/2012.
2 [2009] EWHC 489 (Admin).
3 See also *Brighton and Hove City Council v Woolworths Plc* [2002] EWHC 2565 (Admin).

Crown immunity

4.28 No statute binds the Crown unless its provisions specifically state that this is the case. (See for example, Corporate Manslaughter and Corporate Homicide Act 2007, s 11.) The Post Office, the few remaining nationalised industries, and local authorities[1] do not enjoy this immunity. Hospitals have been held to benefit from crown immunity[2] but the applicability of those decisions to today's more devolved management structure may be questioned.

1 *Re M* [1994] 1 AC, 377, per Lord Templeman at 395.
2 *Nottingham Area No 1 Hospital Management Committee v Owen* [1958] 1 QB 50, [1957] 3 All ER 358; *Pfizer Corporation v Ministry of Health* [1965] AC 512, [1965] 1 All ER 450.

Time limits

4.29 Many of the consumer and trading standards criminal sanctions are subject to strict time limits that must be scrupulously observed – see eg *Staffordshire County Council v Sherratt & Anor*[1]. The rationale for this temporal limitation is 'designed to achieve two important consequences. The first is to provide protection to the citizen who may have committed a criminal offence, and the second is to bring about in the authority having responsibility for the prosecution, an efficient and timely investigation of the offence'[2].

1 [2019] EWHC 1416 (Admin).
2 *Tesco Stores Limited v London Borough of Harrow* [2003] EWHC 2919 (Admin), per Newman J (para 25).

4.30 Similarly, in relation to civil sanctions, Sch 10, CRA 2015 sets out the procedure to be followed by a local weights and measures authority when imposing a financial penalty for a breach of the CRA 2015 secondary ticket provisions and provides a right of appeal against a Final Notice. In *Worldwide Tickets Ltd & Ors v North Yorkshire County Council* (secondary ticketing)[1] it was held that the relevant time limit provisions were not adhered to and the £5,000 penalties imposed by the local authority were quashed.

[1]   [2018] UKFTT PR_2018 0066 (GRC).

The start of the time limit

4.31 Regulatory time limit provisions are typically drafted by reference to two different time periods. A shorter period that runs from prosecution discovery, together with a longstop period that is typically 3 years from the commission of the offence. For example, the limitation period under the CPUTR 2008, reg 14(1) states that no criminal prosecution for an offence may be commenced more than 3 years from the commission of the offence or more than one year after its discovery by the prosecutor, whichever is the earlier. In the case of ongoing offences, time runs from the end date of the period of offending specified in the information, and the prosecutor is not prevented from laying this information merely because they may previously have discovered earlier offending[1].

[1]   *R v Asad Bashir Malik* [2020] EWCA Crim 957 para 15–16.

4.32 A distinction also needs to be drawn between offences framed by reference to the date of '**discovery of the offence** by the prosecutor'[1] or to the 'date on which **evidence which the prosecutor thinks is sufficient** to justify the proceedings comes to his knowledge'[2]. The distinction between the tests of *offence discovery* and *evidential sufficiency* is important. In an *offence discovery* time limit the prosecutor is the local authority, which is fixed with discovery when its officials are first informed of the complaint about an identified suspected offender. There is no requirement that the evidence against this person has been tested or assessed. Discovery does not require that the complaint has been investigated. By contrast, *evidential sufficiency* is a subjective test to be assessed by an individual[3] who is regarded as the prosecutor for that purpose. This does require a subjective judgment of the strength of the evidence. It follows that the time limit for an *offence discovery* provision will usually start well before *evidential sufficiency* has been determined.

[1]   For example, CPUTR 2008, SI 2008/1277, reg 14(1) and the General Product Safety Regulations 2005, SI 2005/1803, reg 41.
[2]   For example, the Animal Welfare Act 2006, s 31.
[3]   *Letherbarrow v Warwickshire County Council* [2014] EWHC 4820 (Admin).

Discovery of the offence provisions

4.33 In *Brooks v Club Continental Ltd* the prosecution case was that a holiday brochure for the South of France included a false statement that a particular hotel had a swimming pool. The consumer was told that the brochure was not accurate before travelling and reported the matter to trading standards. A prosecution was brought for recklessly making a false statement about a service, under the TDA 1968, s 14 (now repealed). The magistrates' court found that that the time limit ran from when the complaint was first made to a trading standards officer, which meant the charges were out of time. The High Court upheld that finding because 'all the facts material to found the relevant charge were disclosed to the appropriate officer'[1]. It follows that discovery is likely to occur when the complaint is first communicated to a local authority, if the basic facts, gist of the offence and identity of the defendant are readily apparent. The fact that it takes more than the permitted period of time to gather evidence to support the facts which have been made known to the prosecutor does not permit the laying of an information outside the permitted time period[2].

[1] Per McNeil J, [1981] Tr L 126 DC See also *R v Thames Metropolitan Stipendiary Magistrate, ex parte Hackney London Borough* (1994) 158 JP 305, *Tesco Stores Ltd v LB of Harrow* [2003] EWHC 2919 (Admin), 167 JP 657.
[2] *R v Beaconsfield Justices, ex p Johnson and Sons Ltd* (1985) 149 JP 535, *Newham London Borough Council v Cooperative Retail Services Ltd* (1984) 149 JP 421.

4.34 In *R (on the application of Donnachie) v Cardiff Magistrates' Court*[1] the High Court considered the time limit under s 19 of the TDA 1968, which is materially the same as other discovery of the offence provisions. The court found that it was the local authority that was the prosecutor for the purposes of the time limit, not the person laying the information. Discovery of the offence had occurred when the local authority's officials had knowledge sufficient to found a reasonable belief that an offence had been committed.

[1] [2003] EWHC 2919 (Admin), (2003) 167 JP 657.

4.35 In *Tesco Stores Ltd v Harrow LBC*[1], a report was made by a consumer that bread rolls containing a piece of metal wire had been purchased from a supermarket. The complainant left a message for an environmental health officer to contact him. On the same day an environmental health officer spoke to the complainant's wife, who confirmed that her husband had complained about the bread rolls. Four days later the investigating officer spoke directly with the complainant and took possession of the contaminated bread rolls. The High Court held that the offence was discovered when the message had been left by the complainant, rather than 4 days later when the investigator spoke directly with him. The test to be applied was whether the facts objectively considered would have led a prosecuting authority to have reasonable grounds to believe that an offence had been committed by some person who had been identified to it.

[1] [2003] EWHC 2919 (Admin), (2003) 167 JP 657.

CONTINUING OFFENCES

4.36 In *R v Malik*[1] the Court of Appeal considered time limits where CPUTR offences were 'ongoing' or 'continuing'. The defendant was a director of companies that provided parking at Gatwick airport. Consumers were misled on a website about the level of security and protection that would be afforded by the parking service provided. Vehicles were stored insecurely in muddy fields and were used to 'ferry' company staff about. The vehicles were sometimes damaged on their return and some customers received parking tickets for infringements whilst on holiday. The defendant was charged with offences under the CPUTR, including two misleading action offences relating to the company website. These were indicted as continuing over a period of time. The Court of Appeal rejected the defendant's argument that they were time barred because they had been commenced after the expiry of the 12 months' time period following discovery by the prosecutor. Coulson LJ stated that:

'In circumstances where there is an ongoing, continuing offence, the 12-month time limit is not triggered by the first time that the offence occurs, but the last.[2]'

[1]   [2021] 1 Cr App R (S) 7.
[2]   Para 16, relying on *Thames Water Utilities v Bromley* [2004] EWHC 301 (Admin).

Evidential sufficiency provisions

4.37 The identification of the prosecutor in offences premised on evidential sufficiency will necessarily require greater focus on the individual responsible for, and capable of, making that decision. It is the individual with responsibility for deciding whether a prosecution should go forward whose thoughts and beliefs are relevant. In *Letherbarrow v Warwickshire County Council*[1] a prosecution was challenged on the basis of time limits by reference to the state of knowledge of the prosecuting body as a whole. Bean LJ rejected the challenge stating that:

'although the prosecutor in the case as a whole is the collective body (here, the County Council), it is the individual with responsibility for deciding whether a prosecution should go forward whose thoughts and beliefs are relevant.'

[1]   [2014] EWHC 4820 (Admin); see also *Riley & Ors v Crown Prosecution Service* [2016] EWHC 2531 at paras 9–17.

4.38 This evidential sufficiency test should not, however, be used as an excuse to shuffle papers between departments. In *RSPCA v Johnson*[1] Pill LJ stated:

'It is right that prosecutors are not entitled to shuffle papers between officers or sit on information so as to extend a time limit. There is, however, a degree of judgment involved in bringing a prosecution, and knowledge, in my judgment, involves an opportunity for those with appropriate skills to consider whether there is sufficient information to justify a prosecution . . . I cannot extract from *Donnachie* any principle of law that time begins to run as soon as some employee of the prosecuting organisation has information. On the other hand, the principle stated by Kennedy LJ in *Morgans v DPP* [1999] 1WLR 968, is, with respect, sound. The prosecuting authority is not entitled, by passing papers from hand to hand and failing to address the issue, to delay the running of time.'

[1]   [2009] EWHC 2702 (Admin).

Commencement of a prosecution

4.39 The commencement of a prosecution normally takes place when the information alleging the offence is received at the offices of the Clerk to the Justices for the relevant area[1]. The person who lays the information is the prosecutor[2]. A prosecution may also take place when the prosecutor causes an amendment to be made to an existing information or indictment after the time limit for bringing a prosecution has expired. This is permissible even when the amendment involves the introduction of a new offence. As long as the offence is founded on the same facts or misdoing, and there is no substantive injustice, such amendments are often allowed by the courts. The outcome of cases will, however, be fact specific[3].

[1]   *R v Dartford Justices, ex parte Dhesi, R v Manchester Stipendiary Magistrate, ex p Hill, R v Edmonton Justices ex p Hughes* [1983] 1 AC 328.

2   *R v Shrewsbury Magistrates' Court ex parte Simon Dudley Ltd* [1996] CCLR 22, CO 3277 94.
3   *R v Newcastle upon Tyne Justices, ex parte John Bryce (Contractors)* [1976] 1 WLR 517, *R v Pain* (1986) 82 Cr App R 141, *R v Scunthorpe Justices, ex parte McPhee* (1998) 162 JP 635, *R v Newcastle Magistrates' Court, ex parte Poundstretcher Ltd* [1998] COD 256, *Shaw v Director of Public Prosecutions* [2007] EWHC 207 (Admin).

4.40 In *Food Standards Agency v Bakers of Nailsea Ltd*[1] the High Court rejected a prosecution appeal against a ruling in the Magistrates' Court that summonses were a nullity because of a failure by the prosecution to 'demonstrate . . . that the application [was] made in time' in compliance with r 7.2 of the Criminal Procedure Rules ('Crim PR') 2015[2]. Although the summonses had been applied for within the relevant statutory time limit, the prosecutor failed to refer to its compliance with those time limits when making the application and had not, therefore, 'demonstrated' that the application was made in time. The decision in the *Bakers*' case is contentious. Its effect is that a largely technical failure to comply with a procedural document obligation renders proceedings a nullity, regardless of whether the prosecution has actually adhered to a relevant time limit or the merit in the prosecution. It can perhaps be explained on the basis that the prosecution in the *Bakers*' case was not fully able to advance arguments concerning the overriding objective in the Crim PR. In particular, the court did not consider properly a series of modern authorities in which procedural errors did not render criminal proceedings a nullity[3].

1   [2020] EWHC 3632 (Admin).
2   Now r 7.3(3)(c) Crim PR 2020.
3   *R v Westbrook (Caron)* [2020] 4 WLR 138 – confiscation order not rendered a nullity by procedural errors; *R v J* [2019] 1 WL 966 – conviction not a nullity despite D being convicted at trial on a different indictment than the indictment arraigned on; *R v Guraj (Lodvik)* [2017] 1 WLR 22 – confiscation proceedings valid despite procedural error; *R v Stocker (Keith Anthony)* [2014] 1 Cr App R 18 – despite indictment specifying incorrect date of statute said procedural error did not render the indictment a nullity; *R v Smith (Joseph Alexander)* [2013] 2 Cr App R 5 – conviction not a nullity where D pleaded guilty to a count that was improperly added to the indictment; *R v Thwaites (Michael John)* [2006] EWCA Crim 3325 – conviction of D safe despite fact D was not given the opportunity to consent to summary trial and *Lawton v Fleming-Brown* [2006] EWHC 3146 (Admin) – proceedings not a nullity despite D not being asked whether he pleaded guilty or not.

4.41 In *R v Newcastle Magistrates, ex parte Poundstretcher*[1] an amendment was allowed to allege a more serious offence. Originally the defendant had faced an information under the General Safety Product Regulations 1994[2], reg 7 in relation to the supply of felt tip pen caps that provided insufficient air flow and were therefore a danger to children. This was later amended outside the 12-month time limit to allege a breach of the Toys (Safety) Regulations 1995[3]. Even though the potential fine was greater under the latter Regulations the Divisional Court held, on appeal, that there was no reason to interfere with the magistrates' decision. The offences were similar in character and *Poundstretcher* had not been prejudiced in its defence. However, in *Shaw v Director of Public Prosecutions*[4] the High Court allowed the defendant's appeal against the decision of the magistrates' court to amend an information outside of the 6-month time limit, from an offence, concerning the custody of a dog, punishable only by a fine to one that was punishable by imprisonment. It was held that, whilst the misdoing was the same, the fact that the new offence rendered the defendant liable to imprisonment rather than a fine was not in the interests of justice.

1   [1998] COD 256.

² SI 1994/2328.
³ SI 1995/204.
⁴ [2007] EWHC 207 (Admin), [2007] 171 JP 254.

4.42 In *R v Begum & Begum v Luton Borough Council*[1], a local authority tried to serve informations on the last day of a 6-month period. The counter at the court had been closed for some months so the informations were left with a sub-contracted court security guard. By the time they reached admin staff they were out of time. The two questions asked were (1) whether a sub-contracted court security guard was a court officer with implied authority to accept the informations and (2) dependent on the answer to the first question, whether the informations were laid in time? The lower court ruled that they were laid in time and the appellants appealed by way of case stated. The High Court held that the answer to both questions was no and allowed the appeal. It was concluded that a court security officer did not have implied authority to accept an information as the Crim PR 2020 nor the practical context required the court to do so. What mattered was the nature of the functions or duties for which the staff member is engaged. The information could be left with a security guard under the contemplation that it would be handed over to more circumscribed group of staff members. The date of service is determined by the provisions of Crim PR Pt 4 so did not hinge on when it was received, opened and date stamped by Her Majesty's Courts and Tribunals Service ('HMCTS') administrative staff. As the answer to the first question was no it followed that the answer to the second was also no. Given the changes in circumstances at many courts it was pointed out that HMCTS may wish to consider reviewing their contractual arrangements so as to confer express authority on security guards to accept informations for the purposes of r 4(3)(1). Although service by electronic means was the obvious and desirable method to follow.

[1] [2018] EWHC 1044 (Admin), [2018] 1 WLR 3792, [2018] 2 Cr App R 18, [2018] Crim LR 756.

4.43 The case of *R v Pain*[1] demonstrates that a prosecutor must take care not to seek amendment out of time to an offence which, although substantially on the same facts, is of a substantially different nature. The case involved a plot to manufacture and market counterfeit perfume. The case had originally been indicted as a conspiracy to defraud. When that allegation was found to be bad the Crown Court allowed an application by the prosecution to amend, out of time, and allege offences under the TDA 1968. The Court of Appeal allowed the appeals holding that, although the facts upon which the counts of conspiracy to defraud were substantially the same facts as the counts of conspiracy to commit offences under the TDA 1968, a prosecution alleging conspiracy to defraud could not properly be described as a prosecution for offences under the TDA 1968. However, the rationale behind the decision was doubted in *Pound-stretcher* on the basis that, in *Pain*, the Crown Court had effectively, and wrongly, permitted the institution of fresh proceedings after an indictment had been quashed rather than by way of amendment of existing proceedings.

[1] (1986) 82 Cr App R 141.

4.44 The statutory time limits will also apply where a summons has been issued within time, but against an incorrect defendant, for example, in relation to separate legal entities within the same corporate group[1].

[1] *Sainsbury's Supermarkets Ltd v HM Courts Service (South West Region, Devon and Cornwall Area) & Ors* [2006] EWHC 1749 (Admin).

4.45 In Scotland, the reference to the date of discovery by the prosecutor is construed as a reference to the date on which evidence sufficient in the opinion of the Lord Advocate to warrant proceedings came to his knowledge.

Primary authority and time limits

4.46 There is an important modification in relation to enforcement time limits in relation to the Primary Authority scheme. Any period that the enforcer was prohibited from taking action by the Primary Authority relationship must be excluded when calculating when a time limit will expire. The provisions of the RESA 2008 (see **Chapter 1**) statutorily require that such periods be excluded[1]. This will include the standard notification period and any further period during which enforcement action was prohibited, including the operation of the RESA 2008, Sch 4A referral process.

[1] RESA 2008, ss 25B(4) and 25C(8).

Certificates

4.47 Many provisions relating to time limits also include a statutory presumption if the prosecutor produces a certificate of the time the offence was discovered. Although this presumption appears to be conclusive[1], it may be challenged on the grounds that it is 'plainly wrong' or the product of prosecution misconduct[2]. There is no statutory requirement that a prosecutor serve such a certificate[3]. However, in *Burwell v Director of Public Prosecutions*[4] it was stated that a prosecutor can only avail himself of the benefits of such a certificate if the certificate complies fully with the requirements of the relevant section[5]. If a certificate is initially defective, a fresh corrected certificate may be issued during the course of proceedings[6]. However, in *Lamont-Perkins v RSPCA*[7] Wyn Williams J stated that:

> 'This case has highlighted the need for all prosecutors to take great care when certifying a date under statutory provisions which have the effect of extending the time limit for bringing criminal proceedings. A prosecutor is exercising a crucial function when certifying such a date and it is incumbent upon the prosecutor to ensure the accuracy of the date.'

[1] See eg *Chesterfield Poultry Ltd v Sheffield Magistrates' Court* [2019] EWHC 2953 (Admin).
[2] *Lamont-Perkins v RSPCA* [2012] EWHC 1002 (Admin), (2012) 176 JP 369, [2012] ACD 64.
[3] *Browning v Lewes Crown Court and RSPCA* [2012] EWHC 1003 (Admin).
[4] [2009] EWHC 1069 (Admin) under the Computer Misuse Act 1990.
[5] See also *RSPCA v Ian James King and Kathleen Patricia King* [2010] EWHC 637 (Admin).
[6] *R v Woodward & Ors* [2017] EWHC 1008 (Admin), [2017] ACD 77.
[7] [2012] EWHC 1002 (Admin).

4.48 In Scotland a certificate signed by the Lord Advocate or on his behalf and stating the date on which evidence came to his knowledge is conclusive evidence of that fact and other presumptions and deeming provisions apply to this process.

Legal identity

4.49 In any prosecution it is of fundamental importance that the correct defendant is identified. The failure to do so has caused significant problems in consumer and trading cases, which are usually the subject of restrictive time limits.

4.50 Most offences permit the prosecution of a 'person', which includes 'anybody of persons corporate or unincorporated'[1]. It follows that individuals, companies and other traders can usually be prosecuted. However, the courts have repeatedly refused applications to amend proceedings to permit a different legal identity to be substituted.

1   Interpretation Act 1978, Sch 1.

4.51 In *Marco (Croydon) Ltd v Metropolitan Police Commissioner*[1] a company hired out builder's skips and left one unlit on the highway at night. A cyclist rode into it and was killed. The skip company responsible was called 'Marco (Croydon) Limited' but traded as 'A & J Bull Containers'. A prosecution was commenced against 'A & J Bull Limited', a different company. The Divisional Court ruled that it had been wrong for the magistrates to permit the information to be amended to identify the correct company[2].

1   [1983] Crim LR 395.
2   See also *Essence Bars (London) Ltd v Wimbledon Magistrates' Court and Royal Borough of Kingston upon Thames* [2014] EWHC 4334 (Admin).

4.52 *R v Greater Manchester Justices ex p Aldi GmbH & Co KG*[1] involved allegations of mispricing offences under the Consumer Protection Act 1987, s 20 at a supermarket. The prosecutor had incorrectly named the wholesale company in a group as the defendant, rather than the retail company. The High Court again rejected the argument that the information could be amended to substitute the retail company.

1   (1994) 159 JP 727.

4.53 In *Sainsbury's Supermarkets Limited v HM Courts Service*[1] the information was laid against 'J Sainsburys plc (trading as Sainsburys Supermarket Ltd)'. Although the actual company name was similar, neither 'J Sainsburys plc' nor 'Sainsburys Supermarket Ltd' existed as a company. It was held to be impermissible to amend the information to substitute the company as the defendant[2].

1   *Sainsbury's Supermarkets Limited v HM Courts Service (South West Region, Devon and Cornwall Area) and Plymouth City Council (Interested Party): J Sainsbury Plc v HM Courts Service (South West Region, Devon and Cornwall Area) and Plymouth City Council* [2006] EWHC 1749 (Admin).
2   See also *British Airways Board v Taylor* [1976] 1 All ER 65 HL where the House of Lords found that there was no legal basis on which the Board could be liable for an offence committed by BOAC even though the Board had subsequently taken over BOAC's business.

4.54 In *Crown Investments Ltd v North East Essex Magistrates' Court*[1] Colchester Borough Council prosecuted Platinum Crown Ltd (PCL), a defunct company which was no longer in existence at the time that the informations were laid, in respect of ten alleged offences, contrary to s 234 of the Housing Act 2004 whereas the true company name was Platinum Crown Investments Ltd (PCIL). Treacy LJ, dismissing the claim for judicial review of the magistrates' decision to permit an amendment (after the expiry of the statutory time limit) stated that, 'This decision shows that a degree of factual inquiry is necessary before the court can distinguish between a mistake as to identity (which cannot be corrected out of time) and a mis-statement of name (which may be corrected out of time).'

¹ [2017] EWHC 2761 (Admin).

4.55 There is, however, a distinction between cases where the wrong corporate defendant is prosecuted and those where the correct individual actually attends court in reply to a summons that incorrectly names him. If the individual attends court after receiving a summons, knowing that it was intended for him, the defective information may be amended where there is no significant prejudice¹.

¹ *Allan v Wiseman* [1975] RTR 217.

LIABILITY

Strict liability

4.56 Usually criminal offences designed to protect consumers are of strict or absolute liability, in that they do not require proof of a mental element such as intention or recklessness (*mens rea*). They are therefore an exception to the criminal law principle that a deed will not make a man guilty unless his mind is guilty.

4.57 In applying this principle to 'truly criminal' offences the courts have shown a reluctance to impose criminal liability without proof of *mens rea*, even when a statute does not expressly require its proof. In the seminal case on strict liability, *Sweet v Parsley*, Lord Reid stated that¹:

'in the absence of a clear indication in the Act that an offence is intended to be an absolute offence, it is necessary to go outside the Act and examine all relevant circumstances in order to establish that this must have been the intention of Parliament.'

¹ [1970] AC 132 at p 149; see also *Gammon (Hong Kong) Ltd v A-G of Hong Kong* [1985] AC 1 PC; *Wings v Ellis* [1985] AC 272 HL. See also *Highbury Poultry Farm Produce Limited v CPS* [2019] CTLC 1 (Admin).

Regulatory offences of strict liability

4.58 The *Sweet v Parsley* principle does not apply, however, when Parliament has intended, or is presumed to have intended, that the offence should not require proof of a *mens rea*. Lord Reid made reference to regulatory offences when he stated that 'it has long been the practice to recognise absolute offences in this class of quasi criminal acts, and one can safely assume that, when Parliament is passing new legislation dealing with this class of offences, its silence as to mens rea means that the old practice is to apply'.

4.59 This is likely to be the position for most consumer and trading standards provisions that have created criminal liability. These regulatory offences generally follow a typical pattern of strict liability. The ingredients of the offence that the prosecution must prove to the criminal standard are counterbalanced with a defence that must be proven by the defendant to the civil standard. It would be difficult to argue that Parliament did not intend this class of offence to be of strict liability when such regulatory provisions have commonly been enforced in that way by the courts over decades.

4.60 The TDA 1968 was the statutory predecessor to the CPUTR 2008 (see Chapter 8 Unfair Commercial Practices) and the main mechanism through which trading offences were prosecuted for 40 years. Although the TDA 1968 (now largely repealed) contained some quasi-*mens rea* offences, in *Wings Ltd v Ellis*[1] Lord Scarman said that 'it is not a truly criminal statute. Its purpose is not the enforcement of the criminal law but the maintenance of trading standards. Trading standards, not criminal behaviour, are its concern'.

[1] [1985] 1 AC 272.

4.61 The rationale for the imposition of strict liability has been explained on the basis that such offences are not *'truly criminal'* or when it is proportionate to an *'issue of social concern'*[1]. Although this might explain the different treatment of relatively minor offences, it is much harder to describe serious imprisonable regulatory offences in those terms. The justification of strict liability for such offences was perhaps better explained by the Court of Appeal in *R v Jackson*, in relation to the offence of 'low flying' under the Air Forces Act 1955, s 51. The Court there found the offence to be of strict liability despite it carrying a maximum penalty of imprisonment. Hooper LJ stated that[2]:

'The rationales behind the creation of such offences is generally that they cover conduct which of itself is potentially dangerous to other members of the public and accordingly the public interest overrides the need to prove knowledge on the part of the alleged offender that he was in fact committing an offence or did the act complained of with any particular *mens rea*. Guilt is to be found in the commission of the act – no particular frame of mind has to be established before guilt is established. This reflects the fact that some conduct – often not truly criminal in the way most people would understand that expression- carries with it such grave risk of endangering public safety or is so heavily the cause of public concern, that it can properly be punished without the need for the establishment of any degree of *mens rea*.'

[1] In the Privy Council case of *Gammon (Hong Kong) Ltd v A-G of Hong Kong* [1985] AC 1 Lord Scarman found justification for strict liability 'where the statute is concerned with an issue of social concern' and 'the creation of strict liability will be effective to promote the objects of the statute by encouraging greater vigilance to prevent the commission of the prohibited act'.
[2] Per Hooper LJ [2007] 1 WLR 1035 at 1040.

Corporate liability

4.62 Where a statute creates an offence for a 'person', that expression includes companies[1]. Where a corporation is charged with a criminal offence, different rules apply in relation to its representation and the procedure by which it can enter a plea. In the magistrates' court, the procedure is governed by the Magistrates' Courts Act 1980, s 46 and Sch 3[2]. The procedure for entering a plea on behalf of a company in the Crown Court is set out in the Criminal Justice Act 1925, s 33. In June 2021, the Law Commission launched a discussion paper seeking views on whether, and how, the law relating to corporate criminal liability could be improved so that they appropriately capture and punish criminal offences committed by corporations, and their directors or senior management. The outcome had not been announced at the time of publication.

[1] Interpretation Act 1978, Sch 1, '"Person" includes a body of persons corporate or unincorporate'.
[2] A representative of the company is defined by reference to the Criminal Justice Act 1925, s 33(6).

4.63 The Crim PR 2020 state that:

46.1 Functions of representatives and supporters
(1) Under these Rules, anything that a party may or must do may be done—
. . .

    (b)   by a person with the corporation's written authority, where that party is a corporation;

Companies in liquidation

4.64 Before a court proceeds in the absence of a plea entered by a corporation it is important to ascertain whether the company is in liquidation, and if so, whether it is in compulsory or voluntary liquidation, because the leave of the High Court will be needed in some cases. In cases of compulsory liquidation, the Insolvency Act 1986, s 130 imposes an automatic stay on proceedings against a company. In the case of a company in voluntary liquidation, there is no automatic stay, but creditors may apply for a stay to be imposed, and so in such cases the position should always be ascertained before proceeding. In *Ratten v Natural Resource Body for Wales*[1] the High Court found that it did not have power to 'stay' criminal proceedings in the Crown Court following a voluntary winding up petition, although it did have a discretion to 'restrain' a prosecutor from pursuing criminal proceedings. It declined to do so in relation to waste disposal offences on the basis that the public interest in prosecuting serious environmental offences outweighed the disadvantage to creditors. In *R v Dickson*[2], a company in liquidation was prosecuted to conviction without the leave of the High Court[3]. However, the argument that this invalidated the conviction of the director under the directors' liability provision of the TDA 1968, s 20 was rejected.

[1] *In the Matter of Paperback Collection & Recycling Ltd Sub Nom (1) Christopher Ratten (2) Lindsey Cooper v Natural Resource Body For Wales* [2019] EWHC 2904. Also known as *Ratten v Natural Resource Body For Wales*.
[2] [1991] BCC 719.
[3] The Insolvency Act 1986 requires leave to be given before proceedings are commenced against a company in administration, or which is the subject of a winding up order or where a provisional liquidator has been appointed.

Corporate liability for offences of strict liability

4.65 The circumstances in which a company is liable for the acts of its employees will depend upon the nature of the offence. A distinction can be drawn, however, between offences that require a *mens rea* (a particular mental state) to be proven and those that do not. For a *strict liability* offence, a company will be criminally liable when the *actus reus* of the offence can properly be attributed to it. In *Mousell Bros Ltd v London and North Western Railway Co*[1], Lord Atkin stated:

'I think that the authorities . . . make it plain that while prima facie a principal is not to be made criminally responsible for the acts of his servants, yet the legislature may prohibit an act or enforce a duty in such words as to make the prohibition or the duty absolute; in which case the principal is liable if the act is in fact done by his servants. To ascertain whether a particular Act of Parliament has that effect or not, regard must be had to the object of the statute, the words used, the nature of the duty laid down, the person upon whom it is imposed, the person by whom it would in ordinary circumstances be performed, and the person upon whom the penalty is imposed . . . When a penalty is imposed for the breach of the duty, it is reasonable to infer that the penalty is imposed for a default of the person by whom the duty would ordinarily be performed.'

1   [1917] 2 KB 836, DC at pp 845–846.

4.66 In construing a statute to ascertain whether it creates vicarious liability for a company, the verb used to create the offence will usually be significant. For example 'selling' or 'supplying' goods is an activity that can reasonably be attributed to a company, even though actually undertaken by its employees[1]. In the consumer and trading standards offences of strict liability it will rarely be difficult to attribute to a company criminal liability for the acts of its employees.

1   See for example *Coppen v Moore (No 2)* [1898] 2 QB 306.

Corporate liability for offences with a mental element

4.67 The corporate liability for offences that involve proof of a mental element (*mens rea*) was discussed in *Tesco Supermarkets Ltd v Nattrass*[1]. Lord Reid considered the nature of a corporate 'personality' stating[2]:

'A living person has a mind which can have knowledge or intention or be negligent and he has hands to carry out his intentions. A corporation has none of these; it must act through living persons, though not always one or the same person. Then the person who acts is not speaking or acting for the company. He is acting as the company and his mind, which directs his acts, is the mind of the company. There is no question of the company being vicariously liable. He is not acting as a servant, representative, agent or delegate. He is an embodiment of the company or, one could say, he hears and speaks through the persona of the company, within his appropriate sphere, and his mind is the mind of the company. If it is a guilty mind then that is the guilt of the company. It must be a question of law whether, once the facts have been ascertained, a person in doing particular things is to be regarded as the company or merely as the company's servant or agent. In that case any liability of the company can only be a statutory or vicarious liability . . .

Normally the board of directors, the managing director and perhaps other superior officers of a company carry out the functions of management and speak and act as the company.'

1   [1971] 2 All ER 127, [1972] AC 153.
2   At pp 131–132.

4.68 A company will only be guilty of an offence requiring proof of a *mens rea*, if the *mens rea* can be attributed to someone who is the directing mind or will of the company. In *R v Andrews Weatherfoil Ltd* it was said that a company was not criminally responsible for the actions of every *'high executive'* or *'agent acting on behalf of the company'*[1].

1   56 Cr App R 31 CA; see also *Leonards Carrying Co Ltd v Asiatic Petroleum Co Ltd* [1915] AC 705 and *HL Bolton (Engineering) Co Ltd v TJ Graham & Sons Ltd* [1957] 1 QB 159.

4.69 In *St Regis Paper Company Ltd v The Crown*[1], a prosecution under the Pollution Prevention and Control (England and Wales) Regulations 2000, the Court of Appeal rejected the argument that the intentional actions of the company's technical manager could be attributed to the company. For the purposes of this specific regulation the question therefore was: '*Was the technical manager in actual control of the relevant operations of the company and not responsible to another person or under that other person's orders?*' The test set out in *Tesco Supermarkets Ltd v Nattrass* was to be followed. The Court held that there was no real sense in which it could be said that the company had delegated its responsibilities under the Regulations to the technical manager. Although he was required to submit the necessary records, that was far removed from the type of delegation necessary to be established. It was emphasised that the extent of delegation is a matter of fact for the jury.

[1]   [2011] EWCA Crim 2527.

Possible exceptions

4.70 This general application of the rule in *Tesco Supermarkets v Nattrass* has been considered in several cases where the courts have sought to avoid a restrictive approach that might allow companies unfairly to escape responsibility, where the employee with the requisite *men rea* was not strictly part of the company's directing mind and will.

4.71 In *Meridian Global Funds Management Asia Ltd v Securities Commission*[1] the chief investment officer of a New Zealand investment management company had used company managed funds to acquire public shares without giving the required notice. The failure to give the notice was a breach of a financial regulation duty, but was not itself a criminal offence. The investment had been made with the company's authority but the company directors did not know about it. The New Zealand Court of Appeal had found the company responsible on the basis that the chief investment officer had been a part of the company's directing mind and will.

[1]   [1995] 3 WLR 413 [1995] 2 AC 500.

4.72 The Privy Council, however, considered that the company could be attributed with the knowledge of the chief investment officer even if he was not a part of the company's directing mind and will. It upheld the decision on the basis that there would be cases where the ordinary rule of attribution to a company would defeat the statutory intention that a company should be responsible for the breach. It was necessary in those cases to apply a special rule of attribution. Lord Hoffmann stated that:

'In such a case, the court must fashion a special rule of attribution for the particular substantive rule. This is always a matter of interpretation: given that it was intended to apply to a company, how was it intended to apply? Whose act (or knowledge, or state of mind) was *for this purpose* intended to count as the act etc. of the company? One finds the answer to this question by applying the usual canons of interpretation, taking into account the language of the rule (if it is a statute) and its content and policy.'

4.73 In *Information Commissioner v Islington LBC*[1] a local authority was prosecuted for an offence of recklessly using data contrary to the Data Protection Act 1998, s 5(5). The offence was committed by *using* data after the expiry of a data protection registration. The conviction was upheld on the basis that the authority's controlling minds had been reckless in failing to register for data protection and that its other employees had thereafter used the data. There was, however, no evidence that any single person had used data whilst actually having the requisite *mens rea* of recklessness.

[1] [2003] LGR 38, DC.

4.74 In *Linnett v Metropolitan Police Commissioner*[1], the conviction of a licensee for 'knowingly permitting disorderly conduct' was upheld, despite him being unaware of it. The rationale of the decision is that the licensee had a special statutory duty to keep an orderly public house which he had delegated to his servant. In those circumstances, the knowledge required by the offence would be imputed to him. It is unlikely that *Linnett* is authority for a general proposition of law and it is probably confined to offences under the Licensing Acts[2].

[1] [1946] KB 290, DC.
[2] In *Vane v Yiannopoullos* [1965] AC 486, the House of Lords doubted any general application of the doctrine. However, in relation to licensing offences, it has since been applied in *R v Winson* [1969] 1 QB 371 and *Howker v Robinson* [1973] 1 QB 178, DC.

4.75 The danger of applying a single inflexible rule of corporate liability in every circumstance is illustrated by *Bilta (UK) Ltd (In liquidation) v Nazir* in the context of civil insolvency proceedings. The Supreme Court in *Bilta* considered a series of cases[1] involving actions by liquidators against directors accused of fraudulent conduct. In simple terms, if the wrongdoing of the directors could be attributed to the company, the individual directors might have a legal defence to the liquidator's action. The reasoning in the judgments in *Bilta* is different, however, for understandable reasons the Supreme Court ruled against the directors. Lord Neuberger PSC stated[2]:

'whether or not it is appropriate to attribute an action by, or a state of mind of, a company director . . . must depend on the nature and factual context of the claim in question.'

[1] Including *Stone & Rolls Ltd v Moore Stephens* [2009] AC 1391, [2009] 3 WLR 455 and *Safeway Stores Ltd v Twigger* [2010] EWCA Civ 1472, [2011] 2 All ER 841.
[2] Paragraph 9 [2015] UKSC 23, [2015] 2 WLR 1168.

Directors' liability

4.76 Consumer and trading standards offences are often based upon individual transactions and consequently the conduct (*actus reus*) that constitutes the offence will be committed by a junior employee within a business. In many cases it is unsatisfactory that those truly responsible for the wrongdoing can hide behind the company 'corporate veil' and most trading standards offences also provide a penal sanction against those persons, charged with functions of management, who can be shown to have been responsible for the commission of a relevant offence by the corporate body (directors' liability).

4.77 In a prosecution using a directors' liability provision it is normal and desirable (although not a mandatory requirement) for the company to be a defendant in the same proceedings. If the company is not prosecuted it is essential for the prosecution to prove that, had the company been prosecuted, it would have been found guilty of the offence. Conversely, a directors' liability provision does not create its own discrete offence and charges need to reflect the principal offence[1].

[1]   *R v Wilson* [2013] EWCA Crim 1780.

4.78 The provision that has generated most case law is TDA 1968, s 20(1) which has been largely replaced by the CPUTR 2008 and in particular reg 15[1].

15 Offences committed by bodies of persons

(1)   Where an offence under these Regulations committed by a body corporate is proved—

(a)   to have been committed with the consent or connivance of an officer of the body, or

(b)   to be attributable to any neglect on his part, the officer as well as the body corporate is guilty of the offence and liable to be proceeded against and punished accordingly.

(2)   In paragraph (1) a reference to an officer of a body corporate includes a reference to—

(a)   a director, manager, secretary or other similar officer; and

(b)   a person purporting to act as a director, manager, secretary or other similar officer.

(3)   Where an offence under these Regulations committed by a Scottish partnership is proved—

(a)   to have been committed with the consent or connivance of a partner, or

(b)   to be attributable to any neglect on his part, the partner as well as the partnership is guilty of the offence and liable to be proceeded against and punished accordingly.

(4)   In paragraph (3) a reference to a partner includes a person purporting to act as a partner.

[1]   SI 2008/1277.

4.79

Precedent: Consent or connivance

Statement of offence

ENGAGING IN AN UNFAIR COMMERCIAL PRACTICE WHICH IS A MISLEADING AC-TION, contrary to regulations 5, 9 and 15(1) of the Consumer Protection from Unfair Trading Regulations 2008.

Particulars of offence

AB was a director of X Limited, a trader, when on [Date] X Limited engaged in a commercial practice, [namely . . .], which was a misleading action in breach of regulations 5 and 9 of the Consumer Protection from Unfair Trading Regulations 2008 in that it contained false information and was therefore untruthful in relation to a matter in regulation 5(4), [. . .], and which caused or was likely to cause the average consumer to take a transactional decision that he would not have taken otherwise.

AND the offence was committed with the consent or connivance of AB by reason of Regulation 15(1) of the Consumer Protection from Unfair Trading Regulations 2008.

4.80

Precedent: Neglect

Statement of offence

ENGAGING IN AN UNFAIR COMMERCIAL PRACTICE WHICH IS A MISLEADING AC-TION, contrary to regulations 5, 9 and 15(1) of the Consumer Protection from Unfair Trading Regulations 2008.

Particulars of offence

A B was a director of X Limited, a trader, when on [date] X Limited, engaged in a commercial practice [namely . . .] which was a misleading action in breach of regulations 5 and 9 of the Consumer Protection from Unfair Trading Regulations 2008 in that it contained false information and was therefore untruthful in relation to a matter in regulation 5(4), [. . .], which caused or was likely to cause the average consumer to take a transactional decision that he would not have taken otherwise.

AND the offence was attributable to the neglect of A B by reason of Regulation 15(1) of the Consumer Protection from Unfair Trading Regulations 2008.

4.81 Directors' liability provisions can be found in most consumer and trading standards legislation that imposes criminal liability[1]. The burden of proving the liability of a director or manager under these provisions is on the prosecution to the criminal standard of proof although evidence can be inferred in appropriate cases[2]. The definition of a company director or company secretary is now governed by the Companies Act 2006 ('CA 2006') and will usually be a matter of public record.

[1] For example, the Consumer Credit Act 1974, s 169; Weights and Measures Act 1985, s 82; Consumer Protection Act 1987, s 40(2); Food Safety Act 1990, s 36; Trade Marks Act 1994, s 101(5); and Copyright, Designs and Patents Act 1988, s 110. If the Companies Act 2006 is a precedent for future legislation these provisions may be simplified. Companies Act 2006, s 1255 merely refers to ' . . . an officer of the body, or a person purporting to act in any such capacity'.

[2] See for example, *Motor Depot Ltd v Kingston-Upon-Hull City Council* [2012] EWHC 3257 (Admin) and *R v X Ltd* [2013] EWCA Crim 818.

4.82 Directors' liability provisions provide for three different modes of liability that will usually overlap. When framing a charge against a director, a question that often arises is whether it is appropriate to include more than one mode of participation in a single count. This issue raises the rule against duplicity in criminal charges and how that should be applied where there is a single offence, but three ways that a director might commit it.

4.83 In *R v Leighton & Town & Country Refuse Collections Limited*[1], the Court of Appeal considered the question of duplicity in the context of offences involving the unlicensed disposal of waste. The case did not primarily consider a directors' liability provision, but different modes by which waste could be deposited, such as 'causing' or 'knowingly permitting'. In giving the judgment of the Court, Auld LJ rejected the duplicity argument by reference to the test of 'whether a statute has created one offence which may be committed in a number of alternative ways or several different offences'. He made the observation that[2]:

> 'it was in principle permissible for the prosecution to charge a single offence stating the various acts of commission in the alternative. To have required it to charge each alternative in a separate count would have resulted in a prolix and unmanageable indictment. We say "in principle" only to make the point that if, in any instance, the prosecution is confident before trial that it can prove the precise mode of committing the offence and/or that it cannot prove one or more of the others, it should specify the particular mode upon which it relies and leave it at that. There would be no point in including alternatives provided by the statute for which there is no evidential support. However, in our view, the nature of the prosecution case here justified the prosecution pleading and relying on the various alternatives.'

[1] [1997] Env LR 411.
[2] [1997] Env LR 411, p 420.

4.84 In our opinion it is unlikely, on the basis of current authority, that a charge that included consent, connivance or neglect would be found to be duplicitous. The *Leighton & Town case* does suggest, however, that it is good practice for a prosecutor to eliminate a mode of participation that will not be advanced[1]. For example, in certain cases it may be appropriate to eliminate consent or connivance where there is no express or implied evidence of the requisite knowledge. In many cases, however, that will simply not be possible. In *Southend Borough Council v White*, the Divisional Court observed that a remedy, where there was insufficient proof of the director's neglect, would have been 'for the justices to allow the amendment of the information so as to include consent or connivance'[2]. In *R v T*[3] the Court of Appeal rejected a different duplicity argument that a charge was bad because it included both an offence against the company and another against the director[4]. The charges were not duplicitous. Indeed, under the directors' liability provision, it was necessary to prove that the company was itself guilty of the offence.

[1] See also *Motor Depot Ltd v Kingston-Upon-Hull City Council* [2012] EWHC 3257 (Admin).
[2] Similarly in *R v P*, the information which alleged that the director's offence was due to his 'consent and/or, connivance and/or neglect' was not challenged despite the court's focus on the difference between consent or connivance and neglect.
[3] [2005] EWCA Crim 3511.
[4] The indictment was worded: 'Statement of offence. Applying a false trade description to goods contrary to the Trade Descriptions Act 1968, s 1(1)(a) and s 20. Particulars of offence [TL] Limited on or before 23 August 2003 in the course of a trade or business applied to goods, namely a BMW motor vehicle registration mark V38 MGJ, a false trade description by means of the vehicle odometer reading of 66,066 miles, whereas the said vehicle had travelled not less than 127,000 miles. The said offence was committed with the consent and connivance of or was attributable to the neglect of [MJT] a Director of the said Company who, by virtue of the Trade Descriptions Act 1968, s 20, is guilty of the said offence'.

4.85 However, in the view of the editors, charging all three modes of participation in a single count can lead to unnecessary difficulties. This is particularly the case where consent or connivance, which often rely on positive acts, are combined with neglect, which is usually premised on the failure to act. In our opinion where the prosecution case is advanced on alternative bases, best practice is to draft two separate counts (see the precedents above) alleging consent and connivance, with a separate alternative count alleging neglect. This provides both clarity in advancing the evidential basis of the prosecution and assists the judge when approaching the issue of sentence. A conviction on the basis of consent or connivance, as opposed to neglect, can make a very real difference to the imposition of an immediate rather than a suspended sentence of imprisonment.

Managerial roles

4.86 The scope of this type of provision in relation to managerial roles that are less formally defined was considered in *R v Boal*[1] where an assistant general manager was in charge of a well-known London bookshop whilst the manager was on holiday. He had been given no training in management and was prosecuted under the Fire Precautions Act 1971, s 23. In quashing his conviction the Divisional Court reviewed a number of previous decisions and concluded that the defendant would only fall within the provision if he had, 'the management of the whole affairs of the company', and was 'entrusted with power to transact the whole affairs of the company' and was 'managing in a governing role the affairs of the company itself'. Simon Brown J went on to say:

> 'The intended scope of section 23 is, we accept, to fix with criminal liability only those who are in a position of real authority, the decision-makers within the company who have both the power and responsibility to decide corporate policy and strategy. It is to catch those responsible for putting proper procedures in place; it is not meant to strike at underlings.'

[1] [1992] 1 QB, applied in *R v Sadighpour* [2012] EWCA Crim 2669.

4.87 The phrase 'any person who was purporting to act in any such capacity' overcomes the difficulty experienced in *Dean v Hiesler*[1] where the defendant was not a validly-appointed director in accordance with the provisions of the Companies Act 1929 but performed some of the duties of a director and even described himself as a director.

[1] [1942] 2 All ER 340.

Consent or connivance

4.88 In considering 'consent' or 'connivance' it should be appreciated that 'neglect' requires a lower level of *mens rea* and therefore proof of 'consent' or 'connivance' will often be an unnecessary hurdle. Idiosyncratically the directors' liability provision that has been considered most by the courts (TDA 1968, s 20) refers to 'consent *and* connivance'[1] in contrast to most other legislative provisions (including reg 15 of the CPUTR 2008) that refer to them in the alternative, 'consent or connivance'. Both words were considered in *Huckerby v Elliott*[2] in proceedings concerning a similar statutory provision[3]. It was stated that:

> 'The learned stipendiary . . . dealt with consent and said: "It would seem that where a director consents to the commission of an offence by his company, he is well aware of what is going on and agrees to it." I agree with the stipendiary . . . The

stipendiary went on: "Where he connives at the offence committed by the company he is equally well aware of what is going on but his agreement is tacit, not actively encouraging what happens but letting it continue and saying nothing about it." . . . I do not disagree with that.'

1   This is widely considered to have been a draftsman's error.
2   [1970] 1 All ER 189.
3   Customs and Excise Act 1952, s 305(3).

4.89 For the purposes of consent, a director must be proved to know the material facts which constitute the offence, however it not necessary to show that the director knew that this was contrary to the law. In *Attorney General's Reference (No 1 of 1995)* the Court of Appeal considered the meaning of director's consent in the context of a company carrying on a deposit taking business without Bank of England authorisation, for the offence under the Banking Act 1987, s 3(1). The Court of Appeal found that where consent is alleged the defendant has to be proved to know the material facts which constitute the offence by the body corporate and to have agreed to its conduct of the business on the basis of those facts. Ignorance of the law and its requirements was no defence. Lord Taylor of Gosforth CJ said[1]:

'A director who knows that acts which can only be performed by the company if it is licensed by the bank are being performed when in fact no licence exists and who consents to that performance is guilty of the offence charged. The fact that he does not know it is an offence to perform them without a licence, ie, ignorance of the law, is no defence . . . [the] suggestion that the director must actively have addressed his mind to the question of licences is wholly unreal. If the two directors, who were wholly responsible for the company's business activity, were ignorant of the need for a licence it can readily be inferred that they knew they did not have one. The concept of a director who is ignorant of the law requiring a licence, focusing his mind on the question of whether he has or has not obtained one is wholly academic. Had anyone approached the defendant directors and asked: "Have you a licence or authorisation from the Bank of England?" the ready answer would have been "No," probably supplemented by "I did not know I needed one." There would have been no need for a search, an inquiry or a focusing of the mind. Since the question had not occurred to them they would know that the company did not have one. The ignorance of the law on the point necessarily must in the context of this case point to the knowledge that the company is operating unlicensed.'

1   [1996] 1 WLR 970, p 980.

4.90 The consent or connivance of a director may be proven by inference where the offence is directed towards the result to be achieved by the company. In *R v Chargot*, the House of Lords considered a directors' liability provision in the Health and Safety at Work etc Act 1974. Lord Hope stated that[1]:

'consent can be established by inference as well as by proof of an express agreement. The state of mind that the words "connivance" and "neglect" contemplate is one that may also be established by inference. [These offences] are directed to the result that must be achieved by the body corporate. Where it is shown that the body corporate failed to achieve or prevent the result that those sections contemplate, it will be a relatively short step for the inference to be drawn that there was connivance or neglect on his part if the circumstances under which the risk arose were under the direction or control of the officer. The more remote his area of responsibility is from those circumstances, the harder it will be to draw that inference.'

1   Per Lord Hope at para 34 in *R v Chargot Limited (trading as Contract Services)* [2008] UKHL 73, [2009] 1 WLR 1.

4.91 In *R v Hutchins and Charalambous*, the Court of Appeal endorsed the language used by both Lord Taylor in *Attorney General's ref (No 1 of 1995)* and Lord Hope in *R v Chargot*. Rix LJ went on to say that[1]:

'it is emphasised that circumstances vary from case to case and that, in truth, no fixed rule can be laid down about what the prosecution must prove in order to establish consent, connivance or neglect. It is explained that in certain circumstances more detailed evidence might be required to fix a manager or director with the necessary knowledge. It is also emphasised that the strategy of provisions of this kind – and we emphasise that the wording in relation to consent, connivance and neglect is to be found in common form in statutes of this kind – is to provide a sanction against persons charged with functions of management.'

[1]   [2011] EWCA Crim 1056.

Neglect

4.92 In this context, neglect[1] requires proof that the director or manager etc failed to do something that reasonably ought to have been done to prevent the offence. The question is objective and does not require proof that the individual director knew that he was under any such duty or obligation. In most consumer protection cases, statutory duties are placed on the trader and, where that is a company, the directors of the company will be under a duty to ensure that the company's statutory duties are met. However, it may well be the case that some directors will have no responsibilities for the conduct complained of. It will be a question of fact, in each case, for the prosecution to prove consent or connivance or neglect against the director charged. It will not necessarily be sufficient simply to allege that mens rea can be inferred against *any* director, regardless of their role. Company directors have a general statutory duty to 'exercise reasonable care, skill and diligence'[2]. The first question will be whether the director had a (or any) responsibility in relation to the part of the business that was at fault. The second question will usually be whether that particular director did all that was reasonable to ensure that the company complied with its statutory duty.

[1]   In the probate case of *Re Hughes, Rea & Black* [1943] Ch 296 the court considered the meaning of the word 'neglect'.
[2]   CA 2006, s 174.

4.93 Where the individual charged is an employee rather than a director, proof of neglect is more problematic. In *R v Boal*[1], it was emphasised that it should only be those with 'real authority' that should be fixed with criminal liability under directors' liability provisions. This illustrates why it may be difficult to show that an employee, even a senior manager, should bear the legal responsibility for his employer's compliance with a consumer protection duty. For employees, it is likely that neglect will be confined to circumstances where the employee is effectively the directing mind of the company, or the statutory provision itself should be properly construed as generating broader employee duties; as is the position, for example, under health and safety and money laundering legislation.

[1]   See above [1992] 1 QB, applied in *R v Sadighpour* [2012] EWCA Crim 2669.

4.94 It has always been the case that a director may delegate certain responsibilities. The question that will then arise is whether the director did all that was reasonable in the circumstances. There is support for the contention that a director of a company cannot be said to be neglectful if he fails to enquire about certain matters which he knows are dealt with by a fellow director or senior manager. In *Huckerby v Elliott*[1] it was stated:

'. . . amongst other things it is perfectly proper for a director to leave matters to another director or to an official of the company, and that he is under no obligation to test the accuracy of anything that he is told by such a person, or even to make certain that he is complying with the law. It was pointed out that business cannot be conducted otherwise than on principles of trust, and accordingly as it seems to me . . . the appellant left matters concerning the licences to her co-director . . . who was the secretary of the company and fully acquainted with the business. One asks oneself this: Has she any reason to distrust [him] or to feel that he was not carrying out his duty? One finds that she had on the evidence produced no reason to distrust him.'

[1] Following Romer J in *Re City Equitable Fire Insurance Co Ltd* [1925] Ch 407 which related the provision of gaming premises without an appropriate licence and an offence under the Customs and Excise Act 1952, s 305(3).

4.95 In *Lewin v Bland*[1] the managing director of a car selling company wrote to a customer enclosing a falsely-compiled replacement service book. He had not looked at the book before sending it out, but relied on a senior employee to have completed it correctly. He was subsequently acquitted of the offence of applying a false trade description under TDA 1968, committed by the company on the basis of his neglect. In rejecting the prosecutor's appeal the Divisional Court said:

'There is nothing peculiar about the circumstances of this case which would mean that the managing director of what cannot be a small company should check the work of his senior staff . . . He was entitled to delegate work to his senior staff and could expect that work to be completed in accordance with the instructions given.'

[1] (1984) 148 JP 69.

4.96 *Motor Depot Ltd v Kingston-Upon-Hull City Council*[1] concerned an allegation of neglect against the director of a motor trader in relation to misleading advertisements placed by an employee of the company. Elias LJ observed:

'In cases like this, it is unlikely in practice that there would be direct evidence as to where exactly the duty lies and to identify who has taken responsibility within an organisation for drafting or checking or placing the advertisements.'

[1] [2012] EWHC 3257 (Admin).

4.97 In *R v P*[1] neglect was considered in the context of a health and safety prosecution of a company director. Latham LJ observed[2]:

'the question, at the end of the day, will always be . . . where there is no actual knowledge of the state of facts, whether nonetheless the officer in question of the company should have, by reason of the surrounding circumstances, been put on enquiry so as to require him to have taken steps to determine whether or not the appropriate safety procedures were in place.'

[1] [2007] EWCA Crim 1937.
[2] See also *Wotherspoon v HM Advocate* [1978] JC 74.

4.98 In *Hirschler v Birch*[1] the defendant, a director of a vehicle parts company, purchasing high level brake lights on the continent, was warned that they were no longer lawful in some countries and likely soon to be banned in others. A fellow director, who was understood by the defendant to be carrying out inquiries on the subject, told the defendant that they were legal in the UK. This was incorrect and the fellow director had not made diligent inquiries on the point. The lights were then imported and sold under the false description that they were fit for use in Britain. Charged with neglect, the defendant was convicted by the magistrates on the basis that he had failed to ensure that an authoritative answer on the lawfulness of the lights had been obtained. The Divisional Court upheld this verdict on the basis that the issue of neglect was one of fact and that there was evidence on which the magistrates were entitled to find neglect because the defendant was on notice as to the question of the legality of the lights[2].

[1]   [1988] BTLC 27, (1986) 151 JP 396.
[2]   For a further case where an offence was held to be attributable to neglect on the part of a director see *Crickitt v Kursaal Casino Ltd (No 2)* [1968] 1 All ER 189, (1969) 113 Sol Jo 1001.

4.99 In *R v Hutchins and Charalambous*[1], (see above) a prosecution under the Private Security Industry Act 2001, s 23, the Court of Appeal held, applying the test set out by Lord Taylor in *Re Attorney General's Reference (No 1 of 1995)*[2] that what had to be proved was that H knew that unlicensed guards were being or would be deployed by X, and that he had agreed to X's conduct of its business on the basis of those facts. The prosecution did not have to prove specific knowledge of each individual offence. That was shown by the broadness of the terms 'consent, connivance and neglect' in the Private Security Industry Act 2001, s 23. It was impossible on the facts of the case to say that H had not consented to, or at least connived in the deployment of unlicensed guards. If directors had to be shown to be aware of specific deployments, that would allow them to shut their eyes to the management of their companies. The nature of regulatory statutes such as the 2001 Act, with the provisions for secondary liability by directors and managers, was to ensure that they were held to proper standards of supervision. The size of the company and the distance of directors from the coal face of individual acts should not, where there was consent, connivance or neglect, afford directors with a 'necessary knowledge' defence.

[1]   [2011] EWCA Crim 1056.
[2]   [1996] 1 WLR 970.

Causal liability

4.100 Consumer protection statutes and regulations usually include a provision making a person liable for causing another to commit an offence. These provisions are also known as 'bypass' provisions because the directly liable party can be bypassed in favour of prosecuting the person who has caused the offence to be committed.

4.101 CPUTR 2008, reg 16 is typical of a provision creating causal liability.

16 Offence due to the default of another person
(1)   This regulation applies where a person 'X'—

(a) commits an offence under regulation 9, 10, 11 or 12, or
(b) would have committed an offence under those regulations but for a defence under regulation 17 or 18,

and the commission of the offence, or of what would have been an offence but for X being able to rely on a defence under regulation 17 or 18[1], is due to the act or default of some other person 'Y'.

(2) Where this regulation applies Y is guilty of the offence, subject to regulations 17 and 18, whether or not Y is a trader and whether or not Y's act or default is a commercial practice.

(3) Y may be charged with and convicted.

[1] Under the Trade Descriptions Act 1968 in *Coupe v Guyett* [1973] 2 All ER 1058 it was held that the fact that A may have a due diligence defence does not prevent him being regarded as having committed the offence for the purposes of the prosecution of B.

4.102

Precedent for misleading actions

Statement of offence

ENGAGING IN AN UNFAIR COMMERCIAL PRACTICE WHICH WAS A MISLEADING ACTION, contrary to regulations 5, 9 and 16(2) of the Consumer Protection from Unfair Trading Regulations 2008.

Particulars of offence

A B on [Date] [supplied a motor vehicle . . .] to X Limited, a trader, which engaged in a commercial practice, [namely . . .], which was a misleading action in breach of regulation 5 and 9 of the Consumer Protection from Unfair Trading Regulations 2008 in that it contained false information and was therefore untruthful in relation to a matter in regulation 5(4) [. . .], and which caused or was likely to cause the average consumer to take a transactional decision that he would not have taken otherwise.

AND the misleading action was due to the act or default of AB by reason of Regulation 16(2) of the Consumer Protection from Unfair Trading Regulations 2008.

4.103 The prosecutor must be able to show a causal connection between the offences committed. In *Tarleton Engineering Co Ltd v Nattrass*[1], the defendants had entered a car for auction on 10 September, but had specifically not guaranteed the stated mileage. They were convicted, under the TDA 1968, s 23, the conviction being based upon the commission of an offence by the auctioneers on 2 November in offering the car for sale with what was, in fact, a false mileage. The Divisional Court held that, where it could not be said with certainty that the defendants had committed an offence on 10 September (since they had specifically not guaranteed the stated mileage) a conviction based upon the later commission of an offence by the auctioneers could not be sustained. On the facts found the offence committed by the auctioneers was unrelated to any act or default of the defendants two months earlier[2].

[1] [1973] 3 All ER 99.
[2] See also *Cottee v Douglas Seaton (Used Cars) Limited* [1972] 3 All ER 750, [1972] 1 WLR 1408; *Naish v Gore* [1971] 3 All ER 737 and *Richmond Upon Thames LB v Motor Sales (Hounslow) Ltd* [1971] RTR 116.

4.104 It is not necessary to prove that the person causing an offence to be committed is a trader. Under the TDA 1968 the conviction of a private person knowingly selling a 'clocked' car to a dealer who then committed an offence when selling the car on was upheld in *Olgeirsson v Kitching*[1].

[1]   [1986] 1 All ER 746.

4.105 In *Padgett Brothers (A-Z) Ltd v Coventry City Council*[1], it was said that causal liability 'does not require that the relevant act should be solely due to the acts or default of the importer but merely that they are due, in part, to that'.

[1]   (1998) 162 JP 673.

General accessory liability

4.106 The general criminal law provides that criminal offences may be committed either by a principal or by secondary party. Under the Accessories and Abettors Act 1861, s 8 and the Magistrates' Courts Act 1980, s 44 aiders, abettors, counsellors and procurers are liable to be charged, tried and sentenced as if they were principals. It is not necessary to prove presence at the location where an offence is committed and a company, which cannot physically be present, may be convicted as a secondary party[1]. The general principles in accessory liability were comprehensively reviewed by the Supreme Court in the case of *R v Jogee (Ameen Hassan)*[2].

[1]   *Provincial Motor Cab Company Ltd v Dunning* [1909] 2 KB 599.
[2]   [2016] UKSC 8, [2017] AC 387, [2016] 2 WLR 681, [2016] 2 All ER 1, [2016] 2 WLUK 496, [2016] 1 Cr App R 31, (2016) 180 JP 313.

4.107 Even for offences of strict liability, a secondary party must know the essential nature of what is being done in order to be found guilty. In *Johnson v Youden* it was stated by the Court of Appeal that[1]:

'Before a person can be convicted of aiding and abetting the commission of an offence he must at least know the essential matters which constitute that offence. He need not actually know that an offence has been committed because he may not know that the facts constitute an offence and ignorance of the law is not a defence. If a person knows all the facts and is assisting another person to do certain things, and it turns out that the doing of those things constitutes an offence, the person who is assisting is guilty of aiding and abetting that offence.'

[1]   *Johnson v Youden* [1950] 1 KB 544, per Lord Goddard CJ; approved in *Churchill v Walton* [1967] 2 AC 224 and *Maxwell v DPP for Northern Ireland* (1979) 68 Cr App R 128 HL.

4.108 The general criminal liability of accessories has also been substantially supplemented by the provisions in Pt 2 of the Serious Crime Act 2007 on encouraging or assisting crime.

The due diligence defence

4.109 As a counterbalance to the strict liability regime of most regulatory offences, there is often an important safeguard in the form of the statutory 'due diligence' defence. Examples of this defence can be found in the Consumer Protection from Unfair Trading Regulations 2008 ('CPUTR 2008'), reg 17, Trade Descriptions Act 1968, s 24 (which has attracted a large amount of case law and academic commentary), the Consumer Credit Act 1974, the Consumer Protection Act 1987 and the Food Safety Act 1990.

4.110 The due diligence defences that run through consumer and trading standards law generally are similar, although not identical. The statutory wording is not consistent but, generally, the defence provides that the person charged has a defence if he can prove (or show) that he took all reasonable precautions (or steps) and exercised all due diligence to avoid the commission of the offence by himself (or by a person under his control). The due diligence defence under the TDA 1968, s 24, has now largely been replaced by CPUTR 2008, reg 17. It is likely that the case law under the TDA 1968 will be equally applicable to the new law and will provide helpful guidance for many of the due diligence defences.

4.111 CPUTR 2008, reg 17 provides a typical example of a due diligence defence.

17 Due diligence defence

(1) In any proceedings against a person for an offence under regulation 9, 10, 11 or 12 it is a defence for that person to prove—

 (a) that the commission of the offence was due to—

  (i) a mistake;
  (ii) reliance on information supplied to him by another person;
  (iii) the act or default of another person;
  (iv) an accident; or
  (v) another cause beyond his control; and

 (b) that he took all reasonable precautions and exercised all due diligence to avoid the commission of such an offence by himself or any person under his control.

(2) A person shall not be entitled to rely on the defence provided by paragraph (1) by reason of the matters referred to in paragraph (ii) or (iii) of paragraph (1)(a) without leave of the court unless—

 (a) he has served on the prosecutor a notice in writing giving such information identifying or assisting in the identification of that other person as was in his possession; and

 (b) the notice is served on the prosecutor at least seven clear days before the date of the hearing.

4.112 CPUTR 2008, reg 17 provides a defence where the defendant can show that the offence was caused by a mistake, or reliance on information supplied to him, or the act or default of any other person, or an accident, or some other cause beyond his control *and* that he took all reasonable precautions *and* exercised all due diligence to avoid the commission of the offence. When due diligence defences are litigated, it is often the case that the prosecution will emphasise the words '*and*' and '*all*', whereas the defence will emphasise the word '*reasonable*'.

4.113 In *Tesco Supermarkets Ltd v Nattrass*[1] Lord Diplock commented (in relation to the TDA 1968, s 24(1)(b)) as follows[2]:

'What amounts to . . . the exercise of due diligence . . . depends on all the circumstances of the business carried on by the principal. It is a question of fact for the justices.'

1   [1972] AC 153, 197.
2   See also *Cambridgeshire CC v Kama* [2006] EWHC 3148 (Admin), where the Divisional Court considered that the failure to maintain a refusals book for underage sales could be a significant failing on the part of a trader.

4.114 Having established the cause of the offence the defendant must go on to prove that he took all reasonable precautions *and* exercised all due diligence to avoid the commission of such an offence.

4.115 Particular problems may arise in cases involving very large businesses where the company cannot undertake the detailed supervision of all employees and delegates supervisory duties to more senior employees. The remarks of Lord Diplock in *Tesco Supermarkets Ltd v Nattrass* are of assistance:

'If the principal has taken all reasonable precautions in the selection and training of servants to perform supervisory duties and has laid down an effective system of supervision and used due diligence to see that it is observed, he is entitled to rely on a default by a superior servant in his supervisory duties as a defence under section 24(1).'

4.116 The *Nattrass* decision has been considered by the Court of Appeal in *R v St Regis Paper Mill Co Ltd*[1]. It was held, in relation to the Pollution Prevention and Control (England and Wales) Regulations 2000[2], reg 32(1)(g), that the *mens rea* of an employee should only be attributed to a company where the 'directing will and mind' could be said to be controlled, wholly or partly, by the employee in question. For example, if the employee was a managing director or senior company officer.

1   [2011] CTLC 291.
2   SI 2000/1973.

4.117 If the prosecution is unable to identify a reasonable precaution that was not taken, it is unlikely that the due diligence defence could be negated. Conversely, a reasonable precaution, identified and implemented after the discovery of an offence, does not necessarily disclose a failure to take all reasonable precautions to avoid the commission of the offence[1]. In *Sherratt v Gerald's The American Jewellers Ltd*[2] a watch described as a 'Diver's Watch' was engraved 'waterproof'. On taking it home the purchaser put the watch in a bowl of water. After an hour it had filled with water and stopped. In the Divisional Court Parker LCJ stated:

'Paragraphs (a) and (b) in s 24(1) have both got to be proved on a balance of probabilities, the burden being on the defendants. That they took no precautions at all is clear; they relied solely on their previous dealings with the wholesalers. . . . To succeed here, they must show on a balance of probabilities that although no precautions were taken, there were no reasonable precautions that could be taken. . . . There is clearly an obligation to take reasonable precautions if there are any precautions which are reasonable that can be taken . . . The elementary precaution which would have prevented this offence from being committed was to dip the watch in a bowl of water as the purchaser did.'

1   *Enfield London Borough Council v Argos Ltd* [2008] EWHC 2597 (Admin).
2   (1970) 68 LGR 256.

4.118 Complete inaction on the part of a defendant is unlikely to provide a basis for a due diligence defence. In *Stainthorpe v Bailey*[1] the Divisional Court stated that:

'the fact is in reality [the defendant] did nothing. In those circumstances . . . appreciating that the burden of proof was on the defendant, there really was no evidence on which the justices could possibly find that [the defendant] did take all reasonable precautions and exercised all due diligence to avoid the commission of an offence.'

[1]   [1980] RTR 7 per Michael Davies J.

4.119 In *London Borough of Croydon v Pinch a Pound (UK) Ltd*[1] the Divisional Court reminded lower courts that the test should be applied in the ordinary language used in the relevant statutory provision. Roderick Evans J stated:

'The defence made available by the Act is couched in ordinary language; the words used are readily understood. For my part, I consider that it will only rarely be necessary for a court to formulate the test in anything other than the language used in the statute.'

[1]   [2010] EWHC 3283 (Admin).

Burden and standard of proof

4.120 The defendant seeking to rely upon the due diligence defence must prove it to the civil standard of proof, that is to say to establish that it is more likely than not that a particular fact exists[1]. The mere assertion of reliance upon such a defence without evidence to support it does not require the prosecution to counter the defence[2]. The burden of proof is on the defendant in respect of *both*:

(a)   the primary fact to be proved; and
(b)   the requirement of due or reasonable diligence[3].

[1]   *R v Carr-Briant* [1943] KB 607.
[2]   *Amos v Melcon (Frozen Foods) Ltd* (1985) 149 JP 712.
[3]   *Wandsworth Borough Council v Fontana* (1984) 148 JP 196.

4.121 The due diligence defence imposes a legal burden on the defendant, rather than merely an evidential burden[1].

[1]   An evidential burden is one that only requires the defendant to adduce sufficient evidence fit for the consideration of a jury.

Reverse burdens and the ECHR

4.122 The courts have considered the compatibility of reverse burdens in criminal offences with Art 6(2) of the European Convention for the Protection of Human Rights ('ECHR'). In some cases the courts have accepted the argument that a reverse burden may be incompatible with the presumption of innocence. In *R v DPP ex parte Kebilene*[1] the House of Lords said that Art 6(2) is not a blanket ban against reverse burdens for criminal charges but that reverse burdens must be confined within reasonable limits[2].

[1]   [2000] 2 AC 326, HL.
[2]   Following the ECHR case law and in particular *Salabiaku v France* 13 EHHR 379.

4.123 Article 6(2) has been used since *Kebilene* to 'read down' legal burdens imposed on defendants in criminal cases and replace them with evidential burdens[1]. Following the decision of the House of Lords in is *R v Johnstone*[2], however, that is unlikely to apply to the due diligence defence in a consumer or trading standards case[3].

[1] See *R v Lambert & Ors* [2002] 2 AC 545, HL (the knowledge burden in ss 28(2) and (3) of the Misuse of Drugs Act 1971), *R v Webster* [2010] EWCA Crim 2819 (Corruption Acts 1889 and 1916), *DPP v Wright, R (Scott, Heard and Summersgill) v Taunton Deane Magistrates' Court* [2009] EWHC 105 (Admin) (s 1 of the Hunting Act 2004); *Sheldrake v DPP, Attorney General's Reference (No 4 of 2002)* [2005] 1 AC 264, HL.

[2] [2003] 1 WLR 1736. The court in *Johnstone* considered another case under the Trade Marks Act 1994 on reverse burdens *R v S (Trade mark defence)* [2002] EWCA Crim 25584.

[3] See also *Attorney General Reference (No 1 of 2004)* [2004] 1 WLR 2111, [2005] 4 All ER 457, [2004] 2 Cr App R 27 [2004] EWCA Crim 1025 where it was stated that the 'Courts should strongly discourage the citation of authority to them other than the decision of the House of Lords in *Johnstone* and this guidance. *Johnstone* is at present the latest word on the subject'.

4.124 In *R v Johnstone* the House of Lords considered the Trade Marks Act 1994, s 92(5), which provides a defence if the defendant can show he '*believed on reasonable grounds*' that usage was not a trade mark infringement. The legal burden imposed was found to be justified and proportionate[1] because it concerned matters within a defendant's own knowledge[2] and the legal burden was necessary in the interests of consumers and traders, to restrain widespread fraudulent trading in counterfeit goods[3].

[1] The opinion was expressly stated to be unnecessary to decide the appeal. But, as there had been conflicting statements in the Court of Appeal, Lord Nichols stated: 'In the events which have happened this issue does not call for decision in the present case. But the House should not leave the law on this point in its present state, with differing views expressed by the Court of Appeal'.

[2] Per Lord Nichols: 'Trade Marks Act 1994 s 92(5) defence relates to facts within the accused person's own knowledge: his state of mind, and the reasons why he held the belief in question. His sources of supply are known to him'.

[3] Per Lord Nicholls: 'Counterfeiting is fraudulent trading. It is a serious contemporary problem. Counterfeiting has adverse economic effects on genuine trade. It also has adverse effects on consumers, in terms of quality of goods and, sometimes, on the health or safety of consumers'.

Alternative elements of the defence

4.125 There are five alternative causes for the commission of the offence which the defendant may rely upon. The case law identified below was mainly generated in relation to the TDA 1968, s 24, but is likely to be applicable generally when considered the merits of a due diligence defence:

(a) **Mistake.** The mistake must be that of the defendant and not of another person[1]. When the defendant is a company, the defence is not made out unless the employee making the mistake is a director, manager, secretary or other similar officer. In *Butler v Keenway Supermarkets Ltd*[2] a junior clerk made a genuine mistake in the pricing of goods. The Divisional Court ruled that she could not advance the defence, which was confined to the category of persons listed in the TDA 1968, s 20. It is clear from this case that the company could have advanced the defence of 'act or default of another person' rather than 'mistake'.

(b) **Reliance on information supplied.** Many commentators have remarked that, despite the statute's silence on the point, reliance cannot be placed on this limb of the defence unless the information is shown to come from a reliable source. The authors suggest that the correct analysis may be that there is no such restriction upon the nature of the information relied upon, but that reliance on information from an unreliable source would obviously fall foul of the due diligence test. Where a defendant claimed reliance on an MOT certificate to show the condition of a vehicle the defence failed since the certificate clearly stated that it should not be relied upon for this purpose[3].

(c) **The act or default of another person.** Where the defendant is a company, the fact that the 'other person' is an employee of the company (as where a company sold a mislabelled turkey through the failure of the manager of one of a chain of shops to read his instructions) does not prevent the company from relying on the statutory defence[4]. On the other hand it is not sufficient simply to name all the persons who might be to blame (for instance all the assistants present in the relevant branch of a chain of shops at the relevant time). The defendant must establish that they have done everything possible to establish the identity of the person to blame: *McGuire v Sittingbourne Co-operative Society Ltd*[5]. Lord Widgery CJ stated:

> 'I think it is important to emphasise . . . that the onus cast upon the defendant under s 24 is not thus easily satisfied. The defendant has to prove on a balance of probabilities that the offence was due to the act or default of another, and that he, the defendant, took all reasonable precautions. The Justices should not accept either of those propositions unless the defendant has carefully examined and investigated the circumstances and done his best to show the justices how the offence was committed and why. Only then, in my judgment, will the onus be discharged and will it be open to the justices to say that the defence under s 24 is made out.'

(d) **Accident.** There is scant authority on the meaning of this word within the context of the either CPUTR 2008, reg 17 or the TDA 1968, s 24. It does not feature in other modern examples of the due diligence defence[6]. It may be that it is appropriate to read it in conjunction with the words '*some other cause beyond his control*', since it is difficult to imagine an accident which would qualify to trigger the defence if it were in fact within the defendant's control.

(e) **Some other cause beyond his control.** In a prosecution under the Weights and Measures Act 1963, which provides a similarly worded statutory defence, it was held that the unanticipated and intermittent malfunction of a machine involved in the filling process of packaged crisps could be a cause beyond the defendant's control[7]. The unexpected illness of an employee has been held to be a cause beyond the defendant's control, although the defence failed on the due diligence test[8].

[1] *Birkenhead and District Co-operative Society Ltd v Roberts* [1970] 3 All ER 391.
[2] [1974] Crim LR 560.
[3] *Barker v Hargreaves* [1981] RTR 197.
[4] *Beckett v Kingston Bros (Butchers) Ltd* [1970] 1 QB 606.
[5] (1976) 140 JP 306, DC.
[6] See, for example, the Licensing Act 2003, s 139.
[7] *Bibby-Cheshire v Golden Wonder Ltd* [1972] 3 All ER 738.
[8] *Marshall v Herbert* [1963] Crim LR 506.

Established systems

4.126 In cases where the defendant proves that he applied an established system of regulation he may advance the 'reliance upon information defence'. In *Hurley v Martinez & Co Ltd*[1] the defendant had relied upon European Regulations in relation to the provision of information about wine. The Divisional Court held that the offence was due to reliance by the defendant on information supplied to him and that the requirement of due diligence was made out, notwithstanding the absence of specific checks by the defendant.

[1] (1990) 154 JP 821 and *Carrick District Council v Taunton Vale Meat Traders Ltd* (1994) 158 JP 347.

Sampling

4.127 Many due diligence cases revolve around the issues of sampling, essentially whether the sample taken was adequate. This topic is also covered in Chapter 15, Product Safety. In *Taylor v Lawrence Fraser (Bristol) Ltd*[1] the defendant supplied toys which were painted with a substance containing lead in excess of the proportions permitted by the Toys (Safety) Regulations 1974[2], and the defence was that the manufacturers had given the defendants a written guarantee that the toys were in compliance with the regulations and invited trading standards officers to take samples for analysis. The Divisional Court found that the defendant had not exercised all due diligence, since they could themselves have taken samples and had the paint analysed, but had failed to do so.

[1] (1977) 121 Sol Jo 757.
[2] SI 1974/1367.

4.128 In *Garrett v Boots the Chemists Ltd*[1] the defendant sold pencils with a higher lead content than permitted by the Pencils and Graphic Instruments (Safety) Regulations 1974[2]. The defence was that in informing their suppliers of the existence of the regulations and requiring, as a condition of their order, that pencils supplied comply with the regulations, the defendants had taken all reasonable precautions. The Divisional Court found that, what was unreasonable for a village shop, was not necessarily so for a concern the size of Boots, and that the failure to take random samples of the pencils supplied meant that the defence must fail.

[1] (1980) 88 ITSA MR 238, July 1980.
[2] SI 1974/226.

4.129 In *Hicks v SD Sullam Ltd*[1] the defendant was prosecuted under TDA 1968, s 23 as the person 'due to whose act or default' British Home Stores ('BHS') committed an offence by supplying a light bulb which was described as 'safe'. The defendant had bought a large number of bulbs in the Far East and had tested none of those supplied to BHS. They had no sampling procedure for safety testing and had not obtained independent testing within the UK. They had arranged for testing to be carried out in the Far East, with satisfactory results. Since the emergence of the problem they had instituted a sampling procedure. The Divisional Court held that the absence of a testing procedure at the relevant time and the failure to obtain independent tests within the UK meant that the defence of due diligence was not made out, despite the evidence of the testing abroad.

[1]   (1983) 91 ITSA MR 122.

4.130 In *Rotherham Metropolitan Borough Council v Rayson (UK) Ltd*[1] a defendant who imported crayons as part of a business which employed 18 people and had a turnover (in 1986) of £4 million was prosecuted under the TDA 1968 as the person 'due to whose act or default' the retailer's offence in selling the crayons had been committed. The crayons were described on the packet as 'poisonless'. One of the crayons in a packet sold by a retailer contained excess amounts of toxic material under the relevant Regulations. The defendants had provided the manufacturers with the requirements for the crayons to comply with the regulations and believed that sampling and analysis was taking place, on the basis that only adverse findings would be reported. In this country the system was that a single packet from the 7 to 10 thousand imported annually would be selected at random for analysis, this sample being found to comply with the Regulations. The Divisional Court held that the system of reporting only adverse findings did not amount to due diligence and nor did the system of sampling just one of many thousands of packets in the UK.

[1]   (1989) 153 JP 37.

4.131 In *P & M Supplies (Essex) Ltd v Devon County Council*[1] the defendant employed 65 to 80 staff with a turnover of £8 million and was responsible for the sale of a toy, manufactured in and imported from China, which failed to conform to safety regulations. The defendant had gone to some lengths to ensure compliance with the regulations, sending a director to the factory to check the methods of manufacture, random in-house testing on approximately 0.5% of all of the toys in a system set up in consultation with the trading standards authority, and external testing by the public analyst at a cost of £13,000. The magistrates rejected a defence of due diligence based on these facts and the decision was upheld by the Divisional Court. Aside from reservations about the care with which the tests were undertaken the Divisional Court said that in such cases the burden was on the defence to provide statistical evidence as to what should be done by a reasonable trader by way of testing.

[1]   (1992) 156 JP 328.

4.132 A general blanket condition in contractual terms that all goods supplied would conform with all requirements imposed by any statute or statutory regulation did not 'come within a mile of establishing or being able to comply with the provisions' in *Riley v Webb*[1] – Watkins LJ saying:

> 'It seems to me to be a minimum requirement, if sampling has not been undertaken, for the establishment of the defence . . . that the sellers of the goods receive from the suppliers a positive assurance that they conform to the specific regulations which govern the sale of them.'

[1]   (1987) 151 JP 372.

Written notice to the prosecutor

4.133 Trade Descriptions Act 1968, s 24(2) requires the defendant to give written notice to the prosecutor if he is seeking to rely upon a s 24(1) defence and to assert that the cause of the offence was the act or default of another person or that he relied on information supplied by another person. CPUTR 2008, reg 17(2) contains a similar provision. No notice is required, it seems, if the cause of the offence is said to be mistake, accident or some other cause beyond the defendant's control.

4.134 The written notice must be given at least 7 clear days before the hearing. There is, on the face of it, a clear conflict between the requirement in CPUTR 2008, reg 17 (and other such provisions) to provide such information *as late as* 7 clear days before trial and the requirement under the Criminal Procedure and Investigations Act 1996 for the defendant to provide in the Crown Court a defence case statement, which would be expected to include such information, in a significantly more timely fashion. The authors' views are that the Crim PR and a marked reluctance by the Courts to tolerate 'ambush' defences should encourage defendants to provide such information sooner rather than later. The written notice must contain such information as is in the defendant's possession which will identify or assist in the identification of the other person. In *McGuire v Sittingbourne Co-operative Society Ltd*[1] it was held that the defendant had a duty to make reasonable inquiries to establish the identity of the other person. Watkins J stated that:

> 'It seems to me that it is incumbent upon the person who serves such a notice to have at least made some reasonable inquiry to establish the identity of the person who is going to be referred to in the course of the hearing of the informations so that at least the field of choice can be limited at the notice stage in cases where no single person can be identified.'

[1]   (1976) 140 JP 306, DC.

ENFORCEMENT POWERS

Introduction

4.135 The use of local authority powers to enter homes and businesses has been a contentious public issue for many years. Between 2006 and 2010 the Conservative peer, Lord Selsdon, introduced five Private Member's Bills that broadly sought to ensure that an official, whether of government or of another organisation, would not be able to enter somebody's property and seize or search without permission or without a court order. The Protection of Freedoms Act 2012 led to a mandatory review of powers of entry under various pieces of legislation and the introduction of a Code of Practice governing powers of entry and associated powers.

4.136 Consumer Rights Act 2015, Sch 5 ('CRA 2015') introduced a generic set of investigatory powers, to replace the powers existing in around 60 different statutes or statutory instruments. This part of the chapter reviews the investigatory powers available to enforcers with a particular focus on the generic set within CRA 2015, Sch 5. It should be borne in mind that the investigatory powers under CRA 2015, Sch 5 only apply to enforcers as defined within the Schedule and for the purposes of enforcing legislation specified in the schedule.

Separate powers still apply, for example, to alcohol and tobacco sales, food and feedstuffs, animal health and welfare and other non-BEIS[1] related subjects.

[1] Department for Business, Energy and Industrial Strategy (formerly known as BIS – Business, Innovation and Skills).

Evidence gathering

4.137 In England and Wales, the provisions of the Criminal Procedure and Investigations Act 1996 ('CPIA 1996'), and its Code of Practice, are applicable to local authority officers (whether investigators, officers in charge of investigations or disclosure officers). Such officers must at all times:

'have regard to any relevant provision of a code which would apply if the investigation were conducted by police officers.' (CPIA 1996, s 26)

4.138 In particular, responsibilities for recording and retaining material are of critical importance. Officers must record any information which they consider may be relevant to an investigation, ie that it has some bearing on *any* offence under investigation, any person being investigated, or on the surrounding circumstances of the case, unless it is incapable of having any impact on the case. In *Leatherland and Pritchard v Powys County Council*[1] the Divisional Court quashed convictions where trading standards officers were found to be in breach of their obligations under the CPIA 1996 and the CPIA 1996 Code of Practice in an animal welfare investigation.

[1] [2007] EWHC 148 (Admin).

4.139 Local authority enforcement officers in England and Wales should also, 'have regard to any relevant provision' of Codes of Practice made under the Police and Criminal Evidence Act 1984, s 67(9) ('PACE 1984') because they are 'Persons other than police officers who are charged with the duty of investigating offences'. The requirement to have regard to relevant provisions does not equate to local authority officers, such as trading standards/environmental health etc officers, or other non-police investigators, being obliged to comply with the provisions of the CPIA 1996, the CPIA 1996 Code or PACE 1984 Codes.

4.140 Local authority officers who conduct investigations in collaboration with police officers need to be aware of the provisions relating to the lawful arrest of a suspected person under PACE 1984. The revisions to PACE 1984 Code G, which came into effect on 12 November 2012, should be particularly noted in their application to PACE 1984, s 24(5)(e) (ie the circumstances where it is necessary to arrest a person in order 'to allow the prompt and effective investigation of the offence or of the conduct of the person in question').

4.141 However, there is an increasing frequency, generally, for challenges to be made regarding the execution of warrants to enter premises and the carrying out of connected enforcement activities. These have resulted, in cases where there has been a failure to comply with statutory requirements, in the entry, search and seizure being held to be unlawful, the material obtained being ordered to be returned and damages being awarded for trespass to property.

4.142 Examples of challenges in relation to the activities of local authorities may be found in *R (on the application of Helidon Vuciterni and Alsat UK Ltd) v Brent Magistrates' Court and Brent and Harrow Trading Standards Service*[1], *R (on the application of Dulai and others) v Chelmsford Magistrates' Court and another*[2] and *R (Ahmed) v York Magistrates' Court and City of York Council*[3]. See also *R (on the application of RSPCA) v Colchester Magistrates' Court*[4].

[1]   [2012] EWCA 2140 (Admin).
[2]   [2012] EWHC 1055 (Admin).
[3]   [2012] EWHC 3636 (Admin).
[4]   [2015] EWHC 1418 (Admin).

4.143 It is particularly important to understand the scope and extent of any statutory enforcement power. For example, in *Najib And Sons Ltd v Crown Prosecution Service*[1] the appellant company operated a slaughterhouse. It was convicted of failing to give an inspector assistance required to take sample[2]. It had refused to participate in a programme under which regular samples were provided to Defra. The High Court quashed the conviction on the basis that there was no power to require the appellant to provide samples. Although there was a statutory power conferred on inspectors to 'take any samples'[3], this was not sufficient. Leggatt LJ stated:

> 'In our view, the language of the Regulations is simply not capable of being interpreted as imposing an obligation on a slaughterhouse operator to comply with a request from an inspector to assist in the taking of samples from sheep slaughtered for human consumption as part of a programme for TSE monitoring.'

[1]   [2018] EWCA Crim 1554.
[2]   Under regulation 17(1) of the Transmissible Spongiform Encephalopathies (England) Regulations 2010 (repealed from 19 July 2018).
[3]   Reg 14(1)(f) (now repealed).

4.144 The evidence gathering methods explored above invariably give rise to issues of retention, disclosure and destruction of exhibits and material. In summary, the current CPIA 1996 regime, regarding prosecution disclosure of unused material before trial, proceeds in stages but involves a single objective test.

4.145 The prosecutor:

*   has an initial duty to disclose prosecution material not previously disclosed that might reasonably be considered capable of undermining the case for the prosecution against the defendant or of assisting the case for the defendant – if there is no such material, then has a duty to give the defendant a written statement to that effect; and then
*   has a continuing duty to disclose any such material:
     (i)   whenever there is any, until the court reaches its verdict or the prosecutor decides not to proceed with the case; and
     (ii)   in particular, after the service of the defence statement.

4.146 Issues of disclosure remain problematic. For example in *R v Joof*[1], Hooper LJ said:

> 'This is a very bad case of non-disclosure. It is to be hoped that the appropriate measures will be taken against those responsible for what appears to us to be a serious

perversion of the course of justice, if those measures have not already been taken. It is to be hoped that lessons will be learnt from this shocking episode.'

1   [2012] EWCA Crim 1475.

4.147 However, as the House of Commons Justice Committee found in its report on criminal disclosure in 2018 'We do not propose any fundamental changes to the legislation, or the principles of disclosure, but failings have arisen in the application of those principles by police officers and prosecutors on the ground'[1].

1   Disclosure of evidence in criminal cases – 17 July 2018.

Covert surveillance

4.148 The use of covert surveillance techniques for test purchasing or other functions carried out by local authorities was not regulated by statute before the enactment of Human Rights Act 1998 and the Regulation of Investigatory Powers Act 2000 ('RIPA 2000'). In Scotland the use of covert surveillance falls under the Regulation of Investigatory Powers (Scotland) Act 2000 ('RIP(S)A 2000'). However, abuse of process principles had developed at common law and evidential rules under the general exclusionary provision in PACE 1984, s 78.

4.149 The House of Lords considered many of these authorities in *R v Looseley and Attorney General's Reference (No 3 of 2000)*[1]. Several general principles can be distilled from the case law:

- there is no defence of entrapment known to English law but it may be ground for mitigating sentence;
- the courts have to perform a balancing exercise and, if they conclude that the conduct of an undercover officer was so unworthy or shameful that it was an affront to the public conscience to allow a trial to proceed, or if it rendered a fair trial impossible, they will stay the proceedings;
- it would be unfair and an abuse of process if a person had been incited or pressurised by an undercover officer into committing a crime that he would not otherwise have committed;
- it would not be objectionable if an undercover officer, behaving as an ordinary member of the public would, gave a person an unexceptional opportunity to commit a crime, and that person freely took advantage of the opportunity;
- when exercising the judicial discretion of whether to exclude evidence of an undercover officer, some (but not an exhaustive list) of the factors to be taken into account are:
  - Was the officer acting as agent provocateur in the sense that he was enticing the defendant to commit an offence that he would not otherwise have committed?
  - What was the nature of any entrapment?
  - Does the evidence consist of admissions to a completed offence, or does it consist of the actual commission of an offence?
  - How active or passive was the officer's role in obtaining the evidence?

- Is there an unassailable record of what happened, or is it strongly corroborated?
- Has the officer abused his undercover role to ask questions which ought properly to have been asked in accordance with the PACE 1984 Codes of Practice (in Scotland the question is one of fairness to the accused and not one governed by PACE 1984)?

[1] [2001] UKHL 53.

4.150 RIPA 2000 regulates the use of a number of covert investigatory techniques, not all of which are available to local authorities. The two types of technique available to local authorities are:

(a) directed surveillance (covert surveillance of individuals in public places); and

(b) covert human intelligence sources ('CHIS') (such as the deployment of undercover officers).

In Scotland RIP(S)A 2000 regulates this conduct – except for the acquisition and disclosure of communications data in which case RIPA 2000 applies.

4.151 The Investigatory Powers Act 2016 ('IPA 2016'), provides an updated framework for the use of investigatory powers to obtain communications and communications data. When brought into force, the IPA 2016 will amend RIPA 2000 in a number of ways, specifically by 'omitting' Chapter 1 of Pt 1 (interception of communications) and Chapter 2 of Pt 1 (acquisition and disclosure of communications data) of RIPA 2000. Pt 2 of RIPA 20000, concerning surveillance and covert human intelligence sources and Pt 3 of RIPA 20000 (investigation of encrypted data) are not significantly amended by the IPA 2016. Also, under IPA 2016, local authorities are, from 1 September 2017, subject to oversight provisions by the Investigatory Powers Commissioner, who replaced the roles previously undertaken by the Chief Surveillance, Interception of Communications, and Intelligence Services Commissioners.

4.152 RIPA 2000 is supported by Codes of Practice[1]. A person exercising any power or duty must, in doing so, have regard to the Code's provisions, as far as applicable. The most recent Codes dealing with 'Covert Surveillance and Property Interference' and 'Covert Human Intelligence Sources' were made under the Investigatory Powers (Codes of Practice and Miscellaneous Amendments) Order 2018[2]. The Code dealing with Acquisition and Disclosure of Communications Data came into force in November 2018.

[1] Made under ss 71 and 72 RIPA 2000.
[2] SI 2018/905.

4.153 Local authority officers considering the deployment of covert enforcement activities should consider the statutory Codes of Practice and the Procedures and Guidance document published in July 2016 by the Office of Surveillance Commissioners ('OSC').

The Investigatory Powers Commissioner's Office has stated:

'Whilst it will take a little time to issue a newly "badged" version of the Guidance, practitioners and interested parties should continue to use the OSC 2016 Guidance to assist with interpretational matters. In due course, the section on procedural arrangements for the judicial oversight process will be updated to take account of changes brought about by the Investigatory Powers Act 2016, and longer term, it is hoped the document will grow in scope to provide the guidance envisaged by section 232(2) of that Act.'

4.154 Recommendations of the Macdonald Review on the use of RIPA 2000 by local authorities, relating to judicial approval, were given statutory effect through the Protection of Freedoms Act 2012 and the Regulation of Investigatory Powers (Directed Surveillance and Covert Human Intelligence Sources) (Amendment) Order 2012[1]. In summary, changes to use of RIPA 2000 by local authorities – which came into effect on 1 November 2012 – require:

- additional judicial approval for all RIPA 2000 authorisations (ie the use of directed surveillance, CHIS and the acquisition and disclosure of communications data); and
- directed surveillance to be confined to cases where the offence under investigation carries a maximum custodial sentence of 6 months or more (unless they relate to investigations into underage sales of alcohol and tobacco, which now includes nicotine-inhaling products).

[1]   SI 2012/1500.

4.155 The procedure, where the application is made in a criminal case, is set out in the Crim PR 2020[1] and, where the application is not made in a criminal case, in the Magistrates' Courts (Regulation of Investigatory Powers) Rules 2012[2]. Applicants should also note the 'Home Office Guidance to local authorities in England and Wales on the judicial approval process for RIPA 2000 and the crime threshold for directed surveillance'.

[1]   Rules 47.51–47.53 of the Crim PR 2020 (wef 5 October 2020).
[2]   SI 2012/2563.

4.156 The regime in Scotland, with the exception of access to communications data, is unchanged.

Intercepting postal items

4.157 In determining the lawfulness of seizing unopened letters suspected to be part of consumer fraud, consideration should be given to the provisions of the Postal Services Act 2000 ('PSA 2000'). In particular, the offence of interfering with the mail under PSA 2000, s 84 and the offence of unlawfully intercepting a communication under the Investigatory Powers Act 2016 ('IPA 2016'), s 3.

   84 Interfering with the mail: general

   (1)   A person commits an offence if, without reasonable excuse, he—

      (a)   intentionally delays or opens a postal packet in the course of its transmission by post, or
      (b)   intentionally opens a mail-bag.

4.158 Section 3(1) IPA 2016 makes it an offence to intentionally intercept, in the United Kingdom, a communication in the course of its transmission without lawful authority. This applies to communications in the course of transmission via a public telecommunications system, a private telecommunications system or a public postal service. This offence previously existed under RIPA 2000. Section 3(2) provides that the criminal offence in s 3(1) does not apply where a person has the right to control the operation or use of the system or has the express or implied consent of such a person to carry out the interception. This is relevant to computer networks in the home or workplace for example.

The term 'in the course of transmission' is a key element of an offence under PSA 2000, s 84 and IPA 2016, s 3. It is defined in the PSA 2000, s 125(3), for the purposes of that Act. It is not defined in IPA 2016.

(a)   a postal packet shall be taken to be in course of transmission by post from the time of its being delivered to any post office or post office letter box to the time of its being delivered to the addressee,

(b)   the delivery of a postal packet of any description to a letter carrier or other person authorised to receive postal packets of that description for the post or to a person engaged in the business of a postal operator to be dealt with in the course of that business shall be a delivery to a post office, and

(c)   the delivery of a postal packet—

(i)   at the premises to which it is addressed or redirected, unless they are a post office from which it is to be collected,

(ii)   to any box or receptacle to which the occupier of those premises has agreed that postal packets addressed to persons at those premises may be delivered, or

(iii)   to the addressee's agent or to any other person considered to be authorised to receive the packet,

shall be a delivery to the addressee.

4.159 For the purposes of the PSA 2000, s 125(3)(c) is likely to mean that a letter is no longer in the course of transmission by post, once it has been delivered to the address of the intermediary or agent appearing on the front of the letter. That will remain the position even if the named recipient person or company is not the occupier of the address. It is the 'premises' address that is critical, because of PSA 2000, s 125(3)(c)(i). Generally, trading standards officers should only intercept or open postal items when they are no longer in the course of transmission. However, in our view it is unlikely that a such an officer, lawfully exercising an enforcement power, would commit an offence under PSA 2000, s 84 or IPA 2016, s 3 because:

(i)   a court is unlikely to consider a delivered letter in the possession of an intermediary to be 'in the course of its transmission by post';

(ii)   it is likely that a court will construe the meaning of 'in the course of its transmission' consistently between the PSA 2000 and IPA 2016. It follows that it is also unlikely that an offence under s 3 IPA 2016 would be committed; and

(iii)   there is also likely to be a 'reasonable excuse' under s 84 PSA 2000 when officers are lawfully exercising an enforcement power for the purposes of an investigation culminating in fraud charges.

Powers under the Consumer Rights Act 2015

4.160 CRA 2015, Sch 5 introduces a consolidated set of investigatory powers which aim to be clear for both enforcers and businesses alike. The revised powers are modelled on the powers under the Consumer Protection from Unfair Trading Regulations 2008[1], but with some differences. The consolidated powers only relate to what can broadly be described as consumer legislation: they do not apply, for example, to investigatory powers in relation to food or animal health and welfare[2]. Further, some certain specific powers contained in product safety and weights and measures legislation are retained and not included within the generic set of powers[3].

1 SI 2008/1277.
2 Although CRA 2015, Sch 5, para 12 does provide the Secretary of State with the power to extend the list of legislation to which Sch 5 applies.
3 See, for example, reg 22(4) of the General Product Safety Regulations 2005, SI 2005/1803 for the power to ask for documentation, such as the product information file, to check compliance or details of the supplier, where the enforcer has reasonable suspicion that the goods have not been placed on the market since they were manufactured or imported; Furniture and Furnishings (Fire) (Safety) Regulations 1988, SI 1988/1324 and under the Weights and Measures Act 1985, ss 38–41.

4.161 CRA 2015, s 77 blandly announces that CRA 2015, Sch 5 'has effect'. The investigatory powers were brought into force from 27 May 2015 as regards the enforcement of duties of letting agents and secondary ticketing under Chapter 3 of Pt 3[1] and Chapter 5 of Pt 3[2] of the Act respectively. The remainder of the provisions were brought into force in October 2015[3]. BIS produced guidance regarding investigatory powers in 2015: 'Investigatory Powers of Law Enforcers – Guidance for Businesses on the Consumer Rights Act 2015'[4].

1 Consumer Rights Act 2015 (Commencement) (England) Order 2015, SI 2015/965.
2 Consumer Rights Act 2015 (Commencement No 1) Order 2015, SI 2015/1333.
3 By the Consumer Rights Act 2015 (Commencement No 3, Transitional Provisions, Savings and Consequential Amendments) Order 2015, SI 2015/1630.
4 www.businesscompanion.info/sites/default/files/Investigatory-powers-of-consumer-law-enforc ers-guidance-for-businesses-on-the-Consumer-Rights-Act-2015-Oct-2015.pdf.

Who can use the investigatory powers to enforce?

4.162 Paragraph 2 of Sch 5, CRA 2015 defines an enforcer as being either a domestic enforcer, a Sch 13 enforcer (previously referred to as an EU enforcer), a public designated enforcer or an unfair contract terms enforcer[1]. This chapter pertains to criminal enforcement and focusses on domestic enforcers. These are listed in CRA 2015, Sch 5, para 3 as being:

(1) In this Schedule "domestic enforcer" means—

    (a) the Competition and Markets Authority,
    (b) a local weights and measures authority in Great Britain,
    (c) a district council in England,
    (d) the Department of Enterprise, Trade and Investment in Northern Ireland,
    (e) a district council in Northern Ireland,
    (f) the Secretary of State,
    (g) the Gas and Electricity Markets Authority,
    (h) the British Hallmarking Council,
    (i) an assay office within the meaning of the Hallmarking Act 1973, or

    (j)   any other person to whom the duty in subsection (1) of section 27 of the Consumer Protection Act 1987 (duty to enforce safety provisions) applies by virtue of regulations under subsection (2) of that section.

[1]   Paragraph 2(2).

Delegation of powers

4.163 The powers described in CRA 2015, Sch 5 refer to an enforcer or an officer of an enforcer. Paragraph 7 defines what is meant by an officer:

(1)   In this Schedule "officer", in relation to an enforcer, means—
    (a)   an inspector appointed by the enforcer to exercise powers under this Schedule, or authorised to do so,
    (b)   an officer of the enforcer appointed by the enforcer to exercise powers under this Schedule, or authorised to do so,
    (c)   an employee of the enforcer (other than an inspector or officer) appointed by the enforcer to exercise powers under this Schedule, or authorised to do so, or
    (d)   a person (other than an inspector, officer or employee of the enforcer) authorised by the enforcer to exercise powers under this Schedule.

(2)   But references in this Schedule to an officer in relation to a particular power only cover a person within sub-paragraph (1) if and to the extent that the person has been appointed or authorised to exercise that power.

The enforcer's legislation

4.164 CRA 2015, Sch 5, para 9(1) defines 'the enforcer's legislation':

(1)   In this Schedule "the enforcer's legislation", in relation to a domestic enforcer, means—
    (a)   legislation or notices which, by virtue of a provision listed in paragraph 10, the domestic enforcer has a duty or power to enforce, and
    (b)   where the domestic enforcer is listed in an entry in the first column of the table in paragraph 11, the legislation listed in the corresponding entry in the second column of that table.

(2)   References in this Schedule to a breach of or compliance with the enforcer's legislation include a breach of or compliance with a notice issued under—
    (a)   the enforcer's legislation, or
    (b)   legislation under which the enforcer's legislation is made.

4.165 The consolidated powers in the CRA 2015 will apply to the legislative provisions listed in Sch 5, paras 10 and 11. Under para 12 the Secretary of State has power to amend the list. There have already been several amendments[1]. In summary, the enforcer's legislation primarily comprises areas concerned with fair trading, product safety, weights and measures, prices, consumer credit, estate agents, package travel, timeshare, video recordings and intellectual property.

[1]   See for example the Consumer Rights Act 2015 (Commencement No 3, Transitional Provisions, Savings and Consequential Amendments) Order 2015, SI 2015/1630, the Consumer Rights Act 2015 (Consequential Amendments) Order 2015, SI 2015/1726.

Using the powers

4.166 Powers under Pt 3 of the Sch 5, CRA 2015(powers in relation to production of information) may be used by each of the enforcers in the circumstances prescribed within that Part.

4.167 The powers under Pt 4 of CRA 2015, Sch 5 are only available to domestic enforcers for the purposes detailed in para 19. Domestic enforcers may exercise any power in paras 21–26 (test purchasing, observing the carrying on of a business, entering premises without a warrant, inspecting products, testing equipment) and in paras 31–34 (power to break open containers, power to enter premises with a warrant, power to require persons on premises to provide assistance) for the purposes of ascertaining compliance with the enforcer's legislation[1].

1   Paragraph 19(2).

4.168 Paragraph 35 of Sch 5, CRA 2015 provides interpretation for phrases used in Pt 4 of CRA 2015, Sch 5, as follows:

"goods" has the meaning given by section 2(8)[1];

"occupier", in relation to premises, means any person an officer of an enforcer reasonably suspects to be the occupier of the premises;

"premises" includes any stall, vehicle, vessel or aircraft;

"product" means—
    (a)   goods,
    (b)   a service,
    (c)   digital content, as defined in section 2(9)[2],
    (d)   immovable property, or
    (e)   rights or obligations.

1   CRA 2015, s 2(8) – 'Goods' means any tangible moveable items, but that includes water, gas and electricity if and only if they are put up for supply in a limited volume or set quantity.
2   CRA 2015, s 2(9) – 'Digital content' means data which are produced and supplied in digital form.

Production of information

4.169 Part 3 of CRA 2015, Sch 5 contains the powers in relation to the production of information. These powers are broadly similar to and replace those under Pt 8 of the Enterprise Act 2002[1] *but now apply to both civil and criminal consumer law enforcement.* Paragraph 13 of Sch 5 CRA 2015 details the purposes for which the powers may be used by domestic enforcers, a Sch 13 enforcer, public designated enforcers and unfair contract terms enforcers.

1   CRA 2015, Sch 6, paras 68–71.

4.170 A domestic enforcer may exercise the powers in Pt 3 CRA 2015 for the purpose of ascertaining whether there has been a breach of the enforcers' legislation[1], but may only use the power to require the production of information for that purpose where an officer of an enforcer reasonably suspects a breach of the legislation, although this does not apply, for example, when the enforcer is acting as a market surveillance authority.

1   Paragraph 13.

4.171 Paragraph 14 Sch 5 CRA 2015 simply states that an enforcer or an officer thereof, may give notice to a person requiring the person to provide the enforcer with information specified in the notice. Exercise of this power may mean that the enforcer does not need to visit the person's premises. Paragraph 15 sets out the procedure by which this is to be done. The notice must be in writing and specify the purpose for which the information is required. The notice may specify the time within which and the manner in which the person to whom it is given must comply with it and the form in which the information is to be provided. The notice may require the creation of documents, or documents of a given description in the notice and the provision of the same to the enforcer or an officer of the enforcer. Such notice cannot require a person to produce documents which would be subject to legal professional privilege.

4.172 Paragraph 16 Sch 5 CRA 2015 provides for enforcement of the notice. Where there is a failure to comply the enforcer may apply to the court for enforcement under para 16. If the court considers that the person has failed to comply with the notice, it may make an order requiring the person to do anything that the court thinks is reasonable for the person to do, for any of the purposes for which the notice was given, to ensure the notice is complied with. Either the person failing to comply or an official of a company, partnership or unincorporated association failing to comply may be required by the court to meet the costs or expenses of the application[1].

[1] Paragraph 15(4), (5). An official is defined in para 16(6) as being a director, manager, secretary or other similar officer for a company, a member in the case of a limited liability partnership, a partner in the case of a partnership and as regards an unincorporated association, a person in management or control of its affairs.

4.173 There are limitations on the use of information[1] provided so as to preserve the right against self-incrimination. Paragraph 17 Sch 5 CRA 2015 makes clear that in criminal proceedings against that person the prosecution may not adduce evidence or ask questions relating to that information. The rule does not apply in proceedings where evidence relating to the information is adduced by or on behalf of the person providing it, or where a question is asked relating to it. Moreover, the restriction on use does not apply where a person is facing proceedings for the obstruction offence under para 36 or a perjury offence under the Perjury Act 1911, s 5 (false statutory declarations).

[1] Including information contained in a document created pursuant to a notice under para 14.

Test purchasing

4.174 'Covert' sampling techniques (or test purchasing), have been part of the tools used to determine compliance with food and weights and measures laws for nearly 150 years. As Lord Nicholls said in *R v Looseley and Attorney General's Reference (No 3 of 2000)*[1]:

'Indeed, conduct of this nature by officials is sometimes expressly authorised by Act of Parliament. The statute creating an offence may authorise officials to make test purchases, as in section 27 of the Trade Descriptions Act 1968.'

[1] [2001] UKHL 53.

4.175 The modern equivalent powers to test purchase are found under para 21 of the CRA 2015, Sch 5. In our view, the vast majority of test purchasing operations are not likely to result in the obtaining of private information about any person (under RIPA 2000, s 26(2) – RIP(S)A 2000, s 1(2)(b)) or to establish or maintain a personal or other relationship with the seller (under RIPA 2000, s 26(8) – RIP(S)A 2000, s 1(8)(b)) so a RIPA 2000/RIP(S)A 2000 authorisation is not required. There will be circumstances when one should be considered and, ultimately, the responsibility for authorising (or not authorising) a test-purchasing operation is that of the authorising Officer.

Children used in test purchases

4.176 In *Ealing London Borough Council v Woolworths plc*[1], the Divisional Court considered a case involving the use of children to make test purchases. An 11-year-old boy had been used in a trading standards test purchase of an 18 category video film at the respondent's shop[2]. The boy had simply bought the video and the sales assistant had made no inquiry of his age. The justices hearing the case at first instance accepted a submission that the evidence be excluded for entrapment under of PACE 1984, s 78 because the defendant had been induced to make the sale when otherwise no such sale would have taken place. The Divisional Court robustly overturned that decision:

> 'If the process employed, which we understand to be a common practice up and down the country, were to fall foul of s 78, it would in my judgment emasculate the enforcement of a sensible piece of legislation which, as earlier indicated, was passed for the express purpose of protecting young people such as the boy employed for the test purchase in this case from being exposed to undesirable influences. I do not accept that what happened was in any sense an entrapment of the respondents, or that the boy acted as an agent provocateur, nor incidentally, did he commit any offence in purchasing the video. He did not incite, aid or abet the commission of an offence by Woolworths. By purchasing the video he was simply playing a part in the situation which rendered Woolworths culpable. Had there been any element of persuasion of the sales girl by the customer, then perhaps different considerations would have prevailed.'

[1]   [1995] Crim LR 58.
[2]   Video Recordings Act 1984, s 11(1) made it an offence to supply the video to a person under the age of 18.

4.177 In *Wm Morrisons Supermarkets plc v Reading Borough Council*[1] a test purchase of cigarettes had been made by a child on behalf of the local authority. The Divisional Court rejected the appellant's argument that there had not been a 'transaction of sale' for the purposes of the Children and Young Persons Act 1933, s 7(1)(a). It was irrelevant whether property had passed to the young person or, as a result of his entering into the transaction, to someone else. What mattered was that the child or young person entered into a contract for the sale of tobacco and that property passed under that contract.

[1]   [2012] EWHC 1358 (Admin), [2012] PTSR 1643, [2012] 2 Cr App R 16, (2012) 176 JP 388, [2012] CTLC 33.

4.178 It should be noted that the Office of Surveillance Commissioners' Procedures and Guidance document, in relation to 'Test Purchase of sales to juveniles', states 'intelligence must be sufficient to prevent "fishing trips"'. Also the non-statutory Age Restricted Products Code of Practice – issued by the Better Regulation Delivery Office in January 2013 and updated in April 2014 – contains a part (paras 13–18) which 'addresses the use of test purchasing by young people as a tactic for conducting spot checks on compliance'.

Power to test purchase under the Consumer Rights Act 2015

4.179 The power to test purchase products for the purpose of ascertaining compliance with the enforcer's legislation is found in CRA 2015, Sch 5, para 21. This power and the power under para 22 to observe the carrying on of a business are akin to the officer acting in the manner of a consumer and in neither case is the officer exercising a power of entry for which a notice or warrant requirement applies.

21 Power to purchase products
(1)   An officer of an enforcer may—
     (a)   make a purchase of a product, or
     (b)   enter into an agreement to secure the provision of a product.
(2)   For the purposes of exercising the power in sub-paragraph (1), an officer may—
     (a)   at any reasonable time, enter premises to which the public has access (whether or not the public has access at that time), and
     (b)   inspect any product on the premises which the public may inspect.
(3)   The power of entry in sub-paragraph (2) may be exercised without first giving notice or obtaining a warrant.

4.180 The BIS guidance suggests that a reasonable time will generally be taken to mean when a business is open for trade but enforcers will need to take account of what is reasonable in the circumstances and for that particular business sector. The definition in CRA 2015, Sch 5, para 7(1)(d) means that, for example, a volunteer, non-employee of a local authority, authorised by the authority to exercise the power of test purchasing under para 20, is an 'officer'.

Power to observe the carrying on of business etc

4.181 CRA 2015, Sch 5, para 22 provides:

22 Power to observe carrying on of business etc
(1)   An officer of an enforcer may enter premises to which the public has access in order to observe the carrying on of a business on those premises.
(2)   The power in sub-paragraph (1) may be exercised at any reasonable time (whether or not the public has access at that time).
(3)   The power of entry in sub-paragraph (1) may be exercised without first giving notice or obtaining a warrant.

4.182 The BIS guidance[1] suggests that the power to observe the carrying on of a business for the purpose of ascertaining compliance with the enforcer's legislation might be used when the business is new to an area or where the enforcer has little intelligence about the business in question. Similar considerations will apply as under para 21 as to what constitutes a reasonable time.

[1]   Reference p 12.

Powers of entry

4.183 The Protection of Freedoms Act 2012 flowed from a Coalition Government declared intent to roll back state intrusion and protect civil liberties. The Act required the review of existing powers of entry and associated powers[1] with a view to:

- repealing them if they are considered to be either unnecessary or inappropriate by the relevant Minister[2];
- adding safeguards such as restrictions as to the times at which the power may be exercised or a requirement for the power of entry to be subject to an authorisation[3]; or
- rewriting them by, for example, consolidating a number of powers of entry exercisable for similar purposes or by a defined category of state officials[4].

[1] Protection of Freedoms Act 2012, s 42.
[2] Protection of Freedoms Act 2012, s 39.
[3] Protection of Freedoms Act 2012, s 40.
[4] Protection of Freedoms Act 2012, s 41.

4.184 The Home Office-coordinated review identified 1,237 separate powers of entry – 749 in primary legislation; 478 in secondary legislation. The Government proposals will leave a total of 91 – with 231 further powers having additional 'safeguards'. Provision is also made in the Act[1] for the exercise of powers of entry and associated powers (which have not been devolved) to be subject to a Code of Practice. The Code of Practice came into force as from 6 April 2015[2]. The Code 'provides guidance and sets out considerations that apply before, during and after powers of entry and associated powers are exercised including those circumstances where entry is exercised with the consent of an occupier. The purpose of the Code is to ensure greater consistency in the exercise of powers of entry and greater clarity for those affected by them while upholding effective enforcement'.

[1] Protection of Freedoms Act 2012, s 47.
[2] Protection of Freedoms Act 2012 (Code of Practice for Powers of Entry and Description of Relevant Persons) Order 2015, SI 2015/240.

4.185 'Relevant persons'[1] must have regard to the Code when exercising any functions to which the Code relates[2]. Not doing so does not create criminal or civil liability for the individual, but it is admissible as evidence in proceedings[3]. Authorities should ensure that all relevant persons are familiar with this Code of Practice[4].

[1] Defined in Protection of Freedoms Act 2012 (Code of Practice for Powers of Entry and Description of Relevant Persons) Order 2015, SI 2015/240 as being any person who is exercising a power of entry or associated power which is not devolved and not subject to another code of practice.
[2] Protection of Freedoms Act 2012, s 51(1).
[3] Protection of Freedoms Act 2012, s 51(2), (3).
[4] Code, para 24.

4.186 The Code mandates the provision of reasonable notice (usually not less than 48 hours or as specified in the relevant legislation), to the landowner or occupier affected by the power of entry. Notice should be considered even where it not required under the relevant legislation, unless to do so would frustrate the purpose of the entry. The Code recognises that there may be a need for unannounced inspections, such that the provision of notice would defeat the purpose of the entry and also that it may not always be practicable to provide notice. The powers of entry under CRA 2015, Sch 5, reflect the Code in terms of the provision of notice but it should be noted that the provisions regarding the notice requirements etc in the Act take precedence over those in the Code.

4.187 The Code also requires the consideration of the number of people needed to affect the entry[1] and where entry without consent or warrant is permitted by legislation, whether the object of the entry could be achieved by less intrusive means[2]. The Code also provides guidance on the conduct of authorised persons exercising powers of entry both during and after the entry and the records which should be maintained.

[1]   Code, para 9.
[2]   Code, para 11.

Powers of entry and the obtaining of warrants

4.188 Various pieces of consumer and trading standards legislation provide officers of enforcing authorities with powers of entry onto premises (dwellings and non-dwellings) either with or without a warrant. Many of these powers have now been consolidated into the generic set of investigatory powers under CRA 2015, Sch 5. Within these consolidated powers, officers have the power to enter but not into premises used wholly or mainly as a dwelling. This power may only be used on provision of two working days' notice, unless prescribed conditions are met. The power of entry to premises with a warrant may only be made after the magistrate hearing the application has been satisfied on receiving written evidence on oath that prescribed conditions have been met. In recent times the exercise of powers of entry, particularly where warrants have been required, has generated considerable case law which provides guidance on how the courts should approach such applications and their execution.

4.189 Officers should first consider whether a warrant is necessary or consider whether notice of entry is required under the legislation governing the power of entry. In *Hargreaves v Brecknock and Radnorshire Magistrates' Court and Powys County Council Trading Standards Department*[1], an application was made to obtain a warrant for entry to premises which were not a dwelling citing both CPUTR 2008, reg 21 (power of entry without a warrant) and reg 22 (power of entry with a warrant). The court observed, 'no warrants were necessary in this case because neither of the premises concerned was used exclusively as a dwelling. We have concluded that everything was done within the scope of CPUTR 2008, reg 21(1)'[2].

[1]   [2015] EWHC 1803 (Admin).
[2]   Per Thirlwall J at para 42.

4.190 In *R (on the application of Redknapp) v Commissioner of the City of London Police*[1] Latham LJ noted[2]:

'The obtaining of a search warrant is never to be treated as a formality. It authorises the invasion of a person's home. All the material necessary to justify the grant of a warrant should be contained in the information provided on the form. If the magistrate . . . does require any further information in order to satisfy himself that the warrant is justified, a note should be made of the additional information so that there is a proper record of the full basis upon which the warrant has been granted.'

1   [2009] 1 WLR 2096.
2   Per Latham LJ at para 13.

4.191 Notwithstanding the fact that CPUTR 2008, reg 21(1) plainly gave the Trading Standards authority power of entry, the court in *Hargreaves* went on to consider the warrant that was issued and in particular whether the court could satisfy itself that the conditions for the granting of a warrant had been met. On quashing the warrant, the court observed:

'What was required was a clear statement in writing that condition A was relied on and the basis upon which it was said that the condition was met. It should have been made plain to the Magistrate that he had first to be satisfied as to Condition A[1] before going on to the second stage of the decision. We are not confident that Condition A was referred to in terms by anyone. It is not on the form (save as part of the Regulation), it is not in the notes and it is not referred to by the Magistrate in his decision.'

1   Condition A stated 'that there are on the premises goods or documents which a duly authorised officer [. . .] has power to inspect and that there evidence is likely to disclose evidence of a breach of these Regulations'.

4.192 The application for a warrant carries with it the duty of full and frank disclosure. In *R (on the application of Helidon Vuciterni and Alsat UK Ltd) v Brent Magistrates' Court and Brent and Harrow Trading Standards Service*[1], Davis LJ stated:

'it must never be forgotten that the granting of a warrant (no less than the making of a search and seize, or Anton Piller, order) is a most extreme and invasive kind of order, not to be granted without great caution and dependent on appropriate full and accurate disclosure by the applicant.'

1   [2012] EWHC 2140 (Admin), [2012] CTLC 171.

4.193 In this case a warrant was obtained under CPUTR 2008, reg 22 (power of entry with a warrant) from the magistrates' court on the basis that the supply in the UK of satellite television decoder cards intended for the Albanian market was likely to constitute an offence under the Copyright, Designs and Patents Act 1988, s 297A as well as the banned practice of stating or otherwise creating the impression that a product could be legally sold when it could not, contrary to CPUTR 2008, Sch 1, para 9.

4.194 The Administrative Court quashed the warrants by reason of material non-disclosure (see paras 24, 29, 34–35 and 38 of the judgment). At the time of the warrants being issued it could not have been fairly represented to the magistrates' court that it was 'likely' that the supplying of such cards would constitute an offence under Copyright, Designs and Patents Act 1988, s 297A given the significant doubts raised about this by the Advocate-General in *QC Leisure* and *Murphy* (by the time of the Administrative Court hearing the CJEU had ruled definitively that it was not an offence)[1].

1   CJEU Cases C-403/03 and C-429–03.

4.195 Parliament did not take the opportunity to make this plain when drafting the generic set of powers under the CRA 2015, however the decision in

Vuciterni is likely to remain good law for the powers of entry under CRA 2015, Sch 5.

4.196 In *Hargreaves* the court ruled that enforcement officer's making a video recording of an entry and search was not unlawful[1]:

'In filming events the officers were not exercising a power . . . They were making a record of the execution of the warrant . . . we consider it would be a proportionate interference with the Article 8 right to respect for private life were the record to be made and retained for the purposes of and the duration of criminal proceedings (subject to any appeals).'

[1]   Per Thirlwall J at paras 40, 41.

Powers of entry under the CRA 2015

ENTRY WITHOUT A WARRANT

4.197 CRA 2015, Sch 5, para 23(1), provides:

(1) An officer of an enforcer may enter premises at any reasonable time.

However, the power under para 23 does not authorise entry to premises which are used wholly or mainly as a dwelling[1].

[1]   Paragraph 23(2).

4.198 In the case of a routine inspection, the power of entry may only be exercised if a notice has been given to the occupier of the premises[1] unless the occupier waives the requirement to give notice[2]. There is no requirement that the waiver of notice be in writing, but clearly, as the BIS Guidance observes, as a matter of best practice, a written communication of waiver (demonstrating understanding of the right to notice which is being waived) should be obtained from the trader and retained by the officer.

[1]   Paragraph 23(3).
[2]   Paragraph 23(5).

4.199 Paragraph 23(4) provides the formal requirements of the notice which are:

(a)   The notice is in writing and given by an officer of the enforcer;
(b)   The notice sets out why the entry is necessary and indicates the nature of the offence of obstruction (under paragraph 36), and
(c)   That there are at least two working days between the date of the receipt of the notice and the date of entry.

4.200 The phrase 'routine inspection' is defined under para 23(6):

(6)   In this paragraph 'routine inspection' means an exercise of the power in sub-paragraph (1) other than where—
    (a)   the power is exercised by an officer of a domestic enforcer who reasonably suspects a breach of the enforcer's legislation,
    (b)   the officer reasonably considers that to give notice in accordance with sub-paragraph (3) would defeat the purpose of the entry,
    (c)   it is not reasonably practicable in all the circumstances to give notice in accordance with that sub-paragraph, in particular because the

officer reasonably suspects that there is an imminent risk to public health or safety, or

(d) the enforcer is a market surveillance authority within the meaning of Article 2(18) of the Regulation on Accreditation and Market Surveillance and the entry is for the purpose of market surveillance within the meaning of Article 2(17) of that Regulation.

4.201 Aside from waiver by the trader or occupier of premises, there remain four situations where notice need not be given. The most common exceptions likely to be used are the reasonable suspicion of the breach of the enforcer's legislation and the defeating of the purpose of the entry. What amounts to reasonable suspicion will turn on the facts and circumstances of each case and can include intelligence material provided by others such as police or other local authorities. In *Hussien v Chong Fook Kam*[1], Lord Devlin stated[2]:

'Suspicion in its ordinary meaning is a state of conjecture or surmise where proof is lacking: "I suspect but I cannot prove". Suspicion arises at or near the starting point of an investigation of which the obtaining of prima facie proof is the end.'

[1] [1970] AC 942.
[2] At 948.

4.202 This passage was approved by Lord Steyn in *O'Hara v Chief Constable of the Royal Ulster Constabulary*[1], where it was said:

'(1) In order to have a reasonable suspicion the constable need not have evidence amounting to a prima facie case. Ex hypothesi one is considering a preliminary stage of the investigation and information from an informer or a tip-off from a member of the public may be enough: *Hussien v Chong Fook Kam* [1970] A.C. 942, 949. (2) Hearsay information may therefore afford a constable reasonable grounds to arrest. Such information may come from other officers: *Hussien's* case, ibid.'

[1] [1997] AC 286.

4.203 Notice is not required where the officer reasonably considers that the giving of notice would defeat the purpose of entry[1]. The most obvious reason why the giving of notice would defeat the purpose of the entry would be that evidence demonstrating a breach of the enforcer's legislation would be concealed, removed or destroyed. For example, an officer may be aware that counterfeit alcohol is being sold within an area, but uses this exception not to give notice as the likelihood would be that the counterfeit alcohol would be removed from the premises when the inspection takes place.

[1] Paragraph 23(6)(b).

4.204 Notice is not required where it is not reasonably practicable in the circumstances, in particular because the enforcer reasonably suspects there is an imminent risk to public health or safety – para 23(6)(c). The BIS Guidance Notes indicate that here may be a number of reasons why it might not be reasonably practicable for the enforcer to give notice to an occupier of a premises. These include situations where the nature of the trading activity makes it impractical for the enforcer to give notice, such as where the trader is a stall holder at an ad hoc market, or where enforcement action needs to be taken quickly to remove unsafe products from sale to reduce the risk to consumers.

4.205 Notice is not required where entry is for market surveillance purposes – para 23(6)(d)). The BIS Guidance Notes emphasise that enforcers do not need to give notice to carry out inspections for European safety legislation market surveillance purposes. However, this does not include inspections to ascertain compliance with domestic legislation which does not implement European law, such as checking the safety of sofas and cushions in accordance with the Furniture and Furnishings (Fire) (Safety) Regulations 1988.

4.206 Where entry is effected other than in the circumstances of a routine inspection, the officer must provide the occupier with a document setting out why the entry is necessary and the nature of the obstruction offence under para 36, but this is not necessary where not practicable to do so[1]. On any entry to premises under para 23, an officer must provide to an occupier evidence of identity and authorisation, but this is not necessary where not practicable to do so[2].

[1]   Paragraph 23(7), (9).
[2]   Paragraph 23(8), (9).

POWER TO ENTER PREMISES WITH A WARRANT

4.207 Paragraph 32 provides for the power of entry into premises with a warrant whilst para 33 addresses the exercise of entry under the warrant.

32 Power to enter premises with warrant

(1)   A justice of the peace may issue a warrant authorising an officer of an enforcer to enter premises if satisfied, on written information on oath given by such an officer, that there are reasonable grounds for believing that—

(a)   condition A or B is met, and
(b)   condition C, D or E is met.

(2)   Condition A is that on the premises there are—

(a)   products which an officer of the enforcer has power to inspect under paragraph 25, or
(b)   documents which an officer of the enforcer could require a person to produce under paragraph 27.

(3)   Condition B is that, on the premises—

(a)   in the case of a domestic enforcer, there has been or is about to be a breach of the enforcer's legislation,
(b)   in the case of an EU enforcer, there has been or is about to be a Community infringement as defined in section 212 of the Enterprise Act 2002, or
(c)   in the case of an EU enforcer, there has been a failure to comply with a measure specified in paragraph 20(3)(b), (c) or (d).

(4)   Condition C is that—

(a)   access to the premises has been or is likely to be refused, and
(b)   notice of the enforcer's intention to apply for a warrant under this paragraph has been given to the occupier of the premises.

(5)   Condition D is that it is likely that products or documents on the premises would be concealed or interfered with if notice of entry on the premises were given to the occupier of the premises.

(6)   Condition E is that—

    (a)   the premises are unoccupied, or

    (b)   the occupier of the premises is absent, and it might defeat the purpose of the entry to wait for the occupier's return.

(7)   In the application of this paragraph to Scotland—

    (a)   the reference in sub-paragraph (1) to a justice of the peace is to be read as a reference to a sheriff, and

    (b)   the reference in that sub-paragraph to information on oath is to be read as a reference to evidence on oath.

(8)   In the application of this paragraph to Northern Ireland—

    (a)   the reference in sub-paragraph (1) to a justice of the peace is to be read as a reference to a lay magistrate, and

    (b)   the reference in that sub-paragraph to written information is to be read as a reference to a written complaint.

4.208 This power of entry extends further than the power under para 23 in that it also applies to domestic premises. This is not specified within the legislation but it follows from the absence of a provision such as that contained in para 23(2) (relating to premises which are used wholly or mainly as a dwelling) and the decision in *R (on the application of Helidon Vuciterni and Alsat UK Ltd) v Brent Magistrates' Court and Brent and Harrow Trading Standards Service*[1], where the Administrative Court made clear that the power under CPUTR 2008, reg 22 (which is in similar terms to the para 32 power) applies to any premises[2].

[1]   [2012] EWHC 2140 (Admin), [2012] CTLC 171.
[2]   Per Davies LJ at para 46.

4.209 A warrant for entry can be obtained where there are two conditions met. First, there must be reasonable grounds for believing that either:

(a)   there are products or documents on the premises which the officer would have power to inspect under para 25, or could require production of under para 27; or

(b)   that there has been or there is about to be a breach of the domestic enforcers legislation[1].

[1]   This paragraph should be contrasted with para 23(6)(a), where entry can be exercised without prior notice by a domestic enforcer who 'reasonably suspects a breach of the enforcer's legislation' and not as in para 32 where there 'has been or is about to be a breach of the enforcer's legislation'.

4.210 Secondly, the court must be satisfied that there are reasonable grounds for believing one of the following:

(a)   that notice of the intention to apply for the warrant has been given to the occupier and access to the premises has been or is likely to be refused;

(b)   that products or documents on the premises would be concealed or interfered with if notice were given;

(c)   the premises are unoccupied or the occupier is absent and it might defeat the purpose of the entry to wait for the occupier's return.

4.211 The obtaining of a warrant for entry under para 32 reproduces the procedural requirements of the CPUTR 2008, reg 22 in similar terms. However, Condition A no longer requires that inspection of the goods/documents is likely to disclose evidence of a breach and the wording of Condition D in CPUTR 2008 was (merely) that an application for admission, or the giving of a notice of intention to apply for a warrant, 'would defeat the object of the entry'.

4.212 Paragraph 33 reads as follows:

33 Entry to premises under warrant

(1)   A warrant under paragraph 32 authorises an officer of the enforcer to enter the premises at any reasonable time, using reasonable force if necessary.

(2)   A warrant under that paragraph ceases to have effect at the end of the period of one month beginning with the day it is issued.

(3)   An officer entering premises under a warrant under paragraph 32 may be accompanied by such persons, and may take onto the premises such equipment, as the officer thinks necessary.

(4)   If the premises are occupied when the officer enters them, the officer must produce the warrant for inspection to an occupier of the premises.

(5)   Sub-paragraph (6) applies if the premises are unoccupied or the occupier is temporarily absent.

(6)   On leaving the premises the officer must—

    (a)   leave a notice on the premises stating that the premises have been entered under a warrant under paragraph 32, and
    (b)   leave the premises as effectively secured against trespassers as the officer found them.

4.213 As to para 33(3), Powers of Entry Code of Practice, para 9 is relevant:

'9.1 Relevant persons should consider the number of persons needed for the exercise of powers of entry and associated powers to be carried out effectively. The number of persons present should reflect what is reasonable and proportionate in the circumstances.'

POWER TO REQUIRE ASSISTANCE FROM PERSON ON PREMISES

4.214 Paragraph 34 provides an officer with the power to require any person on the premises to provide such assistance or information as the officer reasonably considers necessary, (whether the officer has entered premises under the power in para 23(1) or under a warrant under para 32). If the officer has entered the premises under para 23(1) or para 32 for the purposes of the enforcement of the Weights and Measures (Packaged Goods) Regulations 2006[1], (or its Northern Ireland equivalent) the officer has the power to require any person on the premises to provide such information as the person possesses about the name and address of the packer and of any importer of a package which the officer finds on the premises. It should be noted that a person commits an obstruction offence, under para 36(1), if they intentionally fail to comply with a requirement properly imposed by an enforcer or, without good reason fail to give an enforcer assistance or information reasonably required.

[1]   SI 2006/659, or its Northern Ireland equivalent Weights and Measures (Packaged Goods) Regulations (Northern Ireland) 2011, SR 2011/331.

Powers of search and seizure generally

4.215 Powers of seizure were extended under the Criminal Justice and Police Act 2001, ('CJPA 2001'), Pt 2 in relation to legislation within the CJPA 2001, Sch 1, which includes consumer and trading standards legislation. The CRA 2015 amends that Schedule to take account of the generic set of powers under the CRA 2015, Sch 5[1]. In general terms the CJPA 2001, s 50 provides powers for officers lawfully on premises to seize items in order that may be sifted and searched to see whether they are relevant and to seize items which may contain information which would fall within the scope of their entry. This would therefore enable an officer to seize an item containing digital content for example a computer or mobile phone, for the purpose of ascertaining the contents of the item. The CJPA 2001, Sch 1 is amended to include the powers under CRA 2015, Sch 5, paras 27(1)(b), 28(1) and 29(1).

[1]   CRA 2015, Sch 6, para 65.

Powers available on entry under CRA 2015, Sch 5

4.216 The powers under paras 25–31 of Sch 5 only apply where an enforcer has entered under a power of entry under para 23 or with a warrant under para 32[1]. These powers are not free-standing – they are dependent on, and consequential to, entry onto premises through the use of CRA 2015 powers, not entry by consent.

[1]   Paragraph 24.

4.217 In R *(on the application of Helidon Vuciterni and Alsat UK Limited) v Brent Magistrates' Court and Brent and Harrow Trading Standards Service*[1] the defendant submitted that the power to enter premises and to inspect goods under CPUTR 2008 did not, in either case, sanction a search. Davies LJ:

> 'The powers given under Regulation 21(1)(a)–(d) and under Regulation 22(2)(a) and (b) are disjunctive and separate. It is impossible to see how they could be effectively exercised if a power to search is not available: is an enforcement officer, having lawfully obtained entry, confined to standing in the hallway and looking around, by way of 'inspection', for what he can (or cannot) see? Plainly not. The powers conferred necessarily connote a power to, for example, search a desk or cabinet to see if there are relevant documents which may be required to be copied, if a breach has reasonably been suspected; they connote that an enforcement officer may, for example, go into backrooms and store rooms to see if there are goods that should be seized or detained, if there is reasonable cause to believe (not just suspect) a breach; and likewise may search for containers or vending machines. The powers to enter (and inspect) therefore plainly carry with them a power to search, as a matter of sensible construction. It must also not be overlooked that in this area of consumer protection very often thoroughly unscrupulous and disreputable people may be involved (I am again talking generally, not necessarily by reference to this case) and appropriately robust powers are to be expected to be available.'

[1]   [2012] EWCA 2140 (Admin).

Power to inspect products

4.218 Under para 25(1) an officer of a domestic enforcer has the power to inspect any product on the premises[1] and to examine any procedure connected with the production of a product for the purpose of ascertaining compliance with the enforcer's legislation. The power to examine any procedure is, under para 25(3) specifically, also available to an officer acting pursuant to the duty in Consumer Protection Act 1987, s 27(1) or the General Product Safety Regulations 2005, reg 10(1)[2]. Officers acting pursuant to the duty in the Weights and Measures (Packaged Goods) Regulations 2006, reg 10(1)[3] may inspect and take copies of records kept by packers or importers to demonstrate that the weights of packages of products meet the requirements of average quantity legislation[4]. This power is available to officers acting under equivalent Northern Ireland Regulations[5]. Further under para 25(7), (8), there are powers for domestic enforcers acting under duties[6] in the Electromagnetic Compatibility Regulations 2016[7] to inspect any apparatus or fixed installation or to examine any procedure connected with the production of apparatus.

[1]   Paragraph 25(1).
[2]   SI 2005/1803.
[3]   SI 2006/659.
[4]   SI 2006/659, at reg 5(2) or 9(1) or 9(3).
[5]   Weights and Measures (Packaged Goods) (Northern Ireland) Regulations 2011, SR 2011/331.
[6]   Regulation 37(1)(a)(ii) or (b)(ii).
[7]   SI 2016/1091.

Power to test equipment

4.219 Paragraph 26 provides for the power for domestic enforcers to test weighing or measuring equipment for the purpose of ascertaining compliance with relevant legislation.

(1)   An officer of a domestic enforcer may test any weighing or measuring equipment—

    (a)   which is, or which the officer has reasonable cause to believe may be, used for trade or in the possession of any person or on any premises for such use, or

    (b)   which has been, or which the officer has reasonable cause to believe to have been, passed by an approved verifier, or by a person purporting to act as such a verifier, as fit for such use.

(2)   Expressions used in sub-paragraph (1) have the same meaning—

    (a)   as in the Weights and Measures Act 1985, in the case of a domestic enforcer in Great Britain;

    (b)   as in the Weights and Measures (Northern Ireland) Order 1981 (SI 1981/231 (NI 10)), in the case of a domestic enforcer in Northern Ireland.

(3)   The powers in sub-paragraph (4) are available to an officer of a domestic enforcer acting pursuant to—

    (a)   the duty in regulation 10(1) of the Weights and Measures (Packaged Goods) Regulations 2006 (SI 2006/659) ('the 2006 Regulations'), or

    (b)   the duty in regulation 10(1) of the Weights and Measures (Packaged Goods) Regulations (Northern Ireland) 2011 (SR 2011/331) ('the 2011 Regulations').

(4)   The officer may test any equipment which the officer has reasonable cause to believe is used in—

(a) making up packages (as defined in regulation 2) in the United Kingdom, or

(b) carrying out a check mentioned in paragraphs (1) and (3) of regulation 9.

(5) The references in sub-paragraph (4) to regulations are to regulations in the 2006 Regulations in the case of a domestic enforcer in Great Britain or the 2011 Regulations in the case of a domestic enforcer in Northern Ireland.

Power to require the production of documents

4.220 Paragraph 27 provides for the power for an officer, who reasonably suspects a breach of the enforcer's legislation, to require any trader to produce documents and to take copies of them in order to ascertain compliance with the enforcer's legislation. However, where the documents are required as evidence in proceedings or to be held by statute or for market surveillance purposes, the officer can require the documents to be produced etc even when they do not have suspicion of a breach.

27 Power to require the production of documents

(1) The officer may, at any reasonable time—

(a) require a trader occupying the premises, or a person on the premises acting on behalf of such a trader, to produce any documents relating to the trader's business to which the trader has access, and

(b) take copies of, or of any entry in, any such document.

(2) The power in sub-paragraph (1) is available regardless of whether—

(a) the purpose for which the documents are required relates to the trader or some other person, or

(b) the proceedings referred to in paragraph 19(3)(b) or 20(4)(b) could be taken against the trader or some other person.

(3) That power includes power to require the person to give an explanation of the documents.

(4) Where a document required to be produced under sub-paragraph (1) contains information recorded electronically, the power in that subparagraph includes power to require the production of a copy of the document in a form in which it can easily be taken away and in which it is visible and legible.

(5) This paragraph does not permit an officer to require a person to create a document other than as described in sub-paragraph (4).

(6) This paragraph does not permit an officer to require a person to produce any document which the person would be entitled to refuse to produce—

(a) in proceedings in the High Court on the grounds of legal professional privilege, or

(b) in proceedings in the Court of Session on the grounds of confidentiality of communications.

(7) In sub-paragraph (6) 'communications' means—

(a) communications between a professional legal adviser and the adviser's client, or

(b) communications made in connection with or in contemplation of legal proceedings or for the purposes of those proceedings.

(8) In this paragraph 'trader' has the same meaning as in Part 1 of this Act.

4.221 Paragraph 19(3) and (4) prescribe when this power may be used by a domestic enforcer:

> (3) A domestic enforcer may exercise the power in paragraph 27 (power to require the production of documents) for either of the following purposes—
> - subject to sub-paragraph (4), to ascertain compliance with the enforcer's legislation;
> - to ascertain whether the documents may be required as evidence in proceedings for a breach of, or under, the enforcer's legislation.
>
> (4) A domestic enforcer may exercise the power in paragraph 27 for the purpose mentioned in sub-paragraph (3)(a) only if an officer of the enforcer reasonably suspects a breach of the enforcer's legislation, unless—
> - the power is being exercised in relation to a document that the trader is required to keep by virtue of a provision of the enforcer's legislation, or
> - the enforcer is a market surveillance authority within the meaning of Article 2(18) of the Regulation on Accreditation and Market Surveillance and the power is exercised for the purpose of market surveillance within the meaning of Article 2(17) of that Regulation.

4.222 In *Lancashire County Council v Buchanan*[1] a trading standards officer used powers under the Property Misdescriptions Act 1991 to require the production of documents relating to an estate agent's business. The estate agent, Buchanan, had already provided a considerable amount of information and refused to provide any more. He was charged with the obstruction offence under the Act. The issue was whether the officer had reasonable grounds to suspect that an offence had been committed under the Act and so had power to require production of the documents. In a decision upheld by the Administrative Court, it was determined that on the basis of the information that was in the officer's possession, the officer had no reasonable grounds for suspecting an offence had been committed.

[1]   [2007] EWHC 3194 (Admin).

Power to seize and detain goods

4.223 Paragraph 28 provides for the power to seize and detain goods. Paragraph 19(5) prescribes that a domestic enforcer may exercise this power in relation to:

(a)   goods which an officer of the enforcer reasonably suspects may disclose (by means of testing or otherwise) a breach of the enforcer's legislation,

(b)   goods which an officer of the enforcer reasonably suspects are liable to forfeiture under that legislation, and

(c)   goods which an officer of the enforcer reasonably suspects may be required as evidence in proceedings for a breach of, or under, that legislation.

28 Power to seize and detain goods

(1)   The officer may seize and detain goods other than documents (for which see paragraph 29).

(2)   An officer seizing goods under this paragraph from premises which are occupied must produce evidence of the officer's identity and authority to an occupier of the premises before seizing them.

(3)   The officer need not comply with sub-paragraph (2) if it is not reasonably practicable to do so.

(4)   An officer seizing goods under this paragraph must take reasonable steps to—
- inform the person from whom they are seized that they have been seized, and
- provide that person with a written record of what has been seized.

(5)   If, under this paragraph, an officer seizes any goods from a vending machine, the duty in sub-paragraph (4) also applies in relation to—
- the person whose name and address are on the vending machine as the owner of the machine, or
- if there is no such name and address on the machine, the occupier of the premises on which the machine stands or to which it is fixed.

(6)   In determining the steps to be taken under sub-paragraph (4), an officer exercising a power under this paragraph in England and Wales or Northern Ireland must have regard to any relevant provision about the seizure of property made by—
- a code of practice under section 66 of the Police and Criminal Evidence Act 1984, or
- a code of practice under Article 65 of the Police and Criminal Evidence (Northern Ireland) Order 1989 (SI 1989/1341 (NI 12)), (as the case may be).

(7)   Goods seized under this paragraph (except goods seized for a purpose mentioned in paragraph 19(5)(b)) may not be detained—
- for a period of more than 3 months beginning with the day on which they were seized, or
- where the goods are reasonably required to be detained for a longer period by the enforcer for a purpose for which they were seized, for longer than they are required for that purpose.

4.224 Note that the following provisions apply to the power under para 28:

- Paragraph 31: Power to break open container etc.
- Access to seized goods: paragraph 38 applies where anything seized by an officer of an enforcer is detained by the enforcer.
- Notice of testing of goods: paragraph 39 applies where goods seized by an officer of a domestic enforcer under para 28 are submitted to a test.
- Paragraph 40: Appeals against detention of goods and documents.

Power to seize documents

4.225 Paragraph 29 provides the power to seize and detail documents required as evidence and is drafted in similar terms to the power under para 28 for the seizure of goods. Paragraph 19(6) states that a domestic enforcer may exercise the power under para 29 in relation to documents which an officer of the enforcer reasonably suspects may be required as evidence:

(a)   in proceedings for a breach of the enforcer's legislation, or
(b)   in proceedings under the enforcer's legislation.

4.226 Paragraph 29(1) permits an officer to seize and detain documents and there is a requirement to produce to an occupier of the premises evidence of the officer identity and authority[1] (unless it is not reasonably practicable to do so)[2]. Further with due account of relevant codes of practice under PACE 1984, s 66 (or its Northern Ireland equivalent), the officer must take reasonable steps to inform the person from whom the documents have been seized about the seizure and provide that person with a written record of what has been seized. Documents cannot be seized where legal professional privilege applies (or where the person before the Court of Session would be entitled to refuse to produce on the grounds of confidentiality of communications). As with detained goods under para 28, documents may not be detained for longer than 3 months or in the alternative for no longer period than they are reasonably required to be detained by the enforcer for the purposes of the proceedings for which they are seized[3].

1 Paragraph 29(2).
2 Paragraph 29(3).
3 See also *Business Energy Solutions Ltd & Anor v Crown Court at Preston & Anor* [2018] EWHC 1534 (Admin) – data copied from computer devices does amount to 'seized property' for the purposes of s 53 of the Criminal Justice and Police Act 2001.

4.227 Note that the following provisions apply to the power under para 28:

* Paragraph 31 – power to break open container etc.
* Access to seized documents – para 38 applies where anything seized by an officer of an enforcer is detained by the enforcer.
* Paragraph 40 – appeals against detention of goods and documents.

Decommissioning or switching off fixed installations

4.228 Paragraph 30 provides the power to an officer of a domestic enforcer acting pursuant to the duty in the Electromagnetic Compatibility Regulations 2016, reg 52(1)(a)(ii) or (b)(ii)[1] to decommission or switch off any fixed installation (as defined in those regulations) or part of such an installation. Paragraph 19(7) states that this power may be used where an officer of the enforcer reasonably suspects a breach of the regulations and also for the purpose of ascertaining or otherwise whether there has been a breach (whether by means of testing or otherwise.)

1 SI 2016/1091.

Power to break open container etc

4.229 The power under para 31 must be exercised for the purpose of ascertaining compliance with the enforcer's legislation – see para 19(2) – and can only be used where it is reasonably necessary for the purposes for which that power may be exercised – see para 31(3). An enforcer can require a person who has authority to break open a container in order to use the powers of seizure and detention of goods/documents as well as the power to decommission or switch off fixed installations referred to in paras 28–30.

4.230 This power also applies to the opening of a vending machine and accessing information from electronic devices, so that an enforcer can require a person to access information which may be held or stored on, for example, a computer, including those on a network, information held in digital form, such as on USB sticks and held in the Cloud or other electronic networks. The meaning of 'container' in para 31(4) – 'anything in which goods may be stored' – could cover, for example, a shipping container containing goods or a filing cabinet containing documents.

4.231 Where the person fails to comply with such a request, the enforcer can personally break open the container, open the vending machine or access the electronic device. If, as a result of using the power under para 31, the enforcer seizes any goods or documents, the enforcer must adhere to the requirements in paras 28–30, such as taking reasonable steps to inform the person from whom they are seized.

31 Power to break open container etc

(1) The officer may, for the purpose of exercising any of the powers in paragraphs 28 to 30, require a person with authority to do so to—
    (a) break open any container,
    (b) open any vending machine, or
    (c) access any electronic device in which information may be stored or from which it may be accessed.

(2) Where a requirement under sub-paragraph (1) has not been complied with, the officer may, for the purpose of exercising any of the powers in paragraphs 28 to 30—
    (a) break open the container,
    (b) open the vending machine, or
    (c) access the electronic device.

(3) Sub-paragraph (1) or (2) applies if and to the extent that the exercise of the power in that sub-paragraph is reasonably necessary for the purposes for which that power may be exercised.

(4) In this paragraph 'container' means anything in which goods may be stored.

Offences connected with enforcement

4.232 Part 5 of the Schedule details provisions supplementary to Pts 3 and 4. The first two paragraphs detail offences. The offence of obstruction is created by para 36:

36 Offence of obstruction

(1) A person commits an offence if the person—
    (a) intentionally obstructs an enforcer or an officer of an enforcer who is exercising or seeking to exercise a power under Part 4 of this Schedule in accordance with that Part,
    (b) intentionally fails to comply with a requirement properly imposed by an enforcer or an officer of an enforcer under Part 4 of this Schedule, or
    (c) without reasonable cause fails to give an enforcer or an officer of an enforcer any other assistance or information which the enforcer or officer reasonably requires of the person for a purpose for which the enforcer or officer may exercise a power under Part 4 of this Schedule.

(2) A person commits an offence if, in giving information of a kind referred to in sub-paragraph (1)(c), the person—
    (a) makes a statement which the person knows is false or misleading in a material respect, or
    (b) recklessly makes a statement which is false or misleading in a material respect.

(3) A person who is guilty of an offence under sub-paragraph (1) or (2) is liable on summary conviction to a fine not exceeding level 3 on the standard scale.

(4) Nothing in this paragraph requires a person to answer any question or give any information if to do so might incriminate that person.

4.233 Under para 37 a person commits an offence if he is not an officer of an enforcer and purports to act as such using powers under Pt 3 or Pt 4 of the CRA 2015, Sch 5. This offence is punishable on summary conviction with a fine.

Retaining documents and goods

4.234 Paragraphs 38–42 provide for the duties in relation to goods or documents seized and detained. Under para 38, provision is given for a person who had custody or control of goods or documents seized under Pt 4 powers to be allowed supervised access to the thing seized when they request permission to do so. A person must be allowed supervised access to something seized for the purpose of photographing or copying it or have it photographed or copied for them[1]. Such right does not exist where an officer has reasonable grounds for believing that to do so would prejudice the investigation for the purposes of which it was seized[2]. Paragraph 38 is a new provision, not based on any previous consumer law legislation, but reflects provisions contained in PACE 1984 Code B.

[1] Paragraphs 38(3), (4) – if photographed or copied for them this must be supplied within a reasonable time.
[2] Paragraph 38(5).

4.235 Paragraph 39 provides for the notice to be given where goods have been purchased under para 21 (power to purchase products) and are subsequently tested which lead to proceedings being brought for a breach of the enforcers legislation or a notice being served by the enforcer preventing a person from doing anything[1]. This also applies to good seized under para 28[2]. The enforcer must inform the relevant person of the results of the test[3] and, where reasonably practicable to do so, allow the person to have the goods tested. Relevant persons are defined as being the owners of vending machines from which goods were purchased or the occupier of premises where the machine stands[4] (for the purposes of being told the results of test) or those same persons and persons who are either parties to proceedings or who have an interest in the goods (for the purposes of being able to have the goods tested).

[1] Paragraph 39(1).
[2] Paragraph 39(2).
[3] Paragraph 39(3).
[4] For the purposes of being informed of the result of the test.

4.236 Under para 40, where goods or documents have been seized under Pt 4 of the Consumer Rights Act 2015, Sch 5, a person with an interest in the goods or documents may apply to a magistrates' court in England, Wales and Northern Ireland or the Sheriff in Scotland for an order requiring them to be released. The Court or Sheriff may only order release if satisfied that one of two conditions are met. The conditions are:

(6) Condition A is that—
    (a)   no proceedings have been brought—
        (i)   for an offence as the result of the investigation in the course of which the goods or documents were seized, or
        (ii)   for the forfeiture of the goods or documents or (in the case of seized documents) any goods to which the documents relate, and

(b)   the period of 6 months beginning with the date the goods or documents were seized has expired.

(7) Condition B is that—

(a)   proceedings of a kind mentioned in sub-paragraph (6)(a) have been brought, and

(b)   those proceedings have been concluded without the goods or documents being forfeited.

4.237 A right of appeal from a magistrates' court decision lies to the Crown Court in England and Wales or the county court in Northern Ireland. Paragraph 40 is based on the Consumer Protection Act 1987, s 33 (which applied to goods seized and detained in respect of product safety contraventions) but now has much wider application.

4.238 Where a domestic enforcer has seized goods under para 28 which the enforcer reasonably suspects may disclose (by means of testing or otherwise) a breach of the enforcer's legislation[1], then by virtue of para 41(2) the enforcer must pay compensation to any person with an interest in the goods in respect of any loss or damage caused by the detention. This is subject to the following condition:

(3) The condition that is relevant to a domestic enforcer is that—

(a)   the goods have not disclosed a breach of the enforcer's legislation, and

(b)   the power to seize and detain the goods was not exercised as a result of any neglect or default of the person seeking the compensation.

[1]   As per para 19(5)(a).

4.239 Compensation is determined by means of arbitration[1].

[1]   Paragraph 41(5).

CAUTIONS

4.240 This section is not applicable to Scotland.

Simple cautions

4.241 In June 2005 Part 1 of Home Office circular 30/2005 ('Cautioning of Adult Offenders') replaced circular 18/1994. It used the term 'Simple Caution' for the first time – 'to distinguish it from a Conditional Caution', which was to have been the subject for Pt 2 of this circular. Home Office Circular 16/2008 for Simple Cautioning was replaced on 8 April 2013 by the Ministry of Justice's *Simple Caution for Adult Offender guidance*. In *R (on the application of Stratton) v Chief Constable of Thames Valley Police*[1] the decision to administer a simple caution was overturned where the full implications of accepting the caution had not been made clear to the suspect and she had therefore not been able to give informed consent, in accordance with the guidance.

[1]   [2013] EWHC 1561 (Admin).

4.242 When deciding if a simple caution is appropriate, the following criteria must be satisfied:

- the person must have made a clear, reliable and PACE 1984 compliant admission of the offence, either verbally or in writing. In *R (on the application of Rupert Wyman) v The Chief Constable of Hampshire Constabulary*[1] it was held that there was no admission which would justify the claimant being formally cautioned for the alleged offence and the caution was ordered to be quashed. Under no circumstances should suspects be pressed, or induced in any way to admit offences in order to receive a simple caution as an alternative to being charged – see *R v Commissioner of Police of the Metropolis ex parte Thompson*[2];
- there must be a realistic prospect of conviction if the person were to be prosecuted;
- it must be in the public interest to use a simple caution as the means of disposal;
- a simple caution must be appropriate to the offence and the offender.

[1] [2006] EWHC 1904 (Admin).
[2] [1996] 1 WLR 1519.

4.243 A simple caution will not be appropriate where a person has raised a defence or if has refused to accept it. The significance of the admission of guilt in agreeing to accept a simple caution must be fully and clearly explained to the offender before they are cautioned. Repeat cautioning may be acceptable in circumstances where there has been a sufficient lapse of time to suggest that a previous caution has had a significant deterrent effect (2 years or more) and if the current offence is trivial or unrelated to any previous offences, or as part of a mixed disposal.

4.244 Offenders and their legal representatives may be entitled to seek and have disclosure of the evidence before the offender agrees to accept a caution. In *Director of Public Prosecutions v Ara*[1], it was held, on the facts, that disclosure of an interview to a defendant's solicitor was necessary in order to enable informed advice to be given as to whether a caution was agreed. However, Rose LJ made it clear ' . . . that this does not mean that there is a general obligation on the police to disclose material prior to charge'.

[1] [2001] 4 All ER 559.

4.245 Where (i) disclosure is sought and refused, and (ii) consequently a caution is declined because the recipient has been unable to take proper legal advice, and (iii) a subsequent prosecution is instituted to comply with time limits, the case may be (and has at first instance) been stayed as an abuse of process.

4.246 The Criminal Justice and Courts Act 2015, s 17 *places restrictions on the circumstances in which simple cautions may be used*. In essence, the more serious the offence, the greater the restrictions. It also places restrictions on the use of simple cautions for repeat offending. The application of these restrictions does not extend to offences where local authorities may consider issuing a simple caution.

Conditional cautions

4.247 Part 3 of the Criminal Justice Act 2003 makes provision for conditional cautions to be available as a means of dealing with offenders in certain circumstances, as an alternative to prosecution. Conditional cautions may only be given by an authorised person, defined as a constable; a person designated as an investigating officer under the Police Reform Act 2002, s 38; or a person authorised for the purpose by a relevant Prosecutor. A 'person authorised for the purposes' does not include a trading standards officer, a trading standards enforcement officer, nor a local authority.

FINES

4.248 A standard scale of fines for summary offences is contained in the Criminal Justice Act 1982, s 37(2) (as amended) for England and Wales, the Criminal Procedure (Scotland) Act 1995, s 225 for Scotland and in the Fines and Penalties (Northern Ireland) Order 1984[1], art 5 for Northern Ireland.

[1]   SI 1984/703.

4.249 The Legal Aid, Sentencing and Punishment of Offenders Act 2012, s 85(1) ('LASPO 2012'), which applies to England and Wales, provides that a relevant offence which is punishable on summary conviction by a fine or maximum fine of £5,000 or more (however expressed) becomes punishable on summary conviction by a fine of any amount. An offence is relevant if, immediately before the commencement of the LASPO 2012, s 85(1), it was a common law offence or it is contained in an Act or an instrument made under an Act (whether or not the offence is in force at that time). Therefore an offence where the penalty is expressed as eg 'a fine not exceeding level 5 on the standard scale' or 'a fine not exceeding the statutory maximum' is now punishable on summary conviction by a fine of any amount. This provision came into force on 12 March 2015[1] for offences committed on or after that date[2].

[1]   Legal Aid, Sentencing and Punishment of Offenders Act 2012 (Commencement No 11) Order 2015, SI 2015/504 brought LASPO 2012, s 85(1), (2) and (4) into force.
[2]   LASPO 2012, s 85(4)(a).

4.250 The Legal Aid, Sentencing and Punishment of Offenders Act 2012 (Fines on Summary Conviction) Regulations 2015[1], which also came into force on 12 March 2015, make provision in relation to fines and maximum fines which may be imposed on summary conviction, for the purpose of implementing LASPO 2012, s 85. In particular, Pts 1 and 2 of Sch 4 to the LASPO 2012 contain amendments to legislation where the penalty for an offence, punishable on summary conviction, is expressed as a fine or maximum fine in a numerical amount of £5,000 or more. Examples include the Video Recordings Act 1984, ss 9 and 10 and the Animal Welfare Act 2006, s 32 where, in each instance, 'a fine' is substituted for 'a fine not exceeding £20,000'.

[1]   SI 2015/664.

POST-CONVICTION AND ANCILLARY ORDERS

4.251 This section is not relevant to procedures in Scotland.

4.252 The Code for Crown Prosecutors (October 2018)[1], in relation to the selection of charges, states that prosecutors should select charges, *inter alia*, which give the court adequate powers to sentence and impose appropriate post-conviction orders.

1   https://www.cps.gov.uk/publication/code-crown-prosecutors.

4.253 Essentially the types of order that will be relevant to trading standards cases fall into four areas:

- financial matters – such as compensation, confiscation, costs;
- property – such as deprivation, forfeiture;
- relating to the offender – such as anti-social behaviour orders, driving bans and company director disqualifications;
- relating to premises – such as a premises closure order.

Financial orders

4.254 The Proceeds of Crime Act 2002, ss 13 and 97 (Scotland) ('POCA 2002') require the court to have regard to a confiscation order before deciding whether to impose a fine or other order involving payment by a defendant (such as costs) *except* for a compensation order.

Compensation

4.255 The Powers of Criminal Courts (Sentencing) Act 2000, ss 130–134 ('PCC(S)A 2000') provide for a court to make a compensation order, requiring the convicted person to pay compensation for any personal injury, loss or damage resulting from the offence that the person was convicted for, or any other offence which is taken into consideration by the court in determining sentence, instead of or in addition to dealing with him in any other way. An order should only be made where 'the sum claimed by way of compensation is either agreed or proved'.

4.256 The Legal Aid, Sentencing and Punishment of Offenders Act 2012 imposes an express duty to consider making compensation orders where victims have suffered harm or loss.

4.257 The Magistrates' Courts Act 1980, s 40(1) prescribes the maximum amount that a magistrates' court can order. The Crime and Courts Act 2013 amends the PCC(S)A 2000, s 131 to provide that the previous £5,000 limit will only apply in the case of a compensation order imposed on an offender under the age of 18. The effect of the amendment is that there is no limit on the value of a single compensation order handed down to an adult offender by a magistrates' court. This applies to offences committed on or after 11 December 2013.

4.258 The Crown Court has an unlimited power to fine, but should have regard to the means of the offender. The court may make an order whether or not the prosecution apply for it but must give its reasons if it does not do so if an application is made.

4.259 In Scotland the Criminal Procedure (Scotland) Act 1995, ss 249–253 provide for the granting of compensation orders, how they will be determined and enforced. In summary proceedings the Sheriff may make an order up to the prescribed sum and in solemn proceedings the level of compensation is unlimited.

4.260 In *R v Patrick Connors*[1] the defendant pleaded guilty to two offences – one of aggressive commercial practice contrary to CPUTR 2008, reg 11 and the second of fraud. The two offences concerned different householders. He was ordered to pay compensation orders of £16,400 and £1,000. He appealed against the compensation order in respect of the first offence only – contending that it should be £6,500. Mitting J:

'As we have stated in our analysis of the transactions, the complainant got paving which had to be taken up, re-decoration which had to be re-done and had paid for a drain that was neither necessary nor installed. The total damage to him therefore was not the £16,400 in respect of which the compensation order was made, but £19,000. A compensation order in that sum could well have been made.'

The appeal was dismissed.

1   [2012] EWCA Crim 2106.

Confiscation

4.261 Many of the offences enforced by trading standards departments are committed with the purpose of financial gain. Where an offender has benefitted from criminal activity, the Proceeds of Crime Act 2002 ('POCA 2002') may be applicable. POCA 2002 (and the provisions of its predecessors the Criminal Justice Act 1988 and the Drug Trafficking Act 1994) has been the source of much appellate argument in the Court of Appeal, House of Lords and latterly the Supreme Court. This has interpreted significantly the provisions of the Act and the way applications should be brought. This part of the chapter serves as an overview of the basic confiscation provisions following conviction with particular regard to the issues faced by trading standards authorities.

4.262 Practitioners should consider recovering the proceeds of criminal activity from the outset of an investigation, in particular to preserve those assets and prevent the dissipation before a conviction has been obtained and an order for confiscation has been obtained. Application for the recovery of proceeds of crime can be made under POCA 2002, s 6 and applies to criminal activity taking place after 24 March 2003[1]. In *R v Boughton-Fox* the Court of Appeal quashed a confiscation order under POCA 2002 for an indictment alleging offending between 1 March 2003 and 1 June 2008[2]. See also *R v McCool*[3] (a Northern Ireland case following similarly termed transitional provisions) where the Supreme Court determined, for an indictment that included offences committed both before and after 24 March 2003, that the transitional provisions did not prevent the application of POCA to those offences post-dating 24 March 2003.

1   Proceeds of Crime Act 2002 (Commencement No 5, Transitional Provisions, Savings and Amendment) Order 2003, SI 2003/333. For offences prior to this date the provisions of the Criminal Justice Act 1988 are likely to apply but readers should consider specialist texts on the subject.

²   *R v Boughton-Fox* [2014] EWCA Crim 227. However, there was no obstacle 'in principle' why it should not be replaced by an order under the predecessor to POCA 2002, the Criminal Justice Act 1988.
³   [2018] UKSC 23, [2018] 1 WLR 2431, [2018] Crim LR 766.

Production orders

4.263 Information held by banks or other financial institutions will generally not be provided to investigators other than by order of the Court. The POCA 2002, s 345 (production orders) sets out the procedure for investigators to obtain information held by third parties generally. A production order is an order made by a judge of the Crown Court, requiring a person specified in the order to deliver up documents to an appropriate officer to take away or to permit that officer to have access to the material. In a trading standards context, production orders are likely to be obtained where there is either a confiscation investigation or a money laundering investigation¹. A confiscation investigation is an investigation into (a) whether a person has benefitted from his criminal conduct or (b) into the extent or whereabouts of his benefit from criminal conduct or (c) the available amount in respect of the person or the extent or whereabouts of realisable property available for satisfying a confiscation order made in respect of him.

¹   A money laundering investigation is an investigation into whether a money laundering offence has been committed.

4.264 Application is made to the Crown Court by an 'appropriate officer' (defined under the Act as including accredited financial investigators)¹. The application must state that a person specified in the application is subject to a confiscation investigation or a money laundering investigation². The application must also state:

(a)   that the order is sought for the purposes of the investigation;
(b)   the order is sought in relation to material, or material of a description, specified in the application;
(c)   a person specified in the application appears to be in possession or control of the material.

¹   Proceeds of Crime Act 2002, s 378.
²   Note Proceeds of Crime Act 2002, s 345 has been expanded to include civil recovery investigations, detained cash investigations and exploitation proceeds investigations.

4.265 The application would normally give 7 days for the production of documents but the court has power to shorten this¹. The court should only depart from the 7-day period where there are good evidential grounds for doing so².

¹   Proceeds of Crime Act 2002, s 345(5).
²   *R (on the application of Chatwani) v National Crime Agency* [2015] EWHC 1284 (Admin).

4.266 The requirements for making a production order are detailed in the POCA 2002, s 346.

(2)   There must be reasonable grounds for suspecting that—
     (a)   in the case of a confiscation investigation, the person the application for the order specifies as being subject to the investigation has benefited from his criminal conduct;
      . . .

(c) in the case of a money laundering investigation, the person the application for the order specifies as being subject to the investigation has committed a money laundering offence;

. . .

(3) There must be reasonable grounds for believing that the person the application specifies as appearing to be in possession or control of the material so specified is in possession or control of it.

(4) There must be reasonable grounds for believing that the material is likely to be of substantial value (whether or not by itself) to the investigation for the purposes of which the order is sought.

(5) There must be reasonable grounds for believing that it is in the public interest for the material to be produced or for access to it to be given, having regard to—

(a) the benefit likely to accrue to the investigation if the material is obtained;

(b) the circumstances under which the person the application specifies as appearing to be in possession or control of the material holds it.

4.267 Where relevant material is held on a computer, then the order should be read as producing the material in a visible and legible form which the officer can take away[1]. Orders can be made in relation to material held by government departments[2]. The order cannot compel the production of material which is subject to legal privilege[3].

[1] POCA 2002, s 349.
[2] POCA 2002, s 350.
[3] POCA 2002, s 348.

Restraint orders

4.268 In certain cases it is necessary to apply to the court to prevent a suspect from hiding or dissipating assets to avoid them being the subject of an order under Pt 2 of POCA 2002. The power to restrain assets is found under POCA 2002, ss 40 and 41, which are subject to the legislative steer provided in POCA 2002, s 69(2), stating that the powers:

(a) must be exercised with a view to the value for the time being of realisable property being made available (by the property's realisation) for satisfying any confiscation order that has been or may be made against the defendant;

(b) must be exercised, in a case where a confiscation order has not been made, with a view to securing that there is no diminution in the value of realisable property;

. . .

4.269 By POCA 2002, s 40(1), the Crown Court may exercise the powers conferred by POCA 2002, s 41 if any of one of five conditions is satisfied. In the context of this work, the first two conditions are germane:

(2) The first condition is that—

(a) a criminal investigation has been started in England and Wales with regard to an offence, and

(b) there are reasonable grounds to suspect[1] that the alleged offender has benefited from his criminal conduct.

(3) The second condition is that—

(a) proceedings for an offence have been started in England and Wales and not concluded, and

> (b)   there is reasonable cause to believe that the defendant has benefited
> from his criminal conduct.
>
> . . .
>
> (7)   The second condition is not satisfied if the court believes that—
> (a)   there has been undue delay in continuing the proceedings, or
> (b)   the prosecutor does not intend to proceed.

[1]   Note this provision is amended as from 1 June 2015 by virtue of the Serious Crime Act 2015,
s 11, which replaced reasonable to cause to believe with suspicion.

4.270 Where the conditions are satisfied the court may make an order (a
restraint order) under POCA 2002, s 41 prohibiting any specified person from
dealing with any realisable property held by him[1]. A restraint order may
provide that it applies to all realisable property held by the specified person
whether or not the property is described in the order and may provide that it
applies to realisable property transferred to the specified person after the
order is made[2].

[1]   POCA 2002, s 41(1).
[2]   POCA 2002, s 41(2).

4.271 A restraint order may make provision for reasonable living expenses and
legal expenses and make provision for the purpose of enabling any person to
carry on any trade, business, profession or occupation.

4.272 Aside from the statutory provisions, the Prosecutor must consider that
there is a real risk of dissipation of assets before the making of the order. In
Jennings v Crown Prosecution Service[1] Longmore LJ observed[2]:

> 'Fear of dissipation of assets is the reason for seeking a restraint order. Such fear must,
> in fact, exist before an order should be applied for. But in a case where dishonesty is
> charged, there will usually be reason to fear that assets will be dissipated. I do not
> therefore consider it necessary for the prosecutor to state in terms that he fears assets
> will be dissipated merely because he or she thinks there is a good arguable case of
> dishonesty. As my Lord has said, the risk of dissipation will generally speak for itself.
> Nevertheless prosecutors must be alive to the possibility that there may be no risk in
> fact. If no asset dissipation has occurred over a long period, particularly after a
> defendant has been charged, the prosecutor should explain why asset dissipation is
> now feared at the date of application for the order when it was not feared before.'

[1]   [2006] 1 WLR 182.
[2]   At para 61.

4.273 In making applications prosecutors have a duty of full and frank
disclosure. In *Jennings v CPS*, Laws LJ stated:

> 'Thus the court has imposed a duty on the shoulders of the Crown to make disclosure
> of material facts, if it seeks a restraint order without notice, just as a claimant in a
> private civil suit must do if he seeks a freezing order without notice.'

4.274 In *Ashford & Ors v Southampton City Council*[1] the court observed the
importance of providing sufficient court time to consider applications for
restraint orders. Moreover the Court of Appeal approved the comments of
Hooper LJ in *R v Windsor*[2]:

> 'Without being too prescriptive, it is vital that the judge is given material on which he
> can reach the conclusion himself that there is reasonable cause.'

[1]   [2014] EWCA Crim 1244.

² [2011] EWCA Crim 143.

4.275 In *Ashford* the court concluded that the judge was being asked to accept that the investigators had concluded that there was reasonable cause (under POCA 2002, s 40(2)), rather than being presented with evidence sufficient to reach his own conclusion to that effect[1]. It should be borne in mind that when having regard to case law on restraint orders, that the older cases will be based on the first condition as being a 'reasonable cause to believe' and not the 'reasonable grounds to suspect' which is the standard as from 1 June 2015.

¹ At para 31.

Confiscation following conviction

4.276 The criminal confiscation provisions for England and Wales fall under Pt 2 of POCA 2002. The court must proceed[1] under POCA 2002, s 6 where there has been a conviction (or the defendant has been sent to the Crown Court for confiscation[2] and asked the court to proceed under POCA 2002, s 6) or the Court believes that it is appropriate to do so). The steps that the court has to take under POCA 2002, s 6 are as follows[3]:

> (4)   The court must proceed as follows—
>   (a)   it must decide whether the defendant has a criminal lifestyle;
>   (b)   if it decides that he has a criminal lifestyle it must decide whether he has benefited from his general criminal conduct;
>   (c)   if it decides that he does not have a criminal lifestyle it must decide whether he has benefited from his particular criminal conduct.
> (5)   If the court decides under subsection (4)(b) or (c) that the defendant has benefited from the conduct referred to it must—
>   (a)   decide the recoverable amount, and
>   (b)   make an order (a confiscation order) requiring him to pay that amount.
> Paragraph (b) applies only if, or to the extent that, it would not be disproportionate to require the defendant to pay the recoverable amount.

¹ POCA 2002, s 14: The court may postpone determination under Proceeds of Crime Act 2002, s 6 but still proceed to sentence the defendant.
² POCA 2002, s 70, a defendant convicted by a magistrates' court can be committed to the Crown Court for proceedings under Pt 2 of POCA 2002.
³ POCA 2002, s 6(4).

4.277 The reference to 'criminal lifestyle' imports extended benefit provisions: looking at offending beyond the predicate offences. Criminal lifestyle is defined in POCA 2002, s 75.

> (2)   The condition is that the offence (or any of the offences) concerned satisfies any of these tests—
>   (a)   it is specified in Schedule 2[1];
>   (b)   it constitutes conduct forming part of a course of criminal activity[2];
>   (c)   it is an offence committed over a period of at least six months and the defendant has benefited from the conduct which constitutes the offence.

¹ These include intellectual property and money laundering offences.
² Conduct forms part of a course of criminal activity if the defendant has benefited from the conduct and: (a) in the proceedings in which he was convicted he was convicted of three or more other offences, each of three or more of them constituting conduct from which he has benefited,

or (b) in the period of 6 years ending with the day when those proceedings were started (or, if there is more than one such day, the earliest day) he was convicted on at least two separate occasions of an offence constituting conduct from which he has benefited.

4.278 The defendant having a criminal lifestyle is the trigger for the court to be able to look at the defendant's general criminal conduct[1] and it mandates the court to make the following assumptions[2]:

(1) that any property transferred to him after the relevant day[3] was obtained by him as a result of his general criminal conduct and at the earliest time he appears to have held it;

(2) that any property held by him at any time after the date of conviction was obtained by him through his general criminal conduct and at the earliest time he appears to have held it;

(3) that any expenditure incurred by the defendant at any time after the relevant day was met from property obtained by him as a result of his general criminal conduct;

(4) that for the purpose of valuing any property obtained by the defendant he obtained it free of any interests in it.

[1] POCA 2002, s 76(2).
[2] POCA 2002, s 10.
[3] POCA 2002, s 10(8) the relevant day is the first day of the period of 6 years ending with the day that proceedings for the offences concerned were started against him, or where there are two or more proceedings started on different days the earlier of those days.

4.279 The court must not make the required assumption in relation to particular property or expenditure, if the assumption is either shown to be incorrect or there would be a serious risk of injustice if the assumption were made[1]. If the defendant is not regarded as having a criminal lifestyle then the court will consider the benefit obtained from his particular criminal conduct[2] which in broad terms is the conduct which constituted the offences of which he was convicted. A person is deemed to benefit from conduct if he obtains property as a result of or in connection with the criminal conduct[3]. If a person benefits from conduct his benefit is the value of the property obtained[4].

[1] POCA 2002, s 10(6).
[2] POCA 2002, s 76(3).
[3] POCA 2002, s 76(4).
[4] POCA 2002, s 76(7).

4.280 The operation of these provisions has given rise to a considerable body of case law. In *R v May*[1] the House of Lords outlined the principles to be followed (per Lord Bingham):

'(1) The legislation is intended to deprive defendants of the benefit they have gained from relevant criminal conduct, whether or not they have retained such benefit, within the limits of their available means. It does not provide for confiscation in the sense understood by schoolchildren and others, but nor does it operate by way of fine. The benefit gained is the total value of the property or advantage obtained, not the defendant's net profit after deduction of expenses or any amounts payable to co-conspirators.

(2) The court should proceed by asking the three questions posed above: (i) Has the defendant (D) benefited from relevant criminal conduct? (ii) If so, what is the value of the benefit D has so obtained? (iii) What sum is recoverable from

      D? Where issues of criminal life style arise the questions must be modified. These are separate questions calling for separate answers, and the questions and answers must not be elided.

(3)   In addressing these questions the court must first establish the facts as best it can on the material available, relying as appropriate on the statutory assumptions. In very many cases the factual findings made will be decisive.

(4)   In addressing the questions the court should focus very closely on the language of the statutory provision in question in the context of the statute and in the light of any statutory definition. The language used is not arcane or obscure and any judicial gloss or exegesis should be viewed with caution. Guidance should ordinarily be sought in the statutory language rather than in the proliferating case law.

(5)   In determining, under the 2002 Act, whether D has obtained property or a pecuniary advantage and, if so, the value of any property or advantage so obtained, the court should (subject to any relevant statutory definition) apply ordinary common law principles to the facts as found. The exercise of this jurisdiction involves no departure from familiar rules governing entitlement and ownership. While the answering of the third question calls for inquiry into the financial resources of D at the date of the determination, the answering of the first two questions plainly calls for a historical inquiry into past transactions.

(6)   D ordinarily obtains property if in law he owns it, whether alone or jointly, which will ordinarily connote a power of disposition or control, as where a person directs a payment or conveyance of property to someone else. He ordinarily obtains a pecuniary advantage if (among other things) he evades a liability to which he is personally subject. Mere couriers or custodians or other very minor contributors to an offence, rewarded by a specific fee and having no interest in the property or the proceeds of sale, are unlikely to be found to have obtained that property. It may be otherwise with money launderers.'

[1]   [2008] UKHL 28.

Determining benefit in regulatory cases

4.281 In *Sumal and Sons (Properties) Limited v London Borough of Newham*, Davis LJ observed[1]:

'Whether what may be styled a regulatory offence can, when committed, give rise to the availability of a confiscation order will depend on the terms of the statute or regulations creating the offence, read with the terms of the 2002 Act and set in the context of the facts of the case.'

[1]   [2012] EWCA Crim 1840, para 30.

4.282 This was considered further in *R v McDowell and Singh*[1] appeals were made against confiscation orders in what had been referred to as 'regulatory offences'. Pitchford LJ remarked:

'It is not sufficient to treat "regulatory" offences as creating a single category of offence to which POCA is uniformly applied . . . the question whether benefit has been obtained from criminal conduct must first depend upon an analysis of the terms of the statute that creates the offence and, by that means, upon an identification of the criminal conduct admitted or proved. It may be that . . . the wider statutory context of the offence will assist to answer the critical question: what is the conduct made criminal by the statute – is it the activity itself or is it the failure to register, or obtain a licence for, the activity? In our judgment, there is a narrow but critical distinction to be made between an offence that prohibits and makes criminal the very activity admitted by the offender or proved against him (as in *del Basso*[2]) and an offence comprised in the failure to obtain a licence to carry out an activity otherwise lawful (as in *Sumal*[3]).'

[1]   [2015] EWCA Crim 173.
[2]   *R v del Basso* [2010] EWCA Crim 1119, [2011] 1 Cr App R (S) 41.
[3]   *Sumal and Sons (Properties) Limited v London Borough of Newham* [2012] EWCA Crim 1840, [2013] 1 WLR 2078.

4.283 McDowell was an arms trader. He flouted prohibitions on trading in arms under the Trade in Goods (Control) Order 2003[1]. The wording of the order prohibited various acts done in pursuance of trade in arms. The order creates an exception from those prohibitions by the permission to act with a licence. In the absence of the licence the trading is unlawful and *McDowell* was found to have benefited from his criminal conduct and could be the subject of an order under POCA 2002. Singh was a scrap metal dealer, who had failed to register his scrap metal dealing activity as required under the Scrap Metal Dealers Act 1964. The court found the failure to register was criminal activity but that the trading carried out was otherwise lawful and so should not be subject to the confiscation provisions of POCA 2002. It is submitted that the distinction in such cases is a fine one and will require close analysis of the legislation creating the offence.

[1]   SI 2003/2765.

4.284 In *R v Palmer*[1] the defendant had been convicted of engaging in licensable activity otherwise than in accord with a licence contrary to the Private Security Industry Act 2001, s 3 ('PSIA 2001'). The Crown appealed the decision of the Crown Court judge not to make a confiscation order. Paying close analysis to the terms of the statute and considering the judgment in *McDowell and Singh*, the court considered that the PSIA 2001, s 3 created and defined a prohibited act and criminalised the activity of engagement in licensable conduct, not simply failing to obtain a licence.

[1]   [2016] EWCA 1049.

4.285 See also *R v Moss*[1] where a confiscation order imposed following pleas of guilty to record keeping offences under the Cattle Identification Regulations 2007[2] and the Animal By-Products Regulations 2005[3] was quashed.

[1]   [2015] EWCA Crim 713.
[2]   SI 2007/529.
[3]   SI 2005/2347.

Establishing the value of the benefit obtained

4.286 In many cases the value of the benefit obtained by the defendant from criminal conduct is readily ascertainable from the property obtained or pecuniary advantage that has been gained. Particular issues arise when determining benefit in the context of a business. In *R v Waya*[1] the Supreme Court acknowledged in its majority opinion that a legitimate, and proportionate confiscation order may, inter alia, have the effect of requiring a defendant to pay the whole of a sum which he has obtained by crime without enabling to set off expenses of the crime[2]:

> 'These propositions are not difficult to understand. To embark upon an accounting exercise in which the defendant is entitled to set off the cost of committing his crime

would be to treat his criminal enterprise as if it were a legitimate business and confiscation a form of business taxation. To treat (for example) a bribe paid to an official to look the other way, whether at home or abroad, as reducing the proceeds of crime would be offensive, as well as frequently impossible of accurate determination. To attempt to inquire into the financial dealings of criminals as between themselves would usually be equally impracticable and would lay the process of confiscation wide open to simple avoidance. Although these propositions involve the possibility of removing from the defendant by way of confiscation order a sum larger than may in fact represent his net proceeds of crime, they are consistent with the statute's objective and represent proportionate means of achieving it.'

1   [2013] 1 AC 294.
2   At para 26.

4.287 In *R v Beazley*, the court had gone on to consider the decision in *Waya*, explaining that 'a business which is founded entirely on the infringement of other people's property rights, and is a criminal offence, will inevitably attract the consequence of confiscation of the proceeds' and 'it will certainly remove their gross takings from [the] business'[1]. The court confirmed the approach in *Waya* stating:

'There is nothing remotely disproportionate about removing from this unlawful business the proceeds which it has generated. It is not in any way analogous to the kind of double recovery situation contemplated explicitly in *Waya*. The judgment in *Waya* specifically endorses the longstanding approval to the difference for confiscation purposes between gross proceeds on the one hand, which are the measure of benefit, and profit on the other, which is not. That is explicit in paragraph 26. There may be some other special cases in which a confiscation order can properly be described as disproportionate, but the fact that it is based on gross proceeds of crime is not one of them. Nor is there anything in this case which could possibly justify the description "disproportionate", whether under *Waya* or otherwise.'

1   [2013] EWCA Crim 567 at para 17.

4.288 In *R v Bajaj (Arun)*[1], the prosecution had sought to prove that the defendant had received a pecuniary advantage in circumstances where he had admitted offences breaches regulations relating to the overcrowding of a dwelling. Instead of seeking a confiscation order on the basis of the extra rental income that had been generated by the overcrowding of the property, the prosecuting local authority sought to establish a pecuniary advantage on the basis of the money saved by the defendant by not providing proper accommodation for his tenants. In delivering judgment, the Court of Appeal criticised that approach, stating that:

'we do not think it a sustainable proposition that the (notional) costs of providing appropriate, regulation compliant, alternative accommodation for the 12 occupants is to be treated as a saving constituting a pecuniary advantage within the reach of s 76 of the 2002 Act. It is far too broad, indeed speculative, an approach to have sufficient connection with the conduct alleged[2].'

1   [2020] EWCA Crim 1111.
2   Per Davis LJ.

4.289 The defence in *Bajaj* also challenged the confiscation order on the basis that the charges had been particularised for the criminality taking place on a single day. The Court of Appeal, applying the rationale of the decision in *R v Panayi*[1], observed:

187

'The benefit obtained as a result of or in connection with such conduct must be referable to the offence with which the defendant is charged and of which he is convicted. It is not open to a court in confiscation proceedings to find that benefits obtained over an extended period were obtained in connection with the commission of an offence on a single day.'

1 [2019] EWCA 413, [2019] 2 Cr App R (S) 21. In that case, offences in breach of enforcement notices contrary to s 179 of the Town and Country Planning Act 1990 were only charged in relation to a single day, whilst the prosecution argued that a much longer period should apply.

4.290 In *R v Scott King*[1] the defendant who was a used car salesman was convicted of various offences under the CPUTR 2008. He had been selling cars purporting to be a private seller to avoid providing a warranty. The defendant appealed the making of a confiscation order based on gross turnover valued at £109,970 which did not therefore take account of the purchase cost of the vehicles that he had sold, which had rendered him a profit of just £11,140. Having considered the previous authorities, Fulford LJ observed[2]:

'The authorities reveal there is a clear distinction to be drawn between cases in which the goods or services are provided by way of a lawful contract (or when payment is properly paid for legitimate services) but the transaction is tainted by associated illegality (eg the overcharging in Shabir or the bribery in Sale), and cases in which the entire undertaking is unlawful (eg a business which is conducted illegally, as in *Beazley*). When making a confiscation order, the court will need to consider, amongst other things, the difference between these two types of cases. It is to be stressed, however, that this divide is not necessarily determinative because cases differ to a great extent, but it is a relevant factor to be taken into account when deciding whether to make an order that reflects the gross takings of the business . . .

If the transaction is inherently unlawful because of the manner in which it is conducted, that finding militates in favour of making an order that is directed at the gross takings of the business.'

1 [2014] 2 Cr App R (S) 2014.
2 At paras 32, 33.

4.291 The court then determined that in the case of *King* the gross turnover approach had been appropriate, observing that the business was one which had been founded on illegality and that the result was severe but not disproportionate[1]. This approach was followed in *R v Rory J Holbrook Limited*[2] involving breaches of the Environmental Protection Act 1990 and other environmental regulations.

1 At paras 33, 34.
2 [2015] EWCA Crim 1908.

4.292 The Supreme Court had cause to consider this point afresh in *R v Harvey*[1] and in particular the inclusion of sums received by way of VAT being included within the overall turnover as part of the defendant's benefit. Affirming the general principle under POCA 2002 that VAT received should be included within the figure for benefit as being property obtained, the Court then turned to consider the issue of proportionality and Art 1 of Protocol 1 of European Convention on Human Rights[2]:

'This court considered A1P1 in *Waya* at paras 28–33, where it was made clear that, where the proceeds of crime are returned to the loser, it would be disproportionate to treat such proceeds as part of the "benefit obtained" by a defendant as it would amount to "a financial penalty" or "an additional punitive sanction", which should not be imposed through the medium of POCA. Lord Hughes is right in para 71 to say that recognition of the disproportionality of treating property restored to the victim as property "obtained" for the purpose of POCA is not directly in point as it does not concern double recovery. However, given that VAT is effectively collected by a taxpayer as explained above, the two situations are quite similar; furthermore, as Lord Mance points out, the policy behind the principle discussed in *Waya*, paras 28–34 is in part that a defendant who makes good a liability to pay or restore should not be worse off than one who does not . . .

For these reasons, we are of the view that, although it would be appropriate under the terms of POCA as traditionally interpreted, it would be disproportionate, at least when VAT output tax has been accounted for to HMRC (either by remittance or by its being set off against input tax), to make a confiscation order calculated on the basis that that tax, or a sum equivalent to it, has been "obtained" by the defendant for the purposes of POCA.'

1   [2016] 2 WLR 37.
2   At paras 34–36.

4.293 This decision, as noted by Lord Toulson, will involve consideration of the accounting for VAT by a defendant and involves, 'just the sort of accountancy exercise against which the courts have taken a firm stand from the outset'. Practitioners and Crown Court judges will have to determine how best to approach the calculation of benefit in the light of the majority reasoning of the Supreme Court in similar cases.

4.294 Care should be taken to pierce the corporate veil only in cases where it is appropriate to do so. In *R v Boyle Transport (Northern Ireland) Limited*[1] Davis LJ noted:

' . . . even where a company mixed up in relevant wrong doing is solely owned and solely controlled by the (criminal) defendant that does not of itself always necessitate a conclusion in a confiscation case that it is an alter ego company, whose turnover and assets are to be equated with being the property of the defendant himself.'

1   [2016] 4 WLR 63.

4.295 The court rejected the treating of a company's turnover as the benefit of the defendant's in the case involving infringement of driver's hours. See also *R v Jacqueline Powell*[1] in a case where the corporate veil was not pierced where environmental offences had been committed.

1   [2016] EWCA Crim 1043.

Determining the recoverable amount

4.296 Once it has been established that the defendant has benefitted from his criminal conduct, the court has to determine what falls to be recovered from the defendant and then order the payment of that amount[1]. Following the decision in *R v Waya*, the payment of the recoverable amount 'applies only if, or to the extent that, it would not be disproportionate to require the defendant to pay the recoverable amount'[2]. This has now been given statutory force with the amendment to Serious Crime Act 2015, s 6(5).

1   POCA 2002, s 6(5).
2   Amended by Serious Crime Act 2015, Sch 4, para 19.

4.297 The issue of disproportionality was considered in *R v Jon Andrewes*[1], where a confiscation order had been imposed on a Defendant who had admitted to offences of obtaining a pecuniary advantage by deception and fraud by false representation, following his providing false qualifications on three job applications. The confiscation order had been based on a benefit figure established as being the amount of his earnings over the course of the three jobs less statutory deductions for tax and national insurance. There was no dispute that he had performed his duties competently and it was argued on appeal that he had already given full value for his employment, such that it was disproportionate to make the order.

[1] [2020] EWCA Crim 1055.

4.298 The Court of Appeal reviewed all the authorities on the issue of disproportionality and observed[1] that s 6(5) does not re-introduce a level of judicial discretion as to the making of an order, nor is it a matter of balancing factors and competing interests as may occur in a public or family law context[2]. Further, the disproportionality cannot be assessed by reference to the proportion that the available amount bears to the benefit, for this runs contrary to the scheme and purpose of the 2002 Act. According to Davis LJ[3], in assessing disproportionality judges should consider 'whether or the extent to which a confiscation order should be made, ask themselves if such an order is disproportionate to the achievement of the statutory objective of depriving criminals of the proceeds of their criminality'. On the facts of the case, the appellant was found to have given full value for his employment which (notwithstanding his dishonesty) was otherwise lawful and as such the Court found the confiscation order to be disproportionate.

[1] Per Davis LJ at para 79.
[2] *Morrison* [2019] EWCA Crim 351, [2019] 2 Cr App R (S) 25 cited here.
[3] At para 81.

Costs

4.299 Under the Prosecution of Offences Act 1985, s 18 ('POA 1985') – which does not apply to Scotland – where a person is convicted of an offence before a Crown Court or magistrates' court, the court may make such order as to the costs to be paid by the accused to the prosecutor as it considers just and reasonable.

4.300 A local authority is unable to recover its costs in criminal proceedings from central funds (see POA 1985, s 16). The *Practice Direction on Costs in Criminal Proceedings* provides[1]:

'2.6.1 There is no power to order the payment of costs out of Central Funds of any prosecutor who is a public authority, a person acting on behalf of a public authority, or acting as an official appointed by a public authority as defined in the Act.'

[1] Practice Direction (Costs in Criminal Proceedings) 2015 [2015] EWCA Crim 1568 consolidated with Amendment No 1 [2016] EWCA Crim 98.

4.301 Changes to costs that can be obtained from central funds by defendants, including preventing a corporate defendant from obtaining costs from central funds for proceedings commenced after 12 October 2012, may mean that there will be increased costs applications against local authorities in the event of acquittals.

Post-conviction orders relating to property

DEPRIVATION

4.302 The following provision does not apply in Scotland.

4.303 The PCC(S)A 2000, s 143 contains the following:

143 Powers to deprive offender of property used etc for purposes of crime

(1) Where a person is convicted of an offence and the court by or before which he is convicted is satisfied that any property which has been lawfully seized from him, or which was in his possession or under his control at the time when he was apprehended for the offence or when a summons in respect of it was issued—

(a) has been used for the purpose of committing, or facilitating the commission of, any offence, or

(b) was intended by him to be used for that purpose,

the court may (subject to subsection (5) below) make an order under this section in respect of that property.

. . .

(5) In considering whether to make an order under this section in respect of any property, a court shall have regard—

(a) to the value of the property; and

(b) to the likely financial and other effects on the offender of the making of the order (taken together with any other order that the court contemplates making).

FORFEITURE

4.304 Specific provisions exist under trade mark, copyright, video recordings and weights and measures legislation for the forfeiture of items and reference should be made to those sections of this book for details of the relevant provisions.

Post-conviction orders relating to the offender

4.305 In Scotland there are different provisions and applications would be a matter for the Procurators Fiscal/Crown Office.

CRIMINAL BEHAVIOUR ORDERS

4.306 Criminal behaviour orders ('CBO') are made under the Anti-social Behaviour, Crime and Policing Act 2014 and replace, in effect, anti-social behaviour orders ('ASBO'), which were made under the Crime and Disorder Act 1998[1]. A CBO can only be made on the application of the prosecutor following conviction of an offence. The court may make a CBO against the offender if two conditions are met: (i) the court must be satisfied, beyond reasonable doubt, that the offender has engaged in behaviour that caused or was likely to cause harassment, alarm or distress to any person and (ii) the court considers that making the order will help in preventing the offender from engaging in such behaviour. Various provisions of the Anti-social Behaviour, Crime and Policing Act 2014 were brought into force on 20 October 2014 including those relating to CBOs. The Home Office has issued relevant guidance: *Anti-social Behaviour, Crime and Policing Act 2014: Reform of anti-social behaviour powers. Statutory guidance for frontline professionals.*

1   In Scotland the Anti-social Behaviour etc (Scotland) Act 2004.

DISQUALIFICATION FROM DRIVING

4.307 A court by or before which a person is convicted of an offence may, instead of or in addition to dealing with him in any other way, order him to be disqualified, for such period as it thinks fit, for holding or obtaining a driving licence (PCC(S)A 2000, s 146).

4.308 Although the power to disqualify an offender from driving is not limited to any particular offence and it was not necessary that the conviction should be connected in any way with the use of a motor vehicle, the court cannot impose a period of disqualification arbitrarily and there must be a sufficient reason for the disqualification – *R v Cliff*[1].

1   [2004] EWCA Crim 3139.

4.309 In *R v Taylor*[1] the defendant was sentenced to 18 months' imprisonment in respect of offences involving counterfeit CDs, DVDs and MP3 discs. He was also disqualified from driving for 18 months under the PCC(S)A 2000, s 146. The Court of Appeal did not think it appropriate to interfere with the sentence of imprisonment but were ' . . . more troubled by the order for disqualification from driving. Since the appellant was in the habit of travelling to car boot fairs to sell these goods we can understand why the judge took that step, but the effect of the order will be to prevent him from driving for a period of 9 months after his release from prison and that will seriously interfere with his ability to earn his living and rehabilitate himself. In our view an order for disqualification was inappropriate in this case'.

1   [2006] EWCA Crim 2503.

COMPANY DIRECTOR DISQUALIFICATION

4.310 Under the Company Directors Disqualification Act 1986 ('CDDA 1986') the court may make a disqualification order against a person where he is convicted of an indictable offence (whether on indictment or summarily) in connection with the promotion, formation, *management*, liquidation or striking off of a company, or with the receivership of a company's property or with his being an administrative receiver of a company. The maximum period of disqualification is 15 years in the Crown Court and 5 years when imposed in the magistrates' courts. Part 4 of the Deregulation Act 2015 – Disqualification of unfit directors of insolvent companies – amends CDDA 1986, amongst other matters, to enable the Secretary of State or the official receiver to request information relevant to a person's conduct as a director of a company that has been insolvent directly from any person, including from officers of the company themselves.

4.311 As amended by the Insolvency Act 2000, the CDDA 1986 gives the Secretary of State power to accept an undertaking from any person that, for a specified period, that person must not:

(a) without the leave of the court, be a director of a company, act as a receiver of a company's property or in any way take part in the promotion, formation or management of a company; and

(b) act as an insolvency practitioner.

4.312 In *R v Rafi Asghar Sheikh and Sami Asghar Sheikh*[1] the defendants were convicted of intellectual property crimes and sentenced to 6 years' imprisonment. In each case the judge made a disqualification order under CDDA 1986 for a period of 10 years. (The brothers were tried alongside their father, Khalid Asghar Sheikh, who was convicted of conspiracy to acquire criminal property and sentenced to 4 years' imprisonment, was also disqualified for a period of 10 years.) The defendants appealed (only) against the disqualification order. Treacy J stated:

'Given all the circumstances, we are not persuaded that the judge fell into error . . . The term of disqualification imposed was severe but, in our judgment, deservedly so.'

1   [2010] EWCA Crim 921.

Chapter 5

CIVIL ENFORCEMENT

Contents

INTRODUCTION

5.1 The main alternative to criminal law enforcement of consumer legislation is Pt 8 of the Enterprise Act 2002 ('EnA 2002'). This enables certain listed enforcers to bring about the cessation of infringements going forward, and now, with the introduction of Enhanced Consumer Measures[1], also to obtain redress for consumers. It also gives the CMA express powers to seek an order to remove online content[2]. The essential function of enforcers under Pt 8 is to bring about the swift cessation of infringements, as well as to prevent their recurrence[3]. In order to achieve this, they have powers to investigate potential infringements (using the powers in the CRA 2015, Sch 5), obtain court orders, accept undertakings, issue publicity, and to take other steps to hinder infringements from occurring[4].

[1] In November 2012 the then Department for Business, Innovation and Skills ('BIS') published a consultation paper on extending the range of remedies available to courts when public enforcers apply to them for enforcement orders under Pt 8 EnA 2002. Part 3 of the Consumer Rights Act 2015 ('CRA 2015') introduced these new powers for public enforcers to seek:

(i)   Redress for consumers who have been disadvantaged by breaches of consumer law.

(ii)   Remedies from traders who have breached consumer law to improve their compliance and reduce the likelihood of future breaches.

(iii)   Remedies to give consumers more information so they can exercise greater choice and help improve the functioning of the market for consumers and other businesses.

2   The Consumer Protection (Enforcement) (Amendment etc.) Regulations 2020, SI 2020/484 introduced this power, as well as making various other amendments to Part 8.

3   And in the case of Community (or Schedule 13) infringements, to prevent their likely occurrence too. From 1 January 2021, erstwhile Community infringements will be referred to as 'Schedule 13 infringements' (see The Consumer Protection (Enforcement) (Amendment etc) (EU Exit) Regulations 2019, SI 2019/203). However where the infringing conduct took place before the end of the Implementation Period for exiting the EU, the law should be enforced as it was and so for some time yet it is likely that enforcers will need to grapple with both regimes, and plead their cases setting out why conduct was a Community infringement, and is now a Schedule 13 infringement.

4   For example the CMA, under its power of direction in EnA 2002, s 216 can direct that no court action may be taken by a trading standards department, but this does not prevent the CMA from taking 'such other steps it thinks appropriate (apart from making an application [to court]) for the purpose of securing that the infringement is not committed, continued or repeated' (EnA 2002, s 216(3)).

5.2 Part 8 sets out an enforcement mechanism to be used for a very wide range of laws. Enforcement may be directed not only towards the trader directly responsible for malpractice, but also against accessories, major shareholders and related companies. Usually the enforcer will approach the parties under investigation to ask them to bring about the cessation of the infringement voluntarily, and offer Undertakings as to their future conduct. If satisfactory Undertakings are not offered, the enforcer may apply to the court for an Order to secure compliance with the law. The aim of such an application is to ensure that the trader is directed not to continue or repeat the infringing conduct; not to engage in such conduct in the course of his business or another business; not to consent to or connive in the carrying out of such conduct by a body corporate with which he has a special[1] relationship; and to comply with any Enhanced Consumer Measures the court decides to impose. The usual civil law remedies for breach of an order of the court apply to a breach of an enforcement order, and a successful enforcer is generally entitled to recover the costs of the application from the trader.

1   EnA 2002, s 217.

Origin of Pt 8 of the Enterprise Act 2002

5.3 For many years, consumer protection in the UK was achieved through criminal prosecution, particularly through the use of the Trade Descriptions Act 1968. Later, new pieces of legislation, for example the Fair Trading Act 1973, provided for injunctive type relief, but it was not until the introduction of the Injunctions Directive 98/27/EC that there was a comprehensive approach allowing civil enforcement as a clear alternative to criminal enforcement[1]. Part 8 of the EnA 2002 was brought into force on 20 June 2003. It followed the short lived 'Stop Now' regime, which lasted from June 2001 until June 2003 and which need not now be considered in any detail[2].

¹   Part 8 of the EnA 2002 sought to bring fully into UK law the provisions of Directive 98/27/EC of the European Parliament and of the Council of 19 May 1998 on injunctions for the protection of consumers' interests. The Injunctions Directive was amended and largely re-cast in 2009 as Directive 2009/22/EC. References in this chapter are to the wording used in the 2009 Directive.

²   This was the regime under the Stop Now Orders ('EC Directive') Regulations SI 2001/1422.

5.4 The enforcement regime governed by Pt 8 has been substantially required and shaped by the EU Regulations on Consumer Protection Co-operation and Enforcement ('the CPC Regulation')[1]. Part 8 provided the framework for the UK's part in this mutual assistance network, empowering enforcers proactively to share intelligence of cross border infringements, to obtain evidence on behalf of other EEA enforcers, and to take enforcement action to protect consumers from other EEA states[2]. To this end, Pt 8 enforcers are required to possess a minimum set of investigatory powers[3]. Part 8 has continued to grow in importance with the introduction of the Consumer Protection from Unfair Trading Regulations 2008 ('CPUTR 2008'), which has created a set of substantive requirements that can be enforced under Pt 8, along with many other consumer laws.

¹   Initially Council Regulation 2006/2004 on co-operation between national authorities responsible for the enforcement of consumer protection laws, and since 17 January 2020, Regulation (EU) 2017/2394 on co-operation between national authorities responsible for the enforcement of consumer protection laws and repealing Regulation (EC) No 2006/2004. The CPC Regulation has been revoked in the UK as part of the EU exit process (see reg 3(7) of the Consumer Protection (Enforcement) (Amendment etc) (EU Exit) Regulations 2020). However it is still relevant to the correct interpretation of Pt 8 and the CRA 2015, Sch 5.

²   The CPC network requires each state to designate a Single Liaison Office to manage contacts between states (the Competition and Markets Authority, in the UK), and to designate Competent Authorities to enforce the legislation listed in the annex to the CPC Regulation. Other bodies (such as Trading Standards) have often been asked to discharge the responsibilities of a Competent Authority. The UK will be leaving the CPC network as of 1 January 2021.

³   The minimum set of powers are now provided by the CRA 2015, Sch 5.

5.5 Since many of the concepts used in the provisions of Pt 8 of the EnA 2002 are in large part derived from the Injunctions Directive and the CPC Regulation, they were construed in the light of the wording and purpose of that Directive in accordance with the principles laid down by the European Court of Justice in *Marleasing SA v La Comercial de Alimentación SA*[1]. Going forwards the UK courts will provide authoritative and final interpretation of Pt 8, but it is important to recall when interpreting Pt 8 that it gave effect to EU law, and so the purposes of the underlying EU provisions are likely to remain relevant. Further, any future CJEU rulings on the meaning and scope of the CPC Regulation or Injunctions Directive are capable of being taking into account by UK courts[2].

¹   [1990] ECR I-4153 at paras 7–9 and 14.

²   Section 6(2) of the European Union (Withdrawal) Act 2018.

EU Law

5.6 A number of key propositions can be derived from the recitals and articles of the Injunctions Directive and CPC Regulation, which should still guide interpretation of the UK legislative scheme[1]:

(a) Timely resolution of infringing conduct is essential. Recital 3 to the Injunctions Directive explained that a lead reason for harmonisation of the law was because the systems in many member states did not allow infringements to be terminated 'in good time'.

(b) Consultation should be short. Recital 14 and 15 to the Injunctions Directive permit Member States to offer traders an opportunity to bring about voluntary cessation of infringements, but emphasise that after 2 weeks the enforcer should be able to bring an action to court 'without any further delay'.

(c) The obligation to act only arises where there is harm to consumers generally. The enforcement regime is not aimed at the resolution of individual disputes. This is referred to in the Injunctions Directive, Recital 3 and Art 1 as harm to the collective interests of consumers.

(d) Borders should not inhibit enforcement. Recital 5 to the Injunctions Directive stresses the need to prevent traders from evading enforcement by moving across borders, and Art 4 permits enforcers in one Member State to be able to take action in the courts of another Member State[2].

(e) The scheme was designed with cross border enforcement co-operation in mind. Article 6.1 of the 2017 CPC Regulation requires enforcers within a Member State to collaborate, and the whole Regulation sets out a framework to enhance collaboration in order to enforce compliance with EU consumer protection laws, and ensure the smooth functioning of the internal market and in order to enhance the protection of consumers' economic interests (see Art 1).

(f) Enforcers within the EU should share information on their work and investigations to facilitate co-operation[3].

The investigation and enforcement powers of enforcers need to be robust enough to permit effective enforcement and to deter traders from infringing the law, in particular given the prevalence of e-commerce[4]. This means that the court schedule and costs rules must be workable, and that publicity may be used effectively. Article 2 of the Injunctions Directive requires that enforcers must be able to obtain:

'• an order with all due expediency, where appropriate by way of summary procedure, requiring the cessation or prohibition of any infringement;

• where appropriate, measures such as the publication of the decision, in full or in part, in such form as deemed adequate and/or the publication of a corrective statement with a view to eliminating the continuing effects of the infringement;

• insofar as the legal system of the Member State concerned so permits, an order against the losing defendant for payments into the public purse or to any beneficiary designated in or under national legislation, in the event of failure to comply with the decision within a time-limit specified by the courts or administrative authorities, of a fixed amount for each day's delay or any other amount provided for in national legislation, with a view to ensuring compliance with the decisions.'

---

[1] Article 253 of the Treaty Establishing the European Community is the legislative source of the requirement that the reasons for the adoption of a legal act must be recited within the act: legal acts 'shall state the reasons on which they are based'.

[2] Article 4.1 reads 'Each member state shall take the measures necessary to ensure that, in the event of an infringement originating in that member state, any qualified entity from another member state where the interests protected by that qualified entity are affected by the infringement, may apply to the court or administrative authority referred to in Article 2'.

[3] Recital 33 of the 2017 CPC Regulation.

[4] Recital 6 of the 2017 CPC Regulation.

CRITERIA FOR SEEKING AN ENFORCEMENT ORDER

5.7 In order to obtain an enforcement order, very broadly seven criteria need to be satisfied:

(a) the enforcer is entitled to bring proceedings;

(b) the trader has engaged, or is engaging, in conduct which constitutes a domestic or a Community/Schedule 13 infringement, or is likely to engage in conduct which constitutes a Community/Schedule 13[1] infringement;

(c) there is, or has been, or is likely to be, harm to the collective interests of consumers[2];

(d) the defendant is a person against whom an enforcement order may be made;

(e) there has been appropriate consultation that has failed to bring about the cessation of the conduct about which complaint is made or the need to consult has been waived;

(f) where applicable, the enforcer has given correct notice to the CMA;

(g) the court is satisfied that it is appropriate to make an order.

[1] EnA 2002, s 215.

[2] The location or nationality of the consumers is no longer material. Previously the definition of domestic infringements required consumers to be in the UK, however this restriction was repealed by the CRA 2015. Now, where a domestic infringement is alleged it is sufficient if either the trader has a place of business in the UK or the trader is seeking to supply products to a person in the UK – see EnA 2002, s 211(1A).

Enforcers

5.8 There are four types of enforcers, who have been empowered to bring proceedings under Pt 8, originally in compliance with the UK's obligations under the Injunctions Directive and CPC Regulation. These are: general enforcers, designated enforcers, Community enforcers[1] and CPC enforcers (who are from 1 January 2021 referred to as Schedule 13 enforcers). The precise status of an enforcer is important not only for establishing standing to bring proceedings, but also to access certain investigation powers under the CRA 2015, Sch 5, and to be able to seek Enhanced Consumer Measures under Pt 8.

[1] Community enforcers ceased to be able to exercise Pt 8 powers after EU exit IP completion day (ie from 1 January 2021), except they may continue any proceedings which they have already commenced before a court: See The Consumer Protection (Enforcement) (Amendment etc) (EU Exit) Regulations 2019, SI 2019/203, reg 10. We are not aware of any such proceedings which have been so commenced in the UK.

General enforcers

5.9 By the EnA 2002, s 213(1), the following are specifically designated as 'general enforcers', namely the Competition and Markets Authority ('the

CMA')[1]; every local weights and measures authority in Great Britain[2]; and the Department of Enterprise, Trade and Investment in Northern Ireland. A general enforcer may make an application for an enforcement order in respect of any infringement[3].

[1] The CMA replaced the OFT following its abolition by the Enterprise and Regulatory Reform Act 2013, ss 25 and 26.
[2] See the Weights and Measures Act 1985, s 69 – in effect trading standards departments of local authorities.
[3] EnA 2002, s 215(2).

Designated enforcers

5.10 By the EnA 2002, s 213(2), the Secretary of State may by order designate any person or body as a 'designated enforcer' provided that he thinks that person or body has as one of its purposes the protection of the collective interests of consumers, and he is satisfied that it is independent. If the person or body proposed to be designated is not a public body, it must conform to criteria laid down by the Secretary of State by order[1]. A designated enforcer may make an application for an enforcement order in respect of an infringement to which his designation relates[2].

[1] EnA 2002, s 213(4). The Secretary of State's criteria are to be found in the Enterprise Act 2002 (Part 8 Designated Enforcers: Criteria for Designation, Designation of Public Bodies as Designated Enforcers and Transitional Provisions) Order 2003, SI 2003/1399.
[2] EnA 2002, s 215(3).

5.11 The Secretary of State has made a number of orders pursuant to EnA 2002, s 213:

- Enterprise Act 2002 (Pt 8 Designated Enforcers: Criteria for Designation, Designation of Public Bodies as Designated Enforcers and Transitional Provisions) Order 2003[1]. This designates number of **public** bodies in respect of all infringements, namely the Civil Aviation Authority, the Director General of Electricity Supply for Northern Ireland, the Director General of Gas for Northern Ireland, the Office of Communications, the Water Services Regulation Authority, the Gas and Electricity Markets Authority, the Information Commissioner and the Rail Regulator;
- Enterprise Act 2002 (Pt 8) (Designation of the Consumers' Association) Order 2005[2], in respect of all infringements;
- Enterprise Act 2002 (Pt 8) (Designation of the Financial Conduct Authority as a Designated Enforcer) Order 2013[3], in respect of all infringements[4].

Designated bodies that are not public bodies (currently only the Consumers' Association) do not have access to Enhanced Consumer Measures. A power is included in the Act to extend the use of the measures to private designated enforcers provided the following conditions are met[5]:

- The enforcer is specified for the purposes of this section by order made by the Secretary of State[6].
- The enhanced consumer measures do not directly benefit the enforcer or an associated undertaking[7].

[1] SI 2003/1399.
[2] SI 2005/917.

3   SI 2013/478.
4   The Financial Services Authority was previously designated under SI 2004/935.
5   EnA 2002, s 219C as added by para 8 of the CRA 2015, Sch 7.
6   At the time of writing, no orders have been made. The Secretary of State must be satisfied that the criteria set out in EnA 2002, s 219C(6) and (7) are met.
7   See EnA 2002, s 219C(5). Enhanced consumer measures which directly benefit an enforcer or an associated undertaking include, in particular, measures which:(a) require a person to pay money to the enforcer or associated undertaking;(b) require a person to participate in a scheme which is designed to recommend persons supplying or seeking to supply goods or services to consumers and which is administered by the enforcer or associated undertaking; or(c) would give the enforcer or associated undertaking a commercial advantage over any of its competitors.

Community enforcers

5.12 By the EnA 2002, s 213(5):

A Community enforcer was a qualified entity for the purposes of the Injunctions Directive—

(a)   which is for the time being specified in the list published in the Official Journal of the European Communities in pursuance of Article 4.3 of that Directive[1], but

(b)   which is not a general enforcer, a designated enforcer or a CPC enforcer.

1   The UK had 11 entries. All were either general or designated enforcers and so did not qualify as 'Community enforcers' within the meaning of the EnA 2002. Accordingly this provision in practice applied only to enforcers from elsewhere in the EU/EEA.

5.13 This provision was repealed as of 1 January 2021[1]. This provision was required in order to bring Art 4[2] of the Injunctions Directive into force in UK law. Community enforcers are entities from *other* EEA States that are listed in the Official Journal of the European Communities under Art 4.3 and are entitled to make applications for enforcement orders in the courts or other EEA states in respect of intra Community infringements that originate in one Member State but produce effects in the Member State of the enforcer[3]. For example, if defective products were sold by mail order in France and delivered to consumers in Germany, a German qualified entity could apply for an enforcement order in the French courts.

1   The Consumer Protection (Enforcement) (Amendment etc) (EU Exit) Regulations 2019, SI 2019/203, reg 10. Court proceedings already commenced by the enforcer may continue – see reg 3(9) of the Consumer Protection (Enforcement) (Amendment etc) (EU Exit) Regulations 2020.
2   Entitled 'Intra-Community Infringements'.
3   One of the purposes of the Injunctions Directive was to address the situation where the infringement of consumer legislation occurred in one Member State but its effects were felt in another Member State. In those circumstances, the qualified entity of the second State should be empowered to take injunction proceedings in the first State: see recitals (3), (6) and (11).

5.14 Similarly, under the Injunctions Directive, a UK qualified entity could seek injunctive relief in the courts of another Member State where the infringement originated in that Member State but affected UK citizens. Thus, by the EnA 2002, s 221(2), a general enforcer and a designated enforcer, which is a public body, were both empowered to take proceedings in EEA States[1] other than the UK for the cessation or prohibition of a Community infringement. As part of the process of leaving the EU, s 221 was repealed as of 1 January 2021[2]. To date the only enforcer to make use of this ability in the whole EEA is the now defunct Office of Fair Trading, which litigated in Belgium and the Netherlands to tackle traders sending mass marketed mailings into the UK, which were misleading under the Control of Misleading Advertisements Regulations 1989.

1   An EEA State is a State which is a contracting party to the Agreement on the European Economic Area signed at Oporto on 2 May 1992 as adjusted by the Protocol signed at Brussels on 17 March 1993: EnA 2002, s 221(5).
2   The Consumer Protection (Enforcement) (Amendment etc) (EU Exit) Regulations 2019, SI 2019/203, reg 3(14).

5.15 The EnA 2002, s 221(4) provided for cooperation between general enforcers, designated enforcers and CPC enforcers on the one hand and Community enforcers on the other hand for the purpose of assisting the UK enforcer taking proceedings in the EEA State or assisting the Community enforcer taking proceedings in the UK.

Consumer Protection Cooperation ('CPC') enforcers/Schedule 13 enforcers

5.16 The EnA 2002, s 213(5A) lists 'CPC enforcers', namely bodies designated under Art 45(1) of the 2017 CPC Regulation. As of 1 January 2021, these enforcers are known as 'Schedule 13 enforcers[1].' The bodies listed in the EnA 2002, s 213(5A) are the CMA; the Civil Aviation Authority; the Financial Conduct Authority; the Secretary of State for Health; the Department of Health, Social Services and Public Safety in Northern Ireland; the Office of Communications; the Department of Enterprise, Trade and Investment in Northern Ireland; every local weights and measures authority in Great Britain; an enforcement authority within the meaning of the Communications Act 2003, s 120(15) (regulation of premium rate services)[2]; the Information Commissioner; the Department for Infrastructure; the Maritime and Coastguard Agency; the Office of Rail and Road; and the Office for the Traffic Commissioner. A CPC/Schedule 13 enforcer may make an application for an enforcement order in respect of a Community/Schedule 13 infringement[3].

1   The Consumer Protection (Enforcement) (Amendment etc) (EU Exit) Regulations 2019, SI 2019/203, reg 3(4).
2   See para 4 of the CRA 2015, Sch 7.
3   EnA 2002, s 215(4A).

5.17 The EnA 2002, s 213(5A) was inserted by the Enterprise Act 2002 (Amendment) Regulations 2006[1], to give effect to the UK's obligations to create Competent Authorities who could enforce consumer laws, in particular in respect of intra-Community infringements, and have the requisite investigation powers to do so. The government's policy was to ensure that these enforcers could act where a Community infringement is likely, whether or not there is actually a cross border dimension, and therefore the power to enforce, and the availability of the investigation powers in the Consumer Rights Act 2015, Sch 5, extends to UK only investigations for all Community infringements. Where there is an intra-Community infringement however, these bodies had an obligation under EU law to act, but only in respect of infringements of the legislation they are listed as being responsible for, in the Official Journal of the EU[2].

1   SI 2006/3363. Further enforcers were added to s 213(5A) by the Consumer Protection (Enforcement) (Amendment etc) Regulations 2020, SI 2020/484, to give effect to the requirements of the 2017 CPC Regulation.

5.18 CPC enforcers in the EU are also expected to take part in the EU's consumer enforcement programme, which includes annual sweeps to check for non-compliant websites, and they have access to various capability building activities. In recent years, the CPC Network has launched several joint actions to tackle EU wide infringements, for example in respect of children's apps, car rental and social media sites. The UK Competent Authority that took part in these was the CMA.

5.19 The CPC Regulation was revised, with a replacement in force from 17 January 2020, to improve the minimum set of powers available to enforcers and to formalise how joint actions are conducted.

Dual enforcers

5.20 Some bodies are designated as more than one type of enforcer. Where that occurs, the body in question may act as the particular type of enforcer appropriate to the circumstances¹.

¹ EnA 2002, s 235B.

Infringements

5.21 In order to act under Pt 8, an enforcer must be investigating an infringement that is covered by Pt 8. Such infringements are described as domestic infringements and Community/Schedule 13 infringements. In order to qualify as such an infringement, conduct must fall within the scope of the definitions set out in the EnA 2002, ss 211 and 212, and be listed in the appropriate legislation.

Domestic infringements

5.22 By the EnA 2002, s 211:

(1) A domestic infringement is an act or omission which—
    (a)   is done or made by a person in the course of a business,
    (b)   falls within subsection (2), and
    (c)   harms the collective interests of consumers.
(1A) But an act or omission which satisfies the conditions in subsection (1) is a domestic infringement only if at least one of the following is satisfied—
    (a)   the person supplying (or seeking to supply) goods or services has a place of business in the United Kingdom, or
    (b)   the goods or services are supplied (or sought to be supplied) to or for a person in the United Kingdom (see section 232)¹.
(2) An act or omission falls within this subsection if it is of a description specified by the Secretary of State by order and consists of any of the following—
    (a)   a contravention of an enactment which imposes a duty, prohibition or restriction enforceable by criminal proceedings;

(b)   an act done or omission made in breach of contract;

(c)   an act done or omission made in breach of a non-contractual duty owed to a person by virtue of an enactment or rule of law and enforceable by civil proceedings;

(d)   an act or omission in respect of which an enactment provides for a remedy or sanction enforceable by civil proceedings;

(e)   an act done or omission made by a person supplying or seeking to supply goods or services as a result of which an agreement or security relating to the supply is void or unenforceable to any extent;

(f)   an act or omission by which a person supplying or seeking to supply goods or services purports or attempts to exercise a right or remedy relating to the supply in circumstances where the exercise of the right or remedy is restricted or excluded under or by virtue of an enactment;

(g)   an act or omission by which a person supplying or seeking to supply goods or services purports or attempts to avoid (to any extent) liability relating to the supply in circumstances where such avoidance is restricted or prevented under an enactment.

[1]   CRA 2015, Sch 7, para 3(3).

5.23 It can be seen that there are four essential components to be proven when alleging a domestic infringement:

(a)   The infringer is acting in the course of a business.

(b)   The conduct infringes a law that has been listed in an order made under the EnA 2002, s 211(2).

(c)   The conduct harms the collective interests of consumers.

(d)   There is the necessary connection with the UK –either the trader has a place of business in the UK, or where they are based overseas, are seeking to supply at least one person in the UK with goods or services[1].

[1]   The concept of supply of goods is clarified in EnA 2002, s 232 to include buildings, structures, ships, aircraft and hovercraft, and includes lease, hire, hire purchase and construction work. The concept of supply of services is clarified in EnA 2002, s 234 to include the provision for gain or reward of any activity other than the supply of goods, and making arrangements for the use of computer software, or granting access to data that is not readily accessible. It therefore expressly covers all digital content and licensing issues.

Acting in the course of a business

5.24 The requirement that the infringer is acting in the course of a business is not further defined, and it is likely that it is not materially distinct from the general proposition that consumer law in the UK and EU more widely applies to 'traders'. However the EnA 2002, s 210(8) clarifies that:

A business includes—

(a)   a professional practice;

(b)   any other undertaking carried on for gain or reward;

(c)   any undertaking in the course of which goods or services are supplied otherwise than free of charge.

This is intentionally broad, and it encompasses where products are supplied for non-monetary gain, as well as where a 'professional' acts for no remuneration at all.

DOMESTIC INFRINGEMENT ORDERS

5.25 The second component refers to the orders that the Secretary of State has made under s 211[1]. There are two such orders. The bulk of the domestic infringements are listed in Sch 1 to the Enterprise Act 2002 (Part 8 Domestic Infringements) Order 2003[2], as amended by the CPUTR 2008. The Schedule consists of three parts:

- *Part 1: legislation of the UK Parliament.* This is a list of 32 specific Acts and Regulations, and the specific sections of which, may be domestic infringements. This includes, for example, the Consumer Credit Act 1974, the Estate Agents Act 1979, the Misrepresentation Act 1967 and the Unfair Contract Terms Act 1977, which are wholly designated. Specific selections include the Charities Act 1992, ss 60, 61 and 63 (information requirements, cancellation rights and false statements in respect of fundraising); the Pyrotechnic Articles (Safety) Regulations 2010[3], reg 15 (prohibition on supply of category 1 fireworks to persons under 16 years and category 2 or 3 fireworks to persons under 18 years); and the Weights and Measures Act 1985, ss 21–23, 25 (requirements to sell goods by particular quantities etc), 28 (short weight etc), 30 (quantity less than stated), 31 (incorrect statements), 32 (offences due to default of third person), 50(5) and (6) (possession for sale, etc of inadequate regulated package).
- *Part 2: Northern Ireland legislation.* This is a list of 11 Acts and Orders that apply in Northern Ireland. Examples include laws relating to gambling, tobacco advertising, underage sale of fireworks and sale of unroadworthy vehicles.
- *Part 3: entitled 'Rules of Law',* which reads as follows:

    'An act done or omission made in breach of contract for the supply of goods or services to a consumer.

    An act done or omission made in breach of a duty of care owed to a consumer under the law of tort or delict of negligence.'

[1]   EnA 2002, s 211(2)(a)–(g) set out the description of the type of laws that the Secretary of State is permitted to designate as domestic infringements, but this set of subsections is unlikely to require analysis by enforcers: inclusion of a section of legislation in one of the Orders made under EnA 2002, s 211 is likely to be sufficient when pleading out a case.
[2]   SI 2003/1593.
[3]   SI 2010/1554.

5.26 In addition, the Enterprise Act 2002 (Part 8 Domestic Infringements) Order[1] also includes as domestic infringements, acts or omissions in respect of any provision of Pts 1 and 2 of and Chapter 5 of Pt 3 to the Consumer Rights Act 2015, which cover sale of goods and digital content, supply of services, unfair terms and secondary ticketing obligations.

[1]   SI 2015/1727.

HARM TO THE COLLECTIVE INTERESTS OF CONSUMERS

5.27 The concept of harm to the collective interests of consumers is considered below at **5.42** et seq.

CONNECTION WITH THE UK

5.28 Previously the definition of domestic infringement required the consumers to be 'in the UK'. However this has now been replaced with the fourth component, set out in the EnA 2000, s 211(1A). This permits enforcers to take action against UK based traders, even where they are harming the interests of consumers elsewhere in the world. This is important for mutual assistance arrangements with other countries to work effectively, since otherwise it is too straightforward for rogue traders to base themselves in one country and avoid enforcement by directing their activities solely towards consumers in another state.

5.29 This provision also permits enforcers to take action against traders who are not in the UK, where they are seeking to supply goods or services to at least one consumer in the UK. Under the EnA 2000, s 232(4) and (5), this provision also applies where an overseas trader supplies goods or services indirectly to consumers in the UK, where the supply is made through another person who is physically in the UK[1]. It also applies where the consumer seeking the supply is in the UK only temporarily[2].

[1] Section 232(5)(b).
[2] Section 232(5)(a).

5.30 Leaving aside the practicalities of how this is to be done (for example in terms of service of proceedings and enforcement of the subsequent judgment), this provision clarifies that UK courts have jurisdiction and are able to grant an order even if the trader has no place of business, or other assets, in the UK.

Community/Schedule 13 infringements

5.31 In relation to conduct which pre-dates 1 January 2021, by the EnA 2002, s 212:

    (1)   A Community infringement is an act or omission which harms the collective interests of consumers and which—
        (a)   contravenes a listed Directive as given effect by the laws, regulations or administrative provisions of an EEA State,
        (b)   contravenes such laws, regulations or administrative provisions which provide additional permitted protections,
        (c)   contravenes a listed Regulation, or
        (d)   contravenes any laws, regulations or administrative provisions of an EEA State which give effect to a listed Regulation.
    (2)   The laws, regulations or administrative provisions of an EEA State which give effect to a listed Directive provide additional permitted protections if—
        (a)   they provide protection for consumers which is in addition to the minimum protection required by the Directive concerned, and
        (b)   such additional protection is permitted by that Directive.
    (3)   The Secretary of State may by order specify for the purposes of this section the law in the United Kingdom which—
        (a)   gives effect to the listed Directives;
        (b)   provides additional permitted protections, or
        (c)   gives effect to a listed Regulation[1].

[1] Listed Directives and Listed Regulations are defined in s 210 as:
    (7) A Directive is a listed Directive—

(a)   if it is a Directive of the Council of the European Union or of the European Parliament and of the Council, and

(b)   if it is specified in Schedule 13 or to the extent that any of its provisions is so specified.

A Regulation is a listed Regulation—

(a)   if it is a Regulation of the Council of the European Union or of the European Parliament and of the Council, and

(b)   if it is specified in Schedule 13 or to the extent that any of its provisions is so specified.

However ss 210 (7) and (7A) are repealed as of 1 January 2021 – The Consumer Protection (Enforcement) (Amendment etc) (EU Exit) Regulations 2019, SI 2019/203, reg 3(2)(c).

5.32 As of 1 January 2021, EnA 2002, s 212 defines Schedule 13 infringements as:

(1)   In this Part a Schedule 13 infringement is an act or omission which contravenes a listed enactment and which harms the collective interests of consumers.

(2)   References to a listed enactment must be construed in accordance with s 210[1].

[1]   EnA 2002, ss 210 (6), (6A) and (6B) make provision for how to construe the concept of a Schedule 13 infringement.

5.33 There are therefore three components to the analysis of Community infringement:

(a)   The substantive law must be listed in the EnA 2002, Sch 13, and in respect of conduct predating 1 January 2021, the UK implementing provisions set out in an order.

(b)   The substantive law, *as implemented in the UK*, must be consulted to identify if the alleged perpetrator is within the definition of 'trader' in that legislation, and if the conduct is unlawful in that legislation.

(c)   There must be harm to the collective interests of consumers, as defined in the EnA 2002, s 210(6) – namely for conduct predating 31 December 2020 they must be within the scope of that concept as set out either in the Injunctions Directive, or the relevant Directive or Regulation concerned; and in relation to conduct from 1 January 2021 they need only be a consumer for the purposes of the enactment listed in Sch 13.

LEGISLATION LISTED IN SCHEDULE 13

5.34 In relation to conduct which predates 1 January 2021, Part 1 of Sch 13 lists 20 complete Directives and Regulations. These include major cross cutting legislative tools such as the rules on unfair terms in consumer contracts[1]; unfair business-to-consumer commercial practices[2]; consumer rights[3], which amends the rules relating to contracts negotiated away from business premises[4] and the protection of consumers in respect of distance contracts[5]; the indication of the prices of products offered to consumers[6]; the sale of consumer goods and associated[7] guarantees; electronic commerce[8]; and the provision of services in the internal market[9].

[1]   Council Directive 93/13/EEC of 5 April 1993.
[2]   Directive 2005/29/EC of the European Parliament and of the Council of 11 May 2005. This is the important UCPD given force by the CPUTR 2008.
[3]   Directive 2011/83/EU of the European Parliament and of the Council of 25 October 2011.
[4]   Council Directive 85/577/EEC of 20 December 1985.

5   Directive 97/7/EC of the European Parliament and of the Council of 20 May 1997.
6   Directive 98/6/EC of the European Parliament and of the Council of 16 February 1998.
7   Directive 1999/44/EC of the European Parliament and of the Council of 25 May 1999.
8   Directive 2000/31/EC of the European Parliament and of the Council of 8 June 2000.
9   Directive 2006/123/EC of the European Parliament and of the Council of 12 December 2006.

5.35 Part 1 also covers a range of sector specific legislation, such as rules relating to package travel, package holidays and package tours[1]; the protection of consumers in respect of certain aspects of timeshare, long-term holiday product, resale and exchange contracts[2]; the distance marketing of consumer financial services[3]; compensation and assistance to air passengers in the event of denied boarding and of cancellation or long delay of flights[4]; credit agreements for consumers[5]. A number of further items were added in June 2020, to do with passenger rights and cross border portability of online content services[6].

1   Council Directive 90/314/EEC of 13 June 1990.
2   Directive 2008/122/EC of the European Parliament and of the Council of 14 January 2009.
3   Directive 2002/65/EC of the European Parliament and of the Council of 23 September 2002.
4   Regulation (EC) No 261/2004 of the European Parliament and of the Council of 11 February 2004.
5   Directive 2008/48/EC of the European Parliament and of the Council of 23 April 2008.
6   See the Consumer Protection (Enforcement) (Amendment etc) Regulations 2020, SI 2020/484, reg 2(15).

5.36 Part 2 of the Schedule lists parts only of twelve named Directives, including Arts 10–21 on the co-ordination of certain provisions laid down by law, regulation or administrative action in Member States concerning the pursuit of television broadcasting activities[1]; Arts 86–100 on the Community Code relating to medicinal products for human use[2]; Art 13 on privacy and electronic communications[3]; Art 13 on alternative dispute resolution for consumer disputes[4]; Art 14 on online dispute resolution for consumer disputes[5]; and Art 10(4) on interchange fees for card-based payment transactions[6]. Further provisions were added by The Consumer Protection (Enforcement) (Amendment etc) Regulations 2020[7], reg 2(16).

1   Council Directive 89/552/EEC of 3 October 1989.
2   Directive 2001/83/EC of the European Parliament and of the Council of 6 November 2001.
3   Directive 2002/58/EC of the European Parliament and of the Council of 12 July 2002.
4   Directive 2013/11/EU of the European Parliament and of the Council of 21 May 2013. Art 14 of this Directive will be added to Pt 2 of EnA 2002, Sch 13 when the Alternative Dispute Resolution for Consumer Disputes (Amendment) Regulations SI 2015/1392, reg 6 is brought into force.
5   Regulation (EU) No 524/2013 of the European Parliament and of the Council of 21 May 2013.
6   Regulation (EU) 2015/751 of the European Parliament and of the Council of 29 April 2015.
7   SI 2020/484.

5.37 In order to identify which UK laws implement the underlying EU provisions, the Secretary of State has made orders under the EnA 2002, s 212(3), namely[1]:

* The Schedule to the Enterprise Act 2002 (Part 8 Community Infringements Specified UK Laws) Order 2003[2], as amended, which lists 15 Directives or parts of Directives which have been given effect by a UK law. Thus, for example Directive 2005/29/EC of the European Parliament and of the Council of 11 May 2005 concerning unfair business-to-consumer commercial practices in the internal market is specified as having been given effect by the CPUTR 2008.

- The Enterprise Act 2002 (Part 8 Community Infringements Specified UK Laws) Order 2006[3], lists a further one Directive and one Regulation which have respectively been given effect by the UK Price Marking Order 2004 and the Civil Aviation (Denied Boarding, Compensation and Assistance) Regulations 2005[4].
- The Enterprise Act 2002 (Part 8 EU Infringements) Order 2014[5], as amended, lists Directive 2011/83/EU of the European Parliament and of the Council of 25 October 2011 on consumer rights as having been given effect by the Consumer Contracts (Information, Cancellation and Additional Charges) Regulations 2013[6], certain regulations of the Consumer Rights (Payment Surcharges) Regulations 2012[7], and the Consumer Rights Act 2015, ss 5, 11(4)–(6), 12, 19, 28, 29, 36(3) and (4), 37, 38, 42, 50 and 54.
- The Consumer Protection (Enforcement) (Amendment etc) Regulations 2020[8], (see the legislation set out in the Schedule thereto).

[1] These orders are revoked in respect of conduct which occurs after 31 December 2020 by The Consumer Protection (Enforcement) (Amendment) (EU Exit) Regulations 2019, regs 7 and 9.
[2] SI 2003/1374.
[3] SI 2006/3372.
[4] SI 2005/975.
[5] SI 2014/2908.
[6] SI 2013/3134.
[7] SI 2012/3110.
[8] SI 2020/484.

5.38 In relation to conduct which occurs on or after 1 January 2021, Sch 13 lists a large number of enactments (in whole or part), which broadly reflect the laws listed as Community infringements before exit IP completion day, and which include a mixture of UK implementing legislation and retained EU Regulations[1].

[1] Reg 3(10) of the Consumer Protection (Enforcement) (Amendment etc) (EU Exit) Regulations 2020 have added a further 17 pieces of legislation (in full or in part) to Sch 13, largely to do with disabled passengers' rights, rights of passengers on rail, ships, buses and aircraft, airline price advertising, certain financial service rules and rules relating to payment accounts. Several of these pieces of legislation are retained EU regulations.

5.39 It is important to bear in mind the full scope of contraventions that fall within the definition of a Community/Schedule 13 infringement in the EnA 2000, s 212(1), since in many situations there are subtle differences in wording between the underlying Directive or Regulation and the UK implementing legislation, where the UK has set out to provide 'additional permitted protections' in order to provide greater protections for consumers. An example of this is where the UK has extended the protection of the Unfair Commercial Practices Directive to situations where a product is supplied by a consumer to a trader, whereas under the underlying Directive, the scope extends only to where a product is supplied to a consumer.

5.40 The EnA 2002, s 212(1) also permitted enforcers in the UK to enforce the substantive provisions of the laws of other EEA States, before the UK courts where this is necessary – for example where a UK based trader, dealing substantially with consumers in another EEA state is failing to comply with the additional permitted protections provided for in the laws of that state, it may be appropriate to ask a UK court to order compliance with the laws of that other EEA state. However this only applies to conduct which pre-dates 1 January 2021.

5.41 Domestic and Community/Schedule 13 infringements are not necessarily mutually exclusive: conduct which is a domestic infringement may also be a Community/Schedule 13 infringement. It is important that enforcers analyse out properly why conduct amounts to an infringement, since the requirements for proving each type of infringement differ as a matter of law. When drafting pleadings, this is likely to require the enforcer to set out the proof of the underlying facts, and then to articulate separately why those facts amount to domestic and Community/Schedule 13 infringements.

HARM TO THE COLLECTIVE INTERESTS OF CONSUMERS

The concept of consumer

5.42 As noted above, both domestic and Community/Schedule 13 infringements require proof of harm to consumers. The EnA 2002, s 210 sets out how the concept of consumer is to be construed for each of these types of infringements. A person who is a 'consumer' for the purposes of a domestic infringement may not necessarily be a consumer in relation to a Community/Schedule 13 infringement, since the tests technically are different. However these differences ought not to create significant inconsistencies in practice.

5.43 In relation to domestic infringements, a consumer is an individual in respect of whom two conditions are satisfied. First, goods or services are supplied or are sought to be supplied to the individual in the course of a business carried on by the person making the supply. Second, the individual must receive or seek to receive the goods or services otherwise than in the course of a business carried on by him (although he will still be a consumer if the business has not yet commenced)[1]. This means that a person may well be a consumer even if the goods or services are to be used in the course of a business, if he is not the person who will be carrying on that business. The rider in the EnA 2002, s 210(4)(b) in relation to future business activities means that where an individual is purchasing equipment or enrolling for training, but has not yet actually started trading, they will still be treated as a consumer.

[1] EnA 2002, s 210(2)–(4).

5.44 The concept of supplying goods and services must be construed in accordance with the EnA 2002, ss 232–234. 'Goods' include buildings and other structures (including construction work), ships, aircraft and hovercraft, and supply of goods includes supply by way of sale, lease, hire or hire purchase. 'Services' includes any activity that is not the supply of goods, where it is performed for gain or reward. It is therefore a broad concept that is intended to be comprehensive. It also includes rendering services to order, and situations where services are made available to potential users (even where no contract for supply is actually entered into).

5.45 In relation to Community infringements, a consumer is a person who is so defined for the purposes of the Injunctions Directive and the listed Directive or Regulation with which the action is concerned. There is no definition of a consumer in the Injunctions Directive. The listed Directives and Regulations provide, generally speaking, that a consumer is a natural person who acts for purposes outside his trade, business or profession. Thus, for example, Art 2(a) of Directive 2005/29/EC concerning unfair business-to-consumer commercial practices in the internal market defines a consumer as 'any natural person who, in commercial practices covered by this Directive, is acting for purposes which are outside his trade, business, craft or profession'.

5.46 In short, in both cases a consumer may be described as an individual who is not acting in a trading or professional capacity[1]. However there may be inconsistencies where an individual is acting with a view to establishing a business, or is acting for mixed professional and personal purposes –both situations which have required considerable analysis in the case law, and where UK implementation of EU Directives has tended to extend protection beyond that set out in the Directive (see CHAPTER 6 Consumer Rights). However going forward, the position should be simpler, since in relation to Schedule 13 infringements there is no longer any requirement to consider whether the victim is a consumer for the purposes of the original EU legislation it is sufficient that they are a consumer in the UK legislation listed in Sch 13.

[1] See *OFT v MB Designs (Scotland) Ltd* [2005] SLT 69 at [2].

The concept of harm to the collective interests of consumers

5.47 Under the old Fair Trading Act 1973[1], it was necessary for an enforcer to prove 'a course of conduct' before the court could grant an order. In the Enterprise Act 2002, ss 215(1) and 217(1) require the case to be made that a person 'has engaged in *conduct* which constitutes a domestic or Community/Schedule 13 infringement'. This change is significant, in that it is clear that under the Enterprise Act 2002, the enforcer need prove only a single act or omission to succeed in obtaining an order, and need not necessarily adduce an accumulation of instances.

[1] See Fair Trading Act 1973, ss 34 and 37.

5.48 First of all, as a matter of statutory construction, the concept of 'conduct' may be a single act or omission. The proof must be that the conduct 'constitutes' a domestic or Community/Schedule 13 infringement, and each of these concepts is defined as 'an act or omission' etc. This interpretation is supported by the case law, which considered whether a single infringement or breach of the law is enough to warrant making an enforcement order. In *Office of Fair Trading v Vance Miller*[1] where Arden LJ, disagreeing with the Scottish judgment of Lord Drummond-Young[2] said[3]:

'However, I would not for my part agree with Lord Drummond-Young's conclusion . . . that "more than one instance of a defective supply is required before there can be a breach" of an order pursuant to the provisions of the Enterprise Act 2002 now providing for stop orders. It must depend on the facts. A Community infringement is committed when harm is caused to the collective interests of consumers. It is possible that a single supply might be enough, as where a supplier puts on to the market a large consignment of a beverage stated to be a healthy drink for a baby that is wholly unsuitable for this purpose. For this reason, I do not consider that the expression "Community infringement" requires a course of conduct.'

1   [2009] EWCA Civ 34.
2   In *OFT v MB Designs (Scotland) Ltd* [2005] SLT 69.
3   At [44].

5.49 Later[1], she said that a Community infringement 'could in appropriate circumstances be a single act, or several separate acts. They need not be connected in the same way that a course of conduct consists of a series of connected acts, but if they are connected that will be evidence from which the court can conclude that there is damage to the collective interests of consumers'.

1   At [52].

5.50 In the same case, Sedley LJ said[1]:

'In my judgment, while the material provisions do not demand proof of a course of conduct, they do envisage something more than a simple breach of contract. This legislation does not seek to supplant or supplement individual consumers' private law rights; it seeks to protect the body of consumers from commercial malpractice. Accordingly, as it seems to me, infringement envisages a situation such that (at least in a case such as the present) the public cannot safely or confidently deal with the alleged infringer. There is nothing to prevent such a situation arising from a single event.'

1   At [68].

5.51 However the enforcer will still need to set out why a single infringement is sufficient to establish harm to the collective interest of consumers, which is the statutory requirement, although as Arden LJ observed, a single infringement may still have a massive impact on consumers.

5.52 Where there are several infringements, or the infringing activity is capable of impacting on numerous consumers, it seems likely that harm to the collective interests of consumers will more easily be made out. In the same case, Arden LJ said[1]:

'In my judgment, the findings of fact made by the judge on the nine cases show that there were serial episodes of significantly defective supplies of goods. These episodes were not just harmful to the customers concerned, but, by virtue of the risk of repetition, these episodes were also harmful to the collective interests of consumers generally. The judge found that they were not isolated or unconnected incidents. In his judgment they established a consistent pattern of failure to comply with contractual obligations. I do not consider that it is necessary for the court to investigate the level of complaints received by competitors in the industry nor does the limited number of breaches of contract that were proved, when set against the volume of sales, mean that there was no Community infringement.'

In that case, it was held that the evidence of nine complaints (which evidenced infringements) was enough, even when set against the 80,000 kitchens sold over 4 years.

1   At [51].

5.53 Similarly in the *MB Designs* case, Lord Drummond Young recognised that where there are a number of instances of harm, the test is likely to be made out[1]:

'. . . the expression "collective interests" is not something wholly separate from the interests of individual consumers who have been harmed by infringements. "Collective interests" include those interests, but amount to something more than the mere aggregation of those interests. That makes perfectly good sense; it means that the adjective "collective" denotes the generality of consumers, considered as a body, but at the same time recognises that the interests of individual consumers are part of those collective interests, and that harm to the collective interests will normally be inferred from a number of instances of harm to individual interests.'

[1]   At [13].

5.54 As a concept that derives from the Injunctions Directive, the starting point to understand what 'collective interests of consumers' means is to construe the Recitals. However in this case, it seems the English wording is slightly misleading, and it is important to look at the other language versions as well.

5.55 Recital (2)[1] notes:

(2) . . . collective interests mean interests which do not include the cumulation of interests of individuals who have been harmed by an infringement; whereas this is without prejudice to individual actions brought by individuals who have been harmed by an infringement.

[1]   Recital 3 of the 2009 Directive.

5.56 Lord Drummond-Young in *OFT v MB Designs (Scotland) Ltd*[1], concluded in relation to the definition of 'collective interests' that the English translation was 'poorly expressed'. Having considered the French version, he proposed the alternative wording: 'by collective interests, one means interests which are not a *mere* accumulation of the interests of individuals to whom harm has been caused by an infringement' (emphasis added).

[1]   [2005] SLT 691 at [13].

5.57 In this case MB Designs had argued that their actions could not be said to be harmful to the collective interests of consumers in the UK because they operated only in a relatively small geographical area. The judge rejected the argument. The concept of 'harm to the collective interests of consumers', he held, was not based upon percentages of the population, geography or any statistical concept. There was collective harm when there was an infringement and there was potential risk to purchasers of the defective goods or services. The notion of collective interests of consumers indicates that there must be some harm or risk of harm to the public generally, or more precisely to members of the public who may buy the particular goods or service in question.

5.58 A further aspect of the concept of collective harm is that it aims to ensure that the general standards of trading are kept high[1]:

'. . . it is necessary that . . . contravention should harm the collective interests of consumers. The latter expression is of fundamental importance; it makes clear that Part 8 is not concerned with individual breaches of contract or breaches of statutory provisions on the part of traders, but is rather concerned with the enforcement of general standards of trading.'

[1]   *MB Designs* at [1].

5.59 The standard enforcers are seeking to achieve is not that there should never be any infringing conduct, but that the incidence of infringements is kept to a low level: the law recognises that sometimes mistakes happen, and traders should not be unduly penalised for genuine mistakes. Rather the intention of enforcement will often be to improve the practical management and quality control processes used by a business[1]:

> 'The collective interests of consumers, by contrast, are concerned not with the contractual rights of individual consumers but with general trading standards, and in particular with the general standard of goods or services supplied by a particular trader. Part 8 of the 2002 Act is designed to enforce such trading standards. In my opinion a statutory provision of this nature has two important features. First, it is not designed to ensure that no defective product or service is ever supplied; it is rather designed to ensure that the incidence of defective products or services is kept at a low level, and that in cases where a defective product or service is supplied reasonable steps are taken to put matters right. The occasional instance where defective goods or services are supplied cannot be said to harm the collective interests of consumers; it is only when there is an accumulation of a number of such instances that the collective interests can be said to be engaged. Secondly, Part 8 is intended to deal with the overall incidence of defects in a trader's products or services, and it is immaterial for this purpose what the particular defects may be. It is accordingly immaterial that the defects may vary widely in their nature. The existence of a wide range of defects will often be an indication of poor management or poor quality control, and the function of consumer protection legislation is to protect against poor management or quality control just as much as poor fitting or poor manufacturing processes.'

[1]   *MB Designs* at [14].

Potential defendants

5.60 There are three broad categories of person against whom an enforcement order may be sought. These are:

(a)   The person committing the substantive infringement;
(b)   Where the infringer is a body corporate, certain accessories to its conduct[1];
(c)   Where the infringer is a body corporate and a member of a group of interconnected companies, other members of that group[2].

[1]   By virtue of EnA, 2000, s 222.
[2]   By virtue of EnA, 2000, s 223.

The person committing the infringement

5.61 The EnA 2002, s 217 provides that the court may make an order against a person who is named in the application, if it finds that person has engaged (or in the case of a Community/Schedule 13 infringement, also is likely to engage) in conduct which constitutes the infringement. A first point to note is that 'person' is defined in the Interpretation Act 1978 to include individuals, corporate entities and partnerships. It is also important to bear in mind the full range of persons who may be responsible for infringing under the substantive legislation – for example the CPUTR 2008 extends liability to persons acting on the trader's behalf, as well as holding the trader responsible for conduct by those acting on its behalf. All of these people may fall within the scope of persons who may be pursued under Pt 8.

Accessories

5.62 The EnA 2002, s 222 provides:

222 Bodies corporate: accessories

(1)   This section applies if the person whose conduct constitutes a domestic infringement or a Community/Schedule 13 infringement is a body corporate.

(2)   If the conduct takes place with the consent or connivance of a person (an accessory) who has a special relationship with the body corporate, the consent or connivance is also conduct which constitutes an infringement.

5.63 There are three types of accessory who may be pursued alongside, or instead of, an infringer who is a body corporate. These are:

(a)   Company officers.
(b)   Major shareholders.
(c)   Persons who tell the company what to do, despite having no formal role.

5.64 Collectively, these are described as persons with a 'special relationship' with the body corporate. The second and third groups are collectively known as 'controllers'. The purpose of creating potential liability with such breadth is to prevent natural persons from using the separate legal personality of a company they might act through, to evade the effect of an enforcement order – for example by winding up the company, or by setting up or joining a fresh company through which they continue to operate.

5.65 In order to prevent injustice to potentially innocent officers and controllers, who may have been unable to exercise control over rogue actors within the company, in order to secure an order the enforcer must prove that the infringing conduct took place with this defendant's 'consent or connivance'.

Definition of accessories

5.66 The EnA 2002, s 222(3), (4) provides that:

(3) A person has a special relationship with a body corporate if he is—
    (a)   a controller of the body corporate, or
    (b)   a director, manager, secretary or other similar officer of the body corporate or a person purporting to act in such a capacity.
(4) A person is a controller of a body corporate if—
    (a)   the directors of the body corporate or of another body corporate which is its controller are accustomed to act in accordance with the person's directions or instructions, or
    (b)   either alone or with an associate or associates[1] he is entitled to exercise or control the exercise of one third or more of the voting power at any general meeting of the body corporate or of another body corporate which is its controller.

---

[1]   For definitions of 'associates' see EnA 2002, s 222(10)–(13).

5.67 It should be straightforward to identify the official company officers. Identifying those who are controllers may require more forensic investigation. In order to identify whether a shareholder has the requisite 1/3 of the voting power, it is necessary to consider whether their 'associates' also have shares, because it is appropriate to count all of the shareholding of associates in one bloc. The range of people who may be associates of a person under investigation is broad. It includes a person's spouse or partner – whether there is any legal relationship, or they are merely living together in a relationship, and whether the relationship is current or in the past. It also includes a person's 'relatives', who are defined to encompass brother, sister, uncle, aunt, nephew, niece, lineal ancestor or lineal descendant[1]. Finally it includes people with whom the person is in partnership with (even though their partnership may not be under investigation)[2].

[1]   EnA, 2000, s 222(13).
[2]   EnA, 2000, s 222(11).

5.68 The EnA 2002, s 222(12) also makes provision for identifying where a body corporate is an associate of another body corporate, again to ensure that the range of companies that can subjected to orders is broad, to prevent complicated corporate structures from being used to evade responsibility.

5.69 A person may also be a controller of a body corporate if the directors of the company are accustomed to act in accordance with that person's directions or instructions. This may be evidenced by written records of instructions. It may also be that a person, who has no formal role in the company, or appears only to be an employee, holds themselves out as having autonomy, or is in fact able to act without supervision. Collecting evidence that such a person is a controller is likely to require careful observation.

Consent or connivance

5.70 In order to be subjected to an order, an accessory must consent or connive in the infringing conduct. These concepts are not further defined in Pt 8. 'Consent' is likely to involve approving of the conduct, or doing nothing to prevent it, despite having knowledge of it. It could also include wilful blindness. 'Connivance' is likely to involve active planning of the infringement or facilitation of it. In considering these concepts in the context of s 305(3) of the Customs and Excise Act 1952, Ashworth J accepted that 'consent' would include where a director 'is well aware of what is going on and agrees to it', and 'connive' would include where the director 'is equally well aware of what is going on but his agreement is tacit, not actively encouraging what happens, but letting it continue and saying nothing about it.'[1] Where a person is a company officer with responsibility for the area in which the infringements occurred it may be inferred that they are consenting to misconduct by virtue of their legal role, or because they are responsible for policies or practices which give rise to infringements[2].

[1]   *Huckerby v Elliot* [1970] 1 All ER 189 at 194.
[2]   See for example the facts in the criminal prosecution for unfair and aggressive practices set out in *R v Anas Ahmed* [2017] EWCA Crim 1281, where a director of a company failed properly to supervise staff who were misleading consumers and behaving aggressively in complaints

handling. The Court of Appeal noted that 'he failed to carry out his proper duties as an officer of the company' (paras 12–13) and had engaged in 'mismanagement over a sustained period of time' (para 20).

5.71 Facts that may be the basis of a finding of consent or connivance include:

- Evidence the person dealt with complaints by dissatisfied customers, in particular where the manner in which the complaint was dealt with led to further dissatisfaction[1].
- Being a director who was in post at the time of the infringements, and therefore having responsibilities, as a director, for how the company behaved[2].

[1]   As was found to be the case in *MB Designs* at para 32.
[2]   As was found in *OFT v Purely Creative Ltd* [2011] EWHC 106 (Ch) at para 198.

5.72 The fact that a person may no longer be a controller or other accessory at the time of the court order does not necessarily justify not making an order against them. The important test is whether they were an accessory at the time of the infringements. It is for the defendant to show that they no longer pose an appreciable risk of further infringing – perhaps by demonstrating that they have retired, have ill health or have permanently left the UK. Otherwise the risk that they may at some future time re-establish a management role in a similar business to that which infringed is sufficient to justify an order[1].

[1]   *Purely Creative* at para 198.

Interconnected companies

5.73 The EnA 2002, s 223 applies where a court makes an enforcement order against a body corporate, and as a matter of fact, at the time the order is made the defendant is a member of a group of interconnected companies. Companies are interconnected if one is a subsidiary of the other, or both are subsidiaries of a third company[1].

[1]   EnA, 2000, s 223(4). By EnA, 2000, s 223(5), it is stated that 'subsidiary' has the meaning given by the Companies Act 2006, s 1159. Broadly to be treated as a subsidiary of another company, that company must hold a majority of the voting rights in the subsidiary, or have the right to appoint or remove a majority of the subsidiary's Board of Directors. This is therefore a more stringent requirement than the test for a 'controller' under EnA, 2000, s 222.

5.74 It seems that the interconnected companies do not need to be included as defendants when the application is made: it is simply a matter of proving the connection at the time the order is made. Further, under the EnA 2002, s 223(1)(b) and (c), where the corporate family changes after the order has been made, the enforcer may make a further application to the court to direct that the order applies to the companies that are now interconnected.

5.75 There is no need to demonstrate that the interconnected companies pose any particular risk to consumers, or are likely to engage in infringing conduct, or consented or connived in the conduct that gave rise to the order. This seems simply to be a preventative step to ensure the order is not sidestepped.

Consultation

5.76 A key requirement for obtaining an order is that there has been appropriate Consultation that has failed to bring about the cessation of the conduct about which complaint is made, or it is a situation where the CMA thinks that an application for an order should be made without the delay that consultation would entail[1]. The consequence of failing to consult (or obtaining a waiver from the CMA) is that the enforcer 'must not make an application for an enforcement order'[2]. This seems to relate to the enforcer's power to make the application, rather than the court's power to grant an order, so the failure is most likely to risk inviting an application to strike out the claim form, or potentially a judicial review to restrain the proceedings. The chief purpose of consultation seems to be, from Recitals (13) and (14) of the Injunctions Directive[3], to give the trader an opportunity to put things right without the need for any court action to be taken.

> (13) Whereas Member States should be able to require that a prior consultation be undertaken by the party that intends to bring an action for an injunction, in order to give the defendant an opportunity to bring the contested infringement to an end; whereas Member States should be able to require that this prior consultation take place jointly with an independent public body designated by those Member States;

> (14) Whereas, where the Member States have established that there should be prior consultation, a deadline of two weeks after the request for consultation is received should be set after which, should the cessation of the infringement not be achieved, the applicant shall be entitled to bring an action before the competent court or administrative authority without any further delay.

It is clear from this that consultation should be relatively short, and should not be viewed as a requirement to engage in extensive correspondence with the trader about potential legal or other arguments that might justify their conduct. It is also not to be confused with the public law duty to consult – it is a completely different concept.

[1]   EnA 2002, s 214(3).
[2]   EnA 2002, s 214(1).
[3]   Recitals 14 and 15 of the 2009 Directive.

5.77 Some assistance as to the meaning of consultation can also be gained by considering:

(a)   when an enforcer should embark upon consultation;
(b)   what consultation seeks to achieve; and
(c)   how long consultation should last.

When should an enforcer embark upon consultation?

5.78 There is no particular threshold which prevents the enforcer from engaging in consultation, but it is implicit in the concept that the enforcer should have some basis for a belief that the trader has engaged, or is engaging in, conduct which constitutes an infringement, or is likely to engage in conduct which constitutes a Community/Schedule 13 infringement. It is this conduct that the enforcer is asking the trader to address. It is likely therefore that consultation will take place after some investigation into the infringement, but it need not mark the final end of all investigation. For example an enforcer may have obtained complaints about a trader's practices such as to raise concerns about them. It may be appropriate to send an information request to the trader, or to carry out an onsite inspection, to deepen the enforcer's understanding of those practices. This evidence might then form the basis of the case put to the trader in consultation, but further investigation may be necessary before the enforcer is ready to embark on court proceedings.

What does consultation seek to achieve?

5.79 Recital (13) of the Injunctions Directive makes it clear that the sole purpose of consultation is 'to give the defendant an opportunity to bring the contested infringement to an end'. It is to that purpose that the consultation discussions should be directed.

5.80 This purpose is set out in more detail in the EnA 2002, s 214(2):

Appropriate consultation is consultation for the purpose of—

(a)   achieving the cessation of the infringement in a case where an infringement is occurring;

(b)   ensuring that there will be no repetition of the infringement in a case where the infringement has occurred;

(c)   ensuring that there will be no repetition of the infringement in a case where the cessation of the infringement is achieved under paragraph (a);

(d)   ensuring that the infringement does not take place in the case of a Community/Schedule 13 infringement which the enforcer believes is likely to take place.

How long should consultation last?

5.81 Consultation is meant to be a summary, rather than a long drawn out, process. The EnA 2002 aims to balance the inherent urgency of stopping and preventing consumer harm, against the desirable outcome of concluding investigations proportionately and with minimum burden on the court system. To this end, the statutory scheme requires enforcers to engage in appropriate consultation for a minimum period of time before making any application to court. The exception to this requirement is where the CMA thinks that an application for an enforcement order should be made without delay[1]. The sorts of limited situations where the CMA might take this view could include where the trader has a track record of non-cooperation with regulators, and is posing a present risk to consumers, or there is some other good reason why undertakings are unlikely to be a suitable outcome and a court order must be obtained instead.

[1]   EnA 2002, s 214(3).

5.82 The three minimum periods for consultation each run from when the potential defendant receives a request for consultation from the enforcer and are:

- 7 days where an application for an interim enforcement order is to be made[1].
- 14 days where an application for an enforcement order is to be made against a standard defendant.

219

- 28 days where an application for an enforcement order is to be made against a person who is a member of, or is represented by, a 'representative body,' and that body operates an approved consumer code[2].

[1] EnA 2002, s 214(4)(b).
[2] EnA 2002, s 214(4A), which also sets out a description of the various types of body that is able to approve a code for these purposes. EnA 2002, s 214(4B) defines what 'consumer code' and 'representative body' mean.

Consultation procedure

5.83 The date on which a request for consultation is received by the potential defendant, together with whether it was correctly addressed to an appropriate officer of a corporate defendant, is by default a matter for factual proof. However in order to give greater certainty for enforcers, and the court hearing an application for an order, the Enterprise Act 2002 (Part 8 Request for Consultation) Order 2003[1], sets out circumstances where it may be deemed that a request for consultation has been properly addressed and received. Failure to comply with this Order does not invalidate consultation, if it can be proved that consultation has in fact taken place for the purposes of the EnA 2002, s 214. The Order deals with where the enforcement target is an individual, a body corporate, a limited liability partnership, a partnership, an unincorporated body or an association.

- *The method of service*: Article 4 of the Order provides that the initial request for consultation may be posted, sent electronically, or personally delivered.
- *The address for service*: Article 5 sets out what address it may be sent to, according to what type of legal personality the target has –for example it may be sent to the last known place of business, employment or residence of an individual, the registered office of a body corporate, or (for all types of targets) an electronic address which the enforcement subject has held out as an address at which they can be contacted.
- *The individual addressee*: Article 6 lists the specific individuals of each type of legal person to whom the consultation request may be delivered or addressed –for example for a body corporate, it may be sent to a director, secretary, chief executive, treasurer, manager or other officer of the company.
- *The date of service*: Article 7 makes clear, where Arts 4–6 have been complied with, and unless the contrary is proved, what date the request for consultation is deemed to be received. For example, where a request is left at an address, it is deemed received on the next business day, and where it is sent first class post it is deemed received on the second business day after the day on which it was posted. Article 7 also deals with where second class post, electronic communication or personal delivery is used, and it defines what counts as a working day. This is particularly helpful in those cases where an application for an order may be made quite soon after the minimum period of consultation is completed, or where receipt of a request for consultation is disputed.

[1] SI 2003/1375.

5.84 There are no particular formalities that consultation has to take, but it ought to be sufficient for the purposes set out at the EnA 2002, s 214(2). It is suggested that the letter initiating consultation should:

- tell the trader in the clearest terms that the letter is instituting consultation pursuant to Pt 8 of the EnA 2002. Something along the following lines might be appropriate:

  'You should treat this letter as a request for consultation pursuant to section 214 of the Enterprise Act 2002 and The Enterprise Act 2002 (Part 8 Request for Consultation) Order 2003.'

- detail the infringements or breaches that are alleged, so as to enable the trader to know the nature of the case against him. That should be done with as much precision as possible, always remembering that the particulars of the breaches can subsequently be used when drafting the pleadings;
- specify the changes in the trader's conduct or practices that the authority requires in order to achieve the cessation of the infringement and to prevent its recurrence or, in the case of a Community/Schedule 13 infringement, to ensure that the anticipated infringement does not occur. It is useful to append to the letter draft undertakings to be signed by the trader covering those changes;
- explain the enforcer's powers in the event that the trader declines to change his conduct;
- always offer further reasonable discussion;
- specify when the duty to consult will end, using a form of words similar to:

  'By virtue of section 214(4) (a) of the Act, the need for consultation will cease to apply 14 days after receipt of this letter. I would therefore be grateful to receive a substantive response from you by no later than 5pm on [. . .], failing which this Authority will consider applying to the High Court for an Enforcement Order without further notice.'

5.85 The precise form of words in the request will need to be adjusted according to the nature of the trader, local policies and individual preference. An important decision to take early on is what changes the enforcer is likely to be prepared to accept, as a bare minimum, in order not to proceed to court if these are less than those changes set out in the draft undertakings. The appropriateness of consultation is linked closely to the size and nature of the trader's organisation. A sole trader is responsible for everything that happens in his business. A local manager of a national chain may well break the law but consultation solely with him is not likely to satisfy the need for appropriate consultation with the corporation. In the case of large multinational businesses, the relevant staff may be based overseas. Discovering at an early stage the trader's organisational structure – including building up an accurate picture of interconnected companies – will help in deciding how consultation should be handled.

5.86 Three further points are worth making. First, given the stage of the enforcement process, it is probably unnecessary to enter into any prolonged argument as to whether an infringement has occurred or is likely to occur or recur. The enforcer will already be satisfied about those matters, otherwise he would not have commenced consultation. Second, it should always be remembered that consultation is an *attempt* to achieve cessation. Success, while desirable, cannot always be achieved. An enforcer should not spend an inordinate amount of time and valuable resources in trying to achieve a positive response where such a result is unlikely. Third, although it is not the enforcer's job to run or re-model the trader's business, a good understanding of what is workable is likely to be helpful. This is especially the case if the enforcer is minded to ask for enhanced consumer measures.

Dispensing with consultation

5.87 Where a matter of extreme urgency arises and there is no time to engage with the trader or engagement is seen as pointless, the enforcer should ask the CMA for a waiver under the EnA 2002, s 214(3) and make an application to court without further delay. There needs to be a clear and immediate danger of serious consumer harm followed by a prompt application to court. Even where there is some urgency, it is usually best to attempt to engage with the trader, if at all possible.

Undertakings to the enforcer

5.88 By virtue of the provisions of the EnA 2002, s 219(1), an enforcer, if he has power to make an application for an enforcement order, may accept an undertaking from the trader.

5.89 The concept of an 'undertaking' is familiar to all lawyers practising in the civil courts. It means simply 'a promise'. While an undertaking to the court has all the force of an injunction or order of the court, this is a different legal concept, namely a statutory undertaking given to the enforcer. Breach of an undertaking given to the court is punishable as a contempt of court. Failure to comply with an undertaking given to an enforcer has no immediate sanction. However, following any breach, the enforcer may make an application to the court for an enforcement order or for an interim enforcement order and it is suggested that, in those circumstances, the court is likely to be minded to grant such an order[1]. Further, where an undertaking has been given, an enforcer may make use of the investigative powers in the Consumer Rights Act 2015, Sch 5 to investigate potential breach of the undertaking.

[1]   By the EnA 2002, s 217(4) the court must have regard to whether the trader has failed to comply with an undertaking given to the enforcer.

5.90 An undertaking may be accepted from any trader whom the enforcer believes has engaged or is engaging in conduct which constitutes an infringement or is likely to engage in conduct which constitutes a Community/Schedule 13 infringement[1]. Therefore the undertakings should effectively deal with the misconduct that has been identified during the investigation. It is sensible to analyse what exactly is the harm in the trader's conduct, in order to describe what changes the trader needs to make to cure the problem. These changes should be sufficiently specific that the trader knows exactly what they can do, but not so specific that the undertaking can be easily sidestepped. It is very important that careful thought is given to the precise terms of the undertaking before it is accepted –in order to be satisfied that it does indeed cure the harm that the enforcer is concerned about. An inadequate undertaking may be worse than useless, since the court must have regard to whether it is being complied with when deciding whether to grant an order – and so it could become an impediment to dealing effectively with the infringement if it continues. Therefore the enforcer should examine what changes the trader will be making, in practice, to be satisfied that these are adequate.

[1]   EnA 2002, s 219(3). The belief does not have to be shared by the trader, who may give undertakings without admitting wrongdoing.

5.91 There is no duty on the enforcer to accept an undertaking if one is offered. It has an absolute discretion whether or not to do so. However, if, during or after the consultation period, the trader agrees (or promises) to refrain from the infringing or potentially infringing conduct, there is a good prospect that the court may refuse to make an order, since doing so is discretionary. Further, if an undertaking were to be offered but refused and if the enforcer then applied to the court for an enforcement order, which was granted in substantially the same terms as the undertaking offered by the trader, the enforcer would find himself at risk of an adverse costs order. If no undertaking is given, then the only avenue open to the enforcer for resolution is the court. There should therefore be an expectation on the part of the enforcer that, if undertakings are refused, then an application to court will be made promptly.

5.92 The undertaking is that the trader will not continue or repeat the conduct[1], of which complaint is made, will not engage in such conduct in the course of his business or another business, and will not consent to, or connive in, the carrying out of such conduct by a body corporate with which he has a special relationship[2]. All of these restrictions should be included in the rubric of the undertaking.

[1]   That limb does not apply in the case of future conduct likely to amount to a Community/Schedule 13 infringement: see EnA 2002, s 219(5).
[2]   EnA 2002, s 219(4).

5.93 Under the EnA 2002, s 219(5ZA), where there is infringing conduct that has occurred after 1 October 2015[1], the person giving an undertaking may include a further undertaking to take enhanced consumer measures within a period specified in the undertaking and, where such measures are included, to provide information or documents to the enforcer to enable the enforcer to determine if the person is taking those measures. Such an undertaking can be given only to a public body unless a private designated enforcer has satisfied the conditions set out in s 219C[2]. Enhanced consumer measures are described in more detail below. However some points should be made here:

- The full range of measures is available to be included in undertakings, as may be included in a court order.
- Where an enforcer wishes to ask the trader to include such measures in undertakings, the enforcer must be satisfied they are just and reasonable[3].
- In making this assessment, the enforcer must consider whether the proposed measures are proportionate[4].

- If redress is to be sought, this must be only in a situation where the enforcer believes consumers have suffered loss as a result of the trader's conduct, and the enforcer is satisfied that the amount the trader is being asked to pay out does not exceed the sum of the total losses suffered by consumers.

[1] By virtue of the date of the coming into force of the CRA 2015, Sch 7, para 8.
[2] EnA 2002, s 219C.
[3] EnA 2002, s 219B(1).
[4] In assessing proportionality, the enforcer must have regard to the factors set out in EnA 2002, s 219B(2).

5.94 There is no formality required by the EnA 2002. In theory, an undertaking could be given orally, although issues of proof might then arise. Again, in theory, there is no reason why an exchange of correspondence between enforcer and trader should not amount to an undertaking, if, on its proper construction, the correspondence amounts to an agreement or promise on the part of the trader to refrain from doing that which the statute requires him to refrain from doing. However, a degree of formality is probably preferable. It is suggested that a written document should be prepared by the enforcer identifying the infringing, or potentially infringing, conduct and setting out the trader's agreement to refrain from continuing or repeating such conduct. The trader should then be invited to sign the document.

5.95 Earlier editions of this book suggested that possible difficulties could arise when the enforcer wished to require some positive steps to be taken by the trader and it was suggested that the solution might be for the trader to undertake to refrain from the infringing conduct unless he took the positive steps required. However, it is now considered that such difficulties are unlikely to arise, given the provisions in the EnA 2002, ss 219–219B relating to enhanced consumer measures[1]. One such measure, falling within the compliance category, is directed at preventing or reducing the risk of the occurrence or repetition of the impugned conduct. That provision, it is submitted, would enable an enforcer to accept an undertaking requiring the trader to take the positive steps required by the enforcer.

[1] See further below.

Publicity

5.96 There is no general rule preventing publicity of undertakings, and there many good reasons why publicity is helpful – not least to ensure that the public are aware of what the trader has promised to do, in order to hold them to account, as well as to maintain a public record of what the enforcer has done. In line with this aim, the EnA 2002, s 219(5A) provides that where the enforcer is a CPC enforcer, they may accept an undertaking from the trader to publish the terms of the undertaking, or take steps itself to publish the undertaking. The aim of this is to eliminate any continuing effects of the infringement. Such publicity does not constitute an enhanced consumer measure[1].

[1] EnA 2002, s 219A(5)(c).

Notification to the CMA

5.97 Where an undertaking is accepted, the enforcer must notify the CMA, of the terms of the undertaking and the identity of the person who gave it[1]. This is an important measure to ensure the enforcement community has a record of outcomes, and can where appropriate bring a failure to comply with the undertaking to a court's attention.

¹   EnA 2002, s 219(6).

INVESTIGATORY POWERS

5.98 Originally, the EnA 2002, ss 224–227F set out the information gathering powers available to enforcers. Those sections have now been entirely repealed[1]. A new EnA 2002, s 223A headed 'Investigatory Powers' has been inserted into the EnA 2002. It reads:

> For the investigatory powers available to enforcers for the purposes of enforcers' functions under this Part, see Schedule 5 of the Consumer Rights Act 2015[2].

¹   CRA 2015, Sch 6, paras 67–77.
²   CRA 2015, Sch 6, para 78.

5.99 There are three types of investigatory powers:

(a)   Information notices.
(b)   Powers to purchase products and observe business.
(c)   Powers to gather evidence on site.

The powers are set out in Pt 3 and 4 to the CRA 2015, Sch 5. The powers are constructed so that they are available to specified enforcers, where those enforcers are acting for a specified purpose, and certain conditions are fulfilled. A single enforcer may during a single investigation act for several purposes, and therefore have several bases for using investigative powers – but the enforcer should at all times be clear which purposes they are acting for and keep a record of these. In relation to the investigation of infringements which post date, or are suspected to post date EU exit IP completion day (31 December 2020) erstwhile 'EU enforcers' are known as 'Schedule 13 enforcers'[1].

¹   The Consumer Protection (Enforcement) (Amendment etc) (EU Exit) Regulations 2019, SI 2019/203, regs 4 and 9.

Information notices

5.100 Paragraph 14 in Pt 3 of the CRA 2015, Sch 5, enables the CMA and other enforcers to give notice to a person requiring that person to provide the enforcer with the information specified in the notice. By para 15(3), (4) and (5), the enforcer may specify time for compliance and the manner of compliance. The notice may require the creation of documents, as well of course as the production of existing documents, and in order to comply the information must be in legible form. The requirement of legibility means that data held in digital format may need to be printed, or supplied with access to any computer programme required to read the data.

5.101 The power to issue an information notice is the basic power that is available to most enforcers in the widest set of circumstances. For example, the power of the CMA would be exercisable:

(a)   to enable the Authority to exercise or to consider whether to exercise any function it has under Pt 8 of the EnA 2002;

(b)   to enable a private designated enforcer to consider whether to exercise any function it has under that Part;

[(c)   to enable a Community enforcer to consider whether to exercise any function it has under that Part[1];]

(d)   to ascertain whether a person has complied with or is complying with an enforcement order, an interim enforcement order an online interface order or an interim online interface order;

(e)   to ascertain whether a person has complied with or is complying with an undertaking given under the EnA 2002, ss 217(9), 218(10) or 219.

[1]   This power has now been removed as of 1 January 2021 – see The Consumer Protection (Enforcement) (Amendment etc) (EU Exit) Regulations 2019, SI 2019/203, reg 4(6).

5.102 The power of a public designated enforcer, a local weights and measures authority in Great Britain, the Department of Enterprise, Trade and Investment in Northern Ireland or an EU/Schedule 13 enforcer other than the CMA would be exercisable:

(a)   to enable that enforcer to exercise or to consider whether to exercise any function it has under Pt 8 of the EnA 2002;

(b)   to ascertain whether a person has complied with or is complying with an enforcement order or an interim enforcement order made on the application of that enforcer;

(c)   to ascertain whether a person has complied with or is complying with an undertaking given under the EnA 2002, ss 217(9) or 218(10) following such an application;

(d)   to ascertain whether a person has complied with or is complying with an undertaking given to that enforcer under the EnA 2002, s 219.

5.103 An 'EU enforcer' or 'Schedule 13 enforcer' is defined[1] as the CMA, a local weights and measures authority in Great Britain, the Department of Enterprise, Trade and Investment in Northern Ireland, the FCA, the CAA, the Secretary of State, the Department of Health, Social Services and Public Safety in Northern Ireland, the Office of Communications, an enforcement authority within the meaning of the Communications Act 2003, s 120(15) (regulation of premium rate services), the Information Commissioner, the Department for Infrastructure, the Maritime and Coastguard Agency, the Office of Rail and Road and the Office for the Traffic Commissioner.

[1]   CRA 2015, Sch 5, para 4.

5.104 In addition, a domestic enforcer may exercise its information gathering powers for the purpose of ascertaining whether there has been a breach of any legislation listed in paras 10 or 11, which the enforcer separately has the duty or power to enforce. This is an extensive list of laws, at least some of which may also be domestic or Community/Schedule 13 infringements, and so enforceable under Pt 8 (for example the Consumer Protection from Unfair Trading Regulations 2008 are listed, and these are also Community/Schedule 13

Infringements). In order to access this purpose, an officer of the enforcer must generally also reasonably suspect there has been a breach of relevant legislation[1].

> [1]   Paragraph 13(5) – unless the enforcer is a market surveillance authority and para 13(6) applies.

Form

5.105 Under para 15 of the CRA 2015, Sch 5, the following provisions as to the form of the notice apply:

(1)   The notice . . . must be in writing and specify the purpose for which the information is required.

(2)   If the purpose is to enable a person to exercise or to consider whether to exercise a function, the notice must specify the function concerned.

5.106 There is a saving provision which excuses a person from providing any information or creating any document which he would be entitled to refuse to provide or produce:

(a)   in proceedings in the High Court on the grounds of legal professional privilege; or

(b)   in proceedings in the Court of Session on the grounds of confidentiality of communications[1].

Further, any information that a person provides under para 14 may not generally be used in criminal proceedings against them[2]. The exception to this is where the person is being prosecuted for the obstruction offence under para 36 or under the Perjury Act 1911, s 5, for providing misleading information in the notice itself.

> [1]   CRA 2015, Sch 5, para 15(6).
> [2]   Paragraph 17.

5.107 A typical notice might read:

'NOTICE

This is a Notice given under paragraphs 14 and 15 of Schedule 5 to the Consumer Rights Act 2015.

X County Council ('the Council'), being a local weights and measures authority in Great Britain, requires you to provide it with the information specified in this Notice within seven days of receipt of this Notice. The information should be given in writing addressed to: [name and address of officer]

The Council requires the specified information for the purposes of determining whether or not it should exercise any of the following functions that it has under the Act against you, namely:

* Engage in appropriate consultation pursuant to section 214 of the Enterprise Act 2002 ('the Act').
* Apply for an Enforcement Order pursuant to section 215 of the Act.
* Accept undertakings pursuant to section 219 of the Act.

Information Required

Please specify in writing _____ [set out precisely the information required]

Note: you need not provide any information which you would be entitled to refuse to provide or produce in proceedings in the High Court on the grounds of legal professional privilege.

You should be aware that failure to comply with this notice may lead to the local authoritymaking an application to the court seeking an order compelling your compliance. Should such an application be necessary you may be required to meet all, or part, of the costs or expenses incurred by the council in that application.'

The person to be served

5.108 In order to exercise or to consider whether to exercise the specified functions set out in para 13 or to ascertain the specified matters set out in para 13, the enforcer may serve a notice on any person, not just the trader who is the subject of the enquiry. For example, if the enforcer was concerned to discover details of a trader's bank account, his bank could be served with a notice seeking appropriate information Where a person within the UK has control over information stored outside the UK, it is likely that they can be ordered to bring it within the jurisdiction and produce it[1]. The notice may be served on a person who is located outside the UK, where that person has a 'sufficient connection' with the UK[2]. It may also be the case that an information notice could be served on a person without a connection to the UK, however the position is less clear[3]. It remains uncertain whether a UK court could exercise enforcement powers over a person overseas, should an information notice not be complied with. However consideration would need to be given to how the notice should be enforced if no or an inadequate response is received.

[1] See *R (on the application of KBR, Inc) (Appellant) v Director of the Serious Fraud Office (Respondent)* [2021] UKSC 2 para 30.

[2] See the Court of Appeal decision in *The Queen on the Application of Tony Michael Jimenez v The First Tier Tribunal (Tax Chamber), HMRC* [2019] EWCA Civ 51. In deciding that HMRC statutory notices could be served on a person located overseas, the Court of Appeal set out a number of factors which support the proposition that a CRA Sch 5 notice may also be served overseas. These are: a mere request for information needs no authority (para 29); there is no penalty for non-compliance (paras 29, 41, 44, 47, 53); the intention and origin of the legislation envisages engaging with overseas persons (paras 22, 36, 38); the potential availability of enforcement assistance overseas is not decisive (paras 42–43); if service overseas were impossible, the purpose of the legislation would be thwarted (paras 22, 32); the extent to which there is a strong public interest in being able to serve the notice overseas (paras 24, 32).

[3] By analogy to the power to obtain information from an overseas company in a criminal investigation, which was considered by the Supreme Court in *R (on the application of KBR, Inc) (Appellant) v Director of the Serious Fraud Office (Respondent)* [2021] UKSC 2. Absent clear wording in the statute, the court ruled that an intention to legislate over persons outside the UK can be implied where it is clear that the statute was intended to have extra-territorial effect. Such an intention may be implied where the purpose of the legislation could not otherwise be effectively achieved (para 30).

Documents

5.109 There remains an unresolved question as to whether the power to require the production of information under paras 14 and 15 may now also be used to require the production of existing documents in the possession of the party served. This was certainly the position under the statutory predecessor, s 226 of the EA 2002, however, the language and structure of consumer enforcement powers were changed by Sch 5. In particular, the wording of the paras 14 and 15 power does not now include the words 'A notice may require the production of documents'[1]. This was replaced with only the production of 'information' by the 'creation of documents'[2]. This change apparently followed the 2012 Government consultation on enforcement powers which warned against a power, without the threshold of reasonable suspicion, being used for 'fishing expeditions'[3]. A regulator can require the production of existing documents under CRA 2015 para 27, however, this power is subject to the threshold of reasonable suspicion[4] and the person served 'occupying' premises[5] (see below and CHAPTER 4, Criminal Enforcement for further discussion of enforcement powers).

[1]   EA 2002, s 226(5).
[2]   CRA, Sch 5, para 15(4)(a).
[3]   Para 2.31 – BIS Consultation Enhancing Consumer Confidence Through Effective Enforcement: Consultation on consolidating and modernising consumer law enforcement powers, March 2012.
[4]   CRA, Sch 5, para 19(4).
[5]   CRA, Sch 5, para 27(1).

Enforcement

5.110 The only means of enforcing the notice is to apply to the court for an order[1]. If the court is satisfied that the person on whom the notice was served has failed to comply with it, the court may require that person to do anything the court thinks it is reasonable for him to do for any of the purposes for which the notice was given to ensure that the notice is complied with[2]. The court has power to order the person in default or, if that person is a company, partnership or unincorporated association, an official who is responsible for the failure, to pay the costs or expenses of the application. Where enforcement is sought against a person located overseas, consideration must be given to how the court papers may be served on them (eg this may require the consent of the overseas state), and the extent to which a UK court order enforcing the notice would be effective to secure compliance[3].

[1]   CRA 2015, Sch 5, para 16.
[2]   CRA 2015, Sch 5, para 16(2) and (3).
[3]   For a discussion of these issues see *The Queen on the Application of Tony Michael Jimenez v The First Tier Tribunal (Tax Chamber), HMRC* [2019] EWCA Civ 51 at paras 45–54.

5.111 Where the recipient of the notice provides false or misleading information to the enforcer, this may amount to an offence under the Perjury Act 1911, s 5[1].

[1]   Proceedings for this offence are one of the few situations where the information supplied by a person under para 14 may be used in criminal proceedings against them (see para 17(5)).

Further powers

5.112 Part 4 of the CRA 2015, Sch 5 sets out further powers which may be exercised by Domestic Enforcers and EU/Schedule 13 Enforcers. It covers powers to purchase products and observe business conduct, and powers exercisable onsite. Each power is available where the enforcer is acting for the right purpose, the requisite threshold is met, and any relevant conditions are complied with.

5.113 Enforcers may purchase products and observe the carrying on of business for the purpose of ascertaining compliance with a domestic enforcer's legislation, or where acting as an EU/Schedule 13 enforcer, for a purpose related to functions the enforcer has under Pt 8 as a CPC/Schedule 13 enforcer[1]. In order to access the power the EU/Schedule 13 enforcer must first reasonably suspect there has been or is likely to a Community/Schedule 13 infringement, or a failure to comply with an enforcement order, interim enforcement order, online interface order, interim online interface order or an undertaking[2] or be seeking to obtain the product for use as evidence in EnA 2002, Pt 8 proceedings[3].

1   Paragraph 19(2) and 20(2).
2   Paragraph 20(3).
3   CRA 2015, Sch 5, para 20(3A).

5.114 The power to purchase a product, which includes the power to enter into an agreement for the provision of a product, also includes, by necessary implication the ability to carry out those steps that lead up to entering into a contract, such as signing up to a mailing list, making enquiries about a product or visiting the trader's website. The purchase may take place in a shop or online. In order to exercise the test purchase power, para 21(2) explains that the officer of the enforcer may, without giving notice or obtaining a warrant, enter premises that are generally open to the public and inspect any product on the premises which the public may inspect. The officer may do this at any reasonable time, whether or not the public have access to the premises at that time[1]. There is no express power to browse online, but this is because this is not necessary. The power is given to the enforcer to enter the premises so that they cannot be ejected as a trespasser.

1   Paragraph 21.

5.115 A test purchase necessarily involves some degree of concealment of the officer's identity, in order to prevent the trader from adapting their behaviour to evade enforcement. However enforcers must be careful that they do not inadvertently engage the Regulation of Investigatory Powers Act 2000 ('RIPA 2000') by becoming a covert human intelligence source, or conducting directed or intrusive surveillance. If in doubt it is wise to obtain sign off from the relevant authorising officer. Before carrying out the test purchase the officer must also consider the extent to which the exercise is necessary and proportionate, and whether it will involve any collateral intrusion into any person's privacy. As a broad rule of thumb the more the officer interacts with the trader on a personal level, the greater the risk that RIPA 2000 will be engaged.

5.116 Where covert test purchasing occurs online, the enforcer should give consideration to setting up a covert internet connection, and how evidence of the website's behaviour can best be captured (for example by screenshots or filming). It may also be necessary to establish a covert payment account and delivery address if a physical product is to be purchased.

5.117 By para 22, enforcers have power to observe the carrying on of business. As with the power to purchase products, this paragraph makes it lawful for the officer to enter premises to which the public ordinarily have access. Entry may be at any reasonable time, whether or not the public in fact have access at that time, and no notice need be given or warrant obtained first. The power means that the officer may not be ejected as a trespasser.

5.118 Examples of conduct the enforcer may wish to observe include collecting evidence of how shelf edge labelling appears, how sales staff interact with customers and whether a trader is in fact operating from a certain premises.

Onsite powers

5.119 Part 4 also sets out powers that an enforcer may exercise on premises that are not necessarily open to the public. In order to exercise these powers, the enforcer must have entered the premises, which can be achieved either with or without a warrant.

Entry without a warrant

5.120 Under para 23 – where the conditions set out in that paragraph are satisfied – an officer of an enforcer may enter business premises[1] at any reasonable time, taking such persons and equipment with him as he thinks are necessary[2]. The conditions differ depending on whether the visit is a 'routine inspection' or not. In the case of a routine inspection, the officer must first give two working days' notice in writing of his intention to enter, setting out why the entry is necessary and indicating the offence of obstruction.

[1]   As with the former power under the EnA 2002, no authority is given to enter premises used wholly or mainly as a dwelling.
[2]   Paragraph 23(1), (2) and (11).

5.121 By contrast, no notice need be given where <u>one</u> of the situations in para 23(6) applies. These are where:

• the inspection is being carried out by an officer of a domestic enforcer who reasonable suspects a breach of the enforcer's legislation;
• the officer reasonably considers that to give notice would defeat the purpose of the entry;
• it is not reasonably practicable in all the circumstances to give notice, in particular because the officer reasonably suspects that there is an imminent risk to public health or safety;
• the enforcer is a market surveillance authority.

5.122 If a non-routine inspection is carried out, the officer must produce a document to someone on the premises setting out why entry is necessary and explaining the offence of obstruction, and must produce evidence of his identity, unless this is not reasonably practicable.

Entry with a warrant

5.123 Under para 32, an officer of an enforcer may be authorised to enter any premises[1] with a warrant issued by a justice of the peace[2]. The warrant[3] may be issued if the justice of the peace considers that there are reasonable grounds for believing that:

(a)   there are, on the premises, products which an officer of the enforcer has power to inspect or documents which an officer of the enforcer could require a person to produce; or

(b)   on the premises, there has been or is about to be (as the case may be) a breach of a domestic enforcer's legislation or Community infringement or there has been a failure to comply with an enforcement order, an interim enforcement order or an undertaking given to the court;

and either:

(c)   access to the premises has been or is likely to be refused, and notice of the enforcer's intention to apply for a warrant has been given to the occupier of the premises; or

(d)   it is likely that products or documents on the premises would be concealed or interfered with if notice of entry on the premises were given to the occupier of the premises; or

(e)   the premises are unoccupied, or the occupier of the premises is absent, and it might defeat the purpose of the entry to wait for the occupier's return.

1   Note that in this case, 'premises' does not exclude a dwelling.
2   Sheriff in Scotland and lay magistrate in Northern Ireland.
3   'It must never be forgotten that the granting of a warrant is a most extreme and invasive kind of order, not to be granted without great caution and dependent on appropriate full and accurate disclosure by the applicant': see *R (on the application of Vuciterni) v Brent Magistrates' Court* [2012] EWHC 2140 (Admin) at [35]. The warrant may be quashed on an application for judicial review.

5.124 All the material necessary to justify the grant of the warrant should be contained in the information provided on the application form, which must identify which of the conditions specified in para 32 is being relied on by the applicant. If the magistrate requires any further information in order to be satisfied that the issue of a warrant is justified, a note should be made of additional information provided orally, so that there exists a proper record of the full basis upon which the warrant has been granted. Where further documents were considered that also had to be recorded[1].

1   *R (Redknapp) v Commissioner of the City of London Police* [2009] 1 WLR 2091; *Hargreaves v Brecknock and Radnorshire Magistrates Court* [2015] Crim LR 999.

5.125 Under para 33, where a warrant has been issued, the power is to enter the premises at any reasonable time, using reasonable force if necessary. The officer may be accompanied by such persons and may take such equipment, as the officer thinks necessary.

5.126 Paragraph 33 also makes further provision for the execution of the warrant, requiring that:

•   It may not be executed beyond one month from the day it is issued[1].
•   The warrant must be produced to an occupier of the premises for inspection[2].
•   Where the premises are unoccupied, the officer must leave a notice explaining that the premises have been entered under a warrant, and must leave the premises as effectively secured against trespassers as the officer found them[3].

1   Paragraph 33(2).
2   Paragraph 33(4).
3   Paragraph 33(5) and (6).

The powers exercisable on the premises

5.127 Where an officer of an enforcer is lawfully on the premises, either with or without a warrant, para 24 provides that he may exercise the powers set out in paras 25–31. Each power is exercisable where the threshold is met, and where the conditions apply. It is convenient to set these out in a table.

Threshold	*Power*	*Condition*
Reasonably suspect has been or likely to be a Community/Schedule 13 Infringement (para 20(3)(a); Reasonably suspect failure to comply with undertaking or order (para 20(3)(b–d))	*Inspect* any product on the premises (para 25), once lawfully entered premises. *Inspect* held necessarily to imply power to search[1]. Includes the power to examine any procedure connected with the production of a product (para 25(3))	Must be a product, which is Defined in s 35 to mean: goods (defined in s 2(8) –'any tangible movable items'); (for the purposes of these powers, 'goods' appears to include 'documents', where tangible, as expressly excluded elsewhere (eg in Sch 5, Pt 5, para 42)); a *service*; *Digital content* (defined in s 2(9) –'data which are produced and supplied in digital form'); Immovable property; Rights and obligations.
Ascertaining compliance with domestic enforcer's legislation (para 19(2))		
Domestic enforcer ascertaining compliance with enforcer's legislation NB – not usable by EU Enforcers	Test weighing or measuring equipment (para 26)	Is or reasonable cause to believe may be used for trade OR Has been, or reasonable cause to believe has been passed by an approved verifier as fit for use

Threshold	*Power*	*Condition*
Reasonably suspect has been or likely to be a Community/Schedule 13 Infringement (para 20(4)(a) and (3)(a); Reasonably suspect failure to comply with undertaking or order (para 20(4)(a) and (3)(b-d) To ascertain compliance with the domestic enforcer's legislation (if reasonably suspects breach) (para 19(3)(a)) To ascertain whether documents may be required as evidence in proceedings for breach of or under domestic enforcer's legislation (para 19(3)(b))	Require production of documents (para 27): By the trader occupying the premises, or any person on the premises who is acting on the trader's behalf If the trader *has access to* the document (need not be physically on the premises) If document is electronic, may require production in a form in which it can be easily taken away, and in which it is visible and legible (para 27(4))	Must be at a 'reasonable time' (27(1))' Document *includes* information recorded in any form (para 8), so would include digital data and computers'[2] Documents must relate to the trader's business, but the investigation may relate to another trader's business (para 27(2))' 'Trader' means a person acting for purposes relating to that person's business, whether acting personally, or through another person acting in the trader's name or on their behalf (para 27(8) and s 2(2))' May not require production of LPP material.
	Take copies of any document or entry in any document (para 27(1)(b)	
	Require explanation of the document (para 20(3)	

Threshold	Power	Condition
Reasonably suspects good may disclose a Community/Schedule 13 infringement, or failure to comply with Order or Undertaking (para 20(5)(a))	To seize and detain Goods (para 28)	Goods mean 'any tangible movable item' But does not include documents for the purposes of this power
Reasonably suspects good may be required as evidence in Pt 8 proceedings (para 20(5)(b))		Before seizing – produce evidence of the officer's identity AND authority: show these to the occupier (para 28(2) (unless not reasonably practicable – para 28(3))
Reasonably suspects goods may disclose a breach of domestic enforcer's legislation (para 19(5)(a))		Comply with PACE 1984 while seizing goods (para 28(6)
Reasonably suspects goods may be required as evidence in proceedings for a breach of, or under, (para 19(5)(c)) domestic enforcer's legislation		After seizing, take reasonable steps to inform the person from whom they have been seized that they have been seized AND provide that person with a receipt (para 28(4))

Threshold	Power	Condition
Reasonably suspects may be required in evidence in proceedings under Pt 8	Seize documents (para 29)	Document includes information recorded in any form (para 8), so would include digital data and computers
		Does not include LPP material (para 29(6))
Reasonably suspects may be required as evidence in proceedings for breach of or under domestic enforcer's legislation		Before seizing – produce evidence of officers identity and authority to occupier of premises (para 29(2)) – Unless not reasonably practicable (para 29(3))
		Comply with PACE 1984 while seizing goods (para 29(5))
		After seizing, take reasonable steps to inform the person from whom they have been seized that they have been seized AND provide that person with a receipt (para 29(4))
When an enforcer is exercising a power under paras 28 and 30? It is reasonably necessary to exercise the power in order to achieve the purpose (para 31(3))	Break open containers (para 31)	Container means anything in which 'goods' may be stored – this is any tangible movable items
	Access any electronic device In which information may be stored OR From which information may be accessed	Require a person with authority to give access If requirement not complied with, access the container or electronic device yourself
Where the enforcer has already entered premises with or without a warrant (para 34(1))	Require assistance (para 34): From any person on the premises Such assistance as the officer reasonably considers necessary	

[1]   See *R (on the application of Vuciterni) v Brent Magistrates' Court* [2012] EWHC 2140 (Admin) at [48].

[2]   See *R (on the application of Glenn & Co (Essex) Ltd) v HMRC* [2010] EWHC 1469 (Admin).

The offence of obstruction

5.128 Where an enforcer is on the premises, any persons also there are obliged to provide assistance and co-operate. Failing to do so may amount to an offence of obstruction, which is punishable with a fine.

Action by officer	Action by person	Application example
Officer is exercising or seeking to exercise a power in Pt 4	Intentionally obstructs (para 36 (1)(a))	While inspecting a product, seizing a good, or seizing a document
Officer properly imposes a requirement under Pt 4	Intentionally fails to comply (para 36(1)(b))	A requirement to produce a document, provide explanation of document, open a container, or provide assistance
Officer reasonably requires other assistance or information, in order to exercise a power under Pt 4	Fails to give assistance or information without reasonable cause (para 36(1)(c))	Requesting a password to access remote storage
	Gives information, but it is false or misleading in a material respect (para 36(2)): Knowingly OR recklessly	Stating that the person does not have access to material, when this is not true.
The person cannot be prosecuted for failing to answer any question, or give any information, if this might incriminate them (para 36(4))		

TOWARDS AN ENFORCEMENT ORDER

Notice to the CMA

5.129 Along with the requirement to engage in consultation with the potential defendant, the EnA 2002, s 214(1) prohibits any enforcer that is not the CMA from making an application for a court order unless it has given notice to the CMA of its intention to make the application, and the appropriate minimum period has elapsed. The appropriate period is 14 days for an enforcement order, and 7 days for an interim enforcement order.

5.130 The requirement to wait always applies, unless the CMA thinks that the application for an enforcement order should be made without delay[1]. For the purposes of this requirement, the CMA is likely to consider whether this is a case where it is appropriate for the CMA to give directions under the EnA 2002, s 216. This section empowers the CMA to direct that only it or some other enforcer may make the court application (the purpose of this section seems to be to prevent multiple applications for orders being made by several enforcers, against the same trader, potentially for the same factual conduct.

[1]   EnA 2002, s 214(3).

5.131 Where the CMA gives directions, the enforcer (or the CMA) may still accept undertakings from the trader. The CMA may also decide to take some other steps besides accepting undertakings or making a court order, for the purpose of securing that the infringement is not committed, continued or repeated[1].

[1]   EnA 2002, s 216(3).

5.132 It should be noted that under the EnA 2002, s 220(6), if an enforcer wishes to bring further proceedings for breach of an order or undertaking to the court, the enforcer must give further notice to the CMA, of the application and any order the court makes.

Which court?

5.133 Under CRA 2015, Sch 5, para 45, there is the express power for a local authority to bring civil proceedings in relation to infringements occurring outside the local authority's area. Further, the EnA 2002, s 220(2) confirms that any CPC/Schedule 13 enforcer may take action in respect of breach of an order or undertaking to the court, even if the first order or undertaking was obtained as a result of an application by some other enforcer. However this power does not apply to (interim) online interface orders: only the CMA may enforce a breach of these.

England and Wales

5.134 Courts having jurisdiction are the High Court or the county court[1] if the person against whom the order is sought carries on business or has a place of business in England and Wales[2].

[1] Part 2 of the Crime and Courts Act 2013 amended the County Courts Act 1984 by establishing in England and Wales a court called 'the county court' for the purposes of exercising the jurisdiction and powers previously conferred on the several individual county courts.
[2] EnA 2002, s 215(5).

5.135 It is suggested that proceedings should be commenced in the High Court for serious cases and in the county court for less serious cases. However if there is a point of law that it is important to clarify, the High Court may be more appropriate[1].

[1] The High Court should be used where there are complex issues of fact or law, complex remedies or procedures or issues of importance to the public in general.

Scotland

5.136 Courts having jurisdiction in Scotland are the Court of Session or the sheriff if the person against whom the order is sought carries on business or has a place of business in Scotland[1].

[1] EnA 2002, s 215(5).

5.137 Again, it is suggested that proceedings should be commenced in the Court of Session for serious cases and before the sheriff for less serious cases.

Northern Ireland

5.138 Courts having jurisdiction in Northern Ireland are the High Court or a county court if the person against whom the order is sought carries on business or has a place of business in Northern Ireland.

Overseas defendants

5.139 The phrase 'carries on business' should be taken to encompass where the trader is seeking to supply goods or services to at least one person in the relevant jurisdiction, even if they have no actual staff operating there, in order to be consistent with the definition of domestic infringements in the EnA 2002, s 211(1A). Similar reasoning should be applied to Community/Schedule 13 infringements.

5.140 The position where a defendant is within the EU or EEA differs depending on whether the proceedings were commenced before 1 January 2021. Where proceedings were commenced in 2020 or before, the position is governed by European law on jurisdiction and applicable law[1]. Where proceedings are commenced on or after 1 January 2021, they are governed by the principles of UK and private international law. The law governing international disputes is complex and specialist, and is covered in more detail in CHAPTER **3**. However some brief observations may be made here. Within the Brussels regime, the European Court has held that a preventative action brought by a consumer protection association for the purpose of preventing a trader from using terms considered to be unfair in contracts with private individuals, is a matter relating to a tort or delict within the meaning of the Brussels I Regulation[2]. Accordingly it was appropriate for the enforcer to be able to bring proceedings in the courts of the consumer's state, rather than the trader's. Applying this reasoning here, the appropriate UK court would previously have been able to accept jurisdiction even if the trader was domiciled elsewhere in the EU or EEA, as long as there were affected consumers in the UK and the trader directed their activities towards these consumers.

[1] The Brussels I Regulation (44/2001) sets out rules on jurisdiction and recognition and enforcement of judgments in civil and commercial matters. The Rome II Regulation (864/2007) sets out the rules on the law applicable to non-contractual obligations.
[2] *CJEU Verein fur Konsumenteninformation v Henkel* (C-167/00) at para 50.

5.141 The same analysis would have applied to actions covered by the Lugano Convention (applying to Defendants in Norway, Switzerland and Lichtenstein. Service could then have been effected under the Hague Convention.

5.142 However now that the UK has left the EU, and is no longer bound by the Brussels regime on jurisdiction, the only way to bring an overseas trader before the UK courts is to do so in accordance with UK rules on jurisdiction (most commonly by seeking to serve proceedings with the court's permission).

5.143 In order to seek permission to serve on an overseas defendant, an application is made under CPR 6.36 and 6.37. Such an application should be made once the pleadings for the substantive proceedings have been prepared, so that these may be put before the judge hearing the application, who will need to make an assessment of the merits of the claim. The judge also has to consider if there is a gateway under PD6B para 3.1, and finally whether England and Wales is the most appropriate forum for the claim. In the case of *Competition and Markets Authority v Viagogo AG*[1], the court granted permission to serve out against a company based in Switzerland on the basis that there was clearly a serious issue to be tried, that gateway (20)(a) applied (a claim made under an enactment – ie the Enterprise Act 2002 – which allows proceedings to be brought against persons not within England and Wales)[2], and that it was 'plain and obvious that this jurisdiction is the appropriate forum for the litigation of this claim' (para 14).

1   [2018] EWHC 2525 (Ch).
2   See also *Orexim Trading Ltd v Mahavir Port and Terminal Private Limited* [2018] EWCA Civ 1660 para 33.

5.144 In the *Viagogo* case, there was also a concern that service under the Hague Convention would take too long, and also be resisted by the defendant. Therefore an application was made for permission to serve on the defendant's London solicitors. This application was also granted, on the basis that even if the Hague Convention applied, there were good reasons to authorise service as provided for in CPR 6.15 and 6.27. In this case, applying the Court of Appeal's decision in *Cecil v Bayat*[1] para 68, the good reasons were: the claimant was also seeking an Interim Enforcement Order, in part on the basis that Viagogo's competitors had given undertakings to change their practices and non-compliance by Viagogo would disadvantage them; and bringing the proceedings to Viagogo's attention through their lawyers would not be unfair to them (given the extensive involvement of those solicitors in the consultation process), and would enable Viagogo to engage with and react to the proceedings without delay (para 22). As it turned out the judge was correct, because Viagogo settled the matter by consenting to the claimant's order being made.

1   [2011] 1 WLR 3086.

5.145 In this case, the claimant also sought an order excusing them from translating the documents included in the claim. This application was also granted on the basis that many of the documents were the defendant's own documents, which were originally written in English, and the litigation turned in part on whether those words (in English) complied with UK law, so translation would be a distraction. It would also be very slow and expensive to the public purse (para 23).

5.146 Given the lengthy consultation already undertaken, the judge directed that Viagogo should only have 21 days to respond to the claim, notwithstanding the large quantity of material in the claim (para 24).

5.147 The law that applies to such a challenge, under the Rome II Regulations (which are now retained EU law) is the law of the state where the consumers are affected, even if the case is about terms in contracts governed by the law of another EU or EEA state[1]. This means that where a trader based in the EU or EEA is directing their activities towards consumers in the UK, an enforcer may, if they succeed in bringing the trader within the jurisdiction of the UK courts, rely on the Rome II Regulations to bring proceedings under Pt 8 against that trader[2].

1   *CJEU Verein fur Konsumenteninformation v Amazon EU Sarl* (C-191/15) at para 48.
2   Where a challenge is being brought to the fairness of terms under a contract governed by the laws of another EU or EEA state however, this contract must be construed according to the laws of that state, albeit that these may not cause the consumer to lose any mandatory protections they enjoy under their own law, as set out in Art 6(2) of the Rome I Regulation (593/2008) – *CJEU Verein fur Konsumenteninformation v Amazon EU Sarl* (C-191/15) at para 69.

Parties

Claimant

5.148 The enforcer, rather than the investigating officer, will be the claimant. Thus, for example, a local authority trading standards officer, investigating an infringement on behalf of his authority, will institute proceedings in the name of that authority, not in his own name. The officer should ensure that he is authorised to commence proceedings in the name of his authority.

5.149 Part 8 made provision for enforcers in other EU and EEA states to bring proceedings under Pt 8 to enforce the law either as implemented in the UK or as implemented in their own state. However, these provisions of Pt 8 do not apply to proceedings brought after 31 December 2020[1]. Before this date if an application for an enforcement order was made by a Community enforcer, the court was empowered to examine whether the purpose[2] of the enforcer justified its making the application. If the court concluded that there was no such justification, then it could refuse the application on that ground alone[3].

[1]   Any Pt 8 proceedings already commenced by a Community enforcer may continue as long as they are commenced on or before 31 December 2020 – see reg 3(9) of the Consumer Protection (Enforcement) (Amendment etc) (EU Exit) Regulations 2020.
[2]   The purpose of the enforcer is to be construed by reference to the Injunctions Directive: see EnA 2002, s 215(8).
[3]   EnA 2002, s 215(6) and (7).

5.150 If the application is made by an enforcer other than the CMA, then that enforcer must notify the CMA of the result of the application[1].

[1]   EnA 2002, s 215(9).

Defendant

5.151 It is important to identify all parties who have engaged in infringing conduct, as well as those who have consented and connived in them, and those who are interconnected bodies corporate. In principle, all of these should be joined as defendants. See **5.62** on accessories above.

5.152 There are a number of reasons why accessories should be named as defendants:

- it is worth remembering that enforcement orders against, or undertakings from, the corporate body alone will be worthless if the company is subsequently wound up;
- in most cases, it is the accessories that are ultimately responsible for the infringing conduct and often, unless restrained, they will continue to repeat the conduct under other corporate guises. Many traders engage in what is commonly known as 'phoenixing' as a tactic in order to avoid enforcement action.

Pre-action Protocol

5.153 Before issuing proceedings, it is important to check compliance with the Practice Direction on Pre-action Protocol. The aim of this PD is to ensure that the parties have sufficiently narrowed the issues between them, and do not litigate unnecessarily. The PD envisages that key documents that either party is likely to rely on should be exchanged and that correspondence is exchanged swiftly. Assuming the trader has made some sort of offer of undertakings, it is important that the enforcer gives consideration to whether these could avert litigation. Failure to comply with the spirit of the PD could result in adverse costs. A key step that it is usual to take is to send the potential defendant a letter before claim. This may well be in the same terms as the consultation letter, or it may take into account issues raised by the trader during consultation. It is the last opportunity the trader has to provide undertakings before court action commences[1]. Unless there is a particular need for urgency, it is usual to give the trader at least 14 days to respond. In appropriate cases, the consultation process may itself be sufficient to comply with the pre-action process.

[1] Litigants are generally encouraged to consider ADR before commencing court proceedings. However it is unlikely that conduct that gives rise to an application for an enforcement order would be suitable for ADR.

Interim relief

5.154 Even before a claim form has been issued, an enforcer may apply to the court for interim relief in the form of an interim enforcement order. In some circumstances the CMA may also seek an interim online interface order[1].

[1] By virtue of EnA 2002, ss 218ZA–218ZD, discussed in more detail below.

Interim enforcement order

5.155 The EnA 2002, s 218 empowers the court to make an interim enforcement order provided four conditions are satisfied:

. . .

(a) that it is alleged that the person is engaged in conduct which constitutes a domestic or Community/Schedule 13 infringement or is likely to engage in conduct which constitutes a Community/Schedule 13 infringement;

(b) that if the application had been an application for an enforcement order it would be likely to be granted;

(c) that it is expedient that the conduct is prohibited or prevented (as the case may be) immediately; and

(d) if no notice of the application has been given to the person named in the application, that it is appropriate to make an interim enforcement order without notice.

ALLEGATION OF A DOMESTIC OR COMMUNITY/SCHEDULE 13 INFRINGEMENT

5.156 The first condition speaks for itself and is unlikely to cause difficulties. It is sufficient that the enforcer is making the necessary allegation, and it is properly pleaded in the application.

LIKELIHOOD A FINAL ORDER WOULD HAVE BEEN GRANTED

5.157 Given that the court is dealing with a paper application for interim relief where the evidence has not been tested by cross-examination, it manifestly cannot embark on a full trial of the issues. It is suggested that the approach of the court should be as follows: is it more likely than not that, on the evidence presently before the court, a final enforcement order would be made[1].

[1]   See *OFT v MB Designs (Scotland) Ltd* [2005] SLT 69 at [21].

5.158 In the absence of specific references either to the 'serious issue to be tried' or to the 'balance of convenience' tests used in applications for interim injunctions[1], it is probably preferable to approach the grant of an interim enforcement order without reference to those authorities that deal with the grant of interim injunction[2].

[1]   See *American Cyanamid Co v Ethicon Ltd* [1975] AC 396, particularly per Lord Diplock at 406–409.
[2]   A similar view appears to have been taken by Lord Drummond-Young in *OFT v MB Designs (Scotland) Ltd* [2005] SLT 69 at [20].

EXPEDIENT TO PROHIBIT THE CONDUCT IMMEDIATELY

5.159 The third condition requires the enforcer to establish some urgency in the matter – for example, because of the serious and immediate harm being caused or likely to be caused to consumers. If there has been delay in enforcement action on the part of the enforcer, it may be harder to demonstrate this, but it is suggested that the focus ought not to be on the efficiency or otherwise of the enforcer, but the urgency of the risk to consumers. For example there may be many reasons why it takes time to gather sufficient evidence of the infringing conduct, such as where material must be requested from third parties, and in more complex cases there may be a need for detailed legal research. Further, in many cases, the trader will have suffered no prejudice by the enforcer's delay.

IF NO NOTICE HAS BEEN GIVEN, IT IS APPROPRIATE STILL TO MAKE THE ORDER WITHOUT NOTICE

5.160 The fourth condition is considered in further detail in the following section. However, it is suggested that, if the court is not satisfied that the application should have been made without notice, then, rather than dismissing it, the court may decide to adjourn the hearing to enable proper notice to be given.

Procedure for interim order

5.161 An interim enforcement order[1] can be granted at any time before the grant of a final enforcement order[2]. It can be granted before the claim form has been issued. As a general rule, notice of the hearing should be given to the trader[3]. However, an application can be made without notice. Helpful guidance as to when an application can be made without notice is given in the Chancery Guide February 2016 ('the CG'). Paragraph 16.2 suggests that there are four classes of case that are exceptions to the general requirement to give notice. Three are relevant to an interim enforcement notice:

'(a)   where the giving of notice might frustrate the order;
(b)   where there is such urgency that it is truly not possible to give the requisite notice. Even in such a case, however, the applicant should give the respondent informally as much notice of the application as is possible;

(c)   where the applicant cannot identify the respondent by name but only by description.'

¹   Any procedural issues not covered by the statute should be answered by reference to Pts 23 and 25 of the Civil Procedure Rules SI 1998/3132 ('CPR').
²   EnA 2002, s 218(5).
³   Normally three clear days' notice to the other party is required but in an emergency or for other good reason the application can be made without giving the full 3 days' notice. In the Chancery Division, permission to serve on short notice may be obtained on application without notice to the interim applications judge: see para 16.9 of Chancery Guide, as amended.

5.162 An application must be lodged with the court (and served on the defendant, if notice is given). Form N244¹ should be used, either alone or in conjunction with a witness statement. The application:

- must state why the application is being made. The facts of the case, as they are understood by the investigating officer, should be set out in full (preferably in a witness statement). It is on the basis of that evidence that the court will decide whether 'if the application had been an application for an enforcement order it is likely that it would have been granted';
- must make the fullest disclosure. In other words, those facts adverse to the application as well as those in its favour must be given. That is particularly important when the application is made without notice. The EnA 2002, Section 218(6) expressly provides:

    '(6)   An application for an interim enforcement order must refer to all matters—
        (a)   which are known to the applicant, and
        (b)   which are material to the question whether or not the application is granted.'

- if the application is made without notice, must explain why no notice has been² given;
- should set out the order that the enforcer is asking the court to make. It is usual to attach a draft order to the application form;
- if a claim form has not yet been issued, draft particulars of claim can (and probably should, if there is sufficient time to draft them) be exhibited to the witness statement.

¹   All practice forms can be downloaded from www.justice.gov.uk/courts/procedure-rules/civil/forms.
²   EnA 2002, s 218(7).

5.163 A subsequent application may be made by the enforcer or the trader to vary or discharge the order¹.

¹   EnA 2002, s 218(8).

Contents of the interim order

5.164 The court has a discretion whether or not to grant an interim enforcement order. It is suggested that the greater the urgency and potential harm to consumers, the more likely that the court will grant an order.

5.165 An interim enforcement order must:

(a)   indicate the nature of the alleged conduct; and
(b)   direct the person not to continue or to repeat the¹ conduct; not to engage in such conduct in the course of his business or another business; and not

to consent to or connive in the carrying out of such conduct by a body corporate with which he has a special relationship[2].

[1] Unless the allegation is that the trader is likely to engage in conduct which constitutes a Community/Schedule 13 infringement, in which case the inclusion of this clause is meaningless and should be omitted.
[2] EnA 2002, s 218(2) and (3).

5.166 However, if the order is made against an accessory alone, instead of paragraph (b) above, the order must direct the person not to continue or repeat the conduct[1]; in the course of any business carried on by him, not to engage in conduct such as that which constitutes the infringement committed by the body corporate; and not to consent to or connive in the carrying out of such conduct by another body corporate with which he has a special relationship[2].

[1] Except in the case of future conduct likely to amount to a Community/Schedule 13 infringement: see EnA 2002, s 219(5).
[2] EnA 2002, s 222(9).

5.167 An interim enforcement order will be expressed to last either until a specified date or until further order of the court or until the date of the full hearing. If the interim order was made without notice, it will usually contain a provision that the order will last for a limited period only – usually not more than 7 days. The enforcer will then be required to give the trader notice of his intention to apply to the court at the expiration of that period for the order to be continued. In the meantime the trader will be entitled to apply, though generally only after giving notice to the enforcer, for the order to be varied or discharged.

Undertaking

5.168 Instead of making an interim enforcement order, the court may accept an undertaking from the trader to comply in the same terms as for an order (set out in paragraph (b) above) or alternatively an undertaking that he will take such steps as the court believes will secure his compliance with that paragraph[1]. Breach of an undertaking given to the court has more serious consequences than breach of an undertaking given to an enforcer, in that the trader will be in contempt of court and liable to imprisonment, a fine or sequestration of his assets[2].

[1] EnA 2002, s 218(10).
[2] Contempt of court is dealt with below.

Penal notice

5.169 The interim enforcement order and the undertaking should be endorsed with a penal notice in Form N77 explaining the consequence of disobedience.

Cross undertaking as to damages

5.170 Normally an applicant for an interim injunction is required to give the court a cross undertaking as to damages, generally in something like the following terms:

And upon [the Claimant] undertaking to comply with any order that this court may make, if the court later finds that the order for an interim injunction has caused loss to [the defendant] and decides that [the defendant] should be compensated for that loss.

5.171 There is no power under Pt 8 for the court to order an enforcer to give a cross undertaking in damages as a requirement for the grant of any order. However leaving this aside, even where a standard interim injunction is being sought, it is now settled law that a public authority seeking to enforce the law in the interests of the public generally, often in pursuance of a public duty to do so, and enjoying only the resources which have been assigned to it for its functions, generally does not have to give such an undertaking[1].

[1]   See *Kirklees Metropolitan BC v Wickes Building Supplies Ltd* [1993] AC 227 and *FSA v Barclays Bank Ltd* [2013] UKSC 11. See also *Pensions Regulator v Dalriada Trustees Ltd* [2013] EWHC 4346 (Ch) for an application of this principle in the context of a freezing order.

Costs schedule

5.172 This being an interlocutory application and unlikely to last more than one day, each side should serve on the other a written statement of its costs not less than 24 hours before the date fixed for the hearing[1]. At the conclusion of the hearing, the judge will decide what costs order to make and may summarily assess those costs on the basis of the written statement of costs before him.

[1]   See subsection 9 of CPR, Practice Direction 44. The statement of costs should follow as closely as possible Form N260.

Final enforcement order

5.173 When making an application for an enforcement order, either Pt 7 or Pt 8 of the Civil Procedure Rules (CPR) may be used[1].

[1]   Where the CMA is the claimant, in some circumstances it may seek an online interface order, by virtue of EnA 2002, ss 218ZA–218ZD, discussed in more detail below.

5.174 CPR Pt 8 is best suited to any claims where there is no dispute of fact, and the key issue to be addressed is a question of law. It is a quick and simple procedure: the claim (using Form N208) is lodged with a supporting witness statement exhibiting any further evidence. A copy of the draft order sought should be included. All of this paperwork should be served on the defendant. No particulars of claim are required, there is no need to complete allocation questionnaires and there are no disclosure requirements. However there is also no requirement for a defence and no option for judgment in default. The hearing will most likely be purely legal argument with no oral evidence.

5.175 Once served with the proceedings, the defendant must acknowledge service and serve any evidence on which they wish to rely within 14 days (unless the parties agree a short delay). The enforcer then has a further 14 days to put in further evidence in reply.

5.176 Claims under CPR Pt 8 are likely to be most suitably heard in either the Chancery Division or Queen's Bench Division, each of which have further special procedural rules. It is likely that in many if not most trading standards cases there will be a dispute of fact in which case CPR Pt 7 is more suitable. Where in pre-action correspondence it becomes apparent that the defendant believes there is a substantial dispute of fact, this may make it advisable to bring proceedings under Pt 7 in any event, even if the bulk of the evidence being relied on in fact emanates from the defendant, or has been gathered through a thorough investigation. Further, where a key legal issue of the case could involve a factual dispute in order to resolve it, this may become a substantial factual dispute[1]. The rest of this section explains in more detail the Pt 7 process.

1   *Competition and Markets Authority v Care UK* [2019] 10 WLR 96 paras 33–34 & 39–42. Examples of mixed fact and law include the concept of the 'average consumer' under the Consumer Protection from Unfair Trading Regulations 2008.

Particulars of claim

5.177 The first step in CPR Pt 7 proceedings is to issue a claim form[1]. If the defendant is outside the UK, but no permission to serve out is required (for example because service under the Companies Act 2006 is relied on), the claimant must still prepare a notice in Form N510 setting out the grounds on which he is entitled to serve out. This should be filed and served with the claim form[2]. By contrast, if permission to serve out is required, an application must be made before issue of the main claim, using the Pt 23 procedure. Particulars of claim can, and preferably should, be served with the claim form. If not, they may be served separately 14 days after service of the claim form[3]. With some defendants, service may pose practical challenges (for example where they are out of the jurisdiction, itinerant or otherwise seeking to evade service). It is important to use a correct means of service, as set out in CPR 7.5(1) and 6.3 and it may be wise to instruct a process server to produce evidence of service. If the difficulties are causing delay, the court may need to give permission to extend time for service, or even dispense with service altogether. Once service is effected, the claimant must file a certificate of service with the court.

1   See generally CPR Pt 7: practice form N1 must be used.
2   See CPR 6.34(1).
3   See CPR 7.4.

5.178 The particulars of claim must include a concise statement of the facts on which the claimant relies and such other matters as may be set out in the relevant Practice Direction[1]. In the case of an application for an enforcement order, the particulars of claim should include details of the infringement or infringements alleged, and why each defendant either engaged in the conduct, or was an accessory. It should conclude with a request for the grant of an enforcement order, specifying the terms of the order sought.

1   See CPR 16.4. Paragraph 8.2 of Practice Direction 16 – Statements of Case – requires, *inter alia*, that details be given of any allegation of fraud, the fact of any illegality, details of any misrepresentation, notice or knowledge of a fact and details of wilful default.

Defence

5.179 CPR 16.5 provides:

(1)   In his defence, the defendant must state—
   (a)   which of the allegations in the particulars of claim he denies;
   (b)   which allegations he is unable to admit or deny, but which he requires the claimant to prove; and

          (c)   which allegations he admits.
    (2)   Where the defendant denies an allegation—
          (a)   he must state his reasons for doing so; and
          (b)   if he intends to put forward a different version of events from that given by the claimant, he must state his own version.

Reply

5.180 The claimant may serve a reply to the defence if he wishes to allege facts in answer to the defence which were not included in his particulars of claim.

Further interlocutory steps

5.181 Once pleadings are closed, there are further interlocutory steps that must or could be taken. They include:

- Directions as to the course of hearing. Although a case management conference may be held at any time during the course of the proceedings, it is usually held at an early stage when directions will be given such as, for example, a timetable and orders for the exchange of witness statements, for disclosure and for expert evidence[1].
- The filing and exchange of cost budgets, following which a costs management conference may be convened and a costs management order made[2]. Once a costs management order has been made the court, when assessing costs on the standard basis, will have regard to the receiving party's last approved or agreed budget for each phase of the proceedings and will not depart from it unless satisfied that there is good reason to do so.
- Applications for interim or interlocutory orders[3].
- Disclosure and inspection of documents. The recent amendments to the CPR on disclosure alter considerably the extent of disclosure[4].
- Exchange of witness statements, each verified by a statement of truth[5].
- Obtaining the court's permission to call expert evidence[6].

[1] See CPR 3.1 for the court's general powers of management and CPR 3.1A in the case of an unrepresented party.
[2] See CPR 3.12–3.18 for Costs Management.
[3] See CPR Pt 23 for general rules about applications and SI 1998/3132, Pt 25 for applications for interim remedies.
[4] See CPR Pt 31 and in particular r 31.5.
[5] See CPR Pt 32.
[6] See CPR Pt 35.

Evidence from consumers

5.182 Is it essential that one or more consumers be called to testify? The short answer, it is suggested, is no.

5.183 In *OFT v MB Designs (Scotland) Ltd*[1] Lord Drummond-Young said[2]:

'In relation to the evidence, harm to the collective interests of consumers will normally be inferred from an accumulation of individual instances. Evidence relating to those individual instances will generally be provided, however, by officials of the relevant enforcer, such as the present petitioner, or officials in the trading standards departments of local authorities. That is appropriate because it is the collective interests that are relevant, and the individual instances are only adminicles of evidence that go to establish harm to the collective interests.'

1   [2005] SLT 69.
2   At [15].

5.184 The latter passage is of some practical importance. It is unnecessary in every instance for the enforcer to take numerous statements from individual dissatisfied consumers with a view to presenting them at the hearing. It is sufficient for the enforcer to present the evidence of harm to the collective interests of consumers in whatever manner seems most appropriate in the circumstances. That may be from his own and his colleagues' observations; from consumer complaints whether made orally or in writing; or from the direct evidence of the consumers themselves.

5.185 It is instructive to consider the evidence presented in the *MB Designs* case, the sufficiency of which was confirmed by Lord Drummond-Young. It took the form of two affidavits, although (certainly in England) it could have taken the form of two witness statements. One was from an officer of the OFT's Consumer Regulation Enforcement Division and one was from a Divisional Trading Standards Officer of South Lanarkshire Council. Those affidavits were backed up by documentation relating to individual complaints about defective products or services supplied by the trader. It appeared from the documentation that some of the complaints were investigated by independent third parties appointed or recommended by the Consumer and Trading Standards Department of South Lanarkshire Council and found to be justified; others were investigated by tradesmen or surveyors instructed by the householder concerned, or were backed up with photographs. The judge concluded[1]:

'In my opinion the fact that a significant number of complaints have been investigated or documented in this manner is important, because obviously ill-founded complaints are possible. In the present case, I am satisfied that the investigation of complaints relied on by the petitioner relates to a sufficiently large proportion to establish that those complaints are for the most part well-founded.'

1   At [15].

5.186 It is significant that, in that particular case, no consumers gave evidence. A similar approach was taken in other cases litigated by the OFT in *OFT v Foxtons*, although there were a number of complaints about the application of the letting agent's terms, these were all simply exhibited to the claimant's witness statement. Likewise, in *OFT v Ashbourne Management Services*, the consumer complaint evidence was in the form of a series of completed questionnaires. Indeed, using consumer witness evidence should be treated with caution, given that the evidence of just a handful of witnesses may not be considered to be representative of the typical conduct of the business under investigation.

Factual claim

5.187 If an application for an enforcement order or an interim enforcement order is made in respect of a Community/Schedule 13 infringement involving a contravention of the Unfair Commercial Practices Directive (2005/29/EC) and if the trader has made a factual claim as part of his commercial practice[1], the court has power to order the trader to provide evidence as to the accuracy of that claim. If he fails to do so or if he provides inadequate evidence, the court is entitled to infer that the claim was inaccurate[2]. That is a useful provision to be used, for example, to verify claims in a trader's advertising or promotional material.

[1] As defined in CPUTR 2008, SI 2008/1277, reg 2.
[2] EnA 2002, s 218A.

The order

The court's discretion to make an order

5.188 By the EnA 2002, s 217 (as amended by CRA 2015, Sch 7, para 6):

(1) This section applies if an application for an enforcement order is made under section 215 and the court finds that the person named in the application has engaged in conduct which constitutes the infringement.

(2) This section also applies if such an application is made in relation to a Community/Schedule 13 infringement and the court finds that the person named in the application is likely to engage in conduct which constitutes the infringement.

(3) If this section applies the court may make an enforcement order against the person.

(4) In considering whether to make an enforcement order the court must have regard to whether the person named in the application—
    (a) has given an undertaking under section 219 in respect of conduct such as is mentioned in subsection (3) of that section;
    (b) has failed to comply with the undertaking.

5.189 If the court is satisfied that any person named in the application has engaged in conduct which constitutes the infringement or, in the case of a Community/Schedule 13 infringement, that the person named in the application is likely to engage in conduct which constitutes the infringement, it may grant an enforcement order. The infringement does not need to be ongoing, and the mere fact that a trader has made corrections to bring about the cessation of the infringement does not automatically disentitle the enforcer to an order. However, the court has a discretion whether or not to grant the order. In *OFT v Purely Creative Ltd*[1], Briggs J said:

> 'Although the court's power to make an enforcement order is plainly discretionary, the Act gives no further guidance to the court beyond that set out in section 217(4) as to the matters which the court should take into account when deciding whether or not, and if so how, to exercise that discretion.'

It is therefore important that the enforcer is in a position, whether or not the infringement is ongoing, to advance arguments why an order should be made.

[1] [2011] EWHC 106 (Ch) at [25].

5.190 The EnA 2002, s 217(4) refers to the court's obligation to take into account whether the trader has given an undertaking to the enforcer and whether he has failed to comply with it. This is double edged: a trader who has given an undertaking and failed to comply is likely to require an order. However where a trader remains complaint with their undertakings, the court may be less willing to grant an order even if an infringement is proven.

The terms of the order

5.191 By s 217(5):

> (5) An enforcement order must—
>> (a)   indicate the nature of the conduct to which the finding under subsection (1) or (2) relates, and
>> (b)   direct the person to comply with subsection (6).
> (6) A person complies with this subsection if he—
>> (a)   does not continue or repeat the conduct[1];
>> (b)   does not engage in such conduct in the course of his business or another business;
>> (c)   does not consent to or connive in the carrying out of such conduct by a body corporate with which he has a special relationship (within the meaning of section 222(3)).
> (7) But subsection (6) (a) does not apply in the case of a finding under subsection (2).

---

[1]   Where applicable – this will not apply in the case of future conduct likely to amount to a Community/Schedule 13 infringement: see EnA 2002, s 219(5).

5.192 The enforcement order should be directed to the named defendants who have been found to have infringed or be likely to infringe (as the case may be), and set out what each person should or should not do, in order to avoid infringing. Under English law, an injunction whether interim or final, must state with precision what the defendant must or must not do if he is to avoid the peril of imprisonment for contempt of court[1]. A similar rule applies to interdicts in Scotland[2]. These principles should be applied to enforcement orders, in so far as the purposes of the Injunctions Directive may still be achieved – namely to secure the cessation of infringements – but there is inevitably a tension between absolute precision and sufficient generality to prevent avoidance. This tension has been explored in two cases.

---

[1]   See *Lawrence David Ltd v Ashton* [1989] ICR 123, per Balcombe LJ and *CEF Holdings Ltd v Mundey* [2012] FSR 35 per Silber J at [43] and [51], but see the planning case of *Kettering Borough Council v Perkins* [1999] JPL 166, where the court adopted a less rigorous approach.
[2]   See *Webster v Lord Advocate* [1985] SC 173.

5.193 In order to ensure that infringing conduct can be stopped effectively, some degree of generality is possible. In *OFT v MB Designs (Scotland) Ltd*[1] Lord Drummond-Young explained the reasoning why[2]:

> 'Where a trading standard is to be enforced, however, I am of opinion that the same degree of precision is not necessary; nor indeed does it appear possible. The critical point is that the enforcement of provisions such as Pt 8 is not designed to ensure that no defective goods or services are ever supplied; it is rather designed to compel traders to achieve an acceptably low incidence of defects, and to rectify such defects as appear. Any court order of that nature must involve some degree of vagueness about the permissible incidence of defects. The order may also bear some degree of imprecision as to the nature of the defects that are prohibited. This is because the function of trading standards legislation is to minimise defects of every sort, and in cases where management or quality control is poor such defects may take many forms. For that reason I do not think it necessary that the court's order should specify the precise nature of the defects that are covered by it; it is rather designed to cover

251

defects of every sort. Consequently it is not necessary that such an order should be directed against specific acts that are said to be in contravention of Pt 8.'

1   [2005] SLT 69.
2   At [15].

5.194 However reasonable precision is still necessary according to the Court of Appeal in *OFT v Vance Miller*[1]. Having been referred to the Scottish case, Arden LJ said[2]:

'As I see it, in England and Wales the order similarly need not apply only to specific acts and some degree of generality is acceptable, though, in respectful disagreement with Lord Drummond-Young, who thought that a considerable degree of generality was acceptable, I would be reluctant to say more than that "some" degree of generality is permitted. The court should see that what is prohibited is as clearly described as the circumstances permit, taking into account the need to give fair warning to the defendant of the acts that might constitute a breach.'

1   [2009] EWCA Civ 34.
2   At [46].

5.195 As a matter of drafting, the order may therefore contain *some* degree of generality (in order to prevent easy avoidance by minor alterations to the trader's business practices), but it must be sufficiently clear and precise so that the trader knows in what circumstances it will be breached. It is best to avoid an order with the formulation 'such as to harm the collective interests of consumers', since this is too unclear a test for an order[1]. It is suggested that although the court must be satisfied that the trader's conduct harms the collective interests of consumers in order to make the order, the order itself may be drafted in fairly absolute terms, setting out specifically how the trader must behave. Consequently the order should avoid merely restating the law that the trader must comply with in any case, but rather particularise the business activities the trader must engage in, or avoid, in order to comply with the law.

1   *OFT v Vance Miller* [2009] EWCA Civ 34.

Publication of the order

5.196 By s 217(8):

(8) An enforcement order may require a person against whom the order is made to publish in such form and manner and to such extent as the court thinks appropriate for the purpose of eliminating any continuing effects of the infringement—
(a)   the order;
(b)   a corrective statement.

5.197 Requiring publication of the order and any corrective statement is not an enhanced consumer measure, but derives from the Injunctions Directive. There are two significant purposes that publication achieves: first is to ensure the public at large are aware of the requirements that have been imposed on the trader; second is to correct any false information that the trader may have put into the public domain before the order was made. This second aim could require the trader to engage in extensive advertising at considerable expense, if this is appropriate – for example where a trader has purchased misleading ad words, it may be appropriate to force them to purchase a comparable number of ad words to set the record straight.

Undertakings to the Court

5.198 By s 217(9), (10):

> (9) If the court makes a finding under subsection (1) or (2) it may accept an undertaking by the person—
>> (a) to comply with subsection (6), or
>> (b) to take steps which the court believes will secure that he complies with subsection (6).
>
> (10) An undertaking under subsection (9) may include a further undertaking by the person to publish in such form and manner and to such extent as the court thinks appropriate for the purpose of eliminating any continuing effects of the infringement—
>> (a) the terms of the undertaking;
>> (b) a corrective statement.

5.199 Instead of making an order, the court may accept an undertaking from the trader. Such an undertaking appears to have the same effect as an order, and may be enforced in the same way. The chief distinction is simply that the trader is able to take the initiative in drafting the undertaking, and if there is no need for a contested hearing in which an order is made, there may be a saving in costs.

Notification to the CMA

5.200 Section 215(9) requires an enforcer which is not the CMA to notify the CMA of the result of an application under s 215, whether it results in an order or not.

Enhanced consumer measures

5.201 EnA 2002, s 217(10A)–(11) provides:

> (10A) An enforcement order may require a person against whom the order is made to take enhanced consumer measures (defined in section 219A) within a period specified by the court.
>
> (10B) An undertaking under subsection (9) may include a further undertaking by the person to take enhanced consumer measures within a period specified in the undertaking.
>
> (10C) Subsections (10A) and (10B) are subject to section 219C in a case where the application for the enforcement order was made by a designated enforcer which is not a public body.
>
> (10D) Where a person is required by an enforcement order or an undertaking under this section to take enhanced consumer measures, the order or undertaking may include requirements as to the provision of information or documents to the court by the person in order that the court may determine if the person is taking those measures.
>
> (11) If the court—
>> (a) makes a finding under subsection (1) or (2), and
>> (b) accepts an undertaking under subsection (9),
>
> it must not make an enforcement order in respect of the infringement to which the undertaking relates.

What are enhanced consumer measures?

5.202 The EnA 2002, ss 219A–219C[1] deal with enhanced consumer measures[2], which are intended to widen the scope of the measures that a court can impose and to permit the court on a case by case basis to determine the best way of dealing with a breach of the law. They apply only in relation to conduct which occurs, or which is likely to occur, after 1 October 2015 (the commencement of the CRA 2015, s 79)[3]. There were further changes to the regime as of 2 June 2020, which are described more fully below[4]. The EnA 2002, s 219A(1) identifies three categories of enhanced consumer measures, namely:

- the redress category;
- the compliance category;
- the choice category.

Measures in any of these categories may be added to an enforcement order or an undertaking to the court, but not to an interim enforcement order. They may only be used where it is just and reasonable.

[1] Added by CRA 2015, Sch 7, para 8.
[2] There is a useful guide published by the then Department for Business, Innovation and Skills (BIS) in May 2015 entitled 'Enhanced Consumer Measures – Guidance for Enforcers of Consumer Law'.
[3] SI 2015/1630, para 3(e).
[4] Consumer Protection (Enforcement) (Amendment etc.) Regulations 2020, SI 2020/484.

THE REDRESS CATEGORY

5.203 By the EnA 2002, s 219A(2), the measures in the redress category are:

    (a)   measures offering compensation or other redress to consumers:
        (i)   who have suffered loss as a result of the conduct which has given rise to the enforcement order or undertaking, or
        (ii)   where that conduct constitutes a Community/Schedule 13 infringement (which took place after 2 June 2020), who have been affected in any other way by that conduct,
    (b)   where the conduct referred to in paragraph (a) relates to a contract, measures offering such consumers the option to terminate (but not vary) that contract,
    (c)   where such consumers cannot be identified, or cannot be identified without disproportionate cost to the subject of the enforcement order or undertaking, measures intended to be in the collective interests of consumers.

5.204 The redress category enables the court to make provision for compensation to consumers who have suffered loss as a result of the actions of a trader in breach of consumer law, and in relation to Community/Schedule 13 infringements which have taken place since 2 June 2020, to consumers who have simply been affected by that conduct in some way. There is no need to prove loss in respect of such harm. Since the consumers will not be before the court as parties to the action, the order of the court should be directed at the trader ordering him to offer a quantified or quantifiable sum by way of compensation to those consumers who have suffered loss or other harm, for example, by purchasing certain products, paying money or being disadvantaged in some way. In order to assess whether to impose a redress remedy, the court must consider evidence and argument on the following key issues, which are set out in the statutory scheme.

(a)   How have consumers suffered harm? Where the harm post dates 2 June 2020 and was caused by a Community/Schedule 13 infringement, there is no need to demonstrate actual loss. However where the harm predates 2 June 2020 or where it was caused by a domestic infringement after this date, then it is essential to demonstrate some financial loss.

(b)   How can the harm be quantified? In the case of financial loss, this would be how much loss the consumers have suffered. In some cases it may be easier than others to identify the loss per consumer – for example it may be that a product, with a false claim about its attributes, is worth £20 more than its true market value – in which case the loss to consumers would be £20 per purchase. However in more complex situations a more rough and ready calculation may be necessary. Where the harm was caused by a Community/Schedule 13 infringement after 2 June 2020, it is likely that redress will still be most appropriate where the consumer has suffered some loss, but it is sufficient to demonstrate that the consumer was affected by the infringement in some way[1]. At this stage, the court should not factor in any costs the trader will necessarily incur in repaying consumers[2].

(c)   Can the consumers who have suffered loss (or otherwise been affected) be identified and contacted? In many cases, this will no doubt be a matter of analysing the trader's sales records – for example most online sales will be paid for by card, which should permit consumers to be identified. Where there are no records – for example due to payments being made in cash – it may be necessary to publish advertising inviting consumers to come forwards with proof of purchases. If the cost of identifying individual victims is disproportionately large, the loss figure may instead be paid to a charity or some other worthy cause.

(d)   How and when will the redress be paid? How will the measure be policed? It may be necessary to appoint a third party auditor to check compliance, or require the trader to produce documentary evidence to demonstrate they have taken the action as ordered.

[1]   EnA 2002, s 219B(4A).
[2]   EnA 2002, s 219B(4), (5) and (9).

5.205 The court also has the option of permitting consumers to terminate a contract. For example, a consumer might have been misled as to the price of an annual subscription for certain services. They were advertised at one price but, after the consumer entered into the contract, the small print enabled the trader to debit more than the advertised price from the consumer's bank account. This measure allows the court to offer the consumer the option to terminate the contract and, if he accepts that offer, to order that the contract be terminated. That approach would not preclude the court from also making provision for compensation.

5.206 Where appropriate, it may be necessary to ask recipients of redress to agree to a settlement agreement as a condition for getting paid. However this must not prevent them from bringing claims for different infringements to those covered by the application for the enforcement order. Further, the CJEU has ruled that where a consumer is being asked to waive rights to make a claim in the context of an existing dispute, they may only do so on the basis of their free and informed consent. Accordingly, in the case of an unfair term, they must be made aware of the non-binding nature of the term, and of the consequences resulting from it[1]. The scope of the waiver must also be tightly drawn, and not require the consumer to waive any further claims they may wish to bring in the future[2]. Due to its contractual nature, it seems that the waiver agreement may also be assessable for fairness in itself, and so may not in the event provide the protection the trader is looking for[3].

[1] CJEU *XZ v Ibercaja* (C-452/18) paras 29–30.
[2] CJEU *XZ v Ibercaja* (C-452/18) paras 76–77.
[3] CJEU *XZ v Ibercaja* (C-452/18) para 77.

THE COMPLIANCE CATEGORY

5.207 By the EnA 2002, s 219A(3):

> The measures in the compliance category are measures intended to prevent or reduce the risk of the occurrence or repetition of the conduct to which the enforcement order or undertaking relates (including measures with that purpose which may have the effect of improving compliance with consumer law more generally).

5.208 A list of possible measures is not included in the legislation, but the BIS Guidance suggests such measures as a business having to sign up to the Primary Authority Scheme; having to appoint a compliance officer; having to update internal processes to ensure there is no repeat of the breach; or having to improve the training the business gives to its staff to ensure that there is no repeat of the breach[1].

[1] See p 24 of the BIS Guidance 'Enhanced Consumer Measures – Guidance for Enforcers of Consumer Law'.

THE CHOICE CATEGORY

5.209 By the EnA 2002, s 219A(4):

> The measures in the choice category are measures intended to enable consumers to choose more effectively between persons supplying or seeking to supply goods or services.

5.210 This category permits the court to require the trader to provide information that is not strictly a legal requirement, but due to the circumstances of this trader's conduct or products, would be helpful to consumers in exercising choice. Examples could include requiring the trader to provide contact details of competitors offering comparable products, or where consumers can obtain the same product free.

When can enhanced consumer measures be imposed?

5.211 In order to impose an enhanced consumer measure, the court must be satisfied that doing so is just and reasonable[1]. The court may consider any factor that is relevant, but it must at least assess whether the proposed measures are proportionate, taking into account:

(a)   the likely benefit of the measures to consumers;

(b)   the costs likely to be incurred by the subject of the enforcement order or undertaking, such costs being the cost of the measures and the reasonable administrative costs associated with taking the measures[2]; and

(c)   the likely cost to consumers of obtaining the benefit of the measures[3].

[1]   EnA 2002, s 219B(1).
[2]   Where the harm has been caused by a domestic infringement, or took place before 2 June 2020, a redress measure may only be included in the order or undertaking where the amount the trader is being required to pay is not greater than the loss actually caused to consumers: EnA 2002, s 219B(4). However this is no longer a requirement for Schedule 13 infringements.
[3]   EnA 2002, s 219B(2) and (3).

Online interface orders

OVERVIEW AND BACKGROUND

5.212 The CMA (and only the CMA) may bring proceedings for an online interface order or an interim online interface order. This enables it to seek a court order for the removal or alteration of a trader's software content, for example a website or application, where that gives consumers access to the trader's goods and services[1]. An order can be sought where there has been, or is likely to be, a Community/Schedule 13 infringement[2] that occurred on or after 2 June 2020[3].

[1]   EnA 2002, s 218ZD.
[2]   EnA 2002, s 218ZA. It is not available for domestic infringements. Online interface orders and interim online interface orders are be available in relation to Sch 13 infringements, by virtue of reg 3(3)(b) of the Consumer Protection (Enforcement) (Amendment etc) (EU Exit) Regulations 2020.
[3]   The Consumer Protection (Enforcement) (Amendment etc) Regulations 2020, SI 2020/484, reg 8.

5.213 These powers were introduced to ensure the UK's compliance with the 2017 CPC Regulation, but arguably they are unnecessary, since an enforcement order could extend to the removal or alteration of software, either in order directly to address infringing content, or as part of an Enhanced Consumer Measure. The online interface order provisions recognise this, and expressly refrain from limited the operation of Part 8 in relation to enforcement orders, interim enforcement orders and undertakings in respect of Community/Schedule 13 infringements[1]. Therefore it seems likely that other enforcers can broadly achieve the same outcome as the CMA is expressly empowered to do under these provisions. Unlike an application for an enforcement order or interim enforcement order, the court is not able to accept an undertaking from the person against whom an online interface order or interim online interface order is sought.

[1]   EnA 2002, s 218ZD(3). This saving was extended to Sch 13 infringements by virtue of reg 3(3)(b) of the Consumer Protection (Enforcement) (Amendment etc) (EU Exit) Regulations 2020.

WHAT DOES AN ONLINE INTERFACE ORDER DO?

5.214 An online interface order directs a person (who may be the trader under investigation, or another person)[1] to remove or modify content, disable or restrict access to the content, display a warning to consumers who access the content, and/or delete a domain name and register that domain name to the CMA.

[1] EnA 2002, s 218ZA(2). Examples of other persons against whom an online interface order may be obtained include a top level domain name registrar, a business who operates an online platform, an internet service provider.

5.215 Against whom can an online interface order be made? An online interface order may be made against a person who is not in the UK, as long as they can be said to carry on business in a part of the UK. In this respect the territorial scope of the power to make such an order is coextensive with the power of the UK courts to make an enforcement order under Part 8[1].

[1] EnA 2002, s 218ZA(3). See **5.139** above for the concept of 'carries on a business'.

THE CRITERIA TO BE APPLIED

5.216 By EnA 2002, s 218ZB(1) the Court may make an online interface order if it finds:

(a)   there has been or is likely to be a Community/Schedule 13 infringement[1],
(b)   there are *no other available means* of bringing about the cessation or prohibition of the infringement, which would by *themselves be wholly effective* and
(c)   it is necessary to make the order to avoid the risk of serious harm to the collective interests of consumers,
(d)   the order must also be necessary and proportionate.

[1] It is important to remember that where an online interface order is being sought against a trader alleged to be engaging in a practice which is contrary to the Consumer Protection from Unfair Trading Regulations 2008, the court may require them to prove the truth of any factual claim made in their commercial practices. If they fail to do so, the court may find the claim to be false. See EnA 2002, s 218A.

5.217 An online interface order is potentially a very draconian measure, which could severely disrupt a trader's business – therefore it is important for the court to be satisfied that it is necessary to make the order and doing so is a proportionate measure. Assessing whether there are other means which might achieve the cessation of the infringement is essentially asking whether it is necessary to make the order. If some other means would achieve the same result, then it would not be necessary. Proportionality requires that the removal or modification of the content is necessary to stop *serious* harm.

INTERIM ONLINE INTERFACE ORDERS

5.218 The CMA may also make an application for an interim online interface order. By EnA 2002, s 218ZC, the Court may grant this if it appears to the court that:

(a)   it is alleged that there has been or is likely to be a Community/Schedule 13 infringement[1];
(b)   if the application had been for an online interface order it would be likely to be granted[2];

(c)   it is expedient to bring about the cessation of prohibition of the Community infringement/Schedule 13 infringement immediately; and

(d)   if no notice of the application has been given to the person against whom the order is sought that it is appropriate to make an interim online interface order without notice[3].

The process and procedural requirements for seeking an interim online interface order are the same as for seeking an interim enforcement order[4].

[1]   As of 1 January 2021, the test has refered to Sch 13 infringements – see reg 3(3)(b) of the Consumer Protection (Enforcement) (Amendment etc) (EU Exit) Regulations 2020.

[2]   This limb of the test does require the court to assess the evidence for whether the Community/Schedule 13 infringement has occurred or is likely, but to a lower standard – ie on the balance of probabilities the infringement may have occurred. It also requires the court to engage in the necessity and proportionality assessment.

[3]   These last two criteria are the same as those which apply to an interim enforcement order, so are not discussed further here.

[4]   These include the requirement to explain the reasons if no notice is given of the application, and to refer to all matters which are material to the question of whether the application should be granted (see EnA 2002, s 218ZC (4) and (5).

Penal notice

5.219 Breach of an enforcement notice, an interim enforcement notice or an undertaking given to the court renders the defendant in contempt of court and liable to imprisonment, a fine or sequestration of his assets.

5.220 The enforcement order and the undertaking should be endorsed with a penal notice in Form N77 explaining the consequence of disobedience. It should be prominently displayed on the front of the order. Appropriate wording could be:

> '*If you [name of defendant] disobey this order you may be held to be in contempt of court and [if a corporate body, any of your directors] may be imprisoned or fined or your assets may be seized.*'

5.221 Where other persons are likely to assist the defendant in breaching the order in some way, meaning that the order will be served also on them, it is appropriate to add a paragraph stating:

> '*Any other person who knows of this order and does anything which helps or permits the defendant to breach the terms of this order may also be held to be in contempt of court and may be imprisoned, fined or have their assets seized.*'

5.222 Further, the notice must also make clear that the person (whether the defendant or an accessory) must also not effect the breach by employees or agents[1]. It is appropriate to add a paragraph stating:

> '*You must not disobey this order, or assist a person to disobey this order, yourself, or in any other way, whether by others acting on your behalf or on your instructions or with your encouragement. You must not disobey this order or assist a person to disobey this order by your directors, officers, partners, employees, agents, associates or otherwise.*'

[1]   See *OFT v Vance Miller* at para 38.

Action for breach

5.223 *Application of the order*:

Section 217:

> (12) An enforcement order made in a part of the United Kingdom by a court specified in relation to that part in the second or third column of the table has effect in another part of the United Kingdom as if made by a court specified in relation to that other part in the same column of the table—[1].

England and Wales	The High Court	The county court
Scotland	The Court of Session	The sheriff
Northern Ireland	The High Court	A county court.

The effect of this is that an order made in Scotland for example, may be enforced against the defendant in respect of their activities in England, in the same way as an order of a court of the comparable level. Comparable provisions are made for interim enforcement orders (in s 218(11)) and (interim) online interface orders (in s 218ZB(4) and s 218ZC(8)).

[1] This provision, together with the comparable provisions in ss. 218(11), 218ZB(4) and 218ZC(8), a replaced the previous wording as a result of reg 2 of the Consumer Protection (Enforcement)(Amendment etc) (EU Exit) Regulations 2020. The intention of the change was to clarify that where an order is made by a court in one part of the UK, it has the effect in another part of the UK as an order made by a court of the same level.

5.224 The EnA 2002, s 220(2) provides that any CPC/Schedule 13 enforcer has the same right to apply to the court in respect of a failure to comply with the order or undertaking as the enforcer who made the application for the order[1]. This means there should generally be no impediment to any trading standards department for example taking proceedings to enforce an order even if it was obtained by another department.

[1] This does not apply to breach of an online interface order or interim online interface order, which can only be pursued by the CMA.

Construction of the Order

5.225 The starting point for the enforcement of an order is whether the trader's conduct amounts to a breach of order. The correct construction of the language used in the order is important. This is not always straightforward and the courts have set out a number of principles to be applied (a consent order is construed in accordance with the same principles as apply to construction of contracts). In summary these principles are[1]:

- The documentary, factual and commercial context of the order, in particular:
  - The natural and ordinary meaning of the text: this is the key starting point, because the parties have control over this wording, and must have been specifically focussing on this.
  - The other relevant provisions of the order.
  - The overall purpose of the provision, including the statutory or regulatory purposes being given effect to.

- The fact and circumstances known by the parties (and which existed at the time the order was made).
- Commercial common sense.
- But disregarding subjective evidence of any party's intentions.
- The court must consider the quality of the drafting, such that a carefully drafted document is more likely to be given a literal meaning.
- Where unambiguous language is used, the court must apply it, even if it appears to have been an imprudent provision for one party to agree to (for example because their competitors are not subject to comparable requirements), or it goes beyond what is strictly required under the law being enforced. This is particularly important because of the public significance of enforcement orders. It is not for the court to re-write the order after the event.
- Where language is unclear, the court may prefer the construction most consistent with business common sense, as perceived by a reasonable person at the time the order was made.

[1] See *Viagogo AG v Competition and Markets Authority* [2019] EWHC 1706 (Ch) paras 10–11 for these principles, with a discussion of their application to a consent order at paras 12–26.

Contempt proceedings

5.226 Disobedience of an order of the court is punishable. Against an individual, the most severe sanction is a sentence of imprisonment exercised by an order of committal[1]. Against a limited company, it is sequestration exercised by a writ of sequestration[2]. The court may, as an alternative to committal or sequestration, impose a fine[3]. Sentencing for contempt has two purposes: first, punishment for breach of the order because court orders must not be flouted; and secondly, securing compliance with the order in the future. It should always be remembered that contempt must be proved to the criminal standard – in other words, the court must be sure that there was a contempt.

[1] The maximum term is one of 2 years: see Contempt of Court Act 1981, s 14(1).
[2] The writ is addressed to not less than four people named in the writ known as commissioners or sequestrators and directs them to sequestrate (seize) the property of the individual or company in contempt until the contempt is purged.
[3] There is no limit to the amount of the fine. The Contempt of Court Act 1981, s 14(2) does not apply to the County Court, which, by virtue of sub-section (4A) is treated as a superior court.

5.227 The procedure to be followed in order to establish liability for contempt is set out in CPR Pt 81, which applies to proceedings both in the High Court and in the county court[1]. Section II of Pt 81 deals with 'Committal for breach of a judgment, order or undertaking to do or abstain from doing an act'.

[1] County Courts Act 1984, s 38(1) gives the county court power to make any order which could be made by the High Court if the proceedings were in the High Court.

5.228 CPR 81.4(1) provides that where a person required by a judgment or order to do an act does not do it within the time fixed by the judgment or order; or disobeys a judgment or order not to do an act, the judgment or order may be enforced by an order for committal. Because of the wide drafting of the penal notice, a person other than the defendant in the original proceedings may be found in contempt – for example where a third part has assisted breach by the trader (for instance by continuing to host an unlawful website), or where a new company officer has directed the company to act in a way that breaches the order. If the person in contempt (the contemnor) is a company, the committal order may be made against any director or other officer of the company[1]. Section II of CPR Pt 81 applies to undertakings given by a party as it applies to judgments or orders[2].

In order to prove contempt, it must be shown that the contemnor:

- knew the terms of the order;
- acted or failed to act in a manner which amounted to a breach of the order;
- knew of the conduct which amounted to a breach.

[1] CPR 81.4(3). Enforcement against the property of the company or its directors is by a writ of sequestration which can be issued only by the High Court. Section 7 of CPR Pt 81 deals with writs of sequestration. CPR 81.20–81.26 mirror the rules in CPR 81.4–81.10 and are therefore not repeated here. However, enforcement by sequestration requires the permission of the court: CPR 81.20(1).
[2] CPR 81.4(4).

Knew the terms of the order

5.229 As a general rule, a judgment or order may not be enforced unless a copy has been personally served on the defendant[1]. This is because it must be proven that the contemnor knew the terms of the order. Similarly, a copy of the defendant's undertaking must be delivered to him either by handing it to him before he leaves the court or by posting a copy to him or his solicitor[2]. Accordingly, on any application for committal proof of the service of the judgment or order or delivery of the undertaking should be given by the applicant[3].

[1] CPR 81.5 and CPR 81.6. The court may dispense with proof of personal service if satisfied, inter alia that the defendant was present when the judgment or order was given or made: CPR 81.8.
[2] CPR 81.7.
[3] See *The Environment Agency v Bryan Hughes* [2014] EWHC 2484 (QB) at para 31 for an example of a committal application which failed for want of proper service of the order on a company officer.

Acted in a manner which amounted to a breach

5.230 CPR 81.10(1) provides that a committal application should be made by an application notice under CPR Pt 23 in the proceedings in which the judgment or order was made or the undertaking given[1]. The application notice must contain a penal notice similar to the one found in Annex 3 of Practice Direction 81. Precision is vital in contempt proceedings. It is very important that terms of the order are sufficiently unambiguous to warrant enforcement, and that the order is self standing, not requiring a person to go to another document to understand it[2]. This is a key reason why orders must be clear. For example a requirement to use 'best endeavours' may be difficult to enforce in contempt proceedings, likewise mandatory orders should specify a time for compliance[3]. The order must also be capable of being complied with, although it is no defence that the contemnor needed more time to comply, where they did not oppose the granting of the order[4].

CPR 81.10(3) requires the application notice:

(a) To set out **in full** the grounds upon which the application is made and to **identify** each alleged act of contempt including, if known, the date of each of the alleged acts. The detail must be sufficient so the respondent should know the case against them[5].

Some draftsmen like to set out the breaches in tabular form thus:

Order	Breach	Date
'Do not sell any goods not marked . . .'.	Sold goods not marked . . .	27 June 2015

(b) To be supported by one or more **affidavits** containing all the evidence relied upon.

The evidence should demonstrate breach of the order as at the date of the application, but it can include also evidence of breaches which pre-date the application, and have since been rectified[6]. Evidence which post dates the application would be relevant to mitigation, but would not count as further charges the respondent must answer[7].

1 Reference should also be made to Practice Direction 81, paras 8–16.
2 *The Environment Agency v Bryan Hughes* [2014] EWHC 2484 (QB) at para 24.
3 *The Environment Agency v Bryan Hughes* [2014] EWHC 2484 (QB) at para 17.
4 *Westminster City Council v Addbins Ltd* [2012] EWHC 3716 (QB) at para 21.
5 *Westminster City Council v Addbins Ltd* [2012] EWHC 3716 (QB) at para 43.
6 *The Environment Agency v Bryan Hughes* [2014] EWHC 2484 (QB) at para 7.
7 *Westminster City Council v Addbins Ltd* [2012] EWHC 3716 (QB) at para 44.

Knew of the conduct which amounted to a breach

5.231 It is not necessary to show that the contemnor knew the conduct in fact amounted to a breach, or intended to breach the order. The contemnor's motives and thought processes are immaterial. However it does need to be shown that the contemnor knew of the conduct alleged. In some cases, this may be obvious, because they are a sole trader whose conduct is that directly relied on to prove the contempt. Where the contemnor is a corporate entity or a company officer, it will be necessary to show that they actually knew of the conduct – for instance to head off a defence that the conduct was carried out by rogue employees. In order to achieve this, it is helpful to send a letter to the proposed contemnors setting out conduct, which post-dates the coming into force of the order, and which is alleged to breach the order. The enforcer should continue collecting evidence of subsequent breaches as well. Where a contemnor is a director, it may be sufficient to prove that they knew about the order, were responsible for the conduct which amounted to the breach and wilfully failed to take steps to prevent this conduct[1]. It is not necessary to prove facts which are entirely within the respondent's knowledge.

1 *Westminster City Council v Addbins Ltd* [2012] EWHC 3716 (QB) at para 50.

Process

5.232 The application notice and the supporting evidence must be served personally on the respondent[1]. Again, proof of service should be given to the court. A committal application for breach of a solicitor's undertaking cannot be made without first obtaining permission of the court pursuant to CPR 81.11. Likewise an application for a writ of sequestration includes a permission stage[2].

1   CPR 81.10(4).
2   CPR 81.26.

5.233 Section VIII of CPR Pt 81 deals with 'General rules about committal applications, orders for committal and writs of sequestration'. The basic rule is that, unless the court otherwise permits, the applicant is confined to those breaches set out in his application notice and to the evidence served in support[1]. This rule serves to emphasise the need for accuracy and completeness when drafting the application notice and the supporting evidence. The respondent is under no obligation to reply to the application notice or to file evidence. Whether or not he does so, he is entitled to give oral evidence and, with the permission of the court, to call witnesses[2]. If he has a reason which justifies the non-compliance, the respondent must prove this. A court making the committal order may also order that its execution be suspended for such period or on such terms or conditions as it may specify[3]. This power is often exercised. CPR 81.31 and 81.32 deal with the discharge of a person in custody[4]. The general rule is that hearings are carried out in, and judgments and orders are made in, public, and derogations from this rule must be justified and strictly necessary to achieve their purpose. The application notice is also generally available to third parties who wish to see it[5].

1   CPR 81.28(1).
2   CPR 81.28(2).
3   CPR 81.29.
4   See *Swindon Borough Council v Webb* [2016] EWCA Civ 152, where the discharge of the defendant from custody went horribly wrong.
5   Practice Direction: Committal for Contempt of Court – Open Court (26 March 2015).

Sentencing

5.234 Several cases can illustrate the exercise of contempt proceedings and the range of sentences. In *OFT v Vance Miller*[1], the first instance judge was faced with an application to commit Mr Miller in respect of nine breaches of an order prohibiting the sale of goods not conforming to the contractual description or not being of satisfactory quality and prohibiting late delivery of goods. There had been earlier committal proceedings. On that occasion, following a hearing at which Mr Miller had been unrepresented, the judge sentenced Mr Miller to a custodial sentence of 9 months. Subsequently, there was a successful application from Mr Miller to purge his contempt.

1   [2009] EWCA Civ 34.

5.235 In his sentencing remarks in respect of the present application, the judge referred to 'the convoluted tale' which Mr Miller had told about the involvement of others as being 'simply incredible'; he held that the breaches were neither casual nor accidental; and he noted the fact that this was Mr Miller's second appearance for contempt of the same order of the court. As against that, he found that the last complaint had been about 2 years earlier; there was evidence of a significant and continuing reduction in complaints; there was a recent report that he had commissioned from management consultants; and there was evidence that apologies had been given to the complainants. However, the judge concluded that it was a serious case and he ordered that Mr

Miller be committed for contempt for 6 months but suspended the sentence for 2 years and ordered it not to be enforced if Mr Miller complied with the original order. The judge further imposed a fine on Mr Miller of the sum of £90,000[1], and ordered Mr Miller to pay a contribution towards the OFT's costs in the sum of £30,000. On appeal by Mr Miller, the Court of Appeal upheld the sentence, finding that it was not manifestly excessive.

[1]   £10,000 for each complaint. The judge found that the business was making an annual profit of some £200,000. The financial resources of the respondent will always be relevant to the quantum of the fine.

5.236 In *Phillimore v Surrey County Council*[1], Mr Phillimore was a second hand car dealer. There was an injunction against him which restrained him, inter alia, from providing consumers with goods that did not corresponded with their description; selling goods which were not of satisfactory quality; applying a false description to goods or supplying goods to which a false trade description had been applied; selling or offering to supply a vehicle or trailer in an unroadworthy condition; and suppling vehicles that were in an unsafe condition.

[1]   [2010] EWCA Civ 61.

5.237 The first instance judge found that Mr Phillimore had been acting dishonestly as a second-hand car dealer. He had deliberately failed to give his own name and address on business documents, so that customers would find it difficult to pursue him personally by way of legal proceedings when their cars were found to be defective. He had continued to give false descriptions about the vehicles he had sold, as to the mileage, or as to the validity, or extent, of warranties he said he was providing. He had continued to sell cars which he must have known had serious defects. He decided that Mr Phillimore should be committed to prison for 9 months.

5.238 On appeal, the Court of Appeal upheld the sentence. Stanley Burnton LJ said:

'This was a substantial sentence. In my judgment it was well within the range of sentences open to the judge, having regard to the fact that, first, these were repeated breaches of an injunction. Secondly, they must have been deliberate and dishonest breaches of the injunction. Thirdly, the victims were persons who could little afford the losses they suffered as a result of dealing with Mr Phillimore. Fourthly, the breaches were not simply breaches that would lead to financial loss on the part of his victims but could lead to injury or indeed loss of life as, for example, might have occurred when a wheel came off one of the vehicles that he had sold.'

5.239 In *The Royal Borough of Kingston Upon Thames v James Slater*[1], the Court of Appeal approved a 9 months' prison sentence for a trader who had persuaded 16 consumers to agree to have work carried out on their properties. In some cases he took payment in advance, but did not commence any work; in others he commenced work, but then asked for further money; in all cases the work remained unfinished and in many cases was of such poor standard that it had to be redone at extra cost. In total, he owed nearly £50,000 in incomplete work. His case was aggravated by a previous sentence of 6 months for similar behaviour, and his failure to comply with an interim enforcement order requiring him to refund 12 of his victims. The Court of Appeal noted that this sentence was 'entirely justified and well within the reasonable band of sentencing decisions that a Court can come to'.

[1]   [2021] EWCA Civ 1479 at para 20.

5.240 In the case of a breach of an undertaking given to the court, rather than treat the defaulting party as being in contempt, the court has the option of making an enforcement order or an interim enforcement order, but may not accept a further undertaking[1]. Where a person has been committed for contempt and sentenced, it is open to them to apply to the same court[2] to discharge or vary the order – and they should do so rather than appeal since any such appeal is liable to be dismissed[3]. The court should consider all the circumstances and make such order as it thinks fit[4]. By contrast, where the person wishes to challenge the conviction, it would be appropriate for them to appeal to the Court of Appeal.

[1]   EnA 2002, s 220(4).
[2]   *Swindon BC v Webb* [2016] EWCA Civ 152 para 24 stressed that an application for discharge should be listed before the same judge who imposed the order for committal.
[3]   As occurred in *The Royal Borough of Kingston Upon Thames v James Slater* [2021] EWCA Civ 1479.
[4]   CPR 81.10(1) & (3).

Costs

General

5.241 All litigation, whether it be civil or criminal, carries with it exposure to costs[1]. Cases have to be investigated, prepared and fought. It is understood that one of the concerns of enforcers is the risk of being subject to an adverse costs' order should a Pt 8 case be lost. Regrettably, there is no way of obviating that risk. On the other hand, the trader is exposed to the same risk. It is that risk that frequently persuades him to settle the action, by giving acceptable undertakings to the enforcer or to the court.

[1]   Although it is hoped that the recent amendments to the CPR will have some effect on controlling the quantum of costs.

5.242 It is sensible for the enforcer to bring the issue of costs to the attention of the trader at an early stage perhaps in the letter initiating consultation. The letter could include the following passage:

A response to these issues is required by 5pm on [. . .] Should a substantive response or undertaking not be received within that time, I will assume that you are not prepared to comply with the requests made in this letter and my authority will commence court proceedings against you without further notice. In such circumstances, you may be ordered to pay the costs of the court proceedings.

Discretion

5.243 The power to award costs 'of and incidental'[1] to civil proceedings is derived from the Senior Courts Act 1981, s 51. The award of costs and the quantum of costs are in the discretion of the court.

[1]   *Re Gibson's Settlement Trusts* [1981] Ch 179 at 186, Sir Robert Megarry V-C pointed out that the costs 'incidental to' proceedings go beyond those 'of' the proceedings.

5.244 The general rule is that costs follow the event[1]. In the case of an application for an enforcement order, the 'event' is the grant of, or refusal to grant, an enforcement order. Thus the winner is generally entitled to an order that the loser pays his reasonable and proportionate costs[2]. Note the reference to 'reasonable and proportionate costs'. It is rare for the totality of the winning party's costs to be paid by the losing party. There is usually a shortfall between the costs actually incurred by a party and those recoverable from the other party.

[1]   See CPR 44.2(2)(a): 'The general rule is that the unsuccessful party will be ordered to pay the costs of the successful party'.
[2]   See CPR 44.3(2), CRP 44.3(5) and CPR 44.4.

5.245 However, the discretion exists to depart from the general rule that costs follow the event. CPR 44.2(4) and (5) provide:

> (4) In deciding what order (if any) to make about costs, the court must have regard to all the circumstances, including—
>
> (a)   the conduct of all the parties;
> (b)   whether a party has succeeded on part of its case, even if that party has not been wholly successful; and
> (c)   any admissible offer to settle[1] made by a party which is drawn to the court's attention . . .
>
> (5) The conduct of the parties includes—
>
> (a)   conduct before, as well as during, the proceedings . . . ;
> (b)   whether it was reasonable for a party to raise, pursue or contest a particular allegation or issue;
> (c)   the manner in which a party has pursued or defended its case or a particular allegation or issue; and
> (d)   whether a claimant who has succeeded in the claim, in whole or in part, exaggerated its claim.

[1]   It is suggested that 'an offer to settle' would include an offer of an undertaking to the enforcer.

5.246 In *Straker v Tudor Rose*[1] Lord Justice Waller gave helpful guidance on the correct approach:

(a)   Is it appropriate to make an order for costs?
(b)   If so, the general rule is that the unsuccessful party will pay the costs of the successful party.
(c)   Identify the successful party.
(d)   Consider whether there are reasons for departing from the general rule in whole or in part. If so the judge should make clear findings of the factors justifying costs not following the event.

[1]   [2007] EWCA Civ 368.

Recoverable costs

5.247 Assuming that an order for costs has been made, what costs are recoverable? The short answer is that the court has a discretion to award any reasonable and proportionate costs of and incidental to the proceedings.

5.248 Costs normally fall into two categories:

(a)   expenses of a type which solicitors frequently incur when acting on behalf of clients (such as counsel's fees, court fees, witness expenses etc). These are known as 'disbursements'; or

(b)   the fees which a solicitor charges to his client. These are known as 'solicitors' charges' or 'profit costs'.

5.249 Costs incurred before the commencement of proceedings may be properly recoverable if those costs were reasonably incurred in order to obtain material that was, or would have been but for the settlement of the proceedings, of use and service in the claim[1].

[1]   See *Admiral Management Services Ltd v Para-Protect Europe Ltd* [2002] 1 WLR 2722 at [25].

5.250 In criminal cases, it has been accepted that, on the basis of the Prosecution of Offences Act 1985, s 18(1), the costs of the prosecution may include the costs of the prosecuting authority in carrying out investigations with a view to the prosecution of the defendant[1]. It is suggested that the same is not true in civil cases. In general, the work of a party's employees in investigating, formulating and prosecuting a claim by legal proceedings does not qualify for an order for the payment of the costs of and incidental to those proceedings. The exception is where the employees undertake work that would otherwise have been undertaken by an outside expert[2]. It is suggested that, although arguable, it is unlikely that a court would find that a local authority's trading standards officers were performing work that would otherwise have to be done or could lawfully be done by an outside expert.

[1]   See *R v Associated Octel Company Ltd (Costs)* [1997] 1 Cr App R (S) 435.
[2]   See *Admiral Management Services Ltd v Para-Protect Europe Ltd* [2002] 1 WLR 2722; *Sisu Capital Fund Ltd v Tucker (Costs)* [2005] EWHC 2321 (Ch); and *Grant v Ralls* [2016] EWHC 1812 (Ch).

Chapter 6

CONSUMER RIGHTS

Contents

INTRODUCTION

6.1 When the legislation that was to become the Consumer Rights Act 2015 ('CRA 2015') was first conceived, it was intended to become the focal point of consumer law in the UK. It was intended to modernise and rationalise consumer protection and make the law more accessible for consumers. Whilst some of those laudable aims have been at least partially achieved, it is clear that in many respects, consumer law remains as disjointed and inaccessible as ever. One of the most notable issues arose because the legislation that would become the CRA 2015 was not ready in time to implement the EU Consumer Rights Directive 2011/83/EU (the 'CRD')[1]; consequently, the Consumer Contracts (Information, Cancellation and Additional Charges) Regulations 2013 (the 'CCR 2013') were introduced to implement the CRD and, largely, that is where much of the UK law giving effect to the CRD still resides[2]. The CRA 2015 also implements certain parts of the CRD in its consolidation of the contractual rules, ss 11, 12, 36, 37 and 50 (information requirements), s 28 (default rules for the delivery of goods) and s 29 (passing of risk in goods) replacing provisions previously found in the CCR 2013.

[1] The CRD consolidates the EU directives on doorstep selling 85/577/EEC (the 'Doorstep Selling Directive') and distance sales 97/7/EC ('the Distance Sales Directive'). However, with the notable exception of on premises contracts, Art 4 of the CRD now provides for full harmonisation rather than the previous minimal harmonisation. This means that Member States must implement the CRD fully and may not legislate in excess of the CRD's consumer protection measures in the areas that it covers. Guidance on the CRD has been provided by the European Commission Directorate-General for Justice and Consumers (the 'European Commission DG Guidance'). Obviously, subject to any agreement reached with the EU, when the transition period ends on 31 December 2020, the harmonisation restrictions on the UK fall away.

[2] CRD, Art 27 (inertia selling) has been implemented by amendment of the CPUTR 2008, SI 2008/1277, reg 27M.

6.2 Instead of implementing the CRD and consolidating a vast amount of UK consumer law, the CRA 2015 primarily did two things: (1) it consolidated and updated the existing UK law on the sale of goods, the supply of services, the hiring of goods and unfair terms in consumer contracts; and (2) it introduced new rights for 'digital content'. The CRA 2015 came into force on 1 October 2015 and applies to contracts entered into on or after that date; the predecessor legislation remains in force for contracts entered into prior to 1 October 2015. Part 1 of the CRA 2015 is dealt with below at **6.141–6.248**, Part 2 of the CRA is dealt with in **Chapter 9**, Unfair Terms.

6.3 In addition to the CRA 2015, there some other significant pieces of consumer protection legislation in force today, including:

(1)   The CCR 2013 (discussed above);

(2)   The Consumer Protection from Unfair Trading Regulations 2008 ('CPUTR 2008')[1];

(3)   The Consumer Rights (Payment Surcharges) Regulations 2012 ('CR(PS) Regulations')[2];

(4)   The Alternative Dispute Resolution for Consumer Disputes (Competent Authorities and Information) Regulations 2015 (the 'ADR Regulations')[3];

(5)   The Provision of Services Regulations 2009 ('POSR 2009')[4];

(6)   The Supply of Extended Warranties on Domestic Electrical Goods Order 20051 (the '2005 Order')[5];

(7)   The Consumer Credit Act 1974;

(8)   The Data Protection Act 2018;

(9)   The Consumer Protection Act 1987;

(10)   The Package Travel and Linked Travel Arrangements Regulations 2018[6]; and

(11)   The Timeshare, Holiday Products, Resale and Exchange Contracts Regulations 2010[7].

[1]   SI 2008/1277.
[2]   SI 2012/3110.
[3]   SI 2015/542.
[4]   SI 2009/2999.
[5]   SI 2005/37.
[6]   SI 2018/634.
[7]   SI 2010/2960.

6.4 The CCR 2013 came into force on 13 June 2014 and consolidated and revoked the domestic regulations on doorstep[1] and distance selling[2]. These provisions continue to apply, however, to contracts entered into before 13 June 2014. The CCR 2013 principally set down information requirements and, in the case of distance or off premises contracts, consumer cancellation rights. The CCR 2013 are dealt with below at **6.12–6.80**.

[1]   Cancellation of Contracts made in a Consumer's Home or Place of Work etc Regulations 2008, SI 2008/1816.
[2]   Consumer Protection (Distance Selling) Regulations 2000, SI 2000/2334.

6.5 The Consumer Protection from Unfair Trading Regulations 2008 ('CPUTR 2008'), which implemented the EU Unfair Commercial Practices Directive 2005/29/EC and largely replaced the Trade Descriptions Act 1968 are principally dealt with in **Chapter 8**. However, on 1 October 2014, a new Pt 4A was introduced to the CPUTR 2008 which granted consumers a civil cause of action where traders have engaged in misleading actions or aggressive commercial practices. This new civil right of redress is dealt with below at **6.249–6.277**.

6.6 The CR(PS) Regulations came into force on 6 April 2013 and implemented Art 19 of the CRD. They have since been amended[1] to give effect to part of the EU's second Payment Services Directive ('PSD 2') which introduced a wholesale ban on consumer payment surcharges. The CP(PS) Regulations are discussed below at **6.125–6.140**.

1   On 13 January 2018.

6.7 The ADR Regulations came fully into force on 1 October 2015 and implements the EU Alternative Dispute Resolution Directive (2013/11/EU). The Directive principally required Member States to ensure adequate ADR provision and traders to provide consumers with information regarding ADR. The ADR Regulations set out the UK structure for ensuring adequate ADR and impose information requirements on traders. They apply to disputes arising in relation to contracts entered into on or after 9 July 2015 and are discussed in detail below at **6.297–6.305**.

6.8 The POSR 2009 implement an EU Services Directive 2006/123/EC which was introduced to remove barriers to accessing services across the EU. and came into force on 28 December 2009. The Regulations involve a large number of information requirement which are duplicated in the CCR 2013 and ADR Regulations. The Regulations also introduced a ban on discriminating against a service user based on their EU country of residence but it is notable that this provision is due to be revoked on 31 December 2020 when the transition period following Brexit comes to an end. The POSR are discussed below at **6.306–6.316**.

6.9 The 2005 Order was introduced to combat a perceived lack of competition in the sale by retailers of extended warranties on electrical appliances and corresponding consumer detriment. It came into force on 6 April 2005 and sets down certain prohibitions, information requirements and cancellation rights in relation to extended warranties sold in relation to domestic electrical goods. The 2005 Order is discussed below at **6.285–6.288**.

6.10 The consumer rights and protections provided by the Consumer Credit Act 1974 are discussed in CHAPTER **19**, Consumer Credit. The consumer rights and protections provided by the and the Package Travel and Linked Arrangements Regulations 2018 and the Timeshare, Holiday Products, Resale and Exchange Contracts Regulations 2010 are discussed in CHAPTER **16**, Travel).

6.11 As will be apparent from the forgoing, consumer rights law in the UK has a significant European influence. Following Brexit, the UK approach to consumer rights, may diverge from that of Europe but, to date, most changes have been relatively minor and administrative in nature. Those changes are flagged in this discussion below.

INFORMATION AND CANCELLATION

6.12 The CCR 2013[1] primarily sets out the regime under which consumers are provided with the right to specified pre-contract information when contracting with traders, and also to a 14 days' right to cancel certain contracts without reason. The latter is sometimes described as a cooling-off period. The CCR 2013 pre-contract information provisions cover three categories of contracts: 'distance contracts' (eg those made on-line), 'off-premises contracts' (eg those made at the consumer's home) and 'on-premises contracts' (eg those made on retail premises). Cancellation rights apply to distance and off-premises contracts only. How the CCR 2013 cancellation rights apply in practice will depend upon whether the distance or off-premises contract is a 'sales contract' (eg for the supply of goods), a 'services contract' or a contract for online 'digital content'. The CCR 2013 applies throughout the UK with minor modifications for Scotland[2] and Northern Ireland[3].

[1] SI 2013/3134.
[2] SI 2013/3134, regs 20(2)(b) Due diligence notices, 22(3) Directors' liability, 23(3) Duty to enforce, 24(6) Powers and 45(1) Orders.
[3] SI 2013/3134, regs 6(1)(a) NI Gambling legislation, 7(5)(c) NI health service, 23(1)(b) Duty to enforce and 44(3)(b) Complaints to DETI.

6.13 The CCR 2013 is a relatively complex regulation and unhelpfully includes a variety of unclear definitions and exclusions. The language used is a combination of EU law concepts and other terms that are more familiar to domestic regulation. In construing UK legislation, which implements EU provisions it is important to consider the purpose of the underlying EU legislation. In relation to both the pre-contract information provisions and cancellation rights, that purpose has been considered by the courts, by reference to the CRD and the preceding doorstep and distance selling directives, respectively.

6.14 In *Robertson v Swift* the UK Supreme Court considered the Doorstep Selling Directive. Lord Kerr stated that[1]:

> 'since the overall purpose of the Directive is to enhance consumer protection, that overarching principle must guide interpretation of the relevant national legislation.'

[1] [2014] UKSC 50, [2014] 1 WLR 3438 at para 22. See also *Veedfald v Arhus Amtskommune* C-203/99 [2003] 1 CMLR 41 (at para 15) on the general principle that exceptions to consumer protection measures should be construed narrowly.

6.15 The rationale for cancellation rights for doorstep sales is founded on the pressure that consumers feel when they are sold to directly in their home. It has been said that the objective of a cooling-off period is 'to protect the consumer from the element of surprise inherent in doorstep selling'[1]. In *Martin Martin*[2], the ECJ observed that[3]:

> 'the special feature of those contracts is that as a rule it is the trader who initiates the contract negotiations, and the consumer has not prepared for such door-to-door selling by, inter alia, comparing the price and quality of the different offers available.'

[1] *Crailsheimer Volksbank* C-229/04 [2005] ECR I-9273, ECJ.
[2] *Martin Martin v EDP Editores SL* C-227/08 [2010] 2 CMLR 27.
[3] See also *Hamilton v Volksbank Filder eG* C-412/06 [2008] 2 CMLR 46, *Heininger v Bayerische Hypo- und Vereinsbank AG* C-481/99 [2003] 2 CMLR 42 and *E-Friz GmbH v Von der Heyden* C-215/08 [2010] 3 CMLR 23.

6.16 In *Verbraucherzentrale Berlin eV v Unimatic Vertriebs GmbH*[1], when considering the scope of the protection offered by the 'off-premises contract' provisions of the CRD, the CJEU continued to focus on the purpose to protect a consumer from circumstances where they can be taken by 'surprise' or taken 'unawares' by the trader's offer. By reference to recital 21 of the CRD, the Court of Justice found:

'. . . the consumer may be under potential psychological pressure or may be confronted with an element of surprise, irrespective of whether or not the consumer has solicited the trader's visit. To that extent, the EU legislature also intended to include situations where the consumer is personally and individually addressed in an off-premises context but the contract is concluded immediately afterwards on the trader's business premises or through a means of distance communication.'

[1]   C-485/17 [2018] ECL-EU:C:2018:642 at para 33.

6.17 In *Cox v Woodlands Manor Care Home* [2015] the Court of Appeal (Civil Division) stated that the[1]:

'. . . mischief at which [the CCR 2013] are aimed is that consumers in their homes may feel pressured into making a decision which they would not have made if they had an opportunity to reflect in the absence of a trader.'

[1]   *Cox v Woodlands Manor Care Home* [2015] CTLC 53 Court of Appeal (Civil Division) per Underhill LJ.

6.18 The rationale for consumer cancellation rights in distance contracts was explained in *Walbusch Walter Busch*, where the CJEU stated that[1]:

'The right of withdrawal is designed to protect the consumer in the particular situation of mail-order sales, in which he "is not actually able to see the product or ascertain the nature of the service provided before concluding the contract". The right of withdrawal is therefore intended to offset the disadvantage for the consumer resulting from a distance contract by granting him an appropriate period for reflection during which he can examine and test the goods acquired.'

[1]   *Walbusch Walter Busch GmbH & Co KG* (C-430/17) [2019] at para 45 and see by analogy (in the context of the Distance Selling Directive) *Messner v Firma Stefan Krüger* C-489/07 [2009] ECR I-7315 at para 20.

6.19 In *Walbusch Walter Busch*[1], the CJEU also considered the pre-contract information requirements in the context of distance contracts, explaining that:

'The purpose of the . . . [CRD] is to afford consumers extensive protection by conferring on them a number of rights in relation to, inter alia, distance contracts. The objective of the EU legislature is to avoid a situation where the use of means of distance communication leads to a reduction in the information provided to the consumer; see, by analogy *Content Services v Bundesarbeitskammer* (Case C-49/11) [2012] 2 All ER (Comm) 1019, para 36.

The information provided, before a contract is concluded, on the terms of the contract and the consequences of concluding it, is of fundamental importance for a consumer: [reference made to the case of *Wind Tre*[2]]. It is on the basis of that information that the consumer decides whether he wishes to be contractually bound to the trader'.

[1]   *Walbusch Walter Busch GmbH & Co KG* (C-430/17) [2019] at paras 35 and 36.
[2]   *Autorita Garante della Concorrenza e del Mercato v Wind Tre* (Joined Cases C-54/17 and C-55/17) [2019] 1 CMLR 14 at para 46.

SCOPE OF THE CCR 2013

6.20 Certain common contractual arrangements are excluded from the ambit of the CCR 2013 altogether. Under CCR 2013, reg 6(1) obligations expressly do not apply to contracts to the extent that it is for gambling[1], financial services[2], land[3], residential rentals[4], new buildings[5], regular rounds-men[6], package travel[7] and timeshare[8]. Under CCR 2013, reg 6(2) also do not apply to contracts concluded by vending machines[9], by telephone for a telephone service[10] or contracts under which goods are sold by way of execution or otherwise by authority of law, such as the sale of goods after a court order.

[1] SI 2013/3134, reg 6(1)(a) 'gaming, betting and participating in a lottery within the meaning of the Gambling Act 2005' 'or participating in a lottery which forms part of the National Lottery within the meaning of the National Lottery etc. Act 1993' Consumer Contracts (Amendment) Regulations 2015, SI 2015/1629; in Northern Ireland the Betting, Gaming, Lotteries and Amusements (Northern Ireland) Order 1985, SI 1985/1204.

[2] SI 2013/3134, reg 6(1)(b) 'services of a banking, credit, insurance, personal pension, investment or payment nature'. Although these contracts are subject to SI 2013/3134, regs 38(4) (ancillary contracts) and 40(3) (additional payments).

[3] SI 2013/3134, reg 6(1)(c) 'for the creation of immovable property or of rights in immovable property'.

[4] SI 2013/3134, reg 6(1)(d) 'rental of accommodation for residential purposes'.

[5] SI 2013/3134, reg 6(1)(e) 'for the construction of new buildings, or the construction of substantially new buildings by the conversion of existing buildings'.

[6] SI 2013/3134, reg 6(1)(f) 'for the supply of foodstuffs, beverages or other goods intended for current consumption in the household and which are supplied by a trader on frequent and regular rounds to the consumer's home, residence or workplace'.

[7] SI 2013/3134, reg 6(1)(g) as substituted by SI 2018/1326, reg 8(3), with effect from 31 December 2020, as follows: 'which is a package travel contract within the meaning of the Package Travel and Linked Travel Arrangements Regulations 2018'.

[8] SI 2013/3134, reg 6(1)(h) as substituted by SI 2018/1326, reg 8(3), with effect from 31 December 2020, as follows: 'which is a regulated contract within the meaning of the Timeshare, Holiday Products, Resale and Exchange Contracts Regulations 2010'.

[9] SI 2013/3134, reg 6(2)(a) 'concluded by means of automatic vending machines or automated commercial premises'.

[10] SI 2013/3134, reg 6(2)(b) 'concluded with a telecommunications operator through a public telephone for the use of the telephone' and (c) 'concluded for the use of one single connection, by telephone, internet or fax, established by a consumer'.

6.21 Contracts for financial services[1] are excluded from the general scope of the CCR 2013. However where financial services contracts are ancillary to a distance or off-premises contract covered by the Regulations (for example a contract for insurance entered into along with the main purchase of a flight on-line), the financial service contract will be automatically terminated if a consumer exercises their right to withdraw an offer or to cancel the main contract (see **6.101** below). Also, if a payment for financial services does not constitute renumeration for the trader's main obligation under the contract and instead is an additional payment, the provisions of the CCRs 2013 reg 40 will apply (see **6.119**).

[1] Defined as 'services of a banking, credit, insurance, personal pension, investment or payment nature'.

6.22 The CCR 2013 do not apply to contracts for the creation of immovable property or of rights in immovable property. Also, excluded from the CCR 2013 are contracts for residential lettings (eg residential tenancy contracts) and contracts for the construction of a new building or the construction of a substantially new building by the conversion of an existing building. An example of the latter would be where only the façade of an old building is retained.

However, recital 26 of the CRD indicates that the following service contracts between a trader and a consumer fall within the Directive's scope (and so for our purposes are within the scope of the CCR 2013 provisions):

- The construction of annexes to buildings (for example a garage or a veranda);
- Repair and renovation of buildings other than substantial conversion;
- Services provided by estate agents;
- Services relating to the rental of accommodation for non-residential purposes.

CCR 2013 DEFINITIONS

6.23 It is important to consider the definitions in CCR 2013, regs 4 and 5, which also limit the application of the CCR 2013. In particular, the CCR 2013 obligations apply only to contracts between a 'trader' and 'consumer' (CCR 2013, reg 4). As indicated at **6.12** above, the rights available to a consumer will also depend upon whether the contract is a 'distance contract', 'off-premises contract' or 'on premises contract' (CCR 2013, reg 5).

Consumer and trader

6.24 The definitions of 'consumer' and 'trader' are found in CCR 2013, reg 4. These definitions are the same in the CRA 2015, s 2 and under the Consumer Protection from Unfair Trading Regulations 2008[1], ('CPUTR 2008')[2], where they have been the subject of consideration by the courts. The definition of consumer and trader are now considered in CHAPTER 2, Interpreting Consumer Law.

[1]   SI 2008/1277.
[2]   Save for the burden of proof in CRA 2015, s 2(4).

Distance contracts

6.25 The definition of a distance contract in CCR 2013, reg 5 states:

"distance contract" means a contract concluded between a trader and a consumer under an organised distance sales or service-provision scheme without the simultaneous physical presence of the trader and the consumer, with the exclusive use of one or more means of distance communication up to and including the time at which the contract is concluded.

6.26 This is a slightly different definition of distance contract to the one found in the Consumer Protection (Distance Selling) Regulations 2000[1], which was itself a copy of the definition in Art 2(1) of the Distance Selling Directive. The definition of distance contract is perhaps not as clear as it might be, nonetheless, central to its definition are the following elements (a) a contract 'between a trader and a consumer'[2], (b) 'concluded . . . under an organised distance sales or service-provision scheme'[3], (c) 'with the exclusive use of . . . distance communication'[4]. Moreover, some assistance may be found in the recitals to the CRD. Recital 37 of the CRD refers to distance sales in the following way:

'Since in the case of distance sales, the consumer is not able to see the goods before concluding the contract, he should have a right of withdrawal.'

[1] SI 2000/2334, reg 3(1): '"distance contract" means any contract concerning goods or services concluded between a supplier and a consumer under an organised distance sales or service provision scheme run by the supplier who, for the purpose of the contract, makes exclusive use of one or more means of distance communication up to and including the moment at which the contract is concluded'.

[2] See **6.24** above.

[3] See **6.32** below.

[4] See **6.29** to **6.30** below.

6.27 This reflects the central purpose of the protection afforded to consumers in this area. The growth in consumers purchasing goods, services or digital content at a distance, particularly using the internet, has meant that many more products are sold by description. The distance selling provisions in the CRD ensure that consumers are both provided with the key information they need before entering a 'distance contract' and also allow consumers to change their minds about what they have purchased because they will not have had a chance to appraise in person their suitability before the contract was made. Consumers who are supplied products that do not subsequently correspond to their description or are otherwise defective will have their normal rights under the CRA 2015, Pt 1 and such rights are not restricted by the 14-day right to cancel.

6.28 Recital 20 of the CRD provides a number of examples of distance communications, 'mail order, Internet, telephone or fax'. These examples are not exhaustive but suggest a type of transaction that is not immediately fulfilled. The Distance Selling Directive previously provided in Annex 1 an indicative list of the 'means of distance communication'. This included a wide variety of methods through which sales could be made at a distance[1].

[1] Unaddressed printed matter; addressed printed matter; standard letter; press advertising with order form; catalogue; telephone with human intervention; telephone without human intervention (automatic calling machine, audiotext); radio; videophone (telephone with screen); videotex (microcomputer and television screen) with keyboard or touch screen; electronic mail; facsimile machine (fax) and television (teleshopping) (Art 2(4) and Annex I).

6.29 Recital 20 of the CRD also provides that the definition of a distance contract should:

'cover situations where the consumer visits the business premises merely for the purpose of gathering information about the goods or services and subsequently negotiates and concludes the contract at a distance. By contrast, a contract which is negotiated at the business premises of the trader and finally concluded by means of distance communication should not be considered a distance contract. Neither should a contract initiated by means of distance communication, but finally concluded at the business premises of the trader be considered a distance contract. Similarly, the concept of distance contract should not include reservations made by a consumer through a means of distance communications to request the provision of a service from a professional, such as in the case of a consumer phoning to request an appointment with a hairdresser.'

6.30 This clarification is helpful, particularly to the extent it highlights that 'the exclusive use of one or more means of distance communication up to and including the time at which the contract is concluded' should not be reduced to merely asking whether there has been any face to face contact between the trader and the consumer before the contract was entered. Consistent with recital 20 of the CRD, the European Commission DG guidance[1] states:

> 'If the consumer has merely visited the business premises to gather information about the goods or services, the contract that he **subsequently negotiates and concludes with the trader at a distance** should be considered a distance contract' (emphasis added).

For example in the context of a student contract, concluded online or by other distance means, for a place of study at a higher education institution, the relevant CMA's published guidance indicates that these contracts are likely to be 'distance contracts' for the purpose of the CCR 2013. The CMA's view is that this is likely to remain the case even when prospective students have attended open day visits or interviews before entering such contracts, with the CMA noting that such face to face contact pre-contract is unlikely to involve contract negotiations[2].

[1] EC, DG Guidance, June 2014 at p 30.
[2] 'UK higher education providers – advice on consumer protection law', 12 March 2015, CMA 33, at para 4.27.

6.31 The European Commission DG Guidance also states that:

> 'The fact that parties meet each other after concluding the distance contract, typically at the time of delivery or payment, should not change the classification of a contract as a distance contract[1].'

[1] EC DG Guidance, June 2014 at p 30.

6.32 Further the definition of a 'distance contract' refers to a contract between a trader and consumer concluded under 'an organised distance sales or service-provision scheme'. In the European Commission DG Guidance it is stated that the 'Directive only applies to distance contracts concluded under an organised distance sales or service-provision scheme. For example, if a trader only **exceptionally** concludes a contract with a consumer by email or telephone, after being contacted by the consumer, such a contract should not be considered a distance contract under the Directive' [emphasis added][1].

[1] EC DG Guidance, p 30.

6.33 In *Christopher Linnett Ltd and another v Harding*[1], the High Court held that an adjudicator's agreement under which RICS nominates adjudicators to determine disputes as part of its statutory function, in return for a fee, can not be described as an organised distance scheme under the CCR 2013 .

[1] [2018] Bus. LR 179 at paras 86 to 87. However, the limited scope of the Judgment was made clear in the following terms ' . . . the Claimants did not mount a full scale submission to the effect that the [CCR 2013] . . . should not apply to a contract for the provision of dispute resolution services such as this. Any such point will have to be considered on another occasion.'

Business premises

6.34 'Business premises' are defined in CCR 2013, reg 5, as follows:

> "business premises" in relation to a trader means—
>
> (a) any immovable retail premises where the activity of the trader is carried out on a permanent basis, or
>
> (b) any movable retail premises where the activity of the trader is carried out on a usual basis;'

6.35 The CCR 2013 does not provide any further definition of 'retail premises' or what is meant by the 'activity of the trader being carried out on a usual basis'. However, recital 22 of the CRD states that:

> '**Business premises** should include premises in whatever form (such as shops, stalls or lorries) which serve as a permanent or usual place of business for the trader. Market stalls and fair stands should be treated as business premises if they fulfill this condition. Retail premises where the trader carries out his activity on a seasonal basis, for instance during the tourist season at a ski or beach resort, should be considered as business premises as the trader carries out his activity in those premises on a usual basis. Spaces accessible to the public, such as streets, shopping malls, beaches, sports facilities and public transport, which the trader uses on an exceptional basis for his business activities as well as private homes or workplaces should not be regarded as business premises. The business premises of a person acting in the name or on behalf of the trader as defined in this Directive should be considered as business premises within the meaning of this Directive.'

6.36 In *Verbraucherzentrale Berlin eV v Unimatic Vertriebs GmbH*[1], the CJEU confirmed that the approach taken in *Travel-Vac*[2] (where the meaning of 'business premises' for the purposes of the Doorstep Selling Directive 85/577/EEC was considered by the ECJ) remained relevant to the interpretation of 'business premises' under the CRD. The CJEU found that:

> 'It is in light of, inter alia, the fourth recital of Directive 85/577 [the Doorstep Selling Directive] that, in paragraphs 34 and 37 of the judgment of 22 April 1999, Travel Vac . . . , the Court held that the concept of 'business premises' within the meaning of that directive referred to premises in which the trader usually carries on his business and which are clearly identified as premises for sales to the public.

> As it is apparent from recital 22 of Directive 2011/83 [the CRD] that the directive also intends places in which there is no element of surprise if the consumer receives a business solicitation to be covered by the concept of 'business premises', the case law established by that judgment concerning the interpretation of Directive 85/577 [The Doorstep Selling Directive] remains relevant for the purpose of interpreting that concept within the meaning of Directive 2011/83 [the CRD].'

[1] C-485/17 [2018] ECLI-EU:C:2018:642 at paras 37 and 38.
[2] *Travel Vac SL v Snachis* C-423/97 [1999] 2 CMLR 1111.

6.37 In the context of considering whether a stand at a trade fair constitutes 'business premises' within the meaning of Art 2(9)(b) of the CRD, the CJEU clarified the position further in *Verbraucherzentrale Berlin eV v Unimatic Vertriebs GmbH*[1]. The Court stated:

> ' . . . the expression "on a usual basis" within the meaning of Article 2(9)(b) of Directive 2011/83 must be understood as referring to the fact that the activity at issue being carried out on the premises in question is a normal activity.'

On this basis the CJEU held in this case that a stand run by a trader at a trade fair, including one where a trader carries out his business activity for a few days each year:

' . . . constitutes "business premises" within the meaning of that provision if, in light of all the factual circumstances surrounding that activity, in particular the appearance of the stand and the information relayed on the premises of the fair itself, a reasonably well-informed and reasonably observant and circumspect consumer could reasonably assume that the trader is carrying out his activity there and will solicit him in order to conclude a contract . . . '[2]

[1] C-487/17 at para 39.
[2] C-487/17 at para 46.

6.38 With reference to recital 22 of the CRD, the CJEU in *Verbraucherzentrale Berlin eV v Unimatic Vertriebs GmbH*[1] also observed:

' . . . retail premises where the trader carries out his activity on a seasonal basis, for instance during the tourist season at a ski or beach resort, must be regarded as business premises as the trader carries out his activity in those premises on a usual basis. On the other hand, spaces accessible to the public, such as streets, shopping malls, beaches, sport facilities and public transport, which the trader uses on an exceptional basis for his business activities, as well as private homes or workplaces should not be regarded as business premises.'

[1] C-485/17 at para 42.

6.39 In *B & L Elektrogerate GmbH v GC*[1], the CJEU held that the aisle common to the various stands present in an exhibition hall of a trade fair,

'cannot be considered to be "business premises" within the meaning of Article 2(9) of Directive 2011/83 [the CRD], in so far as that aisle provided access to all the trader's stands in that hall.'

The CJEU explained that such an aisle corresponds to spaces accessible to the public, described in recital 22, including streets and shopping malls, which should not be regarded as 'business premises'[2].

[1] Case C-465/19 at para 29.
[2] Case C-465/19 at para 30.

Off-premises contract

6.40 An 'off-premises contract' is defined by CCR 2013, reg 5 as:

"off-premises contract" means a contract between a trader and a consumer which is any of these—
  (a) a contract concluded in the simultaneous physical presence of the trader and the consumer, in a place which is not the business premises of the trader;
  (b) a contract for which an offer was made by the consumer in the simultaneous physical presence of the trader and the consumer, in a place which is not the business premises of the trader;
  (c) a contract concluded on the business premises of the trader or through any means of distance communication immediately after the consumer was personally and individually addressed in a place which is not the business premises of the trader in the simultaneous physical presence of the trader and the consumer;

(d)   a contract concluded during an excursion organised by the trader with the aim or effect of promoting and selling goods or services to the consumer.

6.41 The definition in CCR 2013, reg 5 is broader than its predecessor[1] because, for example, it is capable of covering any venue that is not the trader's business premises and the CCR 2013 apply irrespective of whether the consumer solicits the trader's visit[2]. The definition also now includes the situation where the consumer is 'personally and individually addressed' away from the trader's business premises (eg at the consumer's home), but the contract is immediately concluded on business premises or at a distance. An example of how this might apply is given in the European Commission's DG Guidance[3]:

'The trader's representative approaches the particular consumer in the street with an offer for a subscription to a monthly magazine . . . and the contract is immediately signed on the trader's nearby business premises.'

[1]   Cancellation of Contracts made in a Consumer's Home or Place of Work etc. Regulations 2008, SI 2008/1816.
[2]   Recital 21 of the CRD provides, 'In an off-premises context, the consumer may be under potential psychological pressure or may be confronted with an element of surprise, irrespective of whether or not the consumer has solicited the trader's visit'.
[3]   EC DG Guidance at p 15.

6.42 However, recital 21 of the CRD provides:

'The definition of an off-premises contract should not cover situations in which the trader first comes to the consumer's home strictly with a view to taking measurements or giving an estimate without any commitment of the consumer and where the contract is then concluded only at a later point in time on the business premises of the trader or via means of distance communication on the basis of the trader's estimate. **In those cases, the contract is not to be considered as having been concluded immediately after the trader has addressed the consumer if the consumer has had time to reflect upon the estimate of the trader before concluding the contract**' (emphasis added).

This example covers a fairly common transaction, where a trader visits a consumer's home to talk about home improvements and, after leaving, prepares and sends a written quotation to the consumer. The contract is then entered into later by telephone, email or at the trader's premises. When determining whether a particular transaction of this kind can be regarded as an 'off-premises contract', recital 21 underlines the importance of taking into account whether the period between the trader's visit to the consumer's home and the conclusion of the contract (by distance or at the trader's premises) is sufficient for the consumer to not feel any pressure in entering the contract and has sufficient time to 'reflect'.

6.43 The concept of an excursion has also been changed to apply to one organised by a trader to promote or sell goods or services to the consumer. This appears to be a wider approach to the one adopted in the *Travel Vac* case under the Doorstep Selling Regulations. It implies that the consumer is being taken on some kind of journey only rather than, as in *Travel Vac*[1], where it was considered relevant that both parties were on a journey, the consumer away from their home and the trader away from their trading base. The European Commission's DG Guidance states[2]:

'The notion of "excursion" includes journeys that involve sightseeing or other leisure-related activities rather than just transport to the place where the sale takes place. In applying this notion, it should not matter whether the trader selling the products during an excursion organises the transport himself or has made arrangements with a transport company.'

1   *Travel-Vac SL v Manuel Jose Antelm Sanchis* C-423/97 at para 38.
2   See EC DG Guidance at p 16.

On-premises contract

6.44 An 'on-premises contract' is defined by CCR 2013, reg 5 as:

"on-premises contract" means a contract between a trader and a consumer which is neither a distance contract nor an off-premises contract.

6.45 'On-premises contract' is, therefore, a catch-all definition for every contract that does not fall within the definition of off-premises and distance contracts. The term is, therefore, not very helpful. There is a risk of defining its scope too widely, particularly given the broad scope of 'off-premises contracts'[1]. Clearly 'on-premise contract' will include routine contracts made on retail premises (eg in shops), but it can go beyond this. For example, it is likely to cover a contract which is concluded on the telephone as a 'one off' with the trader ordinarily selling goods from their shop[2].

1   For example, paras (b) and (c) of the CCR 2013 reg 5 definition of off-premises contract are capable of including contracts between a consumer and a trader which are concluded on the trader's premises and paragraph (c) specifically envisages this as it states '**a contract concluded on the business premises of the trader** . . . **immediately after** the consumer was personally and individually addressed in a place which is not the business premises of the trader in the simultaneous physical presence of the trader and the consumer' (emphasis added).
2   In such circumstances, it is unlikely the contract is concluded under 'an organised distance sales or service-provision scheme', for which see **6.32**.

Durable medium

6.46 'Durable medium' is defined by CCR 2013, reg 5 as:

"durable medium" means paper or email, or any other medium that—
(a)   allows information to be addressed personally to the recipient,
(b)   enables the recipient to store the information in a way accessible for future reference for a period that is long enough for the purposes of the information, and
(c)   allows the unchanged reproduction of the information stored;

6.47 Recital 23 of the CRD states that:

'Durable media should enable the consumer to store the information for as long as it is necessary for him to protect his interests stemming from his relationship with the trader. Such media should include in particular paper, USB sticks, CD-ROMs, DVDs, memory cards or the hard disks of computers as well as emails.'

6.48 In *Content Services Ltd*[1] the ECJ rejected the argument that the mere provision of information on a website amounted to a 'durable medium' under the Distance Selling Directive. It was stated that:

' . . . it must be examined whether a website the information of which is accessible to consumers via a link provided by the seller must be regarded as a 'durable medium' within the meaning of Article 5(1) of Directive 97/7 [the Distance Selling Directive].

. . .

Where a medium allows the consumer to store the information which has been addressed to him personally, ensures that its content is not altered and that the information is accessible for an adequate period, and gives consumers the possibility to reproduce it unchanged, that , medium must be regarded as 'durable' within the meaning of that provision.

. . .

There is nothing in the file to indicate that the seller's website, to which the link sent to the consumer connects, allows that consumer to store information which is personally addressed to him in such a way that he can access it and reproduce it unchanged during an adequate period without the seller being able to amend the content unilaterally.

. . .

Leaving aside the question whether the use of . . . an advanced website can meet the requirements of Directive 97/7 [Distance Selling Directive], it is not disputed, and Content Services itself recognises, that it does not use such a site for this activity in question in the main proceedings.

It should be held, therefore, that a website such as that in question in the main proceedings, the information on which is accessible to consumers via a link provided by the seller, cannot be regarded as a "durable medium" within the meaning of Article 5(1) of Directive 97/7 [Distance Selling Directive].'

[1]   *Content Services Ltd v Bundesarbeitskammer* (C-49/11) [2012] 3 CMLR 34 at paras 38–50.

6.49 Following *Content Services Ltd*, The European Commission DG guidance[1] states:

'Accordingly, a consumer's private account on the trader's website where the trader uploads the information addressed to the consumer and cannot remove and change it unilaterally, could be considered a durable medium for the purposes of the Directive. If such an account is the trader's only way of providing contract confirmation, its continued accessibility to the consumer should be ensured for an adequate period also after the consumer's contract with the trader is terminated.'

[1]   See EC DG Guidance at p 35.

Service contracts

6.50 Reg 5 of the CCR 2013 provides:

"service contract" means a contract, other than a sales contract, under which a trader supplies or agrees to supply a service to a consumer and the consumer pays or agrees to pay the price.

Services are defined by reg 5 as follows:

"service" includes–

(a)   the supply of water, gas or electricity if they are not put for sale in a limited volume or a set quantity, and
(b)   the supply of district heating.

The definition of service contract refers to the consumer paying or agreeing to pay the 'price'. The European Commission DG guidance[1] states:

'The reference to "price" in this context [and also sales contracts] would seem to solely relate to a payment in money, which would also include vouchers, gift cards or loyalty points with a specified monetary value. Consequently, the Directive does not seem to apply to gifts or to services provided by the trader for free.'

[1]   EC DG Guidance at p 8.

Sales contracts

6.51 'Sales contract' is defined by CCR 2013, reg 5 as:

"sales contract" means a contract under which a trader transfers or agrees to transfer the ownership of goods to a consumer and the consumer pays or agrees to pay the price, including any contract that has both goods and services as its object.

Reg 5 defines goods as follows:

"goods" means any tangible moveable items, but that includes water, gas and electricity if and only if they are put up for sale in a limited volume or a set quantity.

The final clause of the definition of 'sales contract' reflects the difficulties that can arise in classifying contracts as either a sales contract or service contract where the contract is a mixed contract involving the supply of both goods and services. This is considered further below at **6.89–6.90**.

Digital content contracts

6.52 'Digital content' is defined by CCR 2013, reg 5 as, 'data which are produced and supplied in digital form'. This is directed towards digital content that is supplied in an intangible form. Examples of this include software, mobile phone apps, books, music, film or ringtones that are downloaded or streamed, but not supplied in any tangible form. Recital 19 of the CRD, indicates that while digital content 'supplied on a tangible medium' (for example CDs or DVDs) should be classified as goods for the purpose of the CRD, 'contracts for digital content which is not supplied on a tangible medium should be classified' as digital content.

6.53 When defining the scope of a contract for digital content, no reference is made by the CRD or the CCR 2013 to the payment of a price. As the CCR 2013 regulate contracts, it is relevant that under English common law an essential ingredient of a legally binding contract is consideration. From the consumer's perspective, consideration usually takes the form of monetary payment, but this is not always the case. It is the latter point which appears to be accommodated by the way the Directive and CCRs 2013 define digital content contracts. The European Commission DG guidance[1] provides:

'. . . the Directive distinguishes between sales and service contracts and contracts for the supply of . . . online digital content. Contrary to the definition of sales and service contracts, the Directive does not mention "payment" for the latter . . . types of contracts. Therefore, it would seem to apply also to contracts for the supply of . . . online digital content even if they do not involve payment . . .'

[1]   EC DG Guidance at p 8.

PRE-CONTRACT INFORMATION

6.54 The requirements in Pt 2 (Chapter 1) of the CCR 2013 for traders to provide consumers with pre-contract information apply to on-premises contracts (CCR 2013, reg 9), off-premises contracts (CCR 2013, reg 10) and distance sales (CCR 2013, reg 13) within the scope of the regulations. Recital 34 of the CRD provides:

> 'The trader should give the consumer clear and comprehensible information before the consumer is bound by a distance or off premises contract, a contract other than a distance or an off-premises contract, or any corresponding offer. In providing that information, the trader should take into account the specific needs of consumers who are particularly vulnerable because of their mental, physical or psychological infirmity, age or credulity in a way which the trader could reasonably be expected to foresee. However, taking into account such specific needs should not lead to different levels of consumer protection.'

6.55 Save for criminal proceedings under CCR 2013, reg 19 (that relates to an offence of failing to give the required information relating to the right to cancel 'off-premises contracts' and compliance with any type of enforcement order), it is for the trader to prove that he has complied with the requirements as to provision of information relating to 'off-premises' and 'distance' contracts[1].

[1]   SI 2013/3134, reg 17.

6.56 There are several exceptions to the application of the information requirements. These are set out in CCR 2013, reg 7. The pre-contract information requirements which relate to 'off-premises', 'distance' and 'on-premises' contracts respectively, do not apply to contracts to the extent that they are for medicinal products supplied under a prescription or healthcare products, which are available for free or on prescription and supplied by a health care professional[1]. Save for specific information provisions relating to distance contracts concluded by electronic means[2], passenger transport services including trains and buses are similarly excluded from the information requirements of the CCR 2013[3]. The most significant exception, however, is that the consumer information requirements do not apply to 'off-premises contracts under which the payment to be made by the consumer is not more than £42'[4].

Further CCR 2013, reg 9(2) excludes from the 'on premises contract' information requirements, a contract which involves a day-to day transaction and is performed immediately .

[1]   SI 2013/3134, reg 7(2).
[2]   For which see SI 2013/3134, reg 14(1) to (5) and **6.70** and **6.71** below.
[3]   SI 2013/3134, reg 7(3).
[4]   SI 2013/3134, reg 7(4).

Information for on-premises contracts

6.57 The information requirements for on-premises contracts are set out in CCR 2013, reg 9 and Sch 1. Regulation 9(1) provides:

> 'Before the consumer is bound by an on-premises contract, the trader must give or make available to the consumer the information described in Schedule 1 in a clear and

comprehensible manner, if that information is not already apparent from the context.'

Regulation 8 of the CCR 2013 defines for the purpose of the information provisions, in Part 2 of the CCR 2013, that information will be made available 'only if the consumer can reasonably be expected to know how to access it'.

6.58 Required information given by the trader is treated as included as a term of the contract and any subsequent change (whether before entering the contract or later) is not legally effective unless 'expressly agreed between the consumer and trader'[1]. The same position is reached in relation to the 'supply of digital content other than for a price paid by the consumer' as a consequence of the amendments in the Consumer Contracts (Amendment) Regulations 2015[2].

CCR 2013, Sch 1:

Schedule 1

Information relating to on-premises contracts

The information referred to in regulation 9(1) is—

(a) the main characteristics of the goods, services or digital content, to the extent appropriate to the medium of communication and to the goods, services or digital content;

(b) the identity of the trader (such as the trader's trading name), the geographical address at which the trader is established and the trader's telephone number;

(c) the total price of the goods, services or digital content inclusive of taxes, or where the nature of the goods, services or digital content is such that the price cannot reasonably be calculated in advance, the manner in which the price is to be calculated;

(d) where applicable, all additional delivery charges or, where those charges cannot reasonably be calculated in advance, the fact that such additional charges may be payable;

(e) where applicable, the arrangements for payment, delivery, performance, and the time by which the trader undertakes to deliver the goods, to perform the service or to supply digital content;

(f) where applicable, the trader's complaint handling policy;

(g) in the case of a sales contract, a reminder that the trader is under a legal duty to supply goods that are in conformity with the contract;

(h) where applicable, the existence and the conditions of after-sales services and commercial guarantees;

(i) the duration of the contract, where applicable, or, if the contract is of indeterminate duration or is to be extended automatically, the conditions for terminating the contract;

(j) where applicable, the functionality, including applicable technical protection measures, of digital content;

(k) where applicable, any relevant compatibility of digital content with hardware and software that the trader is aware of or can reasonably be expected to have been aware of.

[1] See CRA 2015, ss 11(4) and 12 (goods), ss 36(3) and (4) and 37 (contracts for digital content for a price) and CRA 2015, s 50(3)–(5) (services). See **6.80** below, for the effect of these provisions if the trader wishes to reserve the right to make changes to any of the required pre-contract information after the contract is entered.

[2] SI 2015/1629, reg 4.

Day-to-day transactions

6.59 Under CCR 2013, reg 9(2) these requirements do not apply to 'day-to-day' transactions that are 'performed immediately at the time when the contract is entered into'. This exception is taken directly from Art 5(3) of the CRD for on-premises contracts 'which involve day-to-day transactions and which are performed immediately at the time of their conclusion'.

6.60 In the European Commission DG Guidance it is stated that[1]:

'By their nature, these transactions are likely to be for low cost items . . . Examples of such possible day-to-day services are: shoe cleaning services provided on the street and cinema services where the ticket is purchased (ie, where the contract is concluded) immediately before the film is watched.'

[1] EC DG Guidance, p 20.

Information for off-premises contracts

6.61 The information requirements for off-premises' contracts[1] are set out in reg 10 and Sch 2 (see below at **6.72**). Regulation 10(1) of the CCR 2013 provides:

Before the consumer is bound by an off-premises contract, the trader—

(a)   must give the consumer the information listed in Schedule 2 in a clear and comprehensible manner, and

(b)   if a right to cancel exists, must give the consumer a cancellation form as set out in Part B of Schedule 3.

For an 'off-premises' contract, the information set out at Sch 2 and any cancellation form must be given on paper or other durable medium[2] (provided the consumer agrees to the latter) and must be legible[3].

Sch 3 Pt A provides model instructions on cancellation which a trader may use to provide the information set out in paras (l), (m) and (n) of Sch 2[4].

[1] Defined in SI 2013/3134, reg 5 and see **6.40–6.43** above.
[2] Defined in SI 2013/3134, reg 5 and see **6.46–6.49** above.
[3] SI 2013/3134, reg 10(2).
[4] SI 2013/3134, reg 10(3). The model instructions for cancellation in Sch 3 was amended with effect from 31 December 2020 by SI 2018/1326, reg 8(4), as follows '£' was substituted for 'EUR'.

6.62 Required information given by the trader is treated as included as a term of the contract and any subsequent change (whether before entering the contract or later) is not legally effective unless 'expressly agreed between the consumer and trader'[1]. The same position is reached in relation to the 'supply of digital content other than for a price paid by the consumer' as a consequence of the amendments in the Consumer Contracts (Amendment) Regulations 2015[2].

[1] CRA 2015, ss 11(4) and (5) and 12 (goods), ss 36(3) and (4) and 37 (contracts for digital content for a price) and CRA 2015, s 50(3)–(5) (services). See **6.80** below, for the effect of these provisions if the trader wishes to reserve the right to make changes to any of the required information after the contract is concluded.
[2] SI 2015/1629, reg 5.

6.63 A copy or confirmation of the off-premises contract must be given to the consumer in accordance with CCR 2013, reg 12. CCR 2013, reg 11 modifies the information requirements where a consumer has requested a trader to carry out an immediate repair or maintenance contract and the payment by the consumer is not more than £170.

Information for distance contracts

6.64 The pre-contract information requirements for distance contracts are set out in Sch 2 (see below at **6.72**) and reg 13 of the CCR 2013. Before the consumer is bound by a distance contract, the trader must give 'or make available'[1] the information to the consumer in a 'clear and comprehensible manner' and 'in a way appropriate to the means of distance communication'[2]. If applicable, the model cancellation form must be given or made available to the consumer as set out in Sch 3 (Pt B). Sch 3 Pt A provides model instructions on cancellation which a trader may use to meet the requirements of paras (l), (m) and (n) of Sch 2[3]. *Verbraucherzentrale Bundesverband eV*[4], the CJEU confirmed that a consumer must receive the pre-contract information (required by Art 6(1) of the CRD) for distance contracts, 'in good time before the contract is concluded and not simply at the stage of concluding the contract, given that the information provided before the contract is concluded is of fundamental importance for a consumer'.

[1]   See SI 2013/3134, reg 8 provides: ' . . . something is made available to a consumer only if the consumer can reasonably be expected to know how to access it'.
[2]   SI 2013/3134, reg 13(1)(a).
[3]   SI 2013/3134, reg 13(3).
[4]   *Bundesverband der Verbraucherzentralen und Verbraucherverbände — Verbraucherzentrale Bundesverband eV v Deutsche Apotheker- und Ärztebank eG* C-380/19 at para 34.

6.65 Required information under CCR 2013, reg 13 given by the trader is treated as having been included as a term of the contract and any subsequent change (whether before entering the contract or later) is not legally effective unless 'expressly agreed between the consumer and trader'[1]. The same position is reached in relation to the 'supply of digital content other than for a price paid by the consumer' as a consequences of the amendments in the Consumer Contracts (Amendment) Regulations 2015[2].

[1]   CRA 2015, ss 11(4) and (5) and 12 (goods), ss 36(3) and (4) and 37 (contracts for digital content for a price) and CRA 2015, s 50(3)–(5) (services). See **6.80** below, for the effect of these provisions if the trader wishes to reserve the right to make changes to any of the required pre-contract information after the contract is concluded.
[2]   SI 2015/1629, reg 6.

6.66 Regulation 13(4) allows information to be split where there is limited space or time for that particular means of distance communication to display all the information in Sch 2:

> (4) Where a distance contract is concluded through a means of distance communication which allows limited space or time to display the information—
>
> (a)   the information listed in paragraphs (a), (b), (f), (g), (h), (l) and (s) of Schedule 2 must be provided on that means of communication in accordance with paragraphs (1) and (2), but
> (b)   the other information required by paragraph (1) may be provided in another appropriate way.

6.67 In *Walbusch Walter Busch*[1] a clothing retailer had distributed a leaflet advertising clothing, which contained a detachable mail order coupon that could be used to make a purchase. The right of withdrawal was referred to on the front and back of the coupon and reference was made to a website where instructions on withdrawal and the model withdrawal form could be found. Action was taken by a German consumer association on the grounds that the model withdrawal form was not attached to the leaflet. The CJEU found that the issue of whether there was 'limited space' or time to display the information had to be decided on a case by case basis, taking into account the inherent nature of the means of communication chosen by the trader and the minimum size of the typeface which is appropriate to use for the average consumer targeted by that communication. However, the CJEU observed that 'the choice made by the trader . . . regarding the development and use of the space and time at its disposal as a result of the means of communication which it decided to use are not relevant' to this assessment[2].

1   *Walbusch Walter Busch GmbH & Co KG* (C-430/17) [2019].
2   *Walbusch Walter Busch GmbH & Co KG* (C-430/17) [2019] at para 39.

6.68 In *Walbusch Walter Busch*, the CJEU held that when if it is found that there is limited space or time to display all the relevant pre-contract information, the consumer must be referred to the other information appropriately before the conclusion of the contract. For example, the trader could provide a toll free telephone number or a hypertext link to a webpage of the trader where the relevant information is directly available and easily accessible[1].

1   *Walbusch Walter Busch GmbH & Co KG* (C-430/17) [2019] at para 37.

6.69 Under CCR 2013, reg 13 the obligation to provide the required information in a durable form does not apply, although there is a legibility requirement for any of the pre-contract information that is provided on a durable medium[1]. However, confirmation of the contract must be given to the consumer under CCR 2013, reg 16 on a durable medium and must include all of the Sch 2 information. Confirmation must be provided within a reasonable time after the conclusion of the contract and, in any event, no later than delivery of goods or performance of a service[2]. If a trader makes a telephone call to a consumer with a view to concluding a distance contract, at the beginning of the conversation he must disclose his identity, any person he acts for and the commercial purpose of the call (CCR 2013, reg 15).

1   SI 2013/3134, reg 13(2).
2   SI 2013/3134, reg 16(4).

Contracts concluded by electronic means

6.70 There are additional requirements in CCR 2013, reg 14 for distance contracts concluded by electronic means, if the contract places the consumer under an obligation to pay. 'Concluded by electronic means' is not further defined in either the CCR 2013 or the CRD[1]. However the explanation for this provision in recital 39 refers only to 'distance contracts concluded through websites'. It would seem plain therefore that any internet purchase would ordinarily fall within the definition. The European Commission DG Guidance suggests that the term ought to be construed by reference to the definition in the Electronic Commerce Directive 98/34/EC, where[2]:

"by electronic means" means that the service is sent initially and received at its destination by means of electronic equipment for the processing (including digital compression) and storage of data, and entirely transmitted, conveyed and received by wire, by radio, by optical means or by other electromagnetic means.

This would suggest that the definition would exclude traders selling by mail order.

[1]   See CRD, Art 8.
[2]   Article 1(2).

6.71 Regulation 14(2) provides that if the contract places the consumer under an obligation to pay, the consumer must be made aware 'in a clear and prominent manner, and directly before the consumer places the order' of the information requirements in Sch 2(a) (the main characteristics), (f) (total price), (g) (additional delivery charges), (h) (for contracts of indeterminate duration the costs per billing period), (s) (contract duration) and (t) (minimum duration of the contract). These information requirements in Sch 2 are highlighted in bold text below. In addition, reg 14(3) provides that when placing an order, the trader must ensure that the consumer explicitly acknowledge that their order implies an obligation to pay. If the order entails (which it normally does) clicking on a button, or similar function, the trader must ensure that the link is labelled in 'an easily legible manner' only with the words 'order with obligation to pay' or similar and unambiguous wording that indicates that placing the order entails an obligation to pay the trader. The European Commission DG Guidance suggests 'buy now' or 'pay now' will suffice for these purposes[1].

[1]   See EC DG Guidance p 32.

Schedule 2

6.72 CCR 2013, Sch 2:

Schedule 2

Information relating to distance and off-premises contracts

(a)   **the main characteristics of the goods, services or digital content, to the extent appropriate to the medium of communication and to the goods, services or digital content**[1];

(b)   the identity of the trader (such as the trader's trading name);

(c)   the geographical address at which the trader is established and, where available, the trader's telephone number, fax number and e-mail address, to enable the consumer to contact the trader quickly and communicate efficiently;

(d)   where the trader is acting on behalf of another trader, the geographical address and identity of that other trader;

(e)   if different from the address provided in accordance with paragraph (c), the geographical address of the place of business of the trader, and, where the trader acts on behalf of another trader, the geographical address of the place of business of that other trader, where the consumer can address any complaints;

(f)   **the total price of the goods, services or digital content inclusive of taxes, or where the nature of the goods, services or digital content is such that the price cannot reasonably be calculated in advance, the manner in which the price is to be calculated;**

(g)   where applicable, all additional delivery charges and any other costs or, where those charges cannot reasonably be calculated in advance, the fact that such additional charges may be payable;

(h)   **in the case of a contract of indeterminate duration or a contract containing a subscription, the total costs per billing period or (where such contracts are charged at a fixed rate) the total monthly costs;**

(i)   the cost of using the means of distance communication for the conclusion of the contract where that cost is calculated other than at the basic rate;

(j)   the arrangements for payment, delivery, performance, and the time by which the trader undertakes to deliver the goods, to perform the services or to supply the digital content;

(k)   where applicable, the trader's complaint handling policy;

(l)   where a right to cancel exists, the conditions, time limit and procedures for exercising that right in accordance with regulations 27 to 38;

(m)   where applicable, that the consumer will have to bear the cost of returning the goods in case of cancellation and, for distance contracts, if the goods, by their nature, cannot normally be returned by post, the cost of returning the goods;

(n)   that, if the consumer exercises the right to cancel after having made a request in accordance with regulation 36(1), the consumer is to be liable to pay the trader reasonable costs in accordance with regulation 36(4);

(o)   where under regulation 28, 36 or 37 there is no right to cancel or the right to cancel may be lost, the information that the consumer will not benefit from a right to cancel, or the circumstances under which the consumer loses the right to cancel;

(p)   in the case of a sales contract, a reminder that the trader is under a legal duty to supply goods that are in conformity with the contract;

(q)   where applicable, the existence and the conditions of after-sale customer assistance, after-sales services and commercial guarantees;

(r)   the existence of relevant codes of conduct, as defined in regulation 5(3)(b) of the Consumer Protection from Unfair Trading Regulations 2008, and how copies of them can be obtained, where applicable;

(s)   **the duration of the contract, where applicable, or, if the contract is of indeterminate duration or is to be extended automatically, the conditions for terminating the contract;**

(t)   **where applicable, the minimum duration of the consumer's obligations under the contract;**

(u)   where applicable, the existence and the conditions of deposits or other financial guarantees to be paid or provided by the consumer at the request of the trader;

(v)   where applicable, the functionality, including applicable technical protection measures, of digital content;

(w)   where applicable, any relevant compatibility of digital content with hardware and software that the trader is aware of or can reasonably be expected to have been aware of;

(x)   where applicable, the possibility of having recourse to an out-of-court complaint and redress mechanism, to which the trader is subject, and the methods for having access to it.

Note: In the case of a public auction, the information listed in paragraphs (b) to (e) may be replaced with the equivalent details for the auctioneer.

[1]   Bold emphasis added for the reg 14 information requirements for contracts concluded by electronic means, see **6.70** and **6.71** above.

6.73 The meaning of 'to enable the consumer to contact the trader quickly and communicate with him efficiently' in Art 6(1)(c) was considered by the CJEU in the *Amazon* case[1]. Amazon offered a variety of means of online communication, but did not offer a fax number. Amazon also utilised an identity verification process before a consumer could telephone Amazon's general helpline number. The CJEU determined. Article 6(1)(c):

> ' . . . does not imply an obligation for traders to establish a telephone or fax line, or to create a new email address to allow consumers to contact them and requires that number, the fax number or their email address to be communicated only where those traders already have those means of communication with consumers.

> Article 6(1)(c) must be interpreted as meaning that, although that provision requires traders to make available to consumers a means of communication capable of satisfying the criteria of direct and effective communication, it does not preclude those traders from providing other means of communication than those listed in that provision in order to satisfy those criteria.'

1 *Bundesverband Der Verbraucherzentralen und Verbraucherverbände – Verbraucherzentrale Bundesverband e V v Amazon EU Sarl* (C-649/17) [2019] at para 53.

Failure to provide required information

6.74 There is the potential for the trader being subject to criminal proceedings for failing to give the pre-contract information relating to the right to cancel in an off-premises contract. Civil enforcement proceedings may also be taken under Pt 8 of the Enterprise Act 2002 for a breach of the regulations including non-compliance with the pre-contract information provisions. Part 8 of the Enterprise Act 2002 provides for an enforcement mechanism which, inter alia, stops the infringing conduct and allows enforcers to seek financial redress for consumers (see CHAPTER 5).

6.75 There is clear overlap between the protection offered by the information provisions of the CCR 2013 and CPUTR 2008. A common purpose shared by both regulations is to ensure that consumers have all the information they need to make informed decisions before entering a contract. Moreover, failure to comply with information provisions under the CCR 2013 may constitute a misleading omission under reg 6 of CPUTR 2008 and/or a misleading action under reg 5 of those regulations. See CHAPTER 8 on Unfair Commercial Practices.

6.76 The consequence of a failure to comply with the consumer information requirements in Pt 2 of CCR 2013 is also set out in CCR 2013, reg 18. The contract is treated as having a term that the trader has complied with his information duties under CCR 2013, regs 9–14 and 16. It follows that the failure will usually amount to a breach of contract and the remedies open to a consumer will depend on the nature and gravity of the breach.

6.77 In addition, specific provisions are made for failure to comply with certain information provisions In the case of distance and off-premises contracts, where the trader has not complied with specific pre-contract information provisions relating to the additional charges or costs to be paid by the consumer, referred to under paragraphs (g), (h) or (m) of Sch 2, then the consumer is not to bear those charges or costs[1]. More severe sanctions are specifically made for non-compliance with regs 14(3) and (4) of the CCR 2013, which apply to distance contracts concluded by electronic means and ensure the consumer understands when placing an order there is an obligation to pay[2]. Reg 14(5) provides the consequence of failing to comply with regs 14(3) and (4) is that 'the consumer is not bound by the contract or order'.

[1]   SI 2013/3134, reg 13(5) and reg 10(4).
[2]   See **6.70–6.71** above.

6.78 A consumer's cancellation rights for off-premises and distance contracts will be preserved until the information requirements are remedied, for a maximum of 12 months (see CCR 2013, reg 31 below at **6.88**).

6.79 Where a consumer exercises his right to cancel a sales contract under the CCRs 2013, ordinarily a trader may recover from a consumer the diminution in value caused by unreasonable handling of delivered goods. However, this does not apply if the trader has failed to provide the consumer with required information about the right to cancel under para (l) of Sch 2[1]. In addition, a consumer is usually responsible for the cost of returning goods to a trader after a contract has been cancelled. However, if a trader has failed to provide the consumer with the required information about the consumer bearing the cost of returning goods under para (m) of Sch 2, the trader will be responsible for those costs (CCR 2013, reg 35(6)). A consumer will also bear no cost for the supply of a service during the cancellation period if the trader failed to provide required Sch 2 information about cancellation rights and the payment of reasonable costs[2].

[1]   SI 2013/3134, reg 34(11).
[2]   SI 2013/3134, Sch 2, paras (l) and (n) and reg 36(6)(a).

Express consent

6.80 As referred to above, the required pre-contract information given by the trader is treated as a term of the contract and any subsequent change (including after the contract is entered) is not legally effective unless 'expressly agreed between the consumer and trader'[1]. This is specifically significant for longer term contracts, where it is common practice for traders to use variation terms in their standard terms and conditions which reserve the right, for example, to change the price or another specific matter which is covered by the CCR 2013 pre-contract information.

The CMA's Unfair Contract Terms Guidance provides the CMA's view that for these types of terms to be effective, inter alia, the trader needs to ensure that any possible change to the pre-contract information must be reflected in the pre-contract information itself. The CMA's guidance states:

> 'The provisions of the CCRs should particularly be borne in mind where clauses could be used to allow changes to be made to any details as to (for instance) the product or its price set out in the Pre-Contract Information. The CMA considers that for such clauses to be legally effective when used with consumers, the Pre-Contract Information must itself reflect the fact that the potential changes envisaged may be made[2].'

Moreover, the CMA's view is that the pre-contract information relating to variation must meet the requirements of fairness under the CRA 2015, Pt 2. See CHAPTER 9 on Unfair Terms.

¹ See **6.58**, **6.62** and **6.65** respectively above.
² See the CMA's 'Guidance on the unfair terms provisions in the Consumer Rights Act 2015', 31 July 2015, CMA37 at **6.36–6.44**.

CANCELLATION RIGHTS

6.81 The origin of cancellation rights in consumer contracts can be found in the Doorstep Selling Directive 85/577/EEC¹ and the Distance Selling Directive 97/7/EC². Both of these Directives were implemented domestically by statutory instrument³.

¹ Council Directive 85/577/EEC to protect the consumer in respect of contracts negotiated away from business premises.
² Directive 97/7/EC on the protection of consumers in respect of distance contracts.
³ Cancellation of Contracts made in a Consumer's Home or Place of Work etc Regulations 2008, SI 2008/1816 and the Consumer Protection (Distance Selling) Regulations 2000, SI 2000/2334 as amended by SI 2005/269.

6.82 Part 3 of the CCR 2013, provides consumers with cancellation rights for off-premises and distance contracts only. The CRD extended the cancellation period to 14 calendar days for both off-premises and distance contracts.

The right to cancel or withdraw

6.83 In determining whether a consumer has a right to cancel a contract it is important to consider the following questions.

(a)   Does the CCR 2013 apply at all?
(b)   Is the contract an 'off-premises contract' or a 'distance contract'?
(c)   Does the contract fall within any of the Pt 3 exceptions?
(d)   Is the contract a 'service', 'sales' or 'digital content' contract?
(e)   Did the consumer cancel within the cancellation period or extended default cancellation period?

Withdrawing an offer and cancellation

6.84 The CCR 2013 refers both to 'cancellation' of a contract and also to a consumer's right to 'withdraw an offer'. Withdrawal covers the position when a consumer has made an offer, but that offer has not yet been accepted by the trader. In that situation there is no contractual agreement until the trader has accepted the offer. The CCR 2013 provides the same right to sever the relationship with a trader for a consumer withdrawing an offer as it does for a consumer cancelling a contract, CCR 2013, regs 31–34.

Exercising the right to cancel or withdraw

6.85 CCR 2013, reg 29 provides a general right to cancel a distance or off-premises contract at any time in the 14 days' cancellation period 'without giving any reason, and without incurring any liability'. The right of not incurring any liability at all upon cancellation is, however, subject to the four circumstances set out at CCR 2013, regs 34–36, these are:

- Under reg 34(3), where the consumer has expressly chosen delivery to them which costs more than the least expensive common and generally acceptable kind of delivery offered by the trader, the trader only has to reimburse the amount of that less expensive delivery offered.
- Under reg 34(9), if in case of a 'sales contract', where the value of the goods is diminished as a result of the consumer handling the goods beyond what is necessary (to establish the nature, characteristic and functioning of the goods), the consumer can be required to pay that amount, up to the contract price.
- Under a 'sales contract', reg 35(5) provides for the consumer paying the direct costs of returning the goods unless the trader has agreed to cover such costs or the trader failed to comply with his obligation to provide the information at Sch 2, para (m), in accordance with the information requirement provision of the CCRs 2013.
- Under reg 36(4), in the case of a 'service contract', where the consumer has made an express request for the supply of the service to begin before the end of the cancellation period but then exercises their right to cancel the contract, the consumer has to pay for the proportion of the service supplied up to the time when the trader is informed of the consumer's decision to cancel[1].

Moreover, there are also numerous exceptions to the right to cancel, which are discussed below.

[1] See also **6.103–6.108**.

6.86 A consumer wishing to withdraw from an offer, or cancel, may do so by informing the trader. Exercising the right to cancel may be done either by using the form set out in Pt B of Sch 3, or by making any other 'clear statement setting out the decision to cancel the contract'[1]. The evidential burden is upon the consumer to show that the contract was cancelled during the cancellation period[2]. CCR 2013, reg 32(5) incorporates the contractual postal rule such that a consumer who sends a letter, or other communication, to the trader will be treated as having cancelled the contract at the time at which the communication is sent, rather than when it is received by the trader.

[1] SI 2013/3134, reg 32.
[2] SI 2013/3134, reg 32(6).

The cancellation period

6.87 The cancellation period starts when the contract is made[1] and, provided that the trader has complied with the information requirements, its end date is defined in CCR 2013, reg 30, depending upon the type of contract that has been entered into[2]. This is summarised in the table below.

Type of contract	Cancellation period
'A service contract'	14 days after the day on which the contract was made

Type of contract	Cancellation period
The supply of digital content not supplied on a tangible medium	14 days after the day on which the contract was made
'A sales contract' *but see below*	14 days after the day on which the goods come into the physical possession of the consumer or the person that she asks you to deliver the goods to
A sales contract consisting of an order for multiple goods which are delivered on different days	14 days after the day on which the last of the goods come into the physical possession of the consumer or the person that she asks to take possession of the goods
A sales contract consisting of an order for multiple lots or pieces which are delivered on different days	14 days after the day on which the last of the lots or pieces come into the physical possession of the consumer or the person that she asks you to deliver the goods to
A sales contract for regular delivery of goods during a period of longer than one day	14 days after the day on which the first of the goods come into the physical possession of the consumer or the person that she asks to take possession of the goods

1   SI 2013/3134, reg 29(2).
2   See **6.50 –6.52** for the definitions of 'service contract', 'sales contract', contract for the supply of 'digital content' and **6.89** below for mixed contracts.

6.88 Under reg 31, the cancellation period is extended, however, if the trader has breached the information requirements in Pt 2 of the CCR 2013, by failing to provide the information required by para (I) of Sch 2, in accordance with Pt 2. The cancellation period continues to run until 14 days after the information failure is remedied by the trader, up to a maximum of 12 months. Note should also be taken of EC Regulation 1182/71[1], which extends the last day of the cancellation period, if it falls on a Saturday, Sunday or Bank Holiday, to the next working day (see CHAPTER 2, at **2.61**).

1   Regulation determining the rules and applicable periods, dates and time limits – see Art 3.4.

Mixed contracts and cancellation rights

6.89 The cancellation rights under the CCR 2013 apply depending on whether the contract entered into by the consumer can be characterised as a 'sales contract', 'service contract' or a contract for the supply of 'digital content'. This raises the issue of how to apply those rights when the contract concerns the supply of two or more of the following: goods, services and digital content.

For these purposes, the European Commission DG guidance[1] suggests the following approach:

'According to the definition under Article 2(5), the criteria for classifying a contract as a 'sales contract' is the transfer of the ownership of goods to the consumer against payment of the price thereof. Therefore, if a contract's main purpose is to transfer of ownership of certain goods, it should be classified as a sales contract even if it also covers related services provided by the seller, such as installation, maintenance or any other processing, irrespective of the relative value of the goods and services.

. . . In contrast if the transfer of the ownership of specific goods is not the main purpose of the mixed contract, the contract should not be considered a sales contract.

. . . In a nutshell, each mixed contract should be classified based on its real main purpose.'

[1]   At p 6 and p 7.

6.90 Further, the European Commission's DG guidance[1] provides a number of practical examples such as contracts for the purchase of a new kitchen, including its installation, should usually be considered as sales contracts for the purpose of the CRD and so too should the purchase of a new mobile handset that is bundled with a subscription to an electronic communications service.

While, 'a contract for the repair, renovation and construction of an annex to a building' and 'a contract for a training course, including delivery of a course book for each participant' should both be regarded as service contracts.

[1]   EC DG Guidance at p 6 and p 7.

Cancelling service contracts

6.91 A trader cannot supply a service during the cancellation period unless the consumer has made an express request and, in the case of an off-premises contract has made the express request in a durable medium[1]. If such a request has been made and properly recorded, the consumer ceases to have the right to cancel[2] a service contract after it has been fully performed, provided that the service began with the consumer's acknowledgment that the right to cancel would be lost[3].

[1]   SI 2013/3134, reg 36(1).
[2]   Other than supply of water, gas electricity or district heating, SI 2013/3134, reg 36(2).
[3]   SI 2013/3134, reg 36(2).

Digital content not on a tangible medium

6.92 CCR 2013, reg 37 provides for an express exception to the right to cancel for the supply of digital content and the consumer consents. For the exception to apply the consumer must have given express *consent* for the supply of the digital content (before the end of the cancellation period) and *acknowledged* that their right to cancel will be lost. The consumer will then cease to have the right to cancel if the supply of the digital content has begun *after* such consent and acknowledgment[1].

[1]   SI 2013/3134, reg 37(1) and (2).

Part 3 cancellation exceptions

6.93 CCR 2013, regs 27 and 28 provide for a number of express exceptions to the right to cancel under Pt 3. These are summarised in the table below.

Regulation	Description	Exception
27(2)(a)	Medicines	Prescription medicinal products 'by administration by a prescriber' or 'under a prescription or directions given by a prescriber'
27(2)(b)	Health products	Products supplied by a health care professional as part of the health service
27(2)(c)	Transport	Passenger transport services
27(3)	Less than £42	Off-premises contracts where the consumer pays less than £42
28(1)(a)	Goods and services where the price is subject to fluctuations in the financial markets	Goods and Services where the price is dependent on fluctuations in the financial market within cancellation period and not controllable by the trader (but not applicable to services for the supply of water, gas, electricity or district heating)
28(1)(b)	Bespoke goods	Supply of goods made to the consumer's specification or are clearly personalised
28(1)(c)	Perishables	Supply of goods liable to deteriorate or expire rapidly
28(1)(d)	Alcohol on market price	Alcoholic beverages, where value is dependent on fluctuations in the market not controllable by the trader, the price is agreed upon conclusion of the contract and delivery can only take place after 30 days
28(1)(e)	Urgent repairs	Urgent repairs or maintenance, where consumer specifically requested a visit from the trader. But see reg 28(2) for services and goods 'in addition'
28(1)(f)	Newspapers	Newspapers, periodicals and magazines, with the exception of subscriptions
28(1)(g)	Public auctions	Contracts concluded at public auction (reg 5 – transparent, competitive bidding procedure run by an auctioneer where consumers are given the possibility to attend in person, and the successful bidder is bound to purchase)
28(1)(h)	Contracts for a specific time	Following services where a specific date or period for performance is contracted: Supply of accommodation eg holiday cottages Transport of goods Vehicle rental service Catering or services related to leisure activities
28(3)(a)	Unhygienic returns*	Sealed products that have been unsealed after delivery and are therefore unsuitable to return for health protection or hygiene reasons
28(3)(b)	Sealed recordings*	Sealed audio recordings, video recordings or computer software unsealed after delivery
28(3)(c)	Mixed goods*	Goods have become mixed inseparably with other items after delivery (thereby resulting in the goods being unable to be returned)

*These contracts are cancellable until the action described occurs, at which point the right to cancel is lost

Bespoke goods

6.94 CCR 2013, reg 28(1)(b) states that the cancellation provisions in Pt 3 do not apply to 'the supply of goods that are made to the consumer's specifications or are clearly personalised'. Whilst goods are defined as 'any tangible moveable items' (see reg 5), the scope of this provision is not further defined in the CCR 2013; however, Art 2(4) of the CRD provides a definition of 'goods made to the consumer's specifications' as 'non-prefabricated goods made on the basis of an individual choice of or decision by the consumer'. Recital 49 of the CRD also states that the 'right of withdrawal should neither apply to goods made to the consumer's specifications or which are clearly personalised such as tailor-made curtains'.

6.95 The European Commission DG Guidance[1] suggests that the exception should be 'interpreted narrowly'.

> 'So, this exception should cover, for example:
> * goods, for which the consumer has provided specifications, such as measurements for furniture or the size of a fabric;
> * goods, for which the consumer has requested specific personalised features, such as a particular design for a car that is made to order or a specific component for a computer, which has to be individually procured for that particular order and which was not part of the trader's general offer to the public;
> * address labels with the consumer's contact information or T-shirts with a personalised print.
>
> Specification/personalisation in this context should be taken to mean that the goods are, in principle, unique and produced according to the individual wishes and requirements stated by the consumer and agreed with the trader.
>
> In contrast, where the consumer simply makes up the goods by picking from the standard (pre-set) options provided by the trader, such as colour or additional equipment in a car, or makes up a set of furniture on the basis of standard elements, it should not be possible to speak of either "specification" or "personalisation" in the narrow sense of this provision.'

[1] EC DG Guidance at p 54.

6.96 The BIS (now BEIS) *Implementing Guidance to the Consumer Contracts Regulations*[1] states that:

> 'An item made up following a consumer order does not necessarily make it a bespoke item which is exempt from cancellation rights. An item, for example a sofa or computer, can be assembled following an order but the component parts may be made up of parts offered from a standard range. So, for instance, a sofa where the consumer chooses a fabric and colour from a range on offer will not be bespoke for the purposes of these Regulations. However, if the consumer asks the trader to source a special finish and which is not in the range generally offered by the trader, that is likely to be a bespoke item.'

[1] BIS Implementing Guidance, December 2013, section H.

6.97 The Guidance from both the European Commission and BIS suggests that the exception should be construed narrowly. The reference in the CRD to 'non-prefabricated goods' suggests that goods assembled from pre-fabricated component parts are less likely to fall within the exception if they are ordinarily available as part of the trader's range. It is likely that a distinction will be drawn between goods that are rendered unique when made up according to a consumer's specification and those that are merely the selection of options that a trader routinely makes available to consumers. Although this distinction may be difficult to draw for products with a vast array of options that, whilst usually made available by the trader, ultimately results in a unique or nearly unique end product.

6.98 A possible rationale for the bespoke goods exception is that it may be difficult for a trader to re-sell goods after they have been personalised or customised in accordance with an individual consumer's specification. The ability of a trader to resell goods may be a factor in determining whether the exception applies. It follows that it may be important to ascertain whether the assembly process is reversible. However, in the context off-premises contracts, the CJEU held in *Mobel Kraft GmbH*[1] that this exception to the consumer's cancellation rights applied 'irrespective of whether the trader has begun to produce' the goods made to the consumer's specifications.

[1] *Mobel Kraft GmbH & Co KG v ML* C-529-19 [2020].

Unhygienic returns

6.99 In *Schlafen leben wohnen GmbH v Sascha Ledowski*[1] the CJEU found that a sealed mattress fell outside this exception because a mattress may come into contact with a human body but it could be made saleable again by means of appropriate cleaning measures by the trader.

[1] *Schlafen leben wohnen GmbH v Sascha Ledowski* C-681-17 [2018].

Effect of cancellation or withdrawal

6.100 A contract that is effectively cancelled will end the contractual obligations of both parties to perform the contract. The same applies if the consumer withdraws an offer to enter into a distance or off-premises contract[1].

[1] SI 2013/3134, reg 33.

6.101 Under CCR 2013 reg 38, ancillary contracts, to the main distance or off-premises contract, are automatically terminated as a consequence of cancellation or withdrawal of the main contract[1]. 'Ancillary contract' is defined as one 'by which the consumer acquires goods or services related to the main contract, where those goods or services are provided' by the trader or a 'third party on the basis of an arrangement between the third party and the trader'[2]. Although excluded by reg 6(1)(b) from CCR 2013, financial services are to be treated as an ancillary contract for the purposes of reg 38, other examples of potential ancillary contracts include insurance contracts and extended warranties.

[1] SI 2013/3134, reg 38(1) and (2). Reg 38(2) makes provision for the trader who is informed of a decision to withdraw or cancel the main contract to inform any 'other trader with whom the consumer has an ancillary contract'.
[2] SI 2013/3134, reg 38(3).

Return of goods following cancellation

6.102 In a sales contract the trader must collect goods that have been delivered to a consumer if he has offered to collect them, or (in the case of an off-premises contract) the goods have been delivered to the consumer's home when the contract was entered and cannot 'by their nature, normally be returned by post' (CCR 2013, reg 35(1)). Otherwise it is the consumer's responsibility to return[1] the goods to the trader without undue delay, and in any event not later than 14 days after cancellation[2].

1   SI 2013/3134, reg 35(2) by sending them back or handing them over. SI 2013/3134, reg 35(3) deals with the appropriate address.
2   SI 2013/3134, reg 35(4).

Reimbursement

6.103 The trader must generally reimburse all payments that have been made by a consumer when a distance or off-premises contract is cancelled under the CCR 2013. No fee may be charged for the reimbursement and it should be made using the same means of payment, unless the consumer has agreed otherwise[1]. Reimbursement must be made without undue delay and no later than 14 days after the trader receives the goods back[2] or has cancelled the contract[3]. This general right to reimbursement, is however, subject to four exceptions in CCR 2013, regs 34–36[4].

1   SI 2013/3134, reg 34(7) and (8).
2   SI 2013/3134, reg 34(5)(a) or if earlier, 14 days after the day on which the consumer supplies evidence of having sent the goods back, reg 34(5)(b).
3   See SI 2013/3134, regs 34(4)–(6).
4   See **6.85** above and **6.104–6.110** below.

NON-STANDARD DELIVERY CHARGES

6.104 The trader must reimburse any payment that the consumer has made for delivery, unless the consumer expressly chose a more expensive delivery service 'costing more than the least expensive common and generally acceptable kind of delivery offered by the trader'[1]. If the consumer has chosen such a more expensive non-standard delivery service, the trader need only reimburse him the amount the trader charges for his standard delivery service[2].

1   SI 2013/3134, reg 34(2).
2   SI 2013/3134, reg 34(3).

VALUE DIMINISHED BY HANDLING

6.105 In a sales contract the trader may make a deduction from the amount to be reimbursed to a consumer if the value of the goods is diminished because of a consumer's handling 'beyond what is necessary to establish the nature, characteristics and functioning of the goods'[1]. This is further defined as handling that 'goes beyond the sort of handling that might reasonably be allowed in a shop'[2].

1   SI 2013/3134, reg 34(9).
2   SI 2013/3134, reg 34(12).

6.106 The reduction made can amount to the entire contract price for the goods and can be deducted from the amount already paid by the consumer. However, if that is insufficient to pay for the diminution in value the consumer can be required to pay the amount to the trader[1]. The provisions permitting a trader to recover the diminution in value do not apply if the trader has failed to provide the consumer with required information about the right to cancel under para (l) of Sch 2[2].

[1]   Under SI 2013/3134, reg 34(10)(b).
[2]   SI 2013/3134, reg 34(11).

COST OF RETURNING GOODS

6.107 In a sales contract the consumer must bear the direct cost of returning goods to the trader after cancellation. This is limited strictly to the actual cost of returning the goods and the consumer is not required to pay any additional amounts[1]. The consumer must pay the costs of returning the goods unless the trader has agreed to bear those costs or has failed to provide the consumer with required information about the consumer bearing such costs under para (m) of Sch 2, in accordance with Pt 2 of the CCR 2013[2]. The contractual term is statutorily implied that the trader must bear the costs of return when he has failed to provide that information.

[1]   SI 2013/3134, reg 35(7).
[2]   SI 2013/3134, reg 35(5)(b).

SERVICES PROVIDED DURING THE CANCELLATION PERIOD

6.108 If a trader legitimately[1] starts to perform a service during the cancellation period, but the consumer cancels before the service has been fully performed, the trader may recover a proportion of the total price he would have charged for the full coverage of the contract[2]. The recoverable amount is proportionate to the total price agreed unless that was 'excessive', in which case the market value is substituted[3].

[1]   A trader cannot supply a service during the cancellation period unless the consumer has made an express request that has also been recorded, in the case of an off-premises contract in a durable medium, SI 2013/3134, reg 36(1) – see **6.91**.
[2]   SI 2013/3134, reg 36(4).
[3]   SI 2013/3134, reg 36(5)(b) market value 'calculated by comparing prices for equivalent services supplied by other traders'.

6.109 In the context of a dispute relating to the amount a consumer should pay after cancelling, within the cancellation period, a 12 month distance contract for dating services, the CJEU[1] held referring to Art 14(3) of the CRD:

'. . . in order to determine the proportionate amount to be paid by the consumer to the trader where that consumer has expressly requested that the performance of the contract concluded begin during the withdrawal period and withdraws from that contract, it is appropriate, in principle, to take account of the price agreed in the contract for the full coverage of the contract and to calculate the amount owed pro rata temporis. It is only where the contract concluded expressly provides that one or more of the services are to be provided in full from the beginning of the performance of the contract and separately, for a price which must be paid separately, that the full price for such a service should be taken into account in the calculation of the amount owed to the trader under Article 14(3) of that directive.

Article 14(3) . . . , read in the light of recital 50 thereof, must be interpreted as meaning that, in order to assess whether the total price is excessive within the meaning of that provision, account should be taken of the price of the service offered by the trader concerned to other consumers under the same conditions and that of the equivalent service supplied by other traders at the time of the conclusion of the contract.'

[1]   *EU v PE Digital GmbH* C-641/19 [2020]

6.110 A consumer will bear no cost for the supply of a service during the cancellation period if the trader failed to provide the Sch 2 information about cancellation rights and costs[1] or the service was not supplied in response to a consumer request recorded in a durable medium[2]. These rules will apply to both service contracts and the service element of a sales contract, if both goods and services have been supplied.

[1]   SI 2013/3134, Sch 2, paras (l) and (n).
[2]   SI 2013/3134, reg 36(6).

Criminal offence

6.111 CCR 2013, reg 19:

19 Offence relating to the failure to give notice of the right to cancel

(1) A trader is guilty of an offence if the trader enters into an off-premises contract to which regulation 10 applies but fails to give the consumer the information listed in paragraph (l), (m) or (n) of Schedule 2 in accordance with that regulation.

6.112 This provision provides for criminal liability for a trader that fails, in an off-premises contract, to give a consumer notice of his cancellation rights. The remainder of the provisions in the CCR 2013 do not of themselves carry criminal sanction, although CPUTR 2008, reg 6(3)(b) (misleading omissions in relation to Community obligations) should be considered in this context, see Chapter 8, Unfair Commercial Practices.

6.113 Enforcement of the CCR 2013 falls upon local weights and measures authorities and the Department for the Economy in Northern Ireland[1]. In England and Wales proceedings for this offence can only be instituted by or on behalf of an enforcement authority.

[1]   SI 2013/3134, reg 23.

6.114 The offence is also subject to a directors' liability provision (CCR 2013, reg 22), a causal liability provision (CCR 2013, reg 21) and a due diligence defence (CCR 2013, reg 20). These types of provision are dealt with in greater detail in Chapter 4, Criminal Enforcement.

Sentencing

6.115 The offence is triable summarily and punishable by a fine[1]. As a consequence of the Legal Aid, Sentencing and Punishment of Offenders Act 2012, s 85(1) the maximum fine is now not limited for offences committed on or after

12 March 2015. At the time of writing there were no appellate authorities on the levels of fines for offences under the CCR 2013, reg 19.

1   SI 2013/3134, reg 19(2).

6.116 It should be remembered, however, that the failure to notify a consumer of their cancellation rights might also generate criminal liability under the CPUTR 2008, see **CHAPTER 8** on Unfair Commercial Practices. In *R v Garfoot* and *Wilsher*[1], a charge contrary to the CPUTR 2008, reg 8 of the (contravening professional diligence) was brought where no cancellation rights were explained or communicated[2].

1   [2011] EWCA Crim 2043.
2   In *R v Lewis Thomas Gilbertson* [2009] EWCA Crim 1715 the defendant pleaded guilty to two misleading omission offences under CPUTR 2008, SI 2008/1277, reg 10 for failing to inform householders of their right to withdraw from a contract made after an unsolicited visit.

CCR 2013 – OTHER MATTERS

6.117 Some provisions of the regulation have been moved to CRA 2015, in particular:

(a)   Regulation 42 – time for delivery of goods – now CRA 2015, s 28.
(b)   Regulation 43 – passing of risk – now CRA 2015, s 29.

Additional payments

6.118 Reg 40 of the CCR 2013 provides that before a consumer is bound by a contract, the trader must have secured the consumer's 'express consent' for any payments which are in addition to the 'remuneration agreed for the trader's main obligation'. Reg 40(2) makes clear that 'express consent' for additional payments cannot be inferred from the consumer not changing a default option. The example is provided of a trader using a pre-ticked box which the consumer must take action to undo.

The CJEU[1] has indicated that the purpose of this provision is to ensure that consumers have expressly chosen to pay for additional payments which are not 'unavoidable and necessary' under the contract.

1   See *ebookers.com Deutschland GmbH v Bundesverband der Verbraucherzentrale und Verbraucherverbande – Verbraucherzentrale Bundesverband e V C-112/11* [2012] at paras 14–16.

6.119 CCR 2013, reg 40 does not apply to financial services, when the financial service is the trader's main obligation under the contract. However, the provisions do apply when financial services are not the trader's main obligation under the contract and attract an additional charge[1]. For example, the provision will apply to an additional charge for insurance under a contract for a flight.

Where a trader receives an additional payment without obtaining the consumer's express consent for it before the contract is entered, the consumer has a right to seek a refund of such a payment. Reg 40(4) provides 'the contract is to be treated as providing for the trader to reimburse the [additional] payment to the consumer'.

1   SI 2013/3134, reg 40(3).

Basic rate help-lines

6.120 Reg 41(1) of the CCR 2013 provides:

> 'Where a trader operates a telephone line for the purpose of consumers contacting the trader by telephone in relation to contracts entered into with the trader, a consumer contacting the trader must not be bound to pay more than the basic rate.'

The provision applies post contract, where the trader makes available to consumers a telephone line to contact them on matters relating to the consumer's contract. The provision is wider than simply providing a customer service line and will also apply to calls for advice about what has been purchased or for amending a contract that has already been entered into.

6.121 Where a trader operates such a telephone line, it must be offered at no more than the 'basic rate'. This is not defined in the CRD or the CCR 2013. With reference to Art 21 of the CRD, the CJEU has observed[1] that 'basic rate' must mean:

> ' . . . that call charges relating to a contract concluded with a trader to a telephone helpline operated by the trader may not exceed the costs of a call to a standard geographic landline or mobile telephone line. Provided that the limit is respected, the fact that the relevant trader makes or does not make a profit through that telephone helpline is irrelevant.'

Consumers have the right to claim back any charge that exceeds the basic rate[2].

1   See *Zentrale zur Bekampfung unlauteren Wettbewerbs Frankfurt am Main eV v comtech GmbH* (C-568/15) [2017] at para 33.
2   SI 2013/3134, reg 41(2).

Civil enforcement

6.122 The CCR 2013 places a duty upon an 'enforcement authority'[1] to consider any complaint regarding its contravention unless the complaint is frivolous or vexatious, or another enforcement authority has notified the CMA that it agrees to consider the complaint. Regulation 45 enables an enforcement authority to apply for an injunction, or in Scotland an interdict or order of specific implement, against any person who appears to be responsible for contravention of the CCR 2013. The CMA must be notified of any undertaking or court action[2]. The CCR 2013 is also prescribed as a community infringement for the purposes of the Enterprise Act 2002 (see CHAPTER 5, Civil Enforcement)[3].

1   A local weights and measures authority in Great Britain and the Department for the Economy in Northern Ireland – SI 2013/3134, reg 44(3).
2   See SI 2013/3134, reg 46.
3   SI 2014/2908.

Review of the CCR 2013

6.123 Regulation 3 requires the Secretary of State to carry a review of the CCR 2013, set out the conclusions of the review and publish a report. The review must assess the extent to which the objectives of the Regulations have been achieved and whether they remain appropriate. In March 2019, BEIS published a call for evidence, to inform their first review[1].

BEIS published a Report on their Review in July 2019[2]. This concluded:

'Our assessment is that there is little scope to change the substantive content or scope of the Regulations themselves whilst the UK continues to be bound by the EU law. The EU itself has proposed amendment to the CRD (which the CCR 2013 implement) through its "New Deal for Consumers" programme and some changes requiring implementation by the UK will follow that work through the Omnibus Directive.'

However BEIS did acknowledge that there were areas requiring clarification or better illustration, many identified in these notes, and that they would work with consumers, business and enforcers so that a common understanding of rights and requirements can be achieved. They indicated that the challenge of consistent enforcement would be considered in the Consumer White Paper.

[1]   'Consumer Contract Regulations Review. Call for evidence' March 2019.
[2]   Statutory Report on the Implementation of the Consumer Contracts (Information, Cancellation and Additional Charges) Regulations 2013: July 2019.

EU Ominbus Directive

6.124 Directive (EU) 2019/2161 was agreed on 27 November 2019. EU Member States had until 28 November 2021 to the put the new measures into domestic legislation, which must apply from 28 May 2022.

The Directive makes a number of changes to 2011/83/EU, including:

•   New definitions are added for 'digital services', 'online market place', 'provider of an online market place', 'compatibility', 'functionality' and 'interoperability'.
•   Pre-contract information for off-premises and distance contracts must include a geographical address **and** a telephone and email contact (currently optional), as well as other means of online contact.
•   Pre-contract information for off-premises and distance contracts must include, where appropriate, that personalised pricing has been provided on the basis of an automated decision-making process.
•   Consumer concluding a contract through an online market place must be given information about the main ranking parameters used to generate the results of their search, whether the third party is a trader or not and whether EU consumer laws apply.
•   Member States are also given the option to extend the cancellation period for unsolicited off-premises contracts to 30 days.

Clearly, it will be a matter for the UK Government to decide the extent to which this Directive is implemented into UK legislation.

PAYMENT SURCHARGES

6.125 Since 6 April 2013, traders have been precluded from charging consumers fees for using a particular payment method which exceeded the cost borne by the trader for the use of that method. That prohibition is set out in reg 4 of the Consumer Rights (Payment Surcharges) Regulations 2012 (CR(PS) Regulations) which implemented Art 19 of the CRD[1]. With effect from 13 January 2018[2], the CR(PS) Regulations were amended[3] to give effect to part of the EU's second Payment Services Directive ('PSD 2')[4] which introduced a wholesale ban on consumer payment surcharges.

[1] Directive 2011/83/EU of the European Parliament and Council on consumer rights.
[2] Subject to the transitional provisions in SI 2017/752, regs 150–154.
[3] By the Payment Services Regulations 2017, SI 2017/752, Sch 8, Pt 3, para 12(6).
[4] Directive 2366/2015/EU on Payment Services in the Internal Market.

6.126 Regulations 6A–6B of the CR(PS) Regulations implemented Art 62 of the PSD 2 on payment surcharges. Regulation 4 continues to prohibit excessive fees that are not caught by the prohibition in reg 6A(1). In summary, regs 6A–6B have the following effect:

(a)   Where the payment service provider, for both the payer and payee, is located within the UK[1], there is a prohibition on fees charged in respect of payment by means of a payment instrument or certain payment services. This will include most credit and debit cards and certain credit transfers or direct debit services[2].

(b)   Where only one of the payment service providers is so located, the fee must be no more than its cost[3].

(c)   Regulations 6A–6B do not apply at all when neither payments service provider is located within the UK. However, the existing reg 4 of the CR(PS) Regulations will continue to apply in those circumstances and where the transaction falls outside the definition in reg 6A(1)[4].

(d)   Payments that do not fall within the definition of 'payment services' are governed under reg 4.

[1] The territorial scope was amended by the Consumer Protection (Amendment etc.) (EU Exit) Regulations 2018, SI 2018/1326, reg 7(3) on 31 December 2020.
[2] SI 2012/3110, reg 6A(1) and 6B(2).
[3] SI 2012/3110, reg 6A(2) and 6B(3).
[4] SI 2012/3110, reg 6B(1).

Payee and payer

6.127 The CR(PS) Regulations must be read alongside the Payment Service Regulations 2017[1] ('PSR 2017'), which implemented the remainder of PSD 2 and provide some of the important new definitions[2].

PSR 2017, reg 2(1):

"payee" means a person who is the intended recipient of funds which have been the subject of a payment transaction;

"payer" means—
(a)   a person who holds a payment account and initiates, or consents to the initiation of, a payment order from that payment account; or

(b)   where there is no payment account, a person who gives a payment order;

. . .

"payment service" means any of the activities specified in Part 1 of Schedule 1 (payment services) when carried out as a regular occupation or business activity, other than any of the activities specified in Part 2 of that Schedule (activities which do not constitute payment services;

'Payment instrument' and 'payment service provider' are also defined widely in reg 2(1) of the PSR 2017 and will include many non-UK financial institutions that are payment service providers with branches located within the UK. Schedule 1, and Pt 2 in particular, is important because it exempts some everyday consumer activities from regs 6A and 6B[3].

[1]   SI 2017/752.
[2]   SI 2012/3110, reg 3 have been amended so that from 13 January 2018 'payee', 'payer', 'payment instrument', 'payment service' and 'payment service provider' have the meanings given in SI 2017/752, reg 2(1).
[3]   Brexit related changes were made to the definitions in reg 2(1) of the PSR 2017 and the listed exemptions in Pt 2 of Sch 1 to the PSR 2017 by Sch 2(2) of the Electronic Money, Payment Services and Payment Systems (Amendment and Transitional Provisions) (EU Exit) Regulations 2018, SI 2018/1201.

The reg 6A prohibitions

6.128 As explained above, regs 6A–6B of the CR(PS) Regulations 2012 came into force on 13 January 2018 and, subject to certain limitations, apply to payments made from that date. The most significant limitation is that, by virtue of reg 1(3) of the CR(PS) Regulations 2012, the prohibition do not apply to charges levied under contracts entered into before the PRS 2017 were made (ie before 18 July 2017). Brexit related amendments were made on 31 December 2020.

6A Fees any payee must not charge any payer

(1)   A payee must not charge a payer any fee in respect of payment by means of—
    (a)   a payment instrument which—
        (i)   is a card-based payment instrument as defined in Article 2(20) of Regulation (EU) 2015/751 of the European Parliament and of the Council of 29th April 2015 on interchange fees for card-based payment transactions; and
        (ii)   is not a commercial card as defined in Article 2(6) of that Regulation; or
    (b)   a payment instrument which—
        (i)   is not a card-based payment instrument as defined in Article 2(20) of that Regulation; and
        (ii)   would not fall within the definition of commercial card at Article 2(6) of that Regulation if, in that definition, the reference to any card-based payment instrument were to any payment instrument and the reference to such cards were to such payment instruments; or
    (c)   a payment service to which Regulation (EU) 260/2012 of the European Parliament and of the Council of 14th March 2012 establishing technical and business requirements for credit transfers and direct debits in euro applies.

(2)   A payee receiving a payment by means of a payment instrument must not charge the payer, in respect of such payment, a fee which exceeds the costs borne by the payee for the use of that specific payment instrument.

6B Application of regulation 6A

(1)   Regulation 6A applies only if the payment service provider of the payer or the payment service provider of the payee is located in the United Kingdom[1].

(2)   Where the payment service providers of both the payee and the payer are located in the United Kingdom[2], regulation 6A(1) and (2) apply.

(3)   Where the payment service provider of either the payer or the payee, but not both, is located in the United Kingdom[3], regulation 6A(2) applies but regulation 6A(1) does not apply.

[1]   Changed from 'located in an EEA State' be reg 7(3) of the Consumer Protection (Amendment etc.) (EU Exit) Regulations 2018, SI 2018/1326.
[2]   Changed from 'located in an EEA State' be reg 7(3) of the Consumer Protection (Amendment etc.) (EU Exit) Regulations 2018, SI 2018/1326.
[3]   Changed from 'located in an EEA State' be reg 7(3) of the Consumer Protection (Amendment etc.) (EU Exit) Regulations 2018, SI 2018/1326.

6.129 Regulation 6A contains two different prohibitions, an absolute prohibition against charging any fee in respect of a payment (reg 6A(1)) and one that is limited to the costs incurred by the payee (reg 6A(2)). Regulation 6B sets out when each prohibition applies according to the location of the relevant payment service providers. Unlike the reg 4 prohibition, the reg 6A prohibitions are not confined to relationships between consumers and traders, however the absolute prohibition in reg 6A(1) does not apply to 'commercial cards' as defined in Art 2(6) of Regulation (EU) 2015/751 of the European Parliament and of the Council of 29 April 2015 on interchange fees for card-based payment transactions[1] and, consequently, most business users remain out of scope of that more stringent provision.

[1]   'Commercial card' means any card-based payment instrument issued to undertakings or public sector entities or self-employed natural persons which is limited in use for business expenses where the payments made with such cards are charged directly to the account of the undertaking or public sector entity or self-employed natural person.

6.130 Regulation 6A(1) prohibits the payee making any charge in respect of the payment instruments covered by the PSR 2017. This will include most personal credit and debit cards used in the EEA. It applies to card-based payment instruments and those that are not card-based. It also applies to certain payment services involving credit transfers and direct debits. The effect of reg 6B(2) is that this prohibition will only apply when the payment service providers for both payee and payer are located within the UK. However, as a result of the breadth of the definitions in the PSR 2017 and, in particular, the application of the PSR 2017 to branches located within its territorial application, even where the legal entity resides elsewhere, the reg 6A(1) prohibition is still likely to have a wide application.

6.131 Regulation 6A(2) prohibits fees, charged in respect of a payment instrument, that 'exceed the costs borne by the payee'. By virtue of regs 6B(2) and (3), this prohibition applies where the payment service provider of both the payer and payee are located within the UK or where only one of the payment service providers is so located. If neither the payer nor payee's provider is located within the UK, neither of the reg 6A prohibitions apply. The scope of reg 6A(2) is similar to that of reg 4, however whilst there is overlap the provisions are not co-extensive.

6.132 The prohibitions in reg 6A only apply to payment services falling within the PSR 2017. Part 2 of Sch 1 lists transactions which do not constitute payment services for the purpose of those Regulations and, consequently, are not subject to the reg 6A prohibitions. The list is long but includes the following day-to-day consumer transactions:

- Wholly cash payments directly between the payer and payee without any intermediary intervention[1].
- Cashback services[2].
- Cash to cash currency exchange[3].
- Cheques, banker's drafts, paper-based vouchers and paper postal orders[4].

These transactions may, nevertheless, be caught by the reg 4 prohibition discussed below.

[1] SI 2017/752, Sch 1, Pt 2(a).
[2] SI 2017/752, Sch 1, Pt 2(e).
[3] SI 2017/752, Sch 1, Pt 2(f).
[4] SI 2017/752, Sch 1, Pt 2(g).

6.133 The government recognised that the prohibitions within reg 6A place increased costs on businesses and the BEIS guidance states[1]:

'Retailers may choose to:
- stop accepting a certain payment method;
- absorb the costs;
- pass on the costs through an increase in headline price of the relevant goods or services which is payable by all customers; or
- negotiate lower fees with their payment service provider.'

Since January 2018, there does not appear to have been a market wide use of any one of these options with different traders choosing different methods of dealing with the increased costs.

[1] Guidance on the Consumer Rights (Payment Surcharges) Regulations 2012 (June 2018).

The reg 4 prohibition

6.134 Given the reg 6A prohibitions discussed above, the reg 4 prohibition is now most relevant where the payment service provider for both the payee and payer are located outside the UK, or the transaction does not fall within the definition of 'payment instrument' or 'payment service' in reg 6A(1). Regulation 4 provides:

4 Excessive charges prohibited

A trader must not charge consumers, in respect of the use of a given means of payment, fees that exceed the cost borne by the trader for the use of that means.

That wording copies exactly the wording set out at Art 19 of the CRD.

6.135 Regulation 4 does not prohibit payment surcharges in their entirety, but aims to ensure that such charges are limited to the costs borne by the trader, ie to ensure that such charges are not used as a 'back-door' method of generating profit for the trader.

6.136 The CR(PS) Regulations do not provide any definition what the costs borne by the trader are, but BEIS Guidance states:

> 'It is important that surcharges can only consist of costs borne by the payee/trader for use of the payment method in question. Importantly, the government's intention is that the general costs of running a business not directly incurred in consequence of use of the payment method in question cannot be included in a surcharge. Consequently, indirect costs, such as general administrative overheads or staff training, equipment installations and set-up fees must not be included in any surcharge[1].'

[1] Guidance on the Consumer Rights (Payment Surcharges) Regulations 2012 (June 2018).

6.137 Regulation 4 applies to business-to-consumer contracts only. The CR(PS) Regulations use the terms 'trader' and 'consumer' which are both defined within reg 2. These are considered in more detail in Chapter 2, Interpreting Consumer Law.

6.138 Further limits on the scope of the reg 4 prohibition are set out in reg 5(1) of The CR(PS) Regulations. Essentially, the payment in question relates to 'a sales or service contract, or a contract . . . for the supply of water, gas, electricity, district heating or digital content' (reg 5(1)(a)) and 'must not be an excluded contract' (reg 5(1)(b)). A specific list of 'excluded' contracts is set out at reg 5(2)(a)–(m) which, notably, includes contracts:

- for social services (reg 5(2)(a));
- for health services provided by health professionals (as defined by Art 3(f) of Directive 2011/24/EU on the application of patents' rights in cross-border healthcare) to patients (reg 5(2)(b));
- for services of a 'banking, credit, insurance, personal pension, investment or payment nature (reg 5(2)(d));
- relating to property including the creation of immovable property, rental of residential property and for the construction of new buildings or substantially new buildings by the conversion of existing buildings (reg 5(2)(e)–(g));
- for the supply of foodstuffs, beverages or other goods intended for current consumption in the household, and which are supplied by a trader on frequent and regular rounds to the consumer's home, residence or workplace (reg 5(2)(i)).

Enforcement

6.139 The CR(PS) Regulations provide two methods of enforcement. The first, under reg 8, is for an enforcement authority (being a local weights and measures authority in Great Britain and the Department for the Economy in Northern Ireland[1]) to apply for a civil injunction against any person who appears to the authority to be responsible for a contravention of regs 4 or 6A. The second, under reg 10, provides consumers with a direct right to redress by making fees unenforceable to the extent that they contravene regs 4 or 6A and implying a term into contracts which renders any contravening fee repayable (to the extent that they contravene regs 4 or 6A).

¹ Formerly the Department of Enterprise, Trade and Industry ('DETI').

6.140 Under reg 7, enforcement authorities are under an obligation to consider complaints about contraventions of regs 4 and 6A unless they appear to be 'frivolous or vexatious' (reg 7(1)(a)) or 'another enforcement authority has notified the CMA that it agrees to consider the complaint' (reg 7(1)(b)). If an enforcement authority has notified the CMA that it agrees to consider a complaint, it then comes under a duty to do so (reg 7(2)) and must decide whether or not to make an application under reg 8 and give reasons for its decision (reg 7(3)). There are no reported cases on either the reg 4 prohibition or the reg 6A prohibition.

SUPPLY OF GOODS, SERVICES AND DIGITAL CONTENT

Introduction

6.141 It has long been considered that UK law on the sale of goods and services was unnecessarily complex and in need of clarification and simplification. Part 1 of the CRA 2015 seeks to remedy that issue for the supply of goods (in Chapter 2), and services by consolidating the provisions as they apply to consumers (in Chapter 4). It also sets out, for the first time, rights and remedies for consumers who are supplied with digital content (in Chapter 3). It applies to contracts (whether written, oral or implied) for the supply of goods, services or digital content by a trader to a consumer. It came into effect on 1 October 2015 for contracts entered into from that date onwards. Brexit means that the CRA 2015 has been subject to some amendment¹.

¹ See the Consumer Protection (Amendments etc) (EU Exit) Regulations 2018, SI 2018/1326 and the Consumer Protection (Enforcement) (Amendment etc) (EU Exit) Regulations 2019, SI 2019/203.

6.142 Part 1 of the CRA 2015 consolidates the main provisions in Sale of Goods Act 1979 ('SGA 1979') and the main statutory provisions relating to the supply of services to consumers¹. The focus of this legislation was to imply terms into consumer contracts to ensure that goods and services provided by a trader were of the agreed quality and description. This legislation will still be applicable, however, for contracts between traders or between consumers.

¹ Supply of Goods (Implied Terms) Act 1973; Supply of Goods and Services Act 1982; Sale and Supply of Goods Act 1994; Sale and Supply of Goods to Consumers Regulations 2002, SI 2002/3045.

6.143 A stated aim of the legislation was to make consumer rights 'more accessible to consumers, business and their advisers'¹. It would improve consumer contract law if the disparate rules provisions could be brought together into a single provision that subjected all consumer supply contracts to the same rights and remedies. It was also suggested that this should be achieved using simpler language, avoiding specialist legal language such as the previous reference to 'implied terms'².

¹ 'Consolidation and Simplification of UK Consumer Law 2010.' Commissioned by BIS.

[2] Instead of using the phrase 'implied terms', the CRA 2015, Pt 1 uses the language of contracts being 'treated as including a [specified] term'. As this is a change in language rather than substance, for the sake of brevity, reference in this text will be made to 'implied terms'.

6.144 Part 1 of the CRA 2015 applies throughout the UK with slight modifications to reflect the different legal system in Scotland[1].

[1] CRA 2015, ss 3(3)(e) and 48(3) (gratuitous contracts); s 27 (consignation); s 30(8)–(10) Guarantees; s 46 (remedies for damage to a digital device) and s 58 (powers of the court).

6.145 The following is a summary of the law in an area that is complex. The legislation should be considered carefully together with the substantial body of case law that was built up around the previous law.

Mixed contracts

6.146 An important aspect of Pt 1 of the CRA 2015 is its application to mixed contracts that involve some combination of the supply of goods, service or digital content. For example, the supply and installation of a central heating system is likely to involve goods (the boiler, radiators etc.) a service (the installation) and also digital content (the programmer). The CRA 2015 makes it clear[1] that each of the three chapters on goods, services and digital content may apply to a mixed contract. It follows that a consumer can take advantage of the applicable rights under each chapter if the contract involves any relevant element.

[1] CRA 2015, s 1(3)–(5).

Definitions

Consumer and trader

6.147 The definitions of 'consumer' and 'trader'[1] are found in the CRA 2015, s 2. These definitions are the same in the unfair terms provisions (Part 2 of the CRA 2015) and under the Consumer Protection from Unfair Trading Regulations ('CPUTR 2008'), where they have been the subject of consideration by the courts. The definition of consumer and trader are now considered in CHAPTER 2, Interpreting Consumer Law.

[1] CRA 2015, s 2(7) 'Business' includes the activities of any government department or local or public authority.

6.148 Under the CRA 2015, s 2(4) the evidential burden of proving that an individual is not a consumer is placed upon the trader.

Goods

6.149 CRA 2015, s 2(8) provides:

(8) "Goods" means any tangible moveable items, but that includes water, gas and electricity if and only if they are put up for supply in a limited volume or set quantity.

6.150 This new definition reflects that found in the 1999 Directive on certain aspects of the law of the sale of consumer goods and associated guarantees (Sale of Consumer Goods and Associated Consumer Guarantees Directive)[1].

[1] 99/44/EC.

Public auctions

6.151 The purchase of second-hand goods at public auction, where individuals have the opportunity to attend in person, is treated as an exception to some of the rights afforded to a consumer in an ordinary sales contract. This exception has its origin in the Sale of Consumer Goods and Associated Consumer Guarantees Directive[1]. The rights that still apply relate to pre-contract information, delivery and risk[2].

[1]   99/44/EC.
[2]   Pre-contract information, CRA 2015, s 11(4) and (5) and s 12; delivery, s 28 and risk, s 29.

Supply of goods

Introduction

6.152 Chapter 2 of the CRA 2015 consolidates the law in relation to the sale and supply of goods by traders to consumers. It seeks to simplify the law and provide consistent remedies for goods supplied under different contract types such as sale, conditional sale, transfer, hire or hire purchase. It introduces a near absolute right for consumers to reject sub-standard goods within the first 30 days and claim a full refund. It also limits the number of repairs or replacements that a trader can offer before consumers can choose to demand their money back.

Goods contracts covered by Chapter 2

6.153 The goods contracts covered by Chapter 2, Pt 1 are set out in CRA 2015, ss 3–8. In addition to a sales contract, Chapter 2 applies to a contract for hire of goods (CRA 2015, s 6), hire purchase (CRA 2015, s 7) and the transfer of goods (CRA 2015, s 8). CRA 2015, s 5 defines a 'sales contract' as one under which the 'trader transfers or agrees to transfer ownership of goods to a consumer', who 'pays or agrees to pay the price'[1]. Conditional sales contracts[2] and contracts for goods to be manufactured or produced (and then supplied and owned by the consumer in return for a price) are also covered within the definition of a 'sales contract'[3].

[1]   CRA 2015, s 5(2) deals with goods.
[2]   CRA 2015, s 5(3).
[3]   CRA 2015, s 5(2).

6.154 Contracts for a 'trader to supply coins or notes (money) to a consumer for use as currency' are excluded, although this will not be the case if money is supplied for another purpose such as a collector's item. Contracts for goods sold by execution or authority of law are not covered, such as goods sold under legal authority to pay off a debt. Chapter 2 also does not apply to contracts intended to operate as a mortgage, pledge, charge or other security. In Scotland it does not apply to a gratuitous contract[1].

[1]   CRA 2015, s 3(3). Also see s 3(3)(d) in England, Wales and Northern Ireland contracts by deed where the only consideration is the presumed consideration imported by the deed are also not covered.

Rights for the supply of goods

6.155 Part 2 of the CRA 2015 is designed to simplify and clarify the implied terms that were previously found in SGA 1979, ss 12–15. CRA 2015, s 14 clarifies the position when a consumer buys goods by reference to a model seen or examined. CRA 2015, ss 15 and 16 provide, respectively, additional rights in relation to installation and goods with digital content.

Satisfactory quality

6.156 CRA 2015, s 9 provides:

9 Goods to be of satisfactory quality

(1) Every contract to supply goods is to be treated as including a term that the quality of the goods is satisfactory.

(2) The quality of goods is satisfactory if they meet the standard that a reasonable person would consider satisfactory, taking account of—

    (a) any description of the goods,

    (b) the price or other consideration for the goods (if relevant), and

    (c) all the other relevant circumstances (see subsection (5)).

(3) The quality of goods includes their state and condition; and the following aspects (among others) are in appropriate cases aspects of the quality of goods—

    (a) fitness for all the purposes for which goods of that kind are usually supplied;

    (b) appearance and finish;

    (c) freedom from minor defects;

    (d) safety;

    (e) durability.

(4) The term mentioned in subsection (1) does not cover anything which makes the quality of the goods unsatisfactory—

    (a) which is specifically drawn to the consumer's attention before the contract is made,

    (b) where the consumer examines the goods before the contract is made, which that examination ought to reveal, or

    (c) in the case of a contract to supply goods by sample, which would have been apparent on a reasonable examination of the sample.

(5) The relevant circumstances mentioned in subsection (2)(c) include any public statement about the specific characteristics of the goods made by the trader, the producer or any representative of the trader or the producer.

(6) That includes, in particular, any public statement made in advertising or labelling.

(7) But a public statement is not a relevant circumstance for the purposes of subsection (2)(c) if the trader shows that—

    (a) when the contract was made, the trader was not, and could not reasonably have been, aware of the statement,

    (b) before the contract was made, the statement had been publicly withdrawn or, to the extent that it contained anything which was incorrect or misleading, it had been publicly corrected, or

    (c) the consumer's decision to contract for the goods could not have been influenced by the statement.

(8) In a contract to supply goods a term about the quality of the goods may be treated as included as a matter of custom.

(9) See section 19 for a consumer's rights if the trader is in breach of a term that this section requires to be treated as included in a contract.

6.157 The implied term that goods should be of satisfactory quality is derived from the requirement in the Sale of Goods Act 1893 that goods should be of 'merchantable quality'. This remained the position in SGA 1979 until 1994 when the standard was amended to the more accessible definition of 'satisfactory quality'[1]. CRA 2015, s 9 also requires that goods sold to consumers be of satisfactory quality and is almost identical to SGA 1979, s 14(2)[2]. It follows that authorities on SGA 1979, s 14 are likely to remain relevant.

[1] Sale and Supply of Goods Act 1994, s 1.
[2] As it was amended by the Sale and Supply of Goods Act 1994.

6.158 The duty to supply goods that are of satisfactory quality is strict. A trader cannot argue that he has taken all possible care or that he had not seen the goods[1]. The responsibility is the trader's and, as against the consumer, he cannot rely on undertakings given by his own supplier[2]. Whether goods are of satisfactory quality is to be determined against an objective test, the standard is what would a 'reasonable person . . . consider satisfactory', taking into account the good's description, the price and all other relevant considerations[3]. The burden of proof under CRA 2015, s 9 remains on the consumer to the civil standard. However, if the goods were not of satisfactory quality during the first 6 months after delivery, there is a statutory presumption that they were not of satisfactory quality when delivered[4].

[1] *Grant v Australian Knitting Mills Ltd* [1936] 1 AC 85.
[2] *Young & Marten Ltd v McManus Childs Ltd* [1969] 1 AC 454.
[3] CRA 2015, s 9(2).
[4] CRA 2015, s 19(14) and (15).

6.159 It is important to recognise that the price at which goods are sold is relevant to the standard that a reasonable person would consider satisfactory[1]. It is plain that this standard might be very different for goods sold brand new, second hand[2] or as scrap. In the Scottish case of *Thain v Anniesland Trade Centre* a second-hand car that developed a faulty gearbox within 2 weeks of purchase was found to have been of satisfactory quality because of its relatively low price[3].

[1] CRA 2015, s 9(2)(b).
[2] See eg, *Bartlett v Sydney Marcus Ltd* [1965] 1 WLR 1013.
[3] 1997 SLT (Sh Ct) 102, 1997 SCLR 991 in the Glasgow Sheriff Court – consumer purchase of a second-hand motorcar with an automatic gear box that had done 80,000 miles and was sold by a trader for £2,995. The consumer had declined a 3-month warranty that was on offer. After about 2 weeks' use of the car the consumer noticed an intermittent droning noise, the source of which was a faulty gearbox. However, it was not economic to replace the gearbox. The trader had offered the consumer a number of alternative cars as a replacement but none was acceptable to her and she insisted that the gearbox should be replaced.

6.160 The requirement to consider 'all the other relevant circumstances' in CRA 2015, s 9(2)(c) reflects the common sense notion that the 'standard that a reasonable person would consider satisfactory' must not be approached artificially without consideration of relevant circumstances. In a case under of SGA 1979, s 14, *Bramhill v Edwards*, the Court of Appeal, made clear that, 'although the test is objective, the reasonable buyer must be attributed with knowledge of all relevant background facts'[1].

1   *Bramhall v Edwards* [2004] EWCA Civ 403 (the sale of a motor home between consumers).

6.161 The requirement that goods be free of 'minor defects' reflects the approach taken in *Rogers v Parish (Scarborough) Ltd*[1], which was decided before SGA 1979, s 14 was amended to include that term. That case involved a defective Range Rover motorcar that had been sold new. Mustill LJ stated that it was 'not merely the buyer's purpose of driving the car from one place to another, but of doing so with an appropriate degree of comfort, ease of handling and reliability and, one may add, of pride in the vehicle's outward and interior purpose'.

1   [1987] QB 933.

6.162 In *Clegg v Andersson (trading as Nordic Marine)*[1], Mr and Mrs Clegg had bought a brand new yacht for £236,000. The yacht had been supplied with a keel, designed for stability that was too heavy. The supplier offered to correct the defect for free. The Court of Appeal rejected the argument that the boat was of satisfactory quality. Hale LJ stated:

'In some cases, such as a high priced quality product, the customer may be entitled to expect that it is free from even minor defects, in other words perfect or nearly so.'

1   [2003] EWCA Civ 320, [2003] 1 All ER (Comm) 721, per Hale LJ.

6.163 *Lamarra v Capital Bank plc*[1] concerned the hire and subsequent purchase of a brand new luxury motor car that had been sold with a number of defects[2], but also a trader warranty. The consumer was entitled to reject the car despite the warranty covering those defects. Although satisfactory quality did not imply perfection in the goods concerned, the Scottish Court of Session found that the warranty was not a justification for the supply of goods that were of unsatisfactory quality. It was held that, while 'the words "all the other relevant circumstances" are potentially of wide scope . . . in the context, they must be seen as referring only to circumstances actually bearing upon the quality of the goods in question'[3].

1   [2006] CSIH 49, 2007 SC 95.
2   Front wheels incorrectly balanced causing excessive tyre wear; road speed related noise; scratch on the ashtray cover; misalignment of the glove box and poorly finished paintwork on parts of the roof.
3   Per Lord Osbourne at para 62.

6.164 'All other relevant circumstances' includes statements made in advertising or labelling, by the trader, producer or their representative[1]. This specific circumstance was added, as the result of the Consumer Goods and Associated Guarantees Directive to the earlier legislation and has been carried across to CRA 2015. This means that a retailer may be responsible for what a consumer has read in advertising or on a manufacturer's website. As consumers, nowadays, are more likely to research many products before buying them this does place a new responsibility on the trader. However the Act does offer some protection that this will not apply to statements of which the trader was not aware, and could not reasonably have been aware of, when the contract was made. Nor will it apply to statements if, before the contract was made, they had publicly been withdrawn or publicly corrected. In addition the consumer cannot rely on information that had not influenced their decision to purchase, for example they read it after the purchase had been made.

[1] CRA 2015, s 9(5)–(7).

6.165 The implied term of satisfactory quality is excluded for faults that are pointed out to a consumer before the contract is made, that should have been apparent from the consumer's examination of the goods, (where the consumer examines the goods), or which would have been apparent from a consumer's reasonable examination of a sample[1]. The Act does not require a consumer to examine goods for faults; the test is whether the examination that they **did carry out** would have revealed that particular defect. The position appears to be different where the goods are supplied by sample, even when the sample was not examined by the consumer, the goods will not be unsatisfactory because of a fault which would have been apparent upon a reasonable examination of the sample[2].

[1] CRA 2015, s 9(4); see also *R & B Customs Brokers v United Dominions Trust* [1988] 1 WLR 321.
[2] CRA 2015, s 9(4)(c).

Fit for particular purpose

6.166 CRA 2015, s 10 provides:

10 Goods to be fit for particular purpose

(1) Subsection (3) applies to a contract to supply goods if before the contract is made the consumer makes known to the trader (expressly or by implication) any particular purpose for which the consumer is contracting for the goods.

(2) Subsection (3) also applies to a contract to supply goods if—

    (a) the goods were previously sold by a credit-broker to the trader,

    (b) in the case of a sales contract or contract for transfer of goods, the consideration or part of it is a sum payable by instalments, and

    (c) before the contract is made, the consumer makes known to the credit-broker (expressly or by implication) any particular purpose for which the consumer is contracting for the goods.

(3) The contract is to be treated as including a term that the goods are reasonably fit for that purpose, whether or not that is a purpose for which goods of that kind are usually supplied.

(4) Subsection (3) does not apply if the circumstances show that the consumer does not rely, or it is unreasonable for the consumer to rely, on the skill or judgment of the trader or credit-broker.

(5) In a contract to supply goods a term about the fitness of the goods for a particular purpose may be treated as included as a matter of custom.

6.167 This provision is very similar to SGA 1979, s 14(3) and it follows that case law concerning that provision is likely to be relevant. The use of the words, 'expressly or by implication', suggest that the surrounding circumstances of a contractual relationship are likely to be considered when determining the particular purpose.

6.168 In *Ashington Piggeries v Christopher Hill Ltd*[1] the House of Lords framed the test as *what could reasonably be foreseen* as the particular purpose. An illustration of this can be found in *Griffiths v Peter Conway Ltd* where the

317

purchaser of a tweed coat developed a skin condition because of her unusually sensitive skin. The seller was not liable as the coat would not have harmed a normal person and the purchaser had not herself realised that she had such a skin condition[2].

[1]   [1972] AC 441.
[2]   [1939] 1 All ER 685, see also *Slater v Finning Ltd* [1997] AC 473.

6.169 There are various examples of consumer goods that the courts have found were not fit for a particular purpose, including *Godley v Perry*[1] (broken plastic catapult); *Priest v Last*[2] (bursting hot water bottle); *Grant v Australian Knitting Mills Ltd*[3] (irritating underwear); *R & B Customs Brokers Ltd v United Dominions Trust Ltd*[4] (car that leaked); *Spencer v Claude Rye Vehicles*[5] (overheating motorcar); *Jackson v Chrysler Acceptances Ltd*[6] (car for holiday) and *Finch Motors Ltd v Quin (No 2)* (car for towing a boat).

[1]   [1960] 1 WLR 9.
[2]   [1903] 2 KB 148.
[3]   [1936] AC 85.
[4]   [1988] 1 WLR 321.
[5]   *The Guardian*, 19 December 1972.
[6]   [1978] RTR 474.

6.170 In *Lambert v Lewis*[1] the House of Lords considered a defective trailer coupling that had led to a fatal accident. Lord Roskill stated in relation to the implied term concerning fitness for purpose that it was:

'a continuing warranty that the goods will continue to be fit for that purpose for a reasonable time after delivery, so long as they remain in the same apparent state as that in which they were delivered, apart from normal wear and tear. What is a reasonable time will depend upon the nature of the goods.'

[1]   [1982] AC 225, at 226.

Goods to be as described

6.171 The CRA 2015, s 11 provides:

11 Goods to be as described

(1)   Every contract to supply goods by description is to be treated as including a term that the goods will match the description.

(2)   If the supply is by sample as well as by description, it is not sufficient that the bulk of the goods matches the sample if the goods do not also match the description.

(3)   A supply of goods is not prevented from being a supply by description just because—
(a)   the goods are exposed for supply, and
(b)   they are selected by the consumer.

(4)   Any information that is provided by the trader about the goods and is information mentioned in paragraph (a) of Schedule 1 or 2 to the Consumer Contracts (Information, Cancellation and Additional Charges) Regulations 2013 (SI 2013/3134) (main characteristics of goods) is to be treated as included as a term of the contract.

(5)   A change to any of that information, made before entering into the contract or later, is not effective unless expressly agreed between the consumer and the trader.

(6) See section 2(5) and (6) for the application of subsections (4) and (5) where goods are sold at public auction[1].

[1] CRA 2015, s 11(7) is identical to CRA 2015, s 9(9) above at **6.156**.

6.172 This provision is similar to SGA 1979, s 13 but now refers to the obligation in the CCR 2013 to provide information about the 'main characteristics of goods'. A failure to supply goods in line with this information is treated as a serious breach of a contract, with the same remedies available as those for breach of the implied terms relating to satisfactory quality and fitness for particular purpose. These remedies are not available, however, in relation to the other CCR 2013 information obligations (see **6.208** below).

Goods to match a sample

6.173 The CRA 2015, s 13 provides:

13 Goods to match a sample

(1) This section applies to a contract to supply goods by reference to a sample of the goods that is seen or examined by the consumer before the contract is made.

(2) Every contract to which this section applies is to be treated as including a term that—

    (a) the goods will match the sample except to the extent that any differences between the sample and the goods are brought to the consumer's attention before the contract is made, and

    (b) the goods will be free from any defect that makes their quality unsatisfactory and that would not be apparent on a reasonable examination of the sample[1].

[1] CRA 2015, s 13(3) is identical to CRA 2015, s 9(9) above at **6.156**.

6.174 This provision covers goods sold by way of a sample, which for example may include a tester pot of paint that is made available before the consumer buys a larger quantity. A term is implied into the contract that the goods will match the sample except for differences that are brought to the consumer's attention before the contract is made and defects that would be apparent on a reasonable examination of the sample, even when the consumer has not examined the sample provided.

Goods to match model seen or examined

6.175 The CRA 2015, s 14 provides:

14 Goods to match a model seen or examined

(1) This section applies to a contract to supply goods by reference to a model of the goods that is seen or examined by the consumer before entering into the contract.

(2) Every contract to which this section applies is to be treated as including a term that the goods will match the model except to the extent that any differences between the model and the goods are brought to the consumer's attention before the consumer enters into the contract[1].

[1] CRA 2015, s 14(3) is identical to CRA 2015, s 9(9) above at **6.156**.

6.176 This provision was new to the Act and extends consumer rights beyond samples that they have seen to actual items, for example inspecting a model of a new car in a showroom from which they decide to purchase a similar item. This would also apply to goods on display in a furniture showroom, when deliveries are made from goods in stock.

OTHER RIGHTS

Installation as part of conformity of the goods

6.177 The CRA 2015, s 15 provides:

15 Installation as part of conformity of the goods with the contract

(1)   Goods do not conform to a contract to supply goods if—
    (a)   installation of the goods forms part of the contract,
    (b)   the goods are installed by the trader or under the trader's responsibility, and
    (c)   the goods are installed incorrectly.
(2)   See s 19 for the effect of goods not conforming to the contract.

Although new, this provision reflects a requirement of the Sale of Consumer Goods and Associated Consumer Guarantees Directive (99/44EC). Logically this provision does not entitle a consumer to exercise a short-term right to reject goods that are not installed properly.

6.178 This illustrates how different provisions of Part 1 of the CRA 2015 will apply to the same situation in a mixed contract, with overlapping but, sometimes, different remedies. As an example, a newly installed patio door that does not lock could fail to conform to the contract under s 15(1) but could also not be of satisfactory quality (CRA 2015, s 9), or might constitute a failure to use reasonable care and skill (CRA 2015, s 49).

Digital content within goods must conform

6.179 The CRA 2015, s 16 states:

16 Goods not conforming if digital content does not conform

(1)   Goods (whether or not they conform otherwise to a contract to supply goods) do not conform to it if—
    (a)   the goods are an item that includes digital content, and
    (b)   the digital content does not conform to the contract to supply that content (for which see section 42(1).
(2)   See section 19 for the effect of goods not conforming to the contract.

Specific protection for goods which include digital content was new to the Act and, unlike the CCR 2013, the CRA 2015 deals with both tangible and intangible digital content (see **6.52** above and **6.233** below). The effect of this provision is that goods which include digital content (such as cars, televisions and DVDs) will not conform to the contract if the digital content is not of satisfactory quality, not fit for a particular purpose or does not match its description[1].

[1] For which see respectively **6.238**, **6.239** and **6.240**.

6.180 CRA 2015, s 12 provides that pre-contract information that a trader is required to give a consumer under the CCR 2013, other than the main characteristics of goods (see CRA 2015, s 11 and **6.171** and **6.172** above), have the status of contractual terms. Further, under s 12(3), a change to any of that information, before or after the consumer enters into a contract, is ineffective unless the consumer gives their express consent to such a change (see **6.80**).

The right to supply

6.181 CRA 2015, s 17 implies a number of contractual terms, which have the effect of protecting the consumer against a trader who does not have the appropriate right to transfer the possession of goods (in the case of hire contracts) or, under any other contract for the supply of goods, who do not have the right to sell or to transfer ownership of the goods supplied[1]. Terms are also implied into the contract relating to the consumer's right to enjoy quiet possession of the goods, free from any charge or encumbrance, except for those disclosed or known to the consumer before entering the contract[2].

[1] CRA 2015, s 17(1).
[2] CRA 2015, s 17(2)–(7).

Delivery and risk

6.182 CRA 2015, s 28 provides for a contractual term that the trader must deliver goods to a consumer unless they have agreed otherwise. Where there has been no agreement about when the goods will be delivered there is included a term in the contract that they must be delivered 'without undue delay' and in any event 'not more than 30 days' after the day on which the contract was entered into[1].

[1] CRA 2015, s 28(2)–(4).

6.183 CRA 2015, s 28 also provides for when a trader does not deliver goods at the agreed time or, where no time is agreed, within the 30 days delivery period implied as a term into the contract. A consumer may treat the contract 'as at an end' if the trader has refused to deliver goods, and:

- either the consumer specified before the contract was entered that the time for delivery is essential,
- or it is essential having regard to the relevant circumstances at the time the contract was entered into[1].

When these circumstances are not applicable, then the consumer can make 'time of the essence' by requiring the trader to deliver the goods before the expiry of a specified period and, if the trader fails to deliver the goods accordingly, the consumer may also treat the contract 'as at an end'[2].

1   CRA 2015, ss 28(5) and (6).
2   CRA 2015, ss 28(7) and (8).

6.184 Following any of the circumstances referred to above, if the consumer treats the contract 'as at an end', the trader must then reimburse all payments made under the contract to a consumer 'without undue delay'[1]. Alternatively, the consumer can cancel goods or reject delivered goods. Following this, the trader must 'without undue delay' reimburse payments made under the contract for those cancelled or rejected goods[2].

1   CRA 2015, s 28(9).
2   CRA 2015, s 28(10).

6.185 CRA 2015, s 26 makes provision for delivery of goods by instalments and provides (inter alia) that the consumer is not bound to accept goods delivered by instalments unless to do so has been agreed[1]. Moreover, if the contract is for goods to be delivered by 'stated instalments, which are to be separately paid for', where goods are not so delivered, the provisions of CRA 2015, s 28 are applicable[2].

1   CRA 2015, s 26(1).
2   CRA 2015, s 26(5).

6.186 CRA 2015, s 29 provides for a term that the goods remain at the trader's risk until they 'come into the physical possession' of the consumer[1]. However, this does not apply if the goods are delivered to a carrier that is commissioned by the consumer and not provided as an option by the trader[2]. CRA 2015, ss 28 and 29 are identical to regs 42 and 43 of the CCR 2013 which were revoked for contracts entered into on or after 1 October 2015[3].

1   CRA 2015, s 29(2) 'or a person identified by the consumer to take possession of the goods'.
2   CRA 2015, s 29(3).
3   Consumer Contracts (Amendment) Regulations 2015, SI 2015/1629.

Delivery of the wrong quantity

6.187 Under CRA 2015, s 25 a consumer has the right to reject goods if the trader delivers a quantity less than was agreed. If he accepts them, however, he must pay for them at the contract rate[1]. If the trader delivers more than the agreed quantity the consumer may reject all of the goods or just the excess. If the consumer accepts all of the goods, he must pay for them (including the larger amount) at the contract rate if he keeps it[2]. In order to reject goods under CRA 2015, s 25 the consumer must indicate to the trader that he is rejecting the goods so that it is 'clear enough to be understood by the trader'[3].

1   CRA 2015, s 25(1).
2   CRA 2015, s 25(2) and (3).
3   CRA 2015, s 25(5) and (6).

Remedies – sale of goods

OVERVIEW OF THE NEW REMEDIES

6.188 A major change that the CRA 2015 sought to introduce was a single, coherent set of remedies in accordance with those required by the Sale of Consumer Goods and Associated Consumer Guarantees Directive[1]. A purpose of the CRA 2015 was to make the language more accessible to consumers and businesses and consequently words such as 'breach' 'rescission' or 'acceptance' are not used.

[1]   1999/44/EC, prior to the CRA 2015 the relevant provisions were implemented in the UK by the Sale of Goods Act, as amended by the Sale of Supply of Goods to Consumers Regulations 2002, SI 2002/3045.

6.189 The main statutory remedies in CRA 2015, ss 19–24 arise when goods do not conform to any of the core standards of:

- satisfactory quality,
- fit for particular purpose,
- as described and match a sample or model[1].

In addition, the main statutory remedies are available for goods that do not conform with the installation standard[2], or included digital content that does not conform to the core standards applicable to digital content, of satisfactory quality, fit for particular purpose and as described, as set down in Chapter 3 of the CRA 2015[3].

[1]   CRA 2015, s 19(3).
[2]   CRA 2015, s 15, save for the short-term right to reject see **6.177** and **6.191**.
[3]   CRA 2015, s 16.

6.190 These new rights and remedies are in addition to other legal rights or remedies available to the consumer under the general law (such as a claim for damages) or for breach of an express term. A consumer can pursue these other legal rights and remedies in addition to, or instead of, those provided for under the CRA 2015, provided the same loss is not claimed twice[1].

However, s 19(12) of the CRA 2015 provides an important limitation to the above approach. If a consumer is claiming a breach of a term implied by the Act into a contract for the supply of goods, goods do not conform with the installation standard or included digital content does not conform to the core standards applicable to digital content, a consumer can only treat the contract as being at an end (repudiated or terminated) if that remedy is available to them under the CRA 2015, rights to reject.

[1]   CRA 2015, ss 19(9)–(11).

6.191 In summary, the effect of the new provisions is that a consumer will usually[1] have a 'short term right to reject' goods (ie during 30 days after receipt of the goods) that do not conform with the core standards relating to goods (see **6.189** above), or those standards relating to digital content (when the goods include digital content), and to claim a full refund. The consumer also has the alterative right to claim a free repair or replacement, which continues after the expiry of the 30 days. If the consumer has exercised this right[2] and the goods still do not conform, the consumer may then choose between a price reduction and the final right to reject the goods. If the consumer chooses the final right to reject the goods, in the first 6 months he will ordinarily be entitled to a full refund (except in the case of motor vehicles). If he rejects the goods after 6 months, a deduction for the usage of the goods may be made from the consumer's refund.

1   Not in the case of defective installation under CRA 2015, s 15.
2   Or it is impossible to undertake repair and replacement, CRA 2015, s 23(4).

6.192 There is a rebuttable presumption that goods which do not conform during the first 6 months, did not conform on the day they were delivered to the consumer[1]. This, reverse burden of proof, is not available if a consumer is exercising their short-term right to reject. Those rights in the CRA 2015 that are not specifically time limited are subject only to the periods set out in the ordinary rules of limitation for civil proceedings[2]. The reversed burden was considered by the CJEU in *Froukje Faber v Autobedrijf Hazet Ochten BV*[3] which held that the consumer must furnish evidence that the goods sold are not in conformity with the contract and such non-conformity became physically apparent within six months of the delivery of goods purchase. The consumer is not required to prove the cause of that lack of conformity or establish that its origin is attributable to the seller.

1   CRA 2015, s 19(14) and (15).
2   The general rule for breach of contract is 6 years from when cause of action accrues, see the Limitation Act 1980, s 5.
3   (Case C-497/13) [2015].

SHORT-TERM RIGHT TO REJECT

6.193 The short-term right to reject applies for a breach of the core standards and when digital content (included in goods) does not conform to the core standards applicable to digital content (s 16) , but not in relation to a breach of CRA 2015, s 15 (defective installation). The 30 days period starts to run the day after all of the following has happened (as applicable):

• the consumer has taken possession or ownership of the goods,
• the goods have been delivered, and
• notification has been given by the trader that installation is completed or that any other action that enables the consumer to use the goods has been taken[1].

It is open to the consumer and the trader to agree a longer period for the consumer to exercise the short-term right to reject[2] but an agreement to reduce the 30 days period is not binding on the consumer[3]. However, a shorter period may apply for perishable goods which can 'reasonably be expected to perish' before the expiry of the 30 days period. Although what the shorter period might be is not further defined[4].

1   CRA 2015, s 22(3), although the consumer may reject at an earlier stage (CRA 2015, s 22(5)).
2   CRA 2015, s 22(1).
3   CRA 2015, s 22(2).
4   CRA 2015, s 22(4).

6.194 If the consumer asks or agrees to the trader repairing or replacing the goods, the short-term period to reject stops running during 'the waiting period'[1]. The period of 30 days period (or the shorter period for perishable goods) starts running again when the 'waiting period' ends (see **6.195** below). The period of waiting begins with the day the consumer requests or agrees to the remedy of repair or replacement and ends on the day when the consumer gets the repaired or replaced goods back[2].

[1]   CRA 2015, s 22(6).
[2]   CRA 2015, s 22(8).

6.195 If the replaced or repaired goods do not conform to the contract, then the consumer can still exercise the short-term right to reject the goods. However this must be done within at least 7 days, beginning with the day after the consumer had the goods returned or, if later, before the expiry of the time remaining under the original period to reject[1].

[1]   CRA 2015, s 22(7).

EFFECTS OF REJECTION GENERALLY

6.196 The contract is treated at an end when a consumer rejects goods under CRA 2015, s 20 by indicating clearly (by words or actions)[1] that he is 'rejecting the goods and treating the contract at an end'. This applies both to the short term and final right to reject goods (see **6.205** below). Under CRA 2015, s 21 there is also the right to partial rejection of goods so that the consumer may reject 'some or all' of the goods.

[1]   Clear enough to be understood by the trader, CRA 2015, s 20(6).

6.197 On rejection the trader then has a duty to refund the consumer in accordance with the provisions in CRA 2015, s 20(9)–(19). If a consumer has paid in money he is entitled to be repaid in the same amount using the same means of payment. The right is qualified where the consumer has not paid in money and it is not possible to return what he has used to pay in its original state (for example where the consumer paid for a new vehicle partly by trading in their current vehicle), although this problem may be resolved by a claim in damages[1]. A refund under the CRA 2015, s 20 must be given without undue delay and in any event within 14 days of the trader agreeing that the consumer is entitled to a refund[2]. If the consumer paid with money, the trader must give the refund using the same means of payment as the consumer used (eg refund a consumer's debit card, if the consumer paid by that card), unless the consumer agrees otherwise[3].

[1]   CRA 2015, ss 20(18) and (19).
[2]   CRA 2015, s 20(15).
[3]   CRA 2015, s 20(16).

6.198 After the consumer has rejected the goods he also has a duty to 'make the goods available for collection by the trader' or, where the consumer has agreed, to return them to the trader. However, in either case the trader must bear any reasonable costs incurred by the consumer, unless they are returning the goods to where they originally took possession of them[1].

[1]   CRA 2015, s 20(7)(b) and (8).

6.199 In *Johnston v R&J Leather (Scotland) Ltd*[1] the Sheriff Appeal Court had to decide whether there was a continuing duty upon the consumer to keep rejected goods for collection by the seller. A suite of furniture was delivered on 30 June 2017 and rejected soon after. Despite numerous communications, the trader did not offer a refund or to collect the rejected goods. Following judgment in their favour, which the trader did not defend, the Johnstons disposed of the furniture in early 2018. *R&J* then argued, in the Sheriff Court and in the Sheriff Court of Appeal that the Johnstons were not entitled to reclaim their money because they no longer had the furniture. *R&J* argued that the obligation to keep rejected goods available for collection did not have a time limit. The Appeal Sheriff, finding in favour of the Johnstons, held that when a consumer exercises a right to reject faulty goods, there was no duty to return the goods to the seller. Rather the duty upon the consumer was to make goods available to the seller. This duty was not an unending one and that the court was entitled to take into account a number of factors, including but not restricted to:

- the timescale in which the rejection was intimated;
- the nature of the goods;
- the practicality of providing storage;
- the nature, extent and frequency of communications sent by the consumers to the seller;
- any response or lack of response from the seller;
- the length of time for which the goods were retained; and
- whether proceedings have been raised.

[1] *Christina Tenant Johnston and Peter Johnston v R&J Leather (Scotland) Ltd* [2019] SAC (Civ) 1.

RIGHT TO REPAIR OR REPLACEMENT

6.200 The statutory right to a repair or a replacement under CRA 2015, s 23 is available from the time that a consumer receives the goods and is not subject to any time limit other than the ordinary limitation period for civil proceedings. Repair or replacement is often referred to as 'the first tier remedies' and are available when goods do not conform to any of the core standards[1], installation standard[2], or included digital content does not conform to the core standards in Chapter 3 (Digital content)[3]. If a consumer exercises this right the trader must repair or replace the goods for free within a reasonable time and without significant inconvenience to the consumer[4].

[1] CRA 2015, s 19(3).
[2] CRA 2015, s 15.
[3] CRA 2015, s 16.
[4] CRA 2015, s 23(2).

6.201 When considering Arts 3(2) and (3) of the Sale of Consumer Goods and Associated Consumer Guarantees Directive (1999/44/EC), the CJEU[1] considered the position where the remedy of replacement is chosen in circumstances where, before the defect became apparent, the consumer had installed the goods, in good faith and in a way consistent with their nature and purpose. In these circumstances, the CJEU held the trader is obliged:

' . . . either to remove the goods from where they were installed and install the replacement goods there or else bear the cost of that removal and installation of the replacement good.'

This obligation exists regardless of whether the trader was obliged under the contract of sale to install the original goods purchased.

1   *Weber GmbH v Wittmer (Jurgen): Putz (Ingrid) v Medianess Electonics GmbH*: C-65/09 and C-87/09 [2011] at para 62.

6.202 A consumer who requires or agrees to the repair of goods cannot require the trader to replace them, or exercise the short-term right to reject (if available to them), without giving the trader a reasonable time to repair them, unless to do so would cause the consumer significant inconvenience[1].

1   CRA 2015, s 23(6) and, similarly vice-versa, if the consumer requires a replacement he cannot require repair or exercise the short term right to reject without giving the trader a reasonable time to replace them (unless to do so would cause them significant inconvenience), CRA 2015, s 23(7).

6.203 Unlike the initial short-term right to reject, there is an element of proportionality built into the repair or replacement remedy. CRA 2015, s 23(3) states that a consumer cannot require a trader to repair or replace the goods (as the case may be) if that remedy is impossible or disproportionate to the other remedy. The chosen remedy (eg replacement) is disproportionate to the other (eg repair or vice-versa) if it imposes costs on the trader which are unreasonable in comparison with the costs of the other remedy, taking into account the value of the goods if they conformed to the contract (eg the price), the significance of the lack of conformity and whether the alternative remedy can be delivered without causing the consumer significant inconvenience[1].

1   CRA 2015, s 23(4).

6.204 The assessment of what is a reasonable time or significant inconvenience should take account of the nature of the goods and the purpose for which they were acquired[1]. A consumer must ordinarily have required the trader to repair or replace goods before he can exercise his right to the 'second tier' remedies of either a price reduction or the final right to reject under CRA 2015, s 24[2]. However, he need only exercise the right once and need not do so if repair and replacement are impossible[3].

1   CRA 2015, s 23(5).
2   CRA 2015, s 24(5)(a), s 24(6) and s 24(7).
3   CRA 2015, s 23(3).

PRICE REDUCTION OR THE FINAL RIGHT TO REJECT

6.205 CRA 2015, s 24 provides for the right to keep the goods and seek a price reduction or a final right to reject the goods and obtain a refund. The remedies are alternatives and the consumer must therefore choose between them. Under CRA 2015, s 24(5) a consumer can only use either remedy if one of three separate circumstances occurs.

- The first is that the goods still do not conform after 'one repair or one replacement'[1]. Not conforming in this context means the failure of the goods to comply with the core standards, the standards for installation[2] or digital content[3] or generally failing to comply with 'requirements that are stated in the contract'[4].

- The second is that the consumer cannot require the trader to either replace or to repair the goods because to do either is impossible[5].

- The third is that the consumer has already required the trader to repair or replace the goods but the trader has failed to do so 'within a reasonable time and without significant inconvenience to the consumer'[6].

[1] As defined by CRA 2015, s 24(6) and (7).
[2] CRA 2015, s 15.
[3] CRA 2015, s 16.
[4] CRA 2015, s 19(1).
[5] For the purpose of CRA 2015, s 23(3).
[6] For the purposes of CRA 2015, s 23(2)(a).

6.206 If any one of those three circumstances apply then the consumer is entitled to choose between the right to a 'price reduction' (where upon the consumer keeps the goods) and the 'final right to reject' (see **6.207** below).

The right to a price reduction is the right to a refund of 'an appropriate amount' from what the consumer has already 'paid, or otherwise transferred'[1]. The amount of the price reduction can be as much as the full amount of the price[2]. The BIS (now BEIS) guidance for goods[3] provides:

> 'The reduction that you offer must be an appropriate amount. This should usually reflect the difference between the value of the goods as they were sold (with the issue) and their value if there had been no fault (i.e. the amount that the consumer paid originally).'

As under CRA 2015 s 20, the right may be qualified where the consumer has not paid in money[4].

[1] CRA 2015, s 24(1).
[2] CRA 2015, s 24(2).
[3] See 'The Consumer Rights Act: Goods, Guidance for Business', September 2015 at p 54.
[4] CRA 2015, s 24(3), which applies s 20(10)–(17) to a consumer's right to receive a refund, and s 24(4).

FINAL RIGHT TO REJECT – DEDUCTION FOR USAGE

6.207 The final right to reject is covered by s 20 (see **6.196–6.199** above) and s 24 of the CRA 2015. In the same way that a consumer who exercises the short-term right to reject is entitled to a refund, so too is the consumer who exercises the 'final right to reject'. However, the refund under the 'final right to reject' is subject to a reduction to take account of the consumer's use of the goods in the period since they were delivered[1]. However, no deduction for usage can be made if; the final right to reject is exercised during the first 6 months[2], save in the case of a motor vehicle[3]. Upon exercising the final right to reject the consumer is under a duty to make the goods available for collection or, if agreed, to return them[4].

[1] CRA 2015, s 24(8).
[2] Defined in CRA 2015, s 24(10) and (11).

3   CRA 2015, s 24(10)(a) and this exception may be supplemented by statutory instrument (s 24(10)(b)). A 'motor' vehicle' is defined in s 24(12) and (13).

4   CRA 2015, s 20(7)(b).

PRE-CONTRACT INFORMATION

6.208 The CRA 2015, s 12 provides for the status of pre-contract information which must be provided under regs 9, 10 or 13 of the CCR 2013 (other than the information relating to the main characteristic of goods[1]) by providing that this pre-contract information is to be 'treated as included as a term of the contract'. The CRA 2015 gives the consumer the right to recover from the trader any costs that they have incurred as a result of breaching this pre-contract information[2].

1   For the information relating to the main characteristics of the goods see para (a) of Schs 1 and 2 of the CCRs 2013 and **6.172** above.

2   CRA 2015, s 19(5).

RIGHT TO SUPPLY

6.209 A consumer will have the right to reject goods if there is a breach of CRA 2015, s 17(1) because the trader did not have the legal right to supply the goods to the consumer[1]. This right is not time limited other than by the ordinary rules of limitation for civil proceedings.

1   CRA 2015, s 19(6) and see **6.181** above.

SUMMARY TABLE

6.210 The remedies under Chapter 1 of the CRA 2015 for contracts for the sale of goods are summarised in the following table.

Type of breach	Remedy
s 9 goods to be of satisfactory quality; s 10 goods to be fit for a particular purpose; s 11 goods to be as described by the trader (including CCR 2013 pre-contract information relating to main characteristics); s 13 goods to match a sample; s 14 goods to match a model; s 16 included digital content to conform with standards in Chapter 3 (Digital content)	The short term right to reject, under s 22 The right to a repair or replacement, under s 23 The right to a price reduction or the final right to reject, under s 24
s 15 goods incorrectly installed by the trader where installation is a part of the contract	The right to a repair or replacement under s 23 The right to a price reduction or final right to reject, under s 24

Type of breach	Remedy
s 12 certain CCR 2013 pre-contract information as terms of the contract (other than main characteristics of goods)	The right to recover any costs incurred by the consumer as a result of the failure to provide certain pre-contract information, up to the price paid, under s 19(5)
s 17 the trader has the right to supply the goods	The right to reject, under s 19(6)
s 28 late delivery of goods	The right to be reimbursed of all payments made under the contract without undue delay, under s 28(9)

Exclusion of liability not permitted

6.211 A term of a contract to supply goods that excludes or restricts any of the supply of goods rights is not binding on a consumer to the extent that it would exclude or restrict a right or remedy, applies restrictive or onerous conditions to the exercise of such rights or remedies, allows the trader to put a consumer pursuing such a right or remedy at a disadvantage, or excluding rules of evidence or procedure[1]. Notwithstanding, that such terms are automatically not binding on a consumer, they can also be assessed for fairness under Pt 2 of the CRA and are highly likely to be found to be unfair. Unfair contract terms are dealt with in CHAPTER 9.

[1]   CRA 2015, s 31(1) and (2).

6.212 Special provision is made for a term in a contract for the hire of goods, which excludes or restricts the trader's liability arising from s 17 of CRA 2015 (the trader's right to supply the goods etc)[1] and also for arbitration clauses[2]. In relation to the latter, s 31(4) of the CRA 2015 provides that a written agreement to subject differences to arbitration is not to be regarded as excluding or restricting any of the consumer's rights or remedies provided under Chapter 2 of the CRA 2015. However, the Arbitration Act 1996 provides that a term which constitutes an arbitration agreement is automatically unfair, if the claim is for less than a specified amount[3]. Further, terms which oblige consumers to take disputes between themselves and the trader to arbitration may be regarded as unfair under Pt 2 of the CRA 2015[4]. Unfair contract terms are dealt with in CHAPTER 9.

[1]   CRA 2015, ss 31(5) and (6).
[2]   CRA 2015, s 31(4).
[3]   Arbitration Act 1996, s 91.
[4]   See CHAPTER 9 on unfair terms.

Services

Introduction

6.213 Chapter 4 provides for rights and remedies in contracts where a trader supplies a service to a consumer. It sets out four basic rights:

- The service is to be performed with reasonable care and skill;
- Information provided about the trader or service is binding;

- If no price is agreed, a reasonable price is to be paid for the service; and
- If no time for performance is agreed, the service is to be performed within a reasonable time.

Provision is also made for the remedies on breach that a consumer is entitled to request and the trader must offer. The two key remedies are the right for a trader to re-perform the service or where that is not possible to make a reduction in the price paid. Chapter 4 does not apply to contracts for employment or apprenticeship (CRA 2015, s 48(2)) or to a gratuitous contract in Scotland (CRA 2015, s 48(3)).

6.214 The service provisions did not apply to 'consumer transport services'[1] when the CRA 2015 came into effect on 1 October 2015. This delay was to allow consideration of the relationship between the provision of the CRA 2015 and statutory compensation provisions for public transport. Consumer transport services fell within the service provisions with regard to contracts entered into from 1 October 2016[2].

[1]   See definition in SI 2015/1630.
[2]   Bought in by SI 2015/1630 as amended by SI 2016/484.

6.215 It should be noted that the Provision of Services Regulations 2009[1] also creates regulatory obligations in relation to services (see below). In particular reg 12 requires that the provider of a service must respond to complaints as quickly as possible and make best efforts to find a satisfactory solution. These provisions can be enforced under Pt 8 of the Enterprise Act 2002 (see CHAPTER 5, Civil Enforcement).

[1]   SI 2009/2999 implementing the Services Directive 2006/123/EC.

Standards for services

REASONABLE CARE AND SKILL

6.216 CRA 2015, s 49 provides that every contract to supply a service is to be treated as including a term that the trader will perform the service with reasonable care and skill. This follows the similar term in the Supply of Goods and Services Act 1982, s 13 and so it is likely that the case law relating to that provision remains relevant when determining what constitutes in a particular case the standard of 'reasonable care and skill'.

SERVICES AND BINDING INFORMATION

6.217 CRA 2015, s 50 provides a new right that 'anything that is said or written to the consumer by or on behalf of the trader, about the trader or service' is to be treated as a term of the contract if the consumer takes it into account when deciding whether to enter into the contract or making any subsequent decision about the service. This is, however, subject to any qualifications made by the trader at the time and any expressly agreed changes[1].

In relation to this new provision, the BIS (now BEIS) guidance for business on services under the CRA, 2015[2] provides:

'The principle behind this requirement is very simple: if you tell a consumer something about yourself or the service, then that "something" should hold true.

. . .

If you provide information to the consumer about yourself or the service, which the consumer then relies on when entering into the contract, or making decisions under the contract, then you should ensure that the service meets this description you gave of it . . . It is for the consumer to prove that they did rely on this information, but if they can then they can assert this right.

However, you can clarify information. For example, if you give a qualification to the information then the consumer cannot ignore that qualification. Similarly if the consumer agrees to any change of the information, this right is not engaged. For example, if you give information in error or circumstances change then you can contact the consumer and if they are still happy to use your services once you have explained that things are not as you thought, then they cannot assert this right for that original error.

This right covers information given by you personally as well as information given by your staff on your behalf.'

1   CRA 2015, s 50(2).
2   Consumer Rights Act Services, Guidance for Business, BIS, September 2015, p 8 and 9.

6.218 Pre-contract information required under the CCR 2013 for on-premises, off-premises and distance contracts[1] is also treated as a contractual term[2]. Further, under s 50(4), a change to any of that information, before or after the consumer enters into a contract, is ineffective unless the consumer gives their express consent to such a change (see **6.80**).

1   SI 2013/3134, regs 9, 10 and 13.
2   CRA 2015, s 50(3).

SERVICES: PRICE AND TIME OF PERFORMANCE

6.219 Section 51 is similar to s 15 of the Supply of Goods and Services Act 1982. The new provision has the effect of implying a term into contract for the supply of service that the consumer must pay a reasonable price for the service, (and no more) when:

- The consumer has not paid a price (or other consideration) already for the service;
- The contract does not expressly fix the price (or other consideration) to be paid and does not say how it will be fixed;
- Anything that is to be treated under s 50 of the CRA 2015 as included as a term in the contract does not fix the price (or other consideration).

It is worth noting that the final point above covers (inter alia) something the trader says to the consumer in conversation which the consumer takes into account when entering the contract (see **6.217**).

6.220 CRA 2015, s 52 makes similar provision for contracts that do not 'expressly fix the time for the service to be performed' by providing an implied term that the trader 'must perform the service within a reasonable time'. The new provision is similar to s 14 of the Supply of Goods and Services Act 1982.

Other laws relating to services

6.221 Terms which are implied into a contract for the supply of services do not affect any other 'enactment or rule of law' that imposes a stricter duty on the trader, or 'defines or restricts the rights, duties or liabilities' arising[1].

¹   CRA 2015, s 53.

Remedies – services

6.222 The remedies provided for in Chapter 4 are additional to any remedies available to a consumer in general contract law[1]. Therefore, where there have been a breach of a term which the CRA, 2015 implies into a contract for the supply of services, a consumer can seek a common law remedy (eg damages) or equitable remedy (eg specific performance) in addition to, or instead of, a remedy provided for under the CRA 2015. This is of course subject to not seeking the same loss twice.

¹   CRA 2015, ss 54(6) and (7).

6.223 There are two key remedies provided under the CRA 2015 in relation to contracts for the supply of services: the right to 'repeat performance' and the right to 'a price reduction'[1].

The right 'to repeat performance' is available when there is a breach of the implied term of reasonable care and skill' (s 49 of the CRA 2015) or a breach of information relating to the performance of the service provided by the trader, which is treated as a contract term under s 50 of CRA 2015[2]. The right to 'repeat performance' is phrased 'as 'a right to require the trader to perform the service again to the extent necessary to complete its performance in conformity with the contract'[3]. This provision suggests that the trader is not required to redo the work completely, but put right those faults in the original performance sufficiently to make it conform with the contract's implied term of reasonable care and skill or a term implied under s 50 of the Act, relating to the performance of the service.

¹   CRA 2015, s 54(3).
²   Also potentially available is the right to a price reduction, see **6.225** and **6.226** below.
³   CRA 2015, s 55(1).

6.224 The trader must undertake repeat performance 'within a reasonable time and without significant inconvenience to the consumer' and must bear all the necessary costs including labour or materials[1]. When deciding what constitutes a 'reasonable time' or 'significant inconvenience', the nature of the service and its purpose are to be taken into account. The BIS (now BEIS) guidance for business on services[2] includes the following example:

> 'You are decorating a room for a party. The consumer inspects the work the day before but tells you it is not in line with the colour scheme she had agreed with your assistant. You phone your assistance who agrees that the consumer did specify the colour scheme. The consumer asks you to re-do the decorating. Due to the purpose the service, you would need to re-do the work before the party to have done so within a "reasonable time".'

The consumer has no right to repeat performance if it is impossible to complete performance of the service in conformity with the contract[3] (ie to complete performance with reasonable care and skill or in accordance with a term of the contract, implied under s 50, relating to the performance of the service).

1   CRA 2015, s 55(2).
2   Consumer Rights Act Services, Guidance for Business, BIS, September 2015 at p 18.
3   CRA 2015, s 55(3).

6.225 Also, where there is a breach of a term implied under ss 49 or 50, the consumer may have the right to require the trader to reduce the price by an appropriate amount, which is referred to as a 'right to price reduction'. Despite its name, a price reduction can be as much as the full price. Where exercising this remedy leads to a (full or partial) refund, this must be given without undue delay and, at the latest, within 14 days from the day on which the trader agreed that the consumer is entitled to a refund[1].

1   CRA 2015, s 56(4).

6.226 The right to repeat performance, to an extent, limits the right of a consumer to an immediate price reduction for breach of the terms implied under the CRA 2015, ss 49 and 50[1]. Where there is a right to repeat performance, a price reduction under CRA 2015, s 56 may only be obtained when repeat performance is impossible[2] or the trader is in breach of the requirement to do the repeat work 'within a reasonable time and without significant inconvenience to the consumer'[3].

1   See **6.223** and **6.224**.
2   CRA 2015, s 56(3)(a) and CRA 2015, s 55(3) 'if completing performance of the service in conformity with the contract is impossible'.
3   CRA 2015, s 56(3)(b) and CRA 2015, s 55(2)(a).

6.227 Breach of a term implied under s 50 of the CRA 2015 which does not relate to the performance of the service gives the consumer the right to pursue the remedy of price reduction under s 56 of the CRA 2015[1]. Similarly, so does breach of an implied term that the service is performed within a reasonable time[2].

1   CRA 2015, s 54(4).
2   CRA 2015, s 54(5).

6.228 The remedies in Chapter 4 in relation to contracts for services are summarised in the table below.

Type of breach	Remedy
s 49 service to be performed with reasonable care and skill s 50 information relating to the performance of the service that s 50 requires to be a term of the contract	The right to require repeat performance, under s 55. The right to a price reduction, under s 56, but only when repeat performance is impossible or after the consumer has required repeat performance but it has not been provided within a reasonable time or without significant inconvenience to the consumer
s 50 information relating to the trader that s 50 requires to be a term of the contract	The right to a price reduction, under s 56. There is no right to repeat performance

Type of breach	Remedy
s 52 Performance within a reasonable time	The right to a price reduction, under s 56. There is no right to repeat performance
s 51 Reasonable price to be paid for a service in the absence of a price being fixed	No special remedy under Chapter 4

Exclusion of liability not permitted

6.229 Firstly, the CRA 2015 provides that terms that exclude the trader's liability to:

- perform the services with reasonable care and skill;
- supply services in accordance with the information supplied under s 50 of the Act (this includes information relating to the trader or performance of the services), which is treated as a contractual term

are not binding on the consumer[1].

1   CRA 2015, s 57(1) and (2).

6.230 Secondly, the CRA 2015 provides that terms are not binding on the consumer to the extent that they restrict the trader's liability for a breach of any of the four statutory implied terms[1] to an amount which is less than the price paid by the consumer (or the value of the consideration provided by the consumer under the contract for the supply of services)[2]. For example, where the contract's price is £50 and the contract includes a term which provides for the trader's liability will not exceed £40 if the services are not provided with reasonable care and skill, that term is not binding on the consumer under the services provisions of the CRA 2015. However, to continue the example, a contract term which limits the trader's liability to £50 would not fall foul of these provisions.

Notwithstanding, terms which are not deemed to be binding on the consumer under Chapter 4 of the CRA 2015 are likely to be assessable for fairness under Pt 2 of the CRA 2015. If they are considered to be unfair under Pt 2 of the CRA 2015, such terms will not be binding on the consumer for this reason. See Chapter 9 for unfair terms.

1   See **6.213** above.
2   CRA 2015, s 57(3). See also s 57(4) which make clear that terms which exclude or restrict liability in the two ways described covers terms which make it difficult for consumers to pursue or enforce those rights.

6.231 Special provision is made for arbitration clauses. CRA 2015, s 57(6) provides that a written agreement to submit differences to arbitration is not a term excluding or restricting any liability. The same provision is included in Chapter 2 in relation to contracts for the supply of goods (see **6.212** above).

Digital content

Introduction

6.232 Chapter 3 of Pt 1 of CRA 2015 seeks to clarify the treatment of digital content as between the different standards that had applied for goods and services. The legal rights of consumers were not clear when digital content proved defective or otherwise unsatisfactory. The new legislation is based on the premise that digital content ought to be treated the same as physical goods 'so far as that is possible'[1].

[1]   R Bradgate (2010) 'Consumer rights in digital products' (report prepared for BIS).

Meaning of digital content

6.233 Digital content is defined as 'data which are produced and supplied in digital form'[1]. This will include a wide variety of digital products such as computer software, mobile phone apps, books, music, film or ringtones that are downloaded or streamed. It will apply to tangible goods that contain data in a digital form such as a compact disc, Blue-ray or DVD. It will also apply to goods that have parts that include data in a digital form such as a mobile phone, television, car, computer or washing machine.

[1]   CRA 2015, s 2(9).

6.234 The provisions in the CRA 2015, s 1 concerning mixed contracts are particularly important in the content of the contracts for the supply of digital content, which will often have elements that are covered by the provisions concerning goods, services and digital content. For example, the supply and fitting of a central heating system will consist of a contract for the heating system (goods), its installation (a service) and digital content (the software within the programmer that can be accessed at home and remotely). Under Pt 1 of the CRA 2015 all of the provisions covering each of the three elements of the contract will apply[1].

In addition to the above clarification, Chapter 2 of the CRA 2015 makes specific provision for when contracts for the supply of goods include digital content[2].

[1]   CRA 2015, s 1(3)–(5).
[2]   CRA 2015, s 16 and **6.179** above.

6.235 A trader does not supply digital content, however, merely because the trader 'supplies a service by which digital content reaches the consumer'[1]. This distinction is not particularly clear; however, the BIS Guidance on Digital Content[2] states:

> 'Digital content is **not** online shopping. Online shopping is just one method by which digital content can be obtained, just as it is a method by which goods can be obtained – so a physical book bought online is not digital content, it is goods.

> Digital content is **not** services delivered online, such as online banking or the website for online grocery shopping. In the same way as the use of a physical bank is not seen as the supply of goods, the use of an online bank is not the supply of digital content. The exception is where a consumer has separately paid for an online banking app – the app itself would be digital content.'

[1]   CRA 2015, s 33(4).

Free digital content

6.236 The starting point is that the rights and remedies in Chapter 3 apply if the digital content is supplied 'for a price paid by the consumer'[1] such that completely free digital content falls outside its ambit. However, digital content that is supplied 'free' with other goods, services or digital content that a consumer pays for are covered if the 'free' digital content is 'not generally available' to consumers unless they pay for it, or pay for other goods, services or digital content supplied with the 'free' digital content[2]. 'Paying a price' means that the consumer has paid with money or using a payment facility which has itself been paid for with money such as a voucher or virtual currency[3].

There is one exception to the above 'paid for' approach and that is a consumer has a statutory remedy under Chapter 3 of the CRA 2015 when digital content causes damage to the consumer's device or other digital content, even when the digital content was free[4].

1 CRA 2015, s 33(1).
2 CRA 2015, s 33(2).
3 CRA 2015, s 33(3).
4 CRA 2015, ss 33(8) and 46.

Standards for digital content

6.237 Under Chapter 3, Pt 1, statutory terms are implied (although the legislation avoids using this word) into a consumer contract for the supply of digital content. These terms broadly mirror those, in Chapter 2, Pt 1 for the sale of goods and will in practice overlap with each other.

The core rights

DIGITAL CONTENT AND SATISFACTORY QUALITY

6.238 CRA 2015, s 34 provides a contractual term that digital content be of satisfactory quality, which includes taking into account any description of the digital content, the price paid for the digital content (as described in **6.236** above) and all other relevant circumstances[1]. The latter may include a consideration of public statements made about the product by the trader, the producer[2] or their representatives. The CRA 2015, s 34(3) provides a non-exhaustive list of other factors to take into account when determining whether the digital content is of satisfactory quality, these include:

• fitness for **all** the purposes for which digital content of that kind is usually supplied;
• freedom from minor defects;
• its safety and durability.

1 CRA 2015, s 34 (1) and (2).
2 CRA 2015, s 59: 'producer', in relation to goods or digital content, means: (a) the manufacturer, (b) the importer into the United Kingdom, or (c) any person who purports to be a producer by placing the person's name, trade mark or other distinctive sign on the goods or

using it in connection with the digital content. 'United Kingdom' was substituted for 'European Economic Area' by the Consumer Protection (Amendments etc) (EU Exit) Regulations 2018, SI 2018/1326, as of 31 December 2020. The amendment applies to contracts made on or after that date.

DIGITAL CONTENT AND FITNESS FOR PARTICULAR PURPOSE

6.239 CRA 2015, s 35 implies a contractual term that the digital content be fit for a particular purpose that the consumer has made known to the trader expressly or by implication before the contract is made. However, such a term will not be implied if it is established (from the circumstances) that the consumer did not rely on the trader's skill or judgment or it is unreasonable for the consumer to place reliance on the trader's skill and judgment.

Save for s 34 (satisfactory quality) and s 35 there are no other implied terms about the quality of the digital content or its fitness for purpose, although these may plainly be specified as express terms of the contract[1].

[1]   CRA 2015, s 38.

DIGITAL CONTENT AND DESCRIPTION

6.240 CRA 2015, s 36 implies contractual term that digital content will match any description given by the trader to the consumer. If a consumer examines a trial version pre-contract, it is insufficient that the digital content that is subsequently obtained matches the trial version, if it does not also match the description given[1]. Section 36 also provides that the CCR 2013, pre-contract information relating to the main characteristics of the digital content, its functionality and compatibility[2] are to be treated as a term of the contract and any change to that information cannot be made unless the consumer expressly agrees (see **6.80** above)[3]. Non-compliance with this information gives the consumer the same remedies as those for breach of the core implied terms of satisfactory quality, fit for a particular purpose and as described (see **6.248** below).

[1]   CRA 2015, s 36(2).
[2]   That is the following pre-contract information in an on-premise contract (reg 9 of CCR 2013) paras (a), (j) or (k) of Sch 1, and for off-premises contracts (reg 10 of CCR 2013) and distance sales (reg 13 of CCR 2013) paras (a), (v) and (w) of Sch 2.
[3]   CRA 2015, s 36(3) and (4).

Information

6.241 CRA 2015, s 37 concerns all the other pre-contract information that a trader is required to give a consumer under the CCR 2013 (see above), providing that such information should be treated as a contractual term and any change to that information cannot be made unless the consumer expressly agrees[1]. A breach of these implied terms gives the consumer a right to more limited remedies than the pre-contract information dealt with under CRA 2015, s 36 (see **6.240** above and **6.248** below).

[1]   CRA 2015, ss 37(2) and (3), which refers to all the pre-contract information, save for – in an on-premise contract (reg 9) paras (a), (j) or (k) of Sch 1, and for off-premises contracts (reg 10) and distance sales (reg 13) paras (a), (v) and (w) of Sch 2.

Transmission of digital content

6.242 CRA 2015, s 39(1) and (2) defines at what point the quality standard of the digital content supplied is to be assessed. The digital content is supplied when the content reaches the consumer's device or, if earlier, when the digital 'content reaches another trader', with whom the consumer has chosen and entered a contract with to provide the service of supplying digital content to their device. For example, when the digital content is transmitted to the consumer across a network, the digital content is supplied when it reaches the consumer's chosen internet service provider. The rationale for this approach is that if the digital content itself is not faulty, and the fault lies with another trader with whom the consumer has a contract, then liability rests with that trader.

6.243 CRA 2015, s 39(3)–(7), covers the situation where after the trader has supplied digital content, the consumer has to have access to a 'processing facility'[1] under the arrangements made by the trader. The BEIS, digital guidance for business[2] gives the following examples of a processing facility:

> 'Some types of digital content may be sold on a disk but then accessed in an online environment for their full functionality (eg a massively multi- user online game, or MMO). Other types of digital content are accessed entirely online such as an online newspaper subscription.'

Unless a time is specified in the contract, a term is implied that the processing facility 'must be available to the consumer for a reasonable time'[3]. Moreover, the digital content must meet all the original core standards (of quality, fitness for a particular purpose and description) on each occasion it is transmitted under the facility[4].

1   As defined in s 39(4).
2   Consumer Rights Act, Digital Content, BIS Guidance for Business, September 2015 at p 23.
3   CRA 2015, s 39(5).
4   CRA 2015, s 39(6).

DIGITAL CONTENT AND MODIFICATIONS

6.244 CRA 2015, s 40 covers the situation where the trader reserves the right to modify the digital content supplied. It provides any modified digital content must meet the core standards as applied to the digital content originally supplied of quality, fitness for a particular purpose and as described[1]. The provision also clarifies that the trader can provide updates which improve, or add new features to, the digital content provided that the digital content continues to match its original description and the pre-contract information relating to the digital content's main characteristics, functionality and compatibility[2].

If the modification leads to a breach of the implied terms relating to any of the core standards, the breach is deemed to have arisen at the time when the digital content was supplied and not at the time the product was modified[3].

1   CRA 2015, s 40(1).
2   CRA 2015, s 40(2).
3   CRA 2015, s 40(3).

Right to supply

6.245 CRA 2015, s 41 implies a contractual term in a contract for the supply of digital content that a trader has the right to supply any digital content. This is directed towards traders that breach intellectual property rights by selling digital content that they do not own or have the legal right to supply to consumers.

Remedies – digital content

6.246 Chapter 3 creates similar remedies when the statutory implied terms for digital content are breached as Chapter 1 does in relation to the sale of goods. The remedies are expressly stated to be in addition to a consumer's existing right to bring a civil claim in contract or tort[1]. However, the provisions do not permit double recovery.

¹   CRA 2015, s 42(7).

6.247 There is a statutory presumption that a contract for digital content did not conform when it was first supplied, if it does not conform at any time during the first 6 months after its supply. Although this can be rebutted if the trader can establish that the digital content did conform, or that the presumption is incompatible with nature of the digital content or how it fails to conform[1].

¹   CRA 2015, s 42(9) and (10).

6.248 The statutory remedies are summarised in the table below.

Type of breach	Remedy
s 34 satisfactory quality; s 35 fit for a particular purpose; or s 36 as described including CCR 2013 pre-contract information relating to main characteristics, functionality and compatibility	The right to a repair or a replacement, under s 43. The right to a price reduction up to the full amount of the price, under s 44.
s 37 certain CCR 2013 pre-contract information (ie all the CCR 2013 pre-contract information other than that referred to above)	The right to recover any costs incurred by the consumer as a result of the breach, up to the price paid, under s 42(4)
s 41 the requirement that a trader has the right to supply the digital content to the consumer	The right to a refund, under s 45
s 46 digital content supplied by a trader to a consumer has caused damage to the consumer's own device or other digital content and the damage would not have occurred had the trader exercised reasonable care and skill	The right to require the trader to repair the damage or compensate the consumer, under s 46(2) The right to bring a civil claim to enforce the right, under s 46(7)

CIVIL REDRESS FOR UNFAIR COMMERCIAL PRACTICES

6.249 The Consumer Protection from Unfair Trading Regulations 2008[1], ('CPUTR 2008') implement the EU Unfair Commercial Practices Directive. The CPUTR 2008 can be enforced by designated enforcers such as local authorities and the OFT in the civil courts using Pt 8 of the Enterprise Act 2002. In *McGuffick v The Royal Bank of Scotland plc*[2] the High Court held that an individual had no locus to enforce the CPUTR 2008 or any cause of action for their breach[3].

[1] SI 2008/1277.
[2] [2009] EWHC 2386 (Comm).
[3] Per Flaux J, it 'is quite clear that the United Kingdom government deliberately excluded any civil law remedies from the Regulations'. See also *Ramsden v Santon Highlands Ltd* [2015] CSOH 65.

6.250 The absence of any private civil redress for breaches of the CPUTR 2008 was the subject of a joint report by the Law Commission and the Scottish Law Commission in March 2012[1]. It was felt that the current law which would apply (including the law of misrepresentation and undue influence) was complex and uncertain and was inaccessible to consumers. The report therefore recommended a new statutory right of redress for a consumer against a trader where there had been a misleading action or misleading omission under CPUTR 2008.

[1] The Law Commission and the Scottish Law Commission Joint Report on 'Consumer Redress For Misleading and Aggressive Practices' March 2012 (Law Com No 332; Scot Law Com No 226).

6.251 The Law Commission's recommendations were largely implemented by the Consumer Protection (Amendment) Regulations 2014[1], which added a new Pt 4A to the CPUTR 2008 and made minor consequential amendments to other legislation. Under Pt 4A, in line with the Law Commission's recommendations, consumers are provided with a right to civil redress against traders who have engaged in misleading or aggressive commercial practices. Part 4A provides consumers with no right of action for misleading omissions or cases where the trader has engaged in a banned practice[2]. The Law Commission had advised against the introduction of a civil right of redress for misleading omissions on the basis that it was too vague a concept with unclear limits. On the other hand, the Law Commission had recommended that the civil right should be extended to the Sch 1 banned practices; however, in one of the rare instances where the legislation did not directly follow the Law Commission's recommendations, this suggestion was not implemented. This Chapter analyses only the civil remedies, the concepts of misleading actions and aggressive commercial practices are dealt with in detail in CHAPTER 8, Unfair Commercial Practices.

[1] SI 2014/870.
[2] For detailed discussion of these concepts, see CHAPTER 8, Unfair Commercial Practices.

The rights

6.252 In certain circumstances, consumers now have the right to unwind their contract, seek a discount and/or seek damages when a trader has engaged in misleading actions or aggressive commercial practices under CPUTR 2008. These civil rights apply only to contracts entered into, or payments made, on or after 1 October 2014[1].

1   Consumer Protection (Amendment) Regulations 2014, SI 2014/870, reg 1(3).

6.253 The existing general provision on damages for misrepresentation under the Misrepresentation Act 1967, s 2 has been restricted if the consumer now has a right to redress under Pt 4A of CPUTR 2008[1]. This amendment was principally introduced to prevent duplicate claims; the Law Commissions having been persuaded by The Council of Her Majesty's Circuit Judges' argument that:

> 'The stated objective is to provide a new and user-friendly alternative for consumers. Litigants and their lawyers are unlikely to opt for the simpler solution – they are much more likely to adopt a "belt and braces approach" and sue in the alternative. This will add to the complexity of proceedings and frustrate the objective. It would be preferable for the new remedies to replace existing law.[2]'

1   Misrepresentation Act 1967, s 2(4): 'This section does not entitle a person to be paid damages in respect of a misrepresentation if the person has a right to redress under Part 4A . . . in respect of the conduct constituting the misrepresentation'.
2   The Law Commission and the Scottish Law Commission Joint Report on 'Consumer Redress For Misleading and Aggressive Practices' March 2012 (Law Com No 332; Scot Law Com No 226) at paras **7.136** and **7.137**. Other consultees also argued in favour of simplification, including the consumer rights group Which?

6.254 In practice this new limitation is often overlooked and damages claims are often pleaded on the basis of misrepresentation when, as a result of the new s 2(4) of the Misrepresentation Act 1967, damages are not available to the consumer on that basis. In most cases where the trader points this out in their defence to the claim, the particulars of claim will be amended and the proceedings will progress on the correct basis. Further, where this issue is not identified at an early stage, county court judges are still likely to be sympathetic to consumers and allow the claim to proceed, provided the evidence is before the Court to enable to judge to decide a Pt 4A claim. This will especially be the case on the small claims track where the rules of procedure do not apply as strictly. However, any pleading based on a cause of action not open to the claimant is at risk of being struck out and consumers, traders and those representing them would be well advised to turn their minds to this issue at an early stage. It should be noted that the new s 2(4) of the Misrepresentation Act 1967 does not prevent a consumer from seeking rescission under that Act or remove the Court's power to award damages in lieu of rescission.

6.255 The new restrictions on consumer misrepresentation claims where the consumer has a right to redress under Pt 4A do not prevent the consumer from bringing a claim under s 75 of the Consumer Credit Act 1974 against their creditor. Whilst s 75 only grants consumers a right of action against their creditor where they have a breach of contract or misrepresentation claim against the supplier, new s 2(5) of the Misrepresentation Act 1967 preserves the consumer's s 75 claim even where they could no longer bring a misrepresentation claim against the supplier. Notably, a proposed amendment to s 75 to provide consumers with a claim against the creditor where the consumer had a claim against the supplier under Pt 4A, thereby extending the scope of s 75, was not enacted[1].

1   For a detailed discussion of s 75 of the Consumer Credit Act 1974, see CHAPTER 19, Consumer Credit.

When do the rights apply?

6.256 Pursuant to reg 27A the rights under Pt 4A apply when there is:

(a)   a sale of a product[1] to a consumer; or
(b)   a purchase of goods[2] from, or payment made by a consumer; and
(c)   payment made by a consumer for the supply of a product;

And a 'prohibited practice'[3] by either:

(a)   a trader; or
(b)   in the case of business to consumer contracts for goods or digital services, a producer[4] (if the trader was or should have been aware of the prohibited practice).

And the prohibited practice was a 'significant factor' in the consumer's transactional decision[5]. However, the Pt 4A rights do not apply to immovable property (save for certain leases)[6] or financial services (save for restricted-use credit agreements which are not secured on land)[7].

1   Defined by reg 2(1) as goods, a service, digital content, immoveable property (albeit this category is largely excluded from the Pt 4A rights by reg 27C) and rights or obligations.
2   Importantly this category is restricted to goods rather than the broader 'products'. Further, it will not apply where the trader also agrees to supply a product to the consumer in part-exchange; the trader's supply of the product in part exchange is, however, likely to fall within the first category in any event.
3   For instance a misleading action under reg 5 or aggressive commercial practice under reg 7 (see 6.258 below).
4   'Producer' is defined in CPUTR, reg 27(5).
5   CPUTR 2008, reg 27A(6).
6   CPUTR 2008, reg 27C.
7   CPUTR 2008, reg 27D; for more detailed discussion of restricted-use credit agreements see CHAPTER 19.

6.257 What amounts to a 'significant factor' is not further defined and will plainly be a fact sensitive question. The decision not to use a formulation of the type 'would not have entered into the contract or made the payment were it not for the prohibited practice' suggests that this test is different to the ordinary test 'but for' causation and this certainly seems to have been the Law Commissions' intention[1]. However, it is unclear how the prohibited practice could ever be said to be a significant factor if the consumer would have entered into the contract or made the payment notwithstanding the practice. Further, if the test is, notwithstanding the forgoing, a lower standard than 'but for' causation that is rather unsatisfactory: as the Bar Council warned during the Law Commissions' consultation:

'Once a consumer is apprised of a misleading practice there is likely to be a natural temptation for that consumer to assume that he or she must have been influenced by it . . . If the requirement is only to show that the practice was a significant factor, rather than a "but for" cause, the difficulty for traders in countering such assertions will be greater.'

In any event, in most cases the nuances of the 'significant factor' test will be academic. Even if the significant factor test is a lower standard than but for causation, due to the parasitic nature of the civil redress rights, the consumer will still have to show 'but for' causation for the average consumer in order to establish the prohibited practice in the first instance (see discussion in CHAPTER 8 on Unfair Commercial Practices). It will be a rare case indeed where a consumer bringing a Pt 4A claim will be able to establish that the average, reasonably well informed, observant and circumspect consumer would not have entered into the transaction but for the commercial practice but is unable to meet that causative test in their own right.

[1]   The Law Commission and the Scottish Law Commission Joint Report on 'Consumer Redress For Misleading and Aggressive Practices' March 2012 (Law Com No 332; Scot Law Com No 226) at paras **7.110** to **7.113**.

The prohibited practice

6.258   As explained above, reg 27B limits the prohibited practices to:

(a)   misleading actions under reg 5; and
(b)   aggressive commercial practices of coercion, undue influence, and harassment under reg 7[1].

The other unfair commercial practices, such as contravening professional diligence, misleading omissions, and banned practices in Sch 1 do not entitle a consumer to redress under Pt 4A.

[1]   It should be noted that the concepts of 'undue influence' and 'harassment' in the CPUTR 2008 do not directly align with the concepts under general UK law. For example, there is no requirement for a special relationship of trust between the trader and consumer for 'undue influence' to arise in the context of the CPUTR 2008. For further discussion see CHAPTER 8, Unfair Commercial Practices.

The right to unwind

6.259   Regulations 27E–27H provide the consumer with a right to unwind contracts where they have met the three threshold conditions discussed in **6.256** above. Under reg 27E, a consumer has the right to unwind a business to consumer contract if the consumer indicates to the trader that the consumer rejects the product, and does so within the relevant period and at a time when the product is capable of being rejected.

6.260   The consumer can indicate that they are rejecting the product by saying or doing something, there is no requirement for the rejection to be in writing but it must be clear[1].

[1]   CPUTR 2008, reg 27E(2).

6.261   The relevant period is 90 days beginning with the later of: the days the consumer enters into the contract; and 'the relevant day'[1]. The relevant day means the day on which good are first delivered, the day on which the performance of the service begins, the day on which the digital content is first supplied, the day on which the lease begins, or the day the right is first exercised[2]. Where the contract involves the provision of more than one type of product (ie goods and a service or goods and digital content), the 'relevant day' means the latest of the possible days[3]. During the Law Commissions' consultation, durations of 30 days and 180 days were also discussed. The Law Commissions accepted the attraction of aligning the duration with the 30 day short term right to reject under the CRA 2015 but ultimately decided that this period was too short for the purposes of the proposed consumer rights as it often took longer than 30 days for consumers to become aware of the prohibited practice. After analysing over 100 case studies submitted during the consultation, the Law Commissions concluded that the vast majority of prohibited practices were discovered within 90 days and, in the interest of certainty, 90 days was preferred to 180 days[4].

[1] CPUTR 2008, reg 27E(3).
[2] CPUTR 2008, reg 27E(4).
[3] CPUTR 2008, reg 27E(5) and (6).
[4] The Law Commission and the Scottish Law Commission Joint Report on 'Consumer Redress For Misleading and Aggressive Practices' March 2012 (Law Com No 332; Scot Law Com No 226) at paras **8.40** to **8.48**.

6.262 A product remains capable of being rejected if the goods have not been fully consumed[1], the service has not been fully performed, the digital content has not been fully consumed[2], the lease has not expired, or the right has not been fully exercised. This is significantly more generous to consumers than the general law where, in broad terms, an inability to return the product to the trader prevents a consumer from rejecting the goods. The Law Commissions opined that a more generous right was appropriate where a trader had committed a misleading action or aggressive commercial practice and, for example, consumers who have been misled about a theatre performance should be entitled to unwind the contract at any point up to the final curtain call[3]. However, where consumers are unable to return any of the goods or digital content that has not been fully consumed, the consumer no longer has a right to reject[4].

[1] Goods have been fully consumed when there is nothing left of them; CPUTR 2008, reg 27E(9)(a).
[2] Digital content has only been fully consumed if the digital content was available to the consumer for a fixed period and that period has expired; CPUTR 2008, reg 27E(9)(b).
[3] The Law Commission and the Scottish Law Commission Joint Report on 'Consumer Redress For Misleading and Aggressive Practices' March 2012 (Law Com No 332; Scot Law Com No 226) at paras **8.78** to **8.81**.
[4] The rationale for this limitation is not explained in the Law Commissions' Joint Report.

6.263 A consumer does not have a right to unwind a business to consumer contract if the consumer has exercised the right to a discount in respect of that contract and the same prohibited practice[1]. This restriction makes logical sense as it prevents the consumer from obtaining an unjustified windfall by exercising their right to a discount and receiving a refund of, for example, 50% of the purchase price, and then exercising their right to unwind the contract and receiving an additional 100% of the purchase price. However, the drafting of reg 27E(10) suggests that a consumer may be able to seek duplicate remedies in relation to the same contract if they can identify distinct prohibited practices.

[1] CPUTR 2008, reg 27E(10). For discussion of the right to a discount, see below at **6.268**.

6.264 Regulation 27F provides that the effect of unwinding such a contract is that:

(a)   The contract comes to an end so that the consumer and the trader are released from their obligations under it;

(b)   The trader has a duty to give the consumer a refund (subject to the qualifications discussed in **6.266** below; and.

(c)   If the contract was wholly or partly for the sale or supply of goods the consumer must make the goods available for collection by the trader.

6.265 The provisions as to a refund are as follows:

•   To the extent that the consumer paid any money under the contract, he is entitled to receive back the same amount of money[1]. If, however, the contract was for the sale or supply of a product on a regular or continuous basis, and the consumer rejected the product after one month, he is only entitled to receive back the amount (if any) found by deducting the market price of the product at the time of rejection from the amount the consumer paid for it[2], unless it is inappropriate to do so having regard to the behaviour of the person who engaged in the prohibited practice, and the impact of the practice on the consumer[3]. Where the product supplied up to the time when the consumer rejected it consists wholly or partly of goods, their market price is only to be taken into account to the extent that they have been consumed[4].

•   To the extent that the consumer transferred anything else under the contract, he is entitled to receive back the same amount as that transferred[5]. If the consumer transferred something for which the same amount of the same thing cannot be substituted the consumer is entitled to receive back in its original state whatever the consumer transferred, or if it cannot be given back in its original state, the consumer is entitled to be paid its market price as at the time when the product was rejected[6].

[1]   CPUTR 2008, reg 27F(3).
[2]   CPUTR 2008, reg 27E(8).
[3]   CPUTR 2008, reg 27E(9).
[4]   CPUTR 2008, reg 27E(10).
[5]   CPUTR 2008, reg 27E(4).
[6]   CPUTR 2008, reg 27E(5).

6.266 Regulation 27G provides that, in the case of a consumer to business contract, where the consumer has met the three threshold conditions discussed in **6.256** above, the consumer has the right to treat the contract as at an end so that the trader and the consumer are released from their obligations under it[1]. In order to treat the contract as at an end, the consumer must indicate to the trader that the contract has ended[2]; the indication does not need to be in writing and can be something said or done but it needs to be clear[3]. Importantly, the consumer's right under reg 27G is not subject to the same 90 day relevant period as in reg 27E and is not subject to any temporal limitation other than the statutory limitation period which would apply to an action founded on contract[4]. The consumer also has a right to the return of the goods, but must repay to the trader the amount (if any) that the trader has paid for the goods[5]. If the goods cannot be returned in the same condition, the consumer is entitled to be refunded any difference between the amount the trader paid and the amount the goods were worth[6].

[1]   CPUTR 2008, reg 27G(2).
[2]   CPUTR 2008, reg 27G(3).

³ CPUTR 2008, reg 27G(4).
⁴ Six years pursuant to CPUTR 2008, reg 27K(5) and Limitation Act 1980, s 6.
⁵ CPUTR 2008, reg 27E(3).
⁶ CPUTR 2008, reg 27E(3).

6.267 Regulation 27H provides that, where they have met the three threshold conditions discussed in **6.256** above, consumers have the right to unwind a payment made following a trader's demand for the consumer required to settle, in full or in part, a purported liability to the trader where that payment was not, in fact, due (ie the consumer was not legally liable to make the payment)[1]. The consumer has a right to receive back the full payment or element of the payment which they were not legally liable to pay[2].

¹ CPUTR 2008, reg 27H(1) by reference back to reg 2(1A) and (1B).
² CPUTR 2008, reg 27H(2).

The right to a discount

6.268 Regulation 27I deals with the right to a discount under a business to consumer contract where the threshold conditions are met and the consumer has made one or more payments for the product[1] to the trader or one or more payments under the contract have not been made, and the consumer has not exercised the right to unwind the contract.

¹ "Product' is defined broadly in CPUTR 2008, reg 2(1).

6.269 If the consumer has made one or more payments, he has the right to receive back from the trader the 'relevant percentage' of the payment or payments[1]; if one or more payments have not been made, the consumer has the right to reduce by the 'relevant percentage' as many of those payments as is appropriate having regard to the seriousness of the prohibited practice or, if reg 27I(6) applies[2], to reduce all of the payments not yet made by the 'relevant percentage'[3].

¹ CPUTR 2008, reg 27I(2).
² See below at **6.272**.
³ CPUTR 2008, reg 27I(2).

6.270 Unless reg 27I(6) applies, the relevant percentages are as follows:

(a) if the prohibited practice is more than minor, 25%;
(b) if the prohibited practice is significant, 50%;
(c) if the prohibited practice is serious, 75%; and
(d) if the prohibited practice is very serious, 100%[1].

Whilst it is not specified in reg 27I(4), it is clear from the graduated structure that where the prohibited practice does not reach the threshold of 'more than minor' no percentage reduction is due; for example, where the practice can be described as either minor or negligible[2].

¹ CPUTR 2008, reg 27I(4).
² See also the discussion in The Law Commission and the Scottish Law Commission Joint Report on 'Consumer Redress For Misleading and Aggressive Practices' March 2012 (Law Com No 332; Scot Law Com No 226) at paras 8.125 to 8.137 especially the inclusion of a 0% band for a prohibited practice which is negligible.

6.271 The seriousness of the prohibited practice is assessed by reference to the behaviour of the trader, the impact of the practice on the consumer and the time which has elapsed since the prohibited practice took place[1]. However, the CPUTRs provide no further definition of 'more than minor', 'significant', 'serious' or 'very serious' and there are no reported cases to provide guidance. Ultimately, which band a prohibited practice falls within will be a fact sensitive question in each and every case and, in the absence of guidance, the scope for argument on the point is significant.

1   CPUTR 2008, reg 27I(5).

6.272 An exception is provided to the standardised discount bands by reg 27I(6)[1]. This exception was introduced following concerns raised in response to the Law Commissions' consultation that the standardised bands could operate unfairly to both consumers and traders in high value cases where there was clear evidence of the difference between what a consumer had paid and what a product was worth: for example, where the customer paid £20,000 but the product was only worth £12,500 (ie the consumer has suffered a £7,500 loss) the pre-set bands would either award £5,000 or £10,000. To address this potential for injustice, reg 27I(6) provides that if the amount payable for the product under the contract exceeds £5,000[2] and the market price of the product, at the time that the consumer entered into the contract, was lower than the amount payable for it under the contract, the relevant percentage is the percentage difference between the market price of the product and the amount payable for it under the contract. Exercising the right to the discount has no effect on any other rights and liabilities under the contract.

1   The Law Commission and the Scottish Law Commission Joint Report on 'Consumer Redress For Misleading and Aggressive Practices' March 2012 (Law Com No 332; Scot Law Com No 226) at paras 8.131 to 8.134.
2   The Law Commission and the Scottish Law Commission Joint Report on 'Consumer Redress For Misleading and Aggressive Practices' March 2012 (Law Com No 332; Scot Law Com No 226) recommended a threshold of £1,000 albeit they did not wish for a specific figure to be included in the legislation; see para 8.134.

6.273 The drafting of reg 27I(6) is, unfortunately, ambiguous. Is the 'relevant percentage' the percentage by which the contract price exceeds the market price or is it the percentage by which the market price is lower than the contract price? In the former construction, the example in **6.272** would provide a relevant percentage of 37.5%, whereas the latter construction the example would provide a relevant percentage of 60%. It is suggested that the former construction is to be preferred as it is plain that the legislature's intention in introducing reg 27I(6) was to avoid a result which was unduly harsh to either party as a result of the standardised bands; it cannot, therefore, have been intended that the calculation under reg 27I(6) would be carried out on the latter basis as it could, as in the example above, provide the consumer with a significant windfall and be unduly punitive to the trader[1]. It is also noteworthy that if the second construction were adopted, reg 27I(6) does not sit comfortably with either reg 27I(2) or (3) as the 'relevant percentage' could potentially exceed 100%.

[1]   This accords with the worked example in the BEIS Guidance (available at: https://assets.publishing.service.gov.uk/government/uploads/system/uploads/attachment_data/file/721872/misleading-aggressive-commercial-practices-guidance.pdf). In contrast, the learned editors of *Benjamin's Sale of Goods* (10th edn) suggest that the latter construction should be preferred on the basis that if the former construction had been intended simpler language could have been used (see para 14–298).

The right to damages

6.274 Under reg 27J, a consumer has a right to damages if he or she has:

(a)   incurred financial loss; or
(b)   suffered alarm, distress, physical inconvenience, or discomfort.

6.275 However, it should be noted that 'financial loss' does not include the difference in value between the market price of the product and the amount payable for it under the contract[1]. This directs the damages right at consequential losses and avoids any overlap with the right to a discount under reg 27I such that in appropriate cases, the consumer can claim both. To be recoverable, damages must have been reasonably foreseeable at the time of the prohibited practice[2]. Further, if the trader can show that the prohibited practice occurred as a result of (i) a mistake; (ii) reliance on information provided by another person; (iii) the act or default of another person; (iv) an accident; or (v) another cause beyond the trader's control; and the trader took all reasonable precautions and exercised all due diligence to avoid the occurrence of the prohibited practice, damages will not be recoverable under reg 27J[3].

[1]   CPUTR 2008, reg 27J(3).
[2]   CPUTR 2008, reg 27J(4). Reasonable foreseeability is not further defined in CPUTR and it is submitted that the it will approached in the same was as under the common law for breach of contract.
[3]   CPUTR 2008, reg 27J(5). For a detailed discussion of "due diligence" see CHAPTER 4.

Proceedings

6.276 Under reg 27K, consumers can bring civil proceedings to enforce their rights to unwind, to a discount or to damages. It is suggested that the county court is likely to be the most appropriate forum to bring such an action in England and Wales, and the Sheriff's Court is likely to be the most appropriate forum in Scotland. The limitation period is 6 years[1]. Regulation 27L makes clear that the new rights to redress do not affect existing causes of action which consumers may have in respect of the same conduct save that they cannot claim compensation under a rule of law or equity, or under an enactment, where they have already been compensated under Pt 4A and vice versa[2]. It is suggested that 'compensation' will be interpreted broadly such that a consumer who has obtained a discount under reg 27I is precluded from recovering a contractual loss under the common law to the extent that it overlaps with this discount even though the right to a discount, is not strictly loss based and is partially a form of civil penalty.

[1]   CPUTR 2008, reg 27K(5).
[2]   CPUTR 2008, reg 27L(2).

Summary of redress rights

6.277 The table below provides a summary of redress rights:

Consumer transaction	Right to redress
Business to consumer contract	The right to unwind (reg 27F) The right to a discount (reg 27I) The right to damages (reg 27J)
Consumer to business contract	The right to unwind (reg 27G) The right to damages (reg 27J)
Consumer payment for product within reg 2(1A) and (1B)	The right to unwind (reg 27H) The right to damages (reg 27J)
Consumer payment for any other type of product	The right to damages

TRADER GUARANTEES AND WARRANTIES

6.278 The product guarantees that traders themselves provide to consumers purchasing goods ('trader guarantees') can be of real value to consumers because they will often provide an easy remedy without the need to resort to a legal claim. However, they have also proven to be contentious. This is primarily because traders sometimes treat their time-limited guarantee as the only right that a consumer has when a product is defective or otherwise unsatisfactory. If the trader guarantee has expired many consumers wrongly believe that they have no remaining rights often extending long after a trader's own guarantee period. There has also been concern about the sale of extended warranties that are of poor value and provide little benefit beyond a consumer's existing statutory rights.

6.279 In response to those concerns limited consumer protection is now provided in relation to both trader guarantees and extended warranties for electrical goods. Although it has to be said that neither of these two measures remedy the central problem that, generally, consumers simply do not understand their statutory rights in this area.

Guarantees under CRA 2015, s 30

6.280 The CRA 2015, s 30 implemented Art 6 (Guarantees) of the Sale of Consumer Goods and Associated Guarantees Directive 1999/44/EC (the 'CSD'). It replaces the Sale and Supply of Goods Regulations 2002, which are revoked by CRA 2015[1].

[1]   SI 2002/3045 revoked by CRA 2015, Sch 1, para 53.

6.281 The CRA 2015, s 30 applies to goods[1] that are the subject of a trader's guarantee. Guarantee is defined in the CRA 2015, s 30(2) as:

> (2) "Guarantee" here means an undertaking to the consumer given without extra charge by a person acting in the course of the person's business (the "guarantor") that, if the goods do not meet the specifications set out in the guarantee statement or in any associated advertising—
>
> (a)   the consumer will be reimbursed for the price paid for the goods, or
>
> (b)   the goods will be repaired, replaced or handled in any way.

One crucial point to draw out from the definition, is that section 30 only applies to guarantees provided free of charge. Where a consumer purchases a guarantee or extended warranty from the trader, or a third party, the consumer will benefit from their usual consumer rights in relation to such a purchase and the guarantee or extended warranty may also be subject to regulation by the Financial Conduct Authority[2]. This distinction was the subject of a number of exchanges between MPs and Jenny Willott (the Parliamentary Under-Secretary of State for Business Innovation and Skills) as it passed through the Public Bill Committee[3]; It is clear from those exchanges that a number of MPs struggled to understand the distinction which does not bode well for wider consumer understanding.

[1]   Defined in CRA 2015, s 2 as 'any tangible moveable items, but that includes water, gas and electricity if and only if they are put up for supply in a limited volume or set quantity'. Importantly, s 30 does not extent to guarantees provided in relation to digital content or services.

[2]   Extended guarantees and warrantees can constitute contracts of insurance. See *Re Digital Satellite Warranty Cover Ltd* [2013] 1 WLR 605.

[3]   In particular, Hansard, February 27, 2014.

6.282 The contents of the guarantee and the essential particulars for making claims under it are required to be set out in plain and intelligible language[1]. This must include the name and address of the guarantor and the guarantee's territorial scope[2]. It must state that a consumer has statutory rights in relation to the goods and that those rights are not affected by the guarantee[3]. Finally, it must be written in English if the goods are offered in the UK[4]. If a consumer requests a copy of the guarantee, a trader must, within a reasonable time, make the guarantee available in writing and in a form accessible to the consumer[5].

[1]   CRA 2015, s 30(4)(a).
[2]   CRA 2015, s 30(5).
[3]   CRA 2015, s 30(4)(b).
[4]   CRA 2015, s 30(4)(c).
[5]   CRA 2015, s 30(6). What is a reasonable time, is a question of fact, CRA 2015, s 30(7).

6.283 A guarantee which falls withing s 30 CRA 2015, takes effect, at the time the goods are delivered, as a contractual obligation owed by the guarantor to the consumer under the conditions set out in the guarantee statement and any associated advertising[1]. Consequently, if a trader fails to honour its obligations under the guarantee, the consumer can bring a breach of contract claim.

[1]   CRA 2015, s 30(3).

6.284 In addition to consumers bringing breach of contract claims against traders, the CMA, or a local weights and measures authority in Great Britain and the Department of Enterprise, Trade and Investment in Northern Ireland can apply to the High Court (or Court of Session as appropriate) for injunctive relief (specific implement in Scotland)[1].

¹   CRA 2015, s 30(8)–(10).

Extended warranties on electrical goods

6.285 The Supply of Extended Warranties on Domestic Electrical Goods Order 2005[1] (the '2005 Order') was introduced following an OFT report[2] about the lack of competition in the sale by retailers of extended warranties on electrical appliances. It was reported that there were few warranty providers other than large electrical retailers that took advantage of a near monopoly and their 'point of sale advantage'. The OFT also concluded that consumers did not shop around, warranties were often not good value and some retailers provided insufficient information unfairly emphasised the potential for goods to develop faults.

¹   SI 2005/37 made under the Fair Trading Act 1973.
²   OFT July 2002, Extended Warranties on Domestic Electrical Goods. See also the Competition Commission Report on the supply of extended warranties on domestic electrical goods within the UK (Cm 6089) (2003).

6.286 The 2005 Order applies only to domestic electrical goods, defined as 'a product designed to be connected to an electricity supply or powered by batteries and used for domestic purposes, but does not include watches, jewellery or fixed installations (other than integrated appliances)'[1]. It does not apply to distance sales or off-premises contracts under the CCR 2013[2].

¹   SI 2005/37, art 1(3).
²   SI 2005/37, art 2 as amended by the CCR 2013, Sch 4, para 5.

6.287 The provider of an extended warranty to a consumer has the obligation to display its price and duration in a manner that is clear, legible and makes clear that its purchase is optional[1]. Subject to limited exceptions[2], a provider must also provide a written quotation for the extended warranty upon the consumer's request[3]or, in any case, where the extended warranty is purchased at the same time, or immediately subsequent to, the purchase of the electrical goods[4]. The written quotation must include: the price and duration of the extended warranty; a statement that the extended warranty can be purchased at the price quoted for a period of 30 days beginning on the day the quote is issued; a statement that extended warranties may be available from other persons; a statement that the extended warranty does not have to be purchased at the same time as the electrical goods to which it relates; the consumer's cancellation and termination rights pursuant to art 8 (see below); and an explanation of whether or not the extended warranty will be terminated in the event of a claim being made[5]. There are further consumer information obligations in relation to advertising[6].

¹   SI 2005/37, art 3(1)(a).
²   SI 2005/37, art 3(3).
³   A consumer request must be made at the time, or immediately subsequent to, the sale of the related electrical goods.
⁴   SI 2005/37, art 3(1)(c).
⁵   SI 2005/37, art 3(4).
⁶   SI 2005/37, arts 4–6.

6.288 The 2005 Order seeks to alleviate the pressure placed on consumers at the point of sale by giving them 30 days to decide whether they will accept the offer of an extended warranty. It is now unlawful for a provider only to offer the warranty at the point of sale so that a consumer has to make the decision immediately[1]. The 2005 Order also gives consumers the right to cancel an extended warranty during the first 45 days after its purchase[2]. After that time, the consumer continues to have the right to cancel the warranty throughout the period it covers and to receive a pro rata refund[3]. The provider must also inform the consumer of these cancellation and termination rights, in writing, at least 20 days before the 45-day period expires[4]. The CMA is given power to direct providers in relation to compliance with the 2005 Order[5]. If a trader provides inaccurate information, an affected consumer may also be able to bring a civil action for misrepresentation or Pt 4A CPUTR 2008.

[1]   SI 2005/37, art 7.
[2]   SI 2005/37, art 8(1)(a) as long as a claim has not been made under the extended warranty.
[3]   SI 2005/37, art 8(1)(b) regardless of whether a valid claim has been made under the extended warranty.
[4]   SI 2005/37, art 8(1)(c).
[5]   SI 2005/37, art 10.

Limitation and trader guarantees

6.289 It is important to understand that the period for which a trader guarantees goods does not limit the consumer's other rights, which will often allow for claims beyond the trader's own guarantee period.

6.290 In England and Wales[1] the limitation periods for civil litigation are primarily set by the Limitation Act 1980 ('LA 1980'). The supply of a defective or unsatisfactory product to a consumer is likely to make a trader liable for breach of contract[2] in a civil claim, ordinarily as a result of a breach of express terms or the terms implied by Pt 1 of the CRA 2015.

[1]   LA 1980, s 41(4).
[2]   It may also generate other liability, for example in the tort of negligence.

6.291 Under the LA 1980, s 5 an action in contract[1] 'shall not be brought after the expiration of 6 years from the date on which the cause of action accrued'. In a simple[2] sale of goods case the cause of action is likely to accrue at the time the product is delivered to, or obtained by, the consumer[3]. Although this may be extended when there has been fraud, concealment or mistake for the purpose of the LA 1980, s 32. It follows that a consumer could conceivably bring a civil claim in contract against a trader if a product becomes defective or unsatisfactory during the 6 years following its delivery. The success of such a claim will depend upon whether there has in fact been a breach of the implied statutory terms and will often turn on whether or not the consumer can adduce evidence that the defect was present at the time of delivery[4]. As will be apparent from the discussion above, this right may well endure far longer than any guarantee or warranty provided by the trader.

[1]   The Latent Damage Act 1980 is unlikely to apply to actions in contract, *Iron Trades Mutual Assurance v JK Buckenham* [1990] 1 All ER 808.
[2]   Caution should be adopted before applying this limitation period in relation to modern transactions, particularly where products are updated after their delivery.
[3]   *Battley v Faulkner* (1820) 3 B & Ald 288, applied in *Lynn v Bamber* [1930] 2 KB 72 at 74.

⁴ See the discussion at **6.192** above for the position in the first six months.

RIGHT TO USE UNSOLICITED GOODS

Introduction

6.292 There has been legislation in the UK concerning unsolicited goods for over 50 years[1]. These measures were designed to combat an unwelcome growth in the practice of 'inertia selling', which involved unsolicited goods being sent to consumers on a speculative basis. Typically, goods would be sent to a random consumer as an offer, with an option to return the goods within a specified period, or failing that an obligation to pay for them. A consumer who did neither would frequently be subjected to demands for payment and threats of legal action.

[1] Unsolicited Goods and Services Act 1971.

Inertia selling

6.293 The prohibition on unsolicited goods is now contained within the list of banned practices in Sch 1 to the CPUTR 2008. The banned practices are dealt with in detail in CHAPTER 8, Unfair Commercial Practices. Paragraph 29 of the Schedule bans inertia selling and applies when a trader demands from a consumer 'immediate or deferred payment for or the return or safekeeping of products supplied by the trader, but not solicited by the consumer'. 'Product' is defined broadly in reg 2 of CPUTR 2008 and includes both goods and services. 'Unsolicited' is not defined in CPUTR 2008, however, it is likely to be construed to mean 'sent or supplied without any prior request made by or on behalf of the recipient', as it was in the Unsolicited Goods and Services Act 1971[1].

[1] Unsolicited Goods and Services Act 1971, s 25(6) (now repealed).

6.294 The provisions in CPUTR 2008 have now been amended by CCR 2013, as a consequence of the CRD. CPUTR 2008, reg 27M[1] now makes further provision in relation to inertia selling.

27M Inertia selling

(1) This regulation applies where a trader engages in the unfair commercial practice described in paragraph 29 of Schedule 1 (inertia selling).

(2) The consumer is exempted from any obligation to provide consideration for the products supplied by the trader.

(3) The absence of a response from the consumer following the supply does not constitute consent to the provision of consideration for, or the return or safekeeping of, the products.

(4) In the case of an unsolicited supply of goods, the consumer may, as between the consumer and the trader, use, deal with or dispose of the goods as if they were an unconditional gift to the consumer.

[1] Previously reg 27A prior to the introduction of the Pt 4A redress measures, upon which it was renumbered to reg 27M.

6.295 The legal effect of this provision is to transfer property in the unsolicited products to a consumer as a gift. The consumer is under no obligation to pay for the goods and may use or dispose of the goods as if the consumer owned them.

It would appear that the right can be exercised by the consumer from the point at which the trader makes a demand for payment, demands the return of goods or demands that a consumer keeps goods safe.

6.296 The drafting of these provisions does not have the clarity of the previous domestic legislation. There appears to be no clear distinction between a trader acting deliberately, taking advantage of consumers, and a trader who sends goods to a consumer mistakenly and merely demands that the consumer returns them or keeps them safe.

ALTERNATIVE AND ONLINE DISPUTE RESOLUTION

Alternative dispute resolution

6.297 Alternative dispute resolution ('ADR') is a method of resolving disputes between consumers and traders that avoids going to court. The common forms of ADR are mediation or conciliation and adjudication or arbitration. Conciliation or mediation involves an independent third party helping the disputing parties to come to a mutually acceptable outcome, a mediator is likely to take a more active role in bringing the two parties together. Adjudication or arbitration is where an independent third party considers the facts and takes a decision that is often binding on one or both parties. In recent years, there has also been a growing prevalence of Early Neutral Evaluations, sometimes referred to as pre-trial settlement hearings, under CPR 3.1(2)(m); this usually involves a judge with suitable expertise expressing an opinion about a dispute or an element of it, The judge's opinion is non-binding will often assist in settlement. Early Neutral Evaluations are most common in family and commercial cases but there is an increasing number occurring in relation to multi-track claims in the county courts, including in relation to consumer disputes[1].

[1]   The judge who conducts the Early Neutral Evaluation will then have no further involvement in the proceedings.

6.298 The Alternative Dispute Resolution Directive (2013/11/EU) (the 'ADR Directive') was implemented[1] in the UK by the Alternative Dispute Resolution for Consumer Disputes (Competent Authorities and Information) Regulations 2015 (the 'ADR Regulations')[2]. The ADR Regulations came fully into force on 1 October 2015 and apply to disputes relating to contracts entered into on, or after, 9 July 2015; they remain in force. The aim of the ADR Directive is set out in Art 1 as:

> 'ensuring that consumers can, on a voluntary basis, submit complaints against traders to entities offering independent, impartial, transparent, effective, fast and fair alternative dispute resolution procedures.'

[1]   Member States were required to implement the requirements of the ADR Directive into national law by 9 July 2015.
[2]   SI 2015/542, as amended by the Alternative Dispute Resolution for Consumer Disputes (Amendment) Regulations 2015, SI 2015/1392. Further amendments are due to be introduced on 31 December 2020 by the Consumer Protections (Amendment etc.) (EU Exit) Regulations 2018, SI 2018/1326 to reflect the end of the transition period. Many of the amendments are mechanical and, for example, substitute 'Secretary of State' in place of 'European Commission' however there are a number of substantive changes, including but not limited to, the removal of

'cross border disputes' from the scope of many provisions and the removal of regs 8A and 19A which require the competent authority and traders to provide information to consumers on the European ODR platform. Unless an agreement is reached, the UK will not have access to the ODR platform from 31 December 2020.

6.299 Regulation 19 of the ADR Regulations requires traders to provide information to consumers where the trader is obliged to use ADR services by any enactment or the rules of a trade association. In those circumstances the trader must provide the name and website address of the ADR entity on his website and his general terms and conditions. Regulation 19(2):

(2) Where a trader has exhausted its internal complaint handling procedure when considering a complaint from a consumer relating to a sales contract or a service contract, the trader must inform the consumer, on a durable medium—

(a) that the trader cannot settle the complaint with the consumer;
(b) of the name and website address of an ADR entity which would be competent to deal with the complaint, should the consumer wish to use alternative dispute resolution; and
(c) whether the trader is obliged, or prepared, to submit to an alternative dispute resolution procedure operated by that ADR entity.

6.300 Regulation 19(2) is the key requirement for a business selling to consumers, that does not belong to a professional body or trade association that obliges them to use and accept the rulings of an ADR scheme. These unattached businesses must simply tell the consumer that they cannot settle their complaint, give them the name of an ADR scheme (which they may or may not be signed up to) and tell the consumer whether they are prepared to submit to the ADR procedure themselves. Breaches of these information are enforceable as Community infringements under Pt 8 of the Enterprise Act 2002[1] (see CHAPTER 5, Civil Enforcement)[2].

[1] SI 2015/542, reg 20 amending the Enterprise Act 2002, Sch 13.
[2] Although note the amendments to Pt 8 due to be made by the Consumer Protection (Enforcement) (Amendment etc.) (EU Exit) Regulations 2019, SI 2019/203 on 31 December 2020 to reflect the end of the transition period. The concept of 'community infringement' will be no more but the power to take enforcement action under Pt 8 will be retained.

6.301 The Chartered Trading Standards Institute ('CTSI') has been appointed to carry out the function of approving ADR entities along with the relevant competent authorities for the regulated sectors – energy, transport, financial services, legal, and communications. At end of August 2021 there were 59 UK certified ADR bodies ranging from some sector specific bodies to some general ADR schemes.

Online dispute resolution

6.302 The EU Regulation on online dispute resolution for consumer disputes (524/2013) (the 'ODR Regulation') came into force[1] on 15 February 2016. The ODR Regulation obliged the EU Commission to establish an online dispute resolution ('ODR') platform for online cross-border disputes. This was designed to facilitate ADR for disputes between consumers and traders in different Member States using a certified ADR provider[2]. Since 1 January 2021, UK consumers have no longer have access to the EU ODR Platform.

[1] Although the requirements relating to the creation of an ODR contact point applied on 9 July 2015.
[2] EU Implementing Regulation 2015/1051 relating to the ODR Platform was published in the Official Journal on 2 July 2015.

Modernising Consumer Markets – Consumer Green Paper

6.303 In April 2018, the Government published their Green Paper. Part of this considered the improvement of enforcement of consumer rights[1]. The Green Paper expressed the view that the system of ADR could be more effective. Take-up was low and awareness was far greater for the statutory schemes, such as the Financial Ombudsman Service (59% awareness), than it was outside the regulated market where 84% of consumers had not heard of the term 'alternative dispute resolution'. In addition, consumers who use ADR tended to be older, more educated and earn more than the average consumer. Research also suggested that the quality of service offered by ADR providers needed to improve.

[1] See CHAPTER 5.

6.304 The Green Paper posed four questions:

- How can we improve consumer awareness and take-up of alternative dispute resolution?
- What model of alternative dispute resolution provision would deliver the best experience for consumers?
- How could we incentivise more businesses to participate in alternative dispute resolution?
- Should there be an automatic right for consumers to access alternative dispute resolution in sectors with the highest levels of consumer harm?[1]

The consultation closed on 4 July.

[1] Second hand cars and home improvements were the two areas identified.

6.305 Despite indications that a White Paper would be forthcoming for the last 18 months, no such paper has materialised. It remains to be seen what, if any, plans the current Government have to reform consumer ADR or any other area of consumer law.

THE PROVISION OF SERVICES REGULATIONS 2009

Purpose and scope

6.306 The Provision of Services Regulations 2009[1] ('POSR 2009') came into force on 28 December 2009, implementing the EU Services Directive[2]. The aim of the Directive is to further open the internal market for services, allowing service providers to trade across the EU without unjustifiable barriers to doing so. The POSR 2009 were amended by the Provision of Services (Amendment etc.) (EU Exit) Regulations 2018[3] on 31 December 2020; the amendments were largely mechanical and, for example, involved inserting references to retained EU Law and limiting the jurisdictional scope of the Regulations to the UK[4].

[1]   SI 2009/2999.
[2]   2006/123/EC.
[3]   SI 2018/1329, not yet in force.
[4]   See the proposed amendment to POSR 2009, reg 5(3).

6.307 Part 2 of the POSR 2009 places duties on service providers regarding the information that they must provide and how they must deal with complaints.

6.308 POSR 2009 applies to providers of a 'service', which is defined as, 'any self-employed economic activity normally provided for remuneration'[1]. POSR 2009 is not confined to consumer protection and applies to any 'recipients' of a regulated service. A 'recipient' is defined as a professional or non-professional person who uses or wishes to use the service[2]. It is therefore important, when considering the requirements of the regulations, to remember that this covers both actual and potential customers, as well as trade and consumer recipients. Breaches of the POSR 2009 are enforceable under Pt 8 of the Enterprise Act 2002 (see CHAPTER 5, Civil Enforcement).

[1]   SI 2009/2999, reg 2(1).
[2]   SI 2009/2999, reg 4.

6.309 The POSR 2009 covers all service providers, unless they fall within the exemptions in reg 2(2) which are listed in the table below.

Regulation	Description	Exception
2(2)(a)	Financial services	Such as banking, credit, insurance and re-insurance, occupational or personal pensions, securities, investment funds, payments and investment advice, including the services listed in Annex 1 to Directive 2006/48/EC[1]
2(2)(b)	Electronic communication services and networks	Including associated facilities and services covered by: Directive 2002/19/EC[2] Directive 2002/20/EC[3] Directive 2002/21/EC[4] Directive 2002/22/EC[5] Directive 2002/58/EC[6]
2(2)(c)	Transport services	Services in the field of transport, including port services
2(2)(d)	Temporary work agencies	Services of temporary work agencies, which includes any employment business as defined in s 13(3) of the Employment Agencies Act 1973
2(2)(e)	Healthcare services	Healthcare services, whether or not they are provided via healthcare facilities and regardless of the ways in which they are organised and financed at national level or whether they are public or private

Regulation	Description	Exception
2(2)(f)	Audiovisual services	Including cinematographic services, whatever their mode of production, distribution and transmission, and radio broadcasting
2(2)(g)	Gambling activities	Activities which involve wagering a stake with pecuniary value in games of chance, including lotteries, gambling in casinos and betting transactions
2(2)(h)	Official authority	Activities which are connected with the exercise of official authority
2(2)(i)	Social services	Relating to social housing, childcare and support of families and persons permanently or temporarily in need which are provided by the State, by providers mandated by the State or by charities recognised as such by the State
2(2)(j)	Private security services	Private security services
2(2)(k)	Notaries of bailiffs	Services provided by notaries or bailiff, if or to the extent that they are appointed by an official act of government to provide those services

1   Relating to the taking up and pursuit of the business of credit institutions.
2   Access to, and interconnection of, electronic communications networks and associated facilities.
3   The authorisation of electronic communications networks and services.
4   A common regulatory framework for electronic communications networks and services.
5   Universal service and users' rights relating to electronic communications networks and services.
6   Processing of personal data and the protection of privacy in the electronic communications sector.

Duty to provide information

6.310 The POSR 2009 set down a number of information requirements (discussed below in **6.312–6.315**). The required information must be provided before the service is provided[1]. It is to be noted that there is some duplication of the information required by POSR 2009 with other legislation such as CCR 2013 and the ADR Regulations.

1   SI 2009/2999, reg 11.

Duty to make contact details available

6.311 Service providers must make their contact details available to enable all recipients of their service to contact them regarding a complaint or to request information regarding their service[1].

The contact details must include:

(a)   a postal address, fax number or e-mail address;
(b)   a telephone number; and
(c)   where the service provider has an official address, that address[2].

Regulation 7 is silent upon how this information should be provided, but guidance provided by BIS[3], suggests that one of the methods listed in reg 8, discussed below, could be used.

1　SI 2009/2999, reg 7(1).
2　An address which a person is required by law to register, notify or maintain for the purpose of receiving notices or other communications; SI 2009/2999, reg 7(3).
3　BIS 'Guidance for Business on the Provision of Services Regulations', October 2009.

Other information to be made available

6.312 Regulation 8(1) of the POSR 2009 provides:

(1)　The provider of a service must make the following information available to a recipient of the service—

(a)　the provider's name;

(b)　the provider's legal status and form;

(c)　the geographic address at which the provider is established and details by which the provider may be contacted rapidly and communicated with directly (including, where the provider may be contacted and communicated with by electronic means, the details of how the provider may be so contacted and communicated with);

(d)　where the provider is registered in a trade or other similar public register, the name of the register and the provider's registration number or equivalent means of identification in that register;

(e)　where the activity is subject to an authorisation scheme in the United Kingdom, the particulars of the relevant competent authority or the electronic facility referred to in regulation 38;

(f)　. . .

(g)　where the provider exercises an activity which is subject to VAT, the identification number referred to in Article 22(1) of the Sixth Council Directive 77/88/EEC of 17 May 1977 on the harmonisation of the laws of the member states relating to turnover taxes – Common system of value added tax: uniform basis of assessment or the registration number as defined in regulation 2(1) of the Value Added Tax Regulations 1995;

(h)　where the provider is carrying on a regulated profession, any professional body or similar institution with which the provider is registered and the professional title;

(i)　the general terms and conditions, if any, used by the provider;

(j)　the existence of contractual terms, if any, used by the provider concerning the competent courts or the law applicable to the contract;

(k)　the existence of any after-sales guarantee not imposed by law;

(l)　the price of the service, where a price is pre-determined by the provider for a given type of service;

(m)　the main features of the service, if not already apparent from the context;

(n)　where the provider is subject to a requirement to hold any professional liability insurance or guarantee, information about the insurance or guarantee and in particular—

(i)　the contact details of the insurer or guarantor, and

(ii)　the territorial coverage of the insurance or guarantee.

6.313 This information can be made available by four means:

- supplied at the provider's initiative;

- made easily accessible to the recipient at the place where the service is provided or where the contract for the service is concluded;
- made easily accessible to the recipient electronically by means of an address supplied by the provider;
- including it in any information document (which gives a detailed description of the service) that has been supplied by the provider to the recipient[1].

[1] SI 2009/2999, reg 8(2).

Information to be supplied on request etc.

6.314 Regulation 9 requires additional information to be supplied upon request from a recipient (an actual or potential customer):

- the price of the service, how it will be calculated or a sufficiently detailed estimate – unless the price of the service is pre-determined;
- if a regulated professional – the rules applicable to the profession and how they can be accessed;
- information about other activities undertaken by the provider, which are directly linked to the service in question, and the measures taken to avoid any conflict of interest;
- any codes of conduct that the provider is subject to and an electronic link to access these.

The information regarding other related activities and how conflicts of interest are avoided must be given in any documents that the provide supplies which contain a detailed description of the service.

Information about dispute resolution

6.315 Service providers who are subject of a code of conduct, trade association or professional body that provides access to an ADR procedure must inform the recipient of this and how to access it. They must also mention this in any information document that gives a detailed description of the service[1]. This requirement is now also found in the ADR Regulations (see above).

[1] SI 2009/2999, reg 10.

Complaints

6.316 Regulation 12 requires service providers to respond to complaints, from recipients of their service, as quickly as possible and to make their best efforts to find a satisfactory solution (unless the complaint is vexatious).

ELECTRONIC COMMERCE

Introduction

6.317 Consumer goods and services are increasingly sold online, often through online platforms such as Amazon, Alibaba and Etsy, with the Covid-19 pandemic cementing the trend. According to the European Commission, online platforms are the most accessed websites in the world, with electronic commerce platforms, search engines and social media receiving the most visits[1].

[1] EC: Commission staff working document: Online Platforms (SWD (2016) 172 final), 25 May 2016. In the UK, 76% of internet users report using a search engine every day or almost every day, half of UK internet users visit a social network site each day, and more than a sixth visit an online marketplace on a daily basis: see TNS opinion and social survey at the request of the European Commission, Special Eurobarometer 447 Report – Online Platforms, April 2016.

6.318 The application of consumer law to goods and services sold through proprietary websites (ie websites operated by the traders supplying the products in question) is relatively straightforward. Such traders are, for instance, required to comply with the pre-contractual requirements in the CCRs and to provide remedies in accordance with the CRA should anything go wrong.

6.319 When it comes to sales through online intermediaries, such as online platforms, however, the position is less straightforward, not least because consumers are often unaware of the underlying contractual relationships. It has been pointed out elsewhere that consumer law is generally premised on a bilateral contractual relationship, whilst transactions that take place through online platform tend to be tripartite, with one contract governing the relationship between the seller and the platform and another governing the relationship between the seller and the consumer[1]. To complicate matters further, there is typically a contractual relationship between the platform and the consumer in respect of the consumer's use of the platform.

[1] See, for instance, Busch et al 'The Rise of the Platform Economy: A New Challenge for EU Consumer Law' 5 (2016) *Journal of European Consumer and Market Law* 3.

6.320 The liability of online intermediaries is governed by Directive 2000/31/EC ('the **E-Commerce Directive**'), which is implemented domestically by the Electronic Commerce (EC Directive) Regulations 2002 ('the **ECRs**'). The ECRs provide for so-called 'safe harbours', or liability exemptions, in respect of third party content, such as advertisements uploaded on online marketplaces by traders.

6.321 In addition, the ECRs impose specific obligations on providers of 'information society services' ('**service providers**'). In particular, service providers are required to supply users with specified information, which, in the consumer context, complement the specific pre-contractual information requirements contained in sectoral consumer measures. In addition to the specific sanctions provided for in the ECRs, the failure to provide specified information to a consumer may constitute a misleading omission under CPUTR.

The e-commerce directive

Information society services

6.322 The ECRs apply to 'information society services', a term that is defined in the ECRs (and in the E-Commerce Directive) by reference to Directive (EU) 2015/1535 ('the Technical Standards Directive')[1]. That Directive, in turn, refers to 'any service normally provided for remuneration, at a distance, by electronic means and at the individual request of a recipient of services'[2]. This covers a wide range of economic activities, including the sale of goods online and online advertising.

1 The E-Commerce Directive and the ECRs refer to Directive 98/34/EC of the European Parliament and of the Council of 22 June 1998 laying down a procedure for the provision of information in the field of technical standards and regulations, as amended by Directive 98/48/EC of 20 July 1998, which was repealed and replaced by Directive (EU) 2015/1535 of the European Parliament and of the Council of 9 September 2015 laying down a procedure for the provision of information in the field of technical regulations and of rules on Information Society services. Article 10 of Directive 2015/1535 confirms that '[r]eferences to the repealed Directive shall be construed as references to [Directive 2015/1535]'.

2 Article 1(2). Directive 98/34/EC also defines each of 'at a distance', 'by electronic means' and 'at the individual request of a recipient of services'.

Information society services

6.323 It is suggested that this concept is broad and is unlikely to require direct payment to be made by the recipient of the service. This interpretation finds support in Recital 18 to the E-Commerce Directive, which states:

'[I]nformation society services are not solely restricted to services giving rise to on-line contracting but also, in so far as they represent an economic activity, extend to services which are not remunerated by those who receive them, such as those offering on-line information or commercial communications, or those providing tools allowing for search, access and retrieval of data.'

6.324 Accordingly, search engines[1], online marketplaces[2], social networks and websites are likely to fall within the definition of information society services, even though the end user is not directly charged for the service[3]. Such services will usually be supported by advertising, sponsorship or other commercial arrangements, thereby bringing them within the definition[4].

1 See, for instance, *Metropolitan International Schools Ltd v Designtechnica Corporation* [2009] EWHC 1765 (QB), where Eady J stated at paras 81–84 that if the phrase 'for remuneration' stood alone, it would imply that the recipient was directly paying for it, but that, given the context, 'on balance' Recital 18 of the Directive indicated that services financed by advertising were covered. It followed, notwithstanding that it did not charge the user directly for its services but instead derived its revenue from advertising, that an internet search engine was an internet society service for the purposes of the ECRs. See also *Davison v Habeeb* [2012] 3 CMLR 6 at para 54: 'The test is whether the service is normally provided for remuneration, which in the circumstances must mean remuneration either from the recipient of the service or from a third party' and *Bunt v Tilley* [2006] EWHC 407 (QB) at para 41.

2 In *McGrath v Dawkins* [2012] EWHC B3 (QB), Amazon was held to be an internet society service for the purposes of the ECRs at para 38.

3 In Case C-291/13, *Sotiris Papasavvas v O Fileleftheros Dimosia Etaireia Ltd* the CJEU clarified that the concept includes a service provided by a provider who is remunerated by advertising income, even though access to the website is free.

4 See, for instance, *Interflora Inc v Marks and Spencer plc* [2009] RPC 22, 808 (Arnold J), where it was assumed that the operator of the website in question was a provider of information society services. Similarly, see *Mulvaney v Sporting Exchange (t/a as Betfair)* [2009] IEHC 133 and Case C-324/09 *L'Oréal SA v eBay International AG* [2012] Bus LR 1369.

At a distance

6.325 The term 'at a distance' is defined in the Technical Standards Directive as 'the service [being] provided without the parties being simultaneously present'[1]. Annex I of the Technical Standards Directive proceeds to provide an indicative list of services not provided at a distance:

Services provided in the physical presence of the provider and the recipient, even if they involve the use of electronic devices:

(a) medical examinations or treatment at a doctor's surgery using electronic equipment where the patient is physically present;

(b) consultation of an electronic catalogue in a shop with the customer on site;

(c) plane ticket reservation at a travel agency in the physical presence of the customer by means of a network of computers;

(d) electronic games made available in a video arcade where the customer is physically present.

[1] Article 1(1)(b)(i).

By electronic means

6.326 The Technical Standards Directive defines 'by electronic means' as 'the service [being] sent initially and received at its destination by means of electronic equipment for the processing (including digital compression) and storage of data, and entirely transmitted, conveyed and received by wire, by radio, by optical means or by other electromagnetic means'.

6.327 The Technical Standards Directive's indicative list of services not provided by electronic means includes the following examples:

— services having material content even though provided via electronic devices:

(a) automatic cash or ticket dispensing machines (banknotes, rail tickets);

(b) access to road networks, car parks, etc., charging for use, even if there are electronic devices at the entrance/exit controlling access and/or ensuring correct payment is made,

— offline services: distribution of CD-ROMs or software on diskettes,

— services which are not provided via electronic processing/inventory systems:

(a) voice telephony services;

(b) telefax/telex services;

(c) services provided via voice telephony or fax;

(d) telephone/telefax consultation of a doctor;

(e) telephone/telefax consultation of a lawyer;

(f) telephone/telefax direct marketing.

6.328 Accordingly, the focus is on the means through which the service is provided. If the means of provision is predominantly physical (eg cash from an ATM), it will be immaterial that the service is supported by electronic infrastructure.

6.329 It may not always be easy to distinguish between the different activities involved in provision of the service. For instance, the sale of goods online is a typical example of a service falling within the definition, whilst delivery of the goods is understood to fall outside it[1].

[1] For a discussion of the distinction in the e-commerce context, see Case C-108/09 *Ker-Optica v ÀNTSZ Dél-dunántúli Regionális Intézete* [2011] 2 CMLR 15, paras 37–39.

Country of origin principle and territorial scope

6.330 Article 3 of the E-Commerce Directive established the digital single market:

(1)   Each Member State shall ensure that the information society services provided by a service provider established on its territory comply with the national provisions applicable in the Member State in question which fall within the coordinated field.

(2)   Member States may not, for reasons falling within the coordinated field, restrict the freedom to provide information society services from another Member State.

Territorial scope

6.331 Article 3(1) makes it clear that the E-Commerce Directive does not apply to service providers established in a third country (ie outside the EEA)[1]. The method for determining a provider's place of establishment is set out in recital 19, which provides:

'The place at which a service provider is established should be determined in conformity with the case-law of the Court of Justice according to which the concept of establishment involves the actual pursuit of an economic activity through a fixed establishment for an indefinite period; this requirement is also fulfilled where a company is constituted for a given period; the place of establishment of a company providing services via an Internet website is not the place at which the technology supporting its website is located or the place at which its website is accessible but the place where it pursues its economic activity; in cases where a provider has several places of establishment it is important to determine from which place of establishment the service concerned is provided; in cases where it is difficult to determine from which of several places of establishment a given service is provided, this is the place where the provider has the centre of his activities relating to this particular service.'

Accordingly, in determining a service provider's place of establishment, the focus is on the centre of the provider's economic activity. This requires a consideration of where the provider carries on its trade, concludes and performs contracts for services, and targets its advertising and offers at consumers[2].

[1]   See also recital 58.
[2]   Jaani Riordan, *The Liability of Internet Intermediaries*, OUP 2016, para 12.18.

Country of origin

6.332 Pursuant to the so-called 'country of origin' principle a service provider established in one EU Member State is permitted to provide services in all other EU Member States. In doing so, it need only comply with the laws of the EU Member State in which it is established.

6.333 The country of origin principle is given effect through regulation 4 of the E-Commerce Regulations. Online service providers established in the UK are required to comply with UK law whether the service they provide is in the UK or elsewhere in the EU[1]. Regulation 4(3), in turn, disapplies UK law in respect of online service providers established in the EU (unless the requirement imposed by UK authorities concerns the protection of public health or consumer interests, as established by EU law).

[1]   Regulation 4(1). Regulation 4(2) requires enforcement authorities in the UK to secure compliance with the relevant requirements.

6.334 The country of origin principle applies to national legal requirements that fall within 'the coordinated field', defined in reg 2(1) as:

> requirements applicable to information society service providers or information society services, regardless of whether they are of a general nature or specifically designed for them, and covers requirements with which the service provider has to comply in respect of—
>
> (a)   the taking up of the activity of an information society service, such as requirements concerning qualifications, authorisation or notification, and
> (b)   the pursuit of the activity of an information society service, such as requirements concerning the behaviour of the service provider, requirements regarding the quality or content of the service including those applicable to advertising and contracts, or requirements concerning the liability of the service provider,
>
> but does not cover requirements such as those applicable to goods as such, to the delivery of goods or to services not provided by electronic means.

6.335 In other words, 'the coordinated field' refers to legal requirements that apply to service providers, regardless of whether these specifically target information society services or are of a general nature[1]. The definition also makes it clear that the country of origin principle does not apply in relation to, for instance, product liability rules[2].

[1]   See Department of Trade and Industry, A Guide for Business to the Electronic Commerce (EC Directive) Regulations 2002 (SI 2002/2013) ('**the DTI Guidance**'), para 2.7.
[2]   See also Recital 21.

6.336 Moreover, the country of origin principle does not apply to the fields set out in the Schedule to the E-Commerce Regulations[1]. These include 'contractual obligations concerning consumer contracts'[2] and 'the permissibility of unsolicited commercial communications by electronic mail'[3].

[1]   Paragraph 4(4).
[2]   Paragraph 3 of the Schedule.
[3]   Paragraph 5 of the Schedule.

6.337 In addition to these carveouts, derogations from the country of origin principle are set out in reg 5, which permits enforcement authorities to restrict the provision of information society services into the UK from elsewhere in the EU, where such measures are necessary for one of the objectives listed in regulation 5 and are proportionate. One such objective is the protection of consumers[1]. In taking any enforcement measures, the enforcement authority will, however, be required to comply with the procedural requirements detailed in reg 5.

[1]   Regulation 5(1)(d).

Interaction with other consumer protection measures

6.338 The E-Commerce Directive makes it clear that it is 'without prejudice' to EU measures for the protection of public health and consumers. Article 1(3) provides:

'3. This Directive complements Community law applicable to information society services without prejudice to the level of protection for, in particular, public health and consumer interests, as established by Community acts and national legislation implementing them in so far as this does not restrict the freedom to provide information society services.'

6.339 Recital 11 provides a long list of EU measures that the E-Commerce Directive is said to be without prejudice to:

'This Directive is without prejudice to the level of protection for, in particular, public health and consumer interests, as established by Community acts; amongst others, Council Directive 93/13/EEC of 5 April 1993 on unfair terms in consumer contracts(5) and Directive 97/7/EC of the European Parliament and of the Council of 20 May 1997 on the protection of consumers in respect of distance contracts(6) form a vital element for protecting consumers in contractual matters; those Directives also apply in their entirety to information society services; that same Community acquis, which is fully applicable to information society services, also embraces in particular Council Directive 84/450/EEC of 10 September 1984 concerning misleading and comparative advertising(7), Council Directive 87/102/EEC of 22 December 1986 for the approximation of the laws, regulations and administrative provisions of the Member States concerning consumer credit(8), Council Directive 93/22/EEC of 10 May 1993 on investment services in the securities field(9), Council Directive 90/314/EEC of 13 June 1990 on package travel, package holidays and package tours(10), Directive 98/6/EC of the European Parliament and of the Council of 16 February 1998 on consumer production in the indication of prices of products offered to consumers(11), Council Directive 92/59/EEC of 29 June 1992 on general product safety(12), Directive 94/47/EC of the European Parliament and of the Council of 26 October 1994 on the protection of purchasers in respect of certain aspects on contracts relating to the purchase of the right to use immovable properties on a timeshare basis(13), Directive 98/27/EC of the European Parliament and of the Council of 19 May 1998 on injunctions for the protection of consumers' interests(14), Council Directive 85/374/EEC of 25 July 1985 on the approximation of the laws, regulations and administrative provisions concerning liability for defective products(15), Directive 1999/44/EC of the European Parliament and of the Council of 25 May 1999 on certain aspects of the sale of consumer goods and associated guarantees(16), the future Directive of the European Parliament and of the Council concerning the distance marketing of consumer financial services and Council Directive 92/28/EEC of 31 March 1992 on the advertising of medicinal products(17); this Directive should be without prejudice to Directive 98/43/EC of the European Parliament and of the Council of 6 July 1998 on the approximation of the laws, regulations and administrative provisions of the Member States relating to the advertising and sponsorship of tobacco products(18) adopted within the framework of the internal market, or to directives on the protection of public health; this Directive complements information requirements established by the abovementioned Directives and in particular Directive 97/7/EC.'

6.340 It has been suggested that the E-Commerce Directive is not intended to abrogate liability rules set out in these measures insofar as they apply to information service providers[1]. The safe harbour regime is thus of limited assistance to service providers who flout consumer law, not least because the safe harbours only apply to third-party content. In the context of unfair commercial practices, the Commission Guidance on the UCPD notes as follows [at 2.3]:

'From a UCPD perspective, what is decisive is whether the relevant on-line interme-diary qualifies as a trader and has or not engaged in a business-to-consumer commercial practice directly connected with the promotion, sale or supply of a product to consumers. It is only if that on-line intermediary qualify as a trader and engages in such commercial practices and does so in a manner that is prohibited under the UCPD that it can be found in breach thereof. In this connection the intermediary cannot invoke the liability exemption of Article 14 of the e-Commerce Directive where those practices concern the intermediary's own activities and not the information stored, nor where the intermediary has knowledge of or control over such information.[2]'

[1]   Jaani Riordan, The Liability of Internet Intermediaries, OUP 2016, para 12.27.
[2]   Available here: https://eur-lex.europa.eu/legal-content/EN/TXT/PDF/?uri=CELEX:52016SC01 63&from=EN

6.341 Moreover, the Commission Guidance on the UCPD points out that the safe harbour regime is distinct from traders' professional diligence duties vis-à-vis consumers under the UCPD. It goes on to state at 5.2.2:

'From a UCPD perspective, whenever an online platform can be considered a "trader" in the sense of the UCPD (Article 2(b) UCPD) it is required to act with a degree of professional diligence (Article 5(2) UCPD), commensurate to its specific field of activity (Article 2(h) UCPD) and not to mislead their users/consumers by either action or omission (particularly with reference to Articles 6(1)(f) and 7(1) and (2) UCPD). Platforms which are considered "traders", should take appropriate measures which – without amounting to a general obligation to monitor or carry out fact-finding (see Article 15(1) e-Commerce Directive) – enable relevant third party traders to comply with EU consumer and marketing law requirements and users to clearly understand with whom they are possibly concluding contracts.'

Provision of information

6.342 Regulations 6 to 9 of the ECRs set out information that must be made available by service providers in specified scenarios (eg when an online contract is concluded). These obligations operate alongside the information require-ments in other EU consumer protection measures, such as those in the CCRs. Regulation 10 expressly confirms that the information requirements in regs 6 to 9(1) have effect 'in addition to any other information requirements in legis-lation giving effect to EU law'. The failure to provide the information specified in the ECRs in a service provider's dealings with consumers is likely to constitute a misleading omission under CPUTR.

General information

6.343 Regulation 6 of the ECRs concerns the 'general information' that must be made available by a service provider. It requires service providers to make available to the recipient of the service, and to any relevant enforcement authority, in a form and manner which is "easily, directly and permanently accessible", the following information:

(a)   the name of the service provider;

(b)   the geographic address at which the service provider is established;

(c)   the details of the service provider, including his electronic mail address, which make it possible to contact him rapidly and communicate with him in a direct and effective manner;

(d)   where the service provider is registered in a trade or similar register available to the public, details of the register in which the service provider is entered and his registration number, or equivalent means of identification in that register;

(e)   where the provision of the service is subject to an authorisation scheme, the particulars of the relevant supervisory authority;

(f)   where the service provider exercises a regulated profession—

    (i)   the details of any professional body or similar institution with which the service provider is registered;

    (ii)   his professional title and the member State where that title has been granted;

    (iii)   a reference to the professional rules applicable to the service provider in the member State of establishment and the means to access them; and

(g)   where the service provider undertakes an activity that is subject to value added tax, the identification number referred to in Article 22(1) of the sixth Council Directive 77/388/EEC of 17 May 1977 on the harmonisation of the laws of the member States relating to turnover taxes— Common system of value added tax: uniform basis of assessment.

(h)   Where a person providing an information society service refers to prices, these shall be indicated clearly and unambiguously and, in particular, shall indicate whether they are inclusive of tax and delivery costs.

Commercial communications

6.344 Regulation 7 specifies the conditions that must be met by commercial communications (including promotional offers, such as discounts, premiums and gifts). It states as follows:

> A service provider shall ensure that any commercial communication provided by him and which constitutes or forms part of an information society service shall—
>
> (a)   be clearly identifiable as a commercial communication;
>
> (b)   clearly identify the person on whose behalf the commercial communication is made;
>
> (c)   clearly identify as such any promotional offer (including any discount, premium or gift) and ensure that any conditions which must be met to qualify for it are easily accessible, and presented clearly and unambiguously; and
>
> (d)   clearly identify as such any promotional competition or game and ensure that any conditions for participation are easily accessible and presented clearly and unambiguously.

The requirement in reg 7 is similar to Art 7(2) of the UCPD, which prohibits the failure to identify the commercial intent of a commercial practice, when this failure is likely to cause the average consumer to take a transactional decision he would not have taken otherwise.

Unsolicited commercial communications

6.345 Unsolicited commercial communications are dealt with in reg 8, which provides:

> A service provider shall ensure that any unsolicited commercial communication sent by him by electronic mail is clearly and unambiguously identifiable as such as soon as it is received.

Information to be provided where contracts are concluded by electronic means

6.346 Regulation 9 specifies the information that must be provided where contracts are concluded electronically. It states as follows:

(1)   Unless parties who are not consumers have agreed otherwise, where a contract is to be concluded by electronic means a service provider shall, prior to an order being placed by the recipient of a service, provide to that recipient in a clear, comprehensible and unambiguous manner the information set out in (a) to (d) below—

     (a)   the different technical steps to follow to conclude the contract;
     (b)   whether or not the concluded contract will be filed by the service provider and whether it will be accessible;
     (c)   the technical means for identifying and correcting input errors prior to the placing of the order; and
     (d)   the languages offered for the conclusion of the contract.

(2)   Unless parties who are not consumers have agreed otherwise, a service provider shall indicate which relevant codes of conduct he subscribes to and give information on how those codes can be consulted electronically.

(3)   Where the service provider provides terms and conditions applicable to the contract to the recipient, the service provider shall make them available to him in a way that allows him to store and reproduce them.

(4)   The requirements of paras (1) and (2) above shall not apply to contracts concluded exclusively by exchange of electronic mail or by equivalent individual communications.

Order

6.347 The term 'order' in reg 9(1)(c) means the contractual offer. With regards to the remainder of reg 9, the term 'may be but need not be the contractual offer'[1].

[1] 'See reg 12 of the ECRs.

Contracting out

6.348 The duties imposed on service providers by reg 9 apply for the benefit of all service recipients, but contracting out is permitted only where the service recipient is not a consumer.

Placing of orders

6.349 Orders placed 'through technological means' (eg in an online shopping scenario) are governed by reg 11, which provides:

(1)   Unless parties who are not consumers have agreed otherwise, where the recipient of the service places his order through technological means, a service provider shall–

    (a)   acknowledge receipt of the order to the recipient of the service without undue delay and by electronic means; and

    (b)   make available to the recipient of the service appropriate, effective and accessible technical means allowing him to identify and correct input errors prior to the placing of the order.

(2)   For the purposes of para (1)(a) above—

    (a)   the order and the acknowledgement of receipt will be deemed to be received when the parties to whom they are addressed are able to access them; and

    (b)   the acknowledgement of receipt may take the form of the provision of the service paid for where that service is an information society service.

(3)   The requirements of para (1) above shall not apply to contracts concluded exclusively by exchange of electronic mail or by equivalent individual communications.

Order

6.350 The term 'order' in reg 11(1)(b) means the contractual offer. With regards to the remainder of reg 11, the term 'may be but need not be the contractual offer'[1].

[1]   See reg 12 of the ECRs.

Enforcement of regs 6–8, 9(1) and 11(1)(a)

6.351 The duties imposed on service providers under regs 6–8, 9(1) and 11(1)(a) are enforceable by the recipient of the service in the tort of breach of statutory duty[1].

[1]   Regulation 13.

6.352 Where the service provider fails to make available means that allow a recipient of the service to identify and correct input errors, contrary to reg 11(1)(b), any contract made may be rescinded, unless a court orders otherwise on the application of the service provider[1]. Apart from this, it would appear that the validity of any contract is not affected by a service provider's failure to comply with any of the other regulations. However, such breaches may attract enforcement measures as 'Community infringements' under Pt 8 of the Enterprise Act 2002[2].

[1]   Regulation 15.
[2]   Sections 210(6) and 212 and Sch 13 Pt 1 para 9 of the Enterprise Act 2002.

Conditional liability exemptions

6.353 The ECRs provide three 'safe harbours' or liability exemptions[1], which protect passive and neutral service providers from liability when they transmit, cache or store information supplied by third parties. The liability exemptions are contained in Arts 12-15 of the E-Commerce Directive, recital 42 of which sets out their scope:

> 'The exemptions from liability established in this Directive cover only cases where the activity of the information society service provider is limited to the technical process of operating and giving access to a communication network over which information made available by third parties is transmitted or temporarily stored, for the sole purpose of making the transmission more efficient; this activity is of a mere technical, automatic and passive nature, which implies that the information society service provider has neither knowledge of nor control over the information which is transmitted or stored.'

¹ The question of whether they are properly described as liability exemptions or remedy restrictions is not straightforward: see Jaani Riordan, *The Liability of Internet Intermediaries* (OUP 2016) paras 12.11 to 12.14.

6.354 In addition to the specific liability exemptions, the E-Commerce Directive prohibits the imposition of general monitoring duties, albeit specific monitoring duties may be imposed. It is worth noting that liability exemptions do not preclude injunctive relief.

Mere conduit: transmission

6.355 Regulation 17 applies where an information society service consists of the transmission in a communication network of information provided by a service recipient or the provision of access to a communication network¹. These acts (transmission and provision of access) include 'the automatic, intermediate and transient storage of the information transmitted' where:

(a) this takes place for the sole purpose of carrying out the transmission in the communication network, and

(b) the information is not stored for any period longer than is reasonably necessary for the transmission².

In other words, in order to fall within this exemption, storage must be (i) automatic, (ii) intermediate, (iii) transient, (iv) for the sole purpose of carrying out the transmission; and (v) be for no longer a period than is reasonably necessary for the transmission. This reflects the need for data to be buffered and stored (normally only for milliseconds) in some form for onward transmission.

¹ Regulation 17(1), which transposes Art 12 of the E-Commerce Directive.
² Regulation 17(2). The DTI Guidance provides that the requirement for the storage to be 'automatic' will be met if it occurs through the ordinary operation of the technology. It will be 'intermediate' if it is made in the course of the transmission (para 6.3).

6.356 A service provider who does no more than transmit or provide access in the manner described in reg 17(1) shall not be liable for damages or for any other pecuniary remedy or for any criminal sanction as a result of that transmission where the service provider:

(a) did not initiate the transmission;

(b) did not select the receiver of the transmission; and

(c) did not select or modify the information contained in the transmission.

6.357 These requirements arguably restrict the 'mere conduit' exemption to transmissions that are both passive and temporary; the service provider should have no involvement with the information that is transmitted[1]. The exemption is commonly applied to 'network layer' services (eg suppliers of internet access services) and 'physical layer' services[2]. Certain activities of 'application layer' services (eg online platforms and marketplaces) could be potentially qualify, but most tend to store information beyond the period needed for transmission[3].

[1] Recital 43.
[2] Network layers are abstractions derived from the Open Systems Interconnection model, which describes the underlying architecture of a communications network as a stack comprising seven independent layers that perform distinct technical functions. The physical layer is that which controls units of electrical hardware used in a network node (i.e. the hardware, cables and related equipment which store and transmit data).
[3] For a discussion of the various categories of intermediaries, see Riordan, paras 12.86 to 12.91.

Initiating a transmission

6.358 The DTI Guidance clarifies that initiating a transmission entails making the decision to carry out the transmission; automatically initiating a transmission at the request of the recipient of the service does not mean that the transmission is 'initiated' in this sense[1].

[1] DTI Guidance, para 6.1(a).

Selecting the receiver of the transmission

6.359 Service providers may still rely on the exemption if they select receivers as an automatic response to a request from the person initiating the transmission, for instance if a user requests to have an email forwarded to a mailing-list broker[1].

[1] DTI Guidance, para 6.1(b).

Selecting or modifying the information contained in the transmission

6.360 A service provider is unlikely to lose the protection offered by reg 17 if it applies technical steps that do not alter the integrity of the information[1], such as error checking, the automatic adding of headers, encryption or the automated removal of viruses from emails[2].

[1] Recital 43.
[2] See DTI Guidance, para 6.1(c).

Irrelevance of actual knowledge

6.361 A service provider will still be able to benefit from the exemption if it has actual or constructive knowledge of unlawful third-party activity (in contrast to the caching and hosting safe harbours), provided it is able to demonstrate neutrality[1]. For instance, a service provider acting as a mere conduit will not be liable for failing to take steps to prevent access to another site which it knows to carry defamatory material[2]. Importantly, however, injunctive relief will still be available to an enforcement authority in such circumstances.

[1] Perhaps unsurprisingly, Recital 44 of the Preamble to the E-Commerce Directive clarifies that where an ISP deliberately collaborates with one of the recipients of his service in order to undertake illegal acts goes beyond the activities of a mere conduit, it cannot benefit from the exemption from liability.

Caching

6.362 Regulation 18 transposes Art 13 of the E-Commerce Directive and provides as follows:

> Where an information society service is provided which consists of the transmission in a communication network of information provided by a recipient of the service, the service provider (if he otherwise would) shall not be liable for damages or for any other pecuniary remedy or for any criminal sanction as a result of that transmission where—
>
> (a) the information is the subject of automatic, intermediate and temporary storage where that storage is for the sole purpose of making more efficient onward transmission of the information to other recipients of the service upon their request, and
>
> (b) the service provider—
>> (i) does not modify the information;
>> (ii) complies with conditions on access to the information;
>> (iii) complies with any rules regarding the updating of the information, specified in a manner widely recognised and used by industry;
>> (iv) does not interfere with the lawful use of technology, widely recognised and used by industry, to obtain data on the use of the information; and
>> (v) acts expeditiously to remove or to disable access to the information he has stored upon obtaining actual knowledge of the fact that the information at the initial source of the transmission has been removed from the network, or access to it has been disabled, or that a court or an administrative authority has ordered such removal or disablement.

6.363 Caching involves creating local copies of third parties' data for the purpose of reducing bandwidth utilisation and access times[1]. It has been described as a 'half-way house between mere transmission and "hosting"'[2]. A service provider wishing to benefit from the exemption must satisfy a number of conditions:

(a) Automatic: caching must be undertaken automatically, rather than manually.

(b) Intermediate: the source and the destination of the information being transmitted must be someone other than the service provider.

(c) Temporary: caching must not be permanent (reflecting the normal use of caching as a means to improve performance on a temporary basis).

(d) For the sole purpose of more efficient onward transmission.

(e) Non-modification of cached information: modification is likely to be construed narrowly, allowing for automatic changes to be made to cached data as part of the technical process of storing it[3].3

(f) Compliance with industry caching rules.

(g) Absence of knowledge or acting expeditiously upon acquiring knowledge: these concepts are discussed below, in the context of the hosting liability exemption. According to the DTI Guidance, what is meant by 'acting expeditiously' may vary according to circumstances. The onus is likely to be on the service provider to demonstrate compliance with this requirement. By contrast, the onus will be on the enforcement authorities to demonstrate that a service provider had 'actual knowledge' but failed to act appropriately upon obtaining it[4].

1   *Gatley on Libel and Slander*, at 6.43, summarising *Bunt v Tilley* [2006] EWHC 407 (QB); [2007] 1 WLR 1243 at [52] explains that caching is the storage of information primarily stored on another computer to make retrieval of a web page more efficient.
2   *Gatley on Libel and Slander*, at para 6.43.
3   See Riordan, para 12.104
4   DTI Guidance, paras 6.5 to 6.6.

Hosting

6.364 The hosting safe harbour is the most important of the three and is the most relevant in the context of consumer and regulatory law. It insulates service providers that store information supplied by others[1].

1   An example provided in Gatley, at 6.44, is the storage on a server of a third-party website.

6.365 Regulation 19 provides:

'Where an information society service is provided which consists of the storage of information provided by a recipient of the service, the service provider (if he otherwise would) shall not be liable for damages or for any other pecuniary remedy or for any criminal sanction as a result of that storage where—

(a)   the service provider—
   (i)   does not have actual knowledge of unlawful activity or information and, where a claim for damages is made, is not aware of facts or circumstances from which it would have been apparent to the service provider that the activity or information was unlawful; or
   (ii)   upon obtaining such knowledge or awareness, acts expeditiously to remove or to disable access to the information, and
(b)   the recipient of the service was not acting under the authority or the control of the service provider.'

Storage of third-party content

6.366 The exemption applies to storage of third-party information; it will not insulate a service provider in respect of its own content. The DTI Guidance gives the example of the provision of server space for a website or newsgroup[1]. Activities going beyond storage – such as the creation of content – will not be covered. It is not always easy to draw a line between storage and activities going beyond storage. In reality, application-layer intermediaries (such as platforms and marketplaces) normally go beyond merely recording third party information; they make it accessible and searchable by users by applying technical processes to, for instance, allow access to the information from mobile devices. Some platforms also offer automated content recommendations or identify relevant or related content. It has been suggested that, in so far as such activities are technical and automatic, and are applied neutrally to hosted information, they ought to be treated as examples of storage activity, thereby bringing them within the hosting exemption[2]. However, it is arguable that such an approach does not sit comfortably with CJEU case law on the hosting exemption, as discussed in the next section.

1   DTI Guidance, para 6.7.

2   Riordan, para 12.114.

Technical, automatic and passive

6.367 As the CJEU clarified in the *Google France* case[1], which concerned Google's 'AdWords' service[2], storage must be 'of a mere technical, automatic and passive nature', such that the intermediary is 'neutral' as regards stored data, as opposed to playing an 'active role of such a kind as to give it knowledge of, or control over, the data stored'[3]. The fact that in operating its AdWords service, Google was 'providing general information to its clients', setting the payment terms and accepting payment, did not prevent it from relying on Art 14. However, the role played by Google in drafting the commercial message accompanying the advertising links or in establishing or selecting keywords was deemed to be relevant to the question of neutrality and control[4]. The issue was ultimately left to be resolved by the national court.

1   Joined Cases C-236/08, C-237/08 and C-238/08, *Google France Sarl v Louis Vuitton Malletier SA* [2010] RPC 19, paras 113 to 114 and 120.
2   In addition to its search engine (whereby Google displays the sites which appear best to correspond to words typed in by an internet user, in decreasing order of relevance), Google operates a paid referencing service called 'AdWords'. That service enables economic operators, by reserving one or more keywords, to obtain the placing, in the event of a correspondence between one or more of those words and that/those entered as a request in the search engine by an internet user, of an advertising link to its site, accompanied by a short commercial message.
3   Note that the term 'neutral' appears solely in relation to cashing and transmission in recital 42 of the E-Commerce Directive, thereby suggesting that neutrality was not intended by the legislator to be an element of the hosting defence. Moreover, Art 14(2) and reg 19(b) refer to control over the recipient of the service, not 'control of the data' being stored.
4   According to Riordan, by 'control' the Court meant the content of the underlying data supplied by the recipient of the service (para 12.124).

6.368 In *L'Oréal SA v eBay International*[1], the CJEU clarified that an intermediary that optimises or promotes certain offers for sale may not be neutral[2], at least insofar as the promoted or optimised content is concerned.

1   Case C-324/09 [2011] ETMR 52.
2   Case C-324/09 *L'Oréal SA v eBay International AG*, paras 114 to 116.

Actual knowledge

6.369 The knowledge held by a service provider must relate to 'unlawful' activity or information. In the context of a claim for damages, it is sufficient that the provider is aware of facts or circumstances from which it would have been apparent[1] to the service provider that the activity or information was unlawful[2]. It would appear, therefore, that mere awareness of such facts or circumstances would not be sufficient for the purposes of a criminal prosecution; actual knowledge of the unlawful activity itself is required.

1   The commentary in Gatley [at 6.44] provides as follows: 'It is clear that he must have actual knowledge (and not merely constructive knowledge) of the facts and circumstances, but it is less clear what is the meaning of "apparent". Arguably something would be "apparent" to the defendant when he has reason to be aware of it; but it may involve a lower standard, something akin to obviousness.'
2   Case C-324/09 *L'Oréal SA v eBay International AG*, para. 120: it is sufficient for a provider to have actual knowledge of facts or circumstances from which a 'diligent economic operator should have identified the illegality in question'. The commentary in Gatley provides [at 6.44] that 'At a minimum, it seems that before one can say that it would be apparent to a defendant that a statement is unlawful he would need to know something of the strength or weakness of available defences.'

6.370 In the civil context, knowledge of unlawfulness is likely to mean that the service provider must have actual knowledge that the material in question is actionable. This takes on particular importance in defamation cases, as a statement may be defamatory without being unlawful (for instance, because it is true or is a statement of honest opinion). Context is also key in copyright, trademark infringement[1], hate speech and terrorist content. It is likely, therefore, that reg 19 requires the service provider to have actual knowledge not only of the stored material, but also the facts or circumstances that make it unlawful.

1   Riordan, paras 12.131 to 12.132.

6.371 Accordingly, it is important that any notice sent to a service provider provides sufficient detail to allow the service provider to ascertain the lawfulness of the impugned content. In *McGrath v Dawkins*, it was suggested that for a defence to fail under reg 19 of the ECRs, a complainant (in that case in a defamation action) had to 'disclose facts or circumstances making it apparent that the postings were unlawful'[1].

1   [2012] 3 WLUK 1003, paras 47 to 48. See also the High Court judgment in *Tamiz v Google Inc* [2012] EWHC 449 (QB) re notifications that are not sufficiently precise and not substantiated – Google was not required to accept notifications 'at face value' to retain protection. The High Court judgment was affirmed on appeal in *Tamiz v Google Inc* [2013] 1 WLR 2151.

6.372 Similarly, in *Davison v Habeeb*, Google was faced with competing allegations in the correspondence received from the claimant and primary author of the allegedly defamatory material, 'between which [Google] was in no position to adjudicate'[1].

1   *Davison v Habeeb*, [2012] 3 CMLR 6, paras 63–68.

6.373 In determining whether a service provider has actual knowledge for the purposes of regs 18 and 19, the following matters shall be taken into account[1]:

> In determining whether a service provider has actual knowledge for the purposes of regulationss 18(b)(v) and 19(a)(i), a court shall take into account all matters which appear to it in the particular circumstances to be relevant and, among other things, shall have regard to—
>
> (a)   whether a service provider has received a notice through a means of contact made available in accordance with regulation 6(1)(c), and
>
> (b)   the extent to which any notice includes—
> > (i)   the full name and address of the sender of the notice;
> > (i)   details of the location of the information in question; and
> > (i)   details of the unlawful nature of the activity or information in question[2].

1   The DTI Guidance, at para 6.12, states that '[t]he Government believes that industry self-regulation and codes of conduct have not yet been shown to be inadequate to the task and that, even if this were to be the case, sectoral approaches would be more appropriate to the different circumstances that will be relevant in each case than the horizontal provisions that would have to be set out in the Regulations.'

2   Regulation 22 of the ECRs. In *CG v Facebook Ireland Ltd* [2016] NICA 54, [2017] EMLR 12, the Northern Ireland Court of Appeal held that reg 6 of the ECRs, which requires service providers to make available to users general information including contact details, requires the provider to set up an easily accessible notice and take down procedure, so as to allow the user to use the reg 22 mechanism to establish actual knowledge and thereby establish an entitlement to damages in the event of failure to take down an unlawful posting (at para 57). The Court

clarified that a complainant cannot be required to give notice in accordance with a provider's procedure: 'The test prescribed by the 2002 Regulations simply requires actual knowledge or awareness of facts and circumstances which make it apparent that the activity or information was unlawful. Actual knowledge is sufficient however acquired.' [at para 58].

6.374 In *Google France* (see above), the act of matching keywords selected by advertisers and search terms entered by internet users was not sufficient of itself to lead to the conclusion that Google had knowledge of, or control over, the data entered into its system by advertisers and stored in memory on its server[1].

[1] *Google France*, para 117.

Negligent failure to make enquiries

6.375 It is arguable that the knowledge standard in reg 19 of the ECRs is in fact higher than that provided for in Art 14 of the E-Commerce Directive, with the latter referring to 'facts or circumstances from which the illegal activity or information is apparent' and the ERCs referring to 'facts or circumstances from which it would have been apparent . . . that the activity or information was unlawful'. Accordingly, the negligent failure to make enquiries might have the effect of denying a service provider the benefit of the hosting exemption (in the context of a claim for damages).

Acting expeditiously

6.376 The question of whether a service provider has acted expeditiously is an objective one, and is likely to depend on a number of circumstances, including the following:

(a) The nature of the unlawful activity or information. The more serious the breach, the more likely it is that a Court would expect the service provider to act expeditiously;

(b) The level of detail provided in the complainant's notification;

(c) The circumstances in which the employee of the service provider became aware of the material in question;

(d) The volume of complaints received by the service provider;

(e) The resources available to the service provider to act on complaints[1].

[1] See Riordan, para 12.145.

Authority or control

6.377 It is not entirely clear what is meant by control in this context. It is arguable that control relates to the content of the information that is stored, rather than the manner in which it is displayed or processed[1].

[1] Riordan, para 12.154.

Voluntary moderation activity

6.378 An issue that has caused some confusion over the years is whether a service provider that voluntarily engages in moderation activity (thereby going beyond storage, eg pursuant to its own terms of use) might forego the benefit of the hosting exemption[1]. This is arguably the implication of *L'Oréal v eBay*, where the Grand Chamber of the CJEU declared that (at 121 and 122):

' . . . if the rules set out in Article 14(1)(a) of Directive 2000/31 are not to be rendered redundant, they must be interpreted as covering every situation in which the provider concerned becomes aware, in one way or another, of such facts or circumstances.

The situations thus covered include, in particular, that in which the operator of an online marketplace uncovers, as the result of an investigation undertaken on its own initiative, an illegal activity or illegal information, as well as a situation in which the operator is notified of the existence of such an activity or such information.'

[1] See *Kaschke v Gray* [2010] EWHC 690 (QB). But cf. *Karim v Newsquest Media Group Ltd* [2009] EWHC 3205 (QB).

Defence in criminal proceedings: burden of proof

6.379 Regulation 21 applies where a service provider charged with a criminal offence seeks to rely on one (or more) of the liability exemptions in regs 17 to 19. Regulation 21(2) provides as follows:

(2) Where evidence is adduced which is sufficient to raise an issue with respect to that defence, the court or jury shall assume that the defence is satisfied unless the prosecution proves beyond reasonable doubt that it is not.

No general obligation to monitor

6.380 Article 15 of the E-Commerce Directive prohibits Member States from imposing on service providers covered by Arts 12, 13 and 14[1] a general obligation to monitor content:

'1. Member States shall not impose a general obligation on providers, when providing the services covered by Articles 12, 13 and 14, to monitor the information which they transmit or store, nor a general obligation actively to seek facts or circumstances indicating illegal activity.

2. Member States may establish obligations for information society service providers promptly to inform the competent public authorities of alleged illegal activities undertaken or information provided by recipients of their service or obligations to communicate to the competent authorities, at their request, information enabling the identification of recipients of their service with whom they have storage agreements.'

[1] Namely providers who (i) act as mere conduits, (ii) provide caching services or (iii) act as hosts.

6.381 Recital 47 makes it clear, however, that Art 15 does not preclude Member States from imposing monitoring obligations in a specific case and, in particular, does not affect orders by national authorities in accordance with national legislation.

Injunctions

6.382 It is important to note that the liability exemptions do not insulate service providers from injunctions; such injunctions can, in particular, consist of orders by courts or administrative authorities requiring the termination or prevention of infringements[1].

[1] Recital 45 of the Preamble to the E-Commerce Directive. See, for instance, Case C-291/13, *Sotiris Papasavvas v O Fileleftheros Dimosia Etaireia Ltd.*

Chapter 7

INFORMATION

Contents

INTRODUCTION

7.1 The short period since 2018 has seen significant changes in the field of information law. Most notably, the Data Protection Act 1998 was retired on 25 May 2018 after 20 years of service, making way for a new data protection regime based on the General Data Protection Regulation and the Data Protection Act 2018. The increased scope for the use (and misuse) of personal data that has been seen over those 20 years has led to a need for greater protection for consumers and data subjects and a more sophisticated data protection regime. This, in turn, has led to what is likely to be a greater regulatory burden on the public authorities responsible for policing the scheme and a greater compliance burden on businesses. However, as more and more business is done in the online space, the need for confidence in those transactions is becoming ever more important for both consumers and businesses.

7.2 However, as an EU Regulation, the GDPR had direct effect without domestic implementing legislation and 2019 saw the possibility that just under 18 months after it came into force in the UK, it would cease to have such effect, with HM Government's stated aim being that the UK would leave the EU on 31 October 2019 with or without a withdrawal agreement in place. The date of the UK's exit was subsequently put back to 31 January 2020, with an implementation period which meant that existing EU law, including the GDPR, would continue to have effect until 31 December 2020. On 1 January 2021 the GDPR became a piece of retained EU legislation, and was incorporated into domestic law as the UK GDPR, a piece of legislation with substantially the same effect, but amended to remove references to EU institutions and mechanisms.

7.3 The latest edition of this chapter reflects the developments which have taken place since the implementation of the GDPR regime – including the impact of Brexit-related developments on information law in the UK – as well as covering the other key information legislation in the consumer and trading standards field.

THE ENTERPRISE ACT 2002

Introduction

7.4 Part 9 of the Enterprise Act 2002 (EnA 2002) introduced restrictions against public authority disclosure of material obtained in connection with certain statutory consumer and competition functions. Since the Pt 9 regime was introduced it has surprisingly never been substantively litigated in the higher courts to any significant degree. The disclosure regime was designed to reflect the 'Government strategy of widening and harmonising the gateways through which information can be disclosed in the UK and overseas and at the same time introduce appropriate safeguards in respect of permitted disclosure of information'.

7.5 Therefore, Pt 9 establishes a set of rigid requirements which have to be met before public authorities can disclose specified information within the United Kingdom or overseas. The importance of complying with these rules is reflected by the fact that criminal offences, attracting sentences of imprisonment, can be committed if the rules are contravened. Although at first glance the rules are strict, the exceptions are wide and Pt 9 is unlikely to prevent enforcers doing anything that they might reasonably want to for the further protection of the public. The rules created by Pt 9 should not be taken to be a complete self-contained code for disclosure. For example, they do not affect a public authority's duties to comply with the requirements of the Data Protection Act 1998 or the Freedom of Information Act 2000.

Specified information

7.6 The core of Pt 9 applies to the disclosure of 'specified information' which is held by a public authority and which relates to the affairs of an individual or of an undertaking. It applies equally to information that has come to the public authority before or after the commencement of the Act. It is therefore deliberately wide ranging in its scope. If a public authority has any other information, the disclosure restrictions in this Part will not apply.

7.7 Specified information is defined in EnA 2002, s 238.

238 Information

(1)   Information is specified information if it comes to a public authority in connection with the exercise of any function it has under or by virtue of—

    (a)   Part 1 [General Functions of the CMA], 3 [Mergers], 4 [Market Studies and Market Investigations], 6 [Cartel Offence], 7 [Miscellaneous Competition Provisions] or 8 [Enforcement of Certain Consumer Legislation];

    (b)   an enactment specified in Schedule 14;

    (c)   such subordinate legislation as the Secretary of State may by order specify for the purposes of this subsection. [The Orders which have been made pursuant to this section are set out in the footnote below.]

Section 238(1)(a): Pt 8

7.8 Part 8 gives enforcers strong powers to obtain court orders against businesses that do not comply with their legal obligations to consumers. These powers include the obtaining of enforcement orders or undertakings, designed to stop businesses from continuing with conduct that harms the collective interests of consumers, along with powers to search premises and retain evidence. The investigatory powers available to enforcers for the purposes of their functions under Pt 8 are now contained in the Consumer Rights Act 2015, Sch 5[1].

1   See, in particular, paras 13–18 – 'Powers in relation to the production of information' – and para 27 – 'Power to require the production of documents'.

Section 238(1)(b): an enactment specified in Sch 14

7.9 This schedule sets out the Acts under which any information obtained by a public authority in connection with the exercise of any statutory function will be 'specified information' for the purposes of Pt 9. It includes both primary and secondary legislation and Scottish and Northern Ireland legislation. Schedule 14 currently contains 21 Acts, which are listed in the footnote below[1].

1   Parts 1, 3, 4, 5, 6, 7, 8 and 11 of the Fair Trading Act 1973; Trade Descriptions Act 1968; Hallmarking Act 1973; Prices Act 1974; Consumer Credit Act 1974; Customs and Excise Management Act 1979; Estate Agents Act 1979; Competition Act 1980; Video Recordings Act 1984; Consumer Protection Act 1987; Consumer Protection (Northern Ireland) Order 1987, SI 1987/2049 (NI 20); Copyright, Designs and Patents Act 1988; Property Misdescriptions Act 1991; Clean Air Act 1993; Value Added Tax Act 1994; Trade Marks Act 1994; Competition Act 1998; Chapter 3 of Pt 10 and Chapter 2 of Pt 18 of the Financial Services and Markets Act 2000 or an order made under s 95 of that Act; Fireworks Act 2003; Compensation Act 2006; Consumers, Estate Agents and Redress Act 2007.

Public authority

7.10 Public authority is defined by EnA 2002, s 238(3) and the Human Rights Act 1998, s 6(3). The definition in the Human Rights Act 1998, s 6(3) does not provide a precise definition for what constitutes 'functions of a public nature'. This has been left to the courts to refine. The House of Lords considered the general approach to this in the case of *YL v Birmingham City Council*[1]. In that case they concluded that the Human Rights Act 1998, s 6 was designed to be given a 'generously wide scope'. They went on to conclude that there was 'no single test of universal application to determine whether a function [was] of a public nature'. However, they held that there were a number of general propositions which were relevant to determining whether a person's functions were 'functions of a public nature'. These propositions reflected the analysis of Lord Nicholls in the case of *Aston Cantlow and Wilmcote with Billesley Parochial Church Council v Wallbank*[2] and are as follows:

- Is the nature of the function public or private?
- What is the role of the State in relation to the function in question[3]?
- What is the extent and nature of any statutory power or duty in relation to the function in question? The absence of any statutory intervention

will tend to indicate parliamentary recognition that the function in question is private.

- To what extent does the state, directly or indirectly, regulate, supervise and inspect the performance of the function in question, and impose criminal penalties on those who fall below publicly promulgated standards in performing it?
- What risk is there that an improper exercise of the function might violate a convention right?
- Does the State ultimately fund the function? The greater the state's involvement in making payment for the function in question, the greater (other things being equal) is its assumption of responsibility.

¹   [2008] 1 AC 95.
²   [2004] 1 AC 546.
³   *YL v Birmingham City Council* [2008] 1 AC 95 at p 105: 'It is also relevant to consider the role and responsibility of the state in relation to the subject matter in question. In some fields the involvement of the state is long-standing and governmental in a strict sense: one might instance defence or the running of prisons. In other fields, such as sport or the arts, the involvement of the state is more recent and more remote. It is relevant to consider the nature and extent of the public interest in the function in question'.

7.11 Conversely the court considered that 'it will not ordinarily matter whether the body in question is amenable to judicial review. The Human Rights Act 1998, s (6)(3)(b) extends the definition of public authority to cover bodies which are not public authorities but certain of whose functions are of a public nature, and it is therefore likely to include bodies which are not amenable to judicial review'[1]. The court also made it clear that the list of considerations were neither comprehensive nor exhaustive and that cases would effectively have to be dealt with on a case by case basis. For example, there will be entities that have both a public and a private function, in which case they would only be a pubic authority for the purposes of its public function. An entity akin to a consumer watchdog is likely to fall into this category.

¹   *XL v Birmingham City Council* [2008] 1 AC 95, p 105.

The general restriction

7.12 Specified information is subject to the general restriction set out in EnA 2002, s 237. If a person discloses information in breach of it, they commit a criminal offence (EnA 2002, s 245).

237 General restriction

(1)   This section applies to specified information which relates to—

   (a)   the affairs of an individual;
   (b)   any business of an undertaking.

(2)   Such information must not be disclosed—

   (a)   during the lifetime of the individual, or
   (b)   while the undertaking continues in existence,

   unless the disclosure is permitted under this Part.

(3)   But subsection (2) does not prevent the disclosure of any information if the information has on an earlier occasion been disclosed to the public in circumstances which do not contravene—

(a)   that subsection;

(b)   any other enactment or rule of law prohibiting or restricting the disclosure of the information.

(4)   Nothing in this Part authorises a disclosure of information which contravenes the Data Protection Act 1998.

(5)   Nothing in this Part affects the Competition Appeal Tribunal[1].

(6)   This Part (except section 244) does not affect any power or duty to disclose information which exists apart from this Part.

---

[1]   For an example of how this exclusion operates, see *Albion Water Limited, Albion Water Group Limited v Water Services Regulation Authority* [2008] CAT 3, where on an application for disclosure of certain redacted information, the Tribunal considered that some of it had to be disclosed because it was relevant and necessary to the issues to be determined. By virtue of the EnA 2002, s 237(5), the restrictions on disclosure of confidential information did not apply to the Tribunal. See also *Umbro Holdings Ltd v Office of Fair Trading (Application for Leniency: Confidentiality)* [2003] CAT 2, for a useful example of where, although the OFT did not disclose what it considered to be confidential information, the Competition Appeal Tribunal took the view that they themselves would have to disclose that information as part of their decision.

Exceptions to the general restriction under EnA 2002, s 237

Information already in the public domain

7.13 The general provision set out above effectively states that, if the information has previously been made public in circumstances which do not contravene EnA 2002, s 237(2) or any other enactment or rule of law, then it may be further disclosed (EnA 2002, s 273(3)). The reason that this is not included as a separate gateway is that, if it has already been properly and publicly disclosed, then clearly there is no need to look for a gateway through which to disclose it again.

7.14 This is an important and wide ranging exception to the rule. Consider for example the effect of the CPR 5.4C:

(1)   The general rule is that a person who is not a party to proceedings may obtain from the court records a copy of—

(a)   statement of case, but not any documents filed with or attached to the statement of case, or intended by the party whose statement it is to be served with it;

(b)   a judgment or order given or made in public (whether made at a hearing or without a hearing), subject to paragraph (1B).

(2)   A non-party may, if the court gives permission, obtain from the records of the court a copy of any other document filed by a party, or communication between the court and a party or another person.

7.15 This rule permits a third party, unconnected to the proceedings, to apply for copies of the statements of case, any rulings that have been given, or judgments that have been made public. So, for instance, if an application for an enforcement order under EnA 2002, s 215 (or s 218 for interim orders) has been filed at court, any member of the public will be able to gain access to the statement of case in which contain the details of the allegations. Therefore, as a general rule, the Pt 9 disclosure rules will cease to apply to any specified information that is included within that documentation once it is filed with a court. A useful example of how the court has approached this issue is *The Asbestos Victims Groups Forum UK [Non-Party] v Concept Limited v Cape Intermediate Holdings PLC*[1]. That case involved the non-party seeking disclosure of litigation documents where the original parties had come to a confidential settlement which included an agreement to destroy all of the documents relating to the case. The court ordered that all material that had been lodged with the court be returned to it to be preserved until a final decision was made.

[1]   [2017] EWHC 811 (QB).

Existing power or duty to disclose

7.16 In the case of *Dumfries and Galloway Council v Dunion, Scottish Information Commissioner*[1] the court had to consider the tension between the restrictions in Pt 9 and the disclosure requirements in other legislation. Although this is a Scottish jurisdiction case, its consideration of the interplay between Pt 9 EnA 2002 and the Freedom of Information (Scotland) Act 2002 ('FI(S)A 2002') is instructive as the provisions of FI(S)A 2002 are very similar to those in the Freedom of Information Act 2000. In that case the court concluded that the FI(S)A 2002 did not justify the disclosure of information in EnA 2002, s 237. A review of that decision assists in understanding how EnA 2002, s 237(6) is likely to be construed.

[1]   [2008] CSIH 12.

7.17 The FI(S)A 2002, s 1(1) provides: 'A person who requests information from a Scottish public authority which holds it is entitled to be given it by the authority'. In Pt 2 FI(S)A 2002, ss 25–41 set out various categories of information which is exempt provided that the information falls within the description applicable to the category in question and the conditions specified in relation to that category are satisfied. The FI(S)A 2002, s 26, which relates to prohibitions on disclosure, provides inter alia:

> Information is exempt information if its disclosure by a Scottish public authority (otherwise than under this Act)—
>
> (a)   is prohibited by or under an enactment; . . .

7.18 The court had to consider the meaning in EnA 2002, s 237(6), of the phrase 'does not affect any power or duty to disclose information which exists apart from Pt 9' along with the meaning, in FI(S)A 2002, s 26, of the words 'information is exempt information if its disclosure . . . (otherwise than under the Act) is *inter alia* prohibited by or under an enactment, such as the Enterprise Act'[1]. In that case, the local council had determined that the information requested by the applicant was exempt absolutely because disclosure was prohibited by Pt 9 EnA 2002. The Commissioner had then held that it was not so exempt, by reason of the EnA 2002, s 237(6). As regards s 237(6), the court held that[2]:

> 'Part 9 does not "affect" any power or duty of disclosure which "exists apart from this Part". In our opinion, contrary to the approach of the Commissioner, these words have a twofold connotation. First, the source of the power or duty in question must be found elsewhere than in Part 9. Second, exercise of the power or performance

of the duty must not be inconsistent with the prohibitions or restrictions imposed by the provisions of Part 9.'

1   Judgment, para 9.
2   Judgment, para 18.

7.19 To illustrate this point they provided a number of examples as follows:

'[19] Information as to an individual's private life may be "specified information" within the meaning of section 238 but will not necessarily be information relating to the "affairs" of that person within the meaning of section 237. Whether it is so or not, the duty of non-disclosure under the Data Protection Act 1998 is consistent with the provisions of Part 9 and is not "affected" by section 237.

[20] Again, where information is "specified information" within the meaning of section 238, but does not relate to the affairs of an individual or any business of an undertaking within the meaning of section 237, section 237 does not constitute a "prohibition" against disclosure for the purposes of section 26 of FOISA. Consequently (except, it seems, in one possible respect) the powers and duties of a public authority under FOISA in relation to disclosure (or non-disclosure) of information are not "affected" by Part 9. (The possible exception relates to section 244 of the Enterprise Act . . .).'

7.20 Applying that reasoning the court concluded that[1]:

'where specified information falls within section 237(1), section 237(2) expressly prohibits disclosure of that information. In that event, exercise of a power or performance of a duty under FOISA to disclose that information would be inconsistent with the provisions of Part 9. It is necessarily affected by the prohibition in section 237(2). Consequently, in our opinion, such a power or duty cannot be said to "exist apart from" Part 9.'

1   Judgment, para 23.

7.21 They therefore held that the Commissioner had erred in law in holding that the EnA 2002, s 237(6) allowed disclosure of the information sought by the applicant in that case.

Permitted disclosure – the six gateways

7.22 If the information does not come within the exceptions to the general restriction set out above, then it will need to go through one of the six gateways before it can be disclosed. All of the gateways are also subject to the public interest test in EnA 2002, s 244.

Consent (s 239)

7.23 If a public authority obtains the consent of the individual concerned, or the consent of the person carrying on the business of the undertaking to which the information relates, then they can disclose the information in question. If the information was obtained by the authority from a person who had the information lawfully, and the authority knows the identity of that person, then the consent of that person is also required. Plainly therefore, if the information in question has been provided by an anonymous source, their consent would not be required.

7.24 If the undertaking is a company, consent may be given by a director, secretary or other officer of the company. If it is a partnership, by a partner and, if it is an unincorporated body or association, then consent can be given by a person concerned in the management or control of that undertaking. It is important therefore, that the correct person is identified and it would be prudent to ensure that any consent is obtained in writing.

Community obligations (s 240)

7.25 This section simply states that, Pt 9 does not prohibit the disclosure of information if the disclosure is required for the purpose of a European Union obligation. Examples of community obligations include Treaty articles, European Directives, Regulations and Decisions which are binding on those to whom they are addressed.

Statutory functions (s 241)

7.26 Under EnA 2002, s 241(1) a public authority may disclose information if it is done to facilitate the exercise of any of its functions it has under, or by virtue of, the EnA 2002 or indeed any other enactment. The word 'enactment' includes a reference to an enactment contained in an Act of the Scottish Parliament, Northern Ireland legislation and subordinate legislation (s 241(5)). It therefore extends to relevant functions that arise under statutory instruments.

7.27 Equally, under EnA 2002, s 241(3) a public authority may disclose information to any other person for the purpose of facilitating the exercise by that person of any function they have under or by virtue of the EnA 2002, an enactment specified in EnA 2002, Sch 15 or any subordinate legislation specified for the purposes of this subsection. So, for example, under this section, one public authority could disclose information to another. The word 'function' in this context has been held to connote 'an act or activity susceptible of being facilitated by disclosure of information', but it cannot be said that disclosure of information itself 'facilitates' disclosure of information[1].

[1] *Dumfries and Galloway Council v Dunion, Scottish Information Commissioner* [2008] CSIH 12.

Civil proceedings (s 241A)

7.28 The EnA 2002, s 241A was added by the Enterprise Act 2002 (Disclosure of Information for Civil Proceedings etc) Order 2007[1]. It permits the disclosure of prescribed information if it is for the purpose of or in connection with, actual or prospective civil proceedings. But it is only in respect of civil proceedings which relate to or arise out of:

- a legal right or obligation of a consumer;
- the infringement of an intellectual property right;
- passing off or the misuse of a trade secret.

[1] SI 2007/2193.

7.29 It also permits disclosure for the purpose of obtaining legal advice in relation to any such proceedings or if it is for the purpose of establishing, enforcing or defending legal rights that are or may be the subject of any such proceedings. This would seem to extend the scope of the section to include the establishment of consumer rights, which may potentially lead to civil litigation by a consumer and is therefore, arguably, an extremely important tool in the protection of consumers and their rights generally.

Criminal proceedings (s 242)

7.30 This section follows the approach taken in other legislation such as the Data Protection Act 1998, namely, that the duties of public authorities should not unduly frustrate the proper process of criminal proceedings. EnA 2002, s 242 allows a public authority to disclose specified information to any person so long as it is in connection with the investigation of a criminal offence in any part of the United Kingdom, or for the purpose of any criminal proceedings. In either case, information can also be disclosed for the purposes of deciding whether to start or end such proceedings.

7.31 Perhaps for obvious reasons, the ambit of this section is very wide. But there is a safeguard in this provision and it is that a public authority must not disclose the information unless it is satisfied that doing so is proportionate to what is sought to be achieved by it (EnA 2002, s 242(3)). The requirement for the public authority to actively consider the aims to be achieved by the proposed disclosure should ensure that global, wide ranging disclosures, are not routinely made. This is perhaps particularly important given that the range of criminal offences to which the section applies is not limited in any way.

Overseas disclosures (s 243)

7.32 EnA 2002, s 243 sets out a restrictive regime relating to the disclosure of information to overseas authorities. Under sub-s (3) certain classes of information cannot be disclosed overseas at all. These include information obtained in a merger or market investigation along with other commercially sensitive information. Outside of this specific limitation, disclosure can only generally be made if it facilitates the investigation, enforcement or bringing of criminal proceedings, or of civil proceedings relating to competition or consumer matters.

The general public interest test (s 244)

7.33 Once the relevant gateway has been identified and the various requirements of it have been met, before any disclosure takes place, the public authority making the decision must have proper regard to the considerations set out in EnA 2002, s 244.

244 Specified information: considerations relevant to disclosure

(1) public authority must have regard to the following considerations before disclosing any specified information (within the meaning of section 238(1),

(2) The first consideration is the need to exclude from disclosure (so far as practicable) any information whose disclosure the authority thinks is contrary to the public interest,

> (3)   The second consideration is the need to exclude from disclosure (so far as practicable)—
>
> > (a)   commercial information whose disclosure the authority thinks might significantly harm the legitimate business interests of the undertaking to which it relates; or
> >
> > (b)   information relating to the private affairs of an individual whose disclosure the authority thinks might significantly harm the individual's interests,
>
> (4)   The third consideration is the extent to which the disclosure of the information mentioned in subsection (3)(a) or (b) is necessary for the purpose for which the authority is permitted to make the disclosure.

7.34 Of course, the application of these principles will be very fact specific and focussed consideration will need to be given to their effect on a case by case basis. If the view is that the information in question meets the relevant requirements in EnA 2002, s 244, then disclosure can be made. For a recent example of how those considerations have applied in practice see *Ryanair Holdings Plc v Competition Commission*[1] where the Commission righty refused to disclose to Ryanair the names and evidence of other airlines which they had taken into account when deciding whether Ryanair's minority shareholding in a rival airline had resulted in a substantial lessening of competition.

[1]   [2015] EWCA Civ 83.

Steps to disclosure

7.35 In analysing whether disclosure is restricted under Pt 9 five questions can be asked:

(1)   Is the information specified information? Has it come to a public authority in connection with the exercise of a function referred to in EnA 2002, s 238?
    If the answer is 'no' the Pt 9 regime does not apply.
    If the answer is 'yes' then consider question (2).

(2)   Has the information already been lawfully disclosed to the public?
    If the answer is 'yes' the information falls within the exception provided by EnA 2002, s 237(3) and the Pt 9 regime does not apply.
    If the answer is 'no' then consider question (3).

(3)   Is there an existing 'power or duty to disclose the information'?
    If the answer is 'yes' then disclosure need not be justified under the gateways, however, the public interest test (question (5)) must still be applied.
    If the answer is 'no' then consider question (4).

(4)   Does the information fall to be disclosed under any of the six gateways?

> (a)   Has the necessary consent been obtained (EnA 2002, s 239)?
> (b)   Is there an EU obligation that applies (EnA 2002, s 240)?
> (c)   Does disclosure facilitate a statutory function (EnA 2002, s 241)?
> (d)   Is the information required for civil proceedings and, if so, are the requirements of EnA 2002, s 241A met?
> (e)   Is the information required for criminal proceedings (EnA 2002, s 242)?
> (f)   Is the disclosure to a public authority overseas and, if so, are all the conditions in EnA 2002, s 243 met?

If the answer is 'no' then the information cannot be disclosed.

(5)   Does disclosure meet the public interest test in EnA 2002, s 244?
      If the answer is 'no' the information cannot be disclosed. If 'yes' then it
      can.

Offences (s 245)

7.36 There are three circumstances relating to the disclosure of information
under Pt 9 in which criminal offences can be committed and they are all offences
of strict liability. The first offence is committed if a person discloses specified
information during the lifetime of the relevant individual or undertaking which
is not otherwise permitted by Pt 9. The second offence is committed if a
disclosure is made to an overseas recipient where the Secretary of State has
directed that no such disclosure should be made[1]. The third offence is committed if, when in receipt of disclosure, the receiver uses the information for a
purpose which is not permitted under Pt 9.

[1]   See EnA 2002, s 243(4).

DATA PROTECTION: GENERAL PROCESSING

Introduction

7.37 Until May 2018, data protection was governed by the Data Protection Act
1998 ('DPA 1998'), an act passed at a time when the legislative and technological landscape as it relates to data was very different to today. Mass use of the
internet for commercial purposes was in its infancy and the tools available to
collect and analyse personal data were nowhere near as diverse or sophisticated
as they are currently. Against this backdrop, Directive 95/46/EC (the 'Data
Protection Directive') was promulgated by the EU to regulate the emerging field
of personal data rights, and implemented in the UK by the DPA 1998.

7.38 The 20 years following the coming into force of the DPA 1998 saw a
revolution in the way in which personal data are collected and used by
corporations and public bodies to the extent that data are now often considered
a valuable commodity in their own right. It was clear, therefore, that data
protection law needed to be brought up to date and made fit to deal with the
revolution in how personal data were being used and the advance of technology.
To this end, Regulation (EU) 2016/679 (the 'General Data Protection Regulation', or GDPR) came into force in the UK on 25 May 2018. Alongside the
GDPR, the Data Protection Act 2018 ('DPA 2018') received royal assent on
23 May 2018, and supplemented the GDPR by making provisions in areas
where the GDPR allowed or required domestic legislation to have effect.

7.39 The effect of the GDPR and the DPA 2018 was to repeal the DPA 1998
and replace it with an entirely new data protection regime. Many features of the
old regime were mirrored and brought up to date in the new one, while several
new features were introduced. In short, the new regime placed greater emphasis
on accountability and record-keeping, took greater account of technology,
increased the onus on data controllers in certain situations (for example, when
obtaining consent for the processing of personal data), and drastically increased
the sanctions available to national enforcers for breaches.

7.40 By virtue of s 3 of the European Union (Withdrawal) Act 2018, the GDPR (along with all other direct EU law, subject to certain specified exemptions) was to be imported into the domestic law of the UK at the point the UK left the EU – ie at 2300 on 31 January 2020. At the same time, the Data Protection, Privacy and Electronic Communications (Amendments etc) (EU Exit) Regulations 2019 was to make amendments to the UK GDPR, the DPA 2018, and other related legislation in order to allow them to stand as pieces of legislation outside of the framework of EU law – for example by removing references to EU institutions and replacing them with the domestic institutions which will take over their competencies. However, as a result of the EU Withdrawal Agreement, which was ratified on 23 January 2020, the EU GDPR continued to have direct effect in the UK until the end of the implementation period. The mechanism for this was ss 1 and 2, para 1(1) of Sch 5 to the European Union (Withdrawal Agreement) Act 2020. Together, these provisions preserved the effect of the GDPR until the end of the implementation period and postponed the commencement of the Data Protection, Privacy and Electronic Communications (Amendments etc) (EU Exit) Regulations 2019 until the end of that period. Following the end of the implementation period, the GDPR, with the amendments made by the Data Protection, Privacy and Electronic Communications (Amendments etc) (EU Exit) Regulations 2019, has now been imported into domestic law as a piece of retained EU legislation. In this form, it will be referred to in this chapter as the UK GDPR. At present, the terms of the UK GDPR are substantially the same as the GDPR, although there is the possibility that the two regimes may diverge in the future.

7.41 While the DPA 1998 applied equally to all processing of personal data, with appropriate exemptions for processing related to law enforcement, the UK GDPR/Pt 2 regime applies to non-law-enforcement-related processing only. Processing related to law enforcement is governed by Pt 3 of the DPA 2018, and forms a self-contained regulatory regime for processing related to law enforcement. This section will deal with general processing under the UK GDPR and Pt 2 of the DPA 2018. For processing relating to law enforcement under Pt 3 of the DPA 2018, see the section entitled 'Data Protection: Law-Enforcement Processing' at **7.146** et seq below.

Scope

7.42 The UK GDPR applies to the automated or structured processing of personal data. This includes processing done in the course of an activity which, immediately before IP completion day, fell outside the scope of EU law and processing done in the course of an activity which, immediately before IP completion date, fell within the scope of Chapter 2 of Title 5 of the Treaty on European Union (common foreign and security policy activities)[1]. Automated or structured processing of personal data covers two types of processing: first, 'the processing of personal data wholly or partly by automated means' and secondly, 'the processing otherwise than by automated means of personal data which forms part of a filing system or is intended to form part of a filing system'[2].

[1]   Art 2(1) of the UK GDPR.
[2]   Art 2(5)(a) of the UK GDPR.

7.43 Additionally, the UK GDPR applies to the manual unstructured processing of personal data held by an FOI public authority[1]. 'Manual unstructured processing of personal data' is defined as the processing of personal data which is not the automated or structured processing of personal data[2]. An FOI public authority is defined in s 21(5) of the DPA 2018 as a public authority as defied in the Freedom of Information Act 2000 or a Scottish public authority as defined in the Freedom of Information (Scotland) Act 2002[3].

[1]   Art 2(1A) of the UK GDPR.
[2]   Art 2(5)(a) of the UK GDPR.
[3]   Art 2(5)(b) of the UK GDPR.

7.44 The UK GDPR does not apply to:

- the processing of personal data by an individual in the course of a purely personal or household activity;
- the processing of personal data by a competent authority for any of the law enforcement;
- the processing of personal data to which Part 4 of the 2018 Act (intelligence services processing) applies[1].

[1]   Art 2(2) of the UK GDPR.

Key concepts and interpretation

7.45 Like the DPA 1998, the UK GDPR is concerned with the processing of personal data by data controllers. However, many of these terms have now been re-defined, and some new terms have been introduced. This section covers the key changes.

Personal data: general

7.46 'Personal data' is defined in Art 4(1) of the UK GDPR as:

'any information relating to an identified or identifiable natural person ('data subject'); an identifiable natural person is one who can be identified, directly or indirectly, in particular by reference to an identifier such as a name, an identification number, location data, an online identifier or to one or more factors specific to the physical, physiological, genetic, mental, economic, cultural or social identity of that natural person.'

7.47 This definition rolls into one the definitions of 'personal data' and 'data subject'. The definition recognises the increased number of types of data which may be generated in respect of data subjects and accounts for advances in technology which have taken place since the definition under the DPA 1998 was drafted.

7.48 Where data are anonymised, they will not fall within the definition of personal data, since it will not be possible to identify a living individual from anonymised data. Whether pseudonymised data is likely to be personal data will depend on how difficult it is to identify the data subject from the pseudonymised data. Pseudonymisation is defined as:

'the processing of personal data in such a manner that the personal data can no longer be attributed to a specific data subject without the use of additional information, provided that such additional information is kept separately and is subject to technical and organisational measures to ensure that the personal data are not attributed to an identified or identifiable natural person.'

7.49 Data relating to companies, associations, and other organisations are not personal data as they do not relate to living individuals. However, in certain circumstances data which ostensibly relate to such organisations may have the effect of identifying a living individual, and therefore falling within the definition of personal data. An example is the company number of a business incorporated by person who trades as a one-man company.

Personal data: sub-types

7.50 Where the DPA 1998 recognised two sub-types of personal data: 'personal data' and 'sensitive personal data', the UK GDPR re-organises this classification into three parts: 'personal data', 'special categories of personal data', and 'personal data relating to criminal convictions and offences'.

The special categories of personal data are set out in Art 9(1) of the UK GDPR as:

'personal data revealing racial or ethnic origin, political opinions, religious or philosophical beliefs, or trade union membership, and the processing of genetic data, biometric data for the purpose of uniquely identifying a natural person, data concerning health or data concerning a natural person's sex life or sexual orientation.'

7.51 No specific definition is given in the UK GDPR for 'personal data relating to criminal convictions and offences', save that Art 10(1) refers to 'personal data relating to criminal convictions and offences or related security measures'. However, it is submitted that these terms are self-explanatory. The term 'convictions and offences' suggests that convictions and offences are distinct concepts, and so data relating to acts which would amount to an offence but did not form the basis for a conviction (eg un-litigated allegations, cautions, and acquittals) fall within this category.

Processing

7.52 'Processing' is defined in Art 4(2) of the UK GDPR as:

'any operation or set of operations which is performed on personal data or on sets of personal data, whether or not by automated means, such as collection, recording, organisation, structuring, storage, adaptation or alteration, retrieval, consultation, use, disclosure by transmission, dissemination or otherwise making available, alignment or combination, restriction, erasure or destruction.'

Data controllers and processors

7.53 A 'controller' is defined in Art 4(7) of the UK GDPR as:

'the natural or legal person, public authority, agency or other body which, alone or jointly with others, determines the purposes and means of the processing of personal data (but see section 6 of the 2018 Act).'

7.54 Section 6(2) of the DPA 2018 provides that where personal data are processed only for purposes required by an enactment, and by means required by that enactment, the person on whom the obligation to process the data is imposed by the enactment is the controller.

7.55 Section 6 of the DPA 2018 also sets out that Art 4(7) is subject to ss 209 and 210 of the DPA 2018, which set out who is considered the controller when personal data are processed by the Crown (including Government departments) and Parliament.

7.56 The controller's responsibilities are set out in Art 24 of the GDPR as follows:

'**Responsibility of the controller**

1. Taking into account the nature, scope, context and purposes of processing as well as the risks of varying likelihood and severity for the rights and freedoms of natural persons, the controller shall implement appropriate technical and organisational measures to ensure and to be able to demonstrate that processing is performed in accordance with this Regulation. Those measures shall be reviewed and updated where necessary.

2. Where proportionate in relation to processing activities, the measures referred to in paragraph 1 shall include the implementation of appropriate data protection policies by the controller.'

7.57 The controller is therefore the person with overall control over how data are to be processed and overall responsibility for ensuring that they are processed in accordance with the UK GDPR and any other applicable law.

7.58 A 'processor' is defined in Art 4(8) of the UK GDPR as:

'a natural or legal person, public authority, agency or other body which processes personal data on behalf of the controller.'

7.59 Art 28 of the UK GDPR sets out the requirements where a processor is engaged (either by a controller or another processor) as follows:

'**Processor**

1. Where processing is to be carried out on behalf of a controller, the controller shall use only processors providing sufficient guarantees to implement appropriate technical and organisational measures in such a manner that processing will meet the requirements of this Regulation and ensure the protection of the rights of the data subject.

2. The processor shall not engage another processor without prior specific or general written authorisation of the controller. In the case of general written authorisation, the processor shall inform the controller of any intended changes concerning the addition or replacement of other processors, thereby giving the controller the opportunity to object to such changes.'

7.60 The engagement of a processor must be governed by 'a contract or other legal act under domestic law'[1].

---

[1]   Art 28(3) of the UK GDPR.

The data protection principles

7.61 Like the DPA 1998, the UK GDPR is centred on a set of data protection principles (DPPs) which regulate the lawfulness of processing of personal data. The DPPs which relate to general (ie non-law-enforcement-related) processing are set out at Art 5(1) of the UK GDPR as follows:

'Principles relating to processing of personal data

1. Personal data shall be:
   (a) processed lawfully, fairly and in a transparent manner in relation to the data subject ('lawfulness, fairness and transparency');
   (b) collected for specified, explicit and legitimate purposes and not further processed in a manner that is incompatible with those purposes; further processing for archiving purposes in the public interest, scientific or historical research purposes or statistical purposes shall, in accordance with Article 89(1), not be considered to be incompatible with the initial purposes ('purpose limitation');
   (c) adequate, relevant and limited to what is necessary in relation to the purposes for which they are processed ('data minimisation');
   (d) accurate and, where necessary, kept up to date; every reasonable step must be taken to ensure that personal data that are inaccurate, having regard to the purposes for which they are processed, are erased or rectified without delay ('accuracy');
   (e) kept in a form which permits identification of data subjects for no longer than is necessary for the purposes for which the personal data are processed; personal data may be stored for longer periods insofar as the personal data will be processed solely for archiving purposes in the public interest, scientific or historical research purposes or statistical purposes in accordance with Article 89(1) subject to implementation of the appropriate technical and organisational measures required by this Regulation in order to safeguard the rights and freedoms of the data subject ('storage limitation');
   (f) processed in a manner that ensures appropriate security of the personal data, including protection against unauthorised or unlawful processing and against accidental loss, destruction or damage, using appropriate technical or organisational measures ('integrity and confidentiality').

2. The controller shall be responsible for, and be able to demonstrate compliance with, paragraph 1 (accountability).'

7.62 Part 3 of the DPA 2018 contains a separate list of DPPs for processing connected to law enforcement (for which, see **7.157–7.166** below).

Lawfulness, fairness, and transparency

7.63 Lawfulness, fairness, and transparency are distinct concepts – in order for the first DPP to be met, processing must meet all three. In order to be lawful, processing must satisfy one or more of the requirements under Art 6 of the GDPR. For special categories and data relating to convictions and offences, there are further requirements for lawful processing. For a detailed discussion of lawfulness, see **7.71–7.79** below.

7.64 Fairness is not defined in the UK GDPR. However, the ICO's website offers the following guidance:

'In general, fairness means that you should only handle personal data in ways that people would reasonably expect and not use it in ways that have unjustified adverse effects on them. You need to stop and think not just about how you can use personal data, but also about whether you should.

Assessing whether you are processing information fairly depends partly on how you obtain it. In particular, if anyone is deceived or misled when the personal data is obtained, then this is unlikely to be fair[1].'

[1]   See https://ico.org.uk/for-organisations/guide-to-the-general-data-protection-regulation-gdpr/principles/lawfulness-fairness-and-transparency/.

7.65 Transparency is largely dealt with by Arts 13 and 14 of the UK GDPR, which require that subjects be provided with information about the identity of the controller and how and why their data are being obtained and processed. Issues of transparency are also addressed in the provisions relating to consent[1] and subject rights[2].

[1]   Art 7 of the UK GDPR.
[2]   Arts 12–22 of the UK GDPR.

Purpose limitation

7.66 The purpose limitation principle requires that controllers be clear about the purpose for which data are to be processed and to then refrain from processing those data for a different purpose where the new purpose is not compatible with the purpose for which the data were originally obtained. The ICO's guidance lists the following factors as relevant to the issue of compatibility:

• any link between your original purpose and the new purpose;
• the context in which you originally collected the personal data – in particular, your relationship with the individual and what they would reasonably expect;
• the nature of the personal data – eg is it particularly sensitive;
• the possible consequences for individuals of the new processing; and
• whether there are appropriate safeguards – eg encryption or pseudonymisation[1].

[1]   https://ico.org.uk/for-organisations/guide-to-the-general-data-protection-regulation-gdpr/principles/purpose-limitation/.

Data minimisation

7.67 The purpose of this principle is to ensure that controllers process only the minimum amount of data they require for the purposes for which the data are processed. This will most obviously be infringed where a controller processes too much data about a subject. However, it could also occur where the controller has too little data – if the data are inadequate for the purpose for which they are to be used, and the controller does not propose to obtain further data to supplement them, then there will be no justification for continuing to retain the inadequate data.

Accuracy

7.68 This principle required controllers to ensure that data they process is accurate. The term 'inaccurate' is defined in the DPA 2018 as 'incorrect or misleading as to any matter of fact'[1].

[1] DPA 2018, s 205(1).

Storage limitation

7.69 This DPP requires that controllers do not keep personal data for longer than necessary. In practice, this means that controllers will generally have to set retention periods for different types of personal data in their data protection policies. The length of such periods will depend on the purpose for which the data are to be retained. Where it is envisaged that the data may be required in the event of future litigation, regard should be had to the limitation period for any foreseen causes of action, with a further period to account for permission being granted to bring claims out of time. Accountancy and auditing purposes, regulatory requirements, and legal obligations may all lead to a need to retain personal data for a set period of time beyond their initial purpose. Organisations should also consider what safeguards are required where data are to be stored for these purposes.

Integrity and confidentiality

7.70 This principle requires that controllers take appropriate steps to ensure the security of data they process and avoid breaches such as accidental destruction or disclosure or cyber-attacks. This principle should be considered in conjunction with Art 32 of the UK GDPR, which states:

'**Security of processing**

1. Taking into account the state of the art, the costs of implementation and the nature, scope, context and purposes of processing as well as the risk of varying likelihood and severity for the rights and freedoms of natural persons, the controller and the processor shall implement appropriate technical and organisational measures to ensure a level of security appropriate to the risk, including inter alia as appropriate:
   (a)   the pseudonymisation and encryption of personal data;
   (b)   the ability to ensure the ongoing confidentiality, integrity, availability and resilience of processing systems and services;
   (c)   the ability to restore the availability and access to personal data in a timely manner in the event of a physical or technical incident;
   (d)   a process for regularly testing, assessing and evaluating the effectiveness of technical and organisational measures for ensuring the security of the processing.

2. In assessing the appropriate level of security account shall be taken in particular of the risks that are presented by processing, in particular from accidental or unlawful destruction, loss, alteration, unauthorised disclosure of, or access to personal data transmitted, stored or otherwise processed.'

Lawfulness

7.71 Art 5(1) (a) of the UK GDPR contains a requirement for data to be processed lawfully. Art 6(1) of the UK GDPR sets out the circumstances in which processing will be lawful as follows:

'**Lawfulness of Processing**

1. Processing shall be lawful only if and to the extent that at least one of the following applies:

(a)   the data subject has given consent to the processing of his or her personal data for one or more specific purposes;

(b)   processing is necessary for the performance of a contract to which the data subject is party or in order to take steps at the request of the data subject prior to entering into a contract;

(c)   processing is necessary for compliance with a legal obligation to which the controller is subject;

(d)   processing is necessary in order to protect the vital interests of the data subject or of another natural person;

(e)   processing is necessary for the performance of a task carried out in the public interest or in the exercise of official authority vested in the controller;

(f)   processing is necessary for the purposes of the legitimate interests pursued by the controller or by a third party, except where such interests are overridden by the interests or fundamental rights and freedoms of the data subject which require protection of personal data, in particular where the data subject is a child.

Point (f) of the first subparagraph shall not apply to processing carried out by public authorities in the performance of their tasks.'

7.72 It is important to note that while Art 6 of the UK GDPR sets out an exhaustive list of gateways for processing to be considered lawful, unlawful processing is not restricted to non-compliance with Art 6. For example, data processed in breach of an injunction, reporting restrictions, intellectual property rights, confidence, contract, or where prohibited by law (eg the Contempt of Court Act 1981) will all be processed unlawfully.

7.73 For the purposes of this work, the two most relevant gateways for lawful processing are consent and official authority. These are discussed in the following sections.

Consent

7.74 One of the conditions for processing to be lawful is consent. Consent is defined in Art 1(11) of the UK GDPR as:

'any freely given, specific, informed and unambiguous indication of the data subject's wishes by which he or she, by a statement or by a clear affirmative action, signifies agreement to the processing of personal data relating to him or her.'

7.75 The effect of this definition is that for consent to be valid, a data subject must be informed of what specific processing he is being asked to consent to and able to freely decide whether or not to give consent. The requirement for consent to be given by a clear affirmative action means that consent can no longer be inferred from silence or inactivity. Consequently, measures such as pre-ticked boxes and clauses stating that a user consents to processing by continuing to use a service (such as browsing a website) are no longer capable of giving rise to valid consent.

7.76 Article 7 of the UK GDPR contains further conditions relating to consent, namely:

- A data controller must be able to demonstrate that a data subject has consented to processing[1].
- Where consent is given in a document which also deals with other matters, the part concerning consent must be easily distinguishable from the rest of the document in clear and plain language[2].
- Consent can be withdrawn at any time, and the data subject must be made aware of this before his consent is sought. Withdrawal of consent must be as easy as giving it. Withdrawal does not affect the lawfulness of processing carried out before the withdrawal of consent[3].

[1]   Art 7(1) of the UK GDPR.
[2]   Art 7(2) of the UK GDPR.
[3]   Art 7(3) of the UK GDPR.

7.77 Article 7(4) of the UK GDPR deals specifically with the issue of conditional consent (ie situations where a contract will not be performed unless consent is given to a form of processing). Where the processing is not necessary for the performance of the contract, 'utmost account' will be given to this factor in considering whether consent really has been given freely. For example, a taxi-hailing app which requires a consumer to consent to the app accessing location data in order to provide the service is likely to fall foul of this provision, since while access to location data may facilitate a booking, it is not necessary for the contract to be performed (as the consumer can instead manually enter the location from which he wishes to be picked up). In those circumstances, the purported consent to access location data is likely to be vitiated, as the consumer's freedom of choice over whether to give it will have been inhibited by the fact that without giving that consent he would be unable to use the services provided through the app.

7.78 The effect of Art 7(4) of the UK GDPR is limited to situations where the processing for which consent is sought is not necessary for the performance of a contract. Where the processing is necessary for contractual performance (for example a mail-order company processing address data in order to make a delivery to a consumer) issues of consent will not arise, as that processing will be lawful under Art 5(1)(b) of the UK GDPR regardless of whether the data subject has given consent.

Public interest and official authority

7.79 Art 5(1)(e) of the UK GDPR provides for processing to be lawful where it is done in the performance of a task carried out in the public interest or in the exercise of official authority vested in the controller. As it relates to the public interest, Art 5(1)(e) of the UK GDPR is supplemented by the DPA 2018, s 8, which sets out five bases on which a task may be considered to be in the public interest, namely:

- the administration of justice;

- the exercise of a function of either House of Parliament;
- the exercise of a function conferred on a person by an enactment or rule of law;
- the exercise of a function of the Crown, a Minister of the Crown or a government department; and
- an activity that supports or promotes democratic engagement.

Processing of special categories of personal data

7.80 Art 9(1) of the UK GDPR contains a general prohibition on the processing of special categories of personal data, which is dis-applied where any of the conditions in Art 9(2) of the UK GDPR are met:

'Processing of Special Categories of Personal Data

. . .

2. Paragraph 1 shall not apply if one of the following applies:

(a) the data subject has given explicit consent to the processing of those personal data for one or more specified purposes, except where domestic law provides that the prohibition referred to in paragraph 1 may not be lifted by the data subject;

(b) processing is necessary for the purposes of carrying out the obligations and exercising specific rights of the controller or of the data subject in the field of employment and social security and social protection law in so far as it is authorised by Union or domestic law or a collective agreement pursuant to Member State law providing for appropriate safeguards for the fundamental rights and the interests of the data subject;

(c) processing is necessary to protect the vital interests of the data subject or of another natural person where the data subject is physically or legally incapable of giving consent;

(d) processing is carried out in the course of its legitimate activities with appropriate safeguards by a foundation, association or any other not-for-profit body with a political, philosophical, religious or trade union aim and on condition that the processing relates solely to the members or to former members of the body or to persons who have regular contact with it in connection with its purposes and that the personal data are not disclosed outside that body without the consent of the data subjects;

(e) processing relates to personal data which are manifestly made public by the data subject;

(f) processing is necessary for the establishment, exercise or defence of legal claims or whenever courts are acting in their judicial capacity;

(g) processing is necessary for reasons of substantial public interest, on the basis of domestic law which shall be proportionate to the aim pursued, respect the essence of the right to data protection and provide for suitable and specific measures to safeguard the fundamental rights and the interests of the data subject;

(h) processing is necessary for the purposes of preventive or occupational medicine, for the assessment of the working capacity of the employee, medical diagnosis, the provision of health or social care or treatment or the management of health or social care systems and services on the basis of domestic law or pursuant to contract with a health professional and subject to the conditions and safeguards referred to in paragraph 3;

(i) processing is necessary for reasons of public interest in the area of public health, such as protecting against serious cross-border threats to health or ensuring high standards of quality and safety of health care and of medicinal products or medical devices, on the basis of domestic law which provides for suitable and specific measures to safeguard the rights and freedoms of the data subject, in particular professional secrecy;

(j)   processing is necessary for archiving purposes in the public interest, scientific or historical research purposes or statistical purposes in accordance with Article 89(1) (as supplemented by section 19 of the 2018 Act) based on domestic law which shall be proportionate to the aim pursued, respect the essence of the right to data protection and provide for suitable and specific measures to safeguard the fundamental rights and the interests of the data subject.'

Substantial public interest

7.81 Where processing is carried out under Art 9(1)(g) of the UK GDPR, the DPA 2018, s 10 sets out the conditions to be met in order for the exemption to be valid. The DPA 2018, s 10(2) states that processing will only be lawful under this exemption if it meets a condition in Pt 2 of Sch 1 to the DPA 2018. The relevant conditions are set out at paras 5–28 of Pt 2 of the Schedule. For the purposes of this publication, the most relevant conditions are as follows:

•   statutory etc. and government purposes[1];
•   administration of justice and parliamentary purposes[2];
•   preventing or detecting unlawful acts[3];
•   protecting the public against dishonesty etc[4]; and
•   regulatory requirements relating to unlawful acts/dishonesty etc[5].

[1]   DPA 2018, Sch 1, Pt 2, para 6.
[2]   DPA 2018, Sch 1, Pt 2, para 7.
[3]   DPA 2018, Sch 1, Pt 2, para 10.
[4]   DPA 2018, Sch 1, Pt 2, para 11.
[5]   DPA 2018, Sch 1, Pt 2, para 12.

7.82 Where processing is carried out under this provision, the controller must have an appropriate policy document in place and the safeguards in Pt 4 of Sch 1 to the DPA 2018 apply[1]. For these, see 'Additional Safeguards' at **7.101–7.103** below.

[1]   DPA 2018, Sch 1, Pt 2, para 5.

7.83 It should be noted that each of these conditions apply only to non-law-enforcement-related processing. Where the processing is done in connection with law enforcement, by a body acting to enforce the law, see **7.167–7.168** below. The exemption as discussed in this part will therefore be of use in two main ways:

•   to enforcers when they seek to process special categories of personal data for the purposes set out above, but in circumstances which fall out with the definition of law-enforcement processing; and
•   to persons and bodies who are not enforcers, who are processing personal data for the purposes of assisting with enforcement action (eg as complainants or witnesses).

Statutory etc. and government purposes

7.84 Paragraph 6 of Pt 2 of Sch 1 to the DPA 2018, provides as follows:

6 Statutory etc and government purposes

(1)   This condition is met if the processing—

    (a)   is necessary for a purpose listed in sub-paragraph (2), and
    (b)   is necessary for reasons of substantial public interest.

(2)   Those purposes are—

    (a)   the exercise of a function conferred on a person by an enactment or rule of law
    (b)   the exercise of a function of the Crown, a Minister of the Crown or a government department.

Administration of justice and parliamentary purposes

7.85 Paragraph 7 of Pt 2 of Sch 1 to the DPA 2018 provides that the processing of special categories of personal data shall be lawful if the processing is necessary for the administration of justice.

Preventing or detecting unlawful acts and protecting against dishonesty

7.86 Paragraph 10 of Pt 2 of Sch 1 to the DPA 2018 provides for processing of special categories of personal data where the processing is done for the purpose of preventing or detecting unlawful acts, while Paragraph 11 makes similar provision for the purposes of protecting against dishonesty and similar conduct. Paragraph 10(1) states as follows:

10 Preventing or detecting unlawful acts

(1)   This condition is met if the processing—

    (a)   is necessary for the purposes of the prevention or detection of an unlawful act,
    (b)   must be carried out without the consent of the data subject so as not to prejudice those purposes, and
    (c)   is necessary for reasons of substantial public interest.

7.87 Enforcers are unlikely to rely on this condition for their own processing, as where they process data for the purpose of preventing or detecting unlawful acts, this will mostly be done under the law-enforcement provisions in Pt 3 of the DPA 2018. Rather, this condition will primarily apply to persons making disclosures or providing evidence to enforcers in the course of an investigation (to whom Pt 3 does not apply). Where a data controller processes special categories of personal data in the course of making such a disclosure, it is not necessary for them to have an appropriate policy document in place[1].

[1]   DPA 2018, Sch 1, Pt 2, para 10(2).

7.88 The language of para 11(1) of Pt 2 of Sch 1 to the DPA 2018 mirrors the language of para 10(1) above, substituting 'the exercise of a protective function' for the prevention or detection of unlawful acts. 'Protective function' is defined as a function intended to protect the public against:

- dishonesty, malpractice or other seriously improper conduct;
- unfitness or incompetence;
- mismanagement in the administration of a body or association; or
- failures in services provided by a body or association[1].

[1] DPA 2018, Sch 1, Pt 2, para 11(2).

7.89 Like the prevention or detection of unlawful acts condition, this condition may be used by persons making reports to enforcers. However, it may also be used by enforcers in connection with acts which merit public protection, but do not amount to criminal activity such as to engage the law-enforcement provisions of Pt 3 of the DPA 2018 (for example in the course of a stand-alone application to disqualify a company director where the misconduct complained of is not criminal). This condition is also likely to be used by informants/witnesses and regulators in the context of professional disciplinary proceedings. For example, in proceedings for professional misconduct against a medical professional, an NHS trust, as data controller, may be entitled to disclose data relating to a patient's health (a special category of personal data) to a regulator for the purposes of the regulator carrying out its functions in protecting the public against unfitness or incompetence.

Regulatory requirements relating to unlawful acts/dishonesty etc.

7.90 Paragraph 12 of Pt 2 of Sch 1 to the DPA 2018 reads as follows:

12 Regulatory requirements relating to unlawful acts and dishonesty etc

(1) This condition is met if—

(a) the processing is necessary for the purposes of complying with, or assisting other persons to comply with, a regulatory requirement which involves a person taking steps to establish whether another person has—
(i) committed an unlawful act, or
(ii) been involved in dishonesty, malpractice or other seriously improper conduct,
(b) in the circumstances, the controller cannot reasonably be expected to obtain the consent of the data subject to the processing, and
(c) the processing is necessary for reasons of substantial public interest.

7.91 The effect of this provision is to provide a gateway for lawful processing of special categories of personal data where regulatory issues are involved. There is a degree of overlap with paras 10 and 11 of Pt 2 of Sch 1 to the DPA 2018, and it is anticipated that this paragraph is only likely to be relied on where the underlying improper conduct falls short of the tests in those paragraphs.

Processing of personal data relating to criminal convictions and offences

7.92 Personal data relating to criminal convictions and offences is treated as a category of data in its own right. Processing of these data is dealt with by Art 10 of the UK GDPR as follows:

'Processing of personal data relating to criminal convictions and offences or related security measures based on Article 6(1) shall be carried out only under the control of official authority or when the processing is authorised by domestic law providing for appropriate safeguards for the rights and freedoms of data subjects. Any comprehensive register of criminal convictions shall be kept only under the control of official authority.'

7.93 For the purposes of Art 10, the relevant authorisation and safeguards come from the DPA 2018, s 10(5), which states:

> **10 Special categories of personal data and criminal convictions etc data**
>
> . . .
>
> (5) The processing meets the requirement in Article 10 of the GDPR for authorisation by the law of the United Kingdom or a part of the United Kingdom only if it meets a condition in Part 1, 2 or 3 of Schedule 1.

7.94 The conditions in Pt 1 of Sch 1 to the DPA 2018 relate to employment, health and social care, public health, and research, and so are unlikely to be relevant in the context of regulatory proceedings.

7.95 Part 2 of the Schedule contains the substantial public interest conditions, the relevant parts of which are discussed at **7.81–7.91** above. Certain of the Pt 2 conditions (for example preventing unlawful acts) contain an express requirement that in order for the condition to be met the processing must be necessary for reasons of substantial public interest. Paragraph 36 of Pt 3 of Sch 1 to the DPA 2018 has the effect of bringing those conditions within the ambit of Pt 3, and in doing so deleting the requirement that processing be necessary for reasons of substantial public interest:

> **36 Extension of conditions in Part 2 of this Schedule referring to substantial public interest**
>
> This condition is met if the processing would meet a condition in Part 2 of this Schedule but for an express requirement for the processing to be necessary for reasons of substantial public interest.

7.96 Part 3 of Sch 1 to the DPA 2018 contains further conditions which, if satisfied, will allow the processing of personal data relating to criminal convictions and offences. The most relevant for the purposes of this publication are discussed below.

Consent

7.97 The considerations here are identical to consent in other contexts. See **7.74–7.78** above.

Personal data in the public domain

7.98 Paragraph 32 of Pt 3 of Sch 1 to the DPA 2018 states that this condition is met if the processing relates to personal data which is manifestly made public by the data subject.

Legal claims

7.99 Paragraph 33 of Pt 3 of Sch 1 to the DPA 2018 reads as follows:

33 Legal claims

This condition is met if the processing—

(a) is necessary for the purpose of, or in connection with, any legal proceedings (including prospective legal proceedings),

(b) is necessary for the purpose of obtaining legal advice, or

(c) is otherwise necessary for the purposes of establishing, exercising or defending legal rights.

Judicial acts

7.100 Paragraph 32 of Pt 3 of Sch 1 to the DPA 2018 states that this condition is met if the processing is necessary when a court or tribunal is acting in its judicial capacity. This paragraph is most likely to apply to judges and court staff performing functions in support of judicial functions, and it allows for processing in order to ensure smooth running of proceedings.

Additional safeguards for special categories and criminal offences

7.101 Part 4 of Sch 1 to the DPA 2018 contains additional safeguards which attach to processing which is done in based on any of the conditions in Pts 1, 2, and 3 which require a controller to have an appropriate policy document in place. What amounts to an appropriate policy document is set out in para 39 of Pt 4, which states:

39 Requirement to have an appropriate policy document in place

The controller has an appropriate policy document in place in relation to the processing of personal data in reliance on a condition described in paragraph 38 if the controller has produced a document which—

(a) explains the controller's procedures for securing compliance with the principles in Article 5 of the GDPR (principles relating to processing of personal data) in connection with the processing of personal data in reliance on the condition in question, and

(b) explains the controller's policies as regards the retention and erasure of personal data processed in reliance on the condition, giving an indication of how long such personal data is likely to be retained.

7.102 Where special categories of personal data or data relating to criminal convictions and offences are processed on the basis of the conditions in Pts 1, 2, or 3 of Sch 1 to the DPA 2018, the policy document must be retained, reviewed (if appropriate), and made available to the Commissioner on request for the period beginning with the commencement of the relevant processing and ending 6 months after the controller ceases to carry out the processing of data of those types[1].

[1] DPA 2018, Sch 1, Pt 4, para 40.

7.103 Paragraph 41 requires a record of processing to be kept as follows:

41 Additional safeguard: record of processing

A record maintained by the controller, or the controller's representative, under Article 30 of the GDPR in respect of the processing of personal data in reliance on a condition described in paragraph 38 must include the following information—

(a)   which condition is relied on,

(b)   how the processing satisfies Article 6 of the GDPR (lawfulness of processing), and

(c)   whether the personal data is retained and erased in accordance with the policies described in paragraph 39(b) and, if it is not, the reasons for not following those policies.

Subject rights

7.104 Chapter 3 of the UK GDPR sets out the rights of which data subjects may avail themselves in respect of their personal data. Articles 13 and 14 deal with information to be provided to subjects when their personal data are obtained. Articles 15–22 contain a list of rights which subjects can assert by way of making requests of controllers. Finally, Art 23 deals with restrictions on subject rights.

General principles

7.105 Any information provided by controllers to subjects under Chapter 3 of the GDPR (whether prescribed information under Arts 13 and 14 or information provided as a result of a request under Arts 15–22) must be provided in a concise, transparent, intelligible and easily accessible form, using clear and plain language[1].

[1]   Art 12(1) of the UK GDPR.

7.106 Subject rights only exist in relation to the personal data of the subject making a request – data subjects cannot assert rights in respect of the personal data of others. In order for a controller to comply with a request by a subject without breaching the personal data of other subjects he therefore needs to know two things:

•   first, the identity of the persons to whom each item of personal data he processes relates; and

•   secondly, the identity of the person making the request.

7.107 In relation to the first of those points, where a controller is processing personal data which does not require a subject to be identified, he may not be able to comply with a request if he does not know that a particular piece of data relates to the subject making the request. In such cases, the onus of demonstrating that a subject right cannot be complied with because the controller cannot identify the subject is on the controller[1].

[1]   Art 12(2) of the UK GDPR.

7.108 As to the second point, if the controller has reasonable doubts concerning the identity of the natural person making a request under Arts 15–21 of the

UK GDPR, the controller may request the provision of additional information necessary to confirm the identity of the data subject[1].

¹ Art 12(6) of the UK GDPR.

7.109 Where a request is made under Arts 15–22 of the UK GDPR the controller must take any action required without undue delay and in any event within one month of the request. If necessary, that period may be extended by a further 2 months, taking into account the complexity and number of requests. If it is so extended, the controller must inform the subject of that fact, together with the reasons for the extension, within the initial one-month period[1].

¹ Art 12(3) of the UK GDPR.

7.110 Where any information is provided under Chapter 3 of the UK GDPR, it must be provided free of charge. There are two exceptions to this rule: first, a controller may charge a fee for any copies of information provided as a result of a request for access under Art 15 of the UK GDPR subsequent to the first (free) copy[1]. Secondly, if any requests are manifestly unfounded or excessive, in particular because of their repetitive character, the controller may either charge a fee or refuse to act on the request[2]. The burden of proving the manifestly unfounded or excessive nature of the request lies on the controller. In both cases, the fee is defined as 'a reasonable fee taking into account the administrative costs of providing the information'. The DPA 2018, s 12 provides that the Secretary of State may specify a limit on fees charged under these provisions.

¹ Art 15(3) of the UK GDPR.
² Art 12(5) of the UK GDPR.

Provision of information

7.111 When collecting personal data, data controllers are required to give certain information to data subjects at the point the data are collected. Where the data are collected from the data subject directly, the requirements are set out at Art 13 of the UK GDPR as follows:

'Information to be provided where personal data are collected from the data subject

1. Where personal data relating to a data subject are collected from the data subject, the controller shall, at the time when personal data are obtained, provide the data subject with all of the following information:
   (a) the identity and the contact details of the controller and, where applicable, of the controller's representative;
   (b) the contact details of the data protection officer, where applicable;
   (c) the purposes of the processing for which the personal data are intended as well as the legal basis for the processing;
   (d) where the processing is based on point (f) of Article 6(1), the legitimate interests pursued by the controller or by a third party;
   (e) the recipients or categories of recipients of the personal data, if any;
   (f) where applicable, the fact that the controller intends to transfer personal data to a third country or international organisation and the existence or absence of relevant adequacy regulations under section 17A of the 2018 Act, or in the case of transfers referred to in Article 46 or 47, or the second subparagraph of Article 49(1), reference to the appropriate or suitable safeguards and the means by which to obtain a copy of them or where they have been made available.

2. In addition to the information referred to in paragraph 1, the controller shall, at the time when personal data are obtained, provide the data subject with the following further information necessary to ensure fair and transparent processing:

(a)   the period for which the personal data will be stored, or if that is not possible, the criteria used to determine that period;

(b)   the existence of the right to request from the controller access to and rectification or erasure of personal data or restriction of processing concerning the data subject or to object to processing as well as the right to data portability;

(c)   where the processing is based on point (a) of Article 6(1) or point (a) of Article 9(2), the existence of the right to withdraw consent at any time, without affecting the lawfulness of processing based on consent before its withdrawal;

(d)   the right to lodge a complaint with the Commissioner;

(e)   whether the provision of personal data is a statutory or contractual requirement, or a requirement necessary to enter into a contract, as well as whether the data subject is obliged to provide the personal data and of the possible consequences of failure to provide such data;

(f)   the existence of automated decision-making, including profiling, referred to in Article 22(1) and (4) and, at least in those cases, meaningful information about the logic involved, as well as the significance and the envisaged consequences of such processing for the data subject.'

7.112 For circumstances in which the data are not obtained from the data subject directly, the required information is set out at Art 14 of the UK GDPR as follows:

'**Information to be provided where personal data have not been obtained from the data subject**

1. Where personal data relating to a data subject are collected from the data subject, the controller shall, at the time when personal data are obtained, provide the data subject with all of the following information:

(a)   the identity and the contact details of the controller and, where applicable, of the controller's representative;

(b)   the contact details of the data protection officer, where applicable;

(c)   the purposes of the processing for which the personal data are intended as well as the legal basis for the processing;

(d)   the categories of personal data concerned;

(e)   the recipients or categories of recipients of the personal data, if any;

(f)   where applicable, the fact that the controller intends to transfer personal data to a third country or international organisation and the existence or absence of relevant adequacy regulations under section 17A of the 2018 Act, or in the case of transfers referred to in Article 46 or 47, or the second subparagraph of Article 49(1), reference to the appropriate or suitable safeguards and the means by which to obtain a copy of them or where they have been made available.

2. In addition to the information referred to in paragraph 1, the controller shall, at the time when personal data are obtained, provide the data subject with the following further information necessary to ensure fair and transparent processing:

(a)   the period for which the personal data will be stored, or if that is not possible, the criteria used to determine that period;

(b)   where the processing is based on point (f) of Article 6(1), the legitimate interests pursued by the controller or by a third party;

(c)   the existence of the right to request from the controller access to and rectification or erasure of personal data or restriction of processing concerning the data subject and to object to processing as well as the right to data portability;

(d)   where processing is based on point (a) of Article 6(1) or point (a) of Article 9(2), the existence of the right to withdraw consent at any time, without affecting the lawfulness of processing based on consent before its withdrawal;

(e)   the right to lodge a complaint with the Commissioner;

(f)   from which source the personal data originate, and if applicable, whether it came from publicly accessible sources;

(g)   the existence of automated decision-making, including profiling, referred to in Article 22(1) and (4) and, at least in those cases, meaningful information about the logic involved, as well as the significance and the envisaged consequences of such processing for the data subject.'

7.113 Where the data are not obtained from the data subject, the controller must provide the relevant information within a reasonable period, but at the latest within one month, having regard to the specific circumstances in which the data are processed. If the data are to be used for communication with the subject or onward disclosure is anticipated, the prescribed information should be provided at the latest at the time of the first communication or disclosure as applicable[1].

[1]   Art 14(3) of the UK GDPR.

7.114 Whether obtained from the subject or not, if the data are to be processed for a purpose other than the one for which they were originally obtained, the controller must, before beginning the new form of processing, inform the subject and provide the information prescribed by para 2 of the relevant Article[1].

[1]   Arts 13(3) and 14(4) of the UK GDPR.

7.115 In certain circumstances the requirements of Arts 13 and 14 of the UK GDPR will be dis-applied. In the case of data obtained from the subject, Art 13(4) of the UK GDPR provides that paras 1–3 of Art 13 do not apply if and to the extent that the subject already has the information. In the case of data not obtained from the subject, the list of exemptions is longer, and is set out at Art 14(5) of the UK GDPR as follows:

'Information to be provided where personal data have not been obtained from the data subject

. . .

5. Paragraphs 1 to 4 shall not apply where and insofar as:

(a)   the data subject already has the information;

(b)   the provision of such information proves impossible or would involve a disproportionate effort, in particular for processing for archiving purposes in the public interest, scientific or historical research purposes or statistical purposes, subject to the conditions and safeguards referred to in Article 89(1) or in so far as the obligation referred to in paragraph 1 of this Article is likely to render impossible or seriously impair the achievement of the objectives of that processing. In such cases the controller shall take appropriate measures to protect the data subject's rights and freedoms and legitimate interests, including making the information publicly available;

(c)   obtaining or disclosure is expressly laid down by a provision of domestic law and which provides appropriate measures to protect the data subject's legitimate interests; or

(d)   where the personal data must remain confidential subject to an obligation of professional secrecy regulated by domestic law, including a statutory obligation of secrecy.'

Right of access

7.116 Article 15 of the UK GDPR creates a right for data subjects to obtain a copy of any personal data which is being processed by a controller, as well as certain information pertaining to those data as follows:

'**GDPR: Right of access by the data subject**

1. the data subject shall have the right to obtain from the controller confirmation as to whether or not personal data concerning him or her are being processed, and, where that is the case, access to the personal data and the following information:

(a)   the purposes of the processing;

(b)   the categories of personal data concerned;

(c)   the recipients or categories of recipient to whom the personal data have been or will be disclosed, in particular recipients in third countries or international organisations;

(d)   where possible, the envisaged period for which the personal data will be stored, or, if not possible, the criteria used to determine that period;

(e)   the existence of the right to request from the controller rectification or erasure of personal data or restriction of processing of personal data concerning the data subject or to object to such processing;

(f)   the right to lodge a complaint with the Commissioner;

(g)   where the personal data are not collected from the data subject, any available information as to their source;

(h)   the existence of automated decision-making, including profiling, referred to in Article 22(1) and (4) and, at least in those cases, meaningful information about the logic involved, as well as the significance and the envisaged consequences of such processing for the data subject.'

7.117 Where a subject makes such a request, the controller may not charge for the first copy of the data provided. For subsequent copies the controller may charge a reasonable fee based on administrative costs[1]. The DPA 2018, s 12 provides that the Secretary of State may specify a limit on fees charged under this provision.

[1]   Art 15(3) of the UK GDPR.

Right to rectification

7.118 Article 16 of the UK GDPR provides that subjects have a right to rectification of inaccurate personal data and completion of incomplete personal data held by a controller without undue delay. Where personal data are rectified as a result of this right, the controller must communicate the fact of the rectification to every person to whom the persona data have been disclosed unless to do so proves impossible or would require disproportionate effort. The controller must also inform the subject of the persons to whom the data have been disclosed if the subject so requests[1].

[1]   Art 19 of the UK GDPR.

Right to erasure

7.119 Article 17 of the UK GDPR creates a right to erasure (often referred to as the right to be forgotten) of personal data in certain circumstances. Article 17 sets out a number of grounds on which erasure may be sought, as well as a number of grounds on which a controller may refuse to comply with a request as follows:

'**Right of erasure ("right to be forgotten")**

1. The data subject shall have the right to obtain from the controller the erasure of personal data concerning him or her without undue delay and the controller shall have the obligation to erase personal data without undue delay where one of the following grounds applies:
   - (a)   the personal data are no longer necessary in relation to the purposes for which they were collected or otherwise processed;
   - (b)   the data subject withdraws consent on which the processing is based according to point (a) of Article 6(1), or point (a) of Article 9(2), and where there is no other legal ground for the processing;
   - (c)   the data subject objects to the processing pursuant to Article 21(1) and there are no overriding legitimate grounds for the processing, or the data subject objects to the processing pursuant to Article 21(2);
   - (d)   the personal data have been unlawfully processed;
   - (e)   the personal data have to be erased for compliance with a legal obligation under domestic law to which the controller is subject;
   - (f)   the personal data have been collected in relation to the offer of information society services referred to in Article 8(1).

2. Where the controller has made the personal data public and is obliged pursuant to paragraph 1 to erase the personal data, the controller, taking account of available technology and the cost of implementation, shall take reasonable steps, including technical measures, to inform controllers which are processing the personal data that the data subject has requested the erasure by such controllers of any links to, or copy or replication of, those personal data.

3. Paragraphs 1 and 2 shall not apply to the extent that processing is necessary:
   - (a)   for exercising the right of freedom of expression and information;
   - (b)   for compliance with a legal obligation which requires processing by domestic law to which the controller is subject or for the performance of a task carried out in the public interest or in the exercise of official authority vested in the controller;
   - (c)   for reasons of public interest in the area of public health in accordance with points (h) and (i) of Article 9(2) as well as Article 9(3);
   - (d)   for archiving purposes in the public interest, scientific or historical research purposes or statistical purposes in accordance with Article 89(1) in so far as the right referred to in paragraph 1 is likely to render impossible or seriously impair the achievement of the objectives of that processing; or
   - (e)   for the establishment, exercise or defence of legal claims.'

7.120 This right has generated some litigation under the previous DPA 1998 regime: in *NT1 & NT2 v Google LLC*[1] the High Court considered claims for the delisting of personal data relating to criminal convictions from Google searches. However, Warby J in that case acknowledged that 'this case is being determined in the twilight of the DP Directive regime, with the first light of the GDPR already visible on the horizon. It seems unlikely that my decision will have an impact on other cases.' At this stage, therefore, it remains to be seen whether subsequent litigation will extend any of the general principles which emerged from the case to the UK GDPR regime².

¹   [2018] EWHC 799 (QB).
²   [2018] EWHC 799 (QB) at [105].

7.121 Where personal data are erased as a result of this right, the controller must communicate the fact of the erasure to every person to whom the persona data have been disclosed unless to do so proves impossible or would require disproportionate effort. The controller must also inform the subject of the persons to whom the data have been disclosed if the subject so requests¹.

¹   Art 19 of the UK GDPR.

Right to restrict processing

7.122 Article 18 of the UK GDPR provides for restrictions on processing by the controller. This right is mostly envisaged to be used as an interim measure pending the resolution of other Chapter 3 rights.

'Right to restriction of processing

1. The data subject shall have the right to obtain from the controller restriction of processing where one of the following applies:
   (a)   the accuracy of the personal data is contested by the data subject, for a period enabling the controller to verify the accuracy of the personal data;
   (b)   the processing is unlawful and the data subject opposes the erasure of the personal data and requests the restriction of their use instead;
   (c)   the controller no longer needs the personal data for the purposes of the processing, but they are required by the data subject for the establishment, exercise or defence of legal claims;
   (d)   the data subject has objected to processing pursuant to Article 21(1) pending the verification whether the legitimate grounds of the controller override those of the data subject.

2. Where processing has been restricted under paragraph 1, such personal data shall, with the exception of storage, only be processed with the data subject's consent or for the establishment, exercise or defence of legal claims or for the protection of the rights of another natural or legal person or for reasons of important public.

3. A data subject who has obtained restriction of processing pursuant to paragraph 1 shall be informed by the controller before the restriction of processing is lifted.'

7.123 Where processing is restricted as a result of this right, the controller must communicate that fact to every person to whom the persona data have been disclosed unless to do so proves impossible or would require disproportionate effort. The controller must also inform the subject of the persons to whom the data have been disclosed if the subject so requests¹.

¹   Art 19 of the UK GDPR.

Right to data portability

7.124 Article 20 provides subjects with the right to be provided with their personal data for the purpose of transferring them to a different controller, or to have the data transferred between controllers directly. This right arises where personal data are processed on the basis of consent or performance of a contract. Article 20(4) of the UK GDPR provides that this right shall not adversely affect the rights and freedoms of others.

Automated decision-making

7.125 Article 22 of the UK GDPR provides that a subject has a right not to be subject to a decision based solely on automated processing in certain circumstances. Article 22(1) of the UK GDPR includes 'profiling' within its ambit, which is defined as:

> 'any form of automated processing of personal data consisting of the use of personal data to evaluate certain personal aspects relating to a natural person, in particular to analyse or predict aspects concerning that natural person's performance at work, economic situation, health, personal preferences, interests, reliability, behaviour, location or movements.'[1]

[1] Art 4(4) of the UK GDPR.

7.126 The prohibition in Art 22 of the UK GDPR is as follows:

'Automated individual decision-making, including profiling

1. The data subject shall have the right not to be subject to a decision based solely on automated processing, including profiling, which produces legal effects concerning him or her or similarly significantly affects him or her.

2. Paragraph 1 shall not apply if the decision:
   (a)   is necessary for entering into, or performance of, a contract between the data subject and a data controller;
   (b)   is required or authorised by domestic law which also lays down suitable measures to safeguard the data subject's rights and freedoms and legitimate interests; or
   (c)   is based on the data subject's explicit consent.

3. In the cases referred to in points (a) and (c) of paragraph 2, the data controller shall implement suitable measures to safeguard the data subject's rights and freedoms and legitimate interests, at least the right to obtain human intervention on the part of the controller, to express his or her point of view and to contest the decision.

4. Decisions referred to in paragraph 2 shall not be based on special categories of personal data referred to in Article 9(2)1), unless point (a) or (g) of Article 9(2) applies and suitable measures to safeguard the data subject's rights and freedoms and legitimate interests are in place.'

7.127 The right not to be subjected to automated decision-making extends only to certain decisions: those which produce legal effects for or similarly significantly affects the data subject. If a decision does have a sufficiently significant effect on either of those tests, para 2 sets out a number of circumstances in which the right can still be dis-applied. The effect of para 2(a) and (c) and para 3 is that where the processing is necessary for a contract or the subject has given his consent, the right can be dis-applied if the controller implements sufficient safeguards.

7.128 Paragraph 2(b) provides that the right not to be subjected to automated decision-making may also be dis-applied where such decision-making is required or authorised by domestic law which also lays down suitable measures to safeguard the such decision-making is required or authorised by domestic law which also lays down suitable measures to safeguard the data subject's rights and freedoms and legitimate interests. In relation to this, provision is made in the DPA 2018, s 14. In order to fall within the exemption in Art 22(2)(b) of the GDPR, the decision in question must be one which the controller is required or authorised by law to make[1]. Where a controller proposes to take such a decision based on automated means, DPA 2018, s 14(4) and (5) set out the relevant safeguards as follows:

14 Automated decision-making authorised by law: safeguards

. . .

(4) Where a controller takes a qualifying significant decision in relation to a data subject based solely on automated processing—

    (a)   the controller must, as soon as reasonably practicable, notify the data subject in writing that a decision has been taken based solely on automated processing, and

    (b)   the data subject may, before the end of the period of 1 month beginning with receipt of the notification, request the controller to—

        (i)   reconsider the decision, or

        (ii)   take a new decision that is not based solely on automated processing.

(5) If a request is made to a controller under subsection (4), the controller must, within the period described in Article 12(3) of the GDPR—

    (a)   consider the request, including any information provided by the data subject that is relevant to it,

    (b)   comply with the request, and

    (c)   by notice in writing inform the data subject of—

        (i)   the steps taken to comply with the request, and

        (ii)   the outcome of complying with the request.

[1]   DPA 2018, s 14(3).

7.129 The timeframes and rules regarding fees set out in Art 12 of the UK GDPR apply to this procedure (for which see **7.109–7.110** above).

Restrictions on protection afforded by the UK GDPR

7.130 Articles 23 and 6(3) of the UK GDPR provide that the Secretary of State law restrict the rights conferred on data subjects under Arts 12–22 (subject rights), Art 34 (communication of a data breach to the subject), and Art 5 (the DPPs) of the UK GDPR. These restrictions are implemented in UK law by the DPA 2018, s 15 and Schs 2, 3, and 4. Of these, the restrictions which are relevant for the purposes of this work are contained in Sch 2. The DPA 2018, Sch 2 is divided into six parts, each of which specifies a list of provisions of the UK GDPR which may be restricted and the grounds upon which such restriction may take place. The relevant parts of the Schedule are discussed below.

Provisions restricted under Pt 1 of Schedule 2 to the DPA 2018

7.131 Part 1 of Sch 2 to the DPA 2018 lists the following provisions of the UK GDPR as the objects of restriction:

1 GDPR provisions to be adapted or restricted: "the listed GDPR provisions"

In this Part of this Schedule "the listed GDPR provisions" means—

(a) the following provisions of the GDPR (the rights and obligations in which may be restricted by virtue of Article 23(1) of the GDPR) —

(i) Article 13(1) to (3) (personal data collected from data subject: information to be provided);

(ii) Article 14(1) to (4) (personal data collected other than from data subject: information to be provided);

(iii) Article 15(1) to (3) (confirmation of processing, access to data and safeguards for third country transfers);

(iv) Article 16 (right to rectification);

(v) Article 17(1) and (2) (right to erasure);

(vi) Article 18(1) (restriction of processing);

(vii) Article 19 (notification obligation regarding rectification or erasure of personal data or restriction of processing);

(viii) Article 20(1) and (2) (right to data portability);

(ix) Article 21(1) (objections to processing);

(x) Article 5 (general principles) so far as its provisions correspond to the rights and obligations provided for in the provisions mentioned in sub-paragraphs (i) to (ix); and

(b) the following provisions of the GDPR (the application of which may be adapted by virtue of Article 6(3) of the GDPR) —

(i) Article 5(1)(a) (lawful, fair and transparent processing), other than the lawfulness requirements set out in Article 6;

(ii) Article 5(1)(b) (purpose limitation).

7.132 Paragraphs 2 and 5 of Pt 1 of Sch 2 to the DPA 2018 set out crime and taxation and legal proceedings as ground on which the listed UK GDPR provisions may be restricted. Each of these are discussed in the following sections.

Crime and taxation

7.133 Paragraph 2 of Pt 1 of Sch 2 to the DPA 2018 reads as follows:

2 Crime and taxation (general)

(1) The listed GDPR provisions and Article 34(1) and (4) of the GDPR (communication of personal data breach to the data subject) do not apply to personal data processed for any of the following purposes—

(a) the prevention or detection of crime,

(b) the apprehension or prosecution of offenders, or

(c) the assessment or collection of a tax or duty or an imposition of a similar nature

to the extent that the application of those provisions would be likely to prejudice any of the matters mentioned in paragraphs (a) to (c).

(2) Sub-paragraph (3) applies where—

(a) personal data is processed by a person ('Controller 1') for any of the purposes mentioned in sub-paragraph (1)(a) to (c), and

(b) another person ('Controller 2') obtains the data from Controller 1 for the purpose of discharging statutory functions and processes it for the purpose of discharging statutory functions.

(3)   Controller 2 is exempt from the obligations in the following provisions of the GDPR—

   (a)   Article 13(1) to (3) (personal data collected from data subject: information to be provided),

   (b)   Article 14(1) to (4) (personal data collected other than from data subject: information to be provided),

   (c)   Article 15(1) to (3) (confirmation of processing, access to data and safeguards for third country transfers), and

   (d)   Article 5 (general principles) so far as its provisions correspond to the rights and obligations provided for in the provisions mentioned in paragraphs (a) to (c),

   to the same extent that Controller 1 is exempt from those obligations by virtue of sub-paragraph (1).

7.134 Paragraph 2(1) of Pt 1 of Sch 2 to the DPA 2018 mirrors the language of the DPA 1998, s 29(1). As such, the principles and authorities relevant to the latter are likely to apply to the former.

7.135 Paragraph 2(1) sets out the purposes for which the data in question must be processed in order to qualify for the exemption. It is the purpose for which the data are being processed, not the nature of the data or the organisation doing the processing, which triggers the exemption. Accordingly, a company investigating (for example) infringements of its IP rights with a view to bringing a private prosecution or passing the evidence to a prosecuting authority will come within the provision.

7.136 Paragraph 2(1) does not provide a blanket restriction in relation to all data processed for one of the purposes described therein. The test is whether the normal application of the one or more of the listed provisions of the UK GDPR would be likely to prejudice the purposes set out in para 2(1). Anybody seeking to rely on para 2(1) should be able to identify the particular listed provision of the UK GDPR which should be restricted, the prejudice in question, and establish a causal link between that prejudice likely to occur and the restriction not being implemented. The question of likelihood was considered in *R (Lord) v SSHD*[1], a case concerning the DPA 1998, s 29, in which it was held that it required 'a degree of probability where there is a very significant and weighty chance to prejudice to the identified public interests'.

[1]   [2003] EWHC 2073 (Admin).

7.137 The effect of para 2(2) and (3) is to extend the effect of the restriction of certain listed provisions of the UK GDPR to controllers who obtain personal data from a controller which has processed those data under para 2(1). This may include enforcing authorities who have obtained data from members of the public, or from another authority.

7.138 Like the DPA 1998, s 29, the effect of para 2 is to disapply what would otherwise be a mandatory requirement. It therefore allows a controller to process data (including disclosing it to enforcers) in ways which would otherwise be prohibited by one of the listed provisions of the UK GDPR. However, this does not equate to a coercive power requiring them to process data in such a way. Like the DPA 1998, s 29, it should be regarded as an empowering, rather than a mandatory, provision.

Legal proceedings

7.139 Paragraph 5 of Sch 2 to the DPA 2018 reads as follows:

5 Information required to be disclosed by law etc or in connection with legal proceedings

(1)   The listed GDPR provisions do not apply to personal data consisting of information that the controller is obliged by an enactment to make available to the public, to the extent that the application of those provisions would prevent the controller from complying with that obligation.

(2)   The listed GDPR provisions do not apply to personal data where disclosure of the data is required by an enactment, a rule of law or an order of a court or tribunal, to the extent that the application of those provisions would prevent the controller from making the disclosure.

(3)   The listed GDPR provisions do not apply to personal data where disclosure of the data—

    (a)   is necessary for the purpose of, or in connection with, legal proceedings (including prospective legal proceedings),

    (b)   is necessary for the purpose of obtaining legal advice, or

    (c)   is otherwise necessary for the purposes of establishing, exercising or defending legal rights,

    to the extent that the application of those provisions would prevent the controller from making the disclosure.

7.140 The effect of this provision is to restrict subject rights and protections where it is necessary to do so in connection with legal proceedings. It will often be the case that a party to proceedings will be a controller of the personal data of the other party. The legal proceedings exemption would (for example) prevent the subject from unfairly gaining an advantage in proceedings by making access or erasure requests of the controller. A further example of the operation of this exemption is where an employer provides information to an enforcer which is investigating an employee – but for the exemption, the employee would be entitled to be told by his employer that his personal data had been processed in that way. If to allow him that right would prejudice the legal proceedings (for example by allowing him to destroy evidence or fabricate a defence), the employer (as controller) may justifiably refuse to comply with the employee's request.

Provisions restricted under Pt 2 of Schedule 2 to the DPA 2018

7.141 Part 2 of Sch 2 to the DPA 2018 lists the following provisions of the UK GDPR as the objects of restriction:

6 GDPR provisions to be adapted or restricted: "the listed GDPR provisions"

In this Part of this Schedule "the listed GDPR provisions" means the following provisions of the GDPR (the rights and obligations in which may be restricted by virtue of Article 23(1) of the GDPR)—

    (a)   Article 13(1) to (3) (personal data collected from data subject: information to be provided);

(b) Article 14(1) to (4) (personal data collected other than from data subject: information to be provided);

(c) Article 15(1) to (3) (confirmation of processing, access to data and safeguards for third country transfers);

(d) Article 16 (right to rectification);

(e) Article 17(1) and (2) (right to erasure);

(f) Article 18(1) (restriction of processing);

(g) Article 19 (notification obligation regarding rectification or erasure of personal data or restriction of processing);

(h) Article 20(1) and (2) (right to data portability);

(i) Article 21(1) (objections to processing);

(j) Article 5 (general principles) so far as its provisions correspond to the rights and obligations provided for in the provisions mentioned in sub-paragraphs (a) to (i).

7.142 Paragraph 7 of Pt 2 of Sch 2 to the DPA 2018 sets out functions designed to protect the public as a ground on which the listed GDPR provisions may be restricted.

Functions designed to protect the public

7.143 Paragraph 7 of Pt 2 of Sch 2 to the DPA 2018 contains a table of functions and conditions which apply to those functions. The listed GDPR provisions do not apply to the extent that their application would be likely to prejudice the proper discharge of the function.

Description of function design	Condition
The function is designed to protect members of the public against— financial loss due to dishonesty, malpractice or other seriously improper conduct by, or the unfitness or incompetence of, persons concerned in the provision of banking, insurance, investment or other financial services or in the management of bodies corporate, or financial loss due to the conduct of discharged or undischarged bankrupts.	The function is— conferred on a person by an enactment, a function of the Crown, a Minister of the Crown or a government department, or of a public nature, and is exercised in the public interest.
The function is designed to protect members of the public against— dishonesty, malpractice or other seriously improper conduct, or unfitness or incompetence.	The function is— conferred on a person by an enactment, a function of the Crown, a Minister of the Crown or a government department, or of a public nature, and is exercised in the public interest.

Description of function design	Condition
The function is designed — to protect charities or community interest companies against misconduct or mismanagement (whether by trustees, directors or other persons) in their administration, to protect the property of charities or community interest companies from loss or misapplication, or to recover the property of charities or community interest companies.	The function is— conferred on a person by an enactment, a function of the Crown, a Minister of the Crown or a government department, or of a public nature, and is exercised in the public interest.
The function is designed — to secure the health, safety and welfare of persons at work, or to protect persons other than those at work against risk to health or safety arising out of or in connection with the action of persons at work.	The function is— conferred on a person by an enactment, a function of the Crown, a Minister of the Crown or a government department, or of a public nature, and is exercised in the public interest.
The function is designed to protect members of the public against— maladministration by public bodies, failures in services provided by public bodies, or a failure of a public body to provide a service which it is a function of the body to provide.	The function is conferred by any enactment on — the Parliamentary Commissioner for Administration, the Commissioner for Local Administration in England, the Health Service Commissioner for England, the Public Services Ombudsman for Wales, the Northern Ireland Public Services Ombudsman, the Prison Ombudsman for Northern Ireland, or the Scottish Public Services Ombudsman.
The function is designed — to protect members of the public against conduct which may adversely affect their interests by persons carrying on a business, to regulate agreements or conduct which have as their object or effect the prevention, restriction or distortion of competition in connection with any commercial activity, or to regulate conduct on the part of one or more undertakings which amounts to the abuse of a dominant position in a market.	The function is conferred on the Competition and Markets Authority by an enactment.

Provisions restricted under Pt 4 of Schedule 2 to the DPA 2018

7.144 Part 4 of Sch 2 to the DPA 2018 lists the following provisions of the UK GDPR as the objects of restriction:

18 GDPR provisions to be restricted: "the listed GDPR provisions"

In this Part of this Schedule "the listed GDPR provisions" means the following provisions of the GDPR (the rights and obligations in which may be restricted by virtue of Article 23(1) of the GDPR)—

(a)   Article 13(1) to (3) (personal data collected from data subject: information to be provided);

(b)   Article 14(1) to (4) (personal data collected other than from data subject: information to be provided);

(c)   Article 15(1) to (3) (confirmation of processing, access to data and safeguards for third country transfers);

(d)   Article 5 (general principles) so far as its provisions correspond to the rights and obligations provided for in the provisions mentioned in sub-paragraphs (a) to (c).

7.145 Paragraphs 19 and 20 of Pt 4 of Sch 2 to the DPA 2018 set out legal professional privilege and self-incrimination as grounds on which the listed UK GDPR provisions may be restricted.

DATA PROTECTION: LAW ENFORCEMENT PROCESSING

Introduction

7.146 While Pt 2 of the DPA 2018 and the UK GDPR set out the regime for general processing, Pt 3 of the DPA 2018 acts as a self-contained regime for processing done in the course of law enforcement. It is based on many of the principles and concepts which feature in Pt 2 of the DPA 2018 and the UK GDPR, modified accordingly to account for the specific requirements of law enforcement.

7.147 Where an enforcing authority is acting for one of the law-enforcement purposes, it will be necessary to have regard to both Pt 3 of the DPA 2018 and the Pt 2/UK GDPR regime. There are two main reasons for this. First, because Pt 3 of the DPA 2018 relates to specifically to processing done by the authority for the purposes of law enforcement, any other processing (such as the provision of information to the enforcement authority by a data controller) will not fall within Pt 3, but the Pt 2/UK GDPR regime. This is because the data controller providing the data is not a competent authority to which Pt 3 of the DPA 2018 applies. However, having obtained the data, the authority's subsequent processing of them will be under Pt 3 of the DPA 2018.

7.148 Secondly, while an authority may initially process data for a law-enforcement purpose, it may need to continue processing those data after the point at which that purpose expires. For example, once a prosecution is concluded and there is no longer a prospect of appeal, the data will cease to be retained for a law-enforcement purpose. However, the authority may wish to retain the data in the event that it needs to defend a legal claim arising from the prosecution, the limitation period for which may expire some years hence. In those circumstances, the justification for retention will shift from the Pt 3 regime to the Pt 2/UK GDPR regime.

Application

7.149 The scope of application of Pt 3 of the DPA 2018 is set out at the DPA 2018, s 29 as follows:

29 Processing to which this Part applies

(1)   This Part applies to—

(a)   the processing by a competent authority of personal data wholly or partly by automated means, and

(b)   the processing by a competent authority otherwise than by automated means of personal data which forms part of a filing system or is intended to form part of a filing system.

Key principles and interpretation

7.150 In addition to the defined terms set out in Art 4 of the UK GDPR, there are a number of terms and principles specific to Pt 3 of the DPA 2018. These are discussed below.

Competent authority

7.151 Part 3 of the DPA 2018 only applies to competent authorities. A competent authority is defined under the DPA 2018, s 30 as follows:

30 Meaning of "competent authority"

(1)   In this Part, "competent authority" means—

(a)   a person specified or described in Schedule 7, and

(b)   any other person if and to the extent that the person has statutory functions for any of the law enforcement purposes.

7.152 Local authority trading standards services are not specified in the DPA 2018, Sch 7. However, they fall within the definition of a competent authority by virtue of the DPA 2018, s 30(1)(b). The NCA, SFO, FCA, HSE, CMA, OFGEM, and FSA (inter alia) are all specified in DPA 2018, Sch 7.

The law enforcement purposes

7.153 The law-enforcement purposes are defined in s 31 of the DPA 2018 as follows:

the purposes of the prevention, investigation, detection or prosecution of criminal offences or the execution of criminal penalties, including the safeguarding against and the prevention of threats to public security.

Data controllers and processors

7.154 The DPA 2018, s 32 defines controllers and processors as follows:

32 Meaning of "controller" and "processor"

(1)   In this Part, "controller" means the competent authority which, alone or jointly with others—

    (a)   determines the purposes and means of the processing of personal data, or

    (b)   is the controller by virtue of subsection (2).

(2)   Where personal data is processed only—

    (a)   for purposes for which it is required by an enactment to be processed, and

    (b)   by means by which it is required by an enactment to be processed,

    (c)   the competent authority on which the obligation to process the data is imposed by the enactment (or, if different, one of the enactments) is the controller.

(3)   In this Part, "processor" means any person who processes personal data on behalf of the controller (other than a person who is an employee of the controller).

7.155 The definition of 'controller' for the purposes of Pt 3 of the DPA 2018 differs from that for general purposes under the UK GDPR in that only competent authorities can be considered to be controllers. Any person (natural or legal) processing data on behalf of such a competent authority is a processor. However, where the definition of 'processor' under the UK GDPR may include an employee of the controller, this is specifically excluded for law-enforcement processing by the DPA 2018, s 32(3).

Sensitive processing

7.156 Part 3 of the DPA 2018 does not refer to special categories of personal data in the way that the UK GDPR does. Instead, it includes the concept of sensitive processing, which is defined in the DPA 2018, s 35 as follows:

35 The first data protection principle

   . . .

(8) In this section, "sensitive processing" means—

    (a)   the processing of personal data revealing racial or ethnic origin, political opinions, religious or philosophical beliefs or trade union membership;

    (b)   the processing of genetic data, or of biometric data, for the purpose of uniquely identifying an individual;

    (c)   the processing of data concerning health;

    (d)   the processing of data concerning an individual's sex life or sexual orientation.

The data protection principles

7.157 The DPA 2018, ss 34–40 set out a separate set of DPPs which apply for the purposes of Pt 3 of the DPA 2018. They share certain features with the DPPs set out under Art 5 of the GDPR, but are designed to better suit the needs of law enforcement.

Lawfulness

7.158 The DPA 2018, s 35 sets out the circumstances in which the processing of personal data will be lawful when carried out under Pt 3 of the DPA 2018. It deals with both non-sensitive and sensitive processing. The lawfulness of sensitive processing is discussed in the section entitles 'Sensitive Processing' at **7.167–7.168** below. For non-sensitive processing, the relevant parts of the section state as follows:

35 The first data protection principle

(1) The first data protection principle is that the processing of personal data for any of the law enforcement purposes must be lawful and fair.

(2) The processing of personal data for any of the law enforcement purposes is lawful only if and to the extent that it is based on law and either—

    (a) the data subject has given consent to the processing for that purpose, or

    (b) the processing is necessary for the performance of a task carried out for that purpose by a competent authority.

7.159 There are two notable differences between the first DPP under Pt 3 of the DPA 2018 and Art 5 of the UK GDPR. First, under Pt 3 of the DPA 2018, processing need only be lawful and fair; the requirement for transparency is absent. This is an inevitable reflection of the fact that transparency can often be inconsistent with the investigation of criminal offences. Secondly, in the absence of consent, the only ground for processing is necessity for the performance of a task carried out for a law enforcement purpose. The test of necessity is arguably wider than the exhaustive list of gateways under the UK GDPR. This reflects the fact that criminal investigations are more intrinsically speculative and serendipitous than commercial processing.

Purpose limitation

7.160 The second DPP is set out in the DPA 2018, s 36 as follows:

36 The second data protection principle

(1) The second data protection principle is that—

    (a) the law enforcement purpose for which personal data is collected on any occasion must be specified, explicit and legitimate, and

    (b) personal data so collected must not be processed in a manner that is incompatible with the purpose for which it was collected.

(2) Paragraph (b) of the second data protection principle is subject to subsections (3) and (4).

(3) Personal data collected for a law enforcement purpose may be processed for any other law enforcement purpose (whether by the controller that collected the data or by another controller) provided that—

(a)   the controller is authorised by law to process the data for the other purpose, and

(b)   the processing is necessary and proportionate to that other purpose.

(4)   Personal data collected for any of the law enforcement purposes may not be processed for a purpose that is not a law enforcement purpose unless the processing is authorised by law.

7.161 The language of the DPA 2018, s 36(1) mirrors that of Art 5 of the UK GDPR. However, DPA 2018, ss 36(3) and (4) make further provision for onward processing. Where data have been obtained under Pt 3 of the DPA 2018, they may be further processed for a different law-enforcement purpose than that for which they were originally obtained (whether by the controller which originally obtained them or a different one), but not for a non-law-enforcement purpose unless such processing is allowed by law.

7.162 The effect of DPA 2018, s 36(4) is to protect against function creep in respect of data obtained under the broader test for lawfulness which is available to law-enforcers.

Data minimisation

7.163 The third DPP simply states that personal data processed for any of the law enforcement purposes must be adequate, relevant and not excessive in relation to the purpose for which they are processed[1].

[1]   DPA 2018, s 37.

Accuracy

7.164 Like its counterpart under the UK GDPR, this DPP requires that personal data be accurate and up-to-date. If further requires that personal data based on facts must, so far as possible, be distinguished from personal data based on personal assessments[1]. It further includes a specific requirement for controllers to make a clear distinction between different classes of data subject, such as:

- persons suspected of having committed or being about to commit a criminal offence;
- persons convicted of a criminal offence;
- persons who are or may be victims of a criminal offence;
- witnesses or other persons with information about offences[2].

[1]   DPA 2018, s 38(2).
[2]   DPA 2018, s 38(3).

Storage limitation

7.165 In addition to stating that data must be kept for no longer than necessary for the purpose for which they are processed, this DPP requires that appropriate time limits be established for the periodic review of the need for the continued storage for any of the law enforcement purposes[1].

[1]   DPA 2018, s 39.

Integrity and confidentiality

7.166 This DPP largely mirrors its counterpart under the UK GPDR in requiring that data be processed in a manner that ensures appropriate security of the personal data, using appropriate technical or organisational measures[1].

[1] DPA 2018, s 40.

Sensitive processing

7.167 For sensitive processing, DPA 2018, s 35 sets out two circumstances in which processing will be lawful for law-enforcement purposes as follows:

> **35 The first data protection principle**
>
> . . .
>
> (3) In addition, where the processing for any of the law enforcement purposes is sensitive processing, the processing is permitted only in the two cases set out in subsections (4) and (5).
> (4) The first case is where—
>
> > (a) the data subject has given consent to the processing for the law enforcement purpose as mentioned in subsection (2)(a), and
> > (b) at the time when the processing is carried out, the controller has an appropriate policy document in place (see section 42).
>
> (5) The second case is where—
>
> > (a) the processing is strictly necessary for the law enforcement purpose,
> > (b) the processing meets at least one of the conditions in Schedule 8, and
> > (c) at the time when the processing is carried out, the controller has an appropriate policy document in place (see section 42).

7.168 The test of 'strict necessity' at DPA 2018, s 35(5)(a) is more stringent than the test of mere necessity. It means that the processing has to relate to a pressing social need, and it cannot reasonably be achieved through less intrusive means. The conditions in the DPA 2018, Sch 8 are as follows:

- Statutory etc. purposes.
- Administration of justice.
- Protecting an individual's vital interests.
- Safeguarding children/individuals at risk.
- Data in public domain.
- Legal claims.
- Judicial acts.
- Preventing fraud.
- Archiving/research.

Processing of personal data relating to criminal convictions and offences

7.169 Part 3 of the DPA 2018 makes no specific provision regarding data relating to criminal convictions and offences. The position therefore defaults to the provisions of the UK GDPR, for which see **7.92** et seq above.

Subject rights

7.170 Chapter 3 of Pt 3 of the DPA 2018 is concerned with the exercise of balancing subject rights with the need to ensure that the law enforcement purposes are not prejudiced. Most obviously, this will involve the curtailment of the rights of anybody under investigation in criminal proceedings. However, the provisions of Chapter 3 acknowledge that notwithstanding this, the existence of criminal proceedings does not automatically lead to an absolute ground for refusing to comply with subject rights in respect of an accused.

7.171 Apart from the person under investigation, competent authorities are also likely to obtain personal data from complainants, witnesses, and other persons in the course of a criminal investigation. Such authorities should have regard in each case to whether the person concerned is a suspect, convicted offender, victim, or witness/informant, and what effect this has on the extent to which the exercise of their subject rights might prejudice the law enforcement purposes.

General duties

7.172 The DPA 2018, s 44 sets out the general duties owed by competent authorities in law enforcement cases. The following information must be provided to data subjects in such cases[1]:

- the identity and the contact details of the controller;
- where applicable, the contact details of the data protection officer;
- the purposes for which the controller processes personal data;
- the existence of the rights of access, rectification, and erasure; and
- the existence of the right to lodge a complaint with the Commissioner and the contact details of the Commissioner.

[1]   DPA 2018, s 44(1).

7.173 The DPA 2018, s 44(1) allows for that information to be provided by making it generally available to the public.

7.174 The DPA 2018, s 44(2) contains a requirement for further information to be provided in certain cases as follows:

44 Information: controller's general duties

. . .

(2) The controller must also, in specific cases for the purpose of enabling the exercise of a data subject's rights under this Part, give the data subject the following—

    (a)   information about the legal basis for the processing;

    (b)   information about the period for which the personal data will be stored or, where that is not possible, about the criteria used to determine that period;

    (c)   where applicable, information about the categories of recipients of the personal data (including recipients in third countries or international organisations);

    (d)   such further information as is necessary to enable the exercise of the data subject's rights under this Part.

(3) An example of where further information may be necessary as mentioned in subsection (2)(d) is where the personal data being processed was collected without the knowledge of the data subject.

7.175 The DPA 2018, s 44(4)–(7) make provision for the requirements to provide information set out in the DPA 2018, s 44(1) and (2) to be disapplied as follows:

44 Information: controller's general duties

. . .

(4) The controller may restrict, wholly or partly, the provision of information to the data subject under subsection (2) to the extent that and for so long as the restriction is, having regard to the fundamental rights and legitimate interests of the data subject, a necessary and proportionate measure to—

- (a) avoid obstructing an official or legal inquiry, investigation or procedure;
- (b) avoid prejudicing the prevention, detection, investigation or prosecution of criminal offences or the execution of criminal penalties;
- (c) protect public security;
- (d) protect national security;
- (e) protect the rights and freedoms of others.

(5) Where the provision of information to a data subject under subsection (2) is restricted, wholly or partly, the controller must inform the data subject in writing without undue delay—

- (a) that the provision of information has been restricted
- (b) of the reasons for the restriction,
- (c) of the data subject's right to make a request to the Commissioner under section 51,
- (d) of the data subject's right to lodge a complaint with the Commissioner, and
- (e) of the data subject's right to apply to a court under section 167.

(6) Subsection (5)(a) and (b) do not apply to the extent that complying with them would undermine the purpose of the restriction.

7.176 The reasons for any restriction under the DPA 2018, s 44(2) must be recorded and provided to the ICO on request[1].

[1]   DPA 2018, s 44(7).

Right of access

7.177 Section 45(1) of the DPA provides that a data subject is entitled to obtain from the controller confirmation as to whether or not his personal data concerning are being processed, and, where that is the case, access those data. In addition the subject is entitled to the following information:

- the purposes of and legal basis for the processing;
- the categories of personal data concerned;
- the recipients or categories of recipients to whom the personal data has been disclosed (including recipients or categories of recipients in third countries or international organisations);

- the period for which it is envisaged that the personal data will be stored or, where that is not possible, the criteria used to determine that period;
- the existence of the data subject's rights of rectification and erasure;
- the existence of the data subject's right to lodge a complaint with the Commissioner and the contact details of the Commissioner; and
- communication of the personal data undergoing processing and of any available information as to its origin.

7.178 Where a request is made, it must be complied with without undue delay, and in any event, within one month[1].

[1] DPA 2018, ss 45(3) and 54.

7.179 The DPA 2018, s 45(4)–(6) allow for the right to access to be restricted as follows:

45 Right of access by the data subject

. . .

(4) The controller may restrict, wholly or partly, the rights conferred by subsection (1) to the extent that and for so long as the restriction is, having regard to the fundamental rights and legitimate interests of the data subject, a necessary and proportionate measure to—

    (a)   avoid obstructing an official or legal inquiry, investigation or procedure;

    (b)   avoid prejudicing the prevention, detection, investigation or prosecution of criminal offences or the execution of criminal penalties;

    (c)   protect public security;

    (d)   protect national security;

    (e)   protect the rights and freedoms of others.

(5) Where the rights of a data subject under subsection (1) are restricted, wholly or partly, the controller must inform the data subject in writing without undue delay—

    (a)   that the rights of the data subject have been restricted

    (b)   of the reasons for the restriction,

    (c)   of the data subject's right to make a request to the Commissioner under section 51,

    (d)   of the data subject's right to lodge a complaint with the Commissioner, and

    (e)   of the data subject's right to apply to a court under section 167.

(6) Subsection (5)(a) and (b) do not apply to the extent that the provision of the information would undermine the purpose of the restriction.

7.180 The controller must record the reasons for any decision to restrict the right of access and make such a record available to the ICO on request[1].

[1] DPA 2018, s 45(7).

Right to rectification

7.181 The DPA 2018, s 46(1) provides that a controller must, if so requested by a data subject, rectify without undue delay inaccurate personal data relating to the data subject. This includes incomplete data. Where data are inaccurate, but must be preserved for the purposes of evidence, processing must be restricted instead[1].

[1] DPA 2018, s 46(4).

7.182 Where a request under this section is made, the DPA 2018, s 48 sets out how the controller must respond as follows:

48 Rights under section 46 or 47: supplementary

(1) Where a data subject requests the rectification or erasure of personal data or the restriction of its processing, the controller must inform the data subject in writing—

    (a) whether the request has been granted, and
    (b) if it has been refused—

        (i) of the reasons for the refusal,
        (ii) of the data subject's right to make a request to the Commissioner under section 51,
        (iii) of the data subject's right to lodge a complaint with the Commissioner, and
        (iv) of the data subject's right to apply to a court under section 167.

7.183 Where a request is made, this process must be complied with without undue delay, and in any event, within one month[1].

[1] DPA 2018, ss 48(2) and 54.

7.184 If a controller rectifies personal data under this section, it must notify the competent authority from which the data originated (if any)[1].

[1] DPA 2018, s 48(7).

Rights to erasure and restriction

7.185 The DPA 2018, s 47(1) states that a controller must erase personal data without undue delay where the controller has an obligation to do so or the processing of the data would infringe any of the following provisions of the DPA 2018:

- section 35 (lawfulness);
- section 36(1)–(3) (purpose limitation);
- section 37 (data minimisation)
- section 38(1) (accuracy);
- section 39(1) (storage limitation);
- section 40 (integrity and confidentiality);
- section 41 (archiving safeguards); or
- section 42 (sensitive processing safeguards).

7.186 Where the obligation to erase would arise but for the requirement to use the data as evidence, processing should be restricted instead[1]. Processing must also be restricted where the accuracy of the data is challenged by the subject and it is not possible to ascertain whether the data are accurate or not[2].

[1] DPA 2018, s 47(2).
[2] DPA 2018, s 47(3).

7.187 Where a request under this section is made, the DPA 2018, s 48 sets out how the controller must respond as follows:

48 Rights under section 46 or 47: supplementary

(1)   Where a data subject requests the rectification or erasure of personal data or the restriction of its processing, the controller must inform the data subject in writing—

    (a)   whether the request has been granted, and

    (b)   if it has been refused-

        (i)   of the reasons for the refusal,

        (ii)   of the data subject's right to make a request to the Commissioner under section 51,

        (iii)   of the data subject's right to lodge a complaint with the Commissioner, and

        (iv)   of the data subject's right to apply to a court under section 167.

7.188 Where a request is made, this process must be complied with without undue delay, and in any event, within one month[1].

[1]   DPA 2018, ss 48(2) and 54.

Restricting the rights to rectification, erasure, and restriction of processing

7.189 Where a request for rectification, erasure, or restriction of processing has been refused by a controller, the controller may wholly or partly restrict the subject's right to the reasons for the refusal under the DPA 2018, s 48(1)(b)(i). This is governed by the DPA 2018, ss 48(3)–(5) as follows:

48 Rights under section 46 or 47: supplementary

. . .

(3) The controller may restrict, wholly or partly, the provision of information to the data subject under subsection (1)(b)(i) to the extent that and for so long as the restriction is, having regard to the fundamental rights and legitimate interests of the data subject, a necessary and proportionate measure to—

    (a)   avoid obstructing an official or legal inquiry, investigation or procedure;

    (b)   avoid prejudicing the prevention, detection, investigation or prosecution of criminal offences or the execution of criminal penalties;

    (c)   protect public security;

    (d)   protect national security;

    (e)   protect the rights and freedoms of others.

(4) Where the rights of a data subject under subsection (1) are restricted, wholly or partly, the controller must inform the data subject in writing without undue delay—

    (a)   that the rights of the data subject have been restricted

    (b)   of the reasons for the restriction,

    (c)   of the data subject's right to make a request to the Commissioner under section 51,

    (d)   of the data subject's right to lodge a complaint with the Commissioner, and

    (e)   of the data subject's right to apply to a court under section 167.

(5) Subsection (4)(a) and (b) do not apply to the extent that the provision of the information would undermine the purpose of the restriction.

7.190 The controller must record the reasons for any decision to restrict the right of access and make such a record available to the ICO on request[1].

1   DPA 2018, s 48(6).

Automated decision-making

7.191 The right not to be subjected to automated decision-making arises in relation to 'significant decisions', which are defined as decisions which produce an adverse legal effect concerning the data subject, or significantly affects the data subject[1]. A controller may not take such a decision based solely on automated processing unless that decision is required or authorised by law[2].

1   DPA 2018, s 49(2).
2   DPA 2018, s 49(1).

7.192 Where automated decision-making of significant decision is required or authorised by law (a 'qualifying significant decision'), the safeguards for such decision-making are set out in the DPA 2018, ss 49(2)–(3) as follows:

49 Right not to be subject to automated decision-making

. . .

(2) Where a controller takes a qualifying significant decision in relation to a data subject based solely on automated processing—

(a)   the controller must, as soon as reasonably practicable, notify the data subject in writing that a decision has been taken based solely on automated processing, and

(b)   the data subject may, before the end of the period of 1 month beginning with receipt of the notification, request the controller to-

(i)   reconsider the decision, or

(ii)   take a new decision that is not based solely on automated processing.

(3) If a request is made to a controller under subsection (2), the controller must, before the end of the period of 1 month beginning with receipt of the request—

(a)   consider the request, including any information provided by the data subject that is relevant to it,

(b)   comply with the request, and

(c)   by notice in writing inform the data subject of-

(i)   the steps taken to comply with the request, and

(ii)   the outcome of complying with the request.

Manifestly unfounded or excessive requests

7.193 The DPA 2018, s 53 makes provision for manifestly unfounded or excessive requests under Chapter 3 of Pt 3 of the DPA 2018 as follows:

53 Manifestly unfounded or excessive requests by the data subject

(1)   Where a request from a data subject under section 45, 46, 47 or 50 is manifestly unfounded or excessive, the controller may—

(a)   charge a reasonable fee for dealing with the request, or

(b)   refuse to act on the request.

(2)   An example of a request that may be excessive is one that merely repeats the substance of previous requests.

(3)   In any proceedings where there is an issue as to whether a request under section 45, 46, 47 or 50 is manifestly unfounded or excessive, it is for the controller to show that it is.

DATA PROTECTION: REGULATORY, ACCOUNTABILITY, AND TECHNICAL REQUIREMENTS

Introduction

7.194 The UK GDPR incorporates a new principle of accountability, which requires controllers to record and be able to prove the basis for their processing and any restriction of subject rights and protections otherwise available. Many of the provisions discussed in the sections above include requirements for records of decisions to be kept and produced to the ICO on requests and/or of controllers to have appropriate policy documents. These provisions are supplemented by a number of general provisions which require organisational measures to be implemented, such as the carrying-out of data protection impact assessments and the appointment of data protection officers. Additionally, the UK GDPR includes provisions about the technical standards to be expected of controllers in order to comply with data protection law. This section will cover some of those provisions.

Data protection by design and default

7.195 One of the hallmarks of the UK GDPR is that it incorporates the technical, as well as the legal, aspects of data protection. Article 25 imposes on controllers a duty to take into account the state of the art and implement appropriate technical and organisational measures to implement the DPPs and other obligations in the GDPR and Member State law:

'Data protection by design and default

1. Taking into account the state of the art, the cost of implementation and the nature, scope, context and purposes of processing as well as the risks of varying likelihood and severity for rights and freedoms of natural persons posed by the processing, the controller shall, both at the time of the determination of the means for processing and at the time of the processing itself, implement appropriate technical and organisational measures, such as pseudonymisation, which are designed to implement data-protection principles, such as data minimisation, in an effective manner and to integrate the necessary safeguards into the processing in order to meet the requirements of this Regulation and protect the rights of data subjects.'

7.196 Controllers should be able to show that they have taken into account the factors set out in Art 25 of the UK GDPR in implementing their systems and be able to justify the decisions they have taken in that regard by reference to Art 25. This will be particularly important in cases where systemic issues have led to a data breach.

7.197 Article 25 of the UK GDPR does not require controllers to implement systems which are on the very cutting-edge of technology – the requirement to consider the state of the art is balanced with cost, the nature of processing, and the risks involved. However, controllers will need to monitor their systems with a view to ensuring they remain sufficiently up-to-date. Where the balancing of the Art 25 factors involves a trade-off, controllers should be prepared to justify the relative weight given to the different factors in coming to their decisions.

Records of processing

7.198 Article 30 of the UK GDPR requires written records to be kept of processing activities, which must be made available to the ICO on request. There are specific record-keeping duties for controllers and processors as follows:

'Records of processing activities

1. Each controller and, where applicable, the controller's representative, shall maintain a record of processing activities under its responsibility. That record shall contain all of the following information:

(a) the name and contact details of the controller and, where applicable, the joint controller, the controller's representative and the data protection officer;

(b) the purposes of the processing;

(c) a description of the categories of data subjects and of the categories of personal data;

(d) the categories of recipients to whom the personal data have been or will be disclosed including recipients in third countries or international organisations;

(e) where applicable, transfers of personal data to a third country or an international organisation, including the identification of that third country or international organisation and, in the case of transfers referred to in the second subparagraph of Article 49(1), the documentation of suitable safeguards;

(f) where possible, the envisaged time limits for erasure of the different categories of data;

(g) where possible, a general description of the technical and organisational security measures referred to in Article 32(1), or, as appropriate, the security measures referred to in section 28(3) of the 2018 Act.

2. Each processor and, where applicable, the processor's representative shall maintain a record of all categories of processing activities carried out on behalf of a controller, containing:

(a) the name and contact details of the processor or processors and of each controller on behalf of which the processor is acting, and, where applicable, of the controller's or the processor's representative, and the data protection officer;

(b) the categories of processing carried out on behalf of each controller;

(c) where applicable, transfers of personal data to a third country or an international organisation, including the identification of that third country or international organisation and, in the case of transfers referred to in the second subparagraph of Article 49(1), the documentation of suitable safeguards;

(d) where possible, a general description of the technical and organisational security measures referred to in Article 32(1), or, as appropriate, the security measures referred to in section 28(3) of the 2018 Act.'

Breach notification

7.199 The UK GDPR contains provisions which require that data breaches be notified to the ICO and any affected subjects. For general processing, a breach is defined in Art 4(12) of the GDPR as follows:

'a breach of security leading to the accidental or unlawful destruction, loss, alteration, unauthorised disclosure of, or access to, personal data transmitted, stored or otherwise processed.'

7.200 This definition is adopted verbatim for law-enforcement processing by the DPA 2018, s 33(3).

Notification to the ICO

7.201 Article 33 of the UK GDPR requires a controller to report a data breach to the ICO 'without undue delay and, where feasible, not later than 72 hours after having become aware of it' unless the breach is unlikely to result in a risk to the rights and freedoms of natural persons. If the breach is notified after more than 72 hours, it must be accompanied by an explanation for the delay. This requirement is transposed into the law-enforcement context by the DPA 2018, s 67.

Notification to the data subject

7.202 Article 34 of the UK GDPR requires a controller to communicate a data breach to the affected data subject(s) without undue delay if the breach is unlikely to result in a high risk to the rights and freedoms of natural persons. This requirement is transposed into the law-enforcement context by the DPA 2018, s 68.

Data protection impact assessments

7.203 Where processing is likely to result in a high risk to the rights and freedoms of natural persons, a controller is required by Art 35(1) of the UK GDPR to carry out a data protection impact assessment (DPIA). Art 35(3) sets out examples of particular cases where a DPIA will be required as:

- a systematic and extensive evaluation of personal aspects relating to natural persons which is based on automated processing, including profiling, and on which decisions are based that produce legal effects concerning the natural person or similarly significantly affect the natural person;
- processing on a large scale of special categories of data referred to in Art 9(1), or of personal data relating to criminal convictions and offences referred to in Art 10; or and
- a systematic monitoring of a publicly accessible area on a large scale.

7.204 The content of a DPIA is dealt with by Art 35(7) of the UK GDPR, which states:

'Data protection impact assessment

. . .

7. The assessment shall contain at least:
(a) a systematic description of the envisaged processing operations and the purposes of the processing, including, where applicable, the legitimate interest pursued by the controller;
(b) an assessment of the necessity and proportionality of the processing operations in relation to the purposes;
(c) an assessment of the risks to the rights and freedoms of data subjects referred to in paragraph 1; and
(d) the measures envisaged to address the risks, including safeguards, security measures and mechanisms to ensure the protection of personal data and to demonstrate compliance with this Regulation taking into account the rights and legitimate interests of data subjects and other persons concerned.'

7.205 Article 35(4) pf the UK GDPR states that the ICO shall make a list of the types of processing which will require a DPIA. The ICO has stated that controllers need a DPIA if they plan to:

- use new technologies;
- use profiling or special category data to decide on access to services;
- profile individuals on a large scale;
- process biometric data;
- process genetic data;
- match data or combine datasets from different sources;
- collect personal data from a source other than the individual without providing them with a privacy notice ('invisible processing');
- track individuals' location or behaviour;
- profile children or target marketing or online services at them; or
- process data that might endanger the individual's physical health or safety in the event of a security breach[1].

[1] https://ico.org.uk/for-organisations/guide-to-the-general-data-protection-regulation-gdpr/accountability-and-governance/data-protection-impact-assessments/.

Data protection officers

7.206 Article 37 of the UK GDPR makes provisions regarding the appointment of a Data Protection Officer (DPO) for general processing purposes. For law-enforcement purposes, the requirements are set out in the DPA 2018, ss 69–71.

Requirement to appoint a DPO

7.207 Article 37(1) of the UK GDPR requires a controller and processor to designate a DPO where:

- the processing is carried out by a public authority or body, except for courts acting in their judicial capacity;
- the core activities of the controller or the processor consist of processing operations which, by virtue of their nature, their scope and/or their purposes, require regular and systematic monitoring of data subjects on a large scale; or
- the core activities of the controller or the processor consist of processing on a large scale of special categories of data pursuant to Art 9 or personal data relating to criminal convictions and offences referred to in Art 10.

7.208 For law-enforcement processing, the controller must designate a data protection officer, unless the controller is a court, or other judicial authority, acting in its judicial capacity[1].

[1] DPA 2018, s 69(1).

Duties of a DPO

7.209 For general processing purposes, the tasks of a DPO are set out in Art 39 of the UK GDPR as follows:

'Tasks of the data protection officer

1. The data protection officer shall have at least the following tasks:
    (a) to inform and advise the controller or the processor and the employees who carry out processing of their obligations pursuant to this Regulation and to other domestic law relating to data protection;
    (b) to monitor compliance with this Regulation, with other domestic law relating to data protection and with the policies of the controller or processor in relation to the protection of personal data, including the assignment of responsibilities, awareness-raising and training of staff involved in processing operations, and the related audits;
    (c) to provide advice where requested as regards the data protection impact assessment and monitor its performance pursuant to Article 35;
    (d) to cooperate with the Commissioner;
    (e) to act as the contact point for the Commissioner on issues relating to processing, including the prior consultation referred to in Article 36, and to consult, where appropriate, with regard to any other matter.

2. The data protection officer shall in the performance of his or her tasks have due regard to the risk associated with processing operations, taking into account the nature, scope, context and purposes of processing.'

7.210 For law enforcement processing, the tasks of the DPO are set out at the DPA 2018, s 71 as follows:

71 Tasks of data protection officer

(1) The controller must entrust the data protection officer with at least the following tasks—
    (a) informing and advising the controller, any processor engaged by the controller, and any employee of the controller who carries out processing of personal data, of that person's obligations under this Part,
    (b) providing advice on the carrying out of a data protection impact assessment under section 64 and monitoring compliance with that section,
    (c) co-operating with the Commissioner,
    (d) acting as the contact point for the Commissioner on issues relating to processing, including in relation to the consultation mentioned in section 65, and consulting with the Commissioner, where appropriate, in relation to any other matter,
    (e) monitoring compliance with policies of the controller in relation to the protection of personal data, and
    (f) monitoring compliance by the controller with this Part.

(2) In relation to the policies mentioned in subsection (1)(e), the data protection officer's tasks include—

        (a)   assigning responsibilities under those policies,
        (b)   raising awareness of those policies,
        (c)   training staff involved in processing operations, and
        (d)   conducting audits required under those policies.

(3)   In performing the tasks set out in subsections (1) and (2), the data protection officer must have regard to the risks associated with processing operations, taking into account the nature, scope, context and purposes of processing.

DATA PROTECTION: ENFORCEMENT, REMEDIES, AND SANCTIONS

Introduction

7.211 Part 6 of the DPA 2018 provides the ICO with a number of tools to enforce the provisions of the UK GDPR and the DPA 2018. These include information notices, assessment notices, enforcement notices, and monetary penalties. The previous limit of £500,000 on monetary penalties under the DPA 1998 has now been increased in certain circumstances to £17.5 million or 4% of global turnover, whichever is the greater, giving the ICO much more extensive enforcement powers than previously. In addition, the DPA 2018 contains various criminal offences relating to the processing of data, proceedings for which may be taken by the ICO or if taken by another body, with the consent of the DPP.

Enforcement by the ICO

7.212 The ICO may investigate infringements of the UK GDPR and DPA 2018 of its own motion or upon a complaint from a data subject. Under Art 77 of the UK GDPR data subjects have the right to lodge a complaint with the ICO, which has a duty to investigate and deal with the complaint under Art 57(1)(f) of the UK GDPR. Depending on the nature of the complaint and the action required, the ICO has a range of enforcement tools available to it, including information notices, assessment notices, enforcement notices, and monetary penalties.

Information notices

7.213 Information notices are dealt with by the DPA 2018, s 14. Such a notice may be served on a controller requiring him to provide the Commissioner with information that the Commissioner reasonably requires for the purposes of carrying out the Commissioner's functions under the data protection legislation, or on any person requiring him to provide the Commissioner with information that the Commissioner reasonably requires:

- for the purposes of investigating a suspected breach of the provisions listed in the DPA 2018, s 149(2) or a suspected offence under the DPA 2018; or
- determining whether the processing of personal data is carried out by an individual in the course of a purely personal or household activity.

7.214 It is an offence to make a false response to an information notice[1].

[1] DPA 2018, s 144.

Assessment notices

7.215 Assessment notices are dealt with under the DPA 2018, s 146 and enable the Commissioner to assess whether a data controller is complying or has complied with data protection law. An assessment notice may require a controller to do one or more of the following:

- permit the Commissioner to enter specified premises;
- direct the Commissioner to documents on the premises that are of a specified description;
- assist the Commissioner to view information of a specified description that is capable of being viewed using equipment on the premises;
- comply with a request from the Commissioner for a copy (in such form as may be requested) of documents and information;
- direct the Commissioner to equipment or other material on the premises which is of a specified description;
- permit the Commissioner to inspect or examine the documents, information, equipment or material to which the Commissioner is directed or which the Commissioner is assisted to view;
- provide the Commissioner with an explanation of such documents, information, equipment or material;
- permit the Commissioner to observe the processing of personal data that takes place on the premises;
- make available for interview by the Commissioner a specified number of people of a specified description who process personal data on behalf of the controller, not exceeding the number who are willing to be interviewed[1].

[1] DPA 2018, s 146(2).

Enforcement notices

7.216 Enforcement notices are dealt with under the DPA 2018, s 149, and are designed to remedy breaches of data protection law by compelling a controller to take, or refrain from taking, specified steps. DPA 2018, ss 149(2)–(5) set out four categories of failing which may give rise to an enforcement notice. Broadly speaking, these deal with processing, codes of conduct, certification, and charges payable to the ICO respectively.

149 Enforcement notices

(1) Where the Commissioner is satisfied that a person has failed, or is failing, as described in subsection (2), (3), (4) or (5), the Commissioner may give the person a written notice (an "enforcement notice") which requires the person—

(a) to take steps specified in the notice, or
(b) to refrain from taking steps specified in the notice,

or both (and see also sections 150 and 151).

(2) The first type of failure is where a controller or processor has failed, or is failing, to comply with any of the following—

      (a)   a provision of Chapter II of the GDPR or Chapter 2 of Part 3 or Chapter 2 of Part 4 of this Act (principles of processing);

      (b)   a provision of Articles 12 to 22 of the GDPR or Part 3 or 4 of this Act conferring rights on a data subject;

      (c)   a provision of Articles 25 to 39 of the GDPR or section 64 or 65 of this Act (obligations of controllers and processors);

      (d)   a requirement to communicate a personal data breach to the Commissioner or a data subject under section 67, 68 or 108 of this Act;

      (e)   the principles for transfers of personal data to third countries, non-Convention countries and international organisations in Articles 44 to 49 of the GDPR or in sections 73 to 78 or 109 of this Act.

(3)   The second type of failure is where a monitoring body has failed, or is failing, to comply with an obligation under Article 41 of the GDPR (monitoring of approved codes of conduct).

(4)   The third type of failure is where a person who is a certification provider—

      (a)   does not meet the requirements for accreditation,

      (b)   has failed, or is failing, to comply with an obligation under Article 42 or 43 of the GDPR (certification of controllers and processors), or

      (c)   has failed, or is failing, to comply with any other provision of the GDPR (whether in the person's capacity as a certification provider or otherwise).

(5)   The fourth type of failure is where a controller has failed, or is failing, to comply with regulations under section 137.

(6)   An enforcement notice given in reliance on subsection (2), (3) or (5) may only impose requirements which the Commissioner considers appropriate for the purpose of remedying the failure.

(7)   An enforcement notice given in reliance on subsection (4) may only impose requirements which the Commissioner considers appropriate having regard to the failure (whether or not for the purpose of remedying the failure).

7.217 Where an enforcement notice is proposed to be issued under the DPA 2018, s 149(2), the ICO must have must consider whether the failure has caused or is likely to cause any person damage or distress[1].

[1]   DPA 2018, s 150(2).

7.218 An enforcement notice must state what the controller has failed to do and give reasons for that assessment[1] and provide information about the consequences of failing to comply with the notice and rights of appeal[2]. The notice may specify a time limit for compliance, which must not expire before the time limit for appealing the notice[3]. If an appeal is brought, the notice need not be complied with until disposal or withdrawal of the appeal[4]. However, the safeguards in DPA 2018, ss 150(6) and (7) are dis-applied if the notice states that compliance is urgent and gives reasons for this. In such cases, compliance may not be required within 24 hours of the issue of the notice[5]. A person served with an enforcement notice may apply to the ICO for it to be varied or cancelled under the DPA 2018, s 153.

[1]   DPA 2018, s 150(1).
[2]   DPA 2018, s 150(5).
[3]   DPA 2018, s 150(4) and (6).
[4]   DPA 2018, s 150(7).
[5]   DPA 2018, s 150(8).

Monetary penalties

7.219 Monetary penalties are available in the same circumstances as enforcement notices (ie those set out in DPA 2018, ss 149(2)–(5) inclusive). Where the failing relates to a provision of the GDPR, the ICO must have regard to the matters set out in Art 83(1) and (2) of the GDPR in determining the amount of the penalty[1].

'**General conditions for imposing administrative fines**

. . .

1. The Commissioner shall ensure that the imposition of administrative fines pursuant to this Article in respect of infringements of this Regulation referred to in paragraphs 4, 5 and 6 shall in each individual case be effective, proportionate and dissuasive.

2. Administrative fines shall, depending on the circumstances of each individual case, be imposed in addition to, or instead of, measures referred to in points (a) to (h) and (j) of Article 58(2). When deciding whether to impose an administrative fine and deciding on the amount of the administrative fine in each individual case due regard shall be given to the following:

(a)   the nature, gravity and duration of the infringement taking into account the nature scope or purpose of the processing concerned as well as the number of data subjects affected and the level of damage suffered by them;

(b)   the intentional or negligent character of the infringement;

(c)   any action taken by the controller or processor to mitigate the damage suffered by data subjects;

(d)   the degree of responsibility of the controller or processor taking into account technical and organisational measures implemented by them pursuant to Articles 25 and 32;

(e)   any relevant previous infringements by the controller or processor;

(f)   the degree of cooperation with the Commissioner, in order to remedy the infringement and mitigate the possible adverse effects of the infringement;

(g)   the categories of personal data affected by the infringement;

(h)   the manner in which the infringement became known to the Commissioner, in particular whether, and if so to what extent, the controller or processor notified the infringement;

(i)   where measures referred to in Article 58(2) have previously been ordered against the controller or processor concerned with regard to the same subject-matter, compliance with those measures;

(j)   adherence to approved codes of conduct pursuant to Article 40 or approved certification mechanisms pursuant to Article 42; and

(k)   any other aggravating or mitigating factor applicable to the circumstances of the case, such as financial benefits gained, or losses avoided, directly or indirectly, from the infringement.'

[1]   DPA 2018, s 155(2).

7.220 For other matters, the ICO must have regard to the factors at the DPA 2018, s 155(3), which are as follows:

155 Penalty notices

. . .

(3) Those matters are—

(a)   the nature, gravity and duration of the failure;

(b)   the intentional or negligent character of the failure;

(c)   any action taken by the controller or processor to mitigate the damage or distress suffered by data subjects;

(d)   the degree of responsibility of the controller or processor, taking into account technical and organisational measures implemented by the controller or processor in accordance with section 57, 66, 103 or 107;

(e)   any relevant previous failures by the controller or processor;

(f)   the degree of co-operation with the Commissioner, in order to remedy the failure and mitigate the possible adverse effects of the failure;

(g)   the categories of personal data affected by the failure;

(h)   the manner in which the infringement became known to the Commissioner, including whether, and if so to what extent, the controller or processor notified the Commissioner of the failure;

(i)   the extent to which the controller or processor has complied with previous enforcement notices or penalty notices;

(j)   adherence to approved codes of conduct or certification mechanisms;

(k)   any other aggravating or mitigating factor applicable to the case, including financial benefits gained, or losses avoided, as a result of the failure (whether directly or indirectly);

(l)   whether the penalty would be effective, proportionate and dissuasive.

7.221 The requirement to have regard to Art 83 of the UK GDPR and the DPA 2018, s 155(3) does not apply if the failing is under the DPA 2018, s 149(5) (charges payable to the ICO by controllers)[1].

1   DPA 2018, s 155(4).

7.222 There are two statutory maxima for penalty notices, depending on the infringement. The 'standard maximum amount' is £8.7 million or 2% of an undertaking's turnover, whichever is the greater (£8.7 million if the controller is not an undertaking)[1]. The 'higher maximum amount' is £17.5 million or 4% of an undertaking's turnover, whichever is the greater (£17.5 million if the controller is not an undertaking)[2]. The table below shows which maximum the various breaches each attract.

Infringements attracting the standard maximum amount	
Provision	**Description**
Art 8 of the UK GDPR	Children's consent in relation to information society services
Art 11 of the UK GDPR	Processing which does not require identification
Arts 25–39 of the UK GDPR	Obligations of controller and processor
Art 41(4) of the UK GDPR	Monitoring of approved codes of conduct
Arts 42–43 of the UK GDPR	Certification
and any provisions of the DPA 2018 not listed in the table below.	

Infringements attracting the higher maximum amount	
Provision	**Description**
Arts 5, 6, 7, and 9 of the UK GDPR	Lawfulness of processing
Arts 12–22 of the UK GDPR	Subject rights
Arts 44–49 of the UK GDPR	International transfers

Infringements attracting the higher maximum amount	
Provision	Description
Arts 58(1) and (2) of the UK GDPR	Improper use of powers by ICO
ss 35–37 DPA 2018	Lawfulness and fairness, purpose limitation, and data minimisation DPPs under Pt 3 of the DPA 2018
s 38(1) DPA 2018	Accuracy under Pt 3 of the DPA 2018
s 39(1) DPA 2018	Storage limitation under Pt 3 of the DPA 2018
s 40 DPA 2018	Integrity and confidentiality under Pt 3 of the DPA 2018
ss 44–49 DPA 2018	Subject rights under Pt 3 of the DPA 2018
ss 52–53 DPA 2018	Provision of information and manifestly unfounded or excessive requests under Pt 3 of the DPA 2018
ss 73–78 DPA 2018	Transfers to third countries under Pt 3 of the DPA 2018
ss 86–91 DPA 2018	Intelligence services processing
ss 93–94 DPA 2018	
s 100 DPA 2018	
s 109 DPA 2018	

1   DPA 2018, s 157(6).
2   DPA 2018, s 157(6).

Appeals

7.223 A person may appeal the imposition of any of the above notices to the Tribunal. In addition, there is a right of appeal in respect of a refusal to cancel or vary an enforcement notice, and a monetary penalty notice may be appealed as to quantum without appealing the notice itself[1]. The test on appeal where the appeal is against a notice or as to quantum of a penalty notice is set out at the DPA 2018, s 163(3) as follows:

163 Determination of appeals

. . .

(3) If the Tribunal considers—

(a)   that the notice or decision against which the appeal is brought is not in accordance with the law, or

(b)   to the extent that the notice or decision involved an exercise of discretion by the Commissioner, that the Commissioner ought to have exercised the discretion differently,
the Tribunal must allow the appeal or substitute another notice or decision which the Commissioner could have given or made.

(4) Otherwise, the Tribunal must dismiss the appeal.

1   DPA 2018, s 162.

7.224 In making its determination, the Tribunal may review any determination of fact on which the notice or decision under appeal was based[1].

1   DPA 2018, s 163(2).

7.225 Where the appeal is against a refusal to vary or cancel an enforcement notice, if the Tribunal considers that the enforcement notice ought to be cancelled or varied by reason of a change in circumstances, the Tribunal must cancel or vary the notice[1].

1   DPA 2018, s 163(5).

Subject remedies

7.226 In addition to enforcement by the ICO, the DPA 2018 provides for data subjects to access remedies directly where they have been affected by a breach of data protection legislation. Articles 78 and 79 of the UK GDPR give them a right to a judicial remedy against the ICO and data controllers respectively, while Art 82 provides for a right to compensation.

Compliance orders

7.227 Pursuant to the right in Art 79 of the UK GDPR, which affords a right to a judicial remedy against a controller, a subject may apply to the court for an order requiring the controller to remedy non-compliance with data protection legislation. The test for such an order is that the court is satisfied that there has been an infringement of the data subject's rights under the data protection legislation in contravention of that legislation[1]. The order may require the controller to take, or to refrain from taking, the steps set out in the order[2].

1   DPA 2018, s 167(1).
2   DPA 2018, s 167(2).

Compensation

7.228 Article 82 of the UK GDPR provides for a right of compensation as follows:

'**Records of processing activities**

1. Any person who has suffered material or non-material damage as a result of an infringement of this Regulation shall have the right to receive compensation from the controller or processor for the damage suffered.

2. Any controller involved in processing shall be liable for the damage caused by processing which infringes this Regulation. A processor shall be liable for the damage caused by processing only where it has not complied with obligations of this Regulation specifically directed to processors or where it has acted outside or contrary to lawful instructions of the controller.

3. A controller or processor shall be exempt from liability under paragraph 2 if it proves that it is not in any way responsible for the event giving rise to the damage.'

7.229 The right to compensation in Art 82 extends only to infringements of the UK GDPR (ie not the DPA 2018 or any regulations made thereunder). It requires non-compliance with a provision of the UK GDPR, causation, and damage. Article 82 of the UK GDPR is supplemented by the DPA 2018, s 168. This states that non-material damage includes distress and provides for applications to be made by, and payments made to, representative bodies appearing on behalf of a data subject.

7.230 The first (and, so far, only) court to rule on an Art 82 claim was the Local Court (Amtsgericht) Diez (in a final decision dated 7 November 2018, case number 8 C 130/18), in a claim under the EU GDPR regime. In that case, the claimant had received an unsolicited e-mail requesting marketing consent. He claimed for €500, but accepted an ex gratia payment of €50. The court ruled that mere infringement of the GDPR in the absence of damage (either material or non-material) would not lead to liability and that for damage to be found, the data subject must have experienced a noticeable disadvantage and it must be an objectively comprehensible impairment of personal rights with a certain weight. The court declined to make a finding of whether the claimant had suffered damage, holding that if non-material damage had been caused, the €50 which the claimant had already accepted would have been appropriate compensation for it. Accordingly, the court dismissed the claim on the basis of quantum. It should also be noted that, being a German case, this case does not account for the supplementary effect of s 168 of the DPA 2018 which would operate in the UK.

7.231 Compensation for infringements of data protection legislation other than the UK GDPR is governed by the DPA 2018, s 169, which reads as follows:

169 Compensation for contravention of other data protection legislation

(1)   A person who suffers damage by reason of a contravention of a requirement of the data protection legislation, other than the GDPR, is entitled to compensation for that damage from the controller or the processor, subject to subsections (2) and (3).

(2)   Under subsection (1)—

(a)   a controller involved in processing of personal data is liable for any damage caused by the processing, and

(b)   a processor involved in processing of personal data is liable for damage caused by the processing only if the processor-

(i)   has not complied with an obligation under the data protection legislation specifically directed at processors, or

(ii)   has acted outside, or contrary to, the controller's lawful instructions.

(3)   A controller or processor is not liable as described in subsection (2) if the controller or processor proves that the controller or processor is not in any way responsible for the event giving rise to the damage.

(4)   A joint controller in respect of the processing of personal data to which Part 3 or 4 applies whose responsibilities are determined in an arrangement under section 58 or 104 is only liable as described in subsection (2) if the controller is responsible for compliance with the provision of the data protection legislation that is contravened.

(5)   In this section, "damage" includes financial loss and damage not involving financial loss, such as distress.

7.232 The combined effect of ss 168 and 169 of the DPA 2018 is to put onto a statutory footing the principle in *Vidal-Hall and others v Google Inc*[1] that an action for distress caused by a data breach can sound in damages even where there is no pecuniary loss. In *Vidal-Hall* the causes of action were the torts of misuse of personal data and breach of privacy; ss 168 and 169 confirm that the principle applies equally in cases where the cause of action is a breach of the statutory duties found in the UK GDPR and DPA 2018.

[1]   [2015] EWCA Civ 311.

7.233 In *Lloyd v Google LLC*[1], which dealt with the DPA 1998 regime, the Court of Appeal held that damages are, in principle, capable of being awarded for loss of control of data, even if there is no pecuniary loss and no distress. This extends the principle, which had been established in breach of privacy cases by *Gulati v MGN Ltd*[2], to cases concerning breaches of data protection legislation. However, it is yet to be tested whether the Court's interpretation of the DPA 1998 in Lloyd will continue to be extended to the DPA 2018 and UK GDPR.

[1]   [2019] EWCA Civ 1599.
[2]   [2015] EWHC 1482 (Ch).

7.234 In *TLT v Secretary of State for the Home Department*[1] the High Court dealt with the issue of quantum in cases where damages for distress are claimed under the DPA 1998. In the absence of case-law relating to ss 168–169 of the DPA 2018, the principles which arise from that case may nonetheless still be of assistance to practitioners and judges. The following principles can be gleaned from the judgment:

(1)   In assessing damages for distress under the DPA 1998, regard should be given to the awards for psychiatric and psychological injury in personal injury cases. Cases involving the unlawful dissemination of information relating to high-profile individuals by the media were not instructive.

(2)   Any degree of distress which is not *de minimis* is capable of sounding in damages.

(3)   Quantum will depend on the duration of the distress, but even the initial shock of discovering that personal data has been misused is likely to attract an award of around £3,000.

(4)   The degree of rationality of any fears or beliefs about the potential consequences of the breach will be relevant to quantum. A claimant who has 'genuine and rational fears' about his safety and/or that of his family members will attract an award at the higher end of the scale.

[1]   [2016] EWHC 2217 (QB).

Criminal offences

7.235 The DPA 2018 creates three criminal offences, each of which are discussed below. Proceedings for offences under the DPA 2018 may only be initiated by the ICO or with the consent of the DPP[1].

[1]   DPA 2018, s 197.

Unlawful obtaining of personal data

7.236 The DPA 2018, s 170 provides for the offence of unlawfully obtaining or disclosing personal data as follows:

170 Unlawful obtaining etc of personal data

(1) It is an offence for a person knowingly or recklessly—

    (a) to obtain or disclose personal data without the consent of the controller,

    (b) to procure the disclosure of personal data to another person without the consent of the controller, or

    (c) after obtaining personal data, to retain it without the consent of the person who was the controller in relation to the personal data when it was obtained.

(2) It is a defence for a person charged with an offence under subsection (1) to prove that the obtaining, disclosing, procuring or retaining—

    (a) was necessary for the purposes of preventing or detecting crime,

    (b) was required or authorised by an enactment, by a rule of law or by the order of a court or tribunal, or

    (c) in the particular circumstances, was justified as being in the public interest.

(3) It is also a defence for a person charged with an offence under subsection (1) to prove that—

    (a) the person acted in the reasonable belief that the person had a legal right to do the obtaining, disclosing, procuring or retaining,

    (b) the person acted in the reasonable belief that the person would have had the consent of the controller if the controller had known about the obtaining, disclosing, procuring or retaining and the circumstances of it, or

    (c) the person acted-

        (i) for the special purposes,

        (ii) with a view to the publication by a person of any journalistic, academic, artistic or literary material, and

        (iii) in the reasonable belief that in the particular circumstances the obtaining, disclosing, procuring or retaining was justified as being in the public interest.

(4) It is an offence for a person to sell personal data if the person obtained the data in circumstances in which an offence under subsection (1) was committed.

(5) It is an offence for a person to offer to sell personal data if the person—

    (a) has obtained the data in circumstances in which an offence under subsection (1) was committed, or

    (b) subsequently obtains the data in such circumstances.

(6) For the purposes of subsection (5), an advertisement indicating that personal data is or may be for sale is an offer to sell the data.

(7) In this section—

    (a) references to the consent of a controller do not include the consent of a person who is a controller by virtue of Article 28(10) of the GDPR or section 59(8) or 105(3) of this Act (processor to be treated as controller in certain circumstances);

(b) where there is more than one controller, such references are references to the consent of one or more of them.

7.237 The offence under the DPA 2018, s 171 is triable either way, and punishable by an unlimited fine whether tried summarily or on indictment[1]. Additionally, the court may order forfeiture and destruction of any document it has been used in connection with the processing of personal data, and it appears to the court to be connected with the commission of the offence[2].

[1] DPA 2018, s 196(2).
[2] DPA 2018, s 196(4).

Re-identification of de-identified personal data

7.238 The DPA 2018, s 171 provides for the offence of re-identifying de-identified personal data as follows:

171 Re-identification of de-identified personal data

(1) It is an offence for a person knowingly or recklessly to re-identify information that is de-identified personal data without the consent of the controller responsible for de-identifying the personal data.

(2) For the purposes of this section and section 172—

(a) personal data is "de-identified" if it has been processed in such a manner that it can no longer be attributed, without more, to a specific data subject;

(b) a person "re-identifies" information if the person takes steps which result in the information no longer being de-identified within the meaning of paragraph (a).

(3) It is a defence for a person charged with an offence under subsection (1) to prove that the re-identification—

(a) was necessary for the purposes of preventing or detecting crime,

(b) was required or authorised by an enactment, by a rule of law or by the order of a court or tribunal, or

(c) in the particular circumstances, was justified as being in the public interest.

(4) It is also a defence for a person charged with an offence under subsection (1) to prove that—

(a) the person acted in the reasonable belief that the person—
(i) is the data subject to whom the information relates,
(ii) had the consent of that data subject, or
(iii) would have had such consent if the data subject had known about the re-identification and the circumstances of it,

(b) the person acted in the reasonable belief that the person—
(i) is the controller responsible for de-identifying the personal data,
(ii) had the consent of that controller, or
(iii) would have had such consent if that controller had known about the re-identification and the circumstances of it,

(c) the person acted—
(i) for the special purposes,
(ii) with a view to the publication by a person of any journalistic, academic, artistic or literary material, and
(iii) in the reasonable belief that in the particular circumstances the

re-identification was justified as being in the public interest, or

(d)   the effectiveness testing conditions were met (see section 172).

(5)   It is an offence for a person knowingly or recklessly to process personal data that is information that has been re-identified where the person does so—

(a)   without the consent of the controller responsible for de-identifying the personal data, and

(b)   in circumstances in which the re-identification was an offence under subsection (1).

(6)   It is a defence for a person charged with an offence under subsection (5) to prove that the processing—

(a)   was necessary for the purposes of preventing or detecting crime,

(b)   was required or authorised by an enactment, by a rule of law or by the order of a court or tribunal, or

(c)   in the particular circumstances, was justified as being in the public interest.

(7)   It is also a defence for a person charged with an offence under subsection (5) to prove that—

(a)   the person acted in the reasonable belief that the processing was lawful,

(b)   the person acted in the reasonable belief that the person-

(i)   had the consent of the controller responsible for de-identifying the personal data, or

(ii)   would have had such consent if that controller had known about the processing and the circumstances of it, or

(c)   the person acted—

(i)   for the special purposes,

(ii)   with a view to the publication by a person of any journalistic, academic, artistic or literary material, and

(iii)   in the reasonable belief that in the particular circumstances the processing was justified as being in the public interest.

(8)   In this section—

(a)   references to the consent of a controller do not include the consent of a person who is a controller by virtue of Article 28(10) of the GDPR or section 59(8) or 105(3) of this Act (processor to be treated as controller in certain circumstances);

(b)   where there is more than one controller, such references are references to the consent of one or more of them.

7.239 The DPA 2018, s 171 creates two forms of the offence: re-identifying de-identified personal data under s 171(1) and processing such data under s 171(5). For both forms of the offence, there is a requirement that the offence be committed knowingly or recklessly.

7.240 The DPA 2018, ss 171(3)–(4) set out the possible defences to an offence under s 171(1). Section 171(3) contains three conditions broadly relating to the public interest and administration of justice. Section 171(4)(a) and (b) provide for a defence where the accused is the subject or controller, or had the consent of the subject or controller, or would have had the consent of the subject or controller had he known of the re-identification and the circumstances of it. Section 171(4)(c) sets out further public interest conditions connected with academic, artistic, literary, and journalistic purposes. Section 171(4)(d) provides for a defence where the accused was engaged in 'effectiveness-testing'. The conditions to be met in order for that defence to be made out are set out in s 172. All of these defences place a burden of proof on the accused.

7.241 The DPA 2018, ss 171(6)–(7) set out the possible defences to an offence under s 171(5). Section 171(6) contains three conditions broadly relating to the public interest and administration of justice. Section 171(7)(a) and (b) provide for a defence where the accused reasonably believed that the processing was lawful or based on consent. Section 171(c) sets out further public interest conditions connected with academic, artistic, literary, and journalistic purposes. All of these defences place a burden of proof on the accused.

7.242 The offence under s 171 is triable either way, and punishable by an unlimited fine whether tried summarily or on indictment[1].

[1]   DPA 2018, s 196(2).

Alteration of personal data to prevent disclosure

7.243 The DPA 2018, s 173 provides for the offence of alteration of personal data as follows:

173 Alteration etc of personal data to prevent disclosure to data subject

(1)   Subsection (3) applies where—

  (a)   a request has been made in exercise of a data subject access right, and
  (b)   the person making the request would have been entitled to receive information in response to that request.

(2)   In this section, "data subject access right" means a right under—

  (a)   Article 15 of the GDPR (right of access by the data subject);
  (b)   Article 20 of the GDPR (right to data portability);
  (c)   section 45 of this Act (law enforcement processing: right of access by the data subject);
  (d)   section 94 of this Act (intelligence services processing: right of access by the data subject).

(3)   It is an offence for a person listed in subsection (4) to alter, deface, block, erase, destroy or conceal information with the intention of preventing disclosure of all or part of the information that the person making the request would have been entitled to receive.

(4)   Those persons are—

  (a)   the controller, and
  (b)   a person who is employed by the controller, an officer of the controller or subject to the direction of the controller.

(5)   It is a defence for a person charged with an offence under subsection (3) to prove that—

  (a)   the alteration, defacing, blocking, erasure, destruction or concealment of the information would have occurred in the absence of a request made in exercise of a data subject access right, or
  (b)   the person acted in the reasonable belief that the person making the request was not entitled to receive the information in response to the request.

7.244 The offence under s 173 is summary-only, and punishable by an unlimited fine[1].

1   DPA 2018, s 196(1).

FREEDOM OF INFORMATION

Introduction

7.245 The purpose of the Freedom of Information Act 2000 ('FIA 2000') is to provide a framework for the release of information held by public bodies. The overall scheme of the Act and the reasons it was considered necessary were set out in the 1997 White Paper *Your Right to Know*. The premise behind the Act is to provide for more open government. This is accomplished by mandating the publication of certain information as well as allowing for requests for information to be made by the public.

7.246 The central concept in the FIA 2000 is the 'general right of access'. This gives rise to two duties on public authorities when a request for information is made: first, the duty to inform the person making the request whether the public authority holds the information requested at all (known as the duty to confirm or deny), and second, if the public authority does hold the information, to communicate it to the person making the request. The general right of access is a qualified right; examples of the qualifications placed upon it include the right of public authorities to charge a fee to deal with requests and the right to refuse requests which are repeated or vexatious. A request may also be refused if it seeks access to information which is exempt. The categories of exempt information are set out at Pt II of the FIA 2000. Part IV of the FIA 2000 provides an enforcement framework.

General right of access

7.247 The general right of access to information is contained in the FIA 2000, s 1, which reads as follows:

1 General right of access to information held by public authorities

(1)   Any person making a request for information to a public authority is entitled—

  (a)   to be informed in writing by the public authority whether it holds information of the description specified in the request, and

  (b)   if that is the case, to have that information communicated to him.

(2)   Subsection (1) has effect subject to the following provisions of this section and to the provisions of sections 2, 9, 12 and 14.

(3)   Where a public authority—

  (a)   reasonably requires further information in order to identify and locate the information requested, and

  (b)   has informed the applicant of that requirement,

  (c)   the authority is not obliged to comply with subsection (1) unless it is supplied with that further information.

(4)   The information—

      (a)   in respect of which the applicant is to be informed under subsection (1)(a), or

      (b)   which is to be communicated under subsection (1)(b),

          is the information in question held at the time when the request is received, except that account may be taken of any amendment or deletion made between that time and the time when the information is to be communicated under subsection (1)(b), being an amendment or deletion that would have been made regardless of the receipt of the request.

(5)   A public authority is to be taken to have complied with subsection (1)(a) in relation to any information if it has communicated the information to the applicant in accordance with subsection (1)(b).

(6)   In this Act, the duty of a public authority to comply with subsection (1)(a) is referred to as "the duty to confirm or deny".

Information

7.248 Per the FIA 2000, s 84, information is defined as 'information which is recorded in any form'. It is not limited to documentary information, and extends to media such as audio or visual recordings. It is also not limited to formal or official items, and can include drafts, notes, and internal communications. However, the FIA 2000, s 1(1)(b) only contains an obligation for the communication of information, not the provision of the original document within which that information is contained. In order to fall within the definition at s 84, the information must be recorded. If it is not recorded, there is no obligation on the public authority in question to create a record or obtain information in response to a request. Further, the obligation to provide the information in s 1(1)(b) only arises if the information is held by the public authority.

Public authorities

7.249 The provisions of the FIA 2000 are only engaged in respect of information held by public authorities. Schedule 1 sets out a list of bodies which are considered public authorities for the purposes of the FIA 2000. Section 4 empowers the Secretary of State to add bodies to, or remove them from, Sch 1. In relation to additions, s 4 provides as follows:

4 Amendment of Schedule 1

(1)   The Secretary of State may by order amend Schedule 1 by adding to that Schedule a reference to anybody or the holder of any office which (in either case) is not for the time being listed in that Schedule but as respects which both the first and the second conditions below are satisfied.

(2)   The first condition is that the body or office—

      (a)   is established by virtue of Her Majesty's prerogative or by an enactment or by subordinate legislation, or

      (b)   is established in any other way by a Minister of the Crown in his capacity as Minister, by a government department or by the Welsh Ministers, the First Minister for Wales or the Counsel General to the Welsh Assembly Government.

(3)   The second condition is—

    (a)   in the case of a body, that the body is wholly or partly constituted by appointment made by the Crown, by a Minister of the Crown, by a government department or by the Welsh Ministers, the First Minister for Wales or the Counsel General to the Welsh Assembly Government, or

    (b)   in the case of an office, that appointments to the office are made by the Crown, by a Minister of the Crown, by a government department or by the Welsh Ministers, the First Minister for Wales or the Counsel General to the Welsh Assembly Government.

Request and response

7.250 To be considered a 'request for information' within the meaning of the Act, a request must be made in writing, state the name of the applicant and an address for correspondence, and describe the information requested[1]. Once a request for information has been received by a public authority, it must comply with FIA 2000, s 1(1) promptly, and in any event, not later than the twentieth working day following receipt of the request[2].

[1]   FIA 2000, s 8(1).
[2]   FIA 2000, s 10(1).

7.251 If, in order to comply with the FIA 2000, s 1(1), the public authority reasonably requires further information in order to identify and locate the information requested, and has informed the applicant of that requirement, the authority is not obliged to comply with the s 1(1) unless it is supplied with that further information[1].

[1]   FIA 2000, s 1(3).

7.252 The authority may charge a fee in order to provide a response, in which case, it must serve a fees notice on the applicant within the compliance period set out at the FIA 2000, s 10(1)[1]. Where this is done, the authority is under no obligation to provide a response unless the fee has been paid within 3 months of the fees notice being served[2]. In cases where a fee is charged, time for compliance starts to run from receipt of the fee[3]. The maximum fee which may be charged is set out at reg 6 of the Freedom of Information and Data Protection (Appropriate Limit and Fees) Regulations 2004[4] as follows:

6 Maximum fee for complying with section 1(1) of the 2000 Act

(1)   Any fee to be charged under section 9 of the 2000 Act by a public authority to whom a request for information is made is not to exceed the maximum determined by the public authority in accordance with this regulation.

(2)   Subject to paragraph (4), the maximum fee is a sum equivalent to the total costs the public authority reasonably expects to incur in relation to the request in—

    (a)   informing the person making the request whether it holds the information, and

    (b)   communicating the information to the person making the request.

(3)   Costs which may be taken into account by a public authority for the purposes of this regulation include, but are not limited to, the costs of—

(a)   complying with any obligation under section 11(1) of the 2000 Act as to the means or form of communicating the information,

(b)   reproducing any document containing the information, and

(c)   postage and other forms of transmitting the information.

(4)   But a public authority may not take into account for the purposes of this regulation any costs which are attributable to the time which persons undertaking activities mentioned in paragraph (2) on behalf of the authority are expected to spend on those activities.

[1]   FIA 2000, s 9(1).
[2]   FIA 2000, s 9(2).
[3]   FIA 2000, s 10(2).
[4]   SI 2004/3244.

Qualifications to the general right of access

7.253 The general right of access is qualified by the FIA 2000, ss 2, 9, 12, and 14[1].

[1]   FIA 2000, s 1(2).

Exempt Information

7.254 The FIA 2000, s 2 provides for certain classes of information (which are set out at Pt II of the Act) to be treated as exempt information. These are dealt with under the heading 'Exempt Information' at **7.262** et seq below.

Fees

7.255 The FIA 2000, s 9 provides that compliance with the FIA 2000, s 1(1) may be subject to a fee being paid. For the provisions relating to the payment of fees and the timescales which apply in such cases, see **7.252** above.

Exceeding the appropriate limit

7.256 The FIA 2000, s 12 removes the obligation to comply with the FIA 2000, s 1(1) if the authority in question estimates that the cost of doing so would exceed the 'appropriate limit'.

12 Exemption where cost of compliance exceeds appropriate limit

(1)   Section 1(1) does not oblige a public authority to comply with a request for information if the authority estimates that the cost of complying with the request would exceed the appropriate limit.

(2)   Subsection (1) does not exempt the public authority from its obligation to comply with paragraph (a) of section 1(1) unless the estimated cost of complying with that paragraph alone would exceed the appropriate limit.

(3)   In subsections (1) and (2) "the appropriate limit" means such amount as may be prescribed, and different amounts may be prescribed in relation to different cases.

(4)   The Secretary of State may by regulations provide that, in such circumstances as may be prescribed, where two or more requests for information are made to a public authority—

(a)   by one person, or

(b)   by different persons who appear to the public authority to be acting in concert or in pursuance of a campaign,

the estimated cost of complying with any of the requests is to be taken to be the estimated total cost of complying with all of them.

(5)   The Secretary of State may by regulations make provision for the purposes of this section as to the costs to be estimated and as to the manner in which they are to be estimated.

7.257 The appropriate limit is set by reg 3 of the Freedom of Information and Data Protection (Appropriate Limit and Fees) Regulations 2004[1], and is £600 in the case of a public authority listed in Pt I of Sch 1 to the FIA 2000, and £450 in the case of all other public authorities (including local authorities, which are listed under Pt II of Sch 1). It is important to note that the duties under s 1(1)(a) and (1)(b) are distinct: if an authority proposes to refuse to comply with s 1(1)(a) (the duty to confirm or deny), it must be because the cost of confirming or denying alone exceeds the appropriate limit[2]. If the cost of confirming that an authority holds the information sought does not exceed the appropriate limit, but the overall cost of confirming and disclosing does, then the authority is still obliged to confirm, but not to disclose.

[1]   SI 2004/3244.
[2]   FIA 2000, s 12(2).

7.258 The provisions for estimating the cost of complying with the FIA 2000, s 1(1) for the purposes of determining whether such costs exceed the appropriate limit are contained in reg 4 of the Freedom of Information and Data Protection (Appropriate Limit and Fees) Regulations 2004[1]:

4 Estimating the cost of complying with a request – general

. . .

(3) In a case in which this regulation has effect, a public authority may, for the purpose of its estimate, take account only of the costs it reasonably expects to incur in relation to the request in—

(a)   determining whether it holds the information,

(b)   locating the information, or a document which may contain the information,

(c)   retrieving the information, or a document which may contain the information, and

(d)   extracting the information from a document containing it.

(4) To the extent to which any of the costs which a public authority takes into account are attributable to the time which persons undertaking any of the activities mentioned in para (3) on behalf of the authority are expected to spend on those activities, those costs are to be estimated at a rate of £25 per person per hour.

[1]   SI 2004/3244.

7.259 The FIA 2000, s 12(4) and reg 5 of the Freedom of Information and Data Protection (Appropriate Limit and Fees) Regulations 2004[1] deal with estimating the cost of compliance in cases where two or more requests for information are made by the same person or by different persons appearing to the authority to be acting on concert or in pursuance of a campaign. In such cases, if the requests relate, to any extent, to the same or similar information AND are received within any period of 60 consecutive working days, the estimated cost of complying with any request is to be taken as the cost of complying with all of them.

¹   SI 2004/3244.

Vexatious and repeated requests

7.260 The FIA 2000, s 14 deals with vexatious and repeated requests as follows:

14 Vexatious or repeated requests

(1)   Section 1(1) does not oblige a public authority to comply with a request for information if the request is vexatious.

(2)   Where a public authority has previously complied with a request for information which was made by any person, it is not obliged to comply with a subsequent identical or substantially similar request from that person unless a reasonable interval has elapsed between compliance with the previous request and the making of the current request.

7.261 In determining what is to be considered a 'reasonable interval' in the case of a repeated request, the ICO's guidance acknowledges that there can be no definitive answer, but two important factors which should be taken into account are: the likelihood that the information will differ significantly from that provided in response to the previous request and the amount of time that has passed (where it is unlikely that the information will differ in any significant way) since the authority complied with the previous request.

Exempt information

7.262 The FIA 2000, s 2 reads as follows:

2 Effect of the exemptions in Part II

(1)   Where any provision of Part II states that the duty to confirm or deny does not arise in relation to any information, the effect of the provision is that where either—

(a)   the provision confers absolute exemption, or
(b)   in all the circumstances of the case, the public interest in maintaining the exclusion of the duty to confirm or deny outweighs the public interest in disclosing whether the public authority holds the information,

section 1(1)(a) does not apply.

(2)   In respect of any information which is exempt information by virtue of any provision of Part II, section 1(1)(b) does not apply if or to the extent that—

(a)   the information is exempt information by virtue of a provision conferring absolute exemption, or
(b)   in all the circumstances of the case, the public interest in maintaining the exemption outweighs the public interest in disclosing the information.

(3)   For the purposes of this section, the following provisions of Part II (and no others) are to be regarded as conferring absolute exemption—

(a)   section 21,
(b)   section 23,
(c)   section 32,
(d)   section 34,
(e)   section 36 so far as relating to information held by the House of Commons or the House of Lords,
  (ea)   in section 37, paras (a) to (ab) of subsection (1), and subsection (2) so far as relating to those paras,
(f)   in section 40—
  (i)   subsection (1), and
  (ii)   subsection (2) so far as relating to cases where the first condition referred to in that subsection is satisfied by virtue of subsection (3)(a)(i) or (b) of that section,
(g)   section 41, and
(h)   section 44.

7.263 Section 2 provides for certain classes of information to be considered 'exempt information'. This removes or qualifies an authority's obligations under s 1(1) in respect of such information. The relevant classes of information, and the particular considerations pertaining to them, are listed at Pt II of the Act. Section 2 designates certain classes of information as being the object of absolute exemption. Where absolute exemption applies, the obligations under s 1(1)(a) and (b) are dis-applied. In the case of exempt information to which absolute exemption does not apply, s 1(1) obligations will be dis-applied if the public interest in doing so outweighs the public interest in complying with the obligations. For regulatory enforcers, the relevant classes of exempt information are likely to be investigations and proceedings conducted by public authorities[1], law enforcement[2], and prohibitions on disclosure[3].

[1]   FIA 2000, s 12(2).
[2]   FIA 2000, s 31.
[3]   FIA 2000, s 44.

Investigations and proceedings conducted by public authorities

7.264 The exemption under the FIA 2000, s 30 may be claimed by a public authority which has a duty or a power to investigate whether a person has committed a criminal offence. The scope of the exemption will depend on whether the authority in question has a duty or a power to investigate, and whether the authority can investigate, bring proceedings, or both. The relevant part of the section reads:

30 Investigations and proceedings conducted by public authorities.

(1)   Information held by a public authority is exempt information if it has at any time been held by the authority for the purposes of—

  (a)   any investigation which the public authority has a duty to conduct with a view to it being ascertained-
    (i)   whether a person should be charged with an offence, or
    (ii)   whether a person charged with an offence is guilty of it,
  (b)   any investigation which is conducted by the authority and in the circumstances may lead to a decision by the authority to institute criminal proceedings which the authority has power to conduct, or
  (c)   any criminal proceedings which the authority has power to conduct.

(2)   Information held by a public authority is exempt information if—

(a)   it was obtained or recorded by the authority for the purposes of its functions relating to-

(i)   investigations falling within subsection (1)(a) or (b),

(ii)   criminal proceedings which the authority has power to conduct,

(iii) investigations (other than investigations falling within subsection (1)(a) or (b)) which are conducted by the authority for any of the purposes specified in section 31(2) and either by virtue of Her Majesty's prerogative or by virtue of powers conferred by or under any enactment, or

(iv) civil proceedings which are brought by or on behalf of the authority and arise out of such investigations, and

(b)   it relates to the obtaining of information from confidential sources.

(3)   The duty to confirm or deny does not arise in relation to information which is (or if it were held by the public authority would be) exempt information by virtue of subsection (1) or (2).

7.265 The exemption in s 30 is class-based: if a piece of information falls into one of the classes described in the section, it will be exempt from the usual duties under the FIA 2000. It is not necessary to establish any prejudice. The exemption under the FIA 2000, s 30(1)(a) can only be claimed in cases where the authority in question has a duty (as opposed to a power) to investigate. The investigation must also be one relating to a criminal charge as opposed to purely civil sanctions. The wording of s 30(1)(a)(i) makes it clear that a charge need not in fact result from the investigation in question, but it must at least be capable of resulting. The exemption under s 30(1)(b) covers authorities with a power to investigate. However, in order for this exemption to apply, the authority in question must not only have the power to investigate, but also to conduct proceedings. Like s 30(1)(a), this section is concerned only with criminal matters, and applies whether or not proceedings are ultimately conducted.

7.266 What amounts to an investigation was considered in *Wynn v Information Commissioner and the Serious Fraud Office*[1]. In that case, the SFO had carried out a vetting procedure it described as the 'pre-investigative stage'. At that stage, it was determined that no charges should be laid. The claimant sought to argue that as a result, no investigation had taken place and the s 30 exemption did not apply. The Tribunal held that notwithstanding that the SFO's internal terminology distinguished between the pre-investigative stage and 'the 'investigative' stage, involving the exercise of powers afforded to the SFO . . . in the Tribunal's clear judgement, the fact that the SFO may use such labels does not in any way conceal the reality that there was . . . an investigation falling squarely within the FIA 2000, s 30(1)'.

[1]   EA/2011/0084 7 September 2012.

7.267 While s 30(1)(a) and (b) relate to investigations, s 30(1)(c) covers all proceedings an authority has a power to conduct. This allows the exemption to cover proceedings regardless of whether the authority conducting them has also conducted the investigation. Section 30(2) is concerned with the protection of confidential sources. For that section to apply, the information in question must have been obtained or recorded within the scope of s 30(2)(a)(i)–(iv) and relate to the obtaining of information from confidential sources. For the list of purposes specified in s 31(2), referred to in s 30(2)(a)(iii), see the section on law enforcement at **7.270** et seq below.

7.268 The FIA 2000, s 30 does not confer absolute exemption, and so the public interest test will apply to any exemptions claimed under this section. Examples of how the Tribunal has applied the public interest test include:

Toms v Information Commissioner[1]: '[freedom of information] should not undermine the investigation, prosecution or prevention of crime, or the bringing of civil or criminal proceedings by public bodies. The investigation and prosecution of crime involve a number of essential requirements. These include the need to avoid prejudicing effective law enforcement, the need to protect witnesses and informers, the need to maintain the independence of the judicial and prosecution processes, and the need to preserve the criminal court as the sole forum for determining guilt'.

Digby-Cameron v the Information Commissioner and Bedfordshire Police and Hertfordshire Police[2]: 'in assessing where the public interest balance lies in section 30(1) case relevant matters are therefore likely to include (a) the stage a particular investigation or prosecution has reached, (b) whether and to what extent the information is already in the public domain, (c) the significance or sensitivity of the information requested and (d) whether there is any evidence that an investigation or prosecution has not been carried out properly which may be disclosed by the information.'

[1] EA/2005/0027 19 June 2006.
[2] EA/2008/0023 and 0025 26 January 2009.

7.269 As an example of the exclusion being dealt with by the Commissioner, see Commissioner's decision of 19 March 2014: the complainant had requested a copy of a report regarding horse meat in Asda Smart Price Corned Beef (where over 50% of horse meat was identified). Leicestershire County Council applied the exemption for investigations and proceedings conducted by public authorities at the FIA 2000, s 30(1)(b). The Commissioner's held that the exemption was correctly engaged but in all the circumstances of the case, the public interest in maintaining the exemption did not outweigh the public interest in disclosure of the information.

Law enforcement

7.270 Information which is not caught by FIA 2000, s 30 may be caught by s 31, which is drafted somewhat more broadly:

31 Law enforcement.

(1) Information which is not exempt information by virtue of section 30 is exempt information if its disclosure under this Act would, or would be likely to, prejudice—

    (a) the prevention or detection of crime,
    (b) the apprehension or prosecution of offenders,
    (c) the administration of justice,
    (d) the assessment or collection of any tax or duty or of any imposition of a similar nature,
    (e) the operation of the immigration controls,
    (f) the maintenance of security and good order in prisons or in other institutions where persons are lawfully detained,
    (g) the exercise by any public authority of its functions for any of the purposes specified in subsection (2),

(h)   any civil proceedings which are brought by or on behalf of a public authority and arise out of an investigation conducted, for any of the purposes specified in subsection (2), by or on behalf of the authority by virtue of Her Majesty's prerogative or by virtue of powers conferred by or under an enactment, or

(i)   any inquiry held under the Fatal Accidents and Sudden Deaths Inquiries (Scotland) Act 1976 to the extent that the inquiry arises out of an investigation conducted, for any of the purposes specified in subsection (2), by or on behalf of the authority by virtue of Her Majesty's prerogative or by virtue of powers conferred by or under an enactment.

(2)   The purposes referred to in subsection (1)(g) to (i) are—

(a)   the purpose of ascertaining whether any person has failed to comply with the law,

(b)   the purpose of ascertaining whether any person is responsible for any conduct which is improper,

(c)   the purpose of ascertaining whether circumstances which would justify regulatory action in pursuance of any enactment exist or may arise,

(d)   the purpose of ascertaining a person's fitness or competence in relation to the management of bodies corporate or in relation to any profession or other activity which he is, or seeks to become, authorised to carry on,

(e)   the purpose of ascertaining the cause of an accident,

(f)   the purpose of protecting charities against misconduct or mismanagement (whether by trustees or other persons) in their administration,

(g)   the purpose of protecting the property of charities from loss or misapplication,

(h)   the purpose of recovering the property of charities,

(i)   the purpose of securing the health, safety and welfare of persons at work, and

(j)   the purpose of protecting persons other than persons at work against risk to health or safety arising out of or in connection with the actions of persons at work.

(3)   The duty to confirm or deny does not arise if, or to the extent that, compliance with section 1(1)(a) would, or would be likely to, prejudice any of the matters mentioned in subsection (1).

7.271 While the FIA 2000, s 30 is class-based, s 31 is prejudice-based. This means that any person seeking to rely on the exemption will need to identify the specific prejudice to the relevant purpose under s 31(1) and a causal link between the normal application of the FIA 2000 and that prejudice. Like s 30, s 31 does not confer absolute exemption, and is subject to the public interest test.

Prohibitions on disclosure

7.272 The FIA 2000, s 44 creates an exemption in the case of information the disclosure of which is prohibited by law extraneous to the FIA 2000. The section confers absolute exemption. The FIA 2000, s 44(1) sets out three classes of prohibition: prohibition under any enactment, incompatibility with any EU obligation, and contempt of court. The FIA 2000, s 44(2) provides that the duty to confirm or deny will not arise if compliance with the duty (as opposed to disclosure of the information itself) would itself fall within any of the prohibitions under s 44(1).

7.273 For examples of how the Commissioner has applied the FIA 2000, s 44, see Commissioner's decisions of 21 May 2013 and 29 July 2013. In each case, the local authority in question relied on the statutory bar to disclosure contained in EnA 2002, s 237 in support of invoking the prohibition of disclosure in s 44(1)(a). In each case, the Commissioner held that the exemption had been correctly applied.

44 Prohibitions on disclosure

    (1)   Information is exempt information if its disclosure (otherwise than under this Act) by the public authority holding it—

        (a)   is prohibited by or under any enactment,
        (b)   is incompatible with any EU obligation, or
        (c)   would constitute or be punishable as a contempt of court.

    (2)   The duty to confirm or deny does not arise if the confirmation or denial that would have to be given to comply with section 1(1)(a) would (apart from this Act) fall within any of paras (a) to (c) of subsection (1).

Enforcement

Decision notices

7.274 Under the FIA 2000, s 50, any person may apply to the ICO for a decision on whether a public authority has dealt with a request for information in accordance with the provisions of the Act. A decision will not be made until any complaints procedure provided by the authority in question has been exhausted. The FIA 2000, s 50(2) sets out the further grounds for the Commissioner to refuse to make a decision, namely that there has been undue delay in making the complaint, the complaint is frivolous or vexatious, or the complaint has been withdrawn. If the Commissioner refuses to make a decision, she must serve notice to that effect on the complainant stating her grounds for refusing. If a decision is made, a decision notice setting out the decision is to be served on the complainant and the authority[1]. If the Commissioner decides that the authority has failed to carry out its obligations under the FIA 2000, ss 1(1), 11, or 17, she must specify in the decision notice the steps which must be taken in order to secure compliance and the period within which those steps must be taken[2].

[1]   FIA 2000, s 50(3).
[2]   FIA 2000, s 50(4).

Information notices

7.275 The FIA 2000, s 51 provides that where the Commissioner has been asked to make a decision under of s 50 or (regardless of whether there has been a request for a decision) she reasonably requires information for the purpose of ascertaining whether an authority has complied with Pt I of the Act or the codes of practice, she may serve an information notice on the authority in question.

The information notice must specify the information which the Commissioner requires the authority to provide. Where a request for a decision has been made under s 50, the information notice must contain a statement to that effect. Where the information notice is issued in order to determine compliance with Pt I of the FIA 2000 or the codes of practice, the notice must state that the Commissioner regards the information specified in the notice as relevant for the determination of such compliance[1]. Section 51(5) contains an exclusion for legally-privileged information.

[1] FIA 2000, s 51(2).

Enforcement notices

7.276 The FIA 2000, s 52 provides that if the Commissioner is satisfied that an authority has failed to comply with its obligations under Pt I of the FIA 2000, she may serve an enforcement notice. An enforcement notice will require the authority to take steps to ensure compliance, and will set a period within which those steps must be taken. An enforcement notice must contain a statement of the requirements of Pt I of the FIA 2000 with which the Commissioner is satisfied the authority has failed to comply.

Failure to comply with notices

7.277 Where an authority has failed to comply with a decision notice requiring it to take action, an information notice, or an enforcement notice, the Commissioner may certify such a failure to the High Court, which then has the power to deal with the non-compliance as if it were a contempt of court[1].

[1] FIA 2000, s 54.

Powers of entry and inspection

7.278 The Commissioner may apply for a warrant in order to enforce compliance. The provisions relating to warrants and powers of entry and inspection are set out at the FIA 2000, Sch 3. An application for a warrant may be made to a circuit judge or a district judge (magistrates' courts).

7.279 Paragraph 1 of Sch 3 to the FIA 2000 sets out the grounds on which a warrant may be granted and the procedural requirements for granting one. The Commissioner must supply information on oath that there are reasonable grounds for suspecting that an authority is breaching or has breached: any of the requirements of Pt I of the FIA 2000, a decision notice requiring steps to be taken, an information notice, or an enforcement notice; or that an offence under FIA 2000, s 77 has been or is being committed, and that evidence of that is to be found on the premises specified in the information[1].

[1] FIA 2000, Sch 6, para 1(1).

7.280 A warrant issued under para 1 of Sch 3 is valid for 7 days and confers on the Commissioner and her staff and officers the power to enter and search the premises specified in the warrant, inspect and seize documents, and inspect, examine, operate, and test any equipment in which information may be recorded[1].

[1] FIA 2000, Sch 6, para 1(2).

7.281 Paragraph 2 of Sch 3 to the FIA 2000 sets out the pre-requisites which must be satisfied before an application for a warrant may be made:

- the Commissioner has given 7 days' notice in writing to the occupier of the premises demanding access;
- access has been demanded at a reasonable hour and unreasonably refused OR access has been granted but the occupier has unreasonably refused a request by the Commissioner or her staff to exercise the powers in para 1; and
- following the refusal, the occupier has been notified of the application for a warrant and given the opportunity to be heard on the matter.

7.282 However, the above pre-requisites will not apply if the judge hearing the warrant application is satisfied that the case is one of urgency or that compliance with those provisions would defeat the object of the entry.

7.283 Paragraph 4 of Sch 3 to the FIA 2000 provides that a person executing a warrant may use such reasonable force as is necessary. Paragraph 5 provides that a warrant must be executed at a 'reasonable hour' unless it appears to the person executing it that there are grounds for suspecting that the evidence in question would not be found. The schedule does not define 'reasonable hour', but most relevant premises are likely to be business premises, some (such as local authority offices) with regular and publicised opening hours. It is therefore unlikely that execution outside of general business hours or publicised opening hours would be considered reasonable.

7.284 Paragraph 9 of Sch 3 to the FIA 2000 provides for legally-privileged information to be exempt from search and seizure.

7.285 Paragraph 12 of Sch 3 to the FIA 2000 creates an offence of obstructing or failing to assist a person executing a warrant:

12 Offences

Any person who—

   (a)   intentionally obstructs a person in the execution of a warrant issued under this Schedule, or

   (b)   fails without reasonable excuse to give any person executing such a warrant such assistance as he may reasonably require for the execution of the warrant,

is guilty of an offence.

7.286 The offence under para 12 is summary-only and a person convicted of such an offence is liable to an unlimited fine.

Appeals

7.287 The FIA 2000, s 53 provides that there is a right of appeal by a complainant or an authority against decision notices made under s 50, and by an authority against information and enforcement notices issued under ss 51 and 52. Appeals lie to the General Regulatory Chamber of the First-Tier Tribunal, and are governed by the Tribunal Procedure (First-Tier Tribunal)

(General Regulatory Chamber) Rules 2009[1]. Where a decision or notice requires that an authority take any action, the period within which that action must be completed may not be within the period in which an appeal may be brought, and where an appeal is brought, no step which is required by the decision or notice need be taken until the appeal is determined or withdrawn[2]. The time limit for lodging an appeal is 28 days from the date the notice or decision being appealed was sent to the appellant[3].

[1] SI 2009/1976.
[2] FIA 2000, ss 50(6), 51(4), and 52(3) for commissioner's decisions, information notices, and enforcement notices respectively.
[3] Tribunal Procedure (First-Tier Tribunal) (General Regulatory Chamber) Rules 2009, SI 2009/1976, r 22(1)(b).

7.288 There are two grounds of appeal under FIA 2000, s 58, namely:

- That the notice against which the appeal is brought is not in accordance with the law;
- To the extent that the notice involved an exercise of discretion by the Commissioner, she should have exercised her discretion differently.

7.289 Where the tribunal allows an appeal, it may substitute any other notice which could have been made by the Commissioner.

7.290 The FIA 2000, s 58(2) provides that the tribunal is entitled to review any finding of fact on which a notice is based.

7.291 An appeal from a decision of the First-Tier Tribunal lies to the Upper Tribunal. An appeal from a decision of the Upper Tribunal is a second appeal, and so must be made to the Court of Appeal and must satisfy the second appeals test, namely that the appeal would raise one important point of principle or practice, or that there is some other compelling reason to hear the appeal.

THE PRIVACY AND ELECTRONIC COMMUNICATIONS (EC DIRECTIVE) REGULATIONS 2003

Introduction

7.292 The Privacy and Electronic Communications (EC Directive) Regulations 2003[1] ('PECR 2003') govern the sending of electronic messages to members of the public for marketing purposes. They set out the circumstances in which such messages may and may not be sent by various media, and provide for the maintenance of registers of persons who do not consent to receiving such communications. The PECR 2003 deal with direct marketing by way of automated calling systems, fax, telephone, and e-mail. The PECR 2003 do not cover direct marketing by post.

[1] SI 2003/2426.

7.293 The PECR 2003 were originally designed to work in conjunction with the DPA 1998. With the repeal of that Act, the PECR 2003 remained in force, but with slight changes to make them compatible with the GDPR. It was intended that the EU would replace the E-Privacy Directive with a new E-Privacy Regulation, which would have had direct effect and replaced the

PECR 2003, sitting alongside the GDPR. However, the UK left the EU before that Regulation was promulgated, and so the PECR remain in force, sitting alongside the UK GDPR.

Direct marketing

7.294 Regulations 19–22 of the PECR 2003 deal with the use of automatic calling systems, fax machines, unsolicited (or 'cold') calls, and e-mail for direct marketing purposes.

Automated calling systems

7.295 Regulation 19 prohibits the use of automated calling systems for direct marketing purposes, save in circumstances where a subscriber has given his consent to be so contacted. Regulation 19(3) prohibits a subscriber from permitting his line to be used in contravention of the regulation and covers subscribers who do not themselves cause transmissions to be made from automated calling systems, but permit their lines to be used for that purpose.

19 Use of automated calling systems

(1)   A person shall neither transmit, nor instigate the transmission of, communications comprising recorded matter for direct marketing purposes by means of an automated calling [or communication] system except in the circumstances referred to in paragraph (2).

(2)   Those circumstances are where—

 (a)   the called line is that of a subscriber who has previously notified the caller that for the time being he consents to such communications being sent by, or at the instigation of, the caller on that line; and

 (b)   the person transmitting, or instigating the transmission of, such communications-

  (i)   does not prevent presentation of the identity of the calling line on the called line; or

  (ii)   presents the identity of a line on which he can be contacted.

(3)   A subscriber shall not permit his line to be used in contravention of paragraph (1).

(4)   For the purposes of this regulation, an automated calling system is a system which is capable of—

 (a)   automatically initiating a sequence of calls to more than one destination in accordance with instructions stored in that system; and

 (b)   transmitting sounds which are not live speech for reception by persons at some or all of the destinations so called.

Fax

7.296 The provisions of reg 20 are somewhat more complicated than those of reg 19 of the PECR 2003. In the case of recipients who are individuals, use of fax machines for direct marketing is prohibited, save with consent. However, in the case of corporate recipients, the prohibition applies once the recipient has notified the caller that such communications should not be sent.

7.297 Regulation 25 provides for a register to be kept of persons who do not consent to being contacted by fax for direct marketing purposes, and for all subscribers (whether individual or corporate), inclusion on the register raises the prohibition on using fax for direct marketing. However, where a recipient has been on the register for under 28 days at the time of the communication being made, no contravention will occur. Additionally, any person on the register may notify a caller that they consent to direct marketing by fax, and no contravention will occur until that consent is withdrawn.

20 Use of facsimile machines for direct marketing purposes

(1) A person shall neither transmit, nor instigate the transmission of, unsolicited communications for direct marketing purposes by means of a facsimile machine where the called line is that of—

    (a) an individual subscriber, except in the circumstances referred to in paragraph (2);

    (b) a corporate subscriber who has previously notified the caller that such communications should not be sent on that line; or

    (c) a subscriber and the number allocated to that line is listed in the register kept under regulation 25.

(2) The circumstances referred to in paragraph (1)(a) are that the individual subscriber has previously notified the caller that he consents for the time being to such communications being sent by, or at the instigation of, the caller.

(3) A subscriber shall not permit his line to be used in contravention of paragraph (1).

(4) A person shall not be held to have contravened paragraph (1)(c) where the number allocated to the called line has been listed on the register for less than 28 days preceding that on which the communication is made.

(5) Where a subscriber who has caused a number allocated to a line of his to be listed in the register kept under regulation 25 has notified a caller that he does not, for the time being, object to such communications being sent on that line by that caller, such communications may be sent by that caller on that line, notwithstanding that the number allocated to that line is listed in the said register.

(6) Where a subscriber has given a caller notification pursuant to paragraph (5) in relation to a line of his—

    (a) the subscriber shall be free to withdraw that notification at any time, and

    (b) where such notification is withdrawn, the caller shall not send such communications on that line.

(7) The provisions of this regulation are without prejudice to the provisions of regulation 19.

Telephone calls for direct marketing purposes

7.298 In the case of telephone calls for direct marketing purposes, there is no distinction between individual and corporate recipients. The conditions for the prohibition to apply are that either the recipient has notified the caller that direct marketing calls should not be made or the recipient is listed in a register of persons who do not consent to receiving unsolicited calls for direct marketing purposes. As in the case of reg 20 above, there is a 28-day grace period from a recipient being listed on the register during which calls may be made without a contravention occurring, and a person on the register may notify a caller that he consents to direct marketing by way of unsolicited calls, and no contravention will occur until that consent is withdrawn. In addition, the persons making or instigating such calls (whether solicited or unsolicited) must not prevent presentation of calling line identity on the called line. Paragraph (6), which was inserted by s 35(2) of the Financial Guidance and Claims Act 2018, and further amended by reg 2 of the Privacy and Electronic Communications (Amendment) (No 2) Regulations 2018, creates an exemption from the prohibition in para (1) in cases which fall within reg 21A (direct marketing calls for claims management services) or reg 21B (direct marketing in relation to pension schemes). For the provisions which apply to these calls, see **7.299** and **7.300** respectively.

21 Calls for direct marketing purposes

(A1) A person shall neither use, nor instigate the use of, a public electronic communications service for the purposes of making calls (whether solicited or unsolicited) for direct marketing purposes except where that person—

(a) does not prevent presentation of the identity of the calling line on the called line; or

(b) presents the identity of a line on which he can be contacted.

(1) A person shall neither use, nor instigate the use of, a public electronic communications service for the purposes of making unsolicited calls for direct marketing purposes where—

(a) the called line is that of a subscriber who has previously notified the caller that such calls should not for the time being be made on that line; or

(b) the number allocated to a subscriber in respect of the called line is one listed in the register kept under regulation 26.

(2) A subscriber shall not permit his line to be used in contravention of paragraphs (A1) or (1)

(3) A person shall not be held to have contravened paragraph (1)(b) where the number allocated to the called line has been listed on the register for less than 28 days preceding that on which the call is made.

(4) Where a subscriber who has caused a number allocated to a line of his to be listed in the register kept under regulation 26 has notified a caller that he does not, for the time being, object to such calls being made on that line by that caller, such calls may be made by that caller on that line, notwithstanding that the number allocated to that line is listed in the said register.

(5) Where a subscriber has given a caller notification pursuant to paragraph (4) in relation to a line of his—

(a) the subscriber shall be free to withdraw that notification at any time, and

(b) where such notification is withdrawn, the caller shall not make such calls on that line.

(6) Paragraph (1) does not apply to a case falling within regulation 21A or 21B

Telephone calls for direct marketing of claims management services

7.299 Regulation 21A deals with direct marketing calls for claims management services. It was inserted by the Financial Guidance and Claims Act 2018. It prohibits calls for the purposes of direct marketing of claims management services except where the subscriber has previously notified the caller that he consents to such calls being made.

21A Calls for direct marketing of claims management services

(1) A person must not use, or instigate the use of, a public electronic communications service to make unsolicited calls for the purposes of direct marketing in relation to claims management services except in the circumstances referred to in paragraph (2).

(2) Those circumstances are where the called line is that of a subscriber who has previously notified the caller that for the time being the subscriber consents to such calls being made by, or at the instigation of, the caller on that line.

(3) A subscriber must not permit the subscriber's line to be used in contravention of paragraph (1).

(4) In this regulation, 'claims management services' means the following services in relation to the making of a claim—

    (a) advice;
    (b) financial services or assistance;
    (c) acting on behalf of, or representing, a person;
    (d) the referral or introduction of one person to another;
    (e) the making of inquiries.

(5) In paragraph (4), 'claim' means a claim for compensation, restitution, repayment or any other remedy or relief in respect of loss or damage or in respect of an obligation, whether the claim is made or could be made—

    (a) by way of legal proceedings,
    (b) in accordance with a scheme of regulation (whether voluntary or compulsory), or
    (c) in pursuance of a voluntary undertaking.

Telephone calls for direct marketing in relation to pension schemes

7.300 Regulation 21B deals with direct marketing calls in relation to pension schemes. It was inserted by the Privacy and Electronic Communications (Amendment) (No 2) Regulations 2018. It prohibits calls in relation to pension schemes except where the circumstances set out in paras (2) and (3) of the regulation exist:

21B Calls for direct marketing in relation to pension schemes

(1) A person must not use, or instigate the use of, a public electronic communications service to make unsolicited calls to an individual for the purpose of direct marketing in relation to occupational pension schemes or personal pension schemes, except where paragraph (2) or (3) applies.

(2) This paragraph applies where—

    (a) the caller is an authorised person or a person who is the trustee or manager of an occupational pension scheme or a personal pension scheme; and
    (b) the called line is that of an individual who has previously notified the caller that for the time being the individual consents to such calls being made by the caller on that line.

(3) This paragraph applies where—

    (a) the caller is an authorised person or a person who is the trustee or manager of an occupational pension scheme or a personal pension scheme;
    (b) the recipient of the call has an existing client relationship with the caller on the line and the relationship is such that the recipient might

reasonably envisage receiving unsolicited calls for the purpose of direct marketing in relation to occupational pension schemes or personal pension schemes; and

(c) the recipient of the call has been given a simple means of refusing (free of charge except for the costs of the transmission of the refusal) the use of the recipient's contact details for the purpose of such direct marketing, at the time that the details were initially collected and, where the recipient did not initially refuse the use of the details, at the time of each subsequent communication.

(4) A subscriber must not permit the subscriber's line to be used in contravention of paragraph (1).

(5) In this regulation—

(a) 'authorised person' has the meaning given in section 31 of the Financial Services and Markets Act 2000;

(b) 'direct marketing in relation to occupational pension schemes or personal pension schemes' includes—

(i) the marketing of a product or service to be acquired using funds held, or previously held, in an occupational pension scheme or a personal pension scheme;

(ii) the offer of any advice or other service that promotes, or promotes the consideration of, the withdrawal or transfer of funds from an occupational pension scheme or a personal pension scheme; and

(iii) the offer of any advice or other service to enable the assessment of the performance of an occupational pension scheme or a personal pension scheme (including its performance in comparison with other forms of investment).

(c) 'existing client relationship' does not include a relationship established at the instigation of the caller primarily for the purpose of avoiding the restriction in paragraph (1); and

(d) 'occupational pension scheme' and 'personal pension scheme' have the meanings given in section 1(1) of the Pension Schemes Act 1993.

E-mail

7.301 In the case of e-mail, there are only two circumstances in which direct marketing may take place: the first is with the consent of the recipient; the second is where the requirements of reg 22(3) (which are cumulative) are met. Regulation 23 prohibits the use of e-mail for direct marketing where the identity of the person on whose behalf the e-mail in question has been sent is disguised or concealed, or where there is no address provided to which a request that the e-mail contact should cease may be sent.

22 Use of electronic mail for direct marketing purposes

(1) This regulation applies to the transmission of unsolicited communications by means of electronic mail to individual subscribers.

(2) Except in the circumstances referred to in paragraph (3), a person shall neither transmit, nor instigate the transmission of, unsolicited communications for the purposes of direct marketing by means of electronic mail unless the recipient of the electronic mail has previously notified the sender that he consents for the time being to such communications being sent by, or at the instigation of, the sender.

(3) A person may send or instigate the sending of electronic mail for the purposes of direct marketing where—

    (a)   that person has obtained the contact details of the recipient of that electronic mail in the course of the sale or negotiations for the sale of a product or service to that recipient;

    (b)   the direct marketing is in respect of that person's similar products and services only; and

    (c)   the recipient has been given a simple means of refusing (free of charge except for the costs of the transmission of the refusal) the use of his contact details for the purposes of such direct marketing, at the time that the details were initially collected, and, where he did not initially refuse the use of the details, at the time of each subsequent communication.

(4)   A subscriber shall not permit his line to be used in contravention of paragraph (2).

23 Use of electronic mail for direct marketing purposes where the identity or address of the sender is concealed

A person shall neither transmit, nor instigate the transmission of, a communication for the purposes of direct marketing by means of electronic mail—

    (a)   where the identity of the person on whose behalf the communication has been sent has been disguised or concealed;

    (b)   where a valid address to which the recipient of the communication may send a request that such communications cease has not been provided.

    (c)   where that electronic mail would contravene regulation 7 of the Electronic Commerce (EC Directive) Regulations 2002 ; or

    (d)   where that electronic mail encourages recipients to visit websites which contravene that regulation.

Enforcement

7.302 Enforcement of the PECR 2003 is covered by regs 30–32. Regulation 30 sets out a right for compensation for any person who has suffered damage caused by a breach, while regs 31–32 deal with enforcement by the ICO. The PECR 2003 adopts the enforcement regime set out in Pt V of the DPA 1998, notwithstanding that that Act has now been repealed for all other purposes.

Compensation (reg 30)

7.303 Regulation 30 provides a right to compensation for any person who has suffered damage by virtue of a contravention of any of the regulations under the PECR 2003. Regulation 30(2) provides a defence that the person in contravention took reasonable care to comply with the regulations.

30 Proceedings for compensation for failure to comply with requirements of the Regulations

(1)   A person who suffers damage by reason of any contravention of any of the requirements of these Regulations by any other person shall be entitled to bring proceedings for compensation from that other person for that damage.

(2)   In proceedings brought against a person by virtue of this regulation it shall be a defence to prove that he had taken such care as in all the circumstances was reasonably required to comply with the relevant requirement.

(3)   The provisions of this regulation are without prejudice to those of regulation 31.

Enforcement by the Information Commissioner

7.304 In addition to the private right to compensation for non-compliance with the Regulations, the Commissioner has jurisdiction to take enforcement action. Regulation 31 extends the enforcement provisions contained in Pt V and the DPA 1998, Schs 6 and 9 to cover non-compliance with the PECR 2003. That regime is modified by the PECR 2003, Sch 1. Many of the modifications in that schedule deal with changing the language of the DPA to reflect that of the PECR 2003 or omitting irrelevant matters. The key substantive differences are as follows:

- When deciding whether to serve an enforcement notice (DPA 1998, s 40) the Commissioner shall consider whether the contravention has caused damage (as opposed to damage or distress).
- A request to the Commissioner for an assessment of compliance (DPA 1998, s 42) cannot be made under the PECR 2003.
- DPA 1998, ss 43(1) and (2) on information notices are modified to remove references to notices issued as a result of a DPA 1998, s 42 request.
- Special information notices are not available under the PECR 2003.

7.305 Regulation 32 provides that the Commissioner's enforcement functions may be exercised on a request by OFCOM, an aggrieved person, or of her own motion.

7.306 An example of the kind of enforcement action taken in a particularly bad case can be found in *Reactiv Media Limited v The Information Commissioner (Privacy & Electronic Communications Regulations 2003)*[1]. That case concerned direct marketing calls to a telephone number whose subscriber has registered with the Telephone Preference Service ('TPS') in contravention of PECR 2003, reg 21. At first instance the Commissioner issued a monetary penalty notice under DPA 1998, s 55A, finding the appellant in serious breach of PECR 2003, reg 21 and imposed a penalty of £50,000. The appellant appealed to the First-tier Tribunal, who found the evidence 'overwhelming' that the company carried on its business 'in conscious disregard of its obligations'. In view of the financial robustness of the company and the aggravating factors in the case, 'a culture of denial . . . weak governance of the company and a tendency to blame others rather than accept responsibility' the penalty originally imposed by the Commissioner was raised by 50% to £75,000.

[1] [2015] UKFTT 2014_0213 (GRC) (13 April 2015).

7.307 On 17 December 2018 the Privacy and Electronic Communications (Amendment) Regulations 2018 came into force. These regulations amended Sch 1 of the PECR so as to allow the ICO to impose monetary penalties of up to £500,000 on directors of companies which breach the PECR, as well as the companies themselves. The mechanism for liability is consent, connivance, or neglect.

THE REGULATION OF INVESTIGATORY POWERS ACT 2000

Introduction

7.308 The Regulation of Investigatory Powers Act 2000 ('RIPA 2000') regulates intelligence-gathering activity and provides a framework for authorising surveillance. It has been amended and supplemented by the Protection of Freedoms Act 2012 ('PFA 2012'), which has reduced the scope of activity which is capable of being authorised under RIPA 2000 for use by local authorities.

Forms of surveillance

7.309 RIPA 2000 distinguishes between three types of intelligence-gathering activity – intrusive surveillance, directed surveillance, and the use of a covert human intelligence sources ('CHIS')[1].

[1]   RIPA 2000, s 26(1).

7.310 Intrusive surveillance is defined as 'covert surveillance that is carried out in relation to anything taking place on any residential premises or in any private vehicle; and involves the presence of an individual on the premises or in the vehicle or is carried out by means of a surveillance device'[1]. Intrusive surveillance may not be authorised by a local authority.

[1]   RIPA 2000, s 26(3).

7.311 Directed surveillance is defined in RIPA 2000, s 26(2) as follows:

(2) Subject to subsection (6), surveillance is directed for the purposes of this Part if it is covert but not intrusive and is undertaken—

    (a)   for the purposes of a specific investigation or a specific operation;

    (b)   in such a manner as is likely to result in the obtaining of private information about a person (whether or not one specifically identified for the purposes of the investigation or operation); and

    (c)   otherwise than by way of an immediate response to events or circumstances the nature of which is such that it would not be reasonably practicable for an authorisation under this Part to be sought for the carrying out of the surveillance.

7.312 A CHIS is defined in RIPA 2000, s 26(8) as follows:

(8) For the purposes of this Part a person is a covert human intelligence source if—

    (a)   he establishes or maintains a personal or other relationship with a person for the covert purpose of facilitating the doing of anything falling within paragraph (b) or (c);

    (b)   he covertly uses such a relationship to obtain information or to provide access to any information to another person; or

    (c)   he covertly discloses information obtained by the use of such a relationship, or as a consequence of the existence of such a relationship.

Directed surveillance

7.313 The key questions in determining whether an activity amounts to directed surveillance are first: whether it is covert (ie whether the subject will be unaware that the activity is taking place); and secondly, whether private information is likely to be obtained. Where an activity does amount to directed surveillance, a directed surveillance authority ('DSA') must be applied for under RIPA 2000, s 28.

7.314 In order for a DSA to be granted, the proposed activity must be necessary for a purpose set out in RIPA 2000, s 28(3), and proportionate to what is sought to be achieved by carrying it out[1]. In the case of DSAs granted by local authorities, the only purpose in RIPA 2000, s 28(3) for which a DSA may be granted is preventing or detecting crime or preventing disorder (at RIPA 2000, s 28(3)(b)).

[1] RIPA 2000, s 28(2).

7.315 In local authority cases, a DSA may only be granted in cases where the offence being investigated carries a maximum sentence of at least 6 months' custody or is an offence relating to the sale of alcohol or tobacco to underage persons.

7.316 RIPA 2000, s 32A, inserted by the PFA 2012, s 38, provides that in addition to being authorised internally, DSAs in local authority cases must be approved by a justice of the peace before they can take effect.

Covert human intelligence sources

7.317 As with a DSA, the necessity and proportionality tests must be met for a CHIS authorisation to be granted[1]. In addition, the matters set out at RIPA 2000, s 29(5) concerning oversight and management of the CHIS must also be met. In local authority cases, preventing or detecting crime or preventing disorder is the only ground on which a CHIS authorisation may be granted.

[1] RIPA 2000, s 29(2)(a) and (b).

7.318 A person will only be a CHIS if he 'establishes or maintains a personal or other relationship'. Mere communication with another may not on its own to amount to a relationship; the nature, duration, and purpose of the contact should all be taken into account in determining whether a relationship is present.

Who may authorise

7.319 In most cases, a DSA or use of a CHIS may be authorised by a Director, Head of Service, or Service Manager. Where directed surveillance or use of a CHIS is likely to obtain confidential information, or the use of a juvenile or vulnerable person as a CHIS is required, authorisation must be by a Head of Paid Service. The required authorising officers are to be found in the Schedule to the Regulation of Investigatory Powers (Directed Surveillance and Covert Human Intelligence Sources) Order 2010[1].

[1]   SI 2010/521.

Judicial approval

7.320 The Home Office has issued guidance on the procedure for judicial approval of DSAs and CHIS authorisations. In summary:

- In order for judicial approval to be granted, an officer will have to attend. The person best placed to answer the questions of the JP is likely to be the investigating officer.
- The hearing will be in private – not open court – but the officer will still have to be sworn and present evidence as required by the JP.
- The forms and supporting papers must by themselves make the case. It is not sufficient for the local authority to provide oral evidence where this is not reflected or supported in the papers provided. Additional information can be noted by a JP, but this should not be information which is fundamental to the case.
- The JP must be satisfied that at the time the application was made, there were reasonable grounds for believing the authorisation was necessary and proportionate.
- They must consider whether there continue to be reasonable grounds.
- They must be satisfied that the person who granted the authorisation or gave the notice was an appropriate designated person within the local authority and the authorisation was made in accordance with any applicable legal restrictions, eg that the crime threshold for directed surveillance has been met.
- If all the above conditions are met, the application should be granted.

Non-authorised surveillance

7.321 Surveillance which is not intrusive and does not amount to directed surveillance or use of a CHIS does not require authorisation under RIPA 2000. Examples include overt use of CCTV and ANPR and covert surveillance which is an immediate response to events, such that it is not practical to obtain an authorisation. However, where surveillance for which authorisation would otherwise be required is carried out without such authorisation, RIPA 2000, s 80 provides as follows:

80 General saving for lawful conduct

Nothing in any of the provisions of this Act by virtue of which conduct of any description is or may be authorised by any warrant, authorisation or notice, or by virtue of which information may be obtained in any manner, shall be construed—

(a)   as making it unlawful to engage in any conduct of that description which is not otherwise unlawful under this Act and would not be unlawful apart from this Act;

(b)   as otherwise requiring—

   (i)   the issue, grant or giving of such a warrant, authorisation or notice, or
   (ii)   the taking of any step for or towards obtaining the authority of such a warrant, authorisation or notice,

before any such conduct of that description is engaged in; or

(c)   as prejudicing any power to obtain information by any means not involving conduct that may be authorised under this Act.

7.322 The effect of RIPA 2000, s 80 is that unauthorised surveillance will not be unlawful unless specifically provided for elsewhere in RIPA 2000, but also that the lack of authorisation is no bar to the surveillance being conducted and information being obtained. The purpose of RIPA 2000 is to ensure that surveillance activity complies with the Human Rights Act 1998 and the ECHR. Surveillance which has passed through the authorisation process will prima facie be so compliant; however, it does not follow that surveillance which has not passed through that process will not be. The compliance of non-authorised surveillance falls to be assessed on its own merits.

7.323 *BA v Chief Constable of Cleveland Police*[1] concerned unauthorised surveillance by the police. Cleveland Police placed a covert silent video recorder in the home of a disabled complainant who suspected her carers of stealing from her. This amounted to intrusive surveillance. Under RIPA 2000, s 32(3), intrusive surveillance may only be authorised in cases of 'serious crime', and the offence of theft does not meet this definition. The surveillance was therefore not only unauthorised, but incapable of being authorised. The evidence obtained led to the conviction of the first claimant for theft. The claimants complained that the placing of the recorder was unlawful and infringed their Art 8 rights. The Tribunal held that any interference with Art 8 ECHR was necessary and justified, and that the conduct of the police was necessary and proportionate.

[1]   IPT/11/129/CH; IPT/11/133/CH & IPT/12/72/CH.

7.324 By contrast, *Wood v Commissioner of Police for the Metropolis*[1] provides an example of surveillance being held to be unlawful. In that case, the Appellant, who was an anti-arms trade campaigner, attended the AGM of a company which organised a trade fair for the arms industry in order to ask a question. As he left, he was photographed by the police in order to assist in ascertaining whether an offence had been committed in the AGM or at the arms fair later. The photograph was retained, but not added to a database of photographs kept by the police for intelligence purposes. The court held that while the bare act of taking a photograph in a public place would not normally engage Art 8 ECHR, the case had to be looked at in context. In the present case, Art 8 was engaged, and it was for the police to justify any interference with that right. Once it was established that the appellant had not committed any offence at the meeting there was no reasonable basis to consider that he might commit an offence at the trade fair. As a result, the interference with the appellant's Art 8 right by way of the taking and retention of the photographs was not justified under Art 8(2).

[1]   [2009] EWCA Civ 414, [2010] 1 WLR 123.

Handling of material obtained through surveillance

7.325 Each public authority must ensure that arrangements are in place for the secure handling, storage and destruction of material obtained through the use of surveillance. Authorising officers, through their relevant Data Controller, must ensure compliance with the appropriate data protection requirements under the DPA 2018 and any relevant codes.

7.326 In *R (on the application of Catt) v Commissioner of the Police of the Metropolis*[1] the Supreme Court considered the proportionality of the retention of data obtained through surveillance in two conjoined appeals. In the *Catt* case, the appellant was a 91-year-old man who had a history of involvement in protests going back to 2005. These protests were organised by a group with a history of violence and criminality, although the appellant had never been convicted of any offence. The appellant asserted that the long-term collection and retention of information about his activities breached his rights under Art 8. The court held that Art 8 was engaged. The court considered the requirements of the DPA, the Code of Practice issued under the Police Act 1996, and the detailed *Guidance on the Management of Police Information issued by the Association of Chief Police Officers*. As the interference was minor, the appellant's inclusion in the police records did not carry any stigma of suspicion or guilt, and the retention of the data was justified by the maintenance of public order and the prevention of crime, the court held that the interference with Art 8 was proportionate.

[1]   [2015] UKSC 9, [2015] 2 WLR 664.

7.327 In the second appeal, the appellant ('T') had been given a warning notice under the Protection from Harassment Act 1997 relating to an incident which she denied. The policy of the police was to retain a copy of the notice for 7 years and a CRIS report of the incident for 12 years. However, both had been deleted after two-and-a-half years on the basis that there were no ongoing concerns. The court held that the policy of retention for 7 and 12 years respectively was disproportionate. However, as the records had been deleted after two-and-a-half years in any event, there had born no interference with T's Art 8 rights.

RIPA 2000 authorisations and disclosure

7.328 In most cases, RIPA 2000 authorisations will form part of the unused material in a criminal case. In such cases, they will usually appear in redacted form on the schedule of non-sensitive unused material, and in their full form on the sensitive schedule. It is not unusual for defence teams to demand their disclosure either within a defence statement or under a CPIA 1996, s 8 disclosure application. Consideration has to be given to whether any part of the documents contain information which could be said to either assist the defence or undermine the prosecution. Whilst this is always a fact specific decision the following decisions give provide instructive examples:

> *R v GS and others*[1]: 'In seeking . . . material, defence counsel did not point to any particular aspects of the authorisation procedure giving them cause for concern. It was essentially a "fishing expedition" to enable them to discover whether they might have a case for seeking exclusion of the recorded conversations as unfair, by reason of unlawfulness of the authorisation procedures adopted or as to compliance with them, or otherwise under section 78 of PACE.' The Judge was not required to accede to the defence requests for disclosure or access to the material underlying those approvals or, in the circumstances, to examine it himself.

R v Jones[2]: ' . . . it is submitted that the Crown should have disclosed all documents relevant to the authorisation of the undercover operation . . . It was relevant, so it is argued, because it would disclose the parameters of the operation and so reveal whether or not the undercover officer had stayed within those parameters . . . Having seen the document, the Judge asserted that the authorisation had been properly given but provided no further assistance. It did not weaken the prosecution case and although it echoed the material provided, so that it was possible to test the officer's actions against the briefing, it did not assist the defence case. On that basis, it did not fall for disclosure.'

[1]   [2005] EWCA Crim 887.
[2]   [2010] EWCA Crim 925.

7.329 In certain cases (particularly those involving a CHIS), PII issues may arise and consideration will have to be given to whether a PII application is necessary in response to a request for disclosure of an authorisation. In such cases, identifying the area of concern raised by the defence is important as this will often determine whether the matter can be resolved by disclosing a suitably redacted document or whether it will be necessary to claim PII.

THE ENVIRONMENTAL INFORMATION REGULATIONS 2004

7.330 The Environmental Information Regulations 2004[1] ('EIR 2004') implement Council Directive 2003/4/EC and provide freedom of access to environmental information held by UK public authorities (except in relation to Scottish public authorities – see the Environmental Information (Scotland) Regulations 2004[2]).

[1]   SI 2004/3391.
[2]   SSI 2004/520.

7.331 The extensive meaning given to 'public authorities' in reg 2(2) includes government departments, local authorities, the NHS, police forces and universities. The Regulations also cover some other bodies that do public work that affects the environment.

7.332 The EIR 2004 enable information to be accessed in two ways:
*   public authorities must make environmental information available pro-actively;
*   a public authority that holds environmental information must generally make it available on request, as soon as possible and no later than 20 working days after the date of receipt of the request. A public authority may charge applicants a reasonable amount for making the information available (subject to certain restrictions).

7.333 Information may only be withheld if an exception to disclosure applies and the public interest in not disclosing the information outweighs the public interest in disclosure. Enforcement powers are given to the Information Commissioner.

OTHER LEGISLATION

Acquisition of information

7.334 Examples of other legislative provisions which enable local authorities to obtain information are given below.

7.335 The Road Vehicles (Registration and Licensing) Regulations 2002[1] enables the Driver and Vehicle Licensing Agency to disclosure vehicle registration and licensing particulars to a local authority for enforcement purposes.

27 Disclosure of registration and licensing particulars
  (1)   The Secretary of State may make any particulars contained in the register available for use—

    (a) by a local authority for any purpose connected with the investigation of an offence or of a decriminalised parking contravention;
    . . .
    (e) by any person who can show to the satisfaction of the Secretary of State that he has reasonable cause for wanting the particulars to be made available to him.
  (2)   Particulars may be provided to such a person as is mentioned in paragraph (1)(e) on payment of such fee, if any, of such amount as appears to the Secretary of State reasonable in the circumstances of the case.

[1]   SI 2002/2742.

7.336 The Postal Services Act 2011 (Disclosure of Information) Order 2012[1] prescribes bodies or other persons, enactments and circumstances and purposes which are exempt from the general prohibition in the Postal Services Act 2011 on disclosure of information obtained by virtue of the exercise of regulatory functions under Pt 3 of that Act.

[1]   SI 2012/1128.

7.337 A local weights and measures authority is a prescribed body and each of the following is a prescribed enactment for the purposes of Postal Services Act 2011, s 56(2)(d) or (f):
•   Trade Descriptions Act 1968.
•   Fair Trading Act 1973.
•   Consumer Credit Act 1974.
•   Estate Agents Act 1979.
•   Consumer Protection Act 1987;
•   Regulation of Investigatory Powers Act 2000.
•   Business Protection from Misleading Marketing Regulations 2008[1].
•   Consumer Protection from Unfair Trading Regulations 2008[2].

[1]   SI 2008/1276.
[2]   SI 2008/1277.

Chapter 8

UNFAIR COMMERCIAL PRACTICES

Contents

INTRODUCTION

8.1 The Consumer Protection from Unfair Trading Regulations 2008[1] ('CPUTR 2008') came into force on 26 May 2008. The CPUTR 2008 replaced most of the criminal offences in the Trade Descriptions Act 1968 and numerous other trading law provisions with a set of new criminal offences based on unfair commercial practices. The same unfair commercial practices now also form the basis for injunctive relief under the Enterprise Act 2002 and consumer rights to civil redress. The scope of the CPUTR 2008 is considerably broader than the legislation it replaced. The distinction between goods and services was swept away and the newer legislation also applies to immovable property, intangible property and financial services.

[1]   SI 2008/1277.

8.2 The CPUTR 2008's history can be traced back to the public consultation undertaken by the European Commission in 2001 on fair trading[1]. In 2005, this consultation resulted in the European Unfair Commercial Practices Directive ('UCPD')[2]; which was implemented into UK law in the form of the CPUTR 2008. The CPUTR 2008 is therefore Directive-based law and its purpose, as set out in Art 1 of the UCPD, is to 'contribute to the proper functioning of the internal market and achieve a high level of consumer protection'[3]. However, Recital 9 of the UCPD makes clear that it is without prejudice to community and national rules on contract law, intellectual property rights, the health and safety aspects of products, on conditions of establishment and authorisation regimes, including those rules which, in conformity with community law, relate to gambling activities, and to community competition rules and the national provisions implementing them. Notwithstanding the UK's exit from the EU,

479

these purposes and exclusions are likely to remain important in interpreting the meaning of the CPUTR 2008, because the legislation was made to give effect to the UCPD.

1   Green Paper on European Union Consumer Protection, COM (2001) 531.
2   Directive 2005/29/EC of the European Parliament and of the Council of 11 May 2005 concerning unfair business-to-consumer commercial practices in the internal market (OJ L149, 11.6.2005, p 22).
3   See also Directive 2005/29/EC, Recital (1) of the preamble.

8.3 At the same time the Business Protection from Misleading Marketing Regulations 2008[1] ('BPR 2008') came into force to implement the European Directive on Misleading and Comparative Advertising[2]. This Directive-based law regulates business-to-business commercial practices and has similar aims to the UCPD.

1   SI 2008/1276.
2   2006/114/EC.

8.4 The UCPD is a maximum harmonisation Directive designed to remove legislative barriers to trade throughout the EU[1] and introduced a general concept of unfair commercial practices, which is applicable throughout the Member States of the EU and EEA. This consumer policy goal needs to be read together with the other principles set out in the European Union's Charter of Fundamental Rights. The Charter was conditionally adopted by the United Kingdom in December 2009 in the Lisbon Treaty. Although its application is confined to EU law, the Charter repeats the obligation of Member States to provide a high level of consumer protection (Art 38). However, it potentially counterbalances this with a requirement that citizens are given freedom to conduct a business (Art 16). The UCPD does restrict free movement of goods, in that it may render the marketing or sale of certain goods impermissible. However, where it is the UCPD itself which prohibits the commercial practice in question, a national court decision to this effect will not be an unlawful obstruction of free movement rights, because EU law in the UCPD necessitates misleading advertising to be prohibited[2].

1   Article 4 of the UCPD.
2   *R (on the application of Actegy Ltd) v ASA* [2019] EWHC 2374 (Admin) para 47.

8.5 The effect of the UK's exit from the EU is that the UK can make laws that would otherwise fall foul of the UCPD's full harmonisation nature, and also refrain from implementing forthcoming amendments to the UCPD. However the UK is required to continue to extend certain rights to consumers, including EU consumers, under the terms of the UK-EU Trade and Co-operation Agreement ('TCA') – in particular in the context of online trade. The CPUTR 2008 must be construed to give effect to these obligations[1]. For example, the UK must continue to:

- restrain fraudulent and deceptive practices;
- require traders to act in good faith and abide by fair commercial practices, including prohibiting charges for unsolicited goods and services;
- require traders to provide consumers with clear and thorough information of their identity, contact details, the transaction, including main

characteristics of the product, full price including all applicable charges and applicable consumer rights; and

• grant consumers access to redress for breaches of their rights, including remedies for where a product is paid for but not delivered[2].

---

[1]   *Lipton & Anr v BA City Flyer Ltd* [2021] EWCA Civ 454 para 77–82, interpreting the EU (Future Relationship) Act 2020 s 29, which the Court of Appeal held requires UK courts to amend or replace a provision of domestic law which incompletely or imperfectly implements an obligation in the TCA.

[2]   Digit 13.1.a and 1B.

8.6 In the UK the CPUTR 2008 is often enforced using the criminal law; however, it is also enforceable under Pt 4A of CPUTR 2008 and Pt 8 of the Enterprise Act 2002 in the civil courts. The key principles concerning construction and the main concepts are common to both the criminal and civil jurisdictions in the UK. The BPR 2008 is considered in Chapter **12**, Advertising. The Consumer Protection (Amendment) Regulations 2014[1] created rights to redress that are enforceable by consumers in relation to contracts entered into, or payments made, on or after 1 October 2014, where certain provisions of the CPUTR 2008 are infringed.

---

[1]   SI 2014/870.

APPROACH TO CONSTRUCTION OF THE CPUTR 2008

8.7 There will always be a tendency for UK regulatory lawyers to focus on the construction of terms using domestic case law and tools of interpretation. Although this may well provide useful assistance in certain cases, it must be remembered that the CPUTR 2008 implemented a maximum harmonisation Directive[1]. In *Office of Fair Trading v Purely Creative*, Briggs J described the process of interpreting the CPUTR 2008[2]:

> 'Domestic regulations designed to implement EU Directives, and in particular maximum harmonisation Directives, must be construed as far as possible so as to implement the purposes and provisions of the Directive. The interpretation of words and phrases is neither a matter of grammar nor dictionaries, nor even a matter of the use of those phrases (or of the underlying concepts) in national law. If similar words and phrases are used in the Directive itself, then they must be interpreted both in the Directive and in the implementing regulations by means of a process of interpretation which is independent of the Member State's national law and, for that matter, independent of any other Member State's national law. For that purpose the primary recourse of the national court is to the jurisprudence of the ECJ. The national court may also obtain assistance from, but is not bound by, guidance issued by the Commission, and by the decisions of other national courts as to the meaning of the relevant Directive.'

---

[1]   See Chapter **2**, Interpretation of Consumer Law, for construction of EU-based legislation.

[2]   [2011] EWHC 106 (Ch), [2011] CTLC 45.

8.8 For as long as the CPUTR 2008 continues substantially to reflect the UCPD, it is suggested that these words should still guide interpretation – albeit that UK courts will not formally be bound by CJEU rulings which are handed down after 31 December 2020. Rulings up to this date will continue to bind most UK courts. Section 6 of the European Union Withdrawal Act 2018 provides that the Supreme Court can depart from retained European Law, and the Secretary of State has also specified by regulations a number of other courts can depart from retained European Law, applying the same test as the Supreme Court would apply when departing from its own case law[1]. These courts include the Court of Appeal of England and Wales, the Inner House of the Court of Session and the Court of Appeal of Northern Ireland. The Supreme Court and the Court of Appeal have emphasised that this power should be used with great caution[2]. In particular, it seems unlikely that the UK courts will feel it is appropriate to depart from retained EU case law where the UCPD and its UK implementation remain substantially unchanged[3].

[1]   The European Union (Withdrawal) Act 2018 (Relevant Court)(Retained EU Case Law) Regulations 2020. The power is set out in the *Practice Statement (Judicial Precedent)* [1966] 1 WLR 1234.
[2]   *Horton v Sadler* [2007] 1 AC 307 at 29; *Peninsula Securities Ltd v Dunnes Stores Ltd (Bangor) Ltd* [2020] UKSC 36 at 49; *Tunein Inc v Warner Music UK Ltd* [2021] EWCA Civ 441 at 73–75.
[3]   See *Tunein Inc v Warner Music UK Ltd* [2021] EWCA Civ 441 at 78–89, 184 and 196–202.

8.9 CJEU rulings from 1 January 2021 are likely to remain persuasive authority, because they interpret the UCPD, which the CPUTR 2008 gives effect to, and s 6(2) of the European Union (Withdrawal) Act 2018 expressly gives UK courts power to have regard to CJEU decisions, so far as they are relevant. CJEU rulings on the UCPD are likely to remain relevant where the CPUTR 2008 continues to reflect the UCPD or the CJEU ruling otherwise builds upon or refines retained EU case law[1]. Over time however, it is likely that the UCPD and UK law will diverge – for example Directive 2019/2161 (the 'Omnibus Directive') regarding better enforcement and modernisation of Union consumer protection rules, will make various amendments to the UCPD. However, as this new Directive must be implemented only from 28 May 2022, there is no guarantee that the UK will choose to make the amendments to the CPUTR 2008 which would be required to reflect the changes[2].

[1]   *Tunein Inc v Warner Music UK Ltd* [2021] EWCA Civ 441 at 90–91.
[2]   The changes being introduced by Directive 2019/2161 are: provisions to deal with dual quality products, rules on online market places (in particular ranking of products), new banned practices (including reselling tickets acquired using automated means; using reviews which purport to be by real consumers without taking steps to verify the origins of the reviews; submitting false consumer reviews), requirement for a private right of redress for UCPD infringements and a requirement for traders to be fined up to at least 4% of their EU turnover for breaches of the UCPD. The UK Government has consulted on changes to the CPUTR 2008, including the adding of several new unfair practices to the blacklist. Some of these changes are similar to those set out in the Omnibus Directive. See Reforming competition and consumer policy – GOV.UK (www.gov.uk) for the consultation.

8.10 The High Court in *Purely Creative* was critical of the OFT's attempt to use differences in the implementation of the UCPD in other Member States as a method of construing the CPUTR 2008[1].

'In my judgment recourse to differences of implementation of a Directive intended to have uniform effect throughout the EU is likely to prove a time-consuming and ultimately fruitless exercise.'

This should not be confused with making use of different language versions of the Directive itself, which is a permissible and often helpful method to construe the true meaning of the text, along with the purpose and overall scheme of the Directive.

¹ An attempt had been made to rely on the Irish Regulations implementing para 31 of Annex 1 to the UCPD.

8.11 On appeal, the Court of Appeal (Civil Division) found that, although it agreed with this statement of practice, such national differences might be relevant to a decision to refer a case to the Court of Justice of the European Union (CJEU)[1]:

'But the different approaches of Member States may well be important to the exercise of this court's discretion whether to refer questions of interpretation of the Directive to the Court of Justice of the European Union.'

The approach of the Court of Appeal to this issue was confirmed when the *Purely Creative* case was later considered by the CJEU[2].

[1] [2011] EWCA Civ 920, [2012] CTLC 40.
[2] *Purely Creative Ltd v Office of Fair Trading* (C-428/11) European Court of Justice (Sixth Chamber), 18 October 2012 [2013] 1 CMLR 35.

8.12 The use of case law from other Member States is dealt with in greater detail in CHAPTER 2, Interpretation of Consumer Law. It is suggested that, although the case law of other Member States is not binding, it can be useful in assisting in the construction of the Directive by providing representative examples. Indeed the CJEU has invoked as part of its reasoning for taking a particular interpretation of the UCPD not only the decisions of national courts of the Member States, but also the position taken in the current Commission Guidance[1]. Some summaries of cases from other EU Member States referred to in this chapter were available from a website maintained by the European Commission, but this is no longer maintained or accessible[2]. The current Commission guidance on the meaning of the UCPD was published on 25 May 2016[3]. A supplementary guidance statement on the application of UCPD to so called dual quality food was also published on 26 September 2017[4].

[1] CJEU *UAB Gelvora* C-357/16 para 26.
[2] The web address was https://webgate.ec.europa.eu/ucp. However, please note that this database has not been kept up to date, and so is not comprehensive. It is hoped that a fresh compendium of case law on the full consumer acquis, including UCPD, will be in place in due course.
[3] See https://ec.europa.eu/info/law/law-topic/consumers/unfair-commercial-practices-law/unfair-commercial-practices-directive_en.
[4] C(2017) 6532 final. See http://ec.europa.eu/newsroom/just/item-detail.cfm?item_id=604475.

PROVISIONS REVOKED BY THE CPUTR 2008

8.13 The CPUTR 2008 replaced most of the criminal offences in the Trade Descriptions Act 1968 ('TDA 1968'), which itself replaced the various Merchandise Marks Acts passed between 1887 and 1953. The CPUTR 2008 does, however, retain a number of key liability concepts found in the TDA 1968 (for example liability of directors). The body of TDA 1968 case law remains relevant when considering these concepts. Schedule 2 of the CPUTR 2008 sets out the amendments to existing legislation. These amendments are too voluminous to set out comprehensively, however the main criminal sanctions that were revoked are as follows:

(a)   under the TDA 1968:
- prohibition of false trade descriptions under the TDA 1968, s 1(1);
- trade descriptions used in advertisements under the TDA 1968, s 5;
- offer to supply under the TDA 1968, s 6;
- false representations concerning services under the TDA 1968, ss 13–15;

(b)   the misleading pricing indication offences under the Consumer Protection Act 1987, ss 20–26[1];

(c)   the Fair Trading Act 1973, ss 29–33 offences[2];

(d)   the Mock Auctions Act 1961;

(e)   the false advertisements offence in the Consumer Credit Act 1974, s 46;

(f)   the misrepresentation offence under the Weights and Measures Act 1985, s 29;

(g)   the Control of Misleading Advertisements Regulations 1988[3];

(h)   the unlawful harassment of debtors offence under the Administration of Justice Act 1970, s 40 is confined to situations not covered by the CPUTR 2008 (for example transactions that do not involve consumers).

Additionally the Property Misdescriptions Act 1991 has now been repealed and the cases that had previously been brought under its provisions will now be dealt with under CPUTR 2008.

[1]   Which additionally resulted in legislation made under the Consumer Protection Act, s 26 – the Price Indications (Method of Payment) Regulations 1991, SI 1991/199 and the Price Indications (Resale of Tickets) Regulations 1994, SI 1994/3248 – ceasing to have effect, although a specific saving was made for the Price Indications (Bureaux de Change) (No 2) Regulations 1992, SI 1992/737.

[2]   The saving for orders made under the Fair Trading Act 1973, contained in the Enterprise Act 2002, also ceased to have effect – and, by this means, the Consumer Transactions (Restrictions on Statements) Order 1976, SI 1976/1813 and the Business Advertisements (Disclosure) Order 1977, SI 1997/1918 were also repealed).

[3]   SI 1988/915, and the amending SI 2000/914 and SI 2003/3183.

THE APPLICATION OF THE CPUTR 2008

Jurisdiction

8.14 The CPUTR 2008 were made pursuant to powers in the European Communities Act 1972, s 2(2), which allows (by order in council) the implementation of, 'any EU obligation of the United Kingdom . . . or of enabling any rights enjoyed or to be enjoyed by the United Kingdom'. The traditional presumption under domestic law was that unless there is an express statutory exception, criminal sanction will usually only extend to acts committed within the jurisdiction[1].

[1]   See eg *Board of Trade v Owen* [1957] AC 602 per Lord Tucker at 625.

8.15 Under the TDA 1968, the courts had already expressed a willingness to extend the geographical jurisdiction of consumer offences. For example, the TDA 1968 was construed to catch descriptions or statements made in travel brochures about holidays abroad, provided that they were read within the UK[1]. By analogy to the TDA 1968, this is very likely to remain the position under the

CPUTR 2008. The modern view of geographical jurisdiction is that, in the absence of express geographical limitation, it should be ascertained by a consideration of the intention of the legislator[2]. Under the European Communities Act 1972, s 2(2) this can only be by reference to the intention and purpose behind the original European provision. It may be observed that it was plainly a purpose of the UCPD to provide uniform protection to consumers throughout the European Union. In the same way, a trader who is outside the EU may infringe the UCPD if they direct their activities towards consumers in any state in the EU and also the CPUTR 2008 if directed towards consumers in the UK.

[1]   *R v Thompson Holidays* [1974] QB 592.
[2]   *Treacy v DPP* [1971] AC 537, per Lord Diplock. For a more recent discussion of the factors to be applied to imply an extra territorial intent to legislation, see the Supreme Court ruling in *R (on the application of KBR, Inc) (Appellant) v Director of the Serious Fraud Office (Respondent)* [2021] UKSC 2.

8.16 The position in respect of the law applying to civil liability under the Enterprise Act 2002 (and for breach of the redress provisions of the CPUTR 2008) was, when the UK was within the EU, governed by the Rome II Regulation on non-contractual obligations, which applies the law of the country where the collective interests of consumers are affected, wherever the trader is located[1]. As of 1 January 2021, this has the status of Retained EU law in the UK[2]. If the business or the affected consumer is within the UK, there is unlikely to be any successful argument against domestic enforcement; the definition of commercial practice under the CPUTR 2008 is broad enough to encompass almost every aspect of consumer trading.

[1]   Article 6(1) of the Rome II Regulation 864/2007.
[2]   It has been amended to reflect that the UK is no longer an EU Member State. See the Law Applicable to Contractual Obligations and Non-Contractual Obligations (Amendment etc) (EU Exit) Regulations 2019, reg 11.

8.17 There remains a question of whether the CPUTR 2008 may potentially be available for criminal offences when both the consumer, and the relevant business, is outside the United Kingdom. For example, if an offence was committed against a UK consumer whilst abroad, could the CPUTR 2008 be used to prosecute the UK consumer's grievance in the UK courts? This might mirror the jurisdictional position for an EU consumer enforcing his civil contractual rights[1]. However, it seems most unlikely that the enforcement authorities would be able to enforce offences outside the UK. There is no express power to do so and it is unlikely that the courts would construe the CPUTR 2008 to allow the domestic prosecution of offences when the circumstances have little or no connection with the United Kingdom. The courts are unlikely to have an appetite for entertaining criminal prosecutions with only a tangential connection to the UK. The most convenient forum for resolving such questions is inevitably the EU country in which the offence occurred. The disadvantage and cost to a defendant of being tried for a consumer offence abroad are likely to be seen as disproportionate, potentially generating abuse of process applications.

[1]   See the Contracts (Applicable Law) Act 1990.

8.18 The CPUTR 2008 will also cover offences by persons if they were committed:

(a)   on board a United Kingdom ship[1];
(b)   on offshore installations[2];
(c)   on board a British controlled aircraft or hovercraft while in flight[3].

[1]   Merchant Shipping Act, ss 686 and 687 as contained in the Merchant Shipping (Registration etc) Act 1993, Sch 4, para 62.
[2]   Installations covered by the Oil and Gas Enterprise Act 1982, s 22.
[3]   Civil Aviation Act 1982, s 92.

Maximum harmonisation

8.19 The UCPD is a maximum harmonisation directive. This means first of all that its provisions must be implemented in the EU Member States, which are not permitted to cut down the scope of protection, for example by granting immunity to certain traders[1]. EU Member States are expected to implement it purposively but must not exceed its provisions (except for financial services and immovable property). This is provided for in Art 4 which states:

> 'Member States shall neither restrict the freedom to provide services nor restrict the free movement of goods for reasons falling within the field approximated by this Directive.'

[1]   See C-421/12 *Commission v Belgium* paras 42–48.

8.20 The CPUTR 2008 has been implemented in the UK in such a way that it is, for the most part, a virtual word-for-word copy of the UCPD. With the UK's exit from the EU, it is free to pass legislation which departs from the standard set in the UCPD, subject to ensuring that the CPUTR 2008 still achieves the effects required by the UK/EU Trade and Co-operation Agreement ('TCA'). However it is still important to set out here a discussion of the full harmonisation nature of the UCPD, both because this shapes how the CPUTR 2008 should be construed, and because any UK traders wishing to deal with EU consumers will need to understand how the EU rules apply. A Member State cannot adopt stricter rules even if the aim is to achieve a higher level of consumer protection. In *Zentrale zur bekampfung unlauteren Wettbewerbs eV v Plus Warenhandelsgesellschaft mbH*[1] the CJEU found that German law had done just this and fell foul of Art 4 because it prohibited promotions where entry to a lottery was on condition of buying goods. This particular case concerned a retailer of lingerie which invited consumers to buy goods in order to obtain free entry into a lottery. The CJEU found that the German law did not have regard to the Directive, under which this practice would not be unfair, and that the law was contrary to Art 4 by implementing a more restrictive national measure.

[1]   *Zentrale zur Bekampfung unlauteren Wettbewerbs eV v Plus Warenhandelsgesellschaft mbH* (C-304/08) European Court of Justice (First Chamber) [2011] 1 All ER (Comm) 658.

8.21 Similarly, in *VTB-VAB NV v Total Belgium*[1] a Belgian law prohibiting combined offers was found by the CJEU to contravene Art 4. In that case, Total had offered a limited free breakdown service to Total Club cardholders with every purchase of a minimum amount of fuel. The Belgian law outlawing such a practice exceeded the provisions of the Directive which would only have required its assessment for fairness.

¹   *VTB-VAB NV v Total Belgium NV* (C-261/07) European Court of Justice (First Chamber) [2010] All ER (EC) 694.

8.22   The European Commission first report on the application of the UCPD¹ refers to other cases where the CJEU has ruled that national provisions are incompatible with the Directive. In *Telekomunikacja Polska²*, another national prohibition on combined offers was found to be incompatible. This concerned a telecom company which had made the conclusion of a contract for the provision of broadband internet access services contingent on the conclusion of a contract for telephone services. *Wamo³* and *Inno⁴* were cases where prohibitions had been made on the announcement of price reductions during the period preceding sales, in so far as the provision in question sought to protect the economic interests of consumers. The provisions were not prohibitions contained in Annex 1 to the UCPD and therefore would be required to be assessed for fairness by the national court. In *Kock⁵* an Austrian trader had announced a 'total clearance' of the products in his shop without applying for an administrative authorisation, as required by national law. The CJEU ruled that a commercial practice not covered by Annex 1 of the Directive cannot be prohibited on the sole ground that the practice had not been the subject of prior authorisation by the competent administrative authority, without an assessment of the unfairness of the practice in question set out in Arts 5–9 of the UCPD. In *Europamur Alimentacion SA⁶* the CJEU ruled that a national provision in Spain containing a general prohibition on offering or selling goods at a loss fell foul of the maximum harmonisation requirements because it was not based on criteria appearing in the UCPD. The case involved sales by wholesalers to small retailers which affected consumers.

¹   European Commission Report First Report on the application of Directive 2005/29/EC COM(2013)139 final (para 31).
²   C-522/08, *Telekomunikacja Polska SA w Warszawie v Prezes Urzedu Komunikacji Elektronicznej* [2010] ECR I-02079.
³   C-288/10, *Wamo BVBA v JBC NV and Modemakers Fashion NV* [2011] ECR I-05835.
⁴   C-126/11, *INNO NV v Unie van Zelfstandige Ondernemers VZW (UNIZO) and Others*, report not published at this time.
⁵   C-206/11 *Georg Köck v Schutzverband gegen unlauteren Wettbewerb*, report not published at this time.
⁶   Case C-295/16.

8.23   However, in *Citroen Benlux NV v Federatie voor Verzekerings en Financiele Tussenpersonen¹*, the CJEU held that a national restriction on combined offers did not contravene Art 4 as at least one component of the offer was a financial service in respect of which the UCPD applies only a minimum harmonisation standard (see Art 3(9)). So long as one component was a financial service, the exception applied and Member States were permitted to impose requirements that were more restrictive or prescriptive than those set out in the Directive. Member States are also permitted to apply more prescriptive protections where there is scope to do so under a *lex specialis* (specific law) provision². However in other respects the UCPD continues to apply, as a safety net, so that mere compliance with a *lex specialis* provision, such as that found in the Consumer Rights Directive, may not guarantee compliance with UCPD³.

¹   C-265/12, [2014] 1 CMLR 26.
²   Recital 15.

[3] Joined cases C-544/13 and C-545/13 at para 82.

8.24 One important exception to the full harmonisation rule relates to authorisation regimes. This includes laws which restrict who is authorised to provide a product (such as to award a degree) and other regulated professions, such as dentists[1]. The CJEU has confirmed that Member States can lay down specific rules governing regulated professions in order to uphold high standards of integrity. The UCPD does not preclude national legislation which protects public health and the dignity of professions[2]. In addition, Member States may pass legislation that impacts on the commercial operations of traders, where the purpose of the legislation is not consumer protection, for example a restriction on Sunday trading aiming to protect small businesses[3]. *Pelckmans Turnhout NV*[4] concerned the compatibility of a Belgian provision with the Directive. The Belgian law prohibited a trader from opening his shop 7 days a week, thereby requiring that he choose a weekly closing day for the shop. The ECJ considered that the provision only aimed to protect the interests of workers and employees in the distribution sector and was not intended to protect consumers. It is also important to note that the UCPD does not impact on rules which govern the validity, formation or effect of a contract[5], nor does it appear to apply where the legal relationship between a trader and a consumer is entirely regulated by national legislation[6]. Finally, of course Member States can extend the protection offered by the Directive into other, non-harmonised, areas (such as business to business transactions).

[1] See CJEU *Kirschstein* C-393/17 (4 July 2019) para 45, in which the Court ruled that a Belgian law which required traders, who award academic qualifications, to be authorised, on pain of criminal prosecution.

[2] CJEU *Luc Vanderborght* C-339/15 at paras 27–30. The Court also considered whether such rules could be prohibited by the E-Commerce Directive (2000/31) or Art 56 of the Treaty for European Union, and concluded that while an absolute ban on online advertising could infringe these laws, specific rules governing the content of such advertisements would in principle be permitted. The CJEU has further considered whether the E-Commerce Directive might prohibit national legislation restricting marketing practices by pharmacists in *V v Daniel B* C-649/18, and concluded that the public health imperative in pharmacists being viewed with respect in society justifies such restrictions, even though they would hinder online pharmacists from marketing as they would wish. This reasoning is likely to apply by analogy to the UCPD.

[3] C-483/12, *Pelckmans Turnhout* at para 24; C-540/08 *Mediaprint* at para 21.

[4] C-483/12, *Pelckmans Turnhout NV v Walter Van Gastel Balen NV and Others*.

[5] Article 3(2) UCPD.

[6] See (post Brexit) CJEU *Stichting Waternet* C-922/19 (3 February 2021) para 39.

Overlap with other EU provisions

8.25 Article 3.4 of the UCPD (which is not directly transposed into the CPUTR 2008) states that:

> 'In the case of conflict between the provisions of this Directive and other Community rules regulating specific aspects of unfair commercial practices, the latter shall prevail and apply to those specific aspects.'

8.26 One reading of this provision is that if a sectoral Directive (eg the Package Travel Directive[1]) covers misleading information provided in respect of a package holiday, then the CPUTR 2008 do not apply at all[2]. However this reading seems not to be correct, given the CJEU jurisprudence on this issue which provides that where sectoral Directives provide for greater protection than the CPUTR 2008 then, by virtue of Art 3.4, they shall take precedence, with the UCPD providing a safety net. This was the position taken in the CJEU case of *Abcur AB v Apoteket AB and Apoteket Farmaci AB*[3] which was a case concerning the overlap between the UCPD and the Medicines Directive. The logic of this position is that where another law lays down specific rules, clearly these must be obeyed, and therefore there is no need to invoke the UCPD unless some element of harm remains unresolved[4]. Rather, what Art 3.4 envisages is the situation where provisions, other than the UCPD, impose on traders, 'in such a way as to leave no margin for discretion, obligations which are incompatible with' those in the UCPD[5]. In accordance with this reasoning, in *Dyson Ltd v BSH Home Appliance*[6] the CJEU ruled that the act of not providing consumers with information on the testing conditions that resulted in the energy classification indicated on the label relating to the energy class of vacuum cleaners did not constitute a misleading omission within the meaning of the UCPD. Directive 2010/30 and delegated Regulation 665/2013 governing vacuum cleaner labelling prevailed over the UCPD in accordance with Article 3.4 because it laid down an absolute rule as to the contents of a label, which could not be deviated from. It was those provisions that must be applied which were to be interpreted as meaning that no information relating to the conditions under which the energy efficiency of vacuum cleaners was measured may be added to the energy label, and strict compliance with this labelling rule could therefore not constitute a misleading omission.

1 Package Travel, Package Holidays and Package Tours Directive 90/314/EEC.
2 This view was preferred by DJ Roger House sitting at Bournemouth Magistrates' Court on 17 April 2013, in dismissing CPUTR 2008 information laid in a Package Travel Context, *Dorset County Council v Alpine Elements Ltd* (unreported).
3 Joined cases C-544/13 and C-545/13. For an application of this reasoning in the context of health claims for food, see the CJEU case of *Konsumentombudsmannen v Mezina AB* C-363/19 para 57–61. The key emphasis in that case is that the specific rules take precedence over the UCPD provisions, and so are to be applied first, where there is conflict between them and the UCPD.
4 This is the effect of the CJEU ruling in *Citroen Commerce GmbH v Zentralvereinigung* C-476/14, which ruled that applying the Price Indications Directive where a car dealer failed to include a pick up fee in the price of a car, was a failure to state the final price as required by that Directive. There was therefore no need to go on to consider if this was a misleading action or omission.
5 CJEU *AGCM v Wind Tre SpA* C-54/17, para 61. In particular, there can be no conflict where sector specific rules are stated to be *'without prejudice to Union rules on consumer protection'*, as in the case, for instance of the Universal Services Directive (para 67).
6 C-632/16 25 July 2018.

8.27 This issue is considered in detail in CHAPTER 2, Interpretation of Consumer Law, but a useful aid to construction is Recital 10 to the UCPD which provides that:

'It is necessary to ensure that the relationship between this Directive and existing Community law is coherent, particularly where detailed provisions on unfair commercial practices apply to specific sectors . . . This Directive accordingly applies only in so far as there are no specific Community law provisions regulating specific aspects of unfair commercial practices, such as information requirements and rules on the way information is presented to the consumer. It provides protection for consumers where there is no specific sectoral legislation at community level and prohibits traders from creating a false impression of the nature of products. This is particularly important for complex products with high levels of risk to consumers, such as certain financial services products. This Directive consequently complements the Community acquis, which is applicable to commercial practices harming consumers' economic interests.'

The Crown

8.28 The Crown may not be criminally liable under the CPUTR 2008 (although individuals serving the Crown may be)[1]. However, if the Crown were to act in breach of the CPUTR 2008, action may be taken against it under Pt 8 of the Enterprise Act 2002[2]. The crucial question is whether an emanation of the Crown is acting as a 'trader' under the UCPD, which is an autonomous concept, not to be restricted by national legal classifications[3]. Hospitals have been held to benefit from Crown immunity[4] but the applicability of those decisions to today's more devolved management structure may be questioned. Local authorities do not benefit from Crown immunity[5].

[1]   CPUTR 2008, SI 2008/1277, reg 28.
[2]   Enterprise Act 2002, s 236.
[3]   C-59/12 *BKK Mobil* at para 26.
[4]   *Nottingham Area No 1 Hospital Management Committee v Owen* [1958] 1 QB 50, *Pfizer Corporation v Ministry of Health* [1965] AC 512.
[5]   *Re M* [1994] 1 AC 377, per Lord Templeman at 395 (defining what is meant by the Crown).

Time limits

8.29 The limitation period under the CPUTR 2008 mirrors the TDA 1968, s 19. Under reg 14(1)(a) and (b), no criminal prosecution for an offence under the CPUTR 2008 may be commenced more than 3 years from the commission of the offence or more than one year after its discovery by the prosecutor, whichever is the earlier. If the prosecutor provides a certificate stating the date he discovered the offence, there is a rebuttable presumption of its correctness under the CPUTR 2008[1]. Time limit provisions are now covered in CHAPTER 4, Criminal Enforcement.

[1]   CPUTR 2008, SI 2008/1277, reg 14(2).

ENFORCERS

The duty to enforce

8.30 CPUTR 2008, reg 19 places a duty on every 'enforcement authority' to enforce the CPUTR 2008. In Great Britain, this includes every 'Local weights and measures authority'[1]. In Northern Ireland, the authority having the duty of enforcement is now the Department for the Economy ('DfE'). For a weights and measures authority, the duty used to extend geographically to within its own area, but the Consumer Rights Act 2015, Sch 5 ('CRA 2015') has removed this limitation in England and Wales.

[1]   Defined in CPUTR 2008, SI 2008/1277, reg 2 by reference to the Weights and Measures Act 1985, s 69. For non-metropolitan counties, the county council. For metropolitan districts, the district council. For London boroughs, the borough council. For Scottish areas, the area council.

8.31 This duty does not automatically mean that formal (civil or criminal) enforcement action will be taken in respect of each and every infringement, nor does it impose any geographical restriction on the powers of officers. Instead the duty will oblige enforcers to take steps to promote compliance by the most appropriate means, in line with their enforcement priorities and consistent with available resources. This is the Government's view as expressed in its reply to the consultation on implementation of the Directive[1]. It should also be noted that the duty of the OFT to enforce CPUTR 2008 has been replaced by a power for the CMA to do so.

1   Government response to the Consultation Paper on Implementing the Unfair Commercial Practices Directive, DTI, December 2006.

8.32   Regulation 19(4) states:

> (4) In determining how to comply with its duty of enforcement every enforcement authority shall have regard to the desirability of encouraging control of unfair commercial practices by such established means as it considers appropriate having regard to all the circumstances of the particular case.

8.33   Regulation 19(4) gives effect to Art 10 of the UCPD, which states that the Directive does not prevent Member States controlling unfair commercial practices using codes of conduct. Although this provision is new, similar wording was contained in the Control of Misleading Advertisements Regulations 1988[1]. After the Government consulted on the appropriate enforcement regime for the implementation of the UCPD it concluded that the provision did not 'substantially alter the current enforcement regime, where the division of responsibilities between enforcers and self-regulatory bodies generally works extremely well'. The 'established means' that an enforcer might have regard to includes referral to a self-regulatory body, such as the Advertising Standards Authority.

1   SI 1988/915.

The right to bring a criminal prosecution

8.34   The right to prosecute is not restricted to a member or officer of an enforcement authority. Any person can bring a prosecution under the CPUTR 2008. In *House of Cars Ltd v Derby Car and Van Contracts Ltd*[1] a private prosecution under the CPUTR 2008 was brought after the OFT and the relevant local authority had declined to do so. The powers of entry and other rights set out in the CRA 2015, Sch 5 to facilitate the gathering of evidence to investigate CPUTR 2008 breaches may not, however, be exercised by a private prosecutor, but only by a duly appointed officer. In *Media Protection Services Ltd v Crawford*[2] it was found that the laying of an information is a reserved legal activity under the Legal Services Act 2007 and can only be undertaken by a private prosecutor himself, or by a person authorised to carry out such a reserved legal activity.

1   [2012] CTLC 62.
2   [2012] EWHC 2373 (Admin), [2013] 1 WLR 1068.

8.35   The Enterprise Act 2002, s 230 requires local weights and measures authorities to give notice to the CMA of intended prosecutions, a summary of the evidence relied upon and their outcome, after they are finally determined. Proceedings are not invalid by reason only of the failure of the authority to comply with the Enterprise Act 2002, s 230.

PROSECUTIONS

8.36 Any person, other than the Crown, may be prosecuted for an offence under the CPUTR 2008. This includes both individuals and bodies corporate. Regulation 15 (directors' liability), reg 16 (causal liability) and general criminal accessory liability are considered in detail in CHAPTER 4, Criminal Enforcement.

ENFORCEMENT POWERS

8.37 The CRA 2015, Sch 5 consolidates enforcement powers in trading standards investigations. Test purchases, the powers of entry, search and seizure and the criminal offences relating to obstruction are now dealt with in detail in CHAPTER 4, Criminal Enforcement. and in CHAPTER 5, Civil Enforcement..

PROHIBITIONS UNDER THE CPUTR 2008

8.38 The prohibitions created by the CPUTR 2008 follow the European wording and the 'principles based' model provided by the UCPD. The CPUTR 2008 essentially uses the framework of the Directive to place into UK domestic legislation the five 'commercial practice' prohibitions, creating criminal offences in respect of each one. The five CPUTR 2008 prohibitions are also made amenable to injunctive relief under the civil jurisdiction of the Enterprise Act 2002[1]. The CPUTR 2008 sweeps away the developed concepts of 'false trade descriptions' under the TDA 1968 and 'misleading price indications' under the Consumer Protection Act 1987. The CPUTR 2008 does, however, retain some of the familiar modes of liability and defences that derive from the TDA 1968 and other domestic trading legislation.

[1] See CHAPTER 5, Civil Enforcement.

8.39 The CPUTR 2008 creates five prohibitions which are all labelled as unfair commercial practices (reg 3). CPUTR 2008 also provides that it is a criminal offence[1] for a trader to engage in any of the prohibited unfair commercial practices[2]. The five prohibitions are as follows:

(a) Contravention of the requirements of professional diligence, reg 3(3) (made a criminal offence, where the requisite element of *mens rea* is proven, by reg 8).

(b) A commercial practice that is a misleading action, reg 5 (made a criminal offence by reg 9)[3].

(c) A commercial practice that is a misleading omission, reg 6 (made a criminal offence by reg 10).

(d) A commercial practice that is an aggressive commercial practice, reg 7 (made a criminal offence by reg 11).

(e) Commercial practices which are in all circumstances considered unfair under Sch 1, paras 1–31 (made a criminal offence by reg 12 except in respect of paras 11 and 28).

When prosecuted criminally, the prohibitions are triable either way, carrying a maximum sentence of 2 years' imprisonment and an unlimited fine when tried on indictment[4]. Following the entry into force of the Legal Aid, Sentencing and Punishment of Offenders Act 2012, s 85, summary conviction is now punishable with an unlimited fine.

[1]   Except for CPUTR 2008, SI 2008/1277, Sch 1, paras 11 and 28 which are only amenable to civil action.
[2]   There are additional enforcement and obstruction offences under CPUTR 2008, SI 2008/1277, regs 21(1), 23(1) and 23(2) that are very similar to those seen in the TDA 1968.
[3]   However, note that while civil liability attaches to the misleading action of failing to comply with a code requirement, this is excluded from the scope of the CPUTR 2008, SI 2008/1277, reg 9 offence.
[4]   CPUTR 2008, SI 2008/1277, reg 13.

Key concepts

8.40 There are three concepts under the CPUTR 2008 that are central to the interpretation of the prohibitions:

(a)   Commercial practice.
(b)   Transactional decision.
(c)   The average consumer.

Proof of a 'commercial practice' is an element of all five of the prohibitions. 'Transactional decision'[1] and the 'average consumer' are elements of all of the prohibitions, save for the Sch 1 banned practices, under which it is only necessary to prove that a trader engaged in a 'commercial practice' of a type described in the 31 specific practices listed.

[1]   In the case of contravention of professional diligence, the threshold condition is 'materially distorts or is likely to materially distort the economic behaviour of the average consumer with regard to the product' CPUTR 2008, SI 2008/1277, reg 3(3)(b) rather than 'transactional decision'.

Commercial practice

8.41 CPUTR 2008, reg 2 provides:

2 Interpretation

"commercial practice" means any act, omission, course of conduct, representation or commercial communication (including advertising and marketing) by a trader, which is directly connected with the promotion, sale or supply of a product to or from consumers, whether occurring before, during or after a commercial transaction (if any) in relation to a product.

The scope of commercial practice

8.42 This concept has been described by the European Court as 'a particularly broad formulation'[1]. There are three main limitations in the definition of 'commercial practice'. Its scope is confined to the relationship between 'traders' and 'consumers' in respect of 'products'. These three concepts are further defined in reg 2. It is considered that the scheme of the CPUTR 2008 is best analysed by first considering the definition of 'commercial practice' and 'trader' together because their respective definitions include reference to each other.

This chapter will first consider those concepts before considering who can be 'consumers' and what can be 'products'.

¹ CJEU *UAB Gelvora* C-357/16 at para 19.

8.43 As a starting point, it is important to recognise that commercial practices are limited to those that might affect consumers and not those that only affect businesses. The definition of 'commercial practice' is purposely broad, including virtually any act or omission that might occur during the course of any transaction, which may affect consumers, even if a consumer is not actually involved. It can apply to transactions between wholesalers and retailers for instance¹. It is intended to cover everything that forms 'part of the commercial strategy of an operator'². This includes 'any measure taken in relation not only to the conclusion of the contract but also its performance, and in particular the measures taken in order to obtain payment for the product'³. It may be a single act, being a specific instance (such as an advertisement, or a statement) not necessarily a modus operandi⁴. It does not depend on the conclusion of a contract or the exchange of money. There need not be a commercial transaction at all⁵. It may be carried out by a third party to whom the original contracting trader has assigned their rights⁶. It does not require the consumer to have acted to his detriment in any way. It may take place before, during, or after any transaction and would also include business practices where the business is buying a product from a consumer. But it does not require a transaction and might concern a mere advertisement.

¹ CJEU *Europamur Alimentacion SA* C-295/16 at para 35.
² C-206/11 *Georg Kock* at para 27.
³ CJEU *UAB Gelvora* C-357/16 at para 21.
⁴ C-388/13 *UPC* para 41.
⁵ *Warwickshire County Council v Halfords Autocentres Ltd (Competition and Markets Authority intervening)* [2018] EWHC 3007 (Admin) para 29.
⁶ CJEU *UAB Gelvora* C-357/16 at paras 25–28. The CJEU in this case considered whether a debt collector, who had taken an assignment of a debt, was covered by the UCPD. In finding that it was, the CJEU found that such post contract activities are necessarily important to consumers' up front decision making, and to rule otherwise would tempt businesses to evade UCPD liability by hiving off the recovery of debts from their normal business operations.

8.44 A commercial practice refers to the specific act or publication (etc) that emanates from a trader, but it does not include a requirement for the trader to be authorised before they can engage in particular activities¹. It concerns all aspects of a consumer relationship including its advertising, marketing, and pricing. In *Deutsche Bank NV v Delta Lloyd Bank NV²*, a type of account was promoted through various media such as radio, a website, and leaflets. The radio advertisement did not mention that the interest rate was dependent on taking other products. It just said it was 'subject to conditions' and referred to a website or leaflets. The court held that the fact that a promotion of the product in one distribution channel is not misleading does not affect its potentially misleading character through another distribution channel, namely the radio. Each channel was found to be a 'commercial practice' and required to be assessed separately for compliance. In that case the condition of buying an additional product was material information needed by an average consumer to make an informed transactional decision.

¹ CJEU *Kirschstein* C-393/17 (4 July 2019) paras 44–47.
² Belgium, Commercial Court of Brussels, 2008.

8.45 The provision of information on a website was found to be a 'commercial practice' by Latvian Courts in *Consumer Rights Protection Centre v Air Baltic Corporation*[1] and *Consumer Rights Protection Centre v Fiji Travel Alma Tour Group*[2]. In the first case, an airline did not identify the final price of an air fare on its website. The trader argued that it was merely a technical issue relating to its website set-up. This was irrelevant and it was not necessary to demonstrate that consumers have actually used the site or entered into a contract. In the latter case, the court decided that it did not need to show detriment by establishing whether anyone had purchased a more expensive tour in order to find that a misleading advert was a commercial practice.

[1] 2009 E03 – REUD-54, Latvia Tribunal First Degree.
[2] 2010, A42774708, Latvia District Court.

8.46 In the Austrian piano case, *Place of production of pianos*[1], a guarantee, usually handed to a consumer after sale, stated that a piano was produced in Austria when it was produced in China. It was held that this misleading statement was a commercial practice even though it had been handed to a consumer after sale. This accords with the definition of 'commercial practice' in reg 2 which provides that it can take place after a commercial transaction, and with the comments of the Court of Criminal Appeal, who have held that the concept 'clearly applies' to sending of letters after a contract is concluded[2]. This analysis is consistent with the position taken by the CJEU, which held that debt collecting activities are clearly within the scope of commercial practices, and remain so even when carried out by a third party[3]. This is consistent with the UK's implementation of the UCPD, where reg 2(1A) of the CPUTR 2008 it is clarified that:

> 'A trader ("T") who demands payment from a consumer ("C") in full or partial settlement of C's liabilities or purported liabilities to T is to be treated for the purposes of these Regulations as offering to supply a product to C.'

[1] Austria Supreme Court, 2008, 4 Ob 42/08t.
[2] *R v Waters & Westminster Recliners Ltd* [2016] EWCA Crim 1112 at para 21.
[3] CJEU *UAB Gelvora* C-357/16.

8.47 Where trader A is promoting products to be supplied by another trader (B), the activities of trader A can still amount to commercial practices. This is especially so where the trader A has the aim of generating profit for itself[1]. Indeed the CJEU has confirmed it is in principle irrelevant whether a trader promotes their own or another person's products[2]. However, the position is different where trader A has no financial interest in the promotion or sales of the product by trader B. The UCPD is not engaged against a publisher of a free newspaper that merely sells advertising space in respect of advertisements placed by other traders in connection with the promotion of their products. Such a publishing practice is not liable to be classified as a 'commercial practice' because it is not directly connected with the promotion, sale or supply of products to consumers[3].

[1] CJEU *Loterie Nationale v Paul Adriaensen* C-667/15 at para 33.
[2] CJEU *Verband Sozialer Wettbwerb v DHL Paket* C-146/16 at para 31. The court held that a platform that merely promotes products, and does not enter into contracts with consumers, is liable for omitting to provide the names of the traders whose products it promotes.
[3] CJEU *RLvS Verlagsgesellschaft v Stuttgarter Wochenblatt GmbH* C-391/12.

One-off acts

8.48 Whether a one-off act can amount to a 'commercial practice' has been the subject of extended debate and litigation. However, recent decisions of the Court of Appeal and the CJEU have added some much needed clarification to the issue, and it is now beyond doubt that the fact that the 'action of the professional concerned took place only on one occasion and affected only one consumer is immaterial'[1]. The concept of commercial practice should, as the definition itself says, be taken to include individual acts and omissions. The CJEU in *UPC* considered the situation where a cable television operator in Hungary charged a customer for television service accidentally provided for 4 days following the termination of the contract. The domestic appeal court held that the company's conduct could not amount to a 'commercial practice' since it was not continuous. The CJEU heard the matter as a preliminary reference from the Hungarian Supreme Court. It held that, on the facts, the communication of erroneous information to a consumer (specifically, that the consumer's cable television service would be terminated on a certain day) could be classified as a 'commercial practice' even though the information only concerned a single consumer.

[1]   *Nemzeti Fogyasztóvédelmi Hatóság v UPC Magyarország Kft* C-388/13 [2015] CTLC 100 at para 41.

8.49 This decision is consistent with, but may go further than, UK case law, where in *R v X Ltd*[1] the Court of Appeal (Criminal Division) held that a commercial practice may be derived from a single incident affecting a sole consumer although it will depend on the circumstances. In that case, X Ltd sold a domestic CCTV security system to a 76-year-old customer who was alleged to be vulnerable and infirm. One of X Ltd's sales representatives had told the customer that burglaries in his postcode had risen by 46.2% in the previous 12 months, when in fact this was untrue. At trial, the defence succeeded in an application of no case to answer on the basis that the one-off communication of erroneous information to a sole consumer could not be a 'commercial practice'. On appeal, the court held that the concept of commercial practice could, depending on the circumstances, cover both a single incident and a pattern of repeated behaviour[2]. In particular the evidence of a single incident could be sufficient 'to infer that the same failure ran at every stage of the process from top to bottom'[3]. Subsequently, the English courts have had no difficulty with accepting that the evidence of a single test purchase by a trading standards officer is sufficient to demonstrate a breach of the CPUTR[4].

[1]   [2013] EWCA Crim 818, [2013] CTLC 145.
[2]   At para 22, Leveson LJ stated 'it is clear that a commercial practice can be derived from a single incident. It will depend on the circumstances'.
[3]   At para 33 – Leveson LJ stressed that it should not be required of trading standards services, given their stretched resources, to find more complaints if one is sufficient.
[4]   *Warwickshire County Council v Halfords Autocentres Ltd (Competition and Markets Authority intervening)* [2018] EWHC 3007 (Admin) para 28.

Traders

8.50 CPUTR 2008, reg 2 provides:

"trader"—

(a)   means a person acting for purposes relating to that person's business, whether acting personally or through another person acting in the trader's name or on the trader's behalf, and

(b)   except in Part 4A, includes a person acting in the name of or on behalf of a trader;

"business" includes—

(a)   a trade, craft or profession, and

(b)   the activities of any government department or local or public authority;

8.51 The five commercial practice offences can only be committed by a 'trader'. Reading the definitions of 'trader' and 'business' together, a trader is a person acting *for purposes relating to his trade, craft or profession*. It has 'a particularly broad meaning', encompassing any natural or legal person carrying out a 'gainful activity,' including public bodies engaging in activities that could in principle be carried out by the private sector[1]. The concept of a trader is intended to be uniform with that used in the Consumer Rights Directive 2011/83 (and it seems the Unfair Terms Directive 93/13), and while it covers all manner of professional activities, it is diametrically opposed to the concept of 'consumer'. It is 'a functional concept, requiring determination of whether the contractual relationship is amongst the activities that a person provides in the course of his trade, business or profession.[2]'

---

[1]   C-59/12 *BKK Mobil* para 41. This was a case that originated from Germany, *Betriebskrankenkasse* Germany, Higher Regional Court, 2010, 13U 173/09, involving a compulsory health care provider set up under public law to administer health funds. The German court considered it to be a trader because it competed for consumers to pay in. The information on its website was not for social purposes, but instead for business purposes.

[2]   CJEU *Komisia za zashtita na potrebitelite v Kamenova* (C-105/17) para 27-33 & 35.

8.52 The broad definition of trader was recognised by the Court of Appeal (Criminal Division) in *R v Scottish and Southern Energy plc*[1] (SSE PLC), which was the first substantive criminal case to be heard at this level in respect of the CPUTR 2008. The prosecution arose out of the doorstep selling of electricity and gas based on a sales script. The PLC and an individual salesman employed by a subsidiary company (the subsidiary) wholly owned by the PLC were defendants. The PLC was convicted of two misleading action offences under CPUTR 2008, reg 5(2) on the basis that:

'Its sales staff and agents were trained to deliver an Energy Script which in its overall presentation . . . deceived or was likely to deceive the average consumer . . . and thereby caused or was likely to cause the average consumer to take a transactional decision he would not have taken otherwise.'

---

[1]   [2012] EWCA Crim 539, [2012] CTLC 1, (2012) 176 JP 241.

8.53 All salesmen were employed by the subsidiary rather than the PLC, which also carried out the salesman's training. It was the subsidiary that was licensed to supply electricity because the PLC was only a holding company. The Court of Appeal found that the definition of 'trader' in reg 2(1) was broad in scope and should be construed purposively. It was possible for more than one trader to be guilty of a specific offence under the Regulations. It found that the mere fact that the subsidiary could be prosecuted as a trader did not mean that the PLC could not also be properly prosecuted for the same offence. At para 28, Davis LJ said:

'It is perfectly possible to have a prosecution of more than one person for the same alleged offence under the 2008 regulations. The very wide definition of "trader" and "commercial practice" demonstrates that: and that is also consistent with the provisions of regulation 16(2), which contemplates that both "X" and "Y" may be traders in relation to the same activity.'

8.54 In construing 'trader' together with 'commercial practice' the court noted the wide definition of both in the Regulations. Even though the PLC was correctly described as a 'non-trading holding company', that did not mean that it was incapable of being a trader within the meaning of the CPUTR 2008. A key factor in the court's decision on this was that there was some evidence that training was carried out with the involvement of the PLC and under its ultimate supervision and control. Davis LJ stated:

'It is important to bear in mind that "trader", for the purposes of the 2008 Regulations, extends to any person who in relation to a commercial practice is acting for purposes relating to his business. The words "any", "in relation to", "acting" and "relating to" are all words with width and elasticity. As to the definition of "commercial practice" that is likewise broadly framed. It is amply sufficient to cover involvement in or supervision or control of training, in appropriate circumstances, as being directly connected with the promotion or sale or supply of a product; and it is also to be noted that the definition of "commercial practice" carefully avoids saying that the promotion or sale or supply has to be made by the trader itself.'

8.55 It can be hard to draw the line between a person engaged in trade and merely engaging in a hobby. Some guidance on this question has been given by the CJEU. In assessing whether a person who lists a few items for sale on a website is a trader, the Court ruled it is relevant to consider the level of organisation they deploy, whether they intend to generate profit (for example by buying items for resale, or selling numerous items of the same type), the scale of their operation (for example whether they are registered for VAT), the regularity of their activities, whether they have technical expertise relating to the product, and whether they received any other financial incentive to sell the items. However the mere fact that a person intends to make a profit, or sells several items, is not enough on its own to render them a trader[1]. This approach seems to be in line with that taken by the High Court in *Reading BC v Younis*[2], which drew on the older TDA 1968 case of *Davies v Sumner*[3]. To be liable as a trader, the court ruled a person must engage in the impugned activities with a *'degree of regularity'* such that they form part of the *'normal practice of a business'*. It is important that the activities should intrinsically be of a business nature. Where individuals engage in activities to satisfy personal needs, they are less likely to be considered a trader, notwithstanding expertise or the regularity of transactions[4]. In a UK competition case, *Durkan Holdings v OFT*[5], the Competition Appeal Tribunal concluded that if a group company gave strategic direction to subsidiaries and exerted its influence then it could be liable as a trader.

[1] CJEU *Komisia za zashtita na potrebitelite v Kamenova* (C-105/17) para 38-42.
[2] [2015] EWHC 3212 (Admin).
[3] [1984] 1 WLR 1301 (HL).
[4] CJEU *AB v Personal Exchange International Ltd* (C-774/19) (10 December 2020) para 45–47.
[5] UK, Competition Appeal Tribunal, 2011, CAT 6.

8.56 The definition of trader also includes anyone 'acting in the name of or on behalf of a trader'. It is arguable that this is broad enough to include an employee if he or she carries out an act or makes a representation on behalf of the employer in relation to a 'commercial practice'. The view of the European Commission is that the definition covers persons, including consumers, who act in the name of or on behalf of another trader, which could include intermediaries, such as online platforms[1]. It would include a media company that places advertisements on behalf of another trader[2], review sites[3], search engines, online market places[4], comparison sites, app stores, group buying sites etc.

1 Commission Staff Working Document Guidance on the Implementation/Application of Directive 2005/29/EC on Unfair Commercial Practices [COM(2016) 320] pp 31 and 119–124. This means that where an intermediary is taken to be a trader, they would not benefit from the defences provided in the E-Commerce Directive (2000/31/EC), since they would not be a 'mere' host. See also a French decision that a price comparison site, by ranking products in exchange for remuneration, was acting as a trader for UCPD purposes – Cass Com 4 Décembre 2012, 11–27729, *Publicité Sté Pewterpassion.com c/ Sté Leguide.com.*

2 Latvian court decision Administratīvās rajona tiesas spriedums lietā Nr. A420632710, 8 March 2012. See also CMA investigation into MyJar, Starcom and Tan Media https://www.gov.uk/cma-cases/online-endorsements-potential-non-disclosure.

3 CMA investigation into trusted trader sites, https://www.gov.uk/cma-cases/review-sites-handling-of-negative-reviews.

4 See the CMA order against Viagogo, an online market place https://www.gov.uk/cma-cases/secondary-ticketing-websites#viagogo-court-order.

8.57 Organisations pursuing charitable or ethical goals may qualify as traders when they engage in commercial activities towards consumers[1]. A charity shop selling goods such a mugs or t-shirts in a commercial capacity would likely be considered to be a trader. However, it is less likely that the mere solicitation for a donation would make a charity a trader, but if it is linked to some form of commercial practice then it could be; for example, when a donation is solicited by a third party paid to fundraise for the charity.

1 Commission Guidance [COM(2016) 320].

8.58 It is possible that a private members club would not be a trader because transactions between it and its members would not be in the course of a 'person's business'. The situation is analogous to the case of *John v Matthews*[1], when referring to the Trade Descriptions Act 1968, Lord Parker CJ said:

'The object of the 1968 Act surely is to protect the public, not a husband from his wife or a club from a member of the club.'

The rationale was that false descriptions in such circumstances would not be in the course of a trade or business. The mere use of the word 'club' in respect of a person or body having none of the features of a club, however, did not prevent the application the TDA 1968[2]. The definition of trader is further considered in CHAPTER 2, Interpretation of Consumer Law.

1 [1970] 2 QB 443.
2 *Cahalne v Croydon London Borough Council* (1985) 149 JP 561.

Consumers

8.59 CPUTR 2008, reg 2 provides:

"business" includes a trade, craft or profession;

. . .

"consumer" means any individual who in relation to a commercial practice is acting for purposes which are outside his business;

8.60 The focus of the CPUTR 2008 is consumer transactions. This is a marked departure from the position under the TDA 1968. Under the TDA 1968, liability extended to trade sales. Offences were not confined to trade descriptions given to consumers, such that an offence would be committed where the transaction was between a person acting in the course of a trade or business and another trader.

8.61 This is a significant difference between the CPUTR 2008 and its predecessors. A part of this lacuna is filled by the Business Protection from Misleading Marketing Regulations 2008[1] ('BPR 2008') which were made at the same time as the CPUTR 2008 (see below at **12.8**). The BPR 2008 provide protection for businesses against misleading and unfair comparative advertising. Under the CPUTR 2008, the definition of 'commercial practice' is concerned only with relationships that are 'directly connected with the promotion, sale or supply of a product to or from consumers'. It follows from this that there will be no 'commercial practice' if the relationship concerns, for example, the sale of a product to a person acting for the purposes of his business. However there is no need to prove that any particular consumer was impacted by the trader's behaviour, since the CPUTR is concerned with practices which are in a broad sense targeted at consumers, rather than practices necessarily connected to a particular consumer transaction[2]. This is significant for investigators seeking to rely on test purchase evidence, since by definition, in such a case the trader would not really have been engaging with a consumer at all, but with an investigator pretending to be a consumer. Nonetheless, where the trader engages in a commercial practice which would otherwise be unlawful under the CPUTR, the offence may be made out: any other approach would be inconsistent with the high level of protection the UCPD seeks to achieve, and the preventative nature of the CPUTR[3].

[1]   SI 2008/1276.
[2]   *Warwickshire County Council v Halfords Autocentres Ltd (Competition and Markets Authority intervening)* [2018] EWHC 3007 (Admin) at para 35(ii).
[3]   *Warwickshire County Council v Halfords Autocentres Ltd (Competition and Markets Authority intervening)* [2018] EWHC 3007 (Admin) at paras 37–40. In this case, the trader sought to argue that the evidence of the test purchase could not demonstrate an offence because the trading standards officer was not a consumer. This argument failed.

8.62 However, where the victim of a commercial practice is acting for purposes that are a mixture of private and business, the CPUTR 2008 will apply, as long as the consumer use is predominant. This is an extension of protection beyond that required by the UCPD, and implemented in some other states, where any professional use of goods or services, even if only to a limited degree, is likely to prevent it being that of a consumer[1].

[1]   *BVAB De Keukiliere Gebroeders v KAAS* (Antwerp Court of Appeal 2009).

8.63 Other difficult situations include where an individual is engaging in activities before setting up their business, or after they have ceased trading, and where they are engaged in profit making activities that may fall short of full trade. This is likely to be particularly acute as an issue where individuals are engaging as suppliers in the collaborative economy. The view of the European Commission is that such a person is not automatically to be viewed as a trader. Account must be taken of the extent to which they have a profit seeking motive, the number, amount and frequency of transactions, the seller's sales turnover and whether they purchase products in order to resell them[1]. Recent CJEU case law however suggests that the crucial question is whether the person is engaging in their professional activity and these other features will be of limited significance if they are not operating professionally[2].

[1] Commission Guidance [COM(2016) 320], para 2.1. See also Commission Communication *A European Agenda for the Collaborative Economy* [COM(2016) 356], para 2.3.
[2] CJEU *AU v Reliantco Investments Ltd* (C-500/18) paras 44–57; CJEU *Petruchova v FIBO Group Holdings Limited* C-208/18

8.64 The definition of 'consumer' is further considered in CHAPTER 2, Interpretation of Consumer Law.

Consumers and causal liability

8.65 Regulation 16 creates liability for those who cause traders to commit CPUTR 2008 offences. Under this mode of liability, the person causing the trader's offence may or may not be a trader himself. It follows that a trader that sold a falsely described motor car to another trader might be guilty (under reg 16) if that motor car was then sold on to a consumer. However, there is no CPUTR 2008 offence committed by either trader until a consumer becomes involved. Causal liability is covered in CHAPTER 4, Criminal Enforcement.

Product

8.66 CPUTR 2008, reg 2:

"product" means—
(a) goods,
(b) a service,
(c) digital content,
(d) immovable property,
(e) rights or obligations, or
(f) a product of the kind mentioned in paragraphs (1A) and (1B),

but the application of this definition to Part 4A is subject to regulations 27C and 27D;

. . .

"digital content" means data which are produced and supplied in digital form;

"goods" means any tangible moveable items, but that includes water, gas and electricity if and only if they are put up for sale in a limited volume or set quantity;

. . .

(1A) a trader ("T") who demands payment from a consumer ("C") in full or partial settlement of C's liabilities or purported liabilities to T is to be treated for the purposes of these Regulations as offering to supply a product to C.

(1B) In such a case the product that T offers to supply comprises the full or partial settlement of those liabilities or purported liabilities.

8.67 The definition of 'product' in the CPUTR 2008 is predominantly directly from the definition in Art 2 of the Unfair Commercial Practices Directive

('UCPD'), although the UK has clarified that the definition also includes digital content and 'liability management services' as set out in reg 2(1A) and (1B). The definition is wide and likely to cover all goods and services, including intangible products such as statutory rights. The CPUTR 2008 offences apply to both goods or services and therefore any combination of the two.

8.68 The BERR/OFT guidance to the CPUTR 2008 states that[1]:

'The CPRs use "**product**" to refer to goods and services in a wide sense, including immovable property, rights and obligations. The prohibitions apply to **commercial practices** relating to products in this wider sense. It is important to note this because the legislation they replace was in many cases narrower in scope, for instance applying to just goods or services. The Trade Descriptions Act 1968 applied to both goods and services but there were different sets of rules applied to goods and to services. The CPRs apply in the same way to both goods and services, and also extend to intangible rights such as cancellation or cashback options.'

[1] Department for Business Enterprise and Regulatory Reform Guidance on the UK Regulations.

8.69 Where a product is supplied completely free of consideration, it is possible that the UCPD will not apply[1]. However, it is necessary to look at the wider context and business model: the CJEU has held in the context of whether a trader is an 'information society service' under the E-Commerce Directive that it is not necessary for the service to be paid for by those for whom it is performed, and in other situations an apparently free product may in fact be incorporated into the price of other goods and services being supplied. The important test is whether the 'free' product represents an economic activity[2]. For example UCPD may well apply where a product is supplied in exchange for consumer data, in the view of the European Commission[3]. The CPUTR 2008 clarify that they apply also where it is the consumer who supplies a product *to* the trader – this is to provide protection in the many circumstances where consumers risk being misled during the course of transactions where a trader is seeking to buy items from the consumer – see for example OFT undertakings obtained from traders purchasing consumers' gold, cars and houses[4].

[1] C-515/12 *4Finance UAB* para 24; C-391/12 *RLvS Verlagsgesellschaft mbH.*
[2] CJEU *Tobias McFadden v Sony Music* C-484/14 at paras 40–42.
[3] Commission Guidance [COM(2016) 320], pp 95–96.
[4] https://www.gov.uk/cma-cases/we-buy-any-car-unfair-practices-by-trader-offering-vehicle-buying-service; and https://webarchive.nationalarchives.gov.uk/20140402160700/http://oft.gov.uk/OFTwork/consumer-enforcement/consumer-enforcement-completed/quick-house-sales/.

Goods

8.70 The definition of 'goods' has been a part of many domestic statutory provisions. In the Consumer Rights Act 2015 it is defined to include 'any tangible moveable items'[1]. The essence of the definition has been to draw a distinction between personal chattels (moveable, tangible articles of property) and interests in land[2]. The definition of 'goods' is not purposive. It does not connote any requirement that the goods be for future sale or supply, nor do they need to be owned by a trade or business[3]. In *Formula One Autocentres v Birmingham City Council*[4] a false representation was made that the servicing of a motor car had been carried out effectively. The motor car was held to be 'goods' for the purpose of the TDA 1968, s 1. The importance of the case is that there was no anticipated transfer of ownership; the contract was simply one of bailment where the vehicle's owner allowed the motor car out of his possession for a short period.

1   Consumer Rights Act 2015, s 2(8).
2   The definition also excludes other interests in freehold and leasehold land (chattels real).
3   *Fletcher v Sledmore* [1973] RTR 371.
4   (1999) 163 JP 234.

Service

8.71 'Service' is not further defined in the CPUTR 2008 or in the UCPD. In *Newell v Hicks*[1] the Divisional Court defined the word 'service' for the purposes of the TDA 1968 as 'doing something for someone'. The CPUTR 2008 does not expressly exclude 'contracts of service' (employment contracts) from the ambit of 'product' in the way that they were excluded from the TDA 1968[2], however these would not be commercial practices directed towards 'consumers', and so would not be covered for this reason. The definition of 'commercial practice' does, however, include 'the supply of a [service] . . . from a consumer'.

1   Reported as *Newell v Taylor* (1983) 148 JP 308.
2   TDA 1968, s 14(4).

Immovable property

8.72 Although the definition of product is straightforward in its application to a simple transaction concerning goods, it is more difficult when considering different forms of property or services over property. The difference between the European concept of 'product' and the British definition of 'goods' is potentially unclear. The background to this may be found in the UCPD itself, which suggests that a Member State, must implement the financial services and immovable property provisions that are already in the UCPD, but may also go further than the UCPD because of their inherent complexity[1]:

> 'Financial services and immovable property, by reason of their complexity and inherent serious risks, necessitate detailed requirements, including positive obligations on traders. For this reason, in the field of financial services and immovable property, this Directive is without prejudice to the right of Member States to go beyond its provisions to protect the economic interests of consumers.'

1   And in Art 3 (scope): 'In relation to "financial services", as defined in Directive 2002/65/EC, and immovable property, Member States may impose requirements which are more restrictive or prescriptive than this Directive in the field which it approximates'.

8.73 The UK did not provide any detailed requirements concerning financial services or immovable property in the CPUTR 2008. But to comply with its treaty obligations the UK did adopt the definition of 'product' in the UCPD, presumably to avoid the suggestion that the Directive had not been properly implemented. The consequence of this rather muddled definition is not satisfactory and raises several practical questions.

Real property

8.74 The expression 'immovable property' is plainly capable of being a reference to real property. The expression which appears in the UCPD, may be intended to be consistent with the definition used in the old European Time-share Directive, which defines the term as follows[1]:

> '"immovable property" shall mean any building or part of a building for use as accommodation to which the right which is the subject of the contract relate.'

[1]   94/47/EC (OJ L280, 29.10.1994, p 83).

8.75 The main provisions of the TDA 1968 did not apply to real property because the TDA 1968, s 1(1) offences (false trade descriptions) applied only to goods and the TDA 1968, s 14 offences (false statements as to services) applied only to 'services, accommodation or facilities'. It is perhaps surprising that the CPUTR 2008 does not expressly deal with real property in the interpretation regulation in the manner of most domestic statutes. It seems unlikely that the words 'immovable property' were intended only to mean services over immovable property, such that it was confined to services such as building or refurbishing accommodation. If that was the correct interpretation of 'product' then the definition would read services 'over' or 'in connection' with immovable property.

8.76 It has become clear that the UCPD should be read so that 'product' includes real property. Parliament repealed the Property Misdescriptions Act 1991 in October 2013, explaining that the 1991 Act had been made redundant by the CPUTR 2008. As a result:

(a)   services in relation to 'immoveable property' are also likely to be considered a 'product', such that the CPUTR 2008 might apply to solicitors or estate agents involved in real property transactions;

(b)   'anything attached to land' is also a 'product', regardless of whether it is a fixture (a part of the land by its attachment to it)[1] or merely a chattel on the land.

[1]   See KJ Gray and SF Gray, *Elements of Land Law* (OUP, 2009) 1246 *et seq* for the distinction.

Intangible property, rights and obligations

8.77 The definition of 'product' in the CPUTR 2008 includes the promotion, sale or supply of 'rights and obligations' to consumers. It is tolerably clear that this was intended by the UCPD to include incorporeal or intangible property such as financial products, which are referred to expressly. In the BERR/OFT guidance (see above) to the CPUTR 2008 it is stated that it applies to intangible rights such as cancellation or cash back options.

8.78 There is, however, no detailed guidance or limit to the rights and obligations that are covered in the CPUTR 2008. The essence of intangible or incorporeal property is that it has a value but lacks any physical presence. This is similar to the concept of 'pecuniary advantage' that the courts have grappled with in the context of the proceeds of crime. Pecuniary advantage has been construed to mean any financial advantage. It would include a chose in action (a bank account) or any financial product such as a pension or investment, but it also extends to the evasion of a debt or tax owed. It would include a consumer guarantee or any other valuable promise. The breadth of the expression 'product' has not yet been fully addressed by the courts. However, on a literal interpretation it is capable of covering a vast array of situations that were not regulated by the TDA 1968 and the other legislation the CPUTR 2008 replaced.

8.79 In the context of tickets for events, the European Free Trade Area (EFTA) Court, in construing the UCPD, has ruled that the concept of 'product' encompasses both the physical chattel/electronic item, and the rights and obligations conferred in accordance with the contract for use in the ticket terms and conditions[1]. The UK courts are likely to treat judgments of the EFTA court in a similar way to the jurisprudence in other Member States (see **8.12** above), although given its supranational role and the fact that its rulings often take into account representations by the European Commission and a range of EU Member States, the weight given to such decisions may be considerable.

[1]   Case E-1/19, *Andreas Gyrre v The Norwegian Government* para 69.

Demanding full or partial settlement of liabilities

8.80 The additions to the definition of product in reg 2(1A) and (1B) clarify that the CPUTR 2008 applies where the 'product' that the consumer takes is in one sense involuntary – such as where their vehicle is clamped, or they are subjected to debt collection or civil recovery.

Digital content

8.81 The CPUTR 2008 now clarify that digital content is within its scope. It was previously thought that digital content might be goods, when supplied through a tangible medium such as a CD ROM, but it was unclear what it was in law when supplied in purely digital form. This uncertainty has now been addressed by the Consumer Rights Act 2015 ('CRA 2015') provisions on digital content, and also by this amendment to the definition of product in the CPUTR 2008.

Transactional decision

8.82 By the CPUTR 2008, reg 2:

"transactional decision" means any decision taken by a consumer, whether it is to act or to refrain from acting, concerning—

(a)   whether, how and on what terms to purchase, make payment in whole or in part for, retain or dispose of a product; or

(b)   whether, how and on what terms to exercise a contractual right in relation to a product;

(but the application of this definition to regulations 5 and 7 as they apply for the purposes of Part 4A is subject to regulation 27B(2)).

8.83 The CPUTR 2008 introduces the concept of a 'transactional decision', which is part of all of the commercial practice offences except the reg 12 (banned practices) offence. This 'transactional decision' element essentially introduces an objective threshold test that, the average consumer might have acted, or not acted, because of the unfair commercial practice.

8.84 A 'transactional decision' is not confined merely to the decision to enter into a binding contract. It is extended to **any** decision the consumer might take about exercising contractual rights or ultimately retaining or disposing of the product. It follows that decisions as diverse as an initial visit to a trader's website, returning a defective product, exercising a guarantee, or suing under the terms of the contract are all potentially transactional decisions.

8.85 In *OFT v Purely Creative Ltd* the High Court found that a transactional decision was a causal decision equivalent to the English standard of the balance of probabilities[1]:

> 'The phrase "to take a transactional decision he would not have taken otherwise" suggests a *sine qua non* test, namely, whether but for the relevant misleading action or omission of the trader, the average consumer would have made a different transactional decision from that which he did make. This may not mean that the misleading act or omission was the sole cause of the average consumer's decision, but it appears to mean that those Regulations will not have been infringed if the court concludes that, but for the misleading act or omission, the average consumer would nonetheless have decided as he did.'

This statement needs to be contrasted with the subsequent CJEU jurisprudence (see below), which suggests that a commercial practice needs only to have influenced the consumer in some way.

[1]   [2011] EWHC 106 (Ch), [2011] CTLC 45.

8.86 This potential breadth of 'transactional decision' is reflected in the 2010 Office of Fair Trading Report: *Online Targeting of Advertising and Prices*, where it is suggested that in relation to the internet and electronic communications[1]:

> 'Both "commercial practice" and "transactional decision" are given a wide definition. In the context of an online environment, the OFT considers that "transactional decision" may include the decision to visit a trader's site in the first place, as opposed to that of its competitors, and the decision to click through to another page on a site to view further content.'[2]

[1]   At para 817, the report summarises the prohibition against unfair commercial practices in the CPUTR 2008.
[2]   In *OFT v Purely Creative Ltd* [2011] EWHC 106 (Ch) Briggs J described the Commission's Guidance (contained in the Commissions Guidance on the Application/Implementation of Directive 2005/29/EC on Unfair Commercial Practices (SEC (2009) 1666)) that a decision such as stepping into a shop is a transactional decision as 'debatable' (para 68). The current Commission Guidance [COM(2016) 320] opines that decisions to travel to a sales outlet, to agree to a sales presentation and to click through a website may be transactional decisions (p 36).

8.87 It is now beyond doubt that a decision to enter a shop is a transactional decision. In the *Trento*[1] case, a consumer complained that a supermarket advertisement was inaccurate because a laptop advertised at a promotional rate was not available in the store when he visited. A dispute arose as to whether the decision to enter the shop was itself a 'transactional decision' distinct from the decision to purchase the laptop. The CJEU held in a preliminary ruling that the concept of 'transactional decision' was broadly defined. The concept covered not only the decision as to whether or not to purchase the laptop, but also related decisions. In this case, the decision to enter the shop was related to the decision to purchase the laptop and, as a result, was a 'transactional decision' within the meaning of the UCPD. The debate concerning whether the mere decision to step into a shop, or to visit a website, is a 'transactional decision' has now been emphatically resolved[2]. It is unnecessary to add any further gloss or require any particular economic consequence to be proven[3]. In the *SSE PLC case* it was held that judge's direction to the jury where he said 'did it cause or was it likely to cause the average consumer to switch suppliers?' was amply sufficient and that to introduce a 'but for exposition' would have been an unnecessary elaboration[4].

1 *Trento Sviluppo srl and Centrale Adriatica Soc. Coop. arl v Autorita Garante della Concorrenza e del Mercato* C-281/12, [2014] CTLC 326.
2 In the CJEU Case C-146/16 *Verband Sozialer Wettbwerb v DHL Paket* at paras 18, 19 and 25 it is abundantly clear that the Court had no difficulty accepting that a decision, based on information in a print advertisement, to visit a trader's website, would be a transactional decision. Further, it considered that the comparative peace of being able to view products on the internet in one's own home did not make a difference to whether the consumer needs the material information before actually visiting the website.
3 In *Competition and Markets Authority v Care UK Health and Social Holdings Ltd* [2021] EWHC 2088 (Ch), Bacon J found that there may not be a transactional decision when a consumer is yet to take 'a provisional decision' to purchase a complex product and was 'merely gathering information so as to inform a subsequent decision of that nature' (para 147–149). CF, the CJEU decision in *Trento* and *DHL Paket*. See also *Ving* (C-122/10) – entry level price for a holiday (paras 64–65) and *Canal Digital* (C-611/14) early stage advertising for complex TV subscription packages would engage the UCPD (para 41).
4 [2012] EWCA Crim 539, [2012] CTLC 1 at paras 43–46. See also the EFTA Court decision in Case E-1/19, *Andreas Gyrre v The Norwegian Government* para 78.

8.88 Clear information is 'imperative for the consumer to be able to make an informed transactional decision'[1]. The CJEU held in *Konsumentombudsmannen v Ving Sverige AB*[2] that it is for the national court to decide whether the information is sufficient so that a consumer can make an informed transactional decision, however it seems from the later CJEU decision in *Canal Digital Danmark*, that certain information, notably pricing information, is so significant that it can be assumed that its omission will impact on transactional decision[3]. In *Nicht Einhaltung Lieferfrist II*[4] it was found that choosing which trader to purchase from can be a transactional decision even before a product is purchased. The *Air Baltic*[5] case further provided that the selection of a business to trade with, before actually buying a product, can be a transactional decision even if the consumer does not go on to buy. Further, in *Competition Authority v Vodaphone Magyarorszag Mobil*[6] corrections to untrue advertisements about airtime contracts were held to have been made too late, as the initial transactional decision had already been taken. Likewise, statements made after the commercial transaction has been completed may also affect transactional decisions (such as to seek a refund, or otherwise enforce rights in relation to a purchased product)[7].

1 Case E-1/19, *Andreas Gyrre v The Norwegian Government* para 76.
2 *Konsumentombudsmannen v Ving Sverige AB* (C-122/10) [2011] ECR I-3903.
3 CJEU *Canal Digital Danmark* (C-611/14) at paras 46–49.
4 Germany Regional Court, 2009, 312 0 74/09.
5 2009 E03 – REUD-54, Latvia Tribunal First Degree.
6 Hungary Competition Tribunal, 2010, Vj/149–041/2009.
7 *R v X Ltd* [2013] EWCA Crim 818 at para 25.

The average consumer

8.89 CPUTR 2008, reg 2:

"average consumer" shall be construed in accordance with paragraphs (2) to (6);

. . .

"materially distort the economic behaviour" means in relation to an average consumer, appreciably to impair the average consumer's ability to make an informed decision thereby causing him to take a transactional decision that he would not have taken otherwise.

. . .

(2) In determining the effect of a commercial practice on the average consumer where the practice reaches or is addressed to a consumer or consumers account shall be taken of the material characteristics of such an average consumer including his being reasonably well informed, reasonably observant and circumspect.

(3) Paragraphs (4) and (5) set out the circumstances in which a reference to the average consumer shall be read as in addition referring to the average member of a particular group of consumers.

(4) In determining the effect of a commercial practice on the average consumer where the practice is directed to a particular group of consumers, a reference to the average consumer shall be read as referring to the average member of that group.

(5) In determining the effect of a commercial practice on the average consumer—

    (a)   where a clearly identifiable group of consumers is particularly vulnerable to the practice or the underlying product because of their mental or physical infirmity, age or credulity in a way which the trader could reasonably be expected to foresee, and

    (b)   where the practice is likely to materially distort the economic behaviour only of that group,

a reference to the average consumer shall be read as referring to the average member of that group.

(6) Paragraph (5) is without prejudice to the common and legitimate advertising practice of making exaggerated statements which are not meant to be taken literally.

8.90 The CPUTR 2008 'average consumer' is a central concept in the consumer protection that the legislation provides. Although it is conceptually similar to the common law reasonable man test, it is derived from European jurisprudence and has a number of differences. In paras 18 and 19 of the preamble to the UCPD it was stated that:

'(18) It is appropriate to protect all consumers from unfair commercial practices; however the Court of Justice has found it necessary in adjudicating on advertising cases since the enactment of Directive 84/450/EEC to examine the effect on a notional, typical consumer. In line with the principle of proportionality, and to permit the effective application of the protections contained in it, this Directive takes as a benchmark the average consumer, who is reasonably well informed and reasonably observant and circumspect, taking into account social, cultural and linguistic factors, as interpreted by the Court of Justice, but also contains provisions aimed at preventing the exploitation of consumers whose characteristics make them particularly vulnerable to unfair commercial practices. Where a commercial practice is specifically aimed at a particular group of consumers, such as children, it is desirable that the impact of the commercial practice be assessed from the perspective of the average member of that group. It is therefore appropriate to include in the list of practices which are in all circumstances unfair a provision which, without imposing an outright ban on advertising directed at children, protects them from direct exhortations to purchase. The average consumer test is not a statistical test. National courts and authorities will have to exercise their own faculty of judgment, having regard to the case-law of the Court of Justice, to determine the typical reaction of the average consumer in a given case.

(19) Where certain characteristics such as age, physical or mental infirmity or credulity make consumers particularly susceptible to a commercial practice or to the underlying product and the economic behaviour only of such consumer is likely to be distorted by the practice in a way that the trader can reasonably foresee, it is appropriate to ensure that they are adequately protected by assessing the practice from the perspective of the average member of that group.'

8.91 The UCPD does not provide a complete definition of the average consumer other than this guidance. The CPUTR 2008 definition can be broken down into three parts:

(a)   the 'ordinary' **average consumer**, under reg 2(2);
(b)   **targeted groups** of consumers, under reg 2(4);
(c)   the **vulnerable consumer**, under reg 2(5).

The ordinary average consumer

8.92 Under reg 2(2), the CPUTR 2008 requires the court to consider the material characteristics of an average consumer, but makes specific reference to three particular characteristics: his being reasonably well informed, reasonably observant, and reasonably circumspect (these three characteristics have been considered above in relation to 'transactional decision'). The CPUTR 2008 essentially enshrines the notion that the average consumer in the United Kingdom is both intelligent and cautious.

8.93 The concept of the average consumer is one that has been derived from the jurisprudence of the European Court of Justice. In 1998, the ECJ gave judgment on a case referred to it by the German courts concerning misleading labelling of eggs – *Gut Springenheide GMBH v Oberkreisdirektor des Krieses Steinfurt*[1]. The ECJ referred with approval to the average consumer test and the line of authorities in which the test had been developed[2]:

'in order to determine whether the description, trade mark or promotional description or statement in question was liable to mislead the purchaser, the Court took into account the presumed expectations of an average consumer who is reasonably well-informed and reasonably observant and circumspect, without ordering an expert's report or commissioning a consumer research poll.'

The average consumer concept is meant to reflect the characteristics and level of knowledge and expertise actually possessed by the consumers to whom the practice is directed, and it is inappropriate to impute specialist knowledge or expertise[3].

[1]   C-210/96 *Gut Springenheide GmbH and Rudolf Tusky v Oberkreisdirektor des Kreises Steinfurt – Amt für Lebensmittelüberwachung* [1998] ECR I-04657.

2   Case C-362/88 *GB-INNO-BM* [1990] ECR I-667, Case C-238/89 *Pall* [1990] ECR I-4827, Case C-126/91 *Yves Rocher* [1993] ECR I-2361, Case C-315/92 *Verband Sozialer Wettbewerb* [1994] ECR I-317, Case C-456/93 *Langguth* [1995] ECR I-1737, and Case C-470/93 *Mars* [1995] ECR I-1923.

3   *The Queen on the application of CityFibre Ltd v The Advertising Standards Authority* [2019] EWHC 950 (Admin) paras 101, 103, 107 and 110.

8.94 The threshold test is objective and therefore the fact that a consumer has actually made a transactional decision based on the unfair practice will not be conclusive of the issue. The question is whether the average consumer would be likely to make the same decision. When assessing the effect of a commercial practice, the court must take into account that the average consumer is deemed (with the exception of the vulnerable consumer provisions) to have the characteristics of being reasonably well informed, observant, and circumspect. However, the court is willing to adapt its approach in appropriate circumstances; for example, 'social, cultural or linguistic factors' of the Member States can be taken into account[1]. Similarly, in a case which concerned the doorstep sales of educational materials, the court had regard to the 'particularly vulnerable consumer' such as those who are 'behind with their education and are seeking to catch up'[2]. Further, the nature of the product in question such as one that is technological- may mean that consumers are assumed to be incapable of taking specific steps such as configuring a device to deactivate pre-installed settings, or be aware of what those settings are[3].

1   Case C-220/98 *Estée Lauder Cosmetics GmbH v Lancaster Group GmbH* [2000] ECR I-117.
2   Case C-382/87 *Ministère Public v Buet* [1989] ECR 1235 at para 13.
3   Case C-54/17 *AGCM v Wind Tre SpA* at para 52.

8.95 The average consumer is therefore, by law, a reasonably intelligent and careful character when making a transactional decision. In *OFT v Purely Creative Ltd*[1], Briggs J commented that the UCPD exists to protect consumers who take reasonable care of themselves, rather than the ignorant, the careless, or the over hasty consumer. The practical reality is, however, that consumers are often not well informed, observant, or circumspect when making purchases. This has been recognised by the CJEU when stressing that the consumer is taken to be the 'target and victim of unfair commercial practices'. He or she is intrinsically in a weaker position and must be considered economically weaker and less experienced in legal matters than the trader[2]. The CJEU has gone on to hold that due to this weakness, when assessing whether the average consumer has been misled, it is not in principle relevant that they could themselves check the veracity of the trader's claim, if it is otherwise misleading[3].

1   [2011] EWHC 106 (Ch), [2011] CTLC 45.
2   C-59/12 *BKK Mobil* at para 36.
3   C-388/13 *UPC* at paras 52–54.

8.96 There is a temptation to assume that purely by providing information a trader can avoid liability for misleading the average consumer. Being informed, observant, and circumspect does not mean the average consumer would read the whole of the text of relevant promotions[1]. It is a fact-intensive issue for the court to decide whether a misleading act or omission has caused a different transactional decision to be taken. However, a court is not limited to considering only the characteristics of being informed, observant, and circumspect. It can consider how consumers behave in relation to the commercial practice in question. In particular this may require evidence of how real consumers in the market in question behave, since the concept is one of mixed fact and law[2].

1   *Purely Creative* at para 66.
2   See *Competition and Markets Authority v Care UK* [2019] 10 WLUK 96 paras 39–42 in the context of care home residents and *The Queen on the application of CityFibre Ltd v The Advertising Standards Authority* [2019] EWHC 950 (Admin) in the context of consumers of broadband.

8.97 The concept of the average consumer requires the courts to identify what information and practices are likely to impact their behaviour. In *Competition Authority v Vodaphone Magyarorszag Mobil*[1] the headline price for a phone contract was untrue. Although later information corrected some of the claim before contracts were signed the first impression given to the average consumer, particularly as regards price, was important and it was untrue. The initial transactional decision had already been made.

1   Hungary Competition Tribunal, 2010, Vj/149–041/2009.

8.98 In *Nicht Einhaltung Lieferfrist II*[1], the court found that a consumer selecting the trader to purchase from could be a transactional decision. The average consumer expects an online shop where offers are updated regularly to have the items in stock and immediately available unless indicated otherwise. Consumers typically expect quick delivery from such online shops. To advertise and take orders for items which were not in stock, and not tell this to consumers, affected their transactional decisions.

1   *Nicht Einhaltung Lieferfrist II*, Regional Court 2009, 312 0 74/09.

8.99 In reg 2(2), the definition of the 'average consumer' is objective. It does not include any subjective element. This is in contrast to most domestic criminal law provisions that have at least some regard to the complainant's actual position and whether they have actually been deceived, cheated, or wronged in some other way.

8.100 Experience suggests that many consumers are cheated because they are commercially naïve or not well informed. It can be argued that under the CPUTR 2008 a naïve consumer who is duped is not protected under reg 2(2) if the reasonably observant or circumspect consumer would not have been duped. However, in *OFT v Purely Creative Ltd*[1] Briggs J drew similarities between the decisions made by the court in passing off cases and those under CPUTR 2008. Where a trader sets out to deceive potential customers it will not be difficult for the court to infer that his deliberate deception has succeeded and affected the transactional decision of the average consumer. The court also rejected a submission that in the real world a regular recipient of a product would soon realise the subtle mischief behind the practice in question. The court said the test to be applied was not that of the habitual user of the product.

1   [2011] EWHC 106 (Ch), [2011] CTLC 45 at para 118.

8.101 In *OFT v Ashbourne Management Services*[1], under the UTCCR 1999, when considering the position of the average consumer the court concluded that the business model was designed to take advantage of the naivety and experience of the average consumer using gym clubs at the lower end of the market. The defendant's standard form agreements contained a trap into which the average consumer was likely to fall. By recommending the use of contracts containing unfair terms, the company contravened the CPUTR 2008.

1   [2011] EWHC 1237 (Ch), [2011] CTLC 237 at para 173.

8.102 Whilst it may be beneficial to introduce witnesses who have been misled by a commercial practice, (see statistical surveys below) the prosecutor need not find a complainant who has actually been wronged to prove a CPUTR 2008 offence. Courts will consider what decisions would have been made based upon the characteristics of the average consumer. Commercial naivety cannot be a material characteristic of the average consumer (see *Unilever v Materne Conflux*)[1]. However, some typical behaviours, such as not closely reading small print, appear to be characteristic of the average consumer[2]. If the impression created by a promotion is misleading to the average consumer paying average attention, then small print requiring meticulous analysis will not save it from being misleading[3]. The question is a matter for each individual case and not appropriate for 'invariable and irrebuttable' presumptions[4].

1   Belgium Court of Appeal 2008 – the average consumer should be deemed to understand that claiming by words and pictures that 100mg of product contains the equivalent of 200mg of fruit should not be taken literally.
2   The use of behavioural insights is likely to increase in litigation to assess the impact of practices on consumers – see the Commission Guidance [COM(2016) 320] p 42.
3   Austria Supreme Court 2008, 4Ob 245/07v and France Supreme Court 2009, 09–83059 *Lionel and Societe ENDIS Telecom*.
4   It does not follow that the trader must in all circumstances give complete disclosure: the average consumer may be taken to do some amount of their own research – see *BIS v PLT Anti-Marketing Ltd* [2015] EWCA Civ 76 at paras 31–32.

Statistical surveys

8.103 The European jurisprudence about the average consumer encourages the court to conduct the exercise so far as possible without recourse to statistical or other expert evidence about typical consumer behaviour, or even the evidence of particular consumers[1]. Recital 18 of the UCPD provides that 'the average consumer test is not a statistical test. National courts and authorities will have to exercise their own faculty of judgment, having regard to the case law of the Court of Justice, to determine the typical reaction of the average consumer in a given case'. The assessment is a question of law, rather than fact[2]. A further rationale for this is recorded in the 2005 *OFT v Officers Club* judgment[3]:

> 'If the evidence is given by too few of them, their views will not be sufficiently representative of the entire range of such consumers; if a large number, intended to cover the full range, gives evidence, the adverse effect on the cost and duration of the trial may be disproportionate to the value of their evidence.'

1   [2011] EWHC 106 (Ch), [2011] CTLC 45.
2   See *Interflora v Marks & Spencer plc* [2014] EWCA Civ 1403 at paras 113–115 and CJEU *Canal Digital Denmark* C-611/14 at para 39.
3   [2005] EWHC 1080 (Ch) at para 146. See also *Competition and Markets Authority v Care UK Health and Social Holdings Ltd* [2021] EWHC 2088 (Ch) paras 67–68, where the judge preferred the evidence of an Ipsos MORI poll to a small number of individual consumer statements.

8.104 This approach was supported in *OFT v Purely Creative Ltd*[1] and the *Austrian Supreme Court*[2]. The question of how the average consumer perceives an advertisement can be answered by the court when everyday experience and knowledge are sufficient to do so. However, this does not mean that real evidence of the effect the practice has on people is irrelevant – and this may be presented through expert or statistical evidence where appropriate[3]. An example of where careful research into the perceptions of real consumers could be relevant is where there is a debate about whether certain specific phrases have an impact on consumers. This is capable of revealing what the 'average' consumer thinks, as opposed to what a person might think if they are specifically educated about a topic: the decision maker ought not to impute specialist knowledge to the average consumer[4]. The approach in relation to the UCPD can be compared with the debate regarding the use of statistical surveys in the context of trademark infringement litigation[5].

[1] Briggs J: 'In accordance with European and English jurisprudence, the parties abstained (wisely in my judgment) from seeking to pursue their cases on that issue by reference either to expert evidence or statistical surveys', [2011] EWHC 1237 (Ch) at para 6.
[2] [2008] 4 Ob 42/08t.
[3] Indeed the CJEU in *Vincent Deroo-Blanquart v Sony* C-310/15 at paras 35–37 accepted that evidence of the expectations of a significant proportion of consumers may be relevant to the national court's assessment of whether the requirements of professional diligence are satisfied.
[4] *The Queen on the application of CityFibre Ltd v The Advertising Standards Authority* [2019] EWHC 950 (Admin) paras 108 and 130. In this case the ASA was held to be correct not to view adverts for part fibre broadband services as misleading, when they described their product as 'fibre'. This was because research commissioned by the ASA showed that describing a product as 'fibre' did not trigger further action by people: it was merely seen as a buzz word, rather than a key differentiator (see para 72 of the judgment).
[5] *(1) Interflora inc (2) Interflora British Unit v Marks and Spencer PLC* [2013] EWCA Civ 319, Official Transcript para 124.

A *characteristic lacuna*

8.105 The 'ordinary' average consumer definition under reg 2(2) makes no reference to characteristics such as age, infirmity, or mental and physical disability. It would appear that this is deliberate because reg 2(4) (targeted groups) and (5) (vulnerable consumers) are both directed towards specific groups or characteristics. However, these two provisions require proof of other elements before they are engaged (see below). If neither of these two provisions is engaged, it would appear that particular characteristics, such as age, infirmity, or mental or physical disability, cannot be considered when applying the test in reg 2(2). It is only the material characteristics of the average consumer that are relevant and the average consumer in reg 2(2) is not particularly young, old, infirm, or disabled[1].

[1] However, see the approach taken in the German Oberlandesgericht Karlsrue (4 U 141/11) and by the Slovak Trade inspectorate (P/0359/07/2010) which found that the average consumer includes those with impaired eyesight, such that using a very small font could be misleading.

TARGETED CONSUMERS

8.106 Under reg 2(3) the 'ordinary' average consumer test *must* be read as meaning the average member of a particular consumer group if either reg 2(4) (targeted groups) or 2(5) (vulnerable consumers) is engaged. The provision is worded mandatorily that the reg 2(2) test 'shall be read as **in addition** referring to the average member of a particular group of consumers'. The words 'in addition' are unlikely to create a two-pronged average consumer test that can be satisfied by *either* the reg 2(2) average consumer, or the alternative average consumer described by reg 2(4) or (5). The wording of reg 2(4) and (5) suggests that (if either provision is engaged) the reg 2(2) test should be modified by the addition of a further material characteristic: that he is an average member of the identified group of consumers.

8.107 Regulation 2(4) requires proof that the commercial practice has been, '*directed* to a particular group of consumers' before it is engaged. If it is engaged, it is the material characteristics of the average member of that particular group that must be considered. This is a subjective element that contrasts with reg 2(5), which asks only objective questions, principally about whether it was reasonably foreseeable that a clearly defined group was 'particularly vulnerable'.

Directed

8.108 The use of the verb 'direct' is likely to be considered a further element in the definition, such that reg 2(4) will not be engaged unless the trader has done something that demonstrates the product was **targeted** at a particular type of consumer. In *OFT v Purely Creative Ltd*[1] the court acknowledged that prize draw letters were sent to the names and addresses of consumers who had previously responded to one or more promotions. It was not, however, targeted at any particular social or economic class. This appears to place a narrow interpretation of 'directed to a particular group of consumers' and arguments for a wider interpretation can be envisaged. This approach may be at variance with that taken in other EU states, such as Sweden, where in the case of advertisements for babies' nappies, the average consumer was taken to be 'parents with small children, not having any special knowledge about allergies'[2].

[1]   [2011] EWHC 106 (Ch) at para 84.
[2]   Decision of 4 July 2012 of the Marknadsdomstolen.

Specialist knowledge

8.109 If the product was directed at a specialist group, should the average consumer be attributed with specialist knowledge that a member of that consumer group would ordinarily have? For example, a rock climbing product is obviously directed at rock climbing consumers. Clearly, the average member of that group is likely to have some rock climbing experience. Does the focus in reg 2(4) on the average member of the group exclude a consumer that is not average, for example the novice or beginner?

8.110 The level of understanding possessed by the average consumer will normally be determined by the courts by reference to everyday experience. Otherwise, factual disputes as to the average consumer's level of understanding will require expert evidence – particularly where the commercial practice is directed to an expert group of consumers[1]. If a beginner buys a falsely described rock climbing product, could it be argued that the average member of the targeted group of rock climbing consumers might not have done so because his experience and specialist knowledge would tell him that the description was misleading? The court must decide whether it can put itself in the position of the average member of rock climbers, without expert assistance, in order to decide the effect of the commercial practice on the transactional decisions of that group.

[1]   Austria Supreme Court 2008, 4 Ob 42/08t.

8.111 This issue is important in applying the CPUTR 2008 because the wording of reg 2(3) makes reg 2(4) mandatory if the product is directed at a particular group of consumers. It is a proposition that might leave consumers who are inexperienced in a particular area unprotected if a more experienced consumer, but still average for the group, would not have made such a transactional decision. This interpretation does not suit the purposive approach of the UCPD to provide a high level of protection for consumers. An argument that could be advanced is that the average member should not be given an artificial amount of knowledge by becoming the statistical 'average'. This is supported within the UCPD where it states that the average consumer test is not a statistical test. In the above example of rock climbing products, the concept of the 'average consumer' has narrowed from the general population to a sub-set of those interested in rock climbing. The court should apply the *transactional decision test* to the 'average consumer' of the new population. This may well alter the degree to which the average consumer is expected to be informed, observant, or circumspect. However, it stops short of expecting the average consumer to possess the statistically 'average' rock climber's level of *specialist knowledge*[1]. A further argument about specialist knowledge is that beginners purchasing products in specialist areas might fall under the protection afforded to vulnerable consumers in reg 2(5), which includes consumers who are vulnerable because of their 'credulity' (see below).

[1]   However, it is legitimate to take into account the social, cultural and linguistic features of the consumers, which might mean that a practice which is misleading in one Member State is not elsewhere – such as where the misleading nature depends on the meaning of a word in one language, which it would not necessarily have in another – see C-220/98 *Estee Lauder* para 29. *Cf* the decision of the CJEU in C-75/15 concerning 'evocation' within the scope of protected geographical indication of spirit drinks. It was held that the national court is required to refer to the perception of the average consumer who is reasonably well informed, observant and circumspect, that concept being understood as concerning European consumers and not only consumers of the Member State in which the product giving rise to the evocation of the protected geographical indication is manufactured.

Vulnerable consumers

8.112 The CPUTR 2008, reg 2(5) is designed to provide consumer protection for vulnerable consumers. It does so by the mechanism of making the average consumer the average member of the vulnerable group of consumers (in the same way that reg 2(4) does for targeted consumers). Before reg 2(5) is engaged, however, it is necessary to prove 4 elements:

(a)   there is a 'clearly identifiable group';
(b)   the group is 'particularly vulnerable' to the commercial practice or underlying product because of its members' mental or physical infirmity, age, or[1] credulity;
(c)   that particular vulnerability is reasonably foreseeable; and

(d)   the commercial practice is, 'likely to distort' **only** the economic behaviour of the 'particularly vulnerable' group.

¹ It is important to note that Recital 19 states that this is not a closed list, and consumers may be vulnerable for further, unspecified, reasons. This wider scope appears to be favoured by the European Commission – Commission Guidance [COM(2016) 320] p 45, where reference is made to a Hungarian decision finding that consumers with a poor credit rating were to be treated as vulnerable (decision Vj-5/2011/73).

8.113 All of these elements are objective so that it does not matter whether the trader has actually directed the commercial practice at the particularly vulnerable group or whether the trader was actually aware that the group of consumers was particularly vulnerable to it. The language used in reg 2(5) has the effect (not necessarily intended) of creating several thresholds:

(a)   the group of consumers must be *clearly* identifiable; and
(b)   the group must be *particularly* vulnerable to the commercial practice or underlying product in a way that the trader could foresee; and
(c)   the commercial practice must be likely to distort *only* the economic behaviour of that vulnerable group; and
(d)   it must not fall within the common and legitimate advertising practice of making exaggerated statements that are not meant to be taken literally.

8.114 In drafting the CPUTR 2008, the vulnerability of child consumers has obviously been important and reg 2(5) reflects that policy consideration. However, these thresholds seem unnecessary and capable of overcomplicating a relatively simple concept. The reason for requiring the group to be 'clearly' defined and 'particularly' vulnerable is not readily apparent. The language will undoubtedly generate legal argument about how clearly the group must be defined and how vulnerable it needs to be. Is a consumer group that is vulnerable, but not 'particularly' vulnerable, excluded? This begs the question whether the paragraph would not have been better drafted without the words 'clearly' and 'particularly'.

Only the vulnerable group

8.115 Equally, it is not obvious why there is a requirement that the commercial practice is likely to distort the economic behaviour of *'only'* the vulnerable group. If a product was likely to affect the economic behaviour of two distinct vulnerable groups, reg 2(5) would not appear to bite. Evidentially, it is potentially difficult to prove that only one group of consumers would be affected by a commercial practice. For example, products that are capable of misleading child consumers may well be capable of misleading consumers with mental impairment. Could it be argued that reg 2(5) does not apply since the commercial practice might mislead two different groups of vulnerable consumers?

8.116 It is not easy to find a linguistic construction of reg 2(5) that overcomes this problem of its literal meaning. It was plainly not an intended consequence in the UCPD, which refers to 'provisions aimed at preventing the exploitation of consumers whose characteristics make them particularly vulnerable to unfair commercial practices'. One possible route to overcoming this might be to use the direction of Briggs J¹: that the interpretation is neither a matter of grammar or dictionaries but must be construed as far as is possible to implement the purposes and provisions of the Directive. Accordingly the provision will bite where the *average* consumer is not impacted, but vulnerable consumers (of whatever class) are likely to be affected.

[1]   [2011] EWHC 106 (Ch), [2011] CTLC 45 at para 40.

Credulity

8.117 Although the noun 'credulity' appears in the English version of the UCPD it is not a word that is in popular English usage. It means the disposition or willingness to believe easily or readily. A credulous consumer is one with a tendency to believe too readily. It is synonymous with the tendency to be naïve or gullible. Its etymology is derived from the Latin verb 'credo' (to believe) and 'credulous' (to believe easily). CPUTR 2008, reg 2(6) provides:

> (6) Paragraph (5) is without prejudice to the common and legitimate advertising practice of making exaggerated statements which are not meant to be taken literally.

8.118 It is important to appreciate that reg 2(6) only applies to the vulnerable average consumer test in reg 2(5). It is not a general exclusion of all 'exaggerated statements which are not meant to be taken literally'. Such statements were generally excluded by the TDA 1968. A statement that was too vague to be treated as definite or one that was obviously not to be taken seriously did not amount to a trade description. In the law of contract such statements are distinguished from contractual terms as mere puffs. However, the scope of the TDA 1968 exclusion went further than this. In *Cadbury v Halliday* the Divisional Court drew the distinction between the TDA 1968, s 2(1) which embraced examples of physical characteristics, and other non-factual concepts upon which opinion could differ[1].

[1]   [1975] 2 All ER 226, the description, 'extra value', was printed on chocolate bars.

8.119 CPUTR 2008, reg 2(6) is plainly not as broad as the rule was under the TDA 1968. It only applies when considering the vulnerable average consumer. The main thrust of the CPUTR 2008 was to enhance consumer rights. This is illustrated by reg 4, which penalises commercial practices that are likely to deceive even if a statement is not actually incorrect. It follows that even opinions of a non-factual type are likely be covered by the CPUTR 2008, subject to misleading the average consumer.

CONTRAVENING PROFESSIONAL DILIGENCE

8.120 **Contravening professional diligence** is made a prohibition by reg 3(3) and an offence by reg 8(1). The reg 17 due diligence defence is not available to a trader charged under reg 8, proof that a trader has contravened professional diligence inevitably means he has not exercised due diligence. The reg 18 (innocent publication defence) is also unavailable in a prosecution under reg 8.

CPUTR 2008, reg 3(3):

3 Prohibition of unfair commercial practices

> (3) A commercial practice is unfair if—

    (a)   it contravenes the requirements of professional diligence; and

    (b)   it materially distorts or is likely to materially distort the economic behaviour of the average consumer with regard to the product.

CPUTR 2008, reg 8(1):

8 Offences relating to unfair commercial practices

(1)   A trader is guilty of an offence if—

    (a)   he knowingly or recklessly engages in a commercial practice which contravenes the requirements of professional diligence under regulation 3(3)(a); and

    (b)   the practice materially distorts or is likely to materially distort the economic behaviour of the average consumer with regard to the product under regulation 3(3)(b).

(2)   For the purposes of paragraph (1)(a) a trader who engages in a commercial practice without regard to whether the practice contravenes the requirements of professional diligence shall be deemed recklessly to engage in the practice, whether or not the trader has reason for believing that the practice might contravene those requirements.

8.121

Precedent for contravening professional diligence

Statement of offence

ENGAGING IN AN UNFAIR COMMERCIAL PRACTICE BY CONTRAVENING THE RE-QUIREMENTS OF PROFESSIONAL DILIGENCE, contrary to Regs 3(3) and 8 of the Consumer Protection from Unfair Trading Regulations 2008.

Particulars of offence

X Limited, a trader, on [date] knowingly or recklessly engaged in an unfair commercial practice in relation to a product, by [. . .], and thereby contravened the requirements of professional diligence, which materially distorted, or was likely to materially distort, the economic behaviour of the average consumer with regard to the product.

Mens rea for the criminal offence

8.122 Unlike the main offences under the TDA 1968, the criminal offence requires proof of *mens rea*, that the offence was committed knowingly or recklessly. Recklessly is statutorily defined in reg 8(2) to include a trader that engaged in the practice 'without regard' to whether it contravened a requirement of professional diligence. This makes the recklessness test entirely objective such that it is not necessary to prove that the trader actually foresaw any risk that the commercial practice might contravene the requirements of professional diligence.

8.123 Regulation 8(2) is very similar to the TDA 1968, s 14(2)(b), which provided that:

(b) a statement made regardless of whether it is true or false shall be deemed to be made recklessly, whether or not the person making it had reasons for believing that it might be false.

8.124 This was considered by the Divisional Court in *MFI Warehouses v Nattrass*[1] where the common law definition of recklessness was rejected[2]. Lord Widgery stated[3]:

'recklessly in the context of the 1968 Act does not involve dishonesty. Accordingly it is not necessary to prove that the statement was made with the degree of irresponsibility which is implied in the phrase 'careless whether it be true or false'. I think it suffices for present purposes if the prosecution can show that the advertiser **did not have regard to the truth or falsity** of his advertisement even if it cannot be shown that he was deliberately closing his eyes to the truth, or that he had any kind of dishonest mind.' (emphasis added)

[1] [1973] 1 WLR 307.
[2] The definition of 'total irresponsibility and a total lack of consideration whether the statement was true or false' per Lord Widgery CJ (taken from *Derry v Peek* (1889) 14 App Cas 337).
[3] At p 768, the Divisional Court rejected the construction of Parker J in *Sunair Holidays v Dodd* [1970] 2 All ER 410 at 411, that the test was the same as *Derry v Peek*, on the basis that the issue had not been fully argued.

8.125 The question is, did the defendant 'have regard' to whether the statement was true or false? In effect this creates a duty upon the maker of a statement to 'have regard' to its truth. What is meant by 'having regard' will depend upon the circumstances, however it will be insufficient to simply address one's mind to the issue of falsity. In *Nattrass* the company chairman had considered a statement before approving it, but had not thought through its implications sufficiently to appreciate that it could be misconstrued. The rationale of the judgment is that he ought to have given *reasonable consideration to whether the practice contravened the requirements of professional diligence* if he is not to be considered reckless.

8.126 In another TDA 1968 case, *Best Travel v Patterson*[1], the defendant company had made a statement in a brochure that a particular hotel had various amenity rooms, which the company knew would not be available until a particular date. A customer made a booking at the hotel after the date when the rooms should have been available, and later found that they were not in fact available. It was held that the company's failure to inquire whether the rooms were available when they took the booking put them in the position that they did not know if the brochure statement was true. The statement had therefore been made recklessly.

[1]   (1987) 151 JP 619.

Attributing recklessness

8.127 The nature of recklessness involves a consideration of the state of an individual's mind. Where recklessness is alleged against non-human corporate entities, a question arises as to whose state of mind must be proven. In the Divisional Court hearing of *Wings v Ellis* case, Mann J stated that[1]:

'a company cannot be guilty of an offence unless the specified state of mind was a state of mind of a person who is or forms part of the directing mind and will of the company.'

Although the House of Lords overturned the decision of the Divisional Court on its construction of the TDA 1968, s 14(1)(a), Lord Hailsham implicitly approved the judgment of Mann J on this issue[2].

1   [1984] 1 All ER 1046.
2   At p 284E. Cf Parker LJ in *Yugotours v Wadsley* [1988] BTLC 300.

8.128 The rationale of Mann J's principle is that a company will not be vicariously responsible for the recklessness of those who do not form part of its directing mind and will. Whether a person forms part of the directing mind and will of a company will depend upon a construction of the responsibility that he holds within the company and his role in the decision making process. The issue was indirectly traversed by the House of Lords in *Tesco Supermarkets Ltd v Nattrass*[1] where it was stated by Lord Reid[2]:

'Normally the board of directors, the managing director and perhaps other superior officers of a company carry out the functions of management and speak and act as the company. Their subordinates do not. They carry out orders from above and it can make no difference that they are given some measure of discretion. But the board of directors may delegate some part of their functions of management giving to their delegate full discretion to act independently of instructions from them. I see no difficulty holding that they have thereby put such a delegate in their place so that within the scope of the delegation he can act as the company.'

1   [1972] AC 153, [1971] 2 All ER 127, see also *Coupe v Guyett* [1973] 2 All ER 1058 a case dealing with an offence being committed under TDA 1968, s 23, where such persons were described as the 'ruling officers'.
2   At pp 132 or 171. See also Viscount Dilhorne at pp 145 or 187 and Lord Diplock at pp 155 or 199.

8.129 It is open to defendant companies to argue that they are not guilty of *mens rea* offences because the 'offender' was not part of the company's controlling mind. This proposition is supported by the TDA 1968 case, *Airtours v Shipley*[1], where a false statement was made by the company's product manager in a holiday brochure. The company's appeal was allowed by the Divisional Court on the principal ground that the product manager was not a director or part of the directing mind of the company; he was merely 'a cog in the machine'. In *Airtours v Shipley*, McCowan LJ said:

'In *Yugotours Ltd v Wadsley* [(1989) 153 JP 345] . . . Parker LJ . . . said . . . "I have no doubt myself that the company can properly be found to have been reckless, notwithstanding the absence of specific evidence of recklessness on the part of somebody who might properly be called part of the directing mind of the company." . . . I find that perfectly acceptable if he meant no more than that a directing mind of the company must in the circumstances have been reckless, even if the particular directing mind cannot be identified. If, on the other hand, he was meaning to say that, an inferior employee being reckless, a directing mind can be vicariously liable therefore in an offence requiring *mens rea*, that would . . . have been a radical departure from principle and authority.'

1   (1994) 158 JP 835.

8.130 Similarly, in *British Airways Board v Taylor*[1] the House of Lords found that the Board was not liable to prosecution in respect of a statement made in a letter, since it had not authorised the writing of the letter. In both cases prosecution of the writer, rather than the company, would have succeeded. For authority to support the proposition that a poor system can found the basis for recklessness to be imputed to the company's controlling mind see *Sunworld Ltd v Hammersmith and Fulham London Borough Council*[2].

1   [1976] 1 WLR 13.
2   [2000] 1 WLR 2102 at 2109F–2110D.

8.131 Further support for the proposition that it is not always necessary to identify the particular controlling mind is found in *R v X Ltd*[1], where Leveson LJ held that an inference could be drawn from the evidence that the way in which the company operated (which must have been through at least one of its controlling minds) demonstrated the requisite recklessness. As a result, it was not important that the prosecution could not prove the identity of a particular controlling mind.

1   [2013] EWCA Crim 818, [2013] CTLC 145.

Professional diligence

8.132 CPUTR 2008, reg 2:

2 Interpretation

"professional diligence" means the standard of special skill and care which a trader may reasonably be expected to exercise towards consumers which is commensurate with either –

(a)   honest market practice in the trader's field of activity, or
(b)   the general principle of good faith in the trader's field of activity.

8.133 The definition of 'professional diligence' in the CPUTR 2008 replicates the definition set out in Art 2(h) of the UCPD. It is essentially defined by the 'reasonable expectation' that traders should behave honestly and in good faith. The concepts of 'honest market practice' and 'good faith' are not defined in the CPUTR 2008, but assistance to their meaning can be found in case law and official guidance.

8.134 Honest market practice in the trader's field of activity is likely to mean no more than *market practices of reasonable and honest traders in that field of activity*. This will inevitably involve a consideration of how traders generally practice in the particular field. However, the fact that a commercial practice is widespread does not make it commensurate with honest practices because there may be many non-compliant traders in that field and it is not by their standards that the practice must be judged. In the OFT/BERR Guidance[1] the following direction is given which supports this view:

'Professional diligence is an objective standard which will vary according to the context. The word "special" is not intended to require more than would reasonably be expected of a trader in their field of activity. However, poor current practice that is widespread in an industry/sector cannot amount to an acceptable objective standard. That is because this is not what a reasonable person would expect from a trader who is acting in accordance with honest market practice or "good faith".'

1   OFT/BERR Guidance on the CPUTR 2008 (August 2008).

8.135 The construction of the unfamiliar concepts of 'honest market practice' and the 'general principle of good faith' was considered in *Tiscali v British Telecommunications Plc*[1] in which Eady J said they:

'are construed in such a way that a breach may be found even in the absence of dishonesty as is traditionally understood in domestic jurisprudence.'

An authoritative exposition of the meaning of 'good faith' in the context of unfair terms was set out by Lord Bingham in *Director General of Fair Trading v First National Bank*[2] where he said:

'The requirement of good faith in this context is one of fair and open dealing. Openness requires that the terms should be expressed fully, clearly and legibly, containing no concealed pitfalls or traps. Appropriate prominence should be given to terms which might operate disadvantageously to the customer. Fair dealing requires that a supplier should not, whether deliberately or unconsciously, take advantage of the consumer's necessity, indigence, lack of experience, unfamiliarity with the subject matter of the contract, weak bargaining position or any other factor . . . Good faith in this context is not an artificial or technical concept . . . It looks to good standards of commercial morality and practice.'

[1]   [2008] EWHC 3129 (QB).
[2]   [2001] UKHL 52, [2002] 1 AC 481 at para 17.

8.136 What amounts to contravention of professional diligence has been considered in the UK and cases from other Member States. A good example is to be found in *OFT v Ashbourne Management Services Ltd*[1] where the High Court found that a gym provider's standard terms were unfair under the Unfair Terms in Consumer Contracts Regulations 1999[2]. One such term provided for the gym receiving the whole of a minimum term subscription in the event of termination for whatever reason:

'in recommending the use of these agreements which are unfair . . . and in seeking payment of subscriptions under them . . . the defendants . . . have not acted in accordance with the standard commensurate with honest market practice and have caused consumers to take transactional decision they would not otherwise have taken.' (per Kitchin J at para 227)

[1]   [2011] EWHC 1237 (Ch), [2011] CTLC 237.
[2]   SI 1999/2083.

8.137 In *Competition Authority v Made in Italy, RVM, Vismara, Cascobene and X Moto*[1] a company produced and distributed motor cycle helmets for adults and children and made declarations on the helmets and in adverts that they were compliant with EU rules. It was not clear whether the helmets did or did not meet the rules, but there was a failure to verify and do all the checks as required under the rules. This was held to constitute a lack of professional diligence. The standard of special skill and care expected was high due to the product being a motor cycle helmet and also because the intended recipients included children and teenagers.

[1]   Italy, Competition Tribunal, 2009, PS 1174.

8.138 In *CHS Tour Services v Team 4 Travel*[1], the CJEU held that there is no automatic infringement of the requirements of professional diligence if a commercial practice is categorised as a misleading commercial practice under

Art 6 of the UCPD. As a result, the two tests for determining whether: (a) an act constitutes a misleading commercial practice, or (b) a failure to meet professional diligence, remain distinct.

¹   C-435/11, [2013] Bus LR 1302, [2014] 1 CMLR 38.

Standard of special skill and care

8.139 The professional diligence test also refers to the 'standard of **special** skill and care'. The word 'special' may be significant in understanding the scope of the professional diligence test. It has the potential to limit professional diligence to those commercial standards that are 'special' to the trader's field, rather than ordinary commercial standards of universal application to traders. Could it be argued that professional diligence was intended only to apply to specialist aspects of a trader's practice? For example, it will cover the standard of skill and care to be expected of a mechanic fitting a car part, but not to the way that he provides written invoices. The *Made in Italy* case, summarised above, discussed the special skill and care required in the making of motor cycle helmets particularly when young people are included as recipients of the product. *Competition Authority v Acea Ato SPA*¹ concerned the supply of water. A water company interrupted or cut off the water supply without warning customers. Due to the essential nature of the product, the Court held that the expected standards, and therefore the degree of expected professional diligence, were higher than for other traders. The failure to inform about the interruption to water supply contravened professional diligence.

¹   Italy, Competition Tribunal, 2009, PS166.

8.140 A construction that avoids this narrowing of the scope of professional diligence might be to confine the word 'special' to merely the 'kind' or 'type' of skill and care associated with traders generally, rather than the skill and care that is special to the trader's particular field. On the other hand, it can be argued that *professional* diligence was intended to apply only to those specific professional duties and that there are several other offences that would cover unfair trading of a general nature¹. Against this narrow wording, several court decisions have tended to take a wider approach – including *R v X*, which held that poor customer service and dismissiveness when dealing with complaints could contravene professional diligence². Likewise providing a service that is generally so poor as to require remedial work infringes this provision³. Requiring airline complainants to use a premium rate phone service has been held to be contrary to professional diligence by the Italian courts⁴, as has the practice of hiding a 'no insurance required' option among a list of potential countries of residence, so that consumers who do not want insurance find it hard to opt out of it⁵.

¹   Where there are specific rules that apply in the trader's field, a failure to comply with those rules may provide the basis for a contravening professional diligence case. For example, an airline failing to present fully inclusive prices as required by Art 23 of the EU Air Services Regulation 1008/2008, see the Italian AGCM decision against Ryanair, referred to in the CJEU ruling C-28/19 *Ryanair Ltd v AGCM* (para 6).
²   *R v X Ltd* [2013] EWCA Crim 818 paras 30–32; see also *R v Asad Bashir Malik* [2020] EWCA Crim 957 for another example of contravening professional diligence – the operator of a secure airport car parking service did not keep vehicles securely, using them to ferry staff members about and on occasion damaging them (para 6).

3   *R v David Hamilton* [2015] EWCA Crim 278. As does carrying out work that is so poorly executed as to be of no value (*R v Neil Jackson* [2017] EWCA Crim 78 at para 9). See also *R v Morrison & Towers* [2017] EWCA Crim 2617 paras 16–20, describing poor workmanship in installing substandard driveways, and failing to honour guarantees subsequently.
4   Decision of the Italian AGCM PS8378, *Ryanair*, 19 January 2015.
5   Decision of the Italian AGCM PS7275, *Ryanair*, 20 December 2013.

Distorting economic behaviour

8.141 CPUTR 2008, reg 2:

2 Interpretation

"materially distort the economic behaviour" means in relation to an average consumer, appreciably to impair the average consumer's ability to make an informed decision thereby causing him to take a transactional decision that he would not have taken otherwise.

8.142 The definitions of 'average consumer' and 'transactional decision' are considered above. The definition of 'materially distort the economic behaviour' can be separated into two parts:

(a)   appreciably impairing the average consumer's ability to make an informed decision; and
(b)   thereby causing him to take a transactional decision he would not have taken otherwise.

8.143 The adjective 'appreciable' means: capable of being estimated, measured, or perceived. The use of the word 'appreciably' creates a threshold test. Examples of what might be considered to be contraventions of professional diligence, which also materially distort economic behaviour, include:

- *Offering products at inflated prices to those you have sold alcohol to.* Even if the test applied is the average drunken consumer, a commercial practice may still lack an operative deception, omission, or aggressive element for the purposes of regs 5, 6 or 7 of the CPUTR 2008. It may, however, contravene the requirements of professional diligence. In such circumstances, the ability of the average drunken consumer to make an informed decision is plainly impaired.
- *A broker selling unfavourable life assurance to hospital patients immediately before medical operations.* Such a practice may lack the requisite undue influence (the application of pressure) for an aggressive commercial practice. However, it could contravene the requirements of professional diligence. The ability of the average patient to make an informed decision about life insurance will probably be impaired when they are just about to go under the surgeon's knife.

8.144 The 'appreciably impairing' test is also supplemented by the requirement that it be sufficient to cause a transactional decision. Under reg 8, the causal test is not whether the average consumer would take a different transactional decision as a consequence of the contravention of professional diligence. It is whether the impairment of his ability to make an informed decision would cause the average consumer to make a different decision. In applying this factually, the question is not whether the average consumer would take a different transactional decision because of the unfair commercial practice, but whether the impairment of the consumer's decision-making ability meant that a different decision was taken.

8.145 The concept of 'materially distorting economic behaviour' is taken directly from the UCPD. It is perhaps not the simplest way that this concept could be expressed. It combines several long and wordy definitions. In combination with the very wide definition of transactional decision, however, it amounts to little more than *whether the average consumer might have, in any way, relied upon the commercial practice as a consumer*. Arguably, it adds little to the standard transactional decision test: the CJEU for example has accepted that infringing national legislation prohibiting the regular resale of event admission tickets is capable of being regarded as an unfair commercial practice, even without any analysis of this concept[1]. The language is also unnecessarily clumsy, which may reflect a failure of the CPUTR 2008's draftsmen to translate the UCPD effectively into plain English. In its present prolix form there is real scope for legal argument, as demonstrated by the two views set out above, that could have been avoided with a simple approach to language.

[1] CJEU *Directeur-Generaal van de Algemene Directie Controlee n Bemiddeling van de FOD Economie v Movic BV* (C-73/19) para 43.

MISLEADING ACTIONS

8.146 Engaging in a commercial practice that is a misleading action is made an offence by regs 5 and 9.

CPUTR 2008, reg 5:

5 Misleading actions

(1) A commercial practice is a misleading action if it satisfies the conditions in either paragraph (2) or paragraph (3).

(2) A commercial practice satisfies the conditions of this paragraph—

    (a) if it contains false information and is therefore untruthful in relation to any of the matters in paragraph (4) or if it or its overall presentation in any way deceives or is likely to deceive the average consumer in relation to any of the matters in that paragraph, even if the information is factually correct; and

    (b) it causes or is likely to cause the average consumer to take a transactional decision he would not have taken otherwise.

(3) A commercial practice satisfies the conditions of this paragraph if—

    (a) it concerns any marketing of a product (including comparative advertising) which creates confusion with any products, trademarks, trade names or other distinguishing marks of a competitor; or

    (b) it concerns any failure by a trader to comply with a commitment contained in a code of conduct which the trader has undertaken to comply with, if—

        (i) the trader indicates in a commercial practice that he is bound by that code of conduct, and

        (ii) the commitment is firm and capable of being verified and is not aspirational, and it causes or is likely to cause the average consumer to take a transactional decision he would not have taken otherwise, taking account of its factual context and of all its features and circumstances.

CPUTR 2008, reg 9:

9 Offences relating to unfair commercial practices

A trader is guilty of an offence if he engages in a commercial practice which is a misleading action under regulation 5 otherwise than by reason of the commercial practice satisfying the condition in regulation 5(3)(b).

8.147

Precedent for misleading action

Statement of offence

ENGAGING IN AN UNFAIR COMMERCIAL PRACTICE WHICH IS A MISLEADING AC-TION, contrary to Regs 5 and 9 of the Consumer Protection from Unfair Trading Regulations 2008.

Particulars of offence

X Limited, a trader, on [date] engaged in a commercial practice which was a misleading action in that its overall presentation deceived, or was likely to deceive, the average consumer in relation to [reg 5(4) matter . . .] by [the practice . . .] thereby causing or being likely to cause the average consumer to take a transactional decision which he would not have taken otherwise.

Falsity

8.148 Regulation 5(2) applies to commercial practices that 'contain' false information or are likely to deceive even if the information is factually correct. It would appear from this that the offence is one of strict liability subject to the CPUTR 2008 defences (mirroring the TDA 1968) that place the evidential burden of proof on the offender. The strict liability of the CPUTR 2008 offence is similar to the TDA 1968, s 1, albeit now covering both goods and services, which also did not require proof of a mental state[1]. It follows that the offence can be committed unknowingly. The test to be applied by the courts for a reg 5 offence is not the degree of falsity but whether the average consumer would have, in reliance, taken a different transactional decision based upon the false or deceptive information[2]. Where a trader misstates the consumer's legal rights – for example by including in their contracts terms which are unfair or otherwise unenforceable – this is likely to be a misleading action[3]. Further, it is likely to be misleading to make a claim that the trader is unable to substantiate because the standard of testing they carried out was insufficient. In civil proceedings under the Enterprise Act 2002, or in the context of an ASA adjudication, the trader may be required to produce the evidence of the testing for examination[4].

[1] *Swithland Motors v Peck* [1991] Crim LR 386 and *Alec Norman Garages v Phillips* (1984) 148 JP 741, *cf Cottee v Douglas Seaton (Used Cars)* [1972] 3 All ER 750, [1972] 1 WLR 1408.

[2] See *Motor Depot Ltd, Philip Wilkinson v Kingston Upon Hull City Council* [2012] EWHC 3257 (Admin).

[3] *OFT v Ashbourne Management Services Ltd* [2011] EWHC 1237 (Ch). See also *R v Christopher Whatcott* [2019] EWCA Crim 1889, where the defendant was prosecuted for seeking to enforce unfair penalties in his contracts. In this case the prosecution succeeded in proving Fraud Act 2006 offences, but the facts could equally have led to Misleading Action offences being pursued.

⁴   R *(Actegy Ltd) v ASA* [2019] EWHC 2374 (Admin) at paras 92–97.

Promises as to the future

8.149 The status of promises as to the future may be the same under CPUTR 2008, reg 5 as it was under the TDA 1968 because the essential question remains one of falsity or deception. Under the TDA 1968, promises that were genuinely made but not actually carried out were not false trade descriptions. In *Beckett v Cohen*, a builder failed to construct a building within an agreed period because he had run out of money. He was prosecuted under the TDA 1968, s 14(1), but it was held that the section had[1]:

'no application to statements which amount to a promise in regard to the future, and which therefore at the time they are made cannot have the character of being either true or false.'

1   [1973] 1 All ER 120, per Widgery LCJ.

8.150 However, in *British Airways Board v Taylor*[1] an airline confirmed a customer's reservation on a flight, but later overbooked the flight so that no seat was available for him. The House of Lords held that there may be an implied statement of fact in a promise: 'A statement of intention may itself be a statement of fact and so capable of being true or false'[2]. These two TDA 1968 cases can be reconciled on the basis that, in *Beckett*, the maker of the statement intended to keep his promise when the statement was made. In *Taylor*, the airline had no intention of maintaining the customer's seat reservation because there was a policy of overbooking.

1   [1976] 1 WLR 13.
2   [1976] 1 WLR 13, per Lord Wilberforce, p 17.

8.151 Where information is false, the fact that it is later corrected may not save it. In a German Federal Supreme Court case, a statement of a price for an espresso machine, on a price comparison site, was held to be misleading, when it did not represent the price that the seller would subsequently offer the item for, even though the price had been accurate three hours previously. A major part of the court's reasoning was that the consumer would be hooked in by the low price claim, and then fail to appreciate that the item might not be the cheapest when they got to the seller's own website[1].

1   Case I ZR 123/08 of 11 March 2010.

Deceived by its overall presentation

8.152 The second route by which the offence can be committed does not require the proof of actual falsity. It is sufficient that the 'overall presentation' of the commercial practice in any way 'deceives' or is likely to deceive the average consumer (in relation to a TDA 1968, s 11 matter). The test is by reference to the average consumer and the use of the word 'deceives' (rather than 'deceived') makes it clear that it is objective. It will not therefore be sufficient to demonstrate that the individual complainant was deceived if the reasonably well informed, observant, and circumspect consumer would not have been deceived (unless the 'targeted consumer' or 'vulnerable consumer' provisions have been engaged under CPUTR 2008, reg 2(4) or (5)). It should be noted that this concept is not the same as the English tort of deceit, and in particular there is no requirement to prove dishonesty[1].

1   *Competition and Markets Authority v Care UK* [2019] 10 WLUK 96 para 29.

8.153 This is a marked broadening of the protection that was afforded to consumers under the TDA 1968 that focused on actual falsity. It reflects the European Community's expressed desire for a high level of consumer protection by tackling traders that operate at the fringes of falsity. This protection allows a prosecutor to consider offences for the aggregate combined effect of all relevant information which may not individually be misleading or satisfy the transactional decision test.

8.154 The provision could provide extra protection from misleading omissions not covered by reg 6[1]. The misleading omissions provision requires the material information to be that which is needed by the average consumer to take, according to context, an informed transactional decision. The omitted information must have been necessary to enable an informed transactional decision to be made[2]. This is not the same as being likely to cause the consumer to take a different transactional decision. No breach of reg 6 occurs where a promotion leaves out information which might assist or be relevant to an average consumer's transactional decision. However, if that promotion, by leaving out the information, was likely to deceive the average consumer and cause him to take a different transactional decision, then there is the potential for a breach of reg 5. Further, the limitations of space or time are likely to be irrelevant when considering if there has been a misleading action[3].

1   See for example CJEU *Canal Digital Danmark* (C-611/14) paras 49 and 64, where the court seems to have expressed a firmer view that omission of important pricing information would be a misleading action, than that it would be a misleading omission.
2   [2011] EWHC 106 (Ch) at para 74.
3   CJEU *Canal Digital Danmark* (C-611/14) at para 42.

8.155 It follows that there may be a misleading action even where the representations made are true but misleading in their presentation[1]. Further, the use of small print to correct a misleading impression created elsewhere on marketing may not a finding of unfairness. Although in some circumstances consumers may look for the small print to clarify headline claims made, this is not a forgone conclusion. A court is likely to assess the expectations that the main labelling creates for the average consumer. It is unlikely that, where the headline claim is deceptive, small print will save it[2]. Examples of deceptive, though literally true, practices from the UK and in other EU Member States include:

- describing a credit product as 'interest free' when there is a cost of[3] credit;
- advertising tickets for sale when the trader cannot guarantee to supply[4] them;
- describing a product as 'travel insurance' when it only covers booking[5] refunds;
- stating a storage capacity for an IT product, which it does not have in practice due to the presence of other[6] software;
- misleading phrases in marketing which a close examination of the mailing would show to be[7] untrue;

- use of reference prices that are far in excess of the market value of work, in order to give the impression that the consumer is being offered a bargain not to be missed[8].
- 'up to' claims in respect of broadband speeds, which cannot be attained by most (that is 80%) of[9] consumers;
- including the price of holiday insurance in the total price of a product, when in fact the insurance policy was optional and not mandatory[10].
- offering a secure car parking service when in fact some cars would be parked in an unsecure muddy field[11].

1   See *OFT v Purely Creative Ltd* [2011] EWHC 106 (Ch).
2   CJEU *Bundesverband der Verbraucherzentralen v Teekanne GmbH* C-195/14 paras 36–43. Where labelling taken as a whole gives the impression that a particular ingredient is in a foodstuff, its absence from the list of ingredients in the small print will not prevent the consumer from being misled.
3   *Motor Depot & Wilkinson v Kingston upon Hull CC* [2012] EWHC 3257 (Admin) at para 33.
4   *OFT v Andreas Gyrre & Euroteam* (High Court, July 2012 unreported).
5   Italy – *AGCM v Ryanair* case PS7245 (17 February 2014).
6   Italy – *AGCM v Samsung* case PS9678 (19 December 2014).
7   Belgium – *Agence de Marketing Applique* Mons Court of Appeal 2011/RG/302.
8   *R v Martin Clifford Evans* [2016] EWCA Crim 2205 at paras 16–17.
9   Denmark – Danish Consumer Ombudsman Marketing Guidelines.
10 Czech Supreme Administrative Court Decision 1 As 59/2001–61 of 22 June 2011 *Blue Style sro v Czech Trade Inspectorate*.
11 *R v Asad Bashir Malik* [2020] EWCA Crim 957.

The eleven matters

8.156 The reg 5(2) offence can only be committed if the deception is in relation to one of the eleven 'matters' identified in reg 5(4). Further definition of these eleven matters is found in reg 5(5), (6), and (7).

5(4) The eleven 'matters' that may be the subject of a deceptive commercial practice		
(a)	the existence or nature of the product;	
(b)	the main characteristics of the product	This is defined further in reg 5(5) which states 'The definition of 'main characteristics of the product' include:
		(a) availability of the product;
		(b) benefits of the product;
		(c) risks of the product;
		(d) execution of the product;
		(e) composition of the[1] product;
		(f) accessories of the product;
		(g) after-sale customer assistance concerning the product;
		(h) the handling of complaints about the product;
		(i) the method and date of manufacture of the product;
		(j) the method and date of provision of the product;

		(k) delivery of the product;
		(l) fitness for purpose of the product;
		(m) usage of the product;
		(n) quantity of the product;
		(o) specification of the product;
		(p) geographical or commercial origin of the[2] product;
		(q) results to be expected from use of the product; and
		(r) results and material features of tests or checks carried out on the product'.
(c)	the extent of the trader's commitments;	
(d)	the motives for the commercial practice;	
(e)	the nature of the sales process;	
(f)	any statement or symbol relating to direct or indirect sponsorship or approval of the trader or the product;	
(g)	the price or the manner in which the price is calculated[3];	
(h)	the existence of a specific price advantage;	
(i)	the need for a service, part, replacement or repair;	
(j)	the nature, attributes and rights of the trader;	This is defined further in para 5(6) which states that 'In paragraph (4)(j), the 'nature, attributes and rights' as far as concern the trader include the trader's: (a) identity; (b) assets; (c) qualification; (d) status; (e) approval; (f) affiliations or connections; (g) ownership of industrial, commercial or intellectual property rights; (h) awards and distinctions'.
(k)	The consumer's rights or the risks he may face[4].	It should be noted that this is further defined in reg 5(7) which states that, 'In paragraph (4)(k) 'consumer's rights' include rights the consumer may have under ss 19 and 23 or 24 of the Consumer Rights Act 2015.

[1] For example, describing furniture as made of 'textile leather' when in fact it does not include any leather – German cases Urteil Az. I-4 U 174/11 OLG Hamm 8 March 2012 and Urteil Az. 3 U 219/11 OLG Bamberg 21 March 2012.

[2] For example, strongly implying that a rum product is from Cuba, when it is in fact not – Court of Appeal of Paris 10 May 2012, *Societe Havana Club v SAS Etablissements* (ref 10/04016). See also Commission Interpretive Notice C-375/5 on indication of origin claims on products from Israel and the Occupied Palestinian Territories, which may be contrasted with the UK Supreme Court decision in *Richardson v DPP* [2014] UKSC 8.

[3] For an example of an analysis of misleading pricing, see the CJEU decision in *Ryanair v AGCM* (C-28/19).

[4] A mere reference to the legal provision setting out the right of withdrawal may not be sufficient – see Prague City Court decision of 11 May 2015 *Bredley & Smith v Czech Trade Inspection Authority*. Likewise, offering a commercial guarantee which in fact duplicates the consumer's statutory protection was found to be misleading in Italy (decision PS7256 of the AGCM upheld on appeal – Consiglio di Stato N 05253.2015 Reg Prov Coll N 05096/2012 Reg Ric).

8.157 The eleven 'matters' identified in the CPUTR 2008 are deliberately broader than the list of essentially physical characteristics under the TDA 1968, s 2(1) that were a requirement for an offence under the TDA 1968, s 1 in relation to goods. It should also be noted that the list for (b) main characteristics of the product and (j) nature attributes and rights of the trader are prefixed by 'include'. This implies that the lists are non-exhaustive. Indeed, while there is no specific reference in any of the listed characteristics to the ecological credentials of a product, there have been numerous rulings and pages of guidance given on the application of the UCPD to so called 'green claims'[1]. They give, by choice of the words used, broad scope to the matters covered under reg 5(2). However, the matter should probably be included where, even though it is not directly mentioned, it goes to the main characteristic, nature, attribute, or right of the trader. The CPUTR 2008, reg 5 applies to 'products' which includes goods and services. It applies to prices[2] and, perhaps most significantly, to non-physical characteristics, such as motive.

1   See Commission Guidance [COM(2016) 320] s 5.1 on Environmental Claims for a comprehensive overview.
2   In its original form, the TDA 1968, s 11 (included prices). This was repealed and replaced by the Consumer Protection Act 1987, s 20 *et seq*. The pricing parts of the CPA 1987 were repealed by the CPUTR 2008, SI 2008/1277.

Non-physical characteristics

8.158 The CPUTR 2008 has introduced several non-physical characteristics into the definition of a misleading act under reg 5, such as a trader's motive for a commercial practice and after sale customer assistance. Its statutory predecessor, the TDA 1968, avoided characteristics that were not susceptible to clear proof, such as future promises or commercial motive. It is doubtful that real consideration was given to these less certain concepts when drafting the CPUTR 2008, which is largely a copy out of the UCPD. It is, however, important as the UK has opted for criminal enforcement. Such subjective concepts are likely to give rise to difficulty in trading cases, particularly when applied to complex corporate organisations (see also reg 6 misleading omissions, failure to disclose commercial intent).

Prices

8.159 The CPUTR 2008 applies to prices[1]. The CPUTR 2008 revoked Pt III of the Consumer Protection Act 1987 ('CPA 1987') which created the main criminal offences for misleading price indications[2]. Prices are now covered in CHAPTER 13.

1   CPUTR 2008, SI 2008/1277, regs 5(4)(g) and (h), 6(4)(d) and (e), Sch 1 paras 5, 6, 7, 15, 18 and 20.
2   The CPA 1987 had in turn removed prices from the ambit of trade descriptions in the Trade Descriptions Act 1968.

Confusing marketing and non-compliance with codes of conduct

8.160 It is a misleading action, under reg 5(3)(a), to market a product in such a way as to create confusion with another trader's product, so that the average consumer takes a different transactional decision. It seems that this is likely to require the average consumer to consider the product is that of the other trader, and so may not cover instances of so called copycat packaging where the consumer is not so deceived as to purchase the wrong product. An example of confusing marketing could be sending out invoices that mimic the other trader's branding, thus creating the impression that a service was rendered by the trader responsible for the invoice[1].

[1]   Swedish Market Court MD 2009:36, 19 November 2009. Another example was the use of yellow designs on the side of Gothenburg taxis, which mimicked the designs of another trader who had been providing taxi services in the Gothenburg area since 1922 (Swedish Market Court MD 2015:9, 11 June 2015).

8.161 Although not criminalised, reg 5(3)(b) makes it unlawful for a trader to fail to comply with commitments in a code of conduct, which the trader has publicly indicated he is bound by, where that commitment is firm and capable of being verified. Such a misleading action may be enforced by civil action, and may form the basis of a claim for redress by the consumer pursuant to Pt 4 CPUTR 2008[1].

[1]   *Bankia SA v Mari Merino* Case C-109/17 the CJEU ruled that the UCPD did not preclude national legislation (in Spain in this case) not providing for an individual contractual remedy for the consumer in circumstances where a trader has not complied with a code of conduct. This ruling was on the basis that the codes of conduct are voluntary non – compliance with which are not in themselves unlawful under the UCPD.

8.162 A code of conduct is defined in reg 2(1) as an agreement or set of rules (which is not imposed by legal or administrative requirements), which defines the behaviour of traders who undertake to be bound by it in relation to one or more commercial practices or business sectors. Examples could be the Property Ombudsman Code for Letting Agents or one of the other CTSI approved codes. It is likely that the display of the relevant code logo would be sufficient to satisfy the public indication test.

MISLEADING OMISSIONS

8.163 Engaging in a commercial practice that is a misleading omission is made an offence by regs 6 and 10.

CPUTR 2008, reg 6:

6 Misleading omissions

(1)   A commercial practice is a misleading omission if, in its factual context, taking account of the matters in paragraph (2)—
    (a)   the commercial practice omits material information,
    (b)   the commercial practice hides material information,
    (c)   the commercial practice provides material information in a manner which is unclear, unintelligible, ambiguous or untimely, or
    (d)   the commercial practice fails to identify its commercial intent, unless this is already apparent from the context,
and as a result it causes or is likely to cause the average consumer to take a transactional decision he would not have taken otherwise.
(2)   The matters referred to in paragraph (1) are—
    (a)   all the features and circumstances of the commercial practice;

(b)   the limitations of the medium used to communicate the commercial practice (including limitations of space or time); and

(c)   where the medium used to communicate the commercial practice imposes limitations of space or time, any measures taken by the trader to make the information available to consumers by other means.

(3)   In paragraph (1) "material information" means—

(a)   the information which the average consumer needs, according to the context, to take an informed transactional decision; and

(b)   any information requirement which applies in relation to a commercial communication as a result of a Community obligation.

(4)   Where a commercial practice is an invitation to purchase, the following information will be material if not already apparent from the context in addition to any other information which is material information under paragraph (3)—

(a)   the main characteristics of the product, to the extent appropriate to the medium by which the invitation to purchase is communicated and the product;

(b)   the identity of the trader, such as his trading name, and the identity of any other trader on whose behalf the trader is acting;

(c)   the geographical address of the trader and the geographical address of any other trader on whose behalf the trader is acting;

(d)   either—
    (i)   the price, including any taxes; or
    (ii)   where the nature of the product is such that the price cannot reasonably be calculated in advance, the manner in which the price is calculated;

(e)   where appropriate, either—
    (i)   all additional freight, delivery or postal charges; or
    (ii)   where such charges cannot reasonably be calculated in advance, the fact that such charges may be payable;

(f)   the following matters where they depart from the requirements of professional diligence—
    (i)   arrangements for payment,
    (ii)   arrangements for delivery,
    (iii)   arrangements for performance,
    (iv)   complaint handling policy;

(g)   for products and transactions involving a right of withdrawal or cancellation, the existence of such a right.

CPUTR 2008, reg 10:

10 Offences relating to unfair commercial practices

A trader is guilty of an offence if he engages in a commercial practice which is a misleading omission under regulation 6.

8.164

Precedent for misleading omission

Statement of offence

ENGAGING IN AN UNFAIR COMMERCIAL PRACTICE WHICH IS A MISLEADING OMISSION, contrary to regs 6 and 10 of the Consumer Protection from Unfair Trading Regulations 2008.

Particulars of offence

X Limited, a trader, on [date] engaged in a commercial practice which was a misleading omission by [practice . . .] which omitted material information, [namely . . .] thereby causing or being likely to cause the average consumer to take a transactional decision he would not have taken otherwise.

8.165 The criminal offence does not require proof of a *mens rea*, however it is subject to the defences set out in the Regulations. Consideration of a misleading omission is subject to the features and circumstances of the commercial practice. This includes limitations of space or time imposed by the medium used and, where there are such limitations, the measures taken to make the information available by other means. This has particular relevance to some electronic mediums. Traders may provide material information by other means where it is not possible to include it because of the 'intrinsic characteristics of the product'[1]. Where it is absolutely necessary to make information available by some alternative means, this is only acceptable insofar as the consumer can easily obtain the information[2].

1   CJEU *Canal Digital Danmark* (C-611/14) at paras 62 and 63. An example of where there may be limitations of space is where an online sales platform is advertised in print medium, and a large number of sales options offered by various traders are presented in that advertisement –it may be difficult to give all the information that is required about those traders and their products (such as their geographical addresses) – see C-146/16 *Verband Sozialer Wettbwerb v DHL Paket* at para 29.
2   C-146/16 *Verband Sozialer Wettbwerb v DHL Paket* at para 30.

Hiding

8.166 There is a clear distinction between omitting and hiding under reg 6. The verb to hide means to keep out of sight, to conceal, or to obscure. It follows that material information may have been included in the commercial practice but has been hidden. This is of particular importance if material information is buried amongst the small print of consumer contracts. The extent to which material information will be considered 'hidden' will depend upon the circumstances.

8.167 In *OFT v Purely Creative Ltd*[1] the court considered whether various pieces of information in prize promotions were omitted or hidden. In a prize award letter the small print stated that premium line telephone calls might take a maximum of 6 minutes at £1.50 per minute. It omitted to say that over 99% of all claims would take 2 seconds less than 6 minutes and, therefore, that almost all consumers would have to pay £8.95. The per minute charge was not hidden, but the actual cost was omitted. However, the actual cost was not misleadingly hidden since it was included in the small print. The small print was intelligible and the actual cost was identified by an asterisk that cross referred to the small print.

1   [2011] EWHC 106 (Ch).

8.168 For an alternative promotion involving scratch cards, the court considered 'by a narrow margin' that the representative quantities of awards were not hidden in the very small print. Part of the consideration was the limitation on

534

space available because of the scratch card format used. On the same basis, information on a cruise that was one of the awards was also not hidden. After having discovered that they had been awarded a cruise, the average consumer would take some trouble looking for the terms and conditions as they would not think an apparently free cruise would be entirely free of conditions.

8.169 Plainly some contracts are necessarily lengthy because detail is necessary in defining the contractual relationship. Important matters, particularly in relation to price or exclusions, should be communicated prominently in the commercial practice to avoid allegations that the matter has been hidden within the pages of the contract. For example, a telephone operator in Finland was found to mislead by omission because it presented the restrictions and conditions of an offer in small print and for only a very short time, in a TV advert. The Supreme Court of Finland held that nothing prevented it from presenting these important facts more clearly[1]. Likewise, a Hungarian trader was guilty of hiding information by informing consumers of their right of withdrawal by setting out the full text of the government decree. This contained conditions not applicable to the contract, and was not plain for consumers to understand[2].

[1]   KKO 2011:65.
[2]   Administrative Court of Gyor, Decision No K. 27.272/2014.

Unclear, unintelligible, ambiguous or untimely

8.170 The use of the words 'unclear, unintelligible, ambiguous or untimely' illustrate the breadth of the CPUTR 2008. It is unlikely that the word 'unintelligible' adds very much to 'unclear' or 'ambiguous'. If a phrase cannot be understood it will also be unclear and ambiguous. However, is 'unintelligible' to be taken literally or purposively? A primary purpose behind the UCPD is to remove barriers to cross-border trade. In this open trading environment there could be promotions in part or totally in a foreign language to the consumer. The words themselves may be clear and unambiguous but they might be unintelligible to those who are not fluent in that language. The court would have to consider the abilities of the average consumer to whom the commercial practice reaches or is addressed. The CPUTR 2008 repeats the UCPD benchmark of the average consumer being reasonably well informed, observant, and circumspect but does not repeat 'taking into account social, cultural and linguistic factors'. As the CPUTR 2008 implements the UCPD, these factors will have to be considered where relevant. Traders willing to engage in cross-border trade will need to make their offers and terms of business clear to all intended customers and overcome any social, cultural, or linguistic barriers.

8.171 The use of the word 'untimely' is significant when combined with the broad definition of transactional decision. The failure of a trader to mention an important matter, before a *transactional decision* is taken, could be considered untimely if the omission concerns material information. Transactional decisions may include decisions made by a consumer before he finally pays or binds himself contractually. For example, it is common practice for many businesses selling goods or services (particularly internet traders) to introduce conditions or extra payments at the end of the transactional process. Visiting a website (or engaging in the process of making a purchase) can amount to a transactional decision, so extra charges or conditions may well be untimely if they are only mentioned at the end of the process.

Commercial intent

8.172 The requirement for traders to identify the commercial intent behind a particular practice has the potential to be significant for any business dealing with consumers. The obligation does not apply if the commercial intent is already apparent from the circumstances, however, UK traders frequently do not disclose what is really behind a specific practice. A recent example is the widespread publicity concerning the provision of boarding passes at airports shops, where the traders' main purpose was to avoid paying tax, rather than provide consumers with discounts. Another unlawful practice is that of hooking the consumer's interest by asking them to take part in a survey, or other presentation, as a prelude to being exposed to marketing[1].

[1]   See eg the Polish Office of Competition and Consumer Protection Decision No RPZ 6/2015, against a trader offering a free health check as part of an 'I care for my health' programme, when in fact the intention was to present products for sale. The practice of inviting consumers to take part in a 'lifestyle survey' (sometimes referred to as 'sugging') may also infringe reg 21 of the Privacy and Electronic Communications Regulations 2003, where conducted over the phone – see the ICO Enforcement Notice issued against Change and Save Ltd on 6 July 2016.

8.173 It is additionally necessary to prove that the trader's failure to identify the commercial intent caused, or was likely to cause, the average consumer to take a different transactional decision. This threshold is likely to be important in the application of this provision because it can be argued the undisclosed commercial intention behind a practice is unlikely to affect a consumer's decision if there is clarity about the subject matter of the contract and its price. However, there may be situations where the consumer would prefer not to engage with a trader at all, if the commercial intent was disclosed – an example being where the purpose of a practice is to harvest consumer's personal data for marketing purposes, when this is not made clear[1].

[1]   See the OFT investigation into a company that offered a free psychic assessment as a means of acquiring personal information www.webarchive.nationalarchives.gov.uk/20100512141327/h ttp://www.oft.gov.uk/news-and-updates/press/2008/130-08.

Material information

8.174 The Regulations set out three categories of 'material information'. The categories are broad and necessarily overlap:

(a)   Under reg 6(3)(a), information the average consumer needs to make an informed transactional decision.

(b)   Under reg 6(3)(b), any information requirement which applies in relation to a commercial communication as a result of a community obligation.

(c)   Under reg 6(4), specific listed information when there is an 'invitation to purchase'.

Informed decision

8.175 A trader must provide all material information that the average consumer would need to take an informed transactional decision. In combination with the broad concept of transactional decision, this is capable of applying to any information that *might make a difference* to the average consumer's decision making, and extends beyond the decision to purchase to all other transactional decisions. However, it is unlikely that the test for materiality is simply a question of causation, as that might encompass information that it would be unreasonable to expect a trader to disclose, such as the lower price of a competitor. The 'concept of need' (see below) is likely to provide the courts with a mechanism for limiting the scope of material information within reasonable bounds. In making the assessment, a court must have regard to the average consumer's perception of the product being advertised, and all the relevant factors of the case, including what is set out in the advert as a whole[1].

[1]   CJEU *Carrefour Hypermarchés SAS* C-562/15 para 31. See also *Competition and Markets Authority v Care UK Health and Social Holdings Ltd* [2021] EWHC 2088 (Ch) paras 119–122, where the judge sought to assess how the average consumer would understand a price which is stated to be indicative, and concluded that the consumer would not expect it to include all possible elements of the price.

8.176 The German Higher Regional Court has decided that an unexpected condition limiting a 'lowest price guarantee' to a €100 cap should have been in a printed advert. In order to take up the offer, consumers would have to go to the company website where the condition became clear. The court considered that merely referring consumers to the terms and conditions on a website would not prevent a misleading omission[1]. The average consumer would not expect such an exclusion and it therefore became material information needed in the consumer's first transactional decisions as to whether to look at the offer further. Similarly, a Spanish court found that limitations on an offer of saving 3% on purchases with a promoted credit card were material, and should have been included in the promotional leaflet and not just in the contract terms[2]. Likewise, important limitations to insurance cover have been found to be misleadingly omitted when not included in the glossy advertising[3].

[1]   Germany, Higher Regional Court 2009, 6U 26/09.
[2]   Audiencia Provincial de Madrid Sentencia No 270/2014.
[3]   Polish Office of Competition and Consumer Protection Decision No DKK 7/2014. See also *Viagogo AG v Competition and Markets Authority* [2019] EWHC 1706 (Ch) para 4: the average consumer needs to know the time limits which apply to a trader's contractual guarantee, since this enables them to decide whether the protection offered is sufficient to justify using the trader's secondary ticket platform.

8.177 The CJEU has held that pricing information is 'in principle, a determining factor in the consumer's mind when making a transactional decision'[1]. For example, where a price comparison is made with a product sold in a different size or format of shop, this must be made clear in the specific advert in which the price comparison is made[2]. Further information about a product may be material, for example where a consumer purchases a ticket on the secondary market for a given price, the face value may also be material, since this enables the consumer to evaluate the quality of the ticket and to understand if they are paying a premium[3].

[1]   CJEU *Canal Digital Danmark* (C-611/14) at para 55.
[2]   CJEU *Carrefour Hypermarchés* C-562/15 at para 38.

[3]   *Viagogo AG v Competition and Markets Authority* [2019] EWHC 1706 (Ch) para 4.

8.178 There is no reasonableness test in the reg 6 obligation to provide material information. The focus is on the consumer's rights to have all relevant information, regardless of whether it is reasonable to expect the particular trader to have provided it. This may prove an onerous burden for smaller traders selling complex products remote from their manufacture. There is a tension between whether material information might have been omitted or just provided in an untimely manner. During a purchase, there can be a number of transactional decisions and the material information relates to that which is needed by the consumer at the time of each decision. For a complex purchase, such as buying a house, the information needed at the start of the process may be very broad and include matters such as location, the number of bedrooms, and the price. As the purchase progresses, the information needed to make an informed decision is likely to narrow to specific matters, such as when the wiring was last checked and whether there have been any problems with neighbours. Rather than remaining silent on an issue, it may be prudent for a trader to be open to expressing, and recording, that they do not know or possess the information. A trader that has failed to provide relevant information may still fall back on the due diligence defence in reg 17. However, proving the defence retrospectively in relation to an omission is often not easy.

The concept of need

8.179 In *Secretary of State for Business, Innovation and Skills v PLT Anti-Marketing Ltd*[1], the Court of Appeal considered the definition of 'material information' for the purposes of reg 6. In that case, the appellant company offered to register customers for a fee with telephone preference services in order to reduce cold calling. However, the company did not inform customers that the telephone preference service was offered independently free of charge to the public. Although the court declined to determine whether the company's practices were in breach of reg 6, it did give some guidance. In determining what is 'material information', the critical question is whether the average consumer *needs* to obtain that information from the trader. Information about alternative products will generally be available in the marketplace, but 'inward-facing' information about the trader's own product is likely to be only available from the trader. As a result, if the consumer could obtain the information by shopping around, then it is unlikely that the information was material. This is because shopping around for information about alternative products is characteristic of the reasonably well-informed, observant, and circumspect consumer. Furthermore, neither CPUTR 2008 nor the UCPD required a trader to disclose to consumers its mark-up or the cost of obtaining the product from a supplier.

[1]   [2015] EWCA Civ 76, [2015] CTLC 8.

8.180 In *Office of Fair Trading v Purely Creative* the High Court considered the extent of the information a consumer needed to make an informed transactional decision. Briggs J stated[1]:

'The starting point under English common law in relation to pre-contractual negotiations is *caveat emptor*. That may be qualified both by statute and even by the common law in relation to particular types of transaction, such as the obligation to disclose latent defects when negotiating a sale of land, and the obligation of utmost good faith on an applicant for insurance. Again, these English law concepts must be put on one side, not least because in systems of civil law widely used in Europe there exist general obligations of good faith in contractual relationships which have no parallel in the common law.

A literal reading of Regulation 6(3)(a) and its equivalent in Article 7.1 of the UCPD might suggest that something approaching an utmost good faith obligation is imposed in relation not merely to the consumer's decision whether to contract, but also to every transactional decision, such as, in the present case, a decision whether to respond to a promotion by post, text message or premium rate telephone call. Although qualified by the causation requirement to which I have referred, I regard that analysis as imposing an excessively high hurdle, and counsel did not suggest otherwise. It cannot have been the intention of the framers of the UCPD to require that level of disclosure, and to do so would indeed cause barriers to the free movement of goods and services beyond that necessary to achieve a high degree of consumer protection.

In my judgment the key to understanding this paragraph is the concept of "need". The question is not whether the omitted information would assist, or be relevant, but whether its provision is necessary to enable the average consumer to take an informed transactional decision.' [emphasis added]

[1] [2011] EWHC 106 (Ch) at paras 73–74.

8.181 The issue of need was explored further in considering the individual promotions in the case. The first transactional decision for the consumer was whether or not to respond to the prize draw letter they had been sent and, if so, whether to respond by premium rate phone line or by post. As the representative quantities of each award was presented to the consumer in the letter they did not need information on their chances of winning in order to decide whether to respond or not. What the consumer did need to know at this stage was the true cost of the premium rate phone call which in 99.9% of cases would be £8.95.

8.182 Other cases support the view that the true cost to consumers needs to be given up front. In a Dutch case[1] a telephone and internet package was promoted at a price of €20 a month. There was a €17 monthly cable network charge that was revealed on the website when signing up. The court found this information was needed by the consumer when they saw the advert or a consumer would consider they could have the whole package at a total cost of €20 a month.

[1] *Tele2 Nederland v UPC Nederland*, Court of Appeal, IER 2010/60.

8.183 The offence has two main tests, the concept of need in order to take an informed decision and the second stage of affecting the transactional decision made by the consumer. However, having proved that the information is needed in order to take an informed decision, it is unlikely that the omission or hiding of that information would not affect the transactional decision of the average consumer.

8.184 In the BERR/OFT guidance[1] to the CPUTR 2008 it is stated that:

'7.16 What information is required will depend on the circumstances, for example what the **product** concerned is, and where and how it is offered for sale. This may range from a very small amount of information for simple **products**, to more information for complex **products**.

7.17 The price of a **product** in most circumstances is material information. Therefore, failing to provide this in a timely fashion before a transactional decision is made is likely to amount to a misleading omission. For example, in restaurants, the prices of the food and drink available will usually need to be given to **consumers** before they order.

7.18 Material information includes any information which causes or is likely to cause the **average consumer** to take a different decision about the **product**.'

[1]   Consumer Protection from Unfair Trading – Guidance on the UK Regulations implementing the Unfair Commercial Practices Directive.

8.185 Examples:

A trader omits to mention that a contract has to run for a minimum period, or that the consumer has to go on making purchases in the future, this would probably be a material omission.

A trader advertises mobile phones for sale. If the phones were second hand and/or had been reconditioned, this would be material information, which would need to be made clear to **consumers**.

A trader operates a car park. If he fails to clearly display the price(s) of parking at a point before the consumer enters the car park and incurs a charge, this would be failing to provide material information.

A trader sells audio visual equipment. He omits to inform the consumer that a particular product includes an analogue tuner, and the implications in the context of the switch from analogue to digital-only television. This is likely to be material information that the consumer needs to make an informed decision[1].

[1]   The European Commission are of the view that where a trader is aware that a product is designed to fail after a period of time (so called planned obsolescence) this could be material information – see Guidance [COM(2016) 320] s 3.4.8.

EU obligations

8.186 Under reg 6(3)(b) 'material information' also includes 'any information requirement which applies in relation to a commercial communication as a result of an EU obligation'. A trader is obliged to provide a consumer with any information that is required by EU law in relation to commercial communications. It follows that this is not limited to obligations about commercial communication with consumers[1].

[1]   It is suggested that going forward this should be taken to refer, in the UK, to obligations set out in retained EU law.

8.187 The failure to advertise airplane ticket prices in accordance with the Air Services Regulations (a community obligation) constituted an unfair commercial practice[1]. The tribunal found it was irrelevant whether consumers had entered into a contract as a result. An advert that merely convinces a consumer to seek further details may be misleading, since the consumer has made a transactional decision to seek those details – even if he or she does not go on to buy a ticket.

[1]   Latvia – *Consumer Rights Protection Centre v Air Baltic Corporation*, 2009 E03 – REUD-54, Latvia Tribunal First Degree. See also CJEU *Ryanair Ltd v AGCM* (C-28/19).

8.188 It is not clear how much extra protection this requirement adds, as the failure to comply with a community obligation is likely to infringe the law that has introduced the obligation, however it may mean that the trader is exposed to a more significant penalty. For example, a failure to give notice of a consumer's cancellation right in a doorstep contract is punishable by a fine only albeit unlimited, whereas as for a CPUTR 2008 breach the trader could also face prison[1]. Likewise, some community information requirements may not carry any other criminal penalty[2].

[1] See *R v Michael Tolliday* [2015] EWCA Crim 603 for an example of a trader prosecuted under the CPUTR 2008 for failing to give notice of doorstep cancellation rights.

[2] An example could be the information requirements for distance contracts under the Consumer Contracts (Information, Cancellation and Additional Charges) Regulations 2013, SI 2013/3134.

Invitation to purchase

8.189 Under reg 6(3)(b), information is deemed to be material information when there is an 'invitation to purchase', which is defined by reg 2(1) (interpretation):

> "invitation to purchase" means a commercial communication which indicates characteristics of the product and the price in a way appropriate to the means of that commercial communication and thereby enables the consumer to make a purchase[1].

[1] The concept of invitation to purchase is also relevant to the meaning of banned practices 5 and 6.

8.190 In the OFT Guidance to the CPUTR 2008 it is stated that:

> '7.25 The following will normally be invitations to purchase where the product's price and characteristics are given:
> *   an advertisement in a newspaper where part of the advertisement is an order form that can be sent to the trader
> *   an interactive TV advertisement through which orders can be directly placed
> *   a page or pages on a web site where consumers can place an order
> *   a menu in a restaurant from which consumers can place an order
> *   a text message promotion to which consumers can directly respond in order to purchase the promoted product
> *   a radio advertisement for a mobile phone ring tone, which provides a word and number to text in order that the consumer can purchase and pay for (via their phone bill) the jingle to be uploaded to their device.
> *   a price on a product in a shop.'

8.191 The CPUTR 2008 define an 'invitation to purchase' as a communication that indicates the characteristics of the product (including its price) and thereby enables a consumer to make a purchase. It will be up to the courts to decide what information about the product and the price is sufficient for a consumer to make a transactional decision. It is clear that the communication does not have to appear at the same time as, or in proximity to, the actual opportunity to make the purchase. This was made clear by the CJEU in the *Ving Sverige* case[1]. A general description of the product with a 'starting from' price is likely to be sufficient to make the commercial practice an invitation to purchase[2]. The CJEU has also held that that a print advertisement describing various products

541

available from different traders on the advertiser's website market place platform can be an invitation to purchase, on the basis that there is pricing information given alongside descriptions of products[3]. However, mere brand advertising would not constitute an invitation to purchase[4].

[1] *Konsumentombudsmannen v Ving Sverige AB* (C-122/10) [2011] ECR I-03903.
[2] The Commission Guidance suggests that a visual representation of the product could be sufficient (COM(2016) 320, p 50.
[3] C-146/16 *Verband Sozialer Wettbwerb v DHL Paket* at para 25.
[4] See for example the Belgian decision of the Commercial Court of Antwerp *Federatie voor verzekerings en financiele tussenpersonen v ING Insurance Services* (29 May 2008).

Deemed 'material information'

8.192 When there is an 'invitation to purchase', all of the categories of information listed in reg 6(4)(a)–(g) are deemed to be material information (where they are applicable). The UK implementation of the UCPD makes clear that this set of information must be given *in addition to* any other information which is material under reg 6(3) because the consumer needs it to take an informed decision or because it is required by an EU obligation[1]. Omitting to provide the reg 6(4) listed information will not automatically be an offence, however, unless the failure to provide it would also cause a different transactional decision to have been taken as required by reg 6(1). However mere provision of this information may not be enough as a commercial practice may still be misleading (for example because the information is not given clearly enough, or because the practice also amounts to a misleading action) even if the invitation to purchase listed information has been given in full[2].

[1] For further discussion of this issue see CJEU Canal Digital C-611/14 at para 68.
[2] CJEU *Canal Digital Danmark* C-611/14 at para 71.

8.193 Especially important is the provision of fully inclusive pricing (ie, a price which includes all taxes and charges). The CJEU has ruled that what is required is the 'overall price of the product, and not the price of each individual component', and the trader is obliged to indicate the overall price to the consumer[1]. The position appears to be comparable to the requirement under the Price Indications Directive to state the 'final price' in advertisements for goods: this price has to include unavoidable and foreseeable components of the price, any components that are necessarily payable by the consumer and elements which in fact constitute the pecuniary consideration for the product[2].

[1] CJEU *Vincent Deroo-Blanquart v Sony Europe Ltd* C-310/15 at para 46. It follows from this that there is no obligation to give a price breakdown (see para 50).
[2] CJEU *Citroen Commerce GmbH v Zentralvereinigung* C-476/14 at para 37.

8.194 In two Polish cases, consumers were misled where contracts did not explicitly state the remuneration including tax. The decision was that consumers presented with net value contracts may consider the price to be beneficial and as a result were likely to be deceived. Price related information is a key condition enabling consumers to make an informed choice[1]. In the second case[2] a price given did not include VAT and was found to contravene the general obligation that all taxes should be included in all communications. Traders need also to be vigilant to include all additional charges. In another Polish case, a telecom operator failed to disclose an activation fee until after the contract was signed[3], and in a Spanish case, an internet service provider wrongly failed to include network charges in its advertised prices[4]. Similarly in a German case, it was unlawful for a trader offering holiday flats to fail to indicate in the price such mandatory costs as cleaning, city taxes and additional service charges for booking[5]. The CJEU has ruled in the context of cable television contracts, that failing to give equal prominence to a 6 monthly charge (in addition to the monthly fee) was likely to be misleading[6].

1   *Office of Competition and Consumer Protection v Grzegorz Daszkowski t/a ETNA*, Poland, 2010, RLO 9/2010.
2   *Office of Competition and Consumer Protection v Eko-Park SA*, Poland, 2010, RWA 25/2010.
3   Polish Office of Competition and Consumer Protection Decision No RBG 38/2014.
4   Tribunal Superior de Justicia de Madrid, Sala de lo Contencioso Administrativo Seccion 10, No 112/2014.
5   OLG Hamm, 06.06.2013, Az. I-4 U 22/13.
6   CJEU *Canal Digital Danmark* (C-611/14).

8.195 Where the nature or the product itself means that the price cannot be calculated in advance, then it must be stated how the price will be calculated. It is considered that this does not permit traders deliberately to create complex pricing, unless the complexity relates to the nature of the product. For example, an invitation to purchase minced meat in a butcher's shop may state the price on a per kilo basis, since by its nature the meat may be sold in many different quantities. By contrast the price of an airline ticket has no complexity which means it cannot be calculated in advance[1].

1   See CJEU *Ryanair v AGCM* (C-28/19) para 32, ruling that payment surcharges are foreseeable, because 'their application results from the air carrier's policy itself'.

8.196 Sometimes there are optional extras. These do not need to be included in the price, as long as they are genuinely optional. For example, where an airline operated a charging structure whereby different payment cards attracted different charges, the OFT considered that it infringed the CPUTR 2008 to fail to include the cost of paying by debit card in the headline price, because this is the payment method most prevalent in the UK[1]. The CJEU has taken a similar, and arguably even firmer stance, in the context of the EU Air Services Regulation 1008/2008 requirement to give fully inclusive pricing. It considered an additional charge applied to transactions made by people who did not hold a Ryanair Mastercard pre-paid card, and ruled that for a charge to qualify as optional, it must be capable of being avoided by every consumer, not just those who had obtained the special payment card. It must be a genuine choice whether or not to accept the additional services and the fact that even the majority of consumers can avoid the fee does not make it optional[2]. The CJEU also considered the practice of charging extra for checking in. It ruled that doing so is acceptable, and the cost need not be added into the headline price, as long as the consumer is also offered a reasonable, free method to check in. This is because it must be open to air carriers to offer a range of check-in options[3]. Likewise an airline cannot charge separately for hand luggage, but it may for checked luggage[4].

1   This is in contrast to the cost of paying by credit card, which the OFT considered to be genuinely optional, and so should be presented no more than one click away from the headline price, along with other genuinely optional add-ons. See the investigation case page: http://webarchiv e.nationalarchives.gov.uk/20140402142426/http:/www.oft.gov.uk/OFTwork/consumer-enfor cement/consumer-enforcement-completed/card-surcharges/.
2   CJEU *Ryanair v AGCM* (C-28/19) para 33–35.

³ CJEU *Ryanair v AGCM* (C-28/19) para 20–25.
⁴ C-487/12 *Vueling Airlines*.

8.197 The presence of an invitation to purchase also triggers the disclosure of the trader's identity and geographical address. This information is important so that the consumer can assess the trader's reputation, as regards the quality and reliability of the products and services it offers and also its economic strength, creditworthiness and liability[1]. This information remains required even where the trader is selling on an online platform which might well have its own branding.

¹ C-146/16 *Verband Sozialer Wettbwerb v DHL Paket* paras 17 and 26.

8.198 This provision must now be read in conjunction with the information requirements set out in the Consumer Contracts Regulations 2013[1], which implement the consumer information obligations in the Consumer Rights Directive, and also the prohibition on additional charges for items going beyond the trader's main contractual obligation. The information provisions in the 2013 Regulations are dealt with in CHAPTER 6, Consumer Rights.

¹ SI 2013/3134.

AGGRESSIVE COMMERCIAL PRACTICES

8.199 Engaging in an aggressive commercial practice is made an offence by CPUTR 2008, regs 7 and 11.

Regulation 7 provides:

7 Aggressive Commercial Practices

(1)   A commercial practice is aggressive if, in its factual context, taking account of all of its features and circumstances—
  (a)   it significantly impairs or is likely significantly to impair the average consumer's freedom of choice or conduct in relation to the product concerned through the use of harassment, coercion or undue influence; and
  (b)   it thereby causes or is likely to cause him to take a transactional decision he would not have taken otherwise.

(2)   In determining whether a commercial practice uses harassment, coercion or undue influence account shall be taken of—
  (a)   its timing, location, nature or persistence;
  (b)   the use of threatening or abusive language or behaviour;
  (c)   the exploitation by the trader of any specific misfortune or circumstance of such gravity as to impair the consumer's judgment, of which the trader is aware, to influence the consumer's decision with regard to the product;
  (d)   any onerous or disproportionate non-contractual barrier imposed by the trader where a consumer wishes to exercise rights under the contract, including rights to terminate a contract or to switch to another product or another trader; and
  (e)   any threat to take any action which cannot legally be taken.

(3)   In this regulation—
  (a)   "coercion" includes the use of physical force; and

(b)   "undue influence" means exploiting a position of power in relation to the consumer so as to apply pressure, even without using or threatening to use physical force, in a way which significantly limits the consumer's ability to make an informed decision.

Regulation 11 provides:

11 Offences relating to unfair commercial practices

A trader is guilty of an offence if he engages in a commercial practice which is aggressive under regulation 7.

8.200

Precedent for aggressive commercial practice

Statement of offence

ENGAGING IN AN AGGRESSIVE COMMERCIAL PRACTICE, contrary to Regs 7 and 11 of the Consumer Protection from Unfair Trading Regulations 2008.

Particulars of offence

X Limited, a trader, on [date] engaged in an aggressive commercial practice which in its factual context taking account of all of its features and circumstances significantly impaired, or was likely to significantly impair, the average consumer's freedom of choice or conduct through the use of harassment, coercion or undue influence, by [practice . . .] and thereby caused or was likely to cause the average consumer to take a transactional decision which he would not have taken otherwise.

The criminal offence

8.201 The reg 7 offence is one of strict liability, being defined by the effect of a commercial practice upon the average consumer rather than any necessary *mens rea*. Although the penalties for committing the offence are the same as for the other commercial practice offences, the label of an 'aggressive' commercial practice that can only be committed when the trader has used 'harassment', 'coercion', or 'undue influence' make it a more serious offence than those under regs 3, 5, and 6. The offence is subject to the defences set out in regs 17 and 18. The meaning of trader, commercial practice, average consumer, and transactional decision are considered above.

The threshold: 'significantly impaired'

8.202 The reg 7 offence includes a threshold that is absent from the regs 3, 5, and 6 offences. Before a reg 7 offence is committed there must be a (likelihood of) *significant* impairment of the average consumer's freedom of choice or conduct. The CPUTR 2008 follows the wording of Art 8 of the UCPD such that a distinct threshold for aggressive commercial practice was deliberate. This is perhaps understandable when the nature of the offence is considered and the potential stigma associated with conviction for such an offence. It seems likely that to be an aggressive practice there should be some active conduct by the trader, which in fact limits the consumer's freedom of choice[1]. However, it seems likely that the threshold is not particularly high for a practice to qualify as aggressive – for example in Latvia the use of pre-ticked boxes has been ruled to be aggressive[2].

[1]   Italian decision of the Consiliglio de Stato, Adunanza Plenaria – Sentenza 11 May 2012, n 14.
[2]   CRPC Decision No E03-PTU-K115–39 of 23 October 2013 against Air Baltic.

8.203 Sending a letter demanding payment where a consumer has exercised their right to cancel a doorstep contract may amount to an aggressive practice, as may including a confidentiality clause in a settlement offer to a consumer, as this inhibits people from taking advice and makes it more difficult for information to get into the public domain[1]. The concept of 'freedom of choice' has been discussed in a CJEU decision on whether telecommunications providers engage in aggressive commercial practices by marketing SIM cards preinstalled with services about which they had not informed consumers[2]. The Court ruled that it is essential for consumers to be given clear and adequate information about the fact of the pre-installation, and the costs connected with using the services and without this it cannot be said that the consumer 'freely chose' the services, even if the consumer could have de-activated the services, and even where in practice the charges might only start to be incurred when the consumer takes some conscious action.

[1]   *R v Waters & Westminster Recliners Ltd* [2016] EWCA Crim 1112 at paras 31 and 17–18.
[2]   *Wind Tre SpA* and *Vodafone Italia SpA* Joined cases C-54/17 and C-55/17 at paras 45–56.

8.204 The imbalance in information and expertise between traders and consumers in the electronic communications sector means traders must be especially diligent. Ultimately the Court considered that this practice also fell within ambit of Banned Practice 29 the prohibition on inertia selling- and was aggressive for that reason especially. All of the trader's sales channels must be examined to see the level of information provided, given that a telesales method might involve less information being provided than where a consumer shops on line[1].

[1]   *Orange Polska* C-628/17 at para 42.

8.205 Can a practice, where clear information is given, still be considered to be aggressive? This would seem to depend on whether the consumer actually has 'freedom of choice' namely if there are circumstances which prevent the consumer from refusing a product, it might not assist the trader merely to provide information about it. In this regard, the CJEU has ruled that it is important that the consumer has a free choice[1]. Where a trader uses practices – even where the consumer has full information – which have the aim of limiting the consumer's freedom of choice, this might be aggressive. For example, where a practice such as insisting on a signature makes the consumer feel uncomfortable and thus confuses his thinking, or where a courier announces that any delay in signing would lead to less favourable contractual conditions, penalties or risk the trader suspending the service[2]. Indeed in some cases, the act of providing the information may be part of the aggressive practice, such as where a trader encourages prompt payment by telling consumers that otherwise the price will go up: seeking to enforce an unlawful contractual penalty, which purported to increase consumers' liability for late payment from £9.95 to £14.95 and then £85, was the subject of a successful prosecution as an aggressive practice[3].

1   *Orange Polska* C-628/17 at para 34.
2   *Orange Polska* C-628/17 at para 46–48.
3   See *R v Christopher Whatcott* [2019] EWCA Crim 1889 paras 2 and 36.

Mandatory considerations

8.206 Regulation 7(2) (following Art 9 of the UCPD) sets out five factors that *must* be considered when deciding whether the commercial practice uses harassment, coercion, or undue influence[1]. These five factors set out features that one might commonly find in a genuinely aggressive commercial practice, such as threatening or abusive language. Although proof of one of the five factors is not an element of the offence, the absence of any of the reg 7(2) factors in the commercial practice may make an allegation under reg 7 difficult. This is because account must be taken of them when determining whether harassment, coercion, or undue influence is present.

1   The wording of SI 2008/1277, reg 7(2) has omitted the words 'including the use of physical force' from Art 9 of the UCPD.

Harassment

8.207 Harassment is not defined in the CPUTR 2008, other than by reference to the five reg 7(2) factors. It should be given an autonomous meaning, which is consistent throughout the EU, but by way of comparison it may be helpful to note that the term 'harassment' has a statutory definition in the Protection from Harassment Act 1997. The *actus reus* under the 1997 Act is 'pursuing a course of conduct . . . which amounts to', 'alarming the person or causing the person distress' 'on at least two occasions'[1]. However, a course of conduct will not amount to harassment if it 'was pursued under any enactment or rule of law' or 'in the particular circumstances the pursuit of the course of conduct was reasonable'[2]. Because the UCPD does not require a 'course of conduct', this definition suggests that the CPUTR 2008 may be infringed even if the harassing event occurs only once.

1   Reading the Protection from Harassment Act 1997, ss 1 and 7 together.
2   Reading the Protection from Harassment Act 1997, s 1(3).

8.208 By excluding conduct amounting to a pursuit under a 'rule of law', the 1997 Act excludes the pursuit of contractual claims and debt[1]. The rationale of this is that the 1997 Act targeted the particular problems of human stalking, anti-social behaviour, and racial harassment. Under the CPUTR 2008, however, the aggressive pursuit of lawful contractual debt etc is not excluded. This is clearly indicated by the fact that threatening to take action that cannot lawfully be taken is only one of the five factors in determining whether harassment, coercion, or undue influence is present, and put beyond doubt by the addition of reg 2(1A), which clarifies that demanding payment to settle a contractual liability is deemed to be a supply of a product to a consumer.

1   *Tuppen v Microsoft Corporation Ltd* (2000) *The Times*, 15 November.

8.209 In *Lisa Maria Angela Ferguson v British Gas Trading Ltd*[1] the claimant successfully argued that British Gas's course of conduct amounted to unlawful harassment contrary to the Protection from Harassment Act 1997. Sedley LJ stated:

> 'Parliament's intention in passing the Protection from Harassment Act 1997 was to criminalise the kind of serious and persistent unwarranted threat which is alleged here, giving a right of civil action as a fallback. In this situation it ought not to be left to hardy individuals to put their savings and homes at risk by suing. *The primary responsibility should rest upon local public authorities which possess the means and the statutory powers to bring alleged harassers, however impersonal and powerful, before the local justices.*'

[1] [2009] EWCA Civ 46, [2010] 1 WLR 785.

8.210 In *OFT v Ashbourne Management Services Ltd*[1] the threat to report customers to credit agencies had no basis because there were no credit agreements, let alone any breach of such agreements. Such threats were therefore aggressive commercial practices. Such conduct was harassment on the basis that there was a threat of action that could not lawfully be taken[2].

[1] [2011] EWHC 1237 (Ch), [2011] CTLC 237.
[2] See also the Italian decision of the AGCM that sending a notice to appear before a judge, who lacked jurisdiction, and had not received any application from the trader, was aggressive (Decision PS8215 no 24117 of 12 December 2012).

Responsible trading practice

8.211 The concept of harassment in the context of commercial activity is problematic because the enforcement of contractual rights, and in particular debts owed by consumers, is inevitably persistent and necessarily robust. If it was not so, many debtors would simply not pay. There is perhaps a fine line between the reasonable but persistent pursuit of a reluctant debtor, and harassment. The focus must surely be upon the reasonableness of the individual trader's conduct. But that remains a rather grey area in which the line has to be drawn. The factors set out in reg 7(2) are too general to help with many cases and reasonableness (on its own) is an uncertain guide to a tribunal's consideration of a hard edged question. One possible solution would be to approach the question of reasonableness on the basis of good practice within the industry. To decide whether conduct amounted to harassment, for example, the question could be asked: *was it reasonable having regard to the practices generally adopted by responsible practitioners in that industry* (in particular traders who are regulated or members of a reputable code scheme)? This approach would at least allow traders to avoid criminal liability by following responsible practice within their own industry.

Coercion

8.212 Coercion is not defined in the CPUTR 2008 other than by the express inclusion of 'the use of physical force'[1]. The ordinary meaning of 'coercion' is forcing a person to do something involuntarily by threats or intimidation. There is currently no guidance on its meaning from the CJEU. However, in the Polish case *Office of Competition and Consumer Protection v WEH Inwestycje sp*[2], a debt recovery business sent uniform letters threatening legal action. These letters were sent ahead of the process and were not legally permissible at that stage. The letters were not easy to understand and the purpose was to convince them to repay the debt. It deprived the consumer of making an autonomous and reasonable decision regarding payment. The business was putting willful pressure on the consumer and the letters were clearly written with the purpose of exerting pressure and using the consumer's inexperience and fear. The facts of this case certainly amounted to harassment. It might also be a marginal example of coercion, in that it involved using threats to force a consumer to act in a certain way. Another example of coercion could be where a trader makes it especially burdensome for customers to terminate their contracts, so that they become trapped in de facto automatic renewals[3].

---

[1] SI 2008/1277, reg 7(3)(b).
[2] 2010, RWR 32/2010, Poland, Office of Competition and Consumer Protection Delegature.
[3] Bulgarian Supreme Court decision of 3 November 2011 (15182/2011, VII d); Italian decisions PS1268 – TELE2 – ostruzionismo migrazione, Provv. n 20266 del 03/09/2009 (Bollettino n. 36/2009); PS1700 – Tiscali-ostruzionismo passaggio a TELECOM, Provv. n 20349 del 01/10/2009 (Bollettino n 40/2009).

8.213 Although not directly determinative in the construction of EU legislation, it is helpful to note that 'coercion' has been defined in other UK legislation. Under the Criminal Justice Act 1925, s 47 (now repealed) it was a defence for a woman to prove that an offence (except murder or treason) was committed, 'in the presence of, and under the **coercion** of, the husband'. This defence was wider than duress because it did not require threats of death or serious injury. In *R v Shortland*[1] it amounted to the wife being 'overborne by the wishes of her husband' so that 'she was forced unwillingly to participate'[2]. Coercing is also used in the Administration of Justice Act 1970, s 40 to define the offence of unlawfully harassing a debtor. It is used in conjunction with various modes (harassment, threats, or false representations) to mean forcing a person to repay a debt.

---

[1] [1996] 1 Cr App R 116.
[2] See also *R v Cairns* [2003] 1 WLR 796, coercion does not require physical force or the threat of physical force.

Undue influence

8.214 'Undue influence' is defined in the CPUTR 2008 as 'exploiting a position of power in relation to the consumer so as to apply pressure, even without using or threatening to use physical force, in a way which significantly limits the consumer's ability to make an informed decision'. It is now clear that this does not require proof that the trader has acted illegally, but merely applied 'influence which, without prejudice to its lawfulness, actively entails, through the application of a certain degree of pressure, the forced conditioning of the consumer's will.'[1]

---

[1] CJEU *Orange Polska* C-628/17 at para 33.

8.215 The reference in reg 7(3)(b) to 'in relation to **the consumer**' and to 'significantly limiting **the consumer's** ability to make an informed decision' does not use to the 'average consumer' test that pervades the CPUTR 2008. This is surprising because Art 8 of the UCPD suggests that the test for aggressive practices should be by reference to the average consumer, which indeed is the test that the CJEU has ruled must be applied[1]. Regulation 7(3) appears to be a domestic gloss on the UCPD, and the effect of the CJEU's rulings is that it should be read as 'in a way which would significantly limit the average consumer's ability to make an informed decision' in order to give full effect to the UCPD.

[1] CJEU *Orange Polska* C-628/17 at paras 30 and 34.

8.216 Given the CJEU's position, it seems it is not (when the allegation is purely one of undue influence) *also* necessary for the prosecution to prove that pressure was applied to an actual consumer (as well as the average consumer) so as to limit significantly his ability to make an informed decision. Put in the negative, would an allegation fail because the pressure did not have this effect on a particularly robust consumer, even though it would have had that effect on the average consumer? The answer to this question seems to be 'No', and it ought not be necessary to show that the actual consumer's ability to make an informed decision was significantly limited.

8.217 In the German *Gravestone Case*[1] a letter advertising gravestones was sent to the deceased's relatives shortly after a death had taken place. It was held that this was an aggressive commercial practice taking advantage of the circumstances. It could be harassment or undue influence, but the relevant factor was the exploitation by the trader of any specific misfortune or circumstance of such gravity as to impair the consumer's judgement (CPUTR 2008, reg 7(2)(c)). A further example of undue influence could be accompanying a consumer to a cash machine to withdraw money[2], or threatening to publish the consumer's name in a newspaper as a defaulter, in order to put pressure on them to pay a debt[3]. In the context of home repairs, it is an aggressive practice to demand upfront payment after work has commenced, and threatening to stop work unless the money is paid[4]. Examples envisaged by the CJEU include telling a consumer that any delay to signing a contract would lead to less favourable conditions, the risk of contractual penalties or the trader suspending the service, and also where an employee says that delay by the consumer could lead to the employee receiving an unfavourable assessment from his employer[5]. However the mere fact that a trader does not provide a consumer with their standard contract before the point of conclusion of the contract is not aggressive, where in fact the purchase was initiated by the consumer, and the terms and conditions are easily available online, and neither is it aggressive merely to ask a consumer to conclude a contract quickly at the point of delivery – assuming the consumer has been properly informed up until that point[6].

[1] Germany, Higher Regional Court, 2009, 6U 90/08.
[2] See *R v Derek Montague* [2015] EWCA Crim 902 at para 7.
[3] Slovakian decision *Krajsky sud v Presove*, 27 October 2011, 2Co/116/2011.
[4] *R v Morrison & Towers* [2017] EWCA Crim 2617 at para 21. See also *R v Christopher Maughan* [2018] EWCA Crim 1885 – aggressive doorstep selling of paving work, cleaning a small area of drive, but leaving a prominent section to put pressure on elderly victims to agree to the rest being done.
[5] *Orange Polska* C-628/17 at para 48. See also the facts in *R v Christopher Whatcott* [2019] EWCA Crim paras 8 and 36.
[6] *Orange Polska* C-628/17 at paras 38–42 and 45.

Undue influence: threatening legal action

8.218 In cases where the trader has threatened to take legal action that he has no right to take (thereby falling within reg 7(2)(e)), undue influence may be easier to identify if it passes the threshold test. *Ashbourne* and *Inwestycje* are examples of cases where such a threat was made. Likewise, failing to carry out a duty that the trader is obliged to comply with (such as to return a deposit when a contract is cancelled under the statutory right of withdrawal) is likely to be aggressive[1].

[1]   *R v Morrison & Towers* [2017] EWCA Crim 2617 at para 22.

8.219 A more difficult question arises when a trader merely threatens legal action that he is entitled to take. It is possible that this could be construed as 'undue influence' if the threat is disproportionate or unjustified, particularly as the trader is often in a position of economic 'power' in relation to a consumer. The real question must be whether the trader's conduct significantly limits the consumer's ability to make an *informed* decision. The threat of legal action does not limit the consumer's ability to make an *informed* decision if it is both justified and does not mislead the consumer about his own rights.

Threshold condition

8.220 For an aggressive commercial practice it is also necessary to show that the impairment:

> 'thereby causes him or is likely to cause him to take a transactional decision he would not have taken otherwise' (reg 7(1)(b)).'

Unlawful harassment of debtors

8.221 The Administration of Justice Act 1970, s 40 (the unlawful harassment of debtors) remains in force after the introduction of the CPUTR 2008, however, it does not now apply to anything that amounts to a commercial practice under the Regulations[1]. This is likely to confine its operation to non-consumer relationships.

40 Punishment for unlawful harassment of debtors

> (1) A person commits an offence if, with the object of coercing another person to pay money claimed from the other as a debt due under a contract, he—
> - (a)   harasses the other with demands for payment which, in respect of their frequency or the manner or occasion of making any such demand, or of any threat or publicity by which any demand is accompanied, are calculated to subject him or members of his family or household to alarm, distress or humiliation;
> - (b)   falsely represents, in relation to the money claimed, that criminal proceedings lie for failure to pay it;
> - (c)   falsely represents himself to be authorised in some official capacity to claim or enforce payment; or
> - (d)   utters a document falsely represented by him to have some official character or purporting to have some official character which he knows it has not.

(2) A person may be guilty of an offence by virtue of subsection (1)(a) above if he concerts with others in the taking of such action as is described in that paragraph, notwithstanding that his own course of conduct does not by itself amount to harassment.

(3) Subsection (1)(a) above does not apply to anything done by a person which is reasonable (and otherwise permissible in law) for the purpose—

    (a)   of securing the discharge of an obligation due, or believed by him to be due, to himself or to persons for whom he acts, or protecting himself or them from future loss; or

    (b)   of the enforcement of any liability by legal process.

(3A) Subsection (1) above does not apply to anything done by a person to another in circumstances where what is done is a commercial practice within the meaning of the CPUTR and the other is a consumer in relation to that practice.

(4) A person guilty of an offence under this section shall be liable on summary conviction to a fine of not more than level 5 on the standard scale.

[1]   Administration of Justice Act 1970, s 40(3A) as amended by the CPUTR 2008.

BANNED PRACTICES

8.222 The CPUTR 2008 create a series of banned practices that are to be regarded as always unfair (reg 3(4)(d)). These are set out in the CPUTR 2008, Sch 1 and follow the wording of Annex 1 of the UCPD, save that items 1–23 are given the sub heading 'Misleading Commercial Practices' and items 24–31 are headed 'Aggressive Commercial Practices' in the UCPD. The subheadings are missing from the CPUTR 2008. Engaging in a commercial practice that is a Sch 1 banned practice is made an offence by reg 12 (except for paras 11 (advertorials) and 28 (children's advertising))[1]. The crucial difference between banned practices and the other CPUTR 2008 unfair commercial practices is that they do not require proof of a causative element such as the objective effect upon the average consumer. A Sch 1 commercial practice will be unfair even if it would not cause the average consumer to make a different transactional decision. It is a closed list, and to be considered unfair in all circumstances, a practice must appear on the list[2].

[1]   It is important to note that to be liable it must be proven that the trader is engaging in a 'commercial practice'. Mere proof of the banned practice is insufficient – see C-391/12 *RL v S* at para 35.

[2]   CJEU *Orange Polska* C-628/17 at para 25.

Mens rea

8.223 Most of the criminal offences created by Sch 1 are of strict liability and the prosecution will bear the burden of proving each element of the offence to the criminal standard. Each offence will need to be considered separately, however, to determine its elements. For example, under reg 13, the prosecution must prove that the trader promoted a product so as 'deliberately to mislead'. The courts are likely to construe such criminal sanctions to require proof of a *mens rea* (see the analysis of strict liability offences in CHAPTER 4, Criminal Enforcement).

Scope

8.224 The scope of Sch 1 is relatively broad for a measure that introduces substantial criminal sanctions using general words or phrases, many of which have not been carefully defined. The drafting of Sch 1 follows the UCPD and is sometimes unclear, but nonetheless the guidance from the CJEU is that these provisions must be read literally[1].

[1]   C-428/11 *Purely Creative* at paras 35, 43 and 45–46.

8.225 Some of the difficulties in interpreting the banned practices may be illustrated by looking at para 9, which makes it a criminal offence for a trader to state or otherwise create 'the impression that a product can legally be sold when it cannot'. There is no definition of what 'legally' means for example there is no distinction made between criminal, regulatory, tortious, or contractual rules in relation to what can 'legally' be sold. The EFTA court has ruled that the infringement will occur when the trader omits information about any legal restriction affecting the sale, possession or use of the product, which is 'likely to contradict the legitimate expectations of the consumer'. This includes where it is illegal to own or use the product in any EEA state and where it is lawful to own the product, but where it may only be marketed and sold under certain conditions or subject to certain restrictions[1].

[1]   Case E-1/19, *Andreas Gyrre v The Norwegian Government* para 73–74.

8.226 On this basis, it is arguable that the prohibition in para 9 may be broader than the High Court found it to be in *R (Vuciterni) v Brent Magistrates Court*[1], where it was held that because it was not a criminal offence under the Copyright, Designs and Patents Act 1988, s 297A to supply decoders in the UK that were meant for the Albanian market that search warrants should be quashed. Once it was decided that there was no underlying criminality, the High Court considered whether the alleged breach of para 9 of Sch 1 to the 2008 Regulations was enough on its own to justify the grant of the warrants. In disagreeing with this Davis LJ said at para 33:

> 'As presented to the District Judge, this case connoted – and was intended to connote – criminal illegality. I find that difficult. Absent s 297A of the 1988 Act, the underlying relevant allegation in its essentials comes down to the claimants selling in the UK decoder cards which they knew were only authorised to be sold in Albania and were only authorised to be for domestic use. That scenario might or might not give rise to a civil liability. But, as at present advised, I think it very debatable as a matter of interpretation whether the word "legally" (by reference to what is "sold") as used in paragraph 9 of Schedule 1 to the 2008 regulations – reflecting the corresponding provision in Annex 1 to Directive 2005/29/EC – extends to such civil wrong doing: the more so when, by Regulation 12, a criminal offence is capable of arising from breach of paragraph 9 of Schedule 1. As put to Mr. Mellor in argument, if a shop owner is subject to a restrictive covenant in his lease not to sell, for example, meat and he, in breach of such a covenant, knowingly proceeds to sell meat to customers is it really to be said that he is in breach of the 2008 Regulations, with a potential criminal sanction? Mr. Mellor himself was disinclined to say that he would be. To the extent that he then sought to say that in the present case the purported sales by Alsat were "nullities", and so – he asserted – within paragraph 9 of Schedule 1, I also found that difficult. On the face of it, and whatever the contractual restrictions purporting to apply, Alsat had property and title in the acquired decoder cards (they were, for example, not stolen or counterfeit) and which on the face of it, it could

transfer to buyers. At all events, nothing was addressed to the District Judge to indicate that, at the very least arguably, something other than criminality under the 2008 regulations might be involved.'

¹   [2012] EWHC 2140 (Admin), [2012] CTLC 171.

8.227 The EFTA court ruling in *Gyrre* suggests that it is not the type of illegality (eg civil or criminal) that is significant, but whether the omission of information about the true legal position deceived the consumer in some way: in particular had they known the true position, would it be 'reasonable to assume that the consumer may consider not to enter into that particular transaction'[1]. This is consistent with the position taken by European Commission, that the prohibition applies both where a trader cannot give good title, and secondly where the product may be marketed only under certain conditions or subject to certain restrictions[2]. An example of the second is where a package travel product is marketed by a trader who has not lodged a guarantee deposit, as required by the Package Travel Directive[3]. In both cases it seems necessary that there should be some potential for unhappy consequences for the consumer, for the banned practice to be made out and mere illegality alone (such as where a trader sells items in breach of covenant to their landlord) will not be sufficient.

CPUTR 2008, Sch 1		Commentary
1	'Claiming to be a signatory to a code of conduct when the trader is not'. reg 2(1): 'code of conduct' means an agreement or set of rules (which is not imposed by legal or administrative requirements), which defines the behaviour of traders who undertake to be bound by it in relation to one or more commercial practices or business sectors.	This makes it automatically unfair to claim to be a signatory to a voluntary code of conduct for business, such as the rules set out by a trade organisation. Rules that are 'imposed by legal or administrative requirements' do not fall within the scope of Paragraph 1. It follows that it would exclude many professional codes of conduct (for example the Bar Code of Conduct) which are imposed by law. Many trade organisations require the trader to pay annual membership fees. The use of the word 'signatory' suggests that the trader's membership of such a scheme would need to be current. It is unlikely to be a defence that the trader was once a signatory to a particular code of conduct; or that he complied by its terms even though he had never been a signatory to it.
2	'Displaying a trust mark, quality mark or equivalent without having obtained the necessary authorisation'.	There is no definition of trust mark or quality mark within the CPUTR 2008 and it is broad enough to cover quality marks that are private without any legal basis. What amounts to the necessary authorisation will depend on the particular organisation and its rules.

CPUTR 2008, Sch 1	Commentary
3	'Claiming that a code of conduct has an endorsement from a public or other body which it does not have'.	This provision targets claims that a code of conduct has the approval by body, when it does not. 'Public or other body' is not defined in the CPUTR 2008. The nature of a public body in law is relatively well understood, however the construction of 'other body' is not. It remains questionable whether 'other body' might also include a private organisation. The language used in para 4 below is 'public or private body'. A question remains about whether it was intended that this would extend to a private company or individual; such as the claim that a code of conduct was approved by a particular company or famous individual.
4	'Claiming that a trader (including his commercial practices) or a product has been approved, endorsed or authorised by a public or private body when the trader, the commercial practices or the product have not or making such a claim without complying with the terms of the approval endorsement or authorisation'.	The example given in the BERR/OFT guidance to the CPUTR 2008 is a plumber claiming he is CORGI-registered when he is not (para 6.1). The expression 'public or private body' does not make it clear that the offence will be committed if the trader refers to an endorsement by an individual. It relates to where the rules lay down requirements to do with the status of the trader or quality of his products[4].

CPUTR 2008, Sch 1	Commentary
5	'Making an invitation to purchase products at a specified price without disclosing the existence of any reasonable grounds the trader may have for believing that he will not be able to offer for supply, or to procure another trader to supply, those products or equivalent products at that price for a period that is, and in quantities that are, reasonable having regard to the product, the scale of advertising of the product and the price offered (bait advertising)'. reg 2(1) 'invitation to purchase' means a commercial communication which indicates characteristics of the product and the price in a way appropriate to the means of that commercial communication and thereby enables the consumer to make a purchase'.	The elements of this offence are convoluted: (a) a trader; (b) made an invitation to purchase; (c) a product; (d) at a specified price; (e) without disclosing any reasonable grounds the trader may have for believing that he will not be able to: (i) offer for supply or procure another trader to supply (ii) those products or equivalent products (iii) at that price; (iv) for a period and in quantities that are reasonable having regard to the product, the scale of advertising and the price offered. The burden of proving all of these elements of the offence are upon the prosecution to the criminal standard. This compares unfavourably to the simpler Misleading Action offence under reg 5 (which includes the availability of the product reg 5(5)(a)). The only real advantage to pursuing a para 5 offence is that the CPUTR 2008 defences are not available. This might be particularly important if the trader blames the unavailability of the product upon a supplier. The BERR/OFT Guidance to the CPUTR 2008 gives the following example of an offence under para 5: *A camera firm advertises nationally using the line 'Digital cameras for £3'. They had only ever planned to have a very small number of such cameras available at that price. This would breach the CPRs because the number of cameras actually available for £3 would not be sufficient to meet the likely level of demand arising from the scale of the advertising and the trader knew this but failed to make clear in the advertisement that only limited numbers were available.*

CPUTR 2008, Sch 1	Commentary
6	Making an invitation to purchase products at a specified price and then: (a) refusing to show the advertised item to consumers, (b) refusing to take orders for it or deliver it within a reasonable time, or (c) demonstrating a defective sample of it, with the intention of promoting a different product (bait and switch). See above for the definition of 'invitation to purchase'.	The BERR/OFT Guidance to the CPUTR 2008 gives the following example of an offence under para 6: *A trader advertises a television in his shop window for £300. When consumers ask him about it, he shows them a model which does not work properly, and then refers them to a different model of television. If the trader intentionally used this practice to promote a different model (for instance one offering a higher profit margin), it would breach the CPRs.*
7	'Falsely stating that a product will only be available for a very limited time, or that it will only be available on particular terms for a very limited time, in order to elicit an immediate decision and deprive consumers of sufficient opportunity or time to make an informed choice'.	The elements of the offence require the prosecution to prove a very specific dual *mens rea*. The false statement must be made 'in order' to: (a) elicit an immediate decision; **and** (b) deprive consumers of sufficient opportunity or time to make an informed choice. 'In order' most likely implies an element of intention. The addition of a complex *mens rea* element will inevitably makes the para 7 offence more difficult to prove, particularly when the offence has been committed by a corporate identity. In most cases it will be simpler to prosecute using the reg 5 (misleading actions) or 6 (misleading omissions) offences. The BERR/OFT Guidance to the CPUTR 2008 gives the following example of an offence under para 7: **'A trader falsely tells a consumer that prices for new houses will be increased in 7 days' time, in order to pressurise him into making an immediate decision to buy'.** There is some discussion of the harm of having a practice of creating unnecessary time limits on sales in *Official Receiver v Wild*[5].

CPUTR 2008, Sch 1	Commentary
8	'Undertaking to provide after-sales service to consumers with whom the trader has communicated prior to a transaction in a language which is not [English (in the case of a trader located in the United Kingdom) or not] an official language of the EEA State where the trader is located and then making such service available only in another language without clearly disclosing this to the consumer before the consumer is committed to the transaction'[6].	The BERR/OFT Guidance to the CPUTR 2008 gives the following example of an offence under para 8: *'A trader based in the UK agrees to provide after-sales service to a consumer with whom he has been communicating in German. The trader then provides after-sales services only in English, without warning the consumer pre-contract that would be the case. This would breach the CPRs'.*
9	'Stating or otherwise creating the impression that a product can legally be sold when it cannot'.	The crux of this prohibition is where the consumer might be misled in some way about the true legal position, such that had they known the truth, it is reasonable to assume they would have considered not entering into the transaction[7]. 'Stating or creating the impression' is likely to include both positive statements and the impression created by the trader. In *Gyrre*, the infringement was made out where the illegality was operative at the time of the sale. The trader's understanding of the law was not relevant[8]. The BERR/OFT Guidance to the CPUTR 2008 gives the following example of an offence under para 9: *'A trader offers goods for sale in circumstances in which the consumer cannot legally become their owner by buying them from him, for instance because they have been stolen and he has no legal title to pass on. This would breach the CPRs'.* It seems unlikely that para 9 will be infringed where the the trader only (and not the consumer) may suffer adverse consequences as a result of para 9 is to casesa restriction on resale but the consumer will be unaffected (such as where a trader sells items in breach of a term of their lease)[9]. It is likely that this prohibition should be restricted to situations where there is a statutory restriction on selling a product[10].

CPUTR 2008, Sch 1	Commentary
10 'Presenting rights given to consumers in law as a distinctive feature of the trader's offer'.	The BERR/OFT Guidance to the CPUTR 2008 gives the following example of an offence under para 10: **'A stationer sells pens. He advertises on the following basis: 'Pens for sale. If they don't work I'll give you your money back or replace them. You won't find this offer elsewhere'. If the pen is faulty at the time of purchase the consumer would be entitled to a refund, repair or replacement under contract law. The trader's emphasis on the unique nature of his offer to refund or replace would breach the CPRs'.**
11 'Using editorial content in the media to promote a product where a trader has paid for the promotion without making that clear in the content or by images or sounds clearly identifiable by the consumer (advertorial)'.	A breach of para 11 is expressly **not** a criminal offence under the CPUTR 2008 (see reg 11). The BERR/OFT Guidance to the CPUTR 2008 gives the following example of an offence under para 11: *'A magazine is paid by a holiday company for an advertising feature on their luxury Red Sea diving school. The magazine does not make it clear that this is a paid-for feature – for example by clearly labelling it 'Advertising Feature' or 'Advertorial'. This would breach the CPRs'.* The CMA has taken enforcement action in relation to unlabelled endorsements of products on social media, whereby social media influencers promote products where they have either been paid, or given a gift or loan of the product, or have some other commercial relationship with the brand, but this is not made clear in the post[11]. The CJEU (post Brexit) has stated that the purpose of this prohibition is to preserve consumer confidence in the neutrality of editorial content and to avoid covert advertising[12]. 'Editorial content' is taken to be anything that is not clearly indicated to be advertising (paras 40–41), and payment covers anything of value (no matter how small) which is liable to influence the content of the publication (paras 41–46).

CPUTR 2008, Sch 1	Commentary
12	'Making a materially inaccurate claim concerning the nature and extent of the risk to the personal security of the consumer or his family if the consumer does not purchase the product'.	The expression 'materially inaccurate' is a different term to the other definitions of misleading statements in the CPUTR 2008. It is not clear whether it will be construed any differently to the tests in reg 5 or 6. The claim must be in relation to 'personal security'. This is not a term that is defined in the CPUTR 2008 but is likely to be confined to claims concerning personal safety, for example protection from offences against the person, rather than a broader meaning to include any risk of personal injury. The BERR/OFT Guidance to the CUPTR gives the following example of an offence under para 12: *'A trader selling video door entry systems tells potential customers 'There have been a lot of doorstep muggings in your street recently. There is clearly a gang at work in this area, and you will probably be mugged on your doorstep too, before very long, unless you purchase one of my door entry systems now'. If the risk of doorstep mugging is materially exaggerated the statement would breach the CPRs'.*
13	'Promoting a product similar to a product made by a particular manufacturer in such a manner as deliberately to mislead the consumer into believing that the product is made by that same manufacturer when it is not'.	The expression 'deliberately to mislead' generates a *mens rea* that the defendant intended to mislead, not only intended to promote a product that did in fact mislead. The prosecution must prove this to the criminal standard. The BERR/OFT Guidance to the CPUTR 2008 gives the following example of an offence under para 13: *'A trader designs the packaging of shampoo A so that it very closely resembles that of shampoo B, an established brand of a competitor. If the similarity was introduced to deliberately mislead consumers into believing that shampoo A is made by the competitor (who makes shampoo B) – this would breach the CPRs'.*

CPUTR 2008, Sch 1	Commentary
14 'Establishing, operating or promoting a pyramid promotional scheme where a consumer gives consideration for the opportunity to receive compensation that is derived primarily from the introduction of other consumers into the scheme rather than from the sale or consumption of products'.	The BERR/OFT Guidance to the CPUTR 2008 gives the following example of an offence under para 14: *'A trader operates a holiday club which offers consumers, on payment of a membership fee, the opportunity of earning large amounts of money by recruiting other consumers to membership of the club. The other benefits of club membership are negligible compared to the potential rewards of earning commission for introducing new members. This practice would breach the CPRs'.* The CJEU gave some guidance on this in *4finance UAB v Valstybine*[13]. It held that a scheme could only come within this paragraph if (1) the members of the scheme gave some financial consideration, but the amount of the consideration was irrelevant (and indeed could be de minimis), and (2) there was a link between the consideration given by new members and the compensation received by existing members. In other words, most of the revenue does not come from real economic activity. The CJEU has further confirmed that the link between the contributions by new members and the compensation paid to existing members need only be indirect to prevent evasion of the prohibition[14]. Examples of unlawful pyramid schemes include three Italian decisions where the compensation was based on the number of new sales agents recruited[15], the registration fee paid by new agents on joining[16], and initial subscriptions to a programme of personal purchases[17]. See also a Polish decision against a scheme where new entrants had to make a cash donation to existing participants[18]. See also an OFT/CMA prosecution of a Bristol based pyramid scheme, involving cash payments by new joiners[19]. Further discussion of this banned practice is contained in the European Commission Guidance[20].

CPUTR 2008, Sch 1	Commentary
15	'Claiming that the trader is about to cease trading or move premises when he is not'.	The BERR/OFT Guidance to the CPUTR 2008 gives the following example of an offence under para 15: *'A trader runs a clothes shop. He puts up a sign in the shop window stating: 'Closing down sale'. Unless the shop was genuinely closing down this would breach the CPRs'.*
16	'Claiming that products are able to facilitate winning in games of chance'.	'Games of chance' are not defined in the CPUTR 2008. It is likely that the provision was designed to cover only those games that are purely games of chance, such as lotteries. It cannot have been intended to criminalise any product that claims to be able to facilitate winning in games that involve an element of both chance and skill, for example card games. The OFT Guidance to the CUPTR gives the following example of an offence under para 16: *'A trader advertises a computer program with the claim: 'This will help you win money on scratchcard lotteries'. This would breach the CPRs'.*

CPUTR 2008, Sch 1	Commentary
17 'Falsely claiming that a product is able to cure illnesses, dysfunction or malformations'.	This provision will require the prosecution to prove that the claim is false to the criminal standard. This could prove to be a complex exercise in many cases, requiring medical evidence to be adduced by the prosecution. 'Malformation' is not defined in the CPUTR 2008 but has a medical usage that equates to a deformity or an abnormal growth or structure. It is likely to be relevant to look at this prohibition in conjunction with other EU legislation on sales of medication[21]. Examples of cases brought in other EU states include a Polish ruling on claims that a massage armchair could cure spine and blood circulation problems[22], and a Lithuanian case against a trader who claimed its products could reduce pain, improve sleep and decrease wrinkles, but could not substantiate its claims[23]. The BERR/OFT Guidance to the CPUTR 2008 gives the following example of an offence under para 17: *'A trader sells orthopaedic beds to the elderly with the advertisement 'Cure your backache once and for all with my special beds'. If untrue, his definitive statement about the curative effects of his product would breach the CPRs'.* The BERR/OFT Guidance goes on to say that: *'The court may order the trader to substantiate such a claim in proceedings'.* The CPUTR 2008 (reg 27) inserted s 218A (Unfair commercial practices: substantiation of claims) into the Enterprise Act 2002. Where an application for an enforcement order is made, the court, for the purposes of considering the application, may require the person named in the application to provide evidence as to the accuracy of any factual claim made as part of a commercial practice of that person if, taking into account the legitimate interests of that person and any other party to the proceedings, it appears appropriate in the circumstances. The court may consider that the factual claim is inaccurate if the person fails to provide such evidence or provides evidence as to the accuracy of the factual claim that the court considers inadequate.

CPUTR 2008, Sch 1	Commentary

18 'Passing on materially inaccurate information on market conditions or on the possibility of finding the product with the intention of inducing the consumer to acquire the product at conditions less favourable than normal market conditions'.	This is a convoluted provision. It requires the prosecution to prove to the criminal standard that the trader:
	(a) passed on;
	(b) materially inaccurate information on;
	   (i) market conditions; or
	   (ii) the possibility of finding a product
	(c) with the intention of inducing a customer to acquire the product at conditions less favourable than normal market conditions.
	The BERR/OFT Guidance to the CPUTR 2008 gives the following example of an offence under para 18:
	'An estate agent tells a consumer that he has recently sold several houses in the same area, just like the one the consumer is viewing, at a certain price. If this is not true and he is making the claim in order to persuade the consumer to buy at an inflated price, the estate agent would breach the CPRs'.

19 'Claiming in a commercial practice to offer a competition or prize promotion without awarding the prizes described or a reasonable equivalent'.	The BERR/OFT Guidance to the CPUTR 2008 gives the following example of an offence under para 19: *'A trader operates a scratch-card prize promotion with a top prize of £10,000. In fact, he does not print any cards that win this top prize (or does print the cards but does not make them available). As this would mean that no prizes of £10,000 could be awarded, this would breach the CPRs'.* A Czech court decision ruled against a practice where a trader gave the false impression that consumers could win a prize of a laptop, by participating in a lottery. However, no such prize could be won[24].

CPUTR 2008, Sch 1	Commentary
20 'Describing a product as 'gratis', 'free', 'without charge' or similar if the consumer has to pay anything other than the unavoidable cost of responding to the commercial practice and collecting or paying for delivery of the item'.	The BERR/OFT Guidance to the CPUTR 2008 gives the following example of an offence under para 20: *'A trader advertises a 'free' gift. He then tells consumers that in order to receive their 'free' gift they need to pay an extra fee. This would breach the CPRs'.* There has been considerable discussion of the application of this prohibition to combined offers. The view of the European Commission is that a combined offer is acceptable as long as the trader does not alter the price of the single item, or the quality of the product being offered. Further, where products are always sold in a combination, one part of that should not be marketed as 'free'[25]. Examples of practices found to have fallen foul of this prohibition include, offering a mobile phone for free as part of a subscription, but then increasing the monthly instalments[26], offering credit as 'free' when the consumer has to purchase credit insurance to get the offered loan, offering a buy one get one free offer when the price of the paid for item had doubled[27], claiming a social media service is free when in fact the trader's revenues are derived from analysing users' private data and selling targeted advertising space[28]. The EU CPC authorities also take the view that it could be contrary to this banned practice to describe an app based or online game as 'free' if in fact it is necessary to make in game purchases in order to play it as the consumer would reasonably expect.
21 'Including in marketing material an invoice or similar document seeking payment which gives the consumer the impression that he has already ordered the marketed product when he has not'.	The BERR/OFT Guidance to the CPUTR 2008 gives the following example of an offence under para 21: *'A trader sends letters to consumers with his marketing material which are or closely resemble invoices for a product that has not been ordered. This would breach the CPRs'.*

CPUTR 2008, Sch 1	Commentary
22 'Falsely claiming or creating the impression that the trader is not acting for purposes relating to his trade, business, craft or profession, or falsely representing oneself as a consumer'.	In order to assess whether the trader has created the impression, the enforcer may consider the 'overall impression' conveyed to the average consumer: is the information available, how is it presented, is it legible, clearly worded, can it be understood by the public targeted by the practice? Clear information is 'imperative for the consumer to be able to make an informed transactional decision'[29]. The BERR/OFT Guidance to the CPUTR 2008 gives the following example of an offence under para 22: *'A second-hand car dealership puts a used car on a nearby road and displays a handwritten advertisement reading 'One careful owner. Good family run-around. £2000 or nearest offer. Call Jack on 01234 56789'. The sign gives the impression that the seller is not selling as a trader, and hence this would breach the CPRs'.* In *R v Scott King*[30] the defendant advertised and sold 58 vehicles as a private seller, whereas the reality was that this formed part of his business activities. The reason that he did this was to avoid providing a guarantee or warranty. He was prosecuted for contravening paragraph 22, pleaded guilty and was sentenced to a community order and was made the subject of a confiscation order in the sum of £109,970. This practice is particularly relevant to the creation of online reviews, which a number of enforcement authorities have investigated. The CMA has taken civil enforcement action under Pt 8 of the Enterprise Act against firms that create fake reviews, which purport to be from consumers[31].
23 'Creating the false impression that after-sales service in relation to a product is available in [the United Kingdom (if the product is sold there) or in] an EEA State other than the one in which the product is sold'[32].	See comments on creating a false impression under banned practice 22 (above). A European Economic Area (EEA) State includes all European Members States and Norway, Iceland, and Liechtenstein.

CPUTR 2008, Sch 1	Commentary
24 'Creating the impression that the consumer cannot leave the premises until a contract is formed'.	See comments on creating a false impression under banned practice 22 (above). There is an overlap in this offence with a reg 7 (aggressive commercial practice) offence. The BERR/OFT Guidance to the CPUTR 2008 gives the following example of an offence under para 24: *'A holiday company advertise sales presentations at hotels. During the presentations, intimidating doormen are posted at all the exits, creating the impression that the consumers cannot leave before buying. This would breach the CPRs'.*
25 'Conducting personal visits to the consumer's home ignoring the consumer's request to leave or not to return, except in circumstances and to the extent justified to enforce a contractual obligation'.	The BERR/OFT Guidance to the CPUTR 2008 gives the following example of an offence under para 25: *'A door to door salesman visits a consumer to sell her some cleaning products. She tells him she is not interested and asks him to leave. He is determined to try and get her to change her mind and continues his sales pitch on her doorstep. This would breach the CPRs'.* This practice also applies to collection of legitimate debts, since it prohibits visits which go beyond 'the extent justified' to enforce the debt.

CPUTR 2008, Sch 1	Commentary
26	'Making persistent and unwanted solicitations by telephone, fax, email or other remote media except in circumstances and to the extent justified to enforce a contractual obligation'.	There may be an overlap with reg 7 aggressive commercial Practices. The BERR/OFT Guidance to the CPUTR 2008 gives the following example of an offence under para 26: *'A direct seller telephones consumers to sell them products, but does not record when consumers have explicitly asked to be removed from their contact lists. The trader calls back consumers several times, who have asked him not to. This would breach the CPRs'.* Note that a consumer who has signed up to the Telephone Preference Service is likely to be regarded as a consumer who does not want unsolicited telephone calls. The recent Commission Guidance[33] reiterates that this ban does not prohibit distance marketing per se, but rather persistent and unwanted solicitations. In an Austrian case an insurance adviser searched for reports of accidents and then sent letters to the victims offering advice. The Austrian Supreme Court ruled that sending a single letter to a person does not qualify as 'persistent and unwanted solicitations' within the meaning of paragraph 26[34].
27	'Requiring a consumer who wishes to claim on an insurance policy to produce documents which could not reasonably be considered relevant as to whether the claim was valid, or failing systematically to respond to pertinent correspondence, in order to dissuade a consumer from exercising his contractual rights'.	The provision creates an offence for an insurance company that deters claims by requiring the production of irrelevant documents by claimants. The language used is clumsy and makes it unclear whether the second part of the provision 'failing systematically to respond' creates a more general offence that applies outside the insurance industry. In our view, it is likely to create two separate offences, the second of which is not confined to consumers making an insurance claim. This is based principally on the use of the words, 'requiring a consumer who wishes to claim on an insurance policy to . . .', which cannot then be read grammatically with, 'failing systematically to respond . . .'.

CPUTR 2008, Sch 1	Commentary
28 'Including in an advertisement a direct exhortation to children to buy advertised products or persuade their parents or other adults to buy advertised products for them'.	A breach of para 11 is expressly not a criminal offence under the CPUTR 2008 (see reg 11). This is a surprisingly broad prohibition. The plain English meaning of 'exhortation' is capable of including both the process of exhorting and persuading or encouraging. However, the broadness of this prohibition is tempered somewhat by the requirement that such exhortation be 'direct'. The prohibition extends to exhortations to buy which made in games, which are directed towards children, or are otherwise likely to appeal to children[35]. The Swedish Market Court found that 'buy more', 'buy here', 'upgrade now' and 'upgrade to superstar' (where each of these involved spending real money in a game) were direct exhortations to children[36]. The OFT previously gave guidance (since adopted by the CMA) on what practices might be more and less likely to comply with this provision[37]. The Commission Guidance[38] provides further discussion of this banned practice and states that the assessment of whether something falls foul of the provision must be carried out on a case-by-case basis. The BERR/OFT Guidance to the CPUTR 2008 gives the following example of an offence under para 28: *'Advertising a comic book for children stating "read about the adventures of Fluffy the Bunny in this new comic book each week – ask your mum to buy it from your local newsagents". This (telling children to ask their mothers) would breach the CPRs'.*

CPUTR 2008, Sch 1	Commentary
29	'Demanding immediate or deferred payment for or the return or safe-keeping of products supplied by the trader, but not solicited by the consumer.	The BERR/OFT Guidance to the CPUTR 2008 gives the following example of an offence under para 29: *'A trader writes to consumers informing them of a new grease eradicating dishcloth which he is selling for £2.99. In the letter the trader encloses one of the cloths for the consumer to inspect and says that if the consumer does not return the cloth within 7 days then action will be taken to collect the £2.99. This would breach the CPRs'.* The CJEU decision in *Wind Tre SpA* and *Vodafone Italia SpA* Joined cases C-54/17 and C-55/17 ruled that this concept covers the pre-installation of internet browsing and voicemail services on a SIM card, where the consumer might be charged for using these services, yet they have not been properly informed of the pre-installation or the costs of using them. The consumer must have a 'free choice' about whether to receive a product to be said to have solicited it, and without 'clear and adequate' information, they cannot be said to have freedom of choice. It does not include the situation where a consumer is required to receive or pay for energy services by virtue of their occupation of an apartment in a block to which district heating is supplied. Their consent to enter into the contract for these services is inferred from their agreement to occupy the apartment[39]. It also does not apply to heavily regulated sectors such as water supply to domestic premises, where under legislation the consumer does not have the choice of supplier, and the legislation sets out how the supplier must structure and present their prices, and the consumer is required to pay for the utility that they have in fact used[40].
30	'Explicitly informing a consumer that if he does not buy the product or service, the trader's job or livelihood will be in jeopardy'.	It would appear that the offence is committed even if the consumer does not purchase the product. Whether or not the trader's claims are accurate is irrelevant.

CPUTR 2008, Sch 1	Commentary
31 'Creating the false impression that the consumer has already won, will win, or will on doing a particular act win, a prize or other equivalent benefit, when in fact either: (a) there is no prize or other equivalent benefit, or (b) taking any action in relation to claiming the prize or other equivalent benefit is subject to the consumer paying money or incurring a cost'.	There are two limbs to this provision – either there is no prize, or it will cost the consumer money to obtain the prize. An example of the first limb is where a trader stated in a letter to a consumer that he had won 18,000 euros, when in fact he had not[41]. The second limb was considered in *OFT v Purely Creative Ltd* [2011] EWHC 106 (Ch) where the OFT argued that the provision would be infringed if (regardless of the value of the prize) the process of claiming the prize involved the 'winner having to post a letter (other than a prepaid letter) or make a minimum charge telephone call or pay for a short bus journey to go and collect it from somewhere too far to reach by walking. This was rejected by the High Court on the basis that the critical requirement in para 31 was that a 'false impression was created'. The imposition of some clearly identified minimal cost was not sufficient to make out the prohibition. However, this was reversed by the CJEU (Case C-428/11, 18 October 2012), the first time that an Annex 1 prohibition had been considered by the CJEU. The court considered that all such practices are prohibited even when the cost imposed on the consumer is minimal (as in the case of a stamp) compared with the value of the prize, and regardless of whether the payment of such costs procures any benefits to the trader. The trader may not even invite the consumer to spend money, or offer any paid claim route, even if there is a free route available (para 50)[42]. The BERR/OFT Guidance to the CPUTR 2008 gives the following example of an offence under para 31:

CPUTR 2008, Sch 1	Commentary
	'A trader sends letters to consumers which, at the top of the letter in large characters, state: 'You have won our top prize of £3,000. 'This is false – only the small print on the back of the letter mentions that the consumer must buy a product before being entered into a draw for the money. This would breach the CPRs'.
	This guidance was provided before the *OFT v Purely Creative* decision.
	The 2016 Commission Guidance[43] further discusses this prohibition and some case law from member states. In relation to the first limb the Prague City Court found that a trader had created the false impression that consumers could win a prize by stating that everyone who participated in a specific lottery would have the chance to win a laptop computer when in reality no such computer could be won[44]. The Spanish *Audencia* case is also discussed[45]. Under the second limb the Netherlands Authority for Consumers and Markets considered the case of a mail order company that sent promotional advertising by post saying that a consumer was guaranteed to receive an electronic product free of charge. In fact, the consumer had to respond within 2 days and pay 19 Euros to cover costs. This was held to give consumer the false impression that they had already won a prize while requiring them to pay a fee and thus contravened paragraph 31.

[1] Case E-1/19, *Andreas Gyrre v The Norwegian Government* para 77–78.
[2] European Commission Guidance [COM(2016) 320, s 4.1.
[3] Swedish decision of the Market Court 2009:17, *Consumer Ombudsman v Casa Nordica* 26 June 2009.
[4] C-206/11 *Kock* at para 39.
[5] [2012] EWHC 4279 (Ch).
[6] Text in square brackets inserted by SI 2018/1326 and applies to practices which occur on or after 1 January 2021.
[7] Case E-1/19, *Andreas Gyrre v The Norwegian Government* para 77–78.
[8] Case E-1/19, *Andreas Gyrre v The Norwegian Government* para 73–83.
[9] *R (Vuciterni) v Brent Magistrates Court* [2012] EWHC 2140 (Admin), [2012] CTLC 171 para 33.
[10] See European Commission Guidance [COM(2016) 320, s 4.1.
[11] See CMA guidance https://www.gov.uk/government/publications/social-media-endorsements-guide-for-influencers/social-media-endorsements-being-transparent-with-your-followers.
[12] (Post Brexit) CJEU *Peek & Cloppenburg KG* (C-371/20) (2 September 2021) at para 29.
[13] C-515/12, [2014] Bus LR 574, [2014] 3 CMLR 33 at paras 20 and 34.
[14] CJEU *Loterie Nationale v Paul Adriaensen* C-667/15 at paras 30–32.
[15] AGCM PS6425 15 December 2010.
[16] AGCM PS4893 2 August 2012.
[17] AGCM PS7621 5 February 2014.
[18] Office of Competition and Consumer Protection decision No RKR 34/2014.
[19] https://www.gov.uk/cma-cases/prosecution-of-a-number-of-individuals-involved-in-an-alleged-unlawful-pyramid-scheme.

20 See Commission Guidance [COM(2016) 320] s 4.2.
21 See Commission Guidance [COM(2016) 320] s 4.3 for a fuller discussion.
22 Office for Competition and Consumer Protection Decision RPZ 2/2012, 13 March 2012.
23 2S-17 Lietuvos Respublikos konkurencijos taryba, 4 November 2011.
24 Prague City Court, 29 October 2014 *Golden Gate Marketing v Czech Trade Inspection Authority*.
25 Commission Guidance [COM(2016) 320] s 4.4.
26 Swedish Market Court joint judgments Dnr B 2/11 and B 3/11 11 May 2012.
27 2S-27 Lietuvos Respublikos konkurencijos taryba 11 November 2010.
28 Germany – *Verbraucherzentrale Bundesverband v Facebook* Landgericht Berlin Az. 160341/15. This case is similar to an Italian decision of the AGCM under Directive 84/450/EEC on misleading advertising, that it is unlawful to offer a service for free when in fact the condition is that the consumer's internet use will be tracked and they have to receive commercial communications – see PI2671.
29 Case E-1/19, *Andreas Gyrre v The Norwegian Government* para 75–76.
30 [2014] 2 Cr App R (S) 54.
31 See CMA case page at https://www.gov.uk/cma-cases/fake-and-misleading-online-reviews and also guidance in the context of social media influencers at https://www.gov.uk/government/pub lications/social-media-endorsements-guide-for-influencers/social-media-endorsements-being-t ransparent-with-your-followers
32 Words in square brackets inserted by SI 2018/1326 and apply to practices which occur on or after 1 January 2021.
33 Commission Guidance [COM(2016) 320] s 4.5.
34 4 Ob 174/09f, OGH (Oberster Gerichtshof), 19 January 2010.
35 The EU CPC authorities took the view in their common position on this matter that the prohibition will apply if the trader could reasonably be expected to foresee that the game is likely to appeal to children.
36 MD 2012:14, Marknadsdomstolen, 6 December 2012, *Stardoll*. This decision was relied on by the Norwegian Market Council, who ruled that encouraging Justin Bieber fans to purchase RIMI cards and concert tickets, was contrary to Practice 28.
37 https://www.gov.uk/government/publications/principles-for-online-and-app-based-games.
38 Commission Guidance [COM(2016) 320] s 4.6.
39 CJEU EVN *Bulgaria Toplofikatsia EAD* (C-708/17 and C-725/17) and see paras 68–70.
40 See (post Brexit) CJEU *Stichting Waternet* C-922/19 (3 February 2021) para 62.
41 Spain – *Audencia Provincial de Barcelona*, 26 June 2014, 323/2014.
42 See also a Dutch case where consumers were told they were 100% guaranteed to receive an electronic product, when in fact they had to respond within 2 days and pay 19.99 euros for 'administration and transport costs.' This practice was held also to fall foul of banned practice 20. Case CA/NB/544/10 *Consumentenautoriteit*, 21 September 2010, Garant-o-Matic BV.
43 Commission Guidance [COM(2016) 320] s 4.7.
44 Prague City Court, 29 October 2014, *Golden Gate Marketing v Czech Trade Inspection Authority*.
45 Commission Guidance [COM(2016) 320] s 4.5.

THE PRIVATE RIGHT TO REDRESS

8.228 The Consumer Protection (Amendment) Regulations 2014[1], provide a private right of redress in respect of certain infringements, where the consumer has entered a contract or paid money after 1 October 2014. It is a civil right enforceable as a breach of contract (reg 27K)[2]. It applies only to misleading actions and aggressive practices, and the practice must have an actual impact on the specific decisions the consumer makes, ie to enter a contract for the trader to supply a product to the consumer (or for the consumer to supply a product to the trader) or to make a payment to the trader (reg 27B)[3]. By contrast with the position under unfair terms, there is no obligation on the courts of member states to assess, of their own motion, whether consumers have been victims of unfair commercial practices – for example where this issue may arise in proceedings brought by a trader to enforce some contractual obligation[4].

1   SI 2014/870.
2   It is considered that absent these provisions, consumers have no other private rights of redress under the CPRs – see *Abbot & Ors v RCI Europe* [2016] EWHC 2602 (Ch) para 56.
3   Where the consumer supplies an item in part exchange for a product from the trader, this is treated as a business to consumer supply.
4   CJEU *Bankia SA v Merino* (C-109/17) paras 31–48.

8.229 There are five steps necessary to prove to establish the right of redress:

(1)   The practice is within scope.
(2)   It is a misleading action or aggressive practice.
(3)   It is carried out by a trader or with the trader's knowledge.
(4)   It was a significant factor in causing the consumer making the complaint to take a specific transactional decision.
(5)   It would have caused the average consumer to take the transactional decision.

8.230 Regulation 27A describes the scope of the redress right, including some exclusions (notably most immovable property and financial services). The requirement that the misleading action or aggressive practice must have a significant impact on the consumer's decision making is set out in reg 27A(6). It does not have to be the only or main cause, but it should be possible to describe how the practice changed the consumer's decision making, and what they would have done otherwise. The requirement to prove the impact on the average consumer is because this is necessary to prove the breach of the CPUTR 2008 in the first place. Depending on the circumstances, it may also be relevant to consider the impact on the average vulnerable or targeted consumer – if the complainant is within one of these categories.

The rights

8.231 Where the consumer establishes that they have a right to redress, these rights are the right to unwind the contract, the right to a discount and the right to damages. Bringing a claim under these provisions exhausts all other rights the consumer might otherwise have against the trader. In order to unwind a contract, the consumer must clearly indicate that the contract is at an end, and the effect is to release both parties from their obligations.

8.232 Where the trader has supplied goods to the consumer:

- The right is only available if the product remains capable of rejection – so not fully consumed or fully performed[1] – and if the consumer has not already exercised their right to a discount.
- The consumer must reject the product within 90 days of delivery or start of performance.
- Any goods must be made available for the trader to collect.
- The trader must refund the consumer any money, and restore any item the consumer has given them, in its original state, or by paying the market price if this is not possible[2].

1   SI 2014/870, reg 27E.

[2] SI 2014/870, reg 27F.

8.233 Where the consumer has supplied an item to the trader:

- The trader must return the goods, unless he is not able to, in which case he must pay the amount by which the market price exceeds the price he paid.
- The consumer must pay back any money they received[1].

[1] SI 2014/870, reg 27G.

8.234 The right to a discount applies where the right to unwind is lost, or not used, and the contract continues to exist. For most contracts involving payments of less than £5,000, it requires an assessment of the seriousness of the practice in order to identify how much the consumer should be reimbursed. The position envisaged by the legislation is that reimbursement will be on a fixed scale of 25% if it is more than minor, 50% if significant, 75% if serious and 100% if very serious. The assessment of seriousness is based on a consideration of the behaviour of the trader, the impact on the consumer and the time elapsed since the practice took place[1].

[1] SI 2014/870, reg 27I.

8.235 Where the contract price is above £5,000, and there is clear evidence of what the market price actually was, the discount must equate to whatever this difference is. So for example if a trader sold a consumer a mobility aid for £6,500, but in fact the market value of that mobility aid was only £3,000 (and there is clear evidence of this), then the right to a discount would be £3,500. If, however, there is not clear evidence of what the market price should be, then it would seem the normal rules would apply, and the discount could be up to 100%.

8.236 The right to damages applies in addition to the rights to unwind or get a refund. It applies where:

- the prohibited practice causes financial loss (beyond that incurred in entering the contract) or alarm, distress or physical inconvenience or discomfort; and
- this harm was reasonably foreseeable at the time of the practice; and
- the trader is unable to prove the due diligence defence set out in reg 27J(5).

Although not set out in the legislation, the government guidance on the right of redress expects these damages to be 'restrained and modest'.

DEFENCES UNDER THE CPUTR 2008

8.237 CPUTR 2008, regs 17, 18:

17 Due diligence defence

   (1)   In any proceedings against a person for an offence under regulation 9, 10, 11 or 12 it is a defence for that person to prove—

        (a)   that the commission of the offence was due to—

            (i)   a mistake;

(ii)   reliance on information supplied to him by another person;
(iii)   the act or default of another person;
(iv)   an accident; or
(v)   another cause beyond his control; and

(b)   that he took all reasonable precautions and exercised all due diligence to avoid the commission of such an offence by himself or any person under his control.

(2)   A person shall not be entitled to rely on the defence provided by paragraph (1) by reason of the matters referred to in paragraph (ii) or (iii) of paragraph (1)(a) without leave of the court unless—

(a)   he has served on the prosecutor a notice in writing giving such information identifying or assisting in the identification of that other person as was in his possession; and

(b)   the notice is served on the prosecutor at least seven clear days before the date of the hearing.

18 Innocent publication of advertisement defence

(1)   In any proceedings against a person for an offence under regulation 9, 10, 11 or 12 committed by the publication of an advertisement it shall be a defence for a person to prove that—

(a)   he is a person whose business it is to publish or to arrange for the publication of advertisements;

(b)   he received the advertisement for publication in the ordinary course of business; and

(c)   he did not know and had no reason to suspect that its publication would amount to an offence under the regulation to which the proceedings relate.

(2)   In paragraph (1) "advertisement" includes a catalogue, a circular and a price list.

The reg 17 defence is now considered in CHAPTER 4, Criminal Enforcement.

SENTENCING UNDER THE CPUTR 2008

8.238 CPUTR 2008, reg 13 provides that:

A person guilty of an offence under regulations 8, 9, 10, 11 or 12 shall be liable—

(a)   on summary conviction, to a fine not exceeding the statutory maximum; or
(b)   on conviction on indictment, to a fine or imprisonment for a term not exceeding two years or both.

It should be noted that the statutory limit on fines imposed after summary conviction was removed by the Legal Aid, Sentencing and Punishment of Offenders Act 2012, s 85. Consequently, on summary conviction offenders now face an unlimited fine.

8.239 There will still be many cases that are suitable for summary disposal in the magistrates' courts. However, where a commercial practice has affected a large number of consumers, or where the behaviour was systemic, coercive, or dishonest, significant sentences can be expected from the Crown Court. There are no guidelines from the Sentencing Guidelines Council in relation to CPUTR 2008 offences, but the Court of Appeal (Criminal Division) has now given some guidance as to the sorts of sentences that may be appropriate through a range of appeal decisions, as well as giving some guidance on general principles. In *R v Stone*[1] it was held that the Sentencing Guidelines for Fraud should not be applied to sentencing under the CPUTR 2008 because the guidance was predicated upon dishonesty, which is not an essential ingredient for CPUTR 2008. In *R v Morrison and Towers*[2] it was ruled that it is appropriate for judges, having considered the criminal conduct in the round, to seek to achieve an overall result which is just and reasonable (in that case 5 years custody for aggressive and misleading selling of substandard driveway work, which involved targeting and bullying of elderly customers over 2 years). In order to do this, it is right to add up the sentences for each offence committed at a different time and consider whether the aggregate length is proportionate[3]. It is also anticipated that (particularly in cases involving large corporate defendants) the courts will adopt a similar approach to that mandated in the sentencing guidelines on health and safety offences, corporate manslaughter, and food safety and hygiene offences. In cases involving a corporate defendant it may also be appropriate to disqualify one or more of the directors. If so, it is important to identify the precise misconduct which justifies this, for example a failure to supervise properly. The mere fact of breach of the CPUTR 2008 alone may not suffice[4].

[1] *R v Stone* and *R v Moore* [2012] EWCA Civ 186.
[2] [2017] EWCA Crim 2617 at paras 36–44.
[3] See in particular the *Definitive Guideline for Offences Taken into Consideration and Totality* (June 2012).
[4] *R v Lloyd Chandler* [2015] EWCA Crim 1825.

8.240 The largest fine imposed under CPUTR 2008 is £1.2m by the Recorder of Guildford in *R v Scottish and Southern Energy PLC*[1]. The facts of this case are set out in the section above on 'scope of commercial practice'. This is a paradigm example of the level of punishment that might be expected for an unfair commercial practice that affected a large number of consumers. In this case, the judge imposed a sentence of this magnitude because the offending script had been used in doorstep sales presentations to 300,000 consumers.

[1] [2012] CTLC 1.

8.241 In *Henry and Victor Mears*[1] the defendants were found guilty of eight offences under CPUTR 2008 following a 10-week trial at Bristol Crown Court in relation to the 'Lapland New Forest'. Both men were sentenced to 13 months' imprisonment and also disqualified for a period of 5 years under the Company Directors Disqualification Act 1986. The Mears were charged with misleading acts contrary to reg 9 and misleading omissions contrary to reg 10 on the grounds that they had allowed the company to give descriptions of various features of the attraction in its advertising material that were either not present at all or which fell far short of what was actually provided. Trading standards officers viewed the company's website, obtained advertising material from local shops, and visited the attraction itself. They considered that the descriptions given in the advertisements were misleading in various respects. This case went to the Court of Appeal (Criminal Division)[2], where the conviction was quashed as a result of jury irregularity.

[1] Before HHJ Horton and a jury [2011] EWCA Crim 2651.
[2] [2011] EWCA Crim 2651, (2011) 108(45) LSG 21.

8.242 In the case of *R v John Lawrence Connolly*[1] a director of a company called Homesure Home Improvements Ltd, which was in the business of replacement windows and doors, was sentenced to 5 months' imprisonment for two CPUTR 2008 offences, including a month's imprisonment for breaching a 2 year conditional discharge for a CPUTR 2008 offence. He was also disqualified for 5 years under the Company Directors Disqualification Act 1986. Both offences involved the use of aggressive tactics during disputes over the quality of his company's jobs. In one instance, he had instructed the fitters to remove the windows unless the customer paid in full. The customer paid, feeling that he had no option. The judge in sentencing found that an incident involving an old age pensioner was an aggressive practice. The trader had demanded payment there and then and put fear into the customer by saying that, if payment was not made, the customer's home would be left without the door and fittings. A similar incident occurred involving a second victim. The tactic of 'pay up or shut up', as the judge described it, was a mean spirited and cruel way to conduct business. The judge, in concluding his sentencing remarks, said: 'This defendant . . . is unfit to be a director in my view and he was responsible for issuing the rather cruel instructions of removing the property. I am told that was on a misunderstanding. I don't think it was at all, it is just called bullying. "Pay up and shut up", that was the manner in which business was conducted by his employees on his direct instruction'. On appeal against sentence, Dobbs J said: 'Looking at the overall sentence and the mitigation, in our judgment, the sentence whilst tough and intentionally so cannot be said to be manifestly excessive. It follows therefore that this appeal against sentence must fail'.

[1] [2012] EWCA Crim 477, Official Transcript.

8.243 In *R v Williams and Stagg*[1] the defendants were charged with offences relating to car clamping activities which involved the extortion of considerable sums of money from members of the public whose vehicles they had clamped by bullying and threatening behaviour. Williams also pleaded guilty to an offence under the CPUTR 2008, contrary to reg 11 and was given a total sentence of 5 years and 6 months' imprisonment (including CPUTR 2008 offence, one year's imprisonment to be served concurrently). On appeal the sentence of 4 years for conspiracy was quashed, and in its place a sentence of 3 years' imprisonment imposed. However, the remaining sentences stood, including the one in respect of the CPUTR 2008 offence.

[1] [2012] EWCA Crim 1483, [2013] 1 Cr App R (S) 70.

8.244 In a case prosecuted by the OFT, Colin Michael Ogle pleaded guilty to five charges under the CPUTR 2008 and eight charges under the Fraud Act 2006, s 2 in relation to his business offering a 'mileage adjustment service'. Ogle also agreed to a further 19 offences being taken into consideration. The matter was committed to Swindon Crown Court[1] for sentence where Ogle was jailed for 9 months. The sentencing judge said:

> 'The second-hand car market affects us all. Mileage significantly affects the market. Consumers rely on mileage when making purchasing decisions. It is the second biggest purchase consumers make after property and for others it is the single biggest purchase. The clocking of cars corrupts the market and brings unjustified suspicion on honest traders.'

[1] His Honour Judge Ambrose.

8.245 In the first private prosecution under the CPUTR 2008 (*House of Cars v Derby Car and Van Contracts Ltd*[1]), an internet car broker pleaded guilty to engaging in a commercial practice that was a misleading omission and was fined £500 and ordered to pay £3,000 in prosecution costs. The defendant sold cars to consumers but registered them initially in the name and address of a third party company in order to obtain a 'fleet car' discount from the car manufacturer. A consumer that purchased a car from the defendants would own and use the car from the outset, however the vehicle would not be DVLA registered in the consumer's name and address until a period of 4 to 6 months had elapsed. The defendant failed to warn purchasers that during this period they were at risk of being prosecuted for an offence under the Vehicle Excise and Registration Act 1994, s 43C or that a claim made against a car insurance policy might be prejudiced by the commercial practice. The defendant argued that no offence was committed under s 43C and that the risk of insurance being prejudiced was notional. The judge indicated the future sentences would be much higher because the unlawfulness was now no longer novel.

[1]   [2012] CTLC 62.

8.246 In *R v Garfoot and Wilsher*[1] Henry Wilsher was a traveller who resided on a caravan park and ran a business, trading as H W Block Paving and Landscaping Specialists. Wilsher was concerned that, if he informed customers of the true business address, they would, prejudicially, not employ him, so he asked his employee, John Garfoot, if he could use his address for the business instead. Garfoot agreed. Flyers were produced bearing this false address and an unregistered pay-as-you-go phone number. Prosecutions were brought by Leicester City Trading Standards in connection with two separate transactions, where the complainants were an 85-year-old woman and (concerning Wilsher alone) a 75-year-old man. Garfoot pleaded guilty to three offences involving his single incident. He was sentenced to 6 months' imprisonment for an offence under CPUTR 2008, reg 8 (in respect of the fact that no cancellation rights were explained or communicated); no separate penalty was passed in respect of two charges of fraud (dishonestly made representations as to the location of the business which gave a false impression as to its pedigree and reputation). The central figure responsible, Wilsher – who had previously been warned by trading standards officers in 2006 and 2007 – was sentenced to 10 months' imprisonment (to run concurrently) for two similar reg 8 matters. Again, no separate penalty was imposed in relation to a count of fraud (the false statement on the flyer). Both appealed against their sentences.

[1]   [2011] EWCA Crim 2043, Official Transcript.

8.247 In Garfoot's case Treacy J said that, although the facts of the case warranted an immediate custodial sentence:

'we are persuaded that taking account of (his) position in the business and what can be viewed as his lesser role, together with his particular personal circumstances.'

8.248 On that basis Garfoot's sentence was reduced to 3 months. Wilsher's appeal had a different foundation. He did plead guilty, but only on the day fixed for his trial and only as set out in a basis of plea document. Treacy J said:

'the central complaint is that the judge took into account matters which were contrary to matters set out in a basis of plea document . . . there is force in the complaint that the sentencing judge was not entitled to find that the works were "shoddy", there was considerable room for debate about him finding that the works were unnecessary but he was perfectly entitled to find that the victims were frail and vulnerable. We have to say that in our judgment insufficient attention was given by prosecuting counsel and the judge to the basis of plea document. There are elements of it which we would regard as unrealistic and elements of it which we consider would not have stood up to any sensible scrutiny. However, that was the basis upon which Mr Wilsher fell to be sentenced and the court having agreed to proceed on that basis should have adhered to the terms of that document.'

Accordingly Wilsher's sentence was reduced to 8 months.

8.249 The issue of compensation to be paid to victims of CPUTR 2008 offences was considered in *R v Patrick Connors*[1]. The Court of Appeal held that it was right in principle when assessing loss or damage in respect of compensation to take no account of any benefit conferred on the victim from any work carried out by the offender. An 81-year-old man had been aggressively persuaded to agree to a series of works to be carried out to his house. He was charged £16,400 and the Crown Court judge made a compensation order in that sum, which was upheld on appeal.

[1]   [2012] EWCA Crim 2106, Official Transcript.

8.250 Another recent case provides a good example of the impact confiscation orders may have on traders that contravene the requirements of the CPUTR 2008. In *R v Scott King*[1], a trader sold motorcars on the false basis that he was selling privately, so as to avoid offering a warranty or guarantee. He pleaded guilty to falsely claiming that he was not acting in the course of business contrary to para 22 of the CPUTR 2008, Sch 1. The Court of Appeal upheld a confiscation order of over £109,000 (representing the turnover of the business) on the basis that it was not disproportionate. Three further cases have recently been considered by the Court of Appeal.

[1]   [2014] EWCA Crim 621.

8.251 In *R v David Philip Hamilton*[1] a trader was sentenced to 12 weeks' imprisonment for contravening professional diligence. He pleaded guilty to a single offence which concerned incompetent building and brick work. He described himself as a good builder and competent brick layer, but the work he did was done very poorly and required to be put right. The Court of Appeal allowed his appeal by suspending the sentence for 12 months observing that whilst the conduct was criminal it did not involve overt bullying or aggression and fell short of being fraudulent.

[1]   [2015] EWCA Crim 278.

8.252 The case of *R v Michael Tolliday*[1] concerned a defendant who had pleaded guilty to 11 counts of fraud and three offences under CPUTR 2008. The fraud aspect of the case concerned serious misrepresentations which caused significant loss to 11 different customers by reason of them not being supplied with the quality of kitchen promised and the failure of the defendant to carry out particular work. The total loss was £42,000. He was sentenced to 30 months' imprisonment for the fraud offences. The CPUTR 2008 offences concerned only two of the customers. Two counts involved the provision of an invoice with logos he was not entitled to use and the third involved a customer not being given written notice of their right to cancel their agreement. He was sentenced to 12 months' imprisonment for each of the three CPUTR 2008 offences consecutive to the fraud sentence giving a total of 42 months' imprisonment. The Court of Appeal allowed the appeal and said that if the CPUTR 2008 offences had stood alone they would not have crossed the custody threshold, but that the context of the repeated frauds could not be ignored. However, the Court held that 12 months' imprisonment for the CPUTR 2008 offences was manifestly excessive and that the sentences should have been 3 months' imprisonment on each to run concurrently with the 30 months' imprisonment for fraud.

[1]   [2015] EWCA Crim 603.

8.253 In *R v Derek Montague*[1] the defendant was sentenced to 42 months' imprisonment after trial on each of four counts of fraud. He was also sentenced to concurrent prison terms of 12 months and 18 months' imprisonment respectively on two CPUTR 2008 offences. The case concerned a sole trader who over the course of 7 months carried out works at the home of a 60-year-old vulnerable woman who lived alone. The quality of work done was poor and the total loss was £25,000. The two CPUTR 2008 offences concerned a professional diligence count and an aggressive commercial practice. The professional diligence matter concerned the appellant's failure to provide a written guarantee for the works being carried out. The aggressive commercial practice concerned the pernicious act of accompanying the victim to her bank where she withdrew £1,200 for work in respect of which he had already been paid £2,000. The Court of Appeal upheld the sentence and all its component parts stating that this was not just a case of overcharging, but involved the deliberate targeting of a vulnerable victim.

[1]   [2015] EWCA Crim 902.

8.254 In *R v Evans*[1] the appellant was a director of a company that installed replacement facia, soffits, guttering and cladding in the Midlands. Together, with Sarah Beadle, a co-director he undertook the day-to day management of the business. They were involved in the development of a misleading pricing structure that was central to the allegations in the case. However, it was Sarah Beadle who had been the prime mover in the sales process which lay at the heart of the criminality. The misleading sales techniques included quoting a grossly overcharged initial price, followed by 'discount' which was still very expensive compared to market rates; falsely stating the property was lucky to get a non-existent subsidy; pretending the property could be a show home; falsely claiming the price was only discounted for that day; discouraging exercise of cancellation rights and selling repair agreements, despite the work being guaranteed. Aggressive sales techniques included cold calling, persistent calling after being asked to stop, repeat visits, lengthy stays (eg 6 hours), refusing to accept cancellation, and threats of litigation when consumers attempted to cancel. There was also use of the banned practice of using a logo on the company's website when not authorised. After a lengthy trial the appellant and Sarah Beadle were both sentenced to 30 months imprisonment. The Court of Appeal accepted that there was an unjust disparity in sentence and reduced the appellants sentence to 2 years.

[1]   [2016] EWCA Crim 2205.

8.255 In *R v Jackson*[1] the appellant appealed against his total sentence of 48 months after a plea of guilty to 2 counts of fraud and 13 counts of contravening professional diligence. He had carried out an extensive course of dishonest trading as a jobbing roofer. The offences were perpetrated against elderly, vulnerable women and would typically involve carrying out shoddy work of no value or less value than he had represented. The Court of Appeal reduced the sentence to 32 months, noting the mean-spirited and dishonest nature of the offences, but finding that the judge had erred in treating the offending as a course of conduct over 2 years rather than one occasion of fraud followed by a later 3 month course of fraudulent conduct.

[1]   [2017] EWCA Crim 78.

8.256 In *R v Christopher Maughan*[1] a sentence of 12 months custody was appropriate as a starting point where there were five elderly victims of a rogue paving operative, who carried out unwanted work, and failed to give any paperwork. There was fraudulent conduct and overt aggression, including damaging one victim's drive with a pickaxe, and becoming aggressive when asked to stop. In *R v Christopher Whatcott*[2] the defendant received a total sentence of 15 months imprisonment for using an aggressive and fraudulent charging structure in his contracts. He introduced consumers to providers of Energy Performance Certificates for a fee of £9.95. If this was not paid within 24 hours, it increased to £14.95. if not paid within 5 days, he sought to charge £85, and subsequently issued letters before claim through his solicitors. He received two consecutive terms of 3 months for two Fraud Act 2006 offences, a consecutive term of 3 months for the aggressive practice and a 6-month consecutive sentence for being in breach of a suspended sentence of 8 and a half months.

[1]   [2018] EWCA Crim 1885.
[2]   [2019] EWCA Crim 1889.

8.257 In *R v Asad Bashir Malik*[1] a sentence of 14 months' imprisonment was appropriate where the trader had contravened professional diligence by falsely advertising a secure airport parking service. The defendant had been a director of two companies that had operated a supposedly secure service, however, vehicles were in fact parked in unsecure muddy fields and in woodland, sometimes unlocked and with keys visible. The vehicles had also been used to ferry staff members about, had incurred parking tickets and some were returned dirty and damaged. The Court of Appeal accepted the judge's finding that the level of culpability and harm was high, not least because the trader had previously been warned by trading standards.

[1]   [2020] EWCA Crim 957.

Sentences under the TDA 1968

8.258 An important principle that emerged from the many sentencing cases under the TDA 1968 was that custodial sentences in trading cases should ordinarily be accompanied by a substantial fine. The rationale for this was that this type of offence will invariably be committed by a trader acting for financial gain. This is clearly illustrated by the leading authority of *R v Gupta*. It should be remembered, however, that these authorities were decided long before the confiscation of the proceeds of crime became mainstream criminal practice.

8.259 In *R v Gupta*[1] the appellant who was of previous good character, pleaded guilty, *inter alia*[2], to a count of applying a false trade description to goods under TDA 1968, s 1(1)(a). He was engaged in the second-hand car business and advertised cars in newspapers without disclosing that he was a dealer. He sold an Austin Maxi motor car which had been 'clocked' from 77,000 miles down to 41,800 and claimed it had had only one previous owner; when it had in fact had three previous owners. The car was sold for an agreed price of £1,000 to a couple who were unaware that he was a second-hand car dealer. When trading standards officers visited him, he refused to discuss the matter at all. He was sentenced to **12 months' imprisonment** in the Crown Court. The Court of Appeal confirmed that sentence but, on account of the appellant's 'comparative youth' and previous good character, varied it partly, to allow 6 months to be suspended. Lawton LJ stated that the offence was one:

> 'which this appellant admitted he had with someone else, or so he said, knowingly committed. Dishonest second-hand car dealers frequently do put the clock back. All too often they claim that they did not know it had been put back and the owner from whom they bought it had put it back. That was not a defence available to this appellant. The problem for the courts, since the passing of the Trade Descriptions Act 1968, has been what kind of sentence should be imposed on second-hand car dealers who "clock" motor cars? This Court has no hesitation whatsoever in adjudging that this kind of fraud calls for a sentence of immediate loss of liberty. It is an offence which is all too prevalent from one end of England and Wales to the other and it is one of which dishonest second-hand car dealers make a great deal of money. It is a matter of observation of this Court reading newspapers, particularly local newspapers, that all too frequently dishonest second-hand car dealers get fined. This appellant had the impudence to suggest, in his application for notice of appeal against conviction, that he expected to get a substantial fine. Dishonest second-hand motor car dealers who "clock" vehicles should expect not to get a substantial fine but a sentence imposing immediate loss of liberty plus a substantial fine. It is very important in these cases that not only should dishonest second-hand car dealers be punished, in the sense of losing their liberty, but the very large profits which they make from this kind of behaviour should be taken away from them by way of substantial fines.'

[1] (1985) 7 Cr App R (S) 172.
[2] There were several other deception offences for which he received concurrent sentences.

Forfeiture of goods

8.260 There may be circumstances where the investigating officer comes into possession of goods which are counterfeit, as part of a CPUTR investigation. In such a case, there will be a question of whether those goods should be forfeited. The relevant law is s 97 of the Trade Marks Act 1994, which applies by virtue of s 97(8)(d) to the CPUTR investigation (see **14.61–14.62**).

Chapter 9

UNFAIR CONTRACT TERMS

Contents

INTRODUCTION

9.1 Initially regulation of unfair terms in the UK came principally from the Unfair Contract Terms Act 1977 ('UCTA 1977'), which focuses on clauses that exclude or limit liability. In 1993 the European Council of Ministers passed the European Unfair Terms Directive 1993/13/EEC ('the Directive') which applies, with exceptions, to unfair terms of any type in consumer contracts in the EU. In 2015 Parliament brought these two regimes together, by re-implementing the

Directive and extending its protections, in Pt 2 and Schs 2 and 3 to the Consumer Rights Act 2015 ('the CRA 2015'). The Unfair Terms in Consumer Contracts Regulations 1999 ('UTCCR 1999'), which previously implemented the Directive in the UK, was revoked[1].

[1] The CRA 2015 came into force on 1 October 2015. The UTCCR 1999 came into force on 1 October 1999. This in turn replaced the UTCCR 1994 which came into force on 1 July 1995. The old legislation, and UCTA 1977 remain in force in respect of contracts entered into during their time of application see Consumer Rights Act 2015 (Commencement No 3, Transitional Provisions, Savings and Consequential Amendments) Order 2015, SI 2015/1630, arts 6(1), (4) and (5). In respect of contracts which predate even the 1994 regulations, there would still appear to be scope for the requirements of the Directive to apply – see CJEU *Kasler* (C-26/13) at para 32, although this was doubted by the Supreme Court in *Arnold v Britton* [2015] UKSC 36 at para 93 (per Lord Carnwath, dissenting on the main issues).

9.2 The CRA 2015 is now the principal provision by which the fairness of terms found in contracts between businesses and *consumers* should be assessed, and UCTA 1977 no longer has application to consumer contracts[1].

[1] UCTA 1977 does, however, continue to apply to business-to-business relationships and employment contracts, whether or not their terms are individually negotiated, and also when notices are used. It restricts exclusions of liability for negligence, and where standard form contracts are used, liability for breach of contract or substandard performance, applying a test of reasonableness. It prohibits exclusions of liability for death or personal injury. Part I of UCTA 1977 applies to England, Wales and Northern Ireland. Part II (ss 15–25) applies to Scotland.

The main changes

9.3 The CRA 2015 was drafted following two reports by the Law Commission that recommended reform, in particular to combine the UTCCR 1999 and UCTA 1977 regimes, and to clarify, and narrow, the main subject matter and price exemption[1]. The key changes to the UTCCR 1999 regime that CRA 2015 has brought are to bring notices and negotiated terms within scope, extending the grey list, and to narrow the core exemption so that to benefit from it terms must not only be transparent, but also be *prominent* and not be on the grey list. Terms which were blacklisted by UCTA 1977 remain prohibited by the CRA 2015.

[1] Law Commission and Scottish Law Commission *Unfair Terms in Contracts: A Joint Consultation Paper* (2005) and *Unfair Terms in Consumer Contracts: Advice to the Department For Business, Innovation and Skills* (2013).

THE CONSUMER RIGHTS ACT 2015, PT 2

9.4 The CRA 2015 applies to contracts concluded between a trader and a consumer, as well as notices that appear to affect rights, obligations or liabilities between a trader and a consumer. It was intended to give effect to the Directive, which has the aim of removing unfair terms from existing contracts, preventing their inclusion in future contracts, and deterring traders from attempting to use them in the first place[1]. The Directive fundamentally requires Member States to put in place a mechanism to ensure that every contractual term may be reviewed to determine whether it is unfair[2]. As primary legislation, the CRA 2015 is not directly affected by the UK's withdrawal from the EU. However the interpretation of the key concepts will be impacted. CJEU rulings made before the end of 2020 are adopted fully into the UK legal system, as retained EU case law, and be binding on most courts in the UK, although the UK Supreme Court, and selected other courts, may depart from retained CJEU jurisprudence, applying the same test that the Supreme Court applies to depart from its own case law[3]. The Supreme Court and the Court of Appeal have emphasised that this power should be used with great caution[4]. It seems unlikely that UK courts will feel it is appropriate to depart from retained EU case law where the Directive and its UK implementation remain substantially unchanged[5].

[1]   CJEU *Banco Espanol de Credito* (C-618/10) at paras 68–69, and 6th and 24th Recitals.
[2]   CJEU *Air Berlin v BVZB* C-290/16 at para 44.
[3]   The European Union (Withdrawal) Act 2018 (Relevant Court)(Retained EU Case Law) Regulations 2020 permits a number of appellate courts (such as the Court of Appeal of England and Wales, the Inner House of the Court of Session and the Court of Appeal of Northern Ireland) to depart from CJEU case law. Such courts must apply the same test as the Supreme Court applies when deciding to depart from its own case law. This power is set out in the Practice Statement (Judicial Precedent) [1966] 1 WLR 1234. These appellate courts will however be bound by retained EU case law so far as there is post-transition case law which modifies or applies that retained EU case law and which is binding on the relevant court.
[4]   *Horton v Sadler* [2007] 1 AC 307 at 29; *Peninsula Securities Ltd v Dunnes Stores Ltd (Bangor) Ltd* [2020] UKSC 36 at 49; *Tunein Inc v Warner Music UK Ltd* [2021] EWCA Civ 441 at 73–75.
[5]   See *Tunein Inc v Warner Music UK Ltd* [2021] EWCA Civ 441 at 78–89, 184 and 196–202.

9.5 CJEU rulings made after 1 January 2021 will no longer be binding on the UK, but UK courts may have regard to them. It is considered that CJEU rulings on the Directive are likely to remain relevant where the CRA 2015 continues to reflect the Directive or the CJEU ruling otherwise builds upon or refines retained EU case law[1]. Therefore while it is suggested that future rulings will clearly be relevant to interpretation of the CRA 2015 (and so capable of being taken into account by UK courts under s 6(2) of the European Union (Withdrawal) Act 2018), UK and EU approaches to unfair terms are liable to diverge.

[1]   *Tunein Inc v Warner Music UK Ltd* [2021] EWCA Civ 441 at 90–91.

9.6 Apart from some limited exemptions, the CRA 2015 requires that terms and notices must be transparent[1], and must be fair[2]. Consumers must not lose protection because they have agreed to a choice of law clause[3]. Unfairness is defined, together with a list of terms that are presumed to be unfair[4]. A term that is unfair will not bind the consumer, however the contract will continue in existence if at all possible[5]. This obligation binds Member States and their courts, which must take steps to ensure that the consumer's rights are protected. In addition to the right of consumers to challenge unfair terms, the CRA 2015 provides a system of collective or pre-emptive challenge, under which a regulator may obtain orders against use of unfair terms[6].

[1]   See the 20th Recital, Arts 4.2 and 5 and s 62.
[2]   See the 14th and 21st Recitals.
[3]   See the 22nd Recital, Art 6.2 and s 74.
[4]   See the 15th to 18th Recitals, Arts 3 and 41 and the Annex and ss 62, 63 and Sch 2.
[5]   See the 21st Recital, Art 6.1 and s 67.
[6]   See the 23rd and 24th Recitals, Arts 7 and 10 and CRA 2015, Sch 3.

9.7 The Directive lays down the minimum level of consumer protection that the UK had to ensure existed[1]. However, in the CRA 2015 the UK consciously went beyond the level of protection required. Accordingly, some UTCCRs case law which previously held terms to be out of scope or exempt from the fairness assessment is not necessarily to be relied on. It is important that the new tests in the CRA 2015 are applied, even though the central unfairness test remains the same.

1   See the Court of Appeal in *London Borough of Newham v Khatun* [2004] EWCA Civ 55 at para 56.

Jurisdiction over unfair terms

9.8 The power to rule a term to be unfair has always been reserved to the national courts, which have a 'significant element of judgment to exercise in the light of the circumstances of each case'[1]. The Court of Justice has competence in the EU only to construe the meaning of an article of the Directive[2]. Indications provided by the CJEU had to be taken into account by the national court in order to assess whether a term is unfair[3]. From 2021, only[4] UK courts will have the power to rule on the meaning of the CRA 2015. Subsequent CJEU rulings are, however, likely to remain important persuasive authority and interpretation of the CRA 2015 will require consideration of the Directive because it was Parliament's intention to give effect to the Directive when it legislated to create Pt 2 of the CRA 2015[5].

1   *Cavendish V El Makdessi, ParkingEye Ltd v Beavis* [2015] UKSC 67 at para 105(1). Only the national court can decide whether a term is unfair in all the circumstances (CJEU *Pannon* (C-243/08) at paras 42–43). Since the Treaty of Lisbon, the CJEU has been renamed the Court of Justice, as part of the Court of Justice for the European Union. For simplicity's sake we refer throughout to the CJEU.
2   CJEU *VB Penzugyi* (C-137/08) at para 37; *OFT v Abbey National* [2009] UKSC 6 per Lord Walker at para 50. See also CJEU *Pannon* (C-243/08) at paras 42–43, CJEU *Caja de Ahorros* (C-484/08) at para 33).
3   *Nemzeti v Invitel* (C-472/10) at para 22.
4   Under Art 86 of the Withdrawal Agreement, the CJEU shall continue to have the power to rule on references made to the CJEU by UK courts before 31 December 2020; according to Art 87 of the Withdrawal Agreement, the Commission can still bring infraction proceedings against the UK for breaches of the Treaty alleged to have occurred before 31 December 2020, for a period of 4 years.
5   See *Lipton & Anr v BA City Flyer Ltd* [2021] EWCA Civ 454 paras 57–70 as to how UK courts should assess the relevance of EU law and CJEU judgments after 1 January 2021. The Court of Appeal made clear that EU legislation and CJEU judgments which were in force up until 31 December 2020 remain binding on courts below the Court of Appeal.

9.9 Under the CRA 2015, s 71 UK courts have a duty to consider the fairness of terms in consumer contracts that are before them, and under s 70 and Sch 3, various regulators have power to ask the courts to rule on the fairness and transparency of terms.

Interpretation

9.10 In interpreting the Directive, it is important to bear in mind that it aims to have a wide application, where one party is acting in a trade, business or professional capacity, and it is meant to apply to every sector of the economy[1]. Where there is any apparent conflict with any other EU law, the Directive's application could only be excluded by clear wording to that effect[2]. The CJEU has ruled it is particularly important that consumers should be protected where the contract relates to their essential needs, involves significant sums or is in a complex legal context, where the professional is likely to have a high degree of technical knowledge or the consumer is likely to find it difficult to judge the quality of the product provided[3]. The sources that may be used to interpret the Directive are numerous and include:

- the Treaty;
- the wording of the Directive and (importantly) its recitals;
- the European Policy programmes that led to the Directive;
- the draft directive and the opinions of the various committees;
- the Commission Explanatory Memorandum;
- the different language versions of the Directive[4];
- case law (especially that of the CJEU, but also Advocate General Opinions, and the case law and administrative decisions of other Member States);
- the current views of the European Commission and UK Government Departments[5].

[1]   CJEU *Ryanair DAC v Delayfix* (C-519/19) para 52.
[2]   CJEU *Air Berlin v Bundesverband der Verbraucherzentralen* (C-290/16) at para 45.
[3]   CJEU *Asbeek Brusse v Jahani BV* (C-488/11) at paras 2932, ruling that tenancy contracts must fall within scope.
[4]   Although only the English language version of the Directive has the status of retained Direct EU legislation (see European Union (Withdrawal) Act 2018, s (4)), where there is doubt as to the scope of the Directive, it will no doubt remain persuasive to consider the scope of the Directive as revealed in other language versions.
[5]   See *London Borough of Newham v Khatun* [2004] EWCA Civ 55 at para 76, where the Court of Appeal stated that 'it is right that in its search for a purposive construction of the Directive, the court should consider all these materials'. See also CJEU *Asbeek Brusse v Jahani BV* (C-488/11) at para 26, where in considering the same issue, the CJEU considered how the intention of the legislator, and the aim of the Directive, is reflected in the different language versions. Contrary to the Court of Appeal's views in *Khatun*, it is not helpful to consider the use of similar concepts in other Directives, or even similar language in other Directives, since different Directives have different purposes – see CJEU *Kasler* (C-26/13) at para 58 and CJEU *BEST Laser Sorters v Bert Peelaers* (C-657/11) at para 51.

9.11 In construing the CRA 2015, it is important to bear in mind[1]:

- The Directive's purposes to improve the functioning of the (European) market place through fair standard contracts and to protect consumers[2].
- The core concepts and scope of the Directive must be given an autonomous and uniform interpretation through the EU[3].
- The Directive is aimed at 'take it or leave it contracts'.
- The Directive treats consumers as presumptively weaker parties, and therefore in need of protection from abuses by stronger contracting parties.
- It is not possible to contract out of the CRA 2015.

[1]   *Director General of Fair Trading v First National Bank* [2001] UKHL 52 at paras 31–32.
[2]   See also *London Borough of Newham v Khatun* [2004] EWCA Civ 55 at para 57. It remains to be seen how UK courts post Brexit will reflect the underlying common market intention of the Directive, but the importance of having a level playing field for traders remains pertinent in the UK.
[3]   CJEU *Kasler* (C-26/13) at paras 37–38. This suggests that UK courts should continue to have close regard to CJEU caselaw on the Directive.

Consumer protection

9.12 Consumer protection is the Directive's 'dominant purpose'[1]. Article 100a of the EC Treaty required the Commission to 'take as its base a high level of protection'[2]. Therefore it follows that the scope is broad, and there must be a clear rationale for excluding transactions involving consumers from its scope[3]. The Directive is premised on[4]:

> 'the idea that the consumer is in a weak position vis-à-vis the trader as regards both his bargaining power and his level of knowledge, which leads to the consumer agreeing to terms drawn up in advance by the trader without being able to influence the content of those terms.[5]'

[1] There are, however, other, subsidiary, purposes which are discussed below, namely the single market, and competition objectives.

[2] In *London Borough of Newham v Khatun* [2004] EWCA Civ 55 (paras 57 and 77), the court noted that Art 100a of the EC Treaty relates to measures which 'have as their object the establishment and functioning of the internal market'. This required that 'in drafting proposals concerning consumer protection with this objective in mind, the Commission will take a 'high level of protection'.' The court stated, 'thus the Directive has the twin purposes of advancing the internal market, and providing a high level of consumer protection'.

[3] *London Borough of Newham v Khatun* [2004] EWCA Civ 55 at para 77.

[4] CJEU *Perenicova* at para 27.

[5] The CJEU has often repeated this purpose which was first developed in the case of *Oceano Groupo* (joined cases C-240/98, 241/98, 242/98, 243/98 and 244/98).

9.13 A central purpose of the Directive is that unfair terms should not be binding on the consumer (Art 6.1)[1]. This aims to 'replace the formal balance which the contract establishes between the parties with an effective balance which re-establishes equality between them'[2]. The imbalance that exists between the trader and the consumer may sometimes only be corrected by 'positive action unconnected with the actual parties to the contract'[3]. Articles 3–6 are intended to grant rights to consumers that they must be able to rely on before the courts[4]. A rationale behind this high level of protection is to enable consumers to shop with confidence, without fearing one-sided terms or unfair exclusion clauses. A trader cannot lawfully abuse its position of power[5]. This aim is important in the furtherance of the other two objectives of the Directive, building the internal market and driving effective competition.

[1] *Pannon* (C-243/08) at paras 21, 23.

[2] CJEU *Nemzeti* at para 34.

[3] CJEU *Asturcom v Nogueira* (C-40/08) at para 31.

[4] CJEU *Commission v Sweden* (C-478/99) at paras 16–18, *Commission v Spain* (C-70/03), CJEU at para 15.

[5] See the 5th, 6th, 8th and 9th Recitals.

The single market

9.14 In *Commission v Sweden* the CJEU stated that the progressive establishment of the EU internal market is supported by confident consumers[1]. The Directive aims, at least partially, to harmonise consumer contract law throughout the EU, and increase consumer awareness of the laws governing contracts in other Member States. It is therefore inappropriate to define the Directive's scope by reference to English legal principles, no matter how well established or useful in the domestic context, because 'European legislation has to be read as a single corpus of law binding across the Member States'. Further, creating arbitrary distinctions in this way could lead to absurdities in the application of the Directive[2]. The concepts of the Directive, as reflected in the CRA 2015, must be given autonomous meaning, so that the Directive has uniform minimum application as far as possible[3]. The test of fairness must be applied by all Member States, no matter what their pre-existing law[4]. The measures and court proceedings Member States use to implement the Directive should not frustrate its purpose[5]. As stated in *Banco Espanol de Credito*[6]:

> 'The directive as a whole constitutes a measure which is essential to the tasks entrusted to the European Union and, in particular, to raising the standard of living and the quality of life throughout the EU.'

It remains to be seen how the UK courts will interpret unfair terms legislation once the UK is no longer part of the single market. However, these CJEU pronouncements emphasise the importance of continuing to look to CJEU jurisprudence after EU exit, because Pt 2 of the CRA 2015 includes the EU legal concepts that the CJEU will continue to interpret.

[1]   See the 1st to 6th Recitals of the Directive.
[2]   *London Borough of Newham v Khatun* [2004] EWCA Civ 55 at para 78. See also *Turner and Co (GB) Ltd v Abi* [2010] EWHC 2078 (QB) at para 42 where the judge emphasised, in considering the European jurisprudence on the definition of a consumer, that the Court of Justice 'has made clear that the concept must be given an autonomous interpretation. By 'autonomous interpretation', I mean an interpretation not grounded in any national law, but which is of general application across the community'.
[3]   *Director General of Fair Trading v First National Bank* [2001] UKHL 52, per Lord Bingham at para 8 and per Lord Steyn at paras 31–32.
[4]   *Director General of Fair Trading v First National Bank* [2001] UKHL 52, per Lord Bingham at para 17.
[5]   *Banco Espanol de Credito* (C-618/10) at paras 55 and 69.
[6]   CJEU *Banco* (C-618/10) at para 67. See also CJEU *Asturcom v Nogueira* (C-40/08) at para 52.

Freedom of competition and choice

9.15   The internal market helps businesses to trade throughout the EU, thus stimulating competition and increasing choice for consumers[1]. Harmonisation of EU contract law aims to give traders greater certainty and reduce the costs of doing business across borders. Disparities in the level of legal protection have the potential to distort competition[2]. Legal certainty means the Directive seeks to preserve, rather than terminate contractual relations[3]. Freedom of competition and choice is the theoretical basis on which contractual terms that relate to the main subject matter of the contract or to the adequacy of the price or remuneration are not reviewed because the consumer is deemed to be adequately protected by competition[4].

[1]   See the 7th Recital. Unfair terms can give an unfair advantage to one trader over another, where they profit by tying consumers into lengthy contracts, preventing switching or increase their income through concealed terms. This hinders competition on quality of product and value for money.
[2]   See the 2nd Recital.
[3]   CJEU *Perenicova* (C-453/10) at para 32 and AG's Opinion at paras 66–68.
[4]   For a fuller discussion see CJEU *Caja de Ahorros* (C-484/08) AG's Opinion at paras 38–40. This also means that where the consumer has not actually been made properly aware of the term, as now explicitly required by the CRA 2015, it is difficult to maintain that they exercised 'freedom of contract' in any meaningful sense.

APPLICATION OF THE CONSUMER RIGHTS ACT 2015

9.16 CRA 2015, s 61:

61 Contracts and notices covered by this Part

(1)   This Part applies to a contract between a trader and a consumer.

(2)   This does not include a contract of employment or apprenticeship.

(3)   A contract to which this Part applies is referred to in this Part as a "consumer contract".

(4)   This Part applies to a notice to the extent that it—

    (a)   relates to rights or obligations as between a trader and a consumer, or

    (b)   purports to exclude or restrict a trader's liability to a consumer.

(5)   This does not include a notice relating to rights, obligations or liabilities as between an employer and an employee.

(6)   It does not matter for the purposes of subsection (4) whether the notice is expressed to apply to a consumer, as long as it is reasonable to assume it is intended to be seen or heard by a consumer.

(7)   A notice to which this Part applies is referred to in this Part as a "consumer notice".

(8)   In this section "notice" includes an announcement, whether or not in writing, and any other communication or purported communication.

9.17 The CRA 2015 applies to terms in **contracts** or **notices**:

- involving **traders** and **consumers**;
- including secondary contracts, no matter who the contracting parties are, if these impact on a consumer contract;
- which do not reflect mandatory statutory or regulatory provisions; or
- the provisions or principles of international conventions to which the state or Community are party; and[1]
- Are not in employment or apprenticeship contracts or notices.

[1]   See CJEU *Caja de Ahorros* (C-484/08) AG's Opinion at para 57.

Consumer

9.18 CRA 2015, s 76(2) and s 2(3):

"Consumer" means an individual acting for purposes that are wholly or mainly outside that individual's trade, business, craft or profession.

The definition of consumer is now considered in Chapter 2, Interpretation of Consumer Law. A person does not automatically cease to be a consumer once the contract they entered into has been performed, since their status as a consumer relates to the point at which contract was entered into. It follows that a consumer may still able to challenge an unfair term even though the contract has been fully performed[1]. Where a consumer has assigned their right to enforce their rights under a contract to a third party who is a professional, such as a claims management company, that third party may still rely on the original consumer's rights under the CRA 2015. This is because the application of the Directive is not dependent on the identities of the parties to the dispute, but rather on the capacity in which they entered the contract[2].

[1]   CJEU SC *Raiffeisen Bank SA v JB* (C-698/18) para 73.

2   CJEU *Ryanair DAC v Delayfix* (C-519/19) para 53. The position may be different however where the consumer has assigned all of their rights and obligations under the original contract (para 63, and see also *R on the application of Emmet Donegan v Financial Services Compensation Scheme Ltd* [2021] EWHC 760 paras 121–122).

Trader

9.19 CRA 2015, s 76 and s 2(2):

"Trader" means a person acting for purposes relating to that person's trade, business, craft or profession, whether acting personally or through another person acting in the trader's name or on the trader's behalf.

The definition of trader is now considered in CHAPTER **2**, Interpretation of Consumer Law. In the context of an unfair terms dispute, however, this concept must be interpreted consistently with that of 'seller or supplier' within the meaning of the Directive[1].

1   CJEU *Karel de Grote v Kuijpers* (C-147/16) at para 42. The Court in this case also ruled that anybody engaged in professional activities, whether publicly or privately owned, or run on a not for profit basis, is within scope (para 51). A higher education establishment can therefore be a trader – in particular where it offers additional services, ancillary to education (para 57). See also CJEU *Henri Pouvin* (C-590/17) at paras 33–36. Further, Where a trader is engaging in activities which are not core to their business, they are still to be treated as governed by the Directive, not least because they still have greater technical information and expertise, and human and material resources, than the natural person with whom they are contracting, but also because these ancillary activities are likely to advance the trader's main business in some way (CJEU *Henri Pouvin* (C-590/17) at paras 36–42).

Contract

9.20 The Directive is stated to apply to all contracts concluded after 31 December 1994[1]. The CRA 2015 applies to both written and oral contracts. It looks to the substance of the agreement, not the form[2]. The formation of a contract is not necessarily defined by the English law. The concept of a contract for the purposes of the Directive is one that applies across the EU[3], and therefore when construing the CRA 2015 post EU exit UK courts are likely to continue to ensure that unfair terms protection is not necessarily ousted where there is no contract (for example) merely because there is a lack of a technical ingredient, such as privity of contract. The CRA 2015 applies to contracts for land and to all tenancies, even though in the assignment of a tenancy there is no privity of contract between assignees, only privity of estate[4]. Where an arrangement is contractual by virtue of a legislative scheme governing arrangements of that sort, then it would seem that this would mean that the Directive applies. For example the CJEU has ruled that where a person boards a train without a ticket, there is nonetheless a 'transport contract' for the purposes of Regulation 1371/2007 on Rail Passengers' Rights, and accordingly the Unfair Terms Directive will apply to that contract[5].

1   Article 10.1. It is unlikely to apply to contracts which were entered into before this date, although where a long lease is re-issued subsequently, the Directive's provisions will apply to the re-issued contract – see *Roundlistic Ltd v Jones & Seymour* [2016] UKUT 325 (LC) para 100 and *Jones & Seymour v Roundlistic Ltd* [2018] EWCA Civ 2284 at para 35. However in this case, on appeal to the Court of Appeal, it was held that where a lease is re-granted under a statutory scheme, and the tenant obtaining the regrant did not seek the removal of potentially

unfair terms, it is no longer open to assignees of the tenant to challenge those terms as unfair – *Jones & Seymour v Roundlistic Ltd* [2018] EWCA Civ 2284 at para 48. This conclusion may however incorrectly fail to take into account the court's own obligation to consider unfairness, on which see below.

2   See the 11th Recital. It is not contingent on whether it is contained in one or many documents.

3   *London Borough of Newham v Khatun* [2004] EWCA Civ 55 at para 78. However where a state has a specific approach to property law, or some other area which is not harmonised at EU level, the Unfair Terms Directive will not override this completely – see *Condominio di Milano, via Meda v Eurothermo SpA* (C-329/19) paras 29–30, which ruled that a commonhold association, which in Italian law is not a natural or legal person, cannot be a consumer under EU law, even though it acted on behalf of consumer residents. EU law will not overrule national rules on property ownership, since this is not a harmonised field (para 27).

4   See the CJEU in *Asbeek Brusse v Jahani BV* (C-488/11) at paras 29–32, holding that the Directive must apply to tenancies.

5   CJEU *NMBS v Kanyeba* (C-349/18) paras 30–53

9.21 In considering whether a contractual arrangement (such as provision of publicly funded educational and ancillary services) falls within scope, the CJEU ruled that the Directive should apply where 'there is, in principle, an inequality between the educational establishment and the student, owing to the asymmetry of information and expertise between the parties [and] . . . the establishment has at its disposal a permanent organization and expertise that the student, acting on a private basis does not.'[1] The CJEU has stressed that the Directive 'is a general regulation for consumer protection, intended to apply in all sectors of economic activity, including the air transport sector'[2].

1   CJEU *Karel de Grote v Kuijpers* (C-147/16) at para 59.

2   CJEU *Ryanair DAC v Delayfix* (C-519/19) para 52.

9.22 The 10th Recital of the Directive sets out a number of obvious exclusions.

'contracts relating to employment, contracts relating to succession rights, contracts relating to rights under family law and contracts relating to the incorporation and organisation of companies or partnership agreements.'

The CRA 2015 expressly excludes, by s 61(2), contracts of employment or apprenticeship. These are contracts which regulate the employment relationship or employment conditions. However contracts – other than their employment contract – which an employee may enter into with their employer are not excluded: this is so even if the product is only available to employees[1].

1   CJEU *Henri Pouvin* (C-590/17) at paras 29–32.

9.23 The CRA 2015 also brings within scope 'secondary contracts' – which are those which 'reduce the rights or remedies or increase the obligations of a person under another contract' ('the main contract')[1]. It does not matter whether the secondary contract is itself a consumer contract, or made between the same persons as the main contract[2]. The effect of this is to bring within scope for example a contract that an individual might make in a trade capacity, if this has a material impact on a consumer contract which they or another consumer has entered into. The terms of such secondary contracts are also assessable for fairness[3].

1   CRA 2015, s 72(1).

2   CRA 2015, s 72(3).

3   CRA 2015, s 72(2).

Term

9.24 Subject to the exclusions below, the CRA 2015 applies to all terms in consumer contracts, whether or not they are individually negotiated by the consumer[1]. It does not apply to mere practices, where there is no contractual term governing the trader's action[2].

[1]   The UTCCRs did not apply to individually negotiated terms. However the threshold, which the trader must cross, for showing that a term was individually negotiated is high: CJEU *Šiba*, (C-537/13), para 31.
[2]   CJEU *Banco Santander v Demba* (C-96/16) at para 39.

9.25 In *Office of Fair Trading v Foxtons Ltd* in the High Court it was said that it was important 'to look at the substance, not the form, and therefore to focus on obligations not precise written terms'[1].

'A "term" comprises all contractual provisions which give rise to a particular obligation, notwithstanding these contractual provisions might be found in various clauses of the contractual documentation.[2]'

A 'term' may also be just part of a clause[3].

[1]   *OFT v Foxtons Ltd* [2009] EWHC 1681 (Ch) at para 41.
[2]   Andrew Smith J in *OFT v Abbey National* [2008] 2 All ER (Comm) 625 at para 431, a part of the judgment which was not appealed.
[3]   *Bankers Insurance Company Ltd v South* [2003] EWHC 380 (QB) at para 35.

9.26 In *Margaret Baybut v Eccle Riggs Country Park Ltd*[1], it was held that implied terms may not be assessed for fairness because an unfair term could never be implied by operation of law or to give effect to the obvious common but unspoken intention of the parties[2]. Neither does the test apply to effects caused by a rule of law[3].

[1]   Unreported, High Court, Manchester District Registry, 2 November 2006.
[2]   This interpretation is consistent with the CJEU's position on the mandatory statutory exemption, which it has held encompasses 'provisions that apply by default, in the absence of other arrangements established by the parties' – CJEU *Banco Santander v Demba* (C-96/16) at para 43.
[3]   *Direct Line Insurance v Khan* [2001] EWCA Civ 1794 at para 36.

Notice

9.27 The CRA 2015 applies to a notice to the extent that it (a) 'relates to rights or obligations as between a trader and a consumer or (b) purports to exclude or restrict a trader's liability to a consumer'[1]. This includes any announcement, and any other communication, as long as it is reasonable to assume it is intended to be seen or heard by a consumer[2]. This provision ensures that a consumer cannot be unfairly disadvantaged where there is a technical reason why they do not have a contract with a trader with whom they are dealing – for example where they are a recipient of a free advice service which excludes liability for negligence.

[1]   CRA 2015, s 61(4).
[2]   CRA 2015, s 61(6) and (8).

9.28 The application to notices ensures that enforcement action can be taken against statements that are not incorporated into any contract, but which a trader may seek to invoke against a consumer. Examples include end user licence agreements, which may not be of contractual status, but define the terms on which the consumer contracts with a vendor of software[1]. Where a notice is incorporated into a contract, it is assessed for fairness as a term.

[1] See the CRA 2015 *Explanatory Notes*, para 296.

Exclusions

9.29 CRA 2015, s 73 provides:

> **73 Disapplication of rules to mandatory terms and notices**
>
> (1) This Part does not apply to a term of a contract, or to a notice, to the extent that it reflects
>
> (a) mandatory statutory or regulatory provisions [which includes rules which, according to law, apply between the parties on the basis that no other arrangements have been established][1], or
>
> (b) the provisions or principles of an international convention to which the United Kingdom or the EU is a party.
>
> (2) In subsection (1) "mandatory statutory or regulatory provisions" includes rules which, according to law, apply between the parties on the basis that no other arrangements have been established.

[1] CRA 2015, s 73(2).

Mandatory statutory provisions

9.30 Provisions that are mandatorily required by primary or secondary legislation fall within this exception, which must be strictly construed[1]. Section 73(2) has clarified that this concept also applies to rules which apply between the parties in the absence of other arrangements, for example terms implied by statute[2]. It only applies 'where the content of the terms is prescribed', not where a statutory scheme merely provides for contracts to be made or re-issued[3]. The terms must apply independent of the parties' choice[4]. Further, the statutory regime in question must be specifically aimed at creating balance between parties in the precise situation covered by the contract in question: a statutory provision which merely provides for the parties to act in accordance with the law, rules of society and established custom, for instance, is not within the exception[5]. A statutory provision which sets an upper limit on what a trader may charge (for example by way of non-interest credit costs) also does not fall within the exception, and does not prevent the court from reviewing the possible unfairness of how the costs are set[6].

[1] CJEU *Ruxandra Andriciuc v Banca Romaneasca SA* (C-186/16) at para 31.
[2] This is consistent with the CJEU in *Barclays Bank v Sara Sancha Garcia* (C-280/13) at paras 39–42 and in *Ruxandra Andriciuc v Banca Romaneasca SA* (C-186/16) at paras 28–29. The exemption also covers statutory provisions which are supplementary in nature and apply by default – see CJEU *Banco Santander v Demba* (C-96/16) at para 43. This includes provisions from which the parties could have derogated, but did not CJEU *NG v SC Banca Transilvania SA* (C-81/19) paras 35–37.
[3] *Jones & Seymour v Roundlistic Ltd* [2018] EWCA Civ 2284 at para 40, which represents the majority view of the Court of Appeal, contrary to that expressed at paras 31–34. This overturns the decision of the Upper Tribunal (Lands Chamber) in the same case, which held erroneously that the exemption applied where a landlord has a statutory obligation to grant a new lease on the same terms as a lease which predated the application of the Unfair Terms Directive (*Roundlistic Ltd v Jones & Seymour* [2016] UKUT 325 (LC) at para 101).

4   CJEU *Aqua Med* (C-266/18) at para 33.
5   CJEU *Dziubak* (C-260/18) at paras 61–62.
6   CJEU *Mikrokasa SA v XO* (C-779/18) paras 56–58.

9.31 Statutory provisions that retroactively operate to change unfair terms in a contract may benefit from this exemption[1]. The rationale for this exception is the presumption that Member States will not require unfair terms to be included in contracts – in both the rules they create and the contracts they themselves enter into[2]. It is presumed that in drafting legislation, Member States 'struck a balance between all the rights and obligations of the parties' to the relevant contracts[3]. However the protections of the Unfair Terms Directive cannot be ousted merely where there is a more specific legislative framework that applies to a sector – in particular more specific EU rules do not oust unfair terms protection unless there is very clear wording to this effect[4]. Further, where a mandatory statutory regime applies, it seems that the effect of this must be set out clearly by the trader in the contract[5]. However, the obligation on a trader to explain how the statutory scheme works is limited only to important core features of the contract, such as how the price may vary or how private international law operates. It should not impose on the trader a burden beyond that which can reasonably be expected[6].

1   CJEU *GT v HS* (C-38/17) at para 25.
2   Recitals 13 and 14. Member States are obliged not to contract with their citizens on unfair terms.
3   CJEU *RWE Vertrieb AG v VBZ Nordrhein Westfalen* Case C-92/11 at para 28.
4   CJEU *Air Berlin v BVZB* C-290/16 at paras 44–45.
5   CJEU *Nemzeti v Invitel* (C-472/10) at para 29 'Where certain aspects of the method of amendment of the fees connected with the service to be provided are specified by mandatory statutory or regulatory provisions within the meaning of Article 1(2) of the Directive, or where those provisions provide, for the consumer, the right to terminate the contract, it is essential that the consumer be informed of those provisions by the seller or supplier'.
6   CJEU *Toth v ERSTE Bank* (C-34/18) paras 68–69. In particular the obligation to explain was held not to apply to rules relating to the burden of proof in the event of a dispute (para 66).

9.32 In *Rochdale Borough Council v Dixon*, the statutory right for a local authority to collect water charges from council tenants was considered. The Court of Appeal stated that 'a term which is expressly authorised by a statutory power . . . is unlikely to be unfair'[1]. However, this was not on its own conclusive. The court went on to consider a range of other factors that led to the conclusion that the term was fair. The CJEU has held that statutory provisions which merely set out arrangements which a trader can choose from do not benefit from the exemption[2].

1   [2011] EWCA Civ 1173 at para 68.
2   CJEU *Aqua Med* (C-266/18) at para 35.

9.33 Where a term merely reproduces a national legal provision (it is not mandatory), it does not fall within the exemption[1]. Likewise, where legislation sets out limitations on parties' conduct it should not be assumed that a term that does not exceed these limits is fair. For example, where statute sets a penalty interest rate ceiling, in particular where this is applicable not only to consumer contracts, this does not prevent assessment of fairness of a term setting the penalty interest rate in a consumer contract, even where this does not exceed the statutory limit[2].

1   CJEU *RWE Vertrieb AG v VBZ Nordrhein Westfalen* Case C-92/11 at paras 29–31.
2   CJEU *Unicaja Banco v Rueda* (C-482/13) at paras 36–40.

International conventions

9.34 Section 73(1) excludes the 'provisions or principles of an international convention to which the United Kingdom or the EU is a party'. The reason or this exclusion is again because it is presumed that states, when negotiating treaties, will not impose unfair terms on their citizens.

Employment contracts

9.35 The CRA 2015 does not apply to contracts of employment or apprenticeship, or notices which relate to rights, obligations or liabilities as between an employer and employee[1]. This is because these are governed by employment law.

[1]   CRA 2015, s 61(2) and (5).

Blacklisted terms

9.36 Some types of term are prohibited, and automatically unfair. They cannot be included in consumer contracts, and are not binding on the consumer. There are three types[1]:

(1)   Those blacklisted in goods, services and digital content contracts by Pt 1 of the CRA 2015.
(2)   Those blacklisted in all contracts by Pt 2 of the CRA 2015.
(3)   Those blacklisted by other legislation.

[1]   In addition, it is open to the national courts to establish blacklisted terms through the development of caselaw, such as a Spanish rule that a default interest rate is unfair where it exceeds the ordinary interest rate in the agreement by more than 2 percentage points – CJEU *Banco Santander v Demba* (C-96/16) at para 71.

Exclusions of liability in goods, digital content and services contracts

9.37 Section 62(8) provides that certain exclusion of liability clauses need not be assessed for fairness in order not to bind consumers. These are exclusions of liability in goods (s 31), digital content (s 47) and services contracts (s 57) (covered in Pt 1), and exclusions of liability for negligence (set out in s 65).

9.38 The Pt 1 exclusions replicate and extend the protections previously afforded consumers by ss 6 and 7 of UCTA 1977. In summary, a trader may not exclude from a goods contract their liability for goods not being of satisfactory quality, fit for purpose, or as described. Goods must conform to pre-contract information that the consumer has relied on, a sample or a model. Goods must be properly installed, and any digital content supplied must also conform to the contract. The trader must have the right to supply the goods and deliver them, and the goods remain at the trader's risk until they come into the physical possession of the consumer.

9.39 Digital content must be of satisfactory quality, fit for purpose, as described, and in conformity with pre-contract information that the consumer has relied on (see **CHAPTER 6**, Consumer Rights). The trader must have the right to supply it. A trader cannot exclude their liability under a service contract for performing it with reasonable care and skill, or for the inaccuracy of information they give that the consumer takes into account when deciding about the service. Unless otherwise agreed, the trader may charge only a reasonable price and must perform the service within a reasonable time. In all of these cases, terms are also not binding on consumers if they make the consumer's rights or remedies subject to onerous or restrictive conditions, allow the trader to put a person at a disadvantage as a result of pursuing a right, or exclude or restrict rules of evidence or procedure[1].

1   Part 1, ss 31(2), 47(2), 57(4).

Exclusion of negligence liability

9.40 Section 65(1) bars a trader from excluding or restricting liability for death or personal injury resulting from negligence.

Other terms that must be regarded as unfair

9.41 Section 63(6) of the CRA 2015 blacklists any term that has the effect of requiring the consumer to bear the burden of proof with regard to compliance with any obligation under the Distance Marketing Directive. This is similar to other prohibitions found in a range of legislation which forbid traders from seeking to contract out of their obligations[1]. In addition, s 91 of the Arbitration Act 1996 renders automatically unfair certain terms which bind a consumer to go to arbitration.

1   For example, reg 14B of the Alternative Dispute Resolution for Consumer Disputes (Competent Authorities and Information) Regulations 2015, SI 2015/542, which prohibits certain agreements to submit to ADR.

Jurisdiction and applicable law terms

Contracts applying law of a country other than the UK

9.42 By s 74 of the CRA 2015, in relation to contracts entered into from 1 January 2021[1]:

(1)   If—
   (a)   the law of a country or territory other than the United Kingdom or any part of the United Kingdom[2] is chosen by the parties to be applicable to a consumer contract, but
   (b)   the consumer contract has a close connection with the United Kingdom,
   this Part applies despite that choice.
(2)   For cases where the law applicable has not been chosen [. . .], see Regulation (EC) No. 593/2008 of the European Parliament and of the Council of 17 June 2008 on the law applicable to contractual obligations [as that Regulation has effect as retained direct EU legislation (including that Regulation as applied by regulation 5 of the Law Applicable to Contractual Obligations (England and Wales and Northern Ireland) Regulations 2009 and regulation 4 of the Law Applicable to Contractual Obligations

(Scotland) Regulations 2009), unless the case is one in respect of which Regulation (EC) No. 593/2008 has effect by virtue of Article 66 of the EU withdrawal agreement, in which case see that Regulation as it has effect by virtue of that Article][3].

[1] This section was amended by The Consumer Protection (Amendment etc) (EU Exit) Regulations 2018, SI 2018/1326, regs 3 and 11.
[2] In relation to contracts which predate 1 January 2021, the text here refers to the law of 'an EEA State'.
[3] In relation to contracts which predate 1 January 2021, s 74(2) said 'For cases where the law applicable has not been chosen [or the law of an EEA State is chosen], see Regulation (EC) No. 593/2008 of the European Parliament and of the Council of 17 June 2008 on the law applicable to contractual obligations.'

9.43 In relation to contracts which pre-date 31 December 2020, the CRA 2015 applies when a contractual terms purports to select the law of a country outside the EEA as long as the contract *'has a close connection with the UK'*[1]. This is designed to protect consumers against the unfair use of foreign jurisdictional clauses to oust the laws of a Member State[2]. Such terms are unfair without the need for an assessment of fairness, and in this sense is similar to the jurisdiction clauses discussed elsewhere in this chapter. Any judgment entered against the consumer in the overseas jurisdiction should not be enforced against the consumer in the EU. Where a contract is entered into on or after 1 January 2021, the references to the EEA are replaced by reference to the UK, with the effect that UK consumer contracts will be governed by UK law, and the law of another EEA state may not oust the protections provided by Pt 2 of the CRA 2015. Section 32 of the CRA 2015 further provides that the protections of Pt 1 of the CRA 2015 may not be ousted either, through a choice of law clause, and is drafted in comparable terms to s 74.

[1] Section 74(1). The concept of 'close connection' was left deliberately vague so that it could be given a wide interpretation – CJEU *Commission v Spain* (C-70/03) at para 33. An example of where there was *not* a close connection is *Chopra v Bank of Singapore Ltd* [2015] EWHC 1549 at para 135 – contracts with a company based in Singapore, to open accounts in Singapore, in order to invest outside the EU (in particular Russia). A further example where there was not a close connection is *Transfer Wise Inc v Decker* [2021] EWHC 1777 at para 75 – a contract made between a US money transfer firm and a person who stated that they lived in California, but was in fact residing in London: the judge ruled there would be no 'close connection' where the trader is led to believe the consumer is not in the UK, and the trader acted on this basis.
[2] See the 6th and 22nd Recitals, CJEU *Commission v Spain* (C-70/03) at para 30.

9.44 Section 74(2) makes clear that where the law of state other than the UK is chosen, (or, in relation to contracts which predate 31 December 2020, the law of another EU/EEA state is chosen), or there is no choice of law clause at all, reference should be made to the Rome I Regulation. This means that it is in principle possible for a consumer to agree that the law of another should apply to the contract[1]. Where such a term is in the small print, and might be a surprise for the consumer however, it may still be unfair, particularly if the effect is to exclude mandatory protections that the consumer has under his own law[2]. In such a case, the trader must set out the implications of this clearly in the contract[3].

[1] CJEU *VFK v Amazon* (C-191/15) at para 66.
[2] CJEU *VFK v Amazon* (C-191/15) at para 59 and Rome I Regulation, Art 6(2).
[3] CJEU *VFK v Treuhand* (C-272/18) para 58.

FAIRNESS

Transparency

9.45 CRA 2015, s 64(3):

> (3) A term is transparent for the purposes of this Part if it is expressed in plain and intelligible language and (in the case of a written term) is legible.

CRA 2015, s 68 provides:

68 Requirement for transparency

(1) A trader must ensure that a written term of a consumer contract, or a consumer notice in writing, is transparent.

(2) A consumer notice is transparent for the purposes of subsection (1) if it is expressed in plain and intelligible language and it is legible.

9.46 The CRA 2015 requires that written terms and notices should be transparent, although lack of transparency does not mean a term is automatically unfair[1]. The trader is under an obligation to ensure they are in plain and intelligible language, and legible[2]. This goes much further than grammatical intelligibility: the average consumer must be able to foresee, on the basis of clear, intelligible criteria, the economic consequences for them that derive from the term[3]. The consumer must be enabled to have 'full knowledge of the terms of future performance of the agreement' and must 'have to hand all the information which could have a bearing on the extent of his liability'[4]. This is assessed according to the standard of the average consumer, who is taken to be reasonably well-informed, and reasonably observant and circumspect[5]. The consumer should also be able clearly to understand the economic reasons for the term, and the term's relationship with other terms[6]. Where there is the potential for the consumer's obligations to change (because they are linked to an external index for instance), the trader must set out the possible variations and the risks inherent in this feature[7]. Where a term requires the consumer to pay a sum of money, it is not enough that the consumer knows the total amount. A consumer must also be able to understand – and be in no doubt about – from the contract as a whole, what and whose services the money is for, in particular to establish that the various charges do not overlap in relation to the services that they cover[8]. Where the trader claims they gave a particular document or explanation to the consumer, it is the trader who bears the burden of proving this is so[9]. The court will need to consider what details the trader can be expected to have specified in the promotional literature, negotiations and the agreement at the time it was concluded[10]. In making this assessment, the court must have regard to all the relevant facts including the following:

1   CJEU *GT v HS* (C-38/17) at para 37.
2   Section 68 and Arts 4.2 and 5, see also Recital 20. For the trader's obligation see CJEU *RWE Vertrieb* (C-92/11) at para 43. Transparency is a broad requirement – CJEU *Kasler* (C-26/13) at para 72.
3   CJEU *Matei v SC Volksbank* Romania (C-143/13) at paras 73–74. This seems to be a more rigorous test than set out in *OFT v Abbey National* [2008] EWHC 875 (Comm) at para 119 that the contractual terms must be 'sufficiently clear to enable the typical consumer to have a proper understanding of them for sensible and practical purposes.'
4   CJEU *EOS KSI Slovensko sro v Danko* (C-488/17) at para 63.
5   CJEU *Ruxandra Andriciuc v Banca Romaneasca SA* (C-186/16) at para 47.
6   CJEU *Kasler* (C-26/13) at para 60.

7   CJEU *OTP Bank Nyrt v Ilyes* (C-51/17) at para 75. In this case, the issue of concern was linking a borrower's obligations to a foreign exchange rate, the fluctuation of which could have significant economic consequences for his financial obligations – and it is this risk that needed to be made clear. This could require inclusion, for example, of worked examples of how much the regular payments would be in different circumstances, and an indication of how the rate has changed over time in the past (see for example (post Brexit) CJEU *VB v BNP Paribas Personal Finance SA* (Joined Cases C-776/19 to C-782/19) paras 73–75, encouraging the use of quantitative simulations, which specifically envisage fluctuations in the exchange rates of the two currencies, and stressing the need to draw the risk of currency fluctuation specifically to the consumer's attention). Similarly, where an exchange rate could be designated by the trader *after* the consumer has agreed to the loan, it will be questionable whether the consumer is enabled to evaluate the total cost of the loan (CJEU *GT v HS* (C-38/17) at para 34). Similarly, where a lender wishes to rely on an interest rate floor clause, they must set out how interest rate fluctuations may mean the consumer could be disadvantaged by the floor clause: CJEU *XZ v Ibercaja* (C-452/18) paras 53–55.

8   CJEU *Kiss* (C-621/77) at para 43. The contract does not however have to specify all the services provided in return for the charges (para 45). See also CJEU *Profi Credit Polska SA v QJ* (C-84/19, C-222/19 & C-252/19) at paras 74–78, which considered three fees charged for a loan (an initial payment fee, a commission fee and a fee for a further financial product). The court stressed that transparency was especially important where there was apparent overlap between charges (para 76) and where the consumer might need to assess whether the fee is for the lender's services or for someone else's (para 77). If there was doubt about these points, the charge would not be transparent (para 78).

9   (Post Brexit) CJEU *VB v BNP Paribas Personal Finance SA* (Joined Cases C-776/19 to C-782/19) paras 84–87.

10   CJEU *GT v HS* (C-38/17) at para 36.

9.47 *The consumer's attributes*

- The level of attention to be expected of the average consumer[1].
- Whether the average consumer would actually understand the implications of the term, given the market and its practices[2].
- The need for the consumer actually to be given the opportunity to examine all the terms of the contract, before concluding it[3].
- A consumer should be able to understand what they are agreeing to[4].

1   CJEU *Matei v SC Volksbank* Romania (C-143/13) at para 75. The average consumer is reasonably well informed, and reasonably observant and circumspect. The consumer is not expected to have the same level of vigilance where concluding a contract that is ancillary to another – such as an insurance contract taken out with a loan (see CJEU *Van Hove v CNP Assurances* (C-96/14) at para 48). Generally UK courts have assumed that the average consumer is able 'to read the relevant documents and to seek to understand the contractual terms from that reading', but there is an acceptance that they do not in fact always read contracts. In *OFT v Ashbourne Management Services Ltd* [2011] EWHC 1237 (Ch) the average consumer was said to be 'a member of the public interested in using a gym club which is not a high end facility and who may be attracted by the relatively low monthly subscriptions' (para 155).

2   CJEU *Kasler* (C-26/13) at para 74. In the case of a loan denominated in foreign currency, this includes being able to predict the sort of fluctuations that might occur, so that he can estimate the total cost of the loan – see CJEU *Ruxandra Andriciuc v Banca Romaneasca SA* (C-186/16) at paras 47 and 50.

3   CJEU *RWE Vertrieb* (C-92/11) at paras 43–44.

4   CJEU *Van Hove v CNP Assurances* (C-96/14) at paras 41 and 43. CJEU *Caja de Ahorros* (C-484/08) AG's Opinion at para 67. Where the consumer did not in fact understand the scope of a term, this is evidence that it was not transparent. See also *OFT v Abbey National* [2009] UKSC 6, per Lord Mance at para 113.

9.48 *The quality of the contract and surrounding literature*

- The fact that terms that form part of the price or main subject matter should be included clearly in the agreement[1].

- The average consumer's expectation that terms correspond to the overall purpose of the contract – and don't create surprising carve outs[2].
- The term should not be *obscure* and it must not be *ambiguous*[3].
- This requires transparency, flagging and explanation that the consumer can also *understand the effect of the term on his rights and obligations*[4]. The true effect of the contract should not be buried in the small print requiring 'some legal mining to bring it to the surface' – 'the typical consumer is not a miner for these purposes'[5].
- The headings and layout used in the contract should facilitate, rather than obscure, understanding[6].
- The promotional material and other information provided by the trader during the negotiations. This is particularly important where it provides the basis on which a consumer decides whether to be bound by the contract[7].

1 CJEU *Ruxandra Andriciuc v Banca Romaneasca SA* (C-186/16) at para 47.
2 CJEU *Van Hove v CNP Assurances* (C-96/14) at para 44.
3 CJEU *Caja de Ahorros* (C-484/08) at para 38; also *Commission v Spain* (C-70/03), AG's Opinion at para 14.
4 *OFT v Abbey National* [2008] EWHC 875 (Comm) at para 103. This formulation was affirmed and adopted also in *OFT v Foxtons Ltd* [2009] EWHC 1681 (Ch) at para 59.
5 *OFT v Foxtons Ltd* [2009] EWHC 1681 (Ch) at para 74.
6 CJEU *Matei v SC Volksbank* Romania (C-143/13) at para 77. In *Andrew Green v Petfre (Gibraltar) Ltd t/a Betfred* [2021] EWHC 842 (at paras 130, 140, 152–153 & 176), the court criticised a contract for iterative and repetitive drafting, inconsistent numbering, typographical mistakes, the need for extensive scrolling, the use of capital letters, text advising the consumer to consult an attorney if in doubt as to the meaning, lack of definitions of key terms, and unclear syntax. The court found that the drafting was so unclear as to fail to bind the consumer.
7 CJEU *Gutiérrez Naranjo and Others*, (C-154/15, C-307/15 and C-308/15), at para 50. See also CJEU *Profi Credit Polska SA v QJ* (C-84/19, C-222/19 & C-252/19) at para 74.

9.49 *The language actually used*

- Terms should not have broad and uncertain application[1].
- The meaning of terms contained in general conditions must not depend 'on which of a number of possible divergent interpretations is placed on them'[2].
- A phrase or word may have many uses in everyday parlance, and if so, the contract must make clear which of these is intended in the contract.
- Crucial information (perhaps especially that expressly required by Retained EU law) must be given and be given correctly[3].
- Terms should not be contradictory. Where they are, the term most favourable to the consumer will prevail[4].
- 'Just because a highly skilled lawyer can find (or contrive) some equivocation in a word, does not make the language lacking in plainness and intelligibility'[5].
- The test is not one of 'absolute and pedantic rigour', and errors that are obvious do not make a term unintelligible[6].

1 Such terms prevent the consumer from predicting their application. For example, variation of an interest rate due to 'significant changes in the money market' does not allow the consumer to foresee when the rate may change: CJEU *Matei v SC Volksbank* Romania (C-143/13) at para 76. Other examples – the terms 'associated' and 'connected' persons are too vague, and 'their scope would puzzle even lawyers'. Terms that, when used in statute, require close definition are likely to be unintelligible if used in contracts. See *OFT v Foxtons Ltd* [2009] EWHC 1681 (Ch) at para 62.
2 *Commission v Spain* (C-70/03), AG's Opinion at para 14.

3   CJEU *EOS KSI Slovensko sro v Danko* (C-488/17) at paras 64–65, which also emphasised the importance of information required by other provisions of EU law. In this case failing to state the APR and interest rate as required by consumer credit legislation was held to be 'decisive evidence' in the assessment as to whether the terms relating to the cost of credit were transparent (para 68). In the post Brexit context, the reference to EU law perhaps should be taken to apply simply to provisions of consumer law which require information to be stated by traders.

4   *Peabody Trust Governors v Reeve* [2008] EWHC 1432 (Ch) at para 31. However, where a collective challenge to a term is brought by an enforcer, the meaning *least* favourable to the consumer will be given.

5   *OFT v Foxtons Ltd* [2009] EWHC 1681 (Ch) at para 63.

6   *OFT v Foxtons Ltd* [2009] EWHC 1681 (Ch) at para 64.

9.50 Other than this, the court is expected to construe the contract as it would usually do for any contractual dispute[1].

CRA 2015, s 69 provides:

69 Contract terms that may have different meanings

(1)   If a term in a consumer contract, or a consumer notice, could have different meanings, the meaning that is most favourable to the consumer is to prevail.

(2)   Subsection (1) does not apply to the construction of a term or a notice in proceedings on an application for an injunction or interdict under paragraph 3 of Schedule 3.

1   *Commission v Spain* (C-70/03), AG's Opinion at para 11.

9.51 If, following the normal principles of construction of contracts, a term in a contract or notice could have different meanings, the interpretation most favourable to the consumer must prevail (s 69(1))[1]. However, where a collective challenge is brought, the meaning *least* favourable to the consumer must be given[2]. This is so that the maximum level of protection is given to consumers. A term that is not transparent is always assessable for fairness, but is not necessarily unfair[3].

1   *Commission v Spain* (C-70/03), CJEU at paras 16–17. See also *AJ Building & Plastering Ltd v Turner* [2013] EWHC 484 at para 53, where it was held that 'there is not material difference between the principle of construction in reg 7(2) and the *contra proferentem* rule'. Both are used only where there is a case of 'genuine interpretative doubt or ambiguity'. See also *West v Ian Finlay & Assocs* [2014] EWCA Civ 316 at paras 30–32. The rule applies where there is a contradiction in the contract, but cannot be deployed where 'a court, having recognised a mistake in the language used, is applying a corrective construction by reading into the clause words, which have not been expressed, to correct the mistake' (which is permissible only where it is clear what a reasonable person would have understood the parties to have meant) – *R&S Pilling (TA Phoenix Engineering) v UK Insurance Ltd* [2019] UKSC 16 para 51. Further, for this provision to apply, there must firstly be actual ambiguity in the meaning of a term – it is not enough that a term merely contradicts another term of the contract – *R on the application of Emmet Donegan v Financial Services Compensation Scheme Ltd* [2021] EWHC 760 paras 150–151. Construction of a contract is for the court, and cannot be dictated by how the sector has historically interpreted a term – *Higgins & Co Lawyers Ltd v Evans* [2019] EWHC 2809 QB para 57.

2   CRA 2015, s 69(2).

3   However, lack of transparency may be a reason why the term is used contrary to the requirements of good faith – *Evans v Cherry Tree Finance Ltd* [2007] EWHC 3523 (Ch) at para 61 and *R on the application of Emmet Donegan v Financial Services Compensation Scheme Ltd* [2021] EWHC 760 para 137–139 and 144.

The core exemption

9.52 CRA 2015, s 64 provides:

64 Exclusion from assessment of fairness

(1)   A term of a consumer contract may not be assessed for fairness under section 62 to the extent that—

(a)   it specifies the main subject matter of the contract, or

(b)   the assessment is of the appropriateness of the price payable under the contract, by comparison with the goods, digital content or services supplied under it.

(2)   Subsection (1) excludes a term from an assessment under section 62 only if it is transparent and prominent.

(3)   A term is transparent for the purposes of this Part if it is expressed in plain and intelligible language and (in the case of a written term) is legible.

(4)   A term is prominent for the purposes of this section if it is brought to the consumer's attention in such a way that an average consumer would be aware of the term.

(5)   In subsection (4) "average consumer" means a consumer who is reasonably well-informed, observant and circumspect.

(6)   This section does not apply to a term of a contract listed in Part 1 of Schedule 2.

9.53 EU Member States do not have to provide for this exemption in their legislation, but where they do, the exemption must be no broader than that set out in the Directive – which must be 'given an autonomous and uniform interpretation throughout the European Union'[1].

[1]   CJEU *Matei v SC Volksbank* Romania (C-143/13) at para 50. This implies that national courts of EU Member States must apply CJEU jurisprudence on this topic, even where it conflicts with the authority of more senior national appellate courts, see CJEU *Ruxandra Andriciuc v Banca Romaneasca SA* (C-186/16) at paras 22 and 33–34.

9.54 The exclusion is narrow and must be strictly interpreted[1], restricted only to the 'essential obligations' of contracts[2]. These could otherwise be referred to as the 'substance of the bargain', 'of central and indispensable importance' to the contract, as distinct from the ancillary 'incidental (if important) terms which surround them'. They represent what, objectively, both parties would view as the core bargain[3], and what in fact is the substance of the bargain[4]. The exclusion does not apply to terms which set out secondary obligations, which apply only on breach of a primary obligation[5]. It is important to look at the substance and reality of the transaction, not at the form[6]. Although the language of the contract is important in this regard, it is not conclusive[7]. The court must also look at the surrounding circumstances or contractual matrix, such as the market generally, the actual negotiation between the parties, and their assumptions, together with the actual package the consumer received, and what he pays for this[8].

[1]   CJEU *Profi Credit Polska SA v QJ* (C-84/19, C-222/19 & C-252/19) at para 66; CJEU *Matei v SC Volksbank* Romania (C-143/13) at para 49; OFT *v Abbey National* [2009] UKSC 6, per Lord Mance at para 104. *Director General of Fair Trading v First National Bank* [2001] UKHL 52, per Lord Bingham at para 12. The CRA reduced the scope of the exemption in several important respects, and therefore the reasoning in the old House of Lords and Supreme Court cases which considered the UTCCR 1999 may not be entirely valid now.

2   CJEU *Caja de Ahorros* (C-484/08) at para 34. These are likely to be the factors on which traders compete: CJEU *Caja de Ahorros* (C-484/08) AG's Opinion at para 40). There should be a functioning market based on competition in respect of price and efficiency (CJEU *Caja de Ahorros* (C-484/08) AG's Opinion at para 62).

3   *OFT v Abbey National* [2009] UKSC 6 per Lord Mance at para 113, *OFT v Foxtons Ltd* [2009] EWHC 1681 (Ch) at para 40 and paras 50–51 (what would the consumer expect instead of being surprised at?). The test does not however consider what the parties actually knew – *OFT v Abbey National* [2009] UKSC 6, per Lord Phillips at para 72.

4   This is what enables the contract to function effectively, and what in fact the consumer receives in exchange for his money: see *Foxtons v O'Reardon* [2011] EWHC 2946 (QB) at paras 60–61, *Smith v Mortgage Express* [2007] CTLC 134 at para 61.

5   *Cavendish V El Makdessi, ParkingEye Ltd v Beavis* [2015] UKSC 67 para 102 – and see also para 32 for discussion of the distinction between primary and secondary obligations.

6   *Bairstow Eves v Smith* [2004] EWHC 263 QB at paras 20 and 28. See also *Smith v Mortgage Express* [2007] CTLC 134 at para 20: 'the core terms of any agreement must be what in substance amounts to the core terms, however so described or not in the agreement'.

7   The fact that an agreement has a subheading 'the main content of the agreement' does not mean these are 'core terms' *Smith v Mortgage Express* [2007] CTLC 134 at para 20.

8   *Bairstow Eves v Smith* [2004] EWHC 263 QB at paras 27–28. Also *Smith v Mortgage Express* [2007] CTLC 134 at para 61.

9.55 Where an element is defined as main subject matter or price by other legislation, it does not follow that it falls within the core exemption – because a purposive interpretation may require the other legislation to be construed more broadly than the Directive[1]. The fact that a term may have been individually negotiated is not a relevant criterion in assessing whether a term falls within the exclusion[2]. The CRA 2015 further constrains the scope of the exclusion by confirming that it does not apply to terms that are listed in the grey list[3].

1   CJEU *Matei v SC Volksbank* Romania (C-143/13) at paras 47–49: elements of the cost of credit that must be included in the APR of a loan might not be 'price' under the Directive, because APR is to be construed broadly, whereas the unfair terms core exemption is to be construed narrowly.

2   CJEU *Kasler* (C-26/13) at para 47.

3   Part 1 of Sch 2. This was also the decision of the CJEU in *Matei v SC Volksbank* Romania (C-143/13) at para 60. Those qualifications to the grey list set out in Part 2 of Sch 2 may still be 'core' terms.

9.56 The exclusion applies only 'to the extent' that terms define the core bargain – so price terms for example may still be attacked for reasons other than the appropriateness of the price – for example the timing of payments, or if they apply in surprising circumstances, or if they have an unfair application to a section of consumers[1].

1   *OFT v Abbey National* [2009] UKSC 6 at paras 29 (per Lord Walker JSC), 57–61 and 78–80 (per Lord Phillips PSC), and 95 and 101 (per Lord Mance JSC).

Requirement for transparency and prominence

9.57 The Directive does not require consumer contracts to represent a 'good deal' for consumers[1]. This is because the Directive preserves freedom of choice and competition[2]. Accordingly, the definition of the 'main subject matter' and the 'appropriateness of price' are excluded from the fairness consideration only if they are *transparent* and *prominent*. Prominence requires that the term be 'brought to the consumer's attention'[3], which implies active flagging and up front presentation in glossy brochures as well as on the face of the contract. The level of prominence is of an objective standard – it is such that 'the average consumer would be aware of the term'[4]. Ultimately the exemption is meant to relate to the essential features of the contract, so it would be surprising if these features were not given appropriate highlighting[5].

1   *OFT v Abbey National* [2009] UKSC 6 per Lord Walker at para 4 and *Director General of Fair Trading v First National Bank* [2001] UKHL 52 per Lord Rodger at para 64.
2   *OFT v Abbey National* [2009] UKSC 6, per Lord Walker at para 44.
3   Section 64(4).
4   Section 64(4). The average consumer is defined as 'a consumer who is reasonably well informed, observant and circumspect' – s 64(5).
5   CJEU *Ruxandra Andriciuc v Banca Romaneasca SA* (C-186/16) at para 47.

Main subject matter

9.58   The main subject matter of a contract is what defines the 'very essence of the contractual relationship'. It is those terms that 'lay down the essential obligations of the contract and, as such, characterise it'[1]. It is the substance of the obligation the trader – and consumer – have agreed to perform –although where a term has been negotiated by the parties, this does not necessarily render it a main subject matter term[2]. It is not defined by the transparency of terms, or whether other rules require certain features to be itemised[3]. The CJEU envisages that it is the content without which the contract would not be capable of existing legally[4]. It does not include terms which are 'ancillary to those that define the very essence of the contractual relationship'[5]. It does not include terms which deal with a contingency[6]. It may be a single item or a multiplicity of items. In the case of a loan, it includes the debtor's obligation to repay[7]. In the case of a bank current account the main subject matter was the package of services supplied, including collection and payment of cheques, money transmission services ATM machines and provision of statements[8]. In the case of a loan involving foreign currency, where the loan is advanced in that currency, and must be repaid in that currency, this constitutes the main subject matter, notwithstanding the economic hardship this may cause to the consumer in the event of currency fluctuations[9]. In the case of insurance, it is the promise to provide the insured, in the event of the risk materialising, with the service agreed when the contract was concluded[10]. In the case of an investment bond, it is payment of the subscription, accrual of interest and repayment upon maturity – but not any provisions about transferability of the bond[11]. Other subjects considered by the courts have included estate agent's duties, gym minimum membership periods, a yearly caravan pitch licence, an e-money payment service, and a disclaimer of what services a seller of land will not carry out[12]. The CJEU has ruled that provisions relating to the security offered for a loan cannot be considered to relate to the main subject matter[13].

1   CJEU *Arpad Kasler* C-26/13 at para 49. See also (post Brexit) CJEU *VB v BNP Paribas Personal Finance SA* (Joined Cases C-776/19 to C-782/19) para 60.
2   CJEU *Arpad Kasler* C-26/13 at para 47.
3   CJEU *Profi Credit Polska SA v QJ* (C-84/19, C-222/19 & C-252/19) at para 69 – charges which are required to be highlighted and itemised under the Consumer Credit Directive (2008/48) concept of total cost of credit are not part of the main subject matter for these reasons alone.
4   CJEU *GT v HS* (C-38/17) para 43.
5   CJEU *Profi Credit Polska SA v QJ* (C-84/19, C-222/19 & C-252/19) at para 67.
6   *Andrew Green v Petfre (Gibraltar) Ltd t/a Betfred* [2021] EWHC 842 at para 182 – here the risk that there is an undetectable flaw in the design of realisation of a game, which shortens the odds in the consumer's favour.

7   CJEU *Matei v SC Volksbank* Romania (C-143/13) at para 54. In CJEU *Profi Credit Polska SA v QJ* (C-84/19, C-222/19 & C-252/19) at para 68 this was described as the sum of money (in the stipulated currency) which must be paid and repaid.

8   *OFT v Abbey National* [2009] UKSC 6, per Lord Walker at paras 39–40, per Lord Phillips at para 53.

9   CJEU *Ruxandra Andriciuc v Banca Romaneasca SA* (C-186/16) at paras 38–41. See also CJEU *GT v HS* (C-38/17) para 30. This is in contrast to where a loan is advanced and repayable in local currency, but denominated in foreign currency, in which case the foreign currency obligation is assessable for fairness (see CJEU *Kasler* C-26/13 at para 59 and discussion in CJEU *Ruxandra Andriciuc v Banca Romaneasca SA* (C-186/16) at para 39).

10 CJEU *Van Hove v CNP Assurances* (C-96/14) at paras 34–35.

11 *R on the application of Emmet Donegan v Financial Services Compensation Scheme Ltd* [2021] EWHC 760 para 143.

12 See *Foxtons v O'Reardon* [2011] EWHC 2946 (QB) at paras 57 and 60; *OFT v Ashbourne Management Services Ltd* [2011] EWHC 1237 (Ch) at para 152; *Margaret Baybut v Eccle Riggs Country Park Ltd* (High Court, Manchester District Registry, 2 November 2006) at para 24; *Alfred Overy v Paypal (Europe) Ltd* [2012] EWHC 2659 (QB) at para 207; and *FSA v Asset LI Inc* [2013] EWHC 178 (Ch) at para 132.

13 CJEU *Profi Credit Polska SA v Wlostowska* (C-419/18) para 56. In this case the security was a blank promissory note, which on default by the consumer, the lender could fill in with the sum of money claimed to be due and seek to enforce without separately proving the original debt.

Price

9.59 The concept of price, although it potentially applies to 'any monetary price . . . payable under the contract'[1], has a 'reduced scope'[2]. The CJEU has stated that in order to qualify, the trader should be providing an 'actual service which could constitute consideration for that charge' – the fact that a payment constitutes an income stream for the trader, 'is in principle irrelevant' to the question of whether it is part of the 'price'[3]. It seems a product should be provided in exchange for the specific fee being charged[4]. Further, the service should be provided 'solely in the consumer's interests'[5]. A penalty cannot be redrafted to be part of the price[6]. Further, it is only the 'appropriateness' of the price (ie whether it 'is adequate as compared with the service provided in return') that is excluded from assessment – other aspects of the price may be assessed[7]. Certain charging elements set out in a contract may fall within the concept of 'price', while others do not. For example, while interest charged on credit may be the price, additional charges such as arrangement fees and administration charges may be assessable for fairness[8]. Terms relating to the consideration provided by a consumer, or which have an impact on the actual price to be paid by the consumer are unlikely to fall within the pricing exemption[9]. It is also possible to have a contract under which the consumer makes no payments at all[10]. As with main subject matter terms, a term cannot be part of the price if it appears on the Grey List, or is lacking in transparency or prominence[11].

1   *OFT v Abbey National* [2009] UKSC 6, per Lord Walker at para 41. The current wording of the exemption in the CRA makes provision only for 'the price' to be exempted. It would appear that ancillary 'revenue' may not fall within the scope of the exemption – a construction which is in line with the CJEU jurisprudence on the price exemption.

2   CJEU *Profi Credit Polska SA v QJ* (C-84/19, C-222/19 & C-252/19) at para 79.

3   CJEU *Matei v SC Volksbank* Romania (C-143/13) at paras 70 and 68. See also CJEU *Kasler* (C-26/13) at para 58.

4   CJEU *Profi Credit Polska SA v QJ* (C-84/19, C-222/19 & C-252/19) at paras 80–81. It seems the concept of price does not have to relate to what the trader supplies as the main subject matter of the contract however (para 82). See also *Competition and Markets Authority v Care UK Health and Social Holdings Ltd* [2021] EWHC 2088 (Ch) paras 93–98: charges incurred in

marketing or showing potential customers round a care home are not permissible services, but activities such as conducting a care needs assessment, liaising with external professionals and taking steps to organise specialist equipment are services for which it was permissible for a care home to charge an up-front administration fee.

⁵ CJEU *Matei v SC Volksbank* Romania (C-143/13) at para 71.
⁶ *OFT v Abbey National* [2009] UKSC 6 per Lord Walker at para 43 (referring to *Bairstowe Eves v* Smith [2004] 263) and Lord Phillips at para 83.
⁷ CJEU *Matei v SC Volksbank* Romania (C-143/13) at paras 56 and 63. CJEU *Caja de Ahorros* (C-484/08) AG's Opinion at para 70, fn 41. CJEU *Profi Credit Polska SA v QJ* (C-84/19, C-222/19 & C-252/19) at para 80.
⁸ CJEU *Mikrokasa SA v XO* (C-779/18) paras 23, 58.
⁹ CJEU *Kiss* (C-621/17) para 35.
¹⁰ *OFT v Abbey National* [2009] UKSC 6, per Lord Mance at para 103.
¹¹ In this respect the High Court case of *Casehub Ltd v Wolf Cola Ltd* [2017] EWHC 1169 (Ch) at paras 41–57) may be wrongly decided. In deciding that an early termination fee for a 1 year cloud storage contract was part of the price, the judge failed to give any consideration to whether the term was transparent or prominent, how it could be reconciled to the Grey List terms set out at paras 5 and 6 of Sch 3 to the CRA 2015, the extent to which it is a disguised penalty clause and the impact of the claim that the reason for the consumers wishing to cancel early was due to the trader's failure actually to provide a cloud storage service (and thus the extent to which the term is blacklisted). The case also failed to engage in any detail with the CJEU case law that has post-dated the *Abbey National* case.

Part of the price?

9.60 The following types of term have been found to fall within the scope of the exemption as it was set out in the UTCCRs, but because of the narrowing in scope of the definition in the CRA 2015, may not fall within the definition now:

- Sums that are an important part of the trader's charging structure, amounting to over 30% of their revenue stream¹.
- Sums the trader relies on in order to be able profitably to provide the services on offer².
- Sums which the vast majority of consumers know about and expect to pay³.
- Bank charges made for various current account services, including interest forgone⁴.
- The price payable for early redemption of a 20-year mortgage within a fixed 3-year period, where the consumer enjoyed a discounted interest rate for the first 2 years⁵.

¹ *OFT v Abbey National* [2009] UKSC 6, per Lord Walker at para 47. As noted above, a revenue stream, which is levied without providing any actual service in exchange seems unlikely to fall within the exemption now.
² *OFT v Abbey National* [2009] UKSC 6 at para 88. According to CJEU case law since the *Abbey National* ruling, the fact a trader relies on an income stream is not relevant to whether it is part of the price.
³ *OFT v Abbey National* [2009] UKSC 6, per Lord Mance at para 105, see also *OFT v Foxtons Ltd* [2009] EWHC 1681 (Ch).
⁴ *OFT v Abbey National* [2009] UKSC 6, per Lord Walker at para 42.
⁵ *Smith v Mortgage Express* [2007] CTLC 134 at para 61.

Not part of the price

9.61 The following terms have been held not to be within the pricing adequacy exemption:

- Interest payments in the event of default by the consumer in breach of contract¹.

- Renewal commission paid by a landlord to a letting agent[2].
- An early redemption charge on a loan[3].
- Provision for the time of payment[4].
- Price escalation clauses[5].
- Any other mechanism for amending the price or a rate of interest, including a price indexation clause[6].
- A sales commission where no selling service was provided[7].
- A regular charge for converting the currency of a loan, due to the loan being tied to a foreign currency, where no foreign exchange service was actually supplied to the consumer – even though this formed part of the APR for a loan[8].
- Terms falling within paras (d), (e), (f) and (l) in Sch 2 para 1[9].
- Sums not necessary to profitable operation, but which are 'adventitious benefits'[10].

[1]   *Director General of Fair Trading v First National Bank* [2001] UKHL 52 at paras 12, 34 and 43.
[2]   *OFT v Foxtons Ltd* [2009] EWHC 1681 (Ch) at para 50. Also conceded by Chesterton Global Ltd in *Chesterton v Finney*.
[3]   *Evans v Cherry Tree Finance Ltd* [2007] EWHC 3523 (Ch), although this point was not argued in this case.
[4]   *Foxtons v O'Reardon* [2011] EWHC 2946 (QB) at para 56. Although on the facts in this case the clause in question was held to relate to the main subject matter of the contract.
[5]   *Bairstow Eves v Smith* [2004] EWHC 263 QB. See also *Director General of Fair Trading v First National Bank* [2001] UKHL 52 at para 34.
[6]   CJEU *Nemzeti v Invitel* (C-472/10) at para 23; CJEU *Matei v SC Volksbank* Romania (C-143/13) at para 57; EFTA *Gunnar Engilbertsson v Islandsbanki* (E-25/13) at para 96.
[7]   *OFT v Foxtons Ltd* [2009] EWHC 1681 (Ch).
[8]   CJEU *Kasler* (C-26/13) at para 58.
[9]   *OFT v Abbey National* [2009] UKSC 6, per Lord Walker at para 43.
[10] *OFT v Foxtons Ltd* [2009] EWHC 1681 (Ch) at para 85. In this case these were letting agent commissions paid when a tenant remained in occupation of a property after the initial fixed period of letting expired.

The fairness test

9.62 Section 62(4) provides that a:

> (4) Term is unfair if, contrary to the requirement of good faith, it causes a significant imbalance in the parties' rights and obligations arising under the contract, to the detriment of the consumer.

Section 62(6) applies the same test to notices.

9.63 The courts in the UK have construed three aspects:

(1)   Is there a significant imbalance in the parties' rights and obligations?
(2)   Is this to the detriment of the consumer?
(3)   Is the detriment in a manner, or to an extent, that is contrary to good faith[1]?

[1]   Lord Bingham in *Director General of Fair Trading v First National Bank* [2001] UKHL 52 at para 17.

9.64 In *UK Housing Alliance (North West) Ltd v Francis* the Court of Appeal stated that[1]:

'the existence of an imbalance caused by the term was held [in First National Bank] not to be enough on its own despite argument that the imbalance of itself demonstrated the absence of good faith.[2]'

¹   *UK Housing Alliance (North West) Ltd v Francis* [2010] EWCA Civ 117 at para 21.
²   See also *Cavendish V El Makdessi, ParkingEye Ltd v Beavis* [2015] UKSC 67 para 107 where the Supreme Court held that a term which created an imbalance was not unfair because it was not contrary to good faith.

9.65 Although the three limbs of the test are separate stages, it is plain that they are interlinked. In *First National Bank* Lord Steyn observed that there was 'a large area of overlap between the concepts of good faith and significant imbalance'[1].

¹   *Director General of Fair Trading v First National Bank* [2001] UKHL 52 at paras 36 and 17 respectively.

9.66 Section 62(5) adds that[1] the unfairness of a contractual term shall be assessed:

- taking into account the nature of the subject matter of the contract; and
- by reference to all the circumstances existing when the term was agreed; and
- to all the other terms of the contract or of any other contract on which it depends.

¹   Section 62(7) applies comparable provisions to the assessment of notices.

9.67 Indeed it is mandatory to take into account all of the terms of the contract, unless the term is being challenged by a regulator[1]. The cumulative effect of all the terms may mean that a term which by itself appears fair enough, is in the context of the contract unfair[2].

¹   CJEU *Banif Plus Bank Zrt v Csaba Csipai* (C-472/11) at paras 40–41, CJEU *Commission v Spain* (C-70/03) at para 16. This is because a regulator brings a challenge to the term which is not dependent on the circumstances in which the term is used.
²   CJEU *A v B* (C-738/19) para 30.

9.68 Section 63(1) creates a presumption that terms falling within the indicative and non-exhaustive list of the terms in Pt 1 of Sch 2 (the grey list) will be regarded as unfair[1]. Section 63(2) confirms that while those terms listed in Pt 2 of Sch 2 are not presumed to be unfair, they may still be assessed for fairness[2].

¹   However, they are not necessarily unfair – *Cavendish V El Makdessi, ParkingEye Ltd v Beavis* [2015] UKSC 67 at para 105.
²   Unless they are otherwise excluded from assessment as core provisions, or mandatory statutory terms.

9.69 In assessing whether terms are unfair, the key tests which have been set out by the Supreme Court are:

- What is the effect of the contract with the term, compared with the effect it would have without it, and whether the term alters the consumer's legal rights[1]?
- Whether the term is appropriate for securing the attainment of the objectives pursued by it, and does not go beyond what is necessary to achieve them[2].

The courts have also taken the following factors into consideration[3]:

- What is the effect of the inclusion of the term on the substance or core of the transaction[4]?
- Whether if it were drawn to his attention, the average consumer would be likely to be surprised by it – in other words, whether the trader, dealing fairly and equitably with the consumer, could reasonably assume they would have agreed to the term in individual contract negotiations.[5].
- Whether the term is a standard term, not merely in non-negotiable consumer contracts, but in commercial contracts freely negotiated between parties acting on level terms and at arm's length[6].
- Whether, in such cases, the party adversely affected by the inclusion of the term or his lawyer might reasonably be expected to object to its inclusion or press for its deletion[7].
- What, if any, protection the consumer has against the unfair application of the term[8].
- The consequences of the term under the law applicable to the contract[9].
- Any benefit to the consumer deriving from the term under challenge[10].

1 See *Mohamed Aziz v Caixa d'Estalvis* (C-415/11) at para 68 and *Cavendish V El Makdessi, ParkingEye Ltd v Beavis* [2015] UKSC 67 at para 105(2). Example of altering the consumer's legal rights include preventing the consumer from transferring a product which they would otherwise be able to sell, and depriving the consumer of regulatory protections which they would have enjoyed absent the term – see *R on the application of Emmet Donegan v Financial Services Compensation Scheme Ltd* [2021] EWHC 760 para 133. The detriment may be caused by reasons extraneous to the contract, if this is triggered by a term in the contract – *R on the application of Emmet Donegan v Financial Services Compensation Scheme Ltd* [2021] EWHC 760 para 134.

2 *Mohamed Aziz v Caixa d'Estalvis* (C-415/11) at paras 71–74 and *Cavendish V El Makdessi, ParkingEye Ltd v Beavis* [2015] UKSC 67 at para 105(4). This may include benefits to the trader, indirectly to the consumer and to other interested parties, see *Cavendish V El Makdessi, ParkingEye Ltd v Beavis* [2015] UKSC 6, at paras 105(4), 106 and 107.

3 And see the speech of Lord Millett in *First National Bank* for the core of this list.

4 In cases where the term is inconsistent with the main object and intent of the contract, this consideration may lead to a term not being incorporated into the contract at all, see *Alexander v West Bromwich Mortgage Company Ltd* [2016] EWCA Civ 496 at para 46.

5 The latter formulation has been repeated in CJEU decisions such as *Mohamed Aziz v Caixa d'Estalvis* (C-415/11) at para 69. Also *Cavendish V El Makdessi, ParkingEye Ltd v Beavis* [2015] UKSC 67 at para 105(3). An example of a term which the consumer would not be taken to have agreed to is a restriction on transferring a bond, which is a provision of no value to purchasers of those bonds, and whose only purpose is to relieve the seller of regulatory obligations – see *R on the application of Emmet Donegan v Financial Services Compensation Scheme Ltd* [2021] EWHC 760 para 135.

6 *FSA v Asset LI Inc* [2013] EWHC 178 (Ch) at para 138(i); *Munkenbeck & Marshall v Harold* [2005] EWHC 356 (TCC) at para 15. Also the Opinion of Advocate General Kokott in *Mohamed Aziz v Caixa d'Estalvis* (C-415/11) at para AG75. This consideration may to some extent excuse a term which is in common use, but the fact that a term is used in commercial transactions may not excuse it completely, because such terms may not be fair in a consumer context.

7 *Director General of Fair Trading v First National Bank* [2001] UKHL 52 at para 54.

8 *Cavendish V El Makdessi, ParkingEye Ltd v Beavis* [2015] UKSC 67 at paras 106 and 111 and AG's Opinion in *Mohamed Aziz v Caixa d'Estalvis* (C-415/11) at para AG75. This might include other rules of law which constrain the trader's application of the term – see *Parker v NFU Mutual Insurance Society Ltd* [2012] EWHC 2156 (Comm) & *Abbot & Ors v RCI Europe* [2016] EWHC 2602 (Ch) at para 46.

9 CJEU *Freiburger* (C-237/02) at para 21.

10 CJEU *Freiburger* (C-237/02) at paras 16 and 23.

All the circumstances of the contract

9.70 This has a wide definition, and includes all the surrounding circumstances including a telesales pitch[1]. Where the trader creates a sense of 'gravity' about the signing of the contract, this will not operate to make unfair terms fair[2]. It could include any unfair commercial practices engaged in by the trader at the time the contract is signed[3]. However it is a narrower test than that of the test for an unfair relationship under s 140A of the Consumer Credit Act 1974[4].

1   *FSA v Asset LI Inc* [2013] EWHC 178 (Ch) at para 134.
2   *FSA v Asset LI Inc* [2013] EWHC 178 (Ch) at para 138(vi).
3   CJEU *Bankia SA v Merino* (C-109/17) at para 48.
4   *Greenlands Trading Ltd v Girolama Pontearso* [2019] EWHC 278 (Ch) at para 50.

Time of the assessment

9.71 The primary focus is on 'all the circumstances existing *when the contract was agreed*'. This includes both the circumstances that were known to the parties at the time, and those that are of such a nature that they could affect the future performance of the contract – and which therefore might give rise to an imbalance which only manifests itself later[1]. So for example when considering an accelerated interest clause, the court must bear in mind what the statutory and market interest rates were at the time of the conclusion of the contract, rather than those that pertained subsequently[2]. It seems to be sufficient that circumstances which could give rise to unfairness 'could have been known by the seller or supplier at the time the agreement was concluded' – thus wilful blindness will not be an excuse, nor is the consumer required to be aware of the problem[3]. Where subsequent legislation replaces certain terms of the agreement with retrospective effect, this should not be factored into the assessment of fairness[4]. However this does not rule out some consideration of later events, such as how the term was enforced[5] or events that demonstrate how the term applies in fact[6]. It is also important to consider the likely effect of a term in the future[7], and the expertise and knowledge of the trader[8]. However the trader's subsequent misuse of a fair term does not render it unfair[9]. Likewise a trader's forbearance when enforcing an unfair term does not exonerate it[10].

1   CJEU *Ruxandra Andriciuc v Banca Romaneasca SA* (C-186/16) at para 54.
2   CJEU *Banco Primus v Garcia* (C-421/14) at para 65.
3   CJEU *GT v HS* (C-38/17) para 40.
4   CJEU *OTP Bank Nyrt v Ilyes* (C-51/17) at para 81.
5   *Du Plessis v Fontgary Leisure Parks Ltd* [2012] EWCA Civ 409 at para 52.
6   See *Clipper Ventures Plc v Boyde* Sheriff Principal's Judgment (Sheriffdom of Lothian and Borders) case A709/11 (24 December 2012).
7   *Director General of Fair Trading v First National Bank* [2001] UKHL 52, per Lord Bingham at para 13 and per Lord Hope of Craighead at para 45.
8   CJEU *Ruxandra Andriciuc v Banca Romaneasca SA* (C-186/16) at para 56 – in this case in order to assess the impact of linking a loan to foreign currency exchange rates, the movements of which a bank might be in a position to predict more accurately than a consumer.
9   *Director General of Fair Trading v First National Bank* [2001] UKHL 52, per Lord Bingham at para 24. Where a term in a lease 'becomes' unfair because parallel terms were not introduced into other properties in the same development, as promised to the tenant who agreed to the term, this has been held not to render the term (in this case a covenant not to sublet the property) unfair *Jones & Seymour v Roundlistic Ltd* [2018] EWCA Civ 2284 para 48.
10   CJEU *Banco Primus v Garcia* (C-421/14) at para 74.

Circumstances existing when the contract was agreed

9.72 Section 62(5)(b) refers to all the circumstances existing when the contract was agreed. However the court should also have regard to circumstances which could have been known to the trader at the time the contract was agreed, and which could affect the future performance of the contract because such later events could reveal a significant imbalance which is latent in the contract[1]. Does it include the personal circumstances of the consumer? In *Tew v BoS*[2], the High Court considered that the comparable wording in the UTCCR 1999 meant that circumstances such as the actual understanding of the individual consumers, and whether the transaction made sense for that consumer, were relevant: courts decide 'individual cases' rather than cases in the abstract. The whole notion of fairness 'involves the impact of matters on a person' and individual circumstances of the consumers (such as how well-heeled, well-informed, well-advised or open-eyed they were) could be relevant. The 'personal circumstances of each individual' had to be considered. This ruling is at odds with that in *Foxtons v O'Reardon*[3] where the High Court ruled that the personal circumstances of the consumers (in terms of vulnerability or ill health, or special requirements that they had) were not relevant to the fairness of terms requiring payment of commission to an estate agent[4].

[1]   (Post Brexit) CJEU *Dexia Nederland BV* (C-229/19) para 53.
[2]   [2010] EWHC 203 (Ch) at para 21.
[3]   [2011] EWHC 2946 (QB) at para 63.
[4]   See also *Harrison v Shepherd Homes Ltd* [2011] EWHC 1811 (TCC).

9.73 In a collective challenge, the courts have to consider the 'typical' circumstances existing when the contract was agreed[1]. This has been taken to include the typical sorts of consumers targeted by a trader, such those who are not financially experienced or sophisticated, and whom the trader discourages from seeking legal advice[2].

[1]   Lord Steyn in *The Director General of Fair Trading v First National Bank plc* at para 33.
[2]   *FSA v Asset LI Inc* [2013] EWHC 178 (Ch) at para 136.

Significant imbalance

9.74 In *Spreadex v Cochrane* it was said that this was about 'the balance between rights and obligations'[1]. However the imbalance is not assessed by weighing the rights and obligations of the parties in the contract as a whole, but simply in respect of the particular term under challenge – thus a term that obliges the consumer to pay a tax that the national law requires to be paid by the trader may create a significant imbalance, even though it is a relatively small sum in comparison to the transaction as a whole[2].

[1]   *Spreadex v Cochrane* [2012] EWHC 1290 (Comm) at para 17.
[2]   CJEU *Constructora Principado SA v Alvarez* (C-226/12) at paras 22–26 and 30. Since Brexit, in *Dexia Nederland BV* (C-229/19) para 49, the CJEU has held that the assessment of significant imbalance should not be based on a comparison between the total value of the transaction and the costs charged under the clause. A significant imbalance may result from a sufficiently serious impairment to the consumer's legal position.

9.75 'The term must be judged by reference to all situations in which it might potentially be applicable'[1]. The term must be considered in context: one which might at first blush appear unfair to the consumer might not cause an imbalance if its effect is mitigated by another term[2]. Likewise, a term which appears to be inoffensive on its own, may in conjunction with other terms in a contract, be unfair (for example where the terms permit the trader to engage in double recovery for some loss)[3]. Where there is a risk that a term might be unfair in certain circumstances, the court should ensure that the term does not result in very unequal sharing of the risks borne by the parties[4].

[1] *Spreadex v Cochrane* [2012] EWHC 1290 (Comm) at para 19. A term may be unfair if the imbalance might occur in certain circumstances, but in others it might benefit the consumer (Post Brexit) CJEU *Dexia Nederland BV* (C-229/19) para 55.
[2] *Director General of Fair Trading v First National Bank* [2001] UKHL 52, per Lord Bingham at para 17.
[3] CJEU *A v B* (C-738/19) para 39.
[4] (Post Brexit) CJEU *Dexia Nederland BV* (C-229/19) paras 59–60. See also (post Brexit) CJEU *VB v BNP Paribas Personal Finance SA* (Joined Cases C-776/19 to C-782/19) paras 95–102, which criticised a term which placed a risk of currency fluctuation solely or substantially on the consumer, when in fact the trader has the knowledge and greater means to foresee how a foreign exchange risk might materialise (see para 100 in particular).

9.76 The CJEU has held that it is particularly relevant to consider whether there are rules of national law that would apply, absent the term under challenge, and if so whether the term puts the consumer in a worse position. This is the main factor in assessing imbalance[1]. The court must also consider whether the consumer is able to use legal means to prevent the application of the term[2]. However mere formal equivalence between the parties may still give rise to a significant imbalance if this does not reflect the dependence of the consumer on the trader's product[3]. Further where legislation imposes constraints on the trader's exercise of a fundamentally unfair term, this does not prevent the court from finding unfairness[4].

[1] CJEU *Mohamed Aziz v Caixa d'Esalvis de Catalunya* (C-415/11) at para 68 and *Cavendish V El Makdessi, ParkingEye Ltd v Beavis* [2015] UKSC 67 para 105(2).
[2] CJEU *Mohamed Aziz v Caixa d'Esalvis de Catalunya* (C-415/11) at para 68. See also *Parker v NFU Mutual Insurance Society Ltd* [2012] EWHC 2156 (Comm).
[3] *Alfred Overy v Paypal (Europe) Ltd* [2012] EWHC 2659 (QB) at para 211. In *Weco Projects Aps v Loro Piana* [2020] EWHC 2150 (Comm) para 109, it was said that formal equivalence between a consumer and trader was enough, in the context of a jurisdiction clause, on the basis that both of them had to operate in a foreign jurisdiction. However this *obiter* decision seems to have been heavily influenced by the fact that the consumer was a billionaire, with staff to assist in the management of his affairs. It is unlikely to have direct application to more typical consumer transactions.
[4] CJEU *Banco Primus v Garcia* (C-421/14) at para 74.

9.77 The illustrative list of terms in Sch 2, Pt 1 *may* be unfair, and those in Pt 2 *may* be fair – but in either case, there must be an assessment of fairness[1].

[1] Section 63(1) and (2). CJEU *RWE Vertrieb AG v VBZ Nordrhein-Westfalen* (Case C-92/11) at paras 46–47.

9.78 Factors that courts have taken into account include:

• What does the consumer get for the term that they are required to submit to? Is it reasonable?[1]
• What risks does the trader take in return for the term, judged at the time the contract was made?[2]
• Whether the term in fact reflects the commercial realities of the transaction[3].

- Whether the term protects the trader's legitimate interests (such as where the trader has given a special discount on a loan for a fixed period of time, and protects their income by means of an early payment charge)[4].
- Whether this legitimate interest could have been protected in a less harmful way, and if the term is drafted too broadly[5].
- Whether the regulatory framework means that the term could not in fact be enforced as broadly as at first appears[6].
- What other rules of law operate to restrain the trader's use of the term (such as a requirement to act with reasonable care and skill)[7].
- Where there is an insurable risk, the context will determine whether the trader or consumer ought to have insured against it[8].

[1]   For example, in *Rochdale Borough Council v Dixon* [2011] EWCA Civ 1173, it was held to be entirely reasonable to require a tenant to pay for water charges as part of their rent, since they made use of the water, and it would be unfair to expect them to get water for free. By contrast, where a consumer is required to pay a fee, but no service, or a disproportionately small service, is provided in exchange, or the description of the fee is misleading, the fee may be unfair (CJEU *Kiss* (C-621/17) para 55). Where the term ensures that a useful service is provided to consumers generally, this may be relevant in assessing whether it is fair to impose an obligation on a consumer in an individual contract – *Higgins & Co Lawyers Ltd v Evans* [2019] EWHC 2809 QB para 101(iii).
[2]   See, eg *UK Housing Alliance (North West) Ltd v Francis* [2010] EWCA Civ 117 at para 27. Where the consumer has control over the risks in fact, it may be more appropriate for the trader to limit their liability if things go wrong – see *West v Ian Finlay & Assocs* [2014] EWCA Civ 316 at paras 53 and 59.
[3]   See, eg in *Du Plessis v Fontgary Leisure Parks Ltd* [2012] EWCA Civ 409 the court considered that it was legitimate for owners of a caravan park to seek to re-grade the pitches, and accordingly to charge certain caravan owners proportionately more money (paras 36–37, 41 and 49).
[4]   *Smith v Mortgage Express* [2007] CTLC 134 at para 63. See also *Higgins & Co Lawyers Ltd v Evans* [2019] EWHC 2809 QB para 101 – a term was held to be fair which protected a solicitor's legitimate interest in being paid in the event that a conditional fee arrangement terminated early as a result of the consumer's death.
[5]   *Spreadex v Cochrane* [2012] EWHC 1290 (Comm) at para 19; *Alfred Overy v Paypal (Europe) Ltd* [2012] EWHC 2659 (QB) at para 210.
[6]   *Parker v NFU Mutual Insurance Society Ltd* [2012] EWHC 2156 (Comm) at para 191.
[7]   *Abbot & Ors v RCI Europe* [2016] EWHC 2602 (Ch) at para 46.
[8]   *West v Ian Finlay & Assocs* [2014] EWCA Civ 316 at para 52.

9.79 Examples of terms which have been held to create a significant imbalance include:

- Making a consumer liable for all trades on a spread betting account, whether authorised or not.
- Terms where the trader assumes no obligations and the consumer has no rights[1].
- Terms making the consumer liable to pay costs on an indemnity basis, plus interest in the event of a dispute, when there is no corresponding liability on the trader[2].
- Terms which lock consumers into long gym contracts, in circumstances where this brings advantages to the gym, but does not significantly benefit the consumer – in particular where the consumer cannot terminate easily if their circumstances change[3].
- Where a loan is granted at a high interest rate to a consumer in need of a swift loan[4].
- Unfair renewal commission charged by a letting agent[5].

- Terms which exclude important legal rights in new house build contracts[6].
- Terms which require the consumer to pay an unknown future sum[7].
- Terms which require an insured consumer promptly to pass information to their insurer, where the effect of not doing so is that they may forfeit all cover where the insurer suffers no prejudice[8].
- Terms which permit a trader to terminate an e-payment service immediately and at will, or for grounds that are not serious[9].
- Terms which exclude liability for statements of telesales staff[10].
- A term which imposes a parking charge in excess of the consumer's liability to the landowner in tort for trespass[11].
- A term which requires the consumer to pay a fee when recovering taxes they have paid to a flight operator when they did not in the end travel[12].
- A term which levies a management charge or disbursement commission in a loan contract for services which cannot reasonably be regarded as services performed in the context of the management or disbursement of a loan, or where the amounts of those charges and commission are disproportionate in relation to the amount of the loan[13].
- A term which prevented the transfer of investment bonds and deprived consumers of important regulatory protections[14].

[1]   *Spreadex v Cochrane* [2012] EWHC 1290 (Comm) at para 17.
[2]   *Munkenbeck & Marshall v Harold* [2005] EWHC 356 (TCC) at paras 12 and 15.
[3]   In *OFT v Ashbourne Management Services Ltd* [2011] EWHC 1237 (Ch).
[4]   *Evans v Cherry Tree Finance Ltd* [2007] EWHC 3523 (Ch) at paras 63–64.
[5]   *OFT v Foxtons Ltd* [2009] EWHC 1681 (Ch) at paras 90–95. The commission was surprising, of a significant amount, and payable even where the agent did no work.
[6]   *Harrison v Shepherd Homes Ltd* [2011] EWHC 1811 (TCC) at paras 107, 115 and 118. See also CJEU *Constructora Principado SA v Alvarez* (C-226/12) at para 28.
[7]   CJEU *Constructora Principado SA v Alvarez* (C-226/12) at para 26.
[8]   *Bankers Insurance Company Ltd v South* [2003] EWHC 380 at para 34. However, see also *Parker v NFU Mutual Insurance Society Ltd* [2012] EWHC 2156 (Comm) at para 191.
[9]   *Alfred Overy v Paypal (Europe) Ltd* [2012] EWHC 2659 (QB) at paras 211–213 and 226.
[10] *FSA v Asset LI Inc* [2013] EWHC 178 (Ch) at paras 135–138.
[11] *Cavendish V El Makdessi, ParkingEye Ltd v Beavis* [2015] UKSC 67 at para 107, although in this case the term was not unfair, because it was not used contrary to good faith. For an application of this reasoning in a context post application of the CRA, see the Scottish Sheriff decision in *Indigo Park Services Ltd v Conor Watson* 6 September 2017 Ref SC67–16 paras 101–110.
[12] See the ruling of the Berlin Regional Court referred to in the CJEU case *Air Berlin v Bundesverband der Verbraucherzentralen* (C-290/16) at para 13.
[13] CJEU *Kiss* (C-621/17) para 55. It does not however create a significant imbalance merely because the term does not unequivocally determine what specific services are provided in return for those charges, as long as the nature of the services actually provided can reasonably be understood from a consideration of the entire contract as a whole (paras 54 & 56).
[14] R *on the application of Emmet Donegan v Financial Services Compensation Scheme Ltd* [2021] EWHC 760 paras 127–146.

Detriment of the consumer

9.80 Terms that clearly operate to the consumer's advantage were held not to fall foul of the UTCCR 1999. Where the consumer has imposed the term either by their own choice or a choice made by their professional agent there appears to be a presumption that there is no detriment to the consumer. A trader has no duty to draw the consumer's attention to the pitfalls in terms which the trader is not offering[1].

[1]   *Mylcrist Builders Ltd v Mrs G Buck* [2008] EWHC 2172 (TCC) at para 51(7), and *Bryen and Langley Ltd v Martin Boston* [2004] EWHC 2450 (TCC) at para 45; see also *Westminster Building Company Lt v Beckingham* [2004] EWHC 138 (TCC).

Good faith

9.81 In the Directive, Recital 16 states that in making an assessment of good faith, particular regard shall be had:

- to the strength of the bargaining positions of the parties[1];
- to whether the consumer had an inducement to agree to the term; and
- to whether the goods or services were sold or supplied to the special order of the consumer.

[1]   In some circumstances, the parties may be of more or less equal strength – see for instance *West v Ian Finlay & Assocs* [2014] EWCA Civ 316 at paras 59–60, where the consumers, who were wealthy professionals, were held to be of 'savvy nature', and therefore in an equal bargaining position. Also *Khurana v Webster Construction Ltd* [2015] EWHC 758 (TCC) at para 53(1), where the consumers were professional persons owning a substantial property, whereas the trader was effectively a modest one man building company. In *Deutsche Bank (Suisse) SA v Gulzar Ahmed Khan* [2013] EWHC 482 (Comm) at para 380, millionaires who were legally advised, during extensive negotiations, conducted assertively by the consumers, to achieve significant terms in the trader's terms, were held not to have been taken advantage of. No lack of good faith was shown. By contrast the experience and competence of a player of internet gambling was held not to outweigh the importance of clearly explaining and signposting exclusions of liability which were relied on to avoid paying out winnings achieved in a defective game – *Andrew Green v Petfre (Gibraltar) Ltd t/a Betfred* [2021] EWHC 842 at paras 177 and 181.

9.82 Recital 16 adds that the requirement of good faith may be satisfied where the seller or supplier 'deals fairly and equitably with the other party whose legitimate interests he has taken into account', which the CJEU has interpreted as including consideration of whether the trader 'could reasonably assume that the [reasonable] consumer would have agreed to such a term in individual contract negotiations'[1]. The UK Supreme Court has also emphasised the need to consider whether the trader has a legitimate interest in imposing the liability (although it is vital that the liability is no more severe than is necessary)[2]. However this does not amount to an inquiry as to whether the trader had an intention to use unfair terms – as the subjective intention of the trader is irrelevant to the test[3]. In *First National Bank* Lord Bingham described good faith as amounting to a requirement of 'fair and open dealing', which he treated as two separate, cumulative criteria. Good faith can never be viewed simply as a matter of being open about objectively imbalanced terms. There must also be consideration of whether the trader is acting fairly. Lord Steyn, described good faith as 'an objective criterion'. It is about whether the trader has dealt fairly and equitably. It is not a procedural requirement to do with the negotiating procedures[4]. Rather it looks also to the trader's motives and the effect of their conduct. It is a question of 'commercial morality'. However, it is not an obligation to check whether the consumer knows what he is doing[5].

[1]   *Mohamed Aziz v Caixa d'Esalvis de Catalunya* (C-415/11) at para 69, applied by the UK Supreme Court as the main factor of the good faith test in *Cavendish V El Makdessi, ParkingEye Ltd v Beavis* [2015] UKSC 67 at paras 105(3) and 108. The Supreme Court stressed that the test is whether the *reasonable* consumer would have agreed to the term, not the

individual challenging the term. In this regard, the fact that a particular consumer, even one who was legally advised, did not challenge the term ought not be taken to be evidence that the term was being used in good faith – contrary to the view taken by the Court of Appeal in *Jones & Seymour v Roundlistic Ltd* [2018] EWCA Civ 2284 para 48.

2   *Cavendish V El Makdessi, ParkingEye Ltd v Beavis* [2015] UKSC 67 at para 107, here the whole aim of the contract was to provide two hours' free parking for shoppers at a retail park, and in order for this system to work, it was imperative to incentivise those shoppers to leave on time.

3   See (post Brexit) CJEU *LH v Profi Credit Slovakia sro* (C-485/19) (22 April 2021) para 65.

4   *Director General of Fair Trading v First National Bank* [2001] UKHL 52 at para 36.

5   *Bryen and Langley Ltd v Martin Boston* [2004] EWHC 2450 at para 46.

Openness

9.83 'Terms should be expressed fully, clearly and legibly, containing no concealed pitfalls or traps. Appropriate prominence should be given to terms which might operate disadvantageously to the consumer[1].' It is not sufficient for individual terms to be presented clearly if their overall effect is not[2].

1   *Director General of Fair Trading v First National Bank* [2001] UKHL 52 at para 17; *Mylcrist Builders Ltd v Mrs G Buck* [2008] EWHC 2172 (TCC) at para 51(4)(a).

2   *R on the application of Emmet Donegan v Financial Services Compensation Scheme Ltd* [2021] EWHC 760 paras 137–139, referring to the CJEU decisions in *Matei* (C-143/13) at para 74 and *Ruxandra* (C-186/16) at para 45.

9.84 The sorts of contractual practices that have been held to lack openness include:

- A term that was only likely to be discovered by a person looking for it[1].
- An onerous and surprising term contained only in the small print[2].
- An important liability that was 'severely camouflaged' by lack of proper headings or signposting in a contract[3].
- A surprising sales commission in the small print, where the consumer would be astonished to find this clause in the contract, and would feel they had been ambushed when it was invoked[4].
- Where the risks of signing a contract with long and onerous liabilities were not spelled out to consumers (and so the term operated as a trap for consumers)[5].
- A surprising term fixing consumer liability found by a web link to a 49-page terms document[6].
- Introducing a term into the contract after the consumer has already paid a deposit[7].
- A term excluding liability to pay winnings in an online gambling game, where the term was set out in obscure language, insufficiently signposted and not clearly explained, and the game was defective[8].

1   *OFT v Foxtons Ltd* [2009] EWHC 1681 (Ch).

2   *OFT v Foxtons Ltd* [2009] EWHC 1681 (Ch).

3   *OFT v Foxtons Ltd* [2009] EWHC 1681 (Ch) at para 98.

4   *OFT v Foxtons Ltd* [2009] EWHC 1681 (Ch) at paras 103–105.

5   *OFT v Ashbourne Management Services Ltd* [2011] EWHC 1237 (Ch). See also *West v Ian Finlay & Assocs* [2014] EWCA Civ 316 at paras 56–58.

6   In *Spreadex v Cochrane* [2012] EWHC 1290 (Comm) at para 21.

7   *FSA v Asset LI Inc* [2013] EWHC 178 (Ch) at paras 137–138. In particular when the sales pitch was contradicted by the term, and there is no compensation for loss of use of the money paid as a deposit.

8   *Andrew Green v Petfre (Gibraltar) Ltd t/a Betfred* [2021] EWHC 842 at para 183.

9.85 By contrast, a term displayed on signs in a car park, imposing a liability to pay £85 for overstaying beyond two hours permitted free parking was held to be fair, the terms 'could not have been briefer, simpler or more prominently proclaimed', such that motorists 'could hardly avoid reading the notice'[1].

[1]   *Cavendish V El Makdessi, ParkingEye Ltd v Beavis* [2015] UKSC 67 at para 108.

Reading the small print

9.86 In *OFT v Foxtons Ltd*[1], it was noted that the 'theory is that the typical consumer . . . will read all the standard terms. But the practice is that even the circumspect one will be unlikely to do so with a great deal of attention'. The consumer expects the small print to contain points of detail to do with things that are not of everyday concern to the consumer. The consumer would not expect important obligations to be tucked away in the small print without prior flagging, notice or discussion[2].

[1]   [2009] EWHC 1681 (Ch) at para 92.
[2]   The key question is likely to be whether the term under challenge is sufficiently surprising or onerous to warrant being flagged to the consumer in this way. This is often a fact sensitive question. For example, a term that required a consumer's estate to pay a solicitor's fees in the event of the consumer's death, even though the consumer entered into a conditional fee arrangement was normal and not unfair because it was contained in a model contract sanctioned by the Law Society. It was necessary to protect solicitors from not being able to recover their fees. Perhaps surprisingly, the judge found that despite the lack of flagging of this term in the pre-contract material or sales process, any defects in this were superseded by inclusion of the term in the contract the consumer signed – see *Higgins & Co Lawyers Ltd v Evans* [2019] EWHC 2809 QB para 101. By contrast see the judgment in *Andrew Green v Petfre (Gibraltar) Ltd t/a Betfred* [2021] EWHC 842 at para 167, which ruled that very obscure drafting of an online contract led to the conclusion that it was 'unreasonable to expect [the consumer] would have found and noted the importance of the key clauses relied upon. This is overwhelmingly obvious in the case of the Game rules, where it is highly unlikely, in my view, he would have gone beyond the description in the earlier part of the document as to what to do to play the Game.'

9.87 Similarly, it has been held to be reasonable for consumers not to read contracts in the context of:

- A contract relating to 'a perfectly ordinary small suburban dwelling house' it was 'not at all surprising' that the full import of the agreement should be missed by the vendors. It was therefore not determinative that the vendors had failed to read the agreement carefully, and they were accordingly not bound by a surprising price escalation clause in an estate agency contract[1].
- A RIBA standard form of agreement for the appointment of an architect, containing onerous costs provisions, that were not pointed out to the consumer, where it was held that 'even a commercial customer . . . might well miss those two unusual and onerous clauses'[2].
- An online contract, where it was held that ticking 'I Agree' to 'terms and conditions', which are closely typed and lengthy, is an entirely inappropriate way to fix a consumer with surprising or onerous liabilities. It is likely therefore to be irrational for a trader to assume that the consumer would read, understand or appreciate the implications of terms set out in such documents. Surprising and onerous terms must be flagged in some other way[3].

[1]   *Bairstow Eves v Smith* [2004] EWHC 263 (QB).

2   *Munkenbeck & Marshall v Harold* [2005] EWHC 356 (TCC) at para 10.
3   *Spreadex v Cochrane* [2012] EWHC 1290 (Comm) at para 21. See also *Andrew Green v Petfre (Gibraltar) Ltd t/a Betfred* [2021] EWHC 842.

9.88 The requirement of openness goes further than the doctrine of incorporation of terms under the common law as set out in *Interfoto Picture Library Ltd v Stiletto Visual Programmes Ltd* which is that the common law requires that reasonable steps are taken to draw the other party's attention to printed conditions, or they would not be part of the contract. Where one condition in a set of printed conditions is particularly onerous or unusual, the party enforcing must show it was fairly brought to the other's attention. If it is not, it will not become part of the contract[1]. Where terms are drafted unclearly, with repetition and obscure language, such that they are not transparent, the court may find they are not incorporated for this reason[2].

1   [1988] 1 All ER 348 (CA) per Dillon LJ at 352.
2   *Andrew Green v Petfre (Gibraltar) Ltd t/a Betfred* [2021] EWHC 842 at paras 166–167.

9.89 Generally 'the more unreasonable a clause is, the greater the notice which must be given of it. Some clauses . . . would need to be printed in red ink on the face of the document with a red hand pointing to it, before the notice could be held to be sufficient'[1]. An example of a term not being incorporated into a consumer contract was where pinning a copy of the rules for a caravan park onto a notice board would not 'come anywhere near being sufficient notice to incorporate the terms into a contract'. There was no evidence that any consumer saw it, or that its existence was drawn to their attention before they paid their site fees, or at all[2]. Likewise, a small print term which is inconsistent with the main purpose of the contract (for example as set out in specifically agreed terms), is not to be treated as a term of the contract[3]. However, where a term is set out in a document which a person actually signs, the usual common law position is that they are taken to have read and be on notice of the term[4]. Where a consumer engages in regular activities over a long period under the trader's terms, it may not be sufficient for the trader to continue to rely on those terms without some sort of reminder[5]. Ultimately if a term is not incorporated into a contract, however, it cannot bind a consumer. It can be assessed for fairness as a notice for enforcement purposes.

1   *Spurling v Bradshaw* [1956] 1 WLR 461 per Denning LJ at 466. It is for the trader to prove the term was incorporated – and the more unusual or onerous it is the harder this task is. See *Picardi v Cuniberti* [2002] EWCA 2923 QB at para 98. Where a term is commonly used in an industry, or is in a model contract provided by an industry body, it is unlikely to be found to be unusual under the common law test – *Higgins & Co Lawyers Ltd v Evans* [2019] EWHC 2809 QB para 86.
2   *Margaret Baybut v Eccle Riggs Country Park Ltd* (High Court, Manchester District Registry, 2 November 2006) (at para 10).
3   *Alexander v West Bromwich Mortgage Company Ltd* [2016] EWCA Civ 496 at paras 46–47. Here small print terms which permitted wide changes to a mortgage interest rate, which was set out in an offer document, were not incorporated.
4   *Higgins & Co Lawyers Ltd v Evans* [2019] EWHC 2809 (QB) at para 75. This is likely especially to be the case where the term under challenge is immediately next to the place the consumer signs the document – *Weco Projects Aps v Loro Piana* [2020] EWHC 2150 (Comm) para 109.
5   *R on the application of Emmet Donegan v Financial Services Compensation Scheme Ltd* [2021] EWHC 760 paras 140–142 – in this case where a term had the effect of removing the stated ISA status of a bond, it was 'obvious' the consumer would not have agreed to the term in individual negotiations.

Fair dealing

9.90 '[A] supplier should not, whether deliberately or unconsciously, take advantage[1] of the consumer's necessity, indigence, lack of experience, unfamiliarity with the subject matter of the contract, weak bargaining position or any other factor listed in or analogous to those' in Recital 16. The supplier should deal fairly and equitably with the consumer[2]. A term that is fully transparent may still be unfair if it takes advantage of the consumer's necessity or weak economic circumstances for instance[3].

[1]   See *Rochdale Borough Council v Dixon* [2011] EWCA Civ 1173.
[2]   *Director General of Fair Trading v First National Bank* [2001] UKHL 52 at para 17, *Mylcrist Builders Ltd v Mrs G Buck* [2008] EWHC 2172 (TCC) at para 51(4)(b).
[3]   *OFT v Ashbourne Management Services Ltd* [2011] EWHC 1237 (Ch).

9.91 Traders should not take advantage of the fact that a consumer is not legally represented to slip unfair terms into their contracts. If a consumer would be surprised by the effect of the clause, and his notional lawyer would press for its deletion, this is indicative of a lack of fair dealing[1]. Where a term objectively serves a useful purpose, and gives real benefits to consumers who might nonetheless be adversely affected by it, it may well be fair, especially if the risk of falling foul of the term is wholly under the consumer's control. This is because the notional reasonable consumer, faced with the term in individual negotiations would be likely to have accepted it[2]. However, where a trader is in a much stronger bargaining position and imposes terms without explaining their reason or practical significance, it may not be assumed the consumer would have agreed to them in individual negotiations[3]. A term which is unfair in one contract, may be fair in another, where there is a fairer balancing of the interests of the parties overall[4].

[1]   *OFT v Foxtons Ltd* [2009] EWHC 1681 (Ch).
[2]   *Cavendish V El Makdessi, ParkingEye Ltd v Beavis* [2015] UKSC 67 at paras 109 and 209. It is relevant also to consider whether the consumer is able to shop around for another supplier, and the relative strengths of the parties bargaining positions (paras 100 and 35).
[3]   *R on the application of Emmet Donegan v Financial Services Compensation Scheme Ltd* [2021] EWHC 760 para 140–142 – in this case where a term had the effect of removing the stated ISA status of a bond, it was 'obvious' the consumer would not have agreed to the term in individual negotiations.
[4]   *Cavendish V El Makdessi, ParkingEye Ltd v Beavis* [2015] UKSC 67 at para 211.

9.92 Fair dealing goes further than[1] the common law principle of an unconscionable bargain set out in *Multiservice Bookbinding Ltd v Marden*[2] under which a party will be freed from a term if it is an objectionable term imposed on them in a morally reprehensible manner. For example, where advantage is taken of a young, inexperienced or ignorant person to introduce a term which no sensible, well-advised person would have accepted.

[1]   An example of the breadth of the UTCCR 1999 protection in contrast to the law on unconscionable bargain is provided by *Evans v Cherry Tree Finance* [2007] EWHC 3523 (Ch) at para 81, where it was held that a term was not unconscionable, not least because the consumer was legally represented. However, it was held that it was unfair.
[2]   [1978] 2 All ER 489 at 502.

Legal advice and process

9.93 Where a consumer is legally advised, unfair terms are not necessarily rendered fair[1]. However, in individual cases, specific legal advice on a term may prevent the consumer from showing that it is unfair, such as where:

- A wealthy individual was advised by lawyers who were able to influence the substance of the terms he was complaining about[2].
- A transaction required the consumer to instruct a solicitor, who in fact made a careful report on the contract, drawing his specific attention to the consequences of the term, and the consumer would have the protection of the court in possession proceedings, which were required before the term under challenge would have effect[3].
- A borrower was assisted by a solicitor and was dealing at arm's length with the lender of a buy to let mortgage[4].
- The consumer, already in a dispute, was represented by solicitors, who provided advice on the merits of agreeing to submit the dispute to adjudication[5].

[1] *Evans v Cherry Tree Finance Ltd* [2007] EWHC 3523 (Ch) (at para 63) – where the term was so opaque that even the lawyer did not understand it.

[2] *Heifer International Inc v Christiansen* [2008] Bus LR D49. The same may be said where a consumer is exceptionally wealthy, and has the assistance of a logistics expert to organise the transport of their yacht – *Weco Projects Aps v Loro Piana* [2020] EWHC 2150 (Comm) para 109

[3] *UK Housing Alliance (North West) Ltd v Francis* [2010] EWCA Civ 117 at para 29. See also *Roundlistic Ltd v Jones & Seymour* [2016] UKUT 325 (LC) at para 105.

[4] *Smith v Mortgage Express* [2007] CTLC 134 at para 62, where there was held to be no lack of good faith.

[5] *Khurana v Webster Construction Ltd* [2015] EWHC 758 (TCC) at para 53(2).

9.94 By contrast, where the consumer's solicitor does not in fact point out the problems with a term, the trader is likely to be held to be acting contrary to good faith[1]. Where the term cannot have application without sanction of a court a term that potentially creates a significant imbalance may be less likely to be held to be unfair[2].

[1] *Harrison v Shepherd Homes Ltd* [2011] EWHC 1811 (TCC) at para 113, although see the contrary view expressed in *Jones & Seymour v Roundlistic Ltd* [2018] EWCA Civ 2284 at para 48.

[2] *UK Housing Alliance (North West) Ltd v Francis* [2010] EWCA Civ 117 at para 24.

THE GREY LIST

9.95 By s 63 of the CRA 2015:

Contract terms which may or must be regarded as unfair

(1) Part 1 of Schedule 2 contains an indicative and non-exhaustive list of terms of consumer contracts that may be regarded as unfair for the purposes of this Part.

(2) Part 1 of Schedule 2 is subject to Part 2 of that Schedule; but a term listed in Part 2 of that Schedule may nevertheless be assessed for fairness under s 62 unless s 64 or 73 applies to it.

9.96 Part 1 of Sch 2 sets out a list ('the grey list') of the terms that are likely to be unfair. The list gives 'concrete form to the high level principles set out in' the fairness test[1]. The grey list also provides a base for the assessment of fairness, in considering the type of factors the court should take into account[2]. It is a 'check list of terms which must be regarded as potentially vulnerable to being unfair'[3] – and accordingly terms listed there cannot benefit from the price or main subject matter exclusion[4]. The grey list is indicative but non-exhaustive. A term that appears in the list is not automatically unfair, in the same way that a term that does not appear in the list may nonetheless be regarded as unfair[5]. It is qualified by Pt 2 to Sch 2, so that while these clarify that a term falling within their terms is not presumed to be unfair, it may still be unfair if it fails to meet the general 'requirements of good faith, balance and transparency'[6]. The CRA 2015 has added three new grey list terms – those in paras 5, 12 and 14. In interpreting the grey list, it may be appropriate to consider guidance issued by the Competition and Markets Authority ('CMA')[7].

1   See CJEU *Commission v Sweden* (C-478/99) AG's Opinion at paras 28–29.
2   CJEU *Nemzeti v Invitel* (C-472/10) at para 26.
3   *Mylcrist Builders Ltd v Mrs G Buck* [2008] EWHC 2172 (TCC) at para 51(5).
4   Section 64(6).
5   CJEU *Freiburger* (C-237/02) at para 20. *Cavendish V El Makdessi, ParkingEye Ltd v Beavis* [2015] UKSC 67 at para 105.
6   CJEU *RWE Vertrieb AG v VBZ Nordrhein-Westfalen* (Case C-92/11) at paras 46–47. See also s 63(2), and *Peabody Trust Governors v Reeve* [2008] EWHC 1432 at para 49.
7   *R on the application of Emmet Donegan v Financial Services Compensation Scheme Ltd* [2021] EWHC 760 para 130. The current CMA guidance on unfair terms is CMA 37 issued in July 2015.

9.97 The sorts of terms in the grey list can be described as relating to exclusions, one sided obligations or rights, compensation payable, lock-ins or auto rollovers, incorporation and variation of terms, dispute resolution, and assignment of rights.

SCHEDULE 2

Consumer contract terms which may be regarded as unfair

Part 1

List of terms

(1)   A term which has the object or effect of excluding or limiting the trader's liability in the event of the death of or personal injury to the consumer resulting from an act or omission of the trader. This does not include a term which is of no effect by virtue of section 65 (exclusion for negligence liability);

(2)   A term which has the object or effect of inappropriately excluding or limiting the legal rights of the consumer in relation to the trader or another party in the event of total or partial non-performance or inadequate performance by the trader of any of the contractual obligations, including the option of offsetting a debt owed to the seller or supplier against any claim which the consumer may have against[1] him;

(3)   A term which has the object or effect of making an agreement binding on the consumer in a case where the provision of services by the trader is subject to a condition whose realisation depends on the trader's will alone;

(4) A term which has the object or effect of permitting the trader to retain sums paid by the consumer where the consumer decides not to conclude or perform the contract, without providing for the consumer to receive compensation of an equivalent amount from the trader where the trader is the party cancelling the contract;

(5) A term which has the object or effect of requiring that, where the consumer decides not to conclude or perform the contract, the consumer must pay the trader a disproportionately high sum in compensation or for services which have not been supplied;

(6) A term which has the object or effect of requiring a consumer who fails to fulfil his obligations under the contract to pay a disproportionately high sum in compensation;

(7) A term which has the object or effect of authorising the trader to dissolve the contract on a discretionary basis where the same facility is not granted to the consumer, or permitting the trader to retain the sums paid for services not yet supplied by the trader where it is the trader who dissolves the contract[2];

(8) A term which has the object or effect of enabling the trader to terminate a contract of indeterminate duration without reasonable notice except where there are serious grounds for doing so. This is subject to paragraphs 21 (financial services) and 24 (sale of securities, foreign currency etc);[3]

(9) A term which has the object or effect of automatically extending a contract of fixed duration where the consumer does not indicate otherwise, when the deadline fixed for the consumer to express his desire not to extend the contract is unreasonably early;

(10) A term which has the object or effect of irrevocably binding the consumer to terms with which the consumer has had no real opportunity of becoming acquainted before the conclusion of the contract;

(11) A term which has the object or effect of enabling the trader to alter the terms of the contract unilaterally without a valid reason which is specified in the contract. This is subject to paragraphs 22 (financial services), 23 (contracts which last indefinitely) and 24 (sale of securities, foreign currency etc);

(12) A term which has the object or effect of permitting the trader to determine the characteristics of the subject matter of the contract after the consumer has become bound by it. This is subject to paragraph 23 (contracts which last indefinitely);

(13) A term which has the object or effect of enabling the trader to alter unilaterally without a valid reason any characteristics of the goods, digital content or services to be provided;

(14) A term which has the object or effect of giving the trader the discretion to decide the price payable under the contract after the consumer has become bound by it, where no price or method of determining the price is agreed when the consumer becomes bound. This is subject to paragraphs 23 (contracts which last indefinitely), 24 (sale of securities, foreign currency etc) and 25 (price index clauses);

(15) A term which has the object or effect of permitting a trader to increase the price of goods, digital content or services without giving the consumer the right to cancel the contract if the final price is too high in relation to the price agreed when the contract was concluded. This is subject to paragraphs 24 (sale of securities, foreign currency etc) and 25 (price index clauses);

(16) A term which has the object or effect of giving the trader the right to determine whether the goods, digital content or services supplied are in conformity with the contract, or giving the trader the exclusive right to interpret any term of the contract[4];

(17) A term which has the object or effect of limiting the trader's obligation to respect commitments undertaken by the trader's agents or making the trader's commitments subject to compliance with a particular[5] formality;

    (18)   A term which has the object or effect of obliging the consumer to fulfil all the consumer's obligations where the trader does not perform the trader's obligations;

    (19)   A term which has the object or effect of allowing the trader to transfer the trader's rights and obligations under the contract, where this may reduce the guarantees for the consumer, without the consumer's agreement;

    (20)   A term which has the object or effect of excluding or hindering the consumer's right to take legal action or exercise any other legal remedy[6], in particular by—

        (a)   requiring the consumer to take disputes exclusively to arbitration not covered by legal provisions,

        (b)   unduly restricting the evidence available to the consumer, or

        (c)   imposing on the consumer a burden of proof which, according to the applicable law, should lie with another party to the contract.

---

[1] *Alfred Overy v Paypal (Europe) Ltd* [2012] EWHC 2659 (QB) at paras 259–260.

[2] This paragraph has been held not to apply to a term which automatically terminated a conditional fee contract on the death of the consumer and obliged the consumer's estate to pay a reasonable sum for work done by a solicitor, *Higgins & Co Lawyers Ltd v Evans* [2019] EWHC 2809 (QB) at para 101(v).

[3] CJEU *Banco Popular Espanol* (C-537/12) at para 70.

[4] See CJEU *Toth v ERSTE Bank* (C-34/18) at paras 73–75 this covers terms which allow the trader to decide unilaterally whether their own performance complies with the contract, but not those under which they can assess whether the consumer's performance complies with the contract.

[5] Entire agreement clauses, see *FSA v Asset LI Ltd* [2013] EWHC 178 (Ch).

[6] It is important to note that the text of the chapeau to para 20 is to be interpreted more widely than the specific examples particularised in the sub paragraphs, and this provision is to be read widely – for example it would include a term which restricts consumer's ability to transfer a product which they have purchased – see *R on the application of Emmet Donegan v Financial Services Compensation Scheme Ltd* [2021] EWHC 760 paras 128–130 and 145.

9.98 The scope of the Grey List is reduced to some degree by Part 2 of Schedule 2, which carves out certain terms from presumed unfairness. Importantly, however, such terms may still be assessed for fairness, assuming they are not within the Core Exemption.

Part 2

Scope of Part 1

Financial services

    (21)   Paragraph 8 (cancellation without reasonable notice) does not include a term by which a supplier of financial services reserves the right to terminate unilaterally a contract of indeterminate duration without notice where there is a valid reason, if the supplier is required to inform the consumer of the cancellation immediately.

    (22)   Paragraph 11 (variation of contract without valid reason) does not include a term by which a supplier of financial services reserves the right to alter the rate of interest payable by or due to the consumer, or the amount of other charges for financial services without notice where there is a valid reason, if—

        (a)   the supplier is required to inform the consumer of the alteration at the earliest opportunity, and

        (b)   the consumer is free to dissolve the contract immediately.

Contracts which last indefinitely

    (23)   Paragraphs 11 (variation of contract without valid reason), 12 (determination of characteristics of goods etc after consumer bound) and 14 (determination of price after consumer bound) do not include a term under which a

trader reserves the right to alter unilaterally the conditions of a contract of indeterminate duration if—

(a)   the trader is required to inform the consumer with reasonable notice, and

(b)   the consumer is free to dissolve the contract.

Sale of securities, foreign currency etc

(24)   Paragraphs 8 (cancellation without reasonable notice), 11 (variation of contract without valid reason), 14 (determination of price after consumer bound) and 15 (increase in price) do not apply to—

(a)   transactions in transferable securities, financial instruments and other products or services where the price is linked to fluctuations in a stock exchange quotation or index or a financial market rate that the trader does not control, and

(b)   contracts for the purchase or sale of foreign currency, traveller's cheques or international money orders denominated in foreign currency.

Price index clauses

(25)   Paragraphs 14 (determination of price after consumer bound) and 15 (increase in price) do not include a term which is a price-indexation clause (where otherwise lawful), if the method by which price varies is explicitly described.

Incorporation – concealed terms

9.99 Paragraph 10 of the Grey list refers to terms which have the object or effect of 'irrevocably binding the consumer to terms with which he had no real opportunity of becoming acquainted before the conclusion of the contract'. This is a particular problem with online 'click-wrap' contracts. The base line for a non-consumer contract is that terms must be 'reasonably accessible', and provided in a durable medium, which allows the terms to be printed and saved[1]. However in a consumer contract, more attention must be given to actively bringing the terms to the consumer's attention.

Examples of such terms that have been held unfair include:

•   A compulsory arbitration clause contained in a guarantee supplied to the consumer after they had already entered into a contract to purchase a new build house[2].

•   An obscure term connected with the early settlement of a loan, the effect of which had not been explained to the consumer[3].

•   A term making the consumer liable for all trades on their account, which was concealed in 49 pages of closely typed, complex paragraphs, and which the consumer accepted by clicking 'agree' on a website[4].

1   *Ang v Reliantco Investments Ltd* [2019] EWHC 879 at paras 74 and 80.

2   *Zealander v Laing* (2000) 2 TCLR 724 at 728.

3   *Evans v Cherry Tree Finance* [2007] EWHC 3523 (Ch) at para 66. By contrast, a term which provided for a consumer's estate to pay a solicitor's reasonable fees under a conditional fee arrangement, in the event that the consumer died, was not held to have been unfairly concealed from the consumer, even though it was not flagged in the literature or pre-contract discussions – *Higgins & Co Lawyers Ltd v Evans* [2019] EWHC 2809 (QB) at para 101.

4   *Spreadex v Cochrane* [2012] EWHC 1290 (Comm) at para 21 – it was 'an entirely inadequate way' to make the consumer liable.

Variation clauses

9.100 Paragraphs 11–15 of the Grey list deal with variation of contracts. Terms which allow for variation of the terms, characteristics of the subject matter, or price cannot fall within the core exemption, and are generally likely to be unfair. All except para 13 (relating to changes to characteristics of the product) are qualified by paragraphs in Pt 2 of Sch 2, which recognises that the trader may have a legitimate interest in being able to vary the terms of service. However where a qualification applies, the term must still be assessed for fairness, unless it falls within the core exemption[1].

[1] *Peabody Trust Governors v Reeve* [2008] EWHC 1432 (Ch) at para 49; CJEU *RWE Vertrieb* (C-92/11) at paras 46–47.

9.101 The courts have laid down how variation terms should be assessed[1].

- The reason for the variation and its method should be set out very clearly in the contract. Without this the term is likely to be unfair. It is not enough if consumers are simply informed of the variation during the life of the contract.
- The terms should be properly brought to the consumer's attention so that the consumer can examine them and appreciate the consequences. It is of 'fundamental importance' that the consumer can foresee on the basis of clear intelligible criteria, what amendments the supplier might make to the price.
- If the method of amendment is governed by mandatory statutory or regulatory provisions, or where these provisions give the consumer the right to terminate the contract, it is 'essential' that the supplier inform the consumer of these.
- Where the trader exercises the right to vary, the consumer must be notified of this in good time, so that they can take the appropriate action.
- The consumer should have a right to terminate the contract, which must not be purely formal, but must be actually exercisable. The court must consider, 'whether the market concerned is competitive, the possible cost to the consumer of terminating the contract, the time between the notification and the coming into force of the new tariffs, the information provided at the time of the notification, and the cost to be borne and the time taken to change supplier'[2]. The consumer's right to cancel must be *more than illusory*. If, in the circumstances it is likely to be impracticable for the consumer to walk away then a trader's right to vary the contract is not likely to be balanced by a corresponding consumer's right to cancel[3].

[1] See in particular CJEU *Nemzeti v Invitel* (C-472/10) at paras 24–31 and CJEU *RWE Vertrieb AG v VBZ Nordrhein-Westfalen* (Case C-92/11) at paras 49–54.
[2] CJEU *RWE Vertrieb AG v VBZ Nordrhein-Westfalen* (Case C-92/11) at para 54.
[3] *Peabody Trust Governors v Reeve* [2008] EWHC 1432 (Ch) at para 57.

9.102 An example of an unfair term was a mortgage interest variation term, permitting the bank to increase their interest to ensure the bank operates 'prudently, efficiently and competitively', where there is no obligation to reduce rates, and no provision for the borrower to exit the contract[1]. Where the contract contains a price indexation clause, this may be fair, but it is crucial that the consumer is given adequate information about its effect before concluding the contract[2]. In *Rochdale Borough Council v Dixon* it was found that a variation clause may be fair where it is set out in a statutory scheme and the variation worked in the best interests of the whole cohort of consumers. The variation must be consulted upon and consumers must have actually agreed to it[3].

[1] *Firstplus Financial Group Plc v Murphy & Dye* (Woolwich County Court, 17 October 2013) at paras 15–18.
[2] EFTA *Gunnar Engilbertsson v Islandsbanki* (E-25/13) at para 141.
[3] *Rochdale Borough Council v Dixon* [2011] EWCA Civ 1173 at para 68. See also *Du Plessis v Fontgary Leisure Parks Ltd* [2012] EWCA Civ 409 at paras 47–54.

Long lock-in contracts

9.103 The new paragraph 5 confirms that charging for services that are not in fact supplied cannot be a price term. This sort of term operates as a quasi-penalty, and its application is illustrated in *OFT v Ashbourne Management Services Ltd*[1], where a term tying consumers to lengthy (1 to 3 year) gym contracts at 'low-end' gyms was found to be unfair. Consumers were attracted by low monthly subscriptions that were discounted from the rolling monthly membership. There was in fact little benefit to the consumer in this discount unless they remained a member for many months. The gyms were aware that many consumers stopped attending gyms after 2 or 3 months. The gyms did not highlight the risks to consumers of signing these contracts, which were, 'designed and calculated to take advantage of the naivety and inexperience of the average consumer using gym clubs at the lower end of the market'[2]. Paragraphs 5 and 6 of the Grey list also have the effect of ensuring consumers are not locked into lengthy contracts to the detriment of competition. In this regard there may be overlap between these provisions and prohibitions in regulated sectors on excessive early termination charges[3].

[1] [2011] EWHC 1237 (Ch).
[2] See paras 162–174.
[3] See *Virgin Media v Ofcom* [2020] CAT 5 for an example of a fine imposed for an excessive early termination charge.

Penalties

9.104 Paragraph 6 presumes terms to be unfair which require 'any consumer who fails to fulfil his obligation to pay a disproportionately high sum in compensation'. This is essentially to prevent a trader benefiting financially from the consumer's breach. This concept is wider than the common law rule that a secondary obligation is void, where it imposes detriment out of all proportion to the legitimate interest of the innocent party in the enforcement of the obligation[1].

[1] See *Cavendish v El Makdessi, ParkingEye Ltd v Beavis* [2015] UKSC 67 at paras 32 and 100 for a summary of the current law on penalties at Common Law, and paras 207 and 309 for the proposition that unfair terms is in principle wider than the rule against penalties. See also *Munkenbeck v Harold* [2005] EWHC 356 at para 16, sum that was not a penalty was still unfair. This is in accordance with the approach taken by the Court of Appeal (Criminal Division) in *R v Christopher Whatcott* [2019] EWCA Crim 1889 para 40, where having found a charge to be a penalty, considered it not need to go on to decide if it was unfair.

9.105 In assessing the imbalance created by a term, the cumulative effect of all the terms which could adversely affect the consumer must be assessed, whether or not they are actually invoked by the trader[1]. It may be relevant also to take into account remedies provided to a trader by statute[2]. In general, when assessing unfairness, the courts have considered whether the consumer received a particular benefit in exchange, whether the sum in question is high compared to other market rates[3], whether it has a surprising impact on the substance of the bargain, whether similar terms are commonly used elsewhere, and whether the term defends a legitimate primary obligation in a proportionate way[4]. It is also important to consider whether the rights of the trader, in the event of breach by the consumer, is proportionate to the breach, if it derogates from a rule of law, and whether the consumer has adequate and effective means under the law to remedy the matter – or whether in fact the term makes it harder for the consumer to exercise his rights[5]. Such an imbalance may be unfair where it is contrary to good faith. In assessing whether a penalty is disproportionately high, significant weight must also be attached to whether several terms relate to the same breach[6]. In assessing whether a parking penalty was unfair, the courts have decided that the significant imbalance created by the term is not contrary to good faith where it could reasonably (objectively) be assumed that the consumer would have agreed to it if individually negotiating. Factors the court takes into account are whether the scale of the charges is exorbitant and out of line with costs, whether there is a good reason for the charges, the extent to which the consumer is in control of whether they pay the charge(s), and whether the imposition of the charge takes advantage of the consumer's circumstances – or whether they in fact have other options[7]. In deciding that a late payment charge was a penalty, the Court of Appeal (Criminal Division) applied the principles in *ParkingEye* to a criminal allegation. It ruled that an interest in ensuring cash flow was not sufficient justification to impose a fee that was well in excess of the actual cost to the business of late payment[8].

[1] CJEU *Radlinger v Finway* (C-377/14) at para 95; CJEU *A v B* (C-738/19) para 30.
[2] CJEU *A v B* (C-738/19) paras 35–38.
[3] *Smith v Mortgage Express* [2007] CTLC 134 at paras 35 and 66–67.
[4] *Director General of Fair Trading v First National Bank* [2001] UKHL 52 at paras 20–24, per Lord Bingham and paras 55–56, per Lord Millett. See also *Parking Eye v Beavis* [2015] EWCA Civ 402 at paras 36–39 and *Cavendish v El Makdessi, ParkingEye Ltd v Beavis* [2015] UKSC 67 at para 109. The CJEU described a similar concept in CJEU *A v B* (C-738/19) para 33, where it considered the extent to which the prohibition 'forms part of the very essence of the contractual relationship'.
[5] *Mohamed Aziz v Caixa d'Esalvis de Catalunya* (C-415/11) at paras 73–75 and *Cavendish v El Makdessi, ParkingEye Ltd v Beavis* [2015] UKSC 67 at paras 108–111. In some situations it will be important for a penalty to make allowances for circumstances, such as to avoid penalising the disabled, or to build in a grace period before it kicks in, and to be appealable, see the dissenting judgment of Lord Toulson at paras 310–311 and the acknowledgement of the relevance of a binding Code of Practice which provided certain protections at paras 100 and 111 of the main judgment.
[6] CJEU *A v B* (C-738/19) para 39.
[7] Scottish Sheriff decision in *Indigo Park Services Ltd v Conor Watson* 6 September 2017 Ref SC67–16 paras 105–107.
[8] *R v Christopher Whatcott* [2019] EWCA Crim 1889 paras 36–38. The fee structure in question was an increase of a 'finders fee' of £9.95 to £14.95 if not paid within 24 hours, followed by an increase to £85 if not paid within 5 days. This was ruled to be disproportionate, extravagant and unconscionable.

9.106 The courts will consider the reality of the situation, rather than the form, for example where a price escalation clause is used[1]. A requirement that a consumer pay an early repayment sum based on 6 months of repayments under an already expensive loan was held to be unfair as a disproportionately high sum in compensation[2]. Where a term imposes an accelerated interest repayment requirement, the CJEU has stated that courts must compare the method of calculation used in that term with the statutory and market terms that applied when the contract was concluded, whether the event that triggers repayment relates to an obligation of 'essential importance' and may only be triggered by sufficiently serious non-compliance, what the rights would be under common law, and whether national law provides for adequate and effective means to the consumer to remedy the effect of the loan being called in[3]. A term may amount to the imposition of a penalty where it requires payment irrespective of what is in fact delivered – for example where a price to be paid for completion of a project is required even if the project is cancelled[4].

[1]   *Bairstow Eves v Smith* [2004] EWHC 263 (QB).
[2]   *Evans v Cherry Tree Finance* [2007] EWHC 3523 (Ch) at para 66.
[3]   CJEU *Banco Primus v Garcia* (C-421/14) at paras 65–66.
[4]   See for example the analysis of the French Cour de Cassation (Supreme Court) in *MB v Societe Civile Immobiliere Pela* [2020] ECC 14 (2019) para 9.

Dispute resolution

9.107 In cases where the trader wishes to reserve the right of unilateral determination, the court must assess whether the term derogates from the rules that would otherwise apply, and whether this makes it more difficult for the consumer, given the procedural means at his disposal, to take legal action and exercise rights of defence[1]. Where a term requires the consumer to contact the trader directly, themselves, rather than via a claims management company, to obtain flight delay compensation, the Court of Appeal have ruled this to be fair. This was on the basis that it did not in fact place a material obstacle in the passenger's route to compensation, the claim could still be made with the minimum of effort, the consumer could still benefit from the assistance of third parties, and if the claim was not dealt with within 30 days, they could use a claims management company if they wished[2].

[1]   *Mohamed Aziz v Caixa d'Estalvis* (C-415/11) at para 75. See also *Toth v ERSTE Bank* (C-34/18) paras 52 and 53.
[2]   *Bott & Co Solicitors Ltd v Ryanair DAC* [2019] EWCA Civ 143 paras 71–72.

9.108 Requiring consumers to bring a claim within a period of time that is shorter than that set out in the Limitation Act 1980 is likely to be unfair by reference to the indicative term in para 20 of the Grey list. This may be so even where such a restriction is common place and a consumer is represented by an experienced solicitor when negotiating the contract[1]. An agreement to waive a claim that a consumer has in an existing dispute about unfair terms may also be unfair by reference to para 20[2].

[1]   See *Allner v Peters & May Group Ltd* [2019] EWHC 3258 (Comm) paras 22–28 and 44–49. For the CMA's view on clauses which seek to limit the time within which a consumer may bring a claim see CMA 37 Unfair Contract Terms Guidance para 5.7.1ff.
[2]   See also CJEU *XZ v Ibercaja* (C-452/18) paras 76–77.

Jurisdiction and applicable law clauses

9.109 Where a consumer contract, with a close connection to the UK, is governed by the law of a non UK state, s 74(1) nonetheless gives UK courts the power to rule that any of its terms are unfair[1]. This could include ruling that the jurisdiction clause itself is unfair. The courts are generally suspicious of terms that require a consumer to submit to an overseas jurisdiction. This is consistent with the policy of the Brussels Regulation concerning the forum for civil litigation. In *Pannon* it was suggested that such a term is likely to be unfair[2]. In *Oceano Groupo* the CJEU appeared to go further, suggesting that such a term is *necessarily* unfair[3] because:

- It may be too far for the consumer to travel to enter an appearance conveniently.
- If the dispute is for a small sum it may be disproportionately costly for the consumer to attend.
- This sort of term has the object or effect of excluding or hindering the consumer's right to take legal action, as set out in para 20 of the grey list.
- By contrast, this sort of term enables the trader to deal with all the litigation relating to his trade in one court, and makes it less onerous for him to enter an appearance.

Where a consumer contract has been assigned to a third party, such as a claims management company, to pursue the consumer's rights against a trader, such as an airline, the CJEU has held that the trader cannot rely on a jurisdiction clause against that third party because the term only has binding effects between the original parties to the contract[4].

[1]   Where the contract was entered into on or before 31 December 2020, the parties were capable of selecting the law of an EEA state – see The Consumer Protection (Amendment etc) (EU Exit) Regulations 2018, SI 2018/1326, regs 3(5) and 11.
[2]   *Pannon* (C-243/08) at para 40.
[3]   CJEU *Oceano Groupo* (C-240/98) at para 22 and CJEU *VB Penzugyi* (C-137/08) at para 54. See also CJEU *Ryanair DAC v Delayfix* (C-519/19) paras 58–61.
[4]   CJEU *Ryanair DAC v Delayfix* (C-519/19) paras 35–47.

9.110 In *Standard Bank London Ltd v Apostolakis (No 2)*[1], the test in *Oceano Group* was applied to an investment contract entered into by a Greek consumer, under which disputes had to be settled in the courts of England and Wales. This was held to be unfair on the basis of the cost and inconvenience suffered by the consumer. The proceedings would be conducted in a language foreign to the consumer. The term also permitted the consumer to be sued in many different countries; however, the trader could only be sued in England. Finally, the impact of the jurisdiction clause was not carefully explained or even translated for the consumer.

[1]   [2002] CLC 939 at paras 49–51.

9.111 Under s 74(1) CCA 2015, where the law of a country other than the UK is chosen, the unfair terms provisions will continue to apply to the consumer contract where it has a close connection with the UK. However, such a term may still be fair where it does not deprive a consumer of the statutory protections afforded by the consumer's own applicable laws[1]. According to the CJEU such a choice of law clause will be unfair where it is not in plain intelligible language, or where the contract fails to inform the consumer of the mandatory statutory provisions that they still enjoy under their own law, notwithstanding the choice of law clause[2]. Such mandatory statutory provisions are all those which cannot be derogated from by agreement, and include provisions transposing the Unfair Terms Directive, which provide a higher standard of protection for the consumer[3]. It would appear from the CJEU decision that a merely general statement along the lines of 'statutory rights are not affected' would not be sufficient – the actual legal provisions must be set out[4]. However, a consumer will not benefit from these mandatory protections when contracting to receive services to be supplied 'exclusively' outside their Member State of habitual residence[5]. This exemption to the general rule will only apply where it is not possible for the consumer to receive the services in their home state, and must travel abroad to receive them[6].

[1] CJEU *VFK v Amazon* (C-191/15) at paras 59 and 66. The determination of which law applies to a consumer contracts, within the EEA, is governed by the Rome I Regulation.
[2] CJEU *VFK v Amazon* (C-191/15) at paras 68 and 69. This is on the basis that it could mislead the consumer into thinking that they have renounced the mandatory protections their own state provides – CJEU *VFK v Treuhand* (C-272/18) para 58.
[3] CJEU *VFK v Amazon* (C-191/15) at paras 70 and 59.
[4] CJEU *VFK v Amazon* (C-191/15) at para 69 and CJEU *Invitel* (C-472/10) at para 29.
[5] Rome I Regulation Art 5(4)(b).
[6] CJEU *VFK v Treuhand* (C-272/18) para 52.

Arbitration clauses

9.112 Paragraph 20 of the Grey list is likely also to apply to arbitration clauses. Such clauses may also be unfair because the arbitration process may be expensive and disproportionate to the size of the sum in dispute, not be able to resolve all matters in dispute, and prevent the consumer from taking legal action[1]. Even where the fact that arbitration will apply to the contract is explained, and the consumer is given information on the likely consequences of this, the term may still be unfair[2]. Where an arbitration scheme is statutory it is not presumed to be unfair[3]. It remains an open question whether an adjudication clause contained in a RIBA proforma contract is unfair, if used in a consumer contract[4]. Terms that fall outside para 20 may still be substantively assessed for fairness[5].

[1] See *Khurana v Webster Construction Ltd* [2015] EWHC 758 (TCC) at para 53(5). The importance of consumers being able to access the courts was stressed by the French Supreme Court (Cour de Cassation) in ruling that a procedural rule which required French courts to respect arbitration awards could be disregarded if this meant the consumer would be subject to unfair terms – *LY v PWC Landwell-PriceWaterhouseCoopers Tax & Legal Services* [2021] ILPr 9 at paras 10–13.
[2] CJEU *Katalin Sebastyen* (C-342/13) at paras 34–36.
[3] See *Zealander v Laing* (2000) 2 TCLR 724 at 729 and *Mylcrist v Buck* at para 54. However, see also CJEU *Asturcom v Nogueira* (C-40/08) at paras 38, 46, 53.
[4] *Beach Homes Ltd v Hazell* [2018] EWHAC 1847 (TCC) para 31, where the court declined to rule that an agreement to submit a dispute to adjudication was unfair, but gave very little reasoning. In *Picardi v Cuniberti* [2003] BLR 487, the Judge stated obiter that he would have found such an adjudication clause unfair.
[5] CJEU *Toth v ERSTE Bank* (C-34/18) paras 44–49.

9.113 There are two types of arbitration clause that are blacklisted by other legislation. Regulation 14B of the Alternative Dispute Resolution for Consumer Disputes (Competent Authorities and Information) Regulations 2015[1] provides that an agreement to submit to ADR is not binding on the consumer if (a) it is concluded before the dispute materialised, and (b) it deprives the consumer of access to court[2].

1   SI 2015/542.
2   This does not cast doubt over the fairness of adjudication clauses – which may have been held to be fair, as in *Domsalla v Dyason* [2007] EWHC 1174 (TCC) at para 92, on the basis that they offer a 'rapid, cheap and temporary legal process which determines the parties' rights'.

9.114 Section 91(1) of the Arbitration Act 1996 provides that[1]:

'a term which constitutes an arbitration agreement is unfair for the purposes of the [CRA 2015 Part 2] so far as it relates to a claim for pecuniary remedy which does not exceed the amount specified by order for the purposes of this section.'

1   SI 1999/2167 sets this at £5,000 as does the corresponding SI for Northern Ireland (SI 2005/219).

9.115 That amount is currently £5,000, such that a clause that referred to arbitration any claim for less than that amount would be automatically unfair[1]. A clause referring a claim of greater than £5,000 may still be unfair[2]. If a consumer is represented by a competent agent, or otherwise requests an arbitration clause, it is unlikely to be unfair[3]. Likewise an agreement to submit to arbitration or adjudication *after* the dispute has arisen is not necessarily unfair[4].

1   In the High Court case of *Mylcrist Builders Ltd v Mrs G Buck* [2008] EWHC 2172 (TCC), it was held that the £5,000 includes VAT, on the basis that on its ordinary meaning 'a pecuniary remedy would relate to the whole of the monetary claim which would include VAT' (para 35).
2   See *Mylcrist Builders Ltd v Mrs G Buck* [2008] EWHC 2172 (TCC) (see paras 54–59); *Zealander v Laing* (2000) 2 TCLR 724; and *Picardi v Cuniberti* [2002] EWHC 2923 QB at para 131.
3   *Heifer International Inc v Christiansen* [2008] Bus LR D49; *Westminster Building Co Ltd v Beckingham* [2004] EWHC 138 (TCC).
4   *Khurana v Webster Construction Ltd* [2015] EWHC 758 (TCC) at para 53. In this case parties already in dispute and advised by solicitors agreed to refer the matter to adjudication.

CONSEQUENCES OF UNFAIRNESS

9.116 CRA 2015, ss 62 and 67:

62 Requirement for contract terms and notices to be fair

(1)   An unfair term of a consumer contract is not binding on the consumer.
(2)   An unfair consumer notice is not binding on the consumer.
(3)   This does not prevent the consumer from relying on the term or notice if the consumer chooses to do so.

. . .

67 Effect of an unfair term on the rest of a contract

Where a term of a consumer contract is not binding on the consumer as a result of this Part, the contract continues, so far as practicable, to have effect in every other respect.

9.117 A term or notice that is held to be unfair is not binding on the consumer[1]. The term must be 'regarded, in principle, as never having existed, so that it cannot have any effect on the consumer'[2]. One caveat to this however is where, after enforcement of the unfair term resulting in the consumer's property being seized by the trader, a third party acquires legal title to the property. In such a case the consumer cannot plead the unfair term against the third party, since this would affect legal certainty[3]. Further, the principle of invalidity does not prevent the consumer from relying on the term if they so choose[4]. A consumer may agree to an unfair term being amended to remove the unfairness. Although, the amendment will only be binding if the consumer understood that the unfair term was not binding[5]. If a court finds that the consumer was not so aware, it may assess the fairness of the original unfair term, and remove it, disregarding the replacement term completely[6]. Where a consumer contract that includes an unfair term is assigned to a trader, that term may continue to have affect[7]. Traders remain bound by their contracts even if this causes them hardship[8]. The term must not be modified and the contract must continue in existence even if this creates disadvantages for the trader[9]. The Directive has a deterrent purpose and otherwise traders might be tempted to try their luck by including unfair terms, in the hope that the court modifies them[10]. In *Spreadex v Cochrane*[11], it was observed that:

'Importantly the Regulations do not operate by precluding reliance on the contractual term in cases where it would be unfair to do so. Their proscription is absolute and binary: the term is either unfair and hence unenforceable, or not.[12]'

[1] CRA 2015, s 62(1) and (2). This is a fundamental objective of the Directive, and a duty on the Member States. See *Banco Espanol de Credito* (C-618/10) at paras 61–62. CJEU *Asbeek Brusse v Jahani BV* (C-488/11) at para 51 where a term is found to be unfair, the court must annul it. Compensation is not in itself sufficient remedy – CJEU *Banco Popular Espanol* (C-537/12) at para 56.

[2] CJEU C-154/15, C-307/15 & C-308/15 *Gutierrez Naranjo & Palacios Martinez* at para 75. See also (Post Brexit) CJEU *Dexia Nederland BV* (C-229/19) para 57 – the unfair term 'must . . . be deemed never to have existed.'

[3] CJEU *Banco Santander SA v Sanches Lopez* C-598/15 at para 45.

[4] CRA 2015, s 62(3). See CJEU *Sinues v Caixabank SA* (C-381/14) at para 25. It seems the default position is for the term to be excluded 'unless the consumer objects' – CJEU C-70/17 & C-179/17 *Abanca Corporacion Bancaria SA v Santos* para 63. CJEU *Dziubak* (C-260/18) para 66 for the process the court should follow.

[5] In other words, they are exercising their 'free and informed consent', CJEU *XZ v Ibercaja* (C-452/18) paras 29–30. Because such novation agreements or other variation proposals are usually made by the trader with whom the contract is made, the obligation to ensure such clarity will generally fall on that trader.

[6] (Post Brexit) CJEU *IW, RW v Bank BPH SA* (C-19/20) (29 April 2021) para 61.

[7] *R on the application of Emmet Donegan v Financial Services Compensation Scheme Ltd* [2021] EWHC 760 paras 120–125.

[8] CRA 2015, s 67 – 'the contract continues, so far as practicable, to have effect in every other respect'.

[9] See CJEU *Asbeek Brusse v Jahani BV* (C-488/11) at para 59 – the court cannot reduce an unfair penalty sum, but must exclude it completely. It may be appropriate to sever only part of a clause (where, on its proper construction, the clause comprises more than one term) – see *Bankers Insurance Company Ltd v South* [2003] EWHC 380 (QB) at para 35 – but the court must ensure it excludes all unfair terms and not merely some or part of them – CJEU *Radlinger v Finway* (C-377/14) at para 100. Where a term is unfair, the whole of that term must be removed (not just the unfair aspects of that term), since otherwise this would amount to amending the term, which is impermissible – (Post Brexit) CJEU *IW, RW v Bank BPH SA* (C-19/20) (29 April 2021) paras 66–68. In particular, the court cannot edit out parts of a term in order to make it fair, since this would weaken the dissuasive effect required – CJEU C-70/17 & C-179/17 *Abanca Corporacion Bancaria SA v Santos* para 55. Further, it seems the trader cannot take advantage of a legislative provision which could fill the gap left by the removal of the unfair term, to entitle the trader to charge money to the consumer, if the contract can otherwise continue in existence – (Post Brexit) CJEU *Dexia Nederland BV* (C-229/19) para 67.

[10] *Banco Espanol de Credito* (C-618/10) at paras 64–66 and 69. This ruling must be borne in mind when reading the judgments in *OFT v Foxtons Ltd* [2009] EWCA Civ 288. It was suggested there that a judge could give an injunction to stop the use of a term in specific circumstances (see paras 73 and 98). It seems rather that if a term is found to be unfair, its use must be prohibited in all circumstances. It is only when the court considers the position of *similar* terms, that it may be possible to rule that such terms are only unfair in certain given circumstances (see the judgment of Waller LJ at para 49.

[11] [2012] EWHC 1290 (Comm) at para 19.

[12] See also the 7th recital and *Perenicova* (C-453/10) at para 32 and AG's Opinion at paras 66–68.

9.118 Equally, the contract should continue to bind the consumer if it is capable of so doing, absent the impugned term(s)[1]. The Directive 'seeks to restore the balance between the parties, and not to cancel all contracts containing unfair terms', but where it is a main subject matter term, the CJEU considers it unlikely that the continuity of the contract would be legally possible, and such a contract cannot be saved by national legislation which seeks to change the main subject matter to make it fair[2]. However, where the deletion of the term would expose the consumer to particularly unfavourable consequences (eg a loan gets called in at once), such that the dissuasive effect resulting from annulment of the term might be jeopardised, the court may substitute a provision from national law. The substitute provision should be one that was designed to create fairness. It may not be possible for courts simply to imply a term to save the contract as this may amount to a revision of the term found to be unfair[3]. It would appear that this power is only available where the invalidity of the term would cause the whole contract to be annulled, and this would be particularly detrimental to the consumer[4]. An example of a term where deletion may not entail the cancellation of the whole contract is a penalty payment clause[5]. If there is however no provision of national law which can be used, it is open to the court to invite the parties to negotiate a replacement term, provided the court sets out the framework for those negotiations, and those negotiations seek to establish an effective balance between the rights and obligations of the parties[6]. Alternatively the consumer could agree to continue to be bound by the unfair term, but before making this decision, it is incumbent on the court to explain, objectively and exhaustively, the legal consequences that removal of the unfair term may entail[8].

[1] CJEU *Perenicova* (C-453/10) at paras 31–32 and 34–36 – the fact that the consumer may benefit from the contract ending is not sufficient reason to terminate it. For example if one part of a trader's claim may be an unfair penalty, the trader should still be able to pursue fair charges made under the contract (see *Britannia Parking Group Ltd v Semark-Jullien* 2020 WL 04353143, decision of Salisbury County Court, para 38). Where the unfair term defines the main subject matter of the contract, it seems unlikely that the contract is capable of continuing – CJEU C-118/17 *Dunai* at para 52.

[2] CJEU *GT v HS* (C-38/17) paras 42–44. Where the main subject matter has been severely modified, the resulting contract unlikely to be what the parties actually agreed to, so continuance is likely to be impossible: CJEU *Dziubak* (C-260/18) at para 40.

[3] CJEU *Kasler* (C-26/13) at paras 81–84. In assessing whether the consumer would be exposed to unfavourable consequences, the court must consider factors such as the national enforcement procedures which would apply if the contract came to an end – CJEU C-70/17 & C-179/17 *Abanca Corporacion Bancaria SA v Santos* para 62. CJEU *Dziubak* (C-260/18) paras 61-62 for the court's inability to imply terms based on general rules of law and usage.

[4] CJEU Joined Cases C-482/13, C-484/13, C-485/13 and C-487/13 *Unicajo Banco* at paras 33–34. See also CJEU *GT v HS* (C-38/17) at para 44.

[5] CJEU *NMBS v Kanyeba* (C-349/18) paras 71–72.

[6] CJEU *Banca B. SA v AAA* (C-269/19) (25 November 2020) paras 42–46. It is unclear how this differs in practice from the court, after hearing argument, implying a replacement term.

[8] (Post Brexit) CJEU *IW, RW v Bank BPH SA* (C-19/20) (29 April 2021) paras 97–98.

9.119 The assessment of whether the nullification of the contract will cause the consumer hardship must be carried out as at the date of the court hearing, not the date of the contract, because it must take into account the real and current situation of the consumer[1]. In carrying out this exercise, the court may need to identify separate terms within a single clause, such as where an initial interest rate or price is increased by an unfair mechanism. In such a case the initial rate or price should remain applicable or operate as a cap on the amount the consumer must pay, if the variation mechanism could lead to the price decreasing from time to time[2]. There may be situations where national law seeks to replace unfair terms with a mandatory replacement. The CJEU has considered this and ruled that while it is possible, this cannot have the effect of weakening the protection of the consumer. In particular, it must not prevent the consumer from being able to seek restitution for the harm that the (pre-amended) unfair term caused[3]. A consumer must remain able to seek the cancellation of the contract where the contract could not continue to exist without the (amended) unfair term[4].

[1]   CJEU *Dziubak* (C-260/18) at para 51.
[2]   CJEU *Banco Santander v Demba* (C-96/16) at paras 76–77, The rationale for treating the terms differently is that they serve different purposes– the default term acting as a penalty, the ordinary price or interest term acting as remuneration.
[3]   CJEU C-118/17 *Dunai* at paras 42–46.
[4]   CJEU C-118/17 *Dunai* at para 56.

9.120 Where a consumer has paid money under a term, subsequently found to be unfair, the obligation on the national court to exclude the application of the unfair term entails a corresponding restitutionary effect in respect of that money. The consumer must be put into the legal and factual position that they would have been in if the unfair term had never existed[1]. It is not open to the national court to impose any temporal limitation on the effect of their finding of unfairness, in order to protect the trader from having to repay money, unless there has already been a court ruling giving rise to *res judicata*[2]. Member States may lay down the precise procedural rules by which the restoration of money to the consumer may take place, which in the UK probably means that the consumer may bring a restitutionary claim to recover their money, as money paid under a mistake of law[3]. In *OFT v Ashbourne Management Services Ltd*[4], it was held that including unfair terms in agreements and enforcing them also amounted to an infringement of the CPUTR 2008 (see **Chapter 8**, Unfair Commercial Practices). Demanding payment of an unlawful penalty has been successfully prosecuted as fraud and an aggressive commercial practice[5].

[1]   CJEU C-154/15, C-307/15 and C-308/15 *Gutierrez Naranjo & Palacios Martinez* at paras 62 and 66.
[2]   CJEU C-154/15, C-307/15 and C-308/15 *Gutierrez Naranjo & Palacios Martinez* at paras 64–75.
[3]   This principle was set out in *Kleinwort Benson v Lincoln City Council* [1999] 2 AC 349, [1998] 4 All ER 513, and applied in an unfair terms context in *Chesterton v Finney* (Lambeth County Court). The High Court has also accepted this is the consequence of unfairness – see *Re Welcome Financial Services Ltd* [2015] EWHC 815 (Ch) at para 106. Such an outcome was also envisaged by the CJEU in *Alexandra Schulz* (C-359/11) at para 55, however the precise consequences of unfairness have not been harmonised at EU level, meaning that the remedy simply has to be no less favourable than under domestic law, and sufficiently effective – CJEU *Sinues v Caixabank SA* (C-381/14) at para 32. See also CJEU C-154/15, C-307/15 and C-308/15 *Gutierrez Naranjo & Palacios Martinez* at paras 66–69 – the time limits and procedures for bring such a claim are generally matters for the Member State, but aside from this, contrary to the position advanced by the Advocate General in that case, no

restriction may be placed on the consumer's ability to achieve restitution. Limitation periods for recovering money paid under an unfair term may run from the date the term was found to be unfair, not from the date of the contract or fulfilment of the contract: CJEU SC *Raiffeisen Bank SA v JB* (C-698/18) paras 75–79.

4   [2011] EWHC 1237 (Ch) at para 227.

5   See *R v Christopher Whatcott* [2019] EWCA Crim 1889 paras 2–3. The defendant received 3 months custody for the aggressive practice, and 3 months custody for the Fraud Act 2006 offence.

ASSESSMENT OF THE COURT'S OWN MOTION

9.121 By s 71 of the CRA 2015:

71 Duty of court to consider fairness of term

(1)   Subsection (2) applies to proceedings before a court which relate to a term of a consumer contract.

(2)   The court must consider whether the term is fair even if none of the parties to the proceedings has raised that issue or indicated that it intends to raise it.

(3)   But subsection (2) does not apply unless the court considers that it has before it sufficient legal and factual material to enable it to consider the fairness of the term.

9.122 A court must assess the fairness of terms even if no party raises the issue[1]. This is so even where the court is dealing with the matter on appeal, and unfairness was not raised in the court below[2]. It is also so where the court is faced with an application for judgment in default[3]. The Directive seeks to re-establish substantive equality between the parties. A consumer is in a weaker bargaining position and may agree to terms he cannot influence[4]. That imbalance may need to be corrected by positive action. If a consumer was required to raise the issue of unfairness himself, in order for him to receive the protection the Directive intends, the aim of Art 6 would not be achieved, in particular because the consumer may not be able or willing to challenge the term[5]. The court must be prepared to investigate potential unfairness even if the consumer is represented by a lawyer, and the lawyer fails to raise the matter[6].

1   CRA 2015, s 71(2) – subject to the court having the necessary legal and factual material before it to do so (s 71(3)). See CJEU *VB Penzugyi* (C-137/08) at paras 46–49. Courts must also construe legislation to give effect to the Directive (CJEU *Oceano Groupo* at para 32), and assess whether any limitation periods are so short as to render the exercise of consumer rights excessively difficult (CJEU *Asturcom v Nogueira* (C-40/08) at paras 41–42).

2   CJEU *Erika Jőrös v Aegon* (C-397/11).

3   CJEU *Karel de Grote v Kuijpers* (C-147/16) at para 36. The court must have this power where it is able to consider whether a claim is contrary to public policy. The CJEU has gone on to rule that any mandatory rule which requires the national court to rule against the consumer, in default of the consumer putting in an appearance, must be interpreted to permit the court to assess whether the term is unfair – and only give judgment if the term is fair: CJEU *Kancelaria Medius SA v RN* (C-495/19) para 48.

4   The obligation to ensure consumers are not bound by unfair terms may extend to officials, such as notaries, who draft official contracts, meaning that they must advise the consumer as to any doubts he has over the fairness of the terms – CJEU *ERSTE Bank Hungary Zrt v Sugar* (C-32/14) at paras 54–58). However, such officials are not obliged to refuse to enforce a potentially unfair term, where the consumer still has recourse to a court – CJEU *ERSTE Bank Hungary Zrt v Sugar* (C-32/14) at paras 62–65.

5   *Pannon* (C-243/08) at paras 23, 28 and 32; *Mostaza Claro* (C-168/05) at para 39; CJEU *VB Penzugyi* (C-137/08) at paras 49–52; and *Banco Espanol de Credito* (C-618/10) at para 54.

6   CJEU *Lintner* (C-511/17) para 40.

9.123 The requirement for the court to have sufficient factual and legal material to enable it to consider the unfairness does not require the consumer to have invoked unfair terms protection in their pleadings, or pleaded their case fully: the court's assessment is independent of the parties' submissions, because otherwise consumers would be disadvantaged by their own lack of awareness of their rights[1]. If there is a lack of factual material before it, a court must initiate investigative measures of its own motion to fill the gaps, for example by asking the parties to provide further evidence[2]. A court ought to ensure that it has before it at least the actual contract terms, the pre-contractual information and evidence of the process by which the consumer was invited to sign the contract[3]. The required assessment does not extend to assessing whether the consumer is entitled to any remedy specifically to address any unfair commercial practice which attended the unfair term, although the incidence of such practices will be relevant to the assessment of unfairness[4]. The court should also limit its assessment to the heads of claim actually pleaded. While it is important to take into account the other terms in the contract, it need not assess their fairness as well[5].

1   CJEU *Froukje Faber* (C-497/13) at paras 46–48. In particular, domestic courts should be reluctant to strike out pleadings which fail to particularise fully unfair terms in consumer contracts, but instead they should assess the consumer's case in the round – CJEU *Lintner* (C-511/17) paras 32–34. It should be noted that this was not the approach taken by the Court of Appeal in *Jones & Seymour v Roundlistic Ltd* [2018] EWCA Civ 2284 para 48 or the Scottish Sheriff's court in *Janice Halvorson v Persimmon Homes Ltd* [2018] SC EDIN 40 at para 39.
2   CJEU *Lintner* (C-511/17) paras 37–38.
3   CJEU *Profi Credit Polska SA v Wlostowska* (C-419/18) paras 56–59.
4   CJEU *Bankia SA v Merino* (C-109/17) at paras 31–48.
5   CJEU *Lintner* (C-511/17) paras 30–31 and 46–48.

9.124 Where the court considers that a term is unfair, it should invite each of the parties to set out their views on the matter (in order to ensure each has the chance to be heard), but it should not need to wait for the consumer to request the term be declared invalid[1]. The court should however bear in mind any potential negative impacts on the consumer of the term being declared invalid, as well as any benefits to the consumer in the term remaining in place – especially if the consumer has had an opportunity to challenge the term and has decided not to do so[2].

1   CJEU *Banif Plus Bank Zrt v Csaba Csipai* (C-472/11) at paras 28–36. In particular it is unlikely to be appropriate for a court to strike out a trader's claim merely because it is based on a term which may be unfair -the court should go on to carry out an actual assessment (see *Britannia Parking Group Ltd v Semark-Jullien* 2020 WL 04353143, decision of Salisbury County Court, paras35–38.
2   CJEU *Banco Santander SA v Sanches Lopez* C-598/15 AG Opinion at paras 79–81. The High Court in *Transfer Wise Inc v Decker* [2021] EWHC 1777 at paras 39–40, considered that where a point on unfairness has not been pleaded, and was raised very late in the proceedings (the day before the hearing), it did not have sufficient legal and factual material to assess the fairness of a term.

PROCEDURAL RULES

9.125 Procedural rules that prevent the court from assessing fairness, where it has the legal and factual elements necessary to do so, or which otherwise prevent consumers from asserting that a term is unfair, are liable to undermine the effectiveness of the Directive, and so fall foul of EU law[1]. Although the UK is no longer bound to achieve outcomes required by EU law, the purpose of the legislation remains to protect consumers. That may not be achieved where procedural rules unduly hinder its application.

[1] *Banco Espanol de Credito* (C-618/10) at paras 52–53; CJEU *BBVA SA v Pedro Penalva Lopez* (C-8/14) at paras 39–41 – where a transitional provision that reasonably allowed consumers to raise an unfairness argument for the first time was struck down because it did not require those consumers to be notified individually of their right.

9.126 This principle applies also where national rules provide for swift enforcement of some security, such as a bill of sale or promissory note, which is ancillary to an agreement containing potentially unfair terms– if the process is such that there is a significant risk that the consumer will be dissuaded from challenging the enforcement for example[1]. The principle also applies to national rules governing where litigation may be conducted, such as where the trader can choose whether to bring a claim in their own place of domicile or the place where the contract was to be performed. These rules will be constrained if they restrict excessively the right of consumers to an effective remedy or to exercise the rights conferred on them by the unfair terms directive. In particular, the time limits, cost and distances involved should not be such as would deter the consumer from entering an appearance in the proceedings[2]. This rule does not preclude national supreme courts from giving binding decisions governing how to interpret the Directive, but these must not prevent a court deciding a case from giving full effect to the Directive, as interpreted by the CJEU[3]. Although there will be no EU law obligation to do so in 2021, in our view it is likely that the UK courts will continue to apply the legislation to prevent the removal of consumer rights by procedural rules.

[1] CJEU *Profi Credit Polska v Mariusz Wawrzosek* (C-176/17) at paras 63-69, in this case considering whether summary enforcement of a promissory note, which secured payment under a credit agreement, was permissible. In considering whether a process is unduly onerous for a consumer to be expected to use, the Court considered the time limits required for lodging an application, the complexity of the pleading required of the consumer, their exposure to costs, and the extent to which they are likely to be aware of their rights anyway.

[2] CJEU *Aqua Med* (C-266/18) at paras 52–54.

[3] CJEU C-118/17 *Dunai* at para 61. This is a further reason why the decision of the High Court in *Casehub Ltd v Wolf Cola Ltd* [2017] EWHC 1169 (Ch) is to be treated with caution, in that the judge ruled that he was bound by Supreme Court decisions even if they conflicted with the jurisprudence of the CJEU.

9.127 In line with the principle of legal certainty, there is a very high threshold for courts to limit the temporal effect of their judgment so that it does not apply to existing contracts, or only applies after a period of time[1]. Similarly the existence of a Scheme of Arrangement made under the Companies Act 2006 does not require consumers who have been subjected to unfair penalties to claim as creditors under the Scheme – they are still able to claim restitution[2].

[1] CJEU *Alexandra Schulz* (C-359/11) at paras 54–64.

[2] *Re Welcome Financial Services Ltd* [2015] EWHC 815 (Ch) at para 106. This is consistent with the CJEU's position in *Radlinger v Finway* (C-377/14) at paras 51–59, where consumers must in insolvency proceedings also be able to challenge unfair terms as a shield.

Limitation periods

9.128 Limitation periods may frustrate the purpose of the Directive if the consumer is time barred from asserting that terms are unfair when a contract is still enforceable by the trader[1]. Likewise, rules which require individual challenges to be stayed pending the outcome of a collective challenge, are liable to be unlawful[2]. Member States may in principle impose limitation periods which stop the consumer from seeking restitution of payments made under an unfair term[3]. However, the CJEU has stated, post-Brexit, that limitation periods which operate to stop a consumer raising unfairness as a defence, or seeking a declaration that a term is unfair, are likely to be incompatible with the principle of effectiveness[4]. Member States remain free to organise their court processes as they wish, and are not required to create processes that make it especially cheap or easy for consumers (or consumer associations) to challenge terms[5]. Further, the right to invoke the Directive's protection is not open ended, and where a consumer has failed to take the opportunity to challenge an unfair term, the courts are not expected to permit further opportunities to be provided outside the usual process in a member state[6].

[1] CJEU *Cofidis v Fredout* (C-473/00) at paras 35–37. However, this does not permit actions to be raised indefinitely – limitation of actions can still apply, particularly if the consumer has not appealed a decision, because of the important principle of *res judicata* – CJEU *Asturcom v Nogueira* (C-40/08) at paras 36–37 and 47.

[2] CJEU *Sinues v Caixabank SA* (C-381/14) at paras 27–39.

[3] (Post Brexit) CJEU *VB v BNP Paribas Personal Finance SA* (Joined Cases C-776/19 to C-782/19) para 39.

[4] (Post Brexit) CJEU *VB v BNP Paribas Personal Finance SA* (Joined Cases C-776/19 to C-782/19) paras 38 and 47. See also (post Brexit) CJEU *LH v Profi Credit Slovakia sro* (C-485/19) (22 April 2021) paras 60–64. In this case, which was in the context of a consumer credit agreement with payments scheduled over 48 months, a limitation period of 3 years from the date of unjust enrichment by a trader was held to be inapplicable. This period meant that even before the loan had been fully repaid, the consumer would already be time barred from recovering payments they made at the start of the repayment period.

[5] As long as the principles of equivalence and effectiveness are satisfied – CJEU *Nora Baczo* (C-567/13) at paras 39–59; CJEU *Asociacion de Consumidores Independientes de Castilla y Leon* (C-413/12) at paras 30–45.

[6] CJEU *Banco Santander SA v Sanches Lopez* C-598/15 at para 49.

INJUNCTIONS

9.129 Section 70 and Sch 3 allow certain regulators[1] to obtain injunctions against any person appearing to be using, proposing or recommending use of a term or notice that is unfair, blacklisted under the CRA 2015, or not transparent[2]. The court may grant an injunction (or interdict in Scotland) against the term or notice under challenge, or against any term or notice of similar kind or with a similar effect[3]. It may be granted in very broad terms[4]. 'Use' of an unfair term covers not just including it in a contract, but also enforcing it in contracts already agreed with consumers[5]. 'Enforcing' includes any reliance on a term, such as demands for payment, letters invoking its existence, or any action, which refers to the unfair term[6]. The trader need not be the person who has actually entered into the contract with the consumer, but may be for example the contracting trader's agent, or another person invoking the term[7]. In addition to seeking an injunction, an enforcer is also entitled to obtain a declaration as to the unfairness of a term – which could be relied on by other persons[8].

1   Listed in Sch 3, para 8.
2   See Sch 3, para 3. This does not oblige the courts to permit consumer associations or other enforcers to intervene as of right in individual challenges however – see CJEU *Pohotovost' s.r.o.* (C-470/12) at paras 53–57.
3   Sch 3, para 5(3). This includes interim injunction or interdict – Sch 3, para 9.
4   Sch 3, para 5(1) and (2). The enforcement power is required to discharge the UK's obligations under the Directive – see *OFT v Foxtons Ltd* [2009] EWCA Civ 288 at para 42.
5   CJEU *Nemzeti v Invitel* (C-472/10) at para 43. A challenge may also be brought against terms not yet in use – CJEU *Commission v Italy* (C-372/99) at para 15 and *Oceano Groupo* (C-240/98) at para 27.
6   *OFT v Foxtons Ltd* [2009] EWCA Civ 288 at para 47.
7   *OFT v Ashbourne Management Services Ltd.*
8   *OFT v Foxtons Ltd* [2009] EWCA Civ 288 at paras 59–61.

9.130 In order to bring a matter to court, the enforcer need not have received any complaints, and the terms need not even have been used in any actual contracts[1].

1   Schedule 3, para 3(6), CJEU *Sinues v Caixabank SA* (C-381/14) at para 29.

Collective challenges

9.131 Regulator action (a 'collective challenge') is a more effective way of preventing the continuing use of unfair terms, and of changing contracting practice, than individual challenges[1]. In a collective challenge the unfair character of a term is assessed *in abstracto* bearing in mind it may be incorporated in contracts that have not yet been concluded[2].

1   *Director General of Fair Trading v First National Bank* [2001] UKHL 52, per Lord Steyn at para 33.
2   CJEU *Commission v Spain* (C-70/03) at para 16.

9.132 Although the meaning of a contract must be given the most favourable interpretation to consumers in an individual challenge, this rule of interpretation does not apply in the context of a collective challenge[1]. The term under challenge must therefore be given the reading *least* favourable to the consumer, since this has the effect of achieving a result that brings about the most favourable result for consumers as a whole[2]. The CJEU has held that this is a 'binding legislative provision which confers rights on consumers, and assists in determining the result which the Directive seeks to achieve'[3].

1   Article 5 and s 69(2).
2   CJEU *Commission v Spain* (C-70/03) at para 16.
3   CJEU *Commission v Spain* (C-70/03) at para 17.

9.133 It is not a defence to a collective challenge that the term could not be enforced due to a rule of law[1]. In a collective challenge, 'it is necessary to consider the position of typical parties when the contract is made'[2]. It is simply assumed that the consumer is in a much weaker bargaining position than a large trader contracting on its own standard form[3].

1   Sch 3, para 5(4). As seen above, this factor may be relevant in an individual challenge.
2   *Director General of Fair Trading v First National Bank* [2001] UKHL 52, per Lord Bingham at para 20. The court has to have regard to 'contemplated or typical relationships between parties' in order to assess any 'substantive unfairness' – per Lord Steyn at para 33.

[3]   *Director General of Fair Trading v First National Bank* [2001] UKHL 52, per Lord Bingham at para 13. There will be little attention paid to factors relevant to individual situations, such as whether the consumer had an inducement to agree to the term, or whether the product was sold or supplied to the special order of the consumer.

9.134 A 'typical consumer' test may be useful in determining the factual basis on which a term's fairness should be assessed in the context of a collective challenge[1]. It has also been used to assess whether a term is in plain intelligible language[2]. However, the Supreme Court has disapproved of its use to identify the price or main subject matter for the purpose of the s 64 exception, finding it was an overly complex addition to what should be an objective test[3].

[1]   As in *OFT v Ashbourne Management Services Ltd* [2011] EWHC 1237 (Ch) at para 128.
[2]   *OFT v Abbey National* [2008] EWHC 875 (Comm) and *OFT v Foxtons Ltd* [2009] EWHC 1681 (Ch) – where it was held that It does not attempt to understand the 'mindset, thinking or attributes' of a typical consumer (at para 34).
[3]   *OFT v Abbey National* [2009] UKSC 6 per Lord Mance at paras 108 and 113.

9.135 The fact that a collective challenge is being brought must not prevent individual consumers from asserting their rights as individuals, since this would contravene the principle of effectiveness[1]. An individual challenge may still be brought if a collective challenge has failed, although the consumer would need to demonstrate why his case was different, drawing on the individual circumstances of their situation[2]. Where a term is found to be unfair in a collective challenge, it is unfair for all purposes and in all circumstances[3]. This could have an impact on traders using the term, who are not before the court[4]. It is also a finding that the term is and always has been unfair – which could lead to serious financial consequences for those traders who have been relying on it[5].

[1]   CJEU *Sinues v Caixabank SA* (C-381/14) at paras 36–40. This also means that individual challenges must not be stayed for administrative reasons to avoid overburdening the court system (para 42).
[2]   CJEU *Sinues v Caixabank SA* (C-381/14) at para 40, *OFT v Foxtons Ltd* [2009] EWCA Civ 288 at para 46.
[3]   CJEU *Nemzeti v Invitel* (C-472/10) at para 43, *Commission v Spain* (C-70/03) at para 16. See also the AG's Opinion at paras 12 and 13, where he states that where in a collective challenge, a term is found to be unfair, its continued use must be prevented. The CJEU therefore supports the position of Waller LJ in *OFT v Foxtons Ltd* [2009] EWCA Civ 288 at para 47, rather than that of Moore-Bick LJ at para 98. However, this does not prevent consumers from submitting to a term, if they wish – CJEU *Sinues v Caixabank SA* (C-381/14) at para 25.
[4]   CJEU *Nemzeti v Invitel* (C-472/10) at para 38, *Director General of Fair Trading v First National Bank* [2001] UKHL 52 at para 9. This appears also to be contemplated by Sch 3, para 5(3)(b). However the CJEU has also confirmed that where a trader was not party to the proceedings in which the finding of unfairness was made, they should have the opportunity to be heard before a court before they are themselves penalised for use of the allegedly unfair term. This is because proceedings to enforce the Unfair Terms Directive are subject to the fundamental rights of the EU legal order (including right to a fair hearing) – see CJEU *Biuro podrozy v Prezes Urzedu* C-119/15 at paras 25–27. The impact of this is that where any form of list of unfair terms exists, on which an enforcer is going to rely to impose a sanction, this must be notified to the Commission, properly publicised, clearly structured and kept up to date (C-119/15 at paras 35–40).
[5]   CJEU *RWE Vertrieb v VBZ Nordrhein Westfalen* (C-92/11) at para 58.

9.136 Where an enforcer wishes to bring proceedings against a trader operating from elsewhere in the EEA, who is directing their activities towards consumers in their Member State, the law that applies to this challenge will be determined under the Rome II Regulation on non-contractual obligations – this is because use of an unfair term is a harmful as a tortious act. Therefore the enforcer may act under Pt 8 of the Enterprise Act 2002 or Sch 3 of the Consumer Rights Act 2015[1]. However the law that applies to the assessment of the fairness of the term will be determined under the Rome I Regulation on contractual relations[2]. This is the same as where a challenge is brought by an individual. The result is that where a choice of law clause validly applies the law of another EEA state, the assessment of fairness may have to be made under the law of that state, rather than of the UK.

[1] CJEU *VFK v Amazon* (C-191/15) at paras 39–48.
[2] CJEU *VFK v Amazon* (C-191/15) at para 49.

9.137 Schedule 3 should be read alongside the enforcement provisions in Pt 8 of the Enterprise Act 2002 (see CHAPTER 5, Civil Enforcement), and the Enhanced Consumer measures in Sch 7 to the CRA 2015 (see CHAPTER 5, Civil Enforcement).

Chapter 10

FRAUD AND MONEY LAUNDERING

Contents

THE FRAUD ACT 2006

Introduction

10.1 In *Reddaway v Banham*[1], Lord MacNaghten stated:

'Fraud is infinite in variety, sometimes it is audacious and unblushing; sometimes it pays a sort of homage to virtue, and then it is modest and retiring; it would be honesty itself if it could only afford it.'

In *Lee Qualter Commercial Reduction Services Ltd & Anor v Crown Court at Preston*[2], Andrew Thomas QC stated:

'Fraud in its various manifestations is the bread and butter work of modern trading standards departments.'

The mechanics for reporting, and investigating fraud, have been found to be inadequate over a number of years and the Home Office policy paper Beating crime plan - published 27 July 2021 – comments:

'We will replace Action Fraud with an improved national fraud and cybercrime reporting system . . . '

[1] [1896] AC 199.
[2] [2019] EWHC 2563 (Admin).

10.2 English criminal law did not include a general offence of 'fraud' until the Fraud Act 2006 ('FA 2006') was introduced. The Act is mainly based on the Law Commission report on fraud, which concluded that the deception offences in the Theft Act 1968 were too specific, overlapping and outdated. In its post-legislative assessment of the FA 2006 published in June 2012 the Ministry of Justice stated: 'Our overall assessment of the Act is that it has been successful in achieving its initial objectives of modernising the former array of deception offences'.

10.3 The Act repealed the following Theft Act 1968 offences:

- s 15 (obtaining property by deception);
- s 15A (obtaining a money transfer by deception);
- s 16 (obtaining pecuniary advantage by deception);
- s 20(2) (procuring the execution of a valuable security by deception).

It also amended s 25 of the Theft Act 1968 (going equipped for burglary, theft or cheat) by removing references to 'cheat'. The FA 2006 came into force on 15 January 2007 in England, Wales and Northern Ireland[1].

[1]   Fraud Act 2006 (Commencement Order) 2006, SI 2006/3200.

Scotland

10.4 The FA 2006 does not apply in Scotland, other than s 10, which increases the maximum sentence for fraudulent trading by a company to 10 years. However, Scotland has the common law crime of fraud, committed when someone achieves a practical result by a false pretence. A reasonable working definition of fraud in Scotland might be:

> 'Fraud consists of a false pretence made to another person in the knowledge of its falsity and with the intention that the other person should be deceived by it into acting in a way which s/he would not otherwise have acted, provided that the other person is so deceived and does act on account of it.'

10.5 A particular form of fraud in Scotland is 'Uttering' – which occurs where a forged document (or instrument) is passed off as real and has a prejudicial effect on another person.

Fraud offences

10.6 Fraud offences are increasingly prosecuted by trading standards services, yet are not offences that attract investigatory powers for trading standards officers or have a long-established track record of being investigated and prosecuted by trading standards services. It is important, in such a context, that the elements of the various fraud offences are properly understood so that the correct offence is identified and pursued from the outset. Under the Fraud Act 2006, s 1, an offence is committed if a person acts dishonestly and breaches any of the three different ways of committing the offence of fraud: by false representation, by failing to disclose information or by abuse of position.

1 Fraud

(1)   A person is guilty of fraud if he is in breach of any of the sections listed in subsection (2) (which provide for different ways of committing the offence).
(2)   The sections are—
   (a)   section 2 (fraud by false representation),
   (b)   section 3 (fraud by failing to disclose information), and

(c)   section 4 (fraud by abuse of position).

10.7 A person who is guilty of an offence under s 1 is liable:

(a)   on summary conviction, to imprisonment for a term not exceeding 12 months or to a fine (or to both);

(b)   on conviction on indictment, to imprisonment for a term not exceeding 10 years or to a fine (or to both).

10.8

Precedent for fraud by false representation

Statement of offence

FRAUD BY FALSE REPRESENTATION, contrary to ss 1 and 2 of the Fraud Act 2006.

Particulars of offence

A B on [date] dishonestly made a representation to C D intending thereby to make a gain for himself or another [or to cause loss to another] [or to expose another to a risk of loss], which was and which he knew was or might be untrue or misleading, namely [. . .].

Section 2 (fraud by false representation)

10.9 FA 2006, s 2 provides:

2 Fraud by false representation

(1)   A person is in breach of this section if he—
    (a)   dishonestly makes a false representation, and
    (b)   intends, by making the representation—
        (i)   to make a gain for himself or another, or
        (ii)   to cause loss to another or to expose another to a risk of loss.

(2)   A representation is false if—
    (a)   it is untrue or misleading, and
    (b)   the person making it knows that it is, or might be, untrue or misleading.

(3)   "Representation" means any representation as to fact or law, including a representation as to the state of mind of—
    (a)   the person making the representation, or
    (b)   any other person.

(4)   A representation may be express or implied.

(5)   For the purposes of this section a representation may be regarded as made if it (or anything implying it) is submitted in any form to any system or device designed to receive, convey or respond to communications (with or without human intervention).

10.10 A representation is defined as false if it is untrue or misleading and the person making it knows that it is, *or might be*, untrue or misleading. It makes no difference if the representation is made to a machine or to a person. A representation may be express or implied; it can be stated in words or communicated by conduct or by omission. There is no limitation on the way in which the representation must be expressed. It could be written, spoken or posted on a website.

10.11 *R v Vig (Deekan)*[1] provides an example of an implied representation. The defendant gave driving lessons using a car with dual pedals and showed pupils documents suggesting he was insured as a driving instructor. He was not a qualified driving instructor and was convicted of fraud under s 2 of the FA 2006. In rejecting his appeal against conviction the Court of Appeal stated:

' . . . in our judgment . . . We do not accept that it had to be shown that the applicant represented himself specifically or expressly as [a driving instructor] only that the implicit representations which were proved amounted in substance to that.'

[1]   [2010] EWCA Crim 2245.

10.12 In *R v Greig*[1] the defendants had done gardening work at the home of a vulnerable elderly consumer who was easily confused. The value of the work was £300, however, the defendants had charged the consumer £6,850, which he paid in three cheques. The defendants were convicted of fraud by the implicit representation that the amounts they had charged 'represented fair payment for gardening work'. The Court of Appeal upheld their convictions.

[1]   [2010] EWCA Crim 1183.

10.13 In *R v Silverman*,[1] it was said that the question of whether a trader has made a false representation in relation to quotations for work or services would always depend on the circumstances. Consumers often rely on tradesmen to act fairly and reasonably towards them. A false representation might be made if a grossly excessive price was charged when there was a relationship of trust between the consumer and tradesmen, even if no pressure to accept the price had been applied by the tradesman.

[1]   86 Cr App R 213, CA.

10.14 The representation must be made dishonestly. The definition of dishonesty was, for many years, established in *R v Ghosh*. In determining whether the accused had acted dishonestly the questions were:

(i)   whether the accused's actions had been dishonest according to the ordinary standards of reasonable and honest people; and, if so
(ii)   whether the accused himself had realised that his actions were, according to those standards, dishonest.

10.15 The definition of dishonesty was, however, re-considered by the Supreme Court in the case of *Ivey v Genting Casinos UK Ltd (t/a Crockfords Club)*[1]. Lord Hughes, giving the judgment of the court, stated that the subjective element of the test for dishonesty in *R v Ghosh* did not correctly represent the law and directions based on it should no longer be given.

The court stated that the proper approach is to first ascertain the actual state of the individual's knowledge or belief as to the facts. Once that is established, the question of whether the conduct was honest or dishonest was to be determined by applying the standards of ordinary decent people. There was, importantly, no requirement that the defendant must appreciate that the conduct was dishonest by those standards.

¹   [2017] UKSC 67.

10.16 Accordingly, the test for dishonesty that has been applied in criminal cases for decades has been changed. Some commentators suggested that the circumstances of the case of *Ivey* and the fact that the comments on the test for dishonesty were obiter meant the criminal courts must continue to apply the *Ghosh* test. The issue was considered in *DPP v Patterson*¹, in which Sir Brian Leveson stated:

'. . . . These observations (from Ivey) were clearly obiter, and as a matter of strict precedent the court is bound by Ghosh, although the Court of Appeal could depart from that decision without the matter returning to the Supreme Court.

Given the terms of the unanimous observations of the Supreme Court expressed by Lord Hughes, who does not shy from asserting that Ghosh does not correctly represent the law, it is difficult to imagine the Court of Appeal preferring Ghosh to Ivey in the future.'

¹   [2018] 1 Cr App R 28.

10.17 Sir Brian Leveson's judgement on which test would be preferred was finally proved correct in the very recent case of *R v Barton*¹, when the Court of Appeal affirmed that the test for dishonesty in the criminal context was that set by the Supreme Court in *Ivey*, thereby ending any possible confusion.

¹   [2020] EWCA Crim 575,

10.18 The proper approach to dishonesty now in all criminal cases is as set out in *Ivey*:

(i)   Ascertain the defendant's actual state of knowledge or belief as to the facts;

(ii) Determine whether the conduct was honest or dishonest by applying the standards of ordinary decent people.

10.19 In *R v Hayes*¹ (considering the *Ghosh* test) it was made clear that the objective part of the test must not be modified to reflect the standards of a particular market or group of traders. However, the context in which a trader is working may be relevant to the defendant's actual state of knowledge.

¹   [2015] EWCA Crim 1944.

10.20 The person must make the representation with the intention of making a gain or causing loss or risk of loss to another. It is not necessary to prove an actual gain or loss. Section 5 defines 'gain' and 'loss' in the same way as s 34(2)(a) of the Theft Act 1968:

5 "Gain" and "loss"

(2) "Gain" and "loss"—
  (a)   extend only to gain or loss in money or other property;
  (b)   include any such gain or loss whether temporary or permanent;
and "property" means any property whether real or personal (including things in action and other intangible property).

(3) "Gain" includes a gain by keeping what one has, as well as a gain by getting what one does not have.

(4) "Loss" includes a loss by not getting what one might get, as well as a loss by parting with what one has.

10.21 It is a matter for the decision-maker, on the facts of each case, whether the causative link between the intention and the making of the false representation, required by the section, is established, *R v Gilbert (Stephanie Rae)*.[1] Unlike its predecessor, s 15 of the Theft Act 1968, it is no longer necessary to prove that any victim was actually deceived by the defendant's behaviour. In *R v Lee*[2] the defendant was an itinerant seller of misdescribed upholstered furniture who would say 'practically anything' to ensure a sale. The Court of Appeal rejected his appeal against conviction on the grounds that there was no evidence of reliance on his false statements.

[1] [2012] EWCA Crim 2392.
[2] [2010] EWCA Crim 268.

10.22 A single offence under s 1 may sometimes be charged where numerous false representations are made. In *R v Downing*[1] the defendant pleaded guilty to one offence of fraud covering 47 false claims for payment. In *R (on the application of Burns) v Woolwich Crown Court*[2] the single offence involved persuading a 76-year-old man that his property was in urgent need of repair and obtaining three banker's drafts totalling £140,000 from him. The offence was said to have taken place over 3 months and reflected the cumulative effect of false representations made on different occasions.

[1] [2010] EWCA Crim 739.
[2] [2010] EWHC 129 (Admin).

Section 3 (fraud by failing to disclose information)

10.23 The FA 2006, s 3 provides:

3 Fraud by failing to disclose information

A person is in breach of this section if he—

(a) dishonestly fails to disclose to another person information which he is under a legal duty to disclose, and

(b) intends, by failing to disclose the information—

(i) to make a gain for himself or another, or

(ii) to cause loss to another or to expose another to a risk of loss.

10.24

Precedent for fraud by failing to disclose

Statement of offence

FRAUD BY FAILURE TO DISCLOSE INFORMATION, contrary to sections 1 and 3 of the Fraud Act 2006.

Particulars of offence

A B on [date] dishonestly and intending thereby to make a gain for himself or another [or to cause loss to another] [or to expose another to a risk of loss], failed to disclose to C D information which he was under a legal duty to disclose, namely [. . .].

10.25 The section is apparently not limited to *statutory or regulatory* disclosure obligations. A legal duty to disclose information may include duties under oral contracts as well as written contracts.

10.26 The Law Commission's Report on Fraud explained the concept of 'legal duty' in the following terms:

'7.28 Such a duty may derive from statute (such as the provisions governing company prospectuses), from the fact that the transaction in question is one of the utmost good faith (such as a contract of insurance), from the express or implied terms of a contract, from the custom of a particular trade or market, or from the existence of a fiduciary relationship between the parties (such as that of agent and principal).

7.29 For this purpose there is a legal duty to disclose information not only if the defendant's failure to disclose it gives the victim a cause of action for damages, but also if the law gives the victim a right to set aside any change in his or her legal position to which he or she may consent as a result of the non-disclosure. For example, a person in a fiduciary position has a duty to disclose material information when entering into a contract with his or her beneficiary, in the sense that a failure to make such disclosure will entitle the beneficiary to rescind the contract and to reclaim any property transferred under it.'

10.27 In *R v Razoq (Adil)*,[1] Hallett LJ said:

'The Fraud Act contains no definition as to what constitutes a legal duty. The question is one of law for the judge who should then direct the jury that if they find certain facts proved they could conclude that a duty to disclose existed in all the circumstances.'

[1] [2012] EWCA Crim 674.

10.28 It follows that the repeated non-provision of cancellation notices under the Consumer Contracts (Information, Cancellation and Additional Charges) Regulations 2013[1] may constitute a breach of s 3. A single failure to provide notice of cancellation rights now constitutes a criminal offence under reg 19 of the 2013 Regulations; however, the maximum sentence is limited to a fine. In *R v Jason Armstrong*[2], the appellant was convicted of fraud contrary to s 3, for failing to disclose to a consumer her right to cancel the contract. It was argued that the prosecution needed to prove that the appellant had specific knowledge of his legal obligations under the relevant cancellation regulations, and that in the absence of such evidence the judge should have withdrawn that count from the jury. The Court of Appeal disagreed, with Sharp LJ stating:

'It is common ground that the prosecution were required to establish that the appellant was aware he was under a legal duty. What is not required however . . . is for the prosecution to establish specific knowledge of the Regulations which imposes it. To put it another way, if the appellant knew, or the prosecution established that he knew, he was under a relevant legal duty, then this was sufficient. It was neither here nor there whether the prosecution could prove his knowledge of the precise statutory framework and the Regulations that gave rise to that duty.

As to the half-time ruling and the appellants awareness that he was under such a duty, the judge decided, and ultimately directed the jury, that such knowledge could be inferred from this among other things: the appellant had clearly been trading for some time, the Regulations had been in force for some considerable time, it could be inferred that a trader would be aware of the Regulations, it is a requirement of anyone starting a business to know the Regulations; and if this was not the case, no trader could ever be convicted of their first offence. Contrary to the appellants submissions, we think this approach was not a flawed one nor that it confused "knew" with "ought to have known". As was observed during the course of argument . . . , the fact that a trader ought to know of Regulations can be evidence from which it can be inferred, depending on the circumstances, that he did have such knowledge. The issue at half time was whether there was evidence from which a jury, properly directed, could infer actual knowledge. In our view, there plainly was.'

It is worth noting, however, that a legal duty to disclose facts cannot be inferred merely because they give rise to financial liability. In the case of *R v D*[3], a local authority argued that in the absence of any statutory provision a legal duty to disclose nevertheless arose implicitly due to the financial obligation to pay council tax. The Court of Appeal disagreed stating that it was wrong to equate a liability to pay with a liability to notify.

1   SI 2013/3134.
2   [2018] EWCA Crim 2363.
3   [2019] EWCA Crim 209.

Section 4 (fraud by abuse of position)

10.29 The FA 2006, s 4 provides:

4 Fraud by abuse of position

(1)   A person is in breach of this section if he –
    (a)   occupies a position in which he is expected to safeguard, or not to act against, the financial interests of another person,
    (b)   dishonestly abuses that position, and
    (c)   intends, by means of the abuse of that position –
        (i)   to make a gain for himself or another, or
        (ii)   to cause loss to another or to expose another to a risk of loss.
(2)   A person may be regarded as having abused his position even though his conduct consisted of an omission rather than an act.

10.30

Precedent for fraud by abuse of position

Statement of offence

FRAUD BY ABUSE OF POSITION, contrary to sections 1 and 4 of the Fraud Act 2006.

Particulars of offence

A B on [date] dishonestly and intending thereby to make a gain for himself or another [or to cause loss to another] [or to expose another to a risk of loss], abused his position [...] in which he was expected to safeguard [or not act against] the financial interests of C D, namely [. . .].

10.31 The FA 2006, s 4 applies in situations where the defendant has been put in a privileged position, and by virtue of this position is expected to safeguard another's *financial* interests or not act against those interests.

10.32 There is no express requirement that a defendant must know that he is expected to safeguard or not to act against the financial interests of the other person, or to know that his act (or failure to act) constitutes such an abuse. 'Abuse' is not defined in the FA 2006. The current CPS Guidance on the FA 2006 gives as an example of the type of conduct that would give rise to a charge under FA 2006, s 4:

> 'a tradesman who helps an elderly person with odd jobs, gains influence over that person and removes money from their account.'

10.33 In *Valujevs*[1] gangmasters had assumed control of collecting wages of vulnerable migrant workers. The Court of Appeal held that the defendants could arguably have been under a duty to avoid acting against the interests of the migrant workers and the defendants consequently fell within the ambit of this offence.

[1]   [2015] QB 745.

10.34 In considering how to frame a charge of fraud by abuse of position it may be appropriate to allege a 'general deficiency' of funds misappropriated over a period of time rather than specific financial transactions, see the case of *R v TJC*.[1]

[1]   [2015] EWCA Crim 1276.

Other offences

Articles used in fraud

10.35 The FA 2006, ss 6 and 7 provide:

6 Possession etc. of articles for use in frauds

(1)   A person is guilty of an offence if he has in his possession or under his control any article for use in the course of or in connection with any fraud.

7 Making or supplying articles for use in frauds

(1)   A person is guilty of an offence if he makes, adapts, supplies or offers to supply any article –

    (a)   knowing that it is designed or adapted for use in the course of or in connection with fraud, or

    (b)   intending it to be used to commit, or assist in the commission of, fraud.

10.36 Note that the offence in s 6 does not relate to an article 'made or adapted' for use in fraud (compared with s 7). The wording of s 6 follows s 25 of the Theft Act 1968 (although s 6 also applies to articles found in an offender's home). Case law on s 25 is therefore likely to continue to be relevant.

10.37 In *R v Ellames*,[1] the court said that:

'In our view, to establish an offence under s 25(1) the prosecution must prove that the defendant was in possession of the article, and intended the article to be used in the course of or in connection with some future burglary, theft or cheat. But it is not necessary to prove that he intended it to be used in the course of or in connection with any specific burglary, theft or cheat; it is enough to prove a general intention to use it for some burglary, theft or cheat; we think that this view is supported by the use of the word "any" in s 25(1). Nor, in our view, is it necessary to prove that the defendant intended to use it himself; it will be enough to prove that he had it with him with the intention that it should be used by someone else.'

[1]   [1974] 3 All ER 130.

10.38 In *R v Nimley (Emmanuel)*[1] the defendant was jailed for 6 months for illegally recording Hollywood movies at a cinema. He then distributed them using his iPhone on the day of their official release. He was charged under ss 6 and 7 of the FA 2006 and s 107(1)(e) Copyright, Designs and Patents Act 1988. The defendant uploaded the recordings to a file-sharing website where viewers could access the material free of charge. On appeal, his sentence was reduced to a 12-month community order and 120 hours of unpaid work.

[1]   [2010] EWCA Crim 2752.

10.39 Possession and control are not defined in the FA 2006 but the Court of Appeal has observed that case law on possession of drugs or firearms may assist, and liability may arise even where a defendant lacks physical possession or control of the article in question[1].

[1]   *R v Tarley* [2012] EWCA Crim 464.

10.40 In *R v Rasoul (Hana Kadir)*[1] the defendant was an Iraqi national who, in an attempt to gain permission to remain in the UK, attempted to have forged documents submitted on his behalf to the government. He pleaded guilty to the offence but appealed on the basis that, in fact, he had never had 'possession' of the relevant documents for the purposes of s 6. The appeal was dismissed on the basis that s 6 requires proof of possession *or control*.

[1]   [2012] EWCA Crim 1248.

10.41 The phrase 'for use in the course of or in connection with any fraud' applies to articles that were used to mislead, but also articles created later in order to disguise or mask fraud. In the case of *R v Smith*[1], the defendant operated a gardening business and having agreed to undertake some gardening work for the victim failed to inform them of their cancellation rights. He subsequently created a false cancellation notice, complete with a forged signature from the victim, in order to cover up the fraud. The Court of Appeal held that there was nothing in the authorities to the effect that the relevant fraud could not be one which had been committed in the past.

[1]   [2020] EWCA Crim 38.

10.42 In *R v Ryan*[1] the defendant was convicted of conspiracy to defraud and controlling an article for use in fraud. He was sentenced to a total of 30 months' imprisonment. One of the other four co-accused was convicted of conspiracy to defraud and sentenced to 51 weeks' imprisonment suspended for 2 years; three other co-accused were found not guilty or verdicts of not guilty were entered. Ryan, was the head of a fraudulent operation Car Clamping Securities which defrauded motorists by tampering with a pay and display machine, fitting it with a computer chip so although it accepted two-pound coins and issued a ticket, no credit was given to the motorist. Motorists would leave their cars thinking they had paid the right amount only to return and discover their car had been taken to the company's compound in Ladywood where they usually had to pay over £300 to get it back.

[1]   [2011] EWCA Crim 1425.

10.43 It is also important to note, as per *R v Sakalaukas*[1] that '[a]ny article in s 6(1) meant any article the defendant had with him for the purpose or intention of using in the course of or in connection with any fraud' and use necessarily related to use in the future and *not* articles which had been used in the past.

[1]   [2013] EWCA Crim 2278.

10.44 The maximum sentence for a s 6 offence, which is triable either way, is 5 years imprisonment, whereas the s 7 offence, also triable either way, is 10 years imprisonment.

Fraudulent trading

10.45 Fraudulent trading is effectively a general fraud offence. The Companies Act 2006 creates liability for a corporate defendant. The provision extends to Scotland. The FA 2006 creates a parallel offence for non-corporate traders such as sole traders and partnerships.

10.46 The FA 2006, s 993 provides:

Companies Act 2006, s 993

993 Offence of fraudulent trading

(1)   If any business of a company is carried on with intent to defraud creditors of the company or creditors of any other person, or for any fraudulent purpose, every person who is knowingly a party to the carrying on of the business in that manner commits an offence.

(2)   This applies whether or not the company has been, or is in the course of being, wound up.

10.47

Precedent for fraudulent trading

Statement of offence

FRAUDULENT TRADING, contrary to section 993(1) of the Companies Act 2006.

Particulars of offence

A B between [date] and [date] was knowingly a party to the carrying on of the business of X Limited for a fraudulent purpose, namely [. . .]

10.48

Precedent for fraudulent trading (defrauding creditors)

Statement of offence

FRAUDULENT TRADING, contrary to section 993(1) of the Companies Act 2006.

Particulars of offence

AB between [date] and [date] was knowingly a party to the carrying on of the business of X Limited with intent to defraud creditors of that company.

10.49 The FA 2006, s 9 provides:

Fraud Act 2006, s 9[1]

9 Participating in fraudulent business carried on by sole trader etc

(1)   A person is guilty of an offence if he is knowingly a party to the carrying on of a business to which this section applies.
(2)   This section applies to a business which is carried on—
    (a)   by a person who is outside the reach of [section 993 of the Companies Act 2006]; and
    (b)   with intent to defraud creditors of any person or for any other fraudulent purpose.

10.50

Precedent for fraudulent trading (sole trader)

Statement of offence

FRAUDULENT TRADING, contrary to section 9 of the Fraud Act 2006.

Particulars of offence

AB between [date] and [date] was knowingly a party to the carrying on of a business called XY for a fraudulent purpose, namely [. . .]

10.51 The term 'fraudulent purpose' connotes an intention to go 'beyond the bounds of what ordinary decent people engaged in business would regard as honest' – *R v Grantham*[1]. 'The words "defraud" and "fraudulent purpose" are words which connote actual dishonesty involving, according to current notions of fair trading among commercial men, real moral blame' – *Re Patrick and Lyon Ltd*[2].

[1]   [1984] 3 All ER 166.
[2]   [1933] All ER 590.

10.52 Dishonesty is an essential element of the offence. This may include 'blind eye knowledge', a firmly grounded suspicion that relevant facts exist and a deliberate decision to avoid confirming their existence: *Re Bank of Credit and Commerce International SA; Morris v State Bank of India*[1].

[1]   [2003] BCC 735, Ch D.

10.53 Some helpful guidance on the application of s 9 is given in:

(a) Home Office Circular 42/2006 – 'section 9 is an "activity" offence, meaning that it captures a course of conduct, and is not limited to specific transactions . . . An example of fraudulent trading would be a pattern of behaviour by a dishonest roof repairer who consistently inflated bills and charged for work he had not done'.

(b) the Crown Prosecution Service Legal Guidance – which includes: 'Prosecutors should consider charges under (s 9) where . . . a business is being run for a fraudulent purpose, for example, rogue "cold calling" traders who regularly submit inflated bills to customers for shoddy work (and who often target the elderly or vulnerable)'.

10.54 In *R v Stansfield*[1] the director of a company called One Food Limited, was sentenced – with two others – to 27 months' imprisonment, after pleading guilty to an offence under s 993 of the Companies Act 2006 for fraudulent trading. In addition, he was disqualified under s 2 of the Company Directors Disqualification Act 1986 from acting as a director of a company for a period of 6 years. Refusing a renewed application for leave to appeal against sentence Stanley Burnton LJ said:

> 'This was a prolonged period of fraud. It was exacerbated not only by the deliberateness of the fraud, but by the involvement of staff, including (your) own wife, in what were frauds involving forgery and false accounting.'

[1] [2010] EWCA Crim 528.

10.55 In *R v Waring*[1] the defendant was sentenced to a total of 5 years' imprisonment in relation to 10 offences of fraudulent trading. Refusing leave to appeal the judge said:

> 'This was a long running fraudulent course of trading in which in effect you ran a scheme whereby largely bogus companies sent totally bogus invoices to other companies which were in a number of instances paid without challenge. By this means the prosecution says you profited to the tune of nearly £1 million. Your own estimate was £630,000 and the exact figure was a difficult one to ascertain. The fraudulent trading was fraudulent virtually from the beginning.'

[1] [2011] EWCA Crim 1567.

10.56 In *R v Ventriglia (Walter)*[1] the defendant pleaded guilty under s 9, following a trading standards enquiry into letters sent by him to members of the public which included misleading information about the requirements for a valid will, along with an invitation to redraft for a fee. The sentence of 14 months' imprisonment was upheld on appeal.

[1] [2011] EWCA Crim 2912.

10.57 In *R v Boakes*[1] the Court of Appeal upheld a sentence of 10 years in relation to two counts of fraudulent trading, one under the Companies Act 1985 (the previous statute) and one under the Companies Act 2006. The Court commented that 10 years' imprisonment for a large number of unpleasant offences against vulnerable people, taking away much or all of their savings, was not a day too long.

[1] [2015] EWCA Crim 2288.

10.58 In *R v Saini*[1] a post office manager who sold a significant number of counterfeit DVDs was prosecuted for fraudulent trading as well as offences under the Trade Marks Act 1994 and was given a 25–month custodial sentence.

[1]   [2017] EWCA Crim 234.

10.59 It should be noted that fraudulent trading, which carries a maximum sentence of 10 years imprisonment, is not included in the Definitive Sentencing Guidelines for Fraud, Bribery and Money Laundering Offences (see Sentencing below), although it is appropriate to pay regard to them where there are similarities to an offence to which the guidelines do apply,[1] which is almost invariably the case. The fact that the guidelines do not apply is no doubt due to the wide spectrum of mechanisms by which the offence can be committed. However, relevant factors to sentencing have been held to be:

* the value of the fraud;
* the manner in which it was committed;
* the period over which it was committed;
* the position of the offender and his measure of control within the company;
* any abuse of trust;
* any effect on public confidence in the integrity of commercial life;
* any loss to investors;
* any personal benefit.

[1]   *R McCrae* [2013] 1 Cr App R (S) 1.

Directors' liability

10.60 Section 12 creates liability for directors etc, which is covered in CHAPTER 4, Criminal Enforcement.

Enforcement

10.61 There is no duty of enforcement or any powers for enforcement officers under the Fraud Act 2006.

Sentencing

10.62 In October 2014 the Sentencing Council issued a *Definitive Guideline for Fraud, Bribery and Money Laundering Offences*. It applies to all individual offenders aged 18 and older and to organisations sentenced after 1 October 2014, regardless of the date of the offence. The Guidelines require the Court to assess the culpability and the harm. The level of culpability is determined by weighing up all the factors of the case to determine the offender's role, the extent to which the offending was planned and the sophistication with which it was carried out.

10.63 Harm is initially assessed by the actual, intended or risked loss as may arise from the offence. The court should then take into account the level of harm caused to the victim(s) or others to determine whether it warrants the sentence being moved up to the corresponding point in the next category or further up the range of the initial category. For example in relation to FA 2006, s 1 offences, one of the indicators of high impact is where the victim is particularly vulnerable (due to factors including but not limited to their age, financial circumstances, mental capacity). This can be particularly relevant in cases such as doorstep crime, which are often perpetrated against vulnerable people and where the non-financial harm caused is recognised by the courts frequently imposing longer sentences than under previous regimes. For an illustration of this point see *R v Montague*.

10.64 In *R v Holt & Holt*[1], it was made clear that harm was not to be measured only in terms of money, but also in terms of disappointment and anguish on the behalf of customers.

[1] [2017] EWCA Crim 720.

10.65 In *R v Ali*[1], three defendants, all variously responsible for the management of fraudulently run letting agencies were sentenced to 28 months' imprisonment for offences of fraudulent trading. The principal criminality related to failing to protect tenancy deposits, taking rent from tenants and failing to pass it on to landlords, and failing to return holding deposits. The sentencing judge considered it appropriate to have 'more than some regard' to the Sentencing Guidelines for Fraud, even though they did not strictly apply to fraudulent trading, and the Court of Appeal, in dismissing all three appeals, agreed. The Court of Appeal noted in particular that fraud and fraudulent trading carry the same maximum of 10 years' imprisonment and the factual circumstances of the case made the offending similar to substantive fraud with the factors outlined in the Guidelines being relevant to sentencing for fraudulent trading.

[1] [2019] EWCA Crim 1263.

10.66 The case of *R v Tolliday* has been described as a 'textbook application of the sentencing guidelines for fraud' in the context of a trading standards investigation. The case is also noteworthy for the manner in which the Court of Appeal addressed the issue of consecutive over concurrent sentences for CPUTR offences related to the overarching fraud.

10.67 The prosecution should always consider obtaining a Victim Personal Statement ('VPS') in any fraud allegation. The VPS provides an opportunity for a victim to explain how the crime has affected them, physically, emotionally, psychologically, financially or in any other way. The use of a VPS was considered in *R v Perkins, Bennett and Hall*.[1] It was stated that such statements:

> 'allow victims a more structured opportunity to explain how they have been affected by the crime or crimes of which they were victims. They provide a practical way of ensuring that the sentencing court will consider, in accordance with s 143 CJA 2003, "any harm which the offence caused", reflecting on the evidence of the victim about the specific and personal impact of the offence or offences, or in the cases of homicide, on the family of the deceased. The statements may, albeit incidentally to the purposes of the sentencing court, identify a need for additional or specific support or protection for the victims of crime, to be considered at the end of the sentencing process. At the same time, the process does not create or constitute an opportunity for the victim of

crime to suggest or discuss the type or level of sentence to be imposed. The distinction is important, and is sometimes misunderstood.'

[1]   [2013] EWCA Crim 323.

10.68 There is now a practice direction on impact statements for businesses.[1] Where a victim is a business or enterprise, including charities but excluding public sector bodies, a nominated representative may make an impact statement.

[1]   Criminal Practice Directions (Amendment No 1) [2013] EWCA Crim 2328.

CONSPIRACY (TO DEFRAUD)

10.69 There are now two types of conspiracy, statutory and the common law offence of conspiracy to defraud.

Statutory conspiracy

10.70 The Criminal Law Act 1977 ('CLA 1977'), s 1 states:

1 The offence of conspiracy

(1)   Subject to the following provisions of this part of this Act, if a person agrees with any other person or persons that a course of conduct shall be pursued which, if the agreement is carried out in accordance with their intentions, either –

(a)   will necessarily amount to or involve the commission of any offence or offences by one or more of the parties to the agreement, or

(b)   would do so but for the existence of facts which render the commission of the offence or any of the offences impossible

he is guilty of conspiracy to commit the offence or offences in question.

10.71

Precedent for conspiracy to defraud

Statement of offence

CONSPIRACY TO DEFRAUD, contrary to common law.

Particulars of offence

A B and C D between [date] and [date] conspired together [and with others unknown] to defraud persons by:

(i)   dishonestly and falsely representing that a product would create significant savings on household bills;

(ii)   [. . .]

10.72 The penalties for conspiracy to commit an offence mirror the sentence of the statutory offence which was the object of the conspiracy. The time limit for the institution of legal proceedings also mirrors that of the statutory offence.

Common law conspiracy to defraud

10.73 The offence of conspiracy to defraud was preserved as a common law offence by s 5(2) CLA 1977. Proceedings for the offence are indictable only. A conspiracy is an agreement between two or more persons to do an unlawful act or to do a lawful act by unlawful means. In addition to direct communication links, it may take the form of a 'wheel' or 'chain' where no contact is made (possible) between all members – there is no need to show that co-conspirators know the identity of the other conspirators, only that they knew there were other parties to the agreement. When the parties to the conspiracy enter into the agreement the offence of conspiracy is complete. It is not necessary for any action to be performed in pursuance of it (*R v Mulcahy*)[1].

[1]   (1868) LR 3 HL 306.

10.74 In *R v Mehta*[1] It was stated:

'The authorities establish the following propositions: 1. A conspiracy requires that the parties to it have a common unlawful purpose or design. 2. A common design means a shared design. It is not the same as similar but separate designs. 3. In criminal law (as in civil law) there may be an umbrella agreement pursuant to which the parties enter into further agreements which may include parties who are not parties to the umbrella agreement.'

[1]   [2012] EWCA Crim 2824.

10.75 Following this, in *R v Shillam*[1] the Court said:

'Conspiracy requires a single joint design between the conspirators within the terms of the indictment . . . it is always necessary that for two or more persons to be convicted of a single conspiracy each of them must be proved to have shared a common purpose or design.'

[1]   [2013] EWCA Crim 160.

10.76 A company can conspire with its directors as long as there are at least two in the conspiracy and a company can be prosecuted for conspiracy in the absence of a directing mind. See the case of *A Ltd (2016)*,[1] in which the Divisional Court stated:

' . . . a corporation can only operate through its directing mind or minds and the directors' knowledge is, and must remain, the knowledge of the corporation. The presence or otherwise of a directing mind at the trial is irrelevant. Were it otherwise, as the judge observed, had the directing mind died, become incapacitated, it would not be possible to prosecute the relevant corporation however egregious the conduct.'

[1]   [2016] EWCA Crim 1469.

10.77 The offence has been successfully used by Trading Standards Services in a wide range of prosecutions in relation to, amongst others, doorstep crime, counterfeiting and rogue car dealing. However, prosecuting such offences *can* cause difficulties in terms of the drafting of charges, which will often be said to lack particularity, and the appropriateness of the charge at all. Legal arguments are frequently raised about whether a conspiracy charge is properly included on an indictment. As a general rule, where there is an effective and sufficient charge of a substantive offence, a charge of conspiracy is undesirable[1].

[1]   *Verrier v DPP* [1967] 2 AC 195, HL; *R v Watts, The Times*, 14 April 1995, CA.

10.78 Consideration was given to abolishing the common law offence, following the introduction of the FA 2006. However, the Ministry of Justice in 2012 stated that:

'With regard to conspiracy to defraud, taking account of the comments and experience provided by the key prosecution practitioners, we have concluded that this offence continues to be an effective and essential tool in combating fraud. This is particularly pertinent where there are various levels of criminal activity involved and the court would not otherwise be aware of the full extent of criminality involved. Whilst it would be possible to consider codifying the common law offence in statute, the evidence strongly suggests that the current situation is working perfectly satisfactorily and therefore we have concluded that we should leave matters as they are.'

10.79 Conspiracy charges are perhaps most useful where the criminality of the agreement is more serious than the act itself.

MONEY LAUNDERING

10.80 The majority of trading standards investigations centre on offences perpetrated in order to make financial gain. Consequently, in many, if not most circumstances, those committing substantive offences are also committing offences against the money laundering provisions of the Proceeds of Crime Act 2002 ('POCA 2002').

10.81 POCA 2002, ss 327–329 (which extend to Scotland and Northern Ireland) create the principal money laundering offences, namely:

- concealing, disguising, converting, transferring or removing criminal property (s 327);
- entering into or becoming concerned in a money laundering arrangement (s 328);
- acquiring, using or possessing criminal property (s 329).

10.82 These offences came into force on 24 February 2003. All of the offences are either way and carry a maximum sentence of 14 years. Offences under s 327 and s 328 are listed in Schs 2 (England and Wales), 4 (Scotland) and 5 (Northern Ireland) to the Act and therefore attract the criminal lifestyle assumptions in confiscation proceedings.

10.83 There are no powers for trading standards officers under any of these provisions but, as with the Fraud Act 2006, trading standards departments are increasingly considering the use of money laundering offences. For example, in *R v Coyle*,[1] the defendant allowed his bank accounts to be used to launder money that had been defrauded by others from three elderly and vulnerable victims. He pleaded guilty to three counts of money laundering, one count of transferring a criminal property and five counts of converting criminal property. His sentence, of 42 months' imprisonment imposed on each count, was reduced, on appeal, to 2½ years on each count.

---

[1] [2011] EWCA Crim 36.

10.84 Careful consideration must always be given before charging money laundering offences. Whilst acquisitive crime will almost always be accompanied by a money laundering offence, common sense should be applied. In *R v GH*[1] Lord Toulson said that the 'courts should be willing to use their powers to discourage inappropriate use of the provisions of POCA 2002 to prosecute conduct which is sufficiently covered by substantive offences . . . '.

[1]   [2015] UKSC 24.

10.85 The appropriateness of using money laundering charges was considered further in the case of *R v Ogden*[1]. The Court of Appeal accepted that every person who buys illicit drugs, even for their own personal use, may in fact be guilty of conspiring to convert criminal property. However, the court commented that the spectre of the authorities charging in that way was unreal because 'good sense' would prevail.

[1]   [2016] EWCA Crim 6.

Criminal property

10.86 Under POCA 2002, money laundering does not just relate to money, but instead to a concept of 'criminal property', that is that the property constitutes or represents a person's benefit from criminal conduct. The concept of criminal property is common to all of the money laundering offences and is central to each of them. It is defined, along with criminal conduct, in s 340.

Section 340 Interpretation

(1)   This section applies for the purposes of this Part.

(2)   Criminal conduct is conduct which—
   (a)   constitutes an offence in any part of the United Kingdom, or
   (b)   would constitute an offence in any part of the United Kingdom if it occurred there.

(3)   Property is criminal property if—
   (a)   it constitutes a person's benefit from criminal conduct or it represents such a benefit (in whole or part and whether directly or indirectly), and
   (b)   the alleged offender knows or suspects that it constitutes or represents such a benefit.

(4)   It is immaterial—
   (a)   who carried out the conduct;
   (b)   who benefited from it;
   (c)   whether the conduct occurred before or after the passing of this Act.

(5)   A person benefits from conduct if he obtains property as a result of or in connection with the conduct.

(6)   If a person obtains a pecuniary advantage as a result of or in connection with conduct, he is to be taken to obtain as a result of or in connection with the conduct a sum of money equal to the value of the pecuniary advantage.

(7)   References to property or a pecuniary advantage obtained in connection with conduct include references to property or a pecuniary advantage obtained in both that connection and some other.

(8)   If a person benefits from conduct his benefit is the property obtained as a result of or in connection with the conduct.

(9)   Property is all property wherever situated and includes—
   (a)   money;
   (b)   all forms of property, real or personal, heritable or moveable;

> (c)   things in action and other intangible or incorporeal property.
>
> (10)   The following rules apply in relation to property—
>
>   (a)   property is obtained by a person if he obtains an interest in it;
>
>   (b)   references to an interest, in relation to land in England and Wales or Northern Ireland, are to any legal estate or equitable interest or power;
>
>   (c)   references to an interest, in relation to land in Scotland, are to any estate, interest, servitude or other heritable right in or over land, including a heritable security;
>
>   (d)   references to an interest, in relation to property other than land, include references to a right (including a right to possession).

10.87 An essential point to note is that, in seeking to prove that property is criminal property, the prosecution do not have to prove the exact offence from which it is derived. This is a significant change from previous legislation. In *R v Anwoir*[1] the court stated 'there are two ways in which the Crown can prove the property derives from crime, (a) by showing that it derives from conduct of a specific kind or kinds and that conduct of that kind or those kinds is unlawful, or (b) by evidence of the circumstances in which the property is handled which are such as to give rise to the irresistible inference that it can only be derived from crime'. This approach has been reinforced more recently in *R v Smith*.[2]

[1]   [2008] 2 Cr App R 36.
[2]   [2015] EWCA Crim 333.

10.88 This point is illustrated by *R v F*[1] where two passengers at an airport had four suitcases in their possession. When asked if there was any money in the suitcases one of them said no and one said yes. The suitcases were actually found to contain in excess of one million pounds. At interview their answer was that they had been asked by a friend to carry the money. One of the defendants stated that he had done it two or three times before and had been paid for each trip. He did not know where the money was coming from but knew that it was wrong and only did it because he was on benefits and had financial problems. The Court of Appeal upheld their convictions, stating that there was no procedural unfairness just because the prosecution were unable to point to any particular criminality.

[1]   [2009] Crim LR 45.

10.89 Failure to declare legitimately earned income, does not automatically convert legitimate profits into criminal property – see *R v Gabriel*[1], where the defendant was charged with possession of criminal property (s 329) in respect of money which he had obtained from legitimate trading but which he had not declared for revenue or benefits purposes, although, of course, other offences may have been committed on the facts.

[1]   [2007] 1 WLR 2272.

10.90 Each case must, however, be considered on its own facts. In *R v K(I)*[1] it was found that the failure to declare profits from dealing in legitimate goods might give rise to an offence if a *prima facie* case of cheating the Revenue was made out. The trader would have obtained a pecuniary advantage as a result of criminal conduct and by reason of s 340(6) would be taken to have obtained a sum of money equal to the amount of tax of which the Revenue had been deprived.

¹   [2007] 2 Cr App R 10.

10.91   The prosecution must prove that the defendant 'knows or suspects' that the property constitutes or represents benefit from criminal conduct. The question of what is meant by the word 'suspect' was considered in *R v Da Silva*¹ where it was stated:

> 'the defendant must think that there is a possibility, which is more than fanciful, that the relevant facts exist. A vague feeling of unease would not suffice. But the statute does not require the suspicion to be "clear" or "firmly grounded and targeted on specific facts", or based upon "reasonable grounds".'

¹   [2006] EWCA Crim 1654.

Concealing etc

10.92   POCA 2002, s 327 makes the following provision:

Section 327 Concealing etc

  (1)   A person commits an offence if he—
      (a)   conceals criminal property;
      (b)   disguises criminal property;
      (c)   converts criminal property;
      (d)   transfers criminal property;
      (e)   removes criminal property from England and Wales or from Scotland or from Northern Ireland.
  (2)   But a person does not commit such an offence if—
      (a)   he makes an authorised disclosure under section 338 and (if the disclosure is made before he does the act mentioned in subsection (1)) he has the appropriate consent;
      (b)   he intended to make such a disclosure but had a reasonable excuse for not doing so;
      (c)   the act he does is done in carrying out a function he has relating to the enforcement of any provision of this Act or of any other enactment relating to criminal conduct or benefit from criminal conduct.
  (3)   Concealing or disguising criminal property includes concealing or disguising its nature, source, location, disposition, movement or ownership or any rights with respect to it.

10.93

Precedent for money laundering (converting criminal property)

Statement of offence

CONVERTING CRIMINAL PROPERTY, contrary to section 327(1) of the Proceeds of Crime Act 2002.

Particulars of offence

A B on [date] converted property, namely [. . .] which he knew or suspected constituted or represented others' benefit, directly or indirectly, in whole or in part, from criminal conduct.

10.94 For an offence under s 327 to be committed, the property that is concealed, disguised, converted or transferred, must be criminal property at the time it is concealed, disguised, converted or transferred. If the property is not criminal property at the time the laundering act takes place, the offence is not committed (*R v Loizou*[1]).

[1] [2005] 2 Cr App R 37.

10.95 In *R v Fazal* it was said that the meaning of 'converting' under POCA is not necessarily the same as the civil tort of conversion, but it cannot be far removed from its nature. Conversion in the civil law is a broad tort which is essentially concerned with the taking, receiving, retaining or parting with someone else's property[1].

[1] *R v Fazal* [2010] 1 Cr App R 6.

Arrangements

10.96 POCA 2002, s 328 provides:

Section 328 Arrangements

(1) A person commits an offence if he enters into or becomes concerned in an arrangement which he knows or suspects facilitates (by whatever means) the acquisition, retention, use or control of criminal property by or on behalf of another person.

(2) But a person does not commit such an offence if—
   (a) he makes an authorised disclosure under section 338 and (if the disclosure is made before he does the act mentioned in subsection (1)) he has the appropriate consent;
   (b) he intended to make such a disclosure but had a reasonable excuse for not doing so;
   (c) the act he does is done in carrying out a function he has relating to the enforcement of any provision of this Act or of any other enactment relating to criminal conduct or benefit from criminal conduct.

10.97

Precedent for money laundering arrangement

Statement of offence

BECOMING CONCERNED IN A MONEY LAUNDERING ARRANGEMENT, contrary to section 328 of the Proceeds of Crime Act 2002.

Particulars of offence

A B between [date] and [date] entered into or became concerned in an arrangement which he knew or suspected facilitated the acquisition, retention, use or control of criminal property, namely [. . .].

10.98 It is necessary for the arrangement to relate to property which has already become criminal property[1]:

'As section 340(3)(b) makes clear, the mental element of the offence includes knowledge or suspicion on the part of the defendant that the property in question is criminal property, but that cannot be the case until it has been acquired by means of criminal conduct. In order for an offence under section 328 to be committed, therefore, the arrangement into which the defendant enters, or in which he becomes involved, must be one which facilitates the acquisition, retention, use or control by another of property which has already become criminal property at the time when it becomes operative. That requirement is not satisfied if the only arrangement into which he enters is one by which the property in question first acquires its criminal character.'

[1] *Kensington International v Republic of Congo* [2008] 1 WLR 1144.

10.99 In *R v Geary*[1] it was stated, when referring to ss 327, 328 and 329:

'In each case the natural meaning of the statutory language is that in each case the property in question must have become criminal property as a result of some conduct which occurred prior to the act which is alleged to constitute the offence, whether that be concealing, disguising, converting, transferring or removing it contrary to section 327 or entering into or becoming concerned in an arrangement which facilitates its acquisition, retention, use or control by another contrary to section 328.'

[1] [2011] 1 Cr App R 8.

10.100 And in *R v Amir and Akhtar*[1] the question considered was whether property was 'criminal property for the purposes of s 328 only after some other offence has been committed, or is it to be characterised as criminal property because of the criminal objective which the arrangements were designed to achieve?' In allowing the appeal against conviction of the appellant who had knowingly submitted false mortgage applications, the court stated:

'They (ss 327, 328, 329) are all concerned in one way or another with dealing with criminal property. By section 340(3) that is property which in fact constitutes a person's benefit from criminal conduct or represents such a benefit and the offender knows or suspects that that is so. The definition does not embrace property which the accused intends to acquire by criminal conduct and the language of the statute is not capable of construing the definition in that way. Property is not criminal property because the wrongdoing intends that it should be so.'

[1] [2011] 1 Cr App R 37.

10.101 This requirement for the property to constitute criminal property prior to the arrangement coming into operation for the commission of an offence under the POCA 2002, s 328 has been confirmed and clarified in *R v GH*.

Acquisition, use and possession

10.102 POCA 2002, s 329 provides:

Section 329 Acquisition, use and possession

(1) A person commits an offence if he—
    (a) acquires criminal property;
    (b) uses criminal property;
    (c) has possession of criminal property.
(2) But a person does not commit such an offence if—
    (a) he makes an authorised disclosure under section 338 and (if the disclosure is made before he does the act mentioned in subsection (1)) he has the appropriate consent;
    (b) he intended to make such a disclosure but had a reasonable excuse for not doing so;
    (c) he acquired or used or had possession of the property for adequate consideration;
    (d) the act he does is done in carrying out a function he has relating to the enforcement of any provision of this Act or of any other enactment relating to criminal conduct or benefit from criminal conduct.
(3) For the purposes of this section—
    (a) a person acquires property for inadequate consideration if the value of the consideration is significantly less than the value of the property;
    (b) a person uses or has possession of property for inadequate consideration if the value of the consideration is significantly less than the value of the use or possession;
    (c) the provision by a person of goods or services which he knows or suspects may help another to carry out criminal conduct is not consideration.

10.103

Precedent for acquiring criminal property

Statement of offence

ACQUIRING CRIMINAL PROPERTY, contrary to section 329(1) of the Proceeds of Crime Act 2002.

Particulars of offence

A B on [date] acquired criminal property, namely [cash], which he knew or suspected constituted or represented others' benefit, directly or indirectly, in whole or in part, from criminal conduct.

10.104 This section differs from the preceding ones in that it is not a Sch 2 'lifestyle' offence and there is an additional defence, namely if the person acquires, uses or has possession of criminal property for 'adequate consideration'. 'Inadequate' consideration is defined in s 329(3). In *Hogan v DPP*[1] the defendant had scaffolding in his possession which was worth over £6,000 and for which he had paid £1,100 in cash. He did not have a receipt, did not get the surname or contact details of the seller and did not record the purchase in his business records. The court stated that in most cases there will be an evidential burden on the defence in relation to adequate consideration and that once raised it should be regarded as an element of the offence to be proved by the prosecution to the normal criminal standard. However, it is also clear that even if it can be shown that the property is criminal property, and, the suspect knew that goods were stolen, if he has given adequate consideration then he does not commit an offence under this section.

¹ [2007] 1 WLR 2944.

Sentencing for money laundering

10.105 The Sentencing Council has issued a definitive guideline for the sentencing of offences contrary to POCA 2002, ss 327–329. The levels of culpability and harm should be assessed having regard to the following major factors:

- the value;
- the role played by the offender;
- abuse of power or trust;
- significant planning or sophisticated offence;
- period of offending;
- proximity to the underlying criminal act(s);
- the level of harm associated with the underlying offence.

Confiscation

10.106 Fraud and money laundering offences will often generate criminal confiscation proceedings under Part 2 of POCA 2002. Criminal confiscation, restraint orders and the related investigatory powers for accredited financial investigators are now covered in Chapter **4**, Criminal Enforcement.

Chapter 11

UNFAIR TRADING

Contents

11.1 In this chapter we cover a wide variety of unfair trading legislation that falls outside the other main chapter areas. The chapter could perhaps best be described as a miscellany of other consumer protection laws and, for this reason, the topics are covered in alphabetical order.

BUSINESS NAMES

Introduction

11.2 The disclosure of business identities is a key part of consumer protection. If consumers cannot identify the correct legal identity of a trader, they may be unable to enforce their consumer rights. The Business Names Act 1985 has been repealed and replaced by the Companies Act 2006 and the Regulations made under it. Following a BIS consultation and response during the course of 2013, the Company, Limited Liability Partnership and Business Names (Sensitive Words and Expressions) Regulations 2014[1] ('SWER 2014') and Company, Limited Liability Partnership and Business (Names and Trading Disclosures) Regulations 2015[2] ('NTDR 2015') were introduced from 31 January 2015. These regulations revoke and consolidate various other secondary legislation, most notably the Companies (Trading Disclosure) Regulations 2008[3].

[1] SI 2014/3140.
[2] SI 2015/17.
[3] SI 2008/495.

Companies

11.3 The Companies Act 2006 ('CA 2006') allowed for the repeal of the Business Names Act 1985 from 1 October 2008. In particular, the NTDR 2015 creates criminal liability for failure to properly disclose a company's identity. Regulations 20–29 set out disclosure obligations for a variety of circumstances. It broadly replicates the former Companies (Trading Disclosure) Regulations 2008[1] as follows:

20 Legibility of displays and disclosures

Any display or disclosure of information required by this Part must be in characters that can be read with the naked eye.

21 Requirement to display registered name at registered office and inspection place

(1)   A company shall display its registered name at—
       (a)   its registered office; and
       (b)   any inspection place.
(2)   But paragraph (1) does not apply to any company which has at all times since its incorporation been dormant.
(3)   Paragraph (1) shall also not apply to the registered office or an inspection place of a company where—
       (a)   in respect of that company, a liquidator, administrator or administrative receiver has been appointed; and
       (b)   the registered office or inspection place is also a place of business of that liquidator, administrator or administrative receiver.

22 Requirement to display registered name at other business locations

(1)   This regulation applies to a location other than a company's registered office or any inspection place.
(2)   A company shall display its registered name at any such location at which it carries on business.
(3)   But paragraph (2) shall not apply to a location which is primarily used for living accommodation.
(4)   Paragraph (2) shall also not apply to any location at which business is carried on by a company where—
       (a)   in respect of that company, a liquidator, administrator or administrative receiver has been appointed; and
       (b)   the location is also a place of business of that liquidator, administrator or administrative receiver.
(5)   Paragraph (2) shall also not apply to any location at which business is carried on by a company of which every director who is an individual is a relevant director.
(6)   In this regulation—
       (a)   "administrative receiver" has the meaning given—
          (i)   in England and Wales or Scotland, by section 251 of the Insolvency Act 1986, and
          (ii)   in Northern Ireland, by Article 5 of the Insolvency (Northern Ireland) Order 1989
       (b)   "credit reference agency" has the meaning given in section 243(7) of the Act;
       (c)   "protected information" has the meaning given in section 240 of the Act; and
       (d)   "relevant director" means an individual in respect of whom the registrar is required by regulations made pursuant to section 243(4) of the Act to refrain from disclosing protected information to a credit reference agency.

23 Manner of display of registered name

(1)   This regulation applies where a company is required to display its registered name at any office, place or location.

(2)   Where that office, place or location is shared by no more than five companies, the registered name—

       (a)   shall be so positioned that it may be easily seen by any visitor to that office, place or location; and

       (b)   shall be displayed continuously.

(3)   Where any such office, place or location is shared by six or more companies, each such company must ensure that either—

       (a)   its registered name is displayed for at least fifteen continuous seconds at least once every three minutes; or

       (b)   its registered name is available for inspection on a register by any visitor to that office, place or location.

24 Registered name to appear on communications

(1)   Every company shall disclose its registered name on—

       (a)   its business letters, notices and other official publications;

       (b)   its bills of exchange, promissory notes, endorsements and order forms;

       (c)   cheques purporting to be signed by or on behalf of the company;

       (d)   orders for money, goods or services purporting to be signed by or on behalf of the company;

       (e)   its bills of parcels, invoices and other demands for payment, receipts and letters of credit;

       (f)   its applications for licences to carry on a trade or activity; and

       (g)   all other forms of its business correspondence and documentation.

(2)   Every company shall disclose its registered name on its websites.

25 Further particulars to appear in business letters, order forms and websites

(1)   Every company shall disclose the particulars set out in paragraph (2) on—

       (a)   its business letters;

       (b)   its order forms; and

       (c)   its websites.

(2)   The particulars are—

       (a)   the part of the United Kingdom in which the company is registered;

       (b)   the company's registered number;

       (c)   the address of the company's registered office;

       (d)   in the case of a limited company exempt from the obligation to use the word "limited" as part of its registered name under section 60 of the Act, the fact that it is a limited company;

       (e)   in the case of a community interest company which is not a public company, the fact that it is a limited company; and

       (f)   in the case of an investment company within the meaning of section 833 of the Act, the fact that it is such a company.

(3)   If, in the case of a company having a share capital, there is a disclosure as to the amount of share capital on—

       (a)   its business letters;

       (b)   its order forms; or

       (c)   its websites,

that disclosure must be as to paid up share capital.

26 Disclosure of names of directors

(1)   Where a company's business letter includes the name of any director of that company, other than in the text or as a signatory, the letter must disclose the name of every director of that company.

(2)   In paragraph (1), "name" has the following meanings—

    (a)   in the case of a director who is an individual, "name" has the meaning given in section 163(2) of the Act; and

    (b)   in the case of a director who is a body corporate or a firm that is a legal person under the law by which it is governed, "name" means corporate name or firm name.

27 Disclosures relating to registered office and inspection place

(1)   A company shall disclose—

    (a)   the address of its registered office;

    (b)   any inspection place; and

    (c)   the type of company records which are kept at that office or place, to any person it deals with in the course of business who makes a written request to the company for that information.

(2)   The company shall send a written response to that person within five working days of the receipt of that request.

[1]   SI 2008/495.

11.4 Under reg 28, a failure to comply with any of the requirements under regs 20–27 results in the commission of a criminal offence by the company and all officers in default. The offences are summary only and punishable by a fine not exceeding level 3 on the standard scale, and for continuing defaults, a daily sum not exceeding one-tenth of level 3 on the standard scale.

11.5

Precedent for failing to disclose business name

Information

X Ltd, on [date], without reasonable excuse failed to comply with a requirement in Regulation 24 of the Company, Limited Liability Partnership and Business (Names and Trading Disclosures) Regulations 2015 requiring the registered name of the company to appear in communications namely by failing to disclose its registered name on its website, contrary to Regulation 28 of the Business (Names and Trading Disclosures) Regulations 2015.

Directors' addresses

11.6 The Companies (Disclosure of Address) Regulations 2009 came into force on 1 October 2009[1]. It requires all companies to provide a service address for every director in their register of directors.

[1]   SI 2009/214. Subsequently amended by the Companies (Disclosure of Address) (Amendment) Regulations 2010, SI 2010/2156.

Protected names

11.7 Sensitive words and expressions such as 'Queen', 'Council' or 'University' are protected against use in the commercial sector by the Sensitive Words and Expressions Regulations 2014[1] ('SWER 2014'). The relevant lists of words and expressions are set out in Pts 1 and 2 of Sch 1 to SWER 2014. Following a Government consultation in 2013, words and expressions that were previously restricted have been removed from the lists in Sch 1, such as 'board', 'national' and 'watchdog'.

[1] Company, Limited Liability Partnership and Business Names (Sensitive Words and Expressions) Regulations 2014, SI 2014/3140.

Public authorities

11.8 The CA 2006, s 54 requires that a company which wishes to use a name 'suggesting a connection' with a HM government, a local authority or a specified public authority must apply to the Secretary of State for approval. Schedule 4 to the NTDR 2015 sets out the public authorities which are specified for the purposes of s 54.

Misleading names

11.9 The Secretary of State has power[1] to direct a company to change a misleading name, regardless of how long the company has had the name. Before such a direction can be given (in writing) he must first be of the opinion that:

(a) the name gives a misleading indication of the nature of the company's activities; and also
(b) that the public are likely to suffer harm as a result.

[1] Companies Act 2006, ss 1197 and 1198.

11.10 If a company fails to comply with such direction an offence is committed by both the company and every officer of the company who is in default punishable on summary conviction by a fine not exceeding level 3 on the standard scale and, for continued contravention, a daily default fine not exceeding one-tenth of level 3 on the standard scale. However, there is a right of appeal for the company by which the decision can be set aside. A CA 2006, s 76 direction can also be made to an LLP. In addition, regulated consumer credit firms must not use business names which contravene the obligation to communicate with customers in a manner which is 'clear, fair and not misleading' under CONC 3.3.3R, as set out in the Financial Conduct Authority's Handbook.

Overseas companies

11.11 The Overseas Companies Regulations 2009[1] require overseas companies that trade in the UK to register at Companies House. Every company incorporated in a country outside the UK that operates its business in the UK through at least one establishment (that is to say either a branch or a place of business that is not a branch) and is not a UK-incorporated subsidiary company, must register its particulars with the Registrar of Companies. Regulation 6 sets out the particulars of the company which are to be included in the return to Companies House. After the 31 December 2020 these particulars are amended[2]. In addition, regs 12–15 of the NTDR 2015 set out certain provisions relating to the names of overseas companies registered in the UK.

¹ SI 2009/1801.
² Companies, Limited Liability Partnerships and Partnerships (Amendment etc.) (EU Exit) Regulations 2019, SI 2019/348.

Limited liability partnerships

11.12 A new corporate vehicle, the limited liability partnership ('LLP'), was created by the Limited Liability Partnerships Act 2000. LLPs have flexibility in relation to their internal arrangements in much the same way as conventional partnerships, but they are bodies corporate with limited liability, and are accordingly subject to the provisions of CA 2006 Act by regs 14 and 15 of the Limited Liability Partnerships (Application of Companies Act 2006) Regulations 2009[1]. Regulation 11 of the NTDR 2015 also extends the restriction on names suggesting a connection with a public authority to LLPs.

¹ SI 2009/1804.

Sole traders, partnerships etc

11.13 The disclosure requirements for non-corporate businesses are set out in Pt 41 CA 2006, ss 1192–1208 and came into force on 1 October 2009[1]. The key provisions relating to business names are set out below:

1200 Application of this Chapter

(1) This Chapter applies to an individual or partnership carrying on business in the United Kingdom under a business name. References in this Chapter to "a person to whom this Chapter applies" are to such an individual or partnership.

(2) For the purposes of this Chapter a "business name" means a name other than—
  (a) in the case of an individual, his surname without any addition other than a permitted addition;
  (b) in the case of a partnership—
    (i) the surnames of all partners who are individuals, and
    (ii) the corporate names of all partners who are bodies corporate,
  without any addition other than a permitted addition.

(3) The following are the permitted additions—
  (a) in the case of an individual, his forename or initial;
  (b) in the case of a partnership—
    (i) the forenames of individual partners or the initials of those forenames, or
    (ii) where two or more individual partners have the same surname, the addition of "s" at the end of that surname;
  (c) in either case, an addition merely indicating that the business is carried on in succession to a former owner of the business.

1201 Information required to be disclosed

(1)   The "information required by this Chapter" is—
      (a)   in the case of an individual, the individual's name;
      (b)   in the case of a partnership, the name of each member of the partnership;
    and, in relation to each person so named, an address at which service of any document relating in any way to the business will be effective.

(2)   If the individual or partnership has a place of business in the United Kingdom, the address must be in the United Kingdom.

(3)   If the individual or partnership does not have a place of business in the United Kingdom, the address must be an address at which service of documents can be effected by physical delivery and the delivery of documents is capable of being recorded by the obtaining of an acknowledgement of delivery.

1202 Disclosure required: business documents etc

(1)   A person to whom this Chapter applies must state the information required by this Chapter, in legible characters, on all—
      (a)   business letters,
      (b)   written orders for goods or services to be supplied to the business,
      (c)   invoices and receipts issued in the course of the business, and
      (d)   written demands for payment of debts arising in the course of the business.
    This subsection has effect subject to section 1203 (exemption for large partnerships if certain conditions met).

(2)   A person to whom this Chapter applies must secure that the information required by this Chapter is immediately given, by written notice, to any person with whom anything is done or discussed in the course of the business and who asks for that information . . .

[*Section 1203 concerns the exemption for large partnerships if certain conditions are met.*]

1204 Disclosure required: business premises

(1)   A person to whom this Chapter applies must, in any premises—
      (a)   where the business is carried on, and
      (b)   to which customers of the business or suppliers of goods or services to the business have access,
    display in a prominent position, so that it may easily be read by such customers or suppliers, a notice containing the information required by this Chapter . . .

1205 Criminal consequences of failure to make required disclosure

(1)   A person who without reasonable excuse fails to comply with the requirements of—
    •   section 1202 (disclosure required: business documents etc), or
    •   section 1204 (disclosure required: business premises),
    commits an offence.

(2)   Where an offence under this section is committed by a body corporate, an offence is also committed by every officer of the body who is in default.

(3)   A person guilty of an offence under this section is liable on summary conviction to a fine not exceeding level 3 on the standard scale and, for continued contravention, a daily default fine not exceeding one-tenth of level 3 on the standard scale.

(4)   References in this section to the requirements of section 1202 or 1204 include the requirements of regulations under that section.

¹   However, note that the substituted CA 2006, s 1201 came into force on 28 December 2009 under the Companies Act 2006 (Substitution of Section 1201) Regulations 2009, SI 2009/3182.

11.14

Precedent for failing to state name and address of business partners

Information

X (partnership) on [date] being a partnership without reasonable excuse failed to comply with the requirements of section 1202 of the Companies Act 2006 by failing to state on all business letters the name of each member of the partnership, and, in relation to each such person, the address at which service of any document relating in any way to the business will be effective, contrary to section 1205 of the Companies Act 2006.

CAT AND DOG FUR

11.15 The Cat and Dog Fur (Control of Import, Export and Placing on the Market) Regulations 2008[1] introduce criminal sanction for breach of an EC Regulation banning the commercial import, export and sale of cat and dog fur. There will be amendments made after the 31 December 2020 making it clear that import and export refers to the United Kingdom and references to the 'Community' are deleted[2]. Regulation 2 makes contravention of Art 3 of the EC Regulation a criminal offence, punishable on indictment with a maximum penalty of £75,000 and on summary conviction with an unlimited fine[3]. At the time of publication these amendments were not yet in force. A duty[4] is imposed on local weights and measures authorities (in Great Britain) and district councils (in Northern Ireland) to enforce reg 2 but reg 3(2) excludes from this duty the enforcement of the Regulations within areas where the goods are under the supervision of Her Majesty's Revenue and Customs, in which areas enforcement will be the responsibility of Her Majesty's Revenue and Customs.

¹   SI 2008/2795.
²   Cat and Dog Fur (Control of Import, Export and Placing on the Market) (Amendment) (EU Exit) Regulations 2019, SI 2019/830.
³   Legal Aid, Sentencing and Punishment of Offenders Act 2012, s 85 for offences committed after 12 March 2015.
⁴   SI 2008/2795, reg 3(1).

11.16 Regulation 3(3) provides (and remains unchanged after the 31 December 2020):

3 Powers of investigation and enforcement

. . .

(3) For the purposes of enforcing these Regulations, an officer may at any reasonable hour and on production, if required, of evidence that he is an officer—
  (a)   inspect any goods;
  (b)   enter any premises (including any place or vehicle) other than premises occupied only as a dwelling;
  (c)   purchase any goods for the purposes of inspection;

(d)   examine any procedure connected with the production of any goods;
(e)   require any person carrying on a business, or employed in connection with a business, to produce any records relating to the business;
(f)   seize and detain any goods or records where there are reasonable grounds for believing that they may be—
    (i)   required as evidence in proceedings for an offence under regulation 2; or
    (ii)   (in relation to goods only) liable to be forfeited;
(g)   take copies of, or of any entry in, any records produced by virtue of sub-paragraph (e) or seized by way of sub-paragraph (f);
(h)   require any person having authority to do so to open any container; and
(i)   where a requirement made under sub-paragraph (h) has not been complied with, open or break open any container.

11.17 Powers are granted to local weights and measures authorities (in England and Wales) and district councils (in Northern Ireland) to apply to court for forfeiture orders in respect of goods which contravene the reg 2 prohibition (reg 4). In Scotland, the Proceeds of Crime (Scotland) Act 1995 will apply following a conviction for a breach of the Regulations. Regulation 5 makes it a criminal offence for a person intentionally to obstruct or fail to co-operate with an officer exercising powers granted under reg 4. The penalty on summary conviction is a fine not exceeding level 3 on the standard scale.

CRYSTAL GLASS

11.18 The Crystal Glass (Descriptions) Regulations 1973[1] were made under the European Communities Act 1972. It is an offence under reg 3 for a person in the course of a trade or business, to supply or offer to supply in the United Kingdom, glass to which there is applied 'a description' (see reg 4), 'symbol' (see reg 5), 'trade mark, name or other inscription' (see reg 6) in contravention of the Regulations. From 31 December 2020, nothing in these regulations shall apply in relation to glass which is intended for export from the United Kingdom[2] (see reg 7).

[1]   SI 1973/1952.
[2]   Consumer Protection (Amendment etc.) (EU Exit) Regulations 2018, SI 2018/1326.

11.19 By virtue of reg 8, certain provisions of the Trade Description Act 1968 are applied (with necessary modifications) to the Regulations – the Trade Description Act 1968, ss 4, 5, 18, 19, 20, 23, 24, 25 and 26. Notwithstanding their repeal by the CPUTR 2008, the Trade Descriptions Act 1968, ss 5, 19(4)(b) and (c) and s 24(3) will continue to apply for the purposes of reg 8. The enforcement powers in the CRA 2015, Sch 5 apply to the Regulations; see CHAPTER 4, Criminal Enforcement.

EDUCATIONAL DEGREES AND AWARDS

11.20 The vast majority of the provisions of the Education Reform Act 1988 ('ERA 1988') have now been repealed. However, a limited number of sections under Pt II remain in force for the purpose of regulating, through criminal sanctions, the provision of education within the UK. The following deals only with the key remaining aspects of the ERA 1988.

11.21 Universities and some colleges in the UK are given the power to grant degrees under an Act of Parliament or by Royal Charter. There are over 150 institutions in the UK that are permitted to award a wide variety of degrees by the UK government and other institutions. These are known as 'recognised bodies'[1]. The degrees that recognised bodies grant are referred to as 'recognised UK degrees'[2]. It is only recognised bodies can award genuine UK degree. There are over 850 educational establishments – colleges and other organisations providing higher education, in full or part – within the UK, which do not grant degrees but run courses in preparation for a degree to be granted by a Recognised Body. These are known as 'Listed Bodies' and are defined in ERA 1988, s 216. Both ERA 1988, ss 214 and 216 have been amended by Higher Education and Research Act 2017 which came into force on the 1 April 2018.

1   Defined in ERA 1988, s 214(2).
2   In addition, the Secretary of State may, by Order, designate recognised awards – for example the Education (Recognised Awards) (Richmond The American International University in London) Order 2017, SI 2017/1185.

11.22 In Northern Ireland, art 3(1) of the Education (Unrecognised Degrees) (Northern Ireland) Order 1988,[1] makes it an offence to grant, offer to grant or issue any invitation relating to certain degrees and awards. This does not apply to anything done in relation to a recognised award. A 'recognised award' means:

(a)   any award granted or to be granted by a university, college or other body which is authorised by Royal Charter or Act of Parliament to grant degrees; or

(b)   any award granted or to be granted by anybody for the time being permitted by anybody falling within sub-paragraph (a) to act on its behalf in the granting of degrees.

1   SI 1988/1989.

11.23 The Education (Listed Bodies) (Northern Ireland) Order 2004, was repealed on the 11 January 2018. The Education (Listed Bodies) Order (Northern Ireland) 2018[1] contains, within the Explanatory Note, the preservation of the list of the names of each body which is not a recognised body within art 3(2)(a) or (b) of the 1988 Order but which either:

(a)   provides any course which is in preparation for a degree to be granted by a recognised body and is approved by or on behalf of the recognised body; or

(b)   is a constituent college, school, or hall or other institution of a university which is a recognised body.

1   SI 2018/9.

Offence and related provisions

11.24 ERA 1988, s 214(1) provides:

214 Unrecognised degrees

(1)   Any person who, in the course of business, grants, offers to grant or issues any invitation relating to any award—
  (a)   which may reasonably be taken to be an award granted or to be granted by a United Kingdom institution; and
  (b)   which either—
    (i)   is described as a degree; or
    (ii)   purports to confer on its holder the right to the title of bachelor, master or doctor and may reasonably be taken to be a degree;
  shall be guilty of an offence and liable on summary conviction to a fine not exceeding level 5 on the standard scale.

11.25   ERA 1988, s 214(1) above does not apply as respects anything done in relation to any 'recognised award' – which means a recognised UK degree (or such other award which has been designated by Order). It is not an offence for overseas organisations to offer their own awards in the UK, as long as they make it clear that they are not qualifications from a UK institution and that accreditation is from overseas and ERA 1988, s 214(4)–(6) provide specific, but limited, statutory defences.

11.26   ERA 1988, s 214(7) permits the prosecution and conviction of any 'director, manager, secretary or other similar officer' of a company or 'any person who was purporting to act in such a capacity' where an offence under ERA 1988, s 214 has been committed by the company 'with the consent and connivance' of that person or as a result of that person's neglect. Directors' liability is now covered in CHAPTER 4, Criminal Enforcement. Importantly, ERA 1988, s 214(8) provides that proceedings for an offence under ERA 1988, s 214 cannot be instituted in England and Wales, except by or on behalf of a local weights and measures authority or the chief officer of police for a police area.

Enforcement

11.27   Enforcement powers are now covered by the CRA 2015, Sch 5; see CHAPTER 4, Criminal Enforcement. In Northern Ireland, it is the duty of the Department of Economic Development to enforce the provisions of art 3 of the Education (Unrecognised Degrees) (Northern Ireland) Order 1988[1] and a duly authorised officer of the Department has similar powers to those described above.

[1]   SI 1988/1989.

ESTATE AGENTS

Introduction

11.28   The Estate Agents Act 1979 ('EAA 1979') applies throughout the UK and regulates the work of those persons engaging in 'estate agency work' – referred in this chapter as 'estate agents'.

11.29   The EAA 1979[1]:

'was the culmination of many attempts begun as long ago as 1888 to regulate the activities of estate agents by legislation. During the 90 years before the Act was passed, public concern had been expressed that neither Parliament nor the profession itself had made provision for registration, for minimum standards of competence and for safeguards to protect clients against defaulting practitioners. In short, any person could adopt the title of, and act as, an "estate agent" though he had no specific qualification and the public had no assurance that he was skilled, competent or even honest. After many unsuccessful attempts by private members to introduce legislation to regulate estate agency practices, a Bill introduced by a private member Mr Bryan Davies in 1978 was adopted by the government to become the Estate Agents Act 1979. The Act did not introduce any system of registration but provided means by which an estate agent could be judged unfit to practice.'

[1] *Antonelli v Secretary of State for Trade and Industry* [1997] EWCA 2282, [1998] 1 All ER 1997, per Beldam LJ.

11.30 The main features of EAA 1979 are that it:

- covers commercial, industrial and agricultural property as well as residential homes;
- applies to those engaged in 'estate agency work' (not necessarily 'estate agents' in the normal sense);
- creates a statutory framework whereby a failure to comply with its requirements may result in criminal proceedings, civil action or action by the lead enforcement authority (to warn or prohibit unfit persons from engaging in estate agency work);
- places obligations on estate agents to maintain proper financial arrangements and provide information;
- prohibits bankrupts from carrying on an estate agency business (but they may work for one).

11.31 EAA 1979 imposes a 'negative licensing' regime in that there is no requirement to demonstrate any particular qualification or competence in order to set up as an 'estate agent' (in fact, the provision of the Act dealing with standards of competence (EAA 1979, s 22) has not been brought into force – nor have others relating to insurance cover for clients' money, regulation of pre-contract deposits outside Scotland). Article 5 of the Public Bodies (Abolition of the National Consumer Council and Transfer of the Office of Fair Trading's Functions in relation to Estate Agents etc) Order 2014[1] transferred the functions of the OFT, in relation to the regulation of estate agents in the EAA 1979, to Powys County Council, the 'lead enforcement authority'.

[1] SI 2014/631.

11.32 The National Trading Standards Estate Agency Team ('NTSEAT'), hosted by Powys County Council, as the 'lead enforcement authority', is responsible under the EAA 1979 for:

- issuing banning or warning orders to businesses or individuals found to be unfit to engage in estate agency work in the UK;
- maintaining a public register of such banning or warning orders;
- approving and monitoring consumer redress schemes;
- providing specific advice and guidance to businesses and consumers about their rights and obligations.

11.33 The lead enforcement authority is also a Competent Authority in this sector for the purposes of the Alternative Dispute Resolution for Consumer Disputes (Competent Authorities and Information) Regulations 2015[1].

1   SI 2015/542.

11.34 The Consumers, Estate Agents and Redress Act 2007 ('CEAR 2007') amended EAA 1979 in a number of respects, including a requirement for estate agents who deal in residential property to join an independent redress scheme, the provision of additional powers to enforcers and an increase of the grounds under which the lead enforcement authority can issue warning and prohibition orders.

Estate agency work

11.35 The meaning of 'estate agency work' is given in EAA 1979, s 1. In practical terms, it means introducing to someone else a person who wishes to buy, sell or lease land or property, and being involved in negotiating the subsequent deal. The work must be in the course of business, whether as employer or employee, and as a result of instructions from a client. The land or property may be freehold or leasehold (or their Scottish equivalents) and may be commercial, industrial, agricultural or residential. EAA 1979, s 1 also details property-related work which is not covered by EAA 1979 (for example 'things done . . . in the course of his profession by a practising solicitor or a person employed by him or by an incorporated practice (within the meaning of the Solicitors (Scotland) Act 1980) or a person employed by it').

11.36 The Enterprise and Regulatory Reform Act 2013 amended EAA 1979, s 1 by extending the exemption of 'estate agency work' to exclude businesses, such as private sales internet portals, which provide a means for prospective parties to a property transaction to make contact in response to an advertisement or property information. The exemption applies provided that such businesses do 'no other things which fall within EAA 1979, s 1(1)', eg they do not otherwise participate in the transaction by advising, negotiating or providing other services.

Connected persons

11.37 The meaning of 'connected person', in relation to an estate agent, is given in art 1 of the Estate Agents (Undesirable Practices) (No 2) Order 1991[1]; it means any of the following:

(a)   his employer or principal, or
(b)   any employee or agent of his, or
(c)   any associate of his or of any person mentioned in (a) and (b) above.

1   SI 1991/1032.

11.38 EAA 1979, s 32 sets out the meaning of 'associate'. The combined effect of the Estate Agents (Undesirable Practices) (No 2) Order 1991[1] and EAA 1979, s 2 is that the 'connected persons' of an estate agent are likely to be numerous – this is of critical importance, for example, when dealing with the 'personal interest' obligations in EAA 1979, s 23.

1   SI 1991/1032.

Estate agent obligations

11.39 The obligations on estate agents are summarised below:

(i)   Open client account(s) to hold deposits[1]; provide receipts for deposits with all the necessary details; keep records of money paid into and out of client accounts; arrange for an annual audit of client accounts; be able to produce the latest auditor's report on demand; failure to comply is an offence.

(ii)   Pay interest on deposits if appropriate[2]; failure to comply is a trigger condition for a prohibition/warning order and may form the basis of a civil claim.

(iii)   Provide advance written information about fees and charges[3]; make written statements of when fees become payable; provide written information about changes to fees and charges; give written definitions of terms in contracts or agreements; tell clients in writing if the estate agent or a connected person or another person will offer services to a potential buyer; explain the terms 'sole selling rights', 'sole agency' and 'ready, willing and able purchaser' if they are used; failure to comply is a trigger condition for a prohibition/warning order and means that the contract is not enforceable without a court order. However, the courts are willing to imply the necessary terms into an informal estate agency agreement that is clearly intended to have legal effect – see *Wells v Devani*[4].

(iv)   Not to accept a pre-contract deposit in Scotland[5]; it is illegal to do so in Scotland.

(v)   Tell all potential buyers in writing about any existing personal interest (including that of connected persons); tell clients in writing about possible future personal interests (including those of connected persons)[6]; failure to comply is a trigger condition for a prohibition/warning order and but does not render the estate agent liable to any criminal penalty or constitute ground for any civil claim.

(vi)   Belong to an approved redress scheme[7].

[1]   EAA 1979, s 14 – 'Keeping of clients' accounts' and the Estate Agents (Accounts) Regulations 1981, SI 1981/1520.

[2]   EAA 1979, s 15 – 'Interest on clients' money' and the Estate Agents (Accounts) Regulations 1981, SI 1981/1520.

[3]   EAA 1979, s 18 – 'Information to clients of prospective liabilities' and the Estate Agents (Provision of Information) Regulations 1991, SI 1991/859.

[4]   [2019] UKSC 4; [2019] 2 WLR 617.

[5]   EAA 1979, s 20 – 'Prohibition of pre-contract deposits in Scotland'.

[6]   EAA 1979, s 21 – 'Transactions in which an estate agent has a personal interest' and the Estate Agents (Undesirable Practices) (No 2) Order 1991, SI 1991/1032.

[7]   EAA 1979, s 23A and Sch 3 'Redress schemes', the Estate Agents (Redress Scheme) Order 2008 and the Estate Agents (Redress Scheme) (Penalty Charge) Regulations 2008, SI 2008/1713.

Redress schemes

11.40 CEAR 2007 amended EAA 1979 to require that residential estate agents join an approved redress scheme that deals with complaints about the buying and selling of residential property. Estate agents that fail to join an approved scheme are subject to a £1,000 penalty charge, which can be repeated if necessary, and will ultimately be banned from carrying out estate agency work if they refuse to sign up. Following the withdrawal of Ombudsman Services:

Property on 6 August 2018 there remain two redress schemes – The Property Ombudsman and The Property Redress Scheme.

Prohibition and warning orders

11.41 EAA 1979, s 3 provides power for the 'lead enforcement authority'[1] to make a prohibition order banning any person (including a limited company) from doing any estate agency work at all, or of a description specified in the order, but only if it is satisfied that particular 'triggering' conditions have been met and that the person is unfit to engage in estate agency work. The triggering conditions which may lead to prohibition order are set out in EAA 1979, s 3(1). The lead enforcement authority must be satisfied that the person:

- has 'committed' (but not necessarily been convicted of) a criminal offence:
  - involving fraud or other dishonesty or violence;
  - under EAA 1979, s 23(4) ('Bankrupts not to engage in estate agency work');
  - listed in the Estate Agents (Specified Offences) (No 2) Order 1991[2], as amended (for example regs 8–12 and 23 of the CPUTR 2008);
- has committed discrimination in the course of estate agency work;
- has failed to comply with either an undertaking or an enforcement order – in respect of estate agency work – made under the Pt 8 of the Enterprise Act 2002;
- has failed to comply with any obligation imposed by any of the following sections of EAA 1979:
  - section 15 – Interest on clients' money;
  - section 18 – Information to clients of prospective liabilities;
  - section 19 – Regulation of pre-contract deposits outside Scotland (not in force);
  - section 20 – Prohibition of pre-contract deposits in Scotland;
  - section 21 – Transactions in which an estate agent has a personal interest;
- has failed to join an estate agents redress scheme approved by the lead enforcement authority (under EAA 1979, s 23A);
- has engaged in a practice listed in the Estate Agents (Undesirable Practices) (No 2) (Order) 1991[3] – for example, failing to pass on an offer to the seller promptly and in writing (except where the client has indicated that he does not want particular types of offer to be passed on), or to misrepresent an offer.

[1]   EAA 1979, s 33(1) defines the 'lead enforcement authority'.
[2]   SI 1991/1091.
[3]   SI 1991/1032.

11.42 Note that EAA 1979, Sch 1 supplements the provisions outlined in the first two trigger points above – those relating to previous convictions (reworded by CEAR 2007; spent convictions may not be relied upon) and discrimination (this part was amended by the Equality Act 2010 (Consequential Amendments, Saving and Supplementary Provisions) Order 2010[1] to extend EAA 1979 to apply not just to sex and race but to discrimination because of all the protected characteristics.) In basic terms, a warning order under EAA 1979, s 4 can be made by the lead enforcement authority if it is satisfied that the person has engaged in any of the conduct or practices, during the course of estate agency work, which would lead to a prohibition order and that, if the person repeated this conduct or practice, the lead enforcement authority would consider him unfit and proceed to make a prohibition order. EAA 1979, ss 5–8 and EAA 1979, Sch 2 make supplementary provisions for prohibition and warning orders, including the procedure for appeals and the maintenance of a register by the lead enforcement authority containing details of all orders made.

[1]   SI 2010/2279.

11.43 In *Littlewood v Powys County Council*[1] it was held that the procedure, which Powys County Council proposed to adopt in their consideration of whether or not to make prohibition orders in relation to either or both of the claimants, did not comply with the requirements of the EAA 1979 and was unlawful. For the purposes of EAA 1979, Sch 2, where the making of an order under EAA 1979, s 3, prohibiting an unfit person from acting as an estate agent had been delegated to an adjudicator, it was that adjudicator who personally had to hear oral representations from the person affected.

[1]   [2015] EWHC 2125 (Admin).

Offences

11.44 The main sanctions employed under EAA 1979 are warning and prohibition orders but offences, which may be committed by estate agents, are, in summary form, where:

- A person fails without reasonable excuse to comply with a prohibition order – punishable on conviction on indictment or on summary conviction to a fine[1].
- The offence under EAA 1979, s 9 has been repealed and replaced with the provisions of Pt 3 of the Consumer Rights Act 2015, Sch 5. Under para 14 an enforcer or an officer of an enforcer may give notice to a person requiring the person to provide the enforcer with the information specified in the notice. If the person fails to provide the information specified in the notice then the enforcer may make an application to the court under para 16 for an order. An order may require the person to meet the costs or expenses of the application. Paragraph 15 sets out the requirements to be followed for a notice under para 14.
- A person contravenes the provisions of EAA 1979 or of the Estate Agents (Accounts) Regulations 1981[2] as to the manner in which clients' money is to be dealt with or accounts and records relating to such money are to be kept, or fails to produce an auditor's report when required to do so by those Regulations – punishable on summary conviction to a fine not exceeding level 4 on the standard scale.

[1]   EAA 1979, s 3(8); see also Legal Aid, Sentencing and Punishment of Offenders Act 2012, s 85 for offences committed after 12 March 2015.
[2]   SI 1981/1520.

11.45

Precedent: Failing to comply with prohibition order, s 3(8)

Information

A B, on [date], did fail without reasonable excuse to comply with an order of the [lead enforcement authority], issued on [date] pursuant to section 3 of the Estate Agents Act 1979 prohibiting him from doing any estate agency work at all [or from doing estate agency work of a description specified in the order] namely [. . .], contrary to Section 3(8) of the Estate Agents Act 1979.

11.46

Precedent: Contravening client money requirement, s 14(8)

Information

A B, on [date], did contravene section [...] of the Estate Agents Act 1979 as to the manner in which clients' money is to be dealt with or accounts and relating to such money are to be kept, namely [. . .], contrary to Section 14(8) of the Estate Agents Act 1979.

Due diligence defence

11.47 EAA 1979, s 28(1) states:

(1) In any proceedings for an offence under this Act it shall be a defence for the person charged to prove that he took all reasonable precautions and exercised all due diligence to avoid the commission of an offence by himself or any person under his control.

Directors' liability

11.48 EAA 1979, s 28(2) states:

(2) Where an offence under this Act committed by a body corporate is proved to have been committed with the consent or connivance of, or to be attributable to any neglect on the part of, any director, manager, secretary or other similar officer of the body corporate, or any person who was purporting to act in any such capacity, he as well as the body corporate shall be guilty of that offence and shall be liable to be proceeded against and punished accordingly.

11.49 The meanings of 'business associate' and 'controller', given in EAA 1979, s 31, are also relevant in the determination of liability in respect of corporate bodies and partnerships. Directors' liability is covered in CHAPTER 4, Criminal Enforcement.

Enforcement

11.50 Investigatory powers are now contained in the CRA 2015, Sch 5, see CHAPTER 4, Criminal Enforcement.

FOOTWEAR COMPOSITION

11.51 The Footwear Composition (Indication of Composition) Labelling Regulations 1995[1] were made under the European Communities Act 1972. The Regulations require the manufacturer or the responsible person (either the manufacturer, the manufacturer's authorised representative or the person who first supplies footwear in the Community) to ensure that footwear placed on the market complies with certain labelling requirements (reg 4). The information may be provided by way of pictogram or written indication (reg 5). Retailers must ensure that footwear is labelled in accordance with the requirements of the Regulations and that consumers are informed of the meaning of the pictograms (reg 6). Under reg 8, failure to comply with the requirements of reg 4 or 6 of the Regulations is an offence. An offence under reg 8 is triable either way and subject to a fine.

[1] SI 1995/2489.

11.52 By virtue of reg 10, certain provisions of the Trade Description Act 1968 are applied (with necessary modifications) to the Regulations – Trade Descriptions Act 1968, ss 19, 20, 23, 24 and 26. Notwithstanding their repeal by the Consumer Protection from Unfair Trading Regulations 2008[1], the Trade Descriptions Act 1968, ss 19(4)(b) and (c) and s 24(3) will continue to apply for the purposes of reg 10. The enforcement powers in the CRA 2015, Sch 5 apply to the Regulations; see CHAPTER 4, Criminal Enforcement. However, under reg 9, before taking enforcement action, trading standards officers may serve a compliance notice (as set out in Sch 3) to give an opportunity for footwear labelling to be brought into line with the requirements of the Regulations – the provisions of the Trade Descriptions Act 1968 'shall not be applied until such a notice has been so served and the person upon whom it has been served has failed to comply with its requirements'.

From 31 December 2020, references in these Regulations to the European Union will be replaced with references to the United Kingdom.

[1] SI 2008/1277.

LEGAL ACTIVITIES

11.53 The Legal Services Act 2007, s 14 makes it an offence for a person who is not entitled to carry on 'a reserved legal activity' to carry out that activity. The LSA 2007, s 16 provides that if an employer carries on 'a reserved legal activity' through a manager or employee who is not entitled to carry on that activity, the employer will commit an offence, even if the employer is so entitled, unless the employer has taken all reasonable precautions and exercised all due diligence to avoid committing the offence. Both offences are subject to imprisonment of 12 months and/or a fine and imprisonment of 2 years and/or an unlimited fine on conviction on indictment (LSA 2007, ss 14(3) and 16(5)). For offences committed prior to the commencement of para 24(2) of Sch 22 the Sentencing Act 2020 the reference to 12 months is to be read as six months. LSA 2007, s 198 has the same effect as the Solicitors Act 1974, s 22A (repealed as of 1 January 2010) and provides that a local weights and measures authority may institute proceedings for an offence under LSA 2007, s 14 or under LSA 2007, s 16 if the activity which it is alleged that the accused person was not entitled to carry on constitutes a specific type of 'reserved legal activity', namely 'reserved instrument activities' (which are defined in LSA 2007, Sch 2).

11.54

Precedent for unlawfully carrying on reserved legal activity

Statement of offence

UNLAWFULLY CARRYING ON A RESERVED LEGAL ACTIVITY, contrary to section 14(1) of the Legal Services Act 2007.

Particulars of offence

A B, on [date], carried on an activity, namely [. . .] which was a reserved legal activity when he was not entitled to do so.

11.55 Article 23 of the Solicitors (Northern Ireland) Order 1976 provides for an offence where an unqualified person, either directly or indirectly, prepares certain Northern Ireland instruments etc, in a manner equivalent to the reserved instrument activities described below. The Department of Economic Development 'may institute proceedings' for an offence under art 23.

LSA 2007, Sch 2, para 5:

> 5(1) "Reserved instrument activities" means—
>
> (a)   preparing any instrument of transfer or charge for the purposes of the Land Registration Act 2002;
>
> (b)   making an application or lodging a document for registration under that Act;
>
> (c)   preparing any other instrument relating to real or personal estate for the purposes of the law of England and Wales or instrument relating to court proceedings in England and Wales.
>
> (2) But "reserved instrument activities" does not include the preparation of an instrument relating to any particular court proceedings if, immediately before the appointed day, no restriction was placed on the persons entitled to carry on that activity.
>
> (3) In this paragraph "instrument" includes a contract for the sale or other disposition of land (except a contract to grant a short lease), but does not include—
>
> (a)   a will or other testamentary instrument,
>
> (b)   an agreement not intended to be executed as a deed, other than a contract that is included by virtue of the preceding provisions of this sub-paragraph,
>
> (c)   a letter or power of attorney, or
>
> (d)   a transfer of stock containing no trust or limitation of the transfer.
>
> (4) In this paragraph a "short lease" means a lease such as is referred to in section 54(2) of the Law of Property Act 1925 (short leases).

11.56 The LSA 2007, s 198 also provides a 'weights and measures officer' (an officer of a local weights and measures authority who is authorised by the authority) with detailed powers to investigate offences under the LSA 2007, ss 14 and 16. The LSA 2007, 198(4)–(9) provides:

(4) A weights and measures officer who has reasonable cause to suspect that a relevant offence may have been committed may, at any reasonable time—

    (a)   enter any premises which are not used solely as a dwelling;

    (b)   require any officer, agent or other competent person on the premises who is, or may be, in possession of information relevant to an investigation of the suspected offence to provide such information;

    (c)   require the production of any document which may be relevant to such an investigation;

    (d)   take copies, or extracts, of any such documents;

    (e)   seize and retain any document which the weights and measures officer has reason to believe may be required as evidence in proceedings for a relevant offence.

(5) Any person exercising a power given by subsection (4) must, if asked to do so, produce evidence that that person is a weights and measures officer.

(6) A justice of the peace may issue a warrant under this section if satisfied, on information on oath given by a weights and measures officer, that there is reasonable cause to believe that a relevant offence may have been committed and that—

    (a)   entry to the premises concerned, or production of any documents which may be relevant to an investigation of the relevant offence, has been or is likely to be refused to a weights and measures officer, or

    (b)   there is reasonable cause to believe that, if production of any such document were to be required by the weights and measures officer without a warrant having been issued under this section, the document would not be produced but would be removed from the premises or hidden, tampered with or destroyed.

(7) A warrant issued under this section must authorise the weights and measures officer accompanied, where that officer considers it appropriate, by a constable or other person—

    (a)   to enter the premises specified in the information, using such force as is reasonably necessary, and

    (b)   to exercise any of the powers given to the weights and measures officer by subsection (4).

(8) It is an offence for a person ("P")—

    (a)   intentionally to obstruct a weights and measures officer in the exercise of any power under this section;

    (b)   intentionally to fail to comply with any requirement properly imposed on P by a weights and measures officer in the exercise of any such power;

    (c)   to fail, without reasonable excuse, to give a weights and measures officer any assistance or information which the weights and measures officer may reasonably require of P for the purpose of exercising any such power; or

    (d)   in giving to a weights and measures officer any information which P has been required to give a weights and measures officer exercising any such power, to make any statement which P knows to be false or misleading in a material particular.

(9) A person who is guilty of an offence under subsection (8) is liable on summary conviction to a fine not exceeding level 3 on the standard scale.

(10) Nothing in this section is to be taken to require any person to answer any question put to that person by a weights and measures officer, or to give any information to such an officer, if to do so might incriminate that person.

There are two other areas where the provisions of the Legal Services Act 2007 may impact on the future operational activities of trading standards officers.

Will writing

11.57 On 13 February 2013, the Legal Services Board ('LSB') concluded a 2-year investigation by recommending to the Lord Chancellor that the list of reserved legal activities be amended to include will-writing activities, so that the significant risks consumers currently face when using these critical services is reduced. The LSB found comprehensive evidence that the market was working contrary to the statutory regulatory objectives outlined in the Legal Services Act 2007 and to the detriment of consumers and providers alike.

11.58 An example of the market working 'to the detriment of consumers' was illustrated in *R v Ventriglia*[1]. Jackson LJ commented:

> 'The fraud committed by the appellant was a particularly pernicious one because he was preying upon customers or clients in the later stages of life, who were obviously concerned about how their assets and their estate would be distributed after death. They were obviously concerned that their dependents and descendants should be provided for in a fair and proper way. In our view, this was a particularly unpleasant form of breach of trust, the character of which the judge rightly had in mind.'

[1]   [2011] EWCA Crim 2912.

11.59 Jackson LJ also hoped:

> ' . . . that this judgment will receive some publicity in whatever journal may be published for and read by will writers. If such persons fraudulently prey upon the fears of vulnerable clients for their own personal gain, they can expect to get caught, because their letters may well go to the Trading Standards Office, and they can expect to receive substantial prison sentences.'

11.60 On 14 May 2013 it was announced that the Government and the Lord Chancellor had decided not to accept the recommendation of the LSB that will-writing activities should be made subject to regulation.

Scotland

11.61 Note that the majority of the Legal Services Act 2007 does not apply in Scotland (except LSA 2007, ss 195, 196(1) and Sch 20) but that provisions regulating legal activities are contained in the Solicitors (Scotland) Act 1980 and the Legal Services (Scotland) Act 2010. In particular the Solicitors (Scotland) Act 1980, s 23 provides an offence to practise without a practising certificate.

LETTING AGENTS

Introduction

11.62 The size of the private rented sector in England is rapidly increasing – up from 2.4m households in 2005 to 4.5m in 2017 – with around 1 million of these households moving every year. The majority of these moves include a letting agent, who is a person appointed by a landlord to find a tenant or who is instructed by a prospective tenant who wants to find a property, or who is both. A report published by the Office of Fair Trading in February 2013 identified several consumer protection issues in the lettings market. Common complaints about lettings and property management in the private rented sector are around how agents handle the security and holding deposits, missed appointments, pressuring tenants to take tenancies, poor customer service, out of date and misleading adverts and opaque and variable fees. Many landlords also appoint an agent to manage their properties on their behalf with common complaints about how the property is managed being around repairs not being carried out in a timely manner or to a satisfactory standard, general customer service and notice and conduct of visits from agents.

11.63 There are a number of non-statutory measures aimed at raising standards, eg the DCLG guide for local authorities: *Improving the private rented sector and tackling bad practice: a guide for local authorities*, which was updated in March 2015. A guide entitled 'How to rent' was published in June 2014 and last updated on 21 July 2021. Also, *Guidance for lettings professionals on consumer protection law*, published by the Competition and Markets Authority in June 2014 and updated in October 2019, is relevant to lettings professionals in England, Wales, Scotland and Northern Ireland (highlighting national variations in legislation) and is intended 'to complement existing industry schemes such as those operated by industry bodies and codes of conduct, which help lettings professionals keep up-to-date with changes to the law, achieve compliance, and provide good quality services to tenants and landlords'. A database of rogue landlords and property agents came into force on the 6 April 2018. On Easter Sunday 2018 the Government announced plans to crack down on rogue letting agents by the introduction of a mandatory code of practice and a nationally recognised qualification. At least one member in any business will be required to obtain a higher qualification. The code will also contain provisions whereby a leaseholder will be able to challenge unfair fees; and a requirement for letting agents to undertake continuing professional development and training. A criminal offence will be created for letting agents who break the code and a new regulator will be set up. The regulator will be able to ban letting agents from trading and serious code breaches will be the subject of prosecution.

11.64 Since November 2013 the Committee of Advertising Practice ('CAP') has required lettings agents and private landlords to make sure that fees are prominently displayed in advertisements alongside rental prices. CAP's guidance was triggered by an Advertising Standards Authority ruling against rental advertisements on an internet property portal. The Government has stated that it does not intend to introduce regulation in this sector, but there have been legislative developments in the areas of redress schemes and publication of fees. A Bill was introduced into the Commons for first reading on the 1 May 2018 names the Tenant Fees Bill 2018. The Tenant Fees Act 2019 was brought into force on the 15 April 2019. The Act makes provision prohibiting landlords and letting agents from requiring certain payments to be made or certain other steps to be taken; to make provision about the payment of holding deposits; to make provision about enforcement and about the lead enforcement authority; to amend the provisions of the Consumer Rights Act 2015 about information to be provided by letting agents and the provisions of the Housing and Planning Act 2016 about client money protection schemes; and for connected purposes. Breach of the prohibitions applying to landlords and letting agents set out in s 1 and s 2 of the Tenants Fees Act 2019 is an offence by s 12 and subject on summary conviction to a fine. The Act makes amendments to the Consumer Rights Act 2015, ss 83 and 87 in relation to the duty to publicise fees and enforcement. The Government consultation pursuant to the Housing and Planning Act 2016 on the 'Mandatory client money protection scheme for property agents' closed on the 13 December 2017 and the Government response was published on the 1 April 2018. Enforcement of this scheme will rest at County Council level and therefore be dealt with by Trading Standards Departments in order to provide consistency with other letting agent regulation. Civil penalties of up to £30,000 will be available but creation of a criminal offence was found to be disproportionate. The Government intends to lay two sets of affirmative regulations in Parliament as soon as parliamentary time allows.

Requirement to join a redress scheme

11.65 The Enterprise and Regulatory Reform Act 2013 ('ERRA 2013') introduced powers to require persons who engage in lettings agency work and property management work in respect of dwelling-houses in England to join an approved redress scheme or a government administered redress scheme. The ERRA 2013, s 83(1) provides for an order-making power to require persons who engage in 'lettings agency work' to belong to such a scheme. Similar provision is made in the ERRA 2013, s 84(1) in respect of persons who engage in 'property management work'. The ERRA 2013, s 85 enables the Secretary of State to make provision for enforcement. The Tenant Fees Act 2019 added the following provisions to s 85:

> (4A) A person on whom functions are conferred under subsection (4) must have regard to any guidance issued by the Secretary of State or the lead enforcement authority (if not the Secretary of State) relating to the enforcement of an order under section 83(1) or 84(1).
> (6) For provisions about enforcement of an order under section 83(1) or 84(1) by the lead enforcement authority, see sections 24 to 26 of the Tenant Fees Act 2019.
> (7) In this section *'lead enforcement authority'* has the meaning given by section 24(1) of the Tenant Fees Act 2019.

11.66 The Redress Schemes for Lettings Agency Work and Property Management Work (Approval and Designation of Schemes) (England) Order 2013[1] (the 'Approval Order') sets out the procedure relating to applications for approval; the conditions a scheme must meet before the Secretary of State may approve the scheme or designate it as a government administered redress scheme; and for the procedure relating to the withdrawal of approval or designation from such schemes. Three redress schemes had been approved under the Approval Order – The Property Ombudsman; Ombudsman Services Property; and The Property Redress Scheme.

[1]   SI 2013/3192.

11.67 The Redress Schemes for Lettings Agency Work and Property Management Work (Requirement to Belong to a Scheme etc) (England) Order 2014[1] (the 'Requirement Order') makes it a legal requirement for a person engaged in letting agency work to be a member of a redress scheme 'for dealing with complaints' with effect from 1 October 2014. 'Lettings agency work', in the ERRA 2013, s 83(7), essentially means things done by an agent in the course of a business in response to instructions from:

- a private rented sector landlord who wants to find a tenant; or
- a tenant who wants to find a property in the private rented sector.

There are, however, a number of areas which are not to be regarded as 'lettings agency work'[2].

[1]   SI 2014/2359.
[2]   Set out in ERRA 2013, s 83(8) and (9) and art 4 of the Requirement Order, SI 2014/2359.

Enforcement

11.68 Article 7 of the Requirement Order[1] makes provision for enforcement by an enforcement authority, which is defined as 'a district council, a London Borough Council, the Common Council of the City of London in its capacity as a local authority, or the Council of the Isles of Scilly'. In practice, enforcement will be by local housing authorities. Section 26 of the Tenant Fees Act 2019 takes effect in respect of enforcement by the lead enforcement authority. The lead enforcement authority is Bristol City Council.

[1]   SI 2014/2359.

11.69 Article 8 provides that an enforcement authorities may impose a monetary penalty of up to £5,000 (with a right of appeal to the First-tier Tribunal under art 9) where it is satisfied, on the balance of probability, that someone is engaged in letting or management work and is required to be a member of a redress scheme, but has not joined. The Requirement Order[1] also provides for procedures for the imposition and recovery of the monetary penalty.

[1]   SI 2014/2359.

Duty of letting agents to publicise fees etc

11.70 The provisions in Chapter 3 of Pt 3 to the Consumer Rights Act 2015, ss 83–88 ('CRA 2015') and CRA 2015, Sch 9 provide a framework for requiring letting agents to publicise relevant fees and for enforcement. There are also requirements, for letting agents who are obliged by law to be a member of a redress scheme, for such persons to display details of that redress scheme, and, for certain agents who hold client money, to display a statement of whether or not they are a member of a client money protection scheme.

11.71 Enforcement of these duties will be by a local weights and measures authority in England and Wales. A new section is added by the Tenant Fees Act 2019:

> (1A) The duty in subsection (1) is subject to section 26 (enforcement by the lead enforcement authority) of the Tenant Fees Act 2019.

11.72 Chapter 3 of Pt 3 was brought into force on 27 May 2015 by the Consumer Rights Act 2015 (Commencement) (England) Order 2015[1]. The Order also brought into force on the same date the investigatory powers provisions (contained in CRA 2015, s 77 and Sch 5 in relation to the enforcement of this area) and CRA 2015, Sch 9 which deals with financial penalties. See Chapter **4**, Criminal Enforcement for details of the investigatory powers provisions.

¹   SI 2015/965.

The duty

11.73 Having been amended by the Tenant Fees Act 2019, the CRA 2015, s 83 provides:

   (1)   A letting agent must, in accordance with this section, publicise details of the agent's relevant fees.

   (2)   The agent must display a list of the fees—

        (a)   at each of the agent's premises at which the agent deals face-to-face with persons using or proposing to use services to which the fees relate, and

        (b)   at a place in each of those premises at which the list is likely to be seen by such persons.

   (3)   The agent must publish a list of the fees on the agent's website (if it has a website).

   (3A)   Subsection (3C) applies to an agent who—

        (a)   is carrying on letting agency work in relation to a dwelling-house in England, and

        (b)   advertises the dwelling-house on a third party website as a dwelling-house which a landlord is seeking to let on a tenancy.

   (3B)   Subsection (3C) also applies to an agent who, on a third party website, advertises letting agency work carried on by the agent in relation to dwelling houses in England.

   (3C)   The agent must ensure that—

        (a)   a list of the agent's relevant fees is published on the third party website, or

        (b)   there is a link on that website to a part of the agent's website where a list of those fees is published.

   (4)   A list of fees displayed or published in accordance with subsection (2) [(3) or (3C)] must include—

        (a)   a description of each fee that is sufficient to enable a person who is liable to pay it to understand the service or cost that is covered by the fee or the purpose for which it is imposed (as the case may be),

        (b)   in the case of a fee which tenants are liable to pay, an indication of whether the fee relates to each dwelling-house or each tenant under a tenancy of the dwelling-house, and

        (c)   the amount of each fee inclusive of any applicable tax or, where the amount of a fee cannot reasonably be determined in advance, a description of how that fee is calculated.

   (5)   Subsections (6) and (7) apply to a letting agent engaging in letting agency or property management work in relation to dwelling-houses in England.

   (6)   If the agent [is required to be a member of a client money protection scheme for the purposes of] that work, the duty imposed on the agent by subsection (2) [, (3) or 3C)] includes a duty to display or publish, with the list of fees, a statement [that—]

        (a)   indicates that the agent is a member of a client money protection scheme, and

        (b)   gives the name of the scheme.

(7)   If the agent is required to be a member of a redress scheme for dealing with complaints in connection with that work, the duty imposed on the agent by subsection (2) [, (3) or (3C)] includes a duty to display or publish, with the list of fees, a statement—

(a)   that indicates that the agent is a member of a redress scheme, and

(b)   that gives the name of the scheme.

(8)   The appropriate national authority may by regulations specify—

(a)   other ways in which a letting agent must publicise details of the relevant fees charged by the agent or (where applicable) a statement within subsection (6) or (7);

(b)   the details that must be given of fees publicised in that way.

(9)   In this section—

"client money protection scheme" means a scheme which enables a person on whose behalf a letting agent holds money to be compensated if all or part of that money is not repaid to that person in circumstances where the scheme applies;

"redress scheme" means a redress scheme for which provision is made by order under section 83 or 84 of the Enterprise and Regulatory Reform Act 2013[;]

"third party website", in relation to a letting agent, means a website other than the agent's website.

Letting agents to which the duty to publicise fees applies

11.74 The CRA 2015, s 84 specifies those who are covered by the duty and CRA 2015, s 86 provides the meanings of 'Letting agency work and property management work'. The meaning of 'Letting agency work' follows that contained in ERRA 2013, s 83(7) and, similarly, describes activities which are not to be regarded as 'lettings agency work'. The broad definition of a letting agent includes members of the legal profession acting in a professional legal capacity on lettings-related work, for example if a landlord instructs a solicitor to draft a tenancy agreement. The Duty of Letting Agents to Publicise Fees etc. (Exclusion) (England) Regulations 2015[1] which came into force on 27 May 2015 exclude legal professionals from the requirement to publicise their fees etc when they engage only in legal activity within the meaning of Legal Services Act 2007, s 12.

[1]   SI 2015/951.

11.75 The CRA 2015, s 85 defines the 'relevant fees' which must be disclosed under CRA 2015, s 83. A letting agent must include, in its list of fees, any fees which are payable to it by a landlord or a tenant in respect of letting agency or property management work or otherwise in connection with an assured tenancy of a dwelling-house (including a proposed assured tenancy). Guidance on the duty of letting agents to publicise fees etc can be found in Annex D to the DCLG guide for local authorities *Improving the private rented sector and tackling bad practice: a guide for local authorities*.

Redress information

11.76 The ERRA 2013, s 83(7) provides that, if the agent is required to be a member of a redress scheme under ERRA 2013, there is also a duty to display or publish, with the list of fees, a statement indicating that the agent is a member of a (named) redress scheme. Under ERRA 2013, s 83(6), if the agent holds money on behalf of persons to whom the agent provides services as part of that work, there is also a duty to display or publish, with the list of fees, a statement of whether the agent is a member of a 'client money protection scheme' (which means a scheme that enables a person on whose behalf a letting agent holds money to be compensated if all or part of that money is not repaid to that person in circumstances where the scheme applies).

Enforcement

11.77 The CRA 2015, s 87 provides for enforcement of the duties. The amendments in the Tenant Fees Act 2019 will not alter this duty but adds an amendment.

87 Enforcement of the duty

(1)   It is the duty of every local weights and measures authority in England and Wales to enforce the provisions of this Chapter in its area.

(1A)   The duty in subsection (1) is subject to section 26 (enforcement by the lead enforcement authority) of the Tenant Fees Act 2019.

11.78 The CRA 2015, s 87 provides for the imposition of a financial penalty of up to £5,000 on a letting agent who has breached a duty in s 83, subject to any statutory guidance issued and an appeals process. Schedule 9 provides for the procedure for, and appeals against, financial penalties.

Wales

11.79 The CRA 2015 provisions relating to letting agents apply only to England and Wales. Part 1 of the Housing (Wales) Act 2014 also relates to the Regulation of Private Rented Housing and includes provisions prohibiting letting and management without registration and licence. Part 1 includes a requirement for most landlords of dwellings let, or to be let, under domestic tenancies, to register with the relevant designated licensing authority. Similarly, persons engaged in letting or managing such dwellings, are required to obtain a licence from the relevant designated licensing authority.

Scotland

11.80 The law in Scotland was clarified in 2012 so that all tenant charges, other than rent and a refundable deposit, are illegal. The Private Rented Housing (Scotland) Act 2011, s 32 was brought into force by the Private Rented Housing (Scotland) Act 2011 (Commencement No 4) Order 2012[1], amending the definition of 'premium' in the Rent (Scotland) Act 1984, s 90 to make clear that it includes any service or administration fee or charge. The Letting Agent Code of Practice (Scotland) Regulations 2016[2] came into effect on 31 January 2018.

[1]   SI 2012/267.
[2]   SI 2016/331.

MOBILE HOMES

11.81 The Mobile Homes Act 2013 ('MHA 2013') received Royal Assent on 26 March 2013. The MHA 2013 amends current legislation – in particular the Mobile Homes Act 1983 – and brings the licensing regime that applies to mobile home sites more closely in line with other local authority licensing regimes. The MHA 2013 also introduces new requirements about site rules, provides a framework for better transparency on pitch fee reviews and inserts into the Caravan Sites and Control of Development Act 1960 a power to enable the Secretary of State to introduce by way of secondary legislation a 'fit and proper' person requirement. This power came into force on 15 June 2020.

11.82 The legal position in relation to Wales is unaltered by the Mobile Homes Act 2013 but, on 21 February 2013, a report published by the National Assembly for Wales Communities, Equality and Local Government Committee supported the general principles of a parallel Bill – the Regulated Mobile Homes Sites (Wales) Bill – to modernise the legal framework in Wales. The Bill – proposed by Peter Black AM – the first non-government Member Bill to come before the Assembly. The Mobile Homes (Wales) Act 2013 came into force on 1 October 2014. All mobile homes sites must have a site licence issued by the local authority on a park with relevant planning permission. Local authorities had 6 months from the MHA 2013 coming into force to revoke and relicense all sites and site owners have 12 months to make and lodge new site rules (by 1 October 2015). The MHA 2013 does not apply to holiday caravans. The DCLG is carrying out a 'Review of park homes legislation' specifically to gather evidence around the effectiveness of the Mobile Homes Act 2013. The call for evidence part 2 closed on the 16 February 2018. A summary of the responses was published on the 25 May 2018 and the Government response was published in October 2018.

11.83 The main features of the MHA 2013 are:

- Site owners will be required to apply for a licence from their local authority to operate a site. The licence will last up to 5 years.
- Site managers will need to pass a 'fit and proper person' test before being awarded a licence. This provision has been in force since 15 June 2020.
- Site owners will no longer be able to block the sale of a mobile home. The mobile home owner will be free to sell their home to whomever they wish.
- Local authorities will be able to inspect sites and issue a fixed penalty notice to site owners if conditions on the site are not kept properly.
- In more serious instances, local authorities will be able to issue the site owners with a compliance notice to make sure that site conditions are upheld.
- Pitch fees can only be increased in line with the Consumer Prices Index.
- Site owners and residents will be able to appeal to the Residential Property Tribunal in certain circumstances.

11.84 The Caravans (Northern Ireland) Act 2011 introduced, for the first time in Northern Ireland, specific legislation controlling the dealings between caravan park owners and those renting holiday caravan pitches for more than 28 days.

PEDLARY AND STREET TRADING

Pedlary

11.85 In summary, a person must obtain a certificate from the police under the Pedlars Act 1871 ('PA 1871') in order to trade as a pedlar throughout the United Kingdom. The definition of a pedlar in the PA 1871, in essence, means that that the person must trade on the move, not from a static location, and carry their goods with him: see *Jones v Bath and North East Somerset Council*[1] (below). A pedlar is required on demand to show his certificate to the police, to a justice of the peace, to any person to whom he offers his goods for sale and to any person on whose private property the pedlar is found. It is an offence not to produce the certificate in these circumstances. The only manner in which a pedlar can be deprived of his certificate is by order of the court under the PA 1871, s 16; there are no provisions for the police to seize, suspend or revoke certificates – see *R (on the application of Jones) v Chief Constable of Cheshire Police*[2]. A person may appeal against the refusal to grant a certificate by virtue of the PA 1871, s 15.

[1]   [2012] EWHC 1361 (Admin).
[2]   [2005] EWHC 2457 (Admin).

Offences

11.86 The PA 1871 creates several offences. Under the PA 1871, s 10 a pedlar to whom a certificate is granted must not lend, transfer or assign the same to another person. By the PA 1871, s 11 no person may borrow or make use of a certificate granted to another and it is an offence under the PA 1871, s 12 to make representations with a view to obtaining a certificate under the Act. All of these offences are punishable on summary conviction by a fine not exceeding level 1 on the standard scale. Any subsequent offence under the PA 1871, s 12 is punishable by a maximum of 6 months' imprisonment. Any convictions under this Act must be indorsed on the certificate.

Street trading

11.87 The Local Government (Miscellaneous Provisions) Act 1982 ('LG(MP)A 1982') provides local authorities in England and Wales with the option of adopting powers to regulate street trading. Pedlars are exempt from the LG(MP)A 1982. Those councils that adopt the LG(MP)A 1982 powers can designate streets in their area as prohibited, consent or license streets for street trading purposes. Councils can then require street traders to apply for licences in order to trade in designated streets and apply the consequent penalties for not being licensed for trading in those streets. Street trading for the purposes of the LG(MP)A 1982 is defined as the selling or exposing or offering for sale of any article (including a living thing) in a street. Thus, street trading under the LG(MP)A 1982 regulates the sale of goods only. Paragraph 4 of the LG(MP)A 1982, Sch 4 allows Local Authorities to attach such conditions as they think reasonable to the licence.

11.88 In Scotland, the Civic Government (Scotland) Act 1982 gives local authorities powers to regulate street trading by requiring persons selling or offering to sell goods and services in a public place (whether from a kiosk, vehicle, moveable stall or otherwise) to hold a licence. See *McCluskey v North Lanarkshire Council*[1] where an appeal against a condition attached to a licence which prohibited trading within a distance of 250 m from all secondary schools between 8 am and 5 pm on any school day during term time was allowed on the basis that Parliament could not have intended local licensing authorities to have the implied power to attach a condition with such a significant effect on the commercial contracts of street traders, regardless of the aim of the condition.

[1]   2016 SLT (Sh Ct) 31.

11.89 The policy objectives of the Street Trading Act (Northern Ireland) 2001 are to enable district councils to control and regulate street trading in their districts in such a way as to prevent undue nuisance, interference and inconvenience to persons and vehicles. The Act includes measures to allow councils to control the activities of those trading without a licence or outside the conditions of their licence. The London Local Authorities (No 2) Act 1990 (as amended), which has been adopted by all 32 London boroughs, gives bespoke powers in respect of licensing, enforcement, seizure, retention and forfeiture of goods. The LLA(No 2)A 1990, s 6 in relation to liquor licensing has been repealed by the Licensing Act 2003. Some local authorities have obtained private Acts of Parliament – for example, in 2013, Canterbury City Council, Leeds City Council, Nottingham City Council and Reading Borough Council. These Acts generally contain provisions to extend the regulation of street trading to the provisions of services, as well as trade in goods, and provide additional powers in relation to enforcement against illegal street trading (such as the imposition of fixed penalties and the seizure of goods).

Offences

11.90 Paragraph 10 of Sch 4 to the LG(MP)A 1982 creates offences thus:

(1)   A person who—
    (a)   engages in street trading in a prohibited street; or
    (b)   engages in street trading in a licence street or a consent street without being authorised to do so under this Schedule; or
    (c)   contravenes any of the principal terms of a street trading licence; or
    (d)   being authorised by a street trading consent to trade in a consent street, trades in that street—
        (i)   from a stationary van, cart, barrow or other vehicle; or
        (ii)   from a portable stall,
        without first having been granted permission to do so under paragraph 7(8) above; or
    (e)   contravenes a condition imposed under paragraph 7(9) above, shall be guilty of an offence.
(2)   It shall be a defence for a person charged with an offence under sub-paragraph (1) above to prove that he took all reasonable precautions and exercised all due diligence to avoid commission of the offence.

(3) Any person who, in connection with an application for a street trading licence or for a street trading consent, makes a false statement which he knows to be false in any material respect, or which he does not believe to be true, shall be guilty of an offence.

(4) A person guilty of an offence under this paragraph shall be liable on summary conviction to a fine not exceeding level 3 on the standard scale.

11.91

Precedent for unlawful street trading

Information

A B, on [date], engaged in street trading on a prohibited street, namely [X Street], contrary to paragraph 10(1)(a) of Schedule 4 to the Local Government (Miscellaneous Provisions) Act 1982.

11.92 In *Jones v Bath and North East Somerset Council*[1] the defendant was convicted of 'street trading' without a local authority licence under LG(MP)A 1982. He unsuccessfully appealed on the basis of the statutory exception of being a person acting as a pedlar under the authority of a pedlar's certificate granted under the Pedlars Act 1871. It was undisputed that the defendant had parked his car in a nearby street from which he was able to replenish his stock (of umbrellas) during a day on which it was either raining or drizzling. Mitting J stated:

' . . . absent any authority to the contrary, it seems to me that the definition of pedlar . . . requires that the pedlar is both peripatetic and ambulatory . . . In modern times someone who drives with his goods in his own van or car to a town or city to offer goods for sale, is not acting as a pedlar. He is not acting as a pedlar because he is not travelling there on foot. The requirement that he conducts his activities on foot applies both to travel and trade.'

[1] [2012] EWHC 1361 (Admin).

Proposals for reform

11.93 The Department for Business, Enterprise and Regulatory Reform published a consultation document – 'Street Trading and Pedlar Laws – A joint consultation on modernising Street Trading and Pedlar Legislation, and on draft guidance on the current regime' – on 6 November 2009, seeking views on the case for, and possible options for amending and modernising the law as it applies to the control of street trading and the certification of pedlars. However, it was subsequently recognised that new legislation, containing authorisation schemes (such as those applied to pedlars or street traders), would need to satisfy the requirements of the European Services Directive 2006/123/EC.

11.94 A joint consultation between the UK and Scottish governments and the Northern Ireland Executive – 'Street Trading and Pedlary Laws – Compliance with the European Services Directive' – was published in November 2012. The consultation sets out proposals and draft regulations to:

• repeal the Pedlars Act 1871 and 1881 in relation to the whole of the United Kingdom, in order to ensure compliance with the Directive;

- set-out a new definition of pedlary in the LG(MP)A 1982, Sch 4 to provide a new legal basis for the exemption of pedlars from the national street trading regime; and
- amend 'national' street trading legislation for England and Wales and for Northern Ireland to ensure that the legislation complies fully with the requirements of the Directive

11.95 On 16 October 2014 the Government's response to the consultation on reform of the street trading regimes in England, Wales and Northern Ireland and the pedlary regime across the UK was announced. In summary, the Government intends to make the minimum changes required to bring the regime into compliance with the Services Directive:

- the Pedlars Acts will be retained. The certification process will be amended to remove a requirement for prior residency in an area and to make the required good character check an objective one that can be applied consistently across the UK;
- there will be no changes to the definition of pedlary or to the exemption in the Local Government (Miscellaneous Provisions) Act 1982, Sch 4 ('LG(MP)A 1982');
- other changes to the LG(MP)A 1982, Sch 4, necessary to bring the regime into compliance with the Services Directive, will be made. These concern the application process, the duration of licences and the grounds for refusing or revoking a licence or consent as well as consequential changes to other parts of the Schedule. Secondary legislation to effect these changes will be brought forward as soon as the Parliamentary timetable allows;
- no action will be taken in relation to two additional proposals in the consultation – for an additional power to designate streets for established traders only and for new discretionary grounds for refusing a licence based on the suitability of the street.

11.96 On the 23 December 2014 the public responses were published and on the 3 March 2015 the public feedback from police divisions was added. These changes mainly affect England, Wales and Scotland because Northern Ireland's separate street trading regime effectively negates the pedlary regime; however, Northern Ireland's Social Development Minister has since confirmed that changes will be made to the application procedures for street trading licences, which are granted by local councils and the type of street trading allowed. At the time of publication the Secretary of State had not published any Guidance on the application of the PA 1871.

SUNDAY TRADING

Introduction

11.97 The Sunday Trading Act 1994 ('STA 1994') was enacted to reform the complex rules in relation to Sunday trading. The STA 1994 does not apply to Scotland or Northern Ireland.

Offences

11.98 The principal offence created by the STA 1994 is one of unlawful Sunday trading[1]. Although the offence is summary only it carries a maximum penalty of an unlimited fine. There is no specified extended time period for prosecutions so the 6-month time period for laying informations for summary offences must be observed.

[1] STA 1994, Sch 1, para 7.

11.99 The STA 1994, Sch 1, paras 2 and 7(1) provides:

2 Restrictions on Sunday opening of large shops

(1)   Subject to sub-paragraphs (2) and (3) below, a large shop shall not be open on Sunday for the serving of retail customers.

(2)   Sub-paragraph (1) above does not apply in relation to—

    (a)   any of the shops mentioned in paragraph 3(1) below, or

    (b)   any shop in respect of which a notice under paragraph 8(1) of Schedule 2 to this Act (shops occupied by persons observing the Jewish Sabbath) has effect.

(3)   Sub-paragraph (1) above does not apply in relation to the opening of a large shop during any continuous period of six hours on a Sunday beginning no earlier than 10 am and ending no later than 6 pm, but this sub-paragraph has effect subject to sub-paragraph (4) below.

(4)   The exemption conferred by sub-paragraph (3) above does not apply where the Sunday is Easter Day.

(5)   Nothing in this paragraph applies where the Sunday is Christmas Day (the opening of large shops on Christmas Day being prohibited by section 1 of the Christmas Day (Trading) Act 2004).

. . .

7 Offences

(1)   If paragraph 2(1) above is contravened in relation to a shop, the occupier of the shop shall be liable on summary conviction to a fine.

Other offences

11.100 Other offences under the STA 1994:

- STA 1994, Sch 1, para 7(2) creates an offence of failure to display a STA 1994, Sch 1, para 4 notice (a notice inside and outside a large shop detailing the permitted Sunday opening hours) which is punishable by a fine (maximum level 2 on the standard scale).

- STA 1994, Sch 2, para 8(10) creates an offence of making a false statement in a notice of intention to keep a shop closed on the Jewish Sabbath. This is punishable by a fine.

- STA 1994, Sch 3, para 9 creates an offence of the occupier of a large shop, loading or unloading on a Sunday morning before 9am, without local authority consent which is punishable by a fine.

STA 1994, Sch 2, Pt II, para 8:

8 Shops occupied by persons observing the Jewish Sabbath

(1)   A person of the Jewish religion who is the occupier of a large shop may give to the local authority for the area in which the shop is situated a notice signed by him stating—
(a)   that he is a person of the Jewish religion, and
(b)   that he intends to keep the shop closed for the serving of customers on the Jewish Sabbath.

Defences

11.101   STA 1994, Sch 1, para 8:

8 The half hour defence

Where a person is charged with having contravened paragraph 2(1) above, in relation to a large shop which was permitted to be open for the serving of retail customers on the Sunday in question, by reason of his having served a retail customer after the end of the period during which the shop is permitted to be open by virtue of paragraph 2(3) above, it shall be a defence to prove that the customer was in the shop before the end of that period and left not later than half an hour after the end of that period.

STA 1994, Sch 2, paras 5–7:

5 Offences due to the act or default of another

Where the commission by any person of an offence under this Act is due to the act or default of some other person, that other person shall be guilty of the offence, and a person may be charged with and convicted of the offence by virtue of this paragraph whether or not proceedings are taken against the first-mentioned person.

6 Offences by body corporates

(1)   Where an offence under this Act committed by a body corporate is proved to have been committed with the consent or connivance of, or to be attributable to any neglect on the part of, any director, manager, secretary or other similar officer of the body corporate, or any person who was purporting to act in any such capacity, he as well as the body corporate shall be guilty of the offence and shall be liable to be proceeded against and punished accordingly.

. . .

7 Defence of due diligence

(1)   In any proceedings for an offence under this Act it shall, subject to sub-paragraph (2) below, be a defence for the person charged to prove that he took all reasonable precautions and exercised all due diligence to avoid the commission of the offence by himself or by a person under his control.
(2)   If in any case the defence provided by sub-paragraph (1) above involves the allegation that the commission of the offence was due to the act or default of another person, the person charged shall not, without leave of the court, be entitled to rely on that defence unless, at least seven clear days before the hearing, he has served on the prosecutor a notice in writing giving such information identifying or assisting in the identification of that other person as was then in his possession.

The burden of proving this defence is on the defendant to the civil standard.

Definitions within the STA 1994

11.102 The definitions are provided in the STA 1994, Sch 1:

- 'shop' means any premises where there is carried on a trade or business consisting wholly or mainly of the sale of goods;
- 'large shop' means a shop which has a relevant floor area exceeding 280 square metres;
- 'relevant floor area', in relation to a shop, means the internal floor area of so much of the shop as consists of or is comprised in a building, but excluding any part of the shop which, throughout the week ending with the Sunday in question, is used neither for the serving of customers in connection with the sale of goods nor for the display of goods.

11.103 The definition of 'relevant floor area' is rather ambiguous and has been the subject of litigation. It is commercially advantageous for a shop to fall outside the definition of a 'large shop' and there has been some wrangling over the floor areas that can be legitimately excluded. The essence of the definition is the 'internal' floor area comprised in a building:

(a) The internal floor area of part of a shop that has been temporarily closed should be included in the definition. A retailer cannot avoid the legislation by closing part of a 'large shop' on a Sunday, so that the remaining part that is open to the public is then smaller than 280 square metres. In *Haskins Garden Centres v East Dorset District Council*[1], the main building of the garden centre had been closed, leaving a smaller covered area open. The Divisional Court held that the shop was a 'large shop' despite the part of the building that was open having a floor area of less than 280 square metres. On the rationale of *Haskins*, if the relevant floor area of a shop is over 280 square metres during weekdays, the shop will be a 'large shop' on a Sunday.

(b) The external area of a shop, which is not 'internal floor area . . . comprised in a building' shall be excluded from the definition. Areas that are not comprised within a building fall outside the definition, such that a garden centre consisting of a building with less than 280 square metres of floor space would fall outside the definition, even if it was built on 100 acres of land, as long as the land did not comprise of buildings with a floor space that would aggregate to greater than 280 square metres.

(c) Parts of the shop that are used for the sale of meals, refreshments or intoxicating liquor[2] are excluded. The area used for customer restaurant or food takeaway area, is therefore excluded from the relevant floor space.

(d) Areas that are not[3] used for 'serving customers in connection with the sale of goods' or for the 'display of goods' are excluded from the relevant floor area. Whereas an area used for the display of goods can be readily identified, the definition of an area used for serving customers is not as simple. It is tolerably clear that areas such as staff and customer amenity rooms would be excluded[4] It is less clear whether area used solely for the storage of goods are excluded from the definition. It depends upon whether a storage area is used for 'serving' customers. There is no definition of 'serving' in the STA 1994 and the ordinary meaning of the word includes attending to a customer and supplying him with goods[5].

There is no requirement that a serving area is one that the public have access to, and when a sales assistant goes to a storage area to collect requested goods, that is an area used for serving the customer that is connected with the sale of goods[6].

1   [1998] NPC 75, DC.
2   STA 1994, Sch 1, para 1 Interpretation of 'sale of goods'.
3   '. . . throughout the week ending with the Sunday in question'.
4   Staff rooms, staff canteens, staff or customer toilets, customer lounges, customer care facilities, playrooms etc.
5   OED definition of 'serving' includes 'supply goods to a customer'.
6   STA 1994, Sch 1, para 1.

'For the serving of retail customers'

11.104 A 'retail customer' is defined in the STA 1994 to mean, 'a person who purchases goods retail'; and a 'retail sale' means 'any sale other than a sale for use or resale in the course of a trade or business'[1]. The STA 1994 does not apply therefore to shops selling only to trade customers and to any businesses that supply only a service, rather than goods. The definition of 'shop' (wholly or mainly the sale of goods) prevents the STA 1994 applying to a business that principally supplies a service, which incidentally includes the supply of goods as a minor part of the service.

1   STA 1994, Sch 1, para 1.

The paragraph 3 exemptions

11.105 The legislation does not apply to any of the shops referred to in para 3 of Sch 1 to the STA 1994[1] which are laid out below. In determining whether a shop falls within the definitions provided, consideration should be given to the nature of the trade or business that is carried on during the week[2].

3 Exemptions

(1)   The shops referred to in paragraph 2(2)(a) above are—
　　(a)   any shop which is at a farm and where the trade or business carried on consists wholly or mainly of the sale of produce from that farm,
　　(b)   any shop where the trade or business carried on consists wholly or mainly of the sale of alcohol,
　　(c)   any shop where the trade or business carried on consists wholly or mainly of the sale of any one or more of the following—
　　　　(i)   motor supplies and accessories, and
　　　　(ii)   cycle supplies and accessories,
　　(d)   any shop which—
　　　　(i)   is a registered pharmacy, and
　　　　(ii)   is not open for the retail sale of any goods other than medicinal products, veterinary medicinal products and medical and surgical appliances,
　　(e)   any shop at a designated airport which is situated in a part of the airport to which sub-paragraph (3) below applies,
　　(f)   any shop in a railway station,
　　(g)   any shop at a service area within the meaning of the Highways Act 1980,
　　(h)   any petrol filling station,

(i) any shop which is not open for the retail sale of any goods other than food, stores or other necessaries required by any person for a vessel or aircraft on its arrival at, or immediately before its departure from, a port, harbour or airport, and

(j) any stand used for the retail sale of goods during the course of an exhibition.

(2) In determining whether a shop falls within sub-paragraph (1)(a), (b) or (c) above, regard shall be had to the nature of the trade or business carried on there on weekdays as well as to the nature of the trade or business carried on there on Sunday.

(3) This sub-paragraph applies to every part of a designated airport, except any part which is not ordinarily used by persons travelling by air to or from the airport.

(4) In this paragraph *"designated airport"* means an airport designated for the purposes of this paragraph by an order made by the Secretary of State, as being an airport at which there appears to him to be a substantial amount of international passenger traffic.

¹ STA 1994, Sch 1, para 2(2)(a).
² STA 1994, Sch 1, para 3(2).

Enforcement powers

11.106 The STA 1994, Sch 2, paras 3 (powers of entry) and 4 (obstruction of inspectors) have been repealed and replaced with powers in the Consumer Rights Act 2015. The STA 1994, Sch 1 contains the 'Restrictions on Sunday opening of large shops'. The STA 1994, Sch 3 contains the provisions regarding 'Loading and unloading at large shops on a Sunday morning' and Pt II concerns 'Shops occupied by persons occupying the Jewish Sabbath'. Investigatory powers are now covered in CHAPTER 4, Criminal Enforcement.

TEXTILE PRODUCTS

11.107 The Textile Products (Labelling and Fibre Composition) Regulations 2012¹ were made under the European Communities Act 1972. They came into force on 8 May 2012 and replace the Textile Products (Indications of Fibre Content) Regulations 1986 in their entirety. Products are excluded from the scope of the Regulations if they were placed on the market in the UK before 8 May 2012, remain available on the market in the UK until 9 November 2014 and complied with the 1986 Regulations as amended (reg 1)).

¹ SI 2012/1102.

11.108 The Regulations require any person who makes a textile product¹ available on the market in the UK to ensure that their product meets the requirements set out in Sch 2.

¹ As defined by Art 3(1)(a) of Regulation (EU) No 1007/2011.

11.109 It is an offence for any person to make a product available on the market in the UK in breach of Sch 2 (reg 5(1)) unless they are either a person working in their home, to whom products are contracted out or an independent firm that carries out work from materials supplied without property being transferred for consideration (reg 5(2)(a)); or, a self-employed tailor making up customised products (reg 5(2)(b)). An offence under reg 5 is triable either way and subject to a fine. The Regulations provide for a due diligence defence (reg 10) and, subject to it, the person as a result of whose acts or omissions the offence was committed, will be guilty of that offence (reg 9). The Department of Business Innovation and Skills[1] ('BIS') issued guidance notes to business on the Regulations in July 2012. Enforcement powers are now covered by the CRA 2015, Sch 5; see CHAPTER 4, Criminal Enforcement.

[1] Now the Department of Business Energy and Industrial Strategy.

TICKET RESELLING

Introduction

11.110 With few exceptions (such as the offence for an unauthorised person to sell or otherwise dispose of a ticket for a designated football match under the Criminal Justice and Public Order Act 1994) the law in the UK does not generally prohibit the re-sale of event tickets. Secondary ticket platforms may be simply described as a means by which individuals or businesses can re-sell tickets they have bought from 'authorised' sellers – often at a different price to the face value of the ticket.

11.111 Significant problems have arisen in the secondary ticketing market due to the rise of traders purchasing tickets using 'bot' technology and bulk buying techniques. The consequence is that tickets sell out very quickly on primary sites only to reappear, sometimes within minutes, on secondary platforms at prices vastly higher than the face value of the ticket. In May 2016 *the Guardian* newspaper reported that tickets for Adele at the O2 with a face value of £85 were being advertised on a secondary ticketing marketplace for £22,000 (£24,840 once fees were included). The market is dominated by four main secondary ticketing platforms, and 'genuine fan-to-fan' sites which will only allow the re-sale of tickets at face value are often overlooked by purchasers.

11.112 In May 2015 the CMA obtained undertakings from the four main secondary ticketing platforms by which they agreed to build upon existing practices and give improved information to buyers about the listed tickets. In the same month the CMA published an open letter to business sellers reminding them of their obligations and pointing out that if a secondary ticketing platform prevented them from being in compliance, for example, by not providing the opportunity to make sure purchasers were aware they were a trader then they should consider only using platforms which did.

11.113 In furtherance of the CRA 2015, s 94(3) a comprehensive review on the secondary ticketing market was commissioned and 'The Waterson Review' was published in May 2016. This highlighted the lack of knowledge amongst purchasers as to the difference between primary and secondary ticket sites. The CMA published a response to the Waterson Review in March 2017 and then issued a press release on the 28 November 2017 stating that enforcement action would be taken against secondary ticketing websites in respect of breaches of legislation.

11.114 National Trading Standards began an investigation and on the 13 December 2017 issued a press release that raids had been conducted at a number of properties across the UK and four people had been arrested under suspicion of breaches of the Consumer Protection from Unfair Trading Regulations 2008[1].

[1] SI 2008/1277.

11.115 On 28 April 2018, the CMA announced that three of the four main secondary ticketing platforms had formally committed to ensuring better information was given about tickets being resold through their platforms. The CMA notified the fourth platform, Viagogo, that it would take action through the courts unless their concerns are promptly and satisfactorily addressed. An enforcement order pursuant to Pt 8 of the Enterprise Act 2002 was obtained on the 27 November 2018. On the 5 March 2019 the CMA warned Viagogo that it was still not compliant with the court order requiring information to be displayed about the tickets listed for re-sale on its site. Action for contempt of court was contemplated. On 5 September 2019, the CMA was satisfied that Viagogo had addressed the concerns about how information was presented to customers, and suspended court action. Independent reviews of Viagogo's website are ongoing until 2023.

11.116 On 16 August 2021, the CMA published recommendations to government to improve consumer protection in the online secondary tickets market. These recommendations included:

- A ban on platforms allowing resellers to sell more tickets for an event than they can legally buy from the primary market;
- Ensuring platforms are fully responsible for incorrect information about tickets that are listed for sale on their websites; and
- A new system of licensing for platforms that sell secondary tickets that would enable sanctions such as taking down websites, withdrawing a business's right to operate in the sector, and the imposition of substantial fines.

11.117 A Government press release issued on the 31 December 2017 announced new regulations to be made under the Digital Economy Act 2017, s 106. These regulations, entitled The Breaching of Limits on Ticket Sales Regulations 2018[1], apply where tickets for a recreational, sporting or cultural event in the UK are offered for sale; a purchase may be made wholly or partly by a process completed using an electronic communications network or service; and the offer is subject to conditions that limit the number of tickets a purchaser may buy. The regulations create a criminal offence where a person uses anything that enables or facilitates completion of any part of the process with intent to obtain tickets in excess of a limit imposed by the conditions of sale. The offence is triable summarily and punishable by an unlimited fine only in England and Wales and a fine up to £50,000 in Scotland. The new regulations came into force on the 5 July 2018.

[1] SI 2018/735.

11.118 Regulations 3 and 4 of the Breaching of Limits on Ticket Sales Regulations 2018 provide:

3.   It is an offence for a person to—
    (a)   use software that is designed to enable or facilitate completion of any part of a process within regulation 2(b); and
    (b)   do so with intent to obtain tickets in excess of the sales limit, with a view to any person obtaining financial gain.
4.   For the purposes of regulation 3 it does not matter whether the offer in regulation 2(a) is made, or anything is done to obtain tickets, in or outside the United Kingdom.

11.119

Precedent for using software to exceed ticket sales limit

Information

A B, on [date], with a view to obtaining a financial gain and with intent to obtain tickets, namely [. . .] in excess of the sales limit, used software designed to enable or facilitate completion of any part of the process for purchasing the tickets using an electronic communications network or an electronic communications service, contrary to Regulation 3 of the Breaching of Limits on Ticket Sales Regulations 2018.

Secondary ticketing

11.120 Chapter 5 of Pt 3 (ss 90–95) of and Sch 10 to CRA 2015 regulate online secondary ticketing marketplaces where tickets for sporting, recreational and cultural events are re-sold. They set out:
(i)   details of information to be provided when a ticket is offered for re-sale;
(ii)   certain protections that will apply to the re-sale of tickets;
(iii)   the duty to report criminal activity;
(iv)   the requirement for a review to be established to consider the consumer protection measures in relation to the secondary ticketing market;
(v)   provisions for enforcement by local weights and measures authorities and the imposition of financial penalties.

11.121 Chapter 5 of Pt 3 was brought into force on 27 May 2015[1]. The Order also brought into force on the same date the investigatory powers provisions (contained in CRA 2015, s 77 and Sch 5 in relation to the enforcement of this area) and Sch 10 which deals with financial penalties. See CHAPTER 4, Criminal Enforcement for details of the investigatory powers provisions. Consumer Rights Act: Secondary Ticketing Guidance for Business ('BIS Guidance') was published in May 2015 and an independent review of consumer protection measures concerning online secondary ticketing facilities was published in May 2016 (Professor Michael Waterson).

[1]   Consumer Rights Act 2015 (Commencement No 1) Order 2015, SI 2015/1333.

Duty to provide information about tickets

11.122 The CRA 2015, s 90 applies where a person re-sells a ticket for a recreational, sporting or cultural event in the United Kingdom through a 'secondary ticketing facility', which means 'an internet-based facility for the resale of tickets for recreational, sporting or cultural events' (CRA 2015, s 95). This includes both ordinary consumers selling on a ticket they no longer want and traders who operate as more frequent re-sellers of tickets. The buyer of the ticket must be given the information specified, where this is applicable to the ticket.

11.123 The information that is required is the detail of the seat itself (including the name of the area in which the seat or standing area is located, information to identify the part of that area, the row and precise seat number); any restriction which limits use of the ticket to persons of a particular description (for example students, wheelchair user); the face value of the ticket – namely the price stated on the ticket. In addition, under the CRA 2015, s 90(6) the buyer must be told where the seller is in fact the secondary ticketing facility operator (or connected in certain ways to that operator), or the organiser of the event itself. A new provision was added to by the Digital Economy Act 2017, s 90 which provides that where a Unique Ticket Number is provided this must also be given to the purchaser. The required information must be given in a clear and comprehensible manner, and before the buyer is bound by the contract for the sale of the ticket.

11.124 The provision of this information does not exhaust the legal responsibility of the seller and platform to provide information, since they will have further duties under the Consumer Protection from Unfair Trading Regulations 2008[1] and under the Consumer Contracts (Information, Cancellation and Additional Charges) Regulations 2013[2]. These duties are likely to require them to reveal where a seller is acting for business purposes, state other 'material information' that the consumer needs to take an informed transactional decision – such as where a ticket holder will only be allowed to enter if they bring additional id- and provide a fully inclusive price from the outset of the booking process.

[1]   SI 2008/1277.
[2]   SI 2013/3134.

11.125 In March 2018 the ASA upheld complaints against GETMEIN, Stubhub, Viagogo and Seatwave. The CAP Code rules on misleading advertising and pricing required that, to avoid misleading consumers, quoted prices must include non-optional taxes and fees that applied to all or most buyers and should also state the applicable delivery fee except where those fees could not be calculated in advance. These are the fixed fees which apply for every sale and are the same for every sale, eg the postage costs. They found that the presentation of the pricing information concerning the additional ticket fees and charges was misleading. In all cases the ticket price did not include booking and delivery fees at the outset[1].

[1]   https://www.asa.org.uk/codes-and-rulings/rulings.html?q=secondary+ticketing.

11.126 The duty to provide the information required under the CRA 2015, s 90 rests on both the seller of the ticket and the operator of the facility. This means the platform will need to take some proactive steps to ensure the information is provided and is accurate. According to the undertakings given to the CMA by three of the major platforms, this includes not only ensuring that sellers are able to upload the correct information, but also carrying out their own pre-set up checks when creating an event page, conducting regular auto-mated checks of the information being uploaded by sellers, and taking steps to remove content that is non-compliant. These undertakings were given under Pt 8 of the Enterprise Act 2002, which is one means to enforce the secondary ticketing provisions (since they are listed as domestic infringements). Where enforcement takes place under the CRA itself, the secondary ticketing facility may benefit from a defence, where the information uploaded is inaccurate, on the basis that it was supplied to them by the seller, and the platform took all reasonable precautions and exercised all due diligence to avoid the breach. It is arguable that steps which fall short of the undertakings given to the CMA would not be sufficient to prove the defence.

11.127 In *Viagogo AG v Competitions and Markets Authority*[1] the claimant applied for declarations that it was complying with its obligations under certain clauses in a consent enforcement order. The company had complied with its obligations to supply information to customers about the face value of tickets. Although customers were required to hover their mouse cursors over an icon on the company's website to make the information visible, the order expressly permitted that method of display. The same could not be said for the display of information about the company's guarantee, which, absent an express provision to the contrary, had to be prominently displayed without requiring customers to take any action to access it.

[1]   [2019] EWHC 1706 (Ch).

Prohibition on cancellation or blacklisting

11.128 The CRA 2015, s 91, which applies in the same circumstances as the CRA 2015, s 90, provides that an event organiser cannot cancel a ticket merely because it is re-sold or offered for re-sale; nor may an organiser blacklist a person who re-sells or offers to re-sell a ticket. The BIS Guidance on the CRA 2015, s 91 states:

> 'This restriction (on cancellation and blacklisting) will always apply unless the event organiser has met two conditions:
> (i)   It must have been clearly set out as a term of the contract under which the original buyer purchased the ticket from the event organiser that cancellation of the ticket and/or blacklisting of the seller may occur as a consequence of that ticket being resold or offered for resale.
> (ii)   The term of the contract under which the original buyer purchased the ticket from the event organiser must not be unfair . . . This is a significant requirement. Contract law ordinarily allows a purchaser to transfer to someone else what they have bought. Terms that prohibit resale are considered to be open to scrutiny for fairness and therefore must meet the principles of fair and open dealing, ensuring that their substance, expression and use respects consumers' legitimate interests. Those terms which are not fair cannot be enforced against a consumer.'

Duty to report criminal activity

11.129 The CRA 2015, s 92 requires an operator of a secondary ticketing facility, who knows that a person has used or is using the facility in such a way that an offence has been or is being committed, and the offence relates to the re-sale of a ticket for a recreational, sporting or cultural event in the UK, to disclose certain matters to 'an appropriate person' (the police) and an organiser of the event. This would therefore apply to situations where, for example, the fraudulent sale of non-existent tickets is taking place.

Enforcement of Chapter 5

11.130 The CRA 2015, s 93 provides:

(1) A local weights and measures authority in Great Britain may enforce the provisions of this Chapter in its area.

(2) The Department of Enterprise, Trade and Investment may enforce the provisions of this Chapter in Northern Ireland.

(3) Each of the bodies referred to in subsections (1) and (2) is an "enforcement authority" for the purposes of this Chapter.

11.131 An enforcement authority, if is satisfied on the balance of probabilities that a person has breached a duty or prohibition imposed by Chapter 5, may impose a financial penalty, not exceeding £5,000, on the person in respect of that breach (CRA 2015, s 93(4)) but a 'due diligence' defence applies in relation to a breach of either CRA 2015, ss 90 or 91 (CRA 2015, s 93(5)). The CRA 2015, Sch 10 provides a detailed procedure to be followed when issuing financial penalties including service of notices and the right to make representations. It also lays out the provisions relating to appeals against financial penalties.

CRA 2015, Sch 10, Pt 5 provides:

(1) A person on whom a final notice is served may appeal against that notice—

    (a) in England and Wales and Scotland, to the First-tier Tribunal;
    (b) in Northern Ireland, to a county court.

(2) The grounds for an appeal under this paragraph are that—

    (a) the decision to impose a financial penalty was based on an error of fact,
    (b) the decision was wrong in law,
    (c) the amount of the financial penalty is unreasonable, or
    (d) the decision was unreasonable for any other reason.

(3) If a person appeals under this paragraph, the final notice is suspended until the appeal is finally determined or withdrawn.

(4) On an appeal under this paragraph the First-tier Tribunal or the court may quash, confirm or vary the final notice.

(5) The final notice may not be varied under sub-paragraph (4) so as to make it impose a financial penalty of more than £5,000.

As it can be seen one of the grounds for appeal is that the financial penalty was unreasonable. This suggests that consideration should be given to the amount of any penalty to be imposed rather than imposing a blanket £5000 in every case. The latest guidance under the CRA 2015 published in February 2018 states 'The enforcer will assess on a case-by-case basis what constitutes a breach (eg failure to provide information on each ticket or a single listing) and the appropriate size of any fine'.

11.132 The importance of complying with time limits was outlined in *World-wide Tickets Limited v North Yorkshire CC*[1]. A local authority's service of formal requests for information that had already been received informally did not restart the clock with regard to the statutory time limit of six months within which to serve Notices of Intent under the Consumer Rights Act 2015, Sch 10, para 1(2). In setting penalties at the statutory maximum, the local authority had not had the power to take into consideration historic breaches of the secondary ticketing legislation so its action had been procedurally unfair, particularly as those historic breaches had not been notified to the recipients.

[1]   [2019] 4 WLUK 418.

TRADE DESCRIPTIONS

Introduction

11.133 The offence provisions of the Trade Descriptions Act 1968 ('TDA 1968') were substantially repealed by the Consumer Protection from Unfair Trading Regulations 2008[1] ('CPUTR 2008') but other provisions continue to apply to legislation such as the Hallmarking Act 1973, the Crystal Glass (Descriptions) Regulations 1973[2], the Textile Products (Indications of Fibre Content) Regulations 2012[3], and the Footwear (Indication of Composition) Labelling Regulations 1995[4]. A considerable body of case law has been established under the TDA 1968; however, that has relevance to other legislation.

[1]   SI 2008/1277.
[2]   SI 1973/1952.
[3]   SI 2012/1102.
[4]   SI 1995/2489.

Territorial jurisdiction

11.134 The TDA 1968 is applicable throughout the United Kingdom.

Offences

11.135 The only remaining offences are contained in TDA 1968, s 12 (False representations as to royal approval or award, etc) which is amended by the addition of TDA 1968, s 12(3) and now states:

12 False representations as to royal approval or award, etc
(1)   If any person, in the course of any trade or business, gives, by whatever means, any false indication, direct or indirect, that any goods or services supplied by him or any methods adopted by him are or are of a kind supplied to or approved by Her Majesty or any member of the Royal Family, he shall, subject to the provisions of this Act, be guilty of an offence.
(2)   If any person, in the course of any trade or business, uses, without the authority of Her Majesty, any device or emblem signifying the Queen's Award to Industry or anything so nearly resembling such a device or emblem as to be likely to deceive, he shall, subject to the provisions of this Act, be guilty of an offence.

(3)   A person shall not be guilty of an offence under subsection (1) or (2) by reason of doing anything that is a commercial practice unless the commercial practice is unfair.

In this subsection "commercial practice" and "unfair" have the same meaning as in the Consumer Protection from Unfair Trading Regulations 2008.

11.136 When Royal Patronage is granted, for instance a Tradesmen's Warrant, the Royal Arms may be displayed in circumstances laid down in the Lord Chamberlain's Rules for holders of a Tradesmen's Warrant. However, they may not be used as a trade mark and should only be displayed for the duration of the grant of a Royal Warrant.

Defences

11.137 The TDA 1968, s 24(1) provides a defence where the defendant can show that the offence was caused by a mistake, or reliance on information supplied to him, or the act or default of any other person, or an accident, or some other cause beyond his control *and* that he took all reasonable precautions *and* exercised all due diligence to avoid the offence. The TDA 1968, s 25 provides a defence where the allegation is of an offence committed by the publication of an advertisement. It is a defence for the defendant to show that he is a person whose business is to publish or arrange for the publication of advertisements *and* that the advertisement in question was received in the ordinary course of business *and* that he did not know *and* had no reason to suspect that its publication would amount to an offence under the TDA 1968. Statutory defences of this nature are considered in detail in Chapter 4, Criminal Enforcement.

Restrictions on proceedings

Time limits

11.138 The TDA 1968, s 19 makes provision as to the time limit for prosecutions under the Act:

19 Time limit for prosecutions
(1)   No prosecution for an offence under this Act shall be commenced after the expiration of three years from the commission of the offence or one year from its discovery by the prosecutor, whichever is the earlier.
(2)   Notwithstanding anything in section 127(1) of the Magistrates' Courts Act 1980, a magistrates' court may try an information for an offence under this Act if the information was laid at any time within twelve months from the commission of the offence.
(3)   Notwithstanding anything in section 23 of the Summary Jurisdiction (Scotland) Act 1954 (limitation of time for proceedings in statutory offences) summary proceedings in Scotland for an offence under this section may be commenced at any time within twelve months from the time when the offence was committed, and subsection (2) of the said section 23 shall apply for the purposes of this subsection as it applies for the purposes of that section.
(4)   Subsections (2) and (3) of this section do not apply where—

(a)   the offence was committed by the making of an oral statement . . .

The importance of compliance with the requirements of the Criminal Procedure Rules ('Crim PR') r 7.2 whereby it is mandatory to ensure that on application for a summons that compliance with the times limits is 'demonstrated' were the subject of the case of *Food Standards Agency v Bakers of Nailsea Limited*[1].

1   [2020] EWHC 3632 (Admin).

11.139 In relation to Scotland it is worth noting the comments of Lord Justice General Hope in *Hamilton v HM Advocate*[1]: 'No analogy can usefully be drawn as to what may be the correct application of the wording of the TDA 1968, s 19(1) to Scottish procedure for what may happen south of the border' and the fact that time limits for offences are also covered by the Criminal Procedure (Scotland) Act 1995. No prosecution for an offence under the TDA 1968 may be commenced more than 3 years from the commission of the offence or more than 1 year after its discovery by the prosecutor, whichever is the earlier[2]. The shorter time limit in the case of an offence allegedly committed by the making of an oral statement apparently provided by the TDA 1968, s 19(4) has been held to be of no effect since the passing of the Magistrates' Courts Act 1980[3]. Time limits are considered in detail in CHAPTER 4, Criminal Enforcement.

1   1997 SLT 31 at pp 34G–34H.
2   TDA 1968, s 19(1).
3   *R v Dacorum Magistrates ex p Michael Gardner* (1985) 149 JP 677 (transcript CO/1219/84).

11.140 Although the TDA 1968, s 19(4)(b) and (c) were repealed by CPUTR 2008 they continue to have effect for certain legislation made under the European Communities Act 1972[1].

19 Time limit for prosecutions
    (4) Subsections (2) and (3) of this section do not apply where—

        (b) the offence was one of supplying goods to which a false trade description is applied, and the trade description was applied by an oral statement; or
        (c) the offence was one where a false trade description is deemed to have been applied to goods by virtue of section 4(3) of this Act and the goods were supplied in pursuance of an oral request.

1   CPUTR 2008, SI 2008/1277, Sch 3, para 2.

Prosecutions

11.141 Any person, other than the Crown, may be prosecuted for an offence under the Act. This includes both individuals and bodies corporate.

Directors' liability

11.142 The TDA 1968, s 20 provides:

20 Offences by corporations
    (1)   Where an offence under this Act which has been committed by a body corporate is proved to have been committed with the consent and connivance of, or to be attributable to any neglect on the part of, any director, manager, secretary or other similar officer of the body corporate, or any person who was purporting to act in any such capacity, he as well as the body corporate shall be guilty of that offence and shall be liable to be proceeded against and punished accordingly.

(2)   In this section "director", in relation to anybody corporate established by or under any enactment for the purpose of carrying on under national ownership any industry or part of an industry or undertaking, being a body corporate whose affairs are managed by the members thereof, means a member of that body corporate.

The liability of directors etc is considered in detail in CHAPTER **4**, Criminal Enforcement.

Causal liability

11.143 The TDA 1968, s 23 provides

23 Offences due to fault of other person

Where the commission by any person of an offence under this Act is due to the act or default of some other person that other person shall be guilty of the offence, and a person may be charged with and convicted of the offence by virtue of this section whether or not proceedings are taken against the first-mentioned person.

Causal liability is considered in CHAPTER **4**, Criminal Enforcement.

Duty to enforce

11.144 The TDA 1968, s 26(1) places a duty on every local 'weights and measures authority' to enforce within their area the provisions of the TDA 1968 but the section does not permit a local weights and measures authority in Scotland to institute proceedings for an offence.

Powers of enforcement officers

11.145 Enforcement powers are now covered by the CRA 2015, Sch 5, see CHAPTER **4**, Criminal Enforcement.

Sentencing

11.146 The TDA 1968, s 18 deals with maximum sentences for offences under the TDA 1968, s 12. On summary conviction, the maximum is a fine not exceeding the prescribed sum[1]. On indictment, the maximum penalty is a fine and/or 2 years' imprisonment. It follows that the Crown Court may impose a lesser community sentence if considered appropriate. The Criminal Procedure (Scotland) Act 1995, s 238 allows for the imposition of a community service order instead of a period of imprisonment.

---

[1]   The 'prescribed sum' is now unlimited upon summary conviction in the Magistrates' Court (Magistrates' Courts Act 1980, s 32(10); Legal Aid, Sentencing and Punishment of Offenders Act 2012, s 85).

UNSOLICITED PRODUCTS

Unsolicited goods

Introduction

11.147 The Unsolicited Goods and Services Act 1971 ('UGSA 1971') was enacted to combat an unwelcome growth in the trade practice of 'inertia selling', which involved unsolicited goods being sent to consumers on a speculative basis. Typically, goods would be sent to a random consumer as an offer, with an option to return the goods within a specified period, or failing that an obligation to pay for them. A consumer who did neither would frequently be subjected to demands for payment and threats of legal action. The rights of a recipient of unsolicited goods are now dealt with by reg 27M of the CPUTR 2008 (see CHAPTER 6, Consumer Rights). Criminal liability for a trader demanding immediate or deferred payment for, or the return or safekeeping of, unsolicited products to consumers is also covered by the CPUTR 2008.

Offences

BUSINESS-TO-BUSINESS OFFENCES

11.148 The UGSA 1971, s 2 provides for business-to-business offences in relation to demands and threats regarding payment concerning unsolicited goods ('unsolicited' means, in relation to goods sent to any person, that they are sent without any prior request made by him or on his behalf). The UGSA 1971, s 2(1) makes it an offence for a person who, not having reasonable cause to believe there is a right to payment, in the course of any trade or business makes a demand for payment, or asserts a present or prospective right to payment, for what he knows are unsolicited goods sent to another person with a view to his acquiring them for the purposes of his trade or business.

11.149 In *Barking & Dagenham (LB of) v Jones* (1999/035/1) Brooke LJ observed:

' . . . Without going into the matter at any length, it appears to me that an offence of demanding payment for unsolicited goods, if made over the telephone, is committed both at the place where the demand is made and in the place where the demand is received.'

11.150 A case brought under the UGSA 1971, s 2(1) – *Eiman v London Borough of Waltham Forest*[1] – considered the issue as to whether a council worker, who, as a hobby, compiled and privately printed a book of verse in Urdu at his own expense – and sought payment for unsolicited copies – did so in the course of a trade or business. The Divisional Court did not interfere with the Crown Court's conclusion that the activity was in the course of business. Omerod LJ has opined that, in general, the word 'business' in statutes should be given its widest possible meaning so as to meet the mischief at which the legislation is aimed.

[1]   (1982) 90 ITSA MR 204.

11.151 The UGSA 1971, s 2(2) makes it an offence for a person who, not having reasonable cause to believe there is a right to payment, in the course of any trade or business and with a view to obtaining any payment for what he knows are unsolicited goods sent to another person with a view to his acquiring them for the purposes of his trade or business:

(a) threatens to bring any legal proceedings; or

(b) places or causes to be placed the name of any person on a list of defaulters or debtors or threatens to do so; or

(c) invokes or causes to be invoked any other collection procedure or threatens to do so.

BUSINESS-TO-CONSUMER OFFENCES

11.152 The Consumer Protection (Distance Selling) Regulations 2000[1] provided for business-to-consumer offences in relation to demands and threats regarding payment concerning unsolicited goods and these were worded in similar terms to the UGSA 1971, s 2 offences. However these provisions of the Regulations were revoked by the CPUTR 2008.

[1] SI 2000/2334.

11.153 Regulation 12 of the Consumer Protection from Unfair Trading Regulations 2008[1] provides that a trader is guilty of an offence if he engages in a commercial practice set out in any of paras 1–10, 12–27 and 29–31 of Sch 1 (Commercial practices which are in all circumstances considered unfair). The commercial practice in para 29 of Sch 1 is:

> Demanding immediate or deferred payment for or the return or safekeeping of products supplied by the trader, but not solicited by the consumer.

[1] SI 2008/1277.

11.154 The detailed provisions of the CPUTR 2008 are set out in CHAPTER **8**, Unfair Commercial Practices.

Reasonable cause to believe there is a right to payment

11.155 As the burden of proof on this issue has not been statutorily placed upon the defence, it is for the prosecution to discharge it to the criminal standard. Whether the sender has a reasonable cause to believe there is a right to payment is a question of fact. It is however, an objective question and it is submitted that a seller's mistaken understanding of his legal rights would not amount to a reasonable cause; which would be contrary to the policy of UGSA 1971.

11.156 A mistaken understanding of the facts, as opposed to the law, was considered in *Readers Digest Association v Pirie*[1] which concerned the billing for copies of a magazine sent to customers after they had cancelled their subscriptions by letter. A junior employee at the company had failed to enter the cancellations onto computer records and the bills had been sent out in error. The High Court of Justiciary decided that it had not been proven that the company did not have a reasonable belief that there was a right to payment. Lord Kissen opined that there could be no breach, 'if the person in question had an honest belief which was based on circumstances which would lead an ordinary prudent man to the same conclusion'.

¹   1973 SLT 170.

11.157 The rationale of the decision in *Readers Digest* was that the company had established a system that would ordinarily have prevented the unwarranted demands for payment. There had been nothing to indicate that the system was not functioning properly and liable to cause mistakes. It was therefore not unreasonable for the company to rely upon the accuracy of the system. The defender in *Readers Digest* was the company and the analysis must be on the basis of whether the company had reasonable cause to believe. The fact that a junior employee had no reasonable cause to believe the company had a right to payment was not enough to make the company liable. This approach reflects decisions in other trading standards areas about the nature of corporate liability when there is a mental element to the offence.

Territorial jurisdiction

11.158 The parts of UGSA 1971 relating to unsolicited goods apply to Great Britain.

Defences

11.159 There are no statutory defences to the offences in UGSA 1971, s 2.

Restrictions on proceedings

11.160 The offences in UGSA 1971, s 2 are summary only – there is therefore a 6-month time limit, from the time when the offence was committed (see Magistrates' Courts Act 1980, s 127). In Scotland, as the offences in UGSA 1971, s 2 can only be tried under summary procedure, the time limits are established under the Criminal Procedure (Scotland) Act 1995, s 136 – within 6 months after the contravention occurred.

Prosecutions

11.161 The nature of the offences in UGSA 1971, s 2 mean that, for the most part, prosecutions will be brought against principals of businesses or corporate bodies.

11.162 The UGSA 1971, s 5 permits the prosecution and conviction of any 'director, manager, secretary or other similar officer' of a company or 'any person who was purporting to act in such a capacity' where an offence under the UGSA 1971 has been committed by the company 'with the consent and connivance' of that person or as a result of that person's neglect. Where the affairs of the body corporate are managed by its members, the provisions apply in relation to the acts and defaults of 'a member in connection with his functions of management as if he were a director of the body corporate'. Directors' liability is considered in detail in CHAPTER 4, Criminal Enforcement.

Sentencing

11.163 A person guilty of a UGSA 1971, s 2(1) offence is liable to a fine not exceeding level 4 on the standard scale and a person guilty of a UGSA 1971, s 2(2) offence is liable to an unlimited fine[1].

[1]   Legal Aid, Sentencing and Punishment of Offenders Act 2012, s 85.

Unsolicited directory entries

Introduction

11.164 Other than the provision relating to the non-application of UGSA 1971 prior to its commencement (UGSA 1971, s 3(4)), the entire provisions of the Act relating to unsolicited directory entries have been amended, at least once, since it was enacted. The provisions apply to charging for the inclusion in a directory of entry relating to a person or his trade or business. Unless the provisions of UGSA 1971 are complied with, a person has no liability to make any payment and is entitled to recover any payment made. The definition of 'directory' under UGSA 1971, s 3 has been considered in civil proceedings in *Re Supporting Link Alliance Ltd*[1]. There, annual business guides, in which the company had sold advertising space through cold calling, were held not to be 'directories' on the basis that the editorial content was not a list of people or things listed by reference to any category or in any order, alphabetical or otherwise.

[1]   [2004] 1 WLR 1549.

11.165 Four methods of legitimately charging for a directory entry are specified UGSA 1971, s 3(1)(a)–(d):
(a)   where there has been signed by the purchaser or on his behalf an order complying with UGSA 1971, s 3(3)(a); or
(b)   where there has been signed by the purchaser or on his behalf a note complying with UGSA 1971, s 3(3)(b) of his agreement to the charge and before the note was signed, a copy of it was supplied, for retention by him, to him or a person acting on his behalf; or
(c)   where there has been transmitted by the purchaser or a person acting on his behalf an electronic communication which includes a statement that the purchaser agrees to the charge and the relevant condition is satisfied in relation to that communication; or
(d)   where the charge arises under a contract in relation to which the conditions set out in UGSA 1971, s 3B(1) – which relates to renewed and extended contracts – are met.

Territorial jurisdiction

11.166 The parts of UGSA 1971 relating to unsolicited directory entries apply to Great Britain.

Offence

11.167 The UGSA 1971, s 3(2) creates an offence in a case where a payment in respect of a charge would be recoverable from him in accordance with the terms of UGSA 1971, s 3(1), the person demands payment, or asserts a present or prospective right to payment, of the charge or any part of it, without knowing or having reasonable cause to believe that:

(a) the entry to which the charge relates was ordered in accordance with UGSA 1971, s 3(1)(a);
(b) a proper note of the agreement has been duly signed; or
(c) the requirements set out in UGSA 1971, s 3(1)(c) or (1)(d) above have been met.

Defences

11.168 There are no statutory defences to the offence in UGSA 1971, s 3(2).

Restrictions on proceedings

11.169 There are no time limit restrictions to the offence in UGSA 1971, s 3(2) as it is an either-way matter by virtue of the Unsolicited Goods and Services (Amendment) Act 1975, s 3 and no time limits are contained in UGSA 1971.

Prosecutions

11.170 The nature of the offences in UGSA 1971, s 3(2) mean that, for the most part, prosecutions will be brought against principals of businesses or corporate bodies.

11.171 The UGSA 1971, s 5 permits the prosecution and conviction of any 'director, manager, secretary or other similar officer' of a company or 'any person who was purporting to act in such a capacity' where an offence under the Act has been committed by the company 'with the consent and connivance' of that person or as a result of that person's neglect. Where the affairs of the body corporate are managed by its members, the provisions apply in relation to the acts and defaults of 'a member in connection with his functions of management as if he were a director of the body corporate'. Directors' liability is considered in detail in CHAPTER 4, Criminal Enforcement.

Sentencing

11.172 A person guilty of a UGSA 1971, s 3(2) offence punishable on summary conviction is liable to an unlimited fine. By virtue of the Unsolicited Goods and Services (Amendment) Act 1975, s 3(1) an offence under UGSA 1971, s 3(2) may be prosecuted on indictment; and a person convicted shall be liable to a fine.

Unsolicited publications

11.173 The UGSA 1971, s 4 provides:

4 Unsolicited publications
(1) A person shall be guilty of an offence if he sends or causes to be sent to another person any book, magazine or leaflet (or advertising material for any such publication) which he knows or ought reasonably to know is unsolicited and which describes or illustrates human sexual techniques.

(2)   A person found guilty of an offence under this section shall be liable on summary conviction to a fine not exceeding level 5 on the standard scale.

(3)   A prosecution for an offence under this section shall not in England and Wales be instituted except by, or with the consent of, the Director of Public Prosecutions.

11.174 In *DPP v Beate UHSE (UK) Ltd*[1] the defendant's contention was that no offence is committed under UGSA 1971, s 4 unless the advertising material itself describes or illustrates human sexual techniques. The advertising material in this case was for a catalogue that described or illustrated human sexual techniques but the advertising material itself did not give any such descriptions or illustrations. On appeal against conviction Widgery LCJ said:

'It is . . . clearly within the mischief of this legislation that there should be a prohibition of advertising material . . . even though [it] does not of itself contain a description or illustration of human sexual techniques . . . On the construction urged by the defendant . . . the reference to advertising material would be wholly unnecessary . . . because, if such material itself illustrated the technique in question, it would in any event when so illustrating those techniques come within the opening words of s 4(1)).'

[1]   [1974] 1 QB 158.

Chapter 12

ADVERTISING

Contents

INTRODUCTION

12.1 Advertising in the United Kingdom is governed by a combination of regulation and self-regulation. Self-regulation in the advertising sector dates back to the 1960s, when the advertising industry rejected calls for an American-style Federal Trade Commission to regulate advertising by statute. An official report on Consumer Protection by the Molony Committee declared:

> 'We are satisfied that the wider problem of advertising ought to be, and can be, tackled by effectively applied voluntary controls. We stress, however, that our conclusion depends on the satisfactory working of the new scheme, and in particular on the continued quality and independence of the Authority at its pinnacle[1].'

[1] Molony Committee, 'The Final report of the Committee on Consumer Protection', 1962. The Molony Committee had been set up in July, 1959, under Mr JT Molony to review existing consumer protection legislation.

12.2 The Advertising Association formed the Committee of Advertising Practice ('CAP') in 1961 and the Advertising Standards Authority ('the ASA') came into existence the following year. The ASA was tasked with overseeing the implementation of the first Code of Advertising Practice in 1962, which only covered non-broadcast advertising. Since 2004, the ASA has also been in charge of regulating certain aspects of broadcast advertising, since the Office of Communications ('Ofcom'), the communications regulator, contracted out responsibility for handling and resolving complaints relating to certain TV and radio advertisements to the ASA[1]. The advertising industry set up the Advertising Standards Board of Finance ('ASBOF') in 1974, which was to secure funding for the ASA's activities through a levy. The ASA continues to be funded by the ASBOF levy today.

1   Crucially, however, Ofcom has only contracted out powers relating to breaches of the UK Broadcast Advertising Standards Code ('BCAP') and the relevant provisions of the Medicines (Advertising) Regulations 1994, SI 1994/1932. Ofcom retains powers in relation to complaints relating to political advertising, unsuitable sponsorship, discrimination between advertisers and the scheduling of advertisements (with some exceptions). Please see: https://www.asa.org.uk/a sset/07CFEEFF-BA43-41E7-9F1615DF911A3B82/.

12.3 Legislation to tackle misleading advertising was introduced in 1988 in the form of the Control of Misleading Advertisements Regulations 1988[1] ('the 1988 Regulations'), which implemented the Directive on misleading advertising[2]. The Regulations retained the ASA's role as a non-statutory body, but enabled it, for the first time, to refer persistently non-compliant advertisers to the Director General of Fair Trading (as it then was) for legal action.

1   SI 1988/915.
2   84/450/EEC.

12.4 The 1988 Regulations have since been superseded by the Consumer Protection from Unfair Trading Regulations 2008[1] ('CPUTR 2008'), which implement the Unfair Commercial Practices Directive[2] ('UCPD'), and by the Business Protection from Misleading Marketing Regulations 2008[3] ('BPR 2008'), which implement the Directive on misleading and comparative advertising[4] ('MCAD 2006'). The UCPD regulates unfair and misleading business-to-consumer commercial practices, whilst MCAD 2006 regulates business-to-business advertising and lays down the conditions that must be satisfied in order to engage in lawful comparative advertising. The UCPD is a maximum harmonisation measure, which prevents Member States from maintaining or adopting rules that are more restrictive than those contained in it[5]. The MCAD 2006 is a maximum harmonisation measure in relation to comparative advertising, but a minimum harmonisation measure in relation to misleading advertising[6].

1   SI 2008/1277.
2   2005/29/EC Directive concerning unfair business-to-consumer commercial practices.
3   SI 2008/1276.
4   2006/114/EC.
5   This is considered further in CHAPTER 2, Interpreting Consumer Law.
6   Article 8(1) of the MCAD 2006.

CONSUMER PROTECTION FROM UNFAIR TRADING REGULATIONS 2008

12.5 The definition of 'commercial practice'[1] in the CPUTR 2008 is broad and does not require the conclusion of a transaction[2]. Accordingly, advertisements and website content that is directly connected with the promotion, sale or supply of a product to or from consumers fall within its remit. Whilst the CPUTR 2008 do cover comparative advertising (in the sense, eg that such advertising can constitute a misleading action under reg 5 or a misleading omission under reg 6[3]), the conditions for permissible comparative advertising are to be found in reg 4[4] of the BPR (see below).

[1] 'Commercial practice' is defined in the CPUTR 2008, SI 2008/1277, reg 2(1) as 'any act, omission, course of conduct, representation or commercial communication (including advertising and marketing) by a trader, which is directly connected with the promotion, sale or supply of a product to or from consumers, whether occurring before, during or after a commercial transaction (if any) in relation to a product'.

[2] See, for instance the CJEU case of *Trento Sviluppo srl and Centrale Adriatica Soc Coop arl v Autorita Garante della Concorrenza e del Mercato* (C-281/12) [2014] CTLC 326.

[3] See the express reference to comparative advertising in SI 2008/1277, regs 5(3)(a) and 6(1).

[4] SI 2008/1276, reg 4.

12.6 The main CPUTR 2008 provisions that are of relevance to advertising are misleading actions (reg 5) and misleading omissions (reg 6)[1]. These provisions are deliberately broad and likely to cover most false or deceptive advertisements made to consumers. The CPUTR 2008 is covered in detail in CHAPTER 8.

[1] For a recent CJEU case considering the interplay between the various provisions of the Unfair Commercial Practices Directive 2005, see Case C-611/14 *Canal Digital Danmark A/S*.

12.7 In addition to these provisions, Sch 1 of the CPUTR 2008[1] bans certain advertising practices outright. The provisions that are of particular importance are set out in the table below.

Provision of Schedule 1	Summary of provision
Para 5	Bait advertising[2]
Para 6	Bait and switch advertising[3]
Para 11	Using editorial content in the media to promote a product where a trader has paid for the promotion without making that clear in the content or by images or sounds clearly identifiable by the consumer (advertorial).
Para 17	Falsely claiming that a product is able to cure illnesses, dysfunction or malformations
Para 21	Including in marketing material an invoice or similar document seeking payment which gives the consumer the impression that he has already ordered the marketed product when he has not
Para 28	Including in an advertisement a direct exhortation to children to buy advertised products or persuade their parents or other adults to buy advertised products for them

[1] SI 2008/1277, Sch 1.

[2] Making an invitation to purchase products at a specified price without disclosing the existence of any reasonable grounds the trader may have for believing that he will not be able to offer for supply, or to procure another trader to supply, those products or equivalent products at that price for a period that is, and in quantities that are, reasonable having regard to the product, the scale of advertising of the product and the price offered.

[3] Making an invitation to purchase products at a specified price and then: (a) refusing to show the advertised item to consumers, (b) refusing to take orders for it or deliver it within a reasonable time, or (c) demonstrating a defective sample of it.

BUSINESS PROTECTION FROM MISLEADING MARKETING REGULATIONS 2008

12.8 The BPR came into force on 26 May 2008 and implement MCAD 2006, which seeks to protect traders from misleading advertising and identifies the circumstances in which comparative advertising is permitted, whether that advertising is aimed at consumers or traders. MCAD 2006 replaced the Misleading and Comparative Advertising Directive ('MCAD 1984')[1] which sought to protect both traders and consumers from misleading advertising and which had been amended in 1997 to include comparative advertising[2]. MCAD 1984 was implemented by the Control of Misleading Advertising Regulations 1988[3] ('the 1988 Regulations'). Under the 1988 Regulations, now revoked, the OFT had the power to seek civil injunctions against publishers of misleading advertisements. The 1988 Regulations did not provide for criminal sanctions and were used sparingly. In the UK, the emphasis in this area had previously been on self-regulation using non-statutory bodies such as the ASA.

1 Council Directive 84/450/EEC concerning misleading and comparative advertising.
2 By Directive 97/55/EC.
3 SI 1988/915.

12.9 The BPR provide for criminal sanctions and wider injunctive powers that can be exercised by any 'enforcement authority', which includes any weights and measures authority[1]. Although injunctive relief can only be sought by enforcement authorities, the offence of engaging in misleading advertising under reg 6 can be privately prosecuted.

1 SI 2008/1276, reg 2 defines 'enforcement authority' as the CMA, every local weights and measures authority, the Department of Enterprise, Trade and Investment Northern Ireland (now DfE, the Department for the Economy) and the Gas and Electricity Markets Authority.

12.10 The structure of the BPR closely resembles that of CPUTR 2008[1]:

- reg 7 sets out the applicable penalties (see CPUTR 2008, reg 13).
- reg 8 provides for corporate liability (see CPUTR 2008, reg 15).
- reg 9 covers causal liability (see CPUTR 2008, reg 16).
- reg 10 sets the time limit for prosecutions (see CPUTR 2008, reg 14).
- reg 11 provides the due diligence defence (see CPUTR 2008, reg 17).
- reg 12 provides the innocent publication of an advertisement defence (see CPUTR 2008, reg 18).
- reg 13 sets out the duty to enforce the BPR (equivalent to CPUTR 2008, reg 19).

1 BPR, SI 2008/1276. CPUTR 2008, SI 2008/1277.

12.11 A weights and measures authority that wishes to bring a criminal prosecution under reg 6 of the BPR is required to notify the Competition and Markets Authority ('CMA') under reg 14[1]. This requirement is expressly stated to be directory rather than mandatory, however, and a failure to comply with it will not render the criminal proceedings invalid[2]. Investigatory powers are now covered by the CRA 2015, Sch 5, see CHAPTER 4, Criminal Enforcement.

1 This does not apply in Scotland.
2 SI 2008/1276, reg 14(3). This is equivalent to the requirement to notify the CMA of prosecutions under the CPUTR 2008 under the Enterprise Act 2002, s 230.

Misleading advertising

12.12 Regulation 3[1] prohibits misleading advertising against traders and provides as follows:

3 Prohibition of advertising which misleads traders

(1) Advertising which is misleading is prohibited.

(2) Advertising is misleading which—

(a)   in any way, including its presentation, deceives or is likely to deceive the traders to whom it is addressed or whom it reaches; and by reason of its deceptive nature, is likely to affect their economic behaviour; or

(b)   for those reasons, injures or is likely to injure a competitor.

(3) In determining whether advertising is misleading, account shall be taken of all its features, and in particular of any information it contains concerning—

(a)   the characteristics of the product (as defined in paragraph (4));

(b)   the price or manner in which the price is calculated;

(c)   the conditions on which the product is supplied or provided; and

(d)   the nature, attributes and rights of the advertiser (as defined in paragraph (5)).

(4) In paragraph (3)(a) the "characteristics of the product" include—

(a)   availability of the product;

(b)   nature of the product;

(c)   execution of the product;

(d)   composition of the product;

(e)   method and date of manufacture of the product;

(f)   method and date of provision of the product;

(g)   fitness for purpose of the product;

(h)   uses of the product;

(i)   quantity of the product;

(j)   specification of the product;

(k)   geographical or commercial origin of the product;

(l)   results to be expected from use of the product; or

(m)   results and material features of tests or checks carried out on the product.

(5) In paragraph (3)(d) the "nature, attributes and rights" of the advertiser include the advertiser's—

(a)   identity;

(b)   assets;

(c)   qualifications;

(d)   ownership of industrial, commercial or intellectual property rights; or

(e)   awards and distinctions.

[1]   SI 2008/1276, reg 3.

Advertising

12.13 'Advertising' is defined in reg 2 as 'any form of representation which is made in connection with a trade, business, craft or profession in order to promote the supply or transfer of a product' and 'advertiser' is to be construed accordingly. This broad definition includes any representation that is made to promote the supply or transfer of a 'product'. Product is defined in the same way as it is in CPUTR 2008 and now includes immovable property, rights, and obligations. The term 'advertising' is likely to cover not only print, broadcast and billboard advertising, but also other marketing and promotional activities, such as details in catalogues or websites, descriptions on packaging and oral representations[1].

[1] This was the view taken by the Office of Fair Trading in its Guidance on the BPR, 'Business to business promotions and comparative advertisements – A quick guide to the Business Protection from Misleading Marketing Regulations 2008, SI 2008/1276', 2009. No guidance on the BPR has yet been issued by the CMA.

Misleading

12.14 'Misleading advertising' is defined in reg 3(2) as advertising that in any way, including its presentation, 'deceives or is likely to deceive the traders to whom it is addressed or whom it reaches' and by reason of its deceptive nature: (a) it is likely to affect the economic behaviour of those traders; or (b) it injures or is likely to injure a competitor.

12.15 There is no guidance in the legislation or the case law as to what is meant by deceiving a trader. Some assistance can be derived from the definition given to the term 'trader' in the BPR 2008[1]:

> "trader" means any person who is acting for purposes relating to his trade, craft, business or profession **and anyone acting in the name of or on behalf of a trader.**

It would appear, therefore, that an advertisement could be misleading if it deceives or is likely to deceive an employee of the trader in question (eg the buyer of a retail chain). Even though there is no concept of an 'average trader', this is likely to be an objective test. Further, the wording of reg 3(2) would appear to suggest that the traders to be taken into account are not only those to whom the advertisement is addressed (ie the intended recipients), but also traders reached by the advertisement, which may include unintended recipients.

[1] SI 2008/1276, reg 2(1), emphasis added.

12.16 As specified in reg 3(3), in determining whether advertising is misleading, account shall be taken of all its features, and in particular of any information it contains concerning the characteristics of the product, the price or manner in which the price is calculated, the conditions on which the product is supplied or provided, and the nature, attributes and rights of the advertiser. The OFT Guidance on the BPR 2008 provided the following examples of advertising that could be deceptive:

- advertising that contained a false statement of fact – this may be possible to prove or disprove by evidence;
- advertising that concealed or left out important facts;
- advertising that promised to do something when there was no intention of carrying it out;
- advertising that created a false impression, even if everything stated in it was literally true.

12.17 The BPR 2008 definition of 'misleading' differs from that provided for misleading actions and misleading omissions in CPUTR 2008[1]. In particular:

- Misleading actions and misleading omissions under CPUTR 2008 contain the threshold condition of causing or being likely to cause the average consumer to take a transactional decision he would not have taken otherwise. The BPR 2008 do make reference to affecting the economic behaviour of the traders to whom the advertisement is addressed or who it reaches, but the advertisement may be deemed to be misleading without having this effect – it may be sufficient to demonstrate that it injures or is likely to injure a competitor.

- The CPUTR 2008 require the distortion of a consumer's economic behaviour to be material; there does not appear to be a corresponding requirement in the BPR 2008, although it is arguable that some *de minimis* test ought to be implied into the legislation[2].
- The wording 'even if the information is factually correct' contained in CPUTR 2008, reg 5(2)(b) (misleading actions) is omitted from the BPR 2008. CPUTR 2008 and BPR 2008 were brought into force together and the omission of these words from the BPR 2008 might be taken to have been deliberate. It could be argued, therefore, that advertising could not be deceptive under the BPR 2008 if it is factually correct. Such a conclusion is likely to be contrary to the general purpose of the legislation, however. The BPR 2008 focus on the likelihood of deception, and they specifically identify the manner in which the advertising is presented as being capable of doing that. For instance, a newspaper advertisement might make a bold claim about a product that is only accurate when read together with a disclaimer. If the disclaimer were hidden in small print, the presentation of the advertisement would deceive – regardless of whether the information was factually accurate.

[1] SI 2008/1277, regs 5 and 6, respectively.
[2] This is in contrast to the position under the Trade Descriptions Act 1968, s 1, where the materiality (or de minimis test) related to the falsity rather than the distortion of the economic behaviour. See, for instance, *Harrison v Freezemaster* (1972) 80 MR 75.

Affect a trader's economic behaviour

12.18 Affecting a trader's economic behaviour is left undefined by the BPR 2008, but it is unlikely that this term can be equated with taking a transactional decision under CPUTR 2008. The breadth of the CPUTR 2008 definition[1] was recently the subject of a CJEU ruling[2], where it was held that even the decision to enter the shop was a 'transactional decision' within the meaning of the UCPD. The CJEU would be unlikely to adopt such a broad definition under the MCAD 2006: the MCAD 2006 is not a maximum harmonisation measure in relation to misleading advertising, in contrast to the UCPD, and its purpose is to protect businesses, as opposed to consumers (with the exception of Art 4 on comparative advertising). Accordingly, a lower level of protection would be expected and justified. It is likely that this condition will require proof that a trader entered into or chose not to enter into a binding contract as a result of the deceptive advertisement.

[1] 'Any decision taken by a consumer, whether it is to act or to refrain from acting, concerning . . . whether, how and on what terms to purchase, make payment in whole or in part for, retain or dispose of a product; or . . . whether, how and on what terms to exercise a contractual right in relation to a product . . .'.
[2] *Trento Sviluppo srl and Centrale Adriatica Soc Coop arl v Autorita Garante della Concorrenza e del Mercato* (C-281/12) [2014] CTLC 326.

12.19 This appears to have been the view of the Office of Fair Trading, as it then was, whose Guidance[1] stated that an advertisement 'will be likely to affect the economic behaviour of traders if, for example, it induces or is likely to induce them to part with money for what is being advertised'.

[1]   Office of Fair Trading, 'Business to business promotions and comparative advertisements – A quick guide to the Business Protection from Misleading Marketing Regulations 2008, SI 2008/1276', 2009. No guidance on the BPR has yet been issued by the CMA.

Injure a competitor

12.20 The offence will be committed if the deceptive advertisement does or is likely to 'injure a competitor'. In this context, it is probable that this will require proof that the deceptive advertisement does or is likely to cause a competitor economic or financial harm[1]. In its guidance on the BPR 2008, the OFT, as it then was, provided the following example:

> 'a competitor may be injured as a result of traders being deceived by a misleading advertisement, for example, where an advertiser misleads traders into using their services when the trader actually intended to use the service of company X (a competitor), perhaps by confusing the trader into believing they were actually dealing with company X. This is likely to injure company X (the competitor) as company X loses out on business as a result of the misleading advertisement.'

[1]   For a pre-MCAD analysis of false statements leading to pecuniary loss, see *Emaco Ltd v Dyson Appliances Ltd* [1999] ETMR 903.

Statutory defences

12.21 A trader engaging in advertising which is misleading under reg 3 is guilty of a criminal offence under the BPR 2008 reg 6, with the penalties for the offence set out in reg 7. The BPR 2008 include both a due diligence defence (reg 11) and an innocent publication defence (reg 12). The burden of proof for both rests with the defendant on the balance of probabilities[1]. Due diligence is now covered in CHAPTER 4, Criminal Enforcement.

[1]   See SI 2008/1276, regs 3, 6, 7, 11 and 12

Injunctive relief

12.22 Injunctions to secure compliance with reg 3 can be sought under reg 15 by an enforcement authority if the authority considers that there has been or there is likely to be a breach. Under reg 15(3) an injunction can only be sought by a local weights and measures authority if it has complied with the CMA notice requirements. If more than one local weights and measures authority in Great Britain is contemplating bringing proceedings the CMA may direct which enforcement authority is to bring the proceedings or decide that only the CMA may do so[1].

[1]   SI 2008/1276, reg 17(1).

12.23 In *Oldham Metropolitan Borough Council v Worldwide Marketing Solutions Ltd*[1] an application was made for an injunction against a company accused of engaging in misleading advertising in national telesales. It was argued that the local authority had no power to obtain an injunction because the company was no longer based in the local authority's area. The High Court rejected an argument that the injunction could not be 'expedient for the promotion or protection of the interests' of Oldham's inhabitants for the purposes of the Local Government Act 1972, s 222. Phillips J stated that 'a local authority can properly take into account broader considerations of how to promote or protect the interests of its inhabitants, not limited to situations where unlawful activity is continuing or contemplated within its area'.

[1]   [2014] PTSR 1072.

12.24 This issue is unlikely to be important following the entry into force of the CRA 2015, which now enables civil proceedings to be instituted by a local authority for consumer law breaches that take place outside its area[1]. In *Croydon LBC v Hogarth*[2], an enforcement authority successfully applied for an injunction for a breach of reg 3(2)(a) against a company sending out contracts disguised as invoices.

[1]   CRA 2015, Sch 5, para 45.
[2]   [2011] EWHC 1126 (QB), [2011] CTLC 34.

12.25 Under reg 16 of the BPR 2008, an enforcement authority that considers that there has been or there is likely to be a breach of regs 3, 4 or 5 may resolve the matter by way of undertakings. Under reg 18, the court has the power to order publication of final injunctions and corrective statements.

Comparative advertising

12.26 'Comparative advertising' is defined broadly, in reg 2[1]:

2 Interpretation

> "comparative advertising" means advertising which in any way, either explicitly or by implication, identifies a competitor or a product offered by a competitor.

[1]   SI 2008/1276, reg 2.

12.27 Comparative advertising is permitted, provided it cumulatively meets the conditions set out in reg 4(a)–(i).

4 Comparative advertising

> Comparative advertising shall, as far as the comparison is concerned, be permitted only when the following conditions are met—
>
> (a)   it is not misleading under regulation 3;
> (b)   it is not a misleading action under regulation 5 of the Consumer Protection from Unfair Trading Regulations 2008 or a misleading omission under regulation 6 of those Regulations;
> (c)   it compares products meeting the same needs or intended for the same purpose;
> (d)   it objectively compares one or more material, relevant, verifiable and representative features of those products, which may include price;
> (e)   it does not create confusion among traders—
>   (i)   between the advertiser and a competitor, or
>   (ii) between the trademarks, trade names, other distinguishing marks or products of the advertiser and those of a competitor;
> (f)   it does not discredit or denigrate the trademarks, trade names, other distinguishing marks, products, activities, or circumstances of a competitor;
> (g)   for products with designation of origin, it relates in each case to products with the same designation;

- (h) it does not take unfair advantage of the reputation of a trade mark, trade name or other distinguishing marks of a competitor or of the designation of origin of competing products;
- (i) it does not present products as imitations or replicas of products bearing a protected trade mark or trade name.'

12.28 Regulation 4 implements Art 4 of MCAD 2006. The predecessor provision was Art 3a(1) of MCAD 1984 and was in materially the same terms. Accordingly, the CJEU (or ECJ, as it then was) cases on comparative advertising, which were under MCAD 1984, remain of relevance under MCAD 2006. The CJEU recently confirmed this to be the case in the *Carrefour v ITM Alimentaire* case[1]. Accordingly, the CJEU case law on MCAD 1984 is discussed below.

[1] Case C-526/15, *Carrefour Hypermarchés SAS v ITM Alimentaire International SASU* at para 19.

12.29 The importance of comparative advertising is set out in the recitals to the MCAD 2006:

'(6) The completion of the internal market means a wide range of choice. Given that consumers and traders can and must make the best possible use of the internal market, and that advertising is a very important means of creating genuine outlets for all goods and services throughout the Community, the basic provisions governing the form and content of comparative advertising should be uniform and the conditions of the use of comparative advertising in the Member States should be harmonised. If these conditions are met, this will help demonstrate objectively the merits of the various comparable products. Comparative advertising can also stimulate competition between suppliers of goods and services to the consumer's advantage.

. . .

(8) Comparative advertising, when it compares material, relevant, verifiable and representative features and is not misleading, may be a legitimate means of informing consumers of their advantage. It is desirable to provide a broad concept of comparative advertising to cover all modes of comparative advertising.'

12.30 Recitals 14 and 15 clarify that for comparative advertising to be effective, the use of a competitor's trade mark may be indispensable and that such use is permissible provided it complies with the conditions laid down by MCAD 2006:

'(14) It may, however, be indispensable, in order to make comparative advertising effective, to identify the goods or services of a competitor, making reference to a trade mark or trade name of which the latter is the proprietor.

(15) Such use of another's trade mark, trade name or other distinguishing marks does not breach this exclusive right in cases where it complies with the conditions laid down by this Directive, the intended target being solely to distinguish between them and thus to highlight differences objectively.'

12.31 As the CJEU made clear in *L'Oréal SA v Bellure NV*[1] the purpose of the conditions in Art 4 (albeit the case refers to its predecessor, Art 3a) is:

' . . . to achieve a balance between the different interests which may be affected by allowing comparative advertising. Thus, it is apparent from a reading of recitals 2, 7 and 9 in the preamble to Directive 97/55 that the aim of Article 3a is to stimulate competition between suppliers of goods and services to the consumer's advantage, by allowing competitors to highlight objectively the merits of the various comparable products while, at the same time, prohibiting practices which may distort competition, be detrimental to competitors and have an adverse effect on consumer choice.[2]'

1 Case C-487/07 *L'Oréal SA v Bellure NV* [2009] ECR I-5185 at para 68. L'Oréal brought proceedings against a company that sold non-luxury perfumes in packaging that resembled that of well-known luxury brands. This company had compiled price comparison lists bearing L'Oréal's trademark.
2 See also Case C-159/09 *Lidl SNC v Vierzon Distribution SA* at para 20.

12.32 The leading authority on comparative advertising is the CJEU case of *Lidl SNC v Vierzon*[1]. Lidl objected to an advertisement published by competitor supermarket Vierzon comparing the prices of its products with those of Vierzon and stating that Vierzon's were 'the cheapest'. Lidl alleged that the comparative advertising was unlawful on the ground that it compared products which were different in quality and quantity. The CJEU found the comparison to be lawful and stated the following principles:

- The conditions listed in Art 3a of MCAD 1984 (now Art 4 of MCAD 2006) must be interpreted in the sense most favourable to permitting advertisements which objectively compare the characteristics of goods or services, whilst ensuring at the same time that comparative advertising is not used anti-competitively and unfairly or in a manner which affects the interests of consumers[2].

- MCAD 1984 exhaustively harmonises the conditions under which comparative advertising is permitted. Such a harmonisation implies by its nature that the lawfulness of comparative advertising throughout the EU is to be assessed solely in the light of the criteria laid down by the EU legislature[3].

- The conditions listed in Art 3a are cumulative and so each condition must be satisfied for the comparative advertising in question to be permitted[4].

- If comparative advertising is to be permitted, the comparison must relate to goods or services which meet the same needs or are intended for the same purpose. That condition implies that the goods being compared must display a sufficient degree of interchangeability for consumers[5]. The angle from which the comparison is made (eg price) can have no bearing on whether two products meet the same needs or are intended for the same purpose within the meaning of Art 3a(1)(b)[6].

- It is for the national court to ascertain in the circumstances of each case, and bearing in mind the consumers to which the advertising is addressed, whether the advertising may be misleading[7]. In carrying out the requisite assessment, the national court must, first, take into account the perception of an average consumer of the products or services being advertised. It must also take account of all the relevant factors in the case, the information contained in the advertisement and, more generally, all its features[8].

1 Case C-159/09 *Lidl SNC v Vierzon Distribution SA*.
2 Paragraph 21, citing Case C-487/07 *L'Oréal SA v Bellure NV* [2009] ECR I-5185 at para 68.
3 Paragraph 22, citing Case C-44/01 *Pippig Augenoptik* [2003] ECR I-3095 at para 44.
4 Paragraph 16, citing Case C-487/07 *L'Oréal SA v Bellure NV* [2009] ECR I-5185 at para 67.
5 Paragraph 25, citing *Lidl Belgium GmbH & Co KG v Etablissementen Franz Colruyt NV* (C-356/04) [2007] Bus LR 492 at para 26, and Case C-381/05 *De Landtsheer Emmanuel* [2007] ECR I-3115 at para 44.

6   Paragraph 27.
7   Paragraph 46, citing Case C-356/04 *Lidl Belgium* [2006] ECR I-8501.
8   Paragraphs 47–48, citing *Lidl Belgium* at para 79.

Misleading

12.33 The CJEU recently confirmed that its 'case-law on the interpretation of [MCAD 1984] is fully applicable to situations covered by [MCAD 2006]'[1]. It can be argued, however, that the CJEU case law under MCAD 1984 is of limited assistance on the question of whether an advertisement is misleading, as MCAD 1984 covered advertising that misled or was likely to mislead consumers as well as traders and defined 'misleading advertising' differently[2]:

> 'any advertising which in any way, including its presentation, deceives or is likely to deceive the persons to whom it is addressed or whom it reaches and which, by reason of its deceptive nature, is likely to affect their economic behaviour or which, for those reasons, injures or is likely to injure a competitor.'

1   Case C-526/15, *Carrefour Hypermarchés SAS v ITM Alimentaire International SASU* at para 19.
2   Article 2 of MCAD 1984. This definition has been retained in MCAD 2006, at Art 2, but it is arguably of limited assistance given the new focus of the Directive, namely other traders. This is reflected in the BPR, which replace 'the persons to whom it is addressed' with 'the traders to whom it is addressed' in SI 2008/1276, reg 3(2).

12.34 Two cases under MCAD 1984 are worth a mention nevertheless. In *Lidl Belgium*[1] Lidl objected to the advertisement of another supermarket chain, Colruyt, which compared some of Colruyt's prices with those charged at other supermarket chains, including Lidl. Lidl argued that this gave consumers the impression that Colruyt was always cheaper than its competitors. The CJEU made it clear that such advertising could be misleading if the advertisement:

- does not reveal that the comparison related only to such a sample and not to all the advertiser's products,
- does not identify the details of the comparison made or inform the persons to whom it is addressed of the information source where such identification is possible, or
- contains a collective reference to a range of amounts that may be saved by consumers who make their purchases from the advertiser rather than from his competitors without specifying individually the general level of the prices charged, respectively, by each of those competitors and the amount that consumers are liable to save by making their purchases from the advertiser rather than from each of the competitors.'

1   Case C-356/04 *Lidl Belgium* [2006] ECR I-8501.

12.35 In *Lidl SNC v Vierzon*[1], the CJEU stated, that advertisements that compared prices could be misleading if the national court were to find that:

- A significant number of consumers may make the decision to buy in the mistaken belief that the selection of goods in the advertisement: (a) is representative of the general level of the advertiser's prices compared to those of his competitor, and (b) that the savings of the kind claimed by the advertisement could be made by regularly buying everyday consumer goods from the advertiser rather than from the competitor.

- The decision to buy on the part of a significant number of consumers to whom the advertising is addressed may be made in the mistaken belief that all of the advertiser's products are cheaper than those of his competitor[2].
- The products compared are in fact objectively different and the differences are capable of significantly affecting the consumer's choice. If such differences are not disclosed, such advertising may be perceived by the average consumer as claiming, by implication, that the other characteristics of the products in question are equivalent[3].

[1]   Case C-159/09 *Lidl SNC v Vierzon Distribution SA*.
[2]   Paragraph 50, citing *Lidl Belgium* at paras 83 and 84.
[3]   Paragraphs 51–52.

12.36 Whilst these cases apply a definition of 'misleading' that is out of date, they may nevertheless be of assistance in understanding the manner in which the conditions in reg 4[1] interact with each other. In particular, they make it clear that the question of whether the advertisement is misleading is linked to the question of interchangeability.

[1]   SI 2008/1276, reg 4

12.37 The interplay between the prohibition on misleading advertising and the requirement of objectivity was recently considered by the CJEU in the *Carrefour v ITM Alimentaire* case[1]. Carrefour, a leading supermarket chain in France, ran an advertising campaign comparing the price of products sold in its larger shops with prices charged by its competitors in smaller shops (even in circumstances where Carrefour's competitors operated larger shops). The CJEU was asked whether MCAD 2006 prohibited price comparisons between goods sold in shops of different sizes and formats and whether this fact constituted material information within the meaning of the UCPD.

[1]   *Carrefour Hypermarchés SAS v ITM Alimentaire International SASU* (C-562/15).

12.38 The CJEU noted that whilst MCAD 2006 did not prohibit the comparison of prices charged in different types of shops, differences in shop size and format could distort the objectivity of the comparison. The Court found that the fact that the goods compared were sold in different types of shops was 'material information' within the meaning of the UCPD. Accordingly, such an advertisement would fall foul of the requirements in MCAD 2006, unless the differences in shop size and format were clearly set out in the advertisement itself.

Meeting the same needs or intended for the same purpose

12.39 As noted by the CJEU in *Lidl Belgium*, this condition implies that the goods being compared must display a sufficient degree of interchangeability for consumers[1]. The CJEU made it clear in *Lidl Vierzon* that this required an individual and specific assessment of products that are the subject of the comparison[2]. In *Lidl Vierzon*, the CJEU was specifically asked whether what is now Art 4 of MCAD 2006 precluded the comparison of products (in that case food) on the basis of price where the products differed on the basis of non-price elements. The CJEU concluded that it did not and that the question was one of fact and degree[3]. Accordingly, two products need not be identical in order to be regarded as comparable.

[1] *Lidl Belgium GmbH & Co KG v Etablissementen Franz Colruyt NV* (C-356/04) [2007] Bus LR 492 at para 26. See also Case C-381/05 *De Landtsheer Emmanuel* [2007] ECR I-3115 at para 44 and *Lidl Vierzon* at para 25. Further, the CJEU found, at para 27, that the angle from which the comparison is made (eg price) can have no bearing on whether two products meet the same needs or are intended for the same purpose within the meaning of Art 4.
[2] *Lidl Vierzon* at paras 29–30, 32–33.
[3] Paragraphs 29 and 33.

12.40 This issue recently fell to be determined by the High Court in *R (Sainsbury's Supermarkets Limited) v The Independent Reviewer of ASA Adjudications*[1]. Sainsbury's complained to the ASA regarding Tesco's 'Price Promise' advertisement, which claimed that customers would not 'lose out on big brands, fresh food or own-label' products to Tesco's competitors. Sainsbury's argued that Tesco's comparison failed to factor in a number of key non-price attributes, such as ethical and environmental characteristics and provenance. Its complaint was rejected by the ASA and the Independent Reviewer. The Independent Reviewer had concluded that whilst such characteristics could be material to many customers, it did not mean that the ASA was wrong to conclude that they were not material, essential or important to this particular comparison. The High Court was equally unsympathetic to Sainsbury's argument, dismissing it as unsustainable in light of *Lidl Vierzon*[2].

[1] [2014] EWHC 3680 (Admin).
[2] At paras 153–154.

Verifiability

12.41 The leading authority on verifiability is the CJEU case of *Lidl Belgium*, which established that[1]:

'in order for the prices of the goods comprising a selection of products or the general level of the prices charged by a chain of stores in respect of its selection of comparable goods to be verifiable, it is a necessary precondition that, even though ... the goods whose prices have been thus compared are not required to be expressly and exhaustively listed in the advertisement addressed to the consumer, they must nevertheless be capable of being individually and specifically identified on the basis of the information contained in that advertisement. The prices of goods can necessarily only ever be verified if it is possible to identify the goods.'

[1] *Lidl Belgium GmbH & Co KG v Etablissementen Franz Colruyt NV* (C-356/04) [2007] Bus LR 492 at para 61.

12.42 The CJEU observed that[1]:

'such an obligation makes it possible, in accordance with the objective of consumer protection pursued by the [MCAD 1984], for the persons to whom an advertisement of that kind is addressed to be in a position to satisfy themselves that they have been correctly informed with regard to the purchases of basic consumables which they are prompted to make.'

[1] *Lidl Belgium* at para 72.

12.43 The advertiser is thus under an obligation to indicate, in particular for the attention of the persons to whom the advertisement is addressed, where and how they may readily examine the details of the comparison with a view to verifying their accuracy or having it verified. As the CJEU made clear, however, this[1]:

'does not mean that the accuracy of the features compared must in all circumstances be capable of being verified by those to whom the advertising is addressed acting in person. It is sufficient for the details allowing such verification to be accessible to those persons . . . in such a way that they may, as a general rule, carry out the desired verification themselves or, more exceptionally and if such verification demands a skill which they do not possess, have it carried out by a third party.'

[1] *Lidl Belgium* at para 73.

12.44 It could be argued that these passages, too, are of limited assistance. The Court expressly refers to the objective of MCAD 1984 as being one of consumer protection and this objective clearly formed an important part of the Court's reasoning. The objective of MCAD 2006 is different[1]:

'The purpose of this Directive is to protect traders against misleading advertising and the unfair consequences thereof and to lay down the conditions under which comparative advertising is permitted.'

[1] MCAD 2006, Art 1. The objective of MCAD 1984 was stated to be: 'to protect consumers, persons carrying on a trade or business or practising a craft or profession and the interests of the public in general against misleading advertising and the unfair consequences thereof'. The scope of the Directive was later expanded to include the conditions under which comparative advertising would be permitted.

Discrediting a competitor

12.45 In *Pippig Augenoptik v Hartlauer*[1] the CJEU was asked whether a price comparison entailed discrediting a competitor if the products were chosen in such a way as to obtain a price difference greater than the average price difference and/or the comparisons were repeated continuously, creating the impression that the competitor's prices were excessive. The CJEU had no hesitation in finding that it did not, noting that the 'comparison of rival offers, particularly as regards price, is of the very nature of comparative advertising'[2].

[1] Case C-44/01 *Pippig Augenoptik GmbH & Co. KG v Hartlauer Handelsgesellschaft mbH and Verlassenschaft nach dem verstorbenen Franz Josef Hartlauer.*
[2] Paragraph 80.

12.46 The advertisement that was subject to British Airways' complaint in *British Airways plc v Ryanair Ltd*[1] is an example of what might be regarded as denigration[2].

[1] [2001] ETMR 24.
[2] This was the view taken by the editors of *Halsbury's Laws of England, Trade Marks and Trade Names*, Volume 97A (2014))/2, at 75. A Ryanair advertisement comparing Ryanair's prices to those of British Airways was featured beneath the headline 'EXPENSIVE BA——DS!', the word 'BA——DS!' being an allusion to the word 'BASTARDS'.

Taking unfair advantage

12.47 The CJEU has considered Art 4(f) (or its predecessor, Art 3a(1)(g) of MCAD 1984) in a number of cases:

- When assessing whether the condition laid down in Art 3a(1)(g) of MCAD 1984 (now Art 4(f) of MCAD 2006) has been satisfied, it is necessary to have regard to Recital 15 in the Preamble to Directive 97/55, which states that the use of a trade mark or distinguishing mark does not breach the right to the mark where it complies with the conditions laid down by Directive 84/450, the aim being solely to distinguish between the products and services of the advertiser and those of his competitor and thus to highlight differences objectively[1].

- In *Siemens AG v VIPA*[2] the CJEU found that the use of a core element of the Siemens trade mark by a competitor (here, catalogue numbers) did not take unfair advantage of the reputation of the Siemens mark. The CJEU confirmed that the benefit of comparative advertising to consumers must necessarily be taken into account in answering whether the advertisement complies with Art 4(f). On the other hand, the benefit derived by an advertiser from comparative advertising cannot alone be determinative of its legality[3].

- The expression 'takes unfair advantage' in Art 4(f) is to, in principle, be interpreted in the same way as in Art 5(2) of Directive 89/104[4].

- In order to determine whether the use of a mark takes unfair advantage of the distinctive character or the repute of the mark, it is necessary to undertake a global assessment, taking into account all factors relevant to the circumstances of the case, which include:
  - (i)   the strength of the mark's reputation;
  - (ii)   the degree of distinctive character of the mark;
  - (iii) the degree of similarity between the marks at issue;
  - (iv)   the nature and degree of proximity of the goods or services concerned; and
  - (v)   the likelihood of dilution or tarnishing of the mark[5].

[1]   Case C-112/99 *Toshiba Europe* [2001] ECR I-7945 at para 53.
[2]   Case C-59/05, *Siemens AG v VIPA Gesellschaft für Visualisierung und Prozeßautomatisierung mbH.*
[3]   Paragraphs 24 and 25.
[4]   Case C-487/07, *L'Oréal SA v Bellure NV.* See also Case C-533/06 *O2 Holdings Ltd v Hutchison 3G Ltd* [2008] ECR I-4231.
[5]   Case C-487/07, *L'Oréal SA v Bellure NV* at paras 44–45. See also *Specsavers International Healthcare Ltd v Asda Stores Ltd* [2012] ETMR 17.

Comparative advertising and the law on trademarks

12.48 Comparative advertising often uses competitor trademarks without their consent. Accordingly, comparative advertising that fails to satisfy the requirements of BPR 2008, reg 4 could expose the advertiser to trademark infringement proceedings under the Trade Marks Act 1994 ('TMA 1994'). The TMA has a specific provision intended to relate to comparative advertising[1]. This provision does not add anything of substance to the other provisions of the TMA, however.

[1]   TMA 1994, s 10(6).

Pricing Practices Guide 2016

12.49 The CTSI published its Guidance for Traders on Pricing Practices in December 2016, which is covered in detail in CHAPTER 13, Prices. The Guidance covers matters such as reference pricing and comparative advertising largely repeating the requirements of MCAD and CPUT.

Code owners

12.50 Regulation 5 of BPR 2008 prohibits the promotion of misleading advertising or of non-compliant comparative advertising by a Code Owner in a code of conduct. A similar prohibition can be found in CPUTR 2008, reg 4[1].

> **5 Promotion of misleading advertising and comparative advertising which is not permitted**
>
> A code owner shall not promote in a code of conduct—
>
> (a) advertising which is misleading under regulation 3; or
> (b) comparative advertising which is not permitted under regulation 4.

[1] See SI 2008/1276, reg 5 and SI 2008/1277, reg 4.

12.51 'Code owner' is defined in reg 2 of the BPR 2008 as:

> **2 Interpretation**
>
> "code owner" means a trader or body responsible for—
> (a) the formulation and revision of a code of conduct; or
> (b) monitoring compliance with the code by those who have undertaken to be bound by it.

Enforcement (regs 4 and 5)

12.52 There is no criminal sanction for breach of the comparative advertising requirements (reg 4) or for breach of the provision relating to codes of conduct (reg 5). It follows that there is no provision in the BPR 2008 for a private party to enforce regs 4 or 5. Breaches of these regs would therefore require a qualified regulator to take injunctive action under reg 15.

THE ADVERTISING STANDARDS AUTHORITY

12.53 The Advertising Standards Authority ('ASA') was established in 1962 by the advertising industry, which came together in the 1961 to form the CAP[1] and produced the first edition of the British Code of Advertising Practice. The ASA was to act as the independent adjudicator under the newly-created Code, which covered non-broadcast advertising[2]. This continues to be the ASA's role today. Non-broadcast advertising is governed by the UK Code of Non-broadcast Advertising and Direct and Promotional Marketing ('CAP Code'). All television and radio advertisements are required to comply with the UK Code of Broadcast Advertising ('BCAP Code'). The focus of this Chapter is on the CAP Code, but reference will be made to the BCAP Code, where relevant.

[1] Today, CAP's membership comprises the Television on Demand Industry Forum, Advertising Association, Cinema Advertising Association, Direct Marketing Association, Direct Selling Association, Incorporated Society of British Advertisers, Institute of Practitioners in Advertising, Institute of Promotional Marketing, Internet Advertising Bureau, Mobile UK, News Media Association, Outsmart Out of Home, Professional Publishers Association, Proprietary Association of Great Britain, Royal Mail, Scottish Newspaper Society, Clearcast, Radiocentre.
[2] The ASA's remit has subsequently been extended to cover broadcast advertising.

The CAP Code

12.54 The CAP Code is largely premised on statutory provisions and is intended accurately to reflect EU and domestic consumer protection legislation in respect of misleading and unfair advertising. In particular, it incorporates the requirements of CPUTR 2008, BPR 2008 and Regulation (EC) No 1924/2006 on nutrition and health claims made on foods. It covers matters of general application to advertisers, such as misleading and comparative advertising, as well as sector- and audience-specific topics, such as advertising to children, environmental claims and claims relating to weight control and slimming. It also goes beyond the remit of legislative provisions. For instance, the CAP Code was recently amended to include a ban on harmful gender stereotypes.

12.55 The CAP Code makes it clear that context is key to its application[1]:

'compliance with the Code is assessed according to the marketing communication's probable impact when taken as a whole and in context. That will depend on the medium in which the marketing communication appeared, the audience and its likely response, the nature of the product and any material distributed to consumers'.

[1] CAP Code, Part IV, para c.

12.56 Rule 1.2 of the CAP Code provides that advertisements should reflect 'the spirit, not merely the letter, of the Code'. Accordingly, arguments of a purely technical nature are rarely successful before the ASA.

Scope

12.57 The Scope of the CAP Code is set out in the Code's introductory section. It covers:

- advertisements in newspapers, magazines, brochures, leaflets, circulars, mailings, e-mails, text transmissions, fax transmissions, catalogues, follow-up literature and other electronic or printed material;
- posters and other promotional media in public places, including moving images;
- cinema, video, DVD and Blu-ray advertisements;
- advertisements in non-broadcast electronic media, including online advertisements in paid-for space, paid-for search listings and preferential listings on price comparison sites;
- marketing databases containing consumers' personal information;
- sales promotions in non-broadcast media;
- advertorials;
- advertisements and other marketing communications by or from companies, organisations or sole traders on their own websites, or in other non-paid-for space online under their control, that are directly connected with the supply or transfer of goods, services, opportunities and gifts, or which consist of direct solicitations of donations as part of their own fund-raising activities[1].

[1] The Code's remit was extended beyond sales promotions and paid-for advertisements in March 2011, to cover marketing claims on company websites and in other third party space under their control, such as social media. See 'Scope of the Code', para 1(h).

12.58 The CAP Code also sets out the areas that fall outside its remit. These include (but are not limited to):

- broadcast advertisements (which are covered by the BCAP Code);
- the contents of premium-rate services (which are the responsibility of PhonepayPlus);
- marketing communications in foreign media, even if targeted at UK[1] consumers;
- claims addressed only to medical, dental, veterinary or allied practitioners, that relate to those practitioners' expertise;
- private correspondence, including correspondence between organisations and their customers about existing relationships or past purchases; and
- packages, wrappers, labels, tickets, timetables and price lists unless they advertise another product or a sales promotion or are visible in a marketing communication.

[1] If, however, the relevant authority in the country from which the advertisements originate does not operate a suitable cross-border complaint system, the ASA will take what action it can.

12.59 The CAP Code also makes it clear that if there is doubt as to whether a communication falls within the remit of the Code, the ASA will be more likely to apply the Code if the material complained about is in paid-for space[1]. The ASA recently issued guidance entitled 'Think you know what the CAP Code applies to?' to assist advertisers with understanding the remit of the CAP Code.

[1] CAP Code, Scope of the Code, Part IV, para b.

Key provisions

12.60 This section sets out the key provisions of the CAP Code and provides examples of recent ASA rulings. ASA's previous rulings are not binding on it. They do, however, provide an indication of how the ASA is likely to reason should it be faced with a similar issue in the future.

Part 1 – Legal, decent, honest and truthful

12.61 A core principle of the CAP Code set out in rule 1 is that advertisements must be 'legal, decent, honest and truthful'. This includes the requirement that advertisements, as well as the products being advertised, be lawful. The ASA website includes a list of relevant legislation, although it is made clear that the list is not exhaustive[1].

[1] Available at www.cap.org.uk/Advertising-Codes.

Part 2 – Recognition of marketing communications

12.62 This rule aims to ensure that advertising is clearly separated from editorial content, so that consumers do not confuse the two. The rules in Pt 2 are premised on the requirements of the Electronic Commerce (EC Directive) Regulations 2002[1] and CPUTR 2008[2]. Recent rulings include:

- *Nomad Choice Pty Ltd t/a Flat Tummy Tea*, 5 April 2017: An Instagram post promoting 'Flat Tummy Tea' was found to be a marketing communication on the basis that (a) there was a financial arrangement between the blogger and the advertiser; and (b) the advertiser had control over the content. Although the advertiser did not dictate the content of the blogger's posts, it had control over the blogger's key messages (in this case regarding the tea being available at a reduced rate), as well as the timing of such messages.
- *Wallshield (UK) Ltd*, 3 August 2016: This ruling concerned an envelope sent to recipients, which was completely blank and did not contain any text to alert recipients to the fact that it contained a marketing communication. The ASA concluded that the advertisement was not obviously identifiable as a marketing communication and was in breach of the CAP Code.
- *OfficeMax Australia Ltd*, 11 May 2016: A mailing, which stated 'Best Offers for Office Supplies. Office Supplies Offer' was laid out like an invoice. Small print stated, 'This is a solicitation for the order of goods, services or both and not a bill, invoice or statement of account due . . . '. The ASA concluded that the mailing was not obviously identifiable as a marketing communication and so breached the CAP Code.

[1]   For example, SI 2002/2013, r 2.2.
[2]   For example, SI 2008/1277, rr 2.3 and 2.4.

12.63 The requirement to ensure that marketing communications are obviously identifiable as such extends to the envelope containing the marketing communication in question. Guidance on the use of envelopes was issued by CAP on 23 February 2017, confirming the ASA's view that envelopes form part of the marketing communication. See also the CAP's recent guidance on online affiliate marketing[1], which confirms that the CAP Code applies to affiliate marketing, whether it applies on an affiliate's site or in social media.

[1]   CAP, 'Online Affiliate Marketing', 9 March 2017. Online affiliate marketing includes eg voucher sites and blogs.

PART 3 – MISLEADING MARKETING COMMUNICATIONS

12.64 Misleading marketing communications are dealt with in Pt 3 of the Code, which covers the following:

- Substantiation.
- Qualification.
- Exaggeration.
- Prohibited claims.
- Pricing claims (including the description of a product as 'free' and availability).
- Comparative advertising.
- Endorsements and testimonials.
- Guarantees and after-sales service.

12.65 The core rule is rule 3.1, which provides that marketing communications 'must not materially mislead or be likely to do so'[1]. Misleading by omission is dealt with in rule 3.3 (and expanded upon in rules 3.4 and 3.5)[2]. The wording of these rules fails to fully reflect the wording of the legislation on which they are based, namely regs 5 and 6 of CPUTR 2008 and reg 3 of the BPR 2008[3]. In particular, rules 3.1 and 3.4 fail to incorporate the threshold condition contained in CPUTR 2008, ie that the advertisement must cause or be likely to cause 'the average consumer to take a transactional decision he would not have taken otherwise' and ASA rulings rarely make reference to it. It could be argued, therefore, that the CAP Code goes beyond the remit of CPUTR 2008, which is significant given the maximum harmonisation nature the UCPD. The CAP Code does, however, make reference to the relevant test in Appendix 1.

[1]   An identical rule is contained in the BCAP Code, rule 3.1.
[2]   In the BCAP Code, the relevant rule is 3.2.
[3]   SI 2008/1277, regs 5 and 6 and SI 2008/1276, reg 3.

12.66 Examples of recent rulings include:

- Glyn Hopkin Ltd and Fiat Chrysler Automobiles UK Ltd, 25 October 2017. The ASA upheld a complaint under the CAP Code regarding an advertisement that failed to state that the vehicles being sold were ex-fleet vehicles. The ASA considered such information to have been material to a consumer's purchasing decision and the failure to include it rendered the advertisement misleading.

- *Power Leisure Bookmakers Ltd*, 6 July 2016. The ASA upheld a complaint under the BCAP Code about an advertisement that implied that an offer was available to 'everyone', when there were restrictions as to who could take advantage of it. Although the ruling relates to broadcast advertising, it is likely to be a helpful guide as to how the ASA is likely to approach 'de minimis' arguments on absolute claims.

- *Hutchinson 3G UK's (trading as 3)*, 27 July 2016. A claim on 3's website regarding 'all you can eat data' was found to be misleading, as it failed to refer to any fair use or other limitations on the amount of data available as part of the offer.

SUBSTANTIATION

12.67 Rule 3.7 requires marketers to 'hold documentary evidence to prove claims that consumers are likely to regard as objective and that are capable of objective substantiation'. The ASA may regard claims as misleading in the absence of adequate substantiation[1].

[1]   For the corresponding requirement in the BCAP Code, see rule 3.9.

12.68 This rule is premised on *inter alia* Art 12 of the UCPD[1], which provides:

'Member States shall confer upon the courts or administrative authorities powers enabling them in the civil or administrative proceedings provided for in Article 11:

(a)   to require the trader to furnish evidence as to the accuracy of factual claims in relation to a commercial practice if, taking into account the legitimate interest of the trader and any other party to the proceedings, such a requirement appears appropriate on the basis of the circumstances of the particular case; and

(b) to consider factual claims as inaccurate if the evidence demanded in accordance with (a) is not furnished or is deemed insufficient by the court or administrative authority.'

[1] Implemented by the Enterprise Act 2002, s 218A. Article 7 of MCAD 2006 is in identical terms.

12.69 Examples of recent rulings include:

- *The University of Law*, 16 November 2016. The ASA upheld a complaint against the University of Law in relation to an advertisement that had claimed that 'in the first 5 years of work a lawyer can expect to earn an average of £54,000 a year' in comparison with the 'national average of £26,000'. The ASA found that newspaper articles were insufficient for the purposes of substantiating the claim and that the advertiser should have supplied the original research on which the newspaper articles were based[1].

- *Parcel2Go.com Ltd*, 16 November 2016. Parcel2Go had made a series of absolute price claims on its website, including the claim that it was 'The Cheapest Parcel Delivery in the UK'. The ASA found that Parcel2Go fell foul of the substantiation requirement, in spite of the fact that Parcel2Go's IT system monitored other websites and flagged instances where they were beaten on price (adjusting their prices accordingly) and had provided the ASA with a spreadsheet demonstrating that its prices were either cheaper or the same as those of its competitors. The ASA found Parcel2Go to have breached the CAP Code. Parcel2Go was unable to demonstrate that it compared its prices to those of couriers and direct delivery services, which the ASA deemed relevant. Furthermore, Parcel2Go offered delivery options without additional insurance, whilst such insurance would often be offered by other operators.

- *ASDA Stores Ltd t/a ASDA*, 3 August 2016. ASDA's website claimed that its 'Little Angels Supreme Protection' nappies were their 'most absorbent nappy ever'. ASDA was unable to provide evidence to demonstrate that this was the case and so was found to have breached rule 3.7 of the CAP Code, as well as rule 3.1.

[1] It is worth noting, for completeness, that the University of Law was found to be responsible for the content of the advertisement, even though the advertisement had been published in consultation with a marketing firm, Marketing VF. It was Marketing VF that had supplied the ASA with the relevant substantiation.

12.70 The issue of substantiation was recently considered by the High Court in *R (Actegy Limited) v ASA* which concerned claims made by Actegy Limited in respect of a medical device – the 'Revitive Circulation Booster' – that had been authorised by the Medicines and Healthcare Products Regulatory Agency. The claimant's argument that the evidential requirements imposed on advertisers by the ASA were disproportionate and irrational was rejected by the Court, which stated that:

'It is self-evidently necessary, in the public interest, for there to be assessment of the quality of evidence, regardless of its quantity. Where claims for the efficacy of medical devices are concerned, neither the terms of the UCPD nor the principles of free movement more generally are inconsistent with a requirement for evidence consisting of studies which are both rigorous, in respect of study methodology, and relevant, in respect of equivalence of devices and correspondence between the test parameters and the types of user and types of use contemplated by an advertisement. Since this approach does not go beyond what is contemplated by the UCPD, for the reasons explained above there can be no attack on the proportionality of the approach.[1]'

1   [2019] EWHC 2374 (Admin) [97]–[98].

Disclaimers

12.71 Rule 3.9 requires marketing communications to 'state significant limitations and qualifications' and provides that 'Qualifications may clarify but must not contradict the claims that they qualify'. Accordingly, a potentially misleading claim cannot be remedied by a disclaimer or explanatory text in the small print. This principle is enshrined in CPUTR 2008, which provides that information may be misleading 'if it or its overall presentation in any way deceives or is likely to deceive the average consumer . . . even if the information is factually correct'[1]. A recent example of the application of this Rule by the ASA is The Carphone Warehouse Ltd, 3 August 2016. The complaint challenged claims appearing on Carphone Warehouse's website which alleged that the retailer offered 'UK'S LOWEST PRICE' and 'AT THE BEST PRICE'. The ASA found that the small print at the bottom of the page was insufficient to counteract the overall impression created by the marketing communication in question.

1   SI 2008/1277, reg 5(2)(a). See also *Director General of Fair Trading v Blinkhorn* (1989, unreported), under the Control of Misleading Advertisements Regulations 1988, SI 1988/915, where Vinelott J stated: 'A document may be misleading, though literally everything in it is true, if the way in which what it says is presented carries with it implications and inferences which the ordinary reader would certainly draw'.

Pricing claims

12.72 Pricing claims are dealt with in rules 3.17–3.32 (as well as in the rules governing comparative advertising, as to which please see below). Pricing claims are now covered in Chapter **13**.

Comparative advertising

12.73 Comparative advertising is covered by rules 3.33–3.44, which broadly reflect the requirements of Art 4 of MCAD 2006, as well as reg 5(3)(a) of CPUTR 2008[1] (rule 3.36). The Rules cover comparisons with identifiable and unidentifiable competitors. An area that causes the most difficulty is the verifiability criterion in rule 3.35, which requires comparisons with identifiable competitors to 'objectively compare one or more material, relevant, verifiable and representative feature of those products, which may include price'. Accordingly, in addition to having substantiation to support any claims made, the CAP Code requires advertisers to ensure that consumers are able to verify the comparison themselves.

1   SI 2008/1277, reg 5(3)(a).

12.74 The CAP has published Advertising Guidance on this topic (updated 24 September 2015) which makes express reference to the CJEU case of *Lidl Belgium*[1]. The CAP provides the following guidance:

- Some comparisons are easy for consumers to verify (eg a comparison between two identical products sold by two different retailers could be checked by looking on their websites).

- Other comparisons (eg those that involve many products), could be more difficult[2].

- The most straightforward way to ensure comparisons are verifiable is to direct readers to a website that contains a list of all the features (such as the products and prices) of the comparison, for example by including the claim 'prices can be verified on www.thiswebsite.co.uk/comparisons/date'.

- Marketers should be explicit about how readers can verify the comparison. The mere inclusion of a website or postal address without stating that readers can verify the comparison might be insufficient.

- It might not be sufficient for marketers to cite a third-party website (eg MySupermarket.com) in the case of grocery retailer price comparisons, without informing readers of the products used in the comparison.

[1] *Lidl Belgium GmbH & Co KG v Etablissementen Franz Colruyt NV* (C-356/04) [2007] Bus LR 492. The Advertising Guidance is available at www.cap.org.uk/Advice-Training-on-the-rules.
[2] The Guidance provides the example *ASDA Stores Ltd*, 14 January 2009, where the ASA found the advertisement to be non-compliant on the basis that it gave no way for readers to verify the advertised savings. A further example given is Wren Kitchens Ltd, 30 January 2013. Wren's advertisement for kitchens provided only enough information to verify some aspects of the products being compared, and their respective prices. Whilst some further information could be found on the advertisers' competitors' website it could not be said that all the necessary information was available.

ENDORSEMENTS AND TESTIMONIALS

12.75 Endorsements and testimonials are addressed by rules 3.45–3.52 of the CAP Code and broadly reflect, inter alia, the prohibitions in Sch 1, paras 1–4 of CPUTR 2008[1], which prohibit the following commercial practices:

- Claiming to be a signatory to a code of conduct when the trader is not.
- Displaying a trust mark, quality mark or equivalent without having obtained the necessary authorisation.
- Claiming that a code of conduct has an endorsement from a public or other body which it does not have.
- Claiming that a trader (including his commercial practices) or a product has been approved, endorsed or authorised by a public or private body when the trader, the commercial practices or the product have not or making such a claim without complying with the terms of the approval, endorsement or authorisation.

[1] SI 2008/1277, Sch 1.

12.76 A recent ruling, *ABC Counselling Services*, 3 Aug 2016, concerned directory entries for ABC Counselling Services claiming that the organisation, as well as one of its individual counsellors, was a member of the British Association for Counselling & Psychotherapy, when this was no longer the case. Unsurprisingly, the advertisement was found to fall foul of rules 3.50 and 3.51 of the CAP Code.

GUARANTEES AND AFTER-SALES SERVICE

12.77 Claims relating to guarantees and after-sales services are governed by rules 3.53–3.57 of the CAP Code[1].

[1]   Rules 3.56 and 3.57 broadly reflect the prohibitions contained in CPUTR 2008, SI 2008/1277, Sch 1, paras 8 and 23. Undertaking to provide after-sales service to consumers with whom the trader has communicated prior to a transaction in a language which is not an official language of the EEA State where the trader is located and then making such service available only in another language without clearly disclosing this to the consumer before the consumer is committed to the transaction. Creating the false impression that after-sales service in relation to a product is available in an EEA State other than the one in which the product is sold.

ASA investigations procedure

12.78 The ASA acts on complaints[1] and a single complaint is sufficient to prompt an investigation. It will not normally pursue complaints if the point at issue is subject to legal proceedings. Complaints must be made within 3 months of the advertisement's appearance (although extensions may be granted in exceptional circumstances) and should focus on no more than three of the most important issues (although more issues may be considered in exceptional circumstances). Complaints may be made by anyone, including members of the public, public bodies and the advertiser's competitors. The ASA's 2018 Annual Report recorded that a vast majority (98%) of complaints that year were made by members of the public. Where the complainant is an individual member of the public, their identity will not be disclosed by the ASA without their permission.

[1]   It may, however, initiate an investigation itself where: (a) it believes that there are potential breaches of the CAP Code based on complaints not raised by the complainant; or (b) a potential breach of the CAP Code has been identified through the ASA's formal intelligence gathering process that it believes warrants an investigation.

12.79 Where a complaint is made by a competitor, the ASA requires the complainant to follow a number of 'Inter-Party Resolution steps'. The competitor complainant must raise its concerns with the advertiser in the first instance. The advertiser should then be given five working days to respond. Any subsequent complaint to the ASA must include the original letter setting out the competitor complainant's concerns and the advertiser's response, if any. The ASA makes it clear, however, that it may not always be appropriate to follow this procedure, but such occasions are deemed to be rare[1].

[1]   'Non-broadcast Complaint Handling Procedures', para 6.

12.80 Complainants who provide evidence in support of their complaints must consent to such evidence being shared with the advertiser. If the complainant fails to give consent if and when requested, the ASA Council will not take the evidence into account when making its ruling. If consent is given, the ASA passes on whatever information it deems (during its investigation) to be relevant 'and needs to be disclosed' to the advertiser. The ASA website also clarifies what is meant by 'evidence'[1]:

'For clarity, by "evidence" we mean documentary information supplied in addition to the point of complaint; it doesn't include a simple description of the circumstances that led the complainant to come to the ASA or an expression of the complainant's opinion or interpretation of a claim.'

1   'Update to ASA procedures: Complainants' evidence', 11 February 2016.

12.81 This revision to the ASA's procedures was introduced in February 2016. Whilst it goes some way in achieving transparency, some would argue that it does not go far enough. In particular, the ASA retains a wide discretion as to whether to disclose evidence to the advertiser and whilst its procedures state that the ASA will not take evidence that the complainant has refused to share into account when making its ruling, advertisers would perhaps rightly be somewhat sceptical of this assurance. In her independent audit of the ASA in April 2017, Dame Paraskeva made calls for more transparency. The ASA's final response to the audit was published in 2017[1].

1   Available here: https://www.asa.org.uk/asset/42129F50-BEE5-4EC3-8DF552FD27BABD46/.

12.82 On receipt of a complaint, the ASA may decide to:

- Take no further action (either because the complaint is unfounded or because it falls outside the ASA's remit). According to the ASA website, around 80% of the complaints received by the ASA do not raise any concerns and are responded to without the need to contact the advertiser[1].
- Resolve the matter informally, usually after receiving assurances from the advertiser that the advertisement will be suitably amended or withdrawn. Such cases are not placed before the ASA Council and no ruling is published[2].
- Commence a formal investigation.

In determining whether a potential breach of the CAP Code merits a formal investigation, the ASA employs 'prioritisation principles'[3].

1   https://www.asa.org.uk/resource/non-broadcast-complaint-handling-procedures.html.
2   The ASA does, however, publish on its website the names of those advertisers that have agreed to amend or withdraw advertisements without the need for a formal investigation.
3   See ss 23–24 of complaint handling procedures: https://www.asa.org.uk/uploads/assets/171eb 506-b4ef-4fec-bdcec62dc49e0be2/Non-Broadcast-Complaint-Handling-Procedures.pdf.

12.83 If the ASA proceeds to an investigation, its procedure[1] is as follows:

- An investigations executive is appointed, as the person in charge of the case and the point of contact for complainants and advertisers.
- A summary of the complaint is sent to the advertiser, inviting a written response. The ASA may also raise issues beyond those raised by the complainant.
- An advertiser is given five working days to respond in cases that involve harm, offence or social responsibility, and seven working days in all other cases. The ASA may grant an extension, but the grounds for requesting the same must be set out in writing. Where the claim is capable of objective substantiation, the CAP Code requires the advertiser to submit documentary evidence to substantiate any such claims.
- On receipt of the response and any further written comments or clarification, the Investigations Executive prepares a draft recommendation.

The draft recommendation is circulated to those named in the report, to other relevant parties if appropriate, and to the complainant for comments[2].

- The recommendation is then placed before the ASA Council ('the Council')[3] In exceptional circumstances, advertisers are given the opportunity to provide written submissions (typically limited to 1000 words) directly to the Council. No provision is made for oral hearings.

- The Council is not bound by the recommendation. If it introduces an important argument or point of view to which the advertiser has not yet had a reasonable opportunity to respond, the ASA will 're-present' the case to the advertiser.

- Once the Council has reached a decision, the Investigations Executive sends a letter to the advertiser informing them of the Council's ruling. If the Council finds that a breach of the Code has occurred, the decision letter details the remedial action that the advertiser is required to take.

- Rulings are published on the ASA website[4] within 14 calendar days of the Council's decision and remain on the website for a period of 5 years. In exceptional circumstances, where the advertiser or complainant have indicated they intend to or have requested an Independent Review, the ASA has a discretion to suspend publication.

[1] The ASA's detailed complaints-handling procedure for non-broadcast advertising is set out on its website, 'Non-broadcast Complaint Handling Procedures' available at www.asa.org.uk/res ource/non-broadcast-complaint-handling-procedures.html.

[2] The ASA's 'Non-broadcast Complaint Handling Procedures' state the such comments should relate to 'the factual accuracy of the draft recommendation' and so would tend to suggest that legal representations are not invited at this stage.

[3] The Council is comprised of 13 people, appointed by the ASA Chairman, two-thirds of whom are independent of the advertising industry. ASA Council members serve 3-year terms for a maximum of 6 years and are appointed following public advertisement.

[4] www.asa.org.uk.

Challenging ASA rulings

Independent review of ASA rulings

12.84 Council decisions are subject to review by an Independent Reviewer. The independent reviewer can only accept the request if one or both of the following conditions are satisfied:

- there is a substantial flaw in the Council's ruling or the process by which that ruling was made;
- additional relevant evidence becomes available that could not reasonably have been shared during the investigation.

Full terms of reference of the independent review procedure are set in the CAP Code and in the 'Non-broadcast Complaint Handling Procedures' document[1], for non-broadcast advertisements, and in the BCAP Code for broadcast advertisements.

[1] Paragraphs 48–61, available at https://www.asa.org.uk/resource/non-broadcast-complaint-ha ndling-procedures.html.

12.85 In summary:

- Requests for review may be made by the complainant or the advertiser. The request must be made in writing and must set out a full statement of the grounds for review in a single document; the Independent Reviewer should not be required to cross-refer to previous correspondence.
- The request must be sent within 21 calendar days of the date on the ASA's letter of notification of the formal ruling or the Council decision that a complaint requires no additional investigation. The 21-day time limit may be waived by the Independent Reviewer in exceptional circumstances.
- Requests for review from the advertiser or from a non-public complainant must be signed by the Chairman, Chief Executive or equivalent office holder; requests made only by a solicitor or agency will not be accepted.
- Oral hearings or meetings with the Independent Reviewer will not be granted.
- Publication of a ruling pending the review process will only be suspended in exceptional circumstances[1].
- The Independent Reviewer can request that a ruling be reconsidered by the Council, following a further investigation by the Reviewer or after the Council re-opens its investigation on the Reviewer's recommendation.
- The Independent Reviewer may invite the Council to reconsider its ruling. However, the final decision as to whether to revise its decision in accordance with the Independent Reviewer's recommendation rests with the ASA Council.

[1]   A request for the same must be received no later than 10am on the Friday that immediately precedes the notified publication date.

Judicial review of ASA rulings

12.86 Decisions made by the ASA are susceptible to judicial review. In *R v ASA Ex Parte Insurance Services*[1], the Divisional Court confirmed that the ASA:

' . . . is clearly exercising a public law function which, if the authority did not exist, would no doubt be exercised by the Director General of Fair Trading'[2].

[1]   (1990) 2 Admin LR 77.
[2]   This is in contrast with the court's position on Clearcast, a body that clears advertisements for broadcast: *Diomed Direct Ltd v Clearcast Ltd*. Mr Justice Stewart found that Clearcast ' . . . exercises no statutory/public law power; nor does it exercise any public law function. The fact that private arrangements are used to secure public law objectives is insufficient.' Stewart J found that Clearcast simply assisted with broadcasters' functions and if a broadcaster decided not to approve an advertisement because of a risk of an adverse finding by the ASA due to a lack of BCAP compliance, then that decision would not be amenable to judicial review.

12.87 Both the decisions of the ASA Council and those of the Independent Reviewer can be challenged by way of judicial review. Whilst it is possible to seek to review both at once, the High Court in *R (Actegy Limited) v ASA*[1] queried whether it was necessary to seek judicial review of the Independent Reviewer's decision in that case: 'If these [judicial review] proceedings led to the ASA's decision being quashed, an omission to challenge the IR's rejection of a review request would not resuscitate that decision'. It is worth noting that an application to review the ASA Council decision without engaging with the Independent Review process exposes the claimant to arguments on the failure to exhaust existing remedies[2]. This formed one of the grounds for dismissing an advertiser's application for judicial review in *R (Debt Free Direct Ltd) v ASA*[3]. It is worth noting the strict time limits imposed by the Civil Procedure Rules 1998[4], and the requirement to comply with them will need to be balanced against the risks of having the claim dismissed on alternative remedy grounds.

[1]   [2019] EWHC 2374 (Admin), para 81.
[2]   The general principle was stated by Lord Scarman in *R v Inland Revenue Commissioners, Ex parte Preston* [1985] AC 835, at 852. See also *R v Epping and Harlow General Commissioners, Ex parte Goldstraw* [1983] 3 All ER 257, at 262. See [2007] EWHC 1337 (Admin) on this point.
[3]   [2007] EWHC 1337 (Admin). Note, however, that the court did make it clear that the complaints put forward were suitable for resolution within the Independent Review procedure. It may be that some complaints are considered less suitable for the said procedure.
[4]   CPR 54.5(1).

12.88 The courts will apply ordinary judicial review principles[1]. Whilst some questions are hard-edged questions of law (such as whether the ASA applied the correct legal test), others are susceptible to an assessment on irrationality grounds only[2]. Judicial review is a difficult remedy and it is perhaps unsurprising that challenges of ASA decisions by way of judicial review have only been successful in a handful of cases.

[1]   For recent examples, see *R (on the application of Sainsbury's Supermarkets Ltd) v Independent Reviewer of Advertising Standards Authority Adjudications* [2015] ACD 23 and *R (Actegy Limited) v ASA* [2019] EWHC 2374 (Admin).
[2]   *Associated Provincial Picture Houses Ltd v Wednesbury Corpn* [1948] 1 KB 223. A decision is Wednesbury unreasonable if it is so unreasonable that no reasonable person acting reasonably could have made it.

UNSUCCESSFUL JUDICIAL REVIEW CHALLENGES

12.89 *R v Advertising Standards Authority Ltd Ex p Vernons Organisation Ltd*[1]. The court dismissed the advertiser's application for an order restraining publication of the ASA's decision pending determination of its application for judicial review[2]. Accordingly, publication could take place notwithstanding the fact that there might be errors of law in the decision which might be reversed on review[3]. See also *R (Jamba GmbH) v ASA*[4] on this point.

[1]   [1992] 1 WLR 1289.
[2]   See also *R (Debt Free Direct Ltd) v ASA* and *R (Sainsbury's Supermarkets Ltd) v Independent Reviewer of ASA Adjudications* discussed above.
[3]   Vernons was successfully distinguished in *R v ASA ex parte Direct Line Financial Services Limited* [1998] COD 20.
[4]   [2005] EWHC 2609 (Admin).

12.90 *R v ASA Ex p City Trading Limited*[1]. The advertiser's application for judicial review on Art 10 (freedom of speech) of the European Convention on Human Rights ('ECHR') grounds was dismissed, but it should be noted that this decision pre-dates the Human Rights Act 1998 ('HRA 1998'). For a post-HRA 1998 decision, please see *R v ASA ex parte Matthias Rath BV*[2]; where the court found that whilst the ASA Codes did not have direct statutory effect, they fell within the meaning of Art 10(2) of the ECHR and could therefore form the basis of a restriction on the advertiser's freedom of speech.

[1]   [1997] COD 202.
[2]   [2001] EMLR 22.

12.91 *R v ASA ex parte DSG Retail Limited*[1]. The High Court held that whilst decisions by the ASA were subject to judicial review, the court's role was supervisory such that it could only interfere on the grounds of irrationality, illegality or procedural impropriety.

[1] [1997] COD 232.

12.92 *R v ASA ex parte Charles Robertson (Developments) Limited*[1]. The High Court adopted a light-touch approach, finding that the question of whether a column was an advertisement was for ASA to decide and the court would not intervene unless the decision was manifestly unreasonable. A similar approach was adopted in *R (Coys of Kensington Automobiles Ltd) v ASA*[2], where it was found that the ASA's decision could not be impugned on irrationality grounds; it came from those with expertise within the advertising industry who understood the potential effects of misleading adverts. Similarly, in *Buxton v Advertising Standards Authority*[3], it was noted that the assessment of '[w]hether an advertisement is or is not likely to mislead the public is a matter which is best dealt with by an expert body such as the ASA'. For a recent decision adopting a similar approach, see *R (on the application of Cityfibre Ltd) v Advertising Standards Authority*[4].

[1] [2000] EMLR 463.
[2] [2012] EWHC 902 (Admin).
[3] [2002] EWHC 2433 (Admin).
[4] [2019] EWHC 950 (Admin), [2019] 4 WLUK 241.

12.93 *R (Smithkline Beecham Plc) v ASA*[1]. The court found that there was no real danger of bias on the part of the ASA, even though it had based its decision on the opinion of an ASA consultant who had previously made complaints regarding the products in the advertisement.

[1] [2001] EMLR 23.

Successful judicial review challenges

12.94 Whilst many have no doubt been brought, few applications for judicial review have been successful. The two reported cases that were successful concern procedural impropriety, rather than the substance of the ASA's decisions. An example of a successful challenge to an ASA ruling is that of *R v ASA Ex Parte Insurance Services*[1] regarding the opportunity to comment on the draft recommendation and any other material put before the ASA Council. This case has not been followed in subsequent cases, however. A further example is *R v ASA ex parte Direct Line Financial Services Limited*[2], where it was held that where a body acted in a judicial or quasi-judicial capacity, a duty existed to give all parties ample opportunity to make whatever representations would normally be appropriate in those circumstances.

[1] (1990) 2 Admin LR 77.
[2] [1998] COD 20.

Copy advice

12.95 The CAP provides copy advice, although the ASA website makes it clear that such advice is not binding on the ASA or CAP. It does clarify, however, that the ASA will check, as part of its investigation process, whether copy advice was consulted. The adviser who dealt with the enquiry will then explain the potential problems that were identified and what recommendations were made for changes. If it is evident that the advertiser 'tried to avoid provoking complaints', the ASA will bear that in mind when reaching its decision.

Advertising guidance

12.96 The CAP also publishes 'Advertising Guidance' (previously known as 'Help Notes') on a host of areas to assist advertisers in complying with their obligations. Recent Advertising Guidance notes have covered matters such as:

- affiliate marketing;
- the use of envelopes in marketing communications;
- lowest price claims and promises;
- promotions with prizes;
- retailers' price comparisons;
- marketing of spiritual and psychic services;
- substantiation for health, beauty and slimming claims; and
- ticket pricing.

Again, the CAP makes it clear that its Advertising Guidance is not intended to bind the ASA in the event of a complaint about an advertisement that follows it.

Sanctions

12.97 The ASA does not have the power to impose fines or take legal action against non-compliant advertisers. It does have a number of sanctions at its disposal, however, some of which can have a significant impact on an advertiser's business.

Publication

12.98 ASA rulings are published weekly on the ASA website. An adverse ASA ruling normally comes with a direction to amend or withdraw the advertisement (or website content) in question and not to repeat it in its current form. Once published,rulings remain on the ASA's website for a period of 5 years. These are designed to appear in search engine results when a consumer searches for a company's website. The ASA also publishes a list of non-compliant advertisers (ie those who have continued to make non-compliant advertising claims on their websites, despite repeated requests to amend them) on its website[1].

[1]   www.asa.org.uk/Rulings.

Ad alerts

12.99 The CAP can issue alerts to its members, including the media, advising them to consult the copy advice team before accepting advertisements for publication or, in some circumstances, to withhold their services (eg access to advertising space) from non-compliant advertisers. The alerts can be either general (relating to a general subject or a policy change that results from an ASA ruling) or specific (relating to individual advertisers). The alerts may cover an entire sector if the CAP perceives a widespread problem.

Withdrawal of trading privileges

12.100 An adverse ASA ruling can result in CAP members revoking, withdrawing or temporarily withholding the non-compliant advertiser's recognition and trading privileges. The ASA website provides an example of the Royal Mail withdrawing its bulk mail discount, which can make running direct marketing campaigns prohibitively expensive. In severe cases of non-compliance, CAP members may expel traders from membership.

Pre-vetting

12.101 The ASA can require repeatedly non-compliant advertisers to have their marketing material vetted prior to publication. Advertising agencies (or other CAP members) are effectively ordered not to carry material to which the ASA objects unless it has been pre-vetted by it[1]. The pre-vetting can last for 2 years. French Connection was subject to the pre-vetting procedure in 2004, following an advertisement which stated 'Fcuk FM from Pnuk to Rcok and back. Non-stop Fnuk. Fcuk Fm'. This followed a series of rulings deeming offensive the use of the 'FCUK' trademark where it was used to replace the common expletive.

[1] The ASA provides the following example on its website: CAP's poster industry members can invoke mandatory pre-vetting for advertisers who have broken the CAP Code on grounds of taste and decency or social responsibility.

12.102 The sanction of pre-vetting is a serious one, particularly in light of the fact that the ASA's decision-making procedures cannot be described as elaborate; there is no right to an oral hearing and the evidence submitted by the complainant is usually summarised rather than disclosed. This contrasts with the intricate procedures that must be followed if a regulator, eg the CMA, wishes to obtain an injunction against an advertiser under the Enterprise Act 2002.

Online sanctions

12.103 The ASA also has a number of online sanctions at its disposal. It can ask websites to remove an advertiser's paid-for search advertisements. In addition to featuring details of rulings in search engine results when consumers search for a company's website (see above), the ASA can also place advertisements in search engine results to warn consumers about non-compliant advertisers.

Referral to trading standards

12.104 The Control of Misleading Advertisements Regulations 1988[1] which implemented Directive 84/450/EEC on misleading advertising, provided the

ASA with legal backing from the Office of Fair Trading ('OFT', now the Competition and Markets Authority). The ASA was thereby given the power to refer persistently non-compliant advertisers to the OFT for legal action. The Control of Misleading Advertisements Regulations 1988 have subsequently been replaced with CPUTR 2008 and the BPR 2008 and referrals have, since 2013, been made to Trading Standards, rather than the OFT. National Trading Standards has in turn contracted Buckinghamshire and Surrey Trading Standards department to investigate, and if necessary act on, matters referred to it by the ASA.

[1]   SI 1988/915.

12.105 The first example of such a referral, under predecessor legislation, dates back to 1988 and the case of Tobyward Ltd. The case concerned an advertisement for a slimming product made from guar gum, which the ASA had found to be misleading and therefore in breach of the CAP Code. The matter was referred to the Director General of Fair Trading, who obtained an injunction against Tobyward Ltd. In granting the injunction, Hoffman J observed[1]:

> 'It is . . . desirable and in accordance with the public interest . . . that the courts should support the principle of self-regulation. I think that advertisers would be more inclined to accept the rulings of their self-regulatory bodies if it were generally known that in cases in which their procedures had been exhausted and the advertiser was still publishing an advertisement which appeared to the court to be *prima facie* misleading, an injunction would ordinarily be granted.'

[1]   *Director General of Fair Trading v Tobyward Ltd* [1989] 1 WLR 517, at 522.

12.106 For a recent referral, please see the matter of Viagogo (a secondary ticketing site), which was referred to Trading Standards by the ASA. The ASA's annual report from 2019 revealed that the ASA referred a further nine advertisers to Trading Standards[1]. In relation to broadcast advertising, non-compliant advertisers are referred to Ofcom, as the ASA's co-regulatory partner for broadcast advertising.

[1]   https://www.asa.org.uk/uploads/assets/5d2b832d-8d12-4f28-9e9f5df54f7b93c1/ASA-CAP-2 019-Annual-Report.pdf.

Closing remarks

12.107 The ASA has often been described as 'toothless' by its critics. The reputational, and potentially financial, risks involved in an adverse ruling cannot be underestimated however, and the ASA has, in recent years taken steps to address concerns about its alleged ineffectiveness. It has, for instance referred a number of non-compliant advertisers to Trading Standards and worked with internet search providers to remove non-compliant paid-for search advertisements. Furthermore, the ASA now places its own advertisements into search engine results as a means of warning consumers about non-compliant advertisers. Its 2019 Annual Report highlights the ASA's efforts to have more impact and be more proactive, successfully addressing a number of online challenges. Whilst it is perhaps 'toothless' in comparison with Trading Standards when it comes to the sanctions at its disposal, its work is well-funded and, as a consequence, more wide-ranging.

Chapter 13

PRICES

Contents

INTRODUCTION

13.1 The regulation of prices can be found in various legislative provisions, some of which are general and others sector-based. Most of these domestic provisions were derived from EU law directives. The legislation in this area can be categorised as follows:

(a)   Price marking obligations under the Price Marking Order 2004[1] ('PMO 2004').

(b)   Sectoral provisions for bureaux de change, package travel and consumer credit.

(c)   Misleading prices under the Consumer Protection from Unfair Trading Regulations 2008[2] ('CPUTR 2008').

(d)   Pricing obligations originally derived from EU based consumer rights legislation.

[1]   SI 2004/102.
[2]   SI 2008/1277.

13.2 The following table sets out the main pricing obligations and where they are covered in this work.

Statutory provision			Description	CTSLP Ref
Price Marking Order	Art 4	Selling price	Obligation to indicate the selling price of goods	**13.12**
	Art 5	Unit price	Obligation to indicate the unit price of goods	**13.14**
	Arts 6, 7 & 8	Manner of price indication	Obligation to indicate the price in sterling, legibly etc	**13.18**
	Art 9	General price reductions	Obligation to indicate details of the reduction so it is prominently displayed, unambiguous, easily identifiable and clearly legible	**13.21**
Bureaux de Change (No. 2) Regulations 1992	Regs 5–8	Price indications about exchange rates	Regulation of the manner of price indications about exchange rates by bureaux de change	**13.33**
Consumer Credit (Disclosure of Information) Regulations 2010	Sch 1	Information about the price	Information to be provided about the amount of credit, cash price, interest, total amount payable, AR etc	**19.62**
Consumer Rights Act 2015, Pt 2 (unfair terms)	Part 2	Unfair terms	Fairness of an aspect of the price that falls outside the core exemption for adequacy	**9.95**
	Sch 2, Pt 1, para 6	Grey list: penalties	Requiring a consumer who fails to fulfil his obligations under the contract to pay a disproportionately high sum in compensation	**9.97**
	Sch 2, Pt 1, para 14	Grey list: unilateral price variation	Giving the trader the discretion to decide the price payable under the contract after the consumer has become bound by it, when no price or method of determining the price is agreed when the consumer becomes bound	**9.97**
	Sch 2, Pt 1, para 15	Grey list: price variation without right to cancel	Permitting a trader to increase the price without giving the consumer the right to cancel the contract if the final price is too high	**9.97**

Statutory provision			Description	CTSLP Ref
Consumer Rights (Payment Surcharges Regulations) 2012	Reg 4 and 6A-6B	Credit and debit card fees etc	Reg 6A(1) prohibition on charging consumers a fee for using a credit card or debit card etc when both payment service providers located in the UK. Otherwise limited to the cost of providing that method of payment	6.125
Consumer Contracts (Information, Cancellation and Additional Charges) Regulations 2013	Regs 10–14; Sch 1 and 2	Pre-contractual information	Obligation to provide pre-contractual information about the total price, delivery charges etc	6.54
	Reg 40	Default options on additional fees	Use a default option (such as a pre-ticked box on a website) in order to obtain a consumer's consent to an additional fee or charge	13.90
Consumer Protection from Unfair Trading Regulations 2008	Regs 3, 5, 6 and Sch 1	Unfair commercial practices	These provisions are set out below at **13.41**. These regulations are covered in detail in CHAPTER 8, Unfair Commercial Practices	13.38

PRICE MARKING

Introduction

13.3 The Prices Act 1974 ('PA 1974') was introduced by Harold Wilson's Labour government as a method of controlling inflation. Its main purpose was to allow governmental control over the price of food and other staple products. The PA 1974 also sought to regulate the way that retailers displayed prices, which was seen as a way of reducing inflationary pressures by increasing public awareness of price differentials. The Act's wide powers have, however been largely repealed and its sole function now is to provide the basis for the Price Marking Order 2004[1], which was made under the PA 1974, s 4.

[1] SI 2004/102.

13.4 Other price marking orders made under the Prices Act 1974 – and other Acts – were repealed by the CPUTR 2008, but there was an express saving for the Price Indications (Bureaux de Change) (No 2) Regulations 1992[1].

[1] SI 1992/737 (made under the now-repealed the Consumer Protection Act 1987, s 26).

THE PRICE MARKING ORDER 2004

13.5 The Price Marking Order 2004[1] ('PMO 2004') came into force on 22 July 2004. It replaces the Price Marking Order 1999, which replaced the convoluted provisions of the Price Marking Order 1991. It implemented the EU Price Indications Directive[2]. Equivalent provisions to PMO 2004 are contained in the Price Marking Order (Northern Ireland) 2004[3].

[1]   SI 2004/102.
[2]   Directive 98/6/EC of the European Parliament and of the Council of 16 February 1998 on consumer protection in the indication of the prices of products offered to consumers.
[3]   SR 2004/368.

Application

13.6 The PA 1974 applies across the UK. The territorial extent of the PMO 2004 is not expressly limited, however, the Price Marking Order (Northern Ireland) in virtually identical terms also applies in Northern Ireland[1]. Both provisions are made pursuant to the PA 1974, s 4 which provides for the making of orders about the price that food is sold at, and the manner that prices are displayed for, all goods. The PMO 2004 generally requires traders to indicate the selling price of all products offered for sale to consumers and, for specified products (such as fruit and vegetables sold from bulk), to indicate the unit price of the product. Importantly, PMO 2004 does not cover products which are supplied in the provision of a service and only regulates sales between traders and consumers. Another significant exception is that the obligation to indicate selling price or unit price does not apply to advertisements. Other exceptions are for sales by auction and sales of works of art or antiques.

[1]   SI 2004/368, a separate process for Northern Ireland is required by PA 1974, s 4(5).

13.7 In the *Citroën Commerce case*[1] the CJEU ruled on a complaint about the final price of a motor car in a newspaper advertisement (see below at **13.74**). The case also addressed the relationship between the Price Indications Directive[2], a sectoral provision, and the Unfair Commercial Practices Directive ('UCPD') which generally covers all unfair commercial practices. The CJEU was asked to consider both the Price Indications Directive and whether the advertisement also amounted to an unfair commercial practice. It declined to consider the latter on the basis of the sectoral conflict provision in Art 3(4) of the UCPD, which requires precedence to be given to a specific sectoral requirement in another EU measure. This is potentially an important development because it suggests that the CPUTR 2008, which implements the UCPD, may not be the appropriate provision to use where there are specific obligations under the PMO 2004.

Price Marking Order 2004, art 1[3]:

1 Citation, commencement and interpretation

(2) In this Order—
"advertisement" means any form of advertisement which is made in order to promote the sale of a product but does not include any advertisement by means of which the trader intends to encourage a consumer to enter into a distance contract, a catalogue, a price list, a container or a label;
"consumer" means any individual who buys a product for purposes that do not fall within the sphere of his commercial or professional activity;

"cosmetic products" means any substance or preparation intended to be placed in contact with an external part of the human body, or with the teeth, inside of the mouth or throat with a view exclusively or mainly to one or more of the following purposes: cleaning, perfuming, changing the appearance of, protecting, and keeping in good condition it or them or correcting body odour;

"distance contract" means any contract concerning products concluded between a trader and a consumer, by any means, without the simultaneous physical presence of the trader and the consumer;

"itinerant trader" means any trader who, as a pedestrian, or from a train, aircraft, vessel, vehicle, stall, barrow, or other mobile sales unit, offers products to consumers other than by means of pre-printed material;

"liquid medium" has the meaning given for the purposes of the second subparagraph of point 5 of Annex IX to Regulation (EU) No 1169/2011 of the European Parliament and of the Council on the provision of food information to consumers;

"make-up products" means cosmetic products solely intended temporarily to change the appearance of the face or nails, including (but not limited to) lipsticks, mascaras, eye shadows, blushers and concealers;

"net drained weight" means the weight of a solid food product when it is presented in a liquid medium;

"precious metal" means gold, silver or platinum, or any other metal to which by an order under section 17 of the Hallmarking Act 1973 the provisions of that Act are applied;

"products sold from bulk" means products which are not pre-packaged and are weighed or measured at the request of the consumer;

"relevant floor area" in relation to a shop means the internal floor area of the shop excluding any area not used for the retail sale of products or for the display of such products for retail sale;

"selling price" means the final price for a unit of a product, or a given quantity of a product, including VAT and all other taxes;

"shop" includes a store, kiosk and a franchise or concession within a shop;

"small shop" means any shop which has a "relevant floor area" not exceeding 280 square metres;

"standard of fineness" means any one of the standards of fineness specified in column (2) of paragraph 2 of Schedule 2 to the Hallmarking Act 1973;

"trader" means any person who sells or offers or exposes for sale products which fall within his commercial or professional activity;

"unit price" means the final price, including VAT and all other taxes, for one kilogram, one litre, one metre, one square metre or one cubic metre of a product, except (i) in respect of the products specified in Schedule 1, where unit price means the final price including VAT and all other taxes for the corresponding units of quantity set out in that Schedule; and (ii) in respect of products sold by number, where unit price means the final price including VAT and all other taxes for an individual item of the product.

PMO 2004, art 3[4]:

3 Scope of application of the Order

(1)   This Order shall not apply—

    (a)   to products which are supplied in the course of the provision of a service; or

    (b)   to sales by auction or sales of works of art or antiques.

(2)   The Electronic Commerce (EC Directive) Regulations 2002 shall apply to this Order notwithstanding Regulation 3(2) of those Regulations.

[1]   *Citroën Commerce GMBH v Zentralvereinigung des Kraftfahrzeuggewerbes zur Aufrechterhaltung lauteren Wettbewerbs eV (ZLW)* Case C-476/14, 7 July 2016.

[2]   Directive 98/6/EC of the European Parliament and of the Council of 16 February 1998 on consumer protection in the indication of the prices of products offered to consumers.

[3]   SI 2004/102, art 1.

[4]   SI 2004/102.

13.8 Article 3 defines the application of PMO 2004. The important exclusions are products supplied in the course of the provision of a service; and auction sales of art or antiques; both of which were excluded by the 1991 and 1999 Orders. It is important to note that delivery of a product does not constitute a service for this purpose. A product that can be bought without a service should also indicate its price. Goods manufactured to order do not have to be price marked unless there is only a limited number of choices available.

13.9 The PMO 2004 states that Electronic Commerce (EC Directive) Regulations 2002[1] ('ECR 2002') applies to the PMO 2004 despite the empowering statute (PA 1974) having been made almost 20 years before the Directive. The ECR 2002 are poorly drafted and slavishly follow a series of EC Directives. Definitions and concepts are overcomplicated and the language used offends against basic principles of plain English.

[1]   SI 2002/2013.

13.10 The ECR 2002 apply to those who provide 'information society services', which is defined by reference to Art 2(a) of the amended European Technical Standards Directive ('ETSD')[1]. It is summarised in the recital to the ETSD and in the definitions set out in the ECR as:

'any service normally provided for remuneration, at a distance, by means of electronic equipment for the processing (including digital compression) and storage of data, and at the individual request of a recipient of a service.'

[1]   98/34/EC as amended by Directive 98/48/EC. The key definitions are provided by the amending Directive.

13.11 A list of areas that fall outside the definition of an ISS is set out at annex J of the amended ETSD. The definition is also augmented by the following:

'For the purposes of this definition:

"at a distance" means that the service is provided without the parties being simultaneously present,

"by electronic means" means that the service is sent initially and received at its destination by means of electronic equipment for the processing (including digital compression) and storage of data, and entirely transmitted, conveyed and received by wire, by radio, by optical means or by other electromagnetic means,

"at the individual request of a recipient of services" means that the service is provided through the transmission of data on individual request.'

Obligation to indicate selling price

13.12 PMO 2004, art 4[1]:

4 Obligation to indicate selling price

(1) Subject to paragraph (2) of this article, where a trader indicates that any product is or may be for sale to a consumer, he shall indicate the selling price of that product in accordance with the provisions of this Order.

(2) The requirement in paragraph (1) above shall not apply in respect of—
(a) products sold from bulk; and
(b) an advertisement for a product.

Article 4 provides the general obligation for a trader to indicate the selling price on all goods for sale to a consumer[2], in a manner prescribed by the other provisions of the Order[3]. Products that are not pre-packaged, but weighed or measured at the request of the consumer (sold from bulk) are excluded, in favour of an obligation simply to indicate the unit price[4]. An 'advertisement' for a product is also excluded from the obligation to indicate the price. 'Advertisement' is defined narrowly, however thereby reducing the scope of the exception. It excludes, 'any advertisement by means of which the trader intends to encourage a consumer to enter into a distance contract, a catalogue, a price list, a container or label'[5], such that the Order does apply to catalogues, price lists, containers and labels. In the *Citroën Commerce case*[6] the CJEU considered the meaning of 'final price' in Art 2(a) of the Price Indications Directive (see below at **13.74**).

[1] SI 2004/102.
[2] Defined as the final price including VAT and other taxes.
[3] 'Trader' and 'consumer' are defined in art 1 (see above).
[4] Article 5.
[5] The categories should be read disjunctively.
[6] *Citroën Commerce GMBH v Zentralvereinigung des Kraftfahrzeuggewerbes zur Aufrechterhaltung lauteren Wettbewerbs eV (ZLW)* Case C-476/14, 7 July 2016.

INTERNET ADVERTISING

13.13 PMO 2004 also applies to goods that are advertised for sale over the internet because advertisements encouraging 'distance contracts' are regulated. The definition of a 'distance contract' includes contracts formed 'by any means', without the simultaneous physical presence of the parties.

Unit prices

13.14 PMO 2004, art 5[1]:

5 Obligation to indicate unit price

(1) Subject to paragraph (2), (3) and (4) and article 9, where a trader indicates that any product is or may be for sale to a consumer, he shall indicate the unit price of that product in accordance with the provisions of this Order.

(2) The requirement in paragraph (1) only applies in respect of products sold from bulk or required by or under Parts IV or V of the Weights and Measures Act 1985 to be –
(a) marked with an indication of quantity; or
(b) made up in a quantity prescribed by or under that Act.

(3)   The requirement in paragraph (1) shall not apply in relation to:
    (a)   any product which falls within Schedule 2;
    (b)   any product the unit price of which is identical to its selling price;
    (c)   bread made up in a prescribed quantity which is or may be for sale in a small shop, by an itinerant trader or from a vending machine; or
    (d)   any product which is pre-packaged in a constant quantity which is or may be for sale in a small shop, by an itinerant trader or from a vending machine.

(4)   The requirement in paragraph (1) applies in relation to an advertisement for a product only where the selling price of the product is indicated in the advertisement.

PMO 2004, Sch 2:

SCHEDULE 2

Products in respect of which a trader is exempt from the requirement to unit price

(1)   Any product which is offered by traders to consumers by means of an advertisement which is—
    (a)   purely aural;
    (b)   broadcast on television;
    (c)   shown at a cinema; or
    (d)   inside a small shop.

(2)   Any product the price of which has been reduced from the usual price at which it is sold, on account of—
    (a)   its damaged condition; or
    (b)   the danger of its deterioration.

(3)   Any product which comprises an assortment of different items sold in a single package.

(4)   Any product the unit price of which is 0.0p as a result of article 12 (Decimal places and rounding of unit prices) of this Order.

[1]   SI 2004/102.

13.15 Article 5 provides a simple rule that the unit price must be indicated on goods that are sold from bulk. The unit price is simply the total price[1] for a **metric** unit of the particular product. The obligation to indicate the unit price extends to goods that come within the Weights and Measures Act 1985 (see Chapter 17)[2]. Advertisements for goods sold in bulk[3] do not need to indicate the unit price, unless the actual price is advertised. If the goods are of a type listed in Sch 1 of the Order, the obligation is to indicate the price for the quantity listed in the Schedule (see below).

[1]   To include VAT and all other taxes.
[2]   The obligation applies to goods for which the Weights and Measures Act 1985 prescribes the selling quantity (for example beer), and goods which the Act simply requires the quantity to be indicated.
[3]   Or those under the Weights and Measures Act 1985.

13.16 In 2005 the then-Department for Trade and Industry ('DTI') (now Business, Energy and Industrial Strategy) issued a *Guidance Note on the Price Marking Order 2004*. Although no longer available, it included useful analysis. As to art 5 it stated that:

'The standard units of quantity to be used for unit pricing purposes are one kilogram, litre, metre, square metre or cubic metre and the unit 'one' for goods sold by number. Some exceptions are allowed and the Order contains a list of products that must be unit priced using different units of quantity – usually 100g or 100ml. Similar products should use the same unit for unit pricing purposes to allow consumers to readily compare prices between them. In exceptional circumstances this may mean that a product required to show a unit price per kilogram, for example, could usefully show a further price per 100g.'

Goods that must indicate the price of a specified quantity

13.17 For the types of goods listed in Sch 1 of the Order, the price must be given for the metric amount listed in column 2 of the Schedule[1].

PMO 2004, art 14[2]:

14 Units of Quantity

For the purposes of Schedule 1, the figure denoting the relevant units of quantity in the second column of the table for the corresponding product in the first column of the table refers to a unit indicated by or under the Weights and Measures Act 1985 and unless specified otherwise:

(a)   grams where the product is sold by weight;
(b)   millilitres where the product is sold by volume; and
(c)   either grams or millilitres, as indicated by the manufacturer of the product, where the product may be sold by either weight or volume.

Price Marking Order 2004, Sch 1[3]:

SCHEDULE 1

Relevant unit of quantity for specific products for the purpose of the definition of 'unit price'

PRODUCT	UNITS
Flavouring essences	10
Food colourings	10
Herbs	10
Make-up Products	10 (except where sold by number)
Seeds other than pea, bean, grass and wild bird seeds	10
Spices	10
Biscuits and shortbread	100 (except where sold by number)
Bread	100 (except where sold by number)
Breakfast cereal products	100 (except where required to be quantity marked by number)
Chocolate confectionery and sugar confectionery	100
Coffee	100
Cooked or ready-to-eat fish, seafoods and crustacea	100
Cooked or ready-to-eat meat including game and poultry	100
Cosmetic products other than make-up products	100
Cream and non-dairy alternatives to cream	100

PRODUCT	UNITS
Dips and spreads excluding edible fats	100
Dry sauce mixes	100
Fresh processed salad	100
Fruit juices, soft drinks	100
Handrolling and pipe tobacco	100
Ice cream and frozen desserts	100
Lubricating oils other than oils for internal combustion engines	100
Pickles	100
Pies, pasties, sausage rolls, puddings and flans indicating net quantity	100 (except where sold by number)
Potato crisps and similar products commonly known as snack foods	100
Preserves including honey	100
Ready to eat desserts	100
Sauces, edible oils	100
Soups	100
Tea and other beverages prepared with liquid	100
Waters, including spa waters and aerated waters	100
Wines, sparkling wine, liqueur wine, fortified wine	75 cl
Coal, where sold by the kilogram	50 kg
Ballast, where sold by the kilogram	1,000 kg

[1]   For example, for herbs the metric amount is 10 grams, whereas for hand cream the amount is 100 millilitres.
[2]   SI 2004/102.
[3]   SI 2004/102, Sch 1.

The manner of price indications

13.18   Price Marking Order 2004, arts 6, 7 and 8[1]:

6 Manner of indication of selling price and unit price

(1)   The indication of selling price and unit price shall be in sterling.

(2)   If a trader indicates his willingness to accept foreign currency in payment for a product, he shall, in addition to the required price indications in sterling—

(a)   give an indication of the selling price and any unit price required for the product in the foreign currency in question together with any commission to be charged; or

(b)   clearly identify the conversion rate on the basis of which the foreign currency price will be calculated together with any commission to be charged; and

indicate that such selling price, unit price or conversion rate as the case may be does not apply to transactions via a payment card to be applied to accounts denominated in currencies other than sterling, the conversion rate for which will be that applied by the relevant payment scheme which processes the transaction.

7 Manner of indication of selling price and unit price

(1) An indication of selling price, unit price, commission, conversion rate or a change in the rate or coverage of value added tax given in accordance with article 11 shall be—

(a) unambiguous, easily identifiable and clearly legible;

(b) subject to paragraph 2, given in proximity to—

(i) the product; or

(ii) in the case of distance contracts and advertisements, a visual or written description of the product; and

(c) so placed as to be available to consumers without the need for them to seek assistance from the trader or someone on his behalf in order to ascertain it.

(2) Paragraph (1)(b)(i) does not apply to an indication given in relation to any item of jewellery, item of precious metal, or watch displayed in a window of the premises where it is or may be for sale and the selling price of which is in excess of £3,000.

(3) The indication of any charges for postage, package or delivery of a product shall be unambiguous, easily identifiable and clearly legible.

(4) Where, in addition to a unit price, a price per quantity is indicated in relation to a supplementary indication of quantity the unit price shall predominate and the price per supplementary indication of quantity shall be expressed in characters no larger than the unit price.

(5) In paragraph (4) "supplementary indication of quantity" refers to an indication of quantity expressed in a unit of measurement other than a metric unit as authorised by section 8(5A) of the Weights and Measures Act 1985.

8 Manner of indication of selling price and unit price

In the case of a pre-packaged solid food product presented in a liquid medium, the unit price shall refer to the net drained weight of the product. Where a unit price is also given with reference to the net weight of the product, it shall be clearly indicated which unit price relates to net drained weight and which to net weight.

[1] SI 2004/102, arts 6, 7 and 8.

13.19 The unit price by its definition must be expressed metrically. Like its predecessors, however, PMO 2004 expressly allows supplementary indications given in imperial measures. The restriction that is placed upon additional measurements is that the metric unit price should 'predominate' and imperial price per quantity should, 'be expressed in characters no larger than the unit price'[1]. The unit must also be authorised by the Weights and Measures Act 1985, s 8(5A).

[1] SI 2004/102, art 7(4).

13.20 The DTI *Guidance Note* stated that:

'5. The Order requires that prices must be "unambiguous, easily identifiable and clearly legible" but it is not prescriptive about the way in which those requirements are met. It does, however, require that consumers should not have to ask for assistance in order to be able to see a price. Legibility of price indications in this context means legible to a consumer with normal sight. Traders are, however, reminded of their obligations under the Disability Discrimination Act 1995 and to take account of the special needs of the elderly and disabled groups. When considering the needs of those with less than perfect eyesight, traders are encouraged to take account of the Royal National Institute for the Blind's Clear Print Guidelines.

6. There is no requirement to price mark items individually. Prices can be shown on the goods themselves, on a ticket or notice on or near to them, or grouped together with other prices on a list or catalogue(s) in close proximity to them. If counter catalogues are used then there should be sufficient copies for consumers to refer to. Goods kept out of sight of the consumer are exempt from price marking until an indication is given that they are for sale.

7. Price indications given in the course of conducting a sale by telephone clearly cannot meet the Order's "legibility" requirement. However, such indications must be clearly audible and linked to the subject of the sales transaction if they are to meet the Order's requirements of "unambiguous, easily identifiable" and to be in keeping with the "proximity" requirement.'

Price reduction indications

13.21 Price Marking Order 2004, art 9[1]:

9 Special provisions relating to general reductions

Where a trader proposes to sell products to which this Order applies at less than the selling price or the unit price previously applicable and indicated in accordance with article 7(1), he may comply with the obligations specified in articles 4(1) (to indicate the selling price) and 5(1) (to indicate the unit price) by indicating by a general notice or any other visible means that the products are or may be for sale at a reduction, provided that the details of the reduction are prominently displayed, unambiguous, easily identifiable and clearly legible.

There is longstanding concern among consumer organisations about the practice of traders that advertise reductions in prices, that such reductions are genuine. All price indications must be (among other things) unambiguous under art 7(1) PMO 2004. Under art 9, a price reduction indication will only comply with PMO 2004 requirements if, 'details of the reduction are prominently displayed, unambiguous, easily identifiable and clearly legible'.

[1]   SI 2004/102, art 9.

13.22 The DTI *Guidance Note* stated that:

'8. Where a trader wants to reduce the price of products that are already priced as the Order requires he may indicate the final selling and/or unit price of the product by displaying a general notice (or by any other visible means) that the products are for sale at a reduction, provided that the details of the reduction are prominently displayed, unambiguous, easily identifiable and clearly legible.

9. In the case of products the selling price of which varies from day to day according to the price of the precious metals contained in them, the obligation to indicate the selling price may be complied with by indicating, in a manner which is unambiguous, easily identifiable and clearly legible, the weight, type and standard of fineness of each precious metal contained in the product, the price per unit of weight and any element of the selling price which is not referable to weight.'

Exceptions

13.23 There are several exceptions from the requirement to price mark. These were set out in the DTI *Guidance Note* (also subsequently adopted by certain local authority trading standards departments):

'a. A unit price is not required when the selling and unit price of the product are identical.

b. The Order does not require advertisements to show a selling price but some advertisers might choose to include one. If they do, the advertisement must also show a unit price where one is normally required under the terms of the Order. However, selling and unit prices are always required (notwithstanding any other exemptions) when the advertisement is actually inviting consumers to conclude a distance contract as opposed to merely seeking to encourage them to visit another retail outlet where prices will be displayed. Examples of advertisements that invite consumers to conclude a distance contract are mail order advertisements in newspapers and goods sold direct from the Internet or the media. Catalogues do not fall within the definition of advertisement and are required to show selling and unit prices as relevant.

c. Where unit pricing would not be useful to the consumer or would be confusing, then an exemption from unit pricing only may be allowed. The exemption applies to:

 i. Advertisements (as defined in the Order) with brief exposure times (eg radio and television) and advertisements in a small shop.

 ii. Promotional offers where the price has been reduced because of the damaged condition of the product and/or the danger of its deterioration. In these cases the condition of the product renders comparisons with perfect equivalents less than useful.

 iii. An assortment of different items sold in a single packet – where individual unit prices may be confusing and a single one misleading. This includes different items packaged together from which a mixture is to be prepared (eg a cake mix).

 iv. Any product where the unit price (as a result of the provisions for decimal places and rounding of unit prices) would be 0.0p.

d. Small shops, with an internal sales/display area not exceeding 280 square metres, itinerant traders and vending machines are all exempt from the requirement to unit price pre-packaged products in constant quantities. However, there is no exemption from the requirement to unit price products sold loose from bulk or pre-packaged in variable quantities. In measuring area for the purposes of the small shops exemption only that used for the retail sale or display of products should be included. Concessions operating within larger outlets should additionally be able to demonstrate that they are a separate business and may thus benefit from the exemption.

e. Itinerant traders, includes barrows in shopping malls, and other movable premises and vehicles of all sorts. "Pitching" in markets is allowed by the Order but once the market trader has revealed the final price for which the goods will actually change hands then that price must be given in writing. Catalogues used by itinerant traders must be unit priced but where the trader uses his discretion to offer a selling price different from that shown in the catalogue then a new unit price does not have to be calculated.'

Offence

13.24 The offence, in para 5 of the Schedule to PA 1974, is one of contravening an order made under PA 1974, s 4.

13.25 The offence is triable either way and penalties are limited to a fine[1]. In Scotland the level of the potential fine will depend on which court and under which process the case is heard.

PA 1974, Sch, para 5(1):

> (1)   Any person who contravenes an order under section 4 of this Act shall be guilty of an offence and liable—
> (a)   on conviction on indictment, to a fine;
> (b)   on summary conviction, to a fine not exceeding the prescribed sum.

[1]   Unlimited in the Crown Court, the prescribed limit in the magistrates' court.

13.26

Precedent for failing to indicate price

Statement of offence

FAILING TO INDICATE THE SELLING PRICE OF A PRODUCT in contravention of paragraph 5 of the schedule to the Prices Act 1974 and article 4 of the Price Marking Order 2004.

Particulars of offence

X Limited, a trader, on [date] failed to indicate the selling price for a product in accordance with the requirements of article 4 of the Price Marking Order 2004, namely tins of baked beans without any price marking, when A B had indicated that the product was for sale to consumers by displaying the baked beans on the shelves at its Northshire shop.

Causal liability

13.27 The provisions of the Trade Descriptions Act 1968, s 23 (Offences due to the fault of other person) have effect in relation to offences under PA 1974[1]. Causal liability is considered generally in Cʜᴀᴘᴛᴇʀ 4, Criminal Enforcement.

[1]   PA 1974, Sch 1, para 5(2).

Liability of directors

13.28 Paragraph 13 of the Schedule to PA 1974 enables proceedings to be brought against a director or other senior employee of a company where the company is itself guilty of an offence and it can be shown that offence has been committed with the 'consent or connivance' of the person in question or as a result of his neglect. This provides essentially the same basis of liability for directors as is present in the majority of trading standards statutes. Directors' liability is considered generally in Cʜᴀᴘᴛᴇʀ 4, Criminal Enforcement.

Restriction on proceedings

13.29 Proceedings for offences under PA 1974 can only be instituted by or on behalf of a local weights and measures authority, who have a duty to enforce the provisions of any Order made under the Act within its area[1]. This provision does not apply in Scotland (PA 1974, Sch 1, para 8(4)). In its application to

Northern Ireland, Sch 1 provides that, for any reference to a local weights and measures authority, there shall be substituted a reference to the Department of Commerce for Northern Ireland.

¹ PA 1974, Sch 1, paras 8(1) and 6. An exception is made for Scotland where all prosecutions are undertaken by the Procurator Fiscal.

Procedural requirements

13.30 Paragraph 8 of the Schedule to the PA 1974 creates a requirement, similar to the notice of intended prosecution under the Weights and Measures Act 1985. The requirements are that:

(a) within 30 days of the date of the offence actually occurring (not the date that the offence is discovered by trading standards officers) (para 8(2)(a));

(b) a written notice detailing that:
  (i) the offender has infringed para 5 of the Schedule to PA 1974 and the related statutory instrument; and
  (ii) giving the date of offence; and
  (iii) brief details of its nature (see the example below) (para 8(2)(a));

(c) should be served on the offender either in person or by post to his usual or last known residence or place of business in the United Kingdom, or a company's registered office (para 8(3)).

(d) proceedings must then be issued in within 3 months of the offence occurring.

13.31 *Example of a PA 1974 Notice*

'Notice of Prices Act 1974 offence

Northshire County Council Trading Standards department hereby gives notice that:

Sainco Supermarkets PLC on [date] committed an offence under paragraph 5 of the Schedule to the Prices Act 1974, and article 4 of the Price Marking Order 2004;

in that they failed to indicate in writing the selling price on a bottle of lemonade which was for sale by retail at their Northshire supermarket.

This notice is given this [date] pursuant to paragraph 8 of the Schedule to the Prices Act 1974.'

Defence

13.32 The due diligence defence in the Trade Descriptions Act 1968, s 24 has effect in relation to offences under PA 1974, s 5(2). See CHAPTER 4, Criminal Enforcement for further details.

SECTORAL PROVISIONS

Bureaux de change

13.33 The Price Indications (Bureaux de Change) (No 2) Regulations 1992¹ came into force on 18 May 1992, save for regs 4(2) [travellers' cheques] and 5(3) [clarity of statements] which came into force a year later on 18 May 1993.

The Regulations were made under the Consumer Protection Act 1987, s 26 (CPA 1987). Although CPA 1987, s 26 and the other pricing provisions of CPA 1987 were repealed by the CPUTR 2008, the Regulations were expressly saved[2]. The Regulations apply throughout the UK.

[1] SI 1992/737. The No 2 Regulations immediately repealed the No 1 Regulations of 1992 which contained a printing error.
[2] CPUTR 2008, SI 2008/1277, Sch 3, paras 5 and 6.

13.34 The Regulations regulate the manner in which a person, operating as a bureau de change, gives an indication to consumers of the rate at which business may be done (an 'exchange rate indication') (reg 3). Such indications must state the terms on which transactions will be conducted and provide other specified information, including any commission or other charges. The exchange rate indications and related information must be given clearly and prominently and either legibly or audibly (reg 5). Special provision is made in relation to circumstances where a consumer requests information about the terms on which a particular transaction will be conducted (reg 4(4)) and for coin-operated machines (reg 7). The Regulations require that a receipt setting out the terms of the transaction must be provided to the consumer in all cases except that of a transaction conducted through a machine (reg 6). An exchange rate indication must be accurate and no suggestion may be made that it is not to be relied on (reg 8). The enforcement provisions in the CRA 2015, Sch 5 apply. The defences and allied provisions contained in CPA 1987, ss 24(2), 39 and 40 are specifically applied to the Regulations by reg 9(2), see CHAPTER 4 Criminal Enforcement.

Package travel

13.35 The Package Travel, Package Holidays and Package Tour Regulations 1992[1] create various obligations in relation to price indications. The descriptive matter concerning the price of a package must not contain any misleading information (reg 4). The price of a package must be provided in a way that is legible, comprehensible and accurate (reg 5). These provisions also regulate the terms that permit a variation of the price of a package after a contract has been agreed (reg 11). They are covered in CHAPTER 16, Travel.

[1] SI 1992/3288.

Consumer credit

13.36 The Consumer Credit (Information) Regulations 2010[1] regulate the way that pricing information about regulated consumer credit agreements must be provided. Sch 1 of the Regulations provides detailed rules on how the cash price, interest, total amount payable, and APR must be indicated. These provisions are covered in CHAPTER 19, Consumer Credit.

[1] SI 2010/1013.

MISLEADING PRICES

13.37 Statutory regulation of misleading prices dates back over half a century. In 1964 the abolition of retail price maintenance[1] allowed traders greater flexibility in the prices they charged and the reductions offered consumers. This era of discounting was the background to introduction of the Trade Descriptions Act 1968, s 11 ('TDA 1968'), which first introduced a misleading price offence and required maintenance of a price for at least 28 days before a trader could claim it had been reduced[2]. It was, however, widely recognised that the provision was insufficiently broad to cover the range of misleading pricing practices that developed during the 1970s and 1980s. The TDA 1968, s 11 was therefore repealed in the Consumer Protection Act 1987 ('CPA 1987'), which introduced a broader misleading prices offence[3]. The misleading prices part of the CPA 1987 was repealed when the Consumer Protection from Unfair Trading Regulations 2008 ('CPUTR 2008') came into force in May 2008. The CPUTR 2008 and PMO 2004 are now the primary measures regulating unfair pricing practices.

[1]   The Resale Prices Act 1964.
[2]   The Trade Descriptions Act 1968, s 11(3) (repealed in 1987).
[3]   CPA 1987, s 20.

Unfair pricing practices

13.38 The CPUTR 2008 are broad and likely to cover all forms of representation made about the price, or price promotion, of a product (goods and services) sold by traders to consumers. In particular, there is specific reference in the Regulations to:

- the price of a product;
- the manner in which the price is calculated;
- the existence of a specific price advantage[1].

[1]   Consumer Protection from Unfair Trading Regulations 2008, SI 2008/1277, reg 5(4).

13.39 The CPUTR 2008 also prohibit misleading omissions. Information that is material to a consumer must not be omitted, hidden or presented in a manner which is unclear, unintelligible, ambiguous or untimely. The CPUTR 2008 impose a general obligation on traders not to contravene the requirements of professional diligence, which are defined by reference to the standard of skill and care that is commensurate with honest market practice or the general principle of good faith.

13.40 The relationship between the overlapping requirements of the PMO 2004 and the CPUTR 2008 was considered by the CJEU in the *Citroën Commerce case*[1], in a ruling about the 'final price' of a motor car in a newspaper advertisement (see below at **13.74**). Both provisions implemented EU directives. In *Citroën* the CJEU was asked to consider both the Price Indications Directive and whether the advertisement also amounted to an unfair commercial practice. It declined to consider the latter on the basis of the sectoral conflict provision in Art 3(4) of the UCPD, which requires precedence to be given to a specific sectoral requirement in another EU measure. This is potentially an important development because it suggests that the CPUTR 2008 may not be the appropriate provision to use where the PMO 2004 applies.

¹ *Citroën Commerce GMBH v Zentralvereinigung des Kraftfahrzeuggewerbes zur Aufrechterhaltung lauteren Wettbewerbs eV (ZLW)* Case C-476/14, 7 July 2016.

13.41 The provisions of the CPUTR 2008 that are likely to be relevant to pricing are summarised in the table below. They are covered in further detail in CHAPTER 8, Unfair Commercial Practices.

Statutory provision			Description	CTSLP Ref
Consumer Protection from Unfair Trading Regulations 2008	Reg 3	Contravening professional diligence	Contravening the requirements of professional diligence, defined by reference to the standard of skill and care that is commensurate with honest market practice or the general principle of good faith	8.120
	Reg 5	Misleading actions	False or misleading commercial practices concerning the price, its calculation or a price advantage	8.146
	Reg 6	Misleading omissions	Material information is omitted, hidden or provided in a manner that is unclear, unintelligible, ambiguous or untimely	8.163
	Sch 1, para 5	Bait advertising	Advertising products at a specific price without reason to believe that they will be available in reasonable quantities without making this clear in the promotion	8.227
	Sch 1, para 6	Bait and switch	Advertising a product at an attractive price to encourage interest and then discouraging its purchase in order to persuade the consumer to switch to something different	8.227
	Sch 1, para 7	Time limited offers	Falsely stating that a product will only be available at a particular price for a very limited amount of time in order to persuade the consumer to make an immediate decision and deny them the time or opportunity to make an informed choice	8.227

Statutory provision			Description	CTSLP Ref
	Sch 1, para 15	Closing down sales	Claiming that the business is about to cease trading or move premises when it is not	8.227
	Sch 1, para 20	Describing a product as 'free'	Describing a product as 'free' if the consumer has to pay anything other than the unavoidable cost of re-sponding to the commercial practice and collecting or paying for delivery of the item	8.227

13.42 An important question when considering a pricing practice under CPUTR 2008, reg 5 (misleading actions) is whether the price indication was 'misleading'. This is a now a broad question which is not confined to the indication itself, but takes into account all of the relevant circumstances. A pricing practice may be unfair if it or its overall presentation is likely to deceive consumers, even if the information contained is factually correct. The question must be assessed using the objective standard of the average consumer, which is modified to take into account the characteristics of targeted and vulnerable groups, see Chapter 8 Unfair Commercial Practices, at **8.112**.

The Pricing Practices Guide

13.43 The Guidance for Traders on Pricing Practices ('PPG') is executive guidance for traders on fair pricing practices.

History

13.44 The origin of the PPG can be found in the Consumer Protection Act 1987 ('CPA 1987'), which first introduced a general misleading prices offence[1]. The CPA 1987, s 25 also provided for a statutory code of practice on pricing, under which the Consumer Protection (Code of Practice for Traders on Price Indications) Approval Order 1988 was made ('the code of practice').

[1]   CPA 1987, s 20.

13.45 The code of practice was designed to give 'practical guidance' and promote 'desirable practices' by which traders could avoid making misleading price indications. A contravention did not of itself create liability. However, the CPA 1987, s 25 expressly made breach or compliance admissible in enforcement proceedings[1].

[1]   In 2005 the code was updated and re-published under CPA 1987, s 25: The Consumer Protection (Code of Practice for Traders on Price Indications) Approval Order 2005, SI 2005/2705; in 2006 for Northern Ireland, SI 2006/371.

13.46 In May 2008 the misleading price indications provisions of the CPA 1987 were replaced by CPUTR 2008. BERR[1] published pricing guidance for traders to coincide with its introduction[2]. Although the 2008 publication reflected the new legislation, the practical guidance remained very similar to the code of practice. However, the 2008 Guidance was not issued statutorily under the CPA 1987, s 25, which was also repealed. The PPG was republished by BIS in November 2010.

1   The Department of Business, Enterprise and Regulatory Reform, which was replaced by BIS in 2009 and the Department for Business, Energy & Industrial Strategy in 2016.
2   http://www.berr.gov.uk/files/file46254.pdf – Guidance for traders on good practice on giving information about prices (May 2008).

13.47 In 2013 the CTSI was given the responsibility for updating the PPG as the previous guidance was widely regarded as being outmoded. The CTSI conducted a widespread consultation on misleading pricing and published an updated version of the PPG in December 2016.

Status of the PPG 2016

13.48 The Guidance for Traders on Pricing Practices 2016 ('PPG 2016') is expressly stated to provide practical guidance to traders rather than set out a strict and comprehensive regulatory code. Compliance with the guidance will not automatically determine liability. In the PPG 2016 introduction it is stated that:

> 'Regulators may refer to the guidance when making enforcement decisions about a trader's pricing practices. This guidance is not statutory guidance and a court is not bound to accept it. The decision whether any particular pricing practice is unlawful remains to be judged by all of the relevant circumstances. Only a court can determine whether a trader has breached the law in a specific case.' (PPG 2016)

13.49 Unlike the statutory code of practice issued under the CPA 1987, s 25, there is no equivalent statutory provision providing that the PPG 2016 should automatically be admitted as evidence in criminal or civil court proceedings. Its admissibility in any particular case will depend on the factual circumstances and the ordinary principles of evidential admissibility. For example, the PPG 2016 may be of significant relevance in the consideration of a due diligence defence. When the PPG 2016 is relevant, the courts are likely to give significant weight to the guidance that it provides because of the specific context in which it has been produced[1]. The guidance was given by the CTSI following an extensive consultation process with business, public bodies and other consumer protection organisations.

1   *R (Ali) v Newham LBC* [2012] EWHC 2970 (Admin) (30 October 2012).

13.50 The legal effect of executive guidance generally is covered further in CHAPTER 2, Interpretation of Consumer Law, at **2.23**.

Misleading pricing practices

13.51 We have set out below relevant passages from the PPG 2016 together with any useful case law. There are currently few appellate authorities on misleading prices under the CPUTR 2008. However, previous case law under the CPA 1987, s 20 is likely to be helpful as the focus of that provision was whether the price indication was 'misleading'. The assessment of that question was also by reference to the objective standard of the reasonable man[1]. That is broadly the same approach that reg 5 of CPUTR 2008 requires. The primary requirements of the PMO 2004 in relation to the indication of final price and price reductions (see above) are also relevant in relation this question.

¹   CPA 1987, s 21(1) 'what those consumers might reasonably be inspected to infer'.

13.52 We have also included certain illustrative decisions made by the Advertising Standards Authority ('ASA') and cases decided in European Member States. The approach in these cases focuses on whether the pricing practice was misleading and reflects the general requirements of the CPUTR 2008, which implemented an EU directive. However, they do not represent binding appellate authority and are useful only as an illustration of the type of pricing practices that have been considered misleading and unlawful. In June 2018 the ASA/CAP (Committees of Advertising Practice) published a document 'Promotional Savings Claims' that provides retailers with guidance on how to ensure promotional pricing does not mislead, or is likely to mislead, consumers. The document cites a number of ASA Rulings to illustrate the advice given.

Price comparisons

13.53 The Guidance in the PPG 2016 on reference pricing states:

Using referencing prices

Including a reference price in an offer can create a point which consumers use as a base for estimating the value of the product and might reduce the effort consumers put into shopping around and comparing prices. It follows that reference pricing calls for a high level of trust and integrity. It is unlikely that consumers will have made a record of the reference prices in order to determine for themselves whether the claimed price reduction is genuine.

Any specific price advantage claimed must not be misleading or unfair. It is important to be clear and not to make unfair price comparisons. If your proposed pricing practice explicitly or by implication indicates a saving against another price, you must be able to satisfy yourself that the quoted saving is genuine and is therefore not unfair. Ask yourself whether the average consumer would think that it is a fair comparison.

Below is a non-exhaustive list of issues that should be considered when determining whether a price reduction is genuine.

1.   How long was the product on sale at the higher price compared to the period for which the price comparison is made?

2.   How many, where and what type of outlets will the price comparison be used in, compared to those at which the product was on sale at the higher price?

3.   How recently was the higher price offered compared to when the price comparison is being made?

4.   Where products are only in demand for short periods each year, are you making price comparisons with out-of-season reference prices?

5.   Were significant sales made at the higher price prior to the price comparison being made or was there any reasonable expectation that consumers would purchase the product at the higher price?

Issues to be considered	More likely to comply	Less likely to comply
1. How long was the product on sale at the higher price compared to the period for which the price comparison is made?	The price comparison is made for a period that is the same or shorter than the period during which the higher price was offered.	The price comparison is made for a materially longer period than the higher price was offered.
2. How many, where and what type of outlets will the price comparison be used in, compared to those at which the product was on sale at the higher price?	The retailer makes a price comparison against a reference price that has been offered in the same store as the price comparison is made.	A retailer charges £3 in store A and £2 in store B and then claims 'Was £3 Now £1.50' in store B, referring to a reference price in a store where that price was never charged.
3. How recently was the higher price offered compared to when the price comparison is being made	A travel agent refers to a selling price that was charged fewer than 2 months ago with no intervening prices and therefore gives a genuine indication of the current value of the holiday.	A website refers to previous selling prices that were charged many months ago and therefore no longer represent a genuine indication of the current value of the item.
4. Where products are only in demand for short periods each year, are you making price comparisons with out-of-season reference prices?	An online trader reduces its prices in order to generate sales where demand has fallen away when the sales season for a product has passed.	A trader offers the product at a higher price when the product is out-of-season and then lowers the price in time for the expected product demand.
5. Were significant sales made at the higher price prior to the price comparison being made or was there any reasonable expectation that consumers would purchase the product at the higher price?	The retailer can provide evidence to show significant sales at the higher price or that this was a realistic selling price for the product.	A retailer repeatedly uses a reference price knowing that it had not previously sold a significant number of units at that price.

It is important that price comparisons are genuine. Examples of price comparisons that may not be genuine include:

1. During the period that the product was sold at the higher price, different types of discount were offered, for example, multi-buy.
2. The higher price is not the last price that the product was sold at, for example there have been intervening prices.
3. A series of price claims made against a reference price, where each subsequent claim does not offer a greater discount.

Examples of price comparisons that may not be genuine	More likely to comply	Less likely to comply
During the period that the product was sold at the higher price, different types of discount were offered, for example, multibuy.	An online retailer offers a product for sale with the price claim of 'Was £500 Now £350' for a month. For the preceding month the product was priced at £500 with no price promotions or other price reductions.	An online retailer offers a product for sale with the price claim of 'Was £500 Now £350' for a month. For the preceding month the product was priced at £500 with a volume promotion operating at the same time – Buy 2 get 10% Off.
The higher price was not the last price that the product was sold at, for example there have been intervening prices.	A sofa is offered for sale at £500 immediately before the price promotion 'Was £500 Now £350' is advertised.	A sofa is offered at £500 then reduced to £350 with no claim of saving. A number of weeks later the product is labelled as 'Was £500 Now £350'.
A series of price claims are made against a reference price, where each subsequent claim does not offer a greater discount.	A coat is offered at 'Was £150 Now £99' then a further reduction is made and the item is advertised as 'Was £150 Was £99 Now Half Price £75'.	A coat is offered at 'Was £150 Now Half Price £75' subsequently the same item is advertised as 'Was £150 Now £99'.

13.54 There are overlapping obligations under the PMO 2004 and CPUTR 2008 in relation to representations about price reductions. Where the PMO 2004 is applicable, reg 9 requires that the 'details of the reduction are prominently displayed, unambiguous, easily identifiable and clearly legible'. The relationship between the PMO 2004 and CPUTR 2008 is considered above at **12.7**. In a case decided before the implementation of the CPUTR 2008, *Office of Fair Trading v Officers Club Ltd*[1] the OFT brought civil enforcement proceedings against a chain of retail clothing stores that operated a '70% off' sales strategy. This involved a small number of items being marked at full price in a limited number of stores for 28 days and thereafter being sold in all stores at a 70% discount. There were advertisements placed in the store windows promoting and explaining the 70% discount scheme. The High Court found the advertised discounts to be misleading. Etherington J stated that[2]:

> 'a customer would have regarded the notices as implicitly stating that the higher price was a genuine price as distinct from, and by contrast with, an artificial price . . . it is a facet of a genuine price, in this context, that the seller honestly believes that the price is an appropriate sale price for the goods. I also agree . . . that the notices carried the implied representation that significant quantities of the goods had actually been offered for sale at the higher price . . . . in this context, a "significant" quantity for sale at the higher price involves a comparison with the total number available for sale at any moment of time at the lower price: in other words, it involves a snapshot comparison at a particular moment in time between what had previously been offered for sale at the higher price and what at that later snapshot moment was offered for sale at the discounted price.'

[1] [2005] EWHC 1080 (Ch).
[2] Paragraphs 157–9.

13.55 In *AG Stanley Ltd v Surrey CC*[1] a retailer sold an occasional table in its outlets for £7.99 for a period of 5.5 months. The price was then reduced to

£4.99 for a 5-month period as part of a general promotion. During that 5-month period the retailer also advertised two shorter sales, a 13-day sale and a Christmas sale. At these two shorter sales a sign was displayed saying 'Sale, round occasional table, now £4.99 was £7.99'. The retailer was convicted on the basis that these price comparisons were misleading. The High Court rejected its appeal on the basis that the notices contained a clear message that immediately prior to each of the shorter sales, the table had been on sale at a higher price, when in fact it had not. There is no requirement to pressure the consumer with anything other than time constraints, also possible confusion with reg 7 offences.

[1] (1995) 159 JP 691, (1995) 159 JPN 655.

13.56 The ASA ruling in *Sofa Sofa Ltd*[1] concerned a furniture retailer that advertised a sofa as 'Was £649, now £499'. A consumer complained that the higher price was not genuine because the sofa price had fluctuated and it had previously been sold at the lower price. The retailer was able to show that during the 10 months before the advertisement was published the sofa had been sold at £649 for a total of 7 months (two periods of 2 months, and one of 3 months) and at £490 during two separate 6-week sale periods. There was also evidence to show that a reasonable number of sofas were sold at £649 during each of the full price periods. The ASA did not uphold the complaint. It found that consumers would expect that £649 was the normal price. Despite the fluctuation in price, the higher price had been charged for the majority of the time and could be regarded as the normal price. The advertisement was not therefore found to be misleading.

[1] A14–280247, December 2014.

13.57 In the *Wren Living ASA Ruling*[1] a furniture retailer claimed 'Now only £169 Was £378' for a nest of tables. A competitor complained that the higher price was not a genuine retail price. The product had been sold for approximately 6 months at the time the advertisement was seen. During that time it had been on sale for £378 at all of the retailer's 50 stores (including online) for 28 days in November 2013 and subsequently for 28 days at two stores from March to April 2014. The advert referred to this later period as the basis for the savings claim. The ASA considered that, although the qualification was likely to be seen by consumers, it did not override the general impression that £378 had been the usual selling price for the product. The product had been on sale for the lower price of £169 for five out of the last 6 months at all of the retailer's 50 stores and online, apart from at two stores, for a further 28 days. The ASA considered that consumers would understand from the claim 'Now only £169.00. Was £378.00 – Save £209.00' that £378 was the usual selling price for the product and that the sale price of £169 represented a genuine saving on the usual price. The ASA, ruling found that in fact the normal selling price of the product was £169 and it was misleading to refer to £378 as a 'Was' price.

[1] A14–268611, December 2014.

13.58 The *Humber Imports Ltd ASA Ruling*[1] concerned a website advertised several garden benches with reductions such as 'Westminster Teak Bench Was £319 Now £169'. In smaller print below the listed products it was stated 'All Internet sale prices are based on the discount from our current showroom prices'. The complainant challenged whether the savings claims were misleading and could be substantiated. The retailer provided a video and photographs which they said demonstrated that they had a showroom on their premises. They also provided evidence of sales and a spreadsheet listing the higher showroom prices. The ASA found the price comparison to be misleading. The retailer had not provided any sales history for products sold over the internet. The showroom sales were insufficient to justify a comparison with the website prices. The retailer 'had not demonstrated that the "was" prices were the prices at which the benches were usually sold across all channels and in particular online'.

[1]   A15–308966, November 2015.

13.59 The ASA ruling in *Purpleholidays.com Limited t/a Purple Travel*[1] was regarding the claim by the retailer of '5* All-inclusive Morocco holiday up to 47% off, from £239 WAS £448'. The complainant challenged whether the savings claim was misleading and could be substantiated. The ASA stated the two relevant points from the Chartered Trading Standards Institute's Guidance for Traders on Pricing Practices non-exhaustive list of issues that should be considered when determining whether or not a price reduction was genuine were 'for how long was the product on sale at the higher price compared to the period for which the price comparison is made?' and 'were significant sales made at the higher price prior to the price comparison being made or was there any reasonable expectation that consumers would purchase the product at the higher price?'. Even though the promotion had run for as long as the period for which the higher price was advertised, the ASA considered that the advertisers had not, in this instance, demonstrated that sales, or significant sales, had been made at the higher price or that the retailer had demonstrated that there was any reasonable expectation that consumers had or could have purchased the product at the higher price.

[1]   A16–366290, August 2017.

13.60 The ASA ruling in *HPAS Ltd t/a Safestyle UK*[1] related to claim of '60% off all windows and doors'. Eleven complainants, who understood that Safestyle UK had been offering all their windows and doors at discounted rates throughout 2016, challenged whether the savings claims were misleading and could be substantiated. Safestyle provided the ASA with their promotional calendar and some evidence of sales at the higher prices. Safestyle UK's promotional calendar showed that they operated promotions in a cyclical manner; between 1 January 2016 and 7 November 2016 there were 142 days of discounted prices including 55% off, 60% off or as part of a 'Buy One Get One Free' offer compared to 169 days of non-promotion. The ASA concluded that the retailer's promotional calendar showed that throughout 2016 the periods when a promotion ran were essentially equivalent in length to when there was no promotion running and therefore they considered that the intervening periods between the promotions were insufficient in length to establish that the higher prices of the products were the usual prices of the products. Further the ASA considered that the sales data Safestyle UK provided did not demonstrate that there were significant sales at the higher selling price outside of the promotional period, which the ASA considered relevant in establishing whether the higher prices were the usual selling prices.

[1]   A17–376765, June 2017.

Recommended retail prices

13.61 Some guidance is provided in the PPG 2016 on the use of recommended retail prices.

Recommended Retail Price (RRP)

A recommended retail price ('RRP') is a price that a manufacturer or supplier has independently recommended. The use of RRPs is contentious – there have been calls to prohibit the practice completely. Traders must take extra care when using RRPs to ensure that they do not mislead consumers.

When making comparisons to an RRP, you should clearly and prominently tell consumers that the higher price is an RRP, rather than a price that you have charged. The initials RRP have historically been used in the UK and its meaning is likely to be understood by most consumers. You should avoid using other abbreviations unless you can be sure that consumers will have a clear understanding of their meaning in the context of the sale.

An RRP must not be false; it must not be created purely in order to present the appearance of a discount. An RRP must represent a genuine selling price. You should not recommend your own RRP or influence the price at which your third party supplier or manufacturer sets the RRP.

Traders using RRPs should consider obtaining substantiation from their suppliers or manufacturers that the RRP represents a genuine selling price. The use of RRPs as a reference price without such substantiation leaves the business open to the risk that the RRP is not genuine and may be considered misleading.

Further guidance on the use of RRPs is available from the Committee of Advertising Practice; 'marketers should be aware that while it is acceptable for them to promote RRPs if they are genuine, such price comparisons are likely to mislead if the RRP differs significantly from the price at which the product or service is generally sold'.

13.62 In the Finnish case of *Consumer Ombudsman v Maskun Kalustetaio*[1] a furniture retailer advertised discounts for several months by reference to a higher price, as well as by reference to RRPs charged by other retailers. The Finnish court prohibited a discount that lasted longer than 2 months, as otherwise the price would become the normal price. The court also prohibited the promotion of the same discount for more than 3 months total in a year (in order to prevent 'yo-yo' pricing). The Market Court of Helsinki ruled that the trader should not discount from a price or an RRP that had not been charged at the shop in question.

[1]   Finnish Market Court of Helsinki 2009, MAO 655/09.

13.63 This case should be considered with some caution to the extent that it suggests a general approach to RRPs. It is questionable whether a UK court would be willing to impose such a rigid requirement that retailers should not discount from an RRP, unless they had themselves sold the product at the RRP in the same outlet. The use of an RRP is not a banned practice under Sch 1 of the CPUTR 2008 and a UK court is more likely to approach an RRP case by addressing whether, in the applicable circumstances, the pricing practice was misleading.

Comparison with prices in different circumstances

13.64 Some guidance is provided in the PPG 2016 on how to compare against prices in different circumstances.

Comparison with prices in different circumstances

It may be possible to make a fair price comparison against the price of a product that has been sold in different circumstances. However, it is very important that any material differences in the circumstances are communicated to consumers in a way that is transparent, fair and prominent. Features that differentiate the circumstances must be clear and not hidden in the small print. Any material information must be provided in a clear, intelligible, unambiguous and timely manner.

The comparison must be readily understandable and relevant to the consumer that it is directed towards. The differences between the circumstances must still allow for a fair comparison to be made. The overall impression given to consumers must not be misleading even if the information provided is correct.

Explanatory text (refer to guidance starting on Page 12) may be useful to ensure that the pricing practice can be clearly understood by the average consumer, as long as it is provided in a clear, intelligible, unambiguous and timely manner.

Examples	More likely to comply	Less likely to comply
Comparing pricing models that are not like-for-like.	The website claims 'Save 50% on airport parking' and also states 'When you book in advance compared to the turn up and pay price' in a clear, intelligible, unambiguous and timely manner.	The website claims 'Save 50% on airport parking' with no further details of the basis of the claim of 50% savings.
Comparing products in different conditions.	A car retailer advertises the price of a second hand car and claims a saving against the higher price of the car when new. The origin of the higher price is clearly stated alongside the savings claim.	A car retailer advertises the price of a second hand car and claims a saving against a higher price that was the price of the car when new. This information is not provided.

13.65 In the *Available Car Ltd* ASA Ruling[1] a website contained listings for used cars, comparing their price to the price of a new car, using the words, 'When New £X – You Save £Y'. The 'When New' price was the price paid for the car when it was originally bought new and not the current price for an equivalent model. The trader argued it was important to draw attention to the significant depreciation in the price of cars after they were sold new. The listings also showed a photograph of the car, its year of registration and mileage. The ASA rejected a complaint that this was misleading because it compared the price of a second hand car to a new one. The information was presented sufficiently clearly for readers to understand the basis of the price comparison and to understand that the 'You Save' figure referred to the difference between the price of the car when originally new and the current market value of a used car.

[1]   A15–310623, December 2015.

13.66 Comparisons made with a competitor's price are covered in the PPG 2016 and fall under both CPUTR 2008 and the Business Protection from Misleading Marketing Regulations 2008[1]. These types of claim are covered in **Chapter 12**, Advertising.

[1] SI 2008/1276.

Representations that become misleading

13.67 The Guidance in the PPG 2016 on after-promotion and introductory pricing states:

After Promotion Price

You can make a comparison against a price that you will subsequently charge for a product. However, this type of pricing practice is likely to be considered unfair if the price is not subsequently increased to the advertised after-promotion price at the end of the promotional period or the reference price did not meet the guidance *[see the PPG guidance on reference pricing above]*.

Introductory Price

Traders must consider carefully the use of "new" or "introductory price" in price promotions. You should assess what consumers in your particular sector would consider as new and therefore how long the claim can be made before the new or introductory price becomes the normal selling price. The claim "new" could be used for a longer period where the product is rarely purchased, compared to a regularly purchased product.

This type of pricing practice is likely to be considered unfair if the price of the product is not in fact increased at the end of the promotional period.

13.68 *R v Warwickshire CC Ex p Johnson*[1] concerned a price-beating promise that was said to be misleading under the CPA 1987, s 20(1). A retailer selling televisions displayed a notice stating 'We will beat any TV, Hi-Fi and Video price by £20 on the spot'. A consumer identified the price of a television sold by a local competitor of the retailer at £159.99. However, when the consumer sought to take advantage of the notice and purchase the television from the retailer for £20 less than this price, the shop manager refused. It was accepted that this was an error on the part of the manager. There was no evidence that it was the retailer's normal practice to refuse to honour the price promise. The House of Lords considered the following certified question set by the Divisional Court:

'Whether . . . a statement, which in itself is not misleading on the face of it, can be rendered misleading by virtue of the fact that, even in the absence of evidence to show a general practice or intention to dishonour the offer contained therein, on one occasion the person making the statement declined to enter into a contract within the terms of the statement.'

[1] [1993] AC 583, [1993] 2 WLR 1.

13.69 The House of Lords found that the price promise was misleading, albeit allowing the appeal on a different ground, and endorsed the approach of the Divisional Court, which had found that 'The notice [was] a continuing offer and whether it is misleading or not can only be tested by somebody taking up the offer'. Lord Roskill stated that:

'To hold otherwise would be seriously to restrict the efficacy of this part of the consumer protection legislation. Seemingly innocent notices could be put up and then when such notices were followed by a refusal to honour them by a person acting in the course of his business no offence would be committed.'

13.70 The rationale of *Johnson* is that whether a representation is 'misleading' may be judged objectively on facts occurring after the representation was made, rather than the subjective intent of the person that originally made the indication. Although *Johnson* is a case decided under the now repealed the CPA 1987, s 20(1), the test that the court applied was simply an analysis of whether the price indication was 'misleading'. In our opinion it follows that *Johnson* would be very likely to be determined in the same way under reg 5 of the CPUTR 2008.

13.71 In *DSG Retail Ltd v Oxfordshire County Council*[1] a retailer displayed a notice in one of its electrical stores which read, 'Price check price – we can't be beaten we guarantee to match any local price'. The retailer refused to reduce the price of a £300 music system to £190 to match a competitor. The retailer had always operated a price promise but excluded certain prices, such as mail-order prices. As a matter of policy, they had not included those conditions on the notice that was displayed. The retailer was convicted under the CPA 1987, s 20(1) on the basis that the price indication was misleading. It was argued by the retailer on an appeal before the Divisional Court that there needed to be identified specified goods and a specific price before the indication could be regarded as misleading. This argument was rejected. Kennedy LJ referred to Lord Roskill's judgment in *Johnson*, stating that[2]:

'the transaction, the interplay between the consumer and the store is the evidence by which, in any individual case, it is possible to test whether the notice is in fact misleading. But once it has been tested, it is then established, not that it was misleading from the moment that the test was made, but that it was misleading from the outset.'

[1]   [2001] EWHC Admin 253, [2001] 1 WLR 1765 (DC).
[2]   Per Kennedy LJ at para 29.

13.72 An important distinction of principle can be drawn between the cases of *Johnson* and *DSG Retail*. In *Johnson*, the price promise could not sensibly be regarded as misleading when it was made because there was no evidence that the retailer did not generally intend to honour it. It was only later that an individual error on the part of the manager rendered the original promise misleading. In effect, the House of Lords decided as a matter of policy that the later act deemed the original price indication to be misleading. By contrast, in *DSG Retail* there was a factual inference that the promise was misleading from the outset because the retailer applied general exceptions that were not disclosed to the consumer. It was a case where the practice itself was misleading and the later act was merely evidence of that misleading practice[1].

[1]   It is arguable that the Divisional court failed to appreciate this distinction in *Link Stores Ltd v Harrow London Borough Council* [2001] 1 WLR 1479 where a trader failed to honour a promise to refund the difference if the goods were sold cheaper within 7 days.

Additional charges

13.73 The PPG 2016 guidance on additional charges draws a distinction between three types of additional charge, compulsory fixed charges, compulsory charges that vary and optional charges.

Additional charges

Examples of additional charges are:
- Fixed compulsory charges, which all consumers have to pay.
- Charges for a component of the product or service that is compulsory but where there is a range of possible charges for that compulsory component.
- Additional charges for an optional product or service.

Compulsory charges that are fixed

Additional charges should be included in the up-front price if they are **compulsory**. A failure to include compulsory charges in the up-front price may breach the Regulations.

Examples of compulsory charges:
- A non-optional administration fee that must be paid for a service.
- A compulsory cover charge at a restaurant.
- Mandatory insurance cover required for hiring a car.

Compulsory charges that may vary

Compulsory charges may vary in accordance with the consumer's choices or circumstances. Even if the charge may vary, it is still compulsory if the consumer must always pay something extra for it. For example, a delivery charge might depend on the consumer's location or the size/weight of the product.

Where a compulsory charge may vary, you should alert consumers to the charge at the outset. You should give information about how it will be calculated in a clear, intelligible, unambiguous and timely manner while still allowing the total cost to be easily and readily calculated by the average consumer as soon as possible.

Examples of compulsory charges that vary:
- A charge for a component part of bespoke furniture that may vary according to the material used, such as the fabric chosen.
- A charge for delivery that is compulsory but varies according to location.

Optional charges

It is not necessary to include an **optional** charge within the up-front price. However, the charge must be genuinely optional. Charges that are, in reality, an unavoidable part of the main purchase are not optional. You should ask the question whether the average consumer would consider 'optional' to be a fair description of the charge. Where a charge is optional, it should still be presented to the consumer clearly.

Examples of optional charges
- When booking a flight, a charge for hiring a car at the destination.
- When buying a product, a charge for gift wrapping.

13.74 It is important to appreciate that there are overlapping obligations under the PMO 2004 and CPUTR 2008 in relation to representations concerning the final price of a product. In the *Citroën Commerce case*[1] the CJEU ruled on a German complaint about a newspaper advertisement for a motor car. The advertisement represented the selling price of a motor car was €21,800. This price was footnoted with the words 'Price plus transfer costs of €790' at the foot of the advertisement. This additional fixed fee was a mandatory charge for transferring the car between the manufacturer and dealership. It was not included in the €21,800 price. The CJEU considered the requirement in the Price Marking Directive[2] (implemented in the UK by the PMO 2004) to provide the selling price, defined in Art 2(a) to mean 'the final price for a unit of the product, or a given quantity of the product, including VAT and all other taxes'. The court found that 'having regard to all the features of that advertisement, in the eyes of the consumer it [set] out an offer concerning that vehicle'. The advertisement breached the obligation to give the final price:

'As a final price, the selling price must necessarily include the unavoidable and foreseeable components of the price, components that are necessarily payable by the consumer and constitute the pecuniary consideration for the acquisition of the product concerned.'

[1] *Citroën Commerce GMBH v Zentralvereinigung des Kraftfahrzeuggewerbes zur Aufrechterhaltung lauteren Wettbewerbs eV (ZLW)* Case C-476/14, 7 July 2016.

[2] Directive 98/6/EC on consumer protection in the indication of the prices of products offered to consumers.

13.75 The CJEU distinguished the fixed cost of transferring a car between the manufacturer and dealer, from a charge for delivering the car to a place chosen by the consumer because such a delivery charge could not 'be regarded as an unavoidable and foreseeable component of the price'.

13.76 In *Toyota (GB) Ltd v North Yorkshire CC*[1] a newspaper advertisement suggested that the price for a particular model of car was £11,655. In very small print at the bottom of the advertisement it was noted that a compulsory delivery charge of £445 applied. The Divisional Court rejected the argument that this was not misleading. This case is likely to be decided in the same way under regs 5 or 6 of the CPUTR 2008[2]. In a Hungarian case, *Competition Authority v Vodaphone Magyarorzag Mobil*[3], an airtime contract where the initial price was not the full price, although subsequent information gave details. The Hungarian Competition Court found the initial price is the most important element that consumers consider. The first impression is the most relevant and in this case it was untrue. In *OCCP v Eko-Park SA*[4] the court held that consumers are misled where contracts do not explicitly state the price including tax. When presented with an agreement that only gives net value, consumers may consider the price beneficial to them and be deceived as a result.

[1] Co/0110/98 Divisional Court 11 March 1998, 1998 WL 1043583.
[2] SI 2008/1277, regs 5 and 6.
[3] Hungary Competition Tribunal 2010, Vj/149–041/2009.
[4] Poland, Office of Competition and Consumer Protection Delegature 2010, RWA 25/2010.

13.77 In the ASA ruling in *Bapchild Motoring World (Kent)*[1] the home page of a website for a car dealer featured a number of cars with their starting prices. These were linked to detailed product pages that also displayed the price of each model and other information. Text at the bottom of each page stated 'All cars sold are subject to a buyer's fee of £142.30'. The ASA upheld a complaint that the advertisement was misleading because it did not make the non-optional buyer's fee sufficiently clear. The fee should have been included in the headline price for the vehicles.

[1] A15–314167, December 2015.

13.78 In the *Manchester Airport Group* ASA Ruling[1] the website for an airport included the claim 'By pre-booking your parking you could be SAVING UP TO 70%* . . . *See terms & conditions'. The complainant was quoted pre-booking prices that were higher than the equivalent rates when parking was not pre-booked. The airport argued that the words 'could' and 'up to' in the claim made it clear that not every customer would achieve savings. They explained that booking for certain shorter periods might not benefit from the pre-book savings. Although the ASA accepted that the claim was conditional, it found the advertisement to be misleading because it omitted to say clearly that in some circumstances pre-booking was more expensive.

[1]   A15–308488, November 2015.

Small print

13.79 The guidance on the use of additional text in the PPG 2016 states:

Use of additional text

You must ensure that the presentation of your offer is transparent and clear. You should consider how consumers are likely to understand it, having regard to its overall presentation.

In particular, you should consider the prominence and clarity of any additional text in comparison to the headline text or main message.

You should ensure that the headline or prominent message is truthful, clear and consistent with other information you provide. It should not need explanatory text to make it comply, particularly if that text is not prominent.

Consider how the offer is expressed – a simple offer can be communicated in straightforward terms using direct language. If your offer is more complex you should take care to ensure that it is presented in a way that consumers will fully understand.

Additional information should not contradict the headline claim. It must be given in a clear, intelligible, unambiguous and timely manner. Including material information in the small print in a manner that is not clear and prominent may mean that you do not meet that requirement.

Material information might be:
*   Qualifying statements, for example, "Wednesdays from 6pm".
*   Important conditions of the offer, for example, "minimum 2 diners".
*   Relevant exclusions, for example, "set menu only".

If you operate a website or use other digital communication, you should use technology so that information is communicated to consumers in a way that is transparent and timely. Additional text that is likely to make a difference to the consumer's decision should be prominent and close to the price, headline or main message. You should not delay telling consumers about additional charges or other material information when it is possible to do so from the outset.

It may amount to an unfair practice if your technology requires that consumers take extra steps, such as clicking on a link or scrolling down a page, to obtain material information, such as additional costs. You should consider carefully whether it is possible to provide consumers with material information about the price and additional costs without the need to visit other webpages or to follow links.

13.80 The Dutch case of *Tele2 Nederland v UPC Nederland*[1] concerned a radio campaign for a telephone package at €20 with a reference to a website or phone line for more details. The offer was subject to a €17 per month cable subscription which was explained on the website or when consumers telephoned. In a poster advert for the same package the small print explained the cable subscription. In both situations the promotion was held to be misleading by the Netherlands Court of Appeal because the small print on the poster was overshadowed by the general advert.

[1]   Netherlands Court of Appeal, IER 2010/60.

13.81 The *GAP (Great Britain) Limited t/a Gap* ASA Ruling[1] concerned the headline of an email promoting a sale in the retailer's outlet stores stating 'Everything under the sun. It's all 40% off . . . excluding sale items'. In smaller print at the end of the email it stated '40% off everything; Excluding Sale Items. Offer applies to select products as indicated at participating Gap Outlet stores'. The retailer argued that the prominent qualification of the claims made it clear that the discount applied to everything except sale items. The ASA ruled that the advertisement was misleading because the exclusion of some clothes 'contradicted rather than clarified the nature of the offer, regardless of the prominence of the qualification'.

[1]   A15–302099, August 2015.

13.82 The *Asos.com Limited ASA Ruling*[1] concerned an email sent by ASOS stating '20% off everything + free delivery*' in the subject line. The asterisks linked to text further down in the email which stated 'Selected marked products excluded from promo'. This amounted to 1,100 items which comprised of footwear (mostly branded trainers), sports performance and face and body products. The ASA considered that the claim '20% off everything' in the subject line and body text of the email was misleading and would be understood by consumers to mean that all products on ASOS.com would be reduced by 20%. Although consumers might generally expect that gift vouchers might not be included in the promotion, they would expect that all other products to be included. The text at the bottom of the email footer which stated 'Selected marked products excluded from promo' was not sufficient to counter the overriding impression that all products would be discounted.

[1]   A20–107655 Asos.com Ltd 7.

13.83 In the *Hutchinson 3G UK Ltd* ASA Ruling[1] a mobile telephone company advertised a mobile phone plan using a banner advertisement on mobile devices. It stated 'Scratching around for the best deal sucks. Get the Samsung Galaxy S6 at the UK's lowest price for a limited time only . . . From £35 a month. No upfront cost'. This was qualified in a footnote saying that the price claim was based on the equivalent plans of six other competitors. The complainant found a plan that could be purchased elsewhere for less than £35 per month and challenged whether the claim 'UK's lowest price' was misleading. The retailer argued that the basis of the comparison had been made clear in the small print. The identified six competitors constituted over 95% of the market and the remainder of the market was so fragmented that it was not practical to check the pricing of other small independent retailers. The ASA found that the claim was misleading. It considered that consumers would understand the claim 'the UK's lowest price' to mean that the phone and plan could not be purchased from any other retailer across the UK for less than £35, at the time they viewed the advert. The information in the footnote was not sufficient to counteract the overall impression that the claim related to all retailers.

[1]   A15–307500.

Using the word 'free' in a promotion

13.84 The PPG 2016 includes guidance on using the word free in a price promotion. This reflects the banned practice in para 20 of Sch 1 CPUTR 2008 which prohibits 'Describing a product as "gratis", "free", "without charge" or similar if the consumer has to pay anything other than the unavoidable cost of responding to the commercial practice and collecting or paying for delivery of the item'.

Use of 'Free'

You must not use the term 'free', or similar phrases, unless the consumer pays nothing other than the unavoidable cost of responding to the commercial practice and collecting or paying for delivery of the item[1].

In promotions where an item is described as 'free' traders should be able to show:
- that the free item is genuinely additional to or separable from what is being sold;
- if the consumer complies with the terms of the promotion, the free item will be supplied alongside what the consumer is paying for;
- the stand-alone price of what is being sold is clear and is the same with or without the free item.

Receiving the free product can be conditional on the purchase of a product provided this is made clear. For example:
- The claim 'Free Wall-Chart When You Buy Thursday's Paper' is legitimate if the paper is sold without a wall-chart on other days for the same price.
- A claim of 'Free Travel Insurance For Customers Who Book Their Holiday Online' is legitimate if customers who book the same journey by telephone are offered the same price but not offered free insurance.

The item must, however, be truly free. The cost of the free item should not be recovered by reducing quality or composition or inflating the price of the product that is to be paid for. You should not describe a part of any package as 'free' if it is already included in the package price.

You should not exaggerate the value of any free product or service to persuade consumers to make qualifying purchases.

You should not describe a service as free, if it is not free for consumers that choose not to enter into an agreement with you after receiving the service. For example, you should not use the terms "free valuation" or "free call-out" if there is a one-off charge for a consumer that decides not to proceed with a subsequent purchase or agreement.

[1]   SI 2008/1277, Sch 1, para 20.

13.85 The ASA ruling in *Practical Publishing International Limited t/a moremags.com*[1] concerned a magazine website that offered an 'Exclusive gift worth up to £10' when purchasing a craft magazine. However, the price of the magazine varied according to the value of the gift provided, with a higher price charged for a gift of greater value. The ASA considered that consumers would understand the claim 'gift' to be synonymous with the claim 'free'. In this context the claim was misleading because the promotion did not offer a genuine additional benefit received for purchase of a magazine.

¹   A18-470676.

Volume offers

13.86 It is common to find volume offers in UK supermarkets. They are essentially price promotions that aim to demonstrate good value by reference to the volume, weight or amount of the product purchased, or the purchase of a combination of different products. Examples of volume offers include **multi-buys**, such as the ubiquitous *buy-one-get-one-free* offer; **combination offers**, where a discount is given for buying a combination of products such as a meal deal; **linked offers**, where a free or discounted product is offered for buying something else; **extra value offers**, such as 50% extra free. In April 2015, the Consumers' Association (Which?) made a super-complaint to the CMA on misleading and opaque pricing practices in the grocery market. This included substantial criticism about misleading volume offers. In July 2015, the CMA responded to the super-complaint and noted that it had found examples of pricing and promotional practices that had the potential to mislead consumers. However, the CMA concluded that the breaches were not occurring in large numbers and that retailers were generally taking compliance seriously.

Volume Offers

You should not use this type of price promotion unless the consumer is genuinely getting better value because of the offer. Care must be taken to ensure that any volume offer is not made to be unfair because better value was being offered before the volume promotion or for the same product elsewhere in your business.

The risk of these price promotions being unfair is increased if they are not easy to understand. You must ensure that the price promotion provides all of the material information that the consumer needs to understand it and that this information is provided in a clear, intelligible, unambiguous and timely manner. You should not take advantage of the fact that many consumers will not calculate for themselves whether your price promotion actually offers better value. For example, the price of a combination offer should be cheaper than the total cost of buying the same items separately.

Pre-printed value claims on pack such as "Bigger Pack – Better Value" should be objectively accurate and justifiable.

'Up to' and 'from' claims

13.87 Guidance is provided on 'Up to' and 'from' claims in the PPG 2016. This reflects the general requirement that the overall impression of a pricing practice should not be misleading under reg 5 of the CPUTR 2008. The reference to 'significant proportion' in the guidance has its origin in the language used by Etherington J in *OFT v Officers Club*¹ (see above).

'Up to' and 'from' claims

Care should be taken that general notices such as 'Up to half price sale' or 'From 50% off' are not misleading; they must reflect the reality of the offer. You should only make such a claim if the maximum reduction quoted applies to a significant proportion of the range of products that are included in the promotion. A prominent general claim of a maximum discount such as this, should represent the true overall picture of the price promotion. The 'up to' and 'from' claims are essential to the understanding of the pricing practice so should be shown clearly and prominently.

[1]   [2005] EWHC 1080 (Ch).

Subscriptions

13.88 In respect of subscription, the Guidance provides:

Subscriptions

If your agreement with a consumer requires that repeat payments are made, such as a monthly subscription, the extent of the consumer's financial commitment should be set out clearly and prominently from the outset and the consumer's express consent to these additional payments secured before they are charged. You must not mislead consumers about the extent of their future commitment in order to secure an agreement. If you initially offer a product that is free or heavily discounted, you must inform consumers clearly and prominently of any additional payment obligations that will be incurred, including the duration of any contract.

13.89 In the *Canal Digital case*[1], the CJEU considered a television commercial for a Danish satellite television service. A monthly subscription fee of kr.99 was payable for the service. However, an additional card charge of kr.389 was also payable every 6 months. In the advertisement the monthly subscription fee predominated. The 6-monthly card fee was not mentioned in the commercial's voiceover and referred to in less conspicuous text. The CJEU found that the practice of dividing the price into components and highlighting only one part was a misleading omission. At para 64 it was stated:

'where a trader has opted to state the price for a subscription so that the consumer must pay both a monthly charge and a six-monthly charge, that practice must be regarded as a misleading omission if the price of the monthly charge is particularly highlighted in the marketing, whilst the six-monthly charge is omitted entirely or presented only in a less conspicuous manner, if such failure causes the consumer to take a transactional decision that he would not have taken otherwise.'

[1]   *Canal Digital Danmark* A/S C-611/14 (judgment 26/10/16).

Default options

13.90 The practice of using default options, common for website transactions, to charge an additional fee was prohibited by reg 40 of the Consumer Contracts (information, Cancellation and Additional Charges) Regulations 2013[1] ('CCR 2013').

40 Additional payments under a contract

(1)   Under a contract between a trader and a consumer, no payment is payable in addition to the remuneration agreed for the trader's main obligation unless, before the consumer became bound by the contract, the trader obtained the consumer's express consent.

(2)   There is no express consent (if there would otherwise be) for the purposes of this paragraph if consent is inferred from the consumer not changing a default option (such as a pre-ticked box on a website).

(3)   This regulation does not apply if the trader's main obligation is to supply services within regulation 6(1)(b), but in any other case it applies even if an additional payment is for such services.

(4)   Where a trader receives an additional payment which, under this regulation, is not payable under a contract, the contract is to be treated as providing for the trader to reimburse the payment to the consumer.

[1]   SI 2013/3134, reg 40.

Chapter 14

INTELLECTUAL PROPERTY

Contents

INTRODUCTION

14.1 Per Baroness Neville-Rolfe[1]:

'Intellectual property rights underpin investment in research and manufacturing, reward innovation in design and branding, and support creativity of all types.

But these crucial IP rights are undermined and devalued on all fronts by infringement, whether by the wholesale sharing of digital content through myriad file sharing and streaming websites, deliberate copying of patent or design protected products, or the importation and sale of counterfeit goods on a massive scale.

The harm that this infringement causes is hard to measure, but it is also hard to understate. Infringement of IP rights is not just an economic matter, although it does cause financial loss to legitimate business, and to the exchequer. The harms caused by IP infringement go much further, to the heart of communities and the wellbeing of UK citizens. Unsafe counterfeit goods can pose serious risks to safety.

The prevalence of IP crime such as counterfeiting is closely associated with other serious criminality, and where entire markets are devoted to counterfeits, the chilling effect on legitimate traders can result in entire communities suffering from a lack of investment and the chance to thrive economically.

Infringement of IP rights online also causes harm to consumers, with close links between illegitimate websites and the spread of malware and other cybercrime. The extensive copying and distribution of infringing material also undermines the ability of our world leading creative industries to invest in new content, reducing the payback for creators, and damaging the long term cultural wealth of the nation.'

[1] Baroness Neville-Rolfe, DBE, CMG Minister for Intellectual Property in the Foreword to '*Protecting creativity, supporting innovation: IP enforcement 2020*', the government's strategy for tackling intellectual property infringement, published in May 2016.

14.2 IP crime is widespread and can be found everywhere from the internet to traditional markets. According to a report published 18 March 2019, the value of imported fake goods worldwide is put at \$509 billion[1]. This represents up to 3.3 % of world trade. For the European Union, counterfeit trade represented 6.8% of imports from non-EU countries. These figures do not include domestically produced and consumed fake goods, or pirated products being distributed via the Internet.

[1] Based on 2016 customs seizure data: the OECD and EU Intellectual Property Office – *Trends in Trade in Counterfeit and Pirated Goods*.

14.3 The key findings from the 2019 IPO[1] Report on counterfeit trade in the UK[2] included:

- Imports of counterfeit goods to the UK accounted for as much as £13.6 billion in 2016. 3% of UK imports are fake goods.
- The total volume of lost sales for UK wholesalers and retailers due to counterfeit and pirated products smuggled into the UK was GBP 9.2 billion in 2016.
- Global trade in counterfeit and pirated products that infringed UK tradements amounted to GBP 16.2 billion in 2016 equivalent to 3.3% of UK manufacturing sales.
- Global counterfeiting and piracy resulted in 86,300 lost jobs in the UK, 1.4% of all employees in the UK in 2016.
- Counterfeit trade meant the UK government lost almost £4 billion in tax revenue in 2016.

[1] EUIPO General Additional Guidance for Right Holders and Representatives in view of the end of the Brexit transition period . . . 10th September 2020.
[2] Trade in Counterfeit Products and the UK Economy 2019 IPO Update.

14.4 In the IP Crime and Enforcement Report 2019/2020[1], Amanda Solloway MP, Parliamentary Under Secretary of State and Minister for Universities, Science, Research and Innovation, stated:

'The IP Crime Group represents a world class approach to IP enforcement. The bedrock of this is the investigative work conducted by Police, Trading Standards, Border Force and independent enforcement organisations. Their contributions to this report have, since its inception, demonstrate the empirical, evidenced-based crime prevention activities the Group's work is based upon. To this end, the contribution from the National Trading Standards gives a clear picture of the organisation and implementation of effective, holistic IP protection. Without an effective system, tracking down and prosecuting criminals who infringe IP rights, online and offline, the additional work undertaken by the UK IP Crime Group, internationally, in the field of education, information sharing, public awareness raising, and behavioural change would not be possible.'

1   EUIPO General Additional Guidance for Right Holders and Representatives in view of the end of the Brexit transition period . . . 10 September 2020.

14.5 Our new challenge lies in the realm of behaviour. We no longer live in a world in which intellectual property could be characterised as a rather technical area of legal practice which only made the headlines when high profile legal cases invited attention. UK trade mark applications are growing at a pace every year. Social media has ensured that generation Z brands itself without the need for persuasion. However, a greater use and better understanding of intellectual property rights by society has not resulted in a reduction in IP crime and infringement by consumers.

14.6 IP is covered by many areas of both common and statute law which are not featured in this work – for example, patents, passing off and breach of confidence. The areas that are considered primarily relate to those parts of trade mark, copyright and (to a limited degree) design law which local authority trading standards departments are most likely to be involved. There were major developments in relation to design and patent law with the enactment of the Intellectual Property Act 2014, and the Digital Economy Act 2017 has further strengthened criminal sanctions for copyright infringement.

TRADE MARKS ACT 1994

Introduction

14.7 A trade mark helps identify a business's branding by protecting its business reputation and is a sign which identifies goods or services of a particular source from those of others. Trademarks predominantly take the form of words or logos, or a mixture of both. Trademarks must be distinctive, they must not describe the goods or service being applied for, and must not consist of words that must be left free for others to use. Trade mark protection lasts 10 years, although this can be renewed indefinitely. The EU legal framework on trademarks encompasses the Trade Mark Directive (89/104), which was codified in 2008 (2008/95), together with the Trade Mark Regulation (40/94) which was codified in 2009 (207/2009) and which established the Community Trade Mark and the Office for Harmonisation in the Internal Market (OHIM – now re-named EUIPO). The Trade Marks Act 1994 ('TMA 1994') replaced previous trade mark law and implemented EC Directive 89/104. Details of a European trade mark reform package were published in December 2015. They comprise:

- a new Trade Mark Regulation (2015/2424) which amends Regulation 207/2009 and entered into force on 23 March 2016; and
- a new Trade Mark Directive (2015/2436) which repeals Directive 2008/95 with effect from 15 January 2019. Member States therefore have until 14 January 2019 to transpose the provisions of the new Directive into their national laws.

14.8 The European Union Trade Mark Regulations 2016[1] which came into force 6 April 2016, amend the TMA 1994, ss 51 and 52 and the Community Trade Mark Regulations 2006[2] to reflect, *amongst other matters*, changes in terminology made by new Regulation 2015/2424. Examples include:

- references to 'Community' are replaced by 'European Union';
- 'Community trade mark' is renamed 'European Union trade mark';
- the Office for Harmonisation in the Internal Market ('OHIM') becomes European Union Intellectual Property Office ('EUIPO').

The Trade Marks Regulations 2018[3] came into force 14 January 2019. The changes relate to areas such as: removing the current requirement that the trade mark must be capable of being represented graphically which will, for example permit the presentation of trade marks in an electronic format, such as an mp3 file. This change allows for the filing of, for example, sound or moving image file formats, as well as permitting new multimedia trademarks, which combine both moving images and sound.

[1] SI 2016/299.
[2] SI 2006/1027.
[3] SI 2018/825.

14.9 The TMA 1994, s 92–101 create offences and provide associated provisions concerning the unauthorised use of registered trademarks in relation to goods. The Act places a duty of policing those offences upon local authorities and provides powers of enforcement[1]. Action against unauthorised use of trade marks (whether registered or unregistered) in relation to services (and for unregistered marks in relation to goods) may be considered under the Consumer Protection from Unfair Trading Regulations 2008[2], which implemented the Unfair Commercial Practices Directive into UK law. Two provisions of the Regulations have specific application in this context:

- By virtue of regs 5(3) and 9 of the Regulations, a trader is guilty of an offence if he engages in a commercial practice which concerns any marketing of a product (including comparative advertising) which creates confusion with any products, trademarks, trade names or other distinguishing marks of a competitor; and it causes or is likely to cause the average consumer to take a transactional decision he would not have taken otherwise, taking account of its factual context and of all its features and circumstances.
- Under reg 12 of, and Sch 1, para 13 to the Regulations, a trader is guilty of an offence if he engages in a commercial practice of promoting a product similar to a product made by a particular manufacturer in such a manner as deliberately to mislead the consumer into believing that the product is made by that same manufacturer when it is not.

[1] Duty to enforce is set out in TMA 1994, s 93, now amended by Consumer Rights Act 2015, Sch 6, para 59.
[2] SI 2008/1277.

14.10 In 2014 the Government conducted a Review of the enforcement provisions of the Consumer Protection from Unfair Trading Regulations 2008 in respect of copycat packaging – seeking views on the case for granting businesses a civil injunctive power. The Ministerial Statement, accompanying the outcome of the Review stated[1]: 'Following the review, I conclude there is little clear evidence that the use of similar packaging is causing any significant consumer detriment or hindering competition or innovation. There would be risks of unintended consequences if we changed the status quo, given the uncertainty around the evidence and the effects of the change, particularly in respect of the litigation that would result, and on enforcement. More generally, it would be difficult to reconcile granting this enforcement power with the Government's deregulatory objectives'.

[1]   Published on 13 October 2015.

Territorial jurisdiction

14.11 The TMA 1994, s 108 provides that the Act extends to England and Wales, Scotland, Northern Ireland and the Isle of Man. The TMA 1994, s 102 provides for the particular meaning of words used in the Act in its application to Scotland.

Brexit

14.12 On 31 January 2020 the United Kingdom withdrew from the European Union. At the end of the transition period on the 1 January 2021 EU law ceased to apply in the UK unless explicitly provided for by the Withdrawal Agreement. At the end of the transition period the Intellectual Property Office ('IPO') converted almost 1.4 million EU trade marks and 700,000 EU designs to comparable UK rights.

14.13 EU trade marks and registered community designs (RCDs) that were registered before the end of the transition period are now recognised as new comparable UK rights. For these comparable UK trade marks, the original EUTM filing date and original priority is retained, but the right is now a fully independent UK trade mark that can be challenged, assigned, licensed or renewed separately from the original EUTM (from 1 January 2021). The UK IPO has issued further guidance for new UK trade marks in relation to the registration process, renewals, opt-outs and numbering. Existing EU trade marks remain protected within EU member states and UK businesses can still apply to the EU IPO to register a new EU trade mark. However, proceedings before the EU IPO based on UK rights (such as UK trade marks or passing off) have now been automatically closed. Similarly, RCDs that were re-registered with the UK IPO under the Withdrawal Agreement retain their original filing and priority dates. The re-registered designs are likewise fully independent UK designs that can be challenged, assigned, licensed or renewed separately from the original RCD (from 1 January)[1].

[1]   Law Society – Intellectual property after Brexit 28.7.21.

Transfer to UK trade marks

14.14 On 1 January 2021, the IPO created a comparable UK trade mark for every registered European Union Trade Mark ('EUTM'). Each of these UK rights was recorded on the UK trade mark register and has the same legal status as a right registered under UK law. The original filing date remains, as does original priority or UK seniority dates. The new UK trade mark is a fully independent trade mark that can be challenged, assigned, licensed or renewed separately from the original EUTM.

14.15 It should be noted that prosecutions for trade mark offences must take account of the change in the regime and the creation of UK trade marks in the place of those formerly covered by the EU. Particular attention should be paid to ensuring the correct trade marks certificate is particularised in drafting any criminal charges.

Offences

14.16 The TMA 1994, s 92(1)–(3) sets out the offences in relation to a registered trade mark (in respect of goods, materials and articles).

92 Unauthorised use of trade mark, &c. in relation to goods

(1)   A person commits an offence who with a view to gain for himself or another, or with intent to cause loss to another, and without the consent of the proprietor—

     (a)   applies to goods or their packaging a sign identical to, or likely to be mistaken for, a registered trade mark, or

     (b)   sells or lets for hire, offers or exposes for sale or hire or distributes goods which bear, or the packaging of which bears, such a sign, or

     (c)   has in his possession, custody or control in the course of a business any such goods with a view to the doing of anything, by himself or another, which would be an offence under paragraph (b).

(2)   A person commits an offence who with a view to gain for himself or another, or with intent to cause loss to another, and without the consent of the proprietor—

     (a)   applies a sign identical to, or likely to be mistaken for, a registered trade mark to material intended to be used—

        (i)   for labelling or packaging goods,

        (ii)   as a business paper in relation to goods, or

        (iii)   for advertising goods, or

     (b)   uses in the course of a business material bearing such a sign for labelling or packaging goods, as a business paper in relation to goods, or for advertising goods, or

     (c)   has in his possession, custody or control in the course of a business any such material with a view to the doing of anything, by himself or another, which would be an offence under paragraph (b).

(3)   A person commits an offence who with a view to gain for himself or another, or with intent to cause loss to another, and without the consent of the proprietor—

     (a)   makes an article specifically designed or adapted for making copies of a sign identical to, or likely to be mistaken for, a registered trade mark, or

     (b)   has such an article in his possession, custody or control in the course of a business,

knowing or having reason to believe that it has been, or is to be, used to produce goods, or material for labelling or packaging goods, as a business paper in relation to goods, or for advertising goods.

14.17

Precedent for unauthorised use of a trade mark

Statement of offence

UNAUTHORISED USE OF A TRADE MARK, contrary to section 92(1)b of the Trade Marks Act 1994.

Particulars of offence

A B on [date] with a view to gain for himself or another or with intent to cause loss to another and without the consent of the proprietor X Limited, sold goods namely [details of item . . .] which bore a sign [identifying description of trademarked sign . . .] identical to or likely to be mistaken for a registered trade mark [trade mark registration number . . .].

14.18

Precedent for possession

Statement of offence

POSSESSION OF GOODS WITH AN UNAUTHORISED TRADE MARK, contrary to section 92(1)(c) of the Trade Marks Act 1994.

Particulars of offence

A B on [date] with a view to gain for himself or another or with intent to cause loss to another and without the consent of the proprietor X Limited had in his possession custody or control in the course of a business goods namely [details of item . . .] which bore a sign [identifying description of trademarked sign . . .] identical to or likely to be mistaken for a registered trade mark [trade mark registration number . . .] with a view to selling the said goods either by himself or another.

14.19 Although only the offences in the TMA 1994, s 92 have specific enforcement responsibilities attached to them, there are other criminal offences under the TMA including:

- TMA 1994, s 84 – unregistered person being described as a 'registered trade mark agent';
- TMA 1994, s 94 – making of a false entry in the register of trademarks;
- TMA 1994, s 95 – falsely representing that a mark is a registered trade mark (either by means of the word 'registered' or any other word or symbol);
- TMA 1994, s 99 – unauthorised use of Royal arms.

There are a number of common ingredients of the TMA 1994, s 92 offences which are examined below. Practitioners should exercise great caution when obtaining statements from trade mark proprietors or their representatives to ensure that trademarks certificates are valid and published and that they are accurately reflected in the particulars of offence.

Multiple trademarks oft re-registered can sometimes result in error from the brand representative or in the drafted particulars. Multiple items and potentially more than one action (for example sales) reflecting the same infringed mark may be included on the same count, subject to representations by the defence and the need for greater particularity[1].

1 Criminal Procedure Rules 2020 ('Crim PR'), r 10.2(2) 'more than one incident of the commission of the offence may be included in a count if those incidents taken together amount to a course of conduct having regard to the time place or purpose of commission'.

Mens rea

14.20 Offences under the TMA 1994, s 92 require that a defendant must have either a view to gain for himself or another, or an intent to cause loss to another, and the offending sign must have been used as an indication of trade origin[1]. The words ' . . . with a view to gain for himself or another, or with intent to cause loss to another' appear in the Theft Act 1968 and the meaning given for the purposes of that Act (Theft Act 1968, s 34(2)(a)) is:

' . . .

(a) 'gain' and 'loss' are to be construed as extending only to gain or loss in money or other property, but as extending to any such gain or loss whether temporary or permanent; and

(i) 'gain' includes a gain by keeping what one has, as well as gain by getting what one has not; and

(ii) 'loss' includes a loss by not getting what one might get, as well as a loss by parting with what one has . . . '

1 *R v Johnstone and Others* [2003] 2 Cr App R 33, HL.

14.21 In *R v Zaman*[1] the Court of Appeal considered whether the words 'with a view to' have the same meaning as 'with intent to' in the TMA 1994, s 92 – it concluded, dismissing the appeal, that they do not. The Court of Appeal agreed with the prosecution that the phrase 'with a view to' should simply mean what the defendant has in his contemplation as something that might realistically occur.

1 [2002] EWCA Crim 1862.

Registered trade marks

14.22 All the offences under the TMA 1994, s 92 are concerned with the abuse of 'signs identical to, or likely to be mistaken for, a registered trade mark'. It was confirmed in *R v Boulter*[1] that these heads of liability are distinct. Section 1 defines a trade mark as meaning 'any sign capable of being represented graphically which is capable of distinguishing goods or services of one undertaking from those of other undertakings'[2]. Such a sign may consist of words, names, designs, letters, numerals or the shape of goods or their packaging. Simple colours *are not* capable of being signs: so found the Court of Appeal in overturning the decision of the High Court in the case *Société des Produits Nestlé SA v Cadbury UK Ltd*[3]. In that case the court ruled that a colour – in this case a particular shade of purple – could not, without further definition of application and use in and of itself constitute 'a sign' that was 'represented graphically'. The TMA 1994, s 63 provides for the keeping of a Register of Trademarks and for the supply of certified or uncertified copies, or extracts, of entries in the register.

1   (2009) ETMR 6.
2   Note that, with effect from 14 January 2019, under the new Directive, 2015/2436, the requirement for graphic representability will be removed.
3   [2013] EWCA Civ 1174. See also subsequent case of *Cadbury UK Ltd v Comptroller General of Patents Designs and Trade Marks* [2016] EWHC 796 (Ch).

14.23 An invisible sign is capable of infringing a registered trade mark if it becomes visible on a computer screen: *Reed Executive plc v Reed Business Information Ltd*[1]. It follows from this decision that a sign within the electronic data on an article, such as a DVD or piece of software, could be a sufficient basis for liability under the Act. Support for this conclusion can be found in the Fraud Act 2006. The Fraud Act, ss 6 and 7 set out the offences of possessing, making and supplying articles for use in fraud. The Fraud Act, s 8 defines 'article' for those purposes as including any program or data held in electronic form.

1   [2004] EWCA Civ 159.

14.24 An offence may be committed in respect of goods not covered by the trade mark's registration. The TMA 1994, s 92(4) provides that an offence is committed not only where the goods are goods in respect of which the trade mark is registered, but also where the trade mark has a reputation in the United Kingdom and the use of the sign takes or would take unfair advantage of, or is or would be detrimental to, the distinctive character or the repute of the trade mark. This not a defence provision – the burden of proving that the mark has such a reputation rests with the prosecutor.

14.25 The prosecutor must therefore prove that, on the date of the commission of the alleged offence, the trade mark:

- was registered for the goods in question (or that the circumstances fall within the TMA 1994, s 92(4)); and
- the registration had been published (see the TMA 1994, s 9(3)(b)).

14.26 The equivalent provision for civil liability under the TMA 1994, s 10(2) requires a likelihood of confusion on the part of the public. It is arguable that the criminal test of 'likely to be mistaken for' creates a higher threshold, but there is little guidance in the case law on the issue.

The sign and the goods

14.27 It will be a necessary part of proving any offence under the TMA 1994, s 92 that the sign in question was identical to, or likely to be mistaken for, a registered trade mark. The question is whether the sign (not the item) is likely to be mistaken for that of the registered trade mark proprietor – see *Kensington and Chelsea RLBC v O'Callaghan*[1], where the magistrates erroneously found that there was no case to answer because they were 'not satisfied that either the watches in themselves or the circumstances in which they were offered for sale provided any, other than minimal, evidence that watches were likely to be mistaken for Gucci watches'.

1   [1997] COD 164 CO-2753–96.

14.28 It is usual in prosecuting these offences to obtain a statement from the proprietor of the trademark to confirm that the goods in question were not genuine. This can become increasingly difficult the older the trademark in question as the history of licensing of such items becomes less clear and/or less regulated.

Without consent

14.29 All of the offences under the TMA 1994, s 92 stipulate that the use of the trade mark in question is without the consent of the proprietor of the trade mark. In *Houghton v Liverpool City Council*[1] the question arose as to whether it was incumbent on the prosecution to adduce positive evidence that the proprietor of the trade mark did not consent to the defendant's activities. Laws LJ said:

> 'It is a matter, like so many matters of fact, that may be the subject of proper inferences by the court, never forgetting that the criminal standard of proof applies. In this case . . . the inference is most plainly to be drawn.'

In Scotland, some Procurators Fiscal have expected the registered trade mark owner to provide evidence that they have informed sellers of the infringement.

[1]   [2000] Crim LR 574, [1999] WL 982526.

14.30 Two recent cases have addressed, and finally settled, the application of the TMA 1994, s 92 to so-called 'grey goods'. This term has been used to describe goods which have, or may have had, trademarked signs applied to them at the time of manufacture by a manufacturer who possessed the necessary licence to do so from the trade mark proprietor, only for the goods to enter the UK supply chain through a route which the proprietor had not authorised or licenced. *R v Genis*[1] is an example of a case where this scenario was raised as a defence, and the Court of Appeal found that the use of the trademarks infringed the proprietor's rights as there was no express consent and none had been implied. This reasoning was upheld by the Supreme Court in *R v M and Others*[2], in dismissing the defendants' argument that the TMA 1994, s 92(1) offences were not committed where the goods were originally manufactured with consent. Giving the leading judgment of the court Lord Hughes made clear that the offences set out in the TMA 1994, s 92(1)(a), (b) and (c) are not cumulative, but separate, and that the requirement in the TMA 1994, s 92(1) that the use made of the sign is 'without the consent of the proprietor' applies to each type of use specified – whether it is the application of a trademark to goods; the sale of goods bearing a trademark; or the possession of goods bearing a trademark in the course of a business. This case definitively settled that it is the plain meaning of the TMA that it is unlawful to put 'grey goods' on the market, just as it is to put fake ones on the market: in both cases the infringing trader is setting out to profit from someone else's trademark without permission.

[1]   [2015] EWCA Crim 2043.
[2]   [2017] UKSC 58.

In the course of a business

14.31 By virtue of the TMA 1994, s 103, the words 'business' and 'trade' may be regarded as synonymous. In *R v Johnstone and others*[1] Tuckey LJ said:

'This is not a narrow definition, the use of a mark " . . . even on a single article to be sold or hired out for reward will normally amount to use of the mark 'in the use of trade'" as will its use on orders, invoices, advertisements, brochures and the like . . . '

[1]   [2002] EWCA Crim 194.

14.32 It is ostensibly a requirement, for certain offences under the TMA 1994, s 92, that the offender be acting 'in the course of a business'. However, the combined effect of the decision of the Court of Appeal in *R v Johnstone* (not overturned by the House of Lords and followed in subsequent cases) and the defence in s 92(5) is that those who commit criminal offences under s 92 can only be convicted where there is civil infringement. Since there can be no civil infringement unless the activity under s 10 occurs 'in the course of trade', successful prosecutions of the s 92 offences can therefore only occur where the offender is acting in the course of a trade/business. This causes no injustice – as Lord Nicholls said in *R v Johnstone*[1]:

'. . . it is hard to think of a realistic example of conduct which would attract criminal liability and yet be excluded from civil liability because it would not be "in the course of trade".'

See also the case of *Devlin v Hall*[2] for a helpful exposition by Alliott J of the meaning of 'in the course of trade or business', and the division of such activity into three categories: ' . . . (a) a one-off adventure in the nature of a trade carried through with a view to profit; (b) a transaction which is an integral part of the business carried on, that is to say, part of its normal practice; or (c) a transaction which is merely incidental to the carrying on of the relevant business that is carried on with some degree of regularity'.

[1]   [2003] 1 WLR 1736.
[2]   [1999] RTR 320.

In possession

14.33 TMA 1994, s 92(1)(c), (2)(c) and (3)(b) are offences involving the 'possession custody or control' of particular goods, materials and articles. Possession by an agent will be covered by these provisions – see, for example, *Essex Trading Standards v Singh*[1]. Shop assistants may also be deemed to be in possession, however such cases will turn on their own facts[2].

[1]   [2009] EWHC 520 (Admin).
[2]   *R v Matrix* [1997] Crim LR 901.

14.34 In *R v Kousar (Rukhsana)*[1] the wife of a market trader successfully appealed against her conviction under the TMA 1994, s 92(1)(c) in circumstances where trading standards officers searched their home address and found a large quantity of counterfeit items. The prosecution's case was that she was aware of the counterfeit goods because they were stored in the family home and on this basis it could be said that she also was in possession of them. Quashing the conviction, David Clarke J said[2]:

'The Crown had to prove that her possession of the goods was possession in the course of a business and it seems to us that, if they could not establish that she was involved in the business as a participant, whether paid or otherwise, in the business of dealing with these goods, then they could not establish that element of their case.'

Thus, even if, contrary to our view, her so-called ability or right to control the goods was sufficient to render her in possession of them, this still did not suffice to establish that further element of these offences. Our conclusion, therefore, is that this appellant in truth did not have a case to answer and the learned Recorder fell into error in ruling that she did.'

¹   [2009] EWCA Crim 139.
²   At para 19.

Use as a trade mark

14.35 In *R v Johnstone*¹ Lord Nicholls said:

'. . . section 92 is to be interpreted as applying only when the offending sign is used as an indication of trade origin. This is one of the ingredients of each of the offences created by section 92. It must therefore be proved by the prosecution. Whether a sign is so used is a question of fact in each case.'

Cases since *Johnstone* have shown that an indication to the immediate purchaser that the product is a replica does not of itself exclude a conclusion that the sign in question was indicative of trade origin (*CPS v Gary Robert Morgan*²) – since the essential function of a trade mark is to guarantee the identity of origin of the marked goods or services to the consumer or end user – and that there is no defence even where material bearing the trademarks was of such poor quality that no one could think that its trade origin was that of the trade mark owner (*R v Boulter*³).

¹   [2003] 1 WLR 1736.
²   [2006] EWCA Crim 1742.
³   [2008] EWCA Crim 2375.

Section 92(2) and (3)

14.36 The TMA 1994, s 92(2) and (3) substantially mirror the TMA 1994, s 92(1) in form, however, they are concerned with the creation, possession and application of labelling, packaging or promotional material which infringe registered trademarks, or the means of producing the same, rather than being concerned with the counterfeit goods themselves.

14.37 Where copies of a registered trademark have been electronically stored on a computer or other electronic storage device, in circumstances where it is apparent that it has been used, or is intended to be used, to apply the trademark to unauthorised labels or packaging the person in control of the device risks falling foul of one or other of these sections – provided that the relevant elements of *mens rea* are also present. Given the ubiquitous nature of computers and linked printers, this is an increasingly important matter in relation to seizure and forfeiture of computer equipment. The fact that the computer may also have been used, or that it was intended to be used, for other, lawful, purposes, is irrelevant as the section does not require that the illegal purpose need be an exclusive one.

Defences

14.38 TMA 1994, s 92(5) provides a statutory defence:

(5) It is a defence for a person charged with an offence under this section to show that he believed on reasonable grounds that the use of the sign in the manner in which it was used, or was to be used, was not an infringement of the registered trade mark.

14.39 TMA 1994, s 92(5) requires the accused to prove his defence on the balance of probabilities: see *R v Johnstone*[1]. The statutory defence has been considered in a number of cases – see, in particular, *R v McCrudden*[2], *West Sussex County Council v Habib Kahraman*[3], *Essex Trading Standards v Singh*[4] and *Stockton on Tees Borough Council v Dawn Frost*[5]. They support the view that the section affords a positive and specific defence and does not provide a defence of mere good faith. In *R v Malik*[6] Rix LJ concurred with this concept: ' . . . in *McCrudden* . . . Laws LJ was quite right to say that there was no general defence of good faith in the TMA 1994, s 92(5) . . . '. However, the Court of Appeal allowed the defendant's appeal on the facts of this case, which involved a shop selling counterfeit vodka[7]:

> 'it is very hard for this court to say . . . that purchases from a long-term reputable supplier, which can be proved by records in the form of invoices, purchases of apparently genuine stock at full price, are not evidence capable of providing a defence for the jury's consideration.'

1 [2002] EWCA Crim 194.
2 [2005] EWCA Crim 466.
3 [2006] EWHC 1703 (Admin).
4 [2009] EWHC 520 (Admin).
5 [2010] EWHC 1304 (Admin).
6 [2011] EWCA Crim 1107.
7 At para 17.

Restrictions on proceedings

14.40 There is no statutory time limit for the TMA 1994, s 92 offences. In Scotland, the TMA 1994, s 96 (supplementary provisions as to summary proceedings in Scotland) provides:

96 Supplementary provisions as to summary proceedings in Scotland

(1) Notwithstanding anything in section 136 of the Criminal Procedure (Scotland) Act 1995, summary proceedings in Scotland for an offence under this Act may be begun at any time within six months after the date on which evidence sufficient in the Lord Advocate's opinion to justify the proceedings came to his knowledge.
For this purpose a certificate of the Lord Advocate as to the date on which such evidence came to his knowledge is conclusive evidence.

(2) For the purposes of subsection (1) and of any other provision of this Act as to the time within which summary proceedings for an offence may be brought, proceedings in Scotland shall be deemed to be begun on the date on which a warrant to apprehend or to cite the accused is granted, if such warrant is executed without undue delay.

14.41 Cases such as *Burwell v DPP*[1] and *RSPCA v Ian James King and Kathleen Patricia King*[2] underline the importance of a prosecutor, who wishes to avail himself of the benefits of such a certificate, fully complying with the statutory requirements.

¹ [2009] EWHC 1069 (Admin).
² [2010] EWHC 637 (Admin).

Prosecutions

14.42 Any person (whether an individual or a body corporate), other than the Crown or its servants or agents, can be prosecuted under the Act.

Date of publication

14.43 Practitioners should be aware that whilst protection afforded by registration in the civil law begins on the date of registration, criminal proceedings cannot be commenced in relation to conduct prior to the publication of the registration¹. Practitioners should always check the date of first publication.

¹ TMA 1994, s 9(3)b.

Partnerships

14.44 Under the TMA 1994, s 101 partnerships must be prosecuted in the name of the firm and not that of the partners and any fine imposed following the partnership's conviction must be paid out of partnership assets. Where a partnership is guilty of an offence under the Act, every partner, other than a partner who is proved (on the balance of probabilities) to have been ignorant of or to have attempted to prevent the commission of the offence, is also guilty of the offence and liable to be proceeded against and punished.

14.45 In *R v Wakefield and Purseglove*¹ the defendants contended that the section under which the prosecution purported to proceed – the TMA 1994, s 101(4) – requires there to have been a conviction of the partnership before the partners themselves can have liability. Since there was no longer any partnership (at the time of the hearing – the partnership had been dissolved after the offences were committed), it was argued that the defendants could not be prosecuted as individuals. The Court of Appeal considered that the argument was misconceived – the subsection does not require there to have been a conviction of the partnership, merely that the court be satisfied that the partnership is guilty of an offence. The appeals were dismissed.

¹ [2004] EWCA Crim 2278.

Directors' liability

14.46 The TMA 1994, s 101(5) permits the prosecution and conviction of any 'director, manager, secretary or other similar officer' of a company or 'any person who was purporting to act in such a capacity' where an offence under the Act has been committed by the company 'with the consent and connivance' of that person or as a result of that person's neglect. It is good practice (though not strictly necessary) to include the company as a defendant in the same proceedings as the person prosecuted under the TMA 1994, s 101(5), as it will be necessary to prove that the company could have been found guilty of the offence even if it is not a defendant. Directors' liability provisions are considered in CHAPTER **4**, Criminal Enforcement.

Duty to enforce

14.47 The Trade Marks Act 1994, s 93 Act (as amended by the Consumer Rights Act 2015) provides that:

> **93 Enforcement function of local weights and measures authority**
>
> (1) It is the duty of every local weights and measures authority to enforce within their area the provisions of section 92 (unauthorised use of trade mark, &c. in relation to goods)'
>
> . . .
>
> (5) Nothing in this section shall be construed as authorising a local weights and measures authority to bring proceedings in Scotland for an offence.

14.48 Although the right to prosecute offences under the Act is not restricted to a member or officer of an enforcement authority, powers are only exercisable by specified persons; see *Media Protection Services Ltd v Crawford*[1].

[1]   [2012] EWHC 2373 (Admin).

14.49 The Copyright, etc and Trade Marks (Offences and Enforcement) Act 2002 rationalised legal provisions relating to copyright and trade marks in a number of areas including police search and seizure powers, and continues to supplement the Trade Marks Act 1994. The TMA 1994, s 92A enables a search warrant to be issued to a constable to enter and search premises where there are reasonable grounds for believing:

(a)   that an offence under the TMA 1994, s 92 has been or is about to be committed in any premises; and

(b)   that evidence that such an offence has been or is about to be committed is in those premises.

Enforcement powers for officers of local weights and measures authorities and DETI (Northern Ireland) are now covered by the CRA 2015, Sch 5, see CHAPTER **4**, Criminal Enforcement.

Sentencing

14.50 The TMA 1994, s 92(6), as amended by the Legal Aid, Sentencing and Punishment of Offenders Act 2012 (Fines on Summary Conviction) Regulations 2015[1], which came into force on 12 March 2015, provides:

> (6) A person guilty of an offence under this section is liable—
>> (a)   on summary conviction to imprisonment for a term not exceeding six months or a fine, or both;
>> (b)   on conviction on indictment to a fine or imprisonment for a term not exceeding ten years, or both.

[1]   SI 2015/664.

14.51 Offences under the TMA 1994, s 92 are triable either way. Guidance on sentencing for the s 92 offence was provided by the 'Magistrates' Court Sentencing Guidelines'[1]. The Guidelines indicate that where an offence involves a high number of counterfeit items or involvement in a wider operation (eg manufacture or distribution) then magistrates should consider sending the case to the Crown Court for sentence. Offenders who occupied a central role in large scale operations should also be sent to the Crown Court. Factors indicating a higher level of seriousness include: a high degree of professionalism; high profit levels; and the exposure of purchasers to risk of harm. Mistake or ignorance as to the provenance of goods may indicate a lower level of culpability.

[1] Guidelines effective from 4 August 2008, and current as of the update issued 24 January 2017, see p 97.

14.52 From 21 October 2020 new guidelines published by the Sentencing Council have applied to cases sentenced in the Crown Court. These guidelines are summarised below. For the full guideline see https://www.sentencingcouncil.org.uk/offences/magistrates-court/item/individuals-trade-mark-unauthorised-use-of-etc/.

Sentencing
SC Guideline – Individuals: Trade mark, unauthorised use of etc

INDIVIDUALS: TRADE MARK, UNAUTHORISED USE OF ETC

14.53

Trade Marks Act 1994, s 92

Effective from: 1 October 2021

Triable either way

Maximum: 10 years' custody

Offence range: Discharge – 7 years' custody

Use this guideline when the offender is an individual. If the offender is an organisation, please refer to the Organisations: Trade mark, unauthorised use of etc guideline [at [14.55]].

STEP 1
Determining the offence category

The court should determine the offence category with reference to culpability and harm.

Culpability

The level of culpability is determined by weighing up all the factors of the case to determine the offender's role and the extent to which the offending was **planned** and the **sophistication** with which it was carried out.

A – High culpability

- Sophisticated nature of offence/significant planning (examples **may** include but are not limited to: the use of multiple outlets or trading identities for the sale of counterfeit goods, the use of multiple accounts for receiving payment, the use of

professional equipment to produce goods, the use of a website that mimics that of the trade mark owner or a legitimate trader, offending over a sustained period of time)
- A leading role where offending is part of a group activity
- Involvement of others through coercion, intimidation or exploitation

B – Medium culpability

- Some degree of organisation/planning involved
- A significant role where offending is part of a group activity
- Other cases that fall between categories A or C because:
  - Factors are present in A and C which balance each other out **and/or**
  - The offender's culpability falls between the factors as described in A and C

C – Lesser culpability

- Little or no organisation/planning
- Performed limited function under direction
- Involved through coercion, intimidation or exploitation
- Limited awareness or understanding of the offence

Where there are characteristics present which fall under different levels of culpability, the court should balance these characteristics to reach a fair assessment of the offender's culpability.

Harm

The assessment of harm for this offence involves putting a monetary figure on the offending with reference to the **value of equivalent genuine goods** and assessing **any significant additional harm** suffered by the trade mark owner or purchasers/end users of the counterfeit goods:

1. Where there is evidence of the volume of counterfeit goods sold or possessed:

(a)　The monetary value should be assessed by taking the **equivalent retail value of legitimate versions** of the counterfeit goods involved in the offending.

(b)　Where it would be impractical to assign an equivalent retail value of legitimate versions, an estimate should be used.

2. Where there is no evidence of the volume of counterfeit goods sold or possessed:

(a)　In the case of labels or packaging, harm should be assessed by taking the **equivalent retail value of legitimate goods** to which the labels or packaging could reasonably be applied, taking an average price of the relevant products.

(b)　In the case of equipment or articles for the making of copies of trade marks, the court will have to make an assessment of the scale of the operation and assign an equivalent value from the table below.

Note: the equivalent retail value is likely to be considerably higher than the actual value of the counterfeit items and this is accounted for in the sentence levels. However, in **exceptional** cases where the equivalent retail value is grossly disproportionate to the actual value, an adjustment **may** be made.

The general harm caused to purchasers/ end users (by being provided with counterfeit goods), to legitimate businesses (through loss of business) and to the owners of the trade mark (through loss of revenue and reputational damage) is reflected in the sentence levels at step 2.

Examples of **significant additional harm** may include but are not limited to:

- Substantial damage to the legitimate business of the trade mark owner (taking into account the size of the business).

- Purchasers/end users put at risk of physical harm from counterfeit goods.

Where purchasers/end users are put at **risk of death or serious physical harm** from counterfeit goods, harm should be **at least category 3** even if the equivalent retail value of the goods falls below £50,000.

	Equivalent value of legitimate goods	Starting point based on
Category 1	£1 million or more **or** category 2 value with significant additional harm	£2 million
Category 2	£300,000–£1 million **or** category 3 value with significant additional harm	£600,000
Category 3	£50,000–£300,000 **or** category 4 value with significant additional harm	£125,000
Category 4	£5,000–£50,000 **or** category 5 value with significant additional harm	£30,000
Category 5	Less than £5,000 **and** little or no significant additional harm	£2,500

STEP 2
Starting point and category range

Having determined the category at step 1, the court should use the appropriate starting point to reach a sentence within the category range in the table below. The starting point applies to all offenders irrespective of plea or previous convictions.

Where the value is larger or smaller than the amount on which the starting point is based, this should lead to upward or downward adjustment as appropriate.

For offences where the equivalent retail value is £1 million or more an upward adjustment within the category range should be made for any significant additional harm.

	Culpability		
Harm	A	B	C
Category 1 £1 million or more Starting point based on £2 million	**Starting point** 5 years' custody **Category range** 3 – 7 years' custody	**Starting point** 3 years' custody **Category range** 2 – 5 years' custody	**Starting point** 2 years' custody **Category range** 1 – 3 years' custody
Category 2 £300,000 – £1 million Starting point based on £600,000	**Starting point** 4 years' custody **Category range** 2 – 5 years' custody	**Starting point** 2 years' custody **Category range** 1 – 3 years' custody	**Starting point** 1 year's custody **Category range** 26 weeks' – 2 years' custody
Category 3 £50,000 – £300,000 Starting point based on £125,000	**Starting point** 2 years' custody **Category range** 1 – 3 years' custody	**Starting point** 1 year's custody **Category range** 26 weeks' – 2 years' custody	**Starting point** High level community order **Category range** Low level community order – 26 weeks' custody

Harm	Culpability		
	A	B	C
Category 4 £5,000 – £50,000 Starting point based on £30,000	**Starting point** 1 years' custody **Category range** 26 weeks' – 2 years custody	**Starting point** High level community order **Category range** Low level community order – 26 weeks' custody	**Starting point** Band C fine **Category range** Band B fine – Medium level community order
Category 5 Less than £5,000 Starting point based on £2,500	**Starting point** High level community order **Category range** Low level community order – 26 weeks' custody	**Starting point** Band C fine **Category range** Band B fine – Medium level community order	**Starting point** Band B fine **Category range** Discharge – Band C fine

This is an offence where it may be appropriate to combine a community order with a fine.

The court should then consider further adjustment for any aggravating or mitigating factors. The following list is a non-exhaustive list of additional factual elements providing the context of the offence and factors relating to the offender. Identify whether any combination of these, or other relevant factors, should result in an upward or downward adjustment from the starting point.

Factors increasing seriousness

Statutory aggravating factors:

- Previous convictions, having regard to a) the nature of the offence to which the conviction relates and its relevance to the current offence; and b) the time that has elapsed since the conviction
- Offence committed whilst on bail

Other aggravating factors:

- Purchasers or others put at risk of harm from counterfeit items (where not taken into account at step 1)
- Expectation of substantial financial gain
- Attempts to conceal/dispose of evidence
- Attempts to conceal identity
- Failure to respond to warnings about behaviour
- Blame wrongly placed on others
- Offences taken into consideration
- Failure to comply with current court orders
- Commission of offence whilst under the influence of alcohol/drugs
- Offence committed on licence or post sentence supervision

Factors reducing seriousness or reflecting personal mitigation

- No previous convictions or no relevant/recent convictions
- Remorse
- Good character and/or exemplary conduct
- Offender co-operated with investigation, made early admissions and/or voluntarily reported offending
- Expectation of limited financial gain
- Lapse of time since apprehension where this does not arise from the conduct of the offender
- Serious medical conditions requiring urgent, intensive or long-term treatment
- Age and/or lack of maturity

- Mental disorder or learning disability
- Sole or primary carer for dependent relatives

STEP 3
Consider any factors which indicate a reduction, such as assistance to the prosecution

The court should take into account section 74 of the Sentencing Code (reduction in sentence for assistance to prosecution) and any other rule of law by virtue of which an offender may receive a discounted sentence in consequence of assistance given (or offered) to the prosecutor or investigator.

STEP 4
Reduction for guilty pleas

The court should take account of any potential reduction for a guilty plea in accordance with section 73 of the Sentencing Code and the *Reduction in Sentence for a Guilty Plea* guideline.

STEP 5
Totality principle

If sentencing an offender for more than one offence, or where the offender is already serving a sentence, consider whether the total sentence is just and proportionate to the overall offending behaviour in accordance with the *Totality* guideline.

STEP 6
Confiscation, compensation and ancillary orders

Confiscation orders under the Proceeds of Crime Act 2002 may only be made by the Crown Court. The Crown Court must proceed with a view to making a confiscation order if it is asked to do so by the prosecutor or if the Crown Court believes it is appropriate for it to do so.

Where, following conviction in a magistrates' court, the prosecutor applies for the offender to be committed to the Crown Court with a view to a confiscation order being considered, the magistrates' court must commit the offender to the Crown Court to be sentenced there (section 70 of the Proceeds of Crime Act 2002). Where, but for the prosecutor's application under s 70, the magistrates' court would have committed the offender for sentence to the Crown Court anyway it must say so. Otherwise the powers of sentence of the Crown Court will be limited to those of the magistrates' court.

(Note: the valuation of counterfeit goods for the purposes of confiscation proceedings is not the same as the valuation used for the purposes of assessing harm in this sentencing guideline.)

Where the offence has resulted in loss or damage the court must consider whether to make a **compensation order** and must give reasons if it does not do so (section 55 of the Sentencing Code).

If the court makes both a confiscation order and an order for compensation and the court believes the offender will not have sufficient means to satisfy both orders in full, the court must direct that the compensation be paid out of sums recovered under the confiscation order (section 13 of the Proceeds of Crime Act 2002).

Forfeiture – section 97 of the Trade Marks Act 1994.

The prosecution may apply for forfeiture of goods or materials bearing a sign likely to be mistaken for a registered trademark or articles designed for making copies of such a sign. The court shall make an order for forfeiture only if it is satisfied that a relevant offence has been committed in relation to the goods, material or articles. A court may infer that such an offence has been committed in relation to any goods, material or articles if it is satisfied that such an offence has been committed in relation to goods, material or articles which are representative of them (whether by reason of being of the same design or part of the same consignment or batch or otherwise).

The court may also consider whether to make other ancillary orders. These may include a deprivation order and disqualification from acting as a company director.

• Ancillary orders – Magistrates' Court
• Ancillary orders – Crown Court Compendium, Part II Sentencing

STEP 7
Reasons

Section 52 of the Sentencing Code imposes a duty to give reasons for, and explain the effect of, the sentence.

STEP 8
Consideration for time spent on bail (tagged curfew)

The court must consider whether to give credit for time spent on bail in accordance with section 240A of the Criminal Justice Act 2003 and section 325 of the Sentencing Code.

14.54 The Sentencing Guideline for organisations is summarised below. The full text of the guideline can be found at https://www.sentencingcouncil.org.uk/offences/magistrates-court/item/organisations-trade-mark-unauthorised-use-of-etc/.

Sentencing
SC Guideline – Organisations: Trade mark, unauthorised use of etc

ORGANISATIONS: TRADE MARK, UNAUTHORISED USE OF ETC

14.55

Trade Marks Act 1994, s 92

Effective from: 1 October 2021

Triable either way

Maximum: Unlimited fine

Offence range: £250 fine to £450,000 fine

Use this guideline when the offender is an organisation. If the offender is an individual please refer to the Individuals: Trade mark, unauthorised use of etc guideline [at [14.53]].

Note The penalties in this guideline for sentencing organisations are financial. Courts are required to consider financial penalties in the following order:

• compensation (which takes priority over any other payment);
• confiscation (Crown Court only);
• fine.

Therefore, in this guideline the court is required to consider compensation and confiscation before going on to determine the fine.

STEP 1
Compensation

The court must consider making a compensation order requiring the offender to pay compensation for any personal injury, loss or damage resulting from the offence in such an amount as the court considers appropriate, having regard to the evidence and to the means of the offender.

Where the means of the offender are limited, priority should be given to the payment of compensation over payment of any other financial penalty.

Reasons should be given if a compensation order is not made (section 55 of the Sentencing Code).

STEP 1
Confiscation

Confiscation orders under the Proceeds of Crime Act 2002 may only be made by the Crown Court. Confiscation must be considered by the Crown Court if either the prosecutor asks for it or the Crown Court thinks that it may be appropriate.

Where, following conviction in a magistrates' court, the prosecutor applies for the offender to be committed to the Crown Court with a view to a confiscation order being considered, the magistrates' court must commit the offender to the Crown Court to be sentenced there (section 70 of the Proceeds of Crime Act 2002). Where, but for the prosecutor's application under s 70, the magistrates' court would have committed the offender for sentence to the Crown Court anyway it must say so. Otherwise the powers of sentence of the Crown Court will be limited to those of the magistrates' court.

(Note: the valuation of counterfeit goods for the purposes of confiscation proceedings will not be the same as the valuation used for the purposes of assessing harm in this sentencing guideline.)

Confiscation must be dealt with before, and taken into account when assessing, any other fine or financial order (except compensation).

(See Proceeds of Crime Act 2002 sections 6 and 13.)

STEP 3
Determining the offence category

The court should determine the offence category with reference to culpability and harm.

Culpability

The level of culpability is determined by weighing up all the factors of the case to determine the offender's role and the extent to which the offending was **planned** and the **sophistication** with which it was carried out.

A – High culpability

- Organisation plays a leading role in organised, planned unlawful activity whether acting alone or with others (indicators of planned activity **may** include but are not limited to: the use of multiple outlets or trading identities for the sale of counterfeit goods, the use of multiple accounts for receiving payment, the use of professional equipment to produce goods, the use of a website that mimics that of the trade mark owner or a legitimate trader, offending over a sustained period of time)
- Involving others through pressure or coercion (for example employees or suppliers)

B – Medium culpability

- Organisation plays a significant role in unlawful activity organised by others
- Some degree of organisation/planning involved
- Other cases that fall between categories A or C because:
  - Factors are present in A and C which balance each other out **and/or**
  - The offender's culpability falls between the factors as described in A and C

C – Lesser culpability

- Organisation plays a minor, peripheral role in unlawful activity organised by others
- Involvement through coercion, intimidation or exploitation
- Little or no organisation/planning
- Limited awareness or understanding of the offence

Where there are characteristics present which fall under different levels of culpability, the court should balance these characteristics to reach a fair assessment of the offender's culpability.

Harm

The assessment of harm for this offence involves putting a monetary figure on the offending with reference to the **value of equivalent genuine goods** and assessing **any significant additional harm** suffered by the trade mark owner or purchasers/end users of the counterfeit goods:

1. Where there is evidence of the volume of counterfeit goods sold or possessed:

(a) The monetary value should be assessed by taking the **equivalent retail value of legitimate versions** of the counterfeit goods involved in the offending.

(b) Where it would be impractical to assign an equivalent retail value of legitimate versions, an estimate should be used.

2. Where there is no evidence of the volume of counterfeit goods sold or possessed:

(a) In the case of labels or packaging, harm should be assessed by taking the **equivalent retail value of legitimate goods** to which the labels or packaging could reasonably be applied, taking an average price of the relevant products.

(b) In the case of equipment or articles for the making of copies of trade marks, the court will have to make an assessment of the scale of the operation and assign an equivalent value from the table below.

Note: the equivalent retail value is likely to be considerably higher than the actual value of the counterfeit items and this is accounted for in the sentence levels. However, in **exceptional** cases where the equivalent retail value is grossly disproportionate to the actual value, an adjustment **may** be made.

The general harm caused to purchasers/ end users (by being provided with counterfeit goods), to legitimate businesses (through loss of business) and to the owners of the trade mark (through loss of revenue and reputational damage) is reflected in the sentence levels at step 4.

Examples of **significant additional harm** may include but are not limited to:

- Substantial damage to the legitimate business of the trade mark owner (taking into account the size of the business).
- Purchasers/end users put at risk of physical harm from counterfeit goods.

Where purchasers/end users are put at **risk of death or serious physical harm** from counterfeit goods, harm should be **at least category 3** even if the equivalent retail value of the goods falls below £50,000.

	Equivalent value of legitimate goods	Starting point based on
Category 1	£1 million or more or category 2 value with significant additional harm	£2 million
Category 2	£300,000–£1 million or category 3 value with significant additional harm	£600,000
Category 3	£50,000–£300,000 or category 4 value with significant additional harm	£125,000
Category 4	£5,000–£50,000 or category 5 value with significant additional harm	£30,000
Category 5	Less than £5,000 and little or no significant additional harm	£2,500

STEP 4
Starting point and category range

Having determined the category at step 3, the court should use the appropriate starting point to reach a sentence within the category range in the table below. The starting point applies to all offenders irrespective of plea or previous convictions.

Where the value is larger or smaller than the amount on which the starting point is based, this should lead to upward or downward adjustment as appropriate.

For offences where the equivalent retail value is £1 million or more an upward adjustment within the category range should be made for any significant additional harm.

The fine levels below assume that the offending organisation has an annual turnover of not more than £2 million. In cases where turnover is higher, adjustment may need to be made at Step 5 below including outside the offence range.

Harm	Culpability		
	A	B	C
Category 1 £1 million or more Starting point based on £2 million	Starting point £250,000 Category range £150,000 – £450,000	Starting point £100,000 Category range £50,000 – £200,000	Starting point £50,000 Category range £25,000 – £100,000
Category 2 £300,000 – £1million Starting point based on £600,000	Starting point £150,000 Category range £75,000 – £250,000	Starting point £50,000 Category range £25,000 – £100,000	Starting point £25,000 Category range £15,000 – £50,000
Category 3 £50,000 – £300,000 Starting point based on £125,000	Starting point £50,000 Category range £25,000 – £100,000	Starting point £25,000 Category range £15,000 – £50,000	Starting point £10,000 Category range £5,000 – £25,000
Category 4 £5,000 – £50,000 Starting point based on £30,000	Starting point £25,000 Category range £15,000 – £50,000	Starting point £10,000 Category range £5,000 – £25,000	Starting point £5,000 Category range £2,000 – £10,000

Harm	Culpability		
	A	B	C
Category 5 Less than £5,000 Starting point based on £2,500	Starting point £10,000 Category range £5,000 – £25,000	Starting point £5,000 Category range £2,000 – £10,000	Starting point £1,000 Category range £250 – £5,000

Having determined the appropriate starting point, the court should then consider adjustment within the category range for aggravating or mitigating features. The following list is a non-exhaustive list of additional factual elements providing the context of the offence and factors relating to the offender. Identify whether any combination of these, or other relevant factors, should result in an upward or downward adjustment from the starting point.

Factors increasing seriousness

- Previous relevant convictions or subject to previous relevant civil or regulatory enforcement action
- Organisation or subsidiary set up to commit counterfeiting activity
- Counterfeiting activity endemic within organisation
- Expectation of substantial financial gain
- Purchasers put at risk of harm from counterfeit items (where not taken into account at step 3)
- Attempts to conceal/dispose of evidence
- Attempts to conceal identity
- Failure to respond to warnings
- Blame wrongly placed on others

Factors reducing seriousness or reflecting mitigation

- No previous convictions or previous relevant civil or regulatory enforcement action
- Offender co-operated with investigation, made early admissions and/or voluntarily reported offending
- Little or no actual gain to organisation from offending
- Lapse of time since apprehension where this does not arise from the conduct of the offender

General principles to follow in setting a fine. The court should determine the appropriate level of fine in accordance with section 125 of the Sentencing Code, which requires that the fine must reflect the seriousness of the offence and requires the court to take into account the financial circumstances of the offender.

STEP 5
Adjustment of fine

Note the fine levels above assume that the offending organisation has an annual turnover of not more than £2 million. In cases where turnover is higher, adjustment may need to be made including outside the offence range.

Having arrived at a fine level, the court should consider whether there are any further factors which indicate an adjustment in the level of the fine including outside the category range. The court should 'step back' and consider the overall effect of its orders. The combination of orders made, compensation, confiscation and fine ought to achieve:

- the removal of all gain
- appropriate additional punishment, and
- deterrence

The fine may be adjusted to ensure that these objectives are met in a fair way. The court should consider any further factors relevant to the setting of the level of the fine to ensure that the fine is proportionate, having regard to the size and financial position of the offending organisation and the seriousness of the offence.

The fine must be substantial enough to have a real economic impact which will bring home to both management and shareholders the need to operate within the law. Whether the fine will have the effect of putting the offender out of business will be relevant; in some bad cases this may be an acceptable consequence.

In considering the ability of the offending organisation to pay any financial penalty the court can take into account the power to allow time for payment or to order that the amount be paid in instalments.

The court should consider whether the level of fine would otherwise cause unacceptable harm to third parties. In doing so the court should bear in mind that the payment of any compensation determined at step one should take priority over the payment of any fine.

Below is a **non-exhaustive** list of additional factual elements for the court to consider.

The court should identify whether any combination of these, or other relevant factors, should result in a proportionate increase or reduction in the level of fine.

Factors to consider in adjusting the level of fine

- Fine fulfils the objectives of punishment, deterrence and removal of gain
-
- The value, worth or available means of the offender
- Fine impairs offender's ability to make restitution to victims
- Impact of fine on offender's ability to implement effective compliance programmes Impact of fine on employment of staff, service users, customers and local economy (but not shareholders)
- Impact of fine on performance of public or charitable function

STEP 6
Consider any factors which indicate a reduction, such as assistance to the prosecution

The court should take into account section 74 of the Sentencing Code (reduction in sentence for assistance to prosecution) and any other rule of law by virtue of which an offender may receive a discounted sentence in consequence of assistance given (or offered) to the prosecutor or investigator.

STEP 7
Reduction for guilty pleas

The court should take account of any potential reduction for a guilty plea in accordance with section 73 of the Sentencing Code and the *Reduction in Sentence for a Guilty Plea* guideline.

STEP 8
Totality principle

If sentencing an offender for more than one offence, or where the offender is already serving a sentence, consider whether the total sentence is just and proportionate to the overall offending behaviour in accordance with the *Totality* guideline.

STEP 9
Ancillary orders

Forfeiture – section 97 of the Trade Marks Act 1994

The prosecution may apply for forfeiture of goods or materials bearing a sign likely to be mistaken for a registered trademark or articles designed for making copies of such a sign. The court shall make an order for forfeiture only if it is satisfied that a relevant offence has been committed in relation to the goods, material or articles. A court may infer that such an offence has been committed in relation to any goods, material or articles if it is satisfied that such an offence has been committed in relation to goods, material or articles which are representative of them (whether by reason of being of the same design or part of the same consignment or batch or otherwise).

The court may also consider whether to make other ancillary orders. These may include a deprivation order.

- Ancillary orders – Magistrates' Court
- Ancillary orders – Crown Court Compendium, Part II Sentencing

STEP 10
Reasons

Section 52 of the Sentencing Code imposes a duty to give reasons for, and explain the effect of, the sentence.

Sentencing authorities

14.56 There are numerous Court of Appeal authorities for sentencing under s 92. However, these are likely to be considerably less significant following the publication of the new Crown Court sentencing guidelines. The scale of the enterprise is often a very significant factor in sentencing such cases. In *R v Brayford*[1] the defendant was sentenced to 2 years' imprisonment, upheld on appeal, in relation to the importation into the United Kingdom from China of 25,000 kilograms of washing powder and 2,875 flat pack boxes into which the powder was to be filled. The boxes unlawfully bore the trademark 'Persil'. In *R v Reilly*[2] – where the defendant sold counterfeit cigarettes from his home address – his sentence of 49 days' imprisonment was quashed and a conditional discharge for 2 years was substituted. In *R v Guest (Maxwell)*[3] the defendant's sentence was reduced from 6 to 4 months' imprisonment on appeal, for 10 offences under the TMA 1994, s 92. He sold computers with counterfeit Microsoft software loaded onto them worth £3,000. In *R v Sarbjit Singh*[4] the defendant pleaded guilty to a total of 17 offences contrary to the TMA 1994, s 92(3)(b) and TMA 1994, s 92(1)(a). His offending involved running, together with others, a large scale, sophisticated counterfeiting operation from a screen printing factory and his sentence of 11 months' imprisonment was upheld.

[1]   [2010] EWCA Crim 2329.
[2]   [2010] EWCA Crim 2534.
[3]   [2013] EWCA Crim 1437.
[4]   [2014] EWCA Crim 1803.

14.57 In *R v Manders*[1] the Court of Appeal upheld a sentence of 2 years imprisonment where the defendant had been responsible for the large-scale commercial manufacture of counterfeit DVD's for sale – 32,000 counterfeit discs were seized together with equipment for loading them with content, guilty pleas were entered on the day of trial. In *R v Khan*[2] four defendants pleaded guilty to conspiracy to commit TMA offences arising from the conduct of a company involved in selling counterfeit items of clothing and footwear from two Birmingham shops. They successfully appealed against their sentences which ranged from 2 years' imprisonment to a community order. In his judgment, reducing the sentences, Sweeney J helpfully summarised the factors which commonly arise when sentencing in such case:

'As to the authorities, there is plainly no guideline case as such . . . However, they do make clear that when considering sentence in a case of this type the court must take into account, amongst other things, that: (1) offences of this type are difficult, time consuming and expensive to detect; (2) they undermine reputable companies who are entitled to be protected; (3) the court should consider how professional the offending was; (4) there should be an estimation of the likely or actual profit; (5) the need for an element of deterrence must be borne in mind . . . '

The custodial sentences were reduced by between one-quarter and almost one-half.

1   [2012] EWCA Crim 908.
2   [2013] EWCA Crim 802.

14.58 The Court of Appeal has acknowledged that intellectual property offences, such as those under the TMA 1994, s 92, ' . . . are difficult to detect, that investigations are time-consuming and that cases of this sort are very expensive to bring to court' (Lloyd Jones J, endorsing the observations of the trial judge, in *R v Lee*[1]. These remarks were further endorsed by Sweeney J in *R v Khan*[2]) and that the ' . . . nature of these offences is such that not only do they involve the deception of innocent members of the public, but also such activities impact upon the reputation and profits of legitimate, reputable companies and can in its most extreme form affect the employment prospects of people working or wishing to work for such reputable companies'. Davies J in *R v Edwards (Mark)*[3].

1   [2010] EWCA Crim 268.
2   *R v Khan (Yasar)* [2013] EWCA Crim 802.
3   [2008] EWCA Crim 2705.

14.59 In *R v Harpreet Singh*[1], D was convicted of TMA offences, including the TMA 1994, s 92(1)(c) and sentenced to 6 months' imprisonment suspended for 2 years, with 120 hours unpaid work. He assisted a stallholder in selling goods, but took no part in replenishing stock and did not concern himself with its legitimacy. He admitted that he was aware that 'loads of people at [the event] were selling fake goods'. He was of previous good character. His appeal against sentence was dismissed: it was a serious offence passing the custody threshold. In *R v Alshateri*[2], D was convicted of selling counterfeit tobacco products over a period of 18 months with a profit of between £100,000 and 300,000. The Judge wrongly applied the sentencing guideline for revenue fraud despite the absence of the issue of avoided duty. The Court of Appeal reduced the 36 months' imprisonment to 24 months'.

1   [2012] EWCA Crim 1855.
2   (2016) EWCA Crim 1266.

14.60 In *R v Demir and Ozdemir*[1] D1 and D2 were convicted of selling and possessing with intent to sell infringing goods contrary to s 92(1)(b) and (c). Their commercial premises were searched and over 2000 items of counterfeit designer clothing were seized, which were valued in excess of £74,000. They were found to have sold items over a period in excess of 18 months. D2 had absented himself from his trial. Both were of good character. Sentences of 18 months and 21 months were upheld.

¹   [2018] EWCA Crim 1116.

Forfeiture

14.61 The TMA 1994, s 97 provides that where goods, materials or articles which are connected with 'relevant' offences come into the possession of any person in connection with the investigation or prosecution of a relevant offence, that person may apply for a forfeiture order. This includes articles used in the production or packaging of such goods. The application may be made as part of proceedings or by way of complaint. In Scotland the TMA 1994, s 98 provides that an order for forfeiture may be made following conviction or on an application by the Procurator Fiscal made in the manner specified in the Criminal Procedure (Scotland) Act 1995, s 134.

14.62 The court must be satisfied that a 'relevant offence' has been committed in respect of the goods etc, or a representative sample of them. It may order that the goods etc are to be destroyed or impose conditions for them to be re-manufactured. A decision of the Magistrates' Court in relation to such forfeiture is subject to appeal by 'any person aggrieved' – who need not have been a party to any original proceedings¹. Forfeiture proceedings brought under the TMA 1994, s 97, and any appeal by an aggrieved person to the Crown Court against an order made under that section, are civil proceedings in character, and therefore the Brussels Convention 1968 applies to them². In *R (Drain) v Birmingham Crown Court*³ the High Court dismissed an application to quash a forfeiture order under TMA 1994, s 97. It held that the court had a discretion, not an obligation, to make such an order and could do so even where there had been no prosecution or criminal conviction, if it was satisfied on the balance of probabilities that a relevant offence had been committed. The order under s 97 is made against the goods and not any particular person.

¹   Section 97(5).
²   *R v Harrow Crown Court, ex parte UNIC Centre Sarl* [2000] 1 WLR 2112.
³   [2018] EWHC 1255 (Admin) the criminal prosecution in this case resulted in the jury being unable to reach a verdict and, after consideration, the prosecutor indicated that it intended to offer no further evidence on the grounds that the public interest did not require a retrial.

Proceeds of crime

14.63 The Proceeds of Crime Act 2002 ('POCA 2002') sets out a procedure for a confiscation order to be made against offenders. The criminal lifestyle tests under the Act have particular relevance to IP crime. A person has a criminal lifestyle if he satisfies one or more of the tests set out in the Act – and the first test is that he is convicted of an offence specified in POCA 2002, Schs 2 (England and Wales), 4 (Scotland) or 5 (Northern Ireland) (which includes the Copyright, Designs and Patents Act 1988, ss 107(1) (2), 198(1) and 297A and the TMA 1994, s 92(1), (2) or (3)).

14.64 The Act has been used increasingly in relation to intellectual property offences, with enforcement agencies, industry bodies and private enterprises finding that significant confiscation orders can act as a 'strong deterrent' to involvement in IP crime[1]. In one notable example Victor Tin Yau Cheng pleaded guilty in 2003 to Trade Marks Act 1994 offences and was fined £200 but his confiscation order was £334,793.61 and failure to pay would result in a 5-year prison term. In *R v Priestley*[2], the confiscation order was £2,290,907.52. Local authority IP crime cases considered by the appellate courts where confiscation orders have been made (from England and Wales – the process differs in Scotland) include *Birmingham City Council v Solinder Ram*[3], *R v Jhalman Singh*[4] (in the latter case the amount of the confiscation order was £585,422.63), *R v Banti Sohal*[5], *R v William Kenneth Ross*[6], and *R v Kamran Hameed Ghori*[7].

1   See IPO IP Crime Annual Report 2011–2012, p 62.
2   [2004] EWCA Crim 2237.
3   [2007] EWCA Crim 3084.
4   [2008] EWCA Crim 243.
5   [2012] EWCA Crim 471.
6   [2012] EWCA Crim 750.
7   [2012] EWCA Crim 1115.

14.65 In the case of *R v Beazley*[1] the defendants were a husband and wife who operated a business selling counterfeit branded car wheel trims, and were convicted of unauthorised use of a trade mark contrary to the Trade Marks Act 1994, s 92(1). Confiscation proceedings were commenced against them on the basis that they had been convicted of a 'criminal lifestyle' offence. At first instance in the Crown Court the Recorder stayed confiscation proceedings as being an abuse of the process of the court and oppressive of the prosecution to proceed to confiscation on such a basis. His ruling was made principally on the basis that he considered that it would be stretching the term 'criminal lifestyle' beyond the meaning intended by Parliament to apply it to the defendants in the particular circumstances of the case, where their culpability was relatively low, and they had otherwise been running a largely legitimate business. On appeal it was held that there had been no abuse of process by the prosecution. In his judgment Hughes LJ found that it was not oppressive to apply the POCA 2002 confiscation regime to defendants convicted of Trade Mark Act 1994 offences in such circumstances. Trade mark offences are lifestyle, repeat offences, which cause real damage to those entitled to the profits of a trade mark and deprive the manufacturers of the legitimate fruits of the research and development of their product. It was the generation of criminal proceeds as a result of the offences which was at the heart of the matter rather than a fine measure of the degree of culpability. The stay on proceedings was quashed and the matter was remitted back to the Crown Court for the confiscation proceedings to proceed.

1   [2013] EWCA Crim 567.

14.66 In *R v Jie Yu and Elaine Lin*[1] the appellants were a married couple who had pleaded guilty to TMA offences involving the sale of counterfeit goods and appealed against confiscation orders which had been made against each of them in the sum of £768,508. It was held that the judge had not erred in her calculation of the 'available' amount when making the confiscation order; the defendants had failed to establish that there should be a discount from the available amount for expenses they had incurred. Their appeals were dismissed.

1   [2015] EWCA Crim 1076.

14.67 The lifestyle provisions have more recently been considered in a different context in *R v Andrewes*[1].

[1]   (2020) EWCA Crim 1055.

14.68 Davies LJ considered the issue of proportionality in connection to the lifestyle provisions and the approach to be adopted by the courts and found that where the criminal lifestyle provisions or the tainted gift provisions have been correctly applied: 'the outcome will only exceptionally be capable of being adjudged disproportionate. It will be exceptional just because the statutory provisions on criminal lifestyle (which also include an entitlement to disapply the assumptions) and on tainted gifts are themselves geared to the objective of depriving criminals of the proceeds of their crime'.

14.69 The case of *R (on the application of Virgin Media Ltd) v Zinga (Munaf Ahmed)*[1] provides useful guidance in relation to confiscation proceedings where the case has been brought by a private prosecutor, or there has been a financial arrangement reached between a private prosecutor and a public enforcer[2].

[1]   [2014] EWCA Crim 52.
[2]   See digest of Zinga under 'Enforcement of IP rights: *criminal v civil*' later in this chapter.

COPYRIGHT, DESIGNS AND PATENTS ACT 1988

Introduction

14.70 The Copyright, Designs and Patents Act 1988 ('CDPA 1988') is a piece of legislation of which only small portions are concerned with criminal offences. The bulk of its provisions bear upon the commercial interests of those involved in the world of technical innovation and intellectual property. As will be seen the duty of enforcement on local authorities, and powers of enforcement, relate only to the CDPA 1988, ss 107 and 198 and the focus of this commentary is in relation to those sections. The Digital Economy Act 2017 ('DEA 2017') made amendments to each of these sections[1]. The most significant such changes are that the CDPA 1988, s 107(2A) was amended to add an additional *mens rea* element – that a person must either intend to make a monetary gain for himself or another, or know or have reason to believe that his actions will cause loss to the owner of the right or expose the owner to a risk of loss; the amendment of the CDPA 1988s 198(1A) to replace the pre-existing concept of 'prejudicial effect' with more precise notions of 'gain' and 'loss of money'; and the maximum sentence for offences under the CDPA 1988, ss 107(2A) and 198(1A) was raised from 2 to 10 years, and the £50,000 limit on fines was removed. The amendments made by the DEA 2017, s 32 do not apply to offences committed before that section came into force, on 1 October 2017.

[1]   Digital Economy Act 2017, s 32, in force from 1 October 2017.

14.71 Digital IP crime – the infringement of copyright of content that is stored in electronic form – has dramatically changed the landscape in relation to copyright offending. Technological advances have made it increasingly easy to make unauthorised copies of protected material and to allow expansive, and profitable, access to it. Illegal copying and sharing of material now takes place on a vast scale. The borderless nature of the internet and the extremely widespread participation by individuals in such behaviour exacerbate difficulties faced in detecting breaches and enforcing owners' rights. Digital IP crime represents the most significant challenge facing copyright owners and enforcement agencies in this field today. The law continues to scramble to catch up with technological developments.

14.72 On 9 December 2015, as part of its strategy to harmonise national copyright regimes across the EU and reflect the digital age, the EC published:

- a 'Communication on the modernisation of the European copyright framework' (which sets out the main political objectives and areas of action as well as the timeline, based on a step-by-step approach);
- a draft 'Regulation on ensuring the cross-border portability of online content services' (which aims at ensuring that consumers who buy or subscribe to films, sport broadcasts, music, e-books and games can access them when they travel in other EU countries); and
- a 'Consultation on the enforcement of IP rights within the EU' (which aims at modernising the copyright framework, focusing on allowing for wider online availability of content across the EU, adapting exceptions and limitations to the digital world, and achieving a well-functioning copyright market place).

On 14 September 2016 this was followed up by the publication of a proposal for a directive[1], but so far nothing more concrete than that.

[1]   2016/0278 (COD).

Territorial jurisdiction

14.73 The relevant parts of CDPA 1988 (covering CDPA 1988, ss 107 (and associated sections) and 198 (and associated sections)) extend to England and Wales, Scotland and Northern Ireland by virtue of CDPA 1988, ss 157 and 207 of the Act.

Offences

14.74 The CDPA 1988, s 107 creates criminal offences relating to activities such as making, selling and distributing articles which infringe copyright without the licence of the copyright owner and the CDPA 1988, s 198 provides for similar, but not identical, criminal liability in relation to illicit recordings. All the offences under the CDPA 1988, ss 107 and 198 are *mens rea* offences – for example under the CDPA 1988, s 107(1) the person must know or have reason to believe that the article is an infringing copy of a copyright work. The majority of the offences under these two sections require that there be a commercial dimension to the person's infringement of copyright. Although this is *not* the case with all of the offences[1], the amendments to the CDPA 1988 by the DEA 2017[2] mean that all the offences – including those under the CDPA 1988, s 107(2A) – now require that the person infringing copyright intends a monetary gain to themselves or another, or that they know or have reason to believe it will cause a monetary loss to the copyright owner.

[1]   See, eg, CDPA 1988, s 107(2A)(b).

14.75 Under s 296ZB of the CDPA 1988 it is an offence to knowingly circumvent technological protection measures, or to supply software, equipment or services for that purpose (commonly referred to as 'chipping'). Under s 297A an offence is created in relation to the manufacture, importation, distribution, sale or hire of unauthorised decoders. It should be noted that the CDPA 1988, s 72 – free public showing or playing of broadcast – now only provides a defence against infringement (in the showing or playing of a broadcast) of the rights in a broadcast *per se*, and will not extend to any film rights in the broadcast[1]. The situation in respect of any other underlying rights remains unchanged.

296ZB Devices and services designed to circumvent technological measures

(1)   A person commits an offence if he—

   (a)   manufactures for sale or hire, or

   (b)   imports otherwise than for his private and domestic use, or

   (c)   in the course of a business—

      (i)   sells or lets for hire, or

      (ii)   offers or exposes for sale or hire, or

      (iii)   advertises for sale or hire, or

      (iv)   possesses, or

      (v)   distributes, or

   (d)   distributes otherwise than in the course of a business to such an extent as to affect prejudicially the copyright owner,

any device, product or component which is primarily designed, produced, or adapted for the purpose of enabling or facilitating the circumvention of effective technological measures.

(2)   A person commits an offence if he provides, promotes, advertises or markets—

   (a)   in the course of a business, or

   (b)   otherwise than in the course of a business to such an extent as to affect prejudicially the copyright owner,

a service the purpose of which is to enable or facilitate the circumvention of effective technological measures.

(4)   A person guilty of an offence under subsection (1) or (2) is liable—

   (a)   on summary conviction, to imprisonment for a term not exceeding three months, or to a fine not exceeding the statutory maximum, or both;

   (b)   on conviction on indictment to a fine or imprisonment for a term not exceeding two years, or both.

(5)   It is a defence to any prosecution for an offence under this section for the defendant to prove that he did not know, and had no reasonable ground for believing, that—

   (a)   the device, product or component; or

   (b)   the service,

enabled or facilitated the circumvention of effective technological measures.

[1]   Copyright (Free Public Showing or Playing) (Amendment) Regulations 2016, SI 2016/565 which came into force 15 June 2016.

14.76

Precedent for selling circumvention device

Statement of offence

SELLING A DEVICE DESIGNED TO CIRCUMVENT TECHNICAL MEASURES contrary to section 296ZB(1)(c)(i) of the Copyright Designs and Patents Act 1988.

Particulars of offence

A B on [date] in the course of a business sold a device, product or component namely [. . .] which was primarily designed, produced, or adapted for the purpose of enabling or facilitating the circumvention of effective technological measures to protect a copyright work.

14.77 Section 296ZB is becoming increasingly important as devices proliferate to enable the illegal streaming of pay per view channels and computer games. In *R v Gilham*[1] the defence sought to argue that the sale of modified computer chips which allowed the playing of counterfeit games did not infringe copyright as at no time was the whole of the work played. On appeal, despite disagreeing with the approach of the judge at first instance, the court observed that various drawings resulting in images created during the course of the playing of a game were artistic works protected by copyright.

[1]   [2009] EWCA Crim 2293.

14.78 There is no duty of enforcement or powers for local authority officers in relation to these offences. Nevertheless, it has become an increasingly commercially sensitive area and there have been a number of prosecutions, involving trading standards, concerning the sale and importation of 'modchips' (devices which enable counterfeit games to be played on consoles despite the protective measures taken by manufacturers to prevent such activity) – see for example *R v Higgs*[1], *Nintendo Company Ltd and another v Playables Ltd and another*[2] and *Nintendo Company Ltd v Sky UK Ltd*[3].

[1]   [2008] EWCA Crim 1324.
[2]   [2010] EWHC 1932 (Ch).
[3]   [2019] EWHC 2376 (Ch).

14.79 In the case of *R (on the application of Helidon Vuciterni and Alsat UK Limited) v Brent Magistrates' Court and Brent and Harrow Trading Standards Service*[1] the defendant sold allegedly illegal Albanian decoder cards through his business Alsat UK Ltd (the case was principally brought under CPRs but it was also alleged that there had been a breach of CDPA 1988, s 297A). It was held on appeal to the Divisional Court that foreign decoder devices used outside the permitted geographical area were not 'unauthorised decoders' within CDPA 1988, s 297A. The case was also significant as the court remarked to the effect that it was not necessarily unlawful for proceedings to be indemnified by a private party, though it may be of concern if the prosecution was only brought at the behest of and funded by a powerful, wealthy corporation. The unsatisfactory state of the law in relation to illegal downloading of media outlets content was summed up by Coulson J in his judgment in *R (on the application of Redcar Cleveland BC) v Dady*[2] when he remarked that:

'It would, I think, be difficult to leave this case without expressing surprise and disquiet that the combination of UK and European case law on this topic has got into such a muddle. It is to be hoped that Parliament can amend the relevant statutory provisions to bring them in line with market (mal) practices.'

1   [2012] EWHC 2140 (Admin) and [2013] EWHC 910 (Admin).
2   [2013] EWCA 475 (QB).

14.80 The extracts from the CDPA 1988, s 107 below are printed with the amendments made by the DEA 2017, s 32 – however those amendments do not apply in relation to offences committed before the section came into force on 1 October 2017.

107 Criminal liability for making or dealing with infringing articles, &c.

(1) A person commits an offence who, without the licence of the copyright owner—

    (a)   makes for sale or hire, or

    (b)   imports into the United Kingdom otherwise than for his private and domestic use, or

    (c)   possesses in the course of a business with a view to committing any act infringing the copyright, or

    (d)   in the course of a business—

        (i)   sells or lets for hire, or

        (ii)   offers or exposes for sale or hire, or

        (iii)   exhibits in public, or

        (iv)   distributes, or

    (e)   distributes otherwise than in the course of a business to such an extent as to affect prejudicially the owner of the copyright,

an article which is, and which he knows or has reason to believe is, an infringing copy of a copyright work.

(2) A person commits an offence who—

    (a)   makes an article specifically designed or adapted for making copies of a particular copyright work, or

    (b)   has such an article in his possession,

knowing or having reason to believe that it is to be used to make infringing copies for sale or hire or for use in the course of a business.

(2A)[1] A person ("P") who infringes copyright in a work by communicating the work to the public commits an offence if P—

    (a)   knows or has reason to believe that O is infringing copyright in the work, and

    (b)   either—

        (i)   intends to make a gain for P or another person, or

        (ii)   knows or has reason to believe that communicating the work to the public will cause loss to the owner of the copyright, or will expose the owner of the copyright to a risk of loss.

(2B) For the Purposes of subsection (2A)—

    (a)   "gain" and "loss"—

        (i)   extend only to gain or loss in money, and

        (ii)   include any such gain or loss whether temporary or permanent, and

    (b)   "loss" includes a loss by not getting what one might get.

(3) Where copyright is infringed (otherwise than by reception of a communication to the public)—

    (a)   by the public performance of a literary, dramatic or musical work, or

    (b)   by the playing or showing in public of a sound recording or film,

any person who caused the work to be so performed, played or shown is guilty of an offence if he knew or had reason to believe that copyright would be infringed.

. . .

(6) Sections 104 to 106 (presumptions as to various matters connected with copyright) do not apply to proceedings for an offence under this section; but without prejudice to their application in proceedings for an order under section 108 below.

. . .

198 Criminal liability for making, dealing with or using illicit recordings

(1) A person commits an offence who without sufficient consent—

    (a)   makes for sale or hire, or

    (b)   imports into the United Kingdom otherwise than for his private and domestic use, or

    (c)   possesses in the course of a business with a view to committing any act infringing the rights conferred by this Chapter, or

    (d)   in the course of a business—

        (i)   sells or lets for hire, or

        (ii)   offers or exposes for sale or hire, or

        (iii)   distributes,

    a recording which is, and which he knows or has reason to believe is, an illicit recording.

(1A)[2] A person ("P") who infringes a performer's making available right in a recording commits an offence if P—

    (a)   knows or has reason to believe that p is infringing the right, and

    (b)   either—

        (i)   intends to make a gain for P or another person, or

        (ii)   knows or has reason to believe that infringing the right will cause loss to the owner of the right, or expose the owner of the right to a risk of loss.

(1B) For the Purposes of subsection (1A)—

    (a)   "gain" and "loss"—

        (i)   extend only to gain or loss in money, and

        (ii)   include any such gain or loss whether temporary or permanent, and

    (b)   "loss" includes a loss by not getting what one might get.

commits an offence if he knows or has reason to believe that, by doing so, he is infringing the making available right in the recording.

(2) A person commits an offence who causes a recording of a performance made without sufficient consent to be –

    (a)   shown or played in public, or

    (b)   communicated to the public

thereby infringing any of the rights conferred by this Chapter, if he knows or has reason to believe that those rights are thereby infringed.

[1]   As amended by DEA 2017, s 32.
[2]   As amended by DEA 2017, s 32.

14.81

Precedent for making an infringing copy

Statement of offence

MAKING AN INFRINGING COPY, contrary to section 107(1)(a) of the Copyright, Designs and Patents Act 1988.

Particulars of offence

A B on [date] without the licence of the copyright owner, X Limited, made for sale or hire an article namely [...] which was and which he knew or had reason to believe was an infringing copy of a copyright work.

Copyright

14.82 Copyright is based on the rights of the author, artist, creator or composer to prevent another person from copying an original – it protects the form in which ideas are expressed rather than the ideas themselves to prevent unfair advantage being taken of a person's creative efforts. Definitions of 'copyright' and 'copyright work' are to be found in CDPA 1988, s 1. Copyright is a property right and legal protection exists only for the following descriptions of work: original literary, dramatic, musical or artistic works, databases, sound recordings, films, broadcasts, and the typographical arrangement of published editions. The Copyright (Computer Programs) Regulations 1992[1] extended the rules covering literary works to include computer programs. The CDPA 1988, s 1(2) defines a copyright work as a work of any of the preceding descriptions in which copyright subsists. Part 6 of the Enterprise and Regulatory Reform Act 2013 ('ERRA 2013')[2] has enacted important enabling provisions which mark a decisive step towards greater state intervention in the copyright sphere.

[1]   SI 1992/3233.
[2]   'ERRA 2013' received Royal Assent on 25 April 2013. See 'Commentary' below for detail regarding relevant provisions ERRA 2013, ss 74–78.

COPYRIGHT INFRINGEMENT

14.83 Under CDPA 1988, s 27 an article is an 'infringing copy' if its making constituted an infringement of the copyright of the work in question. Copyright infringement – under civil law – may be either primary or secondary. Primary infringement is direct infringement – doing or authorising an act restricted to the owner of the copyright ('restricted act'). The owner of the copyright in a work has the exclusive right to do the acts set out in CDPA 1988, ss 17–21 in the United Kingdom, for example: copying the work; issuing or communicating copies of the work to the public; or performing, showing or playing the work in public. Secondary infringements (set out in CDPA 1988, ss 22–26) are indirect and cover activities such as importing, possessing or dealing with infringing copy. The principal difference between the two types of infringement is the mental element – for secondary infringement, it must be shown that the infringer ' . . . knows or has reason to believe [that the article] is an infringing copy of the work'.

14.84 In *Allen v Redshaw*[1] it was alleged that artistic works arising from the children's television show 'Button Moon' had been infringed by copying them onto mugs, t-shirts and other merchandise. It decided that there was no defence of parody to a claim of copyright infringement and passing off where there had been a substantial reproduction of a copyright work or works.

[1]   [2013] WL 2110623 a decision at first instance in Patents County Court.

ACTS THAT DO NOT INFRINGE COPYRIGHT

14.85 Chapter III of the Act deals with acts permitted in relation to copyright works. 'Fair dealing' is a term used to describe acts which are permitted to a certain degree (normally copies of parts of a work) without infringing copyright. These acts include making of temporary copies (excludes computer programs and databases); non-commercial research and private study; criticism, review and news reporting; and the incidental inclusion of copyright material, for example in an artistic work[1]. The detail of certain of these provisions was subject to amendment by a series of 2014 Regulations[2].

[1]   CDPA s 28A–31.
[2]   See Copyright (Public Administration) Regulations 2014, SI 2014/1385; Copyright and Rights in Performances (Personal Copies for Private Use) Regulations 2014, SI 2014/2361; Copyright and Rights in Performances (Quotation and Parody) Regulations 2014, SI 2014/2356; Copyright and Rights in Performances (Disability) Regulations 2014, SI 2014/1384; Copyright and Rights in Performances (Research, Education, Libraries and Archives) Regulations 2014, SI 2014/1372.

REGISTRATION

14.86 Copyright is an automatic right and arises whenever an individual or company creates a work. There is no central source of reference to determine the authorship, ownership or duration of copyright in a particular work and there is no requirement, or provision, relating to the formal registration of copyright. The CDPA 1988, ss 104–106 (as amended by the various 2014 Regulations) provide for certain presumptions to apply in respect of literary, dramatic, musical and artistic works, sound recordings, films and works subject to Crown copyright[1].

[1]   These sections do not apply to proceedings for an offence under CDPA 1988, s 107. The CDPA 1988, ss 104–106 do apply in proceedings for a forfeiture order under CDPA 1988, s 108.

DURATION OF COPYRIGHT

14.87 The terms of protection or duration of copyright vary depending on the type of copyright work and are set out in CDPA 1988, ss 12–15A[1].

[1]   The implementation of provisions under ERRA 2013 may have a bearing on the duration of copyright in certain circumstances.

ILLICIT RECORDINGS

14.88 The rights contained in the Act are largely related to the 'recording' of 'performances'. The meaning of 'illicit recording' is given in CDPA 1988, s 197 and includes a recording of the whole or any substantial part of a performance made, otherwise than for private purposes, without the performer's consent. The Act provides for the duration of performers' rights – see CDPA 1988, s 191[1].

[1]   See Copyright and Rights in Performances (Personal Copies for Private Use) Regulations 2014, SI 2014/2361.

14.89 The Magistrates' Courts Act 1980, s 101 may be applied to 'without the licence of the copyright owner' (CDPA 1988, s 107) and 'without sufficient consent' (CDPA 1988, s 198) – the onus is on the accused to show that he had such licence or consent, or that one of the exceptions set out in the various 2014 Regulations applies[1]. In *Musa v Le Maitre*[2], an industry investigator was considered to be an expert witness in the field of copyright infringement of films. The Divisional Court held that magistrates were entitled to infer from his evidence that relevant copies were infringing copies and agreed with the prosecutor's 'well founded' submission, that it was not necessary for the prosecution ' . . . to go as far as calling from distant parts the makers of the original films or, indeed, the current owner of the copyright'. Stephen Brown LJ:

'. . . I can see no practical difficulty to prevent a prosecutor from inviting a defendant to make an admission of fact as to first publication. An obstructive attitude might result in substantial costs. In any event it is unlikely to require the evidence of the actual maker or the holder of the copyright.'

It should be noted that, in Scotland, the Criminal Procedure (Scotland) Act 1995, s 257 requires the prosecutor and the accused to identify facts which are agreed and secure agreement about these. Further, the Crim PR place to onus on the parties to identify at an early stage what is agreed and what is likely to be disputed to include such matters[3].

1   See Regulations listed under [2008] EWCA Crim 1324.
2   (1987) FSR 272.
3   Crim PR 2020, 3.3(2)(c)(ii).

14.90 In the alternative real difficulties can arise in proving the subsistence of copyright. Ideally the individual or a representative of the company which is the proprietor of the copyright works may confirm that the goods are not licenced copies. Such evidential platforms can be particularly difficult when dealing with older artistic works where the full extent of the licensing history is difficult to ascertain.

14.91 This may be done with reference to business records to which the 'hearsay' provisions of s 117 Criminal Justice Act 2003 will need to be applied in the witness's evidence.

ORPHAN WORKS

14.92 Implementing what has become an increasingly important element of the long standing recommendations made under the 'Hargreaves Review'[1], the Copyright and Rights in Performances (Certain Permitted Uses of Orphan Works) Regulations 2014[2] and Copyright and Rights in Performances (Licensing of Orphan Works) Regulations 2014[3] came into force on 29 October 2014. Orphan works are works which are of a nature which renders them subject to protection by copyright, but where one or more right holders cannot be identified or the right holder(s), even if identified, cannot be located. In such circumstances permission to reproduce the works cannot be obtained in the usual way. Under the new scheme, a licence can be granted by the IPO so that such works can be reproduced without infringing copyright, while protecting the rights of owners so they can be remunerated if they come forward at a later date[4].

1   *Digital Opportunity – a review of Intellectual Property and Growth*, available at www.ipo.go
    v.uk/ipreview-finalreport.pdf.
2   SI 2014/2861.
3   SI 2014/2863.
4   The Regulations require an annual report to be completed. During the passage of the Enterprise
    and Regulatory Reform Act 2013 and the Regulations in 2014, the Minister for Intellectual
    Property also committed to a review of the orphan works licensing scheme after 12 months. A
    review – *Orphan works: Review of the first twelve months* – met both of these requirements.
    From 2016, data on the orphan works scheme has been included in the IPO Annual Report.

Defences

14.93 There are no statutory defences relating to CDPA 1988, ss 107 and 198.

Restrictions on proceedings

14.94 The offences in CDPA 1988, ss 107(1)(c), (d)(i), (ii) and (iii) and 198(1)(c), (d)(i) and (ii) are summary-only matters and are subject to a 6-month time limit. The other offences in CDPA 1988, ss 107 and s 198 are triable either way and are not subject to any statutory time limit.

Brexit

14.95 Continued protection for copyright works between the UK and EU is provided by international treaties on copyright. Copyright was not addressed in the Withdrawal Agreement as those conventions ensure ongoing protection beyond the end of the transition period for covered works. The UK–EU Trade and Cooperation Agreement ('TCA') confirmed that certain cross-border copyright arrangements, that are unique to EU member states, ceased to have effect as of 1 January 2021. This includes cross-border portability of online content services, copyright clearance for satellite broadcasts, and the orphan works exception. The UK IPO has produced further guidance on the implications for copyright law[1].

1   Law Society – 'Intellectual Property after Brexit' 28.7.21. UK IPO 'Protecting Copyright in the
    UK and EU' 30.1.20.

Prosecutions

14.96 Any person (whether an individual or a body corporate), other than the Crown or its servants or agents, can be prosecuted under the Act.

Directors' liability

14.97 The CDPA 1988, ss 110 and 202 are Directors' liability provisions (see Chapter 4, Criminal Enforcement).

14.98 In *Thames & Hudson Ltd v Design and Artists Copyright Society Ltd* (1994)[1] – where proceedings were brought under CDPA 1988, ss 107 and 110

– it was said that Parliament had elected to provide that breach of copyright could in certain circumstances constitute an offence and that where such an offence was committed by a body corporate, the directors who connived at such commission were themselves guilty of an offence. No qualification appeared in the statute limiting the types of offender capable of committing the offence to 'pirates'.

¹   [1995] FSR 153.

Duty to enforce

14.99 By virtue of CDPA 1988, ss 107A and 198A, inserted by the Criminal Justice and Public Order Act 1994, s 165, it is the duty of local weights and measures authorities, to enforce CDPA 1988, ss 107 and 198 respectively.

Powers of enforcement officers

14.100 Enforcement powers for officers of local weights and measures authorities and DETI are now covered by the CRA 2015, Sch 5, see Chapter 4, Criminal Enforcement. CDPA 1988, ss 109 and 200 enable a search warrant to be issued to a constable to enter and search premises where there are reasonable grounds for believing:

(a)   that an offence under CDPA 1988, s 107 or CDPA 1988, s 198 has been or is about to be committed in any premises; and

(b)   that evidence that such an offence has been or is about to be committed is in those premises.

14.101 The CDPA 1988, ss 100 and 196 provide for a right of seizure and detention of infringing copies/illicit recordings, by the copyright owner/a person having performer or recording rights or by authorised persons, from premises to which the public have access, provided:

•   notice of the time and place of the proposed seizure is given to a local police station before anything is seized;

•   the seizure is not made from a person at a permanent or regular place of business of his;

•   force is not used;

•   a notice in prescribed form (see Copyright and Rights in Performances (Notice of Seizure) Order 1989¹) is left at the place where the seizure occurs.

¹   SI 1989/1006.

Sentencing

14.102 Following amendments, most recently by the Legal Aid, Sentencing and Punishment of Offenders Act 2012 (Fines on Summary Conviction) Regulations 2015¹, which came into force on 12 March 2015, and the DEA 2017, s 107(4) provides:

> (4) A person guilty of an offence under subsection (1)(a), (b), (d)(iv) or (e) is liable—

(a) on summary conviction to imprisonment for a term not exceeding six months or a fine, or both;

(b) on conviction on indictment to a fine or imprisonment for a term not exceeding ten years, or both.

(4A) A person guilty of an offence under subsection (2A) is liable—

(a) on summary conviction to imprisonment for a term not exceeding three months or a fine, or both;

(b) on conviction on indictment to a fine or imprisonment for a term not exceeding ten[2] years, or both.

(5) A person guilty of any other offence under this section is liable on summary conviction to imprisonment for a term not exceeding three months or a fine not exceeding level 5 on the standard scale, or both.

[1] SI 2015/664.

[2] As amended by DEA 2017, s 32, for offences committed after 1 October 2017.

14.103 Following amendments, most recently by the Legal Aid, Sentencing and Punishment of Offenders Act 2012 (Fines on Summary Conviction) Regulations 2015, which came into force on 12 March 2015, the CDPA 1988, s 198(5) provides:

(5) A person guilty of an offence under subsection (1)(a), (b) or (d)(iii) is liable—

(a) on summary conviction to imprisonment for a term not exceeding six months or a fine or both;

(b) on conviction on indictment to a fine or imprisonment for a term not exceeding ten years, or both.

(5A) A person guilty of an offence under subsection (1A) is liable—

(a) on summary conviction to imprisonment for a term not exceeding three months or a fine, or both;

(b) on conviction on indictment to a fine or imprisonment for a term not exceeding ten[1] years, or both.

(6) A person guilty of any other offence under this section is liable on summary conviction to a fine not exceeding level 5 on the standard scale or imprisonment for a term not exceeding six months, or both.

[1] As amended by DEA 2017, s 32, for offences committed after 1 October 2017.

14.104 Copyright offences have not been covered by the Sentencing Guidelines Council. The Court of Appeal's recent judgment in the case of *R v Evans (Wayne)*[1] contained comprehensive guidance in relation to factors which should be taken into account when courts are sentencing copyright cases. The defendant pleaded guilty to two offences contrary to CDPA 1988, s 107(1)(e) of distributing articles which infringed copyright and a further offence contrary to the Fraud Act, s 6 of possessing and article for use in fraud. His sentence of 12 months immediate imprisonment was upheld on appeal. Evans operated a number of websites which were responsible for the large-scale illegal distribution licensed and copyrighted music. He did not host the material on his websites, but facilitated users directing them to 'torrent' download sites which enabled them to access the material. He did not make significant profits from his enterprise. In delivering judgment David LJ set out the following generally applicable sentencing guidance for CDPA cases[2]:

'The position must be that in offending of this kind the sentencing court must retain flexibility and gear a sentence to the circumstances of the particular offence or offences and to the circumstances of the particular offender. Nevertheless, we would suggest that the following (non-exhaustive) considerations are likely to be relevant in sentencing cases of this particular kind, involving the unlawful distribution of infringing copyright articles:

(1) First, illegal downloading and distribution is very often difficult to investigate and detect. It can give rise to serious problems and losses (none the less real for not being readily quantifiable) to the music and entertainment industry. Deterrent sentencing in such a context is appropriate.

(2) Second, the length of time (and including also any continuation after service of cease and desist notices) of the unlawful activity will always be highly relevant.

(3) Third, the profit accruing to the defendant as a result of the unlawful activity will always be relevant.

(4) Fourth, and whether or not a significant profit is made by the defendant, the loss accruing to the copyright owners so far as it can accurately be calculated will also be relevant: as will be the wider impact upon the music industry even if difficult to quantify in precise financial terms: because wider impact there always is.

(5) Fifth, even though this particular type of offending is not the subject of any Definitive Guideline there may be cases where it will be helpful to a judge to have regard to the Definitive Guidelines on fraud, bribery and money laundering offences. In some cases, such as the present, that will positively be required because one or more of the counts on the indictment, as here, will be a count which comes within the ambit of the guideline itself. But even where that is not the position there may be some cases where a judge, at least if only as a check, may wish to refer to the Definitive Guideline to get a feel, as it were, for the appropriate sentence. However, there will be other cases where the Definitive Guideline may be of marginal, and perhaps no, assistance at all. That will be a matter for the assessment of the judge in the individual case. Where the Definitive Guideline is required to be taken into account because one of the counts on the indictment is within the ambit of the guideline, that of itself will no doubt lend assistance in deciding what the appropriate overall sentence will be.

(6) Sixth, personal mitigation, assistance to the authorities and bases and pleas of guilt are to be taken into account in the usual way.

(7) Seventh, unless the unlawful activity of this kind is very amateur, minor or short-lived, or in the absence of particularly compelling mitigation or other exceptional circumstances, an immediate custodial sentence is likely to be appropriate in cases of illegal distribution of copyright infringing articles.'

[1]   [2017] EWCA Crim 139.
[2]   At para 22.

14.105 The IPO published an interesting study in 2015 of the criminal sanctions for copyright infringement available under the CDPA 1988 entitled 'Penalty Fair?'[1]. The object of the study was to establish whether such sanctions were currently proportionate and correct. Overall the study concluded that[2]:

'While there is no proof that higher sentences would act as a deterrent to online copyright crime, there is evidence to suggest that increasing the maximum sanction could be important in facilitating investigation and prosecution, now that there is a better foundation of civil cases on which courts can make decisions (in the absence of criminal case law precedents).'

[1]   Report was published by the IPO on 4 March 2015.
[2]   'Penalty Fair?' p 5.

14.106 The increased maximum sentences implemented by the DEA 2017 for CDPA 1988, ss 107 (2A) and 198 (1A) offences, along with the 'deterrent' sentence guidance given in Evans[1] have finally demonstrated a determination by Parliament and the courts to deal with CDPA 1988 offences more robustly.

[1]   [2017] EWCA Crim 139.

14.107 *R v Umar Shahzad*[1] is a sentencing case involving an offence under CDPA 1988, s 296ZB(1)(c)(iv). The defendant was convicted on two counts of attempting to handle stolen goods and of possessing a device designed to circumvent effective technological measures contrary to CDPA 1988, s 296ZB(1)(c)(iv). The CDPA charge against him arose from possession of electronic storage devices, including a micro-SD card reader containing 113 pirated games. He was sentenced to a 15-month sentence which was made up of 9 months' imprisonment concurrent on each of the handling charges and 6 months' imprisonment consecutive on CDPA charge. His appeal against the sentence was dismissed.

In *R v Mahoney*[2], D pleaded guilty to offences which related to the creation and operation of a series of websites which enabled people to view films and television programmes for free which infringed copyright. A loss of several million pounds and advertising revenues worth £280,000. Culpability was deemed high, the operation sophisticated and over 6 years involving a large number of victims. A four year sentence of imprisonment was upheld, although it will be noted that the offence was charged as a conspiracy to defraud, which involved dishonesty and not substantive offences under the Act.

[1]   [2013] EWCA Crim 389.
[2]   (2016) NICA 27.

Forfeiture

14.108 The CDPA 1988, ss 108 and 199 empower a court to order infringing copies/illicit recordings to be 'delivered up' as a result of criminal proceedings. The court can make an order for the delivery up of these goods and articles to the copyright owner or such other person as the court may direct. Provision is made for appeals to be made against these orders.

14.109 After delivery up – either under CDPA 1988, s 108 or as a result of an application by the owner of the copyright under s 99 or equivalent for illicit copies – the goods/articles must be retained, pending a court decision on the making of an order for forfeiture or destruction. Goods and articles which have been seized and detained under s 100 may also be made the subject of a forfeiture order under s 114 – and similar provisions for seizures, under s 196, exist in s 204.

14.110 The CDPA 1988, ss 114A and 204A provide that where infringing copies or illicit recordings – which are connected with 'relevant' offences – come into the possession of any person, that person may apply for a forfeiture order. The application may be made as part of proceedings or by way of complaint. The equivalent provisions for Scotland are contained in CDPA 1988, ss 114B and 204B.

REGISTERED DESIGNS

14.111 Design law has been primarily governed in the UK by the Registered Designs Act 1949, as amended ('RDA 1949'). A 'design' in this context refers to the *appearance* of the whole or a part of a product resulting from the features of, and in particular, the lines, contours, colours, shape, texture or materials of the product or its ornamentation[1]. A design can be protected by a UK (or EU) registered design right to the extent that it is:

* *new* – a design shall be considered to be new if no identical design has been made available to the public; *and*
* *has individual character*. In this respect:

> ' . . . in order for a design to be considered to have individual character, the overall impression which that design produces on the informed user must be different from that produced on such a user by one or more earlier designs taken individually and viewed as a whole, not by an amalgam of various features of earlier designs.'

(see the CJEU case of *Karen Millen Fashions Ltd v Dunnes Stores, Dunnes Stores (Limerick) Ltd*[2]).

[1]   RDA 1949, s 1(2).
[2]   Case C-345/13, [2014] Bus LR 756 and [2016] ECDR 13.

Intellectual Property Act 2014

14.112 The Intellectual Property Act 2014 ('IPA 2014') brought sweeping changes to the law in this area. IPA 2014 was designed to modernise IP law and to enhance support for UK businesses in seeking to protect their IP rights both in the UK and abroad. The majority of the provisions of the IPA came into force on 1 October 2014[1]. For present purposes the most significant element of the Act is IPA 2014, s 13, which, by way of amendments to the Registered Designs Act 1949, introduced a new criminal offence of intentionally copying a UK or EU registered design. This now gives registered designs the same level of protection as copyright and trademarks. The offence requires that the relevant acts were done in the course of a business.

[1]   Intellectual Property Act 2014 (Commencement No 3 and Transitional Provisions) Order 2014, SI 2014/2330.

14.113 The new offence can be committed in one of two ways. First, intentionally copying a registered design under the RDA 1949, s 35ZA(1) is made out if a person, in the course of a business, has intentionally copied a design; without the consent of its owner; whilst knowing (or having reason to believe) that the design is registered. The intentional copying must also result in making a product which is exactly like the design in question, or at least where a design has only been very slightly altered: 'with features that differ only in immaterial details'[1]. Second, the offence can also be committed by secondary use of a copied design: under RDA 1949, s 35ZA(3) it is an offence for a person to knowingly use such an intentionally copied design in the course of business to profit from that copying. This includes using, marketing, importing, exporting, or stocking the design for one of those purposes.

[1]   RDA 1949, s 35ZA(1)(a)(ii).

14.114 The relevant acts must be carried out with intent. Accidental use of a copied registered design does not amount to an offence under this section. It is a defence for a person to show that they reasonably believed that the registration of the design was[1] invalid; or that the person either did not infringe the right in the design, or reasonably believed that the person did not do so[2]. Reference to 'using a product in the course of business' does not include circumstances where it has been used for a purpose which is merely incidental to the carrying on of the business (for example: where a copied design of a coffee machine is used to supply drinks to staff, rather than to customers). The offences apply to any intentional copying, or use of such copied designed that take place after 1 October 2014, and then only to designs which were registered at the time of the offence.

[1]   RDA 1949, s 35ZA(4).
[2]   RDA 1949, s 35ZA(5).

14.115 A person convicted of an offence under RDA 1949, s 35ZA is liable to (a) on conviction on indictment to imprisonment up to 10 years or a fine or both; or (b) on summary conviction in England and Wales to imprisonment for up to 6 months or a fine or both (12 months in Scotland)[1].

[1]   RDA 1949, s 35ZA(8).

14.116 Prosecutions under the new provisions can be brought by Trading Standards, or by rights holders privately. There is no duty of enforcement placed on local authorities by the IPA 2014. The investigatory powers available to a local weights and measures authority or DETI in Northern Ireland for the purposes of the enforcement of RDA 1949, s 35ZA, are contained in the CRA 2015, Sch 5. This mirrors the position for the TMA 1994, s 93(2) and the CDPA 1988, ss 107A and 198A. The introduction of the new offence has not led to a flood of prosecutions – there are no reported cases at time of going to print. This is hardly surprising, as the Impact Assessment for the introduction of the offence estimated it was likely to provide the basis for around six prosecution cases per annum in the UK.

14.117 Powers of forfeiture are attached to the offences[1] – upon conviction, or upon satisfying the court that an offence under RDA 1949, s 35ZA has been committed, application may be made for the forfeiture of relevant products or 'relevant articles' – articles which have been specifically designed or adapted for making relevant copies.

IPA 2014, s 13:

13 Offence of unauthorised copying etc. of design in course of business

After section 35 of the Registered Designs Act 1949 insert—

'35ZA Offence of unauthorised copying etc. of design in course of business
(1)   A person commits an offence if—
    (a)   in the course of a business, the person intentionally copies a registered design so as to make a product—
        (i)   exactly to that design, or
        (ii)   with features that differ only in from that design, and
    (b)   the person does so—
        (i)   knowing, or having reason to believe, that the design is a registered design, and

(ii)   without the consent of the registered proprietor of the design.
(2)   Subsection (3) applies in relation to a product where a registered design has been intentionally copied so as to make the product—
(a)   exactly to the design, or
(b)   with features that differ only in immaterial details from the design.
(3)   A person commits an offence if—
(a)   in the course of a business, the person offers, puts on the market, imports, exports or uses the product, or stocks it for one or more of those purposes,
(b)   the person does so without the consent of the registered proprietor of the design, and
(c)   the person does so knowing, or having reason to believe, that—
(i)   a design has been intentionally copied without the consent of the registered proprietor so as to make the product exactly to the design or with features that differ only in immaterial details from the design, and
(ii)   the design is a registered design.
(4)   It is a defence for a person charged with an offence under this section to show that the person reasonably believed that the registration of the design was invalid.
(5)   It is also a defence for a person charged with an offence under this section to show that the person—
(a)   did not infringe the right in the design, or
(b)   reasonably believed that the person did not do so.
(6)   The reference in subsection (3) to using a product in the course of a business does not include a reference to using it for a purpose which is merely incidental to the carrying on of the business.
(7)   In this section 'registered design' includes a registered Community design; and a reference to the registered proprietor is, in the case of a registered Community design, to be read as a reference to the holder.
(8)   A person guilty of an offence under this section is liable—
(a)   on conviction on indictment, to imprisonment for a term not exceeding ten years or to a fine or to both;
(b)   on summary conviction in England and Wales or Northern Ireland, to imprisonment for a term not exceeding six months or to a fine or to both;
(c)   on summary conviction in Scotland, to imprisonment for a term not exceeding 12 months or to a fine or to both.'

[1]   RDA 1949, s 35ZC.

Design Opinions Service

14.118 IPA 2014, s 11 introduced through the addition of the RDA 1949, s 28A the potential of the creation of a Design Opinions Service. It vests in the Secretary of State the power to provide in Regulations for a non-binding opinions service for designs, similar to that which already exists for patents. On 19 March 2015, the IPO launched a consultation seeking views on the detailed implementing Regulations for the Design Opinions Service. The consultation closed on 15 May 2015, and has yet to result in any firm proposals.

Commentary

14.119 With the introduction of IPA 2014 and related regulations the UK finally saw some long overdue radical reform of IP law. This was generally viewed as a practical, commercial and economic necessity in response to fast-changing circumstances, particularly arising from rapid, game-changing technological advances. The Digital Britain White Paper[1] had proposed amendments to UK copyright legislation – especially relating to the illicit use of peer-to-peer (P2P) file-sharing technology and the continuing global legal issues in this area. The Digital Economy Act 2010 subsequently sought to address certain issues arising from rapid technological developments including online infringement of copyright, liability of internet service providers, internet domain registries, copyright and performers' property rights penalties and public lending rights. Although the Deregulation Act 2015, s 56 repeals the Digital Economy Act 2010, ss 17 and 18 (which confer power on the Secretary of State to make regulations about the granting by courts of injunctions requiring the blocking of websites that infringe copyright) the courts have been willing to grant website blocking order under both the Senior Courts Act 1981, s 37(1)[2] and also under the CDPA 1988, s 97A[3].

[1]   Published in June 2009.
[2]   *AG and Others v British Sky Broadcasting Ltd and Others* [2014] EWHC 2254 (Ch).
[3]   *1967 Ltd and others v British Sky Broadcasting Ltd and Others* [2014] EWHC 3444 (Ch).

14.120 In November 2010 the Prime Minister announced an independent review of how the Intellectual Property framework supports growth and innovation. The review – *Digital Opportunity – A review of Intellectual Property and Growth*[1] – reported to Government in May 2011 ('The Hargreaves Review'). The key recommendations, so far as copyright is concerned, included:

- The UK should have a 'Digital Copyright Exchange': a digital market place where licences in copyright content can be readily bought and sold, a form of online copyright shop. This has yet to be implemented. This has yet to be significantly progressed.
- The Government should legislate to permit access to 'orphan works', where the owner cannot be traced. For example some copyrighted works remain locked away and unused because their authors either aren't known or can't be traced to give permission for use. In the worst cases, where one owner cannot be located – just one out of hundreds contained in a film or TV programme – they can effectively hold the interests of others to ransom as it becomes a criminal offence to exploit that work commercially. This has now been implemented, with the advent of the Copyright and Rights in Performances (Certain Permitted Uses of Orphan Works) Regulations 2014[2] and Copyright and Rights in Performances (Licensing of Orphan Works) Regulations 2014[3].
- Updating what it is lawful to copy. This includes copying for private purposes (such as transferring music from a laptop to a smart phone) and copying which does not conflict with the core aims of copyright – for example, digital copying of medical and other journals for computerised analysis in research. For example, an academic working on a cure for malaria could not always draw effectively on previous research through data mining because they may not have been able to get permission to copy the datasets they needed to mine. The 2014 regulations went some considerable way towards addressing these issues.
- The Government's IP policy decisions need to be more closely based on economic evidence and should pay more attention to the impact on

non-rights holders and consumers. There has been real progress in this sphere. There has been genuine 'top down' recognition of the impact of IP law and policy in these regards. However, there plainly needs to be a more nimble approach from Government to respond to the very fast-changing environment of online data product access and sharing.

- Changes to the Intellectual Property Office's ('IPO') powers to enable it to help the IP framework adapt to future economic and technological change. Change in this respect has so far not been as swift or as radical as was hoped for.

1   Available at www.ipo.gov.uk/ipreview-finalreport.pdf.
2   SI 2014/2861.
3   SI 2014/2863

14.121 The Government broadly accepted the proposals in its response (published in August 2011) and launched a Copyright Consultation. The final part of the Government's response to that Consultation was published in December 2012: 'Modernising Copyright: a modern, robust and flexible framework'. Within that response the Government proposes changes to the framework for 'copyright exceptions', including their intention to 'introduce greater freedoms in copyright law to allow third parties to use copyright works for a variety of economically and/or socially valuable purposes without the need to seek permission from copyright owners'. Reassurance is offered that 'protections for the interests of copyright owners and creators are built in to the revised framework'. Steps to implement changes based on the Hargreaves recommendations are finally beginning to gain momentum, however the Government have failed to catch up with rapid developments in the market, never mind keep pace with them.

14.122 The Enterprise and Regulatory Reform Act 2013 ('ERRA 2013') passed into law on 25 June 2013. It ushered in a period of significant change to the law in the area of IP and copyright. Part 6 of the Act, ERRA 2013, ss 74–78, concerns IP. The ERRA 2013, ss 74–78 are all now in force. These are principally enabling provisions, and have been followed by implementing statutory instruments and regulations. The sections of the Act concerning IP include, controversially, endowing the Secretary of State with the power to make changes to copyright exception by Order[1]. The Law Society had voiced concerns that the ramifications of creating new copyright exceptions is sufficiently commercially important that changes to them should be subject to the full scrutiny of primary legislation. So far, the power has been sparingly used. Bodies representing, among others, professional photographers have expressed outrage at the latitude that the Act allows for the use of orphan works, and complain that they grant a licence to wealthy corporate entities to commandeer original work to their own commercial ends without recompensing the rightful owner of the work. This demonstrates the difficulties faced in seeking to balance the societal interests of modernising and liberalising the law of IP and copyright, against the legitimate economic concerns of trademark and copyright holders.

1   ERRA 2013, s 76.

14.123 The following is a summary of the most significant elements of the Act:

- The ERRA 2013, s 74 (fully in force as of 28 July 2016): Repealed the Copyright, Designs and Patents Act 1988, s 52 so as to provide full copyright protection for the period of the author's life plus 70 years where an item has been mass produced (ie more than 50 copies have been made). This is likely to have a significant impact on the market for replicas of iconic designs – for example in the furniture market.

- The ERRA 2013, s 76: Amended the Copyright, Designs and Patents Act 1988, s 170 to give the Secretary of State the power to reduce the duration of copyright in existing works which are unpublished, pseudonymous or anonymous.

- The ERRA 2013, s 77: Made a series of amendments to Copyright, Designs and Patents Act 1988 to allow (through regulations: leading to the introduction of Copyright and Rights in Performances (Certain Permitted Uses of Orphan Works) Regulations 2014[1] and Copyright and Rights in Performances (Licensing of Orphan Works) Regulations 2014[2]) for the introduction of systems for the licensing of 'orphan works' (for both commercial and non-commercial purposes) provided that a user can demonstrate that they had conducted a 'diligent search' for the owner of the orphan work before using it. It also provides for the authorisation of voluntary extended collective licensing schemes. This part also inserts a new Schedule into the Act which conferred power on the Secretary of State to require a licensing body to adopt a code of practice under certain circumstances, and which makes provision regarding licensing of performers' rights.

- The ERRA 2013, ss 75 and 78: Made provision for the implementation of EU Directive 2011/77/EU under the European Communities Act 1972, whilst retaining the current levels of penalty for infringement of copyright.

1   SI 2014/2861.
2   SI 2014/2863.

14.124 The tension between consumer privacy and the rights of copyright holders in the internet age, and the difficulties faced in pitching the level of regulation at the correct level, is demonstrated by the draft Code published by Ofcom in June 2012[1] concerned with ISP's responsibilities in relation to copyright infringement by their customers. Under the Communications Act 2003, s 124D (as inserted by the Digital Economy Act 2010), Ofcom has a duty to issue a code for the purpose of regulating the initial obligations of ISPs to send notifications and provide copyright infringement lists to copyright owners on request. The code was designed to initially cover the largest ISPs who together account for more than 93% of the retail broadband market in the UK. The draft code requires ISPs to send letters to customers, at least a month apart, informing them when their account is connected to reports of suspected online copyright infringement. If a customer receives three letters or more within a 12-month period, anonymous information may be provided on request to copyright owners showing them which infringement reports are linked to that customer's account. The copyright owner may then seek a court order requiring the ISP to reveal the identity of the customer, with a view to taking legal action for infringement under the Copyright, Designs and Patent Act 1988. Further progress on implementation has been long awaited[2]. The Internet Service

Providers Association is a UK trade organisation. They have designed a voluntary code of practice for members[3], which by no means adequately plugs the gap left by Ofcom's failure to generate and implement an obligatory code with teeth.

[1] Consultation in relation to the Code closed in July 2012. It was anticipated that the Code be laid before Parliament by the end of January 2013; however, it has still not been laid at the time of writing in July 2017.

[2] OFCOM reiterated their commitment to implementation in this sphere in their Annual Plan 2013/14 published 28 March 2013, but still no firm schedule for such implementation has been set.

[3] See ISPA Code of Practice at https://www.ispa.org.uk/about-us/ispa-code-of-practice/.

OLYMPIC SYMBOL ETC (PROTECTION) ACT 1995

Introduction

14.125 Various words, terms, logos that are connected with the Olympic or Paralympic movement are protected by law to prevent an unauthorised association between people, goods or services and the movement or the Games.

14.126 The Olympic Symbol etc (Protection) Act 1995 ('OS(P)A 1995') provides for offences, in similar terms to the Trade Marks Act 1994, where 'a controlled representation' is applied.

14.127 Other marks associated with the Olympics and Paralympics are legally protected by a combination of registered trademarks, copyright, registered community designs, and common law.

Territorial jurisdiction

14.128 The Act has application throughout the UK.

Offences

14.129 The offences in the Act are contained in OS(P)A 1995, s 8(1)–(3) and mirror those in the Trade Marks Act 1994, s 92(1)–(3).

> **8 Offences in relation to goods.**
> (1) A person shall be guilty of an offence if with a view to gain for himself or another, or with intent to cause loss to another, and without the consent of the proprietor, he—
>   (a) applies a controlled representation to goods or their packaging,
>   (b) sells or lets for hire, offers or exposes for sale or hire or distributes goods which bear, or the packaging of which bears, such a representation, or
>   (c) has in his possession, custody or control in the course of a business any such goods with a view to the doing of anything, by himself or another, which would be an offence under paragraph (b) above.
> (2) A person shall be guilty of an offence if with a view to gain for himself or another, or with intent to cause loss to another, and without the consent of the proprietor, he—
>   (a) applies a controlled representation to material intended to be used—
>   (i) for labelling or packaging goods,

        (ii)   as a business paper in relation to goods, or

        (iii)   for advertising goods,

    (b)   uses in the course of a business material bearing such a representation for labelling or packaging goods, as a business paper in relation to goods, or for advertising goods, or

    (c)   has in his possession, custody or control in the course of a business any such material with a view to the doing of anything, by himself or another, which would be an offence under paragraph (b) above.

(3)   A person shall be guilty of an offence if with a view to gain for himself or another, or with intent to cause loss to another, and without the consent of the proprietor, he—

    (a)   makes an article specifically designed or adapted for making copies of a controlled representation, or

    (b)   has such an article in his possession, custody or control in the course of a business, knowing or having reason to believe that it has been, or is to be, used to produce goods, or material for labelling or packaging goods, as a business paper in relation to goods, or for advertising goods.

14.130 A 'controlled representation' has the meaning given by OS(P)A 1995, s 3(1) – it is a representation of:

- the Olympic symbol (the symbol of the International Olympic Committee, consisting of five interlocking rings) or the Paralympic symbol (the symbol of the International Paralympic Committee which consists of three 'agitos'); or
- the Olympic motto ('Citius, altius, fortius') or the Paralympic motto ('Spirit in Motion'); or
- a protected word (Olympic, Olympian, Olympiad, Paralympic, Paralympian, Paralympiad their plurals, translations and anything similar to them); or
- a representation of something so similar to the Olympic symbol or the Olympic motto as to be likely to create in the public mind an association with it (such as 'Olympix').

References to the Olympic motto or a protected word include the motto or word in translation into any language.

Defences

14.131 OS(P)A 1995, s 8(4) of the Act provides a statutory defence:

(4) It shall be a defence for a person charged with an offence under this section to show that he believed on reasonable grounds that the use of the representation in the manner in which it was used, or was to be used, was not an infringement of the Olympics association right.

14.132 The defence under OS(P)A 1995, s 8(4) is comparable to the Trade Marks Act 1994, s 92(5), which has been considered in a number of cases that support the view that the section affords a positive and specific defence and does not provide a defence of good faith.

14.133 A person infringes the Olympics association right – subject to the Act's provisions, in particular, OS(P)A 1995, s 4(1)–(10) – if in the course of trade he uses 'a controlled representation' or a word so similar to a protected word as to be likely to create in the public mind an association with the Olympic Games or the Olympic movement (OS(P)A 1995, s 3) and this is done without the consent of 'the proprietor'. The provisions of the Act apply in relation to the Paralympics association right as they apply to the Olympics association right (so a reference to the Olympic Games, the Olympic motto, the Olympic movement and the Olympic symbol are treated as a reference to the Paralympic Games, the Paralympic motto, the Paralympic movement and the Paralympic symbol respectively).

14.134 For the purposes of OS(P)A 1995, s 3:

> . . . a person uses a controlled representation if, in particular, he—
>
> (a) affixes it to goods or the packaging thereof,
> (b) incorporates it in a flag or banner,
> (c) offers or exposes for sale, puts on the market or stocks for those purposes goods which bear it or whose packaging bears it,
> (d) imports or exports goods which bear it or whose packaging bears it,
> (e) offers or supplies services under a sign which consists of or contains it, or
> (f) uses it on business papers or in advertising.

14.135 It will be seen that infringement under OS(P)A 1995, s 3 could only occur where the use is the course of trade – therefore, as with offences under the Trade Marks Act 1994, s 92, those who commit criminal offences under OS(P)A 1995, s 8 can only be convicted where there is civil infringement and where the offender is acting in the course of a trade/business (by virtue of OS(P)A 1995, s 18 these terms are synonymous).

Restrictions on proceedings

14.136 There is no statutory time limit for OS(P)A 1995, s 8 offences. However, the provisions of OS(P)A 1995, s 9 of the Act, relating to Scotland should be noted.

> **9 Supplementary provisions as to summary proceedings in Scotland.**
> (1) Notwithstanding anything in section 136 of the Criminal Procedure (Scotland) Act 1995 section 331 of the Criminal Procedure (Scotland) Act 1975, summary proceedings in Scotland for an offence under this Act may be begun at any time within six months after the date on which evidence sufficient in the Lord Advocate's opinion to justify the proceedings came to his knowledge.
> (2) For the purposes of subsection (1) above—
>   (a) a certificate of the Lord Advocate as to the date mentioned in that subsection shall be conclusive evidence, and
>   (b) proceedings in Scotland shall be deemed to be begun on the date on which a warrant to apprehend or to cite the accused is granted, if such warrant is executed without undue delay.

Prosecutions

14.137 Any person (whether an individual or a body corporate), other than the Crown or its servants or agents, can be prosecuted under the Act. The OS(P)A

1995, s 10 of the Act provides that the Trade Marks Act 1994, s 101 applies to offences under the Act.

Partnerships

14.138 Under the Trade Marks Act 1994, s 101 partnerships must be prosecuted in the name of the firm and not that of the partners and any fine imposed following the partnership's conviction must be paid out of partnership assets. Where a partnership is guilty of an offence, every partner, other than a partner who is proved (on the balance of probabilities) to have been ignorant of or to have attempted to prevent the commission of the offence, is also guilty of the offence and liable to be proceeded against and punished.

Directors' liability

14.139 The Trade Marks Act 1994, s 101(5) contains a Director's liability provision (see CHAPTER 4, Criminal Enforcement).

Duty to enforce

14.140 Whilst not placing a duty of enforcement, as such, the OS(P)A 1995, s 8A(1) provides that: 'A local weights and measures authority may enforce within their area the provisions of section 8'.

Powers of enforcement officers

14.141 The investigatory powers now available to a local weights and measures authority or the DETI for the purposes of the powers in the OS(P)A 1995, s 8A, are contained in the Consumer Rights Act 2015, Sch 5.

> **8A Enforcement by trading standards authority**
> (4) Nothing in this section shall be construed as authorising a local weights and measures authority to bring proceedings in Scotland for an offence.

14.142 The OS(P)A 1995, s 8B provides:

> (2) A constable in Scotland may arrest without warrant a person who the constable reasonably believes is committing or has committed an offence under section 8 of the Olympic Symbol etc. (Protection) Act 1995.
> (3) Subsection (2) is without prejudice to any power of arrest which is otherwise exercisable by a constable in Scotland.

Sentencing

14.143 The penalties for the OS(P)A 1995, s 8 offences, which were increased during a specified period for the London Olympic Games and Paralympic Games, are:
(a)   on summary conviction, to a fine; and
(b)   on conviction on indictment, to a fine.

14.144 The Act also provides for powers of forfeiture. See the OS(P)A 1995, ss 11 and 12.

11 Forfeiture: England and Wales or Northern Ireland.

(1) Section 97 of the Trade Marks Act 1994 (which makes provision about the forfeiture of certain goods, material or articles which come into the possession of any person in connection with the investigation or prosecution of a relevant offence) shall also have effect with the following modifications.

(2) In subsection (1) (which describes the goods, material or articles concerned)—

    (a) in paragraph (a), for 'sign identical to or likely to be mistaken for a registered trade mark' there shall be substituted 'representation within paragraph (a) or (b) of section 3(1) of the Olympic Symbol etc. (Protection) Act 1995', and

    (b) in paragraphs (b) and (c), for 'sign' there shall be substituted 'representation'.

(3) In subsection (7)(a) (power of court to direct release instead of destruction on condition that offending sign erased etc.) for 'sign' there shall be substituted 'representation'.

(4) In subsection (8) (which defines 'relevant offence') for 'section 92 above (unauthorised use of trade mark etc. in relation to goods)' there shall be substituted 'section 8 of the Olympic Symbol etc. (Protection) Act 1995'.

12 Forfeiture: Scotland.

(1) Section 98 of the Trade Marks Act 1994 (which makes provision about the forfeiture of certain goods, material or articles on application by the procurator-fiscal or where a person is convicted of a relevant offence) shall also have effect with the following modifications.

(2) In subsection (1) (which describes the goods, material or articles concerned)—

    (a) in paragraph (a), for 'sign identical to or likely to be mistaken for a registered trade mark' there shall be substituted 'representation within paragraph (a) or (b) of section 3(1) of the Olympic Symbol etc. (Protection) Act 1995', and

    (b) in paragraphs (b) and (c), for 'sign' there shall be substituted 'representation'.

(3) In subsection (13) (power of court to direct release instead of destruction on condition that offending sign erased etc.) for 'sign' there shall be substituted 'representation'.

(4) In subsection (14), in the definition of 'relevant offence', for 'section 92 (unauthorised use of trade mark, &c. in relation to goods)' there shall be substituted 'section 8 of the Olympic Symbol etc. (Protection) Act 1995'.

ENFORCEMENT OF RIGHTS

14.145 Not all cases will be suitable for trial in the criminal courts[1]. Copyright cases in particular may involve the consideration of complex questions concerning technical factual matters, and the proper application of the relevant law to them. *R v Gilham*[2] is an example of a case which concerned the precise use made of complicated electronic devices. Criminal proceedings were brought against the defendant arising from his dealings in 'modchips'. On appeal it was found that the trial judge in the crown court, faced with a highly technical interaction of law and fact, failed to properly direct the jury (the conviction was nevertheless upheld). Similar potential difficulties led Stanley Burnton LJ in *R v Higgs*[3] to recommend that such cases should be tried in the civil courts before specialist judges:

> 'They can be tried so much more efficiently in terms of cost and time than before a jury, and questions of law can if necessary be determined on appeal on the basis of clear findings of fact. In appropriate cases, the Court will grant injunctive relief, and a breach of an injunction will lead to punishment for contempt of court.'

[1]   See Sharp and Smith, 'The interplay between civil and criminal IP litigation in the UK' (2012) 7(8) *Journal of Intellectual Property Law & Practice*.
[2]   [2009] EWCA Crim 2293.
[3]   [2008] FSR 34.

Agreements between a private prosecutor and a public enforcer

14.146   The case of *R (on the application of Virgin Media Ltd) v Zinga (Munaf Ahmed)*[1] was an important decision concerning issues that may arise where a private prosecutor seeks to bring confiscation proceedings, and the propriety of partnerships, and financial agreements, between private prosecutors and public enforcers such as the police. In *Zinga* the criminal prosecution was brought by Virgin Media Ltd against the defendants for selling equipment and software which enabled customers to obtain Virgin's media services without payment. Virgin agreed to donate 25% of any sums recovered under a compensation order to the police. The Court of Appeal confirmed that private prosecutors were entitled to pursue confiscation under POCA 2002; and the agreement that Virgin would donate a proportion of any sum recovered under a confiscation order to the police did not, in the circumstances of the case, amount to an abuse of process.

[1]   [2014] EWCA Crim 52.

14.147   The court remarked that there had been a pattern of increasing private prosecutions, including cases which presented potential conflicts of interest from the interrelationship between the public interest/public bodies, and the private prosecutor[1]. The court emphasised that further guidance from the Home Office should be forthcoming – however, no such guidance has yet materialised. It is clear from the ruling that parties potentially embarking on prosecutions of this kind must be careful to behave with the upmost probity and openness throughout proceedings in so far as any private/public agreements are concerned. The recent case of *R (on application of Haigh) v City of Westminster Magistrates Court*[2] forcefully re-emphasised this point.

[1]   See paras 55–63.
[2]   [2017] EWHC 232 (Admin).

14.148   Regard must also be had to the guidance given in *R v Hounsham (Robin Edward)*[1] if any such financial arrangements under the Police Act 1996, s 93(1) are reached. In *R (on the application of Helidon Vuciterni and Alsat UK Limited) v Brent Magistrates' Court and Brent and Harrow Trading Standards Service*[2] the court remarked to the effect that it was not necessarily unlawful for proceedings to be indemnified by a private party, though it may be of concern if the prosecution was *only* brought at behest of and funded by powerful, wealthy corporation. Prosecutors must ensure that they can justify the cases they bring as being in the public interest.

1 [2005] EWCA Crim 1366.
2 [2012] EWCA 2140 (Admin).

CIVIL INJUNCTIONS

Introduction

14.149 A wide range of civil remedies may be available in civil litigation relating to counterfeit products. These include various forms of interim relief, such as orders for third-party disclosure (known as *Norwich Pharmacal* orders[1]), freezing orders, and claims for damages or an account of profits. However, the most important and the one which will feature in the majority of claims is injunctive relief. Indeed, it is often the case that rights-owners are more concerned to stop the sale of counterfeit goods than to obtain damages or other remedies. It may be that a threat to obtain an injunction will prompt an alleged transgressor to consent to undertakings to refrain from engaging the activity complained about.

1 *Norwich Pharmacal Company & Ors v Customs And Excise* [1973] UKHL 6, [1974] AC 133. See for example *Juul Labs Inc v Quick Juul Ltd* [2018] EWHC 3350 (IPEC), in which an order was made in proceedings relating to alleged counterfeit e-cigarettes for disclosure of documents by a third-party shop which sold such products.

14.150 An injunction is a court order to do or to refrain from doing something, referred to respectively as mandatory and prohibitory injunctions[1]. Very often, in counterfeit cases, it is a prohibitory injunction which is sought.

Both interim and final injunctions are available. The applicable tests and the various practical considerations involved differ, and are considered further below. In all cases, however, the granting of an injunction is discretionary. The remedy is not obtained as of right, and applicants may be denied the relief by factors such as undue delay in taking action, or, if they themselves are guilty of some wrongdoing. As a result of the discretionary nature of the remedy, a judge's first instance decision will be difficult to overturn on appeal.

1 Whether prohibitory or mandatory, the test is the same. The court should do what seems likely to cause the least irremediable prejudice (*National Commercial Bank Jamaica Ltd v Olint Corp Ltd (Practice note)* [2009] UKPC 16).

14.151 Deliberate breach of an injunction, whether interim or final, will be a contempt of court that is punishable by a fine, imprisonment or sequestration of assets (in the case of a corporate defendant). If an injunction is obtained then the next step will often be to monitor carefully the activities of the defendant, to ensure that it is complied with. If it appears that the defendant is failing to adhere to the order then comprehensive evidence of breach should be compiled in order to support an application for contempt of court[1].

1 The procedural rules governing applications and proceedings for contempt of court in the civil courts are found in CPR 81 and Practice Direction (PD) 81.

14.152 An injunction will typically provide that the defendant is prohibited from infringing the claimant's rights, or in interim cases, alleged rights, in specified ways. The injunction must be carefully drafted so that it addresses the full range of the defendant's conduct which is the subject of complaint. Any injunction must be framed with sufficient precision so as to enable a respondent to know what it is, he is to be prevented from doing[1]. The court will not accept vagueness of wording in a draft order which may leave room for doubt[2].

It is possible, in appropriate cases, to obtain an interim injunction against 'persons unknown', who are identified by description, to restrain a threatened infringement[3]. This may assist where the identity of some or all of the parties involved in supplying counterfeit products is unclear. It has been held that whilst in cases involving flagrant infringement of copyright or trade marks broadly drafted injunctions could be the only reasonable way of protecting the plaintiff, such wide ranging relief cannot be justified in every intellectual property case[4]. The purpose of an injunction is to protect the calimant from a continued infringement of his rights by the defendant's threatened activities, but injunctions must also be fair to the defendant.

[1]   *Lawrence David v Ashton* [1989] IRLR 22.
[2]   In *UK Gymnastics Ltd v British Amateur Gymnastics Association* [2021] EWCA Civ 425 the Court of Appeal set aside parts of an injunction granted to restrain the Appellants from passing off their companies as approved by a National Governing Body. That term was not defined and the wording of the order was unclear. It also went beyond the Respondent's pleaded case.
[3]   *Bloomsbury Publishing Group Ltd v News Group Newspapers Ltd* [2003] 1 WLR 1633.
[4]   *Coflexip v Stolt Comex* [1999] FSR 473.

Interim injunctions

14.153 An interim injunction is typically granted to maintain a particular state of affairs until trial, when the rights of the parties can be properly established. This can be vital where an applicant's business will otherwise be seriously damaged by counterfeit products before the matter can be listed for final hearing. It may be the case, however, that obtaining an interim order will effectively dispose of the dispute between the parties. It can therefore be a relatively quick and straightforward way of dealing with a party which is putting counterfeit goods onto the market, or threatening to do so.

14.154 The touchstone for interim relief remains whether granting it would be 'just and convenient' (s 37, SCA 1981). An applicant for interim relief must however also be able to show that it has an underlying cause of action[1].

The leading authority on interim injunctions generally, which will apply equally in cases of alleged counterfeit goods, is *American Cynamid v Ethicon*[2]. It set out the proper approach which the court should take. The applicant for an interim injunction must first satisfy the court that there is 'a serious question to be tried'. Although the test has been described in various ways, this typically amounts to showing that there is a real prospect of success. In other words, showing that the underlying claim that the applicant's rights have been or will be infringed is not frivolous. This is not usually a difficult bar to get over, and the court is not required to enter into a detailed consideration of the merits of the respective parties' positions (indeed, generally it should avoid doing so). Relief is sought before the court has adjudicated on the parties' substantive rights, and it is to avoid embarking upon 'mini-trials' in the absence of full evidence.

1   *The Veracruz* [1992] 1 Lloyd's Rep 353 CA, at 357, and reiterated in *Octagon Overseas Ltd v Coates* [2017] EWHC 877 (Ch).
2   *American Cyanamid v Ethicon Limited* [1975] AC 396.

14.155 If the court is satisfied that there is a serious issue to be tried, it must go on to consider the 'balance of convenience'. This is where applications for interim injunctions will typically be decided. The focus will often be on the parties' relative commercial positions, and the effect which granting or refusing the relief will have upon each. The court will inquire as to whether the inconvenience to the defendant, if the injunction were granted, would outweigh the benefit to the claimant of being granted the remedy until trial. The court is attempting to maintain a fair balance between the rights of the parties pending trial, and much therefore depends on the relative disruption that will be caused to their respective positions by granting, or refusing to grant, interim relief.

14.156 If an award of damages at trial is likely to fully compensate the claimant then this points strongly against granting an injunction. The claimant will typically argue, however, that the supply of counterfeit goods into the market is likely to do wide-ranging damage to its business, which will be difficult or even impossible to quantify. It may also be possible to show that in light of what is known about a defendant's financial position it would probably not be able to pay a substantial award of damages even if ordered to do so following trial.

On the other hand, it will usually be a condition of a claimant obtaining interim relief that it give a 'cross-undertaking in damages' (although this not generally apply to public authorities when seeking injunctive relief[1]). This is a promise to compensate the defendant for any loss caused if it is ultimately established at trial that an injunction should not have been granted. Given that it can take many months to reach trial, during which an injunction may be preventing a defendant from selling a large number of products, such damages can be substantial. The cross-undertaking should not, therefore, be given lightly. The applicant for an interim injunction will have to provide evidence that it has the means to pay damages should they be due under the cross-undertaking. For a corporate claimant this will involve providing up-to-date accounting informa-tion to show that it has the necessary assets, or can obtain them.

If a defendant can show that it will not be properly compensated by damages, should the claim fail and the cross-undertaking be called upon, then this points against granting an injunction.

1   This was the decision of the Supreme Court in *Financial Services Authority (a company limited by guarantee) (Respondent) v Sinaloa Gold plc & ors (Respondents) and Barclays Bank plc (Appellant)* [2013] UKSC 11.

14.157 If following consideration of the adequacy of damages the balance is still unclear then the court will consider other matters. Another important factor will be the status quo. If the considerations relating to damages are evenly balanced, then the court will often look to make an order holding the position until trial. It can therefore be significant whether the defendant has already embarked upon its allegedly infringing course of action or is yet to do so. If it has not, or has only done so very recently, then this would point in favour of granting an injunction.

14.158 If the court is following *American Cynamid* strictly then it is only if all other factors are equally balanced, and is still unclear whether an injunction should be granted after considering those factors, that it may take into consideration the relative merits of the parties' cases. For the reasons set out above, the court will be reluctant to embark upon consideration of the merits after it has been satisfied that the applicant has a real prospect of success.

However, in some cases it may be reasonably clear that the court can take a preliminary view on the strength of a case, to assist in deciding whether to grant an injunction, particularly if there are some facts which it does not appear can be realistically disputed and other factors are finely balanced. The *American Cynamid* tests should not be regarded as a straightjacket which the court is obliged to apply rigidly. The overriding question is what is the just and convenient order to make in the circumstances.

14.159 There may be special cases where the grant of an interim injunction will effectively dispose of the entirety of the proceedings. For instance, it may be clear that if a defendant is restrained whilst awaiting trial for a few months from supplying certain goods to market, then it will be put out of business. In such cases, again, the court may enquire more fully into the merits of each parties' position. In such cases it will require more substantial evidence, to gain an adequate picture of the merits[1].

[1]   *Martin & Co (UK) Ltd v Cedra Ltd* [2015] EWHC 1036 (Ch).

Procedure

14.160 The basic rules for making any applications in the civil courts, including for interim injunctions, are set out in Pt 23 of the CPR. In addition, there are more detailed provisions on interim remedies in CPR Pt 25, and there is extended commentary in Volume II of the White Book. Applicants should also consult the Court Guide for the court in which the application will be made.

14.161 An application will usually consist of an application form[1], a draft order, and supporting evidence in the form of one or more witness statements. It should be served at least three clear days before the hearing, unless there are good reasons for no notice being given (CPR 25.3). In some cases, it may thought that the infringing activity is doing such damage to the applicant's business that an injunction must be obtained on less than three days' notice (often referred to as 'informal notice', if it is given less than three days before the application is heard)[2].

[1]   Form N16A in the County Court, or N244 in the High Court.
[2]   See for example *Chelsea Football Club Limited v Hardiman* (unreported) QBD 8 October 2019, in which a without notice interim injunction was obtained by the applicant against an alleged ticket tout. The applicant had obtained evidence of his activities by carrying out test purchases, similar to those which would typically be carried out by a local authority trading standards department. The court rejected the respondent's submission that this amounted to entrapment.

14.162 If the notice given is insufficient to enable the respondent to properly prepare, the initial hearing may be adjourned for a short period to a 'return' date, usually a in a few days' time. It is often the case that the applicant will be able to obtain an interim injunction pending the return date.

The courts are generally reluctant to allow without notice applications, and they should generally be made only where it can be clearly demonstrated that giving notice would enable the defendant to take steps to defeat the purpose of the injunctions, or there is some exceptional urgency. This will rarely apply in counterfeit cases. If the application was without notice, there will be return date on notice to the respondent.

14.163 If the application is made without notice, or on informal notice of less than three days[1], then the applicant and its legal representatives will have a duty to give full and frank disclosure. This involves giving a fair presentation to the judge of the material facts and relevant law, including those which favour the respondent rather than the applicant. Any material non-disclosure can lead to the injunction subsequently being set aside, or varying the order originally made, often with adverse costs consequences for the applicant.

[1] *CEF Holdings Ltd v Mundey* [2012] EWHC 1524 (QB).

Undertakings

14.164 An alternative to a fully contested application is to agree a form of undertakings with the respondent. For instance, it may be willing to agree to give undertakings to restrict certain allegedly infringing activity, until a full trial can be arranged. Undertakings given to the court have the same status as a court order, in that breach will be a contempt of court which could lead to various sanctions[1]. It may even be possible to agree undertakings which effectively dispose of the entire matter. Undertakings agreed between the parties may have contractual force (assuming the requisite elements of a binding contract are present), but breach will not constitute a contempt of court.

[1] CPR 81.4.

Final injunctions

14.165 Unlike an interim injunction application, which is usually decided by considering which course of action is likely to case the least irremediable prejudice to either party pending trial, final injunctions are awarded after full consideration of the merits of both parties' cases. A final injunction will usually be available if an applicant has proved at trial that its proprietary right has been infringed by sale of counterfeit products, unless the grant of an injunction would be grossly disproportionate to the right protected[1]. The court will usually take the view that the claimant's right is not properly protected by an award in damages alone. Similarly, a final injunction can be obtained to prevent other IP infringement, such as defendants passing off their products as those of others[2].

[1] *Navitaire v EasyJet Airline* [2006] RPC 3, 4.

² For example in *Litecoin Foundation Ltd v Inshallah Ltd* [2021] EWHC 1998 (Ch) a final injunction was granted preventing the defendants from passing off any goods, services or business as the respondent's goods, services or business. The respondent had developed a cryptocurrency called Litecoin.

Orders for delivery up under CDPA 1988

14.166 The court has both an inherent equitable jurisdiction to order delivery up of goods, and (more importantly in most cases) a statutory power under s 99 of the CDPA¹. A copyright owner can seek an order under that provision for delivery up of both (i) infringing copies of the relevant copyright work which a person has in his possession, custody or control in the course of a business, and (ii) articles specifically designed or adapted for making copies of a particular copyright work, which a person has in his possession, custody or control knowing or having reason to believe that it has been or is to be used to make infringing copies.

¹ Orders for delivery up are also available in criminal prosecutions under s 108 CDPA 1988: see **14.108** above.

14.167 Generally, this remedy is not available after the end of the six-year period from the date on which the relevant infringing copy or article was made (s 99(2), CDPA 1988). No order for delivery up will be made unless the court also makes, or it appears to it there are grounds for making, an order for destruction of the goods, or for their forfeiture to the copyright owner, under s 114 of the CDPA 1988 (s 99(2), CDPA 1988). A person to whom the infringing copies or articles are delivered up must retain them pending the making of such an order, or a decision not to make such an order (s 99(3)).

Website blocking orders under CDPA 1988

14.168 Section 97A of the CDPA 1988 gives the court the power to make an order against a 'service provider' when it has actual knowledge of another person using their service to infringe copyright. It must be shown that the defendants are service providers within the meaning of reg 2 of the Electronic Commerce (EC Directive) Regulations 2002 and the website must be targeted at the UK¹. The court has a discretion then as to whether to make an order, and in what terms. A website blocking order has to meet the following criteria:

- it should be necessary, effective and dissuasive,
- not unduly costly or complicated,
- avoid barriers to legitimate trade,
- a fair balance between the fundamental rights engaged,
- proportionate, and
- safeguarded against abuse².

¹ In *Capitol Records v British Telecommunications Plc* [2021] EWHC 409 (Ch) the claimants sought an order under s 97A requiring the defendant internet service providers (ISPs) to take measures to block their subscribers' access to a specified website (Nitroflare). Nitroflare, described by the claimants as a cyberlocker site, was a file storage site which made available unlicensed commercial content, including music files. The court was satisfied that the Nitroflare

site had been targeted at the UK since it used the English language, there were large numbers of UK visitors to it, it allowed payment for premium services in GBP, and advertising on it was in many instances for UK retailers or services.

2   *Nintendo Co Ltd v Sky UK Ltd* [2019] EWHC 2376 (Ch), [2020] 3 All ER 83, [2019] 9 WLUK 74.

Chapter 15

PRODUCT SAFETY

Contents

INTRODUCTION

15.1 The *Guide to the Consumer Protection Act 1987* provides[1]:

'Every day of our lives we consume, use, or simply come into contact with countless different products. We should be able to assume that those products are safe. Not absolutely safe – that remains unattainable. Nor safe at unbearable cost to industry – that would put innovation at risk. But as safe as is reasonable to expect.'

[1] Department of Trade and Industry, revised November 2001.

15.2 At the time of writing there is considerable uncertainty, following Brexit, about the extent of product safety laws applicable in Northern Ireland under the Northern Ireland Protocol. It follows that, in this edition of the Pink Book, the product safety chapter should be considered to apply only in England, Wales and Scotland. Its application to Northern Ireland will be revisited in future editions when the UK's current negotiations with the EU on Northern Ireland Protocol have concluded.

Whilst a member of the European Union UK product safety legislation was mainly derived from European Directives and Regulations transposed into UK legislation via the European Communities Act 1972 (the 'ECA 1972'). The European Union (Withdrawal Act) 2018 and the European Union (Withdrawal Agreement) Act 2020 have repealed the ECA 1972.

However, the Government has stated that it intends to 'maintain its robust programme of risk based market surveillance to ensure that dangerous products do not reach consumers'. In order to fulfil this declaration, EU product safety law will continue in force and has been converted into domestic law by the Product Safety and Metrology etc. (Amendment etc.) (EU Exit) Regulations 2019 and the Product Safety, Metrology and Mutual Recognition Agreement (Amendment) (EU Exit) Regulations 2019. The framework will still ensure regulatory alignment on industrial goods (manufactured goods) by the following:

- Decision 768/2008/EC establishing a common framework for the marketing of products, that is sector-specific legislation;
- General Product Safety Directive 2001/95/EC ('GPSD').
- Regulation 765/2008/EC on accreditation and market surveillance ('RAMS');

15.3 RAMS will still place obligations on the UK to carry out market surveillance and have appropriate measures in place. 'Market surveillance' means the activities carried out and measures taken by public authorities to ensure that products comply with the requirements set out in any relevant enactment so as not to endanger health, safety or any other aspect of public interest protection.

15.4 The GPSD is implemented in the UK by the General Product Safety Regulations 2005 ('GPSR' 2005), which are addressed in more detail below. Following public consultation on the revision of the GPSD, the Commission has made a new Regulation (EU) 2019/1020 on market surveillance and compliance of productswhich came into force July 2021. It makes major improvements to RAMS not least in defining economic operators to include fulfilment houses. It remains to be seen whether the UK will adopt this new Regulation.

Risks	Risk to health and safety of consumers	Other risks (health and safety at the workplace, environment security)
Serious	GPSD (Arts 6–18) RAMS (Arts 16–26)	RAMS (Arts 16–26)
Non-serious	GPSD (Arts 6–18) RAMS (Arts 16–26)	RAMS (Arts 16–26)

15.5 Much of the legislation concerning product safety, therefore, derives from European Directives and Regulations such as that relating to cosmetics, toys, aerosols and electrical appliances. These are known as 'New Approach' Directives but there still exists some national legislation in areas such as furniture, nightwear flammability and plugs and sockets. This chapter outlines the principal legislation that aims to ensure products are safe to use and which creates criminal consequences for those who contravene its provisions. The legislative framework is set out under the following three headings:

- Consumer Protection Act 1987 ('CPA 1987');
- Product Safety and Metrology etc. (Amendment etc.) (EU Exit) Regulations 2019;
- General Product Safety Regulations 2005 ('GPSR 2005').

15.6 This structure was described by Bingham LCJ in *R v Liverpool City Council, Ex parte Baby Products Association and Another*[1] in the following manner:

'It is apparent that these provisions comprise a detailed and carefully-crafted code designed, on the one hand, to promote the very important objective of protecting the public against unsafe consumer products and, on the other, to give fair protection to the business interests of manufacturers and suppliers.'

[1]   (CO/3733/99).

15.7 The European Commission has made a similar statement, reflecting these aims:

'Market surveillance plays a crucial role in the field of consumer product safety as even the best rules are worth little if they are not enforced properly. That is why effective market surveillance is so important; not only to protect consumers from unsafe products but also to ensure a level playing field for reputable businesses.'

The importance of effective market surveillance has been recognised by the UK government which has created a new national oversight body tasked with identifying risks and managing responses to large scale product recalls and repairs – The Office for Product Safety and Standards (OPSS). The Office sits within BEIS.

15.8 This was part of the government's response to the Working Group on Product Recalls and Safety set up in 2016 by the former consumer minister Margot James. The group of experts was brought together to build on the recommendations made by Lynn Faulds Wood in her independent review into consumer product recalls.

15.9 In addition to providing support and advice to local authority Trading Standards teams the Office will co-ordinate work across local authorities where action is needed on a national scale and will ensure the UK continues to carry out appropriate border checks on imported products. Resource has been allocated to local authorities in the form of training, access to British Standards and financial assistance for sampling and testing of products.

15.10 The Office has also worked with the British Standards Institute to provide guidance on product recalls and corrective action in the form of a Publicly Available Specification (PAS). PAS 7100 a code of practice on consumer product safety related recalls and other corrective actions was published in January 2018. This is currently being revised and will be published in 2022 alongside a new PAS 7050 on bringing safe products to market.

They are also researching consumer behaviour to identify the best way to drive up the number of consumers registering appliances with manufacturers.

CONSUMER PROTECTION ACT 1987

Introduction

15.11 The CPA 1987 is the last in a series of statutes designed to ensure the safety of consumer goods in the UK.

15.12 Part I of the CPA 1987 has the effect of implementing the product liability Directive[1] and provides for civil liability where any damage is caused wholly or partly by a defect in a product. This has been extended to cover food sold in its raw state, 'primary agricultural products and game'[2].

[1]   Council Directive 85/374/EEC on the approximation of the laws, regulations and administrative provisions of the Member States concerning liability for defective products.
[2]   Directive 1999/34/EC implemented in England and Wales by the Consumer Protection Act 1987 (Product Liability) (Modification) Order 2000, SI 2000/2771 and in Scotland by the Consumer Protection Act 1987 (Product Liability) (Modification) (Scotland) Order 2001, SSI 2001/265.

15.13 Part II of the Act consolidated previous consumer safety laws and introduced a general safety requirement. This was subsequently repealed and has largely been replaced by the GPSR 2005. The CPA 1987 provides regulation-making powers for the Secretary of State concerning the safety of specific products. Selling or offering for sale those products in breach of any provisions made under Pt II is an offence. The CPA 1987 also introduced new powers to local authorities to issue suspension notices and to apply for forfeiture orders whether or not a person has been convicted of an offence in relation to them. The powers of enforcement in the CPA 1987 have been amended by the Consumer Rights Act 2015 ('CRA 2015').

Application and jurisdiction

15.14 The CPA 1987 applies throughout Great Britain. The CPA 1987, s 11(1) provides for the making of 'safety regulations', which are the key provisions of Pt II of the Act. In broad terms, goods must be safe, unsafe goods must not be made available to persons generally or to particular classes of person and appropriate information must be, and inappropriate information must not be, provided. The meaning of 'safe' is given in the CPA 1987, s 19(1) and (2). The CPA 1987, s 11(2) lists the types of provisions that the 'safety regulations' may contain. Some Regulations were jointly made under the CPA 1987, s 11 and the European Communities Act 1972 – eg the Toys (Safety) Regulations 2011[1]. The Consumer Protection Act 1987 (Commencement No 1) Order 1987[2] made provision for regulations made under previous legislation, including the Consumer Protection Act 1961, to be treated as though they had been made under the CPA 1987, s 11.

[1]   SI 2011/1881.
[2]   SI 1987/1680.

15.15 Much domestic legislation has been repealed as a result of the government's Red Tape Challenge, which led to the implementation of the Product Safety (Revocation) Regulations 2012[1] and the Product Safety Amendment and Revocation Regulations 2012[2]. However, despite the government rhetoric with regard to easing burdens on business, the products concerned still fall within the jurisdiction of general product safety. For example, restrictions on the use of cords in children's clothing are now found in BS EN 14682:2014 'Safety of children's clothing. Cords and drawstrings on children's clothing. Specifications'. Another example is that asbestos products are now controlled via REACH (see later) rather than domestic legislation. A brief summary of the remaining regulations made, or deemed to have been made, under the CPA 1987, s 11 is given below:

[1]   SI 2012/1815.
[2]   SI 2012/2963.

UK secondary legislation

Oil Heaters (Safety) Regulations 1977

15.16 The 1977 Regulations[1] impose controls on domestic oil heaters that must also have warnings against various hazards and specifies construction and mechanical requirements.

[1]   SI 1977/167.

Filament Lamps for Vehicles (Safety) Regulations 1982

15.17 The 1982 Regulations[1] prohibit the supply of lamps for motor vehicles unless they bear the ECE Approval mark.

[1]   SI 1982/444.

Nightwear (Safety) Regulations 1985

15.18 The 1985 Regulations[1] make provision as follow:

- Children's nightdresses and dressing gowns must comply with flammability requirements.
- Pyjamas, babies garments and bath robes and adult nightwear must be labelled:

KEEP AWAY FROM FIRE

or

LOW FLAMMABILITY TO BS 5722

Action may also be taken under the GPSR 2005 since flammability performance requirements for children's nightwear introduced by the European standard: BS EN 14878 *Textiles – Burning behaviour of children's nightwear – Specification*.

It is interesting to note that a voluntary *Code of Practice on the Flammability of Children's Dress Up Clothing* produced by the British Retail Consortium reverts to the more rigorous flammability requirement in this piece of domestic regulation rather than utilising the flammability requirements contained in BS EN 71 2 2011 which currently still offers a presumption of conformity under the Toys Safety Regulations 2011[2].

[1]   SI 1985/2043.
[2]   SI 2011/1881.

Furniture and Furnishings (Fire) (Safety) Regulations 1988

15.19 The 1988 Regulations[1] apply to new and second-hand furniture which contains upholstery intended for private use in a dwelling. All new furniture must carry a display label at the point of sale:

• prominent position;
• clearly visible.

[1]   SI 1988/1324.

15.20 All new furniture must carry a permanent label either full or short which is securely attached on any external surface. Upholstery (except mattresses, bed bases, pillows and cushions) must pass the cigarette test specified in BS 5852: Part 1 1979. Filling material and fillings in all furniture (except pillows and cushions with a primary cover which passes the relevant ignitability test) must pass the relevant ignitability test. Permanent covers on, and loose and stretch covers for all furniture (except mattresses, bed bases, pillows, cushions and baby nests) must pass the match test unless (in the case of permanent covers) an interliner is fitted. The requirements on manufacturers and importers to keep records on testing for 5 years from date of supply and for retailers to keep information on composition, date of manufacture etc has been revoked by art 5 of and the Consumer Rights Act 2015 (Commencement No 3, Transitional Provisions, Savings and Consequential Amendments) Order 2015[1], with effect from 1 October 2015.

[1]   SI 2015/1630, Sch 2.

15.21 In *Northumberland County Council v PR Manufacturing Ltd (t/a Paul Rosco)*[1] the prosecution's methods of testing garden chair cushions, which, it was alleged, did not satisfy the requirements of the Furniture and Fittings (Fire) (Safety) Regulations 1988 were attacked by the defendant as flawed. The defendant relied on subsequent tests on different cushions. The magistrates preferred the defendant's test as the more accurate and dismissed the charges.

The appeal was allowed, the not guilty verdict was ordered to be set aside and the matter will be remitted to a differently constituted Bench for a new trial. Beatson J said:

> 'It is inconsistent and an error of law to conclude that the prosecution's test satisfied the 1988 Regulations and the British Standards and that the Respondent had not complied with regulation 6(2)(b) but that the result of the test could not be relied upon in order to bring in a guilty verdict in respect of the charges brought under section 12(1) of the Consumer Protection Act.'

1   [2004] EWHC 112 (Admin).

Food Imitations (Safety) Regulations 1989

15.22 The 1989 Regulations[1] prohibit supply etc of manufactured goods which are ordinarily intended for private use and are not food but which:

(a)   have a form, odour, colour, appearance, packaging, labelling, volume or size which is likely to cause persons, in particular, children to confuse them with food and in consequence to place them in their mouths or suck them or swallow them; and

(b)   where such action as is mentioned in (a) above is taken in relation to them, may cause death or personal injury.

1   SI 1989/1291.

Motor Vehicle Tyres (Safety) Regulations 1994

15.23 Under the 1994 Regulations[1] new tyres must be marked with an approval notice in accordance with ECE Regulation 30. Retread tyres must conform to an approved type, the carcass must be no more than 7 years old, be permanently marked to enable identification of the original manufacturer and be marked RETREAD. Part worn tyres must not have cuts, internal lumps and bulges, exposed ply, penetration damage when fully inflated and have 2mm grooves. Should be marked PART WORN and bear an approval mark, speed category and load capacity. Both retreads and part worn tyres, if repaired, must be properly repaired.

1   SI 1994/3117.

Plugs and Sockets etc (Safety) Regulations 1994

15.24 Under the 1994 Regulations[1] standard plug must:

• contain a BS 1362 fuse;
• comply with BS 1363 (have insulation on live and neutral pins) or equivalent level of safety;
• be approved by notified body.

All other electrical devices must comply with relevant standards:

Round-pin plugs, sockets or adaptors	BS 546
2-pin reversible plugs or shaver sockets	BS 4573
Fuses intended for standard plugs	BS 1362

Cartridge fuses (up to 5A) for round-pin plugs	BS 646
Adaptors	BS 5733

[1] SI 1994/1768.

15.25 Electrical Appliances must be fitted with:

- BS 1363 plug which has a fuse of the correct rating made to BS 1362;
- non-UK plug complying with IEC 884–1 which is enclosed by a conversion plug which can only be removed with a tool.

This requirement has been repealed but has been replaced by the Electrical Equipment (Safety) Regulations 2016[1] concerning the safe connection of electrical equipment intended for use in the United Kingdom which has simplified the requirements.

[1] SI 2016/1101, reg 35.

15.26 Standard plug or conversion plug must be:

- marked with or bear a label legibly marked with words, marks or abbreviations of name and reference number of the approving organisation eg BEAB, ASTA, BSI;
- be marked with or accompanied by a notice in English which gives information on safe usage;
- must not give false information re approval.

N-Nitrosamines and N-Nitrostable Substances in Elastomer Rubber Teats and Dummies (Safety) Regulations 1995

15.27 Under the 1995 Regulations[1] teats and dummies shall not, after saliva test, release 0.1 mg/kg of N-nitrosamines or N-Nitrostable substances.

[1] SI 1995/1012.

Road Vehicles (Brake Linings) Safety Regulations 1999

15.28 The 1999 Regulations[1] impose prohibition on supply/fitting of brake linings which contain asbestos to a vehicle, except for fitting to a vehicle first used before 1 January 1973 and clearly marked:

'ILLEGAL TO FIT TO POST – 1972 VEHICLES'

[1] SI 1999/2978.

Fireworks Regulations 2004

15.29 The 2004 Regulations[1]:

- Prohibits supply of an excessively loud category 3 firework.
- Prohibits retail supply of > 50 kg unless require certain information and person buying shows licence or registration certificate.
- Prohibits supply between certain dates unless the person holds an all year round licence.

- Provides for a statutory notice re selling to under 18 years.
[1] SI 2004/1836.

15.30 The duty of enforcement is transferred in relation to some aspects of these Regulations from weights and measures authorities to other enforcers. For the Fireworks (Scotland) Regulations 2004[1], it is transferred to the police.
[1] SSI 2004/393.

Aerosol Dispensers Regulations 2009

15.31 The 2009 Regulations[1] prohibit the supply etc of relevant aerosol dispensers which are not marked with the 'compliance mark' to show compliance with Directive and construction requirements.
[1] SI 2009/2824.

Pedal Bicycles (Safety) Regulations 2010

15.32 The 2010 Regulations[1] provide that new bicycles either assembled or unassembled which have a saddle height of 635 mm must have:

- a bell;
- correctly adjusted brakes;
- reflectors front and rear wheels and pedals;
- lights or reflectors front and rear.

The construction requirements are covered by GPSR 2005 using BS EN ISO 4210.
[1] SI 2010/198.

'New Approach' Regulations

15.33 The following Regulations implement European 'New Approach' Directives but were made under the CPA 1987 – the offences, powers etc are therefore under the Act as opposed to the other 'New Approach' statutory instruments, which were made under the European Communities Act 1972, where such matters are self-contained. These are so called 'CE marking' regulations, now UKCA marking.

Medical Devices Regulations 2002

15.34 These Regulations[1] implement three European Community Directives: Council Directive 90/385/EEC on the approximation of the laws of the Member States relating to active implantable medical devices, Council Directive 93/42/EEC concerning medical devices[2], and Directive 98/79/EC of the European Parliament and of the Council on *in vitro* diagnostic medical devices[3] ('the Medical Devices Directives'). Each weights and measures authority shall enforce concurrently with the Secretary of State that part of the regulations (Pt 11) that relate to consumer goods. Enforcement in relation to non-consumer devices falls to the Medical and Healthcare products Regulatory Agency.
[1] SI 2002/618.

²   OJ L169, 12.7.1993, p 1.
³   OJ L331, 7.12.1998, p 1.

Toys (Safety) Regulations 2011

15.35 The Toy Safety Directive 2009/48/EC¹ was one of the first to be aligned into the new framework and has been transposed into the UK by the Toys Safety Regulations 2011². Subject to certain exceptions (eg playground equipment intended for public use), 'Toys are products designed or intended (whether or not exclusively) for use in play by children under 14 years old'. In *PMS International Group plc v North East Lincolnshire Council; In the Pink Ltd v Same*³ the prosecution argued that a stationery set, which included small safety scissors, a small stapler, pens and a craft knife and other objects – the packaging of which displayed a 'CE' mark – was a toy and failed to meet the warning requirements and safety standards of the Toys (Safety) Regulations 1995⁴. The defendants disputed that it was a toy and their appeal against the justices' decision that it was a toy was dismissed. The justices had properly directed themselves – per Beatson J:

> 'It was . . . open to the justices to find that the product was designed or clearly intended for use in play, having regard to the objective characteristics of the product, including appearance and presentation.'

¹   OJ L170, 30.6.2009, p 1.
²   SI 2011/1881.
³   [2005] EWHC 1111 (Admin).
⁴   SI 1995/204.

15.36 The 2011 Regulations¹ place an obligation on manufacturers/importers to only supply toys which comply with essential safety requirements, consisting of general and particular requirements. Users and third parties must be protected when toys are used as intended or in a foreseeable way, bearing in mind the normal behaviour of children. The particular risks cover:

- physical and mechanical properties;
- flammability;
- chemical properties;
- electrical properties;
- hygiene;
- radioactivity.

¹   SI 2011/1881.

15.37 Before a product is placed on the market the manufacturer must compile the technical file, which makes it possible to assess whether the toy complies with the requirements of the Regulations and the Declaration of conformity. A Declaration of conformity must be drawn up in English. Both sets of documents can be kept electronically and must:

- be kept for 10 years;
- be made available for inspection within a reasonable time;
- be held by the importer, the manufacturer or their representative if they have no UK presence.

15.38 Manufacturers also have an obligation to have procedures in place to ensure toys comply with the essential safety requirements. Importers have an obligation to ensure that this has been done and to produce the documentation when required. Distributors have an obligation to verify that the toy bears the correct labelling. Both manufacturers and importers have an obligation to monitor the safety of toys by carrying out sample testing of marketed toys and investigating any complaints. It could be said that in complying with the obligations required under this framework an economic operator is acting with all due diligence and so the traditional statutory defence is redundant.

Offences

15.39 A breach of the 'safety regulations' is not an offence in itself (CPA 1987, s 11(4) – Safety regulations shall not provide for any contravention of the regulations to be an offence). The CPA 1987, s 12 provides for offences where there is a contravention or non-compliance or a failure to provide information in accordance with requirements of the 'safety regulations'.

12 Offences against the safety regulations

(1) Where safety regulations prohibit a person from supplying or offering or agreeing to supply any goods or from exposing or possessing any goods for supply, that person shall be guilty of an offence if he contravenes the prohibition.

(2) Where safety regulations require a person who makes or processes any goods in the course of carrying on a business—

    (a) to carry out a particular test or use a particular procedure in connection with the making or processing of the goods with a view to ascertaining whether the goods satisfy any requirements of such regulations; or

    (b) to deal or not to deal in a particular way with a quantity of the goods of which the whole or part does not satisfy such a test or does not satisfy standards connected with such a procedure,

that person shall be guilty of an offence if he does not comply with the requirement.

(3) If a person contravenes a provision of safety regulations which prohibits or requires the provision, by means of a mark or otherwise, of information of a particular kind in relation to goods, he shall be guilty of an offence.

(4) Where safety regulations require any person to give information to another for the purpose of enabling that other to exercise any function, that person shall be guilty of an offence if—

    (a) he fails without reasonable cause to comply with the requirement; or

    (b) in giving the information which is required of him—

        (a) he makes any statement which he knows is false in a material particular; or

        (b) he recklessly makes any statement which is false in a material particular.

15.40 Under the CPA 1987, s 13(1)(a), the Secretary of State may serve a notice on any person prohibiting him from supplying, offering to supply, exposing for supply, or possessing for supply, any relevant goods which are considered unsafe, except with the consent of the Secretary of State and in accordance with the conditions (if any) on which the consent is given. Under the CPA 1987, s 13(1)(b) the Secretary of State may require a supplier to publish, at his own expense, a warning about any relevant goods which the Secretary of State considers are unsafe. It is an offence under the CPA 1987, s 13(4) for a person to contravene a prohibition notice or a notice to warn.

15.41 An enforcement authority may serve a suspension notice on any person who they have grounds to suspect is contravening any safety provision under the CPA 1987, s 14. This has the effect of prohibiting the person on whom the notice is served from supplying the goods, offering to supply them, agreeing to supply them or exposing them for supply for up to 6 months. A suspension notice may also require the person on whom it is served to keep the enforcement authority informed on the whereabouts of all the goods in question. Any person who contravenes a suspension notice is guilty of an offence under the CPA 1987, s 14(6).

Supply

15.42 The CPA 1987, s 46 extensively sets out the meaning of the word 'supply'. The CPA 1987, s 46(1) states:

46 Meaning of "supply"

(1) Subject to the following provisions of this section, references in this Act to supplying goods shall be construed as references to doing any of the following, whether as principal or agent, that is to say—
    (a) selling, hiring out or lending the goods;
    (b) entering into a hire-purchase agreement to furnish the goods;
    (c) the performance of any contract for work and materials to furnish the goods;
    (d) providing the goods in exchange for any consideration other than money;
    (e) providing the goods in or in connection with the performance of any statutory function; or
    (f) giving the goods as a prize or otherwise making a gift of the goods;
    and, in relation to gas or water, those references shall be construed as including references to providing the service by which the gas or water is made available for use.

(2) For the purposes of any reference in this Act to supplying goods, where a person ("the ostensible supplier") supplies goods to another person ("the customer") under a hire-purchase agreement, conditional sale agreement or credit-sale agreement or under an agreement for the hiring of goods (other than a hire-purchase agreement) and the ostensible supplier—
    (a) carries on the business of financing the provision of goods for others by means of such agreements; and
    (b) in the course of that business acquired his interest in the goods supplied to the customer as a means of financing the provision of them for the customer by a further person ("the effective supplier"),
    the effective supplier and not the ostensible supplier shall be treated as supplying the goods to the customer.

(3) Subject to subsection (4) below, the performance of any contract by the erection of any building or structure on any land or by the carrying out of any other building works shall be treated for the purposes of this Act as a supply of goods in so far as, but only in so far as, it involves the provision of any goods to any person by means of their incorporation into the building, structure or works.

(4) Except for the purposes of, and in relation to, notices to warn, references in this Act to supplying goods shall not include references to supplying goods comprised in land where the supply is effected by the creation or disposal of an interest in the land.

(5) Except in Part I of this Act references in this Act to a person's supplying goods shall be confined to references to that person's supplying goods in the course of a business of his, but for the purposes of this subsection it shall be immaterial whether the business is a business of dealing in the goods.

(6) For the purposes of subsection (5) above goods shall not be treated as supplied in the course of a business if they are supplied, in pursuance of an obligation arising under or in connection with the insurance of the goods, to the person with whom they were insured.

(7) Except for the purposes of, and in relation to, prohibition notices or suspension notices, references in Part 2 or Part 4 of this Act to supplying goods shall not include—

(a) references to supplying goods where the person supplied carries on a business of buying goods of the same description as those goods and repairing or reconditioning them;

(b) references to supplying goods by a sale of articles as scrap (that is to say, for the value of materials included in the articles rather than for the value of the articles themselves).

(8) Where any goods have at any time been supplied by being hired out or lent to any person, neither a continuation or renewal of the hire or loan (whether on the same or different terms) nor any transaction for the transfer after that time of any interest in the goods to the person to whom they were hired or lent shall be treated for the purposes of this Act as a further supply of the goods to that person.

(9) A ship, aircraft or motor vehicle shall not be treated for the purposes of this Act as supplied to any person by reason only that services consisting in the carriage of goods or passengers in that ship, aircraft or vehicle, or in its use for any other purpose, are provided to that person in pursuance of an agreement relating to the use of the ship, aircraft or vehicle for a particular period or for particular voyages, flights or journeys.

15.43 The general definition in the CPA 1987, s 46(1) is qualified by the CPA 1987, s 46(2)–(9). In particular, the CPA 1987, s 46(5) limits the definition of supply to a 'person's supplying goods in the course of a business of his'. The meaning of this phrase was considered by the House of Lords in the price mis-descriptions case of *R v Warwickshire County Council Ex parte Johnson*[1] where Lord Roskill stated that, 'the words "in the course of any business of his" must mean any business of which the defendant is either the owner or in which he has a controlling interest'.

[1] [1993] AC 583.

15.44 Generally the meaning of 'supply' excludes buying goods for repair or recondition and supplying goods as scrap[1]. Where any goods have at any time been supplied by being hired out or lent to any person, neither a continuation or renewal of the hire or loan nor any transaction for the transfer after that time of any interest in the goods to the person shall be treated for the purpose of the Act as a further supply[2].

[1] CPA 1987, s 46(7).
[2] CPA 1987, s 46(8).

15.45 In *Drummond-Rees v Dorset County Council*[1] the defendant was a landlord, prosecuted under the Act for supplying the equipment in breach of the Low Voltage Electrical Supply (Safety) Regulations 1989[2]. Per Hooper J: 'When the landlord lets property, in circumstances similar to those in this case, then the goods which are in the premises and being left there for the use of the tenant are either being hired out or lent' (CPA 1987, s 46(1)(a)).

[1]   (1998) 162 JP 651.
[2]   SI 1989/728.

Due diligence

15.46 The due diligence defence set out in the CPA 1987, s 39(1) applies to the offences in the CPA 1987, ss 12(1), (2), (3), 13(4) and 14(6). The defence is made out if the defendant can show that he took all reasonable steps and exercised all due diligence to avoid committing the offence. Broadly speaking, 'all reasonable steps' will involve setting up a system and safeguards to prevent the offence. Such safeguards may be risk assessment, quality assurance controls and sampling plans. 'All due diligence' is making sure that the system is operated properly.

15.47 In *Balding v Lew-Ways Ltd*[1] the defendant's the CPA 1987, s 39(1) defence relied on certificates, which showed that the offending toy complied with the relevant British Standard. The British Standard, however, was less stringent than the Regulations dealing with toy safety at that time and the certificates did not purport to deal with whether there had been compliance with the Regulations. Per Pill LJ:

> 'The standard to be applied is that laid down by regulations made under the authority of Parliament . . . It is not taking [all reasonable] steps or exercising [all due] diligence to show that you have complied with some other standard, however reputable the organisation which has proclaimed that standard . . . The company were not entitled to assume that British Standards complied with the requirements laid down by Parliament.'

Due diligence is also covered in CHAPTER 4, Criminal Enforcement.

[1]   (1995) 159 JP 541.

Notice

15.48 The CPA 1987, s 39(2) states:

> (2) Where in any proceedings against any person for such an offence the defence provided by subsection (1) above involves an allegation that the commission of the offence was due—
>   (a)   to the act or default of another; or
>   (b)   to reliance on information given by another,
> that person shall not, without the leave of the court, be entitled to rely on the defence unless, not less than seven clear days before the hearing of the proceedings, he has served a notice . . . on the person bringing the proceedings.

15.49 The purpose of the notice period is to allow the prosecutor opportunity to investigate this aspect of the defence before trial. Leave is discretionary and the central question is whether it is fair to proceed when the prosecutor has not had 7 days to investigate the information. If the information has been available to the prosecutor for some time before the hearing, for example in a defence interview or statement, leave is less likely to be given. Companies may avail themselves of this statutory defence. In *Tesco Supermarkets Ltd v Nattrass*[1] it was held that an employee who is not part of the directing mind of the company, can be 'another person'.

[1]   [1972] AC 153.

Sampling

15.50 Most of the 'due diligence' case law revolves around sampling and testing – whether what was undertaken was adequate and demonstrated what is expected of suppliers, ie retailers, wholesalers, manufacturers and importers. This will be a question determined by magistrates. In *Powys County Council v David Halsall International Ltd*[1] – concerning packs of caps which failed BS7114, contrary to the Fireworks (Safety) Regulations 1997 – it was held that it was a question of fact and degree for the magistrates to satisfy themselves that the in-house sampling and testing was sufficient to meet BS7114.

[1]   [2006] EWHC 613 (QB).

15.51 The size of the organisation and the extent of the operation will affect the level of precautions and diligence that may be reasonably expected. In *Garrett v Boots The Chemists Ltd*[1] Lane LCJ said: 'What might be reasonable for a large retailer might not be reasonable for the village shop'. However the smaller trader still has to do the maximum that can be expected of them, having regard to their size and resources. In *Sherratt v Gerald's The American Jewellers Ltd*[2] – a non-safety matter – failure to take an elementary precaution, which would have prevented the offence from being committed, was fatal to the defence being pleaded successfully. A general blanket condition in contractual terms that all goods supplied would conform with all requirements imposed by any statute or statutory regulation did not 'come within a mile of establishing or being able to comply with the provisions' in *Riley v Webb*[3] – Watkins LJ saying:

> 'It seems to me to be a minimum requirement, if sampling has not been undertaken, for the establishment of the defence . . . that the sellers of the goods receive from the suppliers a positive assurance that they conform to the specific regulations which govern the sale of them.'

[1]   (1980) 88 ITSA MR 238.
[2]   (1970) 68 LGR 256.
[3]   (1987) 151 JP 372.

15.52 For importers more is required. In *London Borough of Sutton v David Halsall plc*[1] Kennedy LJ said (in relation to CPA 1987, s 39(1)):

> 'An importer . . . may be able to satisfy the burden of proof if, for example, the importer buys from an established manufacturer who he has reason to trust, who is aware of his requirements, and in particular of the safety requirements laid down by English law, and if the importer then subjects the goods to sampling. The sampling should however itself be properly organised random sampling, with a sufficient

number of samples being properly tested to indicate compliance with the specifications. . . . If the tests were not equivalent [to the British Standard] then it really follows, as the night the day, that [the defendants] have not done all that was reasonably practicable and exercised due diligence to ensure that these goods complied with the flammability test. . . . There simply was no evidence . . . that in relation to consignments two, three and four, an appropriate number of samples had been taken, and there was no evidence . . . that in fact the testing which was done was sufficient in that it complied with or was better than the tests laid down by British Standards.'

[1]   (1995) 159 JP 431.

15.53 In *Taylor v Lawrence Fraser (Bristol) Ltd*[1] the defendant carried out no checks or sampling. Widgery LCJ said:

'I draw particular attention to the practice apparently of (the defendant) of relying on assurances of some kind from their suppliers to satisfy the regulations then in force. Although every case depends on its own facts, I should think there are very few cases of this kind where reliance on certificates by itself is to be treated as sufficient when there is a possibility of professional sampling . . . '

[1]   (1977) 121 Sol Jo 757.

15.54 In this case, the defendant's premises were opposite those of the trading standards department, whose officers, by invitation, took occasional samples – but Peter Pain J said: '(The defendant) can hardly be heard to say that, simply because they have fair and proper relations with the enforcing authority, they can therefore in some way shuffle off on to the enforcing authority their responsibility for taking precautions'. In *Hicks v Sullam Ltd*[1] the defendant company's claim to have taken all reasonable precautions – having relied on their Hong Kong agent's verbal assurance about the quality of the goods which they imported – was rejected in the absence of random sampling by them or their supplier, 'or anything of that kind'. A similar view was taken in *Rotherham MBC v Rayson (UK) Ltd*[2] where the method of reporting back only adverse analysis through agents did not prove such tests were taking place (the company merely assumed that analyses in Hong Kong were all proving favourable) and sampling in the UK of one packet in respect of an importation of a batch of 10,000 dozen crayons was found not to indicate the taking of the standard of care required.

[1]   (1983) 147 JP 493.
[2]   (1989) 153 JP 37.

15.55 Finally, when attempting to justify satisfactory sampling levels in order to establish a defence, the burden is on the defendant to show that his testing system was sufficient for both the type and number of goods involved and that this system was carried out scrupulously. The defendants in *P & M Supplies (Essex) Ltd v Devon County Council*[1] – a case where there was in-house testing levels of allegedly 0.49% and the testing of 18 toys out of 76,960 by an external analyst – failed to produce evidence necessary as to whether that degree of sampling was adequate. Due diligence and sampling are also covered in CHAPTER 4, Criminal Enforcement.

[1]   (1992) 156 JP 328.

Time limits

15.56 As a general rule, the offences under the Act are summary-only – there is therefore a 6 months' time limit, from the time when the offence was committed (see Magistrates' Courts Act 1980, s 127). In Scotland, as the offences can only be tried under summary procedure, the time limits are established under the Criminal Procedure (Scotland) Act 1995, s 136 – within 6 months after the contravention occurred.

15.57 However, it is essential to refer to individual Regulations to determine precise time limits. For example:

(1)   **Toys (Safety) Regulations 2011**[1] – No proceedings for an offence under these Regulations shall be commenced after the earlier of:
(a)   the end of the period of 3 years beginning with the date of the commission of the offence; or
(b)   the end of the period of 1 year beginning with the date of the discovery of the offence by the prosecutor.
(2)   **Pedal Bicycles (Safety) Regulations 2010**[2] – A magistrates' court in England and Wales may try an information if it is laid within 12 months from the time when the offence was committed.

[1]   SI 2011/1881.
[2]   SI 2010/198.

15.58 Summary proceedings for an offence may be brought in Scotland at any time within 12 months from the time when the offence was committed. Time limits are covered generally in CHAPTER 4, Criminal Enforcement.

Prosecutions

Causal liability

15.59 By virtue of the CPA 1987, s 40(1) where the prosecution can show that A has committed an offence under the CPA 1987, ss 12(1), (2) or (3), 13(4) or 14(6) and that the offence has been committed because of the act or default of B in the course of any business of his, then B shall be guilty of the offence and may be proceeded against and convicted even if A is not proceeded against.

15.60 In *Padgett Brothers (A-Z) Ltd v Coventry City Council*[1], concerning a similar provision contained in the General Product Safety Regulations 1994[2], Schiemann LJ said:

'The fact that the goods were in the retailer's hands and were not safe was due, amongst other causes, to the default of the importer [the defendant in this case]. The regulation does not require that the relevant act should be solely due to the acts or default of the importer but merely that they are due, in part, to that.'

[1]   (1998) 162 JP 673.
[2]   SI 1994/2328.

15.61 In proceedings partly brought under the CPA 1987, s 40(1), involving furniture not complying with fire safety standards (whilst purporting to do so), the defendant submitted that it would be an abuse of process for him to be tried for substantially the same allegations in respect of which he had already been acquitted (in Cardiff). The magistrates accepted that argument and stayed the proceedings. However, on appeal – *North Yorkshire Trading Standards Service v Coleman*[1] – it was held not to be an abuse of process for a defendant to be prosecuted in different courts for similar offences (in fact, Burton J expressed his view that it would be difficult to support the conclusions reached by the magistrates in Cardiff).

[1]   (2002) 166 JP 76.

15.62 The UK agent for a German company – which supplied a painted child's toy hammer bench that contained unacceptably high levels of lead and chromium – was convicted of an offence brought under the CPA 1987, s 40(1) in *Scott Kenworthy (t/a K-Play International) v North Tyneside Borough Council*[1]. However, the retailer could only be guilty of an offence under reg 13 of the Toys (Safety) Regulations 1995[2] if the toy 'jeopardised the safety or health of users or third parties when used as intended or in a foreseeable way, bearing in mind the normal behaviour of children' but the magistrates heard no evidence to this effect. On appeal the agent's conviction was quashed – Maurice Kay LJ said:

> '. . . any conviction of him could only be parasitic on the guilt of (the retailer) . . . Her guilt could not be established simply on the basis of non-compliance with the general safety requirements.'

Causal liability is now covered generally in CHAPTER **4**, Criminal Enforcement.

[1]   [2007] EWHC 434 (Admin).
[2]   SI 1995/204, reg 13.

Directors' liability

15.63 The CPA 1987, s 40(2) permits the prosecution and conviction of any director, manager, secretary or other similar officer or any person who was purporting to act in any such capacity, where an offence has been committed by the company with the consent or connivance of, or is found to be attributable to any neglect on the part of that person. Directors' liability is now covered generally in CHAPTER **4**, Criminal Enforcement.

Enforcement powers

15.64 Under the CPA 1987, s 27, it is the duty of every weights and measures authority in Great Britain to enforce within their area 'the safety provisions' (any provision of safety regulations, a prohibition notice or a suspension notice). Nothing in the CPA 1987, s 27 authorises any weights and measures authority to bring proceedings in Scotland for an offence.

15.65 In *Brighton and Hove City Council v Woolworths plc*[1] it was held that the CPA 1987, s 14(1) does not limit the power a local authority to issue a suspension notice only in respect of its area – the notice had countrywide effect. However, in the further judgment of Field J the local authority had no power to prosecute in its own right breaches of the suspension notice which occurred outside its area because:

'such a prosecution could not ex hypothesi be expedient for the promotion or protection of the interests of the inhabitants of its area as required by section 222(1) of the Local Government Act 1972.'

¹   [2002] EWHC 2565 (Admin).

15.66 Although it is arguable that this opinion of Field J was not the correct test, since it is for the local authority to make this judgment, not the court – see *London Borough of Barking & Dagenham v Jones*¹ and *Mole Valley District Council v Smith*² – in subsequent legislation such as General Product Safety Regulations 2005³ and the Pyrotechnic Articles Safety Regulations 2010⁴ it specifically states that a local authority shall have the power to investigate and prosecute for an alleged contravention of any provision imposed in the regulations which was committed outside its area in any part of England and Wales.

¹   (1999/035/1).
²   [1992] 24 HLR 442.
³   SI 2005/1803.
⁴   SI 2010/1554.

15.67 This has been further clarified within the CRA 2015, Sch 5 – a local weights and measures authority in England or Wales may exercise powers in a part of England or Wales which is outside that authority's area. A local weights and measures authority in Scotland may exercise powers in a part of Scotland which is outside that authority's area. The investigatory powers available to an officer for the purposes of the duty imposed by subsection (1), are now found in the CRA 2015, Sch 5; see CHAPTER 4, Criminal Enforcement.

15.68 The requirement to give notice of intention to carry out a routine inspection or to have reasonable suspicion to require the production of information does not apply if the enforcer is a market surveillance authority within the meaning of Art 2(18) of RAMS and the power is exercised for the purpose of market surveillance within the meaning of Art 2(17) of that Regulation. It follows that officers will be exempt from giving notice, under the CRA 2015, when they are undertaking market surveillance activity (inspections, audits, investigations, sampling, advising etc) and there is a corresponding duty to enforce any relevant enactment. A notice is required, however, for domestic UK legislation.

15.69 It is useful to note that the power within the CPA 1987 to inspect, seize and detain goods that have not yet been placed on the market – ie at the port or airport prior to customs clearance or at an enhanced remote transit shed – without the need for suspicion of any contravention of any regulation is still in force.

15.70 Under the CPA 1987, s 16 an enforcement authority in England and Wales or Northern Ireland may apply for an order to a magistrates' court for an order that goods be forfeited or destroyed on the grounds that there has been a contravention in relation to the goods of a safety provision. Such orders may also be made in Scotland by a sheriff under the CPA 1987, s 17. Suppliers can appeal to a magistrates' court against forfeiture (and suspension) of goods. In certain circumstances enforcement authorities are liable to pay compensation for losses to a supplier against whom enforcement action has been taken, if there has been no contravention of a safety provision.

15.71 There are no powers to warn the public of unsafe products beyond those in the statutory code. In *R v Liverpool City Council, ex parte Baby Products Association and Another*[1], it was held, that a particular press release issued by a local authority, without statutory power to do so, was contrary to law as it deprived those affected of their rights and safeguards under the Act. Following the *Liverpool* case – in June 2000 – the Department of Trade and Industry issued guidance to Chief Trading Standards Officers on powers of enforcement authorities to issue press releases relating to product safety. In summary, this guidance confirms that press releases may be used to draw attention to formal enforcement action (including circumstances where a suspension notice has been served ' . . . irrespective of whether the supplier in question is appealing against the suspension notice'). It would also be acceptable to issue stand-alone press releases where the supplier agrees to this course of action or where the intention/effect does not lead to the suspension of the supply of the goods.

[1]   (CO/3733/99).

15.72 This has been superseded by the duty under reg 39 of the General Product Safety Regulations 2005[1] where an authority shall, in general, make available to the public information on risks to consumer health and safety posed by a product:

* nature of risk;
* product identification;
* measures taken in respect of risk.

[1]   SI 2005/1803, reg 39.

Sentencing

15.73 A person guilty of an offence under the CPA 1987, s 12(1), (2), (3) and (4) is liable on summary conviction to imprisonment for a term not exceeding 6 months or to an unlimited fine or to both. A person guilty of an offence under the CPA 1987, s 13(4) or the CPA 1987, s 14(6) is liable on summary conviction to imprisonment for a term not exceeding 3 months or to an unlimited fine or to both.

THE PRODUCT SAFETY AND METROLOGY ETC. (AMENDMENT ETC.) (EU EXIT) REGULATIONS 2019

Introduction

15.74 Previously, New Approach Directives set out the broad essential safety requirements which had to be met before products could be placed on the market in the UK or anywhere else in the EU. The implementation of these Directives in the UK was made through 'New Approach – CE marking regulations' ('The New Approach Regulations') which were themselves made under the s 2(2) of the ECA. These Regulations are now applied in the UK via the Product Safety and Metrology etc. (Amendment etc.) (EU Exit) Regulations 2019[1]. These have been amended by the Product Safety and Metrology etc

(Amendment to Extent and Meaning of Market) (EU Exit) Regulations 2020 to apply to Great Britain only, and not to Northern Ireland.

[1] These Regulations are now applied in the UK via the Product Safety and Metrology etc. (Amendment etc.) (EU Exit) Regulations 2019 and Product Safety, Metrology and Mutual Recognition Agreement (Amendment) (EU Exit) Regulations 2019 which will create a functioning regulated UK market. Additionally for the chemicals regime, Parliament has made the amendments via the REACH etc (Amendment etc) (EU Exit) Regulations 2019, the REACH etc (Amendment etc) (EU Exit) (No 2) Regulations 2019 and the REACH etc (Amendment etc) (EU Exit) (No 3) Regulations 2019 and The REACH etc (Amendment etc) (EU Exit) Regulations 2020.

15.75 Designated standards provide the detailed technical information enabling manufacturers to meet the essential requirements. Prior to 31 December 2020, products which meet the essential requirements are required to display the CE marking as described in the particular Directive, which means that the products can be sold anywhere in the Community/EEA. After this date products already on the market are free to circulate but goods manufactured or imported thereafter into GB will be subject to the new framework. There will be a new UK Conformity Assessed (UKCA) mark which may be used and will become compulsory once the UK stops recognising the CE mark. Products made to Designated Standards – a list is published by UK government – enjoy a presumption of conformity with the essential requirements of the Regulations. On 24 August 2021 the Government announced the transition periods for UKCA marking and UKCA labelling would each be extended until 31 December 2022 and 31 December 2023 respectively. Legislation will be placed before Parliament in the autumn of 2021 to give effect to this.

15.76 The Regulations place a duty on any 'responsible person' who places products on the market to comply with certain requirements. These requirements are that the products must satisfy certain essential safety or health and safety requirements which are applicable to that class or type of product, the appropriate conformity assessment procedures must have been carried out including the drawing up of technical files and a declaration of conformity, UKCA marking must have been correctly affixed and the products must not compromise the safety of individuals – and sometimes domestic animals or property – when properly maintained and used. Contravention of these duties is an offence under the individual Regulations and provision is made for liability of persons other than the principal offender and directors and managers of corporate bodies.

The New Approach Regulations

15.77 The 'New Approach' Regulations are:

- Supply of Machinery (Safety) Regulations 2008[1];
- Pyrotechnic Articles (Safety) Regulations 2015[2];
- Electrical Equipment (Safety) Regulations 2016[3];
- Simple Pressure Vessels (Safety) Regulations 2016[4];
- Pressure Equipment (Safety) Regulations 2016[5];
- Electromagnetic Compatibility Regulations 2016[6];
- Recreational Craft Regulations 2017[7];
- Radio Equipment Regulations 2017[8];

- Gas Appliances (Enforcement) and Miscellaneous Amendments Regulations 2018[9];
- Personal Protective Equipment (Enforcement) Regulations 2018[10].

See also the Regulations implementing 'New Approach' Directives, relating to medical devices and toys, which are made under the CPA 1987.

[1] SI 2008/1597.
[2] SI 2015/1553.
[3] SI 2016/1101.
[4] SI 2016/1092.
[5] SI 2016/1105.
[6] SI 2016/1091.
[7] SI 2017/737.
[8] SI 2017/1206.
[9] SI 2018/389.
[10] SI 2018/390.

Pyrotechnic Articles (Safety) Regulations 2015

15.78 The Regulations[1] implement EC Pyrotechnic Articles Directive 2013/29/EU[2] and place an obligation on manufacturers/importers to only supply fireworks which comply with essential safety requirements. There are also labelling requirements and obligations on distributors to only supply fireworks which bear a valid UKCA mark etc. The provisions relating to sales to young persons are contained in CHAPTER 17, Age Restricted Products. The categories for fireworks are:

(a)   category F1: fireworks which present a very low hazard and negligible noise level and which are intended for use in confined areas, including fireworks which are intended for use inside domestic buildings;
(b)   category F2: fireworks which present a low hazard and low noise level and which are intended for outdoor use in confined areas;
(c)   category F3: fireworks which present a medium hazard, which are intended for outdoor use in large open areas and whose noise level is not harmful to human health;
(d)   category F4: fireworks which present a high hazard, which are intended for use only by persons with specialist knowledge (commonly known as fireworks for professional use) and whose noise level is not harmful to human health.

The market surveillance and enforcement duty in reg 54(1) requires local authorities to carry out regular inspections in relation to category F1, F2 or F3 fireworks following entry into the EU and at storage sites. Enforcement powers are found in Sch 7.

[1] SI 2015/1553.
[2] OJ L154, 14.6.2007, p 1.

Electrical Equipment Safety Regulations 2016

15.79 The Regulations[1] implement Council Directive 2014/35/EU – the Low Voltage Directive (LVD) as modified. It contains a number of principles:

- Only electrical equipment which does not jeopardise the safety of people, domestic animals and property shall be placed on the market.

- Only electrical equipment which satisfies the UKCA marking requirements will be taken as complying with requirements of the LVD.
- Electrical equipment is not required to be tested or marked for approval by an independent third party.

[1]   SI 2016/1101.

15.80 The regulations clearly distinguish between the different economic operators and their corresponding obligations:

- A manufacturer is a person who manufactures an electrical product or has an electrical product designed or manufactured and markets that product under that person's name or trademark.
- An authorised representative is a person established within the UK who has been appointed by written mandate to act on the manufacturers behalf in relation to specified tasks in relation to an electrical product.
- An importer is a person who is established in the UK and places an electrical product from a third country on the UK market.
- A distributor is any other person who is in the supply chain for an electrical product and makes the product available on the market.

15.81 An importer or distributor who modifies the product and by doing so alters the compliance, assumes the responsibilities of the manufacturer. The addition of legal labels to the retail pack does not constitute modified product. Modifications which may affect compliance are changes in materials, colour, age grading etc.

15.82 Before placing electrical equipment on the market, a manufacturer must ensure that it has been designed and manufactured in accordance with the principal elements of the safety objectives such as protection against hazards arising from the electrical equipment by direct or indirect contact and non-electrical dangers caused by the electrical equipment which are revealed by experience such as fire and explosion.

15.83 Before a product is placed on the market the manufacturer must compile the technical file, which makes it possible to assess whether the appliance complies with the requirements of the Regulation and the declaration of conformity. A declaration of conformity must be drawn up in English. Both sets of documents can be kept electronically and must:

- be kept for 10 years;
- be made available for inspection within a reasonable time;
- be held by the importer, the manufacturer or their representative if they have no UK presence.

15.84 In respect of the obligations of economic operators under the Regulations:

- Manufacturers also have an obligation to have procedures in place to ensure appliances comply with the safety objectives.
- Importers have an obligation to ensure that this has been done and to produce the documentation when required.
- Distributors have an obligation to verify that appliances bear the correct labelling.

• Both manufacturers and importers have an obligation to monitor the safety of appliances by carrying out sample testing of marketed appliances and investigating any complaints.

Definitions

15.85 Certain definitions – such as 'placing on the market', 'transposed harmonised standard' and 'responsible person – are important in the context of the Regulations and their meaning is given in the Regulations themselves and/or is defined in RAMS[1].

[1]   2016/C 272/01.

15.86 For the purposes of UK legislation, a product is placed on the market when it is made available for the first time on the UK market. The manufacturer and the importer are the only economic operators who place products on the market. When a manufacturer or an importer supplies a product to a distributor or an end-user for the first time, the operation is always labelled in legal terms as 'placing on the market'. Any subsequent operation, for instance, from a distributor to distributor or from a distributor to an end-user is defined as making available.

15.87 In particular it is worth noting that 'placing on the market' refers to each individual product, not type of product, so occurs each time any product is placed on the market by any economic operator. Consequently, even though a product model or type has been supplied before UK legislation laying down new mandatory requirements entered into force, individual units of the same model or type, which are placed on the market after the new requirements have become applicable, must comply with these new requirements.

Fulfilment houses

15.88 A new business model has emerged involving on–line sellers based outside the UK offering products to UK customers using a fulfilment house company ('FHC'). Products are generally warehoused by the FHC, which is located within the UK to guarantee swift delivery to UK consumers. The FHC will merely distribute products, at the direction of the seller. The FHC does not own or engage in selling the product, either itself or as an agent. The contractual relationship between the seller and UK consumer will not ordinarily involve the FHC.

15.89 The FHC's limited role is essentially to distribute the product for the non-UK seller. On this basis, it is important to distinguish the position of an FHC from traders that engage in the process of selling a product to consumers, either as principal or agent. The criminal liability of an FHC in relation to the UK product safety framework is likely to depend on the offence alleged. The CPA 1987, s 12 offences relating to the contravention of a safety regulation (for example plugs and sockets, electrical equipment, and toys) are contingent on their 'supply' (see above). 'Supply' is defined in the CPA 1987, s 46 to include 'selling' as principal or agent.

15.90 An FHC is unlikely to engage in 'selling' the product to a consumer where it does not own the product, advertise it for sale, enter into a contract of sale with the consumer or otherwise engage in selling it. However other regulations such as for electrical equipment, machinery, cosmetic products and chemicals introduce the concept of placing on the market or making available on the market. For example, under the Cosmetic Product Regulation[1] 'distributor' means any natural or legal person in the supply chain, other than the manufacturer or the importer, who makes a cosmetic product available on the GB market. The FHC would fit within this definition. The regulation goes on to say that:

'A cosmetic product made available on the market shall be safe for human health . . .'

[1]   EU 1223/2009.

15.91 So products stored in such fulfilment houses are considered to have been supplied for distribution, consumption or use in the GB market and thus placed on the UK market. When an online operator uses a fulfilment house, by shipping the products to the fulfilment house in GB the products are in the distribution phase of the supply chain. When made available on the market, products must be in compliance with the UK relevant enactments applicable at the time of placing on the market.

15.92 Finally, there is the distinction between the enforcement provisions in the CPR 1987 and the GPSR 2005. Regulation 2 of the GPSR 2005 extends the meaning of supply to include 'making a product available, in the context of providing a service, for use by consumers'. So the GPSR 2005 could potentially be used to prosecute an FHC, in appropriate circumstances, on the basis that it was a 'distributor' that had breached its duty of care under reg 8. The FHC's duty of care is likely to be breached if it knowingly distributes dangerous products or ought to have known that it was distributing dangerous products.

Duty of enforcement

15.93 Local weights and measures authorities in Great Britain have a duty to enforce the Regulations – in whole or in association with other regulators – within their areas.

Powers

15.94 Each set of Regulations provides for powers of enforcement – in relation to a number of Regulations, the CPA 1987, ss 14, 15, 28–35, 37, 38, 44 and 47 apply.

Time limits

15.95 In general terms, the Regulations require that, in relation to an offence committed under the Regulations or under the CPA 1987, s 12 in relation to a contravention of the Regulations, the information is laid (in the case of England

and Wales) within 12 months from the time when the offence is committed, and (in Scotland) summary proceedings for such an offence may be begun at any time within 12 months from the time when the offence is committed.

15.96 In the Simple Pressure Vessels Regulations, Pressure Equipment Regulations, EMC Regulations, and the Electrical Equipment Safety Regulations, the time limit is 12 months after the date on which evidence sufficient in the opinion of the prosecutor to justify the proceedings comes to the knowledge of the prosecutor.

15.97 The above provisions do not apply to the following Regulations:

Supply of Machinery (Safety) Regulations 2008

15.98 The time limit for offences under the above Regulations is derived from the Health and Safety at Work etc Act 1974, s 34 so that summary proceedings for an offence may be commenced at any time within 6 months from the date on which there comes to the knowledge of a responsible enforcing authority evidence sufficient in the opinion of that authority to justify a prosecution for that offence. In Scotland, summary proceedings for an offence may be commenced at any time within 6 months from the date on which evidence, sufficient in the opinion of the enforcing authority to justify a report to the Lord Advocate with a view to consideration of the question of prosecution, comes to the knowledge of the authority – and the Criminal Procedure (Scotland) Act 1975, s 331(3) has effect.

Technical documentation

15.99 All the Regulations have technical documentation requirements. Each are specific but in the main a manufacturer must retain for at least 10 years from the date on which the last product was manufactured.

Penalties

15.100 Persons guilty of an offence under the Regulations are liable on summary conviction to:

(a)   imprisonment for a term not exceeding 3 months; or
(b)   an unlimited fine,

or both.

Defence of due diligence

15.101 This defence appears in all the Regulations It is expressed in similar terms to that outlined previously under the CPA 1987, s 39. Due diligence defences are now covered in CHAPTER 4, Criminal Enforcement.

Compliance notice

15.102 Except where, in the opinion of an enforcement authority, a product may endanger the safety of persons and, where appropriate, domestic animals or property, where an enforcement authority has reasonable grounds for suspecting that the UKCA marking has been affixed to the product, or its packaging, and in relation to which any provision of the regulations has not been complied with, it may serve notice in writing on the responsible person, and no other action may be taken, and no proceedings may be brought in respect of that product, until such notice has been given and the person to whom it is given has failed to comply with its requirements. This would be used in such instances as not keeping a technical file, not issuing a declaration of conformity etc. Enforcement action can only be taken in respect of the alleged non-compliance if such a notice has been issued and not acted upon within the time specified in the notice.

Duty of enforcement authority to inform Secretary of State of action taken

15.103 Where an enforcement authority takes action to prohibit or restrict the placing (eg issuing a suspension notice or compliance notice) on the market of any product to which the regulations apply which bears the UKCA marking they must inform the Secretary of State of the action taken and the reasons for it.

The Tobacco and Related Products Regulations 2016

15.104 These Regulations[1] implement the Tobacco Products Directive[2]. The regulations deal with the labelling of tobacco products. They require tobacco products for smoking to carry a health warning label including a colour photograph on the front and back surfaces and a general warning and information message on other surfaces. They also deal with emissions and additives, setting maximum tar, nicotine and carbon dioxide levels for cigarettes and prohibit cigarettes and hand rolling tobacco with a characterising flavour, certain additives and tobacco for oral use.

[1] SI 2016/507, which revoke and replace the Tobacco for Oral Use (Safety) Regulations 1992, SI 1992/3134 and the Tobacco Products (Manufacture, Presentation and Sale) (Safety) Regulations 2002, SI 2002/3041.
[2] 2014/40/EU.

15.105 Producers of tobacco products, including herbal products and electronic cigarettes are required to submit ingredients, emissions, sales data and market research information to the Secretary of State. For electronic cigarettes the regulations stipulate safety and quality standards, including a leak-proof refill mechanism and tamper-proof packaging, and the need for consistent nicotine delivery. They limit tank and refill container volume, and nicotine solution concentration. They also restrict marketing, require the provision of product information and stipulate that products cannot be sold to under 18s.

The Medicines and Healthcare Regulatory Authority is the designated 'competent authority' monitoring compliance, with local Trading Standards authorities enforcing compliance. Responsibility to comply lies with producers (those who manufacture or import e-cigarette products or solutions).

15.106 There is a duty on each weights and measures authority in Great Britain and each district council in Northern Ireland to enforce these Regulations within their area and they are to be enforced as if they were safety regulations within the meaning of the Consumer Protection Act 1987. Persons guilty of an offence under these Regulations are liable on summary conviction to:

(a)   imprisonment for a term not exceeding 3 months; or
(b)   an unlimited fine,

or both.

Directly applicable European Regulations

15.107 There is a growing tendency for Europe to produce directly applicable European Regulations rather than directives. These have been implemented by the Product Safety and Metrology etc. (Amendment etc.) (EU Exit) Regulations 2019.

Reach

15.108 The Registration, Evaluation, Authorisation and Restriction of Chemicals Regulation[1] prohibits and restricts, among other requirements, the use of certain chemicals in articles for consumer use such as phthalates in toys and childcare articles, azo dyes in toys and textiles and di-methyl fumarate in leather goods. It is enforced in the UK via the REACH Enforcement Regulations 2008[2] which contain the duties, powers and offences. There is no statutory defence.

[1]   EC Regulation 1907/2006.
[2]   SI 2008/2852.

Classification, Labelling and Packaging Regulation

15.109 The Classification, Labelling and Packaging Regulation[1] lays down requirements for the classification, packaging and labelling of dangerous chemicals such as the requirement for child resistant packaging and tactile devices. It is enforced in the UK via the Biocidal Products and Chemicals (Appointment of Authorities and Enforcement) Regulations 2013[2].

[1]   EC Regulation 1272/2008.
[2]   SI 2013/1506.

Marketing of Construction Products Regulation

15.110 The EU Regulation on the marketing of construction products[1] sets out harmonised basic requirements for construction products and the obligations of manufacturers, importers and distributors. These include conformity assessment procedures, declaration of performance and UKCA marking. They are enforced in the UK via the Construction Products Regulations 2013[2]. These regulations impose duties, grant powers including the issue of a suspension and recall notice, and create offences.

1   EU Regulation 305/2011.
2   SI 2013/1387.

Cosmetic Products Regulation

15.111 The Cosmetic Products Regulation[1] protects public health by prohibiting the use of certain substances in cosmetics and imposing restrictions on the use of others. There is an IT tool for the notification procedure to the UK Secretary of State under this regulation. The responsible person, who is responsible for the safety assessment, is required to notify the Secretary of State of each product placed on the market in detail (there are also separate requirements for products containing nanomaterials). There are also labelling requirements, a prohibition on animal testing and the requirement to produce a product information package. The EU regulation is enforced in the UK via the Cosmetic Products Enforcement Regulations 2013[2] which create offences and allow for a due diligence defence. Enforcement powers are found within the CRA 2015; see Chapter 4, Criminal Enforcement.

1   EC Regulation 1223/2009.
2   SI 2013/1478.

Regulation (EU) No 2016/425 on personal protective equipment

15.112 The regulation applies to PPE that is any device or appliance intended to be worn or held by an individual for use in domestic, leisure and sports activities and professional use for protection against one or more health and safety hazards. There are three categories of PPE:

• Category 1 (simple)
• Category 11 (intermediate)
• Category 111 (complex)

15.113 Conformity assessment procedures differ according to the category of PPE. The EU regulation is enforced in the UK via The Personal Protective Equipment (Enforcement) Regulations 2018[1] which create offences and allow for a due diligence defence. Enforcement powers are found within the CRA 2015; see Chapter 4, Criminal Enforcement. HSE now have responsibility for work related products

1   SI 2018/390.

Regulation (EU) 2016/426 on appliances burning gaseous fuels

15.114 The regulation provides that:

• No manufacturer etc shall supply an appliance which does not satisfy essential safety requirements.
• No person shall supply an appliance which when normally used is not safe.

- No person shall supply an appliance to which the UKCA mark has not been affixed.
- No manufacturer or his authorised representative established in the UK shall supply an appliance or a fitting in respect of which there is not in force at that time a type-examination certificate and a declaration of conformity to type.

15.115 'Appliances' means appliances burning gaseous fuels used for cooking, refrigeration, air-conditioning, space heating, hot water production, lighting or washing.

15.116 The EU regulation is enforced in the UK via The Gas Appliances (Enforcement) and Miscellaneous Amendments Regulations 2018[1] which create offences and allow for a due diligence defence. Enforcement powers are found within the CRA 2015; see CHAPTER 4, Criminal Enforcement. HSE have responsibility for work related products.

[1] SI 2018/389.

GENERAL PRODUCT SAFETY REGULATIONS 2005

Introduction

15.117 The General Product Safety Regulations 2005[1] ('GPSR 2005') – made under the European Communities Act 1972, s 2(2) – implement Directive 2001/95/EC[2]. The GPSR apply to the supply of new and second-hand consumer products, excluding second-hand products supplied as a product to be repaired or reconditioned prior to being used, provided the supplier clearly informs the person to whom he supplies the product to that effect (reg 4).

[1] SI 2005/1803.
[2] OJ L 11, 15.1.2002, p 4.

15.118 The Regulations primarily aim to do the following:

- specify that products placed on the market or supplied by producers and distributors must be safe;
- define a safe product;
- impose obligations on producers and distributors consistent with marketing safe products;
- lay down a framework for assessing safety;
- require and empower enforcement authorities to take action necessary to protect consumers from unsafe products.

Relationship with other regulations

15.119 Regulation 3(2) states:

(2) Where a product is subject to specific safety requirements imposed by any other relevant enactment these Regulations shall apply only to the aspects and risks or category of risks not covered by those requirements. This means that:

(a)   the definition of "safe product" and "dangerous product" in regulation 2 and regulations 5 and 6 shall not apply to such a product in so far as concerns the risks or category of risks covered by the specific rules, and

(b)   the remainder of these Regulations shall apply except where there are specific provisions governing the aspects covered by those regulations with the same objective.

In September 2009 the Department for Business, Innovation and Skills published *Guidance on the interaction between the General Product Safety Regulations 2005 and national safety regulations.* The Conclusion of this document states:

'16. The GPSR therefore act as a safety net to prevent the placing on the market of dangerous products within its scope:
(a)   where there are no specific safety regulations in place covering those products,
(b)   those products do not comply with national safety regulations; or
(c)   which, even if they do comply with national safety regulations, are nevertheless considered to be dangerous.

17. As such, they operate in parallel to relevant national safety regulations and can be used as an alternative means of enforcement.'

15.120 In *Caerphilly County Borough Council v Stripp*[1] the defendant was prosecuted under reg 13(b) of the General Product Safety Regulations 1994[2] for offering to supply a second-hand car which, it was said, was a dangerous product. The magistrates accepted the defendant's submission that the prosecution was an abuse of process, on the basis that reg 3(c) stated that those regulations did not apply to any product where there are specific provisions in rules of Community law governing all aspects of the safety of the product. The magistrates found that the Road Traffic Act 1988, s 75 was such a specific provision governing all aspects of the safety of second-hand vehicles. The prosecutor appealed. Per Butterfield J:

'. . . regulation 13(b) is available legislation under which to bring a prosecution in respect of a dangerous product, namely a second-hand motor vehicle, if that is thought appropriate by the local authority or other prosecuting agency.'

1   [2001] 2 CMLR 5 (CO/609/00).
2   SI 1994/2328, reg 13(b).

15.121 In another case involving this point, *R v Newcastle Upon Tyne Magistrates' Court ex p Poundstretcher Ltd*[1], a prosecution under reg 13 of the General Product Safety Regulations 1994[2] was brought for supplying a dangerous product. The defendant suggested that, having regard in particular to reg 3(c), the prosecution should have been brought under the Toys (Safety) Regulations 1995[3] which specifically deal with the risk from suffocation and which give effect to an EEC Council Directive. Whilst not accepting that argument, the prosecutor successfully applied to amend the information to allege an offence under the 1995 Regulations. Under the Toys (Safety) Regulations 1995 an information must be laid within 12 months of the date of offence. By the time of the application to amend, 12 months had elapsed. The defendant sought judicial review of the decision to amend. Per Dyson J (Bingham LCJ agreeing): 'The decision in this case was very far from being plainly wrong.'

1   (CO/3282/97).
2   SI 1994/2328, reg 13.
3   SI 1995/204.

15.122 The issue before the Administrative Court in *Essex County Council v PMS International Group Plc*[1] actually related to procedural matters under the Criminal Procedure Rules ('Crim PR') and Practice Direction. However, the legal argument that took place before the magistrates concerned whether it was open to Essex County Council to proceed under the GPSR 2005 when proceedings under the Furniture and Furnishings (Fire) (Safety) Regulations 1988 were available to it. The magistrate held that the prosecution under the provisions of the GPSR 2005 was prevented by virtue of the provisions of reg 3(1)[2] ('Each provision of these Regulations applies to a product in so far as there are no specific provisions with the same objective in rules of Community law governing the safety of the product other than the GPS Directive') due to the fact that there was a specific provision governing flammability of cushions contained in the Furniture and Furnishings Fire Safety Regulations 1988.

1   [2012] EWHC 1500 (Admin).
2   SI 1988/1324, reg 3(1).

Key general concepts

15.123 The GPSR 2005 provide a number of definitions of the key concepts of the legislation and the offences created.

Product

15.124 Regulation 2[1] provides for interpretation and gives the following definition:

> "product" means a product which is intended for consumers or likely, under reasonably foreseeable conditions, to be used by consumers even if not intended for them and which is supplied or made available, whether for consideration or not, in the course of a commercial activity and whether it is new, used or reconditioned and includes a product that is supplied or made available to consumers for their own use in the context of providing a service. "Product" does not include equipment used by service providers themselves to supply a service to consumers, in particular equipment on which consumers ride or travel which is operated by a service provider.

1   SI 2005/1803, reg 2.

15.125 This pithy definition can be summarised as all goods that are or could be placed on the market, or supplied or made available, including in the course of providing a service, to consumers for their private use. The fact that the definition includes products that are not intended for consumers means that products that were originally designed and intended for professional use will still be subject to the GPSR 2005 if it is reasonably foreseeable that they will migrate to the consumer market. Producers and distributors must, therefore, be very careful in considering the likelihood of their product, intended for professionals, ending up in the consumer market *and* ensuring that the product is accompanied by sufficient labelling and instruction as to the risks, or inappropriateness of consumer use. If the product is unlikely to ever be considered safe for the consumer market then steps must be taken to ensure the marketing and supply of the product is strictly controlled. Clear markings provide an unambiguous guide for the enforcement authorities about whether a product is intended for professional use or consumer use, and whether the risks to consumers are sufficiently covered so as to meet the general safety requirements.

Supply

15.126 Assistance is again provided by reg 2, where the following meaning is given: 'Supply' in relation to a product includes making it available, in the context of providing a service, for use by consumers. The meaning of supply clearly goes further than that above. The Regulations expressly refer to producers and distributors and the meaning of supply must therefore be seen in that context. Producers make the product and place it on the market for distributors, the first stage of the supply. Distributors, having received the product from the producers, then supply the products to the consumers thereafter, the second stage of the supply. In addition, supply extends to the hire and making a product available for use by consumers in the course of providing a service, an express departure from the previous regulations.

15.127 The following are, however, key features of the GPSR 2005:

- They only apply to commercial supply ie in the course of a business or a trade.
- Each time a product is made available that constitutes a separate supply.
- Preparatory acts of agreeing to supply and possessing any product for supply are caught by the Regulations.
- They do not apply to products used in the workplace by workers.
- They do not apply to products which are exported, or intended to be exported.
- They do not apply to products used or intended only for display at exhibitions or trade fairs.

15.128 The following are examples of how a product can be supplied for the purposes of the Regulations:

- selling, leasing, hiring it out or lending it;
- entering into a hire purchase or other credit agreement for it;
- exchanging it for any consideration other than money;
- giving it as a prize or otherwise making a gift; and
- providing it in the course of the delivery of a service.

15.129 The above examples are self-explanatory with the exception of the previously absent provision of a product in the course of the delivery of a service. The explanatory memorandum to the Regulations prepared by the Department for Trade and Industry provides a useful example of this particular supply of a product:

'A person books into a hotel room that provides a hairdryer for use by the guest. These Regulations apply to that hairdryer as it is provided to the consumer in the course of delivering a service, namely the hotel room. By contrast, a hairdryer used in a hairdresser's by the professional hairdresser at work rather than by the consumer is not covered by the Regulations.'

Meaning of a safe product

15.130 Regulation 2[1] defines a safe product as follows:

"safe product" means a product which, under normal or reasonably foreseeable conditions of use including duration and, where applicable, putting into service, installation and maintenance requirements, does not present any risk or only the minimum risks compatible with the product's use, considered to be acceptable and consistent with a high level of protection for the safety and health of persons. In determining the foregoing, the following shall be taken into account in particular—

(a)   the characteristics of the product, including its composition, packaging, instructions for assembly and, where applicable, instructions for installation and maintenance,

(b)   the effect of the product on other products, where it is reasonably foreseeable that it will be used with other products,

(c)   the presentation of the product, the labelling, any warnings and instructions for its use and disposal and any other indication or information regarding the product, and

(d)   the categories of consumers at risk when using the product, in particular children and the elderly.

[1]   SI 2005/1803, reg 2.

15.131 Reasonable or foreseeable use will include misuse – commonly using a product other than how it is intended. For example, a screwdriver is designed to withstand turning stresses, however, the normal consumer when looking to open a can of paint will often use a handy screwdriver as a lever – therefore to be safe a screwdriver should also withstand such stress as is foreseeable from a consumer's wider use (in this case opening a can of paint). It is important to note that the mere possibility or feasibility of obtaining higher levels of safety or the availability of other products presenting a lesser degree of risk shall not constitute grounds for considering a product to be a dangerous product[1].

[1]   Defined in SI 2005/1803, reg 2 as a product other than a safe product.

Standards of safety

15.132 The assessment of whether a product is safe is manifestly the key consideration in cases arising out of this legislation. As is clear from earlier in this chapter, products are subject to national safety regulations both those made under the CPA 1987, s 11, and those derived from European Directives and Regulations which detail standards required for those particular products (eg the Aerosol Dispensers Regulations 2009). A product will also be presumed safe, in the absence of the above, if it conforms to a voluntary national standard that gives effect to a designated standard, but only so far as the risks are covered by that standard.

15.133 Where, however, neither a specific regulation nor national safety law applies, safety will be assessed according to reg 6(3)[1]:

. . . the conformity of a product to the general safety requirement shall be assessed taking into account—

(a)   any designated standard of the United Kingdom ,
(b)   other national standards drawn up in the United Kingdom,
(c)   recommendations setting guidelines on product safety assessment,
(d)   product safety codes of good practice in the sector concerned,
(e)   the state of the art and technology, and
(f)   reasonable consumer expectations concerning safety.

1   SI 2005/1803, reg 6(3).

15.134 The safety of many consumer products that fall under the General Product Safety Regulations is assessed in accordance with the hierarchy of standards. Obviously when designing products for vulnerable consumers such as children, extra hazards need to be addressed and extra precautions need to be taken. To assist manufacturers of these products the UK has mandated a large range of deignated standards for products, in particular those which are for children's use and care – such as bunk beds, cots, prams and pushchairs. Recent examples also include looped cords in blinds and reduced ignition propensity cigarettes.

15.135 Compliance with one or more of the above will not, however, necessarily mean that the product is automatically a safe product. Indeed, the Regulations give specific consent to enforcement authorities to take appropriate measures where there is evidence that despite such conformity the product is dangerous[1].

1   SI 2005/1803, reg 6(4).

Application

15.136 The GPSR 2005 apply to all UK suppliers of products. However, suppliers for the purposes of the GPSR 2005 may be either 'producers' or 'distributors', but both have particular meanings in the context of the GPSR 2005. It should not be assumed that the words have the meaning attributed by everyday usage. In addition, where it can be shown that an offence has been committed with the aid or consent of, or is attributable to any neglect on the part of any director, manager, secretary or other similar officer of a company, such persons (in addition to the company in question) may also be proceeded against[1].

1   SI 2005/1803, reg 31(2).

Producers

15.137 Regulation 2[1] states that:

'producer' means—

(a)   the manufacturer of a product, when he is established in the UK and any other person presenting himself as the manufacturer by affixing to the product his name, trade mark or other distinctive mark, or the person who reconditions the product;
(b)   when the manufacturer is not established in the UK—
    (i)   if he has a representative established in the UK, the representative,

(ii)   in any other case, the importer of the product from a third country;
(c)   other professionals in the supply chain, insofar as their activities may affect the safety properties of a product.

¹   SI 2005/1803, reg 2.

15.138 A 'producer' for the purposes of the Regulations, therefore, is not simply the manufacturer. It will include any professional in the supply chain whose activities affect the safety of the product. If the relevant person's activity did not affect the safety properties of the product, the original producer will continue to be responsible for its safety.

Distributors

15.139 Regulation 2 states that 'distributor' means a professional in the supply chain whose activity does not affect the safety properties of the product. This can include wholesalers, retailers, agents and auctioneers¹ and also includes a person who makes a product available for the use of a consumer in the course of delivering a service.

¹   Auctioneers are excluded from the Regulations if they are merely acting under instructions in conducting the sale. In those circumstances, it is the owner of the product who is the seller.

Obligations

The general safety requirement

15.140 The general obligation is on producers to supply only products that are safe.

Regulation 5¹ imposes the general safety requirement on producers:

5 General safety requirement

(1)   No producer shall place a product on the market unless the product is a safe product.
(2)   No producer shall offer or agree to place a product on the market or expose or possess a product for placing on the market unless the product is a safe product.
(3)   No producer shall offer or agree to supply a product or expose or possess a product for supply unless the product is safe.
(4)   No producer shall supply a product unless the product is a safe product.

A person who contravenes reg 5 is guilty of an offence and liable on conviction on indictment to imprisonment for a term not exceeding 12 months or to an unlimited fine or to both, or on summary conviction to imprisonment for a term not exceeding 3 months or to an unlimited fine or to both (reg 20(1)).

¹   SI 2005/1803, reg 5.

Producer obligations

15.141 The GPSR 2005 express obligations in addition to the general safety requirement on both producers and distributors alike. Regulation 7¹ sets out the following in relation to obligations of producers:

7 Other obligations of producers

(1) Within the limits of his activities, a producer shall provide consumers with the relevant information to enable them—

    (a) to assess the risks inherent in a product throughout the normal or reasonably foreseeable period of its use, where such risks are not immediately obvious without adequate warnings, and

    (b) to take precautions against those risks.

(2) The presence of warnings does not exempt any person from compliance with the other requirements of these Regulations.

(3) Within the limits of his activities, a producer shall adopt measures commensurate with the characteristics of the products which he supplies to enable him to—

    (a) be informed of the risks which the products might pose, and

    (b) take appropriate action including, where necessary to avoid such risks, withdrawal, adequately and effectively warning consumers as to the risks or, as a last resort, recall.

(4) The measures referred to in paragraph (3) include—

    (a) except where it is not reasonable to do so, an indication by means of the product or its packaging of—

        (i) the name and address of the producer, and

        (ii) the product reference or where applicable the batch of products to which it belongs; and

    (b) where and to the extent that it is reasonable to do so—

        (i) sample testing of marketed products,

        (ii) investigating and if necessary keeping a register of complaints concerning the safety of the product, and

        (iii) keeping distributors informed of the results of such monitoring where a product presents a risk or may present a risk.

[1] SI 2005/1803, reg 7.

15.142

Precedent for placing an unsafe product on the market

Statement of offence

PLACING AN UNSAFE PRODUCT ON THE MARKET, contrary to regulations 5(1) and 20(1) of the General Product Safety Regulations 2005.

Particulars of offence

A B, a producer, on [date] placed on the market a product, namely [...], which was an unsafe product.

15.143 A person who contravenes reg 7(1), (3) (by failing to take any of the measures specified in reg 7(4)) is guilty of an offence, see section 20 below. Producers, it can be seen, must ensure that consumers are provided with all relevant information and warnings, and that they maintain a high level of information about possible risks. However, common sense dictates that the diversity of products and the risks they pose reflects on the extent of action expected and required of producers and distributors alike. Some products are inherently more dangerous than others and producers or distributors are only required to act within the limits of their activities.

Distributor obligations

15.144 Regulation 8 of the Regulations[1] sets out the following in relation to obligations of distributors:

8 Obligations of distributors

(1)   A distributor shall act with due care in order to help ensure compliance with the applicable safety requirements and in particular he—

(a)   shall not expose or possess for supply or offer or agree to supply, or supply, a product to any person which he knows or should have presumed, on the basis of the information in his possession and as a professional, is a dangerous product; and

(b)   shall, within the limits of his activities, participate in monitoring the safety of a product placed on the market, in particular by—

(i)   passing on information on the risks posed by the product,

(ii)   keeping the documentation necessary for tracing the origin of the product,

(iii)   producing the documentation necessary for tracing the origin of the product, and cooperating in action taken by a producer or an enforcement authority to avoid the risks.

(2)   Within the limits of his activities, a distributor shall take measures enabling him to cooperate efficiently in the action referred to in paragraph (1)(b)(iii).

[1]   SI 2005/1803.

15.145

Precedent for supplying a dangerous product

Statement of offence

SUPPLYING A DANGEROUS PRODUCT, contrary to regulations 8(1)(a) and 20(1) of the General Product Safety Regulations 2005.

Particulars of offence

A B, a distributor, on [date] supplied a product, namely [...], which he knew or should have presumed, on the basis of the information in his possession and as a professional, was a dangerous product.

15.146 A person who contravenes reg 8(1)(a) is guilty of an offence and liable on conviction on indictment to imprisonment for a term not exceeding 12 months or to an unlimited fine or to both, or on summary conviction to imprisonment for a term not exceeding 3 months or to an unlimited fine or to both (reg 20(1)). A person who contravenes reg 8(1)(b)(i), (ii) or (iii) is guilty of an offence, see reg 20 below.

Obligations of producers and distributors

15.147 Regulation 9 of the Regulations[1] imposes obligations on both producers and distributors:

9 Obligations of producers and distributors

(1)   Subject to paragraph (2), where a producer or a distributor knows that a product he has placed on the market or supplied poses risks to the consumer that are incompatible with the general safety requirement, he shall forthwith notify an enforcement authority in writing of that information and—

(a)   the action taken to prevent risk to the consumer; and

(b)   where the product is being or has been marketed or otherwise supplied to consumers outside the United Kingdom, of the identity of each Member State in which, to the best of his knowledge, it is being or has been so marketed or supplied.

(2)   Paragraph (1) shall not apply—

(a)   in the case of a second-hand product supplied as an antique or as a product to be repaired or reconditioned prior to being used, provided the supplier clearly informed the person to whom he supplied the product to that effect,

(b)   in conditions concerning isolated circumstances or products.

(3)   In the event of a serious risk the notification under paragraph (1) shall include the following—

(a)   information enabling a precise identification of the product or batch of products in question,

(b)   a full description of the risks that the product presents,

(c)   all available information relevant for tracing the product, and

(d)   a description of the action undertaken to prevent risks to the consumer.

(4)   Within the limits of his activities, a person who is a producer or a distributor shall co-operate with an enforcement authority (at the enforcement authority's request) in action taken to avoid the risks posed by a product which he supplies or has supplied. Every enforcement authority shall maintain procedures for such co-operation, including procedures for dialogue with the producers and distributors concerned on issues related to product safety.

[1]   SI 2005/1803.

15.148 Such notifications should be sent to the Secretary of State. The obligation is to notify the authorities, in writing, if producers or distributors discover that they have placed an unsafe product on the market, and what action they have taken to remove the risk posed. This notification should be done 'forthwith' and is a very important step in ensuring the safety of consumers by taking the appropriate corrective action as soon as possible. The provisions of reg 9 do not apply:

(a)   in the case of a second-hand product supplied as an antique or as a product to be repaired or reconditioned prior to being used, provided the supplier clearly informed the person to whom he supplied the product to that effect,

(b)   in conditions concerning isolated circumstances or products.

A person who contravenes reg 9(1) is guilty of an offence, see reg 20 below.

15.149 A producer or distributor who does not give notice to an enforcement authority under reg 9(1) in respect of a product he has placed on the market or supplied commits an offence where it is proved that he ought to have known that the product poses risks to consumers that are incompatible with the general safety requirement, see reg 20 below.

15.150 For those cases that go to trial, prosecutors should be aware of evidential limitations about notification statements. Regulation 44 sets out the following:

44 Evidence in proceedings for offence relating to regulation 9(1)

(1) This regulation applies where a person has given a notification to an enforcement authority pursuant to regulation 9(1).

(2) No evidence relating to that statement may be adduced and no question relating to it may be asked by the prosecution in any criminal proceedings (other than proceedings in which that person is charged with an offence under regulation 20 for a contravention of regulation 9(1), unless evidence relating to it is adduced, or a question relating to it asked, in the proceedings by or on behalf of that person.

Offence and penalties

15.151 Regulation 20 states:

20 Offences

(1) A person who contravenes regulations 5 or 8(1)(a) shall be guilty of an offence and liable on conviction on indictment to imprisonment for a term not exceeding 12 months or to a fine not exceeding £20,000 or to both, or on summary conviction to imprisonment for a term not exceeding three months or to a fine not exceeding the statutory maximum or to both.

(2) A person who contravenes regulation 7(1) , 7(3) (by failing to take any of the measures specified in regulation 7(4)), 8(1)(b)(i), (ii) or (iii) or 9(1) shall be guilty of an offence and liable on summary conviction to imprisonment for a term not exceeding three months or to a fine not exceeding level 5 on the standard scale or to both.

(3) A producer or distributor who does not give notice to an enforcement authority under regulation 9(1) in respect of a product he has placed on the market or supplied commits an offence where it is proved that he ought to have known that the product poses risks to consumers that are incompatible with the general safety requirement and he shall be liable on summary conviction to imprisonment for a term not exceeding three months or to a fine not exceeding level 5 on the standard scale or to both.

(4) A person who contravenes a safety notice shall be guilty of an offence and liable on conviction on indictment to imprisonment for a term not exceeding 12 months or to a fine not exceeding £20,000 or to both, or on summary conviction to imprisonment for a term not exceeding three months or to a fine not exceeding the statutory maximum or to both.

The sentencing provisions under the GPSR 2005 are the subject of an unfortunate statutory oversight in relation to the maximum fines for offences sentenced in the Crown Court. Since 12 March 2015 fines in the Magistrates' Court are unlimited, with the statutory maximum no longer applying[1]. However, the £20,000 limit for a fine in the Crown Court has not been changed. This was plainly not an intended consequence of the legislative reform. It is likely to lead to defendants electing Crown Court trial to take advantage of the applicable maximum fine. This is particularly the case where the defendant is not at risk of a custodial sentence, such as a corporate defendant that anticipates a fine exceeding £20,000.

[1]   Legal Aid, Sentencing and Punishment of Offenders Act 2012, s 85(1).

Causal and directors' liability

15.152 Regulation 31[1] states:

31 Liability of person other than principal offender

(1) Where the commission by a person of an offence under these Regulations is due to an act or default committed by some other person in the course of a commercial activity of his, the other person shall be guilty of the offence and may be proceeded against and punished by virtue of this paragraph whether or not proceedings are taken against the first-mentioned person.

(2) Where a body corporate is guilty of an offence under these Regulations (including where it is so guilty by virtue of paragraph (1)) in respect of any act or default which is shown to have been committed with the consent or connivance of, or to be attributable to any neglect on the part of, any director, manager, secretary or other similar officer of the body corporate or any person who was purporting to act in any such capacity he, as well as the body corporate, shall be guilty of that offence and shall be liable to be proceeded against and punished accordingly.

(3) Where the affairs of a body corporate are managed by its members, paragraph (2) shall apply in relation to the acts and defaults of a member in connection with his functions of management as if he were a director of the body corporate.

(4) Where a Scottish partnership is guilty of an offence under these Regulations (including where it is so guilty by virtue of paragraph (1)) in respect of any act or default which is shown to have been committed with the consent or connivance of, or to be attributable to any neglect on the part of, a partner in the partnership, he, as well as the partnership, shall be guilty of that offence and shall be liable to be proceeded against and punished accordingly.

Causal and directors' liability provisions are covered in CHAPTER 4, Criminal Enforcement.

[1]   SI 2005/1803, reg 31.

Defences

15.153 A defence of due diligence (expressed in similar terms to the CPA 1987, s 39) is available in relation to all offences under the GPSR 2005 by virtue of reg 29[1]:

29 Defence of due diligence

(1) Subject to the following provisions of this regulation, in proceedings against a person for an offence under these Regulations it shall be a defence for that person to show that he took all reasonable steps and exercised all due diligence to avoid committing the offence.

(2) Where in any proceedings against any person for such an offence the defence provided by paragraph (1) involves an allegation that the commission of the offence was due—

(a)   to the act or default of another, or

(b)   to reliance on information given by another,

that person shall not, without the leave of the court, be entitled to rely on the defence unless, not less than seven clear days before, in England, Wales and Northern Ireland, the hearing of the proceedings or, in Scotland, the trial diet, he has served a notice under paragraph (3) on the person bringing the proceedings.

(3)   A notice under this paragraph shall give such information identifying or assisting in the identification of the person who—

    (a)   committed the act or default, or

    (b)   gave the information,

as is in the possession of the person serving the notice at the time he serves it.

(4)   A person may not rely on the defence provided by paragraph (1) by reason of his reliance on information supplied by another, unless he shows that it was reasonable in all the circumstances to have relied on the information, having regard in particular—

    (a)   to the steps which he took, and those which might reasonably have been taken, for the purpose of verifying the information; and

    (b)   to whether he had any reason to disbelieve the information.

[1]   SI 2005/1803, reg 29.

15.154 Due diligence defences are dealt with generally in CHAPTER 4, Criminal Enforcement. A specific defence applies in respect of the prosecution of a person for the supply, offer or agreement to supply or exposure or possession for supply of second hand products supplied as antiques (reg 30). Regulation 30(2) and (3)[1] states:

(2) It shall be a defence for that person to show that the terms on which he supplied the product or agreed or offered to supply the product or, in the case of a product which he exposed or possessed for supply, the terms on which he intended to supply the product, contemplated the acquisition of an interest in the product by the person supplied or to be supplied.

(3) Paragraph (2) applies only if the producer or distributor clearly informed the person to whom he supplied the product, or offered or agreed to supply the product or, in the case of a product which he exposed or possessed for supply, he intended to so inform that person, that the product is an antique.

[1]   SI 2005/1803, reg 30(2) and (3).

Enforcement

15.155 Primary enforcement of the Regulations falls to local authorities through local trading standards authorities in England, Wales and Scotland, and in Northern Ireland District Council Environmental Health Officers (reg 10). Certain products, however, require enforcement by both Local Authorities and the Health and Safety Executive ('HSE') working cooperatively. This will be required where the product in question is one that is either designed for dual purpose (ie for consumers and professionals), or where it is a product that has migrated to the consumer market. Note that reg 10(5)[1] states:

(5) An enforcement authority shall in enforcing these Regulations act in a manner proportionate to the seriousness of the risk and shall take due account of the precautionary principle. In this context, it shall encourage and promote voluntary action by producers and distributors. Notwithstanding the foregoing, an enforcement authority may take any action under these Regulations urgently and without first encouraging and promoting voluntary action if a product poses a serious risk.

[1]   SI 2005/1803, reg 10(5).

15.156 Enforcement powers are now found under the CRA 2015, Sch 5 (see CHAPTER 4, Criminal Enforcement).

Time limits

15.157 Regulation 41 of the GPSR 2005 extends the time for bringing summary proceedings beyond the normal 6-month time limit in relation to summary only offences contained in the Magistrates' Courts Act 1980, s 127. Time is extended, so that a summary GPSR 2005 offence must be prosecuted within 3 years from the commission of the offence, or 12 months from the discovery of the offence by the prosecutor, whichever is the sooner[1]. There appears to be no such time limit for the either-way offences in the GPSR 2005. In *R v Thames Magistrates' Court ex p Academy International plc*[2] – it was held that the same time limit applied for the causal liability 'by-pass' offence (now contained in reg 31 (Liability of person other than principal offender)) as for the primary offence. Time limits are now covered generally in CHAPTER **4**, Criminal Enforcement.

1   SI 2005/1803, reg 41.
2   (CO/293/99).

15.158 Notwithstanding the Criminal Procedure (Scotland) Act 1995, s 136, summary proceedings in Scotland for an offence under the GPSR 2005 may be commenced within 3 years from the date of the offence or within one year from the discovery of the offence by the prosecutor whichever is the earlier.

Other measures

15.159 Enforcement authorities have access to a range of measures in regs 11–19 which can be employed to remove risk to consumer safety where producers and distributors have not fulfilled their obligations under the GPSR 2005 – these comprise 'safety notices' (which means a suspension notice, a requirement to mark, a requirement to warn, a withdrawal notice or a recall notice) and forfeiture. Generally, it is assumed that where the producer or distributor is already taking the action necessary to remove the risk to consumers it will not be necessary for the enforcement authorities to serve a safety notice.

Safety notices

SUSPENSION NOTICES

15.160 These notices[1] temporarily ban the placing on the market or the supply of a product while tests are undertaken to determine compliance with the Regulations. They can be issued when an authority has reasonable grounds for suspecting that there has been a contravention.

1   SI 2005/1803, reg 11.

REQUIREMENT TO MARK

15.161 These notices allow an authority to make the marketing of a product subject to prior conditions, thereby making it safe or marked with warnings as to the risks. This is a very powerful tool and could be used in circumstances where a product is safe in some hands but not in others, eg a laser pointer for use by a lecturer is safe but not in the hands of teenagers shining it at the pilot of a helicopter. Such a notice could be issued on a retailer to ensure they do not sell laser pointers to under 18s for example. Additionally, a requirement to mark notice can be used on a car forecourt where second-hand cars have been examined and found to be unsafe – such a notice could be served on the trader requiring them not to supply the vehicles unless they have a valid MOT certificate.

REQUIREMENT TO WARN

15.162 These powers allow an authority to insist on a product being marked with suitable warnings[1] where it could pose risks in certain conditions, or require that specific warnings are given to certain at risk individuals (eg the elderly or children). For example, where an air freshener is found to contain a known allergen a requirement to warn notice could be issued to ensure that users of the air fresheners are alerted to the presence of the allergen. The notice can also require a warning to consumers to be published about the risks arising from the use of the product with instructions such as 'Do not use' or 'Unplug from mains' until repair has been carried out.

[1]   SI 2005/1803, regs 12 and 13.

WITHDRAWAL NOTICES

15.163 Authorities can issue a notice to permanently prevent a person from further supplying a product that is believed to be dangerous or from placing it on the market if it has not yet been placed. This notice would effectively remove the product from the entire supply chain. Again, this notice can only be served if the authority has reasonable grounds for believing that a product is dangerous[1].

[1]   SI 2005/1803, reg 14.

RECALL NOTICES

15.164 This requires a person on whom it is served to take such steps as are identified in the notice to organise the return of the product, deemed upon reasonable grounds to be dangerous by an authority, from consumers. The notice may be temporarily suspended if an appeal is to be launched. All safety notices may be subject to an appeal made before the end of the period of 21 days beginning on the day the notice was served[1].

[1]   SI 2005/1803, reg 15.

15.165 The recall appeal process can be via the Chartered Institute of Arbitrators whose decision has to be taken into account but is not binding on the local authority.

15.166 Any recall may require the recall to be effected in accordance with a code of practice applicable to the product concerned. A Code of Practice on Consumer product safety related recalls and other corrective actions (PAS 7100: 2018) has being drawn up by BSI.

15.167 A person who contravenes a safety notice is guilty of an offence and liable on conviction on indictment to imprisonment for a term not exceeding 12 months or to an unlimited fine or to both, or on summary conviction to imprisonment for a term not exceeding 3 months or to an unlimited fine or to both (reg 20(4)).

Forfeiture

FORFEITURE AND DESTRUCTION

15.168 Under reg 18 an enforcement authority in England and Wales or Northern Ireland may apply for an order for the forfeiture of a product on the grounds that the product is a dangerous product. Equivalent provision for a forfeiture order, by a sheriff, in Scotland is contained in reg 19. Both sections contain provisions for appeal against the decision to impose a forfeiture order.

The Psychoactive Substances Act 2016

15.169 The Psychoactive Substances Act 2016 ('PSA 2016') came into force across the United Kingdom on 26 May 2016. The Act is intended to restrict the production, sale and supply of a class of psychoactive substances often previously referred to as 'legal highs'. The background to the legislation is that new psychoactive substances were produced for the market more quickly than Government could regulate them, whether by classifying them as controlled substances or otherwise. According to the European Monitoring Centre for Drugs and Drug Addiction, 101 new substances were identified in the European Union in 2014, up from 24 in 2009. According to a Select Committee Report on the Psychoactive Substances Bill, the UK had the highest usage of any country in Europe.

15.170 The PSA 2016 is based on a piece of Irish legislation, the Criminal Justice (Psychoactive Substances) Act 2010. The Irish Act was not without its critics. To bring a prosecution the authorities had to prove that a substance has a psychoactive effect, usually by way of scientific evidence. This proved difficult to obtain. By 2015 there had been only four successful prosecutions in 5 years. Similar problems may arise with the PSA 2016 because it works in a similar way. Since the PSA 2016 came into force, a substance does not need to be classified in a particular way by the government for its production or supply to be controlled.

15.171 The Act does not replace the Misuse of Drugs Act 1971, so laws around existing illegal (controlled) drugs will remain the same. Temporary Class Drug Orders (TCDOs) can still be applied and the Human Medicines Regulations 2012 will remain the same. However, the Intoxicating Substances Supply Act 1985 has been repealed.

DEFINITION OF 'PSYCHOACTIVE SUBSTANCES'

15.172 The key definition of 'psychoactive substance' is provided in the PSA 2016, s 2:

2 Meaning of "psychoactive substance" etc

(1) In this Act "psychoactive substance" means any substance which—
  (a) is capable of producing a psychoactive effect in a person who consumes it, and
  (b) is not an exempted substance (see section 3).
(2) For the purposes of this Act a substance produces a psychoactive effect in a person if, by stimulating or depressing the person's central nervous system, it affects the person's mental functioning or emotional state; and references to a substance's psychoactive effects are to be read accordingly.
(3) For the purposes of this Act a person consumes a substance if the person causes or allows the substance, or fumes given off by the substance, to enter the person's body in any way.

15.173 Therefore the central issue in deciding whether a substance is caught by the PSA 2016 is what effect, if any, its consumption is capable of having on the central nervous system. The Explanatory Notes to the PSA 2016 elaborate on the PSA 2016, s 2 definition: 'by speeding up or slowing down activity on the central nervous system, psychoactive substances cause an alteration in the individual's state of consciousness by producing a range of effects including, but not limited to: hallucinations; changes in alertness, perception of time and space, mood or empathy with others; and drowsiness'.

15.174 Prior to the coming into force of the Act concerns were raised in various quarters that the definition of 'psychoactive substances' was too broad. This is particularly so given that an effect on a person's 'emotional state' can be caught, if triggered by stimulation of the central nervous system. It remains to be seen how workable it will be in practice and how narrowly or broadly the courts will interpret the definition. The PSA 2016, s 3 provides that any substances listed in the PSA 2016, Sch 1 will be 'exempted substances' for the purposes of the Act. The Secretary of State can by regulations add or vary any description of substance, or remove substances previously added by regulations.

15.175 The PSA 2016, Sch 1 currently lists controlled drugs (within the meaning of the Misuse of Drugs Act 1971), medicinal products, alcohol, nicotine and tobacco products, caffeine and food. In the course of a prosecution the burden of proving that a substance is not an exempt substance will probably fall on the prosecution; the Act is silent on the issue.

15.176 The listed exemptions are potentially broad because they include medicines and other substances with complex definitions. Difficulties in identifying a clear meaning of 'medicinal products', for example, is highlighted by case a decided by the CJEU, C-358/13, D (12 June 2014). This concerned the interpretation of the term 'medicinal product' within the meaning of Art 1(2)(b) of Directive 2001/83/EC. Two German defendants had been charged with selling herb mixtures containing, inter alia, synthetic cannabinoids, which, at the material time, did not fall under the German law on narcotic drugs. The CJEU decided that legal highs were not medicines, but the reasoning behind the decision (paras 38–50 of the judgment) was not entirely clear or easy to apply in future cases.

15.177 One area of controversy during the passage of the Psychoactive Substances Bill through Parliament was whether alkyl nitrates ('poppers') would be caught by the definition of psychoactive substances. The issue was referred to the Advisory Council on the Misuse of Drugs ('ACMD'), who came to the view that they would not, on the basis that alkyl nitrates do not *directly* stimulate or depress the central nervous system. However, the PSA 2016, s 2 definition as drafted does not distinguish between direct and indirect effects. It remains to be seen whether the ACMD's view on indirect effect will be followed by the courts, should the issue arise. It may be that in due course alkyl nitrates need to be added to the list of exempt substances.

15.178 According to the Explanatory Notes with the PSA 2016, nitrous oxide is authorised by EU legislation for use as a propellant, for example, to administer whipped cream given that it will leave traces in the cream and, as such, would not constitute a prohibited ingredient when used in this way. But the consumption of nitrous oxide gas from a canister for its psychoactive effect would not fall within the food exemption and therefore would constitute a psychoactive substance under the Act.

IDENTIFICATION OF PSYCHOACTIVE SUBSTANCES

15.179 When an unknown substance is seized it will need to be tested to determine what it is, and whether it is a 'psychoactive substance' within the meaning of the PSA 2016. If the substance is already known to have the required effect on the central nervous system then this should not be a problem. In the case of novel substances however reliable evidence will need to be produced that they have such an effect.

15.180 The government has acknowledged this issue in a Forensic Strategy published in relation to the PSA 2016. The strategy sets out guidance for Forensic Service Providers (FSPs), law enforcement agencies, prosecuting agencies and expert witnesses to support the operation of the PSA 2016. It recognises that unlike the regime established under the Misuse of Drugs Act 1971, the PSA 2016 'covers substances by virtue of their psychoactive properties, rather than the identity of the drug or its chemical structure. Consequently, there is a requirement for a new forensic capability'. The Home Office has established a programme of in-vitro testing (ie testing outside the body, such as in a test tube). A commercial supplier has been contracted to perform testing 'for a range of Certified Drug Reference Standards (CDRS) of substances detected in the UK'. CDRSs are pure samples of drugs which are used to identify seized substances by their chemical structure. If a seized sample matches a psychoactive CDRS, this will provide evidence that it is a psychoactive substance within the meaning of the Act.

15.181 The problems however are likely to arise when novel substances are seized and sent for testing, and do not match any known CDRS. It will then be incumbent upon the testing service to carry out scientific tests which can be used by a prosecuting authority to prove, beyond reasonable doubt, that the substances are capable of having the required psychoactive effect. The ACMD provided guidance to the Home Office on how to establish its in-vitro testing programme. It has noted that although biochemical tests can show a substance is *likely* to have a psychoactive effect, proving psychoactivity via this method to the standard required for a conviction cannot be guaranteed.

15.182 It therefore remains to be seen, particularly in the case of novel substances, whether evidence from the Home Office's commercial testing supplier will be sufficiently robust to ensure convictions. There is also the question of whether the testing will be able to keep pace with the production of new types of substance, which was the essential problem under the pre-PSA 2016 regime, particularly in light of costs constraints.

OFFENCES

15.183 The PSA 2016 creates offences related to the production, supply or offer to supply, possession with intent to supply and importation or exportation of a psychoactive substance for human consumption. There is no possession offence except in the context of possession inside a custodial institution. The government did not want the legislation to lead to the mass criminalisation of young people. It has however been pointed out that 'importing' a psychoactive substance would include buying one from a non-UK based website. This could lead to individual users being prosecuted. In addition to the criminal offences, the Act also creates four civil sanctions: prohibition notices, premises notices, prohibition orders and premises orders. The PSA 2016, s 4 makes it an offence to produce a psychoactive substance, either for consumption by the producer himself or by some other person. The PSA 2016, s 5 makes it an offence to supply or offer to supply such a substance, and the PSA 2016, s 6 sets out aggravating factors in relation to supply, including committing the offence near a school, use of couriers who are under 18, and supply within a custodial institution. The PSA 2016, s 7 makes it an offence to possess a psychoactive substance with intent to supply. The PSA 2016, s 8 makes creates offences relating to the import and export of such substances.

15.184 Possession of a psychoactive substance in a custodial institution will be an offence under the PSA 2016, s 9. 'Custodial institution' is defined in the PSA 2016, s 6(10), and includes prisons, young offender institutions, removal centres and service custody premises. Use of 'legal highs' has been a particular problem in such institutions in recent years.

15.185 The PSA 2016, s 11 creates 'exceptions to offences'. There will be no offence in relation to the activities prohibited under the PSA 2016, ss 4–9 if 'in the circumstances in which it is carried on by that person, the activity is an exempt activity'. The exempt activities are listed in the PSA 2016, Sch 2, and relate to healthcare and research.

POWERS

15.186 The PSA 2016, s 36 confers powers to stop and search persons on a police or customs officer. The power is engaged where the officer has reasonable grounds to suspect that a person has committed, or is likely to commit, an offence under the PSA 2016, ss 4–9 or 26. There is no power to stop and search where an officer suspects that a person has in his possession a psychoactive substance intended for personal use, given that there is no possession offence under the PSA 2016. The PSA 2016, s 37 provides a similar power to enter and search vehicles.

15.187 The PSA 2016, s 39 provides powers to apply to a justice for a warrant to search premises for evidence of an offence under any of the PSA 2016, ss 4–9 and 26. 'Premises' is defined in the PSA 2016, s 59 to include vehicles or vessels. Applications for a search warrant must be made, in England and Wales and Northern Ireland, by a relevant enforcement officer. Unlike the powers to stop and search persons, vehicles and vessels, the power extends to local authority officers as well as police or customs officers.

15.188 There is a two-stage test for the grant of a search warrant. The first stage is that the court must be satisfied there are reasonable grounds to suspect that evidence of an offence under any of the PSA 2016, ss 4–9 and 26 is to be found on premises. The justice will apply the civil standard of proof. The second element is that any of the conditions in the PSA 2016, s 39(5) are met. The enforcement officer should only seek a warrant where the co-operation of the occupier of the premises is unlikely to be obtained or where the purpose of the search would be frustrated or seriously prejudiced if immediate entry could not be effected using a warrant. Part 2 of the PSA 2016, Sch 3 sets out the procedure for applying for a search warrant under the PSA 2016, s 39 in England and Wales and provides various safeguards.

15.189 The PSA 2016, s 41 enables a relevant enforcement officer searching a vehicle, vessel or premises, to examine anything found, including by testing substances. The PSA 2016, s 42 gives a power to require the production of documents and the PSA 2016, s 43 gives powers of seizure and detention.

SENTENCING

15.190 The PSA 2016, s 10 sets out penalties for those found guilty of committing the offences in the PSA 2016, ss 4–9. On summary conviction for an offence under the PSA 2016, ss 4–8 a person is liable to a fine and/or a prison sentence of up to 12 months. On conviction on indictment the court can impose a prison sentence of up to 7 years, a fine, or both. Upon summary conviction under the PSA 2016, s 9, possession in a custodial institution, a person can be fined and/or imprisoned for up to 12 months. Upon conviction on indictment the term can be up to 2 years.

CIVIL SANCTIONS

15.191 The PSA 2016, ss 12–35 provide for four civil sanctions – prohibition notices, premises notices, prohibition orders and premises orders. Breach of a prohibition or premises order is a criminal offence. These are intended to enable the police and local authorities to adopt a graded response in appropriate cases.

15.192 According to the Explanatory Notes to the PSA 2016, the use of these powers will enable law enforcement officers 'to take action swiftly to nip a problem in the bud or to adopt a more proportionate approach to low level offending. It will be a matter for the relevant law enforcement agency to determine which approach to adopt in any given circumstances. Where there is evidence of a criminal offence under the PSA 2016, ss 4–8, there is no requirement to apply the civil sanctions in the first instance as a criminal prosecution may be the appropriate action to take'.

15.193 A prohibition notice requires a person to desist from carrying out a prohibited activity. The definition of prohibited activity, set out in the PSA 2016, s 12, covers the conduct elements of the offences in the PSA 2016, ss 4, 5 and 8, together with assisting and encouraging those offences. Such a notice may be in general terms or specifically require the recipient to do something, such as stop offering to supply psychoactive substances from a particular website. A prohibition notice will be of indefinite duration unless withdrawn.

15.194 Premises notices provide a means to tackle prohibited activity taking place from premises. These are likely to mainly be used for 'head shops' where NSPs were often sold before the PSA 2016 came into force. If the respondent is the owner of premises being used by a third party for a prohibited activity, a premises notice could be used to compel the owner to take action against the tenant. Unlike prohibition notices a premises notice may only be given to an individual aged 18 or over.

15.195 Prohibition orders can be obtained either on an application to the courts by a relevant law enforcement agency under the PSA 2016, s 18, or on conviction of a person before the criminal courts for an offence under the PSA 2016, ss 4–8 (or an associated secondary offence). They are similar to prohibition notices in that they can place general or specific requirements on the recipient in relation to prohibited activities, but it is a criminal offence to contravene the order. It is also an offence to contravene a premises order. The requirements for obtaining such an order are set out in the PSA 2016, s 20. They will probably usually be obtained in cases where a premises notice has already been served and the recipient has failed to comply.

Chapter 16

TRAVEL

Contents

INTRODUCTION

16.1 Travel law is an area of law that exists because of a common subject matter, rather than by common legislative provisions or legal concepts. It has contractual, tortious and criminal aspects which are complicated by the inherently international character of the arrangements in question. The common thread is that it governs the arrangements between travellers (in this context, consumers) and travel providers, primarily travel agents, holiday operators and airlines. In addition to the large amount of domestic and European legislation on travel, there is also a vast body of case law interpreting and analysing the various provisions.

16.2 Given the breadth of the subject, an entire textbook could be dedicated to it. This chapter aims to give a practical overview of four of the more important aspects: package travel, timeshare agreements, the role of the Civil Aviation Authority ('the CAA') and the Air Travel Organiser's Licensing scheme, and compensation for delay, cancellation and damage.

PACKAGE TRAVEL

Introduction

16.3 Package holidays remain one of the most popular ways of travelling for UK consumers, with nearly half of all holidaymakers booking a package trip annually[1]. Formerly governed by the Package Travel, Package Holidays and Package Tours Regulations 1992[2] ('the PTR 1992'), they are now covered by the Package Travel and Linked Arrangements Regulations 2018[3] ('the PTLAR 2018'). These came into force on 1 July 2018[4] implementing a European Directive[5] and regulate the supply of combinations of travel services when offered for sale at an inclusive price. The Government's Explanatory Memorandum notes that the PTLAR 2018 was intended to 'reflect modern travel booking methods'[6].

[1] Association of British Travel Agent's *Consumer Holiday Trends Report 2014*.
[2] SI 1992/3288.
[3] SI 2018/634.
[4] The PTR 1992 continue to apply to contracts entered into before that date (as to which see previous editions of this work).
[5] Directive (EU) 2015/2302 of the European Parliament and of the Council on package travel and linked travel arrangements.
[6] At para 7.1.

16.4 It is impossible to ensure that a consumer's package holiday will be perfect, or even satisfactory. However, as with the PTR 1992, the PTLAR 2018 ensure that there are clearly defined consequences in the event of a dispute about the package of goods and services provided within the price. They impose detailed obligations on package travel operators in relation to the information given to consumers prior to purchase, the form and content of package travel contracts, and provide for rights of withdrawal for the consumer and cancellation for the travel operator. They also define terms to be implied into all package travel contracts and impose criminal liability upon operators for failure to comply with certain provisions.

16.5 The PTLAR were originally enacted in order to implement an EU directive, and as a result, in their original form, they contained various references to EU-related concepts. The PTLAR were therefore be amended by The Package Travel and Linked Travel Arrangements (Amendment) (EU Exit) Regulations 2018 ('the PTLAR (EU Exit) Regulations') to remove these references. These amendments took effect at the end of the implementation period by virtue of para 1(1) of Sch 5 to the European Union (Withdrawal Agreement) Act 2020. This chapter states, the law as amended by the PTLAR (EU Exit) Regulations, as it stands at 1 November 2021.

Application of the PTLAR 2018

16.6 By virtue of reg 3(1), the PTLAR 2018[1] apply to:

   (a)   packages offered for sale or sold by traders to travellers, and
   (b)   linked travel arrangements,

Excluded from their application are packages and linked travel arrangements for less than 24 hours, unless they include overnight accommodation, those facilitated 'occasionally on a not-for-profit basis for a limited group of travellers', and those purchased 'on the basis of a general agreement' (ie a business-to-business booking contract). Importantly, unlike the PTR 1992, which expressly limited the application to sales 'in the territory of the United Kingdom', there is no equivalent territorial limitation in the PTLAR 2018. Accordingly, they remedy the lacuna identified in previous editions of this work that traders could attempt to avoid the reach of the regulations by operating online from outside the UK.

[1]   SI 2018/634.

16.7 'Package' is defined by reg 2(5) of the PTLAR 2018[1]. The definition is considerably more complex than that which applied under the PTR 1992. It covers:

> . . . a combination of at least two different types of travel services for the purpose of the same trip of holiday, if—
>
> (a)   those services are combined by one trader, including at the request of, in accordance with, the selection of the traveller, before a single contract on all services is concluded; or
> (b)   those services are—
>> (i)   purchased from a single point of sale and selected before the traveller agrees to pay,
>> (ii)   offered, sold or charged at an inclusive or total price,
>> (iii)   advertised or sold under the term "package" or under a similar term,
>> (iv)   combined after the conclusion of a contract by which a trader entitles the traveller to choose among a selection of different types of travel services, or
>> (v)   purchased from separate traders through linked online booking processes where—
>>> (aa) the traveller's name, payment details and e-mail address are transmitted from the trader with whom the first contract is concluded to another trader or traders, and
>>> (bb) a contract with the latter trader or traders is concluded at the latest 24 hours after the confirmation of the booking of the first travel service,
>
> irrespective of whether the traveller concludes separate contracts with one or more travel service providers in respect of the services.

A 'travel service' is defined by reg 2(1) of the PTLAR 2018 as including the carriage of passengers, accommodation not for residential purposes, motor vehicle or equivalent rental or any other 'tourist service' not otherwise within the definition.

[1]   SI 2018/634.

16.8 This definition is considerably wider than that under the PTR 1992. Indeed, that appears to have been largely the intention behind the PTLAR 2018 – the Explanatory Memorandum explains that it broadens the definition 'to encompass new ways of purchasing package travel online.[1]' In particular, there is no longer any reference to a package as a 'pre-arranged combination' by the trader and the requirement of an 'inclusive or total price' is now one of five possible alternatives to bring arrangements within the definition, rather than an absolute requirement of the definition. It also updates the definition to take account of online travel deals which were obviously not considered by the PTR 1992. In short, the new definition now covers many more combined travel arrangements, whether at the customer or trader's instigation. Its effect is likely to be increased consumer protection.

¹ Paragraph 7.3.

16.9 For example, previous editions of this work criticised the decision in *CAA v Travel Republic Ltd*¹, where Travel Republic Ltd successfully argued that it was merely offering separate services for sale at the same time; the single price charged for all was as a matter of convenience. In concluding that it was not a package Elias LJ expressly referred to it as a situation where a customer was merely 'putting together his own combination . . . '. However, such a distinction is unlikely to survive close scrutiny under the PTLAR 2018, which expressly refers to a combination created at the selection of the customer.

¹ [2010] EWHC 1151 (Admin).

16.10 However, the existing jurisprudence relating to the words 'inclusive price' in the PTR 1992 definition of 'package' is likely to be of continuing relevance. In particular, the decision of the ECJ in *Rechberger & Ors v Republic of Austria*¹ should be noted. There, the claimants were newspaper competition winners who had to pay only nominal sums for accommodation and were given 'free' flights. The fact that the price did not reflect the value of the holiday did not matter; the nominal fee was all that was required to constitute an 'inclusive price'. Thus even if one element of the package is free there is still an 'inclusive price' within the meaning of the PTR 1992 since the 'free' element is on offer only in combination with the paid-for component(s).

¹ [1999] ECR I-3499.

16.11 Moreover, the PTLAR 2018 introduces a new concept of a 'linked travel arrangement' which removes the need for a single contract in order to obtain the protection afforded by the legislation. It is defined by reg 2(3) as:

> . . . at least two different types of travel service purchased for the purpose of the same trip or holiday, not constituting a package, resulting in the conclusion of separate contracts with individual service providers, if a trader facilitates—
>
> (a)   on the occasion of a single visit to, or contact with, a trader's point of sale, the separate selection and separate payment of each travel service by travellers; and
>
> (b)   in a targeted manner, the procurement of at least one additional travel service from another trader where a contract with such other trader is concluded at the latest 24 hours after the confirmation of the booking of the first travel service.

As such, the introduction of 'linked travel arrangements' removes a technical loophole which enabled traders to split up the provision of services so as to avoid coming within the PTR 1992. Now, even arrangements with different traders will ensure consumer protection so long as three conditions are met: (i) the services are for the same trip; (ii) they are with the same trader or procured from a different trader by the first; and (iii) if procured from a different trader, are concluded within 24 hours after the first travel service. By and large, linked travel arrangements do not benefit from the same protections as packages and the traveller must look to the service provider (rather than the organiser or trader) for redress. However, they are the subject of the insolvency protections at Pt 5 of the PTLAR 2018.

16.12 Other key definitions in reg 2(1) of the PTLAR 2018 include 'package travel contract', 'retailer' and 'traveller'. A 'package travel contract' is one or more 'covering the travel services included in the package'. Somewhat confusingly the definition also refers to a package 'provided under separate contracts' whereas a package is inherently defined by reference to a 'single contract'. Presumably, however, this must refer to separate contractual arrangements between the consumer and individual service providers, but combined by the package provider into a single deal. For example, a flight, car hire and accommodation from companies A, B and C could all be combined by the travel agent into a single composite 'package'. A definitional distinction is drawn between the 'organiser' and the 'retailer'; the former is a trader which combines and sells packages, while the latter simply sells them. Largely, liability for compliance is imposed upon the organiser rather than the retailer in order to simplify the position for the traveller[1]. Finally, a 'traveller' means any 'individual' who is seeking to conclude a contract or is 'entitled to travel on the basis of a contract concluded', within the scope of the PTLAR 2018.

[1]   See Explanatory Memorandum at para 7.4.

Informational duties

16.13 Unlike the PTR 1992 which included specific obligations about misleading information and brochures, the PTLAR 2018 impose more general informational requirements which attract criminal sanctions under reg 4(5). Anything not covered by this duty, relating to misleading information or aggressive practices, is likely to be within the scope of the Consumer Protection from Unfair Trading Regulations 2008. Pursuant to reg 4(1) these informational duties must be performed by either the organiser or the retailer. In the first instance 'before a package travel contract is concluded', the relevant person must provide the information in Schs 1–4. However, unlike under the PTR 1992, there is no requirement to do so 'in good time' (or similar) before the conclusion of the package. Pursuant to reg 4(4), information must be given in a 'clear, comprehensible and prominent manner' and, if in writing, must be legible.

16.14 Schedule 1 of the PTLAR 2018 imposes 16 specific items of information to be provided as applicable, which are largely self-explanatory. For example: the itinerary for the trip; meals included; any visits or excursions included; if part of a group tour, the approximate size of the group; the trader's details; and any visa requirements. However, of particular note is the requirement to set out the suitability of the trip if the traveller has 'reduced mobility'[1]. This appears to require an individualised statement for any disabled traveller which, in turn, would necessitate an assessment of what would be suitable.

[1]   Paragraph 10 of Sch 1.

16.15 Similarly to other European-based legislation[1] certain of the information to be provided under Sch 1 forms an 'integral part' of the package travel contract and must not be altered save with the traveller's express consent[2]. Thus, a failure to provide a package which matches the pre-contract information is actionable as a breach of an implied condition, giving the traveller a right to repudiate the agreement where possible[3].

[1]   For example the Consumer Contracts (Information, Cancellation and Additional Charges) Regulations 2013, SI 2013/3134.
[2]   SI 2018/634, reg 6(1).
[3]   SI 2018/634, reg 6(4).

16.16 Schedules 2 and 3 set out alternative mechanisms for providing information to the traveller about rights under the PTLAR 2018. The wording and bullet points in Sch 2 must be provided if 'use of hyperlinks is possible', which would cover where the package is arranged online or an email can be sent to the traveller prior to entry into the package travel contract. Schedule 3 sets out an alternative form of that information if it is to be provided otherwise than by way of hyperlink. The difference is that Sch 2 provides for a link to the complete text of the PTLAR 2018, whereas Sch 3 requires the provision of a web address where it can be accessed. In turn, Sch 4 provides wording where the package comes within reg 2(5)(b)(v), ie is purchased from separate traders through linked online booking processes.

16.17 Informational obligations also apply to linked travel arrangements. These are hidden in reg 26 of the PTLAR 2018. The trader facilitating the arrangement must state in a 'clear, comprehensible and prominent manner' that the traveller will not benefit from the protections of the PTLAR 2018 relating to packages but will benefit from the insolvency requirements (see below), and provide the traveller with a copy of the PTLAR 2018[1]. Depending upon the nature of the facilitation provided by the trader, the information provided to the traveller must include the wording at Schs 6, 7, 8, 9 or 10[2]. Failure by a trader to comply with the informational requirements for linked travel arrangements constitutes an offence triable either way and punishable by a fine[3].

[1]   SI 2018/634, reg 26(7).
[2]   SI 2018/634, reg 26(8).
[3]   SI 2018/634, reg 26(10).

The contract

16.18 Regulations 7–8 deal with the content of the package travel contract itself. Pursuant to reg 7(1) it must be in plain and intelligible language and, if in writing, legible. The contract must include the information in Sch 1 (thereby replicating the pre-contract information), as well as that set out in Sch 5. The latter is concerned more specifically with the parties' rights and duties under the agreement. For example, that the organiser is responsible for performance and is required to provide the traveller with assistance in accordance with reg 18, and the traveller must communicate any perceived non-compliance during the performance of the package in accordance with reg 15[1].

[1]   SI 2018/634, Sch 5, paras 2 and 5.

16.19 Regulation 7 also sets out detailed requirements as to when a copy of the package travel contract must be given to the traveller. In most cases, it must be given 'in a durable medium' at the time the agreement is concluded or 'without undue delay' afterwards[1]. If the contract is concluded face-to-face, the traveller has a right to a paper copy. However, if concluded off-premises, the trader can provide either a copy or 'confirmation of that contract'. Where the contract is a package within reg 2(5)(b)(v), ie is purchased from separate traders through linked online booking processes, the relevant person must be given 'the information necessary to comply with their obligations' by the other trader(s) in question[2]. All relevant receipts, vouchers, tickets and information on departure times and check-in must also be given 'in good time before the start of the package'.

1   SI 2018/634, reg 7(3).
2   SI 2018/634, reg 7(6).

16.20 Compliance with the requirements of reg 7(1), (3)–(6) and (9) is also an implied condition of the package travel contract and therefore entitles the traveller to claim repudiation in the event of breach[1]. Additionally, failure to comply with reg 7(2), (7) or (8) is a criminal offence triable either way and subject to a fine[2]. In civil proceedings concerning compliance with reg 7, reg 8(1) imposes a reverse burden of proof such that it is for the organiser or retailer 'to show that the provision was complied with'.

1   SI 2018/634, reg 7(10).
2   SI 2018/634, reg 7(12).

Transfer of booking

16.21 Unlike under the PTR 1992, where the right to transfer was applicable only where the traveller was 'prevented from proceeding with the package', the PTLAR 2018 provide a far wider right of transfer. Regulation 9(1) provides that he may do so to any transferee who 'satisfies all conditions applicable to that contract'. For example, if a traveller must be a minimum age or meet certain physical fitness requirements to undertake a trip, those must also be met by the transferee. Reasonable notice of transfer must be given to the organiser and, in any event, not less than 7 days before the package starts 'is always deemed to be reasonable'[1]. That may potentially be a very tight timescale for package organisers who may have to make considerable amendments to bookings as a result of the transfer. In any event, an organiser may impose reasonable costs in the event of a transfer which 'must not exceed the cost incurred by the organiser'; the transferor and transferee are jointly and severally liable for such costs[2].

1   SI 2018/634, reg 9(2).
2   SI 2018/634, reg 9(4)–(5).

Alteration, withdrawal and cancellation

16.22 Part 3 of the PTLAR 2018 concerns the alteration of the package travel contract and withdrawal by the traveller or cancellation by the organiser. In relation to alteration, the price is treated differently from any other term of the contract. Regulation 10(2) specifically provides that the price may only be increased following conclusion of the contract unless the contract: (i) states an increase may be made; (ii) states increases may to the cost of carriage because of the cost of fuel, taxes or fees on travel services, or exchange rates; (iii) provides that the customer has a right to a price reduction in the event of any corresponding decrease in costs; and (iv) sets out how the revisions to the price are to be calculated. In any event, notification of a price increase cannot be given less than 20 days before the start of the package. In effect, these provisions reflect in this specific context, the general law on unfair contract terms.

16.23 The provisions dealing with the alteration of other terms of the contract are more general but, arguably, more restrictive for the organiser. Regulation 11(2) provides that he cannot unilaterally alter the terms before the start of the package unless the contract allows him to do so, the changes are 'insignificant' and the traveller is notified by a durable medium in a clear, comprehensible and prominent manner. It is the requirement of insignificance which ultimately curtails an organiser's ability to make changes. It is also the provision which is likely to lead to disputes between the parties – what a traveller might consider 'insignificant' could be different to the organiser's view. For example, a change of car hire firm may be considered important to the customer even if the vehicle type, dates and price remain the same. Ultimately, this provision is aimed at allowing only very minor changes; by analogy the common law concept of 'de minimis' may be of some use in considering whether the change is 'insignificant'. The only exception to that general rule is that the main characteristics may be altered as a result of circumstances beyond the organiser's control.

16.24 Special requirements apply to contractual alterations of the main characteristics of the contract and price increases of more than 8%. Where such alterations are proposed, the organiser must inform the traveller in a durable medium of the proposed changes and his rights as to termination or substitution, along with a reasonable time period for responding and the potential consequences of failure to do so[1]. Upon receipt of such information, the traveller may within the period specified by the organiser either accept the changes or terminate the contract without charge. In the event of termination, the traveller is entitled to a full refund without undue delay and, in any event, within 14 days. Alternatively, if offered by the organiser, he may accept an alternative substitute package with a price reduction where appropriate. If the traveller fails to make any response to notification of such alterations, the organiser 'may' terminate and refund all payments made[2]. This latter right appears to be entirely at the organiser's discretion.

[1] SI 2018/634, reg 11(4).
[2] SI 2018/634, reg 11(5)–(8) and (11).

16.25 Both parties have some right to terminate the contract under regs 12 and 13. The traveller can do so at any time before the start of the contract subject to payment of any specified reasonable termination fee[1]. However, the fee is not payable in the event that the termination is the result of 'unavoidable and extraordinary circumstances occurring at the place of destination or its immediate vicinity' which 'significantly affect' performance or carriage[2]. One of the key additions into the PTLAR 2018 is a specific definition of 'unavoidable and extraordinary circumstances'. It is said to refer to a situation 'beyond the control of the party who seeks to rely on such a situation... and the consequences of which could not have been avoided even if all reasonable measures had been taken.'[3]. Thus, it must be the result of some external act or omission which could not have therefore been avoided by the party relying upon it.

Examples might include natural disasters, major terrorism or other events of that magnitude[4]. The traveller's right to terminate is an implied term in all package travel contracts. In the event that the traveller terminates the package contract in accordance with reg 12(2), the organiser must reimburse any payments made (having deducted the fee) without 'undue delay' and in any event not later than 14 days after termination[5].

[1]   SI 2018/634, reg 12(2)–(4).
[2]   SI 2018/634, reg 12(7).
[3]   SI 2018/634, reg 3(1).
[4]   For example, under the PTR, it was held that a SARS outbreak in China did not constitute an 'unavoidable' circumstance because there had been widespread World Health Organisation and FCO warnings against travel to the region before the travellers had booked the trip (*Lambert v Travelsphere Ltd* (unreported) 1 September 2004, Peterborough CC).
[5]   SI 2018/634, reg 14.

16.26 As is to be expected, the organiser's right to terminate is more restricted. It may only do so in one of two circumstances – either if the number of persons enrolled for the package is 'smaller than the minimum amount stated in the contract' or in the event of 'unavoidable and extraordinary circumstances'. If either requirement is met he may terminate with the required notice and give a full refund without any further liability for compensation[1]. In particular, the latter provides an organiser with a defence to any claim for consequential damages, ie for the traveller booking an alternative trip at an increased price or suffering loss or upset as a result.

[1]   SI 2018/634, reg 13(2)–(3).

16.27 However, this restriction on liability applies only to termination in the two specified circumstances. If the organiser seeks to terminate for any other reason (assuming it is contractually entitled to do so), there is no reason why common law compensation should not be recoverable. For example, in *Robson v Thomson Holidays Ltd*[1] (under the PTR 1992) the claimant specifically requested direct flights which the tour operator confirmed it had arranged. However, as a result of an administrative error, it had in fact booked indirect flights (albeit these made no difference to travel time or length of holiday). The consumer treated this as a repudiatory breach (admitted by the defendant) and sought a full refund of over £5,000. When the defendant refused, the claimant instead reserved club class seats for a direct flight. Upon her return she sued the defendant for the additional expense of having done so (some £10,000). It was undisputed that the club class seats were the only direct flights available which conformed to the claimant's existing dates and requirements. On appeal it was held that the consumer had, in effect, put together her own package of superior quality, for which she was entitled to be compensated.

[1]   Unreported, 5 April 2002, Luton CC.

Performance of the package

16.28 As noted above, the organiser has primary responsibility for performance of the package travel contract; that is so irrespective of whether the organiser or a third-party is to provide the services in question[1]. The organiser's obligations are extensive and are set out in regs 15–18 of the PTLAR 2018. The primary obligation at reg 15(4) is, if services are not performed in accordance with the contract, to 'remedy the lack of conformity within a

reasonable period', unless to do so is either 'impossible' or 'entails disproportionate costs, taking into account the extent of the lack of conformity and the
value of the travel services affected'. The latter exception has the potential to
cause some difficulty for organisers since there is no further guidance on when
costs become 'disproportionate'. Although in most situations it will be obvious,
borderline cases may give rise to dispute. For example, a traveller may place a
'value' on the services affected beyond their face cost which justify remediation.

1   SI 2018/634, reg 15(2).

16.29 In the event that the organiser fails to comply with its duty to remedy
within a reasonable period, reg 16 applies[1]. That provision implies as a term in
all package travel contracts a right to a price reduction for any period during
which there is a lack of conformity in the services provided unless proven that
it is 'attributable to the traveller'[2]. In addition, the organiser must, without
undue delay, offer the traveller compensation for damage sustained as a result
save where the organiser can prove that the lack of conformity was attributable
to the traveller, attributable to an unconnected third party and was 'unforeseeable or unavoidable', or was 'due to unavoidable and extraordinary circumstances'[3]. The latter phrase is also governed by the definition in reg 3(1).
Moreover, it is clearly intended to cover a different (and wider) set of circumstances than the 'unforeseeable or unavoidable' acts of a third party under
reg 16(4). For example, there may be instances where strike action is 'unavoidable and extraordinary' under reg 16(4)(b) but is not to be considered as
'unforeseeable and unavoidable' under reg 16(4)(c).

1   SI 2018/634, reg 15(5).
2   SI 2018/634, reg 16(2).
3   SI 2018/634, reg 16(4).

16.30 As noted above, the organiser has primary responsibility for performance of the package travel contract; that is so irrespective of whether the
organiser or a third-party is to provide the services in question[1]. The organiser's obligations are extensive and are set out in regs 15–18 of the PTLAR 2018.
The primary obligation at reg 15(4) is, if services are not performed in
accordance with the contract, to 'remedy the lack of conformity within a
reasonable period', unless to do so is either 'impossible' or 'entails disproportionate costs, taking into account the extent of the lack of conformity and the
value of the travel services affected.' The latter exception has the potential to
cause some difficulty for organisers since there is no further guidance on when
cost become 'disproportionate'. Although in most situations it will be obvious,
borderline cases may give rise to dispute. For example, a traveller may place a
'value' on the services affected beyond their face cost which justify remediation.

1   SI 2018/634, reg 15(2).

16.31 Where the organiser is unable to provide 'a significant proportion' of the
services agreed under the contract, it must offer 'suitable alternative arrangements of, where possible, equivalent or higher quality'[1]. Alternatively, if unable
to do so, a price reduction must be provided to the traveller[2]. In either case a
traveller must accept the alternative arrangements unless 'they are not comparable' or the price reduction is 'inadequate'[3]. The question of comparability is
likely to be a key area for disputes between travellers and organisers. A
consumer may book a particular trip for any number of personal reasons which

may mean, in his or her view, an alternative offered is not comparable. However, ultimately the question of comparability must be objective, ie are the facilities, location, timings and/or additional costs broadly equivalent to the service originally contracted for?

1   SI 2018/634, reg 15(8).
2   SI 2018/634, reg 15(9).
3   SI 2018/634, reg 15(10).

16.32 In the event of a failure by the organiser to remedy within a reasonable period under reg 15(4) the traveller is entitled to terminate the package free-of-charge and, where appropriate, a price reduction, compensation or both under reg 16. Equally, if the traveller rejects the alternative arrangements under reg 15(10), he may be entitled to a price reduction, damages or both in accordance with reg 16 without terminating[1]. If the termination occurs during the course of the trip, the organiser must also arrange repatriation 'without undue delay and at no extra cost'[2]. Further, if the organiser is unable to ensure the traveller's return 'because of unavoidable and extraordinary circumstances' it must 'bear the cost of necessary accommodation' of an equivalent standard where possible for up to 3 nights per traveller[3].

1   SI 2018/634, regs 15(11)–(12).
2   SI 2018/634, reg 15(13).
3   SI 2018/634, reg 15(13).

16.33 As was the case under the PTR 1992, the organiser may impose the same limits on compensation that would apply under applicable international conventions[1]. In addition, save for personal injury or death, which cannot be limited or excluded, the organisation may limit his liability in other cases to 'not less than 3 times the total price of the package.'[2] Further, travellers' rights to compensation under reg 16 are expressly not to affect other rights under EU legislation or international conventions[3]. These provisions reflect the mandatory rights created by international conventions and the requirements of the Consumer Rights Act 2015 ('CRA 2015')[4]. A traveller is therefore able to present a claim under the PTLAR 2018, other relevant EU legislation or international convention[5]. That right would appear to exclude any jurisdictional argument that a claim has been brought under the wrong legislation or must be pursued under one statutory compensation scheme or another. In any event, in light of reg 16(5) and (7), the route to compensation chosen should make no substantive difference either to the traveller's rights or the organiser's liability. The only potential difference may be as to the applicable limitation period[6]. In any event, reg 16(9) requires a deduction from compensation payable under the PTLAR 2018 to take account of any other sums payable under other EU legislation or international conventions so as 'to avoid over-compensation'.

1   SI 2018/634, reg 16(5).
2   SI 2018/634, reg 16(6).
3   'International conventions' are expressly defined as referring to the Carriage of Air Conventions, the Athens Convention of 1974 on the Carriage of Persons and their Luggage by Sea and the Convention of 1980 concerning International Carriage by Rail (COTIF).
4   Formerly in the Unfair Contract Terms Act 1977, s 65(1).
5   SI 2018/634, reg 16(8).
6   See below in relation to Regulation 261/2004.

16.34 However, where the organiser refuses to remedy a lack of conformity, the traveller is entitled to self-help by remedying the lack of conformity and seeking reimbursement of expenses suffered[1].

[1] SI 2018/634, reg 15(6).

16.35 Under the PTLAR 2018 the organiser's obligations extend beyond simply providing the package in accordance with the contract; in addition it must 'give appropriate assistance without undue delay' during the trip if the traveller 'is in difficulty'[1]. Although the word 'difficulty' is somewhat vague, clarification is provided by reg 18(2)(a) which refers to giving information on 'health services, local authorities and consular services'. The provision is therefore clearly aimed at medical emergencies, lost passports or paperwork, legal disputes and the like. A fee can be charged by the organiser for the provision of assistance but it must be 'reasonable'[2].

[1] SI 2018/634, reg 18(2).
[2] SI 2018/634, reg 18(3).

Civil claims for breach of the PTLAR 2018

16.36 Regulation 16 of the PTLAR 2018 is phrased primarily on the assumption that compensation will be payable by the organiser to the traveller without resort to litigation (for example, the reference to 'without undue delay' in reg 16(3)). Inevitably, however, there will be instances where court action must be taken. Unlike the PTR 1992, each of the provisions of the PTLAR 2018 is implied into the parties' contract as a term. Therefore, if (adequate) compensation is not offered or paid by the organiser, the traveller will have separate claims both for non-conformity and failure to properly remedy. Insofar as litigation is necessary, much of the old case law under the PTR 1992 remains relevant. What follows is an overview of the key issues which arose thereunder.

16.37 One of the key issues which arose under the PTR 1992 was the difference between 'strict' and 'fault-based' obligations. It arose from the fact that liability accrued to the package provider irrespective of whether another supplier, further down the chain, had responsibility for the issue in question. That is also the case under the PTLAR 2018. The issue was considered at great length and resolved by the Court of Appeal in *Hone v Going Places Leisure Travel Ltd*[1]. In *Hone* the claimant booked a package holiday with the defendant via its Teletext service. On the return flight, the plane had to make an emergency landing and passengers were required to disembark via emergency inflatable chutes. As the claimant descended the chute he saw a 'huge' woman, estimated to weigh around 25 stone, stuck at the bottom and unable to get up. He collided with her and was struck by his wife as she followed him down the chute. As a result, he suffered serious spinal injuries.

[1] [2001] EWCA Civ 947.

16.38 The claimant sued the defendant alleging inadequate supervision of the evacuation and contended that reg 15 imposed absolute liability on the other party for the injuries sustained. At first instance Douglas Brown J rejected the claim because the claimant had not proven that a party was at fault, for whom the defendant was responsible:

' . . . the claimant has wholly failed to establish that this accident was any-one's fault. Before criticising employees of an airline in respect of failure arising in an emergency crash, I would need to know much more than I am told in evidence in this case.'

16.39 The claimant then appealed to the Court of Appeal which also rejected the arguments advanced on his behalf. Longmore LJ said:

'In the absence of any contrary intention, the normal implication will be that the service contracted for will be rendered with reasonable care and skill. Of course, absolute obligations may be assumed. If the brochure . . . promises a swimming pool, it will be a term of the contract that a swimming pool will be provided. But in the absence of express wording, there would not be an absolute obligation, for example, to ensure that the holiday-maker catches no infection while swimming in the swimming pool.'

16.40 Thus, following *Hone*, a two stage approach was adopted which is also potentially applicable under the new legislation. In the example of a coach which breaks down during an excursion run by a local operator, the first question is whether the coach operator acted with all reasonable care and skill as per the definition of 'extraordinary and unavoidable' at reg 3(1). If not, then it follows that the organiser will be strictly liable. If the local operator did act with reasonable care and skill, however, then no liability accrues to the organiser.

16.41 In *X v Kuoni Travel Ltd*[1], under the PTR 1992, it was held that a claimant must prove:

'either a failure of performance or . . . the improper performance of the contract and that improper performance has to amount to a breach of contract. That is to say that there has been a failure to perform the contract with reasonable care and skill and in the sense that it must be shown that there is a fault on the part of the other party to the contract or the supplier of the relevant service for whose fault the Defendant is responsible. The starting point must be the contract with the Claimant made with the Defendant . . . '

[1]   [2016] EWHC 3090 (QB).

16.42 Thus, a claim for personal injury following sexual assault by an electrician employed by the hotel was rejected. In assaulting the claimant, the employee 'was not discharging any of the duties he was employed to do' and, in any event, the services of an electrician 'were not services which the defendant agreed to provide to the claimant under the contract'. The highest the defendant's contractual obligations could be put was that it would supply electricity during the claimant's stay and do so with reasonable care and skill[1].

[1]   At [44].

16.43 On appeal to the Supreme Court, two issues were raised: first, did the rape and assault of Mrs. X constitute improper performance of the obligations owed by Kuoni under the package travel contract; and secondly, if so, is any of Kuoni's liability excluded by reg 15(2)(c) of the 1992 Regulations? These questions were made the subject-matter of a reference to the CJEU.

16.44 On the first issue, the Supreme Court held that a broad view should be taken of the obligations owed by a package travel operator. Those obligations include not only the provision of transport, accommodation and meals, but also other ancillary services. In the instant case, one of those ancillary services was assisting guests by guiding them from one part of the hotel to another. The Supreme Court rejected the argument that the employee who carried out the rape and assault was a 'supplier of services'; however, the court held that non-performance or improper performance, although caused by acts committed by employees under the control of a supplier of services, is such as to render the organiser liable in accordance with Art 5(1) of the Directive. The rape and assault of Mrs X amounted to a failure to provide that service with proper care. Accordingly, it amounted to a *prima facie* breach by Kuoni.

16.45 As to the second issue, the CJEU had held that the exemption in Art 5(1) (which is implemented by reg 15(2) of the 1992 Regulations) did not apply because the acts or omissions of an employee of a supplier of services cannot be regarded as events which cannot be foreseen or forestalled within the meaning of Art 5(2) of the Directive. Thus, the defence in reg 15(2)(c) of the 1992 Regulations was not available to Kuoni.

16.46 As to the relevant standard to be applied, the key authority is *Wilson v Best Travel Ltd*[1], where it was held that local standards were what the situation had to be benchmarked against:

> 'Save where uniform international Regulations apply, there are bound to be differences in the safety standards applied in respect of many hazards of modern life between one country and another. All civilised countries attempt to cater for those hazards by imposing mandatory Regulations. The duty of care of the tour operator is likely to extend to checking that local safety Regulations are complied with.'

Although this decision related to the law prior to the implementation of the PTR 1992, it has since been affirmed in numerous cases as a generally applicable principle (eg Swinton Thomas LJ in *C (A Child) v Thomson Tour Operations Ltd*[2]).

[1] [1993] 1 All ER 352 (QBD).
[2] [2000] CA BS/1999/1321.

16.47 Under the PTR 1992 relevant matters when considering what is reasonable included local regulations, laws safety standards and customs. The only exception to Philips J's conclusion in *Wilson* is where the local standard is so poor or the absence of a standard so stark that a fully informed and reasonable consumer would decline to stay in the location:

> ' . . . I do not consider that the tour operator owes a duty to boycott a hotel because of the absence of some safety feature which would be found in an English hotel unless the absence of such a feature might leave a reasonable holidaymaker to decline to take a holiday at the hotel in question.'

However, the circumstances in which that might apply are likely to be few and far between.

Insolvency protection

16.48 Part 5 of the PTLAR 2018 deals with insolvency protection for travellers. The requirements are extended versions of those which were inserted into the PTR 1992 by the Package Travel, Package Holidays and Package Tours (Amendment) Regulations 1995[1]. Both the old and new law implement an underlying European directive imposing such requirements[2]. Failure to put in place the appropriate protections is a criminal offence triable either way[3]. The central obligation at reg 19(1) is for the organiser to 'provide effective security', in the event of its insolvency, to cover the 'foreseeable costs' of 'refunding all payments made by or on behalf of all travellers' for services not performed and the carriage of passengers affected as a result. Such security must provide for organisers whether established in the United Kingdom or not, so long as they sell or offer to sell packages in the UK 'or by any means [direct] such activities to the United Kingdom'[4].

1   SI 1995/1648.
2   Article 7 of Directive 90/314 on package travel, package holidays and package tours.
3   SI 2018/634, reg 25.
4   SI 2018/634, reg 19(4).

16.49 The ECJ considered the meaning and purpose of the previous equivalent requirement in *Verein für Konsumenteninformation v Österreichische Kreditversicherrungs AG*[1]. There, Austrian consumers had booked a package through a travel operator, Karthago-Reisen GmbH, and had paid in full in advance for flights and half-board. However, Karthago-Reisen became insolvent and therefore did not pay the hotel. The hotel owner demanded payment directly from the consumers and refused to allow them to leave the resort in the event that they did not do so. When Karthago-Reisen's insurers refused to compensate the consumers, a claim was brought via the Austrian consumer regulator. The question was whether the payment of sums by the consumers in those circumstances constituted 'security for repatriation' within the meaning of the implementing directive.

1   [1998] ECR I-2949.

16.50 At para 19, the court held:

'The security for the "refund of money paid over" covers cases in which the organiser's insolvency becomes known after the contract has been concluded and before it has begun to be performed or cases in which the services are interrupted while the contract is being performed and the consumer must be reimbursed a proportion of the money paid over corresponding to the services which have not been provided. The purpose of the security for the "repatriation of the consumer" is to ensure that the consumer does not become stranded, during the performance of the contract, at the place where he is staying, through the carrier refusing, on account of the organiser's insolvency, to supply the service of transporting the consumer back to his place of departure.'

Accordingly, it was held that the Austrian consumers' situation was within the scope of the relevant provision of the implementing directive.

16.51 Regulations 20 and 21 of the PTLAR 2018 both relate to 'bonding', which refers to payment by an approved body of which the organiser is a member in the event of its insolvency. In effect, an indemnity provided by the organiser's professional body. Regulation 20(1) provides that, if the organiser is to rely upon a bond, it must be sufficient to pay sums payable in accordance with reg 20(3)–(5) as applicable. Regulation 20(3) refers to the sum which may 'reasonably be expected to enable all monies paid by or on behalf of travellers'. Under reg 20(4), that sum is the smaller of either 25% of 'all payments which the organiser estimates [it] will receive . . . in the 12 month period from the date of entry into force of the bond . . . ' or 'the maximum amount of all payments' expected to be held by the organiser for contracts 'which have not been fully performed'. The 25% requirement is a considerable increase on the 10% formerly specified by reg 18(4) of the PTR 1992. Finally, reg 20(5) relates to sums held for the carriage of passengers affected by insolvency. Such sums must be no less than the minimum sum required by (4) plus such additional sums as the organiser 'may reasonably expect' to be needed for 'the reasonably foreseeable costs of repatriating the travellers' and, if necessary, their accommodation prior to repatriation.

16.52 Before a bond is entered into the organiser must inform the approved body which is providing the indemnity of the sum required under reg 19(3)–(5), whereupon the body will notify the organiser whether it considers the sum to be sufficient. If not, it must state a sum which is considered to be sufficient to protect travellers[1].

[1]   SI 2018/634, reg 20(6).

16.53 Regulation 21 deals with bonding where the approved body has a 'reserve fund or insurance'. Whereas reg 20 is concerned with an indemnity payable directly by the approved body, this type of bond relies upon external arrangements made by the approved body to cover such sums. Again, specific minimum sums are required to be covered by such bonds. These are broadly replicate reg 20(3)–(5) save that the relevant sum is 'not less than 10%' of all payments the organiser estimates it will receive in the year from the date of entry into force of the bond[1]. The reserve fund or insurance held by the approved body must be provided by an organisation authorised in the UK, the Channel Islands or the Isle of Man[2].

[1]   SI 2018/634, reg 21(4).
[2]   SI 2018/634, reg 21(7)(a).

16.54 The third alternative to either the provision of security or a bond is insurance. Under reg 22(4), the policy must not contain any condition which would exclude liability upon the occurrence of the events giving rise to the claim and must cover the costs of 'refunding all payments' made by travellers for services not provided as a result of insolvency plus the cost of repatriation if necessary.

16.55 Finally, organisers can also hold money paid by for travellers in trust, to be repaid in the event of insolvency (reg 23). Such monies must be held until the contract has been performed or the sums in question have been repaid or forfeited by the traveller. The person appointed as trustee in relation to such monies must be independent of the organiser. However, where a trust is established in accordance with reg 23, the organiser must also have insurance to cover the costs of repatriating the travellers and, if necessary, financing accommodation prior to repatriation[1]. Insofar as the insurance extends beyond those liabilities to cover the cost of other services provided as part of the package, such sums do not also need to be held on trust by the organiser[2].

1   SI 2018/634, reg 24(2).
2   SI 2018/634, reg 24(4).

16.56 Equivalent obligations to that set out in regs 19–25 also applies for 'linked travel arrangements' facilitated by 'any trader'[1].

1   SI 2018/634, reg 26.

Due diligence defence

16.57 All of the criminal offences created by the PTLAR 2018 are subject to the due diligence defence at reg 32(1):

> . . . it is a defence for that person to show that the person took all reasonable steps and exercised all due diligence to avoid committing the offence.

Where the defendant wishes to allege that ' . . . the offence was due – (a) to the act or default of another; or (b) to reliance on information giving by another' notice must be given identifying the relevant third party not less than 'seven clear days before the hearing of the proceedings . . . '[1]. A full analysis of the defence of due diligence is to be found in CHAPTER 4, Criminal Enforcement[2].

1   SI 2018/634, reg 32(2).
2   See CHAPTER 4, Criminal Enforcement.

TIMESHARES

Introduction

16.58 Timeshares have been traditionally controversial products. In theory, they enable a holidaymaker to enjoy the benefits of ownership of a holiday property for a specified period of each year. However, they are often entered into as the result of high pressure selling techniques and misrepresentations, which has previously led to complex litigation under the Consumer Credit Act 1974, s 75[1]. Timeshare contracts are now governed by the Timeshare, Holiday Products, Resale and Exchange Contracts Regulations 2010[2] ('TSR 2010') which came into force from 23 February 2011 and implement EU Directive 2008/122/EC[3]. The TSR 2010 repealed the Timeshare Act 1992 and revoked various other secondary legislation made under it[4]. As with the PTR 1992, they include both civil and criminal aspects, all of which are considered below. However, their primary focus is threefold: the provision of information, the control of advertising and the creation of a right of withdrawal.

1   *Jarrett v Barclays Bank Ltd* [1999] 1 QB 1.
2   SI 2010/2960.
3   Directive on the protection of consumers for certain aspects of timeshare, long-term holiday product, resale and exchange contracts.
4   TSR 2010, SI 2010/2960, reg 36.

Scope of the TSR 2010

16.59 In fact the TSR 2010 apply not just to timeshares but to any contract which comes within the definition of a 'regulated contract'; that includes any 'holiday accommodation contract' which is not an 'excluded arrangement' (reg 3). A 'holiday accommodation contract' means: a 'timeshare', 'long term holiday product', 'resale' or 'exchange' contract (reg 4). Each of those types of contract is defined in regs 7–10 of the TSR 2010.

16.60 Pursuant to reg 7(1)(a) a 'timeshare contract' means a contract 'between a trader and a consumer . . . under which the consumer, for consideration, acquires the right to use overnight accommodation for more than one period of occupation . . . '. Accommodation 'includes a reference to accommodation within a pool of accommodation'[1]. Accordingly, it does not have to be specific accommodation but, rather, can be one allocated from an identified group or 'floating'. This definition of timeshare improves that found in the Timeshare Act 1992. It no longer refers just to agreements relating to 'immoveable property' and decreases the period of agreements caught to those of one year in duration.

[1]   TSR 2010, SI 2010/2960, reg 7(2).

16.61 Regulation 8(1)(a) defines 'long-term holiday product contract' as a contract 'the main effect of which is that the consumer, for consideration, acquires the right to obtain discounts or other benefits in respect of accommo-dation . . . irrespective of whether the contract makes provision for the consumer to acquire other services'. Therefore, the difference with a timeshare is that a long-term holiday product contract gives no definitive right to use accommodation. Both a timeshare and long-term holiday product contracts must have a duration of more than one year or, alternatively, contain a provision allowing for it to be renewed or extended so as to have a duration of more than one year[1].

[1]   TSR 2010, SI 2010/2960, regs 7(1)(b) and 8(1)(b).

16.62 A 'resale contract' is defined by reg 9 as one to assist a consumer in buying or selling rights under either a timeshare or long-term holiday product contract. Resale contracts are where many complaints are made. Often con-sumers are the subject of an unsolicited telephone call telling them that a 'definite buyer' has been found for their timeshare and a market offer has been made to buy it. They are then required to make an upfront payment of several hundred pounds to cover 'administration costs' or similar. Once payment is made the consumer is then told the sale has fallen through, but that a meeting has been set up with an available corporate buyer. These meetings often take place abroad where the consumer is made to sit through a lengthy high-pressure sale presentation to join a bogus holiday club in exchange for their timeshare contract plus a top-up payment.

16.63 Regulation 10(1) defines an 'exchange contract' as one between a consumer under a timeshare contract and a trader where the consumer joins a 'timeshare exchange system'. A 'timeshare exchange system' is one which allows the consumer to swap with other persons the benefits of other accom-modation or services for use of the consumer's timeshare accommodation[1].

[1]   TSR 2010, SI 2010/2960, reg 10(2).

16.64 Under reg 5, the TSR 2010 only apply to the above holiday accommodation contracts which also fall within reg 5(2)–(4) being contracts which are governed:

- by the law of the UK or part of the UK[1];
- by the law of a non-EEA state relating to accommodation which is immovable property in an EEA state, the parties to which are subject to the jurisdiction of the courts of the UK[2];
- by the law of a non-EEA state not relating to immoveable property but where the trader carries on 'commercial or professional activities' in the UK and the contract falls within those activities[3].

[1] TSR 2010, SI 2010/2960, reg 5(2).
[2] TSR 2010, SI 2010/2960, reg 5(3).
[3] TSR 2010, SI 2010/2960, reg 5(4).

16.65 The TSR 2010 considerably reduce the jurisdictional scope of their protection, in comparison with the old Timeshare Act 1992. In particular, it provides for special rules on consumer contracts for goods and services[1], which may, in practice coincide with the above. In addition, the contract in question cannot be regulated by the TSR 2010 if it is an 'excluded contract'[2]. These include life insurance investment products that incorporate access to holiday accommodation on a timeshare-like basis, but which are regulated by the Financial Services and Markets Act 2000.

[1] Articles 15 and 16.
[2] See SI 2010/2960, reg 6.

16.66 'Trader' and 'consumer' are defined by reference to whether the party is 'acting for the purposes of a trade, business, craft or profession' (reg 11). These concepts are considered in greater detail in CHAPTER 2, Interpretation of Consumer Law.

16.67 Accordingly, the TSR 2010 treat all holiday accommodation contracts which fall within their scope in the same manner and apply the same rights and protections to consumers under all of them. In particular, consumer under all types of holiday accommodation contracts are given the 14-day cooling-off period during which time the taking of accounts or payments is banned (see below). Further, they are all subject to the specified information to be provided before contracting and to be included in the contract. Finally, the TSR 2010 are expressed to be without prejudice to the application of the PTR 1992 (reg 37). Accordingly, if a regulated holiday accommodation contract also falls within the scope of the PTR 1992, both sets of regulations apply.

Pre-contract matters

16.68 Pre-contract matters are dealt with by regs 12–14 under Pt 3 of the TSR 2010[1].

[1] SI 2010/2960, regs 12–14.

Key information

16.69 Regulation 12 deals with 'key information' which must be provided to the consumer by the trader 'in good time before entering into the contract'. The 'key information' is defined by reg 12(3)[1] as:

(a)   the information required by Part 1 of the standard information form . . . ,
(b)   the information set out in Part 2 of that form, and
(c)   any additional information required by Part 2 of that form.

Schedules 1–4 to the TSR 2010 set out the 'key information' for timeshare, long-term holiday accommodation, resale and exchange contracts, respectively. Each of the Schedules is divided into three parts.

[1]   SI 2010/2960, reg 12(3).

16.70 Generally-speaking, Pt 1 of each Schedule relates to the specifics of the contract. These include:

- identity, place of residence and legal status of the trader(s);
- description of the product or services (as applicable);
- duration of the agreement;
- price (including obligatory costs);
- whether the trader has signed up to a code of conduct and, if so, where it can be found.

16.71 Part 2 then requires what is described as 'general information' relating to the consumer's right to withdraw from and terminate the contract, and that the contract may be governed by the law of another country.

16.72 Finally, Pt 3 of each of the Schedules sets out the 'additional information' to which the consumer is entitled. If the trader does not include it within the pre-contract information, it must state 'where it can be obtained specifically (for example, under which chapter of a general brochure) . . . '. The information under Pt 3 includes matters such as:

- information about the rights acquired under the contract, eg conditions governing their exercise;
- information on the properties including details of immovable property and services available, eg refuse collection or water maintenance;
- where applicable, certain information on properties still under construction;
- information on costs and termination of the contract (including the consequences of doing so);
- additional information, eg on maintenance and repairs to the property, languages available for communication and, where available, out-of-court dispute resolution.

16.73 Regard should be had to the relevant Part of the relevant Schedule in any given case to determine what 'key information' ought to have been provided at the pre-contract stage. In any event, the key information must be 'clear, comprehensible and accurate' and 'sufficient to enable the consumer to make an informed decision about whether or not to enter into the contract'[1]. In particular, the latter may present some difficulty since it suggests a subjective test according to the needs of each consumer (by use of the words 'the consumer'). However, it must be the case that the trader needs to simply consider what information would be appropriate for the average consumer in all the circumstances. Further, the 'key information' must be in the standard form in the Schedules (as required by reg 13), in writing, provided free of charge and in a manner which is easily accessible to the consumer[2].

1   TSR 2010, SI 2010/2960, reg 12(4).
2   TSR 2010, SI 2010/2960, reg 12(5)(a)–(d).

Marketing and sales

16.74 Regulation 14 governs the marketing and sale of holiday accommodation contracts. All advertising must now 'indicate how the key information . . . can be obtained'[1]. Further a trader must not offer a consumer to enter into a contract at a promotional or sales event unless the invitation 'clearly indicates the commercial purpose and nature of the event' and 'the key information . . . is made available to the consumer for the duration of the event'[2]. This provision is intended to prevent traders luring in consumers and then applying a hard sell without providing accurate and detailed information on the products being offered for sale.

1   TSR 2010, SI 2010/2960, reg 14(1).
2   TSR 2010, SI 2010/2960, reg 14(2).

Criminal liability

16.75 Breach of regs 12 and 14 is a criminal offence[1]. It was the view of the Department for Business that there would be a considerable overlap between these offences and those created by the Consumer Protection from Unfair Trading Regulations 2008 ('CPUTR 2008')[2]. Failure to provide the 'key information' or failure to provide it in the language required is likely to impact a consumer's transactional decision thereby creating criminal liability under the CPUTR 2008. However, failure to comply with reg 12(5), ie providing the information but in the wrong format, is where reg 12(8) is likely to have most free-standing relevance because, insofar as the key information is still intelligible and unambiguous, it will not affect the consumer's transaction decision. The same was considered to be true under reg 14: there is likely to be dual liability for breach of the requirements as to marketing and sales under both reg 14(5) of the TSR 2010 and the CPUTR 2008.

1   TSR 2010, SI 2010/2960, regs 12(8) and 14(5) triable either way (SI 2010/2960, reg 27).
2   See Chapter 8, Unfair Commercial Practices.

Regulated contract: formalities

16.76 The formalities for a regulated contract are set out at Pt 4 of the TSR 2010 in regs 15–19[1]. Under reg 15, the contract must be in writing and include:

- the identities, place of residence and signature of the parties;
- the date and place of conclusion of the contract;
- the 'key information' required by reg 12 set out as terms of the contract with no changes other than those communicated to the consumer in writing prior to the conclusion of the contract (aka 'permitted changes');

- the standard withdrawal form set out Sch 3 to the TSR 2010.

¹ SI 2010/2960, regs 15–19.

16.77 In order to make the rights of withdrawal effective, the trader is obliged to specifically draw the consumer's attention to the right of withdrawal, the length of the withdrawal period and the prohibition on advance consideration during the withdrawal period¹. Further, the trader must obtain the consumer's signature in each of those sections of the contract² and provide the consumer with a copy of the contract at the time of conclusion³.

¹ TSR 2010, SI 2010/2960, reg 16(1).
² TSR 2010, SI 2010/2960, reg 16(2).
³ TSR 2010, SI 2010/2960, reg 16(3).

16.78 Regulations 17 and 18 deal with the language of the contract. Similarly in relation to the provision of pre-contract information, the contract must be provided to the consumer in the language of EEA state in which he resides or, if there are two or more official languages, that which is nominated by the consumer¹. It must also be drawn up in English if the consumer is resident in the UK or the trader carries on sales activities in the UK². In relation to timeshare contracts for immoveable property in an EEA state, the trader 'must not enter into the contract unless the trader has provided the consumer with a certified translation of the contract in the language, or one of the languages, of that State'³. Accordingly, if the consumer is based in the UK and the timeshare property is in France, the contract must be provided in both English and a certified translation in French. Finally, under reg 19 'a regulated contract is void to the extent that it purports to allow the consumer to waive the rights conferred on them by these Regulations'.

¹ TSR 2010, SI 2010/2960, reg 17(2)–(3).
² TSR 2010, SI 2010/2960, reg 17(4).
³ TSR 2010, SI 2010/2960, reg 18(2).

Sanctions for non-compliance

16.79 Part 4 of the TSR 2010 impose both civil and criminal penalties for failures to comply with the obligations. Breach of regs 15, 16 and 17 results in the unenforceability of the contract as against the consumer. In other legal contexts it has been held that such a sanction does not render an agreement void or of no effect. Accordingly, there is no right to the return of payments made by a consumer voluntarily under an enforceable contract¹. However, it does mean that the trader is prevented from taking court action against the consumer for breach of its terms². Moreover, should be noted that the enforceability is only 'against the consumer'. Accordingly, the consumer could still seek to hold the trader to his contractual obligations under the deal even if no counterclaim would be available to the trader. In addition to those civil sanctions, criminal offences are also created for breaches of regs 15, 16 and 18. Again, these are either way offences pursuant to reg 27.

¹ *Orakpo v Manson Investments Ltd* [1978] AC 95.
² *McGuffick v Royal Bank of Scotland plc* [2010] Bus LR 1108.

Termination of regulated contracts

16.80 Regulations 20–24 in Pt 5 of the TSR 2010[1] deal with rights of withdrawal and termination. They are the key provisions of the legislation and provide important protections for consumers to get out of the contract either shortly after its conclusion or at the time of renewal.

[1] SI 2010/2960.

Withdrawal

16.81 Under reg 20 all that is necessary for the consumer to withdraw from a regulated contract is that he gives written notice to the trader during the withdrawal period. No reason need be provided. The notice is presumed to have been given by the consumer 'at the time it is sent'. Therefore, so long as the notice is sent during the withdrawal period it will be valid, even if received by the trader outside it.

16.82 Regulation 21(1)–(7)[1] provides:

    (1)   The withdrawal period for a regulated contract—
        (a)   begins on the start date, and
        (b)   ends on the date which is 14 days after the start date, subject to the following provisions.
    (2)   The start date is the later of—
        (a)   the date of the conclusion of the contract;
        (b)   the date on which the consumer receives a copy of the contract.
    (3)   Paragraph (4) applies if the standard withdrawal form is not included in the contract in accordance with regulation 15(7).
    (4)   The withdrawal period ends—
        (a)   on the date which is one year and 14 days after the start date, or
        (b)   in a case where the standard withdrawal form is provided to the consumer within the period of one year beginning on the start date, which is 14 days after the day on which the consumer receives the form.
    (5)   Paragraph (6) applies if the key information in relation to the contract is not provided to the consumer in accordance with the requirements in regulation 12(4) to (7).
    (6)   The withdrawal period ends—
        (a)   on the date which is three months and 14 days after the start date, or
        (b)   in a case where the key information is provided to the consumer within the period of three months beginning with on the start date in accordance with the requirements regulations 12(4) to (7), on the date which is 14 days after the day on which the consumer receives the information.
    (7)   In a case where both paragraphs (4) and (6) apply, the withdrawal period ends on the later of the dates determined by those paragraphs.

[1] SI 2010/2960.

16.83 Accordingly, the standard period for withdrawal is 14 days after the consumer received the agreement (if later than the date of completion). However, failure to properly given notice of rights of withdrawal or key information extends the withdrawal period for up to a further 12 or 3 month period, depending upon the nature of the failure (per regs 21(3) and (5)). The purpose of the extension periods is likely to be two-fold. First, they allow for the trader to correct failures to provide the relevant information. Secondly, they ensure that the consumer remains able to take advantage of the key right of withdrawal even if important information about it or the contract itself was not provided when it should have been.

Effect of withdrawal

16.84 The effect of withdrawal is to terminate the consumer's obligations under the contract and, if it is a timeshare or long-term holiday product contract, their obligations under any ancillary contract[1]. Further, upon withdrawal the consumer cannot be liable for any costs or charges in respect the contract or any ancillary contract[2]. It also results in automatic termination of any related credit agreement[3]. Moreover, since no advance payment can be requested in relation to a timeshare, long-term holiday product or exchange contract during the withdrawal period[4], it means that the consumer can withdraw at no cost to himself.

1   TSR 2010, SI 2010/2960, reg 22(2).
2   TSR 2010, SI 2010/2960, reg 22(4).
3   TSR 2010, SI 2010/2960, reg 23.
4   TSR 2010, SI 2010/2960, reg 25(3).

16.85 Therefore, withdrawal allows the consumer to simply walk away from the contract without any further obligation. In an arena where high-pressure sales tactics may be employed and long-term commitments are entered into as a result, the protection afforded by this right is invaluable. Withdrawal from the contract also results in automatic termination of any related consumer credit agreement 'at no cost to the consumer'[1]. If the trader is not also the creditor, he must inform the creditor of the consumer's withdrawal 'without delay'[2].

1   TSR 2010, SI 2010/2960, reg 23(2).
2   TSR 2010, SI 2010/2960, reg 23(3).

Termination of long-term holiday product contracts

16.86 Regulation 24 deals with termination of long-term holiday product contracts. In effect, this is a repetition of the right to withdraw each time when the consumer receives a request for payment of an instalment under the contract. The consumer may terminate the contract within '14 days after any day on which the consumer receives a request for payment of an instalment . . . '[1]. For the avoidance of doubt, 'instalment' does not include the first instalment[2].

1   TSR 2010, SI 2010/2960, reg 24(2).
2   TSR 2010, SI 2010/2960, reg 24(4).

Criminal and civil proceedings under TSR 2010

Criminal proceedings

16.87 As set out above, various provisions provide for criminal liability. Regulation 28 permits the prosecution and conviction of any 'director, manager, secretary, or other similar officer' of a company or 'any person who was purporting to act in such a capacity' where an offence under the TSR 2010 has been committed by the company 'with the consent and connivance' of that person or as a result of that person's neglect. Where the affairs of the body corporate are managed by its members, the provisions apply in relation to the acts and defaults of 'a member in connection with his functions of management as if he were a director of the body corporate'. Regulation 28 also provides for liability where an offence under the TSR 2010 is committed by a Scottish partnership in Scotland.

16.88 Regulation 29 provides for the situation where an offence has been committed due to the default of another. In that circumstance, the other person is also guilty of the offence whether or not he is a trader and whether or not proceedings are also taken against the principal[1].

[1]   See Chapter 4, Criminal Enforcement.

16.89 Regulations 30 and 31 provide for the two primary defences under the TSR 2010. Regulation 30 provides a defence of due diligence in relation to offences under regs 12, 14, 15, 16, 17, 18, 25 and 26[1]. Regulation 31 also provides a defence for the innocent publication of an advertisement in relation to reg 14(3) (marketing a timeshare or long-term holiday product contract as an investment if it would be a regulated contract).

[1]   See Chapter 4, Criminal Enforcement.

16.90 Regulation 27 provides that the offences are punishable by fine, not exceeding the statutory maximum on summary conviction and unlimited on indictment. Although prosecutions are rare, sentences in analogous situations have been substantial. In *R v Goddard & Hill*[1] two defendants defrauded £460,000 from over 50 people, having invited victims on a free mini-break on condition they attend a sales presentation. The victims were put under severe pressure to sign up to timeshares on holiday lodges and were not told of their right to cancel. Many were also required to pay £1,000 at point of purchase. The two defendants were sentenced to 21/2 years' imprisonment after guilty pleas were entered.

[1]   Unreported, November 2009, Mold Crown Court.

Obligations as statutory duties

16.91 Regulation 35 has the effect of rendering certain obligations under the TSR 2010 duties owed by the trader, so that failure to comply would give the consumer a right to bring an action for breach of statutory duty. Under reg 35(5) liability for breach of such duties 'is not to be limited or excluded by any contractual term, by any notice or by any other provision'. This goes further than is required by the CRA 2015. Although anything which attempts to exclude statutory duties would certainly constitute an unfair term, there would ordinarily be scope to include a clause limiting the trader's liability for breach, subject to the usual test under the CRA 2015, s 62. Actions brought pursuant to reg 35 would, however, be subject to the usual requirements for a tortious claim. Namely, a 6-year limitation period from the date the cause of action accrued[1] and the rules on causation, remoteness and loss.

[1]   Limitation Act 1980, s 2.

Liability for quality of services provided under regulated contracts

16.92 Finally, it should be noted that a question mark remains over what rights a consumer has when the timeshare or holiday accommodation provided under a regulated contract is of a sub-standard quality. The TSR 2010 themselves are not concerned with those issues but, instead, focus upon ensuring that the consumer understands the nature of the agreement and has time to reflect upon it and withdraw if appropriate. Where would a consumer direct complaints during the course of the holiday or upon his return? In particular, the structure of timeshare and long-term accommodation product contracts is such that it is often difficult to pinpoint the party who bears responsibility.

16.93 Although the PTR 1992 could provide an answer to such difficulties, despite reg 37 of the TSR 2010 it is in fact unlikely that a contract will ever be governed by both regimes. Once accommodation has been obtained via contract governed by the TSR 2010, the consumer will probably not purchase other holiday services as part of a bundle for an inclusive price. Usually, transport and other similar matters will be arranged separately and privately by the consumer for each visit to the accommodation.

16.94 Ultimately the consumer is most likely to have to claim for breach of contract. However, where the trader is not UK-based this may give rise to preliminary jurisdictional issues under Regulation 44/2001/EC[1].

[1]   Council Regulation (EC) No 44/2001 of 22 December 2000 on jurisdiction and the recognition and enforcement of judgments in civil and commercial matters.

16.95 The solution may be, if the consumer has paid for the timeshare contract (partly or wholly) by credit card, a claim under the Consumer Credit Act 1974, s 75 against their credit card provider[1]. Such claims may be brought in relation to transactions which occurred with suppliers based outside of the jurisdiction[2]. For example, see *Jarrett v Barclays Bank plc*[3].

[1]   See CHAPTER 19, Consumer Credit.
[2]   *Office of Fair Trading v Lloyds TSB Bank plc* [2008] 1 AC 316.
[3]   [1999] 1 QB 1.

REGULATION OF UK AIR TRAVEL

The Civil Aviation Authority

16.96 In 2016, 75.7 million passengers either arrived or departed from London Heathrow, the UK's busiest airport[1]. Air travel is now the fastest, and often the cheapest, way for British holidaymakers to reach their destination. As with all major industries, air travel is subject to intervention by a regulatory body, the Civil Aviation Authority ('CAA'). The CAA is a statutory body. It was created in 1972 under the Civil Aviation Act 1971, following the recommendations of a government committee chaired by Sir Ronald Edwards. It is now governed by the Civil Aviation Act 1982 ('CAA 1982'), Pt I of which deals with the administration of the CAA. It is crucially important in protecting consumers who make use of the UK's airports and travel with the air carriers regulated by it.

[1]   http://www.heathrow.com/company/company-news-and-information/company-information/f acts-and-figures.

Function and purposes of the CAA

Statutory obligations

16.97   The CAA 1982, s 3 sets out the functions of the CAA in relation to civil aviation[1]. Its functions are any conferred upon it by virtue of:

- the CAA 1982, including 'with respect to the licensing of air transport, the licensing of the provision of accommodation in aircraft, the provision of air navigation services and the provision of assistance and information';
- Air Navigation Orders, including 'with respect to the registration of aircraft, the safety of air navigation and aircraft (including airworthiness), the health of persons on board aircraft, the control of air traffic, the certification of operators of aircraft and the licensing of air crews and aerodromes';
- any other act of Parliament from time-to-time.

[1]   This includes civil aviation which takes place on military premises: *R (Oxford Aviation Services t/a London Oxford Airport) v Secretary of State for Defence & Ors* [2014] EWHC 24 (Admin).

16.98   In carrying on those functions, the CAA must work towards the defined purposes as set out in the CAA 1982. The purposes defined by CAA 1982, s 4(1) are to ensure that British air transport 'satisfies all substantial categories of demand . . . at the lowest charges consistent with a high standard of safety . . . ' and 'to further the reasonable interest of air transport users'. On its website the CAA interprets its purposes as being to ensure:

- the aviation industry meets the highest safety standards;
- consumers have choice, value for money, are protected and treated fairly when they fly;
- we drive improvements in airlines and airports' environmental performance;
- the aviation industry manages security risks effectively.

16.99   For example, it ensures that all UK airlines comply with the regulations made by the European Aviation Safety Agency, although it does not itself set safety guidelines. Equally, the CAA can take enforcement action against airlines on behalf of consumers and ensure that ticket prices are transparently displayed, but has no power to order airlines to pay compensation or to regulate fares. Thus, the CAA regulates the air transport market to ensure that consumers are protected physically and economically, and to ensure that the industry complies with wider environment and security obligations.

Consumer enforcement action

16.100 In carrying out its functions the CAA comes within the definition of an 'EU enforcer' under the CRA 2015, Sch 5[1]. It may therefore exercise investigative powers as provided for by that schedule. The CAA is also a 'CPC enforcer' for the purposes of the Enterprise Act 2002[2]. It may therefore bring proceedings under Pt 8 of the Enterprise Act 2002 in respect of Community infringements, in order to protect the collective interest of consumers[3]. Following the Brexit implementation period, the CAA will be a 'Schedule 13 Enforcer' and empowered to bring proceedings under Pt 8 of the Enterprise Act 2002 in respect of 'Sch 13 infringements'[4]. The CAA can also bring criminal prosecutions. While in the main these are used for safety-related infringements, they are available for some consumer protection matters, such as breaches of the Civil Aviation (Air Travel Organisers' Licensing) Regulations 2012.

1   Consumer Rights Act 2015, Sch 5, para 4(e).
2   Enterprise Act 2002, s 13(5A)(b).
3   Enterprise Act 2002, s 215(4A).
4   Consumer Protection (Enforcement) (Amendment etc.) (EU Exit) Regulations 2019, reg 3.

16.101 The CAA's Regulatory Enforcement Policy[1] emphasises that its intention in taking regulatory action is to ensure a 'just culture'. This means that in carrying out its functions as a regulator it must be careful not to undermine the principle, which is a mainstay in aeronautical investigations, that openness on the part of persons and organisations being investigated is paramount and a fear of sanction should not inhibit frank discussions and admissions which could improve safety in future cases. An illustration of the tension between just culture, which seeks to improve systems and procedures, and regulatory action, which seeks to ascribe culpability, can be found in *Rogers v Hoyle*[2]. While just culture is primarily relevant to safety-related matters, enforcement of consumer standards often touches on the economic aspects of running an airline, which can have a knock-on effect on safety; accordingly, aviation regulators need to have regard to just culture in all aspects of regulation in order to avoid better economic protections for consumers coming at the expense of their safety.

1   CAP 1326 *Regulatory Enforcement Policy*.
2   [2015] QB 265.

16.102 According to its Enforcement Policy, three principles underpin the CAA's approach:

- A 'proportionate and risk based approach': The CAA act proportionately to the evidence of risk to consumers. Accordingly, where there is clear evidence of immediate and substantial risk, enforcement action will follow rapidly. However, where there is a concern which is not supported by evidence, the CAA may simply monitor the situation, ready to take further steps if necessary.
- Taking 'independent evidence-based decisions': This is to be achieved by communication with the airline industry and ensuring that the CAA's enforcement actions are consistent across its areas of control. However, it emphasises that it will take any enforcement action it considers to be appropriate and 'will not alter our course just because we have been challenged, whether through a legal case or other action'. Its view is that such challenges are a natural consequence of its role and ensure that 'any

uncertainties or ambiguities in the applicable law are fully tested to the ultimate benefit of consumers . . . '.

• Publicising enforcement where to do so 'is in the interests of the consumer or the public': The CAA considers that publicising its regulatory actions provides a transparent method to let the public and the industry know what work it is doing. Further it has the benefit of possibly acting as a wider deterrent. Full details of what, when and how the CAA will publish details of enforcement action are set out in the Appendix to the Enforcement Policy.

Examples of enforcement activity

16.103 All enforcement actions taken by the CAA are published on its website in chronological order. The CAA's prosecutions between 1 April 2015 and 31 March 2016 included successfully obtaining fines against defendants causing dangerous goods to be delivered for carriage in an aircraft, negligently causing an aircraft to endanger a person, making flight accommodation available without holiday an air travel organiser's licence, and flying within the Glastonbury Festival restricted airspace[1].

[1] *Brooks Discount Ltd t/a Top Brand Discounts 4 U*, 09/04/15, Bournemouth Magistrates Ct; *Anderson*, 08/08/15, Bodmin Magistrates Ct; *Ahmed Sajawal t/a Al-Karem Travel*, 03/09/15, Leicester Magistrates Ct; *Hoare*, 21/01/16, Weston-Super-Mare Magistrates Ct.

16.104 A good example of the first of the CAA's principles of enforcement is provided by a recent prosecution of a hot air balloon owner[1]. The individual was registered as the owner of seven hot air balloons who was therefore required to provide evidence of insurance to the CAA. When he did so, the CAA checked with the insurance broker, which confirmed that the certificates were not genuine and that there had been no such insurance in place since 2011. Accordingly, the CAA placed a 'no-fly' direction against the balloons. However, in breach of that direction the balloons were flown on four subsequent occasions including, on one occasion, with passengers. A prosecution was brought under regs 9 and 12(1) of the Civil Aviation (Insurance) Regulations 2005[2] (knowingly providing the CAA with seven false insurance certificates). The defendant pleaded guilty to three charges and was sentenced to 3 months' imprisonment on each, suspended for 18 months. Further details on the CAA's approach to criminal enforcement can be found in its 'Code of Practice for the Investigations and Enforcement Team'[3].

[1] *R v Nimmo*, 10/12/15, Southwark Crown Ct.
[2] SI 2005/1089.
[3] CAP 1422.

Civil Aviation (Air Travel Organisers' Licensing) Regulations 2012

The 'ATOL' scheme

16.105 The Civil Aviation (Air Travel Organisers' Licensing) Regulations 2012[1] (the 'ATOL Regulations 2012') are perhaps the most important protection for consumers within the remit of the CAA. Their purpose is to enforce the CAA's ATOL scheme which aims to ensure that 'consumers are not stranded abroad or do not lose money paid to the travel organiser for holidays and flights'. In effect the ATOL scheme operates as a form of mandatory insurance for air accommodation providers, to protect consumers against the insolvency of the airline.

1   SI 2012/1017.

16.106 The ATOL scheme was initially developed shortly after the CAA's creation in the 1970s to require airlines to hold a licence. It was then codified into the ATOL Regulations 1995 which were variously amended before being revoked and replaced by the ATOL Regulations 2012[1]. The ATOL Regulations came into force on 29 April 2012 and introduced various new concepts into travel law. The most notable is the concept of 'Flight-Plus' which has had an impact in the realm of package holidays and the PRTs (see below).

1   See reg 3 of and Schedule to the ATOL Regulations (SI 2012/1017).

16.107 Regulation 2 requires the Secretary of State for Transport to carry out a review of the ATOL Regulations from 'time-to-time'[1]. As dealt with below, a consultation and Government response were published in relation to amendments to ATOL to cover the requirements of the Package Travel Directive[2]. That refers to 'a Post Implementation Review (PIR) of the 2012 ATOL reforms' which the Secretary of State planned to publish 'before 30 April 2017'[3]. However, as at the time of writing, that PIR has yet to be published.

1   Art 2(1).
2   DfT's 'ATOL reform consultation – Government response', January 2017.
3   Paragraph 2.62.

Licensing

16.108 The core part of the ATOL Regulations is Pt 4 which covers the licensing provisions. It sets out the process and procedure for applying for and obtaining an ATOL, as well as details on revocation and appeals against CAA decisions. Having an ATOL puts the holder within the direct regulatory control of the CAA and entitles him or her to undertake various other activities regulated by the CAA (see below).

16.109 Under reg 31 the CAA is entitled to publish the requirements for an application for an ATOL. There are six categories of ATOL. Each depends upon the size and nature of the applicant's business and, in some cases, requires a bond to be put up by the licence holder. The purpose of the bond is to meet refund and repatriation costs should the ATOL holder become insolvent. If those costs are greater than the amount of the bond then the shortfall is met by the Air Travel Trust Fund.

16.110 The categories of ATOL are as follows:

• *Standard*: The Standard ATOL is not subject to any trading restrictions. Accordingly, an applicant may have unlimited employees and turnover. It is, however, subject to a £50,000 bond, a personal fitness and competence test and various financial criteria.
• *Small business*: Applicants in this category are limited to 500 passengers per year and £1m licensable turnover for the first 3 years. Again, a £50,000 bond must be paid and the applicant must meet a personal fitness and competence test and various financial criteria. In addition,

the applicant must not have been previously involved in a failed licence holder. The latter is clearly aimed at preventing directors and managers of failed entities trading as start-ups and thereby repeating previous mistakes.

- *ABTA Joint Administration Scheme*: This is available to members of the Association of British Travel Agents ('ABTA') with an estimated licensable turnover of £1.5m or less. The application is via ABTA. Accordingly, although there are personal fitness and competence tests, there is no requirement to pay a bond nor any need to satisfy financial criteria.
- *Franchise*: The Franchise ATOL is restricted to those who have no more than 1,000 passengers per year and is granted on the basis of membership of an approved franchise customer protection scheme. Again, as a result, there is no bond or financial requirement test, although the personal fitness and competence requirements remain in place.
- *Trade*: A Trade ATOL is restricted to those who wish to only deal with other ATOL holders. It is subject to a £50,000 bond plus personal fitness and competence requirements and meeting the financial requirements.
- *Accredited bodies*: In fact, this is not a category of ATOL. Rather, if a person is a member of an accredited body he/she is exempt from the requirement to hold an ATOL and can trade under the body's licence instead.

16.111 Pursuant to reg 32(2) of the ATOL Regulations[1], upon receipt of an application for any of the categories of ATOL, the CAA 'must' refuse the application if not satisfied of any of the following:

(a) that the applicant is competent to make available flight accommodation;

(b) that the resources of the applicant and the financial arrangements made by the applicant are adequate for discharging the actual and potential obligations in respect of the activities in which the applicant is engaged (if any) and in which the applicant may be expected to engage if granted the ATOL;

(c) that it has appointed a person acceptable to the CAA as its accountable person; or

(d) that the applicant has complied with all or any of regulations 7, 8 and 9 of the Civil Aviation (Contributions to the Air Travel Trust) Regulations 2007 which are applicable to it in the circumstances.

[1] SI 2012/1017, reg 32(2).

16.112 Equally the CAA has power to revoke, suspend or vary an ATOL under reg 35. It 'must' do so if it becomes satisfied that the licensee is no longer a 'fit person to make available flight accommodation'. Otherwise it 'may' do so if the licensee either no longer meets the reg 32(2) criteria (above) or fails to comply with a term of its licence. In making a decision to grant, revoke, vary or suspend an ATOL, the person affected by the decision may request a hearing within 10 days of the service of notice by the CAA of its proposed decision.

16.113 The procedure for such hearings is set out under Pt 5 of the ATOL Regulations. Regulation 56 onwards sets out various procedural requirements for such hearings, including the:

- need for 7 days' notice of the time, date and place (reg 57);
- entitlement of the person concerned to be heard (reg 59);

- right to proceed with the hearing in the absence of the person concerned (reg 60);
- right to be represented and present evidence (reg 62);
- procedure during the hearing itself (reg 64).

An appeal from any decision of the CAA lies to the County Court in England and Wales and the Sheriff's Court in Scotland, with the CAA to be named as the respondent to any such appeal (reg 67).

Who is entitled to provide 'flight accommodation'?

16.114 Part II of the ATOL Regulations regulates the provision of accommodation in an aircraft. In effect it ensures that only those who are licensed or exempted by the CAA are able to sell flights. This ensures that the regulator can control who does so and, thereby, protect consumers. The relevant jargon for the sale of air travel is 'flight accommodation'. It is defined by reg 4(1) as 'accommodation for the carriage of persons on flights in any part of the world'.

16.115 Regulation 9 specifies the persons entitled to provide flight accommodation. They are:

- the operator of the aircraft'
- an ATOL holder acting in accordance with the terms of his ATOL'
- a person exempt from holding an ATOL.

16.116 The persons exempted from the requirement to hold an ATOL are set out at reg 10. They include regulatory bodies (such as the CAA), employees and agents of ATOL holders, airline ticket agents and any person making flight accommodation available as part of a Flight-Plus (see below). Under reg 11 it is within the CAA's power to further add to that list provided it is 'satisfied that consumers will receive a level of consumer protection equivalent to that which would otherwise be required under these Regulations'.

16.117 Regulations 12–14 then provide further requirements and details on who may come within the scope of some of the categories of exempt person under reg 10. It is a criminal offence to hold one's self out as being able to make flight accommodation available when not permitted to do so (reg 16).

16.118 Under reg 17(2)[1], when a person provides flight accommodation (whether on its own, as part of a package or as part of a 'Flight-Plus') he must supply the consumer with an ATOL certificate. This must be done when the person:

(a) accepts a first payment, whether in part or in full, for flight accommodation;
(b) makes a booking for the flight accommodation requested by the consumer where payment for such flight accommodation is made by the consumer to the aircraft operator or another ATOL holder; or
(c) accepts a first payment, whether in part or in full, for anything other than the flight accommodation which is or would be a component of a Flight-Plus.

However, a person must not provide an ATOL certificate unless required to do so[2]. The ATOL certificate itself must comply with the form and content of the example published by the CAA[3].

1   SI 2012/1017, reg 17(2).
2   SI 2012/1017, reg 17(3).
3   SI 2012/1017, reg 19.

16.119 Regulation 20[1] requires:

Where a person makes available flight accommodation, that person must provide to the consumer—

(a)   the name of the person who would be accepting the payment;
(b)   the capacity in which that person is making available the flight accommodation;
(c)   if that person is acting as an agent for an ATOL holder and the flight accommodation is not to form part of a Flight-Plus, the name and ATOL number of that ATOL holder;
(d)   if that person is acting as an agent for an ATOL holder and the flight accommodation is to form part of a Flight-Plus, the agent's name and the agent's ATOL number; and
(e)   if that person is a member of an accredited body, the name and ATOL number of that accredited body.

When issued with an ATOL, a person must not contravene any of the terms or conditions of it or any other accreditation (reg 21). Failure to comply with the ATOL Regulations, regs 17, and 21 also constitute criminal offences.

1   SI 2012/1017, reg 20.

'Flight-Plus'

16.120 The concept of 'Flight-Plus' under the ATOL Regulations was created in an attempt to bridge the gap between the PTR 1992 and the ATOL scheme and to ensure that certain consumers were not left without protection in the event of difficulty. It is dealt with at regs 24–30 under Pt 3 of the ATOL Regulations.

16.121 A 'Flight-Plus' is defined by reg 24[1]:

(1)   Subject to paragraphs (3), (4) and (5), a Flight-Plus exists when paragraphs (a) to (d) are satisfied—
       (a)   flight accommodation is made available which includes as a minimum—
              (i)   a flight out of the United Kingdom; or
              (ii)   a flight into the United Kingdom where the consumer has commenced the journey in the United Kingdom and departed the United Kingdom using another means of transport; and
       (b)   living accommodation outside the United Kingdom or self-drive car hire outside the United Kingdom or both is requested to be booked and is supplied by any person under or in connection with the contract for such flight accommodation; and
       (c)   such living accommodation or self-drive car hire is requested to be booked by or on behalf of the consumer on the same day as the consumer requests to book the flight accommodation, the previous day or the next day;

      (d)   the arrangement covers a period of more than twenty-four hours or includes overnight living accommodation.

  (2)   Where a Flight-Plus exists, any other tourist services will be included in the Flight-Plus if such services—

      (a)   are not ancillary to flight accommodation or living accommodation;

      (b)   account for a significant proportion of the Flight-Plus;

      (c)   were supplied under or in connection with the contract for the flight accommodation; and

      (d)   were requested to be booked by or on behalf of the consumer on the same day as the consumer requested to book the flight accommodation, the previous day or the next day.

  (3)   A package is not a Flight-Plus except—

      (a)   where a package does not include flight accommodation, flight accommodation (as described in paragraph (1)(a)) is requested to be booked by or on behalf of the consumer on the same day as the consumer requests to book the package, the previous day or the next day; or

      (b)   where a package does include flight accommodation, living accommodation or self-drive car hire outside the United Kingdom is requested to be booked by or on behalf of the consumer on the same day as the consumer requests to book the package, the previous day or the next day.

  (4)   A flight which begins and ends in the United Kingdom does not form part of a Flight-Plus.

  (5)   A Flight-Plus will cease to exist if—

      (a)   the consumer withdraws from the contract for any component of the Flight-Plus; and

      (b)   as a consequence of that withdrawal, the requirements in paragraph (1) are no longer satisfied.

[1]   SI 2012/1017, reg 24.

16.122 The use of the phrase 'requested to be booked' at various points in reg 24 is noteworthy. It implies that it is the consumer's request for (for example) living accommodation or self-drive car hire outside the UK which makes the arrangement a 'Flight-Plus' as opposed to the existence of those elements per se. Moreover, the 3 day period defined by reg 24(3) is to avoid the arguments in relation to a 'package' that, because certain parts of the deal were not agreed exactly contemporaneously, it is not a 'pre-arranged combination' at an 'inclusive price'.

16.123 Under reg 4[1], 'consumer' is given a broad interpretation under the ATOL Regulations as a person who makes use of or intends to make use of flight accommodation in person or to provide it to another person:

> . . . but is not a person who procures flight accommodation in the course of business while acting as the agent of another person who uses that flight accommodation for travel in person.

[1]   SI 2012/1017, reg 4.

16.124 Thus, booking agents or PAs making travel arrangements would not constitute a 'consumer'. However, a corporate traveller booking for him or herself would not be excluded merely because the trip was not for pleasure. The 'Flight-Plus' arranger (being the person who makes the flight accommodation available to the consumer and has taken any step to including it within the

'Flight-Plus' (reg 25)) has certain defined obligations pursuant to regs 26–29. All four provisions operate by making various obligations implied terms of the 'Flight-Plus' arranger's ATOL. Accordingly, failure to comply will be a criminal offence and may justify the revocation, suspension or variation of the ATOL.

16.125 Regulation 26(1) provides that where a 'Flight-Plus' arranger becomes aware 'that flight accommodation, living accommodation, self-drive car hire or any combination of these forming part of a Flight-Plus' will not be provided, he 'must make suitable alternative arrangements, at no extra cost to the consumer . . . '. Alternatively, if to do so is 'impossible' the arranger must 'refund to the consumer the amount paid by the consumer, on their own behalf or on another consumer's behalf' for those elements. For the purposes of reg 26(1) non-provision of a 'Flight-Plus' includes supplying the flight accommodation which 'varies significantly from that contracted for' (reg 26(2)).

16.126 Regulation 27 deals with each of the various elements of the 'Flight-Plus' individually:

- In relation to the flight accommodation, the arranger 'must provide the consumer, at no extra cost, with suitable alternative transport back to the place of departure, or to another return-point to which the consumer has agreed' (reg 27(a)).
- If there is an issue with living accommodation or self-drive car hire discovered 'after departure', the arranger 'must provide the consumer, at no extra cost, with suitable alternative living accommodation or self-drive car hire, as appropriate' (reg 27(b)).

Again, as with reg 26, if those alternative arrangements are 'impossible' the consumer must have his monies refunded (reg 27(c)).

16.127 Both of regs 26 and 27 are supplemented by reg 28. That provides that the arranger must compensate the consumer for the difference between the flight accommodation, living accommodation or self-drive hire contract for and actually provided; such compensation must include 'any incidental expenses reasonably incurred by the consumer including but not limited to additional living accommodation expenses'.

16.128 Finally, reg 29[1] provides:

. . . in the case of the non-provision of any tourist service forming part of a Flight-Plus other than flight accommodation, living accommodation or self-drive car hire, the Flight-Plus arranger is liable to refund to the consumer the amount paid by the consumer, on their own behalf or on another consumer's behalf, for that tourist service.

[1] SI 2012/1017, reg 29.

Interaction between 'Flight-Plus' and the PTR 1992

16.129 The obligations at regs 26–29 may appear identical to those imposed by regs 13 and 14 of the PTR 1992. However the key difference is the circumstances in which they apply. Under reg 30 of the ATOL Regulations[1]:

A Flight-Plus arranger is not liable to the consumer under regs 26 to 29 . . . except where the reason for the non-availability . . . is—

(a)   the insolvency of any person concerned with its provision; or

(b)   the failure of the ATOL holder who made available the flight accommodation.

Accordingly, they are limited to very specific circumstances of insolvency or failure by an ATOL licensee.

¹   SI 2012/1017, reg 30.

Criminal liability

16.130 The criminal liability created by regs 13(2), 17 and 21 are summary only offences punishable by a fine up to the statutory maximum[1]. However, the offences created by regs 9, 15, 16 or 41 are triable either way. On summary conviction they are punishable by a fine up to the statutory maximum and, on indictment, by a fine or imprisonment for a term of not more than 2 years or both (reg 69(2)). Under regs 9, 13(2) and 15–17 a due diligence defence applies (reg 70). A full analysis of the defence of due diligence can be found in CHAPTER 4, Criminal Enforcement.

¹   SI 2012/1017, reg 69(1).

16.131 Regulation 71 deals with time limits for prosecutions. They are as follows:

- Notwithstanding anything to the contrary in the Magistrates' Courts Act 1980, s 127(1), an information laid under the ATOL Regulations in England and Wales may be so tried if it is laid 'at any time before the end of the period of 12 months beginning with the date of the commission of the offence'.

- Notwithstanding anything to the contrary in the Criminal Procedure (Scotland) Act 1995, s 136, summary proceedings in Scotland may be commenced at any time before 'the end of the period of 12 months beginning with the date of the commission of the offence'. For that purpose, the Criminal Procedure (Scotland) Act 1995, s 136(3) applies.

- Notwithstanding anything to the contrary in Art 19 of the Magistrates' Courts (Northern Ireland) Order 1981[1], a complaint charging an offence in the Magistrates' Court can be tried if made 'at any time before the end of the period of 12 months beginning with the date of the commission of the offence'.

¹   SI 1981/1675.

INTERNATIONAL CONVENTIONS ON CANCELLATION, DELAY AND DAMAGE

Introduction

16.132 In addition to the above regulatory schemes, a major aspect of travel law involves the rules surrounding compensation for incidents which occur in transit, notably in relation to air travel. Such matters are dealt with via international conventions to overcome the complications of cross-border disputes, and have been regulated since the earliest days of air travel. An initial set of rules was drawn up following an international convention in Warsaw in 1929, which were amended in 1955 and further revised in 1963[1].

[1]   Known as the Warsaw Convention as amended at The Hague 1955.

16.133 However, the purpose of those rules was undermined by the creation of new diverging rules governing the EU and the United States, which led to travellers either being governed by more than one set of rules or left without protection.   Accordingly,   the   Montreal   Convention   ('the Montreal Convention') was agreed in 1999, and came into force on 4 November 2003. Upon signing the Montreal Convention, the US Department of Transport described it as 'a comprehensive and up-to-date set of rules defining and governing the liability of air carriers in relation to passengers, baggage and cargo'. The Montreal Convention is given effect in domestic law by the Carriage by Air Acts (Implementation of the Montreal Convention 1999) Order 2002[1], which came into force on 28 June 2004.

[1]   SI 2002/263.

16.134 Much of the Montreal Convention is beyond the scope of this work. However, of interest are those aspects relating to passenger compensation for lost baggage and delay, which are considered below. This section will also consider the application of Regulation 261/2004[1] ('Regulation 261') which governs EU air travel and deals with the same issues of delay and cancellation from a different perspective.

[1]   Originally Regulation (EC) No 261/2004 of the European Parliament and of the Council of 11 February 2004 establishing common rules on compensation and assistance to passengers in the event of denied boarding and of cancellation or long delay of flights, and repealing Regulation (EEC) No 295/91. Following Brexit, Regulation 261 has been assumed into domestic law as a piece of retained EU legislation.

Position at common law

16.135 The earliest cases on travel compensation in English law relate to the familiar problem of cancelled and delayed trains. The analysis was based upon a contractual offer being contained in the rail operator's timetable with acceptance upon purchase of a ticket. A passenger whose journey was subject to delays or cancellation was entitled to compensation for reasonably incurred expenses insofar as the delay was within the control of the train company.

16.136 In *Denton v The Great Northern Railway Co*[1] the defendant's timetable showed a train which left London at 5pm, arrived at Peterborough at 7pm and then proceeded to Hull, arriving at around midnight. The timetable included the following condition: 'The Companies make every exertion that the trains shall be punctual, but their arrival or departure at the times stated will not be guaranteed, nor will the Companies hold themselves responsible for delay or any consequences arising therefrom'. In fact, that part of railway which ran from Peterborough to Hull was not owned by the defendant and the 7pm train to Hull was discontinued by the line operator from 1 March 1855 but no amendment was made to the defendant's timetable.

[1]   (1856) 5 E&B 860.

16.137 The plaintiff had business in Peterborough on 25 March and in Hull on 26 March 1855. In possession of the defendant's timetable, he purchased a ticket from London with the intention that he would travel to Peterborough early on 25 March and then catch the 7pm train from Peterborough to Hull, to be there ready for the following morning. However, as a result of the discontinuation, the plaintiff was unable to make his connection to Hull and issued a writ for damages. Lord Campbell CJ considered that 'timetables cannot be treated as mere waste paper'. He concluded:

> 'It seems to me that, if the Company promised to give tickets for a train, running at a particular hour to a particular place, to anyone who would come to the station and tender the price of the ticket, it is a good contract with anyone who so comes. I take it to be clear that the issuing of the time tables in this way amounts in fact to such a promise; anyone who read them would so understand them . . . the promise is to the public at large, exactly as it is here; it is in effect the same as if made to each individual conditionally; and, on an individual fulfilling the condition, it is an absolute contract with him, and he may sue. That being so, there is, I think, a contract . . . '

On the basis that the timetable had still been in circulation after the defendant came to know it was no longer accurate, the court held that there had been fraudulent misrepresentation and upheld the plaintiff's claim.

16.138 The authority of *Hamlin v Great Northern Railway Co*[1] again illustrates the apparent difficulty of travelling to Hull by train in the mid-ninteeth century. In *Hamlin*, because the advertised evening train from Grimsby to Hull did not in fact exist, the plaintiff was forced to spend the night at Grimsby and purchase a fresh ticket to continue his journey the following morning. On the basis of breach of contract, he successfully claimed compensation for the price of the additional ticket and his overnight expenses. However, he was denied anything other than nominal damages for the trouble and inconvenience caused to him[2].

[1]   (1856) 1 H&N 408.
[2]   In relation to the question of general damages for mental distress, *Hamlin* was subsequently overturned by *Jarvis v Swans Tours Ltd* [1973] QB 233.

16.139 A third and final example of the common law approach is *Le Blanche v London & Northwestern Railway Co*[1], where the plaintiff missed a series of connections from Leeds to Scarborough as a result of delay to his initial train from Liverpool to Leeds. Although the plaintiff had no particular business in Scarborough and no need to arrive at any particular time, he purchased a second ticket for a special train to Scarborough rather than waiting for the next service covered by his ticket. The defendant's timetable included the following statement seeking to limit liability: 'Every attention will be paid to insure punctuality, so far as it is practicable; but the directors give notice that the company do not undertake that the trains shall start or arrive at the time specified in the bills, nor will they be accountable for any loss, inconvenience, or injury which may arise from delays or detention'.

[1]   (1876) 1 CPD 286.

16.140 The court held that the limitation clause meant that the defendant was not liable for delays which were beyond its control. In concluding that the plaintiff's action should fail, Mellish LJ stated:

'The question . . . is, whether, according to the ordinary habits of society, a gentleman in the position of the plaintiff, who was going to Scarborough for the purpose of amusement, and who missed his train at York, would take a special train from York to Scarborough at his own cost, in order that he might arrive at Scarborough an hour or an hour and a half sooner than he would do if he waited at York for the next ordinary train. This question seems to me to admit of but one answer, namely, that no one but a very exceptionally extravagant person would think of taking a special train under such circumstances.'

16.141 By way of modern contrast to the above case law, the Department for Transport has introduced an enhanced consumer redress scheme, which applies the CRA 2015 to train delays from late 2016. The consequence is that consumers can now claim compensation for delays of even a few minutes, compared to the previous graduated compensation structure which required at least a 30-minute delay. Moreover, from 1 October 2016, Chapters 4 and 5 of the CRA 2015 (relating to 'Services') have now been extended to cover contracts for the supply of consumer transport services[1]. Therefore pre-contract information about timetabling could now justify a claim for breach of contract pursuant to CRA 2015, s 50. At the very least it means that consumer transport operators must be more circumspect about how they describe their services. For further information see CHAPTER 6, Consumer Rights.

[1] Consumer Rights Act 2015 (Commencement No 3, Transitional Provisions, Savings and Consequential Amendments) (Amendment) Order 2016, SI 2016/484, art 2(2).

The Montreal Convention

Introduction

16.142 The Montreal Convention covers the international carriage by air of passengers, baggage, and cargo, and creates a scheme for carriers' liability in the event of death, injury, and delay to passengers and loss, damage and delay to baggage and cargo. The Montreal Convention has its roots in the Warsaw Convention and its subsequent reforms, including the Hague Protocol. The purpose of the Warsaw Convention was to create a single scheme for the liability of air carriers, primarily in cases of accidents. As the airline industry matured, and repeated reforms were implemented, the uniformity of the Warsaw/Hague system was slowly eroded. As a result, the Montreal Convention was intended to create a new unified code for airline liability for the new millennium. Parts of the Montreal Convention preserve (sometimes verbatim) certain elements of the Warsaw/Hague system, and its aim remains to create an exhaustive, unified system of air carrier liability in order to protect airlines from the uncertainty intrinsic to operating in multiple jurisdictions and avoid questions of conflict of laws. As a result, much of the case law on the Warsaw/Hague system is still relevant to Montreal Convention issues. Where the Montreal Convention differs from the Warsaw Convention is that whereas the stated aim of the latter was to shield airlines from excessive liability, the former – while not departing from that aim – addresses the rights of consumers explicitly, stating in the preamble that it recognises: 'the importance of ensuring protection of the interests of consumers in international carriage by air and the need for equitable compensation based on the principle of restitution'.

Scope of application

16.143 As of July 2017 there are currently 120 parties to the Montreal Convention including all Member States of the European Union, the USA, China and a substantial number of South American, African and Asian nations. Art 1 of the Montreal Convention deals with its scope:

> 1. This Convention applies to all international carriage of persons, baggage and cargo performed by aircraft for reward. It applies equally to gratuitous carriage by aircraft performed by an air transport undertaking.

'International carriage' is defined as any carriage where 'according to the agreement between the parties' the place of departure and destination are 'situated either within the territories of two States Parties, or within the territory of a single State Party if there is an agreed stopping place within the territory of another State, even if that State is not a State Party'[1]. Cabotage services which cross non-national airspace without landing are therefore excluded from the scope of the Convention.

[1] Article 1(2) of the Montreal Convention.

16.144 Carriage by 'several successive carriers is deemed, for the purposes of the Montreal Convention, to be one undivided carriage if it has been regarded the parties as a single operation, whether it had been agreed upon under the form of a single contract or of a series of contracts . . . '[1].This gives rise to different outcomes depending on whether the carriers operate on a codeshare or an interlining basis. Where there is a codeshare agreement in place, carriage will be regarded as a single operation and the applicability of the Convention will be extended to all parties to the codeshare and governed by Chapter V. Where a mere interlining agreement (or some other arrangement falling short of the definition in Art 1(3)) is in place, Art 39 of the Convention excludes the effect of Chapter V, and such arrangements are instead governed by Art 36. This provides that in respect of accidents and delay the passenger can take action only against the carrier which performed the carriage during which the accident or the delay occurred, save in cases where, by express agreement, the first carrier has assumed liability for the whole journey; and in respect of damage or loss of baggage the first carrier, the last carrier, and the carrier which performed the carriage during which the destruction, loss, damage or delay took place will be jointly and severally liable to the passenger.

[1] Article 1(3) of the Montreal Convention.

16.145 Accordingly, one must look at both the entire journey and the relationship between the carriers involved (if more than one) in considering whether and how the Montreal Convention applies. For example, if a person bought a ticket from Edinburgh to Los Angeles via London, and an incident occurred between Edinburgh and London causing them to disembark in London, it would be covered by the Montreal Convention if the entire journey was either operated by a single carrier or by two carriers under a codeshare, wet lease, or other arrangement sufficient for the journey to be regarded by the parties as a single operation. That is because the 'agreement between the parties' provided for departure and arrival in the territories of two State Parties. However, if the two legs of the journey were operated by different carriers as mere successive carriers (eg with an interlining agreement), the Montreal Convention will not apply, since liability in those circumstances could only lie against the carrier operating the Edinburgh to London leg, which would only be a cabotage service, and thus excluded from the scope of the Convention.

16.146 Unlike Regulation 261, which requires the existence of a contractual relationship, the Montreal Convention covers 'gratuitous carriage' (although only when performed by an air transport undertaking). It is therefore likely to cover deadheading crew members and airline employees and their family members who are entitled to free carriage as a perk of employment. However, working crew members and stowaways are unlikely to meet the definition of being carried gratuitously. The term 'air transport undertaking' is not defined in the Convention. However, in *Lavergne v Atis Corp.*[1], a decision of the US District Court for Puerto Rico, it was held that the term was intended to cover a 'business dedicated to air transport'. In that case, Atis Corp was a company which had been incorporated to own two general aviation aircraft which were used for personal use. It was operated under Pt 91 of the Federal Aviation Regulations (FAR), which governs flights for personal use, and was not certified under Pt 135 of the FAR, which governs commercial flights. As a result, it was not an air transport undertaking for the purposes of the Montreal Convention. Where carriage is not carried out by an air transport undertaking, the Convention will apply only if the carriage is carried out for reward.

[1]   767 F. Supp. 2d 301 (2011).

16.147 Somewhat unexpectedly 'aircraft' is not defined anywhere in the Convention, although under the General Classification of Aircraft in Air Navigation Order 2000[1] it includes airplanes, gyroplanes, gliders, airships and helicopters. It has been held by the Court of Appeal that a paraglider is not an aircraft[2] but that a hot air balloon is[3]. Neither does the Convention define the limits of 'carriage'; the question of whether it encompasses only what happens on board the aircraft in flight or also includes pre-embarkation procedures, or even the course of booking a ticket has been decided inconsistently by courts in different Convention states. At the time of writing, that question is yet to be litigated in the UK courts.

[1]   SI 2000/1562.
[2]   *Disley v Levine* [2001] EWCA Civ 1087, [2002] 1 WLR 785.
[3]   *Laroche v Spirit of Adventure* [2009] EWCA Civ 12, [2009] 3 WLR 351.

16.148 The Montreal Convention imposes liability in four situations:

- death and injury (Art 17(1));
- damage or loss of baggage (Art 17(2)–(3));
- damage to cargo (Art 18);
- delay to passengers and baggage (Art 19).

The focus of this work is upon Arts 17(2)–(3) and 19.

Damage or loss of baggage

16.149 In the first instance, damage to baggage is subject to the provisions at Art 17. Article 17(2) provides the carrier is only liable for damage to baggage 'during any period within which the check baggage was in the charge of the carrier'. However, it will not be liable 'to the extent that the damage resulted from the inherent defect, quality or vice of the baggage'. In the case of unchecked baggage the carrier will be liable only if 'the damage resulted from its fault or that of its servants or agents'. In relation to lost checked luggage, Art 17(3) allows passengers to enforce against carriers if 'the carrier admits the loss . . . or if the checked baggage has not arrived at the expiration of 21 days after the date on which it ought to have arrived'.

16.150 Art 17(2) effectively provides a causation requirement in relation to damaged baggage. The liability of carriers is (understandably) stricter for baggage which has been checked-in. Un-checked bags can only be the subject of claim if the damage was directly the fault of the carrier.

Delay

16.151 As to delay, Art 19 provides:

> The carrier is liable for damage occasioned by delay in the carriage by air of passengers, baggage or cargo. Nevertheless, the carrier shall not be liable for damage occasioned by delay if it proves that its servants and agents took all measures that could reasonably be required to avoid the damage or that it was impossible for it or them to take such measures.

16.152 Notably, unlike Regulation 261(below), the Montreal Convention gives no guidance on what constitutes 'delay'. Presumably *de minimis* delays of no more than a few minutes could be excluded under the usual rules of interpretation. However, many other short or medium term delays will cause little or no damage. Thus the question remains as to what 'delay' is.

16.153 The 'reasonable measures' defence in the second sentence of Art 19 echoes the common law test laid down in *Le Blanche*[1]. For example, force majeures such as severe weather or terrorism will exonerate the carrier from Art 19 liability. Moreover, many carriers will include as a standard term a limitation clause stating that timetables are not guaranteed and liability is not accepted for consequential losses (most commonly this protects them against liability for missed connections).

[1] (1876) 1 CPD 286.

Material and non-material damage

16.154 Over many years 'damage' under the Montreal Convention was repeatedly held in domestic first-instance cases not to include non-material damage. For example, compensation for loss of enjoyment, distress, anxiety or inconvenience. These decisions relied upon other foreign cases on the point including substantial authorities from the United States Supreme Court.

16.155 However, the status quo was thrown into doubt by the decision of the ECJ in *Walz v Clickair*[1]. The court, having failed to refer to any of the other relevant authorities on the point, concluded a very broad-brush analysis by stating that damage 'must be construed as including both material and non-material damage'[2]. It entirely failed to consider the importance of consistent interpretation throughout signatory states (which has been emphasised by various other global decisions relating to the Montreal Convention) and, instead, focussed exclusively upon the position within the EU. The decision was subsequently re-affirmed by the ECJ in *Rodriguez & Ors v Air France SA*[3].

1   [2011] Bus LR 855.
2   Paragraph 29.
3   [2012] 1 CMLR 40.

Limits of liability

16.156 Article 20 of the Montreal Convention imposes a fairly standard contributory negligence provision upon which a carrier can rely if it is able to prove 'that the damage was caused or contributed to by the negligence or other wrongful act or omission of the person claiming compensation . . . '. In those circumstances 'the carrier shall be wholly or partly exonerated from its liability to the claimant . . . '. Article 22(1) relates to limits of liability for delay and damage to baggage and cargo.

16.157 Given that the Montreal Convention operates globally, it deals with financial limits by reference to 'Special Drawing Rights' ('SDR'). The SDR is a notional international currency created by the International Monetary Fund defined by a weighted average of various convertible currencies. Although secondary legislation has been created for the purposes of determining the domestic value of the SDR[1], it can now be easily converted online. It is likely that the valuation of the SDR is to be determined as at the date of the damage, rather than the date of issue or judgment.

1   Carriage by Air (Sterling Equivalents) Order 1999, SI 1998/2881.

16.158 Article 22 provides:

1. In the case of damage caused by delay as specified in Art 19 in the carriage of persons, the liability of the carrier for each passenger is limited to 4,150 Special Drawing Rights.

2. In the carriage of baggage, the liability of the carrier in the case of destruction, loss, damage or delay is limited 1,000 Special Drawing Rights for each passenger unless the passenger has made, at the time when the checked baggage was handed over to the carrier, a special declaration of interest in delivery at destination and has paid a supplementary sum if the case so requires. In that case the carrier will be liable to pay a sum not exceeding the declared sum, unless it proves that the sum is greater than the passenger's actual interest in delivery at destination.

16.159 Article 22(1) therefore limits damages for delay to a value (at the time of writing) of around £4,275[1]. Article 22(2) provides for a general limit (at the time of writing) of around £1,030 in respect of damage to baggage unless the passenger declares a special interest and pays a supplement. In that case the carrier will be liable for the declared sum unless it can be proved that the passenger's actual interest was less. In effect, it allows a passenger to purchase a top-up of the carrier's liability to the actual value of the item in question. This is most often done for baggage with a value greater than the limit of 1,000 SDR which are to be checked-in. For example, expensive musical instruments or sports equipment.

1   As of July 2021, one SDR was worth approximately £1.03.

16.160 However, per Art 22(5), the limit on liability:

shall not apply if it is proved that the damage resulted from the act or omission of the carrier, its servants or agents, done with the intent to cause damage or recklessly with the knowledge that damage would probably result; providing that . . . it is also proved that such agent or servant was acting within the scope of its employment.

16.161 Under Art 25 a carrier may stipulate that higher limits of liability or no limits apply. However, under Art 26, 'any provision tending to relieve the carrier of liability or to fix a lower limit than that which is laid down in this Convention shall be null and void'. Article 29 prohibits 'punitive, exemplary, or other non-compensatory damages'. However, none of those terms is defined in the Convention.

Mutual liability

16.162 Chapter V of the Montreal Convention deals with situations in which the carrier which operates a flight (the 'actual carrier') is a different entity to the carrier with whom the passenger entered into a contract for the provision of air transport services (the 'contracting carrier'). Examples of such situations include flights operated under a codeshare or wet lease. The effect of the provisions in Chapter V is to impose mutual liability under the Convention on both the actual and contracting carriers. The test for whether Chapter V applies is that the actual carrier 'performs, by virtue of authority from the contracting carrier, the whole or part of the carriage'[1]. Mere successive carriers are specifically excluded from the ambit of Chapter V. The respective liability of the actual and contracting carriers is set out at Article 40 as follows:

> 'If an actual carrier performs the whole or part of carriage which, according to the contract referred to in Article 39, is governed by this Convention, both the contracting carrier and the actual carrier shall, except as otherwise provided in this Chapter, be subject to the rules of this Convention, the former for the whole of the carriage contemplated in the contract, the latter solely for the carriage which it performs.'

[1] Article 39 of the Montreal Convention.

16.163 Article 41 of the Montreal Convention provides that the acts and omissions of the actual carrier and of its servants and agents acting within the scope of their employment shall, in relation to the carriage performed by the actual carrier, be deemed to be also those of the contracting carrier and vice versa. However, it also includes the following specific limits to the actual carrier's liability:

- no such act or omission shall subject the actual carrier to liability exceeding the amounts referred to in Arts 21, 22, 23 and 24;
- any special agreement under which the contracting carrier assumes obligations not imposed by the Convention or waives rights or defences conferred by it shall not affect the actual carrier unless the actual carrier has so agreed; and
- any special declaration of interest in delivery at destination contemplated in Art 22 shall not affect the actual carrier unless the actual carrier has so agreed.

16.164 A claimant in a Chapter V case can elect to issue against the actual carrier, the contracting carrier, or both. In the event that he chooses one over the other, the defendant can apply to join the other carrier to the proceedings under the laws of procedure of the state of the court seized of the case[1]. Where both carriers are joined to proceedings, the aggregate damages against both of them cannot exceed the maximum which could have been awarded against either of them[2].

1   Article 45 of the Montreal Convention.
2   Article 44 of the Montreal Convention.

Exclusivity

16.165 Article 29 of the Montreal Convention deals with exclusivity and reads as follows:

'In the carriage of passengers, baggage and cargo, any action for damages, however founded, whether under this Convention or in contract or in tort or otherwise, can only be brought subject to the conditions and such limits of liability as are set out in this Convention without prejudice to the question as to who are the persons who have the right to bring suit and what are their respective rights. In any such action, punitive, exemplary or any other non-compensatory damages shall not be recoverable.'

The effect of Art 29 is to preclude claims based on causes of action outwith the Montreal Convention, and in doing so to give effect to the Convention's purpose (and that of the Warsaw Convention which went before it) to create a single, exhaustive regime for carrier liability and protect carriers who operate internationally from the vagaries of local laws.

16.166 The majority of the authority on the question of exclusivity is derived from Warsaw Convention cases. The prevailing view in those cases is that the Convention will preclude local causes of action where the claim falls within its scope. One question which arises from this is how the scope of the Convention is to be defined. This question was considered by the US Supreme Court in *El Al Israel Airlines Ltd v Tseng*[1]. That case concerned injury suffered by the passenger. The Warsaw Convention provided that for damages for injury to be recoverable, it must have been suffered as the result of an accident. Both parties agreed that the injury in question did not result from an accident: the passenger argued that that meant that the Warsaw Convention did not apply and she was therefore entitled to an alternative remedy, free of the limits imposed by the Convention; the carrier argued that the Convention applied because the flight fell within its scope and therefore no damages at all were recoverable. The court held that the carrier's interpretation was correct.

1   119 S Ct 662 (1999).

16.167 The principle in *Tseng* was also adopted by the House of Lords in *Sidhu v British Airways plc*[1], in which Lord Hope stated:

'The intention seems to be to provide a secure regime, within which the restriction on the carrier's freedom of contract is to operate. Benefits are given to the passenger in return, but only in clearly defined circumstances to which the limits of liability set out by the Convention are to apply. To permit exceptions, whereby a passenger could sue outwith the Convention for losses sustained in the course of international carriage by air, would distort the whole system, even in cases for which the Convention did not create any liability on the part of the carrier. Thus the purpose is to ensure that, in all questions relating to the carrier's liability, it is the provisions of the Convention which apply and that the passenger does not have access to any other remedies, whether under the common law or otherwise, which may be available within the particular country where he chooses to raise his action. The carrier does not need to make provision for the risk of being subjected to such remedies, because the whole matter is regulated by the Convention.'

1   [1997] AC 430.

16.168 In *Hook v British Airways plc*[1], a case decided after the UK's ratification of the Montreal Convention, the UK Supreme Court considered the relationship between the Montreal Convention and other domestic private causes of action (in that case breach of statutory duty). The court held that the fact that a statutory instrument provided for a cause of action did not mean that where such a breach was committed in circumstances to which the Montreal Convention applied, the limitations in the Convention would be removed. At [57] Lord Toulson said:

'There is similarly no dispute about the meaning of the UK Disability Regulations or their compatibility with the Montreal Convention . If the airline is right in its contention that Mr Stott's claim for damages is precluded by article 29 of the Montreal Convention , it follows that the wording of regulation 9(2) is misleading, because it states (supposedly for the avoidance of doubt) that any damages awarded in respect of any infringement of the EC Regulation may include compensation for injury to feelings. It has rightly not been argued that regulation 9(2) should be read as purporting to create a power to award such damages, if it would be inconsistent with article 29 , for that would be ultra vires. The effect of regulation 9 is to make it clear that the Regulations are capable of giving rise to an action for breach of statutory duty, for which damages are unrestricted by the Regulation, but it does not (and could not) remove any limitation resulting from the Montreal Convention.'

1   [2014] AC 1347.

16.169 Accordingly, the test for whether an action can be brought unencumbered by the limitations of the Montreal Convention is whether it lies outwith the scope of the Convention as set out in Art 1. Where the Convention applies, as defined in Art 1, the absence or limitation of a remedy in the Convention should be interpreted as meaning that such a remedy is not available (or not available beyond the specified limit), and not that it is available only via a cause of action outwith the Convention.

Jurisdiction

16.170 Art 33 of the Montreal Convention deals with jurisdiction:

1. An action for damages must be brought, at the option of the plaintiff, in the territory of one of the State Parties, either before the court of the domicile of the carrier or of its principal place of business, or where it has a place of business through which the contract has been made or before the court at the place of destination.

. . .

4. Questions of procedure shall be governed by the law of the court seized of that case.

16.171 Thus, putting aside the additional option in cases of damage resulting from death or injury set down by Art 33(2), proceedings may be issued under the Montreal Convention where:

•   the carrier is ordinarily based;

- the carrier has its principal place of business;
- the carrier has an establishment through which the contract is made; or
- the journey ended.

16.172 In a claim to which Chapter V of the Montreal Convention applies, Art 33(2) will apply to the contracting carrier. In such cases, Art 46 adds a further possible jurisdiction in which a claim may be brought against the actual carrier, namely 'before the court having jurisdiction at the place where the actual carrier has its domicile or its principal place of business'. Certainly in relation to the previous Warsaw-Hague Convention 1955, the claimant's choice of jurisdiction was held to be final and the doctrine of forum non conveniens was thus inapplicable[1].

1   *Milor SrL v British Airways* [1996] QB 702.

16.173 One curious effect of the jurisdiction provisions of the Montreal Convention is that they do not guarantee that the Convention will ultimately be applied by the court hearing the claim, even if the claim falls within its scope. It is not a requirement that the jurisdictions in Arts 33 and 46 must be Convention states. Thus, if a passenger purchased a ticket in Moscow, from British Airways, for a flight from London to New York, the Convention will apply, as the flight was an international flight beginning and ending in a Convention state. The passenger can choose whether to issue a claim in the UK (being the place the carrier is ordinarily based, as well as its principal place of business), the USA (being the place the journey ended), or Russia (being the place where the carrier has an establishment through which the contract was made). However, While the UK and USA have ratified the Montreal Convention, Russia has not. Thus, if the claim is heard in the UK or the USA, the court will apply the Montreal Convention, but if the passenger elects to issue in Russia, the court will apply the Warsaw/Hague rules instead.

Limitation

16.174 The relevant limitation period under the Montreal Convention is 'two years, reckoned from the date of arrival at the destination, or from the date on which the aircraft ought to have arrived, or from the date on which the carriage stopped'. The method of calculating that period is to be determined according to the law of the court seized of the case[1].

1   Art 35 of the Montreal Convention.

16.175 Article 31(2) imposes an additional requirement of timely complaint in respect of damage or delay to baggage. While not a limitation period as such, it creates a condition precedent for the bringing of a claim, failing which no claim will lie against the carrier. It states:

> 'In the case of damage, the person entitled to delivery must complain to the carrier forthwith after the discovery of the damage, and, at the latest, within seven days from the date of receipt in the case of checked baggage and fourteen days from the date of receipt in the case of cargo. In the case of delay, the complaint must be made at the latest within twenty-one days from the date on which the baggage or cargo have been placed at his or her disposal.'

Compensation under Regulation 261

Introduction

16.176 Regulation 261 has its roots in Regulation (EC) 261/2004 ('EC261') is an EU regulation designed to provide for a uniform scheme of compensation and assistance for passengers affected by delay, cancellation, and denied boarding. EC261 originally came into effect as an EU Regulation, and therefore had direct effect in the UK. By virtue of s 3 of the European Union (Withdrawal) Act 2018, EC261 (along with all other directly-effective EU law, subject to certain specified exemptions) was imported into the domestic law of the UK at the point the UK left the EU. At the same time, the Air Passenger Rights and Air Travel Organisers' Licensing (Amendment) (EU Exit) Regulations 2019 ('the ATR Regulations'), made amendments to Regulation 261 and other related legislation in order to allow them to stand as pieces of legislation outside of the framework of EU law – for example by removing references to EU institutions and replacing them with the domestic institutions which were to take over their competencies. Regulation 261 (as amended by the ATR Regulations) has had effect since the end of the Brexit Implementation Period.

16.177 Unlike the Montreal Convention, Regulation 261 is not damages – or fault-based, and requires no loss to be suffered by passengers. Where a situation exists which makes recovery under EU261 prima facie available, an airline can avoid providing the required compensation and/or assistance if it can prove that the situation was caused 'by extraordinary circumstances which could not have been avoided even if all reasonable measures had been taken'. This derogation has been the subject of much case-law at both domestic and European level, and has often led to inconsistent application between EU member states.

Status of pre-Brexit EU law and jurisprudence

16.178 The status of pre-Brexit EU law and authorities of the CJEU and is set out in the judgment of Green LJ in *Lipton and anor. v BA City Flyer Ltd*[1]. His Lordship acknowledged that EC261 has now been incorporated into the domestic law of the UK, with amendments made by reg 8 of the ATR Regulations, and held that the doctrine of supremacy continues to apply to EC261 (at [57]–[62]). The effect of s 5(4) of the European Union (Withdrawal) Act 2018 ('the 2018 Act') is that ' . . . any fundamental rights or principles which exist irrespective of the Charter [of Fundamental Rights]' are incorporated into domestic law. Further, per para 2 of Sch 1 to that Act, general principles of EU law form part of domestic law, provided they were recognised in relevant case law prior to IP completion day (at [63]–[64]).

[1]   [2021] EWCA Civ 454.

16.179 The effect of s 6(1) of the 2018 Act is that the Court is not bound by any principles laid down, or any decisions made by the CJEU, on or after IP completion day, and may not refer any matter to that Court for preliminary ruling. However, the Court can 'have regard to' anything done on or after IP completion day by the CJEU 'so far as it is relevant to any matter before the court or tribunal'. (at [65]). The effect of s 6(3) of the 2018 Act is that lower courts are, in general, bound to decide any question as to the meaning, validity or effect in accordance with decisions of the CJEU made prior to IP completion day. However, this is qualified by reg 4(2) of the European Union (Withdrawal) Act 2018 (Relevant Court) (Retained EU Case Law) Regulations 2020, which provides that:

'a relevant court is bound by retained EU case law so far as there is post-transition case law which modifies or applies that retained EU case law and which is binding on the relevant court'.

Regulation 5 provides in turn that:

'[i]n deciding whether to depart from any retained EU case law by virtue of section 6(4)(ba) of the 2018 Act and these Regulations, a relevant court must apply the same test as the Supreme Court would apply in deciding whether to depart from the case law of the Supreme Court.' (at [66]–[70]).

As retained domestic legislation reg 261 should be interpreted purposively, so as to provide a high level of consumer protection (at [73]–[82]).

Scope of Regulation 261

16.180 As set out above, Regulation 261 covers many of the same situations as the Montreal Convention, ie for denied boarding, delay and cancellation. In *IATA v Department for Transport*[1], a case which considered the scope of EC261, the ECJ concluded that there was no conflict between the two schemes and that the existence of the Montreal Convention did not invalidate EU261. The difference was said to be that the Montreal Convention provided a mechanism for passengers to bring damages claims, whereas EC261 introduced a strict liability scheme of standardised, fixed compensation.

[1] [2006] ECR I-00403.

16.181 Pursuant to Art 3(1), Regulation 261 applies to:

- flights departing from an airport in the UK
- flights departing from an airport in a country other than the UK and arriving at an airport in the UK if the carrier is a UK air carrier or a Community carrier[1], unless the passengers received benefits or compensation and were given assistance in that other country; and
- flights departing from an airport in a country other than the UK and arriving at an airport in an EU member state if the operating air carrier of the flight concerned is a UK air carrier, unless the passengers received benefits or compensation and were given assistance in that other country.

[1] The definitions of 'Community carrier' and 'UK air carrier' in Regulation 261 are to be found in Arts 2(c) and (m) respectively. See **16.188** and **16.190** below.

16.182 To be covered by Regulation 261, passengers must:

- have a confirmed reservation and have presented themselves for check-in at the time stipulated by 'the air carrier, the tour operator or an authorised travel agent'[1];
- if no time is indicated, not later than 45 minutes 'before the published departure time'; or

- have been transferred onto the flight 'irrespective of the reason'[2].

[1] See *Kupeli v Sirketi (t/a Cyprus Turkish Airlines)* [2016] EWHC 930 (QB).
[2] Art 3(2) of Regulation 261.

16.183 Regulation 261 does not cover passengers 'travelling free of charge or at a reduced fare not directly available to the public'[1]. Accordingly, only paying members of the general public are entitled to protection under Regulation 261. Cabin crew or travel agents who travel at a discount would not be entitled to compensation. Presumably, however, a passenger travelling at a reduced fare which was available to the public-at-large is covered. For example, under a frequent flyer scheme or flights purchase in the sale.

[1] Art 3(3) of Regulation 261.

16.184 Unlike the Montreal Convention which does not define 'aircraft' Regulation 261 specifically provides that it 'shall only apply to passengers transported by motorised fixed wing aircraft'[1].

[1] Art 3(4) of Regulation 261.

16.185 Three types of event entitle a passenger to compensation under Regulation 261:

- denied boarding (Art 4);
- cancellation (Art 5);
- delay (Art 6).

Carriers

16.186 The party liable to pay compensation under Regulation 261 is the 'operating air carrier' of the flight in question. 'Operating air carrier' is defined as 'an air carrier that performs or intends to perform a flight under a contract with a passenger or on behalf of another person, legal or natural, having a contract with that passenger'[1]. An operating air carrier must be an 'air carrier', which is defined as 'an air transport undertaking with a valid operating licence'[2].

[1] Art 2(b) of Regulation 261.
[2] Art 2(a) of Regulation 261.

16.187 A passenger's right to relief under Regulation 261 has its roots in a contractual relationship in that the passenger must have entered into a contract either with the operating air carrier or another party on behalf of whom the operating air carrier is carrying the passenger. Where there is no contractual basis for carriage (for example, a deadheading crew member being carried gratuitously or a stowaway), there will be no liability. However, it is not necessary for a contractual relationship to exist between the operating air carrier and the passenger in order for liability to arise, since where an operating air carrier performs a flight on behalf of a third party which did enter into a contract with the passenger, the operating air carrier will still be liable. Article 3(5) of Regulation 261 provides that any operating air carrier providing transport to passengers to whom the Regulation applies will be deemed to be acting on behalf of any third party with whom the passenger contracted, and will thus be liable to the passenger under the Regulation. The corollary to this is that a passenger seeking relief under Regulation 261 must seek it from the operating air carrier, and not the party with whom he contracted.

16.188 Unlike the Montreal Convention, Regulation 261 contains no mutual liability provisions covering situations where the undertaking with whom the passenger has a contract and the undertaking operating the flight are different entities. This is relevant in the following circumstances:

- where an airline operates as a group of companies in which one company (which does not hold an air operator's certificate) sells tickets and handles customer relations, while a different company holds an air operator's certificate and operates the flights. In this scenario the latter will be the operating air carrier;
- where an aircraft is wet- or damp-leased, in which case the lessor will be the operating air carrier by virtue of operating the flight under its air operator's certificate. This may not always be immediately apparent to a passenger if he purchased his ticket from the lessee and the aircraft and crew are wearing the lessee's branding and uniform; and
- where a codeshare is in use. In such a situation, only the airline which is actually operating the flight will be liable, but it will be liable to all passengers on the flight, regardless of which of the codesharing airlines they bought their tickets from.

16.189 A 'Community carrier' is defined in Art 2(c) of Regulation 261 as follows:

> 'an air carrier with a valid operating licence granted by a Member State in accordance with Chapter II of Regulation (EC) No 1008/2008 of the European Parliament and of the Council of 24 September 2008 on common rules for the operation of air services in the Community as it has effect in EU law[1]'.

[1]   Art 2(c) of Regulation 261.

16.190 A UK air carrier is defined as follows:

> 'an air carrier with a valid operating licence granted by the Civil Aviation Authority in accordance with Chapter II of Regulation (EC) No 1008/2008 of the European Parliament and of the Council of 24 September 2008 on common rules for the operation of air services in the United Kingdom.[1]'

[1]   Art 2(m) of Regulation 261.

Denied boarding

16.191 'Denied boarding' is defined under Art 2(j) as:

> a refusal to carry passengers on a flight, although they have presented themselves for boarding under the conditions laid down in Article 3(2), except where there are reasonable grounds to deny them boarding, such as health, safety or security, or inadequate travel documentation.

16.192 Article 4 mandates a three-step process for denied boarding. First, 'where the air carrier reasonably expects to deny boarding on a flight' it must ask for volunteers to 'surrender their reservations in exchange for benefits to be agreed . . . '. Secondly, if there are not enough volunteers, 'the operating air carrier may then deny boarding to passengers against their will'. Thirdly, in the event that boarding is denied to passengers against their will, the air carrier 'shall immediately compensate them in accordance with Article 7 and assist them in accordance with Articles 8 and 9'. The concept most commonly arises as a result of overbooking although it could also cover broad operational reasons such as flight rescheduling[1].

[1]   *Finnair v Lassooy* (Case C-22/11) at para 26.

16.193 Under the definition at Art 2(j), an air carrier's defence is that there were 'reasonable grounds' for denying boarding. Certain concrete examples are given, which have been given a fairly wide interpretation. For example, in *Limbert v My Travel Group plc*[1], the Limberts were denied boarding when the original aircraft was damaged in a runway collision such that a smaller plane had to be employed. They were therefore flown to a different city and put on a coach to their final destination. It was held that the airline had proven that the smaller aircraft was necessary for safety reasons such that there were 'reasonable grounds' and Art 4 of Regulation 261 was inapplicable. Equally, in *Finnair Oyj v Lassooy*[2] it was held that a strike did not constitute 'reasonable grounds'.

[1]   Unreported, 7 June 2006, Pontefract CC.
[2]   Unreported, 7 June 2006, Pontefract CC.

Cancellation

16.194 Cancellation is fairly self-explanatory. Nonetheless it is defined in EU261 as 'the non-operation of a flight which was previously planned and on which at least one place was reserved'[1]. It has been held that 'non-operation' includes not only when a flight fails to operate at all, ie doesn't take off, but also where it has to return before being abandoned[2]. Thus if a flight is scheduled to reach a certain destination, but fails to do so, it is to be considered as non-operational.

[1]   Article 2(l) of Regulation 261.
[2]   *Rodriguez v Air France* [2011] WLR (D) 348 (ECJ).

16.195 Passengers who are subject to cancellations are provided with a variety of rights under Art 5:

- assistance in accordance with Art 8;
- assistance in accordance with Art 9(1)(a) and (2), plus if the replacement flight is more than a day later, assistance in accordance with Art 9(1)(b)–(c);
- to be compensated in accordance with Art 7, unless the passenger is informed of the cancellation:
  - more than 2 weeks before the scheduled departure;
  - between 2 weeks and 7 days before the scheduled departure and are offered re-routing allowing them to depart no more than two hours before the originally scheduled departure and to arrive no more than four hours after the originally scheduled arrival;
  - less than 7 days before the scheduled departure and are offered re-routing allowing departure not more than one hour before the original schedule and arrival not more than two hours after the original arrival.

16.196 The 2-week cut-off period was considered by the CJEU in *Krijgsman v Surinaamse Luchtvaart Maatschappij NV*[1] where the airline (SLM) had informed the online travel agent of the cancellation of the flight more than 2 weeks before the scheduled departure date, but the passenger had only been informed of the cancellation by the agent 10 days beforehand. The court held that the obligations under EC261 apply to bookings made through online agents, as well as to customers who book directly with the airline. As such, SLM was liable to pay compensation in accordance with Art 7.

[1] C-302/16.

16.197 Article 5(3) provides a key defence for the air carrier 'if it can prove the cancellation is caused by extraordinary circumstances which could not have been avoided even if all reasonable measures had been taken'.

Delay

16.198 Delay is perhaps the most significant basis for compensation under Regulation 261. Article 6(1) defines it as when the operating air carrier 'reasonably expects a flight to be delayed beyond its scheduled time of departure . . . '. Different requirements are imposed upon the air carrier depending upon the length of the delay and the distance to be travelled. Per Art 6(1)(a), in order to qualify for assistance, a delay must be:

- for two hours or more in the case of flights of 1,500 kilometres or less;
- for three hours or more in the case of all flights between 1,500 and 3,500 kilometres;
- for four hours or more in the case of all other flights.

16.199 In all of the above circumstances, passengers are entitled to the assistance specified in Art 9(1)(a) (free meals and refreshments in reasonable relation to the waiting time) and Art 9(2) (two free telephone calls, telex or fax messages, or e-mails). In addition, where the reasonably expected time of departure is at least the day after the time of departure previously announced, passengers are entitled to the assistance specified in Arts 9(1)(b) and 9(1)(c) (free hotel accommodation and free transport between the airport and the hotel). Where the delay is five hours or more, passengers are also entitled to the option to be reimbursed the cost of their tickets and a return flight to their first point of departure (if applicable).

16.200 On the face of it, Art 6 only refers to air carriers offering assistance to delayed passengers under Arts 8 and 9. Accordingly, it would appear that no compensation was available for delay. As a result, for many years, air carriers sought to argue that what might otherwise be considered cancellations were, in fact, delays. For example, passengers on a flight scheduled for 20:00hrs on Friday might be told to return to depart at 13:00 on Saturday and, upon re-checking in be allocated different seats etc. On those facts, although an air carrier might present the situation as one of a 17-hour delay so as to avoid having to pay compensation, on a true analysis the first flight was cancelled and the second flight scheduled in its place.

16.201 Such attempts were dealt with by the ECJ in *Sturgeon v Condor Flugdienst GmbH*[1]. The court held that cancellation and delay are two distinct concepts; a flight which is cancelled cannot also be delayed and vice versa. The relevant test is whether the flight departs with its original planning (ie flight number, crew, itinerary, seat allocation, etc). The ECJ then went considerably further and expanded EC261 well beyond its apparent scope by ruling that the right to compensation under Art 7 should also apply to cases of delay for three or more hours. The basis for doing so was that the 'difference in treatment therefore appears to fall foul of the principle of equal treatment'[2]. Further, that the 'primary objective of the Regulation' was 'consumer protection'[3]. While both reasons are commendable and no doubt true, the effect of *Sturgeon* is to expand EC261 well beyond any justifiable meaning to be derived from its text.

[1]   [2010] Bus LR 1206 (ECJ).
[2]   At [62].
[3]   At [63].

16.202 Nonetheless, the decision was upheld following a challenge by British air carriers in *TUI Travel & Ors v Civil Aviation Authority*[1]. The ECJ again concluded in respect of cancellation and long delays that 'the inconvenience suffered by those two groups of passengers is equivalent'[2].

[1]   *TUI Travel & Ors v CAA* (conjoined with *Nelson v Deutsche Lufthansa AG*) [2013] 1 CMLR 42.
[2]   At [36].

16.203 The scope of the right to compensation for delay has most recently been considered domestically by the Court of Appeal in *Gahan & Ors v Emirates*[1], which concerned the application of Art 7 of Regulation 261 to delayed journeys from inside to outside the EU including a connection outside the EU.

[1]   [2017] EWCA Civ 1530. At the time of writing it is understood that permission to appeal to the Supreme Court has been sought.

16.204 The conjoined cases both involved flights from Manchester Airport with Emirates. The first (Ms Gahan) was to Bangkok via Dubai. The first leg of the flight from Manchester to Dubai was nearly four hours late, as a result of which Ms Gahan missed her connection and arrived in Bangkok just over 13 1/2 hours late. The second case (the Buckley family) involved a journey from Manchester to Sydney. The first leg of the flight from Manchester to Dubai was just over 2 hours late, as a result of which they had to be booked on to a connecting flight the following day. After a further delay, the Buckley family arrived in Sydney over 16 1/2 hours late. Accordingly, both sought compensation under EC261 pursuant to the decision in *Sturgeon*.

16.205 In broad terms, Emirates sought to argue that the compensation sought was not payable in either case because the only relevant flights for the purpose of calculating delay under EC261 were the original flights out of the EU Member State (in both cases, 'flight 1' from Manchester to Dubai). Therefore whether compensation was due and, if so, the amount, was determinable only by reference to the delay (if any) during the first leg.

16.206 Arden LJ, giving the lead judgment, rejected that analysis and concluded that the delay over the total trip was the relevant delay for the purpose of Art 7 of EC261. In reaching that conclusion, she relied upon three points. First, the CJEU held in *Sturgeon* and *Air France SA v Folkerts*[1] that the liability for compensation for delay depends on the delay in arriving at the 'final destination'. Where there are multiple flights provided they must be taken together for determining whether there has been a delay of three hours or more[2]. Secondly, Art 7 of EC261 applies to flights by non-Community carriers (such as Emirates) out of EU airspace if even one or more flights provided lands outside the EU. The Regulation is applicable by virtue of the carrier's presence in the EU at the start of the journey and imposes a contingent liability at that point for the entire journey[3]. Finally, Art 19 of the Montreal Convention[4] did not oust the application of EC261 simply because Emirates was a non-Community carrier. The Montreal Convention was ratified by the UK in 2004, after it became a member of the EU. Accordingly it is to be presumed that it takes effect so as to enable the UK to continue to perform its obligations under EU law. Therefore, the CJEU's analysis in *Nelson v Deutsche Lufthansa AG*[5] applied to the effect that compensation was payable under EC261[6].

[1] C-11/11 (2013).
[2] At [73].
[3] At [76].
[4] See above at **16.151**.
[5] See above at **16.151**.
[6] At [82]–[86]. Arden LJ's analysis has since been broadly confirmed by the CJEU in *Wegener v Royal Air Maroc SA* (Case C-537/17).

'Extraordinary circumstances' defence

16.207 As set out above, Art 5(3) provides for a defence to cancellation claims if the air carrier can prove it was caused 'by extraordinary circumstances which could not have been avoided even if all reasonable measures had been taken'. The effect of the ECJ's decision in *Sturgeon* is that if compensation is also available to delayed passengers, the extraordinary circumstances defence must also be available to air carriers facing such claims.

16.208 The ECJ considered the concept in *Sturgeon* and followed an earlier decision of the court[1] to the effect that the defence did not apply to a technical problem with the aircraft 'unless that problem stems from events which, by their nature or origin, are not inherent in the normal exercise of the activity of the air carrier concerned and are beyond its actual control'. The ECJ, in effect, acknowledged that dealing with technical difficulties with airplanes is part of the day-to-day operation of an airline and cannot therefore be considered an 'exceptional circumstance' under Art 5(3) either for the purposes of cancellation or delay.

[1] *Wallentin-Hermann v Alitalia Linee Aeree Italiane SpA* [2009] Bus LR 1016. For a recent analysis reiterating this position, see Case C-501/17 *Germanwings v Wolfgang Pauels*. In that case it was found that damage to an aircraft tyre caused by a foreign object (eg loose debris) lying on an airport runway fell within the notion of 'extraordinary circumstances'. However, in order to be released from its obligation to pay compensation, the carrier had to prove that it deployed all its resources in terms of staff or equipment and the financial means at its disposal in order to prevent the incident from leading to long delay of the flight in question.

16.209 Whether a particular set of circumstances amounts to extraordinary circumstances falls to be determined on a case-by-case basis. Recital 14 of Regulation 261, like its counterpart in EC261, sets sets out an indicative and non-exhaustive list of circumstances which are capable of being extraordinary, but it is not necessarily the case that every instance of the circumstances listed in the recital will always be extraordinary. In *Wallentin-Hermann* the CJEU held that 'the Community legislature did not mean that those events, the list of which is indeed only indicative, themselves constitute extraordinary circumstances, but only that they may produce such circumstances'[1]. The court also held that since the objective of EC261 was to provide a high level of consumer protection, the derogation under Art 5(3) should be strictly interpreted.

[1]   At [33].

16.210 In *Pešková v Travel Service a.s.*[1] the CJEU held that in addition to the inherency and control tests set out in *Sturgeon* and *Wallentin-Hermann* an airline wishing to rely on the Art 5(3) derogation must also show that it had in fact taken all reasonable measures to prevent the extraordinary circumstance with which it was confronted from leading to the cancellation of the flight. As to what was reasonable, the CJEU held that only measures which were actually the responsibility of the airline (as opposed to, for example, the airport operator or air traffic control) should be considered, that the requirement to take such measures did not require the airline to make intolerable sacrifices in light of its capabilities, and that the airline had to prove that it had taken the measures in question.

[1]   [2017] Bus. LR 1134.

16.211 The Court set out the process to be adopted by national courts as follows:

'Thus, in the context of the individual examination which it must carry out . . . the national court must, first of all, assess whether, in particular at the technical and administrative levels, the air carrier concerned was, in circumstances such as those in the main proceedings, actually in a position to take, directly or indirectly, preventative measures likely to reduce and even prevent the risks of possible collisions with birds . . . If it is not, the air carrier is not required to compensate the passengers under article 7 of Regulation No 261/2004. . . . If such measures could actually be taken by the air carrier concerned, it is for the national court, next, in accordance with the case law recalled in para 29 above, to ensure that the measures concerned did not require it to make intolerable sacrifices in the light of the capacities of its undertaking. . . . Finally, if such measures could be taken by the air carrier concerned without making intolerable sacrifices in the light of the capacities of its undertaking, it is for that carrier to show that those measures were actually taken as regards the flight affected[1].'

[1]   At [44]–[47].

16.212 In *van der Lans v KLM*[1] the CJEU considered the inherency limb of the test in the context of mechanical failures. That case concerned a component which had failed within its TBO/TBR, was not defective, did not arise from poor maintenance by the airline, was not discovered as a result of maintenance by the airline, and was not the result of a defect by the manufacturer. This put it in a different category of mechanical failure to that in Wallentin-Hermann, which dealt with failures which arose from poor maintenance or could have been detected during the maintenance process. In *van der Lans*, KLM sought to argue that because the failure was completely unexpected, it should be considered non-inherent in the normal activities of the airline. Rejecting that argument, the CJEU held that just because a circumstance is unexpected does not mean that it will be extraordinary, saying:

' . . . it must be observed, first, that it is true that a breakdown, such as that at issue in the main proceedings, caused by the premature malfunction of certain components of an aircraft, constitutes an unexpected event. Nevertheless, such a breakdown remains intrinsically linked to the very complex operating system of the aircraft, which is operated by the air carrier in conditions, particularly meteorological conditions, which are often difficult or even extreme, it being understood moreover that no component of an aircraft lasts forever.

Therefore, it must be held that, in the course of the activities of an air carrier, that unexpected event is inherent in the normal exercise of an air carrier's activity, as air carriers are confronted as a matter of course with unexpected technical problems[2].'

[1] [2015] Bus LR 1107.
[2] At [41]–[42].

16.213 There is a degree of inconsistency in the CJEU authorities on inherency where the circumstances leading to the delay are caused by factors external to the airline. In *Pešková* the CJEU held that a delay occasioned by a bird strike was extraordinary because bird strikes are not intrinsic to the normal activities of an airline. However, it is worth noting that the Advocate-General came to the opposite conclusion and that the judgment of the Court is primarily concerned with the control limb of the test, providing comparatively sparse reasoning in support of its conclusions on inherency. Conversely, in *Siewert v Condor Flugdienst GmbH*[1] the CJEU appears to have taken a different approach. In that case, the aircraft was damaged in a collision with a set of mobile boarding stairs being driven by an employee of the airport services provider. In holding that such an event was inherent in the normal activities of an airline, the Court said:

'However, as regards a technical problem resulting from an airport's set of mobile boarding stairs colliding with an aircraft, it should be pointed out that such mobile stairs or gangways are indispensable to air passenger transport, enabling passengers to enter or leave the aircraft, and, accordingly, air carriers are regularly faced with situations arising from their use. Therefore, a collision between an aircraft and any such set of mobile boarding stairs must be regarded as an event inherent in the normal exercise of the activity of the air carrier. Furthermore, there is nothing to suggest that the damage suffered by the aircraft which was due to operate the flight at issue was caused by an act outside the category of normal airport services (such as an act of sabotage or terrorism) and would thus, applying the case-law of the Court (judgment in *Wallentin-Hermann*, EU:C:2008:771, paragraph 26), be covered by the term "extraordinary circumstances", which is what Condor had to demonstrate before the referring court in accordance with the case-law cited in paragraph 17 above.

Consequently, such an event cannot be categorised as "extraordinary circumstances" exempting the air carrier from its obligation to pay the passengers compensation in the event of a long delay to a flight.'

[1] [2014] Bus LR 1324.

16.214 In *Krüsemann and Others v TUIfly GmbH*[1] the CJEU considered the issue of industrial action, which is one of the circumstances referred to in Recital 14 as being capable of being extraordinary. In that case, employees of the airline staged a series of wildcat strikes in protest at restructuring measures implemented by the airline. As a result, a number of flights were cancelled. There was no prior notification of the strikes to the airline and no opportunity for negotiations. The mechanism for the strikes was for the employees in question to spontaneously purport to place themselves on sick leave. There was no official ballot and no union involvement. The Court held that in spite of this, the strikes were inherent in the normal activities of an airline, saying:

> 'the restructuring and reorganisation of undertakings are part of the normal management of those entities. Thus, air carriers may, as a matter of course, when carrying out of their activity, face disagreements or conflicts with all or part of their members of staff².'

1 17 April 2018 (ECLI:EU:C:2018:258).
2 At [40]–[41].

16.215 Domestically, the issue of industrial action was considered by the High Court in *CAA v Ryanair*¹, a case which dealt with strikes which had taken place before the end of the Brexit implementation period, but in which the trial was held after the end of the Brexit implementation period. In that case, HHJ Gerald (sitting as a judge of the High Court) reviewed the pre-Brexit authorities of the CJEU and domestic courts in determining whether industrial action initiated at the call of a trade union recognised by the airline in question amounted to extraordinary circumstances. Ultimately, His Lordship held that it did not. At the time of writing, the case is pending appeal.

1 [2021] EWHC 1476 (Ch).

16.216 In coming to his conclusions, HHJ Gerald set out three principles which apply to the question of whether a carrier has established extraordinary circumstances: first, that Art 5 of Regulation 261 should be interpreted so as to provide a high level of consumer protection (at [19]–[21]); secondly, 'extraordinary circumstances' is to be construed strictly or narrowly because it derogates from the high level of intended consumer protection (at [22]–[28]); and thirdly, the exercise of construing whether something is an extraordinary should be a summary procedure. It is not intended to be something that emits or provides an opportunity for a detailed, granular fact-finding exercise (at [29]–[34]).

16.217 His Lordship concluded, at [47], that union-led industrial action was inherent to a carrier's activities:

> ' . . . by recognising the unions and negotiating with them and dealing with them, their involvement was or became an internal part of the carrier's activities, inherent in its normal activities. Whilst some of the positions were initiated by the unions, there is no evidence that they were not approved by the Defendant's employees. Those employees adopted the unions' proposal and it was those employees who drove the unions' negotiating stance. Once that is identified as a simple matter of fact, it cannot be said that the union is an external third party in the sense identified in the authorities because its representatives and proposals had been approved by the employees of the carrier and were merely representing or acting at the behest of its employees.'

16.218 On the question of control, His Lordship held (at [43]):

> 'The fact that control is temporarily lost, for example when all or part of the workforce, whether unionised or not, walks out, or goes on strike, or takes an outlandish position, does not mean that the carrier is not in "control". It merely means that there has been a hitch in negotiations where one side has withdrawn. All of this is inherent or internal, part and parcel of a business or activities of this nature. It is not random or external to an air carrier, like a bird or a screw. "Control", whether termed "actual control" or otherwise, merely means those aspects which are

within the four corners of the business, and not from outside of it, serving to identify the parameters of what is inherent in the carrier's normal activities.'

16.219 At [49], His Lordship went on to say:

' . . . whilst in the narrow sense the Defendant cannot "control" the activities of the union, neither can it in the narrow sense "control" the activities of its employees or their decision to strike or what terms to offer and what to reject. I cannot see why the same position could not have been reached without union recognition. The presence of the union is therefore a red herring: they were acting on the authority of the employees, so the fact that a new ostensible external third party in the form of a union is involved or interposed does not make the negotiation any different from the normal activities of an air carrier negotiating terms and conditions with its employees.'

16.220 In reaching the above conclusions, HHJ Gerald adopted an approach to the relationship between the inherency and control limbs of the test which correlates with the comments of Elias LJ in *Jet2.com Ltd v Huzar* (for which, see **16.227** below), namely that they are distinct, but related.

16.221 Also before the court in the case was the post-Brexit CJEU authority of *Airhelp Limited v Scandinavian Airlines System SAS*[1]. While acknowledging that, if applied, *Airhelp* would determine the case in the Claimant's favour, HHJ Gerald elected not to have regard to it in coming to his decision.

[1] Case C-28/20.

16.222 The authorities on the point have been recently analysed in detail by the Court of Appeal in *Jet2.com Ltd v Huzar*[1]. There, Mr Ronald Huzar and his family were subject to a delay of 27 hours in their flight from Malaga to Manchester and sought compensation under Art 7. The delay had been caused by a fuel advisory light coming on (indicating a possible fault) during the plane's in-bound journey to Malaga. When the plane landed, a spare part was fitted but the warning light remained on. It was not possible to resolve the problem before the airport shut for the night. Accordingly, further investigations were undertaken the following day which revealed that wiring needed to be replaced. To have done so would have required an engineer and parts to be flown from its hangar in Manchester to Malaga. Instead, the air carrier opted to fly a new place into Malaga from Glasgow.

[1] [2014] Bus LR 1324.

16.223 The air carrier argued that those constituted 'extraordinary circumstances' within the meaning of *Sturgeon*. The district judge at first instance accepted the argument on the basis that the delay was unforeseen and unforeseeable. However, that was overturned by HH Judge Platts, from whom an appeal was made to the Court of Appeal.

16.224 Elias LJ noted that the ECJ in *Sturgeon* had defined the defence by two limbs: first, whether the events which caused the problem were not inherent in the normal exercise of the air carrier's obligations; secondly, if so, whether the events were beyond the air carrier's actual control. He declined to consider how those limbs might interact on the basis that, clearly, the defence here failed on the first alone: the event causing the delay had been a mechanical issue which, even if not foreseen, was something inherent in the normal exercise of Jet2.com Ltd's obligations as an airline.

16.225 Nonetheless, in response to arguments put forward by both sides as to how the control limb of the test should be interpreted, Elias LJ made a number of observations which are worthy of note. First, in a decision which would appear to be consistent with the principle that EC261 should be interpreted so as to provide a high degree of consumer protection, His Lordship rejected Jet2's argument that control should be interpreted restrictively, preferring the Respondent's analysis. That analysis was summarised at [33] as follows:

'On this analysis the concept of control does not have the narrow meaning relied upon by the appellant, namely the power to influence events. It has a wider meaning, capturing the notion that the carrier can sensibly be said to be in control of its own operations, even when problems arise which it could not have anticipated.'

16.226 Elias LJ drew support for his decision from the proposition that EC261 claims, which generally deal with relatively small sums, should be accessible to consumers and not require time and resources to be expended disproportionately. At [46] His Lordship said:

'In my judgment, the potential consequences of Mr Lawson's argument also militate against his construction. If he were right, it would open up endless debate about whether a particular technical problem should have been foreseen or not. This could become a critical question in many compensation claims and would potentially involve lengthy litigation with, no doubt, expert witnesses being called on each side. Alternatively, simply by raising the defence a carrier would be likely to discourage inconvenienced passengers from pursuing their claims. I doubt whether the draftsman would have intended the exception to have that effect.'

16.227 At [47]–[48] Elias LJ dealt with the issue of how the two limbs of the test interact. However, in the very next paragraph His Lordship went on to explicitly refuse to rule on the issue, rendering these remarks *obiter*. However, they are nonetheless illuminating:

'In my judgment, therefore, for all these reasons the appeal fails even on the assumption that the concept of extraordinary circumstances should be defined by reference to a single composite test and not two distinct conditions. If the defendant is right about there being a single composite test, then in my judgment it is essentially as the claimant described it. The second limb will take its meaning from the first rather than vice versa. The event causing the technical problem will be within the control of the carrier if it is part of the normal everyday activity which is being carried on and will be beyond the carrier's control if it is not.

I am inclined to think that this is indeed the correct analysis. I recognise that it can be said to render the second limb redundant. But it does not in my view strip the limb of all significance. It helps identify the parameters of those acts which can properly be described as inherent in the carrier's normal activities and those which cannot; and it also chimes with the examples of events identified in recitals 14 and 15 as being potentially capable of constituting extraordinary circumstances. It makes it clear that events which are beyond the control of the carrier because caused by the extraneous acts of third parties, such as acts of terrorism, strikes or air traffic control problems, or because they result from freak weather conditions, cannot be characterised as inherent in the normal activities of the carrier. It is not fanciful to suggest that there may otherwise be an argument that they can be so described; indeed, Mr Lawson advanced that very argument in the course of his submissions. So on this analysis the second limb is intended to help elucidate the scope of the first but is not intended to establish a distinct and independent condition.'

16.228 Unlike Recital 14, which sets out an indicative list of circumstances which are capable of being extraordinary, subject to their particular facts, Recital 15 operates such that extraordinary circumstances are deemed to exist where a cancellation or delay is occasioned by an air traffic management decision (ATMD). Recital 15 was reviewed by the Court of Appeal in *Blanche v EasyJet Airline Company Limited*[1]. In that case, the appellant was booked on a flight from Brussels to Gatwick. The aircraft which was to operate that flight first had to fly the outbound leg of its itinerary from Gatwick to Brussels. However, due to thunderstorms, air traffic control at Gatwick suspended all eastbound departures as a result. Consequently, the aircraft left Gatwick late, arriving in Brussels 5 hours and 42 minutes behind schedule. This caused a knock on delay for the appellant's flight going back in the other direction.

[1]   [2019] EWCA Civ 69.

16.229 At first instance, the appellant's claim for compensation was dismissed by DJ Richard Clarke sitting in Luton County Court, who found that extraordinary circumstances existed. That decision was upheld on appeal by HHJ Melissa Clarke, sitting in Oxford County Court, following which the appellant appealed to the Court of Appeal. The appellant's chief ground of appeal was that the court ought to have looked behind the ATMD and considered whether the circumstances which caused it were extraordinary. This was rejected by Coulson LJ (with whom King LJ and Sir Ernest Ryder agreed) for three reasons. First, that it flew in the face of the clear and unambiguous meaning of Recital 15. At [15] His Lordship said:

'In my view, Recital 15 could not be clearer. It states that, for the purposes of the Regulation, "extraordinary circumstances should be deemed to exist" where an ATMD has (amongst other things) caused a delay to a particular aircraft on a particular day. The use of the expression "should be deemed to exist" is critical, because it leaves no room for doubt or argument: an ATMD which causes a long delay to a particular flight on a particular day should be deemed to be an extraordinary circumstance. That clear guidance is not qualified in any way.'

16.230 Secondly, Coulson LJ held that there was no previous domestic or EU case law which supported the appellant's construction of Recital 13; and thirdly, that policy reasons militated against the appellant's argument. At [31], he said:

'It would be impractical and time-consuming if carriers felt obliged routinely to challenge every ATMD at the time that it was made, because they knew that they would need subsequently to justify that decision in answer to any claims for delay. It would also be impractical for the courts to allow a debate about the merits of a particular ATMD long after the event, and in circumstances where ATC would not be party to the litigation. Such an approach would be disproportionate to the typical value of compensation awarded in cases of this kind.'

16.231 The Court held that the basis for Rectal 15 cases being treated differently to Recital 14 cases is that safety is paramount, and this approach was consistent with the need to provide a high level of consumer protection, since such protection starts with ensuring the safety of consumers. However, it also said that Recital 15 should not be seen as a 'get-out-of-jail-free card' for the airline, since although extraordinary circumstances will be deemed to exist, the airline will still have to show that it took all reasonable measures to avoid the delay. The Court also clarified that because extraordinary circumstances will be deemed to exist, the inherency and control test is not applicable in Recital 15 cases.

16.232 The Court also considered the hypothetical situation in which an ATMD might 'mask a more mundane problem' – in other words, where there exist circumstances (such as a technical problem) which in the absence of the ATMD would have caused a delay and are not extraordinary. In such circumstances, the Court held that the paramountcy of safety considerations required that the deeming effect of Recital 15 should take precedence, saying at [42]:

' . . . although hypothetical examples can be found of circumstances where an ATMD might, on analysis, "hide" a more mundane reason for the delay, it seems to me that that would be a small price to pay to ensure that the safety of all air passengers remained paramount. Indeed, I am confident that this requirement was precisely what the draughtsman had in mind when he or she made Recital 15 a separate and stand-alone provision deeming ATMDs to be "extraordinary circumstances".'

Compensation

16.233 Compensation under Art 7 is now available for denied board, cancellation and delays. The amount of compensation available is tiered according to the distance of the flight. Under Art 7(1) compensation is available as follows:

- £220 for flights of 1,500km or less;
- £350 for all flights between 1,500km and 3,500km; and
- £520 for all other flights.

The distance is to be determined according to 'the last destination at which the denial of boarding or cancellation will delay the passenger's arrival after the scheduled boarding time'.

16.234 Under Art 7(2) compensation can be reduced by 50% in the event that passengers are offered re-routing under Art 8 (see below), the arrival time of which does not exceed the scheduled arrival time of the original flight by:

- two hours in respect of all flights of 1,500km or less;
- three hours in respect of all other flights of between 1,500km and 3,500km; and
- four hours in respect of all other flights.

There are also special rules on compensation where a customer has been upgraded or downgraded from the ticket purchased (Art 10)[1].

[1] For useful analysis of the basis of compensation under Art 10 see *Steef Mennens v Emirates Direktion für Deutschland* (CJEU Case C-255/15).

16.235 Under Art 12 the specific right to compensation under Art 7 is expressly:

. . . without prejudice to a passenger's rights to further compensation. The compensation granted under this Regulation may be deducted from such compensation.

2. Without prejudice to the relevant principles and rules of national law, including case law, paragraph 1 shall not apply to passengers who have voluntarily surrendered a reservation under Article 4(1).

Rights to reimbursement, re-routing and care

16.236 Where Art 8 is referred to under Arts 4–6, passengers must be offered a choice between:

- reimbursement within 7 days of the cost of the ticket or those interrupted parts of the journey and a return flight to the first point of departure at the earliest opportunity;
- re-routing under comparable transport conditions to their final destination at the earliest opportunity;
- re-routing under comparable transport conditions to their final destination at a later date at the passenger's convenience, subject to availability of seats.

16.237 Where Art 9 is referred to under Arts 4–6, passengers must be offered free of charge:

- meals and refreshments in a reasonable relating to the waiting time;
- hotel accommodation if a stay of one or more nights is necessary or a stay additional to that intended by the passenger is necessary;
- transport between the airport and place of accommodation.

Enforcement

16.238 A breach of an operating air carrier's obligations under Regulation 261 is actionable by an individual passenger, usually in the county court. In addition, the CAA may also bring proceedings under Pt 8 of the Enterprise Act 2002 ('EnA 2002'). The CAA is designated as the enforcer responsible for enforcing EU261 in relation to flights from UK airports and flights from third-country airports into the UK under reg 5(1) of the Civil Aviation (Denied Boarding, Compensation and Assistance) Regulations 2005. By virtue of s 213(5A)(b) the CAA is also a Sch 13 enforcer for the purposes of enforcement under Pt 8 of the EnA 2002.

Regulation 261 is a listed enactment in Sch 13 to the EAn02 and a breach is therefore a Sch 13 infringement per s 210(6A) and 212(1) of the EnA 2002. *Per* s 215(4A), the CAA, as a CPC enforcer, may make an application for an enforcement order in respect of Sch 13 infringements.

16.239 A transitional provision at reg 9 of The Consumer Protection (Enforcement) (Amendment etc.) (EU Exit) Regulations 2019 (which made Brexit-related amendments to the EnA 2002) provides that where a Community infringement occurs, or is suspected to have occurred, before the end of the implementation period, the amendments made by reg 3 of those regulations will be treated as if they had not been made, and Pt 8 of the EnA 2002 will apply as previously drafted. Breaches of EC261 which occurred before the end of the implementation period will be caught by this transitional provision.

Jurisdiction

16.240 Regulation 261 contains no provisions in relation to jurisdiction. In *ZX v Ryanair DAC*[1] the CJEU held that as a result, the competent national court fell to be decided in accordance with Regulation (EU) 1215/2012 (The Recast Brussels Regulation). In *Flightright GmbH v Air Nostrum Líneas Aéreas del Mediterráneo*[2] the CJEU held that because the right to relief under EC261 has its roots in a contractual relationship, the relevant jurisdiction is the member state in which the services were, or should have been, rendered. In *Peter Redher v Air Baltic Corporation*[3], the CJEU clarified that this meant that a claimant is free to choose whether to bring his case in the national courts of the place of take-off or landing.

1   Case C-464/2018.
2   Conjoined cases C-274/16, C-447/16, and C-448/16.
3   Case C-204/08.

Limitation

16.241 Regulation 261 contains nothing in relation to limitation. In a 2011 county court case[1] it was decided that the limitation period should be the same as the 2 years that apply under the Montreal Convention. That has now been established as wrong by the ECJ decision in *Moré v Koninklijke Lucktvaart Maatschappij*[2]. There the court concluded that the limitation period could not be the same as under the Montreal Convention. However, it declined to specify a limitation period, stating somewhat unhelpfully that it was to be 'determined in accordance with the rules of each Member State on the limitation of actions'[3].

1   *Schreiber v TUI UK Ltd* (unreported), 28 July 2011, Clerkenwell CC.
2   Case C-139/11.
3   At [33].

16.242 Accordingly, the question remains without a definitive answer for UK passengers. Although there is an argument that it would be a claim on a specialty to which a 12-year limitation period applies[1], the safer assumption (at least for claimants) is that compensation under Regulation 261 is a sum due 'under any enactment' to which a 6-year limitation period applies[2].

1   Eg 'Pioneering Passengers rights: legislation and jurisprudence from the aviation sector' (2012) 12(2) *ERA Reform* 301.
2   Limitation Act 1980, s 9(1).

Civil Aviation (Denied Boarding, Compensation and Assistance) Regulations 2005

16.243 These are domestic Regulations[1] which create criminal liability in relation to breaches of Arts 4–6, 10, 11 or 14 of EC261. Under reg 3(2), such offences are summary only and subject to an unlimited fine. Under reg 4 there is a due diligence defence, namely for 'the air carrier to show that it took all reasonable steps and exercised all due diligence to avoid committing the offence'[2]. Pending amendments to be made by reg 5 of the ATR Regulations will preserve an equivalent effect for breaches of UK261 once in force. Regulation 5(1) also designates the CAA as the UK enforcer for the purposes of Art 16 of Regulation 261, which requires Member States to designate a body for 'the enforcement of this Regulation as regards flights from airports situated on its territory and flights from a third country to such airports'. Article 16 will be amended once EU261 is in force, but the effect of the amendment is that the CAA will remain the designated body for enforcing UK261, just as it was for EU261. Notwithstanding that the UK has now left the EU, these amendments are still yet to be made, as Art 5 of the ATR Regulations is not yet in force and a date for it to come into force is yet to be appointed.

1   SI 2005/975.
2   See CHAPTER 4, Criminal Enforcement.

Chapter 17

AGE RESTRICTED PRODUCTS

Contents

INTRODUCTION

17.1 The principal method of control by successive governments to prevent the sale of potentially harmful consumer products to children has been the creation of criminal liability for traders. However, as the first edition of this book commented:

> 'The law on age-restricted sales is in a lamentable state. There is manifest inconsistency between the elements of the offences, their penalties and the duty of enforcement . . . .'

and proposed:

> '– a single statute containing all of the age-restricted selling offences;
> – all offences to be made strict liability offences with a due diligence defence;
> – an express power to make test purchases;
> – a duty of enforcement should be placed upon trading standards departments.'

17.2 With the exception of the ramifications of Brexit, little has changed since the first edition of this book. In August 2010 the Age-restricted Products Review Group, representing major businesses, trade associations and professional bodies, made twelve recommendations in *Better Regulation of Age-restricted Products: A Retail View*. The recommendations came 'in response to a call from the Local Better Regulation Office ('LBRO') for an independent and evidence-based review of the regulation and enforcement of age-restricted products'. They included the suggestions that:

(a) The current piecemeal legislation should be consolidated into a single piece of legislation to provide simplicity and greater consistency across the product categories with standardisation of offences and defences. This would provide a framework by which any new controls can be easily implemented in a consistent way to ensure future coherent development of the law. The legislation should include a binding code of practice.

(b)   A simple general due diligence defence should be available for retail employees across all product categories to provide fairness where a genuine and reasonable mistake in judging age has been made.

17.3 Following this, the Better Regulation Delivery Office ('BRDO') – which replaced LBRO – held a consultation in September 2012 on a proposed collaborative 'Code of Practice' to be followed by both communities and businesses, as well as regulators and enforcers, in order to better protect children from the hazards of age-restricted products. The consultation framework focused on four areas: prioritisation and targeting of resources to areas which present the most risk, working with businesses and communities to help them fulfil their obligations, the conduct of checks on compliance by local enforcers and how to respond to non-compliance. However, although the (non-statutory) Code of Practice, which was published on 24 January 2013 and only applies to England and Wales, includes the aim that 'an enforcing authority should ensure clear information and guidance on relevant legislation is readily available' the issue of law reform and the need for a more cohesive legislative approach was not addressed at all. The Code was updated in April 2014 to reflect the introduction of the Regulators' Code and changes to Primary Authority that took effect in October 2013. However, its core recommendations were not amended. Thus the law looks set to remain 'piecemeal' in the short term at least.

However, change is potentially on the horizon as the Government turns its attention to tackling the use of certain products in relatively new ways by children. Following a consultation by the Department of Health and Social Care on ending the sale of energy drinks to children, Mr Hancock, the then Health Secretary, is reported in July 2019 to have supported the change in a letter written to Cabinet. However, substantive changes to implement this policy have not yet been taken. Further, the Offensive Weapons Act 2019, the majority of which is not yet in force, seeks (amongst other things) to create an offence of selling a corrosive product to a person who is under the age of 18.

Test purchases

17.4 The enforcement of age restricted sales offences is particularly reliant upon the power to make test purchases. Test purchases are discussed in CHAPTER 4, Criminal Enforcement.

TOBACCO

Introduction

17.5 England, Wales, Scotland and Northern Ireland each have responsibility for their own smoking cessation and health education campaigns. However, UK-wide policy and law applies to taxation, smuggling, advertising and consumer-protection issues such as the provision of health warnings on tobacco packaging.

17.6 The role of Trading Standards in regulating the sale of tobacco is more extensive than age-related sales but it is not possible in a work of this nature to provide detailed reference to all legislative provisions relating to matters such as counterfeit and illicit tobacco, fiscal marks, novel or niche products including tobacco mixtures for use in water pipes (such as shisha) and smokeless tobacco, oral tobacco, smoking accessories and smoke-free places.

17.7 A raft of initiatives has been introduced by Trading Standards authorities and public health bodies over the last few years. For example, in May 2013, Newcastle City Council passed a declaration committing the council to take comprehensive action to address the harm caused by smoking. This has become known as the 'Local Government Declaration on Tobacco Control' and councils across the UK have signed up to it. The Declaration commits councils to a number of actions and has been endorsed by numerous organisations, including the Chartered Trading Standards Institute. In August 2014, a sister document, the 'National Statement of Support', was launched by the NHS to allow public health organisations to show their support for tobacco control.

17.8 More recently, the Local Government Association's report 'Tackling Tobacco and Nicotine Dependency' (February 2015) outlined a number of proposals which would enable councils to engage with the problem, for example: allowing Trading Standards teams to do more proactive work with shopkeepers to ensure they understand the law about underage sales; how to avoid illegal sales; and what penalties they could face if they fail to comply with the law.

17.9 There are also a number of recent wider legislative developments in this area. In May 2016, the Tobacco and Related Products Regulations 2016[1] came into force, enacting Directive 2014/40/EU. The legislation revises the regime for the manufacture, presentation and sale of tobacco products which existed under the 2001 Directive. Amongst other measures, the 2016 Regulations prohibit the sale of cigarettes and tobacco with 'characterising flavours' (such as fruit or chocolate); phases out menthol cigarettes from 2020; and requires stark and sizeable health warnings to appear on tobacco and related products, which must cover 65% of the front and back of cigarette packages. Products produced before 20 May 2016 were permitted to be sold until 20 May 2017. The Government held a consultation on these Regulations between 29 January 2021 and 19 March 2021 and a post-implementation review is due to be published by the end of 2021.

[1]   SI 2016/507.

17.10 Legal challenges to Directive 2014/40/EU were brought by tobacco companies on the grounds that various different articles of the Directive breached EU law, most notably *Poland v European Parliament and Council of the European Union*[1] (concerning flavoured and menthol cigarettes); *Pillbox 38 (UK) Limited (t/a 'Totally Wicked') v Secretary of State for Health*[2] (concerning e-cigarettes and refills); and *R (on the application of Philip Morris Brands Sarl & Others) v Secretary of State for Health and Others*[3] (concerning the presentation of tobacco products). The CJEU delivered judgment in all three matters on 4 May 2016 and dismissed the challenges in each case.

[1]   Case C-358/14.

² Case C-477/14.
³ Case C-547/14.

17.11 These legislative changes are now supported in England by the *Tobacco Control Plan for England (Towards a Smokefree Generation)*, which was published in July 2017 and identifies a plan for 2017–2022. This plan sets out a number of national ambitions including the first smokefree generation, a smokefree pregnancy for all, parity of esteem for those with mental health conditions, and backing evidenced based innovations to support quitting. Four action points, of prevention first, supporting smokers to quit, eliminating variations in smoking rates, and effective enforcement, have been developed to help achieve these ambitions. A comprehensive understanding of the upcoming changes and developments to smoking policy and initiatives in England cannot be achieved without reference to this plan. Following the Health Secretary's commitment in July 2019 to achieving 'smoke-free by 2030', the Government intends to publish a new Tobacco Control Plan by the end of 2021, which will take into account the findings of the Government's review of tobacco legislation and Public Health England's seventh report on vaping.

Scotland, Northern Ireland and Wales

17.12 Legislation relating to the prohibition of sales of tobacco to a person under 18 in Scotland is set out in a separate section later in this chapter.

17.13 Legislation relating to the prohibition of sales of tobacco and related matters in Northern Ireland is contained in:

(a)   Health (Miscellaneous Provisions) Act (Northern Ireland) 2016;

(b)   Tobacco Retailers Act (Northern Ireland) 2014 (and associated secondary regulation);

(c)   Children and Young Persons (Sale of Tobacco etc) Regulations (Northern Ireland) 2008[1];

(d)   Smoking (Northern Ireland) Order 2006[2]; and

(e)   Children and Young Persons (Protection from Tobacco) (Northern Ireland) Order 1991[3].

¹   SR 2008/306.
²   SI 2006/2957.
³   SI 1991/2872.

17.14 Legislation relating to the prohibition of sales of tobacco specifically pertaining to Wales is contained in:

(a)   Public Health (Wales) Act 2017 (received Royal Assent on 3 July 2017, but significant portions of the Act are not yet in force);

(b)   Proxy Purchasing of Tobacco, Nicotine Products etc (Fixed Penalty Notice) Wales Regulations 2015[1].

¹   SI 2015/1663.

Application and territorial jurisdiction

17.15 The Children and Young Persons Act 1933 ('CYPA 1933') (as amended) contains the main offences relating to the sale of tobacco to a person under 18. The Children and Families Act 2014 ('CFA 2014') creates further offences relating to the purchase of tobacco on behalf of a person under 18 and the sale of 'Nicotine Inhaling Products' (electronic cigarettes) to a person under 18, or on behalf of a person under 18. Both acts extend to England and Wales only.

Offences under CYPA 1933

17.16 CYPA 1933, s 7 states:

7 **Sale of tobacco, etc, to persons under eighteen**

(1) Any person who sells to a person under the age of eighteen years any tobacco or cigarette papers, whether for his own use or not, shall be liable, on summary conviction to a fine not exceeding level 4 on the standard scale [. . . .]

(2) If on complaint to a magistrates' court it is proved to the satisfaction of the court that any automatic machine for the sale of tobacco kept on any premises has been used by any person under the age of eighteen years, the court shall order the owner of the machine, or the person on whose premises the machine is kept, to take such precautions to prevent the machine being so used as may be specified in the order or, if necessary, to remove the machine, within such time as may be specified in the order, and if any person against whom such an order has been made fails to comply therewith, he shall be liable, on summary conviction, to a fine not exceeding level 4 on the standard scale.

17.17 For the purposes of CYPA 1933, s 7 the expression 'tobacco' includes cigarettes, any product containing tobacco and intended for oral or nasal use and smoking mixtures intended as a substitute for tobacco. The expression 'cigarettes' includes cut tobacco rolled up in paper, tobacco leaf, or other material in such form as to be capable of immediate use for smoking[1].

[1] CYPA 1933, s 7(5).

17.18 In *Merton LBC v Sinclair Collis Ltd*[1] the prosecution's case was that children had made test purchases of a packet of cigarettes from vending machines, each situated in a different public house, and that these were sales of cigarettes to a child – and, so, on each occasion an offence under CYPA 1933, s 7(1) was committed. The defendant's case was that CYPA 1933, s 7(1) did not apply to purchases from a cigarette vending machine and that the statutory scheme to control the purchase of cigarettes from vending machines was exclusively contained in CYPA 1933, s 7(2). The district judge accepted the defendant's contention. On appeal – Mitting J:

'24 Nothing in the legislative history suggests that the current provision should be construed in any way more favourable to the operators of vending machines than the 1908 Act. If, as I am satisfied, the 1908 Act made it an offence to sell cigarettes to someone who was apparently a child or a young person under 16 by a machine, then those provisions in their re-enacted and amended form continue to have that effect.

25 There is, however, one proviso. I am told that on the machines from which the test purchases were made the statutory notice appeared. D wish to contend that in consequence there could be no sale within the classical definition in section 2 of the Sale of Goods Act 1979: because the transaction effected by the child test purchaser was in breach of the prohibition in the notice, it was not the willing transfer of property in cigarettes to a buyer in consideration for payment of a price but the taking by the child of something which he knew he was not entitled to take in return for something that did not amount to a price. That is an argument which has been canvassed before me but did not form any part of the stated case. It would not be right for me to express any view upon it now, let alone to decide it. It is an argument which remains open.'

Following this case the sale of tobacco to a person under the age of 18 years from a vending machine is capable of being an offence contrary to CYPA 1933, s 7(1).

[1]   [2010] EWHC 3089 (Admin).

17.19 However, note that the Children and Young Persons (Protection from Tobacco) Act 1991, s 3A provides that the appropriate national authority may by regulations make provision prohibiting the sale of tobacco from an automatic machine in England and Wales. Where a prohibition contained in the regulations is breached, any person liable in accordance with the regulations is guilty of an offence[1]. The Protection from Tobacco (Sales from Vending Machines) (England) Regulations 2010[2] is one such regulation and prohibits the sale of tobacco products from vending machines in England from 1 October 2011. The Regulations state:

2 Prohibition of the sale of tobacco from vending machines

(1)   The sale of tobacco from an automatic machine is prohibited.
(2)   The person who controls, or is concerned with the management of, the premises where the automatic machine is located shall be liable for a breach of paragraph (1).

[1]   Children and Young Persons (Protection from Tobacco) Act 1991, s 3A(3).
[2]   SI 2010/864.

17.20 The Protection from Tobacco (Sales from Vending Machines) (Wales) Regulations 2011[1] (as from 1 February 2012), and the Protection from Tobacco (Sales from Vending Machines) Regulations (Northern Ireland) 2012[2] (as from 1 March 2012) and the Tobacco and Primary Medical Services (Scotland) Act 2010 (as from 1 April 2013) are of similar effect. Following these enactments, it was anticipated that there would be a highly reduced number of prosecutions under CYPA 1933, s 7(2) and attempts to prosecute sales of tobacco from vending machines to persons under the age of 18 years under CYPA 1933, s 7(1).

[1]   SI 2011/2498.
[2]   SR 2012/15.

17.21 An attempt to challenge the legitimacy of these regulations was made in *R (on the application of Sinclair Collis Ltd) v Secretary of State for Health*[1]. The Administrative Court dismissed the judicial review challenges and held that the ban on the sale of tobacco from automatic vending machines was appropriate to secure the attainment of the legislative objective of the protection of public health and did not go beyond what was necessary.

¹   [2010] EWHC 3112 (Admin).

17.22 A more concerted attempt to use the Sale of Goods Act 1979, s 2 to escape liability under CYPA 1933, s 7(1) can be seen in the case of *Wm Morrisons Supermarkets v Reading BC*[1]. In that case a 15-year-old child made a test purchase of 10 cigarettes from a tobacco kiosk in a Morrisons' store, and handed them to an officer of the prosecuting authority, who was waiting around the corner. It was argued by the defence that since the child was acting at all times on behalf of the local authority, there was no sale for the purposes of the Sale of Goods Act 1979, because the child acquired no rights in or ownership of the cigarettes. It was further argued that the sale was really between the local authority and Morrisons, the child acting merely as an agent, and therefore no sale to a person under 18 had taken place within the meaning of CYPA 1933, s 7. However, the door left somewhat ajar by Mitting J in *Merton LBC v Sinclair Collis Ltd* was firmly closed by Lloyd Jones J, who stated:

> '20 I can see that difficult questions could arise as to whether property passes to the agent or directly to the undisclosed principal. These have not been argued before us. However, it seems clear that property would pass from the seller either to the young person or to his undisclosed principal as a result of entering into this transaction. That the question of criminal liability might turn on such a nice analysis of the transaction in civil law would perhaps be undesirable but certainly a possibility, as is apparent from some of the authorities to which we have referred earlier in this judgment.

> 21 However, I consider that in this instance such an analysis is not called for. I am persuaded that Parliament did not intend to limit the application of this provision to a case where a child or young person acts as principal and therefore property passes to him. On the contrary, I have come to the clear conclusion that section 7(1) of the 1933 Act applies where a child or young person enters into a transaction of sale, whether as a principal or on behalf of someone else, whether disclosed or undisclosed and whether or not property passes to him.'

¹   [2012] EWHC 1358 (Admin).

Defences

17.23 CYPA 1933, s 7(1A) provides:

> (1A) It shall be a defence for a person charged with an offence under subsection (1) above to prove that he took all reasonable precautions and exercised all due diligence to avoid the commission of the offence.

17.24 *Tesco Stores Ltd v Norfolk County Council*[1] concerned a case where the defendant relied on the CYPA 1933, s 7(1A) defence. It was held that in every case where the statutory defence was raised, the decision would turn on the specific facts of the case. It was further held that in the instant case, the trader had put in place a sound and comprehensive system designed to avoid sales to under age buyers, which was under continual review. Care had also been taken over the selection of staff, training and supervision by staff. That more could have been done (for example, the existence of a till prompt and a refusals book) did not equate to a lack of reasonable precautions. The appeal was allowed and the conviction quashed.

1   [2002] LLR 240.

17.25 Although not a defence, note that CYPA 1933, s 7(4) provides:

(4) Nothing in this section shall make it an offence to sell tobacco or cigarette papers to, or shall authorise the seizure of tobacco or cigarette papers in the possession of, any person who is at the time employed by a manufacturer of or dealer in tobacco, either wholesale or retail, for the purposes of his business, or is a boy messenger in uniform in the employment of a messenger company and employed as such at the time.

Restriction on proceedings

17.26 The offence under CYPA 1933, s 7(1) is summary-only – there is therefore a 6 months' time limit on bringing proceedings, which runs from the time when the offence was committed[1].

1   Magistrates' Courts Act 1980, s 127.

Prosecutions

17.27 The offence under CYPA 1933, s 7(1) can be committed by the actual seller or, where applicable, by his employer. In *St Helens MBC v Hill*[1] the owner of the shop was charged with an offence under CYPA 1933, s 7(1), despite the cigarettes being sold by an assistant in the shop when the owner was in the stockroom. Lloyd LJ said:

'I have no doubt that the offence of selling cigarettes to a child apparently under the age of 16 is an offence of strict liability . . .   The justices were, therefore, wrong to regard the sale as having been a sale by the assistant. In the eye of the law, the sale was made by the [owner of the shop] himself.'

1   (1992) 156 JP 602.

17.28 The decision in *St Helens MBC v Hill* raises a further question of whether the sales assistant who actually sold the cigarettes could have been prosecuted. It might be argued – on the basis of the comments of Lloyd LJ – that a mere employee is not in law the seller, and that the concept of selling is limited to the owner of the business who is the likely owner of the cigarettes. It is our view that this interpretation of the law is unhelpful and that the word 'sells' in CYPA 1933, s 7(1) should not be construed so narrowly. It is not clear from Lloyd LJ's judgment in *St Helens MBC v Hill* that he was attempting to confine liability, however any remarks made about the liability of mere employees are necessarily obiter dicta because it was unnecessary to decide whether the sales assistant was liable to find that the proprietor was liable.

17.29 There are, however several other reasons why such an interpretation is wrong. First, Parliament has not attempted to complicate the notion of selling by reference to ownership, or proprietorship. There will be many occasions when a vendor will sell over-the-counter tobacco goods that he, or his company, does not in law own. Parliament cannot have intended a complex definition of selling, which was attributed only to those who owned the tobacco or premises from which it is sold.

17.30 Secondly, in our view there is no reason why there cannot be more than one seller at the same time, so that there would be concurrent liability of both the proprietor of a shop and sales assistant. This is supported by an earlier decision in *Preston v Albuery*[1] which focused upon the meaning of sells (under the Merchandise Marks Act 1887, since repealed). Although *Preston v Albuery* is not in relation to the same statute, it is a decision on the ordinary construction of the word 'sells' and therefore directly relevant[2]. In *Preston v Albuery* the defendant was an employee of a coal merchant who delivered sacks of short weight to a purchaser. The court held that he had sold the goods, finding that the person who passes the property in the goods was a seller. Ashworth J stated that, 'where in order to complete a sale, property has to be transferred or appropriated, the person who does transfer or appropriate is a person who sells'.

[1]   [1963] 3 All ER 897.
[2]   It is also worth noting that *Albuery* was not cited to the court in *Hill*.

17.31 It is submitted that the wider construction of 'sells' attributed by the court in *Preston v Albuery* should be preferred. There is no reason that a rogue employee who sells cigarettes to children should escape sanction. This is even more important when the employer has a due diligence defence because it cannot have been the policy of the legislation that nobody would be liable in such circumstances. In any case that a corporate defendant is likely to raise the due diligence defence and argue that the employee was acting on a frolic of their own, it is submitted that it would be open to the prosecutor to charge both employee and employer at the same time.

Duty to enforce

17.32 The Children and Young Persons (Protection from Tobacco) Act 1991, s 5 ('CYP(PT)A 1991') provides for enforcement action by defined local authorities in England and Wales in relation to CYPA 1933, s 7. CYP(PT)A 1991, s 5 requires councils to consider, at least once a year, the extent to which it is appropriate for them to carry out in their area a programme of enforcement. Councils must then carry out any programme that is considered to be appropriate. Programmes may include all or any of the following: bringing prosecutions; investigating complaints; taking other measures intended to reduce the incidence of CYPA 1933, s 7 offences; making complaints under CYPA 1933, s 7(2) and monitoring machines for the sale of tobacco.

Sentencing

17.33 A person who commits an offence under CYPA 1933, s 7(1) or 7(2) is liable, on summary conviction to a fine not exceeding level 4 on the standard scale.

Restricted premises orders and restricted sale orders

17.34 The Criminal Justice and Immigration Act 2008, s 143:

(a)   Inserts CYPA 1933, s 12A, enabling a magistrates' court to impose restricted premises orders preventing the sale, either in person or by automatic machine, of tobacco or nicotine products or cigarette papers on certain premises for up to one year. A magistrates' court may make a restricted premises order only if, in addition to the tobacco or nicotine offence on the premises for which the offender has been convicted, the offender has also committed at least two other tobacco or nicotine offences on the premises within a 2-year period (whether or not convicted of those other offences).

(b)   Inserts CYPA 1933, s 12B enabling a magistrates' court to impose restricted sale orders. A restricted sale order is an order which prohibits a specific named person from making any sale of tobacco, nicotine products, or cigarette papers (whether in person or by automatic machine) to any person for up to one year. It also prohibits the person from having management functions in relation to such sales and from keeping any machine on any premises for the purpose of selling tobacco or nicotine products. A magistrates' court may make a restricted sale order only if, in addition to the tobacco or nicotine offence for which the offender has been convicted, the offender has also committed at least two other tobacco or nicotine offences within a 2-year period (whether or not convicted of those other offences).

17.35 A tobacco or nicotine offence means an offence committed under CYPA 1933, s 7(1) or s 7(2), the CYP(PT)A, s 3A[1] and CFA 2014, s 92[2].

[1]   Provides power for the appropriate national authority to prohibit the sale of tobacco from vending machines.
[2]   Provides power for the Secretary of State by regulations to make provisions prohibiting the sale of nicotine products to persons under aged 18.

17.36 If a person fails to comply with a restricted premises order and knew or ought reasonably to have known that the sale was in contravention of the order, or a restricted sales order, the person commits an offence[1]. A person found guilty of breaching a restricted premises order or a restricted sale order is liable to an unlimited fine[2].

[1]   CYPA 1933, ss 12C(1) and 12C(2).
[2]   CYPA 1933, s 12C(4).

Offences under CFA 2014

17.37 The CFA 2014, s 91(1) (as amended) provides:

91 Purchase of tobacco etc. on behalf of persons under 18

(1)   A person aged 18 or over who buys or attempts to buy tobacco, cigarette papers or a relevant nicotine product on behalf of an individual aged under 18 commits an offence.

17.38

Precedent for offence of buying tobacco for a person under 18

Information

A B, a person aged 18 or over, on [date], attempted to buy tobacco, namely a single size 20 pack of cigarettes, on behalf of C D, an individual aged under 18, contrary to section 91 of the Children and Families Act 2014.

17.39 Regulation 2 of the Nicotine Inhaling Products (Age of Sale and Proxy Purchasing) Regulations 2015[1] came fully in to force on 1 October 2015. Regulation 2 amended CFA 2014, s 91 so as to make it an offence for a person to purchase relevant nicotine products on behalf of a person under the age of 18. Tobacco is given the same meaning as in CYPA 1933, s 7[2]. 'Relevant nicotine product' is defined in the Nicotine Inhaling Products (Age of Sale and Proxy Purchasing) Regulations 2015[3] and discussed in more detail later in this section.

1   SI 2015/895, reg 2.
2   CFA 2014, s 91(7); CYPA 1933, s 7(5).
3   SI 2015/895.

17.40 In August 2016 the Chartered Trading Standards Institute ('CTSI') reported that officers had carried out the first national test purchase operation, for the Department of Health, since sales of nicotine e-cigarettes and vaping liquids to under 18s were banned under the Regulations. The operation found compliance was 'disappointingly low, with illegal sales made on 246 occasions', equivalent to 39% of cases, drawn from independent pharmacies, specialist e-cigarette suppliers, discount stores, markets and tobacconists. However, in January 2017 CTSI reported that 80% of the businesses that illegally sold in the first national test purchase operation did not sell when tested again, and of those that did not sell 90% asked for proof of age.

Defences

17.41 CFA 2014, s 91(2) provides:

(2) Where a person is charged with an offence under this section it is a defence—
   (a)   that the person had no reason to suspect that the individual concerned was aged under 18, or
   (b)   in a case where the person has bought or attempted to buy cigarette papers, that the person had no reason to suspect that the individual concerned intended to use the papers for smoking.

Restriction on proceedings

17.42 The offence under CFA 2014, s 91 is summary only: there is therefore a 6-month time limit on bringing proceedings, which runs from the time when the offence was committed[1].

1   Magistrates' Courts Act 1980, s 127.

Duty to enforce

17.43 The CFA 2014, s 91(4) makes it the duty of each local weights and measures authority in England and Wales to enforce the provisions of the section within its area.

Powers of enforcement officers

17.44 The CFA 2014, s 91(6) provides that the powers of entry under the Health Act 2006, s 11 and Sch 2 apply to this section. The powers in the Health Act 2006, Sch 2 include the following: entering premises (not private dwellings) at a reasonable hour; carrying out inspections and examinations; requiring the production of any product or substance, inspecting it, and taking and retaining samples of or extracts from it; taking possession and retaining any substance or product on the premises; requiring any person to give such information, or afford such facilities and assistance as necessary; and, arranging for any substance, product, sample or extract to be analysed.

Sentencing

17.45 The CFA 2014, s 91(3) provides that a person who commits an offence under CFA 2014, s 91(1) is liable on summary conviction to a fine not exceeding level 4 on the standard scale. CFA 2014, s 91(5) further provides that fixed penalty notices can be issued by a person authorised by the local weights and measures authority. The Proxy Purchasing of Tobacco, Nicotine Products etc. (Fixed Penalty Amount) Regulations 2015[1] set the amount of the fine at £90.

[1]   SI 2015/896.

Offences under Nicotine Inhaling Products (Age of Sale and Proxy Purchasing) Regulations 2015

17.46 The CFA 2014, s 92(1) provides that the Secretary of State may make regulations prohibiting the sale of nicotine products to persons aged under 18. The CFA 2014, s 92(2) states that a person breaching any prohibition created by a regulation under CFA 2014, s 92(1) commits an offence. The Nicotine Inhaling Products (Age of Sale and Proxy Purchasing) Regulations 2015[1] ('NIP 2015') is one such regulation and came into force in October 2015. Regulation 3 prohibits the sale of nicotine inhaling products (commonly referred to as e-cigarettes) to persons under the age of 18. The Regulations also set out exceptions for nicotine inhaling products which are licensed as medicines[2].

[1]   SI 2015/895.
[2]   NIP 2015, SI 2015/895, regs 4 and 5.

17.47 A 'nicotine inhaling product' means any nicotine inhaling device (which is used to inhale nicotine through a mouth piece but is not tobacco, cigarette papers or a device intended to be used for the consumption of lit tobacco), nicotine cartridges (which contain nicotine but not tobacco and form part of a nicotine inhaling device) or nicotine refill substances (which contain nicotine but not tobacco and is intended to refill a nicotine inhaling device)[1].

[1]   NIP 2015, SI 2015/895, reg 1.

17.48 Regulation 7 of NIP 2015 provides for a statutory review of the Regulations within 5 years of their coming into force. This review was commenced as part of a wider review of all tobacco legislation coming into force between 2010 and 2016 and included a public consultation which closed on 15 September 2019. Specifically, in relation to NIP 2015, the following questions were asked:

(i)   Do you think NIP 2015 has helped prevent the sale of nicotine inhaling products including e-cigarettes, to under 18s?

(ii)   Has anyone else benefitted from the age restriction and proxy (when an adult buys a product on behalf of a minor) purchasing ban on nicotine inhaling products?

(iii)   What impact has the age restriction and proxy purchasing ban had on the general population, people under the age of 18, people over the age of 18, retailers, manufacturers and other stakeholders?

(iv)   Is the age of sale restriction and ban on proxy purchasing of nicotine inhaling products an effective way to protect young people from harms of nicotine-containing products?

(v)   Were there any economic losses or gains associated with carrying out this regulation in the community?

A response by the Department for Health and Social Care was published in January 2021. This explained that: (i) e-cigarette prevalence amongst 11–15 years olds had increased only slightly since 2014, indicating that the legislation had served to check growth in e-cigarette use; (ii) adult prevalence over the same period had continued to increase; (iii) there was no evidence of significant costs to business from this legislation; (iv) consultation responses from health-related NGOs, public sector bodies and businesses were generally supportive of the legislation. The report concluded that whilst there was limited evidence, there was enough to enable the conclusion that the legislation had achieved its original objective by limiting increases in the use of nicotine inhaling products amongst young people. Accordingly, these regulations will remain in force as they are.

Defences

17.49 The CFA 2014, s 92(3) provides that no offence is committed where at the time of sale, the person to whom the nicotine product is sold is employed by a manufacturer of or dealer in nicotine products, and the purchase is made for the purpose of that business. The CFA 2014, s 92(4) provides a statutory defence where the person took all reasonable precautions and exercised all due diligence to avoid committing the offence.

Restriction on proceedings

17.50 The offence under CFA 2014, s 92 is summary only – there is therefore a 6-month time limit on bringing proceedings which runs from the time when the offence was committed[1].

[1]   Magistrates' Courts Act 1980, s 127.

Prosecutions

17.51 The offence created by CFA 2014, s 92(2) is a strict liability offence which means that not only can the person who made the sale be prosecuted, but so can the owner of the retail outlet where the sale took place.

Duty to enforce

17.52 The Children and Young Persons (Protection from Tobacco) Act 1991, s 5 provides for enforcement action by defined local authorities in England and Wales in relation to CFA 2014, s 92. Further, CYP(PT)A 1991, s 5 requires councils to carry out a programme of enforcement at least once a year and sets out what the programme must involve.

Sentencing

17.53 A person who commits an offence under CFA 2014, s 92 is liable on summary conviction to a fine not exceeding level 4 on the standard scale[1].

[1]   CFA 2014, s 92(5).

Other offences

17.54 The Children and Young Persons (Protection from Tobacco) Act 1991, s 4 makes it an offence for any person who carries on a business involving the sale of tobacco by retail at any premises to fail to exhibit, in a prominent position, a notice displaying the statement 'It is illegal to sell tobacco products to anyone under the age of 18'. The notice must be exhibited where the statement is readily visible to persons at the point of sale of the tobacco. CYP(PT)A 1991, s 4 further creates a similar offence where no notice stating 'This machine is only for the use of people aged 18 or over' is exhibited on every automatic machine for the sale of tobacco which is kept available for use. The Protection from Tobacco (Display of Warning Statements) Regulations 1992[1] prescribe the dimensions of the notice and the size of the statement which must be displayed on such a notice. Currently, there is no legal requirement for retailers to exhibit a similar warning for nicotine inhaling products.

[1]   SI 1992/3228.

Commentary

17.55 Other recent legislative developments, relating to the sale of tobacco, include:

(a)   The implementation of legislation to end tobacco displays in shops. Legislation to end tobacco displays came fully into effect on 6 April 2015[1].

(b)   Legislative developments relating to the plain packaging of tobacco products. The CFA 2014, s 94 provides for the making of regulations relating to the retail packaging of tobacco products in order to reduce the risk of harm to, or to promote, the health and welfare of people under the age of 18. The Standardised Packaging of Tobacco Products Regulations 2015[2] are made under the CFA 2014 and came into force on 20 May 2016. The Regulations are enforced by Local Authority Trading Standards (or environmental health officers in Northern Ireland), using their powers under the Consumer Protection Act 1987, s 18. The Regulations relate to packaging of cigarettes and rolling tobacco and cover the colour and shade of packaging; the material, shape, opening, unit contents of the packets, the appearance of cigarettes and the scent of the tobacco. Regulation 15 creates an either-way offence of breaching any of the requirements in the Regulations, punishable summarily by 3 months' imprisonment and/or fine; and on indictment by 2 years' imprisonment and/or fine. The legality of the Regulations was challenged by a number of manufacturers and suppliers of tobacco products through judicial review proceedings. It was held in *R (on the application of British American Tobacco UK Ltd) v Secretary of State for Health*[3] that the Regulations were lawful and proportionate.

(c)   Legislative developments relating to smoking in cars carrying children. The CFA 2014, s 95 amends the Health Act 2006, s 5, which relates to smoke-free vehicles, inserting subsection (1A) which provides 'Regulations under this section may in particular provide for a private vehicle to be smoke-free where a person under the age of 18 is present in the vehicle'. The Smoke-Free (Private Vehicles) Regulations 2015[4] came into force in October 2015. They require private vehicles in England to be smoke free where they are enclosed; there is more than one person present; and one of those present is under the age of 18. They also place a duty on the driver of a vehicle to stop a person smoking in that vehicle in those circumstances. Regulation 4 provides that a Fixed Penalty Notice may be given by an authorised officer of an enforcement authority where there is reason to believe that a person has committed an offence of failing to prevent smoking in a vehicle that is smoke-free by virtue of the Regulations.

(d)   The Children and Young Persons (Protection from Tobacco) Act 1991, s 3 creates an offence for any person carrying on a retail business to sell cigarettes to any person other than in their original package. Regulation 4(8) of the Standardised Packaging of Tobacco Products Regulations 2015[5] provides that a unit packet of cigarettes must now contain a minimum of 20 cigarettes.

As part of the government's post implementation review of tobacco legislation, along with NIP 2015, the Tobacco Advertising and Promotion (Display) (England) Regulations 2010, the Tobacco Advertising and Promotion (Specialist Tobacconists) (England) Regulations 2010, the Tobacco Advertising and Promotion (Display of Prices) (England) Regulations 2010 and the Smoke-Free (Private Vehicles) Regulations 2015 were being reviewed. The results were published in January 2021 and the Department of Health and Social Care have decided that all of these regulations should remain in force as they are.

1   Tobacco Advertising and Promotion (Display) (England) Regulations 2010, SI 2010/445; Tobacco Advertising and Promotion (Specialist Tobacconists) (England) Regulations 2010, SI 2010/446; Tobacco Advertising and Promotion (Display of Prices) (England) Regulations 2010, SI 2010/863; Tobacco Advertising and Promotion (Display of Prices) (Wales) Regulations 2012, SI 2012/1911; Tobacco Advertising and Promotion (Specialist Tobacconists)

(Wales) Regulations 2012, SI 2012/1287; Tobacco Advertising and Promotion (Display) (Wales) Regulations 2012, SI 2012/1285; Tobacco Advertising and Promotion (Display of Prices) Regulations (Northern Ireland) 2012, SR 2012/341; Tobacco Advertising and Promotion (Display) Regulations (Northern Ireland) 2012, SR 2012/246.

2   SI 2015/829.
3   [2016] EWCA Civ 1182.
4   SI 2015/286.
5   SI 2015/829, reg 4(8).

TOBACCO (SCOTLAND)

Introduction

17.56 Responsibility for tobacco regulation is devolved to the Scottish Parliament. Legal provisions – brought into force during 2010 and 2011 – relating to the prohibition of sales of tobacco to a person under 18 and an offence of purchasing tobacco products by under 18s or by persons aged 18 or over on behalf of under 18s are contained in the Tobacco and Primary Medical Services (Scotland) Act 2010 ('TPMS(S)A 2010').

17.57 TPMS(S)A 2010 also contains a number of other controls on the sale of tobacco, including a ban on the display of tobacco products and on the sale of tobacco products from vending machines, the establishment of a Register of Tobacco Retailers and the introduction of tobacco retailing banning orders. The Act consolidates and updates some tobacco sales legislation (including provisions from the Children and Young Persons (Scotland) Act 1937; the Children and Young Persons (Protection from Tobacco) Act 1991; the Tobacco Advertising and Promotion Act 2002; and the Smoking, Health and Social Care (Scotland) Act 2005).

17.58 In the case of *Petition of Imperial Tobacco Ltd for Judicial Review of sections 1 and 9 of the Tobacco and Primary Medical Services (Scotland) Act 2010*[1], Imperial Tobacco Ltd brought a judicial review seeking a ruling by the Outer House, Court of Session that TPMS(S)A 2010, s 1 (which prohibits the display of tobacco products) and TPMS(S)A 2010, s 9 (which prohibits the use of vending machines) were outside the legislative competence of the Scottish Parliament and therefore were not law. The Court held that TPMS(S)A 2010, ss 1 and 9 were within the competence of the Scottish Parliament and dismissed the petition. This was confirmed by the Supreme Court in *Imperial Tobacco v Lord Advocate*[2].

1   [2010] CSOH 134.
2   [2012] UKSC 61.

17.59 Coinciding with the remainder of the UK, a tobacco display ban in Scotland came into force on 6 April 2015, by virtue of the Sale of Tobacco (Display of Tobacco Products and Prices etc.) (Scotland) Regulations 2013[1].

1   SSI 2013/85.

17.60 The Smoking Prohibition (Children in Motor Vehicles) (Scotland) Act 2016, which fully came into force in December 2016, creates an offence of smoking in a vehicle in which a child is present, bringing it in line with the rest of the UK, where similar legislation has been in force since 2015[1].

[1] Smoking Prohibition (Children in Motor Vehicles) (Scotland) Act 2016 (Commencement) Regulations 2016, SSI 2016/259.

Application

17.61 The TPMS(S)A 2010, s 35 provides that 'tobacco product' means a product consisting wholly or partly of tobacco and intended to be smoked, sniffed, sucked or chewed. A 'nicotine vapour product' is: (a) a device intended to enable the inhalation of nicotine-containing vapour by an individual; (b) a device intended to enable the inhalation of other vapour by an individual but intended to resemble and be operated in a similar way to (a); (c) an item intended to form part of a device in (a) and (b); and (d) a substance intended to be vaporised by a device within (a) or (b)[1]. Note that TPMS(S)A 2010, s 33 raises a presumption in prosecutions for selling tobacco to persons under the age of 18 that the contents of a container (whether sealed or not) conform to the description of the substance on the container. The presumption can be rebutted by any party at trial.

[1] TPMS(S)A 2010, s 35A (as added by the Health (Tobacco, Nicotine etc and Care) (Scotland) Act 2016, s 1).

Offences relating to the sale of tobacco

17.62 The following offences are created by TPMS(S)A 2010 in relation to persons under the age of 18.

17.63 TPMS(S)A 2010, s 4(1) restates (with modifications) the offence in the Children and Young Persons (Scotland) Act 1937, s 18 and provides:

4 Sale of tobacco products to persons under 18

(1) A person who sells a tobacco product or cigarette papers to a person under the age of 18 commits an offence.

17.64 TPMS(S)A 2010, s 5(1) provides:

5 Purchase of tobacco products by persons under 18

(1) A person under the age of 18 who buys or attempts to buy a tobacco product or cigarette papers commits an offence.

17.65 It is not an offence under TPMS(S)A 2010, s 5(1) for a person under the age of 18 to buy or attempt to buy a tobacco product or cigarette papers if the person is authorised to do so by a council officer or a constable for the purpose of determining whether an offence is being committed under TPMS(S)A 2010, s 4[1]. However, a council officer or a constable may only authorise a person under the age of 18 to buy or attempt to buy a tobacco product or cigarette papers if he is satisfied that all reasonable steps have been or will be taken to avoid any risk to the welfare of the person[2].

[1] TPMS(S)A 2010, s 5(2).
[2] TPMS(S)A 2010, s 5(3).

Avoiding any risk to the welfare of the test-purchaser

17.66 *Guidance for Local Authorities on Test Purchasing Age Restricted Products*, first published in October 2010, and most recently updated on 6 June 2016, sets out updated guidance to be adopted by those authorities and agencies that intend to report criminal offences based on evidence obtained through the use of children (or young people) to test-purchase age-restricted goods. The guide is based on the original LACORS/LGR guidance for England and Wales.

17.67 Paragraphs 10.6–10.7 indicates that it may be considered good practice:

'to follow the requirements of the Regulation of Investigatory Powers (Juveniles) (Scotland) Order 2002 (SSI 2002/206) to ensure that:
- the safety and welfare of the child or young person has been fully considered;
- the officer is satisfied that any risk has been properly explained to, and understood by the child or young person;
- a risk assessment has been undertaken, covering the physical dangers and the moral and psychological aspect of the child or young person's deployment;
- a record is kept.

Experience has shown that in the vast majority of test purchase exercises there has been minimal or no risk to the young test purchaser involved.'

17.68 TPMS(S)A 2010, s 6(1) provides:

6 Purchase of tobacco products on behalf of persons under 18

(1)   A person aged 18 or over who knowingly buys or attempts to buy a tobacco product or cigarette papers on behalf of a person under the age of 18 commits an offence.

17.69 The TPMS(S)A 2010, s 8 makes it an offence for tobacco retailers, without reasonable excuse, not to display a warning statement ('It is illegal to sell tobacco products to anyone under the age of 18'), in accordance with prescribed dimensions[1], in a prominent position, at all points of sale where tobacco products are sold. This section is a restatement of the equivalent provision in the Children and Young Persons (Protection from Tobacco) Act 1991, s 4.

[1]   Sale of Tobacco (Display of Warning Statements) (Scotland) Regulations 2011, SSI 2011/132.

17.70 TPMS(S)A 2010 creates a number of other offences:

(a)   displaying or causing to be displayed tobacco products or smoking-related products in a place (other than a website) where tobacco products are offered for sale (TPMS(S)A 2010, s 1(1));

(b)   displaying or causing to be displayed prices of tobacco products or smoking-related products that do not comply with the regulations (TPMS(S)A 2010, s 3(3));

(c)   a person under 18, who is in possession of tobacco products or cigarette papers in a public place, failing to comply with a request from the police to surrender these items or to supply a name and address (TPMS(S)A 2010, s 7(5));

(d)   selling tobacco products from vending machines (TPMS(S)A 2010, s 9(1)). On 25 January 2018, this offence was extended to nicotine vapour products[1];

(e)   carrying on a tobacco or nicotine vapour product[2] business whilst not on the Register of Tobacco Retailers (TPMS(S)A 2010, s 20(1)) or carrying on such a business from unregistered premises (TPMS(S)A 2010, ss 20(2) and 20(2A)). The TPMS(S)A 2010, s 10 requires the Scottish Ministers to keep a register of persons carrying on a tobacco or nicotine vapour product business and TPMS(S)A 2010, ss 11(2) and 11(2A) set out what must be contained in an application to be registered or to add premises to a person's existing entry in the register. The Sale of Tobacco (Register of Tobacco Retailers) Regulations 2010[3] prescribe information which must be contained in such an application;

(f)   a person who is on the register failing to notify certain changes to the Scottish Ministers (TPMS(S)A 2010, s 20(3));

(g)   breaching a tobacco and nicotine vapour product retailing banning order or an ancillary order (TPMS(S)A 2010, s 20(4))[4];

(h)   failing to display a notice relating to a tobacco and nicotine vapour product retailing banning order (TPMS(S)A 2010, s 20(5))[5].

[1]   Words inserted by Sale of Nicotine Vapour Products (Vending Machines) (Scotland) Regulations 2017, SSI 2017/422, reg 2.
[2]   'nicotine vapour product' is inserted by the Health (Tobacco, Nicotine etc and Care) (Scotland) Act 2016, s 11, and is effective from 1 October 2017.
[3]   SSI 2010/407.
[4]   'nicotine vapour product' is inserted by the Health (Tobacco, Nicotine etc and Care) (Scotland) Act 2016, s 11, and is effective from 1 October 2017.
[5]   'nicotine vapour product' is inserted by the Health (Tobacco, Nicotine etc and Care) (Scotland) Act 2016, s 11, and is effective from 1 October 2017.

Offences relating to the sale of nicotine vapour products

17.71 The Health (Tobacco, Nicotine etc and Care) (Scotland) Act 2016 ('H(TNC)(S)A 2016') received Royal Assent on 6 April 2016 and introduces a similar regime of control on the sale of nicotine vapour products.

17.72 TPMS(S)A 2010, s 4A was added by H(TNC)(S)A 2016, s 2(1) and came fully into force on 1 April 2017[1]. The TPMS(S)A 2010, s 4A provides:

4A Sale of nicotine vapour products to persons under 18

(1)   A person who sells a nicotine vapour product to a person under the age of 18 commits an offence.

[1]   Health (Tobacco, Nicotine etc and Care) (Scotland) Act 2016 (Commencement No 1) Regulations 2017, SSI 2017/12, reg 2 and Sch 1.

17.73 The TPMS(S)A 2010, s 4B was added by H(TNC)(S)A 2016, s 3(1) and came into force on 1 April 2017. The TPMS(S)A 2010, s 4B provides:

4B Age verification policy

(1)   (1) A person commits an offence if the person—
        (a)   carries on a tobacco or nicotine vapour product business, and

(b)   fails to operate an age verification policy in respect of premises at which the person carries on the tobacco or nicotine vapour product business.

17.74 Note TPMS(S)A 2010, s 4B does not apply to business premises[1]. An age verification policy is a policy that steps are to be taken to establish the age of a person attempting to buy a tobacco product, cigarette papers, or a nicotine vapour product on the premises if it appears to the person selling the product that the customer may be under the age of 25 (or such older age as may be specified in the policy)[2].

[1]   As defined in TPMS(S)A 2010, s 4B(2).
[2]   TPMS(S)A 2010, s 4B(3).

17.75 The TPMS(S)A 2010, s 4C was added by H(TNC)(S)A 2016, s 4 and came fully into force on 1 April 2017. The TPMS(S)A 2010, s 4C provides:

4C Sale of tobacco or nicotine vapour products by persons under 18

(1)   A responsible person who allows a tobacco product, cigarette papers or a nicotine vapour product to be sold by a person under the age of 18 commits an offence.

17.76 The TPMS(S)A 2010, s 4C(1) does not apply to a sale which is made at premises which are noted in a registered person's entry in the Register and is authorised by the registered person for those premises. Regulation 2 of the Sale of Tobacco and Nicotine Vapour Products by Persons Under 18 (Scotland) Regulations 2017[1] sets out requirements for authorisation.

[1]   SSI 2017/50.

17.77 The TPMS(S)A 2010, s 6A was added by H(TNC)(S)A 2016, s 6 and came into force on 1 April 2017. The TPMS(S)A 2010, s 6A provides:

6A Purchase of nicotine vapour products on behalf of persons under 18

(1)   A person aged 18 or over who knowingly buys or attempts to buy a nicotine vapour product on behalf of a person under the age of 18 commits an offence.

Defences

17.78 The defence that the accused believed the person under the age of 18 to be aged 18 or over, and the accused had taken reasonable steps to establish the customer's age (by being shown acceptable proof of identification which would have convinced a reasonable person as to the customer's age) is available to offences committed under TPMS(S)A 2010, ss 4[1] and 4A[2]. Acceptable proof of identification includes a passport, a UK driving licence (following the coming into force of the Public Health and Tobacco (EU Exit) (Scotland) (Amendment) Regulations 2019), a European Union photocard driving licence, or a document prescribed by Ministers. Regulation 2 of the Sale of Tobacco (Prescribed Documents) (Scotland) Regulations 2013[3] prescribes a Defence Identity Card, a photographic identity card bearing the national Proof of Age Standards Scheme hologram, a national identity card issued by a member state, Norway, Iceland, Liechtenstein or Switzerland (from the coming into force of the Public Health and Tobacco (EU Exit) (Scotland) (Amendment) Regulations 2019), and a Biometric Immigration Document as documents to establish a person's age.

1 TPMS(S)A 2010, s 4(2).
2 TPMS(S)A 2010, s 4A(2).
3 SSI 2013/202, reg 2 (which revoked the Sale of Tobacco (Prescribed Document) Regulations 2010, SSI 2010/406).

17.79 The TPMS(S)A 2010, s 4D, which was added by H(TNC)(S)A 2016, s 5, creates a new defence for persons charged with an offence under TPMS(S)A 2010, ss 4(1), 4A(1) and 4C(1). Under TPMS(S)A 2010, s 4D it is a defence to prove that the person (or any employee or agent of the person) took all reasonable precautions and exercised all due diligence to prevent the offence being committed.

Restriction on proceedings

17.80 As the offences in TPMS(S)A 2010, ss 4–6A can only be tried under summary procedure, the time limits are established under the Criminal Procedure (Scotland) Act 1995, s 136: within 6 months after the contravention occurred.

Prosecutions

17.81 Offences under TPMS(S)A 2010 can be committed by the actual seller or, where applicable, his employer. The TPMS(S)A 2010, s 34 makes provisions where a body corporate, Scottish partnership or other unincorporated association commits an offence under the Act, which is proved to have been committed with the consent or the connivance of a 'relevant individual' or an individual acting as such, or because of neglect by the 'relevant individual'. In these circumstances, the 'relevant individual', as well as the relevant organisation, will be guilty of the offence. The Scottish Government has published *Guidance for Officers in the enforcement of the provisions of Tobacco and Primary Medical Services (Scotland) Act 2010 relating to the sale of tobacco products*. This document states:

'The following enforcement action is available to officers:
  • written warning
  • Fixed Penalty Notice (FPN)
  • report to the Procurator Fiscal
  • application to the sheriff for a tobacco retailing banning order

All action taken should be fair, proportionate and consistent and in accordance with the local authority's own enforcement policy.

The term "person" covers any person including individuals, partnerships, bodies corporate and unincorporated associations. It is the intent of the legislation that vicarious liability should apply. Accordingly, in section 4(1),

"a person" may be a shop assistant, manager and/or controller or the owner of the business.

"Relevant individuals" as well as bodies corporate, partnerships or unincorporated associations may also be liable to proceedings if the offence was proved to be due to their consent, connivance or neglect.

It is not possible to recommend what course of action should be implemented in any set of circumstances but in normal circumstances officers will consider any mitigating circumstances (eg where the retailer has taken all reasonable to steps to prevent a sale but a member of staff ignores their training and company procedures). They will also consider any aggravating circumstances (eg where the seller is advised by the attempted purchaser that they are under age but proceeds with the sale so that a warning or FPN may not be appropriate but merits a report to the PF).'

Duty to enforce

17.82 It is the duty of councils[1] to enforce within their area the provisions relating to age-restricted sales and regulations made under them as described above[2]. The TPMS(S)A 2010 s 26 requires councils to carry out a programme of enforcement at least once a year and sets out what the programme must involve.

[1]   Those constituted under the Local Government etc (Scotland) Act 1994, s 2.
[2]   TPMS(S)A 2010, s 25(1).

Powers of enforcement officers

17.83 The TPMS(S)A 2010, ss 28–32 set out powers of enforcement and related matters. In summary, council officers, in order to establish compliance with requirements set out in TPMS(S)A 2010, may enter non-residential premises, inspect and examine the premises, require the production of documents and records, take possession of documents and records and require other people to provide them with information and assistance (s 28). Police powers to enforce the Act are similar to those provided for in ss 28 and 32. Sections 29 and 30 provide for warrants for entry in specific circumstances including when the officer has been refused entry or expects to be refused entry. Section 31 creates offences for obstructing a council officer or making false statements to such an officer. There exists a defence to the latter charge if the accused did not know that the information was false and had reasonable grounds to believe it was true.

Sentencing

17.84 TPMS(S)A 2010 sets out different levels of penalty for the offences under ss 4–6A, as follows:

Section	Brief description	Mode of trial	Maximum sentence
4(1)	Sale of tobacco products to persons under 18	Summary only	Fine not exceeding level 4 on the standard scale
4A(1)	Sale of nicotine vapour products to persons under 18	Summary only	Fine not exceeding level 4 on the standard scale
4B(1)	Age verification policy	Summary only	Fine not exceeding level 2 on the standard scale

Section	Brief description	Mode of trial	Maximum sentence
4C(1)	Sale of tobacco or nicotine vapour products by persons under 18	Summary only	Fine not exceeding level 1 on the standard scale
5(1)	Purchase of tobacco products by persons under 18	Summary only	Fine not exceeding level 1 on the standard scale
6(1)	Purchase of tobacco products on behalf of persons under 18	Summary only	Fine not exceeding level 5 on the standard scale
6A(1)	Purchase of nicotine vapour products on behalf of persons under 18	Summary only	Fine not exceeding level 5 on the standard scale

Fixed penalty notices

17.85 The TPMS(S)A 2010, s 27 allows council officers and police constables to issue fixed penalty notices for the above offences. Fixed penalty notices may not be issued to under 16s. Schedule 1 makes further provision in relation to the fixed penalty notice regime.

17.86 The Sale of Tobacco (Registration of Moveable Structures and Fixed Penalty Notices) (Scotland) Regulations 2011[1] prescribe that:

(a)   a fixed penalty notice cannot be given after 7 days from the date of the offence[2];

(b)   the amount of the fixed penalty for offences under TPMS(S)A 2010, ss 5 (purchase of tobacco products by persons under 18) and 7 (confiscation of tobacco products from persons under 18) is £50 (and the discounted amount is £30)[3];

(c)   the amount and the discounted amount for all other offences under Chapters 1 and 2 of Pt 1 TPMS(S)A 2010 is £200 (and the discounted amount is £150)[4];

(d)   where the person receiving the fixed penalty notice has already had a fixed penalty or a conviction for a tobacco offence under the Act within the previous 2 years, the amounts are escalated in accordance with the Schedule to the Regulations[5].

[1]   SSI 2011/23.
[2]   SSI 2011/23, reg 5.
[3]   SSI 2011/23, reg 6.
[4]   SSI 2011/23, reg 7.
[5]   SSI 2011/23, reg 7.

Tobacco retailing banning orders

17.87 The TPMS(S)A 2010, s 15 (the amendments to which fully came into force on 1 October 2017[1]) provides that a council may apply to the sheriff for an order banning a tobacco or nicotine vapour product retailer from selling tobacco or nicotine vapour product from specified premises within the council's area. The conditions are that there have been three or more enforcement actions relating to those premises, at least one of the enforcement actions has been within the 2 months preceding the application made by the council, the conduct which gave rise to the enforcement actions all took place within a 2-year period, and the making of the order is necessary to prevent the commission of offences. Enforcement actions can be in the form of a fixed penalty notice, a conviction for an offence under Chapters 1 or 2 of TPMS(S)A 2010, or a conviction for an offence under the Trade Marks Act 1994, ss 92(1)(b) or (c) where the goods are, or include, tobacco products, smoking related products or nicotine vapour products. The enforcement action may be against the person who is the subject of the application or an employee or agent of that person. The ban can be for a period up to 24 months.

[1]   H(TNC)(S)A 2016, s 10.

17.88 The TPMS(S)A 2010, s 16 (the amendments to which fully came into force on 1 October 2017[1]) allows councils to apply to the sheriff for an 'ancillary order' which can be made along with an application for a banning order or at a later date once a banning order is in place. The order can be sought to prevent the person (against whom a TPMS(S)A 2010, s 15 order is being sought or has already been made) from being connected to or seeking to control another person carrying on a tobacco or nicotine vapour product business at the specified premises. In addition, where this person is not an individual (eg is a company or partnership), an order can be sought to ban any person connected to the person from carrying on a tobacco or nicotine vapour product business at the specified premises or being connected to or seeking to control any such person. The conditions are that the order is necessary to prevent the commission of further offences under Chapters 1 or 2 of TPMS(S) 2010 and the sheriff makes the banning order. Any ancillary order ceases to have effect when the banning order to which it relates ceases to have effect.

[1]   H(TNC)(S)A 2016, s 10.

17.89 An appeals process against a tobacco or nicotine vapour product[1] retailing banning order or an ancillary order is set out in TPMS(S)A 2010, s 17. The TPMS(S)A 2010, s 18 requires the sheriff to notify the Scottish Ministers on making a tobacco or nicotine vapour product banning order or ancillary order. The Clerk to the Sheriff Appeal Court[2] must also notify the Scottish Ministers of the outcome of any appeal.

[1]   As amended by H(TNC)(S)A 2016, s 10.
[2]   As amended by the Courts Reform (Scotland) Act 2014 (Relevant Officer and Consequential Provisions) Order 2016, SSI 2016/387, Sch 3(1), para 5.

17.90 Under TPMS(S)A 2010, s 19, a tobacco or nicotine vapour product[1] retailer, in respect of whom a tobacco or nicotine vapour product retailing banning order has been granted, is required to display a notice in the premises specified in the order if the person continues to carry on a retail business at those premises. The TPMS(S)A 2010, s 19 sets out specific requirements of the notice, including the content of the notice, where it is to be displayed and the period in which the notice has to be displayed. The Sale of Tobacco (Register of Tobacco Retailers) Regulations 2010[2] prescribe information that must be contained in such a notice.

[1]   As amended by H(TNC)(S)A 2016, s 10.
[2]   SSI 2010/407.

Commentary

17.91 On 27 March 2013, the Scottish Government published its new *Tobacco Control Strategy – Creating a Tobacco-Free Generation*. The strategy sets out the Scottish Government's ambition for a smoke-free Scotland by 2034. A technical paper accompanies this target. The strategy also sets out a range of actions, many of which have been implemented since the publication of the report, including:

(a)   standardised tobacco packaging;

(b)   smoke-free hospital grounds;

(c)   social marketing campaign on second-hand smoke;

(d)   review of smoking cessation services; and

(e)   a pilot of the ASSIST peer-education programme in schools.

This action plan has subsequently been replaced by the Tobacco Control Action Plan 2018, which sets out a five-year action plan detailing the interventions and policies to help reduce the use of and associated harms from using tobacco.

ALCOHOL

Introduction

17.92 'Protection of children from harm' is one of the 'licensing objectives' set out in the Licensing Act 2003 ('LA 2003')[1] and the LA 2003 contains a number of specific offences relating to children[2]. Although the legal drinking age is 18, a 16 or 17-year-old may drink beer, wine or cider with 'a table meal' on licensed premises, where accompanied by an adult aged 18 years or over[3]. The Licensing Act 2003 (Mandatory Licensing Conditions) Order 2010[4] provides that the premises licence holder or club premises certificate holder must ensure that an age verification policy is adopted in respect of the premises in relation to the sale or supply of alcohol[5]. The policy must require individuals who appear to the responsible person to be under 18 years of age (or such older age as may be specified in the policy) to produce on request, before being served alcohol, identification bearing their photograph, date of birth and either a holographic mark, or an ultraviolet feature[6]. In October 2014, the age verification policy requirements were updated to provide that the designated premises supervisor is personally responsible for ensuring that the supply of alcohol is carried on in accordance with the age verification policy[7]. To assist businesses, the Home Office issued in July 2012 a document entitled *'False ID Guidance'* to provide better understanding of the issues surrounding false IDs and how to deal with them. Further, in April 2018, the Home Office issued revised guidance to licensing authorities on the discharge of their functions under the LA 2003[8].

[1]   LA 2003, s 4.
[2]   LA 2003, ss 145–154.
[3]   LA 2003, ss 149(4) and (5).
[4]   SI 2010/860.
[5]   SI 2010/860, Sch 1, para 3(1).
[6]   SI 2010/860, Sch 1, para 3(3).
[7]   Licensing Act 2003 (Mandatory Licensing Conditions) (Amendment) Order 2014, SI 2014/2440, Sch 1, para 3(2).
[8]   *Revised Guidance issued under section 182 of the Licensing Act 2003* (April 2018).

17.93 In Wales, the Public Health (Minimum Price for Alcohol) (Wales) Act 2018 received Royal Assent on 9 August 2018, however, the majority of the Act came into force on 2 March 2020. The Act makes provision about the minimum price for which alcohol is to be supplied in Wales to a person in Wales and establishes a local authority led enforcement regime. The Act makes it an offence for a person who is an alcohol retailer to supply alcohol, or to authorise the supply of alcohol, from qualifying premises in Wales, to a person in Wales, at a selling price below the applicable minimum price. It does not matter for the purposes of the offence whether the authorisation of the supply of alcohol takes place in Wales or elsewhere. So, for instance, if an alcohol retailer is in England when he or she authorises a supply of alcohol below the applicable minimum price from qualifying premises in Wales, and to a person in Wales, that retailer will (subject to any applicable defence) commit an offence. The Act allows an authorised officer of a local authority to issue a fixed penalty notice to a person that officer has reason to believe has committed an offence under s 2 in the local authority's area.

17.94 In Scotland, only the police can enforce the age restrictions applying to the sale of alcohol, in particular, under the Licensing (Scotland) Act 2005. The Act creates a number of offences including: selling alcohol to a 'child' or a 'young person';[1] selling liqueur confectionary to a child[2]; and a child or young person buying or attempting to buy alcohol (whether for himself or herself or another person)[3]. The Air Weapons and Licensing (Scotland) Act 2015[4] inserts two new offences of supplying alcohol to a child and supplying alcohol to a young person into the Licensing (Scotland) Act 2005[5]. These offences were introduced to tackle drinking in outdoor public places. The Air Weapons and Licensing (Scotland) Act 2015[6] also repealed the Licensing (Scotland) Act 2005, ss 105(4), (5) and (7), thereby removing the offence of knowingly buying or attempting to buy alcohol on behalf of a child or young person, or for consumption on relevant premises by a child or young person. The Alcohol etc (Scotland) Act 2010 makes a number of provisions regulating the sale of alcohol and, specifically, has the effect of imposing a further mandatory condition in premises licences to ensure that there must be an age-verification policy in relation to the sale of alcohol on the premises[7]. Further, minimum price provisions, similar to those implemented in Wales, came into force on 1 May 2018.

[1] Licensing (Scotland) Act 2005, s 102.
[2] Licensing (Scotland) Act 2005, s 104.
[3] Licensing (Scotland) Act 2005, s 105.
[4] Air Weapons and Licensing (Scotland) Act 2015, s 53.
[5] Licensing (Scotland) Act 2005, ss 104A and 104B.
[6] Air Weapons and Licensing (Scotland) Act 2005, s 53.
[7] Alcohol etc (Scotland) Act 2010, s 6(2).

17.95 The Police Service of Northern Ireland ('PSNI') enforces the laws on underage drinking primarily through the Licensing (Northern Ireland) Order 1996[1] (as amended). The legislative scheme in England and Wales does not specifically require premises to display age-related notices but there are obligations to do so in Scotland[2] and Northern Ireland[3].

[1] SI 1996/3158.
[2] Licensing (Scotland) Act 2005, s 110.

³ Licensing (Notice Relating to Age) Regulations (Northern Ireland) SR 2012/24, reg 2 and Sch 1; Registration of Clubs (Notice Relating to Age) Regulations (Northern Ireland) SR 2012/27, reg 2 and Sch 1.

Territorial jurisdiction

17.96 The Licensing Act 2003 extends to England and Wales only.

Offences (England and Wales)

Licensing Act 2003

SALE OF ALCOHOL TO CHILDREN (S 146)

17.97 LA 2003, s 146:

146 Sale of alcohol to children

(1)   A person commits an offence if he sells alcohol to an individual aged under 18.

(2)   A club commits an offence if alcohol is supplied by it or on its behalf—
   (a)   to, or to the order of, a member of the club who is aged under 18, or
   (b)   to the order of a member of the club, to an individual who is aged under 18.

(3)   A person commits an offence if he supplies alcohol on behalf of a club—
   (a)   to, or to the order of, a member of the club who is aged under 18, or
   (b)   to the order of a member of the club, to an individual who is aged under 18.

17.98

Precedent for offence of selling alcohol to a person under 18

Information

A B, on [date], sold alcohol, namely a single 700ml bottle of vodka, to C D, an individual aged under 18, contrary to section 146 of the Licensing Act 2003.

ALLOWING THE SALE OF ALCOHOL TO CHILDREN (S 147)

17.99 LA 2003, s 147:

147 Allowing the sale of alcohol to children

(1)   A person to whom subsection (2) applies commits an offence if he knowingly allows the sale of alcohol on relevant premises to an individual aged under 18.

(2)   This subsection applies to a person who works at the premises in a capacity, whether paid or unpaid, which authorises him to prevent the sale.

(3)   A person to whom subsection (4) applies commits an offence if he knowingly allows alcohol to be supplied on relevant premises by or on behalf of a club—
   (a)   to or to the order of a member of the club who is aged under 18, or
   (b)   to the order of a member of the club, to an individual who is aged under 18.

(4)   This subsection applies to—

      (a)   a person who works on the premises in a capacity, whether paid or unpaid, which authorises him to prevent the supply, and

      (b)   any member or officer of the club who at the time of the supply is present on the relevant premises in a capacity which enables him to prevent it.

PERSISTENTLY SELLING ALCOHOL TO CHILDREN (S 147A)

17.100 LA 2003, s 147A provides[1]:

147A Persistently selling alcohol to children

(1)   A person is guilty of an offence if—

      (a)   on 2 or more different occasions within a period of 3 consecutive months alcohol is unlawfully sold on the same premises to an individual aged under 18;

      (b)   at the time of each sale the premises were either licensed premises or premises authorised to be used for a permitted temporary activity by virtue of Part 5; and

      (c)   that person was a responsible person in relation to the premises at each such time.

(2)   For the purposes of this section alcohol sold to an individual aged under 18 is unlawfully sold to him if—

      (a)   the person making the sale believed the individual to be aged under 18; or

      (b)   that person did not have reasonable grounds for believing the individual to be aged 18 or over.

(3)   For the purposes of subsection (2) a person has reasonable grounds for believing an individual to be aged 18 or over only if—

      (a)   he asked the individual for evidence of his age and that individual produced evidence that would have convinced a reasonable person; or

      (b)   nobody could reasonably have suspected from the individual's appearance that he was aged under 18.

(4)   A person is, in relation to premises and a time, a responsible person for the purposes of subsection (1) if, at that time, he is—

      (a)   the person or one of the persons holding a premises licence in respect of the premises; or

      (b)   the person or one of the persons who is the premises user in respect of a temporary event notice by reference to which the premises are authorised to be used for a permitted temporary activity by virtue of Part 5.

(5)   The individual to whom the sales mentioned in subsection (1) are made may, but need not be, the same in each case.

(6)   The same sale may not be counted in respect of different offences for the purpose—

      (a)   of enabling the same person to be convicted of more than one offence under this section; or

      (b)   of enabling the same person to be convicted of both an offence under this section and an offence under section 146 or 147.

(7)   In determining whether an offence under this section has been committed, the following shall be admissible as evidence that there has been an unlawful sale of alcohol to an individual aged under 18 on any premises on any occasion—

      (a)   the conviction of a person for an offence under section 146 in respect of a sale to that individual on those premises on that occasion;

(b)   the giving to a person of a caution (within the meaning of Part 5 of the Police Act 1997) in respect of such an offence; or

(c)   the payment by a person of a fixed penalty under Part 1 of the Criminal Justice and Police Act 2001 in respect of such a sale.

¹   Inserted by the Violent Crime Reduction Act 2006, s 23 and amended by the Policing and Crime Act 2009, s 28.

OTHER OFFENCES

17.101   There are a number of other offences relating to alcohol and children contained in the LA 2003, which fall outside the ambit of this book by reason of the fact that the relevant prosecuting authorities are either the police or the relevant licensing authority. They are listed below:

(a)   By virtue of LA 2003, s 145 it is an offence to admit children under 16 to certain categories of 'relevant premises' if they are not accompanied by an adult and those premises are open for the supply of alcohol for consumption there.

(b)   There was until May 2015 an offence under LA 2003, s 148 of selling liqueur confectionery to a child under 16. In April 2011 one outcome from the retail sector Red Tape Challenge was a government statement to 'abolish symbolic cases of heavy-handed intervention, such as shops needing an alcohol licence to sell chocolate liqueurs'. By virtue of the Deregulation Act 2015, s 70 that recommendation was adopted and the offence abolished.

(c)   LA 2003, s 149 makes it an offence for a child to purchase or attempt to purchase alcohol, but this does not apply where the child purchases or attempts to purchase the alcohol at the request of a constable or a weights and measures inspector, who is acting in the course of his duty. LA 2003, s 149 also makes it an offence for a person to purchase or attempt to purchase alcohol on behalf of a child and to purchase or attempt to purchase alcohol for consumption on relevant premises by an individual aged under 18.

(d)   LA 2003, s 150 makes it an offence for a child knowingly to consume alcohol on relevant premises (see the definition in LA 2003, s 159), and for a person to knowingly allow the consumption of alcohol on relevant premises by an individual aged under 18.

(e)   LA 2003, s 151 sets out offences relating to the delivery of alcohol to children.

(f)   By virtue of LA 2003, s 152 it is an offence for a person to knowingly send an individual aged under 18 to obtain alcohol but this does not apply where the individual buys or attempts to buy the alcohol at the request of a constable, or a weights and measures inspector, who is acting in the course of his duty.

(g)   LA 2003, s 153 provides for the prohibition of unsupervised sales of alcohol by children.

Defences

Sale of alcohol to children (s 146)

17.102 LA 2003, s 146

(4) Where a person is charged with an offence under this section by reason of his own conduct it is a defence that—
    (a)   he believed that the individual was aged 18 or over, and
    (b)   either—
        (i)   he had taken all reasonable steps to establish the individual's age, or
        (ii)   nobody could reasonably have suspected from the individual's appearance that he was aged under 18.
(5) For the purposes of subsection (4), a person is treated as having taken all reasonable steps to establish an individual's age if—
    (a)   he asked the individual for evidence of his age, and
    (b)   the evidence would have convinced a reasonable person.
(6) Where a person ("the accused") is charged with an offence under this section by reason of the act or default of some other person, it is a defence that the accused exercised all due diligence to avoid committing it.

Due diligence is covered in CHAPTER 4, Criminal Enforcement.

Restrictions on proceedings

17.103 LA 2003, s 186(2) provides that proceedings for offences under LA 2003 may be instituted:

    (a)   except in the case of an offence under section 147A, by a licensing authority,
    (b)   by the Director of Public Prosecutions, or
    (c)   in the case of an offence under section 146, 147 or 147A [. . .], by a local weights and measures authority [. . .]

The LA 2003, s 186(3) extends the limitation period in the Magistrates' Courts Act 1980, s 127(1) for bringing summary proceedings from 6 months to a period of 12 months from the offence being committed.

Prosecutions

17.104 Prior to the Licensing Act 2003, there were many cases in which the liability of licensees and other persons were considered and it was conventional wisdom that only a licensee, either directly or by his servant or agent, may sell intoxicating liquor. However, it is clear from cases such as *Nottingham City Council v Wolverhampton and Dudley Breweries Ltd*[1], where it was held that the proprietor of alcoholic drink could 'sell' under the Food Safety Act 1990, in the same way that he could sell any other type of food, that this notion was limited to licensing legislation.

[1]   [2003] EWHC 2847 (Admin).

17.105 A case under predecessor legislation, the Licensing Act 1964, *Haringey London Borough Council v Marks & Spencer plc/Liverpool City Council v Somerfield Stores Ltd*[1], held that a proprietor of intoxicating liquor was not a 'person' under the provisions of that Act which made it an offence to sell intoxicating liquor to a person under 18.

1   [2004] EWHC 1141 (QBD).

17.106 The LA 2003, s 146 represents a departure from the previous offence in the Licensing Act 1964. Original guidance issued in July 2004 under LA 2003, s 182 (which was approved by Parliament) stated 'It should be noted that a body corporate, partnership or unincorporated association (see LA 2003, s 187) may be the subject of proceedings for an offence under LA 2003, s 146' but subsequent issues (including the recent April 2018 issue) do not contain that statement. The opinion of LACORS/LGR is that a corporate body that sells alcohol may commit an offence of selling alcohol to a person under the age of 18 but that a pub-owning company, using tenants, that has no title to the stock, and does not 'sell', cannot therefore commit an offence under LA 2003, s 146[1].

1   *LACORS' Opinion on Corporate Liability for Underage Sales under Licensing Act 2003* (August 2007).

Duty to enforce

17.107 The LA 2003, s 154 states:

154 Enforcement role for weights and measures authorities

(1) It is the duty of every local weights and measures authority in England and Wales to enforce within its area the provisions of sections 146 and 147, so far as they apply to sales of alcohol made on or from premises to which the public have access.

Powers of enforcement officers

17.108 The LA 2003, s 154(2) provides:

(2) A weights and measures inspector may make, or authorise any person to make on his behalf, such purchases of goods as appear expedient for the purpose of determining whether those provisions [sections 146 and 147] are being complied with.

Sentencing

17.109 The offences of selling alcohol to children (LA 2003, s 146) and allowing the sale of alcohol to children (LA 2003, s 147) are punishable by an unlimited fine[1]. Punishment of the offence of persistently selling alcohol to children (LA 2003, s 147A) is no longer limited to a fine not exceeding £20,000 and is now also punishable by an unlimited fine[2]. It should be noted that underage sales do not necessarily lead to the prosecution of individuals or corporate bodies. There are other possible sanctions: the issuing of fixed penalty notices; the issuing of closure notices; a review of the licence, which could, if evidence of persistent illegal sales were presented, lead to revocation of the licence; and a summary review in serious cases of crime or disorder, which falls outside the ambit of this book as an application for such a review may only be made by the chief officer of police[3].

1 Legal Aid, Sentencing and Punishment of Offenders Act 2012, s 85. See also s 146(7) and s 147(5) LA 2003.
2 Legal Aid, Sentencing and Punishment of Offenders Act 2012 (Fines on summary conviction) Regulations 2015, SI 2015/664, Sch 4(1), para 33(4). See also s 147A(8) LA 2003.
3 LA 2003, s 53A(1).

Fixed penalty notices

17.110 The Police and Justice Act 2006, s 15 inserts into the Police Reform Act 2002, s 41A (Accreditation of weights and measures inspectors) enabling a chief constable to grant accreditation to a weights and measures inspector for the purpose of carrying out specified powers set out in the Police Reform Act 2002, Sch 5A, including the issuing of fixed penalty notices.

Closure notices

17.111 The Violent Crime Reduction Act 2006, s 24 inserted LA 2003, ss 169A and 169B providing for the issuing of closure notices for persistently selling alcohol to children. The LA 2003, s 169A enables the police and trading standards officers to issue a closure notice to a person in relation to whom there is evidence that he has committed an offence under LA 2003, s 147A and for which there is a reasonable prospect of conviction. The closure notice discharges the person from any further criminal liability but prevents him from selling alcohol for the period specified in the notice[1].

1 The Police Reform and Social Responsibility Act 2011, s 118(3)(b) increased the period from a maximum of 48 hours to a period of between 48 hours and 336 hours.

Licensing reviews

17.112 A responsible authority or any other person, which includes a Trading Standards department, may apply to the relevant licensing authority for a review of the licence[1]. Revised guidance issued under the LA 2003, s 182 in April 2018 states that where there is persistent sales of alcohol to children occurring at a particular premises, responsible authorities should consider taking steps to ensure that a review of the licence is the norm in these circumstances, particularly where there has been a prosecution under LA 2003, s 147A or a closure notice has been given.

1 LA 2003, s 51.

17.113 The case of *LIDL UK GmbH v City of Glasgow Licensing Board*[1], is an example of the equivalent procedure in Scotland under the Licensing (Scotland) Act 2005, s 39(1): a premises licence was suspended for 5 days following a single sale to a 16-year-old child authorised by the duty manager. Following the incident, the manager was dismissed for failing to comply with the company's policies and staff were given additional training. The company appealed against the suspension of its licence citing lack of evidence that underage sales at the premises was a recurring problem and that the staff-training programme was of a high standard. The Inner House of the Court of

Session held that it was not open to the Board to have found that a ground for review had been established; and that the decision to suspend the licence was unjustified.

1   [2013] CSIH 25.

17.114 When reviewing a licence to sell alcohol where criminal activity is applicable, it is appropriate and necessary to consider the wider public interest and the furtherance of the licensing objectives contained in LA 2003, which includes the prevention of crime[1].

1   *R(Bassetlaw District Council) v Worksop Magistrates' Court* [2008] EWHC 3530 (Admin); *Carmarthenshire CC v Llanelli Magistrates Court* [2009] EWHC 3016 (Admin).

17.115 *City of Sunderland Council v Dawson*[1]. A 15-year-old girl made a test purchase of a bottle of 'wine', which looked like alcohol and was labelled as such (with a 7.5% alcohol by volume statement) but there was no evidence, such as a certificate of analysis, to prove that the contents were actually alcohol. The Justices accepted the defendant's submission of no case to answer. On appeal it was held that the court can draw such inferences as it thinks proper from a document – defined as 'anything in which information of any description is recorded' – by the Criminal Justice Act 1988, s 24(1)[2]. The case was remitted for a rehearing.

1   [2004] EWHC 2796 (Admin).
2   See the Criminal Justice Act 2003, ss 117 and 134.

17.116 *Davies v Carmarthenshire County Council*[1]. The defendant, who was the manageress and joint licensee of a Spar Store was convicted of an offence under the Licensing Act 1964, s 146 when a sales assistant sold alcohol to a 15-year-old test purchaser. On appeal the court found that justices were not entitled to reject the defence of due diligence in the circumstances of this case.

1   [2005] EWHC 464 (Admin).

17.117 *R (on the application of Paul Verma) v Stratford Magistrates' Court*[1]. In this case, involving the sale of alcohol to a 15-year-old test purchaser, a number of issues arose, including the fact that the test purchaser's witness statement had been served under the Criminal Justice Act 1967, s 9 and a late application was made for the test purchaser to give oral evidence. The justices refused the late application and further declined an application to exclude the evidence under the Police and Criminal Evidence Act 1984, s 78. The defendant was convicted and an application for judicial review was dismissed.

1   [2006] EWHC 715 (Admin).

17.118 *Cambridgeshire County Council v Kama*[1]. The defendant was convicted of an offence under the Licensing Act 1964, s 146 when an employee sold alcohol to a 15-year-old test purchaser. The magistrates dismissed the information on the basis of a 'due diligence' defence. The prosecutor's appeal was dismissed. Treacy J at para 15:

> 'With some hesitation, I have come to the conclusion that the Justices' decision, whilst not one that every court would necessarily have come to, was one to which they were entitled to come in the particular circumstances of this case. This decision is not to be

taken as one which gives a licence to small corner shops, for example, not to have refusals book.'

¹ [2006] EWHC 3148 (Admin).

17.119 In *City of Sunderland Council v Dawson*¹ Thomas LJ said at para 52:

'It is important that licensees who are found guilty of selling alcohol to those underage are dealt with sternly in the light of the fact that the sale of alcohol to those underage is a serious contributor to many social and criminal problems.'

¹ [2004] EWHC 2796 (Admin).

FIREWORKS

Introduction

17.120 As explosives, there are strict rules in place in the UK regulating the sale, possession and use of fireworks. From 17 August 2015, the legislative provisions relating to age-restricted fireworks are contained in the Pyrotechnic Articles (Safety) Regulations 2015¹ which implement two European Directives². The Regulations revoke and replace the Pyrotechnic Articles (Safety) Regulations 2010³. From the coming into force of the Product Safety and Metrology etc. (Amendment etc.) (EU Exit) Regulations 2019⁴, the Regulations were amended to reflect the changes made as a result of Brexit.

¹ SI 2015/1553.
² Directive 2013/29/EU (which recasts Directive 2007/23/EU and sets harmonised rules relating to the safety of pyrotechnic articles) and Directive 2014/58/EU (on setting up a system for the traceability of pyrotechnic articles).
³ SI 2010/1554.
⁴ SI 2019/696.

Territorial jurisdiction

17.121 The Pyrotechnic Articles (Safety) Regulations 2015 ('PA(S)R 2015') are applicable throughout the United Kingdom.

Offences

The Pyrotechnic Articles (Safety) Regulations 2015

17.122 Regulations 31–38 of PA(S)R 2015 set out the obligations that manufacturers, importers and distributors have. Upon the coming into force of the Product Safety and Metrology etc. (Amendment etc.) (EU Exit) Regulations 2019¹, regs 35 and 38 were amended, reg 36 was revoked except in relation to Northern Ireland and regs 38A to 38F were added to reflect the changes made as a result of Brexit. The PA(S)R 2015² creates a prohibition on making specified pyrotechnic articles available to persons younger than the minimum age limit. Regulation 62 of PA(S)R 2015 makes any failure to comply with the requirements of reg 31 an offence.

¹ SI 2019/696.
² SI 2015/1553, reg 31.

17.123 Regulation 31 PA(S)R 2015[1] provides:

31 Prohibition on making available to persons younger than the minimum age limit

An economic operator must not make a pyrotechnic article available on the market in the United Kingdom to a person younger than the following minimum age limits—

(a)   for a Christmas cracker, 12 years;
(b)   for a category F1 firework other than a Christmas cracker, 16 years;
(c)   for a category F2 firework or a category F3 firework, 18 years;
(d)   for a category T1 theatrical pyrotechnic article, 18 years;
(e)   for a category P1 other pyrotechnic article, 18 years.

[1]   SI 2015/1553, reg 31.

17.124 Schedule 1 PA(S)R 2015[1] defines the categories of pyrotechnic articles:

Schedule 1

Categories of pyrotechnic article

Fireworks

1. Category F1 fireworks are fireworks which present a very low hazard and negligible noise level and which are intended for use in confined areas, including fireworks which are intended for use inside domestic buildings.

2. Category F2 fireworks are fireworks which present a low hazard and low noise level and which are intended for outdoor use in confined areas.

3. Category F3 fireworks are fireworks which present a medium hazard, which are intended for outdoor use in large open areas and whose noise level is not harmful to human health.

4. Category F4 fireworks are fireworks which present a high hazard, which are intended for use only by persons with specialist knowledge and whose noise level is not harmful to human health.

Theatrical pyrotechnic articles

5. Category T1 theatrical pyrotechnic articles are theatrical pyrotechnic articles which present a low hazard.

6. Category T2 theatrical pyrotechnic articles are theatrical pyrotechnic articles which are intended for use only by persons with specialist knowledge.

Other pyrotechnic articles

7. Category P1 other pyrotechnic articles are pyrotechnic articles, other than fireworks and theatrical pyrotechnic articles, which present a low hazard.

8. Category P2 other pyrotechnic articles are pyrotechnic articles, other than fireworks and theatrical pyrotechnic articles, which are intended for handling or use only by persons with specialist knowledge.

[1]   SI 2015/1553, Sch 1.

17.125 Regulation 2[1] provides for the interpretation of various terms which are relevant to the prohibition contained in reg 31 and the offence in reg 62:

"economic operator" means a manufacturer, importer or distributor;

"manufacturer" means a person who—

(a)   manufactures a pyrotechnic article, or has such an article designed or manufactured; and

(b)   markets that pyrotechnic article under that person's name or trade mark;

"importer" means any person who—

(a)   is established in the UK and places a pyrotechnic article from a country outside of the UK on the market; or

(b)   is established in Northern Ireland and places a pyrotechnic article on the market that has been supplied to them for distribution, consumption or use in the course of a commercial activity, whether in return for payment or free of charge, from an EEA state[2];

"distributor" means any person in the supply chain, other than the manufacturer or the importer, who makes a pyrotechnic article available on the market;

"firework" means a pyrotechnic article intended for entertainment purposes;

"Christmas cracker" means a paper or foil tube, crimped at each end, enclosing novelties and with one or more snaps running along the length of the tube;

"snap" means two overlapping strips of cardboard or paper, or two strings, with a friction sensitive pyrotechnic composition in sliding contact with an abrasive surface and designed to be held in the hand.

[1]   SI 2015/1553, reg 2.
[2]   Amended following the coming into force of the Product Safety and Metrology etc. (Amendment etc.) (EU Exit) Regulations 2019, SI 2019/696.

17.126 Other relevant provisions in PA(S)R 2015 include, under reg 62(1)(f), it is an offence for a manufacturer to contravene or fail to comply with any requirement of reg 11 (which deals with the labelling of pyrotechnic articles). The required labelling information (contained in Sch 3) must include instructions for use and safety information, which must include the minimum age limit for persons to whom the pyrotechnic article can be made available on the market[1]. Further, the labelling of sparklers must also display the words 'Warning: not to be given to children under 5 years of age'[2].

[1]   Pyrotechnic Articles (Safety) Regulations 2015/1553, Sch 3, para 1(f).
[2]   Pyrotechnic Articles (Safety) Regulations 2015/1553, Sch 3, para 3.

Other offences

17.127 Other firework-related provisions of relevance include:

(a)   Under reg 4 of the Fireworks Regulations 2004[1] it is an offence for persons under 18 to possess adult fireworks in public places. The chief officer of police is responsible for enforcing this offence[2].

(b)   Under reg 10 of the Fireworks Regulations 2004[3] suppliers of fireworks to the public are required to display in a prominent position a notice stating that it is illegal to sell adult fireworks or sparklers to anyone under 18, and that it is also illegal for anyone under 18 to possess adult fireworks in a public place.

[1]   SI 2004/1836, reg 4.
[2]   SI 2004/1836, reg 12.
[3]   SI 2004/1836, reg 10.

Defences

17.128 Regulation 64 of the PA(S)R 2015[1] provides for a defence of due diligence for offences under reg 62:

64 Defence of due diligence

(1)   Subject to paragraph (2), (4) and (6), in proceedings for an offence under regulation 62, it is a defence for a person ("P") to show that P took all reasonable steps and exercised all due diligence to avoid committing the offence.

(2)   P may not rely on a defence under paragraph (1) which involves a third party allegation unless P has—

   (a)   served a notice in accordance with paragraph (3); or

   (b)   obtained the leave of the court.

(3)   The notice must—

   (a)   give any information in P's possession which identifies or assists in identifying the person who—

      (i)   committed the act or default; or

      (ii)   supplied the information on which P relied.

   (b)   be served on the person bringing the proceedings not less than 7 clear days before—

      (i)   in England, Wales and Northern Ireland, the hearing of the proceedings;

      (ii)   in Scotland, the trial diet.

(4)   P may not rely on a defence under paragraph (1) which involves an allegation that the commission of the offence was due to reliance on information supplied by another person unless it was reasonable for P to have relied upon the information, having regard in particular—

   (a)   to the steps that P took, and those which might reasonably have been taken, for the purpose of verifying the information; and

   (b)   to whether P had any reason to disbelieve the information.

(5)   (5) In this regulation, "third party allegation" means an allegation that the commission of the offence was due—

   (a)   to the act or default of another person; or

   (b)   to reliance on information supplied by another person.

(6)   This regulation does not apply in respect of proceedings for offences under regulation 62(6)."

Due diligence provisions are covered in CHAPTER 4, Criminal Enforcement.

[1]   SI 2015/1553, reg 64.

Restriction on proceedings

17.129 Regulation 66 of the PA(S)R 2015[1] provides for the time limit for prosecution of offences:

66 Time limit for prosecution of offences

(1)   Subject to paragraph (4), in England and Wales, an information relating to an offence under regulation 62 that is triable by a magistrates' court may be so tried if it is laid within 12 months after the date on which evidence sufficient in the opinion of the prosecutor to justify the proceedings comes to the knowledge of the prosecutor.

(2)   Subject to paragraph (4), in Scotland—

(a)   summary proceedings for an offence under regulation 62 may be commenced before the end of 12 months after the date on which evidence sufficient in the Lord Advocate's opinion to justify the proceedings came to the Lord Advocate's knowledge; and

(b)   section 136(3) of the Criminal Procedure (Scotland) Act 1995 (time limit for certain offences) applies for the purpose of this paragraph as it applies for the purpose of that section.

(3)   Subject to paragraph (4), in Northern Ireland summary proceedings for an offence under regulation 62 may be instituted within 12 months after the date on which evidence sufficient in the opinion of the prosecutor to justify proceedings comes to the knowledge of the prosecutor.

(4)   No proceedings may be brought more than 3 years after the commission of the offence.

(5)   For the purposes of this regulation a certificate of the prosecutor (or in Scotland, the Lord Advocate) as to the date on which the evidence referred to paragraphs (1), (2) or (3) came to light, is conclusive evidence.

(6)   This regulation has effect subject to paragraphs 1(o) and 2(n) of Schedule 8 (enforcement powers of the Health and Safety Executive under the 1974 Act).

Note also that, under reg 53(6) only the Lord Advocate may prosecute an offence under PA(S)R 2015 in Scotland. Time limits are covered generally in CHAPTER 4, Criminal Enforcement.

[1]   SI 2015/1553, reg 66.

Prosecutions

17.130 Regulation 65 of the PA(S)R 2015[1] provides for liability of persons other than principal offender:

65 Liability of persons other than the principal offender

(1)   Where the commission of an offence by one person ("A") under regulation 62 is due to anything which another person ("B") did or failed to do in the course of business, B is guilty of the offence and may be proceeded against and punished, whether or not proceedings are taken against A.

(2)   Where a body corporate commits an offence, a relevant person is also guilty of the offence where the body corporate's offence was committed—

(a)   with the consent or connivance of the relevant person; or

(b)   as a result of the negligence of the relevant person.

(3)   In paragraph (2), "relevant person" means—

(a)   a director, manager, secretary or other similar officer of the body corporate;

(b)   in relation to a body corporate managed by its members, a member of that body corporate performing managerial functions;

(c)   in relation to a Scottish partnership, a partner; or

(d)   a person purporting to act as a person described in sub-paragraphs (a), (b) or (c).

[1]   SI 2015/1553, reg 65.

Duty to enforce

17.131 Part 5 of the PA(S)R 2015 sets out provisions for market surveillance and enforcement. Regulation 52 identifies the market surveillance authority which has an obligation to enforce PA(S)R 2015 in respect of each category of pyrotechnic article. For categories F1, F2 and F3 fireworks the market surveillance authority in Great Britain, is, within its area, the weights and measures authority and, in Northern Ireland, within its area, the district council.

17.132 Regulation 53 of the PA(S)R 2015[1] provides:

53 Enforcement

(1) The market surveillance authority must enforce these Regulations, and RAMS in its application to pyrotechnic articles, or ensure that they are enforced.

(2) In Great Britain, a GB enforcer other than the market surveillance authority may enforce these Regulations and RAMS in its application to pyrotechnic articles.

(3) In Northern Ireland, a NI enforcer other than the market surveillance authority may enforce these Regulations and RAMS in its application to pyrotechnic articles.

(4) Before taking action under paragraphs (2) or (3) a GB enforcer or NI enforcer must notify the market surveillance authority of the proposed action.

(5) The Secretary of State may appoint a person to act on behalf of the Secretary of State for the purposes of enforcing these Regulations and RAMS in its application to pyrotechnic articles.

(6) In Scotland, only the Lord Advocate may prosecute an offence under these Regulations.

(7) In this regulation—
"GB enforcer" means—
(a) a weights and measures authority;
(b) the Health and Safety Executive; or
(c) the Secretary of State;
"NI enforcer" means—
(a) a district council; or
(b) the Secretary of State.

[1] SI 2015/1553, reg 53.

Powers of enforcement officers

17.133 Regulation 54 and Schs 7, 8 and 9 of the PA(S)R 2015 set out the enforcement powers that the enforcing authorities have. When enforcing PA(S)R 2015, the enforcing authority must exercise its powers in a manner which is consistent with the factors set out in regs 56–61[1]. From the coming into force of the Product Safety and Metrology etc. (Amendment etc.) (EU Exit) Regulations 2019[2], the factor identified in reg 58 (EU safeguard procedure) has been repealed in England, Scotland and Wales, but remains applicable in Northern Ireland. The PA(S)R 2015, reg 62(6) provides for offences of intentional obstruction of an enforcing authority (or officer of such authority) and of knowingly or recklessly providing any statement, information, document or record which is false or misleading in a material respect in purported compliance with any requirement under PA(S)R 2015. It is also an offence under reg 62(7) for a person who is not authorised to act on behalf of an enforcing authority to purport to exercise any of the powers of the enforcing authority under PA(S)R 2015.

¹   SI 2015/1553, reg 55.
²   SI 2019/696.

Sentencing

17.134 Regulation 63 of the PA(S)R 2015¹ sets out the penalties that are to apply for offences under PA(S)R 2015:

63 Penalties

(1)   A person guilty of an offence under regulation 62 in respect of a category F1 firework, a category F2 firework, or a category F3 firework is liable on summary conviction—

(a)   in England and Wales, to a fine or imprisonment for a term not exceeding 3 months or to both;

(b)   in Scotland or Northern Ireland, to a fine not exceeding level 5 on the standard scale or imprisonment for a term not exceeding 3 months or to both.

(2)   (2) A person guilty of an offence under regulation 62 in respect of a pyrotechnic article to which paragraph (1) does not apply is liable—

(a)   on summary conviction—

(i)   in England and Wales, to a fine or imprisonment for a term not exceeding 3 months or to both;

(ii)   in Scotland or Northern Ireland, to a fine not exceeding the statutory maximum or imprisonment for a term not exceeding 3 months or to both;

(b)   on conviction on indictment, to a fine or imprisonment for a term not exceeding 2 years or to both.

¹   SI 2015/1553.

Commentary

17.135 The notable absence of any reported cases decided under the PA(S)R 2015 can perhaps be best explained by the fact that the most onerous provisions of the PA(S)R 2015, which deal with the design of a pyrotechnic article¹, only came into effect on 5 July 2017 (as per the transitional provisions in reg 74). The recent coming into force of these provisions may lead to greater litigation in this area in the near future.

¹   SI 2015/1553, Pt 2.

KNIVES AND OFFENSIVE WEAPONS

Introduction

17.136 The Criminal Justice Act 1988 ('CJA 1988') prohibits the sale of knives and certain articles with blade or point to persons under 18 years of age¹. Legislation such as the Restriction of Offensive Weapons Act 1959 and the

Knives Act 1997 (which are outside of the scope of this work) also create offences in relation to the sale of knives which are completely prohibited and the unlawful marketing of knives.

1 Criminal Justice Act 1988, s 141A.

Territorial jurisdiction

17.137 The offence in CJA 1988, s 141A extends to England, Wales and Scotland. Note that the text of this provision varies slightly between England and Wales, and Scotland. The CJA 1988, s 141A as it applies in Scotland is more extensive than as it applies in England and Wales: the offence extends beyond sale to letting on hire, selling or letting on hire a knife or knife blade designed for domestic use to a person aged 16 or over is excluded from the offence, the section applies to swords, and there exist more demanding requirements for the defence to the offence to be satisfied. However, from 1 January 2021, the articles exempt from s 141A became more limited in Scotland[1]. Article 54 of the Criminal Justice (Northern Ireland) Order 1996[2] contains similar provision to CJA 1988, s 141A and is similarly amended by the Offensive Weapons Act 2019[3] (see below).

1 Offensive Weapons Act 2019, s 34(1)(b).
2 SI 1996/3160.
3 Offensive Weapons Act 2019, s 37.

Offences

17.138 The CJA 1988, s 141A(1)[1], as it applies in England and Wales provides that any person who sells to a person under 18 any of the following articles[2] shall be guilty of an offence:

(a) any knife, knife blade or razor blade;
(b) any axe; and
(c) any other article which has a blade or which is sharply pointed and which is made or adapted for use for causing injury to the person[3].

The CJA 1988, s 141A does not apply to any article described in s 1 of the Restriction of Offensive Weapons Act 1959[4] or an Order made under CJA 1988, s 141A[5] or CJA 1988, s 141(2)[6].

1 Inserted by the Offensive Weapons Act 1996 and amended by the Violent Crime Reduction Act 2006.
2 Subject to CJA 1988, s 141A(3).
3 CJA 1988, s 141A(2).
4 'flick knife', 'flick gun' or 'gravity knife'.
5 See the Criminal Justice Act 1988 (Offensive Weapons) (Exemption) Order 1996, SI 1996/3064, which exempts a folding pocket knife if the cutting edge of its blade does not exceed three inches, and razor blades permanently enclosed in a cartridge or housing where less than two millimeters of any blade is exposed beyond the plane which intersects the highest point of the surfaces preceding and following such blades.
6 Empowers the Secretary of State to direct that the section applies to any description of weapon except (a) any weapon subject to the Firearms Act 1968, and (b) crossbows. This includes knuckledusters, swordsticks, hand claws, and belt buckle knives.

17.139

Precedent for offence of selling a knife to a person under 18

Information

A B, on [date] sold a knife, namely a carving knife, to C D, an individual aged under 18, contrary to section 141A of the Criminal Justice Act 1988.

17.140 As it applies in Scotland, CJA 1988, s 141A also extends to any person who lets on hire an article to which the section applies[1]. Further, the section applies to any sword.

[1] Inserted by the Criminal Justice and Licensing (Scotland) Act 2010.

17.141 In *Regina (Windsor and Maidenhead Royal Borough Council) v East Berkshire Magistrates' Court*[1] it was held that whether an article was a 'knife' within the meaning of CJA 1988, s 141A(2)(a) was not a pure question of fact, but a question of mixed fact and law; and the justices had erred in law in finding that CJA 1988, s 141A did not apply to a grapefruit knife, notwithstanding that it was a cutting instrument consisting of a blade with a handle. Sir Anthony May stated:

'10 Once it is determined by what description the article is and what are its characteristics, it is a matter of law whether it is a knife within the section of the Act . . . An article designed for single use may well be a knife. Some articles with curved blades may be knives. The suppliers' understanding is certainly not determinative and may not be relevant.

13 In my judgment this grapefruit knife is a cutting instrument consisting of a blade with a sharpened longitudinal edge – it has two such edges in fact – fixed in a handle, and in my judgment it is a knife within section 141A(2) of the 1988 Act.

14 I should add for completeness that there is a definition of "knife" in section 10 of the Knives Act 1997 which is consistent with what I have just held, but that is subsequent legislation.'

[1] [2010] EWHC 3020 (Admin).

Defences

17.142 The CJA 1988, s 141A(4), as it applies in England and Wales, creates a defence of taking all reasonable precautions and exercising all due diligence to avoid the commission of the offence. Upon s 35 of the Offensive Weapons Act 2019 (coming into force on a date to be appointed) this defence will be significantly limited and refined through a new s 141B being inserted into the CJA 1988. Section 141B will apply if the seller is charged with an offence under s 141A and was not in the presence of the buyer at the time of the sale. The section provides that the seller is not to be regarded as having proved that they took all reasonable precautions and exercised all due diligence unless, as a minimum, they prove that the following conditions are met:

(i) Condition A: at the time of the alleged offence (a) the seller operated a system for checking that persons who bought articles to which section 141A applied by the same or a similar method of purchase to that used by the buyer were not under the age of 18, and (b) that the system was likely to prevent persons under the age of 18 from buying such articles by that method.

(ii) Condition B: when the package containing the article was dispatched it was clearly marked to indicate (a) that it contained an article with a blade or which was sharply pointed, and (b) that when delivered, it should only be delivered into the hands of a person aged 18 or over.

(iii) Condition C: the seller took all reasonable precautions and exercised all due diligence to ensure that, when finally delivered, the package would be delivered into the hands of a person aged 18 or over.

(iv) Condition D: the seller did not deliver the package, or arrange for its delivery, to a locker[1].

[1] As defined in art 141B(9), CJA 1988.

17.143 The CJA 1988, s 141A(4), as it applies in Scotland, provides:

(4) It is a defence for a person charged with an offence under subsection (1) (referred to in this section as "the accused") to show that—

    (a) the accused believed the person to whom the article was sold or let on hire (referred to in this section as "the purchaser or hirer") to be of or above the relevant age, and

    (b) either—

        (i) the accused had taken reasonable steps to establish the purchaser or hirer's age, or

        (ii) no reasonable person could have suspected from the purchaser or hirer's appearance that the purchaser or hirer was aged under the relevant age.

(4A) For the purposes of subsection (4)(b)(i), the accused is to be treated as having taken reasonable steps to establish the purchaser or hirer's age if and only if—

    (a) the accused was shown any of the documents mentioned in subsection (4B), and

    (b) the document would have convinced a reasonable person.

(4B) Those documents are any documents bearing to be—

    (a) a passport,

    (aa) a UK driving licence[1],

    (b) European Union photocard driving licence, or

    (c) such other document, or a document of such other description, as the Scottish Ministers may by order prescribe.

(4C) In subsection (4), the "relevant age" is—

    (a) in the case where the article is a knife or knife blade designed for domestic use, 16 years, and

    (b) in any other case, 18 years.

[1] This became a permissible form of identification upon the coming into force of the Licensing (Amendment) (EU Exit) (Scotland) Regulations 2019 (SSI 2019/6) on 31 December 2020.

17.144 On 1 January 2021, s 36 of the Offensive Weapons Act 2019 came into force and significantly altered the available defences through the insertion into the CJA 1988 of s 141C. This section applies if the seller is charged with an offence under s 141A and they were not in the presence of the buyer or hirer at the time of the sale or letting on hire. Section 141C(3) provides that it is a defence for the accused to show that the following conditions are met:

(i)   Condition A: at the time of the alleged offence (a) the accused operated a system for checking that purchasers or hirers of articles to which s 141A applied by the same or similar method of purchase or hire to what used by the buyer or purchaser were not under the age of 18, and (b) that system was likely to prevent persons under the age of 18 from buying or hiring such articles by that method.

(ii)   Condition B: when the package containing the article was dispatched it was clearly marked to indicate (a) that it contained an article with a blade or which was sharply pointed, and (b) that when delivered, it should only be delivered into the hands of a person aged 18 or over.

(iii)   Condition C: the seller or hirer took all reasonable precautions and exercised all due diligence to ensure that, when finally delivered, the package would be delivered into the hands of a person aged 18 or over.

(iv)   Condition D: the seller or hirer did not deliver the package, or arrange for its delivery, to a locker[1].

[1]   As defined in art 141C(10), CJA 1988.

17.145 Note, CJA 1988, s 141A, as it applies in Scotland, was amended by the Police, Public Order and Criminal Justice (Scotland) Act 2006, s 75 by inserting:

> (3A) It is not an offence under subsection (1) to sell or let on hire a knife or knife blade to a person if—
> (a)   the person is aged 16 or over; and
> (b)   the knife or blade is designed for domestic use.

17.146 Due diligence provisions are covered in CHAPTER 4, Criminal Enforcement.

17.147 Whilst mainly concerned with the general principle of retrospective precautions taken after an offence has been committed, *Enfield London Borough Council v Argos Ltd*[1] featured a case where the defendant's employee sold a six-piece knife block to a test-purchasing child who was under the age of 16 (the statutory age-limit at the time). The appeal was dismissed and the magistrates' court finding that the company had a clear system to avoid unlawful sales of knives to underage purchasers that used till bulletins and staff training, and therefore was entitled to rely on the defence, was upheld.

[1]   [2008] EWHC 2597 (Admin).

17.148 In *London Borough of Croydon v Pinch a Pound (UK) Ltd*[1] trading standards' volunteers test purchased a Rolson utility knife (an item with a retractable blade similar to a Stanley knife) selected from an open display. The till was operated by an employee of the defendant company, who did not challenge the purchase. The company was convicted of an offence under the Criminal Justice Act 1988, s 141A but successfully appealed to the Crown Court against that conviction. That decision was appealed by way of case stated to the High Court. The issue before the magistrates, and on appeal, was whether the defendant could avail itself of the statutory defence provided by CJA 1988, s 141A(4).

[1]   [2010] EWHC 3283 (Admin).

17.149 It was held that the statutory defence requires proof of two elements: the taking of all reasonable precautions; and, the exercise of all due diligence. These elements are cumulative requirements, although circumstances may arise where they overlap. The defence is couched in ordinary language, so the test applied by the Crown Court was not correct as it did not fully reflect the requirements of CJA 1988, s 141A(4) and ran the risk of importing a mental element. It was also held that the defendant's acquittal on the basis that the CJA 1988, s 141A(4) defence had been proved was inconsistent with the Crown Court's findings that there were serious shortcomings in the precautions taken by the defendant.

17.150 Pill LJ stated:

> '49 In relation to the refusal register, the Crown Court found that it was adhered to in a "less than effective way and not implemented fully. The system needed to be considerably strengthened". As to signs, it found that they were displayed in a "piecemeal, confused and cavalier way, which had led to confusion in the minds of staff members". As to training about legislation, it found that the defendant "needed to recognise" aspects of the matter, indicating that they had not already recognised them. These are serious shortcomings, as Roderick Evans J has found.'

17.151 The creation by CJA 1988, s 141A(4) of a legal burden on the defendant may in the future be challenged in light of the human rights case law regarding 'reverse burdens'. A challenge could potentially be brought on the basis of an incompatibility with Art 6(2) ECHR, which states that 'everyone charged with a criminal offence shall be presumed innocent until proved guilty according to the law'. However, as per *R v Lambert*[1] it is clear that a reverse burden provision does not inevitably give rise to a finding of incompatibility, and instead the court should focus on the particular context of each case, examining the substance and effect of any presumption adverse to the defendant on all the facts and circumstances, and ensuring the particular provision was reasonable[2].

[1] [2002] 2 AC 545 at [87] per Lord Hope.
[2] *Sheldrake v DPP* [2005] 1 AC 264 at [21] per Lord Bingham.

Restriction on proceedings

17.152 The offence under CJA 1988, s 141A is summary-only. There is therefore a 6-month time limit for bringing proceedings, from the time when the offence was committed[1]. In Scotland, as the offence can only be tried under summary procedure, the time limits are established under the Criminal Procedure (Scotland) Act 1995, s 136 – within 6 months after the contravention occurred.

[1] Magistrates' Courts Act 1980, s 127.

Prosecutions

17.153 The offence under CJA 1988, s 141A can be committed by the actual seller or, where applicable, his employer.

Duty to enforce

17.154 Presently, there is no duty of enforcement prescribed for CJA 1988, s 141A. However, when s 64 of the Offensive Weapons Act 2019, on a date to be appointed, comes into force, local weights and measures authorities may enforce CJA 1988, s 141A within their area. The investigatory powers available to local weights and measures authorities are set out in Sch 5 of the Consumer Rights Act 2015. Section 64(4) of the Offensive Weapons Act 2019 makes clear that s.64 of the same Act does not authorise a local weights and measures authority to bring proceedings in Scotland for an offence. However, in Scotland, businesses selling non-domestic knives must be registered with the local authority in which the premises are located[1].

[1]   Civic Government (Scotland) Act 1982, s 27A.

Sentencing

17.155 A person found guilty of an offence under CJA 1988, s 141A is liable on summary conviction to imprisonment for a term not exceeding 6 months, in England and Wales to a fine, in Scotland and Northern Ireland a fine not exceeding level 5 on the standard scale, or both[1].

[1]   CJA 1988, s 141A(1).

Commentary

17.156 New government initiatives on knives are coming thick and fast in an attempt to reduce knife crime. Two such initiatives are the voluntary agreement and Operation Sceptre. A number of high street retailers have signed a voluntary agreement on the sale of knives[1]. Under the agreement retailers agree to:

(a)   ensure age verification checks take place and knives will only be sold (or supplied) once staff are satisfied the customer is 18 or over;
(b)   customers and staff will be reminded that knives are age restricted products and of the need to complete age verification checks before sale;
(c)   ensure knives are displayed and packaged securely;
(d)   train staff selling or approving sales of knives, and refresh this training at least once every year.

[1]   Sale of Knives: voluntary agreement by retailers (updated February 2018).

17.157 The agreement further provides that the government should report back to the signatories on the progress made by working with the police, trading standards, the Better Regulations Delivery Office and relevant codes to carry out test purchases at different retailers. The government also commits to introduce legislation to extend the Primary Authority Scheme to knives and explore the use of online identity exchange. Whilst this agreement is not compulsory, compliance with the terms can be used as evidence that the retailer took all reasonable precautions and exercised due diligence.

17.158 Operation Sceptre was launched in July 2015 with the aim of reducing knife crime and the number of families affected by crime across London. It is an ongoing series of weeks of intensified action on knife crime, the most recent being in April 2021. The operation seeks to target not only those who carry and use knives, but also the supply, access and importation of weapons. A large reliance is placed on test purchases and 700 test purchase operations in shops that sell knives have been conducted since the initiative was launched[1].

[1]   Figures correct as of June 2017.

17.159 Further, on the 18 July 2017 the Home Secretary, Amber Rudd, announced plans to consult on new offences to toughen up knife crime laws. The proposed new action would restrict the online sale of knives and ban possession of dangerous or offensive weapons on private property. A consequence of these proposed measures would be that anyone who bought a knife online would be required to collect it in person, and thus be subject to the usual age checks. These proposals were contained in the Offensive Weapons Bill 2017–19 and final provisions are found in the Offensive Weapons Act 2019, the relevant provisions of which are not yet in force.

Other offices

17.160 Along with amending the CJA 1988, the Offensive Weapons Act 2019, upon coming into force on a date to be appointed, will create a number of new offences in relation to knives, including delivery of a bladed product to a person under the age of 18. Section 39, which creates the offence, applies if:

(a)   the seller sells a bladed product to the buyer;
(b)   the seller and the buyer are not in each other's presence at the time of the sale[1] and the seller is within the UK at that time[2];
(c)   before the sale, the seller entered into an arrangement with a body corporate by which the body corporate agreed to deliver bladed products for the seller;
(d)   the body corporate was aware when they entered into the arrangement that it covered the delivery of bladed products; and
(e)   the body corporate delivers the bladed product to residential premises[3] pursuant to that arrangement.

[1]   As defined in s 39(2) of the Offensive Weapons Act 2019.
[2]   As defined in s 39(3) of the Offensive Weapons Act 2019.
[3]   As defined in ss 39(4) and (5) of the Offensive Weapons Act 2019.

17.161 The body corporate who delivers the bladed product to the residential premises pursuant to the arrangement commits an offence, if when they deliver the bladed product, they do not deliver it into the hands of a person aged 18 or over. A person found guilty of such an offence is liable on summary conviction in England and Wales to a fine and in Scotland and Northern Ireland to a fine not exceeding level 5 on the standard scale. Defences in relation to this offence are set out in ss 40(7) and (8) of the Offensive Weapons Act 2019.

17.162 Further, s 42 creates the offence of delivery of bladed articles to persons under 18. This section applies if:

(a)   the seller sells a bladed article to the buyer;
(b)   the seller and the buyer are not in each other's presence at the time of the sale[1] and the seller is outside of the UK at the time[2];

(c)   before the sale, the seller entered into an arrangement with a body corporate by which the body corporate agreed to deliver bladed articles for the seller;

(d)   the body corporate was aware when they entered into the arrangement that it covered the delivery of bladed articles, and

(e)   the body corporate delivers the bladed article pursuant to that arrangement.

[1]   As defined in s 42(2) of the Offensive Weapons Act 2019.
[2]   As defined in s 42(3) of the Offensive Weapons Act 2019.

17.163 The body corporate commits an offence if, when they deliver the bladed article, they do not deliver it into the hands of a person aged 18 or over. A person found guilty of such an offence is liable on summary conviction in England and Wales to a fine and in Scotland or Northern Ireland to a fine not exceeding level 5 on the standard scale. The available defences, which are different between England, Wales and Northern Ireland, and Scotland are set out in ss 42(5) and (6).

17.164 Per s 64 of the Offensive Weapons Act 2019, local weights and measures authorities may enforce within their area both s 39 (delivery of bladed products to persons under 18) and s 42 (delivery of bladed articles to persons under 18).

VIDEO RECORDINGS

Introduction

17.165 The primary purpose of the Video Recordings Act 1984 ('VRA 1984') is child protection. The Act regulates the supply of films and certain video games in the form of the physical product, such as discs, magnetic tape and other physical storage devices. Some video works are deemed inappropriate for children to view and VRA 1984 gives powers to a designated authority to determine the suitability of a video work and classify it accordingly. This suitability ranges from those works which are suitable for general viewing to those which may only be sold in a licensed sex shop (ensuring that the recipient of the video work is verifiably over 18). The scheme introduced by VRA 1984 requires that videos should have affixed to them a symbol indicating which of the range of classifications the particular video work belongs to.

17.166 The British Board of Film Classification ('BBFC') is the designated Video Works Authority. Under the VRA 1984 all *'video works'* (films, TV programmes, video games, etc) which are supplied on a disc, tape or any other device capable of storing data electronically are required to be classified by the BBFC, unless they fall within the definition of an exempted work. This section deals with the principal offence relating to age-restricted products contained in VRA 1984, s 11, but VRA 1984, ss 9–14 create a number of other offences, including supplying a video recording of unclassified work, possession of a video recording of unclassified work for the purposes of supply, certain video recordings only to be supplied in licensed sex shops, supply of video recordings not complying with requirements as to labels etc., and supply of a video recording containing false indication as to classification, which are outside the scope of this chapter.

Territorial jurisdiction

17.167 The Act has application throughout the UK.

Offences

17.168 The VRA 1984, s 11(1) provides:

11 Supplying video recording of classified work in breach of classification.

(1)   (1) Where a classification certificate issued in respect of a video work states that no video recording, or no video recording described in the certificate, that contains that work is to be supplied to any person who has not attained the age specified in the certificate, a person who supplies or offers to supply such a video recording to a person who has not attained the age so specified is guilty of an offence unless—
(a)   the video work is an exempted work, or
(b)   the supply is, or would if it took place be, an exempted supply.

17.169 In *Ealing London Borough Council v Woolworths plc*[1] the local authority engaged a child of 11 years to purchase an '18' category video film from the defendant company whilst under the observation of trading standards officers.

[1]   [1995] Crim LR 58.

17.170 Russell LJ stated:

'503 The justices in their finding came to the conclusion that the Trading Standards Department's officers had acted in a way that they described as 'ultra vires' by instructing the boy to make the purchase. The justices went on to say that the transaction was contrived and instigated by the Trading Standards Department and that consequently they were at liberty to exclude the evidence under section 78 of the Police and Criminal Evidence Act 1984. I have to say that . . . the justices were fundamentally in error in the approach that they made. Entrapment is not a defence known to English law . . . [at 505] If the process employed, which we understand to be a common practice up and down the country, were to fall foul of section 78, it would . . . emasculate the enforcement of a sensible piece of legislation which . . . was passed for the express purpose of protecting young people such as the boy employed for the test purchase in this case from being exposed to undesirable influences. I do not accept that what happened was in any sense an entrapment of [Woolworths], or that the boy acted as an agent provocateur, nor, incidentally, did he commit any offence in purchasing the video. He did not incite, aid or abet the commission of an offence by Woolworths. By purchasing the video he was simply playing a part in the situation which rendered Woolworths culpable. Had there been any element of persuasion of the sales girl by the customer, then perhaps different considerations would have prevailed.'

17.171 The offence created by VRA 1984, s 11 and the further offences contained in VRA 1984, ss 9–14 all have a number of common ingredients which are examined below.

Video recording

17.172 The VRA 1984, s 1(3) defines a video recording as 'any disc, magnetic tape or any other device capable of storing data electronically containing information by the use of which the whole or part of a video work may be produced'. A video work is defined by VRA 1984, s 1(2) as being 'any series of visual images (with or without sound) – (a) produced electronically by the use of information contained on any disc, magnetic tape or any other device capable of storing data electronically, and (b) shown as a moving picture'.

17.173 Continuity of images is not the deciding factor in whether a sequence of images constitute a moving picture. Where the sequence is long enough to show continuing movement it can be a moving picture[1]. Both the Home Office and LACOTS[2] have expressed the opinion that images designed to simulate motion by the camera rather than the object viewed constitute a moving picture, although this would not be the case if the movement of the still image were created only by the end users manipulation of the image, for instance by the use of 'scroll bars'.

[1] *Kent CC v Multi Media Marketing (Canterbury) Ltd* (1995) *The Times*, 9 May, DC.
[2] LACOTS Circular CO 14 95 5.

17.174 The VRA 1984, s 22(2) provides further interpretation as to the circumstances when a video recording contains a video work: in particular, it states that a video recording contains a video work if it contains information by the use of which the whole or a part of the work may be produced. There is an exception to this: if a video work contains an extract of another video work (for example, a film that includes an extract from another film), the extract is not part of the work of which it is an extract but a part of the video work which contains the extract; and hence the video recording contains that video work including the extract.

17.175 An increasing variety of video recordings are available, some of which contain a mixture of films and video games. The VRA 1984, s 22(2A)[1] provides a power for the Secretary of State to make provision about the circumstances in which a video recording does or does not contain a video work for the purposes of the Act. This allows provision to be made to take account of new formats, such as where a video game contains a whole film within it or a film contains a game within it. To date, no such regulations have been made.

[1] Inserted by the Digital Economy Act 2010.

Supply

17.176 The VRA 1984, s 1(4) states that the question of reward is irrelevant to the concept of supply, which includes supply by way of 'sale, letting on hire, exchange or loan'. Supply by a company may be committed vicariously by an employee acting in the course of his employment[1]. Where the supply is to an under-aged person who is buying on behalf of an undisclosed adult principal, the supply is to the under-aged person[2].

[1] *Tesco Stores Ltd v Brent London Borough Council* [1993] 1 WLR 1037, DC.
[2] *Tesco Stores Ltd v Brent London Borough Council* [1993] 1 WLR 1037, DC.

Exempted works

17.177 The VRA 1984, s 2 defines a video work (other than a video game) as an exempted work if, taken as a whole, it is either:

(a)   designed to inform, educate or instruct; or
(b)   concerned with sport, religion or music.

17.178 New categories in which a video work (other than a video game) is not an exempted work are contained in VRA 1984, s 2(1ZA), as inserted by the Video Recordings Act 1984 (Exempted Video Works) Regulations[1], and relate to:

(a)   violence or threats of violence;
(b)   the immediate aftermath of violence on human or animal characters;
(c)   imitable dangerous activity;
(d)   activities involving illegal drugs or misuse of drugs;
(e)   use of alcohol or tobacco;
(f)   suicide or attempted suicide, or the immediate aftermath of such an event;
(g)   an act of scarification or mutilation of a person, or self-harm, or the immediate aftermath of such an act;
(h)   techniques likely to be useful in the commission of offences or promotion of such activity;
(i)   words or images intended or likely to convey a sexual message;
(j)   human sexual activity[2] or acts of force or restraint associated with such activity;
(k)   human genital organs or human urinary or excretory functions;
(l)   swearing (other than mild bad language);
(m)   words or images that are intended or likely to cause offence, whether on the grounds of race, gender, disability, religion or belief or sexual orientation, or otherwise.

[1]   SI 2014/2097, reg 2(3).
[2]   'Human sexual activity' need not be intercourse or masturbation if what is depicted is designed to stimulate or encourage such activity: *Kent CC v Multi Media Marketing (Canterbury) Ltd* 1995 *The Times*, 9 May, DC.

17.179 A video game is an exempted work if, taken as a whole it is:

(a)   designed to inform, educate or instruct;
(b)   concerned with sport, religion or music; or
(c)   satisfies one or more of the conditions in VRA 1984, s 2A[1].

[1]   VRA 1984, s 2A(1).

17.180 The VRA 1984, s 2A sets out two conditions relating to video games. First, that the video game does not include any depictions or works listed, and secondly, that the designated authority has confirmed in writing that the video game is suitable for viewing by persons under the age of 12.

17.181 According to VRA 1984, ss 2(2) and 2(3), a video game is not an exempted work if, to any significant extent, it depicts: human sexual activity or acts of force or restraint associated with such activity; mutilation or torture of, or other acts of gross violence towards, humans or animals; human genital organs or human urinary or excretory functions; techniques likely to be useful in the commission of offences; and, criminal activity which is likely to any significant extent to stimulate or encourage the commission of offences.

Exempted supplies

17.182 The VRA 1984, s 3 sets out the circumstances in which a supply of a video recording is an exempted supply, even if the film or game contained in the video recording is not exempted. The supply of a video recording is an exempted supply if it is neither:

(a)   a supply for reward, nor
(b)   a supply in the course or furtherance of a business[1].

¹   VRA 1984, s 3(2).

17.183 Where a video is supplied on premises such as a video shop it is to be treated as having been supplied in the course or furtherance of business[1]. There are other specific instances of exempt supplies which are set out below:

(a)   By VRA 1984, s 3(4), the supply of a video recording to a person in the video trade is exempt unless it is made with a view to the eventual supply of that recording to the general public.

(b)   By VRA 1984, s 3(5) (as amended by the 2014 Regulations[2]), the supply of a video work designed to provide a record of an occasion for those who took part or those connected with them, which does not to any significant extent, depict:

(i)   human sexual activity or acts of force or restraint associated with such activity (and is not designed to any significant extent to stimulate or encourage such activity);

(ii)   mutilation or torture of, or other acts of gross violence towards, humans or animals (and is not designed to any extent to stimulate or encourage such activity); or

(iii)   human genital organs or human urinary or excretory functions;

(c)   By VRA 1984, s 3(6) the supply of a video recording for the purpose of showing it in private or where the public are admitted without[3] payment.

(d)   By VRA 1984, s 3(8) the supply of a video recording with a view only to its use for or in connection with a program service within the meaning of the Broadcasting Act 1990.

(e)   By VRA 1984, s 3(9) the supply of a video recording for the issue of a classification certificate or other arrangements by the designated authority.

(f)   By VRA 1984, ss 3(10) and (11) the supply of a video recording for medical training.

(g)   By VRA 1984, s 3(12) the return, otherwise than for reward, of a video recording to person who had previously made an exempt supply of it.

¹   VRA 1984, s 3(3).
²   SI 2014/2097, reg 3.
³   See the Cinemas Act 1985, s 6.

17.184 The Digital Economy Act 2010 amended VRA 1984, s 3 to secure that the supply of video games by means of amusement arcade machines is exempted[1], unless the game includes any of the matters mentioned in VRA 1984, ss 2(2) and (3).

[1]   See VRA 1984, s 3(8A) and (8B).

Classification certificate

17.185 The VRA 1984, s 7 defines a classification certificate as a certificate issued in respect of a video work in pursuance of arrangements made by the designated authority[1]. The certificate must contain the unique title assigned to the video work[2], and either:

(a)   a statement that it is suitable for general viewing and unrestricted supply with or without advice as to the desirability of parental guidance;

(b)   a statement that it is suitable for viewing only by those of the age specified in the certificate and that it is not to be supplied to any younger person; or

(c)   a statement under para (b) above together with a statement that it is only to be supplied in a licensed sex shop.

[1]   The British Board of Film Classification.
[2]   VRA 1984, s 4(1)(b)(ia).

17.186 Where it is necessary to prove that a particular video work has been issued with a particular classification certificate, or that no such certificate has been issued in respect of the work, or that a particular video work differs from another video work, this may be done by means of a certificate signed by a person authorised to make such a statement by the Secretary of State. Such a certificate is admissible only if a copy of it has been served on the defendant not less than 7 days before the hearing[1]. Where an alteration or addition has been made to a video work in respect of which a classification certificate has been issued, the certificate is not valid for the altered work[2].

[1]   VRA 1984, s 19.
[2]   VRA 1984, s 22(3).

Defences

17.187 The VRA 1984, s 11(2) provides for a defence relating to the offence contained in VRA 1984, s 11:

(2)   It is a defence to a charge of committing an offence under this section to prove—

(a)   that the accused neither knew nor had reasonable grounds to believe that the classification certificate contained the statement concerned,

(b)   that the accused neither knew nor had reasonable grounds to believe that the person concerned had not attained that age,

(ba) that the accused believed on reasonable grounds that the video work concerned or, if the video recording contained more than one work to which the charge relates, each of those works was an exempted work, or

(c)   that the accused believed on reasonable grounds that the supply was, or would if it took place be, an exempted supply by virtue of section 3(4) or (5) of this Act.

General defence to offences under this Act

17.188 In addition to the specific defence in VRA 1984, s 11(2) detailed above, a general defence, applicable to all offences in VRA 1984, ss 9–14, is contained in VRA 1984, s 14A.

17.189 The VRA 1984, s 14A provides:

14A General defence to offences under this Act

Without prejudice to any defence specified in the preceding provisions of this Act in relation to a particular offence, it is a defence to a charge of committing any offence under this Act to prove—

(a) that the commission of the offence was due to the act or default of a person other than the accused, and

(b) that the accused took all reasonable precautions and exercised all due diligence to avoid the commission of the offence by any person under his control.

17.190 The VRA 1984, s 14A, added to the original VRA 1984 scheme by the Video Recordings Act 1993, provides a defence of the type that the Court of Appeal were unable to find implicit in VRA 1984, s 11(2) in *Tesco Stores Ltd v Brent London Borough Council*[1], namely a 'due diligence' defence of the type prescribed in the Trade Descriptions Act 1968, s 24.

[1] [1993] 1 WLR 1037, DC.

17.191 In *Tesco Stores Ltd v Brent London Borough Council* (a case decided prior to the introduction, by amendment, of the general defence under VRA 1984, s 14A) the Court of Appeal held that the state of mind relevant to establishing the defence under VRA 1984, s 11(2)(b) was that of the employee making the supply rather than that of her employer, the company. This conclusion followed from the fact that the company could not be expected to have any knowledge or information as to the age of a purchaser of a video film. Since the magistrates had found that the employee had had reasonable grounds to believe that the purchaser, a 14-year-old boy, was under the age of 18, the defence was not available and the appeal was dismissed.

17.192 In *Bilon v WH Smith Trading Ltd*[1] it was held that a defendant is entitled to rely on the defence of due diligence, despite having taken no positive steps to avoid the commission of the offence. The retailer merely had to show that he had acted without negligence.

[1] [2001] EWHC 469 (Admin).

Restrictions on proceedings

17.193 No prosecutions under VRA 1984 may be brought more than 3 years after the offence was committed or one year after the offence was discovered by the prosecutor, whichever is earlier[1].

[1] VRA 1984, s 15(1).

17.194 In Scotland, the reference to the date of discovery by the prosecutor is construed as a reference to the date on which evidence sufficient in the opinion of the Lord Advocate to warrant proceedings came to his knowledge. A certificate signed by the Lord Advocate or on his behalf and stating the date on which evidence came to his knowledge is conclusive evidence of that fact and other presumptions and deeming provisions apply to this process[1]. Cases such as *Burwell v DPP*[2] and *RSPCA v Ian James King and Kathleen Patricia King*[3] underline the importance of a prosecutor, who wishes to avail himself of the benefits of such a certificate, fully complying with the statutory requirements.

1 VRA 1984, ss 15(2) and 15(3).
2 [2009] EWHC 1069 (Admin).
3 [2010] EWHC 637 (Admin).

Prosecutions

17.195 Any person (whether an individual or a body corporate), other than the Crown or its servants or agents, can be prosecuted under VRA 1984. The VRA 1984, s 16 permits the prosecution and conviction of any 'director, manager, secretary or other similar officer' of a company or 'any person who was purporting to act in such a capacity' where an offence under the Act has been committed by the company 'with the consent and connivance' of that person or as a result of that person's neglect. Where the affairs of the body corporate are managed by its members, the provisions apply in relation to the acts and defaults of 'a member in connection with his functions of management as if he were a director of the body corporate'. It is normal and advisable (though not strictly necessary) that the company should be a defendant in the same proceedings as the person prosecuted under VRA 1984, s 16, since even if it is not, it will be necessary to prove that the company could have been found guilty of the offence.

Duty to enforce

17.196 The VRA 1984, s 16A specifies that the functions of a local weights and measures authority, or in Northern Ireland, the Department for the Economy, include the enforcement of VRA 1984 provisions. The right to prosecute is not restricted to a member or officer of an enforcement authority. Any person can bring a prosecution under the Act although the rights contained within the Act to facilitate the gathering of evidence may not be exercised by a private prosecutor.

Powers of enforcement officers

17.197 The investigatory powers available to a local weights and measures authority in Great Britain and the Department for the Economy in Northern Ireland are set out in Sch 5 to the Consumer Rights Act 2015[1]. These powers include the power to require the production of information, purchase products, observe the carrying on of business, enter premises without a warrant, inspect products, and seize and detain goods. Provisions making it an offence to obstruct an enforcer and providing a right to compensation for goods seized are also contained in Sch 5. In addition there are specific powers of entry, search and seizure (upon the issue of a warrant by a magistrate or, in Scotland, by a sheriff)[2], which may only be exercised by police officers. Where a person refuses to give a police officer his name and address, or gives details which the officer reasonably believes to be false, he may be arrested[3].

[1]   VRA 1984, s 16A(4ZA).
[2]   VRA 1984, s 17.
[3]   VRA 1984, s 18 (note this section does not extend to Scotland).

17.198 The CRA 2015[1] removed from the VRA 1984 the provisions that where offences are suspected to be linked with others committed in the area of another trading standards department, then, provided the consent of the relevant trading standards department has been obtained, investigations and prosecutions may be initiated 'out of area'. However, the powers of magistrates' courts to issue summonses and warrants in respect of linked offences under the Act remain extended. Under VRA 1984, s 16B(3) an offence is 'linked' to the supply or possession of video recordings within the area for which a justice acts if:

(a)   the supply or possession of video recordings within his area is likely to be or to have been the result of the offence; or

(b)   the offence is likely to be or to have been the result of the supply or possession of video recordings in his area.

[1]   CRA 2015, Sch 6, paras 27(2) and 27(3)(b).

Sentencing

17.199 The VRA 1984, s 11(3) provides that upon conviction a defendant is liable on summary conviction for imprisonment for a term not exceeding 6 months, or a fine, or both.

Forfeiture

17.200 By VRA 1984, s 21, following conviction the court may order that any video produced to the court and shown to its satisfaction to relate to the offence be forfeited. Before doing so an opportunity must be given to any person claiming to be interested in the video to show cause why an order of forfeiture should not be made. If an order is made it does not take effect until the expiration of the ordinary time for an appeal to be lodged and, if one is lodged or application is made to appeal, until the appeal is finally decided.

Commentary

17.201 The Digital Economy Act 2017 ('DEA 2017'), which sought to restrict access by young people to the same kinds of material as is covered by the VRA 1984, but which is accessed via the internet, received Royal Assent on 27 April 2017. The legislation was due to come into force on 15 July 2019, however, implementation was delayed in June 2019 for around 6 months in order for the European Commission to be notified of the changes. Whilst the majority of the legislation is now in force, significant parts are only partially in force for the purpose of making regulations. The relevant parts of the DEA 2017 are detailed below. The DEA 2017, s 14(1), which is not yet fully in force, states that:

> 14(1) A person contravenes this subsection if the person makes pornographic material available on the internet to persons in the United Kingdom on a commercial basis other than in a way that secures that, at any given time, the material is not normally accessible by persons under the age of 18.

'Pornographic material' is defined in DEA 2017, s 15, but this provision has also not yet fully come into force. The Online Pornography (Commercial Basis) Regulations 2019[1], which have not yet come fully into force, provide that pornographic material is to be regarded as made available on the internet to persons in the UK on a commercial basis if either: (a) access to the pornographic material is available only upon payment; or, (b) subject to exceptions, the pornographic material is made available free of charge but the person who makes it available receives (or reasonably expects to receive) a payment, reward or other benefit in connection with making it available.

[1]   SI 2019/23.

17.202 The DEA 2017, s 16 provides for an age verification regulator. On 21 February 2018 BBFC was formally designated as the regulator for age-verification of pornography. BBFC published draft guidelines on Age-verification arrangements and Ancillary Service Providers for public consultation, however, these were not formally approved by Parliament. The government had decided to allow a period of up to 3 months after the guidance was formally approved before the law moved into force in order to give the industry sufficient time to comply with the legislation. BBFC also intended to launch a voluntary age-verification certification scheme, with the support of the government and in consultation with the Information Commissioner's Office, to provide information to the public to demonstrate how age-verification providers have met high standards of data protection.

17.203 The DEA 2017, s 19, which is not yet in force, provides that the age verification regulator may impose a financial penalty[1] and/or an enforcement notice where it determines that the person is contravening or has contravened DEA 2017, s 14. No financial penalty may be enforced if the contravention has ceased and the limitation period in respect of the contravention has expired. The DEA 2017, s 19(6) states that the limitation period expires 3 years after the contravention began or if sooner, 1 year after the age verification regulator became aware of the contravention. The DEA 2017, s 21 allows the age verification regulator to notify any payment services providers or ancillary service providers if it considers that a person is contravening DEA 2017, s 14(1) or making extreme pornographic material available on the internet to persons in the UK. Further, the regulator has the power to require internet service providers to block access to material in specified circumstances[2].

[1]   DEA 2017, s 20 sets out the available financial penalties.
[2]   DEA 2017, s 23.

17.204 On 16 October 2019, Nicky Morgan, the Digital Secretary, announced that the government would not be 'commencing Pt 3 of the Digital Economy Act 2017 concerning age verification for online pornography'. The legislation is expected to be replaced by a new duty of care to ensure online safety. On

12 February 2020, the government published its Online Harms White Paper – initial consultation response, which is a precursor to its developed policy to address the harms that were originally supposed to be dealt with by the Digital Economy Act 2017. Following a full Government response in December 2020, the draft Online Safety Bill was published on 12 May 2021.

AEROSOL PAINT

Introduction

17.205 The Anti-social Behaviour Act 2003, s 54 ('ABA 2003') makes it an offence to sell aerosol spray paints to persons aged under 16. The objective of ABA 2003 is to reduce the incidence of criminal damage caused by acts of graffiti[1]. A similar offence is created in Scotland by the Antisocial Behaviour etc (Scotland) Act 2004, s 122 ('AB(S)A 2004') and in Northern Ireland by the Clean Neighbourhoods and Environment Act (Northern Ireland) 2011, s 37.

[1] *Imperial Tobacco Ltd, Petitioner* [2012] CSIH 9, paras 135 and 136.

Territorial jurisdiction

17.206 The ABA 2003, s 54 extends to England and Wales only. AB(S)A 2004 applies only to Scotland.

Offence

17.207 The ABA 2003, s 54 creates an offence of selling an aerosol paint container to a person under 16.

17.208 In Scotland AB(S)A 2004, s 122 creates an offence in almost identical terms. However, the Scottish legislation goes further: AB(S)A 2004, s 123 also requires a notice displaying the statement 'It is illegal to sell a spray paint device to anyone under the age of 16' to be exhibited at an appropriate place (ie in a prominent position where the statement is readily visible to persons at the point of sale of spray paint devices) at every retail premises at which spray paint devices are sold. The Sale of Spray Paint (Display of Warning Statement) (Scotland) Regulations 2004[1] prescribe the dimensions of the notice and the size of the statement which must be displayed on such a notice. The AB(S)A 2004, s 123(4) provides that, where a person carries on a business involving the retail of spray paint devices at any premises, and no notice is exhibited at those premises, that person shall be guilty of an offence.

[1] SSI 2004/419, reg 2.

Defences

17.209 The ABA 2003, s 54(4) provides that is a defence for a defendant to prove that he took all reasonable steps to determine the purchaser's age and reasonably believed that the purchaser was not under the age of 16.

17.210 Where the sale is effected by another person than the defendant, ABA 2003, s 54(5) provides that it is a defence to prove the defendant took all reasonable steps to avoid the commission of an offence.

17.211 The AB(S)A 2004, s 122(4) provides that in Scotland:

(4) It shall be a defence for a person charged with an offence under subsection (1) [*selling spray paint to child*] to show that the person took all reasonable precautions and exercised all due diligence to avoid the commission of the offence.

17.212 The AB(S)A 2004, s 123(6) provides that in Scotland:

(6) It shall be a defence for a person charged with an offence under subsection (4) [*failure to display notice*] to show that the person took all reasonable precautions and exercised all due diligence to avoid the commission of the offence.

17.213 It is difficult to see the practical difference between the operation of the AB(S)A 2004, s 54(4) defence, as applicable in England and Wales, and the AB(S)A 2004, s 122(4) defence, as applicable in Scotland, despite the difference in wording. If a defendant (who made the sale) has taken all reasonable steps to determine the purchaser's age, and reasonably believes them to be over 16, this is likely to amount to reasonable precautions to avoid the commission of the offence and *vice versa*.

Restrictions on proceedings

17.214 The offence under ABA 2003, s 54 is summary-only. There is therefore a 6 months' time limit on bringing proceedings, running from the time when the offence was committed[1]. In Scotland, as the offences in AB(S)A 2004, ss 122 and 123 can only be tried under summary procedure, the time limits are established under the Criminal Procedure (Scotland) Act 1995, s 136 and similarly establish a time limit for bringing proceedings of 6 months after the contravention occurred.

[1]   Magistrates' Courts Act 1980, s 127.

Prosecutions

17.215 The offence under ABA 2003, s 54 (or, in Scotland, under either AB(S)A 2004, s 122 or s 123) can be committed by the actual seller or, where applicable, his employer.

Enforcement powers

17.216 There is no specific duty of enforcement nor are there any powers of enforcement (to test purchase etc) in relation to ABA 2003, s 54. However, ABA 2003, s 54A[1] provides for a duty on local weights and measures authorities to consider, at least once a year, the extent to which it is appropriate to carry out a programme of enforcement action in relation to ABA 2003, s 54 and, to that extent, to carry out such a programme. Such a programme involves all or any of the following:

(a)   bringing prosecutions in respect of offences under ABA 2003, s 54;
(b)   investigating complaints in respect of alleged offences under ABA 2003, s 54;
(c)   taking other measures intended to reduce the incidence of offences under ABA 2003, s 54.

There is a similar requirement placed on district councils in Northern Ireland under the Clean Neighbourhoods and Environment Act (Northern Ireland) 2011, s 37.

[1]   Added to ABA 2003 by the Clean Neighbourhoods and Environment Act 2005, s 32.

17.217 In Scotland, AB(S)A 2004, s 124 places a duty on local authorities to enforce AB(S)A 2004, ss 122 and 123. However, AB(S)A 2004, s 124 does not authorise local authorities to institute proceedings for any offences committed under ss 122 and 123[1]. The AB(S)A 2004, s 125 sets out the powers of entry, inspection and seizure available to authorised officers of the local authority.

[1]   AB(S)A 2004, s 124(2).

Sentencing

17.218 The ABA 2003, s 54(3) provides that a person guilty of an offence is liable on summary conviction to a fine not exceeding level 4.

17.219 In Scotland, a person guilty of an offence under AB(S)A 2004, s 122(1) is liable on summary conviction to a fine not exceeding level 3 on the standard scale[1] and a person guilty of an offence under AB(S)A 2004, s 123(4) is liable on summary conviction to a fine not exceeding level 2 on the standard scale[2].

[1]   AB(S)A 2004, s 122(3).
[2]   AB(S)A 2004, s 123(5).

Commentary

17.220 Prohibition on the sale of spray paints to children is of course not the only way in which the problem of graffiti is addressed. Although beyond the scope of this publication, it is worth noting that graffiti is usually regarded as criminal damage under the Criminal Damage Act 1971, s 1(1). Under ABA 2003, s 43, councils may issue a fixed penalty notice to deal with an offence under CDA 1971, s 1(1) 'which involves only the painting or writing on, or the soiling, marking or other defacing of, any property by whatever means'[1]. The Criminal Justice Act 2003, s 1 extends the definition of prohibited articles under the Police and Criminal Evidence Act 1984, s 1 ('PACE 1984') so that it includes articles made, adapted or intended for use in causing criminal damage. It does this by amending the list of offences in PACE 1984, s 1(8) to include offences under the Criminal Damage Act 1971, s 1. The effect is to give police officers power to stop and search where they have reasonable suspicion that a person is carrying, for example, a paint spray can which they intend to use in producing graffiti. The above legal provisions are not applicable in Scotland or Northern

Ireland. In Scotland, graffiti may be dealt with either as malicious mischief at common law or under the Criminal Law (Consolidation) (Scotland) Act 1995, s 52 as a form of vandalism. In Northern Ireland there are provisions for dealing with graffiti in Pt 4 of the Clean Neighbourhoods and Environment Act (Northern Ireland) 2011.

¹   ABA 2003, s 44(1)(c).

CIGARETTE LIGHTER REFILLS

Introduction

17.221 According to NHS statistics in 2017, volatile substance abuse ('VSA') (which includes abuse of gas, glue, aerosols and other solvents) is the second most common form of drug use among children[1]. This is in line with NHS statistics from previous years[2]. There were 46 deaths associated with volatile substance abuse in 2009, bringing the cumulative total of VSA deaths in the UK since 1971 to 2,390[3].

¹   Statistics on drug misuse, England (February 2017).
²   Smoking, drinking and drug use among young people in England in 2014, 2013, 2012.
³   Data from the International Centre for Drug Policy based at St George's, University of London.

17.222 Various legislative initiatives have been instituted to curb the use of volatile substances – including solvents and butane gas. The Intoxicating Substances (Supply) Act 1985 made it an offence to supply or to offer to supply a substance to someone under the age of 18 if the retailer knew or had reasonable cause to believe that the substance would be inhaled to cause intoxication. The 1985 Act was repealed by the Psychoactive Substances Act 2016[1] ('PSA 2016') which prohibits the supply of any substance 'which is capable of producing a psychoactive effect in a person who consumes it [. . .] by stimulating or depressing the person's central nervous system'[2], see CHAPTER 15, Product Safety. It prohibits the supply of such substances not just to those under the age of 18, but to people of any age[3]. However, the Cigarette Lighter Refill (Safety) Regulations are unaffected by the PSA 2016, and remain in force.

¹   PSA 2016, Sch 5, para 1(1).
²   PSA 2016, s 2.
³   PSA 2016, s 5.

Territorial jurisdiction

17.223 The Cigarette Lighter Refill (Safety) Regulations 1999[1] ('CLR(S)R 1999') apply across the United Kingdom.

¹   SI 1994/1844.

Offences

17.224 The CLR(S)R 1999 are 'safety regulations' for the purposes of the Consumer Protection Act 1987, s 11 ('CPA 1987'). Regulation 2 CLR(S)R 1999[1] states:

No person shall supply any cigarette lighter refill canister containing butane or a substance with butane as a constituent part to any person under the age of eighteen years.

1   SI 1999/1844, reg 2.

17.225 The CPA 1987, s 12 provides that where safety regulations prohibit a person from supplying or offering or agreeing to supply any goods or from exposing or possessing any goods for supply, that person shall be guilty of an offence if he contravenes the prohibition.

Defences

17.226 There are no statutory defences under the CLR(S)R 1999. The CPA 1987, s 39 provides a defence of due diligence which is established if the defendant can show he took all reasonable steps and exercised all due diligence to avoid committing the offence.

Restrictions on proceedings

17.227 The offence under the CLR(S)R 1999 is summary-only[1]: there is therefore a 6 months' time limit to bring proceedings, running from the time when the offence was committed[2]. In Scotland, as the offence can only be tried under summary procedure, the time limits are established under the Criminal Procedure (Scotland) Act 1995, s 136: within 6 months after the contravention occurred.

1   CPA 1987, s 12(5).
2   Magistrates' Courts Act 1980, s 127.

Prosecutions

17.228 The CPA 1987, s 39 (and thus, CPA 1987, s 40) applies to an offence under CLR(S)R 1999 and action against a person other than the principal offender can only be taken where the commission of the offence is due to an act or default committed by that person 'in the course of any business of his'. The section also permits the prosecution and conviction of any 'director, manager, secretary or other similar officer' of a company or 'any person who was purporting to act in such a capacity' where an offence under the Act has been committed by the company 'with the consent and connivance' of that person or as a result of that person's neglect. Where the affairs of the body corporate are managed by its members, the CPA 1987, s 40 provisions apply in relation to the acts and defaults of 'a member in connection with his functions of management as if he were a director of the body corporate'.

Duty to enforce

17.229 The CPA 1987, s 27 creates a duty for trading standards authorities in Great Britain and district councils in Northern Ireland to enforce the above provisions.

Powers of enforcement officers

17.230 Powers for the enforcement of Regulations made under CPA 1987, s 11 are contained in Pt IV CPA 1987, ss 29–35.

Sentencing

17.231 By virtue of CPA 1987, s 12, contravention of the CLR(S)R 1999 constitutes an offence punishable on summary conviction by imprisonment for a term not exceeding 6 months or by a fine or by both.

PET ANIMALS

Introduction

17.232 The Pet Animals Act 1951 provided general protection for the welfare of animals sold as pets and, specifically, created offences for selling an animal as a pet to a person under the age of 12 years. The Animal Welfare Act 2006[1] ('AWA 2006') and the Animal Health and Welfare (Scotland) Act 2006[2] ('AHW(S)A 2006') repealed these offences and extended their scope.

[1]   AWA 2006, Sch 4, para 1.
[2]   AHW(S)A 2006, Sch 2, para 9(d).

Territorial jurisdiction

17.233 The AWA 2006 extends to England and Wales only. In Scotland the sale of animals to children is governed by the AHW(S)A 2006. The Welfare of Animals Act (Northern Ireland) 2011, s 15 (Transfer of animals by way of sale or prize to persons under 16) is identically worded to the provisions described below. The meaning of 'animals' – throughout all of this legislation – is 'vertebrates other than man'[1], so the provisions are not restricted to 'pet' animals.

[1]   AWA 2006, s 1(1); AHW(S)A 2006, s 16(1); Welfare of Animals Act (Northern Ireland) 2011, s 1(1).

Offences

17.234 The AWA 2006, s 11(1)–(3) creates the following offences:

(1)   selling (which includes transferring, or agreeing to transfer, ownership of the animal in consideration of entry by the transferee of another transaction) to a person whom he has reasonable cause to believe to be under 16 (AWA 2006, s 11(1)).

(2)   entering into an arrangement with a person where the person has the chance to win an animal as a prize who he has reasonable cause to believe is under 16 (AWA 2006, s 11(3)).

17.235 The offence of selling under AWA 2006, s 11(1) applies equally to the direct sale of an animal and to any indirect sale that may accompany an otherwise legal transaction. In Scotland, AHW(S)A 2006, s 30 provides that a person commits an offence if they sell (which includes transferring, or agreeing to transfer, ownership of the animal in consideration of entry by the transferee into another transaction) an animal to a person under 16.

17.236 It is also an offence under AHW(S)A 2006[1] for a person to offer or give an animal to another person (of any age) as a prize but this does not apply where the prize is offered or given in a family context.

[1] AHW(S)A 2006, s 31.

Defences

17.237 There are no statutory defences in relation to the offences under AWA 2006, ss 11(1) or 11(3). However, the offence under AWA 2006, s 11(3) is not committed if:

(1)   the arrangement is entered into in the presence of the person with whom the arrangement is made and the person has reasonable cause to believe that the person with whom the arrangement is made is accompanied by a person who is not under 16[1].

(2)   the arrangement is entered into otherwise than in the presence of the person with whom the arrangement is made and the person has reasonable cause to believe that a person who has actual care and control of the person with whom the arrangement is made has consented to the arrangement[2].

(3)   the arrangement is entered into in a family context[3].

[1] AWA 2006, s 11(4).
[2] AWA 2006, s 11(5).
[3] AWA 2006, s 11 (6).

17.238 In Scotland, AHW(S)A 2006, s 30 provides a defence for a person charged under AHW(S)A 2006 if the demonstrate that:

(a)   having been shown convincing evidence (for example, a passport or photocard driving license) of the buyer's identity and age; or

(b)   having no reasonable cause to suspect from the buyer's appearance that the buyer was under 16, they believed that the buyer was aged 16 or over.

Restrictions on proceedings

17.239 The AWA 2006, s 31 details the time limits for prosecutions, which are to be commenced by an information being laid:

(a)   before the end of the period of 3 years beginning with the date of the commission of the offence, and

(b)   before the end of the period of 6 months beginning with the date on which evidence which the prosecutor thinks is sufficient to justify the proceedings comes to his knowledge.

17.240 Time limits are covered generally in CHAPTER 4 (Criminal Enforcement). The AWA 2006, s 31(2) provides that if a prosecutor certifies the date on which he learnt of the relevant evidence, that date shall be the starting point for calculating the period within which proceedings must be commenced. A number of issues relating to the AWA 2006, s 31 provision have been litigated in recent years. *RSPCA v Johnson*[1] held that the date on which evidence that the prosecutor thinks is sufficient to justify proceedings comes to his knowledge cannot be avoided or delayed by sitting on an information. However, there is a degree of judgement involved and a public interest in only bringing prosecutions following consideration of the evidence by an expert. *RSPCA v Ian James King* and *Kathleen Patricia King*[2] underlines the importance of a prosecutor, who wishes to avail himself of the benefits of a certificate under AWA 2006, s 31(2), fully complying with the statutory requirements. An unsigned file copy of a missing certificate does not comply with the statutory requirements, even if accompanied by a letter stating that such a certificate was signed and issued.

1   [2009] EWHC 2702 (Admin).
2   [2010] EWHC 637 (Admin).

17.241 The appellant in *Lamont-Perkins v RSPCA*[1] asserted that the RSPCA could not rely on the time-limits set out in s 31 as it was not a 'prosecutor' within the meaning of the Act, and therefore was subject instead to the time limit of 6 months set by the Magistrates Court Act 1980, s 127. This was rejected by Wyn Williams J who found that the term 'prosecutor' was not limited to local authorities simply because they are given express powers in AWA 2006, s 30, but rather the term simply referred to any party bringing a prosecution under the Act. The other issue raised in this case was the circumstances in which a certificate under AWA 2006, s 31 could be challenged and the court confirmed it could be challenged either on the basis that it constituted a fraud or on the basis that it is plainly wrong.

1   [2012] EWHC 1002 Admin.

17.242 The case of *Letherbarrow v Warwickshire County Council*[1] is authority for the proposition that 'prosecutor' for the purposes of AWA 2006, s 31 means a collective body, such as a local authority, but is specifically the individual with responsibility in the body for deciding whether a prosecution should proceed. The decision on whether a prosecution should proceed is not whether there is a prima facie case, but whether the evidence is sufficient to justify a prosecution. This involves a consideration of the interests of justice. Time runs from the moment that responsible individual is in a position to make that nuanced decision, and not, for example, from the time the matter is reported to the trading standards department of a local authority. This case also clarified that a AWA 2006, s 31 certificate could be issued after a challenge had been raised in court proceedings.

1   [2014] EWHC 4820 (Admin).

17.243 *R v Woodward*[1] applies and provides a good summary of the relevant case law regarding AWA 2006, s 31. This case further held that where there was no certificate to be relied on, the court still had to determine whether the prosecution had been brought within the time frame by considering all of the available evidence. In *Downes v Royal Society for the Prevention of Cruelty to Animals*[2] it was held that Magistrates' Courts should deal robustly with suggestions that s 31 certificates were susceptible to challenge. The defence are required to make clear that there is a prima facie case for undermining a certificate.

¹   [2017] EWHC 1008 (Admin).
²   [2017] EWHC 3622 (Admin).

17.244 In Scotland, as the offence under AHW(S)A 2006, s 30 can only be tried under summary procedure¹, the time limits are established under the Criminal Procedure (Scotland) Act 1995, s 136 – within 6 months after the contravention occurred.

¹   AHW(S)A 2006, s 46.

Prosecutions

17.245 The offences in AWA 2006, s 11 can be committed by any person – whether an individual or a corporate body – and there is no requirement that such offences be committed in the course of a trade or business. The AWA 2006, s 57 permits the prosecution and conviction of any 'director, manager, secretary or other similar officer' of a company or 'any person who was purporting to act in such a capacity' where an offence under the Act has been committed by the company 'with the consent and connivance' of that person or as a result of that person's neglect. Where the affairs of the body corporate are managed by its members, the provisions apply in relation to the acts and defaults of 'a member in connection with his functions of management as if he were a director of the body corporate'. In Scotland, AHW(S)A 2006, s 45 makes similar provision to AWA 2006, s 57 above and in addition, AHW(S)A, s 45 provides for liability where an offence is committed by a Scottish partnership in Scotland.

Duty to enforce

17.246 There is no prescribed duty of enforcement for AWA 2006. Although AWA 2006, s 30 provides a power for a local authority to prosecute offences (which may be seen as superfluous in the light of the Local Government Act 1972, s 222) the right to launch private prosecutions derives from the common law and the Act does not limit that right. There is no prescribed duty of enforcement for AHW(S)A 2006.

Powers of enforcement officers

17.247 There are no powers of test purchasing under AWA 2006. The general enforcement powers are set out in AWA 2006, ss 22–29 (and AWA 2006, Sch 2), and include powers of entry and search, seizure of animals and inspection under certain conditions. In Scotland, AHW(S)A 2006, s 49 and AHW(S)A 2006, Sch 1 permit a local authority to appoint inspectors and set out the powers of inspectors in respect of entry, inspection, search and the conditions for obtaining warrants.

Sentencing

17.248 The AWA 2006, ss 32–45 set out the penalties available on conviction, which include imprisonment, fine, deprivation, disqualification, destruction, forfeiture of equipment and cancellation of a licence or registration.

17.249 The AWA 2006, s 32(4) applies to the offences under s 11 and provides that a person guilty of an offence under AWA 2006, s 11 is liable on summary conviction to imprisonment for a term not exceeding 51 weeks, or a fine not exceeding level 4 on the standard scale, or to both.

17.250 The AWA 2006, s 42 also applies to offences under AWA 2006, s 11 and provides for a power for the court to make an order cancelling the licence held by the defendant, or make an order disqualifying him for a period from holding a licence, instead of or in addition to dealing with the defendant in another way.

17.251 In Scotland, AHW(S)A 2006, s 46 states that a person who commits an offence under AHW(S)A 2006, s 30 is liable to imprisonment for a term not exceeding 6 months or to a fine not exceeding level 5 on the standard scale, or to both.

OTHER LEGISLATION

Gambling

Gambling Act 2005

17.252 The Gambling Act 2005 ('GA 2005') introduced a new regulatory system to govern the provision of all gambling in Great Britain, other than the National Lottery and spread betting. In broad terms, people aged under eighteen are not permitted to gamble but, specifically, GA 2005, s 46(1) provides: 'A person commits an offence if he invites, causes or permits a child or young person to gamble'[1].

[1]   Per GA 2005, s 45, 'child' means an individual who is less than 16 years old and 'young person' means an individual who is not a child but who is less than 18 years old.

17.253 The GA 2005, s 46 provides for a number of exceptions to the general prohibition on gambling by children and young people, including participation in all forms of private or non-commercial gaming and betting, lotteries, pool betting on association football, use of gaming machines with the lowest stakes and prizes (Category D), and participation in equal chance prize gaming at certain premises, as provided for under Pt 13 of the Act.

17.254 Children and young persons may not enter a casino, a betting shop or an adult gaming centre at any time when facilities for gambling are being provided on the premises in reliance on the relevant premises licence. A person commits an offence if he invites or permits a child or young person to enter such premises[1].This is subject to the exception that children and young persons may enter the non-gambling area of a regional casino, but they may not enter the gambling area[2]. Further, a person of any age may enter bingo premises, the betting areas of a horse racecourse, a greyhound track, or any other track on days on which races or other sporting events are being run[3], or any area of a family entertainment centre where no Category C gaming machines are provided at that place[4].

[1]   GA 2005, s 47.
[2]   GA 2005, s 47(2).
[3]   GA 2005, s 182.
[4]   GA 2005, s 47(7).

17.255 A young person commits an offence if they gamble[1] (subject to exceptions) or enter a premises in circumstances where a person would commit an offence under GA 2005, s 47 if they invited or permitted the young person to enter[2]. Further offences relating to children and young persons are set out in GA 2005, ss 50–59 but are beyond the scope of this chapter.

[1]   GA 2005, s 48.
[2]   GA 2005, s 49.

17.256 On 31 October2020 a new version of the Gambling Commission's License conditions and codes of practice came into force. This version updates the April 2020, May 2019 and April 2018 Codes of Practice which consolidated all forms of gambling and includes provisions from the social responsibility code and the ordinary code. The updated code includes requirements that *inter alia*:

(a)   licensees must have and put into effect policies and procedures designed to prevent underage gambling;

(b)   a supervisor of a venue entrance must check the age of customers who appear to be underage; refuse entry to anyone unable to produce an acceptable form of identification; and take action when there are unlawful attempts to enter the premises;

(c)   licensees must not deliberately provide facilities for gambling in such a way as to appeal to children or young people;

(d)   licensees must take all reasonable steps to ensure that all staff understand their responsibilities for preventing underage gambling, including appropriate training;

(e)   licensees must conduct test purchasing or take part in collective test purchasing programmes as a means of providing reasonable assurance that they have effective policies and procedures to prevent underage gambling, and must provide their test-purchase results to the Commission.

DEFENCES

17.257 Where a person is charged with an offence under GA 2005 of doing anything in relation to a child or young person it is a defence under GA 2005, s 63 for the person to prove that he took all reasonable steps to determine the relevant person's age and he reasonably believed that the person was not a child or a young person.

SENTENCING

17.258 An adult guilty of any of the above described offences is liable on summary conviction to imprisonment for a term not exceeding 51 weeks

(6 months in Scotland), a fine or both. A young person guilty of any of the above described offences is liable to a fine not exceeding level 3 on the standard scale[1].

[1]   GA 2005, s 62.

USE OF CHILDREN IN ENFORCEMENT OPERATIONS

17.259 The GA 2005, s 64 enables children and young persons to be used in test purchasing operations for the purpose of assessing whether the provisions in Pt 4, prohibiting under-age gambling, are being complied with. For example, a constable, enforcement officer or authorised person will not commit an offence under GA 2005, s 46 if, in the course of their duty, they invite a child or young person to gamble. Equally, a young person will not commit an offence under GA 2005, s 48 if he gambles at the request of a constable, enforcement officer or authorised officer who is acting in the course of his duties. In February 2015 the Gambling Commission published an updated advice note setting out its approach to test purchasing for gambling in England and Wales.

National Lottery etc. Act 1993

17.260 The National Lottery Regulations 1994 ('NLR 1994')[1] were made under the National Lottery etc. Act 1993, s 12 ('NLA 1993'). Regulation 3 of the NLR 1994 provides: 'No National Lottery ticket shall be sold by or to a person who has not attained the age of 16 years'. Regulation 3 is due to be amended on 1 October 2021 by the National Lottery (Amendment) Regulations[2] to increase the age restriction to 18 years' of age. The NLR 1994 also prohibits sales of National Lottery tickets in a street (reg 4) and on certain premises (reg 5), imposes restrictions on the sales tickets by means of vending machines (reg 6)[3] and on sales of tickets at a person's home (reg 7).

[1]   SI 1994/189.
[2]   SI 2020/1475.
[3]   This regulation is also due to be amended on 1 October 2021 by the National Lottery (Amendment) Regulations 2020 (SI 2020/1475) to increase the age restriction from 16 years' of age to 18 years' of age.

17.261 The NLA 1993, s 13 provides that contravention of Regulations made under the NLA 1993, s 12 is an offence. The following persons may be found guilty of an offence:

(a)   the promoter of the lottery, except if the contravention occurred without the consent or connivance of the promoter and the promoter exercised all due diligence to prevent such a contravention;

(b)   any director, manager, secretary or other similar officer of the promoter, or any person purporting to act in such a capacity, if he consented to or connived at the contravention or if the contravention was attributable to any neglect on his part; and

(c)   any other person who was party to the contravention.

17.262 The NLA 1993 has application throughout the UK but the following provisions apply solely to Scotland. Summary proceedings in Scotland for an offence under NLA 1993, s 13 may be commenced within a period of 6 months from the date on which evidence sufficient in the opinion of the procurator fiscal to warrant proceedings came to his knowledge; but no proceedings in Scotland shall be commenced by virtue of NLA 1993, s 13 more than 3 years after the commission of the offence[1]. For the purposes of NLA 1993, s 13, a certificate signed by or on behalf of the procurator fiscal and stating the date on which evidence sufficient in his opinion to warrant the proceedings came to his knowledge shall be conclusive evidence of that fact; and a certificate stating that matter and purporting to be so signed shall be taken to be so signed unless the contrary is proved[2].

[1]   National Lottery etc Act 1993, s 13(3).
[2]   National Lottery etc Act 1993, s 13(4).

17.263 In *Harrow London Borough Council v Shah and another*[1] the defendants were husband and wife who owned a newsagent's shop. An employee, who knew of his obligations not to sell lottery tickets to under 16-year-olds, sold a National Lottery ticket to a 13 ½-year-old. Mitchell J noted:

> '90 This ticket was sold, not by either Mr Shah or Mrs Shah, but by their employee Mr Hobday. Unfortunately, but inevitably, his offence was, at once, their offence, given the principles of vicarious liability . . . The Prosecution does not have to prove, for the purposes of establishing the offence, that the defendant or his agent was either aware of the buyer's age, or was reckless as to his age.'

[1]   [1999] 3 All ER 302.

Tattoos

Tattooing of Minors Act 1969

17.264 The Tattooing of Minors Act 1969 ('TMA 1969') s 1, which applies to Great Britain, creates an offence of tattooing a person under the age of 18 (except where the tattoo is performed for medical reasons). Further, TMA 1969, s 1 creates a statutory defence of having a reasonable cause to believe that the person tattooed was over the age of 18 and did in fact so believe.

17.265 'Tattoo' means the insertion into the skin of any colouring material designed to leave a permanent mark[1]. Any person found committing the TMA 1969, s 1 offence shall be liable on summary conviction to a fine not exceeding level 3 on the standard scale[2].

[1]   Tattooing of Minors Act 1969, s 3.
[2]   Tattooing of Minors Act 1969, s 2.

17.266 In Scotland, this area is also governed by the Civic Government (Scotland) Act 1982[1] and, in particular, the Civic Government (Scotland) Act 1982 (Licensing of Skin Piercing and Tattooing) Order 2006[2] which designates the activity of carrying on a business which provides skin-piercing or tattooing as an activity for which a licence is required[3]. Note that a licence is not required by a member of certain professions that are regulated by law.

[1]   Civic Government (Scotland) Act 1982, s 44.
[2]   SSI 2006/43.
[3]   SSI 2006/43, art 2.

Petroleum

Petroleum (Consolidation) Regulations 2014

17.267 Previously governed by the Petroleum (Consolidation) Act 1928, there was until recently no direct offence of selling petrol to a minor. Sales of petrol to under 16s was dealt with as a breach of licensing conditions established by the Act. The former legislation was abolished by the Petroleum (Consolidation) Regulations 2014[1]. The Regulations replaced the licensing regime with a certification scheme. To store petrol at a filling station a petroleum storage certificate is now required (reg 5), which is issued by the previous licensing authorities (reg 6) (albeit now renamed Petroleum Enforcement Authorities).

[1]   SI 2014/1637.

17.268 Under-age sales are now expressly prohibited by reg 12 which prohibits persons under the age of 16 from operating a dispenser on dispensing premises and prohibits persons from supplying or allowing the supply of petrol to a person under 16.

17.269 However, where previously it was an offence to supply petroleum in breach of the conditions of the licence (which would generally include a condition not to supply to persons under 16), no offence of breaching the regulations is apparently created by the 2014 Regulations. It therefore seems that the only penalty open to enforcers faced with a trader supplying petrol to minors would be to refuse future grants of storage certificates.

Scrap metal

Scrap Metal Dealers Act 2013

17.270 The Scrap Metal Dealers Act 2013 ('SMDA 2013') abolishes the 1964 Act of the same name, which previously introduced a revised regulatory regime for the scrap-metal industry. The previous legislation made it an offence for a scrap metal dealer to *purchase* scrap metal from a person who was apparently under the age of 16 (somewhat of an anomaly in this chapter dealing with the prohibition on *sales* to minors). Presumably the prohibition stemmed from an assumption that scrap metal provided by under 16 would be more likely to come from illegitimate sources.

17.271 There is no directly equivalent offence in the SMDA 2013. The new regime's focus is upon due diligence on the part of the dealer (which includes managers and employees who have been delegated the responsibility to do so): who is now required to verify the supplier's full name and address, from a reliable and independent source, rather than form a view about the supplier's age[1]. The SMDA 2013, s 11(4) makes it an offence for a scrap metal dealer to receive scrap metal in breach of the requirement. The offence is summary only and punishable by a fine not exceeding level 3 on the standard scale[2]. The SMDA 2013, s 12 further creates an offence of paying for scrap metal other than by a cheque or by an electronic transfer of funds, the so-called 'cash prohibition'.

[1]   Scrap Metal Dealers Act 2013 (Prescribed Documents and Information for Verification of Name and Address) Regulations 2013, SI 2013/2276, reg 2.

² SMDA, s 11(6).

17.272 In Scotland, the Civic Government (Scotland) Act 1982, s 34(1) makes it an offence for any metal dealer to dispose of metal to a person apparently under the age of 16, or to acquire metal from such a person. Upon summary conviction, a metal dealer is punishable to a fine not exceeding level 3 on the standard scale.

Sunbeds

Sunbeds (Regulation) Act 2010

17.273 The Sunbeds (Regulation) Act 2010 ('S(R)A 2010') – which extends to England and Wales – seeks to prevent persons aged under 18 from using sunbeds. With a few exceptions, the Act provides for offences where a person who carries on a sunbed business fails to ensure that no person under 18 uses, or is offered the use of, one of the business's sunbeds on the business premises, or fails to ensure that no person aged under 18 is at any time present, other than in the course of providing services for the person carrying on the sunbed business, in a restricted zone (as defined by S(R)A 2010, ss 2(4) and 2(5))[1]. Note, an offence is still committed where the person aged under 18 did not go on to use the sunbed because, for example, the sunbed failed to work or the person changed their mind[2].

¹ S(R)A 2010, s 2.
² Explanatory notes to S(R)A 2010, para 21.

17.274 Under S(R)A 2010, s 2(7) it is a defence for the defendant to show he took all reasonable precautions and exercised all due diligence to avoid committing an offence. The offences are punishable on summary conviction by a fine[1]. A duty of enforcement is placed on local authorities[2] and the powers of authorised officers are set out in S(R)A 2010, Sch 1 and include a provision to make ' . . . such purchases and secure the provision of such services as the officer considers necessary for the purpose of the proper exercise of the officer's functions under this Act'[3].

¹ S(R)A 2010, s 2(6).
² S(R)A 2010, s 7.
³ S(R)A 2010, Sch 1, para 3.

17.275 The S(R)A 2010, ss 4–6 establish wide powers to make secondary legislation introducing further aspects of regulation, including prohibiting or restricting the sale or hire of sunbeds to persons aged under 18, securing that no sunbed to which the business relates is used on domestic premises by a person under 18, and securing that no offer is made by or on behalf of a person who carries on a sunbed business to make a sunbed to which the business relates available for use on domestic premises by a person aged under 18[1]. These powers have been exercised in relation to Wales, but not in England.

¹ S(R)A 2010, s 4.

17.276 The Sunbeds (Regulation) Act 2010 (Wales) Regulations 2011[1] was made under S(R)A 2010, s 4 and applies solely in relation to Wales. The Regulations impose: a duty on a person who carries on a sunbed business on domestic premises to prevent sunbed use on those premises by persons aged under 18 (reg 3); a requirement for a person who carries on a sunbed business to supervise the use of sunbeds on the business's premises (reg 4); a prohibition on the sale or hire of sunbeds to persons aged under 18 (reg 5); requirements for the provision of information to sunbed users (reg 7); and, requirements relating to the use of protective eyewear by sunbed users (reg 8). A person who fails to comply with these regulations commits an offence. It is the duty of the local authority to enforce these regulations (reg 9).

[1]   SI 2011/1130.

SCOTLAND

17.277 In Scotland, Pt 8 of the Public Health etc (Scotland) Act 2008 regulates the use, sale and hire of sunbeds. The Act prohibits operators from: allowing use of sunbeds on their premises by persons under 18 (PH(S)A 2008, s 95); allowing unsupervised use of sunbeds on their premises (PH(S)A 2008, s 98); selling or hiring sunbeds to persons under 18 (PH(S)A 2008, s 96); places a duty upon operators of sunbed premises to display a public information notice (PH(S)A 2008, s 101); and, requires operators to provide customers with information on the health risks associated with sunbed use each time they intend to use a sunbed (PH(S)A 2008, s 100). The information to be provided to customers and to be displayed in sunbed premises (including the form and manner in which it is to be provided) is prescribed by the Public Health etc (Scotland) Act 2008 (Sunbed) Regulations 2009[1]. Any failure to follow the above parts of the Public Health etc (Scotland) Act 2008 constitutes an offence. The Act enables local authority officers – who are given powers of enforcement[2] – to issue a fixed penalty notice to the operator of the premises where the officer has reason to believe an offence has taken place. The fixed penalty notice gives the operator the opportunity of discharging liability to conviction for the offence by payment of the fixed penalty[3].

[1]   SSI 2009/388.
[2]   As set out in Public Health etc (Scotland) Act 2008, ss 102–107.
[3]   Public Health etc (Scotland) Act 2008, s 105.

NORTHERN IRELAND

17.278 The Sunbeds Act (Northern Ireland) 2011 prohibits the use (s 1), sale or hire (s 2) of a sunbed to persons under the age of 18 and provides an exemption for medical treatment (s 10). The Act places a duty on operators of sunbed premises to display an information notice (s 5). It places a duty on sunbed operators and those who hire or sell sunbeds to provide sunbed users, hirers and buyers with information about the risks associated with sunbed use (s 4). It places a duty on operators of sunbed premises and those who hire or sell sunbeds to make protective eyewear available to sunbed users (s 7). It also places a duty on sunbed operators and those who hire or sell sunbeds to secure that those who allow people to use sunbeds are trained to a required standard (s 8) and that all sunbeds for use in sunbeds premises, for hire or for sale, meet required standards (s 9)[1]. The Sunbeds (Information) Regulations (Northern Ireland) 2012[2] outline the wording to be contained in the information leaflet that must be provided to a person who proposes to use a sunbed on sunbed premises, or is hiring or buying a sunbed. The Regulations also outline the wording to be contained in the display notice that sunbed premises must display in a prominent position and the style and format of this notice. Any failure to follow the above parts of the Act constitutes an offence. Schedules 1 and 2 of the Act set out the enforcement powers available to authorised officers and provides for fixed penalties for particular offences.

¹   Sunbeds Act (Northern Ireland) 2011, ss 8 and 9 are not yet in force and no date has been set for commencement.
²   SR 2012/91.

Corrosive substances

Offensive Weapons Act 2019

17.279   The Offensive Weapons Act 2019 ('OWA 2019') received Royal Assent on 16 May 2019 and will come into force on a date to be appointed. It creates, amongst other things, a number of offences in relation to corrosive products. Following a rising number of acid attacks and voluntary bans by a number of DIY stores and supermarkets on the sale of acids to customers under 18 years old, the OWA 2019 will significantly limit the sale of corrosive substances. A person will commit an offence in England and Wales, Scotland and Northern Ireland, if they sell a corrosive product to a person who is under the age of 18[1]. Statutory defences, which differ between England, Wales and Northern Ireland, and Scotland, are detailed in s 1(2)–(3) and OWA 2019, s 2. A person guilty of such an offence is liable in England and Wales on summary conviction to a term of imprisonment not exceeding 6 months[2], to a fine, or both, and in Scotland or Northern Ireland on summary conviction to a term of imprisonment not exceeding 6 months, to a fine not exceeding level 5 on the standard scale, or both[3].

¹   OWA 2019, s 1(1).
²   To increase to 51 weeks after the coming into force of s 281(5) of the Criminal Justice Act 2003 (OWA 2019, s 1(8)).
³   OWA 2019, s 1(7).

17.280   A seller also commits an offence in England and Wales, Scotland and Northern Ireland if:

(a)   The seller sells a corrosive product to the buyer;
(b)   The seller and the buyer are not in each other's presence at the time of the sale[1] and the seller is outside the UK at that time[2];
(c)   Before the sale, the seller entered into an arrangement with a body corporate by which the body corporate agreed to deliver corrosive products for the seller;
(d)   The body corporate was aware when they entered into the arrangement that it covered the delivery of corrosive products;
(e)   The body corporate delivers the corrosive product pursuant to the arrangement;
(f)   When the body corporate delivers the corrosive product, they do not deliver it into the hands of a person aged 18 or over[3].

¹   As defined in OWA 2019, s 4(2).
²   As defined in OWA 2019, s 4(3).
³   OWA 2019, s 4(4).

17.281 A corrosive product is defined in OWA 2019, s 1(11) as a substance listed in the first column of Sch 1 of OWA 2019 or a product which contains a substance listed in the first column of Sch 1 in a concentration higher than the limit set out for that substance in the second column of that Schedule. Schedule 1 is as follows:

Name of substance	Concentration limit (weight in weight)
Ammonium hydroxide	10% w/w
Formic acid	10% w/w
Hydrochloric acid	10% w/w
Nitric acid	3% w/w
Phosphoric acid	70% w/w
Sodium hydroxide	12% w/w
Sulfuric acid	15% w/w

References to a corrosive product do not include substances or products contained in a battery[1].

[1]   OWA 2019, s 1(15).

17.282 Whilst there will be no duty to enforce OWA 2019, s 1 and s 4, per OWA 2019, s 64(1), a local weights and measures authority may enforce within its area, amongst other sections, OWA 2019, s 1(sale of corrosive products to persons under 18) and OWA 2019, s 4 (delivery of corrosive products to persons under 18). The investigatory powers available to local weights and measures authorities for the purpose of enforcing these provisions are detailed in Sch 5 to the Consumer Rights Act 2015.

Chapter 18

METROLOGY AND HALLMARKING

Contents

INTRODUCTION

18.1 The Magna Carta states at Clause 35:

'Let there be one measure of wine throughout the whole kingdom, and one measure of ale and one measure of corn; and one width of cloth.'

The purpose of regulating weights and measures is to ensure that consumers have accurate information in which they can place confidence when making purchasing decisions. However, it is uncontroversial to note that the evolution of the weights and measures regime has been fragmented and complex, and it is almost universally recognised that, as a result of this evolution, the present state of the law is burdensome for commerce and impenetrable for consumers. Over the years, there have been a number of recommendations and proposals to reform and simplify the law. However, whilst there have been provisions, for example, to deregulate controls on packaged goods, allow self-verification after adjustment, remove obsolete regulations from the statute book[1] and to repeal the fixed sizes that products must be sold in[2], there are still no substantive proposals for fundamental reform.

[1] The Weights and Measures (Revocations) Regulations 2015, SI 2015/356.
[2] For example, yarn and unwrapped bread: see Deregulation Act 2015, s 16 and the Weights and Measures (Specified Quantities) (Unwrapped Bread and Intoxicating Liquor) Order 2011, SI 2011/2331 respectively.

18.2 With that in mind, this chapter aims to cut through the complexity and provide practical information on the core elements of the weights and measures regime: the key concepts and offences under Pt II of the Weights and Measures Act 1985 ('WMA 1985'); the commonly committed offences and associated defences that are set out in Pt IV of the WMA 1985, ss 28–37; and other offences contained in regulations made under the WMA 1985 that also fall within the scope of enforcement of local weights and measures authorities. The WMA 1985 consolidated and very largely replaced the previous Acts of the same name of 1963, 1976 and 1979. Its provisions must be complied with whenever weights and measures are 'used for trade'[1], an expression considered in detail below. Whilst the WMA 1985 remains the core piece of legislation that governs the regulation of weights and measures it has been amended in a significant manner on a number of occasions: for example, the WMA was amended in December 2014[2] to align the UK weights and measures regime with the Food Information to Consumers Regulation[3] and in October 2015 to reflect movement of the disparate enforcement powers across the trading standards field into the Consumer Rights Act 2015[4].

[1] WMA 1985, s 7.
[2] Weights and Measures (Food) (Amendment) Regulations 2014, SI 2014/2975.
[3] Regulation (EU) 1169/2011.
[4] Consumer Rights Act 2015, Sch 5.

18.3 Other recent changes include the launch of the 'Office for Product Safety and Standards ('OPS&S') on 21 January 2018, which supersedes the Regulatory Delivery directorate. OPS&S was created by the Department for Business, Energy and Industrial Strategy, to enhance protections for consumers and the environment and drive increased productivity, growth and business confidence. Regulatory Delivery was part of the Department for Business, Energy and Industrial Strategy and brought together the National Measurement and Regulation Office ('NMRO') and Better Regulation Delivery Office ('BRDO'). The NMRO's role and responsibilities in respect of weights and measures were with Regulatory Delivery who worked with businesses and Local Weights and Measures Authorities with the intention of reducing burdens on business, saving public money and ensuring the proper protection of consumers. This now all lies with the OPS&S.

18.4 EU exit regulations have been enacted in order to distinguish the UK from EU Member and EEA States. The two most relevant regulations that have impacted metrology and hallmarking are the Product Safety and Metrology etc. (Amendment etc.) (EU Exit) Regulations 2019[1] and the Weighing and Measuring Equipment and Meters (Amendment of Secondary Legislation) (EU Exit) Regulations 2018[2].

[1] SI 2019/696, as amended by SI 2019/1246, SI 2020/676, SI 2020/852.
[2] SI 2018/1387.

SUMMARY OF THE WMA 1985

18.5 Parts I and II of the WMA 1985 specify the units of measurement and the measures and weights permitted for 'use for trade' as being those set out in WMA 1985, Schs 1 and 3 respectively. Weighing and measuring equipment for use for trade must be inspected and passed as fit for such use and be stamped[1]. The forging of, and interference with, official stamps are offences[2]. The use for trade of unjust equipment and false weights and the fraudulent use of proper equipment are offences[3].

[1] WMA 1985, s 11.
[2] WMA 1985, s 16.
[3] WMA 1985, s 17.

18.6 Under Pt III of the WMA 1985, operators of public weighing machines are required to hold a certificate[1] and misuse of such equipment is an offence[2].

Part IV of the WMA 1985 contains[3] requirements concerned with the sale of a wide variety of goods and commodities. It grants power to the Secretary of State to make Orders and Regulations as to such matters as to the quantities by which particular goods may be sold, the marking of containers of goods specified within the Schedules to the WMA 1985, the units of measurement to be used in marking such containers and the identification of the packer of pre-packed goods.

1   WMA 1985, s 18.
2   WMA 1985, s 20.
3   WMA 1985, ss 21–24 and WMA 1985, Schs 4–7.

18.7 Selling, or offering for sale, goods in breach of the provisions of Pt IV is an offence[1]. Certain goods must have their quantity stated in writing[2]. Since 13 December 2014, Pt IV of the WMA 1985 also made it an offence for relevant Food Business Operators to fail to comply with certain aspects of the Food Information to Consumers Regulation[3]. The Weights and Measures (Packaged Goods) Regulations 2006[4] repealed Pt V of the WMA 1985 and set out a complete regime for the average system of quantity control applied to packaged goods.

1   WMA 1985, s 25.
2   WMA 1985, ss 26 and 27.
3   Arts 8 and 9(1)(e) and WMA 1985, s 31A.
4   SI 2006/659. See also **18.4** and SI 2019/696.

18.8 Parts VI and VII of the WMA 1985 specify the local weights and measures authorities for England, Wales and Scotland, the requirement on the authorities to appoint inspectors and the duties and powers of these authorities and persons. (No section under the WMA 1985 authorises a local weights and measures authority to institute proceedings in Scotland for an offence.) Since 1 October 2015, the investigatory powers available to local weights and measures authorities have been contained in the Consumer Rights Act 2015, Sch 5.

18.9 Whilst only the provisions set out in WMA 1985, Sch 10 extend to Northern Ireland, the legislative position, relating to weights and measures in that country, is reflected by the Explanatory Notes to the Weights and Measures (Amendment) Act (Northern Ireland) 2000. The Notes state: 'The principal policy objective of the Act is to replicate for Northern Ireland those three deregulatory measures contained in the Deregulation (Weights and Measures) Order 1999, which was made by the DTI under the 1994 Act on 1 March 1999. Parity will thus be maintained between the legislative provisions on weights and measures here and those in Great Britain (GB), with Northern Ireland continuing to remain on all fours with the rest of the UK'. Similarly, the Weights and Measures (Packaged Goods) Regulations (Northern Ireland) 2011 and the Weights and Measures (Specified Quantities) (Unwrapped Bread and Intoxicating Liquor) Order (Northern Ireland)[1] – statutory rules made under the Weights and Measures (Northern Ireland) Order 1981 and the European Communities Act 1972 – reformed Northern Ireland legislation in this area in a comparable manner to that adopted in Great Britain by the Weights and Measures (Packaged Goods) Regulations 2006 and the Weights and Measures (Specified

Quantities) (Unwrapped Bread and Intoxicating Liquor) Order 2011 respectively.

¹   SI 2013/261.

PART II WMA 1985 – WEIGHING AND MEASURING FOR TRADE – KEY CONCEPTS

Units and measures

18.10 The WMA 1985, s 8 prescribes the units of measurement which are lawful for use for trade. They are recited in the WMA 1985, Sch 1. They are now almost all metric, the imperial measures having been deleted from the Schedule by Regulations[1]. The WMA 1985, s 8 also prescribes the measures and weights which are lawful for use for trade. The lawful measures are those recited in the WMA 1985, Sch 3. Thus, for example, cloth may be sold by the metre or the centimetre, but not by the millimetre, and traders may use linear measures with prescribed lengths as sub-divisions to achieve this[2]. There are savings for units and measures set out in the WMA 1985, s 8(2)(a)–(d) (relating to precious metals and stones and measures of alcohol), but since 1 January 2000[3] the imperial units and measures or weights are unlawful if used as the sole measurement of weight or quantity. Imperial units and measures are permitted as a 'supplementary indication'[4] provided they accompany an indication of quantity expressed as a metric unit which is the more prominent of the two. The permitted units and measures for 'supplementary' use are set out in WMA 1985, Sch 1, Pt VI.

¹   Units of Measurement Regulations 1994, SI 1994/2867, reg 6(1), (5)(a).
²   WMA 1985, s 10.
³   Units of Measurement Regulations 1995, SI 1995/1804.
⁴   WMA 1985, s 8(5A).

Drugs

18.11 The prohibition on the use of units of measurement other than those set out in the WMA 1985, Sch 1 does not apply to drugs[1], which may continue to be prescribed and dispensed in the existing, non-metric, units.

¹   WMA 1985, s 8(3). The word 'drugs' bears the same meaning as 'controlled drugs' under the Misuse of Drugs Act 1971.

Weighing and measuring equipment

18.12 Offences under the WMA 1985 are frequently concerned with the use or possession of weighing or measuring equipment. This is defined in WMA 1985, s 94(1) as 'equipment for measuring in terms of length, area, volume, capacity, weight or number, whether or not the equipment is constructed to give an indication of the measurement made or other information determined by reference to that measurement'.

Use for trade

18.13 The WMA 1985, s 7 defines the expression 'use for trade', which is an ingredient of almost all the transaction-based offences under the WMA 1985. Only those transactions which involve the transfer of money, or money's worth, in consideration of money, or money's worth, are affected[1].

[1]   WMA 1985, s 7(2).

18.14 The essential words of WMA 1985, s 7 are:

> . . . use in connection with, or with a view to a transaction . . . where—

(a)   the transaction is by reference to quantity or is a transaction for the purposes of which there is made or implied a statement of the quantity of goods to which the transaction relates and,

(b)   the use is for the purpose of the determination or statement of that quantity.

18.15 The kernel of the definition is that where units of weight or quantity, or equipment for weighing or measuring, are used to determine the quantity of the goods involved in a transaction for value then this will be 'use for trade'. Use includes within its meaning causing or permitting use[1], and thus an employer is liable for the WMA 1985 actions of his employee even if the employee has been acting contrary to instructions[2]. If the employer can establish that the employee has acted altogether outside the scope of his authority then he may escape liability[3]. It is not only the seller of goods who may be caught by the provisions of the WMA 1985. Where the buyer checks the weight of goods supplied, the equipment he uses is in 'use for trade'[4] and must comply with the WMA 1985.

[1]   *FE Charman Ltd v Clow* [1974] 3 All ER 371, [1974] 1 WLR 1384.
[2]   *Elder v Bishop Auckland Co-op Society* (1917) 86 LJKB 1412, [1910–1917] All ER 961.
[3]   *Navarro v Moregrand* [1951] 2 TLR 674 at 681, 95 Sol Jo 367, CA, per Denning LJ.
[4]   *Crick v Theobald* (1895) 64 LJMC 216, 72 LT 807.

Wholesaling goods abroad

18.16 The WMA 1985, s 7(3) exempts statements of the quantity of goods for wholesale to destinations outside Great Britain (and outside of Northern Ireland, the Chanel Islands and the Isle of Man)[1] from the definition of 'use for trade', while by WMA 1985, s 7(4) scales and measuring equipment made available for public use and egg grading equipment are always to be treated as equipment in use for trade.

[1]   WMA 1985, s 94(2).

Presumption of use for trade

18.17 The WMA 1985, s 7(5) deems weighing or measuring equipment found on a person carrying on trade or on any premises which are used for trade, to be in 'use for trade' unless the contrary is proved and the same subsection applies as against the occupier of premises on which such equipment is found[1]. This 'reverse onus' provision will have to be tested against the 'fair trial' provisions of Art 6(2) of the ECHR[2]. In the opinion of the authors it is likely to survive[3].

[1]   'Occupier' and 'Premises' are defined in WMA 1985, s 94(1).
[2]   See *R v Lambert & Ors* [2002] QB 1112, [2001] 2 WLR 211.

³   In relation to a reverse onus provision relating to trademarks, see *R v S* [2002] EWCA Crim 2558.

Transaction by reference to quantity

18.18 Goods sold by price alone are outside 'use for trade', because a transaction must bear a reference to quantity to be within WMA 1985, s 7. In *Craig v M'Phee*¹ whisky was for sale in three different containers. There was no reference to the quantity which each contained, only to the price. Customers were invited to buy 'a shilling's worth of whisky'. The court found that a transaction concluded under such arrangements was not a transaction 'by reference to quantity', but rather a 'contract by price' and fell outside the legislation. That case is to be contrasted with *Robinson v Golding*², where milk was sold by filling a can which, although unmarked, did in fact have a capacity of a pint. When questioned by investigating officers the defendant said that he had delivered a pint of milk when he left the can on a doorstep. The court rejected the argument that this was a 'contract by price', finding that the evidence showed that the can was being used as a measure. In essence the distinction between the two cases is that in *Robinson* there was an implied reference to quantity, whereas in *M'Phee* there was not³.

¹   (1883) 48 JP 115.
²   (1910) 74 JP 335, (1910) 103 LT 248, which was given positive judicial treatment in *Eric Gnapp Ltd v Petroleum Board* [1949] 1 All ER 980.
³   See also *Bellamy v Great Western & Metropolitan Dairies* (1908) 98 LT 757.

Being 'in possession'

18.19 Offences under the WMA 1985, ss 8(4), 11(3), 17(1) and 30(1)) may also be committed by a person being 'in possession' of certain items or equipment. In *Bellerby v Carle*¹ the House of Lords ruled on the meaning of the words 'in possession', in the context of a prosecution under the equivalent provisions to the WMA 1985, s 17(1). It was held that two licensees of a Public House were not in possession of unjust beer measuring equipment that was owned, supplied and maintained by the brewery under the terms of a contract between the brewery and the licensees' company. In order for the prosecution to make good an offence of 'being in possession' the law requires proof of an element of control over the item in question, although not necessarily of physical proximity². The same case also established that use for trade and possession for use for trade in the circumstances defined in the relevant sections are two distinct offences and should not be charged as alternative wording within the one alleged offence.

¹   [1983] 2 AC 101, [1983] 1 All ER 1031, HL.
²   See *Warner v Metropolitan Police Commissioner* [1969] 2 AC 256, [1968] 2 WLR 1303.

PART II WMA 1985 – PRINCIPAL OFFENCES

Unlawful units and measures

18.20 The Weights and Measures Act 1985, s 8, provides:

8 Units of measurement, weights and measures lawful for use for trade

(1) No person shall—

- (a) use for trade any unit of measurement which is not included in Parts I to V of Schedule 1 to this Act, or
- (b) use for trade, or have in his possession for use for trade, any linear, square, cubic or capacity measure which is not included in Schedule 3 to this Act, or any weight which is not so included.

(2) No person shall use for trade—

- (a) the ounce troy, except for the purposes of transactions in, or in articles made from, gold, silver or other precious metals, including transactions in gold or silver thread, lace or fringe, or
- (b) the carat (metric), except for the purposes of transactions in precious stones or pearls, or
- (c) a capacity measure of 35, 70, 125, 150 or 175 millilitres, except for the purposes of transactions in intoxicating liquor, or
- (d) the pint except for—
  - (i) the purposes of the sale of draught beer or cider, or
  - (ii) the purposes of the sale of milk in returnable containers.

(3) Subsection (1)(a) above shall not apply to the prescribing of, or the dispensing of a prescription for, drugs.

(4) A person who contravenes subsection (1) or (2) above shall be guilty of an offence, and any measure or weight used, or in any person's possession for use, in contravention of that subsection shall be liable to be forfeited.

(5) The preceding provisions have effect subject to—

- (a) subsection (5A) below, and
- (b) sections 9 and 89 below.

(5A) Nothing in this section precludes the use for trade of any supplementary indication; and for this purpose any indication of quantity ("the imperial indication") is a supplementary indication if—

- (a) it is expressed in a unit of measurement other than a metric unit,
- (b) it accompanies an indication of quantity expressed in a metric unit ("the metric indication") and is not itself authorised for use in the circumstances as a primary indication of quantity, and
- (c) the metric indication is the more prominent, the imperial indication being, in particular, expressed in characters no larger than those of the metric indication.

(6) The Secretary of State may by order—

- (a) amend Schedule 3 to this Act by adding to or removing from it any linear, square, cubic or capacity measure, or any weight;
- (b) add to, vary or remove from subsection (2) above any restriction on the cases or circumstances in which, or the conditions subject to which, a unit of measurement, measure or weight may be used for trade or possessed for use for trade.

(7) An order under subsection (6) above may contain such transitional or her supplemental or incidental provisions as appear to the Secretary of State expedient.

(8) In this section "unit of measurement" means a unit of measurement of length, area, volume, capacity, mass or weight.

18.21 The WMA 1985, s 8(4) makes it an offence to use for trade any unit of measurement not included in the WMA 1985, Sch 1. Thus, since 1 January 2000, traders selling loose vegetables by the pound (formerly an exception to the prohibition) are committing an offence. The same section makes it an offence to use for trade a measure or weight not included in the WMA 1985, Sch 3.

18.22 The WMA 1985, s 10(2) makes it an offence to use for trade any capacity measurement specified in Pt IV of WMA 1985, Sch 3 by means of any division or sub-division marked on it as a capacity measure of any lesser quantity. This is subject to any relevant Regulations. Under the Measuring Equipment (Capacity Measures and Testing Equipment) Regulations[1], capacity measures with said sub-divisions will only be stamped, and thus lawful measures, if the sub-divisions are displayed in the same field of view as the mark of the nominal capacity and are marked with their respective capacity[2]. The measure must also be made of transparent material[3].

[1]   SI 1995/735.
[2]   SI 1995/735, reg 16(5).
[3]   SI 1995/735, reg 16(6). See also **18.4** and SI 2018/1387.

Supplementary indications

18.23 The Units of Measurement Regulations 1986[1] were amended to provide: 'Supplementary indications are authorised to be used in the specified circumstances up to and including 31 December 2009'. Thus, while the use of imperial measures as primary indicators for the sale of loose goods in bulk had ceased to be lawful on 1 January 2000, their use as supplementary indicators was to be permitted until 31 December 2009.

[1]   SI 1986/1082.

18.24 However, the Weights and Measures (Metrication Amendments) Regulations 2009[1] and Units of Measurement Regulations 2009[2] – which came into force on 1 January 2010 – implemented the major changes made by Directive 2009/3/EC[3] to Directive 80/181/EC, to remove:

- the deadline of 31 December 2009 for the end of supplementary indications (where imperial units are used alongside metric ones); and
- any requirement for the UK to end the use of certain imperial units (the mile, yard and foot for road traffic, the pint for draught beer and cider and bottled milk, the troy ounce for precious metals) that are in use as primary indications. (Although the UK had not in fact set any deadlines to end the use of these units).

In summary, imperial units are no longer contained within Pts I to V of the WMA 1985, Sch 1, and thus, their use for trade is prima facie an offence. However, WMA 1985, s 8(5A) permits imperial units to be used as supplementary indicators if the conditions in WMA 1985, s 8(5A) are satisfied ie the metric unit is more prominent that the imperial unit and, in particular, the imperial unit is expressed in characters that are no larger than those used for the metric unit.

[1]   SI 2009/3045.
[2]   SI 2009/3046.
[3]   OJ L114, 7.5.2009, p 10.

Use of unstamped equipment

18.25 Weights and Measures Act 1985, s 11:

11 Certain equipment to be passed and stamped by inspector

(1) The provisions of this section shall apply to the use for trade of weighing or measuring equipment of such classes or descriptions as may be prescribed.

(2) No person shall use any article for trade as equipment to which this section applies, or have any article in his possession for such use, unless that article, or equipment to which this section applies in which that article is incorporated or to the operation of which the use of that article is incidental—

    (a)   has been passed by an inspector or approved verifier as fit for such use, and

    (b)   except as otherwise expressly provided by or under this Act, bears a stamp indicating that it has been so passed which remains undefaced otherwise than by reason of fair wear and tear.

(3) If any person contravenes subsection (2) above, he shall be guilty of an offence and any article in respect of which the offence was committed shall be liable to be forfeited.

(4) Any person requiring any equipment to which this section applies to be passed by an inspector as fit for use for trade shall submit the equipment, in such manner as the local weights and measures authority may direct, to the inspector who (subject to the provisions of this Act and to any regulations under section 15 below) shall—

    (a)   test the equipment by means of such local or working standards and testing equipment as he considers appropriate or, subject to any conditions which may be prescribed, by means of other equipment which has already been tested and which the inspector considers suitable for the purpose,

    (b)   if the equipment submitted falls within the prescribed limits of error and by virtue of subsection (10) below is not required to be stamped as mentioned in paragraph (c) of this subsection, give to the person submitting it a statement in writing to the effect that it is passed as fit for use for trade, and

    (c)   except as otherwise expressly provided by or under this Act, cause it to be stamped with the prescribed stamp.

(4A) An approved verifier may (subject to the provisions of this Act, to any regulations under section 15 below and to any conditions included in his approval)—

    (a)   test any equipment to which this section applies by means of other equipment which has already been tested and which the verifier considers suitable for the purpose,

    (b)   if the equipment being tested falls within the prescribed limits of error and by virtue of subsection (10) below is not required to be stamped as mentioned in paragraph (c) below, make a statement in writing to the effect that it is passed fit for use for trade, and

    (c)   except as otherwise expressly provided for by or under this Act, stamp it with the prescribed stamp.

(5) There shall be charged in respect of any test carried out under subsection (4) above such reasonable fees as the local weights and measures authority may determine.

(6) An inspector shall keep a record of every test carried out by him under subsection (4) above.

(6A) In this Act "approved verifier", in relation to weighing or measuring equipment of any class or description, means a person who is for the time being approved under section 11A below in relation to the testing, passing and stamping of weighing or measuring equipment of that class or description.

(7) Except as otherwise expressly provided by or under this Act, no weight or measure shall be stamped as mentioned in subsection (4)(c) or (4A)(c) above unless it has been marked in the prescribed manner with its purported value.

(8) Subject to subsection (9) below, where any equipment submitted to an inspector under subsection (4) above is of a pattern in respect of which a certificate of approval granted under section 12 below is for the time being in force, the inspector shall not refuse to pass or stamp the equipment on the ground that it is not suitable for use for trade.

(9) If the inspector is of opinion that the equipment is intended for use for trade for a particular purpose for which it is not suitable, he may refuse to pass or stamp it until the matter has been referred to the Secretary of State, whose decision shall be final.

(10) The requirements of subsections (2), (4), (4A) and (7) above with respect to stamping and marking shall not apply to any weight or measure which is too small to be stamped or marked in accordance with those requirements.

(11) Where a person submits equipment to an inspector under this section, the inspector may require the person to provide the inspector with such assistance in connection with the testing of the equipment as the inspector reasonably considers it necessary for the person to provide and shall not be obliged to proceed with the test until the person provides it; but a failure to provide the assistance shall not constitute an offence under section 81 below.

(12) If an inspector refuses to pass as fit for use for trade any equipment submitted to him under this section and is requested by the person by whom the equipment was submitted to give reasons for the refusal, the inspector shall give to that person a statement of those reasons in writing.

(13) In the case of any equipment which is required by regulations made under section 15 below to be passed and stamped under this section only after it has been installed at the place where it is to be used for trade, if after the equipment has been so passed and stamped it is dismantled and reinstalled, whether in the same or some other place, it shall not be used for trade after being so reinstalled until it has again been passed under this section.

(14) If any person—

- (a)   knowingly uses any equipment in contravention of subsection (13) above, or
- (b)   knowingly causes or permits any other person so to use it, or
- (c)   knowing that the equipment is required by virtue of subsection (13) above to be again passed under this section, disposes of it to some other person without informing him of that requirement,

he shall be guilty of an offence and the equipment shall be liable to be forfeited.

(15) Subject to subsection (13) above, a stamp applied to any equipment under this section shall have the like validity throughout Great Britain as it has in the place in which it was originally applied, and accordingly that equipment shall not be required to be re-stamped because it is used in any other place.

(16) If at any time the Secretary of State is satisfied that, having regard to the law for the time being in force in Northern Ireland, any of the Channel Islands or the Isle of Man, it is proper so to do, he may by order provide for any equipment to which this section applies duly stamped in accordance with that law, or treated for the purposes of that law as if duly stamped in accordance with it, to be treated for the purposes of this Act as if it had been duly stamped in Great Britain under this section.

18.26 The WMA 1985, s 11(2) and (3) make it an offence to use for trade any weighing or measuring equipment 'as may be prescribed' unless it has been passed by an inspector[1] or an approved verifier[2] as fit for such use and duly stamped with a stamp which remains undefaced save by reason of fair wear and tear. The same section makes it an offence to have possession for use for trade of such equipment. Where the equipment is marked with the sign of EC pattern approval in relation to a pattern approval certificate issued before 30 November 2015 in relation to standard mass per storage of grain, cold water meters, tire pressure gauges or material measures of length, then it cannot be found to be false or unjust for the purposes of WMA 1985, s 17(1) until 1 October 2025[3]. Further, any equipment or marked with EC initial verification in relation to bar weights, cylindrical weights above medium accuracy weights, and the inaccuracy found is within the prescribed limits of error cannot be found to be unjust until the same date[4]. This is an offence of strict liability, no *mens rea* is required and mistake is no defence. Note that WMA 1985, s 11A(2)(a) permits approved verifiers to be appointed to verify or re-verify equipment which they have manufactured, installed or repaired and the Legislative Reform (Verification of Weighing and Measuring Equipment) Order 2008[5] amended WMA 1985, s 11A so as to permit approved verifiers to be approved for the additional purpose of re-verifying equipment which they have adjusted.

1   As appointed under WMA 1985, s 72(1).
2   Under the Deregulation (Weights and Measures) Order 1999, SI 1999/503.
3   Measuring Instruments (EEC Requirements) Regulations 1988, SI 1988/186 and Weights and Measures (Revocations) Regulations 2015, SI 2015/356, Sch 1, Pt 2, para 5(4). See also **18.4** and SI 2019/696, Sch 5.
4   Weights and Measures (Revocations) Regulations 2015, SI 2015/356, Sch 1, Pt 2, para 5(3).
5   SI 2008/3262.

18.27 In *Thoburn v Sunderland City Council; Hunt v LB Hackney; Harman/Dove v Cornwall County Council; Collins v LB Sutton*[1] – the 'metric martyrs' case – Thoburn was prosecuted for offences under WMA 1985, s 11(2) and (3). The essence of the cases was that certain Weights and Measures legislation and the Price Marking Order 1999 were unlawful and invalid. It was held that the legislation was lawful and the appeals by all defendants were dismissed. When the matters reached the admissibility stage before the European Court of Human Rights – appeals to the House of Lords having been refused – the Court found that the applicants' complaints ' . . . did not disclose any appearance of a violation of the rights and freedoms set out in the convention or its protocols'. The domestic appeal is, however, an important case on the effect of the EU Treaties and EU legislation on the sovereignty of the British Parliament – Laws LJ said:

> 'There is nothing in the [European Communities Act 1972] which allows the [European Court of Justice], or any other institutions of the EU, to touch or qualify the conditions of Parliament's legislative supremacy in the United Kingdom.'

1   [2002] EWHC 195 (Admin), [2003] QB 151.

Prescribed equipment

18.28 The WMA 1985, s 11, and the offences under it, apply only to such weighing or measuring equipment 'as may be prescribed'. Note that many types of weighing and measuring equipment are now tested, approved and placed on market through Old or New Approach Directives which are independent of

WMA 1985, s 11. However, with the New Approach Directives (such as Directive 2009/23/EC on non-automatic weighing instruments (the 'NAWI Directive')[1] or Directive 2004/22/EC (the Measuring Instruments Directive) ('MID')[2]), whilst the initial verification must be performed by a Notified Body any subsequent reverification is carried out under WMA 1985, s 11.

[1]   OJ L122, 16.05.2009, p 6.
[2]   OJ L135, 30.04.2004, p 1.

18.29 There are numerous regulations that are prescribed for the purposes of WMA 1985, s 11(1) under which the use for trade, or the possession for use for trade, of articles or measuring equipment without verification and a stamp of approval would be an offence under WMA 1985, s 11(2). They include the following topics: Cold-Water Meters[1]; Capacity Measures and Testing Equipment[2]; Liquid Fuel and Lubricants[3]; Measures of Length[4]; Beltweighers[5]; Non-automatic weighing machines[6]; and Weights[7]. See also **18.4** and SI 2018/1387.

[1]   Measuring Equipment (Cold-water Meters) Regulations 1988, SI 1988/997.
[2]   Measuring Equipment (Capacity Measures and Testing Equipment) Regulations 1995, SI 1995/735.
[3]   Measuring Equipment (Liquid Fuel and Lubricants) Regulations 1995, SI 1995/1014.
[4]   Measuring Equipment (Measures of Length) Regulations 1986, SI 1986/1682.
[5]   Weighing Equipment (Beltweighers) Regulations 2001, SI 2001/1208.
[6]   Weighing Equipment (Non-automatic Weighing Machines) Regulations 2000, SI 2000/932.
[7]   Weights Regulations 1986, SI 1986/1683.

Using false or unjust equipment

18.30 The WMA 1985, s 17 provides:

17 Offences relating to false or unjust equipment or fraud

(1)   If any person uses for trade, or has in his possession for use for trade, any weighing or measuring equipment which is false or unjust, he shall be guilty of an offence and the equipment shall be liable to be forfeited.

(2)   Without prejudice to the liability of any equipment to be forfeited, it shall be a defence for any person charged with an offence under subsection (1) above in respect of the use for trade of any equipment to show—
  (a)   that he used the equipment only in the course of his employment by some other person, and
  (b)   that he neither knew, nor might reasonably have been expected to know, nor had any reason to suspect, the equipment to be false or unjust.

(3)   If any fraud is committed in the using of any weighing or measuring equipment for trade, the person committing the fraud and any other person party to it shall be guilty of an offence and the equipment shall be liable to be forfeited.

18.31

Precedent for using false or unjust weighing or measuring equipment

Information

AB on [date], used for trade measuring equipment, namely [. . .], which was false or unjust, in that [. . .], contrary to s 17(1) Weights and Measures Act 1985.

18.32 The WMA 1985, s 17(1) makes it an offence to use for trade any weighing or measuring equipment which is false or unjust. This is an offence of strict liability, no *mens rea* is required and mistake is no defence, nor does the fact that the offence was an isolated and untypical occurrence assist the defendant[1]. The allegation should specify whether the equipment is alleged to be 'false' or 'unjust'[2]. Falsity and unjustness are questions of fact for the court[3], but WMA 1985, s 85(1) permits any party to proceedings for an offence under the WMA 1985, or the court itself, to refer the question to the Secretary of State, whose decision will be final. Where the equipment is marked with the sign of EC pattern approval in relation to a pattern approval certificate issued before 30 November 2015 in relation to standard mass per storage of grain, cold water meters, tire pressure gauges or material measures of length, then it cannot be found to be false or unjust for the purposes of WMA 1985, s 17(1) until 1 October 2025[4]. Further, any equipment or marked with EC initial verification in relation to bar weights, cylindrical weights above medium accuracy weights, and the inaccuracy found is within the prescribed limits of error cannot be found to be unjust until the same date[5].

1   *Percival v Hurst* (1931) 39 Monthly Review 176.
2   *Moore v Ray* [1951] 1 KB 98, [1950] 2 All ER 561, DC, *Bastin v Davies* [1950] 2 KB 579, [1950] 1 All ER 1095.
3   *R v Baxendale* (1880) 44 JP 763.
4   Measuring Instruments (EEC Requirements) Regulations 1988, SI 1988/186 and Weights and Measures (Revocations) Regulations 2015, SI 2015/356, Sch 1, Pt 2, para 5(4). See also **18.4** and Regulation 2019/696.
5   Weights and Measures (Revocations) Regulations 2015, SI 2015/356, Sch 1, Pt 2, para 5(3).

18.33 The question of whether the falsity or unjustness gives rise to a deficiency or excess is irrelevant[1], as is the fact that the customer may have requested or acquiesced in the use of the unjust equipment[2]. A weighing machine which, by its construction, is liable to variation and needs adjustment, by means of an appliance provided for that purpose, before use is not 'false' or unjust[3], but the adjustment appliance must be an integral part of the machine rather than an easily detachable device. Where that is the case the machine would be unlawful, even if it were registering correctly at the time of inspection[4]. Thus, even where a machine is inaccurate by an ascertainable amount, and allowance is customarily made for this so that no one has been defrauded, the offence is still committed[5]. Likewise, where an otherwise accurate balance was hung with a four pound weight, so as to deduct that amount from the weight of live pigs sold at market, that being the local custom and no one having been defrauded, an offence was committed[6]. Where a machine used for weighing tea had a piece of paper placed on it to facilitate weighing, thus making it inaccurate by the weight of the paper, the machine was found to be false and[7] unjust; likewise where the pans of a set of scales could be reversed and the weight was inaccurate when this was done[8], or where the balance was incorrect when the article to be weighed was not placed in the centre of the pan[9].

[1]   *Quality Dairies (York) Ltd v Pedley* [1952] 1 KB 275, [1952] 1 All ER 380, DC.
[2]   *LCC v Payne (No 2)* [1905] 1 KB 410, DC.
[3]   *London and North Western Railway Co v Richards* 121 ER 1094, (1862) 2 B&S 326.
[4]   *Carr v Stringer* (1868) LR 3 QB 433.
[5]   *Great Western Railway Co v Bailie* 112 ER 1076, (1864) 5 B & S 928, 34 LJMC 31.
[6]   *Collins v Denny & Sons* (1897) 31 ILT 167.
[7]   *Lane v Rendall* [1899] 2 QB 673.
[8]   *Henton v Radford* (1881) 45 JP 224.
[9]   *R v Baxendale* (1880) 44 JP 763.

18.34 A modern case where no offence was found is *Makinson v Dewhurst*[1] where a butchers shop had in its possession a self-indicating and price-computing weighing machine which, by its construction had a tendency after a time to give short weight. A mechanism was provided for appropriate adjustment. Test purchases were made and the employee concerned failed to zero the machine when this was done. The Divisional Court held that no offence under WMA 1985, s 17(1) was committed since the mechanism provided made the machine a just one. It seems clear that an allegation of an offence of short weight, under WMA 1985, s 28, in similar factual circumstances would have succeeded.

[1]   Unreported, transcript in (1981) 89 Monthly Review 87.

Defence

18.35 It is a defence under WMA 1985, s 17 for the defendant to prove, on the balance of probabilities, that he used the equipment only in the course of his employment by some other person and that he neither knew, nor might reasonably have been expected to know or have any reason to suspect[1] that the equipment was false or unjust[2].

[1]   This is a matter of fact for the court, *McArdle v Egan* (1933) 150 LT 412.
[2]   WMA 1985, s 17(2).

Fraudulent use of equipment

18.36 The WMA 1985, s 17(3) makes it an offence to commit, or be party to, fraud in the use of weighing or measuring equipment for trade, while WMA 1985, s 20(3)(b) creates a similar offence in respect of the use of public weighing or measuring equipment. These offences differ from those examined thus far in that they require a *mens rea* on the part of the person committing them, namely an intention to commit the fraud. To defraud is to induce another to take a course of action by deceit[1]. Typically, therefore, a fraud covered by this subsection would be one whereby the customer was induced to buy a quantity of goods less than he believed he was receiving by means of some manipulation of the weighing or measuring equipment. In contrast to the offences under WMA 1985, s 17(1), evidence of the consent or acquiescence of the customer to the placing of paper on the pan of a set of scales[2], or of a particular trade custom in relation to the WMA 1985 on which it is alleged constitutes a fraud[3] may be of great importance in establishing whether or not an offence has been committed, since such matters are likely to go to the heart of whether or not the defendant has been acting deceitfully or dishonestly.

1   *Re London and Globe Finance Corporation Ltd* [1903] 1 Ch 728.
2   *Harris v Allwood* (1892) 57 JP 7.
3   *King v Spencer* (1904) 91 LT 470, 68 JP 530.

PART IV WMA 1985 – PRINCIPAL OFFENCES

Short weight

Weights and Measures Act 1985, s 28

18.37 The WMA 1985, s 28 states:

28 Short weight, etc

(1)   Subject to sections 33 to 37 below, any person who, in selling or purporting to sell any goods by weight or other measurement or by number, delivers or causes to be delivered to the buyer—
    (a)   a lesser quantity than that purported to be sold, or
    (b)   a lesser quantity than corresponds with the price charged, shall be guilty of an offence.

(2)   For the purposes of this section—
    (a)   the quantity of the goods in a regulated package (as defined by section 68(1) below) shall be deemed to be the nominal quantity (as so defined) on the package, and
    (b)   any statement, whether oral or in writing, as to the weight of any goods shall be taken, unless otherwise expressed, to be a statement as to the net weight of the goods.

(3)   Nothing in this section shall apply in relation to any such goods or sales as are mentioned in section 24(2)(a) or (b) above.

18.38

Precedent for selling goods by weight or measurement of a lesser quantity than purported

Information

A B on [date] in selling goods by measurement, namely [beer . . .], delivered to C D, the buyer, a lesser quantity, namely [a half pint], than that purported to be sold, namely [a pint], contrary to s 28(1) Weights and Measures Act 1985.

18.39 The WMA 1985, s 28 makes it an offence, where goods are sold by weight, or other measurement, or number, to deliver, or cause to be delivered to the buyer, a lesser quantity than that purported to be sold[1] or than corresponds to the price[2]. For the purposes of the section, any statement as to the weight of the goods is to be taken to refer to their net weight[3], that is their weight without wrapping, containers or any other article[4]. This is an offence of strict liability, no *mens rea* is required and mistake is no defence. Again, the question of the purchaser's state of mind is irrelevant[5]. Where an offence of short measure is committed by an employee in the absence of the employer, and without his knowledge, the employer may nevertheless be guilty of causing short measure to be delivered[6]. Thus, where a delivery driver had caused short weight deliveries by stealing some coal after leaving his employer's premises it was no defence for the employer that they did not know of the short weight[7].

[1]   WMA 1985, s 28(1)(a).
[2]   WMA 1985, s 28(1)(b).
[3]   WMA 1985, s 28(2).
[4]   *Tansley v J Sainsbury & Co Ltd* (1941) 105 JP 337, DC.
[5]   *Sopp v Co-op Retail Services* (1969) 68 LGR 106, DC.
[6]   *Sopp v Long* [1970] 1 QB 518, [1969] 1 All ER 855.
[7]   *Winter v Hinckley and District Co-op Society Ltd* [1959] 1 All ER 403, [1959] 1 WLR 182.

18.40 In the case of the sale of draught beer, the court has previously held that a reasonable head of froth is an integral part of the measure purported to be sold[1], if this is in accordance with local customer preference[2]. The position today, almost two decades on, is less clear. Given the eclectic range of beers and customer preferences, it is most likely that a pint of beer means a pint of liquid beer, and a WMA 1985, s 28 offence will likely be committed if less than a pint is delivered to the customer. This is subject to the dispensation permitted in *Bennett v Markham*. However, for the dispensation to apply, the following factors, if applicable, will need to be clearly supported by evidence: (i) the beer is advertised to be served with a head of froth[3] (ii) local customers demand and expect a head of froth and thereby know that they will not receive a pint of liquid beer[4] (iii) the amount of head is not excessive or unreasonable[5] (iv) most if not all customers are aware that they can request a top-up that will not be refused[6].

[1]   *Bennett v Markham* [1982] 3 All ER 641, [1982] 1 WLR 1230.
[2]   *Allied Domecq Leisure Ltd v Cooper* (1999) 163 JP 1, [1999] Crim LR 230.
[3]   *Marshall v Searles* [1964] Crim LR 667, where it was found that a person who ordered a pint of Guinness expected to be supplied with a pint consisting partly of liquid and partly of gas. A contemporary example may be a pint of Stella Artois served in a certified Stella Artois chalice pint glass. The advertising typically includes the iconic pint brim glass with a head of froth which sits neatly at the brim of the glass thanks to a bartender employing a cut-throat razor.
[4]   [1982] 1 WLR 1230 at 1235 [E].
[5]   [1982] 1 WLR 1230 at 1237 [E].
[6]   [1982] 1 WLR 1230 at 1233 [H].

18.41 The 1995 Guidance Notes from the BBPA[1], which may be relevant in a contemporary assessment, note that 1. A measure of a beer served with a head must include a minimum of 95% liquid, 2. The beer should not be made available to the customer until bar staff are satisfied with the measure 3. Requests from customers for top-ups should be received with good grace and never refused, subject to avoiding spillage of liquid. Although clear signage that a customer can always request a top-up which should not be refused will assist the dispensation argument, Sedley J confirmed that if a pint is not supplied, there is no onus on the customer to demand full measure before an offence is committed[2].

[1]   British Beer and Pub Association, Guidance Notes on the dispense of draught beer by free flow and hand pull (Revised November 1995).
[2]   *Allied Domecq Leisure Ltd v Cooper* (1999) 163 JP 1, [1999] Crim LR 230.

Weights and Measures Act 1985, s 30, Quantity less than stated

18.42 The WMA 1985, s 30 provides:

30 Quantity less than stated

(1)   If, in the case of any goods that are pre-packed within the meaning of this Act or are prepacked food within the meaning of the FIC Regulation and (in either case) are in or on a container marked with a statement in writing with respect to the quantity of the goods, the quantity of the goods is at any time found to be less than that stated, then, subject to sections 33 to 37 below—

   (a)   any person who has those goods in his possession for sale shall be guilty of an offence, and

   (b)   if it is shown that the deficiency cannot be accounted for by anything occurring after the goods had been sold by retail and delivered to, or to a person nominated in that behalf by, the buyer, any person by whom or on whose behalf those goods have been sold or agreed to be sold at any time while they were pre-packed within the meaning of this Act or were prepacked food within the meaning of the FIC Regulation and (in either case) were in or on the container in question, shall be guilty of an offence.

(2)   If—

   (a)   in the case of a sale of or agreement to sell any goods which, not being pre-packed within the meaning of this Act or prepacked food within the meaning of the FIC Regulation, are made up for sale or for delivery after sale in or on a container marked with a statement in writing with respect to the quantity of the goods, or

   (b)   in the case of any goods which, in connection with their sale or an agreement for their sale, have associated with them a document containing such a statement,

the quantity of the goods is at any time found to be less than that stated, then, if it is shown that the deficiency cannot be accounted for by anything occurring after the goods had been delivered to, or to a person nominated in that behalf by, the buyer, and subject to sections 33 to 37 below and paragraph 10 of Schedule 4 to this Act, the person by whom, and any other person on whose behalf: the goods were sold or agreed to be sold shall be guilty of an offence.

(3)   Subsections (1) and (2) above shall have effect notwithstanding that the quantity stated is expressed to be the quantity of the goods at a specified time falling before the time in question, or is expressed with some other qualification of whatever description, except where—

   (a)   that quantity is so expressed in pursuance of an express requirement of this Part of this Act or any instrument made under this Part, or

   (b)   the goods, although falling within subsection (1) or subsection (2)(a) above—

      (i)   are not required by or under this Part of this Act to be pre-packed as mentioned in subsection (1) or required by the FIC Regulation to be prepacked food as mentioned in that subsection or, as the case may be, to be made up for sale or for delivery after sale in or on a container only if the container is marked as mentioned in subsection (2)(a), and

      (ii)   are not goods on a sale of which (whether any sale or a sale of any particular description) the quantity sold is required by or under any provision of this Part, of this Act other than section 26 or required by the FIC Regulation, to be made known to the buyer at or before a particular time, or

(c)   the goods, although falling within subsection (2)(b) above, are not required by or under this Part of this Act to have associated with them such a document as is mentioned in that provision.

(4)   In any case to which, by virtue of paragraph (a), (b) or (c) of sub- section (3) above, the provisions of subsection (1) or (2) above do not apply, if it is found at any time that the quantity of the goods in question is less than that stated and it is shown that the deficiency is greater than can be reasonably justified on the ground justifying the qualification in question, then, subject to sections 33 to 37 below—

    (a)   in the case of goods such as are mentioned in subsection (1) above, if it is further shown as mentioned in that subsection, then—

        (i)   where the container in question was marked in Great Britain, the person by whom, and any other person on whose behalf: the container was marked, or

        (ii)   where the container in question was marked outside Great Britain, the person by whom, and any other person on whose behalf: the goods were first sold in Great Britain,

    shall be guilty of an offence;

    (b)   in the case of goods such as are mentioned in subsection (2) above, the person by whom, and any other person on whose behalf: the goods were sold or agreed to be sold shall be guilty of an offence if: but only if: he would, but for paragraph (a), (b) or (c) of subsection (3) above have been guilty of an offence under subsection (2).

(5)   Subsection (2) of section 28 above shall have effect for the purposes of this section as it has effect for the purposes of that section.

(6)   Nothing in this section shall apply in relation to any such goods or sales as are mentioned in section 24(2)(a) or (b) above.

Quantity less than stated (pre-packed goods)

18.43 The WMA 1985, s 30 creates offences in relation to goods which have been packaged in two different circumstances. The WMA 1985, s 30(1) deals with goods pre-packed[1] in or on a container[2] where the quantity of goods is found to be less than that which is indicated by a statement marked on the container. For the purposes of the section, any statement as to the weight of the goods is to be taken to refer to their net weight[3], that is their weight without wrapping, containers or any other article[4]. Where goods have been sold or agreed to be sold in a container so marked, or a person has such goods in his possession for sale[5], and there is a deficiency which can be shown to be not attributable to the buyer, the person who sold or agreed to sell the goods, or any person on whose behalf the goods were sold or agreed to be sold, is guilty of an offence[6].

[1]   Defined in s 94(1) as 'Made up in advance ready for retail sale in or on a container'.
[2]   Defined in s 94(1) as including 'Any form of packaging of goods for sale as a single item . . . .'.
[3]   Section 30(5).
[4]   *Tansley v J Sainsbury & Co Ltd* (1941) 105 JP 337, DC.
[5]   See *Bellerby v Carle* [1983] 2 AC 101, [1983] 1 All ER 1031, HL and the comments in the text above.
[6]   WMA 1985, s 30(1)(b).

18.44 This is an offence of strict liability, no *mens rea* is required and mistake is no defence. It is generally no defence that the statement of quantity marked on the container relates to a particular time or that it is qualified in some other way[1] save where:

(a)   the quantity is expressed as it is to comply with an express requirement of WMA 1985, s 21, or of statutory instruments made under WMA 1985, s 22[2]; or

(b)   the goods are not required by the WMA 1985 or the Food Information to Consumers Regulation to be pre-packed and are not goods on a sale of which the quantity sold is required by the WMA 1985 (other than by virtue of WMA 1985, s 26) or the Food Information to Consumers Regulation to be made known to the buyer[3].

Where (a) or (b) above apply to render the seller's actions lawful, but the deficiency is greater than can reasonably be justified by reason of the qualification to the statement of quantity marked on the packet, then offences may lie against the person who marked the container with the false statement or the first wholesaler to sell the goods in the UK[4].

[1]   WMA 1985, s 30(3).
[2]   WMA 1985, s 30(3)(a).
[3]   WMA 1985, s 30(3)(b).
[4]   WMA 1985, s 30(4)(a).

Quantity less than stated (goods made up for sale or delivery)

18.45 The WMA 1985, s 30(2) deals with non-prepacked goods which are made up, after sale or agreement to sell, in a container marked with a statement with respect to the quantity of the goods. It also deals with statements made in documents associated with the sale of goods. Where there is a deficiency in the quantity of the goods which can be shown to be not attributable to the buyer, the person who sold or agreed to sell the goods, or any person on whose behalf the goods were sold or agreed to be sold, is guilty of an offence[1].

[1]   WMA 1985, s 30(2).

18.46 This is an offence of strict liability, no *mens rea* is required and mistake is no defence. There is an exceptional defence to this offence in respect of ballast carried by road[1]. It is generally no defence that the statement of quantity marked on the container, or set out in the associated document, is said to relate to a particular time or that it is qualified in some other way[2] save where:

(a)   the quantity is expressed as it is to comply with an express requirement of WMA 1985, s 21, or of statutory instruments made under Pt IV of the WMA 1985; or

(b)   any container in which the goods are made up, after sale or agreement to sell, is not required by the WMA 1985 or the Food Information to Consumers Regulation to be marked with a statement of quantity and the goods are not goods on a sale of which the quantity sold is required by the WMA 1985 to be made known to the buyer (other than by virtue of WMA 1985, s 26);[3] or

(c)   in the case of a statement in an associated document, the goods are not required by the WMA 1985 to have such a document[4].

Where (a) or (b) above apply to render the seller's actions prima facie lawful, but the deficiency is greater than can reasonably be justified by reason of the qualification to the statement of quantity marked on the packet, then offences may still lie against the seller.

1   WMA 1985, Sch 4, para 10.
2   WMA 1985, s 30(3).
3   WMA 1985, s 30(3)(b).
4   WMA 1985, s 30(3)(c).

Incorrect statements

18.47 The WMA 1985, s 31 provides:

31 Incorrect statements

(1)   Without prejudice to section 30(2) to (4) above, if in the case of any goods required by or under this Part of this Act to have associated with them a document containing particular statements, that document is found to contain any such statement which is materially incorrect, any person who, knowing or having reasonable cause to suspect that statement to be materially incorrect, inserted it or caused it to be inserted in the document, or used the document for the purposes of this Part of this Act while that statement was contained in the document, shall be guilty of an offence.

(2)   Subsection (2) of section 28 above shall have effect for the purposes of this section as it has effect for the purposes of that section.

(3)   Nothing in this section shall apply in relation to any such goods or sales as are mentioned in section 24 (2) (a) or (b) above.

18.48 Certain goods are required[1], when delivered in connection with a sale, to have associated with them a document containing particular statements. Sand and other ballast and solid fuel are notable examples. Where such a statement is found to be materially incorrect any person who, knowing or having reasonable cause to suspect (which means they had reasonable cause to believe, and did in fact believe ie that the person charged believed on reasonable grounds[2]) it to be so, inserted it or caused it to be inserted in the document is guilty of an offence under the WMA 1985, s 31(1). It is also an offence under WMA 1985, s 31(1) knowingly to use such a document for the purposes of compliance with the WMA 1985 while that statement was contained in it. These offences require the offender to have the requisite *mens rea* and are not ones of strict liability.

1   By WMA 1985, s 21 and WMA 1985, Schs 4 and 5, or statutory instruments made under WMA 1985, s 22.
2   *R v Banks* [1916] 2 KB 621, [1916–1917] All ER 356, *R v Harrison* [1938] 3 All ER 134, 159 LT 95, *Nakkuda Ali v Jayaratne* [1951] AC 66, PC.

Failure to comply with Food Information for Consumers Regulation

18.49 The WMA 1985, s 31A provides:

31A Non-compliance with certain requirements of the FIC Regulation

(1)   Subject to subsection (2) below, a food business operator to which Article 1(3) of the FIC Regulation applies is guilty of an offence if that food business operator fails to comply with—

(a)   any of the provisions of Article 8 of the FIC Regulation (responsibilities of food business operators) applicable to the food business operator, to the extent that the provisions relate to net quantity;

(b)   Article 9(1)(e) of the FIC Regulation (mandatory indication of net quantity of food), except to the extent that it relates to a failure to comply with Article 13(5) of the FIC Regulation; or

(c)   Chapter V of the FIC Regulation (voluntary food information), to the extent that it imposes requirements in respect of net quantity.

(2)   A food business operator is not guilty of an offence under subsection (1) if the food business operator acts in accordance with any of the following—

(a)   an exception contained in Chapter IV of the FIC Regulation;

(b)   a measure adopted by the United Kingdom before IP completion day under Article 40 of Regulation (EU) No 1169/2011 of the European Parliament and of the Council on the provision of food information to consumers4 as it had effect in EU law (milk and milk products: national measures derogating from Arts 9(1) and 10(1));

(ba)   regulations made under Article 40 of the FIC Regulation (milk and milk products: regulations derogating from Arts 9(1) and 10(1));

(c)   a measure permitted to be maintained by Art 42 of the FIC Regulation authority to maintain measures in specified legislation about the expression of net quantity in relation to food in the absence of regulations under Art 23(2));

(d)   transitional measures under Article 54(1) of the FIC Regulation.

(3)   In this section 'food business operator' and 'net quantity' have the same meanings as in the FIC Regulation.

18.50 By virtue of the Food Information to Consumers Regulation[1] food business operators whose activities concern the supply of food information to consumers are (subject to certain limited exceptions)[2] required to ensure that the net quantity[3] of the food appears on the food's pre-packaging or the label attached thereto[4]. A failure to comply with these requirements under the Food Information to Consumers Regulation is an offence under WMA 1985, s 31A(1).

[1]   Implemented into domestic weights and measures law by the Weights and Measures (Food) (Amendment) Regulations 2014, SI 2014/2975.

[2]   For example, where the net quantity is less than 5g or 5ml or the food in question is usually sold by quantity.

[3]   As set out in Art 23.

[4]   Arts 8 and 9(e).

GENERAL DEFENCES TO PT IV OFFENCES

18.51 As a counterbalance to the strict liability regime, within which the majority of the offences created by the WMA 1985 fall, there is an important safeguard in the form of the statutory defences under WMA 1985, ss 33–37.

Warranty

18.52 The WMA 1985, s 33 provides:

33 Warranty

(1)   Subject to the following provisions of this section, in any proceedings for an offence under this Part of this Act or any instrument made under this Part, being an offence relating to the quantity or pre-packing of any goods, it shall be a defence for the person charged to prove—

(a)   that he bought the goods from some other person—

(i)   as being of the quantity which the person charged purported to sell or represented, or which was marked on any container or stated in any document to which the proceedings relate, or

(ii)   as conforming with the statement marked on any container to which the proceedings relate, or with the requirements with respect to the pre-packing of goods of this Part of this Act or any instrument made under this Part,

as the case may require, and

(b)   that he so bought the goods with a written warranty from that other person that they were of that quantity or, as the case may be, did so conform, and

(c)   that at the time of the commission of the offence he did in fact believe the statement contained in the warranty to be accurate and had no reason to believe it to be inaccurate, and

(d)   if the warranty was given by a person who at the time he gave it was resident outside Great Britain and any designated country, that the person charged had taken reasonable steps, to check the accuracy of the statement contained in the warranty, and

(e)   in the case of proceedings relating to the quantity of any goods, that he took all reasonable steps to ensure that, while in his possession, the quantity of the goods remained unchanged and, in the case of such or any other proceedings, that apart from any change in their quantity the goods were at the time of the commission of the offence in the same state as when he bought them,

(2)   A warranty shall not be a defence in any such proceedings as are mentioned in subsection (1) above unless, not later than three days before the date of the hearing, the person charged has sent to the prosecutor a copy of the warranty with a notice stating that he intends to rely on it and specifying the name and address of the person from whom the warranty was received, and has also sent a like notice to that person.

(3)   Where the person charged is the employee of a person who, if he had been charged, would have been entitled to plead a warranty as a defence under this section, subsection (1) above shall have effect—

(a)   with the substitution, for any reference (however expressed) in paragraphs (a), (b), (d) and (e) to the person charged, of a reference to his employer, and

(b)   with the substitution for paragraph (c) of the following—

"(c)   that at the time of the commission of the offence his employer did in fact believe the statement contained in the warranty to be accurate and the person charged had no reason to believe it to be inaccurate,".

(4)   The person by whom the warranty is alleged to have been given shall be entitled to appear at the hearing and to give evidence.

(5)   If the person charged in any such proceedings as are mentioned in subsection (1) above wilfully attributes to any goods a warranty given in relation to any other goods, he shall be guilty of an offence.

(6)   A person who, in respect of any goods sold by him in respect of which a warranty might be pleaded under this section, gives to the buyer a false warranty in writing shall be guilty of an offence unless he proves that when he gave the warranty he took all reasonable steps to ensure that the statements contained in it were, and would continue at all relevant times to be, accurate.

(7)   Where in any such proceedings as are mentioned in subsection (1) above ("the original proceedings") the person charged relies successfully on a warranty given to him or to his employer, any proceedings under subsection

(6) above in respect of the warranty may, at the option of the prosecutor, be taken either before a court having jurisdiction in the place where the original proceedings were taken or before a court having jurisdiction in the place where the warranty was given.

(8)   For the purposes of this section, any statement with respect to any goods which is contained in any document required by or under this Part of this Act to be associated with the goods or in any invoice, and, in the case of goods made up in or on a container for sale or for delivery after sale, any statement with respect to those goods with which that container is marked, shall be taken to be a written warranty of the accuracy of that statement.

18.53 The WMA 1985, s 33(1) makes it a defence for a person charged with an offence under Pt IV of the WMA 1985, or Regulations made thereunder, relating to the quantity or pre-packing of goods to prove, on the balance of probabilities[1]:

(a)   that the goods were bought from another person as being of the quantity represented by that person, or as marked on their container or stated in a document; and

(b)   that the goods were bought with a written warranty that they were of the relevant quantity; and

(c)   that the warranty was believed to be accurate and that there was no reason to believe the warranty was inaccurate (although it is arguable that it is the subjective question of what was actually believed, rather than the objective question of whether there was 'reason to believe' which should apply here[2]); and

(d)   that, if the warranty was given by a person resident outside the United Kingdom or other associated territory, that all reasonable steps were taken to check its accuracy; and

(e)   in cases relating to the quantity of goods, that all reasonable steps were taken to ensure that the quantity remained unchanged while it was in the possession of the defendant and that, apart from any change in quantity, they were at the time of the commission of the offence in the same state as when they were bought[3].

[1]   *R v Carr-Briant* [1943] KB 607.
[2]   *R v Banks* 1916 2 KB 621, [1916–1917] All ER 356, *R v Harrison* [1938] 3 All ER 134, 159 LT 95, *Nakkuda Ali v Jayaratne* [1951] AC 66, PC, *Jones v Bertram* (1894) 58 JP 478, 10 TLR 285, *Blaydon Co-op Society v Young* (1916) 86 LJKB, 115 LT 827.
[3]   For a case where a retailer failed in reliance upon a warranty because of failure to comply with this requirement see *FW Woolworth and Co Ltd v Gray* [1970] 1 All ER 953.

18.54 Any alteration of the goods, however harmless, will prevent the warranty applying as a defence[1]. The defence can only be relied upon where, not later than 3 days before the date of the hearing, a copy of the warranty has been sent to the prosecutor with a notice stating the intention to rely on it and specifying the name and address of the person from whom the warranty was received. The same notice must be sent to the alleged warrantor[2]. Where an employee is charged, the employee can plead this defence, provided the relevant conditions were fulfilled by or in relation to the employer and he personally had no reason to believe that the warranty was false[3]. The person by whom the warranty is alleged to have been given may give evidence at the proceedings[4]. It is an offence both wilfully to attribute to goods a warranty given in relation to other goods[5] and to give a false warranty[6] in writing unless the warrantor proves that he took all reasonable steps to ensure that the warranty was and would remain accurate[7].

1   *Hotchin v Hindmarsh* [1891] 2 QB 181, 60 LJMC 146, *Hennen v Long* (1904) 90 LT 387, 68 JP 237, *Pugh v Williams* (1917) 86 LJKB 1407, 117 LT 191.
2   WMA 1985, s 33(2).
3   WMA 1985, s 33(3).
4   WMA 1985, s 33(4).
5   WMA 1985, s 33(5).
6   *Herman Jennings & Co Ltd v Slatcher* [1942] 2 KB 115, [1942] 2 All ER 1.
7   WMA 1985, s 33(6).

Reasonable precautions and due diligence

18.55 The WMA 1985, s 34 states:

34 Reasonable precautions and due diligence

(1)   In any proceedings for an offence under this Part of this Act or any instrument made under this Part, it shall be a defence for the person charged to prove that he took all reasonable precautions and exercised all due diligence to avoid the commission of the offence.

(2)   If in any case the defence provided by subsection (1) above involves an allegation that the commission of the offence in question was due to the WMA 1985 or default of another person or due to reliance on information supplied by another person, the person charged shall not, without the leave of the court, be entitled to rely on the defence unless, before the beginning of the period of seven days ending with the date when the hearing of the charge began, he served on the prosecution a notice giving such information identifying or assisting the identification of the other person as was then in his possession.

18.56 It is a defence to offences under Pt IV of the WMA 1985 to show that all reasonable precautions were taken and all due diligence was exercised to avoid the commission of an offence. The defence of due diligence is considered in detail in CHAPTER 4, Criminal Enforcement. However, relevant to offences under Pt IV of the WMA 1985, the due diligence defence has been held not to be available to an employer charged with selling underweight food where there was no proper recruitment, instruction or supervision of managerial staff[1]. Although the WMA 1985 due diligence defence is less onerous than the previous WMA 1963 formula, instances of successful defences under the 1963 formula are still useful[2].

1   *Knowsley MBC v Cowan* (1992) 11 Tr LR 44.
2   See *Bibby Cheshire v Golden Wonder Ltd* [1972] 1 WLR 1487; [1972] 3 All ER 738; *Westminster City Council v Turner, Gow Ltd* (1984) 4 Tr L 130; *North Yorkshire County Council v Holmesterne Farm Co Ltd* (1985) 150 JP 124.

Subsequent deficiency

18.57 The WMA 1985, s 35 provides:

35 Subsequent deficiency

(1)   This subsection applies to any proceedings for an offence under this Part of this Act, or any instrument made under this Part, by reason of the quantity—

    (a)   of any goods made up for sale or for delivery after sale (whether by way of pre-packing or otherwise) in or on a container marked with an indication of quantity,

    (b)   of any goods which, in connection with their sale or an agreement for their sale, have associated with them a document purporting to state the quantity of the goods, or

    (c)   of any goods required by or under this Part of this Act to be pre-packed, or to be otherwise made up in or on a container for sale or for delivery after sale, or to be made for sale, only in particular quantities,

being less than that marked on the container or stated in the document in question or than the relevant particular quantity, as the case may be.

(2)   In any proceedings to which subsection (1) above applies, it shall be a defence for the person charged to prove that the deficiency arose—

    (a)   in a case falling within paragraph (a) of subsection (1) above, after the making up of the goods and the marking of the container,

    (b)   in a case falling within paragraph (b) of that subsection, after the preparation of the goods for delivery in pursuance of the sale or agreement and after the completion of the document,

    (c)   in a case falling within paragraph (c) of that subsection, after the making up or making, as the case may be, of the goods for sale,

and was attributable wholly to factors for which reasonable allowance was made in stating the quantity of the goods in the marking or document or in making up or making the goods for sale, as the case may be.

(3)   In the case of a sale by retail of food, other than food pre-packed in a container which is, or is required by or under this Part of this Act or the FIC Regulation to be, marked with an indication of quantity, in any proceedings for an offence under this Part of this Act or any instrument made under this Part, by reason of the quantity delivered to the buyer being less than that purported to be sold, it shall be a defence for the person charged to prove that the deficiency was due wholly to unavoidable evaporation or drainage since the sale and that due care and precaution were taken to minimise any such evaporation or drainage.

(4)   If in any proceedings for an offence under this Part of this Act or any instrument made under-this Part, being an offence in respect of any deficiency in the quantity of any goods sold, it is shown that between the sale and the discovery of the deficiency the goods were with the consent of the buyer subjected to treatment which could result in a reduction in the quantity of those goods for delivery to, or to any person nominated in that behalf by, the buyer, the person charged shall not be found guilty of that offence unless it is shown that the deficiency cannot be accounted for by the subjecting of the goods to that treatment.

18.58 Where the offence involves goods in containers marked with incorrect quantities or goods with associated documents stating incorrect quantities (and thus most often offences under WMA 1985, ss 30, 31 and 31A) it is a defence that the deficiency arose after the container was marked or the document completed, provided that it is additionally proved that the deficiency was wholly attributable to factors for which reasonable allowance was made at the time the marking or document was made[1]. The defence is available to manufacturers, wholesalers and retailers, as well as the person who actually packed and marked the goods[2].

[1]   WMA 1985, s 35(1) and (2).

² *FW Woolworth and Co Ltd v Gray* [1970] 1 All ER 953, [1970] 1 WLR 764, DC.

18.59 Where non-prepacked food[1] is sold by retail (that is to a person buying for his own use or consumption[2]) and the quantity delivered is less than that purported to be sold, it is a defence to prove that the deficiency was due wholly to unavoidable evaporation or drainage since the sale, provided that it can also be shown that due care and precaution were taken to minimise such a deficiency[3].

¹ Food is defined by the Food Safety Act 1990 as including drink, articles and substances of no nutritional value used for human consumption, and articles and substances used as ingredients in the preparation of food, a definition imported into the WMA 1985, s 94(1).
² *Chappell and Co Ltd v Nestle Co Ltd* [1958] Ch 529, [1958] 2 All ER 155 CA, on appeal [1960] AC 87, [1959] 2 All ER 701, HL.
³ WMA 1985, s 35(3).

18.60 Where the defendant shows that, between sale and the discovery of any deficiency in the quantity of the goods the goods were, with the consent of the buyer, subjected to treatment which could result in a reduction in quantity of the goods this is a defence unless it shown that the deficiency cannot be accounted for by such treatment[1].

¹ WMA 1985, s 35(4).

Excess due to precautions

18.61 The WMA 1985, s 36 provides:

36 Excess due to precautions

In any proceedings for an offence under this Part of this Act or any instrument made under this Part, being an offence in respect of any excess in the quantity of any goods, it shall be a defence for the person charged to prove that the excess was attributable to the taking of measures reasonably necessary in order to avoid the commission of an offence in respect of a deficiency in those or other goods.

18.62 Where the offence alleges an excess in the quantity of goods, it is a defence to show that the excess was caused by taking measures reasonably necessary to avoid committing an offence in respect of a deficiency in those or other goods[1].

¹ WMA 1985, s 36.

Reasonable testing

18.63 The WMA 1985, s 37 provides:

37 Provisions as to testing

(1) If proceedings for an offence under this Part of this Act, or any instrument made under this Part, in respect of any deficiency or excess in the quantity—
    (a) of any goods made up for sale (whether by way of pre-packing or otherwise) in or on a container marked with an indication of quantity, or

(b)   of any goods which have been pre-packed or otherwise made up in or on a container for sale or for delivery after sale, or which have been made for sale, and which are required by or under this Part of this Act or the FIC Regulation to be pre-packed, or to be otherwise so made up, or to be so made, as the case may be, only in particular quantities,

are brought with respect to any article, and it is proved that, at the time and place at which that article was tested, other articles of the same kind, being articles which, or articles containing goods which, had been sold by the person charged or were in that person's possession for sale or for delivery after sale, were available for testing, the person charged shall not be convicted of such an offence with respect to that article unless a reasonable number of those other articles was also tested.

(2)   In any proceedings for such an offence as is mentioned in subsection (1) above, the court—

(a)   if the proceedings are with respect to one or more of a number of articles tested on the same occasion, shall have regard to the average quantity in the articles tested,

(b)   if the proceedings are with respect to a single article, shall disregard any inconsiderable deficiency or excess, and

(c)   shall have regard generally to all the circumstances of the case.

(3)   Subsections (1) and (2) above shall apply with the necessary modifications to proceedings for an offence in respect of the size, capacity or contents of a container as they apply to proceedings for an offence in respect of the excess or deficiency in the quantity of certain goods.

(4)   Where by virtue of section 32 above a person is charged with an offence with which some other person might have been charged, the reference in subsection (1) above to articles or goods sold by or in the possession of the person charged shall be construed as a reference to articles or goods sold by or in the possession of that other person.

18.64 Where a test has been conducted on one of a number of articles made up for sale at the same time and place and that article has been found to be deficient, the defendant shall not be convicted unless a reasonable number of the articles available was also tested[1]. If the proceedings are with respect to a single article, the court must also disregard any inconsiderable deficiency or excess[2] and, in all cases, the court must have regard generally to all the circumstances of the case[3]. However, where a person takes an article which he has purchased to an inspector, at some location other than the place of purchase, there is no obligation on the inspector to test other items which were on sale at the same time and place, since 'available' means physically available to the inspector at the time and place of testing[4].

1   WMA 1985, s 37(1).
2   WMA 1985, s 37(2)(b).
3   WMA 1985, s 37(2)(c).
4   *Sears v Smiths Food Group Ltd* [1968] 2 QB 288, [1968] 2 All ER 721, DC.

OFFENCES WITHIN INSTRUMENTS UNDER THE WMA 1985

18.65 Weights and measures authorities are also responsible for enforcing regulations that have been made under the WMA 1985, s 15. Some regulations create specified offences while others create obligations, the contravention of which can amount to an offence by virtue of WMA 1985, s 15(3). This section addresses some of the more common issues and offences.

The three packers' rules

18.66 Under the average quantity system, packers and importers of packaged goods are responsible for ensuring that their packages meet legislative requirements with regard to quantity control, marking, equipment, checks and documentation. The Weights and Measures (Packaged Goods) Regulations 2006[1] repealed and replaced Pt V of the WMA 1985 and the Weights and Measures (Packaged Goods) Regulations 1986[2] as amended. They also removed the statutory effect of provisions contained in the 'Code of Practical Guidance for Packers and Importers' and the 'Manual of Practical Guidance for Inspectors'. The Regulations apply to packages which are packed in constant nominal quantities by weight or volume which are predetermined by the packer and are not less than 5 grams or 5 millilitres and not more than 25 kilograms or 25 litres[3]. They also apply to 'outer containers'[4] containing at least one package and to bread which is unwrapped.

[1] Weights and Measures (Packaged Goods) Regulations 2006, SI 2006/659.
[2] SI 1986/2049.
[3] SI 2006/659, reg 3.
[4] Defined under SI 2006/659, reg 2.

18.67 Regulation 4 sets out the three rules with which packers must comply in making up packages: (a) the contents of the packages shall be not less on average than the nominal quantity; (b) the proportion of packages having a negative error greater than the tolerable negative error shall be sufficiently small for batches of packages to satisfy the requirements specified in Sch 2; (c) no package shall have a negative error greater than twice the tolerable negative error. Compliance with the rules is to be determined by the reference test set out in Sch 2. Regulations 5 and 6 set out the information which must be marked on packages and outer containers and the circumstances in which the E-mark (the form of which is shown in Sch 4) may be marked on a package or outer container. Regulation 7 provides that a person other than a packer or importer who marks an indication of nominal quantity on a package will become liable under the Regulations as though he were a packer or importer. Regulation 8 sets out specific requirements as to the marking of weight or volume on packages. Regulation 9 imposes duties on packers and importers as to the measurement of the contents of packages, the checking of the contents and keeping of records.

18.68 Regulation 13 makes it an offence to fail to comply with any of regs 4–7 and 9 or, with intent to deceive, to alter records or evidence kept for the purposes of these regulations. Regulation 14 lays down offences in respect of the knowing sale of packages containing short measure or of packages which come from a batch that has failed the reference test. Regulation 15 prohibits the marking of the E-mark on packages except as permitted by the Regulations. Regulation 16 makes the unauthorised disclosure of information concerning trade secrets and secret manufacturing processes an offence. regs 17–20 contain provisions supplementary to the offence provisions including penalties and defences.

Clear and unobstructed view

18.69 Under the Measuring Equipment (Capacity Measures and Testing Equipment) Regulations[1], no person shall use a capacity measure for the measurement of intoxicating liquor before its transfer to a container in which the buyer is to receive it, unless the buyer has a clear and unobstructed view of the measurement and transfer[2]. This provision serves to protect consumers who purchase alcoholic drinks such as cocktails that comprise one or more intoxicating liquors, combined with other substances, and are made up before the buyer receives it. Although reg 7 of these Regulations does not itself create an offence, under WMA 1985, s 15(3), it is an offence to contravene Regulations made under WMA 1985, s 15(1), which the 1995 Regulations are. It is arguable that reg 7 titled 'Purpose and manner of use of capacity measures' falls within WMA 1985, s 15(1)(e). Therefore, acting contrary to reg 7 would be an offence under the WMA 1985.

[1]   SI 1995/735. See also **18.4** and SI 2018/1387.
[2]   SI 1995/735, reg 7. This would previously have been governed by the Capacity Serving Measures (Intoxicating Liquor) Regulations 1988, however those regulations were revoked on 25 March 2015 by the Weights and Measures (Revocations) Regulations 2015, SI 2015/356, Sch 1 para 1.

18.70 The Measuring Instruments Regulations 2016[1] para 41 creates a similar offence but one that requires 'use for trade'. Part VI of these Regulations were also made under WMA 1985, s 15(1) and so acting contrary to Sch 6 para 41, compliance of which is compelled under Pt VI, would appear to also be an offence under the WMA 1985.

[1]   SI 2016/1153, Sch 6. See also **18.4** and SI 2019/696.

Serving gin, rum, vodka and whisky, wine and free pouring on premises

18.71 The Weights and Measures (Intoxicating Liquor) Order[1] contains provisions relating to how certain alcohol shall be served by retail for consumption on the premises at which it is sold.

Under art 3(1), unless pre-packed in a securely closed container, certain intoxicating liquor, that is to say gin, rum, vodka and whisky, shall be sold by retail for consumption on the premises at which it is sold only, art 3(1)(a), in, or in a multiple of, quantities of either 25ml or 35ml, and, art 3(1)(b), if there is displayed on those premises, in such a position and manner as to be readily available without special request for inspection by the buyer before the sale is made, a statement in writing showing in which of those quantities those liquors are offered for sale on those premises.

This suggests that what consumers often refer to as a 'single' may either be a 25ml or a 35 ml quantity (not both at the same premises). Hence, art 3(1)(b) imposes an obligation to clarify this to the consumer before the consumer makes a purchase.

[1]   SI 1988/2039. See also **18.4** and SI 2019/696.

18.72 Article 3(1) imposes two requirements to be satisfied, but contravening art 3(1)(b) is a stand-alone offence for the occupier of the premises under art 7(1), where the liability upon summary conviction is a fine not exceeding £2,000.

18.73 Contravening art 3(1)(a) appears to just be, by the language of art 3(3), unlawful. However, contravening art 3(1)(a) is arguably an offence under WMA 1985, s 25(1), as the intoxicating liquor is not pre-packed and is required to be sold only by quantity expressed in a particular manner or only in a particular quantity, and the 1988/2039 Order is made, inter alia, under WMA 1985, s 22(1)(a). The defences available under WMA 1985, ss 33–37, discussed earlier in this chapter, would apply to this offence[1]. Liability upon summary conviction is a fine[2].

[1] WMA 1985, s 25(6).
[2] WMA 1985, s 84(6).

18.74 Article 3 contains further exemptions. Under art 3(2), the intoxicating liquor shall be exempted from the requirements of art 3 when it forms a constituent of a mixture of three or more liquids. This suggests that if the gin, rum, vodka or whisky is to be part of a mix or cocktail of at least 3 different liquids, then the constituent part of gin, rum, vodka or whisky may be a quantity other than 25ml or 35ml. There is a further exemption under art 3(3). The express request of the buyer can circumvent the unlawfulness of serving a non-prescribed quantity under art 3(1)(a).

18.75 It should be noted that gin, rum, vodka and whisky are not defined in the 1988/2039 Order. Under art 3A, which addresses pre-packed intoxicating liquors, there is reference to Sch A1 and 'spirit drinks' as defined by Regulation (EC) No 1576/89. This was repealed by Regulation (EC) No 110/2008, which is presently in force, which contains, at Annex II, definitions of all gin, rum, vodka and whisky. Further, Order 1988/2039 does refer to CN codes, Combined Nomenclature codes, which Regulation (EC) No 110/2008 has regard to under the definition of spirit drinks. The result is that Regulation (EC) No 110/2008 appears to be the most relevant legislation under which gin, rum, vodka and whisky are to be defined for the purposes of Article 3[1].

[1] WMA 1985, s 94.

18.76 As to the common practice of free pouring, as far as specified quantities for intoxicating liquor spirits is concerned, free pouring would not be an offence provided (i) the spirit served does not fall within the definition of gin, rum, vodka and whisky, or (ii) the drink served contains gin, rum, vodka or whisky, but the final drink which is served contains the relevant intoxicating liquor and at least two other liquids.

18.77 The 1988/2039 Order also provides that wine is to be sold in the glass for consumption on the premises only in quantities, or in a multiple of, 125ml and 175ml[1] and that fortified wine for distillation (fortified wine with, inter alia, an a.b.v. of 18-24%. See Chapter 22 of the Combined Nomenclature of the European Union[2]) is to be sold in quantities of either 50ml or 70ml[3]. There is no provision allowing for multiples of the quantity of either 50ml or 70ml in respect of fortified wine for distillation, and the contravention of selling fortified wine as such is a stand-alone offence for the occupier of the premises under article 7(1), where the liability upon summary conviction is a fine not exceeding £2,000. Selling wine contrary to Article 5A(2)(a) is arguably an offence under s 25 WMA 1985: see **18.73** above.

Further, a statement in writing showing the quantities in which the wine or fortified wine is for sale must either be displayed on those premises in such a position and manner as to be readily available without special request for inspection by the buyer before the sale is made, or must be contained in every winelist and menu which is available to the buyer on those premises before the sale is made and which indicates that wine or fortified wine is for sale for consumption on those premises.

1   SI 1988/2039, art 5A(2)(a).
2   Commission Implementing Regulation (EU) 2018/1602 of 11 October 2018 amending Annex I to Council Regulation (EEC) No 2658/87.
3   SI 1988/2039, art 5A(2)(b).

Regulated measuring equipment

18.78 The Measuring Instruments Regulations 2016[1], which implement Directive 2014/32/EU, creates offences in relation to the unauthorised affixing, altering or defacing, or removal of authorised marks[2] in respect of regulated measuring instruments[3]. It is also an offence to affix any other form of marking to a regulated measuring instrument which is likely to deceive any person as to the meaning or form, or both, of an authorised mark[4]. These are strict liability offences, and a defence of due diligence is available[5]. It is further an offence for a person to place on the market or put into use or use for trade a regulated measuring instrument that that the person knows has been the subject of unauthorized affixing, altering or defacing, or removal of an authorised mark[6]. Note that this is wider than just a prohibition on the 'use for trade' of such measuring instruments.

1   SI 2016/1153. See also **18.4** and SI 2019/696. Since 31 December 2020, CE marks are no longer 'authorised marks' for the purposes of the reg 75 offences. CE marks are now replaced by UK marks.
2   SI 2016/1153, reg 75(5) – 'authorised mark' means the CE marking; the M marking; the identification number of the notified body which carried out the conformity assessment procedure in respect of the relevant regulated measuring instrument; a disqualification mark; or a re-qualification mark.
3   SI 2016/1153, reg 75(1).
4   SI 2016/1153, reg 75(1)(d).
5   SI 2016/1153, reg 78.
6   SI 2016/1153, reg 75(3).

18.79 The Measuring Instruments Regulations 2016 are an important part of the Government's New Legislative Framework ('NLF') which is designed to make it easier for economic operators[1] to comply with the legislation, set common performance assessment criteria for the bodies which determine whether or not a product meets the essential requirements of the legislation, and make the legislation easier to understand and use. In August 2017, guidance was published to assist economic operators achieve compliance. The Measuring Instruments Regulations 2016 draws a distinction between persons and economic operators and the offences applicable therein.

1   SI 2016/1153, reg 2 – 'economic operator' means a manufacturer, authorised representative, importer or distributor.

Prohibited determinations of mass and price

18.80 The Non-automatic Weighing Instruments Regulations 2016[1] creates a similar set of offences[2] as those under the Measuring Instruments Regulations 2016 in respect of authorised marks, but they only apply to a 'non-automatic weighing instrument'[3].

[1] SI 2016/1152. See also **18.4** and SI 2019/696.
[2] SI 2016/1152, reg 71.
[3] SI 2016/1152, reg 2 – 'non-automatic weighing instrument' means a weighing instrument that (a) serves to determine the mass of a body by using the action of gravity on that body and which may also serve to determine other mass-related magnitudes, quantities, parameters and characteristics; and (b) requires the intervention of an operator during weighing. This includes common supermarket instruments, which may be freestanding, or connected to scanners and tills as an electronic point of sale (EPOS) system.

18.81 Under the Non-automatic Weighing Instruments Regulations 2016[1], the use and possession for use of non-complying instruments, for the following applications, is prohibited:

(a)   Determination of mass for commercial transactions.

(b)   Determination of mass for the calculation of a toll, tariff, tax, bonus, penalty, remuneration, indemnity or similar type of payment.

(c)   Determination of mass for the application of laws or regulations or for an expert opinion given in court proceedings.

(d)   Determination of mass in the practice of medicine for weighing patients for the purpose of monitoring, diagnosis and medical treatment.

(e)   Determination of mass for making up medicines on prescription in a pharmacy and determination of mass in analyses carried out in medical and pharmaceutical laboratories.

(f)   Determination of price on the basis of mass for the purposes of direct sales to the public and the making up of pre-packages[2].

[1] SI 2016/1152. See also **18.4** and SI 2019/696.
[2] SI 2016/1152, regs 3(2), 55, 72(1)(d) and 72(2).

PROSECUTIONS

18.82 Proceedings in respect of offences under the WMA 1985 in England and Wales can only be instituted by or on behalf of a local weights and measures authority[1] or the police[2]. The authority may appear in and prosecute proceedings through any member or officer authorised to represent it, and such a person need not be a solicitor holding a current practising certificate[3]. In Scotland, proceedings can only be instituted by the Procurator Fiscal/Crown Office. Any person, other than the Crown or its servants or agents[4], can be prosecuted under the WMA 1985.

[1] Defined in WMA 1985, s 69.
[2] WMA 1985, s 83(1).
[3] Local Government Act 1972, s 223.
[4] See CHAPTER 1 on Crown Immunity generally.

Causal liability

18.83 The WMA 1985 s 32 provides for causal liability, which is now covered in CHAPTER 4, Criminal Enforcement. The case of *Allied Domecq Leisure Limited v Cooper*[1] provides a relevant and useful illustration as to how carefully a WMA 1985, s 32 prosecution must be constructed. There was no dispute that a barmaid caused a potentially short measure to be delivered, contrary to s 28 WMA 1985, but connecting this to the default of Allied Domecq Limited, the company which supplied the manageress who was charged with training the barmaid in the particular circumstances, was problematic. There was no real evidence of default by Allied Domecq Limited. It was not enough merely to state that there was a failure to provide training by the company management. In the circumstances, it was not possible to focus on the behaviour of the relief manageress and hold the company vicariously liable for her alleged deficiencies. This was far too wide a proposition.

[1]   (1999) 163 JP 1.

Directors' liability

18.84 The WMA 1985 s 82 permits the prosecution and conviction of any 'director, manager, secretary or other similar officer' of a company or 'any person who was purporting to act in such a capacity'. Directors' liability provisions are now covered in CHAPTER 4, Criminal Enforcement.

TIME LIMITS

18.85 For all offences under the WMA 1985, prosecutions shall not be instituted except by or on behalf of a local weights and measures authority or the chief officer of police for a police area[1]. This is the only limitation on prosecution of offences that do not fall under Pt IV WMA 1985.

However, by the WMA 1985, s 83(3), no proceedings for offences under Pt IV of the WMA 1985[2], which include the commonly committed offences contrary to WMA 1985, ss 28, 30, 31 and 31A (note that WMA 1985, s 29 (Misrepresentation) was repealed by the Consumer Protection from Unfair Trading Regulations 2008[3]), may be instituted unless one of the following conditions is met:

(a)   the defendant has been served with a written notice giving the date and nature of the alleged offence; or

(b)   that written notice was served within 30 days of the date when evidence which the prosecutor considers is sufficient to justify a prosecution came to his knowledge; or

(c)   proceedings are instituted within 12 months from the date given in the written notice or within 3 months from the date in (b) above, whichever first occurs.

The relevant prosecutor must either (i) first serve a written notice which complies with conditions (a) and (b) and then institute proceedings within

3 months of the date that sufficient evidence came to his knowledge or (ii) not serve a written notice but institute proceedings within 12 months of the alleged date of the offence.

1   WMA 1985, s 83(1).
2   With the exception of offences contrary to WMA 1985, s 33(6) or proceedings by virtue of WMA 1985, s 32.
3   SI 2008/1277.

18.86 The notice may be served either in person or by post at the defendant's last known residence or place of business in the UK, or at a company's registered office[1].

1   WMA 1985, s 83(4).

18.87 In Scotland, the Crown Office has issued instructions to weights and measures authorities, in relation to WMA 1985, s 83(3), the relevant parts of which are as follows:

> 'For the sake of uniformity of practice and to ensure that accused persons receive the notice at the earliest opportunity, the Lord Advocate has instructed that, in future, the notice in terms of Section 83(3) should be served by the enforcement officer of the Weights and Measures Authority and not by the Procurator Fiscal. A copy of the notice and certificate of posting or execution of service, should be attached to any relevant report received by the Procurator Fiscal from the local authority department.
>
> In any case where the Procurator Fiscal discovers that no copy notice accompanies the report he or she should contact the Weights and Measures Authority to give them the opportunity to send a notice provided that 30 days have not expired since the Fiscal has received this report.
>
> Once the notice has been served the Procurator Fiscal will have to consider whether either three months have elapsed from the date of receipt of the report or, whether 12 months have elapsed since the date of the offence. If either period has been overrun, proceedings will be time barred.'

ENFORCEMENT POWERS

18.88 The WMA 1985, s 72 deals with the appointment of inspectors of weights and measures. A weights and measures authority must appoint a chief inspector of weights and measures and ' . . . such number of other inspectors of weights and measures, if any . . . as may be necessary for the efficient discharge in the authority's area of the functions conferred or imposed on inspectors by or under this Act'[1].

1   It is worth noting that the number of inspectors actually working in weights and measures fell from 503 in 2011 to 304 in 2013 (NMO Annual Report 2013/2014). This then fell again to 257 in the subsequent year (NMO Annual Report 2014/2015). No further report has been published. However, the WMA 1985, s 70 is permissive as to the publishing of these reports.

18.89 Qualification requirements for inspectors first appeared in Weights and Measures Acts of 1889 and 1904. The WMA 1985, s 73 currently provides for the granting of a certificate of qualification to act as inspector (by the Secretary of State) for those who pass examinations held ' . . . for the purpose of ascertaining whether persons possess sufficient skill and knowledge for the proper performance of the functions of an inspector . . . '. This has been an area considered for change – for example the National Weights and Measures

Laboratory commenced a 'Reform Project' in October 2007 and specifically examined the 'Qualification and Appointment of Inspectors of Weights and Measures'. Options put forward included the possibility that ' . . . Heads of Service would wish to see the statutory requirement removed so that they have more flexibility in their resourcing of staff'. To date, no substantive reforms have been introduced.

18.90 Future proposals will need to take account of the fact that the post of 'Inspector of Weights and Measures' has found itself in non-metrological settings such as the Police Reform Act 2002 and the Licensing Act 2003, in relation alcohol sales to children in England and Wales, and under the Glasgow Commonwealth Games Act 2008 (where the power of designating enforcement officers is restricted to inspectors of weights and measures and to other individuals who meet specified criteria).

Powers of entry and inspection

18.91 The Consumer Rights Act 2015 omits WMA 1985, s 79 (general powers of inspection and entry) and inserts WMA 1985, s 79A. The powers of officers are now contained within that Act:

79A Investigatory powers

For the investigatory powers available to a local weights and measures authority for the purposes of the enforcement of this Act, see Schedule 5 to the Consumer Rights Act 2015.

18.92 Note, in particular, that WMA 1985, s 79 restricted an inspector to exercise the general powers of inspection and entry only within the area for which he was appointed inspector. CRA 2015, Sch 5, paras 43–46 clarify the law to ensure that Trading Standards Services are able to operate across local authority boundaries. In summary, a local weights and measures authority in England or Wales may:

- exercise their consumer law enforcement function;
- bring civil proceedings in respect of specified conduct/applications for specified forfeiture;
- bring proceedings for a consumer offence allegedly committed in a part of England or Wales which is outside that authority's area.

Powers of seizure

18.93 Powers of entry and associated powers, including powers of seizure, are now contained in the Consumer Rights Act 2015, Sch 5 (see CHAPTER 4, Criminal Enforcement).

Offences concerned with officers and their powers

18.94 It is an offence, contrary to WMA 1985, s 75(2), to impersonate an 'inspector' or an approved verifier. It is an offence contrary to WMA 1985, s 75(1) for an inspector knowingly to commit a breach of duty or otherwise misconduct himself. It is an offence contrary to WMA 1985, s 79(7) for any person to disclose information about such secrets obtained as a result of his entry to premises under the powers granted by the WMA 1985, unless the disclosure is in the course of duty. It is an offence contrary to reg 16 of the Weights and Measures (Packaged Goods) Regulations 2006[1] for an officer, or any person who accompanies him, to disclose any information which relates to a trade secret or secret manufacturing process, unless the disclosure is in the course of duty.

[1] SI 2006/659, reg 16. See also **18.4** and SI 2019/696.

Obstruction of officers

18.95 It is an offence, contrary to WMA 1985, s 80, to wilfully obstruct an Officer acting in pursuance of the WMA 1985. The WMA 1985, s 81 creates three offences:

(a)   The WMA 1985, s 81(1)(a) – wilfully failing to comply with a requirement made under the Officers powers of inspection and seizure under the WMA 1985, ss 38–40;

(b)   The WMA 1985, s 81(1)(b) – without reasonable cause failing to give any inspector acting in pursuance of the WMA 1985 any other assistance or information which the inspector may reasonably require of him for the purposes of the performance by the inspector of his statutory functions;

(c)   The WMA 1985, s 81(2) – in purporting to give information required under 1(a) and (b) above, knowingly giving false information.

18.96 The WMA 1985, s 81(3) excuses the person who fails to comply with an Officer's requirements under WMA 1985, s 81(1)(a) and (b) above if his failure to answer a question or give information is based on the fear that it might incriminate him. The use of information provided by a defendant under the compulsion of s 81 in evidence at his trial would, arguably, be a breach of his right to a fair trial[1].

[1] Art 6 of the ECHR.

Test purchases

18.97 The power to make test purchases is now found in the Consumer Rights Act 2015, Sch 5 (see CHAPTER 4, Criminal Enforcement).

PENALTIES AND SENTENCING

Imprisonment

18.98 The only offences under the WMA 1985 for which a sentence of imprisonment can be imposed are those relating to the fraudulent use for trade of weighing or measuring equipment (WMA 1985, s 17(3)), fraud in connection with public weighing machines (WMA 1985, s 20(3)(b)) and deceitfully damping solid fuel (WMA 1985, Sch 5, para 10)[1]. These are summary offences with a maximum sentence of 6 months' imprisonment.

[1]   WMA 1985, s 84(4).

Financial penalties and forfeiture

18.99 All the other offences under the WMA 1985 carry financial penalties only, and the possible forfeiture of equipment or goods connected with the offences. As most of the commonly committed offences in the WMA are summary only offences it should be noted that, in relation to offences committed after 12 March 2015, the old £5,000 limit on the financial penalty that can be imposed in the magistrates' court has been removed[1]. Where anything other than money is forfeited on a conviction by a magistrates' court it must be sold or otherwise disposed of as the court may direct and the proceeds applied as if they were a fine[2]. In Scotland anything used or connected with the commission of an offence may be forfeited under the Proceeds of Crime (Scotland) Act 1995, s 21.

[1]   Legal Aid, Sentencing and Punishment of Offenders Act 2012, s 85.
[2]   Magistrates' Courts Act 1980, ss 140 and 148(1).

HALLMARKING

Introduction

18.100 OPS&S now holds the policy (legislative) responsibility for the hallmarking of precious metal articles, formerly held by Regulatory Delivery. The British Hallmarking Council ('BHC'), established and governed by the Hallmarking Act 1973, is an Executive Non-Departmental Public Body. The Council is funded by the UK's four Assay Offices. The sponsoring body of the BHC is the Office for Product Safety & Standards ('OPSS') which is part of the Department of Business, Energy & Industrial Strategy ('BEIS').

18.101 When the Hallmarking Act 1973 ('HA 1973') came into force it replaced, in whole or in part, some 26 other statutes, many of them dating back to Stuart or Hanoverian times, which were concerned with the regulation of the trade in precious metals. The HA 1973 provides for the composition, assaying, marking and description of articles made from or containing gold, silver and platinum and (since 21 July 2009) palladium[1]. The scheme of criminal liability introduced by the Hallmarking Act 1973 follows the structure of the Trade Descriptions Act 1968 ('TDA 1968') (now largely repealed). The HA 1973 extends to the United Kingdom. Practical guidance in relation to the Hallmarking Act 1973 published by the UK's assay offices was updated in August 2016 to include information on hallmarking Mokume Gane articles containing precious metals.

[1]   Hallmarking Act 1973 (Application to Palladium) Order 2009, SI 2009/2040.

European hallmarks

18.102 The UK remains a signatory to the Convention on the Control and Marking of Articles of Precious Metals signed in Vienna in 1972[1]. The Convention recognises hallmarks applied in another convention country; and as a consequence articles bearing such marks will be hallmarked for the purposes of the HA 1973 and can therefore be described in the United Kingdom as being of the precious metal (gold, silver, platinum or palladium) of which they are made. The Hallmarking (International Convention) Order 2002 also provides for the application in the United Kingdom of similar marks which will be recognised in other convention countries[2]. Refusing to recognise hallmarks of another Member State may also amount to a restriction on the free movement of goods[3].

[1] This is now under the Hallmarking (International Convention) Order 2002, SI 2002/506.
[2] Articles of fineness of only 830 (accepted by some countries but not by the United Kingdom) may have applied to them marks appropriate to articles of that fineness, but may not be described in the United Kingdom as being of silver unless they are intended for despatch to a destination outside the United Kingdom.
[3] See *Commission of the European Communities v Ireland* (C30/99) EU:C:2001:346; [2001] ECR. I-4619; [2001] 3 CMLR. 28, *UAB Juvelta v VI Lietuvos prabavimo rumai* (C-481/12) EU:C:2014:11; [2014] 2 CMLR. 43 and *European Commission v Czech Republic* (C-525/14) EU:C:2016:714.

Time limits

18.103 By para 2 of Sch 3 to the HA 1973, no prosecutions under the HA 1973 may be commenced more than 3 years after the offence was committed or one year after the offence was discovered[1] by the prosecutor, whichever is earlier.

[1] See *Brooks v Club Continental* Transcript DC/345/81 and *R v Beaconsfield JJ, ex p Johnson Sons Ltd* (1985) 149 JP 535.

18.104 Time limits are considered in detail in CHAPTER 4, Criminal Enforcement.

Prosecutions

18.105 The right to prosecute in England and Wales is not restricted to a member or officer of an enforcement authority – any person can bring a prosecution under the HA 1973. In Scotland proceedings may only be taken by the Procurator Fiscal or Lord Advocate (HA 1973, s 9(5)). Any person (whether an individual or a body corporate), other than the Crown or its servants or agents, can be prosecuted under the HA 1973.

Directors' liability

18.106 Paragraph 3 of Sch 3 to the HA 1973 permits the prosecution and conviction of any 'director, manager, secretary or other similar officer' of a company or 'any person who was purporting to act in such a capacity' where an offence under the HA 1973 has been committed by the company 'with the consent and connivance' of that person or as a result of that person's neglect. The liability of directors etc is considered in detail in CHAPTER **4**, Criminal Enforcement.

Causal liability

18.107 By virtue of para 4 of Sch 3 to the HA 1973, where the prosecution can show that A has committed an offence under the HA 1973 and that the offence has been committed because of the 'act or default' of B, then B may be prosecuted and convicted even if A is not proceeded against. The fact that B is a private individual, and thus otherwise not subject to the legislative scheme of the HA 1973 (which generally requires a defendant to have been acting in the course of a trade or business) is no defence to a prosecution under para 4 of Sch 3. The liability of other persons is considered in detail in CHAPTER **4**, Criminal Enforcement.

Offences

18.108 The HA 1973 creates criminal offences contrary to HA 1973, ss 1, 3, 5, 6, 7, and 11. Those under HA 1973, s 1 are the most important. The ingredients of the offences are examined below. Other words commonly used in the HA 1973 are defined in HA 1973, s 22. The case of *Chilvers v Rayner*[1] established that offences under HA 1973, s 1 are absolute offences for which no *mens rea* is required.

[1]   [1984] 1 WLR 328.

Applying a description

18.109 The only descriptions with which the HA 1973 is concerned are those 'indicating that [an article] is wholly or partly made of gold, silver platinum or palladium': HA 1973, s 1(1)(a). By virtue of the HA 1973, s 1(5) and Pt III of the HA 1973, Sch 1, a description indicating that an article, or the metal in an article, is of so many carats is to be presumed to be an indication that the article or metal is of gold and that its fineness is that specified in the following table:

Number of carats	Indicates gold of a standard of fineness of
9	375 parts per thousand
12	500 parts per thousand
14	585 parts per thousand
15	625 parts per thousand
18	750 parts per thousand
22	916.6 parts per thousand

APPLYING

18.110 The HA 1973, s 1(7)(b) imports the definition of applying a trade description set out in TDA 1968, s 4 into the HA 1973. The TDA 1968, s 4 has now been largely replaced by the CPUTR 2008; however, it remains of relevance for prosecutions under the HA 1973.

4 Applying a trade description to goods

   (1)   A person applies a trade description to goods if he—
        (a)   affixes or annexes it to or in any manner marks it on or incorporates it with—
            (i)   the goods themselves, or
            (ii)   anything in, on or with which the goods are supplied; or
        (b)   places the goods in, on or with anything which the trade description has been affixed or annexed to, marked on or incorporated with, or places any such thing with the goods; or
        (c)   uses the trade description in any manner likely to taken as referring to the goods.
   (2)   An oral statement may amount to the use of a trade description.
   (3)   Where goods are supplied in pursuance of a request in which a trade description is used and the circumstances are such as to make it reasonable to infer that the goods are supplied as goods corresponding to that trade description, the person supplying the goods shall be deemed to have applied that description to the goods.

18.111 The TDA 1968, s 4 defines 'applying a trade description'. It is drafted very widely, but generally covers five situations that will in practice overlap:

(1)   When goods are given a description by physically marking them, or affixing a description to them or material supplied with them, for example packaging or instructions (TDA 1968, s 4(1)(a)).

(2)   Placing different goods with goods of a particular trade description, for example a steel ring sold in a display of silver rings (TDA 1968, s 4(1)(b)).

(3)   Using a general trade description in a manner likely to be taken as referring to the goods in question, for example a shop with a hoarding suggesting that it sells only gold, which sells products that look like they are made of gold (TDA 1968, s 4(1)(c)).

(4)   An oral description of goods (TDA 1968, s 4(2)).

(5)   Where goods are supplied in pursuance of a request in which a trade description is used and it is reasonable to infer that the goods are supplied as goods corresponding to that description, the supplier is deemed to have applied the description to the goods (TDA 1968, s 4(3))[1].

It also includes omissions after goods of a particular trade description have been requested. For example a jeweller who is requested to supply an 18 carat gold bracelet, but instead supplies a 9 carat gold bracelet omitting to describe it as such.

[1]   See *Shropshire CC v Simon Dudley Ltd* (1997) 161 JP 224, where TDA 1968, s 4(3) was held to be applicable to the supply of a fire engine not in accordance with the purchaser's specifications. The court noted that the case did not warrant a prosecution and imposed an absolute discharge; civil proceedings for breach of contract would have been a sufficient remedy.

THE TIME OF APPLICATION

18.112 The time that a trade description is applied to goods is when one of the acts described in s 4 takes place. The defendant does not need to be a contracting or contemplated contracting party, and the application does not need to take place before the contract is concluded[1]. The time of the application is not when another person sees the trade description or is misled by it. The moment that a false trade description is, for example, affixed to goods, the offence is complete[2]. This accords with logic as the offence is designed to capture those who make it their business to apply false trade descriptions.

1   *Fletcher v Sledmore* [1973] RTR 371.
2   *Newman v Hackney London Borough Council* [1982] RTR 296.

18.113 There is limited support for the contention that there is an additional requirement to TDA 1968, s 4; that the application of the trade description must be associated with the sale or supply of goods. In *Hall v Wickens Motors (Gloucester) Ltd*[1], 40 days after the appellant sold a car, he described it as having nothing wrong with it. In a decision that was directed specifically towards the merits of the case, Widgery LCJ allowed the appeal on the basis that the application of a false trade description under the TDA 1968 must be, 'associated with the sale or supply of goods'. However, it is doubtful that this case provides a proposition of universal application.

1   [1972] 3 All ER 759, following his decision in *Wycombe Marsh Garages v Fowler* [1972] 3 All ER 248.

18.114 In *Fletcher v Sledmore*, a mechanic agreed to sell a motor car to a dealer. While the mechanic was repairing the car, the dealer brought a buyer to view it. The mechanic falsely told the buyer that it had a good engine. The Divisional Court, which included Widgery LCJ[1], distinguished *Hall v Wickens Motors* and held that the representation was associated with the sale or supply of goods. Eveleigh J, in a judgment with which Widgery LCJ agreed, stated:

> 'There are no qualifications in section 1 [of the TDA] as to the time when the representation is to be made; the only qualification . . . is that it should be in the course of a trade or business, in other words, should be made as part of the business activities of the person charged . . . The question then remains whether or not there is reason to introduce the qualification that the person charged should himself be a contracting party in the matter in which the representation is made. No such limitation appears in the section.'

1   [1973] LGR 179 Widgery LCJ casting doubt over the generality of his words in *Hall v Wickens Motors*.

18.115 In the case of *Telford & Wrekin Council v Jordan*[1] the respondent motor car repairer had replaced the faulty dashboard of a car, with one showing a lower mileage. His contention was that he had not intended to sell the car, but merely use it as a family car. In relation to this point, Wright J stated:

> 'Even if a false odometer reading is applied to a car . . . at a time when he has no intention of selling the car on but merely wishes to have it as a family car for his own or his family's use, nevertheless the offence is committed because the mischief against which the Trade Descriptions Act is directed is to prevent vehicles with odometers so altered ultimately finding their way into the market, as is very likely to happen sooner or later, bearing false readings as to the mileage that the vehicle has in fact covered. It follows therefore that even though [the Respondent] may have had no immediate

intention of releasing the car into the market when he changed the odometer on this car that did not prevent what he did being an offence under section 1(1)(a).'

It is submitted that the decision in *Wickens Motors* is now of limited importance. The essential question is whether a false trade description has been applied in the course of a trade or business, in other words should be made as part of the business activities of the person charged.

[1]   DC, 20/6/2000 CO/1282/00.

TRUTH AND FALSITY

18.116 The HA 1973, by contrast to the TDA 1968, is not concerned with the question of whether such an indication is true or false, only with the question of whether the article to which the description is applied is hallmarked or not. If such an indication is made, true or false, of an unhallmarked article, an offence is committed.

UNHALLMARKED

18.117 The HA 1973, s 2(1) sets out the marks which qualify as 'approved hallmarks'. They are marks struck by assay offices in the UK, or marks struck abroad providing equivalent information. The HA 1973, s 3 sets out the marks which qualify as 'sponsors' marks' (which provide information about the manufacturer of the goods). By HA 1973, s 2(4)(a) an article which does not bear both an approved hallmark *and* a sponsor's mark is regarded as unhallmarked for the purposes of the HA 1973. An article may also become unhallmarked if it has been the subject of any 'improper alteration'[1], as defined by the HA 1973, ss 2(5) and 5.

[1]   HA 1973, s 2(4)(b).

18.118 The Hallmarking (Hallmarking Act Amendment) Regulations 1998 amended HA 1973, s 2 in order to make the HA 1973's provisions consistent with Art 30 of the EC Treaty, in relation to the importation by one Member State of articles made of or comprising precious metals from another Member State, as explained by the European Court of Justice in the case of *Houtwipper*[1]. Essentially, an 'approved hallmark' includes a mark struck in an 'EEA State' other than the UK. By virtue of the Hallmarking Act 1973 (Amendment) Regulations 2007, 'EEA State' now has the meaning given to it in the Interpretation Act 1978, Sch 1 (see also the HA 1973, s 22).

[1]   Case C-293/93 [1994] ECR 1–4249.

18.119 The Legislative Reform (Hallmarking) Order 2013[1] makes a number of amendments to the HA 1973:

- enabling assay offices to strike hallmarks outside the United Kingdom and for items bearing those hallmarks to be treated in the same way as items bearing hallmarks struck in the United Kingdom;
- removing the requirement that a manufacturer's or sponsor's mark, registered under HA 1973, s 3, must include the initial letters of the name or names of the manufacturer or sponsor; and

- allowing articles of silver, gold or platinum bearing a hallmark, to be coated with platinum without having to first obtain the written consent of an assay office.

[1] SI 2013/251.

IN THE COURSE OF A BUSINESS

18.120 It is a requirement of offences under the HA 1973, s 1 that the offender be acting 'in the course of a trade or business'.

POSSESSION CUSTODY AND CONTROL

18.121 The HA 1973, ss 1 and 6 create offences involving the 'possession' or the 'custody or control' of particular things. It appears that possession by an employee will be held to be possession by the employer[1]. In order for offences of possession to be made good the law requires proof of an element of control over the item in question, although not necessarily of physical proximity[2] and thus the use of the word control rather than possession appears to make little difference. There is no authority on whether the inclusion of the word 'custody' obviates the need for the prosecution to prove an element of control. It is submitted that it should not.

[1] *Towers & Co v Gray* [1961] 2 QB 351, [1961] 2 All ER 68, DC.
[2] See *Warner v Metropolitan Police Commissioner* [1969] 2 AC 256, *Bellerby v Carle* [1983] 2 AC 101, [1983] 1 All ER 1031, HL.

DEALERS

18.122 A 'dealer' is defined by the HA 1973, s 22 as a person engaged in the business of making, supplying, selling (including by auction) or exchanging articles of precious metal, or in other dealings in such articles.

Specific offences

Prohibited descriptions of unhallmarked articles

18.123 The HA 1973, s 1(1)(a) makes it an offence for a person, in the course of a trade or business, to apply to an unhallmarked article a description indicating that it is wholly or partly made of gold, silver, platinum or palladium. The HA 1973, s 1(1)(b) creates an offence for such a person to supply or to offer to supply (which includes a person exposing articles for supply, or having articles in his possession for supply – HA 1973, s 1(7)(c)) an unhallmarked article to which such a description is applied.

18.124

Precedent for applying an unlawful description to an unhallmarked item

Statement of offence

APPLYING AN UNLAWFUL DESCRIPTION TO AN UNHALLMARKED ITEM, contrary to s 1(1)(a) of the Hallmarking Act 1973.

Particulars of offence

A B on [date], in the course of a trade or business, applied to an unhallmarked article, namely [. . .], a description indicating that it was wholly or partly made of [. . .].

Striking an article with a mark purporting to be an authorised sponsor's mark

18.125 The HA 1973, s 3 requires that, before an article is sent to the Assay Office for hallmarking, a mark must be struck on the article indicating its manufacturer. This is known as the sponsor's mark. Sponsor's marks have to be authorised by and registered with the relevant Assay Office, and HA 1973, s 3 sets out how this is to be done and what marks are acceptable. By HA 1973, s 3(6), where the Assay Office in question is of the opinion that it would not be justified in requiring a person submitting an article for hallmarking to register a sponsor's mark, it may strike the article with its own sponsor's mark. It is an offence under HA 1973, s 3(8) without authority to strike an article with a mark purporting to be an authorised sponsor's mark.

Altering a hallmarked article

18.126 The HA 1973, s 5(1) makes it an offence to make an addition, alteration or repair to an article bearing approved hallmarks, except in accordance with the written consent of an assay office. There are four standard consents in writing, made by the Joint Committee of the Assay Offices of Great Britain, which allow specified alterations without further application. The scrapping of articles for remanufacture and the recoating of articles in the same fineness of precious metal (including palladium[1]) as the original are exceptions to these offences by virtue of HA 1973, s 5(3) and (5) respectively. Similarly, additions to hallmarked articles which do not change their character and purpose and which comply which specified requirements are excepted by virtue of HA 1973, s 5(4).

---

[1] As inserted into the Hallmarking Act 1973, s 5 (Application to Palladium) Order 2009, SI 2009/2040.

18.127

Precedent for making an unauthorised alteration to a hallmarked item

Statement of offence

MAKING AN UNAUTHORISED ALTERATION TO A HALLMARKED ARTICLE, contrary to s 5(1) Hallmarking Act 1973.

Particulars of offence

A B on [date] made an alteration to an article bearing an approved hallmark, namely [. . .], without the written consent of an assay office.

18.128 The HA 1973, s 5(2) makes it an offence to remove, alter or deface any mark struck on an article, except in accordance with the written consent of the assay office.

Counterfeiting

18.129 The HA 1973, s 6(1)(a) makes it an offence to make a counterfeit of any die or mark. This offence requires the prosecution to prove that the defendant acted with 'intent to defraud or deceive'. The HA 1973, s 6(2) defines a die as any plate, tool or instrument by means whereof any mark is struck on any metal and defines a mark as any mark in the nature of a sponsor's mark or hallmark.

Removal of marks

18.130 The HA 1973, s 6(1)(b) makes it an offence to remove a mark from an article of precious metal with intent to transpose it to any other article whether of precious metal or not, or to affix to any article any mark which has been removed from an article of precious metal.

Uttering counterfeits

18.131 The HA 1973, s 6(1)(c) makes it an offence to utter any counterfeit of a die or any article bearing a counterfeit of a mark. 'Uttering' is defined by HA 1973, s 6(3) as the supply, offer to supply or delivery of the die or article, in the knowledge or belief that it is counterfeit. The uttering of counterfeits has been held to include any attempt to pass the counterfeit as genuine and is thus much wider than the concepts of 'supply' and 'offer to supply' in the HA 1973, s 1[1].

1 *Selby v DPP* [1972] AC 515, [1971] 3 All ER 810, and see *R v Walmsley* (1977) 122 Sol Jo 127, CA.

Possession of counterfeits

18.132 The HA 1973, s 6(1)(d) makes it an offence, without lawful authority or excuse, for a person to have in his custody or under his control anything which is, and which he knows or believes to be, a counterfeit die or an article bearing a counterfeit mark.

Supply of articles bearing marks likely to be confused with hallmarks

18.133 The HA 1973, s 7 deals with the situation where an article comes into the custody of an assay office bearing a mark likely to be confused with a hallmark, but which is not an approved hallmark because it has not been struck by an assay office according to law or because the article appears to have been the subject of improper alteration. The HA 1973, s 7(1) gives the assay office power to cancel or obliterate such a mark. The HA 1973, s 7(6) makes it an offence for any person knowingly, or for any dealer (without any qualifying *mens rea*), to supply or offer to supply an article bearing such a mark, unless the article has first been submitted to an assay office to enable them to cancel, obliterate or deface the mark.

Failure to exhibit a notice as to hallmarks

18.134 The HA 1973, s 11(1) makes it an offence for dealers to fail to keep exhibited in a conspicuous position in the parts of his premises to which those with whom he deals are commonly admitted a notice as to hallmarks in terms approved and in a form supplied by the British Hallmarking Council.

Statutory exceptions

Permitted descriptions

18.135 By virtue of s 1(2) of and Part I of Sch 1 to HA 1973, the use of the word 'gold' will not constitute an offence under HA 1973, s 1, when used to describe an unhallmarked article, where it is qualified by the words 'plated' or 'rolled'. Thus the description of an unhallmarked fountain pen as 'rolled gold' will not constitute an offence under this legislation (but a plainly and unequivocally false description 'rolled gold' may give rise to action under the CPUTR 2008 – see *Kingston-Upon-Thames Royal London BC v FW Woolworth & Co Ltd*[1]. The same section and Schedule make similar exceptions in the case of the descriptions of unhallmarked articles as 'silver plated' and 'platinum plated'.

[1] [1968] 1 QB 802.

Exempted articles

18.136 By virtue of s 1(3) of and Part II of Sch 1 to HA 1973, the offences created by HA 1973, s 1(1) do not apply to a variety of articles. These are set out in the Schedule. The most noteworthy of the articles completely exempt are those for export, articles in the course of consignment from abroad to an assay office in the UK, current or former coinage, articles used or intended to be used for medical, dental, veterinary, scientific or industrial purposes, raw materials or bullion and uncompleted articles. Other articles, such as those manufactured before, and unaltered since, 1950, the mouthpieces of musical instruments, and articles so small that they cannot be hallmarked are exempt provided that their fineness is not less than 375 parts per thousand in the case of gold and 800 parts per thousand in the case of silver. There are also exemptions for specific articles, such as watch chains, again of minimum fineness, manufactured before 1975. By para 18 of Part II of Sch 1 to the HA 1973, where exemption depends upon the date of an article's manufacture, the manufacture shall be presumed to be after that date until the contrary is proved.

Statutory defences

Reliance on information as to exemption supplied by another

18.137 Schedule 3, para 6 provides a defence to offences under the HA 1973, s 1 where the defendant can show that the offence was caused by reliance on information supplied to him by another person which caused him to believe that the article concerned was one which was exempt from hallmarking by virtue of Pt II of Sch 1. The defendant must also satisfy the court that he could not, with reasonable diligence, have ascertained that it was not such an article.

Innocent publication of advertisement

18.138 Schedule 3, para 5 provides a defence where the allegation is of an offence committed by the publication of an advertisement. It is a defence for the defendant to show that he is a person whose business is to publish or arrange for the publication of advertisements and that the advertisement in question was received in the ordinary course of business and that he did not know and had no reason to suspect that its publication would amount to an offence under the HA 1973.

Duty to enforce

18.139 Under the HA 1973, s 9(1) it is the duty of every local weights and measures authority to enforce the provisions of this Act within their area. Under this subsection, the British Hallmarking Council and the assay offices may also enforce the provisions of the HA 1973. The Consumer Rights Act 2015, Sch 6, para 10 inserts the following subsection into the HA 1973, s 9:

> (2A) For the investigatory powers available to a local weights and measures authority, the Council and an assay office for the purposes of the duty in subsection (1) and the power in subsection (2), see Schedule 5 to the Consumer Rights Act 2015.

18.140 The powers of enforcement officers and offences related to the enforcement provisions are considered in detail in Chapter 4, Criminal Enforcement.

Delivery of articles to the Assay Office

18.141 The HA 1973, s 10 permits the court, following a person's conviction of an offence under the HA 1973, to order any article the subject of the proceedings to be delivered to an assay office for hallmarking, before it is returned to the person entitled to it.

Maximum sentences

18.142

Section	Brief description	Mode of trial	Maximum on indictment	Maximum summarily
1(1)(a)	Applying a prohibited description to an unhallmarked article	Either way	2 years and unlimited fine	6 months and unlimited fine
1(1)(b)	Supplying an unhallmarked article with a prohibited description	Either way	2 years and unlimited fine	6 months and unlimited fine
3	Striking an article with a purported sponsor's mark	Either way	2 years and unlimited fine	6 months and unlimited fine
5(1)	Altering a hallmarked article	Either way	2 years and unlimited fine	6 months and unlimited fine
5(2)	Altering a hallmark	Either way	2 years and unlimited fine	6 months and unlimited fine
6(1)(a)	Counterfeiting	Either way	10 years and unlimited fine	6 months and unlimited fine
6(1)(b)	Removal of marks	Either way	10 years and unlimited fine	6 months and unlimited fine
6(1)(c)	Uttering counterfeits	Either way	10 years and unlimited fine	6 months and unlimited fine
6(1)(d)	Possession of Counterfeits	Either way	10 years and unlimited fine	6 months and unlimited fine
7	Supply of articles bearing marks likely to be confused with hallmarks	Either way	2 years and unlimited fine	6 months and unlimited fine
11	Failure to exhibit a notice as to Hallmarks	Either way	2 years and unlimited fine	6 months and unlimited fine

Chapter 19

CONSUMER CREDIT

Contents

INTRODUCTION

19.1 Virtually every adult in the UK will be party to a number of agreements which fall within the scope of consumer credit regulation, from credit card agreements to mobile phone contracts and overdraft arrangements. The importance of the credit industry to the wider economy cannot be over stated and a well functioning credit market can have a positive social impact. However, credit arrangements inherently involve a significant disparity in the strength of the respective parties' positions and the potential for consumer detriment is significant.

19.2 Consequently, the provision of credit has been closely regulated for over a hundred years, although the modern law really started in the early 1970s with the introduction of the Consumer Credit Act 1974 ('CCA 1974') following the recommendations for a new legal structure in the Crowther Committee Report.

19.3 For many years the credit industry was regulated by the Office of Fair Trading ('OFT') and creditors were required to be licenced by the OFT to engage in certain credit related activities. However, on 1 April 2014, the OFT was abolished and regulation of the credit industry transferred to the Financial Conduct Authority ('FCA'). At the same time, consumer credit regulated activities came within the ambit of the Financial Services and Markets Act 2000 ('FSMA 2000') and the Financial Services and Markets Act 2000 (Regulated Activities) Order 2001 (as amended) ('RAO 2001') and the CCA 1974 was amended significantly. From 1 April 2014, the licencing regime has been replaced by FCA authorisation for permission to undertake regulated activities.

19.4 This change aligned the regulation of consumer credit with the wider regulation of the financial services industries but did not result in simplification. On the contrary, the law governing consumer credit activities is arguably more complex and impenetrable than ever: large sections of the CCA 1974 and Regulations made thereunder have been retained and now sit alongside detailed rules in the Consumer Credit Sourcebook chapter of the FCA Handbook ('CONC'). To further complicate matters, some OFT guidance on advertising, debt collection and assessment of affordability has been replicated, and remains informative, whereas other OFT guidance has been ignored and is now of doubtful relevance, no matter how useful it had previously been. To those who do not specialise in the area, it is often impossible to know whether to start with the CCA 1974 or CONC and whether and to what extent other guidance or Regulations are relevant.

19.5 The FCA was required to report to HM Treasury on the retained provisions of the CCA 1974 and whether their repeal, in whole or in part, combined with their replacement, in whole or in part, by FCA rules and guidance in CONC would adversely affect the appropriate degree of protection for consumers[1]. The FCA did so on 25 March 2019 when it submitted its Final Report[2]. In the Final Report, the FCA, *inter alia*, explained that it considers that the rights and protections currently afforded to borrowers are important and should be maintained in some form and a significant number of these rights and protections are ill suited to FCA rules and cannot be moved into the Handbook with the same level of protection. Accordingly, the FCA recommended retaining these provisions but also acknowledged that there are a number of issues with these provisions and these issues merit further consideration. The FCA also suggested certain information requirements could be shifted into the FCA Handbook especially if the existing sanctions in the CCA 1974 were retained for breach of those requirements. Finally, the FCA recognised that there are some problems with the current sanctions framework which can lead to draconian sanctions for minor infringements. The FCA suggests that this merits further consideration whether or not provisions are moved to or replicated in FCA rules. The FCA has now complied with its obligation to review the retained provisions of the CCA 1974 and what, if any, action is taken now falls to Government to decide.

[1] Paragraph 20(8) of Part 5 of the Financial Services and Markets Act 2000 (Regulated Activities) (Amendment) Order 2014, SI 2014/366

[2] Available at https://www.fca.org.uk/publication/corporate/review-of-retained-provisions-of-the-consumer-credit-act-final-report.pdf.

19.6 Another significant change in recent years occurred on 21 March 2016 with the coming into force of the Mortgage Credit Directive Order 2015 ('MCDO 2015'). Amongst other things, the changes brought about by the MCDO 2015 involved the unification of the law relating to first charge and second charge lending: historically, first charge lending had been dealt with by the Financial Services Authority ('FSA') under the FSMA 2000 regime whereas second charge lending had been dealt with by the OFT under the CCA 1974 regime. From 1 April 2014, the FCA took over the regulation of first and second charge lending but there remained a distinction as second charge lending remained subject to the CCA 1974. However, from 21 March 2016, that anomalous disparity has been addressed and second charge lending has been excluded from regulation by the CCA 1974 and is now principally to be found in the Mortgages and Home Finance Conduct of Business sourcebook ('MCOB') of the FCA Handbook. Further discussion of secured lending falls outside the scope of this chapter.

19.7 On 29 April 2021 the Financial Services Act 2021 ('FSA 2021') received Royal Assent. The FSA 2021 addresses a number of aspects of financial services regulation in the UK post-Brexit. In relation to consumer credit it includes provisions as to the application of the CCA 1974 to certain regulated activities (see s 37) and has been used to bring certain buy now pay later agreements, which typically fall outside of the CCA 1974, within the scope of FCA regulation.

19.8 Further and inevitably, this chapter cannot contain a detailed analysis of unsecured consumer credit, but instead offers a basic introduction and guide with footnotes to enable further research. For further detail, Guest and Lloyd's *Encyclopedia of Consumer Credit Law* and *The Law of Consumer Credit and Hire* by *Philpott et al* are recommended.

THE ROLE OF TRADING STANDARDS

19.9 Section 161(1) of the CCA 1974 provides that, in Great Britain, Trading Standards Departments, as the local weights and measures authorities, have a duty – alongside the FCA – to enforce the CCA 1974; in Northern Ireland it is the duty of the Department of Commerce for Northern Ireland.

19.10 Section 3R of FSMA 2000 enables the FCA to enter into arrangements with Trading Standards Departments (of the Department of Enterprise, Trade and Investment ('DETI') in Northern Ireland) for the provision of services in relation certain types of regulated activity (for example, consumer credit). This would allow the FCA to enter into a contract with a Trading Standards Department for that department to carry out compliance checks on behalf of the FCA. Further, the order-making powers of the Treasury in s 107 of the Financial Services Act 2012, include provision for Trading Standards Departments or DETI to commence proceedings for consumer credit related offences under FSMA 2000 without first obtaining the consent of the Director of Public Prosecutions, for such offences.

19.11 Trading Standards Departments are also granted certain investigatory and enforcement powers in order to assist with their duty above. These were previously contained in ss 162 to 165 CCA 1974 but are now found in Sch 5 to the Consumer Rights Act 2015. These powers include the power of entry and inspection and the power to make test purchases.

19.12 Section 230 of the Enterprise Act 2002, requires Trading Standards Departments in England and Wales to give notice to the Consumer and Markets

Authority ('CMA') of intended prosecutions and their outcome under specified enactments and secondary legislation. Article 2 of and Sch 1 to the Enterprise Act 2002 (Pt 8 Notice to OFT of Intended Prosecution Specified Enactments, Revocation and Transitional Provision) Order 2003[1] provides that all offences under CCA 1974 are specified for the purposes of the Enterprise Act 2002 – but proceedings are not invalid by reason only of the failure to comply with this section.

1   SI 2003/1376.

19.13 The FCA is a proactive regulator and will be far more prominent in the enforcement of consumer credit rules than Trading Standards Departments. However, whilst it is unlikely that Trading Standards Departments will engage with consumer credit in the same way as the FCA[1], credit issues often arise in other contexts where Trading Standards involvement is more likely: for example, with smaller unauthorised lenders (who may not even realise they are granting regulated credit) or other traders who are engaging in other activities which generate Trading Standards' interest (for example, potential breaches of the Consumer Protection from Unfair Trading Regulations 2008). Given the forgoing, it is clear that no book on Trading Standards Law and Practice would be complete without a chapter on consumer credit and it is important for those involved in this area to have an understanding of the consumer credit basics or, at least, know where to go for more information. This Chapter aims to provide that basic information, focusing on the areas likely to be of most relevance and signposting to further information where appropriate.

1   For example, Trading Standards Departments are almost certainly not going to engage with large, FCA authorised, financial institutions on technical compliance with detailed requirements under the CCA 1974 and subsidiary Regulations.

CONSUMER CREDIT REGULATION

19.14 The regulation of financial services, including consumer credit is governed by a complex statutory framework. Firstly, it is necessary to determine whether the activity in question is 'specified' by the RAO 2001. Credit related regulated activities specified in the RAO 2001 include: credit broking (art 36A), operating an electronic system in relation to lending (art 36H), debt adjusting (art 39D), debt counselling (art 39E), debt administration (art 39G), entering into regulated credit agreements (art 60B), entering into a regulated hire agreement (art 60N), providing credit information services (art 89A) and providing credit references (art 89B). Reference should be made directly to the RAO 2001 for the definition and scope of each activity listed. The remainder of this chapter will principally relate to the activity specified in article 60B RAO 2001: entering into a regulated consumer credit agreement as lender and/or exercising or having the right to exercise the lender's rights and duties under a regulated credit agreement.

19.15 However, that is not the end of the story; a specified activity (including those listed above) will only be regulated if it is carried on 'by way of business'[1]. Consequently, if the activity is not carried out by way of business it falls outside of the statuary framework and the permission requirements that apply to regulated credit[2]. Guidance as to what is meant by "by way of business" is provided in the FCA's Perimeter Guidance Manual section of the FCA Handbook ('PERG'). Q37 in PERG 14.5 explains that it 'will invariably depend upon the individual circumstances' but the following factors will be relevant:

(1)   The degree of continuity;

(2)   The existence of a commercial element;

(3)   The scale of the activity;

(4)   The proportion to which the activity bears upon the other activities carried on by the person which are not regulated; and

(5)   The nature of the particular regulated activity carried on.

Further guidance can be obtained from the Court of Appeal's judgment in *Helden v Strathmore Ltd*[3] where the Court upheld the first instance decision that a lender had been acting 'by way of business' by reference to eight factors including the size, regularity, formality and commercial objective of the lending.

[1]   FSMA 2000, s 22 (the 'by way of business' test).

[2]   However, the resultant credit agreements will not necessarily be outside of ambit of the CCA 1974. See discussion of "non-commercial agreements" below.

[3]   [2011] Bus LR 1592.

19.16 Parties that will be engaging the credit related regulated activities by way of business will need to have either Full Authorisation or Limited Permission. Full Authorisation is required for 'higher risk' activities such as consumer credit lending, credit brokerage as a primary activity, debt adjusting, debt counselling and debt collection. 'Lower risk' activities which only require limited permission might include consumer credit lending as a secondary activity on an interest and charges free basis.

19.17 There is a prohibition against carrying on a regulated activity in the UK, or to purporting to do so, unless authorised or exempt[1]. It is a criminal offence to carry out a regulated activity without the necessary authorisation[2]. Moreover, it is a criminal offence if an authorised person carries on a credit-related activity in the UK otherwise than in accordance with their permission.

[1]   This 'general prohibition' is set out in FSMA 2000, s 19. Exempt persons are specified on the Financial Services and Markets Act 2000 (Exemption) Order 2001 but are unlikely to be relevant for present purposes as those specified as exempt are principally large national and supranational organisations.

[2]   FSMA 2000, s 23.

19.18 Agreements made by persons in contravention of the general prohibition are unenforceable[1]. Credit agreements made by an authorised person acting without the necessary permission are also unenforceable[2]. Finally, agreements entered into by properly authorised firms are also unenforceable if they were entered into 'in consequence of something said or done' by third parties carrying on regulated activities in contravention of the general prohibition[3]. In any of these cases, the other party is entitled to recover any money or property paid or transferred by that party under the agreement and compensation for any loss sustained by that party as a result of having parted with it.

[1]   FSMA 2000, s 26.

[2]   FSMA 2000, s 26A.

[3]   FSMA 2000, s 27.

19.19 The FCA may allow agreements rendered unenforceable by ss 26, 26A or 27 of the FSMA 2000 to be enforced but in doing so must consider whether the person carrying on the regulated activity concerned reasonably believed that he was not contravening the general prohibition or acting without permission by making the agreement (the FSMA 2000, s 28A)[1].

[1] See *Helden v Strathmore Limited* [2011] EWCA Civ 542, [2011] CTLC 158 the Court of Appeal upheld a decision to permit the enforcement of an agreement entered into contrary to the general prohibition on the basis that it was just and equitable to do so in the circumstances of that case (FSMA 2000, s 28(3)). In *Chickombe v FCA* [2018] UKUT 258 (TCC) the Upper Tribunal considered its powers in relation to a reference in respect of validation order applications under FSMA 2000, s 28A and the extent to which the FCA should take into account consumer detriment when deciding whether to allow otherwise unenforceable agreements to be enforced.

FCA Handbook

19.20 In addition to complying with the rules in the CCA 1974, the associated Regulations and the sector specific CONC rules, the FCA handbook introduces high level principles to the consumer credit industry. The Principle for Business chapter of the Handbook ('PRIN'), in particular PRIN 2.1.1R sets down the eleven high level principle ('the Principles') which act as a general statement of the fundamental obligations of firms under the regulatory system. The Principles are:

(1) A firm must conduct its business with integrity.

(2) A firm must conduct its business with due skill, care and diligence.

(3) A firm must take reasonable care to organise and control its affairs responsibly and effectively, with adequate risk management systems.

(4) A firm must maintain adequate financial resources.

(5) A firm must observe proper standards of market conduct.

(6) A firm must pay due regard to the interests of its customers and treat them fairly.

(7) A firm must pay due regard to the information needs of its clients, and communicate information to them in a way which is clear, fair and not misleading.

(8) A firm must manage conflicts of interest fairly, both between itself and its customers and between a customer and another client.

(9) A firm must take reasonable care to ensure the suitability of its advice and discretionary decisions for any customer who is entitled to rely upon its judgment.

(10) A firm must arrange adequate protection for clients' assets when it is responsible for them.

(11) A firm must deal with its regulators in an open and cooperative way, and must disclose to the appropriate regulator appropriately anything relating to the firm of which that regulator would reasonably expect notice.

Whilst the breach of most rules in the FCA Handbook are actionable at the suit of a "private person"[1] by virtue of s 138D of the FSMA 2000, the contravention of the Principles are not (see PRIN 3.4.4R)[2]. The FCA may, nevertheless, consider disciplinary action (DEPP 6.2.14 G).

[1] The Financial Services and Markets Act 2000 (Rights of Action) Regulations 2001.

2   For further discussion, see *R (British Bankers association) v Financial Services Authority* [2011] EWHC 999.

CONSUMER CREDIT AGREEMENTS

19.21 The terminology used in the CCA 1974 and FSMA 2000 is slightly different; for example, the former refers to 'consumer credit agreements' and the later simply to 'credit agreements'. Nevertheless, by virtue of the definitions provided to the terms, such differences are of form rather than substance. For ease of reference in this chapter, where there is divergence, the terminology used in the CCA 1974 shall be used.

A consumer credit agreement is an agreement between an individual ('the debtor') and any other person ('the creditor') by which the creditor provides the debtor with credit of any amount[1]. Accordingly, it is important to define both 'individual' and 'credit'.

1   CCA 1974, s 8(1) and art 60B(3) RAO 2001.

'Individual'

19.22 An 'individual' includes natural persons, partnerships consisting of two or three persons, not all of whom are bodies corporate and unincorporated bodies of persons which do not consist entirely of bodies corporate[1]. Accordingly, unlike most consumer law, the consumer credit act will actually govern non-business debtors including small businesses. Nevertheless, agreements with companies and other incorporated bodies falls outside the definition of 'individual' and credit agreements entered into by such borrowers will be unregulated. By virtue of s 1(2) of the Limited Liability Partnership Act 2000, Limited Liability Partnerships are corporate bodies and will, therefore, fall outside the definition of 'individual'.

1   See CCA 1974, s 189(1) and the similar definition of 'relevant recipient of credit' in art 60L RAO 2001.

'Credit'

19.23 Section 9 of the CCA 1974 defines 'credit' as 'a cash loan, and any other form of financial accommodation'[1]. This is not a particularly helpful definition. However, in *Dimond v Lovell*[2], the House of Lords gave a well-known gloss on the statutory definition, essentially saying that credit will be provided if the debtor is granted the contractual right to defer payment of a debt[3]. Therefore the crucial question is often whether the debtor is contractually entitled to defer payment from the date it would otherwise be expected.

1   CCA 1974, s 9(1).
2   [2002] 1 AC 384.
3   So that the 'contract provides for the debtor to pay, or gives him the option to pay, later than the time on which payment would otherwise have been earned under the express or implied terms of the contract' ([2002] 1 AC 384, at 395). The deferment must be contractual, mere indulgence will not amount to the granting of credit.

19.24 The following arrangements have been held on their facts not to be credit:

(i)   monthly payments of estimated minimum commission to an employee, pursuant to an employment contract (this was advance remuneration for services, rather than credit)[1];

(ii)   monthly payments pursuant to a gym membership contract (these payments were made for continuing access to the facilities, in relation to each month)[2];

(iii)   requiring an after-the-event insurance premium to be paid at the conclusion of the litigation (simply because the premium was required to be paid in the future, this was not deferment as there was no established practice requiring such premiums to be paid at the inception of the policy)[3];

(iv)   where any obligation to pay is postponed until a future possible indebtedness arises (which might not ever arise)[4];

(v)   forbearance by the lender to sue on a right to immediate payment (although this has the same result)[5];

(vi)   where payment is postponed as security for the performance of some other obligation by the creditor[6];

(vii)   a future payment to enable a lease to be assigned[7].

[1]   *McMillan Williams v Range* [2004] 1 WLR 1858, CA.
[2]   *Office of Fair Trading v Ashbourne Management Services Ltd* [2011] EWHC 1237 (Ch), [2011] CTLC 237.
[3]   *Tilby v Perfect Pizza Ltd* [2003] CCLR 9.
[4]   *Nejad v City Index Ltd* [2000] CCLR 7.
[5]   *Aspinall's Club Ltd v Al-Zayat* [2008] EWHC 2101 (Comm).
[6]   See *Dimond v Lovell* per Lord Hobhouse.
[7]   *Burrell v Helical (Bramshott Place) Ltd* [2016] CTLC 1.

19.25 In *Holyoake v Candy*[1] it was held that a settlement deed which compromised litigation was a credit agreement by providing financial accommodation (para 498). This was in the context of an unfair relationship claim under s 140A of the CCA 1974 and is discussed further below. However, in *Gertner v CFL Finance Ltd*[2] a Tomlin Order which acknowledged a £2,000,000 debt and permitted the debtor to repay by instalments over two years was not credit. Detailed discussion of these two decisions falls outside the scope of this work but it would seem that settlement agreements will not automatically fall outside of the CCA 1974 and careful consideration must be given in each case to whether the settlement agreement provides credit.

[1]   [2017] EWHC 3397 (Ch).
[2]   [2021] EWCA Civ 228.

'Regulated consumer credit agreement'

19.26 An agreement which falls within the definition of 'consumer credit agreement' will be a 'regulated consumer credit agreement' unless it is exempt[1]. The exemptions are discussed further below. If an agreement is documented as a regulated agreement but as a matter of law it is not, it is not to be treated as a regulated agreement[2].

[1]   See CCA 1974, s 15(2) and art 60B(3) RAO 2001.
[2]   *NRAM v McAdam* [2015] CTLC 169.

19.27 As noted above, since 21 March 2016 credit agreements secured on land, both first and second charges, fall outside the scope of consumer credit regulation.

CATEGORISATION OF AGREEMENTS

19.28 As a starting point, when looking at an agreement, one must which of the various categories of agreement it falls within. This is necessary in order to determine which provisions of the CCA are applicable.

Running-account and fixed-sum credit

19.29 Credit agreements must fall into one of these two categories, which are mutually exclusive. Running-account credit (eg credit cards, bank overdrafts and a dealer's stocking plan agreement) is a facility whereby the debtor can receive from time to time cash/goods/services to a value such that, taking into account repayments made by him, the credit limit, if any, is never exceeded[1]. Fixed-sum credit (eg loans, hire-purchase, credit sale and conditional sale agreements) is anything else, even if the credit is paid in instalments.

[1]   CCA 1974, s 10(1).

19.30 A useful check to determine whether an agreement is for running-account or fixed-sum credit, is to ask whether repayments 'refresh' the available credit; for example, in a fixed-sum credit agreement for £2,000 making a repayment of £200 such that £1,800 remains outstanding does not entitle the debtor to re-draw the £200 but in a running-account credit agreement with a £2,000 credit limit it would. If an agreement is truly running-account, individual draw-downs of credit will not be treated as separate fixed-sum credit agreements, even if different repayment terms are applicable to those draw-downs[1]. However, the contractual earmarking of the first draw-down on a running-account for a specific purpose (eg to discharge existing debt, or to purchase an after-the-event insurance premium) may make that draw-down constitute a separate fixed-sum agreement[2].

[1]   See Guest and Lloyd, *Encyclopaedia of Consumer Credit Law*, vol 1, 2-011.
[2]   See *Goshawk Dedicated (No 2) Ltd v The Governor and Company of the Bank of Scotland* [2006] 2 All ER 610.

Restricted-use and unrestricted-use credit

19.31 Credit must also fall into one of these two categories, which are mutually exclusive. Under CCA 1974, s 11(1), there are three sub-categories of restricted-use credit:

(a)   to finance a transaction with the creditor
       (eg hire-purchase, credit sale or conditional sale);
(b)   to finance a transaction with a third party supplier
       (eg loans to finance the purchase of goods; credit cards (which can be used only with a network of suppliers selected by the card issuer); and credit to finance the purchase of payment protection insurance); or

(c)   to refinance existing debt.

The definition of 'finance' in s 189(1) of the CCA 1974 includes partly financing so it does not matter that the debtor has paid some of the purchase price (eg a deposit) in cash.

19.32 For an agreement to be for restricted-use credit there must be a contractual and practical restriction as to what the credit can be used for. Anything short of a contractual restriction, for example a common intention, is insufficient[1]. Further, even where there is a contractual restriction, the credit will not be restricted-use if, in practice, the credit is provided to the debtor in a manner which enables the debtor to use the credit as they please[2].

[1]   *National Westminster Bank plc v Story* [1999] Lloyd's Rep Bank 261.
[2]   See CCA 1974, s 11(3).

19.33 Anything else is unrestricted-use credit (CCA 1974, s 11(2)) (eg cash loans and overdrafts).

Debtor-creditor (DC) and debtor-creditor-supplier (DCS) agreements

19.34 Credit must also fall into one of these two categories, which are mutually exclusive. Under CCA 1974, s 12, DCS agreements have three sub-categories:

(a)   a restricted-use credit agreement where the creditor is also the supplier (ie a CCA 1974, s 11(1)(a) agreement) (this is a two-party arrangement, but still DCS);

(b)   a restricted-use credit agreement with a third party supplier (ie a CCA 1974, s 11(1)(b) agreement) made by the creditor under pre-existing 'arrangements'[1], or in contemplation of future arrangements, between himself and the[2] supplier;

(c)   an unrestricted-use agreement made under pre-existing arrangements between the creditor and the supplier, in the knowledge that the credit is to be used to finance a transaction between the debtor and the supplier (eg if a dealer introduces a customer to a finance company, which knows that the loan will be used to purchase a car from the dealer, even though in theory the loan could be used for other purposes).

Article 60L of the RAO 2001 describes this category as 'borrower-lender-supplier'.

[1]   CCA 1974, s 187 defines 'future arrangements' and 'pre-existing arrangements' for the purposes of CCA 1974, s 12, but there is no definition of the word 'arrangements' itself; in *OFT v Lloyds TSB Bank plc* [2007] QB 1, CA, it was held that where a supplier had been recruited to accept cards of a particular network (eg Visa/Mastercard) by other members of the network (and not by the card issuer in question), there were 'arrangements' between the supplier and the card issuer, because each had agreed (albeit separately) to adhere to the network rules.
[2]   See *Consolidated Finance Ltd v McCluskey* [2012] CTLC 133; *Consolidated Finance Ltd v Collins* [2013] EWCH Civ 475, [2013] CTLC 121.

19.35 Under CCA 1974, s 13, DC agreements also have three sub-categories:

(a)   a restricted-use credit agreement with a third party supplier (ie a CCA 1974, s 11(1)(b) agreement) not made by the creditor under pre-existing arrangements, or in contemplation of future arrangements, between himself and the supplier;

(eg a loan to finance the purchase of goods where the creditor, at the debtor's request, paid the loan directly to the supplier);

(b)   a restricted-use credit agreement to refinance existing debt (ie a CCA 1974, s 11(1)(c) agreement);

(c)   an unrestricted-use agreement not made under pre-existing arrangements between the creditor and the supplier, in the knowledge that the credit is to be used to finance a transaction between the debtor and the supplier

(eg a cash loan or bank overdraft).

Article 60L of the RAO 2001 describes this category as 'borrower-lender'.

Hire and hire-purchase agreements

19.36 Hire agreements are defined by CCA 1974, s 15. There must be a requirement for the hirer to make payment in exchange for the bailment of the goods: gratuitous payments are not included[1]. Hire agreements are not usually credit agreements (as no credit is provided), but hire-purchase agreements are a specifically made a sub-category of credit agreements[2]. However, throughout this chapter 'creditor' is used as shorthand for 'creditor or owner' and 'debtor' as shorthand for 'debtor or hirer'. Other asset finance agreements which fall within the purview of the CCA 1974 include conditional-sale agreements[3] and credit-sale agreements.

[1]   *TRM Copy Centres (UK) Ltd v Lanwell Services Ltd* [2008] 4 All ER 608, [2008] CTLC 182.
[2]   CCA 1974, s 9(3).
[3]   These agreements differ to hire-purchase agreements in that once all of the mandated payments are made ownership transfers to the debtor/hirer; there is no 'option to purchase' and no 'option to purchase fee'.

19.37 There are a number of products on the market which are now referred to as Personal Contract Plans ('PCP') or similar; this is especially prevalent in the financing of car purchases. These agreements are not a new category but are simply hire-purchase agreements where the regular repayments are intended to cover the depreciation and the 'option to purchase fee' or 'balloon payment' is a figure which is estimated to be the market value of the vehicle at the end of the agreement term.

EXEMPT AGREEMENTS

19.38 A consumer credit agreement which would otherwise be a regulated credit agreement is not regulated it is exempt. The exemptions are set out in arts 60C–60H of the RAO 2001. These include the following types of agreement[1]:

(a)   a regulated mortgage contract (art 60C(2))[2];
(b)   where the agreement provides the borrower with credit exceeding £25,000 and the agreement is entered into by the borrower wholly or predominantly for the purposes of a business carried on, or intended to carried on by the borrower (art 60C(3)). This is usually referred to as

'the business purposes exemption'[3]. The new Art 60C(4A) extends this exemption to business purpose loans where the lender providers the borrower with credit of £25,000 or less and the agreement is entered into by the lender and the borrower under the 'Bounce Back Loan Scheme' (operated from 4 May 2020 by the British Business Bank plc on behalf of the Secretary of State);

(c)   a debtor-creditor-supplier agreement for fixed-sum credit where the repayments do not exceed 12 in number or 12 months in duration (starting on the date of the agreement) and the credit is provided without interest or other charges (art 60F);

(d)   a debtor-creditor agreement where the lender is a credit union and the rate of the total charge for credit does not exceed 42.6% and the agreement is not of a type described in Art 3(1) of the Mortgage Credit Directive or it is of such a type but the agreement is of such a kind to which the Mortgage Credit Directive does not apply or the agreement is a bridging loan within the meaning of that directive (art 60G(2));

(e)   Where the borrower is an individual and the agreement is secured by land, or is for credit which exceeds £60,260, and, if entered into after 21 March 2016, is for a purpose other than the renovation of residential property, or to acquire or retain property rights in land or in an existing building project, and the agreement includes a declaration by the borrower which provides that the borrower agrees to forgo the protection and remedies that would be available to the borrower if the agreement were a regulated credit agreement, and which complies with rules made by the FCA for the purposes of this paragraph, and a statement made in relation to the income or assets of the borrower which complies with rules made by the FCA for the purposes of this paragraph was provided to the lender before the agreement was entered into (art 60H). This is usually referred to as the 'high net worth exemption'[4].

[1]   The examples provided are those that are most common and which are most likely to be relevant to situations involving Trading Standards. Reference should be made to the RAO 2001 for the full list.
[2]   Regulated Mortgage Contracts are dealt with by art 61 RAO 2001.
[3]   See *Wood v Capital Credit* [2015] EWCA Civ 451, [2015] CTLC 155.
[4]   For the rules made by the FCA see CONC App 1.4.

Partially excluded agreements

19.39 'Non-commercial agreements', which are not made by the creditor in a course of a business[1] are excluded by CCA 1974, s 74, from the form and content requirements and cancellation provisions of the CCA. However they are not unregulated or exempt agreements and a number of provisions continue to apply[2].2 Overdrafts on a current account are also excluded by CCA 1974, s 74, from these requirements[3].

[1]   *Hare v Schurek* [1991] CCLR 47: one-off or occasional loans by a motor trader were not made in the course of his business and so were 'non-commercial agreements'.
[2]   This is despite the fact that FCA authorisation will not be required (see above). The provisions that continue to apply include ss 56, 77B, 78B, 90, 93, 94–95B, 97, 97A, 105, 106, 129 and 140A–140C.
[3]   Although CCA 1974, s 74(1B)–(1E) provide that certain provisions nevertheless apply, depending on the type of overdraft.

AGREEMENTS SECURED ON LAND

19.40 Since 21 March 2016 agreements secured on residential land within the European Economic Area whether by first, second or subsequent charge will, subject to exemptions, be governed by FSMA 2000 and MCOB as a result of the Mortgage Credit Directive. Article 3(1) of the Directive provides that the Directive applies to:

(a)   credit agreements which are secured either by a mortgage or by another comparable security commonly used in a Member State on residential immovable property or secured by a right related to residential immovable property; and

(b)   credit agreements the purpose of which is to acquire or retain property rights in land or in an existing or projected building[1].

There are a number of exceptions in Art 3(2) which remove agreements from the scope of Art 3(1).

[1]   Interestingly, in order to enter into Art 3(1)(b) agreements, lenders will require consumer credit permission despite the agreements falling outside the scope of the CCA 1974 and being governed by a number of sections of MCOB.

19.41 Entering a mortgage contract as lender is a specified kind of activity (art 61(1) of the RAO 2001) provides that entering into a regulated mortgage contract as a lender is a specified kind of activity. Administering a mortgage contract is also a specified kind of activity where the contract was entered into by way of business on or after 31 October 2004; or the contract was entered into before 31 October 2004, and was a regulated credit agreement immediately before 21 March 2016 (art 61(2) of the RAO 2001). Further discussion of regulated mortgage contracts and other secured lending is outside the scope of this chapter.

CHATTEL SECURITY

19.42 The main legislation dealing with consumer credit which was not repealed by the CCA is that dealing with bills of sale[1]. The legislation remains relevant today. It applies, for example, to 'log-book loans' where credit is granted over the security of a motor vehicle[2]. The application of the legislation was considered in a High Court case dealing with an expensive viola[3]. In 2016 the Law Commission published a report recommending that the Bills of Sale Acts should be repealed and replaced with modern legislation that imposes fewer burdens on lenders and provides more protection for borrowers. In the 2017 the Commission consulted on draft clauses, which were intended to form part of the Goods Mortgages Bill. In September 2017, a full version of the draft Goods Mortgages Bill was published. However in May 2018 the Government said it did not intend to introduce legislation at this time, citing the 'small and reducing market and the wider work on high-cost credit'.

[1]   The most important are the Bills of Sale Act 1878 and the Bills of Sale Act (1878) Amendment Act 1882.
[2]   Considered in *Log Book Loans Ltd v OFT* [2011] UKUT 280 (AAC).
[3]   *Bassano v Toft* [2014] CTLC 117.

GREEN DEAL

19.43 Green Deal[1] credit agreements which are regulated agreements are subject to the CCA and CONC, but significant exceptions and qualifications have been made to the legislation in respect of such agreements[2].

[1] See the Energy Act 2011.
[2] CCA 1974, s 189B.

ADVERTISING

19.44 As well as having to comply with general advertising rules and codes (which are outside the scope of this chapter) as well as the law on misleading actions etc (which are discussed elsewhere) financial promotions[1] which indicate that a business is willing to provide credit are regulated by the FCA and, subject to limited exceptions, must comply with stringent requirements set down in CONC 3. Misleading or otherwise inappropriate advertising is obviously an area which could lead to significant consumer detriment and may be an area which particularly interests Trading Standards Departments, especially if they are already investigating the trader in question for other advertising issues under, for example, the Consumer Protection from Unfair Trading Regulations 2008.

[1] That is an invitation or inducement to enter into a credit agreement (or other 'investment activity'.

19.45 CONC 3 applies to a communication to a person in the UK. It will also apply to an unsolicited real time financial promotion unless the communication is from a place, and for the purposes of a business that is only carried on outside the UK. It is immaterial whether the credit agreement or the consumer hire agreement to which the financial promotion or communication relates is subject to the law of a country outside of the UK.

General requirements for all financial promotions

19.46 A firm must ensure that a communication or a financial promotion is clear, fair, and not misleading[1]. A firm must ensure that the communication:

(a)   uses plain and intelligible language;
(b)   is easily legible (or audible as the case may be);
(c)   Specifies the name of the person making the communication or communicating the financial promotion or the person on whose behalf the financial promotion is made; and
(d)   In relation to credit broking, indicates to the customer the identity of the lender (where it is known).

A firm must not suggest or state, expressly or by implication, that credit is available regardless of the customer's financial circumstances or status.

[1] CONC3.3.1R.

19.47 Examples of practices which the FCA considers likely to contravene the clear, fair and not misleading rule are set out in CONC3.3.10G.

Representative example

19.48 If the promotion includes a rate of interest or an amount relating to the cost of credit, whether expressed as a sum of money or a proportion of a specified amount, the financial promotion must also include a representative example and specify a postal address at which the person making the financial promotion may be contacted (this last point does not apply where the financial promotion is communicated by television or radio)[1].

[1] CONC 3.5.3R.

19.49 The representative example must comprise of the following items of information[1]:

(a)   the rate of interest and whether it is fixed, variable or both;
(b)   the nature and amount of any other charge included in the total charge for credit;
(c)   the total amount of credit;
(d)   the representative APR;
(e)   in the case of credit in the form of a deferred payment for specific goods, services, land or other things, the cash price and the amount of any advance payment;
(f)   the duration of the agreement;
(g)   the total amount payable;
(h)   the amount of each repayment of credit.

[1] CONC 3.5.5R.

19.50 This information must be:

(a)   specified in a clear and concise way;
(b)   accompanied by the words 'representative example';
(c)   presented together with each item of information being given equal prominence; and
(d)   given greater prominence than any other information relating to the cost of credit in the financial promotion, except for any statement relating to an obligation to enter into a contract for an ancillary service referred to in CONC 3.5.10 R and any indication or incentive of a kind referred to in CONC 3.5.7 R.

19.51 A number of sensible variations to these rules are made in respect of certain credit agreements; for example, a financial promotion for a credit agreement with no fixed duration is not required to include the duration of the agreement.

Representative APR

19.52 Other financial promotions[1], which do not require the representative example, will still require a representative APR where it:

(1)   indicates that credit is available to persons who might otherwise consider their access to credit restricted;
(2)   includes a favourable comparison, relating to the credit, either express or implied with another person, product or service;

(3)   includes an incentive to apply for or enter into a credit agreement and where the way in which the credit is offered is more favourable than corresponding ways used in any other case[2].

[1]   Excluding financial promotions relating to authorised non-business overdrafts and agreements in respect of which the APR is 0% (CONC 3.5.7R(3)).
[2]   CONC 3.5.7R.

19.53 The representative APR must be given greater prominence than any indication or incentive. The APR must be shown as %APR. Where it is subject to change it must be accompanied by the word 'variable', and the representative APR must be accompanied by the word 'representative'. The financial promotion must state where a security is required and specify the nature of the security. It must also clearly and concisely state where there is an obligation to enter into a contract for an ancillary service.

Other requirements and prohibitions

19.54 A financial promotion must not use the following words and phrases: overdraft (as describing running-account credit unless it is in relation to a current account overdraft), interest free (except where the total amount payable does not exceed the cash price), no deposit (except where no advance payments are to be made), the expression loan guaranteed or pre-approved/no credit checks (except where the agreement is free of any conditions regarding the credit status of the customer), the expression gift or present (except where there are no conditions which would require the customer to repay the credit or to return the item that is the subject of the claim).

19.55 CONC 3.6.5 provides specific wording that must be included in a financial promotion where security comprises or may comprise a mortgage or charge on the customer's home. Failing to comply with the advertising rules in CONC 3 will not give rise to a right of action under the FSMA 2000, s 138D where reasonable steps have been taken to ensure that the financial promotion is clear, fair and not misleading.

Risk warning for high-cost short-term credit

19.56 In addition to complying with the forgoing requirements, financial promotions in relation to high-cost short-term credit[1] must also contain the following risk warning displayed in a prominent way:

Warning: Late repayment can cause you serious money problems. For help, go to moneyadviceservice.org.uk.

[1]   The definition is provided by The Consumer Credit (Consequential and Supplementary Amendments) Instrument 2014 and involves the APR equalling or exceeding 100% and the duration being no longer than 12 months.

19.57 A firm may include the Money Advice Service's registered logo instead of the website address. A financial promotion must not be communicated where it indicates that a firm is willing to provide credit under a regulated restricted-use credit agreement relating to goods or services to be supplied by any person, when at the time the financial promotion is communicated, the firm or any supplier under such agreement does not hold itself out as prepared to sell the goods or provide the services for cash.

PRE-CONTRACTUAL OBLIGATIONS

Assessment of creditworthiness

19.58 CONC 5.2 provides that before making a regulated credit agreement a firm must undertake an assessment of the creditworthiness of a customer. The firm must consider:

(a)   the potential for the commitments under the regulated credit agreement to adversely impact on the customer's financial situation, taking into account the information of which the firm is aware at the time that the regulated credit agreement is to be made;

(b)   the ability of the customer to make repayments as and when they fall due over the life of the regulated credit agreement, or for such an agreement which is an open-end agreement, to make repayments within a reasonable period.

A creditworthiness assessment must be based on sufficient information obtained from the customer and a credit reference agency where necessary[1].

[1]   In *Kerrigan & 11 ors v Elevate Credit International Limited (t/a Sunny) (in administration)* [2020] EWHC 2169 (Comm), the High Court found that a payday lender systemically breached the requirement to conduct an adequate creditworthiness assessment, principally by failing to consider whether the customer's repeat borrowing from D meant that the cumulative effect of its loans adversely impacted the customer's financial situation.

19.59 The rule does not apply to the following agreements:

(a)   an agreement secured on land;

(b)   a pawn agreement;

(c)   a non-commercial agreement;

(d)   a borrower-lender agreement enabling the borrower to overdraw on a current account unless the current account is an authorised business overdraft agreement or an authorised non-business overdraft agreement, or would be but for the fact that the credit is not repayable on demand or within 3 months.

19.60 The FCA made changes to CONC 5 on 1 November 2018 following a consultation conducted in 2017; the updated rules were intended to more clearly distinguish between the consumer centric 'affordability' test and the firm centric 'credit risk' assessment, to ensure good practices and ensure affordability checks are appropriate and proportionate to individual lending decisions. For further information, see the substance of the rules and FCA policy statement PS18/19.

2010 regime: pre-contract information

19.61 Subject to certain exceptions, the 2010 regime applies to agreements entered into on or after 1 February 2011. However, the 2010 regime does not apply to:

(1)   Agreements secured on land to which s 58 CCA 1974 apply (see below);
(2)   Authorised non-business overdraft agreements which are for credit exceeding £60,260 or are secured on land; and
(3)   All other agreements exceeding £60,260, secured on land or entered into predominantly for business purposes *unless* the creditor has 'opted in' and purported to comply with the 2010 regime;

Pre-contract credit information

19.62 Under the 2010 regime, pre-contract information must be drafted in accordance with the Consumer Credit (Disclosure of Information) Regulations 2010 ('the 2010 Disclosure Regulations')[1]. Such information must generally be disclosed by means of the Pre-contract Credit Information (CCI) (see reg 8 and Sch 1). The CCI must be contained in a written form which the debtor can take away. It must include contact details, key features of the credit product, the cost of the credit, other important legal aspects (eg any right of withdrawal) and additional information in the case of distance marketing. Beyond this, any other information must be provided in a separate document, if it relates to the credit (reg 8(4)).

[1]   For guidance on interpretation, see the BIS's 'Guidance on the regulations implementing the Consumer Credit Directive', August 2010, URN 10/1053.

19.63 Regulation 3 sets out the disclosure requirements for all agreements under the 2010 regime except:

•   telephone contracts (which are governed by reg 4)
      (in relation to telephone distance contracts, where the debtor explicitly consents, an abridged set of information can be disclosed before the agreement is made; in relation to non-distance contracts, an even more abridged set of information can be disclosed before the agreement is made; in all cases the CCI must be disclosed immediately after the agreement is made);
•   non-telephone distance contracts[1] where pre-contract information cannot be provided before the agreement is made (governed by reg 5: the CCI must be disclosed immediately after the agreement is made);
•   excluded pawn agreements (reg 9); and
•   overdraft agreements (regs 10–11). Further amendments are made and exclusions provided in respect of certain business agreements.

[1]   Defined in SI 2010/1013, reg 1(2).

19.64 If reg 3 applies, the CCI must be disclosed by the creditor[1] 'in good time before an agreement is made' (cf the wording under the old regime, which simply says 'before'). There are further provisions for 'distance contracts' in reg 7 (requiring the disclosure of the terms and conditions).

[1]   Unless it has already been disclosed by an intermediary: SI 2010/1013, reg 3(3).

19.65 If there is any non-compliance with the requirements to give pre-contract information, the agreement is only enforceable on a court order (CCA 1974, s 55(2)).

Pre-contractual explanations

19.66 In addition to providing the CCI, creditors entering into agreements which fall under the 2010 regime must also provide certain 'pre-contractual explanations'. CONC 4.2.5[1] provides that before making a regulated credit agreement, the firm must place the customer in a position to assess whether the agreement is adapted to the customer's needs and financial situation by providing the customer with an adequate explanation (orally or in writing) of the following:

(a)   the features of the agreement which may make the credit to be provided under the agreement unsuitable for particular types of use;

(b)   how much the customer will have to pay periodically and, where the amount can be determined, in total under the agreement;

(c)   the features of the agreement which may operate in a manner which could have a significant adverse effect on the customer in a way which the customer is unlikely to foresee;

(d)   the principal consequences for the customer arising from a failure to make payments under the agreement at the times required by the agreement including, where applicable and depending on the type and amount of credit and circumstances of the customer the total cost of the debt growing, default charges, interest for late or missed payment, impaired credit rating and its effect on future access to credit, legal proceedings including reference to charging orders and the associated costs of such proceedings, repossession of the customer's home or other property, where an article is taken in pawn, that the article might be sold, if not redeemed;

(e)   the effect of the exercise of any right to withdraw from the agreement and how and when this right may be exercised.

[1]   Which replaces CCA 1974, s 55A.

19.67 The firm must also advise the customer to consider the draft credit agreement and where the information is disclosed in person, that the customer is able to take it away. The firm must provide the customer with an opportunity to ask questions about the agreement and advise the customer how to ask for further information and explanation. The option of giving the explanation orally or in writing is qualified by CONC 4.2.5(4) which provides that if certain matters are stated orally, certain other matters must also be stated orally.

19.68 Where a firm is credit broking in relation to a regulated credit agreement the firm must:

(a)   disclose to the customer the fee, if any payable by a customer to the firm for its services;

(b)   any fee must be agreed between the customer and the firm, and the agreement must be recorded in writing or other durable medium before a regulated credit agreement is entered into;

(c)   the firm must disclose the fee to the lender, to enable the lender to calculate the annual percentage rate of charge for the credit agreement;

(d)   a firm must disclose to the customer how and when any fee for its service is payable and in what circumstances a refund may be payable.

Section 55C copy of draft agreement

19.69 Before a regulated agreement is made, a creditor is obliged 'if requested' to give the debtor 'without delay' a copy of the prospective agreement (or such of its terms as have at that time been reduced to writing). The obligation does not arise if the creditor is 'unwilling' at the time of the request to proceed with the agreement. In contrast to the other additional pre-contract obligations, it is expressly provided that breach of the CCA 1974, s 55C obligation gives rise to an action for breach of statutory duty (CCA 1974, s 55C(3)).

Old regime: pre-contract information

19.70 Agreements that do not fall within the 2010 regime must comply with the Consumer Credit (Disclosure of Information) Regulations 2004 ('the 2004 Disclosure Regulations'). Such documents look very similar to regulated agreements, save that the signature boxes are omitted. Estimated information may be given if the exact information is as yet unknown[1].

[1]   SI 2004/1481, s 3(2).

19.71 Regulation 3 of the 2004 Disclosure Regulations merely requires the pre-contract information to be given 'before' the agreement is made. Theoretically this permits it to be given to the debtor along with the copy of the agreement for him to sign, although this would render the pre-contract information redundant, as the debtor is also given a CCA 1974, s 62 copy of the unexecuted agreement at this stage. If there is any non-compliance with the requirements to give pre-contract information, the agreement is only enforceable on a court order (CCA 1974, s 55(2)).

Secured agreements

19.72 Secured agreements to which CCA 1974, s 58 applies do not attract the requirement to give pre-contract information, as in such cases the debtor must already be given a consideration copy of the agreement pursuant to CCA 1974, s 58.

19.73 The consideration copy must contain a prescribed notice indicating the debtor's right to withdraw from the prospective agreement. The creditor must also provide a copy of any other document 'referred to' in the unexecuted agreement, such as a legal charge. Following the provision of the consideration documents, there follows a 'consideration period' of 7–14 days during which the creditor must not contact the debtor except in response to a specific request by him (CCA 1974, s 61(2)). On/after the first 7 days of the consideration period, the creditor must send the debtor a copy of the unexecuted agreement for his signature, presuming no notice of withdrawal has been received (CCA 1974, s 61(2)(b) and (d)). The consideration period then expires when the debtor returns the signed agreement or 7 days after the signature copy was sent, whichever is sooner (CCA 1974, s 61(3)).

19.74 In the event of non-compliance with these provisions, the agreement is only enforceable on a court order (CCA 1974, ss 61(2) and 65).

FORM AND CONTENT OF AGREEMENTS

19.75 Save for limited exceptions (for example in the case of overdrafts; see section 74 CCA 1974), credit agreements are required to comply with very detailed provisions regulating the drafting of agreements, set out in subordinate regulations. CCA 1974, s 61(1)(a) provides that a regulated agreement is 'not properly executed' unless it conforms to these regulations. The consequences of an agreement being 'improperly executed' are that it is only enforceable against the debtor on an order of the court (CCA 1974, s 65). In some cases, for agreements entered into pre-6 April 2007, the unenforceability can be irredeemable. Consequently, ensuring that an agreement is properly drafted and complies with form and content requirements can be particularly important.

19.76 This chapter can only offer a rough guide to the extremely detailed legislative provisions on the drafting of credit and hire agreements. At the outset, it should be noted that consumer credit agreements are constructed around several basic financial concepts, which include:

- the amount of credit (ie the amount of the advance in a fixed-sum agreement);
- the total charge for credit ('the TCC') (interest and other charges);
- the total amount payable ('the TAP') (the sum total of the amount of credit and TCC).

These will be discussed in further detail below.

Deciding which regime applies

19.77 As with the disclosure of information, there are now two sets of regulations which govern the form and content of credit agreements: the Consumer Credit (Agreements) Regulations 1983 ('the 1983 Agreements Regulations') and the Consumer Credit (Agreements) Regulations 2010 ('the 2010 Agreements Regulations').

19.78 The 2010 Agreements Regulations implement the Consumer Credit Directive 2008/48/EC ('the CC Directive') and came into force on 1 February 2011. However, there was an earlier 'opt-in' date from 30 April 2010 for creditors who were prepared to implement the new regime in advance[1].

[1] Consumer Credit (EU Directive) Regulations 2010, SI 2010/1010, reg 101: any one of certain conditions must be satisfied in order to opt-in to the new regime early.

19.79 Some types of credit agreements are outside the scope of the CC Directive. The 2010 regime treats these agreements as excluded agreements. These excluded agreements would normally fall within the old, 1983, regime but creditors may once again choose to opt-in to the 2010 regime. This helpfully permits creditors who would be entering into agreements within the new regime and agreements outside the new regime to 'opt in' and align their documentation and processes.

19.80 The following types of agreements are excluded from the scope of the 2010 Agreements Regulations (reg 2(1A) and (3)):

(i)   agreements secured on land to which CCA 1974, s 58 does apply, where the creditor gives the debtor an advance copy of the agreement containing the prescribed notice of his right to withdraw;

(ii)   agreements secured on land to which CCA 1974, s 58 does not apply (mortgages to finance the purchase of the land and agreements for bridging loans in connection with the purchase of land);

(iii)   agreements for credit exceeding £60,260;

(iv)   'business agreements' (entered wholly/predominantly for the purposes of a business carried on/intended to be carried on by the debtor).

In addition, hire agreements are not covered by the 2010 Agreements Regulations, which only refer to 'credit agreements'.

19.81 Accordingly, the 1983 Agreements Regulations[1] apply to the following agreements:

(i)   all credit agreements made before 30 April 2010;

(ii)   credit agreements made between 30 April 2010 and 31 January 2011, unless the creditor has opted to implement the new regime early;

(iii)   credit agreements entered on/after 1 February 2011, where the agreements are outside the scope of the 2010 regime (and the creditor has not 'opted in' to the 2010 regime);

(iv)   all regulated hire agreements, whenever made.

[1]   See SI 1983/1552, reg 8.

19.82 The 2010 regime applies in the following situations:

(i)   all credit agreements made on/after 1 February 2011 which are within the scope of the 2010 regime;

(ii)   credit agreements made between 30 April 2010 and 31 January 2011, where the creditor has opted to implement the new regime early;

(iii)   credit agreements entered on/after 1 February 2011, where the agreements are outside the scope of the 2010 regime and the creditor chooses to 'opt in' to the 2010 regime.

Opting-in

19.83 If an agreement is outside the scope of the 2010 Agreements Regulations, the creditor can nonetheless 'opt-in' (reg 2(2)) by disclosing pre-contract credit information in compliance or purported compliance with the Consumer Credit (Disclosure of Information) Regulations 2010 (rather than in compliance with the predecessor regulations on disclosure). This right to opt-in cannot be exercised for overdraft agreements (reg 2(4)), which broadly only need to comply with the form and content provisions in reg 8.

1983 Agreements Regulations: order and presentation

19.84 Relatively few agreements still fall to be drafted in accordance with the 1983 Regulations and it is relatively rare to see them in practice. Accordingly, this chapter will not dwell on the detailed requirements but will simply highlight some of the most notable differences with the modern, 2010 regime which will be discussed in further detail. If further information is required on the requirements of the old regulations, reference should be made to Guest and Lloyd's *Encyclopedia of Consumer Credit Law and The Law of Consumer Credit and Hire* by Philpott et al.

19.85 In contrast to the 2010 regime, the 1983 regime required certain information to be shown together in a certain order. This group of information was referred to as the 'holy ground and could not be interspersed with other information (except subtotals of sums and cross-references to terms) or preceded by any information (other than trade names, logos and the agreement number). In addition further information was required by various Schedules to the Regulations and certain prescribed statements of protection and remedies under the CCA 1974 which must be exactly replicated. The form and type of signature box was also closely prescribed and there were detailed and complex prominence requirements.

2010 Agreements Regulations: order and presentation

19.86 All regulated consumer credit agreements falling within the new regime must contain all the Sch 1 'information' (in so far as it is applicable to the type of agreement in question) (reg 3(1)). In contrast to the position under the 1983 Agreements Regulations, there is no prescribed order or 'holy ground' within which this information must be set out.

19.87 The Sch 1 information must be presented in a 'clear and concise' manner and 'clear' means inter alia that the wording be 'easily legible' and of a colour which is easily distinguishable from the background (reg 3(2)–(3)). However, there is no express prohibition on interspersing (as under the 1983 Agreements Regulations). Further, the majority[1] of regulated agreements must contain the 'Forms' of Statements of protection and remedies under the CCA available to debtors set out in Sch 2 (reg 3(4)).

[1]   This requirement does not apply to secured agreements to which CCA 1974, s 58 applies, where there are no charges forming part of the TCC.

19.88 The wording of any of the applicable Forms in Sch 2 must be reproduced on the agreement 'without any alteration' (reg 7(1))[1]. In contrast to the 1983 Agreements Regulations, 'additions' are not expressly prohibited. There is no corresponding requirement to reproduce the exact wording of 'information' in Sch 1[2]. Where any such Form uses capital lettering, those words must be afforded more prominence than the other words in the Form, and no less prominence than that given to other information in the agreement (except the heading etc) (reg 7(4)). There are special provisions on the drafting of multiple agreements[3] and modifying agreements[4], which are outside the scope of this chapter.

[1]   Save for the very limited deviations permitted by SI 2010/1014, reg 7(1).
[2]   *Wilson v Hurstanger* [2007] CTLC 59: describing the amount of credit as 'net amount of loan' was permissible.
[3]   See, eg, SI 2010/1014, reg 3(6)–(7).
[4]   SI 2010/1014, reg 5.

Both regimes: comments on various pieces of information

Amount of credit

19.89 All fixed-sum credit agreements must include a term stating the amount of credit[1]. If this figure is wrongly stated, the agreement will be unenforceable without a court order; further, from a trading standards' perspective the consumer may have been significantly misled as to the amount they were borrowing and the nature of the agreement they were entering.

[1]   1983 Agreements Regulations, SI 1983/1552, Sch 1, para 2; 2010 Agreements Regulations, SI 2010/1014, Sch 1, paras 5 and 6.

19.90 The amount of credit does not include any item falling within the TCC, even if time is allowed for its payment (CCA 1974, s 9(4)). Therefore, even if a charge is added to the amount of the advance (as a front-loading charge), it will not be part of the amount of credit.

19.91 In *Wilson v First County Trust Ltd (No 1)*[1], a 'document fee' of £250 was added to the £5,000 advance, as the debtor did not wish to pay it at the outset. The amount of credit was stated to be £5,250, which the Court of Appeal held to be non-compliant, as the document fee was part of the TCC.

[1]   [2001] QB 407.

19.92 Fees deducted from the amount of the advance should also not be included in the amount of credit: the amount of credit must be the net advance made to the debtor. In agreements secured on land premiums for payment protection insurance should be stated as an amount of credit, where the insurance is not required by the creditor as a condition of the loan[1]. Other insurance premiums will also be part of the amount of credit (but mortgage indemnity fees will not)[2].

[1]   CONC Appendix 1.1.5(c).
[2]   *Griffiths v Welcome Financial Services* [2007] CTLC 37.

19.93 In *McGinn v Grangewood Securities Ltd*[1] the small-print of the agreement required any arrears on the debtor's first mortgage to be discharged on/before completion of the loan. The balance of the advance would then be paid to the debtor. The Court of Appeal held that the amount of the advance used to discharge the arrears was part of the TCC and should not have been included in the amount of credit. The 'purpose' of the loan for the debtor was home improvements, not to clear her arrears (which she was unaware existed).

[1]   [2002] EWCA Civ 522.

19.94 *McGinn* was confined to its peculiar facts in the subsequent case of *London North Securities v Meadows*[1], where the debtors were informed that clearing the arrears on their first mortgage was a condition of the loan. The Court of Appeal held that clearing the arrears was one of the 'objective purposes of the transaction' and therefore that payment was properly treated as part of the amount of credit[2].

1   [2005] EWCA Civ 956.
2   See also *Watchtower Investments v Payne* [2001] EWCA Civ 1159: sums advanced to discharge the arrears under a previous agreement were part of the 'credit', as they formed part of the 'objective purpose' of the loan.

19.95 The label 'amount of credit' need not be used. In assessing whether the agreement contains a 'term stating the amount of credit' there is case law to the effect that the document must be considered as a whole and the constituent information need not be in one place: it suffices if the debtor can calculate the amount of credit from the financial information provided and 'knowledge' that the amount of credit excludes items in the TCC[1].

1   *Ocwen v Hughes; Igroup UK Loans Ltd v Freel* [2004] CCLR 4; but cf the stricter approach in *Central Trust plc v Spurway* [2005] CCLR 1 where it was thought a lay reader should not have to attempt his own calculation; both were county court decisions.

19.96 In *Hurstanger Ltd v Wilson*[1], the Court of Appeal held that it was a matter of construction whether the agreement contained a 'term' stating the amount of credit: this was a term 'which the parties (with the benefit of legal advice if necessary) and/or the court can identify within the four corners of the agreement'. However, in that case the agreement did set out a figure which was the amount of credit (albeit described as 'net amount of loan').

1   [2007] 1 WLR 2351, CTLC 59.

Total charge for credit

19.97 All agreements must show a total amount payable figure; this is the total of the amount of credit and the total charge for credit ('TCC'). This figure is obviously important as it allows a debtor to clearly see how much the credit is going to cost them and how much they need to repay. If this figure is incorrectly stated, the agreement will be unenforceable without a court order and, depending on the error, other consumer protection provisions may have been breached.

19.98 The Total Charge for Credit Regulations have been replaced by CONC Appendix 1. The TCC is the total of the amounts determined as at the date of making the credit agreement of such of the following charges:

(a)   the total of the interest on the credit which may be provided under the credit agreement;

(b)   other charges at any time payable under the transaction by or on behalf of the borrower or a relative of his whether to the lender or any other person; and

(c)   (for land secured agreements) a premium under a contract of insurance, payable under the transaction by the borrower or a relative of his, where the making or maintenance of the contract of insurance is required by the lender as a condition of making the credit agreement, and for the sole purpose of ensuring complete or partial repayment of the credit and complete or partial payment to the lender of such of those charges included in the total charge for credit as are payable to him under the transaction, in the event of the death, invalidity, illness or unemployment or the borrower, notwithstanding that the whole part of the charge may be repayable at any time or that the consideration therefore may include matters not within the transaction or subsisting at a time not within the duration of the credit agreement.

19.99 Items excluded from the TCC include:

(a) any charge payable under the transaction to the lender upon failure by the borrower or a relative of his to do or to refrain from doing anything which he is required to do or to refrain from doing, as the case may be;

(b) any charge which is payable by the lender to any person upon failure by the borrower or a relative of his to do or to refrain from doing anything which he is required under the transaction to do or to refrain from doing, as the case may be, and which the lender may under the transaction require the borrower or a relative of his to pay to him or to another person on his behalf;

(c) any charge relating to a credit agreement to finance a transaction of a description referred to in the definition of restricted-use credit agreement, being a charge which would be payable if the transaction were for cash;

(d) any charge (other than a fee or commission charged by a credit broker) not within (c) above of a description which relates to services or benefits incidental to the credit agreement and also to other services or benefits which may be supplied to the borrower, and which is payable pursuant to an obligation incurred by the borrower under arrangements effected before he applies to enter into the credit agreement, not being arrangements under which the borrower is bound to enter into any credit agreement;

(e) any charge under arrangements for the care, maintenance or protection of any land or goods where the services are to be performed after the date of making the credit agreement and the condition of the land or goods becomes or is in immediate danger of becoming such that the land or goods cannot reasonably be enjoyed or used and the charge will not accrue unless the services are performed, or such provision is available under comparable arrangements from a person chosen by the borrower, and if the consent of the lender is required, the transaction provides that such consent may not be unreasonably withheld;

(f) charges for money transmission services relating to an arrangement for a current account, being charges which vary with the use made by the borrower of the arrangement;

(g) any charge for a guarantee other than a guarantee which is required by the lender as a condition of making the credit agreement, and the purpose of which is to ensure complete or partial repayment of the credit, and complete or partial payment to the lender of such of those charges included in the total charge for credit as are payable to him under the transaction, in the event of the death, invalidity, illness or unemployment of the borrower;

(h) charges for the transfer of funds (other than charges within (f) above) and charges for keeping an account intended to receive payments towards the repayment of the credit and the payment of interest and other charges, except where the borrower does not have reasonable freedom of choice in the matter and where such charges are abnormally high; but this sub-paragraph does not exclude from the total charge for credit charges for collection of the payments to which it refers, whether such payments are made in cash or otherwise;

(i) a premium under a contract of insurance other than a contract of insurance referred to in CONC App 1.1.5R(c).

19.100 CONC App 1.2.5 sets down various assumptions for calculations. These include that for running account agreements it is assumed that the entire credit limit is drawn down and repaid in 12 equal monthly instalments. Where the credit limit is not known, it is assumed to be £1,200.

Credit limit

19.101 Agreements for running-account credit do not include any 'amount of credit', but must instead state the credit limit, which may be expressed as[1]:

(a) a sum of money;

(b) a statement that the credit limit will be determined by the creditor from time to time under the agreement (and that notice of it will be given to the debtor)[2];

(c) a sum of money, together with a statement that the creditor may vary the credit limit to such sum as he may from time to time determine under the agreement (and that notice of it will be given to the debtor); or

(d) in a case not within (a), (b) or (c), either a statement indicating the manner in which the credit limit will be determined and that notice of it will be given to the debtor, or a statement indicating that there is no credit limit.

---

[1] 1983 Agreements Regulations, SI 1983/1552, Sch 1, para 8; 2010 Agreements Regulations, SI 2010/1014, Sch 1, para 7.

[2] Whilst the 1983 Regulations were not this flexible, in *Brophy v HFC Bank Ltd* [2011] EWCA Civ 67, [2010] CTLC 10 it was held that a statement that the credit limit will be determined from time to time and notified to the debtor was sufficient.

19.102 Under a running-account agreement, the 'credit limit' is the maximum amount up to which the debtor may draw (CCA 1974, s 10(2)). Therefore it is irrelevant for the purposes of determining the credit limit whether the draw-downs include items which are part of the TCC and are not 'credit'.

APR

19.103 The annual percentage rate or 'APR' is a figure designed to provide debtors with a guide as to how much borrowing will cost them over the course of a year. The APR is calculated using the equation in CONC App 1.2.6 R and the assumptions in CONC App 1.2.5R; given this standardised methodology, the APR is a figure which allows debtors to compare different credit products. Importantly, when a representative APR is used in a financial promotion, it must be an APR 'at or below which the firm communicating or approving the financial promotion reasonably expects, at the date on which the promotion is communicated or approved, that credit would be provided under at least 51% of the credit agreements which will be entered into as a result of the promotion' (the 51% rule)[1].

1   CONC 3.5.6G(1A) and the Glossary definition of 'representative APR'.

Interest rate

19.104 Under the 2010 Agreements Regulations the interest rate[1], APR, charges and total amount payable must all be stated but there is no separate requirements to list the TCC[2].

1   And, where applicable, any rate on which it is based, together with the conditions governing the application of the rate, the period during which the rate will apply and the conditions and procedure for changing the rate.
2   See Sch 1 to the 2010 Regulations.

19.105 Neither the 2010 Agreements Regulations nor the earlier Regulations 'purport to dictate how the interest rate is to be expressed'[1] (eg flat, 'present value', nominal, simple or compound). In order not to mislead, the type of rate should be carefully selected and identified. A flat rate can be misleading, as it takes no account of the reduction of the outstanding balance through repayments over time. On the other hand, a flat rate is more comprehensible to the average debtor.

1   *Sternlight v Barclays Bank plc* [2010] EWHC 1865, [2010] CTLC 115, in relation to the 1983 Agreements Regulations.

19.106 In *Brooks v Northern Rock (Asset Management) plc*[1], it was held that the 1983 Agreements Regulations left the creditor free to cite either a nominal or effective interest rate 'or indeed some other rate'. The court also held that the interest rate could be cited to any number of decimal places and there was no need to round up (but in the case of agreements not secured on land see CONC App 1.1.2.6(3)(f)).

1   Unreported, Oldham County Court, 16 April 2010 (this case concerned the 1983 Regulations but there is no reason why a similar approach would not be taken to the 2010 Regulations).

Timings and amounts of repayments

19.107 Under the 2010 Agreements Regulations, regulated agreements must include the number (if applicable) and frequency of repayments[1] and the amount of each repayment expressed as:

(a)   a sum of money;
(b)   a specified proportion of a specified amount (including the amount outstanding from time to time);
(c)   a combination of (a) and (b) above; or
(d)   in a case where the amount of any repayment cannot be expressed in accordance with (a), (b) or (c), a statement indicating the manner in which the amount will be determined.

1   Sch 1, para 14. In *Home Credit Slovakia as v Biroova* (C-42/15) [2017] CTLC 31 the CJEU held that the agreement need not indicate the specific date on which every payment is to be made providing that the terms allow the consumer to ascertain the dates of those payments without difficulty and with certainty.

19.108 In *Wilson v Hurstanger Ltd*[1], the agreement stated that a £295 charge was repayable upon termination, plus 1.29% interest per month on the charge. Since the agreement had a fixed term, the creditor could theoretically have stated the total sum payable in respect of this charge upon termination (and therefore subparagraph (d) above did not apply). The Court of Appeal held that there was a failure to state the information in this paragraph compliantly, as the debtor was left to make the calculation himself.

[1]   [2007] EWCA Civ 299, [2007] CTLC 59 (this case concerned the 1983 Regulations but there is no reason why a similar approach would not be taken to the 2010 Regulations).

19.109 If subparagraph (d) does apply, it is arguable that the creditor could simply state that the amount of the repayment will be determined at its discretion and notified to the debtor, without providing any formula[1].

[1]   Guest and Lloyd, *Encyclopaedia of Consumer Credit Law*, vol 1, 3136/8–9.

Variable items/rates

19.110 Under the 2010 Agreements Regulations, the paragraphs of Sch 1 relating to the interest rate and charges (paras 11 and 18) both require the agreement to specify the 'conditions' under which a variation may occur. Further, para 13, which relates to the APR, requires the agreement to set out all the assumptions used to calculate that rate.

19.111 The agreement in *Lombard Tricity Finance Ltd v Paton*[1] displayed an asterisk beside certain items indicating that they were 'subject to variation by the creditor from time to time on notification as required by law'. The Court of Appeal held that this satisfied the requirements of para 19 of Sch 1 to the 1983 Agreements Regulations, as the creditor's discretion to vary was genuinely unfettered. This case was disapproved in *Paragon Finance plc v Nash and Staunton*[2], on the ground that the creditor's discretion to vary an interest rate is subject to an implied term that it will not vary it arbitrarily or in a way no reasonable lender would.

[1]   [1989] 1 All ER 918.
[2]   [2002] 1 WLR 685.

19.112 In *McGinn v Grangewood Securities Ltd*[1], the agreement stated that the creditor might defer payment of legal fees 'at its discretion'. In fact, payment of the fees was only deferred on condition that contractual interest was payable on the fees. The agreement was held to be non-compliant, as it failed to state that deferment would be made only on condition that interest was paid, and failed to specify the rate of that interest.

[1]   [2002] EWCA Civ 522 (this case concerned the 1983 Regulations but there is no reason why a similar approach would not be taken to the 2010 Regulations)

Default charges

19.113 Under the 2010 Agreements Regulations, the agreement must identify any 'charges deriving from the credit agreement' (Sch 1, para 18) and any charges and interest applicable upon late payment (Sch 1, para 19). A broad construction of 'charges' was given in *Rank Xerox v Hepple*[1] to include sums payable under an accelerated payment clause and common law damages payable upon default.

[1]   [1994] CCLR 1 (on the old, 1983 Regulations).

Both Agreements Regulations: prescribed terms

19.114 Under the 1983 Regulations the terms specified in Sch 6 were designated 'prescribed terms' by reg 6(1). Those terms are as follows:

(a)   the amount of credit (for fixed-sum credit agreements);

(b)   the credit limit (for running-account credit);

(c)   the interest rate (for running-account credit or limited types of fixed-sum[1] credit);

(d)   a term stating how the repayment obligations must be discharged.

[1]   Those falling within the exceptions in SI 1983/1552, Sch 1, para 9(a)–(c).

19.115 In the 2010 Agreements Regulations, reg 4 designates certain items of Sch 1 information as 'prescribed terms'. These are the same terms as those in Sch 6 to the 1983 Agreements Regulations (save that the interest rate is prescribed for all types of regulated credit agreement).

19.116 In respect of agreements entered prior to 6 April 2007, the 'prescribed terms' had enormous significance, as an agreement which failed to contain all the prescribed terms was 'irredeemably unenforceable' under CCA 1974, s 127(3). However, following the repeal of CCA 1974, s 127(3), for agreements entered after 6 April 2007 it appears that 'prescribed terms' have no different status from any other terms of the agreement.

Single document

19.117 There is a practical question as to whether the full terms and conditions may be provided on a separate sheet from the face of the agreement. CCA 1974, s 61(1)(a) requires a properly executed agreement to be 'a document . . . itself containing all the prescribed terms'. Therefore the prescribed terms must be contained in the same 'document' as the agreement.

19.118 In *Carey v HSBC Bank Plc*[1], HHJ Waksman QC considered the question of what constituted a single document for the purposes of CCA 1974, s 61, and concluded (at paras 171–174) a document need not be a single piece of paper; the question of what constitutes a document is a question of substance and not form; and a physical connection between several pieces of paper is not necessary in order for them to constitute one document. This approach focusing on the substance of the documentation provided is obviously sensible when considering the consumer credit regime within the wider context of consumer protection.

[1]   [2009] EWHC 3417 (QB), [2009] CTLC 103.

19.119 In respect of the other terms and conditions (ie terms which are not 'prescribed'), the requirement is only that they be 'embodied' in the agreement, and not necessarily contained in the same 'document' (CCA 1974, s 61(1)(b)). The CCA 1974, s 189(4) provides:

> (4) A document embodies a provision if the provision is set out either in the document itself or in another document referred to in it.

Therefore the agreement may cross-reference a booklet of full terms and conditions. The terms and conditions which are embodied in the agreement should be all of the express terms which form the relationship between the parties (ie including all terms, including those not required by the Regulations).

Signing

19.120 The agreement must be signed by the debtor/hirer[1] in the designated signature box (for the 2010 regime 'in the space in the document indicated for the purpose')[2]. E-signatures are acceptable[3]. The requirements are more lax for the creditor: the signature may be inserted on its 'behalf' and may be added anywhere on the agreement (as long as it is outside the debtor's signature box)[4]. The creditor's signature is often stamped rather than handwritten.

[1] Subject to CCA 1974, s 61(4) re partnerships.
[2] SI 2010/1014, reg 4(3)(a).
[3] See **19.122** below.
[4] SI 2010/1014, reg 4(3)(b).

19.121 For agreements entered prior to 6 April 2007, the agreement will be irredeemably unenforceable if not signed by the debtor in the prescribed manner (CCA 1974, s 127(3) – there is no equivalent effect if the creditor fails to sign). If any agreement is unsigned by the creditor, or if any agreement entered on/after 6 April 2007 is unsigned by the debtor, the agreement will be enforceable only on an order of the court under CCA 1974, s 127(1). The date of signature should also be inserted by both parties, but this is not a strict requirement where the agreement is not cancellable and the last party to sign[1] dates his signature[2].

[1] Ie the party who makes the agreement 'executed' (usually the creditor).
[2] SI 2010/1014, reg 4(3)(c).

19.122 An agreement will only be 'executed' under CCA 1974, s 61 once it has been signed by both parties, but it may nonetheless be a 'concluded' agreement under the contractual principles of offer and acceptance without the creditor's signature (eg if the creditor has performed some other act such as delivering the subject goods to the customer)[1]. Regulated agreements may be signed by electronic means, but there is no statutory guidance on permissible forms of electronic signatures and an online click should suffice[2].

[1] *Carlyle Finance Ltd v Pallas Industrial Finance Ltd* [1999] 1 All ER (Comm) 659 (such an analysis may be required in order to determine whether and when title to goods has passed).
[2] See the Consumer Credit Act 1974 (Electronic Communications) Order 2004, SI 2004/3236; the CCA definition of 'document' is now 'information recorded in any form'. Guest and Lloyd, *Encyclopaedia of Consumer Credit Law*, vol 1, 2095 and Philpott 'E-commerce and Consumer Credit' [2001] JLFM 131. See also *Bassano v Toft* [2014] CTLC 117.

Copies of agreement: old regime

19.123 Under the old regime, creditors were required, depending on the circumstances, to provide the debtor with various copies of the agreement in accordance with CCA 1974, ss 62 to 64. In particular, the credit was obliged:

(a)   to supply a CCA 1974, s 62 copy of the unexecuted agreement (unless the agreement is presented personally to the debtor for his signature and the creditor has already signed it, or signs at the same time);

(b)   to supply a CCA 1974, s 63 copy of the executed agreement (unless the agreement is sent to the debtor for his signature and the creditor has already signed it).

19.124 These copies were required to include a copy of any other document 'referred to' in the credit agreement (eg a legal charge) and were subject to strict form and content requirements[1] and must contain the prescribed cancellation notices. Overdrafts are again exempt (CCA 1974, s 74).

1   Consumer Credit (Cancellation Notices and Copies of Documents) Regulations 1983.

19.125 Non-compliance with CCA 1974, ss 62, 63 or 64 renders the agreement unenforceable save on a court order (CCA 1974, ss 62–65). In some pre-6 April 2007 situations for cancellable agreements a failure may result in irredeemable unenforceability under the repealed CCA 1974, s 127(4)[1].

1   See *Goshawk Dedicated (No 2) v Bank of Scotland* [2006] 2 All ER 610 and *Bank of Scotland v Euclidian Ltd (No 1)* [2007] CTLC 151.

Copies of agreement: 2010 regime

19.126 Under the new regime, CCA 1974, s 61A obliges the creditor to give the debtor a copy of the 'executed agreement' (and any other document referred to in it). This must be done where the agreement 'has been made' (CCA 1974, s 61A(1)). There is no prescribed time limit.

19.127 The obligation to provide a copy of the executed agreement does not arise if the debtor has already been given an unexecuted copy, which is in identical terms to the executed agreement (CCA 1974, s 61A(2)). In such a case, the creditor must write to the debtor to state this, and inform him of his right to request an executed copy within 14 days (CCA 1974, s 61A(3)).

19.128 Where the creditor signs first and then posts the agreement to the debtor to sign, the natural reading of CCA 1974, s 61A is that, after the debtor returns the signed agreement, the creditor must then either post an executed copy or write to the debtor under CCA 1974, s 61A(3). However, such an interpretation increases the creditor's obligations compared to those under the old regime, where no s 63 executed copy need be provided in this situation[1]. Copies of overdraft agreements are separately dealt with by CCA 1974, s 61B.

1   See Guest and Lloyd, *Encyclopaedia of Consumer Credit Law*, vol 1, 2098.

19.129 The CCA 1974, ss 61A and 61B copies must comply with the Consumer Credit (Cancellation Notices and Copies of Documents) Regulations

1983 (where applicable). Non-compliance with ss 61A and 61B renders the agreement unenforceable save on a court order (CCA 1974, ss 61A, 61B and 65). The CCA 1974, s 61A does not apply to cancellable agreements; the old CCA 1974, ss 62–63 regime applies to such agreements (CCA 1974, s 61A(5)).

WITHDRAWAL AND CANCELLATION

Section 66A withdrawal

19.130 The CCA 1974, s 66A applies from 1 February 2011 to all credit agreements except 'excluded agreements'[1]. It provides a 14-day right of 'withdrawal' to debtors. In order to exercise this right, the debtor must give the creditor oral[2] or written notice of withdrawal within the 14 days beginning with the day after 'the relevant day'. 'The relevant day' is whichever is the latest of (a) the day the agreement is made, (b) the day the creditor first informs the debtor of the credit limit[3] or (c) the day the debtor receives a CCA 1974, ss 61A and 63 copy of the executed agreement, or receives the written CCA 1974, s 61A(3) information[4]. In *JC v Kreissparkasse Saarlouis*[5] the CJEU ruled that consumer credit agreements must include clear and concise information on how the period for withdrawal is to be calculated. Reference to national provisions which require further reference to other provisions would not be suffice for the purposes of providing this information.

[1] Agreements for credit exceeding £60,260; agreements secured on land; hire agreements; restricted-use credit agreements to finance the purchase of land and agreements for bridging loans in connection with the purchase of land (CCA 1974, s 66A(14)).
[2] Oral notice must be given in any manner specified by the agreement: CCA 1974, s 61A(4).
[3] Where the creditor is required to inform the debtor of the credit limit.
[4] If CCA 1974, s 61A/s 63 respectively applies.
[5] Case C-66/19.

19.131 If the debtor exercises his right to withdraw, the credit agreement (and any ancillary service contract)[1] is treated as never having been entered (CCA 1974, s 66A(7)). Crucially, the debtor must repay any advance (plus accrued interest at the contractual rate); this must be repaid within 30 days of giving notice of withdrawal (CCA 1974, s 66A(9) and (10)). Only the credit agreement is erased: if the credit was extended to finance a sale/supply contract, then that contract will remain valid and the purchase price will have to be paid to the supplier by the debtor.

[1] For example, a PPI policy.

19.132 The CCA 1974, s 66A(11) expressly provides that in the case of hire-purchase, conditional sale or credit sale, the debtor who chooses to withdraw and repay the advance (effectively the purchase price) will gain title to the goods 'on the same terms as would have applied had the debtor not withdrawn'. If the debtor fails to repay the credit within 30 days, it is unclear whether (i) the debtor is entitled to retain possession of any goods and (ii) when title will pass to the debtor (eg may title only pass if he makes payment within 30 days, or will title pass whenever payment is finally made?)[1].

[1] For an analysis of this uncertainty, see Guest and Lloyd, *Encyclopaedia of Consumer Credit Law*, vol 1, 2112–3.

Section 67 cancellable agreements

19.133 From 1 February 2011 (when CCA 1974, s 66A came into effect), the CCA 1974, s 67 cancellation rights only apply to[1]:

- regulated agreements where the amount of credit exceeds £60,620; and
- regulated hire agreements.

Even within these two categories, CCA 1974, s 67 does not apply to overdrafts[2], or in cases where the agreement is signed on trade premises[3]. Additionally, CCA 1974, s 67 does not apply to agreements secured on land or to restricted-use agreements to finance the purchase of land or bridging loans to purchase land (CCA 1974, s 67(1)(a)).

[1]   See CCA 1974, ss 66A(14), 67(1)(a) and (2).
[2]   CCA 1974, s 67 does not apply to agreements listed in CCA 1974, s 74, which includes overdrafts and non-commercial agreements.
[3]   CCA 1974, ss 67(1)(b) and s 67 does not apply where the agreement is signed at premises where any of the following is carrying on business: the creditor/owner, any party to a linked transaction, or the negotiator in antecedent negotiations.

19.134 Where CCA 1974, s 67 does apply, the agreement is only cancellable if the 'antecedent negotiations'[1] included 'oral representations[2] made when in the presence of the debtor/hirer' by an 'individual acting as, or on behalf of the negotiator' (ie face-to-face negotiations). The main situations in which an agreement will be cancellable are therefore doorstep sales and where the negotiations occur on trade premises, but the debtor takes the agreement home to sign.

[1]   'Antecedent negotiations' is defined in CCA 1974, s 56(1).
[2]   See *Moorgate Services Ltd v Kabir* [1995] CCLR 74, where the Court of Appeal narrowed the definition of 'representation' to a statement of fact/opinion, or an undertaking as to the future, which was capable of inducing the debtor/hirer to enter the agreement.

19.135 Agreements are only cancellable if the face-to-face negotiations were conducted by the 'negotiator'. Following the definition of 'negotiator' in CCA 1974, s 56(1), this can generally only include a dealer or credit-broker where the agreement is DCS. In the case of DC or hire agreements, only the creditor or its employee can be the 'negotiator' (unless, unusually, the dealer or credit-broker has actual/ostensible authority to act as the agent of the creditor)[1].

[1]   See *Woodchester Leasing Equipment v Clayton (RM) and Clayton (DM) (t/a Sudbury Sports)* [1994] 4 CLY 506: held supplier was acting as agent of hire company when making representations, so agreement was cancellable.

19.136 Where an agreement is cancellable, the debtor must be given a pre-contract document in accordance with the 2010 or 2004 Disclosure Regulations. The agreement itself must include the prescribed[1] notice of cancellation rights and this notice must also be included in the CCA 1974, ss 62–63 copies of the unexecuted and executed agreements given to the debtor (CCA 1974, s 64)[2].

[1]   See the Consumer Credit (Cancellation Notices and Copies of Documents) Regulations 1983, SI 1983/1557.
[2]   Where CCA 1974, s 63(2) does not apply (only one copy of the agreement is required), the cancellation notice must also be sent to the debtor within 7 days after the agreement is entered (CCA 1974, s 64(1)(b)); in the case of credit-token agreements see CCA 1974, s 64(2).

19.137 Sometimes credit agreements are drafted in the form of cancellable agreements (in case there happen to be face-to-face negotiations, causing CCA 1974, s 67 to apply). In such a case, the debtor will have contractual cancellation rights, but the agreement will not be treated as 'cancellable' under the CCA when it comes to sanctions[1].

[1] *Rankine v MBNA Europe Bank Ltd* [2007] EWCA Civ 1273, [2007] CTLC 241.

Distance marketing

19.138 The Financial Services (Distance Marketing) Regulations 2004 apply to credit agreements with consumers which are concluded at a distance. The cancellation rights do not apply to credit agreements secured on land or if there is a right to withdraw under CCA 1974, s 66A[1]. The cooling-off period is 14 days, either from the time the contract is concluded or (if later) from the time the prescribed information[2] is provided[3]. Where an agreement is cancellable under these Regulations, the debtor will need to be given a pre-contract document in accordance with Sch 1. Agreements may also be cancellable under other legislation[4].

[1] See SI 2004/2095, reg 11.
[2] SI 2004/2095 reg 8.
[3] SI 2004/2095, reg 10.
[4] Eg the Consumer Contracts (Information, Cancellation and Additional Charges) Regulations 2013, SI 2013/3134; the Timeshare, Holiday Products, Resale and Exchange Contracts Regulations 2010, SI 2010/2960; the Package Travel, Package Holidays and Package Tour Regulations 1992, SI 1992/3288.

EARLY SETTLEMENT

19.139 Under CCA 1974, s 94, debtors under regulated consumer credit agreements are entitled to repay their credit early at any time by giving notice to the creditor and making the early payment[1]. Since the implementation of the CC Directive on 1 February 2011, debtors have also been able to make partial early settlements[2] by giving notice to the creditor and making payment within 28 days of the day on which the creditor received the notice (or such later date as specified in the notice)[3]. In order to repay the make a full early repayment, the debtor must repay the entire amount outstanding under the agreement together with any compensatory amount claimed by the creditor under s 95A(2) or s 95B(2), less any rebate allowed under s 95[4].

[1] CCA 1974, s 94(1).
[2] CCA 1974, s 94(3).
[3] CCA 1974, s 94(4).
[4] CCA 1974, s 94(1) and (5).

19.140 The rebate to which a debtor is entitled under CCA 1974, s 95 is calculated in accordance with the Consumer Credit (Early Settlement) Regulations 2004[1]. These Regulations set down an actuarial calculation which is designed to ensure that the debtor is not paying the creditor interest for a future period which has not yet been earned: for example, in 'front loaded' loans the entire interest is debited to the loan account at drawdown but if the debtor repays after only half of the term, the interest referable to the remaining half of the term will be covered by the rebate. Under the Regulations, the creditor may postpone the settlement date by either 28 or 58 days, effectively charging an additional 28 or 58 days' interest upon early settlement. The creditor's entitlement to a compensatory amount in s 95A was introduced as part of the CC Directive implementation; despite initially appearing to be a creditor friendly provision, it is subject to stringent restrictions. The compensatory amount must not exceed the costs incurred by the creditor only as a result of the early repayment and is only claimable where: (1) the repayment exceeds £8,000 or partial repayments exceed £8,000 in 12 months; (2) the agreement is not an overdraft agreement; (3) the payment is not made from the proceeds from a contract of payment protection insurance[2]. In addition, the compensatory amount must be fair, objectively justified and must not exceed the lower of 1%[3] of the credit repaid or the amount of interest that would have been paid by the debtor on that sum had it not been repaid early[4].

[1] Certain agreements are excluded form the scope of the Regulations by Regulation 2. This is because for some agreements a rebate is neither required nor appropriate; for example, running account agreements.
[2] CCA 1974, s 95A(2).
[3] 0.5% if the priod is equal to or less than one year.
[4] CCA 1974, s 95A(3).

DEFAULT NOTICES

When required

19.141 Under CCA 1974, s 87, a creditor must serve a default notice before becoming entitled, by reason of any breach of a regulated agreement by the debtor, to:

- terminate the agreement;
- demand earlier payment of any sum;
- recover possession of any goods/land;
- treat any right conferred on the debtor by the agreement as terminated, restricted or deferred; or
- enforce any security.

19.142 Most credit agreements include an acceleration clause, so that if there is a serious breach by the debtor (eg two or more missed repayments), the creditor will immediately become entitled to the entire outstanding balance. If the creditor issues proceedings to recover the outstanding balance in these circumstances, this will amount to 'demanding earlier payment of any sum' and so a valid default notice will need to have been served. However, a default notice need not be served in order to obtain a money judgment solely for arrears (as such a judgment does not compel 'earlier payment' of any sum)[1]. Neither is a default notice required in order for the creditor to sue the debtor for damages for breach of the credit agreement.

[1] *Woodchester Lease Management Services Ltd v Swain & Co (A Firm)* [1999] 1 WLR 263.

19.143 Interestingly, the Court of Appeal has recently held that a default notice is an inherent element of the creditor's cause of action for claims where the service of such a notice is required and, consequently, the limitation period for brining such claims does not begin to run until the expiry of the default notice (rather than upon the breach by the debtor)[1].

1   *Doyle v PRA Group (UK) Ltd* [2019] EWCA Civ 12.

19.144 Immediately after the debtor's breach, without the need for any default notice, the creditor may take steps to prevent the debtor making further drawings of credit (CCA 1974, s 87(2): eg the creditor may warn suppliers not to accept a credit card where the credit limit has been exceeded).

Form and content

19.145 In order to be a valid default notice for the purposes of CCA 1974, s 87, the notice must be compliant with CCA 1974, s 88 and the associated Consumer Credit (Enforcement, Default and Termination Notices) Regulations 1983 ('the Notices Regulations'), which prescribe the form and content of default notices.

19.146 The default notice must specify (i) the nature of the alleged breach (eg missing monthly instalments), (ii) if the breach is capable of remedy, what action is required to remedy it (eg payment of the arrears), by which date and (iii) if the breach is not capable of remedy[1], the sum (if any) required to be paid as compensation, by which date. It must also state what action is intended to be taken by the creditor such as demanding earlier payment of any sum or enforcing any security.

1   Eg where the breach is bankruptcy, or the sale of goods let under a hire-purchase agreement.

19.147 Where the debtor has missed repayment(s) and, pursuant to an acceleration clause, the entire outstanding balance has become due, when identifying the 'breach', the default notice should only refer to the missed repayments, and not refer to the failure to pay the entire balance[1]. However, if the default notice is not complied with and the arrears are not cleared, the creditor may treat non-payment under the acceleration clause as a breach and need not serve a further default notice before seeking to enforce that clause (CCA 1974, s 88(3)). The same is true of any obligation to pay default interest: the default notice should not treat this as part of the breach, but if the original breach is not remedied, the creditor need not serve a further default notice in relation to the failure to pay default interest (CCA 1974, s 88(3)).

1   In *Blackshaw v MFS Portfolio Limited* [2016] EWHC 3708 (Ch) the High Court held, when refusing permission to appeal in bankruptcy proceedings, that a creditor was justified in referring to the entire balance and not simply the arrears but this would appear to be contrary to the Notices Regulations, SI 1983/1561, reg 2 and SI 1983/1561, Sch 2, para 6(b).

19.148 Certain statements must be set out in the notice, using prescribed forms of wording[1]. The lettering of each prescribed form of statement must be afforded more prominence than any other lettering in the notice. Any words shown in capital letters and underlined in the prescribed forms must be afforded yet more prominence[2]. The wording of the statements in the prescribed form must generally be reproduced without alteration or addition[3].

1   Notices Regulations, SI 1983/1561, reg 2 and SI 1983/1561, Sch 2.
2   Notices Regulations, SI 1983/1561, reg 2(5).
3   Notices Regulations, SI 1983/1561, reg 2(6) and (7).

19.149 The default notice must allow the debtor at least 14 days to take the specified action. There has been a considerable amount of litigation concerning whether the full 14 days have been provided. Since CCA 1974, s 88 refers to 14 days 'after the date of service', it is uncontroversial that the date on which the default notice is served should be excluded in counting the 14 days. However, on one view, 14 days also means 14 'clear' days, so that the day on which the prescribed steps must be taken should also be excluded from the count[1].

[1]   'Goode: Consumer Credit Law and Practice' to CCA 1974, s 88 (vol 2, para 5.168).

19.150 Each default notice must include a copy of the current FCA default information sheet (CCA 1974, s 88(4A)). The default notice must be given in paper form, so may not be sent by email[1]. Its lettering must be easily legible and of a colour that is readily distinguishable from the paper[2]. A default notice sent by post may be validly 'served' even though it is never received[3].

[1]   Notices Regulations, SI 1983/1561, reg 2(4A). This precludes creditors from using section 176A CCA 1974 consent to serve default notices electronically.
[2]   Notices Regulations, SI 1983/1561, reg 2(4).
[3]   CCA 1974, s 176(2); *Lombard North Central v Power-Hines* [1994] 8 CL 57.

Obtaining judgment

19.151 If the creditor issues proceedings to recover the outstanding balance before expiry of the term of the agreement, without serving a compliant default notice, the court may refuse to grant judgment, on the basis that there is no valid cause of action[1]. There is some rather dubious case law[2] to the effect that even if a default notice fails to allow 14 days after service to remedy the breach and so is technically defective, this is not relevant if the debtor has suffered no 'prejudice' as a result. The debtor will have suffered no prejudice if (i) he did not attempt to comply with the default notice anyway and (ii) the creditor did not take any enforcement action within 14 days.

[1]   Accordingly, and in light of the Civil Procedure Rules requirement to plead the date of the default notice, if the creditor becomes aware during litigation that the default notice is defective, he is best advised to serve a new default notice, wait for it to expire and then seek permission to amend his claim to plead reliance on this new default notice.
[2]   *Brandon v American Express Services Europe PE Ltd* [2010] CTLC 139, Bristol County Court, the Court of Appeal ([2011] EWCA Civ 1187), [2011] CTLC 177 declined to comment on the merits of this argument save to say that it was not appropriate for a summary judgment application to be decided on that basis (at para 30).

19.152 Generally, however, all the prescribed information must be accurately stated in order for the notice to be compliant. If the arrears figure is overstated on the notice (and the error is not *de minimis*) then the notice will be defective. In *Woodchester Lease Management Services Ltd v Swain & Co*[1], the Court of Appeal refused to grant judgment for the outstanding balance in these circumstances (although it did grant judgment for the arrears). It held that CCA 1974, s 88 required a precise statement of the remedial action to correct the breach.

[1]   [1999] 1 WLR 263.

Sanctions

19.153 Apart from the consequences for obtaining judgment (above), there is no sanction under the CCA against a creditor who fails to serve a default notice when required, or serves a defective notice, or enforces it before the 14 days have expired. Nonetheless, such failures may have knock on effects on the accuracy of other notices (such as notices of sums in arrears) and could be relevant to authorisation considerations, especially if persistent (CCA 1974, s 170(2)), or contribute towards an 'unfair relationship'. Failures to serve statutory notices may also constitute offences under the Consumer Protection from Unfair Trading Regulations 2008 (eg as an 'unfair commercial practice' or a 'misleading omission').

19.154 It is possible that the debtor may be able to obtain an injunction prohibiting the creditor from enforcing the agreement without serving a valid default notice (CCA 1974, s 170(3)). There may be remedies outside the CCA: for instance, a creditor who recovers possession of goods under a hire-purchase or conditional sale agreement without serving a compliant default notice can be sued in conversion[1]. However, there can be no damages claim by a debtor for loss caused by failure to serve a default notice (or service of a defective notice)[2].

1   *Eshun v Moorgate Mercantile Co Ltd* [1971] 1 WLR 722.
2   CCA 1974, s 170(1); enforcement without serving a valid default notice would not amount to a breach of contract (unless it is required by a clause in the credit agreement).

19.155 There is nothing to prevent the creditor from serving multiple default notices before deciding to issue proceedings. However, in such a case it can be difficult to ascertain when the agreement was 'terminated' by the creditor (where no termination notice is served, the agreement may simply terminate upon expiry of the 14-day period specified in the default notice). The limitation period will also start to run from the expiry of the first notice.

Running-account agreements

19.156 There is some authority[1] that where a credit card agreement gives the creditor the contractual right to terminate without relying on the debtor's breach, it is irrelevant if the default notice is defective. In these circumstances the creditor does not need to rely on the debtor's default in order to terminate, and so any default notice complying with CCA 1974, s 88 is redundant. The rationale for this is that a credit card agreement (as opposed to a fixed-sum loan) is open-ended, and so the creditor needs to have a contractual right to terminate at any time, without relying upon the debtor's breach. However, the creditor will still need to have fulfilled any contractual preconditions on its right to terminate (which may include serving a notice, albeit that this does not need to comply with CCA 1974, s 88). It is possible that contractual notice of non-default termination and CCA 1974, s 87 notice of default can be combined within a single notice[2]. It should be noted that the CCA 1974, s 98A requirements for termination notices must now also be complied with, as regards running-account credit agreements.

1   *American Express Services Europe Ltd v Harrison*, unreported, Exeter County Court, 18 February 2009; approved by the Court of Appeal in *Brandon v American Express Services Europe Ltd* [2011] EWCA Civ 1187 at paras 35–36, [2011] CTLC 177.

2   *Brandon* at paras 34–37.

OTHER POST CONTRACTUAL INFORMATION AND NOTICES

19.157 There are a considerable number of statutory notices and pieces of information which are obliged to be supplied in certain circumstances. This is an important, developing area of law, as the failure to comply with these obligations can have severe consequences, and the requirements are detailed. These were introduced by Consumer Credit Act 2006 ('CCA 2006'). In December 2012, it was announced that Northern Rock (Asset Management) plc would be refunding its customers £270m for interest which it was not entitled to charge due to defects in annual statements. Most of the obligations to supply statements and notices do not apply to 'non-commercial' agreements and 'small' agreements[1].

1   See the relevant sections imposing the duties to give statements and notices; a 'non-commercial' agreement is not made by the creditor in the course of a business carried on by him (CCA 1974, s 189); a 'small' agreement is for under £50 – see CCA 1974, s 17.

Assignees

19.158 When credit agreements have been assigned, it is often unclear whether the duties under the CCA to supply information and notices are imposed on the original creditor, or on the assignee. These duties are stated to be imposed on 'the creditor'. CCA 1974, s 189(1) defines 'the creditor' to mean, unless the context otherwise requires, 'the person providing credit under a consumer credit agreement *or* the person to whom his *rights and duties* under the agreement have passed by assignment or operation of law' (emphasis added). The difficulty is that in an ordinary legal assignment, only the 'rights' of the original creditor are transferred to the assignee, and not the duties. Therefore, on the face of it, most assignees will not be obliged to comply with the duties to supply information and notices.

19.159 For a comprehensive analysis of the question, see *The Law of Consumer Credit and Hire* by Philpott et al[1]. The author's view is that it is probable that legal assignees are not subject to the duties to supply information and notices, which can only be transferred from the original creditor if there is a novation. However, it was the OFT's view that legal assignees have a duty to comply with requests for copies of the agreement under CCA 1974, ss 77–79[2]. Moreover, the original creditor has limited interest in providing ongoing notices and statements once it has assigned the debt so if the assignee chooses not to on the basis that it is under no such legal obligation it may nevertheless find itself affected by the consequences of the original creditor not providing the notices (for example unenforceability and lack of entitlement to interest, to which see further below).

1   At para 8.145 *et seq.*
2   CONC 13 Guidance on the duty to give information under the CCA 1974, ss 77–79 (OFT 1272, October 2010).

Joint debtors

19.160 Where there are joint debtors, the creditor must give the required statement/notice to each of them (CCA 1974, s 185). One joint debtor may give the creditor a 'dispensing notice' authorising the creditor only to send periodic statements[1] to his co-debtor (CCA 1974, s 185(2) and (2B)).

1   Under CCA 1974, s 77A or CCA 1974, s 78(4).

Enforcement notices

19.161 Where the duration of a regulated agreement is specified[1] in the agreement and has not yet expired, CCA 1974, s 76 requires the creditor to give the debtor at least 7 days' written notice[2] before becoming entitled to take certain enforcement action. That enforcement action comprises steps to 'enforce'[3] a contractual term by (i) demanding earlier payment of any sum[4], (ii) recover possession of goods/land, or (iii) treat any right conferred on the debtor as terminated, restricted or deferred.

1   An agreement still has a 'specified' duration even if a party can terminate early: s 76(2).
2   The notice must be in the form prescribed by the Consumer Credit (Enforcement, Default and Termination Notices) Regulations 1983, SI 1983/1561, and must be in paper format.
3   'Enforcement' does not include the mere commencement of proceedings: see p 660 below.
4   A creditor whose loan is repayable on demand is not required to serve an enforcement notice prior to demanding payment: *Barclays Bank plc v Brillouet* [1999] GCCR 1541, CA.

19.162 The CCA 1974, s 76 does not apply where the right to enforce arises by reason of any 'breach' of the debtor (CCA 1974, s 76(6)). In this situation, see the requirements for a default notice under CCA 1974, s 87 instead. A CCA 1974, s 76 enforcement notice does not need to be served before terminating the agreement (in such a case, not based on default, see CCA 1974, s 98). A debtor's right to draw credit may be restricted or deferred (but not terminated) without having to serve an enforcement notice (CCA 1974, s 76(4)).

19.163 The form and content requirements are similar to those for default notices. As for default notices, there is no express sanction for failure to serve a valid enforcement notice when required.

Non-default termination notices

19.164 Contrary to popular belief, a termination notice does not need to be served in every case. For instance, where the agreement is terminated upon non-compliance with a default notice, no further notice need be served. CCA 1974, ss 98 and 98A only regulate termination in non-default cases. As for default notices, there is no express sanction for failure to serve a valid termination notice when required.

Agreements of specified duration: s 98

19.165 The CCA 1974, s 98 applies where the agreement is terminated for a reason other than the debtor's breach[1] (so no default notice has been served). Where the agreement is one of a specified duration, if the creditor wishes to terminate it before the end of that duration, it must give the debtor at least 7 days' written notice. A debtor's right to draw further credit may be restricted or deferred (but not terminated) without having to serve a termination notice (CCA 1974, s 98(4)). The form and content requirements are similar to those for default notices. The form and content is prescribed by reg 2(3) and Sch 3 to the Notices Regulations. A CCA 1974, s 98 termination notice and a CCA 1974, s 76 enforcement notice may be combined within a single document[2]. A CCA 1974, s 98 termination notice may also incorporate the CCA 1974, s 86E notice of default sums and/or the CCA 1974, s 130A notice of post-judgment interest[3].

[1] CCA 1974, s 98(6).
[2] Notices Regulations, SI 1983/1561, reg 2(8).
[3] CCA 1974, ss 86E(3) and 130A(5).

Indefinite duration agreements: s 98A

19.166 As of 1 February 2011[1], CCA 1974, s 98A applies to 'open-ended' credit agreements (ie agreements of indefinite duration, which includes most credit card agreements). Agreements secured on land and overdrafts are excluded[2]. The CCA 1974, s 98A(3) limits the creditor's contractual right to terminate such agreements in non-default[3] cases as follows:

(i)   the creditor must terminate the agreement by serving the debtor with written notice (there are no form and content requirements);
(ii)   the termination can only take effect after 2 months, beginning with the day after the day of service of the notice[4].

[1] CCA 1974, s 98A applies as of 1 February 2011 to agreements made at any time.
[2] CCA 1974, s 98A(8).
[3] CCA 1974, s 98A(7).
[4] Or such longer period as the credit agreement stipulates.

19.167 Alternatively, where the creditor wishes to terminate/suspend the debtor's right to draw on credit (whether or not due to default), there are special provisions in CCA 1974, s 98A(4)–(6) (generally, the creditor must serve a notice with objectively justified reasons for taking the step, such as the unauthorised use of credit, or a significantly increased risk of the debtor being unable to repay). If a debtor wishes to terminate an agreement of indefinite duration, he may do so at any time, simply by giving notice (which need not be in writing, unless the creditor requires) (CCA 1974, s 98A(2)). The debtor's right of termination is subject to any contractual notice period, which cannot exceed one month (CCA 1974, s 98A(1)).

Information and copies to be provided on request

Sections 77, 78 and 79: request for copies of agreements

19.168 CCA 1974, s 77 applies to fixed-sum agreements, CCA 1974, s 78 applies to running-account agreements and CCA 1974, s 79 applies to hire agreements. All three sections require the creditor/owner to provide certain information within 12 working days[1] after receiving payment of a £1 fee[2] and a written request. In response to CCA 1974, ss 77, 78 and 79 requests, the creditor must provide:

(a)   a copy of the executed agreement (if any)[3];

(b)   a copy of any other document referred to in the credit agreement; and

(c)   a statement signed by or on behalf of the creditor/owner showing (according to the information to which it is practicable for him to refer):

    (i)   in the case of a fixed-sum agreement: (i) the total sum paid under the agreement, (ii) the total sum which has become payable but which remains unpaid, the various amounts comprised in that total sum, and the date when each became due and (iii) the total sum which is to become payable, the various amounts comprised in that total sum, and the date (or the means of determining the date) when each becomes due[4];

    (ii)   in the case of a running-account agreement: (i) the state of the account, (ii) the amount, if any, currently payable under the agreement and (iii) the amounts and the due dates of any payments which, if there are no further drawings on the account, will later become payable under the agreement;

    (iii)   in the case of a hire agreement: the total sum which has become payable but remains unpaid and the various amounts comprised in that total sum, with the date when each became due.

1   'Working days' is defined in CCA 1974, s 189.
2   Albeit many creditors waive the requirement for this fee as processing the same is uneconomic.
3   'If any' appears to cover agreements which are exempt under CCA 1974, s 74 form and content requirements; if the creditor has lost its copy of the agreement it is still 'obliged' to provide a copy.
4   If the creditor has insufficient information to ascertain the amounts and dates of payments which are yet to become payable (eg because there is a variable interest rate), it may instead state the basis on which they will be ascertained (CCA 1974, ss 77(2) and 78(2)).

19.169 The 'copies' of the documents in (a) and (b) above must be 'true copies' and comply with the requirements in reg 3 of the Consumer Credit (Cancellation Notices and Copies of Documents) Regulations 1983 ('the Copies Regulations') (see CCA 1974, s 180(2)). In particular, the copy of the executed agreement need not include the signature boxes. It follows from this that the copy of the executed agreement need not be a photocopy or microfiche copy of the original document which the debtor signed. A 'reconstituted' copy of the credit agreement is permissible. Moreover, the agreement may be reconstituted from sources other[1] than the actual document which the debtor signed[2].

1   Eg the creditor's database of templates used for different periods.
2   *Carey v HSBC Bank Plc & ors* [2009] EWHC 3417 (QB), [2009] CTLC 103: the primary purpose of the obligations under CCA 1974, ss 77–79 is to provide the debtor with information about the terms of the agreement, not to enable him to prove whether or not he signed a properly executed agreement.

19.170 If the terms of the credit agreement have subsequently been varied, the creditor must supply copies of both the original and the current terms and conditions[1]. The creditor/owner need not respond if the agreement is one under which 'no sum is or will or may become payable by the debtor/hirer' (CCA 1974, ss 77(3), 78(3)and 79(2))[2]. In addition, the creditor/owner need not respond if the request was made less than 1 month after it complied with a previous such request relating to the same agreement (CCA 1974, ss 77(3), 78(3) and 79(2)).

1   *Carey v HSBC*; Copies Regulations, SI 1983/1557, regs 7–9.

2   It was also held by the High Court in *Rankine v Halifax plc* [2009] CCLR 3 that the duty is only
     imposed on a creditor 'under an agreement' and therefore the duty ceases once the agreement
     has been terminated.

19.171 If the creditor/owner fails to comply with the request, then the agreement is temporarily unenforceable until a compliant response is sent (CCA 1974, ss 77(4), 78(6) and 79(3)). There is no scope for any discretionary enforcement. An agreement may effectively become irredeemably, and interest will continue to accrue unenforceable if the request can never be complied with. While the agreement is temporarily unenforceable, the creditor/owner is prevented from taking any steps that amount to 'enforcement'. However, the debtor's repayment obligations remain valid, albeit temporarily unenforceable. Failure to comply with CCA 1974, ss 77, 78 and 79 requests will not, without more, give rise to an 'unfair relationship'[1]. The debtor may seek a declaration from the court that the agreement is temporarily unenforceable. The court may only order such declaratory relief under its general jurisdiction, and not under CCA 1974, s 142[2]. A CCA 1974, ss 77, 78 and 79 response may incorporate the CCA 1974, s 86E notice of default sums and/or the CCA 1974, s 130A notice of post-judgment interest[3].

1   *McGuffick v RBS plc* [2009] EWHC 2386 on s 77, [2010] 1 All ER 634, *Carey v HSBC
     Bank plc* [2009] EWHC 3417 QB on s 78, [2009] CTLC 103.
2   *Carey v HSBC* [2009] EWHC 3417 QB on s 78, [2009] CTLC 103.
3   CCA 1974, ss 86E(3) and 130A(5).

Statement of account

19.172 As of 1 February 2011, there is a further obligation under CCA 1974, s 77B to supply debtors with statements of account upon request. The obligation only applies to fixed-sum agreements of a fixed duration, where the credit is repayable in instalments. Agreements outside the scope of the CC Directive are excluded (agreements secured on land, agreements for credit exceeding £60,260 and 'business' agreements). The creditor must, upon request, send the debtor a written statement of account complying with CCA 1974, s 77B(3)–(5). The statement must be sent 'as soon as reasonably practicable', without charge. The debtor may not request a statement of account if the agreement has terminated, or if the creditor has already complied with a previous request made less than a month before (CCA 1974, s 77B(6)). There is an express sanction: the creditor's non-compliance is actionable as a breach of statutory duty (CCA 1974, s 77B(8)). In addition, breach could be relevant to fitness and/or contribute towards an 'unfair relationship'.

Other requests

19.173 For the obligation to give 'surety' copies of documents, see CCA 1974, s 107 (in relation to fixed-sum agreements), CCA 1974, s 108 (in relation to running-account agreements) and CCA 1974, s 109 (in relation to hire agreements)[1]. For requests by the debtor for a copy of the 'security instrument', see CCA 1974, s 110. For requests by the debtor for early settlement information, see CCA 1974, s 97. For requests by the debtor for a termination statement (confirming that he has discharged his indebtedness) see CCA 1974, s 103.

1   Further, in respect of guarantors and default notices see FCA Guidance FG17/1.

Periodic statements

19.174 There are separate obligations to provide periodic statements for both fixed-sum and running-account credit agreements. The form and content of periodic statements is prescribed by the Consumer Credit (Information Requirements and Duration of Licences and Charges) Regulations 2007 ('the Information Regulations 2007'). In light of the very detailed provisions, it is fortunate that reg 41 of the Information Regulations 2007 provides that an error or omission which does not affect the 'substance' of the information or wording in a periodic statement will not itself constitute a breach.

19.175 The prescribed information must be easily legible and no less prominent than any other information in the document (except names of parties, headings etc)[1]. There are only minor restrictions (regs 37–38) on the ordering and interspersing of information. There are some additional requirements for periodic statements relating to running-account agreements in the Consumer Credit (Running-Account Credit Information) Regulations 1983 ('the Running-Account Information Regulations'). A periodic statement may incorporate the CCA 1974, s 86E notice of default sums and/or the CCA 1974, s 130A notice of post-judgment interest[2].

[1] Information Regulations 2007, SI 2007/1167, regs 39–40.
[2] CCA 1974, s 86E(3) and 130A(5).

Fixed-sum agreements

19.176 The obligation to provide periodic statements in respect of regulated agreements is contained in CCA 1974, s 77A. The statements must relate to consecutive periods, each of which must not exceed 1 year. The first period must commence either with the day the agreement was made, or the day the first movement occurs on the debtor's account[1]. Each statement must be given to the debtor within 30 days, beginning with the day after the end of the period to which the statement relates (CCA 1974, s 77A(1E)).

[1] CCA 1974, s 77A(1B); but see transitional provisions for agreements made before 1 October 2008 (art 5(2) of the Legislative Reform (Consumer Credit) Order 2008, SI 2008/2826 and Information Regulations 2007, SI 2007/1167, regs 36 and 45–49). There is no obligation to give a statement under CCA 1974, s 77A if the agreement was written as if it was a regulated agreement but in fact it was not (*NRAM v McAdam* [2015] CTLC 169).

19.177 In *JP Morgan Chase Bank v Northern Rock (Asset Management) plc*[1], the court found that where a debtor has been provided with a non-compliant CCA 1974, s 77A statement, the period of non-compliance commences on a date to be calculated as if no statement had been served at all (the day following the last day on which a compliant statement could have been given).

[1] [2014] 1 WLR 2197, [2014] CTLC 33.

19.178 Under the Information Regulations 2007, periodic statements must contain a range of information, including the amount of credit, the opening balance at the beginning of the statement period and the amounts and dates of payments. Prescribed statements about early settlement[1] and paying less than the agreed sum must be included.

[1] If the agreement is a hire-purchase/conditional sale, the form of wording about early settlement must be shown together as a whole with a form of wording about termination rights (Information Regulations 2007, SI 2007/1167, reg 37).

19.179 Where any interest rates are 'applicable on a per annum basis'[1], the statement must specify those rates, the periods during which they applied and (if applicable) the element of the credit to which each such rate applied. The amounts and dates of any interest which became due during the statement period must be separately stated.

[1] For the uncertain meaning of this expression, see *The Law of Consumer Credit and Hire* by Philpott et al, paras 8.07–8.11: it is likely that it only includes rates applied so as to oblige the debtor to make one interest payment each year (and possibly rates that are compounded annually).

19.180 Where the interest rates are not 'applicable on a per annum basis', the statement must quote the interest rates on a per annum basis and explain how and when interest charges are calculated. There need be no separate statement of the amounts and dates of any interest which became due during the statement period (unless any movement on the account consisted solely of interest becoming due). The obligation to provide periodic statements ends when the debtor has no further liability under the agreement (CCA 1974, s 77A(4)).

19.181 There are three express sanctions for non-compliance (CCA 1974, s 77A(6)):

(i)   the agreement is temporarily unenforceable during the 'period of non-compliance';
(ii)   the debtor will not be liable to pay any interest calculated by reference to all/part of the 'period of non-compliance';
(iii)   the debtor will not be liable to pay any default sum which would have become payable during the 'period of non-compliance', or would have become payable after the end of that period in connection with a breach which occurred during the period[1].

[1] The debtor is not liable to pay the default sum even if his breach continues after the end of the period of non-compliance.

19.182 The 'period of non-compliance' begins on the 31st day after the end of the period to which the notice should have related (CCA 1974, s 77A(1E), (5) and (7)). It ends once a compliant statement is given (or, if earlier, when the debtor has no further liability under the agreement).

Running-account agreements

19.183 The obligation to provide periodic statements is contained in CCA 1974, s 78(4). The statements must show the state of the account at regular intervals of not more than 12 months. Where the agreement provides for repayments in relation to specified periods[1] (or for the applying of interest/charges in relation to specified periods), the periodic statement must also show the state of the account at the end of each such period during which there is a movement in the account (CCA 1974, s 78(4)(b)).

¹   As, eg, on a credit card.

19.184 The first periodic statement must relate to a period starting on/before the date of the first movement on the account, and each subsequent statement is consecutive[1]. Each statement must be given within a prescribed time after the end of the period to which the statement relates, namely[2]:

(i)   1 month after the end of the period (if the statement includes a demand for payment);

(ii)   12 months after the end of the period (if there is no demand for payment and the statement indicates there is no credit/debit balance at the end of the period);

(iii)   12 months after the date of the first credit/debit balance on the account following the end of the period if there has been no credit/debit balance on the account at any time during the period); or

(iv)   6 months after the end of the period (in any other case).

¹   SI 1983/1570, reg 2 of the Running-Account Information Regulations; there are no transitional provisions for pre-1 October 2008 agreements (as there are for periodic statements relating to fixed-sum agreements).
²   See CCA 1974, s 78(5) and SI 1983/1570, reg 3 of the Running-Account Information Regulations.

19.185 The periodic statement must contain the information prescribed by reg 2(1) of and the Schedule to the Running-Account Information Regulations (eg the opening and closing balances for the period, the date of any movement on the account, the amounts of payments/drawings, any interest/charges applied during the period and information about the calculation of interest and any variation in the rate).

19.186 In addition, the periodic statement must contain the forms of wording prescribed by the Information Regulations 2007. Importantly, where the agreement requires the payment each month of a minimum sum (as for most credit card agreements), the notice must include a form of wording as follows[1]:

Minimum payments

If you make only the minimum payment each month, it will take you longer and cost you more to clear your balance.

If you do not pay off the full amount outstanding, we will allocate your payment to the outstanding balance in a specific order, which is set out [. . .]. The way in which payments are allocated can make a significant difference to the amount of interest you will pay until the balance is cleared completely.

¹   Information Regulations 2007, SI 2007/1167, reg 14 and SI 2007/1167, Sch 2.

19.187 This form of wording must be shown 'together as a whole' with the closing balance for the end of the period[1]. It must be more prominent than any other information/wording in the periodic statement[2]. There is a separate, additional form of wording if the debtor has failed to make the minimum payment.

¹   Information Regulations 2007, SI 2007/1167, reg 38.
²   Information Regulations 2007, SI 2007/1167, reg 40.

19.188 There is no express provision as to when the obligation to provide periodic statements ends (as there is for fixed-sum agreements), but the obligation is stated only to apply where 'credit is provided' under an agreement. Therefore it is unclear whether the obligation ceases (i) upon withdrawal of the credit facility, (ii) upon termination of the credit agreement, or (iii) when no sums remain payable by the debtor. Further, there is no express sanction for non-compliance (as there is for fixed-sum agreements). However, there may be indirect sanctions: failures to serve statutory notices may be relevant to authorisation considerations, especially if persistent (CCA 1974, s 170(2)), or contribute towards an 'unfair relationship'. Such failures may also constitute offences under the Consumer Protection from Unfair Trading Regulations 2008 (eg as an 'unfair commercial practice' or a 'misleading omission').

Interest rate change

19.189 CCA 1794, s 78A imposes a duty to give debtors written information before a change in interest rate can take effect. As from 1 February 2011, this obligation applies to agreements of indefinite duration whenever made. For agreements of fixed duration, the obligation only applies to agreements made on/after 1 February 2011, unless the creditor has chosen to implement the new regime early. Agreements secured on land are excluded[1]. For agreements to which CCA 1974, s 78A does not apply, see the more general 'variation' provisions in CCA 1974, s 82(1).

[1] Consumer Credit (EU Directive) Regulations 2010; SI 2010/1010, regs 27, 100; CCA 1974, s 78A(6).

19.190 The information which must be supplied is set out in CCA 1974, s 78A(3) and comprises the rate variation, the new payment amount (if different) and the new number or frequency of payments (if different). However, the obligation to provide the CCA 1974, s 78A information does not arise where the rate varies according to a publicly available reference rate and the creditor is contractually obliged to inform the debtor periodically in writing of the information in CCA 1974, s 78A(3). There is a more limited obligation in respect of overdrafts (the creditor need only send information of an increase, and can restrict the information to the variation) (CCA 1974, s 78A(4)). There is no express sanction for non-compliance; however, it can be argued that, in the absence of the required notice, the variation did not take effect which can have considerable impact on other required notices to be considered below.

Arrears notices

19.191 There are separate obligations to provide arrears notices for both fixed-sum and running-account credit agreements. The form and content of arrears notices is prescribed by the Information Regulations 2007. In particular, an arrears notice must state that the debtor is behind with the sums payable under the agreement, and encourage him to discuss the state of his account with the creditor. The arrears notice must include a copy of the FCA information sheet on arrears (as updated on 24 May 2021). Again, it should be noted that reg 41 of the Information Regulations 2007 provides that an error or omission which does not affect the 'substance' of the information or wording in a periodic statement will not itself constitute a breach.

19.192 The prescribed information must be easily legible and no less prominent than any other information in the document (except names of parties, headings etc)[1]. An arrears notice may incorporate the CCA 1974, s 86E notice of default sums and/or the CCA 1974, s 130A notice of post-judgment interest[2]. Arrears notices need not be issued where there is an outstanding judgment debt in relation to the agreement[3]. There are transitional provisions for agreements entered before 1 October 2008[4].

1   Information Regulations 2007, SI 2007/1167, regs 39–40.
2   CCA 1974, ss 86E(3) and 130A(5).
3   CCA 1974, ss 86B(1)(e) and 86C(1)(d).
4   See CCA 2006, Sch 3, paras 6–7.

19.193 There are three express sanctions for non-compliance (CCA 1974, s 86D):

(i)   the agreement is temporarily unenforceable during the 'period of non-compliance';

(ii)   the debtor will not be liable to pay any interest calculated by reference to all/part of the 'period of non-compliance';

(iii)   the debtor will not be liable to pay any default sum which would have become payable during the 'period of non-compliance', or would have become payable after the end of that period in connection with a breach which occurred during the period[1].

1   The debtor is not liable to pay the default sum even if his breach continues after the end of the period of non-compliance.

19.194 The 'period of non-compliance' begins on the day after the end of the period within which the arrears notice should have been given (CCA 1974, s 86D(5)). Where the agreement is for running-account credit, the 'period of non-compliance' ends on the day the arrears notice is given. Where the agreement is for fixed-sum credit or hire, the 'period of non-compliance' ends, in the case of a first arrears notice, on the day that notice is given, and in the case of a subsequent notice, on the day that notice is given, or, if earlier, when the debtor 'ceases to be in arrears'[1].

1   'Ceases to be in arrears' is defined by CCA 1974, s 86B(5) to include the case where a default sum payable in respect of a breach other than non-payment remains outstanding.

Fixed-sum credit and hire agreements

19.195 The CCA 1974, s 86B obliges creditors/owners to send arrears notices whenever at least two payments have fallen due, the amount of the shortfall equals or exceeds the sum of the most recent two payments[1] to have fallen due, and the creditor is not already obliged to provide an arrears notice relating to the agreement. Where repayments are due weekly (or more frequently), arrears notices need only be given when there are four missed payments (CCA 1974, s 86B(9))[2].

1   'Payments' does not include default charges, unless (possibly) they can be said to be payable 'at predetermined intervals' (CCA 1974, s 86B(13)).
2   Further, where such an agreement was made more than 20 weeks before the date the most recent payment fell due, see CCA 1974, s 86B(10) and (11).

19.196 The first arrears notice must be given within 14 days of the date the conditions for service of an arrears notice are met (unless arrears notices are already being given, due to the conditions being met previously). After the first notice, subsequent arrears notices must be given at intervals of not more than 6 months, until the customer 'ceases to be in arrears'[1] (or a judgment is given requiring him to pay a sum).

1   'Ceases to be in arrears' is defined by CCA 1974, s 86B(5) to exclude most cases where interest and default charges remain 'owing'; it is unclear whether a customer will be in arrears where interest or default charges have accrued, but are not yet due and payable; it also unclear what the effect of any repayment arrangement will be, where the creditor has agreed to waive its contractual rights to the full repayments.

19.197 If the customer ceases to be in arrears during the 14 days within which the first arrears notice is to be given, that notice must still be sent (CCA 1974, s 86B(3)). The arrears notice must quote the opening balance at the date when the duty to give the notice arose[1], and set out various other financial figures. The first arrears notice must either supply broken down information about the shortfall, or inform the debtor that he can request further information about which payments he failed to make. If such a request is made, the creditor must respond within 15 working days[2].

1   For subsequent arrears notices, it seems that the part of the opening balance which comprises any sum not paid when due (para 7 of the Information Regulations 2007, SI 2007/1167, Sch 3) must be taken from the balance on the day after the previous notice was given; the part of the closing balance which comprises any sum not paid when due (para 12) must be taken from the balance on the last day of the period to which the notice relates (see *The Law of Consumer Credit and Hire* by Philpott et al, para 8.62).
2   Information Regulations 2007, SI 2007/1167, reg 19(2).

19.198 There is much scope for error in the drafting of arrears notices, due to the ambiguous language used in the Information Regulations 2007 to describe various pieces of financial information which must be included. For instance, 'balance' could refer either to the balance on which interest is accruing, or to the total outstanding balance including accrued daily interest which has not yet been debited.

Running-account agreements

19.199 The CCA 1974, s 86C obliges creditors to send arrears notices whenever at least two payments have fallen due, the most recent two payments[1] to have fallen due have not been made[2], and the creditor has not already become obliged to give an arrears notice in relation to either of those two payments. The arrears notice must be given no later than the end of the period within which the creditor is next obliged[3] to give a periodic statement.

1   'Payments' does not include default charges, unless (possibly) they can be said to be payable 'at predetermined intervals' (CCA 1974, s 86C(8)).
2   It is unclear whether 'not been made' encompasses the situation where, although the payments have not been made on time, there are no arrears, because of the way subsequent payments are appropriated to the outstanding balance.
3   Under CCA 1974, s 78(4).

19.200 The arrears notice may be incorporated into the periodic statement, or into any other CCA statement/notice relating to the agreement (CCA 1974, s 86C(4)). In accordance with the Information Regulations 2007, the arrears notice must set out various pieces of financial information (unless the two missed payments are minimum monthly payments which do not exceed £2)[1].

1   Information Regulations 2007, SI 2007/1167, reg 26.

Notice of default sums

19.201   CCA 1974, s 86E imposes a duty to issue notices of any default sums that become payable, within 35 days of the sum becoming payable. A 'default sum' is any sum[1] (other than interest) payable by the debtor in connection with a breach by him of the agreement (CCA 1974, s 187A). It only includes sums 'payable' as a result of a breach, not sums where the obligation to pay is merely accelerated due to breach.

1   Potentially including legal costs.

19.202   The form and content of notices of default sums is prescribed by the Information Regulations 2007. In particular, the notice must state that it relates to default sums and set out the amount, nature and date of each default sum (and the total amount). The notice must state that it does not take account of default sums which were the subject of a previous notice, whether or not they remain unpaid.

19.203   There is a special form of wording where interest is payable in connection with the default sums (referring to the fact that interest on default sums may not be charged for the first 28 days after the notice is given – CCA 1974, s 86E(4)). It should also be noted that a creditor can only charge simple interest on default sums (s 86F). Again, it should be noted that reg 41 of the Information Regulations 2007 provides that an error or omission which does not affect the 'substance' of the information or wording in a periodic statement will not itself constitute a breach.

19.204   The prescribed information must be easily legible and no less prominent than any other information in the document (except names of parties, headings etc)[1]. There are transitional provisions for agreements entered before 1 October 2008[2].

1   Information Regulations 2007, SI 2007/1167, regs 39–40.
2   See CCA 1974, Sch 3, paras 8–9.

19.205   A notice of default sums may incorporate the CCA 1974, s 130A notice of post-judgment interest[1]. The notice of default sums may itself be incorporated into a periodic statement, or into any other CCA statement/notice relating to the agreement (CCA 1974, s 86E(3)). There are two express sanctions for non-compliance (CCA 1974, s 86E(4) and (5)):

(i)   the agreement is temporarily unenforceable until the notice is given; and
(ii)   no interest is recoverable on a default sum until 28 days have elapsed after the sending of a compliant notice.

1   CCA 1974, s 130A(5).

Current account overdrafts

19.206 Where the account-holder may be allowed to incur an overdraft that is not pre-arranged, or to exceed a pre-arranged overdraft limit ('overrunning'), the current account agreement must provide the information listed in CONC 4.7.2R(2). Unless this overrunning would be secured on land, the creditor must also inform the account-holder of this information annually (CONC 6.3.3R). Where the account-holder overdraws on the current account without a pre-arranged overdraft, or exceeds a pre-arranged overdraft limit, for a period exceeding 1 month; and the amount of that overdraft or excess is significant throughout that period; the overdraft or excess is a regulated credit agreement and a firm must inform the account holder in writing of the matters in CONC 6.3.4 R(2) without delay.

19.207 The matters in CONC 6.3.4 R(2) are:

(a)   the fact that the account is overdrawn or the overdraft limit has been exceeded;
(b)   the amount of that overdraft or excess;
(c)   the rate of interest charged on it; and
(d)   any other charges payable by the customer in relation to it (including any penalties and any interest on those charges).

19.208 On 7 June 2019, the FCA announced significant changes it was making to its rules on overdrafts. The new rules, to be inserted into CONC, will be in force by 6 April 2020 and will, *inter alia*, require firms to:

(a)   charge the same rates for arranged and unarranged overdrafts;
(b)   price overdrafts by a simple annual interest rate rather than fixed daily, weekly or monthly rates;
(c)   advertise arranged overdrafts with an APR to help customers compare different products;
(d)   take greater steps to identify customers showing risks of financial strain and take steps to reduce repeat overdraft use.

Notices of post-judgment interest

19.209 No statutory interest is payable on a judgment given in proceedings to recover money due under a regulated agreement[1]. However, contractual interest may be payable. CCA 1974, s 130A obliges notice to be given if the creditor wishes to recover post-judgment contractual interest.

[1]   Article 2(3) of the County Court (Interest on Judgment Debts) Order 1991, SI 1991/1184. A contractual term providing for post judgment interest under a regulated agreement is not an unfair term (*Director of Fair Trading v First National Bank Plc* [2002]1 AC 481).

19.210 The first notice must be given after the judgment (no time limit is imposed, but post-judgment interest is irrecoverable until it is given) and subsequent notices must be given at intervals of no more than 6 months. The form and content of notices of post-judgment interest is prescribed by the Information Regulations 2007. In particular, the notice must set out the amount on which post-judgment interest is being charged and the rate of that interest. It must include special forms of wording. Subsequent notices must set out the total amount of interest charged since the date of the last notice. Again, it should be noted that reg 41 of the Information Regulations 2007 provides that an error or omission which does not affect the 'substance' of the information or wording in a periodic statement will not itself constitute a breach.

19.211 The prescribed information must be easily legible and no less prominent than any other information in the document (except names of parties, headings etc)[1]. There are transitional provisions for agreements entered before 1 October 2008[2]. The notice of post-judgment interest may be incorporated into a periodic statement, or into any other CCA statement/notice relating to the agreement (CCA 1974, s 130A(5)). If the notices are not given, the debtor is not liable to pay any post-judgment interest for any period when the creditor has not complied with the CCA 1974, s 130A requirements (CCA 1974, s 130A(2) and (3)).

1   Information Regulations 2007, SI 2007/1167, regs 39–40.
2   See CCA 1974, Sch 3, para 13.

ENFORCEABILITY OF AGREEMENT

19.212 In default of many of the CCA obligations imposed on a creditor, the agreement is 'improperly executed'. CCA 1974, s 65 provides that an 'improperly executed' agreement is enforceable against the debtor only on an order of the court[1]. Applications for enforcement orders are dealt with in accordance with CCA 1974, s 127. Alternatively, a debtor may consent to enforcement under CCA 1974, s 173(3).

1   See **19.9–19.11** above for the effect on the enforceability of agreements where there is a breach of FSMA.

Effect of unenforceability

19.213 Where an agreement is unenforceable, the debtor's repayment obligations remain valid contractual obligations, and are not void[1]. Letters sent by a creditor requesting payment in such circumstances would not result in an unfair relationship between the creditor and the debtor[2]. Accordingly, default will still affect the debtor's credit rating (even if the creditor cannot obtain judgment for the outstanding balance without the granting of an enforcement order). There is no provision in the CCA for the debtor to recover payments made pursuant to an unenforceable agreement[3].

1   *Wilson v First County Trust Ltd (No 2)* [2003] UKHL 40, [2004] 1 AC 816.
2   *Re London Scottish Finance Ltd (In Administration)* [2014] Bus LR 424, [2013] CTLC 231. However care should be exercised not to mislead debtors as to the status of the account or misrepresent the position as if the creditor could take legal action without first obtaining the necessary enforcement order.
3   *Barclays Bank plc v Lee* [1993] CLY 474: payments made under an unenforceable credit agreement are not recoverable unless there has been a total failure of consideration. Cf *Wilson v Howard Pawnbrokers* [2005] EWCA Civ 147 and the possibility of an unjust enrichment claim. The issue of recoverability was considered in *Re London Scottish Finance Ltd* [2013] CTLC 231. When dealing with unenforceable agreements under the Money Lenders Act 1927, Lord Diplock in *Orakpo v Manson Investments Ltd* [1978] AC 95 said that they were not devoid of all legal effect. Payments made voluntarily pursuant to their terms are not recoverable.

19.214 Where the creditor has not applied for an enforcement order (or its application has been dismissed), the court may grant a CCA 1974, s 142 declaration that the agreement should not be enforced. In relation to a secured agreement, where a CCA 1974, s 142 declaration has been granted, or the creditor's application for an enforcement order has been dismissed[1], the security shall be treated as never having effect[2]. The creditor must ensure any registered charge is removed[3]. Further, any amount received by the creditor on 'realisation' of the security shall (so far as referable to the agreement) be repaid[4].

[1] Except on technical grounds only.
[2] CCA 1974, ss 113 and 106(a); see also CCA 1974, s 177 (saving for proprietor of charge for valuable consideration, without notice of the defect).
[3] CCA 1974, s 106(c).
[4] CCA 1974, s 106(d): in *Wilson v Howard Pawnbrokers* [2005] All ER (D) 61 the Court of Appeal held (dubiously) that 'realisation' of the security included sums paid by the debtor by way of instalments, as well as the proceeds of sale of the security.

19.215 Enforcement of an improperly executed agreement by the creditor without a court order (ie in breach of CCA 1974, s 65) does not incur any sanction, but may be taken into consideration by the FCA when exercising their powers under CCA (CCA 1974, s 170(2)). Further, where goods are wrongfully repossessed without a court order, the debtor/hirer may have a cause of action against the creditor for wrongful interference, or may be able to apply for a mandatory injunction[1].

[1] See CCA 1974, s 170(3).

What constitutes enforcement

19.216 In *McGuffick v RBS plc*[1], a narrow interpretation was given to the concept of 'enforcement' for which an enforcement order was required. It was held that the following steps did not amount to 'enforcement':

(i)   making adverse reports to credit reference agencies, without explaining that the agreement was temporarily unenforceable;
(ii)   disseminating information about the agreement to third parties;
(iii)   issuing demands for payment;
(iv)   issuing default notices;
(v)   threatening legal action or issuing proceedings;
(vi)   instructing a debt collection agency.

[1] [2009] EWHC 2386 (Comm), [2010] 1 All ER 634. Considered in *Grace v Black Horse Limited* [2014] CTLC 312.

19.217 Obtaining judgment for the outstanding balance will amount to 'enforcement' of the agreement, and therefore judgment cannot be obtained where the agreement is improperly executed unless an enforcement order is also granted. It is expressly provided by CCA 1974, s 65(2) that repossession of goods/land to which the agreement relates amounts to 'enforcement'. However, in the case of live hire-purchase, conditional sale and hire agreements, ownership of goods will not yet have passed to the debtor/hirer. Accordingly, it seems that if the debtor/hirer under such an improperly executed agreement wrongfully sells the goods, the creditor/owner may still sue him for conversion without this amounting to 'enforcement' for which a court order is required. Further, if the term of a hire or hire-purchase agreement has expired, the creditor/owner does not need to 'enforce' the agreement in order to repossess the goods, but can rely on its ownership rights[1].

¹ See further Guest and Lloyd, *Encyclopaedia of Consumer Credit Law*, vol 1, 2108.

19.218 However, where an improperly executed agreement remains live, the creditor/owner will need an enforcement order to obtain an order for delivery-up of the goods from the debtor/hirer (eg where there has been no wrongful onward sale).

Applying for an enforcement order

19.219 The granting of an enforcement order is discretionary. CCA 1974, s 127(1) provides that the court shall dismiss an application by the creditor for an enforcement order only if it considers it 'just' to do so, having regard to:

(i)   the 'prejudice'[1] caused to any person 'by the contravention in question'[2];
(ii)   the degree of 'culpability'[3] for the contravention; and
(iii)   the court's powers under CCA 1974, s 127(2)[4] and CCA 1974, ss 135–136[5].

The starting point is that an enforcement order will be granted, so the burden is on the debtor to show that it would be 'just' to dismiss the application. It is rare that an enforcement order is not granted: the debtor can be compensated for any prejudice by the court exercising its powers under CCA 1974, s 127(2), to reduce/discharge any sum payable by him[6].

¹ Eg if the debtor would not otherwise have entered the agreement (see *PB Leasing Ltd v Patel and Patel* [1995] CCLR 82: financial figures not inserted prior to signature and no s 62 copy).
² Ie by the defect which made the agreement improperly executed.
³ Eg deliberate misstating of the APR in order to attract more custom.
⁴ To reduce/discharge any sum payable by the debtor, to compensate him for the prejudice (see *National Guardian Mortgage Corp v Wilkes* [1993] CCLR 1: interest rate reduced where consideration copy of secured agreement not provided, depriving debtor of opportunity to borrow at lower rate elsewhere; *Rank Xerox v Hepple* [1994] CCLR 1: reduction in amount of accelerated payment due to absence of information).
⁵ CCA 1974, s 135 empowers the court to make the operation of a term conditional upon some act, or to suspend a provision of an order; CCA 1974, s 136 empowers the court to amend agreements.
⁶ *National Guardian Mortgage Corp v Wilkes* [1993] CCLR 1: interest rate reduced where consideration copy of secured agreement not provided, depriving debtor of opportunity to borrow at lower rate elsewhere; *Rank Xerox v Hepple* [1994] CCLR 1: reduction in amount of accelerated payment due to absence of information about that payment; *Wilson v Hurstanger* [2007] EWCA Civ 299 [2007] CTLC 59: debtor discharged from liability to pay administration fee plus interest thereon.

Irredeemably unenforceable agreements

19.220 An agreement may be irredeemably unenforceable (ie the court can make no enforcement order in respect of it) if it was entered before 6 April 2007[1] and:

(i)   the agreement omits or misstates a 'prescribed term';
(ii)   the agreement was not signed by the debtor[2]; or

(iii)   the agreement was cancellable and no notice of cancellation rights was given (or no CCA 1974, ss 62 and 63 copy was given)[3].

1   When CCA 1974, s 127(3) and (4) were repealed.
2   Failure to sign by the creditor cannot give rise to irredeemable unenforceability.
3   The creditor could remedy this defect by giving the debtor a copy of the executed agreement before the proceedings commenced (CCA 1974, s 127(4)); the debtor could then exercise his cancellation rights.

19.221 Where an agreement is irredeemably unenforceable, there will be no prospect of the creditor ever being able to 'enforce' the agreement (eg by obtaining judgment for the outstanding balance). However, the debtor's repayment obligations remain valid (albeit unenforceable). There is no provision in the CCA for the debtor to recover payments made pursuant to an irredeemably unenforceable agreement. However, the debtor could conceivably sue at common law for restitution of payments, on the grounds of mistake at law[1].

1   This being a unilateral mistake that the agreement was enforceable.

19.222 In *Grace & Anr v Black Horse Limited*[1] the Court of Appeal held that it would not be accurate to describe a person as a defaulter (to a credit reference agency) once a competent court has decided that the agreement is irremediably unenforceable against him.

1   [2015] 3 All ER 223, [2014] CTLC 312.

CONNECTED LIABILITY: S 75 AND S 75A

Section 75

19.223 CCA 1974, s 75(1) makes the creditor liable in certain circumstances for breaches by the supplier. Where applicable, it provides the consumer with an incredibly valuable remedy where, despite other consumer protection provisions and/or other steps taken by enforcers, including trading standards, the supplier in breach is unwilling or unable to provide the consumer with the appropriate reimbursement or other compensation.

Which agreements are covered

19.224 The CCA 1974, s 75 only applies to debtor-creditor-supplier (DCS) agreements falling within CCA 1974, s 12(b) or (c). Therefore it applies, for instance, to:

•   credit card transactions to purchase goods/services; and
•   loans to purchase goods under pre-existing arrangements (or in contemplation of future arrangements) between the creditor and the supplier.

This is subject to some specific exceptions which exempt the following from the ambit of section 75:

•   electronic funds transfer at place of sale (EFTPOS) transactions section 75[1];
•   'non-commercial' agreements[2];
•   charge card agreements[3];

Moreover, even with agreements that fall within the ambit of s 75, a debtor will not be able to bring a valid claim unless they meet the other pre-conditions (see below).

1   See CCA 1974, s 187(3A).
2   Defined in CCA 1974, s 189.
3   See CCA 1974, s 75(3).

19.225 Where credit cards operate under a 'network' (eg Visa/MasterCard), the creditor's liability under CCA 1974, s 75 is not limited to cover only breaches by suppliers which the creditor has itself enrolled into the network, and with whom the creditor has direct contractual arrangements. There will be sufficient 'arrangements' between the creditor and the supplier if they are both members of the same network[1]. However, it remains an open questions as to whether the definition of 'arrangements' is sufficient to cover modern payment mechanisms[2] involving a 'master merchant' which is a member of the network and a 'sub merchant' who is not (often because they are small trader who would not been the qualifying criteria for membership of the Visa/MasterCard scheme) but has a contractual arrangement with the 'master merchant' which allows them to accept credit card payments[3].

1   *Office of Fair Trading v Lloyds TSB Bank plc* [2006] EWCA Civ 268, [2007] QB 1.
2   For example Square and iZettle.
3   These payments are then processed through the network by the master merchant and the creditor is often unaware of the existence of the sub merchant.

19.226 The CCA 1974, s 75 will still apply even if the debtor has exceeded the credit limit, or breached another term of the credit agreement (CCA 1974, s 75(4)).

Agreements which are not covered

19.227 The CCA 1974, s 75 does not apply to debtor-creditor agreements, hire agreements, exempt agreements or CCA 1974, s 12(a) agreements where the creditor itself is the supplier. For CCA 1974, s 12(a) agreements (eg hire-purchase, conditional sale or credit-sale), the contract for the supply of goods will be directly between the creditor and the debtor. In these situations, the creditor is also acting as the supplier and therefore if there is any breach of the supply contract, the debtor can sue the creditor directly (eg for breach of the implied terms as to title, satisfactory quality or correspondence with description: for hire-purchase, under the Supply of Goods (Implied Terms) Act 1973, or in a sale, under the Consumer Rights Act 2015). In addition, under such agreements, the deemed agency provisions for credit-brokers apply (CCA 1974, s 56).

Other pre-conditions

19.228 Once it is established that the credit agreement is covered by CCA 1974, s 75, there are four pre-conditions in order for CCA 1974, s 75 to apply:

(i)   the claim relates to any item to which the supplier has attached a cash price of more than £100 but not more than £30,000;
(ii)   there is a 'claim' against the supplier;
(iii)   that claim is by the 'debtor';

(iv)   that claim is either for breach of contract or misrepresentation.

(v)   that claim relates to a transaction financed by the credit agreement.

(i)   SINGLE ITEM PRICE

19.229 By virtue of s 75(3)(b) CCA 1974, s 75 liability does not arise in respect of items which have a 'single item' price of £100 or less or more than £30,000. What the single item price is, is a question of fact and can often give rise to some interesting arguments: for example, if a debtor buys 10 separate DVDs for £15 each, s 75 liability will not arise but, if the debtor bought the same 10 DVDs in a box set for £120, s 75 liability would be triggered. Importantly, the question of the single item price is distinct from the amount paid by the debtor using their credit agreement and s 75 still applies to the entire transaction even if the debtor only pays a portion (even as little as one pence) using their credit agreement.

(ii)   LIKE 'CLAIM' AGAINST SUPPLIER

19.230 In *Durkin v DSG Retail Limited*[1], the Supreme Court held that the law implied a term into a restricted use debtor-creditor-supplier agreement, making it conditional upon the survival of the supply agreement. A debtor, on rescinding the supply agreement for breach of contract, could also rescind the credit agreement by invoking that condition. The debtor would then be under an obligation to repay the borrowed funds that he has recovered from the supplier.

[1]   [2014] 1 WLR 1148.

19.231 If the supplier has inserted a valid exclusion or limitation clause in the supply contract, then the debtor's claim against the creditor will suffer from the same exclusion or limitation. If the debtor has settled his claim against the supplier, then the creditor's liability will also be extinguished.

19.232 The CCA 1974, s 75 covers overseas transactions (ie where a UK credit agreement is used to finance a supply transaction which is made or performed abroad and/or governed by foreign law)[1]. The CCA 1974, s 75 claims may also be brought in respect of the financing of timeshare agreements concerning properties abroad[2].

[1]   *Office of Fair Trading v Lloyds TSB Bank plc* [2007] UKHL 48, [2008] 1 AC 316.

[2]   *Jarrett v Barclays Bank plc* [1999] QB 1, which held that Art 16 of the Brussels Convention (which confers exclusive jurisdiction over disputes over property in rem on the courts of the place where the property is situated) did not apply. See now Art 4.4(c) of Rome I.

19.233 In some circumstances, the 'supplier' (who must be the other contractual party to the transaction financed by the credit)[1] may not be the obvious person. For instance, if a debtor has a complaint against a hotel, he may find that he has no recourse under CCA 1974, s 75, as the 'supplier' to whom he paid the monies was a travel agent[2].

[1]   CCA 1974, ss 11(1)(b) and 189.

[2]   However, the debtor may be assisted in such a situation by the Package Travel, Package Holidays and Package Tours Regulations 1992, SI 1992/3288.

(iii) CLAIM BY THE 'DEBTOR'

19.234 It is only the debtor who is provided with rights under s 75 and it is the debtor who must have a claim against the supplied, For example, in the context of credit cards, CCA 1974, s 75 will only give the account-holder a claim against the creditor, and not additional card-holders (who are not 'debtors', unless they are joint borrowers under the credit agreement)[1]. Likewise, the debtor will not usually be able to bring claims for purchases made by an additional card holder where it is the additional cardholder who has/would have had a claim against the supplier[2].

[1] See definition of 'debtor' in CCA 1974, s 189; see also Guest and Lloyd, *Encyclopaedia of Consumer Credit Law*, vol 1, 2139–40.
[2] However, it is possible that an additional card-holder may be acting as agent for the account-holder, who will then have a CCA 1974, s 75 claim in his capacity as principal.

(iv) CLAIM FOR BREACH OF CONTRACT OR MISREPRESENTATION

19.235 The claim against the supplier must be for breach of contract (which includes breach of terms implied into the contract by consumer protection legislation) or misrepresentation. It follows that CCA 1974, s 75 will not apply if the debtor's sole claim against the supplier is for negligence, or for breach of statutory duty for non-compliance with consumer protection legislation.

(v) RELATES TO TRANSACTION FINANCED

19.236 'Financed' means financed either wholly or in part (CCA 1974, s 189). Therefore CCA 1974, s 75 will apply even where a credit card has only been used to pay part of the purchase price, and the rest has been paid in cash. The claim must 'relate' to the transaction financed by the credit: the connection must not be too remote.

Claim against creditor

19.237 Where CCA 1974, s 75 applies, the debtor is given a 'like claim' against the creditor, who is made jointly and severally liable with the supplier. Since liability is joint and several, the creditor cannot require the debtor to exhaust all avenues of redress against the supplier first, before it becomes liable (in contrast to a limited duty to do so under CCA 1974, s 75A). The debtor may choose to pursue the creditor instead of the supplier.

19.238 In general, the debtor's claim against both supplier and creditor will be monetary. Nevertheless, the words 'a like claim' could indicate that if the debtor has a claim to rescind the supply contract, or treat it as repudiated, he should also be entitled to rescission of the credit agreement, or to treat it as repudiated by the creditor. However, this interpretation has its difficulties, and has been rejected by the Scottish courts; whilst agreeing that CCA 1974, s 75 did not give a right to rescind the credit agreement, the Supreme Court held that such a right was derived from an implied term of the credit agreement that it is conditional on the survival of the supply contract[1]. That implied term obviously makes sense in the context of a restricted-use, fixed-sum credit agreement (a 'linked loan') but it is unlikely that such an implied term would also arise in the context of a running account credit agreement where numerous different supply contracts are likely to be involved or envisaged (ie a credit card agreement).

1   *Durkin v DSG Retail Ltd and HFC Bank plc* [2014] 1 WLR 1148; see also Guest and Lloyd, *Encyclopaedia of Consumer Credit Law*, vol 1, 2142 for further analysis.

19.239 The limitation period for a CCA 1974, s 75 claim against the creditor will normally be 6 years (Limitation Act 1980, s 9).

19.240 There is a tricky question of what happens if the credit agreement has been assigned. Guest and Lloyd[1] are of the view that the original creditor would remain liable under CCA 1974, s 75(1), but that if the debtor was sued for the outstanding balance by the assignee, he could still plead a counterclaim under CCA 1974, s 75(1) by way of set off.

1   *Encyclopaedia of Consumer Credit Law*, vol 1, 2144.

Creditor's indemnity against supplier

19.241 The CCA 1974, s 75(2) grants the creditor a right of indemnity against the supplier (subject to any agreement between them). The indemnity covers loss in satisfying its CCA 1974, s 75(1) liability[1] to the debtor and any legal costs reasonably incurred by the creditor in defending those proceedings. When the debtor issues a CCA 1974, s 75(1) claim against the creditor, the creditor will usually issue a Pt 20 claim against the supplier for a CCA 1974, s 75(2) indemnity[2]. The CCA 1974, s 75(2) does not impose any obligation on foreign suppliers to indemnify the creditor[3].

1   Either pursuant to a judgment, or a settlement of the claim; the supplier may, however, contest the question of liability, or dispute the quantum.
2   This is usually advisable unless a separate agreement has been reached in correspondence that the supplier will assist the creditor in defending the claim and will fulfil its obligation to indemnify the credit against any losses (including costs).
3   *Office of Fair Trading v Lloyds TSB Bank plc* [2007] UKHL 48, [2008] 1 AC 316.

Section 75A

19.242 A separate provision for connected lender liability was added on 1 February 2011 to ensure compliance with the CC Directive. This provision applies from 1 February 2011 to credit agreements made on/after 11 June 2010[1]. If the creditor has chosen to implement the new regime early, then it applies from the date of that implementation to credit agreements made on/after 30 April 2010.

1   Consumer Credit (EU Directive) Regulations 2010, SI 2010/1010, reg 100(3)(a) and (4)(a).

19.243 The CCA 1974, s 75A is narrower than CCA 1974, s 75, and only applies in restricted circumstances. In particular:

- CCA 1974, s 75A only applies to transactions where the cash value of the goods/services exceeds £30,000[1];
- CCA 1974, s 75A only applies where the credit agreement 'serves exclusively' to finance an agreement for the supply of 'specific' goods/services[2];

- CCA 1974, s 75A only applies where either the credit agreement expressly identifies the specific goods/services, or the creditor uses the supplier's services in connection with the preparation or making of the credit agreement;
- CCA 1974, s 75A does not apply to agreements outside the scope of the CC Directive (where the amount of credit exceeds £60,260, or the credit agreement is secured on land, or the credit agreement is wholly/predominantly for business purposes)[3].

[1] CCA 1974, s 75A(6)(a).
[2] CCA 1974, s 75A(5): it seems the credit agreement must not be used to finance anything else.
[3] CCA 1974, s 75A(6)(b) and (c) and (8).

19.244 Where CCA 1974, s 75A does apply, it provides that if the debtor has a claim against the supplier for breach of contract, he may pursue that claim against the creditor. The CCA 1974, s 75A only covers claims for breach of contract, and does not extend to misrepresentation.

19.245 In contrast to the position under CCA 1974, s 75, before the creditor becomes liable under CCA 1974, s 75A, the debtor must in some way be unable to obtain satisfaction from the supplier: either (i) the supplier cannot be traced or is insolvent, (ii) the debtor has contacted the supplier but it has not responded, or (iii) the debtor has taken reasonable steps to pursue his claim against the supplier (which need not include litigation) but has not obtained satisfaction (CCA 1974, s 75A(2) and (3)).

UNFAIR RELATIONSHIPS

Which regime applies

19.246 Some credit agreements will still be governed by the predecessor 'extortionate credit bargain' ('E-C-B') regime, rather than the new 'unfair relationship' ('U-R') regime. There are detailed transitional provisions[1], but the principal rules are:

(i) if the agreement was redeemed/settled before 6 April 2008: E-C-B regime;
(ii) if the agreement was entered before 6 April 2007, but not redeemed/settled before 6 April 2008: U-R regime (provided legal proceedings were issued on/after 6 April 2008);
(iii) if the agreement was entered on/after 6 April 2007: U-R regime.

There is a more tricky situation where a credit agreement was entered on/after 6 April 2007 (and so falls under the U-R regime), but consolidates an earlier agreement with the same creditor[2] which would otherwise fall under the E-C-B regime.

[1] CCA 2006, s 22(3) and CCA 2006, Sch 3, paras 1 and 14–16.
[2] Or an 'associate' of the creditor as defined by s 184.

19.247 The High Court has held[1] that although the earlier agreement is a 'related agreement'[2], that does not entitle the court to make it the subject of a U-R order if the earlier agreement does not itself fall within the transitional provisions (ie because it was redeemed before 6 April 2008) – the two regimes are mutually exclusive. However, there is contrasting authority[3] that an order may be made that there is a U-R arising out of the later agreement 'taking into account' the earlier agreement. It may, therefore, resolve to a pleading point.

1   *Soulsby v Firstplus Financial Group plc* [2010] CTLC 177.
2   Under CCA 1974, s 140C(4): this would include an agreement wholly or partly refinanced by the subsequent agreement (CCA 1974, s 140C(7)).
3   *Barnes v Black Horse Ltd* [2011] EWHC 1416 (QB).

Extortionate credit bargains

19.248 The old E-C-B regime can be found in CCA 1974, ss 137–140. An E-C-B was defined as a 'credit bargain'[1] which required the debtor to make 'grossly exorbitant' payments, or otherwise 'grossly contravened ordinary principles of fair dealing'. There was a indicative list of relevant factors, which included prevailing interest rates[2], the debtor's personal characteristics, any financial pressure the debtor was under, the value of any security provided[3] and whether a 'colourable cash price'[4] was quoted for any goods/services included in the credit bargain.

1   'Credit bargain' was defined by CCA 1974, s 137(2) to include the credit agreement and any other transaction to be taken into account in computing the total charge for credit; in *Paragon Finance v Nash* [2001] EWCA Civ 1466, [2002] 1 WLR 685 this definition was used to exclude from consideration interest rate variations occurring after the credit agreement was entered.
2   The case law makes clear that like for like must be compared: sub-prime interest rates cannot be compared with prevailing high street lending rates.
3   What would be considered an extortionate rate for an unsecured advance is very different from what would be considered extortionate in secured lending.
4   Ie where an inflated cash price for goods/services is quoted so as to artificially reduce the interest rate.

19.249 Most E-C-B cases were unsuccessful attempts by consumers to challenge high interest rates. The High Court held that an interest rate of 48% pa on a short-term bridging loan was not extortionate[1], and neither was an interest rate of 12% pa on a mortgage for buy-to-let domestic property[2]. Contraventions of the former OFT's Non-Status Guidelines (failures by the lender to enquire as to the purpose of the loan or check the information provided by the broker, and the processing of the loan without a signed application form) were also held not to 'grossly contravene the ordinary principles of fair dealing'[3]. The threshold was generally recognised to be very high.

1   *A Ketley Ltd v Scott* [1981] ICR 241.
2   *Davies v Directloans Ltd* [1986] 1 WLR 823; see also *Wills v Wood* [1984] CCLR 7 where the CA overturned an E-C-B finding on a 12% pa loan from a solicitors' firm to an inexperienced borrower.
3   *Broadwick Financial Services Ltd v Spencer* [2002] EWCA Civ 35.

Scope of the regime

19.250 The U-R provisions apply to 'credit agreements'[1] rather than 'regulated agreements'. Therefore exempt agreements may fall within the U-R regime, unless they are exempt because they are FSMA 2000 regulated agreements[2]. For the uncertain position of assignees, see CCA 1974, s 140C(2) (on a strict interpretation, legal assignees are not covered). Any acts or omissions by 'associates' and 'former associates' of the creditor are deemed by CCA 1974, s 140A(3) to have been acts or omissions by the creditor (in so far as this is 'appropriate'). 'Associates' are defined broadly in CCA 1974, s 184 to include certain companies with shared directors.

1 Defined in CCA 1974, s 140C: the debtor must be an 'individual'.
2 Ie the U-R provisions do not apply to agreements which are exempt under RAO art 60C(2); see CCA 1974, s 140A(5). However, note that until 21 March 2016, second charge lending was governed by the CCA regime and by virtue of article 19 of the Mortgage Credit Directive Order 2015, those secured agreements which were CCA agreements but became regulated mortgage contracts on 21 March 2016 ('consumer credit back book mortgage contracts') retain the protections that they enjoyed prior to that date (including the U-R provisions).

Ways in which unfair relationship may arise

19.251 The CCA 1974, s 140A(1)–(2) provides:

(1)   The court may make an order under section 140B in connection with a credit agreement if it determines that the relationship between the creditor and the debtor arising out of the agreement (or the agreement taken with any related agreement) is unfair to the debtor because of one or more of the following—

(a)   any of the terms of the agreement or any related agreement;
(b)   the way in which the creditor has exercised or enforced any of his rights under the agreement or any related agreement;
(c)   any other thing done (or not done) by, or on behalf of, the creditor (either before or after the making of the agreement or any related agreement).

(2)   In deciding whether to make a determination under this section the court shall have regard to all matters it thinks relevant (including matters relating to the creditor and matters relating to the debtor).'

Therefore there are three ways in which a U-R can arise, which are listed in CCA 1974, s 140(1)(a)–(c).

Terms of the agreement

19.252 The first limb deals with unfairness arising from contractual terms. There is no exclusion for 'core terms', as under Pt 2 of the Consumer Rights Act 2015. Therefore a U-R can arise due to a high interest rate[1], or cost. However, whether a term is 'unfair' under the CRA 2015 is likely to be 'relevant'. It should be noted that there can also be a U-R arising from the terms of any 'related agreement'[2]. This would not only include an earlier consolidated credit agreement, but would also cover a supply contract for goods/services, or a Payment Protection Insurance (PPI) policy[3]. Therefore there could be a U-R because the price of such items is unfairly high.

1 See *Patel v Patel* [2009] EWHC 3264, [2009] CTLC 249: U-R where interest rate charged by a friend was three times that of retail banks, and was compounded monthly.
2 Defined in CCA 1974, s 140C(4).
3 Provided that the supply contract/PPI policy falls within the s 19 definition of a 'linked transaction'.

Way rights are exercised/enforced

19.253 The post-contract exercise of the creditor's 'rights' is covered by the second limb, eg the amount of any variation to the interest rate, or the manner in which debt-collection activity is undertaken. Unsolicited increases in the credit limit under a credit card agreement could also be covered, in cases where this can be criticised as irresponsible lending. An unsolicited extension in the repayment term could also be described as unfair, where this results in additional interest being payable. Any act or omission which does not literally amount to an exercise of the creditor's 'rights' will fall within the third limb. The steps the creditor takes in relation to unenforceable agreements could also give rise to a U-R, although in *McGuffick v RBS plc*[1], the High Court held that, in the context of a temporarily unenforceable agreement, taking steps which did not actually amount to 'enforcement' did not give rise to a U-R.

1   [2009] EWHC 2386 (Comm), [2010] 1 All ER 634.

Any act or omission 'by or on behalf of the creditor'

19.254 The third way in which a U-R can arise is because of something 'done (or not done) by, or on behalf of the creditor' (CCA 1974, s 140A(1)). Debtors often seek to argue that conduct by a credit broker or motor dealer should be taken into account under this subsection.

19.255 In *Plevin v Paragon Personal Finance Ltd*[1], the Supreme Court held that 'by or on behalf of' should be confined to common law agency and deemed agency. The broker in this case was not acting as Paragon's agent (indeed it was the debtor's agent) and therefore it was not acting 'on behalf of' Paragon for the purposes of the Unfair Relationships test. This is an important limitation on the breadth of s 140A. Restricting 'on behalf of' to agency follows the ordinary meaning of the statutory words, and is supported by cross-referencing other CCA provisions.

> 'The practice by which the agent of a consumer of financial services is remunerated by the supplier of those services has often been criticised. It is, however, an almost universal feature of the business, and it is of the utmost legal and commercial importance to maintain the principle that the source of the commission has no bearing on the identity of the person for whom the intermediary is acting or the nature of his functions.'[2]

1   [2014] 1 WLR 4222.
2   *Plevin v Paragon Personal Finance Limited* [2014] 1 WLR 4222 at para 33.

19.256 However, under s 56 of the CCA, negotiations conducted by a credit-broker or supplier in relation to debtor-creditor-supplier agreements are deemed to be conducted in the capacity of agent of the creditor even if no such agency actually existed. In *Scotland v British Credit Trust Ltd*[1] the Court of Appeal held that section 56 applied such that representations made by the supplier were made on behalf of the creditor. Consequently, the actions of a supplier can be relevant in the context of unfair relationship claims.

1   [2014] EWCA Civ 790.

19.257 It is made explicit in CCA 1974, s 140A(1) that acts/omissions occurring at any time are covered. For instance, the third limb encompasses irresponsible lending decisions[1], any failure to issue statutory notices (or the issue of non-compliant notices), misleading advertising and non-compliance with any other statutory provisions (whether or not express sanctions are also provided in relation to those provisions). In *Carey v HSBC Bank plc*[2], the High Court held that breach of CCA 1974, s 78 (duty to provide information on request) did not, without more, give rise to a U-R.

1   Eg where the creditor fails to take reasonable steps to check that the repayments are affordable, or where an interest-only loan is sold without checking that the debtor has a repayment vehicle in place; however an argument by the debtor that 'you should not have given me the loan I requested' is not attractive.
2   [2009] EWHC 3417, [2009] CTLC 103.

Unfairness and relevant matters

19.258 There is no indicative list of relevant matters (as there is under the E-C-B provisions). The former OFT guidance 'Unfair Relationships – Enforcement Action under Pt 8 of the Enterprise Act 2002'[1] may be considered by the court although it does not appear to have any statutory basis[2]. Matters 'relating to the creditor' will include the scope and content of any regulatory obligations imposed on the creditor. If there has been full compliance with detailed rules specifically governing the area in question, there is unlikely to be a U-R.

1   OFT 854 rev, May 2008 (updated August 2011).
2   CCA 1974, s 140D has been repealed see SI 2013/1881.

19.259 In *Harrison v Black Horse Ltd*[1], the lender selling single premium PPI had failed to disclose to the debtor that it would retain some 87% of the premium as commission. There was no obligation to disclose commission under the Insurance (Conduct of Business) Rules ('ICOB'). The Court of Appeal held (at para 58) that the 'touchstone' for whether there was a U-R must be the standard imposed by the FSA (now FCA) through ICOB, rather than a 'visceral instinct that the relevant conduct is beyond the pale'. It would be 'anomalous' if a creditor was obliged to disclose commission in order to escape a finding of a U-R, yet not obliged to disclose it under ICOB. However, this decision was disapproved in the Supreme Court in the case of *Plevin*.

1   [2011] EWCA Civ 1128, [2011] CTLC 103.

19.260 In *Tamimi v Khodari*[1], the Court of Appeal held that there was no U-R in a context where a 'very large' 10% charge had been imposed on a wealthy compulsive gambler for short-term loans. The credit risk was high, and the gambler 'wanted these loans and could well afford to repay them'. Although the U-R provisions do not explicitly incorporate any causation test, it was noted by the High Court in *Harrison v Black Horse Ltd*[2] that 'the test is still whether there is unfairness as a result'.

1   [2009] EWCA Civ 1109, [2009] CTLC 208.
2   [2010] EWHC 3152 (QB) at para 61, [2011] CTLC 103.

19.261 In *Pontearso v Greenlands Trading Ltd*[1] the High Court upheld a finding that there was no U-R in a six month bridging loan subject to 3% default rate per month which was said to be an industry standard default rate. In

Pilgrim Lock Ltd v Iwaniuk[2] the High Court dismissed an appeal that there was a U-R in respect of a £1.2 million loan at a rate of 6% compounded quarterly rising to 9% in the event of default. The lender had done nothing to enforce its rights for four years whilst interest was accruing at an escalating rate.

[1]   [2019] CTLC 73.
[2]   [2019] CTLC 96.

Gateways to make application

19.262 There are three gateways to make an application for relief (CCA 1974, s 140B(2)):

(a)   on an application made[1] by the debtor/a surety;
(b)   at the instance of the debtor/surety in any enforcement proceedings in any court to which the debtor and creditor are parties[2];
(c)   in any other proceedings in any court where the amount paid/payable under the agreement (or any related agreement) is relevant.

[1]   This must be in the county court: CCA 1974, s 140B(4).
[2]   To enforce the agreement or any related agreement.

Burden of proof

19.263 The CCA 1974, s 140B(9) provides for a reverse burden of proof: once the debtor alleges an U-R, the creditor bears the burden of proving that there is not a U-R. It is likely that the burden on the creditor is a 'persuasive' burden, which only arises once the 'evidential' burden of proof has been discharged by the debtor[1].

[1]   This was the case under the old E-C-B regime: see Guest and Lloyd, *Encyclopaedia of Consumer Credit Law*, vol 1, 2222/83–84, see *Carey v HSBC Bank Plc* [2009] EWHC 3417 (QB), [2010] Bus LR 1142, [2009] CTLC 103.

Powers of the court to order relief

19.264 If the court makes a U-R finding, there are seven categories of powers it has to order relief (CCA 1974, s 140B(1)). Any such order must be with regard to the agreement or any related agreement. Whether to order any relief, and which form of relief to grant is discretionary[1]. The seven categories of relief are:

(i)   an order requiring the creditor[2] to repay (in whole/part) any sum paid[3] by the debtor/surety by virtue of the agreement (or any related agreement);
(ii)   an injunction requiring the creditor[4] to do/not do/cease doing something[5] in connection with the agreement (or any related agreement);
(iii) reduction/discharge[6] of any sum payable by the debtor/surety by virtue of the agreement (or any related agreement);
(iv)   return to surety[7] of any property provided by him for security;
(v)   setting aside (in whole/part) any duty[8] imposed on the debtor/surety by virtue of the agreement (or any related agreement);
(vi)   alteration of the terms[9] of the agreement (or any related agreement);

(vii)   directing accounts to be taken[10].

[1] See the word 'may' in CCA 1974, s 140B(1).

[2] Or any associate/former associate of the creditor.

[3] Whether or not paid to the creditor, eg sums paid to insurers/ brokers (see also CCA 1974, s 140B(3)).

[4] Or any associate/former associate of the creditor.

[5] Eg an order requiring the cessation of debt collection activities, or requiring the creditor to respond to a request for information/documents.

[6] Eg by reducing the interest rate under the agreement.

[7] Defined by CCA 1974, s 189 to include the debtor: therefore the court could order that a mortgage be discharged.

[8] Other than repayment duties (which are covered by (iii)), eg insurance and maintenance obligations.

[9] Eg extension of the repayment period.

[10] Eg if the interest rate is reduced after an agreement has been terminated, an account may be needed to determine how much one party should pay the other.

Limitation

19.265 The leading authority on limitation periods in relation to the old E-C-B provisions is *Rahman v Sterling Credit*[1]. The Court of Appeal held that the limitation period for an E-C-B claim for declaratory relief, or relief from future liability to make payments was 12 years (Limitation Act 1980, s 8). However, the limitation period for an E-C-B claim for repayment of sums already paid was 6 years (Limitation Act 1980, s 9). It was stated obiter in *Rahman* that the 6-year period begins to run from the date of the agreement. However, it is arguable that the 6 years should instead run from the date of the last payment[2].

[1] [2001] 1 WLR 496.

[2] See Guest and Lloyd, *Encyclopaedia of Consumer Credit Law*, vol 1, 2222/84–85.

19.266 Under the U-R provisions, the date from when the 6-year limitation period starts to run may be different. In *Patel v Patel*[1] it was held that the Court must take account of unfairness throughout the 'relationship'. Therefore time only started to run when the 'relationship' ended (usually this will be when the credit agreement is redeemed).

[1] [2009] EWHC 3264 (QB), [2009] CTLC 249.

PPI MISSELLING

19.267 From 2009 onwards, there was a wave of litigation about payment protection insurance (PPI) 'misselling'. PPI is insurance to cover the debtor's credit repayments in the event of death, accident, sickness and/or unemployment. The PPI insurance policy is a separate contract between the debtor and the insurer, but it will usually fall within the CCA 1974, s 19 definition of a 'linked transaction' to the credit agreement[1]. Factually, the most common allegations are:

(i)   the debtor was told he 'had to' purchase the PPI in order to get the loan;

(ii)   PPI was not discussed at all, or inadequately discussed (eg the debtor was not orally informed that it was optional);

(iii) the PPI was unsuitable (eg because the debtor had generous employee benefits, existing insurance, or a pre-existing illness which would have been excluded);

(iv) the required documents were not provided;

(v) non-disclosure of commission[2];

(vi) failure to adequately assess a customer's demands and needs[3].

[1] Single premium PPI financed on credit will fall within CCA 1974, s 19(1)(b); monthly premium PPI may fall within CCA 1974, s 19(1)(c); being a 'linked transaction' will make it a 'related agreement' for the purposes of the unfair relationship test (CCA 1974, s 140C(4)(b)).

[2] In *Plevin v Paragon Personal Finance Limited* [2014] UKSC 61, [2014] 1 WLR 4222 the Supreme Court found that the non-disclosure of commission may render a lenders relationship with a borrower unfair (see para 18), applied in *Doran v Paragon Personal Finance Limited* [2018] WL 03328883.

[3] *Saville v Central Capital Ltd* [2014] CTLC 97.

19.268 As a matter of law, the usual causes of action are:

(i) breach of the FSA's rules (ICOB[1] or ICOBS)[2] giving rise to damages under the FSMA 2000, s 138D[3];

(ii) an 'unfair relationship' under CCA 1974, s 140A;

(iii) negligence or misrepresentation[4];

(iv) misstatement of the amount of credit, rendering the agreement irredeemably unenforceable (only for pre-6 April 2007 agreements, where it can be said that the PPI was 'required by the creditor as a condition' of the loan)[5].

[1] Insurance (Conduct of Business) Rules, in force from 14 January 2005 until 5 January 2008.

[2] Insurance (Conduct of Business) Sourcebook, in force from 6 January 2008.

[3] The Financial Services and Markets Act 2000.

[4] Usually pleaded where the agreement pre-dates the coming into force of ICOB/ICOBS, or (in the case of negligence) where there are limitation difficulties and the 'unfair relationship' regime does not apply (the debtor has a weak argument that the 'date of knowledge' provisions in the Limitation Act 1980, s 14A apply).

[5] The PPI must have been required 'by the creditor', so it seems the amount of credit cannot be misstated where it was a separate party (eg a broker/dealer) who sold the PPI and wrongly told the debtor that it was compulsory.

19.269 Whether there is an 'unfair relationship' will usually be tied to whether there has been a breach of ICOB/ICOBS, but the CCA 1974, ss 140A–140D cause of action offers the debtors the added advantage of a reversed burden of proof and more favourable limitation provisions[1]. In *Scotland v British Credit Trust Ltd*[2], a misrepresentation by a double-glazing salesmen about the need to purchase PPI when taking out a loan was taken into account by the court as something 'done by, or on behalf of, the creditor' when determining whether the relationship between the creditor and the debtor was unfair under the CCA 1974, s 140A.

[1] In *Canada Square Operations Ltd v Potter* [2021] EWCA Civ 399, the Court of Appeal upheld a decision found that a failure by the lender to disclose commission to the borrower amounted to a deliberate concealment for the purposes of s 32(1)(b) of the Limitation Act 1980.

[2] [2015] 1 All ER 708.

19.270 In *Figurasin v Central Capital Limited*[1], the court held that each communication made to a customer must be clear, fair and not misleading (see ICOBS 2.3.3). Therefore, the fact that an agreement contains all of the necessary details did not mitigate against a company that had failed to properly mention the cost of the PPI on a prior telephone call with the customer.

The Financial Guidance and Claims Act 2018 introduces a cap on the amount that claims management companies (CMCs) can charge for regulated CMC services provided in relation to PPI claims, namely 20% of the commission awarded. CMCs will not be able to recover a fee where the claim is unsuccessful. From the 1 April 2019 the FCA shall have regulatory responsibility for CMCs.

1   [2014] 2 All ER (Comm) 257.

19.271 Whilst many PPI claims were litigated, many more were dealt with via complaints to the creditor (resolved under the FCA's DISP rules) and follow on complaints to the Financial Ombudsman Service. However, the FCA put in place a deadline of 29 August 2019 for bringing claims through this mechanism.

SECRET COMMISSIONS

19.272 In *Hurstanger Ltd v Wilson & anor*[1], the Court of Appeal held that the creditor had procured the broker's breach of fiduciary duty by paying it an undisclosed commission, in circumstances where the debtor had also paid the broker a substantial fee. This was a 'half secret' commission (the fact of the possible commission payment was disclosed, but not the amount). The creditor was held to be liable to make equitable compensation to the debtor in the amount of the commission.

1   [2007] 1 WLR 2351, [2007] CTLC 59.

19.273 In *Wood v Commercial First business Ltd & ors* and *Business Mortgage Finance 4 plc v Pengelly*[1] the Court of Appeal upheld the decision that establishing a fiduciary relationship is not a pre-condition for civil liability in respect of bribery or secret commission. It is the content of the duty not the label that matters. A payee must owe a duty to provide disinterested advice or recommendations or information. It is the duty to be honest that matters. As to remedy, rescission of a transaction with the third party is available as of right in cases of secret commission, subject to making counter restitution.

1   [2021] EWCA Civ 471.

SECTION 56 DEEMED AGENCY

19.274 The CCA 1974, s 56(2) provides that certain 'antecedent negotiations' with the debtor are deemed to have been conducted by the negotiator (the credit broker/supplier) as agent of the creditor. The CCA 1974, s 56 deemed agency only arises in the context of DCS agreements: it is inapplicable to DC agreements and hire agreements. In the case of DC agreements and hire agreements, the debtor must rely on common law agency[1]. The CCA 1974, s 56(3) prevents the creditor from contracting out of the deemed agency.

1   At common law, a dealer is not normally an agent of the creditor in respect of representations, even if it receives commission from the creditor (*Branwhite v Worcester Works Finance Ltd* [1969] 1 AC 552), but the creditor may occasionally be held to have held the dealer out as its agent or be estopped from denying representations were made on its behalf (*Lease Management Services Ltd v Purnell Secretarial Services Ltd* [1994] CCLR 127).

Credit brokers

19.275 The CCA 1974, s 56(1)(b) covers negotiations conducted by a credit-broker 'in relation to goods' sold (or proposed to be sold) by the credit-broker to the creditor before forming the subject matter of a CCA 1974, s 12(a) DCS agreement. This would cover, for instance, negotiations conducted by a motor dealer in relation to a vehicle which will become the subject of a hire-purchase, conditional sale or credit sale agreement. If the dealer first sells the goods to another intermediary, who then sells them on to the creditor, the High Court has held that CCA 1974, s 56(1)(b) does not apply to representations by the dealer[1].

---

[1] *Black Horse Ltd v Langford* [2007] EWHC 907, [2007] CTLC 75.

19.276 Only negotiations 'in relation to goods' are covered. Representations about the terms of the hire-purchase or credit agreement itself are not covered[1]. However, the Court of Appeal gave a broad interpretation to the phrase 'in relation to goods' in *Forthright Finance Ltd v Ingate*[2], extending it in the context of hire-purchase to cover discussions about the discharge of an old agreement (even though the value of the old car was equal to the outstanding balance under the old agreement), as 'all the negotiations form part of the one transaction' to acquire the new car[3]. If *Ingate* is followed, representations about any linked insurance product could also be covered, in the face of the natural meaning of CCA 1974, s 56(1)(b).

---

[1] Contrast the wording in s 56(1)(a).
[2] [1997] 4 All ER 99.
[3] See also *UDT v Whitfield and First National Securities* [1987] CCLR 60: dealer's representation that he would discharge the outstanding balance under the old agreement fell within CCA 1974, s 56(1)(b), as it was an integral part of the transaction to purchase the new car.

Suppliers

19.277 The CCA 1974, s 56(1) covers negotiations conducted by the supplier 'in relation to a transaction financed' (or proposed to be financed) by a CCA 1974, s 12(b) or (c) DCS agreement. This would cover, for instance, negotiations conducted by a supplier before the debtor enters a loan agreement with a finance company to finance the purchase of goods/services. Again, representations about the credit agreement itself will not be covered[1].

---

[1] Contrast the wording in CCA 1974, s 56(1)(a).

Effect of deemed agency

19.278 Where a credit-broker/supplier is deemed to have made certain representations as the agent of the creditor (eg representations that the goods are of satisfactory quality), then the debtor may have a cause of action against the creditor for misrepresentation or (if the representations were incorporated as terms) breach of contract. The creditor could also be liable in tort (eg for negligent misstatement by the negotiator). A cause of action for misrepresentation, tort or breach of contract may entitle the debtor to rescission/repudiation of the credit agreement, or damages. The creditor could also be guilty of a statutory offence committed by the negotiator, in contravention of consumer protection legislation. The CCA 1974, s 56 claims may also be brought in respect of the financing of timeshare agreements concerning properties abroad[1].

[1]   *Jarrett v Barclays Bank plc* [1999] QB 1, which held that Art 16 of the Brussels Convention (which confers exclusive jurisdiction over actions in rem under the timeshare agreement on the courts of the place where the property is situated) did not apply. See now Art 4.1(c) of Rome I.

19.279   Section 56 does not confer on the creditor a right to an indemnity from the credit-broker/supplier for any liability it incurs as deemed principal. However, the creditor may be able to rely upon the Civil Liability (Contribution) Act 1978 or any contractual indemnity which it had in place. There is a tricky question of what happens if the credit agreement has been assigned. Guest and Lloyd[1] are of the view that the original creditor would remain liable under CCA 1974, s 56, but that if the debtor was sued for the outstanding balance by the assignee, he could still plead a counterclaim under CCA 1974, s 56 by way of set off.

[1]   Guest and Lloyd, *Encyclopaedia of Consumer Credit Law*, vol 1, 2081.

MISCELLANEOUS

Unilateral variation of agreements

19.280   Most credit agreements will give the creditor the contractual power to unilaterally vary any term of the agreement. Where this power is exercised, then CCA 1974, s 82(1) comes into effect and the variation will not take effect until notice of it has been given to the debtor in the prescribed[1] manner. The general rule is that notice of variation must be served 7 days before the variation takes effect. The CCA 1974, s 78A imposes a duty to give notice of variations in the interest rate under certain types of agreements. For agreements which are outside the scope of CCA 1974, s 78A (eg agreements secured on land), CCA 1974, s 82(1) only applies where the interest rate is varied by the creditor pursuant to a contractual power. This may exclude some automatic changes in interest rate by reference to external factors.

[1]   Consumer Credit (Notice of Variation of Agreements) Regulations 1977, SI 1977/328.

19.281   In *Paragon Finance plc v Nash and Staunton*[1], it was held that the creditor's discretion to vary an interest rate is subject to an implied term that it will not vary it arbitrarily or in a way no reasonable lender would. Variations in rate (or a failure to vary the rate) could form the basis of an unfair relationship claim.

[1]   [2002] 1 WLR 685.

19.282   The creditor's contractual power to vary will be subject to the provisions on unfair terms in the Consumer Rights Act 2015 discussed elsewhere in this book[1]. The FCA has also published guidance on variation terms in the specific context of financial services contracts (including consumer credit)[2].

[1]   See CHAPTER **9**.
[2]   The FCA's finalised guidance was published on 17 May 2018 (FG18/7).

Modifying agreements

19.283 A full analysis of this area is outside the scope of this chapter. The CCA 1974, s 82(2) introduces the concept of a 'modifying agreement', which is a subsequent agreement which varies or supplements an earlier agreement by mutual consent (in contrast to a unilateral variation under CCA 1974, s 82(1)). It is provided that a modifying agreement shall be treated as revoking the earlier agreement and containing provisions reproducing the combined effect of the two agreements (CCA 1974, s 82(2)). There are special form and content requirements for modifying agreements in the 1983 and 2010 Agreements Regulations. The rules surrounding the drafting of modifying agreements are complex and are often best avoided; in practice this is often achieved by drafting the original terms in a flexible manner such that a modification is not required, modifying agreements through the use of a unilateral right rather than by agreements or entirely replacing the old agreement with the new one (see further below).

19.284 Examples of situations where modifying agreements may have to be drafted are where a further advance is made under a loan agreement, where the term of a fixed-term agreement is extended[1], where there is a substitution in the security, or where the goods which are the subject of a hire agreement are changed.

[1] Unless this is simply by way of waiver or forbearance in allowing further time to pay, rather than a contractual variation (*Broadwick Financial Services Ltd v Spencer* [2002] EWCA Civ 35), [2002] CCLR 5.

19.285 There is often an alteration in the amount/number of repayments, or repayment term. In order for there to be a contractual modification of the agreement under CCA 1974, s 82(2), as opposed to a mere concession by the creditor, there must be some consideration provided by the debtor (eg additional payment obligations). Further, there will not be a CCA 1974, s 82(2) modification of the agreement where the changes involve a termination of the earlier agreement and its replacement by a new, separate agreement – that is a novation.

Multiple agreements

19.286 A full analysis of this difficult area is outside the scope of this chapter. A multiple agreement is defined by CCA 1974, s 18(1), as an agreement where:

    (1)   . . . its terms are such as:

        (a)   to place a part of it within one category of agreement mentioned in [the CCA] and another part of it within a different category of agreement so mentioned, or within a category of agreement not so mentioned, or

        (b)   To place it, or a part of it, within two or more categories of agreement so mentioned.

19.287 Section 18(1) therefore applies to agreements where different parts of the agreement fall within different categories of the CCA 1974, agreements which as a whole fall within more than one category ('unitary agreements') and agreements where one part thereof falls within more than one category. Where there is an agreement in parts, each part must be treated as a separate agreement and comply with the requirements of the category it falls within[1]; where there is a unitary agreement it must be treated as an agreement in each of the relevant categories[2]. Whether a 'part' is treated as a separate agreement affects the applicable form and content requirements and compliance with other CCA obligations.

1   CCA 1974, s 18(2).
2   CCA 1974, s 18(3).

19.288 In *Southern Pacific Mortgage Ltd v Heath*[1], the Court of Appeal dismissed the argument that a credit agreement was a multiple agreement where part of the advance was CCA 1974, s 11(2) unrestricted-use credit paid directly to the borrowers, and part was CCA 1974, s 11(1)(c) restricted-use credit used to redeem a prior mortgage. The Court of Appeal held (at para 41) that: 'It is not correct to start from the proposition that more than one disparate category is concerned, and to conclude from this that the agreement must fall into two or more parts'. The correct approach was set out by the Court of Appeal as follows:

> 'the starting point is that it is from the terms of the agreement that one must find out whether the agreement is one under which there are two or more parts.
>
> It is significant that it is the agreement which is to be placed in one or more categories, not the credit provided under the agreement.'

1   [2009] EWCA Civ 1135, [2009] CTLC 20.

19.289 On the facts in *Heath*, the Court of Appeal found that the credit agreement was a single agreement, saying:

> 'It is a single agreement which cannot be dissected into separate parts . . . it is not possible to collect from the document as a whole what amount to the respective terms of two or more separate agreements.'

Retaking of protected hire-purchase goods

19.290 Under a hire-purchase or conditional sale agreement, CCA 1974, s 90 provides that where the debtor is in breach of the agreement, but has paid 'one third or more of the total price of the goods', the creditor can only recover possession of the goods on a court order. The 'total price' means the total sum payable by the debtor under the agreement (including contractual interest on the credit for the goods, but excluding any payment protection premium or default interest). If the creditor proceeds, in breach of CCA 1974, s 90, to recover the goods without a court order, there is a drastic sanction: the agreement will terminate and the debtor may recover all sums he has paid under the agreement (CCA 1974, s 91).

Termination of hire-purchase and hire agreements

Hire-purchase agreements

19.291 The CCA 1974, s 99 gives the debtor the right to terminate a hire-purchase agreement at any time before the final payment falls due, by giving notice. If the creditor terminates the agreement (with the requisite notice) and the outstanding balance thereupon becomes due (under an acceleration clause), it is likely that this will amount to the 'final payment' falling due, so that the debtor cannot thereafter terminate under s 99[1].

[1]   See *Wadham Stringer Finance Ltd v Meaney* [1981] 1 WLR 39.

19.292 The CCA 1974, s 99 termination by the debtor will not affect any liability under the agreement which has already accrued (CCA 1974, s 99(2)). Further, upon termination, the debtor must pay 'the amount (if any) by which half of the total price exceeds the aggregate of the sums paid and the sums due in respect of the total price' (CCA 1974, s 100(1)). The court has the power to make an order that the debtor pay a lesser amount (CCA 1974, s 100(3))[1]. Of course, the debtor must also return the goods.

[1]   If the actual loss sustained by the creditor as a result of the termination is less than the sum payable under (1).

Section 93: increasing interest rate on default

19.293 The CCA 1974, s 93 prevents a creditor charging default interest (interest on 'sums which, in breach of the agreement, are unpaid')[1] at a higher rate than the contractual interest rate. However, it seems CCA 1974, s 93 may be circumvented by drafting the agreement so as to stipulate a certain level of repayments, then sending the debtor a 'concession letter' offering a reduced level of repayments if he makes timely payments (and making clear that such a concession is not contractually binding, or a variation of the agreement)[2].

[1]   This does not include default charges, provided they are paid on time.
[2]   *Broadwick v Spencer* [2002] CCLR 5.

Time orders

19.294 If it considers it 'just', the court may make a 'time order' under CCA 1974, s 129, providing that a debt be paid by reasonably affordable instalments. The court must have regard to the means of the debtor. Time orders are often made in the context of enforcement actions by the creditor, but may also be made in applications by the creditor for an enforcement order, or specific CCA 1974, s 129 applications by the debtor following receipt of a default/enforcement/termination notice, or a notice of sums in arrears[1].

[1]   If the debtor applies for a time order after receipt of a notice of sums in arrears, he must first give the creditor a CCA 1974, s 129A notice of intent, then wait for 14 days.

19.295 A time order can only be made in respect of sums which are already due and payable (unless the agreement is for hire-purchase or conditional sale – CCA 1974, s 130(2)). Therefore a time order can deal with arrears and, if an acceleration clause has been triggered due to default, the accelerated outstanding balance. A time order should usually be made for a fixed period, to accommodate temporary financial difficulty. If the debtor is unlikely to be able to resume the contractual instalments within time, it is more equitable to permit enforcement[1]. Upon the making of a time order, consequential orders may also be made under CCA 1974, s 136 (eg reducing the interest rate).

[1]   *Southern and District Finance plc v Barnes* [1995] CLY 724, [1995] CCLR 62.

No contracting out

19.296 The CCA 1974, s 173(1) provides that a contractual term will be void if, and to the extent that, it is inconsistent with the consumer protection provided by the CCA. This could, for instance, render void clauses stipulating that foreign law applies, or imposing a fee payable upon early settlement. However, CCA 1974, s 173(3) adds that if the CCA provides that an act may be done in relation to any person only on an order of the court/the FCA, that does not preclude that person from consenting to the act, without needing an order. The consent must be given at the time, and cannot be retrospective.

Jurisdiction

19.297 Pursuant to CCA 1974, s 141, the county court has exclusive jurisdiction over actions by the creditor to enforce regulated agreements or linked transactions.

CRIMINAL ENFORCEMENT

Offences

19.298 A large number of offences created by the CCA, as originally drafted, have subsequently been repealed. Most of these offences related to obligations on the part of the creditor/owner to supply appropriate documentation and/or information to the debtor/hirer and were repealed by the Consumer Protection from Unfair Trading Regulations 2008, Sch 4, Pt 1. Breach of the FCA Handbook rules does not give rise to criminal sanctions but may give rise to civil remedies under FSMA 2000, s 138D. In relation to financial promotions, provided that reasonable care is taken to ensure that the promotion is clear, fair and not misleading, a consumer will not have a right to damages under FSMA 2000, s 138D (CONC 3.3.1R).

Directors' liability

19.299 The CAA 1974, s 169 permits the prosecution and conviction of any director, manager, secretary or other similar officer of the company, or any person who was purporting to act in such capacity. These provisions are now covered in CHAPTER 4, Criminal Enforcement.

Statutory defence

19.300 The CAA 1974, s 168 provides a due diligence defence. This is now covered in CHAPTER 4, Criminal Enforcement.

Chapter 20

FOOD AND FEED

Contents

INTRODUCTION

20.1 The safety and composition of food is a matter of public importance, and a series of laws have been passed to ensure consumers can have confidence that the food they buy and eat is safe and is accurately described so that they know what they are eating. The majority of UK food legislation currently in force is derived from European Union law, with domestic legislation historically only providing for its enforcement. (There remain a few instances of 'domestic' food

1177

law – notable examples being the ban, since 1982, of the sale of raw milk in Scotland and the Food Hygiene Rating (Wales) Act 2013, which was passed by the National Assembly for Wales[1] on 22 January 2013 and received Royal Assent on 4 March 2013.)

Following the formal exit of the United Kingdom from the European Union on 31 July 2020, the combined effect of the European Union (Withdrawal) Act 2018 and the European Union (Withdrawal Agreement) Act 2020 was to create a body of retained EU law, subject to powers of amendment by the UK Parliament, incorporating what had previously been directly-applicable EU legislation into UK law[2]. Whilst a series of necessary amendments have been made to the retained legislation to, for example, replace references to the Community with references to the United Kingdom and in relation to procedural matters (such as the replacement of European Agencies by UK ones), the substance of the law in this area and the applicable principles remain and are expected to remain substantially as it did pre-Brexit, at least in the short term.

[1] Renamed Senedd Cymru as from May 2020, see **1.13**.
[2] References to EU Legislation, unless otherwise stated, are to the retained EU legislation as amended and incorporated into UK law.

20.2 Following the process of devolution, food legislation is now commonly made on a separate parallel basis in England, Scotland and Wales (and has been traditionally transferred in Northern Ireland) so that, for example, the Official Feed and Food Controls (England) Regulations 2009[1], the Official Feed and Food Controls (Scotland) Regulations 2009[2] and the Official Feed and Food Controls (Wales) Regulations 2009[3] each provide for the execution and enforcement of the feed and food elements of Regulation (EC) No 882/2004 (which now forms part of the body of retained EU legislation, by virtue of the process referred to above) in the respective countries of Great Britain. Food legislation is enforced in Northern Ireland by district councils, and in Scotland principally by local councils (and delegated to directors/heads of environmental health to manage local service delivery arrangements). In a work of this nature it is not possible to list all parallel provisions that were connected with the transposition of an EU Directive or Regulation into domestic legislation, and which continue to have effect post-Brexit.

[1] SI 2009/3255.
[2] SI 2009/446.
[3] SI 2009/3376.

20.3 At the time of writing there is considerable uncertainty, following Brexit, about the extent of food and feed laws applicable in Northern Ireland under the Northern Ireland Protocol. It follows that, in this edition of the Pink Book, this chapter should be considered to apply only in England, Wales and Scotland. Its application to Northern Ireland will be revisited in future editions when the UK's current negotiations with the EU on Northern Ireland Protocol have concluded.

20.4 The primary legislation presently in force in England and Wales is the Food Safety Act 1990, supported by regulations dealing with the specific and technical details of the various food industries. Since the Food Safety Act 1990 was passed there have been significant changes to food safety law in the United Kingdom, as a result principally of European Union legislation. In particular, the General Food Law Regulation, Regulation (EC) 178/2002[1], which was adopted by the European Union, and which was put into effect in England and Wales by the General Food Regulations 2004[2], effected significant amendments to the Food Safety Act 1990 itself.

[1]   Regulation (EC) No 178/2002 of the European Parliament and of the Council of 28 January 2002 laying down the general principles and requirements of food law, establishing the European Food Safety Authority and laying down procedures in matters of food safety (OJ L31, 1.2.2002, p 1).

[2]   SI 2004/3279.

20.5 Alongside the Food Safety Act 1990 are two important statutory instruments of general application in England, each initially coming into effect as a result of European legislation. This chapter concentrates on the provisions of the Food Safety Act 1990, together with the Food Safety and Hygiene Regulations (England) Regulations 2013[1] (replacing the offences formerly contained in the General Food Regulations 2004 in England[2], and the Food Hygiene (England) Regulations 2006[3], which are repealed in their entirety), and the Food Information Regulations 2014[4]. Whilst this chapter has been expanded to include commentary on nutrition and health claims made in respect of foods, the use of supplements and additives and on novel foods, detailed analysis of the considerable body of other specific legislation covering the composition and safety of food, which are often limited to particular foods or categories of foods and are often highly specific and technical, remains beyond the scope of this work.

[1]   SI 2013/2996.

[2]   The provisions of the General Food Regulations 2004, SI 2004/3279 continue to apply in Scotland and Wales.

[3]   SI 2006/14.

[4]   SI 2014/1855.

20.6 The Food Information to Consumers Regulation, Regulation (EC) No 1169/2011 ('FIC 2011')[1], entered into force on 13 December 2011. The provisions of FIC 2011 in respect of the labelling requirements have applied since 13 December 2014 and came into force on 13 December 2016 in respect of the mandatory nutrition declaration requirements. FIC 2011 modifies the previous legislation in relation to food labelling, and establishes the general principles of, and the requirements and responsibilities of food business operators governing, the provision of food information to consumers, and in particular in relation to food labelling.

[1]   Regulation (EU) No 1169/2011 of the European Parliament and of the Council of 25 October 2011 on the provision of food information to consumers, amending Regulations (EC) No 1924/2006 and (EC) No 1925/2006 of the European Parliament and of the Council, and repealing Commission Directive 87/250/EEC, Council Directive 90/496/EEC, Commission Directive 1999/10/EC, Directive 2000/13/EC of the European Parliament and of the Council, Commission Directives 2002/67/EC and 2008/5/EC and Commission Regulation (EC) No 608/2004 (OJ L304, 22.11.2011, p 18).

20.7 A series of tragic cases has increased public awareness and concern as to the regulation in particular of labelling requirements in relation to allergens. In the case of *R v Zaman*[1], the defendant's conviction for gross negligence manslaughter, and subsequent 6 year sentence of imprisonment were upheld in respect of a restaurant owner who had supplied a meal containing peanuts to a customer with a peanut allergy and who had been assured that the meal was free from peanuts. Whilst in the subsequent case of *R v Kuddus*[2], the Appellant's conviction was overturned in the particular circumstances of that case (where he personally was unaware of the deceased's allergy), the duty of care owed by food businesses to consumers remains something which the Courts will 'rigorously scrutinise'. In appropriate cases, charges of gross negligence manslaughter remain available.

1   [2017] EWCA Crim 1783, [2018] 1 Cr App Rep (S) 177.
2   [2019] EWCA Crim 837.

20.8 Following the tragic death of Natasha Ednan-Laperouse on a flight from London to Nice following an allergic reaction, concern was expressed concerning food labelling requirements as they applied to foods prepared on the premises and pre-packed for direct sale to consumers. As a result of those concerns, the Food Information (Amendment) (England) Regulations 2019[1] were laid before Parliament on the 5 September 2019, which amend the Food Information Regulations 2014 so as to require such foods to carry a label containing the name of the food and a full ingredients list with the specified allergenic ingredients emphasised. Those amendments came into force on 1 October 2021.

1   SI 2019/1218.

20.9 There is increased recognition of the role that animal feed plays in the safety of the food chain, having implications for the composition and quality of products such as milk, meat and eggs. EU legislation applies principally to feed for food-producing animals (ie farmed livestock) but also covers feed for pet animals, farmed and ornamental fish, zoo and circus animals and, in certain circumstances, creatures living freely in the wild. The Directives on the labelling and composition of animal feed cover declarations of the ingredients used (including the additives and the GM varieties which have been authorised for use in feed – but note that the requirement for the ingredients of compound feeds to be declared by their percentage weight of inclusion has been abolished), analytical declarations for protein, fibre, ash, etc, the name and address of the business, the batch number and shelf-life of the feed product, and certain allowable claims.

20.10 Feed legislation also specifies the maximum permitted levels of certain undesirable substances (contaminants), lays down a list of prohibited ingredients which must never be used in feed, and provides a list of permitted dietetic purposes for which certain feeds may be promoted. These provisions are contained in a number of measures which are given force in England by the Animal Feed (England) Regulations 2010[1] which were made under the Agriculture Act 1970 and the European Communities Act 1972. The Regulations also link provisions to the powers already available to local authority enforcement officers under the Feed (Hygiene and Enforcement) (England) Regulations 2005[2]. Separate but parallel legislation applies in Wales – the Animal Feed (Wales) Regulations 2010[3] – in Scotland – the Animal Feed (Scotland) Regulations 2010[4] and in Northern Ireland – the Animal Feed Regulations (Northern Ireland) 2010[5].

1   SI 2010/2503.
2   SI 2005/3280.
3   SI 2010/2652.

4   SSI 2010/373.
5   SR 2010/355.

FOOD SAFETY ACT 1990

Introduction and application

20.11 The Food Safety Act 1990 ('FSA 1990'), as amended, provides the overall legislative framework for food safety in the United Kingdom and operates alongside regulations setting out the detailed and specific requirements for particular industries. The FSA 1990 was amended in significant respects following the adoption into UK law of the European Union General Food Law Regulation – Regulation (EC) No 178/2002.

20.12 Enforcement of the provisions of the Act is the duty of the relevant food authority[1], unless a particular duty is imposed expressly or by necessary implication upon another authority. The Food Authorities in England are the London Borough Councils, District Councils and Non-metropolitan County Councils, the Common Council for the City of London, the Treasurers of the Inner and Middle Temples and the council of the Isles of Scilly[2]. In Wales, the Food Authorities are the County Councils or County Borough Councils, as the case may be[3].

1   Food Safety Act 1990, s 6, as amended.
2   Food Safety Act 1990, s 5(1), as amended.
3   Food Safety Act 1990, s 5(1A), as amended.

20.13 The effect of the definition of a food authority in the Act gives rise to situations in which two different food authorities have responsibility for enforcing provisions of the Act, and therefore to concurrent responsibilities. Where enforcement falls concurrently on both the county council and the district council, the Secretary of State may, by statutory instrument, specify which of the authorities has responsibility for enforcement of any particular power[1].

1   Food Safety Act 1990, s 5(4), as amended.

20.14 The Food Safety (Enforcement Authority) (England and Wales) Order 1990[1] provides that the responsibility for issuing emergency prohibition notices and orders shall be exercised solely by the district council, and that responsibility for enforcing the provisions of FSA 1990, s 15, relating to the false description and presentation of food, shall be the preserve of the county council[2].

1   SI 1990/2462.
2   Food Safety (Enforcement Authority) (England and Wales) Order 1990, SI 1990/2462, art 2. Of less general application, art 2 also provides that the Treasurers of the Middle and Inner Temples shall have responsibility for emergency prohibition notices and orders, and that the Common Council of the City of London shall have responsibility for the enforcement of the provisions of Food Safety Act 1990, s 15.

20.15 The Secretary of State may also direct that certain duties of food authorities shall be exercised either by the Secretary of State or by the Food Standards Agency, rather than by the relevant food authority[1]. The Secretary of State may additionally take over the conduct of proceedings instituted by a food authority[2], or direct that the Food Standards Agency shall take over the conduct of proceedings instituted by a food authority[3]. The Food Standards Agency may also take over the conduct of proceedings without being directed so to do by the Secretary of State, but in those circumstances only with the consent of the person instituting them[4].

[1]   Food Safety Act 1990, s 6(3), as amended.
[2]   Food Safety Act 1990, s 6(5A), as amended.
[3]   Food Safety Act 1990, s 6(5B), as amended.
[4]   Food Safety Act 1990, s 6(5C), as amended.

Key concepts and definitions

'Food'

20.16 'Food' for the purposes of the FSA 1990 has the same meaning as in Regulation (EC) No 178/2002[1]. Article 2 of Regulation (EC) No 178/2002 defines food as 'any substance or product, whether processed, partially processed or unprocessed, intended to be, or reasonably expected to be ingested by humans'. The definition includes drink (including alcoholic drinks), chewing gum and any substance, including water, intentionally incorporated into the food during manufacture, preparation or treatment. 'Food' does not however include animal feed, live animals (unless prepared for placing on the market for human consumption – for example, oysters), plants prior to harvesting, cosmetics, medicinal products, narcotics, tobacco and tobacco products or residues or contaminants[2]. A 'food source' is any growing crop or live animal, bird or fish from which food is intended to be derived (including by harvesting, slaughtering, milking, collecting eggs or by other means)[3].

[1]   Food Safety Act 1990, s 1, as amended.
[2]   Regulation (EC) No 178/2002 of the European Parliament and of the Council of 28 January 2002 laying down the general principles and requirements of food law, establishing the European Food Safety Authority, and laying down procedures in matters of food safety, Art 2.
[3]   Food Safety Act 1990, s 1(3), as amended.

'Food business'

20.17 Certain provisions of the FSA 1990 apply only to 'food businesses'. The FSA 1990, s 1(3) defines a food business as any business in the course of which commercial operations with respect to food or food sources are carried out. The definition of a business includes the operation of canteens, clubs, schools, hospitals or institutions and the undertakings and activities carried on by public or local authorities, whether carried out for profit or not, in addition to commercial enterprises.

20.18 A commercial operation is defined as selling, possessing for sale, offering exposing or advertising for sale; consigning, delivering or serving by way of sale; preparing for sale or presenting, labelling or wrapping for the purpose of sale; storing or transporting for the purpose of sale; importing or exporting; or deriving food from a food source for the purpose of sale or for purposes connected with sale[1].

[1]   Food Safety Act 1990, s 1(3), as amended.

'Sale'

20.19 Where the word 'sale' is used in provisions of the FSA 1990, it bears an extended meaning by virtue of the provisions of FSA 1990, s 2. 'Sale' includes the supply of food otherwise than on sale in the course of a business[1] – see also *Swain v Old Kentucky Restaurants Ltd*[2]. Food offered as a prize or reward or given away, either in connection with any social gathering, amusement, exhibition, performance, game, sport, or trial of skill, or for the purpose of advertisement or in furtherance of business, shall be treated as being exposed for sale by the person concerned in the organisation of the entertainment or by the person offering or giving away the food as the case may be[3]. In *Haringey London Borough Council v Tshilumbe*[4] the magistrates' court concluded there had not been a breach of an emergency prohibition order under the Food Hygiene (England) Regulations 2006, because food, cans of drink, had allegedly been supplied free of charge. On appeal, Pill LJ said:

> 'It may be that their apparent unawareness of s 2(1) FSA1990 which provides that the sale of food in s 1 extends to the supply of food, otherwise than on sale, in the course of a business, contributed to their error.'

This case reinforced the decision in *Graff v Evans*[5], where it was held that no monetary consideration was needed if the supply is in the course of a business.

[1] Food Safety Act 1990, s 2(1), as amended.
[2] (1973) 138 JP JO 84.
[3] Food Safety Act 1990, s 2(2), as amended.
[4] [2009] EWHC 2820 (Admin).
[5] (1882) 8 QBD 373.

20.20 'Sale' also includes exposure for sale and possession for sale. In relation to food law, case law has stated that it is not necessary for the purchaser to see the product for there to be an exposure for sale (*Wheat v Brown*[1], where a product wrapped in paper was still deemed to have been exposed for sale), and goods already sold and in the course of delivery to a purchaser are not in possession for sale (*Rye v Collip Ltd*[2]).

[1] [1892] 1 QB 418.
[2] *Rye v Collip Ltd* (1957) unreported.

Presumption that food intended for human consumption

20.21 Where food is commonly used for human consumption, there is a presumption that where it is sold, offered, exposed or kept for sale, the food was intended for human consumption. The presumption applies until the contrary is proven by the party seeking to establish that the presumption does not apply[1].

[1] Food Safety Act 1990, s 3(2).

20.22 Similarly:

- where food commonly used for human consumption is found on premises used for the preparation, storage or sale of that food, it is presumed that the food was intended for sale for human[1] consumption;
- where an article or substance commonly used in the manufacture of food for human consumption is found on such premises, it is presumed that

the article or substance is intended for manufacturing food for sale for human[2] consumption;

- where an article or substance capable of being used in the composition or preparation of food commonly used for human consumption is found on premises on which that food is prepared it is presumed that the article or substance is intended for such use[3].

[1] Food Safety Act 1990, s 3(3).
[2] Food Safety Act 1990, s 3(3).
[3] Food Safety Act 1990, s 3(4).

Offences

Rendering food injurious to health

20.23 The FSA 1990, s 7 creates the offence of rendering food injurious to health. The FSA 1990, s 7(1) provides as follows:

7 Rendering food injurious to health

(1) Any person who renders any food injurious to health by means of any of the following operations, namely—
(a) adding any article or substance to the food;
(b) using any article or substance as an ingredient in the preparation of the food;
(c) abstracting any constituent from the food; and
(d) subjecting the food to any other process or treatment, with intent that it shall be sold for human consumption, shall be guilty of an offence.

20.24 It must be proved to the criminal standard that the offender:

(a) either added an article or substance to the food, used an article or substance as an ingredient in its preparation, abstracted a constituent from the food, or otherwise subjected the food to some other process or treatment;
(b) which had the effect of rendering the food injurious to health; and
(c) intended that the food should be sold for human consumption.

20.25

Precedent for rendering food injurious to health

Statement of offence

RENDERING FOOD INJURIOUS TO HEALTH, contrary to s 7(1) of the Food Safety Act 1990.

Particulars of offence

A B between [date] and [date] rendered food, namely meat pies, injurious to health by means of using an article or substance as an ingredient in the preparation of the food, namely condemned meat, with intent that it be sold for human consumption.

20.26 The phrase 'injurious to health' is not further defined, but in determining whether the food in question is injurious to health, the court will have regard to certain considerations set out in paras 14(4)(a)–(c) of Regulation (EC) No 178/2002[1]. Regard shall be had:

(a)   not only to the probable immediate and/or short-term and/or long-term effects of that food on the health of a person consuming it, but also on subsequent generations;

(b)   to the probable cumulative toxic effects;

(c)   to the particular health sensitivities of a specific category of consumers where the food is intended for that category of consumers[2].

[1]   Food Safety Act 1990, s 7(2), as amended.
[2]   Regulation (EC) 178/2002, Art 14(4).

Selling food not of the nature or substance or quality demanded

20.27 It is an offence to sell food not of the nature or substance or quality demanded by the purchaser, to the purchaser's prejudice[1]. The FSA 1990, s 14(1) provides as follows:

14 Selling food not of the nature or substance or quality demanded

(1)   Any person who sells to the purchaser's prejudice any food which is not of the nature or substance or quality demanded by the purchaser shall be guilty of an offence.

(2)   In subsection (1) above the reference to sale shall be construed as a reference to sale for human consumption; and in proceedings under that subsection it shall not be a defence that the purchaser was not prejudiced because he bought for analysis or examination.

[1]   Food Safety Act 1990, s 14(1), as amended.

20.28 It must be proved to the criminal standard that the offender:

(a)   sold food for human consumption[1];

(b)   to the purchaser's prejudice;

(c)   which was not of the nature, or substance, or quality demanded as the case may be.

It is no defence to proceedings under that section that the purchaser was not prejudiced because the purchase was for analysis or examination, as in circumstances where an authorised officer makes a test purchase of food[2]. Case law under previous incarnations of this offence specified that there were three distinct offences, and that accordingly an information that pleaded that a sale was not of the nature, substance or quality demanded was bad for uncertainty[3]. Charges under this section should therefore specify only one of the three ways in which the offence is said to be committed. 'Nature' in the context of natural foods is apt to describe the variety or kind demanded (for example, supplying trout instead of salmon). 'Substance' is apt to describe matters of composition, whilst 'quality' refers to commercial quality as opposed to nature[4].

[1]   Sale is to be construed as sale for human consumption – Food Safety Act 1990, s 14(2), as amended.
[2]   Food Safety Act 1990, s 14(2), as amended.
[3]   *Bastin v Davies* [1950] 2 KB 579, [1950] 1 All ER 1095; *Moore v Ray* [1951] 1 KB 98, [1950] 2 All ER 561.

4   *Anness v Grivell* [1915] 3 KB 685; *McDonalds Hamburgers Ltd v Windle* (1987) 151 JP 333. In the latter case a purchaser who was supplied with ordinary cola rather than diet cola was held to have been sold food which was not of the quality demanded.

20.29

Precedent for selling food not of the nature demanded

Statement of offence

SELLING FOOD NOT OF THE NATURE [SUBSTANCE] [QUALITY] DEMANDED, contrary to s 14(1) of the Food Safety Act 1990.

Particulars of offence

A B on [date] sold, to the prejudice of a purchaser, namely C D, food, namely meat which was described as being minced beef, which was not of the nature [substance, quality] demanded, in that the food was in fact horsemeat.

Falsely describing or presenting food

20.30 Where food is sold, offered or exposed for sale with a label, whether or not that label is attached to or printed on the packaging, which either falsely describes the food or is likely to mislead as to the nature or quality of the food, the person selling, offering or exposing the food for sale is guilty of an offence under the FSA 1990, s 15[1]. Further offences are created in respect of the publication of advertisements falsely describing food[2] and in respect of selling, offering or exposing for sale food the presentation of which is likely to mislead as to the nature or substance or quality of the food[3]. The offences are created by FSA 1990, s 15(1), (2) and (3), which provide as follows:

15 Falsely describing or presenting food

(1)   Any person who gives with any food sold by him, or displays with any food offered or exposed by him for sale or in his possession for the purpose of sale, a label, whether or not attached to or printed on the wrapper or container, which—
(a)   falsely describes the food; or
(b)   is likely to mislead as to the nature or substance or quality of the food, shall be guilty of an offence.

(2)   Any person who publishes, or is a party to the publication of, an advertisement (not being such a label given or displayed by him as mentioned in subsection (1) above) which—
(a)   falsely describes any food; or
(b)   is likely to mislead as to the nature or substance or quality of any food, shall be guilty of an offence.

(3)   Any person who sells, or offers or exposes for sale, or has in his possession for the purpose of sale, any food the presentation of which is likely to mislead as to the nature or substance or quality of the food shall be guilty of an offence.

1   Food Safety Act 1990, s 15(1), as amended.
2   Food Safety Act 1990, s 15(2), as amended.
3   Food Safety Act 1990, s 15(3), as amended.

20.31 In relation to the offence contrary to FSA 1990, s 15(1), it must be proved to the criminal standard that the offender:

(a)   sold, offered or exposed for sale, or had in his possession for the purposes of sale, food for human[1] consumption;
(b)   with a label;
(c)   which either falsely describes the food, or is likely to mislead as to the nature or substance or quality of the food.

[1]   References to sale are to be construed as references to sale for human consumption – Food Safety Act 1990, s 15(5), as amended.

20.32

Precedent for selling food which was falsely described

Statement of offence

SELLING FOOD WHICH WAS FALSELY DESCRIBED, contrary to s 15(1) of the Food Safety Act 1990.

Particulars of offence

A B on [date] gave with food sold by him to a purchaser, namely C D, a label which falsely described the food, namely a quantity of eggs, as being free range eggs, when in fact the eggs were not free range but had been laid by battery hens.

20.33   In relation to offences contrary to FSA 1990, s 15(2), it must be proved to the criminal standard that the offender:

(a)   either published or was party to the publication of an advertisement;
(b)   which either falsely describes the food, or is likely to mislead as to the nature or substance or quality of the food.

20.34   In relation to offences contrary to FSA 1990, s 15(1) or (2), the fact that the label or advertisement carried an accurate statement of the composition of the food does not automatically provide a defence. The question remains whether the label or advertisement either falsely describes the food or is likely to mislead as to nature, substance or quality[1].

[1]   Food Safety Act 1990, s 15(4), as amended.

20.35   In relation to offences contrary to FSA 1990, s 15(3), it must be proved to the criminal standard that the offender:

(a)   sold, offered or exposed for sale, or had in his possession for the purpose of sale any food;
(b)   the presentation of which is likely to mislead as to the nature, substance or quality of the food.

Obstruction of officers

20.36 The intentional obstruction of officers or other persons acting in the execution of their duties under the Act is an offence contrary to FSA 1990, s 33. That section also creates offences relating to the failure without reasonable excuse to provide such information or assistance as may be reasonably required of a person by an officer acting in execution of his duties under the Act, or by the furnishing of false information, either knowingly or recklessly.

20.37 The FSA 1990, s 33 provides as follows:

33 Obstruction etc. of officers

(1)   Any person who—

    (a)   intentionally obstructs any person acting in the execution of this Act; or

    (b)   without reasonable cause, fails to give to any person acting in the execution of this Act any assistance or information which that person may reasonably require of him for the performance of his functions under this Act,

    shall be guilty of an offence.

(2)   Any person who, in purported compliance with any such requirement as is mentioned in subsection (1)(b) above—

    (a)   furnishes information which he knows to be false or misleading in a material particular; or

    (b)   recklessly furnishes information which is false or misleading in a material particular,

    shall be guilty of an offence.

(3)   Nothing in subsection (1)(b) above shall be construed as requiring any person to answer any question or give any information if to do so might incriminate him.

20.38 Three offences are created: intentional obstruction of a person acting in execution of the FSA 1990[1]; failing without reasonable cause to provide such information or assistance as is reasonably requested by a person acting in execution of the Act[2]; and furnishing information to a person acting in execution of the Act which he either knows to be false or misleading in a material particular, or which is false or misleading in a material particular and such information is provided recklessly[3].

[1]   An offence contrary to the Food Safety Act 1990, s 33(1)(a).
[2]   An offence contrary to the Food Safety Act 1990, s 33(1)(b).
[3]   An offence contrary to the Food Safety Act 1990, s 33(2).

20.39 In relation to offences contrary to FSA 1990, s 33(1)(a) it must be proved to the criminal standard that the offender:

(a)   intentionally;
(b)   obstructed;
(c)   a person acting in execution of the Act.

20.40 In relation to offences contrary to FSA 1990, s 33(1)(b) it must be proved to the criminal standard that the offender:

(a)   failed to give information or assistance;
(b)   to a person acting in execution of the Act;
(c)   which had been requested by that person;
(d)   that the request was a reasonable request;
(e)   that the failure was without reasonable cause.

20.41 It should be noted that FSA 1990, s 33(3) provides that the right against self-incrimination is expressly preserved. If therefore the request of information or assistance is such as would tend to incriminate the person to whom the request is made, then the person is entitled to refuse to provide such information and assistance, and would have a defence to any charge under FSA 1990, s 33(1)(b). The right is a right against self-incrimination, however – it does not extend the right to a representative of a company refusing to provide information on the grounds that it might incriminate the company[1], nor indeed on that analysis to an employee on the grounds that it might incriminate his employer or anyone else, whether that employer or other person is a company or an individual.

[1]   *Walkers Snack Foods Ltd v Coventry City Council* [1998] 3 All ER 163, [1998] EHLR 260, (1998) *Times*, April 9, DC.

20.42 In relation to offences contrary to FSA 1990, s 33(2), it must be proved to the criminal standard that the offender, having been requested to provide information or assistance by a person acting in execution of the FSA 1990, either:

(a)   provides information which he knows is untrue or misleading in a material particular; or

(b)   recklessly provides information which is untrue or misleading in a material particular.

Penalties

20.43 Under FSA 1990, s 35, offences under the FSA 1990, ss 7, 14 and 15 are triable either way[1]. The maximum sentence on indictment for each of the offences is 2 years' imprisonment, a fine or both[2]. Where an offender is sentenced in the magistrates' court, the maximum sentence is 6 months' imprisonment, a fine or both[3]. The offence contrary to FSA 1990, s 33 of obstruction of an officer is a summary only offence, and carries a maximum sentence of 3 months' imprisonment, a fine or both[4].

[1]   Food Safety Act 1990, s 35, as amended.
[2]   Food Safety Act 1990, s 35(2)(a), as amended.
[3]   Food Safety Act 1990, s 35(2)(b), as amended.
[4]   Food Safety Act 1990, s 35(1), as amended.

Time limits

20.44 Offences contrary to FSA 1990, ss 7, 14 and 15 are subject to specific time limits under FSA 1990, s 34 of the Act. By virtue of that section, no prosecution may be commenced in relation to those offences later than 3 years from the commission of the offence, or one year after its discovery by the prosecutor, whichever is the earlier. Time limits are now covered in detail in CHAPTER 4, Criminal Enforcement.

Causal liability

20.45 The FSA 1990, s 20 provides that:

20 Offences due to fault of another person

Where the commission by any person of an offence under any of the preceding provisions of this Part is due to the act or default of some other person, that other person commits the offence; and a person may be convicted of the offence by virtue of this section whether or not proceedings are taken against the first-mentioned person.

Causal liability is now covered in detail in Chapter 4, Criminal Enforcement.

Defences

The due diligence defence

20.46 In relation to all offences under the FSA 1990, a defence of due diligence applies under FSA 1990, s 21. The due diligence defence is now covered in detail in Chapter 4, Criminal Enforcement. Specific provisions apply in relation to offences under FSA 1990, s 14 (selling food not of the nature or substance or quality demanded) or FSA 1990, s 15 (falsely describing food). In relation to proceedings brought in respect of offences under those sections, if the accused neither prepared the food nor imported it into Great Britain, then the due diligence defence can be established by an accused who satisfies specified requirements under FSA 1990, s 21(3) or (4). In either case, it is for the accused to prove those facts under FSA 1990, s 21(3) or (4) as the case may be. The particular requirements do not supersede the general due diligence defence, but provide that a person who establishes those requirements shall be deemed to have made out the due diligence defence[1].

[1]   Food Safety Act 1990, s 21(2), as amended.

Defence of publication in the course of business

20.47 A further specific defence is provided where the allegation involves the advertising for sale of any food. In those circumstances, it shall be a defence for the accused to prove (to the civil standard) that he is a person whose business it is to publish advertisements, that he had received the advertisement in the ordinary course of business, and that he had no reason to suspect that its publication would amount to an offence under the Act[1].

[1]   Food Safety Act 1990, s 22, as amended.

Powers of enforcement authorities

Inspection and seizure of suspected food

20.48 Under FSA 1990, s 9 authorised officers of an enforcement authority have powers to inspect food intended for human consumption which has been sold, or is offered or exposed for sale, or is in the possession of a person for sale or preparation for sale or which is otherwise placed on the market within the meaning of Regulation (EC) 178/2002[1].

[1]   Food Safety Act 1990, s 9(1), as amended.

20.49 Where it appears to the officer that any food fails to comply with food safety requirements[1], or is likely to cause food poisoning or any communicable disease in humans[2], then such an authorised officer has the power to seize the food and remove it, so that it can be dealt with by a justice of the peace by way of an application for its condemnation, or to issue a notice specifying that it must not be used for human consumption and must not be removed except as specified in the notice[3].

[1]   Food Safety Act 1990, s 9(1), as amended.

²   Food Safety Act 1990, s 9(2), as amended.
³   Food Safety Act 1990, s 9(3), as amended.

20.50 The issue of a notice under FSA 1990, s 9(3)(a) allows an enforcement authority 21 days to determine whether or not the food contravenes food safety requirements. As soon as is practicable, and in any event within 21 days, the notice must either be withdrawn, or the food seized in order for it to be dealt with by a justice of the peace[1]. Knowingly contravening a notice issued under FSA 1990, s 9(3)(a) is a criminal offence[2].

¹   Food Safety Act 1990, s 9(4), as amended.
²   Food Safety Act 1990, s 9(3), as amended.

20.51 If it appears to a justice of the peace upon application by the authorised officer that food contravenes food safety requirements, the food will be ordered to be destroyed or otherwise disposed of to prevent it being used for human consumption, with the expenses of such destruction or disposal to be met by the owner of the food[1]. Once a justice of the peace is satisfied that the food contravenes food safety requirements, there is no discretion not to order destruction of the food – such an order is mandatory[2]. Should he not be so satisfied, or should a notice under FSA 1990, s 9(3)(a) be withdrawn, then the enforcement authority is liable to compensate the owner of the food for losses incurred[3].

¹   Food Safety Act 1990, s 9(6), as amended.
²   *R (on the application of the Food Standards Agency) v Brent Justices* [2004] EWHC 459 (Admin), (2004) 168 JP 241, (2004) 168 JPN 380.
³   Food Safety Act 1990, s 9(7), as amended.

Procurement and analysis of samples

20.52 Authorised officers of enforcement agencies have powers to take samples of foods pursuant to powers contained within FSA 1990, s 29. That section permits an authorised officer to purchase a sample of any food or substance capable of being used in the preparation of food, to take samples of any food which appears to him to be intended for sale, or to have been sold, for human consumption, or which is found by him in premises entered under his powers of entry under FSA 1990, s 32. An officer is also entitled to take samples from any food source or contact material from such premises, or from any substance within such premises which may be required as evidence.

20.53 If considered appropriate by the officer, such a sample may be submitted for analysis or examination. If it is to be analysed, then the sample should be submitted to the public analyst for the area covered by the enforcement authority, or for the area in which the sample was obtained. If it is to be examined, then the sample should be submitted to a food examiner[1]. In either case, the analyst or examiner should provide to the officer a certificate setting out the results of the analysis or examination[2]. Such a certificate is sufficient evidence within subsequent proceedings under the Act of the facts stated within it unless the other party to the proceedings requires the analyst or examiner to give live evidence[3].

¹   Food Safety Act 1990, s 30(1), as amended.
²   Food Safety Act 1990, s 30(6), as amended.
³   Food Safety Act 1990, s 30(8), as amended.

Powers of entry

20.54 Specific powers of entry are given to authorised officers of an enforcement authority by FSA 1990, s 32. Upon production of official identification showing their authority, such officers are entitled to enter premises at all reasonable hours in the circumstances specified and for the purposes specified in FSA 1990, s 32.

20.55 Under that section, authorised officers have the right to enter premises within their own authority's area for the purposes of ascertaining whether there is or has been on the premises any contravention of the provisions of the FSA 1990, or of any regulations made under the Act[1]. Authorised officers also have the right to enter business premises, whether within or outside their own area for the purpose of ascertaining whether there is on those premises evidence of a contravention within the enforcement authority's jurisdiction[2]. Where the officer is an authorised officer of a food authority, he has, in addition, the power to enter any premises for the purpose of the performance of the food authority of their functions under the Act[3].

[1] Food Safety Act 1990, s 32(1)(a), as amended.
[2] Food Safety Act 1990, s 32(1)(b), as amended.
[3] Food Safety Act 1990, s 32(1)(c), as amended.

20.56 In relation to business premises, no prior warning of the proposed exercise of the rights of entry in FSA 1990, s 32 need be given. Where the premises sought to be entered is used only as a private dwelling house, then entry as of right under The FSA 1990, s 32 shall not be demanded unless at least 24 hours' notice has been given to the occupier[1].

[1] Food Safety Act 1990, s 32(1), as amended.

20.57 The right of entry includes the right to inspect any records held relating to a food business, including records held on computer, and to take copies of such records where the officer has reason to believe that they are required as evidence. Where records are held on computer, the officer may require the assistance of the person having control of that computer, and for the records to be made available to him in a suitable format to be taken away[1].

[1] Food Safety Act 1990, ss 32(5) and 32(6), as amended.

20.58 In certain circumstances, officers may apply to a magistrate for a warrant to enter premises. Such a warrant may authorise the use of reasonable force to effect entry. In order for a warrant to be issued, a justice of the peace must be satisfied on sworn evidence that there are reasonable grounds for the entry, and either:

(a) that admission has been refused, or a refusal is anticipated, and notice of an intention to apply for a warrant has been given;
(b) that either a request for admission or notice of intention to apply would defeat the purpose of the warrant;
(c) that the case is one of urgency; or
(d) that the premises are unoccupied or the occupier is temporarily absent.

Prohibition orders

20.59 Under FSA 1990, s 11, where the proprietor of a food business is convicted of an offence under regulations made under the FSA 1990 which make provision for requiring, prohibiting or regulating the use of any process or treatment in the preparation of food; or for securing the observance of hygienic conditions and practices in connection with the carrying out of commercial operations with respect to food or food sources, and the court is satisfied that the health risk requirement is made out, then the court shall (in addition to sentencing the defendant) make a prohibition order[1].

[1]   Food Safety Act 1990, s 11, as amended.

20.60 The health risk requirement is satisfied if there is a risk of injury to health owing to:

(a)   the use, for the purposes of the business, of any process or treatment;
(b)   the construction of any premises used for the purposes of the business, or the use for those purposes of any equipment; and
(c)   the state or condition of any premises or equipment used for the purposes of the business[1].

'Injury' includes any impairment whether temporary or permanent[2].

[1]   Food Safety Act 1990, s 11(2), as amended.
[2]   Food Safety Act 1990, s 11(2A), as amended.

20.61 In those circumstances, the court must make the appropriate order for prohibition:

(a)   in a case falling within para (a) of FSA 1990, s 11(2), as set out above, a prohibition on the use of the process or treatment for the purposes of the business;
(b)   in a case falling within para (b) of that subsection, a prohibition on the use of the premises or equipment for the purposes of the business or any other food business of the same class or description;
(c)   in a case falling within para (c) of that subsection, a prohibition on the use of the premises or equipment for the purposes of any food business[1].

[1]   Food Safety Act 1990, s 11(3), as amended.

20.62 A prohibition order in those terms continues until the enforcement authority issue a certificate, certifying that the proprietor has taken sufficient measures such that the health risk condition was no longer fulfilled[1].

[1]   Food Safety Act 1990, s 11(6), as amended.

20.63 Where the breach of the regulations relate to securing the observance of hygienic conditions and practices in connection with the carrying out of commercial operations with respect to food or food sources, then the court has a discretionary power 'where the court thinks it proper to do so in all the circumstances of the case' to impose a prohibition on the proprietor, or a manager of a food business, participating in the management of any food business, or any food business of a class or description specified in the order[1].

[1]   Food Safety Act 1990, s 11(4), as amended.

20.64 A prohibition order prohibiting a proprietor from participating in the management of a food business continues until a court directs that it shall cease to have effect. A person affected by such an order may apply to the court no sooner than 6 months after the making of such an order for a direction that the prohibition order shall cease to have effect. Such a direction will be made if the court thinks it proper to do so having regard to all the circumstances of the case, including in particular the conduct of the proprietor since the making of the order. If the application is refused no further application can be made within 3 months[1].

[1] Food Safety Act 1990, s 11(8), as amended.

20.65 In *R v Crestdane Ltd*[1], the Court of Appeal considered the circumstances in which it would be appropriate for a court to exercise its discretion where it thinks it proper to do so in all the circumstances of the case to impose a hygiene prohibition order under reg 7(4) of the Food Hygiene (England) Regulations 2006 prohibiting a food business owner or manager from participating in the management of a food business.

[1] [2012] EWCA Crim 958.

20.66 The exercise of the discretion to make a hygiene prohibition order was not limited to circumstances in which the immediate closure of the premises was necessary to safeguard public health, such as would give rise to a hygiene emergency prohibition notice, although the protection of the public from a future risk of harm is clearly a relevant consideration. Where there is an immediate risk to public health that would be a powerful consideration in favour of making such an order, but even if there has been an improvement in conditions such that a hygiene emergency prohibition notice is no longer necessary, it does not follow that a hygiene prohibition order ought not to be made. It would be open to the court to conclude that notwithstanding the present improvement that there remained a sufficient future risk that a hygiene prohibition order ought to be made.

20.67 The number and nature of the breaches in the present case, particularly where they are numerous and long-standing, might give rise to such a concern, although a single breach might also be of such severity that it required the making of a hygiene prohibition order. Previous convictions and failures to heed warnings were also clearly relevant in assessing the level of future risk. Improvements made after the event were relevant, but a court was entitled to view protestations of future good conduct with a degree of scepticism where there was a history of failures to comply. Deterrence too was an important consideration. The imposition of an order was a powerful message to the food industry that strict compliance with rigorous food hygiene regulations was vital.

20.68 In any event, the future risk to human health was but one consideration. The facts of any particular offence might alone justify the imposition of a hygiene prohibition order – whilst the considerations set out above will be relevant, the discretion remains a wide one, and the test remained whether it was proper to impose such an order in all the circumstances of the case. It is likely that similar considerations will apply to the exercise of the court's discretion to make a prohibition order under FSA 1990, s 11.

Improvement notices

20.69 Where an officer has reasonable grounds for believing that the proprietor of a food business is failing to comply with certain regulations to which the section applies, he may issue an improvement notice under FSA 1990, s 10. Such notice should set out the grounds for believing that there is a failure to comply, the matters constituting the failure to comply and the measures necessary to secure compliance. The effect of such a notice is to require those measures to be taken within a specified period, which shall be not less than 14 days. Strict compliance with the requirements of FSA 1990, s 10 is necessary in order for an improvement notice to be enforceable[1]. Failure to comply with an improvement notice constitutes a criminal offence[2].

[1]   *Bexley LBC v Gardiner Merchant* [1993] COD 383.
[2]   Food Safety Act 1990, s 10, as amended.

Emergency prohibition notices and orders

20.70 Where an authorised officer is satisfied that the health risk condition[1] is fulfilled in respect of a food business, an emergency prohibition notice may be issued in respect of that business under FSA 1990, s 12. The risk of injury to health must be 'imminent' for an emergency notice to be issued. Knowingly contravening an emergency prohibition notice constitutes a criminal offence[2].

[1]   Food Safety Act 1990, s 11.
[2]   Food Safety Act 1990, s 12(6), as amended.

20.71 An emergency prohibition notice expires after 3 days unless an application is made to the magistrates' court for an emergency prohibition order. It is not necessary for the court to hear the application within the 3-day period; an application is made for these purposes once a written application is submitted to the court[1]. If such an application is made within 3 days, then the notice continues until the conclusion of such an application[2]. The proprietor of a food business must be given one day's notice of the intention of the officer to apply for such an order[3]. If a magistrates' court is satisfied, on the application of such an officer, that the health risk condition is fulfilled with respect to any food business, the court shall impose the appropriate prohibition[4]. Knowingly contravening an emergency prohibition order is a criminal offence[5].

[1]   *Farrand v Tse and Another* [1992] TLR 3.
[2]   Food Safety Act 1990, s 12(7), as amended.
[3]   Food Safety Act 1990, s 12(3), as amended.
[4]   Food Safety Act 1990, s 12(2), as amended.
[5]   Food Safety Act 1990, s 12(6), as amended.

20.72 An emergency prohibition notice or emergency prohibition order shall cease to have effect on the issue by the enforcement authority of a certificate to the effect that they are satisfied that the proprietor has taken sufficient measures to secure that the health risk condition is no longer fulfilled with respect to the business[1]. Should no application for an order be made, or the application fail, then compensation for the loss caused as a result of the emergency prohibition notice is payable to the proprietor of the food business[2].

[1]   Food Safety Act 1990, s 12(8), as amended.
[2]   Food Safety Act 1990, s 12(10), as amended.

FOOD SAFETY AND HYGIENE (ENGLAND) REGULATIONS 2013

Introduction and application

20.73 The Food Safety and Hygiene (England) Regulations 2013[1] ('FS&HR 2013') revoke and re-enact with some minor changes the Food Hygiene (England) Regulations 2006[2] and certain provisions of the General Food Regulations 2004[3] in relation to England[4]. The Regulations provide for the enforcement of certain European Regulations, namely the General Food Law Regulation (Regulation (EC) No 178/2002)[5] and a number of other regulations, defined in reg 2 of the 2013 Regulations as 'the EU Hygiene Regulations'[6]. Following the exit of the UK from the European Union, as part of the process of creating the body of retained legislation, amendments have been made to the General Food Law Regulation and to the EU Hygiene Regulations as they apply in England by the General Food Law (Amendment etc) (EU Exit) Regulations 2019[7], The General Food Hygiene (Amendment) (EU Exit) Regulations 2019[8] and the Specific Food Hygiene (Amendment) (EU Exit) Regulations 2019[9]. References to the EU Regulations below are to the retained versions as amended following exit from the EU.

[1] SI 2013/2996.
[2] SI 2006/14.
[3] SI 2004/3279.
[4] In Scotland and Wales the relevant provisions of the General Food Regulations 2004, SI 2004/3279 remain in force, as do the Food Hygiene (Wales) Regulations 2006, SI 2006/31 and the Food Hygiene (Scotland) Regulations 2006, SSI 2006/3.
[5] Regulation (EC) No 178/2002 of the European Parliament and of the Council of 28 January 2002 laying down the general principles and requirements of food law, establishing the European Food Safety Authority and laying down procedures in matters of food safety (OJ L31, 1.2.2002, p 1).
[6] Namely Regulation (EC) No 852/2004 of the European Parliament and of the Council on the hygiene of foodstuffs (OJ L139, 30.4.2004, p 1), Regulation (EC) 853/2004 of the European Parliament and of the Council laying down specific hygiene rules for food of animal origin (OJ L139, 30.4.2004, p 55), Regulation (EC) No 854/2004 of the European Parliament and of the Council laying down specific rules for the organisation of official controls on products of animal origin intended for human consumption (OJ L139, 30.4.2004, p 206), Commission Regulation (EC) No 2073/2005 on microbiological criteria for foodstuffs (OJ L338, 22.12.2005, p 1) and Commission Regulation (EC) 2075/2005 laying down specific rules on official controls for Trichinella in meat (OJ L338, 22.12.2005, p 60).
[7] SI 2019/641.
[8] SI 2019/640.
[9] SI 2019/642.

20.74 The General Food Law Regulation (Regulation (EC) No 178/2002) is the European legislation laying down the general principles of food law and laying down procedures in matters of food safety, with the aim of protecting human health and the interests of consumers in respect of food. The provisions relating to the operation of the European Food Safety Authority and the Rapid Alert System, crisis management and emergencies no longer apply to the UK. The Regulation applies at all stages of the commercial production, processing and distribution of food. The provisions of the General Food Regulation had previously been brought into effect in England by the General Food Regulations 2004, now repealed in relation to England and replaced by the provisions of the FS&HR 2013.

The most significant amendments to the General Food Law Regulation in the process of its to allow its incorporation into domestic law include:

(a)   The replacement of all references to 'the Community' with references to 'the United Kingdom';

(b)   Removal of a number of paragraphs which refer to EU aims[1];

(c)   The designation of the Food Standards Agency in England and Wales as the appropriate authority for the areas which were previously the responsibility of the European Food Safety Authority;

(d)   The designation of UK Ministers as taking responsibility for areas which previously fell under the remit of the European Commission.

Deletion of the provisions relating to the operation of the European Food Safety Authority and the Rapid Alert System, crisis management and emergencies, which no longer apply to the UK. Commission Regulation (EU) 16/2011, which implemented the Rapid Alert System for Food and Feed is also revoked

[1]   An example being para 2 of Art 5, which provided that 'Food law shall aim to achieve the free movement in the Community of food and feed manufactured or marketed according to the general principles and requirements in this Chapter'.

20.75 Enforcement of the provisions of the FS&HR 2013 is governed by reg 5, setting out the areas of responsibility of the food authorities and the Food Standards Agency.

Key concepts and definitions

'Food'

20.76 The definition of 'food' in the Food Safety Act 1990, s 1, taken from the definition in Regulation (EC) No 178/2002, applies under the 2013 Regulations as it does under the Act.

Presumption that food is intended for human consumption

20.77 Under reg 3, where food is commonly used for human consumption, there is a presumption that where it is placed on the market, or offered, exposed or kept for placing on the market, the food was intended for human consumption. The presumption applies until the contrary is proven by the party seeking to establish that the presumption does not apply[1]. The Food Safety Act 1990, s 3 sets out the detail in relation to the presumption that food is intended for human consumption, which is in identical terms save for references to 'sale' being replaced by references to 'placing on the market' – see **20.21**.

[1]   SI 2013/2996, reg 3(2).

'Food business'

20.78 A food business is defined as any undertaking, whether for profit or not, and whether public or private, carrying out any of the activities related to any stage of production, processing and distribution of food[1].

[1]   Regulation (EC) No 178/2002, Art 3.

'Food business operator'

20.79 A food business operator is defined as the natural or legal persons responsible for ensuring compliance with food law in the food business under their control[1].

[1] Regulation (EC) No 178/2002, Art 3.

Offences

20.80 Regulation 19 of the FS&HR 2013 provides that contravention of the EU provisions specified in Sch 2 to the Regulations constitutes a criminal offence under the law of England. The General Food Law (Amendment) (EU Exit) Regulations 2019 substituted a new schedule for that which had applied previously. The provisions (in each case as amended by the EU Exit Regulations) now specified in Sch 2 are as follows:

(1)   Article 12 of Regulation (EC) No 178/2002, as it relates to food;
(2)   Article 14(1) of Regulation (EC) No 178/2002;
(3)   Article 16 of Regulation (EC) No 178/2002, as it relates to food;
(4)   Article 18(2) and (3) of Regulation (EC) No 178/2002, as it relates to food business operators;
(5)   Article 19 of Regulation (EC) No 178/2002;
(6)   The provisions of the EU Hygiene Regulations specified in the Schedule.

Exporting in contravention of requirements of food law

20.81 Article 12 of Regulation (EC) 178/2002 provides that:

1. Food and feed exported or re-exported from the United Kingdom for placing on the market of a third country shall comply with the relevant requirements of food law, unless otherwise requested by the authorities of the importing country or established by the laws, regulations, standards, codes of practice and other legal and administrative procedures as may be in force in the importing country.

In other circumstances, except in the case where foods are injurious to health or feeds are unsafe, food and feed can only be exported or re-exported if the competent authorities of the country of destination have expressly agreed, after having been fully informed of the reasons for which and the circumstances in which the food or feed concerned could not be placed on the market in the United Kingdom.

2. Where the provisions of a bilateral agreement concluded between the United Kingdom and a third country are applicable, food and feed exported from the United Kingdom to that third country must comply with those provisions.

20.82 It is an offence therefore to export or re-export food from the UK which does not comply with the requirements of food law. It must be proved to the criminal standard that the offender:

(a)   exported or re-exported food from the UK to a third country;
(b)   which failed to comply with the relevant requirements of food law, unless:
      (i)   the export is in accordance with the law, regulations, standards etc. of the importing country; or

(ii)   the export is with the express agreement of the importing country, having been fully informed of the circumstances of non-compliance with EU Food Law.

Contravention of food safety requirements

20.83 Article 14 of Regulation (EC) No 178/2002 provides that:

1. Food shall not be placed on the market if it is unsafe.

2. Food shall be deemed to be unsafe if it is considered to be:
(a)   injurious to health;
(b)   unfit for human consumption.

20.84 It is an offence therefore to place food on the market which is unsafe. It must be proved to the criminal standard that the offender:

(a)   placed food on the market;
(b)   which is unsafe, in that it is either:
(i)   injurious to health; or
(ii)   unfit for human consumption.

20.85 The question of whether food is unsafe is a question of fact in each case. Further assistance is given in determining that issue in Art 14. In considering whether food is unsafe, regard is to be had to the normal conditions of use of the food by the consumer and at each stage of production, processing and distribution, and to any information provided to the consumer concerning the avoidance of specific adverse health effects from a particular food or foods[1].

[1]   Regulation (EC) No 178/2002, Art 14(3).

20.86 Specific guidance as to whether a food is injurious to health can be found in Art 14 of Regulation (EC) No 178/2002. Regulation 14 is discussed in relation to the offence contrary to the Food Safety Act 1990, s 7 – see **20.23**.

20.87 In considering whether food is unfit for human consumption, regard is to be had to whether the food is unfit for human consumption according to its intended use, as a result of contamination or through putrefaction, deterioration or decay[1]. Where, however, there are specific provisions concerning food safety applicable to the food in question, then compliance with those provisions will mean that the food is deemed to be safe insofar as the aspects covered by the provisions are concerned[2]. A finding that food is unsafe in respect of food which forms part of a batch, lot or consignment will give rise to a presumption that the remainder of the batch, lot or consignment is also unsafe, unless on detailed analysis of the remainder there is no evidence that the remainder is unsafe[3].

[1]   Regulation (EC) No 178/2002, Art 14(5).
[2]   Regulation (EC) No 178/2002, Art 14(7).
[3]   Regulation (EC) No 178/2002, Art 14(6).

Presentation of food

20.88 Article 16 of Regulation (EC) No 178/2002 reads as follows:

Presentation

Without prejudice to more specific provisions of food law, the labelling, advertising and presentation of food or feed, including their shape, appearance or packaging, the packaging materials used, the manner in which they are arranged and the setting in which they are displayed, and the information which is made available about them through whatever medium, shall not mislead consumers.

20.89 It must be proved to the criminal standard that the offender has:

(a)   misled consumers;
(b)   by way of the labelling, advertising or presentation of food.

Traceability of food

20.90 Article 18 imposes obligations upon food business operators to ensure that traceability of all food, feed, food-producing animals and other substances can be established in respect of food. Obligations are imposed upon food and feed business operators to ensure that proper records are kept, both of food and other substances supplied to them, and food and other substances supplied by them to others. The relevant Article reads as follows:

Traceability

1. The traceability of food, feed, food-producing animals, and any other substance intended to be, or expected to be, incorporated into a food or feed shall be established at all stages of production, processing and distribution.

2. Food and feed business operators shall be able to identify any person from whom they have been supplied with a food, a feed, a food-producing animal, or any substance intended to be, or expected to be, incorporated into a food or feed. To this end, such operators shall have in place systems and procedures which allow for this information to be made available to the competent authorities on demand.

3. Food and feed business operators shall have in place systems and procedures to identify the other businesses to which their products have been supplied. This information shall be made available to the competent authorities on demand.

4. Food or feed which is placed on the market or is likely to be placed on the market in the United Kingdom shall be adequately labelled or identified to facilitate its traceability, through relevant documentation or information in accordance with the relevant requirements of more specific provisions.

Specific provision is made for the making of regulations in relation to specific sectors in England, Wales, Scotland and Northern Ireland in accordance with the different procedures applying in those nations in new paras 5 to 16 inserted by the General Food Law (Amendment) (EU Exit) Regulations 2019. Breach of any of the obligations imposed by Art 14 is, if proved to the criminal standard, an offence.

Withdrawal, recall and notification

20.91 Article 19 of Regulation (EC) No 178/2002 covers the responsibilities of food business operators in a situation in which the food business operator considers or has reason to believe that food for which it bears responsibility is unsafe. In those circumstances, the food business operator has a duty to initiate proceedings to withdraw the food and inform the authorities, and to recall the food where the food may have reached consumers. Article 19 provides:

Responsibilities for food: food business operators

1. If a food business operator considers or has reason to believe that a food which it has imported, produced, processed, manufactured or distributed is not in compliance with the food safety requirements, it shall immediately initiate procedures to withdraw the food in question from the market where the food has left the immediate control of that initial food business operator and inform the competent authorities thereof. Where the product may have reached the consumer, the operator shall effectively and accurately inform the consumers of the reason for its withdrawal, and if necessary, recall from consumers products already supplied to them when other measures are not sufficient to achieve a high level of health protection.

2. A food business operator responsible for retail or distribution activities which do not affect the packaging, labelling, safety or integrity of the food shall, within the limits of its respective activities, initiate procedures to withdraw from the market products not in compliance with the food-safety requirements and shall participate in contributing to the safety of the food by passing on relevant information necessary to trace a food, cooperating in the action taken by producers, processors, manufacturers and/or the competent authorities.

3. A food business operator shall immediately inform the competent authorities if it considers or has reason to believe that a food which it has placed on the market may be injurious to human health. Operators shall inform the competent authorities of the action taken to prevent risks to the final consumer and shall not prevent or discourage any person from cooperating, in accordance with national law and legal practice, with the competent authorities, where this may prevent, reduce or eliminate a risk arising from a food.

4. Food business operators shall collaborate with the competent authorities on action taken to avoid or reduce risks posed by a food which they supply or have supplied.

20.92 Failure to comply with those duties is a criminal offence. In the case of a breach of Art 19(1), it must be proved to the criminal standard that the offender:

(a)   was the operator of food business;

(b)   who considered, or had reason to believe, that food which the business had imported, produced, processed, manufactured or distributed is not in compliance with the food safety requirements;

(c)   failed to fulfil his responsibilities under Art 14 in respect of withdrawal, recall and/or notification as the case may be.

Failure to comply with hygiene regulations

20.93 It is an offence contrary to reg 19 of the FS&HR 2013 to contravene or to fail to comply with specified provisions of Regulation (EC) No 852/2004[1], Regulation (EC) No 853/2004[2], Regulation (EC) No 2073/2005[3] and Regulation (EC) No 2075/2005. It must be proved to the criminal standard that the offender:

(a)   was subject to a provision of the EU Hygiene Regulations (as retained legislation in their amended versions) specified in Sch 2; and

(b)   contravened or failed to comply with the requirements of that provision.

[1]   OJ L139, 30.4.2004, p 1.
[2]   OJ L139, 30.4.2004, p 55.
[3]   OJ L139, 30.4.2004, p 206.

Obstruction of officers

20.94 Similar offences to those created by the Food Safety Act 1990, s 33 are created by reg 17 of the FS&HR 2013, which provides as follows:

17 Obstruction etc. of officers

(1)   Any person who—

    (a)   intentionally obstructs a person acting in the execution of the Hygiene Regulations or Regulation 178/2002; or

    (b)   without reasonable cause, fails to give to any person acting in the execution of the Hygiene Regulations or Regulation 178/2002 any assistance or information which that person may reasonably require of them for the performance of their functions under the Hygiene Regulations,

    commits an offence.

(2)   Any person who, in purported compliance with any such requirement as is mentioned in sub-paragraph (b) of paragraph (1)—

    (a)   furnishes information which they know to be false or misleading in a material particular; or

    (b)   recklessly furnishes information which is false or misleading in a material particular,

    commits an offence.

(3)   Nothing in sub-paragraph (b) of paragraph (1) is to be construed as requiring any person to answer any question or give any information if to do so might incriminate them.

The considerations in relation to obstruction of officers under reg 17 are identical to those set out in relation to the Food Safety Act 1990, s 33 – see **20.36**.

Penalties

20.95 Regulation 19(1) provides that a contravention of, or a failure to comply with, any of the specified EU provisions constitutes an offence. Offences contrary to the FS&HR 2013 (other than offences relating to the obstruction of officers contrary to reg 17 and offences under paras 1A or 1B of Sch 6 relating to the sale of raw milk) are offences which are triable either way. The maximum sentence on indictment for such offences is a term of imprisonment not exceeding 2 years, a fine, or both[1]. Where an offender is sentenced in the magistrates' court, the maximum sentence is a fine[2].

[1]   SI 2013/2996, reg 19(2)(b).
[2]   SI 2013/2996, reg 19(2)(a).

20.96 In relation to offences contrary to reg 19(1), the sentencing court must now have regard to the Sentencing Council's Definitive Guideline for Health and Safety Offences, Corporate Manslaughter and Food Safety and Hygiene Offences. Separate guidelines are included within the Definitive Guideline for offences committed by corporate defendants and by individuals. The Definitive Guideline is published on the Sentencing Council's website[1].

[1]   www.sentencingcouncil.org.uk.

20.97 Offences contrary to reg 17 (obstruction of officers) are summary-only offences. The maximum sentence is 3 months' imprisonment, a fine or both[1].

Offences under paras 1A or 1B (relating to the sale of raw milk) are summary-only offences. The maximum sentence is a fine[2].

1   SI 2013/2996, reg 19(3).
2   SI 2013/2996, reg 19(3A).

Hygiene prohibition orders

20.98 Where the proprietor of a food business is convicted of an offence under the FS&HR 2013 then, under reg 7 of the Regulations, the sentencing court has the power to make a hygiene prohibition order. Where the court is satisfied that the health risk requirement is made out, then the court shall (in addition to sentencing the defendant) make a hygiene prohibition order in the appropriate terms[1]. In addition, a hygiene prohibition order may be made at the discretion of the court where 'it thinks it proper to do so in all the circumstances of the case', prohibiting a food business owner or manager from participating in the management of any food business, or any food business of a particular class[2].

1   SI 2013/2996, reg 7(1).
2   SI 2013/2996, reg 7(4).

20.99 The health risk requirement is satisfied if there is a risk of injury to health owing to:

(a)   the use for the purposes of the business of any process or treatment;
(b)   the construction of any premises used for the purposes of the business, or the use for those purposes of any equipment; and
(c)   the state or condition of any premises or equipment used for the purposes of the business[1].

'Injury' includes any impairment whether temporary or permanent[2].

1   SI 2013/2996, reg 7(2).
2   SI 2013/2996, reg 7(2).

20.100 In those circumstances, the court must make the appropriate order for prohibition:

(a)   in a case falling within para (a) of reg 7(2) above, a prohibition on the use of the process or treatment for the purposes of the business;
(b)   in a case falling within para (b) of reg 7(2), a prohibition on the use of the premises or equipment for the purposes of the business or any other food business of the same class or description;
(c)   in a case falling within para (c) of reg 7(2), a prohibition on the use of the premises or equipment for the purposes of any food business[1].

1   SI 2013/2996, reg 7(3).

20.101 A prohibition order in those terms continues until the enforcement authority issue a certificate, certifying that the proprietor has taken sufficient measures such that the health risk condition was no longer fulfilled[1]. In addition to cases in which the health risk condition is fulfilled, the court has a discretionary power to impose a prohibition on the proprietor, or a manager of a food business, participating in the management of any food business, or any food business of a class or description specified in the order. Such an order may be made by the court if it 'thinks it proper to do so in all the circumstances of the case'[2].

[1] SI 2013/2996, reg 7(6)(a).
[2] SI 2013/2996, reg 7(4).

20.102 The circumstances in which the court ought to exercise its discretion under reg 7(4) were considered by the Court of Appeal in *R v Crestdane Ltd*[1]. See **20.66**.

[1] [2012] EWCA Crim 958.

20.103 The number and nature of the breaches in the present case, particularly where they are numerous and long-standing, might give rise to such a concern, although a single breach might also be of such severity that it required the making of a hygiene prohibition order. Previous convictions and failures to heed warnings were also clearly relevant in assessing the level of future risk.

20.104 Improvements made after the event were relevant, but a court was entitled to view protestations of future good conduct with a degree of scepticism where there was a history of failures to comply. Deterrence too was an important consideration. The imposition of an order was a powerful message to the food industry that strict compliance with rigorous food hygiene regulations was vital.

20.105 In any event, the future risk to human health was but one consideration. The facts of any particular offence might alone justify the imposition of a hygiene prohibition order – whilst the considerations set out above will be relevant, the discretion remains a wide one, and the test remained whether it was proper to impose such an order in all the circumstances of the case.

20.106 A prohibition order prohibiting a proprietor from participating in the management of a food business continues until a court directs that it shall cease to have effect[1]. A person affected by such an order may apply to the court no sooner than 6 months after the making of such an order for a direction that the prohibition order shall cease to have effect. Such a direction will be made if the court thinks it proper to do so having regard to all the circumstances of the case, including in particular the conduct of the proprietor since the making of the order. If the application is refused, no further application can be made within 3 months[2].

[1] SI 2013/2996, reg 7(6)(b).
[2] SI 2013/2996, reg 7(8).

Time limits for prosecutions

20.107 Offences contrary to the FS&HR 2013 are subject to specific time limits under reg 18. By virtue of that regulation, no prosecution may be commenced in relation to those offences later than 3 years from the commission of the offence, or 1 year after its discovery by the prosecutor, whichever is the earlier. Time limits are now covered in CHAPTER 4, Criminal Enforcement.

Directors' liability

20.108 Regulation 20 provides for individual responsibility where an offence is committed by a body corporate with the consent or connivance of a director, manager, secretary or similar officer, or the offence is attributable to their neglect. The Regulation is in identical terms to the Food Safety Act 1990, s 36. Directors' liability is now covered in CHAPTER 4, Criminal Enforcement.

Causal liability

20.109 Regulation 11 provides that:

11 Offences due to the fault of another person

Where the commission by any person of an offence under these Regulations is due to the act or default of some other person, that other person commits the offence; and a person may be convicted of the offence by virtue of this regulation whether or not proceedings are taken against the first-mentioned person.

20.110 The provision is in effectively the same terms as the Food Safety Act 1990, s 20 and applies to offences under the FS&HR 2013 as it does under the Act. Causal liability is now dealt with in detail in CHAPTER 4, Criminal Enforcement.

Defences

Due diligence

20.111 The general defence of due diligence applies under reg 12 of the FS&HR 2013 as under the Food Safety Act 1990, s 21. Due diligence defences are now covered generally in CHAPTER 4, Criminal Enforcement.

20.112 Specific considerations apply in relation to offences relating to contraventions of Art 12 or Art 14 of Regulation (EC) No 178/2002. If the accused neither prepared the food nor imported it into the UK, then the due diligence defence can be established by an accused who satisfies specified requirements under reg 12(3) or (4). In either case, it is for the accused to prove those facts under reg 12(3) or (4) as the case may be. The particular requirements do not supersede the general due diligence defence, but provide that a person who establishes those requirements shall be deemed to have made out the due diligence defence[1].

[1]   SI 2013/2996, reg 12(2).

Defence in relation to exports

20.113 Under reg 13 it is a defence to an offence of contravening or failing to comply with food law for the accused to prove that:

(a)   the item in respect of which the offence is alleged to have been committed was intended for export to a country that is not a Member State and that the item could lawfully be exported there under Art 12 of Regulation (EC) No 178/2002; or

(b) the item in respect of which the offence is alleged to have been committed was intended for export to a Member State and that:

   (i) the legislation applicable to that item in that Member State is compatible with the relevant provisions of food law (except in so far as it relates to feed produced for or fed to food producing animals) at EU level, and

   (ii) the item complies with that legislation.

Powers of enforcement authorities

Inspection and seizure of suspected food

20.114 The provisions of the Food Safety Act 1990, s 9 apply for the purpose of the FS&HR 2013 to authorised officers of an enforcement authority under the FS&HR 2013 as to authorised officers of a food authority under the Act[1].

[1] SI 2013/2996, reg 25.

Procurement and analysis of samples

20.115 Equivalent powers in respect of the procurement (in reg 14) and analysis (in reg 15) of samples are given to authorised officers enforcing the food hygiene legislation as are contained within the Food Safety Act 1990, ss 29 and 30. Save for references to the Act being replaced by references to the Regulations, regs 14 and 15 are in identical terms to FSA 1990, ss 29 and 30.

Powers of entry

20.116 Regulation 16 of the FS&HR 2013 provides authorised officers of an enforcement authority in relation to Regulation (EC) No 178/2002 or the EU Hygiene Regulations with comparable powers of entry to those exercised by authorised officers of a food authority under the Food Safety Act 1990, s 32. Save for references to the Act being replaced by references to the EU Regulations and other minor modifications, reg 16 is in identical terms to the Food Safety Act 1990, s 32, and extends identical powers of entry including in relation to the applications for warrants to authorised officers enforcing the provisions of Regulation (EC) No 178/2002 and the EU Hygiene Regulations.

Hygiene improvement notices

20.117 Where an officer has reasonable grounds for believing that the food business operator is failing to comply with the Hygiene Regulations, he may issue an improvement notice under reg 6. Such notice should set out the officer's grounds for believing that there is a failure to comply, the matters constituting the failure to comply and the measures necessary to secure compliance. The effect of such a notice is to require those measures to be taken within a specified period, which shall be not less than 14 days. Failure to comply with a hygiene improvement notice constitutes a criminal offence[1].

[1] SI 2013/2996, reg 6(2).

Hygiene emergency prohibition notices and orders

20.118 The considerations in relation to hygiene emergency prohibition notices and orders are identical to those set out in the section detailing emergency prohibition notices and orders under the Food Safety Act 1990 (see **20.71** above).

Remedial action notices

20.119 Where it appears to an authorised officer that[1] any of the requirements of the Hygiene Regulations is being breached or inspection under the Hygiene Regulations is being hampered, the officer may serve on the food business operator or duly authorised representative a remedial action notice. A remedial action notice may prohibit the use of any equipment or any part of the establishment specified in the notice; impose conditions upon or prohibit the carrying out of any process; or require the rate of operation to be reduced to such extent as is specified in the notice, or to be stopped completely.

[1] In relation to an establishment requiring approval under Art 4(2) of Regulation 853/2004.

20.120 The notice must be served as soon as practicable, and state why it is being served, and if it is served as a result of alleged breaches of the Hygiene Regulations, it must specify the breach and the action needed to remedy it. As soon as the enforcement authority is satisfied that such remedial action has been taken, a further notice should be served, withdrawing the remedial action notice. Any person who fails to comply with a remedial action notice commits an offence.

Detention notices

20.121 An authorised officer may, in relation to an establishment requiring approval under Art 4(2) of Regulation (EC) No 853/2004 serve on the food business operator a detention notice, requiring the detention of any animal or food for the purpose of examination, or the taking of samples. As soon as the enforcement authority is satisfied that detention is no longer required, a further notice should be served, withdrawing the detention notice. Any person who fails to comply with a detention notice commits an offence.

Rights of appeal

20.122 There is a right of appeal against a decision of an authorised officer of an enforcement authority to serve a hygiene improvement notice, a decision of an enforcement authority to refuse to issue a certificate that the health risk condition is no longer fulfilled under para (6) of reg 7 or para (8) of reg 8, or a decision of an authorised officer of an enforcement authority to serve a Remedial Action Notice by way of complaint to a magistrates' court[1]. On appeal, the court may cancel the notice, or affirm it, either in its original form or with such modifications as the court thinks fit[2].

[1] SI 2013/2996, reg 22.
[2] SI 2013/2996, reg 24.

20.123 There is a further right of appeal to the Crown Court following either the dismissal of an appeal under reg 22, or the making of a hygiene prohibition order or emergency hygiene prohibition order by the magistrates' court[1].

[1] SI 2013/2996, reg 23.

THE EU FOOD INFORMATION REGULATION

Introduction and application

20.124 On 25 October 2011, the European Parliament and the Council adopted the Regulation on the Provision of Food Information to Consumers (Regulation (EU) No 1169/2011) ('FIC 2011')[1]. FIC 2011 came into force on 12 December 2011, and enacts significant changes to the existing EU law on the labelling of food.

[1] Regulation (EU) No 1169/2011 of the European Parliament and of the Council of 25 October 2011 on the provision of food information to consumers, amending Regulations (EC) No 1924/2006 and (EC) No 1925/2006 of the European Parliament and of the Council, and repealing Commission Directive 87/250/EEC, Council Directive 90/496/EEC, Commission Directive 1999/10/EC, Directive 2000/13/EC of the European Parliament and of the Council, Commission Directives 2002/67/EC and 2008/5/EC and Commission Regulation (EC) No 608/2004 (OJ L304, 22.11.2011, p 18).

20.125 The requirements of FIC 2011 applied from 1 January 2014 in respect of the provisions relating to the composition of and labelling of minced meat, from 13 December 2014 in respect of the general food labelling requirements, and from 13 December 2016 in respect of the provisions relating to the mandatory provision of nutrition information.

20.126 FIC 2011 required national legislation in order for its provisions to be brought into effect in the UK, and the Food Information Regulations 2014 ('FIR 2014')[1] were implemented in England on 14 July 2014. Equivalent legislation exists in Wales, Scotland and Northern Ireland. The provisions of FIC 2011 replaced the labelling requirements of the Food Labelling Regulations 1996 ('FLR 1996') from 13 December 2014.

[1] SI 2014/1855.

20.127 Most of the FLR 1996 was repealed by the FIR 2014 with effect from 13 December 2014, although some provisions remain in place until 13 December 2018[1]. Equivalent offences to many of the specific offences contained in the FLR 1996 are not included in the FIR 2014, and the initial frontline measure will be the issuing of an improvement notice under the Food Safety Act 1990, s 10. Failure to comply with such a notice constitutes a criminal offence. Such an approach marked a radical departure from the regime which had applied previously.

[1] SI 2014/1855, Sch 6, Pts 1 and 2.

20.128 The Food Safety Act 1990, ss 10 (improvement notices), 20 (offences due to fault of another), 21 (due diligence defence), 35 (punishment of offences) and 37 (appeals) apply with modifications, as do the powers of entry under FSA 1990, s 32[1]. The FSA 1990, ss 3 (presumptions that food is intended for human consumption), 22 (defence of publication in the course of business), 30(8) (which relates to documentary evidence), 33 (obstruction etc of officers), and 36 (offences by bodies corporate) also apply².

1   SI 2014/1855, Sch 4, Pts 1 and 2, 3 and 5.
2   SI 2014/1855, Sch 4, Pt 5.

20.129 Failure to comply with certain articles of FIC 2011 relating to the provision of information in respect of ingredients causing allergies or intolerances is a separate offence, triable summarily with a fine¹.

1   SI 2014/1855, reg 10.

20.130 In appropriate cases, prosecutions may be brought under other legislation – for example, where the labelling of the food is misleading, a prosecution may be brought under reg 19 of the Food Safety and Hygiene (England) Regulations 2013 and Art 16 of Regulation (EC) No 178/2002.

20.131 Specific provision is also made in respect of food sold after the expiry of a 'use by' date, which by virtue of Art 24(1) of FIC 2011 is deemed to be unsafe for the purposes of reg 14 of Regulation (EC) No 178/2002. Accordingly a prosecution can be brought under reg 19 of the Food Safety and Hygiene (England) Regulations 2013, without further proof being required that the food is unsafe.

20.132 The debate as to whether Art 24(1) created merely an evidential presumption or an absolute rule of law, such that a defendant cannot rebut the proposition by adducing evidence that food was not unsafe at the material time has now been resolved by the Divisional Court in the case of *Regina (on the application of Tesco Stores Ltd v Birmingham Magistrates Court and Birmingham City Council)*¹. The Divisional Court held that the language of Art 24(1) was unambiguous and clear. It did not create a presumption that food was unsafe which could be rebutted by evidence, but conclusively established that food which was labelled with a 'use-by' date that had passed was 'unsafe' within the meaning of the Regulation. Accordingly, food that is displayed for sale, or otherwise placed on the market, labelled with a 'use-by' date that has expired is 'unsafe' for the purposes of Art 14 of the Food Safety Regulation, and that fact could not be controverted by evidence. An FBO which is responsible for placing such food on the market acts in breach of Art 14, and is thus (subject to any defence of due diligence) guilty of an offence under reg 19 of the 2013 Regulations. The position therefore remains as it was under the predecessor offence, reg 44(1)(d) of the Food Labelling Regulations 1996¹².

1   [2020] EWHC 799 (Admin).
2   See *Torfaen CBC v Douglas Willis Ltd* [2013] UKSC 59, [2013] 4 All ER 1, [2013] CTLC 136.

20.133 The *Birmingham* case raised an important point of practice in relation to the re-labelling food that is the subject of a use-by date. Hickinbottom LJ stated that:

'Article 24 essentially defines "unsafe" food to include that which, after its use by date, is considered to pose an unacceptable risk to those who might consume it, on a prospective assessment in relation to such a food made by the relevant FBO on the basis of the general characteristics of that food and how it might be treated before consumption. It thus avoids the need to determine, as a matter of evidence in each case, whether specific food is actually "safe to eat" in the circumstances of the particular case. If someone further down the line considers that that assessment is for any reason wrong, the scheme allows him to re-assess the risk (again, prospectively) and re-label the food; but that can only be done on the basis of (microbiological) evidence (general or specific) and on the basis that he (the re-assessor) bears responsibility for his new assessment and labelling.[1]'

This reflects Art 8(4) FIC 2011 which makes the relevant food business operator[2] ('FBO') responsible for any modifications in the food information provided[3]. It follows that a use-by date can be changed by the responsible FBO where it re-assesses on the basis of microbiological evidence. The capacity to re-label would not appear to depend on whether the original use-by date has expired or not.

[1] Paragraph 61, see also Swift J at para 73 'There was no evidence that any of the hard case situations suggested had ever arisen; even if any of them did arise, as explained by Hickinbottom LJ, they could in all likelihood be addressed by the re-labelling provisions contained in the EU Regulations'.
[2] Article 8(1) FIC 2011 ' . . . the operator under whose name or business name the food is marketed . . . '
[3] Article 8(4) FIC 2011 – Food business operators, within the businesses under their control, shall not modify the information accompanying a food if such modification would mislead the final consumer or otherwise reduce the level of consumer protection and the possibilities for the final consumer to make informed choices. Food business operators are responsible for any changes they make to food information accompanying a food.

20.134 The provisions of FIC 2011 apply to any food intended for supply to the final consumer or to mass caterers. In such a case, the food must be accompanied by food information complying with FIC 2011[1]. The responsibility for compliance lies with food business operator under whose name or business name the food is marketed or, if that operator is not established in the Union, the importer into the Union market[2]. Guidance has been produced by Defra in relation to FIC 2011 and the FIR 2014, with the most recent update in October 2016.

[1] Regulation (EU) No 1169/2011, Art 6.
[2] Regulation (EU) No 1169/2011, Art 8.

Key provisions of FIC 2011

Fair information practices

20.135 Article 7 specifies fair information practices in respect of food. It provides that food information must not be misleading, particularly as to the characteristics of the food, by attributing to food properties which it does not possess, by suggesting that the food has some special characteristic where all similar foods possess those characteristics (such as the presence or absence of an ingredient which is common to all similar foods) or by suggesting the presence of a particular ingredient which is not present.

20.136 Food information must be clear, accurate and easy to understand for the consumer. Fair information practices extend to advertising of food, and to the presentation of food.

20.137 Subject to derogations applicable to natural mineral waters and foods for particular nutritional uses, food information must not attribute to any food the property of preventing, treating or curing a human disease, nor refer to such properties.

General labelling requirements

20.138 The general requirements in respect of food labelling of pre-packed goods are contained in Art 9. The food must be labelled with the name of the food, an ingredients list, information in relation to the use of certain foods causing allergies or intolerances, the quantity of certain ingredients, the net quantity of the food, a date mark, any special storage conditions, the name or business name and address of the food business operator under whose name the food is being marketed, the country of origin or place of provenance where required, instructions for use, the alcoholic strength by volume where applicable and, from 13 December 2016, a nutrition declaration[1].

[1]   Regulation (EU) No 1169/2011, Art 9.

20.139 In the case of pre-packed food, the mandatory food information must appear on the package or on a label attached thereto[1], and be prominently displayed so as to be easily visible, clearly legible and, where appropriate, indelible[2]. The provisions of Art 9(1) will not apply to milk or milk products when sold in a glass bottle which is intended for re-use[3]. Articles 17–28 provide detailed particulars in relation to the mandatory information specified in Art 9.

[1]   Regulation (EU) No 1169/2011, Art 12(2).
[2]   Regulation (EU) No 1169/2011, Art 13(1).
[3]   Regulation 3 of the Food Information Regulations 2014.

The name of the food

20.140 The food must be marked with the name of the food. The name of the food shall be its legal name, where such a name exists. In the absence of such a name, the name of the food shall be its customary name, or, if there is no customary name or the customary name is not used, a descriptive name of the food shall be provided. A brand name, trade mark or fancy name cannot be used as the name of the food. In the case of *Verband Sozialer Wettbewerb eV v TofuTown.com Gmbh*[1] the requirements in Art 17(1) of FIC relating to the name of the food were considered following a referral for a preliminary ruling from the Regional Court in Germany to the CJEU. The case concerned the name given to plant-based products, and whilst principally related to the requirements of Regulation (EU) No 1308/2013 establishing a common organisation of the markets in agricultural products, also considered other parallel legislation.

[1]   Case No. C-422/16; ECLI:EU:C:2017:458; https://eur-lex.europa.eu/legal-content/EN/TXT/P DF/?uri=CELEX:62016CJ0422&from=EN.

20.141 A case was brought against TofuTown for using names such as 'soya butter' and 'plant cheese' on their products. The court considered whether the requirements in the legislation must be interpreted as meaning that they preclude the use of the term 'milk' and designations that are reserved exclusively for milk products from being used to designate a purely plant-based product, even if the terms are clarified or further described to indicate the plant-based origins of the product. The court held that the terms 'milk' and 'milk products' were terms that related to animal products in the legislation and cannot lawfully be used to designate a purely plant-based product, even if clarification or further description is used, unless that product appears on a list in Decision 2010/791.

Allergen listing

20.142 Annex II of FIC 2011 specifies a number of allergens or ingredients giving rise to intolerances which must be specified in the list of ingredients. Where it is not obvious from the name of the ingredient, it is necessary to identify the allergen clearly by reference to the particular ingredient, and highlighted by the use of font, style or background colour so as to stand out from the list of ingredients.

Date of minimum durability

20.143 All foods, other than those listed in Annex X 1(d) of FIC 2011, must be marked with a date of minimum durability. In the case of foods which are, from a microbiological point of view, highly perishable and which are therefore likely after a short period to constitute an immediate danger to human health, the food must be marked with a 'use by' date. In other cases, the food should be marked with a 'best before' date.

20.144 After the 'use by' date a food shall be deemed to be unsafe in accordance with Art 14(2) to (5) of Regulation (EC) No 178/2002. Accordingly a prosecution can be brought under reg 19 of the Food Safety and Hygiene (England) Regulations 2013 where food is sold (within the extended definition of sale) after the 'use by' date. By virtue of Art 24 of FIC 2011, the food shall be deemed to be unsafe, without further proof being required.

Mandatory nutrition labelling

20.145 From 13 December 2016, food business operators will need to provide mandatory 'back of pack' nutritional information on all pre-packed food. The mandatory nutritional information required is a declaration of the energy value in kilojoules and kilocalories, together with the amount in grams of fat, saturates, carbohydrates, sugars, protein and salt which the food contains. If nutritional information is given voluntarily as 'front of pack' nutritional information, it must comprise either the energy value alone, or the energy value with the amounts of fat, saturates, sugars and salt in the food. No other combination of nutritional information is permitted. The nutritional information must be expressed per 100g, or per 100ml[1]. Food business operators may also include in addition to per 100g or per 100ml an expression of the nutritional information by reference to the pack or portion size[2].

[1] Regulation (EU) No 1169/2011, Art 32.
[2] Regulation (EU) No 1169/2011, Art 33.

20.146 There are exemptions from the requirement to give mandatory nutrition labelling for certain foods when pre-packed, as set out in Annex V of FIC 2011. Annex V also contains an exemption from nutrition information for food, including handcrafted food, directly supplied by the manufacturer of small quantities of products to the final consumer or to local retail establishments directly supplying the final consumer. Guidance has been issued by the Department of Health to clarify this exemption, in relation to both 'manufacturer of small quantities' and 'local'[1].

The Calorie Labelling (Out of Home Sector) (England) Regulations 2021[2] have been additionally introduced in the wake of the obesity epidemic. These Regulations require qualifying businesses which sell food for immediate consumption, either in a café, restaurant or other catering establishment or as take away food, to provide information relating to the energy content of the food they sell to consumers in kilocalories ('calorie information').

Regulation 3 identifies the food for which calorie information must be displayed. Regulation 4 defines 'exempt food', for which calorie information does not have to be provided. Regulation 5 sets out the information which must be displayed, and where that information must be displayed. Regulation 6 sets how this information is to be displayed where food is sold on a website or through a mobile application. Regulation 7 defines 'qualifying businesses', which are required to display calorie information in relation to food.

Regulations 8 to 12 and the Schedule to the Regulations provide for the enforcement of the Regulations. Regulation 9 applies s 10 of the Food Safety Act 1990 on improvement notices with modifications.

[1]   https://www.gov.uk/government/publications/technical-guidance-on-nutrition-labelling (March 2017).
[2]   SI 2021/909.

Allergen information in food which is not pre-packed

20.147 In general, foods which are not pre-packed are not subject to the labelling requirements of FIC 2011. In the case of the information regarding allergens required by Art 9(1)(c), Art 44 requires FBOs to provide information if any of the foods/ingredients listed in Annex II of FIC 2011 are used in the preparation of foods which they supply, which are not pre-packed or are packed on the sales premises at the customers request.

20.148 In such cases, rather than requiring the use of an attached label, the information can be provided in such manner as the FBO may choose, including orally by a member of staff[1]. Where it is intended that the information be provided orally, it must be indicated to the consumer either by a label attached to the food or by a notice, such as on a menu, indicating that the allergen information can be obtained by asking a member of staff[2].

[1]   SI 2014/1855, reg 5(1).
[2]   SI 2014/1855, reg 5(3).

20.149 Prior to 1 October 2021, food which was prepacked for direct sale to the consumer was subject to the same provisions. From 1 October 2021, pursuant to the amendments to the FIR 2014 made by the Food Information (Amendment)(England) Regulations 2019[1], food which is pre-packed for direct sale must be labelled with the name of the food and a full ingredient list, with allergenic ingredients emphasised[2]. There will be no change to the requirements in respect of foods which are either not pre-packed or which are packed on the premises at the consumer's request.

[1] SI 2019/1218.
[2] See the new reg 5A, FIR 2014.

Food information policy post EU-exit

20.150 On the 23 March 2021 UK Government and devolved administrations published a command paper setting out how they propose to work together on key food compositional standards and labelling policy now the UK has left the EU[1]. There have been a number of new provisions that will impact upon the labelling of certain foods where the UK or its devolved administrations (with the exception of NI) will begin to diverge from EU or develop its own parallel standards[2] due to inoperabilities in retained EU legislation.

[1] See https://assets.publishing.service.gov.uk/government/uploads/system/uploads/attachment_d ata/file/980681/food-compositional-standards-labelling-provisional-common-framework.pdf.
[2] The Food (Amendment and Transitional Provisions) (England) Regulations 2021; The Food and Drink (Miscellaneous Amendments Relating to Food and Wine Composition, Information and Labelling) Regulations 2021; The Common Organisation of the Markets in Agricultural Products (Transitional Arrangements) (Amendment) Regulations 2021.

Offences

20.151 Regulation 10 of the Food Information Regulations 2014 provides as follows:

10 Offence

(1)   A person is guilty of an offence if the person fails to comply with—
    (a)   any provision of FIC specified in paragraph (2), as read with Articles 1(3) and 6 and the first subparagraph of Article 54(1), or
    (b)   regulation 5(5).
(2)   The provisions of FIC are—
    (a)   Article 9(1)(c), as also read with Annex II;
    (b)   Article 21(1)(a), as also read with Articles 9(1)(c) and 18(1) and Annex II;
    (c)   the second subparagraph of Article 21(1), as also read with Articles 9(1)(c) and 19(1) and Annex II; and
(3)   Article 44(1)(a), as also read with Article 9(1)(c) and regulation 5.

Failing to comply with the specified provisions of the Food Information Regulations

20.152 It is an offence for a food business operator to fail to comply with Arts 9(1)(c), 21(1)(a), the second sub-paragraph of Art 21(1) or Art 44(1)(a). It must be proved to the criminal standard that the offender:

(a)   was a food business operator;
(b)   who failed to comply with the specified provisions.

20.153 Article 9(1)(c) requires a food business operator to provide particulars of any ingredient or processing aid listed in Annex II or derived from a substance or product listed in Annex II causing allergies or intolerances used in the manufacture or preparation of a food and still present in the finished product, even if in an altered form.

20.154 Article 21(1)(a) requires a food business operator to indicate the particulars of any ingredient or processing aid listed in Annex II causing allergies or intolerances within the list of ingredients. The second sub-paragraph of Art 21(1) requires a food business operator to specify the particulars of any ingredient or processing aid listed in Annex II causing allergies or intolerances by stating that the product contains that ingredient where there is no list of ingredients on the label.

20.155 Article 44(1)(a) provides that where a food business operator offers food for sale to the final consumer or to mass caterers without pre-packaging, or where foods are packed on the sales premises at the consumer's request or pre-packed for direct sale, the provision of the particulars specified in Art 9(1)(c) above is mandatory.

Failing to comply with reg 5(5)

20.156 It is an offence to fail to comply with reg 5(5) of the FIR 2014. It must be proved to the criminal standard that the offender:

(a)   offered food for sale to the final consumer, or to a mass caterer, otherwise than by means of distance communication, which was either not pre-packed, was packed on the operator's premises at the consumer's request or was pre-packed for direct sale;

(b)   in respect of which he did not give particulars of any ingredient or processing aid listed in Annex II or derived from a substance or product listed in Annex II causing allergies or intolerances used in the manufacture or preparation of a food and still present in the finished product, even if in an altered form.

Penalties

20.157 Offences of failing to comply with the provisions of the FIR 2014 are offences which are triable summarily. The maximum sentence in the magistrates' court is a fine.

Failure to comply with an Improvement Notice

20.158 The initial frontline measure for the enforcement of the other aspects of FIC 2011 is the issuing of an Improvement Notice under the Food Safety Act 1990, s 10. Failure to comply with such a notice will constitute a criminal offence. The maximum penalty for failing to comply with an Improvement Notice where it relates to a breach of the FIR 2014 is a fine. The offence is triable summarily[1].

---

[1]   SI 2014/1855, Sch 4, Pts 1 and 5.

NUTRITION AND HEALTH CLAIMS

Introduction

20.159 The marketing of foods by use of making claims concerning their nutritional or physiological ('health') benefits is closely regulated to seek to protect consumers from misleading or false claims about such benefits, and to identify the circumstances in which such claims may justifiably be made. The Nutrition and Health Claims Regulation, Regulation (EC) No 1924/20006 ('NHCR 2006')[1], governs the making of such claims, and was incorporated into English Law by the Nutrition and Health Claims (England) Regulations 2007[2].

[1] Regulation (EC) No 1924/2006 of the European Parliament and of the Council on nutrition and health claims made on foods.
[2] SI 2007/2080.

20.160 Changes have been made by the European Union (Withdrawal) Act 2018, the Nutrition (Amendment etc) (EU Exit) Regulations 2019[1], and the Nutrition (Amendment etc) (EU Exit) Regulations 2020[2] in England, Scotland, and Wales (Great Britain) from 1 January 2021 following the end of the transition period. Following the end of the transition period, EU Regulations and tertiary legislation relating to nutrition will be retained under the powers contained within the European Union (Withdrawal) Act 2018 as UK law. That retained EU legislation is subsequently amended by the Nutrition (Amendment etc) (EU Exit) Regulations 2019 and the Nutrition (Amendment etc) (EU Exit) Regulations 2020.

[1] SI 2019/651.
[2] SI 2020/1476.

20.161 There will be practical effects of the changes to the legislation for Industry, and the processes and procedures by which food business operators, and other interested parties, must comply in – particularly, in order to deal with responsibilities that previously fell on EU Institutions and organisations such as standing committees and EFSA (the European Food Safety Authority). The Nutrition (Amendment etc) (EU Exit) Regulations 2019 and the Nutrition (Amendment etc) (EU Exit) Regulations 2020 transfer responsibilities from EU organisations involved in the risk assessment and risk management processes covered by nutrition legislation to bodies in Great Britain (GB). They also make practical changes, that result from this transfer, to:

- applications (eg for authorisation of a new health claim);
- frameworks for the scientific evaluation of applications/dossiers/files; and
- the factors taken into consideration when a risk management decision is required.

20.162 On the 14 January 2021 the Department of Health and Social care (DHSC) published a bulletin outlining changes to domestic and European Union (EU) legislation relating to nutrition related labelling, composition, and standards (NLCS). The subject areas covered by the bulletin include nutrition and health claims made on foods (as well the addition of vitamins, minerals and certain other substances to foods; composition and labelling of food supplements; and the composition and labelling of food for specific groups); and provide guidance to businesses seeking to submit applications, scientific dossiers, or files in accordance with the legislation in the GB market after Exit[1]. **In relation to the GB Market, after 1 January 2021 any references to EU legislation should read as only applying to the retained aspects.**

[1] See https://www.gov.uk/government/publications/nutrition-legislation-information-sources/nutrition-legislation-information-sheet--2

20.163 Nutrition and health claims are defined in Art 2 of the NHCR 2006. A 'nutrition claim' is defined as any claim which states, suggests or implies that a food has particular beneficial nutritional properties due to the presence, absence, increased or reduced levels of energy or of a particular nutrient or other substance. Examples include claims such as 'low fat' or" 'high fibre'. The effect of the Regulation is to specify when such a claim may properly be made about a food, for example to maximum or minimum levels of a particular constituent.

20.164 A 'health claim' is defined as any claim that states, suggests or implies that a relationship exists between a food category, a food or one of its constituents and health. Examples include specific claims such as 'calcium helps maintain normal bones', or more general claims such as a food being 'good for you' or 'healthy'. Such health claims may only be made if such a claim has been authorised according to the procedure set out in the NHCR 2006.

20.165 It should be noted that any claim to cure, prevent or treat a human disease is prohibited by Art 7(3) of the Food Information Regulation (see para **20.137** above). No nutrition or health claim may be used in the labelling, presentation and advertising of foods placed on the market unless it complies with the provisions of the NHCR 2006.

Key provisions

Application

20.166 The scope of the NHCR 2006 is broad, covering claims made on food in commercial communications including generic advertising and promotional campaigns. However, it does not apply to claims made in non-commercial communications[1] such as dietary guidelines or advice by public authorities or information in the press or scientific publications. 'Food' for the purposes of the NHCR 2006 bears the same definition as in Regulation (EC) No 178/2002[2].

[1] On 14 July 2016, the CJEU issued its decision in Case C-19/15 *Verband Sozialer Wettbewerb v Innova Vital GmbH* on the application of the NHCR to B2B commercial communications, suggesting a limited exception to this general rule. The CJEU ruled that: Art 1(2) of Regulation (EC) No 1924/2006 of the European Parliament and of the Council of 20 December 2006 on nutrition and health claims made on foods, as amended by Commission Regulation (EU) No 1047/2012 of 8 November 2012, must be interpreted as meaning that nutrition or health claims made in a commercial communication on a food which is intended to be delivered as such to the final consumer, if that communication is addressed not to the final consumer, but exclusively to health professionals, falls within the scope of that regulation.

[2] Article 2(1)(a) of the NHCR 2006.

Claims

20.167 The NHCR 2006 regulates the making of nutrition and health claims about foods. A 'claim'[1] is defined as:

'any message or representation, which is not mandatory under Community or national legislation, including pictorial, graphic or symbolic representation, in any form, which states, suggests or implies that a food has particular characteristics.'

Accordingly, mandatory information (such as mandatory nutrition labelling under FIR 2014) or the name of the food would not be a claim under NHCR; however, trade marks, brand names or fancy names could amount to a claim. There are specific considerations in respect of trade marks, brand names or fancy names.

1   Article 2.2(1) of NHCR 2006.

20.168 A trade mark, brand name or fancy name[1] appearing in the labelling, presentation or advertising of a food which may be construed as a nutrition or health claim may be used without undergoing the authorisation procedures provided for in the NHCR, provided that it is accompanied by a related nutrition or health claim in that labelling, presentation or advertising which complies with the provisions of the NHCR. Products bearing trade marks or brand names existing before 1 January 2005 which do not comply with the NHCR may continue to be marketed until 19 January 2022 after which time the provisions of the NHCR apply[2].

1   For CJEU consideration of this see Case C-299/12, *Green – Swan Pharmaceuticals CR, a.s. v Státní zemědělská a potravinářská inspekce, ústřední inspektorát,*
2   According to the European Food Law Associations consideration of this provision:
   (I)   The Regulation does not require that the trade mark or brand name must be officially registered.
   (II)   Its simple use/presence in the EU market, ie in any of the Member States, before 19 January 2005 is enough for it to be covered by the lengthy transitional measure.
   (III) The use of a trade mark or brand name before 1 January 2005 in at least one EU Member State is a sufficient condition to allow its use until 19 January 2022 across all EU markets, even if it will be subsequently used for the first time in another Member State after 1 January 2005.
   (IV)   This transitional measure applies to the trade marks or brand names themselves, not to the products bearing them. The same trade mark or brand name, existing before 1 January 2005, can be used after that date in new products and across other EU markets.

General principles

20.169 Chapter II of the NHCR 2006 sets out general principles which apply to all nutrition and health claims made under the Regulation. The general principles include a set of general conditions for claims[1], a prohibition on false or misleading claims[2], a requirement that claims be scientifically substantiated[3] and specific requirements concerning nutrition information[4].

1   Article 5 of the NHCR 2006.
2   Article 3 of the NHCR 2006.
3   Article 6 of the NHCR 2006 .
4   Article 7 of the NHCR 2006.

20.170 Article 3 provides[1] that the use of nutrition and health claims must not:

(a)   be false, ambiguous or misleading[2];
(b)   give rise to doubt about the safety and/or the nutritional adequacy of other foods;
(c)   encourage or condone excess consumption of a food;

(d)   state, suggest or imply that a balanced and varied diet cannot provide appropriate quantities of nutrients in general; or

(e)   exploit fear in the consumer.

¹   Without prejudice to certain other requirements related to food labelling and misleading advertising.

²   A key policy aim of NHCR (see recital 11, NHCR) was to avoid a situation where nutrition or health claims mask the overall nutritional status of a food product, which could mislead consumers when trying to make healthy choices. Consequently, the NHCR tasked the Commission by 19 January 2009, to establish specific nutrient profiles that would need to be met as conditions for the use of nutrition and health claims. To date the Commission has not established these – so the provisions relevant to nutrient profiles are currently not operative. On 8 June 2017, the CJEU confirmed that the Commission could refuse to authorise a number of health claims relating to glucose even though EFSA had found these to have been scientifically substantiated [Case C-296/16 P] – the Commission's refusal was on the basis that a health claim on glucose could encourage consumption of sugars for which, on the basis of generally accepted scientific advice, national and international authorities advise consumers to reduce their intake.

20.171 Article 5 of NHCR requires that nutrition and health claims must refer to a beneficial nutritional/ physiological effect; and that the nutrient/substance on which the claim is made must be contained in the final product[1] in a significant quantity as defined in Community legislation or in a quantity to produce the claimed effect. Article 6 of the EU Nutrition and Health Claims Regulation requires scientific substantiation for claims and any health claims made must be based on and substantiated by generally-accepted scientific evidence.

¹   In an amount of food that can reasonably be consumed after preparation in accordance with the manufacturer's instructions – the nutrient or other substance must be in a form readily available to be used by the body.

20.172 A food business operator making a nutrition or health claim must justify the use of the claim, and the competent authorities may request a food business operator or a person placing a product on the market to produce all relevant elements and data establishing compliance with the Regulation. Nutrition and health claims cannot be made on alcoholic beverages (containing more than 1.2 % by volume of alcohol), except to indicate a reduction in alcohol or energy content or low alcohol content[1].

¹   Article 4(3) of the NHCR 2006.

Nutrition claims

20.173 A 'nutrition claim' is[1] any claim which states, suggests or implies that a food has particular beneficial nutritional properties due to:

(a)   the energy (calorific value) it—
  (i)   provides;
  (ii)   provides at a reduced or increased rate; or
  (iii)   does not provide; and/or
(b)   the nutrients or other substances it—
  (i)   contains;
  (ii)   contains in reduced or increased proportions; or
  (iii)   does not contain;

¹   Article 2.2(4) of the NHCR 2006.

20.174 Article 8 NHCR provides that only those nutritional claims conforming with the specified permitted claims listed in the the Annex to NHCR (as amended[1]) and with other NHCR conditions are permitted. Those claims, and the circumstances in which they may lawfully be made are as follows:

Permitted nutrition claims	
LOW ENERGY	A claim that a food is low in energy, and any claim likely to have the same meaning for the consumer, may only be made where the product does not contain more than 40 kcal (170 kJ)/100 g for solids or more than 20 kcal (80 kJ)/100 ml for liquids. For table-top sweeteners the limit of 4 kcal (17 kJ)/portion, with equivalent sweetening properties to 6 g of sucrose (approximately 1 teaspoon of sucrose), applies.
ENERGY-REDUCED	A claim that a food is energy-reduced, and any claim likely to have the same meaning for the consumer, may only be made where the energy value is reduced by at least 30%, with an indication of the characteristic(s) which make(s) the food reduced in its total energy value.
ENERGY-FREE	A claim that a food is energy-free, and any claim likely to have the same meaning for the consumer, may only be made where the product does not contain more than 4 kcal (17 kJ)/100 ml. For table-top sweeteners the limit of 0,4 kcal (1,7 kJ)/portion, with equivalent sweetening properties to 6 g of sucrose (approximately 1 teaspoon of sucrose), applies.
LOW FAT	A claim that a food is low in fat, and any claim likely to have the same meaning for the consumer, may only be made where the product contains no more than 3 g of fat per 100 g for solids or 1,5 g of fat per 100 ml for liquids (1,8 g of fat per 100 ml for semi-skimmed milk).
FAT-FREE	A claim that a food is fat-free, and any claim likely to have the same meaning for the consumer, may only be made where the product contains no more than 0,5 g of fat per 100 g or 100 ml. However, claims expressed as 'X % fat-free' shall be prohibited.
LOW SATURATED FAT	A claim that a food is low in saturated fat, and any claim likely to have the same meaning for the consumer, may only be made if the sum of saturated fatty acids and trans-fatty acids in the product does not exceed 1,5 g per 100 g for solids or 0,75 g/100 ml for liquids and in either case the sum of saturated fatty acids and trans-fatty acids must not provide more than 10% of energy.

Permitted nutrition claims	
SATURATED FAT-FREE	A claim that a food does not contain saturated fat, and any claim likely to have the same meaning for the consumer, may only be made where the sum of saturated fat and trans-fatty acids does not exceed 0,1 g of saturated fat per 100 g or 100 ml.
LOW SUGARS	A claim that a food is low in sugars, and any claim likely to have the same meaning for the consumer, may only be made where the product contains no more than 5 g of sugars per 100 g for solids or 2,5 g of sugars per 100 ml for liquids.
SUGARS-FREE	A claim that a food is sugars-free, and any claim likely to have the same meaning for the consumer, may only be made where the product contains no more than 0,5 g of sugars per 100 g or 100 ml.
WITH NO ADDED SUGARS	A claim stating that sugars have not been added to a food, and any claim likely to have the same meaning for the consumer, may only be made where the product does not contain any added mono- or disaccharides or any other food used for its sweetening properties. If sugars are naturally present in the food, the following indication should also appear on the label: 'CONTAINS NATURALLY OCCURRING SUGARS'.
LOW SODIUM/SALT	A claim that a food is low in sodium/salt, and any claim likely to have the same meaning for the consumer, may only be made where the product contains no more than 0,12 g of sodium, or the equivalent value for salt, per 100 g or per 100 ml. For waters, other than natural mineral waters falling within the scope of Directive 80/777/EEC, this value should not exceed 2 mg of sodium per 100 ml.
VERY LOW SODIUM/SALT	A claim that a food is very low in sodium/salt, and any claim likely to have the same meaning for the consumer, may only be made where the product contains no more than 0,04 g of sodium, or the equivalent value for salt, per 100 g or per 100 ml. This claim shall not be used for natural mineral waters and other waters.
SODIUM-FREE or SALT-FREE	A claim that a food is sodium-free or salt-free, and any claim likely to have the same meaning for the consumer, may only be made where the product contains no more than 0,005 g of sodium, or the equivalent value for salt, per 100 g.

Permitted nutrition claims	
NO ADDED SODIUM/SALT	A claim stating that sodium/salt has not been added to a food and any claim likely to have the same meaning for the consumer may only be made where the product does not contain any added sodium/salt or any other ingredient containing added sodium/salt and the product contains no more than 0,12 g sodium, or the equivalent value for salt, per 100 g or 100 ml.
SOURCE OF FIBRE[2]	A claim that a food is a source of fibre, and any claim likely to have the same meaning for the consumer, may only be made where the product contains at least 3 g of fibre per 100 g or at least 1,5 g of fibre per 100 kcal.
HIGH FIBRE	A claim that a food is high in fibre, and any claim likely to have the same meaning for the consumer, may only be made where the product contains at least 6 g of fibre per 100 g or at least 3 g of fibre per 100 kcal.
SOURCE OF PROTEIN	A claim that a food is a source of protein, and any claim likely to have the same meaning for the consumer, may only be made where at least 12% of the energy value of the food is provided by protein.
HIGH PROTEIN	A claim that a food is high in protein, and any claim likely to have the same meaning for the consumer, may only be made where at least 20% of the energy value of the food is provided by protein.
SOURCE OF [NAME OF VITAMIN/S] AND/OR [NAME OF MINERAL/S]	A claim that a food is a source of vitamins and/or minerals, and any claim likely to have the same meaning for the consumer, may only be made where the product contains at least a significant amount as defined in the Annex to Directive 90/496/EEC or an amount provided for by derogations granted according to Article 6 of Regulation (EC) No 1925/2006 of the European Parliament and of the Council of 20 December 2006 on the addition of vitamins and minerals and of certain other substances to foods.
HIGH [NAME OF VITAMIN/S] AND/OR [NAME OF MINERAL/S]	A claim that a food is high in vitamins and/or minerals, and any claim likely to have the same meaning for the consumer, may only be made where the product contains at least twice the value of 'source of [NAME OF VITAMIN/S] and/or [NAME OF MINERAL/S]'.

Permitted nutrition claims	
CONTAINS [NAME OF THE NUTRIENT³ OR OTHER SUBSTANCE⁴]	A claim that a food contains a nutrient or another substance, for which specific conditions are not laid down in this Regulation, or any claim likely to have the same meaning for the consumer, may only be made where the product complies with all the applicable provisions of this Regulation, and in particular Article 5. For vitamins and minerals the conditions of the claim 'source of' shall apply.
INCREASED [NAME OF THE NUTRIENT]	A claim stating that the content in one or more nutrients has been reduced, and any claim likely to have the same meaning for the consumer, may only be made where the reduction in content is at least 30% compared to a similar product, except for micronutrients, where a 10 % difference in the reference values as set in Directive 90/496/EEC shall be acceptable, and for sodium, or the equivalent value for salt, where a 25% difference shall be acceptable. The claim 'reduced saturated fat', and any claim likely to have the same meaning for the consumer, may only be made: (a) if the sum of saturated fatty acids and of trans-fatty acids in the product bearing the claim is at least 30% less than the sum of saturated fatty acids and of trans-fatty acids in a similar product; and (b) if the content in trans-fatty acids in the product bearing the claim is equal to or less than in a similar product. The claim 'reduced sugars', and any claim likely to have the same meaning for the consumer, may only be made if the amount of energy of the product bearing the claim is equal to or less than the amount of energy in a similar product.
LIGHT/LITE	A claim stating that a product is 'light' or 'lite', and any claim likely to have the same meaning for the consumer, shall follow the same conditions as those set for the term 'reduced'; the claim shall also be accompanied by an indication of the characteristic(s) which make(s) the food 'light' or 'lite'.
NATURALLY/ NATURAL	Where a food naturally meets the condition(s) laid down in this Annex for the use of a nutritional claim, the term 'naturally/natural' may be used as a prefix to the claim.

Permitted nutrition claims	
SOURCE OF OMEGA-3 FATTY ACIDS	A claim that a food is a source of omega-3 fatty acids, and any claim likely to have the same meaning for the consumer, may only be made where the product contains at least 0,3 g alpha-linolenic acid per 100 g and per 100 kcal, or at least 40 mg of the sum of eicosapentaenoic acid and docosahexaenoic acid per 100 g and per 100 kcal.
HIGH OMEGA-3 FATTY ACIDS	A claim that a food is high in omega-3 fatty acids, and any claim likely to have the same meaning for the consumer, may only be made where the product contains at least 0,6 g alpha-linolenic acid per 100 g and per 100 kcal, or at least 80 mg of the sum of eicosapentaenoic acid and docosahexaenoic acid per 100 g and per 100 kcal.
HIGH MONOUN-SATURATED FAT	A claim that a food is high in monounsaturated fat, and any claim likely to have the same meaning for the consumer, may only be made where at least 45% of the fatty acids present in the product derive from monounsaturated fat under the condition that monounsaturated fat provides more than 20% of energy of the product.
HIGH POLYUNSATU-RATED FAT	A claim that a food is high in polyunsaturated fat, and any claim likely to have the same meaning for the consumer, may only be made where at least 45% of the fatty acids present in the product derive from polyunsaturated fat under the condition that polyunsaturated fat provides more than 20% of energy of the product.
HIGH UNSATU-RATED FAT	A claim that a food is high in unsaturated fat, and any claim likely to have the same meaning for the consumer may only be made where at least 70% of the fatty acids present in the product derive from unsaturated fat under the condition that unsaturated fat provides more than 20% of energy of the product.

[1] Regulation (EU) No 1047/2012 amending Regulation (EC) No 1924/2006 with regard to the list of nutrition claims.

[2] Item 12 of ANNEX I of FICR states 'fibre' means carbohydrate polymers with three or more monomeric units, which are neither digested nor absorbed in the human small intestine and belong to the following categories:
  - edible carbohydrate polymers naturally occurring in the food as consumed,
  - edible carbohydrate polymers which have been obtained from food raw material by physical, enzymatic or chemical means and which have a beneficial physiological effect demonstrated by generally accepted scientific evidence,
  - edible synthetic carbohydrate polymers which have a beneficial physiological effect demonstrated by generally accepted scientific evidence.

[3] 'Nutrient' means protein, carbohydrate, fat, fibre, sodium, vitamins and minerals and substances which belong to or are components of one of those categories (Art 2.2 NHCR).

[4] 'Other substance' means a substance other than a nutrient that has a nutritional or physiological effect (Art 2.3 NHCR).

20.175 Comparative claims[1] for example '50% less sugar' may only be made between foods of the same category, taking into consideration a range of foods of that category. The difference in the quantity of a nutrient and/or the energy value must be stated and the comparison must relate to the same quantity of food. The range of foods of the same category used for comparison including foods of other brands, should not have a composition which allows them to bear a claim[2].

[1] Article 9 of NHCR – this is without prejudice to Directive 84/450/EEC concerning misleading and comparative advertising.
[2] The literal wording of the Article could be taken to bar comparison with any food with a composition which allows it to bear any claim in the Annex. However, the question arises whether a more limited construction should be applied that is only in the context of the attribute in respect of which the comparative claim is made. As an indicator of policy, Recital 21 of NHCR is of limited assistance to this question, as it merely states that for comparative claims it is necessary that the products being compared be clearly identified to the final consumer. The FDF has issued some extensive guidance in this area. See https://www.fdf.org.uk/corporate_pu bs/comparative-claims-guidance-doc-v7.pdf.

New GB nutrition claims after EU exit

20.176 The appropriate UK authorities[1] may, after consulting an expert committee, amend the list of permitted nutrition claims contained within the Annex to Regulation (EC) No 1924/2006, as amended, by making regulations. Authorised and rejected nutrition claims will be added to the GB NHC Register. Food Business Operators wishing to apply for a claim to be authorised for use in the GB market will have to contact the appropriate GB authorities via the DHSC mailbox (which will centrally coordinate applications for all GB nations).Contact may also be made directly via the national authorities:

- England only, please contact the competent authority via the DHSC mailbox;
- Scotland only, please contact the competent authority via the Food Standards Scotland mailbox;
- Wales only, please contact the competent authority via the Welsh Government Mailbox.

[1] The Nutrition (Amendment etc.) (EU Exit) Regulations 2019 transfer functions and powers currently held by the European Commission powers to legislate to give effect to a decision, such as whether to authorise applications for new health claims, to the appropriate authorities. The appropriate authorities are in:
- England: The Secretary of State;
- Scotland: the Scottish Ministers;
- Wales: the Welsh Ministers;

20.177 The appropriate authority will consult the United Kingdom Nutrition and Health Claims Committee (UKNHCC)[1], and any other appropriate scientific advisory committee (SAC) when considering a new nutrition claim. If a claim is authorised by the appropriate UK authorities and added to the Annex, any specific conditions associated with that claim will apply. Businesses wishing to make new nutrition claims in the EU or Northern Ireland market following the end of the Transition Period will have to follow EU processes.

[1] The UK Nutrition and Health Claims Committee (UKNHCC) is a committee of independent experts set up to provide scientific advice to the relevant UK authorities on the substantiation of scientific evidence underpinning nutrition and health claim applications. The relevant UK government authorities make decisions on whether to authorise nutrition and health claims.

The UKNHCC is supported in its work by a secretariat with scientific expertise to support the decision-making processes of the committee. One health claim application had been submitted to the UKNHCC at the time of writing (14/9/2021). The committee has 5 months to issue its scientific opinion. The first UKNHCC scientific opinion on a combination of lutein, zeaxanthin and meso-zeaxanthin and improved visual performance was published on 1 September 2021. Information is still awaited as to where the UKNHCC will sit following creation of the National Institute for Health Protection in place of Public Health England. DHSC is redrafting its NHCR Guidance document. Revisions to the Business-to-Business and Business-to-Healthcare Practitioner section are expected to state that all claims for food that is ready for delivery to the final consumer, in the labelling, advertising or other presentation of the food, must comply with the regulations.

Health claims

20.178 A 'health claim'[1] is defined as 'any claim that states, suggests or implies that a relationship exists between a food category, a food or one of its constituents and health'. Under Art 10 of the NHCR 2006, health claims are prohibited unless they comply with the provisions of the Regulation and are claims which are included in the authorised lists of permitted health claims provided for by Arts 13 and 14. No health claim which is not included in the list of permitted claims, or which does not apply to the food in question may lawfully be made. Health claims made must comply with the relevant provisions of the NHCR, such as the general prohibition on false and misleading claims (Art 3) and general conditions (Art 5) applicable to all claims, together with the additional labelling requirements (Art 10).

[1] Article 2.2(5) of the NHCR 2006.

20.179 Article 10(2) imposes requirements in the case of all foods bearing a health claim, namely that the labelling (or if there is no labelling, the presentation and advertising of the food) must include the following features:

(a) a statement indicating the importance of a varied and balanced diet and a healthy lifestyle;

(b) the quantity of the food and pattern of consumption required to obtain the claimed beneficial effect;

(c) where appropriate, a statement addressed to persons who should avoid using the food; and

(d) an appropriate warning for products that are likely to present a health risk if consumed to excess.

General non-specific claims as to benefits for overall health may only be made if accompanied by a specific permitted health claim included in the authorised lists provided for by Arts 13 and 14[1].

[1] Article 10(3) of the NHCR 2006.

20.180 Certain health claims are specifically prohibited by Art 12 of the NHCR 2006, namely:

(a) claims that suggest that health could be affected by not consuming the food;

(b) claims which make reference to the rate or amount of weight loss;

(c) claims which make reference to recommendations of individual doctors or health professionals and other associations (except in the case recommendations of national associations of medical, nutrition or dietetic professionals and health-related charities, which in the absence of specific EU rules are permitted by national rules of the particular member state[1]).

[1]   See Arts 12(c) and 11 of the NHCR 2006.

Permitted health claims

20.181 Articles 13 and 14 provide for the adoption of lists of permitted health claims in accordance with the procedures set out in the Regulation for and for the establishment of a Community Register of permitted health claims[1]. The procedure and lists differ, and there are different considerations which apply in the case of health claims which specifically relate to a reduction in the risk of disease or to the health and development of children (which are governed by Art 14) and other health claims which are governed by Art 13.

[1]   Article 20 of the NHCR requires the Commission to establish and maintain a register of permitted claims.

20.182 By the deadline of 31 January 2008 (as set out in the legislation), Member states provided the European Commission ('the Commission') with lists of approximately 44,000 submissions (diet and health relationships) from food business operators with references to the relevant scientific justification and conditions applying to them. Those submissions were considered by the European Food Safety Authority, and on 25 May 2012 a list of 222 permitted Health Claims were finally published[1]. The 'general' health claims list[2] (health claims other than those referring to the reduction of disease risk and to children's development and health) came into force on 14 December 2012[3].

[1]   A further 1875 claims were classified as non-authorised claims on the Register; at the time of writing this figure stands at 2077.
[2]   The Art 13.1 health claims list.
[3]   Commission Regulation (EU) No 432/2012 of 16 May 2012 establishing a list of permitted health claims made on foods, other than those referring to the reduction of disease risk and to children's development and health.

20.183 Seven further Art 13.1 claims have since been added to the Register. A further 32 claims under Art 13(5) (which provides for the addition of claims which are based on newly developed scientific evidence and/or proprietary data) and Art 14 (Reduction of Risk of Disease / Child Health and Development) have been added[1].

[1]   Commission Regulation (EU) No 40/2014 of 17/01/2014; Commission Regulation (EU) 2015/7 of 06/01/2015; Commission Regulation (EU) 2016/854 of 30/05/2016; Commission Regulation (EU) 2017/672 of 07/04/2017; and Commission Regulation (EU) 2017/676 of 10/04/2017. The current register can be found online at https://ec.europa.eu/food/safety/labell ing_nutrition/claims/register/public/?event=register.home.

Lists and registers after EU exit

20.184 Where EU legislation amended by the Nutrition (Amendment etc) (EU Exit) Regulations 2019 requires a list or register to be established, each 'Appropriate Authority'[1] must produce and maintain a list or register.

[1]   The Nutrition (Amendment etc) (EU Exit) Regulations 2019 transfer functions and powers currently held by the European Commission powers to legislate to give effect to a decision, such as whether to authorise applications for new health claims, to the appropriate authorities. The appropriate authorities are in:

- England: the Secretary of State;
- Scotland: the Scottish Ministers;
- Wales: the Welsh Ministers;

Each appropriate authority may make legislation equivalent to that which the European Commission would have made to amend lists and registers. However, the Nutrition (Amendment etc) (EU Exit) Regulations 2019 also provide concurrent powers for the UK Secretary of State to legislate for the whole of GB where Devolved Administrations in Scotland and Wales agree.

GB Nutrition and Health Claims Register

20.185 All nutrition and health claims that are listed in the Community Register, as of 1 January 2021, will be adopted and included in the Great Britain Nutrition and Health Claims Register (GB NHC Register). A new application must be submitted to the appropriate GB authorities for assessment if the applicant wishes for a claim to be authorised for use in the GB market, where the European Commission has not taken a decision on an application related to a nutrition or health claim after 1 January 2021. All authorised and rejected nutrition and health claims will be listed in the GB NHC Register, other than those health claims authorised on the basis of proprietary data which will be recorded in a separate Annex to the GB NHC Register. The GB NHC Register, and the separate Annex, will be available at GOV.UK, where any future amendments will also be communicated.

New GB health claims

20.186 From 1 January 2021 food business operators wishing to make a new health claim on a product in GB that is not included in the GB NHC Register must submit an application for that claim to be assessed and authorised before it can be used. An application may be made for:

- claims based on newly developed scientific evidence, or those which include a request for the protection of proprietary data; and
- reduction of disease risk claims and claims referring to children's development and health.

Applications seeking authorisation of a claim for use in the GB market should be submitted to the competent authorities via the DHSC mailbox (which will centrally coordinate applications for all GB nations). Contact may also be made directly via the national authorities (see earlier). Food business operators wishing to make new health claims in the EU or Northern Ireland market following the end of the Transition Period will need to follow the EU process.

'On hold' health claims

20.187 There remain however a number of claims, in particular in relation to botanical products which have still not been definitively resolved, and where there is a potential overlap with the EU Directive relating to traditional herbal medicinal products[1]. The assessment of such unresolved claims is that they are 'on hold' and can be made in accordance with the laws within each member state[2]. It should be noted that 'on hold' claims do not appear on the EU Register of health claims authorised under the Regulation, as they have neither been authorised or rejected – instead they appear in EFSA's Register of questions as claims 'under consideration'. In the UK the Department of Health Bulletin (2014) entitled Art 13(1) 'on hold' Health Claims Spreadsheet, (2014 Bulletin)[3] on referenced hold claims which may be used while they are still under consideration, subject to the transition measures in Art (28)(5) of the Nutrition & Health Claims Regulation (EC) 1924/2006 'On hold' remain under consideration in the EU, however, from 1 January 2021 GB will have its own system for authorising claims separate from the EU authorisation system.

[1]   The issue of Directive 2004/24/EC on traditional herbal medicinal products.
[2]   See https://www.gov.uk/government/publications/on-hold-health-claims-on-foods-if-theres-no-eu-exit-deal.
[3]   https://assets.publishing.service.gov.uk/government/uploads/system/uploads/attachment_data/file/307453/DH_BULLETIN_-_Searching_Article_13.1_on_hold_health_claims_acc.pdf.

20.188 Following the end of the transition period, it is understood that the UK Government and Devolved Administrations in Scotland, Wales, and Northern Ireland will launch a call to evidence, seeking information from stakeholders so that the full scale of the 'on hold' claims issue may be understood. Following the call for evidence, a decision will be made on the approach to 'on hold' claims for use in the GB market. As it is the intention of the UK Government and Devolved Administrations in Scotland, Wales to minimise disruption to business following the end of the transition period, it is understood that they will provide business reasonable time to plan accordingly. 'On hold' claims may therefore continue to be used in accordance with the 2014 Bulletin until a decision is made following the call for evidence. DHSC is due to instigate a fresh call for evidence, to understand the full scale of the issue, and will allow a 21-month transition period. A UK consultation and impact assessment is expected in autumn 2021 including consumers and industry; other DHSC consultations impacting labelling and health are also envisaged[1].

[1]   In 2021 DHSC is also due to consult on alcohol labelling with calories (including the on-trade sector), and on the marketing and labelling of commercial food and drink products for infants and young children.

Claims to reduce the risk of disease

20.189 Article 14(2) imposes and additional requirement in cases relating to a claim of a reduction in the risk of disease. In addition to the general requirements, for reduction of disease risk claims the labelling (or, if no such labelling exists, the presentation or advertising) must also bear a statement indicating that the disease to which the claim is referring has multiple risk factors and that altering one of these risk factors may or may not have a beneficial effect.

Offences

20.190 Regulation 5 of the Nutrition and Health Claims (England) 2007 creates the offence of failing to comply with certain specified articles of the NHCR 2006. The offence is triable either way. By virtue of that Regulation, it is an offence for a food business operator to contravene or fail to comply with the specified provisions of the NHCR 2006. It must be proved to the criminal standard that the offender:

(a)   was a food business operator;
(b)   who failed to comply with the specified provisions.

Regulation 6 provides that certain provisions of the Food Safety Act 1990[1] apply for the purposes of the 2007 Regulations as they do in relation to the Food Safety Act.

[1] Including the extended meaning of 'sale'; presumption that food is intended for human consumption; causal liability; due diligence; innocent publication; documentary evidence; time limits; directors' liability.

20.191 The specified provisions are:

(a)   Article 3 (general requirements relating to all claims);
(b)   Article 4(3) (restrictions on claims that may be made on alcoholic beverages);
(c)   Article 6(2) (requirement for use of claims to be justified);
(d)   Article 7 (requirements for nutrition information);
(e)   Article 8(1) (requirements for nutrition claims);
(f)   (Article 9 (requirements for comparative claims);
(g)   Articles 10(1), (2) and (3) (requirements for health claims);
(h)   Article 12 (prohibition of certain health claims); and
(i)   Article 14(2) (requirements for reduction of disease risk claims).

Offences of failing to comply with the provisions of the NHCR 2006 are offences which are triable either way. The maximum sentence con conviction on indictment is 2 years imprisonment, a fine or both. The maximum sentence on summary conviction is 3 months imprisonment, a fine or both.

New GB health claims after EU exit

20.192 From 1 January 2021 food business operators wishing to make a new health claim on a product in GB that is not included in the GB NHC Register must submit an application for that claim to be assessed and authorised before it can be used. Applicants who wish to apply for authorisation of a health claim under Arts 13.5 or 14 of the retained Regulation (EC) No 1924/2006, as amended by the Nutrition (Amendment etc) (EU Exit) Regulations 2019, or for modification of an existing authorisation should complete the Application form for substantiation of a health claim in the UK. The UKNHCC will take a similar approach to that established by EFSA and can therefore be guided by existing EFSA guidance on the scientific requirements for health claims related. An application may be made for:

•   claims based on newly developed scientific evidence, or those which include a request for the protection of proprietary data; and
•   reduction of disease risk claims and claims referring to children's development and health.

Applications seeking authorisation of a claim for use in the GB market should be submitted to the competent authorities via the DHSC (which will centrally coordinate applications for all GB nations). Applications may also be submitted via the GB national competent authorities.

Food business operators wishing to make new health claims in the EU or Northern Ireland market following the end of the Transition Period will need to follow the EU process.

Claims based on new or emerging science or proprietary data post EU exit

20.193 Article 13(5) of retained Regulation (EC) No 1924/2006, as amended, provides for the authorisation of health claims based on newly-developed scientific evidence and/or which include a request for the protection of proprietary data to the GB NHC Register. The process to be used is set out in Article 18 of retained Regulation (EC) No 1924/2006, as amended. Regulation (EC) No 1924/2006, did not define 'newly-developed scientific evidence'. It is understood that the UK's understanding remains that, in this context, a claim based on newly-developed scientific evidence may be a claim that:

- has never been made before; or
- is based on evidence that has become available since 31 January 2008.

Therefore, the process contained in Art 18 of retained Regulation (EC) No 1924/2006, as amended, may be used to submit health claims other than those referring to disease risk reduction or to children's development and health. For example, a new application for a claim which received a negative opinion from EFSA after submission under Art 13(2), and for which relevant information has come to light since 31 January 2008, could be submitted via this route.

20.194 The GB application process is similar to the EU process, but with the United Kingdom Nutrition and Health Claims Committee (UKNHCC) replacing EFSA for the scientific assessment being one of the key differences. From the date that the UKNHCC receives a valid application from a competent GB authority it has 5 months to provide its opinion to the relevant authorities. The UKNHCC has the option to request further information about the application if necessary. If the UKNHCC requests any further information, the overall time limit will be extended by 1 month, with the applicant required to submit the requested information within 15 days. The UKNHCC will forward its opinion to the relevant authorities and the applicant as well as making it public. The applicant and members of the public have 30 days to make comments to the relevant competent GB authority.

20.195 The appropriate UK authorities have two months from receipt of that UKNHCC scientific opinion to decide whether the claim should be authorised. The appropriate UK authorities will take into account the UKNHCC's scientific opinion; relevant provisions in law; any enactments; and other factors relevant to the matter under consideration and will consult one another in reaching a view. Authorised claims will be added to the GB NHC Register together with any conditions of use. Similarly, if the claim is rejected it will be added to the GB NHC Register together with the reasons for the rejection. Once authorised and added to the GB NHC Register the claim will be available for use on any product that meets with the requirements of the Regulation, and any conditions of use specified. If, however, any of the supporting scientific data or other information has been granted data protection, it cannot be used by any other applicant for five years in accordance with Art 21. This is reliant on:

- the scientific data or other information being designated as proprietary by the applicant when the application is made; and
- the prior applicant having exclusive right of reference to the proprietary data at the time the prior application was made; and

- the health claim not being able to be authorised without the submission of the proprietary data by the applicant.

Reduction of disease risk claims post EU exit

20.196 Retained Regulation (EC) No 1924/2006, as amended, requires disease risk reduction claims and claims which refer to children's development and health to be authorised prior to use, and specifies a procedure for such authorisations. Once authorised, a claim will be added to the GB NHC Register and can be used on any product that meets the conditions of the Regulation and the conditions of use specified. To have a claim authorised for use in the GB market an application with supporting information must be submitted to the relevant competent GB authority and in turn reviewed by the UKNHCC under similar processes to the EU, but again with GB authorities and the UKNHCC as the key organisations in the GB.

Claims authorised by the appropriate UK authorities for use in the GB market will be added to the GB NHC Register together with any conditions of use. Rejected claims will also be added to the GB NHC Register together with the reasons for their rejection.

Modification, suspension, and revocation of authorisations post EU exit

20.197 In accordance with Art 19 of retained Regulation (EC) No 1924/2006, as amended, an applicant and/or user of a claim, authorised for the purposes of Art 13 or Art 14, may apply for a modification of that health claim to be authorised: following the procedures set out in Arts 15 to 18. The appropriate GB authorities may also, on their own initiative, request that a claim be reconsidered. Following a request from an appropriate GB authority, the UKNHCC shall issue a scientific opinion on whether a health claim authorised for the purposes of Art 13 or 14 still meets the conditions laid down in retained Regulation (EC) No 1924/2006, as amended. The UKNHCC shall make available its opinion to the appropriate UK authorities, the original applicant of the claim in question, and the public. The applicant, user, or member of the public have 30 days, the publication of the opinion, to make comments to the appropriate UK authorities. The appropriate UK authorities, taking into consideration the opinion of the UKNHCC and any comments received, may by regulations modify or revoke the claim in question. In cases of urgency, the appropriate UK authorities may exercise the power to make regulations to modify or revoke a claim without allowing for the 30-day comment period.

Generic descriptors

20.198 Retained Regulation (EC) No 1924/2006, as amended, continues to allow for appropriate authorities to make regulations granting derogations from Art 1.3 following the receipt of an application for the GB market by business. The Nutrition (Amendment etc) (EU Exit) Regulations 2019 revoked Commission Regulation (EU) No 907/2013 that set out the application procedure for generic descriptors as the provisions where inoperable for UK only applications. Retained Commission Regulation (EU) No 2019/343 which provides for derogations from Art 1(3) of Retained Regulation (EC) No 1924/2006 is now applicable; it will be subsequently amended by the Nutrition (Amendment etc) (EU Exit) Regulations 2020. The Annex to retained Regulation (EU) No 2019/343 will contain all the generic descriptors permitted for use in the GB following the end of the Transition Period. Applications for generic descriptors other than those addressed by Commission Regulation (EU) No 2019/343 currently being considered by the EU are unlikely to be authorised before the end of the transition period. These will need to be submitted for consideration by the UK appropriate authorities for use in the GB market.

VITAMINS AND MINERALS

Introduction

20.199 The EU Regulation on the addition of vitamins, minerals and of certain other substances to foods[1] ('AVMS 2006'), applies to the addition of a wide range of nutrients and other ingredients used in food manufacturing. The effect of the Regulation was to harmonise the rules in the EU and aims to regulate such additions to foods[2] under conditions:

- that result in the ingestion of amounts greatly exceeding those reasonably expected to be ingested under normal conditions of consumption of a balanced and varied diet; and/or
- would otherwise represent a potential risk to consumers[3].

The provisions of the AVMS 2006 also require that the chemical substances used as sources of vitamins and minerals which may be added to foods[4] should be safe and also be bio-available ie available to be used by the body; and establishes a positive list of these substances in Annexes I and II.

[1] Regulation (EC) No 1925/2006 of the European Parliament and of the Council of 20 December 2006 on the addition of vitamins and minerals and of certain other substances to foods.
[2] The provisions of the AVMS 2006 regarding vitamins and minerals do not apply to food supplements covered by Directive 2002/46/EC.
[3] See Recital 2 of AVMS 2006.
[4] Including, but not limited to, vitamins, minerals including trace elements, amino acids, essential fatty acids, fibre, and various plants and herbal extracts.

20.200 Article 3 specifies that only those vitamins or minerals listed in Annex I, in the form listed in Annex II, may be added to foods[1]. Vitamins and minerals cannot be added to unprocessed foodstuffs, including, but not limited to, fruit, vegetables, meat, poultry and fish or to beverages containing more than 1.2% by volume of alcohol (subject to certain historical exceptions. Whilst there has been extensive consultation as to maximum levels of Vitamins and Minerals in accordance with the provisions of Art 6, no proposal has yet been presented 'due to the complex nature of the issue and the divergent views that were expressed'[2].

[1] Annex I and Annex II are amendable, for example, additional substances have been added by Commission Regulations:
- Commission Regulation (EU) 2017/1203.
- Commission Regulation (EU) No 119/2014.
- Commission Regulation (EU) No 1161/2011.
- Commission Regulation (EC) No 1170/2009.
[2] https://ec.europa.eu/food/safety/labelling_nutrition/vitamins_minerals_en.

20.201 The permitted vitamins and minerals are as follows:

VITAMINS AND MIN-ERALS WHICH MAY BE ADDED TO FOODS	VITAMIN FORMULATIONS AND MINERAL SUBSTANCES WHICH MAY BE ADDED TO FOODS
1. Vitamins	
Vitamin A	Retinol, retinyl acetate, retinyl palmitate, beta-carotene
Vitamin D	Cholecalciferol, ergocalciferol
Vitamin E	D-alpha-tocopherol, DL-alpha-tocopherol, D-alpha-tocopheryl acetate, DL-alpha-tocopheryl acetate, D-alpha-tocopheryl acid succinate
Vitamin K	phylloquinone (phytomenadione), menaquinone[1]
Vitamin B1	thiamin hydrochloride, thiamin mononitrate
Vitamin B2	Riboflavin, riboflavin 5'-phosphate sodium
Niacin	nicotinic acid, nicotinamide
Pantothenic acid	D-pantothenate calcium, D-pantothenate sodium, dexpanthenol
Vitamin B6	pyridoxine hydrochloride, pyridoxine 5'-phosphate, pyridoxine dipalmitate
Folic acid	pteroylmonoglutamic acid, calcium-L-methylfolate
Vitamin B12	Cyanocobalamin, hydroxocobalamin
Biotin	D-biotin
Vitamin C	L-ascorbic acid, sodium-L-ascorbate, calcium-L-ascorbate, potassium-L-ascorbate, L-ascorbyl 6-palmitate
2. Minerals	
Boron	boric acid, sodium borate
Calcium	calcium carbonate, calcium chloride, calcium salts of citric acid, calcium citrate malate, calcium gluconate, calcium glycerophosphate, calcium lactate, calcium salts of orthophosphoric acid, calcium malate, calcium hydroxide, calcium oxide, calcium sulphate
Magnesium	magnesium acetate, magnesium carbonate, magnesium chloride, magnesium salts of citric acid, magnesium gluconate, magnesium glycerophosphate, magnesium salts of orthophosphoric acid, magnesium lactate, magnesium hydroxide, magnesium oxide, magnesium potassium citrate, magnesium sulphate
Iron	ferrous bisglycinate, ferrous carbonate, ferrous citrate, ferric ammonium citrate, ferrous gluconate, ferrous fumarate, ferric sodium diphosphate, ferrous lactate, ferrous sulphate, ferric diphosphate (ferric pyrophosphate), ferric saccharate, elemental iron (carbonyl + electrolytic + hydrogen reduced)

VITAMINS AND MINERALS WHICH MAY BE ADDED TO FOODS	VITAMIN FORMULATIONS AND MINERAL SUBSTANCES WHICH MAY BE ADDED TO FOODS
Copper	cupric carbonate, cupric citrate, cupric gluconate, cupric sulphate, copper lysine complex
Iodine	sodium iodide, sodium iodate, potassium iodide, potassium iodate
Zinc	zinc acetate, zinc bisglycinate, zinc chloride, zinc citrate, zinc gluconate, zinc lactate, zinc oxide, zinc carbonate, zinc sulphate
Manganese	manganese carbonate, manganese chloride, manganese citrate, manganese gluconate, manganese glycerophosphate, manganese sulphate
Sodium	sodium bicarbonate, sodium carbonate, sodium citrate, sodium gluconate, sodium lactate, sodium hydroxide, sodium salts of orthophosphoric acid, sodium fluoride
Potassium	potassium fluoride, potassium bicarbonate, potassium carbonate, potassium chloride, potassium citrate, potassium gluconate, potassium glycerophosphate, potassium lactate, potassium hydroxide, potassium salts of orthophosphoric acid
Selenium	sodium selenate, sodium hydrogen selenite, sodium selenite, selenium enriched yeast[2]
Chromium	chromium (III) chloride and its hexahydrate, chromium picolinate, chromium (III) sulphate and its hexahydrate, chromium(III) lactate trihydrate
Molybdenum	ammonium molybdate (molybdenum (VI)), sodium molybdate (molybdenum (VI))
Fluoride	Any sources in this column
Chloride	Any sources in this column
Phosphorus	Any sources in this column

[1] Menaquinone occurring principally as menaquinone-7 and, to a minor extent, menaquinone-6.
[2] Selenium-enriched yeasts produced by culture in the presence of sodium selenite as selenium source and containing, in the dried form as marketed, not more than 2,5 mg Se/g. The predominant organic selenium species present in the yeast is selenomethionine (between 60 and 85 % of the total extracted selenium in the product). The content of other organic selenium compounds including selenocysteine shall not exceed 10 % of total extracted selenium. Levels of inorganic selenium normally shall not exceed 1 % of total extracted selenium.

Other substances

20.202 For the purposes of the Regulation, 'other substance' is defined as 'a substance other than a vitamin or a mineral that has a nutritional value or physiological effect'[1], for example 'trace elements, amino acids, essential fatty acids, fibre, various plants and herbal extracts'. Article 8(5) in conjunction with Art 9(2)(h) allows for a positive list of substances to be developed 'to generally allow the use of a substance'. No such substances have been included on such a list.

[1]   Article 2(2) of AVMS 2006.

20.203 There is a procedure under Art 8 which allows for substances as additives to food to be prohibited, restricted, or placed under scrutiny in the EU as food additives. Annex III contains a list of those substances which have been prohibited, restricted or placed under scrutiny in accordance with that procedure. The Commission, on its own initiative or at the request of a Member State, may initiate the procedure under Art 8[1] VMR 2006 to prohibit, restrict or put a substance under EU scrutiny. Such concern would arise where the use of such substances in foods would result in the ingestion of amounts greatly exceeding those normally expected to be ingested or would otherwise represent a potential risk to consumers[2].

[1]   The conditions for use of the procedure may be found in Commission Implementing Regulation (EU) No 307/2012 establishing implementing rules for the application of Art of Regulation (EC) No 1925/2006.
[2]   For example see Commission Regulation (EU) 2015/403 which places Ephedra herb and its preparations in Pt A of Annex III and Commission Regulation (EU) 2019/650 which places Yohimbe bark and its preparations originating from Yohimbe (Pausinystalia yohimbe (K. Schum.) Pierre ex Beille) in Pt A of Annex III (having previously been placed in Pt C of Annex III.

20.204 The Commission on its own initiative has initiated the procedure under Art 8 of the VMR 2006 for:

(a)   the intake of hydroxyanthracene derivatives (HADs) from all food sources; and
(b)   the intake of monacolins derived from red yeast rice (ie rice fermented with the red yeast *Monascus purpurseus*).

The procedure under Art 8 of the VMR 2006 has also been initiated on the basis of requests by certain EU countries for the intake of green tea catechins, and particularly epigallocatechin-3-gallate (EGCG), from all food sources – this relates to safety concerns that have been raised by those Member States with regard to the intake of these substances.

Changes to requirements of AVMS after EU exit

20.205 However, the Nutrition (Amendment etc) (EU Exit) Regulations 2019 makes a number of practical changes to the GB regulatory framework from 1 January 2021.

On the 18 March 2021 the EU made provisions for Regulation of HADs[1]. Plants containing hydroxyanthracene derivatives are numerous and belong to different botanical families and genera. They are widely used in food supplements. This EU measure added to Part A (BAN) of Annex III of Regulation (EC) No 1925/2006 aloe-emodin, emodin, danthron and all preparations in which these substances are present and preparations of the leaf of Aloe species containing HADs. It also added to Part C (SCRUTINY) of Annex III the preparations from of Rheum, Cassia, and Rhamnus containing HADs. In effect, it bans edible Aloe products in the EU which contain more than a 'trace' of

HADs, and places limits on other species which contain HADs. It is a controversial measure, with questions about its legal basis, its proportionality, and, because of the absence of agreed test methodology to determine 'traces'.

¹ Commission Regulation (EU) 2021/468 amending Annex III to Regulation (EC) No 1925/2006 of the European Parliament and of the Council as regards botanical species containing hydroxyanthracene derivatives.

GB Register of Vitamins, Minerals, and Certain Other Substances

20.206 In preparation for the UK's withdrawal from the EU, the UK Government and Devolved Administrations in Scotland and Wales have adopted the Community Register of Vitamins, Minerals, and Certain Other Substances as it exists on 1 January 2021, as 'the GB VMS Register'. The GB VMS Register lists:

- the vitamins and minerals which may be added to foods as listed in Annex I of retained Regulation (EC) No 1925/2006, as amended; and
- the vitamin formulations and mineral substances which may be added to foods as listed in Annex II of retained Regulation (EC) No 1925/2006, as amended; and
- the maximum and minimum amounts of vitamins and minerals which may be added to foods and any associated conditions set in accordance with Art 6 of retained Regulation (EC) No 1925/2006, as amended; and
- information regarding enactments applicable in any part of Great Britain on:
  - the mandatory addition of vitamins and minerals to specified foods or categories of foods; or
  - the prohibition or restriction on the use of certain other substances in the manufacture of specified foods; and
- any restrictions on the addition of vitamins and minerals as set out in Art 4 of retained Regulation (EC) No 1925/2006, as amended; and
- information about the substances referred to in Annex III of retained Regulation (EC) No 1925/2006, as amended (Part A: prohibited substances, Part B: restricted substances) and the reasons for their inclusions therein; and
- information about the substances listed in Annex III, Part C, of retained Regulation (EC) No 1925/2006, as amended whose use is generally allowed as referred to in Art 8(5).

The GB VMS Register will have effect across the whole of GB from 1 January 2021.

Modifying the GB VMS Register

Modifying Annexes I & II

20.207 Article 3.3 of retained Regulation (EC) No 1925/2006, as amended, allows for the appropriate GB authorities to make regulations to specify modifications to Annex I (vitamins and minerals which may be added to foods) and Annex II (the vitamin formulations and mineral substances which may be added to foods) after taking into consideration the opinion of an expert committee. Prior to making any modifications to the Annexes of retained Regulation (EC) No 1925/2006, as amended, the appropriate UK authorities will consult with interested parties. Food business operators, or other interested parties, that wish for vitamin and mineral substances to be considered for inclusion in the Annexes may submit a scientific dossier concerning the safety and bioavailability of the individual substance for consideration for use in the GB market by the appropriate UK authorities.

Modifying Annex III Part C

20.208 Annex III Part C of retained Regulation (EC) No 1925/2006, as amended, includes other substances where scientific uncertainty exists over the possibility that they represent a risk to health. This is a temporary listing to allow for further scientific data to be gathered. Within four years of a substance being listed in Annex III Part C of retained Regulation (EC) No 1925/2006, as amended, the appropriate UK authorities will, in consultation with one another and taking into consideration an expert committee on any files submitted for evaluation, decide whether to generally allow the substance in question or add it to the list in Annex III Part A or Part B.

20.209 During this period food business operators or any other interested parties that wish to demonstrate the safety of a substance listed in Annex III Part C of retained Regulation (EC) No 1925/2006, as amended, may submit a file to an expert committee; in accordance with the procedures set out in retained Commission Implementing Regulation (EU) No 307/2012, as amended. It is understood that files should continue to be completed in line with administrative guidance produced by the European Commission, until further notice. For submitted dossiers not considered by the EU before the end of the transition period, where the applicant wishes for that modification to also be applicable in the GB market a submission must also be made to the DHSC (which will centrally coordinate dossiers for all GB nations) for consideration by the appropriate UK authorities. The appropriate UK authorities will identify an appropriate scientific advisory committee that the dossier should be sent to for evaluation. Any modification will be made by the GB authorities in a similar manner to that in the EU but acted out or informed by UK bodies:

- Risk assessment - existing scientific advisory committees in the UK will take on the role of providing advice previously provided by the European Food Safety Authority in relation to vitamins, minerals, and certain other substances when the UK was in the EU.
- Risk management functions related to vitamins, minerals, and certain other substances will be assumed by the appropriate UK authorities.

Legislation which provided for enforcement of Regulation (EC) No 1925/2006 in each part of the United Kingdom's prior to its withdrawal from the European Union still applies.

FOOD SUPPLEMENTS

Introduction

20.210 Food supplements are a sub-category of food and are controlled in the EU by means of Directive 2002/46/EC ('FSD 2002')[1]. For the purpose of the FSD 2002 'food supplements' means foodstuffs 'the purpose of which is to supplement the normal diet and which are concentrated sources of nutrients or other substances with a nutritional or physiological effect, alone or in combination, marketed in dose form, namely forms such as capsules, pastilles, tablets, pills and other similar forms, sachets of powder, ampoules of liquids, drop dispensing bottles, and other similar forms of liquids and powders designed to be taken in measured small unit quantities'.

[1] Directive 2002/46/EC of the European Parliament and of the Council of 10 June 2002 on the approximation of the laws of the Member States relating to food supplements.

20.211 The FSD came into force on 1 August 2005 and is implemented by the Food Supplements (England) Regulations 2003, as amended, and equivalent regulations in the UK devolved administrations. The UK Regulations specify compositional and labelling requirements of food supplements, including the vitamin and mineral substances permitted for use in food supplements. Food supplements are therefore foodstuffs that aim to supplement the normal diet. Critically, they are concentrated sources of nutrients or other substances with nutritional or physiological effects, alone or in combination, marketed in dose form to supplement the normal diet. They must be distinguished from fortified foodstuffs which are treated as foods and regulated in respect of certain additions that may be made to them by the VMR 2006.

20.212 With the exception of vitamins and minerals, the Food Supplements Directive (2002/46/EC) does not include specific rules for other nutrients, and 'functional' ingredients such as:

- amino acids;
- essential fatty acids;
- fibre; and
- various plants and herbal extracts.

However, such nutrients and 'functional' ingredients are subject to the labelling requirements of the Directive (2002/46/EC) and control under the VMR 2006 as 'other substances'.

20.213 Food supplements are covered by food law, unless they have a medicinal effect or make a medicinal claim (ie to prevent, treat or cure any disease or medical condition); in the latter case they must be licensed under medicines legislation, which is the responsibility of the Medicines and Healthcare products Regulatory Agency ('MHRA') in the UK, and other similar bodies throughout the EU. Medicines law is not harmonised across the EU and what may be freely sold in one EU Member State as a food may be classified as medicinal in another EU Member State. In addition, many herbal ingredients are classified as medicines and, as such, are also under the jurisdiction of the MHRA and its counterparts in the EU (see CHAPTER 24 Health and Medicines).

20.214 Member States must ensure that food supplements may be marketed within the EU only if they comply with the rules laid down in the Directive[1]. Similar implementing instruments to that in the UK therefore exist throughout the EU Member States.

[1] Article 3 of the Directive requires.

20.215 The Regulations specify compositional and labelling requirements for food supplements, including the vitamin and mineral substances permitted for use in food supplements. Under the Supplements Directive[1] only limited source substances may be used in the manufacture of food supplements characterised by vitamins or minerals. The Supplements Directive stipulates that the values declared on the labelling must be *average values* based on the *manufacturer's analysis* of the product; and official guidance on monitoring compliance in the EU recognises that variation is to be expected, when samples are analysed, both above and below the declared values[2]. Best practice in manufacturing is to target greater amounts of nutrient sources than those claimed so that the consumer can be assured that the product can provide these during the products minimum durability; however care must be taken to ensure that levels remain safe. A new EU Regulation ((EU) 2021/418) amends Annex I of the Food Supplements Directive 2002/46/EC bringing the units for labelling copper into line with those for foods, ie, the units for labelling food supplements will be changed to milligrams rather than micrograms. It will apply across the EU and therefore to Northern Ireland from 30 September 2022. An 18-month transition period allows for products placed on the market or labelled prior to 30 September 2022 to be marketed until existing stocks run out. As this change has occurred since the UK left the EU, it is not clear whether GB will implement the change. According to Sch 1 of The Nutrition (Amendment etc) (EU Exit) Regulations 2019, copper in food supplements should be labelled in micrograms (µg), while under retained Regulation 1169/2011 on food information to consumers, copper added to food products other than food supplements should be labelled in milligrams (mg). The key UK Trade Associations (HFMA, CRN UK and PAGB) have made a formal request for a proportionate approach to UK regulators to prevent creation of a new technical barrier to trade of food supplements between GB and Northern Ireland. A 24-month transition period has been requested, with products placed on the market or labelled prior to the end of the transition period, which do not comply with the changes, able to be marketed until stocks run out.

[1] Directive 2002/46/EC, as amended.

[2] Guidance document for competent authorities for the control of compliance with EU legislation on: Regulation (EU) No 1169/2011 of the European Parliament and of the Council of 25 October 2011 on the provision of food information to consumers, amending Regulations (EC) No 1924/2006 and (EC) No 1925/2006 of the European Parliament and of the Council, and repealing Commission Directive 87/250/EEC, Council Directive 90/496/EEC, Commission Directive 1999/10/EC, Directive 2000/13/EC of the European Parliament and of the Council, Commission Directives 2002/67/EC and 2008/5/EC and Commission Regulation (EC) No 608/2004 and Council Directive 90/496/EEC of 24 September 1990 on nutrition labelling of foodstuffs and Directive 2002/46/EC of the European Parliament and of the Council of 10 June 2002 on the approximation of the laws of the Member States relating to food supplements with regard to the setting of tolerances for nutrient values declared on a label.

EU Mandatory warnings for excessive consumption

20.216 However, there is also a mandatory requirement in the Supplements Directive to warn consumers not to exceed the recommended daily intake. UK industry has agreed maximum levels with the UK Government, including levels where it is appropriate to use warnings.

Offences

20.217 Regulation 8 of the Food Supplements (England) Regulations 2003 creates the offence of contravening any of regs 4, 5, 6 or 7.

(a)   Reg 4 (restriction on sale of food supplements unless pre-packed);
(b)   Reg 5 (restrictions on sale contravening composition requirements);
(c)   Reg 6 (restrictions on sale relating to labelling);
(d)   Reg 7 (sale in contravention of requirements of manner of marking or labelling).

Offences under the Food Supplements (England) Regulations are summary only. The maximum sentence on summary conviction is a fine. Regulation 11 provides that certain provisions of the Food Safety Act 1990[1] apply for the purposes of the 2003 Regulations as they do in relation to the Food Safety Act.

[1]   Including the extended meaning of 'sale'; presumption that food is intended for human consumption; causal liability; due diligence; innocent publication; documentary evidence; time limits; directors' liability.

Food supplements after EU exit

20.218 The NIP means that EU legislation relating to food supplements will continue to be directly applicable in Northern Ireland. For GB the lists of vitamins and minerals that may be used in the manufacture of food supplements, contained as an Annex to Directive 2002/46/EC, have been inserted into the Nutrition (Amendment etc) (EU Exit) Regulations 2019 as Schedules to ensure that they continue to have affect in GB:

•   Schedule 1: vitamins and minerals which may be used in the manufacture of food supplements.
•   Schedule 2: Vitamin and mineral substances which may be used in the manufacture of food supplements.

Supplementary information in Schs 1 and 2

20.219 In light of the different legal systems, Schs 1[1] and 2[2] in the Nutrition (Amendment etc) (EU Exit) Regulations 2019 omit the footnotes in the Annexes to Directive 2002/46/EC because the footnotes set out recommendations rather than legal requirements. It is understood that this difference may be addressed in GB guidance in the near future.

[1]   **Folic acid** (µg) – Folic acid is the term included in Annex I of Commission Directive 2008/100/EC of 28 October 2008 amending Council Directive 90/496/EEC on nutrition labelling for foodstuffs as regards recommended daily allowances, energy conversion factors and definitions for nutrition labelling purposes and covers all forms of folates.

2   **Vitamin E: (f) Mixed Tocopherols**
alpha-tocopherol < 20 %, beta-tocopherol < 10 %, gamma-tocopherol 50–70 % and delta-tocopherol 10–30 %.
Vitamin E: (g) Tocotrienol Tocopherol
Typical levels of individual tocopherols and tocotrienols:
*   115 mg/g alpha-tocopherol (101 mg/g minimum),
*   5 mg/g beta-tocopherol (< 1 mg/g minimum),
*   45 mg/g gamma-tocopherol (25 mg/g minimum),
*   12 mg/g delta-tocopherol (3 mg/g minimum),
*   67 mg/g alpha-tocotrienol (30 mg/g minimum),
*   < 1 mg/g beta-tocotrienol (< 1 mg/g minimum),
*   82 mg/g gamma-tocotrienol (45 mg/g minimum),
*   5 mg/g delta-tocotrienol (< 1 mg/g minimum).
Vitamin K: (b) Menaquinone
Menaquinone occurring principally as menaquinone-7 and, to a minor extent, menaquinone-6.
Vitamin C: (c) Calcium-L-ascorbate
May contain up to 2 % of threonate.
Mineral: Selenium Enriched Yeast
Selenium-enriched yeasts produced by culture in the presence of sodium selenite as selenium source and containing, in the dried form as marketed, not more than 2,5 mg Se/g. The predominant organic selenium species present in the yeast is selenomethionine (between 60 and 85 % of the total extracted selenium in the product). The content of other organic selenium compounds including selenocysteine shall not exceed 10 % of total extracted selenium. Levels of inorganic selenium normally shall not exceed 1 % of total extracted selenium.
Mineral: Silicic Acid
In the form of gel.

Modifying schedules

20.220 The Nutrition (Amendment etc) (EU Exit) Regulations 2019 provides for the appropriate GB authorities to make regulations to amend the schedules, set the purity criteria as well as maximum and minimum amounts of vitamins and minerals that may be added to food supplements. Food business operators, or other interested parties, that wish for vitamin and mineral substances to be considered for inclusion in the Schedules to the Nutrition (Amendment etc) (EU Exit) Regulations 2019 may submit a scientific dossier concerning the safety and bioavailability of the individual substance for consideration for use in the GB market by the appropriate UK authorities to the DHSC (which will centrally coordinate dossiers for all three GB nations) for consideration by the appropriate UK authorities. The appropriate UK authorities will identify an appropriate scientific advisory committee that the dossier should be sent to for evaluation.

20.221 Any modification will be made by the GB authorities in a similar manner to that in the EU but acted out or informed by UK bodies:

*   Risk assessment - existing scientific advisory committees in the UK will take on the role of providing advice previously provided by the European Food Safety Authority in relation to vitamins, minerals, and certain other substances when the UK was in the EU.
*   Risk management functions related to vitamins, minerals, and certain other substances will be assumed by the appropriate UK authorities.

Legislation which provided for enforcement of FSD 2002 in each part of the United Kingdom's prior to its withdrawal from the European Union still applies.

NOVEL FOODS

Introduction

20.222 The concept of 'novel food' can cover a number of different types of food. It can, for example, be newly developed, innovative food, food produced using new technologies and production processes, as well as food which is or has been traditionally eaten outside of the EU. It is food that has:

(a) not been consumed to a significant degree by humans in the EU before 15 May 1997, when the first Regulation (Regulation (EC) No 258/97) on novel food came into force; and

(b) (b) is brought into scope by falling into a category specified in the Regulation.

20.223 The underlying principles[1] underpinning Novel Food Regulation in the European Union are that novel foods must be:

(a) safe for consumers;

(b) properly labelled, so as not to mislead consumers; and

(c) if novel food is intended to replace another food, it must not differ in a way that the consumption of the novel food would be nutritionally disadvantageous for the consumer.

[1] Article 3.1 of Regulation 258/97 stated: Foods and food ingredients falling within the scope of this Regulation must not:
– present a danger for the consumer,
– mislead the consumer,
– differ from foods or food ingredients which they are intended to replace to such an extent that their normal consumption would be nutritionally disadvantageous for the consumer.

20.224 As of 1 January 2018, the new Regulation (EU) 2015/2283 on novel foods (the new Regulation) is applicable. It repeals and replaces Regulation (EC) No 258/97 and related Regulation (EC) No 1852/2001 which were in force until 31 December 2017. According to the Commission, the new Regulation *aims to make it easier to bring new and innovative foods to the EU market, while maintaining a high level of food safety for European consumers.* The novel food definition describes the various situations of foods originating from plants, animals, microorganisms, cell cultures, minerals, etc., specific categories of foods (insects, vitamins, minerals, food supplements, etc.), foods resulting from production processes and practices, and state of the art technologies (eg intentionally modified or new molecular structure, nanomaterials), which were not produced or used before 1997 and thus may be considered to be as novel foods.

20.225 Under the new Regulation new and existing authorisations cease to be treated as applicant-specific, unless based on protected data. Any food business operator can place an authorised novel food on the EU market, provided the authorised conditions of use, labelling requirements, and specifications are respected. Individual authorisation for 5 years can be granted based on protected data to promote innovation. A centralised authorisation procedure is managed by the European Commission online, which will include a safety evaluation of the novel food carried out by EFSA.

20.226 There is an updateable[1] positive list containing all authorised novel foods. A novel food is added to the list, is automatically considered to be authorised for the EU market. The Implementing Regulation establishing the list of novel foods compiles all the authorised novel foods in the European Union to date[2], many arising from the 1997 Regulation, including via 'substantial equivalence'. It includes their conditions of use, labelling requirements, and their specifications. Under the old Regulation (EC) No 258/97 on novel foods, 228 applications have been submitted to the EU countries pursuant to Art 4 and more than 400 notifications (under 'substantial equivalence' rules) pursuant to Art 5 of that Regulation. As a result of this legal commitment, the initial Union list of authorised novel foods contains 125 entries.

[1] By means of Commission Implementing Regulations: Commission Implementing Regulation (EU) 2017/2470 on establishing the Union list of novel foods in accordance with Regulation (EU) 2015/2283 of the European Parliament and of the Council on Novel Foods.

[2] Commission Implementing Regulation (EU) 2017/2470 of 20 December 2017 establishing the Union list of novel foods in accordance with Regulation (EU) 2015/2283 of the European Parliament and of the Council on novel foods.

20.227 To qualify as novel food under the previous and new Regulation (EU) 2015/2283 (the new Novel Food Regulation) the food in question must be food that has not been consumed to a significant degree by humans in the EU before 15 May 1997, such as entirely new food; traditional foods eaten elsewhere in the world, but not in the EU; or foods produced from new processes. But, this only part of the definition; and an assessment against the full definition is very important, as the requirements if, novel are onerous including extensive pre-market safety assessments, authorisation and monitoring.

20.228 Deciding that a food is not novel is easiest where consumption to a significant degree before 15 May 1997 is evident. An informal guide for that purpose exists in the guise of the Novel Foods Catalogue, however it is not definitive and has no legal status[1]. Given its status as an EU guide under the European Commission's editorial control it has an unclear status in the UK (other than perhaps for NI) now the UK has exited the EU. Under the EU definition a food is novel if not used for human consumption to a significant degree within EU before 15 May 1997, *and* falls under at least one of the following categories[2]:

'(i) food with a new or intentionally modified molecular structure, where that structure was not used as, or in, a food in the EU before 15 May 1997;

(ii) food consisting of, isolated from or produced from microorganisms, fungi or algae;

(iii) food consisting of, isolated from or produced from material of mineral origin;

(iv) food consisting of, isolated from or produced from plants or their parts, except when the food has a history of safe food use within the EU and is consisting of, isolated from or produced from a plant or a variety of the same species obtained by:

– traditional propagating practices which have been used for food production within the EU before 15 May 1997; or

– non-traditional propagating practices which have not been used for food production within the Union before 15 May 1997,
where those practices do not give rise to significant changes in the composition or structure of the food affecting its nutritional value, metabolism or level of undesirable substances;

(v)   food consisting of, isolated from or produced from animals or their parts, except for animals obtained by traditional breeding practices which have been used for food production within the Union before 15 May 1997 and the food from those animals has a history of safe food use within the Union;

(vi)   food consisting of, isolated from or produced from cell culture or tissue culture derived from animals, plants, micro-organisms, fungi or algae;

(vii)   food resulting from a production process not used for food production within the Union before 15 May 1997, which gives rise to significant changes in the composition or structure of a food, affecting its nutritional value, metabolism or level of undesirable substances;

(viii)   food consisting of engineered nanomaterials as defined in point (f) of this paragraph;

(ix)   vitamins, minerals and other substances used in accordance with Directive 2002/46/EC, Regulation (EC) No 1925/2006 or Regulation (EU) No 609/2013, where:

–   a production process not used for food production within the Union before 15 May 1997 has been applied as referred to in point (a) (vii) of this paragraph; or

–   they contain or consist of engineered nanomaterials as defined in point (f) of this paragraph;

(x)   food used exclusively in food supplements within the Union before 15 May 1997, where it is intended to be used in foods other than food supplements as defined in point (a) of Art 2 of Directive 2002/46/EC.'

The Novel Food (Amendment) (EU Exit) Regulations 2019 make a minor amendment to this definition which will apply from 1 January 2021 to indicate that the UK has left the EU ie 'novel food' means any food that was not used for human consumption to a significant degree within the EU or the United Kingdom before 15 May 1997.

1   https://ec.europa.eu/food/safety/novel_food/catalogue/search/public/index.cfm.
2   The definition includes some very specific provisions for certain foods stuffs eg the category that relates to vitamins, minerals and other substances used in accordance with Directive 2002/46/EC, Regulation (EC) No 1925/2006 or Regulation (EU) No 609/2013.

20.229   Article 4 of the Novel Food Regulation (EU) 2015/2283 requires food business operators to verify if the food they intend to place on the EU market falls within the scope of the Novel Food Regulation (EU) 2015/2283.; that is, if the food is novel or not. In practice, that verification does not preclude an informal approach to the competent authorities to share their view or the rationale leading to it for additional assurance.

20.230   UK Trading Standards authorities can give informal views on the novel status of foodstuffs. In the UK, Primary Authorities can also approach the central competent authority ie the Food Standards Agency as a 'supporting regulator' in developing 'assured advice' under the primary authority scheme. Where a food business operator is unclear if a food is Novel, the Regulation allows the operator to get a view from an EU Member State, or the European Commission, as to whether the product requires authorisation under the Novel Food Regulation. If after considering all the information available food business operator is still unsure about a foods status as novel or not, they may formally consult the competent authorities of the EU country where they first intend to place the food (called 'the recipient EU country') on the market.

EU exit

20.231 From 1 January 2020 the Novel Food (Amendment) (EU Exit) Regulations 2019 provides for GB that where food business operators are unsure whether or not a food which they intend to place on the market within the United Kingdom is novel they must consult the Food Safety Authority[1]. Food business operators must provide the necessary information to the Food Safety Authority to enable it to determine whether or not a food is novel under the Regulation.

[1] The Food Standards Agency or in Scotland, Food Standards Scotland.

20.232 Art 5 of NFR 2015 provides (subject to checks and balances[1]) the Commission with an implementing power concerning the definition of novel food. The Commission may decide, on its own initiative or upon a request by a Member State, by means of implementing acts, whether or not a particular food falls within the definition of novel food. From 1 January 2020 the Novel Food (Amendment) (EU Exit) Regulations 2019 provide for GB that the ' . . . appropriate authority[2] may prescribe that a particular food is a novel food . . . '.

[1] The examination procedure referred to in Art 30(3) of NFR 2015.
[2] 'appropriate authority' means—
    (i)   in relation to England, the Secretary of State;
    (ii)   in relation to Wales, the Welsh Ministers;
    (iii) in relation to Scotland, the Scottish Ministers;
    (iv)   in relation to Northern Ireland, the Northern Ireland devolved authority;

Requirements for regulated product applications from 1 January 2021

20.233 The UK Food Standards Agency has indicated that it will deal with GB market authorisations for Novel food within its new regulated product authorisation processes[1]. When applying for authorisation of a regulated product in the UK, the administrative, technical and safety information required as part of the application will be the same as is currently required by the European Food Safety Authority (EFSA) and the European Commission (EC). There are two types of authorisation for novel foods which have slightly different requirements on the data to be submitted:

- Full application:
    - Regulation (EC) 2017/2469 – administrative and scientific requirements for novel foods applications[2];
    - EFSA guidance on the preparation and presentation of an application for authorisation of a novel food[3].
- Traditional food notification:
    - Regulation (EC) 2017/2468 – administrative and scientific requirements concerning traditional foods from third countries[4];
    - Regulation (EC) 2017/2468 – administrative and scientific requirements concerning traditional foods from third countries[5].

[1] https://www.food.gov.uk/business-guidance/requirements-for-regulated-product-applications-from-1-january-2021.
[2] Commission Implementing Regulation (EU) 2017/2469 of 20 December 2017 laying down administrative and scientific requirements for applications referred to in Art 10 of Regulation (EU) 2015/2283 of the European Parliament and of the Council on novel foods.
[3] http://dx.doi.org/10.2903/j.efsa.2016.4594.

4   Commission Implementing Regulation (EU) 2017/2468 of 20 December 2017 laying down administrative and scientific requirements concerning traditional foods from third countries in accordance with Regulation (EU) 2015/2283 of the European Parliament and of the Council on novel foods.

5   https://efsa.onlinelibrary.wiley.com/doi/epdf/10.2903/j.efsa.2016.4590.

Offences

20.234 Regulation 4 of the Novel Foods (England) Regulations 2018 creates the offence of failing to comply with certain specified Union Provisions. The specified provisions are those in Sch 1, and relate to:

(a)   Article 6.2 as read with Art 24 (Requirement that only novel foods authorised and included in the Union list may be placed on the market as such, or used in or on foods, in accordance with the conditions of use and labelling requirements specified therein, and with any post-market monitoring requirements) .

(b)   Article 25 (Requirement that any food business operator which has placed a novel food on the market shall immediately inform the Commission of any information of which it becomes aware concerning (a) any new scientific or technical information which might influence the evaluation of the safety of use of the novel food; (b) any prohibition or restriction imposed by a third country in which the novel food is placed on the market-general requirements relating to all claims).

Offences under the Regulations are summary only, and the maximum sentence is a fine. Regulation 7 provides that certain provisions of the Food Safety Act 1990[1] apply for the purposes of the 2018 Regulations as they do in relation to the Food Safety Act. From 1 of January 2020 the Novel Food (Amendment) (EU Exit) Regulations 2019 will amend the offence provisions to ensure continuity of application after EU exit for the GB Novel Foods regime[2].

1   Including the extended meaning of 'sale'; presumption that food is intended for human consumption; causal liability; due diligence; innocent publication; documentary evidence; time limits; directors' liability.

2   Amendment of the Novel Foods (England) Regulations 2018:

'3. The Novel Foods (England) Regulations 2018 are amended as follows.
4. In Schedule 1, in column 2 of the Table—
in the entry which relates to Article 6.2 as read with Article 24, omit "Union";
in the entry which relates to Article 25, for "Commission", substitute "Food Safety Authority".'

Civil Sanctions

20.235 Regulation 5 and Schs 2 and 3 make provision for a scheme of fixed monetary penalties and for the issuing of compliance or stop notices.

FEED LAW

Key definitions and requirements under European legislation

20.236 EC Regulation 178/2002 lays down the principles of food and feed law. Article 3 provides definitions of 'feed', 'feed businesses' and 'feed business operators'. 'Feed' (or 'feeding stuff') means any substance or product, including additives, whether processed, partially processed or unprocessed, intended to be used for oral feeding to animals[1]. 'Feed business' means any undertaking whether for profit or not and whether public or private, carrying out any operation of production, manufacture, processing, storage, transport or distribution of feed including any producer producing, processing, or storing feed for feeding to animals on his own holding[2]. 'Feed business operator' means the natural or legal persons responsible for ensuring that the requirements of food law are met within the feed business under their control.

1   Regulation (EC) 178/2002, Art 3(4).
2   Regulation (EC) 178/2002, Art 3(5).

20.237 Although EC Regulation 178/2002 appears to apply only to food-producing animals, EC Regulation 767/2009 extends its application in respect of feed to non-food producing animals[1]. This is particularly important given the rise in the use of raw and other feed to pets seen in recent years.

1   Regulation (EC) 767/2009, Introductory Text, recitals 7 and 8

20.238 Article 15(1) prohibits the placing of unsafe feed on the market or the feeding of it to any food-producing animal[1]. Feed will be deemed to be unsafe for its intended use if it is considered to have an adverse effect on human or animal health or make the food derived from food-producing animals unsafe for human consumption, Art 15(2). Where a feed which has been identified as not satisfying the feed safety requirement is part of a batch, lot or consignment of feed of the same class or description, it shall be presumed that all of the feed in that batch, lot or consignment is so affected, unless following a detailed assessment there is no evidence that the rest of the batch, lot or consignment fails to satisfy the feed safety requirement[2].

1   Regulation (EC) 178/2002, Art 15(1).
2   Regulation (EC) 178/2002, Art 15(3).

20.239 Feed business operators at all stages of production, processing, and distribution within the businesses under their control must ensure that foods or feeds satisfy the requirements of food law which are relevant to their activities and shall verify that such requirements are met[1].

Further, the requirements of 'traceability' apply equally to feed as it does to food[2].

1   Regulation (EC) 178/2002, Art 17.
2   Regulation (EC) 178/2002, Art 18.

20.240 Article 20 places an obligation to withdraw feed and inform the competent authorities if it considers or has reason to believe that a feed which it has imported, produced, processed, manufactured, or distributed does not satisfy the feed safety requirements and where feed does not satisfy feed safety requirements, to destroy it. The article also places an obligation on the feed business operator to immediately inform the competent authorities if it considers, or has reason to believe, that it has placed on the market which may not satisfy feed safety requirements and to collaborate with the authorities in order to avoid risks posed by any feed they have supplied.

Feed hygiene

20.241 Regulation (EC) 183/2005 sets down rules for hygiene in respect of feed and the conditions and arrangements for ensuring traceability and for the registration and approval of feed establishments. It specifically provides that feed business operators and farmers shall only source and use feed from establishments which are registered and/or approved in accordance with this Regulation[1]. The regulation also sets down standards relating to the transport and storage of feed, maintenance of equipment, the training of personnel, and the keeping of records.

1   Regulation (EC) 183/2005, Art 5(6).

20.242 According to current Food Standards Agency advice, feed businesses will therefore include the following: importers and merchants of feed materials and manufactured feeds – including merchants buying direct from farmers, food manufacturers selling material into the feed chain, road hauliers and transport companies which ship or deliver feed, livestock and some arable farmers, traders who do not hold stock on their premises or brokers. However, a challenge is pending, by way of case stated to the High Court, to the contention that establishments producing and supplying animal by-products to the feed chain are supplying feed at that stage before further processing[1]. Article 2 provides certain exempt categories from the scope of the regulation; this includes the retailing of pet food.

1   *Happy Hounds Ltd v Neath Port Talbot Borough Council*, Swansea Crown Court.

The use of and placing on the market of animal feed

20.243 Regulation (EC) 767/2009 sets out the requirements for the marketing, labelling and composition of animal feeding stuffs and includes provisions intended to safeguard both animal and human health. It requires that feed may be placed on the market and used only if it is safe and does not have a direct adverse effect on the environment or animal welfare.

20.244 The regulation also provides for a Catalogue of Feed Materials and Codes of Practice for labelling. The Catalogue of Feed Materials is published as Regulation 68/2013. The regulation lays down the minimum information to be provided to purchasers on feed labels; introduces a procedure for applications for the authorisation of new nutritional purposes; requires scientific substantiation for claims for a feed's composition or function; covers the names and descriptions to be applied to various feed materials; lists in Annex III, certain materials whose presence in animal feed is either prohibited or restricted; lists in Annex IV permitted tolerances for the compositional labelling of feed materials or compound feed; requires the labelling of contaminated feed being sent for cleaning or detoxification to prevent its diversion back into the feed chain. sets a demarcation between complementary feeds and premixtures by limiting the amount of feed additives in complementary feeds.

20.245 The regulation's objective is stated to be 'to harmonise the conditions for the placing on the market and the use of feed, in order to ensure a high level of feed safety and thus a high level of protection of public health, as well as to provide adequate information for users and consumers and to strengthen the effective functioning of the internal market'[1].

[1]   Regulation (EC) 767/2009, Art 1.

20.246 Feed may only be placed on the market and used if it is safe and does not have a direct adverse effect on the environment or animal welfare[1]. The requirements of Arts 15 and 16 of Regulation (EC) 178/2002 apply to feed for non-food producing animals by virtue of Art 4 of Regulation (EC) 767/2009. Feed business operators placing feed on the market shall ensure that the feed is sound, genuine, unadulterated, fit for its purpose and of merchantable quality and is labelled, packaged, and presented in accordance with the provisions laid down in all applicable Community legislation. Also, feed must comply with technical provisions on impurities and chemicals[2].

[1]   Regulation (EC) 767/2009, Art 4.
[2]   Regulation (EC) 767/2009, Annex 1.

20.247 This regulation makes Arts 18 and 20 of Regulation (EC) No 178/2002 and Art 4(1) of Regulation (EC) No 183/2005 in respect of feed, applicable to non-food producing animals. The regulation also makes it mandatory for the person responsible for the labelling of feed to make available to the competent authorities any information concerning the composition or claimed properties of the feed placed on the market by that person. The purpose is to allow the accuracy of the information given by the labelling to be verified, including the exact percentages by weight of feed materials used in compound feed[1].

[1]   Regulation (EC) 767/2009, Art 5.

20.248 In the event of any urgency relating to human or animal health or to the environment the competent authority may provide the purchaser with information that is made available to it under this article provided that, after having balanced the respective legitimate interests of the manufacturers and the purchasers, it concludes that the provision of such information is justified. In appropriate circumstances, this can be through the signing of a confidentiality clause by the purchaser of the feed. In addition, feed must not contain restricted or prohibited materials[1]. The amount of additives used in feed is restricted and controlled by this regulation and feed intended for particular nutritional purposes may only be marketed as such if its intended use is included in a list of intended uses and only if it meets the essential nutritional characteristics for the respective particular nutritional purpose set out[2].

[1]   Regulation (EC) 767/2009, Art 6.
[2]   Regulation (EC) 767/2009, Arts 8, 9 and 10.

20.249 Strict control is placed upon the labelling and the presentation of feed to prevent the user of it being misled[1]. Feed materials or compound feed marketed in bulk or in unsealed packages or containers, in accordance with Art 23(2), shall be accompanied by a document containing all mandatory labelling particulars required under this Regulation. There are also requirements for the provision of information accompanying sale of feed by distance communication[2]. Articles 11 to 26 set out the requirements and criteria on presentation, composition and packaging and provide for the creation of relevant codes of practice for member states[3].

[1]   Regulation (EC) 767/2009, Art 11.

20.250 Regulation (EC) 1831/2003 provides for rules on additives for use in animal nutrition and in particular; rules on feed additive authorisations; conditions of use for additives; provisions on the labelling of feed additives and their premixtures which must be adhered to.

20.251 Regulation 2020/354 establishes a list of intended uses of feed intended for nutritional purposes. Feed intended for particular nutritional purposes may only be marketed if its intended use is included in the list of intended uses and if it meets the essential nutritional characteristics for the respective particular nutritional purpose set forth in that list.

20.252 Regulation (EC) 1829/2003 establishes a centralised procedure for the scientific assessment and authorisation of genetically modified organisms (GMOs) and GM food and feed. The assessment procedures cover both the GMO itself and food and feed derivatives.

20.253 The Regulation requires labelling of all GM food and feed which contains or consists of GMOs or is produced from or contains ingredients produced from GMOs, regardless of the presence of GM material in the final product.

Official controls

20.254 Regulation 2017/625 sets out the general principles and enabling powers for carrying out official controls and specifies the approach to be adopted by the enforcement authority for checking compliance with feed and food law and animal health and welfare rules.

National legislation

20.255 The Animal Feed (Competition, Marketing and use etc) (England) Regulations 2015 (hereinafter referred to as 'The Marketing Regulations')[1] and the Animal Feed (Hygiene, Sampling etc and Enforcement) (England) Regulations 2015[2] (hereinafter referred to as the Enforcement Regulations) bring the requirements of the relevant European legislation into force domestically. Parallel regulations exist for each of Scotland, Wales, and Northern Ireland.

1 SI 2015/255.
2 SI 2015/454.

Offences

20.256 The Marketing Regulations create an offence of failing to comply with a specified provision of Regulation (EC) 178/2002[1]. A person who contravenes or fails to comply with any of the following, commits an offence: Art 12, in so far as it relates to feed (conditions on export or re-export to third countries); Art 15(1) (prohibition on the placing on the market or feeding to any animal of unsafe feed); Art 16, in so far as it relates to feed (prohibition on misleading labelling, advertising or presentation); Art 18(2) and (3) (requirements that operators must have traceability information and make such information available to competent authorities) in so far as they relate to feed business operators; and Art 20 (responsibilities of feed business operators regarding feed that does not satisfy feed safety requirements). The competent authority for Arts 15 and 18 is the local feed authority which in most cases will be the local county council and for Art 20 it is either the Food Standards Agency or the local feed authority.

[1]   SI 2015/255, reg 4.

20.257 A person who contravenes or fails to comply with a specified provision of Regulation (EC) 1829/2003 commits an offence[1]. The specified provisions are; Art 16(2) (prohibition on placing on the market, using or processing a product referred to in Art 15(1)(1) unless it is covered by an authorisation and satisfies relevant conditions), as read with Art 20(6) (requirement that products in relation to which the commission has adopted a measure under this Article must be withdrawn from the market); Art 21(1) (requirement that the authorisation holder and the parties concerned must comply with conditions imposed in an authorisation for that product, and that the authorisation holder must comply with post-market monitoring requirements); Art 21(3) (requirement that an authorisation holder inform the commission of any new scientific or technical information about a product which might affect the evaluation of the safety of its use in feed, or of any prohibition or restriction on the feed in a third country); and Art 25 (requirement for certain labelling indications). The competent authority is the Food Standards Agency.

[1]   SI 2015/255, reg 7.

20.258 A person who contravenes or fails to comply with a specified provision of Regulation (EC) 1831/2003 commits an offence[1]. The specified provisions are; Art 3(1) (prohibition on placing on the market, processing or using a feed additive unless it is covered by an authorisation and satisfies relevant conditions), as read with para (2) (national authorisation for scientific experimental purposes), para (4) (conditions on mixing of additives) and Art 10 (status of existing products); Art 3(3) (restriction on the persons who may first place on the market certain additives); Art 12(1) (requirement that any person using or placing on the market an additive, or a feed into which it has been incorporated, or any other interested party, must ensure that any conditions which have been imposed are respected); Art 12(2) (requirement on the holder of an authorisation to observe monitoring obligations where they have been imposed, to inform the commission of any new information about a product which might affect the evaluation of the safety of its use in feed, or of any prohibition or restriction on the feed imposed by the competent authority in a third country); Art 16(1), (3) and (4) (prohibition on the placing on the market of feed additives or premixtures unless labelled in the specified manner and with prescribed information), as read with para (2) (derogation for certain flavouring compounds); and Art 16(5) (requirement that additives and premixtures must be marketed only in closed packages or containers which must be closed in such a way that the fastener is damaged on opening and cannot be re-used).

[1]   SI 2015/255, reg 10.

20.259 Subject to the transitional provisions contained in Art 32, a person commits an offence where he contravenes or fails to comply with a provision of Regulation 767/2009 specified in Sch 1[1] (of Regulation (EC) 767/2009) or places on the market or uses a feed that fails to comply with Art 6(1) (feed shall not contain or consist of materials whose placing on the market or use for animal nutritional purposes is restricted or prohibited) or Art 8, (feed materials and complementary feed shall not contain levels of feed additives that are higher than 100 times the relevant fixed maximum content in complete feed or five times in case of coccidiostats and histomonostats)[2]. The local feed authority is the is the competent authority for the purposes of; Arts 5(3), 13(1)(a) and 17(3) and Annex VII, Ch1, para 8; and Art 13(1)(b) as the competent authority that may request scientific substantiation of a claim and to whose attention purchasers have the right to bring doubts regarding the truthfulness of a claim. The Food Standards Agency is the competent authority for the purposes of; Art 26(1)(b); and Art 13(1)(b) as the competent authority that may submit to the commission doubts concerning the scientific substantiation of a claim. The agency and each feed authority in its area or district is a competent authority for the purposes of Art 5(2)[3].

[1] Regulation (EC) 767/2009.
[2] SI 2015/255, reg 12.
[3] SI 2015/255, reg 13.

20.260 A person who places on the market any feed that is specified in column 2 of Annex I or uses any such feed, commits an offence if it contains any undesirable substance listed in column 1 of that Annex in excess of the relevant maximum content specified in column 3[1]. An 'undesirable substance' means any substance or product, not being a pathogenic agent, which is present in or on a feed and constitutes a potential danger to human or animal health or to the environment, or could adversely affect livestock production. A person who places on the market or uses any complementary feed commits an offence if, having regard to the quantity of it recommended for use in a daily ration, it contains any undesirable substance listed in column 1 of Annex I in excess of the maximum content specified for it in column 3 in relation to complete feeds; and there is no provision relating to any complementary feed in the corresponding entry in column 2 of that annex. A person who for the purpose of dilution mixes any feed with a feed that is specified in column 2 of Annex I and which contains any undesirable substance listed in column 1 of that Annex in excess of the maximum content specified for it in column 3 commits an offence. A person who places on the market or uses any feed which is not sound and genuine and of merchantable quality commits an offence. A feed listed in column 2 of Annex I shall be deemed not to be sound, genuine and of merchantable quality if it contains any undesirable substance specified in column 1 of that annex in excess of the maximum content specified in relation to it in column 3. Pursuant to reg 15(6) a person who has, for the purpose of a trade or business, possession or control of any of the feeds specified in para (7) of the regulation must, if required by an inspector, procure and produce to the inspector an analysis in order to demonstrate that the content of inorganic arsenic in the feed specified in that paragraph is less than 2 parts per million. The applicable feeds are; palm kernel expeller; feeds obtained from the processing of fish and other marine animals; seaweed meal and feed materials derived from seaweed; and complete feeds for fish or for fur-producing animals. A person who, without reasonable excuse, fails to comply with a requirement made under para (6) commits an offence. A person who places on the market a feed intended for a particular nutritional purpose commits an offence if the relevant requirements of paras (2) to (9) of reg 17 are not met.

[1] SI 2015/255, reg 15.

Penalties for offences under the Marketing Regulations

20.261 A person found guilty of an offence under regs 4(1), 7(1), 10(1), 12(1), 15(1), (2), (3) or (4) or 17(1) is liable on summary conviction to a term of imprisonment not exceeding 3 months or to a fine not exceeding level 5 on the standard scale, or both . This is an unlimited fine. A person found guilty of an offence under reg 15(8) is liable on summary conviction to a fine not exceeding level 3 on the standard scale.

Registration and approval of feed businesses

20.262 Article 9 of Regulation (EC) 183/2005 provides for the notification and registration of feed businesses. Feed business operators must cooperate with the competent authorities, in accordance with the relevant Community legislation and national law and must: (a) notify the appropriate competent authority of any establishments under their control, active in any of the stages of production, processing, storage, transport or distribution of feed, in the form required by the competent authority with a view to registration; (b) provide the competent authority with up-to-date information on any establishments under their control as referred to in point (a), including notifying the competent authority of any significant change in activities and any closure of an existing establishment. The competent authority must maintain a register or registers of establishments.

20.263 Regulation 6 of the Enforcement Regulations sets out the form of notification with a view to registration:

A person who is required under Art 9 (officials controls, notification and registration) to notify the enforcement authority of the information mentioned in para (2)(a) or (b) of that Article must ensure that any such notification—
(a)   is in writing and signed by that person or on their behalf;
(b)   contains the person's name and, if different, business name;
(c)   contains the person's address and, if different, the address of any establishment to which the notification relates;
(d)   identifies the feed business activities in such form as may be required by the enforcement authority may require; and
(e)   is properly directed to the enforcement authority for the area in which the establishment to which the notification relates is situated.

20.264 Certain businesses are required to be approved pursuant to Art 10 of Regulation (EC) 183/2005 rather than registered under Art 9. Article 10 states:

Feed business operators shall ensure that establishments under their control and covered by this regulation are approved by the competent authority, where:
(1)   such establishments carry out one of the following activities:

(a) manufacturing and/or placing on the market of feed additives covered by Regulation (EC) No 1831/2003 or products covered by Directive 82/471/EEC and referred to in chapter 1 of Annex IV to this regulation;

(b) manufacturing and/or placing on the market of premixtures prepared using feed additives referred to in chapter 2 of Annex IV to this regulation;

(c) manufacturing for placing on the market, or producing for the exclusive requirements of their holdings, compound feedingstuffs using feed additives or premixtures containing feed additives and referred to in chapter 3 of Annex IV to this regulation;

(2) approval is required under the national law of the Member State where the establishment is located; or

(3) approval is required by a delegated regulation that the commission is empowered to adopt in accordance with Art 30A in order to supplement this regulation.

20.265 Where approval of a feed business establishment is required pursuant to Art 10, an application to the enforcement authority for the area in which the establishment is located must be made which[1]:

(a) is in writing and signed by or on behalf of the applicant;

(b) contains the name or business name and the address of the applicant and, if different, the address of the establishment;

(c) identifies which of the feed business activities specified in Art 10(1) or as may be specified pursuant to Art 10(3) the applicant is exercising or intends to exercise and for which approval is sought;

(d) in the case of a person to whom Art 17(2) (exemption from on-site visits) applies, includes a statement to the effect that the establishment is one to which Art 17(1) applies and a declaration of compliance as required by para (2) of that article; and

(e) is properly directed to the enforcement authority for the area in which the establishment to which the declaration relates is situated.

[1]   SI 2015/454, reg 7.

20.266 Pursuant to Art 13 the competent authority shall approve establishments only where an on-site visit, prior to start-up of any activity, has demonstrated that they meet the relevant requirements of this regulation[1]. The competent authority may grant conditional approval if it appears, from the on-site visit, that the establishment meets all the infrastructure and equipment requirements. It shall grant full approval only if it appears, from a new on-site visit carried out within three months of granting conditional approval, that the establishment meets the other requirements referred to in para 1. If clear progress has been made, but the establishment still does not meet all of these requirements, the competent authority may prolong conditional approval. However, conditional approval shall not exceed a total of six months.

[1]   Regulation (EC) 183/2005.

20.267 The competent authority shall temporarily suspend the registration or the approval of an establishment for one, more or all of its activities, where it is shown that the establishment no longer fulfils the conditions applicable to those activities[1].

[1]   Regulation (EC) 183/2005, Art 14.

20.268 Such suspension shall last until the establishment again meets those conditions. Where such conditions are not met within one year, Art 15 shall apply. This provides that the competent authority shall revoke the registration or the approval of an establishment, for one or more of its activities, where: (a) the establishment ceases one or more of its activities; (b) it is shown that the establishment has not fulfilled the conditions applicable to its activities, for a period of one year; (c) it identifies serious deficiencies or has had to stop production at an establishment repeatedly and the feed business operator is still not able to provide adequate guarantees regarding future production. Upon request, the competent authority shall amend the registration or approval of an establishment, where it has demonstrated its capacity to develop activities which are additional to those for which it was first registered or approved, or which replace them[1].

[1] Regulation (EC) 183/2005, Art 16.

Procedure for suspension of registration or approval

20.269 Where an enforcement authority proposes to take action pursuant to Art 14 (temporary suspension of registration or approval) it must serve on the feed business operator a notice[1]. The notice served by the enforcement authority must—

(a) specify the operative date of the notice ('the operative date');
(b) state that on the operative date the enforcement authority intends to suspend the registration or approval of the establishment pursuant to Art 14 and these regulations;
(c) specify the feed business activity or activities to which the notice relates;
(d) identify the remedial action required;
(e) state that unless remedial action has been carried out to the satisfaction of the enforcement authority within one year of the operative date, the registration or approval will be revoked without further notice on the first anniversary of the operative date; and
(f) provide information on the time limit for appealing under reg 12.

[1] SI 2015/454, reg 8.

Procedure for lifting of suspension

20.270 Where the enforcement authority that has served notice on a feed business operator under regulation 8 is satisfied that—

(a) the remedial action required under para (2)(e) of that regulation has been carried out; and
(b) the period for action specified in that sub-paragraph has not expired,

it must immediately lift the suspension and notify the feed business operator to that effect.

Procedure for revocation of registration or approval

20.271 Where an enforcement authority proposes to take action in the circumstances set out in Article 15 (revocation of registration or approval) it must serve on the feed business operator a notice[1].

(2) A notice served under para (1) must—
  (a) specify the operative date of the notice;
  (b) state that the registration or approval as the case may be has been revoked;
  (c) specify the feed business activity or activities to which the revocation relates;
  (d) identify which of the conditions of revocation set out in Art 15 is applicable;
  (e) provide information on the time limits for appealing under reg 12.

(3) Where an enforcement authority has revoked a registration or approval under this regulation it must—
  (a) make the appropriate amendments to its own register of feed business establishments; and
  (b) promptly transmit to the agency the necessary information to ensure compliance with Art 19(3) (updating of national lists).

[1] SI 2015/454, reg 10(1).

Form of application for amendments to registration or approval

20.272 Where a feed business operator wishes to apply for amendments to registration or approval pursuant to Art 16 (amendments to registration or approval of an establishment), an application to the enforcement authority for the area in which the relevant feed business establishment is located must be made and which must comply with various provisions set out in the regulation.

Rights of appeal in connection with registration or approval

20.273 Any person who is aggrieved by the decision of an enforcement authority taken in respect of Arts 13, 14, 15, 16, may appeal to a magistrates' court within one month from which the notice of the decision is served[1]. An appeal is by way of complaint for an order and the Magistrates' Courts Act 1980 applies to the proceedings. Where the magistrates' court determines that the decision of the enforcement authority is incorrect, the authority must give effect to the determination of the court. Where a registration or an approval is suspended or revoked, the feed business operator who, immediately before such suspension or revocation, had been operating the establishment concerned may continue to operate it, subject to any conditions imposed by the enforcement authority for the protection of public health, unless the time limit for appealing against the decision to suspend or revoke registration or approval has expired without an appeal having been brought or where an appeal against that decision has been brought, the appeal has been finally disposed of or abandoned. However, where a prohibition order, feed business emergency prohibition notice or a feed business emergency prohibition order has been imposed that order or notice is not suspended pending any appeal.

[1] SI 2015/454, reg 12.

Fees for approvals or amendments to approvals

20.274 Fees are required to be paid by the feed business operator to the enforcement authority when applying for approval or amendment to an approval and any cost of laboratory analysis incurred by the enforcement authority in connection with the application[1].

[1] SI 2015/454, reg 13.

Procedure relating to samples for analysis

20.275 Regulation 14 mandates the appointment of an agricultural analyst on behalf of the authority. Regulation 15 sets out the procedure in respect of analysing samples. Under para 1:

(1) Where an authorised officer obtains a sample and decides to have it analysed for the purpose of ascertaining whether there is or has been any contravention of specified feed law, the officer must divide the sample into three parts of as near as may be equal size and—

    (a) cause each part to be marked sealed and fastened in the prescribed manner;

    (b) send one part for analysis to the agricultural analyst for the area of the enforcement authority from which the authorised officer derives his authority;

    (c) send another part to the person on whose premises the material was sampled or to that person's agent;

    (d) retain and preserve the remaining part as an officially sealed reference sample.

(2) If the person who manufactured any material sampled under these Regulations is not a person to whom part of the sample should be sent under para (1), that paragraph has effect as if for the reference to three parts there were substituted a reference to four parts, and the authorised officer must within fourteen days of the date of sampling send the fourth part to the manufacturer, unless the officer does not know and is unable to ascertain after making reasonable enquiries the identity or the address in the United Kingdom of the manufacturer.

(3) The part of the sample sent to the agricultural analyst must be accompanied by a statement signed by the authorised officer confirming that the sample was taken in the prescribed manner.

(4) The agricultural analyst must analyse the part of the sample sent under para (1)(b), and send a certificate of analysis to the authorised officer, who must send a copy to—

    (a) the person on whose premises the material was sampled or that person's agent; and

    (b) if a part of the sample was sent under para (2), to the person to whom that part was sent.

(5) Any analysis required to be made under para (4) may be performed by any person acting under the direction of the agricultural analyst.

(6) If the agricultural analyst to whom the sample was sent under para (1)(b) determines that an effective analysis of the sample cannot be performed by him or her or under his or her direction, that analyst must send it to the agricultural analyst for another area, together with any documents received with the sample, and para (4) shall then apply as if the sample had originally been sent to that other analyst.

Secondary analysis by the government chemist

20.276 Regulation 16 sets out the circumstances when the retained part of any sample analysed must be examined by the government chemist. Where a part of a sample sent under reg 15(1)(b) has been analysed and proceedings are intended to be or have been commenced against a person for an offence under specified feed law; and the prosecution intends to adduce evidence of the result of that part of the sample, the authorised officer, may, of his or her own volition and must, if requested by the prosecutor (if a person other than the authorised officer), or must if requested by the defendant, but subject to the appropriate fee being paid, send the retained part of the sample to be analysed by the government chemist.

Offence of tampering with a sample

20.277 A person who tampers with any material so as to procure that any sample of it taken or submitted for analysis under these regulations does not correctly represent the material, or, tampers or interferes with any sample taken or submitted for analysis under these regulations, commits an offence[1].

[1]   SI 2015/454, reg 20.

Feed business improvement notices

20.278 If an authorised officer has reasonable grounds for believing that a feed business operator is failing to comply with specified feed law, the officer may serve a notice on that person, referred to as a 'feed business improvement notice'[1]. The notice must state the officer's grounds for believing that the feed business operator is failing to comply with specified feed law; specify the matters which constitute the feed business operator's failure to comply; specify the measures which, in the officer's opinion, the feed business operator must take in order to secure compliance; and require the feed business operator to take those measures, or measures which are at least equivalent to them, within such period (not being less than 14 days) as may be specified in the notice. The notice must state the right to appeal under reg 25 and the appropriate time limit for bringing any such appeal. A person who fails to comply with a feed business improvement notice commits an offence.

[1]   SI 2015/454, reg 24.

Right of appeal against feed business improvement notices

20.279 A person who is aggrieved by a decision of an authorised officer to serve a feed business improvement notice may appeal to a magistrates' court either within one month from the date on which the notice is served on the person who desires to appeal or if a period for compliance with the measures stated on by the notice is less than that period, that period as set out in the notice. The procedure on an appeal to a magistrates' court is by way of complaint for an order, and the Magistrates' Courts Act 1980 applies to the proceedings[1].

[1] SI 2015/454, reg 25.

Appeals to the Crown Court

20.280 A person who is aggrieved by the decision of a magistrates' court to dismiss an appeal to it under regs 12(1) or 25(1) or any decision of such a court to make a feed business prohibition order or a feed business emergency prohibition order, may appeal to the Crown Court[1]. On an appeal against a feed business improvement notice the court may cancel or affirm the notice and, if it affirms it, may do so either in its original form or with such modifications as the court may in the circumstances think fit[2].

[1] SI 2015/454, reg 26.
[2] SI 2015/454, reg 27.

Feed business prohibition orders

20.281 If a feed business operator is convicted of an offence under specified feed law and the court is satisfied that the health risk condition is fulfilled with respect to the feed business concerned the court must by an order impose the appropriate prohibition[1]. The health risk condition is fulfilled with respect to a feed business if any of the following involves risk of injury to health (including any impairment, whether permanent or temporary), namely, the use for the purposes of the business of any process or treatment; the construction of any premises used for the purposes of the business, or the use for those purposes of any equipment; or the state or condition of any premises or equipment used for the purposes of the business, health means the health of an animal or, through the consumption of the products of such animal, human health. The appropriate prohibition is a prohibition on the use of the process or treatment for the purposes of the business; a prohibition on the use of the premises or equipment for the purposes of the business or any other feed business of the same class or description; and a prohibition on the use of the premises or equipment for the purposes of any feed business. Further, if a feed business operator is convicted of an offence under specified feed law, and the court thinks it proper to do so in all the circumstances of the case, it may impose a prohibition order on the feed business operator participating in the management of any feed business, or any feed business of a class or description specified in the order. Any person who knowingly contravenes such an order commits an offence.

[1] SI 2015/454, reg 28.

20.282 A feed business prohibition order ceases to have effect, either on the issue by the enforcement authority of a certificate to the effect that it is satisfied that the feed business operator has taken sufficient measures to secure that the health risk condition is no longer fulfilled with respect to the feed business or on the giving by the court of a direction to that effect. The enforcement authority must issue a certificate within three days of its being satisfied that the feed business operator has taken sufficient measures to secure that the health risk condition is no longer fulfilled. On an application by the feed business operator for such a certificate, the authority must determine, as soon as is reasonably practicable and in any event within 14 days, whether or not it is so satisfied; and if it determines that it is not so satisfied, give notice to the feed business operator of the reasons for that determination.

Feed business emergency prohibition notices and orders

20.283 Regulation 29 provides for the service of an emergency prohibition notice where an authorised officer of an enforcement authority is satisfied that the health risk condition, as set out in reg 28, is fulfilled, but as if the reference to 'risk to injury' in that regulation were a reference to imminent risk of such injury. If a magistrates' court is satisfied, on the application of such an officer, that the health risk condition is fulfilled with respect to a feed business, the court must, by an order (referred to as a 'feed business emergency prohibition order'), impose the appropriate prohibition. Such an officer may not apply for a feed business emergency prohibition order unless, at least one day before the date of the application, the officer has served notice on the relevant feed business operator of the intention to apply for the order.

20.284 As soon as practicable after the service of a feed business emergency prohibition notice, an authorised officer of an enforcement authority must affix a copy of the notice in a conspicuous position on such premises used for the purposes of the feed business as the officer considers appropriate; and a person who knowingly contravenes such a notice commits an offence. As soon as practicable after the making of a feed business emergency prohibition order, an authorised officer of an enforcement authority must serve a copy of the order on the relevant feed business operator and affix a copy of the order in a conspicuous position on such premises used for the purposes of the feed business as the officer considers appropriate. A person who knowingly contravenes such an order commits an offence.

20.285 A feed business emergency prohibition notice ceases to have effect if no application for a feed business emergency prohibition order is made within the period of three days beginning with the service of the notice, at the end of that period, or, if such an application is so made, on the determination or abandonment of the application. A feed business emergency prohibition notice or a feed business emergency prohibition order ceases to have effect on the issue by the enforcement authority of a certificate to the effect that it is satisfied that the feed business operator has taken sufficient measures to secure that the health risk condition is no longer fulfilled with respect to the feed business. The enforcement authority must issue such a certificate within three days of being satisfied as to the measures taken and on an application by the feed business operator for such a certificate, the authority must determine as soon as is reasonably practicable and in any event within 14 days whether or not it is so satisfied, and, if it determines that it is not so satisfied, give notice to the feed business operator of the reasons for that determination.

20.286 Compensation is payable to a feed business operator on whom a feed business emergency prohibition notice is served, in respect of any loss suffered by reason of complying with the notice unless: an application for a feed business emergency prohibition order is made within the period of three days beginning with the service of the notice; and the court declares itself satisfied, on the hearing of the application, that the health risk condition was fulfilled with respect to the feed business at the time when the notice was served, Any disputed question as to the right to or the amount of any compensation payable under this paragraph is to be determined by arbitration.

Powers of entry and inspection

20.287 Regulation 30 provides for a power of entry to premises to an authorised officer for investigations in respect of undesirable substances in animal feed and in order to execute and enforce specified feed law. It provides for conditions on such an entry and powers to take samples or inspect and obtain copies of records held, once on the premises. It also provides for the power to apply for a warrant to enter under certain circumstances.

Powers of detention and seizure

20.288 Regulation 31 provides for what is the equivalent to s 9 of the Food Safety Act in respect of the detention and seizure of food.

Offences relating to the exercise of powers

20.289 A person who wilfully obstructs an authorised officer in the exercise of the officer's powers under these regulations or fails to comply with a requirement lawfully made in the exercise of such powers commits an offence[1]. A person not being an authorised officer who purports to act as such under these regulations commits an offence. A person who discloses to any other person any information in relation to any manufacturing process or trade secret which has been obtained on premises entered by virtue of these regulations, or any other information obtained in pursuance of these regulations, commits an offence unless the disclosure was made in and for the purpose of the performance of functions under these regulations.

[1]   SI 2015/454, reg 32.

Penalties for offences

20.290 A person guilty of an offence under reg 5, as read with Table 1 of Sch 2, or regs 24(3), 28(5), 29(5) or (6) or 31(2) is liable—
(a)   on summary conviction to a term of imprisonment not exceeding 3 months or to a fine not exceeding the statutory maximum, or both;
(b)   on conviction on indictment to a term of imprisonment not exceeding 2 years or to a fine, or both.

A person guilty of an offence under reg 5, as read with Table 2 of Schedule 2, or regs 20 or 32(1) or (2) is liable on summary conviction to a term of imprisonment not exceeding 3 months or to a fine not exceeding level 5 on the standard scale, or both.

A person guilty of an offence under reg 32(3) is liable on summary conviction to a fine not exceeding level 5 on the standard scale[1].

[1]   SI 2015/454, reg 34.

Defences

20.291 Where the commission by a person of an offence under specified feed law is due to the act or default of some other person, that other person commits the offence and may be accused and convicted of the offence whether or not proceedings are taken against the first-mentioned person[1]. In any proceedings for an offence under specified feed law it shall, subject to para (3), be a defence to prove that the commission of the offence was due to a mistake, or to reliance on information supplied to the accused, or to the act or default of another person, or to an accident or some other cause beyond the control of the accused; and the accused took all reasonable precautions and exercised all due diligence to avoid the commission of such an offence by the accused or any person under their control.

[1]   SI 2015/454, reg 35.

20.292 If in any case the defence involves the allegation that the commission of the offence was due to the act or default of another person or to reliance on information supplied by another person, the person accused shall not, without leave of the court, be entitled to rely on that defence unless—
(a)   at least seven clear days before the hearing; and
(b)   where the accused has previously appeared before a court in connection with the alleged offence, within one month of the first such appearance,

the accused has served on the prosecutor a notice giving any information the accused may have to identify or assist in identifying that other person.

20.293 In any proceedings in which it alleged that a material has contravened or failed to comply with the requirements of specified feed law it is a defence for the person accused to prove that the material in respect of which the offence was alleged to have been committed—
(a)   was feed to which Art 25 of Regulation 183/2005 applies; and
(b)   could lawfully be exported in accordance with the requirements of Art 12 (food and feed exported from the EU) of Regulation (EC) No 178/2002 of the European Parliament and of the council laying down the general principles and requirements of food law, establishing the European Food Safety Authority and laying down procedures in matters of food safety.

Offences by corporate bodies

20.294 Regulation 36 creates an offence under specified feed law where it is committed by a body corporate with the consent or connivance of, or is attributable to any neglect on the part of, any director, manager, secretary or other similar officer of the body corporate or any person who was purporting to act in any such capacity, In such circumstances that person as well as the body corporate shall be deemed to have committed that offence and liable to be proceeded against and punished accordingly.

Institution of and time limit for prosecutions

20.295 Proceedings for an offence under specified feed law may be taken in the place where the person accused resides or carries on business[1]. No prosecution for an offence under the Enforcement Regulations or Marketing Regulations 2015 may be begun after the expiry of—
(a)   three years from the commission of the offence; or
(b)   one year from its discovery by the prosecutor,

whichever is the earlier.

[1]   SI 2015/454, reg 35.

Chapter 21

ENVIRONMENTAL STANDARDS

Contents

INTRODUCTION

21.1 This chapter outlines the roles that legislation and authorities play in regulating the environment at the local level. This is a broad topic that covers many different types of environmental concerns – from plastic packaging to noise pollution.

21.2 This edition now also includes an overview of the law relating to statutory nuisance, fly tipping, and unlawful waste disposal – subjects that occupy a significant share of local authorities' time and resources. An exhaustive analysis of these areas is necessarily beyond the scope of this work. However, it is hoped that by providing an overview of the law this chapter may be useful in providing a springboard for those coming new to the issues surrounding local environmental standards.

21.3 Finally, as in previous editions, this chapter also considers packaging requirements, energy information, and the energy performance of buildings.

STATUTORY NUISANCE

21.4 The law of statutory nuisance is intended to provide a swift and simple procedure for stopping activities that cause harm or nuisance to a person's neighbours. Its scope is defined primarily by the Environmental Protection Act 1990 ('EPA 1990').

21.5 It should be noted at the outset that both local authorities and private citizens may initiate proceedings for statutory nuisance. Only the law relating to local authorities is considered here. Similarly, this chapter does not consider the common law doctrine of nuisance – a system of laws that operates in parallel to statutory nuisance.

What constitutes statutory nuisance?

21.6 EPA 1990, s 79(1) sets out the basic framework of statutory nuisance:

> (1)   Subject to subsections (1A) to (6A) below, the following matters constitute 'statutory nuisances' for the purposes of this Part, that is to say—
>
>   (a) any premises in such a state as to be prejudicial to health or a nuisance;
>   (b) smoke emitted from premises so as to be prejudicial to health or a nuisance;
>   (c) fumes or gases emitted from premises so as to be prejudicial to health or a nuisance;
>   (d) any dust, steam, smell or other effluvia arising on industrial, trade or business premises and being prejudicial to health or a nuisance;
>   (e) any accumulation or deposit which is prejudicial to health or a nuisance;
>   (f) any animal kept in such a place or manner as to be prejudicial to health or a nuisance;
>   (fa) any insects emanating from relevant industrial, trade or business premises and being prejudicial to health or a nuisance;
>   (fb) artificial light emitted from premises so as to be prejudicial to health or a nuisance;
>   (g) noise emitted from premises so as to be prejudicial to health or a nuisance;
>   (ga) noise that is prejudicial to health or a nuisance and is emitted from or caused by a vehicle, machinery or equipment in a street or in Scotland, road;
>   (h) any other matter declared by any enactment to be a statutory nuisance; and it shall be the duty of every local authority to cause its area to be inspected from time to time to detect any statutory nuisances which ought to be dealt with under section 80 below or sections 80 and 80A below and, where a complaint of a statutory nuisance is made to it by a person living within its area, to take such steps as are reasonably practicable to investigate the complaint.

21.7 This section achieves three things. First, it defines ten categories or types of nuisance (as well as one mopping up category). Second, it imposes a continuing obligation on local authorities to inspect their areas for nuisances. Third, it imposes an obligation on local authorities to investigate complaints of nuisance made to them.

The obligation to inspect for nuisances

21.8 It should be noted that the obligation to inspect for nuisances is distinct and in addition to the obligation to investigate complaints of nuisance. Consequently, local authorities should have in place organised programmes of inspection covering their entire areas of responsibility. Failure to do so can result in reference to the Secretary of State under para 4 of EPA 1990, Sch 3. The Secretary of State may then make an order declaring the local authority to be in default and directing it to take certain steps. Failure to comply with those directions may in turn lead to enforcement by mandamus against the authority or assumption of the authority's responsibilities by the Secretary of State.

Categories of nuisance

21.9 (The categories listed below relate to those listed in EPA 1990, s 79(1) at **21.6** above.):

(a) 'State of the premises' – this relates to premises that are in a poor state. It should be noted that it is only the <u>condition</u> of the premises that can constitute a nuisance and not the <u>use</u> of the premises. For example, a building laced with a toxic fungus would fall within this category, but a building being used to store infectious diseases would not[1].

(b) 'Smoke' – note that EPA 1990, s 79(3) creates a number of exceptions to this category: (i) smoke emitted from a chimney of a private dwelling within a smoke control area, (ii) dark smoke emitted from a boiler or industrial plant, (iii) smoke emitted from railway steam engines, and (iv) dark smoke emitted from industrial or trade premises. These forms of smoke are regulated instead by other statutory regimes.

(c) 'Fumes or gasses' – this category applies only to private dwellings[2].

(d) 'Dust, steam, smell or other effluvia' – this category applies only in relation to industrial, trade, or business premises. 'Effluvia' is defined by most dictionaries as an unpleasant or harmful odour or discharge.

(e) 'Any accumulation or deposit' – this could include rubbish or dog excrement. 'Accumulation' suggests a series of deposits, whilst a 'deposit' might occur only once.

(f) 'Any animal' – note that this applies only to animals 'kept' by a person. As a result, a dog barking in a neighbour's garden could be within the scope of this category, whilst a noisy bird nesting in a neighbour's tree would not.

(fa) 'Insects' – this category applies only to industrial, trade, or business premises. However, it is possible that a private dwelling suffering from an insect infestation might be in a poor 'state' falling within category (a).

(fb) 'Artificial light' – EPA 1990, s 79(5B) provides for a number of exceptions to this category, including airports and bus stations.

(g) 'Noise emitted from premises' – this includes vibration[3]. Note that 'premises' can include a vessel, for example a canal boat.

(ga) 'Noise emitted from a vehicle, machine or equipment in a street' – this does not include noise made by normal traffic, the Armed Forces, or political demonstrations (see EPA 1990, s 79(6A)).

(h) 'Any other matter declared by any enactment' – examples include nuisances relating to water courses in the Public Health Act 1936 and dangerous abandoned mines in the Mines and Quarries Act 1954.

---

[1] *Metropolitan Asylum District Manager v Hill* (1881) 6 Cr App Cas 193.

2   The EPA 1990, s 79(4).
3   The EPA 1990, s 79(7).

'PREJUDICIAL TO HEALTH OR A NUISANCE'

21.10 Once an activity is identified as belonging to one of the categories of nuisance listed above, it is then necessary (except in the case of the final mopping up category) to determine whether the activity is 'prejudicial to health or a nuisance'. The activity may be either prejudicial to health or it may be a nuisance; there is no need to prove both elements.

'PREJUDICIAL TO HEALTH'

21.11 The EPA 1990, s 79(7) defines 'prejudicial to health' as meaning 'injurious, or likely to cause injury, to health'. In considering whether something is likely to cause injury to health, the courts will have regard to expert evidence and professional guides/standards (including, for example, guidance from the World Health Organisation)[1]. However, the courts are also entitled to draw common sense conclusions from the facts presented in evidence.

1   See *Murdoch v Glacier Metal Co Ltd* [1998] Env LR 732.

21.12 Despite use of the word 'injury' in the definition of 'prejudicial to health', the courts have held that personal injury is not included. Rather, the term refers to illness or disease[1]. As a result, a house infested with disease carrying rodents might be 'prejudicial to health', but a house with exposed faulty electrical wiring would not be (notwithstanding the fact that it might pose a significant hazard to the wellbeing of its occupants).

1   *R v Bristol City Council, ex p Everett* [1999] 2 All ER 193, CA.

21.13 The effect on a person's health may be indirect (eg an activity that prevents a person from sleeping properly might be 'prejudicial to health')[1]. Note, however, that the risk of injury to health must be assessed objectively; the court is concerned not with the individual characteristics of a particular complainant, but rather with the risk to health generally[2].

1   See *Lewisham v Fenner* [1995] 248 ENDS Report 44 and *R (ex p Fisher) v Durham County Council* [2020] Env LR 28.
2   *Cunningham v Birmingham City Council* [1998] Env LR 1, DC.

'A NUISANCE'

21.14 A 'nuisance' is any interference with the comfort and/or amenity of a person's surroundings that ordinary decent people would consider to be unacceptable. As such, any person who is affected by a nuisance will generally have the right to commence proceedings for statutory nuisance. In this way, statutory nuisance differs significantly from common law nuisance, the latter requiring the claimant to have a legal interest in the affected property[1].

1   See *Hunter v Canary Wharf Ltd* [1997] AC 655.

21.15 A number of factors are relevant in determining whether something is a nuisance:

- *Neighbourhood* – the character of the neighbourhood in which the activity occurs can be highly relevant in assessing whether something is a nuisance. An often-cited example is that a cock crowing in the morning is a perfectly normal part of country life but a nuisance in town. While the character of a neighbourhood may often be easily ascertained, planning decisions and statutory development plans can be evidence of a neighbourhood's character or change in character[1].
- *Convention* – similarly, common or local patterns of behaviour can be influential in assessing whether an activity is a nuisance. For example, the ringing of church bells on a Sunday morning is accepted by convention[2].
- *Duration* – a dog barking to greet its owner home in the evening will be viewed differently by the court than a dog that barks incessantly.
- *Time* – some activities only become nuisances when they are conducted at certain times. For example, mowing a lawn at night is more likely to constitute nuisance than mowing during the day.
- *Frequency* – similarly, while smoke from burning tyres may be accepted in certain areas from time to time, burning tyres every day may well constitute nuisance.
- *Social utility* – the importance of the bothersome activity to society or to the local community is a relevant factor. For example, the sound of sirens may cause annoyance to people living near police stations, but the social utility of permitting their use is generally unquestioned[3].

[1] See *Wheeler v JJ Saunders Ltd* [1996] Ch 19.
[2] See *Leeman v Montagu* [1936] 2 All ER 1677.
[3] See *Kennaway v Thompson* [1981] QB 88.

Abatement notices

21.16 Where, as a result of investigation or routine survey, a nuisance is discovered, a local authority must serve an abatement notice on the person responsible for the nuisance. The EPA 1990, s 80(1) states:

> (1) Subject to subsection (2A) where a local authority is satisfied that a statutory nuisance exists, or is likely to occur or recur, in the area of the authority, the local authority shall serve a notice ('an abatement notice') imposing all or any of the following requirements—
> (a) requiring the abatement of the nuisance or prohibiting or restricting its occurrence or recurrence;
> (b) requiring the execution of such works, and the taking of such other steps, as may be necessary for any of those purposes,
> and the notice shall specify the time or times within which the requirements of the notice are to be complied with.

The requirement to serve an abatement notice

21.17 The local authority is *required* to serve an abatement notice; there is no scope for discretion[1]. Indeed, Defra guidance suggests that an abatement notice must be served even if the local authority considers that the person benefits from a legitimate defence[2]:

> ' . . . local authorities are required to issue an abatement notice once they are satisfied (see 10.35 above) that a statutory nuisance exists or may occur or recur.

There is no provision for the exercise of discretion as to whether or not to take this action, even if the local authority suspects that 'best practicable means' may be in place (only the courts can rule on whether 'best practicable means' are in place).'

¹ See *R v Carrick District Council, ex p Shelley* [1996] Env LR 273, *Barns (NE) Ltd v Newcastle upon Tyne City Council* [2005] EWCA Civ 1274, and *Southampton City Council v Odysseas (Op Co) Ltd* [2017] EWHC 2783 (Admin).
² At para [36].

21.18 However, Defra's interpretation has attracted significant criticism. What purpose can there be in serving an abatement notice where it is bound to be quashed on appeal? Arguably, doing so would be irrational. It is submitted that a better interpretation would be that an abatement notice must be served wherever a local authority is satisfied that a statutory nuisance exists and may not benefit from a defence. Therefore, an abatement notice should be served where there is any doubt as to whether a successful defence may be mounted.

Exceptions relating to noise complaints

21.19 There is one exception to the general rule that an abatement notice must be served. In cases relating to noise complaints (category (g) above), a local authority may choose instead to 'take such other steps as it thinks appropriate for the purpose of persuading the appropriate person to abate the nuisance or prohibit or restrict its occurrence or recurrence'¹.

¹ EPA 1990, s 80(2A)(b).

21.20 If this alternative course is taken, a record should be kept of the reasons for doing so. The authority then has 7 days to negotiate an agreement with the person responsible for the nuisance¹. At the end of this period, the authority must be satisfied that the nuisance will not reoccur; otherwise, an abatement notice must be served. Similarly, the authority must keep under review whether the negotiations are likely to succeed throughout the 7-day period; if they seemed doomed to failure then an abatement notice must be served².

¹ EPA 1990, s 80(2D).
² EPA, s 80(2C)(a).

Appealing an abatement notice

21.21 The most common way to challenge an abatement notice is by appeal to the magistrates' court under EPA 1990, s 80(3). A recipient of an abatement notice has 21 days from service of the notice to lodge a 'complaint' (ie a formal notice of appeal) to the court. In order to succeed on appeal, the appellant must establish one of the grounds stated in reg 2(2) of the Statutory Nuisance (Appeals) Regulations 1995:

(a) the abatement notice is not justified by EPA 1990, s 80 – ie that a nuisance did not in fact exist;
(b) there has been some informality, defect, or error in making the notice;
(c) the authority has:
    (i) refused unreasonably to accept compliance with alternative re-quirements, or
    (ii) served an abatement notice, the requirements of which are un-reasonable or unnecessary;

(d)   sufficient time has not been given in order to comply with the requirements of the abatement notice;

(e)   the 'best practical means' were used to prevent or counteract the effects of the nuisance – note that this ground applies only to certain categories of nuisance (for discussion of the 'best practical means' defence, see the section below on 'Criminal proceedings in the magistrates' courts');

(f)   in the case of noise emitted from premises (see categories (g) and (ga) at **21.9** above), the requirements of the abatement notice are more onerous than the existing rules contained in the Control of Pollution Act 1974;

(g)   in the case of noise emitted vehicles etc (see category (ga) at **21.9** above), the requirements of the abatement notice are more onerous than any condition of a consent given under the Noise and Statutory Nuisance Act 1993;

(h)   the abatement notice should have been served on some person instead of the appellant, being:

    (i)   the person responsible for the nuisance, or

    (ii)   the person responsible for the vehicle, machinery or equipment, or

    (iii)   in the case of a nuisance arising from any defect of a structural character, the owner of the premises, or

    (iv)   in the case where the person responsible for the nuisance cannot be found or the nuisance has not yet occurred, the owner or occupier of the premises;

(i)   the abatement notice might lawfully have been served on some person instead of the appellant being:

    (i)   in the case where the appellant is the owner of the premises, the occupier of the premises, or

    (ii)   in the case where the appellant is the occupier of the premises, the owner of the premises,

and that it would have been equitable for it to have been so served;

(j)   the abatement notice might lawfully have been served on some person in addition to the appellant, being:

    (i)   a person also responsible for the nuisance, or

    (ii)   a person who is also owner of the premises, or

    (iii)   a person who is also an occupier of the premises, or

    (iv)   a person who is also the person responsible for the vehicle, machinery or equipment,

and that it would have been equitable for it to have been so served.

21.22 On hearing the appeal, the magistrates' court may:

(a)   quash the abatement notice,

(b)   vary the abatement notice in favour of the appellant in such manner as it thinks fit, or

(c)   dismiss the appeal[1].

1   SI 1996/2644, reg 2(5).

Other methods of challenging an abatement notice

21.23 Whilst an appeal by the recipient of an abatement notice is the most common way in which abatement notices are challenged. However, as with most actions taken by public authorities, it is also possible to bring an action for judicial review. Since the appeals procedure outlined above is only open to a recipient of an abatement notice, other affected third parties may seek redress by way of judicial review. Exceptionally, a person served with an abatement notice may also pursue judicial review; however, this is generally to be discouraged in favour of the appeals procedure set out by the EPA.

21.24 Finally, it is also open to any affected party to refer the matter to the Local Government Ombudsman. This may be appropriate where it is alleged that the abatement notice has been the subject of maladministration.

Breach of an abatement notice

21.25 Strictly speaking, a local authority is not bound to act if a person breaches an abatement notice. This results in the unusual position where a local authority must issue an abatement notice where a nuisance exists, but the authority need not do anything if the nuisance continues.

21.26 However, a failure to record the reasons for not enforcing an abatement notice may be regarded as maladministration by the Local Government Ombudsman. Furthermore, it might well be argued that local authorities are under a *prima facie* statutory obligation to enforce abatement notices where they are satisfied a breach has occurred[1]. Good practice is therefore for local authorities to keep records of their reasons for forbearing from enforcement of an abatement notice.

[1]   Crime and Disorder Act 1998, s 17.

21.27 Usually, however, breach of an abatement notice will result in some form of action being taken. The options open to a local authority are:

- Direct action by the authority.
- Criminal proceedings in the magistrates' court.
- Civil proceedings in the High Court.

Each of these options is considered below in turn.

'Minded to act' notices

21.28 It has occasionally been the practice of some local authorities to write to persons responsible for nuisances in order to warn them of the authority's view that a nuisance is being committed. These letters are often called 'minded to act' notices.

21.29 Generally speaking, 'minded to act' notices do not reflect best practice. This is because:

(a)   they have no legal basis;

(b)   if a local authority has determined that a nuisance is being caused, then it is under an obligation (discussed above) to serve an abatement notice. A 'minded to act' notice may therefore only serve to demonstrate that the local authority has failed to comply with its statutory duty to serve an abatement notice; and

(c)   there is no requirement that a person responsible for a nuisance be given any warning or notice prior to service of an abatement notice.

21.30 Where a local authority is genuinely unsure as to whether a nuisance exists, best practice is to conduct an investigation. The local authority may of course inform the relevant person that an investigation is being conducted, but in such circumstances it is not necessary to present such a step as a quasi-statutory 'notice'.

Direct action by local authorities

21.31 It is not necessary for a local authority to start court proceedings before taking action to enforce the terms of an abatement notice. If a local authority is satisfied that the notice has been breached, it may choose to take action itself. A common example is that local authority officers may enter premises and take away sound systems that are being used to create a noise nuisance[1]. It is an offence to obstruct an authority from exercising these powers[2].

[1]   EPA 1990, Sch 3, para 2(4)(c).
[2]   EPA 1990, Sch 3, para 3(1).

21.32 It should be noted that local authorities may only take direct action to remedy a nuisance once an abatement notice has been breached. They cannot, for example, take action before the expiry of any time period specified in a notice for remedying the nuisance.

21.33 In the case of residential premises, authorities must give occupiers 24 hours' notice of their intention to enter the premises[1]. However, this does not apply where the situation is deemed an emergency. 'Emergency' is defined as[2]:

'. . . a case where the person requiring entry has reasonable cause to believe that circumstances exist which are likely to endanger life or health and that immediate entry is necessary to verify the existence of those circumstances or to ascertain their cause and to effect a remedy.'

[1]   EPA 1990, Sch 3, para 2(3).
[2]   EPA 1990, Sch 3, para 2(7).

21.34 The power to enter premises does not extend automatically to forcible entry. Where an authority wishes to gain forcible entry to a property, it will need first to obtain a warrant from a Justice of the Peace. A warrant will only be issued if the court is satisfied:

(a)   that admission to the premises has been refused (or that refusal is anticipated), **or** that the premises are unoccupied or the occupier is temporarily absent, **or** that the case is one of emergency, **or** that an application for admission would defeat the object of the entry; **and**
(b)   that there is reasonable ground for entry into the premises[1].

[1]   EPA 1990, Sch 3, para 2(3).

21.35 A local authority can recover the reasonably incurred expenses of this action from the person responsible for the nuisance[1].

[1]   EPA 1990, s 81(4).

Criminal proceedings in the magistrates' court

21.36 Prosecution in the magistrates' court is the most common method of criminal enforcement of an abatement notice in England and Wales. However, it should be noted that London Borough Councils and local authorities in Scotland are also able to serve a fixed penalty notice on the person responsible for the nuisance as an alternative to prosecution[1].

[1] See London Local Authorities Act 2004 and EPA 1990, s 80ZA.

The offence

21.37 The EPA 1990, s 80(4) creates the offence of failing to comply with an abatement notice:

> (4) If a person on whom an abatement notice is served, without reasonable excuse, contravenes or fails to comply with any requirement or prohibition imposed by the notice, he shall be guilty of an offence.

21.38 The offence is summary only. On conviction, it is punishable by an unlimited fine plus a further fine of £500 for each day on which the offence continues after conviction[1].

[1] See EPA 1990, s 80(5) and the Legal Aid, Sentencing and Punishment of Offenders Act 2012, s 85.

21.39 In order to succeed in a prosecution under EPA 1990, s 80(4), it must be proved that:

(a)   the defendant was served with a copy of the abatement notice;
(b)   the defendant failed to comply with a requirement of the notice; and
(c)   there was no reasonable excuse for failing to comply with the notice.

21.40 Service of the notice is an essential element of the offence. As a result, care should be taken in service of the abatement notice and records kept of how service was effected. A failure to provide evidence at trial of how and when the abatement notice was served may result in the collapse of an otherwise sound prosecution.

21.41 In common with other regulatory prosecutions, care must also be taken in identifying the correct defendant (especially in the context of corporate defendants). For more information on this and generally on criminal enforcement, see CHAPTER 4.

The defence of 'reasonable excuse'

21.42 Although the lack of a 'reasonable excuse' has been included above as an ingredient of the prosecution case, it is more properly a defence that is relevant only where it is raised by the defendant. Once a defendant has established an arguable case of reasonable excuse (including the provision of some evidence), the burden of proof then shifts so that it is for the prosecution to show to the criminal standard that the excuse is not a reasonable one[1].

[1] *Polychronakis v Richards and Jeromm Ltd* [1998] Env LR 346.

21.43 Commenting on the scope of the 'reasonable excuse' defence in *Wellingborough DC v Gordon*, Taylor LJ stated that[1]:

' . . . the defence of reasonable excuse is not available to a defendant who contravenes the notice deliberately and intentionally in circumstances wholly under his control. It would have been available, however, if the contravention occurred in an emergency or in circumstances beyond his control. If, for example, a man devoted to DIY had made a habit of hammering through the night and notice was served prohibiting noise nuisance of that kind, he could plead reasonable excuse if a window had broken during the night in a storm and, to exclude the elements, he hammered some boarding into position.'

Ultimately, however, what constitutes a 'reasonable excuse' will always be a question of fact and degree taking all of the circumstances of the case into account[2].

1   [1993] Env LR 218 (at 221).
2   See also *Waltham Forest LBC v Mitoo* [2016] EWHC 2159 (Admin).

The defence of 'best practical means'

21.44 This defence is provided by EPA 1990, s 80(7). It states:

(7) Subject to subsection (8) below, in any proceedings for an offence under subsection (4) above in respect of a statutory nuisance it shall be a defence to prove that the best practicable means were used to prevent, or to counteract the effects of, the nuisance.

21.45 As with the defence of 'reasonable excuse', what constitutes the 'best practical means' is a question of fact and degree. However, in assessing whether the 'best practical means' have been used, the courts will apply the following interpretation:

(a)   'practicable' means reasonably practicable having regard to local conditions and circumstances, technical knowledge, and the financial implications, among other things;

(b)   the 'means' to be employed include the design, installation, maintenance and manner and periods of operation of plant and machinery, and the design, construction and maintenance of buildings and structures;

(c)   the test is to apply only so far as compatible with any duty imposed by law; and

(d)   the test is to apply only so far as compatible with safety and safe working conditions, and with the exigencies of any emergency or unforeseeable circumstances[1].

Furthermore, regard will also be given to any relevant code of practice issued under the Control of Pollution Act 1974, s 71.

1   EPA 1990, s 79(9).

21.46 It should be noted that this defence is not available in respect of the nuisances listed in sub-s (8), namely:

•   fumes or gasses emitted from premises
•   smoke, unless the smoke is emitted from a chimney;

- dust, steam, smell, effluvia, accumulations, deposits, animals, insects, or noise – except where they arise on industrial, trade, or business premises; and
- artificial light emitted from premises – unless emitted (a) from industrial, trade, or business premises, or (b) by lights used for illuminating 'an outdoor relevant sports facility'.

Civil proceedings in the High Court

21.47 As an alternative to criminal prosecution in the magistrates' court, a local authority may apply to the High Court for an injunction either mandating or prohibiting certain activities in order to enforce compliance with an abatement notice.

21.48 A local authority may only start proceedings in the High Court for an injunction where it is satisfied that criminal proceedings would result in an 'inadequate remedy'[1]. It is not sufficient that High Court proceedings would merely be more convenient or otherwise preferable to the prosecuting authority[2]. The justification for this is clear: failure to comply with a High Court injunction is contempt of court, which is punishable by a term of imprisonment.

[1]   EPA 1990, s 81(5).
[2]   *Vale of the White Horse District Council v Allen & Partners* [1997] Env LR 212.

21.49 It should be noted that service of an abatement notice is usually an essential pre-requisite to obtaining an injunction[1]. However, it is also possible to obtain an interim injunction. An interim injunction is usually made in situations requiring a significant degree of urgency and may be prospective – ie made prior to the existence of a nuisance (for example where it is feared that a planned concert will cause significant disruption to the local community). In such circumstances, the application for an interim injunction may be made without notice to the person responsible for the apprehended nuisance, although that person will inevitably be given the opportunity to make representations subsequently at the substantive hearing.

[1]   *East Dorset District Council v Eaglebeam Ltd* [2006] EWHC 2378 (QB).

FLY TIPPING AND UNLAWFUL WASTE DISPOSAL

21.50 This section considers the related issues of fly tipping and unlawful waste disposal. 'Fly tipping' generally covers all illegal deposits of waste onto land that is not designated for that purpose. It is, unfortunately, a pervasive practice that blights both urban and rural communities.

21.51 The people responsible for the production of waste are not always those responsible for fly tipping. Rogue waste disposal businesses are known to solicit waste from naïve individuals and businesses. These criminal enterprises then deposit the waste into unlicensed landfills, lakes, and rivers, causing significant harm to the environment.

21.52 The law criminalises both fly tipping and unlicensed waste disposal. Local authorities, together with national regulators, are responsible for enforcing these laws, either by serving a waste removal notice or by bringing criminal proceedings. Both fly tipping and unlawful waste disposal are considered below.

Fly tipping

What constitutes fly tipping?

21.53 Fly tipping is:

- the 'deposit'
- of 'controlled waste' or 'extractive waste'
- in a manner prohibited by the EPA 1990, s 33(1).

Each of these concepts is considered below in turn.

'Deposit'

21.54 Generally speaking, to 'deposit' is to set something down. In the context of fly tipping, the meaning of 'deposit' is coloured by the concept of 'discarded' objects included in the definition of 'waste' (see below). As a result, waste that is 'deposited' is waste that has been left somewhere.

21.55 It should be noted that waste may be deposited even if it has been left behind only temporarily; there is no requirement that the deposit be permanent[1].

[1]   *R v Metropolitan Stipendiary Magistrate, ex p London Waste Regulation Authority & ors* [1993] 3 All ER 113.

'Controlled waste' and 'extractive waste'

21.56 'Controlled waste' is defined by EPA 1990, s 75(4) as 'household, industrial and commercial waste or any such waste'. The burden falls on the defendant to prove that waste is not 'controlled waste'.

21.57 'Extractive waste' is waste resulting from the prospecting, extraction, treatment, and storage of mineral resources and the working of quarries, as defined by Art 2(1) of the Mining Waste Directive 2006/21/EC. By virtue of the new s 75A of the EPA 1990, this position continues unaltered save that the now-onshored legislation is known simply as 'the Mining Waste Directive'.

'Waste'

21.58 Central to both 'controlled waste' and 'extractive waste' is the concept of 'waste'. Although a determination of what constitutes 'waste' should be a fairly simple application of common sense, the law has had some difficulty formulating a definition.

21.59 'Waste' is defined by article 3(1) of the Waste Framework Directive 2008/98/EC as 'any substance or object which the holder discards or intends or is required to discard'. Again, s 75A of the EPA 1990 leaves the position much the same as it existed prior to Brexit. Unfortunately, however, the Directive provides no definition of 'discard'. Perhaps unsurprisingly, this has led to much controversy, academic debate, and litigation.

21.60 In *Mayer Parry Recycling Ltd v Environment Agency*, Carnwath J shed some light on the term 'discard'[1]:

> 'The general concept is now reasonably clear. The term 'discard' is used in a broad sense equivalent to 'get rid of'; but it is coloured by the examples of waste given in Annex I and the Waste Catalogue, which indicate that it is concerned generally with materials which have ceased to be required for their original purpose, normally because they are unsuitable, unwanted or surplus to requirements. That broad category is however limited by the context, which shows that the purpose is to control disposal and recovery of such materials. Accordingly, materials which are to be re-used (rather than finally disposed of), but which do not require any recovery operation before being put to their new use, are not treated as waste. Similarly, materials which are made ready for re-use by a recovery operation, cease to be waste when the recovery operation is complete.'

[1] [1999] CMLR 963 (at [46]).

21.61 As noted by Carnwath J, the definition of 'waste' is supplemented by the European Waste Catalogue. This wonderfully labyrinthine document represents an attempt by the European Commission to categorise almost every conceivable type of waste. It consists of twenty chapters, each relating to a different type of waste. These chapters are then divided into a variety of sub-types of waste. Notably, the Catalogue has been onshored by s 75A of the EPA 1990 and remains a curious feature of the UK regulatory landscape post Brexit. The Catalogue may be useful in proving that an item or substance falls within the definition of 'waste'. Clearly, however, it is possible for an item to constitute 'waste' for the purposes of fly tipping legislation without appearing in the Catalogue.

'In a manner prohibited by s 33(1)'

21.62 Fly tipping is prohibited by EPA 1990, s 33(1). The section states:

(1)   Subject to subsections (1A), (1B), (2) and (3) below a person shall not—
  (a)   deposit controlled waste or extractive waste, or knowingly cause or knowingly permit controlled waste or extractive waste to be deposited in or on any land unless an environmental permit authorising the deposit is in force and the deposit is in accordance with the permit;
  (b)   submit controlled waste, or knowingly cause or knowingly permit controlled waste to be submitted, to any listed operation (other than an operation within subsection (1)(a)) that—
    (i)   is carried out in or on any land, or by means of any mobile plant, and
    (ii)   is not carried out under and in accordance with an environmental permit;
  (c)   treat, keep or dispose of controlled waste or extractive waste in a manner likely to cause pollution of the environment or harm to human health.

21.63

Precedent for unauthorised depositing of controlled waste

Statement of offence

UNAUTHORISED DEPOSITING OF CONTROLLED WASTE contrary to s 33(1)(a) and s 33(6) of the Environmental Protection Act 1990.

Particulars of offence

A B, on [date], deposited controlled waste, namely [. . .], on land at [. . .], otherwise than in accordance with an environmental permit.

21.64 Whilst EPA 1990, s 33(1)(a) covers the classic forms of fly tipping (for example, where a rogue dumps waste from his van on the verge of a small country road in the middle of the night), the section also covers a wide variety of other related activities. The EPA 1990, s 33(1)(a) applies equally to 'knowingly permitting' the deposit. As a result, a farmer who knowingly permits waste to be dumped in his fields will commit fly tipping exactly as if he had dumped the waste himself.

21.65 Note also that EPA 1990, s 33(1)(c) does not distinguish between licensed and unlicensed land. As a result, an individual with an environmental permit authorising the deposit of waste on his land might still contravene EPA 1990, s 33(1)(c) where the method of disposal is likely to cause pollution or harm to human health. While in reality the terms of the environmental permit are likely to ensure that the waste is deposited safely, EPA 1990, s 33(1)(c) imposes a general overarching obligation on the regulated person to ensure that waste is disposed of safely.

Enforcement of fly tipping regulation

21.66 The enforcement of the law relating to fly tipping is the responsibility of each local authority together with the relevant national regulator. The national regulators are the Environment Agency, the Natural Resources Body for Wales, and the Scottish Environment Protection Agency.

21.67 Broadly, there are two options for enforcing a contravention of EPA 1990, s 33(1). They are:

(a)   criminal prosecution under EPA 1990, s 33(6); and
(b)   service of a waste removal notice under EPA 1990, s 59(1) requiring the removal of waste or certain other steps be taken.

Each of these options is considered below.

Criminal prosecution under s 33(6)

21.68 A person who contravenes EPA 1990, s 33(1) commits an offence under EPA 1990, s 33(6). This is subject to two defences, one of due diligence (EPA 1990, s 33(7)(a)) and one of acting to avoid danger to human health in an emergency (EPA 1990, s 33(7)(c)):

> (7) It shall be a defence for a person charged with an offence under this section to prove—
>
>> (a) that he took all reasonable precautions and exercised all due diligence to avoid the commission of the offence; or
>>
>> . . .
>>
>> (c) that the acts alleged to constitute the contravention were done in an emergency in order to avoid danger to human health in a case where—
>>> (i) he took all such steps as were reasonably practicable in the circumstances for minimising pollution of the environment and harm to human health; and
>>> (ii) particulars of the acts were furnished to the waste regulation authority as soon as reasonably practicable after they were done.

For analysis of the due diligence defence, as well as commentary on criminal enforcement generally, see CHAPTER 4.

21.69 The offence of fly tipping contrary to EPA 1990, s 33(1) is triable either way. On summary conviction, it is punishable by an unlimited fine and/or up to 12 months' imprisonment. On conviction on indictment, it is punishable by an unlimited fine and/or up to 5 years' imprisonment[1].

[1] EPA 1990, s 33(8). See also *R v Channer* [2021] EWCA Crim 696 and *R v Lawrence* [2020] EWCA Crim 1465.

21.70 However, where a defendant is charged under EPA 1990, s 33(1)(c), and where the waste was disposed of within the curtilage of a residential property (and where the waste was 'household waste' originating from that property), the maximum sentence either way is an unlimited fine; a term of imprisonment is not permitted[1].

[1] EPA 1990, ss 33(9) and 33(10).

21.71 It should be noted that the offence proscribed by EPA 1990, s 33(6) is distinct from that set out in EPA 1990, s 59(1) (relating to failure to comply with a waste removal notice – see below). It is not necessary to first serve a notice under EPA 1990, s 59(1) in order to mount a successful conviction under EPA 1990, s 33(6).

Service of a waste removal notice

21.72 Where a local authority (or a national regulator) is satisfied that a person has contravened the requirements of s 33(1), it may issue a notice under EPA 1990, s 59(1) requiring that person to:

(a)   remove waste from a specified place within a period of time set out in the notice (being not less than 21 days from service of the notice); and/or

(b)   take specified steps to eliminate or reduce the consequences of the deposit of the waste within a period of time set out in the notice (being not less than 21 days from service of the notice).

21.73 The enforcement of a waste removal notice is in many ways analogous to the enforcement of an abatement notice – ie failure to comply with the requirements of a waste removal notice amounts to a summary-only offence subject to a defence of 'reasonable excuse' (see above on 'reasonable excuse' in relation to abatement notices)[1]. Where an occupier has failed to comply with a waste removal notice, the local authority may also take direct action to remove the waste itself and recover the expenses it reasonably incurs in so doing[2].

1   EPA 1990, s 59(5).
2   EPA 1990, s 59(6).

21.74 On conviction, the offence is punishable with an unlimited fine as well as a further fine of £500 for each day on which the offence continues after conviction.

Unlawful waste disposal

What constitutes 'unlawful waste disposal'?

21.75 Unlawful waste disposal is the operation of a waste disposal facility or service without a permit. It is prohibited by reg 12(1) of the Environmental Permitting (England and Wales) Regulations 2016 ('EPR 2016'). Regulation 12(1) states:

(1)   A person must not, except under and to the extent authorised by an environmental permit—
        (a)   operate a regulated facility, or
        (b)   cause or knowingly permit a water discharge activity or groundwater activity.

'Regulated facility'

21.76 'Regulated facility is defined by reg 8 of the EPR 2016:

(1)   In these Regulations, 'regulated facility' means any of the following—
        (a)   an installation;
        (b)   mobile plant;
        (c)   a waste operation;
        (d)   a mining waste operation;
        (e)   a radioactive substances activity;
        (f)   a water discharge activity;
        (g)   a groundwater activity;
        (h)   a small waste incineration plant;
        (i)   a solvent emission activity;
        (j)   a flood risk activity.

21.77 Each of the above categories is then further defined by reg 2 of the EPR 2016. In overview, however, most types of waste removal, processing, and disposal businesses will be 'regulated facilities'. This includes mobile operations, such as rubbish vans.

Enforcement against unlawful waste disposal

21.78 As with fly tipping, enforcing authorities generally have two options in dealing with unlicensed waste disposal prohibited by reg 12(1) of the EPR 2016:

(a)   criminal prosecution under reg 38(1) of the EPR 2016; and
(b)   service of a waste removal notice under EPA 1990, s 59(1) requiring the removal of waste or certain other steps be taken (considered in relation to fly tipping above).

Criminal prosecution under reg 38(1) of the EPR 2016

21.79 Regulation 38(1) of the EPR 2016 creates the offences of:

(a)   contravening reg 12(1) of the EPR 2016, or
(b)   knowingly causing or knowingly permitting a regulated facility to be operated without a permit.

21.80 The offence is triable either way and subject to one defence of acting to avoid danger to human health in an emergency. The defence is set out in reg 40(1) of the EPR 2016:

> (1)   It is a defence for a person charged with an offence under regulation 38(1), (2) or (3) to prove that the acts alleged to constitute the contravention were done in an emergency in order to avoid danger to human health in a case where—
>
> > (a)   the person took all such steps as were reasonably practicable in the circumstances for minimising pollution, and
> > (b)   particulars of the acts were furnished to the regulator as soon as reasonably practicable after they were done.

21.81 On summary conviction, the offence is punishable by an unlimited fine and/or up to 12 months' imprisonment. On conviction on indictment, it is punishable by an unlimited fine and/or up to 5 years' imprisonment.

PACKAGING REQUIREMENTS

The Packaging and Waste Directive

21.82 The Packaging and Waste Directive 94/62/EC requires[1]:

•   packaging to be minimised;
•   packaging to be designed for recovery and re-use;
•   recovery targets for waste packaging to be met by the UK; and
•   heavy metals in packaging to be restricted.

[1]   Directive 94/62/EC, Arts 9 and 11.

21.83 The Directive has been transposed into UK law by two regulations:

•   the Producer Responsibility Obligations (Packaging Waste) Regulations 2007 ('PROPWR 2007')[1];

- the Packaging (Essential Requirements) Regulations 2015 ('PERR 2015')[2].

[1] SI 2007/871.
[2] SI 2015/1640.

21.84 The PERR 2015 are enforced by the Trading Standards Departments of local weights and measures authorities in Great Britain and by the Department of Enterprise, Trade and Investment ('DETI') in Northern Ireland. The PERR are examined in detail below. The PROPWR 2007 are the responsibility of the Department for Environment, Food and Rural Affairs ('Defra') and are enforced by the Environment Agency ('EA') in England, the Natural Resources Body for Wales, the Scottish Environment Protection Agency, and the Northern Ireland Environment Agency.

The Producer Responsibility Obligations (Packaging Waste) Regulations 2007

21.85 The most significant provisions of the PROPWR 2007 may be summarised as follows:

- the Directive imposes recycling and recovery targets for packaging waste on the UK and the aim of the PROPWR 2007 is to meet those targets through the principle of producer responsibility;
- companies with an annual turnover of £2m and handling more than 50 tonnes of packaging a year must pay for a certain amount of the UK obligation to recycle packaging;
- companies' obligations are met by purchasing Packaging Waste Recovery Notes ('PRNs') or Packaging Waste Export Recovery Notes ('PERNs');
- companies can either join a compliance scheme to deal with their obligations for them or register directly with enforcement authorities.

The Packaging (Essential Requirements) Regulations 2015

21.86 The PERR 2015[1] came into force on 1 October 2015. They replace the Packaging (Essential Requirements) Regulations 2003 which implemented the Packaging and Waste Directive[2]. They define a 'responsible person' in respect of the packaging of products and place upon that person a duty to satisfy essential requirements as to the manufacturing and composition of the packaging, its reusability, and its suitability for recycling, energy recovery, or composting. Further duties are placed upon the responsible person in respect of the presence of heavy metals in packaging and the production of technical documentation. Contravention of these duties is an offence under PERR 2015.

[1] SI 2015/1640.
[2] 94/62/EC, Arts 9 and 11.

21.87 In June 2009, a new Government strategy published by Defra, with input from BIS and the Devolved Administrations – Making the Most of Packaging, A strategy for a low-carbon economy – considered the direction for packaging policy for the next 10 years and acknowledged the enforcement difficulties for Trading Standards in proving that the amount of packaging used is excessive under PERR 2003:

'The UK would like to see clearer language on this in the Directive to aid enforcement. We have already raised this formally with the Commission, and intend to continue pressing them for a review of this wording.'

Despite this, the wording remains the same in the PERR 2015.

THE GENERAL DUTY UNDER PERR 2015

21.88 Regulation 4 of PERR 2015 sets out a general duty to comply with the 'essential requirements' of packaging:

(1) A responsible person must not place any packaging on the EU market unless it complies with the essential requirements.

(2) Reused packaging is not considered to be placed on the market for the purposes of this regulation.

(3) Packaging complies with the essential requirements—
    (a) if it satisfies national standards which implement the relevant harmonised standards; or
    (b) where there are no relevant harmonised standards, if it satisfies national standards which have been communicated to the Commission pursuant to Article 9(3) of the Directive and which are notified by the Commission to the member States as being deemed to comply with the essential requirements.

(4) In paragraph (3), 'harmonised standard' means the standard the reference number of which is published in the Official Journal of the European Union in accordance with Article 9(2)(a) of the Directive.

21.89 Regulation 5 of PERR 2015 also creates specific requirements relating to concentration levels of regulated metals present in packaging.

CRIMINAL PROSECUTION UNDER PERR 2015

21.90 Regulation 8 of PERR 2015 creates the offence of contravening, or failing to comply with, regs 4 and 5.

21.91 Regulation 7 imposes a duty upon every local weights and measures authority[1] in Great Britain (and DfE in Northern Ireland) to enforce the Regulations within their areas. The Regulations do not authorise any enforcement authority to bring proceedings in Scotland for an offence (Sch 4, para 2) – only the Crown Office and Procurator Fiscal Service ('COPFS') may do so.

[1]   Defined in the Weights and Measures Act 1985, s 69(1).

21.92 The right to prosecute is not restricted to enforcement authorities. Any person can bring a prosecution under the Regulations, although the rights contained within the PERR 2015 to facilitate the gathering of evidence may not be exercised by such a private prosecutor.

21.93 A defence of due diligence is provided by reg 10(1) of PERR 2015. For detailed discussion of the defence of due diligence, and for criminal enforcement generally, see CHAPTER 4.

21.94 There are a variety of offences created by PERR 2015 in addition to that discussed above. The maximum sentences are set out below:

Provision	Description	Mode of Trial	Maximum Penalty on Indictment	Maximum Penalty on Summary Conviction
reg 4	Failing to comply with the essential requirements	Summary only (England and Wales) Either way (Scotland and Northern Ireland)	Unlimited fine	Unlimited fine (England and Wales) Level 5 fine (Scotland and Northern Ireland)
reg 5	Exceeding concentration levels of heavy metals	Summary only (England and Wales) Either way (Scotland and Northern Ireland)	Unlimited fine	Unlimited fine
reg 6(1)	Failing to supply/keep technical documentation	Summary only		Unlimited fine (England and Wales Level 5 fine (Scotland and Northern Ireland)
reg 6(2)	Failing to submit a report/annual declaration	Summary only		Unlimited fine (England and Wales) Level 5 fine (Scotland and Northern Ireland)
s 14 CPA 1987	Contravening a suspension notice	Summary only		6 months imprisonment and/or unlimited fine

ENERGY INFORMATION

21.95 The aim of the Energy Information Regulations 2011 ('EIR 2011') is to facilitate the labelling of energy-related products (such as washing machines and televisions) so that the power consumption of one model can be easily compared to another, allowing consumers to make informed purchasing decisions. The Regulations introduced a new enforcement regime of civil sanctions, as well as cost sharing.

21.96 The EIR 2011 transposed European Directive 2010/30/EU (on the indication by labelling and standard product information of the consumption of energy and other resources by energy-related products). That directive has now been replaced by Regulation (EU) 2017/1369 ('the EU Energy Labelling Regulation'). The EIR 2011 continues to apply to products that have a significant direct or indirect impact on energy consumption and other re-sources[1], subject to the amendments made by the Energy Information (Amendment) Regulations 2018[2]. The products to which the EU measures apply are set out in Sch 1 to the EIR 2011.

[1]   SI 2011/1524, reg 3.
[2]   SI 2018/255.

Duties under EIR 2011

21.97 The key duties created by the EIR 2011, and enforceable by local authorities, were previously set out in regs 8 and 9. However, these have now been superseded by the obligations set out in the EU Energy Labelling Regulation and cited in the (now amended) reg 4 of the EIR 2011.

Criminal prosecution under the EIR 2011

21.98 Local authorities bear the responsibility of enforcing the articles of the EU Labelling Regulation that are listed in reg 4 of the EIR 2011. Failure to comply with the requirements of these regulations is an offence under reg 11.

21.99 The offence is triable either way. It is punishable with an unlimited fine in both cases. However, a 12-month time limit applies to summary proceedings (calculated from the day on which the regulator has sufficient evidence on which to justify bringing proceedings) by virtue of reg 13.

Civil sanctions

21.100 A parallel regime of civil sanctions exists under Sch 4 of the EIR 2011. These powers allow the authority to require compliance with:

- a compliance notice;
- a stop notice;
- an enforcement undertaking; or
- payment of a variable monetary penalty or non-compliance penalty.

21.101 Para 6 enables a person to make representations and objections to the authority in respect of a proposed compliance notice or variable monetary penalty. Grounds for appeal in respect of a stop notice are found at para 15(2). The requirement to compensate a person for loss suffered as a result of a stop notice that has been withdrawn or successfully appealed is detailed at para 17(1). Failure to comply with a stop notice within the time limit is an offence punishable on summary conviction with an unlimited fine (para 18). Non-compliance with an enforcement undertaking also allows the authority to bring criminal proceedings at any time up to 6 months from the date of notification of failure to comply.

21.102 If a person fails to comply with a compliance notice, stop notice, third party undertaking or enforcement undertaking then the authority may serve a notice on that person imposing a monetary penalty (a 'non-compliance penalty'

– para 25(1)). The penalty amount is determined by the authority and must be a percentage (up to 100%, if appropriate) of the costs of fulfilling the remaining requirements of the notice, third party undertaking or enforcement undertaking (para 25(2) and (3)). Grounds of appeal are set out at para 25(7).

21.103 Part 5 of the Schedule enables the withdrawal of the various notices available to the authority. Under Pt 6, any appeal under the Schedule must be made to the First-tier Tribunal General Regulatory Chamber (Environment) and must be made within 28 days of the date on which the notice or decision is received. Pt 7 imposes an obligation on the authority to publish guidance about its use of civil sanctions.

ENERGY PERFORMANCE OF BUILDINGS

21.104 On 19 May 2010, the European Parliament and Council published Directive 2010/31/EU[1] on the energy performance of buildings ('EPBD'). The EPBD is a recast version of the old Directive 2002/91/EC, which had been transposed into English law by the (now repealed) Energy Performance of Buildings (Certificates and Inspections) (England and Wales) Regulations 2007.

[1] OJ L153, 18.6.2010, p 13.

21.105 The broad terms of the EPBD, amongst other matters, require that Member States:

- ensure that when buildings are constructed, sold or rented out, an energy performance certificate is made available to the owner or by the owner to the prospective buyer or tenant (Art 11);
- ensure that an energy certificate is prominently displayed in buildings with a total useful floor area over 250m2 occupied by public authorities and frequently visited by the public (Art 13);
- regularly inspect air-conditioning systems with an effective rated output of more than 12 kW (Art 15). An inspection report must be issued after each inspection (Art 16);
- ensure that the certification of buildings, drafting of recommendations, and the inspection of air-conditioning systems are carried out in an independent manner by qualified experts (Art 17).

England and Wales

21.106 This has been implemented in England and Wales by the Energy Performance of Buildings (England and Wales) Regulations 2012[1]. The Energy Performance of Buildings (England and Wales) (Amendment) Regulations 2016[2] make a number of changes to the principal regulations, consolidate existing requirements, and make amendments to the existing domestic arrangements and processes for lodging and accessing energy performance of buildings data on the registers. The Energy Performance of Buildings (England and Wales) (Amendment) (No 2) Regulations 2016[3] update certain references that were overlooked in earlier amendments; make provision for the disclosure from the register of energy performance certificates of data used to prepare certificates to stated persons and bodies for purposes related to Government policy to promote the energy efficiency of buildings; and amend the lists of data items from the register that may be published on a website.

¹ SI 2012/3118.
² SI 2016/284.
³ SI 2016/888.

Scotland

21.107 In Scotland, implementation of the EPBD has been made through the Building (Scotland) Act 2003, legislation made under that Act, and the Energy Performance of Buildings (Scotland) Regulations 2008¹ (as amended). The Building (Energy Performance of Buildings) (Scotland) Amendment Regulations 2016² amend the Building (Scotland) Regulations 2004³ to insert requirements in relation to the inspection of air-conditioning systems in buildings and nearly zero-energy buildings. The Assessment of Energy Performance of Non-domestic Buildings (Scotland) Regulations 2016⁴ make provision for the assessment of the energy performance of non-domestic buildings and of the emission of greenhouse gases from such buildings. The Regulations also provide for the circumstances in which the owners of non-domestic buildings are required to take steps to improve the energy performance of such buildings and reduce such emissions.

¹ SSI 2008/309.
² SSI 2016/71.
³ SSI 2004/406.
⁴ SSI 2016/146.

Northern Ireland

21.108 The EPBD is implemented in Northern Ireland by the Energy Performance of Buildings (Certificates and Inspections) Regulations (Northern Ireland) 2008¹ (as amended). The 2008 Regulations implement Arts 11 (energy performance certificate), 15 (inspection of air-conditioning systems) and 17 (independent experts) of the EPBD. The enforcement authority is the relevant district council.

¹ SR 2008/170.

The Energy Performance of Buildings (England and Wales) Regulations 2012

21.109 The Energy Performance of Buildings (England and Wales) Regulations 2012¹ (EPBR 2012), which extend to England and Wales, came into force on 9 January 2013. The recast EPBD (2010/31/EU) is transposed in the EPBR 2012.

¹ SI 2012/3118.

Regulatory framework

21.110 The effect of the EPBR 2012 is to require:

- energy performance certificates (EPCs) and recommendations for improvement of the energy performance of the building to be produced when buildings are constructed sold, rented out or marketed;
- property advertisements to include details of the EPC rating where available;
- commercial premises larger that 500m2 that are frequently visited by the public to display an EPC (where an EPC has been previously issued on sale, rent or construction);
- display energy certificates (DECs) to be displayed in public buildings larger than 250m2 that are frequently visited by the public; and the production of reports with recommendations for improvement of the energy performance of the building;
- air-conditioning systems to be inspected at regular intervals not exceeding 5 years; and
- energy assessors producing the certificates or carrying out the inspections to be accredited.

Breach of the Regulations

21.111 By virtue of reg 36, an enforcement officer may give a penalty charge notice if he believes that a person has committed a breach of any duty under regs 6(2), 6(5), 7(2)–(5), 10(2), 11(2), 14(3), 18(1), 20, 21 or 35(5) or the EPC construction duty. A person in breach of these Regulations will be liable to a civil penalty; breach of these provisions is not a criminal offence.

21.112 By virtue of reg 43, a person who obstructs an enforcement officer or who, not being an enforcement officer, purports to act as one, commits a criminal offence and is liable on summary conviction to an unlimited fine.

Penalty charge notices

21.113 Regulation 36(2) provides that a penalty charge notice may not be given after the end of the period of 6 months beginning with the day on which the breach was committed (or, in the case of a continuing breach, the last day). Regulation 36(3) lists the information that must be included in a penalty charge notice. This includes the requirement that the recipient respond by either (i) paying the charge, or (ii) requesting a review by the enforcement authority. Either way, the response must be given within 28 days beginning with the day after the penalty charge notice (reg 36(4)) – although this period can be extended at the discretion of the enforcement authority if it considers it appropriate to do so (reg 36(5)).

21.114 The enforcement authority

- may withdraw the penalty charge notice, if the authority considers that the notice ought not to have been given (reg 36(6));
- must withdraw a penalty charge notice where the recipient can demonstrate that he took all reasonable steps and exercised all due diligence to avoid breaching the duty (reg 36(7) or a reg 37 defence applies).

21.115 The receipt of a penalty charge does not remove the need to comply with the duty in respect of which it was given. If a penalty notice is withdrawn, the enforcement authority must refund any charge already paid. A pro-forma penalty charge notice is given in Appendix C of the Communities and Local Government fact sheet *Advice to Local Weights and Measures Authorities on Enforcement of Energy Certificates and Air-Conditioning Inspections for Buildings.*

21.116 The amount of the penalty charge is set out in reg 38(1):

(1)   The penalty charge specified in the notice shall be—

    (a)   in relation to a breach of a duty under regulation 6(2) , 6(5) , 7(2), 7(3), (4), 7(5) , 7A(2) or 7A(3)—

        (i)   where the building is a dwelling, £200;

        (ii)   where the building is not a dwelling, calculated in accordance with the formula in paragraph (2);

    (b)   in relation to a breach of a duty under regulation 14(3)(a), £1000;

    (c)   in relation to a breach of a duty under regulation 10(2) or 14(3)(b) 2, £500;

    (d)   in relation to a breach of a duty under regulation 18(1), 20(1), 20(2) or 21, £300; and

    (e)   in relation to a breach of a duty under regulation 11(2) or 35(5), £200.

Reviews and appeals

21.117 Regulation 39 provides that, when the recipient of a penalty charge notice has asked the notice authority to review the decision to issue it, the authority must consider any representations etc and withdraw the notice if it is not satisfied that:

(a)   the recipient committed the breach of duty specified in the notice; or

(b)   the notice was issued within time (allowed by reg 36(2)) and contained the necessary particulars; or

(c)   in the circumstances of the case it was appropriate for the notice to be given to the recipient.

21.118 If the recipient of the penalty notice is not satisfied with the review, he may appeal to the County Court under reg 40 within 28 days after having the penalty charge confirmed. Such an appeal can only be made on one or more of the following grounds:

(a)   the recipient did not commit the breach of duty specified in the penalty charge notice;

(b)   the notice was not given within the period specified (by reg 36(2)), or did not contain the necessary particulars;

(c)   in the circumstances of the case it was inappropriate for the notice to be given to the recipient.

Chapter 22

ANIMAL HEALTH AND WELFARE

Contents

INTRODUCTION

22.1 This chapter concentrates principally on the domestic and farmed animal health and welfare laws that are designed to:

- prevent, control and eradicate farm animal diseases;
- safeguard human health from transmitted diseases;
- protect the welfare of farm animals in transit and at markets.

The effect of Brexit

22.2 The position since the UK left the European Union on 31 January 2020 is that EU law continues to remain in force, but has been converted into UK statute or statutory instruments. The Department for Environment, Food and Rural Affairs ('DEFRA') has already introduced a raft of such measures[1] in relation to animal welfare. Currently s 6 of the European Union (Withdrawal) Act provides that the Supreme Court will be able to depart from previous decisions of the CJEU. It also provides that by regulation the secretary of state can empower other courts to depart from such decisions. At the time of writing the Government is consulting on the question of whether the Court of Appeal and the High Court should have that power.

[1] Animal Health and Welfare (Miscellaneous Amendments) (England) (EU Exit) Regulations 2018; Animal Health and Welfare (Miscellaneous Amendments) (Wales) (EU Exit) Regulations 2019 (as amended); Livestock (Records, Identification and Movement) (England) (Amendment) (EU Exit) Regulations 2019 (and see also the various regional Regulations); Official Controls (Animals, Feed and Food) (England) (Amendment) (EU Exit) Regulations 2018; Official Controls (Animals, Feed and Food) (Northern Ireland) (Amendment) (EU Exit) Regulations 2019; Transmissible Spongiform Encephalopathies and Animal By-Products (Amendment etc.) (EU Exit) Regulations 2019; Veterinary Surgeons and Animal Welfare (Amendment) (EU Exit) Regulations 2019; Farriers and Animal Health (Amendment) (EU Exit) Regulations 2019; Animal Health, Plant Health, Seeds and Seed Potatoes (Amendment) (EU Exit) Regulations 2019; Livestock (Records, Identification and Movement) (Amendment) (EU Exit) Regulations 2019; Animal Health, Alien Species in Aquaculture and Invasive Non-native Species (Amendment) (EU Exit) Regulations 2019; Animal Welfare (Amendment) (EU Exit) Regulations 2019; Trade in Animals and Related Products (Amendment) (EU Exit) Regulations 2019; Zoonotic Disease Eradication and Control (Amendment) (EU Exit) Regulations 2019; Official Controls for Feed, Food and Animal Health and Welfare (Amendment etc.) (EU Exit) Regulations 2019; Equine (Records, Identification and Movement) (Amendment) (EU Exit) Regulations 2019; Animals (Legislative Functions) (EU Exit) Regulations 2019.

22.3 The way in which EU law is to be retained or replaced following the United Kingdom's departure from the EU was prefaced in earlier DEFRA statements as set out below.

The Minister of State, Department for Environment, Food and Rural Affairs, George Eustice in answer to a Parliamentary Question on 19 September 2017, said:

'The government intends to retain our existing high standards of animal welfare once we have left the European Union. Defra is exploring how the principles of Art 13 of the Treaty of the Functioning of the European Union can apply in the United Kingdom after we have left the European Union. Currently the European Union (Withdrawal) Bill will convert the existing body of direct European Union animal welfare law into United Kingdom law, and this European Union law takes into account the principles of Article 13.'

In February 2018 the Department for Environment, Food and Rural Affairs launched a consultation entitled 'Health and Harmony: the future for food, farming and the environment in a Green Brexit' which closed 8 May 2018. The opening paragraphs of the Foreword state:

'Leaving the European Union (EU) provides a once-in-a-generation opportunity to reform agriculture. This paper outlines how we plan to change the way we use the land, so as better to promote health and harmony. For more than 40 years, the EU's Common Agricultural Policy (CAP) has decided how we farm our land, the food we grow and rear and the state of the natural environment. Over that period, the environment has deteriorated, productivity has been held back and public health has been compromised. Now we are leaving the EU we can design a more rational, and sensitive agriculture policy which promotes environmental enhancement, supports profitable food production and contributes to a healthier society.'

The Government's plan to set out a new post EU Agricultural Policy was enacted into law on the 11th November with the Agriculture Act 2020. It sets out how farmers and land managers in England will in the future be rewarded with public money. It includes measures for rewarding animal welfare improvements and provision of transparency and fair dealing in the supply chain and places a statutory obligation for the monitoring, investigation and dealing with non-compliance within the agri-food chain.

22.4 The Animal Welfare (Sentencing) Act 2021 came into force in England and Wales on the 29 June 2021 and increases the maximum penalty for specific offences related to animal welfare – namely ss 4, 5, 6(1), 6(2), 7 and 8 Animal Welfare Act 2006. The Act extends the maximum penalty, specified under Animal Welfare Act 2006, of six months and/or an unlimited fine to a penalty of five years and/or an unlimited fine. These offences therefore become triable either way and may be heard in the Magistrates' Court or the Crown Court. The maximum penalties do not apply to s 9 duty of care offences, however a breach of either s 4 or s 9 may both result in a disqualification being applied by the courts.

22.5 An Action Plan for Animal Welfare was published by the Department for the Environment Food and rural Affairs on the 12 May 2021 and sets out Government plans, aims and ambitions across 5 key areas including sentience and enforcement, international trade and advocacy, farm animals, pets and sporting animals and wild animals. In the opening title the Minister of State, George Eustice states:

> 'Our departure from the EU has provided us with an opportunity to do things better. We can take action to ban the live exports of animals for slaughter 4 Our Action Plan for Animal Welfare and fattening, take forward legislation on puppy smuggling and now we are an independent trading nation and have regained our own voice on wildlife conventions, world forums and organisations we can take a more assertive role on the world stage. This action plan sets the foundation for this, laying out our aims and ambitions for animal welfare domestically and internationally.'

The Animal Welfare Plan for Wales 2021–26 was published on 4 November 2021. It includes:

> 'Our ambition is for animal welfare in Wales to be recognised for its exemplary standards, its adoption and sharing of best practice, its engagement with key stakeholders, its development of effective, supportive and sustainable mechanisms for enforcement, its contribution to research, and its championing of education and responsible ownership for the benefit of our own and future generations.'

22.6 The Animal Welfare (Kept Animals) Bill was introduced to the House of Commons and given its First Reading on 8 June 2021 and will seek to raise animal welfare standards in five key areas:

- *Puppy smuggling*: The Government will introduce new powers to tackle the unethical trade of puppy smuggling by reducing the number of pets (dogs, cats and ferrets) that can travel under pet travel rules. It will also include powers for the Government to bring in further restrictions on the movement of pets on welfare grounds, for example by increasing the minimum age of imported puppies and restricting the import of pregnant dogs and dogs with mutilations such as cropped ears and tails.
- *Live exports*: Live animals can endure excessively long journeys during export, causing distress and injury. EU rules prevented any changes to these journeys, but the UK Government is now free to pursue plans which would see a ban on the export of live animals for slaughter and fattening. We will become the first European country to end this practice.
- *Banning keeping primates as pets*: Primates are highly intelligent animals with complex needs and require specialist care. The Government will deliver on its manifesto commitment to introduce a ban on keeping them as pets, ensuring that all primates being kept privately in England are being kept at zoo-level standards and that those unable to meet the standards are phased out.
- *Livestock worrying*: The Bill will give new powers to the police to provide greater protection to livestock from dangerous and out of control dogs. The Bill will also extend this protection to other species such as llamas, ostriches and game birds.
- *Zoos*: The Zoo Licensing Act will be amended to improve zoo regulations and ensure that zoos are doing more to contribute to conservation.

CCTV in slaughterhouses was made mandatory from 5 November 2018 by virtue of The Mandatory Use of Closed Circuit Television in Slaughterhouses (England) Regulations 2018[1].

[1]   SI 2018/556.

22.7 In February 2018, the Secretary of State announced that a Farm Inspection Review would be carried out. The purpose of the Review is 'to identify opportunities before and after EU exit for improving farming-related regulation and enforcement (including inspections), in order to reduce burdens on farmers, while maintaining and enhancing our animal, environmental and plant health standards'. The review, conducted by Dame Glenys Stacey, will apply only to England. Recommendations include:

'We appreciate there is a cadre of capable and dedicated local authority animal health and welfare staff, albeit numbers are most likely reducing. We propose the regulator should be empowered to commission regulatory activities (such as the first response to welfare complaints) from individual local authorities or other suitable bodies but should do so only where that would be effective as well as efficient. In that way, local authorities that retain animal health and welfare competence and capability may choose to play a role, in line with the regulator's priorities and expectations.

We propose that the government should review local authority statutory obligations relating to the health and welfare of farmed animals. Of course, local authorities have much wider responsibilities than just animal health and welfare on farm, and will wish to continue to investigate and prosecute within their own areas. In exotic disease outbreaks and other emergency situations they have, and will continue to have, an important and valued role.'

To date there is no response from Government on the recommendations.

22.8 An example of the how the UK might enforce in this area, after leaving the EU, is demonstrated by the Bovine Tuberculosis ('BTB') strategy. In November 2018 Professor Charles Godfray's review of the 25-year Bovine TB strategy for England was published. Government published its response on the 5 March 2020 and a list of priorities including the development of a deployable cattle BTB vaccine and improving badger control by increased support for vaccination and diagnostic testing. As part of the Government's response to the Godfray review, in February 2021 a new TB Partnership was established to encourage shared ownership, coordination and decision-making surrounding England's 25 year BTB eradication strategy.

ANIMAL HEALTH

22.9 Animal health is concerned with preventing the spread of disease among animals. Human health is affected where animal diseases pass through to humans. A report from the Department of Environment, Farming and Rural Affairs ('Defra') in 2011 noted[1]:

> 'The health and welfare of animals concerns not just livestock owners or government, but all of us. There have been over 14 exotic disease outbreaks in the last 10 years including foot and mouth disease, avian influenza and bluetongue. The costs of disease outbreaks range from £2 million to over £3 billion with knock-on effects in other economic sectors.'

Never before has the issue of zoonotic disease been more relevant than with the origin of the current Coronavirus pandemic having its genesis in animal species. The large costs attributed to other exotic disease outbreaks pale into insignificance when contrasted with the health and economic consequences of the pandemic.

[1] See www.defra.gov.uk/consult/files/110318-animal-disease-plan-condoc.pdf.

22.10 The regulation of animal health in Great Britain is part of an international and European framework. Internationally, the UK is one of 178 members of the World Organisation for Animal Health – the Office International des Epizooties (OIE). The OIE develops and regularly updates standards for the animal health services of its members. The Community Animal Health Policy covers the health of all animals in the EU kept for food, farming, sport, companionship, entertainment and in zoos. The vision of the EU Animal Health Strategy (2007–13) is to work in partnership to increase the prevention of animal health related problems before they happen: 'Prevention is better than cure'.

22.11 In March 2016 a new EU Regulation[1] on transmissible animal diseases was introduced. The Regulation was published in the Official Journal on 31 March but will not be applicable for 5 years. The new law is designed to consolidate and simplify a vast number of separate provisions. It also provides for the use of new technologies, the early detection, monitoring and control of animal diseases. Every local authority must appoint as many inspectors and other officers as they think necessary for the execution and enforcement of the

Act[2]. The Regulation came into force across Europe on the 21 April 2021 and as a result of Brexit, it is no longer directly applicable to the UK. It is unclear as yet on how this regulation will be adopted in the future.

In March 2017 Regulation (EU) 2017/625 was introduced for the official controls and other official activities performed to ensure the application of food and feed law and rules on animal health and welfare. This has been directly applicable from the 19 December 2019 and is retained EU regulation.

[1] Regulation (EU) 2016/429.
[2] Animal Health Act 1981, s 52(1).

22.12 The National Animal Health and Welfare Panel ('NAHWP') is a national[1] public body that provides technical and operational policy support to local authorities by helping to co-ordinate good practice. The NAHWP provides expert advice on animal health and welfare matters and enforcement. In 2015 the NAHWP agreed and promoted the use of the term 'local authority animal health function' ('LAAHF'). The purpose of the LAAHF is to work 'in partnership with all relevant government agencies and Animal Health and welfare organisations to provide pro-active support to the local farming community with the aim of ensuring compliance with the statutory rules'.

[1] The NAHWP invites representatives from around the UK including Scotland and Northern Ireland.

Animal Health Act 1981

22.13 The main legislation governing animal health in Great Britain is the Animal Health Act 1981 ('AHA 1981'), as amended by:

- the Animal Health and Welfare Act 1984, which amongst other matters, relates to the seizure of things for the purpose of preventing the spread of disease, powers of entry and declarations as to places infected with a disease;
- the Animal Health (Amendment) Act 1998, which relates to improving the welfare of animals in quarantine;
- the Animal Health Act 2002 which, amongst other matters, provides additional powers to tackle foot and mouth disease and for these powers to be extendable to other animal diseases;
- the Animal Health and Welfare (Scotland) Act 2006, which makes provisions for both the health and welfare of animals in Scotland.

22.14 In addition there around 200 statutory instruments applying to animal health issues – either made under the AHA 1981 or under the European Communities Act 1972 in order to transpose an EU Directive or Regulation into domestic legislation (for example the Animal By-Products (Enforcement) (England) Regulations 2013[1] and the African Horse Sickness (England) Regulations 2012[2]). The following list is illustrative of the wide range of diseases etc which are subject to legislative control (it is not intended to be comprehensive and it should be emphasised that some diseases have never occurred in Great Britain).

African Swine Fever	Infectious Diseases of Horses
Anthrax	Pleuro-Pneumonia
Aujesky's Disease	Psittacosis or Ornithosis
Avian Influenza and Newcastle Disease	Rabies
Bluetongue	Salmonella
Cattle Plague	Sheep Scab
Classical Swine Fever	Swine Vesicular Disease
Enzootic Bovine Leukosis	Transmissible Spongiform Encephalopathies
Equine Viral Arteritis	Tuberculosis
Equine Infectious Anaemia	Warble Fly
Foot and Mouth Disease	Zoonoses

[1]   SI 2013/2952.
[2]   SI 2012/2629.

22.15 In a work of this nature it is not possible to provide a complete analysis of the legislative requirements relating to animal health (or welfare) matters and an attempt has therefore been made to focus on those areas which have most significance to local authority trading standards departments During 2018 legislative intervention covered matters such as Transmissible Spongiform Encephalopathies, Avian influenza, Bovine TB and Tuberculosis (Non-bovine animals)). Nor is it possible to list all parallel provisions which are connected with the transposition of an EU Directive or Regulation into domestic legislation within England, Wales, Scotland and Northern Ireland.

22.16 A recent judgement *R(Helen Jane MacDonald) v Secretary of State for Environment Food and Rural Affairs*[1] held that the Secretary of State is the expert decision maker entrusted by Parliament to control diseases in animals and, in the absence of any public law error, the Secretary's decision must be respected by the courts. This case concerned an application by the owner of an alpaca named Geronimo for judicial review of the Secretary of State's decision to slaughter the animal because it had twice tested positively for bovine tuberculosis. This was despite it being possible that results confirming the disease were false positives. The Secretary of State had taken into account the claimant's representations and evidence and given reasons for rejecting the criticisms it made of the Government's evidence.

[1]   [2019] EWHC 1783 (Admin).

Territorial jurisdiction

22.17 Unless otherwise specified the parts of the AHA 1981 referred to in this work apply to Great Britain.

Northern Ireland

22.18 The principal legislation relating to Northern Ireland is the Welfare of Animals Act (Northern Ireland) 2011 and the Diseases of Animals (Northern Ireland) Order 1981[1], which has been amended considerably, most recently by the Disease of Animals Act (Northern Ireland) 2010. The Department of Agriculture and Rural Development ('DARD') has the enforcement responsibility in respect of farmed animals (defined as any animal bred or kept for the production of food, wool or skin or for other farming purposes), licensing of riding establishments, boarding kennels, pet shops and zoos and enforcement of any welfare issues within these premises. District councils have responsibility for enforcement in respect of other (non-farmed) animals, ie domestic pets of any vertebrate species and equines (eg horses and donkeys etc). The All-Island Animal Health and Welfare Strategy – formally agreed in 2010 – enhances North-South co-operation on animal health and welfare issues and has the potential to help reduce and prevent the spread of animal disease.

1   SI 1981/1115 (NI 22).

Application

22.19 Animals are defined under the AHA 1981, s 87 as being (unless the context otherwise requires): (a) cattle, sheep and goats; and (b) all other ruminating animals and swine. The AHA 1981 has effect in relation to poultry as it does in relation to animals. Poultry is defined under AHA 1981, s 87(4) as being: (a) domestic fowls, turkeys, geese, ducks, guinea fowls and pigeons; and (b) pheasants and partridges. Ministers by order may extend the definition of the term 'animals' for all or any of the purposes of the AHA 1981 to include any mammal except man and any four footed beast which is not a mammal[1]. Similarly under AHA 1981, s 87(4) the definition of poultry may by Order be extended to include any other species of bird. So, for example, in the Foot and Mouth Disease (England) Order 2006[2], the definition of animals is extended to include 'all four footed beasts' and the definition of poultry to include 'all birds', within the terms of that Order.

1   Animal Health Act 1981, s 87(2).
2   SI 2006/182.

22.20 The AHA 1981, s 88 provides a definition of the term 'disease':

88 Meaning of "disease"

(1)   In this Act, unless the context otherwise requires, "disease" means cattle plague, pleuro-pneumonia, foot-and-mouth disease, sheep-pox, sheep scab, or swine fever, subject to subsection (2) below.

(2)   The Ministers may by order for all or any of the purposes of this Act extend the definition of "disease" in subsection (1) above so that it shall for those or any of those purposes comprise any other disease of animals.

(3)   In this Act, in so far as it applies to poultry, and unless the context otherwise requires, "disease" means—
   (a)   fowl pest in any of its forms, including Newcastle disease and fowl plague; and
   (b)   fowl cholera, infectious bronchitis, infectious laryngotracheitis, pullorum disease, fowl typhoid, fowl pox and fowl paralysis, subject to subsection (4) below.

(4)   The Ministers may by order for all or any of the purposes of this Act—
   (a)   extend the definition of "disease" in subsection (3) above so that it shall for those or any of those purposes comprise any other disease of birds; or
   (b)   restrict that definition so that it shall for those or any of those purposes exclude any of the diseases mentioned in paragraph (b) of subsection (3).

There are numerous statutory instruments made under AHA 1981, s 88(2) and (4), examples being, Disease of Poultry (England) Order 2003[1], the Specified Animal Pathogens Order 2008[2] and the African Horse Sickness (Scotland) Order 2012[3].

1   SI 2003/1078.
2   SI 2008/944.
3   SSI 2012/178.

Offences

22.21 The main offence provisions are contained in AHA 1981, ss 72 and 73 and, for practical enforcement purposes, relate to breaches of Orders made under the AHA 1981.

22.22 The AHA 1981, s 72 provides:

72 Offences made and declared by and under this Act

A person is guilty of an offence against this Act who, without lawful authority or excuse, proof of which shall lie on him—

(a)   does or omits anything the doing or omission of which is declared by this Act or by an order of the Minister to be an offence by that person against this Act; or

(b)   does anything which by this Act or such an order is made or declared to be not lawful.

22.23 Within the AHA 1981 itself, there are a number of acts or omissions declared as being 'offences against the Act' or other matters referred to simply as offences. The offences referred to in the AHA 1981 include:

- obstructing or impeding inspectors;
- refusing access or failing to assist when required to do so (see for example AHA 1981, ss 4(2), 16, 36G, 66);
- failing to keep diseased animals separate and notifying the authorities promptly (AHA 1981, s 15(7));
- disposal in watercourses or on the foreshore of diseased animal carcasses (AHA 1981, s 35(4));
- offences relating to equine exports (AHA 1981, ss 40, 41, 42 and 45); and
- offences relating to the falsification, use or improper obtaining of licences under the Act (AHA 1981, ss 66–71).

This list is not exhaustive and it should be noted that the Animal Health and Welfare (Scotland) Act 2006 amends the AHA 1981, to create different definitions and separate offences applicable in Scotland.

22.24 A general power for Ministers to make orders is expressed under AHA 1981, s 1 for the better execution of the AHA 1981 and for the purpose of preventing the spread of disease. Other specific powers for Ministers to regulate exist under the AHA 1981, an example being AHA 1981, s 8 which provides the power for Ministers to make orders regulating the movement of animals. Under this section the Welfare of Animals (Transport) (England) Order 2006[1] was enabled which creates a series of offences against the AHA 1981 relating to the transport of animals, enforceable under AHA 1981, s 72(a).

¹   SI 2006/3260.

22.25 In an example of proceedings brought under AHA 1981, s 72(a), *R (Clement) v Durham County Magistrates' Court*¹, which related to breaches of the Pigs (Records, Identification and Movement) Order 1995², Silber J said:

'Before turning to the questions for the opinion of this court, it is necessary to point out that the Order is a complicated Order and so I have great sympathy with the magistrates when considering the task that confronted them when dealing with this case.'

¹   [2003] EWHC 1154 (Admin).
²   SI 1995/11 (now repealed).

22.26 As if to demonstrate the complexities of this area of law, that Order (which specifically stated that breaches of the Order are offences against the AHA 1981), has been revoked and replaced by the Pigs (Records, Identification and Movement) Order 2011¹. This later Order is made under the AHA 1981 but no longer specifies offences as being against s 72(a) of the AHA 1981 and anticipates prosecutions under AHA 1981, s 73.

¹   SI 2011/2154.

22.27 The AHA 1981, s 79 deals with certain aspects of evidence and procedure, including:

79 Evidence and procedure

(2) Where the owner or person in charge of an animal is charged with an offence against this Act relative to disease or to any illness of the animal, he shall be presumed to have known of the existence of the disease or illness unless and until he shows to the court's satisfaction that—
 (a)   he had no knowledge of the existence of that disease or illness, and
 (b)   he could not with reasonable diligence have obtained that knowledge.
(3) Where a person—
 (a)   is charged with an offence against this Act in not having duly cleansed or disinfected any place, vessel, aircraft, vehicle or thing belonging to him or under his charge, and
 (b)   a presumption against him on the part of the prosecution is raised,
it shall lie on him to prove the due cleansing and disinfection mentioned in paragraph (a)¹.

¹   The section as reproduced applies in England and Wales. An alternative AHA 1981, s 79 applies in Scotland, as amended by the Animal Health and Welfare (Scotland) Act 2006.

General offences

22.28 The AHA 1981, s 73 provides:

73 General offences

A person is guilty of an offence against this Act who, without lawful authority or excuse, proof of which shall lie on him—

 (a)   does anything in contravention of this Act, or of an order of the Minister, or of a regulation of a local authority; or

(b)   fails to give, produce, observe or do any notice, licence, rule or thing which by this Act or such an order or regulation he is required to give, produce, observe or do.

Care should be taken to establish under which Act the secondary legislation was made. For example the Animal By-Products (Enforcement) (England) Regulations 2013[1] and the African Horse Sickness (England) Regulations 2012[2] are both made under the European Communities Act 1972, s 2(2) and both contain specific self-contained offence provisions, not invoking the Animal Health Act 1981. Previously, secondary legislation on Animal By-Products had been created under the powers granted by the AHA 1981 (see, for example, the Animal By-Products Order 1999, breach of which formed the basis of a prosecution under AHA 1981, s 73(b) in *R (North Yorkshire Trading Standards) v Nicholson*[3]).

[1]   SI 2013/2952.
[2]   SI 2012/2629.
[3]   [2003] EWHC 1022 (Admin).

Time limits

22.29 The AHA 1981, s 71A provides:

71A Prosecutions: time limit

(1)   Despite anything in section 127(1) of the Magistrates' Courts Act 1980 an information relating to an offence under this Act which is triable by a magistrates' court in England and Wales may be so tried if it is laid at any time—
  (a)   within the period of three years starting with the date of the commission of the offence, and
  (b)   within the period of six months starting with the day on which evidence which the prosecutor thinks is sufficient to justify the proceedings comes to his knowledge.
(2)   A certificate by the prosecutor as to the date on which such evidence came to his knowledge is conclusive evidence of that fact.

Note the commentary (below) on time limits under the Animal Welfare Act 2006, s 31, which is drafted in similar terms. Time limits are dealt with generally in Chapter 4, Criminal Enforcement.

Enforcement

22.30 The AHA 1981, ss 60–66A deal extensively with enforcement and AHA 1981, s 52 provides that every local authority 'shall appoint as many inspectors and other officers as the local authority think necessary for the execution and enforcement of this Act'. The AHA 1981, ss 60–62 provide enforcement powers under the Act for police officers (including under AHA 1981, ss 61–62 as regards rabies). The AHA 1981, s 63 of the Act provides an inspector with all the powers afforded to a police officer in the place where the inspector is acting, save for the powers under AHA 1981, ss 61 and 62 (powers of entry and arrest as regards rabies). In addition, relevant officers should have regard to the Home Office Powers of Entry Code; see Chapter 4, Criminal Enforcement.

Penalties

22.31 The penalties for offences committed under AHA 1981, ss 72 and 73 are contained in AHA 1981, s 75:

> (2) A person guilty of an offence to which this section applies is liable on summary conviction to imprisonment for a term not exceeding six months or to a fine or to both.

ANIMAL WELFARE

Introduction

22.32 The United Kingdom has a long history of protecting animals from cruelty. In 1822, Richard Martin MP piloted the first parliamentary legislation for animal welfare in the world, making it an offence to 'beat, abuse, or ill-treat any horse, mare, gelding, mule, ass, ox, cow, heifer, steer, sheep or other cattle'. The current general principles of animal welfare were set out in the Protection of Animals Acts, the first of which was passed in 1911, which made it an offence to cause any unnecessary suffering to an animal. In June 2004, Defra, the Scottish Executive and the Welsh Assembly Government published 'Animal Health and Welfare Strategy for Great Britain'. The aim of the strategy was to 'develop a new partnership in which we can make a lasting and continuous improvement in the health and welfare of kept animals while protecting society, the economy, and the environment from the effect of animal disease'. The strategy has as its scope all animals which are under people's control, but did not address angling, hunting or the use of animals in science.

22.33 The strategic outcomes included 'Promoting the benefits of animal health and welfare: Prevention is better than cure' which has at its heart an understanding that animals that are cared for appropriately and in accordance with existing welfare standards are more likely to be healthy, and less likely to contract or spread disease. A further strategic outcome was for 'Understanding and accepting roles and responsibilities', calling for individuals to understand and accept the duty they have to provide an acceptable standard of health and welfare for the animals in their care.

22.34 The Animal Welfare Act 2006 ('AWA 2006') supports the implementation of that strategy as regards welfare of animals in England and Wales. It replaced the Protection of Animals Act 1911, the welfare provisions of the Animal Health Act 1981 and consolidated more than 20 other pieces of legislation. The Animal Health and Welfare (Scotland) Act 2006 ('AHW(S)A 2006') also supports the 2004 Strategy. Part 1 of the AHW(S)A 2006 amends the Animal Health Act 1981 to provide additional powers to prevent the spread of animal diseases whilst Pt 2 of the Act addresses animal welfare.

22.35 Within the EU, following the signing of the Lisbon Treaty, acknowledgement of animals as sentient beings and the need to take regard of their welfare requirements, has been enshrined as a governing principle when formulating and implementing EU policies. Article 13 TFEU (2009) reads:

'In formulating and implementing the Union's agriculture, fisheries, transport, internal market, research and technological development and space policies, the Union and the Member States shall, since animals are sentient beings, pay full regard to the welfare requirements of animals, while respecting the legislative or administrative provisions and customs of the Member States relating in particular to religious rites, cultural traditions and regional heritage.'

22.36 The Animal Welfare (Sentience) Bill had its first reading in the House of Lords 13 May 2021 and makes provision for an Animal Sentience Committee with functions relating to the effect of government policy on the welfare of animals as sentient beings, capable of feeling emotions and experiencing pain. In effect, the Bill enshrines the recognition of the sentience of vertebrate animals into domestic law. The Bill provides that an 'animal' under the terms of the legislation means any vertebrate other than homo sapiens.

22.37 The Animals (Penalty Notices) Bill is a Private Members' Bill introduced on 16 June 2021 by Andrew Rosindell MP. It is backed by the Government and will create a system of a financial penalties of up to £5,000 for animal health and welfare offences. The penalties, which could include on-the-spot fines, can be issued to individuals who have cruelly mistreated pets, zoo animals or livestock.

Animal Welfare Act 2006

22.38 The welfare provisions of the AWA 2006 and the AHW(S)A 2006 are drafted in broadly similar terms. Equivalent sections (and differences) under AHW(S)A 2006 are indicated as applicable.

Territorial jurisdiction

22.39 The AWA 2006 extends to England and Wales. It extends to Scotland only in respect of AWA 2006, s 46, enabling disqualification orders made in England and Wales to have force in Scotland; AWA 2006, ss 47–50, making provision for Scottish courts to enforce disqualification orders made under the AWA 2006; the repeal of certain legislation and commencement orders. The AWA 2006, s 1, provides that the Act applies only to vertebrate animals, being the only demonstrably sentient animals. Provision is made under AWA 2006, s 1(3) for the appropriate national authority[1] to extend cover for invertebrates in the future if satisfied on the basis of scientific evidence that these too are capable of experiencing pain and suffering. The equivalent provision under AHW(S)A 2006 is contained in AWA 2006, s 16(1) and (3) empowering Scottish Ministers to extend by regulation the Act in similar terms.

[1]   Defined in AHA 2000, s 62(1) as being the Secretary of State as regards England and the Welsh National Assembly (renamed Senedd Cymru) as regards Wales.

'Protected animal'

22.40 The AWA 2006, s 2 provides that an animal is a 'protected animal' if:

(a)   it is of a kind which is commonly domesticated in the British Islands,

(b)   it is under the control of man whether on a permanent or temporary basis, or

(c)   it is not living in a wild state.

The AHW(S)A 2006, s 17 is framed in virtually identical terms. Animals of a kind not commonly domesticated in the British Islands are only 'protected animals' to the extent that they are under the control of man or are not living independently in the wild. 'Under control' is intended to be a broader expression than 'captive animal' under the Protection of Animals Act 1911, which had been narrowly interpreted by the courts.

'Responsibility for animals'

22.41 Certain offences under AWA 2006[1] and AHW(S)A 2006[2] can only be committed by persons who are 'responsible for an animal'. Section 3 of the AWA 2006 (and the AHW(S)A 2006, s 18) provide that references to a person responsible for an animal under the AWA 2006 are to a person responsible on a permanent or temporary basis and references to being responsible include being in charge. The owner of an animal shall always be regarded as being responsible under the AWA 2006 and a person will be treated as responsible for any animal for which a child under the age of 16 of which he has care and control is responsible.

[1]   AHA 2006, ss 4(2), 5(2), 6(2), 7(2) and 9.
[2]   AHW(S)A 2006, ss 19(2), 20(2), 21(2), 22(2) and 24.

22.42 Responsibility for an animal is only intended to arise where a person can be said to have assumed responsibility for its day-to-day care or for its care for a specific purpose or by virtue of owning it. This includes a person taking responsibility for an animal temporarily, for example a veterinary surgeon taking responsibility for animals kept in the surgery overnight or staff at boarding premises or animal sanctuaries. The AHW(S)A 2006, s 18(5) adds that 'a person does not relinquish responsibility for an animal by reason only of abandoning it'.

Offences

22.43 The AWA 2006, ss 4–8 and the AHW(S)A 2006, ss 19–23 address the prevention of harm by setting out offences relating to cruelty and animal fighting. The AWA 2006, s 9 and the AHW(S)A 2006, s 24 create offences where a person responsible for an animal does not ensure its welfare. In a work of this nature it is not possible to cover all offences arising under the Acts or the secondary legislation, so an attempt is made to address the areas of most significance.

Unnecessary suffering

22.44 The AWA 2006, s 4 sets out offences relating to unnecessary suffering, but provides, in AWA 2006, s 4(4), that nothing in the section applies to the destruction of an animal in an appropriate and humane manner. Also the AWA 2006, s 59 states: 'Nothing in this Act applies in relation to anything which occurs in the normal course of fishing'. Under the Protection of Animals Act 1911, it had been an offence to cause unnecessary suffering to any domestic or captive animal, with limited exceptions (for example suffering caused under the Animals (Scientific Procedures) Act 1986). The AWA 2006, s 4 seeks to replicate the protection under the 1911 Act, but to simplify and update the legislation. 'Suffering' means physical or mental suffering – the AWA 2006, s 62 (the AHW(S)A 2006, s 48 states: 'In this Part, references to suffering include physical or mental suffering').

22.45 The offence under AWA 2006, s 4(1) is applicable to any person and applies to acts and omissions.

> (1) A person commits an offence if—
>
>   (a) an act of his, or a failure of his to act, causes an animal to suffer,
>   (b) he knew, or ought reasonably to have known, that the act, or failure to act, would have that effect or be likely to do so,
>   (c) the animal is a protected animal, and
>   (d) the suffering is unnecessary.

The inclusion of the phrase 'ought reasonably to have known', introduces an objective mental element, such that it is not necessary to prove whether the person actually knew his act or failure to act would cause suffering.

22.46 In *Gray v Aylesbury Crown Court*[1], Toulson LJ in considering this section stated that 'knew or ought reasonably to have known' is a common expression in English law and does not require to be glossed. He rejected the argument that there needed to be some form of actual or constructive knowledge on the part of the defendant and that negligence was not sufficient, stating[2]:

> 'That submission does not accord with a natural reading of the subsection. Its plain effect is to impose criminal liability for unnecessary suffering caused to an animal either by an act or omission which the person responsible knew would, or was likely to, cause unnecessary suffering, or by a negligent act or omission.'[3]

[1] [2013] EWHC 500 (Admin).
[2] At para 26.
[3] The judge also rejected use of previous reported cases under the Protection of Animals Act 1911, stating (at para 28): 'It would be wrong in principle to construe the provisions of the 2006 Act by reference to differently worded provisions of the repealed legislation'.

22.47 The AHW(S)A 2006 offences relating to unnecessary suffering are contained in AHW(S)A 2006, s 19 and include an exception for the humane destruction of an animal[1]. Fishing is also excluded from applying to this part of the Act[2].

[1] AHW(S)A 2006, s 19(5).
[2] AHW(S)A 2006, s 47(b).

22.48 The offence under AHW(S)A 2006, s 19(1) applies to any person but is restricted to positive acts and not a failure to act as covered under the AWA 2006. This is addressed under AHW(S)A 2006, s 19(2) but only as against a person responsible for an animal (as to which see AHW(S)A 2006, s 18). The objective mental element under the AWA 2006 is replicated.

> (1) A person commits an offence if—
>
>   (a) the person causes a protected animal unnecessary suffering by an act, and

      (b)   the person knew, or ought reasonably to have known, that the act would have caused the suffering or be likely to do so.

  (2)   A person who is responsible for an animal commits an offence if—

      (a)   the person causes the animal unnecessary suffering by an act or omission, and

      (b)   the person knew, or ought reasonably to have known, that the act or omission would have caused the suffering or be likely to do so.

22.49

Precedent for causing unnecessary suffering to a protected animal

Information

A B on [date] at [premises], caused unnecessary suffering to a protected animal, namely [. . .], by failing to obtain veterinary treatment for the said animal, and he knew, or ought reasonably to have known, that the failure to act would have that effect or be likely to do so, contrary to s 4(1) of the Animal Welfare Act 2006.

UNNECESSARY

22.50 The AWA 2006, s 4(3) sets out the considerations to which the courts should have regard in determining whether the suffering is unnecessary, these include:

  (a)   whether the suffering could reasonably have been avoided or reduced;

  (b)   whether the conduct which caused the suffering was in compliance with any relevant enactment or any relevant provisions of a licence or code of practice issued under an enactment;

  (c)   whether the conduct which caused the suffering was for a legitimate purpose, such as—

      (i)   the purpose of benefiting the animal, or

      (ii)   the purpose of protecting a person, property or another animal;

  (d)   whether the suffering was proportionate to the purpose of the conduct concerned;

  (e)   whether the conduct concerned was in all the circumstances that of a reasonably competent and humane person.

On 8 June 2019 the Animal Welfare (Service Animals) Act 2019 came into force. It provided increased protection for service animals by amending s 4(3) of the Animal Welfare Act 2006. It inserted a new sub-s (3A) which provides that in determining whether suffering is unnecessary, in a case where it was caused for a purpose mentioned in sub-s (3)(c)(ii), the fact that the conduct was for that purpose is to be disregarded if the animal was under the control of an officer and being used in the course of the officer's duties in a way that was reasonable in all the circumstances and that the officer was not a defendant. This law was passed to make it harder for those who harm service animals such as police dogs and horses to claim they were acting in self-defence. Known as 'Finns Law' it was passed partly following a campaign after Finn, a police dog was stabbed in the head and chest whilst his handler was confronted by a knife-wielding robber in 2016.

22.51 The AHW(S)A 2006, s 19(4) sets out, in identical terms to the AWA 2006, s 4(3) above, the considerations to which regard is to be had in determining, for the purposes of the AHW(S)A 2006, s 19(1)–(3), whether suffering is unnecessary.

OTHER OFFENCES OF UNNECESSARY SUFFERING

22.52 The AWA 2006, s 4(2) and the AHW(S)A 2006, s 19(3), create offences where people responsible for animals permit or fail to intervene where another person causes an animal to suffer. The AWA 2006, Section 4(2) states:

> (2) A person commits an offence if—
> (a)   he is responsible for an animal,
> (b)   an act, or failure to act, of another person causes the animal to suffer,
> (c)   he permitted that to happen or failed to take such steps (whether by way of supervising the other person or otherwise) as were reasonable in all the circumstances to prevent that happening, and
> (d)   the suffering is unnecessary.

In *Riley v Crown Prosecution Service*[1] partners in a slaughterhouse business appealed against their convictions under AWA 2006, s 4(2)(c) for 'failing to take such steps as were reasonable in all the circumstances to prevent an animal . . . from suffering unnecessarily by failing to stop the continued handling and movement of the said bovine using ropes'. The High Court rejected the prosecution argument that the offences were of strict liability. A mental element (mens rea) must be proven that of the circumstances which determined what steps would be reasonable.

[1]   [2016] EWHC 2531 (Admin).

22.53 The AHW(S)A 2006, s 19(3) states:

> (3) A person ("person A") who is responsible for an animal commits an offence if—
> (a)   another person causes the animal unnecessary suffering by an act or omission, and
> (b)   person A—
> (i)   permits that to happen, or
> (ii)   fails to take such steps (whether by way of supervising the other person or otherwise) as are reasonable in the circumstances to prevent that happening.

Suffering is as defined under the AWA 2006, s 62 and the AHW(S)A 2006, s 48 and the courts in both jurisdictions are to have regard to the same factors as under the primary offences. No interpretation of the words 'permitted' or 'permits' appears under either the AWA 2006 or AHW(S)A 2006.

Other cruelty offences

Mutilation

22.54 The AWA 2006, s 5(1) makes it an offence for a person to carry out or cause to be carried out a prohibited procedure on a protected animal save as specified under regulations under AWA 2006, s 5(4)[1]. The carrying out of a prohibited procedure is a procedure which interferes with the sensitive tissues or bone structure of the animal, otherwise than for the purposes of its medical treatment.

[1]   See Mutilation (Permitted Procedures) (England) Regulations 2007, SI 2007/1100 (as amended by SI 2008/1426 and SI 2010/3034) and Mutilation (Permitted Procedures) (Wales) Regulations 2007, SI 2007/1029 (as amended by SI 2008/3094 and SI 2010/2712).

22.55 The AHW(S)A 2006, s 20(1) and (2) create like offences, and there is a further offence under AHW(S)A 2006, s 20(3) of taking (or causing to be taken) an animal from Scotland to have a prohibited procedure carried out outside Scotland. There is a similar power under AHW(S)A 2006, s 20(5)[1] to exempt by regulation specified procedures from falling under AHW(S)A 2006, s 20(1)–(3). The AHW(S)A 2006, s 21 also creates an offence of performing an operation on a protected animal without due care and humanity.

[1]   See the Prohibited Procedures on Protected Animals (Exemptions) (Scotland) Regulations 2010, SSI 2010/387 (as amended by SSI 2011/164 and SSI 2012/40).

Docking of dogs tails

22.56 The AWA 2006, s 6(1) makes it an offence for a person to remove (or cause to be removed by another person) the whole or any part of a dog's tail, otherwise than for the purpose of its medical treatment. The AWA 2006, s 6(2) creates an offence for a person responsible for a dog to permit or fail to take such steps as are reasonable to prevent another from removing the whole or part of the dog's tail, otherwise than for the purpose of its medical treatment. The offence is not committed where the dog is a certified working dog (as specified under regulations[1]) not more than 5 days old[2].

[1]   AWA 2006, s 6(4), the Docking of Working Dogs' Tails (England) Regulations 2007, SI 2007/1120 and Docking of Working Dogs' Tails (Wales) Regulations 2007, SI 2007/1028.
[2]   AWA 2006, s 6(3).

22.57 There is no like offence under the AHW(S)A 2006, but docking of dog's tails is not preserved under the AHW(S)A 2006, s 20 as under the AWA 2006, s 5, and so would amount to an offence under that section unless permitted by regulation made under s 20(5)[1].

[1]   See the Prohibited Procedures on Protected Animals (Exemptions) (Scotland) Regulations 2010, SSI 2010/387 (as amended by SSI 2011/164 and SSI 2012/40).

Administration of poisons

22.58 The AWA 2006, s 7(1) and the AHW(S)A 2006, s 22(1) are similarly drafted and create an offence where a person, without lawful authority or reasonable excuse, administers to or causes to be taken by a protected animal any poisonous or injurious drug or substance, knowing it to be poisonous or injurious. The AWA 2006, s 7(2) and AHW(S)A 2006, s 22(2) create offences where a person responsible for an animal permits another to administer poison, in similar terms as to the foregoing sections. Reference to a poisonous or injurious drug or substance includes where a drug or substance either through the quantity taken or the manner in which it is administered, has the effect of being poisonous or injurious[1]. Neither provision requires that it be shown that the animal actually suffered as a result of having received a poisonous drug or substance.

1   AWA 2006, s 7(3) and AHW(S)A 2006, s 22(3).

Animal fights

22.59 The AWA 2006, s 8(1) creates a series of offences regarding animal fighting, from keeping or training an animal to fight, causing an animal to fight, keeping premises for animal fights through to publicising proposed fights, providing information about animal fights to encourage attendance and betting on animal fights. Under AWA 2006, s 8(2) it is an offence simply to attend an animal fight. An animal fight is defined[1] as an occasion on which a protected animal is placed with an animal, or with a human, for the purpose of fighting, wrestling or baiting.

1   AWA 2006, s 8(7).

22.60 In *RSPCA v McCormick*[1] the defendants went into the countryside at night with lurcher-type dogs with the intention of seeking out wild animals, including deer, foxes and badgers. They set their dogs free and allowed them to pursue, attack and kill wild animals. It was held that this did not amount to the offence because the animal, with which a protected animal is placed, must be the subject of some control or restraint by a person connected with that activity or some other artificial constraint so that its ability to escape is prevented. The court observed that s 8 is aimed at organised and controlled animal fights, such as dog fights. The AHW(S)A 2006, s 23, whilst drafted in different terms, creates similar offences in relation to animal fights.

1   [2016] EWHC 928 (Admin).

Welfare offences

22.61 The 2004 Animal Health and Welfare Strategy document stated[1]:

'This strategy is not simply concerned with ensuring the absence of cruelty and disease. Quite often problems are caused by complacency, lack of skills or knowledge, or a failure to treat animals humanely and as sentient beings for which we have an ethical responsibility. Anyone who takes ownership of an animal, whether for food, farming, sport, companionship, entertainment or zoos, has a duty of care to meet acceptable animal health and welfare standards.'

1   Paragraph 31, p 16 of the Animal Health and Welfare Strategy for Great Britain http://archiv e.defra.gov.uk/foodfarm/policy/animalhealth/strategy/ahws.pdf.

22.62 The AWA 2006, ss 9–12 set out specific offences which relate to the promotion of welfare. Foremost of these is AWA 2006, s 9 which sets out the duty of a person responsible for an animal to ensure its welfare.

22.63 The AWA 2006, s 9(1) states:

(1)   A person commits an offence if he does not take such steps as are reasonable in all the circumstances to ensure that the needs of an animal for which he is responsible are met to the extent required by good practice.

22.64

Precedent for failing to ensure the needs of a protected animal are met

Information

A B on [date] at [premises], failed to take such steps as were reasonable in all the circumstances to ensure that the needs of a protected animal for which he was responsible, namely [. . .], were met to the extent required by good practice in that the animal was not provided with a suitable diet, contrary to s 9(1) of the Animal Welfare Act 2006.

22.65 In *Gray v Aylesbury Crown Court*[1], this section was considered and it was stated that the section sets 'a purely objective standard of care which a person responsible for an animal is required to provide'[2]. The court also confirmed that an indictment would not be bad for duplicity where a person was charged with the AWA 2006, ss 4 and 9 offences arising out of the same facts, given that the offence under AWA 2006, s 4 needs proof of unnecessary suffering, which is not required for proving the offence under AWA 2006, s 9.

1   [2013] EWHC 500 (Admin).
2   Paragraph 31.

22.66 Under AWA 2006, s 9(3), the circumstances which it is relevant to have regard to under AWA 2006, s 9(1) include in particular any lawful purpose for which the animal is kept and any lawful activity undertaken in relation to the animal. As to good practice, regard should be had to codes of practice issued under AWA 2006, s 14(1).

22.67 The Act sets out in AWA 2006, s 9(2) what an animal's needs[1] shall be taken to include, being:

(a)   its need for a suitable environment;
(b)   its need for a suitable diet;
(c)   its need to be able to exhibit normal behaviour patterns;
(d)   any need it has to be housed with, or apart from, other animals;
(e)   its need to be protected from suffering, injury and disease.

1   These needs are derived from the five freedoms for animals referred to in the 2004 Strategy document.

22.68 The AWA 2006 repeals the Abandonment of Animals Act 1960[1] and it is intended that this offence applies where a person abandons an animal for which they are responsible without taking reasonable steps to ensure that it is capable of fending for itself and living independently. Should the animal suffer unnecessarily through abandonment, then it is likely that an offence under AWA 2006, s 4 will have been committed[2].

1   See AWA 2006, s 65 and AWA 2006, Sch 4.
2   Note the AHW(S)A 2006 has a specific offence of abandonment of animals at AHW(S)A 2006, s 29.

22.69 The AHW(S)A 2006, s 24, creates a like offence in virtually identical terms. Neither section applies to the destruction of animals in an appropriate and humane manner[1]. The AWA 2006, s 10 provides an inspector with the power to issue improvement notices where he is of the opinion that a person is failing to comply with AWA 2006, s 9(1). The AWA 2006, s 11 and the AHW(S)A 2006, s 30 create offences with regard to the sale of animals to persons under the age of 16.

¹ AWA 2006, s 9(4) and AHW(S)A 2006, s 24(4).

Regulations

22.70 The appropriate national authority¹ is given a general power under AWA 2006, s 12(1) to, by regulation, make such provision for the purpose of promoting the welfare of animals for which a person is responsible, or the progeny of such animals, including the creation of non-indictable offences arising out of the breach of regulations². The AHW(S)A 2006, s 26 provides for making of regulations to secure the welfare of animals for which a person is responsible. The AWA 2006, s 13 provides powers for the making of regulations regarding the licensing and registration of activities involving animals³.

*R (on the application of The Electronic Collar Manufacturers Association & Anor v The Secretary of State for the Environment, Food and Rural Affairs*⁴ concerned the judicial review of a decision 'to implement a ban on the use of remote-controlled hand-held electronic collar devices for cats and dogs in England' (referred to as both 'e-collars' and 'shock collars') by means of statutory instrument made under s 12 Animal Welfare Act 2006. It was held that the proposed ban on these collars was neither irrational, nor violated ECHR property rights.

¹ The Secretary of State as regards England, the Welsh National Assembly (renamed Senedd Cymru) as regards Wales.
² Punishable by no more than 51 weeks' custody or a fine, AWA 2006, s 12(3)(a).
³ AHW(S)A 2006, s 27.
⁴ [2021] EWCA Civ 666.

Codes of practice

22.71 AWA 2006 provides that codes of practice may be issued (or revised) by an appropriate national authority for the purpose of providing practical guidance in respect of any provision made by or under the Act (AWA 2006, s 14(1))¹. A failure to comply with a code of practice does not of itself render a person liable to any proceedings of any kind (AWA 2006, s 14(3)).

¹ The equivalent power is found at the AHW(S)A 2006, s 37.

22.72 Codes of practice had been issued previously in relation to farmed animals (cattle, sheep, pigs, poultry, goats, rabbits, deer, turkeys and ratites), which have not been replaced and continue to apply in England, with the caveat that references to legislation within them are now out of date¹. In 2013 Defra consulted on replacing statutory based farming welfare codes of practice with industry led drafted guidance, The Government's interim response to the consultation was that it needed further time to consider the responses provided but, in April 2016, a decision was made to retain them in their current statutory format. Revised Codes of Practice for the Welfare of Cats, Dogs, and Horses, Ponies, Donkeys and their Hybrids, for the Welfare of Meat Chickens and Meat

Breeding Chickens and for the Welfare of Laying Hens and Pullets were published in 2018 as was a consultation on updating the Code of Practice for the welfare of pigs.

¹ These can be found on the Defra website.

22.73 Following commencement of AWA 2006, s 14, codes of practice for England have been issued with effect from 6 April 2010 for dogs, cats, privately kept non-human primates and horses, ponies and donkeys (Wales and Scotland have equivalent codes). A code of practice relating to gamebirds was issued in January 2011. All can be located on the .gov website¹.

¹ See https://www.gov.uk/guidance/animal-welfare.

22.74 Regard should be had to AWA 2006, s 14(4) which reads:

(1)   In any proceedings against a person for an offence under this Act or an offence under regulations under section 12 or 13—
  (a)   failure to comply with a relevant provision of a code of practice issued under this section may be relied upon as tending to establish liability, and
  (b)   compliance with a relevant provision of such a code of practice may be relied upon as tending to negative liability.

Time limits for prosecutions

22.75 The AWA 2006, s 31 sets out the time limits for prosecutions being brought (and is in similar terms to the Animal Health Act 1981, s 71A).

31 Time limits for prosecutions

(1)   Notwithstanding anything in section 127(1) of the Magistrates' Courts Act 1980 (c. 43), a magistrates' court may try an information relating to an offence under this Act if the information is laid—
  (a)   before the end of the period of three years beginning with the date of the commission of the offence, and
  (b)   before the end of the period of six months beginning with the date on which evidence which the prosecutor thinks is sufficient to justify the proceedings comes to his knowledge.
(2)   For the purposes of subsection (1)(b)—
  (a)   a certificate signed by or on behalf of the prosecutor and stating the date on which such evidence came to his knowledge shall be conclusive evidence of that fact, and
  (b)   a certificate stating that matter and purporting to be so signed shall be treated as so signed unless the contrary is proved.

For commentary about time limits in general see CHAPTER 4, Criminal Enforcement.

22.76 In *R v King & King*¹, the RSPCA were unsuccessful in seeking to rely on a certificate purporting to be issued under AWA 2006, s 31(2), but which in fact was unsigned. Dismissing the appeal, Toulson LJ stated:

'Given that a certificate in proper form is conclusive, subject to limited qualifications recognised in the case law, the court should not adopt a loose approach to the formal requirements of the subsection.'

There is no requirement under AWA 2006, s 31 for the certificate to be dated or served at the same time as the information is laid or the summons issued[2].

[1]   [2010] EWHC 637 (Admin).
[2]   *Browning v Lewes Crown Court* [2012] EWHC 1003 (Admin), per Wynn Williams J at para 12, approved in *Letherbarrow v Warwickshire County Council* [2015] EWHC 4820 (Admin).

22.77 In *RSPCA v Johnson*[1], the defendant challenged the validity of the date of information coming into the knowledge of the prosecutor, arguing that an earlier date applied thus rendering the information invalid as not properly laid within the 6-month time limit of AWA 2006, s 31(1)(b). In allowing an appeal against the District Judge's decision to dismiss the information as being out of time, Pill LJ stated[2]:

'In my judgment . . . the prosecutor is the RSPCA . . . (but) It appears to be clear . . . that Mr Fletcher was signing on behalf of the RSPCA . . . There is no principle of law that knowledge in a prosecutor begins immediately any employee of that prosecutor has the relevant knowledge . . . It is right that prosecutors are not entitled to shuffle papers between officers or sit on information so as to extend a time limit. There is, however, a degree of judgment involved in bringing a prosecution, and knowledge, in my judgment, involves an opportunity for those with appropriate skills to consider whether there is sufficient information to justify a prosecution.'

[1]   [2009] EWHC 2702 (Admin).
[2]   See also *Letherbarrow v Warwickshire County Council* [2015] EWHC 4820 (Admin), where it was said that the prosecuting authority was the county council but that it is the individual with responsibility for deciding whether a prosecution should go forward whose thoughts and beliefs are relevant.

22.78 The appropriateness of the time taken to issue proceedings in this case was influenced by the actions of the defendant, 'the respondent made concerted efforts to avoid and hide from Mr Jackman [the RSPCA investigator] . . . the more elusive someone is, the more likely an Inspector is want (sic) to have the clearest evidence in case some point is taken – an unforeseen point – by the elusive person when charged. Mr Jackman made very considerable efforts to get to the bottom of things'.

22.79 This approach was followed in *Letherbarrow v Warwickshire County Council*[1] where Bean LJ commented[2]:

'What the section does show is that Parliament expected the consideration of a prosecution under this section to be the subject of careful consideration. The decision which the prosecutor has to make under this subsection is not whether there is a prima facie case but whether the evidence is sufficient to justify a prosecution.'

Thus it was said that the test is not simply the time at which investigations are concluded, but rather the test as set out in the legislation.

[1]   [2015] EWHC 4820 (Admin).
[2]   At para 17.

22.80 In *Lamont-Perkins v RSPCA*[1], the Divisional Court confirmed that AWA 2006, s 31 applies to all prosecutors whether by a public body or private prosecutors. Moving to consider challenges that could be made to certificates Wyn Williams J stated:

'It seems to me to be clear that a certificate issued under section 31(2) of the 2006 Act and which conforms to the criteria specified in section 31(2) can be challenged on two bases alone. First, it can be challenged on the basis that it constitutes a fraud; second, it can be challenged on the basis that it is plainly wrong.'

[1]   [2012] EWHC 1002 (Admin).

22.81 The court was asked to consider the procedure that should be adopted where the certificate is 'plainly wrong' (even where this has occurred innocently). Having concluded that the magistrates have no jurisdiction to hear a summons laid out of time (absent a valid certificate under AWA 2006, s 31(2)), Wynn Williams J stated:

'A certificate under section 31(2) is conclusive evidence of the facts stated therein unless it is demonstrated that the certificate is plainly wrong. If the certificate is plainly wrong it has no effect and the magistrates must disregard it. They will then be left to determine whether or not the prosecutor has initiated proceedings within the time limit permitted by section 31(1) and if he has not the magistrates will have no jurisdiction to hear the summons in question.'

22.82 In *Chesterfield Poultry Limited v Sheffield Magistrates' Court*[1] the Administrative Court said absent fraud or reference to extraneous evidence showing that it is wrong or even plainly wrong . . . 'a prosecutor's certificate is not merely conclusive evidence of the date when particular pieces of evidence came to the prosecutor's knowledge. A certificate in proper form is conclusive evidence of the relevant date from which the six-month period begins to run'.

[1]   [2019] EWHC 2953 (Admin), [2020] 1 WLR 499, [2019] 11 WLUK 46, [2020] 1 Cr App R 26, [2020] LLR 25, [2020] Crim LR 182, [2020] ACD 10.

22.83 In *R v Woodward & Ors*[1] the prosecutor was successful in its appeal, after prosecutions of five defendants for offences under s 4 AWA 2006 were dismissed on the basis that the proceedings were brought out of time. The case concerned evidence obtained covertly by an agent of Animal Aid who had entered an abattoir and installed a digital video recorder to record the slaughtering practices there. The evidence was passed to the Food Standards Agency ('FSA'). The case was subsequently referred by the FSA to the Crown Prosecution Service. The appeal was allowed and the case was remitted to the magistrates' court with a direction that it refuses the application to dismiss the proceedings.

[1]   [2017] EWHC 1008 (Admin).

22.84 Hickinbottom LJ considered that a number of propositions, relating to AWA 2006, s 31, drawn from the cases, are clear. In particular – in cases where there is a time issue, it is for the prosecutor to show, to the relevant standard of proof, that there has been compliance with AWA 2006, s 31(1)(b). If there has been non-compliance, the prosecution is invalid. Where reliance is placed upon a certificate, then the certificate must strictly comply with the statutory requirements; and it must comply on its face, in the sense that deficiencies cannot be remedied by reference to extrinsic evidence.

22.85 A challenge to the jurisdiction of the court would be normally decided as a preliminary issue. In Scotland, the time limits for offences under the AHW(S)A 2006 (except for proceedings for animal fighting offences committed under AHW(S)A 2006, s 23) are established under the Criminal Procedure (Scotland) Act 1995, s 136 – within 6 months after the contravention occurred.

22.86 In *Staffordshire County Council v Sherratt and Sigley*[1] the High Court held that the summary offences in the Welfare of Farm Animals (England) Regulations 2007 were subject to the 6-month time limit from the commission of the offence as provided for under s 127 of the Magistrates' Court Act 1980. The court said that 'before the time limit in s 127 of the Magistrates' Court Act 1980 can be disapplied there must be an express enactment in the relevant legislation for a different time limit'. No such express reference applied and the time limit under s 31 of the Animal Welfare Act 2006 could not be imported into the 2007 Regulations.

[1] [2019] EWHC 1416 (Admin).

22.87 In *Garrett v Chief Constable of West Midlands Police*[1] on the facts of the case the 6-month time limit for bringing a complaint under s 4B(1)(a) of the Dangerous Dogs Act 1991, as amended, ran from the date of the police's seizure of the defendant's Rottweiler (at the earliest) not from the date of the incident which had provided the grounds for the complaint. Accordingly, it was held that a district judge had correctly held that the respondent Chief Constable had brought a complaint applying for an order of the destruction of the dog within the relevant 6-month time limit and the defendant's appeal was dismissed.

[1] [2020] EWHC 1416.

Enforcement

22.88 There is no prescribed duty of enforcement for the AWA 2006 or AHW(S)A 2006. However Regulation EC 2017/625 on the official controls and other official activities performed to ensure the application of food and feed law, rules on animal health and welfare, plant health and plant protection products does include animal welfare in its scope. As this is retained EU regulation, it is directly applicable. Article 78 of EC 2017/625 makes it a requirement that 'Member States shall ensure that adequate financial resources are available to provide the staff and other resources necessary for the competent authorities to perform official controls and other official activities'.

22.89 Although the AWA 2006, s 30 provides a power for a local authority in England Wales to prosecute offences (which may be seen as superfluous in the light of the Local Government Act 1972, s 222) the right to launch private prosecutions derives from the common law and the AWA 2006 does not limit that right. Powers can be exercised by a constable or an inspector. An inspector is a person appointed either by the appropriate national authority (either the Secretary of State or the National Assembly for Wales (renamed Senedd Cymru), for the AWA 2006, or the Scottish Ministers for the AHW(S)A 2006) or by a local authority for AWA/AHW(S)A.

22.90 The enforcement powers available to constables/inspectors are found in AWA 2006, ss 18–29, 51–56 and AWA 2006, Sch 2 (AHW(S)A 2006, ss 32, 49(7) and AHW(S)A 2006, Sch 1); they include emergency powers in relation to animals in distress, powers of entry and search, seizure of animals and inspection under certain conditions. In regard to the powers of entry and search, the court in *R (on the application of the RSPCA) v Colchester Magistrates' Court*[1] admonished the use of a warrant granted to enter under the Environmental Protection Act 1990 to effectively establish a case of animal cruelty, even though the application for a warrant under the AWA 2006 had been refused.

[1]   [2015] EWHC 1418 (Admin).

22.91 The AWA 2006, s 51(5) provides immunity for inspectors for actions taken outside their powers, so long as in purporting to act under their powers, they acted reasonably and in good faith:

> (5) An inspector shall not be liable in any civil or criminal proceedings for anything done in the purported performance of his functions under this Act if the court is satisfied that the act was done in good faith and that there were reasonable grounds for doing it.

22.92 The AHW(S)A 2006, s 49(4) is framed in similar terms:

> (4) An inspector incurs no civil or criminal liability for anything which the inspector does in purported exercise of any functions conferred on the inspector by a provision of this Part, or by regulations made under this Part, where the inspector acts on reasonable grounds and in good faith.

Sentencing

22.93 The AWA 2006, ss 32–45 set out the penalties available on conviction, which include imprisonment, fine, deprivation, disqualification, destruction, forfeiture of equipment and cancellation of a licence or registration.

22.94 The AWA 2006, s 32(1) provides that for the offences under the AWA 2006, ss 4–8[1]:

> (1)   A person guilty of an offence . . . shall be liable on summary conviction
> to—
> (a)   imprisonment for a term not exceeding 51 weeks, or
> (b)   a fine,
> or to both.

For an offence under the AWA 2006, s 9, the sentence on summary conviction is imprisonment not exceeding 51 weeks or an unlimited fine or both[2].

As stated in para **22.4** Animal Welfare (Sentencing) Act 2021 increases the sentencing powers of the courts to 5 years' imprisonment and make the offence triable either way for some offences.

[1]   Not including AWA 2006, s 6(8), (9) or (12).
[2]   References to 51 weeks should be read as 6 months pending the implementation of the Criminal Justice Act 2003, s 281(5).

22.95 The AWA 2006, s 34 provides the power to disqualify following conviction under the Act:

34 Disqualification

(1)   If a person is convicted of an offence to which this section applies, the court by or before which he is convicted may, instead of or in addition to dealing with him in any other way, make an order disqualifying him under any one or more of subsections (2) to (4) for such period as it thinks fit.

(2)   Disqualification under this subsection disqualifies a person—
   (a)   from owning animals,
   (b)   from keeping animals,
   (c)   from participating in the keeping of animals, and
   (d)   from being party to an arrangement under which he is entitled to control or influence the way in which animals are kept.

(3)   Disqualification under this subsection disqualifies a person from dealing in animals.

(4)   Disqualification under this subsection disqualifies a person—
   (a)   from transporting animals, and
   (b)   from arranging for the transport of animals.

(5)   Disqualification under subsection (2), (3) or (4) may be imposed in relation to animals generally, or in relation to animals of one or more kinds.

22.96 In *R (on the application of the RSPCA) v Guildford Crown Court*[1], the RSPCA sought judicial review of the decision of a Crown Court judge to vary the terms of a disqualification under AWA 2006, s 34(2) so as to not disqualify him from the participation in the keeping of animals under AWA 2006, s 34(2)(c). The Divisional Court found that in imposing a disqualification under AWA 2006, s 34(2), (3) or (4), the sentencing judge has no discretion to relax or vary any of the statutory terms of that disqualification. In *R (on the application of Patterson & Patterson) v RSPCA*[2], Blake J considered that the prohibition under AWA 2006, s 34(2) was not 'so wide as preventing any form of contact with a dog or with an animal or control of an animal'. For there to be a breach of a disqualification order[3]:

'it is not sufficient that you are <u>able</u> to control or influence the way in which animals are kept, you must be <u>entitled</u> to control or influence the way in which they are kept under an arrangement to which you are party.'

[1]   [2012] EWHC 3392 (Admin).
[2]   [2013] EWHC 4531 (Admin).
[3]   Blake J at paras 24–25.

22.97 Disqualification is only available for offences under the AWA 2006. This may cause a difficulty in obtaining an order prohibiting a defendant from owning or keeping animals if the offences are framed under other legislation.

22.98 The AHW(S)A 2006, ss 39–43 prescribe for post-conviction deprivation and disqualification orders for relevant offences (which include the AHW(S)A 2006, s 19). The AHW(S)A 2006, Section 46 provides that a person who commits an offence under the AHW(S)A 2006, s 19 is liable on summary conviction to imprisonment for a term not exceeding 12 months or to a fine not exceeding £20,000 or to both.

Commentary

22.99 In December 2010 the Memorandum to Environment, Food and Rural Affairs Committee Post-Legislative Assessment of the Animal Welfare Act 2006 was published as part of the process set out in the document Post-Legislative Scrutiny[1]. The Conclusions of the Memorandum noted that the main criticisms of the 2006 Act focused on three specific issues: the way in which it has been enforced, the delay in introducing the secondary legislation that had originally been envisaged and the lack of public awareness surrounding the new responsibilities for pet owners and the functions of the AWA 2006. The report concluded that whilst there was still more to do to achieve higher standards of animal welfare, improvements had occurred and the objectives of harmonising farm and companion welfare and consolidating and simplifying animal welfare legislation had been met.

[1] Cm 7320.

WELFARE OFFENCES CREATED UNDER REGULATIONS

22.100 It is not intended to provide an exhaustive list of all offences created under secondary legislation, but rather to highlight regulations of note.

Welfare of farmed animals

22.101 The Welfare of Farmed Animals (England) Regulations 2007[1] is made under the AWA 2006, s 12, replacing the 2000 Regulations[2] of the same name. The order implements EU directives on the protection of animals for farming purposes and those setting minimum standards for the protection of laying hens, calves and pigs[3].

[1] SI 2007/2078, amended by Welfare of Farmed Animals (England) (Amendment) Regulations 2010, SI 2010/3033.
[2] SI 2000/1870.
[3] Council Directive 98/58/EC concerning the protection of animals kept for farming purposes, Council Directive 99/74/EC laying down minimum standards for the protection of laying hens, Council Directive 91/629/EEC laying down minimum standards for the protection of calves, as amended by Council Directive 97/2/EC and Commission decision 97/182/EC, and Council Directive 91/630/EEC laying down minimum standards for the protection of pigs, as amended by Council Directive 2001/88/EC and Council Directive 2001/93/EC.

22.102 Under reg 3, a 'farmed animal' means an animal bred or kept for the production of food, wool or skin or other farming purposes, but does not include:

(a)   a fish, reptile or amphibian;
(b)   an animal whilst at, or solely intended for use in, a competition, show or cultural or sporting event or activity;
(c)   an experimental or laboratory animal; or
(d)   an animal living in the wild.

22.103 Regulation 4(1) imposes a duty upon a person responsible for a farmed animal to take all reasonable steps to ensure that the conditions under which it is bred or kept comply with specified standards set out at Sch 1 of the Regulations. Further specific duties lie under reg 5 for poultry, laying hens, calves, cattle, pigs, rabbits. Under reg 6, a person responsible for a farmed animal must not attend to the animal unless he is acquainted with any relevant code of practice and has access to the code while attending to the animal and must take all reasonable steps to ensure that a person employed or engaged by him does not attend to the animal unless that other person is acquainted with any relevant code of practice, has access to the code while attending to the animal and has received instruction and guidance on the code[1]. By reg 7 it is an offence for a person without lawful authority or excuse to contravene or fail to comply with a duty in regs 4, 5 or 6. The local authority is prescribed the power to prosecute under reg 8(1). Equivalent regulations exist for Wales and Scotland.

1 SI 2007/2078, reg 6.

Welfare of animals in transport

22.104 Notwithstanding the repeal of the welfare provisions under the Animal Health Act 1981, some secondary legislation made under that Act continues to apply to welfare issues in England and Wales (and offences are created under that Act for breaches). The Welfare of Animals (Transport) (England) Order 2006[1] and the Welfare of Animals (Transport) (Wales) Order 2007[2] are created under the Animal Health Act 1981 and breach of the regulations are offences under AHA 1981, s 73. Each create under reg 4(1) offences of transporting any animal in a way which causes, or is likely to cause, injury or unnecessary suffering to that animal.

1 SI 2006/3260.
2 SI 2007/1047.

22.105 Amongst other offences under the orders:

'A person who fails to comply with any of the following provisions of Council Regulation (EC) No 1/2005 is guilty of an offence against the Act—
(a)   Article 3 (general conditions for the transport of animals) . . . '

22.106 Council Regulation (EC) No 1/2005 applies to the transport of animals taking place in connection with an economic activity but not where the transport of animals relates to veterinary treatment. Article 3 states:

General conditions for the transport of animals

No person shall transport animals or cause animals to be transported in a way likely to cause injury or undue suffering to them.

In addition, the following conditions shall be complied with:
(a)   all necessary arrangements have been made in advance to minimise the length of the journey and meet animals' needs during the journey;
(b)   the animals are fit for the journey;
(c)   the means of transport are designed, constructed, maintained and operated so as to avoid injury and suffering and ensure the safety of the animals;
(d)   the loading and unloading facilities are adequately designed, constructed, maintained and operated so as to avoid injury and suffering and ensure the safety of the animals;
(e)   the personnel handling animals are trained or competent as appropriate for this purpose and carry out their tasks without using violence or any method likely to cause unnecessary fear, injury or suffering;
(f)   the transport is carried out without delay to the place of destination and the welfare conditions of the animals are regularly checked and appropriately maintained;

(g)   sufficient floor area and height is provided for the animals, appropriate to their size and the intended journey;

(h)   water, feed and rest are offered to the animals at suitable intervals and are appropriate in quality and quantity to their species and size.

22.107 The Welfare of Animals (Transport) (Scotland) Regulations 2006[1] were made under the European Communities Act 1972 and a person who fails to comply with, for example, Art 3 (general conditions for the transport of animals) of Council Regulation (EC) No 1/2005, as set out above, is guilty of an offence under the Animal Health Act 1981. Enforcement under the orders is expressed for the local authority.

[1]   SSI 2006/606.

Welfare of animals at markets

22.108 The welfare of animals at markets is regulated by the Welfare of Animals at Markets Order 1990[1] and make it an offence against the Animal Health Act 1981 to contravene any provision of the Order including[2]:

- permitting an unfit animal to be exposed for sale (art 5)[3];
- being party to injury or unnecessary suffering to an animal, including the exposure to adverse weather conditions (art 6);
- mishandling animals at market, prohibiting lifting, dragging or inappropriate tying of an animal (art 7);
- using excessive force to control an animal; the use of sticks, whips, crops and goads are also restricted (art 8).

[1]   SI 1990/2628, made under the Animal Health Act 1981.
[2]   Article 20(c).
[3]   The prosecution must prove the animal is unfit and that the defendant knowingly allowed that unfit animal to be exposed for sale, *Davidson v Strong* (1997) *The Times*, 20 March.

Welfare of animals at the time of killing

22.109 Hitherto the welfare of animals at the point of slaughter has been governed by the Welfare of Animals (Slaughter or Killing) Regulations 1995[1]. This legislation makes it an offence to cause or permit an animal avoidable excitement, pain or suffering. There are also specific rules on handling, stunning, slaughter or killing of animals.

[1]   SI 1995/731.

22.110 This was replaced by EU Regulation from 1 January 2013[1], which applies to the killing of all animals bred and kept for the production of food, wool, skin, fur or other products in slaughterhouses or on farms as well as the killing of animals for disease control purposes. The Regulation applies to all vertebrate animals including poultry and fish, but excluding reptiles and amphibians. All animals must be spared avoidable pain, distress or suffering during killing and related operations. For all animals (other than fish) specific requirements apply requiring them to be killed by a method that leads to instant death or death after stunning.

[1]   EU Council Regulation (EC) No 1099/2009 on the protection of animals at the time of killing.

22.111 The Regulation places a responsibility on the business operator not to permit welfare abuses and stipulates that animals are to be 'spared any avoidable pain, distress or suffering during killing and related operations'. The key requirements include:

- With the exception of certain low throughput businesses, business operators must have suitably trained and qualified animal welfare officers to ensure that standard operating procedures are developed and implemented, and animal welfare rules are properly understood, applied and reviewed.
- Standard operating procedures are explicitly required for stunning, killing, and all related operations – such as the restraint or handling of animals.
- Individuals carrying out slaughter operations must hold a certificate of competence for the operations they perform.
- Animal welfare officers are required to hold a certificate of competence for all the tasks they are responsible for.
- The keeping of records of maintenance and also routine checks for one year.

The Regulation also encourages the development of guides to good practice.

22.112 In England Defra consulted on implementing the Regulation during 2012 on what became the Welfare of Animals at the Time of Killing Regulations 2014[1]. These regulations were revoked on 19 May 2014[2], the day they were due to come into force as it was decided that the potential impact on some aspects of religious slaughter needed further consideration. The Welfare of Animals at the Time of Killing (England) Regulations 2015[3] came into force on 5 November 2015.

[1] SI 2014/1240.
[2] Welfare of Animals at the Time of Killing (Revocation) Regulations 2014, SI 2014/1258.
[3] SI 2015/1782.

22.113 In August 2016, the Bureau of Investigative Journalism published an article stating that ' . . . vets and meat hygiene inspectors working for the FSA inside abattoirs reported a total of 9,511 animal welfare breaches between July 2014 and June 2016 . . . ' according to data released by the Food Standards Agency under the Freedom of Information Act 2000. Subsequently, the Food Standards Agency Board Meeting, on 21 September 2016, received a paper setting out its current and proposed activities in England and Wales as part of its ongoing programme to 'Deter, Prevent, Detect and Enforce' animal welfare breaches.

22.114 In Scotland, the Regulation is implemented as from 22 November 2012 through the Welfare of Animals at the Time of Killing (Scotland) Regulations 2012[1], in Wales it is implemented under the Welfare of Animals at the Time of Killing (Wales) Regulations 2014[2] and in Northern Ireland, Welfare of Animals at the Time of Killing (Northern Ireland) Regulations 2014[3]. Each of these regulations were made under of the European Communities Act 1972, s 2(2).

[1] SSI 2012/321.
[2] SI 2014/951.
[3] SI 2014/107.

22.115 In *R (Highbury Poultry Farm Produce Ltd) v Telford Magistrates' Court*[1], the Divisional Court considered whether certain offences under the 2015 regulations required proof of a mental element (mens rea). The court held that offences under reg 30(1)(g) of contravening Art 3(1) of EU regulation 1099/2099 requiring that animals be 'spared avoidable pain' during their killing and, contravening Art 15 of Regulation 1099/2099 requiring compliance with slaughter house rules for bleeding out animals, were strict liability offences. The case concerned chickens that had been put into a scalding tank whilst still alive because their necks had not been cut by a certified operative. The Divisional Court certified a point of law of public importance whether proof of an offence contrary to reg 30(1)(g) requires proof of mens rea and/or some culpable act or omission on the part of the business operator. The Supreme Court granted permission to appeal on 22 May 2018[2]. The appeal was heard in the Supreme Court on 25 June 2020. At the time of writing the decision is still awaited.

1 [2018] EWHC 3122.
2 SC citation UKSC 2018/0231.

OTHER ANIMAL WELFARE LEGISLATION

22.116 The Animal Welfare (Licensing of Activities Involving Animals) (England) Regulations 2018[1], which came into force 1 October 2018, introduced an updated licensing system in England for five activities involving animals: selling animals as pets, providing for or arranging for the provision of boarding for cats or dogs, hiring out horses, dog breeding and keeping or training animals for exhibition. This licensing system is enforced by local authorities. Schedule 1 describes each type of licensable activity. Schedule 2 sets out the general conditions that apply to all licensable activities and Schs 3 – 7 set out the specific conditions that apply to each licensable activity. Any person wishing to carry on any of these activities in England must obtain a licence from their local authority under the Regulations. The provisions replace the requirements, in England, to be registered under the Performing Animals (Regulation) Act 1925 or to obtain a licence under the Pet Animals Act 1951; the Animal Boarding Establishments Act 1963; the Riding Establishments Act 1964 or the Breeding of Dogs Act 1973. There are a number of repeals of, and consequential amendments to, these Acts, the principal ones of which are indicated below. The general conditions for licensing include a requirement that the licence holder is required to keep as a condition of the licence, certain records which must be available for inspection by an inspector in a visible and legible form or, where any such records are stored in electronic form, in a form from which they can readily be produced in a visible and legible form. The licence holder must keep all such records for at least 3 years beginning with the date on which the record was created. Note that, in Scotland, the following Acts were repealed by the Animal Health and Welfare (Scotland) Act 2006.

1 SI 2018/486.

Performing animals

22.117 The welfare of performing animals is provided for in the general provisions of the Animal Welfare Act 2006. In addition, trainers and exhibitors of performing animals must be registered with the local authority under this Act. Offences are created, including where a person:

- not being registered under the Act, exhibits or trains any performing animal; or
- being registered under the Act, exhibits or trains any performing animal with respect to which or in a manner with respect to which he is not registered.

As a consequence of the Animal Welfare (Licensing of Activities Involving Animals) (England) Regulations 2018, PA(R)A 1925, s 1(1) (restriction on exhibition and training of performing animals) ceases to have effect in relation to England.

22.118 Under the Act, police officers and officers of local authorities, have power to enter premises where animals are being trained and exhibited, and if cruelty and neglect is detected, magistrates' courts can prohibit or restrict the training or exhibition of the animals and suspend or cancel the registration granted under the Act.

22.119 Note that the Welfare of Wild Animals in Travelling Circuses (England) Regulations 2012 require all operators of travelling circuses in England that use wild animals to be licensed. The Government confirmed its intention to introduce legislation to ban the use of wild animals in circuses 'when parliamentary time allows' and in April 2013 the Government proposed a draft Wild Animals in Circuses Bill that would prohibit the use of wild animals in travelling circuses in England. Although introduced before Parliament in 2014, the Bill did not become law before the end of that Parliamentary session, but has now resulted in the Wild Animals in Circuses Act 2019. It came into force on 20 January 2020 and provides that a circus operator may not use a wild animal in a travelling circus in England. The penalty for contravention of the prohibition will be an unlimited fine on summary conviction. When the Act comes into force, the 2012 regulations will expire because their introduction was an interim measure until an outright legislative ban. The Wild Animals in Travelling Circuses (Scotland) Act 2018, which came into force 28 May 2018 makes it an offence for a circus operator to use, or to cause or permit another person to use, a wild animal in a travelling circus in Scotland. Similar legislation will come into force in Wales on 1 December 2020 after the Wild Animals and Circuses (Wales) Bill was passed into law.

Pet shops

22.120 The Pet Animals Act 1951 requires any person keeping a pet shop (carrying on at premises of any nature – including a private dwelling – of a business of selling animals as pets) to be licensed by the local authority. Before granting a licence the local authority must be satisfied that the animals are kept in accommodation that is suitable as respects size, temperature, lighting, ventilation and cleanliness; that they are supplied with appropriate food and drink; and are adequately protected from disease and fire. The local authority may attach any conditions to the licence, may inspect the licensed premises at all reasonable times and may refuse a licence if the conditions at the premises are unsatisfactory or if the terms of the licence are not being complied with. Offences are created for persons who trade without a licence or in breach of licensing conditions[1].

[1] Pet Animals Act 1951, s 1(7).

England

22.121 As a consequence of the Animal Welfare (Licensing of Activities Involving Animals) (England) Regulations 2018[1], PAA 1951, s 1(1) (restriction on keeping a pet shop) ceases to have effect in relation to England. These regulations came into force on 1 October 2018. They provide for the licensing of persons involved in England in selling animals as pets, providing or arranging for the provision of boarding for cats or dogs, hiring out horses, breeding dogs and keeping or training animals for exhibition. Any person who carries out any of these activities without a licence commits an offence under s 13(6) of the AWA 2006 and is liable to imprisonment for a term of up to 6 months, a fine or both.

[1] SI 2018/486.

Animal boarding establishments

22.122 The Animal Boarding Establishments Act 1953 requires any person keeping a boarding establishment for animals (carrying on at premises of any nature – including a private dwelling – of a business of providing accommodation for other people's cats or dogs) to be licensed by the local authority. The licence is granted at the discretion of the local authority which may take into account the suitability of the accommodation and whether the animals are well fed, exercised and protected from disease and fire. The local authority may attach any conditions to the licence, may inspect the licensed premises at all reasonable times and may refuse a licence if the conditions at the premises are unsatisfactory. Offences are created for persons who trade without a licence or in breach of licensing conditions. As a consequence of the Animal Welfare (Licensing of Activities Involving Animals) (England) Regulations 2018, ABEA 1963, s 1(1) (licensing of boarding establishments for animals) ceases to have effect in relation to England. From 6 April 2020 those who hold a licence to sell pets will be prohibited from selling puppies and kittens aged under six months, that they have not bred themselves[1].

[1] Animal Welfare (Licensing of Activities Involving Animals) (England) (Amendment) Regulations 2019 SI 2019/1093.

Riding establishments

22.123 The Riding Establishments Acts of 1964 and 1970 requires any person keeping a riding establishment (carrying on of a business of keeping horses for prescribed purposes) to be licensed by the local authority. The local authority can impose conditions on the licence. The local authority, in the exercise of its discretion, may take into account the suitability of the applicant/manager, the accommodation and pasture, adequacy of the provision for the horses' health, welfare and exercise, precautions against fire and disease and the suitability of the horses as regards the reasons for which they are kept. (Under the 1970 Act – which also amends the 1964 Act – if the local authority is not satisfied that, having regard to all the circumstances they would be justified in granting a licence, they may grant a provisional licence.) Offences are committed where persons trade without a licence, in breach of licensing conditions and also hiring out or uses for the purposes of instruction, a horse where its condition is such that its riding is likely to cause it suffering. As a consequence of the Animal Welfare (Licensing of Activities Involving Animals) (England) Regulations 2018[1], REA 1964, s 1(1) of the Act (licensing of riding establishments) ceases to have effect in relation to England.

[1]   SI 2018/486.

Breeding of dogs

22.124 As a consequence of the Animal Welfare (Licensing of Activities Involving Animals) (England) Regulations 2018, the Breeding of Dogs Act 1973, the Breeding of Dogs Act 1991 and the Breeding and Sale of Dogs (Welfare) Act 1999 are repealed.

22.125 Schedule 6 of the Regulations provides for 'Specific conditions: breeding dogs'. These conditions comprise detailed and specific requirements relating to: Advertisements and sales; Suitable environment; Suitable diet; Monitoring of behaviour and training; Housing with or apart from other dogs; Protection from pain, suffering, injury and disease. For example:

(3) The licence holder must ensure that no bitch—
    (a)   is mated if aged less than 12 months;
    (b)   gives birth to more than one litter of puppies in a 12-month period;
    (c)   gives birth to more than six litters of puppies in total;
    (d)   is mated if she has had two litters delivered by caesarean section.

22.126 A Defra Call for Evidence in relation to a ban on commercial third party sales of puppies and kittens in England closed 2 May 2018. Subsequently as set out in para **22.116** a strict system for the licensing of the sale of puppies was established. Further to that and on 6 April 2020 'Lucy's Law' came into force as The Animal Welfare (Licensing of Activities involving Animals) (England) (Amendment) Regulations 2019. Lucy was a mistreated dog rescued from a puppy farm. The commercial sale of puppies was already a licensable activity, but the amendment means that licensed pet sellers will no longer be able to sell puppies or kittens under the age of 6 months unless they themselves have bred the animals.

22.127 A Pet Theft Taskforce was established by the Department for Environment, Food and Rural Affairs, Home Office and Ministry of Justice on the 8th May 2021. The objectives the taskforce has been commissioned for is to:

- Gather, research and commission work to build a clear evidence base of the scale of any issue.

- Consider the issue from end to end, including causes, prevention, reporting, enforcement and prosecution.
- Make clear and timely recommendations on ways to improve the situation around pet theft.

22.128 The Breeding of Dogs (Licensing Records) (Scotland) Regulations 1999[1], which apply to Scotland only, prescribe the form in which records must be kept.

[1] SI 1999/176.

Control of horses

22.129 The Control of Horses Act 2015 applies only in England and has been introduced to tackle the problem of 'fly-grazing', namely the practice of deliberately leaving horses to graze on land without the landowner's permission. The Act, which came into force on 26 May 2015, amends the Animals Act 1971 to provide as CHA 2015, s 7A for the power of local authorities to detain a horse which is in any public place within its area, providing that (a) the local authority has reasonable grounds for believing the horse is there without lawful authority, and (b) where the land is lawfully occupied by a person, that person consents to the detention of the horse or the local authority has reasonable grounds for believing that the person would consent to the detention of the horse. If the prescribed notice provisions have been complied with, then under CHA 2015, s 7C, the local authority has the power to dispose of the horse in whatever way it sees fit including by selling it or having it destroyed.

Wales

22.130 The Control of Horses (Wales) Act 2014 became law in Wales on 27 January 2014. The Act provides local authorities with the powers to:

- seize and impound horses which are on land without consent;
- sell the horses or dispose of them, including destruction by humane means if appropriate;
- recover costs reasonably incurred from the owners of horses in such circumstance.

Microchipping of dogs

22.131 The Microchipping of Dogs (England) Regulations 2015[1] provide for the compulsory microchipping of dogs and the recording of each dog's identity and its keeper's contact details on a database. Local authorities have the power under reg 11(2) to authorise in writing any person to act for the purpose of enforcing the regulations. The authorised person may under reg 12 serve a notice on a keeper to microchip their dog, to microchip a dog and recover the cost of doing so from the keeper and to take possession of a dog for the purpose of microchipping it. The regulations apply only in England.

[1] SI 2015/108.

Chapter 23

HEALTH AND
SAFETY ENFORCEMENT

Contents

INTRODUCTION

23.1 There is, rightly, a fundamental belief in this country that everyone has the right to work in places that are safe, where the risks of injury and suffering are properly considered and controlled. However, achieving such control is far from easy, given the number and variety of working environments, all requiring

1327

workers with different skills, training and qualifications, using different equipment and tools. The consequence is a wide spectrum of potential risk and harm arising from working environments. Inevitably, given the above, the legal and regulatory framework that seeks to manage and ensure levels of safety is possessed with a degree of complication. This chapter does not set out to provide a comprehensive analysis of all applicable health and safety law and practice, but rather outline key legislation, concepts, investigatory powers and offences to provide a practical overview.

KEY LEGISLATION

The Health and Safety at Work etc. Act 1974

23.2 The Health and Safety at Work etc. Act 1974 ('HSWA 1974'), which regulates almost all work activity in the UK with an expressly stated purpose[1] of:

(a)   Securing the health, safety and welfare of persons at work;

(b)   Protecting persons other than persons at work against risks to health and safety arising out of or in connection with the activities of persons at work;

(c)   Controlling the keeping and use of explosive or highly flammable or otherwise dangerous substances, and generally preventing the unlawful acquisition, possession and use of such substances.

[1]   HSWA 1974, s 1(1).

23.3 In general terms, the HSWA 1974 contains provisions setting out the following of key importance:

(a)   The general, non-delegable duties on persons, by virtue of their status as employer, self-employed, person in control of works or occupier, to secure health and safety;

(b)   The power to make secondary health and safety regulations;

(c)   The power to prepare and approve codes of practice;

(d)   The definition and scope of investigative and enforcement powers of health and safety inspectors.

Health and safety regulations

23.4 The existence of differing working environments, all with their own potential risks of harm, make it extremely difficult for a single piece of legislation to adequately cover all likely eventualities, particularly when standards of health and safety change over time. The HSWA 1974 envisages this and provides for the making of secondary regulations[1], of which there are over 150.

[1]   HSWA 1974, s 15.

Approved codes of practice and guidance

23.5 In addition, the HSWA 1974 empowers the Health and Safety Executive ('HSE') to publish Approved Codes of Practice ('ACOPs')[1], which generally offer regulation or industry specific, practical examples of good practice and advice on how to comply with the overarching regulatory regime. It is important to note that unlike the HSWA general duties and health and safety regulations, the ACOPs do not impose any legally enforceable duty. Failure to comply may, however, be taken by a court in criminal proceedings as evidence of failure to comply with the requirements of the HSWA 1974 or health and safety regulations, unless the defendant can show that the requirements were complied with in an equally effective way[2]. Failure to comply with an ACOP is, thus, akin, assuming the ACOP was relevant, to the creation of a rebuttable presumption of a breach of the HSWA 1974 or health and safety regulations.

[1] HSWA 1974, s 16.
[2] HSWA 1974, s 17.

23.6 There is additional guidance published by the HSE to assist in the understanding of and compliance with health and safety law. The principal benefit of the guidance, if followed, is that enforcers generally take the view that the law has been complied with and enforcement action is unlikely to result. So, in effect, there is a three-tiered legislative framework with the HSWA 1974 at the top, health and safety regulations beneath it and finally ACOPs and guidance.

INVESTIGATING AND ENFORCING BODIES

23.7 There are three key bodies responsible for the investigation and enforcement of health and safety issues for the vast majority of working environments: the Health and Safety Executive ('HSE'); local authorities and the Crown Prosecution Service ('CPS').

The Health and Safety Executive

23.8 The HSE is a non-departmental public body, sponsored by the Department for Work and Pensions, with specific statutory functions relating to workplace health, safety and welfare and a stated mission to 'prevent death, injury and ill heath to those at work and others affected by work activities in Great Britain'[1]. It is an independent regulator established by the HSWA 1974[2] with the following primary statutory duties:

- proposing and setting necessary standards for health and safety performance, including submitting proposals to the relevant Secretary of State for health and safety regulations and codes of practice;
- securing compliance with these standards, including making appropriate arrangements for enforcement;
- making such arrangements as it considers appropriate for the carrying out of research and for the publication of the results of research and for encouraging research by others;

- making such arrangements as it considers appropriate for the provision of an information and advisory service, ensuring relevant groups are kept informed of and adequately advised on matters related to health and safety;
- providing Ministers on request with information and expert advice.

¹ See para 1.2 of the HSE Framework Document.
² HSWA 1974, s 10.

23.9 The HSE is the primary enforcing body, easily responsible for the largest number of prosecutions each year, with enforcement carried out by Health and Safety Inspectors. The HSE is not, however, the only enforcing body, with jurisdiction allocated to each by primary and secondary legislation. In essence, the nature of the work activity being conducted dictates which enforcing body will be responsible, although the HSE retains a discretion to investigate 'any accident, occurrence, situation or other matter whatsoever which it thinks it necessary or expedient to investigate for any of the general purposes of this Part or with a view to the making of regulations for those purposes'[1].

¹ HSWA 1974, s 14.

23.10 The HSE will be the enforcing authority for the following <u>work activities</u>:

- Any activity in a mine or quarry.
- Any activity in premises occupied by a radio, television or film undertaking in which the activity of broadcasting, recording or filming is carried on.
- Any activity in a fairground.
- Work undertaken by independent contractors for certain construction works.
- The installation, maintenance or repair of any gas system or any work in relation to gas fitting when undertaken by an independent contractor.
- The installation, maintenance or repair of electricity systems when undertaken by an independent contractor.
- Certain work with ionising radiation when undertaken by an independent contractor.
- The use of ionising radiations for medical exposure.
- Any activity in radiography premises where work with ionising radiation is carried out.
- Agricultural activities including any activities at an agricultural show involving the handling of livestock or working with agricultural equipment.
- Any activity on-board a seagoing ship.
- Any activity in relation to a ski slope, ski lift, ski tow or cable car.
- Fish, maggot and game breeding, except in a zoo.
- The manufacture and supply of industrial products.
- Factories.
- Any activity in relation to a pipeline.
- The operation of a trolley vehicle system.
- Stevedores and other shore-based activities on dock premises.

23.11 The HSE is the enforcing authority for the following <u>bodies</u>, regardless of the work activity undertaken:

- Local authorities.
- Police authorities.
- Parish and community councils.
- Fire and rescue authorities.
- United Kingdom Atomic Energy Authority.
- International headquarters and defence organisations and visiting forces.
- The Crown.

23.12 The HSE will be the enforcing authority for the following <u>premises</u>, regardless of the work activity undertaken:

- Airport land.
- Offshore installations.
- University, college, school campuses and any other educational establishment.
- The common parts of domestic premises.
- Channel Tunnel.
- Building or construction sites.
- Hospitals and doctors' surgeries.
- Certain areas within an airport.

Generally speaking, industrial premises are monitored by the HSE and commercial premises by local authorities[1].

[1] See the Health and Safety (Enforcing Authority) Regulations 1998.

Local authorities

23.13 Each local authority is responsible for the enforcement of safety laws within certain premises and for certain activities in its jurisdictional area. There are over 300 such areas and consistency of approach is, consequently, difficult to achieve. The National Enforcement Code ('the Code'), introduced in May 2013[1], sought to address this issue by recognising the broader focus of many local authorities, allowing for greater involvement of the HSE in directing local authority enforcement activity to balance this, but also setting out four main objectives for local authorities:

(1) Clarifying the roles and responsibilities of business, regulators and professional bodies to ensure a shared understanding on the management of risk;

(2) The adoption of a risk-based regulatory approach with reference to the Code and the HSE's Enforcement Policy Statement, which local authorities are expected to follow and abide by;

(3) Setting out the need for the training and competence of local authority Health and Safety regulators linked to the authorisation and use of the HSWA powers;

(4)   Explaining the arrangements for collection and publication of local authority data and peer review to give an assurance on meeting the requirements of the Code.

¹   With a statutory footing by virtue of s 18 of the HSWA 1974.

23.14 Local authorities will generally be the enforcing authority for the following work activities:

(1)   Sale of goods or the storage of goods for retail or wholesale distribution including warehousing.

(2)   The provision of permanent or temporary residential accommodation including the provision of a site for caravans or campers.

(3)   The display or demonstration of goods at an exhibition for the purposes of offer or advertisement for sale.

(4)   Office activities.

(5)   Catering services including restaurants.

(6)   Consumer services provided in a shop except dry cleaning or radio or television repairs.

(7)   Cleaning coin-operated units in launderettes and similar premises.

(8)   The use of a bath, sauna or solarium, massaging, hair transplanting, skin piercing, manicuring or other cosmetic services and therapeutic treatments except where these activities are carried out under the supervision or control of a registered medical practitioner, dentist, physiotherapist, osteopath or chiropractor.

(9)   The hiring out of pleasure craft for use on inland waters.

(10)   The practice or presentation of the arts, sports, games, entertainment or other cultural or recreational activities except where the main activity is the exhibition of a cave to the public.

(11)   The acre, treatment, accommodation or exhibition of animals, birds or other creatures, except where the main activity is horse breeding or horse training at a stable, or is an agricultural activity or veterinary surgery.

(12)   The activities of undertakers, except where the main activity is embalming or the making of coffins.

(13)   Church worship or religious meetings.

(14)   The provision of car parking facilities within the perimeter of an airport.

(15)   The provision of child care or playgroup or nursery facilities.

(16)   Certain activities relating to the manufacture and storage of explosives.

It is important to note that the responsibility for enforcement can be transferred between the HSE and a local authority by agreement, and the Health and Safety Local Authority Enforcement Liaison Committee ('HELA') exists to assist with consistency in approach and to facilitate cooperation between the HSE and local authorities.

The CPS

23.15 Although the HSE and local authorities are the main enforcing bodies for health and safety legislation, there are a number of others: Fire and Rescue Authorities, the Office of Rail and Road, the Civil Aviation Authority, the Care Quality Commission, for example, and the CPS. Proceedings under the HSWA 1974 shall not be instituted in England and Wales except by an inspector, the

Environment Agency, or by or with the consent of the Director of Public Prosecutions. Accordingly, it is open to the CPS to institute proceedings and given that any death that occurs in the workplace is investigated in accordance with the Work-Related Death Protocol, the CPS often institutes proceedings for manslaughter, accompanied by alternative health and safety offences. Whilst supported by the HSE, local authorities or other relevant enforcement agencies, the police will have primacy of the investigation in these circumstances until they are satisfied, through consultation with the CPS, that no homicide charges against an individual or organisation should be brought. Further guidance can be found in the Work-Related Deaths Protocol[1] which provides practical guidance on the interrelationship between the assorted bodies that investigate fatalities within the workplace.

[1]   https://www.hse.gov.uk/pubns/wrdp2.pdf.

INVESTIGATORY POWERS

Health and safety inspectors

23.16 The principal investigatory powers[1] available to health and safety in-spectors appointed by an enforcing authority[2] are contained within the HSWA 1974[3]. In summary, the powers include the power to:

- Enter premises[4] where there is reason to believe it is necessary.
- Require the premises to remain undisturbed.
- Take measurements and photographs and make recordings.
- Require the production of documents (and to take copies).
- Seize certain articles for examination.
- Question any person whom he has reasonable cause to believe to be able to give relevant information[5].
- Require assistance from any person with respect to matters within that person's control.

[1]   The police have separate powers under the Police and Criminal Evidence Act 1984.
[2]   HSWA 1974, s 19.
[3]   HSWA 1974, s 20.
[4]   'Premises' is widely defined by HSWA 1974, s 53 to include 'any place'.
[5]   This should not be exercised in order to question persons regarding their suspected involvement in an offence.

23.17 In addition, there is an umbrella power of 'any other power which is necessary'[1]. Whilst this power is only exercisable if necessary to carry into effect any of the statutory provisions of the HSWA 1974, it affords an inspector an extremely wide discretion as to steps they can take. Inspectors are also empowered to deal with imminent causes of danger by seizing and, if necessary, destroying it[2]. Inspectors also have the power to issue improvement and prohibition notices, which are dealt with later in this chapter. It is important to note that inspectors are created by statute and as such have only those powers provided to them by statute or through the operation of the common law. They, for instance, have no power of arrest and are not expressly empowered to search, and any use of their powers must be necessary, justified and proportionate. However, obstructing an inspector, contravening inspector imposed requirements, preventing others from answering questions from an inspector or knowingly/recklessly providing false statements are separate criminal offences[3].

1   HSWA 1974, s 20(2)(m).
2   HSWA 1974, s 25.
3   See HSWA 1974, ss 33(1)(h), (e), (f) and (k) respectively.

RIDDOR

23.18 There is a legal obligation under the Reporting of Injuries, Diseases and Dangerous Occurrences Regulations 2013 ('RIDDOR') for 'responsible persons' to report the following to the HSE:

(1)   serious work place accidents;
(2)   occupational diseases; and
(3)   dangerous occurrences.

The definition of a 'responsible person' includes employers, the self-employed and people in control of work premises[1]. Once an incident is reported, the HSE will consider whether an investigation of that incident is required.

1   RIDDOR 2013, reg 3.

Serious work place accidents

23.19 A RIDDOR report must be submitted to the HSE when the accident is:

•   'work-related'; and
•   results in an injury of a type which is reportable.

An accident is 'work-related' if it is an accident arising out of or in connection with work[1].

1   RIDDOR 2013, reg 2.

Types of reportable injury

23.20 There are several types of reportable injury:

Specified Injuries to workers[1] – RIDDOR sets out a list of 'specified injuries' which are reportable when suffered by any person at work. The specified injuries are:

–   fractures, other than to fingers, thumbs and toes;
–   amputations;
–   any injury likely to lead to permanent loss of sight or reduction in sight;
–   any crush injury to the head or torso causing damage to the brain or internal organs;
–   serious burns (including scalding) which:
    •   covers more than 10% of the body; or

- causes significant damage to the eyes, respiratory system or other vital organs;
- any scalping requiring hospital treatment;
- any loss of consciousness caused by head injury or asphyxia; and
- any other injury arising from working in an enclosed space which:
  - leads to hypothermia or heat-induced illness; or
  - requires resuscitation or admittance to hospital for more than 24 hours.

Incapacitation for more than 7 days[2] – If any person at work is unable to work as a result of a work-related injury for more than seven consecutive days then this must be reported to the HSE.

The death of any person[3] – If any person dies as a result of a work-related accident, exposure, or to a biological agent or if an employee suffers a reportable injury under regulation 4 which is a cause of death within one year of the accident, a report must be submitted to the HSE.

Non-fatal accidents to non-workers[4] – If a non-worker is injured and this results in them being taken directly to hospital for treatment or they suffer a specified injury on hospital premises, a report must be submitted to the HSE.

[1] RIDDOR 2013, reg 4(1).
[2] RIDDOR 2013, reg 4(2).
[3] RIDDOR 2013, reg 6.
[4] RIDDOR 2013, reg 5.

23.21 Following the COVID-19 pandemic, the HSE has confirmed that a report should be made under RIDDOR when one of the following circumstances applies. It has noted that the reporting requirements only apply in relation to COVID-19 to occupational exposure:

- an accident or incident at work has, or could have, led to the release or escape of coronavirus (SARS-CoV-2). This must be reported as a dangerous occurrence;
- a person at work (a worker) has been diagnosed as having COVID-19 attributed to an occupational exposure to coronavirus. This must be reported as a case of disease;
- a worker dies as a result of occupational exposure to coronavirus. This must be reported as a work-related death due to exposure to a biological agent.

Occupational diseases

23.22 Responsible persons (broadly, employers and self-employed people are obligated under RIDDOR to submit a report to the HSE if specific occupational diseases are diagnosed as a result of exposure to certain hazards in the workplace[1]. The following occupational diseases are reportable:

- Carpal Tunnel Syndrome;
- cramp of the hand or forearm;
- Occupational dermatitis;
- Hand Arm Vibration Syndrome;

–   occupational asthma;
–   tendonitis or tenosynovitis
–   any occupational cancer; and
–   any disease attributed to an occupational exposure to a biological agent.

These reportable diseases must be diagnosed by a doctor and employees need to evidence the diagnosis by providing their employer with a written note. A verbal diagnosis from a doctor is sufficient for self-employed workers.

[1]   RIDDOR 2013, regs 3(1)(b), 8 and 9.

Dangerous occurrences

23.23 In addition to reporting serious accidents and cases of occupational diseases, the HSE also requires responsible persons to report dangerous occurrences which arise out of or in connection with work. The purpose of reporting near misses is to inform the HSE of circumstances that could cause a serious injury or death so that these situations can be prevented. Schedule 2 of RIDDOR has six parts which set out the different types of reportable dangerous occurrences. The most frequently reported dangerous occurrences are featured in Pt 1 of Sch 2. Part 1 sets out general incidents occurring in the workplace related to: lifting equipment, pressure systems, overhead electric lines, electrical incidents causing explosion or fire, explosions, biological agents, radiation generators and radiography, breathing apparatus, diving operations, collapse of scaffolding, train collisions, wells and pipelines or pipeline works. Further detail regarding dangerous occurrences can be found in the remaining parts of Sch 2, which include dangerous occurrences which are reportable in relation to a mine, quarry, relevant transport system and offshore workplace.

Reporting procedure

23.24 When a serious work place accident, occupational disease or dangerous occurrence arises, it is the duty of a responsible person to report it. The responsible person must notify the HSE of the incident without delay and fill out the appropriate online report. In most situations, the report must be submitted to the HSE within ten days of the incident[1]. Further details in relation to specific scenarios can be found in Schedule 1 of RIDDOR. Also, it should be noted that if the accident causes a fatality or is classed as a specific injury, the responsible person can also report to the HSE by calling the contact centre.

[1]   RIDDOR 2013, Sch 1.

NOTICES

23.25 The HSWA 1974 provides that the HSE and local authorities have the power to serve statutory notices on organisations and individuals to enforce health and safety standards. The two main types of notices available to enforcement bodies are improvement notices and prohibition notices. It is also worth noting that, because the sections of the HSWA 1974 relating to improvement notices and prohibition notices do not apply to Crown bodies, there is a non-statutory equivalent notice called a Crown enforcement notice that enforcing authorities can use to ensure that Crown bodies are upholding the health and safety standards required by the HSWA 1974.

Improvement notices

23.26 Improvement notices are issued when a health and safety inspector is of the view that a duty holder is contravening health and safety legislation or has contravened health and safety legislation in circumstances that indicate that the contravention is likely to continue or be repeated. The improvement notice requires the duty holder to remedy the alleged breach within a set period of time. The notice should contain the following information:

(1)   **Details of the alleged breach** – including the opinion of the Inspector, the specific provisions that appear to have been breached and the reasons why the inspector believes that there has been a breach.

(2)   **Details the requirement to remedy the breach** – the notice cannot require the duty holder to go beyond what is legally required of them, and there should be a discussion between the duty holder and the inspector about how they can comply with the notice.

(3)   **The timescales within which the duty holder must comply with the notice** – this should not be less than 21 days from the date the notice was served.

Prohibition notices

23.27 By issuing a prohibition notice, an inspector can require unsafe activities to be stopped immediately (either on a permanent or temporary basis) until sufficient safety improvements have been made if they consider there to be a serious and imminent risk of personal injury. Alternatively, an inspector can issue a deferred prohibition notice if there is no imminent risk of personal injury and additional risks are likely to arise by immediately stopping the activity. Due to its strict nature, the effect of a prohibition notice can significantly interfere with business activities. A prohibition notice should contain the following details:

(1)   **Details of the alleged breach** – including the opinion of the health and safety inspector and specific information relation to the activity that has given rise to the risk.

(2)   **Instructions to the duty holder to stop the unsafe activity** until the issue has been remedied.

23.28 Following the case of *Harris v Evans*[1], it is unlikely that HSE inspectors owe any duty of care to duty holders when advising on health and safety matters. HSE inspectors cannot ordinarily be liable for negligent misstatement if they give erroneous advice which may lead to the business suffering economic loss.

[1]   *Harris v Evans* [1998] WLR 1285.

Service of notices

23.29 Notices are often directly served on the individual by hand, at their workplace (on site). In circumstances where a notice is served on an employee instead of the person in control, a senior officer of the company must also be informed that the notice has been served. Details of the ways in which a notice can be served are set out in the HSWA 1974[1]. For example, HSWA 1974 provides that service of a notice can take place by post, hand delivery or leaving it at the recipient's proper address or office. For large companies, or organisations with multiple sites, the notice should be served at their registered office to ensure that senior officers are made aware of the notice. The HSE advise that there may also be other ways to serve notices that fall outside of the scope of HSWA 1974. For example, a notice can be served by email, as long as it is addressed to the company director or appropriate senior officer and a request for a receipt of personal acknowledgement is included. If the recipient does not return a receipt of acknowledgement, then the notice should be served again via a method set out in HSWA 1974.

[1]   HSWA 1974, s 46.

Enforcement Notice Register

23.30 The HSE maintain an online public database containing details of any enforcement notices that they issue. Entries appear on the database 5 weeks after they are served (to account for the appeals process) and remain on the database for a period of 5 years.

Non-compliance

23.31 It is a criminal offence to fail to comply with the requirements of either an improvement or prohibition notice[1]. If the recipient of an enforcement notice does not comply with an enforcement notice (and does not appeal it within the relevant timeframe), it cannot challenge the terms of the notice if it is later prosecuted for a failure to comply. The question for a court to consider is whether or not the notice was complied with. It is not required to determine whether or not the notice was validly served or whether the defendant had done all that was reasonably practicable to meet the requirements of the legislation in the first place[2].

[1]   HSWA 1974, s 33(1)(e).
[2]   *Deary v Mansion Hide Upholstery* [1983] ICR 610.

23.32 The Health and Safety (Offences) Act 2008 ('HS(O)A 2008') increased the penalties for breaches of HSWA 1974 for such non-compliance. Non-compliance with health and safety notices is punishable by a fine or imprisonment. In the magistrates' court the maximum sentence for imprisonment is 6 months and, since 12 March 2015, the magistrates' court may impose an unlimited fine. In the Crown Court, an unlimited fine can also be imposed, but there is an increased maximum sentence of imprisonment of 2 years. Since HSOA has been introduced, more offences have been tried in the Crown Court as the aim of the legislation was to impose harsher penalties for health and safety breaches, so that employers and organisations are held accountable for unsafe working practices and therefore take health and safety responsibilities more seriously.

Fees for intervention ('FFI')

23.33 The HSE has the power to recover the costs of their time spent, at an hourly rate, dealing with 'material breaches' of health and safety legislation under the Fees for Intervention Scheme (FFI). Under the Health and Safety and Nuclear (Fees) Regulations 2021, HSE's fees and charges have had an inflationary increase of 2.2% from 1 April 2021[1]. The current hourly rate is £160. FFI aims to encourage compliance with health and safety law and businesses or organisations to remedy issues quickly when they are in believed to be in breach of health and safety legislation.

[1] SI 2021/33.

Appeals

23.34 If a person or organisation receives an Improvement or Prohibition notice they have the right to appeal it within 21 days, starting from the date the notice was served upon them. The appeal must be made to the local Employment Tribunal. When an improvement notice is appealed, the operation of the notice is suspended until the appeal is disposed of or withdrawn[1]. However, when a prohibition notice is appealed, suspension only occurs if the tribunal directs as such following an application from the appellant[2].

[1] HSWA 1974, s 24(3)(a).
[2] HSWA 1974, s 24(3)(b).

23.35 On appeal, the burden of proof falls on the inspector to satisfy the tribunal that, on the balance of probabilities, there was a risk to health and safety[1]. Whilst it must have regard to the expertise of the inspector, the tribunal is required to conduct its own review (de novo) as to whether the decision of the inspector was genuinely held and/or reasonable[2]. It is, therefore, open to the Employment Tribunal to reach its own decision on appeal[3], and the Employment Tribunal can have regard, on appeal, to all available evidence relevant to the state of affairs at the time the notice was served, including information coming to light afterwards[4]. If the notice is successfully appealed it may be cancelled. Alternatively, the tribunal may decide to modify the notice or, if they agree with it in its entirety, they can uphold it[5].

Unless there is a real risk of substantial prejudice which may lead to injustice, an Employment Tribunal is entitled to refuse an application to stay appeals against enforcement notices on the basis that criminal proceedings, in relation to the same set of circumstances, are pending[6].

[1] *Readmans and Another v Leeds City Council* [1992] COD 419.
[2] *Railtrack v Smallwood* [2001] ICR 714.
[3] *Chilcott v Thermal Transfer Limited* [2009] EWHC 2086.
[4] *HM Inspector of Health and Safety v Chevron North Sea Ltd* [2018] UKSC 7, [2018] 2 All ER 295, [2018] 1 WLR 964.
[5] HSWA 1974, s 24(2).
[6] *Shiva Limited v Boyd* [2021] EWHC 371.

CORE OFFENCES

Breach of the employer's general duties under the HSWA 1974

23.36 Section 33(1) HSWA 1974 creates a number of offences. The most commonly prosecuted offences under HSWA are in relation to the employer's general duties under ss 2 and 3. Section 33(1) of the Act provides:

> 'It is an offence for a person a) to fail to discharge a duty to which he is subject to by virtue of ss 2 to 7'.

Section 2 HSWA

23.37 Section 2(1) HSWA 1974 imposes a duty on employers to ensure, so far as is reasonably practicable, the health, safety and welfare at work of all its employees.

This general duty is further particularised in s 2(2) and extends to:

(a)   the provision and maintenance of plant and systems of work that are, so far as is reasonably practicable, safe and without risks to health;

(b)   arrangements for ensuring, so far as is reasonably practicable, safety and absence of risks to health in connection with the use, handling, storage, and transport of articles and substances;

(c)   the provision of such information, instruction, training and supervision as is necessary to ensure, so far as is reasonably practicable, the health and safety at work of his employees;

(d)   so far as is reasonably practicable as regards any place of work under the employer's control, the maintenance of it in a condition that is safe and without risks to health and the provision and maintenance of means of access to and egress from it that are safe and without such risks;

(e)   the provision and maintenance of a working environment for his employees that is, so far as is reasonably practicable, safe, without risks to health, and adequate as regards facilities and arrangements for their welfare at work.

Section 53 HSWA 1974 sets out the definition of an employee[1]. It is a question a fact as to whether a person is deemed an 'employee' for the purpose of s 2(1) of HSWA 1974. A casual worker who had been working on the building of a house extension was sufficiently controlled by his employer to qualify as an employee under s 53 of HSWA 1974. Accordingly, the employer was liable for offences under s 33(1)(a) and s 33(1)(c) when the worker suffered severe brain injuries when he fell from a raised platform at the site[2].

---

[1]   'Employee' means an individual who works under a contract of employment or is treated by s 51A as being an employee.

[2]   *R v Pola (Shah Nawaz)* [2009] EWCA Crim 655, [2010] 1 Cr App R (S).

23.38

Example offence

Statement of offence

EMPLOYER FAILING TO DISCHARGE ITS DUTY TO ENSURE THE SAFETY OF ITS EMPLOYEES, contrary to section 33(1)(a) and section 2(1) of the Health and Safety at Work etc. Act 1974.

Particulars of offence

On [date] X Limited, an employer, failed to discharge the duty imposed on it by section 2(1) of the Health and Safety at Work etc. Act 1974 to ensure so far as was reasonably practicable, the health safety and welfare at work of its employees, in that [Particulars].

Section 3 HSWA 1974

23.39 Section 3 HSWA 1974 imposes a duty on the employer to conduct his undertaking in such a way to ensure, so far as is reasonably practicable, that persons not in his employment who may be affected thereby are not thereby exposed to risks to their health or safety. Both duties under ss 2 and 3 HSWA 1974 seek only to create criminal liability and are non-delegable duties. When establishing its case against an employer, the prosecution does not have to prove that harm resulted from the breach. In relation to s 2, the prosecution must simply prove, beyond all reasonable doubt, that the defendant is the employer and that it exposed its employee(s) at work to a material risk to their health and safety[1]. Causation between the breach and any resulting accident does not need to be proven. It is simply that there was a 'risk' to the employees' safety[2]. More often than not, evidence of an accident is sufficient to demonstrate that there was a material risk. In relation to s 3, the position is very similar in that the prosecution must prove that the defendant is the employer and that it failed to conduct its undertaking in a way to ensure that persons not in his employment were exposed to risks to their health and safety.

[1]   *R v Chargot* [2009] 2 All ER 645.
[2]   *R v Board of Trustees of the Science Museum* [1993] 3 All ER 853.

23.40 In *R v Associated Octel Co Ltd*[1] the House of Lords considered the question of whether the activity causing the harm, or risk of harm, formed part of an organisation's undertaking. The defendant was a chemicals company that had engaged a firm of independent contractors to repair the lining of a chemical tank. In the course of repair, an employee of the contractor was seriously injured. The judge at first instance held that the repair of the tank was part of Associated Octel's undertaking, even though it had been sub-contracted out. The House of Lords dismissed the appeal, holding that there is a difference between an employer's vicarious liability, which in general required that the tortfeasor be an employee acting under his contract of employment, and the duty imposed on the employer himself under s 3 of the HSWA 1974. Whether the tasks the contractor was engaged in formed part of the employer's undertaking was ultimately a question of fact for the jury.

[1]   *R v Associated Octel Co Ltd* [1996] 1 WLR 1543.

23.41

Example offence

Statement of offence

EMPLOYER FAILING TO DISCHARGE ITS DUTY TO ENSURE THE SAFETY OF AFFECTED PERSONS, contrary to section 33(1)(a) and section 3(1) of the Health and Safety at Work etc. Act 1974.

Particulars of offence

On [date] X Limited, an employer, failed to discharge the duty imposed on it by section 3(1) of the Health and Safety at Work etc. Act 1974 to conduct its undertaking in such a way as to ensure, so far as was reasonably practicable, that persons not in its employment who may have been affected thereby were not exposed to risks to their health or safety, in that X Limited failed to [particulars].

Breach of the general duties under the HSWA 1974

23.42 In addition to the general employer duties under ss 2 and 3 referred to above, s 33(1) HSWA 1974 also created 3 general duties, namely, s 4, 6 and 7 HSWA 1974[1].

[1] HSWA 1974, s 5 (repealed).

Section 4 HSWA 1974

23.43 Section 4 HSWA 1974 imposes a duty on persons concerned with premises in relation to those who:

(a) are not their employees; but
(b) use non-domestic premises made available to them as a place of work or as a place where they may use plant or substances provided for their use there.

23.44 Section 4(2) states that it shall be the duty of each person who has, to any extent, control of premises to which this section applies or of the means of access thereto or egress therefrom or of any plant or substance in such premises to take such measures as it is reasonable for a person in his position to take to ensure, so far as is reasonably practicable, that the premises, all means of access thereto or egress therefrom available for use by persons using the premises, and any plant or substance in the premises or, as the case may be, provided for use there, is or are safe and without risks to health. The duty is owed to non-employees in non-domestic premises by those persons who have a degree of control over the premises. For example, this duty would be applicable to a person who has control over the premises by way of a tenancy or lease and may have an obligation in relation to maintenance, for example. A duty is imposed on that person to ensure the premises are safe and without risks to health. There may be more than one duty holder that owes this duty.

23.45

Example offence

Statement of offence

FAILING TO DISCHARGE DUTY TO ENSURE THE SAFETY OF PREMISES, contrary to section 33(1)(a) and section 4(2) of the Health and Safety at Work etc. Act 1974.

Particulars of offence

On [date] X Limited had control of the premises at [address] and X Limited failed to discharge the duty imposed on it by section 4 of the Health and Safety at Work etc. Act 1974 to take such measures as were reasonable for a person in its position to take to ensure, so far as was reasonably practicable, that the premises were safe and without risk to health, namely [detail].

Section 6 HSWA 1974

23.46 Section 6 HSWA 1974 imposes a duty on any person who designs, manufactures, imports or supplies any article for use at work or any article of fairground equipment:

(a) to ensure, so far as is reasonably practicable, that the article is so designed and constructed that it will be safe and without risks to health at all times when it is being set, used, cleaned or maintained by a person at work;

(b) to carry out or arrange for the carrying out of such testing and examination as may be necessary for the performance of the duty imposed on him by the preceding paragraph;

(c) to take such steps as are necessary to secure that persons supplied by that person with the article are provided with adequate information about the use for which the article is designed or has been tested and about any conditions necessary to ensure that it will be safe and without risks to health at all such times as are mentioned in paragraph (a) above and when it is being dismantled or disposed of; and

(d) to take such steps as are necessary to secure, so far as is reasonably practicable, that persons so supplied are provided with all such revisions of information provided to them by virtue of the preceding paragraph as are necessary by reason of its becoming known that anything gives rise to a serious risk to health and safety.

23.47 The s6 offence extends only to things done in the course of a trade, business or other undertaking and to matters within his control. Furthermore, for an offence to be created under s 6, the way in which the risk arises must be one that could have reasonably be foreseen by the person in control.

Section 7 HSWA 1974

23.48 Section 7 HSWA 1974 imposes a duty on every employee while at work-

(a) to take reasonable care for the health and safety of himself and of other persons who may be affected by his acts or omissions at work; and

(b)   as regards any duty or requirement imposed on his employer or any other person by or under any of the relevant statutory provisions, to co-operate with him so far as is necessary to enable that duty or requirement to be performed or complied with.

23.49 In recent years, there has been an increase in prosecutions of employees under s 7. While it remains the case that the focus is largely on the employer and the discharge of its duties, the HSE and Local authorities look at the entire management chain when assessing breaches of health and safety legislation. The duty placed on an employee is different to the general duty placed on an employer in so far as the employee must fail to take reasonable care by way of an act or omission. If there is an omission to act, then that omission must be part of the employee's duty or responsibility to act in such a way as part of his work.

Breach of other health and safety regulations

23.50 As mentioned in the key legislation section above, the HSWA 1974 provides for the making of secondary regulations of which there are over 150. Section 33(1)(c) makes it an offence to contravene any health and safety regulations. Liability for a breach of health and safety regulations is different to a breach of one of the general duties set out above. Many health and safety regulations are absolute and impose strict liability duties on employers. Some health and safety regulations are qualified by 'reasonable practicability' i.e. similar to the duties under ss 2 and 3 HSWA 1974. Whereas other regulations, create a defence involving 'reasonable practicability' and due diligence. For example, it may be defence for a person to prove that it took all reasonable precautions and exercised all due diligence to avoid the commission of the offence.

23.51 When relying on the defence of reasonable practicability and due diligence, it is important to note regulation 21 of the Management of Health and Safety at Work Regulations 1999 which states that an employer will not be afforded a defence in any criminal proceedings for a contravention of health and safety provisions by reason of any act or default of an employee of the employer. The obligation is therefore on the employer to demonstrate reasonable practicability and all due diligence. It cannot place blame at the door of its employees.

23.52 At the time of writing, the UK population is in the process of returning to work following the lockdown measures applied by the government in response to the Covid-19 global pandemic. In order to ensure a workplace is 'Covid-secure', the government has issued a number of guidance documents to assist employers. The guidance requires employers to carry out Covid specific risk assessments and to take appropriate measures to guard against the risk of the spread of disease amongst employees and members of the public. The HSWA 1974 was drafted in order to reduce or eliminate risks arising from the 'undertaking' or workplace. With a virus that is so prevalent in the community, it will be interesting to see what, if any, Covid-19 specific enforcement action is taken over the coming months and how the HSE approach it.

Most frequently enforced regulations

23.53 Most often, criminal proceedings for health and safety breaches are brought under the general duties outlined above in ss 2 and 3 HSWA 1974. Where a prosecution is not brought under one of the general duties, a prosecution can be brought in relation to a specific breach under one of the many sets of health and safety regulations. Such regulations are specific to a particular aspect of workplace safety.

23.54 For specific regulatory breaches, the most frequently enforced regulations are:

- The Management of Health and Safety at Work Regulations 1999[1] (duty to conduct suitable and sufficient risk assessments, safe systems of work, manage risk responsibly, provide sufficient training and instruction)
- The Construction (Design and Management) Regulations 2015[2] (duty to ensure construction projects are carried out in a way that secures health and safety)
- The Control of Asbestos Regulations 2012[3] (ensures those responsible for maintaining a non-domestic premises manage the risks of exposure to asbestos)
- The Work at Height Regulations 2005[4] (duty to keep employees safe at height, provide suitable equipment, plan work appropriately)
- Lifting Operations and Lifting Equipment Regulations 1998[5] (duty to maintain lifting equipment)
- Provision and Use of Work Equipment Regulations 1998[6] (provision and maintenance of work equipment)
- Electricity at Work Regulations 1989[7] (safe management of electrical equipment at work)
- The Control of Substances Hazardous to Health Regulations 2002[8] (safe management of chemical substances in the workplace)

[1] SI 1999/3242.
[2] SI 2015/51.
[3] SI 2012/632.
[4] SI 2005/735.
[5] SI 1998/2307.
[6] SI 1998/2306.
[7] SI 1989/635.
[8] SI 2002/2677.

LIABILITY OF DIRECTORS

23.55 It is an offence under s 37(1) HSWA 1974 if a breach of any relevant statutory provision committed by a body corporate is proved to have been committed with the consent or connivance of, or to have been attributable to any neglect on the part of, any director, manager, secretary or other such similar officer of the body corporate or a person who was purporting to act in such a capacity. Directors' liability is covered in detail in Chapter 4 Criminal Enforcement.

DEFENCES

23.56 Unlike many criminal offences, in a health and safety offence under ss 2 and 3 HSWA 1974, once the prosecution has established that an employer exposed an employee or third party to a material risk through the conduct of its undertaking, it is for the employer to establish, on the balance of probabilities, that it had taken all reasonably practicable steps to reduce or eliminate the risk. The burden of proof therefore shifts to the employer[1]. There is no requirement for the prosecution to prove that a person who was the company's 'directing mind' had failed to take reasonable precautions. It is sufficient that those precautions had not been taken by the servants and agents of the company on its behalf[2]. Furthermore, in asking the jury to consider whether a defendant had established that it had done all that was reasonably practicable, the defendant is permitted to adduce evidence in support of its case that it had taken all reasonable steps to eliminate the likelihood of the relevant risk eventuating[3].

[1]   HSWA 1974, s 40.
[2]   *R v Gateway Foodmarkets Ltd* [1997] 3 All ER 78.
[3]   *R v HTM* [2006] EWCA Crim 1156, [2007] 2 All ER 665.

23.57 Section 40 requires:

'In any proceedings for an offence under any of the relevant statutory provisions consisting of a failure to comply with a duty or requirement to do something so far as is practicable or so far as is reasonably practicable, or to use the best practicable means to do something, it shall be for the accused to prove (as the case may be) that it was not practicable or not reasonably practicable to do more than was in fact done to satisfy the duty or requirement, or that there was no better practicable means than was in fact used to satisfy the duty or requirement.'

23.58 The defence was considered in the lead authority *R v Chargot Ltd. Trading as Contract Services, Ruttle Contracting Ltd.*, George Henry Ruttle[1]. Where it was stated that:

'Section (2 and) 3 impose a duty to ensure a state of affairs, so far as is reasonably practicable. Section 33 makes a breach of the duty an offence; but s 40 imposes the obligation on the defence to establish that they had done everything reasonably necessary to ensure that state of affairs'.

[1]   Per Latham J. (2007) EWCA Crim 3032.

23.59 Risk has been considered at length by the appellate court. *R v Porter*[1] considered whether there was a 'risk' arising from the use of a set of steps at a child's school playground which had been in use for generations.

'We acknowledge that the fact that an accident is unavoidable goes primarily to the reasonable practicability of the measures which a defendant might take, rather than the risk to safety. But that is not exclusively so. As we have said, that the risk is part of the everyday incidence of life goes to the issue as to whether an injured person was exposed to risk. Where the risk can truly be said to be part of the incidence of everyday life, it is less likely that the injured person could be said to have been exposed to by the conduct of the operations in question. The judge fairly put that to the jury in his summing-up: He said: "What you must decide is whether there was an unacceptable risk. The trivial risks of everyday life are not unacceptable. They are simply a fact of life, are they not?"'

[1]   (2008) EWCA Crim 1271.

23.60 In *Chargot*, Lord Hope of Craighead stated:

' . . . when the legislation refers to risk it is not contemplating risks that are trivial or fanciful. It is not its purpose to impose burdens on employers that are wholly unreasonable. Its aim is to spell out the basic duty of an employer to create a safe working environment . . . . The law does not aim to create an environment that is entirely risk free. It concerns itself with risks that are material. That, in effect, is what the word "risk" which the statute uses means. It is directed at situations where there is a material risk to health and safety, which any reasonable person would appreciate and take stapes to guard against'.

23.61 The restriction of the employer duty under ss 2 and 3 HSWA 1974 for ensuring safety 'so far as is reasonably practicable' was challenged by the Commission of the European Communities in Case C-127/05 EEC. The Commission was of the view that restricting the duty to 'so far as is reasonably practicable' made it incompatible with the EC's Framework Directive[1] which required employers to 'ensure the safety and health of workers in every aspect related to the work'[2]. The Court rejected this argument. The assessment of what is 'reasonably practicable' has often been referred to as a cost-benefit analysis. However, it is more than that. It is an assessment of the risk, on one hand, which includes the likelihood of the harm that may be caused, and the severity of any injury weighed against the sacrifice, whether that be time, money, effort, or resources on the other hand. These two factors need to be weighed against each other in order to determine whether there is a gross disproportion between them in order to make the step not a reasonably practicable one to take.

[1] 89/391/EEC.
[2] Article 5(1) Framework Directive (89/391/EEC).

23.62 The determination of what is 'reasonably practicable' is far from easy. It is generally a question of fact in each case. Foreseeability of risk is an important aspect when considering the extent of the reasonably practicable measures an employer could have taken. If the risk is not foreseeable, it therefore seems unlikely that it could be reasonably practicable to take steps to guard against it[1]. As set out above, this will ultimately be a jury question in each case.

[1] *R v Tangerine Confectionary Ltd* (2012) 176 JP 349.

MANSLAUGHTER

23.63 In relation to offences of manslaughter arising out of workplace fatalities, there are two relevant offences:

- Gross negligence manslaughter;
- Corporate manslaughter.

23.64 The offence of gross negligence manslaughter is an offence committed by an individual and is subject to common law principles. An individual is guilty of gross negligence manslaughter if he or she owed a duty of care in negligence to the deceased; was in gross breach of that duty of care; and that such breach is a substantial cause of that person's death. The prosecution must prove all elements of the offence to the criminal standard of proof. It is a hard test to meet and the jury must be sure that the defendant's conduct was 'so bad in all the circumstances as to amount to a criminal act or omission'[1].

[1]   *R v Adomako* [1995] 1 AC 171.

23.65 Up until 2008, the offence of corporate manslaughter was a common law offence whereby, in order to secure a conviction against the company, the prosecution had to prove that an individual of the company was its 'guiding mind'. Since the introduction of the Corporate Manslaughter and Corporate Homicide Act 2007 ('CMA'), which came into force on 6 April 2008, there is no longer the need to identify a 'guiding mind' of the company. The new statutory offence[1] is committed by an organisation where:

- the organisation owed a relevant duty of care to the deceased; and
- the way in which its activities are managed or organised:
  - caused a person's death; and
  - amounted to a gross breach of that duty of care owed by the organisation to the deceased.

[1]   CMA 2007, s 1.

23.66 The organisation is only guilty of the offence if the way in which its activities are managed or organised by its senior management is a substantial element of the breach. Senior management is defined as those who play significant roles in:

- the making of decisions about how the whole or a substantial part of its activities are to be managed or organised; or
- the actual managing or organising of the whole or a substantial part of those activities.

There is no definition in the CMA as to what amounts to 'substantial' both in the sense of the extent to which the activities need to be a 'substantial' part of the organisation and the extent in which the activities are managed by senior management is a 'substantial' element of the breach.

CORONER'S INQUESTS

23.67 Any work related death will be reported to the Coroner. A Coroner's inquest is an entirely separate inquiry to any police investigation. An inquest is a fact finding process to establish the answers to four questions: who died; where they died; when they died; and how they died. The decision as to 'how a deceased came by his/her death can often be contentious. The Coroner or jury can only reach a conclusion that does not apportion any blame (criminal or civil) on any person. The conclusion must be a factual conclusion.

SENTENCING

Corporate manslaughter and health and safety

23.68 For many years, sentences applied to breaches of health and safety legislation were considered to be too low, inconsistently delivered across different courts and were not sufficiently adequate to 'bring the message' home to shareholders about the importance of health and safety compliance. In 2016, the Sentencing Council issued the Definitive Sentencing Guidelines for Health and Safety Offences which applied to all cases sentenced on or after 1 February 2016. The Guideline applies to all health and safety offences committed by organisations and individuals. It also applies to corporate manslaughter offences. There is a separate guideline in place for gross negligence manslaughter – see below.

Health and safety offences

23.69 When sentencing for health and safety offences, the court is required to adopt the guideline which comprises 9 separate steps.

Step 1 – Culpability and harm

CULPABILITY

23.70 There are four ranges of culpability; very high, high, medium; and low. As you would expect, for flagrant disregard or deliberate breaches of health and safety, you might expect the defendant's culpability would be placed at the highest level. In cases where the defendant has made significant efforts to address the risk to health and safety and, on one occasion only, fell short of the appropriate standard you might expect the court to assess such a case as low culpability. What often remains open to great debate between the prosecution and defence (and ultimately decided by the sentencing judge) is where the level of culpability rests. The difference between whether a defendant fell short or far short of the appropriate standard is not always clear cut and can include a combination of both medium and high levels of culpability.

HARM

23.71 The second stage of step 1 is determining the level of harm category. The assessment of harm is a two-stage process whereby the court must consider:

• The seriousness of harm risked (A, B or C) by the offender's breach; and
• The likelihood of that harm arising (high, medium or low).

In relation to seriousness, this is split into three categories – A, B and C. Level A is the risk of death or physical or mental impairment resulting in lifelong dependency on third party care for basic needs, and significantly reduced life expectancy. Level B is physical or mental impairment, not amounting to level A, which has a substantial and long-term effect on the sufferer's ability to carry out normal day-to-day activities or on their ability to return to work; a progressive, permanent or irreversible condition. Level C is all other cases not falling within level A or level B.

23.72 In relation to likelihood of harm, there are three categories; high, medium, and low. The court then assesses the seriousness of the harm risked balanced against the likelihood of that harm arising. This gives an overall harm category ranging from 1 to 4, with 1 being the most serious. It is important to note that an assessment of harm is in relation to the harm 'risked'. There does not need to be actual harm caused. When assessing the likelihood of the harm arising, it has become more common to obtain expert evidence in relation to this. In *R v Squibb Group Ltd*[1] the defendant had adduced expert evidence in relation to the risk of its employees contracting an asbestos related disease as a result of their likely level of exposure. The trial judge disagreed (without explanation) with the appellant's expert's statistical evidence of risk and the Court of Appeal found the trial judge was wrong to do so.

[1]   *R v Squibb Group Ltd* [2019] EWCA Crim 227.

23.73 Once the harm category has been determined, the court must then consider 2 further factors in assigning the final harm category:

•   whether the offence exposed a number of workers or members of the public to the risk of harm;
•   whether the offence was a significant cause of actual harm.

If one or both of these factors apply, the court must consider moving up a harm category or substantially moving up within the category.

Step 2 – Turnover

23.74 Having determined the offence category, the court must then look at the turnover of the organisation in order to determine a starting point for any fine. Organisations are categorised as follows in accordance with their turnover:

•   Micro: Turnover not more than £2m
•   Small: Turnover between £2m and £10m
•   Medium: Turnover between £10m and £50m
•   Large: Turnover £50m and over

For an organisation with a turnover that very greatly exceeds the threshold for large organisations, the Sentencing Guideline states that it may be necessary to move outside the suggested range to achieve a proportionate sentence.

23.75 Once the turnover category is determined, a starting point and sentencing range is set out in a tabular format which assists the court in assessing where the level of fine should be pitched in accordance with the previously determined levels of culpability and harm determined at step 1. The court will then move up and down within the sentencing range depending on the aggravating and mitigating features of the offence. Aggravating features include relevant previous convictions; failure to heed warnings; cost cutting at the expense of safety. Mitigating features include a good health and safety record; high levels of co-operation with the investigation.

Step 3 – 'Step back' and review

23.76 In order to ensure the fine is proportionate to the overall means of the offender and that it fulfils the objectives of sentencing, the court should 'step back' and review the fine. Factors that may be taken into consideration are, for example, where an organisation has a large turnover but a very small profit margin. The court may adjust the fine upwards or downwards, including outside the range. In *R v Whirlpool Appliances*[1] it was noted that the guidelines did not dictate an arithmetic approach to the calculation of a fine for a very large organisation, there should be no linear approach.

[1] *R v Whirlpool Appliances* [2017] EWCA Crim 2186.

Step 4 – Other factors that may warrant adjustment

23.77 Having gone through steps 1–3, the court must then consider any wider impacts of the fine within the organisation or on third parties. This is likely to be relevant to charities or public sector organisations where the money spent on a fine is likely to impact on the organisation's ability to improve conditions in the organisation in order to comply with the law or impact on staff or the local economy.

Step 5 – Assistance to the prosecution

23.78 At step 5, there is a further ability for the court to further reduce the fine if there has been assistance provided to the prosecution. This is different to co-operation with the authorities identified at step 2 and is unlikely in most cases.

Step 6 – Reduction for guilty plea

23.79 Any fine should be reduced in accordance with the Sentencing Council's guideline on 'Reduction in Sentence for a Guilty Plea'. A guilty plea entered at the first available opportunity is entitled to a reduction of one third off the fine. A sliding scale is applied for guilty pleas entered after the first available opportunity.

Step 7 – Ancillary orders

23.80 At this step, the court is required to consider whether any ancillary orders should be made such as compensation to a victim; remediation; or forfeiture. As with step 5, it is unlikely that this will apply in many cases.

Step 8 – Totality

23.81 At this stage, the court will consider the overall penalty and ensure that it is just and proportionate in all the circumstances. This will include a case whereby there is more than one charge that is being sentenced. Rather than applying a separate substantial penalty for each offence, the court will look at the totality of offending to ensure the fine is reasonable.

Step 9 – Reasons

23.82 The court is required to give reasons for its decision.

Corporate manslaughter offences

23.83 The approach to sentencing offences of corporate manslaughter is very similar to the approach set out above in relation to health and safety offences. The key difference is the basis upon which the court assesses the level of culpability of the offender. By definition, the harm and culpability involved in corporate manslaughter will be very serious. Factors that affect the level of seriousness include:

- How foreseeable was the serious injury?
- How far short of the appropriate standard did the offender fall?
- How common is this kind of breach in this organisation?
- Was there more than one death, or a high risk of further deaths, or serious personal injury in addition to death?

Where the answers to the above questions indicate a high level of harm or culpability, the offence is category A. Where the culpability and harm is lower, the category is B. Organisations are then fined in accordance with their turnover and the other factors taken into account at steps 2–9 above.

Gross negligence manslaughter

23.84 Individuals convicted of gross negligence manslaughter are sentenced in accordance with the Sentencing Council's Guidelines for Gross Negligence Manslaughter. As one might expect the principles set out above in relation to the sentencing of organisations for corporate manslaughter and health and safety offences are very similar to those set out in the guideline for gross negligence manslaughter. It is important to note that the guideline applies to all types of gross negligence manslaughter and not just those offences arising out of workplace fatalities. Culpability is set out in accordance with levels of very high; high; medium; and low. At step 2, rather than levels of fine, the guideline sets out appropriate periods of custody. As such, the guideline also considers how 'dangerous' the offender is and whether time spent on bail should be taken into account. The most serious offences can see periods of imprisonment of up to 18 years.

SCHEDULES OF MATTERS IN AGREEMENT/DISAGREEMENT

23.85 Health and safety prosecutions are often complex and involve many variables. The criminal courts have sought to simplify the sentencing process by requiring the preparation of detailed schedules by the parties setting out their respective positions. In the case of *R v Friskies Petcare (UK) Ltd*[1] Bedlam LJ stated:

'Problems can, however, arise when there is dispute as to whether the lower court sentenced upon the basis on which the case was presented to it. This case illustrates that problem very well and we recommend, that in this type of case, when the Health and Safety Executive commence proceedings, it should list in writing for the assistance of the court not merely the facts of the case, but the aggravating features, as set out in the Howe case, which it says exist in the particular case. That document can be served upon the Court and upon the defendants for the latter to consider. If it be, as very frequently is the case, that the defendants plead guilty, the defendants themselves should submit a similar document in writing outlining the mitigating features that the court is to take into account. It may well be — and no doubt in many cases is — the case that by the time the matter comes to court there is agreement between the parties as to which are the relevant mitigating and aggravating features that the court should take into account. If the plea therefore is upon an agreed basis, that agreed basis should be put into writing so that there is no doubt whatever what is the proper basis upon which the court should pass sentence.'

Following the case of *R v Kenneth Thelwall*[2], both the prosecution and defence are discouraged from relying on previous case law during the sentencing exercise. It is the sentencing guideline that should now be followed, rather than factual comparisons to previous authority.

1   *R v Friskies Petcare (UK) Ltd* (2003) 3 WLUK 273.
2   *R v Kenneth Thelwall* [2016] EWCA Crim 1755.

BREXIT

23.86 Inevitably, consideration must be given to the current and potential future consequences of Brexit on the health and safety landscape. On 24 December 2020, the UK and EU signed a deal on the Trade Co-Operation Agreement (EU-UK TCA). This does not have a significant impact on the regulation and enforcement of health and safety policy and statute. The HSWA 1974 is of British rather than EU origin and has, therefore, remained the UK's primary source of health and safety law. The HSE has also made clear that the legal duties to protect health and safety of people affected by work will not change with Brexit. However, certain health and safety regulations do make reference to EU law.

23.87 This has been dealt with by new statutory instruments that simply convert references to those EU regulations into domestic law:

- Chemicals (Health and Safety) and Genetically Modified Organisms (Contained Use) (Amendments etc) (EU Exit) Regulations 2019[1].
- Health and Safety (Amendment) (EU Exit) Regulations 2018[2].
- Health and Safety (Amendment) (Northern Ireland) (EU Exit) Regulations 2018[3].

The EU, however, will no longer be involved in the setting of safety standards for the UK, which may have an impact on those future standards.

1   SI 2019/720.
2   SI 2018/1370.
3   SI 2018/1377.

COVID-19

23.88 The COVID-19 pandemic has seen an unprecedented change in the way in which health and safety is approached. From a regulatory perspective, whilst there has been an expectation on those that can work from home to do so, health and safety principles have continued to be upheld by the relevant authorities. Although a significant proportion of employees did not enter their employment premises during the height of the COVID pandemic, employers' legal duties and obligations continued regardless. For instance, the s 2(1) HSWA 1974 duty to ensure, so far as is reasonably practicable, the health, safety and welfare at work of all its employees remains applicable. This applies to both the workplace and the home working environment.

Risk assessments are critical to health and safety compliance and given the high transmissibility of the disease, have become increasingly more important. It is crucial that any risk assessment contemplates all risks and implements the most reasonably practicable control measures to reduce the spread of the disease in the workplace. This will include controls such as adequate ventilation, sufficient cleaning and good hand hygiene. Whilst 19 July 2021 saw a number of COVID restrictions end (such as the social distancing guidance), the risk of transmission remains significant, and businesses will need to continue to protect themselves and their employees from potential outbreaks. This means regular reviews and updates to correspond with any changes in the law. Failing to complete a COVID-19 risk assessment or put into place the measures resulting from a risk assessment could constitute a breach of the HSWA 1974.

The HSE has continued to undertake random spot-checks on all types of businesses to ensure that they remain COVID-secure. Refusing to participate in a spot check could lead to enforcement action being taken. The HSE's approach to regulating health and safety is based on principles published in its Enforcement Policy Statement, which requires 'enforcement action to be proportionate to the risk and to the seriousness of the breach'[1]. It also relies on guidance from its Enforcement Management Model (EMM) to ascertain hazards and control measures observed during visits to determine actual risks and compliance levels. This has been used for over 20 years and has not changed as a result of the pandemic.

It is anticipated that health and safety enforcement of COVID-19 will continue to apply until the virus is no longer a threat to public health in a workplace setting. Expect guidance to be continually updated and reviewed for the foreseeable future.

[1]   Enforcement Policy Statement (hse.gov.uk).

23.89 In respect of local authorities, since 2 December 2020, additional powers have been granted that enable enforcement action against businesses who do not comply with COVID-secure rules, such as mask wearing and social distancing. There are three types of enforcement notice:

- Coronavirus Improvement Notice:
  - Seen as a 'first step' in non-compliance to remedy non-safe practices. Applied for a minimum of 48 hours. Failure to comply could lead to a £2,000 fine.

- Coronavirus Restriction Notice:
  - — A breach of the relevant COVID regulations has occurred which has opened the business to an exposure of the virus. Application of the notice last for 7 days. Failure to comply will lead to a £4,000 fine or Coronavirus Immediate Restriction Notice being issued.
- Coronavirus Immediate Restriction Notice:
  - — Immediate action is required to stop the spread of the virus. Closure of the premises is mandated for a minimum of 48 hours. Failure to comply will result in a £4,000 fine.

Chapter 24

HEALTH AND MEDICINE

Contents

COSMETICS

Introduction

24.1 The regulation of cosmetic products is governed by the EU Cosmetic Products Regulation 2009[1] ('EUCPR'), which now forms part of the body of retained EU law, as amended by Sch 34 to the Product Safety and Metrology etc. (Amendment) Regulations 2019[2]. The enforcement provisions are provided by the Cosmetic Products Enforcement Regulations 2013[3] ('CPER 2013').

[1]   (EC) No 1223/2009.
[2]   SI 2019/696.
[3]   SI 2013/1478.

24.2 EUCPR, Art 2(1)(a), defines cosmetic products as follows:

'Any substance or mixture intended to be placed in contact with the external parts of the human body (epidermis, hair system, nails, lips and external genital organs) or with the teeth and the mucous membranes of the oral cavity with a view exclusively or mainly to cleaning them, perfuming them, changing their appearance, protecting them, keeping them in good condition or correcting body odours.'

24.3 'Substance' means a chemical element and its compounds in the natural state or obtained by any manufacturing process, including any additive necessary to preserve its stability and any impurity deriving from the process used but excluding any solvent which may be separated without affecting the stability of the substance or changing its composition[1]. 'Mixture means a mixture or solution composed of two or more substances[2]. A non-corrective colour contact lens was not a cosmetic product that fell within the EUCPR, notwithstanding an express statement on the packaging that the product was a 'cosmetic eye accessory, subject to the EU Cosmetics Directive', as (1) lenses could not be said to be either a substance or a mixture, (2) the cornea is not one of the parts of the body listed in Art 2(1)(a), and (3) the function of the lens was not to clean, perfume, change the appearance of, protect or keep in good condition any of the parts of the body that are listed[3].

[1]   (EC) No 1223/2009, Art 2(1)(b).
[2]   (EC) No 1223/2009, Art 2(1)(c).
[3]   *Colena AG v Karnevalservice Bastian GmbH* Case C-321/14.

Safety

Definition of safety

24.4 EUCPR, Art 3 provides that cosmetic products made available on the market shall be safe for human health when used under normal or reasonable foreseeable conditions of use, taking account of their presentation, labelling, instructions for use and any other indication or information provided.

Composition

24.5 EUCPR, Art 14 makes provision as to substances that cosmetic products shall not contain. Annex II makes provision as to substances which are prohibited in cosmetic products. Annex III makes provision as to substances which cosmetic products must not contain, except subject to the restrictions laid down. Annex IV makes provision as to colorants allowed. Annex V makes provision as to preservatives allowed. Annex VI makes provision as to UV filters allowed. EUCPR, Art 16 makes provision as to cosmetic products that contain nanomaterials.

Animal testing

24.6 EUCPR, Art 18 prohibits placing on the market any cosmetic product where the final formulation, or the ingredients or combinations of ingredients, have been the subject of animal testing in order to meet the requirements of EUCPR, and prohibits the undertaking of any such testing in the United Kingdom. The prohibition on placing on the market in these circumstances extends to animal testing carried out overseas[1].

[1]   *European Federation for Cosmetic Ingredients v Secretary of State for Business, Innovation and Skills* C-592/14.

24.7 A cosmetic product made available on the market shall be safe for human health when used under normal or reasonably foreseeable conditions of use, taking account, in particular, of the following:

Responsible persons and distributors

24.8 EUCPR, Art 4 prohibits the placing of a cosmetic product on the market unless there is a responsible person for the product established in the United Kingdom:

– Where a product is manufactured, and the manufacturer is established, in the United Kingdom, and the product is not exported and re-imported prior to being placed on the market, then the manufacturer is the responsible person

– Where an importer places the product on the market, then the importer is the responsible person. Such a manufacturer or importer may by written mandate designate another person established in the United Kingdom to be the responsible person, and if they accept that designation in writing, then they shall be the responsible person.

– Where a product is manufactured in the United Kingdom, and not exported and re-imported, but the manufacturer is established outside of the United Kingdom, the manufacturer must ensure that a person in the United Kingdom is designated in writing to be responsible, and that the person has accepted that designation in writing.

– Where a distributor places a product on the market under their own name or trademark, or modifies a product placed on the market in such a way that compliance with the requirements of EUCPR may be affected, the distributor is the responsible person.

24.9 EUCPR, Art 5 provides that responsible persons should ensure compliance with the articles set out in Art 5(1); that if they have reason to believe a cosmetic product which has been placed on the market does not comply with the Regulation, they must immediately take measures to bring it into conformity, to withdraw it, or to recall it; that if it presents a risk to human health, inform the competent authority; and must cooperate with any request of the competent authority as to action to eliminate risks posed by products placed on the market. EUCPR, Art 7 provides that at the requirement of a competent authority, responsible persons shall identify distributors to whom they supply a cosmetic product for a period of 3 years following the supply.

24.10 The responsible person for a cosmetic product is required to ensure that the product has undergone a safety assessment, in accordance with the requirements set out in Art 10, and that a cosmetic product safety report is set up in accordance with Annex I, EUCPR[1]. The responsible person for a cosmetic product must keep a product information file for a period of 10 years following the date on which the last batch of the cosmetic product was placed on the market, which must contain the information set out in Art 11.

[1] (EC) No 1223/2009, Art 12(1).

24.11 EUCPR, Art 6 provides that when making a cosmetic product available on the market, distributors shall act with due care and attention in relation to applicable requirements of EUCPR; that before making a product available, they shall verify the requirements set out in Art 6(2) are met; that if they consider or have reason to believe that a product is not in conformity with the requirement of EUCPR, they shall not make the product available until it has been brought into conformity, and if they have already made the product available, they will make such corrective measures to bring it into conformity, withdraw it, or recall it; that if such a product presents a risk to human health, they shall immediately inform the competent authority and the responsible person; that they must ensure that whilst the product is under their responsibility, that the storage or transportation of it does not jeopardise compliance with the requirements of EUCPR; and must cooperate with any request of the competent authority as to action to eliminate risks posed by products placed on the market. EUCPR, Art 7 provides that at the requirement of a competent authority, a distributor shall identify the distributor or the responsible person from whom, and the distributors to whom, the cosmetic product was supplied for a period of 3 years following the supply.

Notification

24.12 EUCPR, Art 13 makes provision for the notification of information to the Secretary of State.

Labelling

Requirements

24.13 Cosmetic products must be labelled in accordance with the requirements of EUCPR, Art 19. The information required by EUCPR, Art 19(1)(b)–(d), (f) and (2)–(4) must be provided in English[1].

[1]   SI 2013/1478, reg 5(3).

Prohibited claims

24.14 EUCPR, Art 20 prohibits, when making available on the market and advertising of cosmetic products, the use of text, names, trade marks, pictures and figurative or other signs to imply that the products have characteristics or functions which they do not have. The responsible person may refer to the fact that no animal tests have been carried out, only if the manufacturer and his suppliers have not carried out or commissioned any animal tests on the finished cosmetic product, or its prototype, or any of the ingredients contained in it, or used any ingredients that have been tested on animals by others for the purpose of developing new cosmetic products.

Enforcement

24.15 EUCPR, Art 25 makes provision for competent authorities to take appropriate measures to ensure compliance with the regulations, including requiring action to bring products into conformity, withdrawing the product from the market or recalling the product. Where the responsible person does not take all appropriate measures within the time limit specified, or where immediate action is necessary in the event of serious risk to human health, the competent authority shall take all appropriate measures to prohibit or restrict the making available on the market of the cosmetic product or to withdraw the product from the market or to recall it. EUCPR, Art 26 makes similar provision for competent authorities to make requirements of distributors.

24.16 EUCPR, Art 27 provides that when a product is non-compliant in a way set out in Art 25(1), and an enforcement authority ascertains, or has reasonable grounds for concern, that a cosmetic product or products made available on the market present or could present a serious risk to human health, it shall take all appropriate provisional measures in order to ensure that the product or products concerned are withdrawn, recalled or their availability is otherwise restricted. An enforcement authority who is not the Secretary of State must obtain authorisation to do so from the Secretary of State prior to taking provisional measures.

24.17 CPER 2013, reg 8 requires a written notice, that complies with EUCPR, Art 28, to be provided when requiring measures to be undertaken under Arts 25–27, or making a request under Art 5(3) or Art 6(5).

Forfeiture

24.18 CPER 2013, reg 20 makes provision for an enforcement authority to apply for the forfeiture of any cosmetic product if a breach of EUCPR, Art 3 has occurred.

Appeals

24.19 CPER 2013, reg 14 makes provision for a responsible person, distributor, or other person having an interest in the product in respect of which a notice is issued by an enforcement authority under reg 8 to apply for an order to vary or set aside the notice. An application must be made within the period of 21 days beginning with the day on which the enforcement authority's notice was served on the responsible person or distributor. The court may only set aside the measures if satisfied that no contravention of the EUCPR has occurred, or that the measures required were not proportionate to the breach. The court may vary the terms of the notice as it considers appropriate. If proceedings have been brought for an offence contrary to reg 12, or if forfeiture proceedings have been brought under reg 20 or reg 21, an application is to be made to the court dealing with those proceedings, otherwise the appeal is to be made to a magistrates' court. A person aggrieved by a decision of a magistrates' court may appeal to the Crown Court.

Compensation

24.20 CPER 2013, reg 17 makes provision for an enforcement authority to pay compensation. Where an enforcement authority takes, or requires a responsible person or distributor to take, certain measures in accordance with Arts 25, 26 or 27 of the EUCPR, the authority shall be liable to pay compensation to any person having an interest in the goods in respect of any loss or damage caused by reason of the taking of those measures if no contravention of the EUCPR has occurred or is likely to occur and the exercise of the power is not attributable to any neglect or default by that person.

Offences

24.21 CPER 2013, reg 12(1) provides that it is an offence to contravene a provision of EUCPR set out in Sch 4[1]. CPER 2013, reg 12(2) provides that is an offence to intentionally obstruct any person acting in the execution or enforcement of the EU Cosmetics Regulation, to fail without reasonable cause to give to any such person any assistance or information which that person may reasonably require for those purposes, knowingly or recklessly to furnish to any such person any information knowing it to be false or misleading in a material particular, or to fail to produce a document or record to any such person when required to do so. CPER 2013, reg 12(3) provides that it is an offence to fail to comply with any of the requirements made by the enforcement authority acting under Arts 25, 26 or 27 of the EUCPR.

¹ EUCPR, Arts 3, 5–7, 10–11, 13–16, 18–21, and 23–24.

Liability of directors etc

24.22 CPER 2013, reg 24 provides that where an offence under CPER 2013 committed by a body corporate is proved to have been committed with the consent or connivance of, or to be attributable to any neglect on the part of, any director, manager, secretary or other similar officer of the body corporate, or a person purporting to act in any such capacity, that person is also guilty of the offence and liable to be proceeded against and punished accordingly. Directors' liability is covered in CHAPTER 4 Criminal Enforcement.

Causal liability

24.23 CPER 2013, reg 24 provides that where the commission of an offence under CPR is due to anything which another person did or failed to do in the course of a business, that other person is also guilty of the offence, and proceedings may be brought against that other person irrespective of whether proceedings are brought against the first person. Causal liability is covered in CHAPTER 4 Criminal Enforcement.

Duty to enforce

24.24 The Secretary of State, and a local weights and measures authority, are enforcement authorities. CPER 2013, reg 6 provides that it is the duty of the enforcement authority to enforce the EUCR and the CPER 2013 and to carry out market surveillance activities, and that an enforcement authority in England and Wales has the power to investigate and prosecute an alleged contravention of the obligations imposed by the EUCR and the CPER 2013 committed outside of its area in any part of England and Wales. EUCPR, Art 4 provides that the Secretary of State and the enforcement authority are the competent authorities for the purposes of EUCPR, and that the Secretary of State may nominate any other person

Time limits

24.25 CPER 2013, reg 22 provides that a magistrates' court may try any information alleging an offence under the CPER 2013 within 12 months from the date on which evidence sufficient in the opinion of the prosecutor to justify the proceedings comes to the knowledge of the prosecutor. No proceedings may be brought more than 3 years after the commission of the offence. A certificate of the prosecutor as to the date on which such evidence came to their notice is conclusive evidence. Time Limits are covered in Chapter 4 Criminal Enforcement.

24.26 CPER 2013, reg 12(4) provides that proceedings must not be commenced against a responsible person or a distributor under reg 12(1) where an enforcement authority has required the responsible person or the distributor to take measures under Art 25(1) or Art 26 of the EU Cosmetics Regulation in terms of the non-compliance, until the time period for compliance specified by the enforcement authority in the notice served under reg 8 when requesting those measures has expired.

Due diligence defence

24.27 CPER 2013, reg 23 provides that where a person is charged with an offence under the CPER 2013, it is a defence for a person to show that they took all reasonable steps and exercised all due diligence to avoid committing the offence. Due diligence defences are covered in Chapter 4 Criminal Enforcement.

Sentencing

24.28 CPER 2013, reg 13 provides that an offence contrary to reg 12 is punishable as follows:

– For an offence contrary to reg 12(1), in respect of breaches of breach of Arts 3, 5, 6, 7, 10, 14, 15, 18, 19, 20, or 23 only, or an offence contrary to reg 12(3), on summary conviction by up to 3 months' imprisonment, or a fine[1], or both, or on conviction on indictment by up to 12 months' imprisonment, or a fine not exceeding £20,000, or both.
– For an offence contrary to reg 12(1), in respect of a breach of any other article, on summary conviction by up to 3 months' imprisonment or a fine.
– For an offence contrary to reg 12(2), on summary conviction by a fine.

[1] Expressed in the regulation as a fine not exceeding the statutory maximum, which by virtue of s 85 of the Legal Aid, Sentencing and Punishment of Offenders Act 2012 is an unlimited fine. This creates the unusual situation in which the magistrates' court can impose a fine in excess of that which could be imposed by the Crown Court, and thus provides an incentive to a defendant to elect to be dealt with on indictment.

24.29 CPER 2013, reg 18 makes provision for the court to make a remediation order, where an offence relates to a matter which it appears to the court to be a matter which it is in the persons power to remedy. Such an order must specify the steps that the person must take to remedy any of the matters for which that person has been convicted and the period within which those steps must be taken. A remediation order may be made in addition to, or instead of, any penalty. The court has a discretion, upon an application to the court being made, to extend the period specified in a remediation order. During the period, or the extended period, in which a remediation order is in force, the person subject to the order is not liable to be prosecuted for an offence contrary to reg 12.

24.30 An enforcement authority may apply for an order for the forfeiture of any cosmetic product on the grounds that a breach of Art 3 EUCR has occurred[1], where proceedings have been brought in respect of an offence relating to that product[2], where an application in respect of the product has been made to the court under regs 14 or 15[3], or where no such application has been made in either of the aforementioned circumstances by way of complaint[4]. A forfeited product shall be destroyed in accordance with such directions as the court may give[5].

[1] SI 2013/1478, reg 20(1).
[2] SI 2013/1478, reg 20(2)(a).
[3] SI 2013/1478, reg 20(2)(b).
[4] SI 2013/1478, reg 20(2)(c).
[5] SI 2013/1478, reg 20(6). A person aggrieved by the making of, or a decision not to make, a forfeiture order may appeal against that order or decision to the Crown Court, and such an order may contain such provision as appears to the court to be appropriate for delaying the coming into force of an order pending the making and determination of any appeal: SI 2013/1478, reg 20(5).

24.31 CPER 2013, reg 19 provides that where a court convicts a person of an offence or makes an order for forfeiture under CPER 2013, the court may, in addition to any other order it may make as to costs or expenses, order the person to reimburse the enforcement authority for any expenditure which the authority has reasonably incurred in connection with investigation.

MEDICINES

Introduction

24.32 Medicinal products for use in humans are regulated by the Human Medicines Regulations 2012[1] ('HMR 2012'), which implement the Directive relating to medicinal products for human use[2], as amended by the Human Medicines (Amendment etc.) (EU Exit) Regulations 2019[3].

[1] SI 2012/1916.
[2] SI 2012/1916, reg 2(1)(a).
[3] SI 2019/775.

24.33 HMR 2012, reg 2 provides two routes through which a product can be a medicinal product. The first is by presentation: 'any substance or combination of substances presented as having properties of preventing or treating disease in human beings'. The second is by function: 'any substance or combination of substances that may be used by or administered to human beings either with a view to restoring, correcting or modifying physiological functions by exerting a pharmacological, immunological or metabolic action, or to taking a medical diagnosis'[1].

[1] SI 2012/1916, reg 2(1)(b).

24.34 The functional limb covers products 'whose pharmacological properties have been scientifically observed and which are genuinely designed to make a medical diagnosis or to restore, correct or modify physiological functions'[1]. It does not cover 'substances whose effects merely modify physiological functions and which are not such as to entail immediate or long-term beneficial effects for human health'[2]. A case-by-case approach is required, which requires considering in particular the characteristics of the product, the manner in which it is used, the extent of its distribution, its familiarity to consumers and the risks which its use may entail[3]. The case-by-case-approach 'entails the possibility that different products with precisely the same chemical composition may fall within or outside the definition of medicinal product depending on the circumstance'; nitrous oxide is an example of a product that can in different circumstances be both a medicinal and non-medicinal product[4].

[1]   *Commission of the European Communities v Federal Republic of Germany* (C-319/05).
[2]   *D & G* (C-358/13, C-181/4).
[3]   *HLH Warenvertriebs* (C-211/03).
[4]   *Chapman* [2017] EWCA Crim 1743.

Sale and supply of unauthorised medicinal products

Requirement for authorisation

24.35 HMR 2012, reg 46(1) provides that the sale, supply and advertisement of medicinal product is prohibited unless there is a UK marketing authorisation, an EU marketing authorisation, a certificate of registration, a traditional herbal registration or an Article 126a authorisation in force for the product. HMR 2012, reg 46(2) provides that the sale, supply or advertisement is prohibited unless it is in accordance with the terms of the authorisation or registration in force.

24.36 A person may not possess an unauthorised medicinal product if they know or have reasonable cause to believe that the product is intended to be sold or supplied with the UK or the EEA[1], and must not manufacture or assemble, or procure the sale, supply, manufacture or assembly of, a medicinal product they know or have reasonable cause to believe is intended to be sold or supplied in breach of reg 46(1)[2]. Various exceptions to reg 46 apply, including the sale, supply, or offer for sale or supply, of a medicinal product to a person outside the United Kingdom or European Economic Area.

[1]   SI 2012/1916, reg 46(3).
[2]   SI 2012/1916, reg 46(4).

Offences

24.37 HMR 2012, reg 47(1) provides that a person who breaches the prohibitions in reg 46 commits an offence. It is to be presumed for the purposes of reg 46(3) that a person ('P') who knows or has reasonable cause to believe that a person to whom a medicinal product is to be sold or supplied knows or has reasonable cause to believe that the person to whom the sale or supply is to take place is within the UK or EEA, unless P proves that P did not know or have reasonable cause to believe that the person was within the UK or EEA[1].

[1]   SI 2012/1916, reg 47(3).

Defence

24.38 If the holder of an authorisation or registration is charged with an offence under this regulation in respect of anything that has been manufactured

or assembled to the holder's order by another person and has been so manufactured or assembled so as not to comply with the terms of the authorisation or
registration, it is a defence for the holder to prove that the holder communicated
the terms of the authorisation, certificate or registration to the other person and
that the holder did not know and could not by the exercise of reasonable care
have known that those terms had not been complied with[1].

[1]   SI 2012/1916, reg 47(6)–(7).

Sentencing

24.39 HMR 2012, reg 47(2) provides that an offence contrary to reg 47(1) is
punishable on summary conviction by a fine, or on indictment by a fine or by
imprisonment for a term not exceeding 2 years or both.

Sale and supply of medicinal products
Prescription only medications

24.40 HMR 2012, reg 214(1) provides that a person may not sell or supply a
prescription only medicine, except in accordance with a prescription given by
an appropriate practitioner[1], or where a doctor or dentist sells or supplies a
prescription only medicine to their patient[2], or in the course of the business of
a hospital in accordance with specified conditions[3]. A person may not parenterally administer a prescription only medicine, otherwise than to himself or
herself, unless the person is an appropriate practitioner other than an EEA
health professional, or is acting in accordance with the directions of an
appropriate practitioner other than an EEA health professional[4]. A supplementary prescriber may only give a prescription for, parenterally administer or give
directions of the parenteral administration of a prescription only medication if
the conditions set out in reg 215 are met, or if the circumstances set out in
reg 216 apply.

[1]   A doctor, dentist, supplementary prescriber, nurse independent prescriber or pharmacy inde-
      pendent prescriber: SI 2012/1916, reg 214(3); and a podiatrist independent prescriber, physio-
      therapist independent prescriber, therapeutic independent prescriber, paramedic independent
      prescriber in the circumstances set out in SI 2012/1916, reg 214(5A)–(5D). An EEA health
      professional is an appropriate practitioner in relation to any prescription only medicine other
      than a product subject to special medical prescription: reg 214(6).
[2]   SI 2012/1916, reg 223(1).
[3]   SI 2012/1916, reg 227.
[4]   SI 2012/1916, reg 214(2).

24.41 HMR 2012, reg 244–226A provide for exemptions from reg 214(1) in
the case of emergencies where a relevant prescriber is unable to provide a
prescription immediately, where there is an immediate need and it is impracticable for the patient to obtain a prescription without undue delay, in certain
circumstances relating to pandemic diseases, and in accordance with a serious
shortage protocol.

24.42 HMR 2012, regs 217–219A makes provision as to the requirements of
prescriptions.

24.43 The prohibition on the sale or supply of a prescription only medication
by a person other than in accordance with a prescription does not apply:

–   In the case of a supply by a pharmacist where the prescription was given by a person who is not an appropriate or supplementary practitioner, but the pharmacist, having exercised all due diligence, believes they are such a practitioner[1].

–   In the case of a supply by a pharmacist if the pharmacist, having exercised all due diligence, believes on reasonable grounds that the prescription is genuine[2].

–   If the person, having exercised all due diligence, believes that the product is not a prescription only medicine[3].

–   Where the requirements of regs 217–219A are not met, but the person selling or supplying the prescription only medicine, having exercised all due diligence, believes on reasonable grounds that the requirements are met.[4]

[1]   SI 2012/1916, reg 228.
[2]   SI 2012/1916, reg 245.
[3]   SI 2012/1916, reg 244(1).
[4]   SI 2012/1916, reg 246.

24.44 A person lawfully conducting a retail pharmacy business must, in respect of every sale or supply of a prescription only medicine, make or cause to be made an entry in a written or computerised record kept for that purpose, in accordance with the requirements of HMR 2012, reg 253.

Medicines not subject to general sale

24.45 HMR 2012, reg 5(1) provides that a medicinal product is subject to general sale if it is a product which is nor a prescription only or pharmacy medicine, but is covered by an authorisation of which permits it to be provided on a general sale.

24.46 A person may not sell or supply, or offer for sale or supply, a medicinal product that is not subject to general sale, unless that person is (a) lawfully conducting a retail pharmacy business, (b) the sale, supply or offer takes place on premises that are a registered pharmacy, and (c) the person either is, or is acting under the supervision of, a pharmacist[1]. A medicinal product which is not subject to general sale may not be sold or offered for sale by means of an automatic machine[2].

[1]   SI 2012/1916, reg 220.
[2]   SI 2012/1916, reg 222.

24.47 HMR 2012, reg 244(2) provides that the prohibition on the sale or supply of, or the offering to sell or supply, a medicinal product that is not subject to general sale by a person does not apply if the person, having exercised all due diligence, believes on reasonable grounds that the product is not subject to general sale, the belief is due to the act or default of another person, and the conditions that apply to the sale or supply of, or offering to sell or supply, a medicinal product that is subject to general sale in HMR 2012, reg 211 are met.

Medicines subject to general sale

24.48 HMR 2012, reg 221(1) provides that a person may not sell or supply, or offer for sale or supply, a medicinal product that is subject to general sale other than a retail pharmacy business, unless (a) the place at which the medicinal product is sold, supplied, or offered for sale or supply, consists of premises of which the person is the occupier and which the person is able to close so as to exclude the public[1], (b) the medicine was not made up for sale in its immediate and outer packaging at that place and the immediate and outer packaging has not been opened since the product was made up for sale in it[2], and (c) in the case of medicinal products listed in HMR 2012, Sch 30, the medicinal product is listed for sale in accordance with the requirements specified in the schedule for a product of that kind[3].

[1]   SI 2012/1916, reg 221(2).
[2]   SI 2012/1916, reg 221(3).
[3]   SI 2012/1916, reg 221(4).

Presumptions

24.49 Where a medicinal product is found on a vehicle from which medicinal products are sold, it is to be presumed, unless the contrary is proved, that the person in charge of the vehicle offered the medicinal product for sale[1].

[1]   SI 2012/1916, reg 340(1)–(2).

24.50 Where a person is charged with an offence contrary to regs 268, 269 or 276, and a medicinal product is found on premises at which that person carries on a business consisting of or including the sale or supply of medicinal products, it is to be presumed, unless the contrary is proved, that the person charged possessed the medicinal product for the purpose of sale or supply[1].

[1]   SI 2012/1916, reg 340(3)–(5).

Exemptions

24.51 The prohibitions in HMR 2012, regs 220 and 221, do not apply to:

–   The sale, offer for sale or supply of a medicinal product by a doctor or dentist to a patient of a doctor or dentist, or to a person under whose care such a patient is[1];
–   Specified supplies in the course of the business of a hospital of heath centre[2];
–   The sale or supply of a specified medicinal products by a registered midwife in the course of their professional practice, or delivered or administered by a registered midwife upon being supplied the product under arrangements made by a Minister[3]; and
–   The supply of a medicinal product in the event or anticipation of pandemic disease[4].

[1]   SI 2012/1916, reg 223(2).
[2]   SI 2012/1916, reg 223(3).
[3]   SI 2012/1916, reg 223(4)–(5).
[4]   SI 2012/1916, reg 247.

24.52 HMR 2012, regs 229–234 makes provision for exemptions in relation to supplies by national health services bodies, local authorities and under patient group directions. HMR 2012, reg 235 and Sch 17 make provision for exemptions in relation to sales, supplies or administration by certain specified persons. HMR 2012, reg 235 makes provision for exemptions in relation to the sale of specific prescription only medicines by certain categories of person, as set out in Sch 17. HMR 2012, regs 236–243 makes provision for exemptions in relation to specific kinds of products.

24.53 HMR 2012, reg 248 makes provision for making and execution of arrangements for the collection and delivery of medicinal products.

Wholesale supplies

24.54 HMR 2012, reg 249(3) provides that the holder of an authorisation or registration, and a person in the course of a business consisting (wholly or partly) of manufacturing medicinal products or of selling medicinal products by way of wholesale dealing, may not sell or supply a prescription only medicine or a pharmacy medicine by way of wholesale dealing, except to a person listed in HMR 2012, Sch 22. HMR 2012, reg 250 makes provision for certain exceptions from the prohibition on wholesale dealing other than to persons listed in HMR 2012, Sch 22.

Distance sales

24.55 The provisions of HMR 2012, Pt 12A in respect of sales of medicines the public at a distance no longer apply, except in relation to Northern Ireland[1].

[1]   Human Medicines (Amendment etc.) (EU Exit) Regulations 2019, SI 2019/775, reg 197.

Offences

24.56 A person is guilty of an offence if the person:

–   Breaches any provision of HMR 2012, regs 214(1), 214(2), 220, 249, 251 or 254[1];
–   Is an appropriate practitioner and give a prescription or directions in respect of medicinal product in relation to which the person is not an appropriate practitioner[2];
–   Gives a prescription or directions or administers a medicinal product without meeting the conditions for doing so that apply to that person by virtue of reg 215[3];
–   Has in their possession a medicinal product to which reg 214(1) applies with the intent to supply it otherwise than in accordance with a prescription[4];
–   Breaches reg 221 or reg 222[5]; or
–   Breaches reg 253[6].

[1]   SI 2012/1916, reg 254 relates to the requirements for the traceability of treatments of patients with advanced therapy medicinal products.
[2]   SI 2012/1916, reg 255(2).
[3]   SI 2012/1916, reg 255(3).
[4]   SI 2012/1916, reg 255(4).
[5]   SI 2012/1916, reg 255(6).
[6]   SI 2012/1916, reg 255(8).

Sentencing

24.57 An offence contrary to reg 255(1)–(4) is punishable on summary conviction by a fine, or on indictment by a fine or by imprisonment for a term not exceeding 2 years or both[1]. An offence contrary to reg 255(6) is punishable on summary conviction by a fine not exceeding level 3 on the standard scale[2]. An offence contrary to reg 255(6) is punishable on summary conviction by a fine not exceeding £400[3].

[1]   SI 2012/1916, reg 255(5).
[2]   SI 2012/1916, reg 255(7).
[3]   SI 2012/1916, reg 255(9).

24.58 HMR 2012, reg 256 makes provision for a person convicted of any offence under reg 255(8) to be disqualified from using the premises where the offence was committed for a period not exceeding 2 years.

Homeopathic medicinal products and traditional herbal medicines

Homeopathic medicinal products

24.59 HMR 2012, reg 102 provides that a homeopathic medicinal product is registrable if it is administered orally or externally, no therapeutic indication appears on the labelling of the product or in any information supplied with the product, the product contains no more than one part per 10,000 of the mother tincture and, in a case where the product's active substance is a relevant allopathic substance[1], the product contains no more than 1/100th of the smallest concentration of that substance used in allopathy[2].

[1]   A relevant allopathic substance is an active substance whose presence in an allopathic medicinal product means that the product is only available on prescription: SI 2012/1916, reg 102(4). An allopathic medicinal product is a medicinal product other than a homoeopathic medicinal product, and allopathy is treatment using an allopathic medicinal product: SI 2012/1916, reg 102(5).
[2]   Allopathy is treatment using an allopathic medicinal product: SI 2012/1916, reg 102(5).

Traditional herbal medicines

24.60 HMR 2012, reg 2 defines a herbal medicinal product as a medical product whose only active ingredients are herbal substances, or herbal preparations, or both. A herbal substance is a plant or part of a plant, algae, fungi or lichen, or an unprocessed exudate of a plant, defined by the plant part used and the botanical name of the plant, either fresh or dried, but otherwise unprocessed. A herbal preparation is a preparation obtained by subjecting herbal substances to processes such as extraction, distillation, expression, fractionation, purification, concentration or fermentation, and includes a comminuted or powdered herbal substance, a tincture, an extract, an essential oil, an expressed juice or a processed exudate.

24.61 HMR 2012, reg 125 provides that a herbal medicinal product is a traditional herbal medicinal product, and falls within Pt 7 of the regulations if the following five conditions are met:

–   That by virtue of its composition and indications the product is appropriate for use without the need for a medical practitioner to diagnose the condition to be treated by the product, prescribe the product, or monitor the product's use;
–   That the product is intended to be administered at a particular strength and in accordance with a particular posology.

– That the product is intended to be administered externally, orally or by inhalation.

– That the product has been in medicinal use for a continuous period of at least 30 years, and the product has been in medicinal use in the United Kingdom (or, depending on the circumstances, another country listed in reg 215A or in the European Union) for a continuous period of at least 15 years (and it is immaterial whether during those periods the sale or supply of the product has been based on a specific authorisation, or there has been a reduction in the number or quantity of the ingredients).

– That there is sufficient information about the traditional use of the product such as to establish that the traditional use of the product is not harmful and that the pharmacological effects or efficacy of the product are plausible on the basis of long-standing use and experience.

24.62 HMR 2012, reg 126 provides that the addition to a traditional herbal medicinal product of a vitamin or mineral does not prevent a traditional herbal registration from being granted for the product if there is well-documented evidence of the safety of the vitamin or minerals and the action of the vitamin or mineral is ancillary to the action of the product's active herbal ingredients in connection with the use authorised by the traditional herbal registration.

Packaging and leaflets

Packaging requirements

24.63 HMR 2012, reg 257(1)–(3) provides that the information set out in Pt 1 of Sch 24 must appear on the outer packaging of a medicinal product, and must also appear on the immediate packaging of the product, unless the packaging is in the form of a blister pack and is placed in outer packaging which complies contains the information, or the immediate packaging is too small to contain the information. Where the immediate packaging is in the form of a blister pack, the information set out in Pt 2 of Sch 24 must appear on it[1], and where the immediate packaging is too small to contain the information set out in Pt 1 of Sch 24, it must contain the information set out in Pt 3 of Sch 24.[2]

[1]   SI 2012/1916, reg 257(4).
[2]   SI 2012/1916, reg 257(5).

24.64 Information required to be included on the packaging of a product must be easily legible, comprehensible and indelible[1]. HMR 2012, reg 259 makes provision for the name of a medicinal product to be expressed in Braille format on the outer packaging of the product, or, if there is no outer packaging, on the immediate packaging of the product, and for the holder of an authorisation or registration to ensure that the package leaflet is made available on request in formats suitable for blind and partially-sighted persons.

[1]   SI 2012/1916, reg 257(6).

24.65 The requirements of reg 257, Sch 24 and reg 259 do not apply to registered homoeopathic medicinal products[1].

[1]   SI 2012/1916, regs 257(7) and 259(3).

Package Leaflets

24.66 HMR 2012, reg 260(1) provides that a package leaflet for a medicinal product must be drawn up in accordance with the summary of the product characteristics and must contain information specified in Sch 24, in the order that it appears in the schedule. A package leaflet must be included in the packaging of a medicinal product unless all of the information that is required to be included in a package leaflet is conveyed on the outer packaging or the immediate packaging of the product[1].

[1]   SI 2012/1916, reg 260(2).

24.67 A package leaflet for a medicinal product must be legible, clear and easy to use, and the applicant for, or holder of, an authorisation or registration relating to a product must ensure that target patient groups are consulted in order to achieve this[1].

[1]   SI 2012/1916, Sch 27, para.

24.68 The requirements in relation to package leaflets do not apply to registrable homoeopathic medicinal products[1].

[1]   SI 2012/1916, reg 260(6).

Language and use of pictures and symbols

24.69 Information given on packaging and in package leaflets must be given in English, unless either or both of the requirements in reg 266(2) and (3) are met[1].

[1]   SI 2012/1916, reg 266(1).

24.70 The outer packaging and the package leaflet of a medicinal product may include symbols, diagrams, and pictures designed to clarify information mentioned in Sch 24 or Sch 27, and other information, compatible with the summary of the product characteristics, which is useful to the patient[1]. Such symbols, diagrams, pictures or additional information that are so included must not include any element of a promotional nature[2]. These provisions do not apply to registrable homoeopathic products[3].

[1]   SI 2012/1916, reg 261(1).
[2]   SI 2012/1916, reg 261(2).
[3]   SI 2012/1916, reg 261(3).

Traditional herbal medicines

24.71 HMR 2012, reg 265 provides that in addition to other applicable requirements, the packaging of traditional herbal medicinal products must comply with the requirements of Sch 29.

Radionuclides

24.72 HMR 2012, reg 262 makes provision in relation to labelling requirements for radionuclides. HMR 2012, reg 263 makes provision in relation to leaflets to be provided with radionuclides.

Child safety

24.73 Regulated products[1] may be sold only in containers which are opaque or dark tinted, and child resistant[2]. This is with the exception of (1) retail sales, and supplies in circumstances corresponding to retail sale, carried out by or under the supervision of a pharmacist on premises which are a registered pharmacy and either in accordance with a prescription given by an appropriate practitioner where it is not reasonably practicable to provide the regulated medicinal products in containers that are both opaque or dark tinted and child resistant, or at the request of a person who is aged 16 or over and specifically requests that the regulated medicinal products not be contained in a child resistant container[3]. Also exempt is (2) a sale or supply by a doctor or dentist to a patient, or the patient's carer, for the patient's use[4], (3) a sale or supply by a doctor or dentist to a person who is an appropriate practitioner, at the request of that person, for administration to a patient of that person[5], and (4) a sale or supply in the course of the business of a hospital or health centre, where the sale or supply is for the purposes of administration, whether in the hospital or health centre or elsewhere, in accordance with the directions of an appropriate practitioner[6].

1   A medicinal product containing aspirin, paracetamol or more than 24mg of elemental iron, in the form of tablets, capsules, pills, lozenges, suppositories or oral liquids, but does not include effervescent tablets containing not more than 25% of aspirin or paracetamol by weight, medicinal products in sachets or other sealed containers which hold only one dose, medicinal products which are not intended for retail sale or for supply in circumstances corresponding to retail sale, or medicinal products which are for export only: SI 2012/1916, reg 272.
2   SI 2012/1916, reg 273(1). SI 2012/1916, reg 273(2)–(3) makes provision as to the circumstances in which reclosable and non-reclosable containers are to be treated as child resistant.
3   SI 2012/1916, reg 274(2)(a)–(c).
4   SI 2012/1916, reg 274(3)(a).
5   SI 2012/1916, reg 274(3)(b).
6   SI 2012/1916, reg 274(3)(c).

24.74 The sale or supply of a medicinal product that contains aspirin or paracetamol, and that is a product for children aged 12 or under, is prohibited if it is in a colour other than white and, in the case of paracetamol, it is in a solid form (including tablets, capsules, pills, lozenges, pastilles or suppositories)[1].

1   SI 2012/1916, reg 275.

Exemptions

24.75 Where a medicinal product is not intended to be delivered directly to a patient, or where there are severe problems in respect of the availability of a medicinal product, the licensing authority may grant an exemption from the obligation for certain particulars to appear on the outer and immediate packaging and in the package leaflet of the medicinal product, and from the obligation for that information to be given in English[1].

1   SI 2012/1916, reg 266(4).

Offences

24.76 The holder of an authorisation or registration[1], and persons who are not holders of authorisations or registrations[2], are guilty of offences if the person sells or supplies, offers to sell or supply, or possesses for the purposes of sale or supply, a medicinal product to which the authorisation or registration relies, if the product is not accompanied by a package leaflet when one is required, or the package or package leaflet is non-compliant[2].

1   SI 2012/1916, reg 268.
2   SI 2012/1916, reg 269.

24.77 The holder of an authorisation or registration who fails to comply with a notice under reg 270(1) is guilty of an offence[1].

1   SI 2012/1916, reg 270(3).

24.78 A person who, in the course of a business, sells or supplies, or possesses for the purposes of sale or supply, a regulated medicinal product that fails to comply with the requirements of reg 273, or that is prohibited by reg 275, is guilty of an offence[1].

1   SI 2012/1916, reg 276(1).

Sentencing

24.79 An offence contrary to regs 268–270, or reg 276, is punishable on summary conviction by a fine, or on indictment by a fine or by imprisonment for a term not exceeding 2 years or both[1].

1   SI 2012/1916, regs 271 and 276(2).

Advertising

Definition

24.80 HMR 2012, reg 7 broadly defines advertising as anything designed to promote the prescription, supply, sale or use of that product[1]. Advertising does not include a medicinal product's package or package leaflet, reference material and announcements of a factual and informative nature, provided that no product claim is made, or correspondence, which may be accompanied by material of a non-promotional nature, answering a specific question about a medicinal product.

1   It specifically provides that this includes door-to-door canvassing, visits by medical sales representatives to persons qualified to prescribe or supply medicinal products, the supply of samples, the provision of inducements to prescribe or supply medicinal products by the gift, offer or promise of any benefit or bonus, whether in money or in kind, except where the intrinsic value of such inducements is minimal, the sponsorship of promotional meetings attended by persons qualified to prescribe or supply medicinal products, and the sponsorship of scientific congresses attended by persons qualified to prescribe or supply medicinal products, including the payment of their travelling and accommodation expenses in that connection.

Restrictions on advertisements

24.81 HMR 2012, reg 279 provides that a person may not publish an advertisement for a medical product unless a relevant authorisation is in force.

24.82 HMR 2012, reg 280 provides that if a relevant authorisation is in force, a person may not publish an advertisement unless it complies with the particulars listed in the summary of the product characteristics, the advertisement encourages the rational use of the product by presenting it objectively and without exaggerating its properties, and it is not misleading.

24.83 HMR 2012, regs 282–290 set out a series of prohibitions on advertisement that relates to a medicinal product and are wholly or mainly directed at members of the public. The publication of any advertisement likely to lead to the use of a prescription only medicine is prohibited. The publication of an advertisement is also prohibited if it is likely to lead to the use of a medicinal product for the purpose of inducing an abortion; relates to a medicinal product that is listed in specified schedules to the Narcotic Drugs and Psychotropic Substances Convention, states or implies that a medical consultation or surgical operation is unnecessary; offers to provide a diagnosis or suggest a treatment by post or by means of an electronic communications network; might, by a description or detailed representation of a case history, lead to erroneous self-diagnosis; suggests that the effects of taking a medicinal product are guaranteed, better than or equivalent to those or another identifiable treatment or medicinal product, or are not accompanied by any adverse reaction; uses pictorial representations of changes in the human body caused by disease or injury, or the action of the medicinal product on the human body, in terms that are misleading or likely to cause alarm; refers in terms that are misleading or likely to cause alarm to claims of recovery; suggests that the health of a person who is not suffering from any disease or injury could be enhanced by taking a medicinal product; suggests that the health of a person could be affected by not taking a medicinal product; suggests that a medicinal product is a foodstuff, cosmetic or other consumer product that is not a medicinal product; suggests that the safety or efficacy of medicinal product is due to the fact that it is natural; refers to a recommendation of a medicinal product by scientists, health care professionals, or persons who because of their celebrity status could encourage use of the medicinal product; or contains any material that is directed principally at children.

24.84 HMR 2012, regs 291–292 provides that an advertisement must be presented so that it is clear that it is an advertisement; clearly identify the product as a medicinal product; provide the name of the medicinal product; if the product includes only one active ingredient, include the common name of the active ingredient; include information necessary for the current use of the medicinal product; and explicitly and clearly invite the consumer to read carefully the instructions.

24.85 HMR 2012, reg 291A makes provision for exceptions in relation to campaigns relating to the spread of pathogens, toxins, chemical agents or nuclear radiation. HMR 2012, reg 292 provides exceptions for advertisements as part of vaccination campaigns.

Requirements for advertisements directed at prescribers

24.86 HMR 2012, reg 293 provides that a medicinal product may not be sold or supplied for a promotional purpose by the holder of an authorisation or registration to a person or by a person who carries on a medicines business who is not qualified to prescribe medicinal product, regardless of whether the promotional purpose is that of the seller or supplier or of a third party.

24.87 HMR 2012, reg 294 provides that a person may not publish an advertisement that relates to a medicinal product, and that is wholly or mainly directed at persons qualified to prescribe or supply such products, unless it contains the particulars set out in HMR 2012, Sch 30.

24.88 By way of an exception to the aforementioned requirements, a person may publish an advertisement that relates to a pharmacy medicine or a medicinal product subject to general sale if it contains[1]:

- the particulars set out in HMR 2012, Sch 30, paras 2–6[2];
- the statement 'Information about this product, including adverse reactions, precautions, contra-indications, and method of use can be found at' and a website address that corresponds to that statement, which much either contain the matters set out in Sch 30 or a copy of the summary of the product characteristics[3].

[1]   SI 2012/1916, reg 294(2A).
[2]   SI 2012/1916, reg 294(2A)(a).
[3]   SI 2012/1916, reg 294(2A)(b)–(c) and (2B).

24.89 Where an advertisement is not a written advertisement, the required particulars may alternatively be made available in written form to all persons to whom the advertisement is made available[1].

[1]   SI 2012/1916, reg 294(3).

24.90 The requirements in at **24.87–24.89** do not apply to abbreviated advertisements[1] and oral representations made by medical sales representatives[2]. They are subject to exceptions for advertisements intended as a reminder[3] and advertisements for registered homeopathic medicinal products[4].

[1]   As set out in SI 2012/1916, reg 295: SI 2012/1916, reg 294(4)(a).
[2]   As set out in SI 2012/1916, reg 299: SI 2012/1916, reg 299(4)(b).
[3]   As set out in SI 2012/1916, reg 296: SI 2012/1916, reg 294(4)(c).
[4]   As set out in SI 2012/1916, reg 301: SI 2012/1916, reg 294(4)(c).

Requirements for abbreviated advertisements directed at prescribers

24.91 An abbreviated advertisement is an advertisement, other than a loose insert, that does not exceed 420 square centimetres in size and appears in a publication sent or delivered wholly or mainly to persons qualified to prescribe or supply medicinal products[1]. A person may not publish an advertisement that relates to a medicinal product, and that is wholly or mainly directed at persons qualified to prescribe or supply such products, unless it contains the following particulars[2]:

- The particulars set out in HMR 2012, Sch 30, paras 2–6[3];
- The statement 'Information about this product, including adverse reactions, precautions, contra-indications, and method of use can be found at' and a website address that corresponds to that statement, which much either contain the matters set out in Sch 30 or a copy of the summary of the product characteristics[4]; and
- The name and address of the holder of the marketing authorisation or registration, or the business name and address of the part of the holder's business that is responsible for its sale or supply[5].

[1]   SI 2012/1916, reg 295(4).

² SI 2012/1916, reg 295(2).
³ SI 2012/1916, reg 295(2)(a).
⁴ SI 2012/1916, reg 295(2)(b)–(d) and (3).
⁵ SI 2012/1916, reg 295(d).

Advertisements intended as a reminder

24.92 Regulation 296 provides an exception from the requirements for advertisements for an advertisement relating to a medicinal product that is intended solely as a medical requirement that consists solely of:

- In relation to a product other than a homoeopathic medicinal product to which a certificate of registration relates, its name, international non-proprietary name or trademark[1].
- In relation to a homoeopathic medicinal product to which a certificate of registration relates, its name, international non-proprietary name, invented name or trademark or the scientific name of the stock or stocks from which it is derived[2].

¹ SI 2012/1916, reg 296(a).
² SI 2012/1916, reg 296(b).

Written material accompanying promotions

24.93 A person may not as part of the promotion of a medicinal product send or deliver any written material to a person qualified to prescribe or supply medicinal products unless the material contains the particulars set out in HMR 2012, Sch 30, and states the date on which it was drawn up or last revised[1]. A person may not include any information in any such written material unless it is accurate, up-to-date, verifiable and is sufficiently complete to enable the recipient to form an opinion of the therapeutic value of the product to which it relates[2]. A person may not include any illustrative material[3] in any such written material unless the illustrative material is accurately reproduced and the written material indicates the precise source of the illustrative material[4].

¹ SI 2012/1916, reg 297(1).
² SI 2012/1916, reg 297(2).
³ A quotation, table or any other illustrative material taken from a medical journal or other scientific work: SI 2012/1916, reg 297(4).
⁴ SI 2012/1916, reg 297(3).

Medical sales representatives and provision of free samples

24.94 A person may not supply a free sample of a medicinal product to another person unless the recipient is qualified to prescribe medicinal products, receives the sample for the purpose of acquiring experience in dealing with the product in question, and the other conditions set out in HMR 2012, reg 298 are met.

24.95 HMR 2012, reg 299 provides that where a medical sales representative of medicinal products engages in the promotion of products to persons qualified to prescribe or supply such products, the representative must either give to, or have available to give to, each person visited a copy of the summary of the product characteristics for each product promoted.

24.96 Regulation 300 makes provision restricting the provision of gifts and hospitality in the course of the promotion of medicinal products.

Traditional herbal medicine products

24.97 HMR 2012, reg 302 provides that a person may not publish an advertisement that relates to a traditional herbal medicinal product unless it contains the word 'traditional herbal medicinal product for use in', followed by a statement of one or more therapeutic indications for the product consistent with the terms of the registration; followed by the words 'exclusively based on long standing use'.

Offences

24.98 A person is guilty of an offence if that person commits a breach of any provision of regs 282–302[1].

[1]   SI 2012/1916, reg 303(1).

Sentencing

24.99 An offence contrary to reg 303(1) consisting of a breach of regs 298(1), 299(2), 299(3) or 300(4) is punishable on summary conviction by a fine[1]. An offence contrary to reg 303(1) consisting of a breach of any other regulation is punishable on summary conviction by a fine, or on indictment by a fine or by imprisonment for a term not exceeding 2 years or both[2].

[1]   SI 2012/1916, reg 303(4)–(5).
[2]   SI 2012/1916, reg 303(3).

Enforcement

Validity of and challenges to decisions

24.100 HMR 2012, reg 322 provides that any decision of the licensing authority and any licence, authorisation, certificate or registration granted may not be questioned in any legal proceedings, other than by means of proceedings in the High Court in accordance with that regulation.

Duty to enforce

24.101 HMR 2012, reg 323 provides that it is the duty of the Secretary of State to enforce or secure the enforcement of the HMR 2012, and that the Secretary of State may make arrangements for the General Pharmaceutical Council ('GPhC') or a drugs authority for an area[1] to enforce specified provisions[2]. The drugs authority is the council of a non-metropolitan county, metropolitan district or London borough, and the Common Council of the City of London[3].

[1]   SI 2012/1916, reg 323(2).
[2]   SI 2012/1916, reg 323(3)–(9).
[3]   SI 2012/1916, reg 323(10).

Restrictions on proceedings

24.102 HMR 2012, reg 339(1) provides that a magistrates' court may try any information alleging an offence under the HMR 2012 that is triable only summarily if the information was laid at any time within the period of 12 months beginning with the commission of the offence.

24.103 HMR 2012, reg 339(4) provides that the General Pharmaceutical Council or a drugs authority may not institute proceedings for an offence under the HMR 2012 which it may or must enforce unless it has given no less than 28 days' notice of its intention to do so, together with a summary of the facts on which the charges are founded, to the Secretary of State.

Powers of entry and inspection

24.104 HMR 2012, reg 325 provides an inspector with a power to enter premises[1] at any reasonable time for purposes that include determining whether there has been a contravention of a provision of these Regulations which the enforcement authority is required or empowered to enforce by virtue of regs 323 and 324. The power cannot be exercised in premises used only as a private dwelling unless 24 hours' notice has been given to the occupier.

[1]   Including any place, a ship, aircraft, hovercraft or vehicle: SI 2012/1916, reg 323(1).

24.105 A justice of the peace may issue a warrant authorising an inspector to enter premises, including if necessary by force, if satisfied that there are reasonable grounds for entering the premises by virtue of the enforcement authority's functions under these Regulations, an inspector has a right to enter them by virtue of reg 325, and that one of the four conditions specified in para (3) is satisfied[1]. The four conditions are (a) that admission to the premises has been refused or is expected to be refused, and notice of the intention to apply for a warrant has been given to the occupier, (b) that a request for admission, or the giving of notice, would defeat the object of entry, (c) that the case is one of urgency, or (d) that the premises are unoccupied or the occupier is temporarily absent[2]. A warrant continues in force for a period of 30 days beginning with the day on which the warrant is granted[3]. Where an inspector enters premises pursuant to a warrant and the property is unoccupied or the occupier is absent, the inspector must leave the premises as effectively secured against trespass as they were before the inspector entered[4].

[1]   SI 2012/1916, reg 326(1)–(2).
[2]   SI 2012/1916, reg 326(3).
[3]   SI 2012/1916, reg 326(3).
[4]   SI 2012/1916, reg 334(2).

24.106 An officer inspector exercising a power of entry may be accompanied by such persons, and take such equipment, as the inspector thinks appropriate[1].

[1]   SI 2012/1916, reg 334(1).

24.107 HMR 2012, reg 327 makes provision for an inspector to exercise powers of inspection, sampling and seizure. An inspector exercising, or attempting, to exercise such a right must produce identification on request[1]. A inspector who seizes any item must, where practicable, inform any person from whom it was seized and the occupier of the premises from which it was seized[2], and in relation to anything seized from a vending machine, must inform the person whose name and address are stated on the machine to be the machine's owner, or in the absence of a name and address, the occupier of the premises on which the machine stands or to which it is affixed[3].

1 SI 2012/1916, reg 328(2).
2 SI 2012/1916, reg 328(1)(a).
3 SI 2012/1916, reg 328(1)(b).

24.108 HMR 2012, reg 329 makes provision, where a substance or article is seized, for a sample to be preserved and made available.

24.109 Where a person other than an inspector or other person authorised by an enforcement authority purchases an active substance or a medicinal product, HMR 2012, reg 330, makes provision for that person to submit a sample for analysis to a public analyst.

24.110 HMR 2012, reg 331 makes provision as to the steps to be taken where the outcome of an inspection identifies non-compliance.

24.111 A person must not disclose to another person, otherwise than in performance of their functions, any information relating to a manufacturing process or trade secret obtained on premises which have been entered under a power of entry, or any information obtained or provided in pursuance of these Regulations[1], unless that person is or is acting on behalf of, a public authority for the purposes of the Freedom of Information Act 2000 and the information is not held by the authority on behalf of another person[2].

1 SI 2012/1916, reg 322(1).
2 SI 2012/1916, reg 322(2).

24.112 HMR 2012, reg 322 imposes restrictions on the disclosure of information obtained on premises which have been entered under a power of entry, or any information obtained or provided in pursuance of the HMR 2012, except to persons who are acting on behalf of a public authority and the information is not held by the authority on behalf of another person.

24.113 HMR 2012, reg 333 provides that an inspector is not personally liable in respect of actions done in the execution or purported execution of a function under the HMR 2012, provided the inspector had an honest belief that the HMR 2012 required or permitted it.

24.114 HMR 2012, reg 334(4) provides that a person is not required under the HMR 2012 to answer a question or to give information if doing so might incriminate that person or the spouse or civil partner of that person.

Offences

24.115 HMR 2012, reg 33(6) provides that it is an offence for a person to disclose information in breach of the prohibition on disclosing information set out in reg 332(1).

24.116 HMR 2012, reg 333(3) provides that it is an offence for a person to intentionally obstruct an inspector, to intentionally fail to comply with a requirement properly made under reg 327, or to without reasonable cause fail to give to an inspector any other information or assistance which the inspector may reasonably require in order to perform a function under the HMR 2012.

24.117 HMR 2012, reg 333(5) provides that it is an offence for a person required under reg 334(3)(c) to give an inspector assistance or information to make a false statement.

Causal liability

24.118 Where a person charged with specified offences[1] contrary to the HMR 2012 commits that offence by reason of the act or omission of another, that other person is also guilty of the offence and proceedings may be brought against that other person irrespective of whether proceedings are brought against the first person[2].

1   SI 2012/1916, regs 251, 268, 269, 273, 275, 305(4), 306(6), 06(8) and any prohibition or requirement in Pt 14, Chapter 2.
2   SI 2012/1916, reg 335(1)–(3) and (6).

Offences by bodies corporate

24.119 Where an offence under HMR 2012 committed by a body corporate is proved to have been committed with the consent or connivance of, or to be attributable to any neglect on the part of, any director, manager, secretary or other similar officer of the body corporate, or a person purporting to act in any such capacity, that person is also guilty of the offence and liable to be proceeded against and punished accordingly[1]. Where the affairs of a body corporate are managed by its members, a member can be proceeded against in connection with his functions of management as if he were a director[2].

1   SI 2012/1916, reg 338(1).
2   SI 2012/1916, reg 338(2).

Defences

24.120 Where a person is charged with an offence contrary to the HMR 2012 involving the contravention of a specified prohibition[1], it is a defence for the person to show that they exercised all due diligence to avoid contravening the provision and that the contravention was due to the act or omission of another[2]. A person may not rely on such a defence unless not less than seven clear days before the hearing of the proceedings, the person has served a notice on the person bringing the proceedings[2] which must give the information of the person serving the notice which identifies or assisting in identifying the person who committed the act or omission[3].

1   SI 2012/1916, regs 251, 268, 269, 273, 275, 305(4), 306(6), 306(8) and any prohibition or requirement in Pt 14, Chapter 2.
2   SI 2012/1916, reg 335(4).
3   SI 2012/1916, reg 335(5).

24.121 HMR 2012, reg 336 makes provision for it to be a defence for a person to prove that the commission of an offence was as a result of his reliance on a written warranty. HMR 2012, reg 337 creates offences where a person seeks to rely on a warranty providing in relation to a different substance or article, and where a person intentionally or recklessly gives a purchaser a false warranty.

Sentencing

24.122 An offence contrary to reg 334(3) is punishable on summary conviction by a fine not exceeding level 3 on the standard scale[1]. An offence contrary to reg 334(5) or (6) is punishable on summary conviction by a fine, or on indictment by a fine or by imprisonment for a term not exceeding 2 years or both[2].

[1]   SI 2012/1916, reg 334(4).
[2]   SI 2012/1916, reg 334(7).

MEDICAL DEVICES

Introduction

24.123 Medical devices are regulated by the Medical Devices Regulations 2002[1] ('MDR 2002'), as amended by the Medical Devices (Amendment etc.) (EU Exit) Regulations 2019[2], Medical Devices (Amendment etc.) (EU Exit) Regulations 2020[3] and Medical Devices (Amendment) (EU Exit) Regulation 2021[4], and by the Medicines and Medical Devices Act 2021 ('MMDA 2021'). The amended regulations revoke, subject to exceptions in relation to Northern Ireland, provisions of retained EU law relating to medical devices, but the MDR 2002 continue to reference Directive 90/385, notwithstanding that Directive was repealed on 26 May 2021 by Regulation[5].

[1]   SI 2002/618.
[2]   SI 2019/791.
[3]   SI 2020/1478.
[4]   SI 2021/873.
[5]   SI 2017/745.

24.124 MDR 2002, reg 3 provides that the MDR 2002 do not apply to medicinal products, human blood, human blood products, plasma or blood cells of human origin, devices that incorporate, at the time of placing on the market, human blood, blood products, plasma or blood cells of human origin, transplants or tissues or cells of human origin or products incorporating or derived from tissues or cells of human origin, transplants or tissues or cells of animal origin, and cosmetic product.

24.125 The regulations distinguish between general medical devices active implantable medical devices, and in vitro diagnostic medical devices. The effect of MDR 2002, reg 2 and 6 is that:

–   General medical devices are medical devices and accessories, single-use combination products and systems and procedure packs, other than active implantable medical devices and accessories to such devices, and in vitro diagnostic medical devices and accessories to such devices.
–   An active implantable device is a medical device which relies for its functioning on a source of electrical energy or a source of power other than that generated directly by the human body or by gravity and is intended to be totally or partially introduced into the human body

(whether surgically or medically, including being introduced into a natural orifice) and which is intended to remain in the human body after completion of the surgical or medical procedure during which it is introduced, even if it is intended to administer a medicinal product or incorporates as an integral part a substance which, if used separately, would be a medicinal product.

– An *in vitro* diagnostic device is a device which is a reagent, reagent product, calibrator, control material kit, instrument, apparatus, equipment or system, whether used alone or in combination and is intended by the manufacturer to be used *in vitro* for the examination of specimens, including blood and tissue donations, derived from the human body, solely or principally for the purpose of providing information concerning a physiological or pathological state, concerning a congenital abnormality, to determine the safety and compatibility of donations, including blood and tissue donations, with potential recipients or to monitor therapeutic measures. This includes a specimen receptacle but not a product for general laboratory use, unless that product, in view of its characteristics, is specifically intended by its manufacturer to be used for *in vitro* diagnostic examination.

24.126 In *Hyaltech Ltd v Medicines and Healthcare Products Regulatory Agency*[1], the Inner House of the Court of Session held that in determining whether a product was a medicinal product or a medicinal device, a purposive approach should be adopted.

[1] [2008] CSIH 64.

Requirements

24.127 General medical devices are governed by MDR 2002, Pt II; active implantable medical devices by MDR 2002, Pt III and in vitro diagnostic medical devices by MDR 2002, Pt IV.

24.128 No person may place a general, active implantable or in vitro diagnostic medical device on the market unless they are established in Great Britain and comply with the relevant registration requirements[1].

[1] SI 2002/618, regs 7A, 21A and 33A.

24.129 No person may place a general, active implantable or in vitro diagnostic medical devices on the market, or put such a device into service, or supply such a device if that supply is also a putting into service, or if that supply is of a device that has been placed on the market or put into service, unless they are established in Great Britain and comply with the relevant registration requirements[1].

[1] SI 2002/618, regs 10, 24 and 36.

Enforcement

Duty to enforce

24.130 MDR 2002, reg 61(1A) imposes a duty on the Secretary of State to enforce the regulations in relation to relevant devices and devices for performative evaluation. MDR 2002, reg 61(1B) imposes a concurrent duty on each weights and measures authority to enforce the regulations in its area in relation to relevant devices that are ordinarily intended for private use or consumption.

Enforcement notices

24.131 MMDA 2021, s 21(1A) defines, for the purposes of s 21 to 41, 'medical devices provision' as including provisions in the MDR 2002 and in any regulations made under MMDA 2021, s 15.

24.132 Where the enforcement authority has reasonable grounds to a suspect that a person involved in marketing or supplying a medical device is not complying with a medical devices provision, MMDA 2021, s 21(1) empowers the authority to issue a compliance notice, which identifies the relevant provision, sets out the grounds for suspecting that the person is not complying with the provision, requires the person to comply with the provision, and to provide evidence to the satisfaction of the enforcement authority of the compliance, within a specified period of at least 28 days beginning with the day on which the notice is served, and to within such a period take any other measures that may be specified in order to comply with the provision.

24.133 Where the enforcement authority considers that it may be necessary to restrict the availability of a medical device in order to protect health or safety:

- MMDA 2021, s 22 empowers the authority to issue a suspension notice, prohibiting the person from supplying, offering or agreeing to, or exposing or possessing for supply, the device without the consent of the enforcement authority. A suspension notice must set out the enforcement authority's grounds for considering that it may be necessary to restrict the availability of the device and specify the period for which the notice has effect, which may not be more than 6 months after the day on which the suspension notice is served.
- MMDA 2021, s 23 empowers the authority to issue a safety notice, imposing prohibitions or requirements that the authority considers necessary. The prohibitions that may be imposed including prohibiting the person from supplying, offering or agreeing to, or exposing or possessing for supply, the device without the consent of the enforcement authority. The requirements that may be imposed include requirements to publish warnings at the persons expense, and organising or cooperating with the enforcement authority as to the recall of the device.

24.134 Where the enforcement authority considers that a person has information which the authority needs for the purpose of deciding whether to serve or revoke a compliance notice or suspension notice, or to serve, vary or revoke a safety notice, MMDA 2021, s 24 empowers the authority to serve a information notice. An information notice may require the person to disclose to the enforcement authority information specified in the notice, or to produce specified records, within a specified period of at least 28 days beginning with the day on which the notice is served.

24.135 A person affected by a compliance, suspension or safety notice, and a person on whom an information notice has been served, may apply to the magistrates' court to set aside or vary the notice in accordance with MMDA 2021, s 25. Where an order is varied or set aside, the applicant may apply under MMDA 2021, s 26 for an order requiring the enforcement authority to pay compensation in respect of loss or damage caused by reason of the notice. A person aggrieved by a decision made under s 25 or s 26 may appeal to the Crown Court in accordance with MMDA 2021, s 27.

Recall

24.136 MMDA 2021, s 35 provides that where the enforcement authority considers it to be necessary to restrict the availability of a medical device that has already been supplied or made available to members of the public, in order to protect health or safety, the authority may take such steps as it considers necessary to organise the return of the device. The authority may do so regardless of whether it issues a safety notice requiring another person to organise or cooperate in organising the recall, but may only do so if it is satisfied that no alternative steps that did not involve recalling the device would sufficiently protect health or safety.

Offences

24.137 From a date to be appointed, MMDA 2021, Sch 3 will make it an offence to breach various provisions of the MDR 2002. Until that schedule is brought into force, the MDR 2002 continue to be recognised as safety regulations for the purposes of the Consumer Protection Act 1987.

24.138 MMDA 2021, s 28 provides a person commits an offence if they breach a compliance notice, a suspension notice, a safety notice or an information notice. An offence is punishable on summary conviction by imprisonment for a term not exceeding 6 months, a fine or both.

Defences

24.139 MMDA 2021, s 29(1) provides that it is a defence for a person charged with an offence contrary to s 28 to show that the person took all reasonable steps and exercised all due diligence to avoid commission of the offence. A person is not entitled to rely on that defence without leave of the court if it involves an allegation that the commission of the offence was due to an act or default of another person, or reliance on information given by another person, unless at least seven clear days before the hearing of the proceedings, the defendant has served on the prosecutor a notice giving such information identifying or assisting in the identification of that other person as was then in the defendant's possession[1]. A person is not entitled to rely on that defence by reason of their reliance on information supplied by another, unless they show that it was reasonable in all the circumstances to rely on the information, having regard to the steps which the defendant took or might reasonably have taken to verify the information and whether the defendant had any reason to disbelieve the information[2].

1   MMDA 2021, s 29(2)–(3).
2   MMDA 2021, s 29(4).

Offences by bodies corporate

24.140 Where an offence under MMDA 2021 committed by a body corporate is proved to have been committed with the consent or connivance of, or to be attributable to any neglect on the part of, any director, manager, secretary or other similar officer of the body corporate, or a person purporting to act in any such capacity, that person is also guilty of the offence and liable to be proceeded against and punished accordingly[1]. Where the affairs of a body corporate are managed by its members, a member can be proceeded against in connection with his functions of management as if he were a director[2].

1   MMDA 2021, s 30(1).
2   MMDA 2021, s 30(3).

Forfeiture

24.141 MMDA 2021, s 32 allows a magistrates' court, on application by the enforcement authority, to order the forfeiture of a medical device it is satisfied that there has been a contravention of a medical devices provision in relation to the device. MDMA, s 32 provides a right of appeal to any person claiming to be entitled to make a medical device which is subject to a forfeiture order, and to the enforcement authority against any decision to refuse to make an order.

Civil sanctions

24.142 From a date to be appointed, MMDA 2021, s 31 will bring into force Sch 2 which makes provision for civil sanctions in relation to the commission of offences to do with medical devices.

Civil proceedings

24.143 MMDA 2021, s 38 provides that an obligation imposed by a medical devices provision is to be treated as a duty owed to any person who may be affected by a breach of the obligation and that, subject to any contrary provision, a breach of such an obligation gives rise to a right of action for breach of statutory duty.

TOBACCO AND VAPING

The manufacture, labelling, packaging and sale of tobacco

Introduction

24.144 Since 20 May 2016, the manufacture, labelling, packaging and sale of Tobacco is governed on a Community-wide basis by the Tobacco Products

Directive[1] ('TPD'). The TPD is implemented in domestic law by the Tobacco and Related Products Regulations 2016[2] ('TRPR 2016').

[1]   2014/40/EU.
[2]   SI 2016/507.

Labelling and packaging

24.145 The effect of TRPR 2016, regs 5 and 7 is that a unit pack and any container pack of a tobacco product for smoking must not be supplied unless it carries a combined health warning, a general warning and an information message. A combined health warning must consist of one of the text warning, and the corresponding colour paragraph, as specified in schedule A1, and the phrase 'Get help to stop smoking at www.nhs.uk/quit'. The combined health warning must comply with the presentational requirements in reg 5(4)–(9). The selection of photographs must be in accordance with reg 6. The general warning consists of the phrase 'Smoking kills – quit now' and the information message the text 'Tobacco smoke contains over 70 substances known to cause cancer'. The general warning and information message must comply with the presentational requirements in reg 7(3) and, in respect of unit packs of cigarettes other than shoulder boxes and unit packs of hand rolling tobacco which are cuboid in shape, but not a shoulder box, with reg 8.

24.146 These requirements do not apply to large cigars and individually wrapped cigars and cigarillos, which must instead comply with the requirements of reg 9, or to smokeless tobacco products, with must comply with reg 10. A unit pack and any container pack of a smokeless tobacco product must contain the health warning 'this tobacco product damages your health and is addictive'[1] and comply with the presentational requirements in reg 10(3)–(4).

[1]   SI 2016/507, reg 10(1)–(2).

24.147 Health warnings required by regs 5, 7, 9 and 10 must also comply with the presentational requirements in reg 1.

Standardised packaging

24.148 Since 20 May 2016, the Standardised Packaging of Tobacco Products Regulations 2015[1] ('SPTPR 2015') set out the standard packaging requirements for cigarettes and hand rolling tobacco. They effectively supplement the provisions set out in the TRPR 2016, providing further detail as to the colour, structure and material of packaging.

[1]   SI 2015/829.

24.149 SPTPR 2015, reg 10 sets out general provisions which apply to both cigarettes and rolling tobacco. The labelling of the packaging in which a tobacco product is, or is intended to be, presented for retail sale or the product itself may not contain any element or feature which:

(a)   promotes a tobacco product or engages its consumption by creating an erroneous impression about its characteristics, health effects, risks or emissions;

(b)   includes any information about the nicotine, tar or carbon monoxide content of a tobacco product;

(c)   suggests that a particular tobacco product is less harmful than others, aims to reduce the effect of some harmful components of smoke, has vitalising, energising, healing, rejuvenating, natural or organic properties or any other health or lifestyle benefits;

(d)   refers to taste, smell or any flavourings or other additives, or the absence of any such thing;

(e)   resembles a food or a cosmetic product; or

(f)   suggests that a particular tobacco product has improved biodegradability or other environmental damages.

24.150 The packaging in which a tobacco product is, or is intended to be, presented for retail sale may not contain any element or feature which suggests economic advantage by including printed vouchers or offering discounts, free distribution, two-for-one or other similar offers. The elements and features referred to here and above include but are not limited to texts, symbols, names, trade marks, figurative signs and other types of sign.[1]

[1]   SI 2015/829, reg 10.

24.151 SPTPR 2015, reg 11 provides that no person may produce or supply any cigarettes or hand rolling tobacco if any part of the packaging in which the product is, or is intended to be, presented for retail sale makes a noise or contains or produces a smell that is not normally associated with the packaging of cigarettes or, as the case may be, hand rolling tobacco. There is no prohibition on any smell in the packaging which results from any manufacturing process which is designed to give the cigarettes or hand-rolling tobacco a characterising flavour that is not prohibited.

24.152 SPTPR 2015, reg 12 provides that no person may produce or supply any cigarettes or hand rolling tobacco if the packaging in which the product is, or is intended to be, presented for retail sale includes any features which are designed to change the packaging after retail sale.

24.153 In relation to the packaging of cigarettes, no person may produce or supply any cigarettes in breach of any of the provisions of reg 3 or Sch 1. The only colour or shade permitted on or for the external packaging of a unit packet or container packet of cigarettes is Pantone 448 C with a matt finish, and the only colour or shade permitted on or for the internal packaging of a unit packet or container packet of cigarettes is either white or Pantone 448 C with a matt finish, subject to reg 4 below and Sch 1 of the regulations[1].

[1]   SI 2015/829, reg 3.

24.154 SPTPR 2015, reg 5 provides that the only colour or shade permitted on or for the paper, casing, filter or other material forming part of a cigarette is plain white with a matt finish, except for any paper or casing that surrounds the end of the cigarette that is not designed to be lit may be coloured in such a way as to imitate cork, and text printed in accordance with the regulation to identify the brand name and variant name of the cigarette.

24.155 The only colour or shade permitted on or for the external packaging of a unit packet or container packet of hand rolling tobacco is Pantone 448C with a matt finish, and the only colour or shade permitted on or for the internal packaging of a unit packet or container packet of hand rolling tobacco is either white or Pantone 448 C with a matt finish[1].

1   SI 2015/829, reg 7(2)–(3).

24.156 SPTPR 2015, regs 4 and 8 make provisions as to the physical nature of unit packets of cigarettes and hand rolling tobacco. No person may produce or supply any cigarettes in breach of any of these provisions.

24.157 In relation to the packaging of both cigarettes and hand rolling to-bacco, there is no prohibition on any warning, statement, text, picture, image, symbol or marking which is required by any enactment (whenever passed or made) other than the SPTPR 2015 regulations. Paragraph 3 of Sch 1 imposes conditions (the name and address of the producer) in relation to any text required in accordance with reg 7(4)(a)(i) of the General Product Safety Regulations 2005[1].

1   SI 2015/829, regs 3(4) and 7(4).

24.158 It is an offence to breach any regulations of the SPTPR 2015[1]; the sentencing provisions are the same under the TRPR 2016, reg 51, see **24.170** below. The only defence for an offence under the SPTPR 2015 is that the person supplying the tobacco product in breach of these regulations neither knew nor had reasonable grounds for suspecting that the tobacco product was supplied in breach of that provision[2].

1   SI 2015/829, reg 15.
2   SI 2015/829, reg 17.

24.159 In *R (on the application of BAT) v Secretary of State for Health*[1], the High Court rejected a challenge to the making of the SPTPR 2015.

1   [2016] EWHC 1169.

Emissions levels

24.160 No person may produce, supply or manufacture for export any cigarettes with emissions levels greater than 10 milligrams of tar per cigarette; 1 milligram of nicotine per cigarette and 10 milligrams of carbon monoxide per cigarette[1]. TRPR 2016, reg 14 makes provision in relation to the measurement of tar, nicotine and carbon monoxide emissions.

1   SI 2016/507, reg 13(1).

Flavourings, vitamins, colourings and prohibited additives

24.161 No person may produce or supply cigarettes or hand rolling tobacco with a characterising flavour[1]. No person may produce or supply cigarettes or hand rolling tobacco with a filter, paper, package, capsule or other component containing flavourings[2]; a filter paper or capsule containing tobacco or nicotine[3]; or a technical feature allowing the consumer to modify the smell, taste, or smoke intensity of the product[4].

1   SI 2016/507, reg 15(1). A characterising flavour means a smell or taste other than one of tobacco which is clearly noticeable before or during consumption of the product and results from an additive or a combination of additives, including, but not limited to, fruit, spice, herbs, alcohol, candy, menthol or vanilla: SI 2016/507, reg 2.

2   SI 2016/507, reg 15(2)(a).
3   SI 2016/507, reg 15(2)(b).
4   SI 2016/507, reg 15(2)(c).

24.162 No person may produce or supply a tobacco product containing vitamins or other additives that create the impression that a tobacco product has a health benefit or presents reduced health risks; caffeine, taurine or other additives and stimulant compounds that are associated with energy and vitality; additives which have colouring effects on emissions; or in the case of tobacco products for smoking, additives that facilitate inhalation or nicotine uptake[1]. No person may produce or supply a tobacco product containing additives that have CMR properties[2] in unburnt form, or additives in quantities that increase, to a significant or measurable degree, the toxic or addictive effect or CMR properties of the product when it is consumed[3]. Exceptions are provided in relation to the use of an additive which is essential for the manufacture of a tobacco product[4].

1   SI 2016/507, reg 16(1).
2   SI 2016/507, reg 16(2).
3   CMR properties means properties which are carcinogenic, mutagenic or toxic for reproduction: SI 2016/507, reg 2.
4   SI 2016/507, reg 16(3).

Tobacco for oral use

24.163 TRPR 2016, reg 17 provides that no person may produce or supply tobacco for oral use. In *Swedish Match AB v Secretary of State for Health* (C-151/17), the CJEU held that this prohibition was a proportionate means of protecting public health.

Offences

24.164 TRPR 2016, reg 48 provides as follows:

A person is guilty of an offence if that person—
(a)   breaches a provision of—
       (i)   Part 2 (labelling),
       (ii)   Part 3 (emissions, additives etc.) except regulation 14(3) (approved laboratories), or
       (iii)   regulation 27 (no supply of products where reporting obligations not complied with);
(b)   fails to submit information to the Secretary of State in accordance with a provision of Part 4 (reporting about tobacco products) or regulation 29 (ingredients information for herbal products for smoking);
(c)   breaches regulation 28 (labelling and presentation of herbal products for smoking) or regulation 30(2) (no supply where reporting obligation not complied with);
(d)   breaches any provision of Part 6 (electronic cigarettes) except regulations 32(5) (annual reporting requirement) and 34 (Secretary of State duty to publish notifications);
(e)   breaches any provision of regulations 42, 43 or 44 (advertising and sponsorship); or
(f)   supplies a product in breach of regulation 47 (cross border distance sales of tobacco products and electronic cigarettes etc.).

24.165 A producer or retailer who provides information pursuant to any obligation in TRPR 2016 is guilty of an offence if the information is false or misleading in a material particular and the producer or retailer who provides the information either knows that, or is reckless as to whether, it is false or misleading in a material particular[1].

[1]   SI 2016/507, reg 49.

Defences

24.166 TRPR 2016, reg 50 provides as follows:

(1)   In any proceedings for an offence under these Regulations brought against a person who supplies any tobacco product or related product in breach of these Regulations, it is a defence that the supplier exercised all due diligence to avoid committing the offence.

(2)   In any proceedings for an offence against a person under regulations 42, 43 or 44 (advertising and sponsorship) it is a defence that the person exercised all due diligence to avoid committing the offence.

(3)   In any proceedings for an offence against a person under regulations 42(1) or 43 it is a defence that the person did not know and had no reason to suspect that the advertisement was an electronic cigarette advertisement.

(4)   In proceedings for an offence against a person under regulation 42(2), it is a defence that the person did not know and had no reason to suspect that the newspaper, periodical or magazine contained an electronic cigarette advertisement.

(5)   A defendant may not, without permission of the court, rely on the defence provided by paragraph (1) or (2) on the basis that the commission of the offence was due to the act or default of another person or the defendant's reliance on information given by another person, unless the defendant has served on the prosecutor the notice mentioned in paragraph (6).

(6)   That notice is notice in writing, giving such information identifying or assisting in the identification of that other person as is in the defendant's possession and which is served not less than seven clear days before the date of the hearing.

(7)   A defendant may not rely on the defence provided by paragraph (1) or (2) by reason that the defendant relied on information given by another person, unless the defendant shows that it was reasonable in all the circumstances to have relied on that information.

Duty to enforce

24.167 It is the duty of each weights and measures authority in Great Britain to enforce the TRPR 2016 within their area[1], except in relation reg 14(4); Pt 4, with the exception of reg 27; reg 29; reg 31 and reg 32, where the duty is transferred to the Secretary of State[2]. The duty in relation to reg 27, reg 30(2), reg 35 and reg 40(5) is also transferred to the Secretary of State, but each weights and measures authority is not relieved of that duty[3]. The Secretary of State may direct in relation to cases of a particular description or a particular case, that the enforcement duty is to be discharged by the Secretary of State[4].

[1]   SI 2016/507, reg 53(1).
[2]   SI 2016/507, reg 53(6).

24.168 TRPR 2016, reg 53(3) makes provision for provisions of the TRPR 2016 to be treated as safety regulations or the purpose of the Consumer Protection Act 1987.

Offences by bodies corporate

24.169 TRPR 2016, reg 52 provides that where an offence under TRPR 2016 committed by a body corporate is proved to have been committed with the consent or connivance of, or to be attributable to any neglect on the part of, any director, manager, secretary or other similar officer of the body corporate, or a person purporting to act in any such capacity, that person is also guilty of the offence and liable to be proceeded against and punished accordingly. Where the affairs of a body corporate are managed by its members, a member can be proceeded against in connection with his functions of management as if he were a director. Directors liability is covered in CHAPTER 4 Criminal Enforcement.

Sentencing

24.170 TRPR 2016, reg 51 provides that an offence contrary to TRPR 2016 is punishable on summary conviction by imprisonment for a term not exceeding 3 months or a fine or both, or on conviction on indictment by imprisonment for a term no exceeding 2 years or a fine or both.

The smoking of tobacco in premises
Smoke-free premises, places and vehicles

24.171 Health Act 2006 ('HA 2006'), s 1 prohibits smoking in certain premises, places and vehicles. The effect of s 2(1)–(2) is that premises are smoke free if they are open to the public, when open to the public; and all the time, if they are used as a place of work by more than one person or where members of the public might attend for the purpose of seeking or receiving goods or services. Section 2(3) provides that if only part of premises is used as a place of work falling within s 2(2), they are smoke-free only in the relevant part.

24.172 HA 2006, s 2(4) provides that premises are smoke-free only in those areas which are enclosed or substantially enclosed. Premises are enclosed if they have a ceiling or roof, and except for doors, windows and passageways, are wholly enclosed either permanently or temporarily[1]. Premises are substantially enclosed if they have a ceiling or room, but there is an opening in the walls, or an aggregate area of openings in the walls, which is less than half of the area of the walls, including other structures serving the purpose of walls and constituting the perimeter of the premises[2]. Regulation 11 of the Smoke-free (Exemptions and Vehicles) Regulations 2007[3] make provision as to when a vehicle is smoke-free. Limited exceptions are provided for certain premises: private accommodation; accommodation for guests and members of clubs; other residential accommodation; performers; specialist tobacconists; offshore installations; research and testing facilities; and mental health units[4].

¹   SI 2006/3368, reg 2(1).

² SI 2006/3368, reg 2(2).
³ SI 2007/765.
⁴ SI 2007/765, regs 3–10.

24.173 The smoke-free provisions of the HA 2006 do not bind the Crown and so do not apply in state-run prisons: *R (Black) v Secretary of State for Justice*[1]. They do not contravene the ECHR: *R (Howitt) v Preston Magistrates' Court*[2].

¹ [2017] UKSC 81.
² [2009] EWHC 1284 (Admin).

24.174 HA 2006, s 6(1) imposes a duty on any person who occupies or is concerned in the management of smoke-free premises to display no-smoking signs. The Smoke-free Signs Regulations 2012 ('SFSR') imposes a corresponding duty on any person with management responsibilities for a vehicle that is smoke-free. Regulation 3 of the SFSR provides that at least one legible no-smoking sign must be displayed in smoke-free premises.

Offences

24.175 HA 2006, s 7(2) creates an offence of smoking in a smoke-free place. Section 7(3) provides an exception for performers in relevant premises. Section 7(6) provides that a person guilty of an offence is liable on summary conviction to a fine not exceeding a level on the standard scale specified in regulations. The Smoke-free (Penalties and Discounted Amounts) Regulations 2007[1], reg 2(2) specifies level 1.

¹ SI 2007/764.

24.176 HA 2006, s 8 creates an offence of failing to prevent smoking in smoke-free place. It is the duty of any person who controls or is concerned in the management of smoke-free premises to cause a person smoking there to stop smoking. It is an offence to fail to comply with that duty, punishable on summary conviction by a fine not exceeding level 4[1].

¹ HA 2006, s 8 and SI 2007/764, r 2(3).

24.177 HA 2006, s 6(5) creates an offence where a person fails to comply with a duty under s 6(1) or under the SFSR. Section 6(8) provides that a person guilty of an offence is liable on summary conviction to a fine not exceeding a level on the standard scale specified in regulations. The Smoke-free (Penalties and Discounted Amounts) Regulations 2007, reg 3 specifies level 3.

Defences

24.178 It is a defence for a person charged with an offence under s 7(2) to show that he did not know, and could not reasonably have been expected to know, that it was a smoke-free place[1]. It is a defence for a person charged with an offence under s 8 to show that he took reasonable steps to cause the person in question to stop smoking, that he did not know, and could not reasonably have been expected to know, that the person in question was smoking, or that on other grounds it was reasonable for him not to comply with the duty[2].[3]

¹ HA 2006, s 7(4).
² HA 2006, s 8(5).

3   HA 2006, s 7(5) and 8(6).

24.179 It is a defence for a person charged with an offence under s 6(5) to show that he did not know, and could not reasonably have been expected to know, that the premises, place or vehicle were smoke-free (or, as the case may be, that the place or vehicle was smoke-free)[1], that he did not know, and could not reasonably have been expected to know, that no-smoking signs complying with the requirements of this section were not being displayed in accordance with the requirements of this section[2], or that on other grounds it was reasonable for him not to comply with the duty[3].

1   HA 2006, s 6(6)(a).
2   HA 2006, s 6(6)(b).
3   HA 2006, s 6(6)(c).

24.180 Where evidence is adduced which is sufficient to raise an issue with respect to these defences, the court or jury shall assume that the defence is satisfied unless the prosecution proves beyond reasonable doubt that it is not[1].

1   HA 2006, s 6(7), 7(5) and s 8(6).

Duty to enforce

24.181 Unitary authorities, district councils that are not unitary authorities, London borough councils, port health authorities, the Common Council of the City of London, the Sub-Treasurer of the Inner Temple, the Under Treasurer of the Middle Temple and the Council of the Isles of Scilly are designated enforcement authorities[1]. A port health authority has enforcement functions within the district for which it is a port health authority and other authorities have authority in the area for which it is a local authority other than any part of that area which falls within the district of a port health authority[2]. The Chief Officer of each police force is designated as an enforcement authority[3]. The enforcement functions of a Chief Officer of police relate to smoke-free vehicles which are within the police area for which the police force in question is maintained[4]. The Secretary of State may direct, in relation to cases of a particular description, or in relation to a particular case, that the duty of an enforcement authority is to instead be discharged by the Secretary of State[5]. Where more than one enforcement authority is investigating an offence relating to smoke free premises, they may arrange for the transfer of enforcement functions[6].

1   SI 2006/3368, r 3(1).
2   SI 2006/3368, r 3(3).
3   SI 2006/3368, r 3(6).
4   SI 2006/3368, r 3(7).
5   HA 2006, s 10(4).
6   SI 2006/3368, r 3(5).

24.182 HA 2006, s 11 creates offences relating to the obstruction of officers, punishable on summary conviction by a fine not exceeding level 3 on the standard scale.

Fixed penalties

24.183 HA 2006, s 9 provides that an officer of an enforcement authority who has reason to believe a person has committed an offence under s 6(5), s 7(2) or s 8(4) may issue a penalty notice, offering a person the opportunity to discharge any liability to conviction for the offence to which the notice relates by paying a penalty. HA 2006, Sch 1, para 1–4 makes provision as to the contents of penalty notices and the periods of time in which the amount, or the discounted amount, due must be paid. In respect of an offence alleged under s 6(5), the amount specified is £200 and the discounted amount specified is £150. In respect of an offence specified under s 7(2) or s 8(4), the amount specified is £50 and the discounted amount specified is £30[1].

[1] SI 2007/764, reg 2(4)–(5).

The advertising and marketing of tobacco

Introduction

24.184 The advertising and promotion of tobacco products is principally restricted by the Tobacco Advertising and Promotion Act 2002 ('TAPA 2002'), supplemented by a number of statutory instruments and the Broadcast Committee on Advertising Practice Code (BCAP).

Prohibition on advertising, giveaways and sponsorship

24.185 TAPA 2002, s 1 defines a tobacco advertisement as 'an advertisement (a) whose purpose is to promote a tobacco product, or (b) who effect is to do so', and a tobacco product as 'a product consisting wholly or partly of tobacco and intended to be smoked, sniffed, sucked or chewed.

24.186 TAPA 2002, s 2(1) provides as follows:

(1) A person who in the course of a business publishes a tobacco advertisement, or causes on to be published, in the United Kingdom is guilty of an offence.
(2) A person who in the course of a business prints, devises or distributes in the United Kingdom a tobacco advertisement which is published in the United Kingdom, or causes such an advertisement to be so printed, devised or distributed, is guilty of an offence.
(3) Distributing a tobacco advertisement includes transmitting it in an electronic form, participating in doing so, and providing the means of transmission.

24.187 TAPA 2002, s 3 provides that if a tobacco advertisement is published in a newspaper, periodical or other publication in the United Kingdom, any proprietor or editor of the publication is guilty of an offence, any person who (directly or indirectly) procured the inclusion of the advertisement in the publication is guilty of an offence, and any person who sells the publication, or offers it for sale, or otherwise makes it available to the public, is guilty of an offence. The same applies to the advertisement of tobacco by means of an information society service[1].

[1] TAPA 2002, s 3A.

24.188 TAPA 2002, s 4 provides certain exclusions from the prohibitions in s 2 and s 3 for advertisements, including in relation to tobacco trade publications, communications made in a reply to a particular request for information made by an individual, advertisements contained in publications other than in-flight magazines which are printed outside of the United Kingdom and whose principal market is not the United Kingdom, and advertisements published by means of an information society service by a person who does not carry on business in the United Kingdom and it is not intended to be accessed principally by persons in the United Kingdom. No offence is committed in relation to advertising in a specialist tobacconist where the conditions set out in reg 2, the Tobacco Advertising and Promotion (Specialist Tobacconists) (England) Regulations 2010[1], are met.

[1]   SI 2010/446.

24.189 TAPA 2002, s 9(1) creates an offence where a person, in the course of a business, gives any, and cause or permits to be given away, a product or coupon to the public, where the purpose or effect of doing so is to promote a tobacco product. Section 9(3) provides exceptions where products are given away to the tobacco trade. Section 9(5)(a) creates a defence, where it is alleged that the purpose of the product being given away was to promote a tobacco product, where the person did not know and had no reason to suspect that this was the purpose. Section 9(5)(b) creates a defence, where it is alleged that the effect of the product being given away was to promote a tobacco product, where the person could not reasonably have foreseen that that would be its effect.

24.190 TAPA 2002, s 10 creates an offence of being party to a sponsorship agreement where the purpose or effect of the agreement is to promote a tobacco product in the United Kingdom.

24.191 The Tobacco Advertising and Promotion (Brandsharing) Regulations 2004[1] prohibit promotions of names that are the same as, or similar to tobacco products, where the purpose or effect is to promote a tobacco product in the United Kingdom. TAPA 2002, s 11(4) provides that the breach of the provisions of the regulations is an offence. The requirements are subject to exceptions set out in reg 4 and defences provided in reg 5.

[1]   SI 2004/1824.

24.192 Where TAPA 2002 does not otherwise render such activity unlawful, no person may publish or cause to be published in the course of a business an image of a unit pack or container pack of a tobacco product in connection with an offer for sale to a consumer, unless the pack depicted in the image complies with the labelling and packaging requirements for the lawful supply of the product concerned which are imposed by TRPR 2016, Pt 2[1] and regs 4, 8 and 10 of the Standardised Packaging of Tobacco Products Regulations 2015[2].

[1]   SI 2016/507, reg 1.
[2]   SI 2015/829.

Prohibition of tobacco displays

24.193 TAPA 2002, s 7A(1) provides that it is an offence to display or cause tobacco products to be displayed in a place in the course of business in a 'place'. 'Place' means for the purposes of the regulations any premises in which tobacco products are offered for sale in the course of a business, other than premises which are accessible only to persons who are engaged in, or employed by, a business which is part of the tobacco trade, and from which the prices of tobacco products are not visible from the outside of the premises[1].

1   Tobacco Advertising and Promotion (Display) (England) Regulations 2010, SI 2010/445 ('TAPDR 2010'), reg 3.

24.194 No offence is committed under s 7A:

–   Where tobacco products are displayed in the course of a business which is part of the tobacco trade, for the purpose of that trade, and the display is accessible only to persons who are engaged in, or employed by, a business which is also part of that trade[1].

–   By a display of tobacco products in bulk and specialist tobacconists, if the display is not visible from outside of the premises[2].

–   Where a product is displayed as a result of, or in consequence of, a request to display it[3].

–   Where the display is incidental to the ordinary course of business[4].

–   Where the display is requested by an authorised officer of an enforcement authority, a constable or an officer of Revenue and Customs acting in the course of their duty[5].

1   TAPA 2002, s 7B(1).
2   Tobacco Advertising and Promotion (Specialist Tobacconists) (England) Regulations 2010, reg 3 and SI 2010/445, reg 5.
3   TAPA 2002, s 7B(2) and SI 2010/445, reg 4.
4   SI 2010/445, reg 6.
5   SI 2010/445, reg 7.

24.195 TAPDR 2010, reg 8 makes provision as what may permissibly indicated on storage units. Regulation 8(2) provides that no offence under s 2 of the TAPA 2002 is committed where an indication on a storage unit complies with the requirements set out in reg 8(3).

24.196 In *R (BAT and Others) v Secretary of State for Health*[1], the Administrative Court (McCombe J) rejected a challenge to the predecessor regulations to the TAPDR 2010, the Tobacco Advertising and Promotion (Point of Sale) Regulations 2004, holding that the regulations were a proportionate response to a legitimate objective.

1   [2004] EWHC 2493 (Admin).

Display of prices of tobacco products

24.197 The Secretary of State is permitted to make regulations in relation to the display of the prices of tobacco products in a place in England and Wales or Northern Ireland[1], and to make provision as to the meaning of place[2]. To display or cause to be display prices of tobacco products in breach of a requirement contained in the regulations is an offence[3]. 'Place means premises in England where tobacco products are offered for sale in the course of a business, other than premises which are accessible only to persons engaged in or employed by a tobacco trade business and from which the prices are not visible from outside of the premises[4]. Where a display of products complies with the requirements of the regulations, it is to be treated as a display of prices and not as an advertisement, notwithstanding that it would otherwise also amount to an advertisement[5]. Save in relation to specialist and bulk tobacconists[6], the display of prices of tobacco products must comply with regs 5–8, Tobacco Advertising and Promotion (Display of Prices) (England) Regulations 2010 ('TAPDPER 2010').

1   TAPA 2002, s 7C(1).
2   TAPA 2002, s 7C(3).
3   TAPA 2002, s 7C(2).
4   SI 2010/863, reg 3.
5   SI 2010/863, reg 4(3).
6   SI 2010/863, reg 9(1).

24.198 TAPDPER 2010, regs 5–8 set various limitations on and prescribe numerous conditions for the display of prices of tobacco products

24.199 The Secretary of State is permitted to make regulations in relation to the display in the course of a business of tobacco products or their prices on a website where tobacco products are offered for sale[1]. To display or cause to be displayed prices of tobacco products in breach of a requirement contained in the regulations is an offence[2]. No such regulations have been made.

1   TAPA 2002, s 7D(1).
2   TAPA 2002, s 7D(2).

Defences

24.200 TAPA 2002, s 5 provides as follows:

(1)   A person does not commit an offence under section 2, section 3(a) or (b), or section 3A(1)(a), in connection with an advertisement whose purpose is to promote a tobacco product, if he did not know, and had no reason to suspect, that the purpose of the advertisement was to promote a tobacco product.

(2)   A person does not commit such an offence in connection with an advertisement whose effect is to promote a tobacco product if he could not reasonably have foreseen that that would be the effect of the advertisement.

(3)   A person does not commit an offence under section 2(2), 3(a) or (b) or 3A(1)(a) if he did not know, and had no reason to suspect, that the tobacco advertisement would be published in the United Kingdom.

(4)   A person does not commit an offence under section 2(2) of distributing or causing the distribution of a tobacco advertisement, otherwise than as mention in section 2(3), if he did not know, and had no reason to suspect, that what he distributed or caused to be distributed was, or contained, a tobacco advertisement.

(5)   In relation to a tobacco advertisement which is distributed as mentioned in section 2(3), a person does not commit an offence under section 2(2) of distributing it or causing its distribution if—

(a)   he was unaware that what he distributed or caused to be distributed was, or contained, a tobacco advertisement,

(b)   having become aware of it, it was not reasonably practicable for him to prevent its further distribution,

(c)   in relation to transmission by means of information society services, he did not carry on business in the United Kingdom at the relevant time, or

(d)   in relation to transmission by any other means of electronic transmission, he did not carry on business in the United Kingdom at the relevant time.

(6)   A person does not commit an offence under section 3(c) if he did not know,

and had no reason to suspect, that the publication contained a tobacco advertisement.'

24.201 TAPA 2002, s 6 provides as follows:

(1)   A person does not commit an offence under section 2 if the tobacco advertisement—
   (a)   was in, or fixed to the outside of the premises of, a specialist tobacconist,
   (b)   was not for cigarettes or hand-rolling tobacco, and
   (c)   complied with any requirements specified by the appropriate Minister in regulations in relation to tobacco advertisements on the premises of specialist tobacconists.

(2)   A specialist tobacconist is a shop selling tobacco products by retail (whether or not it also sells other things) more than half of whose sales on the premises in question derive from the sale of cigars, snuff, pipe tobacco and smoking accessories.

(3)   The sales referred to in subsection (2) are to be measured by sale price–
   (a)   during the most recent period of twelve months for which accounts are available, or
   (b)   during the period for which the shop has been established, if it has not been established long enough for twelve months' accounts to be available.

(4)   'Shop', in subsections (2) and (3), includes a self-contained part of a shop; and, in that case, 'premises' in subsections (1) and (2) means that self-contained part of the shop.

24.202 Where a person relies on a defence under s 5(1) to (6), s 6(1), s 7B(5) and (7), s 9(5), s 10(3) and (4) and s 15(3) and evidence is adduced which is sufficient to raise an issue with respect to that defence, the court or jury shall assume that the defence is satisfied unless the prosecution proves beyond reasonable doubt that it is not[1].

[1]   TAPA 2002, s 17.

24.203 Where a person is charged with an offence under s 7A, it is a defence that D believed the individual was aged 18 or over, and that either D had taken all reasonable steps to establish the individuals age or from the individual's appearance nobody could reasonably have suspected that the individual was aged under 18[1]. A person is treated as having taken all reasonable steps to establish and individual's age if the person asked the individual for evidence of the individual's age and the evidence would have convinced a reasonable person[2].

[1]   TAPA 2002, s 7B(5).
[2]   TAPA 2002, s 7B(6).

24.204 Where a person is charged with an offence under s 7A, it is a defence that D exercised all due diligence to avoid committing the offence.[1]

[1]   TAPA 2002, s 7B(7).

Broadcast media

24.205 The Act does not apply to anything included in specified broadcast services[1]. All Ofcom-licensed television and radio broadcasters are required to comply with the Broadcast Committee of Advertising Practice Code issued by the Advertising Standards Authority with the Approval of Ofcom[2]. The BCAP Code prohibits the advertising of tobacco products[3]. Advertisements must not promote smoking or the use of tobacco products[4]. Non-tobacco products or services that share a name, emblem or other feature with a tobacco product, rolling papers and filters may not be advertised, unless the advertisement is obviously targeted at an adult audience, does not make or imply a reference to smoking or a tobacco product, does not promote tobacco or smoking and does not include a design, etc., that the audience might associate with a tobacco product[5]. Advertisements that might be of particular interest to children or teenagers may only refer to tobacco or smoking if the reference obviously forms part of an anti-smoking or anti-drugs message[6]. Product placement of cigarettes and other tobacco product, and product placement by or on behalf of an undertaking whose principal activity is the manufacture or sale of cigarettes of other tobacco products, is prohibited[7].

[1] TAPA 2002, s 12.
[2] Section 319 of the Communications Act 2003 and the Contracting Out (Functions Relating to Broadcast Advertising) and Specification of Relevant Functions Order 2004.
[3] Para 10.1.3, BCAP Code.
[4] Para 10.3, BCAP Code.
[5] Para 10.1.3 and 10.4, BCAP Code.
[6] Para 10.5, BCAP Code.
[7] Para 9.11, Ofcom Broadcasting Code.

Duty to enforce

24.206 It is the duty of an enforcement authority (in England and Wales, a weights and measures authority[1]) to enforce TAPA 2002 and regulations made under it within its area[1]. The Secretary of State may take over the conduct of any proceedings which are instituted in England and Wales by another person under any provision of TAPA 2002 or regulations made under TAPA 2002 in respect of an offence committed in England[2], and the Welsh Ministers may take over the conduct of any such proceedings in respect of an offence committed in Wales[3].

[1] TAPA 2002, s 13(1)(a) and (2).
[2] TAPA 2002, s 13(5).
[3] TAPA 2002, s 13(5A).

Powers of enforcement authorities

24.207 TAPA 2002, s 14 makes provision for a duly authorised officer of an enforcement authority to enter premises, carry out inspections, require the production or take possession of documentation, and request certain information as considered necessary. A person subject to the above action by an officer is not obliged to answer any question or provide any document which he would be entitled to refuse to answer or to produce for the purposes of court proceedings in England and Wales. TAPA 2002, s 14 also provides for the issuing of warrants by justices of the peace.

24.208 It is an offence to intentionally obstruct a duly authorised officer of an enforcement authority acting in the proper exercise of his functions[1]. It is an offence for a person, without reasonable cause, to fail to comply with any requirement made of him by a duly authorised officer of an enforcement authority acting in the proper exercise of his functions[2]. It is an offence for a person to make a statement which is false in a material particular whilst giving any information which is properly required of him by a duly authorised officer of an enforcement authority[3]. A person who did not know that the material particular was false and had reasonable grounds to believe that it was true has a defence[4].

1   TAPA 2002, s 15(1)(a).
2   TAPA 2002, s 15(1)(b).
3   TAPA 2002, s 15(2).
4   TAPA 2002, s 15(3).

Offences by bodies corporate

24.209 Where an offence under TAPA 2002 committed by a body corporate is proved to have been committed with the consent or connivance of, or to be attributable to any neglect on the part of, any director, manager, secretary or other similar officer of the body corporate, or a person purporting to act in any such capacity, that person is also guilty of the offence and liable to be proceeded against and punished accordingly[1]. Where the affairs of a body corporate are managed by its members, a member can be proceeded against in connection with his functions of management as if he were a director[2]. Directors' liability is covered in CHAPTER 4 Criminal Enforcement.

1   TAPA 2002, s 18(1)–(2).
2   TAPA 2002, s 18(3).

Sentencing

24.210 An offence contrary to s 15(1) is punishable on summary conviction by a fine not exceeding level 3 on the standard scale[1]. An offence contrary to any other provision of TAPA 2002 is punishable on summary conviction by imprisonment for a term not exceeding 6 months or a fine or both, or on conviction on indictment by imprisonment for a term no exceeding 2 years or a fine or both[2].

1   TAPA 2002, s 16(1).
2   TAPA 2002, s 16(2).

Electronic cigarettes and vaping

Introduction

24.211 TRPR 2016 extends to cover electronic cigarettes and herbal products for smoking. An electronic cigarette is a product, that is not a medicinal product or medical device, that can be used for the consumption of nicotine-containing vapour via a mouthpiece, or any component of that product, including a cartridge, a tank and the device without cartridge or tank (regardless of whether the product is disposable or refillable by means of a refill container and a tank, or rechargeable with single use cartridges)[1]. A herbal product for smoking is a product based on plants, herbs or fruits which contains no tobacco and that can be consumed via a consumption process[2].

1   SI 2016/507, reg 2.
2   SI 2016/507, reg 2.

Electronic cigarettes

24.212 No person may produce or supply an electronic cigarette or refill container unless it complies with the requirements set out in reg 36.

24.213 No person may produce or supply an electronic cigarette or refill container unless it complies the product requirements set out in reg 37 and the information and labelling requirements set out in reg 38.

24.214 A producer of electronic cigarettes or refill containers must establish and maintain a system for collecting information about all of the suspected adverse effects on human health of the product[1]. Where a producer of electronic cigarettes or refill containers considers or has reason to believe that an electronic cigarette or refill container which is in its possession and is intended to be supplied, or which has been supplied, is not safe, of good quality, or in conformity with Pt 6 of the TRPR 2016[2], the producer must, either immediately take the corrective action necessary to bring the product into conformity with this Part of the Regulations, withdraw the product, or recall the product[3]. The producer must notify the Secretary of State and the competent authority of any other member state in which the product has been supplied or intended to be supplied[4]. The Secretary of State or the competent authority of any other member state may request additional information and the producer must comply with a request made of it by the date reasonably required by the Secretary of State[5].

[1]   SI 2016/507, reg 39(1).
[2]   SI 2016/507, reg 39(2).
[3]   SI 2016/507, reg 39(3).
[4]   SI 2016/507, reg 39(4).
[5]   SI 2016/507, reg 39(5)–(6).

24.215 The Secretary of State may take appropriate provisional measures to address the risk to human health[1], including prohibiting the supply of the electronic cigarette or refill container, or the type of electronic cigarette or refill container, and requiring each supplier of the electronic cigarette or refill container, or the type of electronic cigarette or refill container, to recall the product[2], where the Secretary of State has reasonable grounds to believe that an electronic cigarette or refill container, or a type of electronic cigarette or refill container, could present a serious risk to human health[3].

[1]   SI 2016/507, reg 40(2).
[2]   SI 2016/507, reg 40(3).
[3]   SI 2016/507, reg 40(1).

24.216 TRPR 2016, reg 31 requires a producer who supplies or intends to supply electronic cigarettes or refill containers to notify the Secretary of State at least 6 months prior to the date on which the producer first intends to supply the product or modified product. A producer must not supply the product if the producer has not done so[1].

[1]   SI 2016/507, reg 35.

24.217 An electronic cigarette advertisement is an advertisement with the aim of promoting an electronic cigarette or refill container, or the direct or indirect effect of promoting one[1]. No person may, in the course of a business, publish, or procure the publication of, an electronic cigarette advertisement in a news-paper, periodical or magazine, or sell, offer for sale or otherwise make available to the public such a publication an electronic cigarette advertisement[2], except in a newspaper, periodical or magazine which is intended exclusively for professionals in the trade of electronic cigarettes or refill containers, or in such a publication which is printed and published in a third country and is not principally intended for the Union market[3].

1   SI 2016/507, reg 41(1).
2   SI 2016/507, reg 42(1)–(2).
3   SI 2016/507, reg 42(3).

24.218 With the exception of information society services intended exclusively for professionals in the electronic cigarette trade and advertisements not principally intended for the Union market[1], no person may include or procure the inclusion of an electronic cigarette advertisement in the course of a business in an information society service provided to a recipient in the UK.[2] This also applies to recipients in an EEA state,[3] unless it is necessary for the purposes of public policy, the protection of public health, the protection of consumers or unless it relates to an information society service that prejudices consumer protection.[4] Information society services are services normally provided for remuneration at a distance by electronic means and at the individual request of the recipient of those services[5].

1   SI 2016/507, reg 43(5).
2   SI 2016/507, reg 43(1).
3   SI 2016/507, reg 43(2).
4   SI 2016/507, reg 43(4).
5   Directive 98/48/EC.

24.219 In enforcing regs 42–43, every enforcement authority must have regard to the desirability of encouraging control of advertising by such established means as it considers appropriate, having regard to all the circumstances of the particular case[1].

1   SI 2016/507, reg 53(5).

24.220 No person may, in the course of a business, provide electronic cigarette sponsorship[1] to a cross-border event or activity[2] or to an individual taking part in a cross-border event or activity[3].

1   Electronic cigarette sponsorship means any form of public or private contribution to any event, activity or individual, with the aim of or direct or indirect effect of promoting an electronic cigarette or refill container: SI 2016/507, reg 44(2).
2   SI 2016/507, reg 44(1)–(2).
3   SI 2016/507, reg 44(1).

Herbal products for smoking

24.221 No person may produce or supply a herbal product for smoking unless it complies with the labelling and presentation requirements set out in TRPR 2016, reg 28. A producer may not supply a herbal product unless they have complied with the requirement in reg 29 to notify specified information to the Secretary of State[1].

1   SI 2016/507, reg 30(2).

Offences

24.222 TRPR 2016, reg 48 applies in relation to electronic cigarettes and herbal products for smoking.

Index

Index